EDITIONS

CASSELL has published outstanding dictionaries for virtually every major foreign language. Now, for the first time, many of them are being made available in compact, paperback editions. Besides the present German–English, English–German dictionary, the Dell series includes the Cassell's New Compact French–English, Spanish–English, and Latin–English dictionaries. These handy reference books are invaluable aids for students in foreign-language courses or for those who want to polish up their language skills on their own. Additionally, they are designed for the traveler and the reader of contemporary literature, newspapers, and magazines.

CASSELL'S NEW COMPACT

German-English
English-German
Dictionary

Compiled by
H.-C. SASSE, M.A., M.Litt.
Lecturer in German at the
University of Newcastle upon Tyne

DR. J. HORNE
Lecturer in German at the
University of Birmingham

DR. CHARLOTTE DIXON

Published by
Dell Publishing Co., Inc.
1 Dag Hammarskjold Plaza, New York, N.Y. 10017
Copyright © 1966 by Cassell & Co. Ltd.
First published in the United States
in 1966 by Funk & Wagnalls.
All Rights Reserved
Laurel ® TM 674623, Dell Publishing Co., Inc.

ISBN: 0-440-31100-4

Reprinted by arrangement with Funk & Wagnalls,
A division of Reader's Digest Books, Inc.
Printed in the United States of America
First Printing—March 1971
Second Printing—June 1971
Third Printing—August 1972
Fourth Printing—January 1973
Fifth Printing—January 1974
Sixth Printing—September 1974
Seventh Printing—August 1975
Eighth Printing—March 1976
Ninth Printing—February 1977

Contents

Preface

Among the difficulties that arise in the compilation of a Compact Dictionary that of the selection of words is undoubtedly the most formidable one. The decision as to what to include and, much more difficult, what to exclude, must to a considerable extent depend on the type of student of a foreign language who is most likely to use it. Primarily a dictionary of this kind is intended for the student in the earlier stages of learning German, whether at school or university. As the study of German, even at an early stage, is likely to include the reading of literary texts from the eighteenth century onwards, it was felt that some attention at least must be paid to the inclusion of words no longer in common use today but frequently found in the prescribed texts, whether poetry, drama or prose. That in this respect severe limitations are imposed by the very concept of a 'Compact' Dictionary is of course obvious, but an attempt has been made to include at least some of the most common literary and poetical terms. However, the main emphasis throughout must of course be on straightforward contemporary German. In addition to the needs of the student, those of the traveller and the tourist, of the reader of contemporary literature and of newspapers and magazines, have been kept in mind. It is hoped that the student of science and technology too will find the dictionary useful, though in his case additional reference must of course be made to one of the growing number of specialized works dealing with the technical vocabulary of his particular discipline.

The aim of a Compact Dictionary must be to achieve some kind of viable compromise between conciseness on the one hand and completeness on the other. To make the dictionary as helpful as possible—given only a limited amount of space—certain economies were called for. Omissions were inevitable. What is similarly inevitable is that, except in the most obvious cases, no two experts are likely

to agree as to what may safely be omitted unless (as was attempted here) one makes frequency of usage and general usefulness the main criteria.

It should be remembered, lastly, that this is a concise dictionary which cannot remotely hope to do justice to all the finer meanings and nuances of two highly developed and complex languages. But it is hoped that the student and reader of German, especially in the earlier stages of learning the language, will find here all the help he needs.

For more detailed reference the user will find Cassell's New German Dictionary (ed. Dr. H. T. Betteridge) of considerable help, while the Duden works of reference on German are regarded as the authoritative last word on matters of controversy. In the final analysis there will always be areas of doubt and dispute. That is the prerogative of a living and developing language.

Finally, thanks are due on behalf of the publishers to Prof. W. E. Collinson, late of the University of Liverpool, who acted in a consultative capacity.

H.-C. Sasse

Advice to the User

As a guide to the nature of words which have inevitably been omitted from a dictionary of this size, it may be helpful to state that, when a German *Fremdwort* is identical with the corresponding English term and possesses no grammatical peculiarities, it appears only in the English–German section. For example, it was felt that the word *Atom* (and *a fortiori* derivative compounds such as *Atomphysik*) was unlikely to perplex any English reader and it has therefore been omitted from the German–English, but included in the English–German, section. For the same reason, a somewhat similar plan has been followed with regard to the names of countries. These have mostly been given in German–English only, whereas the corresponding nouns and adjectives of nationality or race are given in English–German only.

Arrangement of Entries

Strict alphabetical order seemed to be most helpful in a dictionary intended primarily for readers in the earlier stages of acquiring a knowledge of German. Within the entries themselves literal meanings and frequency of usage determine the sequence of definitions. Admittedly the second criterion is to a considerable extent a matter of personal linguistic judgment, indeed of *Sprachgefühl*, but it is hoped that in most cases the reader will thereby more readily discover the meaning of any particular word. It can generally be assumed that definitions separated by commas have much the same meaning, whereas differences in meaning or usage are marked by semicolons. Where it was thought desirable and feasible to include idiomatic phrases, relative frequency of usage appeared a more helpful criterion than strict alphabetic sequence.

Words which are spelt alike but are etymologically distinct

Zur Benutzung des Wörterbuches

Ein Hinweis auf die Art der Wörter, auf die in einem Taschenwörterbuch unweigerlich verzichtet werden muss, wird dem Leser die Anwendung dieses Nachschlagwerkes gewiss erleichtern: Ein deutsches Fremdwort, das mit dem entsprechenden englischen Ausdruck identisch ist und keine grammatikalischen Besonderheiten aufweist, erscheint als Stichwort nicht in beiden Sprachen, sondern wird nur im englisch–deutschen Teil aufgeführt. Man darf wohl annehmen, dass ein Wort wie z.B. *Atom* (und *a fortiori* abgeleitete Zusammensetzungen wie *Atomphysik*) einen englischen Leser kaum verwirren wird, weshalb es denn auch im deutsch–englischen Teil weggelassen, indessen im englisch–deutschen Teil berücksichtigt wurde. Aus dem gleichen Grunde wurde bei den Namen von Ländern ein ähnliches Prinzip beachtet. Diese wurden in der Regel nur im deutsch–englischen Teil aufgeführt, während die entsprechenden Substantive und Adjektive der Nationalität oder Rasse nur im englisch–deutschen Teil erscheinen.

Anordnung der Stichwörter

Die strikte alphabetische Reihenfolge schien vorteilhaft für ein Nachschlagwerk, das in erster Linie für Lernende gedacht ist, die die deutsche Sprache noch nicht völlig beherrschen. Bei den gegebenen Übersetzungen eines Stichwortes bestimmen die wörtliche Übertragung sowie die Häufigkeit des Gebrauches die Folge der Definitionen. Gewiss ist das zweite Kriterium weitgehend eine Angelegenheit der persönlichen linguistischen Beurteilung, in der Tat des Sprachgefühls. Doch ist zu hoffen, dass der Leser in den meisten Fällen gerade dadurch der Bedeutung eines Begriffes näher kommt. Allgemein gilt, dass durch ein Komma getrennte Wörter eine annähernd gleiche Bedeutung haben, während Unterschiede in Bedeutung oder Anwendung

have been given separate, numbered entries for the sake of clarity.

A word should be added on the subject of compounds. Most students of German come to realize before long that the notoriously long German nouns, far from complicating the understanding of the language, are merely a matter of syntactical and grammatical convenience, a device for structural conciseness within a given sentence construction. In a 'Compact' Dictionary only such compounds can be given which have a meaning which can be arrived at only with difficulty or not at all. Where a compound is not given, the constituent parts of the word should be looked up. The meaning should then become self-evident.

Grammar

Parts of Speech. These are indicated by abbreviations in italics (*adj., v.a.* etc.), the meaning of which will be found in the List of Abbreviations. It has not been felt necessary to indicate the nature of English proper names.

Genders. In the German-English section nouns are denoted by their gender (*m., f.* or *n.*). In the English-German section gender is shown by the definite article preceding the noun; in a series of nouns the gender is sometimes omitted when it is the same as that of the preceding noun or nouns.

Declension. The Genitive singular and Nominative plural of German nouns are given in parentheses after the gender. The plurals of English nouns are not given, except for certain very irregular forms. The cases governed by prepositions have been included.

Verbs. In both German and English the indication *irr.* refers the user to the tables of Irregular Verbs. Where a compound irregular verb is not given, its forms are identical with those of the simple irregular verb in the table. "To" is omitted from English infinitives throughout. German inseparable verbs are described as such only when there is any possibility of doubt, *e.g.* in the case of prepositional prefixes. Where prefixes are axiomatically always part of an

durch ein Semikolon markiert sind. Wo es als notwendig und durchführbar erachtet wurde, idiomatische Redewendungen zu zitieren, schien die relative Häufigkeit der Anwendung ein nützlicheres Kriterium als die strenge alphabetische Folge. Orthographisch gleiche Wörter, die sich durch ihre etymologische Herkunft unterscheiden, wurden um der Klarheit willen als einzelne Stichwörter aufgeführt und mit Ziffern versehen. Noch ein Wort zum Thema der Wortzusammensetzungen: Die meisten Deutschlernenden werden bald erkennen, dass die berüchtigt langen deutschen Substantive das Verständnis der Sprache keineswegs erschweren. Sie sind lediglich eine Sache syntaktischer und grammatikalischer Vereinfachung, ein Hilfsmittel zu struktureller Kürze und Prägnanz innerhalb einer gegebenen Satzbildung. In einem Taschenwörterbuch können allein solche Wortverbindungen berücksichtigt werden, die nur mit Mühe oder überhaupt nicht abzuleiten sind. Ist eine Wortverbindung nicht angeführt, so sollten die einzelnen Bestandteile nachgesehen werden. Auf diese Weise wird sich der Sinn der Zusammensetzung von selbst ergeben.

Grammatik

Wortarten. Sie sind in abgekürzter Form durch Kursivschrift gekennzeichnet (*adj.*, *v.a.* etc.). Eine Erläuterung der Abkürzungen findet sich im Verzeichnis der Abkürzungen. Es wurde nicht für nötig befunden, die Zugehörigkeit von Eigennamen anzuzeigen.

Geschlecht. Im deutsch–englischen Teil sind die Substantive mit ihrem Geschlecht (*m.*, *f.* oder *n.*) gekennzeichnet. Im englisch–deutschen Teil ist das Geschlecht durch den bestimmten Artikel vor dem Substantiv angegeben. In einer Reihe aufeinanderfolgender Definitionen wurde der Artikel dort weggelassen, wo er mit dem vorhergehenden übereinstimmt.

Deklination. Die Endungen des Genitiv Singular und des Nominativ Plural deutscher Substantive sind in Klammern nach der Bezeichnung des Geschlechtes eingefügt. Der

inseparable verb (*be-*, *ent-*, *zer-* etc.) no such information is given, as it is assumed that the student will be familiar with the function of these prefixes long before he comes to use a dictionary.

Phonetics. Phonetic transcriptions, using the symbols of the International Phonetic Association, are given throughout for all entries in both sections of the dictionary as a help to correct pronunciation. The mark ′ precedes the syllable which carries the stress. The glottal stop is not indicated.

Numbers. Only the most common numerals appear in the body of the dictionary. However, fuller coverage is given in the separate Numerical Tables.

Zur Benutzung des Wörterbuches

Plural englischer Substantive wurde nicht berücksichtigt ausser bei einigen stark unregelmässigen Formen. Fälle, die von Präpositionen regiert werden, wurden aufgenommen.

Verben. Im Deutschen wie im Englischen weist die Anmerkung *irr.* den Leser auf die Tabellen unregelmässiger Verben hin. Ist ein zusammengesetztes Verb nicht angeführt, so sind seine Formen mit denen des einfachen Verbs in der Tabelle identisch. "To" vor englischen Infinitivformen wurde durchgehend weggelassen. Deutsche untrennbare Verben werden nur dort als solche gekennzeichnet, wo Zweifel möglich sind, also bei Verben mit präpositionalen Vorsilben. Wo Vorsilben grundsätzlich Teile eines untrennbaren Verbes (*be-*, *ent-*, *zer-* etc.) bilden, ist kein solcher Hinweis angebracht, da angenommen werden darf, dass der Lernende die Funktion dieser Vorsilben kennt, lange bevor er dazu kommt, ein Wörterbuch zu konsultieren.

Phonetik. Jedes einzelne Stichwort ist auch in seiner phonetischen Transkription wiedergegeben. Dabei wurden die phonetischen Symbole der *International Phonetic Association* benutzt. Der Akzent ' steht jeweils unmittelbar vor der betonten Silbe. Der Knacklaut ist indessen nicht markiert.

Zahlwörter. Nur die gebräuchlichsten Zahlen erscheinen im Hauptteil des Wörterbuches. Eine ausführliche Zusammenstellung findet sich in den besonderen Zahlentabellen.

Key to Pronunciation

Vowels

Phonetic Symbol	German Example	Phonetic Symbol	English Example
a	lassen ['lasən]	i:	seat [si:t]
a:	haben ['ha:bən], Haar [ha:r]	i	finish ['finiʃ], physic ['fizik]
ɛ	häßlich ['hɛsliç], Geld [gɛlt]	e	neck [nɛk]
ɛ:	Märchen ['mɛ:rçən], Zähne ['tsɛ:nə]	æ	man [mæn], malefactor ['mælifæktə]
e	Medizin [medi'tsi:n]	ɑ	father ['fɑ:ðə], task [tɑ:sk]
e:	leben ['le:bən], See [ze:], lehnen ['le:nən]	ɔ	block [blɔk], waddle [wɔdl]
ə	rufen ['ru:fən]	ɔ:	shawl [ʃɔ:l], tortoise ['tɔ:təs]
ɪ	Fisch [fɪʃ], Mystik ['mɪstɪk]	o	domain [do'mein]
i	Militär [mili'tɛ:r]	u	good [gud], July [dʒu'lai]
i:	Berlin [bɛr'li:n], Liebe ['li:bə], ihm [i:m]	u:	moon [mu:n], tooth [tu:θ]
ɔ	Kopf [kɔpf]	ʌ	cut [kʌt], somewhere ['sʌmwɛə]
o	mobil [mo'bi:l]	ə:	search [sə:tʃ], surgeon ['sə:dʒən]
o:	Rose ['ro:zə], Boot [bo:t], ohne ['o:nə]	ə	cathedral [kə'θi:drəl], never ['nevə]
œ	Mörder ['mœrdər]		
ø	möblieren [mø'bli:rən]		
ø:	Löwe ['lø:və], Röhre ['rø:ʀə]		
u	Hund [hunt]		
u:	gut [gu:t], Uhr [u:r]		
y	fünf [fynf], Symbol [zym'bo:l]		
y:	Lübeck ['ly:bɛk], Mühe ['my:ə]		

Diphthongs

aɪ	Eis [aɪs], Waise ['vaɪzə]	ei	great [greit]
au	Haus [haus]	ou	show [ʃou]
ɔy	Beute ['bɔytə], Gebäude [gə'bɔydə]	ai	high [hai]
		au	crowd [kraud]
		ɔi	boy [bɔi]
		iə	steer [stiə]
		ɛə	hair [hɛə]
		uə	moor [muə]

Consonants

Phonetic Symbol	German Example	Phonetic Symbol	English Example
ç	Blech [blɛç], ich [ɪç]	p	paper ['peipə]
f	Vater ['fa:tər]	b	ball [bɔ:l]
j	ja [ja:]	t	tea [ti:], train [trein]
ŋ	bringen ['brɪŋən]	d	deed [di:d]
s	beißen ['baɪsən], wißen ['vɪsən], los [lo:s]	k	cake [keik], quest [kwest]
ʃ	schon [ʃo:n]	g	game [geim]
ts	Cäcilie [tsɛ'tsi:ljə], Zimmer ['tsɪmər]	m	mammoth ['mæməθ]
		n	nose [nouz], nanny ['næni]
v	weiß [vais]	ŋ	bring [briŋ], finger ['fiŋgə]
x	Bach [bax], kochen ['kɔxən], ruchbar ['ru:xba:r]	f	fair [fɛə], far [fɑ:]
		v	vine [vain]
z	lesen ['le:zən]	θ	thin [θin], bath [bɑ:θ]
b	Biene ['bi:nə]	ð	thine [ðain], bathe [beið]
d	Dach [dax]		
g	geben ['ge:bən]	s	since [sins]
h	hier [hi:r]	z	busy ['bizi]
k	Koch [kɔx], quartieren [kwar'ti:rən]	l	land [lænd], hill [hil]
l	Lied [li:t]	ʃ	shield [ʃi:ld], sugar ['ʃugə]
m	Mirakel [mi'ra:kəl]	ʒ	vision ['viʒən]
n	Nase ['na:zə]	r	rat [ræt], train [trein]
p	Probe ['pro:bə]	h	here [hiə], horse [hɔ:s]
r	rot [ro:t]	x	coronach ['kɔrənæx], loch [lɔx]
t	Tisch [tɪʃ]		

Semi-Consonants

j	yellow ['jelou], yes [jes]
w	wall [wɔ:l]

List of Abbreviations

abbr.	abbreviation (of), abbreviated	*m.*	masculine
Acc.	Accusative	*Maths.*	Mathematics
adj.	adjective	*Meas.*	Measurement
adv.	adverb	*Mech.*	Mechanics
Agr.	agriculture	*Med.*	Medicine
Am.	American(ism)	*Met.*	Meteorology
Anat.	Anatomy	*Metall.*	Metallurgy
Archæol.	Archæology	*Mil.*	Military
Archit.	Architecture	*Min.*	Mining
Arith.	Arithmetic	*Motor.*	Motoring
art.	article	*Mount.*	Mountaineering
Astrol.	Astrology	*Mus.*	Music
Astron.	Astronomy	*Myth.*	Mythology
Austr.	Austrian	*n.*	neuter
aux.	auxiliary	*Naut.*	Nautical
Aviat.	Aviation	*Nav.*	Navigation
Bibl.	Biblical	*o.('s)*	one('s)
Bot.	Botany	*o.s.*	oneself
Br.	British	*obs.*	obsolete
Build.	Building	*Orn.*	Ornithology
Carp.	Carpentry	*p.*	person
Chem.	Chemistry	*Parl.*	Parliament
coll.	colloquial	*part.*	particle
collec.	collective	*pej.*	pejorative
Comm.	Commerce	*pers.*	person(al)
comp.	comparative	*Phil.*	Philosophy
conj.	conjunction	*Phonet.*	Phonetics
Cul.	Culinary	*Phot.*	Photography
Dat.	Dative	*Phys.*	Physics
def.	definite	*Physiol.*	Physiology
defect.	defective	*pl.*	plural
dem.	demonstrative	*Poet.*	Poetical
dial.	dialect	*Pol.*	Political
Eccl.	Ecclesiastical	*poss.*	possessive
Econ.	Economics	*p.p.*	past participle
Elec.	Electricity	*prec.*	preceded
emph.	emphatic	*pred.*	predicative
Engin.	Engineering	*prep.*	preposition
Ent.	Entomology	*pron.*	pronoun
excl.	exclamation	*Psych.*	Psychology
f.	feminine	*r.*	reflexive
fig.	figurative	*Rad.*	Radio
Fin.	Finance	*Railw.*	Railways
Footb.	Football	*reg.*	regular
Genit.	Genitive	*Rel.*	Religion
Geog.	Geography	*rel.*	relative
Geol.	Geology	*s.*	substantive
Geom.	Geometry	*Sch.*	School
Gram.	Grammar	*Scot.*	Scottish
Gymn.	Gymnastics	*sing.*	singular
Her.	Heraldry	*sl.*	slang
Hist.	History	*s.th.*	something
Hunt.	Hunting	*Tail.*	Tailoring
imper.	imperative	*Tech.*	Technical
impers.	impersonal	*Teleph.*	Telephone
Ind.	Industry	*temp.*	temporal
indecl.	indeclinable	*Text.*	Textiles
indef.	indefinite	*Theat.*	Theatre
infin.	infinitive	*Theol.*	Theology
insep.	inseparable	*Transp.*	Transport
int.	interjection	*Typ.*	Typography
interr.	interrogative	*Univ.*	University
intim.	intimate	*us.*	usually
iron.	ironical	*v.a.*	active *or* transitive verb
irr.	irregular	*v.n.*	neuter *or* intransitive verb
Ling.	Linguistics	*v.r.*	reflexive verb
Lit.	Literary	*Vet.*	Veterinary Science
Log.	Logic	*vulg.*	vulgar
		Zool.	Zoology

A

A, a [a:], *n. das A* (des **—s,** die **—s**) the
letter A; (*Mus.*) the note A; *A Dur*, A
major; *A Moll*, A minor.

Aal [a:l], *m.* (**—s,** *pl.* **—e**) eel.

Aas [a:s], *n.* (**—es,** *pl.* **Äser** *or* **—e**) carcass, carrion.

ab [ap], *adv.* off; down; away; (*Theat.*)
exit *or* exeunt, — *und zu*, now and
again, occasionally; *auf und —,* up
and down, to and fro. — *prep.* from;
— *Hamburg*, from Hamburg.

abändern ['apɛndərn], *v.a.* alter.

Abart ['apa:rt], *f.* (**—,** *pl.* **—en**) variety,
species.

Abbau ['apbau], *m.* (**—s,** *no pl.*) demolition, dismantling; reduction (of staff).

abberufen ['apbəru:fən], *v.a. irr.* recall.

abbestellen ['apbəʃtɛlən], *v.a.* countermand, annul, cancel (an order).

Abbild ['apbɪlt], *n.* (**—es,** *pl.* **—er**) copy,
image.

Abbildung ['apbɪlduŋ], *f.* (**—,** *pl.* **—en**)
illustration.

Abbitte ['apbɪtə], *f.* (**—,** *pl.* **—n**)
apology; — *leisten*, — *tun*, apologise.

abblenden ['apblɛndən], *v.a.* dim
(lights).

Abbruch ['apbrux], *m.* (**—s,** *pl.* **—e**)
breaking off; demolition; *einer Sache
— tun*, damage s.th.

abdanken ['apdaŋkən], *v.n.* resign,
abdicate, retire (from office).

abdecken ['apdɛkən], *v.a.* uncover, un-
roof; clear (the table).

Abdruck ['apdruk], *m.* (**—s,** *pl.* **—e**)
impression, copy, reprint, cast.

Abend ['a:bənt], *m.* (**—s,** *pl.* **—e**)
evening, eve.

Abendbrot ['a:bəntbro:t], *n.* (**—s,** *no
pl.*) evening meal, (*Am.*) supper.

Abendland ['a:bəntlant], *n.* (**—es,** *no
pl.*) occident, west.

Abendmahl ['a:bəntma:l], *n.* (**—s,** *no
pl.*) supper; *das heilige —*, Holy Communion, the Lord's Supper.

abends ['a:bənts], *adv.* in the evening, of
an evening.

Abenteuer ['a:bəntɔyər], *n.* (**—s,**
pl. **—**) adventure.

aber ['a:bər], *conj.* but, however;
(*emphatic*) — *ja!* yes, indeed! of
course! — *prefix.* again, once more.

Aberglaube ['a:bərɡlaubə], *m.* (**—ns,**
no pl.) superstition.

abermals ['a:bərma:ls], *adv.* again,
once more.

Abessinien [abɛ'si:njən], *n.* Abyssinia.

abfahren ['apfa:rən], *v.n. irr.* (*aux.* sein)
set out, depart, drive off.

Abfall ['apfal], *m.* (**—s,** *pl.* **—e**) scrap,
remnant; secession; slope; (*pl.*) waste,
refuse.

abfallen ['apfalən], *v.n. irr.* (*aux.* sein)
fall off; desert; slope.

abfällig ['apfɛlɪç], *adj.* derogatory.

abfangen ['apfaŋən], *v.a. irr.* intercept,
catch.

abfärben ['apfɛrbən], *v.n.* (*colours*)run;
stain; lose colour.

abfassen ['apfasən], *v.a.* compose, draft.

abfertigen ['apfɛrtɪɡən], *v.a.* despatch;
deal with, serve (a customer *or*
client).

abfeuern ['apfɔyərn], *v.a.* fire (off),
launch (rocket, missile).

abfinden ['apfɪndən], *v.a. irr.* indemnify,
compound with (o.'s creditors). — *v.r.
sich — mit*, put up with, come to
terms with.

Abflug ['apflu:k], *m.* (**—s,** *pl.* **—e**) take-
off, departure (by air).

Abfluß ['apflus], *m.* (**—sses,** *pl.* **—sse**)
flowing off; drain.

Abfuhr ['apfu:r], *f.* (**—,** *pl.* **—en**)
removal, collection (of refuse); (*coll.*)
rebuff.

abführen ['apfy:rən], *v.a.* arrest, lead
away. —*v.n.* (*Med.*) act as a purgative.

Abführmittel ['apfy:rmɪtəl], *n.* (**—s,**
pl. **—**) purgative, laxative.

Abgabe ['apɡa:bə], *f.* (**—,** *pl.* **—n**)
delivery, tax, duty, levy.

abgabepflichtig ['apɡa:bəpflɪçtɪç], *adj.*
taxable, subject to duty.

Abgang ['apɡaŋ], *m.* (**—(e)s,** *pl.* **—e**)
wastage, loss; departure; *Schul—*,
school-leaving.

abgängig ['apɡɛŋɪç], *adj.* lost, missing;
(*of goods*) saleable.

abgeben ['apɡe:bən], *v.a. irr.* deliver,
cede; give (an opinion). — *v.r. sich mit
etwas, —* concern o.s. with s.th.

abgedroschen ['apɡədrɔʃən], *adj.*
(*phrases etc.*) trite, hackneyed.

abgefeimt ['apɡəfaɪmt], *adj.* cunning,
crafty.

abgegriffen ['apɡəɡrɪfən], *adj.* well
thumbed, worn.

abgehen ['apɡe:ən], *v.n. irr.* (*aux.* sein)
leave, retire; branch off; (*Theat.*) make
an exit.

abgelebt ['apɡəle:pt], *adj.* (*of humans*)
decrepit, worn out.

abgelegen ['apɡəle:ɡən], *adj.* remote,
distant.

abgemacht ['apɡəmaxt], *adj., int.*
agreed! done!

abgeneigt ['apɡənaɪkt], *adj.* disinclined, averse.

Abgeordnete ['apɡəɔrdnətə], *m., f.*
(**—n,** *pl.* **—n**) political representative,
deputy, Member of Parliament.

Abgesandte ['apɡəzantə], *m., f.* (**—n,**
pl. **—n**) delegate, ambassador.

abgeschieden

abgeschieden [ˈapgəʃiːdən], *adj.* secluded, remote; deceased.

abgeschmackt [ˈapgəʃmakt], *adj.* insipid.

abgesehen [ˈapgəzeːən], *adv.* — *von*, apart from, except for.

abgespannt [ˈapgəʃpant], *adj.* worn out, run down, exhausted.

abgestorben [ˈapgəʃtɔrbən], *adj.* dead, numb.

abgetan [ˈapgətaːn], *adj.* finished, over, done with; *damit ist die Sache* —, that finishes the matter.

abgetragen [ˈapgətraːgən], *adj.* (*clothes*) shabby, threadbare.

abgewöhnen [ˈapgəvøːnən], *v.a. einem etwas* —, free (rid) s.o. from (of) a habit, wean from.

abgrasen [ˈapgraːzən], *v.a.* (*animals*) graze.

Abgrund [ˈapgrunt], *m.* (—es, *pl.* ⁙e) abyss, precipice.

Abguss [ˈapgus], *m.* (—es, *pl.* ⁙e) cast, plaster-cast, mould.

abhalten [ˈaphaltən], *v.a. irr.* restrain, hold back; hold (meeting etc.).

abhandeln [ˈaphandəln], *v.a. einem etwas* —, bargain for s.th.

abhanden [apˈhandən], *adv.* mislaid; — *kommen*, get lost.

Abhandlung [ˈaphandluŋ], *f.* (—, *pl.* —en) treatise, dissertation; (*pl.*) proceedings.

Abhang [ˈaphaŋ], *m.* (—es, *pl.* ⁙e) slope; declivity.

abhängen [ˈaphɛŋən], *v.a. irr.* take off, unhook; *von etwas oder jemandem* —, depend on s.th. or s.o.

abhärten [ˈaphɛrtən], *v.a.* inure against rigours, toughen.

abheben [ˈapheːbən], *v.a. irr.* draw (money from bank).

abhold [ˈaphɔlt], *adj.* averse to (*Dat.*).

abholen [ˈaphoːlən], *v.a. etwas* —, fetch, collect s.th.; *einen* —, meet s.o. (at the station etc.).

Abitur [abiˈtuːr], *n.* (—s, *no pl.*) matriculation examination.

Abiturient [abituˈrjɛnt], *m.* (—en, *pl.* —en) matriculation candidate.

Abkehr [ˈapkeːr], *f.* (—, *no pl.*) turning away, renunciation.

abklären [ˈapklɛːrən], *v.a.* (*Chem.*) filter, clear.

Abkommen [ˈapkɔmən], *n.* (—s, *pl.* —) treaty, agreement, contract.

Abkömmling [ˈapkœmliŋ], *m.* (—s, *pl.* —e) descendant.

abkühlen [ˈapkyːlən], *v.a.* cool, chill.

Abkunft [ˈapkunft], *f.* (—, *no pl.*) descent, origin.

abkürzen [ˈapkyrtsən], *v.a.* shorten, abridge, curtail.

abladen [ˈapladən], *v.a. irr.* unload, dump.

Ablaß [ˈaplas], *m.* (—sses, *pl.* ⁙sse) (*Eccl.*) indulgence.

ablassen [ˈaplasən], *v.n. irr. von etwas* —, desist from, refrain from s.th.— *v.a. einem etwas billig* —, reduce the price of s.th. for s.o.

Ablauf [ˈaplauf], *m.* (—es, *no pl.*) (*water*) drainage; (*ticket*) expiration; lapse (of time); (*bill*) maturity.

ablaufen [ˈaplaufən], *v.n. irr.* (*aux.* sein) (*water*) run off; (*ticket*) expire; *gut* —, turn out well.

Ableben [ˈapleːbən], *n.* (—s, *no pl.*) decease, death.

ablegen [ˈapleːgən], *v.a.* (*clothes*) take off; (*documents*) file; *Rechenschaft* —, account for; *eine Prüfung* —, take an examination.

Ableger [ˈapleːgər], *m.* (—s, *pl.* —) (*Hort.*) cutting.

Ablegung [ˈapleːguŋ], *f.* (—, *no pl.*) making (of a vow); taking (of an oath).

ablehnen [ˈapleːnən], *v.a.* refuse, decline.

ableiten [ˈaplaitən], *v.a.* divert, draw off; (*water*) drain; (*words*) derive from.

ablenken [ˈaplɛŋkən], *v.a.* (*aux.* haben) *einen von etwas* —, divert s.o.'s attention from s.th., distract.

ablesen [ˈapleːzən], *v.a. irr.* (*meter*) read off; (*field*) glean.

abliefern [ˈapliːfərn], *v.a.* deliver.

ablösen [ˈapløːzən], *v.a. einen* —, take the place of s.o., (*Mil.*) relieve; detach (a stamp from a letter etc.).

abmachen [ˈapmaxən], *v.a.* undo, detach; settle, arrange.

abmagern [ˈapmaːgərn], *v.n.* (*aux.* sein) get thinner, waste away.

Abmarsch [ˈapmarʃ], *m.* (—es, *no pl.*) (*Mil.*) marching off.

abmelden [ˈapmɛldən], *v.r. sich* —, give notice of departure.

abmessen [ˈapmɛsən], *v.a. irr.* measure (off), gauge.

abmühen [ˈapmyːən], *v.r. sich* —, exert o.s., strive.

Abnahme [ˈapnaːmə], *f.* (—, *pl.* —n) decline, loss of weight; (*moon*) waning; (*goods*) taking delivery.

abnehmen [ˈapneːmən], *v.n. irr.* lose weight; (*moon*) wane. — *v.a.* (*hat*) take off; *einem etwas* —, relieve s.o. (of trouble or work).

Abneigung [ˈapnaiguŋ], *f.* (—, *pl.* —en) antipathy, dislike.

abnutzen [ˈapnutsən], *v.a.* wear out by use.

Abonnement [abɔnəˈmaŋ], *n.* (—s, *pl.* —s) (*newspaper*) subscription; (*railway*) season-ticket.

Abonnent [abɔˈnɛnt], *m.* (—en, *pl.* —en) subscriber.

abonnieren [abɔˈniːrən], *v.a.* subscribe to (a paper).

Abordnung [ˈapɔrdnuŋ], *f.* (—, *pl.* —en) delegation, deputation.

Abort [aˈbɔrt], *m.* (—s, *pl.* —e) lavatory, toilet.

Abortus [aˈbɔrtus], *m.* (—us, *no pl.*) (*Med.*) abortion.

abplagen [ˈapplaːgən], *v.r. sich* —, slave, toil.

abprallen [ˈappralən], *v.n.* (*aux.* sein) *von etwas* —, bounce off, rebound.

abquälen ['apkvɛ:lən], v.r. sich —, toil, make o.s. weary (mit, with).

abraten ['apra:tən], v.n. irr. einem von etwas —, dissuade s.o. from, advise or warn s.o. against.

abräumen ['aprɔymən], v.a. remove; den Tisch —, clear the table.

abrechnen ['aprɛçnən], v.a. reckon up. — v.n. mit einem —, settle accounts with s.o., (coll.) get even with s.o.

Abrede ['apre:də], f. (—, pl. —n) agreement, arrangement; in — stellen, deny.

abreißen ['apraɪsən], v.a. irr. tear off.

abrichten ['apriçtən], v.a. (dogs) train, (horses) break in.

abriegeln ['apri:gəln], v.a. bolt, bar.

Abriß ['aprɪs], m. (—sses, pl. —sse) sketch; summary, synopsis.

abrollen ['aprɔlən], v.a. uncoil. — v.n. (aux. sein) roll off.

abrücken ['aprykən], v.a. move away. —v.n. (aux. sein) (Mil.) march off.

Abruf ['apru:f], m. (—es, no pl.) recall (from a post).

abrunden ['aprundən], v.a. round off.

abrupfen ['aprupfən], v.a. (feathers) pluck; (flowers) pluck off.

abrüsten ['aprystən], v.n. disarm.

Abrüstung ['aprystuŋ], f. (—, no pl.) disarmament.

abrutschen ['aprutʃən], v.n. (aux. sein) slide, slither down.

Absage ['apza:gə], f. (—, pl. —n) cancellation, refusal.

absagen ['apza:gən], v.n. refuse, beg to be excused, decline (an invitation).

Absatz ['apzats], m. (—es, pl. ˙e) (shoe) heel; (letter) paragraph; (Comm.) guter —, ready sale.

abschaffen ['apʃafən], v.a. abolish, do away with.

abschälen ['apʃɛ:lən], v.a. peel. — v.r. sich —, peel off.

abschätzen ['apʃɛtsən], v.a. estimate, appraise; (taxes) assess.

Abschaum ['apʃaum], m. (—es, no pl.) scum.

Abscheu ['apʃɔy], m. (—s, no pl.) abhorrence, detestation, loathing.

abscheulich ['apʃɔyliç], adj. abominable, repulsive.

abschieben ['apʃi:bən], v.a. irr. shove off, push off; schieb ab! scram!

Abschied ['apʃi:t], m. (—s, pl. —e) leave, departure, farewell; discharge; resignation.

abschießen ['apʃi:sən], v.a. irr. shoot off; discharge; (gun) fire; den Vogel —, win the prize.

abschinden ['apʃindən], v.r. irr. sich —, exhaust o.s. with hard work.

abschirren ['apʃirən], v.a. unharness.

abschlagen ['apʃla:gən], v.a. irr. (attack) beat off; (branches) lop off; einem etwas —, deny s.o. s.th.; eine Bitte —, refuse a request.

abschlägig ['apʃlɛgiç], adj. negative.

Abschlagszahlung ['apʃlaktsa:luŋ], f. (—, pl. —en) payment by instalments.

abschleifen ['apʃlaifən], v.a. irr. grind off.

abschleppen ['apʃlɛpən], v.a. (car) tow (away). — v.r. sich —, wear o.s. out by carrying heavy loads.

abschließen ['apʃli:sən], v.a. irr. lock up; (work) conclude; (accounts) balance; einen Vertrag —, conclude an agreement.

Abschluß ['apʃlus], m. (—sses, pl. ˙sse) settlement, winding-up.

abschneiden ['apʃnaidən], v.a. irr. cut off. — v.n. gut —, come off well.

Abschnitt ['apʃnit], m. (—es, pl. —e) section; (book) paragraph.

abschnüren ['apʃny:rən], v.a. lace up, tie up.

abschrecken ['apʃrɛkən], v.a. deter, frighten.

abschreiben ['apʃraibən], v.a. irr. copy, transcribe; crib; eine Schuld —, write off a debt.

Abschrift ['apʃrift], f. (—, pl. —en) copy, transcript, duplicate; beglaubigte —, certified copy.

Abschuß ['apʃus], m. (—sses, pl. ˙sse) act of firing (a gun), shooting down (aircraft).

abschüssig ['apʃysiç], adj. steep.

abschütteln ['apʃytəln], v.a. shake off, cast off.

abschwächen ['apʃvɛçən], v.a. weaken, diminish.

abschweifen ['apʃvaifən], v.n. (aux. sein) digress (from), deviate.

abschwenken ['apʃvɛŋkən], v.n. (aux. sein) wheel off (or aside).

abschwören ['apʃvø:rən], v.a. irr. abjure, renounce by oath.

absehbar ['apze:ba:r], adj. imaginable, conceivable, foreseeable.

absehen ['apze:ən], v.a., v.n. irr. einem etwas —, copy s.th. from s.o.; auf etwas —, aim at s.th.; von etwas —, waive s.th.; refrain from s.th.

abseits ['apzaits], adv., prep. (Genit.) aside; — von, away from.

Absender ['apzɛndər], m. (—s, pl.—) sender; (Comm.) consigner.

absetzen ['apzɛtsən], v.a. set down; dismiss, deprive of office; depose; (Comm.) sell, dispose of.

Absicht ['apziçt], f. (—, pl. —en) intention, purpose, aim.

absondern ['apzɔndərn], v.a. separate, set apart; (Med.) secrete. — v.r. sich —, seclude o.s. from.

abspannen ['apʃpanən], v.a. unharness.

absparen ['apʃpa:rən], v.n. sich etwas vom Munde —, stint o.s. for s.th.

abspenstig ['apʃpɛnstiç], adj.—machen, alienate s.o.'s affections, entice s.o. away; — werden, desert.

absperren ['apʃpɛrən], v.a. (door) lock, shut up; (street) close, barricade; (gas, water) turn off.

absprechen ['apʃprɛçən], v.a. irr. einem das Recht —, deprive s.o. of the right to do s.th.

3

abspülen ['apʃpyːlən], *v.a.* wash up, rinse.

abstammen ['apʃtamən], *v.n.* (*aux.* sein) descend from, originate from.

Abstand ['apʃtant], *m.* (—es, pl. ⁻e) distance; *von etwas* — *nehmen*, refrain from doing s.th.

abstatten ['apʃtatən], *v.a. einen Besuch* —, pay a visit; *einen Bericht* —, report on; *Dank* —, return thanks.

abstechen ['apʃtɛçən], *v.a. irr. Tiere* —, slaughter animals. — *v.n. von etwas* —, contrast with s.th.

Abstecher ['apʃtɛçər], *m.* (—s, pl. —) short trip, excursion; detour.

abstecken ['apʃtɛkən], *v.a.* mark off, peg out.

absteigen ['apʃtaɪgən], *v.n. irr.* (*aux.* sein) descend, alight, dismount.

abstellen ['apʃtɛlən], *v.a.* put s.th. down; (*gas, water*) turn off.

absterben ['apʃtɛrbən], *v.n. irr.* (*aux.* sein) wither; die.

Abstieg ['apʃtiːk], *m.* (—es, *no pl.*) descent.

Abstimmung ['apʃtimuŋ], *f.* (—, pl. —en) (*Parl.*) division; referendum, voting.

abstoßen ['apʃtoːsən], *v.a. irr.* push off, kick off. —*v.n.* (*Naut.*) set sail.

abstoßend ['apʃtoːsənt], *adj.* repulsive, repugnant.

abstreifen ['apʃtraɪfən], *v.a. irr.* strip off, pull off; cast, shed.

abstufen ['apʃtuːfən], *v.a.* grade.

abstumpfen ['apʃtumpfən], *v.a.* blunt, dull, take the edge off.

abstürzen ['apʃtyrtsən], *v.n.* (*aux.* sein) (*person*) fall; fall down; (*Aviat.*) crash.

Abt [apt], *m.* (—es, pl. ⁻e) abbot.

Abtei ['aptaɪ], *f.* (—, pl. —en) abbey.

Abteil ['aptaɪl], *n.* (—s, pl. —e) compartment.

abteilen ['aptaɪlən], *v.a.* divide, partition.

Abteilung [ap'taɪluŋ], *f.* (—, pl. —en) section, department.

Äbtissin [ɛp'tɪsɪn], *f.* (—, pl. —nen) abbess.

abtöten ['aptøːtən], *v.a.* mortify, deaden.

abtragen ['aptraːgən], *v.a. irr.* carry away; (*building*) demolish; (*dress, shoes*) wear out; *eine Schuld* —, pay a debt.

abtreiben ['aptraɪbən], *v.a. irr.* (*cattle*) drive off; procure an abortion. —*v.n.* (*aux.* sein) (*ship*) drift off.

Abtreibung ['aptraɪbuŋ], *f.* (—, pl. —en) abortion.

abtrennen ['aptrɛnən], *v.a.* (*s.th. sewn*) unpick; separate.

Abtretung ['aptreːtuŋ], *f.* (—, pl. —en) cession; conveyance.

Abtritt ['aptrɪt], *m.* (—es, pl. —e) W.C.; (*Theat.*) exit *or* exeunt.

abtrocknen ['aptrɔknən], *v.a.* dry.

abtrünnig ['aptrynɪç], *adj.* disloyal, faithless.

aburteilen ['apurtaɪlən], *v.a.* pass judgment on.

abwägen ['apvɛːgən], *v.a. gegeneinander* —, weigh against each other.

abwälzen ['apvɛltsən], *v.a. etwas von sich* —, clear o.s. from s.th.

abwandeln ['apvandəln], *v.a.* change; (*verbs*) conjugate; (*nouns*) decline.

abwärts ['apvɛrts], *prep., adv.* downward.

abwaschen ['apvaʃən], *v.a. irr.* wash up.

abwechseln ['apvɛksəln], *v.a.* vary, alternate.

Abweg ['apveːk], *m.* (—es, pl. —e) wrong way; *auf* —*e geraten*, go astray.

abwehren ['apveːrən], *v.a.* ward off, parry.

abweichen ['apvaɪçən], *v.n. irr.* (*aux.* sein) — *von*, deviate from.

abweisen ['apvaɪzən], *v.a. irr.* refuse admittance to, rebuff.

abwenden ['apvɛndən], *v.a. irr.* avert, prevent. — *v.r. sich* —, turn away from.

abwesend ['apveːzənt], *adj.* absent.

Abwesenheit ['apveːzənhaɪt], *f.* (—, pl. —en) absence.

abwickeln ['apvɪkəln], *v.a.* uncoil; (*business*) wind up.

abwischen ['apvɪʃən], *v.a.* wipe clean; *sich die Stirn* —, mop o.'s brow.

abzahlen ['aptsaːlən], *v.a.* pay off; pay by instalments.

abzehren ['aptseːrən], *v.n.* (*aux.* sein) waste away.

Abzeichen ['aptsaɪçən], *n.* (—s, pl. —) badge, insignia.

abzeichnen ['apsaɪçnən], *v.a.* sketch, draw from a model. — *v.r. sich* —, become clear.

abziehen ['aptsiːən], *v.a. irr.* deduct, subtract; (*knife*) sharpen; strip (a bed). — *v.n.* (*aux.* sein) depart; (*Mil.*) march off.

Abzug ['aptsuːk], *m.* (—es, pl. ⁻e) retreat, departure; photographic copy; — *der Kosten*, deduction of charges; (*steam, air*) outlet.

abzweigen ['aptsvaɪgən], *v.n.* (*aux.* sein) fork off, branch off.

Achsel ['aksəl], *f.* (—, pl. —n) shoulder; *die* —*n zucken*, shrug o.'s shoulders.

Acht [axt], *f.* (—, *no pl.*) attention, care, caution, heed; *acht geben*, pay attention; *sich in* — *acht nehmen*, be careful; ban, excommunication, outlawry; *in* — *und Bann tun*, outlaw, proscribe.

acht [axt], *num. adj.* eight; *in* — *Tagen*, in a week; *vor* — *Tagen*, a week ago.

achtbar ['axtbaːr], *adj.* respectable.

achten ['axtən], *v.a.* hold in esteem, value; — *auf*, pay attention to, keep an eye on.

ächten ['ɛxtən], *v.a.* ban, outlaw, proscribe.

achtlos ['axtloːs], *adj.* inattentive, negligent.

achtsam ['axtzaːm], *adj.* attentive, careful.

Achtung ['axtuŋ], *f.* (—, *no pl.*) esteem, regard; (*Mil.*) attention!

Ächtung ['ɛxtuŋ], *f.* (—, *no pl.*) ban, proscription.

achtzehn ['axtseːn], *num. adj.* eighteen.

achtzig ['axtsıç], *num. adj.* eighty.

ächzen ['ɛçtsən], *v.n.* groan.

Acker ['akər], *m.* (—s, *pl.* ⁼) field, arable land; *den — bestellen*, till the soil.

ackern ['akərn], *v.n.* till (the land).

addieren [a'di:rən], *v.a.* add, add up.

Adel ['a:dəl], *m.* (—s, *no pl.*) nobility, aristocracy.

ad(e)lig ['a:dlıç], *adj.* of noble birth, aristocratic.

Ader ['a:dər], *f.* (—, *pl.* —n) vein; *zu — lassen*, bleed s.o.

Adler ['a:dlər], *m.* (—s, *pl.* —) eagle.

Adresse [a'drɛsə], *f.* (—, *pl.* —n) address.

adrett [a'drɛt], *adj.* neat, adroit, smart.

Affe ['afə], *m.* (—n, *pl.* —n) ape, monkey; *(fig.)* fool.

affektiert [afɛk'ti:rt], *adj.* affected, giving o.s. airs.

äffen ['ɛfən], *v.a.* ape, mimic.

Afghanistan [af'ganistan], *n.* Afghanistan.

Afrika ['a:frika], *n.* Africa.

After ['aftər], *m.* (—s, *pl.* —) anus.

Agentur [agɛn'tu:r], *f.* (—, *pl.* —en) agency.

Agraffe [a'grafə], *f.* (—, *pl.* —n) brooch, clasp.

Agrarier [a'gra:rjər], *m.* (—s, *pl.* —) landed proprietor.

Ägypten [ɛ'gyptən], *n.* Egypt.

Ahle ['a:lə], *f.* (—, *pl.* —n) awl, bodkin.

Ahn [a:n], *m.* (—en, *pl.* —en) ancestor, forefather.

ahnden ['a:ndən], *v.a.* avenge, punish.

Ahne ['a:nə] *see* **Ahn**.

ähneln ['ɛ:nəln], *v.a.* resemble, look like.

ahnen ['a:nən], *v.a., v.n.* have a presentiment, foresee, have a hunch.

ähnlich ['ɛ:nlıç], *adj.* resembling, like, similar.

Ahnung ['a:nuŋ], *f.* (—, *pl.* —en) foreboding, presentiment, idea, *(Am.)* hunch.

Ahorn ['a:hɔrn], *m.* (—s, *pl.* —e) *(Bot.)* maple.

Ähre ['ɛ:rə], *f.* (—, *pl.* —n) ear of corn.

Akademiker [aka'de:mɪkər], *m.* (—s, *pl.* —) university graduate.

akademisch [aka'de:mɪʃ], *adj.* academic; *— gebildet*, with a university education.

Akazie [a'ka:tsjə], *f.* (—, *pl.* —n) *(Bot.)* acacia.

akklimatisieren [aklimati'zi:rən], *v.r. sich —*, become acclimatised.

Akkord [a'kɔrt], *m.* (—es, *pl.* —e) *(Mus.)* chord; *in — arbeiten*, work on piece-rates.

Akt [akt], *m.* (—es, *pl.* —e) deed, action; *(Theat.)* act; *(Art)* (depiction of) the nude.

Akte ['aktə], *f.* (—, *pl.* —n) document, deed; *(pl.)* records, files; *zu den —n legen*, pigeonhole, shelve.

Aktenstück ['aktənʃtyk], *n.* (—es, *pl.* —e) official document, file.

Aktie ['aktsjə], *f.* (—, *pl.* —n) *(Comm.)* share, *(Am.)* stock.

Aktiengesellschaft ['aktsjəngəzɛlʃaft], *f.* (—, *pl.* —en) joint stock company.

Aktionär [aktsjo'nɛ:r], *m.* (—s, *pl.* —e) shareholder, *(Am.)* stockholder.

Aktiv ['akti:f], *n.* (—s, *pl.* —e) *(Gram.)* active voice.

Aktiva [ak'ti:va], *n. pl.* *(Comm.)* assets.

aktuell [aktu'ɛl], *adj.* topical.

akzentuieren [aktsɛntu'i:rən], *v.a.* accentuate, stress, emphasize.

Albanien [al'ba:njən], *n.* Albania.

albern ['albərn], *adj.* silly, foolish.

Aliment [ali'mɛnt], *n.* (—es, *pl.* —e) *(usually pl.*—e) alimony, maintenance.

Alkali [al'ka:li], *n.* (—s, *pl.* —en) alkali.

Alkohol ['alkoho:l], *m.* (—s, *no pl.*) alcohol.

Alkoholiker [alko'ho:lıkər], *m.* (—s, *pl.* —) drunkard, alcoholic.

All [al], *n.* (—s, *no pl.*) the universe, (outer) space.

all [al], *adj.* all, entire, whole; every, each, any.

alle ['alə], *adj.* all, everybody; *— beide*, both of them.

Allee [a'le:], *f.* (—, *pl.* —n) tree-lined walk, avenue.

allein [a'laın], *adj.* alone, sole. *— adv.* solely, only, merely. *—conj. (obs.)* only, but, however.

alleinig [a'laınıç], *adj.* sole, only, exclusive.

allenfalls [alən'fals], *adv.* possibly, perhaps, if need be.

allenthalben [alənt'halbən], *adv.* everywhere, in all places.

allerdings [alər'dıŋs], *adv.* of course, indeed, nevertheless.

allerhand [alər'hant], *adj.* of all sorts *or* kinds, various; *das ist ja —!* I say!

Allerheiligen [alər'haılıgən], *pl.* All Saints' Day.

allerlei [alər'laı], *adj.* miscellaneous, various.

allerliebst [alər'li:pst], *adj.* *(Am.)* cute; charming.

allerseits ['alərzaıts], *adv.* generally, on all sides, universally.

alles ['aləs], *adj.* everything, all.

allgemein [algə'maın], *adj.* universal, common, general.

alliieren [ali'i:rən], *v.a., v.n.* ally (o.s.).

allmächtig [al'mɛçtıç], *adj.* omnipotent.

allmählich [al'mɛ:lıç], *adj.* by degrees, gradual.

allseitig ['alzaıtıç], *adj.* universal, *(Am.)* all-round.

Alltag ['alta:k], *m.* (—s, *pl.* —e) working day, week-day.

allwissend [al'vısənt], *adj.* omniscient.

allzu ['altzu:], *adv.* too, much too.

Alm [alm], *f.* (—, *pl.* —en) Alpine meadow.

Almosen [al'mo:zən], *n.* (—s, *pl.* —) alms, charity.

Alp [alp], *f.* (—, *pl.* —en) *(mostly pl.*) mountain(s), Alps.

Alpdrücken ['alpdrykən], *n.* (—s, *no pl.*) nightmare.

5

als [als], *conj.* than; *(after comparatives)* than; as, like; but; *er hat nichts — Schulden*, he has nothing but debts; *(temp.)* when, as.

alsbald [als'balt], *adv.* forthwith.

also ['alzo:], *adv.* thus, so, in this manner. — *conj.* consequently, therefore.

Alt [alt], *m.* (—s, *pl.* —e) *(Mus.)* alto.

alt [alt], *adj.* old, ancient; aged; antique.

Altan [al'ta:n], *m.* (—s, *pl.* —e) balcony, gallery.

Altar [al'ta:r], *m.* (—s, *pl.* ⸚e) altar.

altbacken ['altbakən], *adj.* stale.

Alter ['altər], *n.* (—s, *no pl.*) age, old age; epoch.

altern ['altərn], *v.n.* (*aux.* sein) grow old.

Altertum ['altərtu:m], *n.* (—s, *pl.* ⸚er) antiquity.

Altistin [al'tɪstɪn], *f.* (—, *pl.* —nen) *(Mus.)* contralto.

altklug ['altklu:k], *adj.* precocious.

ältlich ['ɛltlɪç], *adj.* elderly.

Altweibersommer [alt'vaɪbərzɔmər], *m.* (—s, *pl.* —) Indian summer.

Amboß ['ambɔs], *m.* (—sses, *pl.* —sse) anvil.

Ameise ['a:maɪzə], *f.* (—, *pl.* —n) *(Ent.)* ant.

Amerika [a'me:rika], *n.* America.

Amme ['amə], *f.* (—, *pl.* —n) wet nurse.

Ammoniak [amon'jak], *n.* (—s, *no pl.*) ammonia.

Ampel ['ampəl], *f.* (—, *pl.* —n) (hanging) light, lamp, lantern; traffic light.

Ampfer ['ampfər], *m.* (—s, *pl.* —) *(Bot.)* sorrel, dock.

Amsel ['amzəl], *f.* (—, *pl.* —n) *(Orn.)* blackbird.

Amt [amt], *n.* (—es, *pl.* ⸚er) office, post, employment; administration, domain, jurisdiction; place of public business.

amtlich ['amtlɪç], *adj.* official.

Amtmann ['amtman], *m.* (—s, *pl.* ⸚er) bailiff.

Amtsblatt ['amtsblat], *n.* (—es, *pl.* ⸚er) official gazette.

Amtsgericht ['amtsgərɪçt], *n.* (—s, *pl.* —e) county court; *(Am.)* district court.

amüsieren [amy'zi:rən], *v.a.* amuse.— *v.r. sich* —, enjoy o.s.

an [an], *prep.* (*Dat.* or *Acc.*), at, to, on.

analog [ana'lo:k], *adj.* analogous.

Ananas ['ananas], *f.* (—, *pl.* —) pineapple.

Anatom [ana'to:m], *m.* (—en, *pl.* —en) anatomist.

anbahnen ['anba:nən], *v.a.* initiate, open up, pave the way for.

anbändeln ['anbɛndəln], *v.n.* — *mit*, flirt with, make up to.

Anbau ['anbau], *m.* (—s, *pl.* —ten) *(grain)* cultivation; annex(e), wing (of building).

anbauen ['anbauən], *v.a.* cultivate; add to a building.

anbei [an'baɪ], *adv.* enclosed (in letter).

anbeißen ['anbaɪsən], *v.a. irr.* bite at,

take a bite of. — *v.n.* (*fish*) bite; *(coll.)* take the bait.

anbelangen ['anbəlaŋən], *v.a.* concern.

anberaumen ['anbəraumən], *v.a.* fix (a date).

anbeten ['anbe:tən], *v.a.* worship, adore, idolise.

anbiedern ['anbi:dərn], *v.r. sich mit einem* —, chum up with s.o.

anbieten ['anbi:tən], *v.a. irr.* offer.

anbinden ['anbɪndən], *v.a. irr.* tie on, bind to; *kurz angebunden sein*, be curt.

Anblick ['anblɪk], *m.* (—s, *no pl.*) view, sight, aspect, spectacle.

anbrechen ['anbrɛçən], *v.a. irr.* begin; break; start on. —*v.n.* dawn.

anbrennen ['anbrɛnən], *v.a. irr.* light, set fire to, burn. — *v.n.* (*aux.* sein) catch fire; burn.

anbringen ['anbrɪŋən], *v.a. irr.* fit to, place.

Anbruch ['anbrux], *m.* (—s, *no pl.*) beginning; — *der Nacht*, night-fall.

anbrüllen ['anbrylən], *v.a.* roar at.

Andacht ['andaxt], *f.* (—, *pl.* —en) *(Eccl.)* devotion(s).

andächtig ['andɛxtɪç], *adj.* devout.

andauern ['andauərn], *v.n.* last, continue.

Andenken ['andɛŋkən], *n.* (—s, *pl.* —) memory; keepsake; souvenir.

anderer ['andərər], *adj.* other, different; *ein* —, another.

andermal ['andərma:l], *adv. ein* —, another time.

ändern ['ɛndərn], *v.a.* alter, change.

andernfalls ['andərnfals], *adv.* otherwise, or else.

anders ['andərs], *adv.* differently, in another manner, otherwise.

anderthalb ['andərthalp], *adj.* one and a half.

anderweitig ['andərvaɪtɪç], *adj.* elsewhere.

andeuten ['andɔytən], *v.a.* hint at, intimate, indicate.

Andrang ['andraŋ], *m.* (—es, *no pl.*) throng, crowd.

aneignen ['anaɪgnən], *v.r. sich etwas* —, appropriate s.th.; *(an opinion)* adopt.

anekeln ['ane:kəln], *v.a.* disgust.

Anerbieten ['anɛrbi:tən], *n.* (—s, *pl.* —) offer.

anerkennen ['anɛrkɛnən], *v.a. irr.* acknowledge, appreciate, recognize, accept.

anfachen ['anfaxən], *v.a.* kindle (a flame).

Anfahrt ['anfa:rt], *f.* (—, *pl.* —en) drive; *(down a mine)* descent; *(Am.)* drive-way.

Anfall ['anfal], *m.* (—s, *pl.* ⸚e) attack, assault; *(Med.)* seizure, fit; *(mood)* fit, burst.

anfallen ['anfalən], *v.a. irr. einen* —, attack s.o.

Anfang ['anfaŋ], *m.* (—s, *pl.* ⸚e) beginning, start, commencement.

anfangen ['anfaŋən], *v.a. irr.* begin, start. — *v.n.* begin, originate.

Anfänger ['anfɛŋər], *m.* (—s, *pl.* —) beginner, novice.

anfänglich ['anfɛŋlɪç], *adv.* in the beginning, at first, initially.

anfassen ['anfasən], *v.a.* take hold of; touch; seize.

anfechtbar ['anfɛçtba:r], *adj.* disputable, refutable, debatable.

anfechten ['anfɛçtən], *v.a.* (*a will, a verdict*) contest; (*jurors*) challenge.

anfeinden ['anfaɪndən], *v.a.* show enmity to.

anfertigen ['anfɛrtɪgən], *v.a.* make, manufacture, prepare; (*a list*) draw up.

anflehen ['anfle:ən], *v.a.* implore, beseech.

Anflug ['anflu:k], *m.* (—s, *pl.* ⸚e) (*Aviat.*) approach; (*beard*) down; touch.

anfordern ['anfɔrdərn], *v.a.* demand, claim.

Anfrage ['anfra:gə], *f.* (—, *pl.* —n) enquiry.

anfügen ['anfy:gən], *v.a.* join to, annex.

anführen ['anfy:rən], *v.a.* lead; adduce, quote (examples), cite; *einen* —, dupe s.o., take s.o. in.

Anführungszeichen ['anfy:ruŋstsaɪçən], *n.* (—s, *pl.* —) inverted commas, quotation marks.

anfüllen ['anfylən], *v.a. wieder* —, replenish.

Angabe ['anga:bə], *f.* (—, *pl.* —n) declaration, statement; data; instruction; bragging.

angeben ['ange:bən], *v.a. irr.* declare, state; *den Ton* —, lead the fashion; *den Wert* —, declare the value of.— *v.n. groß* —, brag, show off.

Angeber ['ange:bər], *m.* (—s, *pl.* —) informer; braggart.

Angebinde ['angəbɪndə], *n.* (—s, *pl.* —) (*obs.*) present, gift.

angeblich ['ange:plɪç], *adj.* ostensible, alleged, so-called.

angeboren ['angəbo:rən], *adj.* innate, inborn.

Angebot ['angəbo:t], *n.* (—es, *pl.* —e) offer, tender, bid; (*Comm.*) — *und Nachfrage,* supply and demand.

angebracht ['angəbraxt], *adj.* apt, appropriate, opportune.

angedeihen ['angədaɪən], *v.n. einem etwas* — *lassen,* bestow s.th. on s.o.

angegossen ['angəgɔsən], *adj. sitzt wie* —, it fits like a glove.

angehen ['ange:ən], *v.a. irr. einen um etwas* —, apply to s.o. for s.th.; *das geht Dich nichts an,* that is none of your business.

angehören ['angəhø:rən], *v.n.* belong to.

Angehörige ['angəhø:rɪgə], *m., f.* (—n, *pl.* —n) near relative; next of kin.

Angeklagte ['angəkla:ktə], *m., f.* (—n, *pl.* —n) the accused, defendant, prisoner at the bar.

Angel ['aŋəl], *f.* (—, *pl.* —n) fishing-rod;

(*door*) hinge, pivot; *zwischen Tür und* —, in passing.

angelegen ['angəle:gən], *adj. sich etwas* — *sein⸗lassen,* interest o.s. in s.th., concern o.s. in s.th.; *ich werde es mir* — *sein lassen,* I shall make it my business.

Angelegenheit ['angəle:gənhaɪt], *f.* (—, *pl.* —en) concern, matter, affair.

angeln ['aŋəln], *v.a.* fish, angle.

angemessen ['angəmɛsən], *adj.* proper, suitable, appropriate.

angenehm ['angəne:m], *adj.* acceptable, agreeable, pleasing, pleasant.

angenommen ['angənɔmən], *conj.* — *daß,* given that, supposing that, say.

Anger ['aŋər], *m.* (—s, *pl.* —) grass-plot; green, common.

angesehen ['angəze:ən], *adj.* respected, esteemed, distinguished.

Angesicht ['angəzɪçt]. *n.* (—s, *pl.* —er) face, countenance.

angestammt ['angəʃtamt], *adj.* ancestral, hereditary.

Angestellte ['angəʃtɛltə], *m., f.* (—n, *pl.* —n) employee; (*pl.*) staff.

Angler ['aŋlər], *m.* (—s, *pl.* —) angler, fisherman.

angliedern ['angli:dərn], *v.a.* annex, attach.

Anglist [aŋ'glɪst], *m.* (—en, *pl.* —en) (*Univ.*) professor or student of English.

angreifen ['angraɪfən], *v.a. irr.* handle, touch; (*capital*) break into; attack, assail; *es greift mich an,* it taxes my strength.

angrenzen ['angrɛntsən], *v.n.* border upon, adjoin.

Angriff ['angrɪf], *m.* (—s, *pl.* —e) offensive, attack, assault.

Angst [aŋst], *f.* (—, *pl.* ⸚e) anxiety; fear; anguish.

ängstigen ['ɛŋstɪgən], *v.a.* alarm, frighten. — *v.r. sich* —, feel uneasy, be afraid.

angucken ['angukən], *v.a.* look at.

anhaben ['anha:bən], *v.a. irr.* have on, be dressed in, wear; *einem etwas* —, hold s.th. against s.o.

anhaften ['anhaftən], *v.n.* stick to, adhere to.

Anhalt ['anhalt], *m.* (—es, *no pl.*) support, basis.

anhalten ['anhaltən], *v.a. irr. einen* — stop s.o. — *v.n.* stop, pull up, halt; *um ein Mädchen* —, ask for a girl's hand in marriage. — *v.r. sich an etwas halten,* cling to, hang on to s.th.

Anhaltspunkt ['anhaltspuŋkt], *m.* (—es, *pl.* —e) clue, (*Am.*) lead.

Anhang ['anhaŋ], *m.* (—s, *pl.* ⸚e) appendix, supplement.

anhängen ['anhɛŋən], *v.a. irr.* hang on, fasten to, attach.

Anhänger ['anhɛŋər], *m.* (—s, *pl.* —) follower, adherent; (*Footb.*) supporter; pendant (on a necklace); label; (*Transp.*) trailer.

anhänglich ['anhɛŋlɪç], *adj.* attached, affectionate.

Anhängsel

Anhängsel ['anhɛŋsəl], *n.* (—**s**, *pl.* —) appendage.

anhauchen ['anhauxən], *v.a.* breathe upon.

anhäufen ['anhɔyfən], *v.a.* heap up, pile up, amass. —*v.r.* sich —, accumulate.

anheben ['anhe:bən], *v.a. irr.* lift. — *v.n.* (*obs.*) begin.

anheim [an'haɪm], *adv.* — *stellen*, leave to s.o.'s discretion.

anheimeln ['anhaɪməln], *v.a.* remind one of home.

anheischig ['anhaɪʃɪç], *adj.* sich — *machen*, undertake, pledge o.s.

Anhieb ['anhi:p], *m.* (—**s**, *pl.* —**e**) (*fencing*) first stroke; auf —, at the first attempt.

Anhöhe ['anhø:ə], *f.* (—, *pl.* —**n**) hill, rising ground.

anhören ['anhø:rən], *v.a.* listen to; tell by s.o.'s voice *or* accent.

animieren [ani'mi:rən], *v.a.* instigate, egg on.

ankämpfen ['ankɛmpfən], *v.n. gegen etwas* —, struggle against s.th.

ankaufen ['ankaufən], *v.a.* purchase, buy. — *v.r.* sich irgendwo —, buy land somewhere.

Anker ['aŋkər], *m.* (—**s**, *pl.* —) (*Naut.*) anchor; *den* — *auswerfen*, cast anchor.

ankern ['aŋkərn], *v.a., v.n.* anchor, cast anchor.

Anklage ['ankla:gə], *f.* (—, *pl.* —**n**) accusation; *gegen einen* — *erheben*, bring a charge against s.o.

Ankläger ['anklɛ:gər], *m.* (—**s**, *pl.* —) accuser, prosecutor; plaintiff.

Anklang ['anklaŋ], *m.* (—**s**, *pl.* ⁻**e**) reminiscence; — *finden*, please, meet with approval.

ankleben ['ankle:bən], *v.a.* stick to, glue to, paste on.

ankleiden ['anklaɪdən], *v.a.* dress. — *v.r.* sich —, dress o.s., get dressed.

anklingeln ['anklɪŋəln], *v.a.* (*coll.*) *einen* —, ring s.o. up (on the telephone.)

anklopfen ['anklɔpfən], *v.n.* knock.

anknüpfen ['anknypfən], *v.a.* tie; join on to; *ein Gespräch* —, start a conversation; *wieder* —, resume.

ankommen ['ankɔmən], *v.n. irr.* (*aux.* sein) arrive; *es kommt darauf an*, it depends upon.

ankreiden ['ankraɪdən], *v.a.* chalk up.

ankündigen ['ankyndɪgən], *v.a.* announce, advertise, give notice of, proclaim.

Ankunft ['ankunft], *f.* (—, *no pl.*) arrival.

ankurbeln ['ankurbəln], *v.a.* (*Motor.*) crank up.

Anlage ['anla:gə], *f.* (—, *pl.* —**n**) (*capital*) investment; *enclosure* (*with a letter*); (*industrial*) plant; (*building*) lay-out; *öffentliche* —, pleasure grounds; talent.

anlangen ['anlaŋən], *v.n.* (*aux.* sein) arrive; concern; *was das anlangt*, as far as this is concerned.

Anlaß ['anlas], *m.* (—**sses**, *pl.* ⁻**sse**) cause, occasion, motive.

anlassen ['anlasən], *v.a. irr.* keep on; (*Motor.*) start. — *v.r.* sich gut —, promise well.

Anlasser ['anlasər], *m.* (—**s**, *pl.* —) (*Motor.*) starter.

anläßlich ['anlɛslɪç], *prep.* (*Genit.*) à propos of, on the occasion of.

Anlauf ['anlauf], *m.* (—**s**, *pl.* ⁻**e**) start, run, (*Aviat.*) take-off run.

anlaufen ['anlaufən], *v.n. irr.* tarnish; call at (port).

anlegen ['anle:gən], *v.a. Geld* —, invest money; *Kleider* —, don clothes; *einen Garten* —, lay out a garden; *Hand* —, give a helping hand; *auf einen* —, take aim at s.o.; (*Naut.*) land, dock.

Anlegestelle ['anle:gəʃtelə], *f.* (—, *pl.* —**n**) landing place.

anlehnen ['anle:nən], *v.r.* sich an etwas —, lean against s. th.

Anleihe ['anlaɪə], *f.* (—, *pl.* —**n**) loan, *öffentliche* —, government loan; *eine* — *machen*, raise a loan.

anleiten ['anlaɪtən], *v.a.* train, instruct.

anlernen ['anlɛrnən], *v.a. einen* —, train, apprentice s.o. (in a craft).

anliegen ['anli:gən], *n.* (—**s**, *pl.* —) request, petition, concern.

anmachen ['anmaxən], *v.a.* fix, fasten; light (a fire).

anmaßen ['anma:sən], *v.a.* sich etwas —, arrogate s.th.

anmaßend ['anma:sənt], *adj.* arrogant.

anmelden ['anmɛldən], *v.a.* announce, (*claim*) give notice of. — *v.r.* sich —, notify o.'s arrival, make an appointment; sich — *lassen*, send in o.'s name.

Anmeldungsformular [an'mɛlduŋsformula:r], *n.* (—**s**, *pl.* —**e**) registration form.

Anmerkung ['anmɛrkuŋ], *f.* (—, *pl.* —**en**) remark, annotation, footnote.

anmessen ['anmɛsən], *v.a. irr.* measure (s.o. for a garment).

Anmut ['anmu:t], *f.* (—, *no pl.*) grace, charm.

annähen ['annɛ:ən], *v.a.* sew on (to).

annähern ['annɛ:ərn], *v.r.* sich —, approach, draw near; (*Maths.*) approximate.

Annäherung ['annɛ:əruŋ], *f.* (—, *pl.* —**en**) approach; (*Maths.*) approximation.

Annahme ['anna:mə], *f.* (—, *pl.* —**n**) acceptance; assumption, hypothesis.

annehmbar ['anne:mba:r], *adj.* acceptable; *ganz* —, passable.

annehmen ['anne:mən], *v.a. irr.* take, accept, take delivery of; suppose, assume, presume; *an Kindes Statt* —, adopt.

Annehmlichkeit ['anne:mlɪçkaɪt], *f.* (—, *pl.* —**en**) amenity, comfort.

Annonce [an'nɔ̃:sə], *f.* (—, *pl.* —**n**) (classified) advertisement (in newspaper).

anordnen ['anɔrdnən], *v.a.* arrange, regulate; order, direct.

anorganisch ['anɔrga:nɪʃ], *adj.* inorganic.

anpacken ['anpakən], *v.a.* get hold of, seize, grasp.

anpassen ['anpasən], *v.a.* fit, suit. — *v.r. sich —*, adapt o.s.

anpflanzen ['anpflantsən], *v.a.* plant, grow.

Anprall ['anpral], *m.* (**—s**, *no pl.*) impact, bounce, shock.

anpumpen ['anpumpən], *v.a.* (*coll.*) *einen —*, borrow money from s.o.

anrechnen ['anreçnən], *v.a. einem etwas —*, charge s.o. with s.th.; *einem etwas hoch —*, think highly of a person for s.th.

Anrecht ['anreçt], *n.* (**—es**, *no pl.*) *— auf*, title to, claim to.

Anrede ['anre:də], *f.* (**—**, *pl.* **—n**) (form of) address, title.

anreden ['anre:dən], *v.a.* address (s.o.).

anregen ['anre:gən], *v.a.* stimulate (s.o.); suggest (s.th.).

Anregung ['anre:gun], *f.* (**—**, *pl.* **—en**) suggestion, hint.

Anreiz ['anraits], *m.* (**—es**, *no pl.*) incentive; impulse.

Anrichte ['anrɪçtə], *f.* (**—**, *pl.* **—n**) dresser, sideboard.

anrichten ['anrɪçtən], *v.a.* (*meal*) prepare, serve (up); *Unheil —*, make mischief.

anrüchig ['anry:çıç], *adj.* disreputable.

anrücken ['anrykən], *v.a.* bring near to. — *v.n.* (*aux.* sein) approach.

Anruf ['anru:f], *m.* (**—s**, *pl.* **—e**) (*by sentry*) challenge; telephone call.

anrufen ['anru:fən], *v.a. irr.* call to, challenge; implore; ring up; *Gott —*, invoke God.

anrühren ['anry:rən], *v.a.* handle, touch; (*Cul.*) mix.

Ansage ['anza:gə], *f.* (**—**, *pl.* **—n**) announcement.

ansagen ['anza:gən], *v.a.* announce, notify.

Ansager ['anza:gər], *m.* (**—s**, *pl.* **—**) announcer; compere.

ansammeln ['anzaməln], *v.a.* accumulate, gather. — *v.r. sich —*, gather, foregather, congregate, collect.

ansässig ['anzɛsıç], *adj.* domiciled, resident; *sich — machen*, settle.

Ansatz ['anzats], *m.* (**—es**, *pl.* **—e**) start; (*Maths.*) construction; disposition (to), tendency (to).

anschaffen ['anʃafən], *v.a.* buy, purchase, get.

anschauen ['anʃauən], *v.a.* look at, view.

anschaulich ['anʃaulıç], *adj.* clear; *einem etwas — machen*, give s.o. a clear idea of s.th.

Anschauung ['anʃauun], *f.* (**—**, *pl.* **—en**) view, perception; *nach meiner —*, in my opinion.

Anschein ['anʃaın], *m.* (**—s**, *no pl.*) appearance, semblance.

anscheinend ['anʃaınənt], *adj.* apparent, ostensible, seeming.

anschicken ['anʃıkən], *v.r. sich — zu*, prepare for, get ready for.

anschirren ['anʃırən], *v.a.* (*horses*) harness.

Anschlag ['anʃla:k], *m.* (**—s**, *pl.* **—e**) poster, placard; *— auf das Leben*, attempt at assassination.

Anschlagbrett ['anʃla:kbret], *n.* (**—es**, *pl.* **—er**) notice-board.

anschlagen ['anʃla:gən], *v.a. irr.* (*keys of piano or typewriter*) strike, touch; (*knitting*) cast on; *zu hoch —*, overestimate.

anschließen ['anʃli:sən], *v.a. irr.* fasten with a lock. — *v.r. sich —*, join in; (*club*) join.

Anschluß ['anʃlus], *m.* (**—sses**, *pl.* **—sse**) (*Railw., telephone*) connection; (*Pol.*) annexation.

Anschlußpunkt ['anʃluspuŋkt], *m.* (**—es**, *pl.* **—e**) junction; (*Elec.*) inlet point, power point.

anschmiegen ['anʃmi:gən], *v.r. sich —*, nestle closely to.

anschmieren ['anʃmi:rən], *v.a. einen —*, (*coll.*) deceive, cheat s.o.

anschnallen ['anʃnalən], *v.a.* buckle on.

anschnauzen ['anʃnautsən], *v.a.* snarl at, snap at.

anschneiden ['anʃnaıdən], *v.a. irr.* cut into; *ein Thema —*, broach a subject.

Anschrift ['anʃrıft], *f.* (**—**, *pl.* **—en**) address.

anschwellen ['anʃvelən], *v.n.* (*aux.* sein) swell.

Ansehen ['anze:ən], *n.* (**—s**, *no pl.*) respect; reputation; authority.

ansehen ['anze:ən], *v.a. irr.* look at or upon, consider, regard.

ansehnlich ['anze:nlıç], *adj.* considerable, appreciable.

anseilen ['anzaılən], *v.a.* (*Mount.*) rope together.

ansetzen ['anzetsən], *v.a.* join to; (*Maths.*) start, write out (an equation).

Ansicht ['anzıçt], *f.* (**—**, *pl.* **—en**) opinion; view; (*Comm.*) approval.

ansichtig ['anzıçtıç], *adj. — werden*, get a glimpse of.

Ansichts(post)karte ['anzıçts(pɔst)-karta], *f.* (**—**, *pl.* **—n**) picture postcard.

ansiedeln ['anzi:dəln], *v.r. sich —*, settle (down), colonize.

Ansinnen ['anzınən], *n.* (**—s**, *pl.* **—**) demand, suggestion.

anspannen ['anʃpanən], *v.a.* tighten yoke, stretch; harness.

anspielen ['anʃpi:lən], *v.n.* (*Game, Sport*) lead off; *auf etwas —*, allude to s.th.

Ansporn ['anʃpɔrn], *m.* (**—s**, *no pl.*) spur, incentive.

Ansprache ['anʃpra:xə], *f.* (**—**, *pl.* **—n**) address, speech, talk.

ansprechen ['anʃprɛçən], *v.a. irr.* address, accost; please.

anspringen ['anʃprıŋən], *v.a. irr.* leap at. — *v.n.* (*Motor.*) start.

Anspruch ['anʃprux], *m.* (—s, *pl.* ⁔e) (*Law*) claim, title.

anspruchsvoll ['anʃpruxsfɔl], *adj.* demanding, hard to please.

anstacheln ['anʃtaxəln], *v.a.* goad, prod.

Anstalt ['anʃtalt], *f.* (—, *pl.* —en) institution, establishment; —en treffen, make arrangements (for).

Anstand ['anʃtant], *m.* (—es, *no pl.*) propriety; politeness, good manners, good grace; decency; (*Hunt.*) stand, butts.

anständig ['anʃtɛndɪç], *adj.* decent, proper, respectable.

Anstandsbesuch ['anʃtantsbəzu:x], *m.* (—es, *pl.* —e) formal visit.

anstandshalber ['anʃtantshalbər], *adv.* for decency's sake.

anstandslos ['anʃtantslo:s], *adv.* unhesitatingly.

anstarren ['anʃtarən], *v.a.* stare at.

anstatt [an'ʃtat], *prep.* (*Genit.*), *conj.* instead of, in lieu of, in the place of.

anstecken ['anʃtɛkən], *v.a.* pin on; set fire to; infect.

Ansteckung ['anʃtɛkuŋ], *f.* (—, *pl.* —en) infection, contagion.

anstehen ['anʃteːən], *v.n. irr.* stand in a queue; — lassen, put off, delay.

ansteigen ['anʃtaigən], *v.n. irr.* (*aux.* sein) rise, increase.

anstellen ['anʃtelən], *v.a. einen* —, appoint s.o. to a post; employ; *Betrachtungen* —, speculate. — *v.r. sich* —, form a queue, line up.

anstellig ['anʃtelɪç], *adj.* able, skilful, adroit.

Anstellung ['anʃteluŋ], *f.* (—, *pl.* —en) appointment, employment.

anstiften ['anʃtiftən], *v.a.* instigate.

anstimmen ['anʃtimən], *v.a.* intone.

Anstoß ['anʃtoːs], *m.* (—es, *pl.* ⁔e) (*Footb.*) kick-off; — erregen, give offence; *den* — *geben zu*, initiate, give an impetus to; *Stein des* —es, stumbling block; — *nehmen*, take offence.

anstoßen ['anʃtoːsən], *v.a. irr.* knock against, push against; give offence; clink (glasses); border on; *mit der Zunge* —, lisp.

anstößig ['anʃtøːsɪç], *adj.* shocking, offensive.

anstreichen ['anʃtraiçən], *v.a. irr.* paint; *Fehler* —, mark wrong.

Anstreicher ['anʃtraiçər], *m.* (—s, *pl.* —) house-painter.

anstrengen ['anʃtrɛŋən], *v.a.* strain exert; *eine Klage gegen einen* —, bring an action against s.o. — *v.r. sich* —, exert o.s.

Anstrengung ['anʃtrɛŋuŋ], *f.* (—, *pl.* —en) exertion, effort.

Anstrich ['anʃtrɪç], *m.* (—s, *pl.* —e) coat of paint.

Ansturm ['anʃturm], *m.* (—s, *no pl.*) attack, assault, charge.

Ansuchen ['anzu:xən], *n.* (—s, *pl.* —) application, request, petition.

ansuchen ['anzu:xən], *v.n. bei einem um etwas* —, apply to s.o. for s.th.

Anteil ['antail], *m.* (—s, *pl.* —e) share, portion; sympathy.

Anteilnahme ['antailnaːmə], *f.* (—, *no pl.*) sympathy.

Antenne [an'tɛnə], *f.* (—, *pl.* —n) aerial; antenna.

antik [an'ti:k], *adj.* antique, ancient, classical.

Antike [an'ti:kə], *f.* (—, *pl.* —en) (classical) antiquity; ancient work of art (statue etc.).

Antiquar [anti'kva:r], *m.* (—s, *pl.* —e) second-hand dealer; antiquary.

Antiquariat [antikva'rja:t], *n.* (—s, *pl.* —e) second-hand bookshop.

antiquarisch [anti'kva:rɪʃ], *adj.* antiquarian, second-hand.

Antlitz ['antlɪts], *n.* (—es, *pl.* —e) countenance, (*Poet.*) face.

Antrag ['antra:k], *m.* (—s, *pl.* ⁔e) proposition, proposal, application; *einen* — *stellen*, bring in a motion; make application.

antragen ['antra:gən], *v.a. irr.* propose, make a proposal, offer to.

Antragsformular ['antra:ksfɔrmula:r], *n.* (—s, *pl.* —e) (*Insurance*) proposal form; application form.

Antragsteller ['antra:kʃtelər], *m.* (—s, *pl.* —) applicant, mover of a resolution.

antreten ['antre:tən], *v.a. irr. ein Amt* —, enter upon an office; *eine Reise* —, set out on a journey. — *v.n.* (*aux.* sein) (*Mil.*) fall in.

Antrieb ['antri:p], *m.* (—s, *pl.* —e) impulse, motive; incentive; *aus eigenem* —, voluntarily.

Antritt ['antrɪt], *m.* (—s, *no pl.*) start, commencement.

Antrittsvorlesung ['antrɪtsforleːzuŋ], *f.* (*Univ.*) inaugural lecture.

antun ['antu:n], *v.a. irr. einem etwas* —, do s.th. to s.o.

Antwort ['antvɔrt], *f.* (—, *pl.* —en) answer, reply; *abschlägige* —, refusal, rebuff.

antworten ['antvɔrtən], *v.a.* answer, reply to.

anvertrauen ['anfɛrtrauən], *v.a. einem etwas* —, entrust s.o. with s.th.; confide in s.o.

anverwandt ['anfɛrvant] *see* **verwandt**.

Anwalt ['anvalt], *m.* (—s, *pl.* ⁔e) lawyer, barrister, solicitor, attorney, advocate.

anwandeln ['anvandəln], *v.a.* befall.

Anwandlung ['anvandluŋ], *f.* (—, *pl.* —en) fit, turn.

Anwartschaft ['anvartʃaft], *f.* (—, *pl.* —en) (*Law*) reversion; candidacy.

anweisen ['anvaizən], *v.a. irr.* instruct, direct; *angewiesen sein auf*, depend upon.

Anweisung ['anvaizuŋ], *f.* (—, *pl.* —en) instruction, advice, method; (*Comm.*) voucher, credit voucher, cheque.

anwenden ['anvɛndən], *v.a. irr.* use, make use of, apply.

anwerben ['anvɛrbən], *v.a. irr. (Mil.)* recruit; *sich — lassen*, enlist.

anwesend ['anve:zənt], *adj.* at hand, present.

Anwesenheit ['anve:zənhaɪt], *f.* (—, *no pl.*) presence, attendance.

anwidern ['anvi:dərn], *v.a.* disgust.

Anzahl ['antsa:l], *f.* (—, *no pl.*) number, quantity.

anzahlen ['antsa:lən], *v.a.* pay a deposit.

Anzahlung ['antsa:luŋ], *f.* (—, *pl.* —en) deposit.

Anzeichen ['antsaɪçən], *n.* (—s, *pl.* —) indication, omen.

Anzeige ['antsaɪgə], *f.* (—, *pl.* —n) notice, (classified) advertisement; denunciation; — *erstatten*, to lay information.

anzeigen ['antsaɪgən], *v.a.* point out, indicate; announce; notify; advertise; denounce.

Anzeiger ['antsaɪgər], *m.* (—s, *pl.* —) indicator; (*newspaper*) advertiser.

anzetteln ['antsɛtəln], *v.a.* plot, contrive.

anziehen ['antsi:ən], *v.a. irr.* pull, draw tight, give a tug; attract; stretch; dress; (*screws*) tighten. —, *v.r. sich —*, dress, put on o.'s clothes.

anziehend ['antsi:ənt], *adj.* attractive.

Anziehung ['antsi:uŋ], *f.* (—, *no pl.*) attraction.

Anzug ['antsu:k], *m.* (—s, *pl.* ⁼e) (man's) suit; approach.

anzüglich ['antsy:klɪç], *adj.* allusive; suggestive; — *werden*, become offensive.

anzünden ['antsyndən], *v.a.* kindle, ignite.

apart [a'part], *adj.* charming, delightful; (*Am.*) cute.

Apfel ['apfəl], *m.* (—s, *pl.* ⁼) apple.

Apfelmost ['apfəlmɔst], *m.* (—s, *no pl.*) cider.

Apfelsine [apfəl'zi:nə], *f.* (—, *pl.* —n) orange.

Apostel [a'pɔstəl], *m.* (—s, *pl.* —) apostle.

Apotheke [apo'te:kə], *f.* (—, *pl.* —n) dispensary, pharmacy, chemist's shop; (*Am.*) drugstore.

Apparat [apa'ra:t], *m.* (—(e)s, *pl.* —e) apparatus; radio *or* television set; telephone.

appellieren [apɛ'li:rən], *v.n.* — *an*, appeal to.

appetitlich [ape'ti:tlɪç], *adj.* appetising, dainty.

Aprikose [aprɪ'ko:zə], *f.* (—, *pl.* —en) apricot.

Aquarell [akva'rɛl], *n.* (—s, *pl.* —e) water-colour (painting).

Ära ['ɛːra], *f.* (—, *no pl.*) era.

Arabien [a'ra:bjən], *n.* Arabia.

Arbeit ['arbaɪt], *f.* (—, *pl.* —en) work, labour; *an die — gehen*, set to work.

arbeiten ['arbaɪtən], *v.a., v.n.* work, labour, toil.

Arbeiter ['arbaɪtər], *m.* (—s, *pl.* —) worker, workman, labourer, hand.

Arbeiterschaft ['arbaɪtərʃaft], *f.* (—, *no pl.*) working men; workers.

arbeitsam ['arbaɪtza:m], *adj.* industrious, diligent.

Arbeitsamt ['arbaɪtsamt], *n.* (—s, *pl.* ⁼er) labour exchange.

arbeitsfähig ['arbaɪtsfɛ:ɪç], *adj.* capable of working, able-bodied.

arbeitslos ['arbaɪtslo:s], *adj.* unemployed, out of work.

Arbeitslosigkeit ['arbaɪtslo:zɪçkaɪt], *f.* (—, *no pl.*) unemployment.

Arbeitsnachweis ['arbaɪtsnaxvaɪs], *m.* (—es, *no pl.*) labour exchange; (*Am.*) labour registry-office.

Arbeitssperre ['arbaɪtsʃpɛrə], *f.* (—, *pl.* —n) (*Ind.*) lock-out.

Archäologe [arçɛo'lo:gə], *m.* (—n, *pl.* —n) archaeologist.

Arche ['arçə], *f.* (—, *pl.* —n) ark.

Archipel [arçi'pe:l], *m.* (—s, *pl.* —e) archipelago.

architektonisch [arçɪtɛk'to:nɪʃ], *adj.* architectural.

Archivar [arçi'va:r], *m.* (—s, *pl.* —e) keeper of archives.

arg [ark], *adj.* bad, wicked, mischievous.

Argentinien [argən'ti:njən], *n.* Argentina.

Ärger ['ɛrgər], *m.* (—s, *no pl.*) anger, annoyance.

ärgerlich ['ɛrgərlɪç], *adj.* annoying, aggravating, vexing; angry.

ärgern ['ɛrgərn], *v.a.* annoy, vex, make angry. — *v.r. sich —*, get annoyed.

Ärgernis ['ɛrgərnɪs], *n.* (—ses, *pl.* —se) scandal, nuisance.

arglistig ['arklɪstɪç], *adj.* crafty, sly.

arglos ['arklo:s], *adj.* unsuspecting, guileless, naive.

Argwohn ['arkvo:n], *m.* (—s, *no pl.*) mistrust, suspicion.

argwöhnisch ['arkvø:nɪʃ], *adj.* suspicious, distrustful.

Arie ['a:rjə], *f.* (—, *pl.* —n) (*Mus.*) aria.

Arm [arm], *m.* (—s, *pl.* —e) arm.

arm [arm], *adj.* poor, indigent, needy.

Armaturenbrett [arma'tu:rənbrɛt], *n.* (—s, *no pl.*) dashboard.

Armband ['armbant], *n.* (—s, *pl.* ⁼er) bracelet.

Armbanduhr ['armbantu:r], *f.* (—, *pl.* —en) wrist-watch.

Armbrust ['armbrust], *f.* (—, *pl.* —e) cross-bow.

Ärmel ['ɛrməl], *m.* (—s, *pl.* —) sleeve.

Ärmelkanal ['ɛrməlkana:l], *m.* (—s, *no pl.*) English Channel.

Armenien [ar'me:njən], *n.* Armenia.

Armenhaus ['armənhaus], *n.* (—es, *pl.* ⁼er) poor-house, almshouse.

Armenpfleger ['armənpfle:gər], *m.* (—s, *pl.* —) almoner.

Armesündermiene [armə'zyndər-mi:nə], *f.* (—, *pl.* —n) hangdog look.

ärmlich ['ɛrmlɪç], *adj.* poor, shabby, scanty.

armselig ['armze:lɪç], *adj.* poor, miserable, wretched; paltry.

Armut

Armut ['armu:t], *f.* (—, *no pl.*) poverty; *in* — *geraten*, be reduced to penury.

Arsch [arʃ], *m.* (—es, ⸚e) (*vulg.*) arse.

Arsen(ik) [ar'ze:n(ik)], *n.* (—s, *no pl.*) arsenic.

Art [a:rt], *f.* (—, *pl.* —en) kind, species; race; sort; method, way, manner.

artig ['a:rtiç], *adj.* well-behaved, civil.

Artigkeit ['a:rtiçkait], *f.* (—, *pl.* —en) politeness, courtesy.

Artikel [ar'ti:kəl], *m.* (—s, *pl.* —) article; commodity.

Artist [ar'tist], *m.* (—en, *pl.* —en) artiste (circus, variety).

Arznei [arts'nai], *f.* (—, *pl.* —en) medicine.

Arzneimittel [arts'naimitəl], *n.* (—s, *pl.*—) medicine, drug.

Arzt [artst], *m.* (—es, *pl.* ⸚e) doctor, physician; *praktischer* —, general practitioner.

ärztlich ['ɛrtstliç], *adj.* medical.

As (1) [as], *n.* (—ses, *pl.* —se) (*Mus.*) A flat; — *Dur*, A flat major, — *Moll*, A flat minor.

As (2) [as], *n.* (—sses, *pl.* —sse) (*Sport, cards*) ace.

Asbest [as'bɛst], *m.* (—s, *no pl.*) asbestos.

Asche ['aʃə], *f.* (—, *no pl.*) ashes.

Aschenbecher ['aʃənbɛçər], *m.* (—s, *pl.* —) ash-tray.

Aschenbrödel ['aʃənbrø:dəl] or **Aschenputtel** ['aʃənputəl], *n.* Cinderella.

Aschkraut ['aʃkraut], *n.* (—s, *pl.* ⸚er) (*Bot.*) cineraria.

Askese [as'ke:zə], *f.* (—, *no pl.*) asceticism.

Asket [as'ke:t], *m.* (—en, *pl.* —en) ascetic.

Assessor [a'sɛsɔr], *m.* (—s, *pl.* —en) assistant; assistant judge.

Ast [ast], *m.* (—es, *pl.* ⸚e) branch, bough.

Aster ['astər], *f.* (—, *pl.* —n) (*Bot.*) aster.

Astronaut [astro'naut], *m.* (—en, *pl.*—en) astronaut.

Astronom [astro'no:m], *m.* (—en, *pl.* —en) astronomer.

Asyl [a'zy:l], *n.* (—s, *pl.* —e) asylum, sanctuary.

Atem ['a:təm], *m.* (—s, *no pl.*) breath, breathing, respiration.

Atemzug ['a:təmtsu:k], *m.* (—s, *pl.* ⸚e) breath.

Äthiopien [ɛti'o:pjən], *n.* Ethiopia.

Atlas (1) ['atlas], *m.* (—sses, *pl.* —sse *and* **Atlanten**) atlas, book of maps.

Atlas (2) ['atlas], *m.* (—sses, *pl.* —asse) satin.

atmen ['a:tmən], *v.n.* breathe.

atomar [ato'ma:r], *adj.* atomic.

Attentat [atɛn'ta:t], *n.* (—s, *pl.* —e) attempt on s.o.'s life.

Attest [a'tɛst], *n.* (—s, *pl.* —e) (*Med.*) certificate.

ätzen ['ɛtsən], *v.a.* corrode; (*Art*) etch; (*Med.*) cauterise.

auch [aux], *conj.*, *adv.* also, too, likewise, as well.

Au(e) ['au(ə)], *f.* (—, *pl.* —en) green meadow, pasture.

auf [auf], *prep.* on, upon; — *der Straße*, in the road; — *deine Gefahr*, at your own risk; — *Befehl*, by order; — *einige Tage*, for a few days; — *dem Lande*, in the country; — *keinen Fall*, on no account.

aufatmen ['aufa:tmən], *v.n.* breathe a sigh of relief.

Aufbau ['aufbau], *m.* (—s, *no pl.*) building; (*Lit.*) composition, structure.

aufbauen ['aufbauən], *v.a.* erect, build, construct.

aufbäumen ['aufbɔymən], *v.r. sich* —, (*horses*) rear.

aufbewahren ['aufbəva:rən], *v.a.* keep, store; (*luggage*) take charge of.

Aufbewahrung ['aufbəva:ruŋ], *f.* (—, *pl.* —en) storage, safe keeping.

aufbieten ['aufbi:tən], *v.a. irr.* call up for service; exert (*energies*).

aufbinden ['aufbindən], *v.a. irr.* untie; *einem einen Bären* —, to hoax s.o.

aufblähen ['aufblɛ:ən], *v.a.* puff up, swell, inflate.

aufblühen ['aufbly:ən], *v.n.* (*aux.* sein) flourish, unfold.

aufbrausen ['aufbrauzən], *v.n.* (*aux.* sein) fly into a rage.

aufbringen ['aufbriŋən], *v.a. irr.* bring up; afford; annoy (s.o.).

Aufbruch ['aufbrux], *m.* (—s, *no pl.*) departure.

aufbürden ['aufbyrdən], *v.a. einem eine Last* —, burden s.o. with a thing.

aufdecken ['aufdɛkən], *v.a.* uncover, unveil.

aufdonnern ['aufdɔnərn], *v.r. sich* — dress up showily.

aufdrängen ['aufdrɛŋən], *v.a. einem etwas* —, press s.th. upon s.o. — *v.r. sich* —, force o.'s company on.

aufdrehen ['aufdre:ən], *v.a.* (*tap*) turn on.

aufdringlich ['aufdriŋliç], *adj.* importunate, officious, obtrusive.

Aufdruck ['aufdruk], *m.* (—s, *pl.* —e) imprint.

aufdrücken ['aufdrykən], *v.a.* press open; press on s.th.

Aufenthalt ['aufɛnthalt], *m.* (—s, *pl.* —e) stay, sojourn; delay; stop.

auferlegen ['auferle:gən], *v.a.* impose; enjoin.

auferstehen ['aufɛrʃte:ən], *v.n. irr.* (*aux.* sein) (*Rel.*) rise from the dead.

auffahren ['auffa:rən], *v.n. irr.* (*aux.* sein) start (from o.'s sleep); mount; flare up (in anger).

Auffahrt ['auffa:rt], *f.* (—, *pl.* —en) ascent; approach to a house, drive.

auffallen ['auffalən], *v.n. irr.* (*aux.* sein) strike the ground; *einem* —, strike s.o., astonish.

auffangen ['auffaŋən], *v.a. irr.* (*ball*) catch; (*blow*) parry, ward off; (*letter*) intercept.

auffassen ['auffasən], *v.a.* take in, comprehend.

12

Auffassung ['auffasuŋ], f. (—, pl. —en) conception, interpretation; view.

aufflackern ['aufflakərn],v.n. (aux. sein) flare up, flicker.

auffordern ['auffɔrdərn], v.a. summon, request, ask, invite.

aufforsten ['auffɔrstən], v.a. afforest.

auffressen ['auffrɛsən], v.a. irr. devour; (of animals) eat up.

auffrischen ['auffrɪʃən], v.a. renew, redecorate; (fig.) brush up.

aufführen ['auffy:rən], v.a. (Theat.) perform; einzeln —, specify, particularise. — v.r. sich —, behave, conduct o.s.

Aufführung ['auffy:ruŋ], f. (—, pl. —en) (Theat.) performance.

Aufgabe ['aufga:bə], f. (—, pl. —n) giving up, abandonment; (letters, telegrams) posting, despatch; (work) task; (Sch.) exercise; (Maths.) problem.

aufgabeln ['aufga:bəln], v.a. (sl.) pick up.

Aufgang ['aufgaŋ], m. (—s, pl. ⁀e) ascent, stairs.

aufgeben ['aufge:bən], v.a. irr. give up, abandon, relinquish; (Am.) quit; (luggage) check.

aufgeblasen ['aufgəbla:zən], adj. conceited, stuck up.

Aufgebot ['aufgəbo:t], n. (—s, pl. —e) (marriage) banns; (Mil.) levy; mit — aller Kräfte, with the utmost exertion.

aufgebracht ['aufgəbraxt], adj. angry, annoyed.

aufgedunsen ['aufgədunzən], adj. bloated, sodden.

aufgehen ['aufge:ən], v.n. irr. (aux. sein) (knot) come undone; (sun) rise; (dough) swell, rise; (Maths.) leave no remainder, cancel out.

aufgehoben ['aufgəho:bən], adj. gut — sein, be in good hands.

aufgelegt ['aufgəle:kt], adj. disposed, inclined.

aufgeräumt ['aufgərɔymt], adj. merry, cheerful, in high spirits.

aufgeweckt ['aufgəvɛkt], adj. bright, clever, intelligent.

aufgießen ['aufgi:sən], v.a. irr. Kaffee —, make coffee.

aufgreifen ['aufgraɪfən], v.a. irr. seize.

Aufguß ['aufgus], m. (—sses, pl. ⁀sse) infusion.

aufhalsen ['aufhalzən], v.a. einem etwas —, (coll.) saddle s.o. with s.th.

aufhalten ['aufhaltən], v.a. irr. (door) hold open; einen —, delay s.o. — v.r. sich an einem Ort —, stay at a place; sich über etwas —, find fault with s.th.

aufhängen ['aufhɛŋən], v.a. irr. hang (up).

aufhäufen ['aufhɔyfən], v.a. pile up. — v.r. sich —, accumulate.

Aufheben ['aufhe:bən], n. (—s, no pl.) lifting up; ado; viel —s machen, make a great fuss.

aufheben ['aufhe:bən], v.a. irr. lift (up), pick up; keep, preserve; (laws) repeal, abolish; (agreements) rescind, annul.

Aufhebung ['aufhe:buŋ], f. (—, pl. —en) abolition, abrogation, annulment, repeal.

aufheitern ['aufhaɪtərn], v.a. cheer up; amuse. — v.r. sich —, (weather) brighten, clear up.

aufhelfen ['aufhɛlfən], v.n. irr. einem —, help s.o. up.

aufhellen ['aufhɛlən], v.r. sich —, (weather) clear up; (face) brighten up.

aufhetzen ['aufhɛtsən],v.a. rouse (s.o.); einen — gegen, incite s.o. against.

aufhorchen ['aufhɔrçən], v.n. prick up o.'s ears.

aufhören ['aufhø:rən], v.n. cease, stop; (Am.) quit; ohne aufzuhören, incessantly; da hört sich doch alles auf! that is the limit!

aufklären ['aufklɛ:rən], v.a. enlighten; clear up; einen —, enlighten s.o. —v.r. sich —, (weather) brighten.

Aufklärung ['aufklɛ:ruŋ], f. (—, no pl.) (age of) Enlightenment.

aufknacken ['aufknakən], v.a. crack (open).

aufknöpfen ['aufknœpfən], v.a. unbutton; aufgeknöpft sein, be in a talkative mood.

aufkommen ['aufkɔmən], v.n. irr. (aux. sein) come into use, spring up; für etwas —, pay for s.th.; einen nicht — lassen, give s.o. no chance.

aufkrempeln ['aufkrɛmpəln],v.a. (coll.) roll up (o.'s sleeves).

aufkündigen ['aufkyndɪgən], v.a. (money) recall; einem die Freundschaft —, break with s.o.

Auflage ['aufla:gə], f. (—, pl. —n) (tax) impost, duty, levy; (book) edition, impression; circulation.

auflassen ['auflasən], v.a. irr. leave open; (Law) cede.

auflauern ['auflauərn], v.n. einem —, lie in wait for s.o., waylay s.o.

Auflauf ['auflauf], m. (—s, pl. ⁀e) tumult, noisy street gathering; soufflé.

auflaufen ['auflaufən], v.n. irr. (aux. sein) swell, increase; (ship) run aground.

aufleben ['aufle:bən], v.n. (aux. sein) wieder —, revive.

auflegen ['aufle:gən], v.a. irr. lay upon, put on; (book) publish; (tax, punishment) impose, inflict.

auflehnen ['aufle:nən], v.r. sich gegen einen (or etwas) —, rebel against, mutiny, oppose.

auflesen ['aufle:zən], v.a. irr. pick up, gather.

aufleuchten ['auflɔyçtən], v.n. light up; (eyes) shine.

auflockern ['auflɔkərn], v.a. loosen.

auflodern ['auflo:dərn], v.n. (aux. sein) flare up, blaze up.

auflösen

auflösen ['auflø:zən], *v.a.* dissolve, loosen; (*puzzle*) solve, guess; (*meeting*) break up; (*business*) wind up; (*partnership*) dissolve; (*army*) disband. — *v.r. sich* —, melt, dissolve, be broken up.

aufmachen ['aufmaxən], *v.a.* (*door, packet*) open; (*knot*) undo; *gut* —, pack nicely. — *v.r. sich* —, get going, set out for.

Aufmachung ['aufmaxuŋ], *f.* (—, *pl.* —en) outward appearance, make-up, get-up.

Aufmarsch ['aufmarʃ], *m.* (—es, *pl.* ⁓e) (*Mil.*) parade.

aufmerksam ['aufmɛrkza:m], *adj.* attentive, observant; civil, kind; *einen* — *machen auf*, draw s.o.'s attention to.

aufmuntern ['aufmuntərn], *v.a.* encourage, cheer up.

Aufnahme ['aufna:mə], *f.* (—, *pl.* —n) reception; (*Phot.*) snap, photograph; (*Geog.*) mapping out, survey; (*Mus.*) recording.

aufnehmen ['aufne:mən], *v.a. irr.* take up; receive, give shelter to; (*Phot.*) photograph, film; (*Mus.*) record; (*money*) raise, borrow; (*minutes*) draw up; *den Faden wieder* —, take up the thread; *die Arbeit wieder* —, return to work, resume work; *die Fährte* —, (*Hunt.*) recover the scent; *es mit einem* —, be a match for s.o.; (*Comm.*) *Inventar* —, take stock, draw up an inventory.

aufnötigen ['aufnø:tɪgən], *v.a. einem etwas* —, force s.th. upon s.o.

aufpassen ['aufpasən], *v.n.* attend to, pay attention to, take notice of, take care of.

aufpeitschen ['aufpaɪtʃən], *v.a.* whip up.

aufpflanzen ['aufpflantsən], *v.a.* mount, erect. — *v.r. sich vor einem* —, plant o.s. in front of s.o.; *mit aufgepflanztem Bajonett*, with bayonets fixed.

Aufputz ['aufputs], *m.* (—es, *no pl.*) finery, trimmings.

aufraffen ['aufrafən], *v.a.* snatch up, rake up. — *v.r. sich wieder* —, pull o.s. together.

aufräumen ['aufrɔymən], *v.a.* put in order, clear away; (*room*) tidy up; *mit etwas* —, make a clean sweep of s.th.; *aufgeräumt sein*, be in a jolly mood.

aufrechnen ['aufrɛçnən], *v.a.* reckon up; set off against.

aufrecht ['aufrɛçt], *adj.* upright, erect; *etwas* — *erhalten*, maintain s.th.; (*opinion*) stick to, adhere to, uphold.

Aufrechterhaltung ['aufrɛçtərhaltuŋ], *f.* (—, *no pl.*) maintenance, preservation.

aufregen ['aufre:gən], *v.a.* excite, enrage.

aufreiben ['aufraɪbən], *v.a. irr.* rub sore; (*Mil.*) destroy, wipe out. — *v.r. sich* —, exhaust o.s. with worry (*or* work).

aufreizen ['aufraɪtsən], *v.a.* incite, provoke.

aufrichten ['aufrɪçtən], *v.a.* raise, erect, set upright; (*fig.*) comfort, console. — *v.r. sich* —, rise, sit up.

aufrichtig ['aufrɪçtɪç], *adj.* sincere, frank.

aufriegeln ['aufri:gəln], *v.a.* unbolt.

Aufriß ['aufrɪs], *m.* (—sses, *pl.* —sse) sketch, draft; (*Archit.*) elevation, section.

aufrücken ['aufrykən], *v.n.* (*aux.* sein) rise, be promoted (in rank), advance.

Aufruf ['aufru:f], *m.* (—s, *pl.* —e) summons, proclamation, appeal; (*Law*) citation.

aufrufen ['aufru:fən], *v.a. irr.* summons; (*Sch.*) call upon.

Aufruhr ['aufru:r], *m.* (—s, *pl.* —e) uproar, riot, tumult, rebellion, mutiny.

aufrühren ['aufry:rən], *v.a.* stir up, agitate, rouse to rebellion.

Aufrüstung ['aufrystuŋ], *f.* (—, *no pl.*) (*Mil.*) (re-)armament.

aufrütteln ['aufrytəln], *v.a.* rouse, shake s.o. out of his lethargy.

aufsagen ['aufza:gən], *v.a.* recite.

aufsässig ['aufzɛsɪç], *adj.* refractory, rebellious.

Aufsatz ['aufzats], *m.* (—es, *pl.* ⁓e) top, head-piece, table centre-piece; (*Sch.*) composition, essay; (*newspaper*) article.

aufscheuchen ['aufʃɔyçən], *v.a.* flush (game), startle.

aufschichten ['aufʃɪçtən], *v.a.* stack, pile up in layers.

aufschieben ['aufʃi:bən], *v.a. irr.* push open; delay, postpone, adjourn; (*Parl.*) prorogue.

Aufschlag ['aufʃla:k], *m.* (—s, *pl.* ⁓e) impact, striking; (*sleeve*) cuff; turn-up; (*uniform*) facings; (*Comm.*) increase in price; (*Tennis*) service.

aufschlagen ['aufʃla:gən], *v.n. irr.* (*aux.* sein) hit, strike (open); (*Tennis*) serve. — *v.a. die Augen* —, open o.'s eyes; *ein Lager* —, pitch camp; *ein Buch* —, open a book.

aufschlitzen ['aufʃlɪtsən], *v.a.* rip open, slit open.

Aufschluß ['aufʃlus], *m.* (—sses, *pl.* —sse) disclosure, information.

aufschneiden ['aufʃnaɪdən], *v.a. irr.* cut open. — *v.n.* brag, boast.

Aufschneider ['aufʃnaɪdər], *m.* (-s, *pl.* —) swaggerer, braggart.

Aufschnitt ['aufʃnɪt], *m.* (—s, *no pl.*) slice of cold meat *or* sausage.

aufschnüren ['aufʃny:rən], *v.a.* unlace, untie.

Aufschrei ['aufʃraɪ], *m.* (—s, *pl.* —e) outcry, screech, scream, shout, shriek.

Aufschrift ['aufʃrɪft], *f.* (—, *pl.* —en) inscription, address; heading.

Aufschub ['aufʃu:p], *m.* (—s, *pl.* ⁓e) delay, adjournment, postponement.

aufschütten ['aufʃytən], *v.a.* (*liquid*) pour upon; (*dam*) raise.

14

aufschwingen [ˈaufʃvɪŋən], *v.r. irr.*
sich —, soar, rise; *ich kann mich dazu
nicht —,* I cannot rise to that.

Aufschwung [ˈaufʃvuŋ], *m.* (—s, *no
pl.*) flight, rising; (*Comm.*) improvement, boom.

Aufsehen [ˈaufzeːən], *n.* (—s, *no pl.*)
sensation, stir.

Aufseher [ˈaufzeːər], *m.* (—s, *pl.* —)
overseer, inspector.

aufsein [ˈaufzaɪn], *v.n. irr.* (*aux.* sein)
be out of bed, be up and about.

aufsetzen [ˈaufzɛtsən], *v.a.* (*hat*) put on;
(*letter, essay*) draft.

Aufsicht [ˈaufzɪçt], *f.* (—, *no pl.*)
inspection, supervision, control.

Aufsichtsrat [ˈaufzɪçtsraːt], *m.* (—s,
pl. -e) (*Comm.*) board of directors.

aufsitzen [ˈaufzɪtsən], *v.n. irr.* sit up,
wait up at night; (*horse*) mount.

aufspannen [ˈaufʃpanən], *v.a.* (*umbrella*)
put up; (*tent*) pitch.

aufspeichern [ˈaufʃpaɪçərn], *v.a.* store
(up), warehouse.

aufsperren [ˈaufʃpɛrən], *v.a.* open
wide, unlock.

aufspielen [ˈaufʃpiːlən], *v.n. zum Tanz
—,* play music for dancing. — *v.r.
sich groß —,* give o.s. airs.

aufspießen [ˈaufʃpiːsən], *v.a.* pierce on
a spit; (*joint*) skewer.

aufspringen [ˈaufʃprɪŋən], *v.n. irr.*
(*aux.* sein) leap up, jump up; (*door*)
fly open; (*hands in winter*) chap.

aufspüren [ˈaufʃpyːrən], *v.a.* track, trace.

aufstacheln [ˈaufʃtaxəln], *v.a.* goad,
incite.

Aufstand [ˈaufʃtant], *m.* (—s, *pl.* -e)
insurrection, revolt, sedition.

aufstapeln [ˈaufʃtaːpəln], *v.a.* pile up,
stack, store.

aufstechen [ˈaufʃtɛçən], *v.a. irr.* (*Med.*)
lance.

aufstehen [ˈaufʃteːən], *v.n. irr.* (*aux.*
sein) (*door*) stand open; stand up; get
up (from bed); rise (from a chair).

aufstellen [ˈaufʃtɛlən], *v.a.* set up,
arrange; erect; (*Pol.*) put forward
(candidate).

Aufstellung [ˈaufʃtɛluŋ], *f.* (—, *pl.*
—en) arrangement; statement; inventory; (*Pol.*) nomination.

aufstemmen [ˈaufʃtɛmən], *v.a.* prise
open.

Aufstieg [ˈaufʃtiːk], *m.* (—s, *pl.* —e)
ascent, rise.

aufstöbern [ˈaufʃtøːbərn], *v.a.* stir (up);
start; (*fig.*) discover, ferret out.

aufstoßen [ˈaufʃtoːsən], *v.a. irr.* push
open; bump against. — *v.n.* belch.

aufstreben [ˈaufʃtreːbən], *v.n.* soar;
(*fig.*) aspire.

aufstreichen [ˈaufʃtraɪçən], *v.a. irr.*
(*paint*) lay on; (*butter*) spread.

aufstülpen [ˈaufʃtylpən], *v.a.* turn up;
(*hat*) clap on o.'s head.

auftakeln [ˈauftaːkəln], *v.a.* (*Naut.*)
rig.

Auftakt [ˈauftakt], *m.* (—s, *pl.* —e)
(*Mus.*) arsis; (*fig.*) opening, prelude.

auftauchen [ˈauftauxən], *v.n.* (*aux.*
sein) appear, emerge, surface.

auftauen [ˈauftauən], *v.n.* (*aux.* sein)
thaw; (*fig.*) lose o.'s reserve.

auftischen [ˈauftɪʃən], *v.a.* dish up.

Auftrag [ˈauftraːk], *m.* (—s, *pl.* -e)
assignment, commission, errand; *im
— von,* on behalf of.

auftragen [ˈauftraːgən], *v.a. irr.* (*food*)
serve up; (*paint*) apply; *einem etwas
—,* charge s.o. with a job; *stark —,*
lay it on thick.

auftreiben [ˈauftraɪbən], *v.a. irr.* raise
(*money*); procure, obtain. — *v.n.*
(*aux.* sein) (*ship*) run aground.

auftrennen [ˈauftrɛnən], *v.a.* unstitch;
(*hem*) unpick.

Auftreten [ˈauftreːtən], *n.* (—s, *no pl.*)
(*Theat.*) appearance; behaviour.

auftreten [ˈauftreːtən], *v.n. irr.* (*aux.*
sein) tread upon, step upon; (*Theat.*)
appear, come on; *energisch —,* take
strong measures, put o.'s foot
down.

Auftritt [ˈauftrɪt], *m.* (—s, *pl.* —e)
(*Theat.*) scene; altercation, row.

auftun [ˈauftuːn], *v.a. irr.* open; *den
Mund —,* speak. — *v.r. sich —,* (*abyss*)
yawn.

auftürmen [ˈauftʏrmən], *v.a.* pile up,
heap up. — *v.r. sich —,* tower.

aufwachen [ˈaufvaxən], *v.n.* (*aux.* sein)
awake, wake up.

aufwallen [ˈaufvalən], *v.n.* (*aux.* sein)
boil up, bubble up, rage.

Aufwand [ˈaufvant], *m.* (—s, *no pl.*)
expense, expenditure; sumptuous-
ness.

aufwarten [ˈaufvartən], *v.n.* wait upon,
attend on.

aufwärts [ˈaufvɛrts], *adv.* upward(s),
aloft.

Aufwartung [ˈaufvartuŋ], *f.* (—, *pl.*
—en) attendance; *seine — machen,* pay
a (formal) visit.

aufwaschen [ˈaufvaʃən], *v.a. irr.* wash
the dishes.

aufweisen [ˈaufvaɪzən], *v.a. irr.* show,
produce.

aufwenden [ˈaufvɛndən], *v.a. irr.*
spend upon, expend upon.

aufwickeln [ˈaufvɪkəln], *v.a.* wind up;
unwind.

aufwiegeln [ˈaufviːgəln], *v.a.* stir up,
incite to rebellion.

aufwiegen [ˈaufviːgən], *v.a. irr.* outweigh, counter-balance, make up
for.

aufwischen [ˈaufvɪʃən], *v.a.* wipe away,
mop up.

aufwühlen [ˈaufvyːlən], *v.a.* dig, root
up, (*fig.*) stir.

aufzählen [ˈauftsɛːlən], *v.a.* count up,
enumerate, list.

aufzäumen [ˈauftsɔymən], *v.a.* bridle
(horses).

aufzehren [ˈauftseːrən], *v.a.* eat up,
consume.

aufzeichnen [ˈauftsaɪçnən], *v.a.* write
down, take a note of, record.

15

aufziehen ['auftsi:ən], *v.a. irr.* draw up, pull up; pull open; (*pennant*) hoist; (*clock*) wind up; (*child*) bring up, rear; *einen* —, tease s.o.; *gelindere Saiten* —, be more lenient.

Aufzucht ['auftsuxt], *f.* (—, *no pl.*) breeding, rearing.

Aufzug ['auftsu:k], *m.* (—s, *pl.* ⁻e) lift; (*Am.*) elevator; (*Theat.*) act; dress, array, attire.

aufzwingen ['auftsvɪŋən], *v.a. irr. einem etwas* —, force s.th. on s.o.

Augapfel ['aukapfəl], *m.* (—s, *pl.* ⁻) eye-ball; (*fig.*) apple of o.'s eye.

Auge ['augə], *n.* (—s, *pl.* —n) eye; *aus den* —*n, aus dem Sinn*, out of sight, out of mind; *mit einem blauen* — *davonkommen*, escape by the skin of o.'s teeth, get off cheaply; *es wird mir schwarz vor den* —*n*, I feel faint.

Augenblick ['augənblɪk], *m.* (—s, *pl.* —e) moment, instant; *jeden* —, at any moment.

augenblicklich [augən'blɪklɪç], *adj.* momentary, instantaneous.— *adv.* at present, for the moment, immediately.

Augenbraue ['augənbrauə], *f.* (—, *pl.* —n) eye-brow.

augenfällig ['augənfɛlɪç], *adj.* visible, evident, conspicuous.

Augenglas ['augənglas], *n.* (—es, *pl.* ⁻er) eye-glass.

Augenhöhle ['augənhø:lə], *f.* (—, *pl.* —n) eye-socket.

Augenlicht ['augənlɪçt], *n.* (—s, *no pl.*) eye-sight.

Augenlid ['augənli:t], *n.* (—s, *pl.* —er) eye-lid.

Augenmaß ['augənma:s], *n.* (—es, *no pl.*) *gutes* —, good measuring ability with the eye, a sure eye.

Augenmerk ['augənmɛrk], *n.* (—s, *no pl.*) *sein* — *auf etwas richten*, focus o.'s attention on s.th.

Augenschein ['augənʃaɪn], *m.* (—s, *no pl.*) appearance; *in* — *nehmen*, view.

augenscheinlich ['augənʃaɪnlɪç], *adj.* apparent, evident.

Augenweide ['augənvaɪdə], *f.* (—, *pl.* —n) delight to the eye, s.th. lovely to look at.

Augenwimper ['augənvɪmpər], *f.* (—, *pl.* —n) eye-lash.

Augenzeuge ['augəntsɔygə], *m.* (—n, *pl.* —n) eye-witness.

August [au'gust], *m.* (—s, *no pl.*) (*month*) August.

Augustiner [augus'ti:nər], *m.* (—s, *pl.* —) (*Eccl.*) Augustinian.

auktionieren [auktsjo'ni:rən], *v.a.* auction(eer); sell by auction.

Aula ['aula], *f.* (—, *pl.* —len) (*Sch., Univ.*) great hall; auditorium maximum.

Aurikel [au'ri:kəl], *f.* (—, *pl.* —n) (*Bot.*) auricula.

aus [aus], *prep.* (*Dat.*) from, out of, of, off. — *adv.* out, over, finished, done with, spent; *es ist alles* —, it is over and done with; *ich weiß weder ein noch* —, I am at my wits' end.

ausarten ['ausartən], *v.n.* (*aux.* sein) degenerate; (*fig.*) deteriorate.

Ausbau ['ausbau], *m.* (—s, *no pl.*) enlargement, extension.

ausbauen ['ausbauən], *v.a.* enlarge (a house); improve on.

ausbedingen ['ausbədɪŋən], *v.a. sich etwas* —, stipulate.

ausbessern ['ausbɛsərn], *v.a.* (*garment*) mend, repair.

Ausbeute ['ausbɔytə], *f.* (—, *no pl.*) gain, profit, produce.

Ausbeutung ['ausbɔytuŋ], *f.* (—, *no pl.*) exploitation, sweating; (*Min.*) working.

ausbezahlen ['ausbətsa:lən], *v.a.* pay in full.

ausbilden ['ausbɪldən], *v.a.* develop, train; (*Mil.*) drill.

Ausbildung ['ausbɪlduŋ], *f.* (—, *pl.* —en) training, education.

ausbleiben ['ausblaɪbən], *v.n. irr.* (*aux.* sein) fail to appear, be absent.

Ausblick ['ausblɪk], *m.* (—s, *pl.* —e) view (from window); (*fig.*) prospect, outlook.

ausborgen ['ausbɔrgən], *v.a.* (*sich*) *etwas* —, borrow s.th. from.

ausbreiten ['ausbraɪtən], *v.a.* spread (things); stretch out (o.'s arms). — *v.r. sich* —, spread, extend.

Ausbreitung ['ausbraɪtuŋ], *f.* (—, *no pl.*) spreading, extension, distribution, expansion.

ausbringen ['ausbrɪŋən], *v.a. irr. einen Toast auf einen* —, drink s.o.'s health.

Ausbruch ['ausbrux], *m.* (—s, *pl.* ⁻e) breaking out, outbreak, eruption, burst (of laughter).

ausbrüten ['ausbry:tən], *v.a.* hatch; (*fig.*) plot.

Ausbund ['ausbunt], *m.* (—s, *pl.* ⁻e) paragon, embodiment.

Ausdauer ['ausdauər], *f.* (—, *no pl.*) perseverance, persistence, stamina.

ausdehnen ['ausde:nən], *v.a.* extend, stretch, distend; (*fig.*) prolong, protract. — *v.r. sich* —, expand, extend, stretch.

Ausdehnung ['ausde:nuŋ], *f.* (—, *pl.* —en) extension, expansion; dilation; (*Phys.*) dimension.

ausdenken ['ausdɛŋkən], *v.a. irr.* think out. — *v.r. sich etwas* —, devise s.th., invent s.th.; *das ist gar nicht auszudenken*, that is unimaginable, inconceivable.

Ausdeutung ['ausdɔytuŋ], *f.* (—, *pl.* —en) interpretation, explanation.

ausdörren ['ausdœrən], *v.a.* parch, dry (up).

ausdrehen ['ausdre:ən], *v.a.* (*gas, light, water*) turn off, switch off.

Ausdruck ['ausdruk], *m.* (—s, *pl.* ⁻e) expression, phrase.

ausdrücken ['ausdrykən], *v.a.* squeeze out, press out; (*fig.*) express.

ausdrücklich ['ausdryklɪç], *adj.* express, explicit.

ausholen

Ausdrucksweise ['ausdruksvaɪzə], f. (—, pl. —n) enunciation, manner of speech, (mode of) expression, style.

ausdünsten ['ausdynstən], v.a. exhale, perspire.

auseinander [ausaɪn'andər], adv. asunder, apart.

Auseinandersetzung [ausaɪn'andərzɛtsuŋ], f. (—, pl. —en) altercation; discussion, explanation.

auserkoren ['ausɛrkoːrən], adj. elect, chosen, selected.

auserlesen ['ausɛrleːzən], adj. choice, picked, excellent, first class.

auserwählen ['ausɛrvɛːlən], v.a. choose, select.

Ausfahrt ['ausfaːrt], f. (—, pl. —en) drive; gateway; exit.

Ausfall ['ausfal], m. (—s, pl. ⸚e) falling out; (radioactivity) fall-out; sortie, sally; deficiency, loss, cancellation; result, outcome.

ausfallen ['ausfalən], v.n. irr. (aux. sein) drop out, fall out; be cancelled, be omitted, fail to take place; turn out (well etc.).

ausfallend ['ausfalənt], adj. offensive, abusive; — werden, become insulting.

ausfertigen ['ausfɛrtɪgən], v.a. despatch, draw up, make out, issue.

ausfindig ['ausfɪndɪç], adj. — machen, find out, locate, discover.

ausflicken ['ausflɪkən], v.a. mend, patch.

Ausflucht ['ausfluxt], f. (—, pl. ⸚e) evasion, excuse, subterfuge.

Ausflug ['ausfluːk], m. (—s, pl. ⸚e) trip, excursion, outing.

Ausfluß ['ausflus], m. (—sses, pl. ⸚sse) (Engin.) outflow, outlet; (Med.) discharge, suppuration.

ausfragen ['ausfraːgən], v.a. einen —, question, quiz s.o.

Ausfuhr ['ausfuːr], f. (—, pl. —en) export.

ausführbar ['ausfyːrbaːr], adj. practicable, feasible; exportable.

ausführen ['ausfyːrən], v.a. take out; lead out; export; carry out, perform, fulfil; point out.

ausführlich [aus'fyːrlɪç], adj. detailed, full.

Ausführung ['ausfyːruŋ], f. (—, pl. —en) execution, carrying out; finish; workmanship.

ausfüllen ['ausfylən], v.a. (forms) fill up, fill in, complete.

ausfüttern ['ausfytərn], v.a. line (a dress).

Ausgabe ['ausgaːbə], f. (—, pl. —en) issue, distribution; (goods) dispatch, issuing counter; delivery; (book) edition; (pl.) expenses, expenditure.

Ausgang ['ausgaŋ], m. (—s, pl. ⸚e) going out; exit; result, upshot; end, conclusion; time off (from duty).

Ausgangspunkt ['ausgaŋspuŋkt], m. (—s, pl. ⸚e) starting-point; point of departure.

ausgären ['ausgɛːrən], v.n. irr. (aux. sein) ferment; ausgegoren sein, have fermented.

ausgeben ['ausgeːbən], v.a. irr. (work) give out, distribute; (money) expend, spend; (tickets) issue. —v.r. sich — für, pass o.s. off as.

ausgebreitet ['ausgəbraɪtət], adj. extensive, widespread.

Ausgeburt ['ausgəburt], f. (—, pl. —en) monstrosity; — des Hirns, figment of the imagination.

ausgefahren ['ausgəfaːrən], adj. (street) rutted, well-worn.

ausgehen ['ausgeːən], v.n. irr. (aux. sein) go out; (hair) to fall out; (colour) come off, fade; (breath, patience, money) become exhausted; result, end in.

ausgelassen ['ausgəlasən], adj. boisterous, exuberant, frolicsome, merry, jolly, unbridled.

ausgemacht ['ausgəmaxt], adj. arranged, settled, decided; eine —e Sache, a matter of course, a foregone conclusion; ein —er Schurke, a downright scoundrel.

ausgeschlossen ['ausgəʃlɔsən], p.p. das ist —, that is impossible, out of the question.

ausgewachsen ['ausgəvaksən], adj. full-grown, fully grown.

ausgezeichnet ['ausgətsaɪçnət], adj. excellent, first rate, distinguished.

ausgiebig ['ausgiːbɪç], adj. abundant, plentiful; (soil) fertile, rich.

ausgießen ['ausgiːsən], v.a. irr. pour out.

Ausgleich ['ausglaɪç], m. (—s, no pl.) settlement, compromise, compensation, equalisation.

ausgleichen ['ausglaɪçən], v.a. irr. make even, balance, equalise, compensate; (sport) equalise, draw.

ausgraben ['ausgraːbən], v.a. irr. dig out, dig up, excavate, exhume.

Ausguck ['ausguk], m. (—s, pl. —e) look-out; (Naut.) crow's nest.

Ausguß ['ausgus], m. (—sses, pl. ⸚sse) sink, gutter.

aushalten ['aushaltən], v.a. irr. sustain, endure, bear, stand.

aushändigen ['aushɛndɪgən], v.a. deliver up, hand over.

Aushang ['aushaŋ], m. (—s, pl. ⸚e) sign, sign-board, placard.

ausharren ['ausharən], v.n. persevere, hold out, wait patiently.

aushecken ['aushɛkən], v.a. hatch (a plot).

aushelfen ['aushɛlfən], v.n. irr. help out.

Aushilfe ['aushɪlfə], f. (—, pl. —n) help, aid, assistance.

aushilfsweise ['aushɪlfsvaɪzə], adv. temporarily, as a stop-gap.

aushöhlen ['aushøːlən], v.a. hollow out, excavate.

ausholen ['aushoːlən], v.a. pump, sound s.o. — v.n. strike out; weit —, go far back (in a narration).

17

auskehren

auskehren [ˈauskeːrən], *v.a.* sweep out.
auskennen [ˈauskɛnən], *v.r.* *i'r. sich in etwas* —, know all about s.th.
auskleiden [ˈausklaɪdən], *v.a.* undress.
ausklingen [ˈausklɪŋən], *v.n. irr.* (*aux. sein*) (*sound*) die away.
ausklügeln [ˈauskly:gəln], *v.a.* puzzle out, contrive.
auskneifen [ˈausknaɪfən], *v.n. irr.* (*aux. sein*) (*coll.*) bolt, run away.
Auskommen [ˈauskɔmən], *n.* (—s, *no pl.*) sufficiency, subsistence, livelihood; *mit dem ist kein* —, there is no getting on with him.
auskommen [ˈauskɔmən], *v.n. irr.* (*aux. sein*) *mit etwas* —, have enough or sufficient of s.th., manage; *mit einem gut* —, be on good terms with s.o., get on well with s.o.
auskömmlich [ˈauskœmlɪç], *adj.* sufficient.
auskosten [ˈauskɔstən], *v.a.* taste *or* enjoy to the full.
auskramen [ˈauskraːmən], *v.a.* rummage out; (*fig.*) reminisce; talk freely.
auskundschaften [ˈauskuntʃaftən], *v.a.* spy out, reconnoitre, explore.
Auskunft [ˈauskunft], *f.* (—, *pl.* ⁓e) information; (*Tel.*) enquiries; (*Mil.*) intelligence, enquiry.
auslachen [ˈauslaxən], *v.a.* laugh at, deride.
ausladen [ˈauslaːdən], *v.a. irr.* unload, discharge; cancel (invitation).
Auslage [ˈauslaːgə], *f.* (—, *pl.* —n) outlay, expenses, advance; shopwindow display.
Ausland [ˈauslant], *n.* (—s, *no pl.*) foreign country; *ins — fahren,* go abroad.
Ausländer [ˈauslɛndər], *m.* (—s, *pl.* —) foreigner, alien.
auslassen [ˈauslasən], *v.a. irr.* let off (steam); let out (a dress); melt (butter); leave off, omit. — *v.r. sich über etwas* —, speak o.'s mind about s.th.
Auslassung [ˈauslasuŋ], *f.* (—, *pl.* —en) utterance; omission.
auslaufen [ˈauslaufən], *v.n. irr.* (*aux. sein*) run out, leak out; (*ship*) put to sea; (*result*) turn out.
Ausläufer [ˈauslɔyfər], *m.* (—s, *pl.* —) errand boy; (*mountain*) spur.
Auslaut [ˈauslaut], *m.* (—s, *pl.* —e) (*Phonet.*) final sound.
auslegen [ˈausleːgən], *v.a.* lay out, spread out, display; interpret; (*money*) advance.
ausleihen [ˈauslaɪən], *v.a. irr.* lend, hire out. — *v.r. sich etwas* —, borrow s.th.
auslernen [ˈauslɛrnən], *v.n.* end o.'s apprenticeship.
ausliefern [ˈausliːfərn], *v.a.* hand over, deliver; surrender, give up, extradite.
auslöschen [ˈauslœʃən], *v.a.* extinguish, put out (fire).
auslosen [ˈausloːzən], *v.a.* raffle, draw lots for.

auslösen [ˈausløːzən], *v.a.* redeem, ransom, recover; (*fig.*) produce; arouse.
Auslosung [ˈausloːzuŋ], *f.* (—, *pl.* —en) raffle, draw.
Auslösung [ˈausløːzuŋ], *f.* (—, *pl.* —en) ransom.
auslüften [ˈauslyftən], *v.a.* air, ventilate.
ausmachen [ˈausmaxən], *v.a.* decide, settle; amount to; *etwas mit einem* —, arrange s.th. with s.o.; *es macht nichts aus,* it does not matter; *wieviel macht das aus?* how much is this? *würde es Ihnen etwas* —? would you mind?
Ausmaß [ˈausmaːs], *n.* (—es, *pl.* —e) dimension, amount, extent, scale.
ausmeißeln [ˈausmaɪsəln], *v.a.* chisel out, carve out.
ausmerzen [ˈausmɛrtsən], *v.a.* expunge, eradicate.
ausmisten [ˈausmɪstən], *v.a.* clean, clear up (mess).
ausmustern [ˈausmustərn], *v.a.* eliminate, reject; (*Mil.*) discharge.
Ausnahme [ˈausnaːmə], *f.* (—, *pl.* —n) exception.
ausnehmen [ˈausneːmən], *v.a. irr.* except, exclude; (*poultry*) draw; (*fish*) clean.
ausnutzen [ˈausnutsən], *v.a.* make the most of s.th.; take advantage of s.th.
ausnützen [ˈausnytsən], *v.a.* exploit.
auspacken [ˈauspakən], *v.a.* unpack. — *v.n.* talk freely; (*coll.*) open up.
auspfeifen [ˈauspfaɪfən], *v.a. irr.* (*Theat.*) hiss at, cat-call.
auspolstern [ˈauspɔlstərn], *v.a.* stuff.
ausprägen [ˈauspreːgən], *v.a.* stamp, impress, coin.
ausprobieren [ˈausprobiːrən], *v.a.* try out.
Auspuff [ˈauspuf], *m.* (—s, *no pl.*) (*Motor.*) exhaust.
auspusten [ˈauspuːstən], *v.a.* blow out.
ausputzen [ˈausputsən], *v.a.* clean out; adorn.
ausquartieren [ˈauskvartiːrən], *v.a.* (*Mil.*) billet out.
ausquetschen [ˈauskvɛtʃən], *v.a.* squeeze out.
ausradieren [ˈausradiːrən], *v.a.* erase.
ausrangieren [ˈausranʒiːrən], *v.a.* cast off, sort out.
ausräuchern [ˈausrɔyçərn], *v.a.* fumigate.
ausraufen [ˈausraufən], *v.a.* (*obs.*) tear *or* pull out (hair).
ausräumen [ˈausrɔymən], *v.a.* clear out, clear away.
ausrechnen [ˈausrɛçnən], *v.a.* reckon, compute, calculate; *ausgerechnet du,* (*emph.*) you of all people.
ausrecken [ˈausrɛkən], *v.a. sich den Hals* —, crane o.'s neck.
Ausrede [ˈausreːdə], *f.* (—, *pl.* —n) evasion, excuse, subterfuge.
ausreden [ˈausreːdən], *v.a. einem etwas* —, dissuade s.o. from s.th. — *v.n.* finish speaking; *einen — lassen,* allow s.o. to finish speaking.

18

ausreichen ['ausraɪçən], *v.n.* suffice.

ausreißen ['ausraɪsən], *v.a. irr.* pluck, pull out. — *v.n.* (*aux.* sein) run away, bolt.

ausrenken ['ausrɛŋkən], *v.a.* dislocate, sprain.

ausrichten ['ausrɪçtən], *v.a.* adjust, make straight; deliver (a message); accomplish; (*Mil.*) dress.

ausrotten ['ausrɔtən], *v.a.* root up; exterminate, extirpate.

ausrücken ['ausrʏkən], *v.n.* (*aux.* sein) (*Mil.*) march out; (*coll.*) decamp.

Ausruf ['ausruːf], *m.* (—s, *pl.* —e) exclamation, interjection, outcry; (*public*) proclamation.

Ausruf(ungs)zeichen ['ausruːf(uŋs)-tsaɪçən], *n.* (—s, *pl.* —) exclamation mark.

ausruhen ['ausruːən], *v.r. sich* —, rest, take a rest.

ausrüsten ['ausrʏstən], *v.a.* furnish, fit out, equip.

Ausrutschen ['ausrutʃən], *v.n.* (*aux.* sein) slip.

Aussage ['auszaːgə], *f.* (—, *pl.* —n) declaration, statement, evidence; (*Law*) deposition, affidavit; (*Gram.*) predicate.

aussagen ['auszaːgən], *v.a.* say, state, utter, declare; (*Law*) depose, give evidence.

Aussatz ['auszats], *m.* (—es, *no pl.*) leprosy.

Aussätzige ['auszɛtsɪgə], *m.* (—n, *pl.* —n) leper.

aussaugen ['auszaugən], *v.a.* suck dry.

ausschalten ['ausʃaltən], *v.a.* switch off.

Ausschank ['ausʃaŋk], *m.* (—s, *no pl.*) pub, bar.

Ausschau ['ausʃau], *f.* (—, *no pl.*) watch; — *halten*, look out for.

ausscheiden ['ausʃaɪdən], *v.a. irr.* separate; (*Med.*) secrete. — *v.n.* (*aux.* sein) withdraw from, retire, secede.

Ausscheidung ['ausʃaɪduŋ], *f.* (—, *pl.* —en) retirement, withdrawal; (*Med.*) secretion.

Ausschlag ['ausʃlaːk], *m.* (—s, *pl.* ⸚e) turn (of the scales); deflection (of the magnetic needle); (*Med.*) rash, eczema; *den* — *geben*, clinch the matter; give the casting vote.

ausschlagen ['ausʃlaːgən], *v.a. irr.* knock out; refuse, decline (an invitation); *das schlägt dem Faß den Boden aus*, that is the last straw. — *v.n.* (*aux.* sein) (*Hort.*) bud, shoot; *gut* —, turn out well.

ausschlaggebend ['ausʃlaːkgeːbənt], *adj.* decisive; (*vote*) casting.

ausschließen ['ausʃliːsən], *v.a. irr.* lock out; exclude.

ausschließlich ['ausʃliːslɪç], *adj.* exclusive, sole.

ausschlüpfen ['ausʃlʏpfən], *v.n.* (*aux.* sein) hatch out.

Ausschluß ['ausʃlus], *m.* (—sses, *pl.* ⸚sse) exclusion; *unter* — *der Öffentlichkeit*, in camera.

ausschmücken ['ausʃmʏkən], *v.a.* adorn, decorate, embellish.

Ausschnitt ['ausʃnɪt], *m.* (—s, *pl.* —e) cutting out; (*newspaper*) cutting; (*dress*) neck (line).

ausschreiben ['ausʃraɪbən], *v.a. irr.* write down in full; make out a bill; advertise (post) as vacant.

ausschreiten ['ausʃraɪtən], *v.n. irr.* (*aux.* sein) step out, stride along.

Ausschreitungen ['ausʃraɪtuŋən], *f. pl.* rioting; excesses.

Ausschuß ['ausʃus], *m.* (—sses, *pl.* ⸚sse) dross, refuse, rejects, low quality goods; committee, commission, board.

ausschweifend ['ausʃvaɪfənt], *adj.* extravagant; licentious, dissolute.

aussehen ['auszeːən], *v.n. irr.* look; look like, appear.

außen ['ausən], *adv.* outside, abroad, outward, without.

Außenhandel ['ausənhandəl], *m.* (—s, *no pl.*) export trade.

Außenministerium ['ausənmɪnɪsteːrjum], *n.* (—s, *pl.* —terien) Ministry of Foreign Affairs; (*U.K.*) Foreign Office, (*U.S.*) State Department.

Außenstände ['ausənʃtɛndə], *m. pl.* outstanding claims, liabilities.

außer ['ausər], *prep.* (*Dat.*) in addition to, besides, apart from; out of, at the outside of, beside, without; — *Dienst*, retired. — *conj.* except, save, but.

außerdem ['ausərdeːm], *adv.* besides, moreover, furthermore.

Äussere ['ɔysərə], *n.* (—n, *no pl.*) exterior.

außerehelich ['ausəreːəlɪç], *adj.* illegitimate.

außergewöhnlich ['ausərgəvøːnlɪç], *adj.* unusual, exceptional.

außerhalb ['ausərhalp], *prep.* outside.

äußerlich ['ɔysərlɪç], *adj.* external.

Äußerlichkeit ['ɔysərlɪçkaɪt], *f.* (—, *pl.* —en) formality.

äußern ['ɔysərn], *v.a.* utter, express. — *v.r. sich zu etwas* —, give o.'s opinion on some question; express o.s. on some subject.

außerordentlich [ausər'ɔrdəntlɪç], *adj.* extraordinary, unusual; (*Univ.*) —*er Professor*, senior lecturer *or* reader; (*Am.*) associate professor.

äußerst ['ɔysərst], *adj.* outermost, most remote; extreme, utmost.

außerstande ['ausərʃtandə], *adj.* unable.

Äußerung ['ɔysəruŋ], *f.* (—, *pl.* —en) utterance, remark, observation.

aussetzen ['auszetsən], *v.a.* set out, put out; offer (a reward); suspend; *etwas an einer Sache* —, find fault with s.th.; *sich einer Gefahr* —, expose o.s. to danger, run a risk. — *v.n.* pause, discontinue; (*Motor.*) stop, misfire.

Aussicht ['auszɪçt], *f.* (—, *pl.* —en) view, panorama; prospect, chance; *etwas in* — *stellen*, hold out the prospect of s.th.; *in* — *nehmen*, intend.

aussinnen [ˈauszɪnən],*v. a. irr.* imagine, invent, devise.

aussöhnen [ˈauszo:nən], *v.r. sich mit einem —*, become reconciled with s.o.

aussondern [ˈauszɔndərn], *v.a.* single out.

ausspannen [ˈausʃpanən], *v.a. (animals)* unharness. — *v.n. (coll.)* relax.

ausspeien [ˈausʃpaiən], *v.a.* spit out, vomit.

aussperren [ˈausʃpɛrən], *v.a.* shut out; *(industrial)* lock out.

ausspielen [ˈausʃpi:lən], *v.n.* finish playing; *(Sport, Game)* lead (off).

Aussprache [ˈausʃpra:xə], *f.* (—, *no pl.*) pronunciation; discussion; confidential talk.

aussprechen [ˈausʃprɛçən], *v.a. irr.* have o.'s say; utter; pronounce. — *v.r. sich —*, speak o.'s mind.

Ausspruch [ˈausʃprux], *m.* (—s, *pl.* ⁼e) utterance, dictum.

ausspüren [ˈausʃpy:rən], *v.a. (Hunt.)* track down.

ausstaffieren [ˈausʃtafi:rən],*v.a.*furnish, equip.

Ausstand [ˈausʃtant], *m.* (—s, *pl.* ⁼e) *(industry)* strike; *(pl.)* outstanding debts, arrears.

ausständig [ˈausʃtɛndɪç], *adj.* outstanding; on strike.

ausstatten [ˈausʃtatən], *v.a.* endow with, provide with, equip.

Ausstattung [ˈausʃtatuŋ], *f.* (—, *pl.* —en) outfit; (bridal) trousseau; *(coll.)* get-up.

ausstechen [ˈausʃtɛçən], *v.a. irr.* pierce; *einen —*, *(fig.)* excel s.o.

ausstehen [ˈausʃte:ən], *v.n. irr.* stand out; *(money)* be overdue. — *v.a.* endure, suffer, bear, undergo; *ich kann ihn nicht —*, I cannot stand him.

aussteigen [ˈausʃtaigən], *v.n. irr. (aux. sein)* get out, alight; disembark.

ausstellen [ˈausʃtɛlən], *v.a.* exhibit; display; make out (bill etc.).

Aussteller [ˈausʃtɛlər], *m.* (—s, *pl.* —) drawer (of a cheque); exhibitor.

Ausstellung [ˈausʃtɛluŋ], *f.* (—, *pl.* —en) exhibition; *(Am.)* exposition.

Aussteuer [ˈausʃtɔyər], *f.* (—, *pl.* —n) trousseau.

ausstopfen [ˈausʃtɔpfən], *v.a.* stuff.

ausstoßen [ˈausʃtosən], *v.a. irr.* push out, expel; utter.

Ausstrahlung [ˈausʃtra:luŋ], *f.* (—, *pl.* —en) radiation.

ausstrecken [ˈausʃtrɛkən], *v.a.* stretch out, reach out, extend.

ausstreichen [ˈausʃtraiçən], *v.a. irr.* strike out, erase, delete; smoothe.

ausstreuen [ˈausʃtrɔyən], *v.a.* scatter, spread, sprinkle; *Gerüchte —*, circulate rumours.

ausstudieren [ˈausʃtudi:rən], *v.n.* finish o.'s studies, graduate.

aussuchen [ˈauszu:xən], *v.a.* select.

Austausch [ˈaustauʃ], *m.* (—es, *pl.* —e) barter, exchange; *(thoughts, letters)* interchange.

austauschen [ˈaustauʃən], *v.a.* barter, exchange; *(thoughts, letters)* interchange.

austeilen [ˈaustailən], *v.a.* distribute, allocate.

Auster [ˈaustər], *f.* (—, *pl.* —n) oyster.

Austerbank [ˈaustərbaŋk], *f.* (—, *pl.* ⁼e) oyster-bed.

austilgen [ˈaustɪlgən], *v.a.* exterminate, eradicate, extirpate.

Australien [auˈstra:ljən], *n.* Australia.

austreiben [ˈaustraibən], *v.a. irr.* drive out, expel; exorcise.

austreten [ˈaustre:tən], *v.a. irr.* tread out; stretch (shoes) by walking; *ausgetretene Stufen*, worn steps. — *v.n. (aux. sein)* retire (from business); withdraw (from a club); *(coll.)* go to the lavatory.

Austritt [ˈaustrɪt], *m.* (—s, *pl.* —e) withdrawal, retirement.

ausüben [ˈausy:bən], *v.a.* exercise, practise; exert, commit.

Ausverkauf [ˈausfɛrkauf], *m.* (—s, *pl.* ⁼e) selling-off, clearance sale.

Auswahl [ˈausva:l], *f.* (—, *pl.* —en) choice, selection.

Auswanderer [ˈausvandərər], *m.* (—s, *pl.* —) emigrant.

auswärtig [ˈausvɛrtɪç], *adj.* foreign, away.

auswärts [ˈausvɛrts], *adv.* outward(s), away from home.

auswechseln [ˈausvɛksəln], *v.a.* exchange; fit (spare parts).

Ausweg [ˈausve:k], *m.* (—s, *pl.* —e) expedient; way out; *ich weiß keinen —*, I am at my wits' end.

ausweichen [ˈausvaiçən], *v.n. irr. (aux. sein)* give way; evade, parry.

Ausweis [ˈausvais], *m.* (—es, *pl.* —e) proof of identity, identity card.

ausweisen [ˈausvaizən], *v.a. irr.* turn out, banish, exile, deport. — *v.r. (aux. haben) sich —*, show proof of o.'s identity.

auswendig [ˈausvɛndɪç], *adj.* by heart.

auswirken [ˈausvɪrkən], *v.r. sich gut —*, work out well, have a good effect.

Auswuchs [ˈausvu:ks], *m.* (—es, *pl.* ⁼e) sprouting, outgrowth, *(fig.)* excrescence.

Auswurf [ˈausvurf], *m.* (—s, *pl.* ⁼e) excretion; expectoration; — *der Menschheit*, scum of the earth.

auszählen [ˈaustsɛ:lən], *v.n.* count, number. — *v.a.* count out.

Auszahlung [ˈaustsa:luŋ], *f.* (—, *pl.* —en) payment.

auszanken [ˈaustsaŋkən], *v.a.* scold, chide.

auszehren [ˈaustse:rən], *v.n. (aux. sein)* waste away, be consumed.

auszeichnen [ˈaustsaiçnən], *v.a.* mark out, honour, decorate. — *v.r. sich —*, distinguish o.s.

Auszeichnung [ˈaustsaiçnuŋ], *f.* (—, *pl.* —en) distinction, medal.

ausziehen ['austsi:ən], *v.a. irr.* undress, take off (clothes); (*Chem.*) extract; stretch. — *v.n.* (*aux.* sein) move out. — *v.r. sich* —, undress.

auszischen ['austsɪʃən], *v.a.* (*Theat.*) hiss, cat-call.

Auszug ['austsu:k], *m.* (—s, *pl.* ⁓e) removal (from home); marching off; exodus; extract (from a book), abstract (from a deed).

Auto ['auto], *n.* (—s, *pl.* —s) motor-car, (*Am.*) automobile.

Autogramm [auto'gram], *n.* (—s, *pl.* —e) autograph.

Automat [auto'ma:t], *m.* (—en, *pl.* —en) slot machine.

Autor ['autor], *m.* (—s, *pl.* —en) author, writer.

Autorität [autori'tɛ:t], *f.* (—, *pl.* —en) authority.

avisieren [avi'zi:rən], *v.a.* notify, advise.

Axt [akst], *f.* (—, *pl.* ⁓e) axe.

Azur [a'tsu:r], *m.* (⁓s, *no pl.*) azure.

B

B [be:], *n.* (—s, *pl.*—s) the letter B; (*Mus.*) B flat; — *Dur*, B flat major; — *Moll*, B flat minor.

Bach [bax], *m.* (—es, *pl.* ⁓e) brook, rivulet.

Bachstelze ['baxʃteltsə], *f.* (—, *pl.* —n) wagtail.

Backe ['bakə], *f.* (—, *pl.* —n) cheek.

backen ['bakən], *v.a.* bake.

Backenstreich ['bakənʃtraɪç], *m.* (—s, *pl.* —e) box on the ear.

Bäcker ['bɛkər], *m.* (—s, *pl.* —) baker.

Backfisch ['bakfɪʃ], *m.* (—es, *pl.* —e) (*fig.*) teenage girl.

Backhuhn ['bakhu:n], *n.* (—s, *pl.* ⁓er) fried chicken.

Backobst ['bakopst], *n.* (—es, *no pl.*) dried fruit.

Backpfeife ['bakpfaɪfə], *f.* (—, *pl.* —n) box on the ear.

Backpflaume ['bakpflaumə], *f.* (—, *pl.* —n) prune.

Backstein ['bakʃtaɪn], *m.* (—s, *pl.* —e) brick.

Backwerk ['bakvɛrk], *n.* (—s, *no pl.*) pastry.

Bad [ba:t], *n.* (—es, *pl.* ⁓er) bath; spa, watering-place.

Badeanstalt ['ba:dəanʃtalt], *f.* (—, *pl.* —en) public baths.

baden ['ba:dən], *v.n.* bathe, have a bath.

Badewanne ['ba:dəvanə], *f.* (—, *pl.* —n) bath-tub.

Bagage [ba'ga:ʒə], *f.* (—, *no pl.*) luggage; (*Am.*) baggage; (*sl.*) mob, rabble.

Bagger ['bagər], *m.* (—s, *pl.* —) dredger, dredging-machine.

baggern ['bagərn], *v.a.* dredge.

Bahn [ba:n], *f.* (—, *pl.* —en) road, path, course; (*Astr.*) orbit; railway(-line). — *brechen*, open a path.

bahnbrechend ['ba:nbrɛçənt], *adj.* pioneering, epoch-making.

bahnen ['ba:nən], *v.a.* make passable; pave (the way).

Bahngleis ['ba:nglaɪs], *n.* ⁓(—es, *pl.* —e) railway-line, railway-track; (*Am.*) railroad-line, railroad-track.

Bahnhof ['ba:nho:f], *m.* (—s, *pl.* ⁓e) railway-station, (*Am.*) depot.

Bahnsteig ['ba:nʃtaɪk], *m.* (—s, *pl.* —e) platform.

Bahnwärter ['ba:nvɛrtər], *m.* (—s, *pl.* —) signal-man.

Bahre ['ba:rə], *f.* (—, *pl.* —n) litter, stretcher; bier.

Bahrtuch ['ba:rtu:x], *n.* (—s, *pl.* ⁓er) pall, shroud.

Bai [baɪ], *f.* (—, *pl.* —en) bay, cove.

Baisse ['bɛsə], *f.* (—, *pl.* —n) (*Comm.*) fall in share prices.

Bakkalaureat [bakalaure'a:t], *n.* (—s, *pl.* —e) bachelor's degree.

Bakterie [bak'te:rjə], *f.* (—, *pl.* —n) bacterium.

bald [balt], *adv.* soon, shortly, directly, presently.

Baldachin ['baldaxɪn], *m.* (—s, *pl.* —e) canopy.

baldig ['baldɪç], *adj.* quick, speedy; *auf —es Wiedersehen*, see you again soon.

Baldrian ['baldria:n], *m.* (—s, *no pl.*) valerian.

Balearen, die [bale'a:rən, di:], *pl.* Balearic Islands.

Balg (1) [balk], *m.* (—s, *pl.* ⁓e) skin, slough, husk; bellows (of organ *or* forge).

Balg (2) [balk], *n.* (—s, *pl.* ⁓er) brat; naughty child.

balgen ['balgən], *v.r. sich* —, (*children*) fight, romp.

Balgerei ['balgəraɪ], *f.* (—, *pl.* —en) scuffle, scrimmage.

Balken ['balkən], *m.* (—s, *pl.* —) beam, joist, rafter.

Balkenwerk ['balkənvɛrk], *n.* (—s, *no pl.*) building-frame, timbers, wood-work.

Balkon [bal'kɔ̃], *m.* (—s, *pl.* —s, —e) balcony.

Ball [bal], *m.* (—s, *pl.* ⁓e) ball; globe; sphere; dance.

ballen ['balən], *v.a.* form into a ball; clench (o.'s fist).

Ballen ['balən], *m.* (—s, *pl.* —) bale, bundle, package; ball (of the hand *or* foot).

ballförmig ['balfœrmɪç], *adj.* spherical.

Ballistik [ba'lɪstɪk], *f.* (—, *no pl.*) ballistics.

Ballon [ba'lɔ̃], *m.* (—s, *pl.* —s, —e) balloon.

Balsam ['balza:m], *m.* (—s, *pl.* —e) balm, balsam.

Baltikum ['baltikum], *n.* (—s, *no pl.*) the Baltic countries.

Bambusrohr

Bambusrohr ['bambusro:r], *n.* (—s, *pl.* —e) bamboo (cane).

Banane [ba'na:nə], *f.* (—, *pl.* —n) banana.

Banause [ba'nauzə], *m.* (—n, *pl.* —n) narrow-minded person, philistine.

Band (1) [bant], *n.* (—s, *pl.* ¨er) ribbon, riband, tape; string; (*Bot.*) band; hoop (*for a cask*); (*Anat.*) ligament, tendon.

Band (2) [bant], *n.* (—s, *pl.* —e) (*fig.*) bond, fetter, chain, (*pl.*) bonds, ties (*of friendship*).

Band (3) [bant], *m.* (—es, *pl.* ¨e) volume.

Bändchen ['bɛntçən], *n.* (—s, *pl.* —) small ribbon, small piece of string; (*book*) small volume.

Bande ['bandə], *f.* (—, *pl.* —n) horde, gang, set.

bändigen ['bɛndɪgən], *v.a.* tame, subdue.

Bandmaß ['bantma:s], *n.* (—es, *pl.* —e) tape-measure.

Bandwurm ['bantvurm], *m.* (—s, *pl.* ¨er) (*Zool.*) tape-worm.

bange ['baŋə], *adj.* afraid, worried, alarmed.

Bangigkeit ['baŋɪçkaɪt], *f.* (—, *no pl.*) uneasiness, anxiety.

Bank (1) [baŋk], *f.* (—, *pl.* ¨e) bench, seat (in a park); *auf die lange — schieben*, delay, shelve; *durch die —*, without exception.

Bank (2) [baŋk], *f.* (—, *pl.* —en) bank; *die — sprengen*, break the bank.

Bänkelsänger ['bɛŋkəlzɛŋər], *m.* (—s, *pl.* —) ballad singer.

bank(e)rott [baŋk'rɔt], *adj.* bankrupt.

Bankett [baŋ'kɛt], *n.* (—s, *pl.* —e) banquet.

Bankkonto ['baŋkkɔnto], *n.* (—s, *pl.* —ten) bank-account.

Bann [ban], *m.* (—s, *no pl.*) ban, exile; (*Eccl.*) excommunication; *in den — tun*, outlaw, (*Eccl.*) excommunicate; (*fig.*) charm, spell.

bannen ['banən], *v.a.* banish, exile, cast out.

Banner ['banər], *n.* (—s, *pl.* —) banner, standard.

Bannmeile ['banmaɪlə], *f.* (—, *pl.* —n) boundary.

bar [ba:r], *adv.* in cash, ready money.

Bar [ba:r], *f.* (—, *pl.* —s) bar (for selling drinks etc.).

Bär [bɛ:r], *m.* (—en, *pl.* —en) (*Zool.*) bear; *einem einen —en aufbinden*, to lead s.o. up the garden-path.

Barauslagen ['barausla:gən], *f. pl.* cash expenses.

Barbar [bar'ba:r], *m.* (—en, *pl.* —en) barbarian, vandal.

barbarisch [bar'ba:rɪʃ], *adj.* barbarous.

Barbestand ['ba:rbaʃtant], *m.* (—s, *pl.* ¨e) cash reserve, cash balance.

bärbeißig ['bɛ:rbaɪsɪç], *adj.* surly, morose.

Barchent ['barçənt], *m.* (—s, *no pl.*) fustian.

Barde ['bardə], *m.* (—n, *pl.* —n) bard, minstrel.

Bärenfell ['bɛ:rənfɛl], *n.* (—s, *pl.* —e) bear-skin.

Bärenmütze ['bɛ:rənmytsə], *f.* (—, *pl.* —n) (*Mil.*) busby.

Bärenzwinger ['bɛ:rəntsvɪŋər], *m.* (—s, *pl.* —) bear-garden.

Barett [ba'rɛt], *n.* (—s, *pl.* —e) cap, beret; (*Eccl.*) biretta.

barfuß ['barfus], *adj.* barefoot(ed).

Bargeld ['bargɛlt], *n.* (—(e)s, *no pl.*) cash.

barhäuptig ['barhɔyptɪç], *adj.* bareheaded.

Barkasse [bar'kasə], *f.* (—, *pl.* —n) launch.

Barke ['barkə], *f.* (—, *pl.* —n) barge, lighter.

barmherzig [barm'hɛrtsɪç], *adj.* merciful, charitable, compassionate.

Barock [ba'rɔk], *n.* (—s, *no pl.*) Baroque.

Baronin [ba'ro:nɪn], *f.* (—, *pl.* —nen) baroness.

Barren ['barən], *m.* (—s, *pl.* —) parallel bars.

Barsch [barʃ], *m.* (—es, *pl.* —e) (*Zool.*) perch.

barsch [barʃ], *adj.* rough, harsh, sharp, abrupt, unfriendly.

Barschaft ['ba:rʃaft], *f.* (—, *pl.* —en) ready money.

Bart [ba:rt], *m.* (—s, *pl.* ¨e) beard; (*key*) ward.

Bartflechte ['ba:rtflɛçtə], *f.* (—, *pl.* —n) barber's itch.

bärtig ['bɛ:rtɪç], *adj.* bearded.

Basalt [ba'zalt], *m.* (—s, *pl.* —e) (*Min.*) basalt.

Base ['ba:zə], *f.* (—, *pl.* —n) female cousin; (*Chem.*) base.

Basis ['ba:zɪs], *f.* (—, *pl.* **Basen**) base, foundation.

Baskenmütze ['baskənmytsə], *f.* (—, *pl.* —n) tam-o'-shanter, beret.

Baß [bas], *m.* (—sses, *pl.* ¨sse) (*Mus.*) bass.

Baßschlüssel ['basʃlysəl], *m.* (—s, *pl.* —) (*Mus.*) bass-clef.

Bassin [ba'sɛ̃], *n.* (—s, *pl.* —s) basin, reservoir.

Bast [bast], *m.* (—es, *pl.* —e) inner bark, fibre (*of trees etc.*); bast.

basta ['basta], *int.* and that's that!

Bastei [bas'taɪ], *f.* (—, *pl.* —en) bastion.

basteln ['bastəln], *v.a.* work on a hobby, tinker.

Batist [ba'tɪst], *m.* (—s, *pl.* —e) cambric.

Bau [bau], *m.* (—es, *pl.* —ten) building, structure, edifice; act of building; *im — begriffen*, in course of construction.

Bauart ['bauart], *f.* (—, *pl.* —en) (architectural) style, structure.

Bauch [baux], *m.* (—es, *pl.* ¨e) belly, stomach.

Bauchfell ['bauxfɛl], *n.* (—s, *pl.* —e) peritoneum.

bauchig [ˈbauçɪç], *adj.* bulgy.
Bauchredner [ˈbauxreːdnər], *m.* (—s, *pl.* —) ventriloquist.
bauen [ˈbauən], *v.a.* build, construct, erect. — *v.n. auf etwas* —, (*fig.*) rely on s.th., count on s.th.
Bauer (1) [ˈbauər], *m.* (—n, *pl.* —n) farmer, peasant; (*chess*) pawn.
Bauer (2) [ˈbauər], *n.* (—s, *pl.* —) (*bird*) cage.
Bauernfänger [ˈbauərnfɛŋər], *m.* (—s, *pl.* —) sharper, rook, confidence-trickster.
Bäuerin [ˈbɔyərɪn], *f.* (—, *pl.* —nen) farmer's wife.
Bauernstand [ˈbauərnʃtant], *m.* (—s, *pl.* ˑe) peasantry.
baufällig [ˈbaufɛlɪç], *adj.* dilapidated, ramshackle.
Baugerüst [ˈbaugəryst], *n.* (—s, *pl.* —e) scaffolding.
Baugewerbe [ˈbaugəvɛrbə], *n.* (—s, *no pl.*) building trade.
Baukunst [ˈbaukunst], *f.* (—, *no pl.*) architecture.
Baum [baum], *m.* (—(e)s, *pl.* ˑe) tree.
Baumeister [ˈbaumaistər], *m.* (—s, *pl.* —) architect; master-builder.
baumeln [ˈbauməln], *v.n.* dangle.
Baumkuchen [ˈbaumkuːxən], *m.* (—s, *pl.* —) pyramid-cake.
Baumschule [ˈbaumʃuːlə], *f.* (—, *pl.* —n) plantation of trees, orchard, tree nursery.
Baumstamm [ˈbaumʃtam], *m.* (—s, *pl.* ˑe) stem, trunk.
Baumwolle [ˈbaumvɔlə], *f.* (—, *pl.* —n) cotton.
Bauriß [ˈbauris], *m.* (—sses, *pl.* —sse) plan, architect's drawing.
Bausch [bauʃ], *m.* (—es, *pl.* ˑe) pad, bolster; *in* — *und Bogen*, in the lump: all at once.
bauschig [ˈbauʃɪç], *adj.* baggy.
Bauwerk [ˈbauvɛrk] *see* **Gebäude**.
Bayern [ˈbaiərn], *n.* Bavaria.
Bazar [baˈzaːr], *m.* (—s, *pl.* —e) bazaar, fair, emporium.
beabsichtigen [bəˈapzɪçtɪgən], *v.a.* aim at, intend, have in view.
beachten [bəˈaxtən], *v.a.* observe, pay attention to.
Beamte [bəˈamtə], *m.* (—n, *pl.* —n) official, officer, civil servant.
Beamtin [bəˈamtɪn], *f.* (—, *pl.* —nen) female official, female civil servant.
beängstigen [bəˈɛŋstɪgən], *v.a.* alarm, make afraid.
beanspruchen [bəˈanʃpruxən], *v.a.* demand, claim, lay claim to.
beanstanden [bəˈanʃtandən], *v.a.* object to, raise objections to, query.
beantragen [bəˈantraːgən], *v.a.* move, apply, lodge an application.
beantworten [bəˈantvɔrtən], *v.a.* answer, reply to.
bearbeiten [bəˈarbaitən], *v.a.* work (on); (*book, play*) adapt, arrange, revise; (*Agr.*) cultivate; (*fig.*) *einen* —, try to influence s.o., try to convince s.o.

Bearbeitung [bəˈarbaituŋ], *f.* (—, *pl.* —en) working, manipulation, operation; (*Agr.*) culture, cultivation; (*book, play*) adaptation, revision, arrangement.
beargwöhnen [bəˈarkvøːnən], *v.a.* suspect, view with suspicion.
beaufsichtigen [bəˈaufzɪçtɪgən], *v.a.* control, supervise, superintend.
beauftragen [bəˈauftraːgən], *v.a.* commission, charge, authorize.
bebauen [bəˈbauən], *v.a.* build upon; (*Agr.*) cultivate.
beben [ˈbeːbən], *v.n.* shake, quake, tremble; *vor Kälte* —, shiver with cold.
Becher [ˈbɛçər], *m.* (—s, *pl.* —) beaker, cup, goblet, mug; (*dice*) box.
Becken [ˈbɛkən], *n.* (—s, *pl.* —) basin, bowl; (*Anat.*) pelvis; (*Mus.*) cymbal.
Bedacht [bəˈdaxt], *m.* (—s, *no pl.*) consideration; *mit* —, deliberately; *ohne* —, thoughtlessly.
bedächtig [bəˈdɛçtɪç], *adj.* circumspect, deliberate, cautious, slow.
bedanken [bəˈdaŋkən], *v.r. sich für etwas* —, thank s.o. for s.th., decline with thanks (*also iron.*).
Bedarf [bəˈdarf], *m.* (—s, *no pl.*) need, requirement, demand.
bedauerlich [bəˈdauərlɪç], *adj.* regrettable, deplorable.
bedauern [bəˈdauərn], *v.a.* pity, commiserate, regret; *ich bedaure, daß*, I am sorry that . . .
bedecken [bəˈdɛkən], *v.a.* cover (up); *sich mit Ruhm* —, cover o.s. with glory.
bedeckt [bəˈdɛkt], *adj.* (*sky*) overcast.
bedenken [bəˈdɛŋkən], *v.a. irr.* consider, bear in mind. — *v.r. sich* —, deliberate, hesitate; *sich anders* —, change o.'s mind.
bedenklich [bəˈdɛŋklɪç], *adj.* (*persons*) doubtful, dubious; (*things*) risky, delicate, precarious; (*illness*) serious, grave.
Bedenkzeit [bəˈdɛŋktsait], *f.* (—, *pl.* —en) time to consider, respite.
bedeuten [bəˈdɔytən], *v.a.* signify, mean, imply; direct, order.
bedeutend [bəˈdɔytənt], *adj.* important, eminent, considerable, outstanding.
bedeutsam [bəˈdɔytzaːm], *adj.* significant.
Bedeutung [bəˈdɔytuŋ], *f.* (—, *pl.* —en) significance, meaning; consequence, importance; *nichts von* —, nothing to speak of.
bedienen [bəˈdiːnən], *v.a.* serve, attend to, wait on; (*machine*) operate; (*Cards*) follow suit. —*v.r. sich* —, help o.s., make use of.
Bediente [bəˈdiːntə], *m.* (—n, *pl.* —n) servant, attendant, footman, lackey.
Bedienung [bəˈdiːnuŋ], *f.* (—, *pl.* —en) service, attendance.
bedingen [bəˈdiŋən], *v.a.* stipulate, postulate, condition, cause.

23

bedingt

bedingt [bə'dıŋkt], *adj.* conditional.

Bedingung [bə'dıŋuŋ], *f.* (—, *pl.* —en) stipulation, condition, term; *unter keiner* —, on no account.

bedingungsweise [bə'dıŋuŋsvaızə], *adv.* on condition, conditionally.

bedrängen [bə'drɛŋən], *v.a.* oppress; press hard, afflict.

Bedrängnis [bə'drɛŋnıs], *n.* (—ses, *pl.* —se) oppression, distress.

bedrohen [bə'dro:ən], *v.a.* threaten, menace.

bedrohlich [bə'dro:lıç], *adj.* threatening, menacing, ominous.

bedrücken [bə'drykən], *v.a.* oppress, harass, depress.

Beduine [bedu'i:nə], *m.* (—n, *pl.* —n) Bedouin.

bedünken [bə'dyŋkən], *v.a.* appear, seem; *es bedünkt mich*, methinks.

bedürfen [bə'dyrfən], *v.n. irr.* want, need, be in need of.

Bedürfnis [bə'dyrfnıs], *n.* (—ses, *pl.* —se) want, need, requirement, necessity; *es ist mir ein* —, I cannot but; *einem dringenden* — *abhelfen*, meet an urgent want *or* need; *ein* — *haben*, (*coll.*) need to relieve o.s.

Bedürfnisanstalt [bə'dyrfnısanʃtalt], *f.* (—, *pl.* —en) public lavatory, public convenience.

bedürftig [bə'dyrftıç], *adj.* needy, indigent, poor.

beeidigen [bə'aıdıgən], *v.a.* confirm by oath, swear in.

beeifern [bə'aıfərn], *v.r. sich* —, exert o.s., strive, be zealous.

beeilen [bə'aılən], *v.r. sich* —, hurry, hasten, make haste.

beeindrucken [bə'aındrukən], *v.a.* impress.

beeinflussen [bə'aınflusən], *v.a.* influence.

beeinträchtigen [bə'aıntrɛçtıgən], *v.a.* injure, lessen, diminish, detract from, curtail.

beenden [bə'ɛndən], *v.a.* end, finish, terminate, conclude.

beendigen [bə'ɛndıgən], *v.a.* end, finish, terminate, conclude.

beengen [bə'ɛŋən], *v.a.* cramp, narrow.

beerben [bə'ɛrbən], *v.a.* einen —, inherit from s.o.

beerdigen [bə'e:rdıgən], *v.a.* bury, inter.

Beere ['be:rə], *f.* (—, *pl.* —n) berry.

Beet [be:t], *n.* (—es, *pl.* —e) (flower) bed.

befähigen [bə'fɛ:ıgən], *v.a.* fit, enable, qualify.

Befähigung [bə'fɛ:ıguŋ], *f.* (—, *pl.* —en) qualification, capacity, aptitude.

befahren [bə'fa:rən], *v.a. irr.* pass over, travel over; (*Naut.*) navigate.

befallen [bə'falən], *v.a. irr.* befall, fall on; *von Traurigkeit* — *sein*, be overcome by sadness.

befangen [bə'faŋən], *adj.* biased, prejudiced; bashful, embarrassed.

befassen [bə'fasən], *v.a.* touch, handle. — *v.r. sich mit etwas* —, occupy o.s. with s.th.

befehden [bə'fe:dən], *v.a.* make war upon, show enmity towards.

Befehl [bə'fe:l], *m.* (—s, *pl.* —e) order, command; (*Mil.*) *zu* —, very good, sir; (*Mil.*) *den* — *führen über*, command.

befehlen [bə'fe:lən], *v.a. irr.* order, command.

befehligen [bə'fe:lıgən], *v.a.* (*Mil.*) command, head.

Befehlshaber [bə'fe:lsha:bər], *m.* (—s, *pl.* —) commander, commanding officer, chief.

befehlswidrig [bə'fe:lsvi:drıç], *adj.* contrary to orders.

befestigen [bə'fɛstıgən], *v.a.* fasten, fix, attach, affix; (*Mil.*) fortify; strengthen.

befeuchten [bə'fɔyçtən], *v.a.* wet, moisten, dampen.

Befinden [bə'fındən], *n.* (—s, *no pl.*) state of health.

befinden [bə'fındən], *v.a. irr.* think, deem, find. — *v.r. sich an einem Ort* —, be in some place; *sich wohl* —, feel well.

befindlich [bə'fıntlıç], *adj.* existing — *sein*, be contained in.

beflecken [bə'flɛkən], *v.a.* stain, spot, blot; defile, pollute.

befleißigen [bə'flaısıgən], *v.r. sich* —, devote o.s., take pains to.

beflissen [bə'flısən], *adj.* eager to serve, assiduous.

beflügeln [bə'fly:gəln], *v.a.* give wings; (*fig.*) accelerate, animate.

befolgen [bə'fɔlgən], *v.a.* follow, obey; *einen Befehl* —, comply with an order.

befördern [bə'fœrdərn], *v.a.* despatch, forward, send, post, mail, transmit; promote, advance.

Beförderung [bə'fœrdəruŋ], *f.* (—, *pl.* —en) forwarding, transmission; (*office*) promotion, advancement.

Beförderungsmittel [bə'fœrdəruŋsmitəl], *n.* (—s, *pl.* —) conveyance, means of transport.

befragen [bə'fra:gən], *v.a.* question, interrogate, examine.

befreien [bə'fraıən], *v.a.* free, liberate.

befremden [bə'frɛmdən], *v.a.* appear strange, astonish, surprise.

befreunden [bə'frɔyndən], *v.a.* befriend. — *v.r. sich mit einem* —, make friends with s.o.

befriedigen [bə'fri:dıgən], *v.a.* content, satisfy; appease, calm.

befruchten [bə'fruxtən], *v.a.* fertilise; impregnate.

Befugnis [bə'fu:knıs], *f.* (—, *pl.* —se) authority, right, warrant.

Befund [bə'funt], *m.* (—s, *pl.* —e) (*Med.*) diagnosis, findings.

befürchten [bə'fyrçtən], *v.a.* fear, be afraid of.

befürworten [bə'fy:rvɔrtən], *v.a.* support, second.

24

begabt [bə'ga:pt], *adj.* gifted, talented, able.

Begabung [bə'ga:buŋ], *f.* (—, *pl.* —en) ability, talent, gift.

begaffen [bə'gafən], *v.a.* stare at, gape at.

begatten [bə'gatən], *v.r. sich* —, (Zool.) copulate.

begeben [bə'ge:bən], *v.r. irr. sich an einen Ort* —, go to a place, betake o.s. to a place; happen, occur.

Begebenheit [bə'ge:bənhaɪt], *f.* (—, *pl.* —en) happening, event, occurrence.

begegnen [bə'ge:gnən], *v.n.* (*aux.* sein) meet, meet with, encounter, befall, happen.

begehen [bə'ge:ən], *v.a. irr.* (*road*) walk along, go over; (*festival*) celebrate; (*crime*) commit, perpetrate.

begehren [bə'ge:rən], *v.a.* desire, wish, covet, want.—*v.n. nach etwas* —, long for s.th.

begehrlich [bə'ge:rlɪç], *adj.* covetous, greedy, desirous.

begeifern [bə'gaɪfərn], *v.a.* spit at; (*fig.*) vilify, besmirch.

begeistern [bə'gaɪstərn], *v.a.* inspire, fill with enthusiasm, enrapture.— *v.r. sich für etwas* —, become enthusiastic about s.th.

Begier(de) [bə'gi:r(də)], *f.* (—, *pl.* —den) desire, lust, appetite.

begierig [bə'gi:rɪç], *adj.* desirous, lustful; anxious; curious (for news).

begießen [bə'gi:sən], *v.a. irr.* (*plants*) water; (*meat etc.*) baste; *etwas festlich* —, celebrate s.th. by drinking; *sich die Nase* —, (coll.) get tight.

Beginn [bə'gɪn], *m.* (—s, *no pl.*) beginning, commencement, start.

beginnen [bə'gɪnən], *v.a., v.n. irr.* begin, commence, start.

beglaubigen [bə'glaubɪgən], *v.a.* attest; certify, verify; accredit (an ambassador).

Beglaubigungsschreiben [bə'glaubɪguŋsʃraɪbən], *n.* (—s, *pl.* —) credentials.

begleichen [bə'glaɪçən], *v.a. irr.* (*bill*) pay, settle.

begleiten [bə'glaɪtən], *v.a.* accompany, escort, see s.o. off, home etc.

Begleiter [bə'glaɪtər], *m.* (—s, *pl.* —) companion, escort; (Mus.) accompanist.

Begleiterscheinung [bə'glaɪtərʃaɪnuŋ], *f.* (—, *pl.* —en) concomitant; (Med.) complication, attendant symptom.

Begleitung [bə'glaɪtuŋ], *f.* (—, *pl.* —en) company; (Mus.) accompaniment.

beglücken [bə'glʏkən], *v.a.* make happy.

beglückwünschen [bə'glʏkvʏnʃən], *v.a.* congratulate.

begnadet [bə'gna:dət], *adj.* highly talented.

begnadigen [bə'gna:dɪgən], *v.a.* pardon, reprieve.

begnügen [bə'gny:gən], *v.r. sich mit etwas* —, content o.s. with s.th.

Begonie [bə'go:njə], *f.* (—, *pl.* —n) (Bot.) begonia.

begraben [bə'gra:bən], *v.a. irr.* bury, inter.

Begräbnis [bə'grɛ:pnɪs], *n.* (—ses, *pl.* —se) burial, funeral, interment.

begreifen [bə'graɪfən], *v.a. irr.* understand, comprehend, conceive.

begreiflich [bə'graɪflɪç], *adj.* comprehensible, conceivable, understandable.

begrenzen [bə'grɛntsən], *v.a.* bound, border, limit.

Begriff [bə'grɪf], *m.* (—s, *pl.* —e) notion, concept, idea, conception; *im* — *sein*, be about to . . . .

begriffen [bə'grɪfən], *adj.* — *sein in*, be engaged in.

begriffsstutzig [bə'grɪfsʃtutsɪç], *adj.* obtuse, dense, slow in the uptake.

begründen [bə'grʏndən], *v.a.* base on, justify, found, establish.

begrüßen [bə'gry:sən], *v.a.* greet, salute, welcome.

begünstigen [bə'gʏnstɪgən], *v.a.* favour, prefer.

Begutachter [bə'gu:taxtər], *m.* (—s, *pl.* —) expert; (Sch.) assessor, second examiner.

Begutachtung [bə'gu:taxtuŋ], *f.* (—, *pl.* —en) expert opinion, assessment, report.

begütert [bə'gy:tərt], *adj.* wealthy, rich, well-to-do.

behaart [bə'ha:rt], *adj.* covered with hair, hairy.

behäbig [bə'hɛ:bɪç], *adj.* comfortable; corpulent, portly.

behaften [bə'haftən], *v.a.* charge, burden.

behagen [bə'ha:gən], *v.n.* please, be agreeable; *es behagt mir nicht*, I do not like it.

behaglich [bə'ha:klɪç], *adj.* cosy, comfortable, snug.

behalten [bə'haltən], *v.a. irr.* retain, keep.

Behälter [bə'hɛltər], *m.* (—s, *pl.* —) container; box, bin; (*water*) reservoir; tank.

behandeln [bə'handəln], *v.a.* treat, use; (Med.) treat; (*subject*) treat; handle.

Behandlung [bə'handluŋ], *f.* (—, *pl.* —en) treatment, use; (Med.) treatment.

Behang [bə'haŋ], *m.* (—es, *pl.* ¨e) hanging(s); appendage.

behängen [bə'hɛŋən], *v.a. irr.* festoon with, drape.

beharren [bə'harən], *v.n.* persevere; persist, insist.

beharrlich [bə'harlɪç], *adj.* persevering, persistent, constant, firm.

behauen [bə'hauən], *v.a.* (*stones*) hew, cut.

behaupten [bə'hauptən], *v.a.* claim, assert, affirm, maintain.

Behauptung

Behauptung [bə'hauptuŋ], *f.* (—, *pl.* —en) claim, assertion, affirmation.

Behausung [bə'hauzuŋ], *f.* (—, *pl.* —en) habitation, housing.

behelfen [bə'hɛlfən], *v.r. irr. sich — mit*, make do with.

behelfsmäßig [bə'hɛlfsmɛːsɪç], *adj.* makeshift, temporary.

behelligen [bə'hɛlɪgən], *v.a.* trouble, molest, disturb.

behend(e) [bə'hɛndə], *adj.* quick, nimble, agile.

beherbergen [bə'hɛrbɛrgən], *v.a.* give shelter to, put up, harbour.

beherrschen [bə'hɛrʃən], *v.a.* rule, govern, dominate; *eine Sache —*, master a subject. — *v.r. sich —*, control o.s.

Beherrschung [bə'hɛrʃuŋ], *f.* (—, *pl.* (*rare*) —en) domination, sway; (*subject*) grasp; (*languages*) command.

beherzigen [bə'hɛrtsɪgən], *v.a.* take to heart, follow, heed.

Beherztheit [bə'hɛrtsthaɪt], *f.* (—, *no pl.*) courage, spirit.

behexen [bə'hɛksən], *v.a.* bewitch.

behilflich [bə'hɪlflɪç], *adj.* helpful, useful.

behindern [bə'hɪndərn], *v.a.* hinder, hamper.

Behörde [bə'hœrdə], *f.* (—, *pl.* —n) the authorities.

behufs [bə'huːfs], *prep.* (*Genit.*) in order to, with a view to.

behüten [bə'hyːtən], *v.a.* guard, protect; *Gott behüte!* Heaven forbid!

behutsam [bə'huːtzaːm], *adj.* careful, cautious.

bei [baɪ], *prep.* (*Dat.*) (*locally*) near by, close by, next to, at.

beibehalten ['baɪbəhaltən], *v.a. irr.* keep, retain.

Beiblatt ['baɪblat], *n.* (—s, *pl.* ⁓er) supplement (to a newspaper).

beibringen ['baɪbrɪŋən], *v.a. irr.* adduce (proof); produce (witnesses); (*fig.*) teach; impart to.

Beichte ['baɪçtə], *f.* (—, *pl.* —n) confession.

Beichtstuhl ['baɪçtʃtuːl], *m.* (—s, *pl.* ⁓e) confessional.

beide ['baɪdə], *adj.* both, either, the two.

beiderlei ['baɪdərlaɪ], *adj.* of both kinds.

beidrehen ['baɪdreːən], *v.n.* (*Naut.*) heave to.

Beifall ['baɪfal], *m.* (—s, *no pl.*) (*verbal*) approbation; (*shouting*) acclamation, acclaim; (*clapping*) applause.

beifällig ['baɪfɛlɪç], *adj.* favourable, approving, assenting.

beifügen ['baɪfyːgən], *v.a.* enclose, attach.

Beifuß ['baɪfuːs], *m.* (—es, *no pl.*) (*Bot.*) mugwort.

beigeben ['baɪgeːbən], *v.a. irr.* add, join to. — *v.n.*, *klein —*, give in.

Beigeschmack ['baɪgəʃmak], *m.* (—s, *no pl.*) aftertaste, tang.

beigesellen ['baɪgəzɛlən], *v.r. sich —*, associate with.

Beihilfe ['baɪhɪlfə], *f.* (—, *pl.* —n) aid, assistance, subsidy.

beikommen ['baɪkɔmən], *v.n. irr.* (*aux.* sein) *einer Sache —*, to grapple with s.th.; *ich kann ihm nicht —*, I cannot catch him out, get at him.

Beil [baɪl], *n.* (—s, *pl.* —e) hatchet, axe.

Beilage ['baɪlaːgə], *f.* (—, *pl.* —n) enclosure (with a letter); supplement (to a newspaper); *Braten mit —*, joint with vegetables.

beiläufig ['baɪlɔyfɪç], *adv.* by the way, incidentally.

beilegen ['baɪleːgən], *v.a.* add, join; enclose (in letter).

beileibe [baɪ'laɪbə], *int.* *— nicht!* on no account!

Beileid ['baɪlaɪt], *n.* (—s, *no pl.*) condolence, sympathy.

beiliegen ['baɪliːgən], *v.n. irr.* be enclosed with.

beimengen ['baɪmɛŋən], *v.a.* (*Cul.*) mix with, add.

beimessen ['baɪmɛsən], *v.a. irr. einem etwas —*, impute s.th. to s.o.; *einem Glauben —*, credit s.o., give credence to.

Bein [baɪn], *n.* (—s, *pl.* —e) leg; *einem auf die —e helfen*, give a helping hand to s.o.

beinahe [baɪ'naːə], *adv.* almost, nearly.

Beiname ['baɪnaːmə], *m.* (—ns, *pl.* —n) surname; nickname.

Beinbruch ['baɪnbrux], *m.* (—s, *pl.* ⁓e) fracture of the leg; (*coll.*) *Hals- und Beinbruch!* good luck!

Beinkleider ['baɪnklaɪdər], *n. pl.* (*obs.*) pants, trousers.

beipflichten ['baɪpflɪçtən], *v.n. einem —*, agree with s.o.

beirren [bə'ɪrən], *v.a. sich nicht — lassen*, not let o.s. be dissuaded *or* put off.

beisammen [baɪ'zamən], *adv.* together.

Beischlaf ['baɪʃlaːf], *m.* (—s, *no pl.*) cohabitation, coition.

Beisein ['baɪzaɪn], *n.* (—s, *no pl.*) *im — von*, in the presence of.

beiseite [baɪ'zaɪtə], *adv.* apart, aside; (*Theat.*) aside.

beisetzen ['baɪzɛtsən], *v.a.* bury, inter, entomb.

Beispiel ['baɪʃpiːl], *n.* (—s, *pl.* —e) example, instance; *zum —* (*abbr.* z.B.), for instance, for example.

beißen ['baɪsən], *v.a. irr.* bite; (*pepper, smoke*) burn, sting.

Beißzange ['baɪstsaŋə], *f.* (—, *pl.* —n) pair of pincers *or* nippers.

Beistand ['baɪʃtant], *m.* (—s, *pl.* ⁓e) assistance, help; (*Law*) counsel; *— leisten*, give assistance.

beistehen ['baɪʃteːən], *v.n. irr. einem —*, stand by s.o., help s.o.

beisteuern ['baɪʃtɔyərn], *v.a. zu etwas —*, contribute to s.th.

beistimmen ['baɪʃtɪmən], *v.n.* agree with, assent.

Beistrich ['baɪʃtrɪç], *m.* (—(e)s, *pl.* —e) comma.

beitragen ['baɪtraːgən], *v.a. irr.* contribute; be conducive to.

beitreten ['baɪtreːtən], *v.n. irr.* (*aux.* sein) join (a club); enter into partnership with (a firm).

Beitritt ['baɪtrɪt], *m.* (—s, *no pl.*) accession, joining.

Beiwagen ['baɪvaːgən], *m.* (—s, *pl.* —) trailer, sidecar (on motor cycle).

beiwohnen ['baɪvoːnən], *v.n.* be present at, attend.

Beiwort ['baɪvɔrt], *n.* (—s, *pl.* ˙er) adjective, epithet.

Beize ['baɪtsə], *f.* (—, *pl.* —n) caustic fluid; (*wood*) stain.

beizeiten [baɪ'tsaɪtən], *adv.* betimes, early, in good time.

beizen ['baɪtsən], *v.a.* cauterise; (*wood*) stain.

bejahen [bə'jaːən], *v.a.* answer in the affirmative.

bejahrt [bə'jaːrt], *adj.* aged, elderly, old.

bejammern [bə'jamərn], *v.a.* bemoan, bewail.

bekannt [bə'kant], *adj.* known, well-known; — mit, acquainted with.

Bekannte [bə'kantə], *m.* (—n, *pl.* —n) acquaintance.

bekanntlich [bə'kantlɪç], *adv.* as is well known.

Bekanntmachung [bə'kantmaxuŋ], *f.* (—, *pl.* —en) publication, announcement.

Bekanntschaft [bə'kantʃaft], *f.* (—, *pl.* —en) — mit einem machen, strike up an acquaintance with s.o.

bekehren [bə'keːrən], *v.a.* convert. — *v.r. sich* —, be converted *or* become a convert (to); reform.

bekennen [bə'kɛnən], *v.a. irr.* confess, profess; admit, own up to.

Bekenner [bə'kɛnər], *m.* (—s, *pl.* —) Confessor (as title).

Bekenntnis [bə'kɛntnɪs], *n.* (—ses, *pl.* —se) confession (of faith), avowal, creed.

beklagen [bə'klaːgən], *v.a.* lament, bewail, deplore. — *v.r. sich* — *über,* complain of.

Beklagte [bə'klaːktə], *m.* (—n, *pl.* —n) (*Law*) defendant.

bekleiden [bə'klaɪdən], *v.a.* clothe, dress, cover; (*office*) hold.

Bekleidung [bə'klaɪduŋ], *f.* (—, *no pl.*) clothing, clothes; (*office*) administration, holding, exercise.

beklemmen [bə'klɛmən], *v.a. irr.* oppress.

Beklemmung [bə'klɛmuŋ], *f.* (—, *pl.* —en) oppression, anguish.

beklommen [bə'klɔmən], *adj.* anxious, uneasy.

bekommen [bə'kɔmən], *v.a. irr.* obtain, get, receive.

bekömmlich [bə'kœmlɪç], *adj.* beneficial; digestible, wholesome.

beköstigen [bə'kœstɪgən], *v.a.* board; feed.

bekräftigen [bə'krɛftɪgən], *v.a.* aver, corroborate, confirm.

bekränzen [bə'krɛntsən], *v.a.* wreathe, crown (with a garland).

bekreuzigen [bə'krɔytsɪgən], *v.r. sich* —, make the sign of the cross, cross o.s.

bekriegen [bə'kriːgən], *v.a.* make war on.

bekritteln [bə'krɪtəln], *v.a.* criticise, carp at, find fault with.

bekritzeln [bə'krɪtsəln], *v.a.* scrawl on, doodle on.

bekümmern [bə'kymərn], *v.a.* grieve, distress, trouble. — *v.r.* trouble o.s. about, grieve over.

bekunden [bə'kundən], *v.a.* manifest, show; declare.

beladen [bə'laːdən], *v.a. irr.* load.

Belag [bə'laːk], *m.* (—s, *pl.* ˙e) covering, layer; spread (on sandwiches); fur (on the tongue).

belagern [bə'laːgərn], *v.a.* besiege.

Belang [bə'laŋ], *m.* (—s, *pl.* —e) importance; von —, of great moment *or* consequence; (*pl.*) concerns, interests.

belangen [bə'laŋən], *v.a.* (*Law*) sue, prosecute.

belanglos [bə'laŋloːs], *adj.* of small account; irrelevant, unimportant.

belassen [bə'lasən], *v.a. irr. es dabei* —, leave things as they are.

belasten [bə'lastən], *v.a.* load, burden; (*Comm.*) debit, charge; (*Law*) incriminate.

belästigen [bə'lɛstɪgən], *v.a.* bother, pester, molest.

Belastung [bə'lastuŋ], *f.* (—, *pl.* —en) load, burden; (*Comm.*) debiting; (*house*) mortgage; erbliche —, hereditary disposition.

Belastungszeuge [bə'lastuŋstsɔygə], *m.* (—n, *pl.* —n) witness for the prosecution.

belaubt [bə'laupt], *adj.* covered with leaves, leafy.

belaufen [bə'laufən], *v.r. irr. sich* — *auf,* amount to, come to.

belauschen [bə'lauʃən], *v.a.* eavesdrop, overhear.

beleben [bə'leːbən], *v.a.* animate, enliven.

Belebtheit [bə'leːpthaɪt], *f.* (—, *no pl.*) animation, liveliness.

Beleg [bə'leːk], *m.* (—s, *pl.* —e) document, proof, receipt, voucher.

belegen [bə'leːgən], *v.a.* cover, overlay; reserve, book (*seat*); support by documents, authenticate, prove.

Belegschaft [bə'leːkʃaft], *f.* (—, *pl.* —en) workers, personnel, staff; (*Min.*) gang, shift.

belegt [bə'leːkt], *adj.* (*tongue*) furred; —es Brot, sandwich.

belehnen [bə'leːnən], *v.a.* enfeoff; invest (with a fief).

belehren [bə'leːrən], *v.a.* instruct, advise, inform.

Belehrung [bə'le:ruŋ], *f.* (—, *pl.* —en) information, instruction, advice.

beleibt [bə'laɪpt], *adj.* stout, corpulent, obese.

beleidigen [bə'laɪdɪgən], *v.a.* insult, offend, give offence to.

belesen [bə'le:zən], *adj.* well-read.

beleuchten [bə'lɔyçtən], *v.a.* illumine, illuminate; (*fig.*) throw light on, elucidate.

Beleuchtungskörper [bə'lɔyçtuŋskœr-pər], *m.* (—s, *pl.* —) lighting fixture, lamp.

Belgien ['bɛlgjən], *n.* Belgium.

belichten [bə'lɪçtən], *v.a.* (*Phot.*) expose.

belieben [bə'li:bən], *v.a.*, *v.n.* please, like, choose.

beliebig [bə'li:bɪç], *adj.* optional; any, whatever.

beliebt [bə'li:pt], *adj.* popular, well-liked.

Beliebtheit [bə'li:pthaɪt], *f.* (—, *no pl.*) popularity.

bellen ['bɛlən], *v.n.* bark.

beloben [bə'lo:bən], *v.a.* praise, approve.

belohnen [bə'lo:nən], *v.a.* reward, recompense.

belügen [bə'ly:gən], *v.a. irr. einen* —, tell lies to s.o., deceive s.o. by lying.

belustigen [bə'lustɪgən], *v.a.* amuse, divert, entertain.

bemächtigen [bə'mɛçtɪgən], *v.r. sich einer Sache* —, take possession of s.th.

bemäkeln [bə'mɛ:kəln], *v.a.* find fault with.

bemalen [bə'ma:lən], *v.a.* paint (over).

bemängeln [bə'mɛŋəln], *v.a.* find fault with.

bemannen [bə'manən], *v.a.* man.

bemänteln [bə'mɛntəln], *v.a.* cloak, hide.

bemeistern [bə'maɪstərn], *v.a.* master.

bemerkbar [bə'mɛrkba:r], *adj.* perceptible, noticeable.

bemerken [bə'mɛrkən], *v.a.* observe, perceive, notice.

Bemerkung [bə'mɛrkuŋ], *f.* (—, *pl.* —en) remark, observation, note.

bemessen [bə'mɛsən], *v.a. irr.* measure; curtail.

bemitleiden [bə'mɪtlaɪdən], *v.a.* pity, be sorry for.

bemittelt [bə'mɪtəlt], *adj.* well-off, well-to-do.

bemoost [bə'mo:st], *adj.* mossy.

bemühen [bə'my:ən], *v.a.* trouble, give trouble (to). — *v.r. sich* —, take pains, strive, endeavour.

bemüht [bə'my:t], *adj.* studious; — *sein*, endeavour, try to.

bemuttern [bə'mutərn], *v.a.* mother.

benachbart [bə'naxba:rt], *adj.* neighbouring, adjacent.

benachrichtigen [bə'naxrɪçtɪgən], *v.a.* inform, give notice of, notify.

benachteiligen [bə'naxtaɪlɪgən], *v.a.* prejudice, discriminate against, handicap.

benagen [bə'na:gən], *v.a.* gnaw at.

benebeln [bə'ne:bəln], *v.a.* befog, cloud; (*fig.*) dim, intoxicate.

benedeien [bene'daɪən], *v.a.* bless, glorify.

Benediktiner [benedɪk'ti:nər], *m.* (—s, *pl.* —) (monk) Benedictine; Benedictine liqueur.

Benefiz [bene'fi:ts], *n.* (—es, *pl.* —e) benefit; benefit performance.

Benehmen [bə'ne:mən], *n.* (—s, *no pl.*) conduct, behaviour.

benehmen [bə'ne:mən], *v.r. irr. sich* —, behave, conduct o.s.

beneiden [bə'naɪdən], *v.a. einen* — *um*, envy s.o. (s.th.).

benennen [bə'nɛnən], *v.a.* name.

benetzen [bə'nɛtsən], *v.a.* moisten.

Bengel ['bɛŋəl], *m.* (—s, *pl.* —) naughty boy, scamp; rascal, lout.

benommen [bə'nɔmən], *adj.* dazed, giddy.

benötigen [bə'nø:tɪgən], *v.a.* be in need of, require.

benutzen [bə'nutsən], *v.a.* make use of, utilise.

Benzin [bɛnt'si:n], *n.* (—s, *no pl.*) benzine; (*Motor.*) petrol; (*Am.*) gas, gasoline.

beobachten [bə'o:baxtən], *v.a.* watch, observe.

bequem [bə'kve:m], *adj.* comfortable, easy; convenient; indolent, lazy.

bequemen [bə'kve:mən], *v.r. sich* —, condescend (to), comply (with).

Bequemlichkeit [bə'kve:mlɪçkaɪt], *f.* (—, *pl.* —en) convenience, ease; indolence.

beraten [bə'ra:tən], *v.a. irr.* advise, assist with advice, counsel. — *v.r. sich* — *mit*, confer with, consult with.

beratschlagen [bə'ra:tʃla:gən], *v.n.* deliberate with.

Beratung [bə'ra:tuŋ], *f.* (—, *pl.* —en) council, deliberation, consultation.

berauben [bə'raubən], *v.a.* rob, deprive (s.o.) of (s.th.).

berauschen [bə'rauʃən], *v.a.* intoxicate.

berechnen [bə'rɛçnən], *v.a.* compute, charge, calculate, estimate.

berechtigen [bə'rɛçtɪgən], *v.a. einen zu etwas* —, entitle s.o. to s.th.; authorise s.o. to have or do s.th.

beredsam [bə're:tza:m], *adj.* eloquent.

beredt [bə're:t], *adj.* eloquent.

Bereich [bə'raɪç], *m. & n.* (—s, *pl.* —e) extent, realm, sphere, scope.

bereichern [bə'raɪçərn], *v.a.* enrich, enlarge.

bereisen [bə'raɪzən], *v.a.* travel over or through, tour (a country).

bereit [bə'raɪt], *adj.* ready, prepared.

bereiten [bə'raɪtən], *v.a.* prepare, get ready.

bereits [bə'raɪts], *adv.* already.

Bereitschaft [bə'raɪtʃaft], *f.* (—, *no pl.*) readiness, preparedness.

bereitwillig [bə'raɪtvɪlɪç], *adj.* willing, ready, obliging.

28

bereuen [bəˈrɔʏən], *v.a.* repent, be sorry for, regret.

Berg [bɛrk], *m.* (**—es,** *pl.* **—e**) mountain, hill.

bergab [bɛrkˈap], *adj.* downhill.

Bergamt [ˈbɛrkamt], *n.* (**—s,** *pl.* **⁻er**) mining-office, mine authority.

bergan [bɛrkˈan], *adj.* uphill.

Bergarbeiter [ˈbɛrkarbaɪtər], *m.* (**—s,** *pl.* **—**) miner, collier.

bergauf [bɛrkˈauf], *adj.* uphill.

Bergbau [ˈbɛrkbau], *m.* (**—s,** *no pl.*) mining, mining industry.

bergen [ˈbɛrgən], *v.a. irr.* shelter, protect, save; (*flotsam*) save, recover, salvage.

bergig [ˈbɛrgɪç], *adj.* mountainous, hilly.

Bergkristall [ˈbɛrkkrɪstal], *m.* (**—s,** *pl.* **—e**) rock-crystal.

Bergleute [ˈbɛrklɔʏtə], *pl.* miners, colliers.

Bergmann [ˈbɛrkman], *m.* (**—s,** *pl.* **Bergleute**) miner, collier.

Bergpredigt [ˈbɛrkpreːdɪçt], *f.* (**—,** *no pl.*) Sermon on the Mount.

Bergschlucht [ˈbɛrkʃluxt], *f.* (**—,** *pl.* **—en**) ravine, gorge.

Bergsteiger [ˈbɛrkʃtaɪgər], *m.* (**—s,** *pl.* **—**) mountaineer.

Bergstock [ˈbɛrkʃtɔk], *m.* (**—s,** *pl.* **⁻e**) alpenstock.

Bergsturz [ˈbɛrkʃturts], *m.* (**—es,** *pl.* **⁻e**) landslip, landslide.

Bergung [ˈbɛrguŋ], *f.* (**—,** *pl.* **—en**) sheltering, salvaging; rescue operation.

Bergwerk [ˈbɛrkvɛrk], *n.* (**—s,** *pl.* **—e**) mine, pit.

Bericht [bəˈrɪçt], *m.* (**—s,** *pl.* **—e**) report, account, statement; — *erstatten,* report, give an account of.

Berichterstatter [bəˈrɪçtərʃtatər], *m.* (**—s,** *pl.* **—**) reporter.

berichtigen [bəˈrɪçtɪgən], *v.a.* set right, correct, rectify, amend.

berieseln [bəˈriːzəln], *v.a.* irrigate.

beritten [bəˈrɪtən], *adj.* mounted on horseback.

Berlin [bɛrˈliːn], *n.* Berlin; **—er Blau,** Prussian blue.

Bern [bɛrn], *n.* Berne.

Bernhardiner [bɛrnharˈdiːnər], *m.* (**—s,** *pl.* **—**) Cistercian monk; Newfoundland dog, St. Bernard dog.

Bernstein [ˈbɛrnʃtaɪn], *m.* (**—s,** *no pl.*) amber.

bersten [ˈbɛrstən], *v.n. irr.* (*aux.* sein) burst.

berüchtigt [bəˈrʏçtɪçt], *adj.* notorious, infamous.

berücken [bəˈrʏkən], *v.a.* enchant, fascinate.

berücksichtigen [bəˈrʏksɪçtɪgən], *v.a.* have regard to, take into consideration, allow for.

Beruf [bəˈruːf], *m.* (**—s,** *pl.* **—e**) profession, occupation, calling, trade.

berufen [bəˈruːfən], *v.a. irr.* (*meeting*) call, convene; appoint (to an office). **— v.r. sich — auf,** appeal to, refer to. **— adj.** competent, qualified.

berufsmäßig [bəˈruːfsmɛːsɪç], *adj.* professional.

Berufung [bəˈruːfuŋ], *f.* (**—,** *pl.* **—en**) call, vocation, appointment; (*Law*) appeal.

beruhen [bəˈruːən], *v.n. auf etwas —,* be based on, be founded on.

beruhigen [bəˈruːɪgən], *v.a.* calm, pacify; comfort, console, set at rest.

Beruhigung [bəˈruːɪguŋ], *f.* (**—,** *pl.* **—en**) reassurance, quieting, calming.

berühmt [bəˈryːmt], *adj.* famous, celebrated, illustrious, renowned.

berühren [bəˈryːrən], *v.a.* touch, handle; (*subject*) mention, touch upon; *peinlich berührt,* unpleasantly affected.

berußt [bəˈruːst], *adj.* sooty.

Beryll [beˈryl], *m.* (**—s,** *pl.* **—e**) beryl.

besagen [bəˈzaːgən], *v.a.* mean, signify.

besagt [bəˈzaːkt], *adj.* aforesaid, above-mentioned.

besaiten [bəˈzaɪtən], *v.a.* fit with strings.

Besan [bəˈzaːn], *m.* (**—s,** *pl.* **—e**) (*Naut.*) miz(z)en.

besänftigen [bəˈzɛnftɪgən], *v.a.* calm, appease, pacify.

Besatz [bəˈzats], *m.* (**—es,** *pl.* **⁻e**) trimming, border.

Besatzung [bəˈzatsuŋ], *f.* (**—,** *pl.* **—en**) crew; (*Mil.*) garrison, occupation.

besaufen [bəˈzaufən], *v.r. irr.* (*vulg.*) *sich —,* get drunk.

beschädigen [bəˈʃɛːdɪgən], *v.a.* damage.

beschaffen [bəˈʃafən], *v.a.* procure, get. **— adj.** conditioned, constituted.

Beschaffenheit [bəˈʃafənhaɪt], *f.* (**—,** *no pl.*) nature, kind, quality, condition.

beschäftigen [bəˈʃɛftɪgən], *v.a.* occupy, employ.

beschämen [bəˈʃɛːmən], *v.a.* make ashamed, shame.

beschatten [bəˈʃatən], *v.a.* shade, shadow; follow (s.o.).

Beschau [bəˈʃau], *f.* (**—,** *no pl.*) examination; inspection.

beschauen [bəˈʃauən], *v.a.* view, look at.

beschaulich [bəˈʃaulɪç], *adj.* tranquil, contemplative.

Beschaulichkeit [bəˈʃaulɪçkaɪt], *f.* (**—,** *pl.* **—en**) tranquillity, contemplation.

Bescheid [bəˈʃaɪt], *m.* (**—s,** *pl.* **—e**) answer, information; (*Law*) decision; **— wissen,** know o.'s way about; know what's what.

bescheiden [bəˈʃaɪdən], *v.a. irr.* inform (s.o.); *einen zu sich —,* send for s.o. **— adj.** modest, unassuming.

Bescheidenheit [bəˈʃaɪdənhaɪt], *f.* (**—,** *no pl.*) modesty.

bescheinen [bəˈʃaɪnən], *v.a. irr.* shine upon.

bescheinigen [bəˈʃaɪnɪgən], *v.a. einem etwas —,* attest, certify.

beschenken [bəˈʃɛŋkən], *v.a.* give a present to.

bescheren [bə'ʃe:rən], *v.a.* give (a present to), bestow (s.th. on s.o.).

Bescherung [bə'ʃe:ruŋ], *f.* (—, *pl.* —en) giving (of present); *das ist eine schöne* —, (*fig.*) this is a nice mess!

beschicken [bə'ʃikən], *v.a. eine Ausstellung* —, contribute to an exhibition.

beschießen [bə'ʃi:sən], *v.a. irr.* shoot at, fire upon, bombard.

beschiffen [bə'ʃifən], *v.a.* navigate, sail.

beschimpfen [bə'ʃimpfən], *v.a.* insult, abuse, revile.

beschirmen [bə'ʃirmən], *v.a.* protect, shelter, defend.

Beschlag [bə'ʃla:k], *m.* (—s, *pl.* ⸚e) mounting; metal fitting; (*on stick*) ferrule; *etwas mit — belegen*, or *in — nehmen*, sequestrate, confiscate, seize.

beschlagen [bə'ʃla:gən], *v.a. irr.* shoe (a horse). — *v.n.* (*window*) mist over.

Beschlagnahme [bə'ʃla:kna:mə], *f.* (—, *pl.* —n) confiscation, seizure.

beschleunigen [bə'ʃlɔynɪgən], *v.a.* hasten, speed up, accelerate.

beschließen [bə'ʃli:sən], *v.a. irr.* shut, lock up; close, conclude, finish; decide, resolve upon.

Beschluß [bə'ʃlus], *m.* (—sses, *pl.* ⸚sse) determination, resolution, decree.

beschmieren [bə'ʃmi:rən], *v.a.* soil, smear.

beschmutzen [bə'ʃmutsən], *v.a.* soil, dirty, foul.

beschneiden [bə'ʃnaɪdən], *v.a. irr.* cut, clip; (*Hort.*) lop, prune; (*animals*) crop; circumcise.

Beschneidung [bə'ʃnaɪduŋ], *f.* (—, *pl.* —en) lopping, pruning; circumcision.

beschönigen [bə'ʃø:nɪgən], *v.a.* palliate, excuse.

beschränken [bə'ʃrɛnkən], *v.a.* limit, restrict.

beschränkt [bə'ʃrɛŋkt], *adj.* limited; *etwas* —, a little stupid; *Gesellschaft mit —er Haftung*, limited (liability) company.

Beschränkung [bə'ʃrɛŋkuŋ], *f.* (—, *pl.* —en) limitation, restriction.

beschreiben [bə'ʃraɪbən], *v.a. irr.* describe; write upon.

beschreiten [bə'ʃraɪtən], *v.a. irr.* tread on.

beschuldigen [bə'ʃuldɪgən], *v.a.* charge (s.o.), accuse.

beschützen [bə'ʃytsən], *v.a.* protect, shelter, guard.

Beschützer [bə'ʃytsər], *m.* (—s, *pl.* —) protector, defender.

Beschwerde [bə'ʃve:rdə], *f.* (—, *pl.* —en) trouble, hardship, difficulty; complaint, grievance.

beschweren [bə'ʃve:rən], *v.a.* make heavier, weight. — *v.r. sich über etwas* —, complain of s.th.

beschwerlich [bə'ʃve:rlɪç], *adj.* burdensome, hard, troublesome.

beschwichtigen [bə'ʃvɪçtɪgən], *v.a.* soothe, appease, still.

beschwindeln [bə'ʃvɪndəln], *v.a.* cheat, swindle (s.o.).

beschwingt [bə'ʃvɪŋkt], *adj.* winged, light-footed.

beschwipst [bə'ʃvɪpst], *adj.* (*coll.*) tipsy.

beschwören [bə'ʃvø:rən], *v.a. irr.* testify on oath; *einen* —, implore s.o.; conjure (up) (ghosts etc.); exorcise.

beseelen [bə'ze:lən], *v.a.* animate.

besehen [bə'ze:ən], *v.a. irr.* look at, inspect.

beseitigen [bə'zaɪtɪgən], *v.a.* remove.

beseligt [bə'ze:lɪçt], *adj.* enraptured, beatified.

Besen ['be:zən], *m.* (—s, *pl.* —) broom, besom.

Besenstiel ['be:zənʃti:l], *m.* (—s, *pl.* —e) broom-stick.

besessen [bə'zɛsən], *adj.* possessed, obsessed, mad.

besetzen [bə'zɛtsən], *v.a.* (*dress*) trim, lace; (*Mil.*) occupy, garrison; (*office*) fill; (*Theat.*) cast; (*seat*) occupy, take; *besetzt*, engaged.

Besetzung [bə'zɛtsuŋ], *f.* (—, *pl.* —en) lacing, trimming; appointment (to post); (*Theat.*) cast.

besichtigen [bə'zɪçtɪgən], *v.a.* view, go over, inspect, examine.

besiedeln [bə'zi:dəln], *v.a.* colonise.

besiegeln [bə'zi:gəln], *v.a.* seal, set o.'s seal to.

besiegen [bə'zi:gən], *v.a.* vanquish, conquer, overcome.

besinnen [bə'zinən], *v.r. irr.* reflect; *sich auf etwas* —, recollect, remember, think of.

besinnungslos [bə'zinuŋslo:s], *adj.* insensible, unconscious.

Besitz [bə'zits], *m.* (—es, *no pl.*) possession, property.

besitzanzeigend [bə'zitsantsaɪgənt], *adj.* (*Gram.*) possessive.

besitzen [bə'zitsən], *v.a. irr.* possess, own, have.

Besitzergreifung [bə'zitsɛrgraɪfuŋ], *f.* (—, *no pl.*) occupation, taking possession (of).

besoffen [bə'zɔfən], *adj.* (*vulg.*) drunk.

besohlen [bə'zo:lən], *v.a.* sole (shoes).

besolden [bə'zɔldən], *v.a.* give a salary to, pay.

besonder [bə'zɔndər], *adj.* special, particular.

Besonderheit [bə'zɔndərhaɪt], *f.* (—, *pl.* —en) particularity, peculiarity, strangeness.

besonders [bə'zɔndərs], *adv.* especially.

besonnen [bə'zɔnən], *adj.* prudent, cautious, collected, circumspect.

besorgen [bə'zɔrgən], *v.a.* take care of, provide, procure.

Besorgnis [bə'zɔrknɪs], *f.* (—, *pl.* —se) care, concern, anxiety, fear.

besorgt [bə'zɔrkt], *adj.* apprehensive, anxious, worried.

Besorgung [bə'zɔrguŋ], *f.* (—, *pl.* —en) care, management; purchase, commission; —en machen, go shopping.

bespannen [bə'ʃpanən], *v.a.* string (a musical instrument); put horses (to a carriage).

bespötteln [bə'ʃpœtəln], *v.a.* ridicule.

besprechen [bə'ʃprɛçən], *v.a. irr.* discuss, talk over; (book) review. — *v.r. sich — mit*, confer with.

bespritzen [bə'ʃprɪtsən], *v.a.* sprinkle, splash.

besser ['bɛsər], *adj.* better; um so —, so much the better; je mehr desto —, the more the better; — sein als, be better than, be preferable to; — werden, (weather) clear up; (health) improve.

bessern ['bɛsərn], *v.a.* better, improve. — *v.r. sich —*, reform, improve, mend o.'s ways.

Besserung ['bɛsəruŋ], *f.* (—pl. —en) improvement, amendment, reform; (Med.) recovery; gute —, get well soon.

Besserungsanstalt ['bɛsəruŋsanʃtalt], *f.* (—, *pl.* —en) reformatory.

best ['bɛst], *adj.* best.

bestallen [bə'ʃtalən], *v.a.* appoint.

Bestand [bə'ʃtant], *m.* (—s, *pl.* ˙e) continuance, duration; stock; balance of cash; — haben, endure.

Bestandaufnahme [bə'ʃtantaufna:mə], *f.* (—, *pl.* —n) (Comm.) stocktaking.

beständig [bə'ʃtɛndɪç], *adj.* continual, perpetual; (persons) steady, steadfast, constant.

Bestandteil [bə'ʃtanttaɪl], *m.* (—s, *pl.* —e) constituent part, component, ingredient, essential part.

bestärken [bə'ʃtɛrkən], *v.a.* confirm, strengthen.

bestätigen [bə'ʃtɛːtɪgən], *v.a.* confirm, ratify, bear out, sanction; den Empfang eines Briefes —, acknowledge receipt of a letter.

bestatten [bə'ʃtatən], *v.a.* bury, inter.

bestäuben [bə'ʃtɔybən], *v.a.* cover with dust, spray; (Bot.) pollinate.

bestechen [bə'ʃtɛçən], *v.a. irr.* bribe, corrupt; (fig.) captivate.

bestechlich [bə'ʃtɛçlɪç], *adj.* corruptible.

Bestechung [bə'ʃtɛçuŋ], *f.* (—, *pl.* —en) corruption, bribery.

Besteck [bə'ʃtɛk], *n.* (—s, *pl.* —e) set of knife, fork and spoon; set or case (of instruments).

Bestehen [bə'ʃteːən], *n.* (—s, *no pl.*) existence.

bestehen [bə'ʃteːən], *v.a. irr.* undergo, endure, pass (an examination). — *v.n.* exist; aus etwas —, consist of s.th.; be composed of s.th.; auf (Dat.) —, insist upon s.th.

besteigen [bə'ʃtaɪgən], *v.a. irr.* ascend, mount, climb.

bestellen [bə'ʃtɛlən], *v.a.* order, book; appoint; put in order; (letter, message) deliver; (field) till.

Bestellung [bə'ʃtɛluŋ], *f.* (—, *pl.* —en) order, commission, delivery (of letter); tilling (of field); appointment; auf —, to order.

bestens ['bɛstəns], *adv.* in the best manner.

besteuern [bə'ʃtɔyərn], *v.a.* tax.

bestialisch [bɛstɪ'aːlɪʃ], *adj.* beastly, bestial.

Bestie ['bɛstjə], *f.* (—, *pl.* —n) beast, brute.

bestimmen [bə'ʃtɪmən], *v.a.* fix, settle; decide (s.th.); determine, define.

bestimmt [bə'ʃtɪmt], *adj.* decided, fixed, appointed; ganz —, positively, most decidedly.

Bestimmtheit [bə'ʃtɪmthaɪt], *f.* (—, *no pl.*) certainty.

Bestimmung [bə'ʃtɪmuŋ], *f.* (—, *pl.* —en) settlement, decision, determination; provision; destiny.

bestrafen [bə'ʃtraːfən], *v.a.* punish, chastise.

bestrahlen [bə'ʃtraːlən], *v.a.* irradiate; (Med.) treat by radiotherapy.

bestreben [bə'ʃtreːbən], *v.r. sich —*, exert o.s., strive (for), endeavour.

Bestrebung [bə'ʃtreːbuŋ], *f.* (—, *pl.* —en) effort, endeavour, exertion.

bestreichen [bə'ʃtraɪçən], *v.a. irr.* spread.

bestreiten [bə'ʃtraɪtən], *v.a. irr.* contest, deny, dispute; defray (costs).

bestreuen [bə'ʃtrɔyən], *v.a.* sprinkle, strew, powder.

bestricken [bə'ʃtrɪkən], *v.a.* ensnare, entangle.

bestürmen [bə'ʃtyrmən], *v.a.* storm, assail; (fig.) importune.

bestürzen [bə'ʃtyrtsən], *v.a.* dismay, confound, perplex.

Besuch [bə'zuːx], *m.* (—s, *pl.* —e) visit; (person) visitor.

besuchen [bə'zuːxən], *v.a.* visit, call on; attend; frequent.

besudeln [bə'zuːdəln], *v.a.* soil, foul.

betagt [bə'taːkt], *adj.* aged, elderly.

betätigen [bə'tɛːtɪgən], *v.a.* practise, operate. — *v.r. sich —*, take an active part, work, participate (in).

betäuben [bə'tɔybən], *v.a.* deafen; stun, benumb, anaesthetize.

Betäubung [bə'tɔybuŋ], *f.* (—, *pl.* —en) stupor, stupefaction; örtliche —, local anaesthetic.

beteiligen [bə'taɪlɪgən], *v.a.* einen an etwas —, give s.o. a share of s.th. — *v.r. sich an etwas —*, participate in s.th.; (Comm.) have shares in s.th.

Beteiligte [bə'taɪlɪçtə], *m.* (—n, *pl.* —n) person concerned.

Beteiligung [bə'taɪlɪguŋ], *f.* (—, *pl.* —en) participation, interest.

beten ['beːtən], *v.n.* pray, say o.'s prayers.

beteuern [bə'tɔyərn], *v.a.* aver, affirm solemnly.

betiteln [bə'tiːtəln], *v.a.* entitle, name.

Beton [be'tõ], *m.* (—s, *no pl.*) concrete.

betonen [bə'to:nən], *v.a.* accentuate, stress, emphasise.

Betonung [bə'to:nuŋ], *f.* (—, *pl.* —en) accentuation, emphasis, stress.

betören [bə'tø:rən], *v.a.* delude, infatuate.

Betracht [bə'traxt], *m.* (—s, *no pl.*) consideration, respect, regard.

betrachten [bə'traxtən], *v.a.* consider, look at, view; *etwas aufmerksam* —, contemplate s.th.

beträchtlich [bə'trɛçtlɪç], *adj.* considerable.

Betrachtung [bə'traxtuŋ], *f.* (—, *pl.* —en) contemplation, consideration.

Betrag [bə'tra:k], *m.* (—s, *pl.* ˑe) amount, sum total.

betragen [bə'tra:gən], *v.a. irr.* amount to, come to. — *v.r. sich* —, behave, conduct o.s.

Betragen [bə'tra:gən], *n.* (—s, *no pl.*) behaviour, conduct, demeanour.

betrauen [bə'trauən], *v.a. einen mit etwas* —, entrust s.o. with s.th.

betrauern [bə'trauərn], *v.a.* mourn for, bemoan.

Betreff [bə'trɛf], *m.* (—s, *no pl.*) reference; *in* —, with regard to.

betreffen [bə'trɛfən], *v.a. irr.* concern, affect, relate to.

Betreiben [bə'traɪbən], *n.* (—s, *no pl.*) *auf* — *von*, at the instigation of.

betreiben [bə'traɪbən], *v.a. irr.* (*business*) carry on; (*factory*) run; (*trade*) follow, practise.

Betreten [bə'tre:tən], *n.* (—s, *no pl.*) entry, entering.

betreten [bə'tre:tən], *v.a. irr.* step upon, set foot on, enter. — *adj.* disconcerted, embarrassed.

betreuen [bə'trɔyən], *v.a.* care for, attend to.

Betrieb [bə'tri:p], *m.* (—s, *pl.* —e) management, business, factory, plant; *den* — *einstellen*, close down; *in* — *sein*, be in operation; *in* — *setzen*, start working.

betriebsam [bə'tri:pza:m], *adj.* active, busy, industrious, diligent.

Betriebsamkeit [bə'tri:pza:mkaɪt], *f.* (—, *pl.* —en) activity, industry, bustle.

betriebsfertig [bə'tri:psfɛrtɪç], *adj.* ready for service; operational.

Betriebsmaterial [bə'tri:psmaterja:l], *n.* (—s, *pl.* —ien) (*Railw.*) rolling-stock; (*factory*) working-stock.

Betriebspersonal [bə'tri:pspɛrzona:l], *n.* (—s, *no pl.*) workmen, employees, staff.

betrinken [bə'trɪŋkən], *v.r. irr. sich* —, get drunk.

betroffen [bə'trɔfən], *adj.* perplexed, confounded.

betrüben [bə'try:bən], *v.a.* afflict, grieve.

Betrübnis [bə'try:pnɪs], *f.* (—ses, *pl.* —se) affliction, grief, distress, sorrow.

betrübt [bə'try:pt], *adj.* sad, grieved.

Betrug [bə'tru:k], *m.* (—s, *pl.* ˑereien) fraud, deceit, deception, imposture; *einen* — *begehen*, commit a fraud.

betrügen [bə'try:gən], *v.a. irr.* cheat, deceive.

Betrüger [bə'try:gər], *m.* (—s, —) swindler, cheat, deceiver, impostor.

betrunken [bə'truŋkən], *adj.* drunk, drunken, tipsy.

Bett [bɛt], *n.* (—(e)s, *pl.* —en) bed; (*river*) bed, channel.

Bettdecke ['bɛtdɛkə], *f.* (—, *pl.* —n) counterpane; (*Am.*) bedspread; *wollene* —, blanket; *gesteppte* —, quilt.

Bettel ['bɛtəl], *m.* (—s, *no pl.*) trash, trifle.

bettelarm ['bɛtəlarm], *adj.* destitute.

Bettelei [bɛtə'laɪ], *f.* (—, *pl.* —en) begging, beggary, penury.

betteln ['bɛtəln], *v.a.* beg, ask alms.

betten ['bɛtən], *v.a.* bed, lay to rest. — *v.r.* (*fig.*) *sich* —, make o.'s bed.

bettlägerig ['bɛtlɛgərɪç], *adj.* bedridden.

Bettlaken ['bɛtla:kən], *n.* (—s, *pl.* —) sheet.

Bettler ['bɛtlər], *m.* (—s, *pl.* —) beggar.

Bettstelle ['bɛtʃtɛlə], *f.* (—, *pl.* —n) bedstead.

Bettvorleger ['bɛtfo:rle:gər], *m.* (—s, *pl.* —) bedside-carpet *or* rug.

Bettwäsche ['bɛtvɛʃə], *f.* (—, *no pl.*) bed linen, bed clothes.

Bettzeug ['bɛttsɔyk], *n.* (—s, *no pl.*) bedding.

beugen ['bɔygən], *v.a.* bend, bow. — *v.r. sich* —, bend down, stoop.

Beugung ['bɔyguŋ], *f.* (—, *pl.* —en) (*Gram.*) inflection.

Beule ['bɔylə], *f.* (—, *pl.* —n) bruise, bump, swelling, boil.

beunruhigen [bə'unru:ɪgən], *v.a.* alarm, trouble, disquiet.

beurkunden [bə'u:rkundən], *v.a.* authenticate, verify.

beurlauben [bə'u:rlaubən], *v.a.* grant leave of absence. — *v.r. sich* —, take leave.

beurteilen [bə'urtaɪlən], *v.a.* judge, criticise.

Beute ['bɔytə], *f.* (—, *no pl.*) booty, loot; (*animals*) prey; (*Hunt.*) bag.

Beutel ['bɔytəl], *m.* (—s, *pl.* —) bag; (*money*) purse; (*Zool.*) pouch.

Beuteltier ['bɔytəlti:r], *n.* (—s, *pl.* —e) marsupial.

bevölkern [bə'fœlkərn], *v.a.* people, populate.

Bevölkerung [bə'fœlkəruŋ], *f.* (—, *pl.* —en) population.

bevollmächtigen [bə'fɔlmɛçtɪgən], *v.a.* empower, authorise.

bevor [bə'fo:r], *conj.* before, ere, beforehand.

bevormunden [bə'fo:rmundən], *v.a. insep.* act as guardian to; (*fig.*) browbeat.

bevorrechtigt [bə'fo:rrɛçtɪçt], *adj.* privileged.

bevorstehen [bə'fo:rʃte:ən], *v.n. irr.* impend, lie ahead, be imminent; *einem —*, be in store for s.o.

bevorzugen [bə'fo:rtsu:gən], *v.a. insep.* prefer, favour.

bewachen [bə'vaxən], *v.a.* watch over, guard.

bewachsen [bə'vaksən], *adj.* overgrown.

bewaffnen [bə'vafnən], *v.a.* arm, supply with arms.

Bewahranstalt [bə'va:ranʃtalt], *f.* (—, *pl.* —en) kindergarten, nursery.

bewahren [bə'va:rən], *v.a.* preserve, keep, take care of.

bewähren [bə'vɛ:rən], *v.r. sich —*, prove o.s.

bewahrheiten [bə'va:rhaItən], *v.r. sich —*, come true.

bewährt [bə'vɛ:rt], *adj.* proved.

Bewährung [bə'vɛ:ruŋ], *f.* (—, *no pl.*) proof, verification.

Bewährungsfrist [bə'vɛ:ruŋsfrIst], *f.* (—, *no pl.*) probation.

bewaldet [bə'valdət], *adj.* wooded, woody.

bewältigen [bə'vɛltIgən], *v.a.* overcome; manage, master; cope *or* deal with.

bewandert [bə'vandərt], *adj.* versed, skilled, experienced, conversant.

bewandt [bə'vant], *adj.* such; *damit ist es so —*, it is like this.

Bewandtnis [bə'vantnIs], *f.* (—, *pl.* —se) circumstance, condition, state; *es hat damit folgende —*, the circumstances are as follows.

bewässern [bə'vɛsərn], *v.a.* water, irrigate.

bewegen [bə've:gən], *v.a., v.r.* move, stir; take exercise. — *v.a. irr.* persuade, induce.

Beweggrund [bə've:kgrunt], *m.* (—es, *pl.* —e) motive, reason, motivation.

beweglich [bə've:klIç], *adj.* movable; agile, brisk, sprightly.

Bewegung [bə've:guŋ], *f.* (—, *pl.* —en) motion, movement; (*mind*) emotion, agitation.

beweinen [bə'vaInən], *v.a.* lament, bemoan, deplore.

Beweis [bə'vaIs], *m.* (—es, *pl.* —e) proof, evidence; (*Maths.*) demonstration.

beweisen [bə'vaIzən], *v.a. irr.* prove, show, demonstrate.

Beweiskraft [bə'vaIskraft], *f.* (—, *no pl.*) (*Law*) probative force.

Beweismittel [bə'vaIsmItəl], *n.* (—s, *pl.* —) evidence, proof.

Bewenden [bə'vɛndən], *n.* (—s, *no pl.*) *es hat damit sein —*, there the matter rests.

bewenden [bə'vɛndən], *v.n. irr. es dabei — lassen*, leave it at that.

bewerben [bə'vɛrbən], *v.r. irr. sich um etwas —*, apply for s.th.

Bewerber [bə'vɛrbər], *m.* (—s, *pl.* —) applicant, candidate; (*marriage*) suitor.

Bewerbung [bə'vɛrbuŋ], *f.* (—, *pl.* —en) application, candidature; (*marriage*) courtship.

bewerkstelligen [bə'vɛrkʃtɛlIgən], *v.a.* perform, bring about.

bewerten [bə'vɛrtən], *v.a.* estimate, value.

bewilligen [bə'vIlIgən], *v.a.* grant, allow, permit.

bewillkommnen [bə'vIlkɔmnən], *v.a.* welcome.

bewirken [bə'vIrkən], *v.a.* effect, bring about.

bewirten [bə'vIrtən], *v.a.* entertain, act as host (to).

bewirtschaften [bə'vIrtʃaftən], *v.a.* manage.

bewohnen [bə'vo:nən], *v.a.* inhabit, occupy.

Bewohner [bə'vo:nər], *m.* (—s, *pl.* —) inhabitant, tenant, resident.

bewölken [bə'vœlkən], *v.r. sich —*, become overcast, become cloudy.

bewundern [bə'vundərn], *v.a.* admire.

bewundernswert [bə'vundərnsvɛrt], *adj.* admirable.

bewußt [bə'vust], *adj.* conscious, aware; *es war mir nicht —*, I was not aware of.

bewußtlos [bə'vustlo:s], *adj.* unconscious; — *werden*, faint, lose consciousness.

Bewußtsein [bə'vustzaIn], *n.* (—s, *no pl.*) consciousness; *einem etwas zum — bringen*, bring s.th. home to s.o.

bezahlbar [bə'tsa:lba:r], *adj.* payable.

bezahlen [bə'tsa:lən], *v.a.* pay; (*bill*) settle.

bezähmen [bə'tsɛ:mən], *v.a.* tame, restrain. — *v.r. sich —*, restrain o.s., control o.s.

bezaubern [bə'tsaubərn], *v.a.* bewitch, enchant, fascinate.

bezeichnen [bə'tsaIçnən], *v.a.* mark, denote, indicate, designate.

bezeichnend [bə'tsaIçnənt], *adj.* indicative, characteristic, significant.

bezeigen [bə'tsaIgən], *v.a.* manifest, show.

bezeugen [bə'tsɔygən], *v.a.* attest, bear witness, testify.

bezichtigen [bə'tsIçtIgən], *v.a.* accuse (s.o.) of (s.th.).

beziehbar [bə'tsi:ba:r], *adj.* (*goods*) obtainable; (*house*) ready for occupation.

beziehen [bə'tsi:ən], *v.a. irr.* cover; (*house etc.*) move into; (*instrument*) string; make up (a bed); *die Wache —*, mount guard. — *v.r. sich —*, (*sky*) cloud over; *sich auf etwas —*, refer to s.th.

Bezieher [bə'tsi:ər], *m.* (—s, *pl.* —) customer; (*newspaper*) subscriber.

Beziehung [bə'tsi:uŋ], *f.* (—, *pl.* —en) relation, connection; reference, bearing; *in dieser —*, in this respect: (*Comm.*) *unter — auf*, with reference to.

beziehungsweise [bə'tsi:uŋsvaIzə], *adv.* respectively, as the case may be, or.

beziffern

beziffern [bə'tsifərn], *v.a.* number.
Bezirk [bə'tsirk], *m.* (—s, *pl.* —e) district; (*Am.*) precinct; (*Parl.*) constituency; (*Law*) circuit.
Bezirksgericht [bə'tsirksgərɪçt], *n.* (—s, *pl.* —e) county court.
Bezug [bə'tsuːk], *m.* (—s, *pl.* ⁓e) (*pillow*) case, cover; (*goods*) order, purchase; (*fig.*) relation; — *haben auf*, refer to; *mit* — *auf*, referring to; (*pl.*) emoluments, income.
bezüglich [bə'tsyːklɪç], *adj.* with regard to, regarding.
Bezugnahme [bə'tsuːknaːmə], *f.* (—, *pl.* —n) reference; *unter* — *auf*, with reference to.
Bezugsbedingung [bə'tsuːksbədɪŋuŋ], *f.* (—, *pl.* —en) (*usually pl.*) (*Comm.*) conditions *or* terms of delivery.
Bezugsquelle [bə'tsuːkskvɛlə], *f.* (—, *pl.* —n) source of supply.
bezwecken [bə'tsvɛkən], *v.a.* aim at, intend.
bezweifeln [bə'tsvaɪfəln], *v.a.* doubt, question.
bezwingen [bə'tsvɪŋən], *v.a. irr.* subdue, conquer. — *v.r. sich* —, restrain o.s.
Bibel ['biːbəl], *f.* (—, *pl.* —n) Bible.
Bibelauslegung ['biːbəlausleːɡuŋ], *f.* (—, *pl.* —en) (Biblical) exegesis.
Biber ['biːbər], *m.* (—s, *pl.* —) (*Zool.*) beaver.
Bibliothek [biblio'teːk], *f.* (—, *pl.* —en) library.
Bibliothekar [biblioteˈkaːr], *m.* (—s, *pl.* —e) librarian.
biblisch ['biːblɪʃ], *adj.* biblical, scriptural.
Bickbeere ['bɪkbeːrə], *f.* (—, *pl.* —n) bilberry.
bieder ['biːdər], *adj.* upright, honest, decent.
Biederkeit ['biːdərkaɪt], *f.* (—, *no pl.*) uprightness, probity.
Biedermann ['biːdərman], *m.* (—s, *pl.* ⁓er) honourable man; (*iron.*) Philistine.
biegen ['biːɡən], *v.a. irr.* bend, bow. — *v.n.* (*aux.* sein) *um die Ecke* —, turn the corner. — *v.r. sich* —, curve; — *oder brechen*, by hook or by crook.
biegsam ['biːkzaːm], *adj.* flexible, supple, pliant.
Biegung ['biːɡuŋ], *f.* (—, *pl.* —en) curve, bend; (*Gram.*) inflexion.
Biene ['biːnə], *f.* (—, *pl.* —n) bee.
Bienenhaus ['biːnənhaus], *n.* (—es, *pl.* ⁓er) apiary.
Bienenkorb ['biːnənkɔrp], *m.* (—s, *pl.* ⁓e) beehive.
Bienenzüchter ['biːnəntsyçtər], *m.* (—s, *pl.* —) apiarist, bee-keeper.
Bier ['biːr], *n.* (—(e)s, *pl.* —e) beer.
Bierkanne ['biːrkanə], *f.* (—, *pl.* —n) tankard.
Biest [biːst], *n.* (—es, *pl.* —er) brute, beast.
bieten ['biːtən], *v.a. irr.* offer; (*auction*) bid.

Bieter ['biːtər], *m.* (—s, *pl.* —) (*auction*) bidder.
Bigotterie [bɪɡɔtəˈriː], *f.* (—, *no pl.*) bigotry.
Bijouterie [bɪʒutəˈriː], *f.* (—, *pl.* —n) trinkets, dress-jewellery.
Bilanz [bi'lants], *f.* (—, *pl.* —en) (*Comm.*) balance; (financial) statement.
Bild [bɪlt], *n.* (—es, *pl.* —er) picture, painting, portrait, image; idea; (*coins*) effigy; (*Cards*) court card; (*books*) illustration; (*speech*) figure of speech, metaphor.
bilden ['bɪldən], *v.c.* form, shape; (*mind*) cultivate. — *v.r. sich* —, improve o.'s mind, educate o.s.
bildend ['bɪldənt], *adj.* instructive, civilising; *die* —*en Künste*, the fine arts.
bilderreich ['bɪldəraɪç], *adj.* —*e Sprache*, flowery language, figurative style.
Bilderschrift ['bɪldərʃrɪft], *f.* (—, *pl.* —en) hieroglyphics.
Bilderstürmer ['bɪldərʃtyrmər], *m.* (—s, *pl.* —) iconoclast.
Bildhauer ['bɪlthauər], *m.* (—s, *pl.* —) sculptor.
bildhübsch ['bɪlthypʃ], *adj.* as pretty as a picture.
bildlich ['bɪltlɪç], *adj.* figurative.
Bildnis ['bɪltnɪs], *n.* (—ses, *pl.* —se) portrait, figure, image, effigy.
bildsam ['bɪltzaːm], *adj.* plastic, ductile.
bildschön ['bɪltʃøːn], *adj.* very beautiful.
Bildseite ['bɪltzaɪtə], *f.* (—, *pl.* —n) (*coin*) face, obverse.
Bildung ['bɪlduŋ], *f.* (—, *pl.* (*rare*) —en) formation; (*mind*) education, culture; knowledge, learning, accomplishments, attainments.
Billard ['bɪljart], *n.* (—s, *pl.* —s) billiards.
Billett [bɪl'jɛt], *n.* (—s, *pl.* —s) ticket.
billig ['bɪlɪç], *adj.* cheap, inexpensive; equitable, just, fair, reasonable.
billigen ['bɪlɪɡən], *v.a.* sanction, approve of, consent to.
Billigkeit ['bɪlɪçkaɪt], *f.* (—, *no pl.*) cheapness; fairness, equitableness, reasonableness.
Billigung ['bɪlɪɡuŋ], *f.* (—, *no pl.*) approbation, approval, sanction.
Bilsenkraut ['bɪlzənkraut], *n.* (—s, *pl.* ⁓er) henbane.
bimmeln ['bɪmən], *v.n.* (*coll.*) tinkle.
Bimsstein ['bɪmsʃtain], *m.* (—s, *pl.* —e) pumice stone.
Binde ['bɪndə], *f.* (—, *pl.* —n) band, bandage; tie; ligature; sanitary towel.
Bindeglied ['bɪndəɡliːt], *n.* (—s, *pl.* —er) connecting link.
Bindehaut ['bɪndəhaut], *f.* (—, *pl.* ⁓e) (*Anat.*) conjunctiva.
Bindehautentzündung ['bɪndəhautɛntsynduŋ], *f.* (—, *pl.* —en) conjunctivitis.

binden ['bɪndən], *v.a. irr.* bind, tie, fasten.

Bindestrich ['bɪndəʃtrɪç], *m.* (—(e)s, *pl.* —e) hyphen.

Bindewort ['bɪndəvɔrt], *n.* (—s, *pl.* ⁓er) conjunction.

Bindfaden ['bɪntfaːdən], *m.* (—s, *pl.* ⁓) string, twine.

Bindung ['bɪnduŋ], *f.* (—, *pl.* —en) binding, bond; obligation; (*Mus.*) ligature.

binnen ['bɪnən], *prep.* (*Genit. & Dat.*), *adv.* within.

Binnenhafen ['bɪnənhaːfən], *m.* (—s, *pl.* ⁓) inland harbour.

Binnenhandel ['bɪnənhandəl], *m.* (—s, *no pl.*) inland trade.

Binse ['bɪnzə], *f.* (—, *pl.* —n) (*Bot.*) rush, reed.

Biographie [biogra'fiː], *f.* (—, *pl.* —n) biography.

Birke ['bɪrkə], *f.* (—, *pl.* —n) (*Bot.*) birch, birch-tree.

Birma ['bɪrmaː], *n.* Burma.

Birnbaum ['bɪrnbaum], *m.* (—s, *pl.* ⁓e) pear-tree.

Birne ['bɪrnə], *f.* (—, *pl.* —n) pear; (*Elec.*) bulb.

birnförmig ['bɪrnfœrmɪç], *adj.* pear-shaped.

bis [bɪs], *prep.* (*time*) till, until; by; (*place*) to, up to; — *auf*, with the exception of — *conj.* till, until.

Bisam ['biːzam], *m.* (—s, *pl.* —e) musk.

Bischof ['bɪʃɔf], *m.* (—s, *pl.* ⁓e) bishop.

bischöflich ['bɪʃœflɪç], *adj.* episcopal.

Bischofsstab ['bɪʃɔfsʃtaːp], *m.* (—s, *pl.* ⁓e) crosier.

bisher ['bɪsheːr], *adv.* hitherto, till now.

bisherig [bɪs'heːrɪç], *adj.* up to this time, hitherto existing.

Biskayischer Meerbusen [bɪs'kaːɪʃər 'meːrbuːzən], Bay of Biscay.

Biß [bɪs], *m.* (—sses, *pl.* —sse) bite, sting.

Bißchen ['bɪsçən], *n.* (—s, *pl.* —) morsel; little bit.

Bissen ['bɪsən], *m.* (—s, *pl.* —) bite, morsel.

bissig ['bɪsɪç], *adj.* biting, cutting; sharp, vicious; sarcastic.

Bistum ['bɪstuːm], *n.* (—s, *pl.* ⁓er) bishopric, diocese; see.

bisweilen [bɪs'vaɪlən], *adv.* sometimes, now and then, occasionally.

Bitte ['bɪtə], *f.* (—, *pl.* —n) request, entreaty.

bitte ['bɪtə], *int.* please.

bitten ['bɪtən], *v.a. irr.* ask; request.

bitter ['bɪtər], *adj.* bitter.

Bitterkeit ['bɪtərkaɪt], *f.* (—, *no pl.*) bitterness.

bitterlich ['bɪtərlɪç], *adv.* (*fig.*) bitterly.

Bittersalz ['bɪtərzalts], *n.* (—es, *no pl.*) Epsom salts.

Bittgang ['bɪtgaŋ], *m.* (—(e)s, *pl.* ⁓e) (*Eccl.*) procession.

Bittsteller ['bɪtʃtɛlər], *m.* (—s, *pl.* —) petitioner, suppli(c)ant.

Biwak ['biːvak], *m.* (—s, *pl.* —s) bivouac.

blähen ['blɛːən], *v.a.* inflate, puff up, swell.

Blähung ['blɛːuŋ], *f.* (—, *pl.* —en) (*Med.*) flatulence.

blaken ['blaːkən], *v.n.* smoulder; smoke.

Blamage [bla'maːʒə], *f.* (—, *pl.* —n) shame, disgrace.

blamieren [bla'miːrən], *v.a., v.r.* make (o.s.) ridiculous, make a fool of o.s.

blank [blaŋk], *adj.* shining, bright, smooth, polished.

Bläschen ['blɛːsçən], *n.* (—s, *pl.* —) little bubble, blister; (*Med.*) vesicle.

Blase ['blaːzə], *f.* (—, *pl.* —n) (*soap*) bubble; (*skin*) blister; (*Anat.*) bladder.

Blasebalg ['blaːzəbalk], *m.* (—s, *pl.* ⁓e) pair of bellows.

blasen ['blaːzən], *v.a. irr.* blow; (*Mus.*) sound.

Bläser ['blɛːzər], *m.* (—s, *pl.* —) (*glass*) blower; (*Mus.*) wind player.

blasiert [bla'ziːrt], *adj.* blasé, haughty.

Blasrohr ['blaːsroːr], *n.* (—s, *pl.* —e) blow-pipe, pea-shooter.

blaß [blas], *adj.* pale, wan, pallid.

Blässe ['blɛsə], *f.* (—, *no pl.*) paleness, pallor.

Blatt [blat], *n.* (—s, *pl.* ⁓er) leaf; (*paper*) sheet; blade.

Blatter ['blatər], *f.* (—, *pl.* —n) pustule; (*pl.*) smallpox.

blättern ['blɛtərn], *v.a.* turn the leaves (of a book).

Blätterteig ['blɛtərtaɪk], *m.* (—s, *no pl.*) puff pastry.

Blattgold ['blatgɔlt], *n.* (—es, *no pl.*) gold-leaf.

Blattlaus ['blatlaus], *f.* (—, *pl.* ⁓e) (*Ent.*) plant-louse.

Blattpflanze ['blatpflantsə], *f.* (—, *pl.* —n) leaf-plant.

blau [blau], *adj.* blue; —*en Montag machen*, stay away from work; *sein* —*es Wunder erleben*, be amazed.

blauäugig ['blauɔygɪç], *adj.* blue-eyed.

Blaubeere ['blaubeːrə], *f.* (—, *pl.* —n) bilberry, blueberry.

blaublütig ['blaublyːtɪç], *adj.* aristocratic.

bläuen ['blauən], *v.a.* dye blue, rinse in blue.

bläulich ['blɔylɪç], *adj.* pale blue, bluish.

Blausäure ['blauzɔyrə], *f.* (—, *no pl.*) prussic acid.

Blaustrumpf ['blauʃtrumpf], *m.* (—s, *pl.* ⁓e) blue-stocking.

Blech [blɛç], *n.* (—s, *pl.* —e) tinplate, sheet metal.

blechen ['blɛçən], *v.n.* (*coll.*) fork out money.

blechern ['blɛçərn], *adj.* made of tin, tinny.

Blechinstrument ['blɛçɪnstrumɛnt], *n.* (—s, *pl.* —e) (*Mus.*) brass instrument.

35

Blei

Blei [blaɪ], *n.* (**—s,** *no pl.*) lead.
bleiben ['blaɪbən], *v.n. irr.* (*aux.* sein) remain, stay.
bleich [blaɪç], *adj.* pale, wan, pallid.
Bleiche ['blaɪçə], *f.* (**—,** *pl.* **—n**) pallor; (*laundry*) bleaching-place.
bleichen ['blaɪçən], *v.a. irr.* bleach, whiten.
Bleichsucht ['blaɪçzuxt], *f.* (**—,** *no pl.*) chlorosis, anaemia.
bleiern ['blaɪərn], *adj.* leaden.
Bleiglanz ['blaɪglants], *m.* (**—es,** *no pl.*) (*Min.*) lead sulphide.
Bleisoldat ['blaɪzɔldaːt], *m.* (**—en,** *pl.* **—en**) tin soldier.
Bleistift ['blaɪʃtɪft], *m.* (**—s,** *pl.* **—e**) pencil.
Blende ['blɛndə], *f.* (**—,** *no pl.*) blind; (*Min.*) blende; (*Phot.*) shutter.
blenden ['blɛndən], *v.a.* dazzle, blind.
Blendlaterne ['blɛntlatɛrnə], *f.* (**—,** *pl.* **—n**) dark-lantern.
Blendung ['blɛnduŋ], *f.* (**—,** *pl.* **—en**) blinding, dazzling.
Blendwerk ['blɛntvɛrk], *n.* (**—s,** *no pl.*) (optical) illusion, false show.
Blick [blɪk], *m.* (**—s,** *pl.* **—e**) glance, look, glimpse.
blicken ['blɪkən], *v.n.* look, glance.
blind [blɪnt], *adj.* blind, sightless; **—er Passagier,** stowaway.
Blinddarm ['blɪntdarm], *m.* (**—s,** *pl.* **—e**) appendix.
Blinddarmentzündung ['blɪntdarmɛntsynduŋ], *f.* (**—,** *pl.* **—en**) appendicitis.
Blindekuh [blɪndəˈkuː], *f.* (**—,** *no pl.*) blind man's buff.
Blindgänger ['blɪntgɛŋər], *m.* (**—s,** *pl.* **—**) misfire, dud, blind.
Blindheit ['blɪnthaɪt], *f.* (**—,** *no pl.*) blindness.
blindlings ['blɪntlɪŋs], *adv.* blindly; at random.
Blindschleiche ['blɪntʃlaɪçə], *f.* (**—,** *pl.* **—n**) (*Zool.*) blind-worm.
blinken ['blɪŋkən], *v.n.* blink, flash, glitter, gleam.
blinzeln ['blɪntsəln], *v.n.* blink.
Blitz [blɪts], *m.* (**—es,** *pl.* **—e**) lightning, flash.
Blitzableiter ['blɪtsaplaɪtər], *m.* (**—s,** *pl.* **—**) lightning-conductor.
blitzblank ['blɪtsblaŋk], *adj.* as bright as a new pin; shining.
blitzen ['blɪtsən], *v.n.* flash; *es blitzt,* it is lightning; glitter, shine.
Blitzesschnelle -['blɪtsəsʃnɛlə], *f.* (**—,** *no pl.*) lightning-speed.
Blitzlicht ['blɪtslɪçt], *n.* (**—s,** *no pl.*) flashlight.
Blitzschlag ['blɪtsʃlaːk], *m.* (**—s,** *pl.* **—e**) flash of lightning.
Blitzstrahl ['blɪtsʃtraːl], *m.* (**—s,** *pl.* **—en**) flash of lightning.
Block [blɔk], *m.* (**—s,** *pl.* **—e**) block, log; pad.
Blockhaus ['blɔkhaus], *n.* (**—es,** *pl.* **—er**) log-cabin.

blockieren [blɔˈkiːrən], *v.a.* block (up); (*Mil.*) blockade.
blöde ['bløːdə], *adj.* stupid, dull, thick-headed, dim.
Blödsinn ['bløːtsɪn], *m.* (**—s,** *no pl.*) nonsense, idiocy.
blöken ['bløːkən], *v.n.* bleat; (*cows*) low.
blond [blɔnt], *adj.* blond, fair, fair-headed.
bloß [bloːs], *adj.* naked, uncovered; bare, mere.
Blöße ['bløːsə], *f.* (**—,** *pl.* **—n**) nakedness, bareness; (*fig.*) weak point.
bloßlegen ['bloːsleːgən], *v.a.* uncover, lay bare; (*fig.*) reveal, expose.
bloßstellen ['bloːsʃtɛlən], *v.a.* compromise, show up. **—** *v.r. sich* **—,** compromise o.s.
blühen ['blyːən], *v.n.* bloom, blossom, flower, flourish.
Blümchen ['blyːmçən], *n.* (**—s,** *pl.* **—**) small flower.
Blume ['bluːmə], *f.* (**—,** *pl.* **—n**) flower, bloom; (*wine*) bouquet; (*beer*) froth.
Blumenblatt ['bluːmənblat], *n.* (**—s,** *pl.* **ᵉer**) petal.
Blumenerde ['bluːməneːrdə], *f.* (**—,** *no pl.*) garden mould.
Blumenkelch ['bluːmənkɛlç], *m.* (**—es,** *pl.* **—e**) calyx.
Blumenkohl ['bluːmənkoːl], *m.* (**—s,** *pl.* **—e**) cauliflower.
Blumenstaub ['bluːmənʃtaup], *m.* (**—s,** *no pl.*) pollen.
Blumenstrauß ['bluːmənʃtraus], *m.* (**—es,** *pl.* **ᵉe**) bunch of flowers, posy, nosegay.
Blumenzucht ['bluːməntsuxt], *f.* (**—,** *no pl.*) floriculture.
Bluse ['bluːzə], *f.* (**—,** *pl.* **—n**) blouse.
Blut [bluːt], *n.* (**—es,** *no pl.*) blood.
blutarm ['bluːtarm], *adj.* anaemic; (*fig.*) very poor.
Blutbad ['bluːtbaːt], *n.* (**—es,** *pl.* **ᵉer**) massacre.
blutdürstig ['bluːtdyrstɪç], *adj.* bloodthirsty.
Blüte ['blyːtə], *f.* (**—,** *pl.* **—n**) blossom, flower, bloom.
Blutegel ['bluːteːgəl], *m.* (**—s,** *pl.* **—**) leech.
bluten ['bluːtən], *v.n.* bleed.
Bluterguß ['bluːtɛrgus], *m.* (**—es,** *pl.* **ᵉe**) effusion of blood.
Blutgefäß ['bluːtgəfɛːs], *n.* (**—es,** *pl.* **—e**) blood-vessel.
blutig ['bluːtɪç], *adj.* bloody; cruel.
blutjung ['bluːtjuŋ], *adj.* very young.
Blutkörperchen ['bluːtkœrpərçən], *n.* (**—s,** *pl.* **—**) blood-corpuscle.
Blutlassen ['bluːtlasən], *n.* (**—s,** *no pl.*) (*Med.*) bloodletting.
Blutrache ['bluːtraxə], *f.* (**—,** *no pl.*) vendetta.
Blutsauger ['bluːtzaugər], *m.* (**—s,** *pl.* **—**) vampire.
Blutschande ['bluːtʃandə], *f.* (**—,** *no pl.*) incest.

blutstillend ['blu:ʃtɪlənt], *adj.* styptic, blood-stanching.

Blutsturz ['blu:tʃturts], *m.* (—es, *no pl.*) haemorrhage; *einen — haben*, burst a blood-vessel.

Blutsverwandte ['blu:tsfɛrvantə], *m. or f.* (—n, *pl.* —n) blood-relation.

Blutvergießen ['blu:tfɛrgi:sən], *n.* (—s, *no pl.*) bloodshed.

Blutvergiftung ['blu:tfɛrgɪftuŋ], *f.* (—, *pl.* —en) blood poisoning.

Blutwurst ['blu:tvurst], *f.* (—, *pl.* ⸚e) black-pudding.

Blutzeuge ['blu:ttsɔygə], *m.* (—n, *pl.* —n) martyr.

Bö [bø:], *f.* (—, *pl.* —en) (*Naut.*) squall, gust of wind.

Bock [bɔk], *m.* (—s, *pl.* ⸚e) buck; he-goat; (*Gymn.*) horse; (*horse-drawn carriage*) box seat.

bockbeinig ['bɔkbaɪnɪç], *adj.* bow-legged; pigheaded, obstinate.

Bockbier ['bɔkbi:r], *n.* (—s, *no pl.*) bock beer.

bocken ['bɔkən], *v.n.* kick, be refractory; sulk.

Bockfell ['bɔkfɛl], *n.* (—s, *pl.* —e) buckskin.

bockig ['bɔkɪç], *adj.* pigheaded, obstinate.

Bocksbeutel ['bɔksbɔytəl], *m.* (—s, *pl.* —) leather bag; Franconian wine (bottle).

Bockshorn ['bɔkshɔrn], *n.* (—s, *pl.* ⸚er) buck horn; *einen ins — jagen*, intimidate s.o.

Boden ['bo:dən], *m.* (—s, *pl.* ⸚) ground, bottom, soil, floor; garret, loft.

Bodenfenster ['bo:dənfɛnstər], *n.* (—s, *pl.* —) attic window.

Bodenkammer ['bo:dənkamər], *f.* (—, *pl.* —n) garret, attic.

bodenlos ['bo:dənlo:s], *adj.* bottomless; (*fig.*) unimaginable, enormous.

Bodensatz ['bo:dənzats], *m.* (—es, *pl.* ⸚e) sediment, dregs, deposit.

Bodensee ['bo:dənze:], *m.* Lake Constance.

Bogen ['bo:gən], *m.* (—s, *pl.* —, ⸚) arch, vault, curve; (*Maths.*) arc; (*violin*) bow; (*paper*) sheet; (*Mus.*) ligature.

bogenförmig ['bo:gənfœrmɪç], *adj.* arch-shaped, arched.

Bogenführung ['bo:gənfy:ruŋ], *f.* (—, *no pl.*) (*Mus.*) bowing (technique).

Bogengang ['bo:gəngaŋ], *m.* (—es, *pl.* ⸚e) arcade.

Bogenlampe ['bo:gənlampə], *f.* (—, *pl.* —n) arc-lamp.

Bogenschütze ['bo:gənʃytsə], *m.* (—n, *pl.* —n) archer.

bogig ['bo:gɪç], *adj.* bent, curved, arched.

Bohle ['bo:lə], *f.* (—, *pl.* —n) board, plank.

Böhmen ['bø:mən], *n.* Bohemia.

Bohne ['bo:nə], *f.* (—, *pl.* —n) bean; *grüne —n*, French (*Am.* string) beans; *dicke —n*, broad beans; *blaue —n*, (*fig.*) bullets.

Bohnenstange ['bo:nənʃtaŋə], *f.* (— *pl.* —n) bean-pole.

Bohnerbürste ['bo:nərbyrstə], *f.* (—, *pl.* —n) polishing-brush.

bohnern ['bo:nərn], *v.a.* polish, wax.

bohren ['bo:rən], *v.a.* bore, pierce, drill.

Bohrer ['bo:rər], *m.* (—s, *pl.* —) gimlet; drill.

Bohrturm ['bo:rturm], *m.* (—s, *pl.* ⸚e) derrick.

Boje ['bo:jə], *f.* (—, *pl.* —n) (*Naut.*) buoy.

Bolivien [bo'li:vjən], *n.* Bolivia.

Böller ['bœlər], *m.* (—s, *pl.* —) (*Mil.*) small mortar.

Bollwerk ['bɔlvɛrk], *n.* (—s, *pl.* —e) bulwark.

Bolzen ['bɔltsən], *m.* (—s, *pl.* —) bolt, arrow, pin; (*smoothing iron*) heater.

Bombe ['bɔmbə], *f.* (—, *pl.* —n) bomb, bomb-shell.

Bombenerfolg ['bɔmbənerfɔlk], *m.* (—(e)s, *pl.* —e) (*Theat.*) smash hit.

Bonbon [bɔ̃'bɔ̃], *m.* (—s, *pl.* —s) sweet(s), bonbon; (*Am.*) candy.

Bonbonniere [bɔ̃bɔ'njɛ:rə], *f.* (—, *pl.* —n) box of sweets.

Bonze ['bɔntsə], *m.* (—n, *pl.* —n) (*coll.*) bigwig, (*Am.*) big shot.

Boot [bo:t], *n.* (—es, *pl.* —e) boat.

Bootsanker ['bo:tsaŋkər], *m.* (—s, *pl.* —) grapnel.

Bootsleine ['bo:tslaɪnə], *f.* (—, *pl.* —n) tow-rope.

Bor [bo:r], *n.* (—s, *no pl.*) (*Chem.*) boron.

Bord [bɔrt], *m.* (—s, *pl.* —e) rim; (*Naut.*) board.

Bordell [bɔr'dɛl], *n.* (—s, *pl.* —e) brothel.

borgen ['bɔrgən], *v.a., v.n.* borrow; borrow (*von*, from); lend (*Dat.*, to).

Borke ['bɔrkə], *f.* (—, *pl.* —n) bark, rind.

Born [bɔrn], *m.* (—es, —e) (*Poet.*) bourn, spring, well, source.

borniert [bɔr'ni:rt], *adj.* narrow-minded.

Borsäure ['bo:rzɔyrə], *f.* (—, *no pl.*) boric acid.

Börse ['bœrzə], *f.* (—, *pl.* —n) purse; (*Comm.*) stock-exchange, bourse.

Börsenbericht ['bœrzənbərɪçt], *m.* (—s, *pl.* —e) stock-market report.

Borste ['bɔrstə], *f.* (—, *pl.* —n) bristle.

borstig ['bɔrstɪç], *adj.* bristly; (*fig.*) irritable.

Borte ['bɔrtə], *f.* (—, *pl.* —n) order, trimming.

bösartig ['bø:sartɪç], *adj.* malevolent, malicious, vicious; (*disease*) malignant.

Böschung ['bøʃuŋ], *f.* (—, *pl.* —en) slope, scarp.

böse ['bø:zə], *adj.* bad, wicked; evil; angry, cross (with, *Dat.*); — *auf* (*Acc.*), angry with s.o., (*Am.*) mad at s.o.

Bösewicht ['bø:zəvɪçt], *m.* (—s, *pl.* —er) villain, ruffian; wretch.

37

boshaft

boshaft ['bo:shaft], *adj.* spiteful, malicious.

Bosheit ['bo:shaɪt], *f.* (—, *pl.* —en) malice.

böswillig ['bø:svɪlɪç], *adj.* malevolent.

Botanik [bo'ta:nɪk], *f.* (—, *no pl.*) botany.

Botaniker [bo'ta:nɪkər], *m.* (—s, *pl.* —) botanist.

Botanisiertrommel [botanɪ'zi:rtrɔməl], *f.* (—, *pl.* —n) specimen-box.

Bote ['bo:tə], *m.* (—n, *pl.* —n) messenger.

Botengang ['bo:təngaŋ], *m.* (—s, *pl.* ⁖e) errand.

botmäßig [bo:tmɛ:sɪç], *adj.* subject, subordinate.

Botschaft ['bo:tʃaft], *f.* (—, *pl.* —en) message; (*Pol.*) embassy; *gute* —, glad tidings.

Botschafter ['bo:tʃaftər], *m.* (—s, *pl.* —) ambassador.

Böttcher ['bœtçɔr], *m.* (—s, *pl.* —) cooper.

Bottich [bɔtɪç], *m.* (—s, *pl.* —e) vat, tub.

Bouillon [bul'jɔ̃], *f.* (—, *no pl.*) broth, meat soup.

Bowle ['bo:lə], *f.* (—, *no pl.*) bowl; spiced wine.

boxen ['bɔksən], *v.n.* box.

brach [bra:x], *adj.* fallow, unploughed, untilled.

Brand [brant], *m.* (—es, *pl.* ⁖e) burning, fire, combustion, conflagration; (*Med.*) gangrene.

Brandblase ['brantbla:zə], *f.* (—, *pl.* —n) blister.

branden ['brandən], *v.n.* surge, break (waves).

brandig ['brandɪç], *adj.* blighted; (*Med.*) gangrenous.

Brandmal ['brantma:l], *n.* (—s, *pl.* —e) burn mark; brand (cattle); (*fig.*) stigma.

brandmarken ['brantmarkən], *v.a.* brand; (*fig.*) stigmatise.

Brandmauer ['brantmauər], *f.* (—, *pl.* —n) fire-proof wall.

brandschatzen ['brantʃatsən], *v.a.* levy contributions (from); pillage, plunder.

Brandsohle ['brantzo:lə], *f.* (—, *pl.* —n) inner sole, welt (of shoe).

Brandstifter ['brantʃtɪftər], *m.* (—s, *pl.* —e) incendiary, fire-raiser.

Brandstiftung ['brantʃtɪftuŋ], *f.* (—, *pl.* —en) arson.

Brandung ['branduŋ], *f.* (—, *pl.* —en) breakers, surf, surge (of sea).

Branntwein ['brantvaɪn], *m.* (—s, *pl.* —e) brandy.

Brasilien [bra'zi:ljən], *n.* Brazil.

Braten ['bra:tən], *m.* (—s, *pl.* —) roast (meat), joint.

braten ['bra:tən], *v.a. reg. & irr.* roast, broil, bake, fry, grill. — *v.n.* (*coll.*) bask (in sun), roast.

Brathering ['bra:the:rɪŋ], *m.* (—s, *pl.* —e) grilled herring.

Brathuhn ['bra:thu:n], *n.* (—s, *pl.* ⁖er) roast chicken.

Bratkartoffeln ['bra:tkartɔfəln], *f. pl.* roast *or* fried potatoes.

Bratpfanne ['bra:tpfanə], *f.* (—, *pl.* —n) frying pan.

Bratsche ['bra:tʃə], *f.* (—, *pl.* —n) (*Mus.*) viola.

Bratspieß ['bra:tʃpi:s], *m.* (—es, *pl.* —e) spit (roasting).

Bratwurst ['bra:tvurst], *f.* (—, *pl.* ⁖e) sausage for frying; fried sausage.

Brau [brau], **Bräu**, [brɔy], *n. & m.* (—s, *no pl.*) brew.

Brauch [braux], *m.* (—es, *pl.* ⁖e) usage, custom, habit.

brauchbar ['brauxba:r], *adj.* useful, serviceable.

brauchen ['brauxən], *v.a.* make use of, employ; need, require, want; (*time*) take.

Braue ['brauə], *f.* (—, *pl.* —n) brow, eye-brow.

brauen ['brauən], *v.a.* brew.

Brauer ['brauər], *m.* (—s, *pl.* —) brewer.

Brauerei ['brauəraɪ], *f.* (—, *pl.* —en) brewery.

Brauhaus ['brauhaus], *n.* (—es, *pl.* ⁖er) brewery.

braun [braun], *adj.* brown.

bräunen ['brɔynən], *v.a.* make brown, tan.

Braunkohl ['braunko:l], *m.* (—s, *no pl.*) (*Bot.*) broccoli.

Braunschweig ['braunʃvaɪk], *n.* Brunswick.

Braus [braus], *m.* (—es, *no pl.*) bustle, tumult; *in Saus und — leben*, lead a riotous life.

Brause ['brauzə], *f.* (—, *pl.* —n) shower (bath); effervescence, (*coll.*) fizzy drink.

Brausekopf ['brauzəkɔpf], *m.* (—es, *pl.* ⁖e) hothead.

Brauselimonade ['brauzəlimona:də], *f.* (—, *pl.* —n) effervescent *or* fizzy lemonade.

brausen ['brauzən], *v.n.* roar, bluster, rush; effervesce.

Brausepulver ['brauzəpulvər], *n.* (—s, *pl.* —) effervescent powder.

Braut [braut], *f.* (—, *pl.* ⁖e) bride, betrothed, fiancée.

Brautführer ['brautfy:rər], *m.* (—s, *pl.* —) best man.

Bräutigam ['brɔytɪgam], *m.* (—s, *pl.* —e) bridegroom, betrothed, fiancé.

Brautjungfer ['brautjuŋfər], *f.* (—, *pl.* —n) bridesmaid.

bräutlich ['brɔytlɪç], *adj.* bridal.

Brautpaar ['brautpa:r], *n.* (—es, *pl.* —e) engaged couple.

Brautschau ['brautʃau], *f.* (—, *no pl.*) (*obs.*) search for a wife.

brav [bra:f], *adj.* honest, upright, worthy, honourable; well-behaved, good.

bravo! ['bra:vo], *int.* well done!

38

Bravourstück [bra′vu:rſtyk], *n.* (—s, *pl.* —e) feat of valour.

Brechbohnen [′brɛçbo:nən], *f. pl.* kidney-beans.

Brecheisen [′brɛçaɪzən], *n.* (—s, *pl.* —) jemmy.

brechen [′brɛçən], *v.a. irr.* break; (*flowers*) pluck, pick; vomit. — *v.n.* (*aux.* sein) break.

Brechmittel [′brɛçmɪtəl], *n.* (—s, *pl.* —) emetic.

Brechruhr [′brɛçru:r], *f.* (—, *no pl.*) cholera.

Brechstange [′brɛçſtaŋə], *f.* (—, *pl.* —n) crow-bar.

Brechung [′brɛçuŋ], *f.* (—, *pl.* —en) breaking; (*Phys.*) refraction.

Brei [braɪ], *m.* (—s, *pl.* —e) pap, pulp, porridge.

breiartig [′braɪa:rtɪç], *adj.* pulpy.

breiig [′braɪɪç], *adj.* pappy.

breit [braɪt], *adj.* broad, wide.

breitbeinig [′braɪtbaɪnɪç], *adj.* straddle-legged.

Breite [′braɪtə], *f.* (—, *pl.* —n) breadth, width; (*Geog.*) latitude.

Breitengrad [′braɪtəngra:t], *m.* (—es, *pl.* —e) (*Geog.*) degree of latitude.

Breitenkreis [′braɪtənkraɪs], *m.* (—es, *pl.* —e) (*Geog.*) parallel.

breitschultrig [′braɪtſultrɪç], *adj.* broad-shouldered.

Bremse [′brɛmzə], *f.* (—. *pl.* —n) (*Ent.*) gad-fly; (*Motor.*) brake; (*horse*) barnacle.

bremsen [′brɛmzən], *v.a.* brake, pull up.

brennbar [′brɛnba:r], *adj.* combustible.

Brenneisen [′brɛnaɪzən], *n.* (—s, *pl.* —) branding iron.

brennen [′brɛnən], *v.a. irr.* burn; (*Med.*) cauterise; (*alcohol*) distil; (*hair*) curl; (*coffee*) roast; (*coal*) char; (*bricks*) bake. — *v.n.* burn; (*fig.*) sting; (*eyes*) smart.

Brenner [′brɛnər], *m.* (—s, *pl.* —) (*person*) distiller; (*Tech.*) burner.

Brennerei [brɛnə′raɪ], *f.* (—, *pl.* —en) distillery.

Brennessel [′brɛnnɛsəl], *f.* (—, *pl.* —n) stinging nettle.

Brennholz [′brɛnhɔlts], *n.* (—es, *no pl.*) firewood.

Brennmaterial [′brɛnmaterja:l], *n.* (—s, *pl.* —ien) fuel.

Brennofen [′brɛno:fən], *m.* (—s, *pl.* ′n) kiln.

Brennpunkt [′brɛnpuŋkt], *m.* (—s, *pl.* —e) focus.

Brennschere [′brɛnſe:rə], *f.* (—, *pl.* —n) curling-irons.

Brennstoff [′brɛnſtɔf], *m.* (—(e)s, *pl.* —e) fuel.

brenzlich [′brɛntslɪç], *adj.* smelling (or tasting) of burning; (*fig.*) ticklish.

Bresche [′brɛſə], *f.* (—, *pl.* —n) breach, gap.

Brett [brɛt], *n.* (—s, *pl.* —er) board, plank, shelf.

Brettspiel [′brɛtſpi:l], *n.* (—s, *pl.* —e) table-game.

Brevier [bre′vi:r], *n.* (—s, *pl.* (*rare*) —e) breviary.

Brezel [′bre:tsəl], *f.* (—, *pl.* —n) cracknel, pretzel.

Brief [bri:f], *m.* (—es, *pl.* —e) letter; epistle.

Briefanschrift [′bri:fanſrɪft], *f.* (—, *pl.* —en) address.

Briefbeschwerer [′bri:fbəſve:rər], *m.* (—s, *pl.* —) letter-weight, paper-weight.

Briefbogen [′bri:fbo:gən], *m.* (—s, *pl.* —) sheet of notepaper.

Briefkasten [′bri:fkastən], *m.* (—s, *pl.* ∹) (*house*) letter-box; (*street*) pillar-box, (*Am.*) post-box.

brieflich [′bri:flɪç], *adv.* by letter, in writing.

Briefmarke [′bri:fmarkə], *f.* (—, *pl.* —n) postage stamp.

Briefpapier [′bri:fpapi:r], *n.* (—s, *no pl.*) notepaper.

Briefporto [′bri:fpɔrto], *n.* (—s, *pl.* —ti) postage.

Brieftasche [′bri:ftaſə], *f.* (—, *pl.* —n) portfolio, wallet; (*Am.*) pocket-book.

Brieftaube [′bri:ftaubə], *f.* (—, *pl.* —n) carrier pigeon.

Briefträger [′bri:ftrɛ:gər], *m.* (—s, *pl.* —) postman.

Briefumschlag [′bri:fumſla:k], *m.* (—s, *pl.* ∹e) envelope.

Briefwechsel [′bri:fvɛksəl], *m.* (—s, *no pl.*) correspondence.

Brillant [brɪl′jant], *m.* (—en, *pl.* —en) brilliant, diamond. — *adj.* brilliant.

Brille [′brɪlə], *f.* (— *pl.* —n) spectacles, glasses.

Brillenschlange [′brɪlənſlaŋə], *f.* (—, *pl.* —n) (*Zool.*) hooded cobra.

bringen [′brɪŋən], *v.a. irr.* bring, fetch, carry to, take to, conduct to.

Brise [′bri:zə], *f.* (—, *pl.* —n) breeze, light wind.

Britannien [brɪ′tanjən], *n.* Britain.

bröckeln [′brœkəln], *v.a., v.n.* crumble.

Brocken [′brɔkən], *m.* (—s, *pl.* —) bit, piece, fragment, scrap; (*bread*) crumb.

bröcklig [′brœklɪç], *adj.* crumbling.

brodeln [′bro:dəln], *v.n.* bubble, simmer.

Brodem [′bro:dəm], *m.* (—s, *no pl.*) (*Poet.*) steam, vapour, exhalation.

Brokat [bro′ka:t], *m.* (—s, *pl.* —e) brocade.

Brom [bro:m], *n.* (—s, *no pl.*) (*Chem.*) bromine.

Brombeere [′brɔmbe:rə], *f.* (—, *pl.* —n) blackberry, bramble.

Bronze [brɔ̃:sə], *f.* (—, *pl.* —n) bronze.

Brosamen [′bro:za:mən], *pl.* crumbs.

Brosche [′broʃə], *f.* (—, *pl.* —n) brooch.

Broschüre [brɔ′ʃy:rə], *f.* (—, *pl.* —n) pamphlet, brochure, folder.

Brösel [′brø:zəl], *m.* (—s, *pl.* —) crumb.

Brot [bro:t], *n.* (—s, *pl.* —e) bread, loaf; (*fig.*) livelihood.

Brötchen [′brø:tçən], *n.* (—s, *pl.* —) roll, bread-roll.

Broterwerb

Broterwerb [ˈbroːtərvɛrp], *m.* (—s, *no pl.*) livelihood.

Brotgeber [ˈbroːtgeːbər], *m.* (—s, *pl.* —) employer, master.

Brotherr [ˈbroːthɛr], *m.* (—n, *pl.* —en) employer, master.

Brotkorb [ˈbroːtkɔrp], *m.* (—s, *pl.* ˙e) bread-basket.

brotlos [ˈbroːtloːs], *adj.* unemployed; (*fig.*) unprofitable.

Brotneid [ˈbroːtnaɪt], *m.* (—s, *no pl.*) professional jealousy.

Bruch [brux], *m.* (—s, *pl.* ˙e) breakage; rupture; (*Med.*) fracture, rupture, hernia; (*Maths.*) fraction.

Bruchband [ˈbruxbant], *f.* (—es, *pl.* ˙er) abdominal belt, truss.

brüchig [ˈbryçɪç], *adj.* brittle, full of flaws.

Bruchlandung [ˈbruxlanduŋ], *f.* (—, —en) (*Aviat.*) crash-landing.

Bruchrechnung [ˈbruxrɛçnuŋ], *f.* (—, *pl.* —en) (*Arith.*) fractions.

Bruchstück [ˈbruxʃtyk], *n.* (—s, *pl.* —e) fragment, scrap.

Bruchteil [ˈbruxtaɪl], *m.* (—s, *pl.* —e) fraction.

Brücke [ˈbrykə], *f.* (—, *pl.* —n) bridge.

Brückenpfeiler [ˈbrykənpfaɪlər], *m.* (—s, *pl.* —) pier.

Bruder [ˈbruːdər], *m.* (—s, *pl.* ˙) brother; (*Eccl.*) friar.

brüderlich [ˈbryːdərlɪç], *adj.* fraternal, brotherly.

Bruderschaft [ˈbruːdərʃaft], *f.* (—, —en) fraternity, brotherhood.

Brügge [ˈbrygə], *n.* Bruges.

Brühe [ˈbryːə], *f.* (—, *pl.* —n) broth, meat-soup.

brühen [ˈbryːən], *v.a.* scald.

Brühkartoffeln [ˈbryːkartɔfəln], *f. pl.* potatoes cooked in broth.

brüllen [ˈbrylən], *v.n.* roar, howl, yell; (*cows*) low, bellow.

Brummbaß [ˈbrumbas], *m.* (—sses, *pl.* ˙sse) (*Mus.*) double-bass.

Brummeisen [ˈbrumaɪzən], *n.* (—s, *pl.* —) Jew's harp.

brummen [ˈbrumən], *v.n.* growl, grumble, hum.

Brummer [ˈbrumər], *m.* (—s, *pl.* —) (*Ent.*) blue-bottle.

Brunnen [ˈbrunən], *m.* (—s, *pl.* —) well, fountain, spring.

Brunnenkur [ˈbrunənkuːr], *f.* (—, *pl.* —en) taking of mineral waters.

Brunst [brunst], *f.* (—, *pl.* ˙e) (*Zool.*) rut, heat.

Brust [brust], *f.* (—, *pl.* ˙e) breast; chest; bosom.

Brustbein [ˈbrustbaɪn], *n.* (—s, *pl.* —e) breastbone, sternum.

Brustbild [ˈbrustbɪlt], *n.* (—s, *pl.* —er) half-length portrait.

brüsten [ˈbrystən], *v.r. sich* —, boast, brag, plume o.s.

Brustfell [ˈbrustfɛl], *n.* (—s, *pl.* —e) pleura.

Brustfellentzündung [ˈbrustfɛlɛntsynduŋ], *f.* (—, *no pl.*) pleurisy.

Brusthöhle [ˈbrusthøːlə], *f.* (—, *pl.* —n) thoracic cavity.

Brustkasten [ˈbrustkastən], *m.* (—s, *pl.* ˙n) chest.

Brusttee [ˈbrustteː], *m.* (—s, *no pl.*) pectoral (herbal) tea.

Brüstung [ˈbrystuŋ], *f.* (—, *pl.* —en) parapet.

Brustwarze [ˈbrustvartsə], *f.* (—, *pl.* —n) nipple.

Brustwehr [ˈbrustveːr], *f.* (—, *pl.* —en) breastwork, parapet.

Brut [bruːt], *f.* (—, *no pl.*) brood; (*fish*) fry.

brutal [bruˈtaːl], *adj.* brutal.

brüten [ˈbryːtən], *v.a.* brood, hatch.

Brutofen [ˈbruːtoːfən], *m.* (—s, *pl.* ˙) incubator.

brutto [ˈbruto], *adv.* (*Comm.*) gross.

Bube [ˈbuːbə], *m.* (—n, *pl.* —n) boy, lad; (*cards*) knave, (*Am.*) jack; rogue, rascal.

Bubenstreich [ˈbuːbənʃtraɪç], *m.* (—s, *pl.* —e) boyish prank; knavish trick.

Bubikopf [ˈbuːbɪkɔpf], *m.* (—(e)s, *pl.* ˙e) bobbed hair.

Buch [buːx], *n.* (—s, *pl.* ˙er) book; quire (of paper).

Buchdruckerei [ˈbuːxdrukəraɪ], *f.* (—, —en) printing works, printing office.

Buche [ˈbuːxə], *f.* (—, *pl.* —n) beech (tree).

buchen [ˈbuːxən], *v.a.* book, enter, reserve; (*fig.*) score.

Bücherei [byːçəˈraɪ], *f.* (—, *pl.* —en) library.

Buchesche [ˈbuːxɛʃə], *f.* (—, *pl.* —n) hornbeam.

Buchfink [ˈbuːxfɪŋk], *m.* (—en, *pl.* —en) (*Orn.*) chaffinch.

Buchhalter [ˈbuːxhaltər], *m.* (—s, *pl.* —) book-keeper.

Buchhändler [ˈbuːxhɛndlər], *m.* (—s, *pl.* —) bookseller.

Buchmarder [ˈbuːxmardər], *m.* (—s, *pl.* —) (*Zool.*) pine-marten.

Buchsbaum [ˈbuksbaum], *m.* (—s, *pl.* ˙e) (*Bot.*) box-tree.

Büchse [ˈbyksə], *f.* (—, *pl.* —n) box, case; tin, can; rifle, gun.

Büchsenfleisch [ˈbyksənflaɪʃ], *n.* (—es, *no pl.*) tinned meat.

Büchsenlauf [ˈbyksənlauf], *m.* (—s, *pl.* ˙e) gun-barrel.

Büchsenöffner [ˈbyksənœfnər], *m.* (—s, *pl.*—) tin-opener.

Buchstabe [ˈbuːxʃtaːbə], *m.* (—n, *pl.* —n) letter, character; *großer* —, capital (letter).

Buchstabenrätsel [ˈbuːxʃtaːbənrɛtsəl], *n.* (—s, *pl.* —) anagram.

buchstabieren [buːxʃtaˈbiːrən], *v.a.* spell (out).

buchstäblich [ˈbuːxʃtɛplɪç], *adj.* literal.

Bucht [buxt], *f.* (—, *pl.* —en) inlet, bay, creek, bight.

Buchung [ˈbuːxuŋ], *f.* (—, *pl.* —en) (*Comm.*) entry (in a book); booking (of tickets).

Buchwissen ['buːxvɪsən], *n.* (—s, *no pl.*) book-learning.

Buckel ['bukəl], *m.* (—s, *pl.* —) hump, humpback; boss, stud; (*coll.*) back.

bücken ['bykən], *v.r. sich* —, stoop, bow.

bucklig ['buklɪç], *adj.* humpbacked.

Bückling ['byklɪŋ], *m.* (—s, *pl.* —e) smoked herring; kipper.

buddeln ['budəln], *v.n.* (*coll.*) dig.

Bude ['buːdə], *f.* (—, *pl.* —n) shack, stall; (*coll.*) room; (*student's*) digs.

Büfett [by'fɛt], *n.* (—s, *pl.* —s) sideboard; buffet.

Büffel ['byfəl], *m.* (—s, *pl.* —) buffalo.

büffeln ['byfəln], *v.n.* (*coll.*) cram (for an examination), swot.

Bug [buːk], *m.* (—s, *pl.* ̈e, —e) (*Naut.*) bow, (*Aviat.*) nose.

Buganker ['buːkaŋkər], *m.* (—s, *pl.* —) bow-anchor.

Bügel ['byːgəl], *m.* (—s, *pl.* —) coathanger; (*trigger*) guard; (*horse*) stirrup.

bügeln ['byːgəln], *v.a.* iron, smoothe, press.

bugsieren [buk'siːrən], *v.a.* tow.

Bugspriet ['buːkʃpriːt], *n.* (—s, *pl.* —e) bowsprit.

Buhle ['buːlə], *m.* or *f.* (—n, *pl.* —n) (*Poet.*) paramour, lover.

buhlen ['buːlən], *v.n.* (*Poet.*) woo, make love (to).

buhlerisch [buːlərɪʃ], *adj.* (*Poet.*) amorous, wanton, lewd.

Bühne ['byːnə], *f.* (—, *pl.* —n) (*Theat.*) stage; scaffold, platform.

Bühnenbild ['byːnənbɪlt], *n.* (—es, *pl.* —er) scenery.

Bukett [bu'kɛt], *n.* (—s, *pl.* —s) bunch of flowers, bouquet; bouquet (*wine*).

Bulgarien [bul'gaːrjən], *n.* Bulgaria.

Bulldogge ['buldɔgə], *f.* (—, *pl.* —n) bulldog.

Bulle (1) ['bulə], *m.* (—n, *pl.* —n) bull, bullock.

Bulle (2) ['bulə], *f.* (—, *pl.* —n) (*Eccl.*) (Papal) Bull.

bumm [bum], *int.* boom! bang!

Bummel ['buməl], *m.* (—s, *pl.* —) stroll.

Bummelei [bumə'laɪ], *f.* (—, *pl.* —en) idleness, negligence, casualness, carelessness.

bummeln ['buməln], *v.n.* lounge, waste o.'s time, dawdle; stroll.

Bummelzug ['buməltsuːk], *m.* (—s, *pl.* ̈e) slow train.

bums [bums], *int.* bang! crash!

Bund (1) [bunt], *m.* (—es, *pl.* ̈e) bond, tie, league, alliance, federation, confederacy; (*Eccl.*) covenant.

Bund (2) [bunt], *n.* (—es, *pl.* —e) bundle, bunch (of keys).

Bündel ['byndəl], *n.* (—s, *pl.* —) bundle, package.

Bundesgenosse ['bundəsgənɔsə], *m.* (—n, *pl.* —n) confederate, ally.

Bundesstaat ['bundəsʃtaːt], *m.* (—es, *pl.* —en) federal state; federation.

Bundestag ['bundəstaːk], *m.* (—es, *pl.* —e) federal parliament.

Bundeswehr ['bundəsveːr], *f.* (—, *no pl.*) federal defence; armed forces.

bündig ['byndɪç], *adj.* binding; *kurz und* —, concise, terse, to the point.

Bündnis ['byntnɪs], *n.* (—ses, *pl.* —se) alliance.

Bundschuh ['buntʃuː], *m.* (—s, *pl.* —e) clog, sandal.

bunt [bunt], *adj.* many-coloured, chequered, variegated, motley; *das ist mir zu* —, this is going too far.

buntscheckig ['buntʃɛkɪç], *adj.* dappled, spotted.

Buntspecht ['buntʃpɛçt], *m.* (—s, *pl.* —e) (*Orn.*) (spotted) woodpecker.

Bürde ['byrdə], *f.* (—, *pl.* —n) load, burden.

Bure ['buːrə], *m.* (—n, *pl.* —n) Boer.

Burg [burk], *f.* (—, *pl.* —en) castle, fortress, citadel, stronghold.

Bürge ['byrgə], *m.* (—n, *pl.* —n) surety, bail, guarantee; *einen* —n *stellen*, offer bail.

bürgen ['byrgən], *v.n.* give security, vouch (for), go bail (for).

Bürger ['byrgər], *m.* (—s, *pl.* —) citizen, townsman, bourgeois, commoner.

bürgerlich ['byrgərlɪç], *adj.* civic; middle-class, bourgeois; —e *Küche*, plain cooking.

Bürgermeister ['byrgərmaɪstər], *m.* (—s, *pl.* —) burgomaster, mayor.

Burggraf ['burkgraːf], *m.* (—en, *pl.* —en) burgrave.

Bürgschaft ['byrkʃaft], *f.* (—, *pl.* —en) bail, surety, guarantee; — *leisten*, provide security.

Burgund [bur'gunt], *n.* Burgundy.

Burgvogt ['burkfoːkt], *m.* (—s, *pl.* —e) (*obs.*) castellan, bailiff.

Burgwarte ['burkvartə], *f.* (—, *pl.* —n) watch-tower.

Büro [by'roː], *n.* (—s, *pl.* —s) office, bureau, (professional) chambers.

Bursche ['burʃə], *m.* (—n, *pl.* —n) lad, boy, fellow; student; (*Mil.*) batman.

Burschenschaft ['burʃənʃaft], *f.* (—, *pl.* —en) students' association.

Bürste ['byrstə], *f.* (—, *pl.* —n) brush.

Burundi [bu'rundi], *n.* Burundi.

Busch [buʃ], *m.* (—es, *pl.* ̈e) bush, shrub, copse, thicket.

Büschel ['byʃəl], *n.* (—s, *pl.* —) bunch; (*hair*) tuft.

buschig ['buʃɪç], *adj.* bushy, tufted.

Buschklepper ['buʃklɛpər], *m.* (—s, *pl.* —) bushranger.

Busen ['buːzən], *m.* (—s, *pl.* —) bosom, breast; (*Geog.*) bay, gulf.

Bussard ['busart], *m.* (—s, *pl.* —e) (*Orn.*) buzzard.

Buße ['buːsə], *f.* (—, *pl.* —n) penance; repentance; penalty.

büßen ['byːsən], *v.a., v.n.* repent, atone, expiate, make amends.

bußfertig ['buːsfɛrtɪç], *adj.* penitent, repentant.

Büste ['bystə], *f.* (—, *pl.* —n) bust.
Büstenhalter ['bystenhaltər], *m.* (—s, *pl.* —) brassière.
Bütte ['bytə], *f.* (—, *pl.* —n) tub.
Büttel ['bytəl], *m.* (—s, *pl.* —) beadle; bailiff.
Büttenpapier ['bytənpapi:r], *n.* (—s, *no pl.*) hand-made paper.
Butter ['butər], *f.* (—, *no pl.*) butter.
Butterblume ['butərblu:mə], *f.* (—, *pl.* —n) buttercup.
Butterbrot ['butərbro:t], *n.* (—s, *pl.* —e) bread and butter.
buttern ['butərn], *v.a.*, *v.n.* smear with butter; churn.
Butterteig ['butərtaik], *m.* (—es, *pl.* —e) puff-pastry.
Butzenscheibe ['butsənʃaibə], *f.* (—, *pl.* —n) bull's-eyed pane.
Byzanz [by'tsants], *n.* Byzantium, Constantinople.

C

C [tse:], *n.* (—s, *pl.* —s) the letter C; (*Mus.*) *C dur,* C major; *C Moll,* C minor; *C-Schlüssel,* C clef.
Cäsar ['tsε:zar], *m.* Cæsar.
Ceylon ['tseilon], *n.* Ceylon.
Chaiselongue [ʃε:zə'lɔ̃:g], *f.* (—, *pl.* —s) couch, settee, sofa.
Champagner [ʃam'panjər], *m.* (—s, *pl.* —) champagne.
Champignon [ʃampin'jɔ̃], *m.* (—s, *pl.* —s) mushroom.
chaotisch [ka'o:tiʃ], *adj.* chaotic.
Charakter [ka'raktər], *m.* (—s, *pl.* —e) character; mental make-up, disposition.
Charakteristik [karaktər'istik], *f.* (—, *pl.* —en) characterisation.
charakteristisch [karaktər'istiʃ], *adj.* characteristic; typical.
Charge ['ʃarʒə], *f.* (—, *pl.* —n) office, appointment; (*pl.*) (*Mil.*) non-commissioned officers.
Chaussee [ʃɔ'se:], *f.* (—, *pl.* —n) main road, highway.
Chef [ʃεf], *m.* (—s, *pl.* —s) chief, head, employer; (*coll.*) boss.
Chefredakteur ['ʃefredaktø:r], *m.* (—s, *pl.* —e) editor-in-chief.
Chemie [çe'mi:], *f.* (—, *no pl.*) chemistry.
Chemikalien [çemi'ka:ljən], *f. pl.* chemicals.
Chemiker ['çe:mıkər], *m.* (—s, *pl.* —) (analytical) chemist.
chemisch ['çe:mıʃ], *adj.* chemical; *— gereinigt,* dry-cleaned.
Chiffre ['ʃıfər], *f.* (—, *pl.* —n) cipher.
chiffrieren [ʃı'fri:rən], *v.a.* encipher.
Chile ['tʃi:lə, 'çi:lə], *n.* Chile.

China ['çi:na], *n.* China.
Chinarinde [çi:na'rındə], *f.* (—, *no pl.*) Peruvian bark.
Chinin [çi'ni:n], *n.* (—s, *no pl.*) quinine.
Chirurg [çi'rurk], *m.* (—en, *pl.* —en) surgeon.
Chirurgie [çirur'gi:], *f.* (—, *no pl.*) surgery.
Chlor [klo:r], *n.* (—s, *no pl.*) chlorine.
Chlorkalk ['klo:rkalk], *m.* (—s, *no pl.*) chloride of lime.
Chlornatrium [klo:r'na:trjum], *n.* (—s, *no pl.*) sodium chloride.
Choleriker [ko'le:rıkər], *m.* (—s, *pl.* —) irascible person.
Chor [ko:r], *m.* (—s, *pl.* ⁀e) chorus; choir; (*Archit.*) choir, chancel.
Choral [ko'ra:l], *m.* (—s, *pl.* ⁀e) hymn, chorale.
Choramt ['ko:ramt], *n.* (—s, *pl.* ⁀er) cathedral service.
Chorgesang ['ko:rgəsaŋ], *m.* (—s, *pl.* ⁀e) chorus, choral singing.
Chorhemd ['ko:rhεmt], *n.* (—s, *pl.* —en) surplice.
Chorherr ['ko:rhεr], *m.* (—n, *pl.* —en) canon, prebendary.
Christ [krıst], *m.* (—en, *pl.* —en) Christian.
Christbaum ['krıstbaum], *m.* (—s, *pl.* ⁀e) Christmas tree.
Christentum ['krıstəntu:m], *n.* (—s, *no pl.*) Christendom, Christianity.
Christkind ['krıstkınt], *n.* (—s, *no pl.*) Infant Christ, Christ child.
christlich ['krıstlıç], *adj.* Christian.
Christmette ['çe:mıʃ, 'krıstmεtə], *f.* (—, *pl.* —n) Christmas matins; midnight mass.
Christus ['krıstus], *m.* (—i) Christ; *vor —, B.C.; nach —, A.D.*
Chrom [kro:m], *n.* (—s, *no pl.*) chrome.
chromatisch [kro'ma:tıʃ], *adj.* chromatic.
chromsauer ['kro:mzauər], *adj.* — chromate of; *—es Salz,* chromate.
Chronik ['kro:nık], *f.* (—, *pl.* —en) chronicle.
chronisch ['kro:nıʃ], *adj.* chronic.
Chronist [kro'nıst], *m.* (—en, *pl.* —en) chronicler.
Chrysantheme [kryzan'te:mə], *f.* (—, *pl.* —n) chrysanthemum.
Cis [tsıs]. (*Mus.*) C sharp.
Clique ['klıkə], *f.* (—, *pl.* —n) clique, set.
Coeur [kø:r], *n.* (*Cards*) hearts.
coulant [ku'lant], *adj.* polite, friendly; (*Comm.*) fair, obliging.
Couleur [ku'lø:r], *f.* (—, *pl.* —en) colour; students' corporation.
Coupé [ku'pe:], *n.* (—s, *pl.* —s) (*train*) compartment.
Couplet [ku'ple:], *n.* (—s, *pl.* —s) comic song.
Coupon [ku'pɔ̃], *m.* (—s, *pl.* —s) coupon, check, dividend voucher.
Cour [ku:r], *f.* (—, *no pl.*) *einem Mädchen die — machen,* court a girl.

Danzig

Courtage [kur'ta:ʒə], *f.* (—, *pl.* —n) brokerage.

Cousin [ku'zɛ̃], *m.* (—s, *pl.* —s) cousin.

Cousine [ku'zi:nə], *f.* (—, *pl.* —n) (female) cousin.

Cutaway ['katave:], *m.* (—s, *pl.* —s) morning coat.

Czar [tsa:r], *m.* (—en, *pl.* —en) Tsar, Czar.

D

D [de:], *n.* (—s, *pl.* —s) the letter D; (*Mus.*) D *dur*, D major; *D moll*, D minor; *D-Zug*, express train.

da [da:], *adv.* (*local*) there; here; (*temporal*) then, at that moment; (*Mil.*) *wer* —? who goes there? (*Poet. obs.*) where. — *conj.* (*temporal*) when, as; (*causal*) as, because, since.

dabei [da'baɪ], *adv.* nearby; besides, moreover; as well; —*sein*, be present, be about to (*infin.*); — *bleiben*, persist in.

Dach [dax], *n.* (—es, *pl.* ⁻er) roof.

Dachboden ['daxbo:dən], *m.* (—s, *pl.* ⁻) loft.

Dachdecker ['daxdɛkər], *m.* (—s, *pl.* —) slater, tiler.

Dachgiebel ['daxgi:bəl], *m.* (—s, *pl.* —) gable.

Dachluke ['daxlu:kə], *f.* (—, *pl.* —n) dormer window.

Dachpappe ['daxpapə], *f.* (—, *pl.* —n) roofing felt.

Dachrinne ['daxrɪnə], *f.* (—, *pl.* —n) gutter.

Dachs [daks], *m.* (—es, *pl.* —e) badger.

Dachstube ['daxʃtu:bə], *f.* (—, *pl.* —n) garret, attic (room).

Dachtraufe ['daxtraufə], *f.* (—, *pl.* —n) eaves.

dadurch [da'durç], *adv.* (*local*) through it; in that way; (*causal*) thereby.

dafür [da'fy:r], *adv.* for it; instead of it, in return for it; *ich kann nichts* —, it is not my fault, I can't help it.

Dafürhalten [da'fy:rhaltən], *n.* (—s, *no pl.*) opinion.

dagegen [da'ge:gən], *adv.* against it, compared to it. — *conj.* on the other hand.

daheim [da'haɪm], *adv.* at home.

daher [da'he:r], *adv.* thence, from that. — *conj.* therefore, for that reason.

dahin [da'hɪn], *adv.* thither, to that place; there; *bis* —, (*local*) thither; (*temporal*) till then; over, past, lost, gone.

dahinbringen [da'hɪnbrɪŋən], *v.a. irr.* *jemanden* —, induce s.o. to; *es* —, succeed in, manage to.

dahinsiechen [da'hɪnzi:çən], *v.n.* (*aux. sein*) pine away, be failing (in health).

dahinter [da'hɪntər], *adv.* behind that.

Dahlie ['da:ljə], *f.* (—, *pl.* —n) (*Bot.*) dahlia.

Dahome ['daome:], *n.* Dahomey.

damalig [da'maltç], *adj.* then; of that time; past.

damals ['da:mals], *adv.* then, at that time.

Damast [da'mast], *m.* (—s, *no pl.*) damask.

Damaszener [damas'tse:nər], *m.* (—s, *pl.* —) Damascene. — *adj.* — *Stahl*, Damascus steel, dagger.

Dame ['da:mə], *f.* (—, *pl.* —n) lady; (*cards, chess*) queen; draughts (*game*).

damit [da'mɪt], *adv.* therewith, with that, with it; *und* — *basta!* and that's all there is to it. — *conj.* in order that, so that; — *nicht*, lest.

dämlich ['dɛ:mlɪç], *adj.* (*coll.*) foolish, silly.

Damm [dam], *m.* (—es, *pl.* ⁻e) dam, dyke, mole; (*street*) roadway, causeway; (*rail*) embankment.

dämmen ['dɛmən], *v.a.* dam; (*fig.*) stop, restrain.

dämmerig ['dɛmərɪç], *adj.* dusky.

dämmern ['dɛmərn], *v.n.* grow dusky; dawn.

dämonisch [dɛ'mo:nɪʃ], *adj.* demoniac(al), demonlike.

Dampf [dampf], *m.* (—es, *pl.* ⁻e) vapour, steam, mist, fume; smoke.

dampfen ['dampfən], *v.n.* smoke, fume, steam.

dämpfen ['dɛmpfən], *v.a.* damp, smother, steam; subdue, deaden, muffle, soften down.

Dampfer ['dampfər], *m.* (—s, *pl.* —) steamer.

Dämpfer ['dɛmpfər], *m.* (—s, *pl.* —) damper; (*Mus.*) mute.

Dampfkessel ['dampfkɛsəl], *m.* (—s, *pl.* —) boiler.

Dämpfung ['dɛmpfuŋ], *f.* (—, *pl.* —en) damping, smothering, suppression; (*Aviat.*) stabilization.

danach [da'na:x], *adv.* after that, thereafter; accordingly, according to that.

daneben [da'ne:bən], *adv.* near it, by it, close by; *es geht* —, it goes amiss. — *conj.* besides.

Dänemark ['dɛ:nəmark], *n.* Denmark.

Dank [daŋk], *m.* (—es, *no pl.*) thanks, gratitude; reward; *Gott sei* —, thank heaven!

dank [daŋk], *prep.* (*Dat.*) owing to, thanks to.

dankbar ['daŋkba:r], *adj.* grateful; thankful.

danken ['daŋkən], *v.n.* (*Dat.*) thank. — *v.a.* owe.

Dankgebet ['daŋkgəbe:t], *n.* (—s, *pl.* —e) (prayer of) thanksgiving.

dann [dan], *adv.* then, at that time, in that case; — *und wann*, now and then, occasionally.

Danzig ['dantsɪç], *n.* Dantzig.

43

daran

daran, dran [da'ran, dran], *adv.* on it, at it, near that; thereon, thereby; *was liegt —?* what does it matter?

darauf, drauf [da'rauf, drauf], *adv.* (*local*) upon it, on it; (*temporal*) thereupon, thereon, thereafter.

daraufhin [darauf'hɪn], *adv.* thereupon; on the strength of that.

daraus, draus [da'raus, draus], *adv.* therefrom, hence, from that; *ich mache mir nichts —,* I do not care for it.

darben ['darbən], *v.n.* suffer want, go short; famish.

darbieten ['da:rbi:tən], *v.a. irr.* offer, tender, present.

Darbietung ['da:rbi:tuŋ], *f.* (—, *pl.* —en) offering, presentation, performance.

darbringen ['da:rbrɪŋən], *v.a. irr.* bring, present, offer.

darein, drein [da'raɪn, draɪn], *adv.* into it, therein.

darin, drin [da'rɪn, drɪn], *adv.* therein, in it, within.

darinnen, drinnen [da'rɪnən, 'drɪnən], *adv.* inside, in there.

darlegen ['da:rle:gən], *v.a.* demonstrate, explain; expound.

Darlehen ['da:rle:ən], *n.* (—s, *pl.* —) loan.

Darm [darm], *m.* (—s, *pl.* ⁻e) gut; (*pl.*) intestines, bowels.

Darmsaite ['darmzaɪtə], *f.* (—, *pl.* —n) catgut, gut-string.

darob [da'rɔp], *adv.* (*obs.*) on that account, on account of it.

darreichen ['da:raɪçən], *v.a.* offer, tender; present; (*Eccl.*) administer (sacraments).

darstellen ['da:rʃtɛlən], *v.a.* represent, delineate; (*Theat.*) perform.

Darstellung ['da:rʃtɛluŋ], *f.* (—, *pl.* —en) representation, exhibition, presentation; (*Theat.*) performance.

dartun ['da:rtu:n], *v.a. irr.* prove, demonstrate.

darüber, drüber [dar'y:bər, 'dry:bər], *adv.* over that, over it; concerning that.

darum, drum [da'rum, drum], *adv.* around it, around that, thereabout; therefore, for that reason.

darunter, drunter [da'runtər, 'druntər], *adv.* under that; thereunder; among; — *und drüber,* topsy-turvy.

das [das], *def. art. n.* the. — *dem. pron., dem. adj.* that, this. —*rel. pron.* which.

Dasein ['da:zaɪn], *n.* (—s, *no pl.*) presence, being, existence.

daselbst [da:'zɛlpst], *adv.* there, in that very place.

daß [das], *conj.* that; *es sei denn —,* unless; — *nicht,* lest.

dastehen ['da:ʃte:ən], *v.n. irr.* stand (there).

datieren [da'ti:rən], *v.a.* date, put a date to.

Dativ ['da:ti:f], *m.* (—s, *pl.* —e) dative.

dato ['da:to], *adv. bis —,* till now, hitherto.

Dattel ['datəl], *f.* (—, *pl.* —n) (*Bot.*) date.

Datum ['da:tum], *n.* (—s, *pl.* **Daten**) date (*calendar*).

Dauer ['dauər], *f.* (—, *no pl.*) duration, length of time; continuance; permanence.

dauerhaft ['dauərhaft], *adj.* durable, lasting; (*colours*) fast.

Dauerkarte ['dauərkartə], *f.* (—, *pl.* —n) season ticket; (*Am.*) commutation ticket.

dauern ['dauərn], *v.n.* continue; last, endure.— *v.a.* move to pity; *er dauert mich,* I am sorry for him.

Dauerpflanze ['dauərpflantsə], *f.* (—, *pl.* —n) perennial plant.

Dauerwelle ['dauərvɛlə], *f.* (—, *pl.* —n) permanent wave, (*coll.*) perm.

Daumen ['daumən], *m.* (—s, *pl.* —) thumb; *einem den — halten,* wish s.o. well, keep o.'s fingers crossed for s.o.

Daune ['daunə], *f.* (—, *pl.* —n) down.

davon [da'fɔn], *adv.* thereof, therefrom, from that; off, away.

davonkommen [da'fɔnkɔmən], *v.n. irr.* (*aux. sein*) get off; *mit einem blauen Auge —,* get off lightly.

davor [da'fo:r], *adv.* before that, before it.

dawider [da'vi:dər], *adv.* against it.

dazu [da'tsu:], *adv.* thereto, to that, to it; in addition to that; for that purpose; *noch —,* besides.

dazumal ['da:tsuma:l], *adv.* then, at that time.

dazwischen [da'tsvɪʃən], *adv.* between, among; — *kommen,* intervene, interfere; — *treten,* intervene.

debattieren [deba'ti:rən], *v.a., v.n.* debate.

Debet ['de:bɛt], *n.* (—s, *pl.* —s) debit.

Debüt [de'by:], *n.* (—s, *pl.* —s) first appearance, début.

Dechant [de'çant], *m.* (—en, *pl.* —en) (*Eccl.*) dean.

dechiffrieren [deʃɪf'ri:rən], *v.a.* decode, decipher.

Deck [dɛk], *n.* (—s, *pl.* —e) (*Naut.*) deck.

Deckbett ['dɛkbɛt], *n.* (—s, *pl.* —en) coverlet.

Deckblatt ['dɛkblat], *n.* (—s, *pl.* ⁻er) (*Bot.*) bractea; (*cigar*) wrapper.

Decke ['dɛkə], *f.* (—, *pl.* —n) cover; blanket, rug; (*bed*) coverlet; (*room*) ceiling.

Deckel ['dɛkəl], *m.* (—s, *pl.* —) lid, top; (*book*) cover; (*coll.*) hat.

decken ['dɛkən], *v.a.* cover; (*Comm.*) secure, reimburse. — *v.r. sich —,* (*Maths.*) coincide; (*fig.*) square, tally.

Deckfarbe ['dɛkfarbə], *f.* (—, *pl.* —n) body colour.

Deckmantel ['dɛkmantəl], *m.* (—s, *pl.* ⁻) cloak, disguise.

Deckung ['dɛkuŋ], *f.* (—, *pl.* —en) covering, protection; (*Comm.*) reimbursement; security; (*Mil.*) cover.

dedizieren [dedi'tsi:rən], *v.a.* dedicate.

44

deduzieren [dedu'tsi:rən], *v.a.* deduce.

defekt [de'fɛkt], *adj.* defective, incomplete, imperfect.

defilieren [defi'li:rən], *v.n.* (*Mil.*) pass in review, march past.

definieren [defi'ni:rən], *v.a.* define.

Degen ['de:gən], *m.* (—s, *pl.* —) sword; (*fig.*) brave warrior.

degradieren [degra'di:rən], *v.a.* degrade, demote.

dehnbar ['de:nba:r], *adj.* extensible, ductile.

dehnen ['de:nən], *v.a.* extend, expand, stretch. — *v.r. sich* —, stretch o.s.

Deich [daɪç], *m.* (—es, *pl.* —e) dike, dam, embankment.

Deichsel ['daɪksəl], *f.* (—, *pl.* —n) thill, shaft, pole.

deichseln ['daɪksəln], *v.a.* (*fig.*) engineer; (*coll.*) manage; wangle.

dein [daɪn], *poss. adj.* your; (*Poet.*) thy. — *poss. pron.* yours; (*Poet.*) thine.

deinesgleichen [daɪnəs'glaɪçən], *adj. pron.* the like of you, such as you.

deinethalben ['daɪnəthalbən], *adv.* on your account, for your sake, on your behalf.

deinetwegen ['daɪnətve:gən], *adv.* because of you, on your account, for your sake, on your behalf.

deinetwillen ['daɪnətvɪlən], *adv. um* —, on your account, for your sake, on your behalf.

deinige ['daɪnɪgə], *poss. adj.* your; (*Poet.*) thy. — *poss. pron.* yours; (*Poet.*) thine.

Dekan [de'ka:n], *m.* (—s, *pl.* —e) (*Eccl., Univ.*) dean.

Dekanat [deka'na:t], *n.* (—s, *pl.* —e) (*Eccl., Univ.*) deanery, office of dean.

deklamieren [dekla'mi:rən], *v.a., v.n.* recite, declaim.

deklarieren [dekla'ri:rən], *v.a.* declare (for customs duty).

Deklination [deklina'tsjo:n], *f.* (—, —en) (*Gram.*) declension; (*Phys.*) declination.

deklinieren [deklɪ'ni:rən], *v.a.* (*Gram.*) decline.

dekolletiert [dekɔle'ti:rt], *adj.* décolleté, low-necked.

Dekret [de'kre:t], *n.* (—s, *pl.* —e) decree, edict, official regulation.

dekretieren [dekre'ti:rən], *v.a.* decree, ordain.

delegieren [dele'gi:rən], *v.a.* delegate.

Delegierte [dele'gi:rtə], *m.* (—n, *pl.* —n) delegate.

delikat [deli'ka:t], *adj.* subtle, dainty; tasty; (*coll.*) tricky, difficult.

Delikatesse [delika'tɛsə], *f.* (—, *pl.* —n) delicacy, dainty; (*pl.*) (*Am.*) delicatessen.

Delikt [de'lɪkt], *n.* (—s, *pl.* —e) (*Law*) crime; misdemeanour.

Delle ['dɛlə], *f.* (—, *pl.* —n) dent.

Delphin [dɛl'fi:n], *m.* (—s, *pl.* —e) dolphin.

deltaförmig ['dɛltafœrmɪç], *adj.* deltoid.

dem [de:m], *def. art. Dat.* to the. —*dem. adj.* to this, to that: — *dem. pron.* to this, to that; *wie* — *auch sei*, however that may be. — *rel. pron.* to whom, to which.

demarkieren [demar'ki:rən], *v.a.* mark, demarcate.

Dementi [de'mɛnti], *n.* (—s, *pl.* —s) (*official*) denial.

dementieren [demɛn'ti:rən], *v.a.* (*Pol.*) deny, contradict.

demgemäß ['de:mgəmɛ:s], *adv.* accordingly.

demnach ['de:mnax], *conj.* therefore, consequently, in accordance with that.

demnächst ['de:mnɛ:çst], *adv.* shortly, soon, in the near future.

demokratisch [demo'kra:tɪʃ], *adj.* democratic.

demolieren [demo'li:rən], *v.a.* demolish.

demonstrieren [demɔn'stri:rən], *v.a., v.n.* demonstrate.

Demut ['de:mu:t], *f.* (—, *no pl.*) humility, meekness.

demütig ['de:mytɪç], *adj.* humble, meek, submissive.

demütigen ['de:mytɪgən], *v.a.* humble, humiliate, subdue.

Denkart ['dɛŋka:rt], *f.* (—, *pl.* —en) way of thinking.

denken ['dɛŋkən], *v.a., v.n. irr.* think, reflect (upon); imagine; (*coll.*) guess.

Denker ['dɛŋkər], *m.* (—s, *pl.* —) thinker, philosopher.

Denkmal ['dɛŋkma:l], *n.* (—s, *pl.* ⁓er) monument.

Denkmünze ['dɛŋkmyntsə], *f.* (—, *pl.* —n) (commemorative) medal.

Denkschrift ['dɛŋkʃrɪft], *f.* (—, *pl.* —en) memorandum, memoir.

Denkspruch ['dɛŋkʃprux], *m.* (—s, *pl.* ⁓e) aphorism, maxim, motto.

Denkungsart ['dɛŋkuŋsart], *f.* (*pl.* —en) *see* Denkart.

Denkweise ['dɛŋkvaɪzə], *f.* (—, *pl.* —n) *see* Denkart.

denkwürdig ['dɛŋkvyrdɪç], *adj.* memorable.

Denkzettel ['dɛŋktsɛtəl], *m.* (—s, *pl.* —) (*fig.*) reminder, punishment, lesson; *einem einen* — *geben*, give s.o. s.th. to think about *or* a sharp reminder.

denn [dɛn], *conj.* for. — *adv.* then; (*after comparatives*) than; *es sei* — *dass*, unless.

dennoch ['dɛnɔx], *conj.* yet, nevertheless, notwithstanding.

Denunziant [denun'tsjant], *m.* (—en, *pl.* —en) informer.

denunzieren [denun'tsi:rən], *v.a.* inform against, denounce.

Depesche [de'pɛʃə], *f.* (—, *pl.* —n) dispatch; telegram, wire.

deponieren [depo'ni:rən], *v.a.* deposit; (*Law*) depose.

Depositenbank [depo'zi:tənbaŋk], *f.* (—, *pl.* —en) deposit-bank.

deprimieren

deprimieren [deprɪˈmiːrən], v.a. depress.

Deputierte [depuˈtiːrtə], m. (—n, pl. —n) deputy.

der [deːr], def. art. m. the. — dem. adj., dem. pron. this, that. — rel. pron. who, which, that.

derart [ˈdeːraːrt], adv. so, in such a manner.

derartig [ˈdeːraːrtɪç], adj. such.

derb [dɛrp], adj. firm, solid, coarse, blunt, uncouth; strong, robust.

dereinst [deːrˈaɪnst], adv. one day (in future).

derenthalben [ˈdeːrənthalbən], adv. for her (their) sake, on her (their) account, on whose account.

derentwegen [ˈdeːrəntveːgən], adv. see **derenthalben**.

derentwillen [ˈdeːrəntvɪlən], adv. see **derenthalben**.

dergestalt [ˈdeːrgəʃtalt], adv. in such a manner; so.

dergleichen [deːrˈglaɪçən], adv. such, such as, suchlike.

derjenige [ˈdeːrjeːnɪgə], dem. adj., dem. pron. that, this; — welcher, he who.

derlei [deːrˈlaɪ], adj. of that sort.

dermaßen [ˈdeːrmaːsən], adv. to such an extent, to such a degree.

derselbe [deːrˈzɛlbə], pron. the same.

derweilen [deːrˈvaɪlən], adv. meanwhile.

Derwisch [ˈdɛrvɪʃ], m. (—(e)s, pl. —e) dervish.

derzeit [ˈdeːrtsaɪt], adv. at present.

Des [dɛs], n. (—, pl. —) (Mus.) D flat; — Dur, D flat major; — Moll, D flat minor.

des [dɛs], def. art. m. & n. Genit. sing. of the.

desgleichen [dɛsˈglaɪçən], adj. such, suchlike. — adv. likewise, ditto.

deshalb [ˈdeshalp], adv., conj. therefore.

desinfizieren [dɛsɪnfɪtˈsiːrən], v.a. disinfect.

dessen [ˈdɛsən], dem. pron. m & n. Genit. sing. of it, of that. — rel. pron. m. & n. Genit. sing. whose, of whom, of which, whereof.

dessenungeachtet [dɛsənungəˈaxtət], conj. notwithstanding that, for all that, despite all that.

Destillateur [dɛstɪlaˈtøːr], m. (—s, pl. —e) distiller.

destillieren [dɛstɪˈliːrən], v.a. distil.

desto [ˈdesto], adv. the; — besser, so much the better; je . . . —, the . . . the.

deswegen [ˈdɛsveːgən], adv., conj. therefore.

Detaillist [detaˈjɪst], m. (—en, pl. —en) retailer.

deucht [dɔʏçt] see **dünken**; (obs.) mich deucht, methinks.

deuten [ˈdɔʏtən], v.a. point to, show; explain, interpret.

deutlich [ˈdɔʏtlɪç], adj. clear, distinct; evident, plain.

deutsch [dɔʏtʃ], adj. German.

Deutschland [ˈdɔʏtʃlant], n. Germany.

Deutschmeister [ˈdɔʏtʃmaɪstər], m. (—s, pl. —) Grand Master of the Teutonic Order.

Deutschtum [ˈdɔʏtʃtuːm], n. (—s, no pl.) German nationality, German customs, German manners.

Deutung [ˈdɔʏtuŋ], f. (—, pl. —en) explanation, interpretation.

Devise [deˈviːzə], f. (—, pl. —n) device, motto; (pl.) foreign currency.

devot [deˈvoːt], adj. submissive, respectful, humble.

Dezember [deˈtsɛmbər], m. December.

dezent [deˈtsɛnt], adj. modest, decent; unobtrusive.

Dezernent [detsɛrˈnɛnt], m. (—en, pl. —en) head of section in ministry or city administration.

dezimieren [detsɪˈmiːrən], v.a. decimate, reduce.

Diagramm [diaˈgram], n. (—s, pl. —e) diagram, graph.

Diakon [diaˈkoːn], m. (—s, pl. —e) (Eccl.) deacon.

Diakonisse, Diakonissin [diakoˈnɪsə, diakoˈnɪsɪn], f. (—, pl. —nen) deaconess.

Dialektik [diaˈlɛktɪk], f. (—, no pl.) dialectics.

Diamant [diaˈmant], m. (—en, pl. —en) diamond.

diametral [diameˈtraːl], adj. diametrical.

Diapositiv [diapoziˈtiːf], n. (—s, pl. —e) (lantern, Phot.) slide.

Diät [diˈɛːt], f. (—, pl. —en) diet; (pl.) daily allowance.

dich [dɪç], pers. pron. you. — refl. pron. yourself.

dicht [dɪçt], adj. tight; impervious (to water); dense, compact, solid, firm; — bei, hard by, close to.

Dichte [ˈdɪçtə], f. (—, no pl.) density.

dichten [ˈdɪçtən], v.a., v.n. write poetry, compose (verses etc.); (Tech.) tighten; (Naut.) caulk.

Dichter [ˈdɪçtər], m. (—s, pl. —) poet.

dichterisch [ˈdɪçtərɪʃ], adj. poetic(al).

Dichtigkeit [ˈdɪçtɪçkaɪt], f. (—, no pl.) closeness, compactness, thickness, density.

Dichtkunst [ˈdɪçtkunst], f. (—, no pl.) (art of) poetry.

Dichtung [ˈdɪçtuŋ], f. (—, pl. —en) poetry, poem; fiction; (Tech.) caulking; washer, gasket.

dick [dɪk], adj. thick; fat; (books) bulky; voluminous, stout, obese, corpulent.

Dicke [ˈdɪkə], f. (—, no pl.) thickness, stoutness.

dickfellig [ˈdɪkfɛlɪç], adj. thick-skinned.

Dickicht [ˈdɪkɪçt], n. (—s, pl. —e) thicket.

die [diː], def. art. f. & pl. the. — dem. adj., dem. pron. f. & pl. this, these. — rel. pron. f. & pl. who, that which.

Dieb [diːp], m. (—s, pl. —e) thief.

Diebstahl [ˈdiːpʃtaːl], m. (—s, pl. ˙e) theft.

Diele ['di:lə], *f.* (—, *pl.* —n) floor; (entrance) hall.

dielen ['di:lən], *v.a.* board, floor.

dienen ['di:nən], *v.n. einem* —, serve (s.o.); help (s.o.).

Diener ['di:nər], *m.* (—s, *pl.* —) servant, attendant; (*coll.*) bow.

dienlich ['di:nlıç], *adj.* serviceable, useful; *für* — *halten*, think fit.

Dienst [di:nst], *m.* (—es, *pl.* —e) service, employment, duty; — *haben*, be on duty.

Dienstag ['di:nsta:k], *m.* (—s, *pl.* —e) Tuesday.

Dienstalter ['di:nstaltər], *n.* (—s, *pl.* —) seniority.

dienstbar ['di:nstba:r], *adj.* subject, subservient.

Dienstbarkeit ['di:nstba:rkaıt], *f.* (—, *no pl.*) bondage, servitude.

dienstbeflissen ['di:nstbəflısən], *adj.* assiduous.

Dienstbote ['di:nstbo:te], *m.* (—n, *pl.* —n) domestic servant.

dienstfertig ['di:nstfertıç], *adj.* obliging, ready to serve.

Dienstleistung ['di:nstlaıstuŋ], *f.* (—, *pl.* —en) service.

dienstlich ['di:nstlıç], *adj.* official.

Dienstmädchen ['di:nstmɛ:tçən], *n.* (—s, pl. —) maidservant.

Dienstmann ['di:nstman], *m.* (—s, *pl.* -er) commissionaire, porter.

Dienstpflicht ['di:nstpflıçt], *f.* (—, *no pl.*) official duty, liability to serve; (*Mil.*) (compulsory) military service.

Dienststunden ['di:nstʃtundən], *f. pl.* office hours.

diensttauglich ['di:nsttauklıç], *adj.* (*Mil.*) fit for service.

Dienstverhältnis ['di:nstfɛrhɛltnıs], *n.* (—ses, *pl.* —se) (*pl.*) terms of service.

dies [di:s], *abbr.* dieses.

diesbezüglich ['di:sbətsy:klıç], *adj.* concerning this, relating to this matter.

diese ['di:zə], *dem. adj., dem. pron. f. & pl.* this, these.

dieser ['di:zər], *dem. adj., dem. pron. m.* this.

dieses ['di:zəs], *dem. adj., dem. pron. n.* this.

diesjährig ['di:sjɛ:rıç], *adj.* of this year, this year's.

diesmal ['di:sma:l], *adv.* this time, for this once.

Dietrich (1) ['di:trıç], *m.* Derek.

Dietrich (2) ['di:trıç], *m.* (—s, *pl.* —e) pick lock, master-key, skeleton key.

Differentialrechnung [dıfərɛnts'ja:l-rɛçnuŋ], *f.* (—, *pl.* —en) differential calculus.

Differenz [dıfə'rɛnts], *f.* (—, *pl.* —en) difference; quarrel.

Diktat [dık'ta:t], *n.* (—s, *pl.* —e) dictation.

diktatorisch [dıkta'to:rıʃ], *adj.* dictatorial.

Diktatur [dıkta'tu:r], *f.* (—, *pl.* —en) dictatorship.

diktieren [dık'ti:rən], *v.a.* dictate.

Ding [dıŋ], *n.* (—s, *pl.* —e) thing, object, matter.

dingen ['dıŋən], *v.a.* hire, engage (a manual worker).

dingfest ['dıŋfɛst], *adj.* — *machen*, arrest.

dinglich ['dıŋlıç], *adj.* real.

dinieren [di'ni:rən], *v.n.* dine.

Diözese [diø'tse:zə], *f.* (—, *pl.* —n) diocese.

Diphtherie [dıftə'ri:], *f.* (—, *no pl.*) diphtheria.

Diplom [di'plo:m], *n.* (—s, *pl.* —e) diploma.

Diplomatie [dıploma'ti:], *f.* (—, *no pl.*) diplomacy.

dir [di:r], *pers. pron. Dat.* to you.

direkt [di'rɛkt], *adj.* direct; —*er Wagen*, (*railway*) through carriage; — *danach*, immediately afterwards.

Direktion [dirɛk'sjo:n], *f.* (—, *pl.* —en) direction, management.

Direktor [di'rɛktɔr], *m.* (—s, *pl.* —en) (managing) director, manager; headmaster, principal.

Direktorium [dirɛk'to:rjum], *n.* (—s. *pl.* —rien) directorate, board ol directors.

Direktrice [dirɛk'tri:sə], *f.* (—, *pl.* —n) manageress.

Dirigent [diri'gɛnt], *m.* (—en, *pl.* —en) (*Mus.*) conductor; (*Austr. Admin.*) head of section in Ministry.

dirigieren [diri'gi:rən], *v.a.* direct, manage; (*Mus.*) conduct.

Dirndl ['dırndl], *n.* (—s, *pl.* —) (*dial.*) young girl, country wench; (*fig.*) peasant dress, dirndl.

Dirne ['dırnə], *f.* (—, *pl.* —n) (*Poet.*) girl; prostitute.

Dis [dıs], *n.* (—, *no pl.*) (*Mus.*) D sharp.

disharmonisch [dıshar'mo:nıʃ], *adj.* discordant.

Diskant [dıs'kant], *m.* (—s, *pl.* —e) (*Mus.*) treble, soprano.

Diskont [dıs'kɔnt], *m.* (—(e)s, *pl.* —e) discount, rebate.

diskret [dıs'kre:t], *adj.* discreet.

Diskurs [dıs'kurs], *m.* (—es, *pl.* —e) discourse.

diskutieren [dısku'ti:rən], *v.a.* discuss, debate.

Dispens [dıs'pɛns], *m.* (—es, *pl.* —e) dispensation.

dispensieren [dıspɛn'zi:rən], *v.a.* dispense (from), exempt (from).

disponieren [dıspo'ni:rən], *v.n.* — *über*, dispose of; make plans about.

Dissident [dısi'dɛnt], *m.* (—en, *pl.* —en) dissenter, nonconformist.

distanzieren [dıstan'tsi:rən], *v.r. sich* — *von*, keep o.'s distance from; dissociate o.s. from.

Distel ['dıstəl], *f.* (—, *pl.* —n) thistle.

Distelfink ['dıstəlfıŋk], *m.* (—s, *pl.* —e) (*Orn.*) gold-finch.

disziplinarisch [dıstsipli'na:rıʃ], *adj.* diciplinary.

dito ['di:to], *adv.* ditto.

dividieren

dividieren [dɪvɪˈdiːrən], *v.a.* divide.

Diwan [ˈdiːvan], *m.* (—s, *pl.* —e) divan, sofa, couch.

doch [dɔx], *adv.*, *conj.* however, though, although, nevertheless, yet, but; after all, (*emphatic*) yes.

Docht [dɔxt], *m.* (—es, *pl.* —e) wick.

Dock [dɔk], *n.* (—s, *pl.* —s, —e) dock.

Dogge [ˈdɔgə], *f.* (—, *pl.* —n) bulldog, mastiff; Great Dane.

Dogmatiker [dɔgˈmaːtɪkər], *m.* (—s, *pl.* —) dogmatist.

dogmatisch [dɔgˈmaːtɪʃ], *adj.* dogmatic, doctrinal.

Dohle [ˈdoːlə], *f.* (—, *pl.* —n) (*Orn.*) jackdaw.

Doktor [ˈdɔktɔr], *m.* (—s, *pl.* —en) doctor; physician, surgeon.

Dolch [dɔlç], *m.* (—es, *pl.* —e) dagger, dirk.

Dolde [ˈdɔldə], *f.* (—, *pl.* —n) (*Bot.*) umbel.

Dolmetscher [ˈdɔlmɛtʃər], *m.* (—s, *pl.* —) interpreter.

dolmetschen [ˈdɔlmɛtʃən], *v.a.* interpret.

Dolomiten [doloˈmiːtən], *pl.* Dolomites.

Dom [doːm], *m.* (—s, *pl.* —e) cathedral; dome, cupola.

Domherr [ˈdoːmhɛr], *m.* (—n, *pl.* —en) canon, prebendary.

dominieren [domiˈniːrən], *v.a.* dominate, domineer.

Dominikaner [dominiˈkaːnər], *m.* (—s, *pl.* —) Dominican friar.

dominikanische Republik [dominiˈkaːnɪʃə repuˈbliːk], *f.* Dominican Republic.

Domizil [domiˈtsiːl], *n.* (—s, *pl.* —e) domicile, residence, address.

Domkapitel [ˈdoːmkapiːtəl], *n.* (—s, *pl.* —) dean and chapter.

Dompfaff [ˈdoːmpfaf], *m.* (—s, *pl.* —en) (*Orn.*) bullfinch.

Dompropst [ˈdoːmproːpst], *m.* (—es, *pl.* ⁓e) provost.

Donau [ˈdoːnau], *f.* (—, *no pl.*) Danube.

Donner [ˈdɔnər], *m.* (—s, *no pl.*) thunder.

donnern [ˈdɔnərn], *v.n.* thunder; (*fig.*) storm, rage.

Donnerschlag [ˈdɔnərʃlaːk], *m.* (—s, *pl.* ⁓e) thunderclap.

Donnerstag [ˈdɔnərstaːk], *m.* (—s, *pl.* —e) Thursday; *Grün* —, Maundy Thursday.

Donnerwetter [ˈdɔnərvɛtər], *n.* (—s, *pl.* —) thunderstorm; *zum —* (*nochmal*)! hang it all, confound it!

doppeldeutig [ˈdɔpəldɔytɪç], *adj.* ambiguous.

Doppelgänger [ˈdɔpəlgɛŋər], *m.* (—s, *pl.* —) double.

Doppellaut [ˈdɔpəllaut], *m.* (—s, *pl.* —e) diphthong.

doppeln [ˈdɔpəln] *see* **verdoppeln**.

doppelsinnig [ˈdɔpəlzɪnɪç] *see* **doppeldeutig**.

doppelt [ˈdɔpəlt], *adj.* double, twofold.

Doppelzwirn [ˈdɔpəltsvɪrn], *m.* (—s, *no pl.*) double-thread.

Dorf [dɔrf], *n.* (—es, *pl.* ⁓er) village.

dörflich [ˈdœrflɪç], *adj.* rural, rustic.

dorisch [ˈdoːrɪʃ], *adj.* Doric.

Dorn [dɔrn], *m.* (—s, *pl.* —en) thorn, prickle; (*Bot.*) spine; (*buckle*) tongue.

dornig [ˈdɔrnɪç], *adj.* thorny.

Dornröschen [ˈdɔrnröːsçən], *n.* (—s, *pl.* —) Sleeping Beauty.

Dorothea [doroˈteːa], *f.* Dorothea, Dorothy.

dorren [ˈdɔrən] *see* **verdorren**.

dörren [ˈdœrən], *v.a.* dry, make dry, parch.

Dörrobst [ˈdœrrɔbst], *n.* (—es, *no pl.*) dried fruit.

Dorsch [dɔrʃ], *m.* (—es, *pl.* —e) cod, codfish.

dort [dɔrt], (*Austr.*) **dorten** [ˈdɔrtən], *adv.* there, yonder; *von — aus*, from that point, from there.

dorther [ˈdɔrtheːr], *adv.* from there, therefrom, thence.

dorthin [ˈdɔrthɪn], *adv.* to that place, thereto, thither.

dortig [ˈdɔrtɪç], *adj.* of that place, local.

Dose [ˈdoːzə], *f.* (—, *pl.* —n) box, tin, can.

dösen [ˈdøːzən], *v.n.* doze, daydream.

Dosis [ˈdoːzɪs], *f.* (—, *pl.* **Dosen**) dose.

Dotter [ˈdɔtər], *m.* (—s, *pl.* —) yolk (of egg).

Dozent [doˈtsɛnt], *m.* (—en, *pl.* —en) university lecturer; (*Am.*) Assistant Professor.

dozieren [doˈtsiːrən], *v.n.* lecture.

Drache [ˈdraxə], *m.* (—n, *pl.* —n) dragon; kite; (*fig.*) termagant, shrew.

Dragoner [draˈgoːnər], *m.* (—s, *pl.* —) dragoon.

Draht [draːt], *m.* (—es, *pl.* ⁓e) wire.

drahten [ˈdraːtən], *v.a.* wire, telegraph.

Drahtgewebe [ˈdraːtgəveːbə], *n.* (—s, *pl.* —) wire-gauze.

Drahtgitter [ˈdraːtgɪtər], *n.* (—s, *pl.* —) wire grating.

drahtlos [ˈdraːtloːs], *adj.* wireless.

Drahtseilbahn [ˈdraːtzaɪlbaːn], *f.* (—, *pl.* —en) cable (funicular) railway.

Drahtzange [ˈdraːttsaŋə], *f.* (—, *pl.* —n) pliers.

drall [dral], *adj.* buxom, plump.

Drama [ˈdraːma], *n.* (—s, *pl.* —**men**) drama.

Dramatiker [draˈmaːtɪkər], *m.* (—s, *pl.* —) dramatist.

dramatisch [draˈmaːtɪʃ], *adj.* dramatic.

dran [dran] *see* **daran**.

Drang [draŋ], *m.* (—s, *no pl.*) urge; rush; throng; pressure; impulse.

drängeln [ˈdrɛŋəln], *v.a.* jostle.

drängen [ˈdrɛŋən], *v.a.* press, urge; *die Zeit drängt*, time presses; *es drängt mich*, I feel called upon.

Drangsal [ˈdraŋzaːl], *f.* or *n.* (—s, *pl.* —e *or* —en) distress, misery.

drapieren [draˈpiːrən], *v.a.* drape.

drastisch ['drastɪʃ], *adj.* drastic.

drauf [drauf] *see* **darauf**.

Draufgänger ['draufgɛŋər], *m.* (—s, *pl.* —) daredevil.

draußen ['drausən], *adv.* outside, without, out of doors.

drechseln ['drɛksəln], *v.a.* turn (on a lathe); *Phrasen* —, turn phrases.

Drechsler ['drɛkslər], *m.* (—s, *pl.* —) turner.

Dreck [drɛk], *m.* (—s, *no pl.*) dirt, mire, dust, filth, dung.

dreckig ['drɛkɪç], *adj.* dirty, filthy, muddy.

drehbar ['dre:ba:r], *adj.* revolving, swivelling.

Drehbuch ['dre:bu:x], *n.* (—s, *pl.* ̈er) (*film*) script.

drehen ['dre:ən], *v.a.* turn; (*film*) shoot. — *v.n.* turn round, veer.

Drehorgel ['dre:ɔrgəl], *f.* (—, *pl.* —n) barrel-organ.

Drehrad ['dre:ra:t], *n.* (—s, *pl.* ̈er) fly-wheel.

Drehung ['dre:uŋ], *f.* (—, *pl.* —en) rotation, turn, revolution.

drei [draɪ], *num. adj.* three.

dreiblätterig ['draɪblɛtərɪç], *adj.* trifoliate.

Dreieck ['draɪɛk], *n.* (—s, *pl.* —e) triangle.

dreieckig ['draɪɛkɪç], *adj.* triangular, three-cornered.

dreieinig [draɪ'aɪnɪç], *adj.* (*Theol.*) triune.

dreifach ['draɪfax], *adj.* threefold, triple.

Dreifaltigkeit [draɪ'faltɪçkaɪt], *f.* (—, *no pl.*) (*Theol.*) Trinity.

Dreifuß ['draɪfu:s], *m.* (—es, *pl.* ̈e) tripod.

dreijährlich ['draɪjɛrlɪç], *adj.* triennial.

Dreikönigsfest [draɪ'kø:nɪksfɛst], *n.* (—es, *no pl.*) Epiphany.

dreimonatlich ['draɪmo:natlɪç], *adj.* quarterly.

Dreirad ['draɪra:t], *n.* (—s, *pl.* ̈er) tricycle.

dreiseitig ['draɪzaɪtɪç], *adj.* trilateral.

dreißig ['draɪsɪç], *num. adj.* thirty.

dreist [draɪst], *adj.* bold, audacious; impudent.

dreistellig ['draɪʃtɛlɪç], *adj.* —*e Zahl*, number of three figures.

dreistimmig ['draɪʃtɪmɪç], *adj.* for three voices.

Dreistufenrakete ['draɪʃtu:fənra'ke:tə], *f.* (—, *pl.* —n) three-stage rocket.

dreistündig ['draɪʃtyndɪç], *adj.* lasting three hours.

dreitägig ['draɪtɛ:gɪç], *adj.* lasting three days.

dreiteilig ['draɪtaɪlɪç], *adj.* tripartite; three-piece.

dreizehn ['draɪtse:n], *num. adj.* thirteen.

Drell [drɛl], *m.* (—s, *no pl.*) *see* **Drillich**.

Dresche ['drɛʃə], *f.* (—, *no pl.*) thrashing, beating.

dreschen ['drɛʃən], *v.a. irr.* (*corn*) thresh; (*person*) thrash.

Dreschflegel ['drɛʃfle:gəl], *m.* (—s, *pl.* —) flail.

dressieren [drɛ'si:rən], *v.a.* (*animal*) train; break in.

Dressur [drɛ'su:r], *f.* (—, *pl.* —en) training, breaking-in.

Drillbohrer ['drɪlbo:rər], *m.* (—s, *pl.* —) drill.

drillen ['drɪlən], *v.a.* (*a hole*) bore; (*soldiers*) drill.

Drillich ['drɪlɪç], *m.* (—s, *pl.* —e) drill, canvas.

Drilling ['drɪlɪŋ], *m.* (—s, *pl.* —e) three-barrelled gun; (*pl.*) triplets.

drin [drɪn] *see* **darin**.

dringen ['drɪŋən], *v.n. irr.* penetrate, force o.'s way through; *auf etwas* —, insist on s.th.

dringlich ['drɪŋlɪç], *adj.* urgent, pressing.

drinnen ['drɪnən], *adv.* inside, within.

drittens ['drɪtəns], *adv.* thirdly.

droben ['dro:bən], *adv.* up there, above, aloft, overhead.

Droge ['dro:gə], *f.* (—, *pl.* —n) drug.

Drogerie [dro:gə'ri:], *f.* (—, *pl.* —n) druggist's shop, chemist's; (*Am.*) drugstore.

drohen ['dro:ən], *v.a., v.n.* threaten, menace.

Drohne ['dro:nə], *f.* (—, *pl.* —n) drone.

dröhnen ['drø:nən], *v.n.* boom, roar.

Drohung ['dro:uŋ], *f.* (—, *pl.* —en) threat, menace.

drollig ['drɔlɪç], *adj.* droll, odd, quaint.

Dromedar [dromə'da:r], *n.* (—s, *pl.* —e) dromedary.

Droschke ['drɔʃkə], *f.* (—, *pl.* —n) cab, hansom, taxi.

Drossel ['drɔsəl], *f.* (—, *pl.* —n) thrush.

Drosselader ['drɔsəla:dər], *f.* (—, *pl.* —n) jugular vein.

Drosselbein ['drɔsəlbaɪn], *n.* (—s, *pl.* —e) collar-bone.

drosseln ['drɔsəln], *v.a.* throttle. *See also* **erdrosseln**.

drüben ['dry:bən], *adv.* over there, on the other side.

drüber ['dry:bər] *see* **darüber**.

Druck [druk], *m.* (—s, *pl.* ̈e, —e) pressure, squeeze; (*Phys.*) compression; (*Typ.*) impression, print; (*fig.*) hardship.

Druckbogen ['drukbo:gən], *m.* (—s, *pl.* —) proof-sheet, proof.

Druckbuchstabe ['drukbu:xʃta:bə], *m.* (—n, *pl.* —n) letter, type.

Drückeberger ['drykəbɛrgər], *m.* (—s, *pl.* —) slacker, shirker.

drucken ['drukən], *v.a.* print.

drücken ['drykən], *v.a.* press, squeeze; trouble, oppress. — *v.r. sich* —, sneak away, shirk.

Drucker ['drukər], *m.* (—s, *pl.* —) printer.

Drücker ['drykər], *m.* (—s, *pl.* —) (*door*) handle, latch; (*gun*) trigger.

Druckerei ['drukəraɪ], *f.* (—, *pl.* —en) printing shop.

49

Druckerschwärze

Druckerschwärze ['drukərʃvɛrtsə], *f.* (—, *no pl.*) printing-ink.

Druckfehler ['drukfe:lər], *m.* (—s, *pl.* —) misprint, printer's error.

druckfertig ['drukfɛrtɪç], *adj.* ready for press.

Drucksache ['drukzaxə], *f.* (—, *pl.* —n) (*Postal*) printed matter.

drum [drum] *see* **darum**.

drunten ['druntən], *adv.* down there, below.

drunter ['druntər] *see* **darunter**.

Drüse ['dry:zə], *f.* (—, *pl.* —n) gland.

Dschungel ['dʒuŋəl], *m.* or *n.* (—s, *pl.* —) jungle.

du [du:], *pers. pron.* thou, you.

ducken ['dukən], *v.a.* bring down, humble. — *v.r. sich* —, duck, stoop, crouch.

dudeln ['du:dəln], *v.n.* play the bagpipes; tootle.

Dudelsack ['du:dəlzak], *m.* (—s, *pl.* ¨e) bagpipe(s).

Duft [duft], *m.* (—s, *pl.* ¨e) scent, odour, fragrance, aroma, perfume.

duften ['duftən], *v.n.* be fragrant.

duftig ['duftɪç], *adj.* fragrant, odoriferous, perfumed.

dulden ['duldən], *v.a.* suffer, endure, bear, tolerate.

duldsam ['dultza:m], *adj.* tolerant, indulgent, patient.

dumm [dum], *adj.* stupid, foolish, dull.

Dummheit ['dumhaɪt], *f.* (—, *pl.* —en) stupidity, folly.

dumpf [dumpf], *adj.* musty; (*air*) close; (*sound*) hollow; (*fig.*) gloomy.

dumpfig ['dumpfɪç], *adj.* damp, musty, stuffy.

Düne ['dy:nə], *f.* (—, *pl.* —n) dune, sand-hill.

Düngemittel ['dyŋəmɪtəl], *n.* (—s, *pl.* —) fertilizer.

düngen ['dyŋən], *v.a.* manure, fertilize.

Dünger ['dyŋər], *m.* (—s, *no pl.*) compost, artificial manure.

dunkel ['duŋkəl], *adj.* dark; (*fig.*) obscure, mysterious.

Dünkel ['dyŋkəl], *m.* (—s, *no pl.*) conceit, arrogance.

dünkelhaft ['dyŋkəlhaft], *adj.* conceited, arrogant.

Dunkelheit ['duŋkəlhaɪt], *f.* (—, *no pl.*) darkness, obscurity.

dunkeln ['duŋkəln], *v.n.* grow dark.

dünken ['dyŋkən], *v.n.* (*rare*) seem, appear. — *v.r. sich* —, fancy o.s., imagine o.s.

dünn [dyn], *adj.* thin, slim, weak.

Dunst [dunst], *m.* (—es, *pl.* ¨e) vapour, fume; exhalation; haze; (*fig.*) *einem blauen* — *vormachen*, humbug a p.

dünsten ['dynstən], *v.a.* stew.

dunstig ['dunstɪç], *adj.* misty, hazy.

Dunstkreis ['dunstkraɪs], *m.* (—es, *pl.* —e) atmosphere.

Dunstobst ['dunsto:pst], *n.* (—es, *no pl.*) stewed fruit.

duodez [duo'de:ts], *adj.* (*Typ.*) duodecimo (12mo).

Duodezfürst [duo'de:tsfyrst], *m.* (—en, *pl.* —en) petty prince, princeling.

Dur [du:r], *n.* (*Mus.*) major; sharp.

durch [durç], *prep.* (*Acc.*) (*local*) through, across; (*temporal*) during, throughout; (*manner*) by means of, by. — *adv.* thoroughly, through.

durchaus [durç'aus], *adv.* throughout, quite, by all means, absolutely.

Durchblick ['durçblɪk], *m.* (—s, *pl.* —e) vista, view.

durchbohren [durç'bo:rən], *v.a. insep.* perforate, pierce.

durchbrennen ['durçbrɛnən], *v.n. irr.* (*aux. sein*) abscond, bolt.

durchbringen ['durçbrɪŋən], *v.a. irr.* bring through, get through; squander (money); pull (a sick person) through. — *v.r. sich redlich* —, make an honest living.

Durchbruch ['durçbrux], *m.* (—s, *pl.* ¨e) breach, break-through.

durchdrängen ['durçdrɛŋən], *v.r. sich* —, force o.'s way through.

durchdringen ['durçdrɪŋən], *v.n. irr. sep.* (*aux. sein*) get through. — [durç'drɪŋən], *v.a. irr. insep.* penetrate, pierce, permeate, pervade.

durchdrücken ['durçdrykən], *v.a.* press through; (*fig.*) carry through.

durcheilen [durç'aɪlən], *v.a. insep.* hurry through.

Durcheinander [durçaɪn'andər], *n.* (—s, *no pl.*) confusion, muddle.

durcheinander [durçaɪn'andər], *adv.* in confusion, pell-mell.

Durchfall ['durçfal], *m.* (—s, *no pl.*) diarrhoea; (*exams etc.*) failure.

durchfallen ['durçfalən], *v.n. irr.* (*aux. sein*) fall through, come to nought; (*exams etc.*) fail.

durchflechten [durç'flɛçtən], *v.a. irr.* interweave, intertwine.

durchfliegen [durç'fli:gən], *v.a. irr.* fly through; read superficially, skim through.

durchforschen [durç'fɔrʃən], *v.a. insep.* explore, scrutinise, examine thoroughly.

Durchfuhr ['durçfu:r], *f.* (—, *pl.* —en) passage, transit.

durchführbar [durç'fy:rba:r], *adj.* practicable, feasible.

durchführen ['durçfy:rən], *v.a.* escort through; (*fig.*) execute, bring about, carry through.

Durchgang ['durçgaŋ], *m.* (—s, *pl.* ¨e) passage, thoroughfare; (*Comm.*) transit.

Durchgänger ['durçgɛŋər], *m.* (—s, *pl.* —) runaway horse, bolter; (*fig.*) hothead.

durchgängig ['durçgɛŋɪç], *adj.* general, universal.

durchgehen ['durçge:ən], *v.n. irr.* (*aux. sein*) go through; (*fig.*) abscond; (*horse*) bolt; (*proposal*) be carried. — *v.a. irr.* (*aux. sein*) peruse, review, go over.

durchgreifen ['durçgraıfən], v.n. irr. act decisively, take strong action.

durchhauen ['durçhauən], v.a. cut through; einen —, flog s.o.

durchkommen ['durçkɔmən], v.n. irr. (aux. sein) get through; (exams etc.) pass.

durchkreuzen - [durç'krɔytsən], v.a. insep. cross out; (fig.) thwart.

durchlassen ['durçlasən], v.a. irr. let pass.

Durchlaucht ['durçlauxt], f. (— pl. —en) Highness.

durchleuchten [durç'lɔyçtən], v.a. insep. (Med.) X-ray.

durchlöchern [durç'lœçərn], v.a. insep. perforate, riddle.

durchmachen ['durcmaxən], v.a. go through, suffer.

Durchmesser ['durcmɛsər], m. (—s, pl. —) diameter.

durchnässen [durç'nɛsən], v.a. insep. wet to the skin, soak.

durchnehmen ['durçne:mən], v.a. irr. go over or cover (a subject).

durchpausen ['durçpauzən], v.a. trace, copy.

durchqueren [durç'kve:rən], v.a. insep. cross, traverse.

Durchsage ['durçza:gə], f. (—, pl. —n) (radio) announcement.

durchschauen [durç'ʃauən], v.a. insep. einen —, see through s.o.

durchscheinend ['durçʃaınənt], adj. transparent, translucent.

Durchschlag ['durçʃla:k], m. (—s, pl. ⁻e) strainer, sieve, colander, filter; carbon copy.

durchschlagen ['durçʃla:gən], v.a. irr. insep. strain, filter. — v.r. irr. sich —, fight o.'s way through.

durchschlagend ['durçʃla:gənt], adj. thorough, complete, effective.

Durchschnitt ['durçʃnıt], m. (—s, pl. —e) average; (Med. etc.) cross section.

durchschnittlich ['durçʃnıtlıç], adj. average; ordinary.

durchschossen [durç'ʃɔsən], adj. inter-leaved; interwoven.

durchseihen ['durçzaıən], v.a. see **durchsieben**.

durchsetzen [durç'zɛtsən], v.a. insep. intersperse; ['durçzɛtsən], v.a. sep. have o.'s way (with s.o.). — v.r. sep. sich —, make o.'s way successfully, succeed.

Durchsicht ['durçzıçt], f. (—, no pl.) revision, inspection, perusal.

durchsichtig ['durçzıçtıç], adj. trans-parent.

durchsickern ['durçzıkərn], v.n. (aux. sein) trickle through, ooze through.

durchsieben ['durçzi:bən], v.a. strain, filter, sift.

durchsprechen ['durçʃprɛxən], v.a. irr. talk over, discuss.

durchstöbern [durç'ʃtø:bərn], v.a. insep. rummage through.

durchstreichen ['durçʃtraıçən], v.a. irr. cross out, delete.

durchstreifen [durç'ʃtraıfən], v.a. insep. roam (through).

durchströmen [durç'ʃtrø:mən], v.a. insep. flow through, permeate.

durchsuchen [durç'zu:xən], v.a. insep. search thoroughly, examine closely.

durchtrieben [durç'tri:bən], adj. artful, sly, cunning, crafty.

durchweben [durç've:bən], v.a. inter-weave.

durchweg(s) ['durçvɛk(s)], adv. with-out exception, every time, throughout.

durchwühlen [durç'vy:lən], v.a. insep. search; ransack.

durchziehen [durç'tsi:ən], v.a. irr. insep. wander through, traverse; ['durçtsi:ən], v.a. irr. sep. interlace (with threads); draw through.

durchzucken [durç'tsukən], v.a. insep. flash through, convulse.

Durchzug ['durçtsu:k], m. (—s, no pl.) passage, march through; (air) draught.

dürfen ['dyrfən], v.n. irr. be permitted; be allowed; may be likely.

dürftig ['dyrftıç], adj. paltry, insuffi-cient, poor.

dürr [dyr], adj. dry, arid, withered; (wood) dead; (persons) thin, gaunt.

Dürre ['dyrə], f. (—, pl. —n) aridity, dryness; drought; (persons) thinness.

Durst [durst], m. (—es, no pl.) thirst.

dürsten ['dyrstən], v.n. thirst.

durstig ['durstıç], adj. thirsty.

Dusche ['du:ʃə], f. (—, pl. —n) shower (bath).

Düse ['dy:zə], f. (—, pl. —n) jet.

duselig ['du:zəlıç], adj. drowsy; silly.

düster ['dy:stər], adj. dark, gloomy; sad, mournful; sombre.

Dutzend ['dutsənt], n. (—s, pl. —e) dozen.

Duzbruder ['du:tsbru:dər], m. (—s, pl. ⁻) crony, chum; close friend.

duzen ['du:tsen], v.a. be on close terms with.

dynamisch [dy'na:mıʃ], adj. dyna-mic(al).

E

E [e:], n. (—s, pl. —s) the letter E; (Mus.) E Dur, E major; E Moll, E minor.

Ebbe ['ɛbə], f. (—, pl. —n) ebb, low tide; — und Flut, the tides.

ebben ['ɛbən], v.n. ebb.

eben ['e:bən], adj. even, level, plane; (fig.) plain. — adv. precisely, exactly.

Ebenbild ['e:bənbılt], n. (—es, pl. —er) likeness, image.

ebenbürtig ['e:bənbyrtıç], adj. of equal birth or rank; equal.

51

ebenda

ebenda ['e:bəndɑ:], *adv.* in the same place.

ebendeswegen ['e:bəndɛsve:gən], *adv.* for that very reason.

Ebene ['e:bənə], *f.* (—, *pl.* —n) plain; level ground; (*Maths.*) plane; *schiefe* —, inclined plane.

ebenfalls ['e:bənfals], *adv.* likewise, also, too, as well.

Ebenholz ['e:bənhɔlts], *n.* (—es, *no pl.*) ebony.

Ebenmaß ['e:bənmɑ:s], *n.* (—es, *pl.* —e) symmetry.

ebenmäßig ['e:bənmɛ:sɪç], *adj.* symmetrical.

ebenso ['e:bənzo:], *adv.* in the same way; — *wie*, just as . . .

Eber ['e:bər], *m.* (—s, *pl.* —) (*Zool.*) boar.

Eberesche ['e:bərɛʃə], *f.* (—, *pl.* —n) (*Bot.*) mountain ash, rowan.

ebnen ['e:bnən], *v.a.* even out, level; smoothe.

echt [ɛçt], *adj.* genuine, real, true, authentic, pure.

Ecke ['ɛkə], *f.* (—, *pl.* —en) corner, nook.

eckig ['ɛkɪç], *adj.* angular.

Eckzahn ['ɛktsɑ:n], *m.* (—s, *pl.* ⁓e) eye tooth; canine tooth.

Eckziegel ['ɛktsi:gəl], *m.* (—s, *pl.* —) (*Build.*) header.

edel ['e:dəl], *adj.* noble; well-born, aristocratic; (*metal*) precious.

Edelmann ['e:dəlman], *m.* (—s, *pl.* **Edelleute**) nobleman, aristocrat.

Edelmut ['e:dəlmu:t], *m.* (—s, *no pl.*) generosity, magnanimity.

Edelstein ['e:dəlʃtain], *m.* (—s, *pl.* —e) precious stone, jewel.

Edeltanne ['e:dəltanə], *f.* (—, *pl.* —n) (*Bot.*) silver fir.

Edelweiß ['e:dəlvais], *n.* (—sses, *no pl.*) (*Bot.*) edelweiss; lion's foot.

Eduard ['e:duart], *m.* Edward.

Efeu ['e:fɔy], *m.* (—s, *no pl.*) (*Bot.*) ivy.

Effekten [e'fɛktən], *m. pl.* goods and chattels; effects; stocks, securities.

Effektenbörse [e'fɛktənbœrzə], *f.* (—, *pl.* —n) Stock Exchange.

Effekthascherei [e'fɛkthaʃərai], *f.* (—, *pl.* —en) sensationalism, clap-trap.

effektuieren [efɛktu'i:rən], *v.a.* (*Comm.*) execute, effectuate.

egal [e'gɑ:l], *adj.* equal; all the same.

Egge ['ɛgə], *f.* (—, *pl.* —n) harrow.

Egoismus [ego'ismus], *m.* (—, *no pl.*) selfishness, egoism.

egoistisch [ego'ɪstɪʃ], *adj.* selfish, egoistic(al).

Ehe ['e:ə], *f.* (—, *pl.* —n) marriage.

ehe ['e:ə], *conj.* before; *adv.* formerly; *je* —*r, desto besser*, the sooner, the better.

Ehebrecher ['e:əbrɛçər], *m.* (—s, *pl.* —) adulterer.

Ehebruch ['e:əbrux], *m.* (—s, *pl.* ⁓e) adultery.

Ehefrau ['e:əfrau], *f.* (—, *pl.* —en) wife, spouse, consort.

Ehegatte ['e:əgatə], *m.* (—n, *pl.* —n) husband, spouse.

ehelich ['e:əlɪç], *adj.* matrimonial; (*children*) legitimate.

Ehelosigkeit ['e:əlo:zɪçkait], *f.* (—, *no pl.*) celibacy.

ehemalig ['e:əmɑ:lɪç], *adj.* former, late.

ehemals ['e:əmɑ:ls], *adv.* formerly, once, of old.

Ehemann ['e:əman], *m.* (—s, *pl.* ⁓er) husband.

ehern ['e:ərn], *adj.* brazen; of brass, of bronze.

Ehestand ['e:əʃtant], *m.* (—s, *no pl.*) matrimony.

ehestens ['e:əstəns], *adv.* as soon as possible.

Ehre ['e:rə], *f.* (—, *pl.* —n) honour, reputation, respect, distinction, glory.

ehren ['e:rən], *v.a.* honour, respect, esteem; *sehr geehrter Herr*, dear Sir.

Ehrenbezeigung ['e:rənbətsaiguŋ], *f.* (—, *pl.* —en) mark of respect; (*Mil.*) salute.

Ehrenbürger ['e:rənbyrgər], *m.* (—s, *pl.* —) honorary citizen *or* freeman.

Ehrendame ['e:rəndɑ:mə], *f.* (—, *pl.* —n) maid of honour.

Ehrenerklärung ['e:rənɛrklɛ:ruŋ], *f.* (—, *pl.* —en) reparation, apology.

Ehrengericht ['e:rəngərɪçt], *n.* (—s, *pl.* —e) court of honour.

ehrenhaft ['e:rənhaft], *adj.* honourable, worthy.

Ehrenpreis ['e:rənprais], *m.* (—es, *pl.* —e) prize; (*no pl.*) (*Bot.*) speed-well.

Ehrenrettung ['e:rənrɛtuŋ], *f.* (—, *pl.* —en) vindication.

ehrenrührig ['e:rənry:rɪç], *adj.* defamatory, calumnious.

ehrenvoll ['e:rənfɔl], *adj.* honourable.

ehrenwert ['e:rənvɛrt], *adj.* honourable, respectable.

ehrerbietig ['e:rərbi:tɪç], *adj.* reverential, respectful.

Ehrfurcht ['e:rfurçt], *f.* (—, *no pl.*) reverence, awe.

Ehrgefühl ['e:rgəfy:l], *n.* (—s, *no pl.*) sense of honour.

Ehrgeiz ['e:rgaits], *m.* (—es, *no pl.*) ambition.

ehrlich ['e:rlɪç], *adj.* honest; — *währt am längsten*, honesty is the best policy.

ehrlos ['e:rlo:s], *adj.* dishonourable, infamous.

ehrsam ['e:rzɑ:m], *adj.* respectable, honourable.

Ehrwürden ['e:rvyrdən], *m. & f.* (*form of address*) *Euer* —, Reverend Sir, Your Reverence.

ehrwürdig ['e:rvyrdɪç], *adj.* venerable, reverend.

Ei [ai], *n.* (—s, *pl.* —er) egg, ovum.

ei [ai], *int.* ay, indeed.

Eibe ['aibə], *f.* (—, *pl.* —n) (*Bot.*) yew.

Eichamt ['aiçamt], *n.* (—s, *pl.* ⁓er) office of weights and measures; (*Am.*) bureau of standards.

52

Eichapfel ['aɪçapfəl], *m.* (—s, *pl.* ⁀) oak apple.

Eiche ['aɪçə], *f.* (—, *pl.* —n) (*Bot.*) oak.

Eichel ['aɪçəl], *f.* (—, *pl.* —n) acorn; (*Anat.*) glans; (*Cards*) clubs.

eichen ['aɪçən], *v.a.* gauge, calibrate. — *adj.* made of oak.

Eichhörnchen ['aɪçhœrnçən] or **Eichkätzchen** ['aɪçkɛtsçən], *n.* (—s, *pl.* —) squirrel.

Eid [aɪt], *m.* (—es, *pl.* —e) oath; *falscher* —, perjury.

Eidam ['aɪdam], *m.* (—s, *pl.* —e) (*obs.*) son-in-law.

eidbrüchig ['aɪtbryçɪç], *adj.* guilty of perjury.

Eidechse ['aɪdɛksə], *f.* (—, *pl.* —n) lizard.

Eidesleistung ['aɪdəslaɪstuŋ], *f.* (—, *pl.* —en) affidavit.

Eidgenosse ['aɪtgənɔsə], *m.* (—n, *pl.* —n) confederate.

Eidgenossenschaft ['aɪtgənɔsənʃaft], *f.* (—, *pl.* —en) confederacy.

eidlich ['aɪtlɪç], *adj.* by oath, sworn.

Eidotter ['aɪdɔtər], *m. & n.* (—s, *pl.* —) yolk of an egg.

Eierbecher ['aɪərbɛçər], *m.* (—s, *pl.* —) egg cup.

Eierkuchen ['aɪərkuːxən], *m.* (—s, *pl.* —) omelet(te), pancake.

Eierschale ['aɪərʃaːlə], *f.* (—, *pl.* —n) egg shell.

Eierspeise ['aɪərʃpaɪzə], *f.* (—, *pl.* —n) dish prepared with eggs.

Eierstock ['aɪərʃtɔk], *m.* (—s, *pl.* ⁀e) ovary.

Eifer ['aɪfər], *m.* (—s, *no pl.*) zeal, eagerness, ardour, haste, passion, vehemence.

Eiferer ['aɪfərər], *m.* (—s, *pl.* —) zealot.

eifern ['aɪfərn], *v.n.* be zealous; *gegen einen* —, inveigh against s.o.

eiförmig ['aɪfœrmɪç], *adj.* oval, egg-shaped.

eifrig ['aɪfrɪç], *adj.* zealous, ardent, eager.

Eigelb ['aɪgɛlp], *n.* (—s, *no pl.*) yolk of (an) egg.

eigen ['aɪgən], *adj.* own; particular, peculiar.

Eigenart ['aɪgənaːrt], *f.* (—, *pl.* —en) peculiarity; idiosyncrasy.

eigenhändig ['aɪgənhɛndɪç], *adj.* with o.'s own hand.

Eigenheit ['aɪgənhaɪt], *f.* (—, *pl.* —en) peculiarity; idiosyncrasy.

eigenmächtig ['aɪgənmɛçtɪç], *adj.* arbitrary, autocratic, high-handed.

Eigenname ['aɪgənnaːmə], *m.* (—ns, *pl.* —n) proper name.

Eigennutz ['aɪgənnuts], *m.* (—es, *no pl.*) self-interest, selfishness.

eigennützig ['aɪgənnytsɪç], *adj.* selfish, self-interested, self-seeking.

eigens ['aɪgəns], *adv.* particularly, specially.

Eigenschaft ['aɪgənʃaft], *f.* (—, *pl.* —en) quality, peculiarity; property.

Eigenschaftswort ['aɪgənʃaftsvɔrt], *n.* (—s, *pl.* ⁀er) (*Gram.*) adjective.

Eigensinn ['aɪgənzɪn], *m.* (—s, *no pl.*) obstinacy.

eigentlich ['aɪgəntlɪç], *adj.* true, real; exact, literal.

Eigentum ['aɪgəntuːm], *n.* (—s, *pl.* ⁀er) property, possession, estate.

Eigentümer ['aɪgəntyːmər], *m.* (—s, *pl.* —) owner, proprietor.

eigenwillig ['aɪgənvɪlɪç], *adj.* self-willed.

eignen ['aɪgnən], *v.r. sich* — *für* (*zu*), suit, fit, be suitable *or* fit for (to).

Eilbote ['aɪlboːtə], *m.* (—n, *pl.* —n) special messenger.

Eile ['aɪlə], *f.* (—, *no pl.*) haste, hurry.

eilen ['aɪlən], *v.n.* (*aux.* sein), *v.r.* (*sich* —), hasten, hurry; be urgent.

eilends ['aɪlənts], *adv.* hastily.

eilfertig ['aɪlfɛrtɪç], *adj.* hasty.

Eilgut ['aɪlguːt], *n.* (—s, *pl.* ⁀er) express goods.

eilig ['aɪlɪç], *adj.* hasty, speedy; pressing, urgent.

Eilzug ['aɪltsuːk], *m.* (—s, *pl.* ⁀e) fast train.

Eimer ['aɪmər], *m.* (—s, *pl.* —) pail, bucket.

ein(e) ['aɪn(ə)], *indef. art,* a, an; *was für* — , what kind of a(n). — *num. adj.* one; — *jeder,* each one.

einander [aɪn'andər], *adv.* each other, one another.

einarbeiten ['aɪnarbaɪtən], *v.a.* train, familiarise s.o. with. —*v.r.* (*aux.* haben) *sich* —, familiarize o.s.

einäschern ['aɪnɛʃərn], *v.a.* reduce to ashes, incinerate; cremate.

einatmen ['aɪnaːtmən], *v.a.* breathe in, inhale.

einätzen ['aɪnɛtsən], *v.a.* etch in.

einäugig ['aɪnɔygɪç], *adj.* one-eyed.

Einbahnstraße ['aɪnbaːnʃtraːsə], *f.* (—, *pl.* —n) one-way street.

Einband ['aɪnbant], *m.* (—s, *pl.* ⁀e) binding, cover of book.

einbändig ['aɪnbɛndɪç], *adj.* in one volume.

einbauen ['aɪnbauən], *v.a.* build in.

einbegreifen ['aɪnbəgraɪfən], *v.a. irr.* include, comprise.

einberufen ['aɪnbəruːfən], *v.a. irr.* convene, convoke; (*Mil.*) call up.

einbeziehen ['aɪnbətsiːən], *v.a. irr.* include.

einbiegen ['aɪnbiːgən], *v.n. irr.* turn into (road).

einbilden ['aɪnbɪldən], *v.r. sich* —, imagine, fancy.

Einbildung ['aɪnbɪlduŋ], *f.* (—, *no pl.*) imagination, fancy, delusion; conceit.

einbinden ['aɪnbɪndən], *v.a. irr.* (*book*) bind.

Einblick ['aɪnblɪk], *m.* (—s, *no pl.*) insight.

Einbrecher ['aɪnbrɛçər], *m.* (—s, *pl.* —) burglar; intruder.

Einbrenne

Einbrenne [ˈaɪnbrɛnə], *f.* (—, *pl.* —n) thickening of soup.

einbringen [ˈaɪnbrɪŋən], *v.a. irr.* bring in, yield, fetch (a price); *wieder* —, retrieve.

einbrocken [ˈaɪnbrɔkən], *v.a.* crumble; *einem etwas* —, (*fig.*) get s.o. into trouble.

Einbruch [ˈaɪnbrux], *m.* (—s, *pl.* ⁻e) breaking-in; burglary, house-breaking.

Einbuchtung [ˈaɪnbuxtuŋ], *f.* (—, *pl.* —en) bight, bay.

einbürgern [ˈaɪnbyrgərn], *v.a.* naturalise.

Einbuße [ˈaɪnbuːsə], *f.* (—, *pl.* —n) loss.

einbüßen [ˈaɪnbyːsən], *v.a.* suffer a loss from, lose, forfeit.

eindämmen [ˈaɪndɛmən], *v.a.* dam in (*or* up).

Eindecker [ˈaɪndɛkər], *m.* (—s, *pl.* —) (*Aviat.*) monoplane.

eindeutig [ˈaɪndɔytɪç], *adj.* unequivocal, unambiguous.

eindrängen [ˈaɪndrɛŋən], *v.r. sich* —, intrude (into), force o.'s way in(to), interfere.

eindrillen [ˈaɪndrɪlən], *v.a. einem etwas* —, drum s.th. into s.o.

eindringen [ˈaɪndrɪŋən], *v.n. irr.* (*aux. sein*) enter, intrude; invade; penetrate.

eindringlich [ˈaɪndrɪŋlɪç], *adj.* forceful, urgent; impressive.

Eindruck [ˈaɪndruk], *m.* (—s, *pl.* ⁻e) impression.

eindrücken [ˈaɪndrykən], *v.a.* press in, squeeze in.

eindrucksfähig [ˈaɪndruksfɛːɪç], *adj.* impressionable.

einengen [ˈaɪnɛŋən], *v.a.* compress, limit, confine, cramp.

Einer [ˈaɪnər], *m.* (—s, *pl.* —) (*Maths.*) digit, unit.

einerlei [ˈaɪnərlaɪ], *adj.* the same, all the same.

einerseits [ˈaɪnərzaɪts], *adv.* on the one hand.

einfach [ˈaɪnfax], *adj.* single; simple, plain, uncomplicated; modest, homely.

einfädeln [ˈaɪnfɛːdəln], *v.a.* thread.

einfahren [ˈaɪnfaːrən], *v.n. irr.* (*aux. sein*) drive in, enter. — *v.a.* run in (new car).

Einfahrt [ˈaɪnfaːrt], *f.* (—, *pl.* —en) entrance, gateway, drive; (*Min.*) descent.

Einfall [ˈaɪnfal], *m.* (—s, *pl.* ⁻e) falling-in, downfall, fall; (*Mil.*) invasion; (*fig.*) idea, inspiration.

einfallen [ˈaɪnfalən], *v.n. irr.* (*aux. sein*) fall in, fall into; (*Mil.*) invade; (*fig.*) occur to s.o.

Einfalt [ˈaɪnfalt], *f.* (—, *no pl.*) simplicity; silliness.

Einfaltspinsel [ˈaɪnfaltspɪnzəl], *m.* (—s, *pl.* —) simpleton, dunce.

einfangen [ˈaɪnfaŋən], *v.a. irr.* catch, get hold of.

einfarbig [ˈaɪnfarbɪç], *adj.* of one colour; monochrome.

einfassen [ˈaɪnfasən], *v.a.* border, trim; (*diamonds*) set.

Einfassung [ˈaɪnfasuŋ], *f.* (—, *pl.* —en) bordering, trimming, edging, framing.

einfetten [ˈaɪnfɛtən], *v.a.* grease, lubricate.

einfinden [ˈaɪnfɪndən], *v.r. irr. sich* —, appear, be present.

einflechten [ˈaɪnflɛçtən], *v.a. irr.* plait; (*fig.*) insert.

einfließen [ˈaɪnfliːsən], *v.n. irr.* (*aux. sein*) flow in; — *lassen*, (*fig.*) mention casually, slip in (a word).

einflößen [ˈaɪnfløːsən], *v.a.* infuse; (*fig.*) instil, inspire with.

Einfluß [ˈaɪnflus], *m.* (—sses, *pl.* ⁻sse) influx; (*fig.*) influence.

einflußreich [ˈaɪnflusraɪç], *adj.* influential.

einflüstern [ˈaɪnflystərn], *v.n.* suggest, insinuate.

einförmig [ˈaɪnfœrmɪç], *adj.* uniform; monotonous.

einfriedigen [ˈaɪnfriːdɪgən], *v.a.* fence in, enclose.

einfügen [ˈaɪnfyːgən], *v.a.* insert, include, fit in. — *v.r. sich* —, adapt o.s., become a part of.

Einfühlungsvermögen [ˈaɪnfyluŋsfɛrmøːgən], *n.* (—s, *no pl.*) (*Phil.*) empathy, sympathetic understanding.

Einfuhr [ˈaɪnfuːr], *f.* (—, *pl.* —en) importation, import.

einführen [ˈaɪnfyːrən], *v.a.* introduce; (*goods*) import.

Einführung [ˈaɪnfyːruŋ], *f.* (—, *pl.* —en) introduction; (*goods*) importation.

einfüllen [ˈaɪnfylən], *v.a.* fill in, pour into, bottle.

Eingabe [ˈaɪngaːbə], *f.* (—, *pl.* —n) petitition; application.

Eingang [ˈaɪngaŋ], *m.* (—s, *pl.* ⁻e) entry, entrance; arrival.

eingangs [ˈaɪngaŋs], *adv.* in *or* at the beginning.

eingeben [ˈaɪngeːbən], *v.a. irr.* inspire (with); (*petition*) present, deliver; (*claim*) file; (*complaint*) bring; (*medicine*) administer.

eingeboren [ˈaɪngəboːrən], *adj.* native; (*Theol.*) only-begotten.

Eingeborene [ˈaɪngəboːrənə], *m.* (—n, *pl.* —n) native.

Eingebrachte [ˈaɪngəbraxtə], *n.* (—n, *no pl.*) dowry.

Eingebung [ˈaɪngeːbuŋ], *f.* (—, *pl.* —en) inspiration.

eingedenk [ˈaɪngədɛŋk], *prep.* (*Genit.*) mindful of, remembering.

eingefleischt [ˈaɪngəflaɪʃt], *adj.* inveterate, confirmed.

eingehen [ˈaɪngeːən], *v.n. irr.* (*aux. sein*) (*Comm.*) arrive; *auf etwas* —, enter into s.th., agree to s.th.; *auf etwas näher* —, enter into the details of s.th.; (*animals, plants*) die; (*cloth*) shrink.

eingehend ['aɪnɡeːənt], *adj.* thorough, exhaustive.

Eingemachte ['aɪnɡəmaxtə], *n.* (—n, *no pl.*) preserve.

eingenommen ['aɪnɡənɔmən], *adj.* enthusiastic for, infatuated with; — *von sich,* conceited.

Eingeschlossenheit ['aɪnɡəʃlɔsənhaɪt], *f.* (—, *no pl.*) isolation, seclusion.

eingeschrieben ['aɪnɡəʃriːbən], *adj.* registered (letter).

eingesessen ['aɪnɡəzɛsən], *adj.* old-established; resident.

Eingeständnis ['aɪnɡəʃtɛntnɪs], *n.* (—ses, *pl.* —se) confession.

eingestehen ['aɪnɡəʃteːən], *v.a. irr.* confess to, avow.

Eingeweide ['aɪnɡəvaɪdə], *n. pl.* bowels, intestines.

eingewöhnen ['aɪnɡəvøːnən], *v.r. sich* —, accustom o.s. to, get used to.

eingießen ['aɪnɡiːsən], *v.a. irr.* pour in; pour out.

eingleisig ['aɪnɡlaɪzɪç], *adj.* single-track.

eingliedern ['aɪnɡliːdərn], *v.r. sich* —, adapt o.s., fit in.

eingreifen ['aɪnɡraɪfən], *v.n. irr.* intervene in; interfere with, encroach on.

Eingriff ['aɪnɡrɪf], *m.* (—s, *pl.* —e) intervention, encroachment, infringement; (*Med.*) operation.

Einguß ['aɪnɡus], *m.* (—sses, *pl.* ⸚sse) infusion; enema.

einhaken ['aɪnhaːkən], *v.a.* hook in. — *v.r. sich* —, (*fig.*) take a p.'s arm.

Einhalt ['aɪnhalt], *m.* (—s, *no pl.*) stop, check, prohibition, cessation; — *gebieten,* check, suppress.

einhalten ['aɪnhaltən], *v.a. irr.* observe, adhere to.

einhändigen ['aɪnhɛndɪɡən], *v.a.* hand in, deliver.

einhauen ['aɪnhauən], *v.a.* hew in, break open.

Einhebung ['aɪnheːbuŋ], *f.* (—, *pl.* —en) (*taxes*) collection.

einheften ['aɪnhɛftən], *v.a.* sew in, stitch in; (*papers*) file.

einhegen ['aɪnheːɡən], *v.a.* fence in, hedge in.

einheimisch ['aɪnhaɪmɪʃ], *adj.* native; (*Bot.*) indigenous.

einheimsen ['aɪnhaɪmzən], *v.a.* reap.

Einheit ['aɪnhaɪt], *f.* (—, *pl.* —en) unit, unity.

einheitlich ['aɪnhaɪtlɪç], *adj.* uniform, consistent.

einheizen ['aɪnhaɪtsən], *v.a., v.n.* heat the stove, light the fire.

einhellig ['aɪnhɛlɪç], *adj.* unanimous, harmonious.

einher [aɪn'heːr], *adv.* forth, along, on.

einholen ['aɪnhoːlən], *v.a.* obtain; catch up with. — *v.n.* go shopping.

Einhorn ['aɪnhɔrn], *n.* (—s, *pl.* ⸚er) unicorn.

einhüllen ['aɪnhylən], *v.a.* wrap up, cover, envelop.

einig ['aɪnɪç], *adj.* at one. — *adv.* in agreement.

einige ['aɪnɪɡə], *adj.* some, several.

einigemal ['aɪnɪɡəmaːl], *adv.* several times.

einigen ['aɪnɪɡən], *v.a.* unite. — *v.r. sich* — *mit,* come to an agreement with.

einigermaßen [aɪnɪɡər'maːsən], *adv.* to a certain extent.

Einigkeit ['aɪnɪçkaɪt], *f.* (—, *no pl.*) union; unity, unanimity, harmony.

Einigung ['aɪnɪɡuŋ], *f.* (—, *no pl.*) agreement.

einimpfen ['aɪnɪmpfən], *v.a.* inoculate, vaccinate.

einjährig ['aɪnjɛːrɪç], *adj.* one-year-old, annual.

einkassieren ['aɪnkasiːrən], *v.a.* cash (*cheque*), collect (*money*).

Einkauf ['aɪnkauf], *m.* (—s, *pl.* ⸚e) purchase, buy.

einkaufen ['aɪnkaufən], *v.a.* purchase, buy. — *v.n.* go shopping.

Einkäufer ['aɪnkɔyfər], *m.* (—s, *pl.* —) (*Comm.*) purchaser, buyer.

Einkehr ['aɪnkeːr], *f.* (—, *no pl.*) stopping (at an inn); (*fig.*) meditation.

einkehren ['aɪnkeːrən], *v.n.* (*aux. sein*) stop *or* put up (at an inn).

einkerkern ['aɪnkɛrkərn], *v.a.* imprison.

einklagen ['aɪnklaːɡən], *v.a.* (*Law*) sue for (money).

einklammern ['aɪnklamərn], *v.a.* bracket, enclose in brackets.

Einklang ['aɪnklaŋ], *m.* (—s, *no pl.*) accord, unison, harmony.

einkleben ['aɪnkleːbən], *v.a.* paste in.

einkleiden ['aɪnklaɪdən], *v.a.* clothe; (*fig.*) invest; *sich — lassen,* (*Eccl.*) take the veil.

einklemmen ['aɪnklɛmən], *v.a.* squeeze in, jam in.

einkochen ['aɪnkɔxən], *v.a.* preserve. — *v.n.* (*aux. sein*) boil down.

Einkommen ['aɪnkɔmən], *n.* (—s, *no pl.*) income, revenue.

einkommen ['aɪnkɔmən], *v.n. irr.* (*aux. sein*) *bei einem wegen etwas* —, apply to s.o. for s.th.

einkreisen ['aɪnkraɪzən], *v.a.* encircle, isolate.

Einkünfte ['aɪnkynftə], *pl.* income, revenue; emoluments.

einladen ['aɪnlaːdən], *v.a. irr.* load in; invite.

Einlage ['aɪnlaːɡə], *f.* (—, *pl.* —en) (*letter*) enclosure; (*Theat.*) addition to programme; (*game*) stake; (*Comm.*) investment.

einlagern ['aɪnlaːɡərn], *v.a.* (*goods*) store, warehouse; (*Mil.*) billet, quarter.

Einlaß ['aɪnlas], *m.* (—sses, *no pl.*) admission, admittance; (*water*) inlet.

einlassen ['aɪnlasən], *v.a. irr.* admit, allow in; let in. — *v.r. sich auf etwas* —, engage in s.th., enter into s.th.

Einlauf ['aɪnlauf], *m.* (—s, *no pl.*) entering; (*Med.*) enema.

einlaufen

einlaufen [ˈaɪnlaʊfən], *v.n. irr.* (*aux.* sein) (*Naut.*) enter harbour, put into port; (*material*) shrink.

einleben [ˈaɪnleːbən], *v.r. sich* —, grow accustomed to, settle down, acclimatise o.s.

einlegen [ˈaɪnleːgən], *v.a.* put in, lay in; enclose; (*money*) deposit; (*food*) pickle, preserve; *Fürbitte* —, intercede; *eingelegte Arbeit*, inlaid work.

einleiten [ˈaɪnlaɪtən], *v.a.* begin, introduce; institute.

Einleitung [ˈaɪnlaɪtʊŋ], *f.* (—, *pl.* —en) introduction; (*book*) preface; (*Mus.*) prelude; (*Law*) institution.

einlenken [ˈaɪnlɛŋkən], *v.n.* turn in; give in, come round.

einleuchten [ˈaɪnlɔʏçtən], *v.n.* become clear.

einlösen [ˈaɪnløːzən], *v.a.* redeem; (*bill*) honour; (*cheque*) cash.

einmachen [ˈaɪnmaxən], *v.a.* preserve.

einmal [ˈaɪnmaːl], *adv.* once; *es war* —, once upon a time; *auf* —, suddenly; *noch* —, once more; *nicht* —, not even.

Einmaleins [ˈaɪnmaːlaɪns], *n.* (—es, *no pl.*) multiplication table.

einmalig [ˈaɪnmaːlɪç], *adv.* unique, unrepeatable.

Einmaster [ˈaɪnmastər], *m.* (—s, *pl.* —) (*Naut.*) brigantine, cutter.

einmauern [ˈaɪnmaʊərn], *v.a.* wall in, immure.

einmengen [ˈaɪnmɛŋən], *v.r. sich* —, meddle with, interfere.

einmieten [ˈaɪnmiːtən], *v.r. sich* —, take lodgings.

einmischen [ˈaɪnmɪʃən], *v.r. sich* —, meddle (with), interfere.

einmütig [ˈaɪnmyːtɪç], *adj.* unanimous, in harmony, united.

Einnahme [ˈaɪnnaːmə], *f.* (—, *pl.* —n) income, revenue; receipts; (*Mil.*) occupation, capture.

einnehmen [ˈaɪnneːmən], *v.a. irr.* take in; (*money*) receive; (*medicine*) take; (*taxes*) collect; (*place*) take up, occupy; (*Mil.*) occupy, conquer; (*fig.*) captivate, fascinate.

einnehmend [ˈaɪnneːmənt], *adj.* fetching, engaging, charming.

einnicken [ˈaɪnnɪkən], *v.n.* (*aux.* sein) nod *or* doze off.

einnisten [ˈaɪnnɪstən], *v.r. sich* —, nestle down; (*fig.*) settle in a place.

Einöde [ˈaɪnøːdə], *f.* (—, *pl.* —n) desert, solitude.

einordnen [ˈaɪnɔrdnən], *v.a.* place in order, file, classify.

einpauken [ˈaɪnpaʊkən], *v.a.* cram.

einpferchen [ˈaɪnpfɛrçən], *v.a.* pen in, coop up.

einpökeln [ˈaɪnpøːkəln], *v.a.* salt, pickle.

einprägen [ˈaɪnprɛːgən], *v.a.* imprint; impress.

einquartieren [ˈaɪnkvartiːrən], *v.a.* (*Mil.*) quarter, billet.

einrahmen [ˈaɪnraːmən], *v.a.* frame.

einräumen [ˈaɪnrɔʏmən], *v.a.* stow (things) away; (*things*) concede s.th. to s.o.

Einrede [ˈaɪnreːdə], *f.* (—, *pl.* —n) objection.

einreden [ˈaɪnreːdən], *v.a. einem etwas* —, persuade s.o. to. — *v.r. sich etwas* —, get s.th. into o.'s head.

einreichen [ˈaɪnraɪçən], *v.a.* hand in, deliver; tender.

einreihen [ˈaɪnraɪən], *v.a.* place in line, arrange.

einreihig [ˈaɪnraɪɪç], *adj.* consisting of a single row; (*Tail.*) single-breasted (suit).

einreißen [ˈaɪnraɪsən], *v.a. irr.* make a tear in; (*houses*) pull down. — *v.n.* (*fig.*) gain ground.

einrenken [ˈaɪnrɛŋkən], *v.a.* (*Med.*) set; (*fig.*) settle.

einrichten [ˈaɪnrɪçtən], *v.a.* put in order, arrange; equip, set up; furnish.

Einrichtung [ˈaɪnrɪçtʊŋ], *f.* (—, *pl.* —en) arrangement, management; furnishing; (*pl.*) facilities; equipment, amenities.

einrücken [ˈaɪnrykən], *v.n.* (*aux.* sein) march in. — *v.a.* insert (in the newspaper).

Eins [aɪns], *f.* (—, *pl.* —en, —er) one; (*Sch.*) top marks.

eins [aɪns], *num.* one; *es ist mir alles* —, it is all the same to me.

einsalzen [ˈaɪnzaltsən], *v.a.* salt, pickle, cure.

einsam [ˈaɪnzaːm], *adj.* lonely, solitary, secluded.

Einsamkeit [ˈaɪnzaːmkaɪt], *f.* (—, *no pl.*) loneliness, solitude, seclusion.

Einsatz [ˈaɪnzats], *m.* (—es, *pl.* ⁀e) (*game*) stake, pool; (*dress*) lace inset; (*Mus.*) entry (of a voice), starting intonation; (*Mil.*) sortie, mission.

einsaugen [ˈaɪnzaʊgən], *v.a.* suck in; (*fig.*) imbibe.

einsäumen [ˈaɪnzɔʏmən], *v.a.* hem (in).

einschalten [ˈaɪnʃaltən], *v.a.* insert, interpolate; switch on; put in gear.

einschärfen [ˈaɪnʃɛrfən], *v.a.* impress s.th. on s.o.

einschätzen [ˈaɪnʃɛtsən], *v.a.* assess.

einschenken [ˈaɪnʃɛŋkən], *v.a.* pour in *or* out, fill.

einschieben [ˈaɪnʃiːbən], *v.a.* push in; interpolate, insert.

Einschiebsel [ˈaɪnʃiːpsəl], *n.* (—s, *pl.* —) interpolation; interpolated part.

einschiffen [ˈaɪnʃɪfən], *v.a.* embark; (*goods*) ship. — *v.r. sich* —, go aboard, embark.

einschlafen [ˈaɪnʃlaːfən], *v.n. irr.* (*aux.* sein) fall asleep, go to sleep.

einschläfern [ˈaɪnʃlɛːfərn], *v.a.* lull to sleep.

Einschlag [ˈaɪnʃlaːk], *m.* (—s, *pl.* ⁀e) cover, envelope; (*weaving*) woof, weft; explosion; strike; (*fig.*) streak (of character); touch.

einschlagen [ˈaɪnʃlaːgən], v.a. irr. knock in; (nail) drive in; (parcel) wrap up; (road) take. — v.n. (lightning) strike; be a success.

einschlägig [ˈaɪnʃlɛːgɪç], adj. bearing on (the subject), pertinent.

einschleppen [ˈaɪnʃlɛpən], v.a. (disease) bring in, introduce.

einschließen [ˈaɪnʃliːsən], v.a. irr. lock in or up; (enemy) surround; (fig.) include.

einschlummern [ˈaɪnʃlumərn], v.n. (aux. sein) doze off, fall asleep.

Einschluß [ˈaɪnʃlus], m. (—sses, pl. ˙-sse) inclusion; mit — von, inclusive of.

einschmeicheln [ˈaɪnʃmaɪçəln], v.r. sich bei einem —, ingratiate o.s. with s.o.

einschmelzen [ˈaɪnʃmɛltsən], v.a. irr. melt down.

einschmieren [ˈaɪnʃmiːrən], v.a. smear, grease, oil; (sore) put ointment on.

einschneidend [ˈaɪnʃnaɪdənt], adj. important, sweeping, incisive, trenchant.

einschneidig [ˈaɪnʃnaɪdɪç], adj. single-edged.

Einschnitt [ˈaɪnʃnɪt], m. (—s, pl. —e) incision, cut, notch; (verse) caesura.

einschnüren [ˈaɪnʃnyːrən], v.a. lace up; (parcel) tie up.

einschränken [ˈaɪnʃrɛŋkən], v.a. confine, limit, restrict. — v.r. sich —, curtail o.'s expenses, economize.

einschrauben [ˈaɪnʃraubən], v.a. screw in.

einschreiben [ˈaɪnʃraɪbən], v.a. irr. write in or down, inscribe; (letter) register. — v.r. sich —, enter o.'s name; enrol.

Einschreibesendung [ˈaɪnʃraɪbəzɛnduŋ], f. (—, pl. —en) registered letter, registered parcel.

einschreiten [ˈaɪnʃraɪtən], v.n. irr. (aux. sein) step in, intervene.

einschrumpfen [ˈaɪnʃrumpfən], v.n. (aux. sein) shrink, shrivel.

einschüchtern [ˈaɪnʃyçtərn], v.a. intimidate, overawe.

Einschuß [ˈaɪnʃus], m. (—sses, pl. ˙-sse) share, advance of capital; (weaving) woof, weft.

einsegnen [ˈaɪnzeːgnən], v.a. consecrate, bless; (Eccl.) confirm.

Einsehen [ˈaɪnzeːən], n. (—s, no pl.) realisation; ein — haben, be reasonable.

einsehen [ˈaɪnzeːən], v.a. irr. look into, glance over; (fig.) comprehend, realise.

einseifen [ˈaɪnzaɪfən], v.a. soap, lather; (fig.) take s.o. in.

einseitig [ˈaɪnzaɪtɪç], adj. one-sided; (fig.) one-track (mind).

Einsenkung [ˈaɪnzɛŋkuŋ], f. (—, pl. —en) depression (of the ground).

einsetzen [ˈaɪnzɛtsən], v.a. put in, set in; institute, establish; (money) stake; (Hort.) plant; (office) install s.o. — v.n. begin.

Einsetzung [ˈaɪnzɛtsuŋ], f. (—, pl. —en) (office) investiture, installation; institution.

Einsicht [ˈaɪnzɪçt], f. (—, no pl.) inspection, examination; insight, understanding.

einsichtig [ˈaɪnzɪçtɪç], adj. intelligent, sensible, judicious.

Einsichtnahme [ˈaɪnzɪçtnaːmə], f. zur —, (Comm.) on approval, for inspection.

Einsiedler [ˈaɪnziːdlər], m. (—s, pl. —) hermit, recluse.

einsilbig [ˈaɪnzɪlbɪç], adj. monosyllabic; (fig.) taciturn, laconic.

einspannen [ˈaɪnʃpanən], v.a. stretch in a frame; harness; (coll.) put to work.

Einspänner [ˈaɪnʃpɛnər], m. (—s, pl. —) one-horse vehicle; one-horse cab, fiacre.

einsperren [ˈaɪnʃpɛrən], v.a. lock in, shut up, imprison.

einspinnen [ˈaɪnʃpɪnən], v.r. irr. sich —, spin a cocoon.

einsprengen [ˈaɪnʃprɛŋən], v.a. sprinkle.

einspringen [ˈaɪnʃprɪŋən], v.n. irr. (aux. sein) auf einen —, leap at; (lock) catch, snap; für einen —, deputize for s.o.

Einspruch [ˈaɪnʃprux], m. (—s, pl. ˙-e) objection, protest; — erheben, protest; (Law) appeal (against).

einspurig [ˈaɪnʃpuːrɪç], adj. (Railw.) single-track line.

einst [aɪnst], adv. (past) once, once upon a time; (future) some day.

Einstand [ˈaɪnʃtant], m. (—s, no pl.) (Tennis) deuce.

einstecken [ˈaɪnʃtɛkən], v.a. put in; pocket; post (a letter).

einstehen [ˈaɪnʃteːən], v.a. irr. zu etwas —, answer for s.th.; für einen —, stand security for s.o.

einsteigen [ˈaɪnʃtaɪgən], v.n. irr. (aux. sein) get in, climb on; board.

einstellen [ˈaɪnʃtɛlən], v.a. put in; (persons) engage, hire; adjust; (work) stop, strike; (payments) stop; (hostilities) suspend, cease fire. — v.r. sich —, turn up, appear.

einstellig [ˈaɪnʃtɛlɪç], adj. (Maths.) of one digit.

Einstellung [ˈaɪnʃtɛluŋ], f. (—, pl. —en) putting in; (persons) engagement, hiring; adjustment; (work) stoppage, strike; (payments) suspension; (hostilities) suspension, cessation; (fig.) opinion, attitude.

einstig [ˈaɪnstɪç], adj. (past) former, late, erstwhile; (future) future, to be, to come.

einstimmen [ˈaɪnʃtɪmən], v.n. join in, chime in.

einstimmig [ˈaɪnʃtɪmɪç], adj. (Mus.) (for) one voice, unison; (fig.) unanimous.

einstmals [ˈaɪnstmaːls], adv. once, formerly.

57

einstöckig

einstöckig [ˈaɪnʃtœkɪç], *adj.* one-storied.

einstreichen [ˈaɪnʃtraɪçən], *v.a. irr.* (*money*) take in, pocket.

einstreuen [ˈaɪnʃtrɔyən], *v.a.* strew; (*fig.*) intersperse.

einstudieren [ˈaɪnʃtudiːrən], *v.a.* study; (*Theat., Mus.*) rehearse.

einstürmen [ˈaɪnʃtyrmən], *v.n. (aux. sein) auf einen* —, rush at, fall upon.

Einsturz [ˈaɪnʃturts], *m.* (—es, *pl.* ⁀e) fall, crash; subsidence, collapse.

einstürzen [ˈaɪnʃtyrtsən], *v.n. (aux. sein)* fall in, fall into ruin, fall to pieces, collapse.

einstweilen [ˈaɪnstvaɪlən], *adv.* in the meantime, meanwhile, for the time being, provisionally.

einstweilig [ˈaɪnstvaɪlɪç], *adj.* temporary, provisional.

eintägig [ˈaɪntɛːgɪç], *adj.* one-day, ephemeral.

Eintagsfliege [ˈaɪntaːksfliːgə], *f.* (—, *pl.* —n) dayfly.

eintauschen [ˈaɪntauʃən], *v.a.* — *gegen*, exchange for, barter for.

einteilen [ˈaɪntaɪlən], *v.a.* divide; distribute; classify.

eintönig [ˈaɪntøːnɪç], *adj.* monotonous.

Eintracht [ˈaɪntraxt], *f.* (—, *no pl.*) concord, harmony.

einträchtig [ˈaɪntrɛçtɪç], *adj.* united, harmonious.

Eintrag [ˈaɪntraːk], *m.* (—s, *pl.* ⁀e) entry (in a book); prejudice, damage, detriment.

eintragen [ˈaɪntraːgən], *v.a. irr.* enter (in a book), register; bring in, yield.

einträglich [ˈaɪntrɛklɪç], *adj.* profitable, lucrative.

Eintragung [ˈaɪntraːguŋ], *f.* (—, *pl.* —en) entry (in a book); enrolment.

einträufeln [ˈaɪntrɔyfəln], *v.a.* instil.

eintreffen [ˈaɪntrɛfən], *v.n. irr. (aux. sein)* arrive; happen, come true.

eintreiben [ˈaɪntraɪbən], *v.a. irr.* drive home (*cattle*); collect (debts etc.).

eintreten [ˈaɪntreːtən], *v.n. irr. (aux. sein)* step in, enter; happen, take place; *in einen Verein* —, join a club; *für einen* —, speak up for s.o.

eintrichtern [ˈaɪntrɪçtərn], *v.a. einem etwas* —, cram s.th. into s.o.

Eintritt [ˈaɪntrɪt], *m.* (—s, *no pl.*) entry, entrance; beginning; *kein* —, no adr ission.

eintrocknen [ˈaɪntrɔknən], *v.n. (aux. sein)* shrivel, dry up.

einüben [ˈaɪnyːbən], *v.a.* practise, exercise.

einverleiben [ˈaɪnfɛrlaɪbən], *v.a.* incorporate in, embody in.

Einvernahme [ˈaɪnfɛrnaːmə], *f.* (—, *pl.* —n) (*Austr.*) *see* **Vernehmung**.

Einvernehmen [ˈaɪnfɛrneːmən], *n.* (—s, *no pl.*) understanding; *im besten* —, on the best of terms.

einvernehmen [ˈaɪnfɛrneːmən], *v.a.* (*aux. haben*) (*Austr.*) *see* **vernehmen**.

einverstanden [ˈaɪnfɛrʃtandən], (*excl.*)

agreed! — *adj.* — *sein*, agree.

Einverständnis [ˈaɪnfɛrʃtɛntnɪs], *n.* (—ses, *no pl.*) consent, agreement, accord.

Einwand [ˈaɪnvant], *m.* (—s, *pl.* ⁀e) objection, exception; — *erheben*, raise objections.

einwandern [ˈaɪnvandərn], *v.n. (aux. sein)* immigrate.

einwandfrei [ˈaɪnvantfraɪ], *adj.* irreproachable, unobjectionable.

einwärts [ˈaɪnvɛrts], *adv.* inward(s).

einwechseln [ˈaɪnvɛksəln], *v.a.* change, exchange.

einweichen [ˈaɪnvaɪçən], *v.a.* steep in water, soak.

einweihen [ˈaɪnvaɪən], *v.a.* dedicate; (*Eccl.*) consecrate; open (formally), inaugurate; initiate (into).

Einweihung [ˈaɪnvaɪuŋ], *f.* (—, *pl.* —en) (*Eccl.*) consecration; inauguration, formal opening; initiation.

einwenden [ˈaɪnvɛndən], *v.a. irr.* object to, raise objections, urge against.

einwerfen [ˈaɪnvɛrfən], *v.a. irr.* throw in; smash in; interject.

einwickeln [ˈaɪnvɪkəln], *v.a.* wrap up, envelop.

einwilligen [ˈaɪnvɪlɪgən], *v.n.* consent, assent, agree, accede.

einwirken [ˈaɪnvɪrkən], *v.n. auf einen* —, influence s.o.

Einwohner [ˈaɪnvoːnər], *m.* (—s, *pl.* —) inhabitant.

Einwohnerschaft [ˈaɪnvoːnərʃaft], *f.* (—, *no pl.*) population, inhabitants.

Einwurf [ˈaɪnvurf], *m.* (—s, *pl.* ⁀e) (*letter box*) opening, slit; slot; objection.

einwurzeln [ˈaɪnvurtsəln], *v.r. sich* —, take root; *eingewurzelt*, deep-rooted.

Einzahl [ˈaɪntsaːl], *f.* (—, *no pl.*) singular.

einzahlen [ˈaɪntsaːlən], *v.a.* pay in, deposit.

einzäunen [ˈaɪntsɔynən], *v.a.* fence in.

einzeichnen [ˈaɪntsaɪçnən], *v.a.* draw in, sketch in. — *v.r. sich* —, enter o.'s name, sign.

Einzelhaft [ˈaɪntsəlhaft], *f.* (—, *no pl.*) solitary confinement.

Einzelheit [ˈaɪntsəlhaɪt], *f.* (—, *pl.* —en) detail, particular.

einzeln [ˈaɪntsəln], *adj.* single; isolated, detached, apart.

einziehen [ˈaɪntsiːən], *v.a. irr.* draw in, retract; (*Law*) confiscate, impound; (*debts*) collect, call in; (*bill of sight*) discount, cash; (*money*) withdraw (from circulation); (*sails*) furl; (*Mil.*) call up.

einzig [ˈaɪntsɪç], *adj.* sole, single; unique, only.

Einzug [ˈaɪntsuːk], *m.* (—s, *pl.* ⁀e) entry, entrance; move (into new house).

einzwängen [ˈaɪntsvɛŋən], *v.a.* force in, squeeze in.

Eis [aɪs], *n.* (—es, *no pl.*) ice; ice-cream.

E-is [ˈeːɪs], *n.* (—, *pl.* —) (*Mus.*) E sharp.

Eisbahn [′aɪsba:n], *f.* (—, *pl.* —en) ice-rink, skating-rink.

Eisbär [′aɪsbɛ:r], *m.* (—en, *pl.* —en) polar bear, white bear.

Eisbein [′aɪsbaɪn], *n.* (—s, *pl.* —e) pig's trotters.

Eisberg [′aɪsbɛrk], *m.* (—s, *pl.* —e) iceberg.

Eisblumen [′aɪsblu:mən], *f. pl.* frost patterns (*on glass*).

Eisen [′aɪzən], *n.* (—s, *pl.* —) iron; *altes* —, scrap iron.

Eisenbahn [′aɪzənba:n], *f.* (—, *pl.* —en) railway.

Eisenfleck [′aɪzənflɛk], *m.* (—s, *pl.* —e) iron mould.

Eisengießerei [′aɪzəngi:səraɪ], *f.* (—, *pl.* —en) iron foundry, iron forge.

Eisenguß [′aɪzəngus], *m.* (—sses, *pl.* ˑsse) cast-iron.

Eisenhändler [′aɪzənhɛndlər], *m.* (—s, *pl.* —) ironmonger.

Eisenhütte [′aɪzənhytə], *f.* (—, *pl.* —n) *see* Eisengießerei.

Eisenschlacke [′aɪzənʃlakə], *f.* (—, *no pl.*) iron dross, iron slag.

eisern [′aɪzərn], *adj.* made of iron; (*coll. & fig.*) strong; strict.

Eisgang [′aɪsgaŋ], *m.* (—s, *pl.* ˑe) drift of ice.

eisgrau [′aɪsgrau], *adj.* hoary.

eiskalt [′aɪskalt], *adj.* icy cold.

Eislauf [′aɪslauf], *m.* (—s, *no pl.*) ice-skating.

Eismeer [′aɪsme:r], *n.* (—s, *pl.* —e) polar sea; *nördliches* —, Arctic Ocean; *südliches* —, Antarctic Ocean.

Eispickel [′aɪspɪkəl], *m.* (—s, *pl.* —) ice axe.

Eisvogel [′aɪsfo:gəl], *m.* (—s, *pl.* ˑ) (*Orn.*) kingfisher.

Eiszapfen [′aɪstsapfən], *m.* (—s, *pl.* —) icicle.

eitel [′aɪtəl], *adj.* vain, frivolous, conceited; (*obs.*) pure.

Eiter [′aɪtər], *m.* (—s, *no pl.*) (*Med.*) pus, matter.

Eitergeschwür [′aɪtərgəʃvy:r], *n.* (—s, *pl.* —e) abscess.

eitern [′aɪtərn], *v.n.* suppurate.

Eiterung [′aɪtəruŋ], *f.* (—, *pl.* —en) suppuration.

eitrig [′aɪtrɪç], *adj.* purulent.

Eiweiß [′aɪvaɪs], *n.* (—es, *no pl.*) white of egg; albumen.

Ekel [′e:kəl], *m.* (—s, *no pl.*) nausea, disgust, distaste, aversion.

ekelhaft [′e:kəlhaft], *adj.* loathsome, disgusting, nauseous.

ekeln [′e:kəln], *v.r. sich — vor*, be disgusted (by), feel sick, loathe.

Ekuador [ɛkua′dɔr], *n.* Ecuador.

Elan [e′lã], *m.* (—s, *no pl.*) verve, vigour.

elastisch [e′lastɪʃ], *adj.* elastic, flexible, buoyant.

Elastizität [elastɪtsɪ′tɛ:t], *f.* (—, *no pl.*) elasticity; (*mind*) buoyancy.

Elch [ɛlç], *m.* (—s, *pl.* —e) (*Zool.*) elk.

Elegie [ele′gi:], *f.* (—, *pl.* —n) elegy.

elektrisieren [elɛktri′zi:rən], *v.a.* electrify.

Elektrizität [elɛktritsɪ′tɛ:t], *f.* (—, *no pl.*) electricity.

Elend [′e:lɛnt], *n.* (—s, *no pl.*) misery, distress, wretchedness.

elend [′e:lɛnt], *adj.* miserable, wretched, pitiful; weak; *sich — fühlen*, feel poorly.

elendiglich [′e:lɛndɪklɪç], *adv.* miserably, wretchedly.

Elentier [′e:lɛnti:r], *n.* (—s, *pl.* —e) (*Zool.*) elk.

elf [ɛlf], *num. adj.* eleven.

Elfe [′ɛlfə], *f.* (—, *pl.* —n) fairy.

Elfenbein [′ɛlfənbaɪn], *n.* (—s, *no pl.*) ivory.

Elisabeth [e′li:zabɛt], *f.* Elizabeth.

Ellbogen [′ɛlbo:gən], *m.* (—s, *pl.* —) elbow.

Elle [′ɛlə], *f.* (—, *pl.* —n) yard, ell.

Elritze [′ɛlrɪtsə], *f.* (—, *pl.* —n) minnow.

Elsaß [′ɛlzas], *n.* Alsace.

Elster [′ɛlstər], *f.* (—, *pl.* —n) magpie.

Eltern [′ɛltərn], *pl.* parents.

Emaille [e′ma:j], *n.* (—s, *no pl.*) enamel.

emailliert [ema(l)′ji:rt], *adj.* covered with vitreous enamel, enamelled.

Empfang [ɛm′pfaŋ], *m.* (—s, *pl.* ˑe) receipt; reception.

empfangen [ɛm′pfaŋən], *v.a. irr.* receive, accept, take.

Empfänger [ɛm′pfɛŋər], *m.* (—s, *pl.* —) recipient, receiver.

empfänglich [ɛm′pfɛŋlɪç], *adj.* susceptible, impressionable.

Empfängnis [ɛm′pfɛŋnɪs], *f.* (—, *no pl.*) conception.

empfehlen [ɛm′pfe:lən], *v.a. irr.* commend, recommend; give compliments to. — *v.r. sich —*, take leave.

empfinden [ɛm′pfɪndən], *v.a. irr.* feel, perceive.

empfindlich [ɛm′pfɪntlɪç], *adj.* sensitive, susceptible; touchy, thin-skinned.

empfindsam [ɛm′pfɪntsa:m], *adj.* sentimental.

Empfindung [ɛm′pfɪnduŋ], *f.* (—, *pl.* —en) sensation, feeling, sentiment.

empor [ɛm′po:r], *adv.* upward(s), up.

Empore [ɛm′po:rə], *f.* (—, *pl.* —n) gallery (*in church*).

empören [ɛm′po:rən], *v.a.* excite, enrage, shock. — *v.r. sich —*, revolt, rebel.

Emporkömmling [ɛm′po:rkœmlɪŋ], *m.* (—s, *pl.* —e) upstart.

empört [ɛm′po:rt], *adj.* furious, shocked, disgusted.

Empörung [ɛm′pø:ruŋ], *f.* (—, *pl.* —en) rebellion, revolt, mutiny, insurrection; indignation, disgust.

emsig [′ɛmzɪç], *adj.* assiduous, industrious, busy.

Emsigkeit [′ɛmzɪçkaɪt], *f.* (—, *no pl.*) assiduity, diligence.

Ende [′ɛndə], *n.* (—s, *pl.* —n) end, conclusion.

enden ['ɛndən], *v.n.* end, finish, conclude. — *v.a.* terminate, put an end to.

endgültig ['ɛntgyltɪç], *adj.* definitive, final.

Endivie [ɛn'di:vjə], *f.* (—, *pl.* —n) (*Bot.*) endive.

endlich ['ɛntlɪç], *adj.* finite, final, ultimate. — *adv.* at last, at length, finally.

endlos ['ɛntloːs], *adj.* endless, neverending, boundless.

Endung ['ɛnduŋ], *f.* (—, *pl.* —en) (*Gram.*) ending, termination.

Endziel ['ɛntsiːl], *n.* (—s, *pl.* —e) final aim.

Energie [enɛr'giː], *f.* (—, *pl.* —n) energy.

energisch [e'nɛrgɪʃ], *adj.* energetic.

eng [ɛŋ], *adj.* narrow, tight; tightfitting.

engagieren [ãga'ʒiːrən], *v.a.* engage, hire.

Enge ['ɛŋə], *f.* (—, *pl.* —n) narrowness, lack of space; *einen in die* — *treiben* drive s.o. into a corner.

Engel ['ɛŋəl], *m.* (—s, *pl.* —) angel.

engelhaft ['ɛŋəlhaft], *adj.* angelic.

Engelschar ['ɛŋəlʃaːr], *f.* (—, *pl.* —en) angelic host.

Engelwurzel ['ɛŋəlvurtsəl], *f.* (—, *pl.* —n) angelica.

engherzig ['ɛŋhɛrtsɪç], *adj.* narrowminded.

England ['ɛŋlant], *n.* England.

englisch (1) ['ɛŋlɪʃ], *adj.* (*obs.*) angelic.

englisch (2) ['ɛŋlɪʃ], *adj.* English; —*e Krankheit,* rickets.

Engpaß ['ɛŋpas], *m.* (—sses, *pl.* ⁻e) defile, narrow pass; (*fig.*) bottleneck.

engros [ã'groː], *adj.* wholesale.

engstirnig ['ɛŋʃtɪrnɪç], *adj.* narrowminded.

Enkel ['ɛŋkəl], *m.* (—s, *pl.* —) grandchild, grandson.

enorm [e'nɔrm], *adj.* enormous; (*coll.*) terrific.

entarten [ɛnt'artən], *v.n.* (*aux.* sein) degenerate.

entäußern [ɛnt'ɔysərn], *v.r. sich einer Sache* —, part with s.th.

entbehren [ɛnt'beːrən], *v.a.* lack, be in want of; spare.

entbehrlich [ɛnt'beːrlɪç], *adj.* dispensable, unnecessary, superfluous.

Entbehrung [ɛnt'beːruŋ], *f.* (—, *pl.* —en) privation, want.

entbieten [ɛnt'biːtən], *v.a. irr. Grüße* —, send o.'s respects.

entbinden [ɛnt'bɪndən], *v.a. irr. einen von etwas* —, release or dispense s.o. from s.th.; (*Med.*) deliver (a woman of a child).

Entbindung [ɛnt'bɪnduŋ], *f.* (—, *pl.* —en) (*Med.*) delivery, child-birth.

entblättern [ɛnt'blɛtərn], *v.a.* strip of leaves.

entblößen [ɛnt'bløːsən], *v.a., v.r. (sich)* —, uncover (o.s.), bare (o.s.).

entdecken [ɛnt'dɛkən], *v.a.* discover, detect.

Ente ['ɛntə], *f.* (—, *pl.* —n) duck; *junge* —, duckling; (*fig.*) hoax, fictitious newspaper report.

entehren [ɛnt'eːrən], *v.a.* dishonour, disgrace; deflower, ravish.

enterben [ɛnt'ɛrbən], *v.a.* disinherit.

Enterich ['ɛntərɪç], *m.* (—s, *pl.* —e) drake.

entfachen [ɛnt'faxən], *v.a.* set ablaze, kindle.

entfahren [ɛnt'faːrən], *v.n. irr.* (*aux.* sein) slip off, escape.

entfallen [ɛnt'falən], *v.n. irr.* (*aux.* sein) escape o.'s memory; be left off.

entfalten [ɛnt'faltən], *v.a.* unfold; display. — *v.r. sich* —, develop, open up, expand.

entfärben [ɛnt'fɛrbən], *v.r. sich* —, lose colour, grow pale.

entfernen [ɛnt'fɛrnən], *v.a.* remove. — *v.r. sich* —, withdraw.

Entfernung [ɛnt'fɛrnuŋ], *f.* (—, *pl.* —en) removal; distance.

entfesseln [ɛnt'fɛsəln], *v.a.* unfetter; let loose.

Entfettungskur [ɛnt'fɛtuŋskuːr], *f.* (—, —en) slimming-cure.

entflammen [ɛnt'flamən], *v.a.* inflame.

entfliegen [ɛnt'fliːgən], *v.n. irr.* (*aux.* sein) fly away.

entfliehen [ɛnt'fliːən], *v.n. irr.* (*aux.* sein) run away, escape, flee.

entfremden [ɛnt'frɛmdən], *v.a.* estrange, alienate.

entführen [ɛnt'fyːrən], *v.a.* abduct, carry off; kidnap; elope with.

entgegen [ɛnt'geːgən], *prep.* (*Dat.*), *adv.* against, contrary to; towards.

Entgegenkommen [ɛnt'geːgənkɔmən], *n.* (—s, *no pl.*) obliging behaviour, courtesy.

entgegenkommen [ɛnt'geːgənkɔmən], *v.n. irr.* (*aux.* sein) come towards s.o., come to meet s.o.; do a favour, oblige.

entgegennehmen [ɛnt'geːgənneːmən], *v.a. irr.* receive, accept.

entgegensehen [ɛnt'geːgənzeːən], *v.n. irr.* await, look forward to.

entgegnen [ɛnt'geːgnən], *v.a.* reply, retort.

Entgegnung [ɛnt'geːgnuŋ], *f.* (—, *pl.* —en) reply, retort, rejoinder.

entgehen [ɛnt'geːən], *v.n. irr.* (*aux.* sein) (*Dat.*) escape; — *lassen,* let slip.

Entgelt [ɛnt'gɛlt], *n.* (—s, *no pl.*) remuneration, recompense.

entgelten [ɛnt'gɛltən], *v.a. irr. einen etwas* — *lassen,* make s.o. pay for s.th. or suffer.

entgleisen [ɛnt'glaɪzən], *v.n.* (*aux.* sein) run off the rails, be derailed.

enthaaren [ɛnt'haːrən], *v.a.* depilate.

enthalten [ɛnt'haltən], *v.a. irr.* hold, contain. — *v.r. sich* —, abstain from, refrain from.

enthaltsam [ɛnt'haltzaːm], *adj.* abstinent, abstemious, temperate.

Enthaltung [ɛnt'haltuŋ], *f.* (—, *no pl.*) abstention.

enthaupten [ɛnt'hauptən], *v.a.* behead, decapitate.

entheben [ɛnt'he:bən], *v.a. irr. einen einer Sache —,* exempt *or* dispense from, suspend from, relieve of.

entheiligen [ɛnt'haɪlɪgən], *v.a.* profane, desecrate.

enthüllen [ɛnt'hylən], *v.a.* unveil; (*fig.*) reveal.

entkleiden [ɛnt'klaɪdən], *v.a.* unclothe, undress, strip.

entkommen [ɛnt'kɔmən], *v.n. irr. (aux. sein)* escape, get off.

entkräften [ɛnt'krɛftən], *v.a.* enfeeble, debilitate, weaken; (*fig.*) refute (an argument).

entladen [ɛnt'la:dən], *v.a. irr.* unload, discharge. — *v.r. sich —,* burst; (*gun*) go off.

Entladung [ɛnt'la:duŋ], *f.* (—, *pl.* —en) unloading, discharge, explosion.

entlang [ɛnt'laŋ], *prep.* along.

entlarven [ɛnt'larfən], *v.a.* unmask; expose.

Entlarvung [ɛnt'larfuŋ], *f.* (—, *pl.* —en) unmasking, exposure.

entlassen [ɛnt'lasən], *v.a. irr.* dismiss; (*Am.*) fire; discharge; pension off.

Entlastung [ɛnt'lastuŋ], *f.* (—, *no pl.*) exoneration; credit (to s.o.'s bank account).

entlaufen [ɛnt'laufən], *v.n. irr. (aux. sein)* run away.

entlausen [ɛnt'lauzən], *v.a.* delouse.

entledigen [ɛnt'le:dɪgən], *v.r. sich einer Sache —,* rid o.s. of *or* get rid of a thing; *sich einer Aufgabe —,* perform a task; discharge a commission.

entleeren [ɛnt'le:rən], *v.a.* empty.

entlegen [ɛnt'le:gən], *adj.* remote, distant, far off.

entlehnen [ɛnt'le:nən], *v.a.* borrow from.

entleihen [ɛnt'laɪən], *v.a. irr.* borrow.

entlocken [ɛnt'lɔkən], *v.a.* elicit from.

entmannen [ɛnt'manən], *v.a.* castrate, emasculate.

entmündigen [ɛnt'myndɪgən], *v.a.* place under care of a guardian *or* (*Law*) trustees.

Entmündigung [ɛnt'myndɪguŋ], *f.* (—, *no pl.*) placing under legal control.

entmutigen [ɛnt'mu:tɪgən], *v.a.* discourage, dishearten.

Entnahme [ɛnt'na:mə], *f.* (—, *pl.* —n) (*money*) withdrawal.

entnehmen [ɛnt'ne:mən], *v.a. irr.* (*money*) withdraw; understand, gather *or* infer from.

entnerven [ɛnt'nɛrfən], *v.a.* enervate.

entpuppen [ɛnt'pupən], *v.r. sich —,* burst from the cocoon; (*fig.*) turn out to be.

enträtseln [ɛnt'rɛ:tsəln], *v.a.* decipher, make out.

entreißen [ɛnt'raɪsən], *v.a. irr.* snatch away from; *einer Gefahr —,* save *or* rescue from danger.

entrichten [ɛnt'rɪçtən], *v.a.* pay (off).

entrinnen [ɛnt'rɪnən], *v.n. irr. (aux. sein)* escape from.

entrückt [ɛnt rykt], *adj.* enraptured.

entrüsten [ɛnt'rystən], *v.a.* make angry, exasperate. — *v.r. sich —,* become angry, fly into a passion.

entsagen [ɛnt'za:gən], *v.n.* renounce; waive; abdicate.

Entsatz [ɛnt'zats], *m.* (—es, *no pl.*) (*Mil.*) relief.

entschädigen [ɛnt'ʃɛ:dɪgən], *v.a.* indemnify, compensate.

entscheiden [ɛnt'ʃaɪdən], *v.a. irr.* decide. — *v.r. sich für,* come to a decision for, decide in favour of.

Entscheidung [ɛnt'ʃaɪduŋ], *f.* (—, *pl.* —en) decision; verdict.

entschieden [ɛnt'ʃi:dən], *adj.* decided, determined, resolute, peremptory.

Entschiedenheit [ɛnt'ʃi:dənhaɪt], *f.* (—, *no pl.*) resolution, firmness, determination.

entschlafen [ɛnt'ʃla:fən], *v.n. irr. (aux. sein)* fall asleep; (*fig.*) die, depart this life.

entschleiern [ɛnt'ʃlaɪərn], *v.a.* unveil.

entschließen [ɛnt'ʃli:sən], *v.r. irr. sich —,* decide (upon), resolve, make up o.'s mind.

Entschlossenheit [ɛnt'ʃlɔsənhaɪt], *f.* (—, *no pl.*) resoluteness, determination.

entschlummern [ɛnt'ʃlumərn], *v.n.* (*aux.* sein) fall asleep.

entschlüpfen [ɛnt'ʃlypfən], *v.n. (aux. sein)* slip away; escape.

Entschluß [ɛnt'ʃlus], *m.* (—sses, *pl.* -̈sse) resolution; *einen — fassen,* resolve (to).

entschuldigen [ɛnt'ʃuldɪgən], *v.a.* excuse. — *v.r. sich —,* apologise.

entschwinden [ɛnt'ʃvɪndən], *v.n. irr. (aux.* sein) disappear, vanish.

entseelt [ɛnt'ze:lt], *adj.* inanimate, lifeless.

entsenden [ɛnt'zɛndən], *v.a. irr.* send off, despatch.

Entsetzen [ɛnt'zɛtsən], *n.* (—s, *no pl.*) horror, terror.

entsetzen [ɛnt'zɛtsən], *v.a.* (*Mil.*) relieve; frighten, shock, fill with horror. — *v.r. sich — über,* be horrified at.

entsetzlich [ɛnt'zɛtslɪç], *adj.* horrible, terrible, dreadful, awful.

entsiegeln [ɛnt'zi:gəln], *v.a.* unseal.

entsinnen [ɛnt'zɪnən], *v.r. sich einer Sache —,* recollect, remember, call s.th. to mind.

entspannen [ɛnt'ʃpanən], *v.a., v.r. (sich) —,* relax.

entspinnen [ɛnt'ʃpɪnən], *v.r. irr. sich —,* arise, begin.

entsprechen [ɛnt'ʃprɛçən], *v.n. irr.* respond to, correspond to, meet, suit.

entsprechend [ɛnt'ʃprɛçənt], *adj.* corresponding, suitable.

entsprießen [ɛnt'ʃpri:sən], *v.n. irr.* (*aux.* sein) spring up, sprout.

entspringen [ɛnt'ʃprɪŋən], *v.n. irr.* (*aux.* sein) escape, originate from; (*river*) have its source at, rise.

61

entstammen

entstammen [ɛntˈʃtamən], v.n. (aux. sein) spring from, originate from.

entstehen [ɛntˈʃteːən], v.n. irr. (aux. sein) arise, originate, begin, result, spring from.

Entstehung [ɛntˈʃteːʊŋ], f. (—, no pl.) origin, rise.

entstellen [ɛntˈʃtɛlən], v.a. disfigure, deform, distort; (fig.) garble.

entsühnen [ɛntˈzyːnən], v.a. free from sin, purify, purge.

enttäuschen [ɛntˈtɔyʃən], v.a. disappoint.

entthronen [ɛntˈtroːnən], v.a. dethrone.

entvölkern [ɛntˈfœlkərn], v.a. depopulate.

entwachsen [ɛntˈvaksən], v.n. irr. (aux. sein) grow out of, outgrow.

entwaffnen [ɛntˈvafnən], v.a. disarm.

entwässern [ɛntˈvɛsərn], v.a. drain.

entweder [ɛntˈveːdər], conj. either; — ......oder, either ...... or.

entweichen [ɛntˈvaɪçən], v.n. irr. escape, run away.

entweihen [ɛntˈvaɪən], v.a. profane, desecrate.

entwenden [ɛntˈvɛndən], v.a. take away, steal, embezzle.

entwerfen [ɛntˈvɛrfən], v.a. irr. design, sketch, plan, draw up.

entwerten [ɛntˈvɛrtən], v.a. reduce in value, depreciate; (stamps) cancel.

entwickeln [ɛntˈvɪkəln], v.a. unfold, develop; (ideas) explain, explicate. — v.r. sich —, develop (into), evolve.

Entwicklung [ɛntˈvɪklʊŋ], f. (—, pl. —en) unfolding, development, evolution.

entwinden [ɛntˈvɪndən], v.a. irr. wrench from, wrest from.

entwirren [ɛntˈvɪrən], v.a. unravel, disentangle.

entwischen [ɛntˈvɪʃən], v.n. (aux. sein) slip away, escape.

entwöhnen [ɛntˈvøːnən], v.a. disaccustom; break off a habit; (baby) wean.

entwürdigen [ɛntˈvyrdɪgən], v.a. disgrace, degrade.

Entwurf [ɛntˈvurf], m. (—s, pl. ∵e) sketch, design, draft, plan, project.

entwurzeln [ɛntˈvurtsəln], v.a. uproot.

entziehen [ɛntˈtsiːən], v.a. irr. withdraw, take away, deprive of.

entziffern [ɛntˈtsɪfərn], v.a. decipher.

entzücken [ɛntˈtsykən], v.a. enchant, delight, charm.

entzündbar [ɛntˈtsyntbaːr], adj. inflammable.

entzünden [ɛntˈtsyndən], v.a. set on fire, light the fire; (fig.) inflame. — v.r. sich —, catch fire, ignite; (Med.) become inflamed.

Entzündung [ɛntˈtsyndʊŋ], f. (—, pl. —en) kindling, setting on fire; (Med.) inflammation.

entzwei [ɛntˈtsvaɪ], adv. in two, broken.

entzweien [ɛntˈtsvaɪən], v.a. disunite.

Enzian [ˈɛntsjan], m. (—s, pl. —e) (Bot.) gentian.

Enzyklopädie [ɛntsyklopɛˈdiː], f. (—, pl. —n) encyclopædia.

Epidemie [epiˈdeːmiː], f. (—, pl. —en) epidemic.

epidemisch [epiˈdeːmɪʃ], adj. epidemic(al).

Epik [ˈeːpɪk], f. (—, no pl.) epic poetry.

episch [ˈeːpɪʃ], adj. epic.

Epos [ˈeːpɔs], n. (—, pl. Epen) epic poem.

Equipage [ekviˈpaːʒə], f. (—, pl. —n) carriage.

er [eːr], pers. pron. he.

Erachten [ɛrˈaxtən], n. (—s, no pl.) opinion, judgment; meines —s, in my opinion.

erachten [ɛrˈaxtən], v.a. think, consider.

erarbeiten [ɛrˈarbaɪtən], v.a. gain or achieve by working.

erb [ˈɛrb], adj. (in compounds) hereditary.

erbarmen [ɛrˈbarmən], v.r. sich —, have mercy (on), take pity (on).

erbärmlich [ɛrˈbɛrmlɪç], adj. miserable, pitiful; contemptible.

erbauen [ɛrˈbauən], v.a. build, erect; (fig.) edify.

erbaulich [ɛrˈbaulɪç], adj. edifying.

Erbauung [ɛrˈbauʊŋ], f. (—, no pl.) building, erection; (fig.) edification.

Erbbesitz [ˈɛrpbazɪts], m. (—es, pl. —e) hereditary possession.

Erbe [ˈɛrbə], m. (—n, pl. —n) heir. n. (—s, no pl.) inheritance; heritage.

erbeben [ɛrˈbeːbən], v.n. (aux. sein) shake, tremble, quake.

erbeigen [ˈɛrpaɪgən], adj. inherited.

erben [ˈɛrbən], v.a. inherit.

erbeten [ɛrˈbeːtən], v.a. sich etwas —, ask for s.th. by prayer; request.

erbetteln [ɛrˈbɛtəln], v.a. obtain by begging.

erbeuten [ɛrˈbɔytən], v.a. take as booty.

Erbfeind [ˈɛrpfaɪnt], m. (—s, pl. —e) sworn enemy.

Erbfolge [ˈɛrpfɔlgə], f. (—, no pl.) succession.

erbieten [ɛrˈbiːtən], v.r. irr. sich —, offer to do s.th.; volunteer; Ehre —, do homage.

Erbin [ˈɛrbɪn], f. (—, pl. —nen) heiress.

erbitten [ɛrˈbɪtən], v.a. irr. beg, request, ask for, gain by asking.

erbittern [ɛrˈbɪtərn], v.a. embitter, anger, exasperate.

erblassen [ɛrˈblasən], v.n. (aux. sein) turn pale.

Erblasser [ˈɛrplasər], m. (—s, pl. —) testator.

erbleichen [ɛrˈblaɪçən], v.n. irr. (aux. sein) turn pale, lose colour.

erblich [ˈɛrplɪç], adj. hereditary, congenital.

erblicken [ɛrˈblɪkən], v.a. perceive, behold, catch sight of.

erblinden [ɛrˈblɪndən], v.n. (aux. sein) turn blind.

erblos [ˈɛrploːs], adj. disinherited; without an heir.

62

erblühen [ɛr'bly:ən], *v.n.* (*aux.* sein) blossom (out).

Erbmasse ['ɛrpmasə], *f.* (—, *no pl.*) estate.

erbosen [ɛr'bo:zən], *v.a.* make angry. — *v.r.* *sich* —, become angry.

erbötig [ɛr'bø:tɪç], *adj.* — *sein*, be willing, be ready.

Erbpacht ['ɛrppaxt], *f.* (—, *pl.* —en) hereditary tenure.

erbrechen [ɛr'brɛçən], *v.a. irr.* break open, open by force. — *v.r. sich* —, vomit.

Erbrecht ['ɛrprɛçt], *n.* (—s, *no pl.*) law (*or* right) of succession.

Erbschaft ['ɛrpʃaft], *f.* (—, *pl.* —en) inheritance, heritage, legacy.

Erbse ['ɛrpsə], *f.* (—, *pl.* —n) pea.

Erbstück ['ɛrpʃtyk], *n.* (—s, *pl.* —e) heirloom.

Erbsünde ['ɛrpzyndə], *f.* (—, *no pl.*) original sin.

Erbteil ['ɛrptaɪl], *n.* (—s, *pl.* —e) portion of inheritance.

Erdapfel ['ɛr:tapfəl], *m.* (—s, *pl.* ⸚) (*Austr.*) potato.

Erdbahn ['ɛr:tba:n], *f.* (—, *no pl.*) orbit of the earth.

Erdball ['ɛr:tbal], *m.* (—s, *no pl.*) terrestrial globe.

Erdbeben ['ɛr:tbe:bən], *n.* (—s, *pl.* —) earthquake.

Erdbeere ['ɛr:tbe:rə], *f.* (—, *pl.* —n) strawberry.

Erde ['ɛr:də], *f.* (—, *pl.* —n) earth, soil ground.

erden ['ɛr:dən], *v.a.* (*Rad.*) earth.

erdenken [ɛr'dɛŋkən], *v.a. irr.* think out; invent. — *v.r. sich etwas* —, invent s.th., devise s.th.

erdenklich [ɛr'dɛŋklɪç], *adj.* imaginable, conceivable.

Erdenleben ['ɛr:dənle:bən], *n.* (—s, *no pl.*) life on this earth.

Erdfall ['ɛr:tfal], *m.* (—s, *pl.* ⸚e) landslip.

Erdfläche ['ɛr:tflɛçə], *f.* (—, *no pl.*) surface of the earth.

Erdgeschoß ['ɛr:tgəʃɔs], *n.* (—sses, *pl.* —sse) ground floor.

Erdhügel ['ɛr:thy:gəl], *m.* (—s, *pl.* —) mound of earth.

erdichten [ɛr'dɪçtən], *v.a.* think out, invent, feign.

Erdkunde ['ɛr:tkundə], *f.* (—, *no pl.*) geography.

Erdleitung ['ɛr:tlaɪtuŋ], *f.* (—, *pl.* —en) earth circuit, earth connexion.

Erdmaus ['ɛr:tmaus], *f.* (—, *pl.* ⸚e) field mouse.

Erdmolch ['ɛr:tmɔlç], *m.* (—s, *pl.* —e) salamander.

Erdnuß ['ɛr:tnus], *f.* (—, *pl.* ⸚sse) groundnut, peanut.

Erdöl ['ɛr:tø:l], *n.* (—s, *no pl.*) petroleum, mineral oil.

erdolchen [ɛr'dɔlçən], *v.a.* stab (with a dagger).

Erdpech ['ɛr:tpɛç], *n.* (—s, *no pl.*) bitumen.

erdreisten [ɛr'draɪstən], *v.r. sich* —, dare, have the audacity.

erdrosseln [ɛr'drɔsəln], *v.a.* strangle, throttle.

erdrücken [ɛr'drykən], *v.a.* crush to death.

Erdrutsch ['ɛ:rtrutʃ], *m.* (—es, *no pl.*) landslip, landslide.

Erdschicht ['ɛ:rtʃɪçt], *f.* (—, *pl.* —en) (*Geol.*) layer, stratum.

Erdschnecke ['ɛ:rtʃnɛkə], *f.* (—, *pl.* —n) slug, snail.

Erdscholle ['ɛ:rtʃɔlə], *f.* (—, *pl.* —n) clod (of earth).

Erdsturz ['ɛ:rtʃturts], *m.* (—es, *no pl.*) landslide.

erdulden [ɛr'duldən], *v.a.* suffer, endure.

Erdumseg(e)lung ['ɛ:rtumzɛːg(ə)luŋ], *f.* (—, *pl.* —en) circumnavigation of the earth.

ereifern [ɛr'aɪfərn], *v.r. sich* —, become heated, get excited.

ereignen [ɛr'aɪgnən], *v.r. sich* —, happen, come to pass.

Ereignis [ɛr'aɪknɪs], *n.* (—ses, *pl.* —se) event, occurrence, happening.

ereilen [ɛr'aɪlən], *v.a.* overtake, befall.

Eremit [ere'mi:t], *m.* (—en, *pl.* —en) hermit, recluse.

erfahren [ɛr'fa:rən], *v.a. irr.* learn, hear; experience. — *adj.* experienced, practised; conversant with, versed in.

Erfahrenheit [ɛr'fa:rənhaɪt], *f.* (—, *no pl.*) experience, skill.

Erfahrung [ɛr'fa:ruŋ], *f.* (—, *pl.* —en) experience, knowledge, expertness, skill: *in* — *bringen*, ascertain, come to know.

erfahrungsgemäß [ɛr'fa:ruŋsgəmɛːs], *adj.* based on *or* according to experience.

erfahrungsmäßig [ɛr'fa:ruŋsmɛːsɪç], *adj.* based on experience; empirical.

erfassen [ɛr'fasən], *v.a.* get hold of, seize, comprehend, grasp.

erfinden [ɛr'fɪndən], *v.a. irr.* invent, contrive.

erfinderisch [ɛr'fɪndərɪʃ], *adj.* inventive, ingenious.

Erfindung [ɛr'fɪnduŋ], *f.* (—, *pl.* —en) invention; contrivance.

Erfolg [ɛr'fɔlk], *m.* (—s, *pl.* —e) success; result; effect; — *haben*, succeed, be successful; *keinen* — *haben*, fail.

erfolgen [ɛr'fɔlgən], *v.n.* (*aux.* sein) ensue, follow, result.

erfolgreich [ɛr'fɔlkraɪç], *adj.* successful.

erforderlich [ɛr'fɔrdərlɪç], *adj.* necessary, required.

erfordern [ɛr'fɔrdərn], *v.a.* demand, require.

Erfordernis [ɛr'fɔrdərnɪs], *n.* (—ses, *pl.* —se) necessity, requirement, requisite.

erforschen [ɛr'fɔrʃən], *v.a.* explore, investigate, conduct research into.

erfragen [ɛr'fra:gən], *v.a.* find out by asking, ascertain.

erfreuen [ɛr'frɔyən], *v.a.* gladden, cheer, delight. — *v.r. sich* — *an*, enjoy, take pleasure in.

63

erfreulich [ɛr'frɔylıç], *adj.* pleasing, gratifying.

erfrieren [ɛr'fri:rən], *v.n. irr.* (*aux.* sein) freeze to death, die of exposure; become numb.

erfrischen [ɛr'frıʃən], *v.a.* refresh.

erfüllen [ɛr'fylən], *v.a.* fulfil, keep (promise); comply with; perform; *seinen Zweck —*, serve its purpose. — *v.r. sich —*, come true, be fulfilled.

Erfüllung [ɛr'fylun], *f.* (—, *no pl.*) fulfilment; granting; performance; *in — gehen*, come true, be realised.

ergänzen [ɛr'gɛntsən], *v.a.* complete, complement.

Ergänzung [ɛr'gɛntsuŋ], *f.* (—, *pl.* —en) completion; complement, supplement.

ergattern [ɛr'gatərn], *v.a.* pick up.

ergeben [ɛr'ge:bən], *v.a. irr.* give, yield, prove, show. — *v.r. sich —*, surrender (to), acquiesce (in); happen, result, follow. — *adj.* devoted, submissive, humble, obedient.

Ergebenheit [ɛr'ge:bənhaıt], *f.* (—, *no pl.*) devotion, obedience, humility, fidelity.

ergebenst [ɛr'ge:bənst], *adj. Ihr —er* (*letter ending*), yours very truly, your obedient servant. — *adv.* respectfully.

Ergebnis [ɛr'ge:pnıs], *n.* (—ses, *pl.* —se) outcome, result; (*Agr.*) yield.

Ergebung [ɛr'ge:buŋ], *f.* (—, *no pl.*) submission, resignation; surrender.

Ergehen [ɛr'ge:ən], *n.* (—s, *no pl.*) health, condition, well-being.

ergehen [ɛr'ge:ən], *v.n. irr.* (*aux.* sein) be promulgated *or* issued; — *lassen*, issue, publish; *etwas über sich — lassen*, submit to *or* suffer s.th. patiently. — *v.r. sich —*, (*obs.*) take a stroll.

ergiebig [ɛr'gi:bıç], *adj.* rich, productive, fertile, profitable.

ergießen [ɛr'gi:sən], *v.r. irr. sich —*, discharge, flow into.

erglänzen [ɛr'glɛntsən], *v.n.* (*aux.* sein) shine forth, sparkle.

erglühen [ɛr'gly:ən], *v.n.* (*aux.* sein) glow; blush.

ergötzen [ɛr'gœtsən], *v.a.* (*obs.*) amuse, delight. — *v.r. sich — an*, delight in.

ergrauen [ɛr'grauən], *v.n.* (*aux.* sein) become grey; grow old.

ergreifen [ɛr'graıfən], *v.a. irr.* seize, grasp, get hold of; move, touch, affect; *Maßnahmen —*, take measures.

Ergreifung [ɛr'graıfuŋ], *f.* (—, *no pl.*) seizure; (*measure*) adoption.

ergriffen [ɛr'grıfən], *adj.* moved, touched, impressed.

Ergriffenheit [ɛr'grıfənhaıt], *f.* (—, *no pl.*) emotion.

ergrimmen [ɛr'grımən], *v.n.* (*aux.* sein) grow angry, be enraged.

ergründen [ɛr'gryndən], *v.a.* get to the bottom of, investigate, fathom.

Erguß [ɛr'gus], *m.* (—sses, *pl.* -sse) outpouring; (*fig.*) effusion.

erhaben [ɛr'ha:bən], *adj.* sublime, exalted; majestic, elevated.

Erhabenheit [ɛr'ha:bənhaıt], *f.* (—, *no pl.*) majesty, sublimity.

erhalten [ɛr'haltən], *v.a. irr.* receive, obtain, get, preserve; maintain, keep up. — *v.r. sich — von*, subsist on.

erhältlich [ɛr'hɛltlıç], *adj.* obtainable.

Erhaltung [ɛr'haltuŋ], *f.* (—, *no pl.*) preservation, conservation; (*family*) maintenance.

erhärten [ɛr'hɛrtən], *v.a.* make hard; (*fig.*) prove, confirm.

erhaschen [ɛr'haʃən], *v.a.* catch, snatch.

erheben [ɛr'he:bən], *v.a. irr.* lift up, raise; (*fig.*) elevate, exalt; *Klage —*, bring an action; *Geld —*, raise money; *Steuern —*, levy taxes. — *v.r. sich —*, rise, stand up.

erheblich [ɛr'he:plıç], *adj.* considerable, weighty, appreciable.

Erhebung [ɛr'he:buŋ], *f.* (—, *pl.* —en) elevation; (*taxes*) levying; revolt, rebellion, rising.

erheischen [ɛr'haıʃən], *v.a.* (*rare*) require, demand.

erheitern [ɛr'haıtərn], *v.a.* cheer, exhilarate.

erhellen [ɛr'hɛlən], *v.a.* light up, illuminate; (*fig.*) enlighten. — *v.n.* become evident.

erhitzen [ɛr'hıtsən], *v.a.* heat; (*fig.*) inflame, excite. — *v.r. sich —*, grow hot; grow angry.

erhöhen [ɛr'hø:ən], *v.a.* heighten, raise, intensify, increase; (*value*) enhance.

erholen [ɛr'ho:lən], *v.r. sich —*, recover, get better; relax (after work); take a rest.

erholungsbedürftig [ɛr'ho:luŋsbədyrftıç], *adj.* in need of a rest.

erhören [ɛr'hø:rən], *v.a.* hear, vouchsafe, grant.

Erich ['e:rıç], *m.* Eric.

erinnerlich [ɛr'ınərlıç], *adj.* remembered; *soweit mir — ist*, as far as I can remember.

erinnern [ɛr'ınərn], *v.a.* remind. — *v.r. sich —*, remember, recollect, recall, call to mind.

Erinnerung [ɛr'ınəruŋ], *f.* (—, *pl.* —en) remembrance; recollection; reminiscences.

erjagen [ɛr'ja:gən], *v.a.* hunt (down), chase.

erkalten [ɛr'kaltən], *v.n.* (*aux.* sein) grow cold.

erkälten [ɛr'kɛltən], *v.r. sich —*, catch cold.

Erkältung [ɛr'kɛltuŋ], *f.* (—, *pl.* —en) cold, chill.

erkämpfen [ɛr'kɛmpfən], *v.a.* obtain by fighting; obtain by great exertion.

erkaufen [ɛr'kaufən], *v.a.* purchase; bribe, corrupt.

erkennen [ɛr'kɛnən], *v.a. irr.* recognise, perceive, distinguish, discern; (*Comm.*) credit; *zu — geben*, give to understand; *sich zu — geben*, make o.s. known. — *v.n.* (*Law*) judge; — *auf*, (*Law*) announce verdict, pass sentence.

erkenntlich [ɛr'kɛntlɪç], *adj.* grateful; (*fig.*) *sich — zeigen*, show o.s. grateful.

Erkenntlichkeit [ɛr'kɛntlɪçkaɪt], *f.* (—, *no pl.*) gratitude.

Erkenntnis [ɛr'kɛntnɪs], *f.* (—, *pl.* —e) perception, knowledge, comprehension, understanding; realisation, (*Phil.*) cognition.

Erkennung [ɛr'kɛnuŋ], *f.* (—, *no pl.*) recognition.

Erker ['ɛrkər], *m.* (—s, *pl.* —) alcove, bay, turret.

Erkerfenster ['ɛrkərfɛnstər], *n.* (—s, *pl.* —) bay-window.

erklären [ɛr'klɛːrən], *v.a.* explain, expound, account for; make a statement on, declare, state.

erklärlich [ɛr'klɛːrlɪç], *adj.* explicable.

Erklärung [ɛr'klɛːruŋ], *f.* (—, *pl.* —en) explanation; declaration, statement; (*income tax*) return.

erklecklich [ɛr'klɛklɪç], *adj.* considerable.

erklettern [ɛr'klɛtərn], *v.a.* climb.

erklimmen [ɛr'klɪmən], *v.a. irr.* climb.

erklingen [ɛr'klɪŋən], *v.n. irr.* (*aux.* sein) sound, resound.

erkoren [ɛr'koːrən], *adj.* select, chosen.

erkranken [ɛr'kraŋkən], *v.n.* (*aux.* sein) fall ill.

erkühnen [ɛr'kyːnən], *v.r. sich —*, dare, make bold, venture.

erkunden [ɛr'kundən], *v.a.* explore, find out; (*Mil.*) reconnoitre.

erkundigen [ɛr'kundɪgən], *v.r. sich —*, enquire (about), make enquiries.

erlaben [ɛr'laːbən], *v.r. sich —*, (*obs.*) refresh o.s.

erlahmen [ɛr'laːmən], *v.n.* (*aux.* sein) become lame; lose o.'s drive; grow tired.

erlangen [ɛr'laŋən], *v.a.* reach, gain, obtain; acquire; attain.

Erlaß [ɛr'las], *m.* (—sses, *pl.* ᷿sse) remission, exemption, release, dispensation; (*Comm.*) deduction; (*Law, Pol.*) proclamation, edict, decree, writ; (*Eccl.*) indulgence; remission.

erlassen [ɛr'lasən], *v.a. irr.* remit, release, let off; (*Law, Pol.*) enact, promulgate.

erläßlich [ɛr'lɛslɪç], *adj.* remissible, dispensable, venial.

erlauben [ɛr'laubən], *v.a.* permit, allow; *sich etwas —*, take the liberty of, make bold to; have the impertinence to.

Erlaubnis [ɛr'laupnɪs], *f.* (—, *no pl.*) permission, leave, permit; *die — haben*, be permitted; *um — bitten*, beg leave; *mit Ihrer —*, by your leave.

erlaucht [ɛr'lauxt], *adj.* illustrious, noble.

erlauschen [ɛr'lauʃən], *v.a.* overhear.

erläutern [ɛr'lɔytərn], *v.a.* explain, illustrate, elucidate.

Erle ['ɛrlə], *f.* (—, *pl.* —n) (*Bot.*) alder.

erleben [ɛr'leːbən], *v.a.* live to see; go through, experience.

Erlebnis [ɛr'leːpnɪs], *n.* (—sses, *pl.* —sse) experience, adventure, occurrence.

erledigen [ɛr'leːdɪgən], *v.a.* settle, finish off, clear up; dispatch; execute (commission etc.).

erledigt [ɛr'leːdɪçt], *adj.* (*coll.*) worn-out; exhausted.

erlegen [ɛr'leːgən], *v.a.* slay; pay down.

erleichtern [ɛr'laɪçtərn], *v.a.* lighten, ease, facilitate.

erleiden [ɛr'laɪdən], *v.a. irr.* suffer, endure, bear, undergo.

erlernen [ɛr'lɛrnən], *v.a.* learn, acquire.

erlesen [ɛr'leːzən], *v.a. irr.* select, choose. — *adj.* select, choice.

erleuchten [ɛr'lɔyçtən], *v.a.* illumine, illuminate, floodlight; (*fig.*) enlighten, inspire.

erliegen [ɛr'liːgən], *v.n. irr.* (*aux.* sein) succumb.

Erlkönig ['ɛrlkøːnɪç], *m.* (—s, *pl.* —e) fairy-king, elf-king.

erlogen [ɛr'loːgən], *adj.* false, untrue; trumped-up.

Erlös [ɛr'løːs], *m.* (—es, *no pl.*) proceeds.

erlöschen [ɛr'lœʃən], *v.n. irr.* (*aux.* sein) be extinguished, die out; (*fire*) go out; (*contract*) expire.

erlösen [ɛr'løːzən], *v.a.* redeem; release, save, deliver.

ermächtigen [ɛr'mɛçtɪgən], *v.a.* empower; authorise.

ermahnen [ɛr'maːnən], *v.a.* admonish, exhort, remind.

ermäßigen [ɛr'mɛːsɪgən], *v.a.* reduce.

ermatten [ɛr'matən], *v.a.* weaken, weary, tire. — *v.n.* (*aux.* sein) grow weak, become tired.

Ermessen [ɛr'mɛsən], *n.* (—s, *no pl.*) judgment, opinion.

ermitteln [ɛr'mɪtəln], *v.a.* ascertain, find out.

ermöglichen [ɛr'møːklɪçən], *v.a.* make possible.

ermorden [ɛr'mɔrdən], *v.a.* murder.

ermüden [ɛr'myːdən], *v.a.* tire, fatigue. — *v.n.* (*aux.* sein) get tired, grow weary.

ermuntern [ɛr'muntərn], *v.a.* encourage, cheer up.

ermutigen [ɛr'muːtɪgən], *v.a.* encourage.

ernähren [ɛr'nɛːrən], *v.a.* nourish, feed.

ernennen [ɛr'nɛnən], *v.a. irr.* nominate, appoint.

erneuern [ɛr'nɔyərn], *v.a.* renew, repair, renovate.

erniedrigen [ɛr'niːdrɪgən], *v.a.* humble, humiliate, degrade. — *v.r. sich —*, humble o.s., abase o.s.

Ernst (1) [ɛrnst], *m.* Ernest.

Ernst (2) [ɛrnst], *m.* (—es, *no pl.*) earnestness, seriousness.

ernst [ɛrnst], *adj.* earnest, serious.

Ernte ['ɛrntə], *f.* (—, *pl.* —n) harvest, crop.

ernüchtern [ɛr'nyçtərn], *v.a.* sober; (*fig.*) disenchant, disillusion.

erobern [ɛr'oːbərn], *v.a.* (*Mil.*) conquer; take, win.

eröffnen [ɛr'œfnən], *v.a.* open, inaugurate; inform, reveal.

erörtern [ɛr'œrtərn], *v.a.* discuss, debate, argue.

65

erpicht [ɛr'pɪçt], *adj.* eager for, bent on.

erpressen [ɛr'prɛsən], *v.a.* extort, blackmail.

erquicken [ɛr'kvɪkən], *v.a.* refresh.

erraten [ɛr'ra:tən], *v.a. irr.* guess.

erregen [ɛr're:gən], *v.a.* cause; stir up, excite, agitate; provoke.

erreichen [ɛr'raɪçən], *v.a.* reach, arrive at; (*fig.*) attain, reach.

erretten [ɛr'rɛtən], *v.a.* save, rescue.

errichten [ɛr'rɪçtən], *v.a.* erect, raise, build.

erringen [ɛr'rɪŋən], *v.a. irr.* obtain (by exertion), achieve.

erröten [ɛr'rø:tən], *v.n.* (*aux.* sein) blush, redden.

Errungenschaft [ɛr'ruŋənʃaft], *f.* (—, *pl.* —en) achievement, acquisition.

Ersatz [ɛr'zats], *m.* (—es, *no pl.*) substitute; compensation, amends; (*Mil. etc.*) replacement.

erschallen [ɛr'ʃalən], *v.n.* (*aux.* sein) resound, sound.

erschaudern [ɛr'ʃaudərn], *v.n.* (*aux.* sein) be seized with horror.

erscheinen [ɛr'ʃaɪnən], *v.n. irr.* (*aux.* sein) appear, make o.'s appearance; seem; be published.

erschießen [ɛr'ʃi:sən], *v.a. irr.* shoot dead.

erschlaffen [ɛr'ʃlafən], *v.n.* (*aux.* sein) flag, slacken.

erschlagen [ɛr'ʃla:gən], *v.a. irr.* slay, kill.

erschließen [ɛr'ʃli:sən], *v.a. irr.* open up.

erschöpfen [ɛr'ʃœpfən], *v.a.* exhaust.

erschrecken [ɛr'ʃrɛkən], *v.a. irr.* startle, shock, terrify. — *v.n.* (*aux.* sein) be startled, be frightened, be terrified.

erschüttern [ɛr'ʃytərn], *v.a.* shake; (*fig.*) move, affect strongly.

erschweren [ɛr'ʃve:rən], *v.a.* (*fig.*) aggravate, make more difficult.

erschwingen [ɛr'ʃvɪŋən], *v.a. irr.* afford, be able to pay.

erschwinglich [ɛr'ʃvɪŋlɪç], *adj.* attainable, within o.'s means.

ersehen [ɛr'ze:ən], *v.a. irr.* — *aus,* gather (from).

ersehnen [ɛr'ze:nən], *v.a.* long for, yearn for.

ersetzen [ɛr'zɛtsən], *v.a.* replace, take the place of; restore, make good; repair; (*money*) refund.

ersichtlich [ɛr'zɪçtlɪç], *adj.* evident.

ersinnen [ɛr'zɪnən], *v.a. irr.* think out; imagine, devise, contrive.

ersparen [ɛr'ʃpa:rən], *v.a.* save.

ersprießlich [ɛr'ʃpri:slɪç], *adj.* useful, profitable, beneficial.

erst [e:rst], *num. adj.* first. — *adv.* first, at first, only, but; — *jetzt,* only now; *nun — recht,* now more than ever.

erstatten [ɛr'ʃtatən], *v.a.* reimburse, compensate, repay; *Bericht —,* report.

Erstattung [ɛr'ʃtatuŋ], *f.* (—, *pl.* —en) reimbursement, restitution.

Erstaufführung ['e:rstauffy:ruŋ], *f.* (—, *pl.* —en) (*Theat.*) first night; première.

Erstaunen [ɛr'ʃtaunən], *n.* (—s, *no pl.*) amazement, astonishment, surprise.

erstechen [ɛr'ʃtɛçən], *v.a. irr.* stab.

erstehen [ɛr'ʃte:ən], *v.n.* (*aux.* sein) rise, arise. — *v.a.* buy, purchase.

ersteigen [ɛr'ʃtaɪgən], *v.a. irr.* climb, mount, ascend.

ersticken [ɛr'ʃtɪkən], *v.a. irr.* choke, stifle, suffocate. — *v.n.* (*aux.* sein) choke, suffocate.

erstmalig ['e:rstma:lɪç], *adj.* first. — *adv.* for the first time.

erstreben [ɛr'ʃtre:bən], *v.a.* strive after.

erstrecken [ɛr'ʃtrɛkən], *v.r. sich —,* extend, reach to.

ersuchen [ɛr'zu:xən], *v.a.* request, ask.

ertappen [ɛr'tapən], *v.a.* catch, detect.

erteilen [ɛr'taɪlən], *v.a.* bestow, impart; *einen Auftrag —,* issue an order; *Unterricht —,* instruct; *die Erlaubnis —,* give permission.

ertönen [ɛr'tø:nən], *v.n.* (*aux.* sein) sound, resound.

Ertrag [ɛr'tra:k], *m.* (—s, *pl.* -̈e) produce; returns, yield; output; (*sale*) proceeds.

ertragen [ɛr'tra:gən], *v.a. irr.* bear, suffer, endure.

ertränken [ɛr'trɛnkən], *v.a.* drown.

ertrinken [ɛr'trɪŋkən], *v.n. irr.* (*aux.* sein) drown, be drowned.

erübrigen [ɛr'y:brɪgən], *v.a.* save, spare.

erwachen [ɛr'vaxən], *v.n.* (*aux.* sein) awake, wake up.

erwachsen [ɛr'vaksən], *adj.* grown-up, adult. — *v.n. irr.* grow up; ensue, follow, arise.

erwägen [ɛr've:gən], *v.a. irr.* weigh, ponder, consider.

erwähnen [ɛr'vɛ:nən], *v.a.* mention.

erwärmen [ɛr'vɛrmən], *v.a.* warm (up), make warm.

erwarten [ɛr'vartən], *v.a.* expect, await.

Erwartung [ɛr'vartuŋ], *f.* (—, *pl.* —en) expectation.

erwecken [ɛr'vɛkən], *v.a.* wake up, awaken, raise; rouse.

erwehren [ɛr've:rən], *v.r. sich —* (*Genit.*), defend o.s.; *ich kann mich des Lachens nicht —,* I cannot help laughing.

erweichen [ɛr'vaɪçən], *v.a.* soften.

erweisen [ɛr'vaɪzən], *v.a. irr.* prove, show; demonstrate.

erweitern [ɛr'vaɪtərn], *v.a.* widen, enlarge, expand.

erwerben [ɛr'vɛrbən], *v.a. irr.* acquire.

erwidern [ɛr'vi:dərn], *v.a.* reply, answer; return.

erwirken [ɛr'vɪrkən], *v.a.* effect, secure.

erwischen [ɛr'vɪʃən], *v.a. see* ertappen.

erwünschen [ɛr'vynʃən], *v.a.* desire, wish for.

erwürgen [ɛr'vyrgən], *v.a.* strangle, throttle.

Erz [ɛrts], (—es, *pl.* —e) ore; brass, bronze.

erzählen [ɛr'tsɛ:lən], *v.a.* narrate, relate, tell.

Erzbischof ['ɛrtsbɪʃɔf], *m.* (—s, *pl.* ⁓e) archbishop.

erzeugen [ɛr'tsɔygən], *v.a.* engender; beget; produce; (*Elec.*) generate.

Erzherzog ['ɛrtshɛrtso:k], *m.* (—s, *pl.* ⁓e) archduke.

erziehen [ɛr'tsi:ən], *v.a. irr.* educate, train, bring up, rear.

Erziehungsanstalt [ɛr'tsi:uŋsanʃtalt], *f.* (—, *pl.* —en) approved school, reformatory.

erzielen [ɛr'tsi:lən], *v.a.* obtain; fetch, realize (a price); *Gewinn* —, make a profit.

erzittern [ɛr'tsɪtərn], *v.n.* (*aux.* sein) tremble, shake.

Erzofen ['ɛrtso:fən], *m.* (—s, *pl.* ⁓n) furnace.

erzürnen [ɛr'tsyrnən], *v.a.* make angry. — *v.r. sich* —, grow angry.

Erzvater ['ɛrtsfa:tər], *m.* (—s, *pl.* ⁓) patriarch.

erzwingen [ɛr'tsvɪŋən], *v.a. irr.* enforce, force, compel.

es [ɛs], *pron.* it; — *gibt*, there is; — *sind*, there are; — *lebe*, long live!

Es [ɛs], *n.* (—, *pl.* —) (*Mus.*) E flat.

Esche ['ɛʃə], *f.* (—, *pl.* —n) (*Bot.*) ash, ashtree.

Esel [e:zəl], *m.* (—s, *pl.* —) ass, donkey.

Eselsohr ['e:zəlso:r], *n.* (—s, *pl.* —en) (*fig.*) dog's ear.

Eskadron [ɛska'dro:n], *f.* (—, *pl.* —en) squadron.

Espe ['ɛspə], *f.* (—, *pl.* —n) (*Bot.*) asp, aspen.

eßbar ['ɛsba:r], *adj.* edible.

Esse ['ɛsə], *f.* (—, *pl.* —n) chimney, forge.

Essen ['ɛsən], *n.* (—s, *no pl.*) meal; eating.

essen ['ɛsən], *v.a. irr.* eat, have a meal.

Essenz [ɛ'sɛnts], *f.* (—, *pl.* —en) essence.

Essig ['ɛsɪç], *m.* (—s, *no pl.*) vinegar.

Eßlöffel ['ɛslœfəl], *m.* (—s, *pl.* —) table-spoon.

Estland ['ɛstlant], *n.* Estonia.

Estrade [ɛ'stra:də], *f.* (—, *pl.* —n) platform.

Estrich ['ɛstrɪç], *m.* (—s, *no pl.*) floor, flooring, plaster-floor.

etablieren [eta'bli:rən], *v.a.* establish, set up (business).

Etagenwohnung [e'ta:ʒənvo:nuŋ], *f.* (—, *pl.* —en) flat; (*Am.*) apartment.

Etappe [e'tapə], *f.* (—, *pl.* —n) stage; (*Mil.*) lines of communication.

Etat [e'ta:], *m.* (—s, *pl.* —s) (*Parl.*) estimates, budget; (*Comm.*) statement, balance sheet.

ethisch ['e:tɪʃ], *adj.* ethical.

Etikett [eti'kɛt], *n.* (—s, *pl.* —s) label, ticket, tag.

Etikette [eti'kɛtə], *f.* (—, *no pl.*) etiquette; ceremonial.

etikettieren [etikɛ'ti:rən], *v.a.* label.

etliche ['ɛtlɪçə], *pl. adj. & pron.* some, several, sundry.

Etui [e'tvi:], *n.* (—s, *pl.* —s) small case, small box.

etwa ['ɛtva], *adv.* nearly, about; perhaps, perchance, in some way.

etwaig ['ɛtvaɪç], *adj.* possible, any, eventual.

etwas ['ɛtvas], *indef. pron.* some, something. — *adj.* some, any. — *adv.* a little, somewhat.

Etzel ['ɛtsəl], *m.* Attila.

euch [ɔyç], *pers. pron. pl. Dat. & Acc.* you, yourselves.

euer ['ɔyər], *poss. adj.* your. — *poss. pron.* yours.

Eule ['ɔylə], *f.* (—, *pl.* —n) owl.

eurige ['ɔyrɪgə], *poss. pron. der, die, das* —, yours.

Europa [ɔy'ro:pa], *n.* Europe.

Euter ['ɔytər], *n.* (—s, *pl.* —) udder.

evangelisch [evan'ge:lɪʃ], *adj.* Evangelical, Protestant.

Evangelium [evan'ge:ljum], *n.* (—s, *pl.* —lien) gospel.

eventuell [evɛntu'ɛl], *adj.* possible.

ewig ['e:vɪç], *adj.* eternal; perpetual.

Ewigkeit ['e:vɪçkaɪt], *f.* (—, *pl.* —en) eternity.

explodieren [ɛksplo'di:rən], *v.n.* explode; detonate.

exponieren [ɛkspo'ni:rən], *v.a.* set forth, explain at length.

Extemporale [ɛkstɛmpo'ra:lə], *n.* (—s, *pl.* —lien) unprepared exercise.

extrahieren [ɛkstra'hi:rən], *v.a.* extract.

Extremitäten [ɛkstremɪ'tɛ:tən], *f. pl.* extremities.

F

F [ɛf], *n.* (—s, *pl.* —s) the letter F; (*Mus.*) *F Dur*, F major; *F Moll*, F minor.

Fabel ['fa:bəl], *f.* (—, *pl.* —n) fable; (*fig.*) tale, fiction; (*drama*) plot, story.

fabelhaft ['fa:bəlhaft], *adj.* fabulous; phenomenal, gorgeous.

fabeln ['fa:bəln], *v.n.* tell fables; talk nonsense.

Fabrik [fa'bri:k], *f.* (—, *pl.* —en) factory; plant, works.

Fabrikant [fabri'kant], *m.* (—en, *pl.* —en) manufacturer.

fabrizieren [fabri'tsi:rən], *v.a.* manufacture, make.

fabulieren [fabu'li:rən], *v.n.* tell fables; (*fig.*) tell tall stories.

Fach [fax], *n.* (—s, *pl.* ⁓er) compartment; pigeon-hole, drawer; (*fig.*) subject of study, department, branch.

Fachausdruck ['faxausdruk], *m.* (—s, *pl.* ⁓e) technical term.

67

Fächer

Fächer ['fɛçər], m. (—s, pl. —) fan.

Fächertaube ['fɛçərtaubə], f. (—, pl. —n) fantail.

Fachmann ['faxman], m. (—s, pl. ⁻er or **Fachleute**) expert, specialist.

Fachschule ['faxʃuːlə], f. (—, pl. —n) technical school.

fachsimpeln ['faxzimpəln], v.n. talk shop.

Fachwerk ['faxvɛrk], n. (—s, no pl.) timbered framework.

Fackel ['fakəl], f. (—, pl. —n) torch.

fade ['faːdə], adj. tasteless; boring, insipid.

Faden ['faːdən], m. (—s, pl. ⁻) thread; (measure) fathom.

fadenscheinig ['faːdənʃainiç], adj. threadbare.

Fagott [fa'gɔt], n. (—s, pl. —e) (Mus.) bassoon.

fähig ['fɛːiç], adj. able, capable; talented, gifted, competent.

fahl [faːl], adj. pale, sallow.

Fähnchen ['fɛːnçən], n. (—s, pl. —) small banner; pennon; (Mil.) (obs.) small troop.

fahnden ['faːndən], v.a. search for (officially).

Fahne ['faːnə], f. (—, pl. —n) flag, banner, standard, colours; (weather) vane; (Typ.) galley proof.

Fahnenflucht ['faːnənfluxt], f. (—, no pl.) (Mil.) desertion.

Fähnrich ['fɛːnriç], m. (—s, pl. —e) ensign.

Fahrbahn ['faːrbaːn], f. (—, pl. —en) traffic lane, roadway.

fahrbar ['faːrbaːr], adj. passable, navigable, negotiable.

Fähre ['fɛːrə], f. (—, pl. —n) ferry, ferry-boat.

fahren ['faːrən], v.a. irr. drive. — v.n. (aux. sein) (vehicle) ride (in), be driven; (vessel) sail; go, travel.

Fahrer ['faːrər], m. (—s, pl. —) driver, chauffeur.

Fahrgast ['faːrgast], m. (—s, pl. ⁻e) passenger.

fahrig ['faːriç], adj. absent-minded, giddy, thoughtless.

Fahrkarte ['faːrkartə], f. (—, pl. —n) ticket.

fahrlässig ['faːrlɛsiç], adj. negligent, careless.

Fährmann ['fɛːrman], m. (—s, pl. ⁻er) ferry-man.

Fahrplan ['faːrplaːn], m. (—s, pl. ⁻e) timetable, railway-guide.

fahrplanmäßig ['faːrplanmɛːsiç], adj. according to the timetable, scheduled.

Fahrpreis ['faːrprais], m. (—es, pl. —e) cost of ticket, fare.

Fahrrad ['faːrraːt], n. (—s, pl. ⁻er) cycle, bicycle.

Fahrschein ['faːrʃain], m. (—s, pl. —e) ticket.

Fahrstraße ['faːrʃtraːsə], f. (—, pl. —n) roadway.

Fahrstuhl ['faːrʃtuːl], m. (—s, pl. ⁻e) lift; (Am.) elevator.

Fahrt [faːrt], f. (—, pl. —en) drive, ride, journey; (sea) voyage, cruise.

Fährte ['fɛːrtə], f. (—, pl. —n) track, trace, trail.

Fahrzeug ['faːrtsɔyk], n. (—s, pl. —e) vehicle, conveyance; vessel, craft.

faktisch ['faktiʃ], adj. real, actual.

Faktor ['faktɔr], m. (—s, pl. —en) foreman, overseer, factor; (Maths.) factor, component part.

Faktura [fak'tuːra], f. (—, pl. —ren) (Comm.) invoice.

fakturieren [faktu'riːrən], v.a. (Comm.) invoice.

Fakultät [fakul'tɛːt], f. (—, pl. —en) (Univ.) faculty.

fakultativ [fakulta'tiːf], adj. optional.

Falbel ['falbəl], f. (—, pl. —n) flounce, furbelow.

Falke ['falkə], m. (—n, pl. —n) (Orn.) falcon, hawk.

Fall [fal], m. (—s, pl. ⁻e) fall, falling; case; (Geog.) decline, incline, gradient; (fig.) fall, decline, downfall, failure.

Fallbaum ['falbaum], m. (—s, pl. ⁻e) tollbar, turnpike.

Fallbeil ['falbail], n. (—s, pl. —e) guillotine.

Fallbrücke ['falbrykə], f. (—, pl. —n) draw-bridge.

Falle ['falə], f. (—, pl. —n) trap, snare.

fallen ['falən], v.n. irr. (aux. sein) fall, drop; (Mil.) be killed.

fällen ['fɛlən], v.a. fell, cut down, hew down; ein Urteil —, (Law) pronounce judgment.

Fallensteller ['falənʃtɛlər], m. (—s, pl. —) trapper.

fallieren [fa'liːrən], v.n. become bankrupt.

fällig ['fɛliç], adj. due, payable.

Fälligkeit ['fɛliçkait], f. (—, pl. —en) (Comm.) maturity.

Fallobst ['faloːpst], n. (—es, no pl.) windfall (of fruit).

falls [fals], conj. in case, if.

Fallschirm ['falʃirm], m. (—s, pl. —e) parachute.

Fallstrick ['falʃtrik], m. (—s, pl. —e) snare, trap.

Fallsucht ['falzuxt], f. (—, no pl.) (Med.) epilepsy.

Falltür ['faltyːr], f. (—, pl. —en) trap-door.

Fällung ['fɛluŋ], f. (—, pl. —en) cutting down.

falsch [falʃ], adj. false, incorrect, wrong; disloyal; counterfeit.

fälschen ['fɛlʃən], v.a. falsify, forge, tamper with.

Falschheit ['falʃhait], f. (—, pl. —en) falsehood, deceit, disloyalty.

fälschlich ['fɛlʃliç], adv. wrongly, falsely.

Fälschung ['fɛlʃuŋ], f. (—, pl. —en) falsification; forgery.

Falte ['faltə], f. (—, pl. —n) fold, pleat; (face) wrinkle.

falten ['faltən], v.a. fold, plait, pleat; wrinkle.

Falter ['faltər], *m.* (—s, *pl.* —) (*Ent.*) butterfly.

-fältig [fɛltiç], *suffix* (*following numbers*). –fold (*e.g.* vierfältig, fourfold).

Falz [falts], *m.* (—es, *pl.* —e) groove, notch; joint.

Falzbein ['faltsbaɪn], *n.* (—s, *pl.* —e) paper-folder, paper-knife.

Falzmaschine ['faltsmaʃiːnə], *f.* (—, *pl.* —n) folding-machine.

familiär [famil'jɛːr], *adj.* familiar, intimate.

Familie [fa'miːljə], *f.* (—, *pl.* —n) family.

famos [fa'moːs], *adj.* (*coll.*) excellent, splendid.

fanatisch [fa'naːtiʃ], *adj.* fanatic(al), bigoted.

Fanatismus [fana'tɪsmus], *m.* (—, *no pl.*) fanaticism.

Fang [faŋ], *m.* (—es, *pl.* ⁓e) catch, capture; (*bird*) talon, claw.

fangen ['faŋən], *v.a. irr.* catch, seize.

Fangzahn ['faŋtsaːn], *m.* (—s, *pl.* ⁓e) fang, tusk.

Fant [fant], *m.* —s, *pl.* —e) fop, cockscomb.

Farbe ['farbə], *f.* (—, *pl.* —n) colour, hue, paint, dye.

färben ['fɛrbən], *v.a.* dye, stain.

Farbenbrett ['farbənbrɛt], *n.* (—s, *pl.* —er) palette.

Farb(en)druck ['farpdruk, farbəndruk], *m.* (—s, *pl.* —e) colour-printing.

Farbenspiel ['farbənʃpiːl], *n.* (—s, *no pl.*) iridescence.

Färber ['fɛrbər], *m.* (—s, *pl.* —) dyer.

farbig ['farbiç], *adj.* coloured.

Farbstift ['farpʃtɪft], *m.* (—s, *pl.* —e) crayon.

Farbstoff ['farpʃtɔf], *m.* (—es, *pl.* —e) dye.

Farbton ['farptoːn], *m.* (—s, *pl.* ⁓e) hue, tone, tinge, shade.

Farn [farn], *m.* (—s, *pl.* —e) (*Bot.*) fern.

Färse ['fɛrzə], *f.* (—, *pl.* —n) (*Zool.*) heifer.

Fasan [fa'zaːn], *m.* (—s, *pl.* —e) (*Orn.*) pheasant.

Fasching ['faʃɪŋ], *m.* (—s, *no pl.*) (Shrovetide) carnival.

Faschismus [fa'ʃɪsmus], *m.* (—s, *no pl.*) fascism.

Faselei [faːzə'laɪ], *f.* (—, *pl.* —en) silly talk, drivel.

faseln ['faːzəln], *v.n.* drivel.

Faser ['faːzər], *f.* (—, *pl.* —n) thread; string; fibre, filament.

fasern ['faːzərn], *v.n.* fray.

Faß [fas], *n.* (—sses, *pl.* ⁓sser) barrel, vat, tun, tub, cask, keg; *Bier vom* —, draught beer; *Wein vom* —, wine from the wood.

Fassade [fa'saːdə], *f.* (—, *pl.* —n) façade.

faßbar ['fasbaːr], *adj.* tangible.

Faßbinder ['fasbɪndər], *m.* (—s, *pl.* —) cooper.

fassen ['fasən], *v.a.* seize, take hold of, grasp; (*jewels*) set; contain, hold. — *v.r.* (*aux.* haben) *sich* —, compose o.s.; *sich kurz* —, be brief.

faßlich ['fasliç], *adj.* comprehensible, understandable.

Fasson [fa'sõ], *f.* (—, *pl.* —s) fashion; (*fig.*) cut, style.

Fassung ['fasuŋ], *f.* (—, *pl.* —en) (*jewels*) setting; (*speech*) wording, version; (*fig.*) composure.

fassungslos ['fasuŋsloːs], *adj.* bewildered, disconcerted; distraught, speechless.

fast [fast], *adv.* almost, nearly.

fasten ['fastən], *v.n.* fast.

Fastenzeit ['fastəntsaɪt], *f.* (—, *pl.* —en) time of fasting; Lent.

Fastnacht ['fastnaxt], *f.* (—, *no pl.*) Shrove Tuesday; Shrovetide.

fauchen ['fauxən], *v.n.* spit, hiss.

faul [faul], *adj.* (*food*) rotten, putrid, decayed; (*persons*) lazy, idle.

Fäule ['fɔylə], *f.* (—, *no pl.*) rot.

faulen ['faulən], *v.n.* (*aux.* sein) rot.

faulenzen ['faulɛntsən], *v.n.* laze, idle.

Faulenzer ['faulɛntsər], *m.* (—s, *pl.* —) idler, sluggard, lazybones.

Faulenzerei ['faulɛntsəraɪ], *f.* (—, *pl.* —en) idleness, laziness.

Faulheit ['faulhaɪt], *f.* (—, *no pl.*) idleness, laziness, sluggishness.

faulig ['fauliç], *adj.* putrid, rotten.

Fäulnis ['fɔylnɪs], *f.* (—, *no pl.*) rottenness, putridity.

Faust [faust], *f.* (—, *pl.* ⁓e) fist.

Fäustchen ['fɔystçən], *n.* (—s, *pl.* —) small fist; *sich ins* — *lachen*, laugh in o.'s sleeve.

Faustkampf ['faustkampf], *m.* (—es, *pl.* ⁓e) boxing (match).

Faxen ['faksən], *f. pl.* foolery; — *machen*, play the buffoon.

Fazit ['fatsɪt], *n.* (—s, *no pl.*) sum, amount.

Februar ['feːbruaːr], *m.* (—s, *no pl.*) February.

fechten ['fɛçtən], *v.n. irr.* fight; fence; (*fig.*) beg.

Feder ['feːdər], *f.* (—, *pl.* —n) (*bird*) feather; (*hat*) plume; (*writing*) pen; (*antique*) quill; (*Tech.*) spring.

Federball ['feːdərbal], *m.* (—s, *pl.* ⁓e) shuttle-cock.

federig ['feːdəriç], *adj.* feathery; (*Tech.*) springy, resilient.

Federlesen(s) ['feːdərleːzən(s)], *n.* (—s, *no pl.*) *nicht viel* — *machen*, make short work of.

Fee [feː], *f.* (—, *pl.* —n) fairy.

feenhaft ['feːənhaft], *adj.* fairy-like, magical.

Fegefeuer ['feːgəfɔyər], *n.* (—s, *no pl.*) purgatory.

fegen ['feːgən], *v.a.* clean, sweep. — *v.n.* (*aux.* sein) tear along.

Fehde ['feːdə], *f.* (—, *pl.* —n) feud, quarrel.

Fehdehandschuh ['feːdəhantʃuː], *m.* (—s, *pl.* —e) gauntlet.

fehlbar ['fe:lba:r], *adj.* fallible.
Fehlbetrag ['fe:lbətra:k], *m.* (—s, *pl.* ⁓e) deficit.
fehlen ['fe:lən], *v.a.* miss. — *v.n.* err, do wrong; be absent; be wanting; *er. fehlt mir*, I miss him.
Fehler ['fe:lər], *m.* (—s, *pl.* —) fault, defect; mistake, error.
Fehlgeburt ['fe:lgəburt], *f.* (—, *pl.* —en) miscarriage.
Fehlschlag ['fe:lʃla:k], *m.* (—s, *pl.* ⁓e) failure, disappointment.
feien ['faɪən], *v.a. einen — gegen*, charm s.o. against; *gefeit*, proof.
Feier ['faɪər], *f.* (—, *pl.* —n) celebration, festival, holiday, festive day.
Feierabend ['faɪəra:bənt], *m.* (—s, *pl.* —e) time for leaving off work; — *machen*, knock off (work).
feierlich ['faɪərlɪç], *adj.* festive, solemn, stately.
feiern ['faɪərn], *v.a.* celebrate; honour, praise. — *v.n.* rest from work.
Feiertag ['faɪərta:k], *m.* (—s, *pl.* —e) holiday, festive day.
feig [faɪk], *adj.* cowardly.
Feige ['faɪgə], *f.* (—, *pl.* —n) (*Bot.*) fig.
Feigheit ['faɪkhaɪt], *f.* (—, *pl.* —en) cowardice, cowardliness.
Feigling ['faɪklɪŋ], *m.* (—s, *pl.* —e) coward.
Feigwurz ['faɪkvurts], *m.* (—es, *no pl.*) (*Bot.*) fennel.
feil [faɪl], *adj.* (*obs.*) for sale; venal.
feilbieten ['faɪlbi:tən], *v.a.* offer for sale.
Feile ['faɪlə], *f.* (—, *pl.* —n) file.
feilen ['faɪlən], *v.a.* file.
feilhalten ['faɪlhaltən], *v.a.* have for sale, be ready to sell.
feilschen ['faɪlʃən], *v.n.* bargain, haggle.
Feilspäne ['faɪlʃpe:nə], *m. pl.* filings.
fein [faɪn], *adj.* fine; neat, pretty, nice; delicate; (*clothes*) elegant; (*behaviour*) refined, polished.
Feinbäckerei ['faɪnbɛkəraɪ], *f.* (—, *pl.* —en) confectioner's shop.
Feind [faɪnt], *m.* (—es, *pl.* —e) enemy, foe, adversary.
Feindschaft ['faɪntʃaft], *f.* (—, *pl.* —en) enmity, hostility.
feindselig ['faɪntze:lɪç], *adj.* hostile, malignant.
feinfühlend ['faɪnfy:lənt], *adj.* delicate, sensitive.
Feinheit ['faɪnhaɪt], *f.* (—, *pl.* —en) fineness, elegance, politeness, delicacy.
Feinschmecker ['faɪnʃmɛkər], *m.* (—s, *pl.* —), gourmet.
Feinsliebchen ['faɪns'li:pçən], *n.* (—s, *pl.* —) (*Poet. obs.*) sweetheart.
feist [faɪst], *adj.* fat, obese.
Feld [fɛlt], *n.* (—es, *pl.* —er) field, plain; (*chess*) square; (*fig.*) sphere, province.
Feldbett ['fɛltbɛt], *n.* (—s, *pl.* —en) camp-bed.
Feldherr ['fɛlthɛr], *m.* (—n, *pl.* —en) commander, general.

Feldmesser ['fɛltmɛsər], *m.* (—s, *pl.* —) land-surveyor.
Feldscher ['fɛltʃe:r], *m.* (—s, *pl.* —e) army-surgeon.
Feldstecher ['fɛltʃteçər], *m.* (—s, *pl.* —) field-glass(es).
Feldwebel ['fɛltve:bəl], *m.* (—s, *pl.* —) sergeant-major.
Feldzug ['fɛlttsu:k], *m.* (—es, *pl.* ⁓e) campaign, expedition.
Felge ['fɛlgə], *f.* (—, *pl.* —n) (*wheel*) felloe, felly, rim.
Fell [fɛl], *n.* (—s, *pl.* —e) hide, skin, pelt.
Felsabhang ['fɛlsaphaŋ], *m.* (—s, *pl.* ⁓e) rocky slope.
Felsen ['fɛlzən], *m.* (—s, *pl.* —) rock, cliff.
Felsengebirge ['fɛlzəngəbɪrgə], *n.* Rocky Mountains.
Felsenriff ['fɛlzənrɪf], *n.* (—s, *pl.* —e) reef.
felsig ['fɛlzɪç], *adj.* rocky.
Feme ['fe:mə], *f.* (—, *pl.* —n) secret tribunal.
Fenchel ['fɛnçəl], *m.* (—s, *no pl.*) (*Bot.*) fennel.
Fenster ['fɛnstər], *n.* (—s, *pl.* —) window.
Fensterbrett ['fɛnstərbrɛt], *n.* (—s, *pl.* —er) window-sill.
Fensterflügel ['fɛnstərfly:gəl], *m.* (—s, *pl.* —) (window) casement.
Fensterladen ['fɛnstərla:dən], *m.* (—s, *pl.* ⁓) shutter.
Fensterscheibe ['fɛnstərʃaɪbə], *f.* (—, *pl.* —n) pane.
Ferien ['fe:rjən], *pl.* holidays.
Ferkel ['fɛrkəl], *n.* (—s, *pl.* —) young pig, piglet.
Fermate [fɛr'ma:tə], *f.* (—, *pl.* —n) (*Mus.*) pause, fermata.
fern [fɛrn], *adj.* far, distant, remote.
Fernbleiben ['fɛrnblaɪbən], *n.* (—s, *no pl.*) absence.
Ferne ['fɛrnə], *f.* (—, *pl.* —n) distance, remoteness.
ferner ['fɛrnər], *adv.* further, furthermore, moreover.
fernerhin ['fɛrnərhɪn], *adv.* henceforth.
Ferngespräch ['fɛrngəʃprɛx], *n.* (—s, *pl.* —e) long-distance telephone call, trunk call.
Fernglas ['fɛrngla:s], *n.* (—es, *pl.* ⁓er) binoculars.
fernhalten ['fɛrnhaltən], *v.a. irr.* keep away.
fernher ['fɛrnhe:r], *adv. von —*, from afar.
fernliegen ['fɛrnli:gən], *v.n. irr.* be far from.
Fernrohr ['fɛrnro:r], *n.* (—s, *pl.* —e) telescope.
Fernschreiber ['fɛrnʃraɪbər], *m.* (—s, *pl.* —) teleprinter.
Fernsehen ['fɛrnze:ən], *n.* (—s, *no pl.*) television.
fernsehen ['fɛrnze:ən], *v.n. irr.* watch television.

Fernsehgerät ['fɛrnze:gərɛ:t], *n.* (—s, —e) television set.

Fernsprechamt ['fɛrnʃprɛçamt], *n.* (—s, *pl.* ⁛er) telephone exchange.

Fernsprecher ['fɛrnʃprɛçər], *m.* (—s, *pl.* —) telephone.

Fernstehende ['fɛrnʃte:əndə], *m.* (—n, *pl.* —n) outsider.

Fernverkehr ['fɛrnfɛrke:r], *m.* (—s, *no pl.*) long-distance traffic.

Ferse ['fɛrzə], *f.* (—, *pl.* —n) heel.

Fersengeld ['fɛrzəngɛlt], *n.* (—s, *no pl.*) — *geben*, take to o.'s heels.

fertig ['fɛrtiç], *adj.* ready, finished: (*coll.*) worn-out, ruined, done for.

Fertigkeit ['fɛrtiçkaɪt], *f.* (—, *pl.* —en) dexterity, skill.

Fes [fɛs], *n.* (—, *pl.* —) (*Mus.*) F flat.

fesch [fɛʃ], *adj.* smart, stylish; (*dial.*) good-looking.

Fessel ['fɛsəl], *f.* (—, *pl.* —n) fetter, shackle.

Fesselballon ['fɛsəlbalɔ̃], *m.* (—s, *pl.* —s) captive balloon.

Fesselbein ['fɛsəlbaɪn], *n.* (—s, *pl.* —e) pastern-joint.

fesseln ['fɛsəln], *v.a.* fetter, shackle, chain; (*fig.*) captivate.

Fest [fɛst], *n.* (—es, *pl.* —e) feast, festival.

fest [fɛst], *adj.* fast, firm; solid, hard; sound; fixed; constant, steadfast.

Feste ['fɛstə], *f.* (—, *pl.* —n) fortress, stronghold.

festigen ['fɛstɪgən], *v.a.* make firm; strengthen.

Festland ['fɛstlant], *n.* (—es, *pl.* ⁛er) continent.

festlich ['fɛstlɪç], *adj.* festive, solemn.

festmachen ['fɛstmaxən], *v.a.* fasten.

Festnahme ['fɛstna:mə], *f.* (—, *no pl.*) apprehension, arrest.

festnehmen ['fɛstne:mən], *v.a. irr.* seize, arrest.

Festrede ['fɛstre:də], *f.* (—, *pl.* —n) formal address.

festschnallen ['fɛstʃnalən], *v.a.* buckle on, fasten.

Festschrift ['fɛstʃrɪft], *f.* (—, *pl.* —en) commemorative volume (in honour of a person or an occasion).

festsetzen ['fɛstzɛtsən], *v.a.* fix, decree.

Festspiel ['fɛstʃpi:l], *n.* (—s, *pl.* —e) festival (play).

feststehen ['fɛstʃte:ən], *v.n. irr.* stand firm; *es steht fest*, it is certain.

feststellen ['fɛstʃtɛlən], *v.a.* ascertain; state; find; determine; diagnose; establish.

Festtag ['fɛstta:k], *m.* (—s, *pl.* —e) feast-day, holiday.

Festung ['fɛstuŋ], *f.* (—, *pl.* —en) fortress, stronghold, citadel.

festziehen ['fɛsttsi:ən], *v.a. irr.* tighten.

Festzug ['fɛsttsu:k], *m.* (—s, *pl.* ⁛e) procession.

Fett [fɛt], *n.* (—s, *pl.* —e) fat, grease, lard.

fett [fɛt], *adj.* fat, greasy.

fettartig ['fɛtartɪç], *adj.* fatty.

fetten ['fɛtən], *v.a.* oil, grease.

Fettfleck ['fɛtflɛk], *m.* (—s, *pl.* —e) spot of grease.

fettgedruckt ['fɛtgədrukt], *adj.* in heavy type.

fetthaltig ['fɛthaltɪç], *adj.* greasy; adipose.

fettig ['fɛtɪç], *adj.* greasy.

fettleibig ['fɛtlaɪbɪç], *adj.* corpulent, obese.

Fetzen ['fɛtsən], *m.* (—s, *pl.* —) piece, rag, tatter, shred.

feucht [fɔʏçt], *adj.* moist; (*weather*) muggy, wet; (*room*) damp.

Feuchtigkeit ['fɔʏçtɪçkaɪt], *f.* (—, *no pl.*) moisture, humidity, dampness, wetness.

feudal [fɔʏ'da:l], *adj.* feudal; (*coll.*) distinguished, magnificent.

Feuer ['fɔʏər], *n.* (—s, *pl.* —) fire; (*jewels*) brilliancy; (*fig.*) ardour, passion.

feuerbeständig ['fɔʏərbəʃtɛndɪç], *adj.* fire-proof.

Feuerbestattung ['fɔʏərbəʃtatuŋ], *f.* (—, *pl.* —en) cremation.

Feuereifer ['fɔʏəraɪfər], *m.* (—s, *no pl.*) ardour.

feuerfest ['fɔʏərfɛst], *adj.* fire-proof, incombustible.

feuergefährlich ['fɔʏərgəfɛ:rlɪç], *adj.* inflammable.

Feuerlilie ['fɔʏərli:ljə], *f.* (—, *pl.* —n) tiger lily.

Feuermal ['fɔʏərma:l], *n.* (—s, *pl.* —e) burn, burn-mark.

Feuermauer ['fɔʏərmauər], *f.* (—, *pl.* —n) fire-proof wall, party-wall.

Feuermelder ['fɔʏərmɛldər], *m.* (—s, *pl.* —) fire-alarm.

feuern ['fɔʏərn], *v.a.* (*Mil.*) fire, discharge; (*coll.*) fire, sack.

Feuerprobe ['fɔʏərpro:bə], *f.* (—, *pl.* —n) ordeal by fire.

Feuerrad ['fɔʏəra:t], *n.* (—s, *pl.* ⁛er) Catherine wheel.

Feuerrohr ['fɔʏəro:r], *n.* (—s, *pl.* —e) gun, matchlock.

Feuersbrunst ['fɔʏərsbrunst], *f.* (—, *pl.* ⁛e) (*rare*) fire, conflagration.

Feuerspritze ['fɔʏərʃprɪtsə], *f.* (—, *pl.* —n) fire-engine.

Feuerstein ['fɔʏərʃtaɪn], *m.* (—s, *no pl.*) flint.

Feuertaufe ['fɔʏərtaufə], *f.* (—, *pl.* —n) baptism of fire.

Feuerwarte ['fɔʏərvartə], *f.* (—, *pl.* —en) beacon; lighthouse.

Feuerwehr ['fɔʏərve:r], *f.* (—, *no pl.*) fire-brigade.

Feuerwerk ['fɔʏərvɛrk], *n.* (—, *no pl.*) fireworks.

Feuerwerkskunst ['fɔʏərvɛrkskunst], *f.* (—, *no pl.*) pyrotechnics.

Feuerzange ['fɔʏərtsaŋə], *f.* (—, *pl.* —n) fire-tongs.

Feuerzeug ['fɔʏərtsɔʏk], *n.* (—s, *pl.* —e) match-box; cigarette-lighter.

feurig ['fɔʏrɪç], *adj.* fiery, burning; (*fig.*) ardent, impassioned, fervent; (*wine*) heady.

Fiaker [fi'akər], *m.* (—s, *pl.* —)
(*Austr.*) cab, hansom; (*Am.*) coach.

Fiasko [fi'asko:], *n.* (—s, *pl.* —s)
failure.

Fibel ['fi:bəl], *f.* (—, *pl.* —n) primer,
spelling-book.

Fiber ['fi:bər], *f.* (—, *pl.* —n) fibre.

Fichte ['fɪçtə], *f.* (—, *pl.* —n) (*Bot.*)
pine, pine-tree.

fidel [fi'de:l], *adj.* merry, jolly.

Fidibus ['fi:dibus], *m.* (—ses, *pl.* —se)
spill, fidibus.

Fidschi ['fɪdʒi:], Fiji.

Fieber ['fi:bər], *n.* (—s, *no pl.*) fever.

fieberhaft ['fi:bərhaft], *adj.* feverish,
vehement.

fieberig ['fi:bərɪç], *adj.* feverish, racked
by fever.

Fieberkälte ['fi:bərkɛltə], *f.* (—, *no pl.*)
chill, shivering (fit).

fiebern ['fi:bərn], *v.n.* have a fever;
(*fig.*) rave.

fiebrig ['fi:brɪç], *see* **fieberig**.

Fiedel ['fi:dəl], *f.* (—, *pl.* —n) (*Mus.*)
fiddle, violin.

Figur [fi'gu:r], *f.* (—, *pl.* —en) figure,
statue, sculpture; chessman.

figürlich [fi'gy:rlɪç], *adj.* figurative.

Filet [fi'le:], *n.* (—s, *pl.* —s) netting,
net-work; (*meat*) fillet.

Filiale [fil'ja:lə], *f.* (—, *pl.* —n)
branch, branch-establishment, branch-
office.

Filigran [fili'gra:n], *n.* (—s, *no pl.*)
filigree.

Film [film], *m.* (—s, *pl.* —e) film;
(motion) picture.

Filter ['fɪltər], *m.*·(—s, *pl.* —) filter.

filtrieren [fɪl'tri:rən], *v.a.* filter.

Filz [fɪlts], *m.* (—es, *pl.* —e) felt;
(*fig.*) niggard, miser, skinflint.

Filzlaus ['fɪltslaus], *f.* (—, *pl.* ∵e)
crab-louse.

Finanzamt [fi'nantsamt], *n.* (—s, *pl.*
∵er) income-tax office; revenue-
office.

Finanzen [fi'nantsən], *f. pl.* finances,
revenue.

Findelkind ['fɪndəlkɪnt], *n.* (—s, *pl.*
—er) foundling.

finden ['fɪndən], *v.a. irr.* find. — *v.r.*
sich —, *das wird sich* —, we shall
see.

Finder ['fɪndər], *m.* (—s, *pl.* —)
finder.

findig ['fɪndɪç], *adj.* resourceful, ingenious.

Findling ['fɪntlɪŋ], *m.* (—s, *pl.* —e)
foundling.

Finger ['fɪŋər], *m.* (—s, *pl.* —) finger.

Fingerabdruck ['fɪŋərapdruk], *m.* (—s,
pl. ∵e) finger-print.

fingerfertig ['fɪŋərfɛrtɪç], *adj.* nimble-
fingered.

Fingerhut ['fɪŋərhu:t], *m.* (—s, *pl.* ∵e)
thimble; (*Bot.*) foxglove.

fingern ['fɪŋərn], *v.a.* touch with the
fingers, finger.

Fingersatz ['fɪŋərzats], *m.* (—es, *pl.*
∵e) (*Mus.*) fingering.

Fingerspitze ['fɪŋərʃpɪtsə], *f.* (—, *pl.*
—n) finger-tip.

Fingerzeig ['fɪŋərtsaɪk], *m.* (—s, *pl.*
—e) hint.

fingieren [fɪŋ'gi:rən], *v.a.* sham.

fingiert [fɪŋ'gi:rt], *adj.* fictitious.

Fink [fɪŋk], *m.* (—en, *pl.* —en) (*Orn.*)
finch.

Finne (1) ['fɪnə], *m.* (—n, *pl.* —n) Finn.

Finne (2) ['fɪnə], *f.* (—, *pl.* —n)
pimple; (*fish*) fin.

finnig ['fɪnɪç], *adj.* pimpled; (*fish*)
finny.

Finnland ['fɪnlant], *n.* Finland.

finster ['fɪnstər], *adj.* dark, obscure;
(*fig.*) gloomy, sinister.

Finsternis ['fɪnstərnɪs], *f.* (—, *no pl.*)
darkness, gloom.

Finte ['fɪntə], *f.* (—, *pl.* —n) feint;
(*fig.*) pretence, trick.

Firlefanz ['fɪrləfants], *m.* (—es, *no pl.*)
foolery.

Firma ['fɪrma], *f.* (—, *pl.* —men)
(*business*) firm, company.

Firmung ['fɪrmuŋ], *f.* (—, *pl.* —en)
(*Eccl.*) confirmation.

Firnis ['fɪrnɪs], *m.* (—ses, *pl.* —se)
varnish.

firnissen ['fɪrnɪsən], *v.a.* varnish.

First [fɪrst], *m.* (—es, *pl.* —e) (*house*)
roof-ridge; (*mountain*) top.

Fis [fɪs], *n.* (—, *pl.* —) (*Mus.*) F sharp.

Fisch [fɪʃ], *m.* (—es, *pl.* —e) fish.

Fischadler ['fɪʃa:dlər], *m.* (—s, *pl.* —)
osprey, sea-eagle.

Fischbein ['fɪʃbaɪn], *n.* (—s, *no pl.*)
whalebone.

fischen ['fɪʃən], *v.a., v.n.* fish, angle.

Fischer ['fɪʃər], *m.* (—s, *pl.* —)
fisherman, fisher.

Fischerei [fɪʃə'raɪ], *f.* (—, *no pl.*)
fishing; fishery.

Fischergerät ['fɪʃərgərɛ:t], *n.* (—s, *pl.*
—e) fishing-tackle.

Fischgräte ['fɪʃgrɛ:tə], *f.* (—, *pl.* —n)
fish-bone.

Fischkelle ['fɪʃkɛlə], *f.* (—, *pl.* —n)
fish-slice.

Fischlaich ['fɪʃlaɪç], *m.* (—s, *no pl.*)
spawn.

Fischmilch ['fɪʃmɪlç], *f.* (—, *no pl.*)
soft roe, milt.

Fischotter ['fɪʃotər], *m.* (—s, *pl.* —n)
common otter.

Fischreiher ['fɪʃraɪər], *m.* (—s, *pl.* —)
(*Orn.*) heron.

Fischreuse ['fɪʃrɔyzə], *f.* (—, *pl.* —n)
bow-net; weir.

Fischrogen ['fɪʃro:gən], *m.* (—s, *no
pl.*) roe.

Fischschuppe ['fɪʃʃupə], *f.* (—, *pl.*
—n) scale.

Fischtran ['fɪʃtra:n], *m.* (—s, *no pl.*)
train-oil.

Fischzucht ['fɪʃtsuxt], *f.* (—, *no pl.*)
fish-breeding, pisciculture.

Fiskus ['fɪskus], *m.* (—, *pl.* —ken)
Treasury, Exchequer.

Fisole [fi'zo:lə], *f.* (—, *pl.* —n) (*Austr.*)
French bean.

Fistelstimme ['fɪstəlʃtɪmə], *f.* (—, *no pl.*) (*Mus.*) falsetto.

Fittich ['fɪtɪç], *m.* (—es, *pl.* —e) (*Poet.*) wing, pinion.

fix [fɪks], *adj.* quick, sharp; — *und fertig*, quite ready.

Fixum ['fɪksum], *n.* (—s, *pl.* —xa) fixed amount; regular salary.

flach [flax], *adj.* flat, plain, smooth, level; (*water*) shallow.

Fläche ['flɛçə], *f.* (—, *pl.* —n) plain; (*Maths.*) plane; (*crystal*) face.

Flächeninhalt ['flɛçənɪnhalt], *m.* (—s, *no pl.*) area.

Flächenmaß ['flɛçənma:s], *n.* (—es, *pl.* —e) square-measure.

Flächenraum ['flɛçənraum], *m.* (—es, *no pl.*) surface area.

Flachheit ['flaxhaɪt], *f.* (—, *no pl.*) flatness; (*fig.*) shallowness.

Flachs [[flaks], *m.* (—es, *no pl.*) flax.

flackern ['flakərn], *v.n.* flare, flicker.

Fladen ['fla:dən], *m.* (—s, *pl.* —) flat cake; cow-dung.

Flagge ['flagə], *f.* (—, *pl.* —n) flag.

Flame ['fla:mə], *m.* (—n, *pl.* —n) Fleming.

flämisch ['flɛ:mɪʃ], *adj.* Flemish.

Flamme ['flamə], *f.* (—, *pl.* —n) flame; blaze.

flammen ['flamən], *v.n.* flame, blaze, sparkle.

Flammeri ['flaməri:], *m.* (—s, *pl.* —s) blanc-mange.

Flandern ['flandərn], *n.* Flanders.

Flanell [fla'nɛl], *m.* (—s, *pl.* —e) flannel.

Flaneur [fla'nø:r], *m.* (—s, *pl.* —e) lounger, stroller.

flanieren [fla'ni:rən], *v.n.* lounge, stroll.

Flanke ['flaŋkə], *f.* (—, *pl.* —n) flank; *in die — fallen*, (*Mil.*) attack in the flank.

Flasche ['flaʃə], *f.* (—, *pl.* —en) bottle, flask.

Flaschenzug ['flaʃəntsu:k], *m.* (—es, *pl.* —e) pulley.

flatterhaft ['flatərhaft], *adj.* fickle, inconstant, flighty.

flattern ['flatərn], *v.n.* flutter.

flau [flau], *adj.* insipid, stale; (*fig.*) dull.

Flaum [flaum], *m.* (—s, *no pl.*) down.

Flausch [flauʃ], *m.* (—es, *no pl.*) pilot-cloth.

Flaute ['flautə], *f.* (—, *pl.* —n) (*Nav.*) calm; (*fig.*) (*Comm.*) depression.

Flechte ['flɛçtə], *f.* (—, *pl.* —n) twist, plait, braid; (*Med.*) eruption, ringworm; (*Bot.*) lichen.

flechten ['flɛçtən], *v.a. irr.* plait; wreathe.

Flechtwerk ['flɛçtvɛrk], *n.* (—s, *no pl.*) wicker-work, basketry.

Fleck [flɛk], *m.* (—s, *pl.* —e) spot; place, piece (of ground); (*fig.*) stain, blemish.

Flecken ['flɛkən], *m.* (—s, *pl.* —) market town, small town.

fleckenlos ['flɛkənlo:s], *adj.* spotless.

fleckig ['flɛkɪç], *adj.* spotted, speckled.

Fledermaus ['fle:dərmaus], *f.* (—, *pl.* :-e) (*Zool.*) bat.

Flederwisch ['fle:dərvɪʃ], *m.* (—es, *pl.* —e) feather-duster.

Flegel ['fle:gəl], *m.* (—s, *pl.* —) flail; (*fig.*) boor.

flegelhaft ['fle:gəlhaft], *adj.* boorish, churlish, rude.

Flegeljahre ['fle:gəlja:rə], *n. pl.* years of indiscretion; teens, adolescence.

flehen ['fle:ən], *v.a., v.n.* implore, supplicate, entreat.

Fleisch [flaɪʃ], *n.* (—es, *no pl.*) (raw) flesh; (*for cooking*) meat; (*fruit*) pulp.

Fleischbrühe ['flaɪʃbry:ə], *f.* (—, *pl.* —n) broth, beef-tea.

Fleischer ['flaɪʃər], *m.* (—s, *pl.* —) butcher.

fleischfressend ['flaɪʃfrɛsənt], *adj.* carnivorous.

Fleischhacker ['flaɪʃhakər], **Fleischhauer** ['flaɪʃhauər], *m.* (—s, *pl.* —) butcher.

fleischlich ['flaɪʃlɪç], *adj.* fleshly, carnal.

fleischlos ['flaɪʃlo:s], *adj.* vegetarian.

Fleischpastete ['flaɪʃpaste:tə], *f.* (—, *pl.* —n) meat-pie.

Fleiß [flaɪs], *m.* (—es, *no pl.*) diligence, assiduity, industry.

fleißig ['flaɪsɪç], *adj.* diligent, assiduous, industrious, hard-working.

fletschen ['flɛtʃən], *v.a. die Zähne —*, show o.'s teeth.

Flicken ['flɪkən], *m.* (—s, *pl.* —) patch.

flicken ['flɪkən], *v.a.* patch, repair, mend; (*shoes*) cobble; (*stockings*) darn.

Flieder ['fli:dər], *m.* (—s, *pl.* —) (*Bot.*) elder, lilac.

Fliege ['fli:gə], *f.* (—, *pl.* —n) (*Ent.*) fly; (*beard*) imperial.

fliegen ['fli:gən], *v.n. irr.* (*aux.* sein) fly; (*coll.*) get the sack, be fired. — *v.a.* fly, pilot (an aircraft).

Flieger ['fli:gər], *m.* (—s, *pl.* —) airman, aviator; pilot.

fliehen ['fli:ən], *v.n. irr.* (*aux.* sein) flee, run away; *zu einem —*, take refuge with s.o. — *v.a. irr.* avoid, shun (s.o.).

Fliehkraft ['fli:kraft], *f.* (—, *no pl.*) centrifugal force.

Fliese ['fli:zə], *f.* (—, *pl.* —n) floor-tile, flagstone.

Fließband ['fli:sbant], *n.* (—(e)s, *pl.* :-er) (*Ind.*) assembly line.

fließen ['fli:sən], *v.n. irr.* (*aux.* sein) flow.

Fließpapier ['fli:spapi:r], *n.* (—s, *no pl.*) blotting-paper.

Flimmer ['flɪmər], *m.* (—s, *no pl.*) glittering, sparkling, glimmer.

flimmern ['flɪmərn], *v.n.* glisten, glitter.

flink [flɪŋk], *adj.* brisk, agile, quick, sharp, nimble.

73

Flinte

Flinte ['flɪntə], f. (—, pl. —n) gun, musket, rifle.

Flitter ['flɪtər], m. (—s, no pl.) tinsel, spangle, frippery.

Flitterwochen ['flɪtərvɔxən], f. pl. honeymoon.

flitzen ['flɪtsən], v.n. (aux. sein) vorbei —, flit or rush past, dash along.

Flocke ['flɔkə], f. (—, pl. —n) (snow) flake; (wool) flock.

Floh [flo:], m. (—s, pl. ⁻e) (Ent.) flea.

Flor [flo:r], m. (—s, pl. —e) bloom; gauze, crape; in —, blossoming, blooming.

Florenz [flo'rents], n. Florence.

Florett [flo'rɛt], n. (—s, pl. —e) (fencing) foil.

florieren [flo'ri:rən], v.n. flourish.

Florstrumpf ['flo:rʃtrumpf], m. (—s, pl. ⁻e) lisle stocking.

Floskel ['flɔskəl], f. (—, pl. —n) rhetorical ornament; oratorical flourish; phrase.

Floß [flo:s], n. (—es, pl. ⁻e) raft.

Flosse ['flɔsə], f. (—, pl. —n) fin.

flößen ['flo:sən], v.a. float.

Flößer ['flo:sər], m. (—s, pl. —) raftsman.

Flöte ['flo:tə], f. (—, pl. —n) (Mus.) flute.

Flötenzug ['flo:təntsu:k], m. (—es, pl. ⁻e) (organ) flute-stop.

flott [flɔt], adj. (Naut.) afloat, floating; (fig.) gay, jolly, lively, smart; — leben, lead a fast life.

Flotte ['flɔtə], f. (—, pl. —n) fleet, navy.

Flottille [flɔ'tiljə], f. (—, pl. —n) flotilla, squadron.

Flöz [flo:ts], n. (—es, pl. —e) layer, stratum; (coal) seam.

Fluch [flu:x], m. (—es, pl. ⁻e) curse, spell; (verbal) curse, oath, swearword.

fluchen ['flu:xən], v.n. curse, swear.

Flucht [fluxt], f. (—, pl. —en) flight, fleeing; suite (of rooms).

flüchten ['flyçtən], v.n. (aux. sein), v.r. flee, run away, escape.

flüchtig ['flyçtɪç], adj. fugitive; (Chem.) volatile; (fig.) superficial; evanescent; hasty; slight.

Flüchtling ['flyçtlɪŋ], m. (—s, pl. —e) fugitive, refugee.

Flug [flu:k], m. (—s, pl. ⁻e) (Aviat.) flight.

Flugblatt ['flu:kblat], n. (—s, pl. ⁻er) broadsheet, leaflet.

Flügel ['fly:gəl], m. (—s, pl. —) wing; (Mus.) grand piano; (door) leaf.

Flügelschlag ['fly:gəlʃla:k], m. (—s, pl. ⁻e) wing-stroke.

Flügeltür ['fly:gəlty:r], f. (—, pl. —en) folding-door.

flügge ['flygə], adj. fledged.

Flughafen ['flu:kha:fən], m. (—s, pl. ⁻) airport; aerodrome.

Flugpost ['flu:kpɔst], f. (—, no pl.) air mail.

flugs [fluks], adv. quickly, instantly; (Lit., obs.) anon.

Flugsand ['flu:kzant], m. (—s, no pl.) quicksand, drifting sand.

Flugzeug ['flu:ktsɔyk], n. (—s, pl. —e) aeroplane; (Am.) airplane.

Flugzeugführer ['flu:ktsɔykfy:rər], m. (—s, pl. —) (Aviat.) pilot.

Fluidum ['flu:idum], n. (—s, pl. —da) fluid; (fig.) atmosphere.

Flunder ['flundər], f. (—, pl. —n) (fish) flounder.

Flunkerer ['fluŋkərər], m. (—s, pl. —) (coll.) fibber, story-teller.

Flur (1) [flu:r], f. (—, pl. —en) field, plain; auf weiter —, in the open.

Flur (2) [flu:r], m. (—s, pl. —e) (house) hall, vestibule; corridor.

Flurschaden ['flu:rʃa:dən], m. (—s, pl. ⁻) damage to crops.

Fluß [flus], m. (—sses, pl. ⁻sse) river, stream; flow, flowing; flux.

Flußbett ['flusbɛt], n. (—s, pl. —en) channel, riverbed.

flüssig ['flysɪç], adj. fluid, liquid; —e Gelder, ready cash; liquid assets.

flüstern ['flystərn], v.a. whisper.

Flut [flu:t], f. (—, pl. —en) flood; high-tide, high water; torrent; deluge.

fluten ['flu:tən], v.n. flow.

Focksegel ['fɔkze:gəl], n. (—s, pl. —) foresail.

Fockmast ['fɔkmast], m. (—s, pl. —en) foremast.

Föderalismus [fø:dəra'lɪsmus], m. (—, no pl.) federalism.

Fohlen ['fo:lən], n. (—s, pl. —) foal.

fohlen ['fo:lən], v.n. foal.

Föhn [fo:n], m. (—s, pl. —e) (warm) Alpine wind.

Föhre ['fo:rə], f. (—, pl. —n) (Bot.) fir, fir-tree.

Folge ['fɔlgə], f. (—, pl. —n) succession; series, sequence; continuation; consequence.

folgen ['fɔlgən], v.n. (aux. sein) follow; succeed; result from, be the consequence of; obey.

folgendermaßen ['fɔlgəndərma:sən], adv. as follows.

folgenschwer ['fɔlgənʃve:r], adj. momentous, portentous.

folgerichtig ['fɔlgərɪçtɪç], adj. consistent, logical.

folgern ['fɔlgərn], v.a. draw a conclusion, infer, conclude, deduce.

Folgerung ['fɔlgəruŋ], f. (—, pl. —en) induction, deduction, inference.

folglich ['fɔlklɪç], conj. consequently, therefore.

folgsam ['fɔlkza:m], adj. obedient.

Foliant [fo:l'jant], m. (—en, pl. —en) folio-volume, tome.

Folie ['fo:ljə], f. (—, pl. —n) foil.

Folter ['fɔltər], f. (—, pl. —n) rack, torture.

Folterbank ['fɔltərbaŋk], f. (—, pl. ⁻e) rack.

Fond [fõ:], m. (—s, pl. —s) back seat.

Fraktion

Fontäne [fɔ̃'tɛːnə], *f.* (—, *pl.* —n) fountain.

foppen ['fɔpən], *v.a.* chaff, banter, tease.

Fopperei [fɔpə'raɪ], *f.* (—, *pl.* —en) chaff, banter, teasing.

forcieren [fɔr'siːrən], *v.a.* strain, overdo.

Förderer ['fœrdərər], *m.* (—s, *pl.* —) promoter, backer.

Förderkarren ['fœrdərkarən], *m.* (—s, *pl.* —) (*Min.*) truck, trolley.

förderlich ['fœrdərlɪç], *adj.* useful, conducive (to).

Fördermaschine ['fœrdərmaʃiːnə], *f.* (—, *pl.* —n) hauling-machine.

fordern ['fɔrdərn], *v.a.* demand, claim, ask for; (*duel*) challenge.

fördern ['fœrdərn], *v.a.* further, advance, promote, back; hasten; (*Min.*) haul.

Förderschacht ['fœrdərʃaxt], *m.* (—s, *pl.* ˉe) (*Min.*) winding shaft.

Forderung ['fɔrdərʊŋ], *f.* (—, *pl.* —en) demand, claim; (*duel*) challenge.

Förderung ['fœrdərʊŋ], *f.* (—, *no pl.*) furtherance, promotion, advancement; (*Min.*) hauling.

Forelle [fo'rɛlə], *f.* (—, *pl.* —n) trout.

Forke ['fɔrkə], *f.* (—, *pl.* —n) pitch-fork, garden-fork.

Form [fɔrm], *f.* (—, *pl.* —en) form, shape, figure; manner; condition; (*casting*) mould; (*grammar*) form, voice.

Formalien [fɔr'maːljən], *pl.* formalities.

Formalität [fɔrmalɪ'tɛːt], *f.* (—, *pl.* —en) formality, form.

Format [fɔr'maːt], *n.* (—s, *pl.* —e) (*book, paper*) size; format; (*fig.*) stature.

Formel ['fɔrməl], *f.* (—, *pl.* —n) formula.

formell [fɔr'mɛl], *adj.* formal.

Formfehler ['fɔrmfeːlər], *m.* (—s, *pl.* —) faux pas, breach of etiquette.

formieren [fɔr'miːrən], *v.a.* form. — *v.r. sich* —, fall into line.

förmlich ['fœrmlɪç], *adj.* formal; downright.

formlos ['fɔrmloːs], *adj.* shapeless; (*fig.*) unconventional, informal, unceremonious.

Formular [fɔrmu'laːr], *n.* (—s, *pl.* —e) (printed) form, schedule.

formulieren [fɔrmu'liːrən], *v.a.* formulate, word.

formvollendet ['fɔrmfɔlɛndət], *adj.* well-rounded, well-finished.

forsch [fɔrʃ], *adj.* dashing.

forschen ['fɔrʃən], *v.n.* search, enquire (after), do research.

Forschung ['fɔrʃʊŋ], *f.* (—, *pl.* —en) research, investigation; search, exploration.

Forst [fɔrst], *m.* (—es, *pl.* —e) forest.

Förster ['fœrstər], *m.* (—s, *pl.* —) forester, forest-keeper; (*Am.*) ranger.

Forstfrevel ['fɔrstfreːfəl], *m.* (—s, *no pl.*) infringement of forest-laws.

Forstrevier ['fɔrstreviːr], *n.* (—s, *pl.* —e) section of forest.

Forstwesen ['fɔrstveːzən], *n.* (—s, *no pl.*) forestry.

Forstwirtschaft ['fɔrstvɪrtʃaft], *f.* (—, *no pl.*) forestry.

fort [fɔrt], *adv.* away; lost, gone, forth, forward.

Fort [foːrt], *n.* (—s, *pl.* —s) fort.

fortan [fɔrt'an], *adv.* henceforth.

fortbilden ['fɔrtbɪldən], *v.r. sich* —, improve o.s., receive further education.

fortbleiben ['fɔrtblaɪbən], *v.n. irr.* (*aux.* sein) stay away.

Fortdauer ['fɔrtdauər], *f.* (—, *no pl.*) continuance, duration.

fortfahren ['fɔrtfaːrən], *v.n. irr.* (*aux.* sein) drive off; (*Naut.*) set sail; (*fig.*) continue, go on.

Fortgang ['fɔrtgaŋ], *m.* (—s, *no pl.*) going away, departure; (*fig.*) continuation, progress.

Fortkommen ['fɔrtkɔmən], *n.* (—s, *no pl.*) advancement, progress; (*fig.*) livelihood.

fortkommen ['fɔrtkɔmən], *v.n. irr.* (*aux.* sein) *gut* —, prosper, succeed.

fortlassen ['fɔrtlasən], *v.a. irr.* allow to go; leave out, omit; *nicht* —, detain.

fortlaufen ['fɔrtlaufən], *v.n. irr.* (*aux.* sein) run away.

fortpflanzen ['fɔrtpflantsən], *v.r. sich* —, propagate, multiply; (*sickness*) spread.

forträumen ['fɔrtrɔymən], *v.a.* clear away, remove.

fortschaffen ['fɔrtʃafən], *v.a.* carry away, get rid of.

fortscheren ['fɔrtʃeːrən], *v.r. sich* — (*coll.*) beat it, go away.

fortscheuchen ['fɔrtʃɔyçən], *v.a.* scare away.

fortschreiten ['fɔrtʃraɪtən], *v.n. irr.* (*aux.* sein) progress, advance.

Fortschritt ['fɔrtʃrɪt], *m.* (—s, *pl.* —e) progress, advancement, proficiency.

fortsetzen ['fɔrtzɛtsən], *v.a.* continue, carry on.

fortwährend ['fɔrtvɛːrənt], *adj.* continual, perpetual, unceasing.

Fracht [fraxt], *f.* (—, *pl.* —en) freight, cargo, load.

Frack [frak], *m.* (—s, *pl.* —s, ˉe) dress-suit, evening dress.

Frage ['fraːgə], *f.* (—, *pl.* —n) question, query.

Fragebogen ['fraːgəboːgən], *m.* (—s, *pl.* —) questionnaire.

fragen ['fraːgən], *v.a.* ask, enquire, question.

Fragesteller ['fraːgəʃtɛlər], *m.* (—s, *pl* —) interrogator, questioner.

fraglich ['fraːklɪç], *adj.* questionable, problematic(al).

fragwürdig ['fraːkvyrdɪç], *adj.* doubtful, questionable.

Fraktion [frak'tsjoːn], *f.* (—, *pl.* —en) (*Pol.*) party group.

Frakturschrift

Frakturschrift [frak'tu:rʃrɪft], *f.* (—, *no pl.*) (*lettering*) Gothic type, Old English type, Black Letter type.

Frank [fraŋk], *m.* (—**en**, *pl.* —**en**) (*money*) franc.

Franke ['fraŋkə], *m.* (—**n**, *pl.* —**n**) Frank, Franconian.

frankieren [fraŋ'ki:rən], *v.a.* (*post*) prepay, frank.

franko ['fraŋko], *adj.* post-paid; *gratis und* —, gratuitously.

Frankreich ['frankraıx], *n.* France.

Franse ['franzə], *f.* (—, *pl.* —**n**) fringe.

Franzose [fran'tso:zə], *m.* (—**n**, *pl.* —**n**) Frenchman.

französisch [fran'tso:zıʃ], *adj.* French.

frappant [fra'pant], *adj.* striking.

frappieren [fra'pi:rən], *v.a.* strike, astonish.

Fraß [fra:s], *m.* (—**es**, *no pl.*) (*animals*) feed, fodder; (*sl.*) grub.

Fratz [frats], *m.* (—**es**, *pl.* —**en**) brat, little monkey.

Fratze ['fratsə], *f.* (—, *pl.* —**en**) grimace, caricature.

Frau [frau], *f.* (—, *pl.* —**en**) woman, wife, lady; (*title*) Mrs.; *gnädige* —, Madam.

Frauenkirche ['frauənkırçə], *f.* (—, *no pl.*) Church of Our Lady.

Frauenzimmer ['frauəntsımər], *n.* (—**s**, *pl.* —) (*pej.*) woman, female.

Fräulein ['frɔylaın], *n.* (—**s**, *pl.* —) young lady; (*title*) Miss.

frech [frɛç], *adj.* insolent, impudent, cheeky, pert, saucy.

Frechheit ['frɛçhaıt], *f.* (—, *pl.* —**en**) insolence, impudence.

Fregatte [fre'gatə], *f.* (—, *pl.* —**n**) frigate.

frei [fraı], *adj.* free, exempt, unhampered, independent, disengaged; vacant; candid, frank.

Freibeuter ['fraıbɔytər], *m.* (—**s**, *pl.* —) freebooter, pirate.

Freibrief ['fraıbri:f], *m.* (—**s**, *pl.* —**e**) patent, licence; permit.

freien ['fraıən], *v.a.* woo, court.

Freier ['fraıər], *m.* (—**s**, *pl.* —) (*obs.*) suitor.

Freigabe ['fraıga:bə], *f.* (—, *no pl.*) release.

freigeben ['fraıge:bən], *v.a. irr.* release.

freigebig ['fraıge:bıç], *adj.* liberal, generous.

Freigebigkeit ['fraıgə:bıçkaıt], *f.* (—, *no pl.*) liberality, munificence, generosity.

Freigut ['fraıgu:t], *n.* (—**s**, *pl.* "**er**) freehold.

Freiheit ['fraıhaıt], *f.* (—, *pl.* —**en**) freedom, liberty, immunity, privilege.

Freiherr ['fraıhɛr], *m.* (—**n**, *pl.* —**en**) baron.

Freikorps ['fraıko:r], *n.* (—, *no pl.*) volunteer-corps.

Freilauf ['fraılauf], *m.* (—**s**, *no pl.*) (*bicycle*) free-wheel.

freilich ['fraılıç], *adv.* to be sure, it is true, indeed, of course.

Freilicht- ['fraılıxt], *adj.* (*in compounds*) open-air.

Freimarke ['fraımarkə], *f.* (—, *pl.* —**n**) postage stamp.

freimütig ['fraımy:tıç], *adj.* frank, open, candid.

Freisprechung ['fraıʃprɛçuŋ], *f.* (—, *no pl.*) acquittal; absolution.

Freistätte ['fraıʃtɛtə], *f.* (—, *pl.* —**n**) refuge, asylum.

Freistoß ['fraıʃto:s], *m.* (—**es**, *pl.* "**e**) (*Footb.*) free-kick.

Freitag ['fraıta:k], *m.* (—**s**, *pl.* —**e**) Friday.

Freitreppe ['fraıtrɛpə], *f.* (—, *pl.* —**n**) outside staircase.

Freiübung ['fraıy:buŋ], *f.* (—, *pl.* —**en**) (*mostly pl.*) physical exercises, gymnastics.

freiwillig ['fraıvılıç], *adj.* voluntary, of o.'s own accord; spontaneous.

Freiwillige ['fraıvılıgə], *m.* (—**n**, *pl.* —**n**) (*Mil.*) volunteer.

fremd [frɛmt], *adj.* strange, foreign, outlandish; odd.

fremdartig ['frɛmtartıç], *adj.* strange, odd.

Fremde (1) ['frɛmdə], *f.* (—, *no pl.*) foreign country; *in die* — *gehen*, go abroad.

Fremde (2) ['frɛmdə], *m.* (—**n**, *pl.* —**n**) stranger, foreigner.

Fremdheit ['frɛmthaıt], *f.* (—, *no pl.*) strangeness.

Freßbeutel ['frɛsbɔytəl], *m.* (—**s**, *pl.* —) nose-bag.

Fresse ['frɛsə], *f.* (—, *pl.* —**n**) (*vulg.*) mouth, snout.

fressen ['frɛsən], *v.a. irr.* (*animals*) eat; (*also fig.*) devour.

Fresserei ['frɛsəraı], *f.* (—, *no pl.*) gluttony.

Frettchen ['frɛtçən], *n.* (—**s**, *pl.* —) (*Zool.*) ferret.

Freude ['frɔydə], *f.* (—, *pl.* —**n**) joy, joyfulness, gladness, enjoyment, delight, pleasure.

Freudenfest ['frɔydənfɛst], *n.* (—**s**, *pl.* —**e**) feast, jubilee.

Freudenhaus ['frɔydənhaus], *n.* (—**es**, *pl.* "**er**) brothel.

Freudenmädchen ['frɔydənmɛːtçən], *n.* (—**s**, *pl.* —) prostitute.

freudig ['frɔydıç], *adj.* joyful, cheerful, glad.

freudlos ['frɔytlo:s], *adj.* joyless.

freuen ['frɔyən], *v.r. sich* —, rejoice (at), be glad (of); *sich auf etwas* —, look forward to s.th.

Freund [frɔynt], *m.* (—**es**, *pl.* —**e**) friend.

freundlich ['frɔyntlıç], *adj.* friendly, kind, affable, pleasing, cheerful, pleasant, genial.

Freundschaft ['frɔyntʃaft], *f.* (—, *pl.* —**en**) friendship.

Frevel ['fre:fəl], *m.* (—**s**, *pl.* —) crime, misdeed, offence.

freveln ['fre:fəln], *v.n.* do wrong, trespass, commit an outrage.

Friede(n) ['fri:də(n)], *m.* (**—ns**, *no pl.*) peace.

friedfertig ['fri:tfertɪç], *adj.* peaceable.

Friedhof ['fri:tho:f], *m.* (**—s**, *pl.* ⸚e) churchyard, cemetery.

friedlich ['fri:tlɪç], *adj.* peaceful.

friedliebend ['fri:tli:bənt], *adj.* peaceable, peace-loving.

Friedrich ['fri:drɪç], *m.* Frederic(k).

friedselig ['fri:tze:lɪç], *adj.* peaceable.

frieren ['fri:rən], *v.n. irr.* feel cold, freeze.

Fries [fri:s], *m.* (**—es**, *pl.* **—e**) frieze.

Friese ['fri:zə], *m.* ⸚(**—n**, *pl.* **—n**) Frisian.

frisch [frɪʃ], *adj.* fresh; new; (*weather*) crisp; (*fig.*) lively, brisk, gay.

Frische ['frɪʃə], *f.* (**—**, *no pl.*) freshness, liveliness, gaiety.

Friseur [fri'zo:r], *m.* (**—s**, *pl.* **—e**) hairdresser, barber.

Friseuse [fri'zo:zə], *f.* (**—**, *pl.* **—n**) female hairdresser.

frisieren [fri'zi:rən], *v.a.* dress (s.o.'s) hair.

Frist [frɪst], *f.* (**—**, *pl.* **—en**) time, term, period; (fixed) term; delay, respite.

fristen ['frɪstən], *v.a. das Leben* **—**, gain a bare living.

Frisur [fri'zu:r], *f.* (**—**, *pl.* **—en**) coiffure, hair-style.

frivol [fri'vo:l], *adj.* frivolous.

Frivolität [frivo:li'tɛ:t], *f.* (**—**, *pl.* **—en**) frivolity.

froh [fro:], *adj.* glad, joyful, joyous.

frohgelaunt ['fro:gəlaunt], *adj.* good-humoured, cheerful.

fröhlich ['frø:lɪç], *adj.* gay, merry.

frohlocken [fro:'lɔkən], *v.n.* (*rare*) exult.

Frohsinn ['fro:zɪn], *m.* (**—s**, *no pl.*) good humour, gaiety.

fromm [frɔm], *adj.* pious, religious, devout.

frommen ['frɔmən], *v.n.* (*obs.*) be of advantage (to s.o.).

Frömmigkeit ['frœmɪçkaɪt], *f.* (**—**, *no pl.*) piety, devoutness.

Fron [fro:n], *f.* (**—**, *no pl.*) (feudal) service; statute labour.

frönen ['frø:nən], *v.n.* (*fig.*) be a slave to; indulge in (*Dat.*).

Fronleichnam [fro:n'laɪxna:m], *m.* (*Eccl.*) (feast of) Corpus Christi.

Front [frɔnt], *f.* (**—**, *pl.* **—en**) front, forepart; (*building*) elevation; (*Mil.*) front line.

Frosch [frɔʃ], *m.* (**—es**, *pl.* ⸚e) (*Zool.*) frog.

Frost [frɔst], *m.* (**—es**, *pl.* ⸚e) frost; coldness, chill.

Frostbeule ['frɔstbɔylə], *f.* (**—**, *pl.* **—n**) chilblain.

frösteln ['frœstəln], *v.n.* feel a chill, shiver.

frostig ['frɔstɪç], *adj.* frosty; cold, chilly.

frottieren [frɔ'ti:rən], *v.a.* rub (down).

Frottiertuch [frɔ'ti:rtu:x], *n.* (**—s**, *pl.* ⸚er) Turkish towel, bath towel.

Frucht [fruxt], *f.* (**—**, *pl.* ⸚e) fruit; (*fig.*) result, effect; (*Med.*) fœtus.

fruchtbar ['fruxtba:r], *adj.* fruitful, productive, fertile.

fruchten ['fruxtən], *v.n.* produce fruit; (*fig.*) be effectual.

Fruchtknoten ['fruxtkno:tən], *m.* (**—s**, *pl.* **—**) (*Bot.*) seed-vessel.

früh(e) [fry:(ə)], *adj.* early.

Frühe ['fry:ə], *f.* (**—**, *no pl.*) early morning, dawn.

früher ['fry:ər], *adv.* earlier (on), formerly.

frühestens ['fry:əstəns], *adv.* at the earliest (possible moment).

Frühjahr ['fry:ja:r], *n.*, **Frühling** ['fry:lɪŋ], *m.* (**—s**, *pl.* **—e**) spring.

frühreif ['fry:raɪf], *adj.* precocious.

Frühschoppen ['fry:ʃɔpən], *m.* (**—s**, *pl.* **—**) morning pint (beer *or* wine).

Frühstück ['fry:ʃtyk], *n.* (**—s**, *pl.* **—e**) breakfast; *zweites* **—**, lunch.

Fuchs [fuks], *m.* (**—es**, *pl.* ⸚e) fox; chestnut (horse); (*fig.*) cunning chap; (*student*) freshman.

Fuchsbau ['fuksbau], *m.* (**—s**, *pl.* **—e**) fox-hole.

Fuchseisen ['fuksaɪzən], *n.* (**—s**, *pl.* **—**) fox-trap.

fuchsen ['fuksən], *v.r. sich* **—** *über*, be annoyed about.

Fuchsie ['fuksjə], *f.* (**—**, *pl.* **—n**) (*Bot.*) fuchsia.

fuchsig ['fuksɪç], *adj.* (*coll.*) very angry.

Füchsin ['fyksɪn], *f.* (**—**, *pl.* **—innen**) vixen.

fuchsrot ['fuksro:t], *adj.* fox-coloured, sorrel.

Fuchsschwanz ['fukʃvants], *m.* (**—es**, *pl.* ⸚e) fox-brush; pad saw.

Fuchtel ['fuxtəl], *f.* (**—**, *pl.* **—n**) sword blade; rod, whip.

Fuder ['fu:dər], *n.* (**—s**, *pl.* **—**) load, cart-load; wine measure (c. 270 gallons).

Fug [fu:k], *m.* (**—s**, *no pl.*) (*rare*) right, justice; *mit* **—** *und Recht*, with every right.

Fuge (1) ['fu:gə], *f.* (**—**, *pl.* **—n**) joint, groove.

Fuge (2) ['fu:gə], *f.* (**—**, *pl.* **—n**) (*Mus.*) fugue.

fügen ['fy:gən], *v.a.* fit together, join, dovetail. — *v.r. sich* **—**, submit (to), accommodate o.s. (to).

fügsam ['fy:kza:m], *adj.* pliant, submissive, yielding.

Fügung ['fy:gun], *f.* (**—**, *pl.* **—en**) co-incidence; dispensation (of Providence); Providence.

fühlbar ['fy:lba:r], *adj.* perceptible; tangible; *sich* **—** *machen*, make o.s. felt.

fühlen ['fy:lən], *v.a.* feel, touch, sense, be aware of.

Fühler ['fy:lər], *m.* (**—s**, *pl.* **—**) tentacle, feeler.

Fühlhorn

Fühlhorn ['fy:lhɔrn], *n.* (—s, *pl.* ⁻er) feeler, antenna, tentacle.

Fühlung ['fy:luŋ], *f.* (—, *no pl.*) — *haben mit*, be in touch with.

Fuhre ['fu:rə], *f.* (—, *pl.* —n) conveyance, vehicle, cart-load.

führen ['fy:rən], *v.a.* lead, guide, conduct, command; (*pen*) wield; (*law-suit*) carry on; (*conversation*) have, keep up; (*name, title*) bear; (*goods*) stock, deal in; *Krieg* —, wage war; *etwas im Schilde* —, have a plan; *das Wort* —, be spokesman; *einen hinters Licht* —, cheat s.o.

Führer ['fy:rər], *m.* (—s, *pl.* —) leader, guide; head, manager; conductor; driver, pilot.

Führerschaft ['fy:rərʃaft], *f.* (—, *no pl.*) leadership.

Führerschein ['fy:rərʃain], *m.* (—s, *pl.* —e) driving-licence.

Führersitz ['fy:rərzits], *m.* (—es, *pl.* —e) driver's seat; pilot's cockpit.

Fuhrlohn ['fu:rlo:n], *m.* (—s, *no pl.*) cartage, carriage.

Fuhrmann ['fu:rman], *m.* (—s, *pl.* ⁻er) carter, carrier.

Führung ['fy:ruŋ], *f.* (—, *no pl.*) guidance; leadership; conducted tour; management, direction; behaviour, conduct.

Führungszeugnis ['fy:ruŋtsɔyknis], *n.* (—sses, *pl.* —sse) certificate of good conduct.

Fuhrwerk ['fu:rverk], *n.* (—s, *pl.* —e) carriage, vehicle, waggon.

Fuhrwesen ['fu:rve:zən], *n.* (—s, *no pl.*) transport services, transportation.

Fülle ['fylə], *f.* (—, *no pl.*) fullness; abundance, plenty.

Füllen ['fylən], *n.* (—s, *pl.* —) foal.

füllen ['fylən], *v.a.* fill, fill up; stuff.

Füllfederhalter ['fylfe:dərhaltər], *m.* (—s, *pl.* —) fountain-pen.

Füllung ['fyluŋ], *f.* (—, *pl.* —en) filling; stuffing; (*door*) panel.

fummeln ['fuməln], *v.n.* fumble.

Fund [funt], *m.* (—es, *pl.* —e) find; discovery.

Fundbüro ['funtbyro], *n.* (—s, *pl.* —s) lost property office.

Fundgrube ['funtgru:bə], *f.* (—, *pl.* —n) gold-mine, source, treasure-house.

fundieren [fun'di:rən], *v.a.* found; establish.

fünf [fynf], *num. adj.* five.

Fünfeck ['fynfɛk], *n.* (—s, *pl.* —e) pentagon.

Fünffüßler ['fynffy:slər], *m.* (—s, *pl.* —) (*Poet.*) pentameter.

fünfjährig ['fynfjɛ:riç], *num. adj.* five-year-old.

fünfjährlich ['fynfjɛ:rliç], *num. adj.* quinquennial, five-yearly.

fünfzehn ['fynftse:n], *num. adj.* fifteen.

fünfzig ['fynftsiç], *num. adj.* fifty.

fungieren [fuŋ'gi:rən], *v.n.* — *als*, act as, officiate as.

Funk [funk], *m.* (—s, *no pl.*) radio; wireless; telegraphy.

Funke ['funkə], *m.* (—n, *pl.* —n) spark, sparkle.

funkeln ['funkəln], *v.n.* sparkle, glitter; (*stars*) twinkle.

funkelnagelneu ['funkəlna:gəlnɔy], *adj.* (*coll.*) brand-new.

funken ['funkən], *v.a.* flash (messages); telegraph, broadcast.

Funker ['funkər], *m.* (—s, *pl.* —) wireless operator.

Funksender ['funkzɛndər], *m.* (—s, *pl.* —) radio-transmitter.

Funkspruch ['funkʃprux], *m.* (—s, *pl.* ⁻e) wireless-message.

Funktelegramm ['funktelegram], *n.* (—s, *pl.* —e) radio telegram.

für [fy:r], *prep.* (*Acc.*) for, instead of; *ein — allemal*, once and for all; *an und — sich*, in itself.

Fürbitte ['fy:rbitə], *f.* (—, *pl.* —n) intercession.

Furche ['furçə], *f.* (—, *pl.* —n) furrow; (*face*) wrinkle.

furchen ['furçən], *v.a.* furrow; (*face*) wrinkle.

Furcht [furçt], *f.* (—, *no pl.*) fear, worry, anxiety; dread, fright, terror, apprehension.

furchtbar ['furçtba:r], *adj.* dreadful, terrible, frightful.

fürchten ['fyrçtən], *v.a.* fear, be afraid of. — *v.r. sich — vor*, be afraid of.

fürchterlich ['fyrçtərliç], *adj.* terrible, horrible, awful.

furchtsam ['furçtza:m], *adj.* timid, fearful, apprehensive.

Furie ['fu:rjə], *f.* (—, *pl.* —n) fury, virago.

fürlieb [fyr'li:p], *adv.* — *mit etwas — nehmen*, put up with, be content with s.th.

Furnier [fur'ni:r], *n.* (—s, *pl.* —e) veneer, inlay.

Furore [fu'ro:rə], *n.* (—s, *no pl.*) — *machen*, cause a sensation, create an uproar.

Fürsorge ['fy:rzɔrgə], *f.* (—, *no pl.*) solicitude; provision; welfare.

fürsorglich ['fy:rzɔrgliç], *adj.* thoughtful, with loving care.

Fürsprache ['fy:rʃpra:xə], *f.* (—, *no pl.*) advocacy, intercession.

Fürst [fyrst], *m.* (—en, *pl.* —en) prince, sovereign.

Furt [furt], *f.* (—, *pl.* —en) ford.

Furunkel [fu'runkəl], *m.* (—s, *pl.* —) furuncle, boil.

Fürwort ['fy:rvɔrt], *n.* (—s, *pl.* ⁻er) pronoun.

Fusel ['fu:zəl], *m.* (—s, *no pl.*) bad liquor, (*Am.*) hooch (*sl.*).

Fuß [fu:s], *m.* (—es, *pl.* ⁻e) (*human*) foot; (*object*) base.

Fußangel ['fu:saŋəl], *f.* (—, *pl.* —n) man-trap.

Fußball ['fu:sbal], *m.* (—s, *pl.* ⁻e) football.

Fußboden ['fu:sbo:dən], *m.* (—s, *pl.* ∴) floor.
fußen ['fu:sən], *v.n.* — *auf,* be based upon.
fußfrei ['fu:sfraɪ], *adj.* ankle-length.
Fußgänger ['fu:sgɛŋər], *m.* (—s, *pl.* —) pedestrian.
Fußgestell ['fu:sgəʃtɛl], *n.* (—s, *pl.* —e) pedestal.
Fußpflege ['fu:spfle:gə], *f.* (—, *no pl.*) chiropody.
Fußpunkt ['fu:spuŋkt], *m.* (—s, *no pl.*) nadir.
Fußtritt ['fu:strɪt], *m.* (—s, *pl.* —e) kick.
futsch [futʃ], *excl.* (*coll.*) gone, lost.
Futter ['futər], *n.* (—s, *no pl.*) (*dress*) lining; (*animals*) fodder, feed.
Futteral [futə'ra:l], *n.* (—s, *pl.* —e) case; sheath.
Futterkräuter ['futərkrɔytər], *n. pl.* herbage.
futtern ['futərn], *v.n.* (*coll.*) feed, stuff o.s.
füttern ['fytərn], *v.a.* feed; (*garment*) line.

G

G [ge:], *n.* (—s, *pl.* —s) the letter G; (*Mus.*) *G Dur,* G major; (*Mus.*) *G Moll,* G minor; (*Mus.*) — *-Saite,* G string.
Gabe ['ga:bə], *f.* (—, *pl.* —n) gift, present; donation; *barmherzige* —, alms; (*fig.*) gift, talent.
Gabel ['ga:bəl], *f.* (—, *pl.* —n) fork; (*deer*) antler; (*cart*) shafts.
gabelig ['ga:bəlɪç], *adj.* forked.
Gabelung ['ga:bəluŋ], *f.* (—, *pl.* —en) bifurcation, branching (of road).
Gabelzinke ['ga:bəltsɪŋkə], *f.* (—, *pl.* —n) prong, tine.
Gabun [ga'bu:n], *n.* Gaboon.
gackern ['gakərn], *v.n.* cackle; (*fig.*) chatter.
gaffen ['gafən], *v.n.* gape (at), stare.
Gage ['ga:ʒə], *f.* (—, *pl.* —n) salary, pay, fee.
gähnen ['gɛ:nən], *v.n.* yawn, gape.
Galan [ga'la:n], *m.* (—s, *pl.* —e) lover, gallant.
galant [ga'lant], *adj.* polite, courteous; —*es Abenteuer,* love affair.
Galanterie [galantə'ri:], *f.* (—, *pl.* —n) courtesy.
Galanteriewaren [galantə'ri:va:rən], *f. pl.* fancy goods.
Galeere [ga'le:rə], *f.* (—, *pl.* —n) galley.
Galerie [galə'ri:], *f.* (—, *pl.* —n) gallery.
Galgen ['galgən], *m.* (—s, *pl.* —) gallows, gibbet; scaffold.

Galgenfrist ['galgənfrɪst], *f.* (—, *no pl.*) short delay, respite.
Galgenhumor ['galgənhumo:r], *m.* (—s, *no pl.*) wry or grim humour.
Galgenvogel ['galgənfo:gəl], *m.* (—s, *pl.* ∴) gallows-bird.
Galizien [ga'li:tsjən], *n.* Galicia.
Gallapfel ['galapfəl], *m.* (—s, *pl.* ∴) gall-nut.
Galle ['galə], *f.* (—, *pl.* —n) gall, bile.
Gallenblase ['galənbla:zə], *f.* (—, *pl.* —n) gall-bladder.
Gallert ['galərt], *n.* (—s, *no pl.*) jelly.
Gallien ['galjən], *n.* Gaul.
gallig ['galɪç], *adj.* bilious.
galvanisieren [galvanɪ'zi:rən], *v.a.* galvanize.
Gamaschen [ga'maʃən], *f. pl.* spats, gaiters.
Gang [gaŋ], *m.* (—es, *pl.* ∴e) walk, gait; (*horse*) pace; (*house*) passage, corridor; (*meal*) course, dish; (*action*) progress, course; (*sport*) round, bout; (*machine*) motion; stroke; (*Motor.*) gear.
gang [gaŋ], *adj.* — *und gäbe,* customary, usual, common.
Gangart ['gaŋa:rt], *f.* (—, *pl.* —en) gait; (*horse*) pace.
gangbar ['gaŋba:r], *adj.* marketable, saleable; (*road*) passable; practicable.
Gans [gans], *f.* (—, *pl.* ∴e) goose.
Gänseblümchen ['gɛnzəbly:mçən], *n.* (—s, *pl.* —) daisy.
Gänsefüßchen ['gɛnzəfy:sçən], *n. pl.* (*coll.*) inverted commas, quotation marks.
Gänsehaut ['gɛnzəhaut], *f.* (—, *no pl.*) goose-flesh, goose-pimples.
Gänserich ['gɛnzərɪç], *m.* (—s, *pl.* —e) (*Orn.*) gander.
ganz ['gants], *adj.* whole, entire, all; complete, total.
gänzlich ['gɛntslɪç], *adj.* whole, total, entire, full, complete.
gar [ga:r], *adj.* sufficiently cooked, done. — *adv.* very, quite.
garantieren [garan'ti:rən], *v.a.* guarantee, warrant.
Garaus ['ga:raus], *m.* (—, *no pl.*) *einem den* — *machen,* finish s.o., kill s.o.
Garbe ['garbə], *f.* (—, *pl.* —n) sheaf.
Garde ['gardə], *f.* (—, *pl.* —n) guard, guards.
Garderobe [gardə'ro:bə], *f.* (—, *pl.* —n) wardrobe; cloak-room; (*Theat.*) dressing-room.
Gardine [gar'di:nə], *f.* (—, *pl.* —n) curtain.
Gardist [gar'dɪst], *m.* (—en, *pl.* —en) guardsman.
gären ['gɛ:rən], *v.n.* ferment; effervesce.
Garn [garn], *n.* (—s, *pl.* —e) yarn, thread.
Garnele [gar'ne:lə], *f.* (—, *pl.* —n) (*Zool.*) shrimp; *große* —, prawn.
garnieren [gar'ni:rən], *v.a.* trim, garnish.
Garnison [garni'zo:n], *f.* (—, *pl.* —en) garrison.

Garnitur

Garnitur [garni'tu:r], *f.* (—, *pl.* **—en**) trimming; set.

Garnröllchen [ˈgarnrœlçən], *n.* (**—s**, *pl.* —) reel of thread.

garstig [ˈgarstiç], *adj.* nasty, loathsome, ugly.

Garten [ˈgartən], *m.* (**—s**, *pl.* ⁓) garden.

Gartenlaube [ˈgartənlaubə], *f.* (—, *pl.* **—n**) bower, arbour.

Gärtner [ˈgɛrtnər], *m.* (**—s**, *pl.* —) gardener.

Gärtnerei [gɛrtnəˈraɪ], *f.* (—, *pl.* **—en**) horticulture; market-garden; (plant) nursery.

Gärung [ˈgɛːruŋ], *f.* (—, *pl.* **—en**) fermentation, effervescence.

Gas [gaːs], *n.* (**—es**, **—e**) gas; — geben, (*Motor.*) accelerate.

gasartig [ˈgaːsartiç], *adj.* gaseous.

Gäßchen [ˈgɛsçən], *n.* (**—s**, *pl.* —) narrow alley; lane.

Gasse [ˈgasə], *f.* (—, *pl.* **—n**) alleyway, lane; (*rare*) street.

Gassenbube [ˈgasənbuːbə] *see* **Gassenjunge.**

Gassenhauer [ˈgasənhauər], *m.* (**—s**, *pl.* —), street-song, vulgar ballad; pop song.

Gassenjunge [ˈgasənjuŋə], *m.* (**—n**, *pl.* **—n**) street-urchin.

Gast [gast], *m.* (**—s**, *pl.* ⁓e) guest, visitor.

gastfrei [ˈgastfraɪ], *adj.* hospitable.

Gastfreund [ˈgastfrɔynt], *m.* (**—s**, *pl.* **—e**) guest; host.

Gastfreundschaft [ˈgastfrɔyntʃaft], *f.* (—, *no pl.*) hospitality.

Gastgeber [ˈgastgeːbər], *m.* (**—s**, *pl.* —) host.

Gasthaus [ˈgasthaus], *n.* (**—es**, *pl.* ⁓er), **Gasthof** [ˈgasthoːf], *m.* (**—es**, *pl.* ⁓e) inn, hotel, public house.

gastieren [gasˈtiːrən], *v.n.* (*Theat.*) appear as a guest artist; star.

gastlich [ˈgastliç], *adj.* hospitable.

Gastmahl [ˈgastmaːl], *n.* (**—s**, *pl.* **—e**) banquet, feast.

Gastrecht [ˈgastrɛçt], *n.* (**—s**, *no pl.*) right of hospitality.

Gastspiel [ˈgastʃpiːl], *n.* (**—s**, *pl.* **—e**) (*Theat.*) performance by visiting company.

Gaststätte [ˈgaststɛtə], *f.* (—, *pl.* **—n**) restaurant.

Gaststube [ˈgastʃtuːbə], *f.* (—, *pl.* **—n**) hotel lounge; guest room.

Gastwirt [ˈgastvirt], *m.* (**—s**, *pl.* **—e**) landlord.

Gastwirtin [ˈgastvirtin], *f.* (—, *pl.* **—nen**) landlady.

Gastzimmer [ˈgasttsimər], *n.* (**—s**, *pl.* —) *see* **Gaststube**; spare bedroom.

Gatte [ˈgatə], *m.* (**—n**, *pl.* **—n**) husband, spouse, consort.

Gatter [ˈgatər], *n.* (**—s**, *pl.* —) grate, lattice, grating.

Gattin [ˈgatin], *f.* (—, *pl.* **—nen**) wife, spouse, consort.

Gattung [ˈgatuŋ], *f.* (—, *pl.* **—en**) kind, species, sort, class; breed, genus; (*Lit.*) genre.

Gau [gau], *m.* (**—s**, *pl.* **—e**) district, province.

gaukeln [ˈgaukəln], *v.n.* juggle. — *v.a.* dazzle.

Gaul [gaul], *m.* (**—s**, *pl.* ⁓e) (old) horse, nag; *einem geschenkten — sieht man nicht ins Maul,* never look a gift horse in the mouth.

Gaumen [ˈgaumən], *m.* (**—s**, *pl.* —) palate.

Gauner [ˈgaunər], *m.* (**—s**, *pl.* —) rogue, sharper, swindler, cheat.

gaunern [ˈgaunərn], *v.n.* cheat, trick, swindle.

Gaunersprache [ˈgaunərʃpraːxə], *f.* (—, *no pl.*) thieves' slang.

Gaze [ˈgaːzə], *f.* (—, *pl.* **—n**) gauze.

Gazelle [gaˈtsɛlə], *f.* (—, *pl.* **—n**) (*Zool.*) gazelle, antelope.

Geächtete [gəˈɛçtətə], *m.* (**—n**, *pl.* **—n**) outlaw.

Geächze [gəˈɛçtsə], *n.* (**—s**, *no pl.*) moaning, groaning.

Geäder [gəˈɛːdər], *n.* (**—s**, *no pl.*) veins, arteries, veining.

geädert [gəˈɛdərt], *adj.* veined, streaked, grained.

-geartet [gəˈaːrtət], *adj.* (*suffix in compounds*) -natured.

Gebäck [gəˈbɛk], *n.* (**—s**, *no pl.*) pastry, rolls, cakes.

Gebälk [gəˈbɛlk], *n.* (**—s**, *no pl.*) timber-work, timber-frame.

Gebärde [gəˈbɛːrdə], *f.* (—, *pl.* **—n**) gesture.

gebärden [gəˈbɛːrdən], *v.r. sich* —, behave.

Gebaren [gəˈbaːrən], *n.* (**—s**, *no pl.*) demeanour.

gebären [gəˈbɛːrən], *v.a. irr.* bear, bring forth, give birth to, be delivered of.

Gebärmutter [gəˈbɛːrmutər], *f.* (—, *no pl.*) womb, uterus.

Gebäude [gəˈbɔydə], *n.* (**—s**, *pl.* —) building, edifice.

Gebein [gəˈbaɪn], *n.* (**—s**, *pl.* **—e**) bones, skeleton; (*fig.*) remains.

Gebell [gəˈbɛl], *n.* (**—s**, *no pl.*) barking.

geben [ˈgeːbən], *v.a. irr.* give, present; confer, bestow; yield; (*cards*) deal. — *v.r. sich* —, show o.s., behave; abate; *das gibt sich,* that won't last long; *es gibt . . .,* there is . . .; *was gibt's?* what's the matter?

Geber [ˈgeːbər], *m.* (**—s**, *pl.* —) giver, donor.

Gebet [gəˈbeːt], *n.* (**—s**, *pl.* **—e**) prayer; *sein — verrichten,* say o.'s prayers; *ins — nehmen,* question s.o. thoroughly.

Gebiet [gəˈbiːt], *n.* (**—s**, *pl.* **—e**) district, territory; (*Am.*) precinct; jurisdiction; (*fig.*) province, field, sphere, domain.

gebieten [gəˈbiːtən], *v.a. irr.* command, order.

Gebieter [gəˈbiːtər], *m.* (**—s**, *pl.* —) lord, master, ruler.

Gebilde [gə'bɪldə], n. (—s, pl. —) form, thing; formation, structure; figment.

gebildet [gə'bɪldət], adj. educated, cultured, refined.

Gebirge [gə'bɪrgə], n. (—s, pl. —) mountains.

Gebirgskamm [gə'bɪrkskam], m. (—s, pl. ⁓e) mountain-ridge.

Gebiß [gə'bɪs], n. (—sses, pl. —sse) set of (false) teeth, denture; (horse) bit.

Gebläse [gə'blɛːzə], n. (—s, pl. —) bellows; blower.

Gebläsemaschine [gə'blɛːzəmaʃiːnə], f. (—, pl. —n) blower.

Gebläseofen [gə'blɛːzəoːfən], m. (—s, pl. ⁓) blast-furnace.

geblümt [gə'blyːmt], adj. flowered.

Geblüt [gə'blyːt], n. (—s, no pl.) blood; race, line, lineage, stock.

geboren [gə'boːrən], adj. born.

geborgen [gə'bɔrgən], adj. saved, hidden, sheltered, rescued.

Gebot [gə'boːt], n. (—s, pl. —e) order, decree, command; (Bibl.) Commandment.

geboten [gə'boːtən], adj. necessary, advisable.

Gebräu [gə'brɔy], n. (—s, no pl.) brew, concoction, mixture.

Gebrauch [gə'braux], m. (—s, pl. ⁓e) use; employment; custom, usage, habit, practice; (rare) rite.

gebrauchen [gə'brauxən], v.a. use, make use of, employ.

gebräuchlich [gə'brɔyçlɪç], adj. usual, customary, common.

Gebrauchsanweisung [gə'brauxsan-vaizuŋ], f. (—, pl. —en) directions for use.

gebraucht [gə'brauxt], adj. used, second-hand.

Gebrechen [gə'brɛçən], n. (—s, pl. —) infirmity.

gebrechen [gə'brɛçən], v.n. irr. es gebricht mir an, I am in want of, I lack.

gebrechlich [gə'brɛçlɪç], adj. infirm, frail, weak.

gebrochen [gə'brɔxən], adj. broken; —es Deutsch, broken German.

Gebrüder [gə'bryːdər], m. pl. (Comm.) brothers.

Gebrüll [gə'bryl], n. (—s, no pl.) roaring; (cows) lowing.

Gebühr [gə'byːr], f. (—, pl. —en) charge, due; fee; tax, duty.

gebühren [gə'byːrən], v.n. be due to s.o. — v.r. sich —, wie es sich gebührt, as it ought to be, as is right and proper.

gebunden [gə'bundən], adj. (fig.) bound, committed; (Poet.) metrical.

Geburt [gə'buːrt], f. (—, pl. —en) birth.

gebürtig [gə'byrtɪç], adj. a native of.

Geburtsfehler [gə'buːrtsfeːlər], m. (—s, pl. —) congenital defect.

Geburtshelfer [gə'buːrtshɛlfər], m. (—s, pl. —) obstetrician.

Geburtshelferin [gə'buːrtshɛlfərɪn], f. (—, pl. —nen) midwife.

Geburtsort [gə'buːrtsɔrt], m. (—s, pl. —e) birthplace.

Geburtsschein [gə'buːrtsʃain], m. (⁓(e)s, pl. —e) birth certificate.

Geburtswehen [gə'buːrtsveːən], f. pl. birthpangs; labour pains.

Gebüsch [gə'byʃ], n. (—es, pl. —e) bushes, thicket; underwood.

Geck [gɛk], m. (—en, pl. —en) fop, dandy; (carnival) fool.

geckenhaft ['gɛkənhaft], adj. foppish, dandyish.

Gedächtnis [gə'dɛçtnɪs], n. (—ses, no pl.) memory; remembrance, recollection; im — behalten, keep in mind.

Gedanke [gə'daŋkə], m. (—ns, pl. —n) thought, idea.

Gedankenfolge [gə'daŋkənfɔlgə], f. (—, no pl.), **Gedankengang** [gə'daŋ-kəngaŋ], m. (—s, pl. ⁓e) sequence of thought, train of thought.

Gedankenstrich [gə'daŋkənʃtrɪç], m. (—s, pl. —e) dash; hyphen.

Gedärm [gə'dɛrm], n. ⁓(—s, pl. —e) bowels, intestines, entrails.

Gedeck [gə'dɛk], n. (—s, pl. —e) cover; menu; place laid at a table.

gedeihen [gə'daiən], v.n. irr. (aux. sein) thrive, prosper; progress.

gedeihlich [gə'dailɪç], adj. thriving, salutary.

gedenken [gə'dɛŋkən], v.n. irr. (Genit.) think of, remember; — etwas zu tun, intend to do s.th.

Gedenken [gə'dɛŋkən], n. (—s, no pl.) remembrance.

Gedenkfeier [gə'dɛŋkfaiər], f. (—, pl. —n) commemoration.

Gedicht [gə'dɪçt], n. (—s, pl. —e) poem.

gediegen [gə'diːgən], adj. solid, sound, genuine, true, honourable, sterling.

Gedränge [gə'drɛŋə], n. (—s, no pl.) crowd, throng; crush.

Gedrängtheit [gə'drɛnkthait], f. (—, no pl.) conciseness.

gedrungen [gə'druŋən], adj. thick-set, stocky; compact; concise (style).

Geduld [gə'dult], f. (—, no pl.) patience, forbearance.

gedulden [gə'duldən], v.r. sich —, be patient.

geduldig [gə'duldɪç], adj. patient, forbearing, indulgent.

Geduld(s)spiel [gə'dult(s)ʃpiːl], n. (—s, pl. —e) puzzle; (Cards) patience.

gedunsen [gə'dunzən], adj. bloated.

geeignet [gə'aignət], adj. suitable, fit, appropriate, apt.

Gefahr [gə'faːr], f. (—, pl. —en) danger, peril, hazard, risk; — laufen, run the risk.

gefährden [gə'fɛːrdən], v.a. endanger, imperil, jeopardise.

gefährlich [gə'fɛːrlɪç], adj. dangerous, perilous.

Gefährt [gə'fɛːrt], n. (—s, pl. —e) (obs.) vehicle, conveyance.

Gefährte [gə'fɛːrtə], m. (—en, pl. —en) comrade, companion, fellow.

Gefälle

Gefälle [gəˈfɛlə], *n.* (**—s**, *pl.* **—e**) fall, descent, incline, gradient.

Gefallen [gəˈfalən], *m.* (**—s**, *no pl.*) pleasure, liking; favour, kindness.

gefallen (1) [gəˈfalən], *v.n. irr.* please; *es gefällt mir*, I like it; *wie gefällt Ihnen . . .*; how do you like . . . .

gefallen (2) [gəˈfalən], *adj.* (*Mil.*) fallen, killed in action.

gefällig [gəˈfɛlɪç], *adj.* pleasing, accommodating, obliging, anxious to please; *was ist* —? what can I do for you?

Gefälligkeit [gəˈfɛlɪçkaɪt], *f.* (**—**, *pl.* **—en**) courtesy; favour, service, good turn.

gefälligst [gəˈfɛlɪçst], *adv.* if you please.

Gefallsucht [gəˈfalzuxt], *f.* (**—**, *no pl.*) coquetry.

gefallsüchtig [gəˈfalzyçtɪç], *adj.* coquettish.

gefangen [gəˈfaŋən], *adj.* in prison, imprisoned, captive.

Gefangene [gəˈfaŋənə], *m.* (**—n**, *pl.* **—n**) prisoner, captive.

Gefangennahme [gəˈfaŋənnaːmə], *f.* (**—**, *no pl.*) arrest, capture.

Gefangenschaft [gəˈfaŋənʃaft], *f.* (**—**, *no pl.*) captivity, imprisonment, detention; *in — geraten*, be taken prisoner.

Gefängis [gəˈfɛŋnɪs], *n.* (**—sses**, *pl.* **—sse**) prison, gaol.

Gefäß [gəˈfɛːs], *n.* (**—es**, *pl.* **—e**) vessel.

gefaßt [gəˈfast], *adj.* collected, composed, ready; calm; *sich auf etwas — machen*, prepare o.s. for s.th.

Gefecht [gəˈfɛçt], *n.* (**—s**, *pl.* **—e**) fight, battle, combat; action, engagement.

gefeit [gəˈfaɪt], *adj.* proof against.

Gefieder [gəˈfiːdər], *n.* (**—s**, *no pl.*) plumage, feathers.

Gefilde [gəˈfɪldə], *n.* (**—s**, *pl.* **—**) (*Poet.*) fields, plain.

Geflecht [gəˈflɛçt], *n.* (**—s**, *no pl.*) wicker-work, texture.

geflissentlich [gəˈflɪsəntlɪç], *adj.* intentional, wilful, with a purpose.

Geflügel [gəˈflyːgəl], *n.* (**—s**, *no pl.*) fowls, poultry.

geflügelt [gəˈflyːgəlt], *adj.* winged; *—e Worte*, household word, familiar quotation.

Geflüster [gəˈflystər], *n.* (**—s**, *no pl.*) whispering, whisper.

Gefolge [gəˈfɔlgə], *n.* (**—s**, *no pl.*) retinue, following.

gefräßig [gəˈfrɛːsɪç], *adj.* voracious, gluttonous.

Gefreite [gəˈfraɪtə], *m.* (**—n**, *pl.* **—n**) (*Mil.*) lance-corporal.

gefrieren [gəˈfriːrən], *v.n. irr.* (*aux.* sein) freeze; congeal.

Gefrierpunkt [gəˈfriːrpuŋkt], *m.* (**—s**, *no pl.*) freezing point, zero.

Gefrorene [gəˈfroːrənə], *n.* (**—n**, *no pl.*) ice-cream.

Gefüge [gəˈfyːgə], *n.* (**—s**, *no pl.*) joints, structure, construction; frame.

gefügig [gəˈfyːgɪç], *adj.* pliant; docile; *einen — machen*, make s.o. amenable, persuade s.o.

Gefühl [gəˈfyːl], *n.* (**—s**, *pl.* **—e**) feeling, sense, sensation.

gegen [ˈgeːgən], *prep.* (*Acc.*) against; towards; about, near; in comparison with; in the direction of; opposed to; in exchange for; — *Quittung*, against receipt. — *adv.*, *prefix.* counter, opposing, contrary.

Gegend [ˈgeːgənt], *f.* (**—**, *pl.* **—en**) region, country, part.

Gegengewicht [ˈgeːgəngəvɪçt], *n.* (**—s**, *pl.* **—e**) counterweight, counterpoise.

Gegengift [ˈgeːgəngɪft], *n.* (**—s**, *pl.* **—e**) antidote.

Gegenleistung [ˈgeːgənlaɪstuŋ], *f.* (**—**, *pl.* **—en**) return; service in return; *Leistung und* —, give and take.

Gegenrede [ˈgeːgənreːdə], *f.* (**—**, *pl.* **—n**) contradiction; objection.

Gegensatz [ˈgeːgənzats], *m.* (**—es**, *pl.* **̈e**) contrast, opposition, antithesis.

gegensätzlich [ˈgeːgənzɛtslɪç], *adj.* contrary, adverse.

Gegenseite [ˈgeːgənzaɪtə], *f.* (**—**, *pl.* **—n**) opposite side; (*coin*) reverse.

gegenseitig [ˈgeːgənzaɪtɪç], *adj.* reciprocal, mutual.

Gegenstand [ˈgeːgənʃtant], *m.* (**—s**, *pl.* **̈e**) object; subject, matter.

gegenstandslos [ˈgeːgənʃtantsloːs], *adj.* superfluous, irrelevant.

Gegenstück [ˈgeːgənʃtyk], *n.* (**—s**, *pl.* **—e**) counterpart.

Gegenteil [ˈgeːgəntaɪl], *n.* (**—s**, *no pl.*) contrary; *im* —, on the contrary.

gegenüber [geːgənˈyːbər], *prep.* (*Dat.*) opposite to, facing. — *adv.* opposite.

Gegenüberstellung [geːgənˈyːbərʃtɛluŋ], *f.* (**—**, *pl.* **—en**) confrontation.

Gegenwart [ˈgeːgənvart], *f.* (**—**, *no pl.*) presence; (*Gram.*) present tense.

Gegenwehr [ˈgeːgənveːr], *f.* (**—**, *no pl.*) defence, resistance.

Gegenwirkung [ˈgeːgənvɪrkuŋ], *f.* (**—**, *pl.* **—en**) reaction, counter-effect.

gegenzeichnen [ˈgeːgəntsaɪçnən], *v.a.* countersign.

Gegner [ˈgeːgnər], *m.* (**—s**, *pl.* **—**) opponent, adversary, antagonist.

gegnerisch [ˈgeːgnərɪʃ], *adj.* adverse, antagonistic.

Gegnerschaft [ˈgeːgnərʃaft], *f.* (**—**, *no pl.*) antagonism; opposition.

Gehalt (1) [gəˈhalt], *m.* (**—s**, *no pl.*) contents; (*fig.*) value, standard.

Gehalt (2) [gəˈhalt], *n.* (**—s**, *pl.* **̈er**) salary, stipend; pay.

Gehaltszulage [gəˈhaltstsuːlaːgə], *f.* (**—**, *pl.* **—n**) rise (in salary); increment; (*Am.*) raise.

gehaltvoll [gəˈhaltfɔl], *adj.* substantial.

Gehänge [gəˈhɛŋə], *n.* (**—s**, *pl.* **—**) slope; festoon, garland.

geharnischt [gəˈharnɪʃt], *adj.* armoured, steel-clad; (*fig.*) severe.

gehässig [gəˈhɛsɪç], *adj.* malicious, spiteful.

Gehäuse [gə'hɔyzə], *n.* (—s, *pl.* —) casing, case; (*snail*) shell.

Gehege [gə'he:gə], *n.* (—s, *pl.* —) enclosure; *einem ins* — *kommen*, trespass on s.o.'s preserves.

geheim [gə'haɪm], *adj.* secret, clandestine.

Geheimnis [gə'haɪmnɪs], *n.* (—ses, *pl.* —se) secret, mystery.

geheimnisvoll [gə'haɪmnɪsfɔl], *adj.* mysterious.

Geheimrat [gə'haɪmra:t], *m.* (—s, *pl.* ·e) Privy Councillor.

Geheimschrift [gə'haɪmʃrɪft], *f.* (—, *pl.* —en) cryptography.

Geheimsprache [gə'haɪmʃpra:xə], *f.* (—, *pl.* —en) cipher.

Geheiß [gə'haɪs], *n.* (—es, *no pl.*) command, order, bidding.

gehen ['ge:ən], *v.n. irr.* (*aux.* sein) go, walk; (*Mach.*) work, function; (*goods*) sell; (*dough*) rise; *er lässt sich* —, he lets himself go; *er lässt es sich gut* —, he enjoys himself; *einem an die Hand* —, lend s.o. a hand, assist s.o.; *in Erfüllung* —, come true; *in sich* —, reflect; *wie geht es dir?* how are you? *es geht mir gut*, I am well.

geheuer [gə'hɔyər], *adj.* (*only in neg.*) *nicht ganz* —, creepy, eerie, uncanny; (*coll.*) fishy.

Gehilfe [gə'hɪlfə], *m.* (—n, *pl.* —n) assistant, helper.

Gehirn [gə'hɪrn], *n.* (—s, *pl.* —e) brain, brains.

Gehirnhautentzündung [gə'hɪrnhautɛntsynduŋ], *f.* (—, *pl.* —en) meningitis, cerebral inflammation.

Gehirnschlag [gə'hɪrnʃla:k], *m.* (—s, *pl.* ·e) apoplexy.

Gehöft [gə'hœft], *n.* (—es, *pl.* —e) farmstead.

Gehör [gə'hø:r], *n.* (—s, *no pl.*) hearing; *gutes* —, musical ear.

gehorchen [gə'hɔrçən], *v.n.* obey; *nicht* —, disobey.

gehören [gə'hø:rən], *v.n.* belong. — *v.r. sich* —, be the proper thing to do.

gehörig [gə'hø:rɪç], *adj. dazu* —, belonging to, referring to; due, fit, proper, thorough; (*fig.*) sound.

Gehörn [gə'hœrn], *n.* (—s, *pl.* —e) horns, antlers.

gehörnt [gə'hœrnt], *adj.* horned; (*fig.*) duped (husband).

Gehorsam [gə'ho:rza:m], *m.* (—s, *no pl.*) obedience; — *leisten*, show obedience; *den* — *verweigern*, refuse to obey.

gehorsam [gə'ho:rza:m], *adj.* obedient, dutiful, submissive.

Gehrock ['ge:rɔk], *m.* (—s, *pl.* ·e) frock-coat.

Geier ['gaɪər], *m.* (—s, *pl.* —) (*Orn.*) vulture.

Geifer ['gaɪfər], *m.* (—s, *no pl.*) saliva, drivel; (*animals*) foam; (*fig.*) venom, rancour.

geifern ['gaɪfərn], *v.n.* slaver, drivel; (*fig.*) foam at the mouth; give vent to o.'s anger.

Geige ['gaɪgə], *f.* (—, *pl.* —n) violin, fiddle.

Geigenharz ['gaɪgənha:rts], *n.* (—es, *no pl.*) colophony; rosin.

Geigensteg ['gaɪgənʃte:k], *m.* (—s, *pl.* —e) bridge of a violin.

Geiger ['gaɪgər], *m.* (—s, *pl.* —) violin-player, violinist.

geil [gaɪl], *adj.* rank; lecherous, lascivious.

Geisel ['gaɪzəl], *f.* (—, *pl.* —n) hostage.

Geiß [gaɪs], *f.* (—, *pl.* —en) goat, she-goat.

Geißblatt ['gaɪsblat], *n.* (—s, *no pl.*) (*Bot.*) honeysuckle.

Geißbock ['gaɪsbɔk], *m.* (—s, *pl.* ·e) billy-goat.

Geißel ['gaɪsəl], *f.* (—, *pl.* —n) scourge.

geißeln ['gaɪsəln], *v.a.* scourge, whip, flagellate.

Geist [gaɪst], *m.* (—es, *pl.* —er) spirit, mind; brains, intellect; wit; apparition, ghost.

Geisterbeschwörung ['gaɪstərbəʃvø:ruŋ], *f.* (—, *pl.* —en) evocation (of spirits); necromancy; exorcism.

geisterhaft ['gaɪstərhaft], *adj.* ghostly, spectral, weird.

Geisterwelt ['gaɪstərvɛlt], *f.* (—, *no pl.*) world of spirits.

geistesabwesend ['gaɪstəsapve:zənt], *adj.* absent-minded.

Geistesfreiheit ['gaɪstəsfraɪhaɪt], *f.* (—, *no pl.*) freedom of thought.

Geistesgegenwart ['gaɪstəsge:gənvart], *f.* (—, *no pl.*) presence of mind.

Geisteskraft ['gaɪstəskraft], *f.* (—, *pl.* ·e) faculty of the mind.

Geistesstörung ['gaɪstəsʃtø:ruŋ], *f.* (—, *pl.* —en) mental aberration.

Geistesverfassung ['gaɪstəsfɛrfasuŋ], *f.* (—, *no pl.*) state of mind.

geistesverwandt ['gaɪstəsfɛrvant], *adj.* congenial.

Geistesverwirrung ['gaɪstəsfɛrvɪruŋ], *f.* (—, *no pl.*) bewilderment.

Geisteswissenschaften ['gaɪstəsvɪsənʃaftən], *f.pl.* (*Univ.*) Arts, Humanities.

Geisteszerrüttung ['gaɪstəstsɛrytuŋ], *f.* (—, *no pl.*) mental derangement, insanity.

geistig ['gaɪstɪç], *adj.* intellectual, mental; spiritual; —*e Getränke*, alcoholic liquors.

geistlich ['gaɪstlɪç], *adj.* spiritual; religious; ecclesiastical, clerical; —*er Orden*, religious order; —*er Stand*, holy orders, the Clergy.

Geistliche ['gaɪstlɪçə], *m.* (—n, *pl.* —n) priest, clergyman, cleric; minister of religion.

Geistlichkeit ['gaɪstlɪçkaɪt], *f.* (—, *no pl.*) clergy.

geistlos ['gaɪstlo:s], *adj.* dull, stupid.

geistreich ['gaɪstraɪç], *adj.* clever, witty.

Geiz [gaɪts], *m.* (—es, *no pl.*) avarice, covetousness.

geizen ['gaɪtsən], *v.n.* be miserly.

Geizhals ['gaɪtshals], *m.* (—es, *pl.* ⁓e) miser, niggard.

Geizkragen ['gaɪtskra:gən], *m.* (—s, *pl.* —) *see* **Geizhals**.

Gekreisch [gə'kraɪʃ], *n.* (—es, *no pl.*) screaming, shrieks.

Gekritzel [gə'krɪtsəl], *n.* (—s, *no pl.*) scrawling, scribbling.

Gekröse [gə'krø:zə], *n.* (—s, *no pl.*) tripe; (*Anat.*) mesentery.

gekünstelt [gə'kynstəlt], *adj.* artificial, affected.

Gelächter [gə'lɛçtər], *n.* (—s, *no pl.*) laughter.

Gelage [gə'la:gə], *n.* (—s, *pl.* —) (*obs.*) feast, banquet.

Gelände [gə'lɛndə], *n.* (—s, *pl.* —) terrain, region; landscape.

Geländer [gə'lɛndər], *n.* (—s, *pl.* —) railing, balustrade, banister.

gelangen [gə'laŋən], *v.n.* (*aux.* sein) arrive, come (to).

Gelaß [gə'las], *n.* (—sses, *pl.* —sse) (*obs.*) room, chamber.

gelassen [gə'lasən], *adj.* calm, composed, collected.

geläufig [gə'lɔyfɪç], *adj.* fluent.

gelaunt [gə'launt], *adj.* disposed.

Geläute [gə'lɔytə], *n.* (—s, *no pl.*) ringing, chiming; bells.

geläutert [gə'lɔytərt], *adj.* purified, cleansed.

gelb [gɛlp], *adj.* yellow, amber.

Gelbschnabel ['gɛlpʃna:bəl], *m.* (—s, *pl.* ⁓) fledg(e)ling; greenhorn.

Gelbsucht ['gɛlpzuxt], *f.* (—, *no pl.*) jaundice.

Geld [gɛlt], *n.* (—es, *pl.* —er) money, currency, coin; *bares* —, ready money, hard cash; *kleines* —, small change.

Geldanweisung ['gɛltanvaɪzuŋ], *f.* (—, *pl.* —en) money-order.

Geldbuße ['gɛltbu:sə], *f.* (—, *pl.* —n) fine.

Geldkurs ['gɛltkurs], *m.* (—es, *pl.* —e) rate of exchange.

Geldmittel ['gɛltmɪtəl], *n. pl.* pecuniary resources, financial resources.

Geldschrank ['gɛltʃraŋk], *m.* (—s, *pl.* ⁓e) safe.

Geldstrafe ['gɛltʃtra:fə], *f.* (—, *pl.* —n) fine.

Geldverlegenheit ['gɛltfɛrle:gənhaɪt], *f.* (—, *pl.* —en) pecuniary embarrassment, financial difficulty.

Geldwährung ['gɛltvɛ:ruŋ], *f.* (—, *pl.* —en) currency.

Geldwechsel ['gɛltvɛksəl], *m.* (—s, *no pl.*) exchange.

Gelee [ʒə'le:], *n.* (—s, *pl.* —s) jelly.

gelegen [gə'le:gən], *adj.* situated, situate; *das kommt mir gerade* —, that suits me; *mir ist daran* —, *dass,* I am anxious that.

Gelegenheit [gə'le:gənhaɪt], *f.* (—, *pl.* —en) occasion, chance, opportunity; facility; *bei* —, one of these days.

Gelegenheitskauf [gə'le:gənhaɪtskauf], *m.* (—s, *pl.* ⁓e) bargain.

gelegentlich [gə'le:gəntlɪç], *adj.* occasional.

gelehrig [gə'le:rɪç], *adj.* docile, tractable.

Gelehrsamkeit [gə'le:rza:mkaɪt], *f.* (—, *no pl.*) learning, erudition.

gelehrt [gə'le:rt], *adj.* learned, erudite.

Gelehrte [gə'le:rtə], *m.* (—n, *pl.* —n) scholar, man of learning, savant.

Geleise [gə'laɪzə], *n.* (—s, *pl.* —) *see* **Gleis.**

Geleit [gə'laɪt], *n.* (—s, *no pl.*) escort, accompaniment; (*Naut.*) convoy; *sicheres* —, safe conduct.

geleiten [gə'laɪtən], *v.a.* accompany, conduct, escort.

Gelenk [gə'lɛŋk], *n.* (—s, *pl.* —e) (*human*) joint; (*chain*) link.

Gelenkentzündung [gə'lɛŋkɛnttsyn-duŋ], *f.* (—, *pl.* —en) (*Med.*) arthritis.

gelenkig [gə'lɛŋkɪç], *adj.* flexible, pliant, nimble, supple.

Gelenkrheumatismus [gə'lɛŋkrɔyma-tɪsmus], *m.* (—, *no pl.*) (*Med.*) rheumatoid arthritis, rheumatic gout.

Gelichter [gə'lɪçtər], *n.* (—s, *no pl.*) riff-raff.

Geliebte [gə'li:ptə], *m.* (—n, *pl.* —n) lover, sweetheart, beloved. — *f.* (—n, *pl.* —n) mistress; beloved.

gelinde [gə'lɪndə], *adj.* soft, smooth, gentle, mild; — *gesagt,* to say the least.

Gelingen [gə'lɪŋən], *n.* (—s, *no pl.*) success.

gelingen [gə'lɪŋən], *v.n. irr.* (*aux.* sein) succeed; *es gelingt mir,* I succeed.

gellen ['gɛlən], *v.n.* yell; shrill.

geloben [gə'lo:bən], *v.a.* (*aux.* haben) promise solemnly, vow; *das Gelobte Land,* the Promised Land.

Gelöbnis [gə'lø:pnɪs], *n.* (—ses, *pl.* —se) vow, promise.

gelt [gɛlt], *inter.* (*coll.*) isn't it? don't you think so?

gelten ['gɛltən], *v.a. irr.* be worth, cost. — *v.n.* count (as), be valid.

Geltung ['gɛltuŋ], *f.* (—, *no pl.*) value, importance.

Gelübde [gə'lypdə], *n.* (—s, *pl.* —) vow, solemn promise *or* undertaking.

gelungen [gə'luŋən], *adj.* (*coll.*) funny, capital.

Gelüst [gə'lyst], *n.* (—s, *pl.* —e) appetite, desire.

gelüsten [gə'lystən], *v.a.* — *nach,* long for, covet.

Gemach [gə'ma:x], *n.* (—es, *pl.* ⁓er) (*Poet.*) chamber, room; apartment.

gemach [gə'ma:x], *adv.* slowly, softly, by degrees.

gemächlich [gə'mɛçlɪç], *adj.* slow, soft, easy, unhurried, leisurely.

Gemahl [gə'ma:l], *m.* (—s, *pl.* —e) spouse, husband, consort.

Gemahlin [gə'ma:lɪn], *f.* (—, *pl.* —nen) spouse, wife, consort.

Gemälde [gə'mɛ:ldə], *n.* (—s, *pl.* —) picture, painting. (portrait.)

gemäß [gə'mɛ:s], *prep.* (*Dat.*) in accordance with, according to.

gemäßigt [gə'mɛ:sɪçt], *adj.* temperate, moderate; —*es Klima,* temperate climate.

Gemäuer [gə'mɔyər], *n.* (—s, *no pl.*) ancient walls, ruins.

gemein [gə'maɪn], *adj.* common, mean, low, vulgar, base.

Gemeinde [gə'maɪndə], *f.* (—, *pl.* —n) community, parish, municipality; (*Eccl.*) congregation.

Gemeindevorstand [gə'maɪndeforʃtant], *m.* (—es, *no pl.*) town *or* borough council.

gemeingefährlich [gə'maɪngəfɛ:rlɪç], *adj.* dangerous to the public.

Gemeinheit [gə'maɪnhaɪt], *f.* (—, *pl.* —en) meanness; baseness; dirty trick.

gemeinhin [gə'maɪnhɪn], *adv.* commonly.

Gemeinplatz [gə'maɪnplats], *m.* (—es, *pl.* ∸e) commonplace, truism.

gemeinsam [gə'maɪnza:m], *adj.* common, joint; *der — Markt,* (*Pol.*) Common Market; —*e Sache machen,* make common cause; — *adv.* together.

Gemeinschaft [gə'maɪnʃaft], *f.* (—, *pl.* —en) community; association; *in — mit,* jointly; *in — haben,* hold in common.

gemeinschaftlich [gə'maɪnʃaftlɪç], *adj.* common. — *adv.* in common, together.

Gemeinsinn [gə'maɪnzɪn], *m.* (—s, *no pl.*) public spirit.

Gemeinwesen [gə'maɪnve:zən], *n.* (—s, *no pl.*) community.

Gemeinwohl [gə'maɪnvo:l], *n.* (—s, *no pl.*) common weal; common good.

Gemenge [gə'mɛŋə], *n.* (—s, *no pl.*) mixture; (*fig.*) scuffle.

Gemengsel [gə'mɛŋsəl], *n.* (—s, *no pl.*) medley, hotchpotch.

gemessen [gə'mɛsən], *adj.* deliberate.

Gemessenheit [gə'mɛsənhaɪt], *f.* (—, *no pl.*) precision, deliberation.

Gemetzel [gə'mɛtsəl], *n.* (—s, *no pl.*) slaughter, massacre.

Gemisch [gə'mɪʃ], *n.* (—es, *pl.* —e) mixture, motley.

Gemme ['gɛmə], *f.* (—, *pl.* —n) gem, cameo.

Gemse ['gɛmzə], *f.* (—, *pl.* —n) chamois.

Gemüse [gə'my:zə], *n.* (—s, *pl.* —) vegetables, greens.

Gemüsehändler [gə'my:zəhɛndlər], *m.* (—s, *pl.* —) greengrocer.

gemustert [gə'mustərt], *adj.* patterned, figured; (*Comm.*) —*e Sendung,* delivery as per sample.

Gemüt [gə'my:t], *n.* (—s, *pl.* —er) mind, soul, heart; disposition, nature, spirit, temper; feeling.

gemütlich [gə'my:tlɪç], *adj.* cosy, snug, comfortable; genial, friendly, pleasant.

Gemütlichkeit [gə'my:tlɪçkaɪt], *f.* (—, *no pl.*) cosiness, snugness; *da hört die — auf,* that is more than I will stand for.

gemütlos [gə'my:tlo:s], *adj.* unfeeling.

Gemütsart [gə'my:tsa:rt], *f.* (—, *no pl.*) disposition; character.

Gemütsbewegung [gə'my:tsbəve:guŋ], *f.* (—, *pl.* —en) emotion.

gemütskrank [gə'my:tskraŋk], *adj.* sick in mind; melancholy.

Gemütsleben [gə'my:tsle:bən], *n.* (—s, *no pl.*) emotional life.

Gemütsmensch [gə'my:tsmɛnʃ], *m.* (—en, *pl.* —en) man of feeling *or* sentiment; (*pej.*) sentimentalist.

gemütvoll [gə'my:tfɔl], *adj.* full of feeling, sympathetic.

gen [gɛn], *prep. contraction* of **gegen,** (*Poet.*) towards, to (*Acc.*).

Genannte [gə'nantə], *m.* (—n, *pl.* —n) named person, aforesaid.

genäschig [gə'nɛʃɪç], *adj.* fond of sweets, sweet-toothed.

genau [gə'nau], *adj.* precise, exact, accurate; strict, parsimonious.

Genauigkeit [gə'nauɪçkaɪt], *f.* (—, *no pl.*) accuracy, exactitude, precision.

Gendarm [ʒã'darm], *m.* (—en, *pl.* —en) policeman, constable.

genehm [gə'ne:m], *adj.* agreeable, acceptable, convenient.

genehmigen [gə'ne:mɪgən], *v.a.* approve of, agree to, permit; (*contract*) ratify.

geneigt [gə'naɪkt], *adj.* inclined (to), disposed (to), prone (to); *einem — sein,* be well disposed towards s.o.; (*Lit.*) *der —e Leser,* gentle reader.

Geneigtheit [gə'naɪkthaɪt], *f.* (—, *no pl.*) inclination, proneness, propensity; favour, kindness.

General [genə'ra:l], *m.* (—s, *pl.* —e, ∸e) general.

Generalfeldmarschall [genə'ra:lfɛltmarʃal], *m.* (—s, *pl.* ∸e) field marshal.

Generalkommando [genə'ra:lkɔmando], *n.* (—s, *pl.* —s) general's headquarters; (corps) headquarters.

Generalkonsul [genə'ra:lkɔnzul], *m.* (—s, *pl.* —e) consul-general.

Generalnenner [genə'ra:lnɛnər], *m.* (—s, *pl.* —) (*Maths.*) common denominator.

Generalprobe [genə'ra:lpro:bə], *f.* (—, *pl.* —n) dress-rehearsal.

Generalvollmacht [genə'ra:lfɔlmaxt], *f.* (—, *pl.* —en) (*Law*) general power of attorney.

generell [genə'rɛl], *adj.* general, common.

generös [genə'rø:s], *adj.* generous, magnanimous.

genesen [gə'ne:zən], *v.n. irr.* (*aux.* sein) recover, be restored to health; convalesce.

Genf [gɛnf], *n.* Geneva.

genial [gen'ja:l], *adj.* ingenious; extremely gifted.

Genick [gə'nɪk], *n.* (—s, *pl.* —e) nape, neck.

Genickstarre [gə'nɪkʃtarə], *f.* (—, *no pl.*) (*Med.*) (cerebrospinal) meningitis.

Genie [ʒe'ni:], *n.* (—s, *pl.* —s) genius.

genieren

genieren [ʒeˈniːrən], v.a. trouble, embarrass, disturb. — v.r. sich —, feel embarrassed; sich nicht —, make o.s. at home.

genießbar [gəˈniːsbaːr], adj. eatable, edible, palatable; drinkable; (fig.) pleasant, agreeable.

genießen [gəˈniːsən], v.a. irr. enjoy; have the use of; (food) eat, partake of; Ansehen —, enjoy respect.

Geniestreich [ʒeˈniːʃtraɪç], m. (—s, pl. —e) stroke of genius.

Genitiv [ˈgeːnɪtiːf], m. (—s, pl. —e) (Gram.) genitive.

Genosse [gəˈnɔsə], m. (—n, pl. —n) comrade, mate, colleague; (crime) accomplice.

Genossenschaft [gəˈnɔsənʃaft], f. (—, pl. —en) association, company, confederacy, co-operative, union.

Genre [ˈʒãrə], n. (—s, pl. —s) genre; style, kind.

Gent [gɛnt], n. Ghent.

Genua [ˈgeːnua], n. Genoa.

genug [gəˈnuːk], indecl. adj. enough, sufficient; —! that will do!

Genüge [gəˈnyːgə], f. (—, no pl.) zur —, sufficiently; einem — leisten, give satisfaction to s.o.

genügen [gəˈnyːgən], v.n. be enough, suffice; sich etwas — lassen, be content with s.th.

genügsam [gəˈnyːkzaːm], adj. easily satisfied; temperate, sober.

Genügsamkeit [gəˈnyːkzaːmkaɪt], f. (—, no pl.) contentedness, moderation; temperateness, sobriety.

Genugtuung [gəˈnuːktuːuŋ], f. (—, no pl.) satisfaction; reparation; atonement.

Genuß [gəˈnus], m. (—sses, pl. ¨sse) enjoyment; use; (food) consumption.

Genußmittel [gəˈnusmɪtəl], n. (—s, pl. —) (mostly pl.) luxuries; (Am.) delicatessen.

genußreich [gəˈnusraɪç], adj. enjoyable, delightful.

Genußsucht [gəˈnussuxt], f. (—, no pl.) thirst for pleasure.

Geograph [geoˈgraːf], m. (—en, pl. —en) geographer.

Geographie [geograˈfiː], f. (—, no pl.) geography.

Geologe [geoˈloːgə], m. (—n, pl. —n) geologist.

Geologie [geoloˈgiː], f. (—, no pl.) geology.

Geometer [geoˈmeːtər], m. (—s, pl. —) geometrician; land-surveyor.

Geometrie [geomeˈtriː], f. (—, no pl.) geometry.

Georg [geˈɔrk], m. George.

Georgine [geɔrˈgiːnə], f. (—, pl. —n) (Bot.) dahlia.

Gepäck [gəˈpɛk], n. (—s, no pl.) luggage; (Am.) baggage.

Gepäckaufbewahrung [gəˈpɛkaufbəvaːruŋ], f. (—, pl. —en) left luggage office.

Gepäckträger [gəˈpɛktrɛːgər], m. (—s, pl. —) porter.

Gepflogenheit [gəˈpfloːgənhaɪt], f. (—, pl. —en) habit, custom, wont.

Geplänkel [gəˈplɛnkəl], n. (—s, pl. —) (rare) skirmish.

Geplärr [gəˈplɛr], n. (—s, no pl.) bawling.

Geplauder [gəˈplaudər], n. (—s, no pl.) chatting; small talk.

Gepräge [gəˈprɛːgə], n. (—s, no pl.) impression, stamp.

Gepränge [gəˈprɛŋə], n. (—s, no pl.) pomp, ceremony, splendour.

Ger [geːr], m. (—s, pl. —e) (rare) spear, javelin.

Gerade [gəˈraːdə], f. (—n, pl. —n) (Maths.) straight line.

gerade [gəˈraːdə], adj. straight, direct, erect, even; (fig.) upright, honest. — adv. quite, just; jetzt —, now more than ever; fünf — sein lassen, stretch a point; — heraus, in plain terms.

geradeaus [gəˈraːdəaus], adv. straight on.

gerädert [gəˈrɛːdərt], adj. (fig.) fatigued, exhausted, worn out.

geradeswegs [gəˈraːdəsveːks], adv. straightaway, immediately.

geradezu [gəˈraːdətsuː], adv. frankly, downright; das ist — scheußlich, this is downright nasty.

Geradheit [gəˈraːthaɪt], f. (—, no pl.) straightness; (fig.) straightforwardness.

geradlinig [gəˈraːtlɪnɪç], adj. rectilinear.

geradsinnig [gəˈraːtzɪnɪç], adj. honest, upright.

gerändert [gəˈrɛndərt], adj. with a milled edge.

Geranie [gəˈraːnjə], f. (—, pl. —n) (Bot.) geranium.

Gerät [gəˈrɛːt], n. (—s, pl. —e) tool, implement, device; appliance; (radio, television) set; apparatus.

geraten [gəˈraːtən], v.n. irr. (aux. sein) turn out; gut —, turn out well; — auf, come upon.

Geräteturnen [gəˈrɛːtəturnən], n. (—s, no pl.) gymnastics with apparatus.

Geratewohl [gəˈraːtəvoːl], n. (—s, no pl.) aufs —, at random.

geraum [gəˈraum], adj. —e Zeit, a long time.

geräumig [gəˈrɔymɪç], adj. spacious, large, wide, roomy.

Geräusch [gəˈrɔyʃ], n. (—es, pl. —e) noise; sound.

gerben [ˈgɛrbən], v.a. tan, taw; einem die Haut —, give s.o. a hiding.

Gerber [ˈgɛrbər], m. (—s, pl. —) tanner.

Gerbsäure [ˈgɛrpsɔyrə], f. (—, no pl.) tannin.

gerecht [gəˈrɛçt], adj. just, fair; (Bibl.) righteous; einem — werden, do justice to s.o.

Gerechtigkeit [gəˈrɛçtɪçkaɪt], f. (—, no pl.) justice, fairness; (Bibl.) righteousness.

Gerede [gə're:də], n. (—s, no pl.) talk, rumour, gossip.

gereichen [gə'raiçən], v.n. turn out to be; *einem zur Ehre* —, redound to s.o.'s honour.

gereizt [gə'raitst], adj. irritated, annoyed.

gereuen [gə'rɔyən] *see* **reuen.**

Gerhard ['ge:rhart], m. Gerard, Gerald.

Gericht [gə'riçt], n. (—s, pl. —e) court of justice, tribunal; (*food*) course, dish; *das Jüngste* —, Last Judgment.

gerichtlich [gə'riçtliç], adj. judicial, legal; *einen — belangen,* sue s.o.

Gerichtsbarkeit [gə'riçtsbarkait], f. (—, no pl.) jurisdiction.

Gerichtsdiener [gə'riçtsdi:nər], m. (—s, pl. —) (*law court*) usher.

Gerichtshof [gə'riçtsho:f], m. (—es, pl. ⁇e) court of justice.

Gerichtskanzlei [gə'riçtskantslai], f. (—, pl. —en) record office.

Gerichtskosten [gə'riçtskɔstən], f. pl. (*Law*) costs.

Gerichtsordnung [gə'riçtsɔrdnuŋ], f. (—, pl) legal procedure.

Gerichtstermin [gə'riçtstermi:n], m. (—s, pl. —e) day fixed for a hearing.

Gerichtsverhandlung [gə'riçtsfer-handluŋ], f. (—, pl. —en) hearing; trial.

Gerichtsvollzieher [gə'riçtsfɔltsi:ər], m. (—s, pl. —) bailiff.

gerieben [gə'ri:bən], adj. ground; crafty, cunning.

gering [gə'riŋ], adj. small, little, mean, petty, unimportant, of little value, trifling; low, base.

geringfügig [gə'riŋfy:giç], adj. small, petty, insignificant.

geringschätzig [gə'riŋʃetsiç], adj. contemptuous, disdainful, supercilious; derogatory.

gerinnen [gə'rinən], v.n. irr. (*aux.* sein) coagulate, clot; curdle.

Gerinnsel [gə'rinzəl], n. (—s, pl. —) embolism (of the blood); clot.

Gerippe [gə'ripə], n. (—s, pl. —) skeleton; frame; (*Aviat.*) air-frame.

gerippt [gə'ript], adj. ribbed, fluted.

gerissen [gə'risən], adj. (*coll.*) sharp, cunning.

Germane [gɛr'ma:nə], m. (—n, pl. —n) Teuton.

Germanist ['gɛrmanist], m. (—en, pl. — en) (*Univ.*) student of *or* expert in German language and/or literature.

gern [gɛrn], adv. gladly, willingly, readily, with pleasure; — *haben*, like.

Geröll [gə'rœl], n. (—s, no pl.) boulders, rubble.

Gerste ['gɛrstə], f. (—, no pl.) (*Bot.*) barley.

Gerstenschleim ['gɛrstənʃlaim], m. (—s, no pl.) barley water.

Gerte ['gɛrtə], f. (—, pl. —n) whip, switch, rod.

Geruch [gə'ru:x], m. (—s, pl. ⁇e) smell, odour, scent; *guter* —, fragrance, aroma.

geruchlos [gə'ru:xlo:s], adj. scentless, odourless, without smell.

Geruchsinn [gə'ru:xzin], m. (—es, no pl.) sense of smell.

Gerücht [gə'ryçt], n. (—s, pl. —e) rumour, report.

Gerümpel [gə'rympəl], n. (—s, no pl.) lumber, trash.

Gerundium [gə'rundjum], n. (—s, pl. —dien) (*Gram.*) gerund.

Gerüst [gə'ryst], n. (—es, pl. —e) scaffolding.

Ges [gɛs], n. (—, pl. —) (*Mus.*) G flat.

gesamt [gə'zamt], adj. entire, all, complete.

Gesamtheit [gə'zamthait], f. (—, no pl.) totality.

Gesandte [gə'zantə], m. (—n, pl. —n) messenger; ambassador, envoy; *päpstlicher* —, papal nuncio.

Gesandtschaft [gə'zantʃaft], f. (—, pl. —en) embassy, legation.

Gesang [gə'zaŋ], m. (—s, pl. ⁇e) song, air; hymn; (*Lit.*) canto.

Gesangbuch [gə'zaŋbu:x], n. (—s, pl. ⁇er) hymnal, hymn-book.

Gesäß [gə'zɛ:s], n. (—es, pl. —e) seat, buttocks.

Geschäft [gə'ʃeft], n. (—s, pl. —e) business; trade, commerce; affairs; occupation; shop; (*Am.*) store.

geschäftig [gə'ʃeftiç], adj. active, bustling, busy.

geschäftlich [gə'ʃeftliç], adj. concerning business. — adv. on business.

Geschäftsführer [gə'ʃeftsfy:rər], m. (—s, pl. —) manager.

Geschäftshaus [gə'ʃeftshaus], n. (—es, pl. ⁇er) firm; business premises.

geschäftskundig [gə'ʃeftskundiç], adj. experienced in business.

Geschäftslokal [gə'ʃeftsloka:l], n. (—s, pl. —e) business premises, shop.

Geschäftsordnung [gə'ʃeftsɔrdnuŋ], f. (—, pl. —en) standing orders; agenda.

Geschäftsträger [gə'ʃeftstrɛ:gər], m. (—s, pl. —) (*Comm.*) agent; (*Pol.*) chargé d'affaires.

Geschäftsverkehr [gə'ʃeftsferke:r], m. (—s, no pl.) business dealings.

Geschehen [gə'ʃe:ən], n. (—s, no pl.) happening.

geschehen [gə'ʃe:ən], v.n. irr. (*aux.* sein) happen, occur; take place; be done; *das geschieht dir recht,* it serves you right.

gescheit [gə'ʃait], adj. clever, intelligent.

Geschenk [gə'ʃeŋk], n. (—s, pl. —e) gift, present, donation.

Geschichte [gə'ʃiçtə], f. (—, pl. —n) tale; story; history.

Geschichtenbuch [gə'ʃiçtənbu:x], n. (—es, pl. ⁇er) story-book.

geschichtlich [gə'ʃiçtliç], adj. historical.

Geschichtsschreiber [gə'ʃiçtsʃraibər], m. (—s, pl. —) historian.

Geschick [gə'ʃik], n. (—es, no pl.) fate, destiny; dexterity, skill, knack, aptitude.

Geschicklichkeit [gə'ʃɪklɪçkaɪt], f. (—, pl. —en) dexterity, adroitness, skill.

geschickt [gə'ʃɪkt], adj. skilled, skilful, clever, able.

Geschirr [gə'ʃɪr], n.(—s,no pl.) crockery, plates and dishes; (horses) harness.

Geschlecht [gə'ʃlɛçt], n. (—s, pl. —er) sex; kind, race, species, extraction, family; (Gram.) gender.

geschlechtlich [gə'ʃlɛçtlɪç], adj. sexual; generic.

Geschlechtsart [gə'ʃlɛçtsa:rt], f. (—, pl. —en) generic character.

Geschlechtskrankheit [gə'ʃlɛçtskraŋk-haɪt], f. (—, pl. —en) venereal disease.

Geschlechtskunde [gə'ʃlɛçtskundə], f. (—, no pl.) genealogy.

Geschlechtsreife [gə'ʃlɛçtsraɪfə], f. (—, no pl.) puberty.

Geschlechtsteile [gə'ʃlɛçtstaɪlə], m. pl. genitals.

Geschlechtstrieb [gə'ʃlɛçtstri:p], m. (—s, no pl.) sexual instinct.

Geschlechtswort [gə'ʃlɛçtsvɔrt], n. (—s, pl. ⸚er) (Gram.) article.

geschliffen [gə'ʃlɪfən], adj. polished; (glass) cut.

Geschmack [gə'ʃmak], m. (—s, pl. ⸚er) taste, flavour.

geschmacklos [gə'ʃmaklo:s], adj. tasteless, insipid; in bad taste.

Geschmacksrichtung [gə'ʃmaksrɪç-tuŋ], f. (—, pl. —en) prevailing taste; vogue; tendency.

Geschmeide [gə'ʃmaɪdə], n. (—s, pl. —) jewels, jewellery; trinkets.

geschmeidig [gə'ʃmaɪdɪç], adj. flexible, pliant, supple; (Tech.) malleable.

Geschmeiß [gə'ʃmaɪs], n. (—es, no pl.) dung; vermin; (fig.) rabble.

Geschnatter [gə'ʃnatər], n. (—s, no pl.) cackling.

geschniegelt [gə'ʃni:gəlt], adj. spruce, dressed up.

Geschöpf [gə'ʃœpf], n. (—es, pl. —e) creature.

Geschoß [gə'ʃɔs], n. (—sses, pl. —sse) shot, shell, projectile, missile; (house) storey.

geschraubt [gə'ʃraupt], adj. (style) stilted, affected.

Geschrei [gə'ʃraɪ], n. (—s, no pl.) shrieking, shouting, screaming; (fig.) stir, great noise.

Geschreibsel [gə'ʃraɪpsəl], n. (—s, no pl.) scrawl, scribbling.

Geschütz [gə'ʃyts], n. (—es, pl. —e) artillery, guns; schweres — auffahren, bring o.'s guns into play.

Geschützweite [gə'ʃytsvaɪtə], f. (—, no pl.) calibre.

Geschwader [gə'ʃva:dər], n. (—s, pl.—) squadron.

Geschwätz [gə'ʃvɛts], n. (—es, no pl.) chatter, gossip, prattle, tittle-tattle.

geschweige [gə'ʃvaɪgə], adv. let alone, to say nothing of.

geschwind [gə'ʃvɪnt], adj. quick, nimble, fast, swift, fleet.

Geschwindigkeitsmesser [gə'ʃvɪndɪç-kaɪtsmɛsər], m. (—s, pl. —) (Motor.) speedometer.

Geschwister [gə'ʃvɪstər], pl. brothers and sisters.

geschwollen [gə'ʃvɔlən], adj. stilted, turgid, pompous.

Geschworene [gə'ʃvo:rənə], m. (—n, pl. —n), juror, juryman; (pl.) jury.

Geschwulst [gə'ʃvulst], f. (—, pl. ⸚e) swelling, tumour.

Geschwür [gə'ʃvy:r], n. (—s, pl. —e) sore, ulcer, abscess.

Geselle [gə'zɛlə], m. (—n, pl. —n) journeyman; companion, comrade, mate.

gesellen [gə'zɛlən], v.a., v.r. join, associate with, keep company with.

gesellig [gə'zɛlɪç], adj. sociable, companionable; gregarious.

Gesellschaft [gə'zɛlʃaft], f. (—, pl. —en) society; community; (formal) party; company, club; geschlossene —, private party; einem — leisten, keep s.o. company; (Comm.) — mit beschränkter Haftung, (abbr.) GmbH, limited company, (abbr.) Ltd.

gesellschaftlich [gə'zɛlʃaftlɪç], adj. social.

Gesellschaftsanzug [gə'zɛlʃaftsan-tsu:k], m. (—s, pl. ⸚e) evening dress.

Gesellschaftsspiel [gə'zɛlʃaftsʃpi:l], n. (—s, pl. —e) round game, party game.

Gesellschaftsvertrag [gə'zɛlʃaftsfer-tra:k], m. (—es, pl. ⸚e) (Law) partnership agreement; deed of partnership.

Gesellschaftszimmer [gə'zɛlʃaftstsɪ-mər], n. (—s, pl. —) drawing-room, reception room.

Gesetz [gə'zɛts], n. (—es, pl. —e) law, statute, regulation.

Gesetzbuch [gə'zɛtsbu:x], n. (—es, pl. ⸚er) code of laws; statute book.

Gesetzentwurf [gə'zɛtsentvurf], m. (—es, pl. ⸚er) (Parl.) draft bill.

gesetzgebend [gə'zɛtsge:bənt], adj. legislative.

gesetzlich [gə'zɛtslɪç], adj. lawful, legal.

Gesetzlichkeit [gə'zɛtslɪçkaɪt], f. (—, no pl.) lawfulness, legality.

gesetzlos [gə'zɛtslo:s], adj. lawless, anarchical.

gesetzmäßig [gə'zɛtsmɛ:sɪç], adj. conforming to law, lawful, legitimate.

gesetzt [gə'zɛtst], adj. steady, sedate, staid; von —em Alter, of mature age; — daß, supposing that.

Gesetztheit [gə'zɛtsthaɪt], f. (—, no pl.) sedateness, steadiness.

gesetzwidrig [gə'zɛtsvi:drɪç], adj. illegal, unlawful.

Gesicht (1) [gə'zɪçt], n. (—s, pl. —er) face, physiognomy, look.

Gesicht (2) [gə'zɪçt], n. (—s, pl. —e) sight; vision, apparition.

Gesichtsausdruck [gə'zɪçtsausdruk], m. (—s, no pl.) face, mien; expression.

Gesichtsfeld [gə'zɪçtsfɛlt], *n.* (**—es,** *pl.* **—er**) field of vision.

Gesichtskreis [gə'zɪçtskraɪs], *m.* (**—es,** *pl.* **—e**) horizon.

Gesichtspunkt [gə'zɪçtspuŋkt], *m.* (**—es,** *pl.* **—e**) point of view.

Gesichtszug [gə'zɪçtstsu:k], *m.* (**—s,** *pl.* **—e**) feature.

Gesims [gə'zɪms], *n.* (**—es,** *pl.* **—e**) cornice, moulding, ledge.

Gesinde [gə'zɪndə], *n.* (**—s,** *no pl.*) (domestic) servants.

Gesindel [gə'zɪndəl], *n.* (**—s,** *no pl.*) mob, rabble.

gesinnt [gə'zɪnt], *adj.* disposed.

Gesinnung [gə'zɪnuŋ], *f.* (**—,** *pl.* **—en**) disposition, sentiment; conviction.

gesinnungslos [gə'zɪnuŋslo:s], *adj.* unprincipled.

gesinnungstreu [gə'zɪnuŋstrɔy], *adj.* loyal, staunch.

Gesinnungswechsel [gə'zɪnuŋsvɛksəl], *m.* (**—s,** *no pl.*) change of opinion, volte-face.

gesittet [gə'zɪtət], *adj.* civilised, well-mannered.

Gesittung [gə'zɪtuŋ], *f.* (**—,** *no pl.*) (*rare*) civilisation, good manners.

gesonnen [gə'zɔnən] *see* **gesinnt.**

Gespann [gə'ʃpan], *n.* (**—s,** *pl.* **—e**) team, yoke (oxen etc.).

gespannt [gə'ʃpant], *adj.* stretched; intense, thrilled; tense; filled with suspense.

Gespanntheit [gə'ʃpanthaɪt], *f.* (**—,** *no pl.*) tension, strain, suspense.

Gespenst [gə'ʃpɛnst], *n.* (**—es,** *pl.* **—er**) ghost, spectre, apparition.

gespenstisch [gə'ʃpɛnstɪʃ], *adj.* ghostly, spectral.

Gespiele [gə'ʃpi:lə], *m.* (**—n,** *pl.* **—n**) playmate.

Gespielin [gə'ʃpi:lɪn], *f.* (**—,** *pl.* **—innen**) (girl) playmate.

Gespinst [gə'ʃpɪnst], *n.* (**—es,** *pl.* **—e**) web.

Gespött [gə'ʃpœt], *n.* (**—s,** *no pl.*) mocking, mockery, jeering, derision; (*fig.*) laughing stock.

Gespräch [gə'ʃprɛ:ç], *n.* (**—s,** *pl.* **—e**) conversation, discourse, talk; (*phone*) call; *ein — anknüpfen,* start a conversation.

gesprächig [gə'ʃprɛ:çɪç], *adj.* talkative, communicative.

gespreizt [gə'ʃpraɪtst], *adj.* wide apart; (*fig.*) affected, pompous.

gesprenkelt [gə'ʃprɛŋkəlt], *adj.* speckled.

gesprungen [gə'ʃpruŋən], *adj.* cracked (glass etc.).

Gestade [gə'ʃta:də], *n.* (**—s,** *pl.* **—**) shore, coast, bank.

Gestalt [gə'ʃtalt], *f.* (**—,** *pl.* **—en**) form, figure, shape; configuration; stature; fashion; manner, way.

gestalten [gə'ʃtaltən], *v.a.* form, shape, fashion, make. **—***v.r. sich* **—,** turn out.

Gestaltung [gə'ʃtaltuŋ], *f.* (**—,** *pl.* **—en**) formation; arrangement; planning.

geständig [gə'ʃtɛndɪç], *adj.* confessing; *— sein,* confess.

Geständnis [gə'ʃtɛntnɪs], *n.* (**—ses,** *pl.* **—se**) confession, admission.

Gestank [gə'ʃtaŋk], *m.* (**—s,** *no pl.*) stink, stench.

gestatten [gə'ʃtatən], *v.a.* permit, allow, grant; *wir — uns,* we beg leave to; *— Sie !* pardon me, excuse me.

Geste ['gɛstə], *f.* (**—,** *pl.* **—n**) gesture, gesticulation.

gestehen [gə'ʃte:ən], *v.a. irr.* confess, admit, own; *offen gestanden,* quite frankly.

Gestein [gə'ʃtaɪn], *n.* (**—s,** *pl.* **—e**) (*Poet.*) rock; (*Geol.*) rocks, minerals.

Gestell [gə'ʃtɛl], *n.* (**—s,** *pl.* **—e**) rack, frame; (*table*) trestle; (*books*) stand.

Gestellung [gə'ʃtɛluŋ], *f.* (**—,** *no pl.*) (*Mil.*) reporting for service.

gestern ['gɛstərn], *adv.* yesterday; *— abend,* last night.

gestiefelt [gə'ʃti:fəlt], *adj.* booted; *der —e Kater,* Puss in Boots.

gestielt [gə'ʃti:lt], *adj.* (*axe*) helved; (*Bot.*) stalked, stemmed.

gestikulieren [gɛstiku'li:rən], *v.n.* gesticulate.

Gestirn [gə'ʃtɪrn], *n.* (**—s,** *pl.* **—e**) star, constellation.

gestirnt [gə'ʃtɪrnt], *adj.* starred, starry.

Gestöber [gə'ʃtø:bər], *n.* (**—s,** *pl.* **—**) (*snow, dust*) drift, storm, blizzard.

Gesträuch [gə'ʃtrɔyç], *n.* (**—es,** *no pl.*) bushes, shrubs; thicket.

gestreift [gə'ʃtraɪft], *adj.* striped.

gestreng [gə'ʃtrɛŋ], *adj.* (*obs.*) strict, severe.

gestrig ['gɛstrɪç], *adj.* of yesterday.

Gestrüpp [gə'ʃtryp], *n.* (**—s,** *no pl.*) bushes, underwood, shrubs, shrubbery.

Gestüt [gə'ʃty:t], *n.* (**—s,** *pl.* **—e**) stud (-farm).

Gestüthengst [gə'ʃty:thɛŋst], *m.* (**—es,** *pl.* **—e**) stallion.

Gesuch [gə'zu:x], *n.* (**—s,** *pl.* **—e**) petition, request, application.

gesucht [gə'zu:xt], *adj.* in demand; (*style*) far-fetched; affected; studied.

gesund [gə'zunt], *adj.* healthy, wholesome; *der —e Menschenverstand,* common sense.

Gesundbrunnen [gə'zuntbrunən], *m.* (**—s,** *pl.* **—**) mineral waters; spa.

gesunden [gə'zundən], *v.n.* (*aux. sein*) recover o.'s health.

Gesundheit [gə'zunthaɪt], *f.* (**—,** *no pl.*) health.

Gesundheitslehre [gə'zunthaɪtsle:rə], *f.* (**—,** *no pl.*) hygiene.

Getäfel [gə'tɛ:fəl], *n.* (**—s,** *no pl.*) wainscot, wainscoting, panelling.

Getändel [gə'tɛndəl], *n.* (**—s,** *no pl.*) (*rare*) flirting, dallying.

Getier [gə'ti:r], *n.* (**—s,** *no pl.*) (*collective term*) animals.

Getöse [gə'tø:zə], *n.* (**—s,** *no pl.*) loud noise, din.

89

Getränk

Getränk [gə'trɛŋk], *n.* (—s, *pl.* —e) drink, beverage.

getrauen [gə'trauən], *v.r. sich* —, dare, venture.

Getreide [gə'traɪdə], *n.* (—s, *pl.* —) corn, grain.

getreu [gə'trɔy], *adj.* faithful, true, loyal.

getreulich [gə'trɔylɪç], *adv.* faithfully, truly, loyally.

Getriebe [gə'tri:bə], *n.* (—s, *pl.* —) machinery; (*Motor.*) gear; drive; *das — der Welt,* the bustle of life.

getrieben [gə'tri:bən], *adj.* (*Tech.*) chased (work.)

Getrödel [gə'trø:dəl], *n.* (—s, *no pl.*) dawdling.

getrost [gə'tro:st], *adj.* confident, cheerful; — *sein,* be of good cheer.

Getto ['gɛto], *n.* (—s, *pl.* —s) ghetto.

Getue [gə'tu:ə], *n.* (—s, *no pl.*) pretence, fuss.

Getümmel [gə'tyməl], *n.* (—s, *no pl.*) bustle, turmoil.

geübt [gə'y:pt], *adj.* skilled, versed.

Geübtheit [gə'y:pthaɪt], *f.* (—, *no pl.*) skill, experience, dexterity.

Gevatter [gə'fatər], *m.* (—s, *pl.* —) (*obs.*) godfather.

gevierteilt [gə'fi:rtaɪlt], *adj.* quartered.

Gewächs [gə'vɛks], *n.* (—es, *pl.* —e) plant, growth; (*Med.*) excrescence.

gewachsen [gə'vaksən], *adj. einem (einer Sache) — sein,* be equal to s.o. (s.th.).

Gewächshaus [gə'vɛkshaus], *n.* (—es, *pl.* ̈er) green-house, hot-house, conservatory.

gewagt [gə'va:kt], *adj.* risky, hazardous; daring.

gewählt [gə'vɛ:lt], *adj.* choice, select.

gewahr [gə'va:r], *adj. einer Sache — werden,* become aware of s.th., perceive s.th.

Gewähr [gə've:r], *f.* (—, *no pl.*) surety; guarantee; warranty; — *leisten,* guarantee.

gewahren [gə'va:rən], *v.a.* perceive, see, become aware of.

gewähren [gə've:rən], *v.a.* allow, grant; *einen — lassen,* let s.o. do as he pleases, let be.

Gewährleistung [gə've:rlaɪstuŋ], *f.* (—, *pl.* —en) grant of security (*or* bail); guarantee.

Gewahrsam [gə'va:rza:m], *m.* (—s, *no pl.*) safe-keeping, custody.

Gewährsmann [gə've:rsman], *m.* (—es, *pl.* ̈er) authority; informant.

Gewährung [gə've:ruŋ,] *f.* (—, *no pl.*) granting (of request).

Gewalt [gə'valt], *f.* (—, *pl.* —en) power, force, might; authority; violence; *höhere —,* (*Law*) act of God, force majeure; *sich in der — haben,* have control over o.s.

Gewalthaber [gə'valtha:bər], *m.* (—s, *pl.* —) tyrant; despot, autocrat; person in authority.

gewaltig [gə'valtɪç], *adj.* powerful, mighty, enormous, stupendous.

gewaltsam [gə'valtza:m], *adj.* forcible, violent.

Gewaltstreich [gə'valtʃtraɪç], *m.* (—s, *pl.* —e) bold stroke; coup d'état.

Gewalttat [gə'valtta:t], *f.* (—, *pl.* —en) violent action, violence, outrage.

gewalttätig [gə'valttɛ:tɪç], *adj.* violent, fierce, outrageous.

Gewand [gə'vant], *n.* (—es, *pl.* ̈er) (*Lit.*) garment, dress; (*Eccl.*) vestment.

gewandt [gə'vant], *adj.* nimble, deft, clever; (*mind*) versatile.

gewärtig [gə'vɛrtɪç], *adj. einer Sache — sein,* expect s.th. to happen.

Gewäsch [gə'vɛʃ], *n.* (—es, *no pl.*) stuff and nonsense; rubbish.

Gewässer [gə'vɛsər], *n.* (—s, *pl.* —) waters.

Gewebe [gə've:bə], *n.* (—s, *pl.* —) (*Physiol., Text.*) tissue; web, weft, texture.

geweckt [gə'vɛkt], *adj.* smart, wide-awake.

Gewehr [gə've:r], *n.* (—s, *pl.* —e) gun, fire-arm, rifle.

Gewehrlauf [gə've:rlauf], *m.* (—s, *pl.* ̈e) barrel.

Geweih [gə'vaɪ], *n.* (—s, *pl.* —e) horns, antlers.

geweiht [gə'vaɪt], *adj.* consecrated; holy.

gewellt [gə'vɛlt], *adj.* corrugated, wavy.

Gewerbe [gə'vɛrbə], *n.* (—s, *pl.* —) trade, profession, business; calling; industry.

Gewerbekunde [gə'vɛrbəkundə], *f.* (—, *no pl.*) technology.

Gewerbeschein [gə'vɛrbəʃaɪn], *m.* (—s, *pl.* —e) trade-licence.

gewerblich [gə'vɛrplɪç], *adj.* industrial.

gewerbsmäßig [gə'vɛrpsmɛ:sɪç], *adj.* professional.

Gewerkschaft [gə'vɛrkʃaft], *f.* (—, *pl.* —en) trade union.

Gewicht [gə'vɪçt], *n.* (—s, *pl.* —e) weight; *schwer ins — fallen,* carry great weight, weigh heavily.

gewichtig [gə'vɪçtɪç], *adj.* weighty, ponderous; (*fig.*) momentous, important, strong.

gewiegt [gə'vi:kt], *adj.* experienced, clever.

gewillt [gə'vɪlt], *adj.* willing.

Gewimmel [gə'vɪməl], *n.* (—s, *no pl.*) milling crowd, swarm, throng.

Gewinde [gə'vɪndə], *n.* (—s, *pl.* —) (*screw*) thread; (*flowers*) garland.

Gewinn [gə'vɪn], *m.* (—s, *pl.* —e) gain, profit; (*lottery*) prize; (*gambling*) winnings.

gewinnen [gə'vɪnən], *v.a. irr.* win, gain, obtain, get, earn.

gewinnend [gə'vɪnənt], *adj.* prepossessing; engaging.

Gewinnung [gə'vɪnuŋ], *f.* (—, *no pl.*) (*Ind., Chem.*) extraction; output, production.

Gewinsel [gə'vɪnzəl], *n.* (—s, *no pl.*) whimpering.

Gewinst [gə'vɪnst], *m.* (—es, *pl.* —e) (*obs.*) gain, profit.

Gewirr [gə'vɪr], *n.* (—s, *no pl.*) entanglement, confusion.

gewiß [gə'vɪs], *adj.* (*Genit.*) certain, sure. — *adv.* indeed.

Gewissen [gə'vɪsən], *n.* (—s, *no pl.*) conscience.

gewissenhaft [gə'vɪsənhaft], *adj.* conscientious, scrupulous.

gewissenlos [gə'vɪsənlo:s], *adj.* unscrupulous.

Gewissensbiß [gə'vɪsənsbɪs],*m.*(—sses, *pl.* —sse) (*mostly pl.*) pangs of conscience.

gewissermaßen [gə'vɪsərma:sən], *adv.* to a certain extent, so to speak.

Gewißheit [gə'vɪshaɪt], *f.* (—, *no pl.*) certainty.

gewißlich [gə'vɪslɪç], *adv.* surely.

Gewitter [gə'vɪtər], *n.* (—s, *pl.* —) thunderstorm.

gewittern [gə'vɪtərn], *v.n.* thunder.

gewitzigt, gewitzt [gə'vɪtsɪçt, gə'vɪtst], *adj.* knowing, clever; shrewd.

gewogen [gə'vo:gən], *adj.* kindly disposed, favourable; *einem* — *sein,* be favourably inclined towards s.o.

Gewogenheit [gə'vo:gənhaɪt], *f.* (—, *no pl.*) kindness, favour.

gewöhnen [gə'vø:nən], *v.a.* accustom to. — *v.r. sich* — *an,* get used to, accustom o.s. to.

Gewohnheit [gə'vo:nhaɪt], *f.* (—, *pl.* —en) (*general*) custom, usage; (*personal*) habit.

gewohnheitsmäßig [gə'vo:nhaɪtsmɛ:sɪç], *adj.* habitual. — *adv.* by force of habit.

Gewohnheitsrecht [gə'vo:nhaɪtsrɛçt], *n.* (—s, *no pl.*) common law.

gewöhnlich [gə'vø:nlɪç], *adj.* customary, usual; (*fig.*) common, mean, vulgar.

gewohnt [gə'vo:nt], *adj.* accustomed to, used to.

Gewöhnung [gə'vø:nuŋ], *f.* (—, *no pl.*) habit, use, habituation.

Gewölbe [gə'vœlbə], *n.* (—s, *pl.* —) vault, arch.

Gewölk [gə'vœlk], *n.* (—s, *no pl.*) clouds, cloud formation.

Gewühl [gə'vy:l], *n.* (—s, *no pl.*) crowd, throng, bustle.

gewunden [gə'vundən], *adj.* tortuous.

Gewürm [gə'vyrm], *n.* (—s, *no pl.*) reptiles, worms; vermin.

Gewürz [gə'vyrts], *n.* (—es, *pl.* —e) spice.

Gewürznelke [gə'vyrtsnɛlkə], *f.* (—, *pl.* —n) clove.

Gezänk [gə'tsɛŋk], *n.* (—s, *no pl.*) quarrelling, bickering.

Gezeiten [gə'tsaɪtən], *f. pl.* tides.

Gezeter [gə'tse:tər], *n.* (—s, *no pl.*) screaming, yelling; (*fig.*) outcry.

geziemen [gə'tsi:mən], *v.r. sich für einen* —, befit *or* become s.o.

geziert [gə'tsi:rt], *adj.* affected.

Gezischel [gə'tsɪʃəl], *n.* (—s, *no pl.*) whispering.

Gezücht [gə'tsyçt], *n.* (—s, *no pl.*) brood, breed.

Gezweig [gə'tsvaɪk], *n.* (—s, *no pl.*) branches, boughs.

Gezwitscher [gə'tsvɪtʃər], *n.* (—s, *no pl.*) chirping.

Gezwungenheit [gə'tsvuŋənhaɪt], *f.* (—, *no pl.*) constraint.

Gicht [gɪçt], *f.* (—, *no pl.*) (*Med.*) gout.

gichtbrüchig [gɪçtbryçɪç], *adj.* (*obs.*) paralytic; gouty.

gichtig ['gɪçtɪç], *adj.* gouty.

Giebel ['gi:bəl], *m.* (—s, *pl.* —) gable.

Giebelfenster ['gi:bəlfɛnstər], *n.* (—s, *pl.*—) gable-window, dormer-window.

gieb(e)lig ['gi:b(ə)lɪç], *adj.* gabled.

Gier [gi:r], *f.* (—, *no pl.*) greediness, eagerness.

gieren ['gi:rən], *v.n.* (*rare*) — *nach,* thirst for, yearn for.

gierig ['gi:rɪç], *adj.* eager, greedy.

Gießbach ['gi:sbax], *m.* (—s, *pl.* —e) mountain-torrent.

gießen ['gi:sən], *v.a. irr.* (*liquids*) pour, shed; (*metal*) cast, found.

Gießer ['gi:sər], *m.* (—s, *pl.* —) founder.

Gießerei [gi:sə'raɪ], *f.* (—, *pl.* —en) foundry.

Gießform ['gi:sfɔrm], *f.* (—, *pl.* —en) casting-mould.

Gießkanne ['gi:skanə], *f.* (—, *pl.* —n) watering-can.

Gift [gɪft], *n.* (—es, *pl.* —e) poison, venom; (*fig.*) virulence; (*coll.*) *darauf kannst du* — *nehmen,* you can bet your life on it.

Giftbaum ['gɪftbaum], *m.* (—s, *pl.* —e) upas-tree.

Giftdrüse ['gɪftdry:zə], *f.* (—, *pl.* —n) poison-gland.

giftig ['gɪftɪç], *adj.* poisonous; (*fig.*) venomous; (*Med.*) toxic.

Giftlehre ['gɪftle:rə], *f.* (—, *no pl.*) toxicology.

Giftpilz ['gɪftpɪlts], *m.* (—es, *pl.* —e) poisonous toadstool.

Giftschlange ['gɪftʃlaŋə], *f.* (—, *pl.* —n) poisonous snake.

Giftstoff ['gɪftʃtɔf], *m.* (—es, *pl.* —e) poison, virus.

Gigant [gɪ'gant], *m.* (—en, *pl.* —en) giant.

Gigerl ['gi:gərl], *m.* (—s, *pl.* —) (*Austr. dial.*) fop, coxcomb.

Gilde ['gɪldə], *f.* (—, *pl.* —n) guild, corporation.

Gimpel ['gɪmpəl], *m.* (—s, *pl.* —) (*Orn.*) bullfinch, chaffinch; (*fig.*) simpleton.

Ginster ['gɪnstər], *m.* (—s, *no pl.*) (*Bot.*) gorse, furze, broom.

Gipfel ['gɪpfəl], *m.* (—s, *pl.* —) summit, peak; (*fig.*) acme, culmination, height.

gipfeln ['gɪpfəln], *v.n.* culminate.

Gips [gɪps], *m.* (—es, *no pl.*) gypsum, stucco, plaster of Paris.

Gipsabdruck ['gɪpsapdruk], *m.* (—s, *pl.* —e) plaster-cast.

Gipsbild ['gɪpsbɪlt], *n.* (—s, *pl.* —er) plaster-figure.

Gipsverband ['gɪpsfɛrbant], *m.* (—es, *pl.* ⁓e) (*Med.*) plaster of Paris dressing.

girieren [ʒɪ'riːrən], *v.a.* (*Comm.*) endorse (a bill).

Girlande [gɪr'landə], *f.* (—, *pl.* —n) garland.

Girobank ['ʒiːrobaŋk], *f.* (—, *pl.* —en) tránsfer *or* clearing bank.

Gis [gɪs], *n.* (—, *pl.* —) (*Mus.*) G sharp; — *Moll*, G sharp minor.

gischen ['gɪʃən], *v.n.* foam, froth.

Gischt [gɪʃt], *f.* (—, *pl.* —e) foam, froth; spray.

Gitarre [gi'tarə], *f.* (—, *pl.* —n) guitar.

Gitter ['gɪtər], *n.* (—s, *pl.* —) trellis, grate, fence; railing; lattice; (*colour-printing*) screen.

Gitterwerk ['gɪtərverk], *n.* (—s, *no pl.*) trellis-work.

Glacéhandschuh [gla'se:hantʃu:], *m.* (—s, *pl.* —e) kid-glove.

Glanz [glants], *m.* (—es, *no pl.*) brightness, lustre, gloss; polish, sheen; (*fig.*) splendour.

glänzen ['glɛntsən], *v.n.* shine, glitter, glisten; (*fig.*) sparkle.

glänzend ['glɛntsənt], *adj.* glossy; (*fig.*) splendid, magnificent.

Glanzfirnis ['glantsfɪrnɪs], *m.* (—ses, *pl.* —se) glazing varnish.

Glanzleder ['glantsle:dər], *n.* (—s, *no pl.*) patent leather.

Glanzleinwand ['glantslaɪnvant], *f.* (—, *no pl.*) glazed linen.

glanzlos ['glantslo:s], *adj.* lustreless, dull.

glanzvoll ['glantsfɔl], *adj.* splendid, brilliant.

Glanzzeit ['glantstsaɪt], *f.* (—, *pl.* —en) golden age.

Glas [gla:s], *n.* (—es, *pl.* ⁓er) glass, tumbler.

glasartig ['gla:sa:rtɪç], *adj.* vitreous, glassy.

Glaser ['gla:zər], *m.* (—s, *pl.* —) glazier.

Glaserkitt ['gla:zərkɪt], *m.* (—s, *no pl.*) putty.

gläsern ['glɛ:zərn], *adj.* vitreous, glassy, made of glass.

Glashütte ['gla:shytə], *f.* (—, *pl.* —n) glass-works.

glasieren [gla'zi:rən], *v.a.* glaze; (*cake etc.*) ice.

glasiert [gla'zi:rt], *adj.* glazed; (*Cul.*) frosted, iced; (*Art.*) varnished.

Glasröhre ['gla:srø:rə], *f.* (—, *pl.* —n) glass-tube.

Glasscheibe ['gla:sʃaɪbə], *f.* (—, *pl.* —n) glass-pane, sheet of glass.

Glassplitter ['gla:sʃplɪtər], *m.* (—s, *pl.* —) splinter of glass.

Glasur [gla'zu:r], *f.* (—, *pl.* —en) (*potter's*) glaze, glazing; enamel, varnish; (*cake*) icing.

glatt [glat], *adj.* smooth, sleek; even, plain, glossy; glib; downright. — *adv.* entirely; — *rasiert*, close-shaven.

Glätte ['glɛtə], *f.* (—, *no pl.*) smoothness, evenness, slipperiness; polish.

Glatteis ['glataɪs], *n.* (—es, *no pl.*) slippery ice; sheet ice; (*Am.*) glaze; *einen aufs* — *führen*, lead s.o. up the garden path.

glätten ['glɛtən], *v.a.* smooth; (*dial.*) iron.

Glatze ['glatsə], *f.* (—, *pl.* —n) bald head.

glatzköpfig ['glatskœpfɪç], *adj.* bald, bald-pated.

Glaube(n) ['glaubə(n)], *m.* (—ns, *no pl.*) faith, belief; creed, religion.

glauben ['glaubən], *v.a.* believe; think, suppose. — *v.n. an etwas* (*Acc.*) —, believe in s.th.

Glaubensbekenntnis ['glaubənsbəkentnɪs], *n.* (—ses, *pl.* —se) confession of faith; creed.

Glaubensgericht ['glaubənsgərɪçt], *n.* (—es, *no pl.*) inquisition.

Glaubersalz ['glaubərzalts], *n.* (—es, *no pl.*) phosphate of soda, Glauber's salts.

glaubhaft ['glauphaft], *adj.* credible, authentic.

gläubig ['glɔybɪç], *adj.* believing, faithful; (*Eccl.*) *die Gläubigen*, the faithful.

Gläubiger ['glɔybɪgər], *m.* (—s, *pl.* —) creditor.

glaublich ['glauplɪç], *adj.* credible, believable.

glaubwürdig ['glaupvyrdɪç], *adj.* authentic, worthy of belief; plausible.

gleich [glaɪç], *adj.* same, like, equal, even; *auf* —*e Weise*, likewise; *es ist mir ganz* —, it is all the same to me. — *adv.* alike, at once; almost; just as; *ich komme* —, I shall be there in a moment; — *und* — *gesellt sich gern*, birds of a feather flock together.

gleichaltrig ['glaɪçaltrɪç], *adj.* of the same age.

gleichartig ['glaɪça:rtɪç], *adj.* of the same kind, homogeneous.

gleichberechtigt ['glaɪçbərɛçtɪçt], *adj.* entitled to equal rights.

Gleiche ['glaɪçə], *n.* (—n, *pl.* —n) the like; the same; *etwas ins* — *bringen*, straighten s.th. out.

gleichen ['glaɪçən], *v.n. irr.* be like, resemble, be equal to.

gleichermaßen ['glaɪçərma:sən], *adv.* in a like manner, likewise.

gleichfalls ['glaɪçfals], *adv.* likewise, equally, as well; *danke* —, thanks, the same to you.

gleichförmig ['glaɪçfœrmɪç], *adj.* uniform; monotonous.

gleichgesinnt ['glaɪçgəzɪnt], *adj.* congenial, of the same mind.

Gleichgewicht ['glaɪçgəvɪçt], *n.* (—s, *no pl.*) balance, equilibrium.

gleichgültig ['glaɪçgyltɪç], *adj.* indifferent; *es ist mir* —, it's all the same to me.

Gleichheit ['glaɪçhaɪt], *f.* (—, *pl.* —en) equality, likeness.

Glyzerin

Gleichklang ['glaɪçklaŋ], *m.* (—s, *pl.* -e) consonance.

gleichmachen ['glaɪçmaxən], *v.a.* level, equate; *dem Erdboden —,* raze to the ground.

Gleichmaß ['glaɪçmaːs], *n.* (—es, *no pl.*) proportion, symmetry.

gleichmäßig ['glaɪçmɛːsɪç], *adj.* proportionate, symmetrical.

Gleichmut ['glaɪçmuːt], *m.* (—s, *no pl.*) equanimity, calm.

gleichmütig ['glaɪçmyːtɪç], *adj.* even-tempered, calm.

gleichnamig ['glaɪçnaːmɪç], *adj.* homonymous.

Gleichnis ['glaɪçnɪs], *n.* (—ses, *pl.* —se) simile; (*Bibl.*) parable.

gleichsam ['glaɪçzaːm], *adv.* as it were, as if.

gleichschenklig ['glaɪçʃɛŋklɪç], *adj.* (*Maths.*) isosceles.

gleichseitig ['glaɪçzaɪtɪç], *adj.* (*Maths.*) equilateral.

Gleichsetzung ['glaɪçzɛtsuŋ], *f.* (—, *no pl.*), **Gleichstellung** ['glaɪçʃtɛluŋ], *f.* (—, *pl.* —en) equalisation.

Gleichstrom ['glaɪçʃtroːm], *m.* (—s, *no pl.*) (*Elec.*) direct current.

gleichtun ['glaɪçtuːn], *v.a. irr. es einem —,* emulate s.o.

Gleichung ['glaɪçuŋ], *f.* (—, *pl.* —en) (*Maths.*) equation.

gleichwohl ['glaɪçvoːl], *adv., conj.* nevertheless, however, yet.

gleichzeitig ['glaɪçtsaɪtɪç], *adj.* simultaneous, contemporary.

Gleis [glaɪs], *n.* (—es, *pl.* —e) (*Railw.*) track; rails; (*Am.*) track.

gleiten ['glaɪtən], *v.n. irr.* (*aux.* sein) glide, slide, slip.

Gleitflug ['glaɪtfluːk], *m.* (—es, *pl.* -e) (*Aviat.*) gliding.

Gletscher ['glɛtʃər], *m.* (—s, *pl.* —) glacier.

Gletscherspalte ['glɛtʃərʃpaltə], *f.* (—, *pl.* —n) crevasse.

Glied [gliːt], *n.* (—es, *pl.* —er) limb, joint; member; link; rank, file.

Gliederlähmung ['gliːdərlɛːmuŋ], *f.* (—, *no pl.*) paralysis.

gliedern ['gliːdərn], *v.a.* articulate, arrange, form.

Gliederreißen ['gliːdərraɪsən], *n.* (—s, *no pl.*) pain in the limbs, rheumatism, arthritis etc.

Gliederung ['gliːdəruŋ], *f.* (—, *pl.* —en) articulation, disposition, structure, arrangement, organisation.

Gliedmaßen ['gliːtmaːsən], *f. pl.* limbs.

glimmen ['glɪmən], *v.n. irr.* glimmer, glow, burn faintly; *—de Asche,* embers.

Glimmer ['glɪmər], *m.* (—s, *no pl.*) (*Min.*) mica.

glimpflich ['glɪmpflɪç], *adj.* gentle.

glitschen ['glɪtʃən], *v.n.* (*aux.* sein) (*coll.*) slide.

glitschig ['glɪtʃɪç], *adj.* (*coll.*) slippery.

glitzern ['glɪtsərn], *v.n.* glisten, glitter.

Globus ['gloːbus], *m.* (—ses, *pl.* —se) globe.

Glöckchen ['glœkçən], *n.* (—s, *pl.* —) small bell; hand-bell.

Glocke ['glɔkə], *f.* (—, *pl.* —n) bell; *etwas an die große — hängen,* make a great fuss about s.th.

Glockenblume ['glɔkənbluːmə], *f.* (—, *pl.* —n) (*Bot.*) bluebell.

Glockengießer ['glɔkəngiːsər], *m.* (—s, *pl.* —) bell-founder.

glockenklar ['glɔkənklaːr], *adj.* as clear as a bell.

Glockenläuter ['glɔkənlɔytər], *m.* (—s, *pl.* —) bell-ringer.

Glockenspiel ['glɔkənʃpiːl], *n.* (—s, *pl.* —e) chime; (*Mus.*) glockenspiel, carillon.

Glockenstuhl ['glɔkənʃtuːl], *m.* (—s, *pl.* -e) belfry.

Glockenzug ['glɔkəntsuːk], *m.* (—s, *pl.* -e) bell-rope; (*Mus.*) bell-stop.

Glöckner ['glœkner], *m.* (—s, *pl.* —) bellringer, sexton.

glorreich ['gloːraɪç], *adj.* glorious.

Glosse ['glɔsə], *f.* (—, *pl.* —n) gloss, comment, annotation; *—n machen über,* comment upon; find fault with; scoff at.

glotzen ['glɔtsən], *v.n.* stare wide-eyed; gape.

Glück [glyk], *n.* (—s, *no pl.*) luck, good luck, fortune, happiness; *— haben,* be in luck; *auf gut —,* at random; *zum —,* fortunately, luckily; *viel —,* good luck.

Glucke ['glukə], *f.* (—, *pl.* —n) (sitting) hen.

glücken ['glykən], *v.n.* succeed; *es ist mir geglückt,* I have succeeded in.

glücklich ['glyklɪç], *adj.* fortunate, lucky, happy.

glückselig [glyk'zeːlɪç], *adj.* blissful, happy.

glucksen ['gluksən], *v.n.* gurgle.

Glücksfall ['glyksfal], *m.* (—es, *pl.* -e) lucky chance, windfall, stroke of good fortune.

Glückspilz ['glykspɪlts], *m.* (—es, *pl.* —e) (*coll.*) lucky dog.

glückverheißend ['glykfɛrhaɪsənt], *adj.* auspicious, propitious.

Glückwunsch ['glykvunʃ], *m.* (—es, *pl.* -e) congratulation; felicitation.

glühen ['glyːən], *v.a.* make red-hot; (*wine*) mull. — *v.n.* glow, be red-hot.

glühend ['glyːənt], *adj.* glowing, burning; red-hot; (*coal*) live; (*fig.*) ardent, fervent.

Glühstrumpf ['glyːʃtrumpf], *m.* (—es, *pl.* -e) incandescent mantle.

Glühwein ['glyːvaɪn], *m.* (—s, *no pl.*) mulled wine.

Glut [gluːt], *f.* (—, *no pl.*) glowing fire; heat; (*fig.*) ardour.

glutrot ['gluːtroːt], *adj.* fiery red.

Glyzerin ['glyːtsəriːn], *n.* (—s, *no pl.*) glycerine.

Gnade

Gnade ['gna:də], *f.* (—, *pl.* —n) grace; favour; pardon, clemency, mercy; kindness; *Euer* —n, Your Grace.

Gnadenakt ['gna:dənakt], *m.* (—s, *pl.* —e) act of grace.

Gnadenbrot ['gna:dənbro:t], *n.* (—s, *no pl.*) *das* — *essen*, live on charity.

Gnadenfrist ['gna:dənfrıst], *f.* (—, *pl.* —en) respite.

Gnadenort ['gna:dənɔrt], *m.* (—(e)s, *pl.* —e) place of pilgrimage.

Gnadenstoß ['gna:dənʃto:s], *m.* (—es, *pl.* ⁀e) finishing stroke, coup de grâce, death-blow.

gnadenvoll ['gna:dənfɔl], *adj.* merciful, gracious.

Gnadenweg ['gna:dənve:k], *m.* (—es, *no pl.*) act of grace; *auf dem* —, by reprieve (as an act of grace).

gnädig ['gnɛːdıç], *adj.* gracious, merciful, kind; —*e Frau*, Madam; —*er Herr*, Sir.

Gnostiker ['gnɔstıkər], *m.* (—s, *pl.* —) gnostic.

Gnu [gnu:], *n.* (—s, *pl.* —s) (*Zool.*) gnu.

Gold [gɔlt], *n.* (—(e)s, *no pl.*) gold.

Goldammer ['gɔltamər], *f.* (—, *pl.* —n) (*Orn.*) yellow-hammer.

Goldamsel ['gɔltamzəl], *f.* (—, *pl.* —n) (*Orn.*) yellow-thrush.

Goldarbeiter ['gɔltarbaıtər], *m.* (—s, *pl.* —) goldsmith.

Goldbarren ['gɔltbarən], *m.* (—s, *pl.* —) ingot of gold.

Goldbergwerk ['gɔltbɛrkvɛrk], *n.* (—s, *pl.* —e) gold-mine.

Goldfisch ['gɔltfıʃ], *m.* (—es, *pl.* —e) goldfish.

Goldgewicht ['gɔltgəvıçt], *n.* (—s, *no pl.*) gold-weight, troy-weight.

Goldgrube ['gɔltgru:bə], *f.* (—, *pl.* —n) gold-mine.

goldig ['gɔldıç], *adj.* golden; (*fig.*) sweet, cute, charming.

Goldklumpen ['gɔltklumpən], *m.* (—s, *pl.* —) nugget (of gold).

Goldlack ['gɔltlak], *m.* (—s, *no pl.*) gold-coloured varnish; (*Bot.*) wall-flower.

Goldmacher ['gɔltmaxər], *m.* (—s, *pl.* —) alchemist.

Goldregen ['gɔltre:gən], *m.* (—s, *pl.* —) (*Bot.*) laburnum.

Goldscheider ['gɔltʃaıdər], *m.* (—s, *pl.* —) gold-refiner.

Goldschmied ['gɔltʃmi:t], *m.* (—s, *pl.* —e) goldsmith.

Goldschnitt ['gɔltʃnıt], *m.* (—s, *no pl.*) gilt edge.

Golf (1) [gɔlf], *m.* (—s, *pl.* —e) gulf.

Golf (2) [gɔlf], *n.* (—s, *no pl.*) golf.

Gondel ['gɔndəl], *f.* (—, *pl.* —n) gondola.

gondeln ['gɔndəln], *v.n.* (*aux.* sein) ride in a gondola; (*coll.*) travel, get about.

gönnen ['gœnən], *v.a. einem etwas* —, not grudge s.o. s.th.; *wir* — *es ihm*, we are happy for him.

Gönner ['gœnər], *m.* (—s, *pl.* —) patron, protector.

gönnerhaft ['gœnərhaft], *adj.* patronising.

Gönnerschaft ['gœnərʃaft], *f.* (—, *no pl.*) patronage.

gordisch ['gɔrdıʃ], *adj.* Gordian; *der* —*e Knoten*, the Gordian knot.

Göre ['gøːrə], *f.* (—, *pl.* —n) (*coll.*) brat; (*Am.*) kid.

Gosse ['gɔsə], *f.* (—, *pl.* —n) gutter.

Gote ['go:tə], *m.* (—n, *pl.* —n) Goth.

Gotik ['go:tık], *f.* (—, *no pl.*) Gothic style (architecture etc.).

gotisch ['go:tıʃ], *adj.* Gothic.

Gott [gɔt], *m.* (—es, *pl.* ⁀er) God, god; — *befohlen*, goodbye; *grüß* — *!* (*Austr.*) good day; — *sei Dank*, thank God, thank heaven.

gottbegnadet ['gɔtbəgna:dət], *adj.* favoured by God, inspired.

Götterbild ['gœtərbılt], *n.* (—s, *pl.* —er) image of a god.

gottergeben ['gɔtɛrge:bən], *adj.* submissive to God's will, devout.

Götterlehre ['gœtərle:rə], *f.* (—, *pl.* —n) mythology.

Götterspeise ['gœtərʃpaızə], *f.* (—, *pl.* —n) ambrosia.

Götterspruch ['gœtərʃprux], *m.* (—s, *no pl.*) oracle.

Göttertrank ['gœtərtraŋk], *m.* (—s, *pl.* ⁀e) nectar.

Gottesacker ['gɔtəsakər], *m.* (—s, *pl.* —) God's acre, churchyard.

Gottesdienst ['gɔtəsdi:nst], *m.* (—es, *pl.* —e) divine service, public worship.

gottesfürchtig ['gɔtəsfyrçtıç], *adj.* God-fearing, pious.

Gottesgelehrsamkeit ['gɔtəsgəle:rza:mkaıt], *f.* (—, *no pl.*) (*rare*) theology, divinity.

Gottesgericht ['gɔtəsgərıçt], *n.* (—s, *pl.* —e) ordeal.

Gotteshaus ['gɔtəshaus], *n.* (—es, *pl.* ⁀er) house of God; (*rare*) church.

Gotteslästerer ['gɔtəslɛstərər], *m.* (—s, *pl.* —) blasphemer.

Gottesleugner ['gɔtəslɔygnər], *m.* (—s, *pl.* —) atheist.

Gottfried ['gɔtfri:t], *m.* Godfrey, Geoffrey.

gottgefällig ['gɔtgəfɛlıç], *adj.* pleasing to God.

Gottheit ['gɔthaıt], *f.* (—, *pl.* —en) deity, divinity.

Göttin ['gœtın], *f.* (—, *pl.* —nen) goddess.

göttlich ['gœtlıç], *adj.* divine, godlike; (*fig.*) heavenly.

gottlob! [gɔt'lo:p], *excl.* thank God!

gottlos ['gɔtlo:s], *adj.* godless, ungodly, impious; (*fig.*) wicked.

gottvergessen ['gɔtfɛrgɛsən], *adj.* reprobate, impious.

gottverlassen ['gɔtfɛrlasən], *adj.* God-forsaken.

Götze ['gœtsə], *m.* (—n, *pl.* —n) idol, false deity.

94

Götzenbild [ˈgœtsənbɪlt], *n.* (—es, *pl.* —er) idol.

Götzendienst [ˈgœtsəndi:nst], *m.* (—es, *no pl.*) idolatry.

Gouvernante [guvɛrˈnantə], *f.* (—, *pl.* —n) governess.

Gouverneur [guvɛrˈnøːr], *m.* (—s, *pl.* —e) governor.

Grab [gra:p], *n.* (—s, *pl.* ⁻er) grave, tomb; sepulchre.

Graben [ˈgra:bən], *m.* (—s, *pl.* ⁻) ditch, trench.

graben [ˈgra:bən], *v.a. irr.* dig.

Grabgeläute [ˈgra:pgəlɔytə], *n.* (—s, *no pl.*) death-knell.

Grabhügel [ˈgra:phy:gəl], *m.* (—s, *pl.* —) tumulus, mound.

Grablegung [ˈgra:ple:guŋ], *f.* (—, *no pl.*) (*rare*) burial, interment.

Grabmal [ˈgra:pma:l], *n.* (—s, *pl.* —e, ⁻er) tomb, sepulchre, monument.

Grabschrift [ˈgra:pʃrɪft], *f.* (—, *pl.* —n) epitaph.

Grabstichel [ˈgra:pʃtɪçəl], *m.* (—s, *pl.* —) graving-tool.

Grad [gra:t], *m.* (—s, *pl.* —e) degree; rank; grade; extent; point; *in gewissem —e,* to a certain degree; *im höchsten —e,* in the highest degree, extremely.

Gradeinteilung [ˈgra:taɪntaɪluŋ], *f.* (—, *pl* —en) gradation, graduation.

Gradmesser [ˈgra:tmɛsər], *m.* (—s, *pl.* —) graduator; (*fig.*) index.

gradweise [ˈgra:tvaɪzə], *adv.* gradually, by degrees.

Graf [gra:f], *m.* (—en, *pl.* —en) count, earl.

Gräfin [ˈgrɛfɪn], *f.* (—, *pl.* —en) countess.

gräflich [ˈgrɛflɪç], *adj.* belonging to a count *or* earl.

Grafschaft [ˈgra:fʃaft], *f.* (—, *pl.* —en) county, shire.

Gral [gra:l], *m.* (—s, *no pl.*) Holy Grail.

Gram [gra:m], *m.* (—s, *no pl.*) grief, sorrow.

grämen [ˈgrɛ:mən], *v.a.* grieve. — *v.r. sich —,* grieve, fret, worry.

gramgebeugt [ˈgra:mgəbɔykt], *adj.* prostrate with grief.

grämlich [ˈgrɛ:mlɪç], *adj.* sullen, morose, ill-humoured.

Gramm [gram], *n.* (—s, *pl.* —e) gramme (15.438 grains) (*Am.*) gram.

Grammatik [graˈmatɪk], *f.* (—, *pl.* —en) grammar.

grammatikalisch, grammatisch [gramatɪˈka:lɪʃ, graˈmatɪʃ], *adj.* grammatical.

Gran [gra:n], *n.* (—s, *pl.* —e) (*weight*) grain.

Granat [graˈna:t], *m.* (—s, *pl.* —e) garnet.

Granatapfel [graˈna:tapfəl], *m.* (—s, *pl.* ⁻) (*Bot.*) pomegranate.

Granate [graˈna:tə], *f.* (—, *pl.* —n) shell, grenade.

Grande [ˈgrandə], *m.* (—n, *pl.* —n) grandee.

Grandezza [granˈdɛtsa], *f.* (—, *no pl.*) grandeur; sententiousness; pomposity.

grandios [grandiˈo:s], *adj.* grand.

Granit [graˈni:t], *m.* (—s, *pl.* —e) granite.

Granne [ˈgranə], *f.* (—, *pl.* —n) (*corn*) awn, beard.

graphisch [ˈgra:fɪʃ], *adj.* graphic.

Graphit [graˈfi:t], *m.* (—s, *no pl.*) blacklead.

Gras [gra:s], *n.* (—es, *pl.* ⁻er) grass; *ins — beißen,* bite the dust.

grasartig [ˈgra:sa:rtɪç], *adj.* gramineous.

grasen [ˈgra:zən], *v.n.* graze.

Grasfleck [ˈgra:sflɛk], *m.* (—s, *pl.* —e) grass-stain.

Grashalm [ˈgra:shalm], *m.* (—s, *pl.* —e) grass-blade.

Grashüpfer [ˈgra:shypfər], *m.* (—s, *pl.* —) (*Ent.*) grass-hopper.

grasig [ˈgra:zɪç], *adj.* grassy.

Grasmäher [ˈgra:smɛ:ər], *m.* (—s, *pl.* —) lawn-mower.

Grasmücke [ˈgra:smykə], *f.* (—, *pl.* —n) (*Orn.*) hedge-sparrow.

grassieren [graˈsi:rən], *v.n.* (*epidemics etc.*) spread, rage.

gräßlich [ˈgrɛslɪç], *adj.* hideous, horrible, ghastly.

Grasweide [ˈgra:svaɪdə], *f.* (—, *pl.* —n) pasture.

Grat [gra:t], *m.* (—s, *pl.* —e) edge, ridge.

Gräte [ˈgrɛ:tə], *f.* (—, *pl.* —n) fish-bone.

Grätenstich [ˈgrɛ:tənʃtɪç], *m.* (—s, *pl.* —e) (*embroidery*) herring-bone stitch.

grätig [ˈgrɛ:tɪç], *adj.* full of fishbones; (*fig.*) grumpy.

gratis [ˈgra:tɪs], *adj.* gratis; — *und franko,* for nothing.

Gratulation [gratula'tsjo:n], *f.* (—, *pl.* —en) congratulation.

gratulieren [gratuˈli:rən], *v.n. einem zu etwas —,* congratulate s.o. on s.th.

grau [grau], *adj.* grey; (*Am.*) gray; *vor —en Zeiten,* in times of yore.

Grauen [ˈgrauən], *n.* (—s, *no pl.*) horror, aversion.

grauen [ˈgrauən], *v.n.* (*morning*) dawn; *es graut mir vor,* I shudder at.

grauenhaft [ˈgrauənhaft], *adj.* horrible, awful, ghastly.

graulen [ˈgraulən], *v.r. sich —,* shudder, be afraid (of ghosts etc.).

graulich [ˈgraulɪç], *adj. mir ist ganz —,* I shudder.

Graupe [ˈgraupə], *f.* (—, *pl.* —n) groats, peeled barley.

graupeln [ˈgraupəln], *v.n. imp.* (*coll.*) drizzle, sleet.

Graus [graus], *m.* (—es, *no pl.*) horror, dread.

grausam [ˈgrauza:m], *adj.* cruel.

Grauschimmel [ˈgrauʃɪməl], *m.* (—s, *pl.* —) grey (horse).

grausen [ˈgrauzən], *v.n. es graust mir vor,* I shudder at.

grausig [ˈgrauzɪç], *adj.* dread, gruesome, horrible.

Graveur [gra'vø:r], *m.* (—s, *pl.* —e) engraver.

gravieren [gra'vi:rən], *v.a.* engrave.

Gravität [gravi'tɛ:t], *f.* (—, *no pl.*) gravity.

gravitätisch [gravi'tɛ:tɪʃ], *adj.* grave, solemn.

Grazie ['gra:tsjə], *f.* (—, *pl.* —n) grace, charm; (*goddess*) Grace.

graziös [gra'tsjø:s], *adj.* graceful.

Greif [graɪf], *m.* (—(e)s, *pl.* —e) griffin.

greifbar ['graɪfba:r], *adj.* to hand; (*fig.*) tangible, palpable.

greifen ['graɪfən], *v.a. irr.* grasp, seize, touch, handle; *etwas aus der Luft* —, invent s.th.; *um sich* —, gain ground.

greinen ['graɪnən], *v.n.* (*dial. & coll.*) cry, blubber.

Greis [graɪs], *m.* (—es, *pl.* —e) old man.

greisenhaft ['graɪzənhaft], *adj.* senile.

grell [grɛl], *adj.* (*colour*) glaring; (*light*) dazzling; (*tone*) shrill, sharp.

Grenadier [grena'di:r], *m.* (—s, *pl.* —e) grenadier.

Grenadiermütze [grena'di:rmʏtsə], *f.* (—, *pl.* —n) busby, bearskin.

Grenze ['grɛntsə], *f.* (—, *pl.* —n) boundary; frontier; borders; (*fig.*) limit.

grenzen ['grɛntsən], *v.n.* — *an*, border on; (*fig.*) verge on.

Grenzlinie ['grɛntsli:njə], *f.* (—, *pl.* —n) boundary-line, line of demarcation.

Greuel ['grɔyəl], *m.* (—s, *pl.* —) horror, abomination; *das ist mir ein* —, I abominate it.

Greueltat ['grɔyəlta:t], *f.* (—, *pl.* —en) atrocity.

greulich ['grɔylɪç], *adj.* horrible, dreadful, shocking, heinous.

Griebe ['gri:bə], *f.* (—, *pl.* —n) (*mostly pl.*) greaves.

Griebs ['gri:ps], *m.* (—es, *pl.* —e) (*dial.*) (*apple*) core.

Grieche ['gri:çə], *m.* (—n, *pl.* —n) Greek.

Griechenland ['gri:çənlant], *n.* Greece.

Griesgram ['gri:sgra:m], *m.* (—s, *pl.* —e) grumbler.

griesgrämig ['gri:sgrɛ:mɪç], *adj.* morose, grumbling.

Grieß ['gri:s], *m.* (—es, *no pl.*) groats, semolina.

Grießbrei ['gri:sbraɪ], *m.* (—s, *pl.* —e) gruel.

Griff [grɪf], *m.* (—s, *pl.* —e) grip, hold, handle.

griffbereit ['grɪfbəraɪt], *adj.* handy.

Grille ['grɪlə], *f.* (—, *pl.* —n) (*Ent.*) cricket; (*fig.*) whim; —*n haben*, be capricious; —*n fangen*, be crotchety, be depressed.

grillenhaft ['grɪlənhaft], *adj.* whimsical; capricious.

Grimasse [gri'masə], *f.* (—, *pl.* —n) grimace.

Grimm [grɪm], *m.* (—s, *no pl.*) fury, rage, wrath.

Grimmen ['grɪmən], *n.* (—s, *no pl.*) gripes; (*Med.*) colic.

grimmig ['grɪmɪç], *adj.* fierce, furious; grim.

Grind [grɪnt], *m.* (—s, *pl.* —e) scab, scurf.

grinsen ['grɪnzən], *v.n.* grin.

Grippe ['grɪpə], *f.* (—, *pl.* —n) influenza, grippe.

Grips [grɪps], *m.* (—es, *no pl.*) (*coll.*) sense, brains; *einen beim* — *nehmen*, take s.o. by the scruff of his neck.

grob [grɔp], *adj.* coarse; rough; gross; rude, crude, uncouth, impolite; (*jewels*) rough, unpolished.

Grobheit ['grɔphaɪt], *f.* (—, *pl.* —en) rudeness; abusive language.

Grobian ['gro:bja:n], *m.* (—s, *pl.* —e) boor, rude fellow.

Grobschmied ['grɔpʃmi:t], *m.* (—s, *pl.* —e) blacksmith.

Grog [grɔk], *m.* (—s, *pl.* —s) grog, toddy.

grölen ['grø:lən], *v.n.* (*coll.*) scream, squall, bawl.

Groll [grɔl], *m.* (—s, *no pl.*) resentment, anger, rancour; *einen* — *gegen einen haben*, bear s.o. a grudge.

grollen ['grɔlən], *v.n.* (*thunder*) rumble; *einem* —, bear s.o. ill-will; (*Poet.*) be angry (with).

Grönland ['grø:nlant], *n.* Greenland.

Gros (1) [grɔs], *n.* (—ses, *pl.* —se) gross; twelve dozen.

Gros (2) [gro:], *n.* (—s, *no pl.*) bulk, majority; *en* —, wholesale.

Groschen ['grɔʃən], *m.* (—s, *pl.* —) small coin, penny; one 100th of an Austrian shilling; ten-pfennig piece; *einen schönen* — *verdienen*, make good money.

groß [gro:s], *adj.* great, big, large; tall; vast; eminent, famous; intense; —*e Augen machen*, stare; *Grosser Ozean*, Pacific (Ocean).

großartig ['gro:sa:rtɪç], *adj.* grand, sublime, magnificent, splendid.

Großbetrieb ['gro:sbətri:p], *m.* (—s, *pl.* —e) large business; large (industrial) concern.

Großbritannien [gro:sbri'tanjən], *n.* Great Britain.

Größe ['grø:sə], *f.* (—, *pl.* —n) size, largeness, greatness; height; quantity; power; celebrity, star; importance.

Großeltern ['gro:sɛltərn], *pl.* grandparents.

Großenkel ['gro:sɛŋkəl], *m.* (—s, *pl.* —) great-grandson.

Größenverhältnis ['grø:sənferhɛltnɪs], *n.* (—ses, *pl.* —se) proportion, ratio.

Größenwahn ['grø:sənva:n], *m.* (—s, *no pl.*) megalomania; delusion of grandeur.

Großfürst ['gro:sfyrst], *m.* (—en, *pl.* —en) grand-duke.

Großfürstin [ˈgroːsfyrstɪn], *f.* (—, *pl.* —nen) grand-duchess.

Großgrundbesitz [ˈgroːsgruntbəzɪts], *m.* (—es, *pl.* —e) large landed property, estates.

Großhandel [ˈgroːshandəl], *m.* (—s, *no pl.*) wholesale business.

großherzig [ˈgroːshɛrtsɪç], *adj.* magnanimous.

Grossist [grɔˈsɪst], *m.* (—en, *pl.* —en) wholesale merchant.

großjährig [ˈgroːsjɛːrɪç], *adj.* of age; — werden, come of age.

großmächtig [ˈgroːsmɛçtɪç], *adj.* (*fig.*) high and mighty.

großmäulig [ˈgroːsmɔylɪç], *adj.* bragging, swaggering.

Großmut [ˈgroːsmuːt], *f.* (—, *no pl.*) magnanimity, generosity.

Großmutter [ˈgroːsmutər], *f.* (—, *pl.* ˙) grandmother.

Großsiegelbewahrer [groːsˈziːgəlbəvaːrər], *m.* (—s, *pl.* —) Lord Chancellor; Keeper of the Great Seal.

Großstadt [ˈgroːsʃtat], *f.* (—, *pl.* ˙e) large town, city, metropolis.

Großtat [ˈgroːstaːt], *f.* (—, *pl.* —en) achievement, exploit, feat.

Großtuer [ˈgroːstuːər], *m.* (—s, *pl.* —) boaster, braggart.

großtun [ˈgroːstuːn], *v.r. irr. sich — mit*, brag of; show off, parade.

Großvater [ˈgroːsfaːtər], *m.* (—s, *pl.* ˙) grandfather.

großziehen [ˈgroːstsiːən], *v.a. irr.* bring up, rear.

großzügig [ˈgroːstsyːgɪç], *adj.* boldly conceived; grand, generous.

Grotte [ˈgrɔtə], *f.* (—, *pl.* —n) grotto.

Grübchen [ˈgryːpçən], *n.* (—s, *pl.* —) dimple.

Grube [ˈgruːbə], *f.* (—, *pl.* —n) hole, pit; (*Min.*) mine; *in die — fahren*, (*Bibl.*) go down to the grave.

Grübelei [ˈgryːbəlaɪ], *f.* (—, *pl.* —en) brooding, musing.

grübeln [ˈgryːbəln], *v.n.* brood (over s.th.)

Grubenarbeiter [ˈgruːbənarbaɪtər], *m.* (—s, *pl.* —) miner.

Grubengas [ˈgruːbəngaːs], *n.* (—es, *pl.* —e) fire-damp.

Grubenlampe [ˈgruːbənlampə], *f.* (—, *pl.* —n) miner's lamp.

Gruft [gruft], *f.* (—, *pl.* ˙e) tomb, sepulchre; vault, mausoleum.

grün [gryːn], *adj.* green; *grüne Bohnen*, French beans, runner beans; (*fig.*) unripe, immature, inexperienced; *am —en Tisch*, at the conference table; (*fig.*) in theory; *auf einen —en Zweig kommen*, thrive, get on in the world; *einem nicht — sein*, dislike s.o.

Grund [grunt], *m.* (—s, *pl.* ˙e) ground, soil; earth; land; bottom; foundation, basis; valley; reason, cause, argument; motive.

Grundbedeutung [ˈgruntbədɔytuŋ], *f.* (—, *pl.* —en) primary meaning, basic meaning.

Grundbesitz [ˈgruntbəzɪts], *m.* (—es, *no pl.*) landed property.

Grundbuch [ˈgruntbuːx], *n.* (—s, *pl.* ˙er) land register.

grundehrlich [ˈgrunteːrlɪç], *adj.* thoroughly honest.

Grundeigentum [ˈgruntaɪgəntuːm], *n.* (—s, *pl.* ˙er) landed property.

Grundeis [ˈgruntaɪs], *n.* (—es, *no pl.*) ground-ice.

gründen [ˈgryndən], *v.a.* found, establish, float (a company). — *v.r. sich — auf*, be based on.

grundfalsch [ˈgruntfalʃ], *adj.* radically false.

Grundfarbe [ˈgruntfarbə], *f.* (—, *pl.* —n) primary colour.

Grundfläche [ˈgruntflɛçə], *f.* (—, *pl.* —n) basic base.

Grundherr [ˈgrunthɛr], *m.* (—n, *pl.* —en) lord of the manor, freeholder.

grundieren [grunˈdiːrən], *v.a.* prime, size, paint the undercoat.

Grundkapital [ˈgruntkapitaːl], *n.* (—s, *no pl.*) original stock.

Grundlage [ˈgruntlaːgə], *f.* (—, *pl.* —n) foundation, basis.

Grundlegung [ˈgruntleːguŋ], *f.* (—, *no pl.*) laying the foundation.

gründlich [ˈgryntlɪç], *adj.* thorough, solid.

grundlos [ˈgruntloːs], *adj.* bottomless; groundless, unfounded, without foundation.

Grundmauer [ˈgruntmauər], *f.* (—, *pl.* —n) foundation wall.

Gründonnerstag [ˈgryːnˈdɔnərstaːk], *m.* (—s, *pl.* —e) Maundy Thursday.

Grundpfeiler [ˈgruntpfaɪlər], *m.* (—s, *pl.* —) (main) pillar.

Grundriß [ˈgruntrɪs], *m.* (—sses, *pl.* —sse) design, groundplan; compendium, elements; blueprint.

Grundsatz [ˈgruntzats], *m.* (—es, *pl.* ˙e) principle, maxim; axiom.

grundschlecht [ˈgruntʃlɛçt], *adj.* thoroughly bad.

Grundschuld [ˈgruntʃult], *f.* (—, *pl.* —en) mortgage (on land).

Grundstein [ˈgruntʃtaɪn], *m.* (—s, *pl.* —e) foundation-stone.

Grundsteuer [ˈgruntʃtɔyər], *f.* (—, *pl.* —n) land-tax.

Grundstoff [ˈgruntʃtɔf], *m.* (—es, *pl.* —e) raw material.

Grundstück [ˈgruntʃtyk], *n.* (—s, *pl.* —e) real estate; plot of land; lot.

Grundtugend [ˈgrunttuːgənt], *f.* (—, *pl.* —en) cardinal virtue.

Gründung [ˈgrynduŋ], *f.* (—, *pl.* —en) foundation, establishment.

grundverschieden [ˈgruntfɛrʃiːdən], *adj.* radically different.

Grundwasser [ˈgruntvasər], *n.* (—s, *no pl.*) underground water.

Grundzahl [ˈgrunttsaːl], *f.* (—, *pl.* —en) cardinal number.

Grundzug [ˈgrunttsuːk], *m.* (—s, *pl.* ˙e) characteristic; distinctive feature.

Grüne ['gry:nə], *n.* (**—n**, *no pl.*) greenness, verdure; *ins — gehen*, take a walk in the open country.

grünen ['gry:nən], *v.n.* become green; (*fig.*) flourish.

Grünfutter ['gry:nfutər], *n.* (**—s**, *no pl.*) green food.

Grünkohl ['gry:nko:l], *m.* (**—s**, *no pl.*) green kale.

Grünkramhändler ['gry:nkra:mhɛndlər], *m.* (**—s**, *pl.* **—**) greengrocer.

Grünschnabel ['gry:nʃna:bəl], *m.* (**—s**, *pl.* ˙) greenhorn.

Grünspan ['gry:nʃpa:n], *m.* (**—s**, *no pl.*) verdigris.

Grünspecht ['gry:nʃpɛçt], *m.* (**—s**, *pl.* **—e**) (*Orn.*) green woodpecker.

grunzen ['gruntsən], *v.n.* grunt.

Grünzeug ['gry:ntsɔyk], *n.* (**—s**, *no pl.*) greens, herbs.

Gruppe ['grupə], *f.* (**—**, *pl.* **—n**) group.

gruppieren [gru'pi:rən], *v.ä.* group.

gruselig ['gru:zəlɪç], *adj.* creepy, uncanny.

gruseln ['gru:zəln], *v.a. es gruselt mir* I shudder, it gives me the creeps.

Gruß [gru:s], *m.* (**—es**, *pl.* ˙e) salutation, greeting; (*pl.*) regards; *mit herzlichem —*, with kind regards; *einen — ausrichten*, convey s.o.'s regards.

grüßen ['gry:sən], *v.a.* greet; *einen — lassen*, send o.'s regards to s.o.; *— Sie ihn von mir*, remember me to him.

Grütze ['grytsə], *f.* (**—**, *pl.* **—n**) peeled grain, groats; (*fig.*) (*coll.*) gumption, brains.

Guatemala [guatə'ma:la], *n.* Guatemala.

gucken ['gukən], *v.n.* look, peep.

Guinea [gɪ'ne:a], *n.* Guinea.

Gulasch ['gulaʃ], *n.* (**—s**, *no pl.*) goulash.

Gulden ['guldən], *m.* (**—s**, *pl.* **—**) florin, guilder.

gülden ['gyldən], *adj.* (*Poet.*) golden.

gültig ['gyltɪç], *adj.* valid; (*money*) current, legal (tender).

Gummi ['gumi:], *m.* (**—s**, *no pl.*) gum, rubber.

Gummiarabikum [gumia'ra:bɪkum], *n.* gum arabic.

gummiartig ['gumia:rtɪç], *adj.* gummy; like rubber.

Gummiball ['gumibal], *m.* (**—s**, *pl.* ˙e) rubber-ball.

Gummiband ['gumibant], *n.* (**—s**, *pl.* ˙er) rubber-band, elastic.

Gummielastikum [gumie'lastʌkum], *n.* indiarubber.

gummieren [gu'mi:rən], *v.a.* gum.

Gummireifen [gumiaɪfən], *m.* (**—s**, *pl.* **—**) tyre; (*Am.*) tire.

Gummischuhe ['gumiʃu:ə], *m. pl.* galoshes; (*Am.*) rubbers.

Gunst [gunst], *f.* (**—**, *no pl.*) favour; *zu seinen —en*, in his favour.

Gunstbezeigung ['gunstbətsaɪguŋ], *f.* (**—**, *pl.* **—en**) favour, kindness, goodwill.

günstig ['gynstɪç], *adj.* favourable, propitious.

Günstling ['gynstlɪŋ], *m.* (**—s**, *pl.* **—e**) favourite.

Gurgel ['gurgəl], *f.* (**—**, *pl.* **—n**) gullet, throat.

gurgeln ['gurgəln], *v.n.* gargle; gurgle.

Gurke ['gurkə], *f.* (**—**, *pl.* **—n**) (*Bot.*) cucumber; (*pickled*) gherkin.

Gurt [gurt], *m.* (**—es**, *pl.* **—e**) belt; strap; harness.

Gürtel ['gyrtəl], *m.* (**—s**, *pl.* **—**) girdle, belt; (*Geog.*) zone.

Guß [gus], *m.* (**—sses**, *pl.* ˙sse) gush, downpour; founding; cast; (*Cul.*) icing.

Gut [gu:t], *m.* (**—(e)s**, *pl.* ˙er) good thing, blessing; property, possession; country seat; estate; (*pl.*) goods.

gut [gu:t], *adj.* good; beneficial; kind; virtuous. *— adv.* well; *es — haben*, be well off; *—er Dinge sein*, be of good cheer; *kurz und —*, in short.

Gutachten ['gu:taxtən], *n.* (**—s**, *pl.* **—**) expert opinion, expert evidence.

gutartig ['gu:ta:rtɪç], *adj.* good-natured; benign.

Güte ['gy:tə], *f.* (**—**, *no pl.*) goodness, kindness, quality.

Güterabfertigung ['gy:tərapfɛrtɪguŋ], *f.* (**—**, *pl.* **—en**) (*Railw.*) goods-depot, goods-office.

Güterabtretung ['gy:təraptre:tuŋ], *f.* (**—**, *pl.* **—en**) cession of goods; (*Law*) surrender of an estate.

gutgelaunt ['gu:tgəlaunt], *adj.* in good spirits, good-humoured.

gutgemeint ['gu:tgəmaɪnt], *adj.* well-meant, well-intentioned.

gutgesinnt ['gu:tgəzɪnt], *adj.* well-intentioned.

Guthaben ['gu:tha:bən], *n.* (**—s**, *pl.* **—**) credit-balance, assets.

gutheißen ['gu:thaɪsən], *v.a. irr.* approve.

gütig ['gy:tɪç], *adj.* kind, benevolent.

gütlich ['gy:tlɪç], *adj.* amicable, friendly; *—er Vergleich*, amicable settlement; *sich — tun*, indulge o.s.

gutmachen ['gu:tmaxən], *v.a. etwas wieder —*, make amends for s.th., compensate.

gutmütig ['gu:tmy:tɪç], *adj.* good-natured, good-tempered.

Gutsbesitzer ['gu:tsbəzɪtsər], *m.* (**—s**, *pl.* **—**) landowner; proprietor of an estate.

gutschreiben ['gu:tʃraɪbən], *v.a. irr. einem etwas —*, enter a sum to s.o.'s credit.

Gutsverwalter ['gu:tsfɛrvaltər], *m.* (**—s**, *pl.* **—**) land-steward, agent, bailiff.

gutwillig ['gu:tvɪlɪç], *adj.* willing, of o.'s own free will.

Gymnasialbildung [gymnaz'ja:lbɪlduŋ], *f.* (**—**, *no pl.*) classical *or* grammar school education.

Gymnasiast [gymnaz'jast], *m.* (**—en**, *pl.* **—en**) grammar-school pupil.

Gymnasium [gym′na:zjum], *n.* (—s, *pl.* —sien) high school.
Gymnastik [gym′nastık], *f.* (—, *no pl.*) gymnastics.
gymnastisch [gym′nastıʃ], *adj.* gymnastic(al); —e *Übungen*, physical exercises.

H

H [ha:], *n.* (—s, *pl.* —s) the letter H; (*Mus.*) *H Dur*, B major; *H Moll*, B minor.
ha! [ha:], *excl.* ha!
Haag, Den [ha:k, de:n], *m.* The Hague.
Haar [ha:r], *n.* (—s, *pl.* —e) hair; wool; nap; *aufs* —, exactly, to a hair; *um ein* —, very nearly, within a hair's breadth.
haaren [′ha:rən], *v.r. sich* —, shed o.'s hair.
haargenau [′ha:rgənau], *adj.* (very) exactly; to a nicety.
haarig [′ha:rıç], *adj.* hairy.
Haarlocke [′ha:rlɔkə], *f.* (—, *pl.* —n) curl, ringlet.
Haarnadel [′ha:rna:dəl], *f.* (—, *pl.* —n) hairpin.
Haaröl [′ha:rø:l], *n.* (—s, *no pl.*) hair-oil.
Haarpinsel [′ha:rpınzəl], *m.* (—s, *pl.* —) camel-hair brush.
Haarröhrchen [′ha:rrø:rçən], *n.* (—s, *pl.* —) capillary tube.
Haarschleife [′ha:rʃlaıfə], *f.* (—, *pl.* —en) bow in the hair.
Haarschnitt [′ha:rʃnıt], *m.* (—s, *pl.* —e) hair-cut.
Haarschuppen [′ha:rʃupən], *f. pl.* dandruff.
Haarspalterei [′ha:rʃpaltərai], *f.* (—, *pl.* —en) hair-splitting.
haarsträubend [′ha:rʃtrɔybənt], *adj.* hair-raising, monstrous.
Haarwäsche [′ha:rvɛʃə], *f.* (—, *no pl.*) shampooing.
Haarwickel [′ha:rvıkəl], *m.* (—s, *pl.* —) curler.
Haarzange [′ha:rtsaŋə], *f.* (—, *pl.* —n) tweezers.
Habe [′ha:be], *f.* (—, *no pl.*) property, belongings, effects; *Hab und Gut*, all o.'s belongings, goods and chattels.
Haben [′ha:bən], *n.* (—s, *no pl.*) credit; *Soll und* —, debit and credit.
haben [′ha:bən], *v.a. irr.* have, possess; *da hast du's*, there you are; *es ist nicht zu* —, it is not available.
Habenichts [′ha:bənıçts], *m.* (—es, *no pl.*) have-not.
Habgier [′ha:pgi:r], *f.* (—, *no pl.*) greediness, avarice, covetousness.

habhaft [′ha:phaft], *adj. einer Sache* — *werden*, get possession of a thing.
Habicht [′ha:bıçt], *m.* (—s, *pl.* —e) (*Orn.*) hawk.
Habichtsinseln [′ha:bıçtsınzəln], *f. pl.* the Azores.
Habichtsnase [′ha:bıçtsna:zə], *f.* (—, *pl.* —n) hooked nose, aquiline nose.
Habilitation [habilita′tsjo:n], *f.* (—, *pl.* —en) admission *or* inauguration as a university lecturer.
habilitieren [habili′ti:rən], *v.r. sich* —, qualify as a university lecturer.
Habseligkeiten [′ha:pzelıçkaıtən], *f. pl.* property, effects, chattels.
Habsucht [′ha:pzuxt], *f.* (—, *no pl.*) avarice, greediness.
Hackbeil [′hakbaıl], *n.* (—s, *pl.* —e) cleaver, chopping-knife.
Hackbrett [′hakbrɛt], *n.* (—s, *pl.* —er) chopping-board.
Hacke [′hakə], *f.* (—, *pl.* —n) hoe, mattock; heel.
Hacken [′hakən], *m.* (—s, *pl.* —) heel; *sich auf die* — *machen*, be off, take to o.'s heels.
hacken [′hakən], *v.a.* hack, chop, hoe; mince; (*birds*) peck.
Hacker [′hakər], *m.* (—s, *pl.* —) chopper.
Häckerling [′hɛkərlıŋ], *m.* (—s, *no pl.*) chopped straw.
Hackfleisch [′hakflaıʃ], *n.* (—es, *no pl.*) minced meat
Häcksel [′hɛksəl], *n.* (—s, *no pl.*) chopped straw.
Hader [′ha:dər], *m.* (—s, *no pl.*) quarrel, dispute.
hadern [′ha:dərn], *v.n.* quarrel, have a dispute.
Hafen [′ha:fən], *m.* (—s, *pl.* ″) harbour, port; refuge, haven.
Hafendamm [′ha:fəndam], *m.* (—s, *pl.* ″e) jetty, mole, pier.
Hafensperre [′ha:fənʃperə], *f.* (—, *pl.* —n) embargo, blockade.
Hafenzoll [′ha:fəntsol], *m.* (—s, *no pl.*) anchorage, harbour due.
Hafer [′ha:fər], *m.* (—s, *no pl.*) oats; *es sticht ihn der* —, he is getting cheeky, insolent.
Haferbrei [′ha:fərbrai], *m.* (—s, *no pl.*) porridge.
Hafergrütze [′ha:fərgrytsə], *f.* (—, *no pl.*) ground-oats, oatmeal.
Haferschleim [′ha:fərʃlaim], *m.* (—s, *no pl.*) oat-gruel, porridge.
Haff [haf], *n.* (—s, *pl.* —e) bay, lagoon.
Haft [haft], *f.* (—, *no pl.*) custody, imprisonment, arrest.
haftbar [′haftba:r], *adj.* answerable; (*Law*) liable.
Haftbefehl [′haftbəfe:l], *m.* (—s, *pl.* —e) warrant for arrest.
haften [′haftən], *v.n.* stick, cling, adhere; *für einen* —, go bail for s.o.; *für etwas* —, answer for, be liable for s.th.

Häftling

Häftling [ˈhɛftlɪŋ], *m.* (—s, *pl.* —e) prisoner.

Haftpflicht [ˈhaftpflɪçt], *f.* (—, *no pl.*) liability.

Haftung [ˈhaftuŋ], *f.* (—, *no pl.*) liability, security; (*Comm.*) *Gesellschaft mit beschränkter* —, limited liability company, (*abbr.*) Ltd.

Hag [ha:k], *m.* (—es, *pl.* —e) hedge, enclosure.

Hagebuche [ˈha:gəbu:xə], *f.* (—, *pl.* —n) hornbeam.

Hagebutte [ˈha:gəbutə], *f.* (—, *pl.* —n) (*Bot.*) hip, haw.

Hagedorn [ˈha:gədɔrn], *m.* (—s, *no pl.*) (*Bot.*) hawthorn.

Hagel [ˈha:gəl], *m.* (—s, *no pl.*) hail.

hageln [ˈha:gəln], *v.n.* hail.

Hagelschauer [ˈha:gəlʃauər], *m.* (—s, *pl.* —) hailstorm.

hager [ˈha:gər], *adj.* thin, lean, lank, gaunt.

Häher [ˈhɛ:ər], *m.* (—s, *pl.* —) (*Orn.*) jay.

Hahn [ha:n], *m.* (—s, *pl.* ˙˙e) (*Orn.*) cockerel, cock; (*water, gas*) cock, tap, faucet; — *im Korbe sein*, rule the roost; *da kräht kein — danach*, nobody cares two hoots about it.

Hahnenbalken [ˈha:nənbalkən], *m.* (—s, *pl.* —) cock-loft; hen-roost.

Hahnenfuß [ˈha:nənfu:s], *m.* (—es, *no pl.*) (*Bot.*) crow-foot.

Hahnensporn [ˈha:nɛnʃpɔrn], *m.* (—s, *no pl.*) cockspur.

Hahnentritt [ˈha:nəntrɪt], *m.* (—s, *no pl.*) cock's tread.

Hahnrei [ˈha:nrai], *m.* (—s, *pl.* —e) cuckold; *einen zum — machen*, cuckold s.o.

Hai [hai], *m.* (—s, *pl.* —e) (*Zool.*) shark.

Haifisch [ˈhaifɪʃ], *m.* (—es, *pl.* —e) (*Zool.*) shark.

Hain [hain], *m.* (—s, *pl.* —e) (*Poet.*) grove, thicket.

Haiti [ha'iti], *n.* Haiti.

Häkchen [ˈhɛ:kçən], *n.* (—s, *pl.* —) small hook, crotchet; apostrophe.

häkeln [ˈhɛ:kəln], *v.a. v.n.* crochet; (*fig.*) tease; (*Am.*) needle (*coll.*).

Haken [ˈha:kən], *m.* (—s, *pl.* —) hook, clasp; (*fig.*) hitch, snag.

Hakenkreuz [ˈha:kənkrɔyts], *n.* (—es, *pl.* —e) swastika.

halb [halp], *adj.* half; *halb neun*, half past eight.

halbieren [hal'bi:rən], *v.a.* halve, divide into halves; (*Maths.*) bisect.

Halbinsel [ˈhalpInzəl], *f.* (—, *pl.* —n) peninsula.

Halbmesser [ˈhalpmɛsər], *m.* (—s, *pl.* —) radius.

halbpart [ˈhalppart], *adj.* — *mit einem machen*, go halves with s.o.

halbstündig [ˈhalpʃtyndɪç], *adj.* lasting half an hour.

halbstündlich [ˈhalpʃtyntlɪç], *adj.* half-hourly, every half-hour.

halbwegs [ˈhalpve:ks], *adv.* (*coll.*) reasonably, tolerably.

Halbwelt [ˈhalpvɛlt], *f.* (—, *no pl.*) demi-monde.

halbwüchsig [ˈhalpvy:ksɪç], *adj.* teenage.

Halde [ˈhaldə], *f.* (—, *pl.* —n) declivity, hill; (*Min.*) waste-heap, slag-heap.

Hälfte [ˈhɛlftə], *f.* (—, *pl.* —n) half; (*obs.*) moiety.

Halfter [ˈhalftər], *f.* (—, *pl.* —n) halter.

Hall [hal], *m.* (—s, *no pl.*) sound, echo.

Halle [ˈhalə], *f.* (—, *pl.* —n) hall, vestibule; portico; porch.

hallen [ˈhalən], *v.n.* sound, resound; clang.

Halm [halm], *m.* (—es, *pl.* —e) stalk; (*grass*) blade.

Hals [hals], *m.* (—es, *pl.* ˙˙e) neck, throat; — *über Kopf*, head over heels, hastily, hurriedly.

Halsader [ˈhalsa:dər], *f.* (—, *pl.* —n) jugular vein.

Halsbinde [ˈhalsbIndə], *f.* (—, *pl.* —n) scarf, tie.

Halsentzündung [ˈhalsɛntsynduŋ], *f.* (—, *pl.* —en) inflammation of the throat.

Halskrause [ˈhalskrauzə], *f.* (—, *pl.* —n) frill, ruff.

halsstarrig [ˈhalsʃtarɪç], *adj.* stubborn, obstinate.

Halsweh [ˈhalsve:], *n.* (—s, *no pl.*) sore throat.

Halt [halt], *m.* (—es, *no pl.*) halt; stop; hold; (*also fig.*) support.

haltbar [ˈhaltba:r], *adj.* durable, strong; tenable, valid.

halten [ˈhaltən], *v.a. irr.* hold; keep; detain; deliver (speech, lecture); observe, celebrate. — *v.n.* stop; stand firm; insist; *halt!* stop! stop it! — *v.r. sich* —, hold out, keep, behave.

haltlos [ˈhaltlo:s], *adj.* unprincipled; floundering, unsteady.

Haltung [ˈhaltuŋ], *f.* (—, *pl.* —en) carriage, posture, attitude; (*fig.*) behaviour, demeanour; attitude.

Halunke [ha'luŋkə], *m.* (—n, *pl.* —n) scoundrel, rascal, scamp.

hämisch [ˈhɛ:mɪʃ], *adj.* malicious, spiteful.

Hammel [ˈhaməl], *m.* (—s, *pl.* —) (*meat*) mutton.

Hammelkeule [ˈhaməlkɔylə], *f.* (—, *pl.* —n) leg of mutton.

Hammer [ˈhamər], *m.* (—s, *pl.* ˙˙) hammer; *unter den — kommen*, be sold by auction.

Hämorrhoiden [hɛmo'ri:dən], *f. pl.* (*Med.*) piles, haemorrhoids.

Hand [hant], *f.* (—, *pl.* ˙˙e) hand.

Handarbeit [ˈhantarbait], *f.* (—, *pl.* —en) manual labour; needlework.

Handel [ˈhandəl], *m.* (—s, *no pl.*) trade, commerce; — *treiben*, carry on trade, do business.

Händel [ˈhɛndəl], *m. pl.* quarrel, difference, dispute.

handeln ['handəln], *v.n.* act; — *in*, deal in; *es handelt sich um . . .* it is a question of . . . ; *es handelt von . . .* , it deals with . . . .

handelseinig ['handəlsaınıç], *adj.* — *werden*, come to terms.

Handelsgenossenschaft ['handəls-gənɔsənʃaft], *f.* (—, *pl.* —en) trading company.

Handelsgeschäft ['handəlsgəʃeft], *n.* (—es, *pl.* —e) commercial transaction.

Handelsgesellschaft ['handəlsgəzel-ʃaft], *f.* (—, *pl.* —en) trading company; joint-stock company.

Handelskammer ['handəlskamər], *f.* (—, *pl.* —n) chamber of commerce.

Handelsmarke ['handəlsmarkə], *f.* (—, *pl.* —n) trade-mark.

Handelsreisende ['handəlsraızəndə], *m.* (—n, *pl.* —n) commercial traveller.

händelsüchtig ['hendəlzyçtıç], *adj.* quarrelsome; litigious.

Handelsvertrag ['handəlsfertra:k], *m.* (—es, *pl.* ⁀e) commercial treaty; contract.

Handelszweig ['handəlstsvaık], *m.* (—es, *pl.* —e) branch of trade.

Handfeger ['hantfe:gər], *m.* (—s, *pl.* —) hand-broom, handbrush.

Handfertigkeit ['hantfertıçkaıt], *f.* (—, *no pl.*) dexterity, manual skill; handicrafts.

Handfessel ['hantfesəl], *f.* (—, *pl.* —n) handcuff.

handfest ['hantfest], *adj.* robust, strong.

Handgeld ['hantgelt], *n.* (—es, *no pl.*) earnest; (*money*) advance.

Handgelenk ['hantgələŋk], *n.* (—s, *pl.* —e) wrist.

handgemein ['hantgəmaın], *adj.* — *werden*, come to blows.

Handgemenge ['hantgəmeŋə], *n.* (—s, *no pl.*) fray, scuffle.

handgreiflich ['hantgraıflıç], *adj.* palpable; evident, plain.

Handgriff ['hantgrıf], *m.* (—es, *pl.* —e) handle; (*fig.*) knack.

Handhabe ['hantha:bə], *f.* (—, *pl.* —n) (*fig.*) hold, handle.

handhaben ['hantha:bən], *v.a.* handle, manage; operate.

Handlanger ['hantlaŋər], *m.* (—s, *pl.* —) helper, carrier.

Händler ['hendlər], *m.* (—s, *pl.* —) dealer, merchant.

handlich ['hantlıç], *adj.* handy, manageable.

Handlung ['handluŋ], *f.* (—, *pl.* —en) shop; (*Am.*) store; commercial house, mercantile business; action, act, deed; (*Lit.*) plot.

Handrücken ['hantrykən], *m.* (—s, *pl.* —) back of the hand.

Handschelle ['hantʃelə], *f.* (—, *pl.* —n) manacle, handcuff.

Handschlag ['hantʃla:k], *m.* (—s, *pl.* ⁀e) handshake.

Handschuh ['hantʃu:], *m.* (—s, *pl.* —e) glove; (*of iron*) gauntlet.

Handstreich ['hantʃtraıç], *m.* (—es, *pl.* —e) (*Mil.*) surprise attack, coup de main.

Handtuch ['hanttu:x], *n.* (—es, *pl.* ⁀er) towel.

Handumdrehen ['hantumdre:ən], *n.* (—s, *no pl.*) *im* —, in no time, in a jiffy.

Handwerk ['hantverk], *n.* (—s, *pl.* —e) handicraft, trade, craft.

Handwörterbuch ['hantvœrtərbu:x], *n.* (—es, *pl.* ⁀er) compact dictionary.

Handwurzel ['hantvurtsəl], *f.* (—, *pl.* —n) wrist.

Hanf [hanf], *m.* (—es, *no pl.*) hemp.

Hänfling ['henflıŋ], *m.* (—s, *pl.* —e) (*Orn.*) linnet.

Hang [haŋ], *m.* (—es, *pl.* ⁀e) slope, declivity; (*fig.*) (*no pl.*) inclination, propensity.

Hängematte ['heŋəmatə], *f.* (—, *pl.* —n) hammock.

hängen ['heŋən], *v.a. irr.* hang, suspend. — *v.r. sich* —, hang o.s. — *v.n.* hang, be suspended; be hanged (*execution*).

Hannover [ha'no:fər], *n.* Hanover.

Hänselei ['henzəlaı], *f.* (—, *pl.* —en) chaffing, leg-pulling, teasing.

hänseln ['henzəln], *v.a.* tease, chaff.

Hantel ['hantəl], *f.* (—, *pl.* —n) dumb-bell.

hantieren [han'ti:rən], *v.n.* busy o.s., work, occupy o.s. (with).

hapern ['ha:pərn], *v.n.* lack, be deficient; *da hapert es*, that's the snag.

Häppchen ['hepçən], *n.* (—s, *pl.* —) morsel.

Happen ['hapən], *m.* (—s, *pl.* —) mouthful.

happig ['hapıç], *adj.* greedy; excessive.

Härchen ['he:rçən], *n.* (—s, *pl.* —) short hair.

Harfe ['harfə], *f.* (—, *pl.* —n) (*Mus.*) harp.

Harke ['harkə], *f.* (—, *pl.* —n) rake.

Harm [harm], *m.* (—es, *no pl.*) grief; sorrow; injury, wrong.

härmen ['hermən], *v.r. sich* — *um*, grieve over.

harmlos ['harmlo:s], *adj.* harmless, innocuous.

Harmonielehre [harmo'ni:le:rə], *f.* (—, *pl.* —n) (*Mus.*) harmonics; harmony.

harmonieren [harmo'ni:rən], *v.n. mit einem* —, be in concord with s.o., agree with s.o.

Harmonika [har'mo:nıka], *f.* (—, *pl.* —ken) (*Mus.*) accordion, concertina; mouth-organ.

Harn [harn], *m.* (—s, *no pl.*) urine.

Harnisch ['harnıʃ], *m.* (—es, *pl.* —e) harness, armour; *in* — *bringen*, enrage.

Harpune [har'pu:nə], *f.* (—, *pl.* —n) harpoon.

harren ['harən], *v.n.* wait for, hope for.

harsch [harʃ], *adj.* harsh; rough; unfriendly.

hart [hart], *adj.* hard, severe, cruel, austere.

Härte ['hɛrtə], *f.* (—, *pl.* —n) hardness, severity.

härten ['hɛrtən], *v.a.* harden.

hartleibig ['hartlaɪbɪç], *adj.* constipated.

hartnäckig ['hartnɛkɪç], *adj.* stubborn, obstinate; undaunted.

Harz (1) [harts], *m.* (Geog.) (—es, *no pl.*) the Hartz mountains.

Harz (2) [harts], *n.* (—es, *pl.* —e) resin, rosin.

harzig ['hartsɪç], *adj.* resinous.

Hasardspiel [ha'zartʃpi:l], *n.* (—es, *pl.* —e) game of chance, gamble.

Haschee [ha'ʃe:], *n.* (—s, *pl.* —s) puree, hash, mash.

haschen ['haʃən], *v.a.* catch, snatch, seize. — *v.n.* — nach, strain after, snatch at.

Häschen ['hɛːsçən], *n.* (—s, *pl.* —) (Zool.) small hare, leveret.

Häscher ['hɛʃər], *m.* (—s, *pl.* —) bailiff.

Hase ['ha:zə], *m.* (—n, *pl.* —n) (Zool.) hare.

Haselrute ['ha:zəlru:tə], *f.* (—, *pl.* —n) hazel-switch.

Hasenfuß ['ha:zənfu:s], *m.* (—es, *no pl.*) coward.

Hasenklein ['ha:zənklaɪn], *n.* (—s, *no pl.*) jugged hare.

Hasenscharte ['ha:zənʃartə], *f.* (—, *pl.* —n) hare-lip.

Haspe ['haspə], *f.* (—, *pl.* —n) hasp, hinge.

Haspel ['haspəl], *f.* (—, *pl.* —n) reel.

haspeln ['haspəln], *v.a.* wind on a reel; (*fig.*) rattle off.

Haß [has], *m.* (—sses, *no pl.*) hatred, hate, detestation.

hassen ['hasən], *v.a.* hate, detest.

haßerfüllt ['hasərfʏlt], *adj.* full of — spite, full of hatred.

häßlich ['hɛslɪç], *adj.* ugly, repulsive; (*fig.*) unpleasant, unkind; unseemly.

Hast [hast], *f.* (—, *no pl.*) haste, hurry, hastiness, rashness.

hastig ['hastɪç], *adj.* hasty, hurried.

hätscheln ['hɛtʃəln], *v.a.* pamper, caress, fondle.

Hatz [hats], *f.* (—, *pl.* —en) baiting; hunt; revelry.

Haube ['haubə], *f.* (—, *pl.* —n) bonnet, cap; (Motor.) bonnet, (Am.) hood.

Haubenlerche ['haubənlɛrçə], *f.* (—, *pl.* —n) (Orn.) crested lark.

Haubitze [hau'bɪtsə], *f.* (—, *pl.* —n) howitzer.

Hauch [haux], *m.* (—es, *no pl.*) breath, whiff; (*fig.*) touch, tinge.

hauchdünn ['haux'dyn], *adj.* extremely thin.

hauchen ['hauxən], *v.n.* breathe.

Hauchlaut ['hauxlaut], *m.* (—es, *pl.* —e) (Phonet.) aspirate.

Haudegen ['haude:gən], *m.* (—s, *pl.* —) broad-sword; *ein alter* —, an old bully.

Haue ['hauə], *f.* (—, *no pl.*) (coll.) thrashing.

hauen ['hauən], *v.a.* hew; cut; strike; hit; give a hiding to. — *v.n. über die Schnur* —, kick over the traces.

Hauer ['hauər], *m.* (—s, *pl.* —) hewer, cutter; (*animal*) fang, tusk.

Häuer ['hɔyər], *m.* (—s, *pl.* —) miner.

Haufen ['haufən], *m.* (—s, *pl.* —) heap, pile.

häufen ['hɔyfən], *v.a.* heap, pile. — *v.r. sich* —, accumulate, multiply, increase.

häufig ['hɔyfɪç], *adj.* frequent, abundant. — *adv.* frequently, often.

Häufung ['hɔyfuŋ], *f.* (—, *pl.* —en) accumulation.

Haupt [haupt], *n.* (—es, *pl.* ⸚er) head; leader; chief, principal; (*compounds*) main—; *aufs* — *schlagen*, inflict a total defeat on; *ein bemoostes* —, an old student.

Hauptaltar ['hauptalta:r], *m.* (—s, *pl.* —e) (Eccl.) high altar.

Hauptbuch ['hauptbu:x], *n.* (—es, *pl.* ⸚er) ledger.

Häuptling ['hɔyptlɪŋ], *m.* (—s, *pl.* —e) chieftain.

Hauptmann ['hauptman], *m.* (—s, *pl.* ⸚er, Hauptleute) (Mil.) captain.

Hauptnenner ['hauptnɛnər], *m.* (—s, *pl.* —) (Maths.) common denominator.

Hauptquartier ['hauptkvarti:r], *n.* (—es, *pl.* —e) headquarters.

Hauptsache ['hauptzaxə], *f.* (—, *pl.* —n) main thing, substance, main point; *in der* —, in the main.

hauptsächlich ['hauptzɛçlɪç], *adj.* chief, main, principal, essential.

Hauptsatz ['hauptzats], *m.* (—es, *pl.* ⸚e) (Gram.) principal sentence.

Hauptschriftleiter ['hauptʃrɪftlaɪtər], *m.* (—s, *pl.* —) editor-in-chief.

Hauptschule ['hauptʃu:lə], *f.* (—, *pl.* —n) intermediate school.

Hauptstadt ['hauptʃtat], *f.* (—, *pl.* ⸚e) capital, metropolis.

Hauptton ['hauptto:n], *m.* (—s, *pl.* ⸚e) (Mus.) key-note; (Phonet.) primary accent.

Haupttreffer ['haupttrefər], *m.* (—s, *pl.* —) first prize; jackpot.

Hauptverkehrsstunden ['hauptferke:rsʃtundən], *f. pl.* (traffic etc.) rush-hour.

Hauptwache ['hauptvaxə], *f.* (—, *pl.* —n) central guardroom.

Hauptwort ['hauptvɔrt], *n.* (—es, *pl.* ⸚er) noun, substantive.

Hauptzahl ['haupttsa:l], *f.* (—, *pl.* —en) cardinal number.

Haus [haus], *n.* (—es, *pl.* ⸚er) house, home; household; firm; *zu* —e, at home; *nach* —e, home.

Hausarbeit ['hausarbaɪt], *f.* (—, *pl.* —en) housework, domestic work; homework.

Hausarrest [ˈhausarɛst], *m.* (—es, *no pl.*) house arrest.

Hausarzt [ˈhausartst], *m.* (—es, *pl.* ˙e) family doctor.

hausbacken [ˈhausbakən], *adj.* homemade; homely; humdrum.

Häuschen [ˈhɔysçən], *n.* (—s, *pl.* —) small house, cottage; *ganz aus dem — sein*, be beside o.s.

Hausen [ˈhauzən], *m.* (—s, *pl.* —) sturgeon.

hausen [ˈhauzən], *v.n.* reside, be domiciled; *übel —*, play havoc among.

Hausflur [ˈhausfluːr], *m.* (—s, *pl.* —e) entrance hall (of a house), vestibule.

Hausfrau [ˈhausfrau], *f.* (—, *pl.* —en) housewife, mistress of the house.

Hausfriedensbruch [ˈhausfriːdənsbrux], *m.* (—es, *pl.* ˙e) (*Law*) intrusion, trespass.

Hausgenosse [ˈhausgənɔsə], *m.* (—n, *pl.* —n) fellow-lodger.

Haushalt [ˈhaushalt], *m.* (—es, *no pl.*) household.

Haushaltung [ˈhaushaltuŋ], *f.* (—, *no pl.*) housekeeping.

Hausherr [ˈhaushɛr], *m.* (—n, *pl.* —en) master of the house, householder.

Haushofmeister [ˈhaushofmaistər], *m.* (—s, *pl.* —) steward; butler.

hausieren [hauˈziːrən], *v.n.* peddle, hawk.

Hauslehrer [ˈhausleːrər], *m.* (—s, *pl.* —) private tutor.

Häusler [ˈhɔyslər], *m.* (—s, *pl.* —) cottager.

häuslich [ˈhɔyslɪç], *adj.* domestic, domesticated.

Hausmädchen [ˈhausmɛdçən], *n.* (—s, *pl.* —) housemaid.

Hausmannskost [ˈhausmanskɔst], *f.* (—, *no pl.*) plain fare.

Hausmeister [ˈhausmaistər], *m.* (—s, *pl.* —) house-porter, caretaker.

Hausmittel [ˈhausmɪtəl], *n.* (—s, *pl.* —) household remedy.

Hausrat [ˈhausraːt], *m.* (—s, *no pl.*) household furnishings, household effects.

Hausschlüssel [ˈhausʃlysəl], *m.* (—s, *pl.* —) latch-key.

Hausschuh [ˈhausʃuː], *m.* (—s, *pl.* —e) slipper.

Hausstand [ˈhausʃtant], *m.* (—es, *pl.* ˙e) household.

Haustier [ˈhaustiːr], *n.* (—s, *pl.* —e) domestic animal.

Hausvater [ˈhausfaːtər], *m.* (—s, *pl.* ˙) paterfamilias.

Hausverwalter [ˈhausfɛrvaltər], *m.* (—s, *pl.* —) steward, caretaker; (*Am.*) janitor.

Hauswesen [ˈhausveːzən], *n.* (—s, *no pl.*) household management *or* affairs.

Hauswirt [ˈhausvɪrt], *m.* (—es, *pl.* —e) landlord.

Hauswirtin [ˈhausvɪrtɪn], *f.* (—, *pl.* —nen) landlady.

Hauswirtschaft [ˈhausvɪrtʃaft], *f.* (—, *no pl.*) housekeeping, domestic economy.

Haut [haut], *f.* (—, *pl.* ˙e) (*human*) skin; (*animal*) hide; (*fruit*) peel; (*on liquid*) skin; membrane; film; *aus der — fahren*, flare up.

Hautausschlag [ˈhautausʃlaːk], *m.* (—s, *pl.* ˙e) rash, eczema.

Häutchen [ˈhɔytçən], *n.* (—s, *pl.* —) cuticle, pellicle, membrane.

häuten [ˈhɔytən], *v.a.* skin, flay, strip off the skin. — *v.r. sich —*, cast off (skin) *or* slough.

Hebamme [ˈheːpamə], *f.* (—, *pl.* —n) midwife.

Hebel [ˈheːbəl], *m.* (—s, *pl.* —) lever.

heben [ˈheːbən], *v.a. irr.* raise, lift, hoist, heave; elevate; improve; *aus der Taufe —*, be godfather (godmother) to (s.o.).

Heber [ˈheːbər], *m.* (—s, *pl.* —) siphon.

Hebräer [heˈbrɛːər], *m.* (—s, *pl.* —) Hebrew.

Hechel [ˈhɛçəl], *f.* (—, *pl.* —n) hackle, flax-comb.

hecheln [ˈhɛçəln], *v.a.* dress flax; hackle; (*fig.*) taunt, heckle.

Hecht [hɛçt], *m.* (—es, *pl.* —e) (*Zool.*) pike; (*swimming*) dive.

Hechtsprung [ˈhɛçtʃpruŋ], *m.* header.

Heck [hɛk], *n.* (—s, *pl.* —e) (*Naut.*) stern; (*Motor.*) rear; (*Aviat.*) tail.

Heckbord [ˈhɛkbɔrt], *m.* (—s, *pl.* —e) (*Naut.*) taffrail.

Hecke [ˈhɛkə], *f.* (—, *pl.* —n) hedge.

hecken [ˈhɛkən], *v.n.* breed, bring forth.

Heckpfennig [ˈhɛkpfɛnɪç], *m.* (—s, *pl.* —e) lucky sixpence.

heda! [ˈheːdaː], *excl.* hey, you!

Heer [heːr], *n.* (—es, *pl.* —e) army; multitude; *stehendes —*, regular army.

Heeresmacht [ˈheːrəsmaxt], *f.* (—, *pl.* ˙e) armed forces, troops.

Heerschar [ˈheːrʃaːr], *f.* (—, *pl.* —en) host; corps, legion; (*Bibl.*) *der Herr der —en*, the Lord of Hosts.

Heerschau [ˈheːrʃau], *f.* (—, *pl.* —en) review, muster, parade.

Heerstraße [ˈheːrʃtraːsə], *f.* (—, *pl.* —en) military road; highway; (*Am.*) highroad.

Heerwesen [ˈheːrveːzən], *n.* (—s, *no pl.*) military affairs.

Hefe [ˈheːfə], *f.* (—, *no pl.*) yeast; dregs, sediment.

Hefeteig [ˈheːfətaik], *m.* (—s, *pl.* —e) leavened dough.

Heft [hɛft], *n.* (—es, *pl.* —e) exercise-book, copy-book; haft, handle, hilt.

heften [ˈhɛftən], *v.a.* fasten; baste, stitch, fix, pin.

heftig [ˈhɛftɪç], *adj.* vehement, violent.

Heftnadel [ˈhɛftnaːdəl], *f.* (—, *pl.* —n) stitching-needle.

hegen [ˈheːgən], *v.a.* enclose, protect, preserve; (*fig.*) cherish; entertain; hold; *— und pflegen*, nurse carefully.

Hehl

Hehl [he:l], *n.* (**—es**, *no pl.*) concealment, secret.

hehlen [ˈheːlən], *v.n.* receive stolen goods.

Hehler [ˈhəːlər], *m.* (**—s**, *pl.* **—**) receiver of stolen goods, (*sl.*) fence.

hehr [heːr], *adj.* (*Lit.*) exalted, august, sublime.

Heide (1) [ˈhaɪdə], *m.* (**—n**, *pl.* **—n**) heathen, pagan.

Heide (2) [ˈhaɪdə], *f.* (**—**, *pl.* **—n**) heath.

Heidekraut [ˈhaɪdəkraut], *n.* (**—es**, *no pl.*) heath, heather.

Heidelbeere [ˈhaɪdəlbeːrə], *f.* (**—**, *pl.* **—n**) (*Bot.*) bilberry; (*Am.*) blueberry.

Heidenangst [ˈhaɪdənaŋst], *f.* (**—**, *no pl.*) (*coll.*) mortal fear.

Heidenlärm [ˈhaɪdənlɛrm], *m.* (**—es**, *no pl.*) hullabaloo.

Heidenröschen [ˈhaɪdənrøːsçən], *n.* (**—s**, *pl.* **—**) (*Bot.*) sweet-briar.

Heidentum [ˈhaɪdəntuːm], *n.* (**—s**, *no pl.*) paganism.

heidnisch [ˈhaɪdnɪʃ], *adj.* pagan, heathen.

Heidschnuke [ˈhaɪtʃnuːkə], *f.* (**—**, *pl.* **—n**) moorland sheep.

heikel [ˈhaɪkəl], *adj.* delicate, sensitive, critical.

Heil [haɪl], *n.* (**—(e)s**, *no pl.*) safety, welfare; (*Theol.*) salvation; *sein — versuchen*, have a try, try o.'s luck. *— int.* hail! *— der Königin*, God save the Queen.

heil [haɪl], *adj.* unhurt, intact.

Heiland [ˈhaɪlant], *m.* (**—s**, *no pl.*) Saviour, Redeemer.

Heilanstalt [ˈhaɪlanʃtalt], *f.* (**—**, *pl.* **—en**) sanatorium, convalescent home; (*Am.*) sanitarium.

heilbar [ˈhaɪlbaːr], *adj.* curable.

heilbringend [ˈhaɪlbrɪŋənt], *adj.* salutary.

heilen [ˈhaɪlən], *v.a.* cure, heal. *— v.n.* (*aux.* sein) heal.

heilig [ˈhaɪlɪç], *adj.* holy, sacred; *der Heilige Abend*, Christmas Eve; *— sprechen*, canonise; (*before name*) *der, die —e*, Saint.

Heiligenschein [ˈhaɪlɪgənʃaɪn], *m.* (**—s**, *pl.* **—e**) halo; (*clouds*) nimbus.

Heiligkeit [ˈhaɪlɪçkaɪt], *f.* (**—**, *no pl.*) holiness, sanctity, sacredness.

Heiligtum [ˈhaɪlɪçtuːm], *n.* (**—s**, *pl.* **-er**) sanctuary, shrine; holy relic.

Heiligung [ˈhaɪlɪgun], *f.* (**—**, *pl.* **—en**) sanctification, consecration.

heilkräftig [ˈhaɪlkrɛftɪç], *adj.* curative, salubrious.

Heilkunde [ˈhaɪlkundə], *f.* (**—**, *no pl.*) therapeutics.

heillos [ˈhaɪlloːs], *adj.* wicked, mischievous; (*fig.*) awful.

Heilmittel [ˈhaɪlmɪtəl], *n.* (**—s**, *pl.* **—**) remedy.

heilsam [ˈhaɪlzaːm], *adj.* salubrious, salutary.

Heilsamkeit [ˈhaɪlzaːmkaɪt], *f.* (**—**, *no pl.*) salubrity, salubriousness.

Heilsarmee [ˈhaɪlsarmeː], *f.* (**—**, *no pl.*) Salvation Army.

Heilslehre [ˈhaɪlsleːrə], *f.* (**—**, *pl.* **—n**) doctrine of salvation.

Heiltrank [ˈhaɪltraŋk], *m.* (**—es**, *no pl.*) (medicinal) potion.

Heim [haɪm], *n.* (**—es**, *pl.* **—e**) home.

heim [haɪm], *adv. prefix* (*to verbs*) home.

Heimat [ˈhaɪmat], *f.* (**—**, *no pl.*) native place, home, homeland.

Heimatschein [ˈhaɪmatʃaɪn], *m.* (**—es**, *pl.* **—e**) certificate of origin *or* domicile.

Heimchen [ˈhaɪmçən], *n.* (**—s**, *pl.* **—**) (*Ent.*) cricket.

heimführen [ˈhaɪmfyːrən], *v.a.* bring home (a bride); (*fig.*) marry.

Heimgang [ˈhaɪmgaŋ], *m.* (**—es**, *no pl.*) going home; (*fig.*) decease, death.

heimisch [ˈhaɪmɪʃ], *adj.* native, indigenous; *sich — fühlen*, feel at home.

heimkehren [ˈhaɪmkeːrən], *v.n.* return (home).

heimleuchten [ˈhaɪmlɔyçtən], *v.n. einem —*, tell s.o. the plain truth, give s.o. a piece of o.'s mind.

heimlich [ˈhaɪmlɪç], *adj.* secret, clandestine, furtive.

heimsuchen [ˈhaɪmzuːxən], *v.a.* visit; afflict, punish.

Heimtücke [ˈhaɪmtykə], *f.* (**—**, *no pl.*) malice.

heimwärts [ˈhaɪmvɛrts], *adv.* homeward.

Heimweh [ˈhaɪmveː], *n.* (**—s**, *no pl.*) homesickness; nostalgia.

heimzahlen [ˈhaɪmtsaːlən], *v.a.* pay back, retaliate.

Hein [haɪn], *m.* (*coll.*) *Freund —, Death.*

Heinzelmännchen [ˈhaɪntsəlmɛnçən], *n.* (**—s**, *pl.* **—**) goblin, brownie, imp.

Heirat [ˈhaɪraːt], *f.* (**—**, *pl.* **—en**) marriage, wedding.

heiraten [ˈhaɪraːtən], *v.a.* marry, wed.

Heiratsgut [ˈhaɪraːtsguːt], *n.* (**—es**, *pl.* **-er**) dowry.

heischen [ˈhaɪʃən], *v.a.* (*Poet.*) ask, demand.

heiser [ˈhaɪzər], *adj.* hoarse.

heiß [haɪs], *adj.* hot; (*fig.*) ardent; (*climate*) torrid.

heißen [ˈhaɪsən], *v.a. irr.* bid, command. *— v.n.* be called; be said; signify, mean; *es heißt*, it is said; *das heißt (d.h.)*, that is to say; *wie — Sie?* what is your name?

heißgeliebt [ˈhaɪsgəliːpt], *adj.* dearly beloved.

heiter [ˈhaɪtər], *adj.* clear; serene; cheerful.

Heiterkeit [ˈhaɪtərkaɪt], *f.* (**—**, *no pl.*) serenity; cheerfulness.

heizen [ˈhaɪtsən], *v.a. v.n.* heat.

Heizkissen [ˈhaɪtskɪsən], *n.* (**—s**, *pl.* **—**) electric pad *or* blanket.

Heizkörper [ˈhaɪtskœrpər], *m.* (**—s**, *pl.* **—**) radiator; heater.

Heizung [ˈhaɪtsun], *f.* (**—**, *pl.* **—en**) heating.

hektisch [ˈhɛktɪʃ], *adj.* hectic.

hektographieren [hɛktograˈfiːrən], *v.a.*
stencil, duplicate.

Hektoliter [ˈhɛktoliːtər], *m.* (—s, *pl.* —)
hectolitre (22 gallons).

Held [hɛlt], *m.* (—en, *pl.* —en) hero.

Heldengedicht [ˈhɛldəngədɪçt], *n.*
(—es, *pl.* —e) heroic poem, epic.

heldenhaft [ˈhɛldənhaft], *adj.* heroic.
— *adv.* heroically.

Heldenmut [ˈhɛldənmuːt], *m.* (—es,
no pl.) heroism.

helfen [ˈhɛlfən], *v.n. irr.* (*Dat.*) help,
aid, assist.

Helfershelfer [ˈhɛlfərshɛlfər], *m.* (—s,
pl. —) accomplice, accessory.

Helgoland [ˈhɛlgolant], *n.* Heligo-
land.

hell [hɛl], *adj.* clear, bright, light;
(*coll.*) clever, wide awake.

Helldunkel [ˈhɛlduŋkəl], *n.* (—s, *no pl.*)
twilight; (*Art*) chiaroscuro.

Helle [ˈhɛlə], *f.* (—, *no pl.*) clearness;
brightness; daylight.

Heller [ˈhɛlər], *m.* (—s, *pl.* —) small
coin, farthing.

hellhörig [ˈhɛlhøːrɪç], *adj.* keen of
hearing.

Helligkeit [ˈhɛlɪçkaɪt], *f.* (—, *no pl.*)
clearness; daylight.

Hellseher [ˈhɛlzeːər], *m.* (—s, *pl.* —)
clairvoyant.

hellsichtig [ˈhɛlzɪxtɪç], *adj.* clairvoyant;
clear-sighted.

Helm [hɛlm], *m.* (—es, *pl.* —e)
helmet.

Helmbusch [ˈhɛlmbuʃ], *m.* (—es, *pl.*
—e) crest (of helmet).

Helmgitter [ˈhɛlmgɪtər], *n.* (—s, *pl.*
—) eye-slit (in helmet).

Helsingfors [ˈhɛlzɪŋfors], *n.* Helsinki.

Helsingör [hɛlzɪŋˈøːr], *n.* Elsinore.

Hemd [hɛmt], *n.* (—es, *pl.* —en) shirt;
vest.

Hemdenstoff [ˈhɛmdənʃtɔf], *m.* (—es,
pl. —e) shirting.

hemmen [ˈhɛmən], *v.a.* stop, hamper,
hinder, restrain; (*fig.*) inhibit.

Hemmschuh [ˈhɛmʃuː], *m.* (—s, *pl.*
—e) brake; (*fig.*) drag, obstruction.

Hemmung [ˈhɛmuŋ], *f.* (—, *pl.* —en)
stoppage, hindrance, restraint; (*watch*)
escapement; (*fig.*) inhibition, reluctance.

Hengst [hɛŋkst], *m.* (—es, *pl.* —e)
stallion.

Henkel [ˈhɛŋkəl], *m.* (—s, *pl.* —)
handle.

henken [ˈhɛŋkən], *v.a* hang (s.o.).

Henker [ˈhɛŋkər], *m.* (—s, *pl.* —)
hangman, executioner.

Henne [ˈhɛnə], *f.* (—, *pl.* —n) (*Zool.*)
hen; *junge* —, pullet.

her [heːr], *adv.* hither, here, to me;
(*temp.*) since, ago; *von alters* —, from
olden times; *von je* —, from time
immemorial; *wo kommst du* —?
where do you come from? *wie lange
ist es* —? how long ago was it?

herab [hɛˈrap], *adv.* downwards, down
to; *die Treppe* —, downstairs.

herablassen [hɛˈraplasən], *v.r. irr.
sich* — *etwas zu tun,* condescend to
do s.th.

herabsehen [hɛˈrapzeːən], *v.n. irr.*
look down; (*fig.*) look down upon s.o.

herabsetzen [hɛˈrapzɛtsən]; *v.a.* put
down; degrade; (*value*) depreciate;
(*price*) reduce, lower; (*fig.*) disparage.

herabwürdigen [hɛˈrapvyrdɪgən], *v.a.*
degrade, abase.

herabziehen [hɛˈraptsiːən], *v.a. irr.*
pull down.

Heraldik [heˈraldɪk], *f.* (—, *no pl.*)
heraldry.

heran [hɛˈran], *adv.* up to, on, near.

heranbilden [hɛˈranbɪldən], *v.a.* train.
— *v.r. sich* —, train, qualify.

herangehen [hɛˈrangeːən], *v.n. irr.*
(*aux.* sein) approach, sidle up (to); *an
etwas* —, set to work on s.th.

heranmachen [hɛˈranmaxən], *v.r. sich
an etwas* —, set to work on s.th., set
about s.th.

herannahen [hɛˈrannaːən], *v.n.* (*aux.*
sein) approach, draw near.

heranrücken [hɛˈranrykən], *v.a.* move
near. — *v.n.* (*aux.* sein) advance,
draw near.

heranschleichen [hɛˈranʃlaɪçən], *v.r.
irr. sich* — *an,* sneak up to.

heranwachsen [hɛˈranvaksən], *v.n.
irr.* (*aux.* sein) grow up.

heranwagen [hɛˈranvaːgən], *v.r. sich*
—, venture near.

heranziehen [hɛˈrantsiːən], *v.a. irr.*
draw near; *als Beispiel* —, cite as an
example; (*fig.*) enlist (s.o.'s aid). —
v.n. (*aux.* sein) draw near, approach.

herauf [hɛˈrauf], *adv.* up, upwards.

heraufbeschwören [hɛˈraufbeʃvøːrən],
v.a. conjure up.

heraus [hɛˈraus], *adv.* out, out of.

herausfordern [hɛˈrausfordərn], *v.a.*
challenge.

Herausgabe [hɛˈrausgaːbə], *f.* (—, *pl.*
—n) delivery; (*book*) publication;
editing.

herausgeben [hɛˈrausgeːbən], *v.a. irr.*
give out, deliver; (*money*) give
change; (*book*) publish, edit.

Herausgeber [hɛˈrausgeːbər], *m.* (—s,
pl. —) publisher; editor.

heraushaben [hɛˈraushaːbən], *v.a. irr.
etwas* —, have the knack of s.th.

herausputzen [hɛˈrausputsən], *v.r.
sich* —, dress up.

herausrücken [hɛˈrausrykən], *v.n. mit
Geld* —, fork out money; *mit der
Sprache* —, speak out, come out with.

herausschlagen [hɛˈrausʃlaːgən], *v.a.
irr. die Kosten* —, recover expenses;
viel —, make the most of; profit by.

herausstellen [hɛˈrausʃtɛlən], *v.a.* put
out, expose. — *v.r. sich* — *als,* turn
out to be.

herausstreichen [hɛˈrausʃtraɪçən], *v.a.
irr.* extol, praise.

heraussuchen [hɛˈrauszuːxən], *v.a.*
pick out.

herauswollen

herauswollen [hɛˈrausvɔlən], *v.n. nicht mit der Sprache* —, hesitate to speak out.

herb [hɛrp], *adj.* sour, sharp, tart, acrid; (*fig.*) austere, harsh, bitter; (*wine*) dry.

herbei [hɛrˈbaɪ], *adv.* hither, near.

herbeischaffen [hɛrˈbaɪʃafən], *v.a.* procure.

herbeiströmen [hɛrˈbaɪʃtrøːmən], *v.n.* (*aux. sein*) crowd, flock.

Herberge [ˈhɛrbɛrgə], *f.* (—, *pl.* —n) shelter, lodging, inn.

Herbst [hɛrpst], *m.* (—es, *pl.* —e) autumn; (*Am.*) fall.

Herbstrose [ˈhɛrpstroːzə], *f.* (—, *pl.* —n) (*Bot.*) hollyhock.

Herbstzeitlose [ˈhɛrpsttsaɪtloːzə], *f.* (—, *pl.* —n) (*Bot.*) meadow-saffron.

Herd [heːrt], *m.* (—es, *pl.* —e) hearth, fireplace; cooking-stove; (*fig.*) focus.

Herde [ˈheːrdə], *f.* (—, *pl.* —n) flock, herd; (*fig.*) troop.

herein [heˈraɪn], *adv.* in, inside. — *int.* —*!* come in!

hereinbrechen [heˈraɪnbrɛçən], *v.n. irr.* (*aux. sein*) *über einen* —, befall s.o., overtake s.o.; (*night*) close in.

hereinfallen [heˈraɪnfalən], *v.n. irr.* (*aux. sein*) (*fig.*) be taken in, fall for s.th.

herfallen [ˈheːrfalən], *v.n. irr.* (*aux. sein*) *über einen* —, go for s.o., set upon s.o.

Hergang [ˈheːrgaŋ], *m.* (—es, *no pl.*) proceedings, course of events; circumstances; story, plot.

hergeben [ˈheːrgeːbən], *v.a. irr.* give up, surrender.

hergebracht [ˈheːrgəbraxt], *adj.* traditional, time-honoured.

hergehen [ˈheːrgeːən], *v.n. irr.* (*aux. sein*) proceed; *es geht lustig her*, they are having a gay time.

hergelaufen [ˈheːrgəlaufən], *adj. ein —er Kerl*, an adventurer, an upstart.

herhalten [ˈheːrhaltən], *v.n. irr.* suffer, serve (as a butt).

Hering [ˈheːrɪŋ], *m.* (—s, *pl.* —e) (*Zool.*) herring; *geräucherter* —, smoked herring, bloater; *gesalzener* —, pickled herring.

herkommen [ˈheːrkɔmən], *v.n. irr.* (*aux. sein*) come here; be derived from, descend from.

herkömmlich [ˈheːrkœmlɪç], *adj.* traditional, customary, usual.

Herkunft [ˈheːrkunft], *f.* (—, *no pl.*) descent, extraction; origin.

herleiern [ˈheːrlaɪərn], *v.a.* recite monotonously; reel off.

herleiten [ˈheːrlaɪtən], *v.a.* derive from.

Hermelin [hɛrməˈliːn], *m.* (—s, *no pl.*) ermine (*fur*).

hermetisch [hɛrˈmeːtɪʃ], *adj.* hermetical.

hernach [hɛrˈnaːx], *adv.* after, afterwards; hereafter.

hernehmen [ˈheːrneːmən], *v.a. irr.* take, get (from); take (s.o.) to task.

hernieder [hɛrˈniːdər], *adv.* down.

Herr [hɛr], *m.* (—n, *pl.* —en) master; lord; nobleman; gentleman; (*Theol.*) Lord; principal, governor; *mein* —, Sir; *meine Herren*, gentlemen; — *Schmidt*, Mr. Smith; *einer Sache* — *werden*, master s.th.

Herrenhaus [ˈhɛrənhaus], *n.* (—es, *pl.* —er) mansion, manor house; (*Parl.*) House of Lords.

Herrenhof [ˈhɛrənhoːf], *m.* (—es, *pl.* —e) manor, country-seat.

Herrenstand [ˈhɛrənʃtant], *m.* (—es, *no pl.*) nobility, gentry.

Herrenzimmer [ˈhɛrəntsɪmər], *n.* (—s, *pl.* —) study.

Herrgott [ˈhɛrgɔt], the Lord God.

herrichten [ˈheːrrɪçtən], *v.a.* prepare, fix up.

Herrin [ˈhɛrɪn], *f.* (—, *pl.* —innen) mistress, lady.

herrisch [ˈhɛrɪʃ], *adj.* imperious, lordly.

herrlich [ˈhɛrlɪç], *adj.* magnificent, splendid, glorious, excellent.

Herrnhuter [ˈhɛrnhuːtər], *m.* (—s, *pl.* —) Moravian; (*pl.*) Moravian brethren.

Herrschaft [ˈhɛrʃaft], *f.* (—, *pl.* —en) mastery, rule, dominion; master, mistress; *meine —en!* ladies and gentlemen!

herrschaftlich [ˈhɛrʃaftlɪç], *adj.* belonging to a lord; (*fig.*) elegant, fashionable, distinguished.

herrschen [ˈhɛrʃən], *v.n.* rule, govern, reign.

Herrscher [ˈhɛrʃər], *m.* (—s, *pl.* —) ruler.

herrühren [ˈheːrryːrən], *v.n.* come from, originate in.

hersagen [ˈheːrzaːgən], *v.a.* recite, reel off.

herschaffen [ˈheːrʃafən], *v.a.* procure.

herstammen [ˈheːrʃtamən], *v.n.* come from, stem from, originate from; be derived from.

herstellen [ˈheːrʃtelən], *v.a.* place here; manufacture; *wieder* —, restore; (*sick person*) restore to health.

Herstellung [ˈheːrʃteluŋ], *f.* (—, *no pl.*) manufacture, production.

herstürzen [ˈheːrʃtyrtsən], *v.n.* (*aux. sein*) *über einen* —, rush at s.o.

herüber [heˈryːbər], *adv.* over, across; — *und hinüber*, there and back.

herum [heˈrum], *adv.* round, about; around.

herumbalgen [heˈrumbalgən], *v.r. sich* —, scrap; scuffle.

herumbekommen [heˈrumbəkɔmən], *v.a. irr.* (*coll.*) talk s.o. over, win s.o. over.

herumbummeln [heˈrumbumən], *v.n.* loaf about.

herumstreichen [heˈrumʃtraɪçən], *v.n. irr.* (*aux. sein*) gad about.

herumtreiben [heˈrumtraɪbən], *v.r. irr. sich* —, loaf about, gad about.

herumzanken [heˈrumtsaŋkən], *v.r. sich* —, squabble, quarrel; live like cat and dog.

herumziehen [hɛˈrumtsiːən], *v.a. irr.* drag about. — *v.n.* (*aux.* sein) wander about, move from place to place.

herunter [hɛˈruntər], *adj.* down, downward; *ich bin ganz* —, I feel poorly.

heruntergekommen [hɛˈruntərgəkɔmən], *adj.* decayed, broken down; in straitened circumstances; depraved.

herunterhandeln [hɛˈruntərhandəln], *v.a. einem etwas* —, beat s.o. down (in price).

herunterwürgen [hɛˈruntərvyrgən], *v.a.* swallow s.th. with dislike.

hervor [hɛrˈfoːr], *adv.* forth, forward, out.

hervorheben [hɛrˈfoːrheːbən], *v.a. irr.* emphasize, stress.

hervorragen [hɛrˈfoːrraːgən], *v.n.* stand out, project; (*fig.*) be distinguished, excel.

hervorragend [hɛrˈfoːrraːgənt], *adj.* prominent; (*fig.*) outstanding, excellent.

hervorrufen [hɛrˈfoːrruːfən], *v.a. irr.* call forth; (*fig.*) evoke, bring about, create, cause.

hervorstechen [hɛrˈfoːrʃteçən], *v.n. irr.* be predominant, stand out.

hervortun [hɛrˈfoːrtuːn], *v.r. irr. sich* —, distinguish o.s.

Herz [hɛrts], *n.* (—ens, *pl.* —en) heart; courage; mind; spirit; feeling; core; (*Cards*) hearts; (*coll.*) darling; *einem etwas ans* — *legen*, impress s.th. upon s.o.; *von* —*en gern*, with all my heart; *sich etwas zu* —*en nehmen*, take s.th. to heart.

herzählen [ˈhɛːrtsɛːlən], *v.a.* enumerate.

Herzanfall [ˈhɛrtsanfal], *m.* (—s, *pl.* ˙e) (*Med.*) heart attack.

Herzbube [ˈhɛrtsbuːbə], *m.* (—n, *pl.* —n) (*Cards*) knave or jack of hearts.

Herzdame [ˈhɛrtsdaːmə], *f.* (—, *pl.* —n) (*Cards*) queen of hearts.

Herzeleid [ˈhɛrtsəlait], *n.* (—es, *no pl.*) heartbreak, sorrow, anguish, grief.

herzen [ˈhɛrtsən], *v.a.* hug.

Herzenseinfalt [ˈhɛrtsənsainfalt], *f.* (—, *no pl.*) simple-mindedness.

Herzensgrund [ˈhɛrtsənsgrunt], *m.* (—es, *no pl.*) *aus* —, with all my heart.

Herzenslust [ˈhɛrtsənslust], *f.* (—, *no pl.*) heart's delight; *nach* —, to o.'s heart's content.

Herzfehler [ˈhɛrtsfeːlər], *m.* (—s, *pl.* —) (*Med.*) cardiac defect; organic heart disease.

Herzfell [ˈhɛrtsfɛl], *n.* (—s, *pl.* —e) pericardium.

herzförmig [ˈhɛrtsfœrmiç], *adj.* heart-shaped.

herzhaft [ˈhɛrtshaft], *adj.* stouthearted; courageous, bold; resolute; hearty.

herzig [ˈhɛrtsiç], *adj.* lovely, charming, sweet; (*Am.*) cute.

Herzkammer [ˈhɛrtskamər], *f.* (—, *pl.* —n) ventricle (of the heart).

Herzklappe [ˈhɛrtsklapə], *f.* (—, *pl.* —n) valve of the heart.

Herzklopfen [ˈhɛrtsklɔpfən], *n.* (—s, *no pl.*) palpitations.

herzlich [ˈhɛrtsliç], *adj.* hearty, cordial, affectionate; — *gern*, with pleasure; —*e Grüße*, kind regards.

Herzog [ˈhɛrtsoːk], *m.* (—s, *pl.* ˙e) duke.

Herzogtum [ˈhɛrtsoːktuːm], *n.* (—s, *pl.* ˙er) duchy, dukedom.

Herzschlag [ˈhɛrtsʃlaːk], *m.* (—es, *pl.* ˙e) heartbeat; (*Med.*) heart attack, cardiac failure.

Hetäre [heˈtɛːrə], *f.* (—, *pl.* —n) courtesan.

Hetzblatt [ˈhɛtsblat], *n.* (—s, *pl.* ˙er) gutter press.

Hetze [ˈhɛtsə], *f.* (—, *pl.* —n) chase, hunt, hurry, rush; agitation.

hetzen [ˈhɛtsən], *v.a.* bait, fluster, chase, hunt, incite. — *v.n. herum* —, rush around.

Hetzer [ˈhɛtsər], *m.* (—s, *pl.* —) instigator, rabble-rouser.

Heu [hɔy], *n.* (—s, *no pl.*) hay.

Heuboden [ˈhɔyboːdən], *m.* (—s, *pl.* ˙) hayloft.

Heuchelei [hɔyçəˈlai], *f.* (—, *pl.* —en) hypocrisy.

heucheln [ˈhɔyçəln], *v.n.* play the hypocrite, dissemble. — *v.a.* simulate, affect, feign.

Heuchler [ˈhɔyçlər], *m.* (—s, *pl.* —) hypocrite.

Heuer [ˈhɔyər], *f.* (—, *pl.* —n) (*Naut.*) engagement; hire, wages.

heuer [ˈhɔyər], *adv.* (*dial.*) this year, this season.

heuern [ˈhɔyərn], *v.a.* (*Naut.*) engage, hire.

Heugabel [ˈhɔygaːbəl], *f.* (—, *pl.* —n) pitchfork.

heulen [ˈhɔylən], *v.n.* howl; roar; cry, yell, scream.

Heupferd [ˈhɔypfɛrt], *n.* (—es, *pl.* —e) (*Ent.*) grasshopper.

heurig [ˈhɔyriç], *adj.* of this year, this year's (*wine etc.*).

Heuschnupfen [ˈhɔyʃnupfən], *m.* (—s, *no pl.*) hay-fever.

Heuschober [ˈhɔyʃoːbər], *m.* (—s, *pl.* —) hayrick.

Heuschrecke [ˈhɔyʃrɛkə], *f.* (—, *pl.* —n) (*Ent.*) locust.

heute [ˈhɔytə], *adv.* today, this day; — *in acht Tagen*, today week, a week today; — *abend*, tonight.

heutig [ˈhɔytiç], *adj.* today's, this day's; modern.

heutzutage [ˈhɔytsutaːgə], *adv.* nowadays.

Hexe [ˈhɛksə], *f.* (—, *pl.* —n) witch, sorceress, hag.

hexen [ˈhɛksən], *v.n.* use witchcraft; practise sorcery.

Hexenschuß [ˈhɛksənʃus], *m.* (—sses, *no pl.*) (*Med.*) lumbago.

Hexerei [hɛksəˈraɪ], *f.* (—, *pl.* —**en**) witchcraft, sorcery, juggling.

hie [hiː], *adv.* (*dial.*) here.

Hieb [hiːp], *m.* (—**es**, *pl.* —**e**) cut, stroke; hit, blow; (*pl.*) a thrashing.

hienieden [hiːˈniːdən], *adv.* here below, down here.

hier [hiːr], *adv.* here, in this place.

Hiersein [ˈhiːrzaɪn], *n.* (—**s**, *no pl.*) presence, attendance.

hiesig [ˈhiːzɪç], *adj.* of this place, of this country, local.

Hifthorn [ˈhɪfthɔrn], *n.* (—**s**, *pl.* ̈**er**) hunting-horn.

Hilfe [ˈhɪlfə], *f.* (—, *pl.* —**n**) help, aid, assistance, succour, relief.

hilflos [ˈhɪlfloːs], *adj.* helpless.

hilfreich [ˈhɪlfraɪç], *adj.* helpful.

Hilfsmittel [ˈhɪlfsmɪtəl], *n.* (—**s**, *pl.* —) expedient, remedy.

Hilfsschule [ˈhɪlfsʃuːlə], *f.* (—, *pl.* —**n**) school for backward children.

Hilfszeitwort [ˈhɪlfstsaɪtvɔrt], *n.* (—**s**, *pl.* ̈**er**) (*Gram.*) auxiliary verb.

Himbeere [ˈhɪmbeːrə], *f.* (—, *pl.* —**n**) raspberry.

Himmel [ˈhɪməl], *m.* (—**s**, *pl.* —) heaven, heavens; sky; firmament.

himmelan [hɪməlˈan], *adv.* heavenward.

himmelangst [ˈhɪməlaŋkst], *adv.* *ihm war* —, he was panic-stricken.

Himmelbett [ˈhɪməlbɛt], *n.* (—**s**, *pl.* —**en**) fourposter.

himmelblau [ˈhɪməlblau], *adj.* sky-blue.

Himmelfahrt [ˈhɪməlfaːrt], *f.* (—, *no pl.*) Ascension.

Himmelschlüssel [ˈhɪməlʃlysəl], *m.* (—**s**, *pl.* —) (*Bot.*) primrose.

himmelschreiend [ˈhɪməlʃraɪənt], *adj.* atrocious, revolting.

Himmelsgewölbe [ˈhɪməlsɡəvœlbə], *n.* (—**s**, *pl.* —) firmament.

Himmelsstrich [ˈhɪməlsʃtrɪç], *m.* (—**s**, *pl.* —**e**) climate, zone.

Himmelszeichen [ˈhɪməlstsaɪçən], *n.* (—**s**, *pl.* —) sign of the zodiac.

himmelweit [ˈhɪməlvaɪt], *adj.* enormous; — *entfernt*, poles apart.

himmlisch [ˈhɪmlɪʃ], *adj.* celestial, heavenly.

hin [hɪn], *adv.* there, towards that place; finished, gone; ruined; — *und her*, to and fro.

hinab [hɪnˈap], *adv.* down.

hinan [hɪnˈan], *adv.* up.

hinarbeiten [ˈhɪnarbaɪtən], *v.n. auf etwas* —, work towards s.th.

hinauf [hɪnˈauf], *adv.* up, up to.

hinaus [hɪnˈaus], *adv.* out, out of; *es kommt auf dasselbe* —, it comes to the same thing.

hinauswollen [hɪnˈausvɔlən], *v.n.* wish to go out; (*fig.*) *hoch* —, aim high.

hinausziehen [hɪnˈaustsiːən], *v.a. irr.* draw out; (*fig.*) protract.

Hinblick [ˈhɪnblɪk], *m.* (—**es**, *no pl.*) *im* — *auf*, in consideration of, with regard to.

hinbringen [ˈhɪnbrɪŋən], *v.a. irr.* bring to; escort; *Zeit* —, while away time.

hinderlich [ˈhɪndərlɪç], *adj.* obstructive, cumbersome.

hindern [ˈhɪndərn], *v.a.* hinder, obstruct, hamper, impede.

hindeuten [ˈhɪndɔytən], *v.n. auf etwas* —, point to s.th., hint at s.th.

Hindin [ˈhɪndɪn], *f.* (—, *pl.* —**innen**) (*Poet.*) hind.

hindurch [hɪnˈdurç], *adv.* through; throughout; *die ganze Zeit* —, all the time.

hinein [hɪnˈaɪn], *adv.* in, into; *in den Tag* — *leben*, live for the present, lead a life of carefree enjoyment.

hineinfinden [hɪnˈaɪnfɪndən], *v.r. irr. sich in etwas* —, reconcile *or* adapt o.s. to s.th.

hinfällig [ˈhɪnfɛlɪç], *adj.* frail, feeble, weak; shaky, void, invalid.

Hingabe [ˈhɪnɡaːbə], *f.* (—, *no pl.*) surrender; (*fig.*) devotion.

hingeben [ˈhɪnɡeːbən], *v.a. irr.* give up, surrender. — *v.r. sich einer Sache* —, devote o.s. to a task.

hingegen [hɪnˈɡeːɡən], *adv.* on the other hand.

hinhalten [ˈhɪnhaltən], *v.a. irr.* (*thing*) hold out; (*person*) keep in suspense, put off.

hinken [ˈhɪŋkən], *v.n.* limp.

hinlänglich [ˈhɪnlɛŋlɪç], *adj.* sufficient.

hinlegen [ˈhɪnleːɡən], *v.a.* lay down, put away. — *v.r. sich* —, lie down, go to bed.

hinnehmen [ˈhɪnneːmən], *v.a. irr.* take, submit to, accept.

hinreichen [ˈhɪnraɪçən], *v.a.* pass to. — *v.n.* suffice, be sufficient.

Hinreise [ˈhɪnraɪzə], *f.* (—, *pl.* —**n**) outward journey.

hinreißen [ˈhɪnraɪsən], *v.r. irr. sich* — *lassen*, allow o.s. to be carried away.

hinreißend [ˈhɪnraɪsənt], *adj.* charming, ravishing, enchanting.

hinrichten [ˈhɪnrɪçtən], *v.a.* execute, put to death.

hinscheiden [ˈhɪnʃaɪdən], *v.n. irr.* die, pass away.

hinschlängeln [ˈhɪnʃlɛŋəln], *v.r. sich* —, meander, wind along.

Hinsicht [ˈhɪnzɪçt], *f.* (—, *no pl.*) view, consideration, regard.

hinsichtlich [ˈhɪnzɪçtlɪç], *prep.* (*Genit.*) with regard to.

hinstellen [ˈhɪnʃtɛlən], *v.a.* put down; make out to be.

hinten [ˈhɪntən], *adv.* behind; *von* —, from behind.

hinter [ˈhɪntər], *prep.* (*Dat.*) behind, after.

Hinterachse [ˈhɪntəraksə], *f.* (—, *pl.* —**n**) (*Motor.*) rear-axle.

Hinterbein [ˈhɪntərbaɪn], *n.* (—**s**, *pl.* —**e**) hind-leg; (*fig.*) *sich auf die* —**e** *stellen*, get up on o.'s hind-legs.

Hinterbliebene [hɪntər'bliːbənə], *m.* (—n, *pl.* —n) survivor; mourner; (*pl.*) the bereaved.

hinterbringen [hɪntər'brɪŋən], *v.a. irr.* give information about, (*coll.*) tell on.

Hinterdeck ['hɪntərdɛk], *n.* (—s, *no pl.*) (*Naut.*) quarter deck.

hinterdrein ['hɪntərdraɪn], *adv.* afterwards, after; behind.

hintereinander [hɪntəraɪn'andər], *adv.* in succession, one after another.

Hintergedanke ['hɪntərɡədaŋkə], *m.* (—n, *pl.* —n) mental reservation, ulterior motive.

hintergehen [hɪntər'ɡeːən], *v.a. irr.* deceive, circumvent.

Hintergrund ['hɪntərɡrunt], *m.* (—es, *pl.* ⁻e) background; (*Theat.*) back-cloth, back-drop.

Hinterhalt ['hɪntərhalt], *m.* (—s, *pl.* —e) ambush; (*fig.*) reserve.

hinterhältig ['hɪntərhɛltɪç], *adj.* furtive, secretive; insidious.

hinterher [hɪntər'heːr], *adv.* behind; in the rear; afterwards.

Hinterindien ['hɪntərɪndjən], *n.* Indo-China.

Hinterkopf ['hɪntərkɔpf], *m.* (—es, *pl.* ⁻e) occiput, back of the head.

Hinterlader ['hɪntərlaːdər], *m.* (—s, *pl.* —) breech-loader.

hinterlassen [hɪntər'lasən], *v.a. irr.* leave (a legacy), bequeath; leave (word).

Hinterlassenschaft [hɪntər'lasənʃaft], *f.* (—, *pl.* —en) inheritance, bequest.

Hinterlegung [hɪntər'leːɡuŋ], *f.* (—, *pl.* —en) deposition.

Hinterlist ['hɪntərlɪst], *f.* (—, *no pl.*) fraud, deceit; cunning.

hinterrücks [hɪntər'ryks], *adv.* from behind; (*fig.*) treacherously, behind s.o.'s back.

Hintertreffen ['hɪntərtrɛfən], *n.* (—s, *no pl.*) ins — geraten, be left out in the cold, fall behind.

hintertreiben [hɪntər'traɪbən], *v.a. irr.* prevent, frustrate.

Hintertreppe ['hɪntərtrɛpə], *f.* (—, *pl.* —n) back-stairs.

Hintertreppenroman ['hɪntərtrɛpənromaːn], *m.* (—s, *pl.* —e) (*Lit.*) cheap thriller.

hinterziehen ['hɪntərtsiːən], *v.a. irr. insep.* defraud.

hinträumen ['hɪntrɔymən], *v.n. vor sich —*, daydream.

hinüber [hɪn'yːbər], *adv.* over, across.

hinunter [hɪn'untər], *adv.* down; *den Berg —*, downhill.

hinweg [hɪn'vɛk], *adv.* away, off.

hinwegsetzen [hɪn'vɛkzɛtsən], *v.r. sich über etwas —*, make light of s.th.

Hinweis ['hɪnvaɪs], *m.* (—es, *pl.* —e) hint, indication, reference; *unter — auf*, with reference to.

hinweisen ['hɪnvaɪzən], *v.a. irr. auf etwas —*, refer to, point to s.th.

hinwerfen ['hɪnvɛrfən], *v.a. irr.* throw down; *hingeworfene Bemerkung*, casual remark.

hinziehen ['hɪntsiːən], *v.a. irr.* draw along; attract. — *v.n.* (*aux.* sein) march along. — *v.r. sich —*, drag on.

hinzielen ['hɪntsiːlən], *v.n. auf etwas —*, aim at s.th., have s.th. in mind.

hinzu [hɪn'tsuː], *adv.* to, near; besides, in addition.

hinzufügen [hɪn'tsuːfyːɡən], *v.a.* add.

hinzukommen [hɪn'tsuːkɔmən], *v.n. irr.* (*aux.* sein) be added.

hinzuziehen [hɪn'tsuːtsiːən], *v.a. irr.* include, add; call in (expert).

Hiobsbotschaft ['hiːɔpsbotʃaft], *f.* (—, *no pl.*) bad news.

Hirn [hɪrn], *n.* (—es, *pl.* —e) brain, brains. *See also* **Gehirn**.

Hirngespinst ['hɪrnɡəʃpɪnst], *n.* (—es, *pl.* —e) fancy, chimera, illusion, figment of the imagination.

hirnverbrannt ['hɪrnfɛrbrant], *adj.* crazy, insane, mad; (*coll.*) crack-brained.

Hirsch [hɪrʃ], *m.* (—es, *pl.* —e) (*Zool.*) stag, hart.

Hirschbock ['hɪrʃbɔk], *m.* (—s, *pl.* ⁻e) (*Zool.*) stag.

Hirschfänger ['hɪrʃfɛŋər], *m.* (—s, *pl.* —) hunting-knife.

Hirschgeweih ['hɪrʃɡəvaɪ], *n.* (—s, *pl.* —e) horns, antlers.

Hirschhorn ['hɪrʃhɔrn], *n.* (—s, *no pl.*) (*Chem.*) hartshorn.

Hirschkäfer ['hɪrʃkɛːfər], *m.* (—s, *pl.* —) (*Ent.*) stag beetle.

Hirschkeule ['hɪrʃkɔylə], *f.* (—, *pl.* —n) haunch of venison.

Hirschkuh ['hɪrʃkuː], *f.* (—, *pl.* ⁻e) (*Zool.*) hind, doe.

Hirse ['hɪrzə], *f.* (—, *no pl.*) (*Bot.*) millet.

Hirt [hɪrt], *m.* (—en, *pl.* —en) shepherd, herdsman.

Hirtenbrief ['hɪrtənbriːf], *m.* (—s, *pl.* —e) (*Eccl.*) pastoral letter.

His [hɪs], *n.* (—, *pl.* —) (*Mus.*) B sharp.

Historiker [hɪ'stoːrɪkər], *m.* (—s, *pl.* —) historian.

historisch [hɪ'stoːrɪʃ], *adj.* historical.

Hitzblase ['hɪtsblaːzə], *f.* (—, *pl.* —n) blister, heat-rash.

Hitze ['hɪtsə], *f.* (—, *no pl.*) heat, hot weather.

hitzig ['hɪtsɪç], *adj.* hot-headed, hasty, passionate.

Hitzschlag ['hɪtsʃlaːk], *m.* (—es, *pl.* ⁻e) sunstroke, heat-stroke.

Hobel ['hoːbəl], *m.* (—s, *pl.* —) (*tool*) plane.

Hoch [hoːx], *n.* (—s, *no pl.*) toast (*drink*); (*Met.*) high.

hoch, hoh [hoːx, hoː], *adj.* high; (*fig.*) eminent, sublime.

Hochachtung ['hoːxaxtuŋ], *f.* (—, *no pl.*) esteem, regard, respect.

hochachtungsvoll ['hoːxaxtuŋsfɔl], *adj., adv.* (*letters*) yours faithfully.

109

Hochamt ['ho:xamt], *n.* (—es, *pl.* ¨er) (*Eccl.*) High Mass.

Hochbau ['ho:xbau], *m.* (—s, *pl.* —ten) superstructure.

hochbetagt ['ho:xbəta:kt], *adj.* advanced in years.

Hochburg ['ho:xburk], *f.* (—, *pl.* —en) (*fig.*) stronghold, citadel.

Hochebene ['ho:xe:bənə], *f.* (—, *pl.* —n) table-land, plateau.

hochfahrend ['ho:xfa:rənt], *adj.* haughty, high-flown; (*coll.*) stuck-up.

Hochgefühl ['ho:xgəfy:l], *n.* (—s, *no pl.*) exaltation.

Hochgenuß ['ho:xgənus], *m.* (—sses, *pl.* ¨sse) exquisite enjoyment; treat.

Hochgericht ['ho:xgəriçt], *n.* (—s, *pl.* —e) place of execution, scaffold.

hochherzig ['ho:xhɛrtsiç], *adj.* magnanimous.

Hochmeister ['ho:xmaistər], *m.* (—s, *pl.* —) Grand Master.

Hochmut ['ho:xmu:t], *m.* (—s, *no pl.*) haughtiness, pride.

hochnäsig ['ho:xnɛ:ziç], *adj.* supercilious, stuck-up.

hochnotpeinlich ['ho:xno:tpainliç], *adj.* (*obs.*) penal, criminal; —es Verhör, criminal investigation.

Hochofen ['ho:xo:fən], *m.* (—s, *pl.* ¨) blast-furnace.

Hochschule ['ho:xʃu:lə], *f.* (—, *pl.* —n) academy; university.

Hochschüler ['ho:xʃy:lər], *m.* (—s, *pl.* —) student, undergraduate.

höchst [hœ:çst], *adj.* highest, most. — *adv.* most, extremely.

Hochstapler ['ho:xʃta:plər], *m.* (—s, *pl.* —) confidence trickster, swindler.

höchstens ['hœ:çstəns], *adv.* at most, at best.

hochtrabend ['ho:xtra:bənt], *adj.* (*horse*) high-stepping; (*fig.*) high-sounding, bombastic.

hochverdient ['ho:xfɛrdi:nt], *adj.* highly meritorious.

Hochverrat ['ho:xfɛra:t], *m.* (—s, *no pl.*) high treason.

Hochwild ['ho:xvilt], *n.* (—es, *no pl.*) deer; big game.

hochwohlgeboren ['ho:xvo:lgəbo:rən], *adj.* (*obs.*) noble; Euer Hochwohlgeboren, Right Honourable Sir.

hochwürden ['ho:xvyrdən], *adj.* Euer Hochwürden, Reverend Sir.

Hochzeit ['ho:xtsait], *f.* (—, *pl.* —en) wedding; nuptials.

hochzeitlich ['ho:xtsaitliç], *adj.* nuptial, bridal.

Hochzeitsreise ['ho:xtsaitsraizə], *f.* (—, *pl.* —n) honeymoon.

Hocke ['hɔkə], *f.* (—, *pl.* —n) squatting posture; shock, stook.

hocken ['hɔkən], *v.n.* crouch, squat; zu Hause —, be a stay-at-home.

Hocker ['hɔkər], *m.* (—s, *pl.* —) stool.

Höcker ['hœkər], *m.* (—s, *pl.* —) hump.

höckerig ['hœkəriç], *adj.* hump-backed, hunch-backed.

Hode ['ho:də], *f.* (—, *pl.* —n) testicle.

Hof [ho:f], *m.* (—es, *pl.* ¨e) yard, courtyard; farm(stead); (*royal*) court; (*moon*) halo; einem den — machen, court s.o.

Hofarzt ['ho:fartst], *m.* (—es, *pl.* ¨e) court physician.

hoffähig ['ho:ffɛ:iç], *adj.* presentable at court.

Hoffart ['hɔfart], *f.* (—, *no pl.*) pride, arrogance.

hoffärtig ['hɔfɛrtiç], *adj.* proud, arrogant.

hoffen ['hɔfən], *v.n.* hope; fest auf etwas —, trust.

hoffentlich ['hɔfəntliç], *adv.* as I hope, I trust that.

Hoffnung ['hɔfnuŋ], *f.* (—, *pl.* —en) hope, expectation, anticipation, expectancy; guter — sein, be full of hope; be expecting a baby; sich — machen auf, cherish hopes of.

hoffnungslos ['hɔfnuŋslo:s], *adj.* hopeless, past hope.

hofieren [ho'fi:rən], *v.a.* court.

höfisch ['hø:fiʃ], *adj.* courtlike, courtly.

höflich ['hø:fliç], *adj.* courteous, civil, polite.

Hoflieferant ['ho:fli:fərant], *m.* (—en, *pl.* —en) purveyor to His or Her Majesty.

Höfling ['hø:fliŋ], *m.* (—s, *pl.* —e) courtier.

Hofmarschall ['ho:fmarʃal], *m.* (—s, *pl.* —e) Lord Chamberlain.

Hofmeister ['ho:fmaistər], *m.* (—s, *pl.* —) (*obs.*) steward; tutor.

Hofnarr ['ho:fnar], *m.* (—en, *pl.* —en) court jester, court fool.

Hofrat ['ho:fra:t], *m.* (—s, *pl.* ¨e) Privy Councillor.

Hofschranze ['ho:fʃrantsə], *m.* (—n, *pl.* —n) courtier; flunkey.

Hofsitte ['ho:fzitə], *f.* (—, *pl.* —n) court etiquette.

Höhe ['hø:ə], *f.* (—, *pl.* —n) height, altitude; bis zur — von, up to the level of; in die —, upwards; in die — fahren, give a start, get excited.

Hoheit ['ho:hait], *f.* (—, *pl.* —en) grandeur; sovereignty; (*title*) Highness.

Hohelied [ho:ə'li:t], *n.* (—s, *no pl.*) Song of Solomon.

Höhenmesser ['hø:ənmɛsər], *m.* (—s, *pl.* —) (*Aviat.*) altimeter.

Höhensonne ['hø:ənzɔnə], *f.* (—, *pl.* —n) Alpine sun; (*Med.*) ultra-violet lamp.

Höhenzug ['hø:əntsu:k], *m.* (—s, *pl.* ¨e) mountain range.

Höhepunkt ['hø:əpuŋkt], *m.* (—s, *pl.* —e) climax, culmination, acme; peak.

höher ['hø:ər], *comp. adj.* higher.

hohl [ho:l], *adj.* hollow; (*tooth*) decayed, hollow.

Höhle ['hø:lə], *f.* (—, *pl.* —n) cave, cavern, den.

hohlgeschliffen [ˈhoːlgəʃlɪfən], *adj.* concave, hollow-ground.

Hohlheit [ˈhoːlhaɪt], *f.* (—, *no pl.*) hollowness.

Hohlleiste [ˈhoːllaɪstə], *f.* (—, *pl.* —n) groove, channel.

Hohlmaß [ˈhoːlmaːs], *n.* (—es, *pl.* —e) dry measure.

Hohlmeißel [ˈhoːlmaɪsəl], *m.* (—s, *pl.* —) gouge.

Hohlsaum [ˈhoːlzaum], *m.* (—s, *pl.* ⸚e) hemstitch.

Hohlspiegel [ˈhoːlʃpiːgəl], *m.* (—s, *pl.* —) concave mirror.

Höhlung [ˈhøːluŋ], *f.* (—, *pl.* —en) hollow, cavity.

Hohlziegel [ˈhoːltsiːgəl], *m.* (—s, *pl.* —) hollow brick.

Hohn [hoːn], *m.* (—s, *no pl.*) scorn, derision, mockery; sneer.

höhnen [ˈhøːnən], *v.a.* deride, sneer at; *see* **verhöhnen**.

Höker [ˈhøːkər], *m.* (—s, *pl.* —) hawker, huckster.

hold [hɔlt], *adj.* kind, friendly; gracious; graceful; sweet.

Holder [ˈhɔldər] *see* **Holunder**.

holdselig [ˈhɔltzeːlɪç], *adj.* sweet, charming, gracious.

holen [ˈhoːlən], *v.a.* fetch, collect, get.

Holland [ˈhɔlant], *n.* Holland.

Hölle [ˈhœlə], *f.* (—, *no pl.*) hell.

Holm [hɔlm], *m.* (—es, *pl.* —e) islet, holm; (*Gymn.*) bar.

holperig [ˈhɔlpərɪç], *adj.* rough, bumpy.

holpern [ˈhɔlpərn], *v.n.* jolt, stumble; (*fig.*) falter.

Holunder [hoˈlundər], *m.* (—s, *pl.* —) (*Bot.*) elder; *spanischer* —, lilac.

Holz [hɔlts], *n.* (—es, *pl.* ⸚er) wood, timber; (*Am.*) lumber; (*no pl.*) forest; bush.

Holzapfel [ˈhɔltsapfəl], *m.* (—s, *pl.* ⸚) (*Bot.*) crab-apple.

holzartig [ˈhɔltsartɪç], *adj.* woody, ligneous.

holzen [ˈhɔltsən], *v.a.* cut *or* gather wood.

hölzern [ˈhœltsərn], *adj.* wooden; (*fig.*) stiff.

Holzhändler [ˈhɔltshɛndlər], *m.* (—s, *pl.* —) timber-merchant; (*Am.*) lumber merchant.

Holzhauer [ˈhɔltshauər], *m.* (—s, *pl.* —) wood-cutter.

holzig [ˈhɔltsɪç], *adj.* woody, wooded; (*asparagus*) woody, hard; (*beans*) stringy.

Holzkohle [ˈhɔltskoːlə], *f.* (—, *no pl.*) charcoal.

Holzscheit [ˈhɔltsʃaɪt], *n.* (—s, *pl.* —e) log of wood.

Holzschlag [ˈhɔltsʃlaːk], *m.* (—es, *pl.* ⸚e) clearing; felling area.

Holzschnitt [ˈhɔltsʃnɪt], *m.* (—es, *pl.* —e) wood-cut.

Holzschuh [ˈhɔltsʃuː], *m.* (—s, *pl.* —e) clog.

Holzweg [ˈhɔltsveːk], *m.* (—s, *pl.* —e) timbertrack; (*fig.*) *auf dem — sein*, be on the wrong tack.

Holzwolle [ˈhɔltsvɔlə], *f.* (—, *no pl.*) wood shavings.

homogen [homoˈgeːn], *adj.* homogeneous.

homolog [homoˈloːg], *adj.* homologous.

honett [hɔˈnɛt], *adj.* (*obs.*) respectable, genteel.

Honig [ˈhoːnɪç], *m.* (—s, *no pl.*) honey.

Honigkuchen [ˈhoːnɪçkuːxən], *m.* (—s, *pl.* —) ginger-bread.

Honigwabe [ˈhoːnɪçvaːbə], *f.* (—, *pl.* —n) honeycomb.

Honorar [honoˈraːr], *n.* (—s, *pl.* —e) remuneration; (*professional*) fee; honorarium.

Honoratioren [honoraˈtsjoːrən], *m. pl.* people of rank; dignitaries.

honorieren [honoˈriːrən], *v.a.* pay a fee to, remunerate.

Hopfen [ˈhɔpfən], *m.* (—s, *no pl.*) (*Bot.*) hop, hops; *an dem ist — und Malz verloren*, he is beyond help.

Hopfenstange [ˈhɔpfənʃtaŋə], *f.* (—, *pl.* —n) hop-pole; (*fig.*) tall thin person.

hopsen [ˈhɔpsən], *v.n.* (*aux.* sein) (*coll.*) hop, jump.

hörbar [ˈhøːrbaːr], *adj.* audible.

horchen [ˈhɔrçən], *v.n.* listen, eavesdrop.

Horde [ˈhɔrdə], *f.* (—, *pl.* —n) horde.

hören [ˈhøːrən], *v.a., v.n.* hear.

Hörer [ˈhøːrər], *m.* (—s, *pl.* —) listener; (*Univ.*) student; (*telephone*) receiver.

Hörerin [ˈhøːrərɪn], *f.* (—, *pl.* —innen) female listener; (*Univ.*) woman student.

Hörerschaft [ˈhøːrərʃaft], *f.* (—, *no pl.*) audience.

Hörgerät [ˈhøːrgereːt], *n.* (—es, *pl.* —e) hearing aid.

hörig [ˈhøːrɪç], *adj.* in bondage, a slave to.

Horizont [horiˈtsɔnt], *m.* (—es, *pl.* —e) horizon.

Horizontale [horitsɔnˈtaːlə], *f.* (—, *pl.* —n) horizontal line.

Horn [hɔrn], *n.* (—s, *pl.* ⸚er) horn; (*Mus.*) French horn.

Hörnchen [ˈhœrnçən], *n.* (—s, *pl.* —) French roll, croissant.

hörnern [ˈhœrnərn], *adj.* horny, made of horn.

Hornhaut [ˈhɔrnhaut], *f.* (—, *pl.* ⸚te) horny skin; (*eye*) cornea.

Hornhautverpflanzung [ˈhɔrnhautfɛrpflantsuŋ], *f.* (—, *no pl.*) corneal graft.

hornig [ˈhɔrnɪç], *adj.* hard, horny.

Hornisse [hɔrˈnɪsə], *f.* (—, *pl.* —n) (*Ent.*) hornet.

horrend [hɔˈrɛnt], *adj.* exorbitant; stupendous.

Hörrohr [ˈhøːrroːr], *n.* (—s, *pl.* —e) ear trumpet.

Hörsaal [ˈhøːrzaːl], *m.* (—s, *pl.* —säle) auditorium, lecture room.

Hörspiel

Hörspiel [ˈhøːrʃpiːl], *n.* (—s, *pl.* —e) radio play.

Horst [hɔrst], *m.* (—es, *pl.* —e) eyrie.

Hort [hɔrt], *m.* (—es, *pl.* —e) (*Poet.*) treasure; stronghold.

Hortensie [hɔrˈtɛnzjə], *f.* (—, *pl.* —n) (*Bot.*) hydrangea.

Hose [ˈhoːzə], *f.* (—, *pl.* —n) trousers, pants, breeches; (*women*) slacks.

Hosenband [ˈhoːzənbant], *n.* (—es, *pl.* ⁓er) garter.

Hosenträger [ˈhoːzəntreːgər], *m. pl.* braces, suspenders.

Hospitant [hɔspiˈtant], *m.* (—en, *pl.* —en) (*Univ.*) temporary student, non-registered student.

hospitieren [hɔspiˈtiːrən], *v.n.* attend lectures as a visitor.

Hostie [ˈhɔstjə], *f.* (—, *pl.* —n) (*Eccl.*) the Host.

hüben [ˈhyːbən], *adv.* on this side; — und drüben, on either side.

hübsch [hypʃ], *adj.* pretty, attractive; handsome; good-looking.

Hubschrauber [ˈhuːpʃraubər], *m.* (—s, *pl.* —) (*Aviat.*) helicopter.

huckepack [ˈhukəpak], *adv.* — tragen, carry pick-a-back.

Huf [huːf], *m.* (—es, *pl.* —e) hoof.

Hufe [ˈhuːfə], *f.* (—, *pl.* —n) hide (of land).

Hufeisen [ˈhuːfaizən], *n.* (—s, *pl.* —) horseshoe.

Huflattich [ˈhuːflatiç], *m.* (—s, *pl.* —e) (*Bot.*) colt's foot.

Hufschlag [ˈhuːfʃlaːk], *m.* (—s, *pl.* ⁓e) (*of a horse*) hoof-beat.

Hüfte [ˈhyftə], *f.* (—, *pl.* —n) (*Anat.*) hip; (*animals*) haunch.

Hügel [ˈhyːgəl], *m.* (—s, *pl.* —) hill, hillock.

hügelig [ˈhyːgəliç], *adj.* hilly.

Huhn [huːn], *n.* (—s, *pl.* ⁓er) fowl; hen.

Hühnchen [ˈhyːnçən], *n.* (—s, *pl.* —) pullet, chicken.

Hühnerauge [ˈhyːnəraugə], *n.* (—s, *pl.* —n) corn (*on the foot*).

Huld [hult], *f.* (—, *no pl.*) grace, favour.

huldigen [ˈhuldigən], *v.n.* pay homage.

huldvoll [ˈhultfɔl], *adj.* gracious.

Hülle [ˈhylə], *f.* (—, *pl.* —n) cover, covering; veil; in — und Fülle, in abundance, in profusion.

hüllen [ˈhylən], *v.a.* cover, veil, wrap.

Hülse [ˈhylzə], *f.* (—, *pl.* —n) hull, husk, shell; cartridge-case.

Hülsenfrucht [ˈhylzənfruxt], *f.* (—, *pl.* ⁓e) (*Bot.*) leguminous plant.

human [huˈmaːn], *adj.* humane.

humanistisch [humaˈnistiʃ], *adj.* classical; humanistic.

Hummel [ˈhuməl], *f.* (—, *pl.* —n) (*Ent.*) bumble-bee.

Hummer [ˈhumər], *m.* (—s, *pl.* —) (*Zool.*) lobster.

Humor [huˈmoːr], *m.* (—s, *no pl.*) humour.

humoristisch [humoˈristiʃ], *adj.* humorous, witty.

humpeln [ˈhumpəln], *v.n.* hobble, limp.

Humpen [ˈhumpən], *m.* (—s, *pl.* —) deep drinking-cup, bowl, tankard.

Humus [ˈhuːmus], *m.* (—, *no pl.*) garden-mould, humus.

Hund [hunt], *m.* (—es, *pl.* —e) dog; (*hunting*) hound; (*fig.*) rascal, scoundrel.

Hundehaus [ˈhundəhaus], *n.* (—es, *pl.* ⁓er) dog-kennel.

hundert [ˈhundərt], *num. adj.* a hundred, one hundred.

Hündin [ˈhyndin], *f.* (—, *pl.* —innen) bitch.

Hundstage [ˈhuntstaːgə], *m. pl.* dog days (July to August).

Hundszahn [ˈhuntstsaːn], *m.* (—es, *pl.* ⁓e) (*Bot.*) dandelion.

Hüne [ˈhyːnə], *m.* (—n, *pl.* —n) giant, colossus; (*fig.*) tall man.

Hünengrab [ˈhyːnəngraːp], *n.* (—es, *pl.* ⁓er) tumulus, burial mound, barrow, cairn.

Hunger [ˈhuŋər], *m.* (—s, *no pl.*) hunger; starvation.

hungern [ˈhuŋərn], *v.n.* hunger, be hungry.

Hungertuch [ˈhuŋərtuːx], *n.* (—es, *no pl.*) am — nagen, go without food; live in poverty.

hungrig [ˈhuŋriç], *adj.* hungry; (*fig.*) desirous (of).

Hupe [ˈhuːpə], *f.* (—, *pl.* —n) motor-horn, hooter (of a car).

hüpfen [ˈhypfən], *v.n.* (*aux.* sein) hop, skip.

Hürde [ˈhyrdə], *f.* (—, *pl.* —n) hurdle.

Hure [ˈhuːrə], *f.* (—, *pl.* —n) whore, prostitute, harlot; (*coll.*) tart.

hurtig [ˈhurtiç], *adj.* nimble, agile; quick, speedy, swift.

Husar [huˈzaːr], *m.* (—en, *pl.* —en) hussar.

husch! [huʃ], *excl.* quick!

huschen [ˈhuʃən], *v.n.* (*aux.* sein) scurry, slip away.

hüsteln [ˈhyːstəln], *v.n.* cough slightly; clear o.'s throat.

husten [ˈhuːstən], *v.n.* cough.

Hut (1) [huːt], *m.* (—es, *pl.* ⁓e) hat; steifer —, bowler.

Hut (2) [huːt], *f.* (—, *no pl.*) guard, keeping, care.

hüten [ˈhyːtən], *v.a.* guard, tend, care for; Kinder —, baby-sit; das Bett —, be confined to o.'s bed, be ill in bed. — *v.r.* sich — vor, be on o.'s guard against, beware of.

Hüter [ˈhyːtər], *m.* (—s, *pl.* —) guardian, keeper; (*cattle*) herdsman.

Hutkrempe [ˈhuːtkrɛmpə], *f.* (—, *pl.* —n) hat-brim.

Hütte [ˈhytə], *f.* (—, *pl.* —n) hut, cottage; (*Tech.*) furnace, forge, foundry.

Hüttenarbeiter [ˈhytənarbaitər], *m.* (—s, *pl.* —) smelter, foundry worker.

Hyäne [hyˈɛːnə], *f.* (—, *pl.* —n) (*Zool.*) hyena.

112

Hyazinthe [hyat'sɪntə], f. (—, pl. —n) (Bot.) hyacinth.

Hyperbel [hy'pɛrbəl], f. (—, pl. —n) hyperbola.

hypnotisch [hyp'no:tɪʃ], adj. hypnotic.

hypnotisieren [hypnoti'zi:rən], v.a. hypnotise.

Hypochonder [hypo'xɔndər], m. (—s, pl. —) hypochondriac.

Hypothek [hypo'te:k], f. (—, pl. —en) mortgage.

Hysterie [hyste'ri:], f. (—, no pl.) hysterics, hysteria.

hysterisch [hys'te:rɪʃ], adj. hysterical.

I

I [i:], n. (—, no pl.) the letter I. — excl. i wo! (dial.) certainly not, of course not.

ich [ɪç], pers. pron. I, myself.

ideal [ide'a:l], adj. ideal.

idealisieren [ideali'zi:rən], v.a. idealise.

Idealismus [idea'lɪsmus], m. (—, no pl.) idealism.

Idee [i'de:], f. (—, pl. —n) idea, notion, conception.

identifizieren [idɛntifi'tsi:rən], v.a. identify.

identisch [i'dɛntɪʃ], adj. identical.

Identität [idɛnti'tɛ:t], f. (—, no pl.) identity.

idiomatisch [idio'ma:tɪʃ], adj. idiomatic.

Idyll [i'dyl], n. (—s, pl. —e) idyll.

Idylle [i'dylə], f. (—, pl. —n) idyll.

idyllisch [i'dylɪʃ], adj. idyllic.

Igel [i'gəl], m. (—s, pl. —) (Zool.) hedgehog.

ignorieren [ɪgno'ri:rən], v.a. ignore, take no notice of.

ihm [i:m], pers. pron. Dat. to him, it.

ihn [i:n], pers. pron. Acc., him, it.

Ihnen ['i:nən], pers. pron. Dat. you, to you.

ihnen ['i:nən], pers. pron. pl. Dat. them, to them.

Ihr [i:r], poss. adj. your; of your. —, poss. pron. yours.

ihr [i:r], pers. pron. to her; (pl.) (intim.) you. — poss. adj. her, their. — poss. pron. hers, theirs.

Ihrer ['i:rər], pers. pron. of you. — poss. adj. of your.

ihrer ['i:rər], pers. pron. of her, of it; (pl.) of them. — poss. adj of her; to her; (pl.) of their.

ihresgleichen ['i:rəsglaɪçən], adv. of her, its or their kind.

ihrethalben ['i:rəthalbən], adv. for her sake, for their sake, on her account, on their account.

ihretwegen ['i:rətve:gən] see **ihrethalben**.

ihretwillen ['i:rətvɪlən] see **ihrethalben**.

Ihrige [i:rɪgə], poss. pron. yours.

ihrige ['i:rɪgə], poss. pron. hers, its, theirs.

illegitim [ɪlegi'ti:m], adj. illegitimate.

illuminieren [ɪlumi'ni:rən], v.a. illuminate, floodlight.

illustrieren [ɪlu'stri:rən], v.a. illustrate.

Iltis ['ɪltɪs], m. (—ses, pl. —se) (Zool.) polecat, fitchet.

im [ɪm], contraction of in dem, in the.

Imbiß ['ɪmbɪs], m. (—sses, pl. —sse) snack, refreshment, light meal.

Imker ['ɪmkər], m. (—s, pl. —) beekeeper.

immatrikulieren [ɪmmatriku'li:rən], v.a. (Univ.) matriculate, enrol.

Imme ['ɪmə], f. (—, pl. —n) (dial., Poet.) bee.

immer ['ɪmər], adv. always, ever; — mehr, more and more; — noch, still; — wieder, time and again: — größer, larger and larger; auf —, for ever.

immerdar ['ɪmərda:r], adv. for ever.

immerhin ['ɪmərhɪn], adv. nevertheless, still, after all.

immerzu ['ɪmərtsu:], adv. always, constantly.

Immobilien [ɪmo'bi:ljən], pl. real estate.

Immortelle [ɪmɔr'tɛlə], f. (—, pl. —n) (Bot.) everlasting flower.

immun [ɪ'mu:n], adj. immune.

impfen ['ɪmpfən], v.a. vaccinate, inoculate; (Hort.) graft.

imponieren [ɪmpo'ni:rən], v.n. impress.

Import [ɪm'pɔrt], m. (—s, pl. —e) import, importation.

imposant [ɪmpo'zant], adj. imposing, impressive.

imstande [ɪm'ʃtandə], adv. capable, able; — sein, be able.

in [ɪn], prep. (Dat., Acc.) in, into; at; within.

Inangriffnahme [ɪn'angrɪfna:mə], f. (—, no pl.) start, beginning, inception.

Inbegriff ['ɪnbəgrɪf], m. (—es, no pl.) essence, epitome.

inbegriffen ['ɪnbəgrɪfən], adv. inclusive.

Inbrunst ['ɪnbrunst], f. (—, no pl.) ardour, fervour.

indem [ɪn'de:m], adv. meanwhile. — conj. while, whilst; as, because, in that.

indessen [ɪn'dɛsən], adv. meanwhile, in the meantime. — conj. however, nevertheless, yet.

Indien ['ɪndjən], n. India.

Individualität [ɪndividuali'tɛ:t], f. (—, pl. —en) individuality, personality.

individuell [ɪndividu'ɛl], adj. individual.

Individuum [ɪndi'vi:duum], n. (—s, pl. —duen) individual.

Indizienbeweis

Indizienbeweis [ɪnˈdiːtsjənbəvaɪs], *m.* (—es, *pl.* —e) (*Law*) circumstantial evidence *or* proof.

indossieren [ɪndɔˈsiːrən], *v.a.* endorse.

Industrie [ɪndusˈtriː], *f.* (—, *pl.* —n) industry; manufacture.

industriell [ɪndustriˈɛl], *adj.* industrial.

Industrielle [ɪndustriˈɛlə], *m.* (—n, *pl.* —n) manufacturer, industrialist.

ineinander [ɪnaɪˈnandər], *adv.* into each other, into one another.

infam [ɪnˈfaːm], *adj.* infamous.

Infantin [ɪnˈfantɪn], *f.* (—, *pl.* —en) Infanta.

infizieren [ɪnfiˈtsiːrən], *v.a.* infect.

infolge [ɪnˈfɔlgə], *prep.* (*Genit.*) in consequence of, owing to.

informieren [ɪnfɔrˈmiːrən], *v.a.* inform, advise.

Ingenieur [ɪnʒənˈjøːr], *m.* (—s, *pl.* —e) engineer.

Ingrimm [ˈɪngrɪm], *m.* (—s, *no pl.*) anger, rage, wrath.

Ingwer [ˈɪŋvər], *m.* (—s, *no pl.*) ginger.

Inhaber [ˈɪnhaːbər], *m.* (—s, *pl.* —) possessor, owner; proprietor; occupant.

inhaftieren [ɪnhafˈtiːrən], *v.a.* imprison; arrest.

inhalieren [ɪnhaˈliːrən], *v.a.* inhale.

Inhalt [ˈɪnhalt], *m.* (—(e)s, *no pl.*) content; contents; tenor.

Inhaltsverzeichnis [ˈɪnhaltsfɛrtsaɪçnɪs], *n.* (—ses, *pl.* —se) (table of) contents; index.

inhibieren [ɪnhiˈbiːrən], *v.a.* inhibit, prevent.

Inkasso [ɪnˈkaso], *n.* (—s, *pl.* —s) encashment.

inklinieren [ɪnkliˈniːrən], *v.n.* be inclined to.

inklusive [ɪnkluˈziːvə], *adv.* inclusive of, including.

inkonsequent [ˈɪnkɔnzəkvɛnt], *adj.* inconsistent.

Inkrafttreten [ɪnˈkrafttreːtən], *n.* (—s, *no pl.*) enactment; coming into force.

Inland [ˈɪnlant], *n.* (—s, *no pl.*) inland, interior.

Inländer [ˈɪnlɛndər], *m.* (—s, *pl.* —) native.

Inlett [ˈɪnlɛt], *n.* (—s, *pl.* —e) bed-tick, ticking.

inliegend [ˈɪnliːgənt], *adj.* enclosed.

inmitten [ɪnˈmɪtən], *prep.* (*Genit.*) in the midst of.

innehaben [ˈɪnhaːbən], *v.a.* irr. possess; occupy; hold.

innehalten [ˈɪnhaltən], *v.a.* irr. (*conditions*) keep to, observe; (*time*) come promptly at. — *v.n.* stop, pause.

innen [ˈɪnən], *adv.* within; *nach* —, inwards; *von* —, from within.

Innenminister [ˈɪnənmɪnɪstər], *m.* (—s, *pl.* —) Minister for Internal Affairs; Home Secretary; (*Am.*) Secretary of the Interior.

inner [ˈɪnər], *adj.* inner, interior, internal; intrinsic.

innerhalb [ˈɪnərhalp], *prep.* (*Genit.*) within.

innerlich [ˈɪnərlɪç], *adj.* internal; inside o.s.; inward.

innerste [ˈɪnərstə], *adj.* inmost, innermost.

innewerden [ˈɪnəveːrdən], *v.a.* irr. (*aux.* sein) perceive, become aware of.

innewohnen [ˈɪnəvoːnən], *v.n.* be inherent in.

innig [ˈɪnɪç], *adj.* heartfelt, cordial.

Innung [ˈɪnuŋ], *f.* (—, *pl.* —en) guild, corporation.

Insasse [ˈɪnzasə], *m.* (—n, *pl.* —n) inmate; occupant.

insbesondere [ɪnsbəˈzɔndərə], *adv.* especially, particularly, in particular.

Inschrift [ˈɪnʃrɪft], *f.* (—, *pl.* —en) inscription.

Insel [ˈɪnzəl], *f.* (—, *pl.* —n) island.

Inserat [ɪnzəˈraːt], *n.* (—es, *pl.* —e) classified advertisement; (*coll.*) (small) ad.

inserieren [ɪnzəˈriːrən], *v.a.* advertise; insert.

insgeheim [ɪnsgəˈhaɪm], *adv.* privately, secretly.

insgesamt [ɪnsgəˈzamt], *adv.* altogether, in a body.

insofern [ɪnzoˈfɛrn], *conj.* — *als*, in so far as, inasmuch as, so far as.

inspirieren [ɪnspiˈriːrən], *v.a.* inspire.

installieren [ɪnstaˈliːrən], *v.a.* install, fit.

instandhalten [ɪnˈʃtanthaltən], *v.a.* irr. maintain, preserve, keep in repair.

inständig [ˈɪnʃtɛndɪç], *adj.* urgent; fervent.

instandsetzen [ɪnˈʃtantzɛtsən], *v.a.* restore, repair; *einen — etwas zu tun*, enable s.o. to do s.th.

Instanz [ɪnˈstants], *f.* (—, *pl.* —en) (*Law*) instance; *letzte —*, highest court of appeal, last resort.

Institut [ɪnstiˈtuːt], *n.* (—es, *pl.* —e) institute, institution, establishment; (*Univ.*) department.

instruieren [ɪnstruˈiːrən], *v.a.* instruct.

Insulaner [ɪnzuˈlaːnər], *m.* (—s, *pl.* —) islander.

inszenieren [ɪnstseˈniːrən], *v.a.* put on the stage, produce.

Inszenierung [ɪnstseˈniːruŋ], *f.* (—, *pl.* —en) (*Theat.*) production, staging.

intellektuell [ɪntɛlɛktuˈɛl], *adj.* intellectual.

Intendant [ɪntɛnˈdant], *m.* (—en, *pl.* —en) (*Theat.*) director.

interessant [ɪntərɛˈsant], *adj.* interesting.

Interesse [ɪntəˈrɛsə], *n.* (—s, *pl.* —n) interest.

Interessent [ɪntərɛˈsɛnt], *m.* (—en, *pl.* —en) interested party.

interessieren [ɪntərɛˈsiːrən], *v.a.* interest. — *v.r. sich* —, be interested (in).

intern [ɪnˈtɛrn], *adj.* internal.

Internat [ɪntɛrˈnaːt], *n.* (—es, *pl.* —e) boarding-school.

Interne [ɪn'tɛrnə], *m.* (—n, *pl.* —n) resident (pupil *or* doctor), boarder.

Internist [ɪntɛr'nɪst], *m.* (—en, *pl.* —en) specialist in internal diseases.

interpunktieren [ɪntərpunk'tiːrən], *v.a.* punctuate.

Interpunktion [ɪntərpunkts'joːn], *f.* (—, *pl.* —en) punctuation.

intim [ɪn'tiːm], *adj.* intimate; *mit einem — sein*, b : on close terms with s.o.

intonieren [ɪnto'niːrən], *v.n.* intone.

Intrigant [ɪntri'gant], *m.* (—en, *pl.* —en) intriguer, schemer.

intrigieren [ɪntri'giːrən], *v.n.* intrigue, scheme.

Inventar [ɪnvɛn'taːr], *n.* (—s, *pl.* —e) inventory; *ein — aufnehmen*, draw up an inventory.

Inventur [ɪnvɛn'tuːr], *f.* (—, *pl.* —en) stock-taking.

inwärts ['ɪnvɛrts], *adv.* inwards.

inwendig ['ɪnvɛndɪç], *adj.* inward, internal, inner.

inwiefern [ɪnviː'fɛrn], *adv.* to what extent.

inwieweit [ɪnviː'vaɪt], *adv.* how far.

Inzucht ['ɪntsuxt], *f.* (—, *no pl.*) in-breeding.

inzwischen [ɪn'tsvɪʃən], *adv.* meanwhile, in the meantime.

Irak [i'raːk], *m., n.* Iraq.

Iran [i'raːn], *n.* Iran.

irden ['ɪrdən], *adj.* earthen.

irdisch ['ɪrdɪʃ], *adj.* earthly, worldly; terrestrial, temporal.

irgend ['ɪrgənt], *adv.* any, some; *wenn es — geht*, if it can possibly be done.

irgendein [ɪrgənt'aɪn], *pron.* any, some.

Irland ['ɪrlant], *n.* Ireland.

ironisch [i'roːnɪʃ], *adj.* ironic, ironical.

Irre (1) ['ɪrə], *f.* (—, *no pl.*) *in die — gehen*, go astray.

Irre (2) ['ɪrə], *m.* (—n, *pl.* —n) madman, lunatic.

irre ['ɪrə], *adj.* astray; wrong, confused; crazy, demented.

irren ['ɪrən], *v.n.* err, go astray, be wrong. — *v.r. sich —*, be mistaken.

Irrenarzt ['ɪrənartst], *m.* (—es, *pl.* ⁻e) psychiatrist.

Irrenhaus ['ɪrənhaus], *n.* (—es, *pl.* ⁻er) lunatic asylum, mental hospital.

Irrfahrt ['ɪrfaːrt], *f.* (—, *pl.* —en) wandering.

Irrglaube ['ɪrglaubə], *m.* (—ns, *no pl.*) heresy.

irrig ['ɪrɪç], *adj.* erroneous.

irritieren [ɪri'tiːrən], *v.a.* irritate.

Irrlicht ['ɪrlɪçt], *n.* (—s, *pl.* —er) will-o'-the-wisp.

Irrsinn ['ɪrzɪn], *m.* (—s, *no pl.*) madness, insanity, lunacy.

irrsinnig ['ɪrzɪnɪç], *adj.* insane, deranged.

Irrtum ['ɪrtuːm], *m.* (—s, *pl.* ⁻er) error, mistake, fault, oversight.

Irrweg ['ɪrveːk], *m.* (—s, *pl.* —e) wrong track.

Irrwisch ['ɪrvɪʃ], *m.* (—es, *pl.* —e) will-o'-the-wisp.

Ischias ['ɪsçias], *f., m.* (*Med.*) sciatica.

Isegrim ['iːzəgrɪm], *m.* (—s, *pl.* —e) (*fable*) the wolf; a bear (with a sore head) (*also fig.*).

Island ['iːslant], *n.* Iceland.

isolieren [izo'liːrən], *v.a.* (*Electr.*) insulate; (*fig.*) isolate.

Isolierung [izo'liːruŋ], *f.* (—, *pl.* —en) (*Electr.*) insulation; (*fig.*) isolation.

Italien [i'taːljən], *n.* Italy.

J

J [jɔt], *n.* (—, *no pl.*) the letter J.

ja [jaː], *adv., part.* yes; indeed, certainly; even; — *doch*, to be sure; — *freilich*, certainly.

Jacht [jaxt], *f.* (—, *pl.* —en) yacht.

Jacke ['jakə], *f.* (—, *pl.* —n) jacket, tunic.

Jackett [ja'kɛt], *n.* (—s, *pl.* —s) jacket, short coat.

Jagd [jaːkt], *f.* (—, *pl.* —en) hunt, hunting; shooting; chase.

Jagdhund ['jaːkthunt], *m.* (—es, *pl.* —e) retriever, setter; hound.

Jagdrevier ['jaːktreviːr], *n.* (—s, *pl.* —e) hunting-ground.

jagen ['jaːgən], *v.a.* hunt; chase; (*fig.*) tear along.

Jäger ['jɛːgər], *m.* (—s, *pl.* —) hunter, huntsman; game-keeper.

Jägerei [jɛːgə'raɪ], *f.* (—, *no pl.*) huntsmanship.

jäh [jɛː], *adj.* abrupt; steep, precipitous; (*fig.*) hasty, rash, sudden.

jählings ['jɛːlɪŋs], *adv.* abruptly, suddenly, hastily.

Jahr [jaːr], *n.* (—es, *pl.* —e) year.

jähren ['jɛːrən], *v.r. sich —*, (*anniversary*) come round.

Jahresfeier ['jaːrəsfaɪər], *f.* (—, *pl.* —n) anniversary.

Jahresrente ['jaːrəsrɛntə], *f.* (—, *pl.* —n) annuity.

Jahreszeit ['jaːrəstsaɪt], *f.* (—, *pl.* —en) season.

Jahrgang ['jaːrgaŋ], *m.* (—s, *pl.* ⁻e) age group; class; year of publication; vintage.

Jahrhundert [jaːr'hundərt], *n.* (—s, *pl.* —e) century.

jährig ['jɛːrɪç], *adj.* year-old.

jährlich ['jɛːrlɪç], *adj.* yearly, annual. — *adv.* every year.

Jahrmarkt ['jaːrmarkt], *m.* (—s, *pl.* ⁻e) annual fair.

Jahrtausend [jaːr'tauzənt], *n.* (—s, *pl.* —e) millennium.

Jahrzehnt [jaːr'tseːnt], *n.* (—s, *pl.* —e) decade.

Jähzorn ['jɛːtsɔrn], *m.* (—s, *no pl.*) irascibility.

Jalousie [ʒaluˈziː], f. (—, pl. —n) Venetian blind.

Jamaika [jaˈmaika], n. Jamaica.

Jambus [ˈjambus], m. (—, pl. —ben) (Poet.) iambic foot.

Jammer [ˈjamər], m. (—s, no pl.) lamentation; misery; (fig.) pity.

jämmerlich [ˈjɛmərlɪç], adj. lamentable, miserable, wretched, piteous.

jammerschade [ˈjamərʃaːdə], adv. a thousand pities.

Jänner [ˈjɛnər] (Austr.) see **Januar**.

Januar [ˈjanuaːr], m. (—s, pl. —e) January.

Japan [ˈjaːpan], n. Japan.

Jaspis [ˈjaspɪs], m. (—ses, pl. —se) jasper.

jäten [ˈjɛːtən], v.a. weed.

Jauche [ˈjauxə], f. (—, pl. —n) liquid manure.

jauchzen [ˈjauxtsən], v.n. exult, shout with joy.

Jauchzer [ˈjauxtsər], m. (—s, pl. —) shout of joy.

jawohl [jaˈvoːl], int. yes, indeed! certainly, of course.

je [jeː], adv. ever; at any time; at a time; each; von — her, always; — nachdem, it depends; — zwei, in twos; — eher — besser, the sooner the better.

jedenfalls [ˈjeːdənfals], adv. at all events, in any case, at any rate, anyway.

jeder, -e, -es [ˈjeːdər], adj. every, each; — beliebige, any. — pron. each, each one; everybody.

jederlei [ˈjeːdərlaɪ], adj. of every kind.

jedoch [jeˈdɔx], adv., however, nevertheless, yet, notwithstanding.

jeglicher, -e, -es [ˈjeːklɪçər], adj. every, each. — pron. every man, each.

jemals [ˈjeːmals], adv. ever, at any time.

jemand [ˈjeːmant], pron. somebody, someone; anybody, anyone.

Jemen [ˈjeːmən], n. Yemen.

jener, -e, -es [ˈjeːnər], dem. adj. that, (Poet.) yonder. — dem. pron. that one, the former.

Jenseits [ˈjɛnzaɪts], n. (—, no pl.) the next world, the hereafter, the life to come.

jenseits [ˈjɛnzaɪts], prep. (Genit.) on the other side, beyond.

jetzig [ˈjɛtsɪç], adj. present, now existing, current, extant.

jetzt [jɛtst], adv. now, at this time, at present.

jeweilig [ˈjeːvaɪlɪç], adj. momentary; actual, for the time being.

Joch [jɔx], n. (—es, pl. —e) yoke.

Jochbein [ˈjɔxbaɪn], n. (—s, pl. —e) cheek-bone.

Jockei [ˈjɔkaɪ], m. (—s, pl. —s) jockey.

Jod [joːt], n. (—s, no pl.) iodine.

jodeln [ˈjoːdəln], v.n. yodel.

Jodler [ˈjoːdlər], m. (—s, pl. —) (person) yodeler; (sound) yodelling.

Johannisbeere [joˈhanɪsbeːrə], f. (—, pl. —n) (Bot.) red currant.

Johannisfest [joˈhanɪsfɛst], n. (—s, pl. —e) Midsummer Day, St. John the Baptist's Day (June 24th).

Johanniskäfer [joˈhanɪskɛːfər], m. (—s, pl. —) (Ent.) glow-worm.

Johannisnacht [joˈhanɪsnaxt], f. (—, pl. ̈e) Midsummer Eve.

johlen [ˈjoːlən], v.n. bawl.

Joppe [ˈjɔpə], f. (—, pl. —n) shooting jacket.

Jota [ˈjoːta], n. (—s, pl. —s) iota, jot.

Journalismus [ʒurnaˈlɪsmus], m. see **Journalistik**.

Journalistik [ʒurnaˈlɪstɪk], f. (—, no pl.) journalism.

jubeln [ˈjuːbəln], v.n. rejoice, exult.

Jubilar [juːbiˈlaːr], m. (—s, pl. —e) person celebrating a jubilee.

Jubiläum [juːbiˈlɛːum], n. (—s, pl. —läen) jubilee.

jubilieren [juːbiˈliːrən], v.n. exult, shout with joy.

juchhe [juxˈheː], excl. hurrah!

Juchten [ˈjuxtən], m. (—, no pl.) Russian leather.

jucken [ˈjukən], v.a. scratch. — v.n. itch.

Jude [ˈjuːdə], m. (—n, pl. —n) Jew, Israelite.

Judentum [ˈjuːdəntuːm], n. (—s, no pl.) Judaism.

Judenviertel [ˈjuːdənfiːrtəl], n. (—s, pl. —) Jewish quarter, ghetto.

Jüdin [ˈjyːdɪn], f. (—, pl. —innen) Jewess.

jüdisch [ˈjyːdɪʃ], adj. Jewish.

Jugend [ˈjuːgənt], f. (—, no pl.) youth.

jugendlich [ˈjuːgəntlɪç], adj. youthful, juvenile.

Jugoslawien [jugoˈslaːvjən], n. Jugoslavia.

Julfest [ˈjuːlfɛst], n. (—es, pl. —e) Yule.

Juli [ˈjuːli], m. (—s, pl. —s) July.

jung [juŋ], adj. young.

Junge (1) [ˈjuŋə], m. (—n, pl. —n) boy, lad.

Junge (2) [ˈjuŋə], n. (—n, pl. —n) young animal.

jungenhaft [ˈjuŋənhaft], adj. boyish.

Jünger [ˈjyŋər], m. (—s, pl. —) disciple, devotee, follower.

Jungfer [ˈjunfər], f. (—, pl. —n) (obs.) virgin, maid, maiden; lady's maid.

jüngferlich [ˈjyŋfərlɪç], adj. maidenly, coy, prim.

Jungfrau [ˈjuŋfrau], f. (—, pl. —en) virgin.

Junggeselle [ˈjuŋgəzɛlə], m. (—n, pl. —n) bachelor; eingefleischter —, confirmed bachelor.

Jüngling [ˈjyŋlɪŋ], m. (—s, pl. —e) young man.

jüngst [jyŋst], adv. lately, recently.

Juni [ˈjuːni], m. (—s, pl. —s) June.

Junker [ˈjuŋkər], m. (—s, pl. —) country squire; titled landowner.

Jura [ˈjuːra], n. pl. jurisprudence, law; (Univ.) — studieren, read law.

Jurisprudenz [juːrɪspruˈdɛnts], f. (—, no pl.) jurisprudence.

Jurist [juːˈrɪst], m. (—en, pl. —en) lawyer, jurist.

juristisch [ju:'rɪstɪʃ], *adj.* juridical; legal.

just [just], *adv.* just now.

Justiz [jus'ti:ts], *f.* (—, *no pl.*) administration of the law *or* of justice.

Justizrat [jus'ti:tsra:t], *m.* (—s, *pl.* ⸚e) (*Law*) Counsellor; King's (Queen's) Counsel.

Jute ['ju:tə], *f.* (—, *no pl.*) jute.

Juwel [ju've:l], *n.* (—s, *pl.* —en) jewel; (*pl.*) jewellery; (*Am.*) jewelry.

Juwelier [juvə'li:r], *m.* (—s, *pl.* —e) jeweller, goldsmith.

K

K [ka:], *n.* (—, *no pl.*) the letter K.

Kabel ['ka:bəl], *n.* (—s, *pl.* —) cable.

Kabeljau [kabəl'jau], *m.* (—s, *pl.* —e) (*Zool.*) cod, codfish.

kabeln ['ka:bəln], *v.n.* cable, send a cablegram.

Kabine [ka'bi:nə], *f.* (—, *pl.* —n) cabin, cubicle.

Kabinett [kabi'nɛt], *n.* (—s, *pl.* —e) closet; cabinet.

Kabinettsrat [kabi'nɛtsra:t], *m.* (—s, *pl.* ⸚e) cabinet *or* ministerial committee; political adviser.

Kabüse [ka'by:zə], *f.* (—, *pl.* —n) ship's galley.

Kachel ['kaxəl], *f.* (—, *pl.* —n) glazed tile.

Kadaver [ka'da:vər], *m.* (—s, *pl.* —) carrion, carcass; corpse.

Kadenz [ka'dɛnts], *f.* (—, *pl.* —en) (*Mus.*) cadenza.

Kadett [ka'dɛt], *m.* (—en, *pl.* —en) cadet.

Käfer ['kɛ:fər], *m.* (—s, *pl.* —) (*Ent.*) beetle, (*Am.*) bug.

Kaffee ['kafe], *m.* (—s, *no pl.*) coffee.

Käfig ['kɛ:fɪç], *m.* (—s, *pl.* —e) cage.

kahl [ka:l], *adj.* bald; (*trees*) leafless; (*landscape*) barren; — *geschoren*, closecropped.

Kahn ['ka:n], *m.* (—s, *pl.* ⸚e) boat; punt.

Kai [kai], *m.* (—s, *pl.* —s) quay, wharf, landing-place.

Kaimeister ['kaimaistər], *m.* (—s, *pl.* —) wharfinger.

Kaiser ['kaizər], *m.* (—s, *pl.* —) emperor; *um des* —*s Bart streiten*, quarrel about nóthing.

kaiserlich ['kaizərlɪç], *adj.* imperial.

Kaiserschnitt ['kaizər∫nɪt], *m.* (—es, *pl.* —e) (*Med.*) Caesarean operation.

Kajüte [ka'jy:tə], *f.* (—, *pl.* —n) cabin.

Kakadu ['kakadu:], *m.* (—s, *pl.* —s) (*Orn.*) cockatoo.

Kakao [ka'ka:o], *m.* (—s, *no pl.*) cocoa.

Kalauer ['ka:lauər], *m.* (—s, *no pl.*) pun; stale joke.

Kalb [kalp], *n.* (—es, *pl.* ⸚er) calf; (*roe*) fawn; (*fig.*) colt, calf.

Kalbfleisch ['kalpflaiʃ], *n.* (—es, *no pl.*) veal.

Kälberei [kɛlbə'rai], *f.* (—, *pl.* —en) friskiness.

kälbern ['kɛlbərn], *v.n.* frisk, frolic.

Kalbsbraten ['kalpsbra:tən], *m.* (—s, *pl.* —) roast veal.

Kalbshaxe ['kalpshaksə], *f.* (—, *pl.* —n) knuckle of veal.

Kalbskeule ['kalpskɔylə], *f.* (—, *pl.* —n) leg of veal.

Kalbsmilch ['kalpsmɪlç], *f.* (—, *no pl.*) sweetbread.

Kaldaunen [kal'daunən], *f. pl.* (*dial.*) tripe.

Kalesche [ka'leʃə], *f.* (—, *pl.* —n) chaise, light carriage.

Kali ['ka:li], *n.* (—s, *no pl.*) potash.

Kaliber [ka'li:bər], *n.* (—s, *pl.* —) calibre; (*fig.*) sort, quality.

kalibrieren [kali'bri:rən], *v.a.* (*Tech.*) calibrate, graduate, gauge.

Kalifornien [kali'fɔrnjən], *n.* California.

Kalium ['ka:ljum], *n.* (—s, *no pl.*) (*Chem.*) potassium.

Kalk [kalk], *m.* (—s, *pl.* —e) lime; *gebrannter* —, quicklime; *mit* — *bewerfen*, rough-cast.

kalkartig ['kalka:rtɪç], *adj.* calcareous.

Kalkbewurf ['kalkbəvurf], *m.* (—es, *pl.* ⸚e) coat of plaster.

kalken ['kalkən], *v.a.* whitewash; (*Agr.*) lime.

kalkig ['kalkɪç], *adj.* limy, calcareous.

kalkulieren [kalku'li:rən], *v.n.* calculate, reckon.

kalt [kalt], *adj.* cold, frigid; *mir ist* —, I am cold.

kaltblütig ['kaltbly:tɪç], *adj.* coldblooded, cool.

Kälte ['kɛltə], *f.* (—, *no pl.*) cold, coldness.

Kaltschale ['kalt∫a:lə], *f.* (—, *pl.* —n) cold beer (*or* wine) soup.

Kambodscha [kam'bɔt∫a], *f.* Cambodia.

Kamee [ka'me:], *f.* (—, *pl.* —n) cameo.

Kamel [ka'me:l], *n.* (—s, *pl.* —e) (*Zool.*) camel.

Kamelziege [ka'me:ltsi:gə], *f.* (—, *pl.* —n) (*Zool.*) Angora-goat, llama.

Kamerad [kamə'ra:t], *m.* (—en, *pl.* —en) comrade, companion, mate.

Kameradschaft [kamə'ra:t∫aft], *f.* (—, *pl.* —en) comradeship, fellowship.

Kamerun [kamə'ru:n], *n.* the Cameroons.

Kamille [ka'mɪlə], *f.* (—, *pl.* —n) camomile.

Kamin [ka'mi:n], *m.* (—s, *pl.* —e) chimney; funnel; fireplace, fireside.

Kaminaufsatz [ka'mi:naufzats], *m.* (—es, *pl.* ⸚e) mantel-piece, overmantel.

Kaminfeger [ka'mi:nfe:gər], *m.* (—s, *pl.* —) chimney-sweep.

Kaminsims

Kaminsims [ka'mi:nzɪms], *m.* or *n.* (—es, *pl.* —e) mantel-piece.

Kamm [kam], *m.* (—es, *pl.* ⁀e) comb; (*cock*) crest; (*mountains*) ridge.

kämmen ['kɛmən], *v.a.* comb; (*wool*) card.

Kammer ['kamər], *f.* (—, *pl.* —n) chamber, small room; (*Am.*) closet; (*authority*) board; (*Parl. etc.*) chamber.

Kammerdiener ['kamərdi:nər], *m.* (—s, *pl.* —) valet.

Kämmerer ['kɛmərər], *m.*, *s., pl.* —) Chamberlain, Treasurer.

Kammergericht ['kamərgərɪçt], *n.* (—s, *pl.* —e) Supreme Court of Justice.

Kammergut ['kamərgu:t], *n.* (—s, *pl.* ⁀er) domain, demesne; crown land.

Kammerherr ['kamərhɛr], *m.* (—n, *pl.* —en) chamberlain.

Kammersänger ['kamərzɛŋər], *m.* (—s, *pl.* —) court singer; title given to prominent singers.

Kammgarn ['kamgarn], *n.* (—s, *no pl.*) worsted.

Kammwolle ['kamvɔlə], *f.* (—, *no pl.*) carded wool.

Kampagne [kam'panjə], *f.* (—, *pl.* —n) (*Mil.*) campaign.

Kämpe ['kɛmpə], *m.* (—n, *pl.* —n) (*Poet.*) champion, warrior; *alter* —, old campaigner.

Kampf [kampf], *m.* (—es, *pl.* ⁀e) combat, fight, struggle; (*fig.*) conflict.

kämpfen ['kɛmpfən], *v.n.* fight, combat, struggle.

Kampfer ['kampfər], *m.* (—s, *no pl.*) camphor.

Kämpfer ['kɛmpfər], *m.* (—s, *pl.* —) fighter, combatant.

kampfunfähig ['kampfunfɛ:ɪç], *adj.* (*Mil.*) disabled; — *machen*, disable, put out of action.

kampieren [kam'pi:rən], *v.n.* be encamped, camp.

Kanada ['kanada], *n.* Canada.

Kanal [ka'na:l], *m.* (—s, *pl.* ⁀e) (*natural*) channel; (*artificial*) canal; sewer; *der Ärmelkanal*, the English Channel.

kanalisieren [kanali'zi:rən], *v.a.* canalise; (*streets*) drain by means of sewers.

Kanapee ['kanape:], *n.* (—s, *pl.* —s) sofa, divan.

Kanarienvogel [ka'na:rjənfo:gəl], *m.* (—s, *pl.* ⁀) (*Orn.*) canary.

Kanarische Inseln [ka'na:rɪʃə 'ɪnzəln], *f.pl.* Canary Islands.

Kandare [kan'da:rə], *f.* (—, *pl.* —n) bridle, bit.

Kandelaber [kandə'la:bər], *m.* (—s, *pl.* —) candelabrum, chandelier.

kandidieren [kandi'di:rən], *v.n.* be a candidate (for), apply (for) (*post*); (*Parl.*) stand (for), (*Am.*) run (for election).

kandieren [kan'di:rən], *v.a.* candy.

Kandiszucker ['kandɪstsukər], *m.* (—, *no pl.*) sugar-candy.

Kanevas ['kanəvas], *m.* (—ses, *pl.* —se) canvas.

Känguruh ['kɛŋguru:], *n.* (—s, *pl.* —s) (*Zool.*) kangaroo.

Kaninchen [ka'ni:nçən], *n.* (—s, *pl.* —) (*Zool.*) rabbit.

Kaninchenbau [ka'ni:nçənbau], *m.* (—s, *pl.* —e) rabbit-warren, burrow.

Kanne ['kanə], *f.* (—, *pl.* —n) can, tankard, mug; jug; pot; quart.

Kannegießer ['kanəgi:sər], *m.* (—s, *pl.* —) pot-house politician.

kannelieren [kanə'li:rən], *v.a.* flute; channel.

Kannibale [kani'ba:lə], *m.* (—n, *pl.* —n) cannibal.

Kanoe [ka'nu:], *n. see* **Kanu**.

Kanone [ka'no:nə], *f.* (—, *pl.* —n) cannon, gun; *unter aller* —, beneath contempt; beneath criticism.

Kanonier [kano'ni:r], *m.* (—s, *pl.* —e) gunner.

Kanonikus [ka'no:nikus], *m.* (—, *pl.* —ker) canon, prebendary.

kanonisieren [kanoni'zi:rən], *v.a.* canonise.

Kante ['kantə], *f.* (—, *pl.* —n) edge, rim, brim, brink, ledge; (*cloth*) list, selvedge.

Kanten ['kantən], *m.* (—s, *pl.* —) (*bread*) crust.

kanten ['kantən], *v.a.* edge, tilt.

Kanthaken ['kantha:kən], *m.* (—s, *pl.* —) cant-hook; grapple; grappling hook.

kantig ['kantɪç], *adj.* angular.

Kantine [kan'ti:nə], *f.* (—, *pl.* —n) canteen, mess.

Kanton [kan'to:n], *m.* (—s, *pl.* —e) (*Swiss*) canton; district, region.

Kantonist [kanto'nɪst], *m.* (—en, *pl.* —en) *unsicherer* —, shifty fellow.

Kantor ['kantor], *m.* (—s, *pl.* —en) precentor, organist; cantor.

Kanu [ka'nu:], *n.* (—s, *pl.* —s) canoe.

Kanzel ['kantsəl], *f.* (—, *pl.* —n) pulpit; (*Aviat.*) cockpit.

Kanzlei [kants'laɪ], *f.* (—, *pl.* —en) office, secretariat; chancellery; chancery office; lawyer's office.

Kanzleipapier [kants'laɪpapi:r], *n.* (—s, *no pl.*) foolscap (paper).

Kanzleistil [kants'laɪʃti:l], *m.* (—s, *no pl.*) legal jargon.

Kanzler ['kantslər], *m.* (—s, *pl.* —) Chancellor.

Kanzlist [kants'lɪst], *m.* (—en, *pl.* —en) chancery clerk; copying clerk.

Kap [kap], *n.* (—s, *pl.* —s) (*Geog.*) cape, promontory.

Kapaun [ka'paun], *m.* (—s, *pl.* —e) capon.

Kapazität [kapatsi'tɛ:t], *f.* (—, *pl.* —en) capacity; (*fig.*) (*person*) authority.

Kapelle [ka'pɛlə], *f.* (—, *pl.* —n) chapel; (*Mus.*) band.

Kapellmeister [ka'pɛlmaɪstər], *m.* (—s, *pl.* —) (*Mus.*) band leader, conductor.

Kaper ['ka:pər], *f.* (—, *pl.* —n) (*Bot.*) caper.

kapern ['ka:pərn], *v.a.* capture, catch.

kapieren [ka'pi:rən], *v.a.* (*coll.*) understand, grasp.

Kapital [kapi'ta:l], *n.* (—s, *pl.* —ien) (*money*) capital, stock.

Kapitäl, Kapitell [kapɪ'tɛ:l, kapɪ'tɛl], *n.* (—s, *pl.* —e) (*Archit.*) capital.

Kapitalanlage [kapi'ta:lanla:gə], *f.* (— *pl.* —n) investment.

kapitalisieren [kapitali'zi:rən], *v.a.* capitalise.

kapitalkräftig [kapi'ta:lkrɛftɪç], *adj.* wealthy, moneyed, affluent; (*business, firm*) sound.

Kapitalverbrechen [kapi'ta:lfɛrbrɛçən], *n.* (—s, *pl.* —) capital offence.

Kapitän [kapi'tɛ:n], *m.* (—s, *pl.* —e) captain (of a ship), master.

Kapitel [ka'pɪtəl], *n.* (—s, *pl.* —) chapter.

Kapitulation [kapitulats'jo:n], *f.* (—, *pl.* —en) surrender.

kapitulieren [kapitu'li:rən], *v.n.* surrender; capitulate.

Kaplan [kap'la:n], *m.* (—s, *pl.* ⁻e) chaplain; assistant priest.

Kapotte [ka'pɔtə], *f.* (—, *pl.* —n) hood.

Kappe ['kapə], *f.* (—, *pl.* —n) cap, bonnet; (*shoe*) toe-cap.

Käppi ['kɛpi], *n.* (—s, *pl.* —s) military cap.

Kapriole [kapri'o:lə], *f.* (—, *pl.* —n) caper.

kaprizieren [kapri'tsi:rən], *v.r. sich auf etwas —*, set o.'s heart on s.th., be obstinate about s.th.

kapriziös [kapri'tsjø:s], *adj.* whimsical, capricious.

Kapsel [kapzəl], *f.* (—, *pl.* —n) capsule.

kaputt [ka'put], *adj.* broken, ruined, done for; — *machen*, break, ruin.

Kapuze [ka'pu:tsə], *f.* (—, *pl.* —n) hood; monk's cowl.

Kapuziner [kaput'si:nər], *m.* (—s, *pl.* —) Capuchin (friar); (*coffee*) cappuccino.

Kapuzinerkresse [kaput'si:nərkrɛsə], *f.* (—, *no pl.*) (*Bot.*) nasturtium.

Karabiner [kara'bi:nər], *m.* (—s, *pl.* —) (*rifle*) carbine.

Karaffe [ka'rafə], *f.* (—, *pl.* —n) carafe; decanter.

Karambolage [karambo'la:ʒə], *f.* (—, *pl.* —n) collision; (*billiards*) cannon.

Karawane [kara'va:nə], *f.* (—, *pl.* —n) convoy; caravan.

Karbol [kar'bo:l], *n.* (—s, *no pl.*) carbolic acid.

Karbunkel [kar'buŋkəl], *m.* (—s, *pl.* —) (*Med.*) carbuncle.

Karfreitag [kar'fraita:k], *m.* Good Friday.

Karfunkel [kar'fuŋkəl], *m.* (—s, *pl.* —) (*Min.*) carbuncle.

karg [kark], *adj.* scant; meagre; parsimonious.

kargen ['kargən], *v.n.* be stingy, be niggardly.

kärglich ['kɛrklɪç], *adj.* sparing, scanty, poor, paltry.

karieren [ka'ri:rən], *v.a.* checker.

kariert [ka'ri:rt], *adj.* checked, checkered.

Karikatur [karika'tu:r], *f.* (—, *pl.* —en) caricature, cartoon.

karikieren [kari'ki:rən], *v.a.* caricature, distort.

Karl [karl], *m.* Charles; — *der Grosse*, Charlemagne.

Karmeliter [karme'li:tər], *m.* (—s, *pl.* —) Carmelite (friar).

karminrot [kar'mi:nro:t], *adj.* carmine.

karmoisin [karmoa'zi:n], *adj.* crimson.

Karneol [karne'o:l], *m.* (—s, *pl.* —e) (*Min.*) cornelian, carnelian.

Karneval ['karnəval], *m.* (—s, *pl.* —s) carnival; Shrovetide festivities.

Karnickel [kar'nɪkəl], *n.* (—s, *pl.* —) rabbit; *er war das* —, he was to blame.

Kärnten ['kɛrntən], *n.* Carinthia.

Karo ['ka:ro], *n.* (—s, *pl.* —s) check, square; (*cards*) diamonds.

Karosse [ka'rɔsə], *f.* (—, *pl.* —n) statecoach.

Karosserie [karɔsə'ri:], *f.* (—, *pl.* —n) (*Motor.*) body(-work).

Karotte [ka'rɔtə], *f.* (—, *pl.* —n) (*Bot.*) carrot.

Karpfen ['karpfən], *m.* (—s, *pl.* —) (*fish*) carp.

Karre ['karə], *f.* (—, *pl.* —n) cart, wheelbarrow.

Karren ['karən], *m.* (—s, *pl.* —) cart, wheelbarrow, dray.

Karrete [ka're:tə], *f.* (—, *pl.* —n) (*Austr.*) rattletrap, rickety coach.

Karriere [ka'rje:rə], *f.* (—, *pl.* —n) career; — *machen*, get on well.

Kärrner ['kɛrnər], *m.* (—s, *pl.* —) (*obs.*) carter.

Karst [karst], *m.* (—s, *pl.* —e) mattock.

Karthago [kar'ta:go], *n.* Carthage.

Kartätsche [kar'tɛ:tʃə], *f.* (—, *pl.* —n) grape-shot, shrapnel.

Kartäuser [kar'tɔyzər], *m.* (—s, *pl.* —) Carthusian (monk).

Karte ['kartə], *f.* (—, *pl.* —n) card; ticket; map; chart; (*pl.*) pack ((*Am.*) deck) of cards.

Kartei [kar'tai], *f.* (—, *pl.* —en) card index.

Kartell [kar'tɛl], *n.* (—s, *pl.* —e) cartel; ring; syndicate.

Kartoffel [kar'tɔfəl], *f.* (—, *pl.* —n) (*Bot.*) potato.

Kartoffelpuffer [kar'tɔfəlpufər], *m.* (—s, *pl.* —) potato-pancake.

Karton [kar'tɔŋ], *m.* (—s, *pl.* —s) carton, cardboard-box; (*material*) cardboard, paste-board; cartoon.

Kartusche [kar'tuʃə], *f.* (—, *pl.* —n) cartridge.

Karussell [karu'sɛl], *n.* (—s, *pl.* —e) merry-go-round.

Karwoche ['ka:rvɔxə], *f.* Holy Week.

Karzer ['kartsər], *m.* (—s, *pl.* —) lock-up, prison.

Kaschmir ['kaʃmi:r], *m.* (—s, *no pl.*) cashmere.

Käse

Käse [ˈkɛːzə], *m.* (—s, *pl.* —) cheese.
käseartig [ˈkɛːzəˌrtɪç], *adj.* like cheese; caseous.
Kaserne [kaˈzɛrnə], *f.* (—, *pl.* —n) barracks.
kasernieren [kazɛrˈniːrən], *v.a.* put into barracks.
Käsestoff [ˈkɛːzəʃtɔf], *m.* (—s, *pl.* —e) casein.
käseweiß [ˈkɛːzəvaɪs], *adj.* deathly pale.
käsig [ˈkɛːzɪç], *adj.* cheese-like, cheesy, caseous; (*fig.*) sallow.
Kasperle [ˈkaspɛrlə], *n.* (—s, *pl.* —) Punch.
Kasperl(e)theater [ˈkaspərl(ə)teaːtər], *n.* (—s, *pl.* —) Punch-and-Judy show.
Kaspisches Meer [ˈkaspɪʃəsmeːr], *n.* Caspian Sea.
Kasse [ˈkasə], *f.* (—, *pl.* —n) money-box, till; cash-desk; box-office; cash, ready money.
Kassenanweisung [ˈkasənanvaɪzuŋ], *f.* (—, *pl.* —en) treasury-bill; cash voucher.
Kassenbuch [ˈkasənbuːx], *n.* (—es, *pl.* ⸚er) cash-book.
Kassenschrank [ˈkasənʃraŋk], *m.* (—s, *pl.* ⸚e) strong-box, safe.
Kasserolle [kasəˈrɔlə], *f.* (—, *pl.* —n) stew-pot, casserole.
Kassette [kaˈsɛtə], *f.* (—, *pl.* —n) deed-box; casket; (*Phot.*) plate-holder.
kassieren [kaˈsiːrən], *v.a.* cash, collect (money); cashier, annul, discharge.
Kassierer [kaˈsiːrər], *m.* (—s, *pl.* —) cashier; teller.
Kastanie [kasˈtanjə], *f.* (—, *pl.* —n) (*Bot.*) chestnut, (*coll.*) conker; chestnut-tree.
Kästchen [ˈkɛstçən], *n.* (—s, *pl.* —) casket, little box.
Kaste [ˈkastə], *f.* (—, *pl.* —n) caste.
kasteien [kaˈstaɪən], *v.r. sich —*, castigate *or* mortify o.s.
Kastell [kaˈstɛl], *n.* (—s, *pl.* —e) citadel, small fort; castle.
Kastellan [kastɛˈlaːn], *m.* (—s, *pl.* —e) castellan; caretaker.
Kasten [ˈkastən], *m.* (—s, *pl.* ⸚) box, chest, case, crate.
Kastengeist [ˈkastəngaɪst], *m.* (—es, *no pl.*) exclusiveness; class consciousness.
Kastilien [kaˈstiːljən], *n.* Castile.
Kastrat [kaˈstraːt], *m.* (—en, *pl.* —en) eunuch.
kastrieren [kaˈstriːrən], *v.a.* castrate.
Katafalk [kataˈfalk], *m.* (—s, *pl.* —e) catafalque.
katalogisieren [kataloɡiˈziːrən], *v.a.* catalogue.
Katarakt [kataˈrakt], *m.* (—es, *pl.* —e) cataract; waterfall.
Katasteramt [kaˈtastəramt], *n.* (—es, *pl.* ⸚er) land-registry office.
katechisieren [kateçiˈziːrən], *v.a.* catechise, instruct.

kategorisch [kateˈɡoːrɪʃ], *adj.* categorical, definite.
Kater [ˈkaːtər], *m.* (—s, *pl.* —) tom-cat; (*fig.*) hangover; *der gestiefelte —*, Puss-in-Boots.
Katheder [kaˈteːdər], *n.* (—s, *pl.* —) desk; rostrum; lecturing-desk; (*fig.*) professorial chair.
Kathedrale [kateˈdraːlə], *f.* (—, *pl.* —n) cathedral.
Katholik [katoˈliːk], *m.* (—en, *pl.* —en) (Roman) Catholic.
katholisch [kaˈtoːlɪʃ], *adj.* (Roman) Catholic.
Kattun [kaˈtuːn], *m.* (—s, *pl.* —e) calico, cotton.
Kätzchen [ˈkɛtsçən], *n.* (—s, *pl.* —) kitten; (*Bot.*) catkin.
Katze [ˈkatsə], *f.* (—, *pl.* —n) cat; *die — im Sack kaufen*, buy a pig in a poke; *für die —*, no good at all, useless.
katzenartig [ˈkatsənaːrtɪç], *adj.* cat-like, feline.
Katzenauge [ˈkatsənaugə], *n.* (—s, *pl.* —n) cat's-eye.
Katzenbuckel [ˈkatsənbukəl], *m.* (—s, *pl.* —) arched back of a cat.
Katzenjammer [ˈkatsənjamər], *m.* (—s, *pl.* —) hangover.
Katzenmusik [ˈkatsənmuziːk], *f.* (—, *no pl.*) caterwauling; cacophony, discordant music.
Katzensprung [ˈkatsənʃpruŋ], *m.* (—es, *no pl.*) (*fig.*) stone's throw
Kauderwelsch [ˈkaudərvɛlʃ], *n.* (—es, *no pl.*) gibberish, double-Dutch.
kauen [ˈkauən], *v.a., v.n.* chew.
kauern [ˈkauərn], *v.n.* cower, squat, crouch.
Kauf [kauf], *m.* (—es, *pl.* ⸚e) purchase, buy; bargain.
Kaufbummel [ˈkaufbuməl], *m.* (—s, *no pl.*) shopping-spree.
kaufen [ˈkaufən], *v.a.* (*things*) buy, purchase; (*persons*) bribe.
Käufer [ˈkɔyfər], *m.* (—s, *pl.* —) buyer, purchaser.
Kaufhaus [ˈkaufhaus], *n.* (—es, *pl.* ⸚er) department store, emporium.
Kaufladen [ˈkauflaːdən], *m.* (—s, *pl.* ⸚) shop.
käuflich [ˈkɔyflɪç], *adj.* (*things*) purchasable, marketable; (*persons*) open to bribery, venal.
Kaufmann [ˈkaufman], *m.* (—s, *pl.* **Kaufleute** [ˈkaufləytə]) merchant; shopkeeper; (*Am.*) store-keeper.
kaufmännisch [ˈkaufmɛnɪʃ], *adj.* commercial, mercantile.
Kaugummi [ˈkauɡumi], *m.* (—s, *no pl.*) chewing gum.
Kaukasus [ˈkaukazus], *m.* Caucasus (Mountains).
Kaulquappe [ˈkaulkvapə], *f.* (—, *pl.* —n) (*Zool.*) tadpole.
kaum [kaum], *adv.* scarcely, hardly; no sooner.
Kaurimuschel [ˈkaurimuʃəl], *f.* (—, *pl.* —n) (*Zool.*) cowrie shell.

120

Kautabak ['kautabak], *m.* (—s, *no pl.*) chewing-tobacco.

Kaution [kau'tsjo:n], *f.* (—, *pl.* —en) security, bail, surety; *eine — stellen*, go, give *or* stand bail.

Kautschuk ['kautʃuk], *m.* (—s, *no pl.*) caoutchouc, India-rubber.

Kauz [kauts], *m.* (—es, *pl.* ⁒e) (*Orn.*) screech-owl; (*fig.*) *komischer —*, queer customer.

Käuzchen ['kɔytsçən], *n.* (—s, *pl.* —) little owl; (*fig.*) imp.

Kavalier [kava'li:r], *m.* (—s, *pl.* —e) gentleman; lady's man.

keck [kɛk], *adj.* bold, daring; pert, saucy.

Kegel ['ke:gəl], *m.* (—s, *pl.* —) ninepin, skittle; (*Geom.*) cone; *mit Kind und —*, bag and baggage.

Kegelbahn ['ke:gəlba:n], *f.* (—, *pl.* —en) skittle-alley, bowling-alley.

kegelförmig ['ke:gəlfœrmiç], *adj.* conical.

kegeln ['ke:gəln], *v.n.* bowl, play at ninepins.

Kehle ['ke:lə], *f.* (—, *pl.* —n) throat, windpipe.

Kehlkopf ['ke:lkɔpf], *m.* (—es, *pl.* ⁒e) larynx.

Kehllaut ['ke:llaut], *m.* (—es, *pl.* —e) (*Phonet.*) guttural sound.

Kehlung ['ke:luŋ], *f.* (—, *pl.* —en) channel, flute, groove.

Kehraus ['ke:raus], *m.* (—, *no pl.*) last dance; (*fig.*) break-up, end.

kehren ['ke:rən], *v.a.* sweep; turn; *den Rücken —*, turn o.'s back. — *v.r. sich — an*, pay attention to, regard.

Kehricht ['ke:riçt], *m.* (—s, *no pl.*) sweepings; rubbish.

Kehrreim ['ke:rraim], *m.* (—s, *pl.* —e) refrain.

Kehrseite ['ke:rzaitə], *f.* (—, *pl.* —n) reverse.

kehrtmachen ['ke:rtmaxən], *v.n.* turn around; (*Mil.*) face about; turn back.

keifen ['kaifən], *v.n.* scold, nag.

Keil [kail], *m.* (—s, *pl.* —e) wedge.

Keile ['kailə], *f.* (—, *no pl.*) blows; (*coll.*) hiding; *— kriegen*, get a thrashing.

keilen ['kailən], *v.a.* wedge; (*coll.*) thrash.

Keilerei [kailə'rai], *f.* (—, *pl.* —en) brawl, fight.

keilförmig ['kailfœrmiç], *adj.* wedge-shaped.

Keilschrift ['kailʃrift], *f.* (—, *pl.* —en) cuneiform writing.

Keim [kaim], *m.* (—es, *pl.* —e) germ, seed.

keimen ['kaimən], *v.n.* germinate.

keimfrei ['kaimfrai], *adj.* sterile, germ-free.

keiner, -e, -es [kainər], *adj.* no, not a, not any. — *pron.* no one, none.

keinerlei ['kainərlai], *adj.* no, of no sort, no … whatever.

keineswegs ['kainəsve:ks], *adv.* by no means, on no account.

Keks [ke:ks], *m.* (—es, *pl.* —e) biscuit.

Kelch [kɛlç], *m.* (—es, *pl.* —e) cup; (*Eccl.*) chalice; (*Bot.*) calyx.

Kelchblatt ['kɛlçblat], *n.* (—es, *pl.* ⁒er) sepal.

kelchförmig ['kɛlçfœrmiç], *adj.* cup-shaped.

Kelle ['kɛlə], *f.* (—, *pl.* —n) ladle; (*mason*) trowel.

Keller ['kɛlər], *m.* (—s, *pl.* —) cellar, basement.

Kellergewölbe ['kɛlərgəvœlbə], *n.* (—s, *pl.* —) vault.

Kellner ['kɛlnər], *m.* (—s, *pl.* —) waiter.

keltern ['kɛltərn], *v.a.* press (*grapes*).

Kenia ['ke:nja], *n.* Kenya.

kennbar ['kɛnba:r], *adj.* recognisable, conspicuous.

kennen ['kɛnən], *v.a. irr.* know, be acquainted with.

Kenner ['kɛnər], *m.* (—s, *pl.* —) connoisseur, expert.

Kennkarte ['kɛnkartə], *f.* (—, *pl.* —n) identity card.

kenntlich ['kɛntliç], *adj.* distinguishable.

Kenntnis ['kɛntnis], *f.* (—, *pl.* —se) knowledge; (*language*) command.

Kennzeichen ['kɛntsaixən], *n.* (—s, *pl.* —) characteristic, distinguishing mark; sign; symptom; criterion.

Kenterhaken ['kɛntərha:kən], *m.* (—s, *pl.* —) grappling-iron.

kentern ['kɛntərn], *v.n.* (*aux.* sein) capsize.

keramisch [ke'ra:miʃ], *adj.* ceramic.

Kerbe ['kɛrbə], *f.* (—, *pl.* —n) notch, indentation.

kerben ['kɛrbən], *v.a.* notch.

Kerbholz ['kɛrphɔlts], *n.* (—es, *no pl.*) tally; *auf dem —*, on o.'s conscience, charged against o.

Kerbtier ['kɛrpti:r], *n.* (—es, *pl.* —e) insect.

Kerker ['kɛrkər], *m.* (—s, *pl.* —) prison, jail, gaol; dungeon.

Kerl [kɛrl], *m.* (—s, *pl.* —e) fellow, chap; (*Am.*) guy (*coll.*).

Kern [kɛrn], *m.* (—es, *pl.* —e) (*nut*) kernel; (*fruit*) stone; (*fig.*) heart, crux; pith; (*Phys.*) nucleus.

kerngesund ['kɛrngəzunt], *adj.* hale and hearty, fit as a fiddle.

kernig ['kɛrniç], *adj.* solid, pithy.

Kernphysik ['kɛrnfyzi:k], *f.* (—, *no pl.*) nuclear physics.

Kernpunkt ['kɛrnpuŋkt], *m.* (—es, *pl.* —e) gist, essential point.

Kernwaffe ['kɛrnvafə], *f.* (—, *pl.* —n) nuclear weapon.

Kerze ['kɛrtsə], *f.* (—, *pl.* —n) candle.

Kessel ['kɛsəl], *m.* (—s, *pl.* —) kettle, cauldron; (*steam*) boiler.

Kesselschmied ['kɛsəlʃmi:t], *m.* (—s, *pl.* —e) boiler maker.

Kesselstein ['kɛsəlʃtain], *m.* (—s, *no pl.*) fur, deposit, scale (*on boiler*).

Kette ['kɛtə], *f.* (—, *pl.* —n) chain.

ketten ['kɛtən], *v.a.* chain, fetter.

Kettenstich ['kɛtənʃtiç], *m.* (—es, *pl.* —e) chain stitch; (*Naut.*) chain knot.

Ketzer ['kɛtsər], *m.* (—s, *pl.* —) heretic.
Ketzerei [kɛtsə'raɪ], *f.* (—, *pl.* —en) heresy.
ketzerisch ['kɛtsərɪʃ], *adj.* heretical.
keuchen ['kɔʏçən], *v.n.* pant, puff, gasp.
Keuchhusten ['kɔʏçhu:stən], *m.* (—s, *no pl.*) whooping-cough.
Keule ['kɔʏlə], *f.* (—, *pl.* —n) club; (*meat*) leg.
keusch [kɔʏʃ], *adj.* chaste, pure.
kichern ['kɪçərn], *v.n.* titter, giggle.
Kiebitz ['ki:bɪts], *m.* (—es, *pl.* —e) (*Orn.*) lapwing, peewit; (*fig.*) onlooker; (*coll.*) rubber-neck (at chess *or* cards).
Kiefer (1) ['ki:fər], *m.* (—s, *pl.* —) jaw, jaw-bone.
Kiefer (2) ['ki:fər], *f.* (—, *pl.* —n) (*Bot.*) pine.
Kiel [ki:l], *m.* (—es, *pl.* —e) keel; (*pen*) quill.
Kielwasser ['ki:lvasər], *n.* (—s, *no pl.*) wake.
Kieme ['ki:mə], *f.* (—, *pl.* —n) (*fish*) gill.
Kien [ki:n], *m.* (—s, *no pl.*) pine-resin, resinous pinewood.
Kienspan ['ki:nʃpa:n], *m.* (—s, *pl.* ⁻e) pine-splinter.
Kiepe ['ki:pə], *f.* (—, *pl.* —n) (*dial.*) creel, wicker basket.
Kies [ki:s], *m.* (—s, *no pl.*) gravel.
Kiesel ['ki:zəl], *m.* (—s, *pl.* —) pebble; flint.
Kieselsäure ['ki:zəlzɔʏrə], *f.* (—, *no pl.*) silicic acid.
Kieselstein ['ki:zəlʃtaɪn], *m.* (—s, *pl.* —e) pebble.
Kilogramm ['ki:logram], *n.* (—s, *pl.* —e) kilogram (1000 grammes).
Kilometer ['ki:lome:tər], *m.* (—s, *pl.* —) kilometre; (*Am.*) kilometer (1000 metres).
Kimme ['kɪmə], *f.* (—, *pl.* —n) notch.
Kind [kɪnt], *n.* (—es, *pl.* —er) child; (*law*) infant; — *und Kegel*, bag and baggage.
Kind(e)l ['kɪnd(ə)l], *n.* (—s, *pl.* —) (*dial.*) small child, baby; *Münchner* —, Munich beer.
Kinderei [kɪndə'raɪ], *f.* (—, *pl.* —en) childishness; childish prank.
Kinderfräulein ['kɪndərfrɔʏlaɪn], *n.* (—s, *pl.* —) nurse, (*coll.*) nannie.
Kindergarten ['kɪndərgartən], *m.* (—s, *pl.* ⁻) kindergarten, infant-school.
Kinderhort ['kɪndərhort], *m.* (—s, *pl.* —e) crèche.
kinderleicht ['kɪndərlaɪçt], *adj.* extremely easy, child's play.
Kindermärchen ['kɪndərmɛːrçən], *n.* (—s, *pl.* —) fairy-tale.
Kinderstube ['kɪndərʃtu:bə], *f.* (—, *pl.* —n) nursery; *eine gute* —, a good upbringing.
Kinderwagen ['kɪndərva:gən], *m.* (—s, *pl.* —) perambulator, pram.
Kindesbeine ['kɪndəsbaɪnə], *n. pl. von* —*n an*, from infancy.

Kindeskind ['kɪndəskɪnt], *n.* (—es, *pl.* —er) (*obs.*) grandchild.
Kindheit ['kɪnthaɪt], *f.* (—, *no pl.*) childhood, infancy.
kindisch ['kɪndɪʃ], *adj.* childish.
kindlich ['kɪntlɪç], *adj.* childlike; naïve.
Kinn [kɪn], *n.* (—s, *pl.* —e) chin.
Kinnbacken ['kɪnbakən], *m.* (—s, *pl.* —) (*Anat.*) jaw-bone.
Kinnbackenkrampf ['kɪnbakənkrampf], *m.* (—s, *pl.* ⁻e) (*Med.*) lock-jaw.
Kinnlade ['kɪnla:də], *f.* (—, *pl.* —n) (*Anat.*) jaw-bone.
Kino ['ki:no], *n.* (—s, *pl.* —s) cinema; (*coll.*) pictures; (*Am.*) motion picture theatre; motion pictures, (*coll.*) movies.
Kipfel ['kɪpfəl], *n.* (—s, *pl.* —) (*dial.*) roll, croissant.
kippen ['kɪpən], *v.a.* tilt, tip over.
Kirche ['kɪrçə], *f.* (—, *pl.* —n) church.
Kirchenbann ['kɪrçənban], *m.* (—s, *no. pl.*) excommunication.
Kirchenbuch ['kɪrçənbu:x], *n.* (—es, *pl.* ⁻er) parish-register.
Kirchengut ['kɪrçəngu:t], *n.* (—es, *pl.* ⁻er) church-property.
Kirchenlicht ['kɪrçənlɪçt], *n.* (—es, *pl.* —er) (*fig.*) shining light, bright spark.
Kirchenrecht ['kɪrçənrɛçt], *n.* (—es, *no pl.*) canon law.
Kirchenschiff ['kɪrçənʃɪf], *n.* (—es, *pl.* —e) nave.
Kirchenstuhl ['kɪrçənʃtu:l], *n.* (—es, *pl.* ⁻e) pew.
Kirchenversammlung ['kɪrçənfɛrzamluŋ], *f.* (—, *pl.* —en) synod; convocation.
Kirchenvorsteher ['kɪrçənforʃte:ər], *m.* (—s, *pl.* —) churchwarden.
kirchlich ['kɪrçlɪç], *adj.* ecclesiastic(al), religious.
Kirchspiel ['kɪrçʃpi:l], *n.* (—es, *pl.* —e) parish.
Kirchsprengel ['kɪrçʃprɛŋəl], *m.* (—s, *pl.* —) diocese.
Kirchturm ['kɪrçturm], *m.* (—s, *pl.* ⁻e) steeple.
Kirchweih ['kɪrçvaɪ], *f.* (—, *pl.* —en) consecration (of a church); church fair.
Kirmes ['kɪrmɛs], *f.* (—, *pl.* —sen) *see* **Kirchweih.**
kirre ['kɪrə], *adj.* tame; (*fig.*) amenable.
kirren ['kɪrən], *v.a.* tame, allure. — *v.n.* coo.
Kirsch(branntwein) [kɪrʃ(brantvaɪn)], *m.* (—s, *no pl.*) cherry-brandy.
Kirsche ['kɪrʃə], *f.* (—, *pl.* —n) (*Bot.*) cherry; *mit ihr ist nicht gut* —*n essen*, she is hard to get on with *or* not pleasant to deal with.
Kirschsaft ['kɪrʃzaft], *m.* (—es, *no pl.*) cherry-juice.
Kirschwasser ['kɪrʃvasər], *n.* (—s, *no pl.*) cherry-brandy.
Kissen ['kɪsən], *n.* (—s, *pl.* —) cushion, pillow.

Kiste ['kɪstə], *f.* (—, *pl.* —n) box, case, chest; crate; coffer.

Kitsch [kɪtʃ], *m.* (—es, *no pl.*) trash; rubbish.

Kitt [kɪt], *m.* (—s, *pl.* —e) cement; (*Glazing*) putty.

Kittel ['kɪtəl], *m.* (—s, *pl.* —) smock; overall, tunic; frock.

kitten ['kɪtən], *v.a.* cement, glue.

Kitzchen ['kɪtsçən], *n.* (—s, *pl.* —) kid; fawn; kitten.

Kitzel ['kɪtsəl], *m.* (—s, *no pl.*) tickling, titillation; itch; (*fig.*) desire, appetite.

kitzeln ['kɪtsəln], *v.a.* tickle, titillate.

kitzlich ['kɪtslɪç], *adj.* ticklish; (*fig.*) delicate.

Kladderadatsch ['kladəradatʃ], *m.* (—es, *no pl.*) bang; mess, muddle.

klaffen ['klafən], *v.n.* gape, yawn.

kläffen ['klɛfən], *v.n.* bark, yelp.

Klafter ['klaftər], *f.* (—, *pl.* —n) fathom; (*wood*) cord.

klagbar ['kla:kba:r], *adj.* (*Law*) actionable.

Klage ['kla:gə], *f.* (—, *pl.* —n) complaint; (*Law*) suit, action.

Klagelied ['kla:gəli:t], *n.* (—es, *pl.* —er) dirge, lamentation.

klagen ['kla:gən], *v.n.* complain, lament; (*Law*) sue.

Kläger ['klɛ:gər], *m.* (—s, *pl.* —) complainant; (*Law*) plaintiff.

Klageschrift ['kla:gəʃrɪft], *f.* (—, *pl.* —en) bill of indictment; written complaint.

kläglich ['klɛ:klɪç], *adj.* woeful, pitiful, deplorable.

klaglos ['kla:klo:s], *adj.* uncomplaining.

Klamm [klam], *f.* (—, *pl.* —en) gorge, ravine.

klamm [klam], *adj.* tight, narrow; numb; clammy.

Klammer ['klamər], *f.* (—, *pl.* —n) clamp, clasp, hook; peg; clip; bracket, parenthesis.

klammern ['klamərn], *v.a.* fasten, peg. — *v.r.* *sich* — *an*, cling to.

Klang [klaŋ], *m.* (—es, *pl.* —e) sound, tone; *ohne Sang und* —, unheralded and unsung.

klanglos ['klaŋlo:s], *adj.* soundless.

klangnachahmend ['klaŋnaxa:mənt], *adj.* onomatopoeic.

klangvoll ['klaŋfɔl], *adj.* sonorous.

Klappe ['klapə], *f.* (—, *pl.* —en) flap; (*Tech.*) valve; (*vulg.*) *halt die* —! shut up!

klappen ['klapən], *v.n.* flap; (*fig.*) tally, square; *es hat geklappt*, it worked.

Klapper ['klapər], *f.* (—, *pl.* —n) rattle.

klappern ['klapərn], *v.n.* rattle; (*teeth*) chatter.

Klapperschlange ['klapərʃlaŋə], *f.* (—, *pl.* —n) (*Zool.*) rattle-snake.

Klapphut ['klaphu:t], *m.* (—es, *pl.* ⸚e) opera-hat; chapeau-claque.

Klapps [klaps], *m.* (—es, *pl.* ⸚e) slap, smack; (*fig.*) touch of madness, kink.

Klappstuhl ['klapʃtu:l], *m.* (—s, *pl.* ⸚e) camp-stool, folding-chair.

Klapptisch ['klaptɪʃ], *m.* (—es, *pl.* —e) folding-table.

klar [kla:r], *adj.* clear; bright; (*fig.*) evident; plain, distinct.

Kläranlage ['klɛ:ranla:gə], *f.* (—, *pl.* —n) sewage-farm; filter plant.

klären ['klɛ:rən], *v.a.* clear.

Klarheit ['kla:rhaɪt], *f.* (—, *no pl.*) clearness, plainness.

Klarinette [klari'nɛtə], *f.* (—, *pl.* —n) (*Mus.*) clarinet.

Klärmittel ['klɛ:rmɪtəl], *n.* (—s, *pl.* —) clarifier.

Klärung ['klɛ:ruŋ], *f.* (—, *pl.* —en) clarification; (*fig.*) elucidation.

Klasse ['klasə], *f.* (—, *pl.* —n) class, order; (*Sch.*) form.

klassifizieren [klasifi'tsi:rən], *v.a.* classify.

Klassiker ['klasɪkər], *m.* (—s, *pl.* —) classic.

klassisch ['klasɪʃ], *adj.* classic(al), standard.

Klatsch [klatʃ], *m.* (—es, *no pl.*) gossip, scandal.

klatschen ['klatʃən], *v.n.* clap; gossip; (*rain*) patter; *Beifall* —, applaud.

Klatscherei [klatʃə'raɪ], *f.* (—, *pl.* —en) gossip, scandalmongering.

klauben ['klaubən], *v.a.* pick.

Klaue ['klauə], *f.* (—, *pl.* —n) claw, talon; paw.

klauen ['klauən], *v.a.* steal, (*coll.*) pinch.

Klauenseuche ['klauənzɔyçə], *f.* (—, *pl.* —n) *Maul und* —, foot and mouth disease.

Klause ['klauzə], *f.* (—, *pl.* —n) cell, hermitage; (*coll.*) den.

Klausel ['klauzəl], *f.* (—, *pl.* —n) clause, paragraph.

Klausner ['klausnər], *m.* (—s, *pl.* —) hermit, recluse, anchorite.

Klausur [klau'zu:r], *f.* (—, *pl.* —en) seclusion; written examination.

Klaviatur [klavja'tu:r], *f.* (—, *pl.* —en) keyboard.

Klavier [kla'vi:r], *n.* (—s, *pl.* —e) piano, pianoforte.

Klavierstück [kla'vi:rʃtyk], *n.* (—s, *pl.* —e) piece of piano music.

Klebemittel ['kle:bəmɪtəl], *n.* (—s, *pl.* —) adhesive, glue.

kleben ['kle:bən], *v.a.* paste, stick, glue. — *v.n.* stick, adhere.

klebrig ['kle:brɪç], *adj.* sticky; clammy.

Klebstoff ['kle:pʃtɔf], *m.* (—es, *no pl.*) gum; glue.

Klecks [klɛks], *m.* (—es, *pl.* —e) blot; blotch.

Kleckser ['klɛksər], *m.* (—s, *pl.* —) scrawler; (*painter*) dauber.

Klee [kle:], *m.* (—s, *no pl.*) (*Bot.*) clover, trefoil.

Kleid [klaɪt], *n.* (—es, *pl.* —er) frock, garment, dress, gown; (*Poet.*) garb; (*pl.*) clothes; — *er machen Leute*, clothes make the man.

Kleidchen ['klaɪtçən], *n.* (—s, *pl.* —) child's dress.

kleiden ['klaɪdən], *v.a.* dress, clothe.

Kleiderbügel

Kleiderbügel ['klaɪdərbyːgəl], *m.* (—s, *pl.* —) coat-hanger.

Kleiderpuppe ['klaɪdərpupə], *f.* (—, *pl.* —n) tailor's dummy.

Kleiderschrank ['klaɪdərʃraŋk], *m.* (—s, *pl.* ⁼e) wardrobe.

kleidsam ['klaɪtzaːm], *adj.* becoming; well-fitting, a good fit.

Kleidung ['klaɪduŋ], *f.* (—, *no pl.*) clothing, clothes, dress.

Kleie ['klaɪə], *f.* (—, *no pl.*) bran.

klein [klaɪn], *adj.* little, small; minute; petty; *ein — wenig,* a little bit.

Kleinasien [klaɪn'aːzjən], *n.* Asia Minor.

Kleinbahn ['klaɪnbaːn], *f.* (—, *pl.* —en) narrow-gauge railway.

kleinbürgerlich ['klaɪnbyrgərlɪç], *adj.* (petit) bourgeois.

Kleingeld ['klaɪngɛlt], *n.* (—(e)s, *no pl.*) small change.

kleingläubig ['klaɪnglɔybɪç], *adj.* faint-hearted.

Kleinhandel ['klaɪnhandəl], *m.* (—s, *no pl.*) retail-trade.

Kleinigkeit ['klaɪnɪçkaɪt], *f.* (—, *pl.* —en) trifle, small matter.

Kleinkram ['klaɪnkraːm], *m.* (—s, *no pl.*) trifles.

kleinlaut ['klaɪnlaut], *adj.* subdued, dejected, low-spirited.

kleinlich ['klaɪnlɪç], *adj.* petty; mean; narrow-minded; pedantic.

Kleinmut ['klaɪnmuːt], *m.* (—es, *no pl.*) faint-heartedness; dejection.

Kleinod ['klaɪnoːt], *n.* (—s, *pl.* —ien) jewel; trinket.

Kleinstadt ['klaɪnʃtat], *f.* (—, *pl.* ⁼e) small town.

Kleister ['klaɪstər], *m.* (—s, *no pl.*) paste.

Klemme ['klɛmə], *f.* (—, *pl.* —n) (*Tech.*) vice; clamp; (*fig.*) difficulty, straits; (*coll.*) fix, jam.

klemmen ['klɛmən], *v.a.* pinch, squeeze, jam.

Klemmer ['klɛmər], *m.* (—s, *pl.*—) (*eye*) glasses, pince-nez.

Klempner ['klɛmpnər], *m.* (—s, *pl.*—) tin-smith; plumber.

Klerus ['kleːrus], *m.* (—, *no pl.*) clergy.

Klette ['klɛtə], *f.* (—, *pl.* —n) burdock, bur(r); (*fig.*) hanger-on.

klettern ['klɛtərn], *v.n.* (*aux.* sein) climb, clamber.

Klima ['kliːma], *n.* (—s, *pl.* —s) climate.

Klimaanlage ['kliːmaːanlaːgə], *f.* (—, *pl.* —n) air conditioning plant.

Klimbim ['klɪmˈbɪm], *m.* (—s, *no pl.*) goings-on; festivity; fuss; *der ganze —,* the whole caboodle.

klimpern ['klɪmpərn], *v.n.* (*piano*) strum; (*money*) jingle.

Klinge ['klɪŋə], *f.* (—, *pl.* —n) blade.

Klingel ['klɪŋəl], *f.* (—, *pl.* —n) (*door, telephone*) bell.

Klingelbeutel ['klɪŋəlbɔytəl], *m.* (—s, *pl.*—) collecting-bag.

klingeln ['klɪŋəln], *v.n.* ring, tinkle.

Klingelzug ['klɪŋəltsuːk], *m.* . (—es, *pl.* ⁼e) bell-rope, bell-pull.

klingen ['klɪŋən], *v.n. irr.* sound; (*metals*) clang; (*ears*) tingle; *—de Münze,* hard cash, ready money.

Klinke ['klɪŋkə], *f.* (—, *pl.* —en) (*door*) handle, latch.

klipp [klɪp], *adv. — und klar,* as clear as daylight.

Klippe ['klɪpə], *f.* (—, *pl.* —n) cliff, crag, rock.

klirren ['klɪrən], *v.n.* clatter, rattle.

Klischee [kliˈʃeː], *n.* (—s, *pl.* —s) (*Typ.*) plate, printing-block; (*fig.*) cliché, hackneyed expression, tag.

Klistier [klɪˈstiːr], *n.* (—s, *pl.* —e) (*Med.*) enema.

Kloake [kloˈaːkə], *f.* (—, *pl.* —n) sewer, drain.

Kloben ['kloːbən], *m.* (—s, *pl.* —) log, block (of wood); pulley.

klopfen ['klɔpfən], *v.a., v.n.* knock, beat.

Klöppel ['klœpəl], *m.* (—s, *pl.* —) mallet; (*bell*) tongue, clapper; (*drum*) stick; (*lace*) bobbin.

klöppeln ['klœpəln], *v.a* make (bone) lace.

Klöppelspitze ['klœpəlʃpɪtsə], *f.* (—, *no pl.*) bone-lace.

Klops [klɔps], *m.* (—es, *pl.* —e) meat-dumpling.

Klosett [kloˈzɛt], *n.* (—s, *pl.* —e) lavatory, water-closet, toilet.

Kloß [kloːs], *m.* (—es, *pl.* ⁼e) dumpling.

Kloster ['kloːstər], *n.* (—s, *pl.* ⁼) cloister; monastery; convent.

Klostergang ['kloːstərgaŋ], *m.* (—es, *pl.* ⁼e) cloisters.

Klotz [klɔts], *m.* (—es, *pl.* ⁼e) block, trunk, stump; (*fig.*) *ein grober —,* a great lout.

klotzig ['klɔtsɪç], *adj.* cloddy; lumpish; (*sl.*) enormous.

Klub [klup], *m.* (—s, *pl.* —s) club.

Kluft [kluft], *f.* (—, *pl.* ⁼e) gap; gulf, chasm; (*fig.*) cleavage.

klug [kluːk], *adj.* clever, wise, prudent, judicious, sagacious; *ich kann daraus nicht — werden,* I cannot make head nor tail of it.

klügeln ['klyːgəln], *v.n.* ponder; quibble.

Klugheit ['kluːkhaɪt], *f.* (—, *no pl.*) cleverness, wisdom, prudence, judiciousness.

Klumpfuß ['klumpfuːs], *m.* (—es, *pl.* ⁼e) club-foot.

Klumpen ['klumpən], *m.* (—s, *pl.* —) lump, mass, clod; (*blood*) clot; (*metal*) ingot; (*gold*) nugget.

Klüngel ['klyŋəl], *m.* (—s, *pl.* —) clique, set.

knabbern ['knabərn], *v.n.* nibble.

Knabe ['knaːbə], *m.* (—n, *pl.* —n) boy.

Knäblein ['knɛːblaɪn], *n.* (—s, *pl.* —) (*Poet.*) baby boy, small boy.

knack [knak], *int.* crack! snap!

Knäckebrot ['knɛkəbroːt], *n.* (—es, *no pl.*) crispbread.

knacken ['knakən], *v.a.* crack.

Knackmandel [ˈknakmandəl], *f.* (—, *pl.* —n) shell-almond.

Knackwurst [ˈknakvurst], *f.* (—, *pl.* ⁓e) saveloy.

Knacks [knaks], *m.* (—es, *pl.* —e) crack.

knacksen [ˈknaksən], *v.n.* (*coll.*) crack.

Knall [knal], *m.* (—es, *pl.* —e) report, bang, detonation; — *und Fall*, quite suddenly, then and there.

Knallbüchse [ˈknalbyksə], *f.* (—, *pl.* —n) pop-gun.

Knalleffekt [ˈknalɛfɛkt], *m.* (—s, *pl.* —e) coup de théâtre; sensation.

knallen [ˈknalən], *v.n.* pop, explode, crack.

Knallgas [ˈknalgaːs], *n.* (—es, *no pl.*) oxyhydrogen gas.

knallrot [ˈknalroːt], *adj.* scarlet; glaring red.

knapp [knap], *adj.* tight; scarce, insufficient; (*style*) concise; (*majority*) narrow, bare.

Knappe [ˈknapə], *m.* (—n, *pl.* —n) esquire, shield-bearer; miner.

Knappheit [ˈknaphait], *f.* (—, *no pl.*) scarcity, shortage.

Knappschaft [ˈknapʃaft], *f.* (—, *pl.* —en) miners' association.

Knarre [ˈknarə], *f.* (—, *pl.* —n) rattle.

knarren [ˈknarən], *v.n.* rattle, creak.

Knaster [ˈknastər], *m.* (—s, *pl.* —) tobacco.

knattern [ˈknatərn], *v.n.* crackle.

Knäuel [ˈknɔyəl], *m.*, *n.* (—s, *pl.* —) skein, clew, ball.

Knauf [knauf], *m.* (—es, *pl.* ⁓e) (*stick*) knob, head; (*Archit.*) capital.

Knauser [ˈknauzər], *m.* (—s, *pl.* —) niggard, skinflint.

knausern [ˈknauzərn], *v.n.* be stingy, scrimp.

Knebel [ˈkneːbəl], *m.* (—s, *pl.* —) cudgel; gag.

knebeln [ˈkneːbəln], *v.a.* tie, bind; gag; (*fig.*) muzzle.

Knecht [knɛçt], *m.* (—es, *pl.* —e) servant, farm hand, menial; vassal, slave.

Knechtschaft [ˈknɛçtʃaft], *f.* (—, *no pl.*) servitude, slavery.

kneifen [ˈknaifən], *v.a. irr.* pinch. — *v.n.* (*fig. coll.*) back out (of), shirk.

Kneifer [ˈknaifər], *m.* (—s, *pl.* —) pince-nez.

Kneifzange [ˈknaiftsaŋə], *f.* (—, *pl.* —n) pincers.

Kneipe [ˈknaipə], *f.* (—, *pl.* —n) pub; saloon.

kneten [ˈkneːtən], *v.a.* knead; massage.

knick(e)beinig [ˈknɪk(ə)bainɪç], *adj.* knock-kneed.

knicken [ˈknɪkən], *v.a.* crack, break.

Knicks [knɪks], *m.* (—es, *pl.* —e) curtsy.

knicksen [ˈknɪksən], *v.n.* curtsy.

Knie [kniː], *n.* (—s, *pl.* —) knee; *etwas übers — brechen*, make short work of.

Kniekehle [ˈkniːkeːlə], *f.* (—, *pl.* —n) hollow of the knee.

knien [ˈkniːən], *v.n.* kneel.

Kniescheibe [ˈkniːʃaibə], *f.* (—, *pl.* —n) knee-cap.

Kniff [knɪf], *m.* (—es, *pl.* —e) fold; (*fig.*) trick, knack, dodge.

knipsen [ˈknɪpsən], *v.a.* (*tickets*) clip, punch; (*Phot.*) take a snap of.

Knirps [knɪrps], *m.* (—es, *pl.* —e) pigmy; (*fig.*) urchin.

knirschen [ˈknɪrʃən], *v.n.* crunch, grate, gnash (teeth).

knistern [ˈknɪstərn], *v.n.* crackle.

knittern [ˈknɪtərn], *v.a.* rumple, wrinkle, crinkle, crease.

Knobel [ˈknoːbəl], *m. pl.* dice.

Knoblauch [ˈknoːblaux], *m.* (—s, *no pl.*) (*Bot.*) garlic.

Knöchel [ˈknœçəl], *m.* (—s, *pl.* —) knuckle, joint; ankle.

Knochen [ˈknɔxən], *m.* (—s, *pl.* —) bone.

Knochengerüst [ˈknɔxəngəryst], *n.* (—es, *pl.* —e) skeleton.

knöchern [ˈknœçərn], *adj.* made of bone.

knochig [ˈknɔxɪç], *adj.* bony.

Knödel [ˈknøːdəl], *m.* (—s, *pl.* —) dumpling.

Knollen [ˈknɔlən], *m.* (—s, *pl.* —) lump, clod; (*Bot.*) tuber, bulb.

knollig [ˈknɔlɪç], *adj.* knobby, bulbous.

Knopf [knɔpf], *m.* (—es, *pl.* ⁓e) button; stud; (*stick*) head, knob.

knöpfen [ˈknœpfən], *v.a.* button.

Knorpel [ˈknɔrpəl], *m.* (—s, *pl.* —) gristle, cartilage.

knorplig [ˈknɔrplɪç], *adj.* gristly.

knorrig [ˈknɔrɪç], *adj.* knotty, gnarled.

Knospe [ˈknɔspə], *f.* (—, *pl.* —n) bud.

Knote [ˈknoːtə], *m.* (—n, *pl.* —n) (*fig.*) bounder; lout.

Knoten [ˈknoːtən], *m.* (—s, *pl.* —) knot; (*fig.*) difficulty; (*Theat.*) plot.

Knotenpunkt [ˈknoːtənpuŋkt], *m.* (—es, *pl.* —e) (*Railw.*) junction.

Knotenstock [ˈknoːtənʃtɔk], *m.* (—es, *pl.* ⁓e) knotty stick.

knotig [ˈknoːtɪç], *adj.* knotty, nodular.

knüllen [ˈknylən], *v.a.* crumple.

knüpfen [ˈknypfən], *v.a.* tie; knot; form (a friendship etc.).

Knüppel [ˈknypəl], *m.* (—s, *pl.* —) cudgel.

knurren [ˈknurən], *v.n.* grunt, snarl; (*fig.*) growl, grumble.

knurrig [ˈknurɪç], *adj.* surly, grumpy.

knusprig [ˈknusprɪç], *adj.* crisp, crunchy.

Knute [ˈknuːtə], *f.* (—, *pl.* —n) knout.

knutschen [ˈknuːtʃən], *v.r. sich —*, (*coll.*) cuddle; (*Am.*) neck.

Knüttel [ˈknytəl], *m.* (—s, *pl.* —) cudgel, bludgeon.

Knüttelvers [ˈknytəlfɛrs], *m.* (—es, *pl.* —e) doggerel, rhyme.

Kobalt [ˈkoːbalt], *m.* (—s, *no pl.*) cobalt.

Kobaltblau [ˈkoːbaltblau], *n.* (—s, *no pl.*) smalt.

Koben ['ko:bən], *m.* (—s, *pl.* —) pig-sty.

Kober ['ko:bər], *m.* (—s, *pl.* —) (*dial.*) basket, hamper.

Kobold ['ko:bɔlt], *m.* (—(e)s, *pl.* —e) goblin, hobgoblin.

Koch [kɔx], *m.* (—es, *pl.* ⁓e) cook, chef.

kochen ['kɔxən], *v.a.* cook, boil. — *v.n.* boil; (*fig.*) seethe.

Kocher ['kɔxər], *m.* (—s, *pl.* —) boiler.

Köcher ['kœçər], *m.* (—s, *pl.* —) quiver.

Köchin ['kœçɪn], *f.* (—, *pl.* —innen) (female) cook.

Kochsalz ['kɔxzalts], *n.* (—es, *no pl.*) common salt.

Köder ['kø:dər], *m.* (—s, *no pl.*) bait, lure; (*fig.*) decoy.

ködern ['kø:dərn], *v.a.* bait; (*fig.*) decoy.

Kodex ['ko:dɛks], *m.* (—es, *pl.* —e) codex; old MS.; (*Law*) code.

kodifizieren [ko:difi'tsi:rən], *v.a.* codify.

Koffein [kɔfɔ'i:n], *n.* (—s, *no pl.*) caffeine.

Koffer ['kɔfər], *m.* (—s, *pl.* —) box, trunk, suitcase, portmanteau.

Kofferradio ['kɔfərra:djo], *n.* (—s, *pl.* —s) portable radio.

Kofferraum ['kɔfərraum], *m.* (—s, *no pl.*) (*Motor.*) boot, (*Am.*) trunk.

Kohl [ko:l], *m.* (—s, *no pl.*) (*Bot.*) cabbage; (*fig.*) nonsense, rot.

Kohle ['ko:lə], *f.* (—, *pl.* —n) coal.

Kohlenflöz ['ko:lənflø:ts], *n.* (—es, *pl.* —e) coal-seam.

Kohlenoxyd ['ko:lənɔksy:t], *n.* (—s, *no pl.*) carbon monoxide.

Kohlensäure ['ko:lənzɔyrə], *f.* (—, *no pl.*) carbonic acid.

Kohlenstift ['ko:lənʃtɪft], *m.* (—es, *pl.* —e) charcoal-crayon.

Köhler ['kø:lər], *m.* (—s, *pl.* —) charcoal-burner.

Koje ['ko:jə], *f.* (—, *pl.* —n) (*Naut.*) berth, bunk.

Kokarde [ko'kardə], *f.* (—, *pl.* —n) cockade.

kokett [ko'kɛt], *adj.* coquettish.

Kokette [ko'kɛtə], *f.* (—, *pl.* —n) coquette, flirt.

kokettieren [kokɛ'ti:rən], *v.n.* flirt.

Kokon [ko'kõ], *m.* (—s, *pl.* —s) cocoon.

Kokosnuß ['ko:kɔsnus], *f.* (—, *pl.* ⁓sse) (*Bot.*) coconut.

Koks [ko:ks], *m.* (—es, *no pl.*) coke.

Kolben ['kɔlbən], *m.* (—s, *pl.* —) club; (*rifle*) butt-end; (*engine*) piston; (*Chem.*) retort.

Kolbenstange ['kɔlbənʃtaŋə], *f.* (—, *pl.* —n) piston-rod.

Kolibri ['ko:libri:], *m.* (—s, *pl.* —s) (*Orn.*) humming-bird.

Kolkrabe ['kɔlkra:bə], *m.* (—n, *pl.* —n) (*Orn.*) raven.

Kolleg [kɔ'le:k], *n.* (—s, *pl.* —ien) course of lectures; lecture.

Kollege [kɔ'le:gə], *m.* (—n, *pl.* —n) colleague.

Kollekte [kɔ'lɛktə], *f.* (—, *pl.* —n) collection; (*Eccl.*) collect.

Koller ['kɔlər], *m.* (—s, *no pl.*) frenzy, rage.

kollidieren [kɔli'di:rən], *v.n.* collide.

Köln [kœln], *n.* Cologne.

kölnisch ['kœlnɪʃ], *adj.* of Cologne; —*Wasser*, eau de Cologne.

kolonisieren [koloni'zi:rən], *v.a.* colonise.

Kolonnade [kolo'na:də], *f.* (— *pl.* —n) colonnade.

Koloratur [kolora'tu:r], *f.* (—, *pl.* —n) coloratura.

kolorieren [kolo'ri:rən], *v.a.* colour.

Koloß [ko'lɔs], *m.* (—sses, *pl.* —sse) colossus.

Kolportage [kɔlpɔr'ta:ʒə], *f.* (—, *pl.* —n) colportage, door-to-door sale of books; sensationalism.

Kolportageroman [kɔlpɔr'ta:ʒəroma:n], *m.* (—s, *pl.* —e) penny dreadful, shocker.

kolportieren [kɔlpɔr'ti:rən], *v.a.* hawk; spread, disseminate.

Kombinationsgabe [kɔmbina'tsjo:nsga:bə], *f.* (—, *pl.* —en) power of deduction.

kombinieren [kɔmbi'ni:rən], *v.a.* combine; deduce.

Kombüse [kɔm'by:zə], *f.* (— *pl.* —n) galley, caboose.

Komik ['ko:mɪk], *f.* (—, *no pl.*) comicality; humour; funny side.

Komiker ['ko:mɪkər], *m.* (—s, *pl.* —) comedian.

komisch ['ko:mɪʃ], *adj.* comical, funny; peculiar, strange, odd.

Kommandantur [kɔmandan'tu:r], *f.* (—, *pl.* —en) commander's office; garrison headquarters.

kommandieren [kɔman'di:rən], *v.a.* command.

Kommanditgesellschaft [kɔman'di:tgəzɛlʃaft], *f.* (—, *pl.* —en) limited partnership.

Kommando [kɔ'mando], *n.* (—s, *pl.* —s) command.

kommen ['kɔmən], *v.n. irr.* (*aux.* sein) come, arrive; come about; *um etwas* —, lose s.th.; *zu etwas* —, come by s.th.; *zu sich* —, come to, regain consciousness.

Kommentar [kɔmɛn'ta:r], *m.* (—s, *pl.* —e) comment, commentary.

Kommers [kɔ'mɛrs], *m.* (—es, *pl.* —e) students' festivity; drinking party.

Kommersbuch [kɔ'mɛrsbu:x], *n.* (—es, *pl.* ⁓er) students' song-book.

kommerziell [kɔmɛrts'jɛl], *adj.* commercial.

Kommerzienrat [kɔ'mɛrtsjənra:t], *m.* (—s, *pl.* ⁓e) Councillor to the Chamber of Commerce.

Kommilitone [kɔmili'to:nə], *m.* (—n, *pl.* —n) fellow-student.

Kommis [kɔ'mi:], *m.* (—, *pl.* —) clerk.

Kommiß [kɔ'mɪs], *m.* (—sses, *pl.* —) military fatigue-dress; (*fig.*) military service.

Kommißbrot [kɔ'mɪsbroːt], n. (**—es**, no pl.) (coarse) army bread.

Kommissar [kɔmɪ'saːr], m. (**—s**, pl. —e) commissioner.

Kommissariat [kɔmɪsar'jaːt], n. (**—s**, pl. —e) commissioner's office.

Kommission [kɔmɪs'joːn], f. (**—**, pl. —en) commission, mission, committee.

kommod [kɔ'moːd], adj. (coll.) snug, comfortable.

Kommode [kɔ'moːdə], f. (**—**, pl. —n) chest of drawers.

Kommune [kɔ'muːnə], f. (**—**, pl. —n) (coll.) Communist Party; Reds.

Kommunismus [kɔmu'nɪsmus], m. (**—**, no pl.) Communism.

kommunistisch [kɔmu'nɪstɪʃ], adj. Communist.

Komödiant [kɔmød'jant], m. (**—en**, pl. —en) comedian, player; humbug.

Komödie [kɔ'møːdjə], f. (**—**, pl. —n) comedy, play; make-believe; — spielen, (fig.) sham, pretend, play-act.

Kompagnon ['kɔmpanjɔ̃], m. (**—s**, pl. —s) partner, associate.

Kompanie [kɔmpa'niː], f. (**—**, pl. —n) (Mil.) company; (Comm.) partnership, company.

Kompaß ['kɔmpas], m. (**—sses**, pl. —sse) compass.

Kompaßrose ['kɔmpasroːzə], f. (**—**, pl. —n) compass-card.

kompensieren [kɔmpɛn'ziːrən], v.a. compensate.

komplementär [kɔmpləmɛn'tɛːr], adj. complementary.

komplett [kɔm'plɛt], adj. complete.

komplimentieren [kɔmplimɛn'tiːrən], v.a. compliment, flatter.

Komplize [kɔm'pliːtsə], m. (**—n**, pl. —n) accomplice.

kompliziert [kɔmpli'tsiːrt], adj. complicated.

Komplott [kɔm'plɔt], n. (**—s**, pl. —e) plot, conspiracy.

Komponente [kɔmpo'nɛntə], f. (**—**, pl. —n) component part; constituent.

komponieren [kɔmpo'niːrən], v.a. compose, set to music.

Komponist [kɔmpo'nɪst], m. (**—en**, pl. —en) composer.

Kompositum [kɔm'poːzitum], n. (**—s**, pl. —ta) (Gram.) compound word.

Kompott [kɔm'pɔt], n. (**—s**, pl. —e) stewed fruit, compote; sweet, dessert.

Kompresse [kɔm'prɛsə], f. (**—**, pl. —n) compress.

komprimieren [kɔmpri'miːrən], v.a. compress.

Kompromiß [kɔmpro'mɪs], m. (**—sses**, pl. —sse) compromise, settlement.

kompromittieren [kɔmprɔmɪ'tiːrən], v.a. compromise. — v.r. sich —, compromise o.s.

kondensieren [kɔndɛn'ziːrən], v.a. condense.

Konditor [kɔn'diːtɔr], m. (**—s**, pl. —en) confectioner, pastry-cook.

Konditorei [kɔnditɔ'raɪ], f. (**—**, pl. —en) confectioner's shop, pastry-shop; café.

kondolieren [kɔndo'liːrən], v.n. condole with s.o.

Kondukteur [kɔnduk'tøːr], m. (**—s**, pl. —e) (Swiss & Austr. dial.) guard (on train), conductor (on tram or bus).

Konfekt [kɔn'fɛkt], n. (**—s**, pl. —e) chocolates; (Am.) candy.

Konfektion [kɔnfɛk'tsjoːn], f. (**—**, no pl.) ready-made clothes; outfitting.

Konfektionär [kɔnfɛktsjo'nɛːr], m. (**—s**, pl. —e) outfitter.

Konferenz [kɔnfe'rɛnts], f. (**—**, pl. —en) conference.

konfessionell [kɔnfɛsjo'nɛl], adj. denominational, confessional.

Konfirmand [kɔnfɪr'mant], m. (**—en**, pl. —en) confirmation candidate.

konfirmieren [kɔnfɪr'miːrən], v.a. (Eccl.) confirm.

konfiszieren [kɔnfɪs'tsiːrən], v.a. confiscate.

Konfitüren [kɔnfi'tyːrən], f. pl. confectionery, candied fruit, preserves.

konform [kɔn'fɔrm], adj. in comformity (with).

konfus [kɔn'fuːs], adj. confused, puzzled, disconcerted.

Kongo ['kɔŋgo], m. Congo.

Kongruenz [kɔŋgru'ɛnts], f. (**—**, no pl.) congruity.

König ['køːnɪç], m. (**—s**, pl. —e) king.

Königin ['køːnɪgɪn], f. (**—**, pl. —nen) queen.

königlich ['køːnɪglɪç], adj. royal, regal, kingly, king-like.

Königreich ['køːnɪçraɪç], n. (**—(e)s**, pl. —e) kingdom.

Königsadler ['køːnɪçsaːdlər], m. (**—s**, pl. —) golden eagle.

Königsschlange ['køːnɪçsʃlaŋə], f. (**—**, pl. —n) (Zool.) boa constrictor.

Königstiger ['køːnɪçstiːgər], m. (**—s**, pl. —) (Zool.) Bengal tiger.

Königtum ['køːnɪçtuːm], n. (**—s**, no pl.) kingship.

Konjunktur [kɔnjuŋk'tuːr], f. (**—**, pl. —en) state of the market, (coll.) boom.

Konkordat [kɔnkɔr'daːt], n. (**—s**, pl. —e) concordat.

konkret [kɔn'kreːt], adj. concrete.

Konkurrent [kɔnku'rɛnt], m. (**—en**, pl. —en) competitor, (business) rival.

Konkurrenz [kɔnku'rɛnts], f. (**—**, no pl.) competition.

konkurrieren [kɔnku'riːrən], v.n. compete.

Konkurs [kɔn'kurs], m. (**—es**, pl. —e) bankruptcy.

Konkursmasse [kɔn'kursmasə], f. (**—**, pl. —n) bankrupt's estate, bankrupt's stock.

Können ['kœnən], n. (**—s**, no pl.) ability; knowledge.

können [kœnən], v.a., v.n. irr. be able to, be capable of; understand; ich kann, I can; er kann Englisch, he speaks English.

127

konsequent [kɔnze'kvɛnt], *adj.* consistent.

Konsequenz [kɔnze'kvɛnts], *f.* (—, *pl.* —en) (*characteristic*) consistency; (*result*) consequence.

Konservatorium [kɔnzɛrva'to:rjum], *n.* (—s, *pl.* —rien) (*Mus.*) conservatoire, conservatorium.

Konserve [kɔn'zɛrvə], *f.* (—, *pl.* —n) preserve; tinned, *or* (*Am.*) canned food.

konservieren [kɔnzɛr'vi:rən], *v.a.* preserve.

Konsistorium [kɔnzɪs'to:rjum], *n.* (—s, *pl.* —rien) (*Eccl.*) consistory.

Konsole [kɔn'zo:lə], *f.* (—, *pl.* —n) bracket.

konsolidieren [kɔnzoli'di:rən], *v.a.* consolidate.

Konsonant [kɔnzo'nant], *m.* (—en, *pl.* —en) (*Phonet.*) consonant.

Konsorte [kɔn'zɔrtə], *m.* (—n, *pl.* —n) associate, accomplice.

Konsortium [kɔn'zɔrtsjum], *n.* (—s, *pl.* —tien) syndicate.

konstatieren [kɔnsta'ti:rən], *v.a.* state, note, assert.

konsternieren [kɔnstɛr'ni:rən], *v.a.* dismay, disconcert.

konstituieren [kɔnstitu'i:rən], *v.a.* constitute.

konstitutionell [kɔnstitutsjo'nɛl], *adj.* constitutional.

konstruieren [kɔnstru'i:rən], *v.a.* construct; (*Gram.*) construe.

konsularisch [kɔnzu'la:rɪʃ], *adj.* consular.

Konsulat [kɔnzu'la:t], *n.* (—s, *pl.* —e) consulate.

Konsulent [kɔnzu'lɛnt], *m.* (—en, *pl.* —en) (*Law*) counsel; consultant.

konsultieren [kɔnzul'ti:rən], *v.a.* consult.

Konsum [kɔn'zu:m], *m.* (—s, *no pl.*) (*Econ.*) consumption.

Konsumverein [kɔn'zu:mfɛraɪn], *m.* (—s, *pl.* —e) cooperative society.

konsumieren [kɔnzu'mi:rən], *v.a.* consume.

Konterbande [kɔntər'bandə], *f.* (—, *no pl.*) contraband.

Konterfei [kɔntər'faɪ], *n.* (—s, *pl.* —e) (*obs.*) portrait, likeness.

Kontertanz [kɔn'tərtants], *m.* (—es, *pl.* ⁻e) square dance, quadrille.

kontinuierlich [kɔntinu'i:rlɪç], *adj.* continuous.

Kontinuität [kɔntinui'tɛ:t], *f.* (—, *no pl.*) continuity.

Konto ['kɔnto], *n.* (—s, *pl.* —ten) (*bank*) account; à —, on account.

Kontokorrent [kɔntoko'rɛnt], *n.* (—s, *pl.* —e) current account.

Kontor [kɔn'to:r], *n.* (—s, *pl.* —e) (*obs.*) office.

Kontorist [kɔnto'rɪst], *m.* (—en, *pl.* —en) clerk.

Kontrabaß ['kɔntrabas], *m.* (—sses, *pl.* ⁻sse) double-bass.

Kontrapunkt ['kɔntrapuŋkt], *m.* (—es, *pl.* —e) (*Mus.*) counterpoint.

kontrastieren [kɔntras'ti:rən], *v.a., v.n.* contrast.

kontrollieren [kɔntro'li:rən], *v.a.* check, verify.

Kontroverse [kɔntro'vɛrzə], *f.* (—, *pl.* —n) controversy.

Kontur [kɔn'tu:r], *f.* (—, *pl.* —en) outline, (*pl.*) contours.

Konvent [kɔn'vɛnt], *m.* (—s, *pl.* —e) convention, assembly, congress.

konventionell [kɔnvɛntsjo'nɛl], *adj.* conventional, formal.

Konversationslexikon [kɔnvɛrza-'tsjo:nslɛksɪkɔn], *n.* (—s, *pl.* —s) encyclopaedia.

konvertieren [kɔnvɛr'ti:rən], *v.a., v.n.* convert.

Konvertit [kɔnvɛr'tɪt], *m.* (—en, *pl.* —en) convert.

Konvolut [kɔnvo'lu:t], *n.* (—s, *pl.* —e) bundle; scroll.

konvulsivisch [kɔnvul'zi:vɪʃ], *adj.* convulsive.

konzentrieren [kɔntsɛn'tri:rən], *v.a., v.r.* concentrate; *auf etwas* —, centre upon.

konzentrisch [kɔn'tsɛntrɪʃ], *adj.* concentric.

Konzept [kɔn'tsɛpt], *n.* (—es, *pl.* —e) rough draft, sketch; *aus dem bringen*, unsettle, disconcert.

Konzeptpapier [kɔn'tsɛptpapi:r], *n.* (—s, *no pl.*) scribbling paper.

Konzern [kɔn'tsɛrn], *m.* (—s, *pl.* —e) (*Comm.*) combine.

Konzert [kɔn'tsɛrt], *n.* (—es, *pl.* —e) concert, (musical) recital.

Konzertflügel [kɔn'tsɛrtfly:gəl], *m.* (—s, *pl.* —) grand piano.

konzertieren [kɔntsɛr'ti:rən], *v.n.* give recitals; play in a concert.

Konzertmeister [kɔn'tsɛrtmaɪstər], *m.* (—s, *pl.* —) impresario.

Konzession [kɔntsɛ'sjo:n], *f.* (—, *pl.* —en) concession, licence.

konzessionieren [kɔntsɛsjo'ni:rən], *v.a.* license.

Konzil [kɔn'tsi:l], *n.* (—s, *pl.* —ien) (*Eccl.*) council.

konzipieren [kɔntsi'pi:rən], *v.a.* draft, plan.

Koordinierung [ko:ɔrdi'ni:ruŋ], *f.* (—, *pl.* —en) co-ordination.

Kopf [kɔpf], *m.* (—es, *pl.* ⁻e) head; top; heading; (*fig.*) mind, brains, judgment; *aus dem* —, by heart.

köpfen ['kœpfən], *v.a.* behead, decapitate; (*Bot.*) lop.

Kopfhaut ['kɔpfhaut], *f.* (—, *no pl.*) scalp.

Kopfhörer ['kɔpfhø:rər], *m.* (—s, *pl.* —) headphone, receiver.

Kopfkissen ['kɔpfkɪsən], *n.* (—s, *pl.* —) pillow.

Kopfsalat ['kɔpfzala:t], *m.* (—s, *pl.* —e) (garden) lettuce.

kopfscheu ['kɔpfʃɔy], *adj.* afraid; alarmed, timid; — *machen*, scare; — *werden*, take fright, jib.

Kopfschmerz ['kɔpfʃmɛrts], m. (—es, pl. —en) (mostly pl.) headache.

Kopfsprung ['kɔpfʃpruŋ], m. (—s, pl. ⁻e) (diving) header.

kopfüber [kɔpf'y:bər], adv. head over heels; headlong.

Kopfweh ['kɔpfve:], n. (—s, no pl.) headache.

Kopfzerbrechen ['kɔpftsɛrbrɛçən], n. (—s, no pl.) racking o.'s brains.

Kopie [ko'pi:] f. (—, pl. —n) copy, duplicate.

kopieren [ko'pi:rən], v.a. copy, ape, mimic, take off.

Koppe ['kɔpə], f. see **Kuppe**.

Koppel ['kɔpəl], f. (—, pl. —n) (dogs) couple, leash; (ground) enclosure, paddock.

koppeln ['kɔpəln], v.a. couple, leash.

kopulieren [kopu'li:rən], v.a. (obs.) marry; pair; (Hort.) graft.

Koralle [ko'ralə], f. (—, pl. —n) coral.

Korallenriff [ko'ralənrif], n. (—es, pl. —e) coral-reef.

Korb [kɔrp], m. (—s, pl. ⁻e) basket, hamper; einen — geben, turn s.o. down, refuse an offer of marriage.

Korbweide ['kɔrpvaidə], f. (—, pl. —n) (Bot.) osier.

Kord [kɔrt], m. (—s, no pl.) corduroy.

Kordel ['kɔrdəl], f. (—, pl. —n) cord, twine, thread.

Korea [ko're:a], n. Korea.

Korinthe [ko'rintə], f. (—, pl. —n) (Bot.) currant.

Korken ['kɔrkən], m. (—s, pl. —) cork, stopper.

Korkenzieher ['kɔrkəntsi:ər], m. (—s, pl. —) cork-screw.

Korn [kɔrn], n. (—s, pl. —e, ⁻er) (Bot.) corn, grain, cereal, rye; (gun) sight, aufs — nehmen, take aim at.

Kornblume ['kɔrnblu:mə], f. (—, pl. —n) (Bot.) corn-flower.

Kornbranntwein ['kɔrnbrantvain], m. (—s, no pl.) corn-brandy, whisky.

Kornett [kɔr'nɛt], m. (—s, pl. —e) (Mil., Mus.) cornet.

körnig ['kœrniç], adj. granular, granulous; grained.

Kornrade ['kɔrnra:də], f. (—, pl. —n) (Bot.) corn-cockle.

Kornspeicher ['kɔrnʃpaiçər], m. (—s, pl. —) granary, corn-loft.

Körper ['kœrpər], m. (—s, pl. —) body; (Phys.) solid.

Körperbau ['kœrpərbau], m. (—s, no pl.) build, frame.

Köpergeruch ['kœrpərgəru:x], m. (—s, no pl.) body odour.

körperlich ['kœrpərliç], adj. bodily, physical; —e Züchtigung, corporal punishment.

Körpermaß ['kœrpərma:s], n. (—es, pl. —e) cubic measure.

Körperschaft ['kœrpərʃaft], f. (—, pl. —en) corporation.

Korps [ko:r], n. (—, pl. —) (Mil.) corps; students' corporation.

Korrektheit [kɔ'rɛkthait], f. (—, no pl.) correctness.

Korrektionsanstalt [kɔrɛk'tsjo:nsan-ʃtalt], f. (—, pl. —en) penitentiary, Borstal institution.

Korrektor [kɔ'rɛktər], m. (—s, pl. —en) proof-reader.

Korrektur [kɔrɛk'tu:r], f. (—, pl. —en) correction; proof-correction; revision.

Korrekturbogen [kɔrɛk'tu:rbo:gən], m. (—s, pl.—) (Typ.) proof-sheet, galley.

Korrespondenzkarte [kɔrɛspɔn'dɛnts-kartə], f. (—, pl. —n) post-card.

korrigieren [kɔri'gi:rən], v.a. correct, revise; read (proofs).

Korsett [kɔr'zɛt], n. (—s,· pl. —s) corset, bodice, stays.

Koryphäe [kɔri'fɛ:ə], m. (—n, pl. —n) celebrity, authority, master mind.

Koseform ['ko:zəfɔrm], f. (—, pl. —en) term of endearment, pet-name, diminutive.

kosen ['ko:zən], v.a., v.n. caress, fondle; make love (to).

Kosinus ['ko:zinus], m. (—, pl. —) (Maths.) cosine.

Kosmetik [kɔs'me:tik], f. (—, no pl.) cosmetics.

kosmetisch [kɔs'me:tiʃ], adj. cosmetic.

kosmisch ['kɔzmiʃ], adj. cosmic.

Kosmopolit [kɔsmopo'li:t], m. (—en, pl. —en) cosmopolitan.

kosmopolitisch [kɔsmopo'li:tiʃ], adj. cosmopolitan.

Kost [kɔst], f. (—, no pl.) food, fare; board.

Kostarika [kɔsta'rika], n. Costa Rica.

kostbar ['kɔstba:r], adj. valuable, precious, costly.

Kostbarkeit ['kɔstba:rkait], f. (—, pl. —en) costliness, preciousness; (pl.) (goods) valuables.

Kosten ['kɔstən], pl. cost(s), expenses, charges; (Law) costs.

kosten ['kɔstən], v.a. taste; (money) cost; take, require; was kostet das? how much is this?

Kosten(vor)anschlag ['kɔstən(for)an-ʃla:k], m. (—s, pl. ⁻e) estimate.

Kostenaufwand ['kɔstənaufvant], m. (—s, pl. ⁻e) expenditure.

Kostenersatz ['kɔstənɛrzats], m. (—es, no pl.) refund of expenses, compensation.

kostenfrei ['kɔstənfrai], adj. free (of charge), gratis.

kostenlos ['kɔstənlo:s], see **kostenfrei**.

Kostgänger ['kɔstgɛŋər], m. (—s, pl. —) boarder.

Kostgeld ['kɔstgɛlt], n. (—es, no pl.) maintenance or board allowance.

köstlich ['kœstliç], adj. excellent, precious; delicious; ein — er Witz, a capital joke.

kostspielig ['kɔstʃpi:liç], adj. expensive, costly.

Kostüm [kɔ'sty:m], n. (—s, pl. —e) costume, fancy dress.

Kostümfest [kɔ'sty:mfɛst], n. (—s, pl. —e) fancy-dress ball.

kostümieren [kɔsty'miːrən], *v.a.* dress up.

Kot [koːt], *m.* (—es, *no pl.*) mud, dirt; filth, mire; excrement.

Kotelett [kɔt'lɛt], *n.* (—s, *pl.* —s) cutlet.

Köter ['køːtər], *m.* (—s, *pl.* —) cur, mongrel.

Koterie [koːtə'riː], *f.* (—, *pl.* —n) clique, set, coterie.

Kotflügel ['koːtflyːgəl], *m.* (—s, *pl.* —) (*Motor.*) mudguard.

kotig ['koːtɪç], *adj.* dirty, miry.

kotzen ['kɔtsən], *v.n.* (*vulg.*) vomit.

Koweit ['kɔvaɪt], *n.* Kuwait.

Krabbe ['krabə], *f.* (—, *pl.* —n) (*Zool.*) crab; shrimp; (*fig.*) brat, imp.

krabbeln ['krabəln], *v.n.* crawl.

Krach [krax], *m.* (—es, *pl.* —e) crack, crash; din, noise; (*Comm.*) slump; quarrel, row.

krachen ['kraxən], *v.n.* crack, crash.

krächzen ['krɛçtsən], *v.n.* croak.

Kraft [kraft], *f.* (—, *pl.* ̈e) strength, vigour; force; power, energy; intensity; *in — treten*, come into force.

kraft [kraft], *prep.* (*Genit.*) by virtue of, by authority of, on the strength of.

Kraftausdruck ['kraftausdruk], *m.* (—s, *pl.* ̈e) forcible expression; expletive.

Kraftbrühe ['kraftbryːə], *f.* (—, *pl.* —n) meat-soup, beef-tea.

Kraftfahrer ['kraftfaːrər], *m.* (—s, *pl.* —) motorist.

kräftig ['krɛftɪç], *adj.* strong, powerful, vigorous, energetic; (*food*) nourishing.

Kraftlehre ['kraftleːrə], *f.* (—, *no pl.*) dynamics.

kraftlos ['kraftloːs], *adj.* weak, feeble.

Kraftwagen ['kraftvaːgən], *m.* (—s, *pl.* —) motor car, automobile, car, lorry, truck.

Kragen ['kraːgən], *m.* (—s, *pl.* —) collar; *es geht mir an den —*, it will cost me dearly.

Krähe ['krɛːə], *f.* (—, *pl.* —n) (*Orn.*) crow.

krähen ['krɛːən], *v.n.* crow.

Krähenfüße ['krɛːənfyːsə], *m. pl.* crow's feet (wrinkles).

Krakau ['kraːkau], *n.* Cracow.

krakeelen [kra'keːlən], *v.n.* (*coll.*) kick up a row.

Kralle ['kralə], *f.* (—, *pl.* —n) claw, talon.

Kram [kraːm], *m.* (—s, *no pl.*) small wares (trade); stuff, rubbish, litter; *es paßt mir nicht in den —*, it does not suit my purpose.

kramen ['kraːmən], *v.n.* rummage.

Krämer ['krɛːmər], *m.* (—s, *pl.* —) retailer, general dealer, shopkeeper.

Kramladen ['kraːmlaːdən], *m.* (—s, *pl.* ̈) small retail-shop, general shop *or* store.

Krampe ['krampə], *f.* (—, *pl.* —n) staple.

Krampf [krampf], *m.* (—es, *pl.* ̈) cramp, spasm, convulsion.

Krampfader ['krampfaːdər], *f.* (—, *pl.* —n) varicose vein.

krampfartig ['krampfaːrtɪç], *adj.* spasmodic.

krampfhaft ['krampfhaft], *adj.* convulsive.

Kran [kraːn], *m.* (—s, *pl.* ̈e) (*Engin.*) crane.

Kranich ['kraːnɪç], *m.* (—s, *pl.* —e) (*Orn.*) crane.

krank [kraŋk], *adj.* sick, ill.

kränkeln ['krɛŋkəln], *v.n.* be ailing, be in poor health.

kranken ['kraŋkən], *v.n. an etwas —*, suffer from s.th., be afflicted with s.th.

kränken ['krɛŋkən], *v.a.* vex, grieve; offend, insult.

Krankenbahre ['kraŋkənbaːrə], *f.* (—, *pl.* —n) stretcher.

Krankenhaus ['kraŋkənhaus], *n.* (—es, *pl.* ̈er) hospital.

Krankenkasse ['kraŋkənkasə], *f.* (—, *pl.* —n) sick-fund; health insurance.

Krankenkost ['kraŋkənkɔst], *f.* (—, *no pl.*) invalid diet.

Krankenschwester ['kraŋkənʃvɛstər], *f.* (—, *pl.* —n) nurse.

Krankenstuhl ['kraŋkənʃtuːl], *m.* (—s, *pl.* ̈e) invalid chair.

Krankenversicherung ['kraŋkənfɛrziçəruŋ], *f.* (—, *pl.* —en) health insurance.

Krankenwärter ['kraŋkənvɛrtər], *m.* (—s, *pl.* —) attendant, male nurse.

krankhaft ['kraŋkhaft], *adj.* morbid.

Krankheit ['kraŋkhaɪt], *f.* (—, *pl.* —en) illness, sickness, disease, malady; complaint; *englische —*, rickets.

Krankheitserscheinung ['kraŋkhaɪtsɛrʃaɪnuŋ], *f.* (—, *pl.* —en) symptom.

kränklich ['krɛŋklɪç], *adj.* sickly, infirm, in poor health.

Kränkung ['krɛŋkuŋ], *f.* (—, *pl.* —en) grievance, annoyance; offence, insult.

Kranz [krants], *m.* (—es, *pl.* ̈e) wreath, garland.

Kränzchen ['krɛntsçən], *n.* (—s, *pl.* —) little garland; (*fig.*) (ladies') weekly tea party; circle, club.

kränzen ['krɛntsən], *v.a.* garland, wreathe.

Krapfen ['krapfən], *m.* (—s, *pl.* —) doughnut.

kraß [kras], *adj.* crass, crude.

Krater ['kraːtər], *m.* (—s, *pl.* —) crater.

Kratzbürste ['kratsbyrstə], *f.* (—, *pl.* —n) scraper; (*fig.*) cross-patch, irritable person.

Krätze ['krɛtsə], *f.* (—, *no pl.*) (*Med.*) scabies, itch, mange.

kratzen ['kratsən], *v.a., v.n.* scratch, scrape, itch.

krauen ['krauən], *v.a.* scratch softly.

kraus [kraus], *adj.* frizzy, curly; crisp, fuzzy; creased; (*fig.*) abstruse; *die Stirn — ziehen*, frown, knit o.'s brow.

Krause ['krauzə], *f.* (—, *pl.* —n) ruff.

kräuseln ['krɔyzəln], *v.a., v.r.* crisp, curl; ripple.

Krauskohl ['krauskoːl], *m.* (—s, *no pl.*) Savoy cabbage.

Kraut [kraut], *n.* (—es, *pl.* ̈er) herb; plant; (*dial.*) cabbage; *wie — und Rüben*, higgledy-piggledy.

krautartig ['krauta:rtɪç], *adj.* herbaceous.

Kräuterkäse ['krɔytərkɛ:zə], *m.* (—s, *pl.* —) green cheese.

Kräutertee ['krɔytərte:], *m.* (—s, *no pl.*) herb-tea, infusion of herbs.

Krawall [kra'val], *m.* (—s, *pl.* —e) (*coll.*) row, uproar; shindy.

Krawatte [kra'vatə], *f.* (—, *pl.* —n) cravat, tie.

kraxeln ['kraksəln], *v.n.* (*coll.*) climb, clamber.

Krebs [kre:ps], *m.* (—es, *pl.* —e) (*Zool.*) crayfish, crab; (*Med.*) cancer, carcinoma; (*Geog.*) Tropic of Cancer.

krebsartig ['kre:psa:rtɪç], *adj.* cancerous.

Krebsbutter ['kre:psbutər], *f.* (—, *no pl.*) crab-cheese.

Krebsgang ['kre:psgaŋ], *m.* (—es, *no pl.*) crab's walk, sidling; *den — gehen*, retrograde, decline.

Krebsschaden ['kre:psʃa:dən], *m.* (—s, *pl.* ̈) cancerous sore *or* affection; (*fig.*) canker, inveterate evil.

Kredenz [kre'dɛnts], *f.* (—, *pl.* —en) buffet, serving table, sideboard.

kredenzen [kre'dɛntsən], *v.a.* taste (*wine*); (*obs.*) present, offer.

kreditieren [kredi'ti:rən], *v.a. einem etwas —*, credit s.o. with s.th.

Kreide ['kraɪdə], *f.* (—, *pl.* —n) chalk; (*Art*) crayon.

kreieren [kre'i:rən], *v.a.* create.

Kreis [kraɪs], *m.* (—es, *pl.* —e) circle; (*Astron.*) orbit; district; range; sphere.

Kreisabschnitt ['kraɪsapʃnɪt], *m.* (—s, *pl.* —e) segment.

Kreisausschnitt ['kraɪsausʃnɪt], *m.* (—s, *pl.* —e) sector.

Kreisbogen ['kraɪsbo:gən], *m.* (—s, *pl.* ̈) arc.

kreischen ['kraɪʃən], *v.n.* scream, shriek.

Kreisel ['kraɪzəl], *m.* (—s, *pl.* —) (*toy*) (spinning) top; gyroscope.

kreisen ['kraɪzən], *v.n.* circle, revolve; circulate.

Kreislauf ['kraɪslauf], *m.* (—es, *pl.* ̈e) circular course; (*Astron.*) orbit; (*blood*) circulation.

kreißen ['kraɪsən], *v.n.* (*Med.*) be in labour.

Kreisstadt ['kraɪsʃtat], *f.* (—, *pl.* ̈e) county town.

Kreisumfang ['kraɪsumfaŋ], *m.* (—s, *pl.* ̈e) circumference.

Kreml [kreml], *m.* (—s, *no pl.*) the Kremlin.

Krempe ['krɛmpə], *f.* (—, *pl.* —n) (*hat*) brim.

Krempel ['krɛmpəl], *m.* (—s, *no pl.*) (*coll.*) refuse, rubbish; stuff.

Kren [kre:n], *m.* (—s, *no pl.*) (*Austr.*) horse-radish.

krepieren [kre'pi:rən], *v.n.* (*aux.* sein) (*animals*) die; (*humans*) (*coll.*) perish miserably; explode.

Krepp [krɛp], *m.* (—s, *no pl.*) crape, crêpe.

Kresse ['krɛsə], *f.* (—, *pl.* —n) cress.

Kreta ['kre:ta], *n.* Crete.

Kreuz [krɔyts], *n.* (—es, *pl.* —e) cross, crucifix; (*Anat.*) small of the back; (*fig.*) calamity; affliction; *kreuz und quer*, in all directions.

Kreuzband ['krɔytsbant], *n.* (—es, *pl.* ̈er) wrapper (for printed matter).

kreuzbrav ['krɔytsbra:f], *adj.* as good as gold.

kreuzen ['krɔytsən], *v.a.* cross. — *v.r. sich —*, make the sign of the cross.

Kreuzfahrer ['krɔytsfa:rər], *m.* (—s, *pl.* —) crusader.

kreuzfidel ['krɔytsfide:l], *adj.* jolly, merry, as merry as a cricket.

Kreuzgang ['krɔytsgaŋ], *m.* (—es, *pl.* ̈e) cloisters.

kreuzigen ['krɔytsɪgən], *v.a.* crucify.

Kreuzritter ['krɔItsrɪtər], *m.* (—s, *pl.* —) Knight of the Cross; crusader.

Kreuzschmerzen ['krɔytsʃmɛrtsən], *m. pl.* lumbago.

Kreuzstich ['krɔytsʃtɪç], *m.* (—es, *no pl.*) (*Embroidery*) cross-stitch.

Kreuzung ['krɔytsuŋ], *f.* (—, *pl.* —en) (*road*) crossing; (*animals*) crossbreeding.

Kreuzverhör ['krɔytsfɛrhø:r], *n.* (—s, *pl.* —e) cross-examination.

Kreuzweg ['krɔytsve:k], *m.* (—es, *pl.* —e) crossroads; (*Eccl.*) Stations of the Cross.

Kreuzworträtsel ['krɔytsvɔrtrɛ:tsəl], *n.* (—s, *pl.* —) crossword-puzzle.

Kreuzzug ['krɔytstsu:k], *m.* (—es, *pl.* ̈e) crusade.

kriechen ['kri:çən], *v.n. irr.* (*aux.* sein) creep, crawl; (*fig.*) cringe, fawn.

kriecherisch ['kri:çərɪʃ], *adj.* fawning, cringing.

Kriechtier ['kri:çti:r], *n.* (—s, *pl.* —e) reptile.

Krieg [kri:k], *m.* (—es, *pl.* —e) war.

kriegen ['kri:gən], *v.a.* get, obtain.

Krieger ['kri:gər], *m.* (—s, *pl.* —) warrior.

kriegerisch ['kri:gərɪʃ], *adj.* warlike, martial.

kriegführend ['kri:kfy:rənt], *adj.* belligerent.

Kriegsfuß ['kri:ksfu:s], *m.* (—es, *no pl.*) *auf —*, at logger-heads.

Kriegsgewinnler ['kri:ksgəvɪnlər], *m.* (—s, *pl.* —) war-profiteer.

Kriegslist ['kri:kslɪst], *f.* (—, *pl.* —en) stratagem.

Kriegsschauplatz ['kri:ksʃauplats], *m.* (—es, *pl.* ̈e) theatre of war.

Kriegsschiff ['kri:ksʃɪf], *n.* (—es, *pl.* —e) man-of-war, warship.

Kriegswesen ['kri:ksve:zən], *n.* (—s, *no pl.*) military affairs.

Kriegszug ['kri:kstsu:k], *m.* (—es, *pl.* ̈e) campaign.

Krim [krɪm], *f.* the Crimea.

Kriminalbeamte [krɪmi'na:lbəamtə], *m.* (—n, *pl.* —n) crime investigator.

Kriminalprozeß [krɪmi'naːlprotsɛs], *m.* (—sses, *pl.* —sse) criminal procedure *or* trial.

Krimskrams ['krɪmskrams], *m.* (—, *no pl.*) whatnots, knick-knacks, medley.

Krippe ['krɪpə], *f.* (—, *pl.* —n) crib, manger; crèche.

Krise ['kriːzə], *f.* (—, *pl.* —n) crisis.

Kristall [krɪ'stal], *m.* (—s, *pl.* —e) crystal; cut glass.

kristallartig [krɪ'stalaːrtɪç], *adj.* crystalline.

kristallisieren [krɪstali'ziːrən], *v.a.*, *v.n.* (*aux.* sein), crystallise.

Kristallkunde [krɪ'stalkundə], *f.* (—, *no pl.*) crystallography.

Kriterium [kri'teːrjum], *n.* (—s, *pl.* —rien) criterion, test.

Kritik [kri'tiːk], *f.* (—, *pl.* —en) criticism, review; *unter aller* —, extremely bad.

Kritiker ['kriːtɪkər], *m.* (—s, *pl.* —) critic.

kritisch ['kriːtɪʃ], *adj.* critical; precarious, crucial.

kritisieren [kriti'ziːrən], *v.a.* criticise; review; censure.

kritteln ['krɪtəln], *v.n.* cavil (at), find fault.

Krittler ['krɪtlər], *m.* (—s, *pl.* —) caviller, fault-finder.

Kritzelei [krɪtsə'laɪ], *f.* (—, *pl.* —en) scrawling, scribbling.

kritzeln ['krɪtsəln], *v.a.* scrawl, scribble.

Kroatien [kro'aːtsjən], *n.* Croatia.

Krokodil [kroko'diːl], *n.* (—s, *pl.* —e) (*Zool.*) crocodile.

Kronbewerber ['kroːnbeverbər], *m.* (—s, *pl.* —) aspirant to the crown, pretender.

Krone ['kroːnə], *f.* (—, *pl.* —n) crown; (*Papal*) tiara; (*fig.*) head, top, flower.

krönen ['krøːnən], *v.a.* crown.

Kronerbe ['kroːnerbə], *m.* (—n, *pl.* —n) heir apparent.

Kronleuchter ['kroːnlɔyçtər], *m.* (—s, *pl.* —) chandelier.

Kronsbeere ['kroːnsbeːrə], *f.* (—, *pl.* —n) (*Bot.*) cranberry.

Krönung ['krøːnuŋ], *f.* (—, *pl.* —en) coronation.

Kropf [krɔpf], *m.* (—es, *pl.* ⸚e) (*human*) goitre, wen; (*birds*) crop, craw.

kropfartig ['krɔpfaːrtɪç], *adj.* goitrous.

kröpfen ['krœpfən], *v.a.* (*birds*) cram.

Kropftaube ['krɔpftaubə], *f.* (—, *pl.* —n) (*Orn.*) pouter-pigeon.

Kröte ['krøːtə], *f.* (—, *pl.* —n) toad.

Krücke ['krykə], *f.* (—, *pl.* —n) crutch; (*fig.*) rake.

Krückstock ['krykʃtɔk], *m.* (—s, *pl.* ⸚e) crutch.

Krug [kruːk], *m.* (—es, *pl.* ⸚e) jug, pitcher, mug; (*fig.*) pub, inn.

Krüger ['kryːgər], *m.* (—s, *pl.* —) pub-keeper, tapster.

Krume ['kruːmə], *f.* (—, *pl.* —n) crumb.

krüm(e)lig ['kryːm(ə)lɪç], *adj.* crumbly, crumby.

krümeln ['kryːmeln], *v.n.* crumble.

krumm [krum], *adj.* crooked, curved; *etwas — nehmen*, take s.th. amiss.

krummbeinig ['krumbaɪnɪç], *adj.* bandy-legged.

krümmen ['krymən], *v.a.* crook, bend, curve. — *v.r. sich* —, (*fig.*) writhe, cringe.

Krummholz ['krumhɔlts], *n.* (—es, *no pl.*) (*Bot.*) dwarf-pine.

Krummschnabel ['krumʃnaːbəl], *m.* (—s, *pl.* ⸚) (*Orn.*) curlew, crook-bill.

Krümmung ['krymuŋ], *f.* (—, *pl.* —en) curve; turning, winding.

Krüppel ['krypəl], *m.* (—s, *pl.* —) cripple.

krüppelhaft ['krypəlhaft], *adj.* crippled, lame.

krüpp(e)lig ['kryp(ə)lɪç], *adj.* crippled, lame.

Kruste ['krustə], *f.* (—, *pl.* —n) crust.

Kübel ['kyːbəl], *m.* (—s, *pl.* —) tub, bucket.

Kubikfuß [ku'biːkfuːs], *m.* (—es, *pl.* —) cubic foot.

Kubikinhalt [ku'biːkɪnhalt], *m.* (—s, *no pl.*) cubic content.

Kubismus [ku'bɪsmus], *m.* (—, *no pl.*) cubism.

Küche ['kyçə], *f.* (—, *pl.* —n) (*room*) kitchen; (*food*) cooking, cookery, cuisine.

Kuchen ['kuːxən], *m.* (—s, *pl.* —) cake.

Küchengeschirr ['kyçəngəʃɪr], *n.* (—s, *no pl.*) kitchen utensils.

Küchenherd ['kyçənheːrt], *m.* (—es, *pl.* —e) kitchen-range.

Küchenlatein ['kyçənlataɪn], *n.* (—s, *no pl.*) dog-Latin.

Küchenmeister ['kyçənmaɪstər], *m.* (—s, *pl.* —) chef, head cook.

Küchenschrank ['kyçənʃraŋk], *m.* (—s, *pl.* ⸚e) dresser.

Kuchenteig ['kuːxəntaɪk], *m.* (—s, *pl.* —e) dough (for cake).

Küchenzettel ['kyçəntsetəl], *m.* (—s, *pl.* —) bill of fare.

Küchlein ['kyːçlaɪn], *n.* (—s, *pl.* —) young chicken, pullet.

Kücken ['kykən], *n.* (—s, *pl.* —) young chicken, pullet.

Kuckuck ['kukuk], *m.* (—s, *pl.* —e) (*Orn.*) cuckoo; *scher Dich zum* —! go to blazes!

Kufe ['kuːfə], *f.* (—, *pl.* —n) tub, vat; (*sleigh*) runner; (*cradle*) rocker.

Küfer ['kyːfər], *m.* (—s, *pl.* —) cooper.

Kugel ['kuːgəl], *f.* (—, *pl.* —n) ball, bullet, sphere; globe.

kugelfest ['kuːgəlfest], *adj.* bullet-proof.

kugelförmig ['kuːgəlfœrmɪç], *adj.* spherical, globular.

Kugelgelenk ['kuːgəlgelɛŋk], *n.* (—s, *pl.* —e) ball and socket joint.

Kugellager ['kuːgəllaːgər], *n.* (—s, *pl.* —) ball-bearing.

Kugelmaß ['kuːgəlmaːs], *n.* (—es, *pl.* —e) ball-calibre.

kugeln ['kuːgəln], *v.a.* roll; bowl.

Kugelregen ['ku:gəlre:gən], *m.* (—s, *no pl.*) hail of bullets.

kugelrund ['ku:gəlrunt], *adj.* round as a ball, well-fed.

Kugelschreiber ['ku:gəlʃraibər], *m.* (—s, *pl.* —) ball-point pen.

Kuh [ku:] *f.* (—, *pl.* ⁝e) cow; *junge* —, heifer.

Kuhblattern ['ku:blatərn], *f. pl.* cow-pox.

Kuhblume ['ku:blu:mə], *f.* (—, *pl.* —n) (*Bot.*) marigold.

Kuhfladen ['ku:fla:dən], *m.* (—s, *pl.* —) cow-dung.

Kuhhaut ['ku:haut], *f.* (—, *pl.* ⁝e) cow-hide; *das geht auf keine* —, that defies description.

kühl [ky:l], *adj.* cool, fresh; (*behaviour*) reserved.

Kühle ['ky:lə], *f.* (—, *no pl.*) coolness, freshness; (*behaviour*) reserve.

kühlen ['ky:lən], *v.a.* cool, freshen.

Kühlraum ['ky:lraum], *m.* (—es, *pl.* ⁝e) refrigerating-chamber.

Kühlschrank ['ky:lʃraŋk], *m.* (—s, *pl.* ⁝e) refrigerator, (*coll.*) fridge.

Kühltruhe ['ky:ltru:ə], *f.* (—, *pl.* —n) deep freeze.

Kühlung ['ky:luŋ], *f.* (—, *pl.* —en) refrigeration.

Kuhmist ['ku:mist], *m.* (—s, *no pl.*) cow-dung.

kühn [ky:n], *adj.* bold, daring, audacious.

Kühnheit ['ky:nhait], *f.* (—, *no pl.*) boldness, daring, audacity.

Kujon [ku'jo:n], *m.* (—s, *pl.* —e) bully, scoundrel.

kujonieren [kujo'ni:rən], *v.a.* bully, exploit.

Kukuruz ['kukuruts], *m.* (—es, *no pl.*) (*Austr.*) maize.

kulant [ku'lant], *adj.* obliging; (*terms*) easy.

Kulanz [ku'lants], *f.* (—, *no pl.*) accommodating manner.

Kuli ['ku:li], *m.* (—s, *pl.* —s) coolie.

kulinarisch [kuli'na:riʃ], *adj.* culinary.

Kulisse ['ku'lisə], *f.* (—, *pl.* —n) (*Theat.*) back-drop, side-scene, wings.

Kulissenfieber [ku'lisənfi:bər], *n.* (—s, *no pl.*) stage-fright.

kulminieren [kulmi'ni:rən], *v.n.* culminate.

kultivieren [kulti'vi:rən], *v.a.* cultivate.

Kultur [kul'tu:r], *f.* (—, *pl.* —en) (*Agr.*) cultivation; (*fig.*) culture, civilization.

Kultus ['kultus], *m.* (—, *pl.* **Kulte**) cult, worship.

Kultusministerium ['kultusministe:rjum], *n.* (—s, *pl.* —rien) Ministry of Education.

Kümmel ['kymal], *m.* (—s, *no pl.*) caraway-seed; (*drink*) kümmel.

Kummer ['kumər], *m.* (—s, *no pl.*) grief, sorrow, trouble.

kümmerlich ['kymərliç], *adj.* miserable, pitiful.

kummerlos ['kumərlo:s], *adj.* untroubled.

kümmern ['kymərn], *v.r. sich* — *um*, mind, look after, be worried about, care for.

Kümmernis ['kymərnis], *f.* (—, *pl.* —se) grief, sorrow.

kummervoll ['kumərfɔl], *adj.* sorrowful, painful, grievous.

Kumpan [kum'pa:n], *m.* (—s, *pl.* —e) companion; mate; *lustiger* —, jolly fellow, good companion.

kund [kunt], *adj.* known, public; *etwas* — *tun*, make s.th. public; — *und zu wissen sei hiermit,* (*obs.*) we hereby give notice.

kundbar ['kuntba:r], *adj.* known; *etwas* — *machen*, announce s.th., make s.th. known.

kündbar ['kyntba:r], *adj.* (*loan, capital etc.*) redeemable; capable of being called in, terminable.

Kunde (1) ['kundə], *m.* (—n, *pl.* —n) customer; *ein schlauer* —, an artful dodger.

Kunde (2) ['kundə], *f.* (—, *pl.* —n) news; information, notification; (*compounds*) science.

Kundgebung ['kuntge:buŋ], *f.* (—, *pl.* —en) publication; rally; demonstration.

kundig ['kundiç], *adj.* versed in, conversant with.

Kundige ['kundigə], *m.* (—n, *pl.* —n) expert, initiate.

kündigen ['kyndigən], *v.n.* give notice (*Dat.*).

Kundmachung ['kuntmaxuŋ], *f.* (—, *pl.* —en) publication.

Kundschaft ['kuntʃaft], *f.* (—, *no pl.*) clientele, customers; information, reconnaissance.

kundschaften ['kuntʃaftən], *v.n.* reconnoitre, scout.

künftig ['kynftiç], *adj.* future, prospective, to come.

Kunst [kunst], *f.* (—, *pl.* ⁝e) art; skill.

Kunstbutter ['kunstbutər], *f.* (—, *no pl.*) margarine.

Künstelei [kynstə'lai], *f.* (—, *pl.* —en) affectation, mannerism.

kunstfertig ['kunstfertiç], *adj.* skilled, skilful.

Kunstfreund ['kunstfrɔynt], *m.* (—es, *pl.* —e) art-lover.

kunstgerecht ['kunstgərɛçt], *adj.* workmanlike.

Kunstgewerbe ['kunstgəvɛrbə], *n.* (—s, *no pl.*) arts and crafts.

Kunstgriff ['kunstgrif], *m.* (—es, *pl.* —e) trick, dodge, artifice, knack.

Kunsthändler ['kunsthendlər], *m.* (—s, *pl.* —) art-dealer.

Kunstkenner ['kunstkenər], *m.* (—s, *pl.* —) connoisseur.

Künstler ['kynstlər], *m.* (—s, *pl.* —) artist, performer.

künstlerisch ['kynstləriʃ], *adj.* artistic, elaborate, ingenious.

künstlich ['kynstliç], *adj.* artificial.

kunstlos ['kunstlo:s], *adj.* artless, unaffected.

133

kunstreich

kunstreich [ˈkunstraɪç], *adj.* ingenious.

Kunstseide [ˈkunstzaɪdə], *f.* (—, *no pl.*) artificial silk.

Kunststickerei [ˈkunstʃtɪkəraɪ], *f.* (—, *no pl.*) art needlework.

Kunststoff [ˈkunstʃtɔf], *m.* (—es, *pl.* —e) plastics.

Kunststopfen [ˈkunstʃtɔpfən], *n.* (—s, *no pl.*) invisible mending.

Kunststück [ˈkunstʃtyk], *n.* (—es, *pl.* —e) trick, feat.

Kunstverständige [ˈkunstfɛrʃtɛndɪgə], *m.* (—n, *pl.* —n) art expert.

Küpe [ˈkyːpə], *f.* (—, *pl.* —n) large tub; (dyeing) copper.

Kupfer [ˈkupfər], *n.* (—s, *no pl.*) copper.

Kupferblech [ˈkupfərblɛç], *n.* (—es, *no pl.*) copper-sheet.

Kupferdraht [ˈkupfərdraːt], *m.* (—es, *pl.* ⁻e) copper-wire.

kupferhaltig [ˈkupfərhaltɪç], *adj.* containing copper.

Kupferrost [ˈkupfərrɔst], *m.* (—es, *no pl.*) verdigris.

Kupferstecher [ˈkupfərʃtɛçər], *m.* (—s, *pl.* —) (copperplate) engraver.

kupieren [kuˈpiːrən], *v.a.* (*rare*) (*ticket*) punch; (*Austr.*) (*horse*) dock.

Kuppe [ˈkupə], *f.* (—, *pl.* —n) (*hill*) top, summit.

Kuppel [ˈkupəl], *f.* (—, *pl.* —n) cupola, dome.

kuppeln [ˈkupəln], *v.n.* procure, pimp; make a match.

Kuppler [ˈkuplər], *m.* (—s, *pl.* —) procurer, pimp; matchmaker.

Kupplung [ˈkuplʊŋ], *f.* (—, *pl.* —en) (*Railw.*) coupling, joint; (*Motor.*) clutch.

Kur [kuːr], *f.* (—, *pl.* —en) cure; *eine — machen,* undergo medical treatment.

Kuranstalt [ˈkuːranʃtalt], *f.* (—, *pl.* —en) sanatorium; (*Am.*) sanitarium.

Küraß [ˈkyːras], *m.* (—sses, *pl.* —sse) cuirass.

Kuratel [kuraˈtɛl], *f.* (—, *pl.* —en) guardianship, trusteeship.

Kuratorium [kuraˈtoːrjum], *n.* (—s, *pl.* —rien) board of guardians *or* trustees; council, governing body.

Kurbel [ˈkurbəl], *f.* (—, *pl.* —n) crank, winch.

Kurbelstange [ˈkurbəlʃtaŋə], *f.* (—, *pl.* —n) connecting rod.

Kurbelwelle [ˈkurbəlvɛlə], *f.* (—, *pl.* —n) crankshaft.

Kürbis [ˈkyrbɪs], *m.* (—ses, *pl.* —se) (*Bot.*) pumpkin, gourd.

küren [ˈkyːrən], *v.a. irr.* (*Poet.*) choose, elect.

Kurfürst [ˈkuːrfyrst], *m.* (—en, *pl.* —en) Elector (of the Holy Roman Empire).

Kurhaus [ˈkuːrhaus], *n.* (—es, *pl.* ⁻er) spa; hotel; pump room.

Kurie [ˈkuːrjə], *f.* (—, *pl.* —n) (*Eccl.*) Curia; Papal Court.

Kurier [kuˈriːr], *m.* (—s, *pl.* —e) courier.

kurieren [kuˈriːrən], *v.a.* cure.

kurios [kurˈjoːs], *adj.* curious, queer, strange.

Kuriosität [kurjoziˈtɛːt], *f.* (—, *pl.* —en) curio, curiosity.

Kurort [ˈkuːrɔrt], *m.* (—es, *pl.* —e) spa, watering-place, health-resort.

Kurrentschrift [kuˈrɛntʃrift], *f.* (—, *no pl.*) running hand, cursive writing.

Kurs [kurs], *m.* (—es, *pl.* —e) rate of exchange; quotation; circulation; course.

Kursaal [ˈkuːrzaːl], *m.* (—s, *pl.* —säle) hall, (*spa*) pump-room, casino.

Kursbericht [ˈkursbərɪçt], *m.* (—es, *pl.* —e) market report.

Kursbuch [ˈkursbuːx], *n.* (—es, *pl.* ⁻er) railway-guide, time-table.

Kürschner [ˈkyrʃnər], *m.* (—s, *pl.* —) furrier, skinner.

kursieren [kurˈziːrən], *v.n.* be current, circulate.

Kursivschrift [kurˈziːfʃrift], *f.* (—, *no pl.*) italics.

Kursstand [ˈkursʃtant], *m.* (—es, *no pl.*) rate of exchange.

Kursus [ˈkurzus], *m.* (—, *pl.* **Kurse**) course of lectures).

Kurszettel [ˈkursˌsetəl], *m.* (—s, *pl.* —) quotation-list.

Kurve [ˈkurvə], *f.* (—, *pl.* —n) curve.

kurz [kurts], *adj.* short, brief, concise; curt, abrupt.

kurzangebunden [kurtsˈangəbundən], *adj.* terse, abrupt, curt.

kurzatmig [ˈkurtsaːtmɪç], *adj.* shortwinded, short of breath.

Kürze [ˈkyrtsə], *f.* (—, *no pl.*) shortness, brevity.

kürzen [ˈkyrtsən], *v.a.* shorten, abbreviate, condense; (*Maths.*) reduce.

kürzlich [ˈkyrtslɪç], *adv.* lately, recently, the other day.

Kurzschluß [ˈkurtsʃlus], *m.* (—sses, *pl.* ⁻sse) short circuit.

Kurzschrift [ˈkurtsʃrift], *f.* (—, *no pl.*) shorthand.

kurzsichtig [ˈkurtszɪçtɪç], *adj.* shortsighted.

kurzum [kurtsˈum], *adv.* in short.

Kürzung [ˈkyrtsuŋ], *f.* (—, *pl.* —en) abbreviation, abridgement.

Kurzwaren [ˈkurtsvaːrən], *f. pl.* haberdashery.

kurzweg [kurtsˈveːk], *adv.* simply, offhand, briefly.

Kurzweil [ˈkurtsvaɪl], *f.* (—, *no pl.*) pastime.

kurzweilig [ˈkurtsvaɪlɪç], *adj.* amusing, diverting, entertaining.

kusch! [kuʃ], *excl.* (*to dogs*) lie down!

kuschen [ˈkuʃən], *v.n., v.r.* crouch, lie down.

Kuß [kus], *m.* (—sses, *pl.* ⁻sse) kiss.

küssen [ˈkysən], *v.a., v.n., v.r.* kiss.

Küste [ˈkystə], *f.* (—, *pl.* —n) coast, shore.

Küstenstadt ['kystənʃtat], *f.* (—, *pl.* ⁓e)
seaside town.

Küster ['kystər], *m.* (—s, *pl.* —)
sacristan, sexton, verger.

Kustos ['kustɔs], *m.* (—, *pl.* —oden)
custodian; director of museum.

Kutschbock ['kutʃbɔk], *m.* (—s, *pl.*
⁓e) box(-seat).

Kutsche ['kutʃə], *f.* (—, *pl.* —n)
coach, carriage.

kutschieren [kut'ʃiːrən], *v.n.* drive a
coach.

Kutte ['kutə], *f.* (—, *pl.* —n) cowl.

Kutter ['kutər], *m.* (—s, *pl.* —) (*Naut.*)
cutter.

Kuvert [ku'vɛːr], *n.* (—s, *pl.* —s)
envelope; (*dinner*) place laid.

kuvertieren [kuvɛr'tiːrən], *v.a.* envelop,
wrap.

Kux [kuks], *m.* (—es, *pl.* —e) share in
a mining concern.

Kybernetik [kyːbɛr'neːtɪk], *f.* (—, *no
pl.*) cybernetics.

L

L [ɛl], *n.* (—, *pl.* —) the letter L.

Lab [laːp], *n.* (—es, *pl.* —e) rennet.

labbern ['labərn], *v.a.*, *v.n.* dribble,
slobber; blab.

Labe ['laːbə], *f.* (—, *no pl.*) (*Poet.*) refreshment; comfort.

laben ['laːbən], *v.a.* refresh, restore,
revive.

labil [la'biːl], *adj.* unstable.

Laborant [labo'rant], *m.* (—en, *pl.*
—en) laboratory assistant.

Laboratorium [labora'toːrjum], *n.*
(—s, *pl.* —rien) laboratory.

laborieren [labo'riːrən], *v.n.* experiment; suffer (from).

Labsal ['laːpzaːl], *n.* (—s, *pl.* —e)
restorative, refreshment.

Labung ['laːbuŋ], *f.* (—, *pl.* —en)
refreshment, comfort.

Lache ['laxə], *f.* (—, *pl.* —n) pool,
puddle.

Lächeln ['lɛçəln], *n.* (—s, *no pl.*)
smile; *albernes* —, smirk; *höhnisches*
—, sneer.

lächeln ['lɛçəln], *v.n.* smile.

Lachen ['laxən], *n.* (—s, *no pl.*) laugh,
laughter.

lachen ['laxən], *v.n.* laugh.

lächerlich ['lɛçərlɪç], *adj.* laughable,
ridiculous; preposterous; ludicrous;
sich — machen, make a fool of o.s.;
etwas — machen, ridicule s.th.

Lachgas ['laxgaːs], *n.* (—es, *no pl.*)
nitrous oxide, laughing-gas.

lachhaft ['laxhaft], *adj.* laughable,
ridiculous.

Lachkrampf ['laxkrampf], *m.* (—es,
pl. ⁓e) hysterical laughter, a fit of
laughter.

Lachs [laks], *m.* (—es, *pl.* —e) salmon.

Lachsalve ['laxzalvə], *f.* (—, *pl.* —n)
peal of laughter.

Lack [lak], *m.* (—s, *pl.* —e) lac, lacquer,
varnish.

lackieren [la'kiːrən], *v.a.* lacquer,
varnish.

Lackmus ['lakmus], *n.* (—, *no pl.*)
litmus.

Lackschuh ['lakʃuː], *m.* (—s, *pl.* —e)
patent-leather shoe.

Lackwaren ['lakvaːrən], *f. pl.* japanned
goods.

Lade ['laːdə], *f.* (—, *pl.* —n) box, chest,
case, drawer.

Ladebaum ['laːdəbaum], *m.* derrick.

Ladefähigkeit ['laːdəfɛːɪçkaɪt], *f.* (—,
pl. —en), carrying capacity, loading
capacity; tonnage.

Ladegeld ['laːdəgɛlt], *n.* (—es, *pl.* —er)
loading charges.

Laden ['laːdən], *m.* (—s, *pl.* ⁓) (*window*)
shutter; shop, store.

laden ['laːdən], *v.a. irr.* load; (*Elec.*)
charge; (*Law*) summon, (*fig.*) incur.

Ladenhüter ['laːdənhyːtər], *m.* (—s,
pl. —) unsaleable article.

Ladenpreis ['laːdənpraɪs], *m.* (—es,
pl. —e) retail-price.

Ladentisch ['laːdəntɪʃ], *m.* (—es, *pl.*
—e) counter.

Ladeschein ['laːdəʃaɪn], *m.* (—s, *pl.*
—e) bill of lading.

Ladestock ['laːdəʃtɔk], *m.* (—es, *pl.* ⁓e)
ramrod.

Ladung ['laːduŋ], *f.* (—, *pl.* —en) loading, lading, freight; shipment, cargo;
(*gun*) charge; (*Law*) summons.

Laffe ['lafə], *m.* (—n, *pl.* —n) fop.

Lage ['laːgə], *f.* (—, *pl.* —n) site, position, situation; state, condition;
stratum, layer.

Lager ['laːgər], *n.* (—s, *pl.* —) couch,
bed, divan; (*Geol.*) seam, vein; (*Tech.*)
bearing; (*Comm.*) warehouse, store;
camp.

Lageraufnahme ['laːgəraufnaːmə], *f.*
(—, *pl.* —n) stock-taking, inventory.

Lager(bier) ['laːgər(biːr)], *n.* (—s,
pl. —e) lager.

Lagergeld ['laːgərgɛlt], *n.* (—es, *pl.*
—er) storage charge.

Lagerist [laːgə'rɪst], *m.* (—en, *pl.* —en)
warehouse-clerk.

lagern ['laːgərn], *v.a.* store, warehouse.

Lagerstätte ['laːgərʃtɛtə], *f.* (—, *pl.*—n)
couch, resting-place; camp site.

Lagerung ['laːgəruŋ], *f.* (—, *pl.* —en)
encampment; storage; stratification.

Lagune [la'guːnə], *f.* (—, *pl.* —n)
lagoon.

lahm [laːm], *adj.* lame, paralysed,
crippled.

lahmen ['laːmən], *v.n.* be lame, limp.

lähmen ['lɛːmən], *v.a.* paralyse.

lahmlegen ['laːmleːgən], *v.a.* paralyse.

Lähmung

Lähmung ['lɛ:muŋ], *f.* (—, *pl.* —en) paralysis.

Laib [laɪp], *m.* (—es, *pl.* —e) (*bread*) loaf.

Laich [laɪç], *m.* (—es, *pl.* —e) spawn.

laichen ['laɪçən], *v.n.* spawn.

Laie ['laɪə], *m.* (—n, *pl.* —n) layman, (*pl.*) laity.

Lakai [la'kaɪ], *m.* (—en, *pl.* —en) lackey, flunkey, footman.

Lake ['la:kə], *f.* (—, *pl.* —n) brine, pickle.

Laken ['la:kən], *n.* (—s, *pl.* —) (*bed*) sheet.

lakonisch [la'ko:nɪʃ], *adj.* laconic.

Lakritze [la'krɪtsə], *f.* (—, *pl.* —n) liquorice.

lallen ['lalən], *v.a.*, *v.n.* stammer; babble.

Lama (1) ['la:ma:], *n.* (—s, *pl.* —s) (*animal*) llama.

Lama (2) ['la:ma:], *m.* (—s, *pl.* —s) (*priest*) lama.

lamentieren [lamɛn'ti:rən], *v.n.* lament, wail.

Lamm [lam], *n.* (—es, *pl.* ⁻er) (*Zool.*) lamb.

Lämmchen ['lɛmçən], *n.* (—s, *pl.* —) (*Zool.*) lambkin.

Lämmergeier ['lɛmərgaɪər], *m.* (—s, *pl.* —) (*Orn.*) great bearded vulture.

Lampe ['lampə], *f.* (—, *pl.* —n) lamp.

Lampenfieber ['lampənfi:bər], *n.* (—s, *no pl.*) stage-fright.

Lampenputzer ['lampənputsər], *m.* (—s, *pl.* —) lamplighter.

Lampenschirm ['lampənʃɪrm], *m.* (—s, *pl.* —e) lampshade.

Lampion ['lampˈpjɔ̃], *m. & n.* (—s, *pl.* —s) Chinese lantern.

lancieren [lã'si:rən], *v.a.* thrust; launch.

Land [lant], *n.* (—es, *pl.* —e (*Poet.*) and ⁻er) land, country; state; ground, soil; *das Gelobte* —, the Promised Land; *an* — *gehen*, go ashore; *aufs* — *gehen*, go into the country.

Landadel ['lanta:dəl], *m.* (—s, *no pl.*) landed gentry.

Landarbeiter ['lantarbaɪtər], *m.* (—s, *pl.* —) farm-worker.

Landauer ['landauər], *m.* (—s, *pl.* —) landau.

Landebahn ['landəba:n], *f.* (—, *pl.* —en) (*Aviat.*) runway.

landen ['landən], *v.n.* (*aux. sein*) land, disembark; (*aircraft*) land, touch down.

Landenge ['lantɛŋə], *f.* (—, *pl.* —n) isthmus.

Ländereien ['lɛndəraɪən], *f. pl.* landed property, estate.

Landeserzeugnis ['landəsɛrtsɔyknɪs], *n.* (—sses, *pl.* —sse) home produce.

Landesfürst ['landəsfyrst], *m.* (—en, *pl.* —en) sovereign.

Landesherr ['landəshɛr], *m.* (—n, *pl.* —en) (reigning) prince; sovereign.

Landeshoheit ['landəshohaɪt], *f.* (—, *no pl.*) sovereignty.

Landeskirche ['landəskɪrçə], *f.* (—, *pl.* —n) established church; national church.

Landesschuld ['landəsʃult], *f.* (—, *no pl.*) national debt.

Landessprache ['landəsʃpra:xə], *f.* (—, *pl.* —n) vernacular.

Landestracht ['landəstraxt], *f.* (—, *pl.* —en) national costume.

landesüblich ['landəsy:plɪç], *adj.* conventional, usual, customary.

Landesverweisung ['landəsfɛrvaɪzuŋ], *f.* (—, *pl.* —en) exile, banishment.

landflüchtig ['lantflyçtɪç], *adj.* fugitive.

Landfrieden ['lantfri:dən], *m.* (—s, *no pl.*) King's (*or* Queen's) peace; (*medieval*) public peace.

Landgericht ['lantgərɪçt], *n.* (—es, *pl.* —e) district court; county court.

Landgraf ['lantgra:f], *m.* (—en, *pl.* —en) landgrave, count.

Landhaus ['lanthaus], *n.* (—es, *pl.* ⁻er) country house.

Landjunker ['lantjuŋkər], *m.* (—s, *pl.* —) country squire.

Landkarte ['lantkartə], *f.* (—, *pl.* —n) map.

landläufig ['lantlɔyfɪç], *adj.* customary, conventional.

ländlich ['lɛntlɪç], *adj.* rural, rustic.

Landmann ['lantman], *m.* (—es, *pl.* **Landleute**) rustic, peasant.

Landmesser ['lantmɛsər], *m.* (—s, *pl.* —) surveyor.

Landpartie ['lantparti:], *f.* (—, *pl.* —n) country excursion, picnic.

Landplage ['lantpla:gə], *f.* (—, *pl.* —n) scourge, calamity; *eine richtige* —, a public nuisance.

Landrat ['lantra:t], *m.* (—s, *pl.* ⁻e) district president *or* magistrate.

Landratte ['lantratə], *f.* (—, *pl.* —n) landlubber.

Landrecht ['lantreçt], *n.* (—es, *no pl.*) common law.

Landregen ['lantre:gən], *m.* (—s, *no pl.*) steady downpour; persistent rain.

Landschaft ['lantʃaft], *f.* (—, *pl.* —en) landscape.

landschaftlich ['lantʃaftlɪç], *adj.* scenic.

Landsknecht ['lantsknɛçt], *m.* (—es, *pl.* —e) mercenary; hired soldier.

Landsmann ['lantsman], *m.* (—es, *pl.* **Landsleute**) fellow-countryman, compatriot.

Landspitze ['lantʃpɪtsə], *f.* (—, *pl.* —n) cape, headland, promontory.

Landstraße ['lantʃtra:sə], *f.* (—, *pl.* —n) open road, main road, highway.

Landstreicher ['lantʃtraɪçər], *m.* (—s, *pl.* —) vagabond, tramp, (*Am.*) hobo.

Landstrich ['lantʃtrɪç], *m.* (—es, *pl.* —e) tract of land.

Landsturm ['lantʃturm], *m.* (—s, *no pl.*) (*Milit.*) militia; Home Guard.

Landtag ['lantta:k], *m.* (—s, *pl.* —e) (*Parl.*) diet.

Landung ['landuŋ], *f.* (—, *pl.* —en) landing.

Landvermesser *see* **Landmesser**.

136

Landvogt ['lantfoːkt], *m.* (—es, *pl.* ⁓e) (provincial) governor.

Landweg ['lantveːk], *m.* (—s, *pl.* —e) overland route.

Landwehr ['lantveːr], *f.* (—, *pl.* —en) militia.

Landwirt ['lantvɪrt], *m.* (—s, *pl.* —e) farmer, husbandman.

Landwirtschaft ['lantvɪrtʃaft], *f.* (—, *no pl.*) agriculture.

Landzunge ['lanttsuŋə], *f.* (—, *pl.* —n) spit of land.

lang [laŋ], *adj.* long, tall. — *adv.*, *prep.* (*prec. by Acc.*) for, during, long.

langatmig ['laŋaːtmɪç], *adj.* long-winded.

lange ['laŋə], *adv.* a long time; *wie* —? how long? *so* — *wie*, as long as.

Länge ['lɛŋə], *f.* (—, *pl.* —n) length; (*Geog.*) longitude.

langen ['laŋən], *v.a.* reach, hand, give s.o. s.th. — *v.n.* suffice, be enough.

Längengrad ['lɛŋəngraːt], *m.* (—s, *pl.* —e) degree of longitude.

Längenkreis ['lɛŋənkraɪs], *m.* (—es, *pl.* —e) meridian.

Längenmaß ['lɛŋənmaːs], *n.* (—es, *pl.* —e) linear measure.

Langeweile ['laŋəvaɪlə], *f.* (—, *no pl.*) boredom, ennui.

Langfinger ['laŋfɪŋər], *m.* (—s, *pl.* —) pickpocket.

langjährig ['laŋjɛːrɪç], *adj.* of long standing.

Langlebigkeit ['laŋleːbɪçkaɪt], *f.* (—, *no pl.*) longevity.

länglich ['lɛŋlɪç], *adj.* oblong.

Langmut ['laŋmuːt], *f.* (—, *no pl.*) forbearance, patience.

längs [lɛŋs], *prep.* (*Genit.*, *Dat.*) along.

langsam ['laŋzaːm], *adj.* slow; deliberate.

längst [lɛŋst], *adv.* long ago, long since.

längstens ['lɛŋstəns], *adv.* at the longest; at the latest.

Languste [laŋˈgustə], *f.* (—, *pl.* —n) (*Zool.*) spiny lobster.

langweilen ['laŋvaɪlən],*v.a.*(*insep.*) bore, tire. — *v.r. sich* —, feel bored, be bored.

langwierig ['laŋviːrɪç], *adj.* lengthy, protracted, wearisome.

Lanze ['lantsə], *f.* —, *pl.* —n) lance, spear; *eine* — *brechen*, take up the cudgels, stand up for (s.th. *or* s.o.).

Lanzenstechen ['lantsənʃtɛçən], *n.* (—s, *no pl.*) tournament.

Lanzette [lanˈtsetə], *f.* (—, *pl.* —n) lancet.

Lanzknecht ['lantsknɛçt], *m.* (—es, *pl.* —e) *see* **Landsknecht**.

Laos ['laːɔs], *n.* Laos.

Lappalie [laˈpaljə], *f.* (—, *pl.* —n) trifle.

Lappen ['lapən], *m.* (—s, *pl.* —) rag, duster, patch; (*ear*) lobe.

Läpperschulden ['lɛpərʃuldən], *f. pl.* petty debts.

läppisch ['lɛpɪʃ], *adj.* silly, foolish, trifling.

Lappland ['lapland], *n.* Lapland.

Lärche ['lɛrçə], *f.* (—, *pl.* —n) (*Bot.*) larch.

Lärm [lɛrm], *m.* (—s, *no pl.*) noise, din.

lärmen ['lɛrmən], *v.n.* make a noise, brawl.

Larve ['larfə], *f.* (—, *pl.* —n) mask; (*Ent.*) grub, larva.

lasch [laʃ], *adj.* limp; insipid.

Lasche ['laʃə], *f.* (—, *pl.* —n) flap; (*shoe*) gusset, strip.

lassen ['lasən], *v.a.*, *v.n. irr.* let, allow, suffer, permit; leave; make, cause; order, command; desist.

läßlich ['lɛslɪç], *adj.* (*Eccl.*) venial (*sin*).

lässig ['lɛsɪç], *adj.* indolent, sluggish, inactive.

Lässigkeit ['lɛsɪçkaɪt], *f.* (—, *no pl.*) lassitude, inaction, indolence; negligence.

Last [last], *f.* (—, *pl.* —en) load, burden, weight, charge.

lasten ['lastən], *v.n.* be heavy; weigh (on).

lastenfrei ['lastənfraɪ], *adj.* unencumbered.

Laster ['lastər], *n.* (—s, *pl.* —) vice.

Lästerer ['lɛstərər], *m.* (—s, *pl.* —) slanderer, calumniator; blasphemer.

lasterhaft ['lastərhaft], *adj.* vicious, wicked; corrupt.

Lasterhöhle ['lastərhøːlə], *f.* (—, *pl.* —n) den of vice.

lästerlich ['lɛstərlɪç], *adj.* blasphemous.

lästern ['lɛstərn], *v.a.* slander, defame; blaspheme.

lästig ['lɛstɪç], *adj.* tiresome, troublesome.

Lasttier ['lasttiːr], *n.* (—es, *pl.* —e) beast of burden.

Lastwagen ['lastvaːgən], *m.* (—s, *pl.* —) lorry, (*Am.*) truck.

Lasur [laˈzuːr], *m.* (—s, *pl.* —e) lapis-lazuli; ultramarine.

Latein [laˈtaɪn], *n.* (—s, *no pl.*) Latin.

lateinisch [laˈtaɪnɪʃ], *adj.* Latin.

Laterne [laˈtɛrnə], *f.* (—, *pl.* —n) lantern; (*street*) lamp.

latschen ['laːtʃən], *v.n.* shuffle along.

Latte ['latə], *f.* (—, *pl.* —n) lath, batten; *eine lange* —, lanky person.

Lattich ['latɪç], *m.* (—s, *pl.* —e) lettuce.

Latz [lats], *m.* (—es, *pl.* ⁓e) flap, bib; pinafore.

lau [lau], *adj.* tepid, lukewarm, insipid; (*fig.*) half-hearted.

Laub [laup], *n.* (—es, *no pl.*) foliage, leaves.

Laube ['laubə], *f.* (—, *pl.* —n) arbour, summer-house.

Laubengang ['laubəngaŋ], *m.* (—es, *pl.* ⁓e) arcade, covered walk.

Laubfrosch ['laupfrɔʃ], *m.* (—es, *pl.* ⁓e) (*Zool.*) tree-frog.

Laubsäge ['laupzɛːgə], *f.* (—, *pl.* —n) fret-saw.

Lauch [laux], *m.* (—es, *no pl.*) (*Bot.*) leek.

Lauer ['lauər], *f.* (—, *no pl.*) ambush, hiding-place; *auf der* — *sein*, lie in wait.

lauern

lauern ['lauərn], *v.n.* lurk, lie in wait (for), watch (for).

Lauf [lauf], *m.* (**—es,** *pl.* ‑e) course, run; running; operation; (*river*) current; (*gun*) barrel; (*fig.*) rein.

Laufbahn ['laufbaːn], *f.* (**—,** *pl.* **—en**) career, *die medizinische — einschlagen,* enter upon a medical career.

Laufband ['laufbant], *n.* (**—s,** *pl.* ‑er) (*baby*) rein, leading-string; (*Tech.*) conveyor-belt.

Laufbrücke ['laufbrykə], *f.* (**—,** *pl.* **—n**) gangway.

Laufbursche ['laufburʃə], *m.* (**—n,** *pl.* **—n**) errand-boy.

laufen ['laufən], *v.n. irr.* (*aux.* sein) run; walk; (*wheel*) turn; flow, trickle down.

laufend ['laufənt], *adj.* current.

Läufer ['lɔyfər], *m.* (**—s,** *pl.* **—**) runner; (*carpet*) rug; (*Chess*) bishop; (*Footb.*) half-back.

Lauffeuer ['lauffɔyər], *n.* (**—s,** *no pl.*) wildfire.

Laufgraben ['laufgraːbən], *m.* (**—s,** *pl.* ‑) trench.

läufig ['lɔyfiç], *adj.* (*animals*) ruttish.

Laufpaß ['laufpas], *m.* (**—sses,** *no pl.*) *den — geben,* give (s.o.) the sack.

Laufschritt ['laufʃrit], *m.* (**—es,** *pl.* **—e**) march; *im —,* at the double.

Laufzeit ['lauftsait], *f.* (**—,** *pl.* **—en**) running-time; currency; (*animals*) rutting time.

Lauge ['laugə], *f.* (**—,** *pl.* **—en**) (*Chem.*) lye, alkali.

Lauheit ['lauhait], *f.* (**—,** *no pl.*) tepidity, lukewarmness; (*fig.*) half-heartedness.

Laune ['launə], *f.* (**—,** *pl.* **—n**) humour, temper, mood, whim.

launenhaft ['launənhaft], *adj.* moody.

launig ['launiç], *adj.* humorous.

launisch ['launiʃ], *adj.* moody, fitful, bad-tempered.

Laus [laus], *f.* (**—,** *pl.* ‑e) (*Zool.*) louse.

Lausbub ['lausbuːp], *m.* (**—en,** *pl.* **—en**) young scamp, rascal.

lauschen ['lauʃən], *v.n.* listen, eavesdrop.

Lausejunge ['lauzəjuŋə], *m.* (**—n,** *pl.* **—n**) rascal, lout.

lausig ['lauziç], *adj.* (*vulg.*) sordid, lousy.

laut [laut], *adj.* loud, noisy, audible, clamorous. — *prep.* (*Genit.*) as per, according to, in virtue of.

Laut [laut], *m.* (**—es,** *pl.* **—e**) sound.

lautbar ['lautbaːr], *adj.* — *machen,* make known.

Laute ['lautə], *f.* (**—,** *pl.* **—n**) (*Mus.*) lute.

lauten ['lautən], *v.n.* purport, run, read.

läuten ['lɔytən], *v.a., v.n.* ring; toll; *es läutet,* the bell is ringing.

lauter ['lautər], *adj.* clear, pure; (*fig.*) single-minded; genuine; nothing but. — *adv.* merely.

Lauterkeit ['lautərkait], *f.* (**—,** *no pl.*) clearness, purity; (*fig.*) single-mindedness, integrity.

läutern ['lɔytərn], *v.a.* clear, purify; refine.

Läuterung ['lɔytəruŋ], *f.* (**—,** *pl.* **—en**) clearing, purification; refinement.

lautieren [lau'tiːrən], *v.a.* read phonetically.

Lautlehre ['lautleːrə], *f.* (**—,** *no pl.*) phonetics.

lautlich ['lautliç], *adj.* phonetic.

lautlos ['lautloːs], *adj.* mute, silent; noiseless.

Lautmalerei ['lautmaːlərai], *f.* (**—,** *no pl.*) onomatopoeia.

Lautsprecher ['lautʃpreçər], *m.* (**—s,** *pl.* **—**) loudspeaker.

Lautverschiebung ['lautfərʃiːbuŋ], *f.* (**—,** *pl.* **—en**) sound shift.

lauwarm ['lauvarm], *adj.* lukewarm, tepid; (*fig.*) half-hearted.

Lava ['laːva], *f.* (**—,** *no pl.*) lava.

Lavendel [la'vendəl], *m.* (**—s,** *no pl.*) (*Bot.*) lavender.

lavieren [la'viːrən], *v.n.* tack; (*fig.*) wangle.

Lawine [la'viːnə], *f.* (**—,** *pl.* **—n**) avalanche.

lax [laks], *adj.* lax, loose.

Laxheit ['lakshait], *f.* (**—,** *pl.* **—en**) laxity.

Laxiermittel [lak'siːrmitəl], *n.* (**—s,** *pl.* **—**) laxative, aperient.

Lazarett [latsa'ret], *n.* (**—s,** *pl.* **—e**) infirmary, military hospital.

Lebemann ['leːbəman], *m.* (**—es,** *pl.* ‑er) man about town.

Leben ['leːbən], *n.* (**—s,** *pl.* **—**) life; (*fig.*) existence; activity; animation, bustle, stir.

leben ['leːbən], *v.n.* live, be alive.

lebend ['leːbənt], *adj.* alive, living; (*language*) modern.

lebendig [le'bɛndiç], *adj.* living, alive, quick.

Lebensanschauung ['leːbənsanʃauuŋ], *f.* (**—,** *pl.* **—en**) conception of life, philosophy of life.

Lebensart ['leːbənsaːrt], *f.* (**—,** *no pl.*) way of living; (*fig.*) behaviour; *gute —,* good manners.

lebensfähig ['leːbənsfɛːiç], *adj.* capable of living, viable.

lebensgefährlich ['leːbənsgəfɛːrliç], *adj.* perilous, extremely dangerous.

Lebensgeister ['leːbənsgaistər], *m. pl.* spirits.

lebensgroß ['leːbənsgroːs], *adj.* life-size.

lebenslänglich ['leːbənslɛŋliç], *adj.* lifelong, for life; *—e Rente,* annuity.

Lebenslauf ['leːbənslauf], *m.* (**—es,** *pl.* ‑e) curriculum vitae.

Lebensmittel ['leːbənsmitəl], *n. pl.* food, provisions, victuals.

lebensmüde ['leːbənsmyːdə], *adj.* weary of life.

Lebensunterhalt ['leːbənsuntərhalt], *m.* (**—s,** *no pl.*) livelihood.

Lebenswandel ['leːbənsvandəl], *m.* (**—s,** *no pl.*) conduct, mode of life.

Lebensweise ['le:bənsvaızə], *f.* (—, *no pl.*) habits, way of life.
Leber ['le:bər], *f.* (—, *pl.* —n) liver; *frisch von der — weg*, frankly, without mincing matters.
Leberblümchen ['le:bərbly:mçən], *n.* (—s, *pl.* —) (*Bot.*) liverwort.
Leberfleck ['le:bərflɛk], *m.* (—s, *pl.* —e) mole.
Lebertran ['le:bərtra:n], *m.* (—s, *no pl.*) cod-liver oil.
Leberwurst ['le:bərvurst], *f.* (—, *pl.* ⁓e) liver sausage.
Lebewesen ['le:bəve:zən], *n.* (—s, *pl.* —) living creature.
Lebewohl ['le:bəvo:l], *n.*, *excl.* farewell, good-bye; *— sagen*, bid farewell.
lebhaft ['le:phaft], *adj.* lively, vivacious, brisk, animated.
Lebkuchen ['le:pku:xən], *m.* (—s, *pl.* —) gingerbread.
Lebzeiten ['le:ptsaıtən], *f. pl. zu — von* (*Genit.*), in the lifetime of.
lechzen ['lɛçtsən], *v.n.* be parched with thirst; *nach etwas —*, (*fig.*) long for s.th., pine for s.th.
Leck [lɛk], *n.* (—s, *pl.* —e) leak; *ein — bekommen*, spring a leak.
leck [lɛk], *adj.* leaky.
lecken ['lɛkən], *v.a.* lick, lap.
lecker ['lɛkər], *adj.* delicate, delicious, dainty.
Leckerbissen ['lɛkərbisən], *m.* (—s, *pl.* —) delicacy; dainty, tit-bit.
Leckerei [lɛkə'raı], *f.* (—, *pl.* —en) delicacy.
Leder ['le:dər], *n.* (—s, *no pl.*) leather.
ledern ['le:dərn], *adj.* (of) leather, leathery; (*fig.*) dull, boring.
ledig ['le:dıç], *adj.* unmarried, single; (*fig.*) rid of, free from.
lediglich ['le:dıklıç], *adv.* merely, only, solely.
leer [le:r], *adj.* empty, void; blank; (*fig.*) hollow, futile, empty, vain, inane.
Leere ['le:rə], *f.* (—, *no pl.*) emptiness, void, vacuum.
leeren ['le:rən], *v.a.* empty, evacuate.
Leerlauf ['le:rlauf], *m.* (—s, *no pl.*) (*Motor.*) idling; (*gear*) neutral.
legalisieren [legali'zi:rən], *v.a.* legalise, authenticate.
Legat (1) [le'ga:t], *m.* (—en, *pl.* —en) legate.
Legat (2) [le'ga:t], *n.* (—s, *pl.* —e) legacy, bequest.
Legationsrat [lega'tsjo:nsra:t], *m.* (—s, *pl.* ⁓e) counsellor in a legation.
legen ['le:gən], *v.a.* lay, put, place. *— v.r. sich —*, lie down; cease, subside.
Legende [le'gɛndə], *f.* (—, *pl.* —n) legend.
Legierung [lə'gi:ruŋ], *f.* (—, *pl.* —en) alloy.
Legion [le'gjo:n], *f.* (—, *pl.* —en) legion.
Legionär [le:gjo'nɛ:r], *m.* (—s, *pl.* —e) legionary.
legitim [legi'ti:m], *adj.* legitimate.

Legitimation [legitima'tsjo:n], *f.* (—, *pl.* —en) proof of identity.
legitimieren [legiti'mi:rən], *v.a.* legitimise. *— v.r. sich —*, prove o.'s identity.
Lehen ['le:ən], *n.* (—s, *pl.* —) fief; *zu — geben*, invest with, enfeoff; *zu — tragen*, hold in fee.
Lehensdienst *see* **Lehnsdienst**.
Lehenseid *see* **Lehnseid**.
Lehensmann *see* **Lehnsmann**.
Lehm [le:m], *m.* (—s, *no pl.*) loam, clay, mud.
lehmig ['le:mıç], *adj.* clayey, loamy.
Lehne ['le:nə], *f.* (—, *pl.* —n) support, prop; (*chair*) back, arm-rest.
lehnen ['le:nən], *v.a.*, *v.n.* lean. *— v.r. sich — an*, lean against.
Lehnsdienst ['le:nsdi:nst], *m.* (—es, *pl.* —e) feudal service.
Lehnseid ['le:nsaıt], *m.* (—es, *pl.* —e) oath of allegiance.
Lehnsmann ['le:nsman], *m.* (—es, *pl.* ⁓er) feudal tenant, vassal.
Lehnstuhl ['le:nʃtu:l], *m.* (—s, *pl.* ⁓e) armchair, easy chair.
Lehramt ['le:ramt], *n.* (—es, *pl.* ⁓er) professorship; teaching post *or* profession.
Lehrbrief ['le:rbri:f], *m.* (—es, *pl.* —e) apprentice's indentures; certificate of apprenticeship.
Lehrbuch ['le:rbu:x], *n.* (—es, *pl.* ⁓er) textbook, manual.
Lehre ['le:rə], *f.* (—, *pl.* —n) teaching, advice, rule, doctrine, dogma, moral; (*craft*) apprenticeship.
lehren ['le:rən], *v.a.* teach, inform, instruct; profess.
Lehrer ['le:rər], *m.* (—s, *pl.* —) teacher, instructor, schoolmaster.
Lehrgang ['le:rgaŋ], *m.* (—es, *pl.* ⁓e) course (of instruction).
Lehrgegenstand ['le:rge:gənʃtant], *m.* (—es, *pl.* ⁓e) subject of instruction; branch of study.
Lehrgeld ['le:rgɛlt], *n.* (—es, *pl.* —er) premium for apprenticeship; *— zahlen*, (*fig.*) pay for o.'s experience.
Lehrkörper ['le:rkø:rpər], *m.* (—s, *no pl.*) teaching staff; (*Univ.*) faculty.
Lehrling ['le:rlıŋ], *m.* (—s, *pl.* —e) apprentice.
Lehrmädchen ['le:rme:tçən], *n.* (—s, *pl.* —) girl apprentice.
Lehrmeister ['le:rmaıstər], *m.* (—s, *pl.* —) teacher, instructor, master.
Lehrmittel ['le:rmıtəl], *n.* (—s, *pl.* —) teaching appliance or aid.
lehrreich ['le:rraıç], *adj.* instructive.
Lehrsatz ['le:rzats], *m.* (—es, *pl.* ⁓e) tenet, dogma, rule; (*Maths.*) theorem.
Lehrstuhl ['le:rʃtu:l], *m.* (—s, *pl.* ⁓e) (*Univ.*) chair; professorship.
Lehrzeit ['le:rtsaıt], *f.* (—, *pl.* —en) apprenticeship.
Leib [laıp], *m.* (—es, *pl.* —er) body; abdomen; womb.
Leibarzt ['laıpa:rtst], *m.* (—es, *pl.* ⁓e) court surgeon.

Leibbinde

Leibbinde ['laɪpbɪndə], *f.* (—, *pl.* —n) abdominal belt.

Leibchen ['laɪpçən], *n.* (—s, *pl.* —) bodice, corset; vest.

leibeigen [laɪp'aɪgən], *adj.* in bondage, in thraldom, in serfdom.

Leibeserbe ['laɪbəserbə], *m.* (—n, *pl.* —n) heir, descendant, offspring; (*pl.*) issue.

Leibesfrucht ['laɪbəsfruxt], *f.* (—, *pl.* ⁻e) embryo, foetus.

Leibeskraft ['laɪbəskraft], *f.* (—, *pl.* ⁻e) bodily strength; *aus* —en, with might and main.

Leibesübung ['laɪbəsyːbuŋ], *f.* (—, *pl.* —en) physical exercise; (*pl.*) gymnastic exercises.

Leibgericht ['laɪpgərɪçt], *n.* (—s, *pl.* —e) favourite dish.

leibhaftig [laɪp'haftɪç], *adj.* real, incarnate, in person.

leiblich ['laɪplɪç], *adj.* bodily, corporeal.

Leibrente ['laɪprɛntə], *f.* (—, *pl.* —n) life-annuity.

Leibschmerzen ['laɪpʃmɛrtsən], *m. pl.* stomach-ache.

Leibspeise ['laɪpʃpaɪzə], *f.* (—, *pl.* —n) favourite dish.

Leibwache ['laɪpvaxə], *f.* (—, *no pl.*) body-guard.

Leibwäsche ['laɪpvɛʃə], *f.* (—, *no pl.*) underwear.

Leiche ['laɪçə], *f.* (—, *pl.* —n) (dead) body, corpse; (*dial.*) funeral.

Leichenbegängnis ['laɪçənbəgɛŋnɪs], *n.* (—ses, *pl.* —se) funeral, burial, interment.

Leichenbeschauer ['laɪçənbəʃauər], *m.* (—s, *pl.* —) coroner.

Leichenbestatter ['laɪçənbəʃtater], *m.* (—s, *pl.* —) undertaker; (*Am.*) mortician.

leichenhaft ['laɪçenhaft], *adj.* corpselike, cadaverous.

Leichenschau ['laɪçənʃau], *f.* (—, *no pl.*) post mortem (examination), (coroner's) inquest.

Leichentuch ['laɪçəntuːx], *n.* (—es, *pl.* ⁻er) shroud, pall.

Leichenverbrennung ['laɪçənferbrennuŋ], *f.* (—, *pl.* —en) cremation.

Leichenwagen ['laɪçənvaːgən], *m.* (—s, *pl.* —) hearse.

Leichenzug ['laɪçəntsuːk], *m.* (—es, *pl.* ⁻e) funeral procession.

Leichnam ['laɪçnaːm], *m.* (—s, *pl.* —e) (dead) body, corpse.

leicht [laɪçt], *adj.* light; slight; weak; easy.

leichtfertig ['laɪçtfertɪç], *adj.* frivolous, irresponsible.

leichtgläubig ['laɪçtglɔybɪç], *adj.* credulous, gullible.

leichthin ['laɪçthɪn], *adv.* lightly.

Leichtigkeit ['laɪçtɪçkaɪt], *f.* (—, *no pl.*) ease, facility.

Leichtsinn ['laɪçtzɪn], *m.* (—s, *no pl.*) thoughtlessness, carelessness; frivolity.

Leid [laɪt], *n.* (—es, *no pl.*) sorrow, grief; harm, hurt; *einem etwas zu* —e *tun*, harm s.o.

leid [laɪt], *adj. es tut mir* —, I am sorry; ⁻*du tust mir* —, I am sorry for you.

Leiden ['laɪdən], *n.* (—s, *pl.* —) suffering, misfortune; (*illness*) affliction, complaint; *das* — *Christi*, the Passion.

leiden ['laɪdən], *v.a., v.n. irr.* suffer, bear, endure, undergo.

Leidenschaft ['laɪdənʃaft], *f.* (—, *pl.* —en) passion.

leider ['laɪdər], *adv.* unfortunately.

leidig ['laɪdɪç], *adj.* tiresome, unpleasant.

leidlich ['laɪtlɪç], *adj.* tolerable, moderate.

leidtragend ['laɪttraːgənt], *adj.* in mourning.

Leidtragende ['laɪttraːgəndə], *m. or f.* (—n, *pl.* —n) mourner.

Leidwesen ['laɪtveːzən], *n.* (—s, *no pl.*) *zu meinem* —, to my regret.

Leier ['laɪər], *f.* (—, *pl.* —n) lyre.

Leierkasten ['laɪərkastən], *m.* (—s, *pl.* ⁻) barrel organ.

leiern ['laɪərn], *v.n.* drone, drawl on.

leihen ['laɪən], *v.a. irr. einem etwas* —, lend s.o. s.th.; *von einem etwas* —, borrow s.th. from s.o.

Leim [laɪm], *m.* (—s, *no pl.*) glue; *einem auf den* — *gehen*, be taken in by s.o., fall for s.th.

Leimfarbe ['laɪmfarbə], *f.* (—, *pl.* —en) water-colour, distemper.

Lein [laɪn], *m.* (—s, *pl.* —e) linseed, flax.

Leine ['laɪnə], *f.* (—, *pl.* —n) line, cord.

Leinen ['laɪnən], *n.* (—s, *no pl.*) linen.

Leinöl ['laɪnøːl], *n.* (—s, *no pl.*) linseed oil.

Leintuch ['laɪntuːx], *n.* (—es, *pl.* ⁻er) linen sheet, sheeting.

Leinwand ['laɪnvant], *f.* (—, *no pl.*) linen, sheeting; (*Art*) canvas; (*film*) screen.

leise ['laɪzə], *adj.* low, soft, gentle, faint, slight; delicate.

Leiste ['laɪstə], *f.* (—, *pl.* —n) ledge, border; groin.

Leisten ['laɪstən], *m.* (—s, *pl.* —) (*shoe*) last, forme.

leisten ['laɪstən], *v.a.* do, perform; accomplish; *ich kann es mir nicht* —, I cannot afford it.

Leistenbruch ['laɪstənbrux], *m.* (—es, *pl.* ⁻e) hernia, rupture.

Leistung ['laɪstuŋ], *f.* (—, *pl.* —en) performance, accomplishment, achievement.

leistungsfähig ['laɪstuŋksfɛːɪç], *adj.* efficient.

leiten ['laɪtən], *v.a.* lead, guide, manage; preside over.

Leiter (1) ['laɪtər], *m.* (—s, *pl.* —) leader, manager; conductor; head.

Leiter (2) ['laɪtər], *f.* (—, *pl.* —n) ladder.

Leiterwagen ['laɪtərvaːgən], *m.* (—s, *pl.* —) rack-wagon; (*Austr.*) small hand-cart.

Leitfaden ['laitfɑ:dən], *m.* (—s, *pl.* ∵) (*book*) manual, textbook, guide.

Leitstern ['laitʃtɛrn], *m.* (—s, *pl.* —e) pole-star; (*fig.*) lodestar, guiding star.

Leitung ['laituŋ], *f.* (—, *pl.* —en) management, direction; (*Elec.*) lead, connection; line; (water- *or* gas-) main(s); pipeline; *eine lange — haben*, be slow in the uptake.

Leitungsvermögen ['laituŋsfɛrmø:- gən], *n.* (—s, *no pl.*) conductivity.

Leitwerk ['laitvɛrk], *n.* (—s, *no pl.*) (*Aviat.*) tail unit.

Lektion [lɛkts'jo:n], *f.* (—, *pl.* —en) lesson; *einem eine —, geben*, lecture s.o.

Lektor ['lɛktɔr], *m.* (—s, *pl.* —en) publisher's reader; teacher, lector.

Lektüre [lɛk'ty:rə], *f.* (—, *pl.* —n) reading matter, books.

Lende ['lɛndə], *f.* (—, *pl.* —n) (*Anat.*) loin.

lendenlahm ['lɛndənlɑ:m], *adj.* weak-kneed, lame.

lenkbar ['lɛŋkbɑ:r], *adj.* dirigible, manageable, tractable, governable.

lenken ['lɛŋkən], *v.a.* drive, steer; (*fig.*) direct, rule, manage.

Lenkstange ['lɛŋkʃtaŋə], *f.* (—, *pl.* —n) connecting-rod; (*bicycle*) handle-bar.

Lenz [lɛnts], *m.* (—es, *pl.* —e) (*Poet.*) spring.

Lepra ['le:pra], *f.* (—, *no pl.*) leprosy.

Lerche ['lɛrçə], *f.* (—, *pl.* —n) (*Orn.*) lark, skylark.

lernbegierig ['lɛrnbəgi:rɪç], *adj.* studious, eager to learn.

lernen ['lɛrnən], *v.a.* learn; study; *einen kennen —*, make s.o.'s acquaintance; *auswendig —*, learn by heart.

Lesart ['le:sa:rt], *f.* (—, *pl.* —en) reading, version.

lesbar ['le:sba:r], *adj.* legible; readable.

Lese ['le:zə], *f.* (—, *pl.* —n) gathering (of fruit); vintage.

lesen ['le:zən], *v.a. irr.* gather; glean; read; *die Messe —*, celebrate *or* say mass; *über etwas —*, (*Univ.*) lecture on s.th.

lesenswert ['le:zənsvɛrt], *adj.* worth reading.

Leser ['le:zər], *m.* (—s, *pl.* —) gatherer, gleaner; reader.

leserlich ['le:zərlɪç], *adj.* legible.

Lettland ['lɛtlant], *n.* Latvia.

letzen ['lɛtsən], *v.a.* (*Poet.*) comfort, cheer, refresh.

letzt [lɛtst], *adj.* last, extreme, ultimate, final.

letztens ['lɛtstəns], *adv.* lastly, in the end.

letztere ['lɛtstərə], *adj.* latter.

letzthin ['lɛtsthɪn], *adv.* (*rare*) lately, the other day, recently.

Leu [lɔy], *m.* (—en, *pl.* —en) (*Poet.*) lion.

Leuchte ['lɔyçtə], *f.* (—, *pl.* —n) light, lamp, lantern; (*fig.*) luminary, star.

leuchten ['lɔyçtən], *v.n.* light, shine.

leuchtend ['lɔyçtənt], *adj.* shining, bright; luminous.

Leuchter ['lɔyçtər], *m.* (—s, *pl.* —) candlestick, candelabrum.

Leuchtrakete ['lɔyçtrake:tə], *f.* (—, *pl.* —n) Roman candle; flare.

Leuchtturm ['lɔyçtturm], *m.* (—s, *pl.* ∵e) lighthouse.

leugnen ['lɔygnən], *v.a.* deny, disclaim; *nicht zu —*, undeniable.

Leumund ['lɔymunt], *m.* (—es, *no pl.*) renown, reputation.

Leute ['lɔytə], *pl.* persons, people, men; servants, domestic staff.

Leutnant ['lɔytnant], *m.* (—s, *pl.* —s) lieutenant.

leutselig ['lɔytze:lɪç], *adj.* affable, friendly; condescending.

Levkoje [lɛf'ko:jə], *f.* (—, *pl.* —n) (*Bot.*) stock.

Lexikon ['lɛksɪkɔn], *n.* (—s, *pl.* —s, —ka) dictionary, lexicon, encyclopaedia.

Libanon ['li:banɔn], *m.* Lebanon.

Libelle [li'bɛlə], *f.* (—, *pl.* —n) (*Ent.*) dragonfly.

Liberia [li'be:rja], *n.* Liberia.

Libyen ['li:bɪən], *n.* Libya.

Licht [lɪçt], *n.* (—es, *pl.* —er) light, candle; luminary.

licht [lɪçt], *adj.* light, clear, open.

Lichtbild ['lɪçtbɪlt], *n.* (—es, *pl.* —er) photograph.

Lichtbrechung ['lɪçtbrɛçuŋ], *f.* (—, *pl.* —en) refraction of light.

lichten ['lɪçtən], *v.a.* clear, thin; *den Anker —*, weigh anchor.

lichterloh ['lɪçtərlo:], *adj.* blazing, ablaze.

Lichthof ['lɪçtho:f], *m.* (—s, *pl.* ∵e) well of a court, quadrangle.

Lichtmeß ['lɪçtmɛs], *f.* (—, *no pl.*) (*Eccl.*) Candlemas.

Lichtschirm ['lɪçtʃɪrm], *m.* (—s, *pl.* —e) screen, lamp-shade.

Lichtspieltheater ['lɪçtʃpi:ltea:tər], *n.* (—s, *pl.* —) cinema.

Lichtung ['lɪçtuŋ], *f.* (—, *pl.* —en) glade, clearing.

Lid [li:t], *n.* (—s, *pl.* —er) eye-lid.

lieb [li:p], *adj.* dear; beloved; good; *das ist mir —*, I am glad of it; *der —e Gott*, God; *unsere —e Frau*, Our Lady; *bei einem — Kind sein*, be a favourite with s.o., curry favour with s.o.

liebäugeln ['li:pɔygəln], *v.n. insep.* ogle.

Liebchen ['li:pçən], *n.* (—s, *pl.* —) sweetheart, love, darling.

Liebe ['li:bə], *f.* (—, *no pl.*) love.

Liebelei [li:bə'lai], *f.* (—, *pl.* —en) flirtation.

lieben ['li:bən], *v.a.* love, like, be fond of.

liebenswürdig ['li:bənsvyrdɪç], *adj.* amiable, kind, charming.

lieber ['li:bər], *adv.* rather, better, sooner; *etwas — tun*, prefer to do s.th.

Liebhaber ['li:pha:bər], *m.* (—s, *pl.* —) lover; (*fig.*) amateur, dilettante; (*Theat.*) leading man.

Liebhaberin ['li:phabərɪn], *f.* leading lady.

liebkosen ['li:pko:zən], *v.a.* *insep.* fondle, caress.

lieblich ['li:plɪç], *adj.* lovely, charming, sweet.

Liebling ['li:plɪŋ], *m.* (—s, *pl.* —e) darling, favourite.

lieblos ['li:plo:s], *adj.* hard-hearted; unkind.

Liebreiz ['li:praɪts], *m.* (—es, *no pl.*) charm, attractiveness.

liebreizend ['li:praɪtsənt], *adj.* charming.

Liebschaft ['li:pʃaft], *f.* (—, *pl.* —en) love affair.

Lied [li:t], *n.* (—es, *pl.* —er) song, air, tune; *geistliches* —, hymn.

liederlich ['li:dərlɪç], *adj.* careless, slovenly; dissolute, debauched; —es Leben, profligacy.

Lieferant [li:fə'rant], *m.* (—en, *pl.* —en) supplier, purveyor, contractor; Eingang für —en, tradesmen's entrance.

liefern ['li:fərn], *v.a.* deliver, furnish, supply.

Lieferschein ['li:fərʃaɪn], *m.* (—s, *pl.* —e) delivery note.

liegen ['li:gən], *v.n. irr.* lie; be situated; es liegt mir daran, it is of importance to me, I have it at heart; es liegt mir nichts daran, it is of no consequence to me.

Liegenschaft ['li:gənʃaft], *f.* (—, *pl.* —en) landed property, real estate.

Liga ['li:ga:], *f.* (—, *pl.* —gen) league.

Liguster [li'gustər], *m.* (—s, *no pl.*) privet.

liieren [li'i:rən], *v.r.* (*aux.* haben) sich — mit, unite with, combine with.

Likör [li'kø:r], *m.* (—s, *pl.* —e) liqueur.

lila ['li:la:] *adj.* (*colour*) lilac.

Lilie ['li:ljə], *f.* (—, *pl.* —n) (*Bot.*) lily.

Limonade [limo'na:də], *f.* (—, *pl.* —n) lemonade.

lind [lɪnt], *adj.* soft, gentle, mild.

Linde ['lɪndə], *f.* (—, *pl.* —n) (*Bot.*) lime-tree, linden.

lindern ['lɪndərn], *v.a.* soften, assuage, mitigate, soothe, allay.

Lindwurm ['lɪntvurm], *m.* (—s, *pl.* —er) (*Poet.*) dragon.

Lineal [line'a:l], *m.* (—s, *pl.* —e) ruler, rule.

Linie ['li:njə], *f.* (—, *pl.* —n) line; lineage, descent; in erster —, in the first place.

Linienschiff ['li:njənʃɪf], *n.* (—es, *pl.* —e) (*Naut.*) liner.

lin(i)ieren [lin'(j)i:rən], *v.a.* rule.

linkisch ['lɪŋkɪʃ], *adj.* awkward, clumsy.

links [lɪŋks], *adv.* to the left, on the left-hand side; —um! left about turn!

Linnen ['lɪnən], *n.* (—s, *no pl.*) (*Poet.*) linen.

Linse ['lɪnzə], *f.* (—, *pl.* —n) (*vegetable*) lentil; (*optical*) lens.

linsenförmig ['lɪnzənfœrmɪç], *adj.* lens-shaped.

Linsengericht ['lɪnzəngərɪçt], *n.* (—s, *pl.* —e) (*Bibl.*) mess of pottage.

Lippe ['lɪpə], *f.* (—, *pl.* —n) lip; (*coll.*) eine — riskieren, be cheeky.

Lippenlaut ['lɪpənlaut], *m.* (—s, *pl.* —e) (*Phonet.*) labial.

Lippenstift ['lɪpənʃtɪft], *m.* (—s, *pl.* —e) lipstick.

liquidieren [lɪkvi'di:rən], *v.a.* liquidate, wind up, settle; charge.

lispeln ['lɪspəln], *v.n.* lisp.

Lissabon [lɪsa'bɔn], *n.* Lisbon.

List [lɪst], *f.* (—, *pl.* —en) cunning, craft; trick, stratagem, ruse.

Liste ['lɪstə], *f.* (—, *pl.* —n) list, roll, catalogue.

listig ['lɪstɪç], *adj.* cunning, crafty, sly.

Listigkeit ['lɪstɪçkaɪt], *f.* (—, *no pl.*) slyness, craftiness.

Litanei [lita'naɪ], *f.* (—, *pl.* —en) litany.

Litauen ['lɪtauən], *n.* Lithuania.

Liter ['li:tər], *m. & n.* (—s, *pl.* —) litre.

literarisch [litə'ra:rɪʃ], *adj.* literary.

Literatur [litəra'tu:r], *f.* (—, *pl.* —en) literature, letters.

Litfaßsäule ['lɪtfaszɔylə], *f.* (—, *pl.* —n) advertisement pillar.

Liturgie [litur'gi:], *f.* (—, *pl.* —n) liturgy.

Litze ['lɪtsə], *f.* (—, *pl.* —n) lace, braid, cord; (*Elec.*) flex.

Livland ['li:flant], *n.* Livonia.

Livree [li'vre:], *f.* (—, *pl.* —n) livery.

Lizenz [li'tsɛnts], *f.* (—, *pl.* —en) licence.

Lob [lo:p], *n.* (—es, *no pl.*) praise, commendation.

loben ['lo:bən], *v.a.* praise, commend.

lobesam [lo'bəza:m], *adj.* (*Poet.*) worthy, honourable.

Lobgesang ['lo:pgəzaŋ], *m.* (—s, *pl.* —e) hymn of praise.

Lobhudelei [lo:phu:də'laɪ], *f.* (—, *pl.* —en) adulation, flattery, toadying.

löblich ['lø:plɪç], *adj.* laudable, commendable, meritorious.

lobpreisen ['lo:ppraɪzən], *v.a. insep.* eulogise, extol.

Lobrede ['lo:pre:də], *f.* (—, *pl.* —n) panegyric, eulogy.

Loch [lɔx], *n.* (—es, *pl.* —er) hole.

Lochbohrer ['lɔxbo:rər], *m.* (—s, *pl.*—) auger.

lochen ['lɔxən], *v.a.* perforate, punch.

Locher ['lɔxər], *m.* (—s, *pl.* —) perforator, punch.

löcherig ['lœçərɪç], *adj.* full of holes.

Lochmeißel ['lɔxmaɪsəl], *m.* (—s, *pl.* —) mortice-chisel.

Locke ['lɔkə], *f.* (—, *pl.* —n) curl, lock, ringlet, tress.

locken ['lɔkən], *v.a.* allure, decoy, entice.

locker ['lɔkər], *adj.* loose; slack; spongy; dissolute; nicht — lassen, stick to o.'s guns.

lockern ['lɔkərn], *v.a.* loosen.

lockig ['lɔkɪç], *adj.* curled, curly.

Lockmittel ['lɔkmɪtəl], *n.* (—s, *pl.* —) inducement, lure, bait.

Lockspeise ['lɔkʃpaɪzə], *f.* (—, *pl.* —n) lure, bait.

Lockung ['lɔkuŋ], f. (—, pl. —en) allurement, enticement. *

Lockvogel ['lɔkfoːgəl], m. (—s, pl. ⁓) decoy-bird.

Loden ['loːdən], m. (—s, pl. —) coarse cloth, frieze.

lodern ['loːdərn], v.n. blaze, flame.

Löffel ['lœfəl], m. (—s, pl. —) spoon; (*animal*) ear; *einen über den — barbieren*, take s.o. in.

Logarithmus [loga'rɪtmus], m. (—, pl. —men) logarithm.

Logbuch ['lɔkbuːx], n. (—es, pl. ⁓er) logbook.

Loge ['loːʒə], f. (—, pl. —n) (*Theat.*) box; (*Freemasonry*) lodge.

Logenschließer ['loːʒənʃliːsər], m. (—s, pl. —) (*Theat.*) attendant.

logieren [lo'ʒiːrən], v.n. board (with).

Logis [lo'ʒiː], n. (—, pl. —) lodgings.

logisch ['loːgɪʃ], adj. logical.

Lohe ['loːhə], f. (—, pl. —n) tanning bark; flame.

Lohgerber ['loːgɛrbər], m. (—s, pl. —) tanner.

Lohn [loːn]; m. (—s, pl. ⁓e) wages, pay; reward; recompense.

lohnen ['loːnən], v.a. reward, recompense, remunerate; pay wages to; *es lohnt sich nicht*, it is not worth while.

Lohnstopp ['loːnʃtɔp], m. (—s, pl. —s) pay pause, wage freeze.

Löhnung ['løːnuŋ], f. (—, pl. —en) pay, payment.

Lokal [lo'kaːl], n. (—s, pl —e) locality, premises; inn, pub, café.

lokalisieren [lokali'ziːrən], v.a. localise.

Lokalität [lokali'tɛːt], f. (—, pl. —en) *see* Lokal.

Lokomotive [lokomo'tiːvə], f. (—, pl. —n) (*Railw.*) locomotive, engine.

Lokomotivführer [lokomo'tiːffyːrər], m. (—s, pl. —) (*Railw.*) engine-driver.

Lombard [lɔm'bart], m. (—s, pl. —e) deposit-bank, loan bank.

Lombardei [lɔmbar'daɪ], f. Lombardy.

Lorbeer ['lɔrbeːr], m. (—s, pl. —en) laurel.

Lorbeerbaum ['lɔrbeːrbaum], m. (—s, pl. ⁓e) laurel-tree, bay-tree.

Lorbeerspiritus ['lɔrbeːrʃpiːritus], m. (—, no pl.) bay rum.

Lorgnon [lɔrn'jõ], n. (—s, pl. —s) monocle, eye-glass.

Los [loːs], n. (—es, pl. —e) share, ticket; lot, fate; *das große —*, first prize.

los [loːs], adj. loose, untied; free from, released from, rid of; (*Am.*) quit of; *was ist los ?* what is going on ? what's the matter ? *etwas — werden*, get rid of s.th.; *schieß los !* fire away!

lösbar ['løːsbaːr], adj. (*question, riddle*) soluble.

losbinden ['loːsbɪndən], v.a. irr. untie, unbind, loosen.

losbrechen ['loːsbrɛçən], v.a. irr. break off. — v.n. (aux. sein) break loose.

Löschblatt ['lœʃblat], n. (—es, pl. ⁓er) blotting-paper.

Löscheimer ['lœʃaɪmər], m. (—s, pl. —) fire-bucket.

löschen ['lœʃən], v.a. put out; extinguish; (*debt*) cancel; (*writing*) efface, blot; (*freight*) (*Naut.*) unload; (*thirst*) quench.

Löschpapier ['lœʃpapiːr], n. (—s, no pl.) blotting-paper.

Löschung ['lœʃuŋ], f. (—, pl. —en) (*freight*) (*Naut.*) discharging, landing, unloading.

losdrücken ['loːsdrykən], v.n. discharge, fire.

lose ['loːzə], adj. loose, slack; (*fig.*) dissolute; *—s Maul*, malicious tongue.

Lösegeld ['løːzəgɛlt], n. (—es, pl. ⁓er) ransom.

losen ['loːzən], v.n. draw lots.

lösen ['løːzən], v.a. loosen, untie; absolve, free, deliver; dissolve; solve; (*relations*) break off; (*tickets*) take, buy.

losgehen ['loːsgeːən], v.n. irr. (aux. sein) begin; (*gun*) go off; *auf einen —*, go for s.o.; *jetzt kann's —*, now for it.

loskaufen ['loːskaufən], v.a. redeem, ransom.

loskommen ['loːskɔmən], v.n. irr. (aux. sein) come loose; *von etwas —*, get rid of s.th.

löslich ['løːslɪç], adj. (*Chem.*) soluble.

loslösen ['loːsløːzən], v.a. detach.

losmachen ['loːsmaxən], v.a. free from. — v.r. sich — von, disengage o.s. from.

losreißen ['loːsraɪsən], v.a. irr. pull away, separate. — v.n. (aux. sein), break loose. — v.r. sich — von, tear o.s. away from.

lossagen ['loːszaːgən], v.r. sich — von, renounce s.th., dissociate o.s. from s.th.

losschlagen ['loːsʃlaːgən], v.a. knock loose; let fly; (*fig.*) sell, dispose of.

lossprechen ['loːsʃprɛçən], v.a. irr. (*Eccl.*) absolve; (*Law*) acquit.

lossteuern ['loːsʃtɔyərn], v.n. — auf, make for.

Losung ['loːzuŋ], f. (—, pl. —en) watchword, motto, password, slogan.

Lösung ['løːzuŋ], f. (—, pl. —en) loosening; solution.

losziehen ['loːstsiːən], v.n. irr. (*Mil.*) set out; *gegen einen —*, inveigh against s.o.; (*fig., coll.*) run s.o. down.

Lot [loːt], n. (—es, pl. —e) lead, plummet; (*weight*) half an ounce; (*Maths.*) perpendicular (line).

Löteisen ['løːtaɪzən], n. (—s, pl. —) soldering iron.

loten ['loːtən], v.a., v.n. (*Naut.*) take soundings, plumb.

löten ['løːtən], v.a. solder.

Lothringen ['loːtrɪŋən], n. Lorraine.

Lötkolben ['løːtkɔlbən], m. (—s, pl. —) soldering iron.

Lotleine ['loːtlaɪnə], f. (—, pl. —n) sounding-line.

Lotrechtstarter ['loːtrɛçtʃtartər], m. (—s, pl. —) (*Aviat.*) vertical take-off plane (V.T.O.L.).

143

Lötrohr ['lø:tro:r], n. (—s, pl. —e) soldering-pipe.

Lotse ['lo:tsə], m. (—n, pl. —n) (*Naut.*) pilot.

Lotterbett ['lɔtərbɛt], n. (—es, pl. —en) bed of idleness; (*obs.*) couch.

Lotterie [lɔtə'ri:], f. (—, pl. —n) lottery, sweep-stake.

Lotterleben ['lɔtərle:bən], n. (—s, no pl.) dissolute life.

Löwe ['lø:və], m. (—n, pl. —n) (*Zool.*) lion.

Löwenbändiger ['lø:vənbɛndigər], m. (—s, pl.—) lion tamer.

Löwengrube ['lø:vəngru:bə], f. (—, pl. —n) lion's den.

Löwenmaul ['lø:vənmaul], n. (—s, no pl.) (*Bot.*) snapdragon.

Löwenzahn ['lø:vəntsa:n], m. (—s, no pl.) (*Bot.*) dandelion.

Löwin ['lø:vɪn], f. (—, pl. —nen) (*Zool.*) lioness.

Luchs [luks], m. (—es, pl. —e) lynx.

Lücke ['lykə], f. (—, pl. —n) gap, breach; (*fig.*) omission, defect, blank.

Lückenbüßer ['lykənby:sər], m. (—s, pl. —) stop-gap, stand-in.

lückenhaft ['lykənhaft], adj. fragmentary, incomplete, imperfect.

Luder ['lu:dər], n. (—s, pl. —) (*rare*) carrion; (*vulg.*) beast, trollop; *dummes* —, silly ass, fathead.

Luderleben ['lu:dərle:bən], n. (—s, no pl.) dissolute life.

ludern ['lu:dərn], v.n. lead a dissolute life.

Luft [luft], f. (—, pl. ¨e) air.

Luftbrücke ['luftbrykə], f. (—, no pl.) air-lift.

Lüftchen ['lyftçən], n. (—s, pl. —) gentle breeze.

luftdicht ['luftdɪçt], adj. airtight.

Luftdruck ['luftdruk], m. (—s, no pl.) air pressure, atmospheric pressure; blast.

Luftdruckmesser ['luftdrukmɛsər], m. (—s, pl. —) barometer, pressure-gauge.

lüften ['lyftən], v.a. air, ventilate.

luftförmig ['luftfœrmiç], adj. gaseous.

luftig ['luftiç], adj. airy, windy.

Luftklappe ['luftklapə], f. (—, pl. —n) air-valve.

Luftkurort ['luftku:rɔrt], m. (—s, pl. —e) health resort.

Luftlinie ['luftli:njə], f. (—, pl.—n) bee-line; *in der* —, as the crow flies; (*Aviat.*) airline.

Luftloch ['luftlɔx], m. (—s, pl. ¨er) air-pocket.

Luftraum ['luftraum], m. (—s, no pl.) atmosphere; air space.

Luftröhre ['luftrø:rə], f. (—, pl. —n) windpipe.

Luftschiff ['luftʃif], n. (—es, pl. —e) air-ship.

Luftschiffahrt ['luftʃifa:rt], f. (—, no pl.) aeronautics.

Luftspiegelung ['luftʃpi:gəluŋ], f. (—, pl. —en) mirage.

Luftsprung ['luftʃpruŋ], m. (—s, pl. ¨e) caper, gambol; ¨*e machen*, caper, gambol.

Lüftung ['lyftuŋ], f. (—, no pl.) airing, ventilation.

Lug [lu:k], m. (—s, no pl.) (*obs.*) lie; — *und Trug*, a pack of lies.

Lüge ['ly:gə], f. (—, pl. —n) lie, false-hood, fib; *einen* — *strafen*, give s.o. the lie.

lügen ['ly:gən], v.n. irr. lie, tell a lie.

lügenhaft ['ly:gənhaft], adj. lying, false, untrue.

Lügner ['ly:gnər], m. (—s, pl. —) liar.

Luke ['lu:kə], f. (—, pl. —n) dormer-window; (*ship*) hatch.

Lümmel ['lyməl], m. (—s, pl. —) lout; hooligan.

Lump [lump], m. (—s, —en, pl. —e, —en) scoundrel, blackguard.

Lumpen ['lumpən], m. (—s, pl. —) rag, tatter.

Lumpengesindel ['lumpəngəzindəl], n. (—s, no pl.) rabble, riffraff.

Lumpenpack ['lumpənpak], n. (—s, no pl.) rabble, riffraff.

Lumpensammler ['lumpənzamlər], m. (—s, pl. —) rag-and-bone-man.

Lumperei [lumpə'rai], f. (—, pl. —en) shabby trick; meanness; trifle.

lumpig ['lumpiç], adj. ragged; (*fig.*) shabby, mean.

Lunge ['luŋə], f. (—, pl. —n) (*human*) lung; (*animals*) lights.

Lungenentzündung ['luŋənɛntsyn-duŋ], f. (—, pl. —en) pneumonia.

Lungenkrankheit ['luŋənkraŋkhait], f. (—, pl. —en) pulmonary disease.

Lungenkraut ['luŋənkraut], n. (—s, pl. ¨er) lungwort.

Lungenschwindsucht ['luŋənʃvint-zuxt], f. (—, no pl.) pulmonary consumption, tuberculosis.

lungern ['luŋərn], v.n. idle, loiter.

Lunte ['luntə], f. (—, pl. —n) fuse, slow-match; — *riechen*, smell a rat.

Lupe ['lu:pə], f. (—, pl. —n) magnifying glass, lens; *etwas durch die* — *besehen*, examine s.th. closely, scrutinise s.th.; *unter die* — *nehmen*, examine closely.

lüpfen ['lypfən], v.a. lift.

Lupine [lu'pi:nə], f. (—, pl. —n) (*Bot.*) lupin.

Lust [lust], f. (—, pl. ¨e) enjoyment, pleasure, delight; desire, wish, inclination, liking; — *bekommen zu*, feel inclined to; — *haben auf*, have a mind to, feel like; *nicht übel* — *haben*, have half a mind to.

Lustbarkeit ['lustba:rkait], f. (—, pl. —en) amusement, diversion, entertainment, pleasure.

Lustdirne ['lustdɪrnə], f. (—, pl. —n) prostitute.

lüstern ['lystərn], adj. lustful, lascivious.

lustig ['lustiç], adj, gay, merry, cheerful, amusing, funny; — *sein*, make merry; *sich über einen* — *machen*, poke fun at s.o.

Lüstling ['lystlɪŋ], *m.* (—s, *pl.* —e) libertine, lecher.

Lustmord ['lustmɔrt], *m.* (—es, *pl.* —e) sex murder.

Lustreise ['lustraɪzə], *f.* (—, *pl.* —n) pleasure trip.

Lustschloß ['lustʃlɔs], *n.* (—sses, *pl.* ˝sser) country house, country seat.

Lustspiel ['lustʃpi:l], *n.* (—s, *pl.* —e) comedy.

lustwandeln ['lustvandəln], *v.n. insep.* (*aux.* sein) stroll, promenade.

Lutherisch ['lutərɪʃ], *adj.* Lutheran.

lutschen ['lutʃən], *v.a.* suck.

Lüttich ['lytɪç], *n.* Liège.

Luxus ['luksus], *m.* (—, *no pl.*) luxury.

Luzern [lu'tsɛrn], *n.* Lucerne.

Luzerne [lu'tsɛrnə], *f.* (—, *pl.* —n) (*Bot.*) lucerne.

Lymphe ['lymfə], *f.* (—, *pl.* —n) lymph.

lynchen ['lynçən], *v.a.* lynch.

Lyrik ['ly:rɪk], *f.* (—, *no pl.*) lyric poetry.

lyrisch ['ly:rɪʃ], *adj.* lyric(al).

Lyzeum [ly'tse:um], *n.* (—s, *pl.* Lyzeen) lyceum, grammar school *or* high school for girls.

M

M [ɛm], *n.* (—s, *pl.* —s) the letter M.

Maas [ma:s], *f.* River Meuse.

Maat [ma:t], *m.* (—s, *pl.* —s, —en) (*Naut.*) mate.

Mache ['maxə], *f.* (—, *no pl.*) put-up job, humbug, sham, eyewash.

machen ['maxən], *v.a.* make, do, produce, manufacture; cause; amount to; *mach schon,* be quick; *das macht nichts,* it does not matter; *mach's kurz,* cut it short; *etwas — lassen,* have s.th. made; *sich auf den Weg —,* set off; *sich viel (wenig) aus etwas —,* care much (little) for s.th.; *mach, daß du fortkommst,* get out, scram.

Macherlohn ['maxərlo:n], *m.* (—es, *pl.* ˝e) charge for making s.th.

Macht [maxt], *f.* (—, *pl.* ˝e) might, power; force, strength; authority; *mit aller —,* with might and main.

Machtbefugnis ['maxtbəfu:knɪs], *f.* (—, *pl.* —se) competence.

Machtgebot ['maxtgəbo:t], *n.* (—s, *pl.* —e) authoritative order.

Machthaber ['maxtha:bər], *m.* (—s, *pl.* —) potentate, ruler.

mächtig ['mɛçtɪç], *adj.* mighty, powerful; *einer Sache — sein,* to have mastered s.th.

machtlos ['maxtlo:s], *adj.* powerless.

Machtspruch ['maxtʃprux], *m.* (—s, *pl.* ˝e) authoritative dictum; command; decree.

Machtvollkommenheit ['maxtfɔlkəmənhaɪt], *f.* (—, *pl.* —en) absolute power; sovereignty; *aus eigner —,* of o.'s own authority.

Machtwort ['maxtvɔrt], *n.* (—es, *pl.* —e) word of command, fiat; *ein — sprechen,* bring o.'s authority to bear, speak with authority.

Machwerk ['maxvɛrk], *n.* (—s, *pl.* —e) shoddy product; bad job; concoction; (*story*) pot-boiler.

Madagaskar [mada'gaskar], *n.* Madagascar.

Mädchen ['mɛːtçən], *n.* (—s, *pl.* —) girl; (*servant*) maid; — *für alles,* maid-of-all-work.

mädchenhaft ['mɛːtçənhaft], *adj.* girlish, maidenly.

Mädchenhandel ['mɛːtçənhandəl], *m.* (—s, *no pl.*) white slave trade.

Made ['ma:də], *f.* (—, *pl.* —n) maggot, mite.

Mädel ['mɛːdəl], *n.* (—s, *pl.* —) (*coll.*) *see* **Mädchen.**

madig ['ma:dɪç], *adj.* maggoty.

Magazin [maga'tsi:n], *n.* (—s, *pl.* —e) warehouse, storehouse; journal.

Magd [ma:kt], *f.* (—, *pl.* ˝e) maid, maidservant; (*Poet.*) maiden.

Magen ['ma:gən], *m.* (—s, *pl.* —) (*human*) stomach; (*animals*) maw.

Magengrube ['ma:gəngru:bə], *f.* (—, *pl.* —n) pit of the stomach.

Magensaft ['ma:gənzaft], *m.* (—es, *pl.* ˝e) gastric juice.

mager ['ma:gər], *adj.* lean, thin, slender, slim; (*fig.*) meagre.

Magerkeit ['ma:gərkaɪt], *f.* (—, *no pl.*) leanness, thinness, slenderness.

Magie [ma'gi:], *f.* (—, *no pl.*) magic.

Magier ['ma:gjər], *m.* (—s, *pl.* —) magician.

Magister [ma'gɪstər], *m.* (—s, *pl.* —) schoolmaster; (*Univ.*) Master; — *der freien Künste,* Master of Arts.

Magistrat [magɪs'tra:t], *m.* (—s, *pl.* —e) municipal board, local authority.

magnetisch [mag'ne:tɪʃ], *adj.* magnetic.

magnetisieren [magneti'zi:rən], *v.a.* magnetise.

Magnetismus [magne'tɪsmus], *m.* (—, *pl.* —men) magnetism; (*person*) mesmerism; *Lehre vom —,* magnetics.

Magnifizenz [magnifi'tsɛnts], *f.* (—, *pl.* —en) magnificence; *seine —,* (*Univ.*) title of Vice-Chancellor.

Mahagoni [maha'go:ni], *n.* (—s, *no pl.*) mahogany.

Mahd [ma:t], *f.* (—, *pl.* —en) mowing.

mähen ['mɛːən], *v.a.* mow, v.a. mow.

Mäher ['mɛːər], *m.* (—s, *pl.* —) mower.

Mahl [ma:l], *n.* (—s, *pl.* —e, ˝er) meal, repast.

mahlen ['ma:lən], *v.a.* grind.

Mahlstrom ['ma:lʃtro:m], *m.* (—s, *no pl.*) maelstrom, whirlpool, eddy.

Mahlzahn ['ma:ltsa:n], *m.* (—s, *pl.* ˝e) molar, grinder.

Mahlzeit ['ma:ltsaɪt], *f.* (—, *pl.* —en) meal, repast.

Mähmaschine ['mɛ:maʃi:nə], *f.* (—, *pl.* —n) reaping-machine; lawn-mower.

Mähne ['mɛ:nə], *f.* (—, *pl.* —n) mane.

mahnen ['ma:nən], *v.a.* remind, admonish, warn; (*debtor*) demand payment, dun.

Mähre ['mɛ:rə], *f.* (—, *pl.* —n) mare.

Mähren ['mɛ:rən], *n.* Moravia.

Mai [maɪ], *m.* (—s, *pl.* —e) May.

Maid [maɪt], *f.* (—, *no pl.*) (*Poet.*) maiden.

Maiglöckchen ['maɪglœkçən], *n.* (—s, *pl.* —) (*Bot.*) lily of the valley.

Maikäfer ['maɪkɛ:fər], *m.* (—s, *pl.* —) (*Ent.*) cockchafer.

Mailand ['maɪlant], *n.* Milan.

Mais [maɪs], *m.* (—es, *no pl.*) (*Bot.*) maize, Indian corn.

Majestät [majɛs'tɛ:t], *f.* (—, *pl.* —en) majesty.

majestätisch [majɛs'tɛ:tiʃ], *adj.* majestic.

Major [ma'jo:r], *m.* (—s, *pl.* —e) (*Mil.*) major.

Majoran [majo'ra:n], *m.* (—s, *no pl.*) (*Bot.*) marjoram.

Majorat [majo'ra:t], *n.* (—s, *pl.* —e) primogeniture; entail.

majorenn [majo'rɛn], *adj.* (*obs.*) of age, over twenty-one.

Majorität [majori'tɛ:t], *f.* (—, *pl.* —en) majority.

Makel ['ma:kəl], *m.* (—s, *pl.* —) spot, blot; (*fig.*) blemish, flaw, defect.

Mäkelei [mɛ:kə'laɪ], *f.* (—, *pl.* —en) fault-finding, carping; fastidiousness.

makellos ['ma:kɛllo:s], *adj.* spotless, immaculate.

mäkeln ['mɛ:kəln], *v.n.* find fault (with), cavil (at).

Makkabäer [maka'bɛ:ər], *m.* Maccabee.

Makler ['ma:klər], *m.* (—s, *pl.* —) broker.

Mäkler ['mɛ:klər], *m.* (—s, *pl.* —) fault-finder, caviller.

Maklergebühr [ma:klərgəby:r], *f.* (—, *pl.* —en) brokerage.

Makrele [ma'kre:lə], *f.* (—, *pl.* —n) (*Zool.*) mackerel.

Makrone [ma'kro:nə], *f.* (—, *pl.* —n) macaroon.

Makulatur [makula'tu:r], *f.* (—, *no pl.*) waste paper.

Mal [ma:l], *n.* (—s, *pl.* —e) mark, sign, token; monument; mole, birth-mark; stain; time; *dieses* —, this time, this once; *manches* —, sometimes; *mehrere —e*, several times; *mit einem —*, all of a sudden.

mal [ma:l], *adv. & part.* once; *noch—*, once more; (*coll.*) *hör* —, I say.

Malaya [ma'laɪa], *n.* Malaya.

malen ['ma:lən], *v.a.* paint.

Maler ['ma:lər], *m.* (—s, *pl.* —) painter.

Malerei [ma:lə'raɪ], *f.* (—, *pl.* —en) painting; picture.

malerisch ['ma:ləriʃ], *adj.* picturesque.

Malerleinwand ['ma:lərlaɪnvant], *f.* (—, *no pl.*) canvas.

Malheur [ma'lø:r], *n.* (—s, *pl.* —e) misfortune, mishap.

Mali [ma:li] *n.* Mali.

maliziös [mali'tsjø:s], *adj.* malicious.

Malkasten ['ma:lkastən], *m.* (—s, *pl.* —) paint-box.

Malstein ['ma:lʃtaɪn], *m.* (—s, *pl.* —e) monument; boundary stone.

Malstock ['ma:lʃtɔk], *m.* (—s, *pl.* —e) maulstick, mahlstick.

Malteserorden [mal'te:zərɔrdən], *m.* (—s, *no pl.*) Order of the Knights of Malta.

malträtieren [maltrɛ'ti:rən], *v.a.* ill-treat.

Malve ['malvə], *f.* (—, *pl.* —n) (*Bot.*) mallow.

Malz [malts], *n.* (—es, *no pl.*) malt; *an ihm ist Hopfen und — verloren*, he is hopeless.

Malzbonbon ['maltsbɔbɔ̃], *m.* (—s, *pl.* —s) cough-lozenge, malt drop.

Mälzer ['mɛltsər], *m.* (—s, *pl.* —) maltster.

Mama [ma'ma:], *f.* (—, *pl.* —s) (*fam.*) mummy, mum, (*Am.*) ma.

Mammon ['mamɔn], *m.* (—s, *no pl.*) mammon; *schnöder* —, filthy lucre.

Mammut ['mamut], *n.* (—s, *pl.* —e) mammoth.

Mamsell [mam'zɛl], *f.* (—, *pl.* —en) housekeeper.

man [man], *indef. pron.* one, they, people, men; — *sagt*, they say.

manch [manç], *pron.* (—er, —e, —es) many a, some, several.

mancherlei [mançər'laɪ], *adj.* several; of several kinds.

Manchester [man'çɛstər], *m.* (—s, *no pl.*) corduroy.

manchmal ['mançma:l], *adv.* sometimes.

Mandant [man'dant], *m.* (—en, *pl.* —en) client.

Mandantin [man'dantin], *f.* (—, *pl.* —innen) female client.

Mandarine [manda'ri:nə], *f.* (—, *pl.* —n) mandarin (orange), tangerine.

Mandat [man'da:t], *n.* (—s, *pl.* —e) mandate.

Mandel ['mandəl], *f.* (—, *pl.* —n) almond; (*Anat.*) tonsil; (*quantity*) fifteen; *eine — Eier*, fifteen eggs.

Mandoline [mando'li:nə], *f.* (—, *pl.* —n) mandolin.

Mangan [man'ga:n], *n.* (—s, *no pl.*) (*Chem.*) manganese.

Mangel (1) ['maŋəl], *f.* (—, *pl.* —n) mangle, wringer.

Mangel (2) ['maŋəl], *m.* (—s, *pl.* —) deficiency, defect; blemish; lack, shortage, want; *aus — an*, for want of; — *haben an*, be short of, lack (s.th.).

mangelhaft ['maŋəlhaft], *adj.* defective, imperfect.

mangeln (1) ['maŋəln], *v.a.* (*laundry*) mangle.

mangeln (2) ['maŋəln], *v.n.* be in want of, be short of; *es —t uns an . . .,* we lack . . . .

mangels ['maŋəls], *prep.* (*Genit.*) for lack of, for want of.

Mangold ['maŋɔlt], *m.* (—s, *no pl.*) (*Bot.*) beet, mangel-wurzel.

Manie [ma'ni:], *f.* (—, *pl.* —n) mania, craze.

Manier [ma'ni:r], *f.* (—, *pl.* —en) manner, habit; *gute —en haben,* have good manners.

manieriert [mani'ri:rt], *adj.* affected; (*Art*) mannered.

manierlich [ma'ni:rlɪç], *adj.* well behaved, civil, polite.

manipulieren [manipu'li:rən], *v.a.* manipulate.

Manko ['maŋko:], *n.* (—s, *pl.* —s) deficit, deficiency.

Mann [man], *m.* (—(e)s, *pl.* ̈er, (*Poet.*) —en) man; husband; *etwas an den — bringen,* get s.th. off o.'s hands, dispose of s.th.; *seinen — stellen,* hold o.'s own; *bis auf den letzten —,* to a man.

Mannbarkeit ['manba:rkaɪt], *f.* (—, *no pl.*) puberty; marriageable age.

Männchen ['mɛnçən], *n.* (—s, *pl.* —) little man, manikin; (*Zool.*) male; *mein —,* (*coll.*) my hubby; *— machen,* (*dogs*) sit on the hindlegs, beg.

mannhaft ['manhaft], *adj.* manly, stout, valiant.

mannigfaltig ['manɪçfaltɪç], *adj.* manifold, multifarious.

männlich ['mɛnlɪç], *adj.* male; (*fig.*) manly; (*Gram.*) masculine.

Mannsbild ['mansbɪlt], *n.* (—es, *pl.* —er) (*coll.*) man, male person.

Mannschaft ['manʃaft], *f.* (—, *pl.* —en) men; crew, team.

mannstoll ['manstɔl], *adj.* man-mad.

Mannszucht ['manstsuxt], *f.* (—, *no pl.*) discipline.

Manöver [ma'nø:vər], *n.* (—s, *pl.* —) manoeuvre.

manövrieren [manø'vri:rən], *v.a.* manoeuvre.

Mansarde [man'zardə], *f.* (—, *pl.* —n) garret, attic.

manschen ['manʃən], *v.a., v.n.* dabble; splash (about).

Manschette [man'ʃɛtə], *f.* (—, *pl.* —n) cuff.

Mantel ['mantəl], *m.* (—s, *pl.* ̈) cloak, overcoat, coat, mantle, wrap; *den — nach dem Winde hängen,* be a timeserver.

Manufaktur [manufak'tu:r], *f.* (—, *pl.* —en) manufacture.

Mappe ['mapə], *f.* (—, *pl.* —n) portfolio, case, file.

Mär [mɛ:r], *f.* (—, *pl.* —en) (*Poet.*) tale, tidings, legend.

Märchen ['mɛ:rçən], *n.* (—s, *pl.* —) fairy-tale, fable; fib.

märchenhaft ['mɛ:rçənhaft], *adj.* fabulous, legendary; (*coll.*) marvellous.

Marder ['mardər], *m.* (—s, *pl.* —) (*Zool.*) marten.

Maria [ma'ri:a], *f.* Mary; *die Jungfrau —,* the Virgin Mary.

Marienbild [ma'ri:ənbɪlt], *n.* (—es, *pl.* —er) image of the Virgin Mary.

Marienblume [ma'ri:ənblu:mə], *f.* (—, *pl.* —n) (*Bot.*) daisy.

Marienglas [ma'ri:ənglas], *n.* (—es, *no pl.*) mica.

Marienkäfer [ma'ri:ənkɛ:fər], *m.* (—s, *pl.* —) (*Ent.*) lady-bird.

Marine [ma'ri:nə], *f.* (—, *pl.* —n) navy.

marinieren [mari'ni:rən], *v.a.* pickle.

Marionette [mario'nɛtə], *f.* (—, *pl.* —n) puppet, marionette.

Mark (1) [mark], *n.* (—s, *no pl.*) (*bone*) marrow; (*fruit*) pith, pulp.

Mark (2) [mark], *f.* (—, *pl.* —en) boundary, frontier province.

Mark (3) [mark], *f.* (—, *pl.* —) (*coin*) mark.

markant [mar'kant], *adj.* striking, prominent; (*remark*) pithy.

Marke ['markə], *f.* (—, *pl.* —n) (*trade*) mark, brand; (*postage*) stamp; (*game*) counter.

markieren [mar'ki:rən], *v.a.* mark.

markig ['markɪç], *adj.* marrowlike; (*fig.*) pithy, strong.

Markise [mar'ki:zə], *f.* (—, *pl.* —n) (sun)blind, awning.

Markt [markt], *m.* (—es, *pl.* ̈e) market, market-square, fair.

Marktflecken ['marktflɛkən], *m.* (—s, *pl.* —) borough; (small) market town.

Marktschreier ['marktʃraɪər], *m.* (—s, *pl.* —) cheap-jack, quack, charlatan.

Markus ['markus], *m.* Mark.

Marmel ['marməl], *f.* (—, *pl.* —n) (*obs.*) marble.

Marmelade [marmə'la:də], *f.* (—, *pl.* —n) marmalade, jam.

Marmor ['marmɔr], *m.* (—s, *no pl.*) marble.

Marokko [ma'rɔko], *n.* Morocco.

Marone [ma'ro:nə], *f.* (—, *pl.* —n) sweet chestnut.

Maroquin [maro'kɛ̃], *n.* (—s, *no pl.*) Morocco leather.

Marotte [ma'rɔtə], *f.* (—, *pl.* —n) whim; fad.

Marquise [mar'ki:zə], *f.* (—, *pl.* —n) marchioness.

Marsch (1) [marʃ], *m.* (—es, *pl.* ̈e) march; *sich in — setzen,* set out; march off.

Marsch (2) [marʃ], *f.* (—, *pl.* —en) fen, marsh.

marsch! [marʃ], *int.* march! be off! get out!

Marschboden ['marʃbo:dən], *m.* (—s, *no pl.*) marshy soil, marshland.

marschieren [mar'ʃi:rən], *v.n.* (*aux.* sein) march.

Marstall ['marʃtal], *m.* (—s, *pl.* ̈e) royal stud.

Marter ['martər], *f.* (—, *pl.* —n) torture, torment.

martern [′martərn], *v.a.* torture, torment.

Märtyrer [′mɛrtyrər], *m.* (—s, *pl.* —) martyr.

Martyrium [mar′ty:rjum], *n.* (—s, *pl.* —rien) martyrdom.

März [mɛrts], *m.* (—es, *pl.* —e) (*month*) March.

Masche [′maʃə], *f.* (—, *pl.* —n) mesh; (*knitting*) stitch; (*dial.*) bow tie; (*coll.*) racket.

Maschine [ma′ʃi:nə], *f.* (—, *pl.* —n) machine; engine; *mit der — geschrieben,* typewritten.

Maschinengarn [ma′ʃi:nəngarn], *n.* (—s, *no pl.*) twist.

Maschinerie [maʃinə′ri:], *f.* (—, *pl.* —en) machinery.

Maser [′ma:zər], *f.* (—, *pl.* —n) (*wood*) vein, streak.

Masern [′ma:zərn], *f. pl.* measles.

Maske [′maskə], *f.* (—, *pl.* —n) mask, visor.

Maskerade [maskə′ra:də], *f.* (—, *pl.* —n) masquerade.

maskieren [mas′ki:rən], *v.a.* mask. — *v.r. sich —,* put on a mask.

Maß (1) [ma:s], *n.* (—es, *pl.* —e) measure, size; moderation, propriety; degree, extent; proportion; — *halten,* be moderate; *einem — nehmen,* measure s.o. (for); *in starkem —,* to a high degree; *mit —,* in moderation; *nach —,* to measure; *ohne — und Ziel,* immoderately, with no holds barred; *über alle —en,* exceedingly.

Maß (2) [ma:s], *m. & f.* (—, *pl.* —e) (*drink*) quart.

massakrieren [masa′kri:rən], *v.a.* massacre, slaughter.

Maßarbeit [′ma:sarbaɪt], *f.* (—, *pl.* —en) (*work*) made to measure; bespoke tailoring.

Masse [′masə], *f.* (—, *pl.* —n) mass, bulk; multitude; *eine —,* a lot.

Maßeinheit [′ma:saɪnhaɪt], *f.* (—, *pl.* —en) measuring-unit.

massenhaft [′masənhaft], *adj.* abundant.

Maßgabe [′ma:sga:bə], *f.* (—, *pl.* —n) *nach —,* according to, in proportion to.

maßgebend [′ma:sge:bənt], *adj.* standard; (*fig.*) authoritative.

massieren [ma′si:rən], *v.a.* massage.

mäßig [′mɛ:sɪç], *adj.* moderate, temperate, frugal.

Mäßigkeit [′mɛ:sɪçkaɪt], *f.* (—, *no pl.*) moderation, temperance, frugality.

Mäßigung [′mɛ:sɪguŋ], *f.* (—, *no pl.*) moderation.

Massiv [ma′si:f], *n.* (—s, *pl.* —e) (*mountains*) massif, range.

Maßliebchen [′ma:sli:pçən], *n.* (—s, *pl.* —) (*Bot.*) daisy.

maßlos [′ma:slo:s], *adj.* immoderate; (*fig.*) extravagant.

Maßnahme [′ma:sna:mə], *f.* (—, *pl.* —n) measure; *—n ergreifen,* take steps.

Maßregel [′ma:sre:gəl], *f.* (—, *pl.* —n) measure.

maßregeln [′ma:sre:gəln], *v.a.* reprove, reprimand.

Maßstab [′ma:sʃta:p], *m.* (—es, *pl.* ¨e) standard; (*maps*) scale; *in kleinem (großem) —,* on a small (large) scale.

maßvoll [′ma:sfɔl], *adj.* moderate.

Mast (1) [mast], *m.* (—es, *pl.* —e) mast; pylon.

Mast (2) [mast], *f.* (—, *no pl.*) fattening.

Mastbaum [′mastbaum], *m.* (—s, *pl.* ¨e) mast.

Mastdarm [′mastdarm], *m.* (—s, *pl.* ¨e) rectum.

mästen [′mɛstən], *v.a.* feed, fatten.

Mastkorb [′mastkɔrp], *m.* (—s, *pl.* ¨e) masthead.

Mästung [′mɛstuŋ], *f.* (—, *no pl.*) fattening, cramming.

Materialwaren [mate′rjalva:rən], *f. pl.* groceries; household goods.

materiell [mate′rjɛl], *adj.* material, real; materialistic.

Mathematik [matema′ti:k], *f.* (—, *no pl.*) mathematics.

mathematisch [mate′ma:tɪʃ], *adj.* mathematical.

Matratze [ma′tratsə], *f.* (—, *pl.* —n) mattress.

Matrikel [ma′tri:kəl], *f.* (—, *pl.* —n) register, roll.

Matrize [ma′tri:tsə], *f.* (—, *pl.* —n) matrix, die, stencil.

Matrose [ma′tro:zə], *m.* (—n, *pl.* —n) sailor, seaman.

Matsch [matʃ], *m.* (—es, *no pl.*) slush; mud.

matt [mat], *adj.* tired, exhausted, spent; languid; weak, feeble; (*light*) dim; (*gold*) dull; (*silver*) tarnished; (*Chess*) (check-)mate; — *setzen,* (*Chess*) to (check-)mate.

Matte [′matə], *f.* (—, *pl.* —n) mat, matting.

Matthäus [ma′tɛ:us], *m.* Matthew.

Mattheit [′mathaɪt], *f.* (—, *no pl.*) tiredness, exhaustion, languor, feebleness; (*light*) dimness; (*gold*) dullness.

mattherzig [′mathɛrtsɪç], *adj.* poorspirited, faint-hearted.

Matura [ma′tu:ra], *f.* (—, *pl.* —en) (*Austr.*) school-leaving *or* matriculation examination.

Mätzchen [′mɛtsçən], *n.* (—s, *pl.* —) nonsense; trick; *mach keine —,* don't be silly.

Mauer [′mauər], *f.* (—, *pl.* —n) wall.

Mauerkelle [′mauərkɛlə], *f.* (—, *pl.* —n) trowel.

mauern [′mauərn], *v.a.* build. — *v.n.* lay bricks, construct a wall.

Mauerwerk [′mauərvɛrk], *n.* (—s, *no pl.*) brick-work.

Maul [maul], *n.* (—es, *pl.* ¨er) (*animals*) mouth, muzzle; (*vulg.*) mouth; *das — halten,* shut up, hold o.'s tongue; *ein loses — haben,* have a loose tongue; *nicht aufs — gefallen sein,* have a quick tongue; (*vulg.*) *halt's —,* shut up.

Maulaffe ['maulafə], *m.* (—n, *pl.* —n) booby; —*n feilhalten,* stand gaping.

Maulbeere ['maulbe:rə], *f.* (—, *pl.* —n) (*Bot.*) mulberry.

maulen ['maulən], *v.n.* pout, sulk.

Maulesel ['maule:zəl], *m.* (—s, *pl.* —) (*Zool.*) mule.

maulfaul ['maulfaul], *adj.* tongue-tied; taciturn.

Maulheld ['maulhɛlt], *m.* (—en *pl.* —en) braggart.

Maulkorb ['maulkɔrp], *m.* (—s, *pl.* ⸚e) muzzle.

Maulschelle ['maulʃɛlə], *f.* (—, *pl.* —n) box on the ear.

Maultier ['maulti:r], *n.* (—s, *pl.* —e) (*Zool.*) mule.

Maulwerk ['maulvɛrk], *n.* (—s, *no pl.*) *ein großes — haben,* (*coll.*) have the gift of the gab.

Maulwurf ['maulvurf], *m.* (—s, *pl.* ⸚e) (*Zool.*) mole.

Maurer ['maurər], *m.* (—s, *pl.* —) mason, bricklayer.

Maus [maus], *f.* (—, *pl.* ⸚e) mouse.

Mausefalle ['mauzəfalə], *f.* (—, *pl.* —n) mouse-trap.

mausen ['mauzən], *v.n.* catch mice. — *v.a.* (*fig.*) pilfer, pinch.

Mauser ['mauzər], *f.* (—, *no pl.*) moulting.

mausern ['mauzərn], *v.r. sich* —, moult.

mausetot ['mauzəto:t], *adj.* dead as a door-nail.

mausig ['mauzɪç], *adj. sich — machen,* put on airs.

Maxime [mak'si:mə], *f.* (—, *pl.* —n) maxim, motto, device.

Mazedonien [matsə'do:njən], *n.* Macedonia.

Mäzen [mɛ:'tse:n], *m.* (—s, *pl.* —e) patron of the arts, Maecenas.

Mechanik [me'ça:nɪk], *f.* (—, *no pl.*) mechanics.

Mechaniker [me'ça:nɪkər], *m.* (—s, *pl.* —) mechanic.

mechanisch [me'ça:nɪʃ], *adj.* mechanical.

meckern ['mɛkərn], *v.n.* bleat; (*fig.*) grumble, complain.

Medaille [me'daljə], *f.* (—, *pl.* —n) medal.

Medaillon [medal'jõ], *n.* (—s, *pl.* —s) locket.

meditieren [medi'ti:rən], *v.n.* meditate.

Medizin [medi'tsi:n], *f.* (—, *pl.* —en) medicine, physic.

Mediziner [medi'tsi:nər], *m.* (—s, *pl.* —) physician, medical practitioner, student of medicine.

medizinisch [medi'tsi:nɪʃ], *adj.* medical, medicinal.

Meer [me:r], *n.* (—es, *pl.* —e) sea, ocean; *offnes —,* high seas; *am —,* at the seaside; *auf dem —,* at sea; *übers —,* overseas.

Meerbusen ['me:rbu:zən], *m.* (—s, *pl.* —) bay, gulf, bight.

Meerenge ['me:rɛŋə], *f.* (—, *pl.* —n) straits.

Meeresspiegel ['me:rəsʃpi:gəl], *m.* (—s, *no pl.*) sea-level.

Meerkatze ['me:rkatsə], *f.* (—, *pl.* —n) long-tailed monkey.

Meerrettich ['me:rrɛtɪç], *m.* (—s, *pl.* —e) (*Bot.*) horse-radish.

Meerschaum ['me:rʃaum], *m.* (—s, *no pl.*) sea-foam; (*pipe*) meerschaum.

Meerschwein ['me:rʃvain], *n.* (—s, *pl.* —e) (*Zool.*) porpoise.

Meerschweinchen ['me:rʃvainçən], *n.* (—s, *pl.* —) (*Zool.*) guinea-pig.

Mehl [me:l], *n.* (—es, *no pl.*) flour; meal; dust, powder.

Mehlkleister ['me:lklaistər], *m.* (—s, *no pl.*) flour paste.

Mehlspeise ['me:lʃpaizə], *f.* (—, *pl.* —n) (*dial.*) pudding, sweet.

mehr [me:r], *indecl. adj., adv.* more; *umso —,* all the more; *immer —,* more and more; *— als genug,* enough and to spare.

Mehrbetrag ['me:rbətra:k], *m.* (—s, *pl.* ⸚e) surplus.

mehrdeutig ['me:rdɔytɪç], *adj.* ambiguous.

mehren ['me:rən], *v.r. sich —,* multiply, increase in numbers.

mehrere ['me:rərə], *pl. adj.* several.

mehrfach ['me:rfax], *adj.* repeated.

Mehrheit ['me:rhait], *f.* (—, *pl.* —en) majority.

mehrmals ['me:rma:ls], *adv.* several times.

Mehrzahl ['me:rtsa:l], *f.* (—, *no pl.*) (*Gram.*) plural; majority, bulk.

meiden ['maidən], *v.a. irr.* shun, avoid.

Meierei [maiə'rai], *f.* (—, *pl.* —en) (*dairy*) farm.

Meile ['mailə], *f.* (—, *pl.* —n) mile; league.

Meiler ['mailər], *m.* (—s, *pl.* —) charcoal-kiln, charcoal-pile.

mein(e) ['main(ə)], *poss. adj.* my. — *poss. pron.* mine.

Meineid ['mainait], *m.* (—s, *pl.* —e) perjury; *einen — schwören,* perjure o.s.

meineidig ['mainaidɪç], *adj.* perjured, forsworn.

meinen ['mainən], *v.a.* mean, intend, think.

meinerseits ['mainərzaits], *adv.* I, for my part.

meinethalben ['mainəthalbən], *adv.* on my account, speaking for myself, for my sake; I don't care, I don't mind.

meinetwegen ['mainətve:gən], *adv. see* meinethalben.

meinetwillen ['mainətvilən], *adv. um —,* for my sake, on my behalf.

meinige ['mainigə], *poss. pron.* mine.

Meinung ['mainuŋ], *f.* (—, *pl.* —en) opinion; meaning; notion; *öffentliche —,* public opinion; *der — sein,* be of the opinion, hold the opinion; *einem die — sagen,* give s.o. a piece of o.'s mind; *meiner — nach,* in my opinion.

Meinungsverschiedenheit [ˈmaɪnuŋs-ferʃiːdənhaɪt], *f.* (—, *pl.* —en) difference of opinion, disagreement.

Meise [ˈmaɪzə], *f.* (—, *pl.* —n) (*Orn.*) titmouse.

Meißel [ˈmaɪsəl], *m.* (—s, *pl.* —) chisel.

meißeln [ˈmaɪsəln], *v.a.* chisel, sculpt.

meist [maɪst], *adj.* most. — *adv.* usually, generally.

meistens [ˈmaɪstəns], *adv.* mostly.

Meister [ˈmaɪstər], *m.* (—s, *pl.* —) (*craft*) master; (*sport*) champion; *seinen — finden,* meet o.'s match.

meisterhaft [ˈmaɪstərhaft], *adj.* masterly.

meisterlich [ˈmaɪstərlɪç], *adj.* masterly.

meistern [ˈmaɪstərn], *v.a.* master.

Meisterschaft [ˈmaɪstərʃaft], *f.* (—, *pl.* —en) mastery; (*sport*) championship.

Mekka [ˈmɛka], *n.* Mecca.

Meldeamt [ˈmɛldəamt], *n.* (—s, *pl.* ˙er) registration office.

melden [ˈmɛldən], *v.a.* announce, inform, notify; (*Mil.*) report. — *v.r. sich* —, answer the phone; *sich lassen,* send in o.'s name, have o.s. announced; *sich zu etwas* —, apply for s.th.

Meldezettel [ˈmɛldətsɛtəl], *m.* (—s, *pl.* —) registration form.

meliert [meˈliːrt], *adj.* mixed; (*hair*) iron grey, streaked with grey.

melken [ˈmɛlkən], *v.a. irr.* milk.

Melodie [meloˈdiː], *f.* (—, *pl.* —n) melody, tune.

Melone [meˈloːnə], *f.* (—, *pl.* —n) (*Bot.*) melon; (*coll.*) bowler hat.

Meltau [ˈmeːltau], *m.* (—s, *no pl.*) mildew.

Membrane [mɛmˈbraːnə], *f.* (—, *pl.* —n) membrane, diaphragm.

Memme [ˈmɛmə], *f.* (—, *pl.* —n) coward, poltroon.

memorieren [memoˈriːrən], *v.a.* memorise, learn by heart.

Menage [meˈnaːʒə], *f.* (—, *pl.* —n) household.

Menge [ˈmɛŋə], *f.* (—, *pl.* —n) quantity, amount; multitude, crowd; *eine* —, a lot.

mengen [ˈmɛŋən], *v.a.* mix. — *v.r. sich — in,* interfere in.

Mensch (1) [mɛnʃ], *m.* (—en, *pl.* —en) human being; man; person; *kein* —, nobody.

Mensch (2) [mɛnʃ], *n.* (—es, *pl.* —er) (*vulg.*) wench.

Menschenfeind [ˈmɛnʃənfaɪnt], *m.* (—es, *pl.* —e) misanthropist.

Menschenfreund [ˈmɛnʃənfrɔynt], *m.* (—es, *pl.* —e) philanthropist.

Menschengedenken [ˈmɛnʃəngədɛnkən], *n.* (—s, *no pl.*) *seit* —, from time immemorial.

Menschenhandel [ˈmɛnʃənhandəl], *m.* (—s, *no pl.*) slave-trade.

Menschenkenner [ˈmɛnʃənkɛnər], *m.* (—s, *pl.* —) judge of character.

Menschenmenge [ˈmɛnʃənmɛŋə], *f.* (—, *no pl.*) crowd.

Menschenraub [ˈmɛnʃənraup], *m.* (—s, *no pl.*) kidnapping.

Menschenverstand [ˈmɛnʃənfɛrʃtant], *m.* (—es, *no pl.*) human understanding; *gesunder* —, commonsense.

Menschheit [ˈmɛnʃhaɪt], *f.* (—, *no pl.*) mankind, human race.

menschlich [ˈmɛnʃlɪç], *adj.* human.

Menschwerdung [ˈmɛnʃverduŋ], *f.* (—, *no pl.*) incarnation.

Mensur [mɛnˈzuːr], *f.* (—, *pl.* —en) students' duel.

Mergel [ˈmɛrgəl], *m.* (—s, *no pl.*) marl.

merkbar [ˈmɛrkbaːr], *adj.* perceptible, noticeable.

merken [ˈmɛrkən], *v.a.* note, perceive, observe, notice; *sich etwas* —, bear in mind; *sich nichts — lassen,* show no sign.

merklich [ˈmɛrklɪç], *adj.* perceptible, appreciable.

Merkmal [ˈmɛrkmaːl], *n.* (—s, *pl.* —e) mark, characteristic, feature.

merkwürdig [ˈmɛrkvyrdɪç], *adj.* remarkable, curious, strange.

Merle [ˈmɛrlə], *f.* (—, *pl.* —n) (*dial.*) blackbird.

Mesner [ˈmɛsnər], *m.* (—s, *pl.* —) sexton, sacristan.

meßbar [ˈmɛsbaːr], *adj.* measurable.

Meßbuch [ˈmɛsbuːx], *n.* (—es, *pl.* ˙er) missal.

Messe [ˈmɛsə], *f.* (—, *pl.* —n) (*Eccl.*) Mass; *stille* —, Low Mass; (*Comm.*) fair; (*Mil.*) mess.

messen [ˈmɛsən], *v.a. irr.* measure, gauge. — *v.r. sich mit einem* —, pit oneself against s.o.

Messer (1) [ˈmɛsər], *m.* (—s, *pl.* —) gauge, meter.

Messer (2) [ˈmɛsər], *n.* (—s, *pl.* —) knife.

Messerheld [ˈmɛsərhɛlt], *m.* (—en, *pl.* —en) cut-throat, hooligan, rowdy.

Messias [mɛˈsiːas], *m.* Messiah.

Meßgewand [ˈmɛsgəvant], *n.* (—es, *pl.* ˙er) chasuble, vestment.

Meßkunst [ˈmɛskunst], *f.* (—, *no pl.*) surveying.

Messing [ˈmɛsɪŋ], *n.* (—s, *no pl.*) brass; *aus* —, brazen.

Metall [meˈtal], *n.* (—s, *pl.* —e) metal; *unedle —e,* base metals.

Metallkunde [meˈtalkundə], *f.* (—, *no pl.*) metallurgy.

meteorologisch [meteoroˈloːgɪʃ], *adj.* meteorological.

Meter [ˈmeːtər], *n. & m.* (—s, *pl.* —) (*linear measure*) metre; (*Am.*) meter; (*Poet.*) metre.

methodisch [meˈtoːdɪʃ], *adj.* methodical.

Metrik [ˈmeːtrɪk], *f.* (—, *no pl.*) prosody, versification.

Mette [ˈmɛtə], *f.* (—, *pl.* —n) (*Eccl.*) matins.

Metze ['mɛtsə], f. (—, pl. —n) (obs.) prostitute.

Metzelei [mɛtsə'laɪ], f. (—, pl. —en) slaughter, massacre.

metzeln ['mɛtsəln], v.a. massacre, butcher.

Metzger ['mɛtsgər], m. (—s, pl. —) butcher.

Meuchelmörder ['mɔyçəlmœrdər], m. (—s, pl. —) assassin.

meucheln ['mɔyçəln], v.a. assassinate.

meuchlings ['mɔyçlɪŋs], adv. treacherously, insidiously.

Meute ['mɔytə], f. (—, pl. —n) pack of hounds; (fig.) gang.

Meuterei [mɔytə'raɪ], f. (—, pl. —en) mutiny, sedition.

meutern ['mɔytərn], v.n. mutiny.

Mezzanin ['mɛtsanɪn], n. (—s, pl. —e) half-storey, mezzanine.

miauen [mi'auən], v.n. mew.

mich [mɪç], pers. pron. me, myself.

Michaeli(s) [mɪça'e:li(s)], n. Michaelmas.

Michel ['mɪçəl], m. Michael; deutscher —, plain honest German.

Mieder ['mi:dər], n. (—s, pl. —) bodice.

Miene ['mi:nə], f. (—, pl. —n) mien, air; (facial) expression.

Miete ['mi:tə], f. (—, pl. —n) rent; hire; (corn) rick, stack.

mieten ['mi:tən], v.a. rent, hire.

Mieter ['mi:tər], m. (—s, pl. —) tenant, lodger.

Mietskaserne ['mi:tskazɛrnə], f. (—, pl. —n) tenement house.

Mietszins ['mi:tstsɪns], m. (—es, pl. —e) rent.

Milbe ['mɪlbə], f. (—, pl. —n) mite.

Milch [mɪlç], f. (—, no pl.) milk; (fish) soft roe; abgerahmte —, skim(med) milk; geronnene —, curdled milk.

Milchbart ['mɪlçba:rt], m. (—s, pl. ¨e) milksop.

Milchbruder ['mɪlçbru:dər], m. (—s, pl. ¨) foster-brother.

milchen ['mɪlçən], v.n. yield milk.

Milcher ['mɪlçer], m. (—s, pl. —) (fish) milter.

Milchgesicht ['mɪlçgəzɪçt], n. (—s, pl. —er) baby face; smooth complexion.

Milchglas ['mɪlçglas], n. (—es, no pl.) opalescent glass, frosted glass.

Milchstraße ['mɪlçʃtra:sə], f. (—, no pl.) Milky Way.

Milde ['mɪldə], f. (—, no pl.) mildness, softness; (fig.) gentleness, (rare) charity, generosity.

mildern ['mɪldərn], v.a. soften, alleviate, mitigate, soothe, allay; —de Umstände, extenuating circumstances.

Milderung ['mɪldəruŋ], f. (—, pl. —en) mitigation, moderation; soothing.

mildtätig ['mɪltte:tɪç], adj. charitable, benevolent, munificent.

Militär [mili'tɛ:r], n. (—s, no pl.) military, army; beim — sein, serve in the army.

Miliz [mi'li:ts], f. (—, no pl.) militia.

Milliarde [mɪl'jardə], f. (—, pl. —n) a thousand millions; (Am.) billion.

Million [mɪl'jo:n], f. (—, pl. —en) million.

Millionär [mɪljo'nɛ:r], m. (—s, pl. —e) millionaire.

Milz [mɪlts], f. (—, pl. —en) spleen.

Mime ['mi:mə], m. (—n, pl. —n) mime, actor.

Mimik ['mi:mɪk], f. (—, no pl.) mime, miming.

Mimiker ['mi:mɪkər], m. (—s, pl. —) mimic.

Mimose [mi'mo:zə], f. (—, pl. —n) (Bot.) mimosa.

minder ['mɪndər], adj. lesser, smaller, minor, inferior.

Minderheit ['mɪndərhaɪt], f. (—, pl. —en) minority.

minderjährig ['mɪndərjɛ:rɪç], adj. (Law) under age.

mindern ['mɪndərn], v.a. diminish, lessen.

minderwertig ['mɪndərvɛrtɪç], adj. inferior, of poor quality.

Minderwertigkeitskomplex ['mɪndərvɛrtɪçkaɪtskɔmplɛks], m. (—es, pl. —e) inferiority complex.

mindest ['mɪndəst], adj. least, smallest, minimum, lowest; nicht im —en, not in the least, not at all.

mindestens ['mɪndəstəns], adv. at least.

Mine ['mi:nə], f. (—, pl. —n) mine; (ball point pen) refill; (pencil) lead.

minimal [mini'ma:l], adj. infinitesimal, minimum.

Ministerialrat [minister'ja:lra:t], m. (—s, pl. ¨e) senior civil servant.

ministeriell [mɪnɪster'jɛl], adj. ministerial.

Ministerium [mini'ste:rjum], n. (—s, pl. —rien) ministry.

Ministerpräsident [mi'nɪstərpre:zidɛnt], m. (—en, pl. —en) prime minister; premier.

Ministerrat [mi'nɪstərra:t], m. (—s, pl. ¨e) cabinet, council of ministers.

Ministrant [mini'strant], m. (—en, pl. —en) acolyte; sacristan.

Minne ['minə], f. (—, no pl.) (obs., Poet.) love.

Minnesänger [mɪnə'zɛŋər], m. (—s, pl. —) minnesinger;' troubadour, minstrel.

Minus ['mi:nus], n. (—, no pl.) deficit.

Minze ['mɪntsə], f. (—, pl. —n) (Bot.) mint.

mir [mi:r], pers. pron. to me.

Mirakel [mi'ra:kəl], n. (—s, pl. —) miracle, marvel, wonder.

mischen ['mɪʃən], v.a. mix; (Cards) shuffle; (coffee, tea) blend.

Mischling ['mɪʃlɪŋ], m. (—s, pl. —e) mongrel, hybrid.

Mischrasse [ˈmiʃrasə], *f.* (—, *pl.* —n) cross-breed.

Mischung [ˈmiʃuŋ], *f.* (—, *pl.* —en) mixture, blend.

Misere [miˈzeːrə], *f.* (—, *no pl.*) unhappiness, misery.

Mispel [ˈmɪspəl], *f.* (—, *pl.* —n) (*Bot.*) medlar (tree).

mißachten [mɪsˈaxtən], *v.a.* disregard, despise.

mißarten [mɪsˈaːrtən], *v.n.* (*aux.* sein) degenerate.

Mißbehagen [ˈmɪsbəhaːgən], *n.* (—s, *no pl.*) displeasure, uneasiness.

mißbilligen [mɪsˈbɪlɪgən], *v.a.* object (to), disapprove (of).

Mißbrauch [ˈmɪsbraux], *m.* (—s, *pl.* ⸗e) abuse, misuse.

missen [ˈmɪsən], *v.a.* lack, be without, feel the lack of.

Missetat [ˈmɪsətaːt], *f.* (—, *pl.* —en) misdeed, felony.

mißfallen [mɪsˈfalən], *v.n. irr.* displease.

mißförmig [ˈmɪsfœrmɪç], *adj.* deformed, misshapen.

Mißgeburt [ˈmɪsgəburt], *f.* (—, *pl.* —en) abortion; monster.

mißgelaunt [ˈmɪsgəlaunt], *adj.* ill-humoured.

Mißgeschick [ˈmɪsgəʃɪk], *n.* (—s, *no pl.*) mishap, misfortune.

mißgestimmt [ˈmɪsgəʃtɪmt], *adj.* grumpy, out of sorts.

mißglücken [mɪsˈglykən], *v.n.* (*aux.* sein) fail, be unsuccessful.

Mißgriff [ˈmɪsgrɪf], *m.* (—s, *pl.* —e) blunder, mistake.

Mißgunst [ˈmɪsgunst], *f.* (—, *no pl.*) jealousy, envy.

mißhandeln [mɪsˈhandəln], *v.a.* ill-treat.

Missionar [mɪsjoˈnaːr], *m.* (—s, *pl.* —e) missionary.

mißlich [ˈmɪslɪç], *adj.* awkward; difficult, unpleasant.

mißliebig [ˈmɪsliːbɪç], *adj.* unpopular, odious.

mißlingen [mɪsˈlɪŋən], *v.n. irr.* (*aux.* sein) miscarry, go wrong, misfire, prove a failure, turn out badly.

mißraten [mɪsˈraːtən], *v.n. irr.* (*aux.* sein) miscarry, turn out badly.

Mißstand [ˈmɪsʃtant], *m.* (—es, *pl.* ⸗e) grievance, abuse.

Mißton [ˈmɪstoːn], *m.* (—s, *pl.* ⸗e) dissonance.

mißtrauen [mɪsˈtrauən], *v.n.* distrust, mistrust.

Mißverhältnis [ˈmɪsfɛrhɛltnɪs], *n.* (—ses, *no pl.*) disproportion.

Mißverständnis [ˈmɪsfɛrʃtɛntnɪs], *n.* (—ses, *pl.* —se) misunderstanding.

Mist [mɪst], *m.* (—es, *no pl.*) dung, manure, muck; (*fig.*) rubbish.

Mistel [ˈmɪstəl], *f.* (—, *pl.* —n) (*Bot.*) mistletoe.

Mistfink [ˈmɪstfɪŋk], *m.* (—s, *pl.* —e) (*fig.*) dirty child; mudlark.

mit [mɪt], *prep.* (*Dat.*) with. — *adv.* also, along with.

mitarbeiten [ˈmɪtarbaitən], *v.n.* collaborate, cooperate; (*lit. work*) contribute.

mitbringen [ˈmɪtbrɪŋən], *v.a. irr.* bring along.

Mitbürger [ˈmɪtbyrgər], *m.* (—s, *pl.* —) fellow-citizen.

mitempfinden [ˈmɪtɛmpfɪndən], *v.a. irr.* sympathise with.

Mitesser [ˈmɪtɛsər], *m.* (—s, *pl.* —) (*Med.*) blackhead.

mitfahren [ˈmɪtfaːrən], *v.n. irr.* (*aux.* sein) ride with s.o.; *einen — lassen*, give s.o. a lift.

mitfühlen [ˈmɪtfyːlən], *v.n.* sympathise.

mitgehen [ˈmɪtgeːən], *v.n. irr.* (*aux.* sein) go along (with), accompany (s.o.); *etwas — heißen* or *lassen*, pilfer, pocket, pinch.

Mitgift [ˈmɪtgɪft], *f.* (—, *no pl.*) dowry.

Mitglied [ˈmɪtgliːt], *n.* (—s, *pl.* —er) member, fellow, associate.

mithin [mɪtˈhɪn], *adv., conj.* consequently, therefore.

Mitläufer [ˈmɪtlɔyfər], *m.* (—s, *pl.* —) (*Polit.*) fellow-traveller.

Mitlaut [ˈmɪtlaut], *m.* (—s, *pl.* —e) (*Phonet.*) consonant.

Mitleid [ˈmɪtlait], *n.* (—s, *no pl.*) compassion, sympathy, pity; *mit einem — haben*, take pity on s.o.

Mitleidenschaft [ˈmɪtlaidənʃaft], *f.* (—, *no pl.*) *einen in — ziehen*, involve s.o., implicate s.o.

mitmachen [ˈmɪtmaxən], *v.a., v.n.* join in, participate (in), do as others do; go through, suffer.

Mitmensch [ˈmɪtmɛnʃ], *m.* (—en, *pl.* —en) fellow-man, fellow-creature.

mitnehmen [ˈmɪtneːmən], *v.a. irr.* take along, take with o.; strain, take it out of o., weaken.

mitnichten [mɪtˈnɪçtən], *adv.* by no means.

mitreden [ˈmɪtreːdən], *v.n.* join in a conversation; contribute.

mitsamt [mɪtˈzamt], *prep.* (*Dat.*) together with.

Mitschuld [ˈmɪtʃult], *f.* (—, *no pl.*) complicity.

Mitschüler [ˈmɪtʃyːlər], *m.* (—s, *pl.* —) schoolfellow, fellow-pupil, fellow-student, classmate.

Mittag [ˈmɪtaːk], *m.* (—s, *pl.* —e) midday, noon, noontide; *zu — essen*, have dinner or lunch.

Mittagessen [ˈmɪtaːkɛsən], *n.* (—s, *pl.* —) lunch, luncheon.

Mittagsseite [ˈmɪtaːkszaɪtə], *f.* (—, *no pl.*) south side.

Mittäter [ˈmɪttɛːtər], *m.* (—s, *pl.* —) accomplice.

Mitte [ˈmɪtə], *f.* (—, *no pl.*) middle, midst.

mitteilen [ˈmɪttaɪlən], *v.a.* (*Dat.*) communicate, inform, impart.

mitteilsam ['mɪttaɪlzaːm], *adj.* communicative.

Mitteilung ['mɪttaɪluŋ], *f.* (—, *pl.* —en) communication.

Mittel ['mɪtəl], *n.* (—s, *pl.*) means, expedient, way, resource; remedy; (*pl.*) money, funds; *als — zum Zweck*, as a means to an end; *sich ins — legen*, mediate, intercede.

Mittelalter ['mɪtəlaltər], *n.* (—s, *no pl.*) Middle Ages.

mittelbar ['mɪtəlbaːr], *adj.* indirect.

Mittelding ['mɪtəldɪŋ], *n.* (—s, *pl.* —e) medium; something in between.

Mittelgebirge ['mɪtəlgəbɪrgə], *n.* (—s, *pl.* —) hills; (subalpine) mountains.

mittelländisch ['mɪtəllɛndɪʃ], *adj.* Mediterranean.

mittellos ['mɪtəlloːs], *adj.* penniless, impecunious.

Mittelmaß ['mɪtəlmaːs], *n.* (—es, *pl.* —e) average.

mittelmäßig ['mɪtəlmɛːsɪç], *adj.* mediocre.

Mittelmeer ['mɪtəlmeːr], *n.* (—s, *no pl.*) Mediterranean.

Mittelpunkt ['mɪtəlpuŋkt], *m.* (—s, *pl.* —e) centre; focus.

mittels ['mɪtəls], *prep.* (*Genit.*) by means of.

Mittelschule ['mɪtəlʃuːlə], *f.* (—, *pl.* —n) secondary (intermediate) school; (*Austr.*) grammar school; (*Am.*) high school.

Mittelstand ['mɪtəlʃtant], *m.* (—es, *no pl.*) middle class.

mittelste ['mɪtəlstə], *adj.* middlemost, central.

Mittelstürmer ['mɪtəlʃtyrmər], *m.* (—s, *pl.* —) (*Footb.*) centre-forward.

Mittelwort ['mɪtəlvɔrt], *n.* (—es, *pl.* ⁒er) (*Gram.*) participle.

mitten ['mɪtən], *adv.* in the midst; — *am Tage*, in broad daylight.

Mitternacht ['mɪtərnaxt], *f.* (—, *no pl.*) midnight.

Mittler ['mɪtlər], *m.* (—s, *pl.* —) mediator.

mittlere ['mɪtlərə], *adj.* middle; average; mean.

Mittwoch ['mɪtvɔx], *m.* (—s, *pl.* —e) Wednesday.

mitunter [mɪt'untər], *adv.* now and then, occasionally, sometimes.

mitunterzeichnen ['mɪtuntərtsaɪçnən], *v.a., v.n.* countersign; add o.'s signature (to).

Miturheber ['mɪtuːrheːbər], *m.* (—s, *pl.* —) co-author.

Mitwelt ['mɪtvɛlt], *f.* (—, *no pl.*) the present generation, contemporaries, our own times; the world outside.

mitwirken ['mɪtvɪrkən], *v.n.* cooperate.

Mnemotechnik [mne:mo'tɛçnɪk], *f.* (—, *no pl.*) mnemonics.

Möbel ['møːbəl], *n.* (—s, *pl.* —) piece of furniture; (*pl.*) furniture.

mobil [mo'biːl], *adj.* mobile, active, quick; — *machen*, mobilise, put in motion.

Mobiliar [mobil'jaːr], *n.* (—s, *pl.* **Mobilien**) furniture, movables.

mobilisieren [mobili'ziːrən], *v.a.* mobilise.

möblieren [mø'bliːrən], *v.a.* furnish; *neu —*, refurnish.

Mode ['moːdə], *f.* (—, *pl.* —n) mode, fashion; custom, use; *in der —*, in fashion, in vogue.

Modell [mo'dɛl], *n.* (—s, *pl.* —e) model; — *stehen*, model; (*fig.*) be the prototype.

modellieren [modɛ'liːrən], *v.a.* (*dresses*) model; (*Art*) mould.

Moder ['moːdər], *m.* (—s, *no pl.*) mould.

moderig ['moːdrɪç] *see* **modrig**.

modern (1) ['moːdərn], *v.n.* moulder, rot.

modern (2) [mo'dɛrn], *adj.* modern, fashionable, up-to-date.

modernisieren [modɛrni'ziːrən], *v.a.* modernise.

modifizieren [modifi'tsiːrən], *v.a.* modify.

modisch ['moːdɪʃ], *adj.* stylish, fashionable.

Modistin [mo'dɪstɪn], *f.* (—, *pl.* —nen) milliner.

modrig ['moːdrɪç], *adj.* mouldy.

modulieren [modu'liːrən], *v.a.* modulate.

Modus ['moːdus], *m.* (—, *pl.* **Modi**) (*Gram.*) mood; mode, manner.

mogeln ['moːgəln], *v.n.* cheat.

mögen ['møːgən], *v.n. irr.* like, desire, want, be allowed, have a mind to; (*modal auxiliary*) may, might; *ich möchte gern*, I should like to.

möglich ['møːklɪç], *adj.* possible, practicable; feasible; *sein —stes tun*, do o.'s utmost; *nicht —!* you don't say (so)!

Möglichkeit ['møːklɪçkaɪt], *f.* (—, *pl.* —en) possibility, feasibility, practicability; (*pl.*) potentialities; contingencies, prospects (of career).

Mohn [moːn], *m.* (—es, *no pl.*) poppy (-seed).

Mohr [moːr], *m.* (—en, *pl.* —en) Moor; negro.

Möhre ['møːrə], *f.* (—, *pl.* —n) carrot.

Mohrenkopf ['moːrənkɔpf], *m.* (—es, *pl.* ⁒e) chocolate éclair.

Mohrrübe ['moːrryːbə], *f.* (—, *pl.* —n) carrot.

mokieren [mɔ'kiːrən], *v.r. sich — über*, sneer at, mock at, be amused by.

Mokka ['mɔka], *m.* (—s, *no pl.*) Mocha coffee.

Molch [mɔlç], *m.* (—es, *pl.* —e) (*Zool.*) salamander.

Moldau ['mɔldau], *f.* Moldavia.

Mole ['moːlə], *f.* (—, *pl.* —n) breakwater, jetty, pier.

Molekül [mole'kyːl], *n.* (—s, *pl.* —e) molecule.

Molke ['mɔlkə], *f.* (—, *pl.* —n) whey.

Molkerei [mɔlke'raɪ], *f.* (—, *pl.* —en) dairy.

moll [mɔl], *adj.* (*Mus.*) minor.

Molluske

Molluske [mɔ'luskə], *f.* (—, *pl.* —n) (*Zool.*) mollusc.

Moment (1) [mo'mɛnt], *m.* (—s, *pl.* —e) moment, instant.

Moment (2) [mo'mɛnt], *n.* motive, factor; (*Phys.*) momentum.

Momentaufnahme [mo'mɛntaufna:-mə], *f.* (—, *pl.* —n) snapshot.

momentan [momɛn'ta:n], *adv.* at the moment, for the present, just now.

Monarch [mo'narç], *m.* (—en, *pl.* —en) monarch.

Monarchie [monar'çi:], *f.* (—, *pl.* —n) monarchy.

Monat ['mo:nat], *m.* (—s, *pl.* —e) month.

monatlich ['mo:natlɪç], *adj.* monthly.

Monatsfluß ['mo:natsflus], *m.* (—sses, *pl.* ¨sse) menses.

Monatsschrift ['mo:natsʃrɪft], *f.* (—, *pl.* —en) monthly (*journal*).

Mönch [mœnç], *m.* (—es, *pl.* —e) monk, friar.

Mönchskappe ['mœnçskapə], *f.* (—, *pl.* —n) cowl, monk's hood.

Mönchskutte ['mœnçskutə], *f.* (—, *pl.* —n) cowl.

Mond [mo:nt], *m.* (—es, *pl.* —e) moon; *zunehmender* —, waxing moon; *abnehmender* —, waning moon.

Mondfinsternis ['mo:ntfɪnstərnɪs], *f.* (—, *pl.* —se) eclipse of the moon.

mondsüchtig ['mo:ntzyçtɪç], *adj.* given to sleep-walking; (*fig.*) moon-struck.

Mondwandlung ['mo:ntvandluŋ], *f.* (—, *pl.* —en) phase of the moon.

Moneten [mo'ne:tən], *pl.* (*sl.*) money, cash, funds.

Mongolei [mɔŋgo'laɪ], *f.* Mongolia.

monieren [mo'ni:rən], *v.a.* remind (a debtor); censure.

monogam [mono'ga:m], *adj.* monogamous.

Monopol [mono'po:l], *n.* (—s, *pl.* —e) monopoly.

monoton [mono'to:n], *adj.* monotonous.

Monstrum ['mɔnstrum], *n.* (—s, *pl.* Monstra) monster, monstrosity.

Monsun [mɔn'zu:n], *m.* (—s, *pl.* —e) monsoon.

Montag ['mo:nta:k], *m.* (—s, *pl.* —e) Monday; *blauer* —, Bank Holiday Monday.

Montage [mɔn'ta:ʒə], *f.* (—, *pl.* —n) fitting (up), setting up, installation, assembling.

Montanindustrie [mɔn'ta:nɪndustri:], *f.* (—, *no pl.*) mining industry.

Montanunion [mɔn'ta:nunjo:n], *f.* (—, *no pl.*) (*Pol.*) European Coal and Steel Community.

Monteur [mɔn'tø:r], *m.* (—s, *pl.* —e) fitter.

montieren [mɔn'ti:rən], *v.a.* fit (up), set up, mount, install.

Montur [mɔn'tu:r], *f.* (—, *pl.* —en) uniform, livery.

Moor [mo:r], *n.* (—es, *pl.* —e) swamp, fen, bog.

Moos [mo:s], *n.* (—es, *pl.* —e) moss; (*sl.*) cash.

Moped ['mo:pɛt], *n.* (—s, *pl.* —s) moped, motorised pedal cycle.

Mops [mɔps], *m.* (—es, *pl.* ¨e) pug (dog).

mopsen ['mɔpsən], *v.r. sich* —, feel bored.

Moral [mo'ra:l], *f.* (—, *no pl.*) moral, morals.

moralisch [mo'ra:lɪʃ], *adj.* moral.

Morast [mo'rast], *m.* (—es, *pl.* ¨e) morass, bog, fen, mire.

Moratorium [mora'to:rjum], *n.* (—s, *pl.* —rien) (*payments etc.*) respite.

Morchel ['mɔrçəl], *f.* (—, *pl.* —n) (*Bot.*) morel (edible fungus).

Mord [mɔrt], *m.* (—es, *pl.* —e) murder.

morden ['mɔrdən], *v.a., v.n.* murder.

Mörder ['mœrdər], *m.* (—s, *pl.* —) murderer.

Mordsgeschichte ['mɔrtsgəʃɪçtə], *f.* (—, *pl.* —n) (*coll.*) cock-and-bull story.

Mordskerl ['mɔrtskerl], *m.* (—s, *pl.* —e) devil of a fellow; (*Am.*) great guy.

Mordtat ['mɔrtta:t], *f.* (—, *pl.* —en) murder.

Morelle [mo'rɛlə], *f.* (—, *pl.* —n) (*Bot.*) morello cherry.

Morgen ['mɔrgən], *m.* (—s, *pl.* —) morning, daybreak; (*Poet.*) east; measure of land; *eines* —s, one morning.

morgen ['mɔrgən], *adv.* tomorrow; *— früh*, tomorrow morning; *heute* —, this morning.

Morgenblatt ['mɔrgənblat], *n.* (—s, *pl.* ¨er) morning paper.

morgendlich ['mɔrgəntlɪç], *adj.* of or in the morning; matutinal.

Morgenland ['mɔrgənlant], *n.* (—es, *pl.* —) orient, east.

Morgenrot ['mɔrgənro:t], *n.* (—s, *no pl.*) dawn, sunrise.

morgens ['mɔrgəns], *adv.* in the morning.

morgig ['mɔrgɪç], *adj.* tomorrow's.

Morphium ['mɔrfjum], *n.* (—s, *no pl.*) morphia, morphine.

morsch [mɔrʃ], *adj.* brittle, rotten, decayed.

Mörser ['mœrzər], *m.* (—s, *pl.* —) mortar.

Mörserkeule ['mœrzərkɔylə], *f.* (—, *pl.* —n) pestle.

Mörtel ['mœrtəl], *m.* (—s, *no pl.*) mortar, plaster.

Mörtelkelle ['mœrtəlkɛlə], *f.* (—, *pl.* —n) trowel.

Mosaik [moza'i:k], *n.* (—s, *pl.* —e) mosaic (work); inlaid work.

mosaisch [mo'za:ɪʃ], *adj.* Mosaic.

Moschee [mo'ʃe:], *f.* (—, *pl.* —n) mosque.

Moschus ['mɔʃus], *m.* (—, *no pl.*) musk.

Mosel ['mo:zəl], *f.* Moselle.

Moskau ['mɔskau], *n.* Moscow.

Moskito [mɔs'ki:to], *m.* (—s, *pl.* —s) (*Ent.*) mosquito.

Most [mɔst], *m.* (—es, *no pl.*) new wine, cider.

Mostrich ['mɔstrɪç], *m.* (—s, *no pl.*) mustard.

Motiv [mo'ti:f], *n.* (—es, *pl.* —e) motive; (*Mus.*, *Lit.*) motif, theme.

motivieren [moti'vi:rən], *v.a.* motivate.

Motorrad ['mo:tɔrra:t], *n.* (—es, *pl.* ̈er) motor-cycle.

Motte ['mɔtə], *f.* (—, *pl.* —n) (*Ent.*) moth.

moussieren [mu'si:rən], *v.n.* effervesce, sparkle.

Möwe ['mø:və], *f.* (—, *pl.* —n) (*Orn.*) seagull.

Mucke ['mukə], *f.* (—, *pl.* —n) whim, caprice; obstinacy.

Mücke ['mykə], *f.* (—, *pl.* —n) (*Ent.*) gnat, fly, mosquito.

Muckerei [mukə'raɪ], *f.* (—, *pl.* —en) cant.

mucksen ['muksən], *v.n.* stir, move, budge.

müde ['my:də], *adj.* tired, weary; — machen, tire.

Muff [muf], *m.* (—es, *pl.* —e) muff.

muffig ['mufɪç], *adj.* musty, fusty, stuffy.

Mühe ['my:ə], *f.* (—, *pl.* —n) trouble, pains; effort, labour, toil; *sich* — geben, take pains.

mühelos ['my:əlo:s], *adj.* effortless, easy.

mühen ['my:ən], *v.r. sich* —, exert o.s., take pains.

Mühewaltung ['my:əvaltuŋ], *f.* (—, *pl.* —en) exertion, effort.

Mühle ['my:lə], *f.* (—, *pl.* —n) (*flour*) mill; (*coffee*) grinder; game.

Muhme ['mu:mə], *f.* (—, *pl.* —n) (*obs.*) aunt.

Mühsal ['my:za:l], *f.* (—, *pl.* —e) hardship, misery, toil.

mühsam ['my:za:m], *adj.* troublesome, laborious.

mühselig ['my:ze:lɪç], *adj.* painful, laborious; miserable.

Mulatte [mu'latə], *m.* (—n, *pl.* —n) mulatto.

Mulde ['muldə], *f.* (—, *pl.* —n) trough.

muldenförmig ['muldənfœrmɪç], *adj.* trough-shaped.

Mull [mul], *m.* (—s, *no pl.*) Indian muslin.

Müll [myl], *m.* (—s, *no pl.*) dust, rubbish; (*Am.*) garbage.

Müller ['mylər], *m.* (—s, *pl.* —) miller.

mulmig ['mulmɪç], *adj.* dusty, mouldy, decayed.

multiplizieren [multipli'tsi:rən], *v.a.* multiply.

Mumie ['mu:mjə], *f.* (—, *pl.* —n) (*Archæol.*) mummy.

Mummenschanz ['mumənʃants], *m.* (—es, *no pl.*) mummery, masquerade.

München ['mynçən], *n.* Munich.

Mund [munt], *m.* (—es, *pl.* —e, ̈er) mouth; *den* — halten, keep quiet; *einen großen* — haben, talk big; *sich den* — verbrennen, put o.'s foot in it.

Mundart ['munta:rt], *f.* (—, *pl.* —en) (local) dialect.

Mündel ['myndəl], *m.*, *f. & n.* (—s, *pl.* —) ward, minor, child under guardianship.

mündelsicher ['myndəlzɪçər], *adj.* gilt-edged.

munden ['mundən], *v.n. es mundet mir,* I like the taste, I relish it.

münden ['myndən], *v.n.* discharge (into), flow (into).

mundfaul ['muntfaul], *adj.* tonguetied; taciturn.

mundgerecht ['muntgərɛçt], *adj.* palatable; (*fig.*) suitable.

Mundharmonika ['muntharmo:nɪka], *f.* (—, *pl.* —kas, —ken) mouth organ.

mündig ['myndɪç], *adj.* of age; — werden, come of age.

mündlich ['myntlɪç], *adj.* verbal, oral, by word of mouth; (*examination*) viva voce.

Mundschenk ['muntʃɛŋk], *m.* (—s, *pl.* —e) cupbearer.

mundtot ['muntto:t], *adj.* — machen, silence, gag.

Mündung ['mynduŋ], *f.* (—, *pl.* —en) (*river*) estuary, mouth; (*gun*) muzzle.

Mundvorrat ['muntforra:t], *m.* (—s, *pl.* ̈e) provisions, victuals.

Mundwerk ['muntvɛrk], *n.* (—s, *no pl.*) mouth; (*fig.*) gift of the gab.

Munition [muni'tsjo:n], *f.* (—, *no pl.*) ammunition.

munkeln ['muŋkəln], *v.n.* whisper; *man munkelt,* it is rumoured.

Münster ['mynstər], *n.* (—s, *pl.* —) minster, cathedral.

munter ['muntər], *adj.* awake; lively, active, sprightly, vivacious, cheerful, gay.

Münze ['myntsə], *f.* (—, *pl.* —n) coin.

Münzeinheit ['myntsaɪnhaɪt], *f.* (—, *no pl.*) monetary unit.

Münzfälscher ['myntsfɛlʃər], *m.* (—s, *pl.* —) (counterfeit) coiner.

Münzkunde ['myntskundə], *f.* (—, *no pl.*) numismatics.

Münzprobe ['myntspro:bə], *f.* (—, *pl.* —n) assay of a coin.

mürbe ['myrbə], *adj.* mellow; (*meat*) tender; (*cake*) crisp; brittle; *einen* — machen, soften s.o. up, force s.o. to yield.

Murmel ['murməl], *f.* (—, *pl.* —n) (*toy*) marble.

murmeln ['murməln], *v.n.* murmur, mutter.

Murmeltier ['murməlti:r], *n.* (—s, *pl.* —e) (*Zool.*) marmot; *wie ein* — schlafen, sleep like a log.

murren ['murən], *v.n.* grumble, growl.

mürrisch ['myrɪʃ], *adj.* morose, surly, sulky, peevish, sullen.

Mus [mu:s], *n.* (**—es**, *no pl.*) purée, (apple) sauce; pulp.

Muschel ['muʃəl], *f.* (**—**, *pl.* **—n**) mussel, shell; (*telephone*) ear-piece.

Muse ['mu:zə], *f.* (**—**, *pl.* **—n**) muse.

Muselman ['mu:zəlman], *m.* (**—en**, *pl.* **—en**) Muslim, Moslem.

Musik [mu'zi:k], *f.* (**—**, *no pl.*) music.

musikalisch [muzi'ka:liʃ], *adj.* musical.

Musikant [muzi'kant], *m.* (**—en**, *pl.* **—en**) musician; performer.

Musiker ['mu:zɪkər], *m.* (**—s**, *pl.* **—**) musician.

musizieren [muzi'tsi:rən], *v.n.* play music.

Muskateller [muska'tɛlər], *m.* (**—s**, *no pl.*) muscatel (wine).

Muskatnuß [mus'ka:tnus], *f.* (**—**, *pl.* **¨sse**) nutmeg.

Muskel ['muskəl], *m.* (**—s**, *pl.* **—n**) muscle.

muskelig ['musklɪç] *see* **musklig.**

Muskete [mus'ke:tə], *f.* (**—**, *pl.* **—n**) musket.

Musketier [muske'ti:r], *m.* (**—s**, *pl.* **—e**) musketeer.

musklig ['musklɪç], *adj.* muscular.

muskulös [musku'lø:s], *adj.* muscular.

Muße ['mu:sə], *f.* (**—**, *no pl.*) leisure; *mit —*, leisurely, at leisure.

Musselin [musə'li:n], *m.* (**—s**, *pl.* **—e**) muslin.

müssen ['mysən], *v.n. irr.* have to, be forced, be compelled, be obliged; *ich muß*, I must, I have to.

müßig ['my:sɪç], *adj.* idle, lazy, unemployed.

Müßiggang ['my:sɪçgaŋ], *m.* (**—s**, *no pl.*) idleness, laziness, sloth.

Muster ['mustər], *n.* (**—s**, *pl.* **—**) sample; pattern; (proto-)type; (*fig.*) example.

Musterbild ['mustərbɪlt], *n.* (**—s**, *pl.* **—er**) paragon.

mustergültig ['mustərgyltɪç], *adj.* exemplary; standard; excellent.

musterhaft ['mustərhaft], *adj.* exemplary.

mustern ['mustərn], *v.a.* examine, muster, scan; (*troops*) review, inspect.

Musterung ['mustəruŋ], *f.* (**—**, *pl.* **—en**) review; examination, inspection.

Mut ['mu:t], *m.* (**—es**, *no pl.*) courage, spirit; *— fassen*, take heart, muster up courage.

Mutation [muta'tsjo:n], *f.* (**—**, *pl.* **—en**) change.

mutieren [mu'ti:rən], *v.n.* change; (*voice*) break.

mutig ['mu:tɪç], *adj.* courageous, brave.

mutlos ['mu:tlo:s], *adj.* discouraged, dejected, despondent.

mutmaßen ['mu:tma:sən], *v.a. insep.* surmise, suppose, conjecture.

Mutter ['mutər], *f.* (**—**, *pl.* **¨**) mother; (*screw*) nut.

Mutterkorn ['mutərkɔrn], *n.* (**—s**, *no pl.*) ergot.

Mutterkuchen ['mutərku:xən], *m.* (**—s**, *pl.* **—**) placenta, after-birth.

Mutterleib ['mutərlaɪp], *m.* (**—s**, *no pl.*) womb, uterus.

Muttermal ['mutərma:l], *n.* (**—s**, *pl.* **—e**) birth-mark.

Mutterschaft ['mutərʃaft], *f.* (**—**, *no pl.*) motherhood, maternity.

mutterseelenallein ['mutərze:lənalaɪn], *adj.* quite alone; (*coll.*) all on o.'s own.

Muttersöhnchen ['mutərz:ønçən], *n.* (**—s**, *pl.* **—**) mother's darling, spoilt child.

Mutterwitz ['mutərvɪts], *m.* (**—es**, *no pl.*) mother-wit, native wit, common sense.

Mutwille ['mu:tvɪlə], *m.* (**—ns**, *no pl.*) mischievousness, wantonness.

Mütze ['mytsə], *f.* (**—**, *pl.* **—n**) cap; bonnet; beret.

Myrrhe ['mɪrə], *f.* (**—**, *pl.* **—n**) myrrh.

Myrte ['mɪrtə], *f.* (**—**, *pl.* **—n**) (*Bot.*) myrtle.

Mysterium [mɪs'te:rjum], *n.* (**—s**, *pl.* **—rien**) mystery.

Mystik ['mɪstɪk], *f.* (**—**, *no pl.*) mysticism.

Mythologie [mytolo'gi:], *f.* (**—**, *pl.* **—n**) mythology.

Mythus ['mytus], *m.* (**—**, *pl.* **Mythen**) myth.

N

N [ɛn], *n.* (**—s**, *pl.* **—s**) the letter N.

na [na], *int.* well, now; *—nu!* well, I never! *— und?* so what?

Nabe ['na:bə], *f.* (**—**, *pl.* **—n**) hub.

Nabel ['na:bəl], *m.* (**—s**, *pl.* **—**) navel.

Nabelschnur ['na:bəlʃnu:r], *f.* (**—**, *pl.* **¨e**) umbilical cord.

nach [na:x], *prep.* (*Dat.*) after, behind, following; to, towards; according to, in conformity *or* accordance with; in imitation of. *— adv., prefix.* after, behind; afterwards, later; *— und —*, little by little, by degrees, gradually.

nachäffen ['na:xɛfən], *v.a.* ape, mimic, imitate; (*coll.*) take off.

nachahmen ['na:xa:mən], *v.a.* imitate, copy; counterfeit.

nacharbeiten ['na:xarbaItən], *v.n.* work after hours *or* overtime. *— v.a.* copy (*Dat.*).

nacharten ['na:xa:rtən], *v.n.* (*aux. sein*) resemble, (*coll.*) take after.

Nachbar ['naxba:r], *m.* (**—s**, *pl.* **—n**) neighbour.

Nachbarschaft ['naxba:rʃaft], *f.* (**—**, *no pl.*) neighbourhood, vicinity; (*people*) neighbours.

nachbestellen ['na:xbəʃtɛlən], *v.a.* order more, re-order.

nachbilden ['na:xbɪldən], *v.a.* copy, reproduce.

nachdem [na:x'de:m], *adv.* afterwards, after that. — *conj.* after, when; *je* —, according to circumstances, that depends.

nachdenken ['na:xdɛŋkən], *v.n. irr.* think (over), meditate, muse, ponder.

nachdenklich ['na:xdɛŋklɪç], *adj.* reflective, pensive, wistful; — *stimmen,* set thinking.

Nachdruck ['na:xdrʊk], *m.* (—s, *pl.* —e) reprint; stress, emphasis.

nachdrucken ['na:xdrʊkən], *v.a.* reprint.

nachdrücklich ['na:xdrʏklɪç], *adj.* emphatic; — *betonen,* emphasise.

nacheifern ['na:xaɪfərn], *v.n. einem* —, emulate s.o.

nacheinander ['na:xaɪnandər], *adv.* one after another.

nachempfinden ['na:xɛmpfɪndən], *v.a. irr.* sympathize with, feel for.

Nachen ['naxən], *m.* (—s, *pl.* —) (*Poet.*) boat, skiff.

Nachfolge ['na:xfɔlgə], *f.* (—, *pl.* —n) succession.

nachfolgend ['na:xfɔlgənt], *adj.* following, subsequent.

Nachfolger ['na:xfɔlgər], *m.* (—s, *pl.* —) successor.

nachforschen ['na:xfɔrʃən], *v.a.* search after; enquire into, investigate.

Nachfrage ['na:xfra:gə], *f.* (—, *no pl.*) enquiry; (*Comm.*) demand; *Angebot und* —, supply and demand.

nachfühlen ['na:xfy:lən], *v.a. einem etwas* —, enter into s.o.'s feelings, sympathize with s.o.

nachfüllen ['na:xfʏlən], *v.a.* replenish, fill up.

nachgeben ['na:xge:bən], *v.n. irr.* relax, slacken, yield; give in, relent, give way.

nachgehen ['na:xge:ən], *v.n. irr.* (*aux.* sein) *einem* —, follow s.o., go after s.o.; (*clock*) be slow; follow up, investigate.

nachgerade ['na:xgəra:də], *adv.* by this time, by now; gradually.

nachgiebig ['na:xgi:bɪç], *adj.* yielding, compliant.

nachgrübeln ['na:xgry:bəln], *v.n.* speculate.

Nachhall ['na:xhal], *m.* (—s, *no pl.*) echo, resonance.

nachhaltig ['na:xhaltɪç], *adj.* lasting, enduring.

nachhängen ['na:xhɛŋən], *v.n. irr. seinen Gedanken* —, muse.

nachher ['na:xhe:r], *adv.* afterwards, later on.

nachherig ['na:xhe:rɪç], *adj.* subsequent, later.

Nachhilfestunde ['na:xhɪlfəʃtundə], *f.* (—, *pl.* —n) private coaching.

nachholen ['na:xho:lən], *v.a.* make good; make up for.

Nachhut ['na:xhu:t], *f.* (—, *no pl.*) (*Mil.*) rearguard.

nachjagen ['na:xja:gən], *v.n.* (*aux.* sein) pursue.

Nachklang ['na:xklaŋ], *m.* (—s, *pl.* ¨e) echo; (*fig.*) after-effect, reminiscence.

Nachkomme ['na:xkɔmə], *m.* (—n, *pl.* —n) descendant, offspring.

nachkommen ['na:xkɔmən], *v.n. irr.* (*aux.* sein) come after, follow; *seiner Pflicht* —, do o.'s duty; comply with; *einem Versprechen* —, keep a promise; *seinen Verpflichtungen nicht* — *können,* be unable to meet o.'s commitments.

Nachkommenschaft ['na:xkɔmənʃaft], *f.* (—, *no pl.*) descendants, offspring, issue, progeny.

Nachlaß ['na:xlas], *m.* (—sses, *pl.* ¨sse) inheritance, estate, bequest; remission, discount, allowance.

nachlassen ['na:xlasən], *v.a. irr.* leave behind, bequeath; (*trade*) give a discount of. — *v.n.* abate, subside, slacken.

nachlässig ['na:xlɛsɪç], *adj.* negligent, remiss, careless.

nachlaufen ['na:xlaufən], *v.n. irr.* (*aux.* sein) *einem* —, run after s.o.

Nachlese ['na:xle:zə], *f.* (—, *pl.* —n) gleaning.

nachliefern ['na:xli:fərn], *v.a.* supply subsequently, complete delivery of.

nachmachen ['na:xmaxən], *v.a.* copy, imitate; counterfeit, forge.

nachmals ['na:xma:ls], *adv.* afterwards, subsequently.

Nachmittag ['na:xmɪta:k], *m.* (—s, *pl.* —e) afternoon.

Nachnahme ['na:xna:mə], *f.* (—, *no pl.*) *per* —, cash *or* (*Am.*) collect (payment) on delivery (*abbr.* C.O.D.).

nachplappern ['na:xplapərn], *v.a.* repeat mechanically.

Nachrede ['na:xre:də], *f.* (—, *pl.* —n) epilogue; *üble* —, slander.

Nachricht ['na:xrɪçt], *f.* (—, *pl.* —en) news, information; (*Mil.*) intelligence; — *geben,* send word.

nachrücken ['na:xrʏkən], *v.n.* (*aux.* sein) move up.

Nachruf ['na:xru:f], *m.* (—s, *pl.* —e) obituary.

nachrühmen ['na:xry:mən], *v.a. einem etwas* —, speak well of s.o.

Nachsatz ['na:xzats], *m.* (—es, *pl.* ¨e) concluding clause; postscript.

nachschauen ['na:xʃauən], *v.n. jemandem* —, gaze after s.o.

nachschlagen ['na:xʃla:gən], *v.a. irr.* look up, consult (a book).

Nachschlagewerk ['na:xʃla:gəverk], *n.* (—s, *pl.* —e) work of reference, reference book.

Nachschlüssel ['na:xʃlʏsəl], *m.* (—s, *pl.* —) master-key, skeleton-key.

Nachschrift ['na:xʃrɪft], *f.* (—, *pl.* —en) postscript, (*abbr.* P.S.).

Nachschub ['na:xʃu:p], *m.* (—s, *pl.* ¨e) (fresh) supply; (*Mil.*) reinforcements.

Nachsehen ['na:xze:ən], *n.* (—s, *no pl.*) *das* — *haben,* be left out in the cold.

nachsehen ['naːxzeːən], v.a., v.n. irr. look for, look s.th. up, refer to s.th.; einem etwas —, be indulgent with s.o.

Nachsicht ['naːxzɪçt], f. (—, no pl.) forbearance, indulgence.

Nachsilbe ['naːxzɪlbə], f. (—, pl. —n) suffix.

nachsinnen ['naːxzɪnən], v.n. muse, reflect.

nachsitzen ['naːxzɪtsən], v.n. be kept in after school.

Nachsommer ['naːxzɔmər], m. (—s, pl. —) Indian summer.

Nachspeise ['naːxʃpaɪzə], f. (—, pl. —n) dessert.

nachspüren ['naːxʃpyːrən], v.n. einem —, trace, track.

nächst [nɛːçst], prep. (Dat.) next to, nearest to. — adj. next.

Nächste ['nɛːçstə], m. (—n, pl. —n) fellow-man, neighbour.

nachstehen ['naːxʃteːən], v.n. irr. einem —, be inferior to s.o.; keinem —, be second to none.

nachstehend ['naːxʃteːənt], adv. below, hereinafter. — adj. following.

nachstellen ['naːxʃtelən], v.n. einem —, lie in wait for s.o.

Nachstellung ['naːxʃtelʊŋ], f. (—, pl. —en) persecution, ambush; (Gram.) postposition.

nächstens ['nɛːçstəns], adv. soon, shortly.

nachstöbern ['naːxʃtøːbərn], v.n. rummage.

nachströmen ['naːxʃtrøːmən], v.n. (aux. sein) crowd after.

Nacht [naxt], f. (—, pl. ⁻e) night; die ganze — hindurch, all night; bei —, at night; gute — wünschen, bid goodnight; über —, overnight; in der —, during the night; bei — und Nebel, in the dead of night.

Nachteil ['naːxtaɪl], m. (—s, pl. —e) disadvantage, damage.

Nachtessen ['naːxtesən], n. (—s, pl. —) supper; evening meal.

Nachtfalter ['naːxtfaltər], m. (—s, pl. —) (Ent.) moth.

Nachtgeschirr ['naːxtgəʃɪr], n. (—s, pl. —e) chamber-pot.

Nachtgleiche ['naːxtglaɪçə], f. (—, pl. —n) equinox.

Nachthemd ['naːxtɛmt], n. (—es, pl. —en) night-dress, night-gown.

Nachtigall ['naːxtɪgal], f. (—, pl. —en) (Orn.) nightingale.

nächtigen ['nɛçtɪgən], v.n. spend the night.

Nachtisch ['naːxtɪʃ], m. (—es, pl. —e) dessert.

Nachtlager ['naːxtlaːgər], n. (—s, pl. —) lodgings for the night; (Mil.) bivouac.

Nachtmahl ['naːxtmaːl], n. (—s, pl. —e) (Austr.) supper.

nachtönen ['naːxtøːnən], v.n. resound.

Nachtrag ['naːxtraːk], m. (—s, pl. ⁻e) supplement, postscript, addition; (pl.) addenda.

nachtragen ['naːxtraːgən], v.a. irr. carry after; add; (fig.) einem etwas —, bear s.o. a grudge.

nachträglich ['naːxtrɛːklɪç], adj. subsequent; supplementary; additional; further; later.

Nachtrupp ['naːxtrup], m. (—s, no pl.) rearguard.

Nachtschwärmer ['naxtʃvɛrmər], m. (—s, pl. —) night-reveller.

Nachttisch ['naxttɪʃ], m. (—es, pl. —e) bedside-table.

nachtun ['naːxtuːn], v.a. irr. einem etwas —, imitate s.o., emulate s.o.

Nachtwächter ['naxtvɛçtər], m. (—s, pl. —) night-watchman.

Nachtwandler ['naxtvandlər], m. (—s, pl. —) sleep-walker, somnambulist.

Nachwahl ['naːxvaːl], f. (—, pl. —en) by(e)-election.

Nachwehen ['naːxveːən], f. pl. aftermath; unpleasant consequences.

Nachweis ['naːxvaɪs], m. (—es, pl. —e) proof; (Lit.) reference; agency.

nachweisen ['naːxvaɪzən], v.a. irr. prove, establish; (Lit.) refer.

Nachwelt ['naːxvɛlt], f. (—, no pl.) posterity.

Nachwort ['naːxvɔrt], n. (—es, pl. —e) epilogue.

Nachwuchs ['naːxvuːks], m. (—es, no pl.) coming generation; recruits.

Nachzahlung ['naːxtsaːluŋ], f. (—, pl. —en) additional payment, supplementary payment.

Nachzählung ['naːxtsɛːluŋ], f. (—, pl. —en) recount.

nachziehen ['naːxtsiːən], v.a. irr. drag, tow; tighten; trace, pencil. — v.n. follow.

Nachzügler ['naːxtsyːglər], m. (—s, pl. —) straggler.

Nacken ['nakən], m. (—s, pl. —) nape, scruff of the neck.

nackend ['nakənt], adj. naked.

nackt [nakt], adj. nude, naked; (bird) callow; (fig.) bare; sich — ausziehen, strip.

Nadel ['naːdəl], f. (—, pl. —n) needle, pin; wie auf —n sitzen, be on tenterhooks.

Nadelöhr ['naːdəløːr], n. (—s, pl. —e) eye of a needle.

Nagel ['naːgəl], m. (—s, pl. ⁻) nail; (wooden) peg; (ornament) stud; etwas an den — hängen, lay s.th. aside, give s.th. up.

nagelneu ['naːgəlnɔy], adj. brand new.

nagen ['naːgən], v.a., v.n. gnaw; (fig.) rankle.

Näharbeit ['nɛːarbaɪt], f. (—, pl. —en) sewing, needlework.

nahe ['naːə], adj., adv. near, close, nigh; — bei, close to; — daran sein, be on the point of; es geht mir —, it grieves me, it touches me; einem zu — treten, hurt s.o.'s feelings; es liegt —, it is obvious, it suggests itself.

Nähe ['nɛːə], f. (—, no pl.) nearness, proximity; in der —, at hand, close by.

nahen [ˈnaːən], *v.n.* (*aux.* sein) draw near, approach.

nähen [ˈnɛːən], *v.a.* sew, stitch.

Nähere [ˈnɛːərə], *n.* (—n, *no pl.*) details, particulars.

Näherin [ˈnɛːərɪn], *f.* (—, *pl.* — innen) seamstress, needlewoman.

nähern [ˈnɛːərn], *v.r.* sich —, draw near, approach.

nahestehen [ˈnaːəʃteːən], *v.n.* be closely connected *or* friendly (with s.o.).

Nährboden [ˈnɛːrboːdən], *m.* (—s, *pl.* ∸) rich soil; (*Med., Biol.*) culture-medium.

nähren [ˈnɛːrən], *v.a.* nourish, feed. — *v.r.* sich — von, feed on; (*fig.*) gain a livelihood.

nahrhaft [ˈnaːrhaft], *adj.* nourishing, nutritive, nutritious.

Nährstand [ˈnɛːrʃtant], *m.* (—es, *no pl.*) peasants, producers.

Nahrung [ˈnaːruŋ], *f.* (—, *no pl.*) nourishment.

Nahrungsmittel [ˈnaːruŋsmɪtəl], *n.* (—s, *pl.* —) food, provisions, victuals.

Naht [naːt], *f.* (—, *pl.* ∸e) seam.

Nähzeug [ˈnɛːtsɔyk], *n.* (—s, *no pl.*) sewing kit, work box.

naiv [naˈiːf], *adj.* naïve, artless, guileless.

Naivität [naiviˈtɛːt], *f.* (—, *no pl.*) artlessness, guilelessness, naiveté.

Name [ˈnaːmə], *m.* (—ns, *pl.* —n) name; *guter* —, good name, renown, reputation; *dem* —n *nach*, by name; *etwas beim rechten* —n *nennen*, call a spade a spade.

namens [ˈnaːməns], *adv.* called; by the name of.

Namensvetter [ˈnaːmənsfɛtər], *m.* (—s, *pl.* —n) namesake.

namentlich [ˈnaːməntlɪç], *adj.* by name; particularly.

Namenverzeichnis [ˈnaːmənfɛrtsaɪçnɪs], *n.* (—ses, *pl.* —se) list of names; (*scientific*) nomenclature.

namhaft [ˈnaːmhaft], *adj.* distinguished, renowned; considerable; — *machen*, name.

nämlich [ˈnɛːmlɪç], *adv.* namely, to wit.

Napf [napf], *m.* (—es, *pl.* ∸e) bowl, basin.

Napfkuchen [ˈnapfkuːxən], *m.* (—s, *pl.* —) pound-cake, large cake.

Narbe [ˈnarbə], *f.* (—, *pl.* —n) scar; (*leather*) grain.

Narkose [narˈkoːzə], *f.* (—, *pl.* —n) anaesthesia; narcosis.

Narr [nar], *m.* (—en, *pl.* —en) fool; jester, buffoon; *einen zum* —en *haben*, make a fool of s.o.; *an einem einen* —en *gefressen haben*, dote on, be infatuated with s.o.

Narrheit [ˈnarhaɪt], *f.* (—, *pl.* —en) foolishness, folly.

närrisch [ˈnɛrɪʃ], *adj.* foolish, comical; odd; merry; eccentric, mad; — *werden*, go mad.

Narzisse [narˈtsɪsə], *f.* (—, *pl.* —n) (*Bot.*) narcissus; *gelbe* —, daffodil.

naschen [ˈnaʃən], *v.a.,v.n.* pilfer titbits; nibble at, eat sweets.

Näscherei [nɛʃərˈaɪ], *f.* (—, *pl.* —en) sweets, dainties, sweetmeats.

naschhaft [ˈnaʃhaft], *adj.* sweet-toothed.

Naschkatze [ˈnaʃkatsə], *f.* (—, *pl.* —n) sweet tooth.

Nase [ˈnaːzə], *f.* (—, *pl.* —n) nose; (*animal*) snout; scent; *stumpfe* —, snub nose; *gebogene* —, Roman nose; *immer der* — *nach*, follow your nose; *die* — *hoch tragen*, be stuck-up; *eine feine* (*gute*) — *haben*, be good at; not miss much; *die* — *rümpfen*, turn up o.'s nose; *seine* — *in alles stecken*, poke o.'s nose into everything; *einem etwas unter die* — *reiben*, bring s.th. home to s.o.

näseln [ˈnɛːzəln], *v.n.* speak with a twang.

Nasenbein [ˈnaːzənbaɪn], *n.* (—s, *pl.* —e) nasal bone.

Nasenbluten [ˈnaːzənbluːtən], *n.* (—s, *no pl.*) nose-bleed.

Nasenflügel [ˈnaːzənflyːgəl], *m.* (—s, *pl.* —) side of the nose; nostril.

naseweis [ˈnaːzəvaɪs], *adj.* pert, saucy.

Nashorn [ˈnaːshɔrn], *n.* (—s, *pl.* ∸er) (*Zool.*) rhinoceros.

Naß [nas], *n.* (—sses, *no pl.*) (*Poet.*) fluid.

naß [nas], *adj.* wet, moist, damp.

Nässe [ˈnɛsə], *f.* (—, *no pl.*) wetness, dampness, moisture, humidity.

nationalisieren [natsjonaliˈziːrən], *v.a.* nationalise.

Nationalität [natsjonaliˈtɛːt], *f.* (—, *pl.* —en) nationality.

Natrium [ˈnaːtrjum], *n.* (—s, *no pl.*) sodium.

Natron [ˈnaːtrɔn], *n.* (—s, *no pl.*) sodium carbonate; *doppelkohlensaures* —, sodium bicarbonate; bicarbonate of soda.

Natter [ˈnatər], *f.* (—, *pl.* —n) (*Zool.*) adder, viper.

Natur [naˈtuːr], *f.* (—, *pl.* —en) nature; (*body*) constitution; (*mind*) disposition; *von* —, by nature, constitutionally; *nach der* — *zeichnen*, draw from nature.

naturalisieren [naturaliˈziːrən], *v.a.* naturalise.

Naturalleistung [natuˈraːllaɪstuŋ], *f.* (—, *pl.* —en) payment in kind.

Naturell [natuˈrɛl], *n.* (—s, *pl.* —e) natural disposition, temper.

Naturforscher [naˈtuːrfɔrʃər], *m.* (—s, *pl.* —) naturalist.

naturgemäß [naˈtuːrgəmɛːs], *adj.* natural.

Naturgeschichte [naˈtuːrgəʃɪçtə], *f.* (—, *no pl.*) natural history.

naturgetreu [naˈtuːrgətrɔy], *adj.* true to nature, lifelike.

Naturkunde [naˈtuːrkundə], *f.* (—, *no pl.*) natural history.

Naturlehre [naˈtuːrleːrə], *f.* (—, *no pl.*) natural philosophy; physics.

natürlich [na'ty:rlɪç], *adj.* natural; innate, inherent; unaffected, artless. — *adv.* of course, naturally.

Naturspiel [na'tu:rʃpi:l], *n.* (—**s**, *pl.* —**e**) freak of nature.

Naturtrieb [na'tu:rtri:p], *m.* (—**s**, *no pl.*) natural impulse, instinct.

naturwidrig [na'tu:rvi:drɪç], *adj.* contrary to nature, unnatural.

Naturwissenschaft [na'tu:rvɪsənʃaft], *f.* (—, *pl.* —**en**) (natural) science.

naturwüchsig [na'tu:rvy:ksɪç], *adj.* original; unsophisticated.

Nautik ['nautɪk], *f.* (—, *no pl.*) nautical science.

nautisch ['nautɪʃ], *adj.* nautical.

Nazi ['na:tsi], *abbr.* National Socialist.

Neapel [ne'a:pəl], *n.* Naples.

Nebel ['ne:bəl], *m.* (—**s**, *pl.* —) fog; *leichter* —, haze, mist; *dichter* —, (*London*) pea-souper; (*with soot*) smog.

Nebelschicht ['ne:bəlʃɪçt], *f.* (—, *pl.* —**n**) fog-bank.

neben ['ne:bən], *prep.* (*Dat., Acc.*) near, by, beside, besides, close to, next to; (*in compounds*) secondary, subsidiary, side-. — *adv.* beside, besides.

nebenan [ne:bən'an], *adv.* next door, nearby.

nebenbei [ne:bən'bai], *adv.* besides, by the way, incidentally.

Nebenbuhler ['ne:bənbu:lər], *m.* (—**s**, *pl.* —) rival.

nebeneinander [ne:bənain'andər], *adv.* side by side, abreast.

Nebenfluß ['ne:bənflus], *m.* (—**sses**, *pl.* -**¨sse**) tributary, affluent.

nebenher [ne:bən'he:r], *adv.* by the side of, along with.

Nebenmensch ['ne:bənmɛnʃ], *m.* (—**en**, *pl.* —**en**) fellow creature.

Nebensatz ['ne:bənzats], *m.* (—**es**, *pl.* -**¨e**) (*Gram.*) subordinate clause.

Nebenzimmer ['ne:bəntsɪmər], *n.* (—**s**, *pl.* —) adjoining room.

neblig ['ne:blɪç], *adj.* foggy, misty, hazy.

nebst [ne:pst], *prep.* (*Dat.*) together with, including.

necken ['nɛkən], *v.a.* tease, chaff, banter.

neckisch ['nɛkɪʃ], *adj.*, droll, playful, arch.

Neffe ['nɛfə], *m.* (—**n**, *pl.* —**n**) nephew.

Neger ['ne:gər], *m.* (—**s**, *pl.* —) Negro.

negerartig ['ne:gəra:rtɪç], *adj.* Negroid.

negieren [ne'gi:rən], *v.a.* deny, negate, negative.

nehmen ['ne:mən], *v.a. irr.* take, seize; receive, accept; *einem etwas* —, take s.th. from s.o.; *das lasse ich mir nicht* —, I insist on that, I am not to be done out of that; *ein Ende* —, come to an end; *etwas in die Hand* —, take s.th. in hand; *Schaden* —, suffer damage; *einen beim Wort* —, take s.o. at his word; *sich in acht* —, take care.

Nehrung ['ne:ruŋ], *f.* (—, *pl.* —**en**) narrow tongue of land, spit.

Neid [nait], *m.* (—**es**, *no pl.*) envy, grudge.

Neidhammel ['naithaməl], *m.* (—**s**, *pl.* —) dog in the manger.

neidisch ['naidɪʃ], *adj.* envious, grudging, jealous.

Neige ['naigə], *f.* (—, *pl.* —**n**) remnant, sediment; *zur* — *gehen*, be on the decline, run short, dwindle.

neigen ['naigən], *v.a., v.n.* incline, bow, bend; *zu etwas* —, be inclined to, be prone to. — *v.r. sich* —, bow.

Neigung ['naiguŋ], *f.* (—, *pl.* —**en**) inclination, proneness; affection; (*ground*) dip, slope, gradient; (*ship*) list.

Neigungsfläche ['naiguŋsflɛçə], *f.* (—, *pl.* —**n**) inclined plane.

nein [nain], *adv.* no.

Nekrolog [nekro'lo:k], *m.* (—(**e**)**s**, *pl.* —**e**) obituary.

Nelke ['nɛlkə], *f.* (—, *pl.* —**n**) (*Bot.*) pink, carnation; (*condiment*) clove.

nennen ['nɛnən], *v.a. irr.* name, call by name, term, style.

Nenner ['nɛnər], *m.* (—**s**, *pl.* —) denominator.

Nennung ['nɛnuŋ], *f.* (—, *pl.* —**en**) naming, mentioning.

Nennwert ['nɛnve:rt], *m.* (—**s**, *pl.* —**e**) nominal value.

Nepal ['ne:pal], *n.* Nepal.

Nerv [nɛrf], *m.* (—**s**, *pl.* —**en**) nerve, sinew; *einem auf die* —**en** *gehen*, get on s.o.'s nerves.

Nervenlehre ['nɛrfənle:rə], *f.* (—, *no pl.*) neurology.

nervig ['nɛrvɪç], *adj.* strong; (*fig.*) pithy.

nervös [nɛr'vø:s], *adj.* nervous, irritable, fidgety.

Nerz [nɛrts], *m.* (—**es**, *pl.* —**e**) mink.

Nessel ['nɛsəl], *f.* (—, *pl.* —**n**) nettle.

Nesseltuch ['nɛsəltu:x], *n.* (—**es**, *no pl.*) muslin.

Nest [nɛst], *n.* (—**es**, *pl.* —**er**) nest; (*eagle*) eyrie; *kleines* —, small town.

Nesthäkchen ['nɛsthɛ:kçən], *n.* (—**s**, *pl.* —) youngest child.

nett [nɛt], *adj.* nice, kind, friendly; neat, trim.

netto ['nɛto], *adv.* (*Comm.*) net, clear.

Netz [nɛts], *n.* (—**es**, *pl.* —**e**) net; (*Electr.*) grid; *Eisenbahn* —, railway network *or* system.

netzen ['nɛtsən], *v.a.* (*obs., Poet.*) wet, moisten.

Netzhaut ['nɛtshaut], *f.* (—, *pl.* -**¨e**) retina.

neu [nɔy], *adj.* new, fresh; modern; recent; *aufs* —, *von* —**em**, anew, afresh; —**e**, —**ere** *Sprachen*, modern languages.

Neuenburg ['nɔyənburk], *n.* Neuchâtel.

neuerdings ['nɔyərdɪŋs], *adv.* newly, lately.

Neuerer ['nɔyərər], *m.* (—**s**, *pl.* —) innovator.

neuerlich ['nɔyərlɪç], *adj.* late, repeated.

Neufundland [nɔy'funtlant], *n.* Newfoundland.

Neugier(de) ['nɔygi:r(də)], *f.* (—, *no pl.*) inquisitiveness, curiosity.

neugierig ['nɔygi:rɪç], *adj.* curious, inquisitive.

Neuheit ['nɔyhaɪt], *f.* (—, *pl.* —en) novelty.

Neuigkeit ['nɔyɪçkaɪt], *f.* (—, *pl.* —en) piece of news.

neulich ['nɔylɪç], *adv.* lately, recently.

Neuling ['nɔylɪŋ], *m.* (—s, *pl.* —e) novice, beginner, tyro, newcomer; (*Am.*) greenhorn.

neumodisch ['nɔymo:dɪʃ], *adj.* newfangled, in vogue.

Neumond ['nɔymo:nt], *m.* (—s, *pl.* —e) new moon.

neun [nɔyn], *num. adj.* nine.

Neunauge ['nɔynaugə], *n.* (—s, *pl.* —n) river lamprey.

neunzehn ['nɔyntse:n], *num. adj.* nineteen.

neunzig ['nɔyntsɪç], *num. adj.* ninety.

Neuregelung ['nɔyre:gəluŋ], *f.* (—, *pl.* —en) rearrangement.

Neuseeland [nɔy'ze:lant], *n.* New Zealand.

neutralisieren [nɔytrali'zi:rən], *v.a.* neutralise.

Neutralität [nɔytrali'tɛ:t], *f.* (—, *no pl.*) neutrality.

Neutrum ['nɔytrum], *n.* (—s, *pl.* —ren) (*Gram.*) neuter.

Neuzeit ['nɔytsaɪt], *f.* (—, *no pl.*) modern times.

nicht [nɪçt], *adv.* not; *auch* —, nor; — *doch*, don't; — *einmal*, not even; *durchaus* —, not at all, by no means; — *mehr*, no more, no longer; not any more; *noch* —, not yet; — *wahr*? isn't it? aren't you? (*in compounds*) non-, dis-, a- (*negativing*).

Nichte ['nɪçtə], *f.* (—, *pl.* —n) niece.

nichten ['nɪçtən], *adv.* (*obs.*) *mit*—, by no means, not at all.

nichtig ['nɪçtɪç], *adj.* null, void, invalid.

Nichtigkeit ['nɪçtɪçkaɪt], *f.* (—, *no pl.*) invalidity, nullity.

nichts [nɪçts], *pron.* nothing, nought; — *als*, nothing but.

nichtsdestoweniger [nɪçtsdɛsto've:nɪgər], *adv.* nevertheless.

Nichtsnutz ['nɪçtsnuts], *m.* (—es, *pl.* —e) good for nothing.

Nickel ['nɪkəl], *n.* (—s, *no pl.*) (*metal*) nickel.

nicken ['nɪkən], *v.n.* nod.

nie [ni:], *adv.* never, at no time.

nieder ['ni:dər], *adj.* low, lower, nether; mean, inferior. — *adv.* down.

niedergeschlagen ['ni:dərgəʃla:gən], *adj.* dejected, low-spirited, depressed.

niederkommen ['ni:dərkɔmən], *v.n. irr.* (*aux.* sein) (*rare*) be confined.

Niederkunft ['ni:dərkunft], *f.* (—, *no pl.*) confinement, childbirth.

Niederlage ['ni:dərla:gə], *f.* (—, *pl.* —n) (*enemy*) defeat, overthrow; (*goods*) depot, warehouse; agency.

Niederlande ['ni:dərlandə], *n. pl.* the Netherlands.

niederlassen ['ni:dərlasən], *v.a. irr.* let down. — *v.r. sich* —, sit down, take a seat; settle; establish o.s. in business.

Niederlassung ['ni:dərlasuŋ], *f.* (—, *pl.* —en) establishment; settlement, colony; branch, branch establishment.

niederlegen ['ni:dərle:gən], *v.a.* lay down, put down; (*office*) resign, abdicate. — *v.r. sich* —, lie down.

Niederschlag ['ni:dərʃla:k], *m.* (—s, *pl.* ⁃e) precipitation, sediment, deposit; rain.

niederschlagen ['ni:dərʃla:gən], *v.a. irr.* strike down; (*fig.*) depress, discourage; (*Law*) quash, cancel; (*eyes*) cast down; (*Chem.*) precipitate; (*Boxing*) knock out.

Niedertracht ['ni:dərtraxt], *f.* (—, *no pl.*) baseness, meanness, villainy, beastliness.

Niederung ['ni:dəruŋ], *f.* (—, *pl.* —en) low ground, marsh.

niedlich ['ni:tlɪç], *adj.* pretty, dainty; (*Am.*) cute.

niedrig ['ni:drɪç], *adj.* low; (*fig.*) base, vile.

niemals ['ni:ma:ls], *adv.* never, at no time.

niemand ['ni:mant], *pron.* nobody, no one.

Niere ['ni:rə], *f.* (—, *pl.* —n) kidney.

Nierenbraten ['ni:rənbra:tən], *m.* (—s, *no pl.*) roast loin.

Nierenfett ['ni:rənfɛt], *n.* (—s, *no pl.*) suet.

nieseln ['ni:zəln], *v.n. imp.* drizzle.

niesen ['ni:zən], *v.n.* sneeze.

Nießbrauch ['ni:sbraux], *m.* (—s, *no pl.*) usufruct, benefit.

Niete ['ni:tə], *f.* (—, *pl.* —n) blank; (*Engin.*) rivet; failure.

Niger ['ni:gər], *n.* Niger.

Nigeria [ni'ge:rja], *n.* Nigeria.

Nikaragua [nika'ra:gua], *n.* Nicaragua.

Nikolaus ['nɪkolaus], *m.* Nicholas; *Sankt* —, Santa Claus.

Nil [ni:l], *m.* (—s, *no pl.*) Nile.

Nilpferd ['ni:lpfe:rt], *n.* (—s, *pl.* —e) (*Zool.*) hippopotamus.

nimmer (mehr) ['nɪmər (me:r)], *adv.* never, never again.

nippen ['nɪpən], *v.a., v.n.* sip, (take a) nip (of).

Nippsachen ['nɪpzaxən], *f. pl.* knick-knacks.

nirgends ['nɪrgənts], *adv.* nowhere.

Nische ['ni:ʃə], *f.* (—, *pl.* —n) niche.

Nisse ['nɪsə], *f.* (—, *pl.* —n) nit.

nisten ['nɪstən], *v.n.* nest.

Niveau [ni'vo:], *n.* (—s, *pl.* —s) level, standard.

nivellieren [nivɛ'li:rən], *v.a.* level.

Nixe ['nɪksə], *f.* (—, *pl.* —n) water-nymph, mermaid, water-sprite.

Nizza

Nizza ['nɪtsa], *n.* Nice.
nobel ['no:bəl], *adj.* noble, smart; (*Am.*) swell; munificent, open-handed, magnanimous.
noch [nɔx], *adv.* still, yet; — *einmal,* — *mals,* once more; *weder . . . — . . .,* neither . . . nor . . .; — *nicht,* not yet; — *nie,* never yet, never before.
nochmalig ['nɔxmaːlɪç], *adj.* repeated.
Nomade [no'maːdə], *m.* (**—n,** *pl.* **—n**) nomad.
nominell [nomi'nɛl], *adj.* nominal.
nominieren [nomi'niːrən], *v.a.* nominate.
Nonne ['nɔnə], *f.* (**—,** *pl.* **—n**) nun.
Noppe ['nɔpə], *f.* (**—,** *pl.* **—n**) nap.
Norden ['nɔrdən], *m.* (**—s,** *no pl.*) north.
nördlich ['nœrtlɪç], *adj.* northern, northerly.
Nordsee ['nɔrtzeː], *f.* North Sea.
nörgeln ['nœrgəln], *v.n.* find fault, cavil, carp, nag.
Norm ['nɔrm], *f.* (**—,** *pl.* **—en**) standard, rule, norm.
normal [nɔr'maːl], *adj.* normal, standard.
Norwegen ['nɔrveːgən], *n.* Norway.
Not [noːt], *f.* (**—,** *pl.* **—̈e**) need, necessity; misery, want, trouble, distress; (*in compounds*) emergency.
not [noːt], *pred. adj.* — *tun,* be necessary.
Nota ['noːta], *f.* (**—,** *pl.* **—s**) bill, statement.
Notar [no'taːr], *m.* (**—s,** *pl.* **—e**) notary.
Notdurft ['noːtdurft], *f.* (**—,** *pl.* **—̈e**) want, necessaries, necessity; *seine — verrichten,* ease o.s.
notdürftig ['noːtdyrftɪç], *adj.* scanty, makeshift.
Note ['noːtə], *f.* (**—,** *pl.* **—n**) note; (*Mus.*) note; (*School*) mark(s); *nach —n,* (*fig.*) with a vengeance.
Notenbank ['noːtənbaŋk], *f.* (**—,** *pl.* **—en**) bank of issue.
Notenblatt ['noːtənblat], *n.* (**—s,** *pl.* **—̈er**) sheet of music.
notgedrungen ['noːtgədruŋən], *adj.* compulsory, forced; perforce.
Nothelfer ['noːthɛlfər], *m.* (**—s,** *pl.* **—**) helper in time of need.
notieren [no'tiːrən], *v.a.* note, book; (*Comm.*) quote.
notifizieren [notifi'tsiːrən], *v.a.* notify.
nötig ['nøːtɪç], *adj.* necessary; — *haben,* want, need.
nötigen ['nøːtɪgən], *v.a.* compel, press, force, urge; necessitate; *sich — lassen,* stand upon ceremony.
Notiz [no'tiːts], *f.* (**—,** *pl.* **—en**) note, notice; — *nehmen von,* take notice of; (*pl.*) notes, jottings.
notleidend ['noːtlaɪdənt], *adj.* financially distressed, indigent, needy.
notorisch [no'toːrɪʃ], *adj.* notorious.
Notstand ['noːtʃtant], *m.* (**—s,** *no pl.*) state of distress; emergency.

Notverband ['noːtfɛrbant], *m.* (**—es,** *pl.* **—̈e**) first-aid dressing.
Notwehr ['noːtveːr], *f.* (**—,** *no pl.*) self-defence.
notwendig ['noːtvɛndɪç], *adj.* necessary, essential, needful.
Notzucht ['noːtsuxt], *f.* (**—,** *no pl.*) rape, violation.
Novelle [no'vɛlə], *f.* (**—,** *pl.* **—n**) (*Lit.*) novella, short story, short novel.
Novize [no'viːtsə], *m.* (**—n,** *pl.* **—n**) or *f.* (**—,** *pl.* **—n**) novice.
Nu [nuː], *m. & n.* (**—,** *no pl.*) moment; *im —,* in no time, in an instant.
Nubien ['nuːbjən], *n.* Nubia.
nüchtern ['nyçtərn], *adj.* fasting; sober; jejune; (*fig.*) dry, matter-of-fact, realistic.
Nüchternheit ['nyçtərnhaɪt], *f.* (**—,** *no pl.*) sobriety; (*fig.*) dryness.
Nudel ['nuːdəl], *f.* (**—,** *pl.* **—n**) noodles, macaroni, vermicelli; *eine komische —,* a funny person.
Null [nul], *f.* (**—,** *pl.* **—en**) nought, zero; (*fig.*) nonentity.
null [nul], *adj.* null; nil; — *und nichtig,* null and void; *etwas für — und nichtig erklären,* annul.
numerieren [nume'riːrən], *v.a.* number.
Nummer ['numər], *f.* (**—,** *pl.* **—n**) number, size, issue.
nun [nuːn], *adv., conj.* now, at present; since; —*!* now! well! *von — an,* henceforth; — *und nimmermehr,* nevermore; *was —?* what next?
nunmehr ['nuːnmeːr], *adv.* now, by this time.
Nunzius ['nuntsjus], *m.* (**—,** *pl.* **—zien**) (*Papal*) nuncio.
nur [nuːr], *adv.* only, solely, merely, but; *wenn —,* if only, provided that; — *das nicht,* anything but that; — *zu,* go to it!
Nürnberg ['nyrnbɛrk], *n.* Nuremberg.
Nuß [nus], *f.* (**—,** *pl.* **—̈sse**) nut.
Nußhäher ['nushɛːər], *m.* (**—s,** *pl.* **—**) (*Orn.*) jay.
Nüster ['nystər], *f.* (**—,** *pl.* **—n**) (*horse*) nostril.
Nutzanwendung ['nutsanvɛnduŋ], *f.* (**—,** *pl.* **—en**) practical application.
nutzbar ['nutsbaːr], *adj.* useful, usable, productive.
nütze ['nytsə], *adj.* useful, of use.
Nutzen ['nutsən], *m.* (**—s,** *pl.* **—**) use, utility; profit, gain, advantage, benefit; — *bringen,* yield profit; — *ziehen aus,* derive profit from.
nützen ['nytsən], *v.a.* make use of, use. — *v.n.* be of use, serve, be effective, work.
nützlich ['nytslɪç], *adj.* useful.
nutzlos ['nutsloːs], *adj.* useless.
Nutznießer ['nutsniːsər], *m.* (**—s,** *pl.* **—**) beneficiary, usufructuary.
Nymphe ['nymfə], *f.* (**—,** *pl.* **—en**) nymph.

O

O [o:], *n.* (**—s**, *pl.* **—s**) the letter O.
o! [o:], *excl.* oh!
Oase [o'a:zə], *f.* (**—**, *pl.* **—n**) oasis.
ob [ɔp], *conj.* whether; if; *als* **—**, as if; *und* **—!** rather! yes, indeed! — *prep.* (*Genit., Dat.*) on account of; upon, on.
Obacht ['o:baxt], *f.* (**—**, *no pl.*) heed, care; *— geben*, pay attention, look out.
Obdach ['ɔpdax], *n.* (**—es**, *no pl.*) shelter, lodging.
Obduktion ['ɔpdukts'jo:n], *f.* (**—**, *pl.* **—en**) post-mortem examination.
oben [o:bən], *adv.* above, aloft, on top; (*house*) upstairs; (*water*) on the surface; *von — bis unten*, from top to bottom; *von — herab*, from above; (*fig.*) haughtily, superciliously.
obendrein [o:bən'drain], *adv.* besides, into the bargain.
obengenannt ['o:bəngənant], *adj.* above-mentioned.
Ober ['o:bər], *m.* (**—s**, *pl.* **—**) head waiter; *Herr —!*, waiter!; (*in compounds*) upper, chief.
ober ['o:bər], *adj.* upper, higher; chief; superior.
Oberfläche ['o:bərflɛçə], *f.* (**—**, *pl.* **—n**) surface.
oberflächlich ['o:bərflɛçliç], *adj.* superficial, casual.
oberhalb ['o:bərhalp], *adv., prep.* (*Genit.*) above.
Oberin ['o:bərin], *f.* (**—**, *pl.* **—innen**) (*Eccl.*) Mother Superior; hospital matron.
Oberschule ['o:bərʃu:lə], *f.* (**—**, *pl.* **—n**) high school, secondary school.
Oberst ['o:bərst], *m.* (**—en**, *pl.* **—en**) colonel.
Oberstaatsanwalt ['o:bərʃta:tsanvalt], *m.* (**—s**, *pl.* **-̈e**) Attorney-General.
oberste ['o:bərstə], *adj.* uppermost, highest, supreme.
Oberstimme ['o:bərʃtimə], *f.* (**—**, *pl.* **—n**) (*Mus.*) treble, soprano.
Oberstübchen ['o:bərʃty:pçən], *n.* (**—s**, *pl.* **—**) (*fig.*) *nicht richtig im — sein*, have bats in the belfry.
Obervolta ['o:bərvɔltə], *n.* Upper Volta.
obgleich [ɔp'glaiç], *conj.* though, although.
Obhut ['ɔphu:t], *f.* (**—**, *no pl.*) keeping, care, protection.
obig ['o:biç], *adj.* foregoing, above-mentioned, aforementioned, aforesaid.
objektiv [ɔpjɛk'ti:f], *adj.* objective, impartial, unprejudiced.
Oblate [o'bla:tə], *f.* (**—**, *pl.* **—n**) wafer; (*Eccl.*) Host.

obliegen ['ɔpli:gən], *v.n. irr.* be incumbent upon s.o.; be o.'s duty; apply o.s. to.
Obmann ['ɔpman], *m.* (**—es**, *pl.* **-̈er**) chairman; (*jury*) foreman.
Obrigkeit ['o:briçkait], *f.* (**—**, *pl.* **—en**) authorities.
obschon [ɔp'ʃo:n] *see under* **obwohl**.
Observatorium ['ɔpzɛrva'to:rjum], *n.* (**—s**, *pl.* **—rien**) observatory.
obsiegen ['ɔpzi:gən], *v.n.* (*rare*) be victorious.
Obst [o:pst], *n.* (**—es**, *no pl.*) fruit.
obszön [ɔps'tsø:n], *adj.* obscene.
obwalten ['ɔpvaltən], *v.n.* (*rare*) exist, prevail, obtain; *unter den —den Umständen*, in the circumstances, as matters stand.
obwohl [ɔp'vo:l] (also **obschon** [ɔp'ʃo:n], **obzwar** [ɔp'tsva:r]), *conj.* though, although.
Ochse ['ɔksə], *m.* (**—n**, *pl.* **—n**) (*Zool.*) ox; bullock; (*fig.*) blockhead.
ochsen ['ɔksən], *v.n.* (*sl.*) swot, cram.
Ochsenauge ['ɔksənaugə], *n.* (**—s**, *pl.* **—n**) ox-eye, bull's eye; (*Archit.*) oval dormer window; porthole light.
Ochsenziemer ['ɔksəntsi:mər], *m.* (**—s**, *pl.* **—**) (*obs.*) horse-whip.
Ocker ['ɔkər], *m.* (**—s**, *no pl.*) ochre.
Öde ['ø:də], *f.* (**—**, *pl.* **—n**) wilderness.
öde ['ø:də], *adj.* desolate, bleak, dreary.
Odem ['o:dəm], *m.* (**—s**, *no pl.*) (*Poet.*) breath.
oder ['o:dər], *conj.* or; *— aber*, or else; *— auch*, or rather.
Ofen ['o:fən], *m.* (**—s**, *pl.* **-̈**) stove, oven, furnace.
Ofenpest [o:fən'pɛst], *n.* Budapest.
offen ['ɔfən], *adj.* open; (*fig.*) candid, sincere, frank; *— gestanden*, frankly speaking.
offenbar [ɔfən'ba:r], *adj.* obvious, manifest, evident.
offenbaren [ɔfən'ba:rən], *v.a. insep.* make known, reveal, disclose. — *v.r. sich einem —*, open o.'s heart to s.o.; unbosom o.s.
Offenheit ['ɔfənhait], *f.* (**—**, *pl.* **—en**) frankness, candour.
offenkundig ['ɔfənkundiç], *adj.* obvious, manifest.
offensichtlich ['ɔfənziçtliç], *adj.* obvious; apparent.
öffentlich ['œfəntliç], *adj.* public.
offerieren [ɔfe'ri:rən], *v.a.* offer.
Offerte [ɔ'fɛrtə], *f.* (**—**, *pl.* **—n**) offer, tender.
offiziell [ɔfi'tsjɛl], *adj.* official.
Offizier [ɔfi'tsi:r], *m.* (**—s**, *pl.* **—e**) officer, lieutenant.
Offizierspatent [ɔfi'tsi:rspatɛnt], *n.* (**—s**, *pl.* **—e**) (*Mil.*) commission.
offiziös [ɔfi'tsjø:s], *adj.* semi-official.
öffnen ['œfnən], *v.a.* open.
oft [ɔft], **oftmals** ['ɔftma:ls], *adv.* often, frequently.
öfters ['œftərs], *adv.* often, frequently.

Oheim ['oːhaɪm], m. (—s, pl. —e) (Poet.) uncle.

ohne ['oːnə], prep. (Acc.) without, but for, except.

ohnehin ['oːnəhin], adv. as it is.

Ohnmacht ['oːnmaxt], f. (—, pl. —en) fainting-fit, swoon; impotence; in — fallen, faint.

Ohr [oːr], n. (—es, pl. —en) ear; bis über beide —en, head over heels; die —en spitzen, prick up o.'s ears.

Ohrenbläser ['oːrənblɛːzər], m. (—s, pl. —) tale-bearer.

Ohrensausen ['oːrənzauzən], n. (—s, no pl.) humming in the ears.

Ohrenschmaus ['oːrənʃmaus], m. (—es, no pl.) musical treat.

Ohrfeige ['oːrfaɪɡə], f. (—, pl. —n) box on the ear.

Ohrläppchen ['oːrlɛpçən], n. (—s, pl. —) lobe of the ear.

Ohrmuschel ['oːrmuʃəl], f. (—, pl. —n) auricle.

oktav [ɔk'taːf], adj. octavo.

Oktober [ɔk'toːbər], m. (—s, pl. —) October.

oktroyieren [ɔktroa'jiːrən], v.a. dictate, force s.th. upon s.o.

okulieren [oku'liːrən], v.a. (trees) graft.

Öl [øːl], n. (—s, pl. —e) oil; (rare) olive-oil.

Ölanstrich ['øːlanʃtriç], m. (—s, pl. —e) coat of oil-paint.

ölen ['øːlən], v.a. oil, lubricate; (rare) anoint.

Ölgemälde ['øːlɡəmɛːldə], n. (—s, pl. —) oil painting.

Ölung ['øːluŋ], f. (—, pl. —en) oiling; anointing; (Eccl.) die letzte —, Extreme Unction.

Olymp [o'lymp], m. Mount Olympus.

olympisch [o'lympiʃ], adj. Olympian.

Omelett [ɔmə'lɛt], n. (—s, pl. —s) omelette.

Onkel ['ɔnkəl], m. (—s, pl. —) uncle.

Oper ['oːpər], f. (—, pl. —n) opera.

operieren [opə'riːrən], v.a., v.n. operate (on); sich — lassen, be operated on; undergo an operation.

Opfer ['ɔpfər], n. (—s, pl. —) sacrifice; victim.

opfern ['ɔpfərn], v.a., v.n. offer (up), sacrifice, immolate.

opponieren [ɔpo'niːrən], v.n. oppose.

Optiker ['ɔptikər], m. (—s, pl. —) optician.

oratorisch [ora'toːriʃ], adj. oratorical.

Orchester [ɔr'kɛstər], n. (—s, pl. —) orchestra, band.

orchestrieren [ɔrkɛs'triːrən], v.a. orchestrate, score for orchestra.

Orchidee [ɔrçi'deː], f. (—, pl. —n) (Bot.) orchid.

Orden ['ɔrdən], m. (—s, pl. —) medal; (Eccl.) (religious) order.

ordentlich ['ɔrdəntliç], adj. orderly, tidy, methodical, neat; regular; respectable, steady; sound; —er Professor, (full) professor.

Order ['ɔrdər], f. (—, pl. —s) (Comm.) order.

Ordinarius [ɔrdi'naːrjus], m. (—, pl. —ien) (Univ.) professor; (Eccl.) ordinary.

ordinär [ɔrdi'nɛːr], adj. common, vulgar.

ordnen ['ɔrdnən], v.a. put in order, tidy, arrange, dispose.

Ordnung ['ɔrdnuŋ], f. (—, pl. —en) order, arrangement, disposition, routine; tidiness; class, rank; in —, all right, in good trim; nicht in —, out of order, wrong.

ordnungsgemäß ['ɔrdnuŋsɡəmɛːs], adv. duly.

ordnungsmäßig ['ɔrdnuŋsmɛːsiç], adj. regular.

ordnungswidrig ['ɔrdnuŋsviːdriç], adj. irregular.

Ordnungszahl ['ɔrdnuŋstsaːl], f. (—, pl. —en) ordinal number.

Ordonnanz [ɔrdo'nants], f. (—, pl. —en) ordinance; (Mil.) orderly.

Organ [ɔr'gaːn], n. (—s, pl. —e) organ.

organisieren [ɔrɡani'ziːrən], v.a. organise.

Orgel ['ɔrɡəl], f. (—, pl. —n) (Mus.) organ.

Orgelzug ['ɔrɡəltsuːk], m. (—s, pl. -e) organ-stop.

Orgie ['ɔrɡjə], f. (—, pl. —n) orgy.

orientalisch [ɔrjɛn'taːliʃ], adj. oriental, eastern.

orientieren [ɔrjɛn'tiːrən], v.a. inform, orientate; set s.o. right. — v.r. sich — über, orientate o.s., find out about; get o.'s bearings.

Orkan [ɔr'kaːn], m. (—s, pl. —e) hurricane, gale, typhoon.

Ornat [ɔr'naːt], m. (—es, pl. —e) official robes; vestments.

Ort [ɔrt], m. (—es, pl. —e, -er) place, spot; region; (in compounds) local.

örtlich ['œrtliç], adj. local.

Ortschaft ['ɔrtʃaft], f. (—, pl. —en) place, township, village.

Öse ['øːzə], f. (—, pl. —n) loop; Haken und —n, hooks and eyes.

Ostasien ['ɔstaːzjən], n. Eastern Asia, the Far East.

Ost(en) ['ɔst(ən)], m. (—s, no pl.) east.

ostentativ [ɔstɛnta'tiːf], adj. ostentatious.

Osterei ['oːstəraɪ], n. (—s, pl. —er) Easter egg.

Ostern ['oːstərn], f. pl. (used as n. sing.) Easter.

Österreich ['øːstərraɪç], n. Austria.

Ostindien ['ɔstindjən], n. the East Indies.

östlich ['œstliç], adj. eastern, easterly.

Oxyd [ɔk'syːt], n. (—es, pl. —e) oxide.

oxydieren [ɔksy'diːrən], v.a., v.n. oxidise.

Ozean ['oːtsea:n], m. (—s, pl. —e) ocean, sea; Grosser —, Pacific (Ocean).

Ozon [o'tsoːn], n. (—s, no pl.) ozone.

P

P [peː], n. (—s, pl. —s) the letter P.
Paar [paːr], n. (—es, pl. —e) pair, couple.
paar [paːr], adj. ein —, a few, some.
Pacht [paxt], f. (—, pl. —en) lease; in — nehmen, take on lease.
Pachthof ['paxthoːf], m. (—s, pl. ¨e) leasehold estate, farm.
Pack (1) [pak], m. (—s, pl. ¨e) pack, bale, packet; mit Sack und —, (with) bag and baggage.
Pack (2) [pak], n. (—s, no pl.) rabble, mob.
Päckchen ['pɛkçən], n. (—s, pl. —) pack, packet; (small) parcel.
packen ['pakən], v.a. pack; seize; (fig.) —d, thrilling; pack dich! be off! scram!
pädagogisch [pɛːda'goːgiʃ], adj. educational, pedagogic(al).
paddeln ['padəln], v.n. paddle.
paff [paf], excl. bang! ich bin ganz —, I am astounded.
paffen ['pafən], v.n. puff; draw (at a pipe).
Page ['paːʒə], m. (—n, pl. —n) page-boy.
Paket [pa'keːt], n. (—s, pl. —e) packet, package, parcel.
paktieren [pak'tiːrən], v.n. come to terms.
Palast [pa'last], m. (—es, pl. ¨e) palace.
Palästina [palɛ'stiːna], n. Palestine.
Paletot ['palətoː], m. (—s, pl. —s) overcoat.
Palisanderholz [pali'zandərhɔlts], n. (—es, no pl.) rosewood.
Palme ['palmə], f. (—, pl. —n) (Bot.) palm-tree.
Palmkätzchen ['palmkɛtsçən], n. (—s, pl. —) (Bot.) catkin.
Palmwoche ['palmvɔxə], f. Holy Week.
Pampelmuse ['pampəlmuːzə], f. (—, pl. —n) (Bot.) grapefruit.
Panama ['paːnama], n. Panama.
Panier [pa'niːr], n. (—s, pl. —e) standard, banner.
panieren [pa'niːrən], v.a. dress (meat etc.), roll in bread-crumbs.
Panne ['panə], f. (—, pl. —n) puncture; (Motor.) break-down; mishap.
panschen ['panʃən], v.n. splash about in water. — v.a. adulterate.
Pantoffel [pan'tɔfəl], m. (—s, pl. —n) slipper; unter dem — stehen, be henpecked.
Pantoffelheld [pan'tɔfəlhɛlt], m. (—en, pl. —en) henpecked husband.

Panzer ['pantsər], m. (—s, pl. —) armour, breast-plate, coat of mail; (Mil.) tank.
Papagei [papa'gaɪ], m. (—s, pl. —en) (Orn.) parrot.
Papier [pa'piːr], n. (—s, pl. —e) paper; (Comm.) stocks; (pl.) papers, documents; ein Bogen —, a sheet of paper.
Papierkrieg [pa'piːrkriːk], m. (—s, no pl.) (coll.) red tape.
Papierwaren [pa'piːrvaːrən], f. pl. stationery.
Pappdeckel ['papdɛkəl], m. (—s, pl. —) pasteboard.
Pappe ['papə], f. (—, no pl.) paste, cardboard, pasteboard.
Pappel ['papəl], f. (—, pl. —n) poplar.
pappen ['papən], v.a. stick; glue, paste.
Pappenstiel ['papənʃtiːl], m. (—s, pl. —e) trifle.
papperlapapp ['papərlapap], excl. fiddlesticks! nonsense!
Papst [paːpst], m. (—es, pl. ¨e) Pope.
päpstlich ['pɛːpstlɪç], adj. papal; —er als der Papst, fanatically loyal, outheroding Herod; over-zealous.
Parabel [pa'raːbəl], f. (—, pl. —n) parable; (Maths.) parabola.
paradieren [para'diːrən], v.n. parade, make a show.
Paradies [para'diːs], n. (—es, pl. —e) paradise.
paradox [para'dɔks], adj. paradoxical.
Paragraph [para'graːf], m. (—en, pl. —en) paragraph, article, clause, section.
Paraguay ['paragvaɪ, para'gua:ɪ], n. Paraguay.
Paralyse [para'lyːzə], f. (—, pl. —n) paralysis.
parat [pa'raːt], adj. prepared, ready.
Pardon [par'dɔ̃], m. (—s, no pl.) pardon, forgiveness.
Parfüm [par'fyːm], n. (—s, pl. —e) perfume, scent.
pari ['paːriː], adv. at par.
parieren [pa'riːrən], v.a. parry, keep off. — v.n. obey; aufs Wort —, obey implicitly or to the letter.
Parität [pari'tɛːt], f. (—, no pl.) parity; (religious) equality.
Parkanlagen [park'anlaːgən], f. pl. parks; public gardens.
parken ['parkən], v.a. park.
Parkett [par'kɛt], n. (—s, pl. —e) parquet flooring; (Theat.) stalls.
Parkuhr [park'uːr], f. (—, pl. —en) parking-meter.
Parlament [parla'mɛnt], n. (—s, pl. —e) parliament.
Parlamentär [parlamɛn'tɛːr], m. (—s, pl. —e) officer negotiating a truce.
Parlamentarier [parlamɛn'taːrjər], m. (—s, pl. —) parliamentarian, member of a parliament.
Parole [pa'roːlə], f. (—, pl. —n) watchword, cue, motto, slogan, password.

Partei [par'taɪ], *f.* (—, *pl.* **—en**) party, faction; — *nehmen für,* side with.

Parteigänger [par'taɪgɛŋər], *m.* (**—s,** *pl.* —) partisan.

Parteigenosse [par'taɪgənɔsə], *m.* (**—n,** *pl.* **—n**) party member (especially National Socialist); comrade.

parteiisch [par'taɪɪʃ], *adj.* partial, biased, prejudiced.

Parteinahme [par'taɪnaːmə], *f.* (—, *no pl.*) partisanship.

Parteitag [par'taɪtaːk], *m.* (**—s,** *pl.* **—e**) party conference; congress.

Parterre [par'tɛrə], *n.* (**—s,** *pl.* **—s**) ground floor; (*Theat.*) pit; stalls.

Partie [par'tiː], *f.* (—, *pl.* **—n**) (*Comm.*) parcel; (*marriage*) match; (*chess etc.*) game; (*bridge*) rubber; outing, excursion, trip.

Partitur [parti'tuːr], *f.* (—, *pl.* **—en**) (*Mus.*) score.

Partizip [parti'tsiːp], *n.* (**—s,** *pl.* **—e,** **—ien**) (*Gram.*) participle.

Parzelle [par'tsɛlə], *f.* (—, *pl.* **—n**) allotment, lot, parcel.

paschen ['paʃən], *v.a.* smuggle.

Paß [pas], *m.* (**—sses,** *pl.* **˸sse**) (*mountain*) pass; (*travelling*) passport; (*horse*) amble.

Passagier [pasa'ʒiːr], *m.* (**—s,** *pl.* **—e**) passenger; *blinder* —, stowaway.

Passant [pa'sant], *m.* (**—en,** *pl.* **—en**) passer-by.

Passatwind [pa'saːtvɪnt], *m.* (**—s,** *pl.* **—e**) trade-wind.

passen ['pasən], *v.n.* fit, suit, be suitable, be convenient; (*Cards*) pass.

passieren [pa'siːrən], *v.a.* sieve; (*road*) pass, cross, negotiate. — *v.n.* (*aux.* sein) pass; happen, take place, come about.

Passif, Passivum [pa'siːf *or* 'pasiːf, pa'siːvum], *n.* (**—s,** *pl.* **—e,** **—va**) (*Gram.*) passive voice; (*Comm.*) (*pl.*) debts, liabilities.

Passus ['pasus], *m.* (—, *pl.* —) passage (in book).

Pasta, Paste ['pasta, 'pastə], *f.* (—, *pl.* **—ten**) paste.

Pastell [pa'stɛl], *m.* (**—s,** *pl.* **—e**) pastel, crayon; — *malen,* draw in pastel.

Pastete [pa'steːtə], *f.* (—, *pl.* **—n**) pie, pastry.

Pastille [pa'stɪlə], *f.* (—, *pl.* **—n**) lozenge, pastille.

Pastor ['pastɔr], *m.* (**—s,** *pl.* **—e**) minister, pastor; parson; vicar, rector.

Pate ['paːtə], *m.* (**—n,** *pl.* **—n**) godparent; — *stehen,* be godfather to.

patent [pa'tɛnt], *adj.* fine, grand, (*sl.*) smashing.

Patent [pa'tɛnt], *n.* (**—(e)s,** *pl.* **—e**) patent; charter, licence.

patentieren [patɛn'tiːrən], *v.a.* patent, license.

pathetisch [pa'teːtɪʃ], *adj.* elevated, solemn, moving.

Patin ['paːtɪn], *f.* (—, *pl.* **—innen**) godmother.

patriotisch [patri'oːtɪʃ], *adj.* patriotic.

Patrone [pa'troːnə], *f.* (—, *pl.* **—n**) cartridge; stencil, pattern.

Patrouille [pa'truljə], *f.* (—, *pl.* **—n**) (*Mil.*) patrol.

Patsche ['patʃə], *f.* (—, *pl.* **—n**) (*dial.*) hand; (*fig.*) mess, pickle; *in eine — geraten,* get into a jam.

patschen ['patʃən], *v.n.* (*aux.* sein) splash.

Patt [pat], *n.* (**—s,** *pl.* **—s**) (*Chess*) stalemate.

patzig ['patsɪç], *adj.* rude; cheeky, saucy.

Pauke ['paukə], *f.* (—, *pl.* **—n**) kettledrum; *mit —n und Trompeten,* with drums beating and colours flying.

pauken ['paukən], *v.n.* beat the kettledrum; (*coll.*) swot, plod, grind; fight a duel.

pausbackig ['pausbakɪç], *adj.* chubbyfaced, bonny.

Pauschale [pau'ʃaːlə], *f.* (—, *pl.* **—n**) lump sum.

Pause ['pauzə], *f.* (—, *pl.* **—n**) pause, stop; (*Theat.*) interval; (*Sch.*) playtime, break; (*Tech.*) tracing.

pausen ['pauzən], *v.a.* trace.

pausieren [pau'ziːrən], *v.n.* pause.

Pavian ['paːvjaːn], *m.* (**—s,** *pl.* **—e**) (*Zool.*) baboon.

Pech [pɛç], *n.* (**—es,** *no pl.*) pitch; (*shoemaker's*) wax; (*fig.*) bad luck, rotten luck.

pechschwarz ['pɛçʃvarts], *adj.* black as pitch.

Pechvogel ['pɛçfoːgəl], *m.* (**—s,** *pl.* **˸**) unlucky fellow.

Pedell [pe'dɛl], *m.* (**—s,** *pl.* **—e**) beadle; porter, caretaker; (*Univ. sl.*) bulldog.

Pegel ['peːgəl], *m.* (**—s,** *pl.* —) watergauge.

peilen ['paɪlən], *v.a.,* *v.n.* sound, measure, take bearings (of).

Pein [paɪn], *f.* (—, *no pl.*) pain, torment.

peinigen ['paɪnɪgən], *v.a.* torment; harass, distress.

peinlich ['paɪnlɪç], *adj.* painful, disagreeable; embarrassing; delicate; strict, punctilious; (*Law*) capital, penal.

Peitsche ['paɪtʃə], *f.* (—, *pl.* **—n**) whip.

pekuniär [pekun'jeːr], *adj.* financial.

Pelerine [pelə'riːnə], *f.* (—, *pl.* **—n**) cape.

Pelle ['pɛlə], *f.* (—, *pl.* **—n**) peel, husk.

Pellkartoffeln ['pɛlkartɔfəln], *f. pl.* potatoes in their jackets.

Pelz [pɛlts], *m.* (**—es,** *pl.* **—e**) pelt, fur; fur coat.

pelzig ['pɛltsɪç], *adj.* furry.

Pendel ['pɛndəl], *n.* (**—s,** *pl.* —) pendulum.

pendeln ['pɛndəln], *v.n.* swing, oscillate.

pennen ['pɛnən], *v.n.* (*sl.*) sleep.

Pension [pã'sjo:n], *f.* (—, *pl.* —en) pension; boarding-house; board and lodging.

Pensionat [pãsjo'na:t], *n.* (—s, *pl.* —e) boarding-school.

pensionieren [pãsjo'ni:rən], *v.a.* pension off; *sich — lassen*, retire.

Pensum ['pɛnzum], *n.* (—s, *pl.* —sen) task; curriculum, syllabus.

per [pɛr], *prep. — Adresse*, care of.

Perfekt [pɛr'fɛkt], *n.* (—s, *pl.* —e) (*Gram.*) perfect (tense).

perforieren [pɛrfo'ri:rən], *v.a.* perforate, punch.

Pergament [pɛrga'mɛnt], *n.* (—s, *pl.* —e) parchment, vellum.

Perle ['pɛrlə], *f.* (—, *pl.* —n) pearl; (*glass*) bead; (*fig.*) gem, treasure.

perlen ['pɛrlən], *v.n.* sparkle.

Perlgraupe ['pɛrlgraupə], *f.* (—, *no pl.*) (*Bot.*) pearl-barley.

Perlhuhn ['pɛrlhu:n], *n.* (—s, *pl.* -er) (*Zool.*) guinea-fowl.

Perlmutter ['pɛrlmutər], *f.* (—, *no pl.*) mother-of-pearl.

Perpendikel [pɛrpən'dɪkəl], *m. & n.* (—s, *pl.* —) pendulum.

Perser ['pɛrzər], *m.* (—s, *pl.* —) Persian; *echter —*, genuine Persian carpet.

Persien ['pɛrzjən], *n.* Persia.

Personal [pɛrzo'na:l], *n.* (—s, *no pl.*) personnel, staff.

Personalien [pɛrzo'na:ljən], *n. pl.* particulars (of a person).

Personenverkehr [pɛr'zo:nənfɛrke:r], *m.* (—s, *no pl.*) passenger-traffic.

Personenzug [pɛr'zo:nəntsu:k], *m.* (—s, *pl.* -e) (slow) passenger train.

personifizieren [pɛrzonifi'tsi:rən], *v.a.* personify, embody, impersonate.

Persönlichkeit [pɛr'zø:nlɪçkaɪt], *f.* (—, *pl.* —en) personality, person.

perspektivisch [pɛrspɛk'ti:vɪʃ], *adj.* perspective.

Peru [pe'ru:], *n.* Peru.

Perücke [pɛ'rykə], *f.* (—, *pl.* —n) wig.

Pest [pɛst], *f.* (—, *no pl.*) plague, pestilence.

pestartig ['pɛsta:rtɪç], *adj.* pestilential.

Petersilie [pe:tər'zi:ljə], *f.* (—, *no pl.*) (*Bot.*) parsley.

petitionieren [petitsjo'ni:rən], *v.a.* petition.

Petschaft ['pɛtʃaft], *n.* (—s, *pl.* —e) seal, signet.

Petz [pɛts], *m.* (—es, *pl.* —e) *Meister* —, Bruin (the bear).

petzen ['pɛtsən], *v.n.* tell tales (about), sneak.

Pfad [pfa:t], *m.* (—es, *pl.* —e) path.

Pfadfinder ['pfa:tfɪndər], *m.* (—s, *pl.* —) Boy Scout.

Pfaffe ['pfafə], *m.* (—n, *pl.* —n) (*pej.*) cleric, priest.

Pfahl [pfa:l], *m.* (—s, *pl.* -e) post, stake.

Pfahlbauten ['pfa:lbautən], *m. pl.* lake dwellings.

pfählen ['pfɛ:lən], *v.a.* fasten with stakes; impale.

Pfand [pfant], *n.* (—s, *pl.* -er) pawn, pledge; security; (*game*) forfeit; *ein — einlösen*, redeem a pledge.

pfänden ['pfɛndən], *v.a.* take in pledge; seize.

Pfänderspiel ['pfɛndərʃpi:l], *n.* (—s, *pl.* —e) game of forfeits.

Pfandgeber ['pfantge:bər], *m.* (—s, *pl.* —) pawner.

Pfandleiher ['pfantlaɪər], *m.* (—s, *pl.* —) pawnbroker.

Pfandrecht ['pfantrɛçt], *n.* (—s, *no pl.*) lien.

Pfändung ['pfɛnduŋ], *f.* (—, *pl.* —en) seizure, attachment, distraint.

Pfanne ['pfanə], *f.* (—, *pl.* —n) pan, frying-pan.

Pfannkuchen ['pfanku:xən], *m.* (—s, *pl.* —) pancake; *Berliner —*, doughnut.

Pfarre ['pfarə], *f.* (—, *pl.* —n) living, parish; (*house*) vicarage, parsonage, manse.

Pfarrer ['pfarər], *m.* (—s, *pl.* —) parson; vicar, (parish) priest.

Pfau [pfau], *m.* (—en, *pl.* —en) (*Orn.*) peacock.

Pfauenauge ['pfauənaugə], *n.* (—s, *pl.* —n) (*Ent.*) peacock butterfly.

Pfeffer ['pfɛfər], *m.* (—s, *no pl.*) pepper; *spanischer —*, red pepper, cayenne.

Pfefferkuchen ['pfɛfərku:xən], *m.* (—s, *pl.* —) gingerbread, spiced cake.

Pfefferminz ['pfɛfərmɪnts], *n.* (—, *no pl.*) peppermint.

Pfeife ['pfaɪfə], *f.* (—, *pl.* —n) whistle, fife; pipe.

pfeifen ['pfaɪfən], *v.a., v.n. irr.* whistle, play the fife; (*Theat.*) boo, hiss; (*bullets*) whiz(z).

Pfeifenrohr ['pfaɪfənro:r], *n.* (—s, *pl.* —e) pipe-stem.

Pfeil [pfaɪl], *m.* (—es, *pl.* —e) arrow, dart, bolt.

Pfeiler ['pfaɪlər], *m.* (—s, *pl.* —) pillar.

Pfeilwurz ['pfaɪlvurts], *f.* (—, *no pl.*) (*Bot.*) arrow root.

Pfennig ['pfɛnɪç], *m.* (—s, *pl.* —e) one hundredth of a mark; (*loosely*) penny.

Pferch [pfɛrç], *m.* (—es, *pl.* —e) fold, pen.

Pferd [pfe:rt], *n.* (—es, *pl.* —e) horse; *zu —*, on horseback; *vom — steigen*, dismount.

Pferdeknecht ['pfe:rdəknɛçt], *m.* (—es, *pl.* —e) groom.

Pferdestärke ['pfe:rdəʃtɛrkə], *f.* (—, *no pl.*) horse-power (*abbr.* PS).

Pfiff [pfɪf], *m.* (—s, *pl.* —e) whistle.

Pfifferling ['pfɪfərlɪŋ], *m.* (—s, *pl.* —e) (*Bot.*) mushroom; chanterelle; *einen — wert*, worthless.

pfiffig ['pfɪfɪç], *adj.* cunning, sly, crafty.

Pfiffikus ['pfɪfɪkus], *m.* (—, *pl.* —se) (*coll.*) sly dog.

Pfingsten ['pfɪŋkstən], *n.* Whitsun (-tide), Pentecost.

Pfingstrose ['pfɪŋkstroːzə], *f.* (—, *pl.* (*Bot.*) peony.

Pfirsich ['pfɪrzɪç], *m.* (—s, *pl.* —e) (*Bot.*) peach.

Pflanze ['pflantsə], *f.* (—, *pl.* —n) plant.

pflanzen ['pflantsən], *v.a.* plant.

Pflanzer ['pflantsər], *m.* (—s, *pl.* —) planter.

pflanzlich ['pflantslɪç], *adj.* vegetable, botanical.

Pflänzling ['pflɛntslɪŋ], *m.* (—s, *pl.* —e) seedling, young plant.

Pflanzung ['pflantsuŋ], *f.* (—, *pl.* —en) plantation.

Pflaster ['pflastər], *n.* (—s, *pl.* —) (*Med.*) plaster; (*street*) pavement; *ein teures* —, an expensive place to live in.

Pflaume ['pflaumə], *f.* (—, *pl.* —n) plum; *getrocknete* —, prune.

Pflege ['pfleːgə], *f.* (—, *no pl.*) care, attention, nursing, fostering.

Pflegeeltern ['pfleːgəɛltərn], *pl.* foster-parents.

pflegen ['pfleːgən], *v.a.* nurse, look after, take care of; *Umgang* — *mit*, associate with. — *v.n.* be used to, be in the habit of.

Pflegling ['pfleːklɪŋ], *m.* (—s, *pl.* —e) foster-child, ward.

Pflicht [pflɪçt], *f.* (—, *pl.* —en) duty, obligation.

Pflichtgefühl ['pflɪçtgəfyːl], *n.* (—s, *no pl.*) sense of duty.

pflichtgemäß ['pflɪçtgəmɛːs], *adj.* dutiful.

pflichtschuldig ['pflɪçtʃuldɪç], *adj.* in duty bound.

Pflock [pflɔk], *m.* (—s, *pl.* ⸚e) plug, peg.

pflücken ['pflykən], *v.a.* pluck, pick, gather.

Pflug [pfluːk], *m.* (—es, *pl.* ⸚e) plough.

Pflugschar ['pfluːkʃaːr], *f.* (—, *pl.* —en) ploughshare.

Pforte ['pfɔrtə], *f.* (—, *pl.* —n) gate, door, porch.

Pförtner ['pfœrtnər], *m.* (—s, *pl.* —) door-keeper, porter.

Pfosten ['pfostən], *m.* (—s, *pl.* —) post, stake; (*door*) jamb.

Pfote ['pfoːtə], *f.* (—, *pl.* —n) paw.

Pfriem [pfriːm], *m.* (—es, *pl.* —e) awl.

Pfropf(en ['pfrɔpf(ən)], *m.* (—s, *pl.* —en) cork, stopper; (*gun*) wad.

pfropfen ['pfrɔpfən], *v.a.* graft; cork.

Pfründe ['pfryndə], *f.* (—, *pl.* —n) living, benefice.

Pfuhl [pfuːl], *m.* (—es, *pl.* —e) pool, puddle.

Pfühl [pfyːl], *m.* (—es, *pl.* —e) (*Poet.*) bolster, pillow, cushion.

pfui! [pfui], *excl.* shame! ugh! — *Teufel!* shame! a damned shame!

Pfund [pfunt], *n.* (—es, *pl.* —e) pound.

pfuschen ['pfuʃən], *v.n.* botch; *einem ins Handwerk* —, poach on s.o. else's preserve.

Pfütze ['pfytsə], *f.* (—, *pl.* —n) puddle.

Phänomen [fɛːnoˈmeːn], *n.* (—s, *pl.* —e) phenomenon.

Phantasie [fantaˈziː], *f.* (—, *pl.* —n) fancy, imagination; (*Mus.*) fantasia.

phantasieren [fantaˈziːrən], *v.n.* indulge in fancies; (*sick person*) rave, wander, be delirious; (*Mus.*) improvise.

Phantast [fanˈtast], *m.* (—en, *pl.* —en) dreamer, visionary.

Pharisäer [fariˈzɛːər], *m.* (—s, *pl.* —) Pharisee.

Phase ['faːzə], *f.* (—, *pl.* —n) phase, stage (of process *or* development).

Philippinen [filiˈpiːnən], *f. pl.* Philippines.

Philister [fiˈlɪstər], *m.* (—s, *pl.* —) Philistine.

philisterhaft [fiˈlɪstərhaft], *adj.* philistine, narrow-minded, conventional.

Philologie [filoloˈgiː], *f.* (—, *no pl.*) philology; study of languages.

Philosoph [filoˈzoːf], *m.* (—en, *pl.* —en) philosopher.

Philosophie [filozoˈfiː], *f.* (—, *pl.* —n) philosophy.

Phiole [fiˈoːlə], *f.* (—, *pl.* —n) phial, vial.

Phlegma ['flɛgma], *n.* (—s, *no pl.*) phlegm.

Phonetik [foˈneːtɪk], *f.* (—, *no pl.*) phonetics.

photogen [fotoˈgeːn], *adj.* photogenic.

Photograph [fotoˈgraːf], *m.* (—en, *pl.* —en) photographer.

Photographie [fotograˈfiː], *f.* (—, *pl.* —n) photograph, photo; (*Art*) photography.

photographieren [fotograˈfiːrən], *v.a.* photograph.

Physik [fyˈziːk], *f.* (—, *no pl.*) physics.

physikalisch [fyziˈkaːlɪʃ], *adj.* physical (of physics).

Physiker ['fyːzɪkər], *m.* (—s, *pl.* —) physicist.

Physiologe [fyːzjoˈloːgə], *m.* (—en, *pl.* —en) physiologist.

physiologisch [fyːzjoˈloːgɪʃ], *adj.* physiological.

physisch ['fyːzɪʃ], *adj.* physical.

Picke ['pɪkə], *f.* (—, *pl.* —n) pickaxe, axe.

Pickel ['pɪkəl], *m.* (—s, *pl.* —) pimple.

Piedestal ['pjeːdɛstaːl], *n.* (—s, *pl.* —e) pedestal.

piepen ['piːpən], *v.n.* squeak, chirp.

piepsen ['piːpsən], *v.n.* squeak, chirp.

Pietät [pieˈtɛːt], *f.* (—, *no pl.*) piety, reverence.

Pik [piːk], *n.* (—s, *pl.* —s) (*cards*) spades.

pikant [piˈkant], *adj.* piquant, spicy; (*fig.*) risqué.

Pikee [piˈkeː], *m.* (—s, *pl.* —s) piqué.

pikiert [piˈkiːrt], *adj.* irritated, annoyed, piqued.

Pikkolo ['pɪkolo], *m.* (—s, *pl.* —s) apprentice waiter, boy (waiter); (*Mus.*) piccolo, flute.

Pilger ['pɪlgər], *m.* (—s, *pl.* —) pilgrim.

Pille ['pɪlə], *f.* (—, *pl.* —n) pill.

Pilz [pɪlts], *m.* (—es, *pl.* —e) fungus, mushroom.

Piment [pi'mɛnt], *n.* (—s, *pl.* —e) pimento, Jamaican pepper, all-spice.

pimplig ['pɪmplɪç], *adj.* effeminate.

Pinguin [pɪŋgu'i:n], *m.* (—s, *pl.* —e) (*Orn.*) penguin.

Pinie ['pi:njə], *f.* (—, *pl.* —n) (*Bot.*) stone-pine.

Pinne ['pɪnə], *f.* (—, *pl.* —n) drawing-pin; peg.

Pinscher ['pɪnʃər], *m.* (—s, *pl.* —) terrier.

Pinsel ['pɪnzəl], *m.* (—s, *pl.* —) (*Painting*) brush, pencil; (*fig.*) simpleton.

Pinzette [pɪn'tsɛtə], *f.* (—, *pl.* —n) pincers, tweezers.

Pirsch [pɪrʃ], *f.* (—, *no pl.*) (deer-) stalking.

Piste ['pɪstə], *f.* (—, *pl.* —n) track; (*Aviat.*) runway.

pittoresk [pɪto'rɛsk], *adj.* picturesque.

placken ['plakən], *v.r. sich —*, toil, drudge.

plädieren [plɛ'di:rən], *v.n.* plead.

Plädoyer [plɛ:doa'je:], *n.* (—s, *pl.* —s) speech for the prosecution *or* the defence (in a court of law), plea, pleading.

Plage ['pla:gə], *f.* (—, *pl.* —n) torment, trouble; calamity; plague.

plagen ['pla:gən], *v.a.* plague, trouble, torment, vex. — *v.r. sich —*, toil.

Plagiat [plag'ja:t], *n.* (—es, *pl.* —e) plagiarism.

Plaid [plɛ:t], *n.* (—s, *pl.* —s) travelling-rug.

Plakat [pla'ka:t], *n.* (—(e)s, *pl.* —e) poster, placard, bill.

Plan [pla:n], *m.* (—es, *pl.* ⁻e) plan, scheme, plot; map, ground-plan.

Plane ['pla:nə], *f.* (—, *pl.* —n) awning, cover.

planieren [pla'ni:rən], *v.a.* level, plane down; bulldoze, flatten.

Planke ['plaŋkə], *f.* (—, *pl.* —n) plank, board.

Plänkelei [plɛnkə'laɪ], *f.* (—, *pl.* —en) skirmish.

planmäßig ['pla:nmɛ:sɪç], *adj.* according to plan.

planschen ['planʃən], *v.n.* splash; paddle.

Plantage [plan'ta:ʒə], *f.* (—, *pl.* —n) plantation.

planvoll ['pla:nfɔl], *adj.* systematic, well-planned.

Planwagen ['pla:nva:gən], *m.* (—s, *pl.* —) tilt-cart.

plappern ['plapərn], *v.n.* prattle, chatter.

plärren ['plɛrən], *v.n.* blubber, bawl.

Plastik ['plastɪk], *f.* (—, *pl.* —en) plastic art; plastic (material).

Platane [pla'ta:nə], *f.* (—, *pl.* —n) plane-tree.

Platin ['pla:ti:n], *n.* (—s, *no pl.*) platinum.

platonisch [pla'to:nɪʃ], *adj.* platonic.

plätschern ['plɛtʃərn], *v.n.* splash about.

platt [plat], *adj.* flat, level, even; insipid; downright; —e Redensart, commonplace, platitude; (*coll.*) *ich bin ganz —*, I am astonished *or* dumbfounded.

Plättbrett ['plɛtbrɛt], *n.* (—es, *pl.* —er) ironing board.

plattdeutsch ['platdɔytʃ], *adj.* Low German.

Platte ['platə], *f.* (—, *pl.* —n) plate; dish; board; slab; sheet; ledge; (*fig.*) bald head; (*Mus.*) (gramophone) record.

plätten ['plɛtən], *v.a.* iron (clothes).

Plattfisch ['platfɪʃ], *m.* (—es, *pl.* —e) (*Zool.*) plaice.

Plattfuß ['platfu:s], *n.* (—es, *pl.* ⁻e) flat foot.

Plattheit ['plathaɪt], *f.* (—, *pl.* —en) flatness; (*fig.*) platitude.

Platz [plats], *m.* (—es, *pl.* ⁻e) place, town, spot, site; space, room; (*town*) square; seat; — *nehmen*, take a seat, be seated.

Platzanweiserin ['platsanvaɪzərɪn], *f.* (—, *pl.* —nen) usherette.

Plätzchen ['plɛtsçən], *n.* (—s, *pl.* —) small place; biscuit.

platzen ['platsən], *v.n.* (*aux.* sein) burst, explode.

Platzregen ['platsre:gən], *m.* (—s, *no pl.*) downpour, heavy shower.

Plauderei [plaudə'raɪ], *f.* (—, *pl.* —en) chat.

Plaudertasche ['plaudərtaʃə], *f.* (—, *pl.* —n) chatterbox.

Pleite ['plaɪtə], *f.* (—, *pl.* —n) (*coll.*) bankruptcy; — *machen*, go bankrupt.

Plenum ['ple:num], *n.* (—s, *no pl.*) plenary session.

Pleuelstange ['plɔyəlʃtaŋə], *f.* (—, *pl.* —n) connecting-rod.

Plinsen ['plɪnzən], *f. pl.* (*Austr.*) fritters.

Plissee [plɪ'se:], *n.* (—s, *pl.* —s) pleating.

Plombe ['plɔmbə], *f.* (—, *pl.* —n) lead, seal; (*teeth*) filling.

plombieren [plɔm'bi:rən], *v.a.* seal with lead; (*teeth*) fill.

plötzlich ['plœtslɪç], *adj.* sudden.

plump [plump], *adj.* clumsy, ungainly, awkward; crude, coarse.

plumps [plumps], *excl.* bump! oops!

Plunder ['plundər], *m.* (—s, *no pl.*) lumber, trash.

plündern ['plyndərn], *v.a.* plunder, pillage.

Plüsch [ply:ʃ], *m.* (—es, *no pl.*) plush.

pneumatisch [pnɔy'ma:tɪʃ], *adj.* pneumatic.

Pöbel ['pø:bəl], *m.* (—s, *no pl.*) mob, rabble.

pochen ['pɔxən], *v.a., v.n.* knock, beat, throb.

Pocke

Pocke ['pɔkə], *f.* (—, *pl.* —n) pock-mark; (*pl.*) smallpox.

pockennarbig ['pɔkənnarbɪç], *adj.* pockmarked.

Podagra ['po:dagra:], *n.* (—s, *no pl.*) (*Med.*) gout.

Pointe [po'ε̃tə], *f.* (—, *pl.* —n) (*of a story*) point.

Pokal [po'ka:l], *m.* (—s, *pl.* —e) goblet, cup; trophy.

Pökelfleisch ['pø:kəlflaɪʃ], *n.* (—es, *no pl.*) salted meat.

Pol [po:l], *m.* (—s, *pl.* —e) pole.

polemisch [po'le:mɪʃ], *adj.* pole-mic(al), controversial.

Polen ['po:lən], *n.* Poland.

Police [po'li:sə], *f.* (—, *pl.* —n) insurance policy.

polieren [po'li:rən], *v.a.* polish, furbish, burnish.

Poliklinik ['po:likli:nɪk], *f.* (—, *pl.* —en) (*Med.*) out-patients' department.

Politik [poli'ti:k], *f.* (—, *no pl.*) politics; policy.

politisieren [politi'zi:rən], *v.n.* talk politics.

Politur [poli'tu:r], *f.* (—, *no pl.*) polish, gloss.

Polizei [poli'tsaɪ], *f.* (—, *no pl.*) police.

polizeilich [poli'tsaɪlɪç], *adj.* of the police.

Polizeistunde [poli'tsaɪʃtundə], *f.* (—, *no pl.*) closing time.

Polizeiwache [poli'tsaɪvaxə], *f.* (—, *pl.* —n) police station.

Polizist [poli'tsɪst], *m.* (—en, *pl.* —en) policeman, constable.

Polizze [po'lɪtsə], *f.* (—, *pl.* —n) (*Austr. dial.*) insurance policy.

polnisch ['pɔlnɪʃ], *adj.* Polish.

Polster ['pɔlstər], *n.* (—s, *pl.* —) cushion, bolster.

Polterabend ['pɔltəra:bənt], *m.* (—s, *pl.* —e) wedding-eve party.

Poltergeist ['pɔltərgaɪst], *m.* (—es, *pl.* —er) poltergeist, hobgoblin.

poltern ['pɔltərn], *v.n.* rumble; make a noise; bluster.

Polyp [po'ly:p], *m.* (—en, *pl.* —en) (*Zool.*) polyp; (*Med.*) polypus.

Pomeranze [pomə'rantsə], *f.* (—, *pl.* —n) (*Bot.*) orange.

Pommern ['pɔmərn], *n.* Pomerania.

Pope [po:pə], *m.* (—n, *pl.* —n) Greek Orthodox priest.

Popo [po'po:], *m.* (—s, *pl.* —s) (*coll.*) backside, bottom.

populär [popu'lε:r], *adj.* popular.

porös [po'rø:s], *adj.* porous.

Porree ['pɔre:], *m.* (—s, *no pl.*) leek.

Portefeuille [pɔrt'fœj], *n.* (—s, *pl.* —s) portfolio.

Portier [pɔr'tje:], *m.* (—s, *pl.* —s) doorkeeper, caretaker; porter.

Porto ['pɔrto:], *n.* (—s, *pl.* Porti) postage.

Porzellan [pɔrtsε'la:n], *n.* (—s, *pl.* —e) china, porcelain; *Meißner* —, Dresden

---

Posamenten [poza'mεntən], *n. pl.* trimmings.

Posaune [po'zaunə], *f.* (—, *pl.* —n) (*Mus.*) trombone.

Positur [pozi'tu:r], *f.* (—, *pl.* —en) posture; *sich in* — *setzen*, strike an attitude.

Posse ['pɔsə], *f.* (—, *pl.* —n) (*Theat.*) farce, skit.

Possen ['pɔsən], *m.* (—s, *pl.* —) trick; *einem einen* — *spielen*, play a trick on s.o.

possierlich [pɔ'si:rlɪç], *adj.* droll, funny, comic(al).

Post [pɔst], *f.* (—, *pl.* —en) post, mail; (*building*) post-office.

Postament [pɔsta'mεnt], *n.* (—s, *pl.* —e) plinth, pedestal.

Postanweisung ['pɔstanvaɪzuŋ], *f.* (—, *pl.* —en) postal order, money order.

Posten ['pɔstən], *m.* (—s, *pl.* —) post, station; place; (*goods*) parcel, lot, job lot; (*Comm.*) item; (*Mil.*) outpost; — *stehen*, stand sentry; *nicht auf dem* — *sein*, be unwell.

Postfach ['pɔstfax], *n.* (—es, *pl.* ∸er) post-office box.

postieren [pɔs'ti:rən], *v.a.* post, place, station.

postlagernd ['pɔstla:gərnt], *adj.* poste restante, to be called for.

Postschalter ['pɔstʃaltər], *m.* (—s, *pl.* —) post-office counter.

postulieren [pɔstu'li:rən], *v.a.* postulate.

postwendend ['pɔstvεndənt], *adj.* by return of post.

Postwertzeichen ['pɔstve:rttsaɪçən], *n.* (—s, *pl.* —) stamp.

Potenz [po'tεnts], *f.* (—, *pl.* —en) (*Maths.*) power; *zur dritten* —, cubed, to the power of three.

potenzieren [potεn'tsi:rən], *v.a.* (*Math.*) raise; intensify.

Pottasche ['pɔtaʃə], *f.* (—, *no pl.*) potash.

potzblitz ['pɔtsblɪts], *excl.* good Heavens! good gracious!

potztausend ['pɔtstauzənt], *excl.* great Scott! good Heavens!

Pracht [praxt], *f.* (—, *no pl.*) splendour, magnificence; (*in compounds*) de luxe.

prächtig ['prε:çtɪç], *adj.* splendid, magnificent, sumptuous.

prachtvoll ['praxtfɔl], *adj.* gorgeous, magnificent.

Prädikat [prε:di'ka:t], *n.* (—s, *pl.* —e) mark; (*Gram.*) predicate.

Prag [pra:k], *n.* Prague.

prägen ['prε:gən], *v.a.* coin, mint, stamp.

prägnant [prεg'nant], *adj.* meaningful, precise.

prahlen ['pra:lən], *v.n.* boast, brag, talk big, show off.

Praktikant [praktɪ'kant], *m.* (—en, *pl.* —en) probationer; apprentice.

Praktiken ['praktɪkən], *f. pl.* machi-nations.

praktisch ['praktɪʃ], *adj.* practical; —er *Arzt*, general practitioner.

praktizieren [praktɪ'tsi:rən], *v.a.* practise.

Prall [pral], *m.* (—es, *pl.* —e) impact.

prall [pral], *adj.* tense, tight; (*cheeks*) chubby.

prallen ['pralən], *v.n.* (*aux.* sein) *auf etwas* —, bounce against s.th.

Prämie ['prɛ:mjə], *f.* (—, *pl.* —n) prize; (*insurance*) premium; (*dividend*) bonus.

prangen ['praŋən], *v.n.* shine, glitter, make a show.

Pranger ['praŋər], *m.* (—s, *pl.* —) pillory; *etwas an den* — *stellen*, expose s.th., pillory.

präparieren [prɛpa'ri:rən], *v.a.*, *v.r.* prepare.

Präsens ['prɛ:zɛns], *n.* (—, *pl.* —ntia) (*Gram.*) present tense.

präsentieren [prɛzɛn'ti:rən], *v.a.* present; *präsentiert das Gewehr!* present arms!

prasseln ['prasəln], *v.n.* (*fire*) crackle, rattle.

prassen ['prasən], *v.n.* revel, gorge (o.s.), guzzle, feast.

Prätendent [prɛtɛn'dɛnt], *m.* (—en, *pl.* —en) pretender, claimant.

Präteritum [prɛ'tɛ:ritum], *n.* (—s, *pl.* —ta) (*Gram.*) preterite, past tense.

Praxis ['praksɪs], *f.* (—, *no pl.*) practice.

präzis [prɛ'tsi:s], *adj.* precise, exact.

präzisieren [prɛtsi'zi:rən], *v.a.* define exactly.

predigen ['prɛ:dɪgən], *v.a.*, *v.n.* preach.

Predigt ['prɛ:dɪçt], *f.* (—, *pl.* —en) sermon; (*fig.*) homily, lecture.

Preis [praɪs], *m.* (—es, *pl.* —e) price, rate, value; (*reward*) prize; praise; *um jeden* —, at any price, at all costs; *um keinen* —, not for all the world; *feste* —*e*, fixed prices; no rebate, no discount.

Preisausschreiben ['praɪsausʃraɪbən], *n.* (—s, *pl.* —) prize competition.

Preiselbeere ['praɪzəlbe:rə], *f.* (—, *pl.* —n) (*Bot.*) bilberry, cranberry.

preisen ['praɪzən], *v.a.* irr. praise, laud; glorify.

preisgeben ['praɪsge:bən], *v.a.* irr. give up, abandon, part with; *dem Spott preisgegeben sein*, become a laughing-stock.

Preisunterbietung ['praɪsuntərbi:-tuŋ], *f.* (—, *pl.* —en) under-cutting.

Prellbock ['prɛlbɔk], *m.* (—s, *pl.* ⁻e) buffer (-block).

prellen ['prɛlən], *v.a.* cheat, defraud.

Prellstein ['prɛlʃtaɪn], *m.* (—s, *pl.* —e) kerbstone.

pressant [prɛ'sant], *adj.* (*Austr.*) urgent.

Presse ['prɛsə], *f.* (—, *pl.* —n) press; newspapers; (*coll.*) coaching establishment, crammer.

pressieren [prɛ'si:rən], *v.n.* be urgent.

Preßkohle ['prɛsko:lə], *f.* (—, *no pl.*) briquette(s).

Preßkolben ['prɛskɔlbən], *m.* (—s, *pl.* —) piston.

Preßluft ['prɛsluft], *f.* (—, *no pl.*) compressed air.

Preußen ['prɔysən], *n.* Prussia.

prickeln ['prɪkəln], *v.n.* prick, prickle, sting, tickle.

Prieme ['pri:mə], *f.* (—, *pl.* —n) chew, quid.

Priester ['pri:stər], *m.* (—s, *pl.* —) priest; *zum* — *weihen*, ordain to the priesthood.

Prima ['pri:ma:], *f.* (—, *pl.* **Primen**) highest form at a grammar school (sixth form).

prima ['pri:ma:], *adj.* excellent, splendid, first-rate.

Primaner [pri'ma:nər], *m.* (—s, *pl.* —) pupil in the highest form at a grammar school, sixth form boy.

Primel ['pri:məl], *f.* (—, *pl.* —n) (*Bot.*) primrose, primula.

Primus ['pri:mus], *m.* (—, *no pl.*) (*School*) head boy, captain of the school.

Prinzip [prɪn'tsi:p], *n.* (—s, *pl.* —ien) principle.

Priorität [priori'tɛ:t], *f.* (—, *no pl.*) priority, precedence.

Prise ['pri:zə], *f.* (—, *pl.* —n) pinch of snuff.

Prisma ['prɪsma:], *n.* (—s, *pl.* —men) prism.

Pritsche ['prɪtʃə], *f.* (—, *pl.* —n) plank-bed.

Privatdozent [pri'va:tdotsɛnt], *m.* (—en, *pl.* —en) (*Univ.*) (unsalaried) lecturer.

privatisieren [privati'zi:rən], *v.n.* have private means.

Probe ['pro:bə], *f.* (—, *pl.* —n) experiment, trial, probation, test; (*Theat.*, *Mus.*) rehearsal; sample, pattern; *auf* —, on trial; *auf die* — *stellen*, put to the test *or* on probation.

Probeabzug ['pro:baptsu:k], *m.* (—s, *pl.* ⁻e) (*Printing*) proof.

proben ['pro:bən], *v.a.* rehearse.

probieren [pro'bi:rən], *v.a.* try, attempt; taste.

Probst [pro:pst], *m.* (—es, *pl.* ⁻e) provost.

Produzent [produ'tsɛnt], *m.* (—en, *pl.* —en) producer (of goods), manufacturer.

produzieren [produ'tsi:rən], *v.a.* produce (goods). — *v.r. sich* —, perform, show off.

profanieren [profa'ni:rən], *v.a.* desecrate, profane.

Professur [profɛ'su:r], *f.* (—, *pl.* —en) (*Univ.*) professorship, Chair.

profitieren [profi'ti:rən], *v.a.*, *v.n.* profit (by), take advantage (of).

projizieren [proji'tsi:rən], *v.a.* project.

Prokura [pro'ku:ra:], *f.* (—, *no pl.*) (*Law*) power of attorney.

Prokurist [proku'rɪst], *m.* (—en, *pl.* —en) confidential clerk; company secretary.

prolongieren

prolongieren [prolɔŋˈgiːrən], *v.a.* prolong, extend.

promenieren [proməˈniːrən], *v.n.* take a stroll.

Promotion [promoˈtsjoːn], *f.* (—, *pl.* —en) graduation, degree ceremony.

promovieren [promoˈviːrən], *v.n.* graduate, take a degree.

promulgieren [promulˈgiːrən], *v.a.* promulgate.

Pronomen [proˈnoːmən], *n.* (—s, *pl.* —mina) (*Gram.*) pronoun.

prophezeien [profeˈtsaɪən], *v.a.* prophesy, predict, forecast.

prophylaktisch [profyˈlaktiʃ], *adj.* preventive, prophylactic.

Propst [proːpst], *m.* (—es, *pl.* ⁀e) provost.

Prosa [ˈproːzaː], *f.* (—, *no pl.*) prose.

prosit [ˈproːzit], *excl.* cheers! here's to you! your health!

Prospekt [proˈspɛkt], *m.* (—es, *pl.* —e) prospect; (*booklet*) prospectus.

Prostituierte [prostituˈiːrtə], *f.* (—n, *pl.* —n) prostitute; (*coll.*) tart.

protegieren [proteˈʒiːrən], *v.a.* favour, patronize.

Protektion [protɛkˈtsjoːn], *f.* (—, *no pl.*) patronage, favouritism.

protestieren [protɛsˈtiːrən], *v.n.* make a protest, protest (against s.th.).

Protokoll [protoˈkɔl], *n.* (—s, *pl.* —e) minutes, record; protocol; regulations.

Protokollführer [protoˈkɔlfyːrər], *m.* (—s, *pl.* —) recorder, clerk of the minutes.

Protz [prɔts], *m.* (—en, *pl.* —en) snob, upstart; show-off.

Proviant [proˈvjant], *m.* (—s, *no pl.*) provisions, stores.

provinziell [provɪnˈtsjɛl], *adj.* provincial.

Provinzler [proˈvɪntsler], *m.* (—s, *pl.* —) provincial.

Provision [proviˈzjoːn], *f.* (—, *pl.* —en) (*Comm.*) commission, brokerage.

Provisor [proˈviːzɔr], *m.* (—s, *pl.* —en) dispenser.

provisorisch [proviˈzoːriʃ], *adj.* provisional, temporary.

provozieren [provoˈtsiːrən], *v.a.* provoke.

Prozedur [protseˈduːr], *f.* (—, *pl.* —en) proceedings, procedure.

Prozent [proˈtsɛnt], *m. & n.* (—s, *pl.* —e) per cent.

Prozentsatz [proˈtsɛntzats], *m.* (—es, *pl.* ⁀e) percentage, rate of interest.

Prozeß [proˈtsɛs], *m.* (—es, *pl.* —e) process; lawsuit, litigation; trial; *mit etwas kurzen — machen*, deal summarily with.

Prozeßwesen [proˈtsɛsveːzən], *n.* (—s, *no pl.*) legal procedure.

prüde [ˈpryːdə], *adj.* prudish, prim.

prüfen [ˈpryːfən], *v.a.* test, examine.

Prüfung [ˈpryːfuŋ], *f.* (—, *pl.* —en) trial, test; examination; (*fig.*) temptation, affliction.

Prügel [ˈpryːgəl], *m.* (—s, *pl.* —) cudgel; (*pl.*) thrashing; *eine Tracht —*, a good hiding.

prügeln [ˈpryːgəln], *v.a.* beat, give a hiding to.

Prunk [pruŋk], *m.* (—(e)s, *no pl.*) splendour, ostentation, pomp.

prusten [ˈpruːstən], *v.n.* snort.

Psalm [psalm], *m.* (—es, *pl.* —e) psalm.

Psalter [ˈpsaltər], *m.* (—s, *pl.* —) (*book*) psalter; (*instrument*) psaltery.

Psychiater [psyçiˈaːtər], *m.* (—s, *pl.* —) psychiatrist.

Psychologe [psyçoˈloːgə], *m.* (—n, *pl.* —n) psychologist.

Pubertät [pubɛrˈtɛːt], *f.* (—, *no pl.*) puberty.

Publikum [ˈpuːblɪkum], *n.* (—s, *no pl.*) public; (*Theat.*) audience.

publizieren [publiˈtsiːrən], *v.a.* publish; promulgate.

Pudel [ˈpuːdəl], *m.* (—s, *pl.* —) poodle; *des —s Kern*, the gist of the matter.

Puder [ˈpuːdər], *m.* (—s, *no pl.*) powder, face-powder.

pudern [ˈpuːdərn], *v.a.* powder.

Puff [puf], *m.* (—es, *pl.* ⁀e) cuff, thump.

puffen [ˈpufən], *v.a.* cuff, thump.

Puffer [ˈpufər], *m.* (—s, *pl.* —) buffer.

Puffspiel [ˈpufʃpiːl], *n.* (—s, *pl.* —e) backgammon.

pullen [ˈpulən], *v.n.* rein in (a horse); (*coll.*) piddle.

Pulsader [ˈpulsaːdər], *f.* (—, *pl.* —n) artery; aorta.

pulsieren [pulˈziːrən], *v.n.* pulsate; pulse, throb.

Pulsschlag [ˈpulsʃlaːk], *m.* (—s, *pl.* ⁀e) pulse-beat; pulsation.

Pult [pult], *n.* (—es, *pl.* —e) desk, writing-table; lectern.

Pulver [ˈpulvər], *n.* (—s, *pl.* —) powder.

Pump [pump], *m.* (—s, *no pl.*) (*sl.*) credit; *auf —*, on tick.

pumpen [ˈpumpən], *v.a., v.n.* pump; (*fig.*) (*sl.*) *sich etwas —*, borrow s.th., touch s.o. for s.th.; lend.

Pumpenschwengel [ˈpumpənʃvɛŋəl], *m.* (—s, *pl.* —) pump-handle.

Pumpernickel [ˈpumpərnɪkəl], *m.* (—s, *pl.* —) black bread, Westphalian rye-bread.

Pumphosen [ˈpumphoːzən], *f. pl.* plus-fours.

Punkt [puŋkt], *m.* (—es, *pl.* —e) point, dot, spot; (*Gram.*) full stop.

punktieren [puŋkˈtiːrən], *v.a.* dot; punctuate.

pünktlich [ˈpyŋktlɪç], *adj.* punctual.

punktum [ˈpuŋktum], *excl. und damit —*, that's the end of it; that's it.

Puppe [ˈpupə], *f.* (—, *pl.* —n) doll; (*Ent.*) pupa, chrysalis.

pur [puːr], *adj.* pure, sheer; (*drink*) neat.

172

Puritaner [puri'taːnər], *m.* (—s, *pl.* —) puritan.

Purpur ['purpur], *m.* (—s, *no pl.*) purple.

Purzelbaum ['purtsəlbaum], *m.* (—s, *pl.* ⁀e) somersault.

purzeln ['purtsəln], *v.n.* tumble.

Pustel ['pustəl], *f.* (—, *pl.* —n) pustule.

pusten ['puːstən], *v.n.* puff, blow.

Pute ['puːtə], *f.* (—, *pl.* —n) (*Orn.*) turkey-hen; *dumme* —, silly goose.

Puter ['puːtər], *m.* (—s, *pl.* —) turkey-cock.

puterrot ['puːtərroːt], *adj.* as red as a turkey-cock.

Putsch [putʃ], *m.* (—es, *pl.* —e) coup de main, insurrection, riot.

Putz [puts], *m.* (—es, *no pl.*) finery; cleaning; rough-cast.

putzen ['putsən], *v.a.* polish, shine; clean. — *v.r. sich* —, dress up.

Putzfrau ['putsfrau], *f.* (—, *pl.* —en) charwoman.

Putzmacherin ['putsmaxərɪn], *f.* (—, *pl.* —nen) milliner.

Pyramide [pyra'miːdə], *f.* (—, *pl.* —n) pyramid.

Pyrenäen [pyrɛ'nɛːən], *pl.* Pyrenees; —*halbinsel*, Iberian Peninsula.

Q

Q [kuː], *n.* (—s, *pl.* —s) the letter Q.

quabbeln ['kvabəln], *v.n.* shake, wobble.

Quacksalber ['kvakzalbər], *m.* (—s, *pl.* —) quack, mountebank.

Quacksalberei [kvakzalbə'raɪ], *f.* (—, *pl.* —en) quackery.

Quaderstein ['kvaːdərʃtaɪn], *m.* (—s, *pl.* —e) ashlar, hewn stone.

Quadrat [kva'draːt], *n.* (—es, *pl.* —e) square; *zum* (or *ins*) — *erheben*, square (a number).

Quadratur [kvadra'tuːr], *f.* (—, *pl.* —en) quadrature; *die — des Kreises finden*, square the circle.

quadrieren [kva'driːrən], *v.a.* square.

quaken ['kvaːkən], *v.n.* (*frog*) croak; (*duck*) quack.

quäken ['kvɛːkən], *v.n.* squeak.

Quäker ['kvɛːkər], *m.* (—s, *pl.* —) Quaker.

Qual [kvaːl], *f.* (—, *pl.* —en) anguish, agony, torment.

quälen ['kvɛːlən], *v.a.* torment, torture, vex. — *v.r. sich* —, toil.

qualifizieren [kvalifi'tsiːrən], *v.a.* qualify.

Qualität [kvali'tɛːt], *f.* (—, *pl.* —en) quality.

Qualle ['kvalə], *f.* (—, *pl.* —n) (*Zool.*) jelly-fish.

Qualm [kvalm], *m.* (—es, *no pl.*) dense smoke.

Quantität [kvanti'tɛːt], *f.* (—, *pl.* —en) quantity.

Quantum ['kvantum], *n.* (—s, *pl.* —ten) portion, quantity.

Quappe ['kvapə], *f.* (—, *pl.* —n) (*Zool.*) tadpole.

Quarantäne [kvaran'tɛːnə], *f.* (—, *no pl.*) quarantine.

Quark [kvark], *m.* (—s, *no pl.*) curds; cream-cheese; (*fig.*) trash, rubbish, nonsense, bilge.

Quarta ['kvarta:], *f.* (—, *no pl.*) fourth form.

Quartal [kvar'taːl], *n.* (—s, *pl.* —e) quarter of a year; term.

Quartier [kvar'tiːr], *n.* (—s, *pl.* —e) quarters, lodging; (*Mil.*) billet.

Quarz [kvarts], *m.* (—es, *no pl.*) quartz.

Quaste ['kvastə], *f.* (—, *pl.* —n) tassel.

Quatember [kva'tɛmbər], *m.* (—s, *pl.* —) quarter day; (*Eccl.*) Ember Day.

Quatsch [kvatʃ], *m.* (—es, *no pl.*) nonsense, drivel.

Quecke ['kvɛkə], *f.* (—, *pl.* —n) couch-grass, quick-grass.

Quecksilber ['kvɛkzɪlbər], *n.* (—s, *no pl.*) quicksilver, mercury.

Quelle ['kvɛlə], *f.* (—, *pl.* —n) well, spring, fountain; (*fig.*) source; *aus sicherer* —, on good authority.

Quentchen ['kvɛntçən], *n.* (—s, *pl.* —) small amount, dram.

quer [kveːr], *adj.* cross, transverse, oblique, diagonal. — *adv.* across; *kreuz und* —, in all directions.

Querbalken ['kveːrbalkən], *m.* (—s, *pl.* —) cross-beam.

querdurch ['kveːrdurç], *adv.* across.

querfeldein ['kveːrfɛltaɪn], *adv.* cross-country.

Querkopf ['kveːrkɔpf], *m.* (—es, *pl.* ⁀e) crank.

Quersattel ['kveːrzatəl], *m.* (—s, *pl.* ⁀) side-saddle.

Querschiff ['kveːrʃɪf], *n.* (—es, *pl.* —e) (*church*) transept.

Querschnitt ['kveːrʃnɪt], *m.* (—s, *pl.* —e) cross-section; (*fig.*) average.

Querulant [kveru'lant], *m.* (—en, *pl.* —en) grumbler.

quetschen ['kvɛtʃən], *v.a.* squeeze, crush, mash; bruise.

Queue [køː], *n.* (—s, *pl.* —s) (*Billiards*) cue.

quieken ['kviːkən], *v.n.* squeak.

Quinta ['kvɪntaː], *f.* (—, *no pl.*) fifth form.

Quinte ['kvɪntə], *f.* (—, *pl.* —n) (*Mus.*) fifth.

Quirl [kvɪrl], *m.* (—s, *pl.* —e) whisk; (*Bot.*) whorl.

quitt [kvɪt], *adj.* — *sein*, be quits.

Quitte ['kvɪtə], *f.* (—, *pl.* —n) (*Bot.*) quince.

quittegelb [ˈkvɪtəgɛlp], *adj.* bright yellow.

quittieren [kvɪˈtiːrən], *v.a.* receipt; give a receipt; *den Dienst* —, leave the service.

Quittung [ˈkvɪtuŋ], *f.* (—, *pl.* —en) receipt.

Quodlibet [ˈkvɔdliˌbɛt], *n.* (—s, *pl.* —s) medley.

Quote [ˈkvoːtə], *f.* (—, *pl.* —n) quota, share.

quotieren [kvoˈtiːrən], *v.a.* (*stock exchange*) quote (prices).

R

R [ɛr], *n.* (—s, *pl.* —s) the letter R.

Rabatt [raˈbat], *m.* (—s, *pl.* —e) rebate, discount.

Rabatte [raˈbatə], *f.* (—, *pl.* —n) flower-border.

Rabbiner [raˈbiːnər], *m.* (—s, *pl.* —) rabbi.

Rabe [ˈraːbə], *m.* (—n, *pl.* —n) (*Orn.*) raven; *ein weißer* —, a rare bird.

Rabenaas [ˈraːbənaːs], *n.* (—es, *pl.* —e) carrion.

rabiat [raˈbjaːt], *adj.* furious, rabid.

Rache [ˈraxə], *f.* (—, *no pl.*) revenge, vengeance.

Rachen [ˈraxən], *m.* (—s, *pl.* —) jaws, throat.

rächen [ˈrɛːçən], *v.a.* avenge. — *v.r. sich* —, avenge o.s., take vengeance.

Rachenbräune [ˈraxənbrɔynə], *f.* (—, *no pl.*) croup, quinsy.

Rachitis [raˈxiːtɪs], *f.* (—, *no pl.*) (*Med.*) rickets.

rachsüchtig [ˈraxzʏçtɪç], *adj.* vindictive, vengeful.

rackern [ˈrakərn], *v.r. sich* —, (*coll.*) toil, work hard.

Rad [raːt], *n.* (—es, *pl.* ˝er) wheel; bicycle; *ein* — *schlagen*, turn a cart-wheel; (*peacock*) spread the tail.

Radau [raˈdau], *m.* (—s, *no pl.*) noise, din, shindy.

Rade [ˈraːdə], *f.* (—, *pl.* —n) còrn-cockle.

radebrechen [ˈraːdəbrɛçən], *v.a. insep.* murder a language.

radeln [ˈraːdəln], *v.n.* (*aux.* sein) (*coll.*) cycle.

Rädelsführer [ˈrɛːdəlsfyːrər], *m.* (—s, *pl.* —) ringleader.

rädern [ˈrɛːdərn], *v.a.* break on the wheel; *gerädert sein*, (*fig.*) ache in all o.'s bones, be exhausted.

Radfahrer [ˈraːtfaːrər], *m.* (—s, *pl.* —) cyclist.

radieren [raˈdiːrən], *v.n.* erase; etch.

Radierung [raˈdiːruŋ], *f.* (—, *pl.* —en) etching.

Radieschen [raˈdiːsçən], *n.* (—s, *pl.* —) (*Bot.*) radish.

Radio [ˈraːdjo], *n.* (—s, *pl.* —s) wireless, radio.

raffen [ˈrafən], *v.a.* snatch up, gather up.

Raffinade [rafiˈnaːdə], *f.* (—, *no pl.*) refined sugar.

Raffinement [rafinəˈmãː], *n.* (—s, *no pl.*) elaborateness.

raffinieren [rafiˈniːrən], *v.a.* refine.

raffiniert [rafiˈniːrt], *adj.* refined; elaborate, crafty, wily, cunning.

ragen [ˈraːgən], *v.n.* tower, soar.

Rahm [raːm], *m.* (—es, *no pl.*) cream; *den* — *abschöpfen*, skim; (*fig.*) skim the cream off.

Rahmen [ˈraːmən], *m.* (—s, *pl.* —) frame; milieu, limit, scope, compass; *im* — *von*, within the framework of.

rahmig [ˈraːmɪç], *adj.* creamy.

raisonnieren [rɛzɔˈniːrən], *v.n.* reason, argue; (*fig.*) grumble, answer back.

Rakete [raˈkeːtə], *f.* (—, *pl.* —n) rocket, sky-rocket.

Rakett [raˈkɛt], *n.* (—s, *pl.* —s) (*tennis*) racket.

rammen [ˈramən], *v.a.* ram.

Rampe [ˈrampə], *f.* (—, *pl.* —n) ramp, slope; platform; (*Theat.*) apron.

ramponiert [rampoˈniːrt], *adj.* battered, damaged.

Ramsch [ramʃ], *m.* (—es, *pl.* ˝e) odds and ends; (*Comm.*) job lot.

Rand [rant], *m.* (—es, *pl.* ˝er) edge, border, verge, rim; (*book*) margin; (*hat*) brim; *am* — *des Grabes*, with one foot in the grave; *außer* — *und Band geraten*, get completely out of hand.

randalieren [randaˈliːrən], *v.n.* kick up a row.

Randbemerkung [ˈrantbəmerkuŋ], *f.* (—, *pl.* —en) marginal note, gloss.

rändern [rendərn], *v.a.* border, edge, mill.

Ränftchen [ˈrɛnftçən], *n.* (—s, *pl.* —) crust (of bread).

Rang [raŋ], *m.* (—es, *pl.* ˝e) rank, grade, rate; order, class; standing (in society); (*Theat.*) circle, tier, gallery.

Range [ˈraŋə], *m.* (—n, *pl.* —n) scamp, rascal. — *f.* (—, *pl.* —n) tomboy, hoyden.

rangieren [rãˈʒiːrən], *v.a.* (*Railw.*) shunt. — *v.n.* rank.

Ranke [ˈraŋkə], *f.* (—, *pl.* —n) tendril, shoot.

Ränke [ˈrɛŋkə], *m. pl.* intrigues, tricks.

ranken [ˈraŋkən], *v.r.* (*aux.* haben) *sich* —, (*plant*) climb (with tendrils).

Ränkeschmied [ˈrɛŋkəʃmiːt], *m.* (—es, *pl.* —e) plotter, intriguer.

Ranzen [ˈrantsən], *m.* (—s, *pl.* —) satchel, knapsack, rucksack.

ranzig [ˈrantsɪç], *adj.* rancid, rank.

Rappe [ˈrapə], *m.* (—n, *pl.* —n) black horse.

Rappel ['rapəl], *m.* (—s, *no pl.*) (*coll.*) slight madness; rage, fit.

Rappen ['rapən], *m.* (—s, *pl.* —) small Swiss coin; centime.

rapportieren [rapɔr'tiːrən], *v.a.* report.

Raps [raps], *m.* (—es, *no pl.*) rape-seed.

rar [raːr], *adj.* rare, scarce; exquisite.

rasch [raʃ], *adj.* quick, swift.

rascheln ['raʃəln], *v.n.* rustle.

Rasen ['raːzən], *m.* (—s, *pl.* —) lawn, turf, sod.

rasen ['raːzən], *v.n.* rave, rage, be delirious; rush, speed; *in — der Eile,* in a tearing hurry.

Raserei [raːzə'raɪ], *f.* (—, *pl.* —en) madness; (*fig.*) fury.

Rasierapparat [ra'ziːrapara:t], *m.* (—s, *pl.* —e) (safety-)razor; shaver.

rasieren [ra'ziːrən], *v.a.* shave; *sich — lassen,* be shaved, get a shave.

Rasierzeug [ra'ziːrtsɔyk], *n.* (—s, *no pl.*) shaving-tackle.

Raspel ['raspəl], *f.* (—, *pl.* —n) rasp.

Rasse ['rasə], *f.* (—, *pl.* —n) race; breed; *reine —,* thoroughbred; *gekreuzte —,* cross-breed.

Rassel ['rasəl], *f.* (—, *pl.* —n) rattle.

rasseln ['rasəln], *v.n.* rattle, clank.

Rassendiskriminierung ['rasəndiskrimini:ruŋ], *f.* (—, *no pl.*) racial discrimination.

Rast [rast], *f.* (—, *no pl.*) rest, repose.

rasten ['rastən], *v.n.* rest, take a rest; halt.

Raster ['rastər], *m.* (—s, *pl.* —) (*Phot.*) screen.

rastlos ['rastloːs], *adj.* restless.

Rat (1) [raːt], *m.* (—es, *pl.* —schläge) advice, counsel; deliberation.

Rat (2) [raːt], *m.* (—es, *pl.* ∵e) council, councillor; *mit — und Tat,* with advice and assistance; *einem einen — geben,* give s.o. advice, counsel s.o.; *einen um — fragen,* consult s.o.; *— schaffen,* find ways and means.

Rate ['raːtə], *f.* (—, *pl.* —n) instalment, rate.

raten ['raːtən], *v.a., v.n. irr.* advise; guess, conjecture.

Ratgeber ['raːtgeːbər], *m.* (—s, *pl.* —) adviser, counsellor.

Rathaus ['raːthaus], *n.* (—es, *pl.* ∵er) town-hall.

Ratifizierung [ratifi'tsiːruŋ], *f.* (—, *pl.* —en) ratification.

Ration [ra'tsjoːn], *f.* (—, *pl.* —en) ration, share, portion.

rationell [ratsjo'nɛl], *adj.* rational.

ratlos ['raːtloːs], *adj.* helpless, perplexed.

ratsam ['raːtzaːm], *adj.* advisable.

Ratschlag ['raːtʃlaːk], *m.* (—s, *pl.* ∵e) advice, counsel.

Ratschluß ['raːtʃlus], *m.* (—sses, *pl.* ∵sse) decision, decree.

Ratsdiener ['raːtsdiːnər], *m.* (—s, *pl.* —) beadle, tipstaff, summoner.

Rätsel ['rɛːtsəl], *n.* (—s, *pl.* —) riddle, puzzle, mystery, enigma, conundrum.

Ratsherr ['raːtshɛr], *m.* (—n, *pl.* —en) alderman, (town-)councillor, senator.

Ratte ['ratə], *f.* (—, *pl.* —n) (*Zool.*) rat.

Raub [raup], *m.* (—es, *no pl.*) robbery; booty, prey.

rauben ['raubən], *v.a.* rob, plunder; *es raubt mir den Atem,* it takes my breath away.

Räuber ['rɔybər], *m.* (—s, *pl.* —) robber, thief; highwayman; *— und Gendarm,* cops and robbers.

Raubgier ['raupgiːr], *f.* (—, *no pl.*) rapacity.

Rauch [raux], *m.* (—s, *no pl.*) smoke, vapour.

Rauchen ['rauxən], *n.* (—s, *no pl.*) smoking; *— verboten,* no smoking.

rauchen ['rauxən], *v.a., v.n.* smoke.

räuchern ['rɔyçərn], *v.a.* (*meat, fish*) smoke-dry, cure; (*disinfect*) fumigate. *— v.n.* (*Eccl.*) burn incense.

Rauchfang ['rauxfaŋ], *m.* (—s, *pl.* ∵e) chimney-flue.

Räude ['rɔydə], *f.* (—, *no pl.*) mange.

Raufbold ['raufbɔlt], *m.* (—s, *pl.* —e) brawler, bully.

raufen ['raufən], *v.a.* (*hair*) tear out, pluck. *— v.n.* fight, brawl. *— v.r. sich — mit,* scuffle with, fight, have a scrap with.

rauh [rau], *adj.* rough; (*fig.*) harsh, rude; hoarse; (*weather*) raw, inclement.

Rauheit ['rauhaɪt], *f.* (—, *no pl.*) roughness; hoarseness; (*fig.*) harshness, rudeness; (*weather*) inclemency; (*landscape*) ruggedness.

rauhen ['rauən], *v.a.* (*cloth*) nap.

Raum [raum], *m.* (—es, *pl.* ∵e) space, room; outer space; (*fig.*) scope; *dem Gedanken — geben,* entertain an idea.

räumen ['rɔymən], *v.a.* clear, empty; quit, leave; *das Feld —,* abandon the field, clear out.

Rauminhalt ['raumɪnhalt], *m.* (—s, *no pl.*) volume.

räumlich ['rɔymlɪç], *adj.* spatial; (*in compounds*) space-.

Räumlichkeiten ['rɔymlɪçkaɪtən], *f. pl.* premises.

Raumschiff ['raumʃif], *n.* (—es, *pl.* —e) spaceship, spacecraft.

Räumung ['rɔymuŋ], *f.* (—, *pl.* —en) evacuation.

raunen ['raunən], *v.a., v.n.* whisper.

Raupe ['raupə], *f.* (—, *pl.* —n) (*Ent.*) caterpillar.

Rausch [rauʃ], *m.* (—es, *pl.* ∵e) intoxication; delirium, frenzy; *einen — haben,* be drunk, intoxicated; *seinen — ausschlafen,* sleep it off.

rauschen ['rauʃən], *v.n.* rustle, rush, roar.

Rauschgift ['rauʃgɪft], *n.* (—s, *pl.* —e) drug; narcotic.

Rauschgold ['rauʃgɔlt], *n.* (—es, *no pl.*) tinsel.

räuspern ['rɔyspərn], *v.r. sich —,* clear o.'s throat.

Raute ['rautə], *f.* (—, *pl.* —n) (*Maths.* rhombus; lozenge; (*Bot.*) rue.

Razzia

Razzia ['ratsja], *f.* (—, *pl.* —**zzien**) (police-)raid, swoop.

reagieren [rea'gi:rən], *v.n.* react (on).

realisieren [reali'zi:rən], *v.a.* convert into money, realise.

Realschule [re'a:lʃu:lə], *f.* (—, *pl.* —**n**) technical grammar school; secondary modern school.

Rebe ['re:bə], *f.* (—, *pl.* —**n**) vine.

Rebell [re'bɛl], *m.* (—**en**, *pl.* —**en**) rebel, mutineer, insurgent.

Rebensaft ['re:bənzaft], *m.* (—**s**, *pl.* ⸚e) grape-juice, wine.

Rebhuhn ['re:phu:n], *n.* (—**s**, *pl.* ⸚er) (*Orn.*) partridge.

Reblaus ['re:plaus], *f.* (—, *pl.* ⸚e) (*Ent.*) phylloxera.

Rechen ['rɛçən], *m.* (—**s**, *pl.* —) (*garden*) rake; (*clothes*) rack.

Rechenaufgabe ['rɛçənaufga:bə], *f.* (—, *pl.* —**n**) sum; mathematical *or* arithmetical problem.

Rechenmaschine ['rɛçənmaʃi:nə], *f.* (—, *pl.* —**n**) calculating machine, adding-machine.

Rechenschaft ['rɛçənʃaft], *f.* (—, *no pl.*) account; — *ablegen,* account for; *zur — ziehen,* call to account.

Rechenschieber ['rɛçənʃi:bər], *m.* (—**s**, *pl.* —) slide-rule.

Rechentabelle ['rɛçəntabɛlə], *f.* (—, *pl.* —**n**) ready reckoner.

rechnen ['rɛçnən], *v.a.,* *v.n.* reckon, calculate, do sums, compute; *auf etwas* —, count on s.th.; *auf einen* —, rely on s.o.

Rechnung ['rɛçnuŋ], *f.* (—, *pl.* —**en**) reckoning, account, computation; (*document*) invoice, bill, statement, account; *einer Sache — tragen,* make allowances for s.th.; take s.th. into account; *einem einen Strich durch die — machen,* put a spoke in s.o.'s wheel; *eine — begleichen,* settle an account.

Rechnungsabschluß ['rɛçnuŋsapʃlus], *m.* (—**sses**, *pl.* ⸚sse) balancing of accounts, balance-sheet.

Rechnungsprüfer ['rɛçnuŋspry:fər], *m.* (—**s**, *pl.* —) auditor.

Rechnungsrat ['rɛçnuŋsra:t], *m.* (—**s**, *pl.* ⸚e) member of the board of accountants, (senior government) auditor.

Recht [rɛçt], *n.* (—**es**, *pl.* —**e**) right, justice; claim on, title to; law, jurisprudence; *von —s wegen,* by right; — *sprechen,* administer justice; *die —e studieren,* study law.

recht [rɛçt], *adj.* right; just; real, true; suitable; proper; *zur —en Zeit,* in time; *es geht nicht mit —en Dingen zu,* there is s.th. queer about it; *was dem einen —, ist dem andern billig,* what is sauce for the goose is sauce for the gander; *einem — geben,* agree with s.o.; — *haben,* be (in the) right.

Rechteck ['rɛçtɛk], *n.* (—**s**, *pl.* —**e**) rectangle.

rechten ['rɛçtən], *v.n. mit einem* —, dispute, remonstrate with s.o.

rechtfertigen ['rɛçtfɛrtigən], *v.a. insep.* justify. — *v.r. sich —,* exculpate o.s.

rechtgläubig ['rɛçtglɔybiç], *adj.* orthodox.

rechthaberisch ['rɛçtha:bəriʃ], *adj.* stubborn, obstinate.

rechtlich ['rɛçtliç], *adj.* legal, lawful, legitimate; (*Law*) judicial, juridical.

rechtmäßig ['rɛçtmɛ:siç], *adj.* lawful, legitimate, legal.

rechts [rɛçts], *adv.* to the right, on the right.

Rechtsabtretung ['rɛçtsaptre:tuŋ], *f.* (—, *pl.* —**en**) cession, assignment.

Rechtsanwalt ['rɛçtsanvalt], *m.* (—**s**, *pl.* ⸚e) lawyer, solicitor, attorney.

Rechtsbeistand ['rɛçtsbaiʃtant], *m.* (—**s**, *pl.* ⸚e) (legal) counsel.

rechtschaffen ['rɛçtʃafən], *adj.* upright, honest, righteous.

Rechtschreibung ['rɛçtʃraibuŋ], *f.* (—, *no pl.*) orthography, spelling.

Rechtshandel ['rɛçtshandəl], *m.* (—**s**, *pl.* ⸚) action, case, lawsuit.

rechtskräftig ['rɛçtskrɛftiç], *adj.* legal, valid.

Rechtslehre ['rɛçtsle:rə], *f.* (—, *pl.* —**n**) jurisprudence.

Rechtsspruch ['rɛçtsʃprux], *m.* (—(**e**)**s**, *pl.* ⸚e) verdict.

Rechtsverhandlung ['rɛçtsfɛrhandluŋ], *f.* (—, *pl.* —**en**) legal proceedings.

Rechtsweg ['rɛçtsve:k], *m.* (—(**e**)**s**, *pl.* ⸚e) course of law.

rechtswidrig ['rɛçtsvi:driç], *adj.* against the law, illegal.

Rechtszuständigkeit ['rɛçtstsu:ʃtendiçkait], *f.* (—, *pl.* —**en**) (legal) competence.

rechtwinklig ['rɛçtviŋkliç], *adj.* rectangular.

rechtzeitig ['rɛçttsaitiç], *adj.* opportune. — *adv.* in time, at the right time.

Reck [rɛk], *n.* (—**s**, *pl.* —**e**) horizontal bar.

Recke ['rɛkə], *m.* (—**n**, *pl.* —**n**) (*Poet.*) hero.

recken ['rɛkən], *v.a.* stretch, extend.

Redakteur [redak'tø:r], *m.* (—**s**, *pl.* —**e**) editor (newspaper, magazine).

Redaktion [redak'tsjo:n], *f.* (—, *pl.* —**en**) editorship, editorial staff; (*room*) editorial office.

Rede ['re:də], *f.* (—, *pl.* —**n**) speech, oration; address; *es geht die —, people say; es ist nicht der — wert,* it is not worth mentioning; *eine — halten,* deliver a speech; *zur — stellen,* call to account.

reden ['re:dən], *v.a.* speak, talk, discourse; *einem nach dem Munde —,* humour s.o.; *in den Wind —,* speak in vain, preach to the winds; *mit sich — lassen,* be amenable to reason.

Redensart ['re:dənsa:rt], *f.* (—, *pl.* —en) phrase, idiom; cliché; *einen mit leeren —en abspeisen*, put s.o. off with fine words.

Redewendung ['re:dəvɛnduŋ], *f.* (—, *pl.* —en) turn of phrase.

redigieren [redi'gi:rən], *v.a.* edit.

redlich ['re:tlɪç], *adj.* honest, upright.

Redner ['re:dnər], *m.* (—s, *pl.* —) speaker, orator.

Reede ['re:də], *f.* (—, *pl.* —n) (*Naut.*) roadstead.

Reederei [re:də'raɪ], *f.* (—, *pl.* —en) shipping-business.

reell [re'ɛl], *adj.* honest, fair, sound, bona fide.

Reep [re:p], *n.* (—s, *pl.* —e) (*Naut.*) rope.

Referat [refe'ra:t], *n.* (—s, *pl.* —e) report; paper (to a learned society), lecture.

Referendar [referɛn'da:r], *m.* (—s, *pl.* —e) junior barrister *or* teacher.

Referent [refe'rɛnt], *m.* (—en, *pl.* —en) reporter, reviewer; lecturer; expert (adviser).

Referenz [refe'rɛnts], *f.* (—, *pl.* —en) reference (to s.o. *or* s.th.).

referieren [refe'ri:rən], *v.a., v.n.* report (on), give a paper (on).

reflektieren [reflɛk'ti:rən], *v.a.* reflect. — *v.n. auf etwas* —, be a prospective buyer of s.th., have o.'s eye on s.th.

Reformator [refɔr'ma:tɔr], *m.* (—s, *pl.* —en) reformer.

reformieren [refɔr'mi:rən], *v.a.* reform.

Regal [re'ga:l], *n.* (—s, *pl.* —e) shelf.

rege ['re:gə], *adj.* brisk, lively, animated.

Regel ['re:gəl], *f.* (—, *pl.* —n) rule, precept, principle; *in der —*, as a rule, generally.

regelmäßig ['re:gəlmɛ:sɪç], *adj.* regular.

regeln ['re:gəln], *v.a.* regulate, arrange, order.

Regelung ['re:gəluŋ], *f.* (—, *pl.* —en) regulation.

regelwidrig ['re:gəlvi:drɪç], *adj.* contrary to rule, irregular, foul.

Regen ['re:gən], *m.* (—s, *no pl.*) rain.

regen ['re:gən], *v.r. sich —*, move, stir.

Regenbogen ['re:gənbo:gən], *m.* (—s, *pl.* —) rainbow.

Regenbogenhaut ['re:gənbo:gənhaut], *f.* (—, *pl.* ⸚e) (*eye*) iris.

Regenguß ['re:gəngus], *m.* (—sses, *pl.* ⸚sse) downpour, violent shower.

Regenmantel ['re:gənmantəl], *m.* (—s, *pl.* ⸚) waterproof, raincoat, mac.

Regenpfeifer ['re:gənpfaɪfər], *m.* (—s, *pl.* —) (*Orn.*) plover.

Regenrinne ['re:gənrɪnə], *f.* (—, *pl.* —n) eaves.

Regenschirm ['re:gənʃɪrm], *m.* (—s, *pl.* —e) umbrella.

Regentschaft [re'gɛntʃaft], *f.* (—, *pl.* —en) regency.

Regie [re'ʒi:], *f.* (—, *pl.* —n) stage management, production, direction.

regieren [re'gi:rən], *v.a.* rule, reign over, govern. — *v.n.* reign; (*fig.*) prevail, predominate.

Regierung [re'gi:ruŋ], *f.* (—, *pl.* —en) government; reign.

Regierungsrat [re'gi:ruŋsra:t], *m.* (—s, *pl.* ⸚e) government adviser.

Regiment (1) [regi'mɛnt], *n.* (—s, *pl.* —e) rule, government.

Regiment (2) [regi'mɛnt], *n.* (—s, *pl.* —er) (*Mil.*) regiment.

Regisseur [reʒi'sø:r], *m.* (—s, *pl.* —e) stage-manager, producer, director.

Registrator [regɪs'tra:tɔr], *m.* (—s, *pl.* —en) registrar, recorder; registering machine.

Registratur [regɪstra'tu:r], *f.* (—, *pl.* —en) record office, registry; filing-cabinet.

registrieren [regɪs'tri:rən], *v.a.* register, record, file.

reglos ['re:klo:s], *adj.* motionless.

regnen ['re:gnən], *v.n.* rain; *es regnet in Strömen*, it is raining cats and dogs.

Regreß [re'grɛs], *m.* (—sses, *pl.* —sse) recourse, remedy.

regsam ['re:kza:m], *adj.* quick, alert, lively.

regulieren [regu'li:rən], *v.a.* regulate.

Regung ['re:guŋ], *f.* (—, *pl.* —en) movement; impulse.

Reh [re:], *n.* (—(e)s, *pl.* —e) doe, roe.

rehabilitieren [rehabili'ti:rən], *v.a.* rehabilitate.

Rehbock ['re:bɔk], *m.* (—s, *pl.* ⸚e) (*Zool.*) roe-buck.

Rehkeule ['re:kɔylə], *f.* (—, *pl.* —n) haunch of venison.

reiben ['raɪbən], *v.a. irr.* rub, grate, grind; *einem etwas unter die Nase* —, throw s.th. in s.o.'s teeth, bring s.th. home to s.o.

Reibung ['raɪbuŋ], *f.* (—, *pl.* —en) friction.

Reich [raɪç], *n.* (—(e)s, *pl.* —e) kingdom, realm, empire, state.

reich [raɪç], *adj.* rich, wealthy, opulent.

reichen ['raɪçən], *v.a.* reach, pass, hand; *einem die Hand* —, shake hands with s.o. — *v.n.* reach, extend; be sufficient.

reichhaltig ['raɪçhaltɪç], *adj.* abundant, copious.

reichlich ['raɪçlɪç], *adj.* ample, plentiful.

Reichskammergericht [raɪçs'kamərgərɪçt], *n.* (—s, *no pl.*) Imperial High Court of Justice (*Holy Roman Empire*).

Reichskanzlei ['raɪçskantslaɪ], *f.* (—, *pl.* —en) (Imperial) Chancery.

Reichskanzler ['raɪçskantslər], *m.* (—s, *pl.* —) (Imperial) Chancellor.

Reichsstände ['raɪçsʃtɛndə], *m. pl.* Estates (of the Holy Roman Empire).

Reichstag ['raɪçsta:k], *m.* (—s, *pl.* —e) Imperial Parliament, Reichstag, Diet.

Reichtum ['raiçtu:m], *m.* (—s, *pl.* ꞏer) riches, wealth, opulence.

Reif (1) [raif], *m.* (—s, *no pl.*) hoarfrost.

Reif (2) [raif], *m.* (—s, *pl.* —e) ring.

reif [raif], *adj.* ripe, mature.

Reifen ['raifən], *m.* (—s, *pl.* —) hoop; tyre; — *schlagen*, trundle a hoop.

reifen ['raifən], *v.n.* (*aux.* sein) ripen, mature, grow ripe.

Reifeprüfung ['raifəpry:fuŋ], *f.* (—, *pl.* —en) matriculation examination.

reiflich ['raiflıç], *adj. sich etwas — überlegen*, give careful consideration to s.th.

Reigen ['raigən], *m.* (—s, *pl.* —) round-dance, roundelay.

Reihe ['raiə], *f.* (—, *pl.* —n) series; file; row; progression, sequence; (*Theat.*) tier; *in — und Glied*, in closed ranks; *nach der —*, in turns; *ich bin an der —*, it is my turn.

Reihenfolge ['raiənfɔlgə], *f.* (—, *no pl.*) succession.

Reiher ['raiər], *m.* (—s, *pl.* —) (*Orn.*) heron.

Reim [raim], *m.* (—(e)s, *pl.* —e) rhyme.

rein [rain], *adj.* clean, pure, clear, neat; —*e Wahrheit*, plain truth; *ins —e bringen*, settle, clear up; *ins —e schreiben*, make a fair copy of; *einem —en Wein einschenken*, have a straight talk with s.o.

Reineke ['rainəkə], *m.* (—, *no pl.*) — *Fuchs*, Reynard the Fox.

Reinertrag ['rainɛrtra:k], *m.* (—(e)s, *pl.* ꞏe) net proceeds.

Reinfall ['rainfal], *m.* (—s, *pl.* ꞏe) sell, wild-goose chase; disappointment.

reinfallen ['rainfalən], *v.n. irr.* (*aux.* sein) be unsuccessful.

Reingewinn ['raingəvin], *m.* (—s, *pl.* —e) net proceeds.

Reinheit ['rainhait], *f.* (—, *no pl.*) purity.

reinigen ['rainıgən], *v.a.* clean, cleanse; dry-clean; purge.

Reinigung ['rainıguŋ], *f.* (—, *pl.* —en) cleaning; (*fig.*) purification, cleansing; *chemische —*, dry-cleaning.

reinlich ['rainlıç], *adj.* clean, neat.

Reis (1) [rais], *m.* (—es, *no pl.*) rice.

Reis (2) [rais], *n.* (—es, *pl.* —er) twig, sprig; scion; cutting.

Reisbesen ['raisbe:zən], *m.* (—s, *pl.* —) birch-broom, besom.

Reise ['raizə], *f.* (—, *pl.* —n) tour, trip, journey, travels; voyage; *gute —! bon voyage!*

reisefertig ['raizəfɛrtıç], *adj.* ready to start.

Reisegeld ['raizəgɛlt], *n.* (—es, *pl.* —er) travel allowance.

reisen ['raizən], *v.n.* (*aux.* sein) travel, tour, journey, take a trip.

Reisende ['raizəndə], *m.* (—n, *pl.* —n) traveller; commercial traveller.

Reisig ['raizıç], *n.* (—s, *no pl.*) brushwood.

Reisige ['raizıgə], *m.* (—n, *pl.* —n) (*obs.*) trooper, horseman.

Reißaus [rais'aus], *n.* (—, *no pl.*) — *nehmen*, take to o.'s heels.

Reißbrett ['raisbrɛt], *n.* (—es, *pl.* —er) drawing-board.

reißen ['raisən], *v.a. irr.* tear; rend; pull; snatch; *etwas an sich —*, seize s.th., usurp.

reißend ['raisənt], *adj.* rapid; ravening; carnivorous; (*Comm.*) brisk, rapid (sales).

Reißnagel ['raisna:gəl], *m. see* **Reißzwecke**.

Reißschiene ['raisʃi:nə], *f.* (—, *pl.* —n) T-square.

Reißverschluß ['raisfɛrʃlus], *m.* (—sses, *pl.* ꞏsse) zip-fastener.

Reißzwecke ['raistsvɛkə], *f.* (—, *pl.* —n) drawing-pin.

reiten ['raitən], *v.a. irr.* ride (a horse). — *v.n.* (*aux.* sein) ride, go on horseback.

Reiterei [raitə'rai], *f.* (—, *pl.* —en) cavalry.

Reitknecht ['raitknɛçt], *m.* (—es, *pl.* —e) groom.

Reiz [raits], *m.* (—es, *pl.* —e) charm, attraction, fascination, allure; stimulus; irritation; (*Phys.*) impulse.

reizbar ['raitsba:r], *adj.* susceptible; irritable.

reizen ['raitsən], *v.a.* irritate; stimulate, charm, entice.

reizend ['raitsənt], *adj.* charming.

Reizmittel ['raitsmitəl], *n.* (—s, *pl.* —) stimulant; irritant.

rekeln ['re:kəln], *v.r.* (*dial.*) *sich —*, loll about.

Reklame [re'kla:mə], *f.* (—, *pl.* —n) propaganda, advertisement, advertising, publicity.

reklamieren [rekla'mi:rən], *v.a.* claim, reclaim. — *v.n.* complain.

rekognoszieren [rekɔgnɔs'tsi:rən], *v.a.* reconnoitre.

rekommandieren [rekɔman'di:rən], *v.a.* (*Austr.*) register (a letter).

Rekonvaleszent [rekɔnvalɛs'tsɛnt], *m.* (—en, *pl.* —en) convalescent.

Rekrut [re'kru:t], *m.* (—en, *pl.* —en) recruit.

rekrutieren [rekru'ti:rən], *v.a.* recruit. — *v.r. sich — aus*, be recruited from.

rektifizieren [rɛktifi'tsi:rən], *v.a.* rectify.

Rektor ['rɛktɔr], *m.* (—s, *pl.* —en) (school) principal; (*Univ.*) president.

Rektorat [rɛktoʹra:t], *n.* (—es, *pl.* —e) rectorship, presidency.

relativ [rela'ti:f], *adj.* relative, comparative.

relegieren [rele'gi:rən], *v.a.* expel; (*Univ.*) send down, rusticate.

Relief [rɛl'jɛf], *n.* (—s, *pl.* —s) (*Art*) relief.

religiös [reli'gjø:s], *adj.* religious.

Reliquie [re'li:kvjə], *f.* (—, *pl.* —n) (*Rel.*) relic.

Remise [re′mi:zə], *f.* (—, *pl.* —n) coach-house.

Remittent [remɪ′tɛnt], *m.* (—en, *pl.* —en) remitter.

Renegat [rene′ga:t], *m.* (—en, *pl.* —en) renegade.

Renette [rɛ′netə], *f.* (—, *pl.* —n) rennet(-apple).

renken [′rɛŋkən], *v.a.* wrench, bend, twist.

Rennbahn [′rɛnba:n], *f.* (—, *pl.* —en) race-course; (cinder)-track; (*Motor.*) racing-circuit.

rennen [′rɛnən], *v.n. irr.* (*aux.* sein) run, race, rush.

Renommé [reno′me:], *n.* (—s, *no pl.*) renown, repute, reputation.

renommieren [reno′mi:rən], *v.n.* brag, boast.

renovieren [reno′vi:rən], *v.a.* renovate, restore, redecorate, renew.

rentabel [rɛn′ta:bəl], *adj.* profitable, lucrative.

Rente [′rɛntə], *f.* (—, *pl.* —n) pension, annuity.

Rentier [rɛn′tje:], *m.* (—s, *pl.* —s) rentier, person of independent means.

rentieren [rɛn′ti:rən], *v.r. sich* —, be profitable, be worthwhile, pay.

Rentner [′rɛntnər], *m.* (—s, *pl.* —) pensioner.

Reparatur [repara′tu:r], *f.* (—, *pl.* —en) repair.

reparieren [repa′ri:rən], *v.a.* repair.

Repräsentant [reprɛzɛn′tant], *m.* (—en, *pl.* —en) representative.

Repräsentantenkammer [reprɛzɛn-′tantənkamər], *f.* (—, *pl.* —n) (*Am.*) House of Representatives.

Repressalien [reprɛ′sa:ljən], *f. pl.* reprisals, retaliation.

reproduzieren [reprodu′tsi:rən], *v.a.* reproduce.

Republikaner [republi′ka:nər], *m.* (—s, *pl.* —) republican.

requirieren [rekvi′ri:rən], *v.a.* requisition.

Reseda [re′ze:da], *f.* (—, *pl.* —s) (*Bot.*) mignonette.

Reservat [rezɛr′va:t], *n.* (—es, *pl.* —e) reservation, reserve.

Residenz [rezi′dɛnts], *f.* (—, *pl.* —en) residence, seat of the Court.

residieren [rezi′di:rən], *v.n.* reside.

Residuum [re′zi:duum], *n.* (—s, *pl.* —duen) residue, dregs.

resignieren [rezig′ni:rən], *v.n.*, *v.r.* resign; be resigned (to s.th.); give up.

Respekt [re′spɛkt], *m.* (—es, *no pl.*) respect, regard; *mit — zu sagen*, with all due respect.

respektieren [respɛk′ti:rən], *v.a.* respect, honour.

Ressort [rɛ′so:r], *n.* (—s, *pl.* —s) department, domain.

Rest [rɛst], *m.* (—es, *pl.* —e) rest, residue, remainder; remnant; (*money*) balance.

restaurieren [rɛsto′ri:rən], *v.a.* restore, renovate.

Resultat [rezul′ta:t], *n.* (—es, *pl.* —e) result, outcome.

Resümee [rezy′me:], *n.* (—s, *pl.* —s) résumé, précis, digest, summary, synopsis, abstract.

retten [′rɛtən], *v.a.* save, preserve; rescue, deliver; *die Ehre —*, vindicate o.'s honour.

Rettich [′rɛtiç], *m.* (—s, *pl.* —e) radish.

Rettung [′rɛtuŋ], *f.* (—, *pl.* —en) saving, rescue, deliverance.

retuschieren [retu′ʃi:rən], *v.a.* retouch.

Reue [′rɔyə], *f.* (—, *no pl.*) repentance, remorse, contrition.

reuen [′rɔyən], *v.a.*, *v.n.* repent, regret; *es reut mich*, I am sorry.

Reugeld [′rɔygɛlt], *n.* (—es, *pl.* —er) forfeit-money, penalty.

reüssieren [rey′si:rən], *v.n.* succeed.

Revanche [re′vã:ʃə], *f.* (—, *pl.* —n) revenge; (*fig.*) return.

revanchieren [revã′ʃi:rən], *v.r. sich* —, repay a service, have *or* take o.'s revenge.

Reverenz [reve′rɛnts], *f.* (—, *pl.* —en) bow, curtsy.

revidieren [revi′di:rən], *v.a.* revise, check.

Revier [re′vi:r], *n.* (—s, *pl.* —e) district, precinct, quarter; preserve.

Revisor [re′vi:zor], *m.* (—s, *pl.* —en) accountant, auditor.

revoltieren [revɔl′ti:rən], *v.n.* rise, revolt.

revolutionieren [revolutsjo′ni:rən], *v.a.* revolutionise.

Revolverblatt [re′vɔlvərblat], *n.* (—s, *pl. -*er) gutter press.

Revue [re′vy:], *f.* (—, *pl.* —n) revue; review; *— passieren lassen*, pass in review.

Rezensent [retsɛn′zɛnt], *m.* (—en, *pl.* —en) reviewer, critic.

rezensieren [retsɛn′zi:rən], *v.a.* review.

Rezept [re′tsɛpt], *n.* (—es, *pl.* —e) (*Med.*) prescription; (*Cul.*) recipe.

rezitieren [retsi′ti:rən], *v.a.* recite.

Rhabarber [ra′barbər], *m.* (—s, *no pl.*) (*Bot.*) rhubarb.

Rhein [rain], *m.* (—s, *no pl.*) (*River*) Rhine.

Rhodesien [ro′de:zjən], *n.* Rhodesia.

Rhodus [′ro:dus], *n.* Rhodes.

Rhythmus [′rytmus], *m.* (—, *pl.* —men) rhythm.

Richtbeil [′riçtbail], *n.* (—s, *pl.* —e) executioner's axe.

richten [′riçtən], *v.a.*, *v.n.* direct, point at; prepare; *die Augen — auf*, fix o.'s eyes upon; *einen zugrunde —*, ruin s.o.; judge, try, pass sentence on, condemn. *—v.r. sich nach* (*Dat.*) —, be guided by.

Richter [′riçtər], *m.* (—s, *pl.* —) judge; justice.

richtig [′riçtiç], *adj.* right, correct, exact, true; *nicht ganz — sein*, be not quite right in the head.

Richtlot [ˈrɪçtloːt], n. (—s, pl. —e) plumb-line.

Richtschnur [ˈrɪçtʃnuːr], f. (—, pl. —en) plumb-line; (fig.) rule, precept.

Richtung [ˈrɪçtuŋ], f. (—, pl. —en) direction.

riechen [ˈriːçən], v.a., v.n. irr. smell, scent, reek; Lunte —, smell a rat.

Riege [ˈriːgə], f. (—, pl. —n) row, section.

Riegel [ˈriːgəl], m. (—s, pl. —) bar, bolt; ein — Schokolade, a bar of chocolate.

Riemen [ˈriːmən], m. (—s, pl. —) strap, thong; oar.

Ries [riːs], n. (—es, pl. —e) (paper) ream.

Riese [ˈriːzə], m. (—n, pl. —n) giant.

rieseln [ˈriːzəln], v.n. murmur, babble, ripple, trickle; drizzle.

Riesenschlange [ˈriːzənʃlaŋə], f. (—, pl. —n) anaconda.

Riff [rɪf], n. (—es, pl. —e) reef.

rigoros [rigoˈroːs], adj. strict, rigorous.

Rille [ˈrɪlə], f. (—, pl. —n) groove, small furrow; (Archit.) flute, chamfer.

Rind [rɪnt], n. (—es, pl. —er) ox, cow; (pl.) cattle, horned cattle, head of cattle.

Rinde [ˈrɪndə], f. (—, pl. —n) rind, bark, peel; (bread) crust.

Rinderbraten [ˈrɪndərbraːtən], m. (—s, pl. —) roast beef.

Rindfleisch [ˈrɪntflaɪʃ], n. (—es, no pl.) beef.

Rindvieh [ˈrɪntfiː], n. (—s, no pl.) cattle; (fig.) blockhead, ass.

Ring [rɪŋ], m. (—(e)s, pl. —e) ring; (chain) link; (under the eye) dark circle; (Comm.) syndicate, trust.

Ringelblume [ˈrɪŋəlbluːmə], f. (—, pl. —n) (Bot.) marigold.

ringeln [ˈrɪŋəln], v.r. sich —, curl.

ringen [ˈrɪŋən], v.a. irr. wring. — v.n. wrestle.

Ringer [ˈrɪŋər], m. (—s, pl. —) wrestler.

Ringmauer [ˈrɪŋmauər], f. (—, pl. —n) city or town wall.

rings [rɪŋs], adv. around.

ringsum(her) [rɪŋˈsʊm(heːr)], adv. round about.

Rinne [ˈrɪnə], f. (—, pl. —n) furrow, gutter; groove.

rinnen [ˈrɪnən], v.n. irr. (aux, sein) run, leak, drip.

Rinnsal [ˈrɪnzaːl], n. (—s, pl. —e) channel, water-course.

Rinnstein [ˈrɪnʃtaɪn], m. (—s, pl. —e) gutter.

Rippe [ˈrɪpə], f. (—, pl. —n) rib.

Rippenfellentzündung [ˈrɪpənfɛlɛntsʏnduŋ], f. (—, pl. —en) pleurisy.

Rippenspeer [ˈrɪpənʃpeːr], m. (—s, pl. —e) (Casseler) —, spare-rib, ribs of pork.

Rippenstoß [ˈrɪpənʃtoːs], m. (—es, pl. ⸚e) dig in the ribs, nudge.

Rips [rɪps], m. (—es, no pl.) rep.

Risiko [ˈriːziko], n. (—s, pl. —ken) risk.

riskant [rɪsˈkant], adj. risky.

riskieren [rɪsˈkiːrən], v.a. risk.

Riß [rɪs], m. (—sses, pl. —sse) rent, tear; sketch, design, plan.

rissig [ˈrɪsɪç], adj. cracked, torn.

Ritt [rɪt], m. (—(e)s, pl. —e) ride.

Ritter [ˈrɪtər], m. (—s, pl. —) knight; einen zum — schlagen, dub s.o. a knight.

ritterlich [ˈrɪtərlɪç], adj. knightly; (fig.) chivalrous, valiant, gallant.

Ritterschlag [ˈrɪtərʃlaːk], m. (—(e)s, pl. ⸚e) accolade.

Rittersporn [ˈrɪtərʃporn], m. (—s, pl. —e) (Bot.) larkspur.

rittlings [ˈrɪtlɪŋs], adv. astride.

Rittmeister [ˈrɪtmaɪstər], m. (—s, pl. —) captain (of cavalry).

Ritus [ˈriːtus], m. (—, pl. Riten) rite.

Ritz [rɪts], m. (—es, pl. —e) chink, fissure, cleft, crevice; (glacier) crevasse.

ritzen [ˈrɪtsən], v.a. scratch.

Rivale [riˈvaːlə], m. (—n, pl. —n) rival.

Rivalität [rivaliˈtɛːt], f. (—, pl. —en) rivalry.

Rizinusöl [ˈriːtsinusøːl], n. (—s, no pl.) castor oil.

Robbe [ˈrɔbə], f. (—, pl. —n) (Zool.) seal.

Robe [ˈroːbə], f. (—, pl. —n) dress, robe; gown.

röcheln [ˈrœçəln], v.n. rattle in o.'s throat.

rochieren [rɔˈxiːrən], v.n. (Chess) castle.

Rock [rɔk], m. (—(e)s, pl. ⸚e) (woman) skirt; (man) coat.

rodeln [ˈroːdəln], v.n. (aux. haben & sein) toboggan.

roden [ˈroːdən], v.a. clear, weed, thin out (plants).

Rogen [ˈroːgən], m. (—s, no pl.) (fish) roe, spawn.

Roggen [ˈrɔgən], m. (—s, no pl.) rye.

roh [roː], adj. raw; rough, rude, coarse, crude; ein —er Mensch, a brute; (in compounds) rough-; preliminary, unrefined.

Rohbilanz [ˈroːbilants], f. (—, pl. —en) trial balance.

Roheisen [ˈroːaɪzən], n. (—s, no pl.) pig-iron.

Roheit [ˈroːhaɪt], f. (—, pl. —en) coarseness, rudeness, crudity.

Rohr [roːr], n. (—es, pl. —e, ⸚er) tube, pipe; reed, cane; (gun) barrel.

Rohrdommel [ˈroːrdɔməl], f. (—, pl. —n) (Orn.) bittern.

Röhre [ˈrøːrə], f. (—, pl. —n) tube, pipe; (Radio) valve.

Röhricht [ˈrøːrɪçt], n. (—s, pl. —e) reeds.

Rohrpfeife [ˈroːrpfaɪfə], f. (—, pl. —n) reed-pipe.

Rohrpost [ˈroːrpɔst], f. (—, no pl.) pneumatic post.

Rohrzucker [ˈroːrtsukər], m. (—s, no pl.) cane-sugar.

Rolladen ['rɔladən], *m.* (—s, *pl.* ·:) sliding shutter, roller blind.

Rollbahn ['rɔlba:n], *f.* (—, *pl.* —en) (*Aviat.*) runway.

Rolle ['rɔlə], *f.* (—, *pl.* —n) reel, roll; pulley; (*Theat.*) part; rôle; (*laundry*) mangle.

rollen ['rɔlən], *v.a.* roll, reel; (*laundry*) mangle. — *v.n.* (*aux.* sein) roll (along); (*thunder*) roar, roll.

Roller ['rɔlər], *m.* (—s, *pl.* —) scooter.

Rollmops ['rɔlmɔps], *m.* (—es, *pl.* ·:e) soused herring.

Rollschuh ['rɔlʃu:], *m.* (—s, *pl.* —e) roller-skate.

Rollstuhl ['rɔlʃtu:l], *m.* (—s, *pl.* ·:e) wheel-chair, bath-chair.

Rolltreppe ['rɔltrepə], *f.* (—, *pl.* —n) escalator, moving staircase.

Rom [ro:m], *n.* Rome.

Roman [ro'ma:n], *m.* (—s, *pl.* —e) novel.

romanisch [ro'ma:nɪʃ], *adj.* Romanesque.

Romanliteratur [ro'ma:nlitəratu:r], *f.* (—, *no pl.*) fiction.

Romanschriftsteller [ro'ma:nʃrɪftʃtɛlər], *m.* (—s, *pl.* —) novelist.

Römer ['røːmər], *m.* (—s, *pl.* —) Roman; (*glass*) rummer.

Rondell [rɔn'del], *n.* (—s, *pl.* —e) circular flower-bed.

Röntgenstrahlen ['rœntgənʃtra:lən], *m. pl.* X-rays.

rosa ['ro:za:], *adj.* pink, rose-coloured.

Rose ['ro:zə], *f.* (—, *pl.* —n) rose.

Rosenkranz ['ro:zənkrants], *m.* (—es, *pl.* ·:e) garland of roses; (*Eccl.*) rosary.

Rosenkreuzer ['ro:zənkrɔytsər], *m.* (—s, *pl.* —) Rosicrucian.

Rosine [ro'zi:nə], *f.* (—, *pl.* —n) sultana, raisin.

Rosmarin ['rɔsmari:n], *m.* (—s, *no pl.*) (*Bot.*) rosemary.

Roß [rɔs], *n.* (—sses, *pl.* —sse) horse, steed.

Roßbremse ['rɔsbremzə], *f.* (—, *pl.* —n) (*Ent.*) horsefly, gadfly.

Rössel ['røsəl], *n.* (—s, *pl.* —) (*Chess*) knight.

Roßhaarmatratze ['rɔsha:rmatratsə], *f.* (—, *pl.* —n) hair-mattress.

Roßkastanie ['rɔskasta:njə], *f.* (—, *pl.* —n) (*Bot.*) horse-chestnut.

Rost (1) [rɔst], *m.* (—es, *no pl.*) rust.

Rost (2) [rɔst], *m.* (—s, *pl.* —e) grate; gridiron.

Rostbraten ['rɔstbra:tən], *m.* (—s, *pl.* —) roast meat.

rosten ['rɔstən], *v.n.* go rusty; rust; *alte Liebe rostet nicht,* love that's old rusts not away.

rösten ['røːstən], *v.a.* toast, roast, grill.

rot [ro:t], *adj.* red; — *werden,* redden, blush.

Rotauge ['ro:taugə], *n.* (—s, *pl.* —n) (*Zool.*) roach.

Röte ['røːtə], *f.* (—, *no pl.*) redness, red colour.

Röteln ['røːtəln], *m. pl.* (*Med.*) German measles, rubella.

Rotfink ['ro:tfɪŋk], *m.* (—en, *pl.* —en) (*Orn.*) bullfinch.

Rotfuchs ['ro:tfuks], *m.* (—es, *pl.* ·:e) (*Zool.*) sorrel horse.

rotieren [ro'ti:rən], *v.n.* rotate.

Rotkäppchen ['ro:tkepçən], *n.* Little Red Riding Hood.

Rotkehlchen ['ro:tke:lçən], *n.* (—s, *pl.* —) robin.

Rotlauf ['ro:tlauf], *m.* (—s, *no pl.*) (*Med.*) erysipelas.

Rotschimmel ['ro:tʃɪməl], *m.* (—s, *pl.* —) roan-horse.

Rotspon ['ro:tʃpo:n], *m.* (—s, *no pl.*) (*dial.*) claret.

Rotte ['rɔtə], *f.* (—, *pl.* —n) band, gang, rabble; (*Mil.*) file, squad.

Rotwild ['ro:tvɪlt], *n.* (—s, *no pl.*) red deer.

Rotz [rɔts], *m.* (—es, *no pl.*) (*vulg.*) mucus; snot.

Rouleau [ru'lo:], *n.* (—s, *pl.* —s) sun-blind, roller-blind.

routiniert [ruti'ni:rt], *adj.* smart; experienced.

Rübe ['ry:bə], *f.* (—, *pl.* —n) (*Bot.*) turnip; *rote* —, beetroot; *gelbe* —, carrot.

Rubel ['ru:bəl], *m.* (—s, *pl.* —) rouble.

Rübenzucker ['ry:bəntsukər], *m.* (—s, *no pl.*) beet-sugar.

Rubin [ru'bi:n], *m.* (—s, *pl.* —e) ruby.

Rubrik [ru'bri:k], *f.* (—, *pl.* —en) rubric; title, heading, category, column.

Rübsamen ['ry:pza:mən], *m.* (—s, *no pl.*) rape-seed.

ruchbar ['ru:xba:r], *adj.* manifest, known, notorious.

ruchlos ['ru:xlo:s], *adj.* wicked, profligate, vicious.

Ruck [ruk], *m.* (—(e)s, *pl.* —e) pull, jolt, jerk.

Rückblick ['rykblik], *m.* (—s, *pl.* —e) retrospect, retrospective view.

Rücken ['rykən], *m.* (—s, *pl.* —) back; (*mountains*) ridge; *einem den* — *kehren,* turn o.'s back upon s.o.

rücken ['rykən], *v.a.* move, push. — *v.n.* move along.

Rückenmark ['rykənmark], *n.* (—s, *no pl.*) spinal marrow.

Rückenwirbel ['rykənvɪrbəl], *m.* (—s, *pl.* —) dorsal vertebra.

rückerstatten ['rykərʃtatən], *v.a.* refund.

Rückfahrkarte ['rykfa:rkartə], *f.* (—, *pl.* —n) return ticket.

Rückfall ['rykfal], *m.* (—s, *pl.* ·:e) relapse.

rückgängig ['rykgɛŋɪç], *adj.* — *machen,* cancel, annul, reverse (a decision).

Rückgrat ['rykgra:t], *n.* (—(e)s, *pl.* —e) backbone, spine.

Rückhalt ['rykhalt], *m.* (—s, *no pl.*) reserve; support, backing.

Rückkehr ['rykke:r], *f.* (—, *no pl.*) return.

Rücklicht ['ryklıçt], *n.* (—s, *pl.* —er) (*Motor. etc.*) tail-light.

rücklings ['ryklıŋks], *adv.* from behind.

Rucksack ['rukzak], *m.* (—s, *pl.* ⸚e) rucksack; knapsack.

Rückschritt ['rykʃrıt], *m.* (—es, *pl.* —e) step backward, retrograde step, regression.

Rücksicht ['rykzıçt], *f.* (—, *pl.* —en) consideration, regard.

Rücksprache ['rykʃpra:xə], *f.* (—, *pl.* —n) conference, consultation; — *nehmen mit*, consult, confer with.

rückständig ['rykʃtɛndıç], *adj.* outstanding; old-fashioned; backward.

Rücktritt ['ryktrıt], *m.* (—s, *no pl.*) resignation.

ruckweise ['rukvaızə], *adv.* by fits and starts; jerkily.

Rückwirkung ['rykvırkuŋ], *f.* (—, *pl.* —en) reaction, retroaction.

Rüde ['ry:də], *m.* (—n, *pl.* —n) male (dog, fox etc.).

Rudel ['ru:dəl], *n.* (—s, *pl.* —) flock, herd, pack.

Ruder ['ru:dər], *n.* (—s, *pl.* —) oar, rudder, paddle; *am — sein*, be at the helm; (*Pol.*) be in power.

rudern ['ru:dərn], *v.a., v.n.* row.

Ruf [ru:f], *m.* (—(e)s, *pl.* —e) call; shout; reputation, renown; *einen guten (schlechten) — haben*, have a good (bad) reputation, be well (ill) spoken of.

rufen ['ru:fən], *v.a., v.n. irr.* call, shout; *einen — lassen*, send for s.o.

Rüffel ['ryfəl], *m.* (—s, *pl.* —) (*coll.*) reprimand; (*sl.*) rocket.

Rüge ['ry:gə], *f.* (—, *pl.* —n) censure, blame, reprimand.

Ruhe ['ru:ə], *f.* (—, *no pl.*) rest, repose; quiet, tranquillity; *sich zur — setzen*, retire (from business etc.).

Ruhegehalt ['ru:əgəhalt], *n.* (—es, *pl.* ⸚er) retirement pension, superannuation.

ruhen ['ru:ən], *v.n.* rest, repose, take a rest.

Ruhestand ['ru:əʃtant], *m.* (—es, *no pl.*) retirement.

ruhig ['ru:ıç], *adj.* quiet, tranquil, peaceful, calm; *sich — verhalten*, keep quiet.

Ruhm [ru:m], *m.* (—(e)s, *no pl.*) glory, fame, renown; *einem zum — gereichen*, be *or* redound to s.o.'s credit.

rühmen ['ry:mən], *v.a.* praise, extol, glorify. — *v.r. sich —*, boast.

Ruhr (1) [ru:r], *f.* (River) Ruhr.

Ruhr (2) [ru:r], *f.* (—, *no pl.*) dysentery.

Rührei ['ry:raı], *n.* (—s, *pl.* —er) scrambled egg.

rühren ['ry:rən], *v.a.* stir, move, touch. — *v.r. sich —*, move, stir; get a move on.

rührig ['ry:rıç], *adj.* active, alert.

rührselig ['ry:rze:lıç], *adj.* oversentimental; lachrymose.

Rührung ['ry:ruŋ], *f.* (—, *no pl.*) emotion.

Ruin [ru'i:n], *m.* (—s, *no pl.*) (*fig.*) ruin; decay; bankruptcy.

Ruine [ru'i:nə], *f.* (—, *pl.* —n) ruin(s).

rülpsen ['rylpsən], *v.n.* belch.

Rum [rum], *m.* (—s, *no pl.*) rum.

Rumänien [ru'mɛ:njən], *n.* Rumania.

Rummel ['ruməl], *m.* (—s, *no pl.*) tumult, row, hubbub.

Rumor [ru'mo:r], *m.* (—s, *no pl.*) noise; rumour.

rumoren [ru'mo:rən], *v.n.* make a noise.

Rumpelkammer ['rumpəlkamər], *f.* (—, *pl.* —n) lumber-room, junkroom.

rumpeln ['rumpəln], *v.n.* rumble.

Rumpf [rumpf], *m.* (—(e)s, *pl.* ⸚e) (*Anat.*) trunk; (*ship*) hull; (*Aviat.*) fuselage.

rümpfen ['rympfən], *v.a. die Nase —*, turn up o.'s nose.

rund [runt], *adj.* round, rotund; — *heraus*, flatly; *etwas — abschlagen*, refuse s.th. flatly; — *herum*, round about.

Runde ['rundə], *f.* (—, *pl.* —n) round; (*Sport*) round, bout; *die — machen*, (*watchman*) patrol.

Rundfunk ['runtfuŋk], *m.* (—s, *no pl.*) broadcasting, wireless; radio.

Rundgang ['runtgaŋ], *m.* (—s, *pl.* ⸚e) round, tour (of inspection).

rundlich ['runtlıç], *adj.* plump.

Rundschau ['runtʃau], *f.* (—, *no pl.*) panorama; review, survey.

Rundschreiben ['runtʃraıbən], *n.* (—s, *pl.* —) circular letter.

rundweg ['runtve:k], *adv.* flatly, plainly.

Rune ['ru:nə], *f.* (—, *pl.* —n) rune; runic writing.

Runkelrübe ['ruŋkəlry:bə], *f.* (—, *pl.* —n) beetroot.

Runzel ['runtsəl], *f.* (—, *pl.* —n) wrinkle, pucker.

Rüpel ['ry:pəl], *m.* (—s, *pl.* —) bounder, lout.

rupfen ['rupfən], *v.a.* pluck; *einen —*, (*fig.*) fleece s.o.

Rupie ['ru:pjə], *f.* (—, *pl.* —n) rupee.

ruppig ['rupıç], *adj.* unfriendly, rude; scruffy.

Ruprecht ['ru:prɛçt], *m. Knecht —*, Santa Claus.

Rüsche ['ry:ʃə], *f.* (—, *pl.* —n) ruche.

Ruß [ru:s], *m.* (—es, *no pl.*) soot.

Rüssel ['rysəl], *m.* (—s, *pl.* —) snout; (*elephant*) trunk.

Rußland ['ruslant], *n.* Russia.

rüsten ['rystən], *v.a.* prepare, fit (out); equip; (*Mil.*) arm, mobilise.

Rüster ['rystər], *f.* (—, *pl.* —n) elm.

rüstig ['rystıç], *adj.* vigorous, robust.

Rüstung ['rystuŋ], *f.* (—, *pl.* —en) armour; preparation; (*Mil.*) armament.

Rüstzeug ['rysttsɔyk], *n.* (—s, *no pl.*) equipment.

Rute ['ruːtə], *f.* (—, *pl.* —n) rod, twig; (*fox*) brush.

Rutengänger ['ruːtəŋɛŋər], *m.* (—s, *pl.* —) water-diviner.

rutschen ['rutʃən], *v.n.* (*aux.* sein) slip, slide, skid, slither.

rütteln ['rytəln], *v.a., v.n.* shake, jolt.

S

S [ɛs], *n.* (—s, *pl.* —s) the letter S.

Saal [zaːl], *m.* (—(e)s, *pl.* Säle) hall, large room.

Saat [zaːt], *f.* (—, *pl.* —en) seed; sowing; standing corn.

Sabbat ['zabat], *m.* (—s, *pl.* —e) sabbath.

sabbern ['zabərn], *v.n.* (*sl.*) slaver, drivel.

Säbel ['zɛːbəl], *m.* (—s, *pl.* —) sabre; *krummer* —, falchion, scimitar.

säbeln ['zɛːbəln], *v.a.* sabre, hack at.

sachdienlich ['zaxdiːnlɪç], *adj.* relevant, pertinent.

Sache ['zaxə], *f.* (—, *pl.* —n) thing, matter, affair; (*Law*) action, case; *die* — *ist* (*die*) *daß*, the fact is that; *das gehört nicht zur* —, that is beside the point; *bei der* — *sein*, pay attention to the matter in hand; *das ist meine* —, that is my business; *die* — *der Unterdrückten verteidigen*, take up the cause of the oppressed.

Sachlage ['zaxlaːgə], *f.* (—, *no pl.*) state of affairs.

sachlich ['zaxlɪç], *adj.* pertinent; objective.

sächlich ['zɛçlɪç], *adj.* (*Gram.*) neuter.

Sachse ['zaksə], *m.* (—n, *pl.* —n) Saxon.

Sachsen ['zaksən], *n.* Saxony.

sachte ['zaxtə], *adj.* soft, slow, quiet, careful, gentle.

Sachverhalt ['zaxfɛrhalt], *m.* (—s, *no pl.*) facts (of a case), state of things, circumstances.

sachverständig ['zaxfɛrʃtɛndɪç], *adj.* expert, competent, experienced.

Sachwalter ['zaxvaltər], *m.* (—s, *pl.* —) manager, counsel, attorney.

Sack [zak], *m.* (—(e)s, *pl.* ⸚e) sack, bag; *mit* — *und Pack*, (with) bag and baggage.

Säckel ['zɛkəl], *m.* (—s, *pl.* —) purse.

Sackgasse ['zakgasə], *f.* (—, *pl.* —n) cul-de-sac, blind alley; *einen in eine* — *treiben*, corner s.o.

Sackpfeife ['zakpfaıfə], *f.* (—, *pl.* —n) bagpipe.

Sacktuch ['zaktuːx], *n.* (—es, *pl.* ⸚er) sacking; (*dial.*) pocket-handkerchief.

säen ['zɛːən], *v.a.* sow.

Saffian ['zafjaːn], *m.* (—s, *no pl.*) morocco-leather.

Saft [zaft], *m.* (—(e)s, *pl.* ⸚e) juice; (*tree*) sap; (*meat*) gravy; *ohne* — *und Kraft*, insipid; *im eigenen* — *schmoren*, stew in o.'s own juice.

Sage ['zaːgə], *f.* (—, *pl.* —n) legend, fable, myth; *es geht die* —, it is rumoured.

Säge ['zɛːgə], *f.* (—, *pl.* —n) saw.

sagen ['zaːgən], *v.a.* say, tell; *einem etwas* — *lassen*, send word to s.o.; *es hat nichts zu* —, it does not matter; *was Du nicht sagst!* you don't say (so)!

sägen ['zɛːgən], *v.a., v.n.* saw; (*fig.*) snore.

sagenhaft ['zaːgənhaft], *adj.* legendary, mythical; (*fig.*) fabulous.

Sahne ['zaːnə], *f.* (—, *no pl.*) cream.

Saite ['zaıtə], *f.* (—, *pl.* —n) string; *strengere* —n *aufziehen*, (*fig.*) take a stricter line.

Sakko ['zako], *m.* (—s, *pl.* —s) lounge jacket.

Sakristei [zakrɪ'staı], *f.* (—, *pl.* —en) vestry.

Salat [za'laːt], *m.* (—(e)s, *pl.* —e) salad; (*plant*) lettuce; (*sl.*) mess.

salbadern ['zalbaːdərn], *v.n.* prate, talk nonsense.

Salbe ['zalbə], *f.* (—, *pl.* —n) ointment, salve.

Salbei ['zalbaı], *m.* (—s, *no pl.*) (*Bot.*) sage.

salben ['zalbən], *v.a.* anoint.

salbungsvoll ['zalbuŋsfɔl], *adj.* unctuous.

Saldo ['zaldo], *m.* (—s, *pl.* —s) balance.

Saline [za'liːnə], *f.* (—, *pl.* —n) saltmine, salt-works.

Salkante ['zaːlkantə], *f.* (—, *pl.* —n) selvedge, border.

Salm [zalm], *m.* (—s, *pl.* —e) (*Zool.*) salmon.

Salmiakgeist ['zalmjakgaıst], *m.* (—s, *no pl.*) ammonia.

Salon [za'lɔ̃], *m.* (—s, *pl.* —s) salon; saloon; drawing-room.

salonfähig [za'lɔ̃fɛːɪç], *adj.* presentable, socially acceptable.

salopp [za'lɔp], *adj.* careless, slovenly, shabby, sloppy.

Salpeter [zal'peːtər], *m.* (—s, *no pl.*) nitre, saltpetre.

salutieren [zalu'tiːrən], *v.a., v.n.* salute.

Salve ['zalvə], *f.* (—, *pl.* —n) volley, discharge, salute.

Salz [zalts], *n.* (—es, *pl.* —e) salt.

Salzfaß ['zaltsfas], *n.* (—sses, *pl.* ⸚sser) salt-cellar.

Salzlake ['zaltslaːkə], *f.* (—, *pl.* —n) brine.

Salzsäure ['zaltszɔyrə], *f.* (—, *no pl.*) hydrochloric acid.

Sämann ['zɛːman], *m.* (—s, *pl.* ⸚ner) sower.

Sambia ['zambia], *n.* Zambia.

Same(n)

Same(n) ['zaːmə(n)], *m.* (**—ns**, *pl.* **—n**) seed; sperm; spawn.

Samenstaub ['zaːmənʃtaup], *m.* (**—s**, *no pl.*) pollen.

Sämereien [zɛːməˈraɪən], *f. pl.* seeds, grain.

sämisch ['zɛːmɪʃ], *adj.* chamois.

Sammelband ['zaməlbant], *m.* (**—es**, *pl.* ¨**e**) miscellany, anthology.

sammeln ['zaməln], *v.a.* collect, gather. — *v.r. sich —,* meet; collect o.'s thoughts, compose o.s.

Sammler ['zamlər], *m.* (**—s**, *pl.* **—**) collector; accumulator.

Samstag ['zamstaːk], *m.* (**—s**, *pl.* **—e**) Saturday.

Samt [zamt], *m.* (**—(e)s**, *pl.* **—e**) velvet.

samt [zamt], *adv.* together, all together; *— und sonders,* jointly and severally.— *prep.* (*Dat.*) together with.

sämtlich ['zɛmtlɪç], *adj.* each and every.

Sand [zant], *m.* (**—es**, *no pl.*) sand; *feiner —,* grit; *grober —,* gravel.

Sandtorte ['zanttɔrtə], *f.* (**—**, *pl.* **—n**) sponge-cake, madeira-cake.

Sanduhr ['zantuːr], (**—**, *pl.* **—en**) hour-glass.

sanft [zanft], *adj.* soft, gentle.

Sänfte ['zɛnftə], *f.* (**—**, *pl.* **—n**) sedan-chair.

Sang [zaŋ], *m.* (**—es**, *pl.* **Gesänge**) song; *ohne — und Klang,* (*fig.*) unostentatiously, without fuss, without ceremony.

sanieren [zaˈniːrən], *v.a.* cure; (*company*) reconstruct, put on a sound financial basis.

sanitär [zaniˈtɛːr], *adj.* sanitary.

Sanitäter [zaniˈtɛːtər], *m.* (**—s**, *pl.*—) medical orderly; ambulance man.

Sankt [zaŋkt], *indecl. adj.* Saint; (*abbr.*) St.

sanktionieren [zaŋktsjoˈniːrən], *v.a.* sanction.

Sansibar ['zanziˌbaːr], *n.* Zanzibar.

Sardelle [zarˈdɛlə], *f.* (**—**, *pl.* **—n**) (*Zool.*) anchovy.

Sardinien [zarˈdiːnjən], *n.* Sardinia.

Sarg [zark], *m.* (**—es**, *pl.* ¨**e**) coffin.

sarkastisch [zarˈkastɪʃ], *adj.* sarcastic.

Satellit [zatəˈliːt], *m.* (**—en**, *pl.* **—en**) satellite.

Satiriker [zaˈtiːrɪkər], *m.* (**—s**, *pl.* **—**) satirist.

satt [zat], *adj.* sated, satiated, satisfied; (*colours*) deep, rich; *sich — essen,* eat o.'s fill; *einer Sache — sein,* be sick of s.th., have had enough of s.th.

Sattel ['zatəl], *m.* (**—s**, *pl.* ¨) saddle; *einen aus dem — heben,* (*fig.*) oust s.o.; *fest im — sitzen,* (*fig.*) be master of a situation; *in allen — gerecht,* versatile.

satteln ['zatəln], *v.a.* saddle.

Sattheit ['zathaɪt], *f.* (**—**, *no pl.*) satiety.

sättigen ['zɛtɪgən], *v.a.* satisfy, sate, satiate; (*Chem.*) saturate.

sattsam ['zatzaːm], *adv.* enough, sufficiently.

saturieren [zatuˈriːrən], *v.a.* (*Chem.*) saturate.

Satz [zats], *m.* (**—es**, *pl.* ¨**e**) sentence; proposition; thesis; (*Mus.*) movement; (*Typ.*) composition; (*dregs*) sediment; (*gambling*) stake; *mit einem —,* with one leap (*or* jump *or* bound).

Satzbildung ['zatsbɪlduŋ], *f.* (**—**, *pl.* **—en**) (*Gram.*) construction; (*Chem.*) sedimentation.

Satzlehre ['zatsleːrə], *f.* (**—**, *no pl.*) syntax.

Satzung ['zatsuŋ], *f.* (**—**, *pl.* **—en**) statute.

Satzzeichen ['zatstsaɪçən], *n.* (**—s**, *pl.* **—**) punctuation-mark.

Sau [zau], *f.* (**—**, *pl.* ¨**e**) sow; (*vulg.*) dirty person, slut.

sauber ['zaubər], *adj.* clean, neat, tidy.

säubern ['zɔybərn], *v.a.* clean, cleanse; (*fig.*) purge.

Saubohne ['zauboːnə], *f.* (**—**, *pl.* **—n**) broad bean.

Saudiarabien ['zaudiaraːbjən], *n.* Saudi Arabia.

sauer ['zauər], *adj.* sour, acid; (*fig.*) troublesome; morose.

Sauerbrunnen ['zauərbrunən], *m.* (**—s**, *pl.* **—**) mineral water.

Sauerei [zauəˈraɪ], *f.* (**—**, *pl.* **—en**) (*sl.*) filthiness; mess.

Sauerkraut ['zauərkraut], *n.* (**—es**, *no pl.*) pickled cabbage.

säuerlich ['zɔyərlɪç], *adj.* acidulous.

Sauerstoff ['zauərʃtɔf], *m.* (**—(e)s**, *no pl.*) oxygen.

Sauerteig ['zauərtaɪk], *m.* (**—(e)s**, *pl.* **—e**) leaven.

sauertöpfisch ['zauərtœpfɪʃ], *adj.* morose, peevish.

saufen ['zaufən], *v.a., v.n. irr.* (*animals*) drink; (*humans*) drink to excess.

Säufer ['zɔyfər], *m.* (**—s**, *pl.* **—**) drunkard, drinker, alcoholic.

saugen ['zaugən], *v.a., v.n.* suck.

säugen ['zɔygən], *v.a.* suckle.

Säugetier ['zɔygətiːr], *n.* (**—s**, *pl.* **—e**) mammal.

Saugheber ['zaukheːbər], *m.* (**—s**, *pl.* **—**) suction-pump; siphon.

Säugling ['zɔyklɪŋ], *m.* (**—s**, *pl.* **—e**) suckling, baby.

Saugwarze ['zaukvartsə], *f.* (**—**, *pl.* **—n**) nipple.

Säule ['zɔylə], *f.* (**—**, *pl.* **—n**) pillar, column.

Säulenbündel ['zɔylənbyndəl], *n.* (**—s**, *pl.* **—**) (*Archit.*) clustered column.

Säulenfuß ['zɔylənfuːs], *m.* (**—es**, *pl.* ¨**e**) (*Archit.*) base, plinth.

Säulengang ['zɔyləngaŋ], *m.* (**—s**, *pl.* ¨**e**) colonnade.

Saum [zaum], *m.* (**—(e)s**, *pl.* ¨**e**) seam, hem, border, edge; selvedge.

saumäßig ['zaumɛːsɪç], *adj.* (*sl.*) beastly, filthy, piggish; enormous.

säumen (1) ['zɔymən], *v.a.* hem.

säumen (2) ['zɔymən], *v.n.* delay, tarry.

säumig ['zɔymɪç], *adj.* tardy, slow, dilatory.

Saumpferd ['zaumpfe:rt], *n.* (**—s**, *pl.* **—e**) pack-horse.

saumselig ['zaumze:lɪç], *adj.* tardy, dilatory.

Säure ['zɔyrə], *f.* (**—**, *pl.* **—n**) acid; (*Med.*) acidity.

Saurier ['zaurjər], *m.* (**—s**, *pl.* **—**) saurian.

Saus [zaus], *m.* (**—es**, *no pl.*) rush; revel, riot; *in — und Braus leben,* live a wild life, live riotously.

säuseln ['zɔyzəln], *v.n.* rustle, murmur.

sausen ['zauzən], *v.n.* bluster, blow, howl, whistle; (*coll.*) rush, dash.

Saustall ['zauʃtal], *m.* (**—s**, *pl.* **·̈e**) pigsty.

Schabe ['ʃa:bə], *f.* (**—**, *pl.* **—n**) (*Ent.*) cockroach.

schaben ['ʃa:bən], *v.a.* scrape, shave, rub.

Schabernack ['ʃa:bərnak], *m.* (**—s**, *pl.* **—e**) practical joke, trick.

schäbig ['ʃɛ:bɪç], *adj.* shabby.

Schablone [ʃa'blo:nə], *f.* (**—**, *pl.* **—n**) model, mould, pattern, stencil; (*fig.*) routine.

Schach [ʃax], *n.* (**—(e)s**, *no pl.*) chess; *— bieten,* check; *— spielen,* play chess; *in — halten,* keep in check.

Schacher ['ʃaxər], *m.* (**—s**, *no pl.*) haggling, bargaining, barter.

Schächer ['ʃɛçər], *m.* (**—s**, *pl.* **—**) wretch, felon, robber.

Schacht [ʃaxt], *m.* (**—(e)s**, *pl.* **·̈e**) shaft.

Schachtel ['ʃaxtəl], *f.* (**—**, *pl.* **—n**) box, (cardboard) box, (small) case.

Schachtelhalm ['ʃaxtəlhalm], *m.* (**—s**, *pl.* **—e**) (*grass*) horse-tail.

Schächter ['ʃɛçtər], *m.* (**—s**, *pl.* **—**) (kosher) butcher.

schade ['ʃa:də], *int.* a pity, a shame, unfortunate; *wie —,* what a pity; *sehr —,* a great pity.

Schädel ['ʃɛ:dəl], *m.* (**—s**, *pl.* **—**) skull.

Schaden ['ʃa:dən], *m.* (**—s**, *pl.* **·̈**) damage, injury, detriment; *zu — kommen,* come to grief.

schaden ['ʃa:dən], *v.n.* do harm, do damage, do injury; *es schadet nichts,* it does not matter.

Schadenersatz ['ʃa:dənɛrzats], *m.* (**—es**, *no pl.*) indemnity, compensation, indemnification; (*money*) damages.

Schadenfreude ['ʃa:dənfrɔydə], *f.* (**—**, *no pl.*) malicious pleasure.

Schadensforderung ['ʃa:dənsfɔrdə-ruŋ], *f.* (**—**, *pl.* **—en**) claim (for damages).

schadhaft ['ʃa:thaft], *adj.* defective, faulty.

schädlich ['ʃɛ:tlɪç], *adj.* injurious, noxious, pernicious, noisome.

schadlos ['ʃa:tlo:s], *adj.* indemnified; *einen — halten,* indemnify s.o., compensate s.o.; *sich an einem — halten,* recoup o.s. from s.o.

Schadlosigkeit ['ʃa:tlo:zɪçkaɪt], *f.* (**—**, *no pl.*) harmlessness.

Schaf [ʃa:f], *n.* (**—(e)s**, *pl.* **—e**) sheep.

Schafblattern ['ʃa:fblatərn], *f. pl.* (*Med.*) chicken-pox.

Schafdarm ['ʃa:fdarm], *m.* (**—s**, *pl.* **·̈e**) sheep-gut.

Schäfer ['ʃɛ:fər], *m.* (**—s**, *pl.* **—**) shepherd.

Schäferstündchen ['ʃɛ:fərʃtyntçən], *n.* (**—s**, *pl.* **—**) tryst; rendezvous.

schaffen ['ʃafən], *v.a., v.n. irr.* make, produce, create. *— v.a. reg.* provide; manage; *aus dem Wege —,* remove. *— v.n. reg.* work; *einem zu — machen,* give s.o. trouble.

Schaffner ['ʃafnər], *m.* (**—s**, *pl.* **—**) (*Railw. etc.*) guard, conductor.

Schafgarbe ['ʃa:fgarbə], *f.* (**—**, *pl.* **—n**) (*Bot.*) common yarrow.

Schafhürde ['ʃa:fhyrdə], *f.* (**—**, *pl.* **—n**) sheep-fold.

Schafott [ʃa'fɔt], *n.* (**—(e)s**, *pl.* **—e**) scaffold.

Schafschur ['ʃa:fʃu:r], *f.* (**—**, *pl.* **—en**) sheep-shearing.

Schaft [ʃaft], *m.* (**—(e)s**, *pl.* **·̈e**) shaft; (*gun*) stock.

Schafwolle ['ʃa:fvɔlə], *f.* (**—**, *no pl.*) sheep's wool, fleece.

Schakal [ʃa'ka:l], *m.* (**—s**, *pl.* **—e**) (*Zool.*) jackal.

Schäkerei [ʃɛ:kə'raɪ], *f.* (**—**, *pl.* **—en**) playfulness, teasing, dalliance, flirtation.

Schal [ʃa:l], *m.* (**—(e)s**, *pl.* **—e**) scarf, shawl.

schal [ʃa:l], *adj.* stale, flat, insipid.

Schale ['ʃa:lə], *f.* (**—**, *pl.* **—n**) (*nut, egg*) shell; (*fruit*) peel, rind; dish, bowl; (*Austr.*) cup; (*fig.*) outside.

schälen ['ʃɛ:lən], *v.a.* shell; peel.

Schalk [ʃalk], *m.* (**—(e)s**, *pl.* **—e**) knave; rogue; wag, joker.

Schall [ʃal], *m.* (**—(e)s**, *no pl.*) sound.

Schallbecken ['ʃalbɛkən], *n.* (**—s**, *pl.* **—**) cymbal.

Schallehre ['ʃalle:rə], *f.* (**—**, *no pl.*) acoustics.

schallen ['ʃalən], *v.n.* sound, reverberate.

Schalmei [ʃal'maɪ], *f.* (**—**, *pl.* **—en**) (*Poet., Mus.*) shawm.

Schallplatte ['ʃalplatə], *f.* (**—**, *pl.* **—n**) (gramophone) record.

schalten ['ʃaltən], *v.n.* rule; switch; (*Motor.*) change gear; *— und walten,* manage.

Schalter ['ʃaltər], *m.* (**—s**, *pl.* **—**) (*Elec.*) switch; booking-office; counter.

Schalthebel ['ʃalthe:bəl], *m.* (**—s**, *pl.* **—**) (*Motor.*) gear lever.

Schaltier ['ʃa:lti:r], *n.* (**—s**, *pl.* **—e**) (*Zool.*) crustacean.

Schaltjahr ['ʃaltja:r], *n.* (**—s**, *pl.* **—e**) leap year.

Schalttafel ['ʃaltta:fəl], *f.* (**—**, *pl.* **—n**) switch-board.

Scham [ʃa:m], *f.* (**—**, *no pl.*) shame, modesty; private parts.

schämen ['ʃɛ:mən], *v.r. sich —,* be ashamed (of).

schamlos ['ʃa:mlo:s], *adj.* shameless.

schamrot ['ʃa:mro:t], *adj.* blushing; *— werden,* blush.

185

schandbar ['ʃantba:r], *adj.* ignominious, infamous.

Schande ['ʃandə], *f.* (—, *no pl.*) shame, disgrace; dishonour, ignominy.

schänden ['ʃɛndən], *v.a.* dishonour, disgrace; violate, ravish.

Schandfleck ['ʃantflɛk], *m.* (—s, *pl.* —e) stain, blemish.

schändlich ['ʃɛntliç], *adj.* shameful, disgraceful, infamous.

Schändung ['ʃɛnduŋ], *f.* (—, *pl.* —en) violation.

Schank ['ʃaŋk], *m.* (—s, *no pl.*) sale of liquor.

Schanzarbeiter ['ʃantsarbaɪtər], *m.* (—s, *pl.* —) sapper.

Schanze ['ʃantsə], *f.* (—, *pl.* —n) redoubt, bulwark; *in die* — *schlagen*, risk, venture.

Schar [ʃa:r], *f.* (—, *pl.* —en) troop, band; host.

Scharade [ʃa'ra:də], *f.* (—, *pl.* —n) charade.

scharen ['ʃa:rən], *v.r. sich* — *um*, assemble, congregate, gather round.

Schären ['ʃɛ:rən], *f. pl.* reefs, skerries.

scharf [ʃarf], *adj.* sharp, keen, acute, acrid, pungent; piercing; (*fig.*) severe, rigorous.

Schärfe ['ʃɛrfə], *f.* (—, *no pl.*) sharpness, keenness, acuteness; pungency, acridness; severity, rigour.

schärfen ['ʃɛrfən], *v.a.* sharpen, whet; (*fig.*) strengthen, intensify.

Scharfrichter ['ʃarfrɪçtər], *m.* (—s, *pl.* —) executioner.

scharfsichtig ['ʃarfzɪçtɪç], *adj.* sharpeyed, (*fig.*) penetrating, astute.

scharfsinnig ['ʃarfzɪnɪç], *adj.* clearsighted, sagacious, ingenious.

Scharlach ['ʃarlax], *m.* (—s, *no pl.*) scarlet; (*Med.*) scarlet-fever.

Scharlatan ['ʃarlata:n], *m.* (—s, *pl.* —e) charlatan, humbug.

scharmant [ʃar'mant], *adj.* charming.

Scharmützel [ʃar'mytsəl], *n.* (—s, *pl.* —) skirmish.

Scharnier [ʃar'ni:r], *n.* (—s, *pl.* —e) hinge, joint.

Schärpe ['ʃɛrpə], *f.* (—, *pl.* —n) sash.

Scharpie [ʃar'pi:], *f.* (—, *no pl.*) lint.

scharren ['ʃarən], *v.a., v.n.* scrape, rake.

Scharte ['ʃartə], *f.* (—, *pl.* —n) notch, crack; *eine* — *auswetzen*, repair a mistake, make up for s.th.

Scharteke [ʃar'te:kə], *f.* (—, *pl.* —n) worthless book, trash; *eine alte* —, an old fuddy-duddy, frump.

scharwenzeln [ʃar'vɛntsəln], *v.n.* dance attendance, be obsequious.

Schatten ['ʃatən], *m.* (—s, *pl.* —) shade, shadow.

Schattenbild ['ʃatənbɪlt], *n.* (—s, *pl.* —er) silhouette.

Schattenriß ['ʃatənrɪs], *m.* (—sses, *pl.* -sse) silhouette.

schattieren [ʃa'ti:rən], *v.a.* shade (drawing).

schattig ['ʃatɪç], *adj.* shady.

Schatulle [ʃa'tulə], *f.* (—, *pl.* —n) cashbox; privy purse.

Schatz [ʃats], *m.* (—es, *pl* ⁝e) treasure; (*fig.*) sweetheart, darling.

Schatzamt ['ʃatsamt], *n.* (—s, *pl.* ⁝er) Treasury, Exchequer.

schätzbar ['ʃɛtsba:r], *adj.* estimable.

Schätzchen ['ʃɛtsçən], *n.* (—s, *pl.* —) (*coll.*) sweetheart.

schätzen ['ʃɛtsən], *v.a.* value, estimate; esteem; reckon at.

Schatzkammer ['ʃatskamər], *f.* (—, *pl.* —n) treasury.

Schatzmeister ['ʃatsmaɪstər], *m.* (—s, *pl.* —) treasurer.

Schätzung ['ʃɛtsuŋ], *f.* (—, *pl.* —en) valuation, estimate; (*fig.*) esteem.

Schau [ʃau], *f.* (—, *pl.* —en) show, view, spectacle; *zur* — *stellen*, display, parade.

Schauder ['ʃaudər], *m.* (—s, *pl.* —) shudder, shiver; horror.

schaudern ['ʃaudərn], *v.n.* shudder, shiver.

schauen ['ʃauən], *v.a.* see, view. — *v.n.* look, gaze (*auf*, at), *schau mal*, look here.

Schauer ['ʃauər], *m.* (—s, *pl.* —) shiver, paroxysm; (*fig.*) thrill, awe; (*rain*) shower.

schauern ['ʃauərn], *v.n.* shudder, shiver; (*rain*) shower.

Schauerroman ['ʃauərroma:n], *m.* (—s, *pl.* —e) (*novel*) penny dreadful, thriller.

Schaufel ['ʃaufəl], *f.* (—, *pl.* —n) shovel.

Schaufenster ['ʃaufɛnstər], *n.* (—s, *pl.* —) shop-window.

Schaukel ['ʃaukəl], *f.* (—, *pl.* —n) swing.

schaulustig ['ʃaulustɪç], *adj.* curious.

Schaum [ʃaum], *m.* (—es, *pl.* ⁝e) foam, froth; bubbles; scum; — *schlagen*, whip cream.

schäumen ['ʃɔymən], *v.n.* foam, froth, sparkle.

Schauplatz ['ʃauplats], *m.* (—es, *pl.* ⁝e) scene, stage.

schaurig ['ʃaurɪç], *adj.* grisly, horrid, horrible.

Schauspiel ['ʃauʃpi:l], *n.* (—s, *pl.* —e) spectacle; drama, play.

Schauspieler ['ʃauʃpi:lər], *m.* (—s, *pl.* —) actor, player.

Schaustellung ['ʃauʃtɛluŋ], *f.* (—, *pl.* —en) exhibition.

Scheck [ʃɛk], *m.* (—s, *pl.* —s) cheque.

scheckig ['ʃɛkɪç], *adj.* piebald, spotted, dappled.

scheel [ʃe:l], *adj.* squint-eyed; envious; *einen* — *ansehen*, look askance at s.o.

Scheffel ['ʃɛfəl], *m.* (—s, *pl.* —) bushel.

scheffeln ['ʃɛfəln], *v.a.* rake in; accumulate.

Scheibe ['ʃaɪbə], *f.* (—, *pl.* —n) disc; (*window*) pane; (*shooting*) target; (*bread*) slice.

Scheibenhonig ['ʃaɪbənho:nɪç], *m.* (—s, *no pl.*) honey in the comb.

Scheibenschießen ['ʃaɪbənʃiːsən], *n.* (—s, *no pl.*) target-practice.

Scheich [ʃaɪç], *m.* (—s, *pl.* —e) sheikh.

Scheide ['ʃaɪdə], *f.* (—, *pl.* —n) sheath, scabbard; (*Anat.*) vagina.

Scheidemünze ['ʃaɪdəmyntsə], *f.* (—, *pl.* —n) small coin, change.

scheiden ['ʃaɪdən], *v.a.* irr. divide; separate, divorce; *sich — lassen,* obtain a divorce. — *v.n.* (*aux.* sein) part, depart; *aus dem Amte —,* resign office.

Scheidewand ['ʃaɪdəvant], *f.* (—, *pl.* ˙e) partition-wall.

Scheideweg ['ʃaɪdəveːk], *m.* (—s, *pl.* —e) cross-roads; *am — stehen,* be at the parting of the ways.

Scheidung ['ʃaɪduŋ], *f.* (—, *pl.* —en) divorce.

Schein [ʃaɪn], *m.* (—(e)s, *no pl.*) shine, sheen, lustre, splendour; semblance, pretence; *den — wahren,* keep up appearances; *der — trügt,* appearances are deceptive; (*in compounds*) mock, would-be, apparent; (*pl.* —e) (piece of) paper, chit, note; (*fig.*) attestation, certificate.

scheinbar ['ʃaɪnbaːr], *adj.* apparent; ostensible, specious. — *adv.* seemingly.

scheinen ['ʃaɪnən], *v.n.* irr. shine, sparkle; seem, appear.

scheinheilig ['ʃaɪnhaɪlɪç], *adj.* hypocritical.

Scheinheiligkeit ['ʃaɪnhaɪlɪçkaɪt], *f.* (—, *no pl.*) hypocrisy.

scheintot ['ʃaɪntoːt], *adj.* in a cataleptic trance; seemingly dead.

Scheinwerfer ['ʃaɪnverfər], *m.* (—s, *pl.* —) headlight; searchlight; floodlight.

Scheit [ʃaɪt], *n.* (—(e)s, *pl.* —e) piece of wood, billet.

Scheitel ['ʃaɪtəl], *m.* (—s, *pl.* —) (*hair*) parting; top, vertex.

Scheiterhaufen ['ʃaɪtərhaufən], *m.* (—s, *pl.* —) stake; funeral pyre.

scheitern ['ʃaɪtərn], *v.n.* (*aux.* sein) (*ship*) founder, be wrecked; (*fig.*) miscarry, fail.

Schelle ['ʃɛlə], *f.* (—, *pl.* —n) bell.

Schellen ['ʃɛlən], *f. pl.* (*Cards*) diamonds.

schellen ['ʃɛlən], *v.n.* ring the bell.

Schellfisch ['ʃɛlfɪʃ], *m.* (—es, *pl.* —e) (*Zool.*) haddock.

Schelm [ʃɛlm], *m.* (—(e)s, *pl.* —e) rogue, knave, villain.

schelten ['ʃɛltən], *v.a.* irr. scold, chide, rebuke, reprimand.

Schema ['ʃeːma], *n.* (—s, *pl.* —s) schedule, model, plan, scheme.

Schemel ['ʃeːməl], *m.* (—s, *pl.* —) foot-stool.

Schenk [ʃɛŋk], *m.* (—en, *pl.* —en) cupbearer; publican.

Schenke ['ʃɛŋkə], *f.* (—, *pl.* —n) ale-house, tavern, pub.

Schenkel ['ʃɛŋkəl], *m.* (—s, *pl.* —) thigh; (*Geom.*) side of triangle.

schenken ['ʃɛŋkən], *v.a.* present s.o. with, donate, give.

Schenkstube ['ʃɛŋkʃtuːbə], *f.* (—, *pl.* —n) tap-room.

Scherbe ['ʃɛrbə], *f.* (—, *pl.* —n) potsherd; fragment of glass etc.

Schere ['ʃeːrə], *f.* (—, *pl.* —n) scissors; (*garden*) shears; (*crab*) claw.

scheren ['ʃeːrən], *v.a.* shave; clip, shear; bother, concern. — *v.r. sich —,* clear off; *scher dich zum Teufel!* go to blazes!

Scherereien [ʃerəˈraɪən], *f. pl.* vexation, bother, trouble.

Scherflein ['ʃɛrflaɪn], *n.* (—s, *pl.* —) mite; *sein — beitragen,* contribute o.'s share.

Scherge ['ʃɛrgə], *m.* (—n, *pl.* —n) (*obs.*) beadle.

Scherz [ʃɛrts], *m.* (—es, *pl.* —e) jest, joke; *— beiseite,* joking apart.

scheu [ʃɔy], *adj.* shy, bashful, timid; skittish.

scheuchen ['ʃɔyçən], *v.a.* scare away.

scheuen ['ʃɔyən], *v.a.* shun, avoid, fight shy of, fear. — *v.n.* take fright.

Scheuer ['ʃɔyər], *f.* (—, *pl.* —n) barn.

scheuern ['ʃɔyərn], *v.a.* scour, scrub.

Scheuklappe ['ʃɔyklapə], *f.* (—, *pl.* —n) blinker.

Scheune ['ʃɔynə], *f.* (—, *pl.* —n) barn.

Scheusal ['ʃɔyzaːl], *n.* (—s, *pl.* —e) monster.

scheußlich ['ʃɔyslɪç], *adj.* frightful, dreadful, abominable, hideous.

Schicht [ʃɪçt], *f.* (—, *pl.* —en) layer, stratum, seam; (*society*) class; (*work*) shift.

schick [ʃɪk], *adj.* stylish, chic.

schicken ['ʃɪkən], *v.a.* send, despatch, convey. — *v.r. sich —,* be proper; *sich in etwas —,* put up with s.th., resign o.s. to s.th.

schicklich ['ʃɪklɪç], *adj.* proper, becoming, suitable, seemly.

Schicksal ['ʃɪkzaːl], *n.* (—s, *pl.* —e) fate, destiny, lot.

Schickung ['ʃɪkuŋ], *f.* (—, *pl.* —en) Divine Will, Providence.

schieben ['ʃiːbən], *v.a.* irr. shove, push; *die Schuld auf einen —,* put the blame on s.o.

Schieber ['ʃiːbər], *m.* (—s, *pl.* —) bolt, slide; (*fig.*) profiteer, spiv.

Schiedsgericht ['ʃiːtsgərɪçt], *n.* (—es, *pl.* —e) arbitration tribunal.

Schiedsrichter ['ʃiːtsrɪçtər], *m.* (—s, *pl.* —) referee, umpire, arbiter.

schief [ʃiːf], *adj.* slanting, oblique, bent, crooked; wry; *—e Ebene,* inclined plane; *— gehen,* go wrong.

Schiefe ['ʃiːfə], *f.* (—, *no pl.*) obliquity.

Schiefer ['ʃiːfər], *m.* (—s, *no pl.*) slate.

schiefrig ['ʃiːfrɪç], *adj.* slaty.

schielen ['ʃiːlən], *v.n.* squint, be cross-eyed.

Schienbein ['ʃiːnbaɪn], *n.* (—s, *pl.* —e) shin-bone, shin.

Schiene

Schiene [ˈʃiːnə], f. (—, pl. —n) rail; (*Med.*) splint.

schier [ʃiːr], adj. (*rare*) sheer, pure. — adv. almost, very nearly.

Schierling [ˈʃiːrlɪŋ], m. (—s, pl. —e) (*Bot.*) hemlock.

schießen [ˈʃiːsən], v.a., v.n. irr. shoot, fire, discharge; (*fig.*) rush; *etwas — lassen*, let go of s.th.; *die Zügel — lassen*, loosen o.'s hold on the reins; *ein Kabel — lassen*, pay out a cable; *das ist zum —*, that's very funny.

Schiff [ʃɪf], n. (—(e)s, pl. —e) ship, vessel, boat; (*church*) nave.

schiffbar [ˈʃɪfbaːr], adj. navigable.

Schiffbruch [ˈʃɪfbrux], m. (—s, pl. ⸚e) shipwreck.

Schiffbrücke [ˈʃɪfbrykə], f. (—, pl. —n) pontoon-bridge.

schiffen [ˈʃɪfən], v.n. sail; navigate.

Schiffsboden [ˈʃɪfsboːdən], m. (—s, pl. ⸚) (ship's) hold.

Schiffsmaat [ˈʃɪfsmaːt], m. (—s, pl. —e) shipmate.

Schiffsrumpf [ˈʃɪfsrumpf], m. (—es, pl. ⸚e) hull.

Schiffsschnabel [ˈʃɪfsʃnaːbəl], m. (—s, pl. ⸚) prow, bows.

Schiffsvorderteil [ˈʃɪfsfordərtaɪl], n. (—s, pl. —e) forecastle, prow.

Schiffszwieback [ˈʃɪfstsviːbak], m. (—s, no pl.) ship's biscuit.

Schikane [ʃiˈkaːnə], f. (—, pl. —n) chicanery.

Schild (1) [ʃɪlt], m. (—(e)s, pl. —e) shield, buckler, escutcheon; *etwas im — führen*, have designs on s.th., plan s.th.

Schild (2) [ʃɪlt], n. (—s, pl. —er) signboard, plate.

Schilderhaus [ˈʃɪldərhaus], n. (—es, pl. ⸚er) sentry-box.

Schildermaler [ˈʃɪldərmaːlər], m. (—s, pl. —) sign-painter.

schildern [ˈʃɪldərn], v.a. describe, depict.

Schildknappe [ˈʃɪltknapə], m. (—n, pl. —n) shield-bearer, squire.

Schildkrot [ˈʃɪltkroːt], n. (—s, no pl.) tortoise-shell.

Schildkröte [ˈʃɪltkrøːtə], f. (—, pl. —n) (*Zool.*) turtle, tortoise.

Schildpatt [ˈʃɪltpat], n. (—s, no pl.) tortoise-shell.

Schildwache [ˈʃɪltvaxə], f. (—, pl. —n) sentinel, sentry; — *stehen*, be on sentry duty, stand guard.

Schilf(rohr) [ˈʃɪlf(roːr)], n. (—(e)s, no pl.) (*Bot.*) reed, rush, sedge.

schillern [ˈʃɪlərn], v.n. opalesce, glitter, change colour, be iridescent.

Schilling [ˈʃɪlɪŋ], m. (—s, pl. —e) Austrian coin; shilling.

Schimmel (1) [ˈʃɪməl], m. (—s, pl. —) white horse.

Schimmel (2) [ˈʃɪməl], m. (—s, no pl.) mould, mustiness.

schimmeln [ˈʃɪməln], v.n. (*aux.* sein) go mouldy, moulder.

Schimmer [ˈʃɪmər], m. (—s, pl. —) glitter, gleam; *ich habe keinen —*, I haven't a clue.

schimmlig [ˈʃɪmlɪç], adj. mouldy, musty, mildewed.

Schimpanse [ʃɪmˈpanzə], m. (—n, pl. —n) (*Zool.*) chimpanzee.

Schimpf [ʃɪmpf], m. (—es, no pl.) abuse, affront, insult; *mit — und Schande*, in disgrace.

schimpfen [ˈʃɪmpfən], v.n. curse, swear; — *auf*, (*fig.*) run (s.o.) down. — v.a. insult (s.o.), call (s.o.) names; scold.

Schindel [ˈʃɪndəl], f. (—, pl. —n) shingle.

schinden [ˈʃɪndən], v.a. irr. flay; (*fig.*) grind, oppress, sweat. — v.r. *sich —*, slave, drudge.

Schindluder [ˈʃɪntluːdər], n. (—s, pl. —) worn-out animal; *mit einem — treiben*, exploit s.o.

Schinken [ˈʃɪŋkən], m. (—s, pl. —) ham.

Schinkenspeck [ˈʃɪŋkənʃpɛk], m. (—s, no pl.) bacon.

Schippe [ˈʃɪpə], f. (—, pl. —n) shovel, spade.

Schirm [ʃɪrm], m. (—(e)s, pl. —e) screen; umbrella; parasol, sunshade; lampshade; (*fig.*) shield, shelter, cover.

schirmen [ˈʃɪrmən], v.a. protect (from), shelter.

Schirmherr [ˈʃɪrmhɛr], m. (—n, pl. —en) protector, patron.

Schlacht [ʃlaxt], f. (—, pl. —en) battle; fight; *eine — liefern*, give battle; *die — gewinnen*, carry the day, win the battle.

Schlachtbank [ˈʃlaxtbaŋk], f. (—, pl. ⸚e) shambles; *zur — führen*, lead to the slaughter.

schlachten [ˈʃlaxtən], v.a. kill, butcher, slaughter.

Schlachtenbummler [ˈʃlaxtənbumlər], m. (—s, pl. —) camp follower.

Schlachtfeld [ˈʃlaxtfɛlt], n. (—s, pl. —er) battlefield.

Schlachtruf [ˈʃlaxtruːf], m. (—s, pl. —e) battle-cry.

Schlacke [ˈʃlakə], f. (—, pl. —n) slag, clinker, dross.

Schlackwurst [ˈʃlakvurst], f. (—, pl. ⸚e) (*North German*) sausage.

Schlaf [ʃlaːf], m. (—(e)s, no pl.) sleep; slumber, rest; *in tiefem —*, fast asleep; *in den — wiegen*, rock to sleep.

Schläfchen [ˈʃlɛːfçən], n. (—s, pl. —) nap; *ein — machen*, have forty winks.

Schläfe [ˈʃlɛːfə], f. (—, pl. —n) temple.

schlafen [ˈʃlaːfən], v.n. irr. sleep; *schlaf wohl*, sleep well; — *gehen*, go to bed.

schlaff [ʃlaf], adj. slack, loose, lax, flabby; weak; remiss.

schlaflos [ˈʃlaːfloːs], adj. sleepless.

Schlafmittel [ˈʃlaːfmɪtəl], n. (—s, pl. —) soporific, sleeping tablet, sleeping draught.

schläfrig [ˈʃlɛːfrɪç], adj. drowsy, sleepy.

188

Schlafrock ['ʃlaːfrɔk], s. (—s, pl. ⁓e) dressing-gown; *Äpfel im —,* apple fritters.

schlafwandeln ['ʃlaːfvandəln], v.n. (aux. sein) walk in o.'s sleep, sleepwalk.

Schlag [ʃlaːk], m. (—(e)s, pl. ⁓e) blow, stroke; beat; (*Elec.*) shock; *ein Mann von gutem —,* a good type of man; *vom — gerührt,* struck by apoplexy; *— fünf,* at five o'clock sharp.

Schlagader ['ʃlaːkaːdər], f. (—, pl. —n) artery.

Schlaganfall ['ʃlaːkanfal], m. (—s, pl. ⁓e) stroke, apoplexy.

Schlagballspiel ['ʃlaːkbalʃpiːl], n. (—s, pl. —e) rounders.

Schlagbaum ['ʃlaːkbaum], m. (—s, pl. ⁓e) turnpike.

schlagen ['ʃlaːgən], v.a. irr. beat, strike, hit; (*tree*) fell; (*money*) coin; *Alarm —,* sound the alarm; *ans Kreuz —,* crucify; *ein Kreuz —,* make the sign of the cross. — v.n. (*clock*) strike; (*birds*) warble; *aus der Art —,* degenerate. — v.r. *sich —,* fight; *sich auf Säbel —,* fight with sabres; *sich an die Brust —,* beat o.'s breast.

Schlager ['ʃlaːgər], m. (—s, pl. —) hit, pop song; (*fig.*) success.

Schläger ['ʃlɛːgər], m. (—s, pl. —) rapier; bat; (tennis-)racket; (golf-) club.

Schlägerei [ʃlɛːgə'raɪ], f. (—, pl. —en) fray, scuffle.

schlagfertig ['ʃlaːkfɛrtɪç], adj. quick-witted.

Schlagkraft ['ʃlaːkkraft], f. (—, no pl.) striking power.

Schlaglicht ['ʃlaːklɪçt], n. (—s, pl. —er) strong direct light.

Schlagsahne ['ʃlaːkzaːnə], f. (—, no pl.) double cream, raw cream; whipped cream.

Schlagschatten ['ʃlaːkʃatən], m. (—s, pl. —) deep shadow.

Schlagseite ['ʃlaːkzaɪtə], f. (—, no pl.) — *bekommen,* (*Naut.*) list.

Schlagwort ['ʃlaːkvɔrt], n. (—s, pl. ⁓er) catchword, slogan; trite saying.

Schlagzeile ['ʃlaːktsaɪlə], f. (—, pl. —n) headline.

Schlamm [ʃlam], m. (—(e)s, no pl.) mud, mire.

Schlampe ['ʃlampə], f. (—, pl. —n) slut.

Schlange ['ʃlaŋə], f. (—, pl. —n) snake, serpent; (*fig.*) queue.

schlängeln ['ʃlɛŋəln], v.r. *sich —,* wind, meander.

schlangenartig ['ʃlaŋənaːrtɪç], adj. snaky, serpentine.

schlank [ʃlaŋk], adj. slim, slender.

schlapp [ʃlap], adj. limp, tired, weak, slack; — *machen,* break down, collapse.

Schlappe ['ʃlapə], f. (—, pl. —n) reverse, defeat; *eine — erleiden,* suffer a setback.

Schlappschwanz ['ʃlapʃvants], m. (—es, pl. ⁓e) weakling; milksop.

Schlaraffenland [ʃlaˈrafənlant], n. (—(e)s, pl. ⁓er) land of milk and honey.

schlau [ʃlau], adj. cunning, crafty, sly, shrewd.

Schlauch [ʃlaux], m. (—(e)s, pl. ⁓e) hose; tube.

Schlaukopf ['ʃlaukɔpf], m. (—(e)s, pl. ⁓e) slyboots; (*Am.*) wiseacre.

schlecht [ʃlɛçt], adj. bad, evil, wicked; poor; *mir ist —,* I feel ill; *—e Zeiten,* hard times; *—es Geld,* base money.

schlechterdings ['ʃlɛçtərdɪŋs], adv. simply, positively, absolutely.

schlechthin ['ʃlɛçthɪn], adv. simply, plainly.

Schlechtigkeit ['ʃlɛçtɪçkaɪt], f. (—, pl. —en) wickedness, baseness.

Schlegel ['ʃleːgəl], m. (—s, pl. —) mallet; drumstick; (*bell*) clapper.

Schlehdorn ['ʃleːdɔrn], m. (—s, pl. —e) blackthorn, sloe-tree.

schleichen ['ʃlaɪçən], v.n. irr. (aux. sein) sneak, prowl, slink; —*de Krankheit,* lingering illness.

Schleichhandel ['ʃlaɪçhandəl], m. (—s, pl. ⁓) smuggling, black marketeering.

Schleie ['ʃlaɪə], f. (—, pl. —n) tench.

Schleier ['ʃlaɪər], m. (—s, pl. —) veil.

Schleife ['ʃlaɪfə], f. (—, pl. —n) bow, loop, noose.

schleifen ['ʃlaɪfən], v.a. irr. drag along, trail; grind, polish, sharpen, whet, hone; cut.

Schleim [ʃlaɪm], m. (—(e)s, no pl.) slime, mucus, phlegm.

Schleimhaut ['ʃlaɪmhaut], f. (—, pl. ⁓e) mucous membrane.

Schleimsuppe ['ʃlaɪmzupə], f. (—, pl. —n) gruel.

schleißen ['ʃlaɪsən], v.a. irr. split, slit; (*feathers*) strip.

schlemmen ['ʃlɛmən], v.n. carouse, gormandise.

schlendern ['ʃlɛndərn], v.n. (aux. sein) saunter along, stroll.

Schlendrian ['ʃlɛndriaːn], m. (—s, no pl.) old jog-trot, routine.

schlenkern ['ʃlɛŋkərn], v.a. dangle, swing.

Schleppdampfer ['ʃlɛpdampfər], m. (—s, pl. —) steam-tug, tug-boat, tow-boat.

Schleppe ['ʃlɛpə], f. (—, pl. —n) train (of a dress).

schleppen ['ʃlɛpən], v.a. carry (s.th. heavy), drag, tow.

Schleppenträger ['ʃlɛpəntrɛːgər], m. (—s, pl. —) train-bearer.

Schleppnetz ['ʃlɛpnɛts], n. (—es, pl. —e) dragnet.

Schlesien ['ʃleːzjən], n. Silesia.

Schleuder ['ʃlɔydər], f. (—, pl. —n) sling; catapult.

schleudern ['ʃlɔydərn], v.a. sling, throw, fling away. — v.n. (*Motor.*) skid; (*Comm.*) sell cheaply, undersell.

schleunigst [ˈʃlɔynɪçst], *adv.* very quickly, with the utmost expedition, promptly.

Schleuse [ˈʃlɔyzə], *f.* (—, *pl.* —n) sluice, flood-gate, lock.

Schlich [ʃlɪç], *m.* (—es, *pl.* —e) trick, dodge; *einem hinter seine —e kommen*, be up to s.o.'s tricks.

schlicht [ʃlɪçt], *adj.* plain, simple, homely; *—er Abschied*, curt dismissal.

schlichten [ˈʃlɪçtən], *v.a.* level; (*argument*) settle; adjust, compose.

Schlichtheit [ˈʃlɪçthaɪt], *f.* (—, *no pl.*) plainness, simplicity, homeliness.

schließen [ˈʃliːsən], *v.a. irr.* shut, close; contract; *etwas — aus*, conclude s.th. from; (*meeting*) close; *Frieden —*, make peace; *einen in die Arme —*, embrace s.o.; *etwas in sich —*, imply, entail.

Schließer [ˈʃliːsər], *m.* (—s, *pl.* —) doorkeeper; (*prison*) jailer, turnkey.

schließlich [ˈʃliːslɪç], *adv.* lastly, finally, in conclusion.

Schliff [ʃlɪf], *m.* (—(e)s, *no pl.*) polish, refinement.

schlimm [ʃlɪm], *adj.* bad, evil, ill; sad; serious, sore; disagreeable; naughty; *un so —er*, so much the worse, worse luck.

Schlinge [ˈʃlɪŋə], *f.* (—, *pl.* —n) loop, knot; noose, snare.

Schlingel [ˈʃlɪŋəl], *m.* (—s, *pl.* —) little rascal.

schlingen [ˈʃlɪŋən], *v.a. irr.* sling, wind; swallow, devour.

Schlips [ʃlɪps], *m.* (—es, *pl.* —e) (neck-)tie, cravat.

Schlitten [ˈʃlɪtən], *m.* (—s, *pl.* —) sledge, sled, sleigh.

Schlittschuh [ˈʃlɪtʃuː], *m.* (—s, *pl.* —e) skate; *— laufen*, skate.

Schlitz [ʃlɪts], *m.* (—es, *pl.* —e) slit.

schlohweiß [ˈʃloːvaɪs], *adj.* white as sloe-blossom, snow-white.

Schloß [ʃlɔs], *n.* (—sses, *pl.* ⁻sser) (*door*) lock, padlock; (*gun*) lock; palace, castle; *unter — und Riegel*, under lock and key.

Schloße [ˈʃloːsə], *f.* (—, *pl.* —n) hailstone.

Schlosser [ˈʃlɔsər], *m.* (—s, *pl.* —) locksmith.

Schlot [ʃloːt], *m.* (—(e)s, *pl.* —e) chimney, funnel.

schlottern [ˈʃlɔtərn], *v.n.* wobble, dodder; tremble.

Schlucht [ʃluxt], *f.* (—, *pl.* —en) deep valley, defile, cleft, glen, ravine, gorge.

schluchzen [ˈʃluxtsən], *v.n.* sob.

schlucken [ˈʃlukən], *v.a.* gulp down, swallow. — *v.n.* hiccup.

Schlucker [ˈʃlukər], *m.* (—s, *pl.* —) *armer —*, poor wretch.

Schlummer [ˈʃlumər], *m.* (—s, *no pl.*) slumber.

Schlumpe [ˈʃlumpə], *f.* (—, *pl.* —n) slut, slattern.

Schlund [ʃlunt], *m.* (—(e)s, *pl.* ⁻e) throat, gorge, gullet; gulf, abyss.

schlüpfen [ˈʃlypfən], *v.n.* (*aux.* sein) slip, slide, glide.

Schlüpfer [ˈʃlypfər], *m. pl.* knickers.

schlüpfrig [ˈʃlypfrɪç], *adj.* slippery; (*fig.*) obscene, indecent.

schlürfen [ˈʃlyrfən], *v.a.* drink noisily, lap up. — *v.n.* (*aux.* sein) (*dial.*) shuffle along.

Schluß [ʃlus], *m.* (—sses, *pl.* ⁻sse) end, termination; conclusion.

Schlüssel [ˈʃlysəl], *m.* (—s, *pl.* —) key; (*Mus.*) clef.

Schlüsselbein [ˈʃlysəlbaɪn], *n.* (—s, *pl.* —e) collar-bone.

Schlüsselblume [ˈʃlysəlbluːmə], *f.* (—, *pl.* —n) (*Bot.*) cowslip, primrose.

Schlußfolgerung [ˈʃlusfɔlgərʊŋ], *f.* (—, *pl.* —en) conclusion, inference, deduction.

schlüssig [ˈʃlysɪç], *adj.* resolved, determined; sure; (*Law*) well-grounded; *sich — werden über*, resolve on.

Schmach [ʃmaːx], *f.* (—, *no pl.*) disgrace, ignominy.

schmachten [ˈʃmaxtən], *v.n.* languish, pine.

schmächtig [ˈʃmɛçtɪç], *adj.* slender, slim, spare.

schmackhaft [ˈʃmakhaft], *adj.* tasty, savoury.

schmähen [ˈʃmɛːən], *v.a.* revile, abuse, calumniate.

Schmähschrift [ˈʃmɛːʃrɪft], *f.* (—, *pl.* —en) lampoon.

schmal [ʃmaːl], *adj.* narrow.

schmälen [ˈʃmɛːlən], *v.a.* chide, scold.

schmälern [ˈʃmɛːlərn], *v.a.* lessen, diminish, curtail; detract from, belittle.

Schmalz [ʃmalts], *n.* (—es, *no pl.*) grease, lard, fat.

schmarotzen [ʃmaˈrɔtsən], *v.n.* sponge on others.

Schmarren [ˈʃmarən], *m.* (—s, *pl.* —) trash; (*dial.*) omelette.

Schmatz [ʃmats], *m.* (—es, *pl.* ⁻e) (*dial.*) smacking kiss.

schmauchen [ˈʃmauxən], *v.a.*, *v.n.* smoke.

Schmaus [ʃmaus], *m.* (—es, *pl.* —e) feast, banquet.

schmecken [ˈʃmɛkən], *v.a.* taste. — *v.n.* taste; *es schmeckt mir*, I like it.

Schmeichelei [ʃmaɪçəˈlaɪ], *f.* (—, *pl.* —en) flattery, adulation.

schmeicheln [ˈʃmaɪçəln], *v.n.* flatter; fondle, pet.

schmeißen [ˈʃmaɪsən], *v.a. irr.* throw, hurl, fling; (*sl.*) *ich werde die Sache schon —*, I shall pull it off.

Schmeißfliege [ˈʃmaɪsfliːgə], *f.* (—, *pl.* —n) (*Ent.*) bluebottle.

Schmelz [ʃmɛlts], *m.* (—es, *no pl.*) enamel; melting; (*voice*) mellowness.

schmelzbar [ˈʃmɛltsbaːr], *adj.* fusible.

schmelzen [ˈʃmɛltsən], *v.a. irr.* smelt, melt. — *v.n.* (*aux.* sein) (*ice*) melt; (*fig.*) decrease, diminish.

Schmelztiegel ['ʃmɛltstiːgəl], *m.* (—s, *pl.* —) crucible; melting pot.

Schmelztopf ['ʃmɛltstɔpf], *m. see* **Schmelztiegel.**

Schmerbauch ['ʃmeːrbaux], *m.* (—(e)s, *pl.* ·'e) (*coll.*) paunch, belly.

Schmerz [ʃmɛrts], *m.* (—es, *pl.* —en) ache, pain; grief, sorrow; *einem —en verursachen,* give *or* cause s.o. pain.

schmerzlich ['ʃmɛrtslɪç], *adj.* painful, distressing.

Schmetterling ['ʃmɛtərlɪŋ], *m.* (—s, *pl.* —e) (*Ent.*) butterfly, moth.

schmettern ['ʃmɛtərn], *v.n.* resound; (*trumpets*) blare; (*bird*) warble.

Schmied [ʃmiːt], *m.* (—s, *pl.* —e) (black)smith.

Schmiede ['ʃmiːdə], *f.* (—, *pl.* —n) forge, smithy.

schmiegen ['ʃmiːgən], *v.r. sich —,* bend, yield; *sich an einen —,* cling to s.o., nestle against s.o.

Schmiere ['ʃmiːrə], *f.* (—, *pl.* —n) grease, salve; (*Theat.*) troop of strolling players.

schmieren ['ʃmiːrən], *v.a.* smear, grease, spread; (*fig.*) bribe; (*bread*) butter. — *v.n.* scrawl, scribble.

Schmierfink ['ʃmiːrfɪŋk], *m.* (—en, *pl.* —en) dirty person; muckraker.

Schmiermittel ['ʃmiːrmɪtəl], *n.* (—s, *pl.* —) lubricant.

Schmierseife ['ʃmiːrzaɪfə], *f.* (—, *no pl.*) soft soap.

Schminke ['ʃmɪŋkə], *f.* (—, *pl.* —n) greasepaint; rouge; make-up, cosmetics.

Schmirgel ['ʃmɪrgəl], *m.* (—s, *no pl.*) emery.

Schmiß [ʃmɪs], *m.* (—sses, *pl.* —sse) cut in the face, (duelling) scar; (*fig.*) smartness, verve.

Schmöker ['ʃmøːkər], *m.* (—s, *pl.* —) trashy book.

schmollen ['ʃmɔlən], *v.n.* sulk, pout.

Schmorbraten ['ʃmoːrbraːtən], *m.* (—s, *pl.* —) stewed meat.

Schmuck [ʃmuk], *m.* (—(e)s, *pl.* —stücke) ornament, jewels, jewellery; (*Am.*) jewelry.

schmuck [ʃmuk], *adj.* neat, spruce, dapper, smart.

schmücken ['ʃmʏkən], *v.a.* adorn, embellish.

Schmucksachen ['ʃmukzaxən], *f. pl.* jewels, finery, jewellery, articles of adornment; (*Am.*) jewelry.

schmuggeln ['ʃmugəln], *v.a.* smuggle.

schmunzeln ['ʃmuntsəln], *v.n.* smirk, grin.

Schmutz [ʃmuts], *m.* (—es, *no pl.*) dirt, filth.

schmutzen ['ʃmutsən], *v.n.* get soiled, get dirty.

Schmutzkonkurrenz ['ʃmutskɔnkurɛnts], *f.* (—, *no pl.*) unfair competition.

Schnabel ['ʃnaːbəl], *m.* (—s, *pl.* ·') bill, beak; (*ship*) prow; *halt den —,* keep your mouth shut; *er spricht, wie ihm*

der — gewachsen ist, he calls a spade a spade.

Schnabeltier ['ʃnaːbəltiːr], *n.* (—s, *pl.* —e) duck-bill, duck-billed platypus.

Schnaderhüpfel ['ʃnaːdərhypfəl], *n.* (—s, *pl.* —) (*dial.*) Alpine folk-song.

Schnalle ['ʃnalə], *f.* (—, *pl.* —n) buckle.

schnalzen ['ʃnaltsən], *v.n.* click; snap.

schnappen ['ʃnapən], *v.n.* snap; snatch at s.th.; *nach Luft —,* gasp for breath.

Schnaps [ʃnaps], *m.* (—es, *pl.* ·'e) spirits, brandy, gin.

schnarchen ['ʃnarçən], *v.n.* snore.

Schnarre ['ʃnarə], *f.* (—, *pl.* —n) rattle.

schnattern ['ʃnatərn], *v.n.* cackle; gabble; chatter.

schnauben ['ʃnaubən], *v.n.* puff and blow; snort; *vor Zorn —,* fret and fume.

schnaufen ['ʃnaufən], *v.n.* breathe heavily, pant.

Schnauze ['ʃnautsə], *f.* (—, *pl.* —n) (*animals*) snout; (*vulg.*) mouth, trap; nozzle.

schnauzen ['ʃnautsən], *v.n.* snarl, shout (at).

Schnecke ['ʃnɛkə], *f.* (—, *pl.* —n), (*Zool.*) snail, slug.

Schnee [ʃneː], *m.* (—s, *no pl.*) snow.

Schneegestöber ['ʃneːgəʃtøːbər], *n.* (—s, *pl.* —) snow-storm.

Schneeglöckchen ['ʃneːglœkçən], *n.* (—s, *pl.* —) (*Bot.*) snowdrop.

Schneeschläger ['ʃneːʃlɛːgər], *m.* (—s, *pl.* —) whisk.

Schneetreiben ['ʃneːtraɪbən], *n.* (—s, *no pl.*) snow-storm, blizzard.

Schneewittchen [ʃneːˈvɪtçən], *n.* (—s, *no pl.*) Snow White.

Schneid [ʃnaɪt], *m.* (—s, *no pl.*) go, push, dash, courage.

Schneide ['ʃnaɪdə], *f.* (—, *pl.* —n) edge.

Schneidebohne ['ʃnaɪdəboːnə], *f.* (—, *pl.* —n) French bean, string-bean.

Schneidemühle ['ʃnaɪdəmyːlə], *f.* (—, *pl.* —n) saw mill.

schneiden ['ʃnaɪdən], *v.a. irr.* cut, trim, carve; (*fig.*) ignore, cut; *Gesichter —,* make faces. — *v.r. sich —,* cut o.s.; (*Maths.*) intersect; *sich die Haare — lassen,* have o.'s hair cut.

Schneider ['ʃnaɪdər], *m.* (—s, *pl.* —) tailor.

Schneiderei [ʃnaɪdəˈraɪ], *f.* (—, *no pl.*) tailoring; dressmaking.

Schneidezahn ['ʃnaɪdətsaːn], *m.* (—s, *pl.* ·'e) incisor.

schneidig ['ʃnaɪdɪç], *adj.* dashing.

schneien ['ʃnaɪən], *v.n.* snow.

Schneise ['ʃnaɪzə], *f.* (—, *pl.* —n) (*forest*) glade, cutting.

schnell [ʃnɛl], *adj.* quick, swift, speedy, fast, rapid; *mach —,* hurry up.

Schnelle ['ʃnɛlə], *f.* (—, *pl.* —n) (*river*) rapids.

schnellen ['ʃnɛlən], *v.n.* spring, jump.

Schnelligkeit

Schnelligkeit [ˈʃnɛlɪçkaɪt], *f.* (—, *no pl.*) quickness, speed, swiftness, rapidity; (*Tech.*) velocity.

Schnepfe [ˈʃnɛpfə], *f.* (—, *pl.* —**n**) (*Orn.*) snipe, woodcock.

schneuzen [ˈʃnɔytsən], *v.r. sich (die Nase)* —, blow o.'s nose.

schniegeln [ˈʃniːgəln], *v.r. sich* —, (*coll.*) dress up, deck out; *geschniegelt und gebügelt,* spick and span.

Schnippchen [ˈʃnɪpçən], *n.* (—**s**, *pl.* —) *einem ein — schlagen,* play a trick on s.o.

schnippisch [ˈʃnɪpɪʃ], *adj.* pert, perky.

Schnitt [ʃnɪt], *m.* (—(e)**s**, *pl.* —**e**) cut, incision; section; (*beer*) small glass; (*dress*) cut-out pattern; (*book*) edge.

Schnittbohne [ˈʃnɪtboːnə], *f.* (—, *pl.* —**n**) (*Bot.*) French bean.

Schnitte [ˈʃnɪtə], *f.* (—, *pl.* —**n**) slice (of bread).

Schnitter [ˈʃnɪtər], *m.* (—**s**, *pl.* —) reaper.

Schnittlauch [ˈʃnɪtlaux], *m.* (—**s**, *no pl.*) (*Bot.*) chives.

Schnittmuster [ˈʃnɪtmustər], *n.* (—**s**, *pl.* —) cut-out pattern.

Schnittwaren [ˈʃnɪtvaːrən], *f. pl.* dry goods, drapery.

Schnitzel [ˈʃnɪtsəl], *n.* (—**s**, *pl.* —) (*Cul.*) cutlet; *Wiener* —, veal cutlet; snip; (*pl.*) shavings.

schnitzen [ˈʃnɪtsən], *v.a.* carve (in wood).

schnodd(e)rig [ˈʃnɔd(ə)rɪç], *adj.* (*coll.*) cheeky, insolent.

schnöde [ˈʃnøːdə], *adj.* base, heinous, mean, vile; —*r Mammon,* filthy lucre; —*r Undank,* rank ingratitude.

Schnörkel [ˈʃnœrkəl], *m.* (—**s**, *pl.* —) (*writing*) flourish.

schnorren [ˈʃnɔrən], *v.n.* (*rare*) cadge, beg.

schnüffeln [ˈʃnyfəln], *v.n.* sniff; (*fig.*) pry, snoop.

Schnuller [ˈʃnulər], *m.* (—**s**, *pl.* —) baby's dummy; (*Am.*) pacifier.

Schnupfen [ˈʃnupfən], *m.* (—**s**, *pl.* —) cold (in the head); *den — haben,* have a (running) cold; *den — bekommen,* catch cold.

schnupfen [ˈʃnupfən], *v.a., v.n.* take snuff.

Schnupftuch [ˈʃnupftuːx], *n.* (—(e)**s**, *pl.* ˙ʻer) (*dial.*) (pocket-) handkerchief.

schnuppe [ˈʃnupə], *adj.* (*sl.*) *mir ist alles* —, it is all the same to me, I don't care.

schnuppern [ˈʃnupərn], *v.n.* smell, snuffle.

Schnur [ʃnuːr], *f.* (—, *pl.* —**en**, ˙ʻe) twine, cord, string; (*Elec.*) lead, extension cord.

Schnurrbart [ˈʃnurbaːrt], *m.* (—**s**, *pl.* ˙ʻe) moustache; *sich einen — wachsen lassen,* grow a moustache.

Schnürchen [ˈʃnyːrçən], *f.* (—**s**, *pl.* —) *wie am —,* like clockwork.

schnüren [ˈʃnyːrən], *v.a.* lace, tie up; *sein Ränzel —,* pack o.'s bag.

Schnurre [ˈʃnurə], *f.* (—, *pl.* —**n**) funny story, yarn.

schnurren [ˈʃnurən], *v.n.* purr.

Schnürsenkel [ˈʃnyːrzɛŋkəl], *m.* (—**s**, *pl.* —) (*shoe*) lace.

schnurstracks [ˈʃnuːrʃtraks], *adv.* directly, immediately, on the spot.

Schober [ˈʃoːbər], *m.* (—**s**, *pl.* —) stack, rick.

Schock (1) [ʃɔk], *n.* (—(e)**s**, *pl.* —**e**) sixty, three score.

Schock (2) [ʃɔk], *m.* (—(e)**s**, *pl.* —**s**) shock; blow; stroke.

Schöffe [ˈʃœfə], *m.* (—**n**, *pl.* —**n**) (*Law*) juror; member of jury.

Schokolade [ʃokoˈlaːdə], *f.* (—, *pl.* —**n**) chocolate; *eine Tafel —,* a bar of chocolate.

Scholle [ˈʃɔlə], *f.* (—, *pl.* —**n**) plaice; (*ice*) floe; clod; soil.

schon [ʃoːn], *adv.* already; indeed; yet; *na wenn —,* so what; *— gut,* that'll do; *— gestern,* as early as yesterday.

schön [ʃøːn], *adj.* beautiful, fair, handsome, lovely; —*e Literatur,* belleslettres, good books.

schonen [ˈʃoːnən], *v.a.* spare, save; treat considerately.

Schoner [ˈʃoːnər], *m.* (—**s**, *pl.* —) antimacassar; (*Naut.*) schooner.

Schönheit [ˈʃøːnhaɪt], *f.* (—, *no pl.*) beauty.

Schonung [ˈʃoːnuŋ], *f.* (—, *pl.* —**en**) forbearance, considerate treatment; (*forest*) plantation of young trees.

Schonzeit [ˈʃoːntsaɪt], *f.* (—, *pl.* —**en**) close season.

Schopf [ʃɔpf], *m.* (—**es**, *pl.* ˙ʻe) tuft, head of hair; (*bird*) crest; *das Glück beim —e fassen,* take time by the forelock, make hay while the sun shines.

Schöpfbrunnen [ˈʃœpfbrunən], *m.* (—**s**, *pl.* —) (draw-)well.

schöpfen [ˈʃœpfən], *v.a.* (*water*) draw; derive; *Verdacht —,* become suspicious; *frische Luft —,* get a breath of fresh air; *Mut —,* take heart.

Schöpfer [ˈʃœpfər], *m.* (—**s**, *pl.* —) creator.

Schöpfkelle [ˈʃœpfkɛlə], *f.* (—, *pl.* —**n**) scoop.

Schopflerche [ˈʃɔpflɛrçə], *f.* (—, *pl.* —**n**) (*Orn.*) crested lark.

Schöpfung [ˈʃœpfuŋ], *f.* (—, *pl.* —**en**) creation.

Schoppen [ˈʃɔpən], *m.* (—**s**, *pl.* —) (*approx.*) half a pint.

Schöps [ʃœps], *m.* (—**es**, *pl.* —**e**) (*Zool.*) wether; (*fig.*) simpleton.

Schorf [ʃɔrf], *m.* (—(e)**s**, *pl.* —**e**) scab, scurf.

Schornstein [ˈʃɔrnʃtaɪn], *m.* (—**s**, *pl.* —**e**) chimney; (*ship*) funnel.

Schoß [ʃoːs], *m.* (—**es**, *pl.* ˙ʻe) lap; (*Poet.*) womb; skirt, tail; *die Hände in den — legen,* be idle, fold o.'s arms, twiddle o.'s thumbs.

Schößling [ˈʃœslɪŋ], *m.* (—s, *pl.* —e) shoot, sprig.

Schote [ˈʃoːtə], *f.* (—, *pl.* —n) pod, husk, shell; (*pl.*) green peas.

Schotter [ˈʃɔtər], *m.* (—s, *no pl.*) road-metal, broken stones, gravel.

Schottland [ˈʃɔtlant], *n.* Scotland.

schraffieren [ʃraˈfiːrən], *v.a.* (*Art*) hatch.

schräg [ˈʃrɛːk], *adj.* oblique, sloping, slanting, diagonal.

Schramme [ˈʃramə], *f.* (—, *pl.* —n) scratch, scar.

Schrank [ʃraŋk], *m.* (—(e)s, *pl.* ⁓e) cupboard, wardrobe.

Schranken [ˈʃraŋkən], *f. pl.* barriers, (level crossing) gates, limits, bounds; *in — halten,* limit, keep within bounds.

schränken [ˈʃrɛŋkən], *v.a.* cross; fold.

Schranze [ˈʃrantsə], *m.* (—n, *pl.* —n) sycophant, toady.

Schraube [ˈʃraubə], *f.* (—, *pl.* —n) screw; bolt; propeller.

Schraubengewinde [ˈʃraubəngəvɪndə], *n.* (—s, *pl.* —) thread of a screw.

Schraubenmutter [ˈʃraubənmutər], *f.* (—, *pl.* —n) female screw, nut.

Schraubenzieher [ˈʃraubəntsiːər], *m.* (—s, *pl.* —) screw-driver.

Schraubstock [ˈʃraupʃtɔk], *m.* (—s, *pl.* ⁓e) (*tool*) vise.

Schreck(en) [ˈʃrɛk(ən)], *m.* (—s, *pl.* —) fright, terror, alarm, horror; shock.

Schrecknis [ˈʃrɛknɪs], *n.* (—ses, *pl.* —se) terror, horror.

Schrei [ʃrai], *m.* (—s, *pl.* —e) cry; scream.

Schreiben [ˈʃraibən], *n.* (—s, *pl.* —) letter, missive.

schreiben [ˈʃraibən], *v.a. irr.* write; *ins Reine —,* make a fair copy.

Schreibfehler [ˈʃraipfeːlər], *m.* (—s, *pl.* —) slip of the pen.

Schreibkrampf [ˈʃraipkrampf], *m.* (—(e)s, *pl.* ⁓e) writer's cramp.

Schreibmaschine [ˈʃraipmaʃiːnə], *f.* (—, *pl.* —n) typewriter.

Schreibwaren [ˈʃraipvaːrən], *f. pl.* stationery.

Schreibweise [ˈʃraipvaizə], *f.* (— *pl.* —n) style; spelling.

schreien [ˈʃraiən], *v.a., v.n. irr.* cry, shout, scream, yell.

Schreihals [ˈʃraihals], *m.* (—es, *pl.* ⁓e) cry-baby, noisy child.

Schrein [ʃrain], *m.* (—(e)s, *pl.* —e) box, chest; shrine.

schreiten [ˈʃraitən], *v.n. irr.* (*aux.* sein) stride, step, pace.

Schrift [ʃrɪft], *f.* (—, *pl.* —en) writing; handwriting, calligraphy; publication; type; *Heilige —,* Holy Writ, Holy Scripture.

Schriftführer [ˈʃrɪftfyːrər], *m.* (—s, *pl.* —) secretary.

Schriftgießerei [ˈʃrɪftgiːsərai], *f.* (—, *pl.* —en) type-foundry.

Schriftleiter [ˈʃrɪftlaitər], *m.* (—s, *pl.* —) editor.

schriftlich [ˈʃrɪftlɪç], *adj.* written. — *adv.* in writing, by letter.

Schriftsetzer [ˈʃrɪftzetsər], *m.* (—s, *pl.* —) compositor.

Schriftsteller [ˈʃrɪftʃtɛlər], *m.* (—s, *pl.* —) writer, author.

Schriftstück [ˈʃrɪftʃtyk], *n.* (—s, *pl.* —e) document, deed.

Schriftwechsel [ˈʃrɪftvɛksəl], *m.* (—s, *no pl.*) exchange of notes, correspondence.

Schriftzeichen [ˈʃrɪftsaiçən], *n.* (—s, *pl.* —) character, letter (of alphabet).

schrill [ʃrɪl], *adj.* shrill.

Schritt [ʃrɪt], *m.* (—(e)s, *pl.* —e) step, pace, move; *lange —e machen,* stride; *— halten,* keep pace; *— fahren,* drive slowly, drive at walking pace; *aus dem —,* out of step; *in einer Sache —e tun,* make a move *or* take steps about s.th.

schrittweise [ˈʃrɪtvaizə], *adv.* step by step, gradually.

schroff [ˈʃrɔf], *adj.* steep, precipitous; (*fig.*) gruff, blunt, rough, harsh.

schröpfen [ˈʃrœpfən], *v.a.* (*Med.*) cup; (*fig.*) fleece.

Schrot [ʃroːt], *m. & n.* (—(e)s, *pl.* —e) grape-shot, small shot; *ein Mann vom alten —,* a man of the utmost probity.

Schrotbrot [ˈʃroːtbroːt], *n.* (—es, *no pl.*) wholemeal bread.

Schrott [ʃrɔt], *m.* (—(e)s, *pl.* —e), old iron, scrap metal.

Schrulle [ˈʃrulə], *f.* (—, *pl.* —n) fad, whim.

schrumpfen [ˈʃrumpfən], *v.n.* (*aux.* sein) shrink, shrivel.

Schub [ʃup], *m.* (—s, *pl.* ⁓e) shove, push; batch.

Schubkarren [ˈʃupkarən], *m.* (—s, *pl.* —) wheelbarrow.

Schublade [ˈʃuplaːdə], *f.* (—, *pl.* —n) drawer.

schüchtern [ˈʃʏçtərn], *adj.* shy, bashful, timid.

Schuft [ʃuft], *m.* (—(e)s, *pl.* —e) blackguard, scoundrel.

schuften [ˈʃuftən], *v.n.* work hard, toil.

Schufterei [ʃuftəˈrai], *f.* (—, *no pl.*) drudgery.

schuftig [ˈʃuftɪç], *adj.* rascally, mean.

Schuh [ʃuː], *m.* (—s, *pl.* —e) shoe; *einem etwas in die —e schieben,* lay the blame at s.o.'s door.

Schuhwerk [ˈʃuːvɛrk], *n.* (—s, *no pl.*) footwear.

Schuhwichse [ˈʃuːvɪksə], *f.* (—, *no pl.*) shoe-polish.

Schuld [ʃult], *f.* (—, *pl.* —en) guilt, offence, sin; fault; blame; cause; (*money*) debt; *in —en geraten,* run into debt.

schuld [ʃult], *adj. ich bin —,* it is my fault, I am to blame.

schulden [ˈʃuldən], *v.a.* owe, be indebted to.

schuldig [ˈʃuldɪç], *adj.* guilty, culpable; *sich — bekennen,* plead guilty; *einen — sprechen,* pronounce s.o. guilty;

ihm ist Anerkennung —, appreciation is due to him.

Schuldigkeit ['ʃuldɪçkaɪt], *f.* (—, *no pl.*) obligation, duty.

schuldlos ['ʃultloːs], *adj.* innocent, guiltless.

Schuldner ['ʃuldnər], *m.* (—s, *pl.* —) debtor.

Schule ['ʃuːlə], *f.* (—, *pl.* —n) school; *in die* — *gehen,* go to school, attend school; *die* — *schwänzen,* play truant; *hohe* —, (*Riding*) advanced horsemanship.

schulen ['ʃuːlən], *v.a.* train, instruct.

Schüler ['ʃyːlər], *m.* (—s, *pl.* —) schoolboy, pupil, student, scholar.

Schulklasse ['ʃuːlklasə], *f.* (—, *pl.* —n) class, form.

Schulleiter ['ʃuːllaɪtər], *m.* (—s, *pl.* —) headmaster.

Schulrat ['ʃuːlraːt], *m.* (—s, *pl.* ⸚e) school-inspector.

Schulter ['ʃultər], *f.* (—, *pl.* —n) shoulder.

Schulterblatt ['ʃultərblat], *n.* (—s, *pl.* ⸚er) shoulder-blade.

Schultheiß ['ʃulthaɪs], *m.* (—en, *pl.* —en) village magistrate, mayor.

Schulunterricht ['ʃuːlʊntərrɪçt], *m.* (—s, *no pl.*) school teaching, lessons.

schummeln ['ʃuməln], *v.n.* (*coll.*) cheat.

Schund [ʃunt], *m.* (—(e)s, *no pl.*) trash.

Schuppe ['ʃupə], *f.* (—, *pl.* —n) scale; (*pl.*) dandruff.

Schuppen ['ʃupən], *m.* (—s, *pl.* —) shed.

Schuppentier ['ʃupəntiːr], *n.* (—s, *pl.* —e) (*Zool.*) armadillo.

Schur [ʃuːr], *f.* (—, *pl.* —en) shearing.

schüren ['ʃyːrən], *v.a.* (*fire*) poke, rake; (*fig.*) stir up, fan, incite.

schürfen ['ʃyrfən], *v.a.* scratch. — *v.n.* (*Min.*) prospect.

schurigeln ['ʃuːrɪgəln], *v.a.* bully, pester.

Schurke ['ʃurkə], *m.* (—n, *pl.* —n) scoundrel, villain, blackguard.

Schurz [ʃurts], *m.* (—es, *pl.* —e) apron, overall.

Schürze ['ʃyrtsə], *f.* (—, *pl.* —n) apron, pinafore.

schürzen ['ʃyrtsən], *v.a.* tuck up, pin up.

Schürzenjäger ['ʃyrtsənjeːgər], *m.* (—s, *pl.* —) ladies' man.

Schurzfell ['ʃurtsfɛl], *n.* (—s, *pl.* —e) leather apron.

Schuß [ʃus], *m.* (—sses, *pl.* ⸚sse) shot, report; dash; *weit vom* —, out of harm's way; wide of the mark.

Schüssel ['ʃysəl], *f.* (—, *pl.* —n) dish.

Schußwaffe ['ʃusvafə], *f.* (—, *pl.* —n) fire-arm.

Schuster ['ʃuːstər], *m.* (—s, *pl.* —) shoemaker, cobbler; *auf* —s *Rappen,* on Shanks's pony.

schustern ['ʃuːstərn], *v.n.* cobble, make *or* mend shoes.

Schutt [ʃut], *m.* (—(e)s, *no pl.*) rubbish, refuse; rubble; — *abladen,*

dump refuse.

Schütte ['ʃytə], *f.* (—, *pl.* —n) (*dial.* bundle, truss.

schütteln ['ʃytəln], *v.a.* shake, jolt.

schütten ['ʃytən], *v.a.* shoot, pour; pour out.

schütter ['ʃytər], *adj.* (*dial.*) (*hair*) thin; scarce.

Schutz [ʃuts], *m.* (—es, *no pl.*) protection, shelter, cover; *einen in* — *nehmen gegen,* defend s.o. against.

Schutzbefohlene ['ʃutsbəfoːlənə], *m.* (—n, *pl.* —n) charge, person in o.'s care, ward.

Schutzbündnis ['ʃutsbyntnɪs], *n.* (—ses, *pl.* —se) defensive alliance.

Schütze ['ʃytsə], *m.* (—n, *pl.* —n) rifleman, sharpshooter, marksman; (*Astrol.*) Sagittarius.

schützen ['ʃytsən], *v.a.* protect, shelter, defend. — *v.r. sich* — *vor,* guard o.s. against.

Schützengraben ['ʃytsəngraːbən], *m.* (—s, *pl.* ⸚) trench.

Schutzgebiet ['ʃutsgəbiːt], *n.* (—s, *pl.* —e) protectorate.

Schutzgitter ['ʃutsgɪtər], *n.* (—s, *pl.* —e) grid, guard.

Schutzheilige ['ʃutshaɪlɪgə], *m.* (—n, *pl.* —n) patron saint.

Schützling ['ʃytslɪŋ], *m.* (—s, *pl.* —e) protégé, charge.

Schutzmann ['ʃutsman], *m.* (—s, *pl.* ⸚er, **Schutzleute**) policeman, constable.

Schutzmarke ['ʃutsmarkə], *f.* (—, *pl.* —n) trade-mark.

Schutzzoll ['ʃutstsɔl], *m.* (—s, *pl.* ⸚e) protective duty, tariff.

Schwaben ['ʃvaːbən], *n.* Swabia.

Schwabenstreich ['ʃvaːbənʃtraɪç], *m.* (—s, *pl.* —e) tomfoolery.

schwach [ʃvax], *adj.* weak, frail, feeble; (*noise*) faint; (*pulse*) low; —*e Seite,* foible; —*e Stunde,* unguarded moment.

Schwäche ['ʃvɛçə], *f.* (—, *pl.* —n) weakness, faintness; infirmity.

schwächen ['ʃvɛçən], *v.a.* weaken, debilitate.

Schwächling ['ʃvɛçlɪŋ], *m.* (—s, *pl.* —e) weakling.

Schwachsinn ['ʃvaxzɪn], *m.* (—s, *no pl.*) feeble-mindedness.

Schwächung ['ʃvɛçuŋ], *f.* (—, *pl.* —en) weakening, lessening.

Schwadron [ʃvaˈdroːn], *f.* (—, *pl.* —en) squadron.

Schwadroneur [ʃvadroˈnøːr], *m.* (—s, *pl.* —e) swaggerer.

schwadronieren [ʃvadroˈniːrən], *v.n.* talk big, swagger.

schwafeln ['ʃvaːfəln], *v.n.* (*sl.*) talk nonsense, waffle.

Schwager ['ʃvaːgər], *m.* (—s, *pl.* ⸚) brother-in-law.

Schwägerin ['ʃvɛːgərɪn], *f.* (—, *pl.* —nen) sister-in-law.

Schwalbe ['ʃvalbə], *f.* (—, *pl.* —n) (*Orn.*) swallow.

Schwalbenschwanz [ˈʃvalbənʃvants], *m.* (—es, *pl.* ⁀e) (*butterfly*) swallow's tail; (*joinery*) dovetail.

Schwall [ʃval], *m.* (—(e)s, *no pl.*) flood; (*fig.*) deluge, torrent.

Schwamm [ʃvam], *m.* (—(e)s, *pl.* ⁀e) sponge; fungus, mushroom; dry rot.

schwammig [ˈʃvamiç], *adj.* spongy, fungous.

Schwan [ʃvaːn], *m.* (—(e)s, *pl.* ⁀e) swan; *junger* —, cygnet.

schwanen [ˈʃvaːnən], *v.n. imp. es schwant mir*, I have a foreboding.

Schwang [ʃvaŋ], *m. im* —*e sein*, be in fashion, be the rage.

schwanger [ˈʃvaŋər], *adj.* pregnant.

schwängern [ˈʃvɛŋərn], *v.a.* make pregnant, get with child; (*fig.*) impregnate.

Schwangerschaft [ˈʃvaŋərʃaft], *f.* (—, *pl.* —en) pregnancy.

Schwank [ʃvaŋk], *m.* (—(e)s, *pl.* ⁀e) funny story, joke; (*Theat.*) farce.

schwank [ʃvaŋk], *adj.* flexible, supple; *ein* —*es Rohr*, a reed shaken by the wind.

schwanken [ˈʃvaŋkən], *v.n.* totter, stagger; (*fig.*) waver, vacillate; (*prices*) fluctuate.

Schwanz [ʃvants], *m.* (—es, *pl.* ⁀e) tail.

schwänzeln [ˈʃvɛntsəln], *v.n.* (*animal*) wag the tail; (*fig.*) fawn, cringe.

schwänzen [ˈʃvɛntsən], *v.a. die Schule* —, play truant.

Schwären [ˈʃvɛːrən], *m.* (—s, *pl.* —) ulcer, abscess.

schwären [ˈʃvɛːrən], *v.n.* fester, suppurate.

Schwarm [ʃvarm], *m.* (—(e)s, *pl.* ⁀e) (*insects*) swarm; (*humans*) crowd; (*birds*) flight.

Schwärmerei [ʃvɛrməˈrai], *f.* (—, *pl.* —en) enthusiasm, passion, craze.

Schwarte [ˈʃvartə], *f.* (—, *pl.* —n) rind; crust; *alte* —, (*fig.*) old volume; tome.

schwarz [ʃvarts], *adj.* black.

Schwarzamsel [ˈʃvartsamzəl], *f.* (—, *pl.* —n) (*Orn.*) blackbird.

Schwarzdorn [ˈʃvartsdɔrn], *m.* (—s, *no pl.*) (*Bot.*) blackthorn, sloe.

Schwärze [ˈʃvɛrtsə], *f.* (—, *no pl.*) blackness; printer's ink.

schwärzen [ˈʃvɛrtsən], *v.a.* blacken.

Schwarzkünstler [ˈʃvartskynstlər], *m.* (—s, *pl.* —) magician, necromancer.

Schwarzwald [ˈʃvartsvalt], *m.* Black Forest.

Schwarzwild [ˈʃvartsvilt], *n.* (—(e)s, *no pl.*) wild boar.

schwatzen [ˈʃvatsən], *v.n.* chat, chatter, prattle.

Schwätzer [ˈʃvɛtsər], *m.* (—s, *pl.* —) chatterbox.

Schwatzhaftigkeit [ˈʃvatshaftiçkait], *f.* (—, *no pl.*) loquacity, talkativeness.

Schwebe [ˈʃveːbə], *f.* (—, *pl.* —n) suspense; suspension.

Schwebebaum [ˈʃveːbəbaum], *m.* (—s, *pl.* ⁀e) horizontal bar.

schweben [ˈʃveːbən], *v.n.* be suspended, hover; (*fig.*) be pending; *in Gefahr* —, be in danger; *es schwebt mir auf der Zunge*, it is on the tip of my tongue.

Schwede [ˈʃveːdə], *m.* (—n, *pl.* —n) Swede; *alter* —, (*fig.*) old boy.

Schweden [ˈʃveːdən], *n.* Sweden.

Schwedenhölzer [ˈʃveːdənhœltsər], *n. pl.* (*rare*) matches.

Schwefel [ˈʃveːfəl], *m.* (—s, *no pl.*) sulphur, brimstone.

Schwefelhölzchen [ˈʃveːfəlhœltsçən], *n.* (—s, *pl.* —) (*obs.*) match.

schwefeln [ˈʃveːfəln], *v.a.* impregnate with sulphur, fumigate.

Schwefelsäure [ˈʃveːfəlzɔyrə], *f.* (—, *no pl.*) sulphuric acid.

Schweif [ʃvaif], *m.* (—(e)s, *pl.* —e) tail.

schweifen [ˈʃvaifən], *v.n.* (*aux.* sein) ramble, stray, wander.

schweifwedeln [ˈʃvaifveːdəln], *v.n.* fawn.

Schweigegeld [ˈʃvaigəgɛlt], *n.* (—(e)s, *pl.* —er) (*coll.*) hush-money.

Schweigen [ˈʃvaigən], *n.* (—s, *no pl.*) silence.

schweigen [ˈʃvaigən], *v.n. irr.* be silent; be quiet; *ganz zu* — *von*, to say nothing of.

schweigsam [ˈʃvaikzaːm], *adj.* taciturn.

Schwein [ʃvain], *n.* (—(e)s, *pl.* —e) pig, hog; swine; *wildes* —, boar; (*fig.*) luck, fluke; — *haben*, be lucky.

Schweinekoben [ˈʃvainəkoːbən], *m.* (—s, *pl.* —) pigsty.

Schweinerei [ʃvainəˈrai], *f.* (—, *pl.* —en) filth; (*fig.*) smut, filthiness, obscenity; mess.

Schweineschmalz [ˈʃvainəʃmalts], *n.* (—es, *no pl.*) lard.

Schweinigel [ˈʃvainigəl], *m.* (—s, *pl.* —) (*Zool.*) hedgehog, porcupine; (*fig.*) dirty pig, filthy wretch.

Schweinskeule [ˈʃvainskɔylə], *f.* (—, *pl.* —n) leg of pork.

Schweiß [ʃvais], *m.* (—es, *no pl.*) sweat, perspiration.

schweißen [ˈʃvaisən], *v.a.* weld, solder.

Schweiz [ʃvaits], *f.* Switzerland.

Schweizer [ˈʃvaitsər], *m.* (—s, *pl.* —) Swiss; (*fig.*) dairyman.

Schweizerei [ʃvaitsəˈrai], *f.* (—, *pl.* —en) dairy.

schwelen [ˈʃveːlən], *v.n.* burn slowly, smoulder.

schwelgen [ˈʃvɛlgən], *v.n.* carouse, revel.

Schwelgerei [ʃvɛlgəˈrai], *f.* (—, *pl.* —en) revelry.

schwelgerisch [ˈʃvɛlgəriʃ], *adj.* luxurious, voluptuous.

Schwelle [ˈʃvɛlə], *f.* (—, *pl.* —n) threshold; (*Railw.*) sleeper, tie.

schwellen [ˈʃvɛlən], *v.n. irr.* (*aux.* sein) swell; (*water*) rise.

Schwellung [ˈʃvɛluŋ], *f.* (—, *pl.* —en) swelling.

schwemmen

schwemmen ['ʃvɛmən], v.a. wash, soak, carry off.

Schwengel ['ʃvɛŋəl], m. (—s, pl. —) (bell) clapper; (pump) handle.

schwenken ['ʃvɛŋkən], v.a. swing; shake, brandish; (glasses) rinse.

Schwenkung ['ʃvɛŋkuŋ], f. (—, pl. —en) change; (Mil.) wheeling.

schwer [ʃveːr], adj. heavy; difficult, hard; ponderous; severe; — von Begriff, obtuse, slow in the uptake; —e Speise, indigestible food; einem das Herz — machen, grieve s.o.

schwerblütig ['ʃveːrblyːtɪç], adj. phlegmatic.

Schwere ['ʃveːrə], f. (—, no pl.) weight, heaviness; gravity.

Schwerenöter ['ʃveːrənøːtər], m. (—s, pl. —) gay dog, ladies' man.

schwerfällig ['ʃveːrfɛlɪç], adj. ungainly, cumbrous, unwieldy; (fig.) thickheaded, dense.

Schwergewicht ['ʃveːrgəvɪçt], n. (—s, no pl.) (Sport) heavyweight; (fig.) emphasis.

schwerhörig ['ʃveːrhøːrɪç], adj. hard of hearing, deaf.

Schwerkraft ['ʃveːrkraft], f. (—, no pl.) gravity.

schwerlich ['ʃveːrlɪç], adv. hardly, scarcely.

schwermütig ['ʃveːrmyːtɪç], adj. melancholy.

Schwerpunkt ['ʃveːrpuŋkt], m. (—s, pl. —e) centre of gravity.

Schwert [ʃveːrt], n. (—(e)s, pl. —er) sword.

Schwertgriff ['ʃveːrtgrɪf], m. (—s, pl. —e) hilt.

Schwertlilie ['ʃveːrtliːljə], f. (—, pl. —n) (Bot.) iris; fleur-de-lys.

Schwertstreich ['ʃveːrtʃtraɪç], m. (—(e)s, pl. —e) sword-blow, swordstroke.

schwerwiegend ['ʃveːrviːgənt], adj. weighty.

Schwester ['ʃvɛstər], f. (—, pl. —n) sister; barmherzige —, sister of mercy.

Schwesternschaft ['ʃvɛstərnʃaft], f. (—, pl. —en) sisterhood; (Am.) sorority.

Schwibbogen ['ʃvɪpboːgən], m. (—s, pl. —) (Archit.) flying buttress.

Schwiegersohn ['ʃviːgərzoːn], m. (—s, pl. —e) son-in-law.

Schwiegertochter ['ʃviːgərtɔxtər], f. (—, pl. —) daughter-in-law.

Schwiele ['ʃviːlə], f. (—, pl. —n) hard skin, callus, weal.

schwielig ['ʃviːlɪç], adj. callous, horny.

schwierig ['ʃviːrɪç], adj. difficult, hard.

Schwierigkeit ['ʃviːrɪçkaɪt], f. (—, pl. —en) difficulty; auf —en stoßen, meet with difficulties.

schwimmen ['ʃvɪmən], v.n. irr. (aux. sein) swim, float.

Schwimmer ['ʃvɪmər], m. (—s, pl. —) swimmer.

Schwimmgürtel ['ʃvɪmgyrtəl], m. (—s, pl. —) life-belt.

Schwindel ['ʃvɪndəl], m. (—s, pl. —) giddiness, dizziness, vertigo; swindle, fraud.

Schwindelanfall ['ʃvɪndəlanfal], m. (—s, pl. ⸚e) attack of giddiness, vertigo.

Schwindelei [ʃvɪndə'laɪ], f. (—, pl. —en) swindle, fraud, deceit.

schwindelhaft ['ʃvɪndəlhaft], adj. fraudulent.

schwinden ['ʃvɪndən], v.n. irr. (aux. sein) dwindle; disappear, vanish.

Schwindler ['ʃvɪndlər], m. (—s, pl. —) swindler, humbug, cheat.

schwindlig ['ʃvɪndlɪç], adj. dizzy, giddy.

Schwindsucht ['ʃvɪntzuxt], f. (—, no pl.) (Med.) tuberculosis, consumption.

schwindsüchtig ['ʃvɪntzyçtɪç], adj. (Med.) tubercular.

Schwinge ['ʃvɪŋə], f. (—, pl. —n) wing.

schwingen ['ʃvɪŋən], v.a. irr. brandish. — v.n. swing, vibrate. — v.r. sich —, vault; sich auf den Thron —, usurp or take possession of the throne.

Schwingung ['ʃvɪŋuŋ], f. (—, pl. —en) vibration, oscillation.

Schwips [ʃvɪps], m. (—es, pl. —e) (coll.) tipsiness; einen — haben, be tipsy.

schwirren ['ʃvɪrən], v.n. whir, buzz.

Schwitzbad ['ʃvɪtsbaːt], n. (—es, pl. ⸚er) Turkish bath, steam-bath.

schwitzen ['ʃvɪtsən], v.n. sweat, perspire.

schwören ['ʃvøːrən], v.a., v.n. irr. swear, take an oath; darauf kannst du —, you can be quite sure of that, you bet; falsch —, forswear o.s., perjure o.s.

schwül [ʃvyːl], adj. sultry, close.

Schwüle ['ʃvyːlə], f. (—, no pl.) sultriness.

Schwulst [ʃvulst], m. (—es, no pl.) bombast.

schwülstig ['ʃvylstɪç], adj. bombastic, turgid.

Schwülstigkeit ['ʃvylstɪçkaɪt], f. (—, pl. —en) bombastic style, turgidity.

Schwund [ʃvunt], m. (—(e)s, no pl.) dwindling, decline; shrinkage.

Schwung [ʃvuŋ], m. (—(e)s, pl. ⸚e) swing, leap, bound; (fig.) verve, élan; (Poet.) flight, soaring.

schwunghaft ['ʃvuŋhaft], adj. flourishing, soaring.

Schwungkraft ['ʃvuŋkraft], f. (—, no pl.) centrifugal force; (mental) resilience.

Schwungrad ['ʃvuŋraːt], n. (—s, pl. ⸚er) fly-wheel.

schwungvoll ['ʃvuŋfɔl], adj. spirited.

Schwur [ʃvuːr], m. (—(e)s, pl. ⸚e) oath.

Schwurgericht ['ʃvuːrgərɪçt], n. (—s, pl. —e) (Law) assizes.

sechs [zɛks], num. adj. six.

Sechseck ['zɛksɛk], n. (—s, pl. —e) hexagon.

sechseckig ['zɛksɛkɪç], adj. hexagonal.

Sechser ['zɛksər], *m.* (—s, *pl.* —) coin of small value.

sechsspännig ['zɛksʃpɛnɪç], *adj.* drawn by six horses.

sechzehn ['zɛçtse:n], *num. adj.* sixteen.

sechzig ['zɛçtsɪç], *num. adj.* sixty.

Sediment [zedi'mɛnt], *n.* (—s, *pl.* —e) sediment.

See (1) [ze:], *m.* (—s, *pl.* —n) lake, pool.

See (2) [ze:], *f.* (—, *no pl.*) sea, ocean; *hohe* —, high seas; *zur* — *gehen*, go to sea, become a sailor.

Seeadler ['ze:adlər], *m.* (—s, *pl.* —) (*Orn.*) osprey.

Seebad ['ze:ba:t], *n.* (—s, *pl.* "er) seaside resort; bathe in the sea.

Seebär ['ze:bɛ:r], *m.* (—en, *pl.* —en) (*fig.*) old salt.

Seefahrer ['ze:fa:rər], *m.* (—s, *pl.* —) mariner, navigator.

Seefahrt ['ze:fa:rt], *f.* (—, *pl.* —en) seafaring; voyage, cruise.

seefest ['ze:fɛst], *adj.* (*ship*) seaworthy; (*person*) a good sailor.

Seefischerei ['ze:fɪʃəraɪ], *f.* (—, *no pl.*) deep-sea fishing.

Seeflotte ['ze:flɔtə], *f.* (—, *pl.* —n) navy, fleet.

Seegang ['ze:gaŋ], *m.* (—s, *no pl.*) swell.

Seegras ['ze:gra:s], *n.* (—es, *no pl.*) seaweed.

Seehandel ['ze:handəl], *m.* (—s, *no pl.*) maritime trade.

Seehund ['ze:hunt], *m.* (—s, *pl.* —e) (*Zool.*) seal.

Seeigel ['ze:i:gəl], *m.* (—s, *pl.* —) (*Zool.*) sea-urchin.

Seejungfrau ['ze:juŋfrau], *f.* (—, *pl.* —en) mermaid.

Seekadett ['ze:kadɛt], *m.* (—en, *pl.* —en) midshipman; (*naval*) cadet.

Seekarte ['ze:kartə], *f.* (—, *pl.* —n) chart.

seekrank ['ze:kraŋk], *adj.* seasick.

Seekrieg ['ze:kri:k], *m.* (—s, *pl.* —e) naval war.

Seeküste ['ze:kystə], *f.* (—, *pl.* —n) sea-coast, shore, beach.

Seele ['ze:lə], *f.* (—, *pl.* —n) soul; *mit ganzer* —, with all my heart.

Seelenamt ['ze:lənamt], *n.* (—s, *pl.* "er) (*Eccl.*) office for the dead, requiem.

Seelenangst ['ze:lənaŋkst], *f.* (—, *pl.* "e) anguish, agony.

Seelenheil ['ze:lənhaɪl], *n.* (—s, *no pl.*) (*Theol.*) salvation.

Seelenhirt ['ze:lənhɪrt], *m.* (—en, *pl.* —en) pastor.

seelenlos ['ze:lənlo:s], *adj.* inanimate.

Seelenmesse ['ze:lənmɛsə], *f.* (—, *pl.* —n) requiem; Mass for the dead.

Seelenruhe ['ze:lənru:ə], *f.* (—, *no pl.*) tranquility of mind.

seelenruhig ['ze:lənru:ɪç], *adj.* cool, calm, collected, unperturbed.

Seelenstärke ['ze:lənʃtɛrkə], *f.* (—, *no pl.*) fortitude; composure.

seelenvergnügt ['ze:lənfɛrgny:kt], *adj.* blissfully happy.

Seelenverwandtschaft ['ze:lənfɛrvantʃaft], *f.* (—, *pl.* —en) mental affinity, (mutual) understanding.

seelenvoll ['ze:lənfɔl], *adj.* wistful, soulful.

Seelenwanderung ['ze:lənvandəruŋ], *f.* (—, *no pl.*) transmigration of souls, metempsychosis.

Seeleute ['ze:lɔytə] *see under* **Seemann.**

seelisch ['ze:lɪʃ], *adj.* mental, psychological, psychic(al).

Seelsorge ['ze:lsɔrgə], *f.* (—, *no pl.*) (*Eccl.*) cure of souls; pastoral duties or work.

Seemann ['ze:man], *m.* (—s, *pl.* "er, Seeleute) seaman, sailor, mariner.

Seemeile ['ze:maɪlə], *f.* (—, *pl.* —n) knot, nautical mile.

Seemöwe ['ze:mø:və], *f.* (—, *pl.* —n) (*Orn.*) seagull.

Seemuschel ['ze:muʃəl], *f.* (—, *pl.* —n) sea-shell.

Seepflanze ['ze:pflantsə], *f.* (—, *pl.* —n) marine plant.

Seerabe ['ze:ra:bə], *m.* (—n, *pl.* —n) (*Orn.*) cormorant.

Seeräuber ['ze:rɔybər], *m.* (—s, *pl.* —) pirate.

Seerose ['ze:ro:zə], *f.* (—, *pl.* —n) (*Bot.*) water-lily.

Seesalz ['ze:zalts], *n.* (—es, *no pl.*) bay salt, sea salt.

Seeschlacht ['ze:ʃlaxt], *f.* (—, *pl.* —en) naval engagement, naval battle.

Seestern ['ze:ʃtɛrn], *m.* (—s, *pl.* —e) (*Zool.*) starfish.

Seestille ['ze:ʃtɪlə], *f.* (—, *no pl.*) calm (at sea).

Seetang ['ze:taŋ], *m.* (—s, *no pl.*) (*Bot.*) seaweed.

seetüchtig ['ze:tyçtɪç], *adj.* seaworthy.

Seeuhr ['ze:u:r], *f.* (—; *pl.* —en) marine chronometer.

Seeuntüchtigkeit ['ze:untyçtɪçkaɪt], *f.* (—, *no pl.*) unseaworthiness.

Seewasser ['ze:vasər], *n.* (—s, *no pl.*) sea-water, brine.

Seewesen ['ze:vezən], *n.* (—s, *no pl.*) naval affairs.

Seezunge ['ze:tsuŋə], *f.* (—, *pl.* —n) sole (*fish*).

Segel ['ze:gəl], *n.* (—s, *pl.* —) sail; *großes* —, mainsail; *unter* — *gehen*, set sail, put to sea; *die* — *streichen*, strike sail.

segelfertig ['ze:gəlfɛrtɪç], *adj.* ready to sail; *sich* — *machen*, get under sail.

Segelflugzeug ['ze:gəlflu:ktsɔyk], *n.* (—s, *pl.* —e) glider(-plane).

Segelschiff ['ze:gəlʃɪf], *n.* (—s, *pl.* —e) sailing-vessel.

Segelstange ['ze:gəlʃtaŋə], *f.* (—, *pl.* —n) sail-yard.

Segen ['ze:gən], *m.* (—s, *no pl.*) blessing, benediction; (*fig.*) abundance; — *sprechen*, give the blessing, say grace.

segensreich ['ze:gənsraiç], *adj.* blessed, full of blessings; prosperous.
Segenswunsch ['ze:gənsvunʃ], *m.* (—es, *pl.* ⸚e) good wish.
segnen ['ze:gnən], *v.a.* bless.
sehen ['ze:ən], *v.a. irr.* see, behold, perceive; *etwas gern* —, like s.th., approve of s.th. — *v.n.* look, see; *sich* — *lassen*, parade, show o.s., *wir werden* —, that remains to be seen, we shall see.
sehenswert ['ze:ənsve:rt], *adj.* worth seeing.
Sehenswürdigkeit ['ze:ənsvyrdiçkait], *f.* (—, *pl.* —en) curiosity, object of interest, tourist attraction; (*pl.*) sights.
Seher ['ze:ər], *m.* (—s, *pl.* —) seer, prophet.
Sehne ['ze:nə], *f.* (—, *pl.* —n) sinew, tendon; string.
sehnig ['ze:niç], *adj.* sinewy, muscular; (*meat*) tough.
sehnlich ['ze:nliç], *adj.* earnest, passionate, eager.
Sehnsucht ['ze:nzuxt], *f.* (—, *no pl.*) longing, yearning, desire.
sehr [ze:r], *adv.* very, much, greatly, very much; *zu* —, too much; — *gut*, very good; — *wohl*, very well.
Sehweite ['ze:vaitə], *f.* (—, *no pl.*) range of vision.
seicht [zaiçt], *adj.* shallow, superficial.
Seide ['zaidə], *f.* (—, *pl.* —n) silk.
Seidel ['zaidəl], *n.* (—s, *pl.* —) (*dial.*) mug, tankard; pint.
seiden ['zaidən], *adj.* silk, silken, silky.
Seidenpapier ['zaidənpapi:r], *n.* (—s, *no pl.*) tissue-paper.
Seidenraupe ['zaidənraupə], *f.* (—, *pl.* —n) (*Ent.*) silkworm.
Seidenstoff ['zaidənʃtɔf], *m.* (—es, *pl.* —e) spun silk.
Seife ['zaifə], *f.* (—, *pl.* —n) soap; *ein Stück* —, a cake of soap.
seifen ['zaifən], *v.a.* soap.
Seifenschaum ['zaifənʃaum], *m.* (—s, *no pl.*) lather.
Seifenwasser ['zaifənvasər], *n.* (—s, *no pl.*) soap-suds.
seifig ['zaifiç], *adj.* soapy, saponaceous.
seihen ['zaiən], *v.a.* strain, filter.
Seil [zail], *n.* (—(e)s, *pl.* —e) rope; *straffes* —, taut rope, tight rope; *schlaffes* —, slack rope.
Seilbahn ['zailba:n], *f.* (—, *pl.* —en) funicular railway; cable car.
Seilbrücke ['zailbrykə], *f.* (—, *pl.* —n) rope bridge.
Seiltänzer ['zailtɛntsər], *m.* (—s, *pl.* —) tight-rope walker.
Seilziehen ['zailtsi:ən], *n.* (—s, *no pl.*) tug of war.
Seim [zaim], *m.* (—(e)s, *pl.* —e) strained honey.
Sein [zain], *n.* (—s, *no pl.*) being, existence.
sein (1) [zain], *v.n. irr.* (*aux.* sein) be, exist.
sein (2) [zain], *poss. adj.* his, her, its; one's. — *pers. pron.* his.

seinerseits ['zainərzaits], *adv.* for his part.
seinerzeit ['zainərtsait], *adv.* at that time, at the time, formerly.
seinesgleichen ['zainəsglaiçən], *indecl. adj. & pron.* of his sort, such as he.
seinethalben ['zainəthalbən], *adv.* on his account, for his sake, on his behalf.
seinetwegen ['zainətve:gən], *adv.* on his account, for his sake, on his behalf.
Seinige ['zainigə], *n.* (—n, *pl.* —n) his, his property; (*pl.*) his family, his people; *das* — *tun*, do o.'s share.
seit [zait], *prep.* (*Dat.*) since, for; — *gestern*, since yesterday, from yesterday onwards; — *einiger Zeit*, for some time past. — *conj. see* **seitdem**.
seitdem [zait'de:m], *adv.* since then, since that time. — *conj.* since.
Seite ['zaitə], *f.* (—, *pl.* —n) side, flank; (*book*) page; *etwas auf die* — *bringen*, put s.th. aside; *ich bin auf seiner* —, I side with him, I am on his side; *er hat seine guten* —*n*, he has his good points.
Seitenansicht ['zaitənanziçt], *f.* (—, *pl.* —en) profile.
Seitengleis ['zaitənglais], *n.* (—es, *pl.* —e) (*railway*) siding.
Seitenhieb ['zaitənhi:p], *m.* (—s, *pl.* —e) innuendo, sly hit, dig.
seitens ['zaitəns], *prep.* (*Genit.*) on the part of.
Seitensprung ['zaitənʃpruŋ], *m.* (—s, *pl.* ⸚e) side-leap, caper; (*fig.*) (amorous) escapade.
Seitenstraße ['zaitənʃtra:sə], *f.* (—, *pl.* —n) side-street.
Seitenstück ['zaitənʃtyk], *n.* (—s, *pl.* —e) companion-piece.
Seitenzahl ['zaitəntsa:l], *f.* (—, *pl.* —en) page-number; number of pages.
seither [zait'he:r], *adv.* since that time, since then.
seitlich ['zaitliç], *adj.* lateral.
Sekretär [zekre'tɛ:r], *m.* (—s, *pl.* —e) secretary.
Sekretariat [zekreta'rja:t], *n.* (—s, *pl.* —e) secretariat, secretary's office.
Sekt [zɛkt], *m.* (—s, *pl.* —e) champagne.
Sekte ['zɛktə], *f.* (—, *pl.* —n) sect.
Sektierer [zɛk'ti:rər], *m.* (—s, *pl.* —) sectarian.
Sektion [zɛk'tsjo:n] *f.* (—, *pl.* —en) section; (*Med.*) dissection.
Sekundaner [zekun'da:nər], *m.* (—s, *pl.* —) pupil in the second (highest) form.
Sekundant [zekun'dant], *m.* (—en, *pl.* —en) (*Duelling*) second.
sekundär [zekun'dɛ:r], *adj.* secondary.
Sekunde [ze'kundə], *f.* (—, *pl.* —n) (*time*) second.
Sekundenzeiger [ze'kundəntsaigər], *m.* (—s, *pl.* —) (*clock*) second-hand.
sekundieren [zekun'di:rən], *v.n. einem* —, second s.o.
selber ['zɛlbər], *indecl. adj. & pron.* self.
selb(ig) ['zɛlb(iç)], *adj.* the same.

selbst [zɛlpst], *indecl. adj. & pron.* self; — *ist der Mann*, depend on yourself; *von* —, of its own accord, spontaneously. — *adv.* even; — *wenn*, even if, even though; — *dann nicht*, not even then.

selbständig [ˈzɛlpʃtɛndɪç], *adj.* independent.

Selbstbestimmung [ˈzɛlpstbəʃtɪmuŋ], *f.* (—, *no pl.*) self-determination, autonomy.

selbstbewußt [ˈzɛlpstbəvust], *adj.* self-assertive, self-confident, conceited.

selbstherrlich [ˈzɛlpsthɛrlɪç], *adj.* autocratic, tyrannical.

Selbstlaut [ˈzɛlpstlaut], *m.* (—s, *pl.* —e) vowel.

selbstlos [ˈzɛlpstlo:s], *adj.* unselfish, selfless, altruistic.

Selbstlosigkeit [ˈzɛlpstˈlo:zɪçkaɪt], *f.* (—, *no pl.*) unselfishness, altruism.

Selbstmord [ˈzɛlpstmɔrt], *m.* (—s, *pl.* —e) suicide.

selbstredend [ˈzɛlpstre:dənt], *adj.* self-evident, obvious.

Selbstsucht [ˈzɛlpstzuxt], *f.* (—, *no pl.*) selfishness, ego(t)ism.

selbstsüchtig [ˈzɛlpstzyçtɪç], *adj.* selfish, ego(t)istic(al).

selbstverständlich [ˈzɛlpstfɛrʃtɛntlɪç], *adj.* self-evident. — *adv.* of course, obviously.

Selbstzweck [ˈzɛlpsttsvɛk], *m.* (—s, *no pl.*) end in itself.

selig [ˈze:lɪç], *adj.* blessed, blissful; (*fig.*) delighted; deceased, late; — *sprechen*, beatify.

Seligkeit [ˈze:lɪçkaɪt], *f.* (—, *pl.* —en) bliss, blissfulness; (*Eccl.*) salvation, beatitude.

Seligsprechung [ˈze:lɪçʃprɛçuŋ], *f.* (—, *pl.* —en) beatification.

Sellerie [ˈzɛləri:], *m.* (—s, *pl.* —s) (*Bot.*) celery.

selten [ˈzɛltən], *adj.* rare, scarce; (*fig.*) remarkable. — *adv.* seldom, rarely, infrequently.

Seltenheit [ˈzɛltənhaɪt], *f.* (—, *pl.* —en) rarity, curiosity, scarcity; (*fig.*) remarkableness.

Selterwasser [ˈzɛltərvasər], *n.* (—s, *no pl.*) soda-water.

seltsam [ˈzɛltza:m], *adj.* strange, unusual, odd, curious.

Semester [zeˈmɛstər], *n.* (—s, *pl.* —) university term, semester.

Semit [zeˈmi:t], *m.* (—en, *pl.* —en) Semite, Jew.

semmelblond [ˈzɛməlblɔnt], *adj.* flaxen-haired.

Semmelkloß [ˈzɛməlklo:s], *m.* (—es, *pl.* ⸚e) bread dumpling.

Senator [zeˈna:tɔr], *m.* (—s, *pl.* —en) senator.

senden [ˈzɛndən], *v.a. irr.* send, despatch; (*money*) remit. — *v.a. reg.* (*Rad.*) broadcast.

Sender [ˈzɛndər], *m.* (—s, *pl.* —) sender; (*Rad.*) (broadcasting) station, transmitter.

Sendling [ˈzɛntlɪŋ], *m.* (—s, *pl.* —e) (*Poet.*) emissary.

Sendschreiben [ˈzɛntʃraɪbən], *n.* (—s, *pl.* —) epistle, missive.

Sendung [ˈzɛnduŋ], *f.* (—, *pl.* —en) (*Comm.*) shipment, consignment; (*fig.*) mission; (*Rad.*) broadcast, transmission.

Senegal [ˈze:nəgal], *n.* Senegal.

Senf [zɛnf], *m.* (—s, *no pl.*) mustard.

sengen [ˈzɛŋən], *v.a.* singe, scorch; — *und brennen*, lay waste.

Senkblei [ˈzɛŋkblaɪ], *n.* (—s, *pl.* —e) plummet.

Senkel [ˈzɛŋkəl], *m.* (—s, *pl.* —) shoe-lace.

senken [ˈzɛŋkən], *v.a.* lower, sink. — *v.r. sich* —, sink, go down; dip, slope, subside.

senkrecht [ˈzɛŋkrɛçt], *adj.* perpendicular.

Senkung [ˈzɛŋkuŋ], *f.* (—, *pl.* —en) depression, dip, subsidence.

Senn(e) [ˈzɛn(ə)], *m.* (—n, *pl.* —(e)n) Alpine herdsman.

Sennerin [ˈzɛnərɪn], *f.* (—, *pl.* —nen) Alpine dairy-woman.

Senneschoten [ˈzɛnəʃo:tən], *f. pl.* senna pods.

Sennhütte [ˈzɛnhytə], *f.* (—, *pl.* —n) Alpine dairy; chalet.

sensationell [zɛnzatsjoˈnɛl], *adj.* sensational.

Sense [ˈzɛnzə], *f.* (—, *pl.* —n) scythe.

sensibel [zɛnˈzi:bəl], *adj.* sensitive.

Sentenz [zɛnˈtɛnts], *f.* (—, *pl.* —en) aphorism.

sentimental [zɛntimɛnˈta:l], *adj.* sentimental.

separat [zepaˈra:t], *adj.* separate, special.

September [zɛpˈtɛmbər], *m.* (—s, *pl.* —) September.

Serbien [ˈzɛrbjən], *n.* Serbia.

Serie [ˈze:rjə], *f.* (—, *pl.* —n) series.

Service [zɛrˈvi:s], *n.* (—s, *pl.* —) dinner-set, dinner-service.

servieren [zɛrˈvi:rən], *v.a., v.n.* serve, wait at table.

Serviertisch [zɛrˈvi:rtɪʃ], *m.* (—es, *pl.* —e) sideboard.

Sessel [ˈzɛsəl], *m.* (—s, *pl.* —) arm-chair, easy-chair; (*Austr. dial.*) chair.

seßhaft [ˈzɛshaft], *adj.* settled, domiciled.

setzen [ˈzɛtsən], *v.a.* set, put, place; (*monument*) erect; (*bet*) stake; (*Typ.*) compose. — *v.r. sich* —, sit down; (*coffee*) settle; *sich bei einem in Gunst* —, ingratiate o.s. with s.o.

Setzer [ˈzɛtsər], *m.* (—s, *pl.* —) compositor.

Setzling [ˈzɛtslɪŋ], *m.* (—s, *pl.* —e) young tree, young plant.

Seuche [ˈzɔyçə], *f.* (—, *pl.* —n) pestilence; epidemic.

seufzen [ˈzɔyftsən], *v.n.* sigh.

Seufzer [ˈzɔyftsər], *m.* (—s, *pl.* —) sigh.

Sexta [ˈzɛksta:], *f.* (—, *pl.* —s) (*Sch.*) sixth form, lowest form.

Sextant

Sextant [zɛks'tant], *m.* (**—en,** *pl.* **—en**) sextant.

sexuell [zɛksu'ɛl], *adj.* sexual.

sezieren [ze'tsi:rən], *v.a.* dissect.

Seziersaal [ze'tsi:rza:l], *m.* (**—s,** *pl.* **—säle**) dissecting-room.

Sibirien [zi'bi:rjən], *n.* Siberia.

sich [zɪç], *pron.* oneself, himself, herself, itself, themselves; each other.

Sichel [ˈzɪçəl], *f.* (**—,** *pl.* **—n**) sickle.

sicher [ˈzɪçər], *adj.* certain, sure, secure, safe; confident, positive; *seiner Sache — sein,* be sure of o.'s ground; — *stellen,* secure.

Sicherheit [ˈzɪçərhaɪt], *f.* (**—,** *pl.* **—en**) certainty; security, safety; confidence, positiveness; *in — bringen,* secure.

sichern [ˈzɪçərn], *v.a.* secure, make secure; assure, ensure.

Sicherung [ˈzɪçərunŋ], *f.* (**—,** *pl.* **—en**) securing; (*Elec.*) fuse; (*gun*) safety-catch.

Sicht [zɪçt], *f.* (**—,** *no pl.*) sight.

sichtbar [ˈzɪçtbaːr], *adj.* visible; conspicuous.

sichten [ˈzɪçtən], *v.a.* sift, sort out; sight.

sichtlich [ˈzɪçtlɪç], *adv.* visibly.

Sichtwechsel [ˈzɪçtvɛksəl], *m.* (**—s,** *pl.* **—**) (*Banking*) sight-bill, bill payable on sight.

Sichtweite [ˈzɪçtvaɪtə], *f.* (**—,** *no pl.*) range of vision.

sickern [ˈzɪkərn], *v.n.* (*aux.* sein) leak, ooze, seep.

Sie [ziː], *pron.* (*formal*) you.

sie [ziː], *pers. pron.* she, her; they, them.

Sieb [ziːp], *n.* (**—(e)s,** *pl.* **—e**) sieve; riddle; colander.

sieben (1) [ˈziːbən], *v.a.* (*Cul.*) sift, strain.

sieben (2) [ˈziːbən], *num. adj.* seven; *meine — Sachen,* my belongings.

Siebeneck [ˈziːbənɛk], *n.* (**—s,** *pl.* **—e**) heptagon.

Siebengestirn [ˈziːbəngəʃtɪrn], *n.* (**—s,** *no pl.*) Pleiades.

siebenmal [ˈziːbənmaːl], *adv.* seven times.

Siebenmeilenstiefel [ziːbənˈmaɪlənʃtiːfəl], *m. pl.* seven-league boots.

Siebenschläfer [ˈziːbənʃlɛːfər], *m.* (**—s,** *pl.* **—**) lazy-bones.

siebzehn [ˈziːptseːn], *num. adj.* seventeen.

siebzig [ˈziːptsɪç], *num. adj.* seventy.

siech [ziːç], *adj.* (*rare*) sick, infirm.

siechen [ˈziːçən], *v.n.* be in bad health.

sieden [ˈziːdən], *v.a., v.n.* boil, seethe.

siedeln [ˈziːdəln], *v.n.* settle.

Siedlung [ˈziːdluŋ], *f.* (**—,** *pl.* **—en**) settlement; housing estate.

Sieg [ziːk], *m.* (**—(e)s,** *pl.* **—e**) victory; *den — davontragen,* win the day.

Siegel [ˈziːgəl], *n.* (**—s,** *pl.* **—**) seal; *Brief und —,* sign and seal.

Siegelbewahrer [ˈziːgəlbəvaːrər], *m.* (**—s,** *pl.* **—**) Lord Privy Seal; keeper of the seal.

Siegellack [ˈziːgəllak], *n.* (**—s,** *no pl.*) sealing wax.

siegeln [ˈziːgəln], *v.a.* seal.

siegen [ˈziːgən], *v.n.* conquer, win, be victorious, triumph (over).

Sieger [ˈziːgər], *m.* (**—s,** *pl.* **—**) victor, conqueror.

Siegesbogen [ˈziːgəsboːgən], *m.* (**—s,** *pl.* **⁀**) triumphal arch.

Siegeszeichen [ˈziːgəstsaɪçən], *n.* (**—s,** *pl.* **—**) sign of victory, trophy.

sieghaft [ˈziːkhaft], *adj.* victorious, triumphant.

siegreich [ˈziːkraɪç], *adj.* victorious, triumphant.

siehe! [ˈziːə], *excl.* see! look! lo and behold!

Sierra Leone [ˈsiera leˈoːnə], *f.* Sierra Leone.

Signal [zɪgˈnaːl], *n.* (**—s,** *pl.* **—e**) signal.

Signalement [zɪgnaləˈmãː], *n.* (**—s,** *pl.* **—s**) personal description.

Signalglocke [zɪgˈnaːlglɔkə], *f.* (**—,** *pl.* **—n**) warning-bell.

signalisieren [zɪgnaliˈziːrən], *v.a.* signal.

Signatarmacht [zɪgnaˈtaːrmaxt], *f.* (**—,** *pl.* **⁀e**) signatory power.

signieren [zɪgˈniːrən], *v.a.* sign.

Silbe [ˈzɪlbə], *f.* (**—,** *pl.* **—n**) syllable.

Silbenmaß [ˈzɪlbənmaːs], *n.* (**—es,** *pl.* **—e**) (*Poet.*) metre.

Silbenrätsel [ˈzɪlbənrɛːtsəl], *n.* (**—s,** *pl.* **—**) charade.

Silber [ˈzɪlbər], *n.* (**—s,** *no pl.*) silver; plate.

Silberbuche [ˈzɪlbərbuːxə], *f.* (**—,** *pl.* **—n**) white beech(-tree).

Silberfuchs [ˈzɪlbərfuks], *m.* (**—es,** *pl.* **⁀e**) (*Zool.*) silver fox.

silbern [ˈzɪlbərn], *adj.* made of silver, silvery.

Silberpappel [ˈzɪlbərpapəl], *f.* (**—,** *pl.* **—n**) (*Bot.*) white poplar(-tree).

Silberschimmel [ˈzɪlbərʃɪməl], *m.* (**—s,** *pl.* **—**) grey-white horse.

Silberzeug [ˈzɪlbərtsɔyk], *n.* (**—s,** *no pl.*) (silver) plate.

Silvester [zɪlˈvɛstər], *m.* (**—s,** *pl.* **—**) New Year's Eve.

Similistein [ˈziːmiliʃtaɪn], *m.* (**—s,** *pl.* **—e**) imitation *or* paste jewellery.

Sims [zɪms], *m.* (**—es,** *pl.* **—e**) cornice, moulding, shelf, ledge.

Simulant [zimuˈlant], *m.* (**—en,** *pl.* **—en**) malingerer.

simulieren [zimuˈliːrən], *v.a.* simulate.

simultan [zimulˈtaːn], *adj.* simultaneous.

Singapur [zɪŋgaˈpuːr], *n.* Singapore.

Singdrossel [ˈzɪŋdrɔsəl], *f.* (**—,** *pl.* **—n**) (*Orn.*) common thrush.

singen [ˈzɪŋən], *v.a., v.n. irr.* sing.

Singspiel [ˈzɪŋʃpiːl], *n.* (**—s,** *pl.* **—e**) musical comedy, light opera, opera buffa.

Singular [ˈzɪŋgulaːr], *m.* (**—s,** *pl.* **—e**) singular.

sinken ['zɪŋkən], *v.n. irr.* (*aux.* sein) sink; (*price*) decline, drop, fall; *den Mut — lassen*, lose heart.

Sinn [zɪn], *m.* (—(e)s, *pl.* —e) sense; intellect, mind; consciousness, memory; taste, meaning, purport; wish; *etwas im — haben*, have s.th. in mind, intend s.th.; *leichter —*, lightheartedness; *andern — es werden*, change o's mind; *das hat keinen —*, there is no sense in that; *von —en sein*, be out of o.'s senses; *seine fünf —e beisammen haben*, be in o.'s right mind; *sich etwas aus dem — schlagen*, dismiss s.th. from o.'s mind; *es kommt mir in den —*, it occurs to me.

Sinnbild ['zɪnbɪlt], *n.* (—s, *pl.* —er) symbol, emblem.

sinnen ['zɪnən], *v.n. irr.* meditate, reflect.

Sinnesänderung ['zɪnəsɛndəruŋ], *f.* (—, *pl.* —en) change of mind.

Sinnesart ['zɪnəsaːrt], *f.* (—, *no pl.*) disposition, character.

Sinnesorgan ['zɪnəsɔrgaːn], *n.* (—s, *pl.* —e) sense-organ.

Sinnestäuschung ['zɪnəstɔyʃuŋ], *f.* (—, *pl.* —en) illusion, hallucination.

sinnfällig ['zɪnfɛlɪç], *adj.* obvious, striking.

Sinngedicht ['zɪngədɪçt], *n.* (—es, *pl.* —e) epigram.

sinnig ['zɪnɪç], *adj.* thoughtful, meaningful; judicious, fitting.

sinnlich ['zɪnlɪç], *adj.* sensual, sensuous.

Sinnlichkeit ['zɪnlɪçkaɪt], *f.* (—, *no pl.*) sensuality, sensuousness.

sinnlos ['zɪnloːs], *adj.* senseless, meaningless, pointless.

sinnreich ['zɪnraɪç], *adj.* ingenious.

Sinnspruch ['zɪnʃprux], *m.* (—es, *pl.* ̈e) sentence, maxim, device, motto.

sinnverwandt ['zɪnfɛrvant], *adj.* synonymous.

sinnvoll ['zɪnfɔl], *adj.* meaningful, significant.

sinnwidrig ['zɪnviːdrɪç], *adj.* nonsensical, absurd.

Sintflut ['zɪntfluːt], *f.* (—, *no pl.*) (*Bibl.*) the Flood.

Sinus ['ziːnus], *m.* (—, *pl.* —se) (*Maths.*) sine.

Sippe ['zɪpə], *f.* (—, *pl.* —n) kin, tribe, family, clan.

Sippschaft ['zɪpʃaft], *f.* (—, *pl.* —en) kindred; *die ganze —*, the whole caboodle.

Sirene [ziˈreːnə], *f.* (—, *pl.* —n) siren.

Sirup ['ziːrup], *m.* (—s, *no pl.*) syrup, treacle.

Sitte ['zɪtə], *f.* (—, *pl.* —n) custom, mode, fashion; (*pl.*) manners, morals; *—n und Gebräuche*, manners and customs.

Sittengesetz ['zɪtəngəzɛts], *n.* (—es, *pl.* —e) moral law.

Sittenlehre ['zɪtənleːrə], *f.* (—, *no pl.*) moral philosophy, ethics.

sittenlos ['zɪtənloːs], *adj.* immoral, profligate, licentious.

Sittenprediger ['zɪtənpreːdɪgər], *m.* (—s, *pl.* —) moraliser.

Sittich ['zɪtɪç], *m.* (—s, *pl.* —e) (*Orn.*) budgerigar; parakeet.

sittig ['zɪtɪç], *adj.* well-behaved.

sittlich ['zɪtlɪç], *adj.* moral.

Sittlichkeit ['zɪtlɪçkaɪt], *f.* (—, *no pl.*) morality, morals.

sittsam ['zɪtzaːm], *adj.* modest, demure.

situiert [zituˈiːrt], *adj. gut* (*schlecht*) —, well (badly) off.

Sitz [zɪts], *m.* (—es, *pl.* —e) seat, chair; residence, location, place; (*Eccl.*) see.

Sitzarbeit ['zɪtsarbaɪt], *f.* (—, *pl.* —en) sedentary work.

Sitzbad ['zɪtsbaːt], *n.* (—(e)s, *pl.* ̈er) hip bath.

sitzen ['zɪtsən], *v.n. irr.* sit, be seated; (*fig.*) be in prison; (*dress*) fit; *lassen*, throw over, jilt; *bleiben*, remain seated; (*school*) stay in the same class, not be moved up; be a wallflower; remain unmarried.

Sitzfleisch ['zɪtsflaɪʃ], *n.* (—es, *no pl.*) (*coll.*) *kein — haben*, be restless, lack application.

Sitzplatz ['zɪtsplats], *m.* (—es, *pl.* ̈e) seat.

Sitzung ['zɪtsuŋ], *f.* (—, *pl.* —en) meeting, sitting, session.

Sitzungsprotokoll ['zɪtsuŋsprotokɔl], *n.* (—s, *pl.* —e) minutes (of a meeting).

Sitzungssaal ['zɪtsuŋsaːl], *m.* (—s, *pl.* —säle) board-room, conference room.

Sizilien [ziˈtsiːljən], *n.* Sicily.

Skala ['skaːla], *f.* (—, *pl.* —len) scale; (*Mus.*) gamut.

Skandal [skanˈdaːl], *m.* (—s, *pl.* —e) scandal; row, riot; *— machen*, kick up a row.

skandalös [skandaˈløːs], *adj.* scandalous.

skandieren [skanˈdiːrən], *v.a.* (*Poet.*) scan.

Skandinavien [skandiˈnaːvjən], *n.* Scandinavia.

Skelett [skeˈlɛt], *n.* (—s, *pl.* —e) skeleton.

Skepsis ['skɛpzɪs], *f.* (—, *no pl.*) scepticism, doubt.

skeptisch ['skɛptɪʃ], *adj.* sceptical, doubtful.

Skizze ['skɪtsə], *f.* (—, *pl.* —n) sketch.

skizzieren [skɪˈtsiːrən], *v.a.* sketch.

Sklave ['sklaːvə], *m.* (—n, *pl.* —n) slave; *zum —n machen*, enslave.

Sklavendienst ['sklaːvəndiːnst], *m.* (—es, *no pl.*) slavery.

Sklaverei [sklaːvəˈraɪ], *f.* (—, *no pl.*) slavery, thraldom.

Skonto ['skɔnto], *m. & n.* (—s, *pl.* —s) discount.

Skrupel ['skruːpəl], *m.* (—s, *pl.* —) scruple; *sich — machen*, have scruples.

skrupulös [skrupuˈløːs], *adj.* scrupulous, meticulous.

Skulptur [skulp'tu:r], *f.* (—, *pl.* —en) sculpture.

skurril [sku'ri:l], *adj.* ludicrous.

Slawe ['sla:və], *m.* (—n, *pl.* —n) Slav.

slawisch ['sla:vıʃ], *adj.* Slav, Slavonic.

Slowake [slo'va:kə], *m.* (—n, *pl.* —n) Slovakian.

Slowene [slo've:nə], *m.* (—n, *pl.* —n) Slovenian.

Smaragd [sma'rakt], *m.* (—(e)s, *pl.* —e) emerald.

smaragden [sma'raktən], *adj.* emerald.

Smoking ['smo:kıŋ], *m.* (—s, *pl.* —s) dinner-jacket.

so [zo:], *adv.* so, thus, in this way, like this; —? really? — *ist es*, that is how it is; — *daß*, so that; — ... *wie*, as ... as; *na — was!* well, I never! — *conj.* then, therefore.

sobald [zo'balt], *conj.* as soon as, directly.

Socke ['zɔkə], *f.* (—, *pl.* —n) sock.

Sockel ['zɔkəl], *m.* (—s, *pl.* —) pedestal, plinth, stand, base.

Soda ['zo:da], *n.* (—s, *no pl.*) (carbonate of) soda.

sodann [zo'dan], *adv. conj.* then.

Sodbrennen ['zo:tbrɛnən], *n.* (—s, *no pl.*) heartburn.

soeben [zo'e:bən], *adv.* just now.

sofern [zo'fɛrn], *conj.* if, in case, so far as.

sofort [zo'fɔrt], *adv.* at once, immediately.

Sog [zo:k], *m.* (—(e)s, *pl.* —e) undertow, suction.

sogar [zo'ga:r], *adv.* even.

sogenannt [zogə'nant], *adj.* so-called, would-be.

sogleich [zo'glaıç], *adv.* at once, immediately.

Sohle ['zo:lə], *f.* (—, *pl.* —n) sole; (*minz*) floor.

Sohn [zo:n], *m.* (—(e)s, *pl.* ⁻e) son; *der verlorene* —, the prodigal son.

solange [zo'laŋə], *conj.* as long as.

Solbad ['zo:lba:t], *n.* (—s, *pl.* ⁻er) saline bath.

solch [zɔlç], *adj.*, *dem. pron.* such.

solcherlei ['zɔlçərlaı], *adj.* of such a kind, suchlike.

Sold [zɔlt], *m.* (—(e)s, *no pl.*) army pay.

Soldat [zɔl'da:t], *m.* (—en, *pl.* —en) soldier.

Soldateska [zɔlda'tɛska], *f.* (—, *pl.* —s) soldiery.

Söldner ['zœldnər], *m.* (—s, *pl.* —) mercenary, hireling.

Sole ['zo:lə], *f.* (—, *pl.* —n) salt-water, brine.

Solei ['zo:laı], *n.* (—s, *pl.* —er) pickled egg.

solidarisch [zoli'da:rıʃ], *adj.* joint, jointly responsible; unanimous.

Solidarität [zolidari'tɛ:t], *f.* (—, *no pl.*) solidarity.

Solist [zo'lıst], *m.* (—en, *pl.* —en) soloist.

Soll [zɔl], *n.* (—s, *no pl.*) debit; — *und Haben*, debit and credit.

sollen ['zɔlən], *v.n. irr.* be obliged, be compelled; have to; be supposed to; (*aux.*) shall, should etc.; *ich soll*, I must, I am to; *er soll krank sein*, he is said to be ill; *ich sollte eigentlich*, I really ought to.

Söller ['zœlər], *m.* (—s, *pl.* —) loft, garret, balcony.

Somali ʾzo'ma:li], *n.* Somalia.

somit [zo'mıt], *adv.* consequently, therefore, accordingly.

Sommer ['zɔmər], *m.* (—s, *pl.* —) summer.

Sommerfäden ['zɔmərfɛ:dən], *m. pl.* gossamer.

Sommerfrische ['zɔmərfrıʃə], *f.* (—, *pl.* —n) holiday resort.

Sommergetreide ['zɔmərgətraıdə], *n.* (—s, *no pl.*) spring corn.

Sommersonnenwende ['zɔmərzɔnənvendə], *f.* (—, *pl.* —n) summer solstice.

Sommersprosse ['zɔmərʃprɔsə], *f.* (—, *pl.* —n) freckle.

sonach [zo'na:x], *adv.* therefore, consequently.

Sonate [zo'na:tə], *f.* (—, *pl.* —n) sonata.

Sonde ['zɔndə], *f.* (—, *pl.* —n) sounding-lead, plummet; probe.

sonder ['zɔndər], (*obs.*) *prep.* (*Acc.*) without.

Sonderausgabe ['zɔndərausga:bə], *f.* (—, *pl.* —n) separate edition; special edition.

Sonderausschuß ['zɔndərausʃus], *m.* (—sses, *pl.* ⁻sse) select committee.

sonderbar ['zɔndərba:r], *adj.* strange, odd, queer, singular, peculiar.

sonderlich ['zɔndərlıç], *adj.* special, especial, particular. — *adv. nicht* —, not much.

Sonderling ['zɔndərlıŋ], *m.* (—s, *pl.* —e) freak, odd character, crank.

sondern ['zɔndərn], *v.a.* separate, distinguish, differentiate. — *conj.* but; *nicht nur*, ... — *auch*, not only ... but also.

Sonderrecht ['zɔndərrɛçt], *n.* (—s, *pl.* —e) special privilege.

sonders ['zɔndərs], *adv. samt und* —, all and each, all and sundry.

Sonderstellung ['zɔndərʃtɛluŋ], *f.* (—, *no pl.*) exceptional position.

Sonderung ['zɔndəruŋ], *f.* (—, *pl.* —en) separation.

Sonderzug ['zɔndərtsu:k], *m.* (—s, *pl.* ⁻e) special train.

sondieren [zɔn'di:rən], *v.a.* (*wound*) probe; (*ocean*) plumb; (*fig.*) sound.

Sonett [zo'nɛt], *n.* (—(e)s, *pl.* —e) sonnet.

Sonnabend ['zɔna:bənt], *m.* (—s, *pl.* —e) Saturday.

Sonne ['zɔnə], *f.* (—, *pl.* —n) sun.

sonnen ['zɔnən], *v.r. sich* —, sun o.s., bask in the sun, sunbathe.

Sonnenaufgang ['zɔnənaufgaŋ], *m.* (—s, *pl.* ⁻e) sunrise.

Sonnenbrand ['zɔnənbrant], *m.* (—s, *pl.* ⁻e) sunburn.

Sonnendeck ['zɔnəndɛk], *n.* (—s, *pl.* —e) awning.

Sonnenfinsternis ['zɔnənfɪnstərnɪs], *f.* (—, *pl.* —se) eclipse of the sun.

sonnenklar ['zɔnənkla:r], *adj.* very clear, as clear as daylight.

Sonnenschirm ['zɔnənʃɪrm], *m.* (—s, *pl.* —e) parasol, sunshade.

Sonnenstich ['zɔnənʃtɪç], *n.* (—(e)s, *no pl.*) sunstroke.

Sonnenuhr ['zɔnənu:r], *f.* (—, *pl.* —en) sundial.

Sonnenuntergang ['zɔnənuntərgaŋ], *m.* (—s, *pl.* —e) sunset.

Sonnenwende ['zɔnənvɛndə], *f.* (—, *no pl.*) solstice.

Sonntag ['zɔnta:k], *m.* (—s, *pl.* —e) Sunday.

sonntags ['zɔnta:ks], *adv.* on Sundays, of a Sunday.

Sonntagsjäger ['zɔnta:ksjɛ:gər], *m.* (—s, *pl.* —) amateur sportsman.

sonor [zo'no:r], *adj.* sonorous.

sonst [zɔnst], *adv.* else, otherwise, besides, at other times; — *noch etwas?* anything else?

sonstig ['zɔnstɪç], *adj.* other, existing besides.

sonstwo ['zɔnstvo], *adv.* elsewhere, somewhere else.

Sopran [zo'pra:n], *m.* (—s, *pl.* —e) soprano.

Sorbett ['zɔrbɛt], *n.* (—s, *pl.* —e) sherbet.

Sorge ['zɔrgə], *f.* (—, *pl.* —n) care; grief, worry; sorrow; anxiety; concern; (*pl.*) troubles, worries; — *tragen dass . . .* , see to it that . . . ; — *tragen zu*, take care of — *um*, concern for.

sorgen ['zɔrgən], *v.n.* — *für*, care for, provide for, look after. — *v.r. sich — um*, worry about.

sorgenvoll ['zɔrgənfɔl], *adj.* uneasy, troubled, anxious.

Sorgfalt ['zɔrkfalt], *f.* (—, *no pl.*) care, attention.

sorgfältig ['zɔrkfɛltɪç], *adj.* careful, painstaking; elaborate.

sorglos ['zɔrklo:s], *adj.* careless, irresponsible, unconcerned, indifferent; carefree.

sorgsam ['zɔrkza:m], *adj.* careful, heedful.

Sorte ['zɔrtə], *f.* (—, *pl.* —n) sort, kind, species, brand.

sortieren [zɔr'ti:rən], *v.a.* sort (out).

Sortiment [zɔrti'mɛnt], *n.* (—s, *pl.* —e) assortment; bookshop.

Sortimentsbuchhändler [zɔrti'mɛntsbu:xhɛndlər], *m.* (—s, *pl.* —) retail bookseller.

Soße ['zo:sə], *f.* (—, *pl.* —n) sauce, gravy.

Souffleur [suf'lø:r], *m.* (—s, *pl.* —e) prompter.

Soutane [su'ta:nə], *f.* (—, *pl.* —n) cassock, soutane.

Souterrain [sutɛ'rɛ̃], *n.* (—s, *pl.* —s) basement.

souverän [su:və'rɛ:n], *adj.* sovereign; (*fig.*) supremely good.

Souveränität [su:vərɛ:ni'tɛ:t], *f.* (—, *no pl.*) sovereignty.

soviel [zo'fi:l], *adv.* so much; — *wie*, as much as. — *conj.* so far as; — *ich weiß*, as far as I know.

sowie [zo'vi:], *conj.* as, as well as, as soon as.

Sowjet [sɔv'jɛt], *m.* (—s, *pl.* —s) Soviet.

sowohl [zo'vo:l], *conj.* — *wie*, as well as.

sozial [zo'tsja:l], *adj.* social.

sozialisieren [zotsjali'zi:rən], *v.a.* nationalize.

Sozialwissenschaft [zo'tsja:lvɪsənʃaft], *f.* (—, *pl.* —en) sociology; social science.

Sozietät [zotsje'tɛ:t], *f.* (—, *pl.* —en) partnership.

Sozius ['zotsjus], *m.* (—, *pl.* —se, **Socii**) partner; pillion-rider; —*sitz*, (*motor cycle*) pillion (seat).

sozusagen ['zo:tsuza:gən], *adv.* as it were, so to speak.

Spagat [ʃpa'ga:t], *m.* (—(e)s, *no pl.*) (*dial.*) string, twine; (*Dancing*) the splits.

spähen ['ʃpɛ:ən], *v.n.* look out, watch; (*Mil.*) scout; spy.

Späher ['ʃpɛ:ər], *m.* (—s, *pl.* —) scout; spy.

Spalier [ʃpa'li:r], *n.* (—s, *pl.* —e) trellis; — *bilden*, form a lane (*of people*).

Spalierobst [ʃpa'li:ro:pst], *n.* (—(e)s, *no pl.*) wall-fruit.

Spalt [ʃpalt], *m.* (—(e)s, *pl.* —e) crack, rift, cleft, rent; (*glacier*) crevasse.

Spalte ['ʃpaltə], *f.* (—, *pl.* —n) (*newspaper*) column.

spalten ['ʃpaltən], *v.a.* split, cleave, slit. — *v.r. sich —*, divide, break up, split up; (*in two*) bifurcate.

Spaltholz ['ʃpalthɔlts], *n.* (—es, *no pl.*) fire-wood.

Spaltpilz ['ʃpaltpɪlts], *m.* (—es, *pl.* —e) fission-fungus.

Spaltung ['ʃpaltuŋ], *f.* (—, *pl.* —en) cleavage; (*atomic*) fission; (*fig.*) dissension, rupture; (*Eccl.*) schism.

Span [ʃpa:n], *m.* (—(e)s, *pl.* ⁻e) chip, chippings, shavings.

Spange ['ʃpaŋə], *f.* (—, *pl.* —n) clasp, buckle.

Spanien ['ʃpa:njən], *n.* Spain.

spanisch ['ʃpa:nɪʃ], *adj.* Spanish; —*e Wand*, folding screen; *es kommt mir — vor*, it is Greek to me.

Spann [ʃpan], *m.* (—(e)s, *pl.* —e) instep.

Spanne ['ʃpanə], *f.* (—, *pl.* —n) span; *eine — Zeit*, a short space of time.

spannen ['ʃpanən], *v.a.* stretch, strain, span.

spannend ['ʃpanənt], *adj.* thrilling, tense.

Spannkraft ['ʃpankraft], *f.* (—, *no pl.*) elasticity.

Spannung ['ʃpanuŋ], *f.* (—, *pl.* —en) tension, suspense, strain; (*fig.*) eager expectation, curiosity, suspense, close attention; (*Elec.*) voltage.

Sparbüchse [ˈʃpaːrbyksə], *f.* (—, *pl.* —n) money-box.

sparen [ˈʃpaːrən], *v.a.*, *v.n.* save, economise, put by, lay by.

Spargel [ˈʃpargəl], *m.* (—s, *pl.* —) asparagus.

Spargelder [ˈʃpaːrgɛldər], *n. pl.* savings.

Sparkasse [ˈʃpaːrkasə], *f.* (—, *pl.* —n) savings bank.

spärlich [ˈʃpɛːrlɪç], *adj.* scant, scanty, sparse.

Sparpfennig [ˈʃpaːrpfɛnɪç], *m.* (—s, *pl.* —e) nest-egg.

Sparren [ˈʃparən], *m.* (—s, *pl.* —) spar, rafter; *er hat einen* —, he has a screw loose.

sparsam [ˈʃpaːrzaːm], *adj.* economical, thrifty, frugal.

Spaß [ʃpaːs], *m.* (—es, *pl.* ⁓e) jest, fun, joke; *aus* —, *im* —, *zum* —, in fun; — *verstehen*, take a joke; *es macht mir* —, it amuses me, it is fun for me.

spaßen [ˈʃpaːsən], *v.n.* jest, joke.

spaßhaft [ˈʃpaːshaft], *adj.* funny, facetious, jocular.

Spaßverderber [ˈʃpaːsfɛrdɛrbər], *m.* (—s, *pl.* —) spoil-sport.

Spaßvogel [ˈʃpaːsfoːgəl], *m.* (—s, *pl.* ⁓) wag.

Spat [ʃpaːt], *m.* (—(e)s, *pl.* —e) (*Min.*) spar.

spät [ʃpɛːt], *adj.* late; *wie* — *ist es?* what is the time? *zu* — *kommen*, be late.

Spätabend [ˈʃpɛːtaːbənt], *m.* (—s, *pl.* —e) latter part of the evening, late evening.

Spatel [ˈʃpaːtəl], *m.* (—s, *pl.* —) spatula.

Spaten [ˈʃpaːtən], *m.* (—s, *pl.* —) spade.

Spatenstich [ˈʃpaːtənʃtɪç], *m.* (—(e)s, *pl.* —e) *den ersten* — *tun*, turn the first sod.

später [ˈʃpɛːtər], *adv.* later (on), afterwards.

spätestens [ˈʃpɛːtəstəns], *adv.* at the latest.

Spätling [ˈʃpɛːtlɪŋ], *m.* (—s, *pl.* —e) late arrival; late fruit.

Spätsommer [ˈʃpɛːtzɔmər], *m.* (—s, *pl.* —) Indian summer.

Spatz [ʃpats], *m.* (—en *pl.* —en) (*Orn.*) sparrow.

spazieren [ʃpaˈtsiːrən], *v.n.* (*aux.* sein) walk leisurely, stroll; — *gehen*, go for a walk, take a stroll; — *führen*, take for a walk.

Spazierfahrt [ʃpaˈtsiːrfaːrt], *f.* (—, *pl.* —en) (pleasure-)drive.

Spazierstock [ʃpaˈtsiːrʃtɔk], *m.* (—s, *pl.* ⁓e) walking-stick.

Spazierweg [ʃpaˈtsiːrveːk], *m.* (—s, *pl.* —e) walk, promenade.

Specht [ʃpɛçt], *m.* (—(e)s, *pl.* —e) (*Orn.*) woodpecker.

Speck [ʃpɛk], *m.* (—(e)s, *no pl.*) bacon; *eine Scheibe* —, a rasher of bacon.

speckig [ˈʃpɛkɪç], *adj.* fat.

Speckschwarte [ˈʃpɛkʃvartə], *f.* (—, *pl.* —n) bacon-rind.

Speckseite [ˈʃpɛkzaːtə], *f.* (—, *pl.* —n) flitch of bacon.

spedieren [ʃpeˈdiːrən], *v.a.* forward; despatch.

Spediteur [ʃpediˈtøːr], *m.* (—s, *pl.* —e) forwarding agent, furniture-remover, carrier.

Spedition [ʃpediˈtsjoːn], *f.* (—, *pl.* —en) conveyance; forwarding agency.

Speer [ʃpeːr], *m.* (—(e)s, *pl.* —e) spear, lance.

Speiche [ˈʃpaɪçə], *f.* (—, *pl.* —n) spoke.

Speichel [ˈʃpaɪçəl], *m.* (—s, *no pl.*) spittle, saliva.

Speicher [ˈʃpaɪçər], *m.* (—s, *pl.* —) granary; warehouse, storehouse; loft.

speien [ˈʃpaɪən], *v.a.*, *v.n. irr.* spit; vomit, be sick.

Speise [ˈʃpaɪzə], *f.* (—, *pl.* —n) food, nourishment, dish.

Speisekammer [ˈʃpaɪzəkamər], *f.* (—, *pl.* —n) larder, pantry.

Speisekarte [ˈʃpaɪzəkartə], *f.* (—, *pl.* —n) bill of fare, menu.

speisen [ˈʃpaɪzən], *v.a.* feed, give to eat. — *v.n.* eat, dine, sup, lunch.

Speiseröhre [ˈʃpaɪzərøːrə], *f.* (—, *pl.* —n) gullet.

Speisewagen [ˈʃpaɪzəvaːgən], *m.* (—s, *pl.* —) (*Railw.*) dining-car.

Spektakel [ʃpɛkˈtaːkəl], *m.* (—s, *no pl.*) uproar, hubbub; shindy, rumpus; noise, row.

Spektrum [ˈʃpɛktrum], *n.* (—s, *pl.* Spektren) spectrum.

Spekulant [ʃpekuˈlant], *m.* (—en, *pl.* —en) speculator.

spekulieren [ʃpekuˈliːrən], *v.n.* speculate; theorise.

Spende [ˈʃpɛndə], *f.* (—, *pl.* —n) gift, donation; bounty.

spenden [ˈʃpɛndən], *v.a.* bestow, donate, contribute.

Spender [ˈʃpɛndər], *m.* (—s, *pl.* —) donor, giver, benefactor.

spendieren [ʃpɛnˈdiːrən], *v.a.* (give a) treat, pay for, stand.

Sperber [ˈʃpɛrbər], *m.* (—s, *pl.* —) (*Orn.*) sparrow-hawk.

Sperling [ˈʃpɛrlɪŋ], *m.* (—s, *pl.* —e) (*Orn.*) sparrow.

sperrangelweit [ˈʃpɛraŋəlvaɪt], *adv.* wide open.

Sperre [ˈʃpɛrə], *f.* (—, *pl.* —n) shutting, closing, blockade, blocking; closure; ban; (*Railw.*) barrier.

sperren [ˈʃpɛrən], *v.a.* spread out; (*Typ.*) space; shut, close, block; cut off; *ins Gefängnis* —, put in prison. — *v.r. sich* — *gegen*, offer resistance to.

Sperrhaken [ˈʃpɛrhaːkən], *m.* (—s, *pl.* —) catch, ratchet.

Sperrsitz [ˈʃpɛrzɪts], *m.* (—es, *pl.* —e) (*Theat.*) stall.

Sperrung [ˈʃpɛruŋ], *f.* (—, *pl.* —en) barring, obstruction, block, blockade; (*Comm.*) embargo.

Sperrzeit [ˈʃpɛrtsaɪt], *f.* (—, *pl.* —en) closing-time.

Spesen [ˈʃpeːzən], *f. pl.* charges, expenses.

spesenfrei [ˈʃpeːzənfraɪ], adj. free of charge; expenses paid.
Spezereien [ʃpeˈtsəraɪən], f. pl. spices.
spezial [ʃpeˈtsjaːl], adj. special, particular.
spezialisieren [ʃpetsjaliˈziːrən], v.a. specify. — v.r. sich —; specialise.
Spezialist [ʃpetsjaˈlɪst], m. (—en, pl. —en) specialist, expert.
Spezialität [ʃpetsjaliˈtɛːt], f. (—, pl. —en) speciality, (Am.) specialty.
Spezies [ˈʃpeːtsjɛs], f. (—, pl. —) species; (Maths.) rule.
Spezifikation [ʃpetsifikaˈtsjoːn], f. (—, pl. —en) specification.
spezifisch [ʃpeˈtsiːfɪʃ], adj. specific.
spezifizieren [ʃpetsifiˈtsiːrən], v.a. specify.
Spezifizierung [ʃpetsifiˈtsiːruŋ], f. (—pl. —en) specification.
Spezimen [ˈʃpeːtsimən], n. (—s, pl. —mina) specimen.
Sphäre [ˈsfɛːrə], f. (—, pl. —n) sphere.
sphärisch [ˈsfɛːrɪʃ], adj. spherical.
Spickaal [ˈʃpɪkaːl], m. (—s, pl. —e) smoked eel.
spicken [ˈʃpɪkən], v.a. lard; den Beutel —, fill o.'s purse.
Spiegel [ˈʃpiːgəl], m. (—s, pl. —) mirror, looking-glass.
spiegelblank [ˈʃpiːgəlblaŋk], adj. sparkling, shiny, polished.
Spiegelei [ˈʃpiːgəlaɪ], n. (—s, pl. —er) fried egg.
Spiegelfechterei [ˈʃpiːgəlfɛçtəraɪ], f. (—, pl. —en) shadow-boxing, make-believe.
Spiegelfenster [ˈʃpiːgəlfɛnstər], n. (—s, pl. —) plate-glass window.
spiegeln [ˈʃpiːgəln], v.n. glitter, shine. — v.a. reflect. — v.r. sich —, be reflected.
Spiegelscheibe [ˈʃpiːgəlʃaɪbə], f. (—, pl. —n) plate-glass pane.
Spiegelung [ˈʃpiːgəluŋ], f. (—, pl. —en) reflection; mirage.
Spiel [ʃpiːl], n. (—(e)s, pl. —e) play; game; sport; (Theat.) acting, performance; (Mus.) playing; ehrliches (unehrliches) —, fair (foul) play; leichtes —, walk-over; auf dem — stehen, be at stake; aufs — setzen, stake, risk; die Hand im — haben, have a finger in the pie; gewonnenes — haben, gain o.'s point; ein gewagtes — treiben, play a bold game; sein — mit einem treiben, trifle with s.o.
Spielart [ˈʃpiːlaːrt], f. (—, pl. —en) manner of playing; variety.
Spielbank [ˈʃpiːlbaŋk], f. (—, pl. —en) casino; gambling-table.
Spieldose [ˈʃpiːldoːzə], f. (—, pl. —n) musical box.
spielen [ˈʃpiːlən], v.a., v.n. play; gamble; (Mus.) play; (Theat.) act; eine Rolle —, play a part; mit dem Gedanken —, toy with the idea.
spielend [ˈʃpiːlənt], adv. easily.
Spieler [ˈʃpiːlər], m. (—s, pl. —) player; gambler; gamester.

Spielerei [ʃpiːləˈraɪ], f. (—, pl. —en) child's play; trivialities.
Spielhölle [ˈʃpiːlhœlə], f. (—, pl. —n) gambling-den.
Spielmann [ˈʃpiːlman], m. (—s, pl. Spielleute) musician, fiddler; (Middle Ages) minstrel.
Spielmarke [ˈʃpiːlmarkə], f. (—, pl. —n) counter, chip.
Spielplan [ˈʃpiːlplan], m. (—s, pl. ⁓e) (Theat.) repertory.
Spielplatz [ˈʃpiːlplats], m. (—es, pl. ⁓e) playground.
Spielraum [ˈʃpiːlraum], m. (—s, no pl.) elbow-room; (fig.) scope; margin; clearance.
Spielsache [ˈʃpiːlzaxə], f. (—, pl. —n) toy, plaything.
Spielschule [ˈʃpiːlʃuːlə], f. (—, pl. —n) infant-school, kindergarten.
Spieltisch [ˈʃpiːltɪʃ], m. (—es, pl. —e) card-table.
Spieluhr [ˈʃpiːluːr], f. (—, pl. —en) musical clock.
Spielverderber [ˈʃpiːlfɛrdɛrbər], m. (—s, pl. —) spoilsport.
Spielwaren [ˈʃpiːlvaːrən], f. pl. toys.
Spielzeit [ˈʃpiːltsaɪt], f. (—, pl. —en) playtime; (Theat.) season.
Spielzeug [ˈʃpiːltsɔyk], n. (—s, pl. —e) plaything, toy.
Spieß [ʃpiːs], m. (—es, pl. —e) spear, pike; (Cul.) spit.
Spießbürger [ˈʃpiːsbyrgər], m. (—s, pl. —) Philistine.
spießen [ˈʃpiːsən], v.a. spear, pierce.
Spießer [ˈʃpiːsər], m. (—s, pl. —) Philistine.
Spießgeselle [ˈʃpiːsgəzɛlə], m. (—n, pl. —n) accomplice, companion or partner in crime.
spießig [ˈʃpiːsɪç], adj. (coll.) Philistine, uncultured, narrow-minded.
Spießruten [ˈʃpiːsruːtən], f. pl. — laufen, run the gauntlet.
Spinat [ʃpiˈnaːt], m. (—s, no pl.) spinach.
Spind [ʃpɪnt], n. (—(e)s, pl. —e) cupboard.
Spindel [ˈʃpɪndəl], f. (—, pl. —n) spindle; distaff; (staircase) newel.
spindeldürr [ˈʃpɪndəldyr], adj. as thin as a lath.
Spindelholz [ˈʃpɪndəlhɔlts], n. (—es, no pl.) spindle-tree wood.
Spinett [ʃpiˈnɛt], n. (—s, pl. —e) spinet.
Spinne [ˈʃpɪnə], f. (—, pl. —n) spider.
spinnefeind [ˈʃpɪnəfaɪnt], adj. einander — sein, hate each other like poison.
spinnen [ˈʃpɪnən], v.a. irr. spin. — v.n. (coll.) be off o.'s head, be crazy.
Spinnerei [ʃpɪnəˈraɪ], f. (—, pl. —en) spinning-mill.
Spinngewebe [ˈʃpɪngəveːbə], n. (—s, pl. —) cobweb.
Spinnrocken [ˈʃpɪnrɔkən], m. (—s, pl. —) distaff.
spintisieren [ʃpɪntiˈziːrən], v.n. muse, meditate.

205

Spion

Spion [ʃpiˈoːn], *m.* (—s, *pl.* —e) spy.

spionieren [ʃpioˈniːrən], *v.n.* spy, pry.

Spirale [ʃpiˈraːlə], *f.* (—, *pl.* —n) spiral.

Spirituosen [ʃpirituˈoːzən], *pl.* spirits, liquors.

Spiritus [ˈʃpiːritus], *m.* (—, *pl.* —se) alcohol, spirits of wine; *denaturierter* —, methylated spirits.

Spiritusbrennerei [ˈʃpiːritusbrɛnərai], *f.* (—, *pl.* —en) distillery.

Spiritusgehalt [ˈʃpiːritusgəhalt], *m.* (—s, *pl.* —e) (*alcoholic*) strength, proof.

Spital [ʃpiˈtaːl], *n.* (—s, *pl.* ⁓er) infirmary; hospital.

Spitz [ʃpits], *m.* (—es, *pl.* —e) Pomeranian dog; *einen — haben*, (*coll.*) be slightly tipsy.

spitz [ʃpits], *adj.* pointed; (*fig.*) snappy, biting.

Spitzbart [ˈʃpitsbaːrt], *m.* (—s, *pl.* ⁓e) imperial (beard), pointed beard.

Spitzbogen [ˈʃpitsboːgən], *m.* (—s, *pl.* —) pointed arch, Gothic arch.

Spitzbogenfenster [ˈʃpitsboːgənfɛnstər], *n.* (—s, *pl.* —) lancet window.

Spitzbube [ˈʃpitsbuːbə], *m.* (—n, *pl.* —n) rogue; rascal; scamp.

Spitzbubenstreich [ˈʃpitsbuːbənʃtraiç], *m.* (—(e)s, *pl.* —e) act of roguery, knavery.

spitzbübisch [ˈʃpitsbyːbiʃ], *adj.* roguish.

Spitze [ˈʃpitsə], *f.* (—, *pl.* —n) point; tip; top, peak; extremity; (*pipe*) mouthpiece; (*cigarette*) holder; (*pen*) nib; lace; *etwas auf die — treiben*, carry s.th. to extremes; *an der — stehen*, be at the head of.

Spitzel [ˈʃpitsəl], *m.* (—s, *pl.* —) police-agent; informer.

spitzen [ˈʃpitsən], *v.a.* sharpen; *die Ohren —*, prick up o.'s ears; *sich auf etwas —*, await s.th. eagerly, be all agog for s.th.

Spitzenbelastung [ˈʃpitsənbəlastuŋ], *f.* (—, *pl.* —en) peak load.

Spitzenleistung [ˈʃpitsənlaistuŋ], *f.* (—, *pl.* —en) maximum output; peak performance.

Spitzentuch [ˈʃpitsəntuːx], *n.* (—(e)s, *pl.* ⁓er) lace scarf.

spitzfindig [ˈʃpitsfindiç], *adj.* subtle, crafty; hair-splitting.

Spitzhacke [ˈʃpitshakə], *f.* (—, *pl.* —n) pickaxe.

spitzig [ˈʃpitsiç], *adj.* pointed, sharp; (*fig.*) biting, poignant.

Spitzmaus [ˈʃpitsmaus], *f.* (—, *pl.* ⁓e) (*Zool.*) shrew.

Spitzname [ˈʃpitsnaːmə], *m.* (—ns, *pl.* —n) nickname.

spitzwinklig [ˈʃpitsviŋkliç], *adj.* acute-angled.

spleißen [ˈʃplaisən], *v.a. irr.* split, cleave.

Splitter [ˈʃplitər], *m.* (—s, *pl.* —) splinter, chip.

splitternackt [ˈʃplitərnakt], *adj.* stark naked.

splittern [ˈʃplitərn], *v.n.* (*aux.* sein) splinter.

spontan [ʃpɔnˈtaːn], *adj.* spontaneous.

sporadisch [ʃpoˈraːdiʃ], *adj.* sporadic.

Spore [ˈʃpoːrə], *f.* (—, *pl.* —n) spore.

Sporn [ʃpɔrn], *m.* (—s, *pl.* **Sporen**) spur.

spornstreichs [ˈʃpɔrnʃtraiçs], *adv.* post-haste, at once.

Sportler [ˈʃpɔrtlər], *m.* (—s, *pl.* —) athlete, sportsman.

sportlich [ˈʃpɔrtliç], *adj.* athletic; sporting.

sportsmäßig [ˈʃpɔrtsmɛːsiç], *adj.* sportsmanlike.

Spott [ʃpɔt], *m.* (—(e)s, *no pl.*) mockery; scorn; *Gegenstand des —s*, laughing-stock; *— treiben mit*, mock, deride; *zum Schaden den — hinzufügen*, add insult to injury.

spottbillig [ˈʃpɔtbiliç], *adj.* ridiculously cheap, dirt-cheap.

Spöttelei [ʃpœtəˈlai], *f.* (—, *pl.* —en) sarcasm.

spötteln [ˈʃpœtəln], *v.n.* mock, jeer.

spotten [ˈʃpɔtən], *v.a., v.n.* deride, scoff (at); *es spottet jeder Beschreibung*, it defies description.

Spötter [ˈʃpœtər], *m.* (—s, *pl.* —) mocker, scoffer.

Spötterei [ʃpœtəˈrai], *f.* (—, *pl.* —en) mockery, derision.

Spottgedicht [ˈʃpɔtgədiçt], *n.* (—(e)s, *pl.* —e) satirical poem.

spöttisch [ˈʃpœtiʃ], *adj.* mocking, satirical, ironical, scoffing.

spottlustig [ˈʃpɔtlustiç], *adj.* flippant, satirical.

Spottschrift [ˈʃpɔtʃrift], *f.* (—, *pl.* —en) satire, lampoon.

Sprache [ˈʃpraːxə], *f.* (—, *pl.* —n) speech, language; tongue; expression; diction; discussion; *etwas zur — bringen*, bring a subject up; *zur — kommen*, come up for discussion; *heraus mit der —!* speak out!

Sprachfehler [ˈʃpraːxfeːlər], *m.* (—s, *pl.* —) impediment in o.'s speech.

sprachfertig [ˈʃpraːxfɛrtiç], *adj.* having a ready tongue; a good linguist, fluent.

Sprachgebrauch [ˈʃpraːxgəbraux], *m.* (—(e)s, *no pl.*) (linguistic) usage.

Sprachkenner [ˈʃpraːxkɛnər], *m.* (—s, *pl.* —) linguist.

sprachkundig [ˈʃpraːxkundiç], *adj.* proficient in languages.

Sprachlehre [ˈʃpraːxleːrə], *f.* (—, *no pl.*) grammar.

sprachlich [ˈʃpraːxliç], *adj.* linguistic.

sprachlos [ˈʃpraːxloːs], *adj.* speechless, tongue-tied; *— dastehen*, be dumbfounded.

Sprachrohr [ˈʃpraːxroːr], *n.* (—s, *pl.* —e) megaphone, speaking-tube; (*fig.*) mouthpiece.

Sprachschatz [ˈʃpraːxʃats], *m.* (—es, *no pl.*) vocabulary.

Sprachvergleichung [ˈʃpraːxfɛrglaiçuŋ], *f.* (—, *no pl.*) comparative philology.

Sprachwerkzeug ['ʃpraːxvərktsɔyk], *n.* (—s, *pl.* —e) organ of speech.

Sprachwissenschaft ['ʃpraːxvisənʃaft], *f.* (—, *pl.* —en) linguistics, philology.

sprechen ['ʃprɛçən], *v.a.,v.n. irr.* speak, declare, say; talk; *für einen* —, put in a good word for s.o., speak up for s.o.; *er ist nicht zu* —, he is not available; *auf einen gut zu* — *sein*, feel well disposed towards s.o.; *schuldig* —, pronounce guilty; *das Urteil* —, pass sentence.

sprechend ['ʃprɛçənt], *adj.* expressive; — *ähnlich*, strikingly alike.

Sprecher ['ʃprɛçər], *m.* (—s, *pl.* —) speaker, orator, spokesman; (*Rad.*) announcer.

Sprechstunde ['ʃprɛçʃtundə], *f.* (—, *pl.* —n) consulting hours, surgery hours; office hours.

Sprechzimmer ['ʃprɛçtsimər], *n.* (—s, *pl.*—) consulting-room.

spreizen ['ʃpraitsən], *v.a.* spread open; *die Beine* —, plant o.'s legs wide apart, straddle. — *v.r. sich* —, give o.s. airs.

Sprengbombe ['ʃprɛŋbɔmbə], *f.* (—, *pl.* —n) (high explosive) bomb.

Sprengel ['ʃprɛŋəl], *m.* (—s, *pl.* —) diocese.

sprengen ['ʃprɛŋən], *v.a.* sprinkle; water; burst, explode; burst open, blow up; *eine Versammlung* —, break up a meeting. — *v.n.* (*aux.* sein) ride at full speed, gallop.

Sprengpulver ['ʃprɛŋpulvər], *n.* (—s, *no pl.*) blasting-powder.

Sprengstoff ['ʃprɛŋʃtɔf], *m.* (—es, *pl.* —e) explosive.

Sprengwagen ['ʃprɛŋvaːgən], *m.* (—s, *pl.* —) sprinkler; water-cart.

sprenkeln ['ʃprɛŋkəln], *v.a.* speckle.

Spreu ['ʃprɔy], *f.* (—, *no pl.*) chaff.

Sprichwort ['ʃpriçvɔrt], *n.* (—s, *pl.* ˙˙er) proverb, adage, saying.

sprießen ['ʃpriːsən], *v.n. irr.* sprout, shoot, germinate.

Springbrunnen ['ʃpriŋbrunən], *m.* (—s, *pl.* —) fountain.

springen ['ʃpriŋən], *v.n. irr.* (*aux.* sein) spring, leap, jump; (*glass*) burst; *etwas* — *lassen*, (*coll.*) treat s.o. to s.th.

Springer ['ʃpriŋər], *m.* (—s, *pl.* —) jumper, acrobat; (*Chess*) knight.

Springflut ['ʃpriŋfluːt], *f.* (—, *pl.* —en) spring-tide.

Springtau ['ʃpriŋtau], *n.* (—s, *pl.* —e) skipping-rope; (*Naut.*) slip-rope.

Sprit [ʃprit], *m.* (—s, *pl.* —e) spirit alcohol; (*sl.*) fuel, petrol.

Spritze ['ʃpritsə], *f.* (—, *pl.* —n) squirt, syringe; fire-engine; (*coll.*) injection.

spritzen ['ʃpritsən], *v.a.* squirt, spout, spray, sprinkle; (*coll.*) inject. — *v.n.* gush forth.

Spritzkuchen ['ʃpritskuːxən], *m.* (—s, *pl.* —) fritter.

Spritztour ['ʃpritstuːr], *f.* (—, *pl.* —en) (*coll.*) pleasure trip, outing; (*coll.*) spin.

spröde ['ʃprøːdə], *adj.* (*material*) brittle; (*person*) stubborn; coy, prim, prudish.

Sprödigkeit ['ʃprøːdiçkait], *f.* (—, *no pl.*) (*material*) brittleness; (*person*) stubbornness; coyness, primness, prudery.

Sproß [ʃprɔs], *m.* (—sses, *pl.* —sse) sprout, shoot, germ; (*fig.*) scion, offspring.

Sprosse ['ʃprɔsə], *f.* (—, *pl.* —n) (*ladder*) step, rung.

Sprößling ['ʃprœsliŋ], *m.* (—s, *pl.* —e) scion, offspring.

Sprotte ['ʃprɔtə], *f.* (—, *pl.* —n) sprat.

Spruch [ʃprux], *m.* (—(e)s, *pl.* ˙˙e) saying, aphorism; proverb; (*obs.*) saw; (*judge*) sentence, verdict.

spruchreif ['ʃpruxraif], *adj.* ripe for judgment; ready for a decision.

Sprudel ['ʃpruːdəl], *m.* (—s, *pl.* —) bubbling spring; (*coll.*) soda water.

sprudeln ['ʃpruːdəln], *v.n.* bubble, gush.

sprühen ['ʃpryːən], *v.a.* sprinkle, scatter, spray. — *v.n.* sparkle, emit sparks; (*rain*) drizzle.

sprühend ['ʃpryːənt], *adj.* (*fig.*) sparkling, scintillating, brilliant.

Sprühregen ['ʃpryːreːgən], *m.* (—s, *no pl.*) drizzling rain, drizzle.

Sprung [ʃpruŋ], *m.* (—(e)s, *pl.* ˙˙e) leap, bound, jump; chink, crack; *nur auf einen* — *zu Besuch kommen*, pay a flying visit; *auf dem* — *sein zu*, be on the point of; *sich auf den* — *machen*, cut and run, (*coll.*) fly; *große* ˙˙e *machen*, (*coll.*) live it up, cut a dash.

Sprungfeder ['ʃpruŋfeːdər], *f.* (—, *pl.* —n) spring.

Sprungkraft ['ʃpruŋkraft], *f.* (—, *no pl.*) springiness, elasticity, buoyancy.

Spucke ['ʃpukə], *f.* (—, *no pl.*) spittle, saliva.

spucken ['ʃpukən], *v.a., v.n.* spit.

Spuk [ʃpuːk], *m.* (—s, *pl.* —e) haunting; ghost, spectre, apparition; (*coll.*) spook.

spuken ['ʃpuːkən], *v.n.* haunt; be haunted.

spukhaft ['ʃpuːkhaft], *adj.* uncanny, phantom-like, ghost-like, spooky.

Spule ['ʃpuːlə], *f.* (—, *pl.* —n) spool; (*Elec.*) coil.

Spüleimer ['ʃpyːlaimər], *m.* (—s, *pl.* —) slop-pail.

spülen ['ʃpyːlən], *v.a.* rinse, wash.

Spülicht ['ʃpyːliçt], *n.* (—s, *no pl.*) dish-water.

Spund [ʃpunt], *m.* (—(e)s, *pl.* ˙˙e) bung.

Spundloch ['ʃpuntlɔx], *n.* (—s, *pl.* ˙˙er) bung-hole.

Spur [ʃpuːr], *f.* (—, *pl.* —en) footprint, track, trail; spoor; (*fig.*) trace, vestige; *frische* —, hot scent; *einer Sache auf die* — *kommen*, be on the track of s.th.; *keine* — *von*, not a trace of, not an inkling of.

spüren ['ʃpyːrən], *v.a.* trace, track (down); feel, sense, notice.

Spürhund ['ʃpyːrhunt], *m.* (—s, *pl.* —e) tracker dog, setter, beagle; (*fig.*) spy, sleuth.

spurlos ['ʃpuːrloːs], *adj.* trackless, without a trace; *es ging — an ihm vorüber,* it left no mark on him; *— verschwinden,* vanish into thin air.

Spürsinn ['ʃpyːrzɪn], *m.* (—s, *no pl.*) scent; flair; sagacity, shrewdness.

Spurweite ['ʃpuːrvaɪtə], *f.* (—, *pl.* —n) gauge, width of track.

sputen ['ʃpuːtən], *v.r. sich* —, make haste, hurry.

Staat [ʃtaːt], *m.* (—(e)s, *pl.* —en) state; government; pomp, show, parade; *— machen,* make a show of.

Staatenbund ['ʃtaːtənbunt], *m.* (—(e)s, *pl.* ⁇e) confederacy, federation.

staatlich ['ʃtaːtlɪç], *adj.* belonging to the state, public, national.

Staatsangehörige ['ʃtaːtsangəhøːrɪgə], *m.* (—n, *pl.* —n) citizen (of a country), subject, national.

Staatsangehörigkeit ['ʃtaːtsangəhøːrɪçkaɪt], *f.* (—, *pl.* —en) nationality.

Staatsanwalt ['ʃtaːtsanvalt], *m.* (—s, *pl.* ⁇e) public prosecutor, Attorney-General.

Staatsbeamte ['ʃtaːtsbəamtə], *m.* (—n, *pl.* —n) civil servant, employee of the state.

Staatsbürger ['ʃtaːtsbyrgər], *m.* (—s, *pl.* —) citizen, national.

Staatsdienst ['ʃtaːtsdiːnst], *m.* (—(e)s, *pl.* —e) civil service, government service.

Staatseinkünfte ['ʃtaːtsaɪnkynftə], *f. pl.* public revenue.

Staatsgesetz ['ʃtaːtsgəzɛts], *n.* (—es, *pl.* —e) statute law.

Staatsgewalt ['ʃtaːtsgəvalt], *f.* (—, *no pl.*) executive power.

Staatshaushalt ['ʃtaːtshaushalt], *m.* (—s, *no pl.*) state finances, budget.

Staatshaushaltsanschlag ['ʃtaːtshaushaltsanʃlaːk], *m.* (—s, *pl.* ⁇e) budget estimates.

Staatskanzler ['ʃtaːtskantslər], *m.* (—s, *pl.* —) Chancellor.

Staatskasse ['ʃtaːtskasə], *f.* (—, *no pl.*) public exchequer, treasury.

Staatskörper ['ʃtaːtskœrpər], *m.* (—s, *pl.* —) body politic.

Staatskosten ['ʃtaːtskɔstən], *f. pl. auf* —, (at (the) public expense.

Staatskunst ['ʃtaːtskunst], *f.* (—, *no pl.*) statesmanship; statecraft.

Staatsminister ['ʃtaːtsminɪstər], *m.* (—s, *pl.* —) cabinet minister; minister of state.

Staatsrat ['ʃtaːtsraːt], *m.* (—s, *no pl.*) council of state; (*pl.* ⁇e) councillor of state.

Staatsrecht ['ʃtaːtsrɛçt], *n.* (—(e)s, *no pl.*) constitutional law.

Staatssiegel ['ʃtaːtsziːgəl], *n.* (—s, *pl.* —) Great Seal, official seal.

Staatsstreich ['ʃtaːtsʃtraɪç], *m.* (—(e)s, *pl.* —e) coup d'état.

Staatswirtschaft ['ʃtaːtsvɪrtʃaft], *f.* (—, *no pl.*) political economy.

Staatszimmer ['ʃtaːtstsɪmər], *n.* (—s, *pl.* —) state apartment.

Stab [ʃtaːp], *m.* (—(e)s, *pl.* ⁇e) staff; stick, rod, pole; crosier; mace; (*Mil.*) field-officers, staff; *den — über einen brechen,* condemn s.o. (to death).

stabil [ʃtaˈbiːl], *adj.* steady, stable, firm.

stabilisieren [ʃtabiliˈziːrən], *v.a.* stabilise.

Stabreim ['ʃtaːpraɪm], *m.* (—s, *no pl.*) alliteration.

Stabsarzt ['ʃtaːpsartst], *m.* (—es, *pl.* ⁇e) (*Mil.*) medical officer.

Stabsquartier ['ʃtaːpskvartiːr], *n.* (—s, *pl.* —e) (*Mil.*) headquarters.

Stachel ['ʃtaxəl], *m.* (—s, *pl.* —n) (*animal*) sting; (*plant*) prickle, thorn; (*fig.*) keen edge, sting; stimulus; *wider den — löcken,* kick against the pricks.

Stachelbeere ['ʃtaxəlbeːrə], *f.* (—, *pl.* —n) (*Bot.*) gooseberry.

Stachelschwein ['ʃtaxəlʃvaɪn], *n.* (—s, *pl.* —e) (*Zool.*) hedgehog, porcupine.

stachlig ['ʃtaxlɪç], *adj.* prickly, thorny; (*fig.*) disagreeable.

Stadion ['ʃtaːdjɔn], *n.* (—s, *pl.* —dien) sports-arena, stadium.

Stadium ['ʃtaːdjum], *n.* (—s, *pl.* —dien) stage (of development), phase.

Stadt [ʃtat], *f.* (—, *pl.* ⁇e) town; city.

Stadtbahn ['ʃtatbaːn], *f.* (—, *pl.* —en) metropolitan railway.

Städtchen ['ʃtɛtçən], *n.* (—s, *pl.* —) small town, township.

Städter ['ʃtɛtər], *m.* (—s, *pl.* —) townsman.

Stadtgemeinde ['ʃtatgəmaɪndə], *f.* (—, *pl.* —n) municipality.

städtisch ['ʃtɛtɪʃ], *adj.* municipal.

Stadtmauer ['ʃtatmauər], *f.* (—, *pl.* —n) town wall, city wall.

Stadtrat ['ʃtatraːt], *m.* (—s, *no pl.*) town council; (*pl.* ⁇e) town councillor; alderman.

Stadtteil ['ʃtattaɪl], *m.* (—s, *pl.* —e) ward, district, part of a town.

Stadttor ['ʃtattoːr], *n.* (—s, *pl.* —e) city-gate.

Stadtverordnete ['ʃtatfɛrɔrdnətə], *m.* (—n, *pl.* —n) town councillor.

Stafette [ʃtaˈfɛtə], *f.* (—, *pl.* —n) courier; relay.

Staffel ['ʃtafəl], *f.* (—, *pl.* —n) step, rundle, rung, round; relay; (*fig.*) degree; (*Aviat.*) squadron.

Staffelei [ʃtafəˈlaɪ], *f.* (—, *pl.* —en) easel.

staffeln ['ʃtafəln], *v.a.* grade; differentiate; stagger.

Staffelung ['ʃtafəluŋ], *f.* (—, *pl.* —en) gradation.

stagnieren [ʃtagˈniːrən], *v.n.* stagnate.

Stahl [ʃtaːl], *m.* (—(e)s, *pl.* ⁇e) steel.

stählen ['ʃtɛːlən], *v.a.* steel, harden, temper; brace.

stählern ['ʃtɛːlərn], *adj.* made of steel, steely.

Stahlquelle ['ʃtaːlkvɛlə], *f.* (—, *pl.* —n) chalybeate spring; mineral spring.

Stahlstich ['ʃtaːlʃtɪç], *m.* (—(e)s, *pl.* —e) steel-engraving.

Stählung ['ʃtɛːluŋ], *f.* (—, *no pl.*) steeling; (*fig.*) bracing.

Stahlwaren ['ʃtaːlvaːrən], *f. pl.* hardware, cutlery.

Stall [ʃtal], *m.* (—(e)s, *pl.* ⸚e) stable; (*pig*) sty; (*dog*) kennel.

Stallbursche ['ʃtalburʃə], *m.* (—n, *pl.* —n) stable-boy, groom.

Stallungen ['ʃtaluŋən], *f. pl.* stabling, stables.

Stambul ['ʃtambul], *n.* Istanbul.

Stamm [ʃtam], *m.* (—(e)s, *pl.* ⸚e) (*tree*) trunk; (*people*) tribe, family, race; (*words*) stem; root.

Stammaktie ['ʃtamaktsjə], *f.* (—, *pl.* —n) (*Comm.*) original share.

Stammbaum ['ʃtambaum], *m.* (—s, *pl.* ⸚e) pedigree; family tree.

Stammbuch ['ʃtambuːx], *n.* (—(e)s, *pl.* ⸚er) album.

stammeln ['ʃtaməln], *v.a., v.n.* stammer, stutter; falter.

stammen ['ʃtamən], *v.n.* (*aux.* sein) be descended from, spring from, originate from, stem from; be derived from.

Stammesgenosse ['ʃtaməsgənɔsə], *m.* (—n, *pl.* —n) kinsman, clansman.

Stammgast ['ʃtamgast], *m.* (—es, *pl.* ⸚e) regular customer.

Stammgut ['ʃtamguːt], *n.* (—s, *pl.* ⸚er) family estate.

Stammhalter ['ʃtamhaltər], *m.* (—s, *pl.* —) son and heir; eldest son.

Stammhaus ['ʃtamhaus], *n.* (—es, *pl.* ⸚er) ancestral mansion; (*royalty*) dynasty; (*Comm.*) business headquarters, head office.

stämmig ['ʃtɛmɪç], *adj.* sturdy, strong.

Stammler ['ʃtamlər], *m.* (—s, *pl.* —) stammerer, stutterer.

Stammsilbe ['ʃtamzɪlbə], *f.* (—, *pl.* —n) (*Ling.*) radical syllable.

Stammtafel ['ʃtamtaːfəl], *f.* (—, *pl.* —n) genealogical table.

Stammvater ['ʃtamfaːtər], *m.* (—s, *pl.* ⸚) ancestor, progenitor.

stammverwandt ['ʃtamfɛrvant], *adj.* cognate, kindred.

stampfen ['ʃtampfən], *v.a.* stamp, pound, ram down. — *v.n.* stamp, trample.

Stand [ʃtant], *m.* (—(e)s, *pl.* ⸚e) stand; (*market*) stall; situation, state (of affairs), condition; reading, position; rank, station (in life); (*pl.*) the classes, the estates.

Standarte [ʃtan'dartə], *f.* (—, *pl.* —n) standard, banner.

Standbild ['ʃtantbɪlt], *n.* (—(e)s, *pl.* ⸚er) statue.

Ständchen ['ʃtɛntçən], *n.* (—s, *pl.* —) serenade; *einem ein — bringen*, serenade s.o.

Ständehaus ['ʃtɛndəhaus], *n.* (—es, *pl.* ⸚er) state assembly-hall.

Ständer ['ʃtɛndər], *m.* (—s, *pl.* —) stand, pedestal; post; (upright) desk.

Standesamt ['ʃtandəsamt], *n.* (—s, *pl.* ⸚er) registry office.

Standesbeamte ['ʃtandəsbəamtə], *m.* (—n, *pl.* —n) registrar (of births, marriages and deaths).

Standesbewußtsein ['ʃtandəsbəvustzaɪn], *n.* (—s, *no pl.*) class-feeling, class-consciousness.

Standesperson ['ʃtandəspɛrzoːn], *f.* (—, *pl.* —en) person of rank.

Standgericht ['ʃtantgərɪçt], *n.* (—es, *pl.* —e) court-martial; summary court of justice.

standhaft ['ʃtanthaft], *adj.* constant, firm, steadfast.

standhalten ['ʃtanthaltən], *v.n.* irr. bear up, stand o.'s ground, withstand, resist.

ständig ['ʃtɛndɪç], *adj.* permanent.

ständisch ['ʃtɛndɪʃ], *adj.* relating to the estates (of the realm).

Standort ['ʃtantɔrt], *m.* (—s, *pl.* —e) location; station.

Standpauke ['ʃtantpaukə], *f.* (—, *pl.* —n) (*coll.*) harangue; severe reprimand.

Standpunkt ['ʃtantpuŋkt], *m.* (—(e)s, *pl.* —e) standpoint; point of view; *den — vertreten*, take the line; *einem den — klar machen*, give s.o. a piece of o.'s mind.

Standrecht ['ʃtantrɛçt], *n.* (—(e)s, *no pl.*) martial law.

Standuhr ['ʃtantuːr], *f.* (—, *pl.* —en) grandfather-clock.

Stange ['ʃtaŋə], *f.* (—, *pl.* —n) stick, pole; *bei der — bleiben*, stick to the point, persevere.

Stank [ʃtaŋk], *m.* (—s, *no pl.*) (*dial.*) stench; discord, trouble.

Stänker ['ʃtɛŋkər], *m.* (—s, *pl.* —) (*coll.*) mischief-maker, quarrelsome person.

stänkern ['ʃtɛŋkərn], *v.n.* pick quarrels; ferret about, make trouble.

Stanniol [ʃta'njoːl], *n.* (—s, *no pl.*) tinfoil.

stanzen ['ʃtantsən], *v.a.* punch, stamp.

Stapel ['ʃtaːpəl], *m.* (—s, *pl.* —) pile, heap; (*Naut.*) slipway; *ein Schiff vom — lassen*, launch a ship.

Stapellauf ['ʃtaːpəllauf], *m.* (—s, *pl.* ⸚e) (*Naut.*) launch, launching.

stapeln ['ʃtaːpəln], *v.a.* pile up.

Stapelnahrung ['ʃtaːpəlnaːruŋ], *f.* (—, *no pl.*) staple diet.

Stapelplatz ['ʃtaːpəlplats], *m.* (—es, *pl.* ⸚e) mart, emporium.

Stapelware ['ʃtaːpəlvaːrə], *f.* (—, *pl.* —n) staple goods.

Stapfen ['ʃtapfən], *m.* or *f. pl.* footsteps.

Star (1) ['ʃtaːr], *m.* (—(e)s, *pl.* —e) (*Med.*) cataract; *einem den — stechen*, operate for cataract; (*fig.*) open s.o.'s eyes.

Star (2) ['ʃtaːr], *m.* (—(e)s, *pl.* —en) (*Orn.*) starling.

stark [ʃtark], *adj.* strong, stout; robust; vigorous; heavy; considerable; *—er Esser*, hearty eater. — *adv.* very much.

Stärke

Stärke ['ʃtɛrkə], *f.* (—, *no pl.*) strength, vigour, robustness; strong point; starch.

Stärkekleister ['ʃtɛrkəklaɪstər], *m.* (—s, *no pl.*) starch-paste.

Stärkemehl ['ʃtɛrkəme:l], *n.* (—s, *no pl.*) starch-flour.

stärken ['ʃtɛrkən], *v.a.* strengthen; corroborate; starch. — *v.r. sich* —, take some refreshment.

stärkend ['ʃtɛrkənt], *adj.* strengthening, restorative; —*es Mittel*, tonic.

starkleibig ['ʃtarklaɪbɪç], *adj.* corpulent, stout, obese.

Stärkung ['ʃtɛrkuŋ], *f.* (—, *pl.* —en) strengthening, invigoration; refreshment.

starr [ʃtar], *adj.* stiff, rigid; fixed; inflexible; stubborn; stare at s.o.; *einen* — *ansehen*, stare at s.o.

starren ['ʃtarən], *v.n.* stare.

Starrheit ['ʃtarhaɪt], *f.* (—, *no pl.*) stiffness, rigidity; fixedness; inflexibility; stubbornness.

starrköpfig ['ʃtarkœpfɪç], *adj.* headstrong, stubborn, obstinate, pigheaded.

Starrkrampf ['ʃtarkrampf], *m.* (—(e)s, *no pl.*) (*Med.*) tetanus.

Starrsinn ['ʃtarzɪn], *m.* (—s, *no pl.*) stubbornness, obstinacy.

Station [ʃta'tsjo:n], *f.* (—, *pl.* —en) (*Railw.*) station; (*main*) terminus; stop, stopping-place; (*hospital*) ward; *freie* —, board and lodging found.

stationär [ʃtatsjo'nɛ:r], *adj.* stationary.

stationieren [ʃtatsjo'ni:rən], *v.a.* station.

Stationsvorsteher [ʃtat'sjo:nsfɔrʃte:ər], *m.* (—s, *pl.* —) station-master.

statisch ['ʃta:tɪʃ], *adj.* static.

Statist [ʃta'tɪst], *m.* (—en, *pl.* —en) (*Theat.*) extra, walking-on part; (*pl.*) supers.

Statistik [ʃta'tɪstɪk], *f.* (—, *pl.* —en) statistics.

Statistiker [ʃta'tɪstɪkər], *m.* (—s, *pl.* —) statistician.

Stativ [ʃta'ti:f], *n.* (—s, *pl.* —e) stand, tripod.

Statt [ʃtat], *f.* (—, *no pl.*) place, stead; *an seiner* —, in his place.

statt [ʃtat], *prep.* (*Genit.*) instead of, in lieu of.

Stätte ['ʃtɛtə], *f.* (—, *pl.* —n) place, abode.

stattfinden ['ʃtatfɪndən], *v.n. irr.* take place.

stattgeben ['ʃtatge:bən], *v.n. irr. einer Bitte* —, grant a request.

statthaft ['ʃtathaft], *adj.* admissible, allowable, lawful.

Statthalter ['ʃtathaltər], *m.* (—s, *pl.* —) governor.

stattlich ['ʃtatlɪç], *adj.* stately, handsome, distinguished, comely; portly; considerable; *eine* —*e Summe*, a tidy sum.

statuieren [ʃtatu'i:rən], *v.a.* decree; *ein Exempel* —, make an example of.

Statut [ʃta'tu:t], *n.* (—s, *pl.* —en) statute, regulation.

Staub [ʃtaup], *m.* (—(e)s, *no pl.*) dust, powder; *sich aus dem* — *machen*, take French leave; abscond.

Stäubchen ['ʃtɔypçən], *n.* (—s, *pl.* —) mote, particle of dust.

stauben ['ʃtaubən], *v.n. es staubt*, it is dusty.

Staubgefäß ['ʃtaupgəfɛ:s], *n.* (—es, *pl.* —e) stamen.

staubig ['ʃtaubɪç], *adj.* dusty.

Staubkamm ['ʃtaupkam], *m.* (—s, *pl.* ∸e) fine-tooth comb.

Staublappen ['ʃtauplapən], *m.* (—s, *pl.* —) duster.

Staubmantel ['ʃtaupmantəl], *m.* (—s, *pl.* ∸) overall, smock; dust(er)coat, (*Am.*) duster.

Staubsauger ['ʃtaupzaugər], *m.* (—s, *pl.* —) vacuum cleaner.

Staubtuch ['ʃtauptu:x], *n.* (—es, *pl.* ∸er) duster.

Staubwedel ['ʃtaupve:dəl], *m.* (—s, *pl.* —) feather duster.

Staubwolke ['ʃtaupvɔlkə], *f.* (—, *pl.* —n) cloud of dust.

Staubzucker ['ʃtauptsukər], *m.* (—s, *no pl.*) castor-sugar, icing-sugar.

Staudamm ['ʃtaudam], *m.* (—s, *pl.* ∸e) dam, dyke.

Staude ['ʃtaudə], *f.* (—, *pl.* —n) shrub, bush.

stauen ['ʃtauən], *v.a.* stow; (*water*) dam. — *v.r. sich* —, be congested.

staunen ['ʃtaunən], *v.n.* be astonished, be surprised, wonder (at).

Staupe ['ʃtaupə], *f.* (—, *pl.* —n) (*animals*) distemper.

stäupen ['ʃtɔypən], *v.a.* (*obs.*) scourge, flog.

Stauung ['ʃtauuŋ], *f.* (—, *pl.* —en) stowage; (*water*) damming-up, swell, rising; (*blood*) congestion; (*traffic*) jam, build-up.

stechen ['ʃtɛçən], *v.a. irr.* prick, sting; stab; (*cards*) trump.

stechend ['ʃtɛçənt], *adj.* pungent, biting.

Stechmücke ['ʃtɛçmykə], *f.* (—, *pl.* —n) (*Ent.*) gnat, mosquito.

Stechpalme ['ʃtɛçpalmə], *f.* (—, *pl.* —n) (*Bot.*) holly.

Steckbrief ['ʃtɛkbri:f], *m.* (—s, *pl.* —e) warrant (for arrest).

stecken ['ʃtɛkən], *v.a.* stick into, put, place, fix; (*plants*) set, plant; *in Brand* —, set on fire, set fire to. — *v.n. irgendwo* —, be about somewhere; — *bleiben*, get stuck, break down; *er steckt dahinter*, he is at the bottom of it. — *v.r. sich hinter einen* —, shelter behind s.o.

Stecken ['ʃtɛkən], *m.* (—s, *pl.* —) stick, staff.

Stecker ['ʃtɛkər], *m.* (—s, *pl.* —) (*Elec.*) plug.

Steckkontakt ['ʃtɛkkɔntakt], *m.* (—(e)s, *pl.* —e) (*Elec.*) plug, point.

Stecknadel ['ʃtɛkna:dəl], *f.* (—, *pl.* —n) pin.

Steg [ʃte:k], *m.* (—(e)s, *pl.* —e) plank, foot-bridge; jetty; (*violin*) bridge.

Stegreif [ˈʃteːkraɪf], m. (—s, pl. —e) (obs.) stirrup; aus dem — sprechen, extemporise, improvise.

stehen [ˈʃteːən], v.n. irr. stand; be; stand still; einem gut —, fit or suit s.o. well; mit einem gut —, be on good terms with s.o.; gut —, be in a fair way, look promising; was steht zu Diensten? what can I do for you? — bleiben, stand still, stop, pull up.

stehlen [ˈʃteːlən], v.a. irr. steal.

Steiermark [ˈʃtaɪərmark], f. Styria.

steif [ʃtaɪf], adj. stiff; (grog) strong; awkward; ceremonious, punctilious, formal. — adv. etwas — und fest behaupten, swear by all that's holy.

steifen [ˈʃtaɪfən], v.a. stiffen, starch.

Steifheit [ˈʃtaɪfhaɪt], f. (—, no pl.) stiffness; (fig.) formality.

Steifleinen [ˈʃtaɪflaɪnən], n. (—s, no pl.) buckram.

Steig [ʃtaɪk], m. (—(e)s, pl. —e) path, (mountain) track.

Steigbügel [ˈʃtaɪkbyːgəl], m. (—s, pl. —) stirrup.

Steigen [ˈʃtaɪgən], n. (—s, no pl.) rising, increase; (price) advance, rise; im —, on the increase.

steigen [ˈʃtaɪgən], v.n. irr. (aux. sein) climb, mount, ascend; (barometer) rise; (population) increase; (horse) rear; (price) advance, rise.

Steiger [ˈʃtaɪgər], m. (—s, pl. —) climber, mountaineer; mining-surveyor, overseer.

steigern [ˈʃtaɪgərn], v.a. (price) raise; (fig.) enhance, increase. — v.r. sich —, increase.

Steigerung [ˈʃtaɪgəruŋ], f. (—, pl. —en) raising; (fig.) enhancement; increase; (Gram.) comparison.

Steigung [ˈʃtaɪguŋ], f. (—, pl. —en) gradient.

steil [ʃtaɪl], adj. steep.

Stein [ʃtaɪn], m. (—(e)s, pl. —e) stone, rock; flint; jewel, gem; monument; (Chess) piece, chessman; (Draughts) man; (fruit) stone, kernel; — des Anstoßes, stumbling block; mir fällt ein — vom Herzen, it is a load off my mind; bei einem einen — im Brett haben, be in s.o.'s good books; einem —e in den Weg legen, put obstacles in s.o.'s way; der — des Weisen, the philosopher's stone.

Steinadler [ˈʃtaɪnaːdlər], m. (—s, pl. —) (Orn.) golden eagle.

steinalt [ˈʃtaɪnalt], adj. very old.

Steinbock [ˈʃtaɪnbɔk], m. (—s, pl. ⁻e) ibex; (Astrol.) Capricorn.

Steinbruch [ˈʃtaɪnbrux], m. (—s, pl. ⁻e) stone-pit, quarry.

Steinbutt [ˈʃtaɪnbut], m. (—s, pl. —e) (Zool.) turbot.

Steindruck [ˈʃtaɪndruk], m. (—s, no pl.) lithography.

steinern [ˈʃtaɪnərn], adj. stony; built of stone.

Steingut [ˈʃtaɪnguːt], n. (—s, no pl.) earthenware, stoneware, pottery.

Steinhagel [ˈʃtaɪnhaːgəl], m. (—s, no pl.) shower of stones.

Steinhaue [ˈʃtaɪnhauə], f. (—, pl. —n) pickaxe.

Steinhügel [ˈʃtaɪnhyːgəl], m. (—s, pl. —) cairn.

steinig [ˈʃtaɪnɪç], adj. stony, rocky.

steinigen [ˈʃtaɪnɪgən], v.a. stone.

Steinkalk [ˈʃtaɪnkalk], m. (—s, no pl.) quicklime.

Steinkohle [ˈʃtaɪnkoːlə], f. (—, no pl.) pit-coal.

Steinkrug [ˈʃtaɪnkruːk], m. (—s, pl. ⁻e) stone jar.

Steinmarder [ˈʃtaɪnmardər], m. (—s, pl. —) (Zool.) stone-marten.

Steinmetz [ˈʃtaɪnmɛts], m. (—es, pl. —e) stone-cutter, stone-mason.

Steinobst [ˈʃtaɪnoːpst], n. (—es, no pl.) stone-fruit.

Steinplatte [ˈʃtaɪnplatə], f. (—, pl. —n) slab, flagstone.

steinreich [ˈʃtaɪnraɪç], adj. as rich as Croesus.

Steinsalz [ˈʃtaɪnzalts], n. (—es, no pl.) rock-salt, mineral-salt.

Steinwurf [ˈʃtaɪnvurf], m. (—s, pl. ⁻e) einen — entfernt, within a stone's throw.

Steiß [ʃtaɪs], m. (—es, pl. —e) rump; (coll.) buttocks, posterior.

Stellage [ʃtɛˈlaːʒə], f. (—, pl. —n) stand, frame.

Stelldichein [ˈʃtɛldɪçaɪn], n. (—s, no pl. assignation, rendezvous, tryst; (coll.) date.

Stelle [ˈʃtɛlə], f. (—, pl. —n) place, spot; job, position; situation; (book) passage; figure, digit; department; offene —, vacancy; auf der —, at once, immediately; an deiner —, if I were you; nicht von der — kommen, remain stationary; zur — sein, be at hand.

stellen [ˈʃtɛlən], v.a. put, place, set; richtig —, regulate, correct, amend; (clock) set right; seinen Mann —, play o.'s part, pull o.'s weight. — v.r. sich —, come forward; pretend; sich krank —, feign illness, malinger, pretend to be ill.

Stellenbewerber [ˈʃtɛlənbəverbər], m. (—s, pl. —) applicant (for a job).

Stellengesuch [ˈʃtɛləngəzuːx], n. (—s, pl. —e) application (for a job).

Stellenvermittlung [ˈʃtɛlənfermɪtluŋ], f. (—, pl. —en) employment office, employment exchange.

stellenweise [ˈʃtɛlənvaɪzə], adv. in parts, here and there.

Stellmacher [ˈʃtɛlmaxər], m. (—s, pl. —) wheelwright.

Stellung [ˈʃtɛluŋ], f. (—, pl. —en) position, posture; attitude; situation; job; (Mil.) trenches; — nehmen zu, express o.'s views on.

Stellvertreter [ˈʃtɛlfertreːtər], m. (—s, pl. —) representative, deputy; substitute, supply, proxy, relief; (doctor) locum.

Stelzbein [ˈʃtɛltsbaɪn], n. (—s, pl. —e) wooden leg.

211

Stemmeisen

Stemmeisen ['ʃtɛmaɪzən], *n.* (—s, *pl.* —) crowbar.

stemmen ['ʃtɛmən], *v.a.* (*water*) stem, dam; (*weight*) lift. — *v.r. sich —*
gegen, resist fiercely.

Stempel ['ʃtɛmpəl], *m.* (—s, *pl.* —) stamp, rubber-stamp, die; pounder; (*Bot.*) pistil.

Stempelgebühr ['ʃtɛmpəlgəby:r], *f.* (—, *pl.* —en) stamp-duty.

stempeln ['ʃtɛmpəln], *v.a.* stamp, hallmark; brand; cancel (*postage stamp*). — *v.n.* (*coll.*) — *gehen*, be on the dole.

Stengel ['ʃtɛŋəl], *m.* (—s, *pl.* —) stalk.

Stenografie [ʃtenoɡra'fi:], *f.* (—, *no pl.*) stenography, shorthand.

stenografisch [ʃteno'ɡra:fɪʃ], *adj.* in shorthand.

Stenogramm [ʃteno'ɡram], *n.* (—s, *pl.* —e) shorthand-note.

Stenotypistin [ʃtenoty'pɪstɪn], *f.* (—, *pl.* —nen) shorthand-typist.

Stephan ['ʃtefan], *m.* Stephen.

Steppdecke ['ʃtɛpdɛkə], *f.* (—, *pl.* —n) quilt.

Steppe ['ʃtɛpə], *f.* (—, *pl.* —n) steppe.

steppen ['ʃtɛpən], *v.a.* stitch, quilt.

Sterbeglocke ['ʃtɛrbəɡlɔkə], *f.* (—, *pl.* —n) passing bell, death bell.

Sterbehemd ['ʃtɛrbəhɛmt], *n.* (—(e)s, *pl.* —en) shroud, winding-sheet.

sterben ['ʃtɛrbən], *v.n. irr.* (*aux.* sein) die.

Sterbenswörtchen ['ʃtɛrbənsvœrtçən], *n.* (—s, *pl.* —) *nicht ein* —, not a syllable.

Sterbesakramente ['ʃtɛrbəzakramɛntə], *n. pl.* (*Eccl.*) last sacraments, last rites.

sterblich ['ʃtɛrplɪç], *adj.* mortal; — *verliebt*, desperately in love.

Sterblichkeit ['ʃtɛrplɪçkaɪt], *f.* (—, *no pl.*) mortality.

stereotyp [stereo'ty:p], *adj.* stereotyped.

sterilisieren [sterili'zi:rən], *v.a.* sterilise.

Sterilität [sterili'tɛ:t], *f.* (—, *no pl.*) sterility.

Stern [ʃtɛrn], *m.* (—(e)s, *pl.* —e) star; (*Typ.*) asterisk.

Sternbild ['ʃtɛrnbɪlt], *n.* (—s, *pl.* —er) constellation.

Sterndeuter ['ʃtɛrndɔytər], *m.* (—s, *pl.* —) astrologer.

Sterndeutung ['ʃtɛrndɔytuŋ], *f.* (—, *no pl.*) astrology.

Sternenschimmer ['ʃtɛrnənʃɪmər], *m.* (—s, *no pl.*) starlight.

sternförmig ['ʃtɛrnfœrmɪç], *adj.* star-like, star-shaped.

Sterngucker ['ʃtɛrnɡukər], *m.* (—s, *pl.* —) stargazer.

sternhagelvoll ['ʃtɛrnha:ɡəlfɔl], *adj.* (*coll.*) as drunk as a lord.

Sternkunde ['ʃtɛrnkundə], *f.* (—, *no pl.*) astronomy.

Sternkundige ['ʃtɛrnkundɪɡə], *m.* (—n, *pl.* —n) astronomer.

Sternschnuppe ['ʃtɛrnʃnupə], *f.* (—, *pl.* —n) falling star, shooting star, meteorite.

Sternwarte ['ʃtɛrnvartə], *f.* (—, *pl.* —n) observatory.

stetig ['ʃte:tɪç], *adj.* continual, continuous, constant.

stets [ʃte:ts], *adv.* always, ever, continually.

Steuer (1) ['ʃtɔyər], *n.* (—s, *pl.* —) rudder, helm, steering wheel.

Steuer (2) ['ʃtɔyər], *f.* (—, *pl.* —n) tax; (*local*) rate; (*import*) customs duty.

Steueramt ['ʃtɔyəramt], *n.* (—s, *pl.* ⁻er) inland revenue office, tax office.

Steuerbeamte ['ʃtɔyərbaamtə], *m.* (—n, *pl.* —n) revenue officer, tax collector.

Steuerbord ['ʃtɔyərbɔrt], *n.* (—s, *no pl.*) starboard.

Steuereinnehmer ['ʃtɔyəraɪnne:mər], *m.* (—s, *pl.* —) tax collector.

steuerfrei ['ʃtɔyərfraɪ], *adj.* duty-free, exempt from taxes.

Steuerhinterziehung ['ʃtɔyərhɪntərtsi:uŋ], *f.* (—, *pl.* —en) tax evasion.

steuerlos ['ʃtɔyərlo:s], *adj.* rudderless, adrift.

Steuermann ['ʃtɔyərman], *m.* (—s, *pl.* ⁻er) mate; helmsman.

steuern ['ʃtɔyərn], *v.a.* steer; *einem Unheil* —, avoid *or* steer clear of an evil.

steuerpflichtig ['ʃtɔyərpflɪçtɪç], *adj.* taxable, liable to tax, dutiable.

Steuerrad ['ʃtɔyərra:t], *n.* (—s, *pl.* ⁻er) steering-wheel.

Steuerung ['ʃtɔyəruŋ], *f.* (—, *no pl.*) steering, controls.

Steuerveranlagung ['ʃtɔyərfɛranla:ɡuŋ], *f.* (—, *pl.* —en) tax-assessment.

stibitzen [ʃti'bɪtsən], *v.a.* (*coll.*) pilfer, filch.

Stich [ʃtɪç], *m.* (—(e)s, *pl.* —e) sting; prick; stitch; stab; (*Cards*) trick; (*Art*) engraving; *einen im — lassen*, leave s.o. in the lurch.

Stichel ['ʃtɪçəl], *m.* (—s, *pl.* —) (*Art*) graver.

Stichelei [ʃtɪçə'laɪ], *f.* (—, *pl.* —en) taunt, sneer, gibe.

sticheln ['ʃtɪçəln], *v.a.* taunt, nag.

stichhaltig ['ʃtɪçhaltɪç], *adj.* valid, sound.

Stichhaltigkeit ['ʃtɪçhaltɪçkaɪt], *f.* (—, *no pl.*) validity, cogency.

Stichprobe ['ʃtɪçpro:bə], *f.* (—, *pl.* —n) sample taken at random, sampling.

Stichwahl ['ʃtɪçva:l], *f.* (—, *pl.* —en) second ballot.

Stichwort ['ʃtɪçvɔrt], *n.* (—s, *pl.* —e) key-word; (*Theat.*) cue.

sticken ['ʃtɪkən], *v.a., v.n.* embroider.

Stickerei [ʃtɪkə'raɪ], *f.* (—, *pl.* —en) embroidery.

Stickgarn ['ʃtɪkɡarn], *n.* (—s, *pl.* —e) embroidery cotton or silk.

Stickhusten ['ʃtɪkhu:stən], *m.* (—s, *no pl.*) choking cough.

stickig [ˈʃtɪkɪç], adj. stuffy.
Stickmuster [ˈʃtɪkmustər], n. (—s, pl. —) embroidery-pattern.
Stickstoff [ˈʃtɪkʃtɔf], m. (—(e)s, no pl.) nitrogen.
stieben [ˈʃtiːbən], v.n. (aux. sein) scatter, spray; auseinander —, disperse.
Stiefbruder [ˈʃtiːfbruːdər], m. (—s, pl. ⸚) step-brother.
Stiefel [ˈʃtiːfəl], m. (—s, pl. —) boot.
Stiefelknecht [ˈʃtiːfəlknɛçt], m. (—(e)s, pl. —e) boot-jack.
Stiefelputzer [ˈʃtiːfəlputsər], m. (—s, pl. —) shoe-black; (Am.) shoe-shine; (hotel) boots.
Stiefeltern [ˈʃtiːfɛltern], pl. step-parents.
Stiefmütterchen [ˈʃtiːfmytərçən], n. (—s, pl. —) (Bot.) pansy.
stiefmütterlich [ˈʃtiːfmytərlɪç], adj. like a stepmother; niggardly.
Stiefsohn [ˈʃtiːfzoːn], m. (—s, pl. ⸚e) stepson.
Stiege [ˈʃtiːgə], f. (—, pl. —n) staircase.
Stieglitz [ˈʃtiːglɪts], m. (—es, pl. —e) goldfinch.
Stiel [ʃtiːl], m. (—(e)s, pl. —e) handle; (plant) stalk.
Stier [ʃtiːr], m. (—(e)s, pl. —e) bull; junger —, bullock; (Astrol.) Taurus.
stieren [ˈʃtiːrən], v.n. stare (at), goggle.
Stift (1) [ʃtɪft], m. (—(e)s, pl. —e) tack, pin, peg; pencil; (coll.) apprentice; young chap.
Stift (2) [ʃtɪft], n. (—(e)s, pl. —e) charitable or religious foundation.
stiften [ˈʃtɪftən], v.a. establish, give, donate; found, set on foot, originate; Frieden —, bring about peace.
Stifter [ˈʃtɪftər], m. (—s, pl. —) founder, originator, donor.
Stiftung [ˈʃtɪftuŋ], f. (—, pl. —en) establishment, foundation; institution; charitable foundation; endowment, donation.
Stil [ʃtiːl], m. (—(e)s, pl. —e) style; (fig.) manner.
stilisieren [ʃtiliˈziːrən], v.a. word, draft.
Stilistik [ʃtiˈlɪstɪk], f. (—, no pl.) art of composition.
stilistisch [ʃtiˈlɪstɪʃ], adj. stylistic.
still [ʃtɪl], adj. quiet, still, silent; calm; —er Teilhaber, sleeping partner; im —en, secretly, on the sly.
Stille [ˈʃtɪlə], f. (—, no pl.) silence, quietness, tranquillity; calm, calmness; in der —, silently; in der — der Nacht, at dead of night.
stillen [ˈʃtɪlən], v.a. allay; (blood) staunch; (baby) suckle, feed, nurse; (thirst) quench; (hunger) appease.
stillos [ˈʃtɪlloːs], adj. incongruous; in bad taste.
Stillung [ˈʃtɪluŋ], f. (—, no pl.) allaying; (blood) staunching; (baby) suckling, feeding, nursing; (thirst) quenching; (hunger) appeasing.

stilvoll [ˈʃtiːlfɔl], adj. harmonious; stylish; in good taste.
Stimmband [ˈʃtɪmbant], n. (—s, pl. ⸚er) vocal chord.
stimmberechtigt [ˈʃtɪmbərɛçtɪçt], adj. entitled to vote, enfranchised.
Stimmbruch [ˈʃtɪmbrux], m. (—s, no pl.) breaking of the voice.
Stimme [ˈʃtɪmə], f. (—, pl. —n) voice; (election) vote, suffrage; die — abgeben, vote.
stimmen [ˈʃtɪmən], v.a. (piano) tune; einen günstig —, dispose s.o. favourably towards s.th. — v.n. agree, tally (with), square (with), accord (with); vote.
Stimmeneinheit [ˈʃtɪmənaɪnhaɪt], f. (—, no pl.) unanimity.
Stimmengleichheit [ˈʃtɪmənglaɪçhaɪt], f. (—, no pl.) equality of votes, tie.
Stimmer [ˈʃtɪmər], m. (—s, pl. —) (piano) tuner.
Stimmführer [ˈʃtɪmfyːrər], m. (—s, pl. —) leader, spokesman.
Stimmgabel [ˈʃtɪmgaːbəl], f. (—, pl. —n) tuning fork.
stimmhaft [ˈʃtɪmhaft], adj. (Phonet.) voiced.
Stimmlage [ˈʃtɪmlaːgə], f. (—, pl. —n) (Mus.) register.
stimmlos [ˈʃtɪmloːs], adj. voiceless; (Phonet.) unvoiced.
Stimmrecht [ˈʃtɪmrɛçt], n. (—s, no pl.) suffrage, right to vote; allgemeines —, universal suffrage.
Stimmung [ˈʃtɪmuŋ], f. (—, no pl.) tuning; (fig.) disposition, humour, mood; atmosphere; in guter —, in high spirits, in gedrückter —, in low spirits.
stimmungsvoll [ˈʃtɪmuŋsfɔl], adj. impressive, full of atmosphere.
Stimmwechsel [ˈʃtɪmvɛksəl], m. (—s, no pl.) breaking of the voice.
Stimmzettel [ˈʃtɪmtsɛtəl], m. (—s, pl. —) ballot-paper.
stinken [ˈʃtɪŋkən], v.n. irr. stink, reek, smell.
Stinktier [ˈʃtɪŋktiːr], n. (—s, pl. —e) (Zool.) skunk.
Stipendium [ʃtiˈpɛndjum], n. (—s, pl. —dien) scholarship.
Stirn [ʃtɪrn], f. (—, pl. —en) forehead, brow; die — runzeln, frown, knit o.'s brow; die — haben zu, have the cheek to; einem die — bieten, face s.o., defy s.o.
Stirnhöhle [ˈʃtɪrnhøːlə], f. (—, pl. —en) frontal cavity.
Stirnseite [ˈʃtɪrnzaɪtə], f. (—, pl. —n) front.
stöbern [ˈʃtøːbərn], v.n. rummage about; (snow) drift.
stochern [ˈʃtɔxərn], v.a., v.n. (food) pick (at); (teeth) pick.
Stock (1) [ʃtɔk], m. (—(e)s, pl. ⸚e) stick, cane, walking-stick; über — und Stein, over hedges and ditches.
Stock (2) [ʃtɔk], m. (—es, pl. —werke) storey, floor.

stocken ['ʃtɔkən], *v.n.* stop; (*blood*) run cold; (*linen*) go mildewed; hesitate, falter; (*conversation*) flag.

stockfinster ['ʃtɔkfɪnstər], *adj.* pitch dark.

Stockfisch ['ʃtɔkfɪʃ], *m.* (—es, *pl.* —e) dried cod; dried fish.

stöckisch ['ʃtœkɪʃ], *adj.* obstinate, stubborn.

Stockrose ['ʃtɔkro:zə], *f.* (—, *pl.* —n) (*Bot.*) hollyhock.

Stockschnupfen ['ʃtɔkʃnupfən], *m.* (—s, *no pl.*) heavy *or* chronic cold.

stocksteif ['ʃtɔkʃtaɪf], *adj.* stiff as a poker.

stockstill ['ʃtɔkʃtɪl], *adj.* quite still, stock-still.

stocktaub ['ʃtɔktaup], *adj.* deaf as a post.

Stockung ['ʃtɔkuŋ], *f.* (—, *pl.* —en) stagnation; hesitation; block, blockage; stopping, standstill.

Stockwerk ['ʃtɔkvɛrk], *n.* (—s, *pl.* —e) storey, floor.

Stoff [ʃtɔf], *m.* (—(e)s, *pl.* —e) fabric, material; substance; subject matter.

Stoffwechsel ['ʃtɔfvɛksəl], *m.* (—s, *no pl.*) metabolism.

stöhnen ['ʃtø:nən], *v.n.* groan, moan.

Stoiker ['ʃto:ɪkər], *m.* (—s, *pl.* —) stoic.

Stola ['ʃto:la:], *f.* (—, *pl.* —len) (*Eccl.*) stole.

Stollen ['ʃtɔlən], *m.* (—s, *pl.* —) fruit-cake; (*Min.*) gallery, adit.

stolpern ['ʃtɔlpərn], *v.n.* (*aux.* sein) stumble, trip.

Stolz [ʃtɔlts], *m.* (—es, *no pl.*) haughtiness, pride.

stolz [ʃtɔlts], *adj.* haughty, proud; stuck-up, conceited; (*fig.*) majestic.

stolzieren [ʃtɔl'tsi:rən], *v.n.* (*aux.* sein) strut; prance.

stopfen ['ʃtɔpfən], *v.a.* stuff; fill; darn, mend; *einem den Mund* —, cut s.o. short.

Stopfgarn ['ʃtɔpfgarn], *n.* (—s, *pl.* —e) darning-thread.

Stoppel ['ʃtɔpəl], *f.* (—, *pl.* —n) stubble.

stoppeln ['ʃtɔpəln], *v.a.* glean; *etwas zusammen* —, compile s.th. badly.

Stöpsel ['ʃtœpsəl], *m.* (—s, *pl.* —) stopper, cork; *kleiner* —, little mite.

stöpseln ['ʃtœpsəln], *v.a.* cork.

Stör [ʃtø:r], *m.* (—(e)s, *pl.* —e) (*Zool.*) sturgeon.

Storch [ʃtɔrç], *m.* (—(e)s, *pl.* ⁓e) (*Orn.*) stork.

Storchschnabel ['ʃtɔrçʃna:bəl], *m.* (—s, *pl.* ⁓) stork's bill; (*Tech.*) pantograph.

stören ['ʃtø:rən], *v.a.* disturb, trouble; (*Rad.*) jam. — *v.n.* intrude; be in the way.

Störenfried ['ʃtø:rənfri:d], *m.* (—s, *pl.* —e) intruder, mischief-maker, nuisance.

Störer ['ʃtø:rər], *m.* (—s, *pl.* —) disturber.

stornieren [ʃtɔr'ni:rən], *v.a.* cancel, annul.

störrisch ['ʃtœrɪʃ], *adj.* stubborn obstinate.

Störung ['ʃtø:ruŋ], *f.* (—, *pl.* —en) disturbance, intrusion; (*Rad.*) jamming.

Stoß [ʃto:s], *m.* (—es, *pl.* ⁓e) push, thrust; impact; blow, stroke, jolt; (*papers*) heap, pile; (*documents*) bundle.

Stoßdegen ['ʃto:sde:gən], *m.* (—s, *pl.* —) rapier.

Stößel ['ʃtø:səl], *m.* (—s, *pl.* —) pestle; (*Motor.*) tappet.

stoßen ['ʃto:sən], *v.a. irr.* thrust, push; pound; *vor den Kopf* —, offend. — *v.n.* bump, jolt; — *an,* border upon; *auf etwas* —, come across s.th., stumble on s.th.; *ins Horn* —, blow a horn. — *v.r. sich* —, hurt o.s.; *sich an etwas* —, take offence at s.th., take exception to s.th.

Stoßseufzer ['ʃto:szɔyftsər], *m.* (—s, *pl.* —) deep sigh.

Stoßwaffe ['ʃto:svafə], *f.* (—, *pl.* —n) thrusting *or* stabbing weapon.

stoßweise ['ʃto:svaɪzə], *adv.* by fits and starts.

Stotterer ['ʃtɔtərər], *m.* (—s, *pl.* —) stutterer, stammerer.

stottern ['ʃtɔtərn], *v.n.* stutter, stammer.

stracks [ʃtraks], *adv.* straight away, directly.

Strafanstalt ['ʃtra:fanʃtalt], *f.* (—, *pl.* —en) penitentiary, prison.

Strafarbeit ['ʃtra:farbaɪt], *f.* (—, *pl.* —en) (*Sch.*) imposition.

strafbar ['ʃtra:fba:r], *adj.* punishable, criminal, culpable.

Strafbarkeit ['ʃtra:fba:rkaɪt], *f.* (—, *no pl.*) culpability.

Strafe ['ʃtra:fə], *f.* (—, *pl.* —n) punishment; (*money*) fine, penalty; *bei* — *von,* on pain of.

strafen ['ʃtra:fən], *v.a.* punish, rebuke; (*money*) fine.

Straferlaß ['ʃtra:fərlas], *m.* (—sses, *pl.* —sse) remission of penalty, amnesty.

straff [ʃtraf], *adj.* tight, tense, taut.

Strafgericht ['ʃtra:fgərɪçt], *n.* (—es, *no pl.*) punishment; judgment; (*Law*) Criminal Court.

Strafgesetzbuch ['ʃtra:fgəzɛtsbu:x], *n.* (—(e)s, *pl.* ⁓er) penal code.

sträflich ['ʃtrɛ:flɪç], *adj.* punishable; culpable; reprehensible, blameworthy.

Sträfling ['ʃtrɛ:flɪŋ], *m.* (—s, *pl.* —e) convict.

Strafporto ['ʃtra:fpɔrto], *n.* (—s, *pl.* —ti) excess postage.

Strafpredigt ['ʃtra:fpredɪçt], *f.* (—, *pl.* —en) severe admonition, stern reprimand.

Strafprozeß ['ʃtra:fprotsɛs], *m.* (—es, *pl.* —e) criminal proceedings.

Strafrecht ['ʃtra:frɛçt], *n.* (—(e)s, *no pl.*) criminal law.

Strafverfahren ['ʃtra:ffɛrfa:rən], *n.* (—s, *pl.* —) criminal procedure.

Strahl [ʃtra:l], *m.* (—(e)s, *pl.* —en) beam, ray; (*water etc.*) jet, spout; (*lightning*) flash; —en werfen, emit rays.

Strahlantrieb [ʃtra:lantri:p], *m.* (—s, *no pl.*) (*Aviat.*) jet propulsion.

strahlen [ʃtra:lən], *v.n.* radiate, shine, beam, emit rays; (*fig.*) beam (with joy).

strählen [ʃtrɛ:lən], *v.a.* (*rare*) comb.

Strahlenbrechung [ʃtra:lənbrɛçuŋ], *f.* (—, *pl.* —en) refraction.

strahlenförmig [ʃtra:lənfœrmɪç], *adj.* radiate.

Strahlenkrone [ʃtra:lənkro:nə], *f.* (—, *pl.* —n) aureole, halo.

Strahlung [ʃtra:luŋ], *f.* (—, *pl.* —en) radiation; (*fig.*) radiance.

Strähne [ʃtrɛ:nə], *f.* (—, *pl.* —n) skein, hank; eine — Pech, a spell of bad luck.

Stramin [ʃtra'mi:n], *m.* (—s, *pl.* —e) embroidery canvas.

stramm [ʃtram], *adj.* tight; rigid; sturdy, strapping.

strampeln [ʃtrampəln], *v.n.* struggle; (*baby*) kick.

Strand [ʃtrant], *m.* (—(e)s, *pl.* —e) shore, beach, strand.

stranden [ʃtrandən], *v.n.* be stranded, founder.

Strandkorb [ʃtrantkɔrp], *m.* (—s, *pl.* ̈e) beach-chair.

Strandwache [ʃtrantvaxə], *f.* (—, *no pl.*) coast-guard.

Strang [ʃtraŋ], *m.* (—(e)s, *pl.* ̈e) rope, cord; über die ̈e schlagen, kick over the traces; zum — verurteilen, condemn to be hanged.

strangulieren [ʃtraŋgu'li:rən], *v.a.* strangle.

Strapaze [ʃtra'patsə], *f.* (—, *pl.* —n) over-exertion, fatigue, hardship.

strapazieren [ʃtrapa'tsi:rən], *v.a.* over-exert, fatigue.

strapaziös [ʃtrapa'tsjø:s], *adj.* fatiguing, exacting.

Straße [ʃtra:sə], *f.* (—, *pl.* —n) (*city*) street; (*country*) road, highway; (*sea*) strait; auf der —, in the street; über die — gehen, cross the street.

Straßenbahn [ʃtra:sənba:n], *f.* (—, *pl.* —en) tram; tramcar, (*Am.*) street-car.

Straßendamm [ʃtra:səndam], *m.* (—s, *pl.* ̈e) roadway.

Straßendirne [ʃtra:səndɪrnə], *f.* (—, *pl.* —n) prostitute, street-walker.

Straßenfeger [ʃtra:sənfe:gər], *m.* (—s, *pl.* —) roadman, road-sweeper, scavenger, crossing-sweeper.

Straßenpflaster [ʃtra:sənpflastər], *n.* (—s, *no pl.*) pavement.

Straßenraub [ʃtra:sənraup], *m.* (—s, *no pl.*) highway-robbery.

Stratege [ʃtra'te:gə], *m.* (—n, *pl.* —n) strategist.

sträuben [ʃtrɔybən], *v.r.* sich —, bristle; (*fig.*) struggle (against), oppose.

Strauch [ʃtraux], *m.* (—(e)s, *pl.* ̈er) bush, shrub.

straucheln [ʃtrauxəln], *v.n.* (*aux.* sein) stumble.

Strauchritter [ʃtrauxrɪtər], *m.* (—s, *pl.* —) footpad, vagabond, highwayman.

Strauß (1) [ʃtraus], *m.* (—es, *pl.* ̈e) (*Poet.*) fight, tussle; (*flowers*) bunch, bouquet, nosegay.

Strauß (2) [ʃtraus], *m.* (—es, *pl.* —e) (*Orn.*) ostrich.

Sträußchen [ʃtrɔysçən], *n.* (—s, *pl.* —) small bunch of flowers, nosegay.

Straußfeder [ʃtrausfe:dər], *f.* (—, *pl.* —n) ostrich-feather.

Strazze [ʃtratsə], *f.* (—, *pl.* —n) scrapbook.

Strebe [ʃtre:bə], *f.* (—, *pl.* —n) buttress, prop, stay.

Strebebogen [ʃtre:bəbo:gən], *m.* (—s, *pl.* —) (*Archit.*) arch, buttress; flying buttress.

Streben [ʃtre:bən], *n.* (—s, *no pl.*) ambition, aspiration; effort, endeavour, striving.

streben [ʃtre:bən], *v.n.* strive, aspire, endeavour.

Streber [ʃtre:bər], *m.* (—s, *pl.* —) pushing person, (social) climber. (*Am. coll.*) go-getter.

strebsam [ʃtre:pza:m], *adj.* ambitious, assiduous, industrious.

streckbar [ʃtrɛkba:r], *adj.* ductile, extensible.

Streckbett [ʃtrɛkbɛt], *n.* (—s, *pl.* —en) orthopaedic bed.

Strecke [ʃtrɛkə], *f.* (—, *pl.* —n) stretch, reach, extent; distance; tract; line; zur — bringen, (*Hunt.*) bag, run to earth.

strecken [ʃtrɛkən], *v.a.* stretch, extend; (*metal*) hammer out, roll; make (s.th.) last; die Waffen —, lay down arms.

Streich [ʃtraɪç], *m.* (—(e)s, *pl.* —e) stroke, blow; (*fig.*) prank; trick; dummer —, piece of folly, lark.

streicheln [ʃtraɪçəln], *v.a.* stroke, caress.

streichen [ʃtraɪçən], *v.a. irr.* stroke, touch; paint, spread; cancel; strike; (*sail*) lower. — *v.n.* move past, fly past; wander.

Streichholz [ʃtraɪçhɔlts], *n.* (—es, *pl.* ̈er) match.

Streichinstrument [ʃtraɪçɪnstrumɛnt], *n.* (—s, *pl.* —e) stringed instrument.

Streif [ʃtraɪf], *m.* (—(e)s, *pl.* —e) stripe, strip, streak.

Streifband [ʃtraɪfbant], *n.* (—s, *pl.* ̈er) wrapper.

Streifblick [ʃtraɪfblɪk], *m.* (—s, *pl.* —e) glance.

Streife [ʃtraɪfə], *f.* (—, *pl.* —n) raid; patrol (*police etc*).

Streifen [ʃtraɪfən], *m.* (—s, *pl.* —) stripe, streak; (*Mil.*) bar.

streifen

streifen ['ʃtraɪfən], *v.a.* graze, touch in passing; take off (remove). — *v.n.* (aux. sein) ramble, roam, rove.

streifig ['ʃtraɪfɪç], *adj.* striped, streaky.

Streik [ʃtraɪk], *m.* (—(e)s, *pl.* —s) strike; in den — treten, go on strike.

Streikbrecher ['ʃtraɪkbrɛçər], *m.* (—s, *pl.* —) blackleg.

streiken ['ʃtraɪkən], *v.n.* (workers) strike, be on strike.

Streit [ʃtraɪt], *m.* (—(e)s, *pl.* —e) dispute, quarrel, conflict; (words) argument; einen — anfangen, pick a quarrel.

Streitaxt ['ʃtraɪtakst], *f.* (—, *pl.* ⁻e) battle-axe.

streitbar ['ʃtraɪtbaːr], *adj.* warlike, martial.

streiten ['ʃtraɪtən], *v.n. irr.* quarrel, fight; —de Kirche, Church Militant.

Streitfrage ['ʃtraɪtfraːgə], *f.* (—, *pl.* —n) moot point, point at issue; controversy.

Streithammel ['ʃtraɪthaməl], *m.* (—s, *pl.* —) squabbler.

Streithandel ['ʃtraɪthandəl], *m.* (—s, *pl.* ⁻) law-suit.

streitig ['ʃtraɪtɪç], *adj.* disputable, doubtful, at issue; einem etwas — machen, contest s.o.'s right to s.th.

Streitkräfte ['ʃtraɪtkrɛftə], *f. pl.* (Mil.) forces.

streitlustig ['ʃtraɪtlustɪç], *adj.* argumentative.

Streitschrift ['ʃtraɪtʃrɪft], *f.* (—, *pl.* —en) pamphlet, polemical treatise.

Streitsucht ['ʃtraɪtzuxt], *f.* (—, *no pl.*) quarrelsomeness; (Law) litigiousness.

streitsüchtig ['ʃtraɪtzyçtɪç], *adj.* quarrelsome, litigious.

streng [ʃtrɛŋ], *adj.* severe, strict, rigorous; —e Kälte, biting cold; im —sten Winter, in the depth of winter. — *adv.* —genommen, strictly speaking.

Strenge ['ʃtrɛŋə], *f.* (—, *no pl.*) severity, rigour.

strenggläubig ['ʃtrɛŋglɔybɪç], *adj.* strictly orthodox.

Streu [ʃtrɔy], *f.* (—, *pl.* —en) litter, bed of straw.

Streubüchse ['ʃtrɔybyksə], *f.* (—, *pl.* —n) castor.

streuen ['ʃtrɔyən], *v.a.* strew, scatter, sprinkle.

streunen ['ʃtrɔynən], *v.n.* roam (about).

Streuung ['ʃtrɔyuŋ], *f.* (—, *pl.* —en) strewing; (shot) dispersion.

Streuzucker ['ʃtrɔytsukər], *m.* (—s, *no pl.*) castor-sugar.

Strich [ʃtrɪç], *m.* (—(e)s, *pl.* —e) stroke, line, dash; (land) tract; (Art) touch; region; gegen den —, against the grain; einem einen — durch die Rechnung machen, put a spoke in s.o.'s wheel, frustrate s.o.

Strichpunkt ['ʃtrɪçpuŋkt], *m.* (—s, *pl.* —e) semicolon.

Strichregen ['ʃtrɪçreːgən], *m.* (—s, *pl.* —) passing shower.

Strick [ʃtrɪk], *m.* (—(e)s, *pl.* —e) cord, line, rope; du —, (fig.) you scamp! einem einen — drehen, give s.o. enough rope to hang himself, lay a trap for s.o.

stricken ['ʃtrɪkən], *v.a., v.n.* knit.

Strickerei [ʃtrɪkə'raɪ], *f.* (—, *pl.* —en) knitting; knitting business, workshop.

Strickleiter ['ʃtrɪklaɪtər], *f.* (—, *pl.* —n) rope-ladder.

Strickzeug ['ʃtrɪktsɔyk], *n.* (—s, *pl.* —e) knitting.

Striegel ['ʃtriːgəl], *m.* (—s, *pl.* —) curry-comb.

striegeln ['ʃtriːgəln], *v.a.* curry.

Strieme ['ʃtriːmə], *f.* (—, *pl.* —n) weal, stripe.

Strippe ['ʃtrɪpə], *f.* (—, *pl.* —n) strap, band, string; cord.

strittig ['ʃtrɪtɪç], *adj.* contentious, debatable.

Stroh [ʃtroː], *n.* (—s, *no pl.*) straw; (roof) thatch; mit — decken, thatch; leeres — dreschen, beat the air.

Strohfeuer ['ʃtroːfɔyər], *n.* (—s, *no pl.*) (fig.) flash in the pan; short-lived enthusiasm.

Strohhalm ['ʃtroːhalm], *m.* (—s, *pl.* —e) straw.

Strohhut ['ʃtroːhuːt], *m.* (—s, *pl.* ⁻e) straw-hat.

Strohkopf ['ʃtroːkɔpf], *m.* (—(e)s, *pl.* ⁻e) (coll.) stupid person.

Strohmann ['ʃtroːman], *m.* (—s, *pl.* ⁻er) (coll.) man of straw; (Cards) dummy.

Strohmatte ['ʃtroːmatə], *f.* (—, *pl.* —n) straw-mat.

Strohwitwe ['ʃtroːvɪtvə], *f.* (—, *pl.* —n) grass-widow.

Strolch [ʃtrɔlç], *m.* (—(e)s, *pl.* —e) vagabond; (fig.) scamp.

Strom [ʃtroːm], *m.* (—(e)s, *pl.* ⁻e) river, torrent; (also fig.) flood; stream; (also Elec.) current; (coll.) electricity; gegen den — schwimmen, swim against the current, be an individualist.

stromab ['ʃtroːmap], *adv.* downstream.

stromauf ['ʃtroːmauf], *adv.* upstream.

strömen ['ʃtrøːmən], *v.n.* (aux. sein) flow, stream; (rain) pour; (people) flock.

Stromer ['ʃtroːmər], *m.* (—s, *pl.* —) vagabond, tramp, vagrant.

Stromkreis ['ʃtroːmkraɪs], *m.* (—es, *pl.* —e) (Elec.) circuit.

Stromschnelle ['ʃtroːmʃnɛlə], *f.* (—, *pl.* —n) rapids.

Strömung ['ʃtrøːmuŋ], *f.* (—, *pl.* —en) current; (fig.) tendency.

Strophe ['ʃtroːfə], *f.* (—, *pl.* —n) verse, stanza.

strotzen ['ʃtrɔtsən], *v.n.* be puffed up; overflow, burst, teem.

strotzend ['ʃtrɔtsənt], *adj. vor Gesundheit —,* bursting with health.

Strudel ['ʃtruːdəl], *m.* (—s, *pl.* —) whirl, whirlpool, vortex, eddy; pastry.

Struktur [ʃtruk'tuːr], *f.* (—, *pl.* —en) structure.

Strumpf [ʃtrumpf], *m.* (—(e)s, *pl.* ⸚e) stocking; (*short*) sock.

Strumpfband [ˈʃtrumpfbant], *n.* (—(e)s, *pl.* ⸚er) garter.

Strumpfwaren [ˈʃtrumpfvaːrən], *f. pl.* hosiery.

Strumpfwirker [ˈʃtrumpfvɪrkər], *m.* (—s, *pl.* —) stocking-weaver.

Strunk [ʃtruŋk], *m.* (—(e)s, *pl.* ⸚e) (*tree*) stump, trunk; (*plant*) stalk.

struppig [ˈʃtrupɪç], *adj.* rough, unkempt, frowsy.

Stube [ˈʃtuːbə], *f.* (—, *pl.* —n) room, chamber; sitting-room.

Stubenarrest [ˈʃtuːbənarɛst], *m.* (—s, *pl.* —e) confinement to quarters.

Stubenhocker [ˈʃtuːbənhɔkər], *m.* (—s, *pl.* —) stay-at-home.

Stubenmädchen [ˈʃtuːbənmɛːtçən], *n.* (—s, *pl.* —) housemaid.

Stuck [ʃtuk], *m.* (—(e)s, *no pl.*) stucco, plaster.

Stück [ʃtyk], *n.* (—(e)s, *pl.* —e) piece; part; lump; (*Theat.*) play; *aus freien —en,* of o.'s own accord; *große —e auf einen halten,* think highly of s.o.

Stückarbeit [ˈʃtykarbaɪt], *f.* (—, *pl.* —en) piece-work.

Stückchen [ˈʃtykçən], *n.* (—s, *pl.* —) small piece, morsel, bit.

stückeln [ˈʃtykəln], *v.a.* cut in(to) pieces; patch, mend.

stückweise [ˈʃtykvaɪzə], *adv.* piecemeal.

Stückwerk [ˈʃtykvɛrk], *n.* (—s, *no pl.*) (*fig.*) patchy or imperfect work, a bungled job.

Stückzucker [ˈʃtyktsukər], *m.* (—s, *no pl.*) lump sugar.

Student [ʃtuˈdɛnt], *m.* (—en, *pl.* —en) (*Univ.*) student, undergraduate.

studentenhaft [ʃtuˈdɛntənhaft], *adj.* student-like.

Studentenverbindung [ʃtuˈdɛntənferbɪnduŋ], *f.* (—, *pl.* —en) students' association *or* union.

Studie [ˈʃtuːdjə], *f.* (—, *pl.* —n) study, (*Art*) sketch; (*Lit.*) essay; (*pl.*) studies.

Studienplan [ˈʃtuːdjənplaːn], *m.* (—s, *pl.* ⸚e) curriculum.

Studienrat [ˈʃtuːdjənraːt], *m.* (—s, *pl.* ⸚e) grammar school teacher, assistant master.

studieren [ʃtuˈdiːrən], *v.a., v.n.* study, read (a subject); be at (the) university.

studiert [ʃtuˈdiːrt], *adj.* educated; (*fig.*) affected, deliberate, studied.

Studierte [ʃtuˈdiːrtə], *m.* (*coll.*) egghead.

Studium [ˈʃtuːdjum], *n.* (—s,) *pl.* —dien study, pursuit; university education.

Stufe [ˈʃtuːfə], *f.* (—, *pl.* —n) step; (*fig.*) degree; *auf gleicher — mit,* on a level with.

stufenweise [ˈʃtuːfənvaɪzə], *adv.* gradually, by degrees.

Stuhl [ʃtuːl], *m.* (—s, *pl.* ⸚e) chair, seat; *der Heilige —,* the Holy See.

Stuhlgang [ˈʃtuːlgaŋ], *m.* (—s, *no pl.*) (*Med.*) stool, evacuation (of the bowels), movement, motion.

Stukkatur [ʃtukaˈtuːr], *f.* (—, *no pl.*) stucco-work.

Stulle [ˈʃtulə], *f.* (—, *pl.* —n) (*dial.*) slice of bread and butter.

Stulpe [ˈʃtulpə], *f.* (—, *pl.* —n) cuff.

stülpen [ˈʃtylpən], *v.a.* turn up, invert.

Stulpnase [ˈʃtulpnaːzə], *f.* (—, *pl.* —n) turned-up nose, pug-nose.

Stulpstiefel [ˈʃtulpʃtiːfəl], *m.* (—s, *pl.* —) top-boot.

stumm [ʃtum], *adj.* mute, dumb, silent.

Stumme [ˈʃtumə], *m. & f.* (—n, *pl.* —n) dumb person, mute.

Stummel [ˈʃtuməl], *m.* (—s, *pl.* —) stump; (*cigarette*) end, butt.

Stummheit [ˈʃtumhaɪt], *f.* (—, *no pl.*) dumbness.

Stümper [ˈʃtympər], *m.* (—s, *pl.* —) bungler, botcher.

stümperhaft [ˈʃtympərhaft], *adj.* bungling, botchy.

stümpern [ˈʃtympərn], *v.a., v.n.* bungle, botch.

Stumpf [ʃtumpf], *m.* (—(e)s, *pl.* ⸚e) stump, trunk; *mit — und Stiel ausrotten,* destroy root and branch.

stumpf [ʃtumpf], *adj.* blunt; (*angle*) obtuse; (*fig.*) dull; *— machen,* blunt, dull.

Stumpfsinn [ˈʃtumpfzɪn], *m.* (—s, *no pl.*) stupidity, dullness.

stumpfwinklig [ˈʃtumpfvɪŋklɪç], *adj.* obtuse-angled.

Stunde [ˈʃtundə], *f.* (—, *pl.* —n) hour; lesson.

stunden [ˈʃtundən], *v.a.* give a respite, allow time (to pay up).

Stundenglas [ˈʃtundənglas], *n.* (—es, *pl.* ⸚er) hour-glass.

Stundenplan [ˈʃtundənplaːn], *m.* (—s, *pl.* ⸚e) (*Sch.*) schedule.

Stundenzeiger [ˈʃtundəntsaɪgər], *m.* (—s, *pl.* —) hour-hand.

Stündlein [ˈʃtyntlaɪn], *n.* (—s, *pl.* —) *sein — hat geschlagen,* his last hour has come.

Stundung [ˈʃtunduŋ], *f.* (—, *pl.* —en) respite, grace.

stupend [ʃtuˈpɛnt], *adj.* stupendous.

stur [ʃtuːr], *adj.* obdurate, unwavering, stolid, dour, stubborn.

Sturm [ʃturm], *m.* (—(e)s, *pl.* ⸚e) storm, gale, tempest, hurricane; (*Mil.*) attack, assault; *— und Drang,* (*Lit.*) Storm and Stress; *— im Wasserglas,* storm in a teacup; *— laufen gegen,* storm against.

Sturmband [ˈʃturmbant], *n.* (—s, *pl.* ⸚er) chinstrap.

Sturmbock [ˈʃturmbɔk], *m.* (—s, *pl.* ⸚e) battering-ram.

stürmen [ˈʃtyrmən], *v.a.* storm, take by assault. *— v.n.* be violent, be stormy; (*Mil.*) advance.

Stürmer [ˈʃtyrmər], *m.* (—s, *pl.* —) assailant; (*football*) centre-forward.

Sturmglocke [ˈʃturmglɔkə], *f.* (—, *pl.* —n) tocsin, alarm-bell.

Sturmhaube

Sturmhaube [ˈʃturmhaubə], f. (—, pl. —en) (Mil.) morion, helmet.

stürmisch [ˈʃtyrmɪʃ], adj. stormy, tempestuous; (fig.) boisterous, tumultuous, impetuous; —er Beifall, frantic applause; —e Überfahrt, rough crossing.

Sturmschritt [ˈʃturmʃrɪt], m. (—s, no pl.) double march.

Sturmvogel [ˈʃturmfoːgəl], m. (—s, pl. ¨) (Orn.) stormy petrel.

Sturz [ʃturts], m. (—es, pl. ¨e) fall, tumble; crash; collapse; (Comm.) failure, smash; (government) overthrow.

Sturzacker [ˈʃturtsakər], m. (—s, pl. ¨) freshly ploughed field.

Sturzbach [ˈʃturtsbax], m. (—(e)s, pl. ¨e) torrent.

Stürze [ˈʃtyrtsə], f. (—, pl. —n) pot-lid, cover.

stürzen [ˈʃtyrtsən], v.a. hurl, overthrow; ruin. — v.n. (aux. sein) (person) have a fall; (object) tumble down; (business) fail; crash; plunge; (water) rush. — v.r. throw oneself; sich — auf, rush at, plunge into.

Sturzhelm [ˈʃturtshɛlm], m. (—s, pl. —e) crash-helmet.

Sturzsee [ˈʃturtszeː], f. (—, no pl.) heavy sea.

Sturzwelle [ˈʃturtsvɛlə], f. (—, pl. —n) breaker, roller.

Stute [ˈʃtuːtə], f. (—, pl. —n) mare.

Stutzbart [ˈʃtutsbaːrt], m. (—s, pl. ¨e) short beard.

Stütze [ˈʃtytsə], f. (—, pl. —n) prop, support, stay.

Stutzen [ˈʃtutsən], m. (—s, pl. —) short rifle, carbine.

stutzen [ˈʃtutsən], v.a. (hair) clip, trim; (horse) dock, crop; (tree) prune, lop. — v.n. be taken aback, hesitate.

stützen [ˈʃtytsən], v.a. prop, support; base or found (on). — v.r. sich — auf, lean upon; (fig.) rely upon.

Stutzer [ˈʃtutsər], m. (—s, pl. —) dandy, fop, beau.

stutzerhaft [ˈʃtutsərhaft], adj. dandified.

stutzig [ˈʃtutsɪç], adj. startled, puzzled; — werden, be non-plussed, be taken aback or puzzled.

Stützmauer [ˈʃtytsmauər], f. (—, pl. —n) buttress, retaining wall.

Stützpunkt [ˈʃtytspuŋkt], m. (—s, pl. —e) point of support; foothold; (Mil.) base; (Tech.) fulcrum.

Subjekt [zupˈjekt], n. (—s, pl. —e) subject; (fig.) creature.

subjektiv [zupjekˈtiːf], adj. subjective, personal, prejudiced.

sublimieren [zubliˈmiːrən], v.a. sublimate.

Substantiv [zupstanˈtiːf], n. (—(e)s, pl. —e) (Gram.) substantive, noun.

subtil [zupˈtiːl], adj. subtle.

subtrahieren [zuptraˈhiːrən], v.a. subtract.

Subvention [zupvenˈtsjoːn], f. (—, pl. —en) subsidy, grant-in-aid.

Suche [ˈzuːxə], f. (—, no pl.) search, quest; auf der — nach, in quest of.

suchen [ˈzuːxən], v.a., v.n. seek, look for; attempt, endeavour.

Sucht [zuxt], f. (—, pl. ¨e) mania, addiction, passion.

süchtig [ˈzyxtɪç], adj. addicted (to).

Sud [zuːd], m. (—(e)s, pl. —e) boiling, brewing; suds.

Sudan [ˈzuːdan], m. the Sudan.

sudeln [ˈzuːdəln], v.a., v.n. smear, daub, make a mess (of).

Süden [ˈzyːdən], m. (—s, no pl.) south.

Südfrüchte [ˈzyːtfryçtə], f. pl. Mediterranean or tropical fruit.

südlich [ˈzyːtlɪç], adj. southern, southerly; in —er Richtung, southward.

Südosten [zyːtˈɔstən], m. (—s, no pl.) south-east.

Suff [zuf], m. (—(e)s, no pl.) (sl.) boozing, tippling.

suggerieren [zugeˈriːrən], v.a. suggest.

Sühne [ˈzyːnə], f. (—, no pl.) expiation, atonement.

sühnen [ˈzyːnən], v.a. expiate, atone for.

Sühneopfer [ˈzyːnəɔpfər], n. (—s, pl. —) expiatory sacrifice; atonement.

Suite [ˈsviːtə], f. (—, pl. —n) retinue, train.

sukzessiv [zuktseˈsiːf], adj. gradual, successive.

Sülze [ˈzyltsə], f. (—, pl. —n) brawn, aspic, jelly.

Summa [zuˈmaː], f. (—, pl. **Summen**) — summarum, sum total.

summarisch [zuˈmaːrɪʃ], adj. summary.

Summe [ˈzumə], f. (—, pl. —n) sum, amount.

summen [ˈzumən], v.a. hum. — v.n. buzz, hum.

summieren [zuˈmiːrən], v.a. sum up, add up. — v.r. sich —, mount up.

Sumpf [zumpf], m. (—(e)s, pl. ¨e) bog, morass, marsh, moor, swamp.

sumpfig [ˈzumpfɪç], adj. boggy, marshy.

Sund [zunt], m. (—(e)s, pl. —e) straits, sound.

Sünde [ˈzyndə], f. (—, pl. —n) sin.

Sündenbock [ˈzyndənbɔk], m. (—s, pl. ¨e) scapegoat.

Sündenfall [ˈzyndənfal], m. (—s, no pl.) (Theol.) the Fall (of man).

Sündengeld [ˈzyndəngelt], n. (—(e)s, no pl.) ill-gotten gains; (coll.) vast sum of money.

sündenlos [ˈzyndənloːs], adj. sinless, impeccable.

Sündenpfuhl [ˈzyndənpfuːl], m. (—s, pl. —e) sink of iniquity.

Sünder [ˈzyndər], m. (—s, pl. —) sinner; armer —, poor devil; du alter —, you old scoundrel.

sündhaft [ˈzynthaft], adj. sinful, iniquitous.

sündig [ˈzyndɪç], adj. sinful.

sündigen [ˈzyndɪgən], v.n. sin, err.

Sündigkeit [ˈzyndɪçkaɪt], f. (—, no pl.) sinfulness.

Superlativ [ˈzuːpərlatiːf], m. (—s, pl. —e) superlative (degree).

Suppe ['zupə], f. (—, pl. **—n**) soup; *eingebrannte* —, thick soup; *einem edi — versalzen*, spoil s.o.'s little game.
Suppenfleisch ['zupənflaɪʃ], n. (**—es**, no pl.) stock-meat.
Suppenkelle ['zupənkɛlə], f. (—, pl. **—n**) soup ladle.
Suppenterrine ['zupəntɛriːnə], f. (—, pl. **—n**) tureen.
Surrogat [zuro'gaːt], n. (**—s**, pl. **—e**) substitute.
süß [zyːs], adj. sweet.
Süße ['zyːsə], f. (—, no pl.) sweetness.
süßen ['zyːsən], v.a. sweeten.
Süßholz ['zyːshɔlts], n. (**—es**, no pl.) liquorice; — *raspeln*, talk sweet nothings, pay compliments.
Süßigkeit ['zyːsɪçkaɪt], f. (—, pl. **—en**) sweetness; (pl.) sweets.
süßlich ['zyːslɪç], adj. sweetish; (fig.) fulsome, mawkish, cloying.
Süßspeise ['zyːsʃpaɪzə], f. (—, pl. **—n**) dessert.
Süßwasser ['zyːsvasər], n. (**—s**, no pl.) fresh water.
Symbolik [zym'boːlɪk], f. (—, no pl.) symbolism.
symbolisch [zym'boːlɪʃ], adj. symbolic(al).
symbolisieren [zymbɔliː'ziːrən], v.a. symbolize.
symmetrisch [zy'meːtrɪʃ], adj. symmetrical.
Sympathie [zympa'tiː], f. (—, no pl.) sympathy.
sympathisch [zym'paːtɪʃ], adj. congenial, likeable.
Synagoge [zyna'goːgə], f. (—, pl. **—n**) synagogue.
synchronisieren [zynkroni'ziːrən], v.a. synchronise.
Syndikus ['zyndikus], m. (—, pl. **Syndizi**) syndic.
Synode [zy'noːdə], f. (—, pl. **—n**) synod.
synthetisch [zyn'teːtɪʃ], adj. synthetic.
Syrien [zyːrjən] n. Syria.
systematisch [zyste'maːtɪʃ], adj. systematic(al).
Szenarium [stse'naːrjum], n. (**—s**, pl. **—rien**) scenario, stage, scene.
Szene ['stseːnə], f. (—, pl. **—n**) scene; *in — setzen*, stage, produce; (coll.) get up; *sich in — setzen*, show off.
Szenerie [stsenə'riː], f. (—, pl. **—n**) scenery.
szenisch ['stseːnɪʃ], adj. scenic.
Szepter ['stsɛptər], n. (**—s**, pl. **—**) sceptre, mace.

T

T [teː], n. (—, pl. —) the letter T.
Tabak ['taːbak], m. (**—s**, pl. **—e**) tobacco.

Tabaksbeutel ['taːbaksbɔytəl], m. (**—s**, pl. **—**) tobacco-pouch.
Tabatiere [ta:ba'tjɛːrə], f. (—, pl. **—n**) snuff-box.
tabellarisch [tabɛ'laːrɪʃ], adj. in tables, tabular.
Tabelle [ta'bɛlə], f. (—, pl. **—n**) table, index, schedule.
Tablett [ta'blɛt], n. (**—s**, pl. **—s**) tray.
Tablette [ta'blɛtə], f. (—, pl. **—n**) tablet, pill.
Tabulatur [tabula'tuːr], f. (—, pl. **—en**) tablature, tabling, index.
Tadel ['taːdəl], m. (**—s**, pl. **—**) blame, censure, reproach; (Sch.) bad mark; *ohne —*, blameless.
tadellos ['taːdəlloːs], adj. blameless, faultless, impeccable.
tadeln ['taːdəln], v.a. blame, censure, find fault with; reprimand.
tadelnswert ['taːdəlnsveːrt], adj. blame-worthy, culpable.
Tafel ['taːfəl], f. (—, pl. **—n**) board; (Sch.) blackboard; slate; (fig.) (obs.) dinner, banquet; festive fare; (chocolate) slab, bar.
Täfelchen ['tɛːfəlçən], n. (**—s**, pl. **—**) tablet.
tafelförmig ['taːfəlfœrmɪç], adj. tabular.
tafeln ['taːfəln], v.n. dine, feast.
täfeln ['tɛːfəln], v.a. wainscot, panel.
Täfelung ['tɛːfəluŋ], f. (—, pl. **—en**) wainscoting, panelling.
Taft, Taffet [taft, 'tafət], m. (**—(e)s**, pl. **—e**) taffeta.
Tag [taːk], m. (**—(e)s**, pl. **—e**) day; (fig.) light; *der jüngste —*, Doomsday; *bei —e*, in the daytime, by daylight; *sich etwas bei —e besehen*, examine s.th. in the light of day; — *für —*, day by day; *von — zu —*, from day to day; *dieser —e*, one of these days, shortly; *etwas an den — bringen*, bring s.th. to light; *in den — hinein leben*, live improvidently; —- *und Nachtgleiche*, equinox.
Tagbau ['taːkbau], m. (**—s**, no pl.) opencast mining.
Tageblatt ['taːgəblat], n. (**—s**, pl. **⁻er**) daily paper.
Tagebuch ['taːgəbuːx], n. (**—(e)s**, pl. **⁻er**) diary, journal.
Tagedieb ['taːgədiːp], m. (**—(e)s**, pl. **—e**) idler, wastrel.
Tagelöhner ['taːgəløːnər], m. (**—s**, pl. **—**) day-labourer.
tagen ['taːgən], v.n. dawn; (gathering) meet; (Law) sit.
Tagesanbruch ['taːgəsanbrux], m. (**—s**, pl. **⁻e**) daybreak, dawn.
Tagesbericht ['taːgəsbərɪçt], m. (**—(e)s**, pl. **—e**) daily report.
Tagesgespräch ['taːgəsgəʃprɛːç], n. (**—(e)s**, pl. **—e**) topic of the day.
Tagesordnung ['taːgəsɔrdnuŋ], f. (—, pl. **—en**) agenda.
Tagewerk ['taːgəverk], n. (**—s**, no pl.) day's work, daily round.
täglich ['tɛːklɪç], adj. daily.

tagsüber [ˈtaːksyːbər], *adv.* in the daytime, during the day.

Taille [ˈtaljə], *f.* (—, *pl.* —**n**) waist.

takeln [ˈtaːkəln], *v.a.* tackle, rig.

Takelwerk [ˈtaːkəlvɛrk], *n.* (—**s**, *no pl.*) rigging.

Takt (1) [takt], *m.* (—**es**, *pl.* —**e**) (*Mus.*) time, measure, bar; — *schlagen*, beat time.

Takt (2) [takt], *m.* (—**es**, *no pl.*) tact, discretion.

taktfest [ˈtaktfɛst], *adj.* (*Mus.*) good at keeping time; (*fig.*) firm.

taktieren [takˈtiːrən], *v.n.* (*Mus.*) beat time.

Taktik [ˈtaktɪk], *f.* (—, *pl.* —**en**) tactics.

Taktiker [ˈtaktɪkər], *m.* (—**s**, *pl.* —) tactician.

taktisch [ˈtaktɪʃ], *adj.* tactical.

taktlos [ˈtaktloːs], *adj.* tactless.

Taktmesser [ˈtaktmɛsər], *m.* (—**s**, *pl.* —) metronome.

Taktstock [ˈtaktʃtɔk], *m.* (—**s**, *pl.* ·⁚e) baton.

Tal [taːl], *n.* (—(**e**)**s**, *pl.* ·⁚er) valley, dale, glen.

talab [taˈlˀap], *adv.* downhill.

Talar [taˈlaːr], *m.* (—**s**, *pl.* —**e**) gown.

Talent [taˈlɛnt], *n.* (—(**e**)**s**, *pl.* —**e**) talent, accomplishment, gift.

talentiert [talənˈtiːrt], *adj.* talented, gifted, accomplished.

talentvoll [taˈlɛntfɔl], *adj.* talented, gifted, accomplished.

Taler [ˈtaːlər], *m.* (—**s**, *pl.* —) old German coin; thaler.

Talfahrt [ˈtaːlfaːrt], *f.* (—, *pl.* —**en**) descent.

Talg [talk], *m.* (—(**e**)**s**, *no pl.*) tallow.

Talk [talk], *m.* (—(**e**)**s**, *no pl.*) talc.

Talkerde [ˈtalkeˑrdə], *f.* (—, *no pl.*) magnesia.

Talkessel [ˈtaːlkɛsəl], *m.* (—**s**, *pl.* —) (*Geog.*) hollow, narrow valley.

Talmulde [ˈtaːlmuldə], *f.* (—, *pl.* —**n**) narrow valley, trough.

Talschlucht [ˈtaːlʃluxt], *f.* (—, *pl.* —**en**) glen.

Talsohle [ˈtaːlzoːlə], *f.* (—, *pl.* —**n**) floor of a valley.

Talsperre [ˈtaːlʃpɛrə], *f.* (—, *pl.* —**n**) dam (across valley); barrage.

Tambour [tambuːr], *m.* (—**s**, *pl.* —**e**) drummer.

Tamtam [tamtam], *n.* (—**s**, *no pl.*) tom-tom; (*fig.*) palaver.

Tand [tant], *m.* (—(**e**)**s**, *no pl.*) knick-knack, trifle; rubbish.

Tändelei [tɛndəˈlaɪ], *f.* (—, *pl.* —**en**) trifling, toying; (*fig.*) flirting.

Tändelmarkt [ˈtɛndəlmarkt], *m.* (—**s**, *pl.* ·⁚e) rag-fair.

tändeln [ˈtɛndəln], *v.n.* trifle, dally, toy; (*fig.*) flirt.

Tang [taŋ], *m.* (—**s**, *pl.* —**e**) (*Bot.*) seaweed.

Tanganjika [taŋgaˈnjiːka], *n.* Tanganyika.

Tangente [taŋˈgɛntə], *f.* (—, *pl.* —**n**) tangent.

Tanger [ˈtaŋər], *n.* Tangier.

Tank [taŋk], *m.* (—(**e**)**s**, *pl.* —**e**) tank.

tanken [ˈtaŋkən], *v.n.* refuel; fill up (with petrol).

Tankstelle [ˈtaŋkʃtɛlə], *f.* (—, *pl.* —**n**) filling-station.

Tanne [ˈtanə], *f.* (—, *pl.* —**n**) (*Bot.*) fir.

Tannenbaum [ˈtanənbaum], *m.* (—**s**, *pl.* ·⁚e) (*Bot.*) fir-tree.

Tannenholz [ˈtanənhɔlts], *n.* (—**es**, *no pl.*) (*timber*) deal.

Tannenzapfen [ˈtanəntsapfən], *m.* (—**s**, *pl.* —) (*Bot.*) fir-cone.

Tansania [tanzaˈniːa], *n.* Tanzania.

Tante [ˈtantə], *f.* (—, *pl.* —**n**) aunt.

Tantieme [tãˈtjeːmə], *f.* (—, *pl.* —**n**) royalty, share (in profits), percentage.

Tanz [tants], *m.* (—**es**, *pl.* ·⁚e) dance.

Tanzboden [ˈtantsboːdən], *m.* (—**s**, *pl.* ·⁚) ballroom, dance-hall.

tänzeln [ˈtɛntsəln], *v.n.* skip about, frisk; (*horses*) amble.

tanzen [ˈtantsən], *v.a.*, *v.n.* dance.

tanzlustig [ˈtantslustɪç], *adj.* fond of dancing.

Tapet [taˈpeːt], *n.* (—**s**, *no pl.*) *aufs* — *bringen*, broach, bring up for discussion.

Tapete [taˈpeːtə], *f.* (—, *pl.* —**n**) wall-paper.

tapezieren [tapəˈtsiːrən], *v.a.* paper.

Tapezierer [tapəˈtsiːrər], *m.* (—**s**, *pl.* —) paperhanger; upholsterer.

tapfer [ˈtapfər], *adj.* brave, valiant, gallant, courageous.

Tapferkeit [ˈtapfərkaɪt], *f.* (—, *no pl.*) valour, bravery, gallantry.

Tapisserie [tapɪsəˈriː], *f.* (—, *no pl.*) needlework; tapestry.

tappen [ˈtapən], *v.n.* grope about.

täppisch [ˈtɛpɪʃ], *adj.* clumsy, awkward, unwieldy.

tarnen [ˈtarnən], *v.a.* camouflage.

Tasche [ˈtaʃə], *f.* (—, *pl.* —**n**) pocket; bag, pouch; *in die* — *stecken*, pocket; *in die* — *greifen*, pay, fork out, put o.'s hand in o.'s pocket.

Taschendieb [ˈtaʃəndiːp], *m.* (—(**e**)**s**, *pl.* —**e**) pickpocket; *vor* —*en wird gewarnt*, beware of pickpockets.

Taschenformat [ˈtaʃənfɔrmaːt], *n.* (—**s**, *no pl.*) pocket-size.

Taschenspieler [ˈtaʃənʃpiːlər], *m.* (—**s**, *pl.* —) juggler, conjurer.

Taschentuch [ˈtaʃəntuːx], *n.* (—**s**, *pl.* ·⁚er) (pocket-)handkerchief.

Taschenuhr [ˈtaʃənuːr], *f.* (—, *pl.* —**en**) pocket-watch.

Tasse [ˈtasə], *f.* (—, *pl.* —**n**) cup.

Tastatur [tastaˈtuːr], *f.* (—, *pl.* —**en**) keyboard.

Taste [ˈtastə], *f.* (—, *pl.* —**n**) (*Mus.*) key.

tasten [ˈtastən], *v.n.* grope about, feel o.'s way.

Tastsinn [ˈtastzɪn], *m.* (—**s**, *no pl.*) sense of touch.

technologisch

Tat [ta:t], *f.* (—, *pl.* —en) deed, act, action; feat, exploit; *in der* —, in fact, indeed; *auf frischer* —, in the very act; *einem mit Rat und* — *beistehen*, give s.o. advice and guidance, help by word and deed.

Tatbestand ['ta:tbəʃtant], *m.* (—es, *pl.* ✶e) (*Law*) facts of the case.

Tatendrang ['ta:təndraŋ], *m.* (—(e)s, *no pl.*) urge for action; impetuosity.

tatenlos ['ta:tənlo:s], *adj.* inactive.

Täter ['tɛ:tər], *m.* (—s, *pl.* —) perpetrator, doer; culprit.

tätig ['tɛ:tɪç], *adj.* active, busy.

Tätigkeit ['tɛ:tɪçkaɪt], *f.* (—, *pl.* —en) activity.

Tätigkeitswort ['tɛ:tɪçkaɪtsvɔrt], *n.* (—(e)s, *pl.* ✶er) (*Gram.*) verb.

Tatkraft ['ta:tkraft], *f.* (—, *no pl.*) energy.

tätlich ['tɛ:tlɪç], *adj.* — *werden*, become violent.

tätowieren [tɛ:to'vi:rən], *v.a.* tattoo.

Tatsache ['ta:tzaxə], *f.* (—, *pl.* —en) fact, matter of fact.

tatsächlich ['ta:tzɛçlɪç], *adj.* actual. — *excl.* really!

tätscheln ['tɛ:tʃəln], *v.a.* fondle.

Tatterich ['tatərɪç], *m.* (—s, *no pl.*) (*coll.*) trembling, shakiness.

Tatze ['tatsə], *f.* (—, *pl.* —n) paw.

Tau (1) [tau], *m.* (—s, *no pl.*) thaw; dew.

Tau (2) [tau], *n.* (—s, *pl.* —e) rope, cable.

taub [taup], *adj.* deaf; (*nut*) hollow, empty; — *machen*, deafen; — *sein gegen*, turn a deaf ear to.

Täubchen ['tɔypçən], *n.* (—s, *pl.* —) little dove; (*fig.*) sweetheart.

Taube ['taubə], *f.* (—, *pl.* —n) (*Orn.*) pigeon, dove.

Taubenschlag ['taubənʃla:k], *m.* (—s, *pl.* ✶e) dovecote.

Taubenschwanz ['taubənʃvants], *m.* (—es, *pl.* ✶e) (*Ent.*) hawkmoth.

Tauber ['taubər], *m.* (—s, *pl.* —) (*Orn.*) cock-pigeon.

Taubheit ['tauphaɪt], *f.* (—, *no pl.*) deafness.

Taubnessel ['taupnɛsəl], *f.* (—, *pl.* —n) (*Bot.*) deadnettle.

taubstumm ['taupʃtum], *adj.* deaf and dumb, deaf-mute.

tauchen ['tauçən], *v.n.* (*aux.* haben & sein) dive, plunge. — *v.a.* immerse, dip.

Tauchsieder ['tauçzi:dər], *m.* (—s, *pl.* —) (*Elec.*) immersion heater.

tauen ['tauən], *v.a., v.n.* thaw, melt.

Taufbecken ['taufbɛkən], *n.* (—s, *pl.* —) (baptismal) font.

Taufe ['taufə], *f.* (—, *pl.* —n) baptism, christening; *aus der* — *heben*, stand godparent.

taufen ['taufən], *v.a.* baptise, christen.

Taufkleid ['taufklaɪt], *n.* (—s, *pl.* —er) christening robe.

Täufling ['tɔyflɪŋ], *m.* (—s, *pl.* —e) infant presented for baptism; neophyte.

Taufname ['taufna:mə], *n.* (—ns, *pl.* —n) Christian name.

Taufpate ['taufpa:tə], *m.* (—n, *pl.* —n) godfather, godmother.

Taufstein ['taufʃtaɪn], *n.* (—s, *pl.* —e) (baptismal) font.

taugen ['taugən], *v.n.* be good for, be fit for; *nichts* —, be good for nothing.

Taugenichts ['taugənɪçts], *m.* (—, *pl.* —e) ne'er-do-well, scapegrace, good-for-nothing.

tauglich ['tauklɪç], *adj.* able; useful, fit, suitable.

Taumel ['tauməl], *m.* (—s, *no pl.*) giddiness, dizziness, staggering; (*fig.*) whirl; ecstasy, frenzy, delirium, intoxication.

taumeln ['tauməln], *v.n.* (*aux.* sein) reel, stagger.

Tausch [tauʃ], *m.* (—es, *no pl.*) exchange, barter.

tauschen ['tauʃən], *v.a.* exchange for, barter against, swop; *die Rollen* —, change places.

täuschen ['tɔyʃən], *v.a.* deceive, delude. — *v.r. sich* —, be mistaken.

Tauschhandel ['tauʃhandəl], *m.* (—s, *no pl.*) barter.

Tauschmittel ['tauʃmɪtəl], *n.* (—s, *pl.* —) medium of exchange.

Täuschung ['tɔyʃuŋ], *f.* (—, *pl.* —en) deceit, deception; illusion.

Täuschungsversuch ['tɔyʃuŋsfɛrzu:ç], *m.* (—es, *pl.* —e) attempt at deception; (*Mil.*) diversion.

tausend ['tauzənt], *num. adj.* a thousand.

tausendjährig ['tauzəntjɛ:rɪç], *adj.* millennial, of a thousand years; *das* —*e Reich*, the millennium.

Tausendsasa ['tauzəntzasa], *m.* (—s, *pl.* —s) devil of a fellow.

Tautropfen ['tautrɔpfən], *m.* (—s, *pl.* —) dew-drop.

Tauwetter ['tauvɛtər], *n.* (—s, *no pl.*) thaw.

Taxameter [taksa'me:tər], *m.* (—s, *pl.* —) taximeter.

Taxe ['taksə], *f.* (—, *pl.* —n) set rate, tariff; (taxi)cab; *nach der* — *verkauft werden*, be sold *ad valorem*.

taxieren [tak'si:rən], *v.a.* appraise, value.

Taxus ['taksus], *m.* (—, *pl.* —) (*Bot.*) yew(-tree).

Technik ['tɛçnɪk], *f.* (—, *pl.* —en) technology, engineering; technique; skill, execution.

Techniker ['tɛçnɪkər], *m.* (—s, *pl.* —) technician, technical engineer.

Technikum ['tɛçnɪkum], *n.* (—s, *pl.* —s) technical school, college.

technisch ['tɛçnɪʃ], *adj.* technical; —*er Ausdruck*, technical term; —*e Störung*, technical hitch *or* breakdown.

technologisch [tɛçno'lo:gɪʃ], *adj.* technological.

221

Techtelmechtel ['tɛçtəlmɛçtəl], n. (—s, pl. —) (coll.) love affair, flirtation.

Tee [te:], m. (—s, no pl.) tea.

Teedose ['te:do:zə], f. (—, pl. —n) tea-caddy.

Teekanne ['te:kanə], f. (—, pl. —n) tea-pot.

Teelöffel ['te:lœfəl], m. (—s, pl. —) tea-spoon.

Teemaschine ['te:maʃi:nə], f. (—, pl. —n) tea-urn.

Teer [te:r], m. (—(e)s, no pl.) tar.

Teerleinwand ['te:rlaɪnvant], f. (—, no pl.) tarpaulin.

Teerose ['te:ro:zə], f. (—, pl. —n) (Bot.) tea rose.

Teerpappe ['te:rpapə], f. (—, no pl.) roofing-felt.

teeren ['te:rən], v.a. tar.

Teesieb ['te:zi:p], n. (—(e)s, pl. —e) tea-strainer.

Teich [taɪç], m. (—(e)s, pl. —e) pond.

Teig [taɪk], m. (—(e)s, pl. —e) dough, paste.

teigig ['taɪgɪç], adj. doughy.

Teigrolle ['taɪkrɔlə], f. (—, pl. —n) rolling-pin.

Teil [taɪl], m. & n. (—(e)s, pl. —e) part; portion; piece, component; share; edler —, vital part; zum —, partly; zu gleichen —en, share and share alike.

teilbar ['taɪlba:r], adj. divisible.

Teilchen ['taɪlçən], n. (—s, pl. —) particle.

teilen ['taɪlən], v.a. divide; share; partition off. — v.r. sich —, share in; (road) fork.

Teiler ['taɪlər], m. (—s, pl. —) divider; (Maths.) divisor.

teilhaben ['taɪlha:bən], v.n. irr. (have a) share in, participate in.

Teilhaber ['taɪlha:bər], m. (—s, pl. —) partner.

teilhaftig ['taɪlhaftɪç], adj. sharing, participating; einer Sache — werden, partake of s.th., come in for s.th.

Teilnahme ['taɪlna:mə], f. (—, no pl.) participation; (fig.) sympathy, interest.

teilnahmslos ['taɪlna:mslo:s], adj. unconcerned, indifferent.

Teilnahmslosigkeit ['taɪlna:mslo:zɪçkaɪt], f. (—, no pl.) unconcern; listlessness, indifference.

teilnahmsvoll ['taɪlna:msfɔl], adj. solicitous.

teilnehmen ['taɪlne:mən], v.n. irr. take part (in), participate, partake; (fig.) sympathise.

Teilnehmer ['taɪlne:mər], m. (—s, pl. —) member, participant; (telephone) subscriber.

teils [taɪls], adv. partly.

Teilstrecke ['taɪlʃtrɛkə], f. (—, pl. —n) section (of a railway).

Teilung ['taɪluŋ], f. (—, pl. —en) division, partition; distribution.

Teilungszahl ['taɪluŋstsa:l], f. (—, pl. —en) (Maths.) dividend; quotient.

teilweise ['taɪlvaɪzə], adv. partly, in part.

Teilzahlung ['taɪltsa:luŋ], f. (—, pl. —en) part-payment, instalment.

Teint [tɛ̃], m. (—s, no pl.) complexion.

telephonieren [telefo'ni:rən], v.a., v.n. telephone.

Telegraphie [telegra'fi:], f. (—, no pl.) telegraphy.

telegraphisch [tele'gra:fɪʃ], adj. telegraphic, by telegram.

Telegramm [tele'gram], n. (—s, pl. —e) telegram, wire, cable.

Telegrammadresse [tele'gramadrɛsə], f. (—, pl. —n) telegraphic address.

Telegrammformular [tele'gramformula:r], n. (—s, pl. —e) telegram-form.

Teleskop [teles'ko:p], n. (—s, pl. —e) telescope.

Teller ['tɛlər], m. (—s, pl. —) plate.

Tempel ['tɛmpəl], m. (—s, pl. —) temple.

Temperament [tɛmpəra'mɛnt], n. (—s, pl. —e) temperament, disposition; (fig.) spirits.

temperamentvoll [tɛmpəra'mɛntfɔl], adj. full of spirits, vivacious; lively.

Temperatur [tɛmpəra'tu:r], f. (—, pl. —en) temperature.

Temperenzler [tɛmpə'rɛntslər], m. (—s, pl. —) total abstainer, tee-totaller.

temperieren [tɛmpə'ri:rən], v.a. temper.

Tempo ['tɛmpo:], n. (—s, pl. —s, Tempi) time, measure, speed.

temporisieren [tɛmpori'zi:rən], v.n. temporise.

Tendenz [tɛn'dɛnts], f. (—, pl. —en) tendency.

tendenziös [tɛndɛn'tsjø:s], adj. biased, coloured, tendentious.

Tender ['tɛndər], m. (—s, pl. —) (Railw.) tender.

Tenne ['tɛnə], f. (—, pl. —n) threshing floor.

Tenor [te'no:r], m. (—s, pl. ⸚e) (Mus.) tenor.

Teppich ['tɛpɪç], m. (—s, pl. —e) carpet.

Termin [tɛr'mi:n], m. (—s, pl. —e) time, date, appointed day; einen — ansetzen, fix a day (for a hearing, examination etc.).

Termingeschäft [tɛr'mi:ngəʃɛft], n. (—s, pl. —e) (business in) futures.

Terminologie [tɛrminolo'gi:], f. (—, pl. —n) terminology.

Terpentin [tɛrpɛn'ti:n], n. (—s, no pl.) turpentine.

Terrain [tɛ'rɛ̃], n. (—s, pl. —s) ground, terrain.

Terrasse [tɛ'rasə], f. (—, pl. —n) terrace.

Terrine [tɛ'ri:nə], f. (—, pl. —n) tureen.

territorial [tɛrɪto'rja:l], adj. territorial.

Territorium [tɛrɪ'to:rjum], n. (—s, pl. —torien) territory.

tertiär [tɛr'tsjɛːr], *adj.* tertiary.

Terzett [tɛr'tsɛt], *n.* (—s, *pl.* —e) trio.

Testament [tɛsta'mɛnt], *n.* (—s, *pl.* —e) testament, will; (*Bibl.*) Testament; *ohne* —, intestate.

testamentarisch [tɛstamɛn'taːrɪʃ], *adj.* testamentary.

Testamentseröffnung [tɛsta'mɛntsɛrœfnuŋ], *f.* (—, *pl.* —en) reading of the will.

Testamentsvollstrecker [tɛsta'mɛntsfɔlʃtrɛkər], *m.* (—s, *pl.* —) executor.

teuer ['tɔyər], *adj.* dear; costly, expensive; *einem — zu stehen kommen,* cost s.o. dear.

Teuerung ['tɔyəruŋ], *f.* (—, *pl.* —en) scarcity, dearth.

Teufel ['tɔyfəl], *m.* (—s, *pl.* —) devil, fiend; *armer* —, poor devil; *scher dich zum* —, go to blazes; *den — an die Wand malen,* talk of the devil.

Teufelei [tɔyfə'laɪ], *f.* (—, *pl.* —en) devilry, devilish trick.

teuflisch ['tɔyflɪʃ], *adj.* devilish, diabolical.

Thailand ['taɪlant], *n.* Thailand.

Theater [te'aːtər], *n.* (—s, *pl.* —) theatre, stage.

Theaterkarte [te'aːtərkartə], *f.* (—, *pl.* —n) theatre-ticket.

Theaterkasse [te'aːtərkasə], *f.* (—, *pl.* —n) box-office.

Theaterstück [te'aːtərʃtyk], *n.* (—(e)s, *pl.* —e) play, drama.

Theatervorstellung [te'aːtərfoːrʃtɛluŋ], *f.* (—, *pl.* —en) theatre performance.

Theaterzettel [te'aːtərtsɛtəl], *m.* (—s, *pl.* —) play-bill.

theatralisch [tea'traːlɪʃ], *adj.* theatrical; dramatic; histrionic.

Thema ['teːmaː], *n.* (—s, *pl.* —men, Themata) theme, subject, topic.

Themse ['tɛmzə], *f.* Thames.

Theologe [teo'loːgə], *m.* (—n, *pl.* —n) theologian.

Theologie [teolo'giː], *f.* (—, *no pl.*) theology, divinity.

theoretisch [teo're:tɪʃ], *adj.* theoretical.

theoretisieren [teoreti'ziːrən], *v.n.* theorise.

Theorie [teo'riː], *f.* (—, *pl.* —n) theory.

Therapie [tera'piː], *f.* (—, *no pl.*) therapy.

Therme ['tɛrmə], *f.* (—, *pl.* —n) hot spring.

Thermometer [tɛrmo'meːtər], *n.* (—s, *pl.* —) thermometer.

Thermosflasche ['tɛrmɔsflaʃə], *f.* (—, *pl.* —n) thermos-flask.

These ['teːzə], *f.* (—, *pl.* —n) thesis.

Thron [troːn], *m.* (—(e)s, *pl.* —e) throne; *auf den — setzen,* place on the throne, enthrone; *vom — stoßen,* dethrone, depose.

Thronbesteigung ['troːnbəʃtaɪguŋ], *f.* (—, *pl.* —en) accession (to the throne).

Thronbewerber ['troːnbəvɛrbər], *m.* (—s, *pl.* —) claimant to the throne, pretender.

thronen ['troːnən], *v.n.* sit enthroned.

Thronerbe ['troːnɛrbə], *m.* (—n, *pl.* —n) heir apparent, crown prince.

Thronfolge ['troːnfɔlgə], *f.* (—, *no pl.*) line *or* order of succession.

Thronfolger ['troːnfɔlgər], *m.* (—s, *pl.* —) heir to the throne, heir apparent.

Thronhimmel ['troːnhɪməl], *m.* (—s, *pl.* —) canopy.

Thronrede ['troːnreːdə], *f.* (—, *pl.* —n) speech from the throne.

Thunfisch ['tuːnfɪʃ], *m.* (—es, *pl.* —e) (*Zool.*) tunny, (*Am.*) tuna.

Thüringen ['tyːrɪŋən], *n.* Thuringia.

Thymian ['tyːmjaːn], *m.* (—s, *no pl.*) (*Bot.*) thyme.

ticken ['tɪkən], *v.n.* tick.

tief [tiːf], *adj.* deep, profound, low; far; extreme; (*voice*) bass; (*fig.*) profound; *in —ster Nacht,* in the dead of night; *aus —stem Herzen,* from the bottom of o.'s heart. — *adv.* — *atmen,* take a deep breath; — *in Schulden,* head over ears in debt; — *verletzt,* cut to the quick.

Tiefbau ['tiːfbau], *m.* (—s, *no pl.*) underground workings.

tiefbedrückt ['tiːfbədrykt], *adj.* deeply distressed; very depressed.

tiefbewegt ['tiːfbəveːkt], *adj.* deeply moved.

Tiefe ['tiːfə], *f.* (—, *pl.* —en) depth; (*fig.*) profundity.

tiefgebeugt ['tiːfgəbɔykt], *adj.* bowed down.

tiefgreifend ['tiːfgraɪfənt], *adj.* radical, sweeping.

tiefschürfend ['tiːfʃyrfənt], *adj.* profound; thoroughgoing.

Tiefsee ['tiːfzeː], *f.* (—, *no pl.*) deep sea.

Tiefsinn ['tiːfzɪn], *m.* (—s, *no pl.*) pensiveness, melancholy.

tiefsinnig ['tiːfzɪnɪç], *adj.* pensive, melancholy, melancholic(al).

Tiegel ['tiːgəl], *m.* (—s, *pl.* —) crucible; saucepan.

Tier [tiːr], *n.* (—(e)s, *pl.* —e) animal, beast; *ein großes* —, (*coll.*) a V.I.P., a bigwig; (*Am.*) a swell, a big shot.

Tierart ['tiːraːrt], *f.* (—, *pl.* —en) (*Zool.*) species.

Tierarzt ['tiːraːrtst], *m.* (—es, *pl.* ⁀e) veterinary surgeon.

Tierbändiger ['tiːrbɛndɪgər], *m.* (—s, *pl.* —) animal-tamer.

Tiergarten ['tiːrgartən], *m.* (—s, *pl.* ⁀) zoological gardens, zoo.

tierisch ['tiːrɪʃ], *adj.* animal, brute, brutal, bestial.

Tierkreis ['tiːrkraɪs], *m.* (—es, *no pl.*) zodiac.

Tierkunde ['tiːrkundə], *f.* (—, *no pl.*) zoology.

Tierquälerei ['tiːrkvɛːləraɪ], *f.* (—, *pl.* —en) cruelty to animals.

Tierreich ['tiːrraɪç], *n.* (—(e)s, *no pl.*) animal kingdom.

Tierschutzverein ['tiːrʃutsfəraɪn], *m.* (—s, *pl.* —e) society for the prevention of cruelty to animals.

Tierwärter ['ti:rvɛrtər], *m.* (—s, *pl.* —) keeper (at a zoo).

Tiger ['ti:gər], *m.* (—s, *pl.* —) (*Zool.*) tiger.

Tigerin ['ti:gərɪn], *f.* (—, *pl.* —nen) (*Zool.*) tigress.

tilgbar ['tɪlkba:r], *adj.* extinguishable; (*debt*) redeemable.

tilgen ['tɪlgən], *v.a.* strike out, efface, annul; (*debt*) discharge; (*sin*) expiate, atone for.

Tilgung ['tɪlguŋ], *f.* (—, *pl.* —en) striking out, obliteration; annulment, payment; redemption.

Tilgungsfonds ['tɪlguŋsfɔ] *m.* (—, *pl.* —) sinking fund.

Tingeltangel ['tɪŋəltaŋəl], *m. & n.* (—s, *pl.* —) (*coll.*) music-hall.

Tinktur [tɪŋk'tu:r], *f.* (—, *pl.* —en) tincture.

Tinte ['tɪntə], *f.* (—, *pl.* —n) ink; *in der — sein,* be in a jam, be in the soup.

Tintenfaß ['tɪntənfas], *n.* (—sses, *pl.* ⸚sser) ink-pot, ink-stand.

Tintenfisch ['tɪntənfɪʃ], *m.* (—es, *pl.* —e) (*Zool.*) cuttle-fish.

Tintenfleck ['tɪntənflɛk], *m.* (—s, *pl.* —e) blot, ink-spot.

Tintenklecks ['tɪntənklɛks], *m.* (—es, *pl.* —e) blot.

Tintenstift ['tɪntənʃtɪft], *m.* (—s, *pl.* —e) indelible pencil.

Tintenwischer ['tɪntənvɪʃər], *m.* (—s, *pl.* —) pen-wiper.

tippen ['tɪpən], *v.a.* tap; (*coll.*) type.

Tirol [ti'ro:l], *n.* Tyrol.

Tisch [tɪʃ], *m.* (—es, *pl.* —e) table, board; *den — decken,* lay the table; *zu — gehen,* sit down to dinner.

Tischdecke ['tɪʃdɛkə], *f.* (—, *pl.* —n) tablecloth.

Tischgebet ['tɪʃgəbe:t], *n.* (—s, *pl.* —e) grace.

Tischler ['tɪʃlər], *m.* (—s, *pl.* —) joiner, cabinet-maker, carpenter.

Tischlerei [tɪʃlə'rai], *f.* (—, *no pl.*) joinery, cabinet-making, carpentry.

Tischrede ['tɪʃre:də], *f.* (—, *pl.* —n) after-dinner speech.

Tischrücken ['tɪʃrykən], *n.* (—s, *no pl.*) table-turning.

Tischtennis ['tɪʃtɛnɪs], *n.* (—, *no pl.*) table-tennis, ping-pong.

Tischtuch ['tɪʃtu:x], *n.* (—(e)s, *pl.* ⸚er) tablecloth.

Tischzeit ['tɪʃtsait], *f.* (—, *pl.* —en) mealtime.

Titane [ti'ta:nə], *m.* (—n, *pl.* —n) Titan.

titanenhaft [ti'ta:nənhaft], *adj.* titanic.

Titel ['ti:təl], *m.* (—s, *pl.* —) title; claim; heading, headline.

Titelbild ['ti:təlbɪlt], *n.* (—(e)s, *pl.* —er) frontispiece.

Titelblatt ['ti:təlblat], *n.* (—(e)s, *pl.* ⸚er) title page.

Titelrolle ['ti:təlrɔlə], *f.* (—, *pl.* —n) title role.

titulieren [titu'li:rən], *v.a.* style, address.

toben ['to:bən], *v.n.* rave; rage, roar; be furious; be wild.

tobsüchtig ['to:pzyçtɪç], *adj.* raving, mad.

Tochter ['tɔxtər], *f.* (—, *pl.* ⸚) daughter.

töchterlich ['tœçtərlɪç], *adj.* filial, daughterly.

Tod [to:t], *m.* (—es, *pl.* —esfälle *or* (*rare*) —e) death, decease, demise; *dem — geweiht,* doomed; *Kampf auf — und Leben,* fight to the death; *zum — verurteilen,* condemn to death.

Todesangst ['to:dəsaŋst], *f.* (—, *pl.* ⸚e) agony, mortal terror.

Todesanzeige ['to:dəsantsaigə], *f.* (—, *pl.* —n) announcement of death; obituary notice.

Todesfall ['to:dəsfal], *m.* (—(e)s, *pl.* ⸚e) death, decease; fatality.

Todesgefahr ['to:dəsgəfa:r], *f.* (—, *pl.* —en) mortal danger.

Todeskampf ['to:dəskampf], *m.* (—(e)s, *pl.* ⸚e) death agony.

todesmutig ['to:dəsmu:tɪç], *adj.* death-defying.

Todesstoß ['to:dəsʃto:s], *m.* (—es, *pl.* ⸚e) death-blow.

Todesstrafe ['to:dəsʃtra:fə], *f.* (—, *no pl.*) capital punishment.

Todfeind ['to:tfaint], *m.* (—es, *pl.* —e) mortal enemy.

todkrank ['to:tkraŋk], *adj.* sick unto death, dangerously *or* mortally ill.

tödlich ['tœ:tlɪç], *adj.* mortal, deadly, fatal.

todmüde ['to:tmy:də], *adj.* tired to death.

Todsünde ['to:tzyndə], *f.* (—, *pl.* —n) mortal sin.

Togo ['to:go], *n.* Togo.

Toilette [toa'lɛtə], *f.* (—, *pl.* —n) lavatory, toilet; (*fig.*) dress.

tolerant [tole'rant], *adj.* tolerant.

Toleranz [tole'rants], *f.* (—, *no pl.*) toleration; tolerance.

tolerieren [tole'ri:rən], *v.a.* tolerate.

toll [tɔl], *adj.* mad, frantic; wild; *—er Streich,* mad prank; *zum — werden,* enough to drive o. mad.

Tolle ['tɔlə], *f.* (—, *pl.* —n) (*dial.*) forelock, tuft of hair, top-knot.

Tollhaus ['tɔlhaus], *n.* (—es, *pl.* ⸚er) madhouse, lunatic asylum.

Tollheit ['tɔlhait], *f.* (—, *pl.* —en) foolhardiness, mad prank.

Tollkirsche ['tɔlkɪrʃə], *f.* (—, *pl.* —n) belladonna, deadly nightshade.

Tollwut ['tɔlvu:t], *f.* (—, *no pl.*) frenzy; rabies.

Tolpatsch ['tɔlpatʃ], *m.* (—es, *pl.* —e) clumsy person.

Tölpel ['tœlpəl], *m.* (—s, *pl.* —) blockhead, lout, hobbledehoy.

Tölpelei [tœlpə'lai], *f.* (—, *pl.* —en) clumsiness, awkwardness.

tölpelhaft ['tœlpəlhaft], *adj.* clumsy, doltish, loutish.

Tomate [to'ma:tə], *f.* (—, *pl.* —n) tomato.

Ton (1) [to:n], *m.* (—(e)s, *pl.* ∵e) sound, tone, accent, note; shade; manners; *guter (schlechter)* —, good (bad) form, etiquette; *den* — *angeben,* set the fashion.

Ton (2) [to:n], *m.* (—s, *no pl.*) clay, potter's earth.

Tonabnehmer ['to:nabne:mər], *m.* (—s, *pl.* —) *(gramophone)* pick-up.

tonangebend ['to:nange:bənt], *adj.* leading in fashion, setting the pace; leading, fashionable.

Tonart ['to:na:rt], *f.* (—, *pl.* —en) *(Mus.)* key.

Tonbandgerät ['to:nbantgɛrɛ:t], *n.* (—s, *pl.* —e) tape-recorder.

tönen ['to:nən], *v.n.* sound.

Tonerde ['to:ne:rdə], *f.* (—, *no pl.*) clay.

tönern ['to:nərn], *adj.* earthen.

Tonfall ['to:nfal], *m.* (—s, *no pl.*) cadence, intonation (of voice).

Tonfolge ['to:nfɔlgə], *f.* (—, *pl.* —n) *(Mus.)* succession of notes.

Tonführung ['to:nfy:run], *f.* (—, *no pl.*) modulation.

Tonkunst ['to:nkunst], *f.* (—, *no pl.*) music.

Tonkünstler ['to:nkynstlər], *m.* (—s, *pl.* —) musician.

Tonleiter ['to:nlaɪtər], *f.* (—, *pl.* —n) scale, gamut.

Tonne ['tɔnə], *f.* (—, *pl.* —n) tun, cask, barrel; ton.

Tonnengewölbe ['tɔnəngəvœlbə], *n.* (—s, *pl.* —) cylindrical vault.

Tonpfeife ['to:npfaɪfə], *f.* (—, *pl.* —n) clay-pipe.

Tonsatz ['to:nzats], *m.* (—es, *pl.* ∵e) *(Mus.)* composition.

Tonsur [tɔn'zu:r], *f.* (—, *pl.* —en) tonsure.

Tonwelle ['to:nvɛlə], *f.* (—, *pl.* —n) sound-wave.

Topas [to'pa:s], *m.* (—es, *pl.* —e) topaz.

Topf [tɔpf], *m.* (—(e)s, *pl.* ∵e) pot; *alles in einen* — *werfen,* lump everything together.

Topfblume ['tɔpfblu:mə], *f.* (—, *pl.* —n) pot-plant.

Topfdeckel ['tɔpfdɛkəl], *m.* (—s, *pl.* —) lid of a pot.

Töpfer ['tœpfər], *m.* (—s, *pl.* —) potter.

Töpferarbeit ['tœpfərarbaɪt], *f.* (—, *pl.* —en) pottery.

Töpferscheibe ['tœpfərʃaɪbə], *f.* (—, *pl.* —n) potter's wheel.

Töpferware ['tœpfərva:rə], *f.* (—, *pl.* —n) pottery, earthenware.

Topfgucker ['tɔpfgukər], *m.* (—s, *pl.* —) busybody; inquisitive person.

Topographie [topogra'fi:], *f.* (—, *no pl.*) topography.

Tor (1) [to:r], *m.* (—en, *pl.* —en) *(obs.)* fool, simpleton.

Tor (2) [to:r], *n.* (—(e)s, *pl.* —e) gate; *(Footb.)* goal.

Torangel ['to:raŋəl], *f.* (—, *pl.* —n) hinge.

Tor(es)schluß ['to:r(əs)ʃlus], *m.* (—es, *no pl.*) shutting of the gate; *noch gerade vor* —, at the eleventh hour.

Torf [tɔrf], *m.* (—(e)s, *no pl.*) peat, turf.

Torfgrube ['tɔrfgru:bə], *f.* (—, *pl.* —n) turf-pit.

Torfmoor ['tɔrfmo:r], *n.* (—s, *pl.* —e) peat-bog.

Torfstecher ['tɔrfʃteçər], *m.* (—s, *pl.* —) peat-cutter.

Torheit ['to:rhaɪt], *f.* (—, *pl.* —en) foolishness, folly.

Torhüter ['to:rhy:tər], *m.* (—s, *pl.* —) gate-keeper.

töricht ['tø:rɪçt], *adj.* foolish, silly.

Törin ['tø:rɪn], *f.* (—, *pl.* —nen) *(rare)* foolish woman.

torkeln ['tɔrkəln], *v.n.* *(aux.* sein) *(coll.)* stagger, reel.

Tornister [tɔr'nɪstər], *m.* (—s, *pl.* —) knapsack, satchel.

Torpedo [tɔr'pe:do], *m.* (—s, *pl.* —s) torpedo.

Torso ['tɔrzo], *m.* (—s, *pl.* —s) trunk, torso.

Tort [tɔrt], *m.* (—s, *no pl.*) injury, wrong; *einem einen* — *antun,* wrong s.o.; play a trick on s.o.

Torte ['tɔrtə], *f.* (—, *pl.* —n) cake, pastry, tart.

Tortur [tɔr'tu:r], *f.* (—, *pl.* —en) torture.

Torwächter ['to:rvɛçtər], *m.* (—s, *pl.* —) gate-keeper; porter.

tosen ['to:zən], *v.n.* roar.

tot [to:t], *adj.* dead, deceased.

total [to'ta:l], *adj.* total, complete.

Totalisator [totali'za:tɔr], *m.* (—s, *pl.* —en) totalisator; *(coll.)* tote.

Totalleistung [to'ta:llaɪstun], *f.* (—, *pl.* —en) full effect; total output.

Tote ['to:tə], *m., f.* (—n, *pl.* —n) dead person, the deceased.

töten ['tø:tən], *v.a.* kill, put to death.

Totenacker ['to:tənakər], *m.* (—s, *pl.* ∵) churchyard, cemetery.

Totenamt ['to:tənamt], *n.* (—s, *no pl.*) office for the dead, requiem, Mass for the dead.

Totenbahre ['to:tənba:rə], *f.* (—, *pl.* —n) bier.

Totengräber ['to:təngrɛ:bər], *m.* (—s, *pl.* —) grave-digger.

Totenhemd ['to:tənhɛmt], *n.* (—(e)s, *pl.* —en) shroud, winding-sheet.

Totenklage ['to:tənkla:gə], *f.* (—, *no pl.*) lament.

Totenschein ['to:tənʃaɪn], *m.* (—(e)s, *pl.* —e) death-certificate.

Totenstille ['to:tənʃtɪlə], *f.* (—, *no pl.*) dead calm.

Totenwache ['to:tənvaxə], *f.* (—, *no pl.*) wake.

totgeboren ['to:tgəbo:rən], *adj.* still-born, born dead.

Totschlag ['to:tʃla:k], *m.* (—s, *no pl.*) manslaughter.

totschlagen ['to:tʃla:gən], *v.a.* *irr.* kill, strike dead.

Totschläger ['tо:tʃlɛ:gər], *m.* (—s, *pl.* —) loaded cane, cudgel.

totschweigen ['tо:tʃvaɪgən], *v.a. irr.* hush up.

Tötung ['tо:tuŋ], *f.* (—, *pl.* —en) killing.

Tour [tuːr], *f.* (—, *pl.* —en) tour, excursion; *in einer* —, ceaselessly; *auf* —en *bringen,*(coll.) (*Motor.*) rev up.

Tournee [turˈne:], *f.* (—, *pl.* —n) (*Theat.*) tour.

Trab [tra:p], *m.* (—(e)s, *no pl.*) trot.

Trabant [traˈbant], *m.* (—en, *pl.* —en) satellite.

traben ['tra:bən], *v.n.* (*aux.* sein) trot.

Trabrennen ['tra:prɛnən], *n.* (—s, *pl.* —) trotting-race.

Tracht [traxt], *f.* (—, *pl.* —en) dress, costume; national costume; native dress; *eine* — *Prügel,* a good hiding.

trachten ['traxtən], *v.n.* strive, aspire, endeavour; *einem nach dem Leben* —, seek to kill s.o.

trächtig ['trɛçtɪç], *adj.* (*animal*) pregnant, with young.

Trafik [traˈfīk], *m.* (—s, *pl.*—s) (*Austr.*) tobacco-kiosk.

Tragbahre ['tra:kba:rə], *f.* (—, *pl.* —n) stretcher.

Tragbalken ['tra:kbalkən], *m.* (—s *pl.*, —) girder.

tragbar ['tra:kba:r], *adj.* portable; tolerable.

träge ['trɛ:gə], *adj.* lazy, indolent, inert, sluggish.

tragen ['tra:gən], *v.a. irr.* bear, carry; (*dress*) wear; (*fig.*) bear, endure; *Bedenken* —, hesitate, have doubts; *Zinsen* —, yield interest; *einen auf Händen* —, care lovingly for s.o.

Träger ['trɛ:gər], *m.* (—s, *pl.* —) porter, carrier; girder.

Trägheit ['trɛ:khaɪt], *f.* (—, *no pl.*) indolence, laziness, inertia.

tragisch ['tra:gɪʃ], *adj.* tragic(al).

Tragkraft ['tra:kkraft], *f.* (—, *no pl.*) carrying *or* load capacity; lifting power.

Tragödie [traˈgø:djə], *f.* (—, *pl.* —n) tragedy.

Tragsessel ['tra:kzɛsəl], *m.* (—s, *pl.* —) sedan-chair.

Tragweite ['tra:kvaɪtə], *f.* (—, *no pl.*) significance, importance, range.

trainieren [trɛˈni:rən], *v.a.* train.

Traktat [trakˈta:t], *n.* (—s, *pl.* —e) treatise, tract.

Traktätchen [trakˈtɛ:tçən], *n.* (—s, *pl.* —) (short) tract.

traktieren [trakˈti:rən], *v.a.* treat; treat badly.

trällern ['trɛlərn], *v.n.* trill, hum.

Trambahn ['tramba:n], *f.* (—, *pl.* —en) tram; (*Am.*) streetcar.

Trampel ['trampəl], *n.* (—s, *pl.* —) clumsy person, bumpkin; (*Am.*) hick.

trampeln ['trampəln], *v.n.* trample.

Trampeltier ['trampəlti:r], *n.* (—s, *pl.* —e) camel; (*fig.*) clumsy person.

Tran [tra:n], *m.* (—(e)s, *no pl.*) whale-oil.

tranchieren [trãˈʃi:rən], *v.a.* carve.

Tranchiermesser [trãˈʃi:rmɛsər], *n.* (—s, *pl.* —) carving-knife.

Träne ['trɛ:nə], *f.* (—, *pl.* —n) tear, teardrop; *zu* —n *gerührt,* moved to tears.

tränen ['trɛ:nən], *v.n.* (*eyes*) water.

Tränendrüse ['trɛ:nəndry:zə], *f.* (—, *pl.* —n) lachrymal gland.

tränenleer ['trɛ:nənle:r], *adj.* tearless.

Tränenstrom ['trɛ:nənʃtro:m], *m.* (—s, *pl.* ˙-e) flood of tears.

tränenvoll ['trɛ:nənfɔl], *adj.* tearful.

tranig ['tra:nɪç], *adj.* dull, slow.

Trank [traŋk], *m.* (—(e)s, *pl.* ˙-e) drink, beverage, potion.

Tränke ['trɛŋkə], *f.* (—, *pl.* —n) (*horse*) watering-place.

tränken ['trɛŋkən], *v.a.* give to drink, water; impregnate, saturate.

transitiv ['tranziti:f], *adj.* transitive.

Transitlager ['tranzɪtla:gər], *n.* (—s, *pl.* —) bonded warehouse; transit camp.

transitorisch [tranziˈto:rɪʃ], *adj.* transitory.

transpirieren [transpiˈri:rən], *v.n.* perspire.

transponieren [transpoˈni:rən], *v.a.* transpose.

Transportkosten [transˈpɔrtkɔstən], *f. pl.* shipping charges.

Transportmittel [transˈpɔrtmɪtəl], *n.* (—s, *pl.* —) means of carriage, conveyance, transport.

Trapez [traˈpe:ts], *n.* (—es, *pl.* —e) trapeze; (*Maths.*) trapezoid.

Tratsch [tra:tʃ], *m.* (—es, *no pl.*) (*coll.*) gossip, tittle-tattle.

tratschen ['tra:tʃən], *v.n.* (*coll.*) gossip.

Tratte ['tratə], *f.* (—, *pl.* —n) (*Comm.*) draft, bill of exchange.

Traube ['traubə], *f.* (—, *pl.* —n) (*Bot.*) grape, bunch of grapes.

Traubensaft ['traubənzaft], *m.* (—s, *pl.* ˙-e) grape-juice; (*Poet.*) wine.

traubig ['traubɪç], *adj.* clustered, grape-like.

trauen ['trauən], *v.a.* marry; join in marriage; *sich* — *lassen,* get married. — *v.n. einem* —, trust s.o., confide in s.o. — *v.r. sich* —, dare, venture.

Trauer ['trauər], *f.* (—, *no pl.*) mourning; sorrow, grief.

Trauermarsch ['trauərmarʃ], *m.* (—es, *pl.* ˙-e) funeral march.

trauern ['trauərn], *v.n.* mourn, be in mourning.

Trauerspiel ['trauərʃpi:l], *n.* (—s, *pl.* —e) tragedy.

Trauerweide ['trauərvaɪdə], *f.* (—, *pl.* —n) (*Bot.*) weeping willow.

Traufe ['traufə], *f.* (—, *pl.* —n) eaves; *vom Regen in die* —, out of the frying pan into the fire.

träufeln ['trɔyfəln], *v.a.* drip, drop.

Traufröhre ['traufrø:rə], *f.* (—, *pl.*—n) gutter-pipe.

traulich ['traulɪç], *adj.* familiar, homely, cosy.

Traum [traum], *m.* (—(e)s, *pl.* ⸚e) dream; *das fällt mir nicht im —e ein,* I should not dream of it.

Traumbild ['traumbɪlt], *n.* (—s, *pl.* —er) vision.

Traumdeutung ['traumdɔytuŋ], *f.* (—, *no pl.*) interpretation of dreams.

träumen ['trɔymən], *v.n.* dream; *sich etwas nicht — lassen,* have no inkling of, not dream of s.th.; not believe s.th.

Träumer ['trɔymər], *m.* (—s, *pl.* —) dreamer; (*fig.*) visionary.

Träumerei [trɔymə'raɪ], *f.* (—, *pl.* —en) dreaming, reverie.

traumhaft ['traumhaft], *adj.* dream-like.

traurig ['traurɪç], *adj.* sad, mournful, sorrowful.

Traurigkeit ['traurɪçkaɪt], *f.* (—, *no pl.*) sadness, melancholy.

Trauring ['traurɪŋ], *m.* (—s, *pl.* —e) wedding-ring.

Trauschein ['trauʃaɪn], *m.* (—s, *pl.* —e) marriage certificate.

traut [traut], *adj.* dear, beloved; cosy; *es Heim Glück allein,* east, west, home's best; there's no place like home.

Trauung ['trauuŋ], *f.* (—, *pl.* —en) marriage ceremony.

Trauzeuge ['trautsɔygə], *m.* (—n, *pl.* —n) witness to a marriage.

trecken ['trɛkən], *v.a.* (*dial.*) draw, drag, tug.

Trecker ['trɛkər], *m.* (—s, *pl.* —) tractor.

Treff [trɛf], *n.* (—s, *no pl.*) (*Cards*) clubs.

Treffen ['trɛfən], *n.* (—s, *no pl.*) action, battle, fight; meeting, gathering; *etwas ins — führen,* put s.th. forward, urge s.th.

treffen ['trɛfən], *v.a. irr.* hit, meet; *nicht —,* miss; *wie vom Donner getroffen,* thunderstruck; *ins Schwarze —,* hit the mark, score a bull's eye. *— v.r. sich —,* happen.

treffend ['trɛfənt], *adj.* appropriate, pertinent.

Treffer ['trɛfər], *m.* (—s, *pl.* —) (*lottery*) win, prize; (*Mil.*) hit.

trefflich ['trɛflɪç], *adj.* excellent.

Treffpunkt ['trɛfpuŋkt], *m.* (—s, *pl.* —e) meeting-place.

Treffsicherheit ['trɛfzɪçərhaɪt], *f.* (—, *no pl.*) accurate aim.

Treibeis ['traɪpaɪs], *n.* (—es, *no pl.*) floating-ice, ice floe.

treiben ['traɪbən], *v.a. irr.* drive, urge; incite; (*trade*) carry on, ply; *Studien —,* study; *was treibst du?* what are you doing? *etwas zu weit —,* carry s.th. too far; *einen in die Enge —,* drive s.o. into a corner. *— v.n.* be adrift, drift.

Treiben ['traɪbən], *n.* (—s, *no pl.*) driving; doings; bustle.

Treiber ['traɪbər], *m.* (—s, *pl.* —) (*Hunt.*) driver; beater.

Treibhaus ['traɪphaus], *n.* (—es, *pl.* ⸚er) hothouse, greenhouse.

Treibkraft ['traɪpkraft], *f.* (—, *no pl.*) impulse, driving power.

Treibriemen ['traɪpri:mən], *m.* (—s, *pl.* —) driving-belt.

Treibsand ['traɪpzant], *m.* (—s, *no pl.*) quicksand, shifting sand.

Treibstange ['traɪpʃtaŋə], *f.* (—, *pl.* —en) main rod, connecting-rod.

Treibstoff ['traɪpʃtɔf], *m.* (—(e)s, *pl.* —e) fuel.

treideln ['traɪdəln], *v.a.* (*Naut.*) tow.

Treidelsteig ['traɪdəlʃtaɪk], *m.* (—s, *pl.* —e) towpath.

trennbar ['trɛnbaːr], *adj.* separable.

trennen ['trɛnən], *v.a.* separate, sever. *— v.r. sich —,* part.

Trennung ['trɛnuŋ], *f.* (—, *pl.* —en) separation, segregation; parting; division.

Trennungsstrich ['trɛnuŋsʃtrɪç], *m.* (—es, *pl.* —e) hyphen, dash.

treppab [trɛp'ap], *adv.* downstairs.

treppauf [trɛp'auf], *adv.* upstairs.

Treppe ['trɛpə], *f.* (—, *pl.* —n) stairs, staircase, flight of stairs.

Treppenabsatz ['trɛpənapzats], *m.* (—es, *pl.* —e) (*staircase*) landing.

Treppengeländer ['trɛpəngəlɛndər], *n.* (—s, *pl.* —) balustrade, banisters.

Treppenhaus ['trɛpənhaus], *n.* (—es, *pl.* ⸚er) stair-well, staircase.

Treppenläufer ['trɛpənlɔyfər], *m.* (—s, *pl.* —) stair-carpet.

Treppenstufe ['trɛpənʃtuːfə], *f.* (—, *pl.* —n) step, stair.

Treppenwitz ['trɛpənvɪts], *m.* (—es, *no pl.*) afterthought, esprit de l'escalier.

Tresor [tre'zoːr], *m.* (—s, *pl.* —e) safe, strongroom.

Tresse ['trɛsə], *f.* (—, *pl.* —n) braid, lace, galloon.

treten ['treːtən], *v.a., v.n. irr.* tread, step, trample upon; go; *— Sie näher,* step this way; *in Verbindung — mit,* make contact with; *in den Ehestand —,* get married; *einem zu nahe —,* offend s.o., tread on s.o.'s toes.

treu [trɔy], *adj.* faithful, loyal, true; conscientious.

Treubruch ['trɔybrux], *m.* (—(e)s, *pl.* ⸚e) breach of faith, disloyalty.

Treue ['trɔyə], *f.* (—, *no pl.*) faithfulness, loyalty, fidelity; *meiner Treu!* upon my soul! *auf Treu und Glauben,* on trust.

Treueid ['trɔyaɪt], *m.* (—s, *pl.* —e) oath of allegiance.

Treuhänder ['trɔyhɛndər], *m.* (—s, *pl.* —) trustee.

treuherzig ['trɔyhɛrtsɪç], *adj.* guileless, trusting.

treulich ['trɔylɪç], *adv.* faithfully.

treulos ['trɔyloːs], *adj.* faithless, perfidious; unfaithful.

Treulosigkeit ['trɔylo:ziçkaıt], *f.* (—, *no pl.*) faithlessness, perfidy, disloyalty.

Tribüne [tri'by:nə], *f.* (—, *pl.* —n) tribune, platform; (*racing*) grandstand.

Tribut [tri'bu:t], *m.* (—s, *pl.* —e) tribute.

tributpflichtig [tri'bu:tpfliçtiç], *adj.* tributary.

Trichter ['triçtər], *m.* (—s, *pl.* —) funnel.

trichterförmig ['triçtərfœrmiç], *adj.* funnel-shaped.

Trieb [tri:p], *m.* (—(e)s, *pl.* —e) (*plant*) shoot, growth; instinct, bent, propensity, inclination; (*Psych.*) drive.

Triebfeder ['tri:pfe:dər], *f.* (—, *pl.* —n) mainspring; (*fig.*) motive, guiding principle.

Triebkraft ['tri:pkraft], *f.* (—, *pl.* ⁒e) motive power.

Triebwagen ['tri:pva:gən], *m.* (—s, *pl.* —) rail-car.

Triebwerk ['tri:pvɛrk], *n.* (—s, *pl.* —e) power unit, drive.

triefen ['tri:fən], *v.n. irr. & reg.* trickle, drip; be wet through, be soaking wet.

Trient [tri'ɛnt], *n.* Trent.

Trier [tri:r], *n.* Treves.

Triest [tri'ɛst], *n.* Trieste.

Trift [trift], *f.* (—, *pl.* —en) pasture, pasturage, common, meadow.

triftig ['triftiç], *adj.* weighty, valid, conclusive, cogent.

Trikot [tri'ko:], *m. & n.* (—s, *pl.* —s) stockinet; (*circus, ballet*) tights.

Triller ['trilər], *m.* (—s, *pl.* —) (*Mus.*) trill, shake.

trillern ['trilərn], *v.n.* trill, quaver, shake; warble.

Trinität ['trini'tɛ:t], *f.* (—, *no pl.*) Trinity.

trinkbar ['trıŋkba:r], *adj.* drinkable.

Trinkbecher ['trıŋkbɛçər], *m.* (—s, *pl.* —) drinking-cup.

trinken ['trıŋkən], *v.a., v.n. irr.* drink.

Trinker ['trıŋkər], *m.* (—s, *pl.* —) drinker, drunkard.

Trinkgelage ['trıŋkgəla:gə], *n.* (—s, *pl.* —) drinking-bout.

Trinkgeld ['trıŋkgɛlt], *n.* (—s, *pl.* —er) tip, gratuity.

Trinkhalle ['trıŋkhalə], *f.* (—, *pl.* —n) (*spa*) pump-room.

Trinkspruch ['trıŋkʃprux], *m.* (—(e)s, *pl.* ⁒e) toast.

Trinkstube ['trıŋkʃtu:bə], *f.* (—, *pl.* —n) tap-room.

Tripolis ['tri:polis], *n.* Tripoli.

trippeln ['tripəln], *v.n.* trip (daintily), patter.

Tripper ['tripər], *m.* (—s, *no pl.*) (*Med.*) gonorrhoea.

Tritt [trit], *m.* (—(e)s, *pl.* —e) step, pace; kick.

Trittbrett ['tritbrɛt], *n.* (—s, *pl.* —er) foot-board; carriage-step; (*organ*) pedal.

Triumph [tri'umf], *m.* (—(e)s, *pl.* —e) triumph.

Triumphzug [tri'umftsu:k], *m.* (—(e)s, *pl.* ⁒e) triumphal procession.

Trivialität [trivjali'tɛ:t], *f.* (—, *pl.* —en) triviality, platitude.

trocken ['trɔkən], *adj.* dry, arid; (*fig.*) dull, dry as dust; (*wine*) dry.

Trockenfäule ['trɔkənfɔylə], *f.*, **Trockenfäulnis** ['trɔkənfɔylnıs], *f.* (—, *no pl.*) dry rot.

Trockenboden ['trɔkənbo:dən], *m.* (—s, *pl.* ⁒) loft.

Trockenfutter ['trɔkənfutər], *n.* (—s, *no pl.*) fodder.

Trockenfütterung ['trɔkənfytəruŋ], *f.* (—, *pl.* —en) dry feeding.

Trockenhaube ['trɔkənhaubə], *f.* (—, *pl.* —n) hair drier.

Trockenheit ['trɔkənhaıt], *f.* (—, *no pl.*) dryness; drought.

Trockenschleuder ['trɔkənʃlɔydər], *f.* (—, *pl.* —n) spin-drier.

trocknen ['trɔknən], *v.a., v.n.* dry, air.

Troddel ['trɔdəl], *f.* (—, *pl.* —n) tassel.

Trödel ['trø:dəl], *m.* (—s, *no pl.*) junk, lumber, rubbish.

Trödelladen ['trø:dəlla:dən], *m.* (—s, *pl.* ⁒) junk-shop.

Trödelmarkt ['trø:dəlmarkt], *m.* (—s, *no pl.*) kettle market, jumble sale.

trödeln ['trø:dəln], *v.n.* dawdle, loiter.

Trödler ['trø:dlər], *m.* (—s, *pl.* —) second-hand dealer; (*coll.*) dawdler, loiterer.

Trog [tro:k], *m.* (—(e)s, *pl.* ⁒e) trough.

Troja ['tro:ja], *n.* Troy.

trollen ['trɔlən], *v.r. sich* —, decamp, toddle off, make o.s. scarce.

Trommel ['trɔməl], *f.* (—, *pl.* —n) drum; cylinder, barrel; tin box; *die* — *rühren*, beat the big drum.

Trommelfell ['trɔməlfɛl], *n.* (—s, *pl.* —e) drum-skin; ear-drum.

trommeln ['trɔməln], *v.n.* drum, beat the drum.

Trommelschlegel ['trɔməlʃle:gəl], *m.* (—s, *pl.* —) drumstick.

Trommelwirbel ['trɔməlvırbəl], *m.* (—s, *pl.* —) roll of drums.

Trommler ['trɔmlər], *m.* (—s, *pl.* —) drummer.

Trompete [trɔm'pe:tə], *f.* (—, *pl.* —n) trumpet; *die* — *blasen*, blow the trumpet.

trompeten [trɔm'pe:tən], *v.n.* trumpet, sound the trumpet.

Trompetengeschmetter [trɔm'pe:təngəʃmɛtər], *n.* (—s, *no pl.*) flourish of trumpets.

Tropen ['tro:pən], *f. pl.* the tropics.

Tropenfieber ['tro:pənfi:bər], *n.* (—s, *no pl.*) tropical fever.

tröpfeln ['trœpfəln], *v.a., v.n.* trickle, sprinkle.

Tropfen ['trɔpfən], *m.* (—s, *pl.* —) drop; *steter — höhlt den Stein*, constant dripping wears away a stone.

tropfen ['trɔpfən], *v.n.* drop, drip.

Trophäe [tro'fɛə], f. (—, pl. —n) trophy.

tropisch ['tro:pɪʃ], adj. tropical, tropic.

Troß [trɔs], m. (—sses, pl. -sse) (Mil.) baggage-train; (fig.) hangers-on, camp-followers.

Troßpferd ['trɔspfe:rt], n. (—s, pl. —e) pack-horse.

Trost [tro:st], m. (—es, no pl.) consolation, comfort; geringer —, cold comfort; du bist wohl nicht bei —? have you taken leave of your senses?

trösten ['trø:stən], v.a. comfort, console; tröste dich, cheer up.

Tröster ['trø:stər], m. (—s, pl. —) comforter, consoler; (Theol.) Holy Ghost, Comforter.

tröstlich ['trø:stlɪç], adj. consoling, comforting.

trostlos ['tro:stlo:s], adj. disconsolate, inconsolable; desolate, bleak.

Trostlosigkeit ['tro:stlo:zɪçkaɪt], f. (—, no pl.) disconsolateness; (fig.) wretchedness; dreariness.

Trott [trɔt], m. (—s, no pl.) trot.

Trottel ['trɔtəl], m. (—s, pl. —) (coll.) idiot.

Trottoir [trɔto'a:r], n. (—s, pl. —e) pavement, footpath; (Am.) sidewalk.

trotz [trɔts], prep. (Genit., Dat.) in spite of, despite; — alledem, all the same.

Trotz [trɔts], m. (—es, no pl.) defiance, obstinacy, refractoriness; einem — bieten, defy s.o.; einem etwas zum — machen, do s.th. in defiance of s.o.

trotzdem [trɔts'de:m], conj. notwithstanding that, albeit, although. — adv. nevertheless.

trotzen ['trɔtsən], v.n. defy; sulk, be obstinate; Gefahren —, brave dangers.

trotzig ['trɔtsɪç], adj. defiant; sulky, refractory; headstrong, stubborn, obstinate.

Trotzkopf ['trɔtskɔpf], m. (—(e)s, pl. ˙e) obstinate child; pig-headed person.

trübe ['try:bə], adj. dim, gloomy; (weather) dull, cloudy, overcast; (water) troubled; (glass) misted; —s Lächeln, wan smile.

Trubel ['tru:bəl], m. (—s, no pl.) tumult, turmoil, disturbance.

trüben ['try:bən], v.a. darken, sadden, trouble; (glass) mist; (metal) tarnish; (fig.) obscure.

Trübsal ['try:pza:l], f. (—, pl. —e), n. (—s, pl. —e) misery, trouble, distress; — blasen, mope.

trübselig ['try:pze:lɪç], adj. woeful, lamentable; woebegone, forlorn.

Trübsinn ['try:pzɪn], m. (—s, no pl.) sadness, dejection.

trübsinnig ['try:pzɪnɪç], adj. sad, dejected.

Trüffel ['tryfəl], f. (—, pl. —n) truffle.

Trug [tru:k], m. (—(e)s, no pl.) deceit, fraud; Lug und —, a pack of lies.

Trugbild ['tru:kbɪlt], n. (—es, pl. —er) phantom.

trügen ['try:gən], v.a. irr. deceive.

trügerisch ['try:gərɪʃ], adj. deceptive, illusory, fallacious.

Truggewebe ['tru:kgəve:bə], n. (—s, pl. —) tissue of lies.

Trugschluß ['tru:kʃlus], m. (—sses, pl. ˙sse) fallacy, false deduction.

Truhe ['tru:ə], f. (—, pl. —n) chest, trunk, coffer.

Trumm [trum], m. (—s, pl. ˙er) lump, broken piece.

Trümmer ['trymər], m. pl. fragments, debris, ruins; in — gehen, go to wrack and ruin; in — schlagen, wreck.

Trümmerhaufen ['trymərhaufən], m. (—s, pl. —) heap of ruins, heap of rubble.

Trumpf [trumpf], m. (—(e)s, pl. ˙e) trump, trump-card.

trumpfen ['trumpfən], v.a. trump.

Trumpffarbe ['trumpffarbə], f. (—, pl. —n) trump-suit.

Trunk [truŋk], m. (—(e)s, pl. ˙e) draught, potion, drinking; sich dem — ergeben, take to drink.

trunken ['truŋkən], adj. drunk, intoxicated; (fig.) elated.

Trunkenbold ['truŋkənbɔlt], m. (—s, pl. —e) drunkard.

Trunkenheit ['truŋkənhaɪt], f. (—, no pl.) drunkenness, intoxication.

Trunksucht ['truŋkzuxt], f. (—, no pl.) dipsomania, alcoholism.

trunksüchtig ['truŋkzyçtɪç], adj. dipsomaniac, addicted to drinking.

Trupp [trup], m. (—s, pl. —s) troop, band.

Truppe ['trupə], f. (—, pl. —n) (Mil.) company, troops, forces; (actors) troupe.

Truppengattung ['trupəngatuŋ], f. (—, pl. —en) branch of the armed forces.

Truthahn ['tru:tha:n], m. (—s, pl. ˙e) (Orn.) turkey cock.

Truthenne ['tru:thɛnə], f. (—, pl. —n) (Orn.) turkey hen.

Trtuhühner ['tru:thy:nər], n. pl. (Orn.) turkey-fowl.

Trutz [truts], m. (—es, no pl.) (Poet.) defiance; zum Schutz und —, offensively and defensively.

Tschad [tʃat], n. Chad.

Tschechoslowakei [tʃeçoslova'kaɪ], f. Czechoslovakia.

Tuch (1) [tu:x], n. (—(e)s, pl. ˙er) shawl, wrap.

Tuch (2) [tu:x], n. (—s, pl. —e) cloth, fabric.

Tuchhändler ['tu:xhɛndlər], m. (—s, pl. —) draper, clothier.

tüchtig ['tyçtɪç], adj. able, competent, efficient. — adv. largely, much, heartily.

Tüchtigkeit ['tyçtɪçkaɪt], f. (—, no pl.) ability, competence, efficiency.

Tücke ['tykə], f. (—, pl. —n) malice, spite.

tückisch ['tykɪʃ], *adj.* malicious, insidious.

Tugend ['tu:gənt], *f.* (—, *pl.* —en) virtue.

Tugendbold ['tu:gəntbɔlt], *m.* (—s, *pl.* —e) paragon.

tugendhaft ['tu:gənthaft], *adj.* virtuous.

Tugendlehre ['tu:gəntle:rə], *f.* (—, *no pl.*) ethics, morals.

Tüll [tyl], *m.* (—s, *pl.* —e) tulle.

Tulpe ['tulpə], *f.* (—, *pl.* —n) (*Bot.*) tulip.

Tulpenzwiebel ['tulpəntsvi:bəl], *f.* (—, *pl.* —n) tulip-bulb.

tummeln ['tuməln], *v.r. sich* —, romp about; make haste.

Tummelplatz ['tuməlplats], *m.* (—es, *pl.* ⸚e) playground, fairground.

Tümpel ['tympəl], *m.* (—s, *pl.* —) pond, pool, puddle.

Tun [tu:n], *n.* (—s, *no pl.*) doing; *sein — und Lassen,* his conduct.

tun [tu:n], *v.a. irr.* do, make; put; *tut nichts,* it does not matter; *viel zu — haben,* have a lot to do, be busy; *not —,* be necessary; *Buße —,* repent.

Tünche ['tynçə], *f.* (—, *pl.* —n) whitewash.

tünchen ['tynçən], *v.a.* whitewash.

Tunichtgut ['tu:nɪçtgu:t], *m.* (—s, *no pl.*) ne'er-do-well, scamp.

Tunke ['tuŋkə], *f.* (—, *pl.* —n) sauce, gravy.

tunken ['tuŋkən], *v.a.* dip, steep; (*Am.*) dunk.

tunlich ['tu:nlɪç], *adj.* feasible, practicable, expedient.

tunlichst ['tu:nlɪçst], *adv.* if possible, possibly.

Tunnel ['tunəl], *m.* (—s, *pl.* —) tunnel.

Tunnelbau ['tunəlbau], *m.* (—s, *no pl.*) tunnelling.

tüpfeln ['typfəln], *v.a.* dot, spot.

Tupfen ['tupfən], *m.* (—s, *pl.* —) dot, polka-dot.

Tür [ty:r], *f.* (—, *pl.* —en) door; *einem die — weisen,* show s.o. the door; *vor der — stehen,* be imminent; *kehr vor deiner eigenen —,* mind your own business; *put your own house in order; offene —en einrennen,* flog a willing horse; *zwischen — und Angel stecken,* be undecided.

Türangel ['ty:raŋəl], *f.* (—, *pl.* —n) door-hinge.

Türhüter ['ty:rhy:tər], *m.* (—s, *pl.* —) doorkeeper.

Türkei [tyr'kai], *f.* Turkey.

Türkensäbel ['tyrkənze:bəl], *m.* (—s, *pl.* —) scimitar.

Türkis [tyr'ki:s], *m.* (—es, *pl.* —e) turquoise.

Türklinke ['ty:rkliŋkə], *f.* (—, *pl.* —n) door-handle.

Turm [turm], *m.* (—(e)s, *pl.* ⸚e) tower; spire, steeple; belfry; (*Chess*) castle.

Turmalin [turma'li:n], *m.* (—s, *pl.* —e) tourmaline.

Türmchen ['tyrmçən], *n.* (—s, *pl.* —) turret.

türmen ['tyrmən], *v.a.* pile up. — *v.n.* (*coll.*) bolt, run away. — *v.r. sich* —, rise high, be piled high.

Turmspitze ['turmʃpitsə], *f.* (—, *pl.* —n) spire.

turnen ['turnən], *v.n.* do exercises *or* gymnastics.

Turnen ['turnən], *n.* (—s, *no pl.*) gymnastics, physical training.

Turner ['turnər], *m.* (—s, *pl.* —) gymnast.

Turngerät ['turngərɛ:t], *n.* (—es, *pl.* —e) gymnastic apparatus.

Turnhalle ['turnhalə], *f.* (—, *pl.* —n) gymnasium.

Turnier [tur'ni:r], *n.* (—s, *pl.* —e) tournament.

Turnübung ['turny:buŋ], *f.* (—, *pl.* —en) gymnastic exercise.

Turnverein ['turnfərain], *m.* (—s, *pl.* —e) athletics club, gymnastics club.

Türpfosten ['ty:rpfɔstən], *m.* (—s, *pl.* —) door-post.

Türriegel ['ty:rri:gəl], *m.* (—s, *pl.* —) bolt.

Türschild ['ty:rʃilt], *n.* (—(e)s, *pl.* —e) (door)plate.

Türschloß ['ty:rʃlɔs], *n.* (—sses, *pl.* ⸚sser) lock.

Türschlüssel ['ty:rʃlysəl], *m.* (—s, *pl.* —) door-key, latch-key.

Türschwelle ['ty:rʃvɛlə], *f.* (—, *pl.* —n) threshold.

Tusch [tuʃ], *m.* (—es, *pl.* —e) (*Mus.*) flourish.

Tusche ['tuʃə], *f.* (—, *pl.* —n) water-colour; Indian ink.

tuscheln ['tuʃəln], *v.n.* whisper.

tuschen ['tuʃən], *v.a.* draw in Indian ink.

Tuschkasten ['tuʃkastən], *m.* (—s, *pl.* ⸚) paint-box.

Tüte ['ty:tə], *f.* (—, *pl.* —n) paper bag.

Tutel [tu'te:l], *f.* (—, *no pl.*) guardianship.

tuten ['tu:tən], *v.n.* hoot, honk, blow a horn.

Tütendreher ['ty:təndre:ər], *m.* (—s, *pl.* —) (*sl.*) small shopkeeper.

Typ [ty:p], *m.* (—s, *pl.* —en) type.

Type ['ty:pə], *f.* (—, *pl.* —n) (*Typ.*) type; (*fig.*) queer fish.

Typhus ['ty:fus], *m.* (—, *no pl.*) (*Med.*) typhoid (fever).

typisch ['ty:pɪʃ], *adj.* typical.

Typus ['ty:pus], *m.* (—, *pl.* **Typen**) type.

Tyrann [ty'ran], *m.* (—en, *pl.* —en) tyrant.

Tyrannei [tyra'nai], *f.* (—, *pl.* —en) tyranny, despotism.

tyrannisch [ty'ranɪʃ], *adj.* tyrannical, despotic.

tyrannisieren [tyrani'zi:rən], *v.a.* tyrannize over, oppress, bully.

U

U [u:], *n.* (—**s**, *pl.* —**s**) the letter U.

U-Bahn ['u:ba:n], *f.* (—, *no pl.*) underground (railway) ;(*Am.*)subway.

Übel ['y:bəl], *n.* (—**s**, *pl.* —) evil, trouble ; misfortune ; disease.

übel ['y:bəl], *adj.* evil, ill, bad ; *mir ist* —, I feel sick ; *nicht* —, not too bad ; — *daran sein*, be in a bad way, be in a mess.

übelgesinnt ['y:bəlgəzɪnt], *adj.* evil-minded ; ill-disposed ; *einem* — *sein*, bear s.o. a grudge.

Übelkeit ['y:bəlkaɪt], *f.* (—, *pl.* —**en**) nausea, sickness.

übellaunig ['y:bəllaunɪç], *adj.* ill-humoured, bad-tempered.

übelnehmen ['y:bəlne:mən], *v.a. irr.* take amiss, resent, be offended at.

übelnehmerisch ['y:bəlne:mərɪʃ], *adj.* touchy, easily offended.

Übelstand ['y:bəlʃtant], *m.* (—(**e**)**s**, *pl.* "**e**) inconvenience, drawback ; (*pl.*) abuses.

Übeltat ['y:bəlta:t], *f.* (—, *pl.* —**en**) misdeed.

Übeltäter ['y:bəlte:tər], *m.* (—**s**, *pl.* —) evildoer, malefactor.

übelwollend ['y:bəlvɔlənt], *adj.* malevolent.

üben ['y:bən], *v.a.* practise, exercise ; *Rache* —, wreak vengeance.

über ['y:bər], *prep.* (*Dat., Acc.*) over, above ; across ; about ; more than, exceeding ; via ; by way of ; concerning, on. — *adv.* over, above ; — *und* —, all over ; — *kurz oder lang*, sooner or later ; *heute* —**s** *Jahr*, a year from today.

überall ['y:bəral], *adv.* everywhere, anywhere.

überanstrengen [y:bər'anʃtrɛŋən], *v.a. insep.* overtax s.o.'s strength, strain. — *v.r. sich* —, overtax o.'s strength, overexert o.s.

Überanstrengung [y:bər'anʃtrɛŋuŋ], *f.* (—, *pl.* —**en**) over-exertion, strain.

überantworten [y:bər'antvɔrtən], *v.a. insep.* deliver up, surrender.

überarbeiten [y:bər'arbaɪtən], *v.a. insep.* revise, do again. — *v.r. sich* —, overwork o.s.

überarbeitet [y:bər'arbaɪtət], *adj.* overwrought, overworked.

überaus ['y:bəraus], *adv.* exceedingly, extremely.

überbauen [y:bər'bauən], *v.a. insep.* build over.

überbieten [y:bər'bi:tən], *v.a. irr. insep.* outbid (s.o.) ; (*fig.*) surpass.

Überbleibsel ['y:bərblaɪpsəl], *n.* (—**s**, *pl.* —) remainder, remnant, residue, rest.

Überblick ['y:bərblɪk], *m.* (—(**e**)**s**, *pl.* —**e**) survey, general view.

überblicken [y:bər'blɪkən], *v.a. insep.* survey, look over.

überbringen [y:bər'brɪŋən], *v.a. irr. insep.* bear, deliver, hand in.

Überbringung [y:bər'brɪŋuŋ], *f.* (—, *no pl.*) delivery.

überbrücken [y:bər'brykən], *v.a. insep.* bridge, span.

überdachen [y:bər'daxən], *v.a. insep.* roof (over).

überdauern [y:bər'dauərn], *v.a. insep.* outlast ; tide over.

überdenken [y:bər'dɛŋkən], *v.a. irr. insep.* think over, consider.

überdies [y:bər'di:s], *adv.* besides, moreover.

überdrucken [y:bər'drukən], *v.a. insep.* overprint.

Überdruß ['y:bərdrus], *m.* (—**sses**, *no pl.*) weariness ; disgust ; *zum* —, ad nauseam.

überdrüssig ['y:bərdrysɪç],*adj.* weary of.

Übereifer ['y:bəraɪfər], *m.* (—**s**, *no pl.*) excessive zeal.

übereifrig ['y:bəraɪfrɪç], *adj.* excessively zealous, officious.

übereilen [y:bər'aɪlən], *v.r. insep. sich* —, hurry too much, overshoot the mark.

übereilt [y:bər'aɪlt], *adj.* overhasty, rash.

übereinkommen [y:bər'aɪnkɔmən], *v.n. irr.* (*aux.* sein) agree.

Übereinkunft [y:bər'aɪnkunft], *f.* (—, *pl.* "**e**) agreement, convention.

übereinstimmen [y:bər'aɪnʃtɪmən], *v.n.* agree, concur, harmonize, be of one mind, be of the same opinion ; (*things*) tally, square.

Übereinstimmung [y:bər'aɪnʃtɪmuŋ], *f.* (—, *no pl.*) accord, agreement, conformity, harmony.

überfahren (1) [y:bər'fa:rən], *v.a. irr. insep.* traverse, pass over ; run over (s.o.).

überfahren (2) ['y:bərfa:rən], *v.a. irr. insep.* ferry across. — *v.n.* (*aux.* sein) cross.

überfahren (3) ['y:bərfa:rən], *v.n.* (*aux.* sein) cross.

Überfahrt ['y:bərfa:rt], *f.* (—, *pl.* —**en**) passage, crossing.

Überfall ['y:bərfal], *m.* (—**s**, *pl.* "**e**) sudden attack, raid.

überfallen (1) ['y:bərfalən], *v.n. irr.* (*aux.* sein) (*p.p.* **übergefallen**) fall over.

überfallen (2) [y:bər'falən], *v.a. irr., insep.* (*p.p.* **überfallen**) attack suddenly, raid.

überfliegen [y:bər'fli:gən], *v.a. irr. insep.* fly over ; (*fig.*) glance over, skim.

überfließen ['y:bərfli:sən], *v.n. irr.* (*aux.* sein) overflow.

überflügeln [y:bər'fly:gəln], *v.a. insep.* surpass, outstrip.

Überfluß ['y:bərflus], *m.* (—sses, *no pl.*) abundance, plenty, profusion; surplus; — *haben an*, abound in, have too much of.

überflüssig ['y:bərflysɪç], *adj.* superfluous, unnecessary.

überfluten [y:bər'flu:tən], *v.a. insep.* overflow, flood.

überführen (1) ['y:bərfy:rən], *v.a.* convey, conduct (across).

überführen (2) [y:bər'fy:rən], *v.a. insep.* convict; transport a coffin.

Überführung [y:bər'fy:ruŋ], *f.* (—, *pl.* —en) conviction (for a crime); transport (of a coffin).

Überfüllung [y:bər'fyluŋ], *f.* (—, *no pl.*) overcrowding.

Übergabe ['y:bərga:bə], *f.* (—, *no pl.*) surrender, yielding up; delivery, handing over.

Übergang ['y:bərgaŋ], *m.* (—s, *pl.* ⁀e) passage; (*Railw.*) crossing; (*fig.*) change-over, transition.

übergeben [y:bər'ge:bən], *v.a. irr. insep.* deliver up, hand over. — *v.r. sich* —, vomit.

übergehen (1) ['y:bərge:ən], *v.n. irr.* (*aux. sein*) (*p.p. übergegangen*) go over, change over, turn (into); *zum Feinde* —, go over to the enemy; *in andre Hände* —, change hands.

übergehen (2) [y:bər'ge:ən], *v.a. irr. insep.* (*p.p. übergangen*) pass over, pass by.

Übergehung [y:bər'ge:uŋ], *f.* (—, *no pl.*) omission; passing over.

übergeordnet ['y:bərgəordnət], *adj.* superior.

Übergewicht ['y:bərgəvɪçt], *n.* (—(e)s, *no pl.*) overweight; (*fig.*) preponderance, superiority.

übergießen [y:bər'gi:sən], *v.a. irr. insep.* pour over, douse with.

überglücklich ['y:bərglyklɪç], *adj.* overjoyed.

übergreifen ['y:bərgraɪfən], *v.n. irr.* overlap; encroach (upon); spread.

Übergriff ['y:bərgrɪf], *m.* (—(e)s, *pl.* —e) encroachment.

übergroß ['y:bərgro:s], *adj.* excessively large, overlarge.

überhaben [y:bər'ha:bən], *v.a. irr.* have enough of, be sick of.

überhandnehmen [y:bər'hantne:mən], *v.n. irr.* gain the upper hand; run riot.

überhangen ['y:bərhaŋən], *v.n. irr.* hang over.

überhängen ['y:bərhɛŋən], *v.a. irr.* cover, hang upon.

überhäufen [y:bər'hɔyfən], *v.a. insep.* overwhelm.

überhaupt [y:bər'haupt], *adv.* in general, altogether, at all.

überheben [y:bər'he:bən], *v.r. insep. sich* —, strain o.s. by lifting; (*fig.*) be overbearing.

überheblich [y:bər'he:plɪç], *adj.* overbearing, arrogant.

überheizen [y:bər'haɪtsən], *v.a. insep.* overheat.

überhitzt [y:bər'hɪtst], *adj.* overheated; impassioned.

überholen [y:bər'ho:lən], *v.a. insep.* overtake, out-distance; (*fig.*) overhaul.

überhören [y:bər'hø:rən], *v.a. insep.* hear s.o.'s lessons; ignore, miss (s.th.).

überirdisch ['y:bərɪrdɪʃ], *adj.* celestial, superterrestrial.

Überkleid ['y:bərklaɪt], *n.* (—(e)s, *pl.* —er) outer garment; overall.

überklug ['y:bərklu:k], *adj.* too clever by half, conceited.

überkochen ['y:bərkɔxən], *v.n.* (*aux. sein*) boil over.

überkommen [y:bər'kɔmən], *adj.* — *sein von*, be seized with.

überladen [y:bər'la:dən], *v.a. irr. insep.* overload. — *adj.* overdone, too elaborate; bombastic.

überlassen [y:bər'lasən], *v.a. irr. insep.* leave, relinquish, give up, yield.

überlasten [y:bər'lastən], *v.a. insep.* overburden.

überlaufen (1) ['y:bərlaufən], *v.a. irr.* run over; (*to the enemy*) desert.

überlaufen (2) [y:bər'laufən], *v.a. insep.* (*p.p. überlaufen*) overrun.

Überläufer ['y:bərlɔyfər], *m.* (—s, *pl.* —) deserter, runaway.

überleben [y:bər'le:bən], *v.a. insep.* survive, outlive; (*fig.*) live (s.th.) down; *sich überlebt haben*, be out of date, be dated.

Überlebende [y:bər'le:bəndə], *m.* (—n, *pl.* —n) survivor.

überlegen (1) ['y:bərle:gən], *v.a.* lay over, cover.

überlegen (2) [y:bər'le:gən], *v.a. insep.* (*p.p. überlegt*) think over, consider, turn over in o.'s mind. — *adj.* superior; — *sein*, outdo, be superior to.

Überlegenheit [y:bər'le:gənhaɪt], *f.* (—, *no pl.*) superiority.

Überlegung [y:bər'le:guŋ], *f.* (—, *pl.* —en) consideration, deliberation; *bei näherer* —, on second thoughts, on thinking it over.

überliefern [y:bər'li:fərn], *v.a. insep.* hand down (to posterity); hand on, pass on.

Überlieferung [y:bər'li:fəruŋ], *f.* (—, *pl.* —en) tradition.

überlisten [y:bər'lɪstən], *v.a. insep.* outwit.

Übermacht ['y:bərmaxt], *f.* (—, *no pl.*) superiority, superior force.

übermalen [y:bər'ma:lən], *v.a. insep.* paint over.

übermangansauer [y:bərmaŋ'ga:nzauər], *adj.* permanganate of; —*saueres Kali*, permanganate of potash.

übermannen [y:bər'manən], *v.a. insep.* overpower.

Übermaß ['y:bərma:s], *n.* (—es, *no pl.*) excess; *im* —, to excess.

übermäßig ['y:bərmɛ:sıç], *adj.* excessive, immoderate.

Übermensch ['y:bərmɛnʃ], *m.* (—en, *pl.* —en) superman.

übermenschlich ['y:bərmɛnʃlıç], *adj.* superhuman.

übermitteln [y:bər'mıtəln], *v.a. insep.* convey.

übermorgen ['y:bərmɔrgən], *adv.* the day after tomorrow.

Übermut ['y:bərmu:t], *m.* (—s, *no pl.*) wantonness; high spirits.

übermütig ['y:bərmy:tıç], *adj.* wanton; full of high spirits.

übernachten [y:bər'naxtən], *v.n. insep.* pass *or* spend the night.

übernächtig [y:bər'nɛçtıç], *adj.* haggard, tired by a sleepless night.

Übernahme ['y:bərna:mə], *f.* (—, *no pl.*) taking possession, taking charge.

übernatürlich ['y:bərnaty:rlıç], *adj.* supernatural.

übernehmen [y:bər'ne:mən], *v.a. irr. insep.* take possession of, take upon o.s., take over. — *v.r. sich* —, overtax o.'s strength.

überordnen ['y:bərɔrdnən], *v.a.* place above.

überprüfen [y:bər'pry:fən], *v.a. insep.* examine, overhaul.

überquellen [y:bər'kvɛlən], *v.n. irr. insep.* (aux. sein) bubble over.

überqueren [y:bər'kve:rən], *v.a. insep.* cross.

überragen [y:bər'ra:gən], *v.a. insep.* tower above, overtop; (*fig.*) surpass, outstrip.

überraschen [y:bər'raʃən], *v.a. insep.* surprise, take by surprise.

Überraschung [y:bər'raʃuŋ], *f.* (—, *pl.* —en) surprise.

überreden [y:bər're:dən], *v.a. insep.* persuade, talk s.o. into (s.th.).

Überredung [y:bər're:duŋ], *f.* (—, *no pl.*) persuasion.

überreichen [y:bər'raıçən], *v.a. insep.* hand over, present formally.

überreichlich ['y:bərraıçlıç], *adj.* superabundant.

Überreichung [y:bər'raıçuŋ], *f.* (—, *no pl.*) formal presentation.

überreizen [y:bər'raıtsən], *v.a. insep.* over-excite, over-stimulate.

überrennen [y:bər'rɛnən], *v.a. irr. insep.* take by storm, overrun.

Überrest ['y:bərrɛst], *m.* (—es, *pl.* —e) remainder, remnant, residue.

überrumpeln [y:bər'rumpəln], *v.a. insep.* catch unawares, surprise.

übersättigen [y:bər'zɛtıgən], *v.a. insep.* saturate; surfeit, cloy.

Übersättigung [y:bər'zɛtıguŋ], *f.* (—, *no pl.*) saturation; surfeit.

Überschallgeschwindigkeit ['y:bər-ʃalgəʃvındıçkaıt], *f.* (—, *no pl.*) supersonic speed.

überschatten [y:bər'ʃatən], *v.a. insep.* overshadow.

überschätzen [y:bər'ʃɛtsən], *v.a. insep.* overrate, over-estimate.

überschauen [y:bər'ʃauən], *v.a. insep.* survey.

überschäumen ['y:bərʃɔymən], *v.n.* (aux. sein) bubble over.

überschäumend ['y:bərʃɔymənt], *adj.* ebullient, exuberant.

Überschlag ['y:bərʃla:k], *m.* (—s, *pl.* ∸e) somersault; estimate.

überschlagen [y:bər'ʃla:gən], *v.a. irr. insep.* (*pages*) miss, skip; estimate, compute. — *v.r. sich* —, turn a somersault, overturn. — *adj.* tepid, lukewarm.

überschnappen ['y:bərʃnapən], *v.n.* (aux. sein) snap; (*fig., coll.*) go out of o.'s mind.

überschreiben [y:bər'ʃraıbən], *v.a. irr. insep.* superscribe, entitle.

überschreiten [y:bər'ʃraıtən], *v.a. irr. insep.* cross; go beyond, exceed.

Überschrift ['y:bərʃrıft], *f.* (—, *pl.* —en) heading, headline.

Überschuß ['y:bərʃus], *m.* (—sses, *pl.* ∸sse) surplus.

überschüssig ['y:bərʃysıç], *adj.* surplus, remaining.

überschütten [y:bər'ʃytən], *v.a. insep.* shower with, overwhelm with.

Überschwang ['y:bərʃvaŋ], *m.* (—s, *no pl.*) exaltation, rapture.

überschwemmen [y:bər'ʃvɛmən], *v.a. insep.* flood, inundate.

Überschwemmung [y:bər'ʃvɛmuŋ], *f.* (—, *pl.* —en) inundation, flood, deluge.

überschwenglich [y:bər'ʃvɛŋlıç], *adj.* exuberant, exalted.

Übersee ['y:bərze:], *f.* (—, *no pl.*) overseas.

übersehen [y:bər'ze:ən], *v.a. irr. insep.* survey, look over; overlook, disregard.

übersenden [y:bər'zɛndən], *v.a. irr. insep.* send, forward, transmit; (*money*) remit.

Übersendung [y:bər'zɛnduŋ], *f.* (—, *pl.* —en) sending, forwarding, transmission; remittance.

übersetzen (1) ['y:bərzɛtsən], *v.a.* (*p.p.* übergesetzt) ferry across, cross (a river).

übersetzen (2) [y:bər'zɛtsən], *v.a. insep.* (*p.p.* übersetzt) translate.

Übersetzer [y:bər'zɛtsər], *m.* (—s, *pl.* —) translator.

Übersetzung [y:bər'zɛtsuŋ], *f.* (—, *pl.* —en) translation.

Übersicht ['y:bərzıçt], *f.* (—, *pl.* —en) survey, summary; epitome.

übersichtlich ['y:bərzıçtlıç], *adj.* clearly arranged, readable at a glance, lucid.

übersiedeln [y:bər'zi:dəln], *v.n.* (aux. sein) remove, move, settle in a different place.

Übersiedlung [y:bər'zi:dluŋ], *f.* (—, *pl.* —en) removal.

überspannen [y:bər'ʃpanən], *v.a. insep.* overstretch.

überspannt [y:bər'ʃpant], *adj.* eccentric, extravagant.

233

Überspanntheit

Überspanntheit [y:bər'ʃpanthaıt], *f.* (—, *pl.* —en) eccentricity.

überspringen [y:bər'ʃprıŋən], *v.a. irr. insep.* jump over; (*fig.*) skip.

übersprudeln [y:bər'ʃpru:dəln], *v.n.* (*aux.* sein) bubble over.

überstechen [y:bər'ʃteçən], *v.a. irr.* (*cards*) trump higher.

überstehen [y:bər'ʃte:ən], *v.a. irr. insep.* overcome, endure, get over, weather.

übersteigen [y:bər'ʃtaıgən], *v.a. irr. insep.* exceed, surpass.

überstrahlen [y:bər'ʃtra:lən], *v.a. insep.* outshine, surpass in splendour.

überstreichen [y:bər'ʃtraıçən], *v.a. irr. insep.* paint over.

überströmen [y:bər'ʃtrø:mən], *v.a. insep.* flood, overflow.

Überstunde [y:bər'ʃtundə], *f.* (—, *pl.* —n) extra working time, overtime.

überstürzen [y:bər'ʃtyrtsən], *v.r. insep. sich —*, act in haste.

übertäuben [y:bər'tɔybən], *v.a. insep.* deafen.

überteuern [y:bər'tɔyərn], *v.a. insep.* overcharge.

übertölpeln [y:bər'tœlpəln], *v.a. insep.* cheat.

übertönen [y:bər'tø:nən], *v.a. insep.* (*sound*) drown.

übertragen [y:bər'tra:gən], *v.a. irr. insep.* transfer, hand over; convey; broadcast; translate; (*Comm.*) carry over; *einem ein Amt —*, confer an office on s.o.

Übertragung [y:bər'tra:guŋ], *f.* (—, *pl.* —en) cession; transference; handing over; (*Comm.*) carrying over; (*Rad.*) transmission; (*Med.*) transfusion.

übertreffen [y:bər'trɛfən], *v.a. irr. insep.* surpass, excel, outdo.

übertreiben [y:bər'traıbən], *v.a. irr. insep.* exaggerate.

Übertreibung [y:bər'traıbuŋ], *f.* (—, *pl.* —en) exaggeration.

übertreten (1) [y:bər'tre:tən], *v.n. irr.* (*aux.* sein) go over to; (*river*) overflow; (*religion*) change to, join (*church, party*).

übertreten (2) [y:bər'tre:tən], *v.a. irr. insep.* transgress, trespass against, infringe, violate.

Übertretung [y:bər'tre:tuŋ], *f.* (—, *pl.* —en) transgression, trespass, violation, infringement.

übertrieben [y:bər'tri:bən], *adj.* excessive, immoderate, exaggerated.

Übertritt ['y:bərtrıt], *m.* (—s, *no pl.*) defection, going over; (*Rel.*) change, conversion.

übertünchen [y:bər'tynçən], *v.a. insep.* whitewash, rough-cast; (*fig.*) gloss over.

Übervölkerung [y:bər'fœlkəruŋ], *f.* (—, *no pl.*) overpopulation.

übervoll [y:bər'fɔl], *adj.* overful, brimful, chock-full.

übervorteilen [y:bər'fo:rtaılən], *v.a. insep.* cheat, defraud.

überwachen [y:bər'vaxən], *v.a. insep.* watch over, superintend, supervise.

Überwachung [y:bər'vaxuŋ], *f.* (—, *no pl.*) superintendence, supervision.

überwachsen [y:bər'vaksən], *v.a. irr. insep.* overgrow.

überwältigen [y:bər'vɛltıgən], *v.a. insep.* overcome, overpower, subdue.

überwältigend [y:bər'vɛltıgənt], *adj.* overwhelming.

Überwältigung [y:bər'vɛltıguŋ], *f.* (—, *no pl.*) overpowering.

überweisen [y:bər'vaızən], *v.a. irr. insep.* assign; (*money*) remit.

Überweisung [y:bər'vaızuŋ], *f.* (—, *pl.* —en) assignment; (*money*) remittance.

überwerfen (1) ['y:bərvɛrfən], *v.a. irr.* throw over; (*clothes*) slip on.

überwerfen (2) [y:bər'vɛrfən], *v.r. irr. insep. sich — mit*, fall out with s.o.

überwiegen [y:bər'vi:gən], *v.n. irr. insep.* prevail.

überwiegend [y:bər'vi:gənt], *adj.* paramount, overwhelming, predominant.

überwinden [y:bər'vındən], *v.a. irr. insep.* overcome, conquer. — *v.r. sich —*, prevail upon o.s., bring o.s. (to).

Überwindung [y:bər'vınduŋ], *f.* (—, *no pl.*) conquest; reluctance.

überwintern [y:bər'vıntərn], *v.n. insep.* winter, hibernate.

Überwinterung [y:bər'vıntəruŋ], *f.* (—, *no pl.*) hibernation.

überwölkt [y:bər'vœlkt], *adj.* overcast.

Überwurf ['y:bərvurf], *m.* (—s, *pl.* ⁓e) wrap, shawl, cloak.

Überzahl ['y:bərtsa:l], *f.* (—, *no pl.*) *in der —*, in the majority.

überzählig ['y:bərtse:lıç], *adj.* supernumerary, surplus.

überzeichnen ['y:bərtsaıçnən], *v.a. insep.* (*Comm.*) over-subscribe.

überzeugen [y:bər'tsɔygən], *v.a. insep.* convince. — *v.r. sich—*, satisfy o.s.

Überzeugung [y:bər'tsɔyguŋ], *f.* (—, *no pl.*) conviction.

überziehen (1) ['y:bərtsi:ən], *v.a. irr.* put on (a garment).

überziehen (2) [y:bər'tsi:ən], *v.a. irr. insep.* cover; (*bed*) put fresh linen on; (*Bank*) overdraw.

Überzieher ['y:bərtsi:ər], *m.* (—s, *pl.* —) overcoat.

Überzug ['y:bərtsu:k], *m.* (—s, *pl.* ⁓e) case, cover; bed-tick; coating.

üblich ['y:plıç], *adj.* usual, customary; *nicht mehr —*, out of use, obsolete.

übrig ['y:brıç], *adj.* remaining, left over; *die —en*, the others; — *bleiben*, be left, remain; — *haben*, have left; — *sein*, be left; *im —en*, for the rest; *ein —es tun*, stretch a point; *für einen etwas — haben*, like s.o.

übrigens ['y:brıgəns], *adv.* besides, moreover; by the way.

Übung ['y:buŋ], *f.* (—, *pl.* —en) exercise, practice.

Ufer [ˈuːfər], *n.* (—s, *pl.* —) (*river*) bank; (*sea*) shore, beach.

Uganda [uˈganda], *n.* Uganda.

Uhr [uːr], *f.* (—, *pl.* —en) clock; watch; *elf* —, eleven o'clock; *wieviel — ist es?* what is the time?

Uhrmacher [ˈuːrmaxər], *m.* (—s, *pl.* —) watchmaker, clockmaker.

Uhrwerk [ˈuːrvɛrk], *n.* (—s, *pl.* —e) clockwork.

Uhrzeiger [ˈuːrtsaɪɡər], *m.* (—s, *pl.* —) hand (of clock *or* watch).

Uhu [ˈuːhuː], *m.* (—s, *pl.* —s) (*Orn.*) eagle-owl.

ulkig [ˈʊlkɪç], *adj.* funny.

Ulme [ˈulmə], *f.* (—, *pl.* —en) (*Bot.*) elm, elm-tree.

Ultrakurzwelle [ˈultrakurtsvɛlə], *f.* (—, *pl.* —n) ultra-short wave.

ultrarot [ˈultraroːt], *adj.* infra-red.

Ultrastrahlung [ˈultraʃtraːluŋ], *f.* (—, *pl.* —en) cosmic radiation.

ultraviolett [ˈultraviolet], *adj.* ultra-violet.

um [um], *prep.* (*Acc.*) about, around; approximately, near; for, because of; by; — *Geld bitten,* ask for money; — *5 Uhr,* at five o'clock. — *conj.* to, in order to. — *adv.* up, past, upside down; round about; around.

umarbeiten [ˈumarbaɪtən], *v.a.* do again, remodel, revise; recast.

umarmen [umˈarmən], *v.a. insep.* embrace.

Umarmung [umˈarmuŋ], *f.* (—, *pl.* —en) embrace.

umbauen (1) [ˈumbauən], *v.a.* rebuild.

umbauen (2) [umˈbauən], *v.a. insep.* surround with buildings.

umbiegen [ˈumbiːɡən], *v.a. irr.* bend.

umbilden [ˈumbɪldən], *v.a.* transform, reform, recast, remould.

umbinden [ˈumbɪndən], *v.a. irr. sich etwas* —, tie s.th. around o.s.

umblicken [ˈumblɪkən], *v.r. sich* —, look round.

umbringen [ˈumbrɪŋən], *v.a. irr.* kill, slay, murder.

umdrehen [ˈumdreːən], *v.a.* turn over, turn round, revolve. — *v.r. sich* —, turn round.

Umdrehung [umˈdreːuŋ], *f.* (—, *pl.* —en) revolution, rotation.

umfahren (1) [umˈfaːrən], *v.a. irr. insep.* drive round, circumnavigate.

umfahren (2) [ˈumfaːren], *v.a. irr.* run down.

umfallen [ˈumfalən], *v.n. irr.* (*aux.* sein) fall down, fall over.

Umfang [ˈumfaŋ], *m.* (—s, *pl.* ⁀e) circumference; (*fig.*) extent.

umfangen [umˈfaŋən], *v.a. irr. insep.* encircle, embrace.

umfangreich [ˈumfaŋraɪç], *adj.* extensive, voluminous.

umfassen [umˈfasən], *v.a. insep.* comprise, contain.

umfassend [umˈfasənt], *adj.* comprehensive.

umfließen [umˈfliːsən], *v.a. irr. insep.* surround by water.

umformen [ˈumfɔrmən], *v.a.* transform, remodel.

Umformung [ˈumfɔrmuŋ], *f.* (—, *pl.* —en) transformation, remodelling.

Umfrage [ˈumfraːɡə], *f.* (—, *pl.* —n) enquiry, poll, quiz.

Umfriedung [umˈfriːduŋ], *f.* (—, *pl.* —en) enclosure.

Umgang [ˈumgaŋ], *m.* (—s, *pl.* ⁀e) circuit, procession; (*fig.*) acquaintance, association; relations, connection; — *haben mit,* associate with.

umgänglich [ˈumgɛŋlɪç], *adj.* sociable, companionable.

Umgangsformen [ˈumgaŋsfɔrmən], *f. pl.* manners.

Umgangssprache [ˈumgaŋsʃpraːxə], *f.* (— *pl.* —en) colloquial speech.

umgeben [umˈgeːbən], *v.a. irr. insep.* surround.

Umgebung [umˈgeːbuŋ], *f.* (—, *pl.* —en) environment, surroundings.

umgehen (1) [ˈumgeːən], *v.n. irr.* (*aux.* sein) associate with s.o.; handle s.th.; — *in,* haunt.

umgehen (2) [umˈgeːən], *v.a. irr. insep.* go round; (*flank*) turn; (*fig.*) evade, shirk.

umgehend [ˈumgeːənt], *adv.* immediately; (*letter*) by return mail.

Umgehung [umˈgeːuŋ], *f.* (—, *pl.* —en) shirking, evasion; detour; (*Mil.*) flank movement, turning.

umgekehrt [ˈumgəkeːrt], *adj.* reverse. — *adv.* conversely.

umgestalten [ˈumgəʃtaltən], *v.a.* transform, recast.

Umgestaltung [ˈumgəʃtaltuŋ], *f.* (—, *pl.* —en) transformation; recasting.

umgraben [ˈumgraːbən], *v.a. irr.* dig up.

umgrenzen [umˈgrɛntsən], *v.a. insep.* limit, set bounds to.

Umgrenzung [umˈgrɛntsuŋ], *f.* (—, *pl.* —en) boundary; limitation.

umgucken [ˈumgukən], *v.r. sich* —, look about o.

umhalsen [umˈhalzən], *v.a. insep.* hug, embrace.

Umhang [ˈumhaŋ], *m.* (—s, *pl.* ⁀e) shawl, cloak.

umher [umˈheːr], *adv.* around, round, about.

umherblicken [umˈheːrblɪkən], *v.n.* look round.

umherflattern [umˈheːrflatərn], *v.n.* (*aux.* sein) flutter about.

umherlaufen [umˈheːrlaufən], *v.n. irr.* (*aux.* sein) run about; roam about, ramble, wander.

umherziehend [umˈheːrtsiːənt], *adj.* itinerant.

umhüllen [umˈhylən], *v.a. insep.* envelop, wrap up.

Umkehr [ˈumkeːr], *f.* (—, *no pl.*) return; change; (*fig.*) conversion.

umkehren

umkehren [ˈumkeːrən], *v.a.* turn (back), upset, overturn. — *v.n.* (*aux.* sein) turn back, return.

Umkehrung [ˈumkeːruŋ], *f.* (—, *pl.* —en) inversion.

umkippen [ˈumkɪpən], *v.a.* upset, overturn. — *v.n.* (*aux.* sein) capsize, tilt over.

umklammern [umˈklamərn], *v.a. insep.* clasp; clutch; (*fig.*) cling to.

umkleiden (1) [ˈumklaɪdən], *v.r. sich* —, change o.'s clothes.

umkleiden (2) [umˈklaɪdən], *v.a. insep.* cover.

umkommen [ˈumkɔmən], *v.n. irr.* (*aux.* sein) perish.

Umkreis [ˈumkraɪs], *m.* (—es, *pl.* —e) circumference, compass.

Umlauf [ˈumlauf], *m.* (—s, *no pl.*) circulation; *in — bringen,* put into circulation.

Umlaut [ˈumlaut], *m.* (—s, *pl.* —e) (*Phonet.*) modification of vowels.

umlegen [ˈumleːgən], *v.a.* lay down, move, shift, put about; (*sl.*) kill.

umleiten [ˈumlaɪtən], *v.a.* (*traffic*) divert.

umlernen [ˈumlɛrnən], *v.a., v.n.* relearn; retrain (for new job).

umliegend [ˈumliːgənt], *adj.* surrounding.

ummodeln [ˈummoːdəln], *v.a.* remodel, recast, change, fashion differently.

Umnachtung [umˈnaxtuŋ], *f.* (—, *no pl.*) mental derangement.

umpacken [ˈumpakən], *v.a.* repack.

umpflanzen [ˈumpflantsən], *v.a.* transplant.

Umpflanzung [ˈumpflantsuŋ], *f.* (—, *pl.* —en) transplantation.

umrahmen [ˈumraːmən], *v.a. insep.* frame, surround.

umrändern [umˈrɛndərn], *v.a. insep.* border, edge.

umrechnen [ˈumrɛçnən], *v.a.* (*figures*) reduce, convert.

umreißen (1) [ˈumraɪsən], *v.a. irr.* pull down, break up.

umreißen (2) [umˈraɪsən], *v.a. irr. insep.* sketch, outline.

umrennen [ˈumrɛnən], *v.a. irr.* run down, knock over.

umringen [umˈrɪŋən], *v.a. insep.* encircle, surround.

Umriß [ˈumrɪs], *m.* (—sses, *pl.* —sse) outline, contour.

umrühren [ˈumryːrən], *v.a.* (*Cul.*) stir.

umsatteln [ˈumzatəln], *v.n.* (*fig.*) change o.'s profession.

Umsatz [ˈumzats], *m.* (—es, *pl.* —e) turnover.

umschalten [ˈumʃaltən], *v.a.* (*Elec.*) switch (over); reverse (current).

Umschau [ˈumʃau], *f.* (—, *no pl.*) review, survey; *— halten,* look round, muster, review.

umschauen [ˈumʃauən], *v.r. sich* —, look round.

umschichtig [ˈumʃɪçtɪç], *adv.* turn and turn about, in turns.

umschiffen (1) [ˈumʃɪfən], *v.a.* tranship, transfer (cargo, passengers).

umschiffen (2) [umˈʃɪfən], *v.a. insep.* sail round, circumnavigate.

Umschlag [ˈumʃlaːk], *m.* —(e)s, *pl.* ̈-e) (*weather*) break, sudden change; (*letter*) envelope; (*Med.*) poultice, compress.

umschlagen [ˈumʃlaːgən], *v.n. irr.* (*aux.* sein) (*weather*) change suddenly; capsize; turn sour.

umschließen [umˈʃliːsən], *v.a. irr. insep.* enclose, surround; comprise.

umschlingen [umˈʃliŋən], *v.a. irr. insep.* embrace.

umschnallen [ˈumʃnalən], *v.a.* buckle on.

umschreiben (1) [ˈumʃraɪbən], *v.a. irr. insep.* rewrite, write differently.

umschreiben (2) [umˈʃraɪbən], *v.a. irr. insep.* circumscribe, paraphrase.

Umschreibung [umˈʃraɪbuŋ], *f.* (—, *pl.* —en) paraphrase.

Umschweife [umˈʃvaɪfə], *m.pl.* fuss, talk; circumlocution; *ohne* —, point-blank.

Umschwung [ˈumʃvuŋ], *m.* (—s, *no pl.*) sudden change, revolution.

umsegeln [umˈzeːgəln], *v.a. insep.* sail round.

umsehen [ˈumzeːən], *v.r. irr. sich* —, look round; look out (for); cast about (for).

Umsicht [ˈumzɪçt], *f.* (—, *no pl.*) circumspection.

umsichtig [ˈumzɪçtɪç], *adj.* cautious, circumspect.

umsinken [ˈumzɪŋkən], *v.n. irr.* (*aux.* sein) sink down.

umsonst [umˈzɔnst], *adv.* without payment, gratis, for nothing; in vain, vainly, to no purpose.

umspannen (1) [ˈumʃpanən], *v.a.* change horses.

umspannen (2) [umˈʃpanən], *v.a. insep.* encompass, span.

umspringen [ˈumʃprɪŋən], *v.n. irr.* (*aux.* sein) (*wind*) change suddenly; *mit einem* —, (*fig.*) deal with s.o.

Umstand [ˈumʃtant], *m.* (—s, *pl.* ̈-e) circumstance; fact; factor; (*pl.*) fuss; *in anderen ̈-en sein,* be expecting a baby; *unter keinen ̈-en,* on no account.

umständlich [ˈumʃtentlɪç], *adj.* circumstantial, ceremonious; complicated, fussy.

Umstandswort [ˈumʃtantsvɔrt], *n.* (—es, *pl.* ̈-er) (*Gram.*) adverb.

umstehend [ˈumʃteːənt], *adv.* on the next page.

Umstehenden [ˈumʃteːəndən], *pl.* bystanders.

umsteigen [ˈumʃtaɪgən], *v.n. irr.* (*aux.* sein) change (trains etc.).

umstellen (1) [ˈumʃtelən], *v.a.* place differently, transpose, change over.

umstellen (2) [umˈʃtelən], *v.a. insep.* surround, beset.

Umstellung [ˈumʃtɛluŋ], *f.* (—, *pl.*
—en) transposition; (*Gram.*) inversion; change of position in team.
umstimmen [ˈumʃtimən], *v.a.* turn
s.o. from his opinion, bring s.o.
round to (s.th.).
umstoßen [ˈumʃtoːsən], *v.a. irr.* knock
down, upset, overthrow; (*judgment*)
reverse.
umstricken [um'ʃtrikən], *v.a. insep.*
ensnare.
umstritten [um'ʃtritən], *adj.* controversial, disputed.
umstülpen [ˈumʃtylpən], *v.a.* turn up,
turn upside down.
Umsturz [ˈumʃturts], *m.* (—es, *no pl.*)
downfall; subversion; revolution.
umstürzen [ˈumʃtyrtsən], *v.a.* upset,
overturn; overthrow.
umtaufen [ˈumtaufən], *v.a.* rename,
rechristen.
Umtausch [ˈumtauʃ], *m.* (—s, *no pl.*)
exchange.
umtauschen [ˈumtauʃən], *v.a.* exchange, change.
Umtriebe [ˈumtriːbə], *m. pl.* plots,
goings-on, intrigues.
umtun [ˈumtuːn], *v.r. irr. sich — nach*,
look for, cast about for.
Umwälzung [ˈumvɛltsuŋ], *f.* (—, *pl.*
—en) turning-about; (*fig.*) revolution.
umwandeln [ˈumvandəln], *v.a.* change,
transform; (*Gram.*) inflect.
umwechseln [ˈumvɛksəln], *v.a.* exchange.
Umweg [ˈumveːk], *m.* (—s, *pl.* —e)
roundabout way, detour.
Umwelt [ˈumvɛlt], *f.* (—, *no pl.*)
environment, milieu.
umwenden [ˈumvɛndən], *v.a. irr.* turn
round; turn over. — *v.r. sich* —, turn
round.
umwerben [um'vɛrbən], *v.a. irr. insep.*
court.
umwerfen [ˈumvɛrfən], *v.a. irr.* overturn, knock over, upset.
umwickeln [um'vikəln], *v.a. insep.*
wrap round, wind round.
umwölken [um'vœlkən], *v.r. insep.
sich* —, (*sky*) darken, become overcast.
umzäunen [um'tsɔynən], *v.a. insep.*
hedge in, fence in, enclose.
umziehen (1) [ˈumtsiːən], *v.a. irr.*
change (clothes). — *v.n.* (*aux.* sein)
move (abode).— *v.r. sich* —, change o.'s
clothes.
umziehen (2) [um'tsiːən], *v.r. irr.
insep. sich* —, get overcast, cloud over.
umzingeln [um'tsiŋəln], *v.a. insep.*
surround.
Umzug [ˈumtsuːk], *m.* (—s, *pl.* ⁀e)
procession; removal; move.
unabänderlich [unap'ɛndərliç], *adj.*
unalterable, irrevocable.
Unabänderlichkeit [ˈunapɛndərliç-
kait], *f.* (—, *no pl.*) unchangeableness,
irrevocability.
unabhängig [ˈunaphɛŋiç], *adj.* independent, autonomous; unrelated.

Unabhängigkeit [ˈunaphɛŋiçkait], *f.*
(—, *no pl.*) independence, self-
sufficiency.
unabkömmlich [ˈunapkœmliç], *adj.*
indispensable.
unablässig [ˈunaplɛsiç], *adj.* unceasing, continual, unremitting.
unabsehbar [ˈunapzeːbaːr], *adj.* immeasurable, immense; unfathomable.
unabsichtlich [ˈunapziçtliç], *adj.* unintentional, accidental.
unabwendbar [unap'vɛntbaːr], *adj.*
irremediable; unavoidable.
unachtsam [ˈunaxtzaːm], *adj.* inattentive, inadvertent, negligent, careless.
Unachtsamkeit [ˈunaxtzaːmkait], *f.*
(—, *pl.* —en) inadvertence, in-
attention, negligence, carelessness.
unähnlich [ˈunɛːnliç], *adj.* unlike,
dissimilar.
unanfechtbar [ˈunanfɛçtbaːr], *adj.* indisputable, incontestable.
unangebracht [ˈunangəbraxt], *adj.*
out of place, inapposite.
unangefochten [ˈunangəfɔxtən], *adj.*
undisputed, uncontested.
unangemeldet [ˈunangəmɛldət], *adj.*
unannounced, unheralded.
unangemessen [ˈunangəmɛsən], *adj.*
unsuitable, inappropriate, inadequate.
unangenehm [ˈunangəneːm], *adj.* disagreeable, unpleasant; *einen —
berühren*, jar, grate on s.o.
unangetastet [ˈunangətastət], *adj.* untouched.
unangreifbar [ˈunangraifbaːr], *adj.*
unassailable, secure.
unannehmbar [ˈunanneːmbaːr], *adj.*
unacceptable.
Unannehmlichkeit [ˈunanneːmliç-
kait], *f.* (—, *pl.* —en) unpleasantness,
annoyance.
unansehnlich [ˈunanzeːnliç], *adj.* insignificant; unattractive.
unanständig [ˈunanʃtɛndiç], *adj.* improper, indecent.
Unanständigkeit [ˈunanʃtɛndiçkait], *f.*
(—, *pl.* —en) indecency, immodesty,
impropriety.
unantastbar [ˈunantastbaːr], *adj.* unimpeachable.
unappetitlich [ˈunapetiːtliç], *adj.* distasteful, unsavoury, unappetising.
Unart [ˈunaːrt], *f.* (—, *pl.* —en) bad
habit, naughtiness.
unartig [ˈunaːrtiç], *adj.* ill-behaved,
naughty.
unästhetisch [ˈunɛsteːtiʃ], *adj.* offensive, coarse; inartistic.
unauffällig [ˈunauffɛliç], *adj.* unobtrusive.
unaufgefordert [ˈunaufgəfɔrdərt], *adj.*
unbidden.
unaufgeklärt [ˈunaufgəklɛːrt], *adj.* un-
explained, unsolved.
unaufgeschnitten [ˈunaufgəʃnitən],
adj. uncut.
unaufhaltsam [ˈunaufhaltzaːm], *adj.*
incessant, irresistible.

unaufhörlich ['unaufhø:rlɪç], *adj.* incessant, continual.

unauflöslich ['unauflø:slɪç], *adj.* indissoluble.

unaufmerksam ['unaufmɛrkza:m], *adj.* inattentive.

unaufrichtig ['unaufrɪçtɪç], *adj.* insincere.

unaufschiebbar ['unauf∫i:pba:r], *adj.* urgent, pressing, brooking no delay.

unausbleiblich ['unausblaɪplɪç], *adj.* inevitable, unfailing.

unausführbar ['unausfy:rba:r], *adj.* impracticable.

unausgebildet ['unausgəbɪldət], *adj.* untrained, unskilled.

unausgefüllt ['unausgəfylt], *adj.* not filled up; (*form*) blank.

unausgegoren ['unausgəgo:rən], *adj.* crude; (*wine*) unfermented.

unausgesetzt ['unausgəzɛtst], *adj.* continual, continuous.

unausgesprochen ['unausgə∫prɔxən], *adj.* unsaid; (*fig.*) implied.

unauslöschlich ['unauslø:∫lɪç], indelible, inextinguishable.

unaussprechlich ['unaus∫prɛçlɪç], *adj.* inexpressible, unspeakable.

unausstehlich ['unaus∫te:lɪç], *adj.* insufferable.

unausweichlich ['unausvaɪçlɪç], *adj.* inevitable.

unbändig ['unbɛndɪç], *adj.* intractable, unmanageable; (*fig.*) extreme.

unbarmherzig ['unbarmhɛrtsɪç], *adj.* merciless.

unbeabsichtigt ['unbəapzɪçtɪçt], *adj.* unintentional.

unbeanstandet ['unbəan∫tandət], *adj.* unexceptionable; unopposed; with impunity.

unbeantwortlich ['unbəantvɔrtlɪç], *adj.* unanswerable.

unbeaufsichtigt ['unbəaufzɪçtɪçt], *adj.* unattended to, not looked after; without supervision.

unbebaut ['unbəbaut], *adj.* (*Agr.*) uncultivated; undeveloped (by building).

unbedacht ['unbədaxt], *adj.* thoughtless.

unbedenklich ['unbədɛŋklɪç], *adj.* harmless, innocuous. — *adv.* without hesitation.

unbedeutend ['unbədɔytənt], *adj.* insignificant.

unbedingt ['unbədɪŋkt], *adj.* unconditional, unlimited, absolute. — *adv.* quite definitely; without fail.

unbeeinflußt ['unbəaɪnflust], *adj.* uninfluenced.

unbefahrbar ['unbəfa:rba:r], *adj.* impassable, impracticable.

unbefangen ['unbəfaŋən], *adj.* unbiased, unprejudiced; easy, unselfconscious, unembarrassed, uninhibited; natural.

Unbefangenheit ['unbəfaŋənhaɪt], *f.*

(—, *no pl.*) impartiality; ease of manner, unselfconsciousness, openness, naturalness.

unbefestigt ['unbəfɛstɪçt], *adj.* unfortified.

unbefleckt ['unbəflɛkt], *adj.* immaculate; —*e Empfängnis*, Immaculate Conception.

unbefriedigend ['unbəfri:dɪgənt], *adj.* unsatisfactory.

unbefriedigt ['unbəfri:dɪçt], *adj.* not satisfied, unsatisfied.

unbefugt ['unbəfu:kt], *adj.* unauthorised.

unbegreiflich ['unbəgraɪflɪç], *adj.* incomprehensible, inconceivable.

unbegrenzt ['unbəgrɛntst], *adj.* unlimited, unbounded.

unbegründet ['unbəgryndət], *adj.* unfounded, groundless.

Unbehagen ['unbəha:gən], *n.* (—s, *no pl.*) uneasiness, discomfort.

unbehaglich ['unbəha:klɪç], *adj.* uncomfortable; *sich — fühlen*, feel ill at ease.

unbehelligt ['unbəhɛlɪçt], *adj.* unmolested.

unbeholfen ['unbəhɔlfən], *adj.* awkward, clumsy.

unbeirrt ['unbəɪrt], *adj.* unswerving, uninfluenced, unperturbed.

unbekannt ['unbəkant], *adj.* unknown, unacquainted; *ich bin hier —*, I am a stranger here.

unbekümmert ['unbəkymərt], *adj.* unconcerned, careless, indifferent.

unbelehrt ['unbəle:rt], *adj.* uninstructed.

unbeliebt ['unbəli:pt], *adj.* unpopular.

unbemannt ['unbəmant], *adj.* without crew, unmanned.

unbemerkbar ['unbəmɛrkba:r], *adj.* unnoticeable, imperceptible.

unbemerkt ['unbəmɛrkt], *adj.* unnoticed.

unbemittelt ['unbəmɪtəlt], *adj.* impecunious, poor.

unbenommen ['unbənɔmən], *adj. es bleibt dir —*, you are free to.

unbenutzt ['unbənutst], *adj.* unused.

unbequem ['unbəkve:m], *adj.* uncomfortable, inconvenient, troublesome.

Unbequemlichkeit ['unbəkve:mlɪçkaɪt], *f.* (—, *pl.* —en) inconvenience.

unberechenbar ['unbərɛçənba:r], *adj.* incalculable; (*fig.*) erratic.

unberechtigt ['unbərɛçtɪçt], *adj.* unwarranted, unjustified.

unberücksichtigt ['unbərykzɪçtɪçt], *adj.* disregarded; — *lassen*, ignore.

unberufen ['unbəru:fən], *adj.* unauthorized. — *excl.* touch wood!

unbeschadet ['unbə∫a:dət], *prep.* (*Genit.*) without prejudice to.

unbeschädigt ['unbə∫ɛ:dɪçt], *adj.* undamaged.

unbeschäftigt ['unbə∫ɛftɪçt], *adj.* unemployed, disengaged.

unbescheiden ['unbəʃaɪdən], *adj.* presumptuous, greedy, immodest; unblushing; exorbitant; arrogant.

Unbescheidenheit ['unbəʃaɪdənhaɪt], *f.* (—, *no pl.*) presumptuousness, greed.

unbescholten ['unbəʃɔltən], *adj.* irreproachable, of unblemished character.

Unbescholtenheit ['unbəʃɔltənhaɪt], *f.* (—, *no pl.*) blamelessness, good character, unsullied reputation.

unbeschränkt ['unbəʃrɛŋkt], *adj.* unlimited, unbounded; —*e Monarchie*, absolute monarchy.

unbeschreiblich ['unbəʃraɪplɪç], *adj.* indescribable.

unbeschrieben ['unbəʃriːbən], *adj.* unwritten; *ein* —*es Papier*, a blank sheet of paper.

unbeschwert ['unbəʃveːrt], *adj.* unburdened; easy.

unbeseelt ['unbəzeːlt], *adj.* inanimate.

unbesiegbar [unbə'ziːkbaːr], *adj.* invincible.

unbesoldet ['unbəzɔldət], *adj.* unpaid, unsalaried.

unbesonnen ['unbəzɔnən], *adj.* thoughtless, rash.

Unbesonnenheit ['unbəzɔnənhaɪt], *f.* (—, *pl.* —en) thoughtlessness.

unbesorgt ['unbəzɔrkt], *adj.* unconcerned; *sei* —, never fear.

unbeständig ['unbəʃtendɪç], *adj.* fickle, inconstant; (*weather*) unsettled.

unbestechlich ['unbəʃteçlɪç], *adj.* incorruptible.

unbestellbar ['unbəʃtelbaːr], *adj.* not deliverable; (*letters etc.*) address(ee) unknown.

unbestellt ['unbəʃtelt], *adj.* not ordered; (*Agr.*) uncultivated, untilled.

unbestimmt ['unbəʃtɪmt], *adj.* uncertain, not settled; indefinite; irresolute; vague.

unbestraft ['unbəʃtraːft], *adj.* unpunished; without previous conviction.

unbestreitbar ['unbəʃtraɪtbaːr], *adj.* indisputable, incontestable.

unbestritten ['unbəʃtrɪtən], *adj.* uncontested, undoubted, undisputed.

unbeteiligt ['unbətaɪlɪçt], *adj.* unconcerned, indifferent.

unbeträchtlich ['unbətreçtlɪç], *adj.* inconsiderable, trivial.

unbetreten ['unbətreːtən], *adj.* untrodden, untouched.

unbeugsam ['unbɔykzaːm], *adj.* inflexible, unyielding.

unbewacht ['unbəvaxt], *adj.* unguarded.

unbewaffnet ['unbəvafnət], *adj.* unarmed; *mit* —*em Auge*, with the naked eye.

unbewandert ['unbəvandərt], *adj.* unversed in, unfamiliar with.

unbezahlt ['unbətsaːlt], *adj.* unpaid.

unbezähmbar ['unbətse:mbaːr], *adj.* uncontrollable; indomitable.

unbezwinglich ['unbətsvɪŋlɪç], *adj.* invincible, unconquerable.

Unbildung ['unbɪlduŋ], *f.* (—, *no pl.*) lack of education *or* knowledge *or* culture.

Unbill ['unbɪl], *f.* (—, *pl.* **Unbilden**) injustice, wrong, injury; (*weather*) inclemency.

unbillig ['unbɪlɪç], *adj.* unreasonable, unfair.

Unbilligkeit ['unbɪlɪçkaɪt], *f.* (—, *no pl.*) unreasonableness, injustice, unfairness.

unbotmäßig ['unbo:tmɛːsɪç], *adj.* unruly, insubordinate.

unbußfertig ['unbuːsfertɪç], *adj.* impenitent, unrepentant.

und [unt], *conj.* and; — *nicht*, nor; — *so weiter* (abbr. *u.s.w.*), etc., and so on, and so forth; — *wenn*, even if.

Undank ['undaŋk], *m.* (—s, *no pl.*) ingratitude.

undankbar ['undaŋkbaːr], *adj.* ungrateful; *eine* —*e Aufgabe*, a thankless task.

Undankbarkeit ['undaŋkbaːrkaɪt], *f.* (—, *no pl.*) ingratitude.

undenkbar ['undeŋkbaːr], *adj.* unthinkable, unimaginable, inconceivable.

undenklich ['undeŋklɪç], *adj. seit* —*en Zeiten*, from time immemorial.

undeutlich ['undɔytlɪç], *adj.* indistinct; inarticulate; (*fig.*) unintelligible.

Unding ['undɪŋ], *n.* (—s, *no pl.*) absurdity.

unduldsam ['undultzaːm], *adj.* intolerant.

undurchdringlich ['undurçdrɪŋlɪç], *adj.* impenetrable.

undurchführbar ['undurçfyːrbaːr], *adj.* impracticable, unworkable.

undurchsichtig ['undurçzɪçtɪç], *adj.* opaque, not transparent.

uneben ['uneːbən], *adj.* uneven, rugged; (*coll.*) *nicht* —, not bad.

unecht ['uneçt], *adj.* false, not genuine, spurious, counterfeit.

unedel ['uneːdəl], *adj.* (*metal*) base.

unehelich ['uneːəlɪç], *adj.* illegitimate.

Unehre ['uneːrə], *f.* (—, *no pl.*) dishonour, disgrace, discredit.

unehrlich ['uneːrlɪç], *adj.* dishonest.

Unehrlichkeit ['uneːrlɪçkaɪt], *f.* (—, *pl.* —en) dishonesty.

uneigennützig ['unaɪgənnytsɪç], *adj.* unselfish, disinterested, public-spirited.

uneingedenk ['unaɪngədeŋk], *adj.* (*Genit.*) unmindful, forgetful.

uneingeschränkt ['unaɪngəʃreŋkt], *adj.* unrestrained, unlimited.

uneinig ['unaɪnɪç], **uneins** ['unaɪns], *adj.* disunited, divided; — *werden*, fall out; — *sein*, disagree.

Uneinigkeit ['unaɪnɪçkaɪt], *f.* (—, *pl.* —en) disharmony, discord.

uneinnehmbar ['unaɪnneːmbaːr], *adj.* unconquerable, impregnable.

uneins *see under* **uneinig.**
unempfänglich ['unɛmpfɛŋlɪç], *adj.*
  insusceptible; unreceptive.
unempfindlich ['unɛmpfɪntlɪç], *adj.*
  insensitive, indifferent; unfeeling.
unendlich [un'ɛntlɪç], *adj.* endless,
  infinite.
unentbehrlich ['unɛntbe:rlɪç], *adj.*
  indispensable, (absolutely) essential.
unentgeltlich [unɛnt'gɛltlɪç], *adj.* free
  (of charge).
unentschieden ['unɛntʃi:dən], *adj.* undecided, undetermined; irresolute;
  (*game*) drawn, tied.
unentschlossen ['unɛntʃlɔsən], *adj.*
  irresolute.
Unentschlossenheit ['unɛntʃlɔsən-
  haɪt], *f.* (—, *no pl.*) irresolution,
  indecision.
unentschuldbar ['unɛntʃultba:r], *adj.*
  inexcusable.
unentstellt ['unɛntʃtɛlt], *adj.* undis-
  torted.
unentwegt ['unɛntve:kt], *adj.* steadfast, unflinching, unswerving.
unentwickelt ['unɛntvɪkəlt], *adj.* undeveloped; —e *Länder*, under-
  developed countries.
unentwirrbar ['unɛntvɪrba:r], *adj.* inextricable.
unentzifferbar ['unɛnttsɪfərba:r], *adj.*
  indecipherable.
unentzündbar ['unɛnttsyntba:r], *adj.*
  non-inflammable.
unerachtet ['unɛraxtət], *prep.* (*Genit.*)
  (*obs.*) notwithstanding.
unerbeten ['unɛrbe:tən], *adj.* unsolicited.
unerbittlich ['unɛrbɪtlɪç], *adj.* inexorable.
unerfahren ['unɛrfa:rən], *adj.* inexperienced.
unerforschlich ['unɛrfɔrʃlɪç], *adj.* inscrutable.
unerfreulich ['unɛrfrɔylɪç], *adj.* unpleasant, displeasing, disagreeable.
unerfüllbar ['unɛrfylba:r], *adj.* un-
  realisable.
unerfüllt ['unɛrfylt], *adj.* unfulfilled.
unergründlich ['unɛrgryntlɪç], *adj.*
  unfathomable, impenetrable.
unerheblich ['unɛrhe:plɪç], *adj.*
  trifling, unimportant.
unerhört ['unɛrhø:rt], *adj.* unpre-
  cedented, unheard of, shocking, outrageous; not granted; turned
  down.
unerkannt ['unɛrkant], *adj.* unrecog-
  nised.
unerkennbar ['unɛrkɛnba:r], *adj.* unrecognisable.
unerklärlich ['unɛrklɛ:rlɪç], *adj.* inexplicable.
unerläßlich ['unɛrlɛslɪç], *adj.* indispensable.
unerlaubt ['unɛrlaupt], *adj.* unlawful,
  illicit.
unermeßlich ['unɛrmɛslɪç], *adj.*
  immense, vast.

unermüdlich ['unɛrmy:tlɪç], *adj.* untiring, indefatigable.
unerquicklich ['unɛrkvɪklɪç], *adj.* un-
  edifying, disagreeable.
unerreichbar ['unɛrraɪçba:r], *adj.* un-
  attainable, inaccessible.
unerreicht ['unɛrraɪçt], *adj.* unequalled.
unersättlich ['unɛrzɛtlɪç], *adj.* insatiable, greedy.
unerschöpflich ['unɛrʃœpflɪç], *adj.*
  inexhaustible.
unerschöpft ['unɛrʃœpft], *adj.* unexhausted.
unerschrocken ['unɛrʃrɔkən], *adj.* intrepid, undaunted.
unerschütterlich ['unɛrʃytərlɪç], *adj.*
  imperturbable.
unerschüttert ['unɛrʃytərt], *adj.* un-
  shaken, unperturbed.
unerschwinglich ['unɛrʃvɪŋlɪç], *adj.*
  prohibitive, exorbitant, unattain-
  able.
unersetzlich ['unɛrzɛtslɪç], *adj.* ir-
  replaceable.
unersprießlich ['unɛrʃpri:slɪç], *adj.*
  unprofitable.
unerträglich ['unɛrtrɛ:klɪç], *adj.* intolerable, insufferable.
unerwartet ['unɛrvartət], *adj.* unexpected.
unerwidert ['unɛrvi:dərt], *adj.* (*love*)
  unrequited; (*letter*) unanswered.
unerwünscht ['unɛrvynʃt], *adj.* un-
  desirable, unwelcome.
unerzogen ['unɛrtso:gən], *adj.* un-
  educated; ill-bred, unmannerly.
unfähig ['unfɛ:ɪç], *adj.* incapable,
  unable, unfit.
Unfähigkeit ['unfɛ:ɪçkaɪt], *f.* (—, *no
  pl.*) incapability, inability, unfit-
  ness.
Unfall ['unfal], *m.* (—s, *pl.* ⸚e) accident.
unfaßbar ['unfasba:r], *adj.* incomprehensible, inconceivable.
unfehlbar ['unfe:lba:r], *adj.* inevitable;
  infallible.
Unfehlbarkeit ['unfe:lba:rkaɪt], *f.* (—,
  no pl.) infallibility.
unfein ['unfaɪn], *adj.* indelicate, coarse,
  impolite.
unfern ['unfɛrn], *prep.* (*Genit., Dat.*)
  not far from.
unfertig ['unfɛrtɪç], *adj.* unfinished,
  unready.
unflätig ['unflɛ:tɪç], *adj.* obscene,
  nasty, filthy.
unfolgsam ['unfɔlkza:m], *adj.* disobedient, recalcitrant.
unförmig ['unfœrmɪç], *adj.* deformed,
  ill-shaped, misshapen.
unförmlich ['unfœrmlɪç], *adj.* shapeless; free and easy, unceremonious.
unfrankiert ['unfraŋki:rt], *adj.* (*letter*)
  not prepaid, unstamped, unfranked.
unfrei ['unfraɪ], *adj.* not free; sub-
  jugated; constrained.
unfreiwillig ['unfraɪvɪlɪç], *adj.* involuntary.

unfreundlich ['unfrɔyntlɪç], *adj.* unfriendly, unkind; *(weather)* inclement.

Unfreundlichkeit ['unfrɔyntlɪçkaɪt], *f.* (—, *pl.* —en) unfriendliness, unkindness; *(weather)* inclemency.

Unfrieden ['unfri:dən], *m.* (—s, *no pl.*) discord, dissension.

unfruchtbar ['unfruxtba:r], *adj.* barren, sterile; *(fig.)* fruitless.

Unfug ['unfu:k], *m.* (—s, *no pl.*) disturbance, misconduct; mischief; *grober* —, public nuisance.

unfühlbar ['unfy:lba:r], *adj.* imperceptible.

ungangbar ['unganba:r], *adj.* impassable.

Ungarn ['uŋgarn], *n.* Hungary.

ungastlich ['ungastlɪç], *adj.* inhospitable.

ungeachtet ['ungəaxtət], *prep. (Genit.)* notwithstanding.

ungeahndet ['ungəa:ndət], *adj.* unpunished, with impunity.

ungeahnt ['ungəa:nt], *adj.* unexpected, unsuspected, undreamt of.

ungebändigt ['ungəbɛndɪçt], *adj.* untamed.

ungebärdig ['ungəbɛ:rdɪç], *adj.* unmannerly, refractory.

ungebeten ['ungəbe:tən], *adj.* uninvited, unbidden.

ungebleicht ['ungəblaɪçt], *adj.* unbleached.

ungebraucht ['ungəbrauxt], *adj.* unused.

Ungebühr ['ungəby:r], *f.* (—, *no pl.*) unseemliness, impropriety, excess.

ungebührlich ['ungəby:rlɪç], *adj.* unseemly.

ungebunden ['ungəbundən], *adj.* unbound, in sheets; unrestrained, loose; unlinked; *—e Rede,* prose.

Ungeduld ['ungədult], *f.* (—, *no pl.*) impatience.

ungeduldig ['ungəduldɪç], *adj.* impatient.

ungeeignet ['ungəaɪgnət], *adj.* unfit, unsuitable.

ungefähr ['ungəfɛ:r], *adj.* approximate, rough. — *adv.* approximately, roughly, about, round.

ungefährlich ['ungəfɛ:rlɪç], *adj.* not dangerous, harmless, safe.

ungefällig ['ungəfɛlɪç], *adj.* ungracious, disobliging.

ungefärbt ['ungəfɛrpt], *adj.* uncoloured; *(fig.)* unvarnished.

ungefüge ['ungəfy:gə], *adj.* clumsy.

ungehalten ['ungəhaltən], *adj.* indignant, angry.

ungeheißen ['ungəhaɪsən], *adj.* unbidden. — *adv.* of o.'s own accord.

ungehemmt ['ungəhɛmt], *adj.* unchecked, uninhibited.

ungeheuchelt ['ungəhɔyçəlt], *adj.* unfeigned.

Ungeheuer ['ungəhɔyər], *n.* (—s, *pl.* —) monster, monstrosity.

ungeheuer ['ungəhɔyər], *adj.* huge, immense; atrocious, frightful.

ungehobelt ['ungəho:bəlt], *adj.* unplaned; *(fig.)* boorish, uncultured, unpolished.

ungehörig ['ungəhø:rɪç], *adj.* unseemly, improper.

Ungehorsam ['ungəho:rza:m], *m.* (—s, *no pl.*) disobedience.

ungehorsam ['ungəho:rza:m], *adj.* disobedient; — *sein,* disobey.

Ungehorsamkeit ['ungəho:rza:mkaɪt], *f.* (—, *pl.* —en) disobedience, insubordination.

ungekämmt ['ungəkɛmt], *adj.* unkempt.

ungekünstelt ['ungəkynstəlt], *adj.* artless, unstudied.

ungeladen ['ungəla:dən], *adj. (gun)* unloaded, not charged; uninvited.

ungeläutert ['ungəlɔytərt], *adj.* unrefined; unpurified.

ungelegen ['ungəle:gən], *adj.* inconvenient, inopportune.

Ungelegenheit ['ungəle:gənhaɪt], *f.* (—, *pl.* —en) inconvenience, trouble.

ungelehrig ['ungəle:rɪç], *adj.* intractable, unintelligent.

ungelenk ['ungəlɛŋk], *adj.* clumsy, awkward; ungainly.

ungelöscht ['ungəlœʃt], *adj.* unquenched; *(lime)* unslaked; *(mortgage)* unredeemed.

Ungemach ['ungəma:x], *n.* (—(e)s, *no pl.*) adversity, toil, privation.

ungemein ['ungəmaɪn], *adj.* uncommon, extraordinary. — *adv.* very much, exceedingly.

ungemütlich ['ungəmy:tlɪç], *adj.* uncomfortable, cheerless, unpleasant.

ungeniert ['unʒeni:rt], *adj.* free and easy, unceremonious, unabashed.

ungenießbar ['ungə'ni:sba:r], *adj.* unpalatable, uneatable, inedible.

ungenügend ['ungənygənt], *adj.* insufficient, unsatisfactory.

ungenügsam ['ungəny:kza:m], *adj.* insatiable, greedy.

ungeordnet ['ungəɔrdnət], *adj.* illassorted, confused.

ungepflegt ['ungəpfle:kt], *adj.* uncared for, neglected.

ungerade ['ungəra:də], *adj.* uneven; *Zahl,* odd number.

ungeraten ['ungəra:tən], *adj.* abortive, unsuccessful, spoiled; undutiful; illbred.

ungerecht ['ungərɛçt], *adj.* unjust, unfair.

ungerechtfertigt ['ungərɛçtfertɪçt], *adj.* unwarranted, unjustified.

Ungerechtigkeit ['ungərɛçtɪçkaɪt], *f.* (—, *pl.* —en) injustice.

ungeregelt ['ungərə:gəlt], *adj.* not regulated, irregular.

ungereimt ['ungəraɪmt], *adj.* rhymeless; *—es Zeug,* nonsense, absurdity.

ungern ['ungɛrn], *adv.* unwillingly, reluctantly.

ungerufen ['ungəru:fən], *adj.* un-bidden.

ungerührt ['ungəry:rt], *adj.* unmoved.

ungesäumt ['ungəzɔymt], *adj.* un-seamed, unhemmed; (*fig.*) im-mediate. — *adv.* immediately, without delay.

ungeschehen ['ungəʃe:ən], *adj.* un-done; — *machen*, undo.

Ungeschick ['ungəʃɪk], *n.* (—s, *no pl.*) awkwardness, clumsiness.

Ungeschicklichkeit ['ungəʃɪklɪçkaɪt], *f.* (—, *pl.* —en) awkwardness, clumsi-ness.

ungeschickt ['ungəʃɪkt], *adj.* awkward, clumsy, unskilful.

ungeschlacht ['ungəʃlaxt], *adj.* un-couth, unwieldy; coarse, rude.

ungeschliffen ['ungəʃlɪfən], *adj.* un-polished; (*fig.*) coarse.

Ungeschliffenheit ['ungəʃlɪfənhaɪt], *f.* (—, *no pl.*) coarseness, uncouthness.

ungeschmälert ['ungəʃmɛ:lərt], *adj.* undiminished, unimpaired.

ungeschminkt ['ungəʃmɪŋkt], *adj.* without cosmetics *or* make-up, not made up; (*truth*) plain, unvarnished.

ungeschoren ['ungəʃo:rən], *adj.* un-shorn; *laß mich* —, leave me alone.

ungeschult ['ungəʃu:lt], *adj.* un-trained.

ungeschwächt ['ungəʃvɛçt], *adj.* un-impaired.

ungesellig ['ungəzɛlɪç], *adj.* unsociable.

ungesetzlich ['ungəzɛtslɪç], *adj.* illegal, unlawful, illicit.

ungesetzmäßig ['ungəzɛtsmɛ:sɪç], *adj.* illegitimate, lawless; exceptional; not regular.

ungesiegelt ['ungəzi:gəlt], *adj.* un-sealed.

Ungestalt ['ungəʃtalt], *f.* (—, *no pl.*) deformity.

ungestalt ['ungəʃtalt], *adj.* misshapen, deformed.

ungestempelt ['ungəʃtɛmpəlt], *adj.* unstamped, uncancelled, not post-marked.

ungestillt ['ungəʃtɪlt], *adj.* unquenched, unslaked; not fed, unsatisfied.

ungestört ['ungəʃtø:rt], *adj.* undis-turbed.

ungestraft ['ungəʃtra:ft], *adj.* un-punished. — *adv.* with impunity.

ungestüm ['ungəʃty:m], *adj.* im-petuous.

Ungestüm ['ungəʃty:m], *m. & n.* (—s, *no pl.*) impetuosity.

ungesund ['ungəzunt], *adj.* unwhole-some, unhealthy, sickly; (*fig.*) un-natural, morbid.

ungetan ['ungəta:n], *adj.* not done, left undone.

ungetreu ['ungətrɔy], *adj.* disloyal, faithless.

ungetrübt ['ungətry:pt], *adj.* un-troubled.

ungewandt ['ungəvant], *adj.* unskilful.

ungewaschen ['ungəvaʃən], *adj.* un-washed; (*sl.*) —*es Mundwerk*, mal-icious tongue.

ungeweiht ['ungəvaɪt], *adj.* uncon-secrated.

ungewiß ['ungəvɪs], *adj.* uncertain, doubtful.

Ungewißheit ['ungəvɪshaɪt], *f.* (—, *no pl.*) uncertainty, suspense.

Ungewitter ['ungəvɪtər], *n.* (—s, *pl.* —) storm, thunderstorm.

ungewöhnlich ['ungəvø:nlɪç], *adj.* un-usual, uncommon.

Ungewohntheit ['ungəvo:nthaɪt], *f.* (—, *no pl.*) strangeness; want of practice.

ungezähmt ['ungətsɛ:mt], *adj.* un-tamed; (*fig.*) uncurbed.

Ungeziefer ['ungətsi:fər], *n.* (—s, *pl.* —) vermin.

ungeziert ['ungətsi:rt], *adj.* unaffected, natural.

ungezogen ['ungətso:gən], *adj.* ill-mannered, naughty.

ungezügelt ['ungətsy:gəlt], *adj.* un-bridled; (*fig.*) unruly.

ungezwungen ['ungətsvuŋən], *adj.* unforced; (*fig.*) unaffected.

Ungezwungenheit ['ungətsvuŋənhaɪt], *f.* (—, *no pl.*) naturalness, ease.

Unglaube ['unglaubə], *m.* (—ns, *no pl.*) disbelief.

unglaubhaft ['unglauphaft], *adj.* un-authenticated, incredible.

ungläubig ['unglɔybɪç], *adj.* incredu-lous, disbelieving.

Ungläubige ['unglɔybɪgə], *m.* (—n, *pl.* —n) unbeliever.

unglaublich ['unglauplɪç], *adj.* in-credible, unbelievable.

unglaubwürdig ['unglaupvyrdɪç], *adj.* unauthenticated, incredible.

ungleichartig ['unglaɪtça:rtɪç], *adj.* dissimilar, heterogeneous.

ungleichförmig ['unglaɪtçfœrmɪç], *adj.* not uniform; dissimilar.

Ungleichheit ['unglaɪçhaɪt], *f.* (—, *pl.* —en) inequality; unlikeness, dis-similarity; unevenness.

ungleichmäßig ['unglaɪçmɛ:sɪç], *adj.* unequal, irregular; changeable, fitful.

Unglimpf ['unglɪmpf], *m.* (—(e)s, *no pl.*) harshness; insult.

Unglück ['unglyk], *n.* (—s, *pl.* —sfälle) misfortune, adversity, ill-luck; acci-dent, disaster; distress, sorrow, affliction.

unglückbringend ['unglykbrɪŋənt], *adj.* disastrous, unpropitious.

unglücklich ['unglyklɪç], *adj.* un-fortunate, unhappy, unlucky; —*e Liebe*, unrequited love.

unglücklicherweise ['unglyklɪçər-vaɪzə], *adv.* unfortunately, unluckily.

Unglücksbotschaft ['unglyksbo:tʃaft], *f.* (—, *pl.* —en) bad news.

unglückselig ['unglykze:lɪç], *adj.* luck-less, wretched, unfortunate, calamitous.

Unglücksfall ['unglyksfal], *m.* (—(e)s, *pl.* ⸚e) accident.

Unordnung

Unglücksgefährte [ˈunglyksgəfɛːrtə], *m.* (**—n**, *pl.* **—n**) companion in misfortune.

Ungnade [ˈungnaːdə], *f.* (**—**, *no pl.*) disgrace.

ungültig [ˈungyltiç], *adj.* invalid, void; — *machen*, invalidate, annul.

Ungunst [ˈungunst], *f.* (**—**, *no pl.*) disfavour; unpropitiousness; (*weather*) inclemency.

ungünstig [ˈungynstiç], *adj.* unfavourable, adverse.

ungut [ˈunguːt], *adv. etwas für — nehmen*, take s.th. amiss.

unhaltbar [ˈunhaltbaːr], *adj.* untenable.

Unheil [ˈunhail], *n.* (**—s**, *no pl.*) mischief, harm; disaster.

unheilbar [ˈunhailbaːr], *adj.* incurable.

unheilbringend [ˈunhailbriŋənt], *adj.* ominous, unlucky; disastrous.

Unheilstifter [ˈunhailʃtiftər], *m.* (**—s**, *pl.* **—**) mischief-maker.

unheilvoll [ˈunhailfɔl], *adj.* calamitous, disastrous.

unheimlich [ˈunhaimliç], *adj.* weird, eerie, uncanny.

unhöflich [ˈunhøːfliç], *adj.* impolite, uncivil, discourteous.

Unhold [ˈunhɔlt], *m.* (**—s**, *pl.* **—e**) fiend, monster.

Unhörbarkeit [ˈunhøːrbaːrkait], *f.* (**—**, *no pl.*) inaudibility.

Uniformität [uniˈfɔrmiˈtɛːt], *f.* (**—**, *no pl.*) uniformity.

Unikum [ˈuːnikum], *n.* (**—s**, *pl.* **—s**) unique thing *or* person; eccentric.

Universalmittel [univerˈzaːlmitəl], *n.* (**—s**, *pl.* **—**) panacea, universal remedy.

Universität [univerziˈtɛːt], *f.* (**—**, *pl.* **—en**) university.

Universitätsdozent [univerziˈtɛːtsdotsɛnt], *m.* (**—en**, *pl.* **—en**) university lecturer.

Universum [uniˈvɛrzum], *n.* (**—s**, *no pl.*) universe.

unkaufmännisch [ˈunkaufmɛniʃ], *adj.* unbusinesslike.

Unke [ˈuŋkə], *f.* (**—**, *pl.* **—n**) (*Zool.*) toad; (*fig.*) grumbler, pessimist.

unken [ˈuŋkən], *v.n.* grumble, grouse.

unkenntlich [ˈunkɛntliç], *adj.* indiscernible, unrecognisable.

Unkenntlichkeit [ˈunkɛntliçkait], *f.* (**—**, *no pl.*) *bis zur* **—**, past recognition.

Unkenntnis [ˈunkɛntnis], *f.* (**—**, *no pl.*) ignorance.

unklug [ˈunkluːk], *adj.* imprudent.

Unkosten [ˈunkɔstən], *f. pl.* expenses, costs, charges; overheads.

Unkraut [ˈunkraut], *n.* (**—s**, *no pl.*) weed(s).

unkündbar [ˈunkyntbaːr], *adj.* irredeemable; irrevocable, permanent.

unkundig [ˈunkundiç], *adj.* ignorant (of), unacquainted (with).

unlängst [ˈunlɛŋst], *adv.* recently, lately, not long ago.

unlauter [ˈunlautər], *adj.* sordid, squalid; unfair.

unleidlich [ˈunlaitliç], *adj.* intolerable.

unleserlich [ˈunleːzərliç], *adj.* illegible.

unleugbar [ˈunlɔykbaːr], *adj.* undeniable, indisputable.

unlieb [ˈunliːp], *adj.* disagreeable.

unliebenswürdig [ˈunliːbənsvyrdiç], *adj.* sullen, surly.

unlösbar [ˈunløːsbaːr], *adj.* insoluble.

unlöslich [ˈunløːsliç], *adj.* (*substance*) indissoluble, insoluble.

Unlust [ˈunlust], *f.* (**—**, *no pl.*) aversion, disinclination; slackness.

unlustig [ˈunlustiç], *adj.* averse, disinclined.

unmanierlich [ˈunmaniˈrliç], *adj.* illmannered.

unmännlich [ˈunmɛnliç], *adj.* unmanly, effeminate.

Unmaß [ˈunmaːs], *n.* (**—es**, *no pl.*) excess.

Unmasse [ˈunmasə], *f.* (**—**, *pl.* **—n**) vast quantity.

unmaßgeblich [ˈunmaːsgeːpliç], *adj.* unauthoritative, open to correction; (*fig.*) humble.

unmäßig [ˈunmɛːsiç], *adj.* intemperate, excessive.

Unmenge [ˈunmeŋə], *f.* (**—**, *pl.* **—n**) vast quantity.

Unmensch [ˈunmɛnʃ], *m.* (**—en**, *pl.* **—en**) brute.

unmenschlich [ˈunmɛnʃliç], *adj.* inhuman, brutal; (*coll.*) vast.

unmerklich [ˈunmɛrkliç], *adj.* imperceptible.

unmeßbar [ˈunmɛsbaːr], *adj.* immeasurable.

unmittelbar [ˈunmitəlbaːr], *adj.* immediate, direct.

unmöglich [ˈunmøːkliç], *adj.* impossible.

unmündig [ˈunmyndiç], *adj.* under age, minor.

Unmündige [ˈunmyndigə], *m.* (**—n**, *pl.* **—n**) (*Law*) minor.

Unmündigkeit [ˈunmyndiçkait], *f.* (**—**, *no pl.*) minority.

Unmut [ˈunmuːt], *m.* (**—s**, *no pl.*) ill-humour; displeasure, indignation, petulance.

unmutig [ˈunmuːtiç], *adj.* ill-humoured, petulant, indignant.

unnachahmlich [ˈunnaxaˈmliç], *adj.* inimitable.

unnachgiebig [ˈunnaxgiːbiç], *adj.* relentless, unyielding.

unnachsichtig [ˈunnaxziçtiç], *adj.* unrelenting, relentless.

unnahbar [ˈunnaːbaːr], *adj.* unapproachable, stand-offish.

unnennbar [ˈunnɛnbaːr], *adj.* unutterable.

unnütz [ˈunnyts], *adj.* useless.

unordentlich [ˈunɔrdəntliç], *adj.* untidy, slovenly.

Unordnung [ˈunɔrdnuŋ], *f.* (**—**, *no pl.*) disorder, untidiness, muddle, confusion.

243

unparteiisch ['unpartaɪʃ], *adj.* impartial, unbiased, objective.

unpassend ['unpasənt], *adj.* unsuitable, inappropriate; improper.

unpassierbar ['unpasiːrbaːr], *adj.* impassable.

unpäßlich ['unpɛslɪç], *adj.* indisposed, unwell, out of sorts.

Unpäßlichkeit ['unpɛslɪçkaɪt], *f.* (—, *pl.* —en) indisposition.

unproportioniert ['unprɔpɔrtsjoniːrt], *adj.* disproportionate; unshapely.

unqualifizierbar ['unkvalifitsiːrbaːr], *adj.* unspeakable, nameless.

Unrat ['unraːt], *m.* (—(e)s, *no pl.*) dirt, rubbish.

unratsam ['unraːtzaːm], *adj.* inadvisable.

Unrecht ['unrɛçt], *n.* (—(e)s, *no pl.*) wrong, injustice; — *haben*, be in the wrong.

unrecht ['unrɛçt], *adj.* wrong, unjust.

unrechtmäßig ['unrɛçtmɛːsɪç], *adj.* unlawful, illegal.

unredlich ['unreːtlɪç], *adj.* dishonest.

unregelmäßig ['unreːgəlmɛːsɪç], *adj.* irregular.

unreif ['unraɪf], *adj.* unripe, immature; (*fig.*) crude, raw.

Unreife ['unraɪfə], *f.* (—, *no pl.*) immaturity.

unrein ['unraɪn], *adj.* unclean; (*fig.*) impure.

Unreinheit ['unraɪnhaɪt], *f.* (—, *pl.* —en) impurity.

Unreinlichkeit ['unraɪnlɪçkaɪt], *f.* (—, *no pl.*) uncleanliness.

unrentabel ['unrɛntaːbəl], *adj.* unprofitable.

unrettbar ['unrɛtbaːr], *adj.* irretrievable, hopelessly lost.

unrichtig ['unrɪçtɪç], *adj.* incorrect, erroneous, wrong.

Unrichtigkeit ['unrɪçtɪçkaɪt], *f.* (—, *no pl.*) error, falsity, incorrectness.

Unruhe ['unruːə], *f.* (—, *pl.* —en) unrest, restlessness; disquiet, uneasiness; riot, disturbance; (*clock*) balance.

Unruhestifter ['unruːəʃtɪftər], *m.* (—s, *pl.* —) disturber (of the peace); troublemaker.

unruhig ['unruːɪç], *adj.* restless; troublesome, turbulent, uneasy (about), fidgety.

unrühmlich ['unryːmlɪç], *adj.* inglorious.

uns [uns], *pers. pron.* us, ourselves; to us.

unsachlich ['unzaxlɪç], *adj.* subjective; irrelevant.

unsagbar ['unzaːkbaːr], *adj.* unutterable, unspeakable.

unsanft ['unzanft], *adj.* harsh, violent.

unsauber ['unzaubər], *adj.* unclean, dirty; (*fig.*) squalid.

unschädlich ['unʃeːtlɪç], *adj.* harmless, innocuous.

unschätzbar ['unʃɛtsbaːr], *adj.* invaluable.

unscheinbar ['unʃaɪnbaːr], *adj.* plain, homely, insignificant.

unschicklich ['unʃɪklɪç], *adj.* unbecoming, indecent, improper, unseemly.

unschlüssig ['unʃlysɪç], *adj.* irresolute, undecided.

Unschuld ['unʃult], *f.* (—, *no pl.*) innocence; *verfolgte* —, injured innocence.

unschuldig ['unʃuldɪç], *adj.* innocent, guiltless; chaste; —*es Vergnügen*, harmless pleasure.

unschwer ['unʃveːr], *adv.* easily.

Unsegen ['unzeːgən], *m.* (—s, *no pl.*) misfortune; curse.

unselbständig ['unzɛlpʃtɛndɪç], *adj.* dependent.

unselig ['unzeːlɪç], *adj.* unfortunate, luckless, fatal.

unser ['unzər], *poss. adj.* our. — *pers. pron.* of us.

unsereiner ['unzəraɪnər], *pron.* s.o. in our position; one of us, people in our position.

unserthalben, unsertwegen ['unzərthalbən, unzərtveːgən], *adv.* for our sake, on our account.

unsertwillen ['unzərtvilən], *adv. um* —, for our sake, on our account.

unsicher ['unzɪçər], *adj.* unsafe; uncertain, doubtful; (*route*) precarious; (*hand*) unsteady; (*legs*) shaky.

unsichtbar ['unzɪçtbaːr], *adj.* invisible.

Unsinn ['unzɪn], *m.* (—s, *no pl.*) nonsense.

unsinnig ['unzɪnɪç], *adj.* nonsensical; mad, insane.

Unsitte ['unzɪtə], *f.* (—, *pl.* —n) abuse, nuisance; bad habit.

unsittlich ['unzɪtlɪç], *adj.* immoral.

unstät, unstet ['unʃtɛːt, 'unʃteːt], *adj.* unsteady, inconstant; restless.

unstatthaft ['unʃtathaft], *adj.* illicit.

unsterblich ['unʃtɛrplɪç], *adj.* immortal.

Unsterblichkeit ['unʃtɛrplɪçkaɪt], *f.* (—, *no pl.*) immortality.

unstillbar ['unʃtɪlbaːr], *adj.* unappeasable, unquenchable.

unstreitig ['unʃtraɪtɪç], *adj.* indisputable, unquestionable.

Unsumme ['unzumə], *f.* (—, *pl.* —n) vast amount (of money).

unsympathisch ['unzympaːtɪʃ], *adj.* uncongenial, disagreeable; *er ist mir* —, I dislike him.

untadelhaft, untadelig ['unta:dəlhaft, 'unta:dəlɪç], *adj.* blameless, irreproachable, unimpeachable.

Untat ['untaːt], *f.* (—, *pl.* —en) misdeed, crime.

untätig ['untɛːtɪç], *adj.* inactive, idle, supine.

untauglich ['untauklɪç], *adj.* unfit, useless; incompetent; (*Mil.*) disabled.

unteilbar [un'taɪlbaːr], *adj.* indivisible.

unten ['untən], *adv.* below, beneath; (*house*) downstairs.

unter ['untər], *prep.* (*Dat., Acc.*) under, beneath, below, among, between.

Unterbau ['untərbau], *m.* (—s, *pl.* —ten) substructure, foundation.

Unterbewußtsein ['untərbəvustzaɪn], *n.* (—s, *no pl.*) subconscious mind, subconsciousness.

unterbieten [untər'biːtən], *v.a. irr. insep.* underbid, undersell.

Unterbilanz ['untərbilants], *f.* (—, *pl.* —en) deficit.

unterbinden [untər'bɪndən], *v.a. irr. insep.* tie up, bind up; (*fig.*) prevent, check.

unterbleiben [untər'blaɪbən], *v.n. irr. insep.* (*aux.* sein) remain undone, be left undone, cease.

unterbrechen [untər'brɛçən], *v.a. irr. insep.* interrupt; (*journey*) break; (*speech*) cut short.

Unterbrechung [untər'brɛçuŋ], *f.* (—, *pl.* —en) interruption.

unterbreiten (1) ['untərbraɪtən], *v.a.* spread under.

unterbreiten (2) [untər'braɪtən], *v.a. insep.* submit, lay before.

unterbringen ['untərbrɪŋən], *v.a. irr.* provide (*a place*) for; (*goods*) dispose of; (*money*) invest; (*people*) accommodate, put up.

Unterbringung ['untərbrɪŋuŋ], *f.* (—, *no pl.*) provision for; (*goods*) disposal of; (*money*) investment; (*people*) accommodation.

unterdessen [untər'dɛsən], *adv., conj.* in the meantime, meanwhile.

unterdrücken [untər'drykən], *v.a. insep.* suppress, curb, check; oppress.

Unterdrückung [untər'drykuŋ], *f.* (—, *no pl.*) oppression, suppression.

untereinander [untəraɪn'andər], *adv.* with each other, mutually, among themselves.

unterfangen [untər'faŋən], *v.r. irr. insep.* sich —, dare, venture, presume.

Untergang ['untərgaŋ], *m.* (—s, *pl.* ⸚e) (*sun*) setting; (*ship*) sinking; (*fig.*) decline.

untergeben [untər'geːbən], *adj.* subject, subordinate.

Untergebene [untər'geːbənə], *m.* (—n, *pl.* —n) subordinate.

untergehen ['untərgeːən], *v.n. irr.* (*aux.* sein) (*sun*) go down, set; (*ship*) sink; (*fig.*) perish; decline.

Untergeschoß ['untərgəʃɔs], *n.* (—sses, *pl.* —sse) ground floor.

Untergestell ['untərgəʃtɛl], *n.* (—s, *pl.* —e) undercarriage, chassis.

untergraben [untər'graːbən], *v.a. irr. insep.* undermine.

unterhalb ['untərhalp], *prep.* (*Genit.*) below, under.

Unterhalt ['untərhalt], *m.* (—s, *no pl.*) maintenance, support, livelihood.

unterhalten (1) ['untərhaltən], *v.a. irr.* hold under.

unterhalten (2) [untər'haltən], *v.a. irr. insep.* maintain, keep, support; entertain. — *v.r.* sich —, converse, make conversation; sich gut —, enjoy o.s.

unterhaltend [untər'haltənt], *adj.* entertaining, amusing, lively.

Unterhaltskosten ['untərhaltskɔstən], *f. pl.* maintenance; (*house*) cost of repairs.

Unterhaltung [untər'haltuŋ], *f.* (—, *pl.* —en) maintenance; conversation; amusement, entertainment.

Unterhaltungslektüre [untər'haltuŋslɛktyːrə], *f.* (—, *no pl.*) light reading, fiction.

unterhandeln [untər'handəln], *v.n. insep.* negotiate.

Unterhändler [untər'hendlər], *m.* (—s, *pl.* —) negotiator, mediator.

Unterhandlung [untər'handluŋ], *f.* (—, *pl.* —en) negotiation.

Unterhaus ['untərhaus], *n.* (—es, *pl.* ⸚er) ground floor; (*Parl.*) lower house; House of Commons.

Unterhemd ['untərhɛmt], *n.* (—(e)s, *pl.* —en) vest.

unterhöhlen [untər'høːlən], *v.a. insep.* undermine.

Unterholz ['untərhɔlts], *n.* (—es, *no pl.*) undergrowth, underwood.

Unterhosen ['untərhoːzən], *f. pl.* (*women*) briefs; (*men*) underpants.

unterirdisch ['untərɪrdɪʃ], *adj.* subterranean, underground.

unterjochen [untər'jɔxən], *v.a. insep.* subjugate, subdue.

Unterkiefer ['untərkiːfər], *m.* (—s, *pl.* —) lower jaw.

Unterkleid ['untərklaɪt], *n.* (—s, *pl.* —er) under-garment.

unterkommen ['untərkɔmən], *v.n. irr.* (*aux.* sein) find accommodation *or* shelter; (*fig.*) find employment.

Unterkommen ['untərkɔmən], *n.* (—s, *no pl.*) shelter, accommodation; (*fig.*) employment, place.

Unterkörper ['untərkœrpər], *m.* (—s, *pl.* —) lower part of the body.

unterkriegen ['untərkriːgən], *v.a.* get the better of; lass dich nicht —, stand firm.

Unterkunft ['untərkunft], *f.* (—, *pl.* ⸚e) shelter, accommodation; employment.

Unterlage ['untərlaːgə], *f.* (—, *pl.* —n) foundation, base; blotting pad; (*pl.*) documents, files.

unterlassen [untər'lasən], *v.a. irr. insep.* omit (to do), fail (to do), neglect; forbear.

Unterlassung [untər'lasuŋ], *f.* (—, *pl.* —en) omission, neglect.

Unterlassungssünde [untər'lasuŋszyndə], *f.* (—, *pl.* —n) sin of omission.

Unterlauf ['untərlauf], *m.* (—(e)s, *pl.* ⸚e) (*river*) lower course.

unterlaufen [untər'laufən], *v.n. irr. insep.* (*aux.* sein) run under; (*mistake*) creep in. — *adj.* suffused, blood-shot.

unterlegen (1) ['untərle:gən], *v.a.* lay under; *einen anderen Sinn* —, put a different construction upon.

unterlegen (2) [untər'le:gən], *adj.* inferior.

Unterleib ['untərlaıp], *m.* (—s, *no pl.*) abdomen.

unterliegen [untər'li:gən], *v.n. irr. insep.* (*aux.* sein) succumb, be overcome; be subject (to).

Untermieter ['untərmi:tər], *m.* (—s, *pl.* —) subtenant.

unterminieren [untərmi'ni:rən], *v.a. insep.* undermine.

unternehmen [untər'ne:mən], *v.a. irr. insep.* undertake, take upon o.s., attempt.

Unternehmen [untər'ne:mən], *n.* (—s, *pl.* —) enterprise, undertaking.

unternehmend [untər'ne:mənt], *adj.* bold, enterprising.

Unternehmer [untər'ne:mər], *m.* (—s, *pl.* —) contractor, entrepreneur.

Unteroffizier ['untərəfitsi:r], *m.* (—s, *pl.* —e) (*army*) non-commissioned officer; (*navy*) petty officer.

unterordnen ['untərərdnən], *v.a.* subordinate. — *v.r. sich* —, submit (to).

Unterordnung ['untərərdnuŋ], *f.* (—, *no pl.*) subordination, submission; (*Biol.*) sub-order.

Unterpacht ['untərpaxt], *f.* (—, *no pl.*) sublease.

Unterpfand ['untərpfant], *n.* (—(e)s, *no pl.*) (*obs.*) pawn, pledge.

Unterredung [untər're:duŋ], *f.* (—, *pl.* —en) conference, interview, talk.

Unterricht ['untərrıçt], *m.* (—(e)s, *no pl.*) instruction, tuition, teaching.

unterrichten [untər'rıçtən], *v.a. insep.* instruct, teach.

Unterrichtsanstalt ['untərrıçtsanʃtalt], *f.* (—, *pl.* —en) educational establishment or institution.

Unterrichtsgegenstand ['untərrıçtsge:gənʃtant], *m.* (—s, *pl.* ⁓e) subject of instruction.

Unterrock ['untərrɔk], *m.* (—s, *pl.* ⁓e) petticoat, slip; underskirt.

untersagen [untər'za:gən], *v.a. insep.* forbid; *Rauchen untersagt*, smoking prohibited.

Untersatz ['untərzats], *m.* (—es, *pl.* ⁓e) basis, holder, stand, trestle; saucer.

unterschätzen [untər'ʃɛtsən], *v.a. insep.* underrate, underestimate.

unterscheiden [untər'ʃaıdən], *v.a. irr. insep.* distinguish, discriminate, discern, differentiate. — *v.r. sich* —, differ; *ich kann sie nicht* —, I cannot tell them apart.

Unterscheidung [untər'ʃaıduŋ], *f.* (—, *pl.* —en) distinction, differentiation.

Unterscheidungsmerkmal [untər'ʃaıduŋsmerkma:l], *n.* (—s, *pl.* —e) distinctive mark, characteristic.

Unterscheidungsvermögen [untər'ʃaıduŋsfermø:gən], *n.* (—s, *no pl.*) power of discrimination.

Unterscheidungszeichen [untər'ʃaıduŋstsaıçən], *n.* (—s, *pl.* —) criterion.

Unterschenkel [untər'ʃɛŋkəl], *m.* (—s, *pl.* —) shank, lower part of the thigh.

Unterschicht ['untərʃıçt], *f.* (—, *pl.* —en) substratum, subsoil.

unterschieben (1) ['untərʃi:bən], *v.a. irr.* substitute; interpolate; forge; foist upon.

unterschieben (2) [untər'ʃi:bən], *v.a. irr. insep.* (*fig.*) attribute falsely, pass s.o. off as.

Unterschiebung [untər'ʃi:buŋ], *f.* (—, *pl.* —en) substitution; forgery.

Unterschied ['untərʃi:t], *m.* (—(e)s, *pl.* —e) difference.

unterschiedlich ['untərʃi:tlıç], *adj.* different, diverse.

unterschiedslos ['untərʃi:tslo:s], *adv.* indiscriminately.

unterschlagen [untər'ʃla:gən], *v.a. irr. insep.* embezzle, intercept.

Unterschlagung [untər'ʃla:guŋ], *f.* (—, *pl.* —en) embezzlement.

Unterschlupf ['untərʃlupf], *m.* (—es, *pl.* ⁓e) shelter, refuge.

unterschlüpfen ['untərʃlypfən], *v.n.* (*aux.* sein) find shelter, slip away; (*fig.*) hide.

unterschreiben [untər'ʃraıbən], *v.a. irr. insep.* sign, subscribe to.

Unterschrift ['untərʃrıft], *f.* (—, *pl.* —en) signature.

Unterseeboot ['untərze:bo:t], *n.* (—s, *pl.* —e) submarine.

untersetzt [untər'zɛtst], *adj.* thickset, dumpy.

untersinken ['untərzıŋkən], *v.n. irr.* (*aux.* sein) go down.

unterst ['untərst], *adj.* lowest, undermost, bottom.

Unterstaatssekretär [untər'ʃta:tssekrete:r], *m.* (—s, *pl.* —e) under-secretary of state.

unterstehen (1) ['untərʃte:ən], *v.n. irr.* (*aux.* sein) find shelter (under).

unterstehen (2) [untər'ʃte:ən], *v.n. irr. insep.* be subordinate. — *v.r. sich* —, dare, venture.

unterstellen (1) ['untərʃtɛlən], *v.a.* place under. — *v.r. sich* —, take shelter (under).

unterstellen (2) [untər'ʃtɛlən], *v.a. insep.* put under the authority of; impute (s.th. to s.o.).

Unterstellung [untər'ʃtɛluŋ], *f.* (—, *pl.* —en) imputation, insinuation.

unterstreichen [untər'ʃtraıçən], *v.a. irr. insep.* underline.

Unterstreichung [untər'ʃtraıçuŋ], *f.* (—, *pl.* —en) underlining.

Unterströmung ['untərʃtrø:muŋ], *f.* (—, *pl.* —en) undercurrent.

unterstützen [untər'ʃtytsən], *v.a. insep.* support, assist, aid; (*fig.*) countenance.

Unterstützung [untər'ʃtytsuŋ], f. (—, pl. —en) support, aid, assistance, relief.

Unterstützungsanstalt [untər'ʃtytsuŋsanʃtalt], f. (—, pl. —en) charitable institution.

unterstützungsbedürftig [untər'ʃtytsuŋsbədyrftiç], adj. indigent.

untersuchen [untər'zu:xən], v.a. insep. investigate, examine, look over.

Untersuchung [untər'zu:xuŋ], f. (—, pl. —en) investigation, inquiry; (medical) examination.

Untersuchungshaft [untər'zu:xuŋshaft], f. (—, no pl.) imprisonment pending investigation.

Untersuchungsrichter [untər'zu:xuŋsriçtər], m. (—s, pl. —) examining magistrate.

Untertan ['untərta:n], m. (—s, pl. —en) subject, vassal.

untertan ['untərta:n], adj. subject.

untertänig ['untərtɛ:niç], adj. humble, obsequious, submissive, servile.

Untertasse ['untərtasə], f. (—, pl. —n) saucer.

untertauchen ['untərtauxən], v.a. dip, duck, submerge. — v.n. (aux. sein) dive.

unterwegs [untər've:ks], adv. on the way.

unterweisen [untər'vaizən], v.a. irr. insep. teach, instruct.

Unterweisung [untər'vaizuŋ], f. (—, pl. —en) instruction, teaching.

Unterwelt [untər'vɛlt], f. (—, no pl.) Hades, the underworld.

unterwerfen [untər'vɛrfən], v.a. irr. insep. subject, subdue. — v.r. sich —, submit (to), resign o.s. (to).

Unterwerfung [untər'vɛrfuŋ], f. (—, no pl.) subjection, submission.

unterwühlen [untər'vy:lən], v.a. insep. root up; (fig.) undermine.

unterwürfig [untər'vyrfiç], adj. submissive, subject; obsequious.

Unterwürfigkeit [untər'vyrfiçkait], f. (—, no pl.) submissiveness; obsequiousness.

unterzeichnen [untər'tsaiçnən], v.a. insep. sign.

Unterzeichner [untər'tsaiçnər], m. (—s, pl. —) signatory; (insurance) underwriter.

Unterzeichnete [untər'tsaiçnətə], m. (—n, pl. —n) undersigned.

Unterzeichnung [untər'tsaiçnuŋ], f. (—, pl. —en) signature.

unterziehen [untər'tsi:ən], v.r. irr. insep. sich —, submit to, undertake; (operation) undergo.

Untiefe ['unti:fə], f. (—, pl. —n) shallow water, flat, shoal, sands.

Untier ['unti:r], n. (—s, pl. —e) monster.

untilgbar ['untilkba:r], adj. indelible; (debt) irredeemable.

untrennbar ['untrɛnba:r], adj. inseparable.

untreu ['untrɔy], adj. faithless, unfaithful, disloyal, perfidious.

Untreue ['untrɔyə], f. (—, no pl.) faithlessness, unfaithfulness, disloyalty, perfidy.

untröstlich ['untrø:stliç], adj. inconsolable, disconsolate.

untrüglich ['untry:kliç], adj. unmistakable, infallible.

untüchtig ['untyçtiç], adj. inefficient; incompetent.

unüberlegt ['uny:bərle:kt], adj. inconsiderate, thoughtless; rash.

unübersehbar ['uny:bərze:ba:r], adj. immense, vast.

unübersteiglich ['uny:bərʃtaikliç], adj. insurmountable.

unübertrefflich ['uny:bərtrɛfliç], adj. unsurpassable, unequalled, unrivalled.

unübertroffen ['uny:bərtrɔfən], adj. unsurpassed.

unüberwindlich ['uny:bərvintliç], adj. invincible, unconquerable.

unumgänglich ['unumgɛŋliç], adj. indispensable, unavoidable, inevitable.

unumschränkt ['unumʃrɛŋkt], adj. unlimited, absolute.

unumstößlich ['unumʃtø:sliç], adj. irrefutable.

unumwunden ['unumvundən], adj. frank, plain.

ununterbrochen ['ununtərbrɔxən], adj. uninterrupted, unremitting.

unveränderlich ['unfɛrɛndərliç], adj. unchangeable, unalterable.

unverändert ['unfɛrɛndərt], adj. unchanged, unaltered.

unverantwortlich ['unfɛrantvɔrtliç], adj. irresponsible, inexcusable, unjustifiable.

unveräußerlich ['unfɛrɔysərliç], adj. not for sale; inalienable.

unverbesserlich ['unfɛrbɛsərliç], adj. incorrigible.

unverbindlich ['unfɛrbintliç], adj. not binding, without prejudice, without obligation.

unverblümt ['unfɛrbly:mt], adj. blunt, point-blank.

unverbrennlich ['unfɛrbrɛnliç], adj. incombustible.

unverbrüchlich ['unfɛrbryçliç], adj. inviolable.

unverbürgt ['unfɛrbyrkt], adj. unwarranted, unofficial; unconfirmed.

unverdaulich ['unfɛrdauliç], adj. indigestible.

unverdaut ['unfɛrdaut], adj. undigested.

unverdient ['unfɛrdi:nt], adj. unmerited, undeserved.

unverdientermaßen ['unfɛrdi:ntərma:sən], adv. undeservedly.

unverdorben ['unfɛrdɔrbən], adj. unspoiled, uncorrupted, innocent.

unverdrossen ['unfɛrdrɔsən], adj. indefatigable.

unvereidigt ['unfɛraidiçt], adj. unsworn.

unvereinbar ['unfɛrainba:r], adj. incompatible, inconsistent.

247

Unvereinbarkeit

Unvereinbarkeit [ˈunfɛraɪnbaːrkaɪt], *f.* (—, *no pl.*) incompatibility, inconsistency.

unverfälscht [ˈunfɛrfɛlʃt], *adj.* unadulterated, genuine, pure.

unverfänglich [ˈunfɛrfɛŋlɪç], *adj.* harmless.

unverfroren [ˈunfɛrfroːrən], *adj.* cheeky, impudent.

unvergeßlich [ˈunfɛrgɛslɪç], *adj.* memorable, not to be forgotten, unforgettable.

unvergleichlich [ˈunfɛrglaɪçlɪç], *adj.* incomparable.

unverhältnismäßig [ˈunfɛrhɛltnɪsmɛːsɪç], *adj.* disproportionate.

unverheiratet [ˈunfɛrhaɪraːtət], *adj.* unmarried.

unverhofft [ˈunfɛrhɔft], *adj.* unexpected.

unverhohlen [ˈunfɛrhoːlən], *adj.* unconcealed, undisguised, candid.

unverkennbar [ˈunfɛrkɛnbaːr], *adj.* unmistakable.

unverlangt [ˈunfɛrlaŋkt], *adj.* unsolicited, not ordered.

unverletzlich [ˈunfɛrlɛtslɪç], *adj.* invulnerable; (*fig.*) inviolable.

unverletzt [ˈunfɛrlɛtst], *adj.* (*persons*) unhurt; (*things*) undamaged, intact.

unvermeidlich [ˈunfɛrmaɪtlɪç], *adj.* inevitable, unavoidable.

unvermindert [ˈunfɛrmɪndərt], *adj.* undiminished.

unvermittelt [ˈunfɛrmɪtəlt], *adj.* sudden, abrupt.

Unvermögen [ˈunfɛrmøːgən], *n.* (—s, *no pl.*) inability, incapacity.

unvermögend [ˈunfɛrmøːgənt], *adj.* incapable; impecunious.

unvermutet [ˈunfɛrmuːtət], *adj.* unexpected, unforeseen.

unverrichtet [ˈunfɛrrɪçtət], *adj.* —*er Sache*, empty-handed; unsuccessfully.

unverschämt [ˈunfɛrʃɛːmt], *adj.* impudent, brazen.

unverschuldet [ˈunfɛrʃuldət], *adj.* not in debt, unencumbered; (*fig.*) undeserved.

unversehens [ˈunfɛrzeːəns], *adv.* unexpectedly, unawares.

unversehrt [ˈunfɛrzeːrt], *adv.* (*persons*) unhurt, safe; (*things*) undamaged.

unversiegbar [ˈunfɛrziːkbaːr], *adj.* inexhaustible.

unversiegt [ˈunfɛrziːkt], *adj.* unexhausted.

unversöhnlich [ˈunfɛrzøːnlɪç], *adj.* implacable, irreconcilable.

unversöhnt [ˈunfɛrzøːnt], *adj.* unreconciled.

unversorgt [ˈunfɛrzɔrkt], *adj.* unprovided for.

Unverstand [ˈunfɛrʃtant], *m.* (—(e)s, *no pl.*) want of judgment, indiscretion.

unverständig [ˈunfɛrʃtɛndɪç], *adj.* foolish, unwise, imprudent.

unverständlich [ˈunfɛrʃtɛntlɪç], *adj.* unintelligible, incomprehensible.

unversteuert [ˈunfɛrʃtɔyərt], *adj.* with duty *or* tax unpaid.

unversucht [ˈunfɛrzuːxt], *adj.* untried; *nichts — lassen*, leave no stone unturned.

unverträglich [ˈunfɛrtrɛːklɪç], *adj.* quarrelsome.

unverwandt [ˈunfɛrvant], *adj.* unrelated; fixed, constant; immovable.

unverwundbar [ˈunfɛrvuntbaːr], *adj.* invulnerable.

unverwüstlich [ˈunfɛrvyːstlɪç], *adj.* indestructible.

unverzagt [ˈunfɛrtsaːkt], *adj.* undaunted, intrepid.

unverzeihlich [ˈunfɛrtsaɪlɪç], *adj.* unpardonable.

unverzinslich [ˈunfɛrtsɪnslɪç], *adj.* (*money*) gaining no interest.

unverzollt [ˈunfɛrtsɔlt], *adj.* duty unpaid.

unverzüglich [ˈunfɛrtsyːklɪç], *adj.* immediate.

unvollendet [ˈunfɔlɛndət], *adj.* unfinished.

unvollständig [ˈunfɔlʃtɛndɪç], *adj.* incomplete.

unvorbereitet [ˈunfoːrbəraɪtət], *adj.* unprepared.

unvordenklich [ˈunfoːrdɛŋklɪç], *adj. seit —en Zeiten*, from time immemorial.

unvorhergesehen [ˈunfoːrheːrgəzeːən], *adj.* unforeseen, unlooked for.

unvorsichtig [ˈunfoːrzɪçtɪç], *adj.* imprudent, incautious, careless.

unvorteilhaft [ˈunfɔrtaɪlhaft], *adj.* unprofitable, disadvantageous; — *aussehen*, not look o.'s best.

unwägbar [ˈunvɛːkbaːr], *adj.* imponderable.

unwahr [ˈunvaːr], *adj.* untrue, false.

Unwahrhaftigkeit [ˈunvaːrhaftɪçkaɪt], *f.* (—, *no pl.*) want of truthfulness, unreliability, dishonesty.

Unwahrheit [ˈunvaːrhaɪt], *f.* (—, *pl.* —en) lie, untruth, falsehood.

unwegsam [ˈunveːkzaːm], *adj.* impassable, impracticable.

unweigerlich [ˈunvaɪgərlɪç], *adj.* unhesitating, unquestioning. — *adv.* without fail.

unweit [ˈunvaɪt], *prep.* (*Genit.*) not far from, near.

Unwesen [ˈunveːzən], *n.* (—s, *no pl.*) nuisance; *sein — treiben*, be up to o.'s tricks.

Unwetter [ˈunvɛtər], *n.* (—s, *pl.* —) bad weather, thunderstorm.

unwichtig [ˈunvɪçtɪç], *adj.* unimportant; insignificant, of no consequence.

unwiderleglich [ˈunviːdərleːklɪç], *adj.* irrefutable.

unwiderruflich [ˈunviːdərruːflɪç], *adj.* irrevocable.

unwidersprechlich [ˈunviːdərʃprɛçlɪç], *adj.* incontestable.

unwidersprochen [ˈunviːdərʃprɔxən], *adj.* uncontradicted.

unwiderstehlich [ˈunviːdərʃteːlɪç], *adj.* irresistible.

unwiederbringlich [ˈunviːdərbrɪŋlɪç], *adj.* irrecoverable, irretrievable.

Unwille [ˈunvɪlə], *m.* (—ns, *no pl.*) displeasure, indignation.

unwillkürlich [ˈunvɪlkyːrlɪç], *adj.* involuntary; instinctive.

unwirsch [ˈunvɪrʃ], *adj.* petulant, testy; curt, uncivil.

unwirtlich [ˈunvɪrtlɪç], *adj.* inhospitable.

unwirtschaftlich [ˈunvɪrtʃaftlɪç], *adj.* not economic, uneconomic.

unwissend [ˈunvɪsənt], *adj.* illiterate, ignorant.

Unwissenheit [ˈunvɪsənhaɪt], *f.* (—, *no pl.*) ignorance.

unwissenschaftlich [ˈunvɪsənʃaftlɪç], *adj.* unscholarly; unscientific.

unwissentlich [ˈunvɪsəntlɪç], *adv.* unknowingly, unconsciously.

unwohl [ˈunvoːl], *adj.* unwell, indisposed.

Unwohlsein [ˈunvoːlzaɪn], *n.* (—s, *no pl.*) indisposition.

unwürdig [ˈunvyrdɪç], *adj.* unworthy, undeserving.

Unzahl [ˈuntsaːl], *f.* (—, *no pl.*) vast number.

unzählbar [unˈtsɛːlbaːr], *adj.* innumerable, numberless.

unzählig [unˈtsɛːlɪç], *adj.* innumerable; —*e Male*, over and over again.

unzart [ˈuntsaːrt], *adj.* indelicate, rude, rough; unceremonious.

Unzeit [ˈuntsaɪt], *f.* (—, *no pl.*) *zur* —, out of season, inopportunely.

unzeitgemäß [ˈuntsaɪtgəmɛːs], *adj.* out of date, behind the times; unfashionable.

unzeitig [ˈuntsaɪtɪç], *adj.* unseasonable; untimely, inopportune.

unziemlich [ˈuntsiːmlɪç], *adj.* unseemly, unbecoming.

Unzier [ˈuntsiːr], *f.* (—, *no pl.*) disfigurement; flaw.

Unzucht [ˈuntsuxt], *f.* (—, *no pl.*) unchastity; lewdness; fornication.

unzüchtig [ˈuntsyçtɪç], *adj.* unchaste, lascivious, lewd.

unzufrieden [ˈuntsufriːdən], *adj.* discontented, dissatisfied.

unzugänglich [ˈuntsugɛŋlɪç], *adj.* inaccessible.

unzulänglich [ˈuntsulɛŋlɪç], *adj.* inadequate, insufficient.

Unzulänglichkeit [ˈuntsulɛŋlɪçkaɪt], *f.* (—, *no pl.*) inadequacy.

unzulässig [ˈuntsulɛsɪç], *adj.* inadmissible.

unzurechnungsfähig [ˈuntsurɛçnuŋsfɛːɪç], *adj.* not accountable (for o.'s actions), non compos mentis, insane.

Unzurechnungsfähigkeit [ˈuntsurɛçnuŋsfɛːɪçkaɪt], *f.* (—, *no pl.*) irresponsibility; feeblemindedness.

unzusammenhängend [ˈuntsuzamənhɛŋənt], *adj.* incoherent.

unzuständig [ˈuntsuʃtɛndɪç], *adj.* incompetent, not competent (*Law etc.*).

unzuträglich [ˈuntsutrɛːklɪç], *adj.* unwholesome.

unzutreffend [ˈuntsutrɛfənt], *adj.* inapposite; unfounded; inapplicable.

unzuverlässig [ˈuntsufɛrlɛsɪç], *adj.* unreliable.

unzweckmäßig [ˈuntsvɛkmɛːsɪç], *adj.* inexpedient.

unzweideutig [ˈuntsvaɪdɔytɪç], *adj.* unequivocal, explicit, unambiguous.

üppig [ˈypɪç], *adj.* abundant; opulent; luxurious, luxuriant, voluptuous.

uralt [ˈuːralt], *adj.* very old, old as the hills; ancient.

uranfänglich [ˈuːranfɛŋlɪç], *adj.* primordial, primeval.

Uraufführung [ˈuːrauffyːruŋ], *f.* (—, *pl.* —en) (*Theat.*) first night, première.

urbar [ˈuːrbaːr], *adj.* arable, under cultivation; — *machen*, cultivate.

Urbarmachung [ˈuːrbaːrmaxuŋ], *f.* (—, *no pl.*) cultivation.

Urbild [ˈuːrbɪlt], *n.* (—(e)s, *pl.* —er) prototype; (*fig.*) ideal.

ureigen [ˈuːraɪgən], *adj.* quite original; idiosyncratic.

Ureltern [ˈuːrɛltərn], *pl.* ancestors.

Urenkel [ˈuːrɛŋkəl], *m.* (—s, *pl.* —) great-grandson, great-grandchild.

Urenkelin [ˈuːrɛŋkəlɪn], *f.* (—, *pl.* —nen) great-granddaughter.

Urfehde [ˈuːrfeːdə], *f.* (—, *no pl.*) oath to keep the peace.

Urform [ˈuːrfɔrm], *f.* (—, *pl.* —en) primitive form; original form; archetype.

Urgroßmutter [ˈuːrgroːsmutər], *f.* (—, *pl.* ⸚) great-grandmother.

Urgroßvater [ˈuːrgroːsfaːtər], *m.* (—s, *pl.* ⸚) great-grandfather.

Urheber [ˈuːrheːbər], *m.* (—s, *pl.* —) author, originator.

Urheberrecht [ˈuːrheːbərrɛçt], *n.* (—s, *pl.* —e) copyright.

Urheberschaft [ˈuːrheːbərʃaft], *f.* (—, *no pl.*) authorship.

Urin [uˈriːn], *m.* (—s, *no pl.*) urine.

Urkunde [ˈuːrkundə], *f.* (—, *pl.* —n) document, deed, charter; *zur* — *dessen*, (*obs.*) in witness whereof.

Urkundenbeweis [ˈuːrkundənbəvaɪs], *m.* (—es, *pl.* —e) documentary evidence.

urkundlich [ˈuːrkuntlɪç], *adj.* documentary.

Urlaub [ˈuːrlaup], *m.* (—s, *pl.* —e) leave of absence; vacation; (*Mil.*) furlough.

urplötzlich [ˈuːrplœtslɪç], *adj.* sudden. — *adv.* all at once, suddenly.

Urquell [ˈuːrkvɛl], *m.* (—s, *pl.* —en) fountain-head, original source.

Ursache [ˈuːrzaxə], *f.* (—, *pl.* —n) cause; *keine* —, don't mention it.

Urschrift [ˈuːrʃrɪft], *f.* (—, *pl.* —en) original text.

Ursprache [ˈuːrʃpraːxə], *f.* (—, *pl.* —n) original language.

Ursprung [ˈuːrʃpruŋ], *m.* (—s, *pl.* ⸚e) origin; extraction.

ursprünglich [ˈuːrʃpryŋlɪç], *adj.* original.

Urteil [ˈurtaɪl], *n.* (—s, *pl.* —e) opinion; (*Law*) judgment, verdict, sentence; *ein — fällen*, pass judgment on; *nach meinem —*, in my opinion.

urteilen [ˈurtaɪlən], *v.n.* judge.

Urteilsspruch [ˈurtaɪlsʃprux], *m.* (—s, *pl.* —e) judgment, sentence.

Uruguay [uruˈgwaːɪ], *n.* Uruguay.

Urureltern [ˈuːruːrɛltərn], *pl.* ancestors.

Urvater [ˈuːrfaːtər], *m.* (—s, *pl.* —) forefather.

Urvolk [ˈuːrfɔlk], *n.* (—(e)s, *pl.* —er) primitive people, aborigines.

Urwald [ˈuːrvalt], *m.* (—(e)s, *pl.* —er) primæval forest, virgin forest.

Urwelt [ˈuːrvɛlt], *f.* (—, *no pl.*) primæval world.

Urzeit [ˈuːrtsaɪt], *f.* (—, *pl.* —en) prehistoric times.

V

V [fau], *n.* (—s, *pl.* —s) the letter V.

Vagabund [vagaˈbunt], *m.* (—en, *pl.* —en) vagabond, tramp; (*Am.*) hobo.

vag [ˈvaːk], *adj.* vague.

Vakuumbremse [ˈvaːkuumbrɛmzə], *f.* (—, *pl.* —n) air-brake, vacuum-brake.

Vase [ˈvaːzə], *f.* (—, *pl.* —n) vase.

Vater [ˈfaːtər], *m.* (—s, *pl.* —) father.

Vaterland [ˈfaːtərlant], *n.* (—(e)s, *pl.* —er) mother-country, native country; —*sliebe*, patriotism.

vaterländisch [ˈfaːtərlɛndɪʃ], *adj.* patriotic.

vaterlandslos [ˈfaːtərlantsloːs], *adj.* having no mother country; unpatriotic.

väterlich [ˈfɛːtərlɪç], *adj.* fatherly, paternal. — *adv.* like a father.

vaterlos [ˈfaːtərloːs], *adj.* fatherless.

Vatermord [ˈfaːtərmɔrt], *m.* (—(e)s, *pl.* —e) parricide; patricide.

Vatermörder [ˈfaːtərmœrdər], *m.* (—s, *pl.* —) parricide; (*fig.*) high or stand-up collar.

Vaterschaft [ˈfaːtərʃaft], *f.* (—, *no pl.*) paternity.

Vatersname [ˈfaːtərsnaːmə], *m.* (—ns, *pl.* —n) surname, family name.

Vaterstadt [ˈfaːtərʃtat], *f.* (—, *pl.* —e) native town.

Vaterstelle [ˈfaːtərʃtɛlə], *f.* (—, *pl.* —n) — *vertreten*, act as a father, be a father (to).

Vaterunser [faːtərˈunzər], *n.* (—s, *pl.* —) Lord's Prayer.

Vatikan [vatiˈkaːn], *m.* (—s, *no pl.*) Vatican.

vegetieren [vegeˈtiːrən], *v.n.* vegetate.

Veilchen [ˈfaɪlçən], *n.* (—s, *pl.* —) (*Bot.*) violet.

Vene [ˈveːnə], *f.* (—, *pl.* —n) vein.

Venezuela [venɛtsuˈeːla], *n.* Venezuela.

Ventil [venˈtiːl], *n.* (—s, *pl.* —e) valve.

ventilieren [ventiˈliːrən], *v.a.* ventilate, air; (*fig.*) discuss, ventilate.

verabfolgen [fɛrˈapfɔlgən], *v.a.* deliver, hand over, remit; serve.

Verabfolgung [fɛrˈapfɔlguŋ], *f.* (—, *no pl.*) delivery.

verabreden [fɛrˈapreːdən], *v.a.* agree (upon); stipulate; *etwas mit einem —*, agree on s.th. with s.o. — *v.r. sich mit einem —*, make an appointment with s.o.; (*coll.*) have a date.

Verabredung [fɛrˈapreːduŋ], *f.* (—, *pl.* —en) agreement, arrangement, appointment; (*coll.*) date.

verabreichen [fɛrˈapraɪçən], *v.a.* deliver, dispense.

verabsäumen [fɛrˈapzɔymən], *v.a.* neglect, omit.

verabscheuen [fɛrˈapʃɔyən], *v.a.* detest, loathe, abhor.

Verabscheuung [fɛrˈapʃɔyuŋ], *f.* (—, *no pl.*) abhorrence, detestation, loathing.

verabscheuungswürdig [fɛrˈapʃɔyuŋsvyrdɪç], *adj.* abominable, detestable.

verabschieden [fɛrˈapʃiːdən], *v.a.* dismiss, discharge. — *v.r. sich —*, take leave, say good-bye; (*Pol.*) pass (of an Act).

Verabschiedung [fɛrˈapʃiːduŋ], *f.* (—, *no pl.*) dismissal; discharge; (*Pol.*) passing (of an Act).

verachten [fɛrˈaxtən], *v.a.* despise, scorn.

verächtlich [fɛrˈɛçtlɪç], *adj.* despicable, contemptible; contemptuous, scornful.

Verachtung [fɛrˈaxtuŋ], *f.* (—, *no pl.*) contempt, disdain, scorn.

verallgemeinern [fɛralgəˈmaɪnərn], *v.a., v.n.* generalise.

veralten [fɛrˈaltən], *v.n.* (*aux.* sein) become obsolete, date.

veraltet [fɛrˈaltət], *adj.* obsolete.

Veranda [veˈranda], *f.* (—, *pl.* —den) verandah, porch.

veränderlich [fɛrˈɛndərlɪç], *adj.* changeable, variable; (*fig.*) inconstant, fickle.

verändern [fɛrˈɛndərn], *v.a.* change, alter. — *v.r. sich —*, change, vary; change o.'s job.

verankern [fɛrˈaŋkərn], *v.a.* anchor.

veranlagt [fɛrˈanlaːkt], *adj.* inclined; gifted; having a propensity (to); *gut —*, talented; (*tax*) assessed.

Veranlagung [fɛrˈanlaːguŋ], *f.* (—, *pl.* —en) bent; talent · predisposition; (*tax*) assessment.

veranlassen [fɛrˈanlasən], *v.a.* bring about, cause, motivate; *einen —*, induce s.o., cause s.o.; *etwas —*, bring s.th. about, cause s.th.

Veranlassung [fɛr'anlasuŋ], f. (—, no pl.) cause, motive; occasion; inducement; *auf seine* —, at his suggestion; *ohne irgend eine* —, without the slightest provocation.

veranschaulichen [fɛr'anʃauliçən], v.a. illustrate, make clear.

veranschlagen [fɛr'anʃla:gən], v.a. estimate, assess.

Veranschlagung [fɛr'anʃla:guŋ], f. (—, pl. —en) estimate.

veranstalten [fɛr'anʃtaltən], v.a. organise, arrange.

Veranstalter [fɛr'anʃtaltər], m. (—s, pl. —) organiser.

Veranstaltung [fɛr'anʃtaltuŋ], f. (—, pl. —en) arrangement; entertainment; show; event; (sporting) fixture.

verantworten [fɛr'antvɔrtən], v.a. account for. — v.r. sich —, answer (for), justify o.s.

verantwortlich [fɛr'antvɔrtlɪç], adj. responsible, answerable, accountable.

Verantwortlichkeit [fɛr'antvɔrtlɪçkaɪt], f. (—, no pl.) responsibility.

Verantwortung [fɛr'antvɔrtuŋ], f. (—, no pl.) responsibility, justification, excuse; defence; *auf deine* —, at your own risk; *einen zur — ziehen*, call s.o. to account.

verantwortungsvoll [fɛr'antvɔrtuŋsfɔl], adj. responsible.

verarbeiten [fɛr'arbaɪtən], v.a. manufacture, process; (fig.) digest.

Verarbeitung [fɛr'arbaɪtuŋ], f. (—, no pl.) manufacture; process; finish; (fig.) digestion.

verargen [fɛr'argən], v.a. *einem etwas* —, blame or reproach s.o. for s.th.

verärgern [fɛr'ɛrgərn], v.a. annoy, make angry.

Verarmung [fɛr'armuŋ], f. (—, no pl.) impoverishment.

verausgaben [fɛr'ausga:bən], v.r. sich —, overspend, run short of money; spend o.s., wear o.s. out.

veräußern [fɛr'ɔysərn], v.a. dispose of, sell.

Veräußerung [fɛr'ɔysəruŋ], f. (—, no pl.) sale; alienation.

Verband [fɛr'bant], m. (—s, pl. ̈e) bandage, dressing; association, union; unit.

verbannen [fɛr'banən], v.a. banish, exile, outlaw.

Verbannte [fɛr'bantə], m. (—n, pl. —n) exile, outlaw.

Verbannung [fɛr'banuŋ], f. (—, pl. —en) banishment, exile.

verbauen [fɛr'bauən], v.n. obstruct; build up; use up or spend in building.

verbeißen [fɛr'baɪsən], v.a. irr. sich etwas —, suppress s.th.; sich das Lachen —, stifle a laugh. — v.r. sich in etwas —, stick doggedly to s.th.

verbergen [fɛr'bɛrgən], v.a. irr. conceal, hide.

verbessern [fɛr'bɛsərn], v.a. improve, correct, mend.

Verbesserung [fɛr'bɛsəruŋ], f. (—, pl. —en) improvement; correction.

verbeugen [fɛr'bɔygən], v.r. sich —, bow.

Verbeugung [fɛr'bɔyguŋ], f. (—, pl. —en) bow, obeisance.

verbiegen [fɛr'bi:gən], v.a. irr. twist, distort, bend the wrong way.

verbieten [fɛr'bi:tən], v.a. irr. forbid, prohibit.

verbilligen [fɛr'bɪlɪgən], v.a. cheapen, reduce the price of.

verbinden [fɛr'bɪndən], v.a. irr. tie up, bind up, connect; (Med.) dress, bandage; unite, join; *die Augen* —, blindfold. — v.r. sich —, unite, join; (Chem.) combine.

verbindlich [fɛr'bɪntlɪç], adj. binding; obligatory; obliging; —en Dank, my best thanks.

Verbindlichkeit [fɛr'bɪntlɪçkaɪt], f. (—, pl. —en) liability, obligation; compliment.

Verbindung [fɛr'bɪnduŋ], f. (—, pl. —en) connexion, connection, junction; association; alliance; (Railw.) connection; (Chem.) compound.

Verbindungsglied [fɛr'bɪnduŋsgli:t], n. (—(e)s, pl. —er) connecting link.

Verbindungslinie [fɛr'bɪnduŋsli:njə], f. (—, pl. —n) line of communication.

verbissen [fɛr'bɪsən], adj. obstinate, grim; soured. — adv. doggedly.

verbitten [fɛr'bɪtən], v.a. irr. sich etwas —, forbid s.th. determinedly; insist on s.th. not being done, object to.

verbittern [fɛr'bɪtərn], v.a. embitter.

Verbitterung [fɛr'bɪtəruŋ], f. (—, no pl.) exasperation.

verblassen [fɛr'blasən], v.n. (aux. sein) turn pale.

Verbleib [fɛr'blaɪp], m. (—(e)s, no pl.) whereabouts.

verbleiben [fɛr'blaɪbən], v.n. irr. (aux. sein) remain.

verblenden [fɛr'blɛndən], v.a. dazzle, delude, blind.

Verblendung [fɛr'blɛnduŋ], f. (—, no pl.) infatuation; delusion.

verblüffen [fɛr'blyfən], v.n. amaze, stagger, dumbfound.

Verblüffung [fɛr'blyfuŋ], f. (—, no pl.) bewilderment.

verblühen [fɛr'bly:ən], v.n. (aux. sein) wither, fade.

verblümt [fɛr'bly:mt], adj. veiled.

verbluten [fɛr'blu:tən], v.n. (aux. sein) bleed to death.

verborgen (1) [fɛr'bɔrgən], v.a. lend out.

verborgen (2) [fɛr'bɔrgən], adj. concealed, hidden; im —en, secretly.

Verborgenheit [fɛr'bɔrgənhaɪt], f. (—, no pl.) concealment, seclusion.

Verbot [fɛr'bo:t], n. (—(e)s, pl. —e) prohibition.

verboten [fɛr'bo:tən], adj. forbidden, prohibited.

verbrämen [fɛr'brɛ:mən], v.a. (garment) edge, border.

251

verbrauchen

verbrauchen [fɛrˈbrauxən], *v.a.* consume, use up; spend.

Verbraucher [fɛrˈbrauxər], *m.* (—s, *pl.* —) consumer.

Verbrechen [fɛrˈbrɛçən], *n.* (—s, *pl.* —) crime.

verbrechen [fɛrˈbrɛçən], *v.a. irr.* commit, perpetrate.

Verbrecher [fɛrˈbrɛçər], *m.* (—s, *pl.* —) criminal.

Verbrecheralbum [fɛrˈbrɛçəralbum], *n.* (—s, *no pl.*) rogues' gallery.

verbreiten [fɛrˈbraitən], *v.a.* spread, diffuse.

verbreitern [fɛrˈbraitərn], *v.a.* widen.

Verbreitung [fɛrˈbraituŋ], *f.* (—, *no pl.*) spread(ing), propaganda, extension.

verbrennbar [fɛrˈbrɛnbaːr], *adj.* combustible.

verbrennen [fɛrˈbrɛnən], *v.a. irr.* burn; cremate; *von der Sonne verbrannt*, sunburnt. — *v.n.* (*aux.* sein) get burnt. — *v.r. sich* —, scald o.s., burn o.s.

Verbrennung [fɛrˈbrɛnuŋ], *f.* (—, *pl.* —en) burning, combustion; cremation.

verbrieft [fɛrˈbriːft], *adj.* vested; documented.

verbringen [fɛrˈbriŋən], *v.a. irr.* (*time*) spend, pass.

verbrüdern [fɛrˈbryːdərn], *v.r. sich* —, fraternise.

verbrühen [fɛrˈbryːən], *v.a.* scald.

verbummeln [fɛrˈbuməln], *v.a. die Zeit* —, fritter the time away.

verbunden [fɛrˈbundən], *adj. einem* — *sein*, be obliged to s.o.

verbünden [fɛrˈbyndən], *v.r. sich* — *mit*, ally o.s. with.

Verbündete [fɛrˈbyndətə], *m.* (—n, *pl.* —n) ally, confederate.

verbürgen [fɛrˈbyrgən], *v.a.* warrant, guarantee. — *v.r. sich für etwas* —, vouch for s.th.; guarantee s.th.

Verdacht [fɛrˈdaxt], *m.* (—(e)s, *no pl.*) suspicion.

verdächtig [fɛrˈdɛçtiç], *adj.* suspicious, doubtful, questionable.

verdächtigen [fɛrˈdɛçtigən], *v.a.* throw suspicion on, suspect.

verdammen [fɛrˈdamən], *v.a.* condemn, damn.

verdammenswert [fɛrˈdaməsveːrt], *adj.* damnable.

Verdammung [fɛrˈdamuŋ], *f.* (—, *no pl.*) condemnation.

verdampfen [fɛrˈdampfən], *v.n.* (*aux.* sein) evaporate.

verdanken [fɛrˈdaŋkən], *v.a. einem etwas* —, be indebted to s.o. for s.th.; owe s.th. to s.o.

verdauen [fɛrˈdauən], *v.a.* digest.

verdaulich [fɛrˈdauliç], *adj.* digestible.

Verdauung [fɛrˈdauuŋ], *f.* (—, *no pl.*) digestion.

Verdauungsstörung [fɛrˈdauuŋʃtøː-ruŋ], *f.* (—, *pl.* —en) indigestion.

Verdeck [fɛrˈdɛk], *n.* (—s, *pl.* —e) awning; (*Naut.*) deck.

verdecken [fɛrˈdɛkən], *v.a.* cover, hide.

verdenken [fɛrˈdɛŋkən], *v.a. irr. einem etwas* —, blame s.o. for s.th.

Verderb [fɛrˈdɛrp], *m.* (—s, *no pl.*) ruin, decay.

verderben [fɛrˈdɛrbən], *v.a. irr.* spoil, corrupt, pervert. — *v.n.* (*aux.* sein) decay, go bad.

Verderben [fɛrˈdɛrbən], *n.* (—s, *no pl.*) corruption, ruin.

Verderber [fɛrˈdɛrbər], *m.* (—s, *pl.*—) corrupter, perverter.

verderblich [fɛrˈdɛrpliç], *adj.* ruinous, pernicious, destructive; (*goods*) perishable.

Verderbnis [fɛrˈdɛrpnis], *f.* (—, *no pl.*) corruption, depravity; perversion; perdition.

Verderbtheit [fɛrˈdɛrpthait], *f.* (—, *no pl.*) corruption, perversion, depravity.

verdeutlichen [fɛrˈdɔytliçən], *v.a.* illustrate, clarify.

verdichten [fɛrˈdiçtən], *v.a., v.r.* thicken, condense, liquefy.

Verdichtung [fɛrˈdiçtuŋ], *f.* (—, *no pl.*) condensation; solidification.

verdicken [fɛrˈdikən], *v.a.* thicken; solidify.

verdienen [fɛrˈdiːnən], *v.a.* earn; deserve.

Verdienst (1) [fɛrˈdiːnst], *m.* (—es, *pl.* —e) profit, gain, earnings.

Verdienst (2) [fɛrˈdiːnst], *n.* (—es, *pl.* —e) merit, deserts.

verdienstvoll [fɛrˈdiːnstfɔl], *adj.* meritorious, deserving; distinguished.

verdient [fɛrˈdiːnt], *adj. sich* — *machen um*, deserve well of, serve well (a cause etc.).

verdientermaßen [fɛrˈdiːntərmasən], *adv.* deservedly.

verdingen [fɛrˈdiŋən], *v.r. irr. sich* —, enter service (with), take a situation (with).

verdolmetschen [fɛrˈdɔlmɛtʃən], *v.a.* interpret, translate.

verdoppeln [fɛrˈdɔpəln], *v.a.* double.

verdorben [fɛrˈdɔrbən], *adj.* spoilt; corrupted, depraved, debauched.

verdrängen [fɛrˈdrɛŋən], *v.a.* crowd out; (*Phys.*) displace; (*fig.*) supplant, supersede; (*Psych.*) inhibit, repress.

Verdrängung [fɛrˈdrɛŋuŋ], *f.* (—, *no pl.*) supplanting; (*Phys.*) displacement; (*Psych.*) inhibition, repression.

verdrehen [fɛrˈdreːən], *v.a.* twist (the wrong way); (*fig.*) misrepresent, distort.

verdreht [fɛrˈdreːt], *adj.* cracked, cranky, crazy, queer.

Verdrehtheit [fɛrˈdreːthait], *f.* (—, *no pl.*) crankiness.

Verdrehung [fɛrˈdreːuŋ], *f.* (—, *pl.* —en) distortion; (*fig.*) misrepresentation.

verdrießen [fɛrˈdriːsən], *v.a. irr.* vex, annoy.

verdrießlich [fɛrˈdriːsliç], *adj.* (*thing*) vexatious, tiresome; (*person*) morose, peevish.

verdrossen [fɛr'drɔsən], *adj.* annoyed; fretful, sulky.

Verdrossenheit [fɛr'drɔsənhaɪt], *f.* (—, *no pl.*) annoyance ;fretfulness,sulkiness.

verdrücken [fɛr'drykən], *v.a.* (*sl.*) eat o.'s fill of. — *v.r.* (*coll.*) *sich* —, slink away; sneak away.

Verdruß [fɛr'drus], *m.* (—**sses,** *no pl.*) vexation, annoyance; — *bereiten,* give trouble, cause annoyance.

verduften [fɛr'duftən], *v.n.* (*aux.* sein) evaporate; (*fig.*) (*coll.*) take French leave, clear out.

verdummen [fɛr'dumən], *v.n.* (*aux.* sein) become stupid.

verdunkeln [fɛr'duŋkəln], *v.a.* black-out, obscure; (*fig.*) eclipse.

Verdunk(e)lung [fɛr'duŋk(ə)luŋ], *f.* (—, *no pl.*) darkening, eclipse; black-out.

Verdunk(e)lungsgefahr [vɛr'duŋk(ə)-luŋsgəfaːr], *f.* (—, *no pl.*) (*Law*) danger of prejudicing the course *or* administration of justice.

verdünnen [fɛr'dynən], *v.a.* thin out, dilute.

Verdünnung [fɛr'dynuŋ], *f.* (—, *no pl.*) attenuation; dilution.

verdunsten [fɛr'dunstən], *v.n.* (*aux.* sein) evaporate.

verdursten [fɛr'durstən], *v.n.* (*aux.* sein) die of thirst, perish with thirst.

verdüstern [fɛr'dyːstərn], *v.a.* darken, make gloomy.

verdutzen [fɛr'dutsən], *v.a.* disconcert, bewilder, nonplus.

Veredlung [fɛr'eːdluŋ], *f.* (—, *no pl.*) improvement, refinement.

verehelichen [fɛr'eːəlɪçən], *v.r.* (*obs.*) *sich* —, get married.

verehren [fɛr'eːrən], *v.a.* respect, revere, esteem; worship, adore.

Verehrer [fɛr'eːrər], *m.* (—**s,** *pl.* —) admirer; lover.

verehrlich [fɛr'eːrlɪç], *adj.* venerable.

verehrt [fɛr'eːrt], *adj.* honoured; *sehr* —*er Herr,* dear Sir.

Verehrung [fɛr'eːruŋ], *f.* (—, *no pl.*) reverence, veneration; worship, adoration.

verehrungswürdig [fɛr'eːruŋsvyrdɪç], *adj.* venerable.

vereidigt [fɛr'aɪdɪçt], *adj.* sworn in, bound by oath, under oath; —*er Bücherrevisor,* chartered accountant.

Vereidigung [fɛr'aɪdɪguŋ], *f.* (—, *no pl.*) swearing in; oathtaking.

Verein [fɛr'aɪn], *m.* (—**s,** *pl.* —**e**) union, association, society; club.

vereinbar [fɛr'aɪnbaːr], *adj.* compatible.

vereinbaren [fɛr'aɪnbaːrən], *v.a.* agree upon, arrange.

Vereinbarung [fɛr'aɪnbaːruŋ], *f.* (—, *pl.* —**en**) arrangement, agreement.

vereinen [fɛr'aɪnən], *v.a.* unite.

vereinfachen [fɛr'aɪnfaxən], *v.a.* simplify.

vereinigen [fɛr'aɪnɪgən], *v.a.* unite. — *v.r. sich* — *mit,* associate o.s. with, join with.

Vereinigung [fɛr'aɪnɪguŋ], *f.* (—, *pl.* —**en**) union; association.

vereinnahmen [fɛr'aɪnnaːmən], *v.a.* receive, take (*money*).

vereinsamen [fɛr'aɪnzaːmən], *v.n.* (*aux.* sein) become isolated, become lonely.

vereint [fɛr'aɪnt], *adj.* united, joined. — *adv.* in concert, (all) together.

vereinzelt [fɛr'aɪntsəlt], *adj.* sporadic, isolated. — *adv.* here and there, now and then.

Vereinzelung [fɛr'aɪntsəluŋ], *f.* (—, *pl.* —**en**) isolation; individualization.

vereisen [fɛr'aɪzən], *v.n.* become frozen, freeze; congeal.

Vereisung [fɛr'aɪzuŋ], *f.* (—, *pl.* —**en**) freezing, icing (up).

vereiteln [fɛr'aɪtəln], *v.a.* frustrate, thwart.

Vereitelung [fɛr'aɪtəluŋ], *f.* (—, *pl.* —**en**) frustration, thwarting.

vereitern [fɛr'aɪtərn], *v.n.* suppurate.

Vereiterung [fɛr'aɪtəruŋ], *f.* (—, *pl.* —**en**) suppuration.

verenden [fɛr'ɛndən], *v.n.* (*aux.* sein) (*animal*) die.

verengen [fɛr'ɛŋən], *v.a.* narrow, straighten, constrict.

Verengung [fɛr'ɛŋuŋ], *f.* (—, *pl.* —**en**) narrowing, straightening, contraction.

vererben [fɛr'ɛrbən], *v.a.* leave (by will), bequeath. — *v.r. sich* — *auf,* devolve upon, be hereditary.

vererblich [fɛr'ɛrplɪç],*adj.*(in)heritable, hereditary.

Vererbung [fɛr'ɛrbuŋ], *f.* (—, *no pl.*) heredity.

verewigen [fɛr'eːvɪgən], *v.a.* immortalise.

Verewigte [fɛr'eːvɪçtə], *m.* (—**n,** *pl.* —**n**) (*Poet.*) deceased.

Verfahren [fɛr'faːrən], *n.* (—**s,** *pl.* —) process; (*Law*) procedure; proceedings; *das* — *einstellen,* quash proceedings.

verfahren [fɛr'faːrən], *v.n. irr.* (*aux.* sein) proceed, act, operate. — *v.a.* spend (*money etc.*) on travelling. — *v.r. sich* —, (*Motor.*) lose o.'s way.

Verfall [fɛr'fal], *m.* (—**s,** *no pl.*) decay, decline; downfall, ruin; (*Comm.*) expiration, maturity; *in* — *geraten,* fall into ruin, decay.

verfallen [fɛr'falən], *v.n. irr.* (*aux.* sein) decay; go to ruin; lapse; (*Comm.*) fall due, expire; (*pledge*) become forfeit; *einem* —, become the property of, accrue to, devolve upon s.o.; (*fig.*) become the slave of s.o.; (*health*) decline, fail; *auf etwas* —, hit upon an idea. — *adj.* decayed, ruined.

Verfalltag [fɛr'faltaːk], *m.* (—**s,** *pl.* —**e**) day of payment; maturity.

verfälschen [fɛr'fɛlʃən], *v.a.* falsify; adulterate.

Verfälschung [fɛr'fɛlʃuŋ], *f.* (—, *pl.* —**en**) falsification; adulteration.

verfangen

verfangen [fɛr'faŋən], *v.r. irr. sich* —, get entangled; *sich in ein Lügennetz* —, entangle o.s. in a tissue of lies.

verfänglich [fɛr'fɛŋlɪç], *adj.* risky; insidious.

verfärben [fɛr'fɛrbən], *v.r. sich* —, change colour.

verfassen [fɛr'fasən], *v.a.* compose, write, be the author of.

Verfasser [fɛr'fasər], *m.* (—s, *pl.* —) author, writer.

Verfassung [fɛr'fasuŋ], *f.* (—, *pl.* —en) composition; *(state)* constitution; state, condition, disposition.

verfassungsgemäß [fɛr'fasuŋsgəmɛːs], *adj.* constitutional.

verfassungswidrig [fɛr'fasuŋsviːdrɪç], *adj.* unconstitutional.

verfaulen [fɛr'faulən], *v.n. (aux. sein)* rot, putrefy.

verfechten [fɛr'fɛçtən], *v.a. irr.* defend, advocate; maintain.

verfehlen [fɛr'feːlən], *v.a.* fail, miss; fail to meet; fail to do; *den Weg* —, lose o.'s way.

verfehlt [fɛr'feːlt], *adj.* unsuccessful, false, abortive; *eine* —*e Sache*, a failure.

Verfehlung [fɛr'feːluŋ], *f.* (—, *pl.* —en) lapse.

verfeinern [fɛr'fainərn], *v.a.* refine, improve.

Verfeinerung [fɛr'fainəruŋ], *f.* (—, *pl.* —en) refinement, polish.

verfertigen [fɛr'fɛrtɪgən], *v.a.* make, manufacture.

verfilmen [fɛr'fɪlmən], *v.a.* make a film of, film.

verfinstern [fɛr'fɪnstərn], *v.r. sich* —, get dark; be eclipsed.

verflechten [fɛr'flɛçtən], *v.a. irr.* interweave, interlace. — *v.r. sich* —, (*fig.*) become entangled, become involved.

verfließen [fɛr'fliːsən], *v.n. irr. (aux. sein)* flow away; (*time*) elapse, pass.

verflossen [fɛr'flosən], *adj.* past, bygone.

verfluchen [fɛr'fluːxən], *v.a.* curse, execrate.

verflucht [fɛr'fluːxt], *excl.* damn!

verflüchtigen [fɛr'flyçtɪgən], *v.r. sich* —, become volatile; evaporate; (*coll.*) make off, make o.s. scarce.

Verfluchung [fɛr'fluːxuŋ], *f.* (—, *pl.* —en) malediction, curse.

Verfolg [fɛr'folk], *m.* (—(e)s, *no pl.*) progress, course.

verfolgen [fɛr'folgən], *v.a.* pursue; persecute; prosecute.

Verfolger [fɛr'folgər], *m.* (—s, *pl.* —) pursuer; persecutor.

Verfolgung [fɛr'folguŋ], *f.* (—, *pl.* —en) pursuit; persecution; prosecution.

Verfolgungswahn [fɛr'folguŋsvaːn], *m.* (—s, *no pl.*) persecution mania.

verfrüht [fɛr'fryːt], *adj.* premature.

verfügbar [fɛr'fyːkbaːr], *adj.* available.

verfügen [fɛr'fyːgən], *v.a.* decree, order. — *v.n.* — *über etwas*, have control of s.th., have s.th. at o.'s disposal.

Verfügung [fɛr'fyːguŋ], *f.* (—, *pl.* —en) decree, ordinance; disposition, disposal; *einem zur* — *stehen*, be at s.o.'s service *or* disposal.

verführen [fɛr'fyːrən], *v.a.* seduce.

verführerisch [fɛr'fyːrərɪʃ], *adj.* seductive, alluring; (*coll.*) fetching.

Verführung [fɛr'fyːruŋ], *f.* (—, *no pl.*) seduction.

vergällen [fɛr'gɛlən], *v.a.* spoil, mar.

vergallopieren [fɛrgalo'piːrən], *v.r.* (*coll.*) *sich* —, blunder, overshoot the mark.

vergangen [fɛr'gaŋən], *adj.* past, gone, last.

Vergangenheit [fɛr'gaŋənhait], *f.* (—, *no pl.*) past, time past; (*Gram.*) past tense.

vergänglich [fɛr'gɛŋlɪç], *adj.* transient, transitory.

Vergaser [fɛr'gaːzər], *m.* (—s, *pl.* —) (*Motor.*) carburettor.

vergeben [fɛr'geːbən], *v.a. irr.* give away; forgive, pardon; confer, bestow.

vergebens [fɛr'geːbəns], *adv.* in vain, vainly.

vergeblich [fɛr'geːplɪç], *adj.* vain, futile, fruitless. — *adv.* in vain.

Vergebung [fɛr'geːbuŋ], *f.* (—, *no pl.*) forgiveness, pardon; (*office*) bestowal.

vergegenwärtigen [fɛrge'gən'vɛrtɪgən], *v.a.* bring to mind, imagine.

Vergehen [fɛr'geːən], *n.* (—s, *pl.* —) offence lapse.

vergehen [fɛr'geːən], *v.n. irr.* (*aux. sein*) go away, pass (away); elapse; perish; (*time*) pass. — *v.r. sich* —, go wrong; offend; violate (*Law, person*).

vergelten [fɛr'gɛltən], *v.a. irr.* repay, reward, recompense.

Vergeltung [fɛr'gɛltuŋ], *f.* (—, *no pl.*) requital, retribution; reward, recompense.

vergessen [fɛr'gɛsən], *v.a. irr.* forget; *bei einem* —, leave behind.

Vergessenheit [fɛr'gɛsənhait], *f.* (—, *no pl.*) oblivion.

vergeßlich [fɛr'gɛslɪç], *adj.* forgetful.

vergeuden [fɛr'gɔydən], *v.a.* waste, squander.

vergewaltigen [fɛrgə'valtɪgən], *v.a.* assault criminally, rape, violate; (*fig.*) coerce, force.

Vergewaltigung [fɛrgə'valtɪguŋ], *f.* (—, *no pl.*) criminal assault, rape; (*fig.*) coercion.

vergewissern [fɛrgə'vɪsərn], *v.r. sich* —, ascertain, make sure.

vergießen [fɛr'giːsən], *v.a. irr.* spill; shed.

vergiften [fɛr'gɪftən], *v.a.* poison.

Vergiftung [fɛr'gɪftuŋ], *f.* (—, *pl.* —en) poisoning.

vergilbt [fɛr'gɪlpt], *adj.* yellow with age.

Vergißmeinnicht [fɛr'gɪsmainnɪçt], *n.* (—s, *pl.* —e) (*Bot.*) forget-me-not.

Vergleich [fɛr'glaɪç], *m.* (—(e)s, *pl.* —e) comparison; agreement; (*Law*) compromise.

vergleichbar [fɛr'glaɪçbaːr], *adj.* comparable.

vergleichen [fɛr'glaɪçən], *v.a. irr.* compare.

vergleichsweise [fɛr'glaɪçsvaɪzə], *adv.* by way of comparison; comparatively; (*Law*) by way of agreement.

Vergnügen [fɛr'gnyːgən], *n.* (—s, *no pl.*) pleasure, enjoyment, fun.

vergnügen [fɛr'gnyːgən], *v.a.* amuse, delight.

Vergnügung [fɛr'gnyːguŋ], *f.* (—, *pl.* —en) entertainment, amusement.

vergönnen [fɛr'gœnən], *v.a.* grant, allow; not (be)grudge.

vergöttern [fɛr'gœtərn], *v.a.* idolise, worship.

vergraben [fɛr'graːbən], *v.a. irr.* hide in the ground, bury.

vergrämt [fɛr'grɛːmt], *adj.* careworn.

vergreifen [fɛr'graɪfən], *v.r. irr. sich — an*, lay violent hands on, violate.

vergriffen [fɛr'grɪfən], *adj.* out of stock, out of print.

vergrößern [fɛr'grøːsərn], *v.a.* enlarge, expand; increase; magnify; (*fig.*) exaggerate.

Vergrößerung [fɛr'grøːsəruŋ], *f.* (—, *pl.* —en) magnification, enlargement, increase.

Vergrößerungsglas [fɛr'grøːsəruŋsglas], *n.* (—es, *pl.* ̈er) magnifying glass.

Vergünstigung [fɛr'gynstɪguŋ], *f.* (—, *pl.* —en) privilege, favour, special facility, concession.

vergüten [fɛr'gyːtən], *v.a. einem etwas —*, compensate s.o. for s.th.; reimburse s.o. for s.th.

Vergütung [fɛr'gyːtuŋ], *f.* (—, *pl.* —en) indemnification, compensation, reimbursement.

verhaften [fɛr'haftən], *v.a.* arrest.

Verhaftung [fɛr'haftuŋ], *f.* (—, *pl.* —en) arrest.

verhallen [fɛr'halən], *v.n.* (*aux. sein*) (*sound*) fade, die away.

verhalten [fɛr'haltən], *v.r. irr. sich —*, act, behave.

Verhalten [fɛr'haltən], *n.* (—s, *no pl.*) behaviour, conduct, demeanour.

Verhältnis [fɛr'hɛltnɪs], *n.* (—ses, *pl.* —se) (*Maths.*) proportion, ratio; relation; footing; love-affair, liaison; (*coll.*) mistress.

verhältnismäßig [fɛr'hɛltnɪsmɛsɪç], *adj.* proportionate, comparative.

Verhältniswort [fɛr'hɛltnɪsvɔrt], *n.* (—es, *pl.* ̈er) preposition.

Verhältniszahl [fɛr'hɛltnɪstsaːl], *f.* (—, *pl.* —en) proportional number.

Verhaltungsmaßregel [fɛr'haltuŋsmaːsreːgəl], *f.* (—, *pl.* —n) rule of conduct; instruction.

verhandeln [fɛr'handəln], *v.a.* discuss, transact. — *v.n.* negotiate.

Verhandlung [fɛr'handluŋ], *f.* (—, *pl.* —en) discussion, negotiation, transaction; (*Law*) proceedings.

verhängen [fɛr'hɛŋən], *v.a.* cover with; decree; inflict (a penalty) on s.o.

Verhängnis [fɛr'hɛŋnɪs], *n.* (—ses, *pl.* —se) fate, destiny; misfortune.

Verhängnisglaube [fɛr'hɛŋnɪsglaubə], *m.* (—ns, *no pl.*) fatalism.

verhängnisvoll [fɛr'hɛŋnɪsfɔl], *adj.* fateful, portentous; fatal.

verhärmt [fɛr'hɛrmt], *adj.* careworn.

verharren [fɛr'harən], *v.n.* remain; persist.

Verhärtung [fɛr'hɛrtuŋ], *f.* (—, *pl.* —en) hardening, hardened state; (*skin*) callosity; (*fig.*) obduracy.

verhaßt [fɛr'hast], *adj.* hated, odious.

verhätscheln [fɛr'hɛtʃəln], *v.a.* pamper, coddle.

verhauen [fɛr'hauən], *v.a.* beat, thrash.

Verheerung [fɛr'heːruŋ], *f.* (—, *pl.* —en) devastation.

verhehlen [fɛr'heːlən], *v.a.* conceal, hide.

verheilen [fɛr'haɪlən], *v.n.* (*aux. sein*) heal.

verheimlichen [fɛr'haɪmlɪçən], *v.a.* keep secret, hush up.

verheiraten [fɛr'haɪraːtən], *v.a.* give in marriage, marry off. — *v.r. sich —*, marry, get married.

verheißen [fɛr'haɪsən], *v.a. irr.* promise.

Verheißung [fɛr'haɪsuŋ], *f.* (—, *pl.* —en) promise.

verhelfen [fɛr'hɛlfən], *v.n. irr. einem zu etwas —*, help s.o. to s.th.

Verherrlichung [fɛr'hɛrlɪçuŋ], *f.* (—, *no pl.*) glorification.

Verhetzung [fɛr'hɛtsuŋ], *f.* (—, *pl.* —en) incitement, instigation.

verhexen [fɛr'hɛksən], *v.a.* bewitch.

verhindern [fɛr'hɪndərn], *v.a.* hinder, prevent.

Verhinderung [fɛr'hɪndəruŋ], *f.* (—, *pl.* —en) prevention, obstacle.

verhöhnen [fɛr'høːnən], *v.a.* deride, scoff at, jeer at.

Verhöhnung [fɛr'høːnuŋ], *f.* (—, *pl.* —en) derision.

Verhör [fɛr'høːr], *n.* (—s, *pl.* —e) hearing; (judicial) examination; *ins — nehmen*, question, interrogate, cross-examine.

verhören [fɛr'høːrən], *v.a.* examine judicially, interrogate. — *v.r. sich —*, misunderstand.

verhüllen [fɛr'hylən], *v.a.* cover, wrap up, veil.

verhungern [fɛr'huŋərn], *v.n.* (*aux. sein*) starve.

verhungert [fɛr'huŋərt], *adj.* famished.

verhunzen [fɛr'huntsən], *v.a.* spoil, bungle.

verhüten [fɛr'hyːtən], *v.a.* prevent, avert.

Verhütung [fɛr'hyːtuŋ], *f.* (—, *no pl.*) prevention, warding off.

verirren [fɛr'ɪrən], *v.r. sich —*, go astray, lose o.'s way.

verirrt [fɛr'ɪrt], *adj.* stray, straying, lost.

verjagen [fɛr'jaːgən], *v.a.* drive away, chase away.

verjährt [fɛr'jɛːrt], *adj.* statute-barred; prescriptive; obsolete; old.

verjubeln [fɛr'juːbəln], *v.a.* play ducks and drakes with; squander.

verjüngen [fɛr'jyŋən], *v.a.* make younger; (*Archit.*) taper. — *v.r.* sich ⌐, grow younger.

Verjüngung [fɛr'jyŋuŋ], *f.* (—, *pl.* —en) rejuvenation.

verkannt [fɛr'kant], *adj.* misunderstood.

verkappt [fɛr'kapt], *adj.* disguised, secret, in disguise.

Verkauf [fɛr'kauf], *m.* (—(e)s, *pl.* ⸚e) sale.

verkaufen [fɛr'kaufən], *v.a.* sell.

Verkäufer [fɛr'kɔyfar], *m.* (—s, *pl.* —) seller; shop assistant, salesman.

verkäuflich [fɛr'kɔyflɪç], *adj.* for sale, saleable; mercenary.

Verkaufspreis [fɛr'kaufsprais], *m.* (—es, *pl.* —e) selling-price.

Verkehr [fɛr'keːr], *m.* (—s, *no pl.*) traffic; commerce; intercourse; communication; — *mit*, association with; service (*trains, buses etc.*), transport.

verkehren [fɛr'keːrən], *v.a.* turn upside down; transform; pervert. — *v.n.* frequent (a place), visit, associate (with); run, operate.

Verkehrsstraße [fɛr'keːrsʃtraːsə], *f.* (—es, *pl.* —n) thoroughfare.

Verkehrsstockung [fɛr'keːrsʃtɔkuŋ], *f.* (—, *pl.* —en) traffic jam.

verkehrt [fɛr'keːrt], *adj.* upside down; (*fig.*) wrong.

Verkehrtheit [fɛr'keːrthait], *f.* (—, *pl.* —en) absurdity, piece of folly.

Verkehrung [fɛr'keːruŋ], *f.* (—, *pl.* —en) turning; inversion; perversion; misrepresentation; (*Gram.*) inversion.

verkennen [fɛr'kɛnən], *v.a. irr.* mistake, fail to recognize; misjudge (s.o.'s intentions).

verklagen [fɛr'klaːgən], *v.a.* sue; accuse.

verklären [fɛr'klɛːrən], *v.a.* transfigure, illumine.

verklärt [fɛr'klɛːrt], *adj.* transfigured; radiant.

verkleben [fɛr'kleːbən], *v.a.* paste over.

verkleiden [fɛr'klaidən], *v.a., v.r.* disguise (o.s.).

Verkleidung [fɛr'klaiduŋ], *f.* (— *pl.* —en) disguise.

verkleinern [fɛr'klainərn], *v.a.* make smaller, diminish, reduce; belittle, disparage.

Verkleinerung [fɛr'klainəruŋ], *f.* (—, *pl.* —en) diminution, reduction; belittling, detraction.

Verkleinerungswort [fɛr'klainəruŋsvɔrt], *n.* (—s, *pl.* ⸚er) (*Gram.*) diminutive.

verkneifen [fɛr'knaifən], *v.r. irr.* (*coll.*) *sich etwas* —, deny o.s. s.th.

verkniffen [fɛr'knifən], *adj.* pinched; shrewd; hard-bitten.

verknöchern [fɛr'knœçərn], *v.n.* (*aux.* sein) ossify; (*fig.*) become fossilised *or* inflexible.

Verknöcherung [fɛr'knœçəruŋ], *f.* (—, *pl.* —en) ossification; (*fig.*) fossilisation.

verknüpfen [fɛr'knypfən], *v.a.* tie, connect, link.

verkochen [fɛr'kɔxən], *v.n.* (*aux.* sein) boil away.

verkommen [fɛr'kɔmən], *v.n. irr.* (*aux.* sein) go from bad to worse, go to seed, decay, become depraved. — *adj.* demoralised, down and out, depraved.

Verkommenheit [fɛr'kɔmənhait], *f.* (—, *no pl.*) demoralisation; depravity.

verkörpern [fɛr'kœrpərn], *v.a.* embody.

verkrachen [fɛr'kraxən], *v.r.* sich —, quarrel, (*coll.*) have a row.

verkriechen [fɛr'kriːçən], *v.r. irr.* sich —, creep *or* crawl away; slink away, lie low.

verkümmern [fɛr'kymərn], *v.n.* (*aux.* sein) wear away, waste away; pine away.

verkünden [fɛr'kyndən], *v.a.* proclaim, announce, publish, prophesy.

Verkündigung [fɛr'kyndiguŋ], *f.* (—, *pl.* —en) announcement, proclamation; prediction.

Verkündung [fɛr'kynduŋ], *f.* (—, *pl.* —en) publication, proclamation.

Verkürzung [fɛr'kyrtsuŋ], *f.* (—, *pl.* —en) shortening, curtailment.

verlachen [fɛr'laxən], *v.a.* laugh at, deride.

verladen [fɛr'laːdən], *v.a. irr.* load, ship, freight.

Verladung [fɛr'laːduŋ], *f.* (—, *pl.* —en) loading, shipping.

Verlag [fɛr'laːk], *m.* (—(e)s, *pl.* —e) publication; publishing-house, (firm of) publishers.

Verlagsrecht [fɛr'laːksrɛçt], *n.* (—s, *pl.* —e) copyright.

Verlangen [fɛr'laŋən], *n.* (—s, *no pl.*) demand, request; longing, desire.

verlangen [fɛr'laŋən], *v.a.* ask, demand, request.

verlängern [fɛr'lɛŋərn], *v.a.* lengthen, prolong, extend.

Verlängerung [fɛr'lɛŋəruŋ], *f.* (—, *pl.* —en) lengthening; (*period*) prolongation, extension.

verlangsamen [fɛr'laŋzaːmən], *v.a.* slow down, slacken, decelerate.

Verlaß [fɛr'las], *m.* (—sses, *no pl.*) *es ist kein* — *auf dich*, you cannot be relied on.

verlassen [fɛr'lasən], *v.a. irr.* leave, abandon. — *v.r.* sich — *auf*, rely on, depend upon. — *adj.* forlorn, forsaken, deserted, desolate, lonely.

Verlassenheit [fɛr'lasənhait], *f.* (—, *no pl.*) desolation, loneliness, solitude.

verläßlich [fɛr'lɛslɪç], *adj.* reliable, trustworthy.

Verlauf [fɛr'lauf], *m.* (—(e)s, *no pl.*) lapse, expiration; course.

verlaufen [fɛr'laufən], *v.n. irr.* (aux. sein) (*time*) pass; (*period*) expire, elapse; develop(e), turn out. — *v.r. sich* —, lose o.'s way; (*colour*) run.

verlauten [fɛr'lautən], *v.n.* transpire.

verleben [fɛr'le:bən], *v.a.* pass, spend.

verlebt [fɛr'le:pt], *adj.* worn out; spent; (*Am.*) played out.

verlegen [fɛr'le:gən], *v.a.* (*domicile*) move, remove; (*things*) mislay; (*books*) publish; obstruct; adjourn; change to another date *or* place. — *v.r. sich auf etwas* —, devote o.s. to s.th. — *adj.* embarrassed, ill at ease.

Verlegenheit [fɛr'le:gənhaɪt], *f.* (—, *pl.* —en) embarrassment, perplexity; predicament, difficulty.

Verleger [fɛr'le:gər], *m.* (—s, *pl.* —) publisher.

verleiden [fɛr'laɪdən], *v.a. einem etwas* —, spoil s.th. for s.o.

verleihen [fɛr'laɪən], *v.a. irr.* lend; (*honour, title*) confer; bestow, award.

Verleiher [fɛr'laɪər], *m.* (—s, *pl.* —) lender.

Verleihung [fɛr'laɪuŋ], *f.* (—, *pl.* —en) lending, loan; (*medal, prize*) investiture; grant, conferring.

verleiten [fɛr'laɪtən], *v.a.* mislead, entice, induce; seduce.

Verleitung [fɛr'laɪtuŋ], *f.* (—, *no pl.*) misleading, enticement, inducement; seduction.

verlernen [fɛr'lɛrnən], *v.a.* unlearn; forget.

verlesen [fɛr'le:zən], *v.a. irr.* read aloud, read out, recite. — *v.r. sich* —, misread.

verletzen [fɛr'lɛtsən], *v.a.* injure, hurt, wound, violate.

verletzend [fɛr'lɛtsənt], *adj.* offensive, insulting; cutting.

verletzlich [fɛr'lɛtslɪç], *adj.* vulnerable.

Verletzlichkeit [fɛr'lɛtslɪçkaɪt], *f.* (—, *no pl.*) vulnerability.

Verletzung [fɛr'lɛtsuŋ], *f.* (—, *pl.* —en) hurt, wound; (*Law*) violation.

verleugnen [fɛr'lɔygnən], *v.a.* deny, renounce, disown.

Verleugnung [fɛr'lɔygnuŋ], *f.* (—, *pl.* —en) denial, abnegation.

verleumden [fɛr'lɔymdən], *v.a.* slander, calumniate, traduce.

Verleumdung [fɛr'lɔymduŋ], *f.* (—, *pl.* —en) slander, libel, calumny.

verlieben [fɛr'li:bən], *v.r. sich* — *in*, fall in love with.

Verliebte [fɛr'li:ptə], *m. or f.* (—n, *pl.* —n) person in love, lover.

Verliebtheit [fɛr'li:pthaɪt], *f.* (—, *no pl.*) infatuation, amorousness.

verlieren [fɛr'li:rən], *v.a. irr.* lose.

Verlierer [fɛr'li:rər], *m.* (—s, *pl.* —) loser.

Verlies [fɛr'li:s], *n.* (—(s)es, *pl.* —(s)e) dungeon.

verloben [fɛr'lo:bən], *v.r. sich* — *mit*, become engaged to.

Verlöbnis [fɛr'lø:pnɪs], *n.* (—ses, *pl.* —se) (*rare*) engagement.

Verlobte [fɛr'lo:ptə], *m.* (—n, *pl.* —n) and *f.* (—n, *pl.* —n) fiancé(e), betrothed.

Verlobung [fɛr'lo:buŋ], *f.* (—, *pl.* —en) engagement, betrothal.

verlocken [fɛr'lɔkən], *v.a.* tempt, entice.

verlogen [fɛr'lo:gən], *adj.* lying, mendacious.

Verlogenheit [fɛr'lo:gənhaɪt], *f.* (—, *no pl.*) mendacity.

verlohnen [fɛr'lo:nən], *v. impers.* be worth while.

verlöschen [fɛr'lœʃən], *v.a.* extinguish.

verlosen [fɛr'lo:zən], *v.a.* raffle; draw *or* cast lots for.

Verlosung [fɛr'lo:zuŋ], *f.* (—, *pl.* —en) raffle, lottery.

verlöten [fɛr'lø:tən], *v.a.* solder.

verlottern [fɛr'lɔtərn], *v.n.* (aux. sein) go to the dogs.

Verlust [fɛr'lust], *m.* (—es, *pl.* —e) loss; (*death*) bereavement; (*Mil.*) casualty.

verlustig [fɛr'lustɪç], *adj.* — *gehen*, lose s.th., forfeit s.th.

vermachen [fɛr'maxən], *v.a. einem etwas* —, bequeath s.th. to s.o.

Vermächtnis [fɛr'mɛçtnɪs], *n.* (—ses, *pl.* —sse) will; legacy, bequest; (*fig.*) *heiliges* —, sacred trust.

vermahlen [fɛr'ma:lən], *v.a.* grind (down).

Vermählung [fɛr'mɛ:luŋ], *f.* (—, *pl.* —en) marriage, wedding.

Vermahnung [fɛr'ma:nuŋ], *f.* (—, *pl.* —en) admonition, exhortation.

vermauern [fɛr'mauərn], *v.a.* wall up.

vermehren [fɛr'me:rən], *v.a.* augment, multiply, increase. — *v.r. sich* —, multiply.

Vermehrung [fɛr'me:ruŋ], *f.* (—, *pl.* —en) increase, multiplication.

vermeiden [fɛr'maɪdən], *v.a. irr.* avoid, shun, shrink.

vermeidlich [fɛr'maɪtlɪç], *adj.* avoidable.

Vermeidung [fɛr'maɪduŋ], *f.* (—, *no pl.*) avoidance.

vermeintlich [fɛr'maɪntlɪç], *adj.* supposed, alleged, pretended; (*heir*) presumptive.

vermelden [fɛr'mɛldən], *v.a.* announce, notify.

vermengen [fɛr'mɛŋən], *v.a.* mingle, mix.

Vermerk [fɛr'mɛrk], *m.* (—s, *pl.* —e) entry, notice, note.

vermerken [fɛr'mɛrkən], *v.a.* observe, jot down.

vermessen [fɛr'mɛsən], *v.a. irr.* measure; (*land*) survey. — *adj.* bold, daring, audacious; arrogant.

Vermessenheit [fɛr'mɛsənhaɪt], *f.* (—, *no pl.*) boldness, audacity; arrogance.

Vermesser [fɛr'mɛsər], *m.* (—s, *pl.* —) (*land*) surveyor.

Vermessung

Vermessung [fɛr'mɛsuŋ], *f.* (—, *pl.* —en) (*land*) survey; measuring.

vermieten [fɛr'mi:tən], *v.a.* let, lease, hire out.

Vermieter [fɛr'mi:tər], *m.* (—s, *pl.* —) landlord; hirer.

vermindern [fɛr'mɪndərn], *v.a.* diminish, lessen.

Verminderung [fɛr'mɪndəruŋ], *f.* (—, *pl.* —en) diminution, reduction, decrease, lessening.

vermischen [fɛr'mɪʃən], *v.a.* mix, mingle, blend.

vermissen [fɛr'mɪsən], *v.a.* miss; *vermißt sein,* be missing; *vermißt werden,* be missed.

vermitteln [fɛr'mɪtəln], *v.n.* mediate. — *v.a.* adjust; negotiate, secure.

Vermittler [fɛr'mɪtlər], *m.* (—s, *pl.* —) mediator; agent, middleman.

Vermittlung [fɛr'mɪtluŋ], *f.* (—, *pl.* —en) mediation, intervention.

vermöbeln [fɛr'møːbəln], *v.a.* (*sl.*) *einen* —, thrash s.o.

vermodern [fɛr'moːdərn], *v.n.* (*aux.* sein) moulder, rot.

vermöge [fɛr'møːgə], *prep.* (*Genit.*) by virtue of, by dint of, on the strength of.

Vermögen [fɛr'møːgən], *n.* (—s, *pl.* —) faculty, power; means, assets; fortune, wealth, riches; *er hat* —, he is a man of property; *nach bestem* —, to the best of o.'s ability.

vermögen [fɛr'møːgən], *v.a. irr.* be able to, have the power to, be capable of.

vermögend [fɛr'møːgənt], *adj.* wealthy.

Vermögensbestand [fɛr'møːgənsbəʃtant], *m.* (—s, *pl.* ⁐e) assets.

Vermögenssteuer [fɛr'møːgənsʃtɔyər], *f.* (—, *pl.* —en) property tax.

vermorscht [fɛr'mɔrʃt], *adj.* mouldering, rotten.

vermuten [fɛr'muːtən], *v.a.* suppose, conjecture, surmise, presume; guess.

vermutlich [fɛr'muːtlɪç], *adj.* likely, probable.

Vermutung [fɛr'muːtuŋ], *f.* (—, *pl.* —en) guess, supposition, conjecture.

vernachlässigen [fɛr'naxlɛsɪgən], *v.a.* neglect.

Vernachlässigung [fɛr'naxlɛsɪguŋ], *f.* (—, *pl.* —en) neglect, negligence.

vernarren [fɛr'narən], *v.r. sich* — (*in*, *Acc.*), become infatuated (with).

vernarrt [fɛr'nart], *adj.* madly in love.

vernaschen [fɛr'naʃən], *v.a.* squander (money) on sweets.

vernehmbar [fɛr'neːmbaːr], *adj.* audible; *sich* — *machen,* make o.s. heard.

Vernehmen [fɛr'neːmən], *n.* (—s, *no pl.*) *dem* — *nach,* from what o. hears.

vernehmen [fɛr'neːmən], *v.a. irr.* hear, learn; (*Law*) examine, interrogate.

vernehmlich [fɛr'neːmlɪç], *adj.* audible, distinct, clear.

Vernehmlichkeit [fɛr'neːmlɪçkaɪt], · *f.* (—, *no pl.*) audibility.

Vernehmung [fɛr'neːmuŋ], *f.* (—, *pl.* —en) (*Law*) interrogation, examination.

verneigen [fɛr'naɪgən], *v.r. sich* —, curts(e)y, bow.

Verneigung [fɛr'naɪguŋ], *f.* (—, *pl.* —en) curts(e)y, bow.

verneinen [fɛr'naɪnən], *v.a.* deny, answer in the negative.

Verneinung [fɛr'naɪnuŋ], *f.* (—, *pl.* —en) negation, denial; (*Gram.*) negation, negative.

vernichten [fɛr'nɪçtən], *v.a.* annihilate, destroy utterly, exterminate.

Vernichtung [fɛr'nɪçtuŋ], *f.* (—, *no pl.*) annihilation, extinction, destruction.

vernieten [fɛr'niːtən], *v.a.* rivet.

Vernunft [fɛr'nunft], *f.* (—, *no pl.*) reason, sense, intelligence, judgment; *gesunde* —, common sense; — *annehmen,* listen to reason; *einen zur* — *bringen,* bring s.o. to his senses.

vernünftig [fɛr'nynftɪç], *adj.* sensible, reasonable, rational.

veröden [fɛr'øːdən], *v.n.* (*aux.* sein) become desolate, become devastated.

Verödung [fɛr'øːduŋ], *f.* (—, *no pl.*) devastation, desolation.

veröffentlichen [fɛr'œfəntlɪçən], *v.a.* publish.

Veröffentlichung [fɛr'œfəntlɪçuŋ], *f.* (—, *pl.* —en) publication.

verordnen [fɛr'ɔrdnən], *v.a.* order, command, ordain; (*Med.*) prescribe.

Verordnung [fɛr'ɔrdnuŋ], *f.* (—, *pl.* —en) order; (*Law*) decree, edict, statute; (*Med.*) prescription.

verpassen [fɛr'pasən], *v.a.* lose by delay, let slip; (*train etc.*) miss.

verpfänden [fɛr'pfɛndən], *v.a.* pawn, pledge.

Verpfänder [fɛr'pfɛndər], *m.* (—s, *pl.* —) mortgager.

Verpfändung [fɛr'pfɛnduŋ], *f.* (—, *pl.* —en) pawning, pledging.

verpflanzen [fɛr'pflantsən], *v.a.* transplant.

Verpflanzung [fɛr'pflantsuŋ], *f.* (—, *pl.* —en) transplantation.

verpflegen [fɛr'pfleːgən], *v.a.* board, provide food for, feed; nurse.

Verpflegung [fɛr'pfleːguŋ], *f.* (—, *no pl.*) board, catering; food.

Verpflegungskosten [fɛr'pfleːguŋskɔstən], *f. pl.* (cost of) board and lodging.

verpflichten [fɛr'pflɪçtən], *v.a.* bind, oblige, engage.

verpflichtend [fɛr'pflɪçtənt], *adj.* obligatory.

Verpflichtung [fɛr'pflɪçtuŋ], *f.* (—, *pl.* —en) obligation, duty; liability, engagement.

verplaudern [fɛr'plaudərn], *v.a.* spend (time) chatting.

verplempern [fɛr'plɛmpərn], *v.a.* (*coll.*) spend foolishly, fritter away.

verpönt [fɛr'pøːnt], *adj.* frowned upon; taboo.

verprassen [fɛr'prasən], *v.a.* squander (money) in riotous living.

verpuffen [fɛr'pufən], *v.n.* (*aux.* sein) (*coll.*) fizzle out.

verpulvern [fɛr'pulvərn], *v.a.* fritter away.

Verputz [fɛr'puts], *m.* (**—es**, *no pl.*) plaster.

verquicken [fɛr'kvɪkən], *v.a.* amalgamate; mix up.

Verrat [fɛr'ra:t], *m.* (**—(e)s**, *no pl.*) treachery, treason.

verraten [fɛr'ra:tən], *v.a. irr.* betray; disclose; *das verrät die Hand des Künstlers*, this proclaims the hand of the artist.

Verräter [fɛr'rɛ:tər], *m.* (**—s**, *pl.* **—**) traitor.

verräterisch [fɛr'rɛ:tərɪʃ], *adj.* treacherous, treasonable, perfidious; (*fig.*) tell-tale.

verrauchen [fɛr'rauxən], *v.n.* (*aux.* sein) evaporate; (*fig.*) blow over; cool down.

verräuchern [fɛr'rɔyçərn], *v.a.* smoke, fill with smoke.

verräumen [fɛr'rɔymən], *v.a.* misplace, mislay.

verrauschen [fɛr'rauʃən], *v.n.* (*aux.* sein) (*sound*) die away; pass away.

verrechnen [fɛr'rɛçnən], *v.a.* reckon up. — *v.r. sich* **—**, miscalculate.

Verrechnung [fɛr'rɛçnuŋ], *f.* (**—**, *pl.* **— en**) reckoning-up.

Verrechnungsscheck [fɛr'rɛçnuŋs-ʃɛk], *m.* (**—s**, *pl.* **—e**, **—s**) crossed cheque, non-negotiable cheque.

verregnen [fɛr're:gnən], *v.a.* spoil by rain.

verreiben [fɛr'raɪbən], *v.a. irr.* rub away; rub hard.

verreisen [fɛr'raɪzən], *v.n.* (*aux.* sein) go on a journey.

verrenken [fɛr'rɛŋkən], *v.a.* sprain, dislocate.

Verrenkung [fɛr'rɛŋkuŋ], *f.* (**—**, *pl.* **—en**) sprain, dislocation.

verrichten [fɛr'rɪçtən], *v.a.* do, perform, acquit o.s. of; execute; (*prayer*) say.

verriegeln [fɛr'ri:gəln], *v.a.* bolt.

verringern [fɛr'rɪŋərn], *v.a.* reduce, diminish.

Verringerung [fɛr'rɪŋəruŋ], *f.* (**—**, *no pl.*) diminution, reduction.

verrinnen [fɛr'rɪnən], *v.n. irr.* (*aux.* sein) run off; (*fig.*) pass, elapse.

verrosten [fɛr'rɔstən], *v.n.* (*aux.* sein) rust.

verrottet [fɛr'rɔtət], *adj.* rotten.

verrucht [fɛr'ru:xt], *adj.* villainous, atrocious, heinous, infamous.

Verruchtheit [fɛr'ru:xthaɪt], *f.* (**—**, *no pl.*) villainy.

verrücken [fɛr'rykən], *v.a.* shift, displace.

verrückt [fɛr'rykt], *adj.* crazy, mad.

Verrückte [fɛr'ryktə], *m.* (**—n**, *pl.* **—n**) madman. — *f.* (**—n**, *pl.* **—n**) madwoman.

Verrücktheit [fɛr'rykthaɪt], *f.* (**—**, *pl.* **—en**) craziness; mad act.

Verruf [fɛr'ru:f], *m.* (**—s**, *no pl.*) discredit, ill repute.

verrufen [fɛr'ru:fən], *adj.* notorious, of ill repute.

Vers [fɛrs], *m.* (**—es**, *pl.* **—e**) verse.

versagen [fɛr'za:gən], *v.a. einem etwas* **—**, deny s.o. s.th., refuse s.o. s.th. — *v.n.* fail, break down; (*voice*) falter; *sich etwas* **—**, abstain from s.th., deny o.s. s.th.

Versager [fɛr'za:gər], *m.* (**—s**, *pl.* **—**) misfire; failure, unsuccessful person, flop.

versammeln [fɛr'zaməln], *v.a.* gather around, convene. — *v.r. sich* **—**, assemble, meet.

Versammlung [fɛr'zamluŋ], *f.* (**—**, *pl.* **—en**) assembly, meeting, gathering, convention.

Versand [fɛr'zant], *m.* (**—s**, *no pl.*) dispatch, forwarding, shipping, shipment.

versanden [fɛr'zandən], *v.n.* (*aux.* sein) silt up.

Versandgeschäft [fɛr'zantgəʃɛft], *n.* (**—s**, *pl.* **—e**) export business; mail order business.

Versatzamt [fɛr'zatsamt], *n.* (**—s**, *pl.* **¨er**) pawn-shop.

versauen [fɛr'zauən], *v.a.* (*sl.*) make a mess of.

versauern [fɛr'zauərn], *v.n.* (*aux.* sein) turn sour; (*fig.*) become morose.

versaufen [fɛr'zaufən], *v.a. irr.* (*sl.*) squander (money) on drink, drink away.

versäumen [fɛr'zɔymən], *v.a.* miss, omit, lose by delay; leave undone; neglect.

Versäumnis [fɛr'zɔymnɪs], *n.* (**—ses**, *pl.* **—se**) neglect, omission; (*time*) loss.

Versbau ['fɛrsbau], *m.* (**—s**, *no pl.*) versification; verse structure.

verschachern [fɛr'ʃaxərn], *v.a.* barter away.

verschaffen [fɛr'ʃafən], *v.a.* provide, procure, obtain, get.

verschämt [fɛr'ʃɛ:mt], *adj.* shamefaced, bashful.

verschanzen [fɛr'ʃantsən], *v.a.* fortify.

Verschanzung [fɛr'ʃantsuŋ], *f.* (**—**, *pl.* **—en**) fortification, entrenchment.

verschärfen [fɛr'ʃɛrfən], *v.a.* heighten, intensify, sharpen.

verscharren [fɛr'ʃarən], *v.a.* cover with earth; bury hurriedly.

verscheiden [fɛr'ʃaɪdən], *v.n. irr.* (*aux.* sein) die, pass away.

verschenken [fɛr'ʃɛŋkən], *v.a.* make a present of, give away.

verscherzen [fɛr'ʃɛrtsən], *v.a. sich etwas* **—**, forfeit s.th.

verscheuchen [fɛr'ʃɔyçən], *v.a.* scare away, frighten away; *Sorgen* **—**, banish care.

verschicken [fɛr'ʃɪkən], *v.a.* send on, send out, forward, transmit; evacuate.

Verschickung [fɛr'ʃɪkuŋ], *f.* (**—**, *no pl.*) forwarding, transmission; evacuation; banishment, exile.

verschieben [fɛrˈʃiːbən], *v.a. irr.* shift, move; delay, put off, defer, postpone.

Verschiebung [fɛrˈʃiːbuŋ], *f.* (—, *pl.* —en) removal; postponement; (*fig.*) black marketeering.

verschieden [fɛrˈʃiːdən], *adj.* different, diverse; deceased, departed; (*pl.*) some, several, sundry.

verschie·lenartig [fɛrˈʃiːdənaːrtɪç], *adj.* varied, various, heterogeneous.

verschiedenerlei [fɛrˈʃiːdənərlaɪ], *in-decl. adj.* diverse, of various kinds.

Verschiedenheit [fɛrˈʃiːdənhaɪt], *f.* (—, *pl.* —en) difference; diversity, variety.

verschiedentlich [fɛrˈʃiːdəntlɪç], *adv.* variously, severally; repeatedly.

verschiffen [fɛrˈʃɪfən], *v.a.* export, ship.

verschimmeln [fɛrˈʃɪməln], *v.n.* (*aux.* sein) go mouldy.

verschlafen [fɛrˈʃlaːfən], *v.a. irr.* sleep through, sleep away. — *v.r. sich* —, oversleep. — *adj.* sleepy, drowsy.

Verschlag [fɛrˈʃlaːk], *m.* (—s, *pl.* ⁼e) partition, box, cubicle.

verschlagen [fɛrˈʃlaːgən], *v.a. irr. es verschlägt mir den Atem*, it takes my breath away. — *adj.* cunning, crafty, sly.

verschlechtern [fɛrˈʃlɛçtərn], *v.a.* worsen, make worse. — *v.r. sich* —, deteriorate.

Verschlechterung [fɛrˈʃlɛçtəruŋ], *f.* (—, *no pl.*) deterioration.

verschleiern [fɛrˈʃlaɪərn], *v.a.* veil.

Verschleierung [fɛrˈʃlaɪəruŋ], *f.* (—, *pl.* —en) veiling, concealment; camouflage.

verschleißen [fɛrˈʃlaɪsən], *v.a. irr.* wear out, waste.

verschlemmen [fɛrˈʃlɛmən], *v.a.* squander on eating and drinking.

verschleppen [fɛrˈʃlɛpən], *v.a.* carry off, deport; kidnap; protract, spread; put off, procrastinate.

verschleudern [fɛrˈʃlɔydərn], *v.a.* waste; sell at cut prices.

verschließen [fɛrˈʃliːsən], *v.a. irr.* lock, lock up.

verschlimmern [fɛrˈʃlɪmərn], *v.a.* make worse. — *v.r. sich* —, get worse, worsen, deteriorate.

Verschlimmerung [fɛrˈʃlɪməruŋ], *f.* (—, *no pl.*) worsening, deterioration.

verschlingen [fɛrˈʃlɪŋən], *v.a. irr.* swallow up, devour.

verschlossen [fɛrˈʃlɔsən], *adj.* reserved, uncommunicative, withdrawn.

Verschlossenheit [fɛrˈʃlɔsənhaɪt], *f.* (—, *no pl.*)

verschlucken [fɛrˈʃlukən], *v.a.* swallow, gulp down; (*fig.*) suppress. — *v.r. sich* —, swallow the wrong way.

verschlungen [fɛrˈʃluŋən], *adj.* intricate, complicated.

Verschluß [fɛrˈʃlus], *m.* (—sses. *pl.* ⁼sse) lock; clasp; fastening; *unter* — *haben*, keep under lock and key.

Verschlußlaut [fɛrˈʃluslaut], *m.* (—s, *pl.* —e) (*Phon.*) explosive, plosive, stop.

verschmachten [fɛrˈʃmaxtən], *v.n.* (*aux.* sein) languish, pine; be parched.

Verschmähung [fɛrˈʃmɛːuŋ], *f.* (—, *no pl.*) disdain, scorn, rejection.

Verschmelzung [fɛrˈʃmɛltsuŋ], *f.* (—, *no pl.*) coalescence, fusion, blending.

verschmerzen [fɛrˈʃmɛrtsən], *v.a.* get over; bear stoically, make the best of.

verschmitzt [fɛrˈʃmɪtst], *adj.* cunning, crafty, mischievous.

verschmutzen [fɛrˈʃmutsən], *v.n.* (*aux.* sein) get dirty.

verschnappen [fɛrˈʃnapən], *v.r. sich* —, blurt out a secret, give o.s. away, let the cat out of the bag.

verschneiden [fɛrˈʃnaɪdən], *v.a. irr.* (*wings*) clip; (*trees*) prune; (*animals*) castrate; (*wine*) blend.

verschneien [fɛrˈʃnaɪən], *v.n.* (*aux.* sein) be snowed up, be covered with snow, be snowbound.

Verschnitt [fɛrˈʃnɪt], *m.* (—s, *no pl.*) blended wine, blend.

Verschnittene [fɛrˈʃnɪtənə], *m.* (—n, *pl.* —n) eunuch.

verschnörkelt [fɛrˈʃnœrkəlt], *adj.* adorned with flourishes.

verschnupft [fɛrˈʃnupft], *adj.* — *sein*, have a cold in the head; (*fig.*) be vexed.

verschnüren [fɛrˈʃnyːrən], *v.a.* (*shoes*) lace up; (*parcel*) tie up.

verschonen [fɛrˈʃoːnən], *v.a.* spare, exempt from.

verschönern [fɛrˈʃøːnərn], *v.a.* embellish, beautify.

Verschönerung [fɛrˈʃøːnəruŋ], *f.* (—, *pl.* —en) embellishment, adornment.

Verschonung [fɛrˈʃoːnuŋ], *f.* (—, *no pl.*) exemption; forbearance.

verschossen [fɛrˈʃɔsən], *adj.* faded, discoloured; (*fig.*) madly in love.

verschreiben [fɛrˈʃraɪbən], *v.a. irr.* prescribe. — *v.r. sich* —, make a mistake in writing.

verschrien [fɛrˈʃriːən], *adj.* notorious.

verschroben [fɛrˈʃroːbən], *adj.* cranky, eccentric.

Verschrobenheit [fɛrˈʃroːbənhaɪt], *f.* (—, *pl.* —en) crankiness, eccentricity.

verschrumpfen [fɛrˈʃrumpfən], *v.n.* (*aux.* sein) shrivel up.

verschüchtern [fɛrˈʃyçtərn], *v.a.* intimidate.

verschulden [fɛrˈʃuldən], *v.a.* bring on, be the cause of; be guilty of.

verschuldet [fɛrˈʃuldət], *adj.* in debt.

Verschuldung [fɛrˈʃulduŋ], *f.* (—, *no pl.*) indebtedness.

verschütten [fɛrˈʃytən], *v.a.* spill; bury alive.

verschwägern [fɛrˈʃvɛːgərn], *v.r. sich* —, become related by marriage.

Verschwägerung [fɛrˈʃvɛːgəruŋ], (—, *no pl.*) relationship by marriage.

verschwatzen [fɛrˈʃvatsən], *v.a.* gossip (the time) away, spend o.'s time gossiping.

verschweigen [fɛrˈʃvaɪgən], *v.a. irr.* keep secret, keep (news) from, hush up.

verschwenden [fɛr'ʃvɛndən], v.a. squander, waste.

verschwenderisch [fɛr'ʃvɛndərɪʃ], adj. prodigal, profuse, lavish; wasteful.

Verschwendung [fɛr'ʃvɛnduŋ], f. (—, no pl.) waste, extravagance.

Verschwendungssucht [fɛr'ʃvɛnduŋs-zuxt], f. (—, no pl.) prodigality; extravagance.

verschwiegen [fɛr'ʃviːgən], adj. discreet, close, secretive.

Verschwiegenheit [fɛr'ʃviːgənhaɪt], f. (—, no pl.) discretion, secrecy.

verschwimmen [fɛr'ʃvɪmən], v.n. irr. (aux. sein) become blurred.

verschwinden [fɛr'ʃvɪndən], v.n. irr. (aux. sein) disappear, vanish.

verschwommen [fɛr'ʃvɔmən], adj. vague, blurred.

verschwören [fɛr'ʃvøːrən], v.r. irr. sich —, plot, conspire.

Verschwörer [fɛr'ʃvøːrer], m. (—s, pl. —) conspirator.

Verschwörung [fɛr'ʃvøːruŋ], f. (—, pl. —en) conspiracy.

Versehen [fɛr'zeːən], n. (—s, pl. —) error, mistake, oversight.

versehen [fɛr'zeːən], v.a. irr. provide; perform; fill (an office); einen — mit, furnish s.o. with. — v.r. sich —, make a mistake.

versehren [fɛr'zeːrən], v.a. wound; disable.

versenden [fɛr'zɛndən], v.a. irr. forward, consign, send off.

Versender [fɛr'zɛndər], m. (—s, pl.—) consigner, exporter.

Versendung [fɛr'zɛnduŋ], f. (—, no pl.) transmission, shipping.

Versendungskosten [fɛr'zɛnduŋskɔs-tən], f. pl. forwarding charges.

versengen [fɛr'zɛŋən], v.a. singe, scorch.

versenken [fɛr'zɛŋkən], v.a. sink; (ship) scuttle.

Versenkung [fɛr'zɛŋkuŋ], f. (—, no pl.) sinking; hollow; (ship) scuttling; (Theat.) trap-door.

versessen [fɛr'zɛsən], adj. — sein auf, be bent upon, be mad on.

versetzen [fɛr'zɛtsən], v.a. transplant, remove; give; pawn, pledge; transfer; (pupil) promote to a higher form. — v.r. sich in die Lage eines anderen —, put o.s. in s.o. else's position.

versichern [fɛr'zɪçərn], v.a. assert, declare, aver, assure (s.o. of s.th); insure (s.th.).

Versicherung [fɛr'zɪçəruŋ], f. (—, pl. —en) assurance, assertion; insurance.

Versicherungsgesellschaft [fɛr'zɪçə-ruŋsgəzɛlʃaft], f. (—, pl. —en) insurance company.

Versicherungsprämie [fɛr'zɪçəruŋs-prɛːmjə], f. (—, pl. —n) insurance premium.

versiegbar [fɛr'ziːkbaːr], adj. exhaustible.

versiegeln [fɛr'ziːgəln], v.a. seal (up).

versiegen [fɛr'ziːgən], v.n. (aux. sein) dry up, be exhausted.

versilbern [fɛr'zɪlbərn], v.a. plate with silver; (fig.) convert into money.

versinken [fɛr'zɪŋkən], v.n. irr. sink; (ship) founder; sink; versunken sein, be absorbed (in s.th.).

Versmaß ['fɛrsmaːs], n. (—es, pl. —e) metre.

versoffen [fɛr'zɔfən], adj. (vulg.) drunken.

versohlen [fɛr'zoːlən], v.a. (coll.) thrash (s.o.).

versöhnen [fɛr'zøːnən], v.r. sich mit einem —, become reconciled with s.o.

versöhnlich [fɛr'zøːnlɪç], adj. propitiatory, conciliatory.

Versöhnung [fɛr'zøːnuŋ], f. (—, no pl.) reconciliation.

versorgen [fɛr'zɔrgən], v.a. provide with; take care of; support, maintain.

Versorger [fɛr'zɔrgəɪ], m. (—s, pl. —) provider.

Versorgung [fɛr'zɔrguŋ], f. (—, no pl.) provision, maintenance.

verspäten [fɛr'ʃpɛːtən], v.r. sich —, be late, be behind time; (train) be overdue.

Verspätung [fɛr'ʃpɛːtuŋ], f. (—, no pl.) delay; lateness.

verspeisen [fɛr'ʃpaɪzən], v.a. eat up.

versperren [fɛr'ʃpɛrən], v.a. block up, barricade, close.

verspielen [fɛr'ʃpiːlən], v.a. lose (at play); gamble away. — v.r. sich —, play wrong.

verspielt [fɛr'ʃpiːlt], adj. playful.

verspotten [fɛr'ʃpɔtən], v.a. deride, scoff at.

versprechen [fɛr'ʃprɛçən], v.a. irr. promise. — v.r. sich —, make a slip of the tongue.

Versprechen [fɛr'ʃprɛçən], n. (—s, pl. —) promise.

versprengen [fɛr'ʃprɛŋən], v.a. disperse.

verspüren [fɛr'ʃpyːrən], v.a. feel, perceive.

verstaatlichen [fɛr'ʃtaːtlɪçən], v.a. nationalise.

Verstand [fɛr'ʃtant], m. (—(e)s, no pl.) intellect, intelligence, sense; understanding, reason, mind.

verstandesmäßig [fɛr'ʃtandəsmɛːsɪç], adj. rational, reasonable.

Verstandesschärfe [fɛr'ʃtandəsʃɛrfə], f. (—, no pl.) penetration, acumen.

verständig [fɛr'ʃtɛndɪç], adj. judicious, sensible, reasonable.

verständigen [fɛr'ʃtɛndɪgən], v.a. inform, notify. — v.r. sich mit einem —, come to an agreement with s.o.

Verständigung [fɛr'ʃtɛndɪguŋ], f. (—, pl. —en) understanding, agreement; information; arrangement.

verständlich [fɛr'ʃtɛntlɪç], adj. intelligible, clear, understandable.

Verständnis [fɛr'ʃtɛntnɪs], (—ses, no pl.) comprehension, understanding, perception, insight.

verständnisinnig

verständnisinnig [fɛrˈʃtɛntnɪsɪnɪç], *adj.* sympathetic; having profound insight.

verstärken [fɛrˈʃtɛrkən], *v.a.* strengthen, reinforce, intensify.

Verstärker [fɛrˈʃtɛrkər], *m.* (—s, *pl.* —) amplifier; magnifier.

Verstärkung [fɛrˈʃtɛrkuŋ], *f.* (—, *pl.* —en) strengthening, intensification, amplification; (*Mil.*) reinforcements.

verstauben [fɛrˈʃtaubən], *v.n.* (*aux.* sein) get dusty.

verstauchen [fɛrˈʃtauxən], *v.a.* wrench, sprain, dislocate.

verstauen [fɛrˈʃtauən], *v.a.* stow away.

Versteck [fɛrˈʃtɛk], *n.* (—s, *pl.* —e) hiding-place; place of concealment; —(en) spielen, play hide-and-seek.

verstecken [fɛrˈʃtɛkən], *v.a.* hide, conceal.

versteckt [fɛrˈʃtɛkt], *adj.* indirect, veiled.

verstehen [fɛrˈʃteːən], *v.a. irr.* understand, comprehend.

versteigen [fɛrˈʃtaigən], *v.r. irr.* sich —, climb too high; (*fig.*) go too far.

versteigern [fɛrˈʃtaigərn], *v.a.* sell by auction.

Versteigerung [fɛrˈʃtaigəruŋ], *f.* (—, *pl.* —en) auction, public sale.

versteinern [fɛrˈʃtainərn], *v.n.* (*aux.* sein) turn into stone, petrify.

verstellbar [fɛrˈʃtɛlbaːr], *adj.* adjustable.

verstellen [fɛrˈʃtɛlən], *v.a.* adjust; (*voice*) disguise. — *v.r.* sich —, sham, pretend.

versterben [fɛrˈʃtɛrbən], *v.n. irr.* (*aux.* sein) die (*Poet.*).

versteuern [fɛrˈʃtɔyərn], *v.a.* pay tax on.

verstiegen [fɛrˈʃtiːgən], *adj.* eccentric, extravagant.

verstimmen [fɛrˈʃtɪmən], *v.a.* (*Mus.*) put out of tune; (*fig.*) put out of humour, annoy.

Verstimmtheit [fɛrˈʃtɪmthait], *f.* (—, *no pl.*) ill-humour, ill-temper, pique.

Verstimmung [fɛrˈʃtɪmuŋ], *f.* (—, *pl.* —en) bad temper, ill-feeling.

verstockt [fɛrˈʃtɔkt], *adj.* stubborn, obdurate.

Verstocktheit [fɛrˈʃtɔkthait], *f.* (—, *no pl.*) stubbornness, obduracy.

verstohlen [fɛrˈʃtoːlən], *adj.* surreptitious, clandestine, furtive.

verstopfen [fɛrˈʃtɔpfən], *v.a.* stop up; block (up); *verstopft sein*, be constipated.

Verstopfung [fɛrˈʃtɔpfuŋ], *f.* (—, *pl.* —en) obstruction; constipation.

verstorben [fɛrˈʃtɔrbən], *adj.* deceased, late.

verstört [fɛrˈʃtøːrt], *adj.* troubled, worried; distracted.

Verstörtheit [fɛrˈʃtøːrthait], *f.* (—, *no pl.*) consternation, agitation; distraction; haggardness.

Verstoß [fɛrˈʃtoːs], *m.* (—es, *pl.* ⸚e) blunder, mistake; offence.

verstoßen [fɛrˈʃtoːsən], *v.a. irr.* cast off, disown, repudiate. — *v.n.*

gegen, offend against, act in a manner contrary to.

verstreichen [fɛrˈʃtraiçən], *v.n. irr.* (*aux.* sein) (*time*) elapse, pass away.

verstricken [fɛrˈʃtrɪkən], *v.a.* entangle, ensnare.

Verstrickung [fɛrˈʃtrɪkuŋ], *f.* (—, *pl.* —en) entanglement.

verstümmeln [fɛrˈʃtyməln], *v.a.* mutilate, mangle.

verstummen [fɛrˈʃtumən], *v.n.* (*aux.* sein) grow silent; become speechless.

Verstümmlung [fɛrˈʃtymluŋ], *f.* (—, *pl.* —en) mutilation.

Versuch [fɛrˈzuːx], *m.* (—s, *pl.* —e) attempt, trial, endeavour; (*science*) experiment; (*Lit.*) essay.

versuchen [fɛrˈzuːxən], *v.a.* try, attempt, endeavour; (*food*) taste; *einen* —, tempt s.o.

Versucher [fɛrˈzuːxər], *m.* (—s, *pl.* —) tempter.

Versuchskaninchen [fɛrˈzuːxskaniːnçən], *n.* (—s, *pl.* —) (*fig.*) guinea-pig.

Versuchung [fɛrˈzuːxuŋ], *f.* (—, *pl.* —en) temptation.

versündigen [fɛrˈzyndigən], *v.r.* sich —, sin (against).

Versunkenheit [fɛrˈzuŋkənhait], *f.* (—, *no pl.*) absorption, preoccupation.

vertagen [fɛrˈtaːgən], *v.a.* adjourn, prorogue.

Vertagung [fɛrˈtaːguŋ], *f.* (—, *pl.* —en) adjournment, prorogation.

vertauschen [fɛrˈtauʃən], *v.a.* exchange, barter, mistake, confuse.

verteidigen [fɛrˈtaidigən], *v.a.* defend, uphold, vindicate; (*fig.*) maintain.

Verteidiger [fɛrˈtaidigər], *m.* (—s, *pl.* —) defender; (*Law*) counsel for the defence.

Verteidigung [fɛrˈtaidiguŋ], *f.* (—, *no pl.*) defence; justification.

Verteidigungskrieg [fɛrˈtaidiguŋskriːk], *m.* (—(e)s, *pl.* —e) defensive war.

verteilen [fɛrˈtailən], *v.a.* distribute, allot, allocate.

Verteilung [fɛrˈtailuŋ], *f.* (—, *pl.* —en) distribution, apportionment.

verteuern [fɛrˈtɔyərn], *v.a.* make dearer, raise the price of.

verteufelt [fɛrˈtɔyfəlt], *adj.* devilish. — *adv.* (*coll.*) awfully, infernally.

vertiefen [fɛrˈtiːfən], *v.a.* deepen.

vertieft [fɛrˈtiːft], *adj.* absorbed, deep in thought.

Vertiefung [fɛrˈtiːfuŋ], *f.* (—, *pl.* —en) cavity, recess, hollow; (*knowledge*) deepening; (*fig.*) absorption.

vertilgen [fɛrˈtɪlgən], *v.a.* wipe out, exterminate; (*food*) (*coll.*) polish off.

Vertilgung [fɛrˈtɪlguŋ], *f.* (—, *no pl.*) extermination, extirpation.

Vertrag [fɛrˈtraːk], *m.* (—(e)s, *pl.* ⸚e) contract, agreement; (*Pol.*) treaty, pact, convention.

vertragen [fɛrˈtraːgən], *v.a. irr.* suffer, endure; (*food*) digest. — *v.r.* sich — *mit*, get on well with.

vertraglich [fɛr'tra:klɪç], *adj.* as per contract, according to agreement.

verträglich [fɛr'trɛ:klɪç], *adj.* accommodating, peaceable.

vertragsmäßig [fɛr'tra:ksmɛ:sɪç], *adj.* according to contract.

vertragswidrig [fɛr'tra:ksvi:drɪç], *adj.* contrary to contract.

vertrauen [fɛr'trauən], *v.n.* rely (upon), trust (in).

Vertrauen [fɛr'trauən], *n.* (—s, *no pl.*) confidence, trust, reliance.

vertrauenerweckend [fɛr'trauənɛrvɛkənt], *adj.* inspiring confidence.

Vertrauensbruch [fɛr'trauənsbrux], *m.* (—es, *pl.* ⸗e) breach of faith.

Vertrauensmann [fɛr'trauənsman], *m.* (—s, *pl.* ⸗er) confidant; delegate; person entrusted with s.th.; (*Ind.*) shop steward.

vertrauensselig [fɛr'trauənsze:lɪç], *adj.* confiding, trusting.

Vertrauensvotum [fɛr'trauənsvo:tum], *n.* (—s, *pl.* —ten) vote of confidence.

vertrauenswürdig [fɛr'trauənsvyrdɪç], *adj.* trustworthy.

vertraulich [fɛr'traulɪç], *adj.* confidential; familiar.

Vertraulichkeit [fɛr'traulɪçkaɪt], *f.* (—, *pl.* —en) familiarity.

verträumt [fɛr'trɔymt], *adj.* dreamy.

vertraut [fɛr'traut], *adj.* intimate, familiar; conversant.

Vertraute [fɛr'trautə], *m.* (—n, *pl.* —n) close friend, confidant.

Vertrautheit [fɛr'trauthaɪt], *f.* (—, *no pl.*) familiarity.

vertreiben [fɛr'traɪbən], *v.a. irr.* drive away, expel; eject; (*person*) banish; (*time*) pass, kill; (*goods*) sell.

Vertreibung [fɛr'traɪbuŋ], *f.* (—, *no pl.*) expulsion; banishment.

vertreten [fɛr'tre:tən], *v.a. irr.* represent (s.o.), deputise for (s.o.).

Vertreter [fɛr'tre:tər], *m.* (—s, *pl.* —) representative, deputy; (*Comm.*) agent.

Vertretung [fɛr'tre:tuŋ], *f.* (—, *pl.* —en) representation, agency.

Vertrieb [fɛr'tri:p], *m.* (—s, *pl.* —e) sale; distribution.

vertrinken [fɛr'trɪŋkən], *v.a. irr.* spend *or* waste money on drink.

vertrocknen [fɛr'trɔknən], *v.n.* (*aux.* sein) dry up, wither.

vertrödeln [fɛr'trø:dəln], *v.a.* fritter (o.'s time) away.

vertrösten [fɛr'trø:stən], *v.a.* console; put off; put (s.o.) off with fine words; fob (s.o.) off with vain hopes.

Vertröstung [fɛr'trø:stuŋ], *f.* (—, *pl.* —en) comfort; empty promises.

vertun [fɛr'tu:n], *v.a. irr.* squander, waste.

vertuschen [fɛr'tuʃən], *v.a.* hush up.

verübeln [fɛr'y:bəln], *v.a.* take amiss.

verüben [fɛr'y:bən], *v.a.* commit, perpetrate.

verunehren [fɛr'une:rən], *v.a.* dishonour, disgrace.

verunglimpfen [fɛr'unglɪmpfən], *v.a.* bring into disrepute; defame, calumniate.

Verunglimpfung [fɛr'unglɪmpfuŋ], *f.* (—, *pl.* —en) defamation, detraction, calumny.

verunglücken [fɛr'unglykən], *v.n.* (*aux.* sein) (*person*) meet with an accident; be killed; (*thing*) misfire, fail.

verunreinigen [fɛr'unraɪnɪgən], *v.a.* contaminate.

Verunreinigung [fɛr'unraɪnɪguŋ], *f.* (—, *pl.* —en) contamination.

verunstalten [fɛr'unʃtaltən], *v.a.* disfigure, deface.

Verunstaltung [fɛr'unʃtaltuŋ], *f.* (—, *pl.* —en) disfigurement.

Veruntreuung [fɛr'untrɔyuŋ], *f.* (—, *pl.* —en) embezzlement, misappropriation.

verunzieren [fɛr'untsi:rən], *v.a.* disfigure, spoil.

verursachen [fɛr'u:rzaxən], *v.a.* cause, occasion.

verurteilen [fɛr'urtaɪlən], *v.a.* condemn; (*Law*) sentence.

Verurteilung [fɛr'urtaɪluŋ], *f.* (—, *no pl.*) condemnation; (*Law*) sentence.

vervielfältigen [fɛr'fi:lfɛltɪgən], *v.a.* multiply; duplicate, make copies of.

Vervielfältigung [fɛr'fi:lfɛltɪguŋ], *f.* (—, *pl.* —en) multiplication; duplication, copying.

vervollkommnen [fɛr'fɔlkɔmnən], *v.a.* improve, perfect.

Vervollkommnung [fɛr'fɔlkɔmnuŋ], *f.* (—, *no pl.*) improvement, perfection.

vervollständigen [fɛr'fɔlʃtɛndɪgən], *v.a.* complete.

Vervollständigung [fɛr'fɔlʃtɛndɪguŋ], *f.* (—, *no pl.*) completion.

verwachsen [fɛr'vaksən], *v.n. irr.* (*aux.* sein) grow together; be overgrown. — *adj.* deformed.

verwahren [fɛr'va:rən], *v.a.* take care of, preserve, secure. — *v.r. sich — gegen*, protest against.

verwahrlosen [fɛr'va:rlo:zən], *v.a.* neglect. — *v.n.* (*aux.* sein) be in need of care and protection, be neglected.

Verwahrlosung [fɛr'va:rlo:zuŋ], *f.* (—, *no pl.*) neglect.

Verwahrung [fɛr'va:ruŋ], *f.* (—, *no pl.*) keeping; charge; *in — geben*, deposit, give into s.o.'s charge; *— einlegen gegen*, enter a protest against.

verwalten [fɛr'valtən], *v.a.* manage, administer.

Verwalter [fɛr'valtər], *m.* (—s, *pl.* —) administrator, manager; steward, bailiff.

Verwaltung [fɛr'valtuŋ], *f.* (—, *pl.* —en) administration, management; Civil Service.

Verwaltungsbezirk [fɛr'valtuŋsbətsɪrk], *m.* (—s, *pl.* —e) administrative district.

Verwandlung [fɛr'vandluŋ], *f.* (—, *pl.* —en) alteration, transformation.

Verwandlungskünstler [fɛrˈvandluŋs-kynstlər], *m.* (—s, *pl.* —) quick-change artist.

verwandt [fɛrˈvant], *adj.* related; cognate; congenial.

Verwandte [fɛrˈvantə], *m.* (—n, *pl.* —n) relative, relation; kinsman; *der nächste* —, next of kin.

Verwandtschaft [fɛrˈvantʃaft], *f.* (—, *pl.* —en) relationship; relations, family; congeniality, sympathy.

verwarnen [fɛrˈvarnən], *v.a.* admonish, forewarn.

Verwarnung [fɛrˈvarnuŋ], *f.* (—, *pl.* —en) admonition.

Verwässerung [fɛrˈvɛsəruŋ], *f.* (—, *pl.* —en) dilution.

verwechseln [fɛrˈvɛksəln], *v.a.* confuse; mistake for.

Verwechslung [fɛrˈvɛksluŋ], *f.* (—, *pl.* —en) confusion, mistake.

verwegen [fɛrˈveːgən], *adj.* bold, audacious.

Verwegenheit [fɛrˈveːgənhait], *f.* (—, *pl.* —en) boldness, audacity.

verweichlichen [fɛrˈvaiçliçən], *v.a.* coddle. — *v.n.* (*aux.* sein) become effeminate.

verweigern [fɛrˈvaigərn], *v.a.* refuse, deny; reject.

Verweigerung [fɛrˈvaigəruŋ], *f.* (—, *pl.* —en) refusal, denial; rejection.

verweilen [fɛrˈvailən], *v.n.* remain; tarry; stay (with), dwell (on).

verweint [fɛrˈvaint], *adj.* (*eyes*) red with weeping.

Verweis [fɛrˈvais], *m.* (—es, *pl.* —e) reproof, reprimand, rebuke.

verweisen [fɛrˈvaizən], *v.a. irr.* reprimand; banish, exile; — *auf etwas*, refer to s.th., hint at s.th.

Verweisung [fɛrˈvaizuŋ], *f.* (—, *pl.* —en) banishment, exile; reference.

verweltlichen [fɛrˈvɛltliçən], *v.a.* secularise, profane.

verwenden [fɛrˈvɛndən], *v.a.* use, make use of; apply to, employ in, utilize.

Verwendung [fɛrˈvɛnduŋ], *f.* (—, *pl.* —en) application, use, expenditure, employment.

verwerfen [fɛrˈvɛrfən], *v.a. irr.* reject, disapprove of.

verwerflich [fɛrˈvɛrfliç], *adj.* objectionable.

Verwertung [fɛrˈveːrtuŋ], *f.* (—, *no pl.*) utilisation.

verwesen [fɛrˈveːzən], *v.a.* administer. — *v.n.* (*aux.* sein) rot, decompose, putrefy.

Verweser [fɛrˈveːzər], *m.* (—s, *pl.* —) administrator.

Verwesung [fɛrˈveːzuŋ], *f.* (—, *no pl.*) (*office*) administration; putrefaction, rotting.

verwickeln [fɛrˈvikəln], *v.a.* entangle, involve.

verwickelt [fɛrˈvikəlt], *adj.* intricate, complicated, involved.

Verwicklung [fɛrˈvikluŋ], *f.* (—, *pl.*

—en) entanglement, involvement, complication.

verwildern [fɛrˈvildərn], *v.n.* (*aux.* sein) run wild.

verwildert [fɛrˈvildərt], *adj.* wild, uncultivated, overgrown; (*fig.*) intractable.

Verwilderung [fɛrˈvildəruŋ], *f.* (—, *no pl.*) running wild, growing wild.

verwirken [fɛrˈvirkən], *v.a.* forfeit.

verwirklichen [fɛrˈvirkliçən], *v.a.* realise. — *v.r. sich* —, materialise, come true.

Verwirklichung [fɛrˈvirkliçuŋ], *f.* (—, *no pl.*) realisation, materialisation.

Verwirkung [fɛrˈvirkuŋ], *f.* (—, *no pl.*) forfeiture.

verwirren [fɛrˈvirən], *v.a.* disarrange, throw into disorder, entangle; puzzle, bewilder, confuse, disconcert.

Verwirrung [fɛrˈviruŋ], *f.* (—, *pl.* —en) bewilderment, confusion.

verwischen [fɛrˈviʃən], *v.a.* blot out, smudge, obliterate.

verwittern [fɛrˈvitərn], *v.n.* (*aux.* sein) be weather-beaten.

verwöhnen [fɛrˈvøːnən], *v.a.* spoil, pamper, coddle.

verworfen [fɛrˈvorfən], *adj.* profligate; rejected, reprobate.

verworren [fɛrˈvorən], *adj.* confused, perplexed; intricate; (*speech*) rambling.

verwundbar [fɛrˈvuntbaːr], *adj.* vulnerable.

verwunden [fɛrˈvundən], *v.a.* wound, hurt, injure.

verwundern [fɛrˈvundərn], *v.r. sich* —, be surprised, wonder, be amazed.

Verwunderung [fɛrˈvundəruŋ], *f.* (—, *no pl.*) surprise, astonishment, amazement.

Verwundung [fɛrˈvunduŋ], *f.* (—, *pl.* —en) wounding, wound, injury.

verwunschen [fɛrˈvunʃən], *adj.* enchanted, spellbound, bewitched.

verwünschen [fɛrˈvynʃən], *v.a.* curse; cast a spell on, bewitch.

verwünscht [fɛrˈvynʃt], *excl.* confound it!

Verwünschung [fɛrˈvynʃuŋ], *f.* (—, *pl.* —en) curse, malediction.

verwüsten [fɛrˈvyːstən], *v.a.* devastate, ravage, lay waste.

Verwüstung [fɛrˈvyːstuŋ], *f.* (—, *pl.* —en) devastation.

verzagen [fɛrˈtsaːgən], *v.n.* (*aux.* sein) lose heart, lose courage.

verzagt [fɛrˈtsaːkt], *adj.* fainthearted, discouraged.

Verzagtheit [fɛrˈtsaːkthait], *f.* (—, *no pl.*) faintheartedness.

verzählen [fɛrˈtsɛːlən], *v.r. sich* —, miscount.

verzapfen [fɛrˈtsapfən], *v.a.* sell (liquor) on draught; (*fig.*) tell (a story), talk (nonsense).

verzärteln [fɛrˈtsɛːrtəln], *v.a.* pamper, coddle; spoil.

verzaubern [fɛrˈtsaubərn], *v.a.* bewitch, charm, put a spell on.

Vision

verzehren [fɛr'tseːrən], *v.a.* consume, eat. — *v.r. sich — in,* pine away with, be consumed with.

Verzehrung [fɛr'tseːruŋ], *f.* (—, *no pl.*) (*obs.*) consumption, tuberculosis.

verzeichnen [fɛr'tsaɪçnən], *v.a.* draw badly; note down, register, record.

Verzeichnis [fɛr'tsaɪçnɪs], *n.* (—ses, *pl.* —se) catalogue, list, register.

verzeihen [fɛr'tsaɪən], *v.a. irr.* forgive, pardon.

verzeihlich [fɛr'tsaɪlɪç], *adj.* pardonable, forgivable, excusable, venial.

Verzeihung [fɛr'tsaɪuŋ], *f.* (—, *no pl.*) pardon, forgiveness; *ich bitte um —,* I beg your pardon.

verzerren [fɛr'tsɛrən], *v.a.* distort.

Verzerrung [fɛr'tsɛruŋ], *f.* (—, *pl.* —en) distortion; (*face*) grimace.

verzetteln [fɛr'tsɛtəln], *v.a.* disperse, scatter.

Verzicht [fɛr'tsɪçt], *m.* (—(e)s, *no pl.*) renunciation, resignation.

verzichten [fɛr'tsɪçtən], *v.n.* forgo, renounce.

verziehen [fɛr'tsiːən], *v.a. irr.* distort; spoil (*child*). — *v.n.* (*aux.* sein) go away, move away.

Verzierung [fɛr'tsiːruŋ], *f.* (—, *pl.* —en) decoration, ornament.

verzögern [fɛr'tsøːgərn], *v.a.* delay, defer, retard, protract, procrastinate. — *v.r. sich —,* be delayed.

Verzögerung [fɛr'tsøːgəruŋ], *f.* (—, *pl.* —en) delay, retardation, procrastination; time-lag.

verzollen [fɛr'tsɔlən], *v.a.* pay duty on.

Verzücktheit [fɛr'tsʏkthaɪt], *f.* (—, *no pl.*) ecstasy, rapture.

Verzug [fɛr'tsuːk], *m.* (—s, *no pl.*) delay.

verzweifeln [fɛr'tsvaɪfəln], *v.n.* despair, be desperate.

Verzweiflung [fɛr'tsvaɪfluŋ], *f.* (—, *no pl.*) despair.

verzwickt [fɛr'tsvɪkt], *adj.* complicated, intricate, tricky.

Vesuv [veˈzuːf], *m.* Mount Vesuvius.

Vetter ['fɛtər], *m.* (—s, *pl.* —n) cousin.

Vetternwirtschaft ['fɛtərnvɪrtʃaft], *f.* (—, *no pl.*) nepotism.

Vexierbild [vɛˈksiːrbɪlt], *n.* (—s, *pl.* —er) picture-puzzle.

Vexierspiegel [vɛˈksiːrʃpiːgəl], *m.* (—s, *pl.*—) distorting mirror.

vibrieren [viˈbriːrən], *v.n.* vibrate.

Vieh [fiː], *n.* (—s, *no pl.*) cattle, livestock.

Viehfutter ['fiːfutər], *n.* (—s, *no pl.*) forage, fodder, feeding-stuff.

viehisch ['fiːɪʃ], *adj.* beastly, brutal.

Viehwagen ['fiːvaːgən], *m.* (—s, *pl.* —) cattle-truck.

Viehweide ['fiːvaɪdə], *f.* (—, *pl.* —n) pasture, pasturage.

Viehzüchter ['fiːtsʏçtər], *m.* (—s, *pl.* —) cattle-breeder.

viel [fiːl], *adj.* much, a great deal, a lot; (*pl.*) many.

vielartig ['fiːlartɪç], *adj.* multifarious.

vieldeutig ['fiːldɔytɪç], *adj.* ambiguous, equivocal.

Vieleck ['fiːlɛk], *n.* (—s, *pl.* —e) polygon.

vielerlei ['fiːlərlaɪ], *adj.* of many kinds, various.

vielfältig ['fiːlfɛltɪç], *adj.* manifold.

vielfarbig ['fiːlfarbɪç], *adj.* multicoloured, variegated.

Vielfraß ['fiːlfraːs], *m.* (—es, *pl.* —e) glutton.

vielgeliebt ['fiːlgəliːpt],*adj.* much loved, well-beloved, dearly loved.

vielgereist ['fiːlgəraɪst], *adj.* much travelled.

vielleicht [fiˈlaɪçt],*adv.* perhaps, maybe.

vielmals ['fiːlmaːls], *adv.* many times, frequently, much.

Vielmännerei [fiːlmɛnəˈraɪ], *f.* (—, *no pl.*) polyandry.

vielmehr [fiːlˈmeːr], *adv.* rather, much more. — *conj.* rather, on the other hand.

vielsagend ['fiːlzaːgənt], *adj.* expressive, full of meaning.

vielseitig ['fiːlzaɪtɪç], *adj.* multilateral; (*fig.*) versatile.

Vielseitigkeit ['fiːlzaɪtɪçkaɪt], *f.* (—, *no pl.*) versatility.

vielverheißend ['fiːlfɛrhaɪsənt], *adj.* promising, auspicious.

Vielweiberei [fiːlvaɪbəˈraɪ], *f.* (—, *no pl.*) polygamy.

vier [fiːr], *num. adj.* four.

Viereck ['fiːrɛk], *n.* (—s, *pl.* —e) square, quadrangle.

viereckig ['fiːrɛkɪç], *adj.* square.

vierfüßig ['fiːrfyːsɪç], *adj.* four-footed.

vierhändig ['fiːrhɛndɪç], *adj.* four-handed; — *spielen,* (*piano*) play duets.

vierschrötig ['fiːrʃrøːtɪç], *adj.* robust, thick-set, stocky.

vierseitig ['fiːrzaɪtɪç], *adj.* quadrilateral.

vierstimmig ['fiːrʃtɪmɪç], *adj.* (*Mus.*) four-part; for four voices.

vierteilen ['fiːrtaɪlən], *v.a.* quarter, divide into four parts.

Viertel ['fɪrtəl], *n.* (—s, *pl.* —) quarter, fourth part.

Viertelstunde [fɪrtəlˈʃtundə], *f.* (—, *pl.* —n) quarter of an hour.

viertens ['fiːrtəns], *num. adv.* fourthly, in the fourth place.

Vierwaldstättersee [fiːrˈvaltʃtetərzeː], *m.* Lake Lucerne.

vierzehn ['fɪrtseːn], *num. adj.* fourteen; — *Tage,* a fortnight.

vierzig ['fɪrtsɪç], *num. adj.* forty.

Vietnam [viɛtˈnaːm], *n.* Vietnam.

Violinschlüssel [vioˈliːnʃlʏsəl], *m.* (—s, *pl.* —) (*Mus.*) treble clef.

Virtuosität [vɪrtuoziˈteːt], *f.* (—, *no pl.*) mastery, virtuosity.

Visage [viˈzaːʒə], *f.* (—, *pl.* —n) (*coll.*) face.

Visier [viˈziːr], *n.* (—, *pl.* —e) visor; (*gun*) sight.

Vision [viˈzjoːn], *f.* (—, *pl.* —en) vision.

265

Visionär

Visionär [vizjo'nɛːr], *m.* (—s, *pl.* —e) visionary.

Visitenkarte [vi'ziːtənkartə], *f.* (—, *pl.* —n) card, visiting card.

Visum ['viːzum], *n.* (—s, *pl.* **Visa**) visa.

Vizekönig ['viːtsøːnɪç], *m.* (—s, *pl.* —e) viceroy.

Vlies [fliːs], *n.* (—es, *pl.* —e) fleece.

Vogel ['foːgəl], *m.* (—s, *pl.* ⸚) bird; (*coll.*) fellow; *einen — haben*, be off o.'s head.

Vogelbauer ['foːgəlbauər], *n.* (—s, *pl.* —) bird-cage.

Vogelfänger ['foːgəlfɛŋər], *m.* (—s, *pl.* —) fowler, bird-catcher.

vogelfrei ['foːgəlfrai], *adj.* outlawed, proscribed.

Vogelfutter ['foːgəlfutər], *n.* (—s, *no pl.*) bird-seed.

Vogelhändler ['foːgəlhɛndlər], *m.* (—s, *pl.* —) bird-dealer.

Vogelhaus ['foːgəlhaus], *n.* (—es, *pl.* ⸚er) aviary.

Vogelkenner ['foːgəlkɛnər], *m.* (—s, *pl.* —) ornithologist.

Vogelkunde ['foːgəlkundə], *f.* (—, *no pl.*) ornithology.

Vogelperspektive ['foːgəlpɛrspɛktiːvə], *f.* (—, *no pl.*) bird's-eye view.

Vogelschau ['foːgəlʃau], *f.* (—, *no pl.*) bird's-eye view.

Vogelsteller ['foːgəlʃtɛlər], *m.* (—s, *pl.* —) fowler, bird-catcher.

Vogesen [voˈgeːzən], *pl.* Vosges Mountains.

Vogler ['foːglər], *m.* (—s, *pl.* —) fowler.

Vogt [foːkt], *m.* (—(e)s, *pl.* ⸚e) prefect, bailiff, steward, provost.

Vogtei [foːk'tai], *f.* (—, *pl.* —en) prefecture, bailiwick.

Vokabel [voˈkaːbəl], *f.* (—, *pl.* —n) word, vocable.

Vokabelbuch [voˈkaːbəlbuːx], *n.* (—(e)s, *pl.* ⸚er) vocabulary (book).

Vokal [voˈkaːl], *m.* (—s, *pl.* —e) vowel.

Vokativ [vokaˈtiːf], *m.* (—s, *pl.* —e) (*Gram.*) vocative.

Volk [fɔlk], *n.* (—(e)s, *pl.* ⸚er) people, nation; *das gemeine —,* mob, the common people.

Völkerkunde ['fœlkərkundə], *f.* (—, *no pl.*) ethnology.

Völkerrecht ['fœlkərrɛçt], *n.* (—s, *no pl.*) international law.

Völkerschaft ['fœlkərʃaft], *f.* (—, *pl.* —en) tribe, people.

Völkerwanderung ['fœlkərvandərʊŋ], *f.* (—, *pl.* —en) mass migration.

Volksabstimmung ['fɔlksapʃtɪmʊŋ], *f.* (—, *pl.* —en) referendum.

Volksausgabe ['fɔlksausgaːbə], *f.* (—, *pl.* —n) popular edition.

Volksbeschluß ['fɔlksbəʃlus], *m.* (—sses, *pl.* ⸚sse) plebiscite.

Volksbibliothek ['fɔlksbibliote:k], *f.* (—, *pl.* —en) public library.

Volkscharakter ['fɔlkskaraktər], *m.* (—s, *no pl.*) national character.

Volksentscheid ['fɔlksɛntʃait], *m.* (—s, *pl.* —e) plebiscite.

Volksführer ['fɔlksfyːrər], *m.* (—s, *pl.* —) demagogue.

Volksheer ['fɔlksheːr], *n.* (—s, *pl.* —e) national army.

Volksherrschaft ['fɔlksherʃaft], *f.* (—, *no pl.*) democracy.

Volkshochschule ['fɔlkshoxʃuːlə], *f.* (—, *no pl.*) adult education (classes).

Volksjustiz ['fɔlksjustiːts], *f.* (—, *no pl.*) lynch-law.

Volkskunde ['fɔlkskundə], *f.* (—, *no pl.*) folklore.

Volkslied ['fɔlksliːt], *n.* (—s, *pl.* —er) folk-song.

Volksschicht ['fɔlksʃɪçt], *f.* (—, *pl.* —en) class.

Volksschule ['fɔlksʃuːlə], *f.* (—, *pl.* —n) primary school; elementary school.

Volkssitte ['fɔlksziːtə], *f.* (—, *pl.* —n) national custom.

Volkssprache ['fɔlksʃpraːxə], *f.* (—, *pl.* —n) vernacular.

Volksstamm ['fɔlksʃtam], *m.* (—s, *pl.* ⸚e) tribe.

Volkstracht ['fɔlkstraxt], *f.* (—, *pl.* —en) national costume.

volkstümlich ['fɔlkstyːmlɪç], *adj.* national, popular.

Volksvertretung ['fɔlksfɛrtreːtuŋ], *f.* (—, *no pl.*) representation of the people, parliamentary representation.

Volkswirt ['fɔlksvɪrt], *m.* (—s, *pl.* —e) political economist.

Volkswirtschaft ['fɔlksvɪrtʃaft], *f.* (—, *no pl.*) political economy.

Volkszählung ['fɔlkstseːluŋ], *f.* (—, *pl.* —en) census.

voll [fɔl], *adj.* full, filled; whole, complete, entire.

vollauf ['fɔlauf], *adv.* abundantly.

Vollbart ['fɔlbaːrt], *m.* (—s, *pl.* ⸚e) beard.

vollberechtigt ['fɔlbərɛçtɪçt], *adj.* fully entitled.

Vollbild ['fɔlbɪlt], *n.* (—s, *pl.* —er) full-length portrait, full-page illustration.

Vollblut ['fɔlbluːt], *n.* (—s, *pl.* ⸚er) thoroughbred.

vollblütig ['fɔlblyːtɪç], *adj.* full-blooded, thoroughbred.

vollbringen [fɔl'brɪŋən], *v.a. irr.* accomplish, achieve, complete.

Vollbringung [fɔl'brɪŋuŋ], *f.* (—, *no pl.*) achievement.

Volldampf ['fɔldampf], *m.* (—es, *no pl.*) full steam.

vollenden [fɔl'ɛndən], *v.a.* finish, complete.

vollendet [fɔl'ɛndət], *adj.* finished; accomplished.

vollends ['fɔlɛnts], *adv.* quite, altogether, wholly, entirely, moreover.

Vollendung [fɔl'ɛnduŋ], *f.* (—, *no pl.*) completion; perfection.

Völlerei [fœlə'rai], *f.* (—, *pl.* —en) gluttony.

vollführen [fɔl'fy:rən], *v.a.* execute, carry out.

Vollgefühl ['fɔlgəfy:l], *n.* (—**s**, *no pl.*) consciousness, full awareness.

Vollgenuß ['fɔlgənus], *m.* (—**sses**, *no pl.*) full enjoyment.

vollgültig ['fɔlgyltɪç], *adj.* fully valid; unexceptionable.

Vollheit ['fɔlhaɪt], *f.* (—, *no pl.*) fullness, plenitude.

völlig ['fœlɪç], *adj.* entire, whole, complete.

vollinhaltlich ['fɔlɪnhaltlɪç], *adv.* to its full extent.

volljährig ['fɔljɛ::rɪç], *adj.* of age.

Volljährigkeit ['fɔljɛ:rɪçkaɪt], *f.* (—, *no pl.*) adult years, majority.

vollkommen ['fɔlkɔmən], *adj.* perfect. — *adv.* entirely.

Vollkommenheit [fɔl'kɔmənhaɪt], *f.* (—, *no pl.*) perfection.

Vollmacht ['fɔlmaxt], *f.* (—, *pl.* —**en**) authority; fullness of power; power of attorney.

vollsaftig ['fɔlzaftɪç], *adj.* juicy, succulent.

vollständig ['fɔlʃtɛndɪç], *adj.* complete, full. — *adv.* entirely.

vollstrecken [fɔl'ʃtrɛkən], *v.a.* execute, carry out.

Vollstrecker [fɔl'ʃtrɛkər], *m.* (—**s**, *pl.* —) executor.

volltönig ['fɔltø:nɪç], *adj.* sonorous.

vollwertig ['fɔlvɛrtɪç], *adj.* standard, sterling.

vollzählig ['fɔltsɛ:lɪç], *adj.* complete.

vollziehen [fɔl'tsi:ən], *v.a. irr.* execute, carry out, ratify.

vollziehend [fɔl'tsi:ənt], *adj.* executive.

Vollziehungsgewalt [fɔl'tsi:uŋsgəvalt], *f.* (—, *no pl.*) executive power.

Vollzug [fɔl'tsu:k], *m.* (—**s**, *no pl.*) execution; fulfilment.

Volontär [vɔlɔ̃'tɛ:r], *m.* (—**s**, *pl.* —**e**) volunteer.

von [fɔn] (*von den* becomes **vom**), *prep.* (*Dat.*) by, from; of; on; concerning, about; — *Shakespeare*, by Shakespeare; — *Beruf*, by profession; *er kommt — London*, he comes from London; — *fern*, from afar; — *jetzt an*, from now on; — *einem sprechen*, speak of s.o.; *dein Brief vom 15.*, your letter of the 15th.

vonnöten [fɔn'nø:tən], *adv.* — *sein*, be necessary.

vonstatten [fɔn'ʃtatən], *adv.* — *gehen*, progress; go off.

vor [fo:r], *prep.* (*Dat., Acc.*) (*place*) before, ahead of, in front of; (*time*) before, prior to, earlier than; from; of; with; above; in presence of, because of; more than; — *dem Hause*, in front of the house; — *Sonnenaufgang*, before sunrise; —*zwei Tagen*, two days ago; *sich — einem verstecken*, hide from s.o.; *sich hüten* —, beware of; *starr — Kälte*, stiff with cold; — *allem*, above all. — *adv.* before; *nach wie* —, now as before.

Vorabend ['fo:ra:bənt], *m.* (—**s**, *pl.* —**e**) eve.

Vorahnung ['fo:ra:nuŋ], *f.* (—, *pl.* —**en**) presentiment, foreboding.

voran [fo'ran], *adv.* before, in front, forward, on.

vorangehen [fo'range:ən], *v.n. irr.* (*aux.* sein) take the lead, go ahead.

Voranzeige ['fo:rantsaɪgə], *f.* (—, *pl.* —**n**) advance notice; (*film*) trailer.

Vorarbeiter ['fo:rarbaɪtər], *m.* (—**s**, *pl.* —) foreman.

voraus [fo'raus], *adv.* before, in front, foremost; in advance; *im* or *zum* —, beforehand; (*thanks*) in anticipation.

vorauseilen [fo'rausaɪlən], *v.n.* (*aux.* sein) run ahead.

vorausgehen [fo'rausge:ən], *v.n. irr.* (*aux.* sein) walk ahead; *einem* —, go before; precede s.o.

voraushaben [fo'rausha:bən], *v.n. irr. etwas vor einem* —, have the advantage over s.o.

Voraussage [fo'rausza:gə], *f.* (—, *pl.* —**n**) prediction, prophecy; (*weather*) forecast.

voraussagen [fo'rausza:gən], *v.a.* predict, foretell; (*weather*) forecast.

voraussehen [fo'rausze:ən], *v.a. irr.* foresee.

voraussetzen [fo'rauszɛtsən], *v.a.* presuppose, take for granted.

Voraussetzung [fo'rauszɛtsuŋ], *f.* (—, *pl.* —**en**) supposition, presupposition; *unter der* —, on the understanding.

Voraussicht [fo'rauszɪçt], *f.* (—, *no pl.*) foresight, forethought; *aller* — *nach*, in all probability.

voraussichtlich [fo'rauszɪçtlɪç], *adj.* prospective, presumptive, probable, expected. — *adv.* probably, presumably.

Vorbau ['fo:rbau], *m.* (—**s**, *pl.* —**ten**) frontage.

Vorbedacht ['fo:rbədaxt], *m.* (—**s**, *no pl.*) premeditation; *mit* —, on purpose, deliberately.

vorbedacht ['fo:rbədaxt], *adj.* premeditated.

Vorbedeutung ['fo:rbədɔytuŋ], *f.* (—, *pl.* —**en**) omen.

Vorbehalt ['fo:rbəhalt], *m.* (—**s**, *pl.* —**e**) reservation, proviso.

vorbehalten ['fo:rbəhaltən], *v.a. irr.* reserve; make reservation that.

vorbehaltlich ['fo:rbəhaltlɪç], *prep.* (*Genit.*) with the proviso that.

vorbei [fo:r'baɪ], *adv.* by; along; past, over, finished, gone.

vorbeigehen [fo:r'baɪge:ən], *v.n. irr.* (*aux.* sein) pass by; go past; march past.

vorbeilassen [fo:r'baɪlasən], *v.a. irr.* let pass.

Vorbemerkung ['fo:rbəmɛrkuŋ], *f.* (—, *pl.* —**en**) preface, prefatory note.

vorbereiten ['fo:rbəraɪtən], *v.a.* prepare.

Vorbereitung ['fo:rbəraɪtuŋ], *f.* (—, *pl.* —**en**) preparation.

Vorbesitzer ['foːrbəzɪtsər], *m.* (**—s**, *pl.* **—**) previous owner.

Vorbesprechung ['foːrbəʃprɛçuŋ], *f.* (**—**, *pl.* **—en**) preliminary discussion.

vorbestimmen ['foːrbəʃtɪmən], *v.a.* predestine, predetermine.

Vorbestimmung ['foːrbəʃtɪmuŋ], *f.* (**—**, *no pl.*) predestination.

vorbestraft ['foːrbəʃtraːft], *adj.* previously convicted.

vorbeten ['foːrbeːtən], *v.n.* lead in prayer.

vorbeugen ['foːrbɔygən], *v.n.* prevent, preclude, obviate. — *v.r. sich* **—**, bend forward.

Vorbeugung ['foːrbɔyguŋ], *f.* (**—**, *no pl.*) prevention; prophylaxis.

Vorbeugungsmaßnahme ['foːrbɔyguŋsmaːsnaːmə], *f.* (**—**, *pl.* **—n**) preventive measure.

Vorbild ['foːrbɪlt], *n.* (**—s**, *pl.* **—er**) model, example, pattern, ideal.

vorbildlich ['foːrbɪltlɪç], *adj.* exemplary; typical; — *sein*, be a model.

Vorbildung ['foːrbɪlduŋ], *f.* (**—**, *no pl.*) preparatory training.

Vorbote ['foːrboːtə], *m.* (**—n**, *pl.* **—n**) herald, precursor, forerunner.

vorbringen ['foːrbrɪŋən], *v.a. irr.* produce, proffer; advance, utter, allege, assert, claim.

vordatieren ['foːrdatiːrən], *v.a.* antedate.

vordem [for'deːm], *adv.* (*obs.*) formerly, once.

Vorderachse ['fɔrdəraksə], *f.* (**—**, *pl.* **—n**) front axle.

Vorderansicht ['fɔrdəranzɪçt], *f.* (**—**, *pl.* **—en**) front view.

Vorderarm ['fɔrdərarm], *m.* (**—s**, *pl.* **—e**) forearm.

Vordergrund ['fɔrdərgrunt], *m.* (**—s**, *pl.* **—e**) foreground.

vorderhand ['fɔrdərhant], *adv.* for the present.

Vorderseite ['fɔrdərzaɪtə], *f.* (**—**, *pl.* **—n**) front.

vorderst ['fɔrdərst], *adj.* foremost, first.

Vordertür ['fɔrdərtyːr], *f.* (**—**, *pl.* **—en**) front door.

Vordertreffen ['fɔrdərtrɛfən], *n.* (**—s**, *no pl.*) *ins* — *kommen*, be in the vanguard, come to the fore.

vordrängen ['foːrdrɛŋən], *v.r. sich* **—**, press forward, jump the queue.

vordringen ['foːrdrɪŋən], *v.n. irr.* (*aux.* sein) advance, push forward.

vordringlich ['foːrdrɪŋlɪç], *adj.* urgent; forward, importunate.

Vordruck ['foːrdruk], *m.* (**—s**, *pl.* **—e**) (*printed*) form.

voreilen ['foːraɪlən], *v.n.* (*aux.* sein) rush forward.

voreilig ['foːraɪlɪç], *adj.* over-hasty, rash.

Voreiligkeit ['foːraɪlɪçkaɪt], *f.* (**—**, *no pl.*) hastiness, rashness.

voreingenommen ['foːraɪngənɔmən], *adj.* biased, prejudiced.

Voreingenommenheit ['foːraɪngənɔmənhaɪt], *f.* (**—**, *no pl.*) bias, prejudice.

Voreltern ['foːrɛltərn], *pl.* forefathers, ancestors.

vorenthalten ['foːrɛnthaltən], *v.a. irr. sep. & insep.* withhold.

Vorentscheidung ['foːrɛntʃaɪduŋ], *f.* (**—**, *pl.* **—en**) preliminary decision.

vorerst [foːr'eːrst], *adv.* first of all, firstly; for the time being.

vorerwähnt ['foːrɛrvɛːnt], *adj.* aforementioned.

Vorfahr ['foːrfaːr], *m.* (**—en**, *pl.* **—en**) ancestor.

vorfahren ['foːrfaːrən], *v.n. irr.* (*aux.* sein) drive up (to a house *etc.*).

Vorfall ['foːrfal], *m.* (**—s**, *pl.* **—e**) occurrence, incident.

vorfinden ['foːrfɪndən], *v.a. irr.* find, find present, meet with.

Vorfrage ['foːrfraːgə], *f.* (**—**, *pl.* **—n**) preliminary question.

vorführen ['foːrfyːrən], *v.a.* bring forward, produce.

Vorführung ['foːrfyːruŋ], *f.* (**—**, *pl.* **—en**) production, presentation; performance.

Vorgang ['foːrgaŋ], *m.* (**—s**, *pl.* **—e**) occurrence, event, happening; proceeding, precedent; procedure.

Vorgänger ['foːrgɛŋər], *m.* (**—s**, *pl.* **—**) predecessor.

Vorgarten ['foːrgartən], *m.* (**—s**, *pl.* **—**) front garden.

vorgeben ['foːrgeːbən], *v.a. irr.* pretend; allow (in advance).

Vorgebirge ['foːrgəbɪrgə], *n.* (**—s**, *no pl.*) cape, promontory.

vorgeblich ['foːrgeːplɪç], *adj.* pretended; ostensible.

vorgefaßt ['foːrgəfast], *adj.* preconceived.

Vorgefühl ['foːrgəfyːl], *n.* (**—s**, *pl.* **—e**) presentiment.

vorgehen ['foːrgeːən], *v.n. irr.* (*aux.* sein) advance, walk ahead; proceed; (*clock*) be fast, gain; (*fig.*) take precedence; occur, happen; *was geht hier vor?* what's going on here?

Vorgehen ['foːrgeːən], *n.* (**—s**, *no pl.*) (course of) action, (manner of) procedure.

vorgenannt ['foːrgənant], *adj.* aforenamed.

Vorgericht ['foːrgərɪçt], *n.* (**—s**, *pl.* **—e**) hors d'œuvre, entrée.

Vorgeschichte ['foːrgəʃɪçtə], *f.* (**—**, *no pl.*) prehistory; early history; antecedents.

vorgeschichtlich ['foːrgəʃɪçtlɪç], *adj.* prehistoric.

Vorgeschmack ['foːrgəʃmak], *m.* (**—s**, *no pl.*) foretaste.

Vorgesetzte ['foːrgəzɛtstə], *m.* (**—n**, *pl.* **—n**) superior, senior; boss.

vorgestern ['foːrgɛstərn], *adv.* the day before yesterday.

vorgreifen ['foːrgraɪfən], *v.n. irr.* anticipate, forestall.

Vorhaben ['foːrhaːbən], *m.* (—s, *no pl.*) intention, purpose, design.

vorhaben ['foːrhaːbən], *v.a. irr.* intend; be busy with; *etwas mit einem —,* have designs on s.o.; have plans for s.o.

Vorhalle ['foːrhalə], *f.* (—, *pl.* —n) vestibule, hall, porch.

vorhalten ['foːrhaltən], *v.a. irr.* hold s.th. before s.o.; (*fig.*) remonstrate (with s.o. about s.th.); reproach. — *v.n.* last.

Vorhaltungen ['foːrhaltuŋən], *f. pl.* remonstrances, expostulations.

vorhanden [for'handən], *adj.* at hand, present, in stock, on hand.

Vorhandensein [for'handənzaɪn], *n.* (—s, *no pl.*) existence; availability.

Vorhang ['foːrhaŋ], *m.* (—s, *pl.* ⸗e) curtain.

Vorhängeschloß ['foːrhɛŋəʃlɔs], *n.* (—sses, *pl.* ⸗sser) padlock.

vorher ['foːrheːr], *adv.* before, beforehand, in advance.

vorhergehen [foːr'heːrgeːən], *v.n. irr.* (*aux.* sein) go before, precede.

vorhergehend [foːr'heːrgeːənt], *adj.* foregoing, aforesaid, preceding.

vorherig [foːr'heːrɪç], *adj.* preceding, previous, former.

vorherrschen ['foːrhɛrʃən], *v.n.* prevail, predominate.

vorhersagen [foːr'heːrzaːgən], *v.a.* predict, foretell.

vorhersehen [foːr'heːrzeːən], *v.a. irr.* foresee.

vorheucheln ['foːrhɔyçəln], *v.a. einem etwas —,* pretend s.th. to s.o.

vorhin [foːr'hɪn], *adv.* just before, a short while ago.

Vorhof ['foːrhoːf], *m.* (—s, *pl.* ⸗e) forecourt.

Vorhölle ['foːrhœlə], *f.* (—, *no pl.*) limbo.

Vorhut ['foːrhuːt], *f.* (—, *no pl.*) vanguard.

vorig ['foːrɪç], *adj.* former, preceding.

Vorjahr ['foːrjaːr], *n.* (—s, *pl.* —e) preceding year.

vorjammern ['foːrjamərn], *v.n. einem etwas —,* moan to s.o. about s.th.

Vorkämpfer ['foːrkɛmpfər], *m.* (—s, *pl.* —) champion; pioneer.

vorkauen ['foːrkauən], *v.a.* (*fig.*) predigest; spoon-feed.

Vorkaufsrecht ['foːrkaufsrɛçt], *n.* (—s, *no pl.*) right of first refusal, right of pre-emption.

Vorkehrung ['foːrkeːruŋ], *f.* (—, *pl.* —en) preparation; precaution; (*pl.*) arrangements.

Vorkenntnisse ['foːrkɛntnɪsə], *f. pl.* rudiments, elements, grounding; previous knowledge.

vorkommen ['foːrkɔmən], *v.n. irr.* (*aux.* sein) occur, happen; be found.

Vorkommnis ['foːrkɔmnɪs], *n.* (—ses, *pl.* —se) occurrence, event, happening.

Vorkriegs- ['foːrkriːks], *prefix.* prewar.

Vorladung ['foːrlaːduŋ], *f.* (—, *pl.* —en) summons, writ, subpœna.

Vorlage ['foːrlaːgə], *f.* (—, *pl.* —n) pattern, master-copy.

vorlagern ['foːrlaːgərn], *v.n.* (*aux.* sein) extend (in front of).

Vorland ['foːrlant], *n.* (—s, *pl.* ⸗er) cape, foreland, foreshore.

vorlassen ['foːrlasən], *v.a. irr.* give precedence to; admit, show in.

Vorläufer ['foːrlɔyfər], *m.* (—s, *pl.* —) forerunner, precursor.

vorläufig ['foːrlɔyfɪç], *adj.* provisional, preliminary, temporary. — *adv.* for the time being.

vorlaut ['foːrlaut], *adj.* pert, forward.

Vorleben ['foːrleːbən], *n.* (—s, *no pl.*) antecedents, past life.

vorlegen ['foːrleːgən], *v.a.* put before s.o.; submit, propose; (*food*) serve.

Vorleger ['foːrleːgər], *m.* (—s, *pl.* —) rug, mat.

Vorlegeschloß ['foːrleːgəʃlɔs], *n.* (—sses, *pl.* ⸗sser) padlock.

vorlesen ['foːrleːzən], *v.a. irr.* read aloud, read out.

Vorlesung ['foːrleːzuŋ], *f.* (—, *pl.* —en) lecture.

vorletzte ['foːrlɛtstə], *adj.* last but one, penultimate.

Vorliebe ['foːrliːbə], *f.* (—, *no pl.*) predilection, partiality.

vorliebnehmen [foːr'liːpneːmən], *v.n.* — *mit etwas,* be content with s.th., take pot luck.

vorliegen ['foːrliːgən], *v.n. irr.* (*aux.* sein) be under consideration.

vorlügen ['foːrlyːgən], *v.a. irr. einem etwas —,* tell lies to s.o.

vormachen ['foːrmaxən], *v.a. einem etwas —,* show s.o. how a thing is done; (*fig.*) play tricks on s.o., deceive s.o.

vormalig ['foːrmaːlɪç], *adj.* former, erstwhile, late.

vormals ['foːrmaːls], *adv.* formerly.

Vormarsch ['foːrmarʃ], *m.* (—es, *pl.* ⸗e) (*Mil.*) advance.

vormerken ['foːrmɛrkən], *v.a.* make a note of, take down; book.

Vormittag ['foːrmɪtaːk], *m.* (—s, *pl.* —e) morning, forenoon.

vormittags ['foːrmɪtaːks], *adv.* in the morning; before noon.

Vormund ['foːrmunt], *m.* (—s, *pl.* ⸗er) guardian.

Vormundschaft ['foːrmuntʃaft], *f.* (—, *pl.* —en) guardianship.

Vormundschaftsgericht ['foːrmuntʃaftsgərɪçt], *n.* (—s, *pl.* —e) Court of Chancery.

vorn [forn], *adv.* before, in front of; in front; (*Naut.*) fore.

Vorname ['foːrnaːmə], *m.* (—ns, *pl.*—n) first name, Christian name.

vornehm ['foːrneːm], *adj.* of noble birth, refined; distinguished, elegant.

vornehmen ['foːrneːmən], *v.a. irr.* take in hand; *sich etwas —,* undertake s.th.; plan *or* intend to do s.th.

Vornehmheit ['fo:rne:mhaɪt], *f.* (—, *no pl.*) refinement, distinction.

vornehmlich ['fo:rne:mlɪç], *adv.* chiefly, principally, especially.

vornherein ['fɔrnhɛraɪn], *adv. von* —, from the first; from the beginning.

Vorort ['fo:rɔrt], *m.* (—s, *pl.* —e) suburb.

Vorortsbahn ['fo:rɔrtsba:n], *f.* (—, *pl.* —en) suburban (railway) line.

Vorplatz ['fo:rplats], *m.* (—es, *pl.* ⁓e) forecourt.

Vorposten ['fo:rpɔstən], *m.* (—s, *pl.* —) (*Mil.*) outpost, pickets.

Vorpostengefecht ['fo:rpɔstəngəfɛçt], *n.* (—s, *pl.* —e) outpost skirmish.

Vorprüfung ['fo:rpry:fuŋ], *f.* (—, *pl.* —en) preliminary examination.

Vorrang ['fo:rraŋ], *m.* (—s, *no pl.*) precedence, first place, priority.

Vorrat ['fo:rra:t], *m.* (—s, *pl.* ⁓e) store, stock, provision.

Vorratskammer ['fo:rra:tskamər], *f.* (—, *pl.* —n) store-room; larder.

Vorrecht ['fo:rreçt], *n.* (—s, *pl.* —e) privilege, prerogative.

Vorrede ['fo:rre:də], *f.* (—, *pl.* —n) preface; introduction.

Vorredner ['fo:rre:dnər], *m.* (—s, *pl.* —) previous speaker.

vorrichten ['fo:rrɪçtən], *v.a.* prepare, fix up, get ready.

Vorrichtung ['fo:rrɪçtuŋ], *f.* (—, *pl.* —en) appliance, device, contrivance.

vorrücken ['fo:rrykən], *v.a.* move forward, advance; (*clock*) put on. — *v.n.* (*aux.* sein) (*Mil.*) advance.

Vorsaal ['fo:rza:l], *m.* (—s, *pl.* —säle) hall, entrance hall.

Vorsatz ['fo:rzats], *m.* (—es, *pl.* ⁓e) purpose, design, intention.

vorsätzlich ['fo:rzɛtslɪç], *adj.* intentional, deliberate.

Vorschein ['fo:rʃaɪn], *m.* zum — *kommen*, turn up; appear.

vorschießen ['fo:rʃi:sən], *v.a.* irr. (*money*) advance, lend.

Vorschlag ['fo:rʃla:k], *m.* (—s, *pl.* ⁓e) proposal, offer, proposition.

vorschlagen ['fo:rʃla:gən], *v.a.* irr. put forward, propose, suggest; recommend.

vorschnell ['fo:rʃnɛl], *adj.* hasty, rash, precipitate.

vorschreiben ['fo:rʃraɪbən], *v.a.* irr. write out (for s.o.); (*fig.*) prescribe, order.

Vorschrift ['fo:rʃrɪft], *f.* (—, *pl.* —en) prescription, direction, order, command, regulation.

vorschriftsmäßig ['fo:rʃrɪftsmɛ:sɪç], *adj.* according to regulations.

vorschriftswidrig ['fo:rʃrɪftsvi:drɪç], *adj.* contrary to regulations.

Vorschub ['fo:rʃup], *m.* (—s, *no pl.*) aid, assistance; — *leisten*, countenance, encourage, abet.

Vorschule ['fo:rʃu:lə], *f.* (—, *pl.* —n) preparatory school.

Vorschuß ['fo:rʃus], *m.* (—sses, *pl.* ⁓sse) advance (of cash).

vorschützen ['fo:rʃytsən], *v.a.* use as a pretext, pretend, plead.

vorschweben ['fo:rʃve:bən], *v.n.* be present in o.'s mind.

vorsehen ['fo:rze:ən], *v.r.* irr. sich —, take heed, be careful, look out, beware.

Vorsehung ['fo:rze:uŋ], *f.* (—, *no pl.*) Providence.

vorsetzen ['fo:rzɛtsən], *v.a.* set before; serve; (*word*) prefix.

Vorsicht ['fo:rzɪçt], *f.* (—, *no pl.*) care, precaution, caution, circumspection.

vorsichtig ['fo:rzɪçtɪç], *adj.* cautious, careful, circumspect.

vorsichtshalber ['fo:rzɪçtshalbər], *adv.* as a precautionary measure.

Vorsichtsmaßnahme ['fo:rzɪçtsma:sna:mə], *f.* (—, *pl.* —n) precautionary measure, precaution.

Vorsilbe ['fo:rzɪlbə], *f.* (—, *pl.* —n) prefix.

vorsintflutlich ['fo:rzɪntflu:tlɪç], *adj.* antediluvian; (*fig.*) out-of-date.

Vorsitzende ['fo:rzɪtsəndə], *m.* (—n, *pl.* —n) chairman, president.

Vorsorge ['fo:rzɔrgə], *f.* (—, *no pl.*) care, precaution.

vorsorglich ['fo:rzɔrklɪç], *adj.* provident, careful.

vorspiegeln ['fo:rʃpi:gəln], *v.a. einem etwas* —, deceive s.o., pretend.

Vorspiegelung ['fo:rʃpi:gəluŋ], *f.* (—, *pl.* —en) pretence; — *falscher Tatsachen*, false pretences.

Vorspiel ['fo:rʃpi:l], *n.* (—s, *pl.* —e) prelude; overture.

vorsprechen ['fo:rʃprɛçən], *v.n.* irr. bei einem —, call on s.o. — *v.a. einem etwas* —, say s.th. for s.o.; repeat.

vorspringen ['fo:rʃprɪŋən], *v.n.* irr. (*aux.* sein) leap forward; jut out, project.

Vorsprung ['fo:rʃpruŋ], *m.* (—s, *pl.* ⁓e) projection, prominence; (*fig.*) advantage (over), start, lead.

Vorstadt ['fo:rʃtat], *f.* (—, *pl.* ⁓e) suburb.

vorstädtisch ['fo:rʃtɛtɪʃ], *adj.* suburban.

Vorstand ['fo:rʃtant], *m.* (—s, *pl.* ⁓e) board of directors; director, principal.

Vorstandssitzung ['fo:rʃtantszɪtsuŋ], *f.* (—, *pl.* —en) board meeting.

vorstehen ['fo:rʃte:ən], *v.n.* irr. project, protrude; (*office*) administer, govern, direct, manage.

vorstehend ['fo:rʃte:ənt], *adj.* projecting, protruding; above-mentioned, foregoing.

Vorsteher ['fo:rʃte:ər], *m.* (—s, *pl.* —) director, manager; supervisor.

Vorsteherdrüse ['fo:rʃte:ərdry:zə], *f.* (—, *pl.* —n) prostate gland.

vorstellbar ['fo:rʃtɛlba:r], *adj.* imaginable.

vorstellen ['fo:rʃtɛlən], *v.a.* (*thing*) put forward; (*person*) present, introduce; (*Theat.*) impersonate; represent; (*clock*) put on; *sich etwas* —, visualise s.th., imagine s.th.

vorstellig ['foːrʃtɛlɪç], *adj.* — werden, petition; lodge a complaint.

Vorstellung ['foːrʃtɛluŋ], *f.* (—, *pl.* —en) (*person*) presentation, introduction; (*Theat.*) performance; idea, notion, image; representation.

Vorstellungsvermögen ['foːrʃtɛluŋsfɛrˈmøːgən], *n.* (—s, *no pl.*) imagination, imaginative faculty.

Vorstoß ['foːrʃtoːs], *m.* (—es, *pl.* ⁝e) (*Mil.*) sudden advance, thrust.

vorstoßen ['foːrʃtoːsən], *v.a. irr.* push forward. — *v.n.* (*aux.* sein) (*Mil.*) advance suddenly.

Vorstrafe ['foːrʃtraːfə], *f.* (—, *pl.* —n) previous conviction.

vorstrecken ['foːrʃtrɛkən], *v.a.* stretch forward, protrude; (*money*) advance.

Vorstufe ['foːrʃtuːfə], *f.* (—, *pl.* —n) first step.

Vortänzerin ['foːrtɛntsərɪn], *f.* (—, *pl.* —nen) prima ballerina.

Vorteil ['fortaɪl], *m.* (—s, *pl.* —e) advantage, profit.

vorteilhaft ['fortaɪlhaft], *adj.* advantageous, profitable, lucrative.

Vortrag ['foːrtraːk], *m.* (—s, *pl.* ⁝e) recitation, delivery, rendering; statement, report; talk, speech, lecture.

vortragen ['foːrtraːgən], *v.a. irr.* make a report; (*poem*) recite, declaim; make a request; (*Comm.*) carry forward; lecture on.

Vortragskunst ['foːrtraːkskunst], *f.* (—, *no pl.*) elocution; (art of) public speaking.

vortrefflich [for'trɛflɪç], *adj.* excellent, splendid.

Vortrefflichkeit [for'trɛflɪçkaɪt], *f.* (—, *no pl.*) excellence.

vortreten ['foːrtreːtən], *v.n. irr.* (*aux.* sein) step forward.

Vortritt ['foːrtrɪt], *m.* (—s, *no pl.*) precedence.

vorüber [for'yːbər], *adv.* past, gone, over, finished, done with.

vorübergehen [for'yːbərgeːən], *v.n. irr.* (*aux.* sein) pass by, pass, go past.

vorübergehend [for'yːbərgeːənt], *adj.* passing, temporary, transitory.

Vorübung ['foːryːbuŋ], *f.* (—, *pl.* —en) preliminary exercise.

Voruntersuchung ['foːruntərzuːxuŋ], *f.* (—, *pl.* —en) preliminary inquiry; trial in magistrate's court.

Vorurteil ['foːrurtaɪl], *n.* (—s, *pl.* —e) bias, prejudice.

vorurteilslos ['foːrurtaɪlsloːs], *adj.* impartial, unprejudiced, unbiased.

Vorvater ['foːrfaːtər], *m.* (—s, *pl.* ⁝) progenitor, ancestor.

Vorverkauf ['foːrfɛrkauf], *m.* (—s, *pl.* ⁝e) booking in advance, advance booking.

vorwagen ['foːrvaːgən], *v.r. sich* —, dare to go (or come) forward.

vorwaltend ['foːrvaltənt], *adj.* prevailing, predominating.

Vorwand ['foːrvant], *m.* (—s, *pl.* ⁝e) pretence, pretext; unter dem —, under pretence of.

vorwärts ['forverts], *adv.* forward.

vorwärtskommen ['forvɛrtskɔmən], *v.n. irr.* (*aux.* sein) make headway, get on.

vorweg [for'vɛk], *adv.* before.

vorwegnehmen [for'vɛkneːmən], *v.a. irr.* anticipate.

vorweisen ['foːrvaɪzən], *v.a. irr.* show, produce, exhibit.

Vorwelt ['foːrvɛlt], *f.* (—, *no pl.*) primitive world; former ages.

vorweltlich ['foːrvɛltlɪç], *adj.* primæval, prehistoric.

vorwerfen ['foːrvɛrfən], *v.a. irr. einem etwas* —, blame s.o. for s.th.; charge s.o. with s.th., tax s.o. with s.th.

vorwiegen ['foːrviːgən], *v.n. irr.* prevail.

vorwiegend ['foːrviːgənt], *adv.* mostly, for the most part.

Vorwissen ['foːrvɪsən], *n.* (—s, *no pl.*) foreknowledge, prescience.

Vorwitz ['foːrvɪts], *m.* (—es, *no pl.*) pertness.

vorwitzig ['foːrvɪtsɪç], *adj.* forward, pert, meddlesome.

Vorwort (1) ['foːrvɔrt], *n.* (—s, *pl.* —e) preface.

Vorwort (2) ['foːrvɔrt], *n.* (—s, *pl.* ⁝er) (*Gram.*) preposition.

Vorwurf ['foːrvurf], *m.* (—s, *pl.* ⁝e) reproach; theme, subject.

vorwurfsfrei ['foːrvurfsfraɪ], *adj.* free from blame, irreproachable.

vorwurfsvoll ['foːrvurfsfɔl], *adj.* reproachful.

Vorzeichen ['foːrtsaɪxən], *n.* (—s, *pl.* —) omen, token; (*Maths.*) sign.

vorzeigen ['foːrtsaɪgən], *v.a.* show, produce, exhibit, display.

Vorzeit ['foːrtsaɪt], *f.* (—, *no pl.*) antiquity, olden times.

vorzeiten [for'tsaɪtən], *adv.* (*Poet.*) in olden times, formerly.

vorzeitig ['foːrtsaɪtɪç], *adj.* premature.

vorziehen ['foːrtsiːən], *v.a. irr.* prefer.

Vorzimmer ['foːrtsɪmər], *n.* (—s, *pl.* —) anteroom, antechamber.

Vorzug ['foːrtsuːk], *m.* (—s, *pl.* ⁝e) preference, advantage; excellence, superiority.

vorzüglich [for'tsyːklɪç], *adj.* superior, excellent, exquisite.

Vorzüglichkeit [for'tsyːklɪçkaɪt], *f.* (—, *no pl.*) excellence, superiority.

Vorzugsaktie ['foːrtsuːksaktsjə], *f.* (—, *pl.* —n) preference share.

vorzugsweise ['foːrtsuːksvaɪzə], *adv.* for choice, preferably.

vulgär [vulˈgɛːr], *adj.* vulgar.

Vulkan [vul'kaːn], *m.* (—s, *pl.* —e) volcano.

vulkanisch [vul'kaːnɪʃ], *adj.* volcanic.

W

W [ve:] *n.* (**—s**, *pl.* **—s**) the letter W.

Waage ['va:gə], *f.* (**—**, *pl.* **—n**) balance, pair of scales.

waag(e)recht ['va:g(ə)rɛçt], *adj.* horizontal.

Waagschale ['va:kʃa:lə], *f.* (**—**, *pl.* **—n**) pan of a balance.

Wabe ['va:bə], *f.* (**—**, *pl.* **—n**) honeycomb.

Waberlohe ['va:bərlo:ə], *f.* (**—**, *no pl.*) (*Poet.*) flickering flames, magic fire.

wach [vax], *adj.* awake; alert; *völlig* **—**, wide awake.

Wachdienst ['vaxdi:nst], *m.* (**—es**, *no pl.*) guard, sentry duty.

Wache ['vaxə], *f.* (**—**, *pl.* **—n**) guard, watch; (*person*) sentry, sentinel.

wachen ['vaxən], *v.n.* be awake; guard; *— über*, watch, keep an eye on.

Wacholder [va'xɔldər], *m.* (**—s**, *pl.* **—**) (*Bot.*) juniper.

wachrufen [vax'ru:fən], *v.a. irr.* (*fig.*) call to mind.

Wachs [vaks], *n.* (**—es**, *no pl.*) wax.

wachsam ['vaxza:m], *adj.* watchful, vigilant.

Wachsamkeit ['vaxza:mkaɪt], *f.* (**—**, *no pl.*) watchfulness, vigilance.

Wachsbild ['vaksbɪlt], *n.* (**—s**, *pl.* **—er**) waxen image.

wachsen ['vaksən], *v.n. irr.* (*aux.* sein) grow, increase.

wächsern ['vɛksərn], *adj.* waxen, made of wax.

Wachsfigur ['vaksfigu:r], *f.* (**—**, *pl.* **—en**) wax figure.

Wachsfigurenkabinett ['vaksfigu:rənkabinɛt], *n.* (**—s**, *pl.* **—e**) waxworks.

Wachsleinwand ['vakslaɪnvant], *f.* (**—**, *no pl.*) oil-cloth.

Wachstuch ['vakstu:x], *n.* (**—(e)s**, *no pl.*) oil-cloth; American cloth.

Wachstum ['vakstu:m], *n.* (**—s**, *no pl.*) growth, increase.

Wacht [vaxt], *f.* (**—**, *pl.* **—en**) watch, guard.

Wachtdienst ['vaxtdi:nst] *see* **Wachdienst**.

Wachtel ['vaxtəl], *f.* (**—**, *pl.* **—n**) (*Orn.*) quail.

Wachtelhund ['vaxtəlhunt], *m.* (**—(e)s**, *pl.* **—e**) (*Zool.*) spaniel.

Wächter ['vɛçtər], *m.* (**—s**, *pl.* **—**) watchman, warder, guard.

wachthabend ['vaxtha:bənt], *adj.* on duty.

Wachtmeister ['vaxtmaɪstər], *m.* (**—s**, *pl.* **—**) sergeant.

Wachtparade [vaxtpara:də], *f.* (**—**, *pl.* **—n**) mounting of the guard.

Wachtposten ['vaxtpɔstən], *m.* (**—s**, *pl.* **—**) guard, picket.

Wachtraum ['vaxtraum], *m.* (**—s**, *pl.* **-e**) day-dream, waking dream.

Wachtturm ['vaxtturm], *m.* (**—s**, *pl.* **-e**) watch-tower.

wackeln ['vakəln], *v.n.* totter, shake, wobble.

wacker ['vakər], *adj.* gallant, brave, valiant; upright.

wacklig ['vaklɪç], *adj.* tottering, shaky; (*furniture*) rickety; (*tooth*) loose.

Wade ['va:də], *f.* (**—**, *pl.* **—n**) calf (of the leg).

Wadenbein ['va:dənbaɪn], *n.* (**—s**, *pl.* **—e**) shin-bone.

Waffe ['vafə], *f.* (**—**, *pl.* **—n**) weapon, arm; *die —n strecken*, surrender.

Waffel ['vafəl], *f.* (**—**, *pl.* **—n**) wafer; waffle.

Waffeleisen ['vafəlaɪzən], *n.* (**—s**, *pl.* **—**) waffle-iron.

Waffenbruder ['vafənbru:dər], *m.* (**—s**, *pl.* **-**) brother-in-arms, comrade.

waffenfähig ['vafənfɛ:ɪç], *adj.* able to bear arms.

Waffengewalt ['vafəngəvalt], *f.* (**—**, *no pl.*) *mit —*, by force of arms.

Waffenglück ['vafənglyk], *n.* (**—s**, *no pl.*) fortunes of war.

Waffenrock ['vafənrɔk], *m.* (**—s**, *pl.* **-e**) tunic.

Waffenruf ['vafənru:f], *m.* (**—s**, *no pl.*) call to arms.

Waffenschmied [vafənʃmi:t], *m.* (**—s**, *pl.* **—e**) armourer.

Waffenstillstand ['vafənʃtɪlʃtant], *m.* (**—s**, *no pl.*) armistice, truce.

waffnen ['vafnən], *v.a.* arm.

Wage *see* **Waage**.

Wagebalken ['va:gəbalkən], *m.* (**—s**, *pl.* **—**) scale-beam.

Wagen ['va:gən], *m.* (**—s**, *pl.* **—**) vehicle, conveyance, carriage, coach, car, cab, wagon, cart, truck, van, dray.

wagen ['va:gən], *v.a.*, *v.n.* dare, venture, risk.

wägen ['vɛ:gən], *v.a.*, *irr.* weigh, balance; (*words*) consider.

Wagenverkehr ['va:gənfɛrke:r], *m.* (**—s**, *no pl.*) vehicular traffic.

wagerecht *see* **waagerecht**.

Waggon [va'gɔ̃], *m.* (**—s**, *pl.* **—s**) railway car, goods van, freight car.

waghalsig ['va:khalzɪç], *adj.* foolhardy, rash, daring.

Wagnis ['va:knɪs], *n.* (**—ses**, *pl.* **—se**) venture, risky undertaking; risk.

Wagschale *see* **Waagschale**.

Wahl [va:l], *f.* (**—**, *pl.* **—en**) choice; election; selection; alternative.

Wahlakt ['va:lakt], *m.* (**—s**, *pl.* **—e**) poll, election.

Wahlaufruf ['va:laufru:f], *m.* (**—s**, *pl.* **—e**) manifesto, election address.

wählbar ['vɛ:lba:r], *adj.* eligible.

Wählbarkeit ['vɛ:lba:rkaɪt], *f.* (**—**, *no pl.*) eligibility.

wahlberechtigt ['vaːlbərɛçtɪçt], *adj.* entitled to vote.

wählen ['vɛːlən], *v.a.* choose; (*Parl.*) elect; (*Telephone*) dial.

Wähler ['vɛːlər], *m.* (—s, *pl.* —) elector; constituent.

wählerisch ['vɛːlərɪʃ], *adj.* fastidious, particular.

Wählerschaft ['vɛːlərʃaft], *f.* (—, *pl.* —en) constituency.

wahlfähig ['vaːlfɛːɪç], *adj.* eligible.

Wahlliste ['vaːllɪstə], *f.* (—, *pl.* —n) electoral list, register (of electors).

wahllos ['vaːlloːs], *adj.* indiscriminate.

Wahlrecht ['vaːlrɛçt], *n.* (—s, *no pl.*) franchise.

Wahlspruch ['vaːlʃprux], *m.* (—s, *pl.* ⁀e) device, motto.

wahlunfähig ['vaːlunfɛːɪç], *adj.* ineligible.

Wahlurne ['vaːlurnə], *f.* (—, *pl.* —n) ballot-box.

Wahlverwandtschaft ['vaːlfɛrvantʃaft], *f.* (—, *no pl.*) elective affinity, congeniality.

Wahlzettel ['vaːltsɛtəl], *m.* (—s, *pl.* —) ballot-paper.

Wahn [vaːn], *m.* (—(e)s, *no pl.*) delusion.

Wahnbild ['vaːnbɪlt], *n.* (—s, *pl.* —er) hallucination, delusion; phantasm.

wähnen ['vɛːnən], *v.a.* fancy, believe.

Wahnsinn ['vaːnzɪn], *m.* (—s, *no pl.*) madness, lunacy.

wahnsinnig ['vaːnzɪnɪç], *adj.* insane, mad, lunatic; (*coll.*) terrific.

Wahnsinnige ['vaːnzɪnɪgə], *m.* (—n, *pl.* —n) madman, lunatic.

Wahnwitz ['vaːnvɪts], *m.* (—es, *no pl.*) madness.

wahnwitzig ['vaːnvɪtsɪç], *adj.* mad.

wahr [vaːr], *adj.* true, real, genuine.

wahren ['vaːrən], *v.a.* guard, watch over.

währen ['vɛːrən], *v.n.* last.

während ['vɛːrənt], *prep.* (*Genit.*) during. — *conj.* while, whilst; whereas.

wahrhaft ['vaːrhaft], *adj.* truthful, veracious.

wahrhaftig [vaːr'haftɪç], *adv.* truly, really, in truth.

Wahrhaftigkeit [vaːr'haftɪçkaɪt], *f.* (—, *no pl.*) truthfulness, veracity.

Wahrheit ['vaːrhaɪt], *f.* (—, *pl.* —en) truth; reality; *die — sagen*, tell the truth.

Wahrheitsliebe ['vaːrhaɪtsliːbə], *f.* (—, *no pl.*) love of truth, truthfulness.

wahrlich ['vaːrlɪç], *adv.* truly, in truth.

wahrnehmbar ['vaːrneːmbaːr], *adj.* perceptible.

wahrnehmen ['vaːrneːmən], *v.a. irr.* perceive, observe.

Wahrnehmung ['vaːrneːmuŋ], *f.* (—, *pl.* —en) perception, observation.

wahrsagen ['vaːrzaːgən], *v.n.* prophesy; tell fortunes.

Wahrsager ['vaːrzaːgər], *m.* (—s, *pl.* —) fortune-teller, soothsayer.

wahrscheinlich [vaːr'ʃaɪnlɪç], *adj.* likely, probable; *es wird — regnen*, it will probably rain.

Wahrscheinlichkeit [vaːr'ʃaɪnlɪçkaɪt], *f.* (—, *pl.* —en) likelihood, probability.

Wahrung ['vaːruŋ], *f.* (—, *no pl.*) protection, preservation, maintenance.

Währung ['vɛːruŋ], *f.* (—, *pl.* —en) currency, standard.

Wahrzeichen ['vaːrtsaɪçən], *n.* (—s, *pl.* —) landmark; (*fig.*) sign, token.

Waibling(er) ['vaɪblɪŋ(ər)], *m.* Ghibelline.

Waidmann ['vaɪtman], *m.* (—s, *pl.* ⁀er) huntsman, hunter.

waidmännisch ['vaɪtmɛnɪʃ], *adj.* sportsmanlike.

Waise ['vaɪzə], *f.* (—, *pl.* —n) orphan.

Waisenhaus ['vaɪzənhaus], *n.* (—es, *pl.* ⁀er) orphanage.

Waisenmutter ['vaɪzənmutər], *f.* (—, *pl.* ⁀) foster-mother.

Waisenvater ['vaɪzənfaːtər], *m.* (—s, *pl.* ⁀) foster-father.

Wald [valt], *m.* (—es, *pl.* ⁀er) wood, forest; woodland.

Waldbrand ['valtbrant], *m.* (—s, *pl.* ⁀e) forest-fire.

Waldlichtung ['valtlɪçtuŋ], *f.* (—, *pl.* —en) forest glade, clearing.

Waldmeister ['valtmaɪstər], *m.* (—s, *no pl.*) (*Bot.*) woodruff.

Waldung ['valduŋ], *f.* (—, *pl.* —en) woods, woodland.

Waldwiese ['valtviːzə], *f.* (—, *pl.* —en) forest-glade.

Walfisch ['vaːlfɪʃ], *m.* (—es, *pl.* —e) whale.

Walfischfang ['vaːlfɪʃfaŋ], *m.* (—s, *no pl.*) whaling.

Walfischfänger ['vaːlfɪʃfɛŋər], *m.* (—s, *pl.* —) whaler, whale fisher.

Walfischtran ['vaːlfɪʃtraːn], *m.* (—s, *no pl.*) train-oil.

Walküre [val'kyːrə], *f.* (—, *pl.* —n) Valkyrie.

Wall [val], *m.* (—(e)s, *pl.* ⁀e) rampart, dam, vallum; mound.

Wallach ['valax], *m.* (—s, *pl.* —e) castrated horse, gelding.

wallen ['valən], *v.n.* bubble, boil up; wave, undulate.

Wallfahrer ['valfaːrər], *m.* (—s, *pl.* —) pilgrim.

Wallfahrt ['valfaːrt], *f.* (—, *pl.* —en) pilgrimage.

wallfahrten ['valfaːrtən], *v.n.* (*aux.* sein) go on a pilgrimage.

Walnuß ['valnus], *f.* (—, *pl.* ⁀sse) (*Bot.*) walnut.

Walpurgisnacht [val'purgɪsnaxt], *f.* witches' sabbath.

Walroß ['valrɔs], *n.* (—sses, *pl.* —sse) sea-horse, walrus.

Walstatt ['valʃtat], *f.* (—, *pl.* ⁀en) (*Poet.*) battlefield.

walten ['valtən], *v.n.* rule; *seines Amtes —*, do o.'s duty, carry out o.'s duties.

Walze ['valtsə], *f.* (—, *pl.* —n) roller, cylinder.

walzen ['valtsən], *v.a.* roll. — *v.n.* waltz.

wälzen ['vɛltsən], *v.a.* roll, turn about.

walzenförmig ['valtsənfœrmɪç], *adj.* cylindrical.

Walzer ['valtsər], *m.* (—s, *pl.* —) waltz.

Wälzer ['vɛltsər], *m.* (—s, *pl.* —) tome; thick volume.

Walzwerk ['valtsvɛrk], *n.* (—s, *pl.* —e) rolling-mill.

Wams [vams], *n.* (—es, *pl.* ˙e) (*obs.*) doublet, jerkin.

Wand [vant], *f.* (—, *pl.* ˙e) wall; side.

Wandbekleidung ['vantbəklaiduŋ], *f.* (—, *pl.* —en) wainscot, panelling.

Wandel ['vandəl], *m.* (—s, *no pl.*) mutation, change; behaviour, conduct; *Handel und* —, trade and traffic.

wandelbar ['vandəlba:r], *adj.* changeable, inconstant.

Wandelgang ['vandəlgaŋ], *m.* (—s, *pl.* ˙e) lobby; lounge, foyer; (*in the open*) covered way, covered walk.

wandeln ['vandəln], *v.a.* (*aux.* haben) change. — *v.n.* (*aux.* sein) walk, wander. — *v.r. sich* —, change.

Wanderbursche ['vandərburʃə], *m.* (—n, *pl.* —n) travelling journeyman.

Wanderer ['vandərər], *m.* (—s, *pl.* —) wanderer, traveller; hiker.

Wanderleben ['vandərle:bən], *n.* (—s, *no pl.*) travelling life.

Wanderlehrer ['vandərle:rər], *m.* (—s, *pl.* —) itinerant teacher.

Wanderlust ['vandərlust], *f.* (—, *no pl.*) urge to travel; call of the open.

wandern ['vandərn], *v.n.* (*aux.* sein) wander, travel; migrate.

Wanderschaft ['vandərʃaft], *f.* (—, *no pl.*) wanderings.

Wandersmann ['vandərsman], *m.* (—s, *pl.* ˙er) wayfarer.

Wandertruppe ['vandərtrupə], *f.* (—, *pl.* —n) (*Theat.*) strolling players.

Wanderung ['vandəruŋ], *f.* (—, *pl.* —en) walking tour; hike.

Wandervolk ['vandərfɔlk], *n.* (— (e)s, *pl.* ˙er) nomadic tribe.

Wandgemälde ['vantgəmɛ:ldə], *n.* (—s, *pl.* —e) mural painting, mural.

Wandlung ['vandluŋ], *f.* (—, *pl.* —en) transformation; (*Theol.*) transubstantiation.

Wandspiegel ['vantʃpi:gəl], *m.* (—s, *pl.* —) pier-glass.

Wandtafel ['vantta:fəl], *f.* (—, *pl.* —n) blackboard.

Wange ['vaŋə], *f.* (—, *pl.* —n) cheek.

Wankelmut ['vaŋkəlmu:t], *m.* (—s, *no pl.*) fickleness, inconstancy.

wankelmütig ['vaŋkəlmy:tɪç], *adj.* inconstant, fickle.

wanken ['vaŋkən], *v.n.* totter, stagger; (*fig.*) waver, be irresolute.

wann [van], *adv.* when; *dann und* —, now and then, sometimes.

Wanne ['vanə], *f.* (—, *pl.* —n) tub, bath.

wannen ['vanən], *adv.* (*obs.*) *von* —, whence.

Wannenbad ['vanənba:t], *n.* (—s, *pl.* ˙er) bath.

Wanst [vanst], *m.* (—es, *pl.* ˙e) belly, paunch.

Wanze ['vantsə], *f.* (—, *pl.* —n) (*Ent.*) bug.

Wappen ['vapən], *n.* (—s, *pl.* —) crest, coat-of-arms.

Wappenbild ['vapənbɪlt], *n.* (—s, *pl.* —er) heraldic figure.

Wappenkunde ['vapənkundə], *f.* (—, *no pl.*) heraldry.

Wappenschild ['vapənʃilt], *m.* (—s, *pl.* —e) escutcheon.

Wappenspruch ['vapənʃprux], *m.* (—(e)s, *pl.* ˙e) motto, device.

wappnen ['vapnən], *v.a.* arm.

Ware ['va:rə], *f.* (—, *pl.* —n) article, commodity; (*pl.*) merchandise, goods, wares.

Warenausfuhr ['va:rənausfu:r], *f.* (—, *no pl.*) exportation, export.

Warenbörse ['va:rənbœrzə], *f.* (—, *pl.* —n) commodity exchange.

Wareneinfuhr ['va:rənainfu:r], *f.* (—, *no pl.*) importation, import.

Warenhaus ['va:rənhaus], *n.* (—es, *pl.* ˙er) department store, emporium; (*Am.*) store.

Warenlager ['va:rənla:gər], *n.* (—s, *pl.* —) magazine; stock; warehouse.

Warensendung ['va:rənzɛnduŋ], *f.* (—, *pl.* —en) consignment of goods.

Warentausch ['va:rəntauʃ], *m.* (—es, *no pl.*) barter.

warm [varm], *adj.* warm, hot.

warmblütig ['varmbly:tɪç], *adj.* warm-blooded.

Wärme ['vɛrmə], *f.* (—, *no pl.*) warmth; heat.

Wärmeeinheit ['vɛrməainhait], *f.* (—, *pl.* —en) thermal unit; calorie.

Wärmegrad ['vɛrməgra:t], *m.* (—s, *pl.* —e) degree of heat; temperature.

Wärmeleiter ['vɛrməlaitər], *m.* (—s, *pl.* —) conductor of heat.

Wärmemesser ['vɛrməmesər], *m.* (—s, *pl.* —) thermometer.

wärmen ['vɛrmən], *v.a.* warm, heat.

Wärmflasche ['vɛrmflaʃə], *f.* (—, *pl.* —n) hot-water bottle.

warnen ['varnən], *v.a.* warn; caution.

Warnung ['varnuŋ], *f.* (—, *pl.* —en) warning, caution, admonition; notice.

Warschau ['varʃau], *n.* Warsaw.

Warte ['vartə], *f.* (—, *pl.* —n) watch-tower, belfry, look-out.

Wartegeld ['vartəgɛlt], *n.* (—s, *pl.* —er) half pay; (*ship*) demurrage charges.

warten ['vartən], *v.n.* wait; — *auf* (*Acc.*), wait for, await. — *v.a.* tend, nurse.

Wärter ['vɛrtər], *m.* (—s, *pl.* —) keeper, attendant; warder; male nurse.

Wartesaal ['vartəza:l], *m.* (—s, *pl.* —säle) (*Railw.*) waiting-room.

Wartung ['vartuŋ], *f.* (—, *no pl.*) nursing, attendance; servicing; maintenance.

warum [va'rum], *adv., conj.* why, for what reason.

Warze ['vartsə], *f.* (—, *pl.* —n) wart.

was [vas], *interr. pron.* what? — *rel. pron.* what, that which.

Waschanstalt ['vaʃanʃtalt], *f.* (—, *pl.* —en) laundry.

waschbar ['vaʃbaːr], *adj.* washable.

Waschbär ['vaʃbɛːr], *m.* (—en, *pl.* —en) (*Zool.*) raccoon.

Waschbecken ['vaʃbɛkən], *n.* (—s, *pl.* —) wash-basin.

Wäsche ['vɛʃə], *f.* (—, *no pl.*) washing, wash, laundry; linen.

waschecht ['vaʃɛçt], *adj.* washable; (*fig.*) genuine.

waschen ['vaʃən], *v.a. irr.* wash.

Wäscherin ['vɛʃərin], *f.* (—, *pl.* —nen) washerwoman, laundress.

Waschhaus ['vaʃhaus], *n.* (—es, *pl.* ̈er) wash-house, laundry; (*reg. trade name*) launderette.

Waschkorb ['vaʃkɔrp], *m.* (—s, *pl.* ̈e) clothes-basket.

Waschküche ['vaʃkyçə], *f.* (—, *pl.* —en) wash-house.

Waschlappen ['vaʃlapən], *m.* (—s, *pl.* —) face-flannel, face-cloth, face-washer; (*fig.*) milksop.

Waschleder ['vaʃleːdər], *n.* (—s, *no pl.*) chamois leather, wash-leather.

Waschmaschine ['vaʃmaʃiːnə], *f.* (—, *pl.* ̈n) washing-machine.

Waschtisch ['vaʃtiʃ], *m.* (—es, *pl.* —e) wash-stand.

Waschwanne ['vaʃvanə], *f.* (—, *pl.* —n) wash-tub.

Wasser ['vasər], *n.* (—s, *pl.* —) water; *stille — sind tief,* still waters run deep.

wasserarm ['vasərarm], *adj.* waterless, dry, arid.

Wasserbehälter ['vasərbəhɛltər], *m.* (—s, *pl.* —) reservoir, cistern, tank.

Wasserblase ['vasərblaːzə], *f.* (—, *pl.* —en) bubble.

Wässerchen ['vɛsərçən], *n.* (—s, *pl.* —) brook, streamlet; *er sieht aus, als ob er kein — trüben könnte,* he looks as if butter would not melt in his mouth.

Wasserdampf ['vasərdampf], *m.* (—(e)s, *no pl.*) steam.

wasserdicht ['vasərdiçt], *adj.* water-proof.

Wasserdruck ['vasərdruk], *m.* (—s, *no pl.*) hydrostatic pressure, hydraulic pressure.

Wassereimer ['vasəraimər], *m.* (—s, *pl.* —) pail, water-bucket.

Wasserfall ['vasərfal], *m.* (—s, *pl.* ̈e) waterfall, cataract, cascade.

Wasserfarbe ['vasərfarbə], *f.* (—, *pl.* —n) water-colour.

Wasserheilanstalt ['vasərhailanʃtalt], *f.* (—, *pl.* —en) spa.

wässerig ['vɛsəriç], *adj.* watery; (*fig.*) insipid, flat, diluted.

Wasserkanne ['vasərkanə], *f.* (—, *pl.* —n) pitcher, ewer.

Wasserkessel ['vasərkɛsəl], *m.* (—s, *pl.* —) boiler; kettle.

Wasserkopf ['vasərkɔpf], *m.* (—(e)s, *pl.* ̈e) (*Med.*) hydrocephalus.

Wasserkur ['vasərkuːr], *f.* (—, *pl.* —en) hydropathic treatment.

Wasserleitung ['vasərlaituŋ], *f.* (—, *pl.* —en) aqueduct; water main.

Wasserlinsen ['vasərlinzən], *f. pl.* (*Bot.*) duck-weed.

Wassermann ['vasərman], *m.* (—s, *no pl.*) (*Astron.*) Aquarius.

wässern ['vɛsərn], *v.a.* water, irrigate, soak.

Wassernixe ['vasərniksə], *f.* (—, *pl.* —n) water nymph.

Wassernot ['vasərnoːt], *f.* (—, *no pl.*) drought, scarcity of water.

Wasserrabe ['vasərraːbə], *m.* (—n, *pl.* —n) (*Orn.*) cormorant.

Wasserrinne ['vasərrinə], *f.* (—, *pl.* —n) gutter.

Wasserröhre ['vasərrøːrə], *f.* (—, *pl.* —n) water-pipe.

Wasserscheide ['vasərʃaidə], *f.* (—, *pl.* —n) watershed.

Wasserscheu ['vasərʃɔy], *f.* (—, *no pl.*) hydrophobia.

Wasserspiegel ['vasərʃpiːgəl], *m.* (—s, *pl.* —) water-level.

Wasserspritze ['vasərʃpritsə], *f.* (—, *pl.* —n) squirt; sprinkler.

Wasserstand ['vasərʃtant], *m.* (—s, *no pl.*) water-level.

Wasserstiefel ['vasərʃtiːfəl], *m.* (—s, *pl.* —) wader, gumboot.

Wasserstoff ['vasərʃtɔf], *m.* (—(e)s, *no pl.*) hydrogen.

Wassersucht ['vasərzuxt], *f.* (—, *no pl.*) dropsy.

Wassersuppe ['vasərzupə], *f.* (—, *pl.* —n) water-gruel.

Wässerung ['vɛsəruŋ], *f.* (—, *pl.* —en) watering, irrigation.

Wasserverdrängung ['vasərferdrɛŋuŋ], *f.* (—, *no pl.*) displacement (of water).

Wasserwaage ['vasərvaːgə], *f.* (—, *pl.* —n) water-balance, water-level; hydrometer.

Wasserweg ['vasərveːk], *m.* (—s, *pl.* —e) waterway; *auf dem —,* by water, by sea.

Wasserzeichen ['vasərtsaiçən], *n.* (—s, *pl.* —) watermark.

waten ['vaːtən], *v.n.* (*aux.* sein) wade.

watscheln ['vaːtʃəln], *v.n.* (*aux.* sein) waddle.

Watt (1) [vat], *n.* (—s, *pl.* —e) sand-bank; (*pl.*) shallows.

Watt (2) [vat], *n.* (—s, *pl.* —) (*Elec.*) watt.

Watte ['vatə], *f.* (—, *no pl.*) wadding, cotton-wool.

wattieren [va'tiːrən], *v.a.* pad.

Webe ['veːbə], *f.* (—, *pl.* —n) web, weft.

weben ['veːbən], *v.a.* weave.

Weber ['veːbər], *m.* (—s, *pl.* —) weaver.

Weberei [veːbə'rai], *f.* (—, *pl.* —en) weaving-mill.

Weberschiffchen

Weberschiffchen ['veːbərʃifçən], *n.* (—s, *pl.* —) shuttle.

Wechsel ['vɛksəl], *m.* (—s, *pl.* —) change; turn, variation; vicissitude; (*Comm.*) bill of exchange.

Wechselbalg ['vɛksəlbalk], *m.* (—s, *pl.* ⁚e) changeling.

Wechselbank ['vɛksəlbaŋk], *f.* (—, *pl.* ⁚e) discount-bank.

Wechselbeziehung ['vɛksəlbətsiːuŋ], *f.* (—, *pl.* —en) reciprocal relation, correlation.

Wechselfälle ['vɛksəlfɛlə], *m. pl.* vicissitudes.

Wechselfieber ['vɛksəlfiːbər], *n.* (—s, *pl.* —) intermittent fever.

Wechselfolge ['vɛksəlfɔlgə], *f.* (—, *no pl.*) rotation, alternation.

Wechselgeld ['vɛksəlgɛlt], *n.* (—(e)s, *no pl.*) change.

wechseln ['vɛksəln], *v.a.* change, exchange. — *v.n.* change, alternate, change places.

wechselseitig ['vɛksəlzaɪtɪç], *adj.* reciprocal, mutual.

Wechselstrom ['vɛksəlʃtroːm], *m.* (—s, *no pl.*) alternating current.

Wechselstube ['vɛksəlʃtuːbə], *f.* (—, *pl.* —n) exchange office.

wechselvoll ['vɛksəlfɔl], *adj.* eventful, chequered; changeable.

wechselweise ['vɛksəlvaɪzə], *adv.* reciprocally, mutually; by turns, alternately.

Wechselwinkel ['vɛksəlvɪŋkəl], *m.* (—s, *pl.* —) alternate angle.

Wechselwirkung ['vɛksəlvɪrkuŋ], *f.* (—; *pl.* —en) reciprocal effect.

Wechselwirtschaft ['vɛksəlvɪrtʃaft], *f.* (—, *no pl.*) rotation of crops.

Wecken ['vɛkən], *m.* (—s, *pl.* —) (*dial.*) bread-roll.

wecken ['vɛkən], *v.a.* wake, rouse, awaken.

Wecker ['vɛkər], *m.* (—s, *pl.* —) alarm-clock.

Weckuhr ['vɛkuːr], *f.* (—, *pl.* —en) alarm-clock.

Wedel ['veːdəl], *m.* (—s, *pl.* —) feather-duster, fan; tail.

wedeln ['veːdəln], *v.n. mit dem Schwanz* —, wag its tail.

weder ['veːdər], *conj.* neither; — . . . *noch,* neither . . . nor.

Weg [veːk], *m.* (—(e)s, *pl.* —e) way, path, route, road; walk, errand; *am* —, by the wayside.

weg [vɛk], *adv.* away, gone, off, lost.

wegbegeben ['vɛkbəgeːbən], *v.r. irr. sich* —, go away, leave.

wegbekommen ['vɛkbəkɔmən], *v.a. irr. etwas* —, get the hang of s.th.; get s.th. off or away.

Wegbereiter ['veːkbəraɪtər], *m.* (—s, *pl.* —) forerunner, pathfinder, pioneer.

wegblasen ['vɛkblaːzən], *v.a. irr.* blow away; *wie weggeblasen,* without leaving a trace.

wegbleiben ['vɛkblaɪbən], *v.n. irr.* (*aux. sein*) stay away.

wegblicken ['vɛkblɪkən], *v.n.* look the other way.

wegbringen ['vɛkbrɪŋən], *v.a. irr. einen* —, get s.o. away.

wegdrängen ['vɛkdrɛŋən], *v.a.* push away.

Wegebau ['veːgəbau], *m.* (—s, *no pl.*) road-making.

wegeilen ['vɛkaɪlən], *v.n.* (*aux. sein*) hasten away, hurry off.

wegelagern ['veːgəlaːgərn], *v.a.* waylay.

wegen ['veːgən], *prep.* (*Genit., Dat.*) because of, on account of, owing to, by reason of.

Wegfall ['vɛkfal], *m.* (—s, *no pl.*) omission.

wegfallen ['vɛkfalən], *v.n. irr.* (*aux. sein*) fall off; be omitted; cease.

Weggang ['vɛkgaŋ], *m.* (—s, *no pl.*) departure, going away.

weggießen ['vɛkgiːsən], *v.a. irr.* pour away.

weghaben ['vɛkhaːbən], *v.a. irr. etwas* —, understand how to do s.th, have the knack of doing s.th.

wegkommen ['vɛkkɔmən], *v.n. irr.* (*aux. sein*) get away; be lost.

wegkönnen ['vɛkkœnən], *v.n. irr. nicht* —, not be able to get away.

Weglassung ['vɛklasuŋ], *f.* (—, *pl.* —en) omission.

wegmachen ['vɛkmaxən], *v.r. sich* —, decamp, make off.

wegmüssen ['vɛkmysən], *v.n. irr.* be obliged to go; have to go.

Wegnahme ['vɛknaːmə], *f.* (—, *no pl.*) taking, seizure, capture.

Wegreise ['vɛkraɪzə], *f.* (—, *no pl.*) departure.

Wegscheide ['vɛkʃaɪdə], *f.* (—, *pl.* —n) crossroads, crossways.

wegscheren ['vɛkʃeːrən], *v.a.* clip; shave off. — *v.r. sich* —, be off.

wegschnappen ['vɛkʃnapən], *v.a.* snatch away.

wegsehnen ['vɛkzeːnən], *v.r. sich* —, wish o.s. far away; long to get away.

wegsein ['vɛkzaɪn], *v.n. irr.* (*aux. sein*) (*person*) be gone, be away; have gone off; (*things*) be lost; *ganz* —, (*coll.*) be beside o.s. or amazed.

wegsetzen ['vɛkzɛtsən], *v.a.* put away.

wegspülen ['vɛkʃpyːlən], *v.a.* wash away.

Wegstunde ['veːkʃtundə], *f.* (—, *pl.* —n) an hour's walk.

Wegweiser ['veːkvaɪzər], *m.* (—s, *pl.* —) signpost, road-sign.

wegwenden ['vɛkvɛndən], *v.r. irr. sich* —, turn away.

wegwerfen ['vɛkvɛrfən], *v.a. irr.* throw away.

wegwerfend ['vɛkvɛrfənt], *adj.* disparaging, disdainful.

Wegzehrung ['veːktseːruŋ], *f.* (—, *no pl.*) food for the journey; (*Eccl.*) viaticum.

wegziehen ['vɛktsi:ən], *v.a. irr.* draw away, pull away. — *v.n.* (*aux.* sein) march away; (*fig.*) move, remove.

Wegzug ['vɛktsu:k], *m.* (—s, *no pl.*) removal; moving away.

Weh [ve:], *n.* (—s, *no pl.*) pain; grief, pang; misfortune.

weh [ve:], *adj.* painful, sore; *mir ist — ums Herz,* I am sick at heart; my heart aches. — *adv.* — *tun,* ache; pain, hurt, offend, distress, grieve. — *int.* — *mir!* woe is me!

Wehen ['ve:ən], *n. pl.* birth-pangs, labour-pains.

wehen ['ve:ən], *v.n.* (*wind*) blow.

Wehgeschrei ['ve:gəʃraɪ], *n.* (—s, *no pl.*) wailings.

Wehklage ['ve:kla:gə], *f.* (—, *pl.* —n) lamentation.

wehklagen ['ve:kla:gən], *v.n. insep.* lament, wail.

wehleidig ['ve:laɪdɪç], *adj.* tearful; easily hurt; self-pitying.

wehmütig ['ve:my:tɪç], *adj.* sad, melancholy, wistful.

Wehr (1) [ve:r], *n.* (—s, *pl.* —e) weir.

Wehr (2) [ve:r], *f.* (—, *pl.* —en) defence, bulwark.

wehren ['ve:rən], *v.r. sich* —, defend o.s., offer resistance.

wehrhaft ['ve:rhaft], *adj.* capable of bearing arms, able-bodied.

wehrlos ['ve:rlo:s], *adj.* defenceless, unarmed; (*fig.*) weak, unprotected.

Wehrpflicht ['ve:rpflɪçt], *f.* (—, *no pl.*) compulsory military service, conscription.

Wehrstand ['ve:rʃtant], *m.* (—s, *no pl.*) the military.

Weib [vaɪp], *n.* (—(e)s, *pl.* —er) woman; (*Poet.*) wife.

Weibchen ['vaɪpçən], *n.* (—s, *pl.* —) (*animal*) female.

Weiberfeind ['vaɪbərfaɪnt], *m.* (—s, *pl.* —e) woman-hater, misogynist.

Weiberherrschaft ['vaɪbərhɛrʃaft], *f.* (—, *no pl.*) petticoat rule.

weibisch ['vaɪbɪʃ], *adj.* womanish, effeminate.

weiblich ['vaɪplɪç], *adj.* female, feminine; womanly.

Weiblichkeit ['vaɪplɪçkaɪt], *f.* (—, *no pl.*) womanliness, femininity.

Weibsbild ['vaɪpsbɪlt], *n.* (—s, *pl.* —er) (*sl.*) female; wench.

weich [vaɪç], *adj.* weak; soft; tender, gentle; effeminate; sensitive; — *machen,* soften; — *werden,* relent.

Weichbild ['vaɪçbɪlt], *n.* (—s, *no pl.*) precincts; city boundaries.

Weiche ['vaɪçə], *f.* (—, *pl.* —n) (*Railw.*) switch, points.

weichen (1) ['vaɪçən], *v.a.* steep, soak, soften.

weichen (2) ['vaɪçən], *v.n. irr.* (*aux.* sein) yield, make way, give ground.

Weichensteller ['vaɪçənʃtɛlər], *m.* (—s, *pl.* —) (*Railw.*) pointsman, signalman.

Weichheit ['vaɪçhaɪt], *f.* (—, *no pl.*) softness; (*fig.*) weakness, tenderness.

weichherzig ['vaɪçhɛrtsɪç], *adj.* soft-hearted, tender-hearted.

weichlich ['vaɪçlɪç], *adj.* soft; (*fig.*) weak, effeminate.

Weichling ['vaɪçlɪŋ], *m.* (—s, *pl.* —e) weakling.

Weichsel ['vaɪksəl], *f.* Vistula.

Weichselkirsche ['vaɪksəlkɪrʃə], *f.* (—, *pl.* —n) sour cherry; morello.

Weide ['vaɪdə], *f.* (—, *pl.* —n) pasture, pasturage; (*Bot.*) willow.

Weideland ['vaɪdəlant], *n.* (—s, *pl.* ‐er) pasture-ground.

weiden ['vaɪdən], *v.a., v.n.* pasture, feed.

Weidenbaum ['vaɪdənbaum], *m.* (—s, *pl.* ‐e) willow-tree.

Weiderich ['vaɪdərɪç], *m.* (—s, *pl.* —e) willow-herb, loose-strife, rose bay.

Weidgenosse ['vaɪtgənəsə], *m.* (—n, *pl.* —en) fellow huntsman.

weidlich ['vaɪtlɪç], *adv.* (*rare*) greatly, thoroughly.

Weidmann ['vaɪtman], *m.* (—s, *pl.* ‐er) sportsman, huntsman.

Weidmannsheil! ['vaɪtmanshaɪl], *excl.* tally-ho!

weigern ['vaɪgərn], *v.r. sich* —, refuse, decline.

Weigerung ['vaɪgəruŋ], *f.* (—, *pl.* —en) refusal, denial.

Weih [vaɪ], *m.* (—en, *pl.* —en) (*Orn.*) kite.

Weihbischof ['vaɪbɪʃɔf], *m.* (—s, *pl.* ‐e) suffragan bishop.

Weihe ['vaɪə], *f.* (—, *pl.* —en) consecration; (*priest*) ordination; initiation; (*fig.*) solemnity.

weihen ['vaɪən], *v.a.* bless, consecrate; ordain. — *v.r. sich* —, devote o.s. (to).

Weiher ['vaɪər], *m.* (—s, *pl.* —) pond, fishpond.

weihevoll ['vaɪəfɔl], *adj.* solemn.

Weihnachten ['vaɪnaxtən], *n. or f.* Christmas.

Weihnachtsabend ['vaɪnaxtsa:bənt], *m.* (—s, *pl.* —e) Christmas Eve.

Weihnachtsfeiertag ['vaɪnaxtsfaɪərta:k], *m.* (—s, *pl.* —e) Christmas Day; *zweiter* —, Boxing Day.

Weihnachtsgeschenk ['vaɪnaxtsgəʃɛŋk], *n.* (—s, *pl.* —e) Christmas box, Christmas present.

Weihnachtslied ['vaɪnaxtsli:t], *n.* (—(e)s, *pl.* —er) Christmas carol.

Weihnachtsmann ['vaɪnaxtsman], *m.* (—(e)s, *pl.* ‐er) Santa Claus, Father Christmas.

Weihrauch ['vaɪraux], *m.* (—s, *no pl.*) incense.

Weihwasser ['vaɪvasər], *n.* (—s, *no pl.*) holy water.

weil [vaɪl], *conj.* because, as, since.

weiland ['vaɪlant], *adv.* (*obs.*) formerly, once.

Weile ['vaɪlə], *f.* (—, *no pl.*) while, short time; leisure.

weilen ['vaɪlən], *v.n.* tarry, stay, abide.

Wein [vaɪn], *m.* (—(e)s, *pl.* —e) wine; (*plant*) vine; *einem reinen — einschenken,* tell s.o. the truth.

Weinbau

Weinbau [ˈvaɪnbaʊ], *m.* (—s, *no pl.*) vine growing, viticulture.

Weinbeere [ˈvaɪnbeːrə], *f.* (—, *pl.* —n) grape.

Weinberg [ˈvaɪnbɛrk], *m.* (—s, *pl.* —e) vineyard.

Weinbrand [ˈvaɪnbrant], *m.* (—s, *no pl.*) brandy.

weinen [ˈvaɪnən], *v.n.* weep, cry.

Weinernte [ˈvaɪnɛrntə], *f.* (—, *pl.* —n) vintage.

Weinessig [ˈvaɪnɛsɪç], *m.* (—s, *no pl.*) (wine) vinegar.

Weinfaß [ˈvaɪnfas], *n.* (—sses, *pl.* ∵sser) wine-cask.

Weingeist [ˈvaɪngaɪst], *m.* (—es, *no pl.*) spirits of wine, alcohol.

Weinhändler [ˈvaɪnhɛndlər], *m.* (—s, *pl.* —) wine merchant.

Weinkarte [ˈvaɪnkartə], *f.* (—, *pl.* —n) wine-list.

Weinkeller [ˈvaɪnkɛlər], *m.* (—s, *pl.* —) wine-cellar; wine-tavern.

Weinkellerei [ˈvaɪnkɛləraɪ], *f.* (—, *pl.* —en) wine-store.

Weinkelter [ˈvaɪnkɛltər], *f.* (—, *pl.* —n) wine-press.

Weinkneipe [ˈvaɪnknaɪpə], *f.* (—, *pl.* —n) wine-tavern.

Weinkoster [ˈvaɪnkɔstər], *m.* (—s, *pl.* —) wine-taster.

Weinlaub [ˈvaɪnlaup], *n.* (—s, *no pl.*) vine-leaves.

Weinlese [ˈvaɪnleːzə], *f.* (—, *pl.* —n) vintage, grape harvest.

Weinranke [ˈvaɪnraŋkə], *f.* (—, *pl.* —n) vine-branch, tendril.

Weinschenke [ˈvaɪnʃɛŋkə], *f.* (—, *pl.* —n) wine-house, tavern.

weinselig [ˈvaɪnzeːlɪç], *adj.* tipsy.

Weinstein [ˈvaɪnʃtaɪn], *m.* (—s, *no pl.*) tartar.

Weinsteinsäure [ˈvaɪnʃtaɪnzɔyrə], *f.* (—, *no pl.*) tartaric acid.

Weinstock [ˈvaɪnʃtɔk], *m.* (—s, *pl.* ∵e) vine.

Weintraube [ˈvaɪntraubə], *f.* (—, *pl.* —n) grape, bunch of grapes.

weinumrankt [ˈvaɪnumraŋkt], *adj.* vine-clad.

weise [ˈvaɪzə], *adj.* wise, prudent.

Weise (1) [ˈvaɪzə], *m.* (—n, *pl.* —n) wise man, sage.

Weise (2) [ˈvaɪzə], *f.* (—, *pl.* —n) manner, fashion; method, way; tune, melody.

weisen [ˈvaɪzən], *v.a. irr.* point to, point out, show.

Weiser [ˈvaɪzər], *m.* (—s, *pl.* —) signpost; indicator; (*clock*) hand.

Weisheit [ˈvaɪshaɪt], *f.* (—, *pl.* —en) wisdom, prudence.

Weisheitszahn [ˈvaɪshaɪtstsaːn], *m.* (—s, *pl.* ∵e) wisdom tooth.

weislich [ˈvaɪslɪç], *adv.* wisely, prudently, advisedly.

weismachen [ˈvaɪsmaxən], *v.a. einem etwas —,* (*coll.*) spin a yarn to s.o.; *laß dir nichts —,* don't be taken in.

weissagen [ˈvaɪszaːgən], *v.a. insep.* prophesy, foretell.

Weissager [ˈvaɪszaːgər], *m.* (—s, *pl.* —) prophet, soothsayer.

Weissagung [ˈvaɪszaːguŋ], *f.* (—, *pl.* —en) prophecy.

weiß [vaɪs], *adj.* white, clean, blank.

Weißbuche [ˈvaɪsbuːxə], *f.* (—, *pl.* —n) (*Bot.*) hornbeam.

Weiße [ˈvaɪsə], *f.* (—, *no pl.*) whiteness; (*fig.*) (*dial.*) pale ale.

weißglühend [ˈvaɪsglyːənt], *adj.* at white heat, incandescent, white hot.

Weißnäherin [ˈvaɪsnɛːərɪn], *f.* (—, *pl.* —nen) seamstress.

Weißwaren [ˈvaɪsvaːrən], *f. pl.* linen.

Weisung [ˈvaɪzuŋ], *f.* (—, *pl.* —en) order, direction, instruction; directive.

weit [vaɪt], *adj.* distant, far, far off; wide, broad, vast, extensive; (*clothing*) loose, too big.

weitab [vaɪtˈap], *adv.* far away.

weitaus [vaɪtˈaus], *adv.* by far.

weitblickend [ˈvaɪtblɪkənt], *adj.* far-sighted.

Weite [ˈvaɪtə], *f.* (—, *pl.* —n) width, breadth; distance.

weiten [ˈvaɪtən], *v.a.* widen, expand.

weiter [ˈvaɪtər], *adj.* further, farther, wider.

weiterbefördern [ˈvaɪtərbəfœrdərn], *v.a.* send, forward, send on.

weiterbilden [ˈvaɪtərbɪldən], *v.a.* improve, develop(e), extend.

Weitere [ˈvaɪtərə], *n.* (—n, *no pl.*) rest, remainder.

weiterführen [ˈvaɪtərfyːrən], *v.a.* continue, carry on.

weitergeben [ˈvaɪtərgeːbən], *v.a. irr.* pass on.

weitergehen [ˈvaɪtərgeːən], *v.n. irr.* (*aux.* sein) walk on.

weiterhin [ˈvaɪtərhɪn], *adv.* furthermore; in time to come; in future.

weiterkommen [ˈvaɪtərkɔmən], *v.n. irr.* (*aux.* sein) get on, advance.

Weiterung [ˈvaɪtəruŋ], *f.* (—, *pl.* —en) widening, enlargement.

weitgehend [ˈvaɪtgeːənt], *adj.* far-reaching, sweeping.

weitläufig [ˈvaɪtlɔyfɪç], *adj.* ample, large; detailed, elaborate; distant, widespread; diffuse, long-winded.

weitschweifig [ˈvaɪtʃvaɪfɪç], *adj.* prolix, diffuse, rambling.

weitsichtig [ˈvaɪtzɪçtɪç], *adj.* long-sighted.

weittragend [ˈvaɪttraːgənt], *adj.* portentous, far-reaching.

weitverbreitet [ˈvaɪtferbraɪtət], *adj.* widespread.

Weizen [ˈvaɪtsən], *m.* (—s, *no pl.*) wheat.

Weizengrieß [ˈvaɪtsəngriːs], *m.* (—es, *no pl.*) semolina; grits.

welch [vɛlç], *pron.* what (a).

welcher, -e, -es [ˈvɛlçər], *interr. pron.* which? what? — *rel. pron.* who which, that; (*indef.*) (*coll.*) some.

welcherlei ['vɛlçərlaɪ], *indecl. adj.* of what kind.

Welfe ['vɛlfə], *m.*(—**n**, *pl.* —**n**) Guelph.

welk [vɛlk], *adj.* faded, withered; — *werden*, fade, wither.

welken ['vɛlkən], *v.n.* (*aux.* sein) wither, fade, decay.

Wellblech ['vɛlblɛç], *n.* (—**s**, *no pl.*) corrugated iron.

Welle ['vɛlə], *f.* (—, *pl.* —**n**) wave, billow.

wellen ['vɛlən], *v.a.* wave.

Wellenbewegung ['vɛlənbəve:guŋ], *f.* (—, *pl.* —**en**) undulation.

Wellenlinie ['vɛlənli:njə], *f.* (—, *pl.* —**n**) wavy line.

wellig ['vɛlɪç], *adj.* wavy, undulating.

welsch [vɛlʃ], *adj.* foreign; Italian; French.

Welschkohl ['vɛlʃko:l], *m.* (—**s**, *no pl.*) (*Bot.*) savoy cabbage.

Welschkorn ['vɛlʃkɔrn], *n.* (—**s**, *no pl.*) (*Bot.*) Indian corn.

Welt [vɛlt], *f.* (—, *pl.* —**en**) world, earth; universe; society.

Weltall ['vɛltal], *n.* (—**s**, *no pl.*) universe, cosmos; (outer) space.

Weltanschauung ['vɛltanʃauuŋ], *f.* (—, *pl.* —**en**) view of life, philosophy of life, ideology.

Weltbeschreibung ['vɛltbəʃraɪbuŋ], *f.* (—, *no pl.*) cosmography.

Weltbürger ['vɛltbyrgər], *m.* (—**s**, *pl.* —) cosmopolitan.

welterschütternd ['vɛltərʃytərnt], *adj.* world-shaking.

weltfremd ['vɛltfrɛmt], *adj.* unwordly, unsophisticated.

Weltgeschichte ['vɛltgəʃɪçtə], *f.* (—, *no pl.*) world history.

Weltherrschaft ['vɛlthɛrʃaft], *f.* (—, *no pl.*) world dominion.

Weltkenntnis ['vɛltkɛntnɪs], *f.* (—, *no pl.*) worldly wisdom.

weltklug ['vɛltklu:k], *adj.* astute, worldly-wise.

Weltkrieg ['vɛltkri:k], *m.* (—**es**, *pl.* —**e**) world war.

weltlich ['vɛltlɪç], *adj.* worldly; (*Eccl.*) temporal, secular.

Weltmacht ['vɛltmaxt], *f.* (—, *pl.* —**e**) world power, great power.

Weltmeer ['vɛltme:r], *n.* (—**s**, *pl.* —**e**) ocean.

Weltmeisterschaft ['vɛltmaɪstərʃaft], *f.* (—, *pl.* —**en**) world championship.

Weltordnung ['vɛltɔrdnuŋ], *f.* (—, *pl.* —**en**) cosmic order.

Weltraum ['vɛltraum], *m.* (—**s**, *no pl.*) space.

Weltraumflug ['vɛltraumflu:k], *m.* (—**e**)**s**, *pl.* —**e**) space flight.

Weltraumforschung ['vɛltraumfɔrʃuŋ], *f.* (—, *no pl.*) space exploration.

Weltraumgeschoss ['vɛltraumgəʃɔs], *n.* (—**es**, *pl.* —**e**) space rocket.

Weltruf ['vɛltru:f], *m.* (—**s**, *no pl.*) world-wide renown.

Weltschmerz ['vɛltʃmɛrts], *m.* (—**es**, *no pl.*) world-weariness, Wertherism; melancholy.

Weltsprache ['vɛltʃpra:xə], *f.* (—, *pl.* —**en**) universal language; world language.

Weltstadt ['vɛltʃtat], *f.* (—, *pl.* —**e**) metropolis.

Weltumseglung ['vɛltumze:gluŋ], *f.* (—, *pl.* —**en**) circumnavigation (of the globe).

Weltuntergang ['vɛltuntərgaŋ], *m.* —**s**, *no pl.*) end of the world.

Weltwirtschaft ['vɛltvɪrtʃaft], *f.* (—, *no pl.*) world trade.

wem [ve:m], *pers. pron.* (*Dat. of* **wer**) to whom — *interr. pron.* to whom?

wen [ve:n], *pers. pron.* (*Acc. of* **wer**) whom — *interr. pron.* whom?

Wende ['vɛndə], *f.* (—, *pl.* —**n**) turn, turning(point).

Wendekreis ['vɛndəkraɪs], *m.* (—**es**, *pl.* —**e**) tropic.

Wendeltreppe ['vɛndəltrɛpə], *f.* (—, *pl.* —**n**) spiral staircase.

wenden ['vɛndən], *v.a. reg. & irr.* turn.

Wendepunkt ['vɛndəpuŋkt], *m.* (—**es**, *pl.* —**e**) turning point; crisis.

Wendung ['vɛnduŋ], *f.* (—, *pl.* —**en**) turn, turning; crisis; (*speech*) phrase.

wenig ['ve:nɪç], *adj.* little, few; *ein* —, a little.

weniger ['ve:nɪgər], *adj.* less, fewer.

wenigstens ['ve:nɪçstəns], *adv.* at least.

wenn [vɛn], *conj.* if; when; whenever, in case; — *nicht*, unless.

wenngleich [vɛn'glaɪç], *conj.* though, although.

wer [ve:r], *rel. pron.* who, he who; — *auch*, whoever. — *interr. pron.* who? which? — *da?* who goes there?

Werbekraft ['vɛrbəkraft], *f.* (—, *no pl.*) (*Advertising*) attraction; appeal; publicity value.

werben ['vɛrbən], *v.n. irr.* advertise, canvass; court, woo. — *v.a.* (*soldiers*) recruit.

Werbung ['vɛrbuŋ], *f.* (—, *pl.* —**en**) advertising, publicity, propaganda; recruiting; courtship.

Werdegang ['ve:rdəgaŋ], *m.* (—**s**, *no pl.*) evolution, development.

werden ['ve:rdən], *v.n. irr.* (*aux.* sein) become, get; grow; turn; *Arzt* —, become a doctor; *alt* —, grow old; *bleich* —, turn pale.

werdend ['ve:rdənt], *adj.* becoming; nascent, incipient, budding.

werfen ['vɛrfən], *v.a. irr.* throw, cast.

Werft (1) [vɛrft], *m.* (—(**e**)**s**, *pl.* —**e**) warp.

Werft (2) [vɛrft], *f.* (—, *pl.* —**en**) dockyard, shipyard, wharf.

Werk [vɛrk], *n.* (—(**e**)**s**, *pl.* —**e**) work, action, deed; undertaking; (*Ind.*) works, plant, mill, factory.

Werkführer ['vɛrkfy:rər], *m.* (—**s**, *pl.* —) foreman.

Werkleute ['vɛrkløytə], *pl.* workmen.

Werkmeister ['vɛrkmaɪstər], *m.* (—**s**, *pl.* —) overseer.

werktätig ['vɛrktɛ:tɪç], *adj.* active, practical; hard-working.

279

Werkzeug ['vɛrktsɔyk], *n.* (—s, *pl.* —e) implement, tool, jig, instrument.

Wermut ['ve:rmu:t], *m.* (—s, *no pl.*) absinthe, vermouth.

Wert [ve:rt], *m.* (—(e)s, *pl.* —e) value, worth, price; use; merit; importance.

wert [ve:rt], *adj.* valuable; worth; dear, esteemed.

Wertangabe ['ve:rtanga:bə], *f.* (—, *pl.* —n) valuation; declared value.

Wertbestimmung ['ve:rtbəʃtimuŋ], *f.* (—, *no pl.*) appraisal, assessment, valuation.

Wertbrief ['ve:rtbri:f], *m.* (—s, *pl.* —e) registered letter.

werten ['ve:rtən], *v.a.* value.

Wertgegenstand ['ve:rtgə:gənʃtant], *m.* (—s, *pl.* ⁻e) article of value.

Wertmesser ['ve:rtmɛsər], *m.* (—s, *pl.* —) standard.

Wertpapiere ['ve:rtpapi:rə], *n. pl.* securities.

Wertsachen ['ve:rtzaxən], *f. pl.* valu-ables.

wertschätzen ['ve:rtʃɛtsən], *v.a.* es-teem (highly).

wertvoll ['ve:rtfɔl], *adj.* of great value, valuable.

Wertzeichen ['ve:rttsaiçən], *n.* (—s, *pl.* —) stamp; coupon.

wes [vɛs], *pers. pron. (obs.)* whose.

Wesen ['ve:zən], *n.* (—s, *pl.* —) being, creature; reality; essence, nature, substance; character, demeanour; (*in compounds*) organisation, affairs.

wesenlos ['ve:zənlo:s], *adj.* disem-bodied, unsubstantial, shadowy: trivial.

wesensgleich ['ve:zənsglaiç], *adj.* iden-tical, substantially the same.

wesentlich ['ve:zəntliç], *adj.* essential, material.

weshalb [vɛs'halp], *conj., adv.* where-fore, why; therefore.

Wespe ['vɛspə], *f.* (—, *pl.* —n) (*Ent.*) wasp.

Wespennest ['vɛspənnɛst], *n.* (—s, *pl.* —er,) wasp's nest; *in ein — stechen,* stir up a hornet's nest.

wessen ['vɛsən], *pers. pron.* (*Genit. of* **wer**) whose. — *interr. pron.* whose?

Weste ['vɛstə], *f.* (—, *pl.* —n) waist-coat.

Westen ['vɛstən], *m.* (—s, *no pl.*) west; *nach —,* westward.

Westfalen [vɛst'fa:lən], *n.* Westphalia.

Westindien [vɛst'indjən], *n.* the West Indies.

weswegen [vɛs've:gən] *see* **weshalb**.

Wettbewerb ['vɛtbəvɛrp], *m.* (—s, *pl.* —e) competition, rivalry; *unlau-terer —,* unfair competition.

Wettbewerber ['vɛtbəvɛrbər], *m.* (—s, *pl.* —) rival, competitor.

Wette ['vɛtə], *f.* (—, *pl.* —n) bet, wager; *um die — laufen,* race one another.

Wetteifer ['vɛtaifər], *m.* (—s, *no pl.*) rivalry.

wetteifern ['vɛtaifərn], *v.n. insep.* vie (with), compete.

wetten ['vɛtən], *v.a., v.n.* bet, lay a wager, wager.

Wetter ['vɛtər], *n.* (—s, *pl.* —) weather; bad weather, storm; *schlagende —,* (*Min.*) fire-damp.

Wetterbeobachtung ['vɛtərbəobax-tuŋ], *f.* (—, *pl.* —en) meteorological observation.

Wetterbericht ['vɛtərbəriçt], *m.* (—s, *pl.* —e) weather report *or* forecast.

Wetterfahne ['vɛtərfa:nə], *f.* (—, *pl.* —en) weather-cock, vane; (*fig.*) turncoat.

wetterfest ['vɛtərfɛst], *adj.* weather-proof.

Wetterglas ['vɛtərgla:s], *n.* (—es, *pl.* ⁻er) barometer.

Wetterhahn ['vɛtərha:n], *m.* (—s, *pl.* ⁻e) weather-cock.

Wetterkunde ['vɛtərkundə], *f.* (—, *no pl.*) meteorology.

Wetterleuchten ['vɛtərlɔyçtən], *n.* (—s, *no pl.*) summer lightning; sheet lightning.

wettern ['vɛtərn], *v.n.* be stormy; (*fig.*) curse, swear, thunder (against), storm.

Wettervorhersage ['vɛtərfo:rhe:rza:-gə], *f.* (—, *pl.* —n) weather fore-cast.

wetterwendisch ['vɛtərvɛndiʃ], *adj.* changeable; irritable, peevish.

Wettkampf ['vɛtkampf], *m.* (—(e)s, *pl.* ⁻e) contest, tournament.

Wettlauf ['vɛtlauf], *m.* (—s, *pl.* ⁻e) race.

wettmachen ['vɛtmaxən], *v.a.* make up for.

Wettrennen ['vɛtrɛnən], *n.* (—s, *pl.* —) racing, race.

Wettstreit ['vɛtʃtrait], *m.* (—s, *pl.* —e) contest, contention.

wetzen ['vɛtsən], *v.a.* whet, hone, sharpen.

Wichse ['viksə], *f.* (—, *pl.* —n) blacking, shoe-polish; (*fig.*) thrashing.

wichsen ['viksən], *v.a.* black, shine; (*fig.*) thrash.

Wicht [viçt], *m.* (—(e)s, *pl.* —e) creature; (*coll.*) chap.

Wichtelmännchen ['viçtəlmɛnçən], *n.* (—s, *pl.* —) pixie, goblin.

wichtig ['viçtiç], *adj.* important; weighty; significant; *sich — machen,* put on airs.

Wichtigkeit ['viçtiçkait], *f.* (—, *no pl.*) importance; s g nificance.

Wicke ['vikə], *f.* (—, *pl.* —n) (*Bot.*) vetch.

Wickel ['vikəl], *m.* (—s, *pl.* —) roller; (*hair*) curler; (*Med.*) compress.

Wickelkind ['vikəlkint], *n.* (—s, *pl.* —er) babe in arms.

wickeln ['vikəln], *v.a.* roll, coil; wind; wrap (up); (*babies*) swaddle; (*hair*) curl.

Widder ['vidər], *m.* (—s, *pl.* —) ram; (*Astrol.*) Aries.

wider ['vi:dər], *prep.* (*Acc.*) against, in opposition to, contrary to.

widerfahren [vi:dər'fa:rən], *v.n. irr. insep. (aux. sein)* happen to s.o., befall s.o.; *einem Gerechtigkeit — lassen,* give s.o. his due.

Widerhaken ['vi:dərha:kən], *m.* (—s, *pl.* —) barb.

Widerhall ['vi:dərhal], *m.* (—s, *pl.* —e) echo, resonance; (*fig.*) response.

widerlegen [vi:dər'le:gən], *v.a. insep.* refute, disprove, prove (s.o.) wrong.

Widerlegung [vi:dər'le:guŋ], *f.* (—, *pl.* —en) refutation, rebuttal.

widerlich ['vi:dərlɪç], *adj.* disgusting, nauseating, repulsive.

widernatürlich ['vi:dərnaty:rlɪç], *adj.* unnatural; perverse.

widerraten [vi:dər'ra:tən], *v.a. irr. insep.* advise against; dissuade from.

widerrechtlich ['vi:dərreçtlɪç], *adj.* illegal, unlawful.

Widerrede ['vi:dərre:də], *f.* (—, *pl.* —n) contradiction.

Widerruf ['vi:dərru:f], *m.* (—s, *pl.* —e) revocation, recantation.

widerrufen [vi:dər'ru:fən], *v.a. irr. insep.* recant, retract, revoke.

Widersacher ['vi:dərzaxər], *m.* (—s, *pl.* —) adversary, antagonist.

Widerschein ['vi:dərʃaɪn], *m.* (—s, *no pl.*) reflection.

widersetzen [vi:dər'zɛtsən], *v.r. insep. sich —,* resist, (*Dat.*) oppose.

widersetzlich [vi:dər'zɛtslɪç], *adj.* refractory, insubordinate.

Widersinn ['vi:dərzɪn], *m.* (—s, *no pl.*) nonsense, absurdity; paradox.

widersinnig ['vi:dərzɪnɪç], *adj.* nonsensical, absurd; paradoxical.

widerspenstig ['vi:dərʃpɛnstɪç], *adj.* refractory, rebellious, obstinate, stubborn.

widerspiegeln [vi:dər'ʃpi:gəln], *v.a.* reflect, mirror.

widersprechen [vi:dər'ʃprɛçən], *v.n. irr. insep.* (*Dat.*) contradict, gainsay.

Widerspruch ['vi:dərʃprux], *m.* (—(e)s, *pl.* ⁓e) contradictory.

widerspruchsvoll ['vi:dərʃpruxsfɔl], *adj.* contradictory.

Widerstand ['vi:dərʃtant], *m.* (—s, *pl.* ⁓e) resistance, opposition.

widerstandsfähig ['vi:dərʃtantsfɛ:ɪç], *adj.* resistant, hardy.

widerstehen [vi:dər'ʃte:ən], *v.n. irr. insep.* (*Dat.*) resist, withstand; be distasteful (to).

Widerstreben [vi:dər'ʃtre:bən], *n.* (—s, *no pl.*) reluctance.

widerstreben [vi:dər'ʃtre:bən], *v.n. insep.* (*Dat.*) strive against, oppose; be distasteful to a p.

Widerstreit ['vi:dərʃtraɪt], *m.* (—s, *no pl.*) contradiction, opposition; conflict.

widerwärtig ['vi:dərvɛrtɪç], *adj.* unpleasant, disagreeable, repugnant, repulsive; hateful, odious.

Widerwille ['vi:dərvɪlə], *m.* (—ns, *no pl.*) aversion (to).

widmen ['vɪdmən], *v.a.* dedicate.

Widmung ['vɪdmuŋ], *f.* (—, *pl.* —en) dedication.

widrig ['vi:drɪç], *adj.* contrary, adverse, inimical, unfavourable.

widrigenfalls ['vi:drɪgənfals], *adv.* failing this, otherwise, else.

wie [vi:], *adv. how. — conj.* as, just as, like; — *geht's?* how are you?

wieder ['vi:dər], *adv.* again, anew, afresh; back, in return.

Wiederabdruck ['vi:dərapdruk], *m.* (—s, *pl.* —e) reprint.

Wiederaufbau [vi:dər'aufbau], *m.* (—s, *no pl.*) rebuilding.

Wiederaufnahme [vi:dər'aufna:mə], *f.* (—, *no pl.*) resumption.

Wiederbelebungsversuch ['vi:dərbəle:buŋsfɛrzu:x], *m.* (—es, *pl.* —e) attempt at resuscitation.

Wiederbezahlung ['vi:dərbətsa:luŋ], *f.* (—, *pl.* —en) reimbursement.

wiederbringen ['vi:dərbrɪŋən], *v.a. irr.* bring back, restore.

Wiedereinrichtung ['vi:dəraɪnrɪçtuŋ], *f.* (—, *no pl.*) reorganisation, re-establishment.

Wiedereinsetzung ['vi:dəraɪnzɛtsuŋ], *f.* (—, *pl.* —en) restoration, reinstatement, rehabilitation.

wiedererkennen ['vi:dərɛrkɛnən], *v.a. irr.* recognise.

Wiedererstattung ['vi:dərɛrʃtatuŋ], *f.* (—, *no pl.*) restitution.

Wiedergabe ['vi:dərga:bə], *f.* (—, *no pl.*) restitution, return; (*fig.*) rendering, reproduction.

wiedergeben ['vi:dərge:bən], *v.a. irr.* return, give back; (*fig.*) render.

Wiedergeburt ['vi:dərgəbu:rt], *f.* (—, *no pl.*) rebirth, regeneration, renascence.

Wiedergutmachung [vi:dər'gu:tmaxuŋ], *f.* (—, *no pl.*) reparation.

Wiederherstellung [vi:dər'he:rʃteluŋ], *f.* (—, *no pl.*) restoration; recovery.

Wiederherstellungsmittel [vi:dər'he:rʃteluŋsmɪtəl], *n.* (—s, *pl.* —) restorative, tonic.

wiederholen [vi:dər'ho:lən], *v.a. insep.* repeat, reiterate.

Wiederholung [vi:dər'ho:luŋ], *f.* (—, *pl.* —en) repetition.

Wiederkäuer ['vi:dərkɔyər], *m.* (—s, *pl.* —) ruminant.

Wiederkehr ['vi:dərke:r], *f.* (—, *no pl.*) return; recurrence.

wiederkehren ['vi:dərke:rən], *v.n.* (*aux.* sein) return.

wiederklingen ['vi:dərklɪŋən], *v.n. irr.* reverberate.

wiederkommen ['vi:dərkɔmən], *v.n. irr.* (*aux.* sein) return, come back.

Wiedersehen ['vi:dərze:ən], *n.* (—s, *no pl.*) reunion, meeting after separation; *auf —,* good-bye; so long! see you again!

wiedersehen ['vi:dərze:ən], *v.a. irr.* see again, meet again.

281

wiederum [ˈviːdərum], *adv.* again, anew, afresh.

Wiedervereinigung [ˈviːdərfɛraɪnɪguŋ], *f.* (—, *pl.* —en) reunion, reunification.

Wiedervergeltung [ˈviːdərfɛrgɛltuŋ], *f.* (—, *no pl.*) requital, retaliation, reprisal.

Wiederverkauf [ˈviːdərfɛrkauf], *m.* (—s, *no pl.*) resale.

Wiederverkäufer [ˈviːdərfɛrkɔyfər], *m.* (—s, *pl.* —) retailer.

Wiederversöhnung [ˈviːdərfɛrzøːnuŋ], *f.* (—, *no pl.*) reconciliation.

Wiederwahl [ˈviːdərvaːl], *f.* (—, *no pl.*) re-election.

Wiege [ˈviːgə], *f.* (—, *pl.* —n) cradle.

wiegen [ˈviːgən], *v.a.* rock (the cradle). — *v.r. sich* — *in*, delude o.s. with. — *v.a., v.n. irr.* weigh.

Wiegenfest [ˈviːgənfɛst], *n.* (—es, *pl.* —e) (*Poet., Lit.*) birthday.

Wiegenlied [ˈviːgənliːt], *n.* (—s, *pl.* —er) cradle-song, lullaby.

wiehern [ˈviːərn], *v.n.* neigh.

Wien [viːn], *n.* Vienna.

Wiese [ˈviːzə], *f.* (—, *pl.* —n) meadow.

Wiesel [ˈviːzəl], *n.* (—s, *pl.* —) (*Zool.*) weasel.

wieso [viˈzoː] *adv.* why? how do you mean? in what way?

wieviel [viˈfiːl], *adv.* how much, how many; *den* —*ten haben wir heute?* what is the date today?

wiewohl [viˈvoːl], *conj.* although, though.

Wild [vɪlt], *n.* (—(e)s, *no pl.*) game; venison.

wild [vɪlt], *adj.* wild, savage, fierce; furious.

Wildbach [ˈvɪltbax], *m.* (—s, *pl.* ːe) (mountain) torrent.

Wilddieb [ˈvɪltdiːp], *m.* (—(e)s, *pl.* —e) poacher.

Wilde [ˈvɪldə], *m.* (—n, *pl.* —n) savage.

wildern [ˈvɪldərn], *v.n.* poach.

Wildfang [ˈvɪltfaŋ], *m.* (—s, *pl.* ːe) scamp, tomboy.

wildfremd [ˈvɪltfrɛmt], *adj.* completely strange.

Wildhüter [ˈvɪlthyːtər], *m.* (—s, *pl.* —) gamekeeper.

Wildleder [ˈvɪltleːdər], *n.* (—s, *no pl.*) suède, doeskin, buckskin.

Wildnis [ˈvɪltnɪs], *f.* (—, *pl.* —se) wilderness, desert.

Wildpark [ˈvɪltpark], *m.* (—s, *pl.* —s) game-reserve.

Wildpret [ˈvɪltprɛt], *n.* (—s, *no pl.*) game; venison.

Wildschwein [ˈvɪltʃvain], *n.* (—s, *pl.* —e) wild boar.

Wille [ˈvɪlə], *m.* (—ns, *no pl.*) will, wish, design, purpose.

willenlos [ˈvɪlənloːs], *adj.* weak-minded.

willens [ˈvɪləns], *adv.* — *sein,* be willing, have a mind to.

Willenserklärung [ˈvɪlənsɛrklɛːruŋ], *f.* (—, *pl.* —en) (*Law*) declaratory act.

Willensfreiheit [ˈvɪlənsfraihait], *f.* (—, *no pl.*) free will.

Willenskraft [ˈvɪlənskraft], *f.* (—, *no pl.*) strength of will, will-power.

willentlich [ˈvɪləntlɪç], *adv.* purposely, on purpose, intentionally, wilfully.

willfahren [vɪlˈfaːrən], *v.n. insep.* (*Dat.*) comply with, gratify.

willfährig [ˈvɪlfɛːrɪç], *adj.* compliant, complaisant.

willig [ˈvɪlɪç], *adj.* willing, ready, docile.

willkommen [vɪlˈkɔmən], *adj.* welcome; — *heißen,* welcome.

Willkür [ˈvɪlkyːr], *f.* (—, *no pl.*) free will; discretion; caprice, arbitrariness.

willkürlich [ˈvɪlkyːrlɪç], *adj.* arbitrary.

wimmeln [ˈvɪməln], *v.n.* swarm, teem (with).

wimmern [ˈvɪmərn], *v.n.* whimper.

Wimpel [ˈvɪmpəl], *m.* (—s, *pl.* —) pennon, pennant, streamer.

Wimper [ˈvɪmpər], *f.* (—, *pl.* —n) eyelash; *ohne mit der* — *zu zucken,* without turning a hair, without batting an eyelid.

Wind [vɪnt], *m.* (—(e)s, *pl.* —e) wind, breeze; *von etwas* — *bekommen,* get wind of.

Windbeutel [ˈvɪntbɔytəl], *m.* (—s, *pl.* —) cream puff; (*fig.*) windbag.

Windbüchse [ˈvɪntbyksə], *f.* (—, *pl.* —n) air-gun.

Winde [ˈvɪndə], *f.* (—, *pl.* —n) (*Tech.*) windlass; (*Bot.*) bindweed.

Windel [ˈvɪndəl], *f.* (—, *pl.* —n) (baby's) napkin; (*Am.*) diaper.

windelweich [ˈvɪndəlvaiç], *adj.* very soft, limp; *einen* — *schlagen,* beat s.o. to a jelly.

winden [ˈvɪndən], *v.a. irr.* wind, reel; wring; (*flowers*) make a wreath of. — *v.r. sich* —, writhe.

Windeseile [ˈvɪndəsailə], *f.* (—, *no pl.*) lightning speed.

Windfahne [ˈvɪntfaːnə], *f.* (—, *pl.* —n) weather-cock, vane.

windfrei [ˈvɪntfrai], *adj.* sheltered.

Windhund [ˈvɪnthunt], *m.* (—s, *pl.* —e) greyhound; (*fig.*) windbag.

windig [ˈvɪndɪç], *adj.* windy.

Windklappe [ˈvɪntklapə], *f.* (—, *pl.* —n) air-valve.

Windlicht [ˈvɪntlɪçt], *n.* (—s, *pl.* —er) torch; storm lantern.

Windmühle [ˈvɪntmyːlə], *f.* (—, *pl.* —n) windmill.

Windpocken [ˈvɪntpɔkən], *f. pl.* (*Med.*) chicken-pox.

Windrichtung [ˈvɪntrɪçtuŋ], *f.* (—, *pl.* —en) direction of the wind.

Windrose [ˈvɪntroːzə], *f.* (—, *pl.* —n) compass card; windrose.

Windsbraut [ˈvɪntsbraut], *f.* (—, *no pl.*) gust of wind, squall; gale.

windschief [ˈvɪntʃiːf], *adj.* warped, bent.

Windschutzscheibe [ˈvɪntʃutsʃaibə], *f.* (—, *pl.* —n) (*Motor.*) windscreen.

Windseite [ˈvɪntzaitə], *f.* (—, *pl.* —n) windward side.

Windspiel ['vɪntʃpiːl], *n.* (—s, *pl.* —e) greyhound.

windstill ['vɪntʃtɪl], *adj.* calm.

Windung ['vɪnduŋ], *f.* (—, *pl.* —en) winding; convolution; twist, loop; coil; meandering.

Wink [vɪŋk], *m.* (—(e)s, *pl.* —e) sign, nod; (*fig.*) hint, suggestion.

Winkel ['vɪŋkəl], *m.* (—s, *pl.* —) corner; (*Maths.*) angle.

Winkeladvokat ['vɪŋkəlatvokaːt], *m.* (—en, *pl.* —en) quack lawyer.

Winkelmaß ['vɪŋkəlmaːs], *n.* (—es, *pl.* —e) set-square.

Winkelmesser ['vɪŋkəlmɛsər], *m.* (—s, *pl.* —) protractor.

Winkelzug ['vɪŋkəltsuːk], *m.* (—s, *pl.* ‥e) evasion, trick, shift.

winken ['vɪŋkən], *v.n.* signal, nod, beckon, wave.

winklig ['vɪŋklɪç], *adj.* angular.

winseln ['vɪnzəln], *v.n.* whimper, whine, wail.

Winter ['vɪntər], *m.* (—s, *pl.* —) winter.

Wintergarten ['vɪntərgartən], *m.* (—s, *pl.* ‥) conservatory.

Wintergewächs ['vɪntərgəvɛks], *n.* (—es, *pl.* —e) perennial plant.

Wintergrün ['vɪntərgryːn], *n.* (—s, *no pl.*) evergreen; wintergreen.

wintern ['vɪntərn], *v.n.* become wintry.

Winterschlaf ['vɪntərʃlaːf], *m.* (—s, *no pl.*) hibernation; den — halten, hibernate.

Winzer ['vɪntsər], *m.* (—s, *pl.* —) vine-grower.

winzig ['vɪntsɪç], *adj.* tiny, diminutive.

Wipfel ['vɪpfəl], *m.* (—s, *pl.* —) top (of a tree), tree-top.

Wippe ['vɪpə], *f.* (—, *pl.* —n) seesaw.

wippen ['vɪpən], *v.n.* balance, see-saw.

wir [viːr], *pers. pron.* we.

Wirbel ['vɪrbəl], *m.* (—s, *pl.* —) (*water*) whirlpool, eddy; whirlwind; (*drum*) roll; (*head*) crown; (*back*) vertebra.

wirbeln ['vɪrbəln], *v.a., v.n.* whirl.

Wirbelsäule ['vɪrbəlzɔylə], *f.* (—, *pl.* —n) spine, vertebral column.

Wirbelwind ['vɪrbəlvɪnt], *m.* (—s, *pl.* —e) whirlwind.

Wirken ['vɪrkən], *n.* (—s, *no pl.*) activity.

wirken ['vɪrkən], *v.a.* effect, work; bring to pass; (*materials*) weave; (*dough*) knead. — *v.n.* work.

Wirker ['vɪrkər], *m.* (—s, *pl.* —) weaver.

wirklich ['vɪrklɪç], *adj.* real, actual; true, genuine.

Wirklichkeit ['vɪrklɪçkaɪt], *f.* (—, *no pl.*) reality.

wirksam ['vɪrkzaːm], *adj.* effective, efficacious.

Wirksamkeit ['vɪrkzaːmkaɪt], *f.* (—, *no pl.*) efficacy, efficiency.

Wirkung ['vɪrkuŋ], *f.* (—, *pl.* —en) working, operation; reaction; efficacy; effect, result, consequence; force, in-

fluence; *eine — ausüben auf,* have an effect on; influence s.o. *or* s.th.

Wirkungskreis ['vɪrkuŋskraɪs], *m.* (—es, *pl.* —e) sphere of activity.

wirkungslos ['vɪrkuŋsloːs], *adj.* ineffectual.

wirkungsvoll ['vɪrkuŋsfɔl], *adj.* effective, efficacious; (*fig.*) impressive.

wirr [vɪr], *adj.* tangled, confused; — *durcheinander,* higgledy-piggledy; *mir ist ganz — im Kopf,* my head is going round.

Wirren ['vɪrən], *f. pl.* troubles, disorders, disturbances.

wirrköpfig ['vɪrkœpfɪç], *adj.* muddleheaded.

Wirrsal ['vɪrzaːl], *n.* (—s, *pl.* —e) confusion, disorder.

Wirrwarr ['vɪrvar], *m.* (—s, *no pl.*) jumble, hurly-burly, hubbub.

Wirt [vɪrt], *m.* (—(e)s, *pl.* —e) host; innkeeper; landlord.

Wirtin ['vɪrtɪn], *f.* (—, *pl.* —innen) hostess, landlady, innkeeper's wife.

wirtlich ['vɪrtlɪç], *adj.* hospitable.

Wirtschaft ['vɪrtʃaft], *f.* (—, *pl.* —en) housekeeping; administration; economy; household; housekeeping; inn, ale-house; (*coll.*) mess.

wirtschaften ['vɪrtʃaftən], *v.n.* keep house, housekeep; administer, run; (*coll.*) rummage.

Wirtschafterin ['vɪrtʃaftərɪn], *f.* (—, *pl.* —innen) housekeeper.

wirtschaftlich ['vɪrtʃaftlɪç], *adj.* economical, thrifty.

Wirtschaftlichkeit ['vɪrtʃaftlɪçkaɪt], *f.* (—, *no pl.*) economy; profitability.

Wirtschaftsgeld ['vɪrtʃaftsgɛlt], *n.* (—s, *pl.* —er) housekeeping-money.

Wirtshaus ['vɪrtshaus], *n.* (—es, *pl.* ‥er) inn.

Wisch [vɪʃ], *m.* (—es, *pl.* —e) scrap of paper, rag.

wischen ['vɪʃən], *v.a.* wipe.

wispern ['vɪspərn], *v.a., v.n.* whisper.

Wißbegier(de) ['vɪsbəgiːr(də)], *f.* (—, *no pl.*) craving for knowledge; curiosity.

Wissen ['vɪsən], *n.* (—s, *no pl.*) knowledge, learning, erudition.

wissen ['vɪsən], *v.a. irr.* know, be aware of (a fact); be able to.

Wissenschaft ['vɪsənʃaft], *f.* (—, *pl.* —en) learning, scholarship; science.

wissenschaftlich ['vɪsənʃaftlɪç], *adj.* learned, scholarly; scientific.

wissenswert ['vɪsənsveːrt], *adj.* worth knowing.

Wissenszweig ['vɪsənstsvaɪk], *m.* (—s, *pl.* —e) branch of knowledge.

wissentlich ['vɪsəntlɪç], *adj.* deliberate, wilful. — *adv.* knowingly.

wittern ['vɪtərn], *v.a.* scent, smell; (*fig.*) suspect.

Witterung ['vɪtəruŋ], *f.* (—, *no pl.*) weather; trail; scent.

Witterungsverhältnisse ['vɪtəruŋsfɛrhɛltnɪsə], *n. pl.* atmospheric conditions.

Witterungswechsel

Witterungswechsel [ˈvɪtərʊŋsvɛksəl], *m.* (—s, *no pl.*) change in the weather.

Witwe [ˈvɪtvə], *f.* (—, *pl.* —n) widow.

Witwer [ˈvɪtvər], *m.* (—s, *pl.* —) widower.

Witz [vɪts], *m.,* (—es, *pl.* —e) wit, brains; joke, jest, witticism; funny story.

Witzblatt [ˈvɪtsblat], *n.* (—s, *pl.* ⸚er) satirical *or* humorous journal.

Witzbold [ˈvɪtsbɔlt], *m.* (—es, *pl.* —e) wag; wit.

witzeln [ˈvɪtsəln], *v.n.* poke fun (at).

witzig [ˈvɪtsɪç], *adj.* witty; funny, comical; bright.

wo [voː], *interr. adv.* where? — *conj.* when.

wobei [voːˈbaɪ], *adv.* by which, at which, in connection with which; whereby; in doing so.

Woche [ˈvɔxə], *f.* (—, *pl.* —n) week.

Wochenbericht [ˈvɔxənbərɪçt], *m.* (—s, *pl.* —e) weekly report.

Wochenbett [ˈvɔxənbɛt], *n.* (—s, *no pl.*) confinement.

Wochenblatt [ˈvɔxənblat], *n.* (—s, *pl.* ⸚er) weekly (paper).

Wochenlohn [ˈvɔxənloːn], *m.* (—s, *pl.* ⸚e) weekly wage(s).

Wochenschau [ˈvɔxənʃau], *f.* (—, *no pl.*) newsreel.

Wochentag [ˈvɔxəntaːk], *m.* (—s, *pl.* —e) week-day.

wöchentlich [ˈvœçəntlɪç], *adj.* weekly, every week.

wodurch [voːˈdurç], *adv.* whereby, by which, through which; (*interr.*) by what?

wofern [voːˈfɛrn], *conj.* if, provided that.

wofür [voːˈfyːr], *adv.* for what, for which, wherefore.

Woge [ˈvoːgə], *f.* (—, *pl.* —n) wave, billow.

wogegen [voːˈgeːgən], *adv.* against what, against which, in return for which.

wogen [ˈvoːgən], *v.n.* heave, sway; (*fig.*) fluctuate.

woher [voːˈheːr], *adv.* whence, from what place, how.

wohin [voːˈhɪn], *adv.* whither, where.

wohingegen [voːhɪnˈgeːgən], *conj.* (*obs.*) whereas.

Wohl [voːl], *n.* (—(e)s, *no pl.*) welfare, health; *auf dein* —, your health! cheers!

wohl [voːl], *adv.* well, fit; indeed, doubtless, certainly; *ja* —, to be sure.

wohlan! [voːlˈan], *excl.* well! now then!

wohlauf! [voːlˈauf], *excl.* cheer up! — *sein*, be in good health.

wohlbedacht [ˈvoːlbədaxt], *adj.* well considered.

Wohlbefinden [ˈvoːlbəfɪndən], *n.* (—s, *no pl.*) good health.

Wohlbehagen [ˈvoːlbəhaːgən], *n.* (—s, *no pl.*) comfort, ease, wellbeing.

wohlbehalten [ˈvoːlbəhaltən], *adj.* safe.

wohlbekannt [ˈvoːlbəkant], *adj.* well known.

wohlbeleibt [ˈvoːlbəlaɪpt], *adj.* corpulent, stout.

wohlbestallt [ˈvoːlbəʃtalt], *adj.* duly installed.

Wohlergehen [ˈvoːlɛrgeːən], *n.* (—s, *no pl.*) welfare, wellbeing.

wohlerhalten [ˈvoːlɛrhaltən], *adj.* well preserved.

wohlerzogen [ˈvoːlɛrtsoːgən], *adj.* well bred, well brought up.

Wohlfahrt [ˈvoːlfaːrt], *f.* (—, *no pl.*) welfare, prosperity.

wohlfeil [ˈvoːlfaɪl], *adj.* cheap, inexpensive.

Wohlgefallen [ˈvoːlgəfalən], *n.* (—s, *no pl.*) pleasure, delight, approval.

wohlgefällig [ˈvoːlgəfɛlɪç], *adj.* pleasant, agreeable.

Wohlgefühl [ˈvoːlgəfyːl], *n.* (—s, *no pl.*) comfort, ease.

wohlgelitten [ˈvoːlgəlɪtən], *adj.* popular.

wohlgemeint [ˈvoːlgəmaɪnt], *adj.* well meant.

wohlgemerkt [ˈvoːlgəmɛrkt], *adv.* mind you! mark my words!

wohlgemut [ˈvoːlgəmuːt], *adj.* cheerful, merry.

wohlgeneigt [ˈvoːlgənaɪkt], *adj.* well disposed (towards).

wohlgepflegt [ˈvoːlgəpfleːkt], *adj.* well kept.

wohlgeraten [ˈvoːlgəraːtən], *adj.* successful; well turned out; good, well behaved.

Wohlgeruch [ˈvoːlgəruːx], *m.* (—es, *pl.* ⸚e) sweet scent, perfume, fragrance.

Wohlgeschmack [ˈvoːlgəʃmak], *m.* (—s, *no pl.*) pleasant flavour, agreeable taste.

wohlgesinnt [ˈvoːlgəzɪnt], *adj.* well disposed.

wohlgestaltet [ˈvoːlgəʃtaltət], *adj.* well shaped.

wohlgezielt [ˈvoːlgətsiːlt], *adj.* well aimed.

wohlhabend [ˈvoːlhaːbənt], *adj.* well-to-do, wealthy, well off.

wohlig [ˈvoːlɪç], *adj.* comfortable, cosy.

Wohlklang [ˈvoːlklaŋ], *m.* (—s, *pl.* ⸚e) harmony, euphony.

wohlklingend [ˈvoːlklɪŋənt], *adj.* harmonious, euphonious, sweet-sounding.

Wohlleben [ˈvoːlleːbən], *n.* (—s, *no pl.*) luxurious living.

wohllöblich [ˈvoːllœˑplɪç], *adj.* worshipful.

wohlmeinend [ˈvoːlmaɪnənt], *adj.* well-meaning.

wohlschmeckend [ˈvoːlʃmɛkənt], *adj.* savoury, tasty, delicious.

Wohlsein [ˈvoːlzaɪn], *n.* (—s, *no pl.*) good health, wellbeing.

Wohlstand [ˈvoːlʃtant], *m.* (—s, *no pl.*) prosperity.

Wohltat [ˈvoːltaːt], *f.* (—, *pl.* —en) benefit; kindness; (*pl.*) benefaction, charity; (*fig.*) treat.

Wohltäter ['vo:ltɛ:tər], m. (—s, pl. —) benefactor.
Wohltätigkeit ['vo:ltɛ:tɪçkaɪt], f. (—, no pl.) charity.
wohltuend ['vo:ltu:ənt], adj. soothing.
wohltun ['vo:ltu:n], v.n. irr. do good; be comforting.
wohlweislich ['vo:lvaɪslɪç], adj. wisely.
Wohlwollen ['vo:lvɔlən], n. (—s, no pl.) benevolence; favour, patronage.
wohnen ['vo:nən], v.n. reside, dwell, live.
wohnhaft ['vo:nhaft], adj. domiciled, resident; — sein, reside, be domiciled.
Wohnhaus ['vo:nhaus], n. (—es, pl. ⸚er) dwelling-house.
wohnlich ['vo:nlɪç], adj. comfortable; cosy.
Wohnort ['vo:nɔrt], m. (—s, pl. —e) place of residence.
Wohnsitz ['vo:nzɪts], m. (—es, pl. —e) domicile, abode, residence.
Wohnstätte ['vo:nʃtɛtə], f. (—, pl. —n) abode, home.
Wohnung ['vo:nuŋ], f. (—, pl. —en) residence, dwelling; house, flat, lodging; apartment.
Wohnungsmangel ['vo:nuŋsmaŋəl], m. (—s, no pl.) housing shortage.
Wohnwagen ['vo:nva:gən], m. (—s, pl. —) caravan.
Wohnzimmer ['vo:ntsɪmər], n. (—s, pl. —) sitting-room, living-room.
wölben ['vœlbən], v.r. sich —, vault, arch.
Wölbung ['vœlbuŋ], f. (—, pl. —en) vault, vaulting.
Wolf [vɔlf], m. (—(e)s, pl. ⸚e) wolf.
Wolke ['vɔlkə], f. (—, pl. —n) cloud.
Wolkenbruch ['vɔlkənbrux], m. (—s, pl. ⸚e) cloudburst, violent downpour.
Wolkenkratzer ['vɔlkənkratsər], m. (—s, pl. —) sky-scraper.
Wolkenkuckucksheim [vɔlkən'kukukshaɪm], n. (—s, no pl.) Utopia, cloud cuckoo land.
Wolldecke ['vɔldɛkə], f. (—, pl. —n) blanket.
Wolle ['vɔlə], f. (—, pl. —n) wool.
wollen (1) ['vɔlən], v.a., v.n. irr. wish, want to, be willing, intend; was — Sie, what do you want?
wollen (2) ['vɔlən], ad. woollen, made of wool.
Wollgarn ['vɔlgarn], n. (—s, pl. —e) woollen yarn.
Wollhandel ['vɔlhandəl], m. (—s, no pl.) wool-trade.
wollig ['vɔlɪç], adj. woolly.
Wollsamt ['vɔlzamt], m. (—s, no pl.) plush, velveteen.
Wollust ['vɔlust], f. (—, pl. ⸚e) voluptuousness; lust.
wollüstig ['vɔlystɪç], adj. voluptuous.
Wollwaren ['vɔlva:rən], f. pl. woollen goods.
Wollzupfen ['vɔltsupfən], n. (—s, no pl.) wool-picking.
womit [vo:'mɪt], adv. wherewith, with which; (interr.) with what?

womöglich [vo:'mø:klɪç], adv. if possible, perhaps.
wonach [vo:'na:x], adv. whereafter, after which; according to which.
Wonne ['vɔnə], f. (—, pl. —n) delight, bliss, rapture.
wonnetrunken ['vɔnətruŋkən], adj. enraptured.
wonnig ['vɔnɪç], adj. delightful.
woran [vo:'ran], adv. whereat, whereby; (interr.) by what? at what?
worauf [vo:'rauf], adv. upon which, at which; whereupon; (interr.) on what?
woraufhin [vo:rauf'hɪn], conj. whereupon.
woraus [vo:'raus], adv. (rel. & interr.) whence, from which; by or out of which.
worein [vo:'raɪn], adv. (rel. & interr.) into which; into what.
worin [vo:'rɪn], adv. (rel.) wherein; (interr.) in what?
Wort [vɔrt], n. (—(e)s, pl. ⸚er, —e) word, term; expression, saying.
wortarm ['vɔrtarm], adj. poor in words, deficient in vocabulary.
Wortarmut ['vɔrtarmu:t], f. (—, no pl.) paucity of words, poverty of language.
Wortbildung ['vɔrtbɪlduŋ], f. (—, pl. —en) word-formation.
wortbrüchig ['vɔrtbryçɪç], adj. faithless, disloyal.
Wörterbuch ['vœrtərbu:x], n. (—(e)s, pl. ⸚er) dictionary.
Worterklärung ['vɔrtɛrklɛ:ruŋ], f. (—, pl. —en) definition.
Wortforschung ['vɔrtfɔrʃuŋ], f. (—, no pl.) etymology.
Wortfügung ['vɔrtfy:guŋ], f. (—, no pl.) syntax.
Wortführer ['vɔrtfy:rər], m. (—s, pl. —) spokesman.
Wortgefecht ['vɔrtgəfɛçt], n. (—es, pl. —e) verbal battle.
wortgetreu ['vɔrtgətrɔy], adj. literal, verbatim.
wortkarg ['vɔrtkark], adj. laconic, sparing of words, taciturn.
Wortlaut ['vɔrtlaut], m. (—s, pl. —e) wording, text.
wörtlich ['vœrtlɪç], adj. verbal; literal, word for word.
wortlos ['vɔrtlo:s], adj. speechless. — adv. without uttering a word.
wortreich ['vɔrtraɪç], adj. (language) rich in words; (fig.) verbose, wordy.
Wortreichtum ['vɔrtraɪçtum], m. (—s, no pl.) (language) wealth of words; (fig.) verbosity, wordiness.
Wortschwall ['vɔrtʃval], m. (—s, no pl.) bombast; torrent of words.
Wortspiel ['vɔrtʃpi:l], n. (—s, pl. —e) pun.
Wortversetzung ['vɔrtfɛrzɛtsuŋ], f. (—, pl. —en) inversion (of words).
Wortwechsel ['vɔrtvɛksəl], m. (—s, pl. —) dispute, altercation.
worüber [vo:'ry:bər], adv. (rel.) about which, whereof; (interr.) about what?

285

worunter

worunter [voˈruntər], *adv.* (*rel.*) whereunder; (*interr.*) under what?

woselbst [voːˈzɛlpst], *adv.* where.

wovon [voːˈfɔn], *adv.* (*rel.*) whereof; (*interr.*) of what?

wovor [voːˈfoːr], *adv.* (*rel.*) before which; (*interr.*) before what?

wozu [voːˈtsuː], *adv.* (*rel.*) whereto; (*interr.*) why? for what purpose? to what end?

Wrack [vrak], *n.* (—s, *pl.* —s) wreck.

wringen [ˈvrɪŋən], *v.a.* wring.

Wringmaschine [ˈvrɪŋmaʃiːnə], *f.* (—, *pl.* —n) wringer, mangle.

Wucher [ˈvuːxər], *m.* (—s, *no pl.*) usury.

wucherisch [ˈvuːxərɪʃ], *adj.* usurious, extortionate.

wuchern [ˈvuːxərn], *v.n.* practise usury; (*plants*) luxuriate, grow profusely.

Wucherungen [ˈvuːxəruŋən], *f. pl.* (*Med.*) excrescence, growth.

Wuchs [vuːks], *m.* (—es, *no pl.*) growth; shape, build.

Wucht [vuxt], *f.* (—, *no pl.*) power, force; weight; impetus.

wuchten [ˈvuxtən], *v.n.* (*Poet.*) press heavily. — *v.a.* prise up.

wuchtig [ˈvuxtɪç], *adj.* weighty, forceful.

Wühlarbeit [ˈvyːlarbaɪt], *f.* (—, *pl.* —en) subversive activity.

wühlen [ˈvyːlən], *v.a.*, *v.n.* dig, burrow; (*fig.*) agitate.

Wühler [ˈvyːlər], *m.* (—s, *pl.* —) agitator, demagogue.

Wühlmaus [ˈvyːlmaus], *f.* (—, *pl.* ⸚e) (*Zool.*) vole.

Wulst [vulst], *m.* (—es, *pl.* ⸚e) roll, pad; swelling.

wülstig [ˈvylstɪç], *adj.* padded, stuffed; swollen.

wund [vunt], *adj.* sore, wounded.

Wundarzt [ˈvuntartst], *m.* (—es, *pl.* ⸚e) (*obs.*) surgeon.

Wundbalsam [ˈvuntbalzam], *m.* (—s, *pl.* —e) balm.

Wunde [ˈvundə], *f.* (—, *pl.* —n) wound, hurt.

Wunder [ˈvundər], *n.* (—s, *pl.* —) marvel, wonder, miracle.

wunderbar [ˈvundərbaːr], *adj.* wonderful, marvellous.

Wunderding [ˈvundərdɪŋ], *n.* (—s, *pl.* —e) marvel.

Wunderdoktor [ˈvundərdɔktɔr], *m.* (—s, *pl.* —en) quack doctor.

Wunderglaube [ˈvundərglaubə], *m.* (—ns, *no pl.*) belief in miracles.

wunderhübsch [vundərˈhypʃ], *adj.* exceedingly pretty.

Wunderkind [ˈvundərkɪnt], *n.* (—s, *pl.* —er) infant prodigy.

Wunderlampe [ˈvundərlampə], *f.* (—, *pl.* —n) magic lantern.

wunderlich [ˈvundərlɪç], *adj.* strange, odd, queer.

wundern [ˈvundərn], *v.r. sich — über*, be surprised at, be astonished at.

wundersam [ˈvundərzaːm], *adj.* wonderful, strange.

wunderschön [ˈvundərʃøːn], *adj.* lovely,

gorgeous; exquisite.

Wundertat [ˈvundərtaːt], *f.* (—, *pl.* —en) miraculous deed.

wundertätig [ˈvundərtɛːtɪç], *adj.* miraculous.

Wundertier [ˈvundərtiːr], *n.* (—s, *pl.* —e) monster; (*fig.*) prodigy.

Wunderwerk [ˈvundərvɛrk], *n.* (—s, *pl.* —e) miracle.

Wundmal [ˈvuntmaːl], *n.* (—s, *pl.* —e) scar.

Wunsch [vunʃ], *m.* (—es, *pl.* ⸚e) wish, desire, aspiration.

Wünschelrute [ˈvynʃəlruːtə], *f.* (—, *pl.* —n) divining-rod.

wünschen [ˈvynʃən], *v.a.* wish, desire, long for.

wünschenswert [ˈvynʃənsveːrt], *adj.* desirable.

Wunschform [ˈvunʃfɔrm], *f.* (—, *no pl.*) (*Gram.*) optative form.

wuppdich! [ˈvupdɪç], *excl.* here goes!

Würde [ˈvyrdə], *f.* (—, *pl.* —n) dignity, honour.

Würdenträger [ˈvyrdəntrɛːgər], *m.* (—s, *pl.* —) dignitary.

würdevoll [ˈvyrdəfɔl], *adj.* dignified.

würdig [ˈvyrdɪç], *adj.* worthy (of), deserving, meritorious.

würdigen [ˈvyrdɪgən], *v.a.* honour; *ich weiss es zu —*, I appreciate it.

Würdigung [ˈvyrdɪguŋ], *f.* (—, *pl.* —en) appreciation.

Wurf [vurf], *m.* (—(e)s, *pl.* ⸚e) cast, throw.

Würfel [ˈvyrfəl], *m.* (—s, *pl.* —) die; (*Geom.*) cube; — *spielen*, play at dice.

würfelförmig [ˈvyrfəlfœrmɪç], *adj.* cubic, cubiform.

würfeln [ˈvyrfəln], *v.n.* play at dice.

Wurfgeschoß [ˈvurfgəʃoːs], *n.* (—sses, *pl.* —sse) missile, projectile.

Wurfmaschine [ˈvurfmaʃiːnə], *f.* (—, *pl.* —n) catapult.

Wurfscheibe [ˈvurfʃaɪbə], *f.* (—, *pl.* —n) discus, quoit.

Wurfspieß [ˈvurfʃpiːs], *m.* (—es, *pl.* —e) javelin.

würgen [ˈvyrgən], *v.a.* strangle, throttle. — *v.n.* choke.

Würgengel [ˈvyrgɛŋəl], *m.* (—s, *no pl.*) avenging angel.

Würger [ˈvyrgər], *m.* (—s, *pl.* —) strangler, murderer; (*Poet.*) slayer; (*Orn.*) shrike, butcher-bird.

Wurm [vurm], *m.* (—(e)s, *pl.* ⸚er) worm; (*apple*) maggot.

wurmen [ˈvurmən], *v.a.* vex.

wurmstichig [ˈvurmʃtɪçɪç], *adj.* worm-eaten.

Wurst [vurst], *f.* (—, *pl.* ⸚e) sausage.

wurstig [ˈvurstɪç], *adj.* (*sl.*) quite indifferent.

Wurstigkeit [ˈvurstɪçkaɪt], *f.* (—, *no pl.*) callousness, indifference.

Würze [ˈvyrtsə], *f.* (—, *pl.* —n) seasoning, spice, condiment.

Wurzel [ˈvurtsəl], *f.* (—, *pl.* —n) root.

wurzeln [ˈvurtsəln], *v.n.* be rooted.

würzen [ˈvyrtsən], *v.a.* season, spice.

würzig [ˈvyrtsɪç], *adj.* spicy, fragrant.

Wust [vust], *m.* (**—es**, *no pl.*) chaos, trash.
wüst [vy:st], *adj.* waste, desert; desolate; dissolute.
Wüste [ˈvy:stə], *f.* (**—**, *pl.* **—n**) desert, wilderness.
Wüstling [ˈvy:stlɪŋ], *m.* (**—s**, *pl.* **—e**) profligate, libertine.
Wut [vu:t], *f.* (**—**, *no pl.*) rage, fury, passion.
wüten [ˈvy:tən], *v.n.* rage, storm, fume.
wutentbrannt [ˈvu:təntbrant], *adj.* enraged, infuriated.
Wüterich [ˈvy:tərɪç], *m.* (**—s**, *pl.* **—e**) tyrant; ruthless fellow.
Wutgeschrei [ˈvu:tgəʃraɪ], *n.* (**—s**, *no pl.*) yell of rage.
wutschnaubend [ˈvu:tʃnaubənt], *adj.* foaming with rage.

X

X [ɪks], *n.* (**—s**, *pl.* **—s**) the letter X.
X-Beine [ˈɪksbaɪnə], *n. pl.* knock-knees.
x-beliebig [ˈɪksbəli:bɪç], *adj.* any, whatever (one likes).
Xenie [ˈkse:njə], *f.* (**—**, *pl.* **—n**) epigram.
Xereswein [ˈkse:rəsvaɪn], *m.* (**—s**, *pl.* **—e**) sherry.
x-mal [ˈɪksma:l], *adv.* (*coll.*) so many times, umpteen times.
X-Strahlen [ˈɪksʃtra:lən], *m. pl.* X-rays.
Xylographie [ksylograˈfi:], *f.* (**—**, *no pl.*) wood-engraving.
Xylophon [ksyloˈfo:n], *n.* (**—s**, *pl.* **—e**) (*Mus.*) xylophone.

Y

Y [ˈypsilɔn], *n.* (**—s**, *pl.* **—s**) the letter Y.
Yak [jak], *m.* (**—s**, *pl.* **—s**) (*Zool.*) yak.
Yamswurzel [ˈjamsvurtsəl], *f.* (**—**, *pl.* **—n**) yam.
Ysop [ˈy:zo:p], *m.* (**—s**, *no pl.*) hyssop.

Z

Z [tsɛt], *n.* (**—s**, *pl.* **—s**) the letter Z.
Zabel [ˈtsa:bəl], *m.* (**—s**, *pl.* **—**) (*obs.*) chess-board.

Zacke [ˈtsakə], *f.* (**—**, *pl.* **—n**) tooth, spike; (*fork*) prong.
zackig [ˈtsakɪç], *adj.* pronged, toothed, indented; (*rock*) jagged; (*sl.*) smart.
zagen [ˈtsa:gən], *v.n.* quail, blench, be disheartened, be fainthearted.
zaghaft [ˈtsa:khaft], *adj.* faint-hearted.
Zaghaftigkeit [ˈtsa:khaftɪçkaɪt], *f.* (**—**, *no pl.*) faintheartedness, timidity.
zäh [tsɛ:], *adj.* tough.
Zähigkeit [ˈtsɛ:ɪçkaɪt], *f.* (**—**, *no pl.*) toughness.
Zahl [tsa:l], *f.* (**—**, *pl.* **—en**) number, figure.
zahlbar [ˈtsa:lba:r], *adj.* payable, due.
zählbar [ˈtsɛ:lba:r], *adj.* calculable.
zahlen [ˈtsa:lən], *v.a.* pay; *Ober!* **—**, waiter! the bill, please.
zählen [ˈtsɛ:lən], *v.a.*, *v.n.* count, number.
Zahlenfolge [ˈtsa:lənfɔlgə], *f.* (**—**, *no pl.*) numerical order.
Zahlenlehre [ˈtsa:lənle:rə], *f.* (**—**, *no pl.*) arithmetic.
Zahlenreihe [ˈtsa:lənraɪə], *f.* (**—**, *pl.* **—n**) numerical progression.
Zahlensinn [ˈtsa:lənzɪn], *m.* (**—s**, *no pl.*) head for figures.
Zahler [ˈtsa:lər], *m.* (**—s**, *pl.* **—**) payer.
Zähler [ˈtsɛ:lər], *m.* (**—s**, *pl.* **—**) counter, teller; meter; (*Maths.*) numerator.
Zahlkellner [ˈtsa:lkɛlnər], *m.* (**—s**, *pl.* **—**) head waiter.
Zahlmeister [ˈtsa:lmaɪstər], *m.* (**—s**, *pl.* **—**) paymaster, treasurer, bursar.
zahlreich [ˈtsa:lraɪç], *adj.* numerous.
Zahltag [ˈtsa:lta:k], *m.* (**—s**, *pl.* **—e**) pay-day.
Zahlung [ˈtsa:luŋ], *f.* (**—**, *pl.* **—en**) payment; — *leisten*, make payment; *die —en einstellen*, stop payment.
Zählung [ˈtsɛ:luŋ], *f.* (**—**, *pl.* **—en**) counting, computation; census.
Zahlungseinstellung [ˈtsa:luŋsaɪnʃtɛluŋ], *f.* (**—**, *pl.* **—en**) suspension of payment.
zahlungsfähig [ˈtsa:luŋsfɛ:ɪç], *adj.* solvent.
Zahlungsmittel [ˈtsa:luŋsmɪtəl], *n.* (**—s**, *pl.* **—**) means of payment; *gesetzliches —*, legal tender.
Zahlungstermin [ˈtsa:luŋstɛrmi:n], *m.* (**—s**, *pl.* **—e**) time of payment.
zahlungsunfähig [ˈtsa:luŋsunfɛ:ɪç], *adj.* insolvent.
Zahlwort [ˈtsa:lvɔrt], *n.* (**—s**, *pl.* **ˉer**) (*Gram.*) numeral.
zahm [tsa:m], *adj.* tame; domestic(ated); — *machen*, tame.
zähmen [ˈtsɛ:mən], *v.a.* tame, domesticate.
Zähmer [ˈtsɛ:mər], *m.* (**—s**, *pl.* **—**) tamer.
Zahmheit [ˈtsa:mhaɪt], *f.* (**—**, *no pl.*) tameness.
Zähmung [ˈtsɛ:muŋ], *f.* (**—**, *no pl.*) taming, domestication.
Zahn [tsa:n], *m.* (**—(e)s**, *pl.* **ˉe**) tooth; (*wheel*) cog.

Zahnarzt

Zahnarzt [ˈtsaːnartst], *m.* (—es, *pl.* ⁻e) dentist, dental surgeon.

Zahnbürste [ˈtsaːnbyrstə], *f.* (—, *pl.* —n) tooth-brush.

Zähneklappern [ˈtsɛːnəklapərn], *n.* (—s, *no pl.*) chattering of teeth.

Zähneknirschen [ˈtsɛːnəknɪrʃən], *n.* (—s, *no pl.*) gnashing of teeth.

zahnen [ˈtsaːnən], *v.n.* teethe, cut o.'s teeth.

zähnen [ˈtsɛːnən], *v.a.* indent, notch.

Zahnfleisch [ˈtsaːnflaɪʃ], *n.* (—es, *no pl.*) gums.

Zahnfüllung [ˈtsaːnfyluŋ], *f.* (—, *pl.* —en) filling, stopping (of tooth).

Zahnheilkunde [ˈtsaːnhaɪlkundə], *f.* (—, *no pl.*) dentistry, dental surgery.

Zahnlücke [ˈtsaːnlykə], *f.* (—, *pl.* —n) gap in the teeth.

Zahnpaste [ˈtsaːnpastə], *f.* (—, *no pl.*) tooth-paste.

Zahnpulver [ˈtsaːnpulvər], *n.* (—s, *no pl.*) tooth-powder.

Zahnrad [ˈtsaːnraːt], *n.* (—s, *pl.* ⁻er) cog-wheel.

Zahnradbahn [ˈtsaːnraːtbaːn], *f.* (—, *pl.* —en) rack-railway.

Zahnschmerzen [ˈtsaːnʃmɛrtsən], *m. pl.* toothache.

Zahnstocher [ˈtsaːnʃtɔxər], *m.* (—s, *pl.* —) tooth-pick.

Zähre [ˈtsɛːrə], *f.* (—, *pl.* —n) (*Poet.*) tear.

Zander [ˈtsandər], *m.* (—s, *pl.* —) (*fish*) pike.

Zange [ˈtsaŋə], *f.* (—, *pl.* —n) tongs; pincers; tweezers, nippers; (*Med.*) forceps.

Zank [tsaŋk], *m.* (—es, *pl.* ⁻ereien) quarrel, altercation, tiff.

Zankapfel [ˈtsaŋkapfəl], *m.* (—s, *pl.* ⁻) bone of contention.

zanken [ˈtsaŋkən], *v.r. sich* —, quarrel, dispute.

zänkisch [ˈtsɛnkɪʃ], *adj.* quarrelsome.

Zanksucht [ˈtsaŋkzuxt], *f.* (—, *no pl.*) quarrelsomeness.

zanksüchtig [ˈtsaŋkzyçtɪç], *adj.* quarrelsome, cantankerous.

Zapfen [ˈtsapfən], *m.* (—s, *pl.* —) pin, peg; (*cask*) bung, spigot; (*fir*) cone.

zapfen [ˈtsapfən], *v.a.* tap, draw.

Zapfenstreich [ˈtsapfənʃtraɪç], *m.* (—s, *no pl.*) (*Mil.*) tattoo, retreat.

zapp(e)lig [ˈtsap(ə)lɪç], *adj.* fidgety.

zappeln [ˈtsapəln], *v.n.* kick, struggle, wriggle.

Zar [tsaːr], *m.* (—en, *pl.* —en) Czar, Tsar.

zart [tsart], *adj.* tender, sensitive, delicate, gentle; — *besaitet*, (*iron.*) sensitive, highly strung.

Zartgefühl [ˈtsartgəfyːl], *n.* (—s, *no pl.*) delicacy, sensitivity.

Zartheit [ˈtsarthaɪt], *f.* (—, *no pl.*) tenderness, gentleness.

zärtlich [ˈtsɛːrtlɪç], *adj.* loving, amorous, tender.

Zärtlichkeit [ˈtsɛːrtlɪçkaɪt], *f.* (—, *pl.* —en) tenderness; caresses.

Zartsinn [ˈtsartzɪn], *m.* (—s, *no pl.*) delicacy.

Zauber [ˈtsaubər], *m.* (—s, *no pl.*) charm, spell, enchantment; magic; fascination.

Zauberei [tsaubəˈraɪ], *f.* (—, *pl.* —en) magic, witchcraft, sorcery.

Zauberer [ˈtsaubərər], *m.* (—s, *pl.* —) magician, sorcerer, wizard.

zauberisch [ˈtsaubərɪʃ], *adj.* magical; (*fig.*) enchanting.

Zauberkraft [ˈtsaubərkraft], *f.* (—, *no pl.*) magic power, witchcraft.

Zaubermittel [ˈtsaubərmɪtəl], *n.* (—s, *pl.* —) charm.

zaubern [ˈtsaubərn], *v.n.* practise magic; conjure.

Zauberspruch [ˈtsaubərʃprux], *m.* (—s, *pl.* ⁻e) spell, charm.

Zauberstab [ˈtsaubərʃtaːp], *m.* (—s, *pl.* ⁻e) magic wand.

Zauderer [ˈtsaudərər], *m.* (—s, *pl.* —) loiterer, temporizer, procrastinator.

zaudern [ˈtsaudərn], *v.n.* delay; hesitate, procrastinate.

Zaum [tsaum], *m.* (—(e)s, *pl.* ⁻e) bridle; *im — halten*, check, restrain.

zäumen [ˈtsɔymən], *v.a.* bridle.

Zaun [tsaun], *m.* (—(e)s, *pl.* ⁻e) hedge; fence; *einen Streit vom — brechen*, pick a quarrel.

Zaungast [ˈtsaungast], *m.* (—s, *pl.* ⁻e) onlooker, outsider; intruder.

Zaunkönig [ˈtsaunkøːnɪç], *m.* (—s, *pl.* —e) (*Orn.*) wren.

Zaunpfahl [ˈtsaunpfaːl], *m.* (—s, *pl.* ⁻e) pale, hedge-pole; *mit dem — winken*, give s.o. a broad hint.

Zaunrebe [ˈtsaunreːbə], *f.* (—, *pl.* —n) (*Bot.*) Virginia creeper.

zausen [ˈtsauzən], *v.a.* tousle; (*hair*) disarrange, ruffle.

Zechbruder [ˈtsɛçbruːdər], *m.* (—s, *pl.* ⁻) tippler, toper.

Zeche [ˈtsɛçə], *f.* (—, *pl.* —n) bill (in a restaurant); mine; *die — bezahlen*, foot the bill, pay the piper.

Zeder [ˈtseːdər], *f.* (—, *pl.* —n) (*Bot.*) cedar.

zedieren [tsɛˈdiːrən], *v.a.* cede.

Zehe [ˈtseːə], *f.* (—, *pl.* —n) toe.

Zehenspitze [ˈtseːənʃpɪtsə], *f.* (—, *pl.* —n) tip of the toe, tiptoe.

zehn [tseːn], *num. adj.* ten.

Zehneck [ˈtseːnɛk], *n.* (—s, *pl.* —e) decagon.

Zehnte [ˈtseːntə], *m.* (—n, *pl.* —n) tithe.

zehren [ˈtseːrən], *v.n. von etwas —*, live on s.th., prey upon s.th.

Zehrfieber [ˈtseːrfiːbər], *n.* (—s, *no pl.*) hectic fever.

Zehrgeld [ˈtseːrgɛlt], *n.* (—s, *pl.* —er) subsistence, allowance.

Zehrvorrat [ˈtseːrfoːrraːt], *m.* (—s, *pl.* ⁻e) provisions.

Zehrung [ˈtseːruŋ], *f.* (—, *pl.* —en) consumption; victuals; (*Eccl.*) *letzte —*, viaticum.

Zeichen [ˈtsaɪçən], *n.* (—s, *pl.* —) sign, token, symptom, omen; indication; badge; signal.

Zeichenbrett ['tsaɪçənbrɛt], *n.* (—s, *pl.* —er) drawing-board.

Zeichendeuter ['tsaɪçəndɔytər], *m.* (—s, *pl.* —) astrologer.

Zeichendeuterei [tsaɪçəndɔytəˈraɪ], *f.* (—, *no pl.*) astrology.

Zeichenerklärung ['tsaɪçənɛrklɛ:ruŋ], *f.* (— *pl.*—en) legend, key.

Zeichensprache ['tsaɪçənʃpra:xə], *f.* (—, *no pl.*) sign-language.

Zeichentinte ['tsaɪçəntɪntə], *f.* (—, *no pl.*) marking ink.

zeichnen ['tsaɪçnən], *v.a.* draw; mark; (*money*) subscribe; (*letter*) sign.

Zeichner ['tsaɪçnər], *m.* (—s, *pl.* —) draughtsman, designer.

Zeichnung ['tsaɪçnuŋ], *f.* (—, *pl.* —en) drawing.

Zeigefinger ['tsaɪgəfɪŋər], *m.* (—s, *pl.* —) forefinger, index finger.

zeigen ['tsaɪgən], *v.a.* show, point to, prove.

Zeiger ['tsaɪgər], *m.* (—s, *pl.* —) indicator; hand (of watch, clock).

zeihen ['tsaɪən], *v.a. irr. einen einer Sache* —, tax s.o. with s.th.

Zeile ['tsaɪlə], *f.* (—, *pl.* —n) line; furrow; (*pl.*) letter.

Zeisig ['tsaɪzɪç], *m.* (—s, *pl.* —e) (*Orn.*) siskin.

Zeit [tsaɪt], *f.* (—, *pl.* —en) time; *zur* —, at present; *auf* —, on credit.

Zeitabschnitt ['tsaɪtapʃnɪt], *m.* (—s, *pl.* —e) period; epoch.

Zeitalter ['tsaɪtaltər], *n.* (—s, *pl.* —) age, era.

Zeitdauer ['tsaɪtdauər], *f.* (—, *no pl.*) space of time.

Zeitfrage ['tsaɪtfra:gə], *f.* (—, *pl.* —n) topical question; question of time.

Zeitgeist ['tsaɪtgaɪst], *m.* (—s, *no pl.*) spirit of the age.

zeitgemäß ['tsaɪtgəmɛ:s], *adj.* timely, seasonable, opportune, modern.

Zeitgenosse ['tsaɪtgənɔsə], *m.* (—n, *pl.* —n) contemporary.

zeitig ['tsaɪtɪç], *adj.* early, timely.

zeitigen ['tsaɪtɪgən], *v.a.* engender, generate. — *v.n.* mature, ripen.

Zeitkarte ['tsaɪtkartə], *f.* (—, *pl.* —n) season ticket.

Zeitlauf ['tsaɪtlauf], *m.* (—s, *pl.* ⸚e) course of time, conjuncture.

zeitlebens ['tsaɪtle:bəns], *adv.* for life, (for) all his (or her) life.

zeitlich ['tsaɪtlɪç], *adj.* temporal, earthly; secular; temporary, transient.

zeitlos ['tsaɪtlo:s], *adj.* lasting, permanent.

Zeitmangel ['tsaɪtmaŋəl], *m.* (—s, *no pl.*) lack of time.

Zeitmesser ['tsaɪtmɛsər], *m.* (—s, *pl.* —) chronometer, timepiece; metronome.

Zeitpunkt ['tsaɪtpuŋkt], *m.* (—s, *pl.* —e) moment, date; point of time.

zeitraubend ['tsaɪtraubənt], *adj.* time-consuming.

Zeitraum ['tsaɪtraum], *m.* (—s, *pl.* ⸚e) space of time, period.

Zeitschrift ['tsaɪtʃrɪft], *f.* (—, *pl.* —en) periodical, journal, magazine.

Zeitung ['tsaɪtuŋ], *f.* (—, *pl.* —en) newspaper.

Zeitungsente ['tsaɪtuŋsɛntə], *f.* (—, *pl.* —n) canard, newspaper hoax.

Zeitungskiosk ['tsaɪtuŋskiɔsk], *m.* (—s, *pl.* —e) newspaper-stall.

Zeitungsnachricht ['tsaɪtuŋsna:xrɪçt], *f.* (—, *pl.* —en) newspaper report.

Zeitungswesen ['tsaɪtuŋsve:zən], *n.* (—s, *no pl.*) journalism.

Zeitverlust ['tsaɪtfɛrlust], *m.* (—s, *no pl.*) loss of time; *ohne* —, without delay.

Zeitvertreib ['tsaɪtfɛrtraɪp], *m.* (—s, *no pl.*) pastime, amusement; *zum* —, to pass the time.

zeitweilig ['tsaɪtvaɪlɪç], *adj.* temporary.

zeitweise ['tsaɪtvaɪzə], *adv.* from time to time.

Zeitwort ['tsaɪtvɔrt], *n.* (—s, *pl.* ⸚er) (*Gram.*) verb.

Zelle ['tsɛllə], *f.* (—, *pl.* —n) cell;booth.

Zelt [tsɛlt], *n.* (—(e)s, *pl.* —e) tent.

Zeltdecke ['tsɛltdɛkə], *f.* (—, *pl.* —n) awning, marquee.

Zement [tse'mɛnt], *m.* (—s, *no pl.*) cement.

Zenit [tse'ni:t], *m.* (—s, *no pl.*) zenith.

zensieren [tsɛn'zi:rən], *v.a.* review, censure; (*Sch.*) mark.

Zensor ['tsɛnzɔr], *m.* (—s, *pl.* —en) censor.

Zensur [tsɛn'zu:r], *f.* (—, *pl.* —en) censure; (*Sch.*) report, mark; censorship.

Zentimeter ['tsɛntime:tər], *m.* (—s, *pl.* —) centimetre.

Zentner ['tsɛntnər], *m.* (—s, *pl.* —) hundredweight.

zentral [tsɛn'tra:l], *adj.* central.

Zentrale [tsɛn'tra:lə], *f.* (—, *pl.* —n) control room; head office.

zentralisieren [tsɛntrali'zi:rən], *v.a.* centralise.

Zentrum ['tsɛntrum], *n.* (—s, *pl.* —tren) centre; (*Am.*) center.

Zephir ['tse:fi:r], *m.* (—s, *pl.* —e) zephyr.

Zepter ['tsɛptər], *m. & n.* (—s, *pl.* —) sceptre, mace.

zerbrechen [tsɛr'brɛçən], *v.a., v.n. irr.* (*aux.* sein) break to pieces; shatter; *sich den Kopf* —, rack o.'s brains.

zerbrechlich [tsɛr'brɛçlɪç], *adj.* brittle, fragile.

zerbröckeln [tsɛr'brœkəln], *v.a., v.n.* (*aux.* sein) crumble.

zerdrücken [tsɛr'drykən], *v.a.* crush, bruise.

Zeremonie [tseremo'ni:], *f.* (—, *pl.* —n) ceremony.

zeremoniell [tseremo'njɛl], *adj.* ceremonial, formal.

Zerfahrenheit [tsɛr'fa:rənhaɪt], *f.* (—, *no pl.*) absent-mindedness.

Zerfall [tsɛr'fal], *m.* (—s, *no pl.*) disintegration; decay.

zerfallen [tsɛr'falən], *v.n. irr.* (*aux.* sein) fall to pieces. — *adj.* in ruins.

zerfleischen

zerfleischen [tsɛrˈflaɪʃən], *v.a.* lacerate, tear to pieces.

zerfließen [tsɛrˈfliːsən], *v.n. irr.* (*aux.* sein) dissolve, melt.

zerfressen [tsɛrˈfrɛsən], *v.a. irr.* gnaw, corrode.

zergehen [tsɛrˈgeːən], *v.n. irr.* (*aux.* sein) dissolve, melt.

zergliedern [tsɛrˈgliːdərn], *v.a.* dissect; (*fig.*) analyse.

zerhauen [tsɛrˈhauən], *v.a.* hew in pieces, chop up.

zerkauen [tsɛrˈkauən], *v.a.* chew.

zerkleinern [tsɛrˈklaɪnərn], *v.a.* cut into small pieces; (*firewood*) chop.

zerklüftet [tsɛrˈklyftət], *adj.* rugged.

zerknirscht [tsɛrˈknɪrʃt], *adj.* contrite.

Zerknirschung [tsɛrˈknɪrʃuŋ], *f.* (—, *no pl.*) contrition.

zerknittern [tsɛrˈknɪtərn], *v.a.* crumple.

zerknüllen [tsɛrˈknylən], *v.a.* rumple.

zerlassen [tsɛrˈlasən], *v.a. irr.* melt, liquefy.

zerlegen [tsɛrˈleːgən], *v.a.* resolve; take to pieces; cut up, carve; (*fig.*) analyse.

zerlumpt [tsɛrˈlumpt], *adj.* ragged, tattered.

zermahlen [tsɛrˈmaːlən], *v.a.* grind to powder.

zermalmen [tsɛrˈmalmən], *v.a.* crush.

zermartern [tsɛrˈmartərn], *v.a.* torment; *sich das Hirn* —, rack o.'s brains.

zernagen [tsɛrˈnaːgən], *v.a.* gnaw (away).

zerquetschen [tsɛrˈkvɛtʃən], *v.a.* squash, crush.

zerraufen [tsɛrˈraufən], *v.a.* dishevel.

Zerrbild [ˈtsɛrbɪlt], *n.* (—s, *pl.* —er) caricature.

zerreiben [tsɛrˈraɪbən], *v.a. irr.* grind to powder, pulverise.

zerreißen [tsɛrˈraɪsən], *v.a. irr.* tear, rend, tear up; break; rupture. — *v.n.* (*aux.* sein) be torn; (*clothes*) wear out.

zerren [ˈtsɛrən], *v.a.* pull, tug, drag; strain.

zerrinnen [tsɛrˈrɪnən], *v.n. irr.* (*aux.* sein) dissolve, melt; (*fig.*) vanish.

zerrütten [tsɛrˈrytən], *v.a.* unsettle, disorder, unhinge; ruin, destroy.

zerschellen [tsɛrˈʃɛlən], *v.n.* (*aux.* sein) be dashed to pieces, be wrecked.

zerschlagen [tsɛrˈʃlaːgən], *v.a. irr.* break, smash to pieces, batter.

zerschmettern [tsɛrˈʃmɛtərn], *v.a.* dash to pieces, break, crush; shatter, overwhelm.

zersetzen [tsɛrˈzɛtsən], *v.a., v.r.* break up; disintegrate.

zerspalten [tsɛrˈʃpaltən], *v.a.* cleave, split, slit.

zersprengen [tsɛrˈʃprɛŋən], *v.a.* explode, burst; (*crowd*) disperse; (*Mil.*) rout.

zerspringen [tsɛrˈʃprɪŋən], *v.n. irr.* (*aux.* sein) crack; fly to pieces, split.

zerstampfen [tsɛrˈʃtampfən], *v.a.* crush, pound.

zerstäuben [tsɛrˈʃtɔybən], *v.a.* spray, atomize.

zerstörbar [tsɛrˈʃtøːrbaːr], *adj.* destructible.

zerstören [tsɛrˈʃtøːrən], *v.a.* destroy, devastate.

Zerstörer [tsɛrˈʃtøːrər], *m.* (—s, *pl.* —) destroyer.

Zerstörung [tsɛrˈʃtøːruŋ], *f.* (—, *pl.* —en) destruction.

Zerstörungswut [tsɛrˈʃtøːruŋsvuːt], *f.* (—, *no pl.*) vandalism.

zerstoßen [tsɛrˈʃtoːsən], *v.a. irr.* bruise, pound.

zerstreuen [tsɛrˈʃtrɔyən], *v.a.* scatter, disperse; divert.

zerstreut [tsɛrˈʃtrɔyt], *adj.* absent-minded.

Zerstreuung [tsɛrˈʃtrɔyuŋ], *f.* (—, *pl.* —en) dispersion; amusement, diversion, distraction.

zerstückeln [tsɛrˈʃtykəln], *v.a.* dismember.

Zerstückelung [tsɛrˈʃtykəluŋ], *f.* (—, *no pl.*) dismemberment.

zerteilen [tsɛrˈtaɪlən], *v.a.* divide, separate; disperse, dissipate. — *v.r. sich* —, disperse.

Zertifikat [tsɛrtifiˈkaːt], *n.* (—s, *pl.* —e) certificate, attestation.

zertrennen [tsɛrˈtrɛnən], *v.a.* rip up, unstitch.

zertrümmern [tsɛrˈtrymərn], *v.a.* destroy, break up, demolish.

Zerwürfnis [tsɛrˈvyrfnɪs], *n.* (—ses, *pl.* —se) discord, dissension.

zerzausen [tsɛrˈtsauzən], *v.a.* dishevel, tousle.

zerzupfen [tsɛrˈtsupfən], *v.a.* pick to pieces, pluck.

Zession [tsɛsˈjoːn], *f.* (—, *pl.* —en) cession, assignment, transfer.

Zetergeschrei [ˈtseːtərgəʃraɪ], *n.* (—s, *no pl.*) outcry, hullabaloo.

zetern [ˈtseːtərn], *v.n.* yell; (*coll.*) kick up a row.

Zettel [ˈtsɛtəl], *m.* (—s, *pl.* —) slip of paper; label, chit.

Zettelkasten [ˈtsɛtəlkastən], *m.* (—s, *pl.* ⸚) card-index, filing cabinet.

Zeug [tsɔyk], *n.* (—(e)s, *no pl.*) stuff, material; implements, kit, utensils; (*coll.*) things.

Zeuge [ˈtsɔygə], *m.* (—n, *pl.* —n) witness; *zum* —n *aufrufen*, call to witness.

zeugen [ˈtsɔygən], *v.a.* beget, generate, engender. — *v.n.* give evidence.

Zeugenaussage [ˈtsɔygənauszaːgə], *f.* (—, *pl.* —n) evidence, deposition.

Zeugenbeweis [ˈtsɔygənbəvaɪs], *m.* (—es, *pl.* —e) evidence, proof.

Zeugeneid [ˈtsɔygənaɪt], *m.* (—s, *pl.* —e) oath of a witness.

Zeughaus [ˈtsɔykhaus], *n.* (—es, *pl.* ⸚er) (*obs.*) arsenal.

Zeugin [ˈtsɔygɪn], *f.* (—, *pl.* —innen) female witness.

Zeugnis ['tsɔyknɪs], *n.* (—ses, *pl.* —se) (*Law.*) deposition; testimonial, certificate, reference; character; school report; — *ablegen*, give evidence, bear witness; *einem ein gutes — ausstellen*, give s.o. a good reference.

Zeugung ['tsɔyguŋ], *f.* (—, *pl.* —en) procreation, generation.

Zeugungskraft ['tsɔyguŋskraft], *f.* (—, *no pl.*) generative power.

Zeugungstrieb ['tsɔyguŋstri:p], *m.* (—s, *no pl.*) procreative instinct.

Zichorie [tsɪ'çoːrjə], *f.* (—, *pl.* —n) chicory.

Zicke ['tsɪkə], *f.* (—, *pl.* —n) *dial.* for **Ziege**.

Ziege ['tsiːgə], *f.* (—, *pl.* —n) goat.

Ziegel ['tsiːgəl], *m.* (—s, *pl.* —) (*roof*) tile; (*wall*) brick.

Ziegelbrenner ['tsiːgəlbrenər], *m.* (—s, *pl.* —) tile-maker, tiler; brickmaker.

Ziegelbrennerei ['tsiːgəlbrenəˈraɪ], *f.* (—, *pl.* —en) tile-kiln; brickyard.

Ziegeldach ['tsiːgəldax], *n.* (—s, *pl.* ˙er) tiled roof.

Ziegeldecker ['tsiːgəldekər], *m.* (—s, *pl.* —) tiler.

Ziegelei [tsiːgəˈlaɪ], *f.* (—, *pl.* —en) brickyard, brickworks.

Ziegelerde ['tsiːgələːrdə], *f.* (—, *no pl.*) brick-clay.

Ziegenbart ['tsiːgənbaːrt], *m.* (—s, *pl.* ˙e) goat's beard; (*human*) goatee.

Ziegenleder ['tsiːgənleːdər], *n.* (—s, *no pl.*) kid (leather).

Ziegenpeter ['tsiːgənpeːtər], *m.* (—s, *no pl.*) (*Med.*) mumps.

ziehen ['tsiːən], *v.a. irr.* draw, pull, drag; pull out; cultivate; breed; (*game*) move. — *v.n.* draw, be an attraction; (*aux.* sein) go, move. — *v.r. sich* —, extend.

Ziehkind ['tsiːkɪnt], *n.* (—s, *pl.* —er) foster-child.

Ziehmutter ['tsiːmutər], *f.* (—, *pl.* ˙) foster-mother.

Ziehung ['tsiːuŋ], *f.* (—, *pl.* —en) draw (in a lottery).

Ziehvater ['tsiːfaːtər], *m.* (—s, *pl.* ˙) foster-father.

Ziel [tsiːl], *n.* (—s, *pl.* —e) goal, aim, purpose, intention, end; butt, target; (*Mil.*) objective; (*sports*) winning-post.

zielbewußt ['tsiːlbəvust], *adj.* purposeful; systematic.

zielen ['tsiːlən], *v.n.* aim (at), take aim (at).

Ziellosigkeit ['tsiːllo:zɪçkaɪt], *f.* (—, *no pl.*) aimlessness.

Zielscheibe ['tsiːlʃaɪbə], *f.* (—, *pl.* —en) target, butt.

ziemen ['tsiːmən], *v.r. sich* —, become s.o., behove s.o., be proper for, befit.

Ziemer ['tsiːmər], *n. & m.* (—s, *pl.* —) whip.

ziemlich ['tsiːmlɪç], *adj.* moderate, tolerable, middling, fairly considerable, fair. — *adv.* rather, fairly.

Zier [tsiːr], *f.* (—, *pl.* —den) ornament.

Zieraffe ['tsiːrafə], *m.* (—n, *pl.* —n) fop, affected person.

Zierat ['tsiːraːt], *m.* (—s, *no pl.*) ornament, finery.

Zierde ['tsiːrdə], *f.* (—, *pl.* —n) decoration, embellishment; (*fig.*) credit, pride.

Ziererei [tsiːrəˈraɪ], *f.* (—, *pl.* —en) affectation.

Ziergarten ['tsiːrgartən], *m.* (—s, *pl.* ˙) flower-garden, ornamental garden.

zierlich ['tsiːrlɪç], *adj.* dainty, graceful, pretty.

Zierpflanze ['tsiːrpflantsə], *f.* (—, *pl.* —n) ornamental plant.

Zierpuppe ['tsiːrpupə], *f.* (—, *pl.* —n) overdressed woman.

Ziffer ['tsɪfər], *f.* (—, *pl.* —n) figure, numeral.

Zifferblatt ['tsɪfərblat], *n.* (—s, *pl.* ˙er) dial, face.

ziffernmäßig ['tsɪfərnmɛːsɪç], *adj.* statistical.

Ziffernschrift ['tsɪfərnʃrɪft], *f.* (—, *pl.* —en) code.

Zigarette [tsigaˈrɛtə], *f.* (—, *pl.* —n) cigarette.

Zigarettenetui [tsigaˈrɛtənɛtvi:], *n.* (—s, *pl.* —s) cigarette-case.

Zigarettenspitze [tsigaˈrɛtənʃpitsə], *f.* (—, *pl.* —n) cigarette-holder.

Zigarettenstummel [tsigaˈrɛtənʃtuməl], *m.* (—s, *pl.* —) cigarette-end.

Zigarre [tsiˈgarə], *f.* (—, *pl.* —n) cigar.

Zigarrenkiste [tsiˈgarənkɪstə], *f.* (—, *pl.* —n) cigar-box.

Zigarrenstummel [tsiˈgarənʃtuməl], *m.* (—s, *pl.* —) cigar-end.

Zigeuner [tsiˈgɔynər], *m.* (—s, *pl.* —) gipsy.

Zikade [tsiˈkaːdə], *f.* (—, *pl.* —n) (*Ent.*) grasshopper.

Zimmer ['tsɪmər], *n.* (—s, *pl.* —) room.

Zimmermädchen ['tsɪmərmɛːtçən], *n.* (—s, *pl.* —) chambermaid.

Zimmermann ['tsɪmərman], *m.* (—s, *pl.* **Zimmerleute**) carpenter, joiner.

zimmern ['tsɪmərn], *v.a.* carpenter, construct, build.

Zimmernachweis ['tsɪmərnaːxvaɪs], *m.* (—es, *pl.* —e) accommodation bureau.

Zimmerreihe ['tsɪmərraɪə], *f.* (—, *pl.* —n) suite of rooms.

Zimmervermieter ['tsɪmərfɛrmiːtər], *m.* (—s, *pl.* —) landlord.

zimperlich ['tsɪmpərlɪç], *adj.* simpering; prim; finicky, hypersensitive.

Zimt [tsɪmt], *m.* (—(e)s, *no pl.*) cinnamon.

Zink [tsɪŋk], *n.* (—s, *no pl.*) zinc.

Zinke ['tsɪŋkə], *f.* (—, *pl.* —n) prong, tine.

Zinn [tsɪn], *n.* (—s, *no pl.*) tin; pewter.

Zinnblech ['tsɪnblɛç], *n.* (—s, *no pl.*) tin-plate.

Zinne ['tsɪnə], *f.* (—, *pl.* —n) battlement, pinnacle.

zinnern [ˈtsɪnern], *adj.* made of pewter, of tin.

Zinnober [tsɪnˈoːbər], *m.* (—s, *no pl.*) cinnabar; (*coll.*) fuss.

Zinnsäure [ˈtsɪnzɔyrə], *f.* (—, *no pl.*) stannic acid.

Zins [tsɪns], *m.* (—es, *pl.* —en) duty, tax; rent; (*pl.*) interest.

zinsbar [ˈtsɪnsbaːr], *adj.* tributary; — *anlegen,* invest at interest; — *machen,* force to pay a tribute.

Zinsen [ˈtsɪnzən], *m. pl.* interest.

zinsentragend [ˈtsɪnzəntraːgənt], *adj.* interest-bearing.

Zinseszins [ˈtsɪnzəstsɪns], *m.* (—, *no pl.*) compound interest.

Zinsfuß [ˈtsɪnsfuːs], *m.* (—es, *pl.* ˙e) rate of interest.

zinspflichtig [ˈtsɪnspflɪçtɪç], *adj.* subject to tax.

Zinsrechnung [ˈtsɪnsrεçnuŋ], *f.* (—, *pl.* —en) interest account, calculation of interest.

Zinsschein [ˈtsɪnsʃaɪn], *m.* (—s, *pl.* —e) coupon, dividend warrant.

Zipfel [ˈtsɪpfəl], *m.* (—s, *pl.* —) tassel, edge, point, tip.

Zipperlein [ˈtsɪpərlaɪn], *n.* (—s, *no pl.*) (*coll.*) gout.

zirka [ˈtsɪrka], *adv.* circa, about, approximately.

Zirkel [ˈtsɪrkəl], *m.* (—s, *pl.* —) circle; (*Maths.*) pair of compasses; gathering.

zirkulieren [tsɪrkuˈliːrən], *v.n.* circulate; — *lassen,* put in circulation.

Zirkus [ˈtsɪrkus], *m.* (—, *pl.* —se) circus.

zirpen [ˈtsɪrpən], *v.n.* chirp.

zischeln [ˈtsɪʃəln], *v.n.* whisper.

zischen [ˈtsɪʃən], *v.n.* hiss; sizzle.

Zischlaut [ˈtsɪʃlaut], *m.* (—s, *pl.* —e) (*Phon.*) sibilant.

Zisterne [tsɪsˈtεrnə], *f.* (—, *pl.* —n) cistern.

Zisterzienser [tsɪstεrˈtsjεnzər], *m.* (—s, *pl.* —) Cistercian (monk).

Zitadelle [tsɪtaˈdεla], *f.* (—, *pl.* —n) citadel.

Zitat [tsiˈtaːt], *n.* (—(e)s, *pl.* —e) quotation, reference; *falsches* —, misquotation.

Zither [ˈtsɪtər], *f.* (—, *pl.* —n) zither.

zitieren [tsiˈtiːrən], *v.a.* cite, quote; *falsch* —, misquote.

Zitronat [tsitroˈnaːt], *n.* (—s, *no pl.*) candied lemon peel.

Zitrone [tsiˈtroːnə], *f.* (—, *pl.* —n) lemon.

Zitronenlimonade [tsiˈtroːnənlimonaːdə], *f.* (—, *pl.* —n) lemonade, lemon drink.

Zitronensaft [tsiˈtroːnənzaft], *m.* (—s, *pl.* ˙e) lemon-juice.

Zitronensäure [tsiˈtroːnənzɔyrə], *f.* (—, *no pl.*) citric acid.

Zitronenschale [tsiˈtroːnənʃaːlə], *f.* (—, *pl.* —n) lemon-peel.

zitterig [ˈtsɪtərɪç], *adj.* shaky, shivery.

zittern [ˈtsɪtərn], *v.n.* tremble, shiver, quake.

Zitterpappel [ˈtsɪtərpapəl], *f.* (—, *pl.* —n) (*Bot.*) aspen-tree.

Zivil [tsiˈviːl], *n.* (—s, *no pl.*) civilians, *in* —, in plain clothes; (*coll.*) in civvies *or* mufti.

Zivilbeamte [tsiˈviːlbəamtə], *m.* (—n, *pl.* —n) civil servant.

Zivildienst [tsiˈviːldiːnst], *m.* (—es, *no pl.*) civil service.

Zivilehe [tsiˈviːleːə], *f.* (—, *pl.* —n) civil marriage.

Zivilgesetzbuch [tsiˈviːlgəzεtsbuːx], *n.* (—s, *pl.* ˙er) code of civil law.

Zivilingenieur [tsiˈviːlɪnʒenjøːr], *m.* (—s, *pl.* —e) civil engineer.

Zivilisation [tsivilizaˈtsjoːn], *f.* (—, *pl.* —en) civilisation.

zivilisatorisch [tsivilizaˈtoːrɪʃ], *adj.* civilising.

zivilisieren [tsiviliˈziːrən], *v.a.* civilise.

Zivilist [tsiviˈlɪst], *m.* (—en, *pl.* —en) civilian.

Zivilkleidung [tsiˈviːlklaɪduŋ], *f.* (—, *no pl.*) civilian dress, plain clothes.

Zobel [ˈtsoːbəl], *m.* (—s, *pl.* —) sable.

Zobelpelz [ˈtsoːbəlpεlts], *m.* (—es, *pl.* —e) sable fur; sable-coat.

Zofe [ˈtsoːfə], *f.* (—, *pl.* —n) lady's maid.

zögern [ˈtsøːgərn], *v.n.* hesitate, tarry, delay.

Zögerung [ˈtsøːgəruŋ], *f.* (—, *pl.* —en) hesitation, delay.

Zögling [ˈtsøːklɪŋ], *m.* (—s, *pl.* —e) pupil, charge.

Zölibat [tsøːliˈbaːt], *m. & n.* (—s, *no pl.*) celibacy.

Zoll (1) [tsɔl], *m.* (—s, *no pl.*) inch.

Zoll (2) [tsɔl], *m.* (—s, *pl.* ˙e) customs duty; (*bridge*) toll.

Zollabfertigung [ˈtsɔlapfεrtɪguŋ], *f.* (—, *no pl.*) customs clearance.

Zollamt [ˈtsɔlamt], *n.* (—s, *pl.* ˙er) custom house.

Zollaufschlag [ˈtsɔlaufʃlaːk], *m.* (—s, *pl.* ˙e) additional duty.

Zollbeamte [ˈtsɔlbəamtə], *m.* (—n, *pl.* —n) customs officer.

zollbreit [ˈtsɔlbraɪt], *adj.* one inch wide.

zollen [ˈtsɔlən], *v.a. Ehrfurcht* —, pay o.'s respects; *Beifall* —, applaud; *Dank* —, show gratitude.

zollfrei [ˈtsɔlfraɪ], *adj.* duty-free, exempt from duty.

Zöllner [ˈtsœlnər], *m.* (—s, *pl.* —) tax-gatherer.

zollpflichtig [ˈtsɔlpflɪçtɪç], *adj.* liable to duty, dutiable.

Zollsatz [ˈtsɔlzats], *m.* (—es, *pl.* ˙e) customs tariff.

Zollverein [ˈtsɔlfəraɪn], *m.* (—s, *no pl.*) customs union.

Zollverschluß [ˈtsɔlfεrʃlus], *m.* (—sses, *pl.* ˙sse) bond.

Zone [ˈtsoːnə], *f.* (—, *pl.* —n) zone.

Zoologe [tsoːˈoːloːgə], *m.* (—n, *pl.* —n) zoologist.

Zoologie [tsoːoloˈgiː], *f.* (—, *no pl.*) zoology.

zoologisch [tso:oˈlo:gɪʃ], *adj.* zoological; *—er Garten*, zoological gardens, zoo.

Zopf [tsɔpf], *m.* (—(e)s, *pl.* ˙e) plait, pigtail; (*coll.*) (old-fashioned) pedantry.

Zorn [tsɔrn], *m.* (—(e)s, *no pl.*) wrath, anger, indignation; *seinen — auslassen*, vent o.'s anger; *in — geraten*, get angry.

zornglühend [ˈtsɔrngly:ənt], *adj.* boiling with rage.

zornig [ˈtsɔrnɪç], *adj.* angry, wrathful, irate; *— werden*, get angry.

Zote [ˈtso:tə], *f.* (—, *pl.* —n) smutty story, ribaldry, bawdiness.

zotig [ˈtso:tɪç], *adj.* loose, ribald, smutty.

zottig [ˈtsɔtɪç], *adj.* shaggy.

zu [tsu:], *prep.* (*Dat.*) to, towards; in addition to; at, in, on; for; *— Anfang*. in the beginning; *— Fuß*, on foot; *— Hause*, at home; *— Wasser*, at sea, by sea; *— deinem Nutzen*, for your benefit. *— adv. & prefix*, to, towards; closed; too; *— sehr*, too; *— viel*, too much.

Zubehör [ˈtsu:bəhø:r], *n.* (—s, *no pl.*) accessory, appurtenance.

zubekommen [ˈtsu:bəkɔmən], *v.a. irr.* get in addition.

Zuber [ˈtsu:bər], *m.* (—s, *pl.* —) tub.

zubereiten [ˈtsu:bəraitən], *v.a.* prepare.

Zubereitung [ˈtsu:bəraituŋ], *f.* (—, *no pl.*) preparation.

zubilligen [ˈtsu:bɪlɪgən], *v.a.* allow, grant.

zubleiben [ˈtsu:blaibən], *v.n. irr.* (*aux.* sein) remain shut.

zubringen [ˈtsu:brɪŋən], *v.a. irr. die Zeit —*, spend the time.

Zubringerdienst [ˈtsu:brɪnərdi:nst], *m.* (—es, *pl.* —) shuttle-service, tender-service.

Zubuße [ˈtsu:bu:sə], *f.* (—, *pl.* —n) (additional) contribution.

Zucht [tsuxt], *f.* (—, *no pl.*) race, breed; discipline; breeding, rearing; education, discipline; (good) manners; *in — halten*, keep in hand.

züchten [ˈtsyçtən], *v.a.* cultivate; rear, breed; grow.

Züchter [ˈtsyçtər], *m.* (—s, *pl.* —) (*plants*) nurseryman; (*animals*) breeder.

Zuchthaus [ˈtsuxthaus], *n.* (—es, *pl.* ˙er) penitentiary, convict prison.

Zuchthäusler [ˈtsuxthɔyslər], *m.* (—s, *pl.* —) convict.

Zuchthengst [ˈtsuxthɛŋst], *m.* (—es, *pl.* —e) stallion.

züchtig [ˈtsyçtɪç], *adj.* modest, chaste.

züchtigen [ˈtsyçtɪgən], *v.a.* chastise, lash.

Züchtigkeit [ˈtsyçtɪçkait], *f.* (—, *no pl.*) modesty, chastity.

Züchtigung [ˈtsyçtɪguŋ], *f.* (—, *pl.* —en) chastisement; *körperliche —*, corporal punishment.

Zuchtlosigkeit [ˈtsuxtlo:zɪçkait], *f.* (—, *no pl.*) want of discipline.

Zuchtmeister [ˈtsuxtmaistər], *m.* (—s, *pl.* —) disciplinarian, taskmaster.

Zuchtochse [ˈtsuxtɔksə], *m.* (—n, *pl.* —n) bull.

Zuchtstute [ˈtsuxtʃtu:tə], *f.* (—, *pl.* —n) brood-mare.

Züchtung [ˈtsyçtuŋ], *f.* (—, *pl.* —en) (*plants*) cultivation; (*animals*) rearing, breeding.

Zuchtvieh [ˈtsuxtfi:], *n.* (—s, *no pl.*) breeding stock.

Zuchtwahl [ˈtsuxtva:l], *f.* (—, *no pl.*) (*breeding*) selection.

zucken [ˈtsukən], *v.n.* quiver, twitch; wince; start, jerk.

Zucken [ˈtsukən], *n.* (—s, *no pl.*) palpitation, convulsion, twitch, tic.

Zucker [ˈtsukər], *m.* (—s, *no pl.*) sugar.

Zuckerbäcker [ˈtsukərbɛkər], *m.* (—s, *pl.* —) confectioner.

Zuckerguß [ˈtsukərgus], *m.* (—es, *no pl.*) (sugar-)icing.

Zuckerkandis [ˈtsukərkandɪs], *m.* (—, *no pl.*) sugar-candy.

zuckerkrank [ˈtsukərkraŋk], *adj.* (*Med.*) diabetic.

Zuckerkrankheit [ˈtsukərkraŋkhait], *f.* (—, *no pl.*) (*Med.*) diabetes.

zuckern [ˈtsukərn], *v.a.* sugar.

Zuckerpflanzung [ˈtsukərpflantsuŋ], *f.* (—, *pl.* —en) sugar-plantation.

Zuckerraffinerie [ˈtsukərrafinəri:], *f.* (—, *pl.* —n) sugar-refinery.

Zuckerrohr [ˈtsukərro:r], *n.* (—s, *no pl.*) sugar-cane.

Zuckerrübe [ˈtsukərry:bə], *f.* (—, *pl.* —n) sugar-beet.

Zuckerwerk [ˈtsukərvɛrk], *n.* (—s, *no pl.*) confectionery.

Zuckerzange [ˈtsukərtsaŋə], *f.* (—, *pl.* —n) sugar-tongs.

Zuckung [ˈtsukuŋ], *f.* (—, *pl.* —en) convulsion, spasm.

zudecken [ˈtsu:dɛkən], *v.a.* cover up.

zudem [tsuˈde:m], *adv.* besides, moreover.

Zudrang [ˈtsu:draŋ], *m.* (—s, *no pl.*) crowd(ing); rush (on), run (on).

zudrehen [ˈtsu:dre:ən], *v.a.* turn off.

zudringlich [ˈtsu:drɪŋlɪç], *adj.* importunate; intruding.

zudrücken [ˈtsu:drykən], *v.a.* close (by pressing), shut.

zueignen [ˈtsu:aignən], *v.a.* dedicate.

zuerkennen [ˈtsu:ɛrkɛnən], *v.a. irr.* award, adjudicate.

zuerst [tsuˈe:rst], *adv.* at first, first, in the first instance.

Zufahrt [ˈtsu:fa:rt], *f.* (—, *no pl.*) approach, drive.

Zufall [ˈtsu:fal], *m.* (—s, *pl.* ˙e) chance, coincidence; *durch —*, by chance.

zufallen [ˈtsu:falən], *v.n. irr.* (*aux.* sein) close, fall shut; *einem —*, devolve upon s.o., fall to s.o.'s lot.

zufällig [ˈtsu:fɛlɪç], *adj.* accidental, casual, fortuitous. *— adv.* by chance.

Zuflucht [ˈtsu:fluxt], *f.* (—, *no pl.*) refuge, shelter, haven, recourse.

293

Zufluchtsort

Zufluchtsort ['tsu:fluxtsɔrt], *m.* (—(e)s, *pl.* —e) asylum, shelter, place of refuge.

Zufluß ['tsu:flus], *m.* (—sses, *pl.* ⸚sse) supply; influx.

zuflüstern ['tsu:flystərn], *v.a. einem etwas* —, whisper s.th. to s.o.

zufolge [tsu'fɔlgə], *prep.* (*Genit.*, *Dat.*) in consequence of, owing to, due to, on account of.

zufrieden [tsu'fri:dən], *adj.* content, contented, satisfied; — *lassen*, leave alone.

zufriedenstellen [tsu'fri:dənʃtelən], *v.a.* satisfy.

zufügen ['tsu:fy:gən], *v.a.* add (to); inflict.

Zufuhr ['tsu:fu:r], *f.* (—, *pl.* —en) (*goods*) supplies.

Zug [tsu:k], *m.* (—(e)s, *pl.* ⸚e) drawing, pull, tug; draught; march, procession; (*Railw.*) train; (*face*) feature; (*chess*) move; (*character*) trait; (*pen*) stroke; (*birds*) flight; migration; (*mountains*) range.

Zugabe ['tsu:ga:bə], *f.* (—, *pl.* —n) addition, make-weight, extra; (*concert*) encore; *als* —, into the bargain.

Zugang ['tsu:gaŋ], *m.* (—s, *pl.* ⸚e) approach, entry, entrance, admittance, access.

zugänglich ['tsu:geŋlıç], *adj.* accessible, available; (*person*) affable.

Zugbrücke ['tsu:kbrykə], *f.* (—, *pl.* —n) drawbridge.

zugeben ['tsu:ge:bən], *v.a. irr.* give in addition; concede, admit.

zugegen [tsu'ge:gən], *adv.* present.

zugehen ['tsu:ge:ən], *v.n. irr.* (*aux. sein*) (*door*) shut (of itself), close; happen; *auf einen* —, walk towards s.o.; *so geht es im Leben zu*, such is life; *das geht mit nicht mit rechten Dingen zu*, there is something uncanny about it.

zugehörig ['tsu:gəhø:rıç], *adj.* belonging, appertaining.

zugeknöpft ['tsu:gəknœpft], *adj.* reserved, taciturn.

Zügel ['tsy:gəl], *m.* (—s, *pl.* —) rein, bridle.

zügeln ['tsy:gəln], *v.a.* bridle, curb, check.

zugesellen ['tsu:gəzelən], *v.r. sich* —, associate with, join.

Zugeständnis ['tsu:gəʃtentnıs], *n.* (—sses, *pl.* —sse) admission; concession.

zugestehen ['tsu:gəʃte:ən], *v.a. irr.* admit; concede; *einem etwas* —, allow s.o. s.th.

zugetan ['tsu:gəta:n], *adj.* attached, devoted.

Zugführer ['tsu:kfy:rər], *m.* (—s, *pl.* —) (*Railw.*) guard; (*Mil.*) platoon commander.

zugießen ['tsu:gi:sən], *v.a. irr.* fill up, pour on.

zugig ['tsu:gıç], *adj.* windy, draughty.

Zugkraft ['tsu:kkraft], *f.* (—, *no pl.*) tractive power, magnetic attraction;

(*fig.*) pull, attraction; publicity value.

zugleich [tsu'glaıç], *adv.* at the same time; — *mit*, together with.

Zugluft ['tsu:kluft], *f.* (—, *no pl.*) draught (of air).

zugreifen ['tsu:graıfən], *v.n. irr.* grab; lend a hand; (*at table*) help o.s.

Zugrolle ['tsu:krɔlə], *f.* (—, *pl.* —n) pulley.

zugrunde [tsu'grundə], *adv.* — *gehen*, perish, go to ruin, go to the dogs; — *legen*, base upon.

Zugstück ['tsu:kʃtyk], *n.* (—s, *pl.* —e) (*Theat.*) popular show; (*coll.*) success, hit.

zugucken ['tsu:gukən], *v.n.* look on, watch.

zugunsten [tsu'gunstən], *prep.* (*Genit.*) for the benefit of.

zugute [tsu'gu:tə], *adv.* — *halten*, make allowances.

Zugvogel ['tsu:kfo:gəl], *m.* (—s, *pl.* ⸚) bird of passage.

zuhalten ['tsu:haltən], *v.a. irr.* keep closed.

Zuhälter ['tsu:heltər], *m.* (—s, *pl.* —) souteneur; pimp.

Zuhilfenahme [tsu'hılfəna:mə], *f.* (—, *no pl.*) *unter* —, with the help of, by means of.

zuhören ['tsu:hø:rən], *v.n.* listen to, attend to.

Zuhörerschaft ['tsu:hø:rərʃaft], *f.* (—, *pl.* —en) audience.

zujubeln ['tsu:ju:bəln], *v.n. einem* —, acclaim s.o., cheer s.o.

zukehren ['tsu:ke:rən], *v.a. einem den Rücken* —, turn o.'s back on s.o.

zuknöpfen ['tsu:knœpfən], *v.a.* button (up).

zukommen ['tsu:kɔmən], *v.n. irr.* (*aux. sein*) *auf einen* —, advance towards s.o.; *einem* —, be due to s.o.; become s.o.; reach s.o.

Zukost ['tsu:kɔst], *f.* (—, *no pl.*) (*food*) trimmings, extras.

Zukunft ['tsu:kunft], *f.* (—, *no pl.*) future; prospects.

zukünftig ['tsu:kynftıç], *adj.* future, prospective.

Zukunftsmusik ['tsu:kunftsmuzi:k], *f.* (—, *no pl.*) daydreams, pipe-dreams.

zulächeln ['tsu:leçəln], *v.a. einem* —, smile at s.o.

Zulage ['tsu:la:gə], *f.* (—, *pl.* —n) addition; increase of salary, rise; (*Am.*) raise.

zulangen ['tsu:laŋən], *v.n.* be sufficient; (*at table*) help o.s.

zulänglich ['tsu:leŋlıç], *adj.* sufficient, adequate.

zulassen ['tsu:lasən], *v.a. irr.* leave unopened; allow; admit; permit.

zulässig ['tsu:lesıç], *adj.* admissible; *das ist nicht* —, that is not allowed.

Zulassung ['tsu:lasuŋ], *f.* (—, *pl.* —en) admission.

Zulauf ['tsu:lauf], *m.* (—s, *no pl.*) run (of customers); crowd, throng.

294

zulaufen ['tsu:laufən], v.n. irr. (aux. sein) auf einen —, run towards s.o.; spitz —, taper, come to a point.

zulegen ['tsu:le:gən], v.a. add; increase; sich etwas —, make o.s. a present of s.th.; get s.th.

zuletzt [tsu'lɛtst], adv. last, at last, lastly, finally, eventually, in the end.

zuliebe [tsu'li:bə], adv. einem etwas — tun, oblige s.o.; do s.th. for s.o.'s sake.

zum = zu dem.

zumachen ['tsu:maxən], v.a. shut, close.

zumal [tsu'ma:l], adv. especially, particularly. — conj. especially since.

zumeist [tsu'maɪst], adv. mostly, for the most part.

zumute [tsu'mu:tə], adv. mir ist nicht gut —, I don't feel well.

zumuten ['tsu:mu:tən], v.a. einem etwas —, expect or demand s.th. of s.o.

Zumutung ['tsu:mu:tuŋ], f. (—, pl. —en) unreasonable demand.

zunächst [tsu'nɛ:çst], adv. first, above all.

Zunahme ['tsu:na:mə], f. (—, pl. —n) increase.

Zuname ['tsu:na:mə], m. (—ns, pl. —n) surname, family name.

zünden ['tsyndən], v.n. catch fire, ignite.

Zunder ['tsundər], m. (—s, no pl.) tinder.

Zünder ['tsyndər], m. (—s, pl. —) lighter, detonator, fuse.

Zündholz ['tsynthɔlts], n. (—es, pl. ̈er) match.

Zündkerze ['tsyntkertsə], f. (—, pl. —n) (Motor.) sparking-plug.

Zündstoff ['tsyntʃtɔf], m. (—s, pl. —e) fuel.

Zündung ['tsynduŋ], f. (—, pl. —en) ignition; detonation.

zunehmen ['tsu:ne:mən], v.n. irr. increase, put on weight; (moon) wax.

zuneigen ['tsu:naɪgən], v.r. sich —, incline towards.

Zuneigung ['tsu:naɪguŋ], f. (—, pl. —en) affection, inclination.

Zunft [tsunft], f. (—, pl. ̈e) company, guild, corporation; (fig.) brotherhood.

Zunftgenosse ['tsunftgənɔsə], m. (—n, pl. —n) member of a guild.

zünftig ['tsynftiç], adj. professional; proper.

zunftmäßig ['tsunftmɛ:sɪç], adj. professional; competent.

Zunge ['tsuŋə], f. (—, pl. —n) tongue; (buckle) catch; (fig.) language; (fish) sole.

züngeln ['tsyŋəln], v.n. (flame) shoot out, lick.

Zungenband ['tsuŋənbant], n. (—s, pl. ̈er) ligament of the tongue.

zungenfertig ['tsuŋənfɛrtɪç], adj. voluble, glib.

Zungenlaut ['tsuŋənlaut], m. (—s, pl. —e) (Phon.) lingual sound.

Zungenspitze ['tsuŋənʃpɪtsə], f. (—, pl. —n) tip of the tongue.

zunichte [tsu'nɪçtə], adv. — machen, ruin, undo, destroy; — werden, come to nothing.

zupfen ['tsupfən], v.a. pick, pluck.

zurechnungsfähig ['tsu:rɛçnuŋsfɛ:ɪç], adj. accountable, of sane mind, compos mentis.

zurecht [tsu'rɛçt], adv. aright, right(ly), in order.

zurechtfinden [tsu'rɛçtfɪndən], v.r. irr. sich —, find o.'s way about.

zurechtkommen [tsu'rɛçtkɔmən], v.n. irr. (aux. sein) arrive in (good) time; mit einem gut —, get on well with s.o.

zurechtlegen [tsu'rɛçtle:gən], v.a. put in order, get ready.

zurechtmachen [tsu'rɛçtmaxən], v.a. get s.th. ready, prepare s.th. — v.r. sich—, prepare o.s.; (women) make up; (coll.) put on o.'s face.

zurechtweisen [tsu'rɛçtvaɪzən], v.a. irr. reprove (s.o.), set (s.o.) right; direct.

Zurechtweisung [tsu'rɛçtvaɪzuŋ], f. (—, pl. —en) reprimand.

zureden ['tsu:re:dən], n. (—s, no pl.) encouragement; entreaties.

zureden ['tsu:re:dən], v.n. encourage (s.o.), persuade (s.o.).

zureichen ['tsu:raɪçən], v.a. reach, hand. — v.n. be sufficient, be enough, suffice.

zurichten ['tsu:rɪçtən], v.a. etwas (einen) übel —, maltreat s.th. (s.o.).

zürnen ['tsyrnən], v.n. be angry (with).

zurück [tsu'ryk], adv. back; behind; backwards; — excl. stand back!

zurückbegeben [tsu'rykbəge:bən], v.r. irr. sich —, go back, return.

zurückbehalten [tsu'rykbəhaltən], v.a. irr. retain, keep back.

zurückbekommen [tsu'rykbəkɔmən], v.a. irr. get back, recover (s.th.).

zurückberufen [tsu'rykbəru:fən], v.a. irr. recall.

zurückfordern [tsu'rykfɔrdərn], v.a. demand back, demand the return of.

zurückführen [tsu'rykfy:rən], v.a. lead back; auf etwas —, attribute to; trace back to.

zurückgeblieben [tsu'rykgəbli:bən], adj. retarded, mentally deficient, backward.

zurückgezogen [tsu'rykgətso:gən], adj. secluded, retired.

zurückhalten [tsu'rykhaltən], v.a. irr. keep back, retain.

zurückhaltend [tsu'rykhaltənt], adj. reserved.

zurückkehren [tsu'rykke:rən], v.n. (aux. sein) return.

zurückkommen [tsu'rykkɔmən], v.n. irr. (aux. sein) come back.

zurücklassen [tsu'ryklasən], v.a. irr. leave behind, abandon.

zurücklegen [tsu'ryklɛ:gǝn], *v.a.* lay aside, put by; *eine Strecke* —, cover a distance. — *v.r. sich* —, lean back; *zurückgelegter Gewinn*, undistributed profits.

zurückmüssen [tsu'rykmysǝn], *v.n. irr.* be obliged to return.

zurücknehmen [tsu'rykne:mǝn], *v.a. irr.* take back.

zurückschrecken [tsu'rykʃrɛkǝn], *v.a.* frighten away. — *v.n. irr.* (*aux.* sein) recoil (from).

zurücksehnen [tsu'rykze:nǝn], *v.r. sich* —, long to return, wish o.s. back.

zurücksetzen [tsu'rykzɛtsǝn], *v.a.* put back; slight; discriminate against; neglect.

Zurücksetzung [tsu'rykzɛtsuŋ], *f.* (—, *pl.* —en) slight, rebuff.

zurückstrahlen [tsu'rykʃtra:lǝn], *v.a.* reflect.

zurücktreten [tsu'ryktre:tǝn], *v.n. irr.* (*aux.* sein) stand back, withdraw; resign.

zurückverlangen [tsu'rykfɛrlaŋǝn], *v.a.* demand back, request the return of.

zurückversetzen [tsu'rykfɛrzɛtsǝn], *v.a.* (*Sch.*) put in a lower form. — *v.r. sich* —, turn o.'s thoughts back (to), hark back.

zurückweichen [tsu'rykvaɪçǝn], *v.n. irr.* (*aux.* sein) withdraw, retreat.

zurückweisen [tsu'rykvaɪzǝn], *v.a. irr.* refuse, reject, repulse.

zurückwollen [tsu'rykvɔlǝn], *v.n.* wish to return.

zurückziehen [tsu'ryktsi:ǝn], *v.a. irr.* draw back; (*fig.*) withdraw, retract, countermand. — *v.r. sich* —, retire, withdraw.

Zuruf ['tsu:ru:f], *m.* (—s, *pl.* —e) call, acclaim, acclamation.

Zusage ['tsu:za:gǝ], *f.* (—, *pl.* —n) promise; acceptance.

zusagen ['tsu:za:gǝn], *v.a.* promise; *es sagt mir zu*, I like it. — *v.n.* accept.

zusagend ['tsu:za:gǝnt], *adj.* affirmative; agreeable.

zusammen [tsu'zamǝn], *adv.* together, jointly.

zusammenbeißen [tsu'zamǝnbaɪsǝn], *v.a. irr. die Zähne* —, set o.'s teeth.

zusammenbetteln [tsu'zamǝnbɛtǝln], *v.a. sich etwas* —, collect (by begging).

zusammenbrechen [tsu'zamǝnbrɛçǝn], *v.n. irr.* (*aux.* sein) break down, collapse.

Zusammenbruch [tsu'zamǝnbrux], *m.* (—s, *pl.* ⸚e) breakdown, collapse, débâcle.

zusammendrängen [tsu'zamǝndrɛŋǝn], *v.a.* press together; (*fig.*) abridge, condense.

zusammendrücken [tsu'zamǝndrykǝn], *v.a.* compress.

zusammenfahren [tsu'zamǝnfa:rǝn], *v.n. irr.* (*aux.* sein) collide; give a start.

zusammenfallen [tsu'zamǝnfalǝn], *v.n. irr.* (*aux.* sein) collapse.

zusammenfassen [tsu'zamǝnfasǝn], *v.a.* sum up, summarize.

Zusammenfassung [tsu'zamǝnfasuŋ], *f.* (—, *no pl.*) summing-up, summary.

zusammenfinden [tsu'zamǝnfindǝn], *v.r. irr. sich* —, discover a mutual affinity, come together.

Zusammenfluß [tsu'zamǝnflus], *m.* (—sses, *pl.* ⸚sse) confluence.

zusammengeben [tsu'zamǝnge:bǝn], *v.a. irr.* join in marriage.

Zusammengehörigkeit [tsu'zamǝngǝhø:rɪçkaɪt], *f.* (—, *no pl.*) solidarity; (*Am.*) togetherness.

zusammengesetzt [tsu'zamǝngǝzɛtst], *adj.* composed (of), consisting (of); complicated; (*Maths.*) composite.

zusammengewürfelt [tsu'zamǝngǝvyrfǝlt], *adj.* motley, mixed.

Zusammenhalt [tsu'zamǝnhalt], *m.* (—s, *no pl.*) holding together; unity.

Zusammenhang [tsu'zamǝnhaŋ], *m.* (—s, *pl.* ⸚e) coherence; connection, context.

zusammenhängen [tsu'zamǝnhɛŋǝn], *v.n. irr.* hang together, cohere; (*fig.*) be connected (with).

Zusammenklang [tsu'zamǝnklaŋ], *m.* (—s, *pl.* ⸚e) unison, harmony.

Zusammenkunft [tsu'zamǝnkunft], *f.* (—, *pl.* ⸚e) meeting, convention, conference; reunion.

zusammenlaufen [tsu'zamǝnlaufǝn], *v.n. irr.* (*aux.* sein) crowd together, converge; flock together; (*milk*) curdle; (*material*) shrink.

zusammenlegen [tsu'zamǝnle:gǝn], *v.a.* put together; (*money*) collect; (*letter*) fold up.

zusammennehmen [tsu'zamǝnne:mǝn], *v.a. irr.* gather up. — *v.r. sich* —, get a firm grip on o.s., pull o.s. together.

zusammenpassen [tsu'zamǝnpasǝn], *v.n.* fit together, match; agree; be compatible.

zusammenpferchen [tsu'zamǝnpfɛrçǝn], *v.a.* pen up, crowd together in a small space.

zusammenpressen [tsu'zamǝnprɛsǝn], *v.a.* squeeze together.

zusammenraffen [tsu'zamǝnrafǝn], *v.a.* gather up hurriedly, collect. — *v.r. sich* —, pluck up courage; pull o.s. together.

zusammenrechnen [tsu'zamǝnrɛçnǝn], *v.a.* add up.

zusammenreimen [tsu'zamǝnraɪmǝn], *v.a. sich etwas* —, figure s.th. out.

zusammenrücken [tsu'zamǝnrykǝn], *v.a.* move together, draw closer. — *v.n.* move closer together, move up.

zusammenschießen [tsu'zamǝnʃi:sǝn], *v.a. irr.* shoot to pieces, shoot down; *Geld* —, club together, raise a subscription.

zusammenschlagen [tsu'zamǝnʃla:gǝn], *v.a. irr.* beat up; strike together; clap, fold.

Zustimmung

zusammenschließen [tsu'zamənʃli:-sən], *v.r. irr. sich* —, join, unite, ally o.s. (with).

zusammenschweißen [tsu'zamənʃvaɪ-sən], *v.a.* weld together.

Zusammensein [tsu'zamənzaɪn], *n.* (**—s**, *no pl.*) meeting, social gathering.

Zusammensetzung [tsu'zamənzɛtsuŋ], *f.* (**—**, *no pl.*) construction; composition.

Zusammenspiel [tsu'zamənʃpiːl], *n.* (**—s**, *no pl.*) (*Theat., Mus.*) ensemble.

zusammenstellen [tsu'zamənʃtɛlən], *v.a.* compose, concoct; put together, compile.

Zusammenstellung [tsu'zamənʃtɛluŋ], *f.* (**—**, *pl.* **—en**) combination, compilation; juxtaposition.

zusammenstoppeln [tsu'zamənʃtɔp-əln], *v.a.* string together, patch up.

Zusammenstoß [tsu'zamənʃtoːs], *m.* (**—es**, *pl.* **—e**) clash, conflict; collision.

zusammenstoßen [tsu'zamənʃtoːsən], *v.n. irr.* (*aux.* sein) clash; crash, come into collision, collide.

zusammentragen [tsu'zaməntraːgən], *v.a. irr.* collect, compile.

zusammentreffen [tsu'zaməntrɛfən], *v.n. irr.* meet; coincide.

zusammentreten [tsu'zaməntreːtən], *v.n. irr.* (*aux.* sein) meet.

zusammentun [tsu'zaməntuːn], *v.r. irr. sich* — *mit*, associate with, join.

zusammenwirken [tsu'zamənvɪrkən], *v.n.* cooperate, collaborate.

zusammenwürfeln [tsu'zamənvyr-fəln], *v.a.* jumble up.

zusammenzählen [tsu'zaməntsɛːlən], *v.a.* add up.

zusammenziehen [tsu'zaməntsiːən], *v.n. irr.* (*aux.* sein) move in together. — *v.a.* draw together, contract. — *v.r. sich* —, shrink; (*storm*) gather; *Zahlen* —, add up.

Zusammenziehung [tsu'zaməntsiːuŋ], *f.* (**—**, *no pl.*) contraction.

Zusatz [ˈtsuːzats], *m.* (**—es**, *pl.* **—e**) addition, supplement, admixture; (*will*) codicil.

zuschanzen [ˈtsuːʃantsən], *v.a. einem etwas* —, obtain s.th. for s.o.

zuschauen [ˈtsuːʃauən], *v.n.* look on, watch.

Zuschauer [ˈtsuːʃauər], *m.* (**—s**, *pl.* —) onlooker, spectator.

Zuschauerraum [ˈtsuːʃauərraum], *m.* (**—s**, *pl.* **—e**) (*Theat.*) auditorium.

zuschaufeln [ˈtsuːʃaufəln], *v.a.* shovel in, fill up.

zuschieben [ˈtsuːʃiːbən], *v.a. irr.* push towards; shut; *einem etwas* —, shove (blame) on to s.o.

zuschießen [ˈtsuːʃiːsən], *v.a. irr. Geld* —, put money into (an undertaking).

Zuschlag [ˈtsuːʃlaːk], *m.* (**—s**, *pl.* **—e**) addition; (*Railw.*) excess fare.

zuschlagen [ˈtsuːʃlaːgən], *v.a. irr.* add; (*door*) bang; (*auction*) knock down to (s.o.). — *v.n.* strike hard.

zuschlag(s)pflichtig [ˈtsuːʃlaːk(s)pflɪç-tɪç], *adj.* liable to a supplementary charge.

zuschmeißen [ˈtsuːʃmaɪsən], *v.a. irr.* (*door*) slam to, bang.

zuschneiden [ˈtsuːʃnaɪdən], *v.a. irr.* (*pattern*) cut out; cut up.

Zuschneider [ˈtsuːʃnaɪdər], *m.* (**—s**, *pl.*—) (*Tail.*) cutter.

Zuschnitt [ˈtsuːʃnɪt], *m.* (**—s**, *no pl.*) (*clothing*) cut.

zuschreiben [ˈtsuːʃraɪbən], *v.a. irr. einem etwas* —, impute s.th. to s.o.; attribute *or* ascribe s.th. to s.o.

Zuschrift [ˈtsuːʃrɪft], *f.* (**—**, *pl.* **—en**) communication, letter.

Zuschuß [ˈtsuːʃus], *m.* (**—sses**, *pl.* **—sse**) additional money, supplementary allowance, subsidy.

zuschütten [ˈtsuːʃytən], *v.a.* fill up.

Zusehen [ˈtsuːzeːən], *n.* (**—s**, *no pl.*) *das* — *haben*, be left out in the cold.

zusehen [ˈtsuːzeːən], *v.n. irr.* look on, watch; be a spectator; see to it.

zusehends [ˈtsuːzeːənts], *adv.* visibly.

zusetzen [ˈtsuːzɛtsən], *v.a.* add to, admix; lose. — *v.n. einem* —, pester s.o.; attack s.o.

zusichern [ˈtsuːzɪçərn], *v.a.* promise, assure.

Zusicherung [ˈtsuːzɪçəruŋ], *f.* (**—**, *pl.* **—en**) promise, assurance.

Zuspeise [ˈtsuːʃpaɪzə], *f.* (**—**, *no pl.*) (*dial.*) (*food*) trimmings; vegetables.

zusperren [ˈtsuːʃpɛrən], *v.a.* shut, close, lock up.

zuspitzen [ˈtsuːʃpɪtsən], *v.a.* sharpen to a point. — *v.r. sich* —, come to a climax.

zusprechen [ˈtsuːʃprɛçən], *v.n. irr. dem Wein* —, drink heavily. — *v.a. Mut* —, comfort.

Zuspruch [ˈtsuːʃprux], *m.* (**—s**, *pl.* **—e**) exhortation; consolation.

Zustand [ˈtsuːʃtant], *m.* (**—s**, *pl.* **—e**) condition, state of affairs, situation.

zustande [tsuˈʃtandə], *adv.* — *kommen*, come off, be accomplished; — *bringen*, accomplish.

zuständig [ˈtsuːʃtɛndɪç], *adj.* competent; appropriate.

Zuständigkeit [ˈtsuːʃtɛndɪçkaɪt], *f.* (**—**, *no pl.*) competence.

zustecken [ˈtsuːʃtɛkən], *v.a.* pin up; *einem etwas* —, slip s.th. into s.o.'s hand.

zustehen [ˈtsuːʃteːən], *v.n. irr.* be due to, belong to; be s.o.'s business to.

zustellen [ˈtsuːʃtɛlən], *v.a.* deliver, hand over; (*Law*) serve (a writ).

Zustellung [ˈtsuːʃtɛluŋ], *f.* (**—**, *pl.* **—en**) delivery; (*Law*) service.

zusteuern [ˈtsuːʃtɔyərn], *v.a.* contribute. — *v.n.* (*aux.* sein) steer for; (*fig.*) aim at.

zustimmen [ˈtsuːʃtɪmən], *v.n.* agree to.

Zustimmung [ˈtsuːʃtɪmuŋ], *f.* (**—**, *pl.* **—en**) assent, consent, agreement.

zustopfen

zustopfen [ˈtsuːʃtɔpfən], *v.a.* fill up, stop up, plug; darn, mend.

zustoßen [ˈtsuːʃtoːsən], *v.a. irr.* push to, shut.

zustürzen [ˈtsuːʃtyrtsən], *v.n.* (*aux.* sein) *auf einen* —, rush at or towards s.o.

Zutaten [ˈtsuːtaːtən], *f. pl.* ingredients, garnishings.

zuteil [tsuˈtaɪl], *adv.* — *werden,* fall to s.o.'s share.

zutragen [ˈtsuːtraːgən], *v.a. irr.* report, tell. — *v.r. sich* —, happen.

Zuträger [ˈtsuːtrɛːgər], *m.* (—s, *pl.* —) informer, tale-bearer.

zuträglich [ˈtsuːtrɛːklɪç], *adj.* advantageous, wholesome.

Zutrauen [ˈtsuːtrauən], *n.* (—s, *no pl.*) confidence.

zutrauen [ˈtsuːtrauən], *v.a. einem etwas* —, credit s.o. with s.th.

zutraulich [ˈtsuːtraulɪç], *adj.* trusting; familiar, intimate; tame.

zutreffen [ˈtsuːtrɛfən], *v.n. irr.* prove correct, take place.

zutreffend [ˈtsuːtrɛfənt], *adj.* apposite, pertinent.

Zutritt [ˈtsuːtrɪt], *m.* (—s, *no pl.*) entry; access, admittance; — *verboten,* no admittance.

zutunlich [ˈtsuːtuːnlɪç], *adj.* confiding; obliging.

zuverlässig [ˈtsuːfɛrlɛsɪç], *adj.* reliable; authentic.

Zuversicht [ˈtsuːfɛrzɪçt], *f.* (—, *no pl.*) trust, confidence.

zuversichtlich [ˈtsuːfɛrzɪçtlɪç], *adj.* confident.

zuvor [tsuˈfoːr], *adv.* before, first, formerly.

zuvorkommend [tsuˈfoːrkɔmənt], *adj.* obliging, polite.

Zuwachs [ˈtsuːvaks], *m.* (—es, *no pl.*) increase, accretion, growth.

zuwachsen [ˈtsuːvaksən], *v.n. irr.* (*aux.* sein) become overgrown.

zuwandern [ˈtsuːvandərn], *v.n.* (*aux.* sein) immigrate.

zuwegebringen [tsuˈveːgəbrɪŋən], *v.a. irr.* bring about, effect.

zuweilen [tsuˈvaɪlən], *adv.* sometimes, at times.

zuweisen [ˈtsuːvaɪzən], *v.a. irr.* assign, apportion.

zuwenden [ˈtsuːvɛndən], *v.a.* turn towards; give.

zuwerfen [ˈtsuːvɛrfən], *v.a. irr.* throw towards, cast; (*door*) slam.

zuwider [tsuˈviːdər], *prep.* (*Dat.*) against, contrary to. — *adv.* repugnant.

Zuwiderhandlung [tsuˈviːdərhandluŋ], *f.* (—, *pl.* —**en**) contravention.

zuwiderlaufen [tsuˈviːdərlaufən], *v.n. irr.* (*aux.* sein) be contrary to, fly in the face of.

zuzählen [ˈtsuːtsɛːlən], *v.a.* add to.

zuziehen [ˈtsuːtsiːən], *v.a. irr.* draw together; tighten; consult; (*curtain*) draw. — *v.r. sich eine Krankheit* —, catch a disease.

Zuzug [ˈtsuːtsuːk], *m.* (—s, *no pl.*) immigration; population increase.

zuzüglich [ˈtsuːtsyːklɪç], *prep.* (*Genit.*) in addition to, including, plus.

Zwang [tsvaŋ], *m.* (—s, *no pl.*) coercion, force; compulsion; (*fig.*) constraint; *sich* — *auferlegen,* restrain o.s.; *tu deinen Gefühlen keinen* — *an,* let yourself go.

zwanglos [ˈtsvaŋloːs], *adj.* informal, free and easy.

Zwangsarbeit [ˈtsvaŋsarbaɪt], *f.* (—, *pl.* —**en**) forced labour.

Zwangsjacke [ˈtsvaŋsjakə], *f.* (—, *pl.* —**en**) strait-jacket.

Zwangsmaßnahme [ˈtsvaŋsmaːsnaːmə], *f.* (—, *pl.* —**en**) compulsory measure, compulsion.

Zwangsversteigerung [ˈtsvaŋsfɛrʃtaɪgəruŋ], *f.* (—, *pl.* —**en**) enforced sale.

Zwangsvollstreckung [ˈtsvaŋsfɔlʃtrɛkuŋ], *f.* (—, *pl.* —**en**) distraint.

zwangsweise [ˈtsvaŋsvaɪzə], *adv.* by force, compulsorily.

Zwangswirtschaft [ˈtsvaŋsvɪrtʃaft], *f.* (—, *no pl.*) price control, controlled economy.

zwanzig [ˈtsvantsɪç], *num. adj.* twenty.

zwar [tsvaːr], *adv.* to be sure, indeed, it is true, true; (*Am.*) sure.

Zweck [tsvɛk], *m.* (—(e)s, *pl.* —e) end, object, purpose.

zweckdienlich [ˈtsvɛkdiːnlɪç], *adj.* useful, expedient.

Zwecke [ˈtsvɛkə], *f.* (—, *pl.* —**n**) tack, drawing-pin.

zweckentsprechend [ˈtsvɛkɛntʃprɛçant], *adj.* suitable, appropriate.

zweckmäßig [ˈtsvɛkmɛːsɪç], *adj.* expedient, suitable, proper.

zwecks [tsvɛks], *prep.* (*Genit.*) for the purpose of.

zwei [tsvaɪ], *num. adj.* two.

zweibändig [ˈtsvaɪbɛndɪç], *adj.* in two volumes.

zweideutig [ˈtsvaɪdɔytɪç], *adj.* ambiguous, equivocal; (*fig.*) suggestive.

Zweideutigkeit [ˈtsvaɪdɔytɪçkaɪt], *f.* (—, *pl.* —**en**) ambiguity.

Zweifel [ˈtsvaɪfəl], *m.* (—s, *pl.* —) doubt, scruple; *ohne* —, no doubt.

zweifelhaft [ˈtsvaɪfəlhaft], *adj.* doubtful, dubious.

zweifellos [ˈtsvaɪfəlloːs], *adv.* doubtless.

zweifeln [ˈtsvaɪfəln], *v.n.* doubt, question; *ich zweifle nicht daran,* I have no doubt about it.

Zweifelsfall [ˈtsvaɪfəlsfal], *m.* (—s, *pl.* ⁻e) doubtful matter; *im* —, in case of doubt.

Zweifler [ˈtsvaɪflər], *m.* (—s, *pl.* —) doubter, sceptic.

Zweig [tsvaɪk], *m.* (—(e)s, *pl.* —e) twig, bough, branch.

zweigen [ˈtsvaɪgən], *v.r. sich* —, bifurcate, fork, branch.

Zweigniederlassung [ˈtsvaɪkniːdərlasuŋ], *f.* (—, *pl.* —**en**) branch establishment.

zweihändig ['tsvaɪhɛndɪç], *adj.* two-handed; (*keyboard music*) solo.

Zweihufer ['tsvaɪhuːfər], *m.* (—s, *pl.* —) cloven-footed animal.

zweijährig ['tsvaɪjɛːrɪç], *adj.* two-year-old; of two years' duration.

zweijährlich ['tsvaɪjɛːrlɪç], *adj.* biennial. — *adv.* every two years.

Zweikampf ['tsvaɪkampf], *m.* (— (e)s, *pl.* ⸚e) duel.

zweimal ['tsvaɪmaːl], *adv.* twice; — *soviel*, twice as much.

zweimotorig ['tsvaɪmotoːrɪç], *adj.* twin- (*or* two-) engined.

Zweirad ['tsvaɪraːt], *n.* (—s, *pl.* ⸚er) bicycle.

zweireihig ['tsvaɪraɪɪç], *adj.* (*suit*) double-breasted.

zweischneidig ['tsvaɪʃnaɪdɪç], *adj.* two-edged.

zweiseitig ['tsvaɪzaɪtɪç], *adj.* two-sided, bilateral.

zweisprachig ['tsvaɪʃpraːxɪç], *adj.* bilingual, in two languages.

zweitälteste ['tsvaɪtɛltəstə], *adj.* second (eldest).

zweitbeste ['tsvaɪtbɛstə], *adj.* second best.

zweite ['tsvaɪtə], *num. adj.* second; *aus —r Hand*, secondhand; *zu zweit*, in twos, two of (us, them).

Zweiteilung ['tsvaɪtaɪluŋ], *f.* (—, *pl.* —en) bisection.

zweitens ['tsvaɪtəns], *adv.* secondly, in the second place.

zweitletzte ['tsvaɪtlɛtstə], *adj.* last but one, penultimate.

zweitnächste ['tsvaɪtnɛçstə], *adj.* next but one.

Zwerchfell ['tsvɛrçfɛl], *n.* (—s, *pl.* —e) diaphragm, midriff.

zwerchfellerschütternd ['tsvɛrçfɛlərʃytərnt], *adj.* side-splitting.

Zwerg [tsvɛrk], *m.* (—s, *pl.* —e) dwarf, pigmy.

zwerghaft ['tsvɛrkhaft], *adj.* dwarfish.

Zwetsche ['tsvɛtʃə], *f.* (—, *pl.* —n) (*Bot.*) damson.

Zwickel ['tsvɪkəl], *m.* (—s, *pl.* —) gusset; *komischer —*, (*coll.*) queer fish.

zwicken ['tsvɪkən], *v.a.* pinch, nip.

Zwicker ['tsvɪkər], *m.* (—s, *pl.* —) pince-nez.

Zwickmühle ['tsvɪkmyːlə], *f.* (—, *pl.* —n) *in der — sein*, be on the horns of a dilemma, be in a jam.

Zwickzange ['tsvɪktsaŋə], *f.* (—, *pl.* —n) pincers.

Zwieback ['tsviːbak], *m.* (—s, *pl.* —e) rusk.

Zwiebel ['tsviːbəl], *f.* (—, *pl.* —n) onion; bulb.

zwiebelartig ['tsviːbəlaːrtɪç], *adj.* bulbous.

zwiebeln ['tsviːbəln], *v.a. einen —*, bully, torment s.o.

Zwielicht ['tsviːlɪçt], *n.* (—s, *no pl.*) twilight.

Zwiespalt ['tsviːʃpalt], *m.* (—s, *pl.* —e) difference, dissension; schism.

Zwiesprache ['tsviːʃpraːxə], *f.* (—, *pl.* —n) dialogue; discussion.

Zwietracht ['tsviːtraxt], *f.* (—, *no pl.*) discord, disharmony.

zwieträchtig ['tsviːtrɛçtɪç], *adj.* discordant, at variance.

Zwillich ['tsvɪlɪç], *m.* (—s, *pl.* —e) ticking.

Zwilling ['tsvɪlɪŋ], *m.* (—s, *pl.* —e) twin; (*pl.*) (*Astron.*) Gemini.

Zwingburg ['tsvɪŋburk], *f.* (—, *pl.* —en) stronghold.

Zwinge ['tsvɪŋə], *f.* (—, *pl.* —n) ferrule.

zwingen ['tsvɪŋən], *v.a. irr.* force, compel; master, overcome, get the better of. — *v.r. sich —*, force o.s. (to), make a great effort (to).

zwingend ['tsvɪŋənt], *adj.* cogent, imperative, convincing.

Zwinger ['tsvɪŋər], *m.* (—s, *pl.* —) keep, donjon, fort; bear-pit.

Zwingherrschaft ['tsvɪŋhɛrʃaft], *f.* (—, *pl.* —en) despotism, tyranny.

zwinkern ['tsvɪŋkərn], *v.n.* wink; (*stars*) twinkle.

Zwirn [tsvɪrn], *m.* (—(e)s, *pl.* —e) thread, sewing cotton.

Zwirnrolle ['tsvɪrnrolə], *f.* (—, *pl.* —n) ball of thread, reel of cotton.

zwischen ['tsvɪʃən], *prep.* (*Dat., Acc.*) between; among, amongst.

Zwischenakt ['tsvɪʃənakt], *m.* (—s, *pl.* —e) (*Theat.*) interval.

Zwischenbemerkung ['tsvɪʃənbəmɛrkuŋ], *f.* (—, *pl.* —en) interruption, digression.

Zwischendeck ['tsvɪʃəndɛk], *n.* (—s, *pl.* —e) (*ship*) steerage, between decks.

zwischendurch ['tsvɪʃəndurç], *adv.* in between, at intervals.

Zwischenfall ['tsvɪʃənfal], *m.* (—s, *pl.* ⸚e) incident; episode.

Zwischengericht ['tsvɪʃəngərɪçt], *n.* (—s, *pl.* —e) (*food*) entrée, entremets.

Zwischenglied ['tsvɪʃəngliːt], *n.* (—s, *pl.* —er) link.

Zwischenhändler ['tsvɪʃənhɛndlər], *m.* (—s, *pl.* —) middleman.

Zwischenpause ['tsvɪʃənpauzə], *f.* (—, *pl.* —n) interval; pause.

Zwischenraum ['tsvɪʃənraum], *m.* (—s, *pl.* ⸚e) intermediate space, gap.

Zwischenrede ['tsvɪʃənreːdə], *f.* (—, *pl.* —n) interruption.

Zwischenruf ['tsvɪʃənruːf], *m.* (—s, *pl.* —e) interruption, interjection.

Zwischensatz ['tsvɪʃənzats], *m.* (—es, *pl.* ⸚e) parenthesis; interpolation.

Zwischenspiel ['tsvɪʃənʃpiːl], *n.* (—s, *pl.* —e) interlude, intermezzo.

Zwischenzeit ['tsvɪʃəntsaɪt], *f.* (—, *no pl.*) interval, interim, meantime; *in der —*, meanwhile.

Zwist [tsvɪst], *m.* (—es, *pl.* —e) discord, quarrel, dispute.

Zwistigkeiten ['tsvɪstɪçkaɪtən], *f. pl.* hostilities.

zwitschern ['tsvɪtʃərn], *v.n.* chirp, twitter.

Zwitter ['tsvɪtər], *m.* (**—s**, *pl.* **—**) hybrid, cross-breed, mongrel; hermaphrodite.

zwitterhaft ['tsvɪtərhaft], *adj.* hybrid; bisexual.

zwölf [svœlf], *num. adj.* twelve.

Zwölffingerdarm ['tsvœlffɪŋərdarm], *m.* (**—s**, *pl.* **⸚e**) duodenum.

Zyankali [tsy:anˈkaːli], *n.* (**—s**, *no pl.*) potassium cyanide.

Zyklon [tsyˈkloːn], *m.* (**—s**, *pl.* **—e**) cyclone.

Zyklus ['tsyklus], *m.* (**—**, *pl.* **Zyklen**) cycle; course, series.

zylinderförmig [tsyˈlɪndərfœrmɪç], *adj.* cylindric(al).

Zylinderhut [tsyˈlɪndərhuːt], *m.* (**—s**, *pl.* **⸚e**) top-hat, silk-hat.

zylindrisch [tsyˈlɪndrɪʃ], *adj.* cylindric(al).

Zyniker ['tsyːnɪkər], *m.* (**—s**, *pl.* **—**) cynic.

zynisch ['tsyːnɪʃ], *adj.* cynical.

Zynismus [tsyˈnɪsmus], *m.* (**—**, *no pl.*) cynicism.

Zypern ['tsyːpərn], *n.* Cyprus.

Zypresse [tsyˈprɛsə], *f.* (**—**, *pl.* **—n**) (*Bot.*) cypress.

Cassell's English-German Dictionary

A

A [ei]. das A (*also Mus.*).

a [ə, ei] (**an** [ən, æn] *before vowel or silent* h), *indef. art.* ein, eine, ein; *two at a time*, zwei auf einmal; *many a*, mancher; *two shillings a pound*, zwei Schilling das Pfund.

abacus ['æbəkəs], *s.* das Rechenbrett.

abandon [ə'bændən], *v.a.* (*give up*) aufgeben; (*forsake*) verlassen; (*surrender*) preisgeben.

abandonment [ə'bændənmənt], *s.* das Verlassen (*active*); das Verlassensein (*passive*); die Wildheit, das Sichgehenlassen.

abasement [ə'beismənt], *s.* die Demütigung, Erniedrigung.

abash [ə'bæʃ], *v.a.* beschämen.

abate [ə'beit], *v.n.* nachlassen.

abbess ['æbes], *s.* die Äbtissin.

abbey ['æbi], *s.* die Abtei.

abbot ['æbət], *s.* der Abt.

abbreviate [ə'bri:vieit], *v.a.* abkürzen.

abbreviation [əbri:vi'eifən], *s.* die Abkürzung.

abdicate ['æbdikeit], *v.a.*, *v.n.* entsagen (*Dat.*), abdanken.

abdomen [æb'doumən, 'æbdəmən], *s.* (*Anat.*) der Unterleib, Bauch.

abdominal [æb'dominəl], *adj.* (*Anat.*) Bauch-, Unterleibs-.

abduct [æb'dʌkt], *v.a.* entführen.

abed [ə'bed], *adv.* zu Bett, im Bett.

aberration [æbə'reifən], *s.* die Abirrung; die Verirrung; (*Phys.*) die Strahlenbrechung.

abet [ə'bet], *v.a.* helfen (*Dat.*), unterstützen.

abeyance [ə'beiəns], *s.* die Unentschiedenheit, (der Zustand der) Ungewißheit; *in —*, unentschieden.

abhor [əb'hɔ:], *v.a.* verabscheuen.

abhorrence [əb'hɔrəns], *s.* die Abscheu (*of*, vor, *Dat.*).

abhorrent [əb'hɔrənt], *adj.* widerlich, ekelhaft.

abide [ə'baid], *v.n. irr.* bleiben, verweilen; (*last*) dauern. — *v.a.* aushalten.

ability [ə'biliti], *s.* die Fähigkeit, Tüchtigkeit; (*pl.*) die Geisteskräfte, *f. pl.*

abject ['æbdʒekt], *adj.* elend; (*submissive*) unterwürfig, verächtlich.

ablaze [ə'bleiz], *adj.*, *adv.* in Flammen.

able [eibl], *adj.* fähig; (*clever*) geschickt; (*efficient*) tüchtig.

ablution [ə'blu:fən], *s.* die Abwaschung, Waschung.

abnormal [æb'nɔ:məl], *adj.* abnorm, ungewöhnlich.

abnormality [æbnɔ:'mæliti], *s.* die Ungewöhnlichkeit.

aboard [ə'bɔ:d], *adv.* an Bord.

abode [ə'boud], *s.* der Wohnsitz, Wohnort.

abolish [ə'bɔliʃ], *v.a.* aufheben, abschaffen.

abolition [æbo'lifən], *s.* die Abschaffung, Aufhebung.

abominable [ə'bɔminəbl], *adj.* abscheulich, scheußlich.

abominate [ə'bɔmineit], *v.a.* verabscheuen.

abomination [əbɔmi'neifən], *s.* der Abscheu, Greuel.

aboriginal [æbə'ridʒinəl], *adj.* eingeboren, einheimisch. — *s.* der Eingeborene.

aborigines [æbə'ridʒini:z], *s. pl.* die Eingeborenen, Ureinwohner.

abortion [ə'bɔ:fən], *s.* die Fehlgeburt; die Abtreibung.

abortive [ə'bɔ:tiv], *adj.* mißlungen.

abound [ə'baund], *v.n.* wimmeln von (*Dat.*).

about [ə'baut], *prep.* um; (*toward*) gegen; *about 3 o'clock*, gegen drei; (*concerning*) über, betreffend. — *adv.* umher, herum; (*round*) rund herum; (*nearly*) etwa, ungefähr; (*everywhere*) überall; *to be — to*, im Begriffe sein or stehen zu . . .

above [ə'bʌv], *prep.* über; *— all things*, vor allen Dingen; *this is — me*, das ist mir zu hoch; *— board*, offen, ehrlich. — *adv.* oben, darüber, *over and —*, obendrein; *—mentioned*, obenerwähnt.

abrade [ə'breid], *v.a.* abschaben, abschürfen.

abrasion [ə'breiʒən], *s.* die Abschürfung; Abnutzung.

abreast [ə'brest], *adj.*, *adv.* nebeneinander, Seite an Seite; *keep —*, (sich) auf dem Laufenden halten; Schritt halten (mit).

abridge [ə'bridʒ], *v.a.* (ab)kürzen.

abridgement [ə'bridʒmənt], *s.* die (Ab)kürzung; (*book etc.*) der Auszug.

abroad [ə'brɔ:d], *adv.* im Ausland, auswärts; *to go —*, ins Ausland reisen.

abrogate ['æbrogeit], *v.a.* abschaffen.

abrogation [æbro'geifən], *s.* (*Pol.*) die Abschaffung.

abrupt [ə'brʌpt], *adj.* plötzlich; (*curt*) schroff; kurz; jäh.

abruptness [ə'brʌptnis], *s.* (*speech*) die Schroffheit; (*suddenness*) die Plötzlichkeit; (*drop*) die Steilheit.

abscess ['æbses], *s.* das Geschwür, die Schwellung, der Abszeß.

abscond

abscond [əb'skɔnd], *v.n.* sich davon-machen.

absence ['æbsəns], *s.* die Abwesenheit; *leave of* —, der Urlaub.

absent (1) ['æbsənt], *adj.* abwesend; — *minded*, zerstreut.

absent (2) [æb'sent], *v.r.* — *oneself*, fehlen, fernbleiben; (*go away*) sich ent-fernen.

absentee [æbsən'ti:], *s.* der Abwesende.

absolute ['æbsəlu:t], *adj.* absolut, un-umschränkt.

absolve [əb'zɔlv], *v.a.* freisprechen (*from*, von), lossprechen, entbinden.

absorb [əb'sɔ:b], *v.a.* absorbieren, aufsaugen; (*attention*) in Anspruch nehmen.

absorbed [əb'sɔ:bd], *adj.* versunken.

absorbent [əb'sɔ:bənt], *adj.* absorbie-rend.

absorption [əb'sɔ:pʃən], *s.* (*Chem.*) die Absorption; (*attention*) das Versun-kensein.

abstain [əb'stein], *v.n.* sich enthalten; — *from voting*, sich der Stimme enthalten.

abstainer [əb'steinə], *s.* der Abstinenz-ler, Antialkoholiker.

abstemious [əb'sti:miəs], *adj.* enthalt-sam.

abstention [əb'stenʃən], *s.* die Enthaltung.

abstinence ['æbstinəns], *s.* die Ent-haltsamkeit, das Fasten (*food*).

abstract [æb'strækt], *v.a.* abstrahieren, abziehen; (*summarize*) kürzen, aus-ziehen.—['æbstrækt], *adj.* abstrakt; (*Maths.*) rein. — *s.* der Auszug, Abriß (*of article, book, etc.*).

abstracted [æb'stræktid], *adj.* zerstreut, geistesabwesend.

abstraction [æb'strækʃən], *s.* die Ab-straktion; der abstrakte Begriff.

abstruse [æb'stru:s], *adj.* schwerver-ständlich, tiefsinnig.

absurd [əb'sə:d], *adj.* absurd, töricht; (*unreasonable*) unvernünftig, gegen alle Vernunft; (*laughable*) lächerlich.

absurdity [əb'sə:diti], *s.* die Torheit, Unvernünftigkeit.

abundance [ə'bʌndəns], *s.* die Fülle, der Überfluß.

abundant [ə'bʌndənt], *adj.* reichlich.

abuse [ə'bju:z], *v.a.* mißbrauchen; (*insult*) beschimpfen; (*violate*) schän-den. —[ə'bju:s], *s.* der Mißbrauch; (*language*) die Beschimpfung; (*vio-lation*) die Schändung.

abusive [ə'bju:siv], *adj.* (*language*) grob; schimpfend, schmähend.

abut [ə'bʌt], *v.n.* anstoßen, angrenzen.

abysmal [ə'bizməl], *adj.* bodenlos.

abyss [ə'bis], *s.* der Abgrund, Schlund.

Abyssinian [æbi'sinjən], *adj.* abes-sinisch. — *s.* der Abessinier.

acacia [ə'keiʃə], *s.* (*Bot.*) die Akazie.

academic [ækə'demik], *adj.* akademisch. — *s.* der Akademiker.

academy [ə'kædəmi], *s.* die Akademie.

acajon ['ækəʒu:], *s.* (*Bot.*) der Nieren-baum.

accede [æk'si:d], *v.n.* beistimmen; ein-willigen; — *to the throne*, den Thron besteigen.

accelerate [æk'seləreit], *v.a.* beschleu-nigen. — *v.n.* schneller fahren.

acceleration [ækselə'reiʃən], *s.* die Beschleunigung.

accelerator [æk'seləreitə], *s.* (*Motor.*) der Gashebel, das Gaspedal.

accent (1), **accentuate** [æk'sent, æk-'sentjueit], *v.a.* akzentuieren, betonen.

accent (2) ['æksənt], *s.* (*Phon.*) der Ton, Wortton, die Betonung; der Akzent (*dialect*), die Aussprache.

accentuation [æksentju'eiʃən], *s.* die Aussprache, Akzentuierung, Beto-nung.

accept [æk'sept], *v.a.* annehmen.

acceptable [æk'septəbl], *adj.* angenehm, annehmbar, annehmlich.

acceptance [æk'septəns], *s.* die An-nahme; (*Comm.*) das Akzept.

access ['ækses], *s.* der Zugang, Zutritt.

accessible [æk'sesibl], *adj.* erreichbar, zugänglich.

accession [æk'seʃən], *s.* der Zuwachs; — *to the throne*, die Thronbesteigung.

accessory [æk'sesəri], *adj.* zugehörig; hinzukommend; (*Law*) mitschuldig; (*subsidiary*) nebensächlich. — *s.* (*Law*) der Mitschuldige; (*pl.*) das Zubehör.

accidence ['æksidəns], *s.* (*Gram.*) die Flexionslehre.

accident ['æksidənt], *s.* (*chance*) der Zufall; (*mishap*) der Unfall, Unglücks-fall.

accidental [æksi'dentəl], *adj.* zufällig; (*inessential*) unwesentlich; durch Un-fall.

acclaim [ə'kleim], *v.a.* akklamieren, mit Beifall aufnehmen. — *v.n.* zujubeln. — *s.* der Beifall.

acclamation [æklə'meiʃən], *s.* der Beifall, Zuruf.

acclimatize [ə'klaimətaiz], *v.a.*, *v.r.* akklimatisieren; sich anpassen, einge-wöhnen.

accommodate [ə'kɔmədeit], *v.a.* (*adapt*) anpassen; (*lodge*) unter-bringen, beherbergen, aufnehmen; einem aushelfen; (*with money*) jeman-dem Geld leihen. — *v.r.* — *oneself to*, sich an etwas anpassen, sich in etwas fügen.

accommodating [ə'kɔmədeitiŋ], *adj.* gefällig, entgegenkommend.

accommodation [əkɔmə'deiʃən], *s.* (*adaptation*) die Anpassung; (*dispute*) die Beilegung; (*room*) die Unterkunft.

accompaniment [ə'kʌmpənimənt], *s.* die Begleitung.

accompany [ə'kʌmpəni], *v.a.* begleiten.

accomplice [ə'kʌmplis *or* ə'kɔmplis], *s.* der Komplize, Mitschuldige, Mit-täter.

accomplish [ə'kʌmpliʃ *or* ə'kɔmpliʃ], *v.a.* vollenden, zustandebringen, voll-bringen; (*objective*) erreichen.

accomplished [ə'kʌmpliʃd *or* ə'kɔm-pliʃd], *adj.* vollendet.

accomplishment [əˈkʌmpliʃmənt or əˈkɔmpliʃmənt], s. (of project) die Ausführung; (of task) die Vollendung; (of prophecy) die Erfüllung; (pl.) die Talente, n. pl., Gaben, Kenntnisse, f. pl.

accord [əˈkɔːd], s. (agreement) die Übereinstimmung; (unison) die Eintracht. — v.n. übereinstimmen (with, mit) — v.a. bewilligen.

accordance [əˈkɔːdəns], s. die Übereinstimmung.

according [əˈkɔːdiŋ], prep. — to, gemäß, nach, laut.

accordingly [əˈkɔːdiŋli], adv. demgemäß, demnach, folglich.

accordion [əˈkɔːdiən], s. (Mus.) die Ziehharmonika, das Akkordeon.

accost [əˈkɔst], v.a. ansprechen, anreden.

account [əˈkaunt], s. die Rechnung; (report) der Bericht; (narrative) die Erzählung; (importance) die Bedeutung; (Fin.) das Konto, Guthaben; cash —, die Kassenrechnung; on no —, auf keinen Fall; on his —, seinetwegen, um seinetwillen; on — of, wegen (Genit.); on that —, darum; of no —, unbedeutend. — v.n. — for, Rechenschaft ablegen über (Acc.); (explain) erklären.

accountable [əˈkauntəbl], adj. verrechenbar (item); verantwortlich (person).

accountant [əˈkauntənt], s. der Bücherrevisor, Rechnungsführer; junior —, der Buchhalter.

accredit [əˈkredit], v.a. akkreditieren, beglaubigen; (authorize) ermächtigen, bevollmächtigen.

accretion [əˈkriːʃən], s. der Zuwachs.

accrue [əˈkruː], v.n. (Comm.) zuwachsen, erwachsen, zufallen.

accumulate [əˈkjuːmjuleit], v.a., v.n. anhäufen; sich anhäufen, zunehmen, sich ansammeln.

accumulation [əkjuˈmjuˈleiʃən], s. die Ansammlung, Anhäufung.

accuracy [ˈækjurəsi], s. die Genauigkeit.

accurate [ˈækjurit], adj. genau, richtig.

accursed [əˈkəːsid], adj. verflucht, verwünscht.

accusation [ækjuˈzeiʃən], s. die Anklage.

accusative [əˈkjuːzətiv], s. (Gram.) der Akkusativ.

accuse [əˈkjuːz], v.a. anklagen, beschuldigen (of, Genit.).

accustom [əˈkʌstəm], v.a. gewöhnen (to, an, Acc.).

ace [eis], s. (Cards) das As, die Eins.

acerbity [əˈsəːbiti], s. die Rauheit, Herbheit; (manner) die Grobheit.

acetate [ˈæsiteit], s. das Azetat; essigsaures Salz.

acetic [əˈsiːtik, əˈsetik], adj. essigsauer.

acetylene [əˈsetiliːn], s. das Azetylen.

ache [eik], s. der Schmerz. — v.n. schmerzen, weh(e)tun.

achieve [əˈtʃiːv], v.a. erreichen, erlangen; (accomplish) vollenden; (perform) ausführen; (gain) erlangen, erwerben.

achievement [əˈtʃiːvmənt], s. (accomplishment) die Leistung, der Erfolg; die Errungenschaft; (gain) die Erwerbung.

achromatic [ækroˈmætik], adj. achromatisch, farblos.

acid [ˈæsid], adj. sauer, scharf. — s. (Chem.) die Säure.

acidulated [əˈsidjuleitid], adj. (Chem.) angesäuert.

acknowledge [əkˈnɔlidʒ], v.a. anerkennen; (admit) zugeben; (confess) bekennen; (letter) den Empfang bestätigen.

acknowledgement [əkˈnɔlidʒmənt], s. die Anerkennung, (receipt) Bestätigung, Quittung; (pl.) die Dankesbezeigung; die Erkenntlichkeit.

acme [ˈækmi], s. der Gipfel, Höhepunkt.

acorn [ˈeikɔːn], s. (Bot.) die Eichel.

acoustics [əˈkuːstiks], s. pl. die Akustik; (subject, study) die Schallehre.

acquaint [əˈkweint], v.a. bekanntmachen; (inform) mitteilen (Dat.), informieren; unterrichten.

acquaintance [əˈkweintəns], s. die Bekanntschaft; der Bekannte, die Bekannte (person); die Kenntnis (with, von).

acquiesce [ækwiˈes], v.n. einwilligen, sich fügen.

acquiescence [ækwiˈesəns], s. die Einwilligung (in, in, Acc.), Zustimmung (in, zu, Dat.)

acquiescent [ækwiˈesənt], adj. fügsam.

acquire [əˈkwaiə], v.a. erlangen, erwerben; (language) erlernen.

acquisition [ækwiˈziʃən], s. die Erlangung, Erwerbung.

acquit [əˈkwit], v.a. freisprechen.

acre [ˈeikə], s. der Acker (appr. 0.4 Hektar).

acrid [ˈækrid], adj. scharf, beißend.

acrimonious [ækriˈmouniəs], adj. scharf, bitter.

across [əˈkrɔs, əˈkrɔːs], adv. kreuzweise, (quer) hinüber. — prep. quer durch, über; come —, (zufällig) treffen, come — a problem, auf ein Problem stoßen.

act [ækt], s. (deed) die Tat; (Theat.) der Akt; (Parl. etc.) die Akte. — v.a. (Theat.) spielen. — v.n. handeln (do something); sich benehmen or tun, als ob (act as if, pretend); (Theat.) spielen; (Chem.) wirken (react).

action [ˈækʃən], s. die Handlung (play, deed), Wirkung (effect); (Law) der Prozeß; der Gang.

active [ˈæktiv], adj. (person, Gram.) aktiv; tätig; rührig (industrious); wirksam (effective).

activity [ækˈtiviti], s. die Tätigkeit; (Chem.) Wirksamkeit.

actor [ˈæktə], s. der Schauspieler.

actress [ˈæktrəs], die Schauspielerin.

actual [ˈæktjuəl], adj. tatsächlich, wirklich.

actuality [æktjuˈæliti], s. die Wirklichkeit.

actuary [ˈæktjuari], s. der Aktuar, Versicherungsbeamte.

actuate [ˈæktjueit], v.a. betreiben, in Bewegung setzen.

acuity [əˈkjuːiti], s. der Scharfsinn (mind), die Schärfe (vision etc.).

acute [əˈkjuːt], adj. scharf, scharfsinnig (mind); spitz (angle); fein (sense); — accent, der Akut.

adage [ˈædidʒ], s. das Sprichwort.

adamant [ˈædəmənt], adj. sehr hart, unerbittlich (inexorable).

adapt [əˈdæpt], v.a. anpassen, angleichen; bearbeiten.

adaptable [əˈdæptəbl], adj. anpassungsfähig.

adaptation [ædæpˈteifən], s. die Anpassung, die Bearbeitung (of book).

adaptive [əˈdæptiv], adj. anpassungsfähig.

add [æd], v.a. hinzufügen, (Maths.) addieren.

adder [ˈædə], s. (Zool.) die Natter.

addict [ˈædikt], s. der Süchtige.

addiction [əˈdikfən], s. die Sucht.

addicted [əˈdiktid], adj. verfallen.

addition [əˈdifən], s. die Hinzufügung, Zugabe, (Maths.) Addition.

additional [əˈdifənəl], adj. zusätzlich, nachträglich.

address [əˈdres], s. die Anschrift, Adresse (letter); die Ansprache (speech). — v.a. (letter) adressieren, richten an (Acc.).

addressee [ædreˈsiː], s. der Adressat, der Empfänger.

adduce [əˈdjuːs], v.a. anführen (proof, Beweis).

adenoid [ˈædinɔid], s. (usually pl.) (Med.) die Wucherung.

adept [ˈædept], adj. geschickt, erfahren.

adequacy [ˈædikwəsi], s. die Angemessenheit, das Gewachsensein, die Zulänglichkeit.

adequate [ˈædikwət], adj. gewachsen (Dat.); angemessen, hinreichend (sufficient).

adhere [ədˈhiə], v.n. haften, anhängen; — to one's opinion, bei seiner Meinung bleiben.

adherence [ədˈhiərəns], s. das Festhalten (an, Dat.).

adhesion [ədˈhiːʒən], s. (Phys.) die Adhäsion; das Anhaften.

adhesive [ədˈhiːziv], adj. haftend, klebrig; — plaster, das Heftpflaster.

adipose [ˈædipous], adj. fett, feist.

adjacent [əˈdʒeisənt], adj. naheliegend, benachbart, angrenzend.

adjective [ˈædʒəktiv], s. (Gram.) das Adjektiv; Eigenschaftswort.

adjoin [əˈdʒɔin], v.a. anstoßen, angrenzen.

adjourn [əˈdʒəːn], v.a. vertagen, aufschieben.

adjudicate [əˈdʒuːdikeit], v.a. beurteilen, richten.

adjunct [ˈædʒʌŋkt], s. der Zusatz.

adjust [əˈdʒʌst], v.a. ordnen; (adapt) anpassen; regulieren, einstellen.

adjustable [əˈdʒʌstəbl], adj. verstellbar, einstellbar.

adjustment [əˈdʒʌstmənt], s. die Einstellung, Anpassung; (Law) Schlichtung; Berichtigung.

administer [ədˈministə], v.a. verwalten (an enterprise); verabreichen (medicine); abnehmen (an oath, einen Eid).

administration [ədminisˈtreifən], s. die Verwaltung, Regierung; die Darreichung (sacraments).

administrative [ədˈministrətiv], adj. Verwaltungs-; verwaltend.

admirable [ˈædmirəbl], adj. bewundernswert.

admiral [ˈædmirəl], s. der Admiral.

Admiralty [ˈædmirəlti], s. die Admiralität.

admiration [ædmiˈreifən], s. die Bewunderung.

admire [ədˈmaiə], v.a. bewundern, verehren.

admirer [ədˈmaiərə], s. der Bewunderer, Verehrer.

admissible [ədˈmisibl], adj. zulässig.

admission [ədˈmifən], s. die Zulassung; (entry) der Eintritt; Zutritt; (confession) das Eingeständnis, Zugeständnis.

admit [ədˈmit], v.a. zulassen; aufnehmen; zugeben (deed); gelten lassen (argument).

admittance [ədˈmitəns], s. der Zugang, Eintritt, Zutritt.

admixture [ədˈmikstfə], s. die Beimischung, Beigabe.

admonish [ədˈmɔnif], v.a. ermahnen, mahnen, warnen.

admonition [ædməˈnifən], s. die Ermahnung, Warnung.

ado [əˈduː], s. der Lärm, das Tun, das Treiben; without further —, ohne weiteres.

adolescence [ædoˈlesəns], s. die Adoleszenz, Jugend, Jugendzeit.

adolescent [ædoˈlesənt], s. der Jugendliche. — adj. jugendlich.

adopt [əˈdɔpt], v.a. (Law) annehmen, adoptieren.

adoption [əˈdɔpfən], s. (Law) die Annahme, Adoption.

adoptive [əˈdɔptiv], adj. Adoptiv-, angenommen.

adorable [əˈdɔːrəbl], adj. anbetungswürdig; (coll.) wunderbar, schön.

adoration [ædoˈreifən], s. die Anbetung.

adore [əˈdɔː], v.a. anbeten; verehren.

adorn [əˈdɔːn], v.a. (aus)schmücken, zieren.

Adriatic (Sea) [eidriˈætik (siː)]. das adriatische Meer.

adrift [əˈdrift], adv. treibend; cut o.s. —, sich absondern.

adroit [əˈdrɔit], adj. gewandt, geschickt.

adroitness [əˈdrɔitnis], s. die Gewandtheit, die Geschicklichkeit.

adulation [ædju'leiʃən], s. die Schmeichelei.

adulator ['ædjuleitə], s. der Schmeichler.

adulatory ['ædjuleitəri], adj. schmeichlerisch.

adult [ə'dʌlt or 'ædʌlt], adj. erwachsen. — s. der Erwachsene.

adulterate [ə'dʌltəreit], v.a. verfälschen; verwässern.

adulterer [ə'dʌltərə], s. der Ehebrecher.

adultery [ə'dʌltəri], s. der Ehebruch.

adumbrate [ə'dʌmbreit or 'æd-], v.a. skizzieren, entwerfen, andeuten.

advance [əd'vɑːns], v.a. fördern (a cause); vorschießen (money); geltend machen (claim). — v.n. vorrücken, vorstoßen; (make progress, gain promotion) aufsteigen. — s. der Fortschritt (progress); der Vorschuß (money); in —, im voraus.

advancement [əd'vɑːnsmənt], s. der Fortschritt (progress); der Aufstieg, die Beförderung (promotion); die Förderung (of a cause).

advantage [əd'vɑːntidʒ], s. der Vorteil, Nutzen; (superiority) die Überlegenheit.

Advent ['ædvent]. (Eccl.) der Advent.

advent ['ædvənt], s. die Ankunft.

adventitious [ædven'tiʃəs], adj. zufällig.

adventure [əd'ventʃə], s. das Abenteuer. — v.n. auf Abenteuer ausgehen, wagen.

adventurer [əd'ventʃərə], s. der Abenteurer.

adventurous [əd'ventʃərəs], adj. abenteuerlich, unternehmungslustig.

adverb ['ædvɑːb], s. (Gram.) das Adverb(ium), Umstandswort.

adverbial [əd'vɑːbiəl], adj. adverbial.

adversary ['ædvəsəri], s. der Gegner, Widersacher.

adverse ['ædvɑːs], adj. widrig, feindlich, ungünstig.

adversity [əd'vɑːsiti], s. das Unglück, Mißgeschick; in —, im Unglück.

advert [əd'vɑːt], v.n. hinweisen.

advertise ['ædvətaiz], v.a. anzeigen; annoncieren (in press), Reklame machen.

advertisement [əd'vɑːtizmənt], s. die Anzeige, Annonce; Reklame.

advertiser ['ædvətaizə], s. der Anzeiger.

advice [əd'vais], s. der Rat, Ratschlag; die Nachricht (information).

advise [əd'vaiz], v.a. raten (Dat.), beraten; benachrichtigen (inform); verständigen.

advisable [əd'vaizəbl], adj. ratsam.

advisedly [əd'vaizidli], adv. absichtlich, mit Bedacht.

adviser [əd'vaizə], s. der Berater.

advisory [əd'vaizəri], adj. beratend, ratgebend, Rats-.

advocacy ['ædvəkəsi], s. (Law) die Verteidigung; die Fürsprache (championing of, für, Acc.); die Vertretung (of view).

Aegean (**Sea**) [iː'dʒiːən (siː)]. das ägäische Meer.

aerated ['ɛəreitid], adj. kohlensauer.

aerial ['ɛəriəl], s. (Rad.) die Antenne. — adj. luftig, Luft-.

aerie ['ɛəri, 'iəri], s. see **eyrie**.

aerodrome ['ɛərodroum], s. der Flugplatz, Flughafen.

aeronautical [ɛəro'nɔːtikəl], adj. aeronautisch.

aeronautics [ɛəro'nɔːtiks], s. pl. die Aeronautik, Luftfahrt.

aeroplane, (Am.) **airplane** ['ɛəroplein, 'ɛərplein], s. das Flugzeug.

aesthetic(al) [iːs'θetik(əl)], adj. ästhetisch.

aesthetics [iːs'θetiks], s. die Ästhetik.

afar [ə'fɑː], adv. fern, weit entfernt; from —, von weitem, (von) weit her.

affability [æfə'biliti], s. die Leutseligkeit, Freundlichkeit.

affable ['æfəbl], adj. freundlich, leutselig.

affair [ə'fɛə], s. die Affäre; die Angelegenheit (matter); das Anliegen (concern).

affect [ə'fekt], v.a. beeinflußen; rühren; wirken auf; vortäuschen (pretend); zur Schau tragen (exhibit).

affectation [æfek'teiʃən], s. die Ziererei, das Affektieren, die Affektiertheit.

affected [ə'fektid], adj. affektiert, gekünstelt, geziert; befallen, angegriffen (illness).

affection [ə'fekʃən], s. die Zuneigung, Zärtlichkeit.

affectionate [ə'fekʃənit], adj. zärtlich, liebevoll; (in letters) yours —ly, herzlichst.

affinity [ə'finiti], s. (Chem.) die Affinität; die Verwandtschaft (relationship).

affirm [ə'fɑːm], v.a. behaupten, bestätigen, versichern; bekräftigen (confirm).

affirmation [æfə'meiʃən], s. die Behauptung, Bekräftigung.

affirmative [ə'fɑːmətiv], adj. bejahend, positiv; in the —, bejahend.

affix [ə'fiks], v.a. anheften, aufkleben (stick); anbringen (join to, an, Acc.).

afflict [ə'flikt], v.a. quälen, plagen.

affliction [ə'flikʃən], s. die Plage, Qual; das Mißgeschick; die Not; das Leiden.

affluence ['æfluəns], s. der Überfluß (abundance); der Reichtum.

affluent ['æfluənt], adj. reich, wohlhabend. — s. der Nebenfluß (tributary).

afford [ə'fɔːd], v.a. geben, bieten; (sich) leisten (have money for); gewähren (give); hervorbringen (yield).

afforest [ə'fɔrist], v.a. aufforsten.

affray [ə'frei], s. die Schlägerei.

African ['æfrikən], adj. afrikanisch. — s. der Afrikaner.

affront [ə'frʌnt], s. die Beleidigung. — v.a. beleidigen.

Afghan ['æfgæn], adj. afghanisch. — s. der Afghane.

afield [ə'fiːld], adj., adv. im Felde; weit umher; weit weg.

afire [ə'faiə], adv., adv. in Flammen.

aflame [ə'fleim], *adj.*, *adv.* in Flammen.
afloat [ə'flout], *adj.*, *adv.* schwimmend, dahintreibend.
afoot [ə'fut], *adj.*, *adv.* im Gange.
afore [ə'fɔː], *adv.* vorher.
aforesaid [ə'fɔːsed], *adj.* the —, das Obengesagte, der Vorhergenannte.
afraid [ə'freid], *adj.* ängstlich, furchtsam; be —, fürchten (of s.th., etwas, Acc.); sich fürchten.
afresh [ə'freʃ], *adv.* von neuem.
aft [ɑːft], *adv.* (Naut.) achtern.
after [ɑːftə], *prep.* nach (time); nach, hinter (place); the day — tomorrow, übermorgen. — *adj.* hinter, später. — *adv.* hinterher, nachher (time); darauf, dahinter (place). — *conj.* nachdem.
afternoon [ɑːftə'nuːn], *s.* der Nachmittag.
afterwards ['ɑːftəwədz], *adv.* nachher, daraufhin, später.
again [ə'gein], *adv.* wieder, abermals, noch einmal; zurück (back); dagegen (however); as much —, noch einmal soviel; — and —, immer wieder.
against [ə'geinst], *prep.* gegen, wider; nahe bei (near, Dat.); bis an (up to, Acc.); — the grain, wider or gegen den Strich.
agate ['ægeit], *s.* der Achat.
agave [ə'geivi], *s.* (Bot.) die Agave.
age [eidʒ], *s.* das Alter (person); das Zeitalter (period); die Reife; come of —, volljährig werden; mündig werden; old —, das Greisenalter; for —s, seit einer Ewigkeit. — *v.n.* altern, alt werden.
aged ['eidʒid], *adj.* bejahrt.
agency ['eidʒənsi], *s.* die Agentur (firm); die Mitwirkung (participation); die Hilfe (assistance); die Vermittlung (mediation).
agenda [ə'dʒendə], *s.* das Sitzungsprogramm; die Tagesordnung.
agent ['eidʒənt], *s.* der Agent, Vertreter.
agglomerate [ə'glomereit], *v.a.* zusammenhäufen. — *v.n.* sich zusammenhäufen, sich ballen.
aggrandisement [ə'grændizmənt], *s.* die Überhebung, Übertreibung, Erweiterung.
aggravate ['ægrəveit], *v.a.* verschlimmern; ärgern.
aggravation [ægrə'veiʃən], *s.* die Verschlimmerung (of condition); der Ärger (annoyance).
aggregate ['ægrigit], *adj.* gesamt, vereinigt, vereint. — *s.* das Aggregat.
aggregation [ægri'geiʃən], *s.* (Geol., Chem.) die Vereinigung, Anhäufung, Ansammlung.
aggression [ə'greʃən], *s.* der Angriff, Überfall.
aggressive [ə'gresiv], *adj.* aggressiv, angreifend.
aggressor [ə'gresə], *s.* der Angreifer.
aggrieve [ə'griːv], *v.a.* kränken.

aghast [ə'gɑːst], *adj.* bestürzt; sprachlos; entsetzt.
agile ['ædʒail], *adj.* behend, flink, beweglich.
agitate ['ædʒiteit], *v.a.* bewegen; beunruhigen; aufrühren; stören.
agitation [ædʒi'teiʃən], *s.* (Pol.) die Agitation; die Unruhe (unrest); der Aufruhr (revolt).
agitator ['ædʒiteitə], *s.* (Pol.) der Agitator; der Aufwiegler (inciter).
aglow [ə'glou], *adv.* glühend.
agnostic [æg'nɔstik], *s.* der Agnostiker.
ago [ə'gou], *adv.* vor; long —, vor langer Zeit; not long —, kürzlich; a month —, vor einem Monat.
agog [ə'gɔg], *adj.* erregt, gespannt, neugierig (for, auf, Acc.).
agonize ['ægənaiz], *v.a.* quälen, martern. — *v.n.* Qual erleiden; mit dem Tode ringen or kämpfen.
agonising ['ægənaiziŋ], *adj.* schmerzhaft, qualvoll.
agony ['ægəni], *s.* die Pein, Qual; der Todeskampf; — column, die Seufzerspalte.
agrarian [ə'grɛəriən], *adj.* landwirtschaftlich; — party, die Bauernpartei.
agree [ə'griː], *v.n.* übereinstimmen (be in agreement); übereinkommen (come to an agreement); sich einigen.
agreeable [ə'griːəbl], *adj.* angenehm, gefällig.
agreement [ə'griːmənt], *s.* die Übereinstimmung, das Übereinkommen; der Vertrag, die Verständigung (understanding).
agricultural [ægri'kʌltʃərəl], *adj.* landwirtschaftlich.
agriculture ['ægrikʌltʃə], *s.* die Landwirtschaft.
aground [ə'graund], *adj.*, *adv.* (Naut.) gestrandet; to run —, stranden.
ague ['eigjuː], *s.* (Med.) der Schüttelfrost.
ah! [ɑː], *interj.* ach!; aha! (surprise).
aha! [ɑ'hɑː], *interj.* ach so!
ahead [ə'hed], *adv.* vorwärts, voran (movement), voraus (position), go — (carry on), fortfahren; go — (make progress), vorwärtskommen.
ahoy! [ə'hɔi], *interj.* (Naut.) ahoi!
aid [eid], *v.a.* helfen (Dat.), unterstützen (Acc.), beistehen (Dat.). — *s.* die Hilfe, der Beistand.
aide-de-camp ['eiddə'kɑ̃], *s.* der Adjutant (eines Generals).
ail [eil], *v.n.* schmerzen; krank sein.
ailing ['eiliŋ], *adj.* kränklich, leidend.
ailment ['eilmənt], *s.* das Leiden.
aim [eim], *v.a.* (weapon, blow etc.) richten (at, auf). — *v.n.* zielen (auf, Acc.); trachten (nach, strive for). — *s*, das, Ziel, der Zweck (purpose); die Absicht (intention).
aimless ['eimlis], *adj.* ziellos, zwecklos.

air [ɛə], s. die Luft; die Melodie (*tune*); die Miene (*mien*); *air force*, die Luftwaffe; *air pocket*, das Luftloch; *air raid*, der Luftangriff; *in the open* —, im Freien; *on the* —, im Rundfunk; *to give oneself* —s, vornehm tun. — *v.a.* lüften (*room*); trocknen (*washing*); aussprechen (*views*).

airbase [ˈɛəbeis], s. der Fliegerstützpunkt.

airconditioning [ˈɛəkəndiʃəniŋ], s. die Klimaanlage.

aircraft [ˈɛəkrɑːft], s. das Luftfahrzeug, Flugzeug.

airgun [ˈɛəgʌn], s. die Windbüchse, das Luftgewehr.

[ˈɛərinis], s. die Luftigkeit, ...eit.

...letə], s. der Luftpostbrief.

..., s. das Verkehrs-

..., die Luftpost.

..., s. der Flieger.

aeroplane.

...[ˈɛəpɔːt], s. der Flughafen.

...[ˈɛətait], adj. luftdicht.

...ry [ˈɛəri], adj. luftig.

aisle [ail], s. das Seitenschiff (*church*); der Gang.

Aix-la-Chapelle [ˈeikslaʃæˈpel], Aachen, n.

ajar [əˈdʒɑː], adv. angelehnt, halb offen.

akimbo [əˈkimbou], adv. Hände an den Hüften, Arme in die Seiten gestemmt.

akin [əˈkin], adj. verwandt (*to*, mit, *Dat.*).

alack [əˈlæk], interj. ach! oh, weh! *alas and* —, ach und wehe!

alacrity [əˈlækriti], s. die Bereitwilligkeit; Munterkeit.

alarm [əˈlɑːm], s. der Alarm; Lärm (*noise*); die Warnung; Angst, Bestürzung; — *clock*, der Wecker. — *v.a.* erschrecken.

alas! [əˈlæs], interj. ach, wehe!

Albanian [ælˈbeiniən], adj. albanisch. — s. der Albanier.

album [ˈælbəm], s. das Album.

albumen [ˈælˈbjuːmən], s. das Eiweiß, (*Chem.*) der Eiweißstoff.

albuminous [ælˈbjuːminəs], adj. eiweißhaltig, Eiweiß-.

alchemist [ˈælkimist], s. der Alchimist.

alchemy [ˈælkimi], s. die Alchimie.

alcohol [ˈælkəhɔl], s. der Alkohol.

alcoholic [ælkəˈhɔlik], adj. alkoholisch. — s. der Trinker, Alkoholiker.

alcove [ˈælkouv], s. der Alkoven.

alder [ˈɔːldə], s. (*Bot.*) die Erle.

alderman [ˈɔːldəmən], s. der Ratsherr, der Stadtrat.

ale [eil], s. englisches Bier.

alert [əˈləːt], adj. wachsam, aufmerksam; *on the* —, auf der Hut.

algebra [ˈældʒibrə], s. die Algebra.

Algerian [ælˈdʒiəriən], adj. algerisch. — s. der Algerier.

Algiers [ælˈdʒiəz], Algier, n.

alias [ˈeiliəs], adv. sonst genannt.

alien [ˈeiliən], adj. fremd, ausländisch. — s. der Fremde, Ausländer.

alienate [ˈeiliəneit], v.a. entfremden.

alienation [eiliəˈneiʃən], s. die Entfremdung; — *of mind*, die Geisteserkrankung, Geistesgestörtheit.

alienist [ˈeiliənist], s. der Irrenarzt.

alight (1) [əˈlait], v.n. absteigen (*from horse*); aussteigen (*from carriage etc.*).

alight (2) [əˈlait], adj. brennend, in Flammen.

alike [əˈlaik], adj. gleich, ähnlich. — adv. *great and small* —, sowohl große wie kleine.

alimentary [æliˈmentəri], adj. Nahrungs-, Verdauungs-; — *canal*, (*Anat.*) der Darmkanal.

alimentation [ælimenˈteiʃən], s. die Beköstigung; (*Law*) der Unterhalt.

alimony [ˈæliməni], s. der Unterhaltsbeitrag; (*pl.*) Alimente., *n.pl.*

alive [əˈlaiv], adj. lebendig; — *and kicking*, wohlauf, munter; — *to*, empfänglich für.

alkali [ˈælkəlai], s. (*Chem.*) das Laugensalz, Alkali.

alkaline [ˈælkəlain], adj. (*Chem.*) alkalisch, laugensalzig.

all [ɔːl], adj., pron. all, ganz (*whole*); sämtliche, alle; *above* —, vor allem; *once and for* —, ein für allemal; *not at* —, keineswegs; *All Saints*, Allerheiligen; *All Souls*, Allerseelen. — adv. ganz, gänzlich, völlig; — *the same*, trotzdem; — *the better*, umso besser.

allay [əˈlei], v.a. lindern, beruhigen, unterdrücken.

allegation [æliˈgeiʃən], s. die Behauptung.

allege [əˈledʒ], v.a. behaupten, aussagen.

allegiance [əˈliːdʒəns], s. die Treue, Ergebenheit; Untertanenpflicht.

allegorical [æliˈgɔrikəl], adj. allegorisch, sinnbildlich.

alleviate [əˈliːvieit], v.a. erleichtern, mildern.

alleviation [əliːviˈeiʃən], s. die Erleichterung, Milderung.

alley [ˈæli], s. die Gasse; Seitenstraße; *bowling* —, die Kegelbahn.

alliance [əˈlaiəns], s. (*Pol.*) die Allianz, das Bündnis (*treaty*); der Bund (*league*).

allied [əˈlaid, ˈælaid], adj. verbündet, vereinigt; alliiert; verwandt.

alliteration [əlitəˈreiʃən], s. die Alliteration, der Stabreim.

allocate [ˈæləkeit], v.a. zuweisen, zuteilen.

allot [əˈlɔt], v.a. zuteilen (*assign*); verteilen (*distribute*).

allotment [əˈlɔtmənt], s. der Anteil; die Zuteilung; die Landparzelle; die Laubenkolonie, der Schrebergarten (*garden*).

allow [əˈlau], v.a. gewähren (*grant*); erlauben (*permit*); zulassen (*admit*). — v.n. — *for*, Rücksicht nehmen auf (*Acc.*); in Betracht ziehen.

allowance

allowance [ə'lauəns], *s.* die Rente; das Taschengeld (*money*); die Erlaubnis (*permission*); die Genehmigung (*approval*); die Nachsicht (*indulgence*).

alloy [ə'bi, 'ælɔi], *s.* die Legierung. — *v.a.* (*Metall.*) legieren.

allude [ə'lu:d], *v.a.* anspielen (*to,* auf).

allure [ə'ljuə], *v.a.* locken, anlocken.

allurement [ə'ljuəmənt], *s.* der Reiz, die Lockung.

allusion [ə'lu:ʒən], *s.* die Anspielung.

alluvial [ə'lu:viəl], *adj.* angeschwemmt.

alluvium [ə'lu:viəm], *s.* das Schwemmgebiet, Schwemmland.

ally [ə'lai], *s.* der Verbündete, Bundesgenosse, Alliierte. — [ə'lai], *v.a., v.r.* (sich) vereinigen, (sich) verbünden.

almanac ['ɔ:lmənæk], *s.* der Almanach.

almighty [ɔ:l'maiti], *adj.* allmächtig; *God Almighty!* allmächtiger Gott!

almond ['ɑ:mənd], *s.* (*Bot.*) die Mandel.

almoner ['ælmənə], *s.* der Wohlfahrtsbeamte, die Fürsorgerin.

almost ['ɔ:lmoust], *adv.* fast, beinahe.

alms [ɑ:mz], *s.* das Almosen.

aloe ['ælou], *s.* (*Bot.*) die Aloe.

aloft [ə'lɔft], *adv.* droben, (hoch) oben; empor.

alone [ə'loun], *adj., adv.* allein; *all —,* ganz allein; *leave —,* in Ruhe lassen; *let —,* geschweige (denn).

along [ə'lɔŋ], *adv.* längs, der Länge nach; entlang, weiter; *come —!* komm mit!; *get —* (*with*), auskommen. — *prep.* längs; entlang.

alongside [əlɔŋ'said], *adv.* nebenan. — [ə'lɔŋ'said], *prep.* neben.

aloof [ə'lu:f], *adj., adv.* fern, weitab; *keep —,* sich fernhalten.

aloofness [ə'lu:fnis], *s.* das Sichfernhalten; das Vornehmtun.

aloud [ə'laud], *adj., adv.* laut; hörbar.

alphabet ['ælfəbet], *s.* das Alphabet, Abc.

Alpine ['ælpain], *adj.* alpinisch, Alpen-.

Alps, The [ælps, ði]. die Alpen, *pl.*

already [ɔ:l'redi], *adv.* schon, bereits.

Alsatian [æl'seiʃən], *adj.* elsässisch. — *s.* der Elsässer; (*dog*) der Wolfshund, deutscher Schäferhund.

also [ɔ:lsou], *adv.* (*likewise*) auch, ebenfalls; (*moreover*) ferner.

altar ['ɔ:ltə], *s.* der Altar.

alter ['ɔ:ltə], *v.a.* ändern, verändern. — *v.n.* sich (ver)ändern.

alterable ['ɔ:ltərəbl], *adj.* veränderlich.

alteration [ɔ:ltə'reiʃən], *s.* die Änderung, Veränderung.

altercation [ɔ:ltə'keiʃən], *s.* der Zank, Streit; Wortwechsel.

alternate ['ɔ:ltəneit], *v.a., v.n.* abwechseln lassen, abwechseln.

alternative [ɔ:l'tə:nətiv], *adj.* abwechselnd, alternativ, zur Wahl gestellt. — *s.* die Alternative, die Wahl.

although [ɔ:l'ðou], *conj.* obgleich, obwohl, obschon.

altimeter ['æltimi:tə], *s.* der Höhenmesser.

altitude ['æltitju:d], *s.* die Höhe.

alto ['æltou], *s.* (*Mus.*) die Altstimme, der Alt.

altogether [ɔ:ltu'geðə], *adv.* zusammen, zusammengenommen, allesamt; (*wholly*) ganz und gar, durchaus.

alum ['æləm], *s.* (*Chem.*) der Alaun.

aluminium [ælju'minjəm], (*Am.*) **aluminum** [ə'lu:minəm], *s.* das Aluminium.

always ['ɔ:lweiz], *adv.* immer, stets.

am [æm] *see* **be**.

amalgamate [ə'mælgəmeit], *v.a.* amalgamieren. — *v.n.* sich vereinigen, vermischen.

amalgamation [əmælgə'meiʃən], *s.* die Verbindung, Vereinigung.

amass [ə'mæs], *v.a.* anhäufen, ~~mentragen~~.

amateur [æmə'tə: *or* 'æm~~~~], *s.* der Amateur, Liebhaber~~~~

amatory ['æmətəri~~~~] ~~~~liebt, sinnlich.

amaze [ə'meiz], *v.a.~~~~* Erstaunen versetzen;~~~~ (*baffle*).

amazement [ə'meizmənt], ~~s.~~ Erstaunen, Staunen, die Verw~~~~derung.

amazing [ə'meiziŋ], *adj.* erstaunlich, wunderbar.

Amazon (1) ['æməzən], *s.* (*Myth.*) die Amazone.

Amazon (2) ['æməzən], *s.* (*river*) der Amazonas.

ambassador [æm'bæsədə], *s.* der Botschafter.

ambassadorial [æmbæsə'dɔ:riəl], *adj.* Botschafts-, gesandtschaftlich.

amber ['æmbə], *s.* der Bernstein.

ambidextrous [æmbi'dekstrəs], *adj.* (mit beiden Händen gleich) geschickt.

ambiguity [æmbi'gju:iti], *s.* die Zweideutigkeit, der Doppelsinn.

ambiguous [æm'bigjuəs], *adj.* zweideutig; dunkel (*sense*).

ambit ['æmbit], *s.* der Umkreis, die Umgebung.

ambition [æm'biʃən], *s.* die Ambition, der Ehrgeiz.

ambitious [æm'biʃəs], *adj.* ehrgeizig.

amble [æmbl], *v.n.* schlendern, (gemächlich) spazieren.

ambulance ['æmbjuləns], *s.* der Krankenwagen.

ambush ['æmbuʃ], *v.a.* überfallen (*Acc.*), auflauern (*Dat.*). — *s.* die Falle, der Hinterhalt.

ameliorate [ə'mi:liəreit], *v.a.* verbessern.

amenable [ə'mi:nəbl], *adj.* zugänglich; unterworfen.

amend [ə'mend], *v.a.* verbessern, berichtigen; ändern.

amendment [ə'mendmənt], *s.* die Verbesserung; der Zusatz, die zusätzliche Änderung (*proposal*).

amends [ə'mendz], *s. pl.* der Schadenersatz; *make —,* Schadenersatz leisten; wiedergutmachen.

amenity [ə'mi:niti *or* ə'meniti], *s.* die Behaglichkeit, Annehmlichkeit; (*pl.*) die Vorzüge, *m pl.*; die Einrichtungen, *f. pl.*

American [ə'merikən], *adj.* amerikanisch; — *cloth*, das Wachstuch. — *s.* der Amerikaner.

amiability [eimjə'biliti], *s.* die Liebenswürdigkeit.

amiable ['eimjəbl], *adj.* liebenswürdig.

amicable ['æmikəbl], *adj.* freundschaftlich.

amidst [ə'midst], *prep.* mitten in, mitten unter (*Dat.*), inmitten (*Gen.*).

amiss [ə'mis], *adj., adv.* übel; verkehrt; *take —*, übelnehmen.

amity ['æmiti], *s.* die Freundschaft.

ammonia [ə'mounjə], *s.* das Ammoniak; *liquid —*, der Salmiakgeist.

ammunition [æmju'niʃən], *s.* die Munition.

amnesty ['æmnisti], *s.* die Amnestie, Begnadigung.

among(st) [ə'mʌŋ(st)], *prep.* (mitten) unter, zwischen, bei.

amorous ['æmərəs], *adj.* verliebt.

amorphous [ə'mɔːfəs], *adj.* amorph, gestaltlos, formlos.

amortization [əmɔːti'zeiʃən], *s.* die Amortisierung (*debt*); (*Comm.*) Tilgung, Abtragung.

amount [ə'maunt], *s.* der Betrag (*sum of money*); die Menge (*quantity*). — *v.n.* betragen; — *to*, sich belaufen auf (*Acc.*).

amphibian [æm'fibiən], *adj.* amphibisch. — *s.* (*Zool.*) die Amphibie.

amphibious [æm'fibiəs], *adj.* amphibienhaft.

ample [æmpl], *adj.* weit, breit (*scope*); voll, reichlich; ausgebreitet; genügend.

amplification [æmplifi'keiʃən], *s.* die Ausbreitung; Verbreiterung; Erklärung, Erweiterung; (*Elec.*) die Verstärkung (*sound*).

amplifier ['æmplifaiə], *s.* der Verstärker; der Lautsprecher.

amplify ['æmplifai], *v.a.* erweitern, ausführen, vergrößern; verstärken (*sound*).

amputate ['æmpjuteit], *v.a.* amputieren.

amputation [æmpju'teiʃən], *s.* die Amputation.

amuck [ə'mʌk], *adv.* amok.

amulet ['æmjulit], *s.* das Amulett.

amuse [ə'mju:z], *v.a.* unterhalten, amüsieren.

amusement [ə'mju:zmənt], *s.* die Unterhaltung, das Vergnügen.

an *see under* **a**.

Anabaptist [ænə'bæptist], *s.* der Wiedertäufer.

anachronism [ə'nækrənizm], *s.* der Anachronismus.

anaemia [ə'ni:miə], *s.* (*Med.*) die Blutarmut.

anaemic [ə'ni:mik], *adj.* (*Med.*) blutarm.

anaesthetic [ænəs'θetik], *adj.* schmerzbetäubend. — *s.* die Narkose.

analogous [ə'næləgəs], *adj.* analog.

analogy [ə'nælədʒi], *s.* die Analogie.

analyse ['ænəlaiz], *v.a.* analysieren.

analysis [ə'nælisis], *s.* die Analyse.

anarchic(al) [ə'na:kik(əl)], *adj.* anarchisch.

anarchy ['ænəki], *s.* die Anarchie.

anathema [ə'næθimə], *s.* (*Eccl.*) der Kirchenbann.

anatomical [ænə'tɔmikəl], *adj.* anatomisch.

anatomist [ə'nætəmist], *s.* der Anatom.

anatomize [ə'nætəmaiz], *v.a.* zergliedern, zerlegen.

anatomy [ə'nætəmi], *s.* die Anatomie.

ancestor ['ænsəstə], *s.* der Vorfahre, Ahnherr.

ancestry ['ænsəstri], *s.* die Ahnenreihe, Herkunft, der Stammbaum (*family tree*).

anchor ['æŋkə], *s.* der Anker. — *v.a.* verankern. — *v.n.* ankern.

anchorage ['æŋkəridʒ], *s.* die Verankerung; der Ankerplatz.

anchovy [æn'tʃouvi *or* 'æntʃəvi], *s.* (*Zool.*) die Sardelle.

ancient ['einʃənt], *adj.* alt, uralt, antik; althergebracht (*traditional*). — *s.* (*pl.*) die Alten (Griechen und Römer).

and [ænd], *conj.* und.

Andes, the ['ændi:z, ði], die Anden, *pl.*

anecdote ['ænekdout], *s.* die Anekdote.

anemone [ə'neməni], *s.* (*Bot.*) die Anemone, das Windröschen; (*Zool.*) *sea —*, die Seeanemone.

anew [ə'nju:], *adv.* von neuem.

angel ['eindʒəl], *s.* der Engel.

angelic [æn'dʒelik], *adj.* engelhaft, engelgleich.

anger ['æŋgə], *s.* der Zorn, Unwille, Ärger. — *v.a.* erzürnen, verärgern, ärgerlich machen.

angle [æŋgl], *s.* (*Geom.*) der Winkel; die Angel (*fishing*). — *v.n.* angeln (*for*, nach).

Angles [æŋglz], *s. pl.* die Angeln, *m. pl.*

Anglo-Saxon [æŋglou'sæksən], *adj.* angelsächsisch. — *s.* der Angelsachse.

anglicism ['æŋglisizm], *s.* der Anglizismus (*style*).

anguish ['æŋgwiʃ], *s.* die Qual, Pein.

angular ['æŋgjulə], *adj.* winklig, eckig.

anhydrous [æn'haidrəs], *adj.* wasserfrei, (*Chem.*) wasserlos.

aniline ['ænilain], *s.* das Anilin. — *adj.* — *dye*, die Anilinfarbe.

animal ['æniməl], *s.* das Tier, Lebewesen.

animate ['ænimeit], *v.a.* beleben, beseelen; (*fig.*) anregen.

animated ['ænimeitid], *adj.* belebt; munter.

animation [æni'meiʃən], *s.* die Belebung.

animosity [æni'mɔsiti], *s.* die Feindseligkeit, Abneigung, Erbitterung.

anise ['ænis], *s.* (*Bot.*) der Anis.

ankle [æŋkl], s. (Anat.) der Fußknöchel;
— socks, kurze Socken.

anklet ['æŋklit], s. der Fußring.

annalist ['ænəlist], s. der Chronist,
Geschichtsschreiber.

annals ['ænəlz], s. pl. die Annalen
(f. pl.); die Chronik (sing.).

anneal [ə'ni:l], v.a. ausglühen.

annex [ə'neks], v.a. annektieren, angliedern, sich aneignen.

annex(e) ['æneks], s. der Anhang, der
Anbau.

annexation [ænek'seiʃən], s. die An-
gliederung, Aneignung.

annihilate [ə'naiileit], v.a. vernichten,
zerstören.

annihilation [ənaii'leiʃən], s. die
Vernichtung, Zerstörung.

anniversary [æni'və:səri], s. der Jah-
restag, die Jahresfeier.

annotate ['ænoteit], v.a. anmerken,
mit Anmerkungen versehen.

annotation [æno'teiʃən], s. die Anmerkung, Notiz.

announce [ə'nauns], v.a. melden,
ankündigen; anzeigen; (Rad.) ansagen.

announcement [ə'naunsmənt], s. die
Ankündigung, Bekanntmachung;
(Rad.) die Ansage.

announcer [ə'naunsə], s. (Rad.) der
Ansager.

annoy [ə'nɔi], v.a. ärgern; belästigen.

annoyance [ə'nɔiəns], s. das Ärgernis;
die Belästigung.

annual ['ænjuəl], adj. jährlich, Jahres-.
— s. der Jahresband (serial publication); das Jahrbuch; (Bot.) die
einjährige Pflanze.

annuity [ə'nju:iti], s. die Jahresrente,
Lebensrente.

annul [ə'nʌl], v.a. annullieren, ungültig machen, für ungültig erklären.

annulment [ə'nʌlmənt], s. die Annul-
lierung, Ungültigkeitserklärung.

Annunciation [ənʌnsi'eiʃən], s. (Eccl.)
die Verkündigung.

anode ['ænoud], s. die Anode.

anodyne ['ænodain], adj. schmerz-
stillend.

anoint [ə'nɔint], v.a. salben.

anomalous [ə'nɔmələs], adj. abweichend, unregelmäßig, anomal.

anomaly [ə'nɔməli], s. die Anomalie,
Abweichung, Unregelmäßigkeit.

anon [ə'nɔn], adv. sogleich, sofort.

anonymous [ə'nɔniməs], adj. (abbr.
anon.) anonym; namenlos; unbekannt.

anonymity [æno'nimiti], s. die Anonymi-
tät.

another [ə'nʌðə], adj. & pron. ein
anderer; ein zweiter; noch einer; one
—, einander.

answer ['ɑ:nsə], v.a. beantworten. —
v.n. antworten. — s. die Antwort,
Erwiderung.

answerable ['ɑ:nsərəbl], adj. verantwortlich (responsible); beantwortbar
(capable of being answered).

ant [ænt], s. (Ent.) die Ameise.

antagonise [æn'tægənaiz], v.a. sich
(Dat.) jemanden zum Gegner machen.

antagonism [æn'tægənizm], s. der
Widerstreit, Konflikt; der Antagonis-
mus.

Antarctic [ænt'ɑ:ktik], adj. Südpol-,
antarktisch. — s. der südliche Polar-
kreis.

antecedence [ænti'si:dəns], s. der
Vortritt (rank).

antecedent [ænti'si:dənt], s. (pl.) das
Vorhergehende, die Vorgeschicht

antedate ['æntideit], v.a. vordat~

antediluvian [æntidi'lu:viən]
sintflutlich;(fig.) überh~ zusam-

antelope ['æntiloup]
...nətjuə], s. der
Antilope.

antenna [æn'...
Fühler; (Ro~ adj. Liebes-, ver-

anterior [æn...
space), älter, vo... erstaunen, in
(in time). verblüffen

anteroom ['æntiru:m], ... das
zimmer.

anthem ['ænθəm], s. die Hym~
Hymnus.

anther ['ænθə], s. (Bot.) der Staub-
beutel.

antic ['æntik], s. die Posse; (pl.)
komisches Benehmen.

anticipate [æn'tisipeit], v.a. vorwegnehmen; zuvorkommen; ahnen
(guess); erwarten (await); vorgreifen.

anticipation [æntisi'peiʃən], s. die
Vorwegnahme; die Erwartung.

antidote ['æntidout], s. das Gegengift.

antipathy [æn'tipəθi], s. die Antipathie,
der Widerwille.

antipodal [æn'tipədəl], adj. anti-
podisch; entgegengesetzt.

antiquarian [ænti'kwɛəriən], adj. altertümlich; antiquarisch.

antiquary ['æntikwəri], s. der Alter-
tumsforscher, Antiquar.

antiquated ['æntikweitid], adj. über-
holt, unmodern, veraltet.

antique [æn'ti:k], s. die Antike; das
alte Kunstwerk. — adj. alt, antik;
altmodisch.

antiquity [æn'tikwiti], s. die Antike,
das Altertum; die Vorzeit (period of
history).

antiseptic [ænti'septik], adj. antisep-
tisch — s. das antiseptische Mittel.

antler ['æntlə], s. die Geweihsprosse;
(pl.) das Geweih.

anvil ['ænvil], s. der Amboß.

anxiety [æŋ'zaiəti], s. die Angst (fear);
Besorgnis (uneasiness); Unruhe.

anxious ['æŋkʃəs], adj. ängstlich
(afraid); besorgt (worried); eifrig
bemüht (keen, um, on, Acc.).

any ['eni], adj. & pron. jeder; irgendein;
etwas; (pl.) einige; (neg.) not —, kein.

anybody, anyone ['enibədi, 'eniwan],
pron. irgendeiner, jemand; jeder.

anyhow, anyway ['enihau, 'eniweið],
adv. irgendwie, auf irgendeine Weise;
auf alle Fälle.

anyone see under **anybody**.

anything ['eniθiŋ], s. irgend etwas; alles.

anyway see under **anyhow**.

anywhere ['enihwɛə], adv. irgendwo; überall; not —, nirgends.

apace [ə'peis], adv. geschwind, hurtig, flink.

apart [ə'pɑ:t], adv. für sich, abgesondert; einzeln; poles —, weit entfernt; take —, zerlegen; — from, abgesehen von.

apartment [ə'pɑ:tmənt], s. das Zimmer; (Am.) die Wohnung (flat).

apathy ['æpəθi], s. die Apathie, Interesselosigkeit, Gleichgültigkeit.

apathetic [æpə'θetik], adj. apathisch, uninteressiert; teilnahmslos.

ape [eip], s. (Zool.) der Affe. — v.a. nachäffen, nachahmen.

aperient [ə'piəriənt], adj. (Med.) abführend. — s. (Med.) das Abführmittel.

aperture ['æpətʃə], s. die Öffnung.

apex ['eipeks], s. die Spitze, der Gipfel.

aphorism ['æfərizm], s. der Aphorismus.

apiary ['eipiəri], s. das Bienenhaus.

apiece [ə'pi:s], adv. pro Stück, pro Person.

apologetic [əpɔlə'dʒetik], adj. entschuldigend, reumütig; verteidigend.

apologize [ə'pɔlədʒaiz], v.n. sich entschuldigen (for, wegen; to, bei).

apology [ə'pɔlədʒi], s. die Entschuldigung; Abbitte; Rechtfertigung.

apoplectic [æpə'plektik], adj. (Med.) apoplektisch.

apoplexy ['æpəpleksi], s. (Med.) der Schlagfluß, Schlaganfall (fit).

apostle [ə'pɔsl], s. der Apostel.

apostolic [æpəs'tɔlik], adj. apostolisch.

apostrophe [ə'pɔstrəfi], s. der Apostroph (punctuation); die Anrede (speech).

apostrophize [ə'pɔstrəfaiz], v.a. apostrophieren; anreden (speak to).

apotheosis [əpɔθi'ousis], s. die Apotheose.

appal [ə'pɔ:l], v.a. erschrecken.

appalling [ə'pɔ:liŋ], adj. schrecklich.

apparatus [æpə'reitəs], s. das Gerät, die Apparatur; (coll.) der Apparat.

apparel [ə'pærəl], s. die Kleidung.

apparent [ə'pærənt], adj. scheinbar; offensichtlich; augenscheinlich; heir —, der rechtmäßige Erbe.

apparition [æpə'riʃən], s. die Erscheinung; der Geist, das Gespenst (ghost).

appeal [ə'pi:l], v.n. appellieren (make an appeal); (Law) Berufung einlegen; gefallen (please). — s. (public, Mil.) der Appell; die Bitte (request).

appear [ə'piə], v.n. erscheinen; scheinen; auftreten.

appearance [ə'piərəns], s. die Erscheinung; das Auftreten (stage, etc.); der Schein (semblance); keep up—s, den Schein wahren; to all —s, allem Anschein nach.

appease [ə'pi:z], v.a. besänftigen.

appeasement [ə'pi:zmənt], s. die Besänftigung, (Pol.) die Befriedung.

appellation [æpe'leiʃən], s. die Benennung.

append [ə'pend], v.a. anhängen, beifügen.

appendicitis [əpendi'saitis], s. (Med.) die Blinddarmentzündung.

appendix [ə'pendiks], s. der Anhang; (Med.) der Blinddarm.

appertain [æpə'tein], v.n. gehören (to, zu).

appetite ['æpitait], s. der Appetit.

appetizing ['æpitaiziŋ], adj. appetitlich, appetitanregend.

applaud [ə'plɔ:d], v.a., v.n. applaudieren, Beifall klatschen (Dat.).

applause [ə'plɔ:z], s. der Applaus, Beifall.

apple [æpl], s. der Apfel.

appliance [ə'plaiəns], s. das Gerät, die Vorrichtung.

applicable ['æplikəbl], adj. anwendbar, passend (to, auf).

applicant ['æplikənt], s. der Bewerber (for, um).

application [æpli'keiʃən], s. die Bewerbung (for, um); das Gesuch; die Anwendung (to, auf); letter of —, der Bewerbungsbrief; — form, das Bewerbungsformular.

apply [ə'plai], v.a. anwenden (auf, to, Acc.); gebrauchen. — v.n. sich bewerben (um, for, Acc.); (Dat.) this does not —, das trifft nicht zu; — within, drinnen nachfragen.

appoint [ə'pɔint], v.a. bestimmen; ernennen; ausrüsten.

appointment [ə'pɔintmənt], s. die Festsetzung; die Ernennung; die Bestellung; die Stellung (position); make an —, jemanden ernennen (fill a post), sich verabreden (arrange to meet); by —, Hoflieferant (to, Genit.).

apportion [ə'pɔ:ʃən], v.a. zuteilen, zuweisen, zumessen.

apposite ['æpəzit], adj. passend, angemessen.

appositeness ['æpəzitnis], s. die Angemessenheit.

appraise [ə'preiz], v.a. beurteilen.

appraisal [ə'preizəl], s. die Beurteilung, Abschätzung.

appreciable [ə'pri:ʃəbl], adj. merklich; nennenswert.

appreciate [ə'pri:ʃieit], v.a. würdigen, schätzen.

appreciation [əpri:ʃi'eiʃən], s. die Schätzung, Würdigung.

apprehend [æpri'hend], v.a. verhaften, ergreifen (arrest); befürchten (fear).

apprehension [æpri'henʃən], s. die Verhaftung (arrest); die Befürchtung (fear).

apprehensive [æpri'hensiv], adj. besorgt, in Furcht (for, um), furchtsam.

apprentice [ə'prentis], s. der Lehrling; Praktikant. — v.a. in die Lehre geben (with, bei, Dat.).

apprenticeship

apprenticeship [ə'prentiſip], *s.* die Lehre, Lehrzeit, Praktikantenzeit; *student* —, die Studentenpraxis.

apprise [ə'praiz], *v.a.* benachrichtigen, informieren.

approach [ə'proutʃ], *v.a.*, *v.n.* sich nähern (*Dat.*). — *s.* die Annäherung, das Herankommen, Näherrücken.

approachable [ə'proutʃəbl], *adj.* zugänglich, freundlich.

approbation [æpro'beiʃən], *s.* die (offizielle) Billigung, Zustimmung.

appropriate [ə'proupriit], *adj.* angemessen, gebührend, geeignet (*suitable*). — [ə'prouprieit], *v.a.* requirieren, sich aneignen.

appropriation [əproupri'eiʃən], *s.* die Requisition, Aneignung, Übernahme, Besitznahme.

approval [ə'pru:vəl], *s.* die Billigung, der Beifall, die Zustimmung.

approve [ə'pru:v], *v.a.* loben, billigen; genehmigen; annehmen (*work*).

approved [ə'pru:vd], *adj.* anerkannt.

approximate [ə'prɔksimit], *adj.* ungefähr, annähernd. —*v.n.* & *a.*[ə'prɔksimeit],sich nähern.

approximation [əprɔksi'meiʃən], *s.* die Annäherung.

approximative [ə'prɔksimətiv], *adj.* annähernd.

appurtenance [ə'pə:tənəns], *s.* das (or der) Zubehör.

appurtenant [ə'pə:tənənt], *adj.* zugehörig.

apricot ['eiprikɔt], *s.* (*Bot.*) die Aprikose.

April ['eipril]. der April.

apron ['eiprən], *s.* die Schürze; der Schurz; — *stage*, die Vorbühne, das Proszenium.

apropos [ɑ:prɔ'pou], *adv.* beiläufig; mit Bezug auf, diesbezüglich.

apse [æps], *s.* (*Archit.*) die Apsis.

apt [æpt], *adj.* geeignet, passend; fähig.

aptitude ['æptitju:d], *s.* die Eignung, Fähigkeit.

aptness ['æptnis], *s.* die Angemessenheit, Eignung.

aquatic [ə'kwɔtik or ə'kwætik], *adj.* Wasser-, wasser-; — *display*, Wasserkünste. — *s.* (*pl.*) der Wassersport.

aqueduct ['ækwidʌkt], *s.* die Wasserleitung; der Aquädukt.

aqueous ['eikwiəs], *adj.* (*Chem.*) wässerig.

aquiline ['ækwilain], *adj.* adlerartig, Adler-.

Arab ['ærəb], *s.* der Araber.

Arabian [ə'reibiən], *adj.* arabisch; — *Nights*, Tausend-und-eine-Nacht.

Arabic ['ærəbik], *adj.* arabisch (*language, literature*).

arable ['ærəbl], *adj.* pflügbar, bestellbar.

arbiter ['ɑ:bitə], *s.* der Schiedsrichter.

arbitrary ['ɑ:bitrəri], *adj.* willkürlich.

arbitrate ['ɑ:bitreit], *v.n.* vermitteln.

arbitration [ɑ:bi'treiʃən], *s.* die Vermittlung; Entscheidung; (*Ccmm.*) Arbitrage.

arboriculture ['ɑ:bɔrikʌltʃə], *s.* die Baumzucht.

arbour ['ɑ:bə], *s.* die Laube, Gartenlaube.

arc [ɑ:k], *s.* (*Geom.*) der Bogen; — *lamp*, die Bogenlampe; — *welding*, das Lichtschweißen.

arcade [ɑ:'keid], *s.* die Arkade.

Arcadian [ɑ:'keidiən], *adj.* arkadisch. — *s.* der Arkadier.

arch [ɑ:tʃ], *s.* der Bogen, die Wölbung; —*way*, der Bogengang. — *v.a.*, *v.n.* wölben, sich wölben. — *adj.* schelmisch, listig. — *prefix* oberst; erst Haupt-; -*enemy*, der Erzfeind.

archaeological [ɑ:kiə'lɔdʒikəl], *adj.* archäologisch.

archaeologist [ɑ:ki'ɔlədʒist], *s.* der Archäologe.

archaeology [ɑ:ki'ɔlədʒi], *s.* die Archäologie.

archaic [ɑ:'keiik], *adj.* altertümlich.

archaism ['ɑ:keiizm], *s.* der Archaismus (*style*).

archbishop [ɑ:tʃ'biʃəp], *s.* der Erzbischof.

archduke [ɑ:tʃ'dju:k], *s.* der Erzherzog.

archer ['ɑ:tʃə], *s.* der Bogenschütze.

archery ['ɑ:tʃəri], *s.* das Bogenschießen.

architect ['ɑ:kitekt], *s.* der Architekt, Baumeister.

architecture ['ɑ:kitektʃə], *s.* die Architektur, Baukunst.

archives ['ɑ:kaivz], *s. pl.* das Archiv.

Arctic ['ɑ:ktik], *adj.* arktisch. — *s.* die Nordpolarländer, *n. pl.*

ardent ['ɑ:dənt], *adj.* heiß, glühend, brennend.

ardour ['ɑ:də], *s.* die Hitze, die Inbrunst, der Eifer.

arduous ['ɑ:djuəs], *adj.* schwierig; mühsam.

area ['ɛəriə], *s.* das Areal (*measurement*); das Gebiet, die Zone; die Fläche (*region*).

arena [ə'ri:nə], *s.* die Arena, der Kampfplatz.

Argentine ['ɑ:dʒəntain], *adj.* argentinisch. — (*Republic*), Argentinien, *n.*

Argentinian [ɑ:dʒən'tiniən], *adj.* argentinisch. — *s.* der Argentin(i)er.

argue ['ɑ:gju:], *v.n.* disputieren, streiten; folgern, schließen.

argument ['ɑ:gjumənt], *s.* das Argument; (*Log.*) der Beweis; der Streit (*dispute*).

argumentative [ɑ:gju'mentətiv], *adj.* streitsüchtig.

arid ['ærid], *adj.* trocken, dürr.

aright [ə'rait], *adv.* richtig, zurecht.

arise [ə'raiz], *v.n. irr.* aufstehen; sich erheben; entstehen (*originate*); *arising from the minutes*, es ergibt sich aus dem Protokoll.

aristocracy [æris'tɔkrəsi], *s.* die Aristokratie, der Adel.

aristocratic [æris'o'krætik], *adj.* aristokratisch, adlig.

arithmetic [ə'riθmətik], *s.* die Arithmetik.

arithmetical [æriθ'metikəl], *adj.* arithmetisch.

ark [ɑ:k], *s.* die Arche; — *of the Covenant*, die Bundeslade.

arm (1) [ɑ:m], *s.* (*Anat.*) der Arm.

arm (2) [ɑ:m], *s.* die Waffe; *up in* —*s*, in Aufruhr. — *v.a., v.n.* bewaffnen, sich bewaffnen, rüsten, sich rüsten.

armament ['ɑ:məmənt], *s.* die Rüstung, Bewaffnung.

armature ['ɑ:mətiuə], *s.* die Armatur.

armchair ['ɑ:mtʃɛə], *s.* der Lehnstuhl; der Sessel.

Armenian [ɑ:'mi:niən], *adj.* armenisch. — *s.* der Armenier.

armistice ['ɑ:mistis], *s.* der Waffenstillstand.

armour ['ɑ:mə], *s.* die Rüstung, der Harnisch; —*plated*, gepanzert; —*ed car*, der Panzerwagen.

armourer ['ɑ:mərə], *s.* der Waffenschmied.

armoury ['ɑ:məri], *s.* die Rüstkammer, Waffenschmiede.

army ['ɑ:mi], *s.* die Armee, das Heer.

aroma [ə'roumə], *s.* das Aroma, der Duft.

aromatic [ærə'mætik], *adj.* aromatisch. —*s.* (*Chem.*) das Aromat.

around [ə'raund], *adv.* herum, rund-, ringsherum, umher, im Kreise; *stand* —, herumstehen; *be* —, sich in der Nähe halten. — *prep.* um; bei, um . . . herum.

arouse [ə'rauz], *v.a.* aufwecken, aufrütteln.

arraignment [ə'reinmənt], *s.* die Anklage.

arrange [ə'reindʒ], *v.a.* anordnen, arrangieren, einrichten, vereinbaren.

arrangement [ə'reindʒmənt], *s.* die Anordnung; die Einrichtung; die Vereinbarung (*agreement*); (*Law*) die Vergleichung, der Vergleich.

arrant ['ærənt], *adj.* durchtrieben.

array [ə'rei], *v.a.* schmücken, aufstellen. — *s.* die Ordnung; Aufstellung.

arrears [ə'riəz], *s. pl.* der Rückstand, die Schulden.

arrest [ə'rest], *v.a.* (*Law*) festnehmen, verhaften; festhalten; aufhalten (*hinder*). — *s.* die Festnahme; die Festhaltung.

arrival [ə'raivəl], *s.* die Ankunft.

arrive [ə'raiv], *v.n.* ankommen.

arrogance ['ærəgəns], *s.* die Anmaßung, Überheblichkeit.

arrogant ['ærəgənt], *adj.* anmaßend, hochfahrend, überheblich.

arrow ['ærou], *s.* der Pfeil.

arrowroot ['ærouru:t], *s.* (*Bot.*) die Pfeilwurz.

arsenal ['ɑ:sinəl], *s.* das Arsenal, Zeughaus.

arsenic ['ɑ:sənik], *s.* das Arsen.

arson ['ɑ:sən], *s.* die Brandstiftung.

art [ɑ:t], *s.* die Kunst; *fine* —, schöne Kunst; (*Univ.*) —*s faculty*, die philosophische Fakultät; —*s* (*subject*), das humanistische Fach, die Geisteswissenschaften.

arterial [ɑ:'tiəriəl], *adj.* Pulsader-, Schlagader-; — *road*, die Hauptverkehrsader, die Hauptstraße.

artery ['ɑ:təri], *s.* die Pulsader, Schlagader; der Hauptverkehrsweg.

artesian [ɑ:'ti:ʒən], *adj.* artesisch.

artful ['ɑ:tful], *adj.* listig, schlau.

article ['ɑ:tikl], *s.* (*Gram.*, *Law*, *Press*) der Artikel; der Posten (*item in list*). — *v.a. be* —*d to a solicitor*, bei einem Advokaten assistieren.

articulate [ɑ:'tikjuleit], *v.a.* artikulieren (*pronounce clearly*). — [—lit], *adj.* deutlich (*speech*).

articulation [ɑ:tikju'leiʃən], *s.* die Artikulation, deutliche Aussprache.

artifice ['ɑ:tifis], *s.* der Kunstgriff, die List.

artificer [ɑ:'tifisə], *s.* der Handwerker.

artificial [ɑ:ti'fiʃəl], *adj.* künstlich, Kunst-; — *silk*, die Kunstseide.

artillery [ɑ:'tiləri], *s.* die Artillerie.

artisan [ɑ:ti'zæn], *s.* der Handwerker.

artist ['ɑ:tist], *s.* der Künstler, die Künstlerin.

artistic [ɑ:'tistik], *adj.* künstlerisch.

artless ['ɑ:tlis], *adj.* arglos, natürlich, naiv.

Aryan ['ɛəriən], *adj.* arisch. — *s.* der Arier.

as [æz], *adv.*, *conj.* so, als, wie, ebenso; als, während, weil; — *big* —, so groß wie; — *well* —, sowohl als auch; *such* —, wie; — *it were*, gleichsam.

asbestos [æz'bestɔs], *s.* der Asbest.

ascend [ə'send], *v.a.*, *v.n.* ersteigen, besteigen; emporsteigen.

ascendancy, -ency [ə'sendənsi], *s.* der Aufstieg; der Einfluß; das Übergewicht.

ascendant, -ent [ə'sendənt], *s. in the* —, aufsteigend.

ascent [ə'sent], *s.* der Aufstieg, die Besteigung.

ascension [ə'senʃən], *s.* (*Astron.*) das Aufsteigen; *Ascension Day*, Himmelfahrt(stag).

ascertain [æsə'tein], *v.a.* in Erfahrung bringen, erkunden, feststellen.

ascertainable [æsə'teinəbl], *adj.* erkundbar, feststellbar.

ascetic [ə'setik], *adj.* asketisch.

asceticism [ə'setisizm], *s.* die Askese.

ascribe [ə'skraib], *v.a.* zuschreiben.

ascribable [ə'skraibəbl], *adj.* zuzuschreiben, zuschreibbar.

ash (1) [æʃ], *s.* (*Bot.*) die Esche.

ash (2) [æʃ], *s.* die Asche.

ashamed [ə'ʃeimd], *adj.* beschämt; *be* —, sich schämen.

ashcan ['æʃkæn] (*Am.*) *see* **dustbin**.

ashen ['æʃən], *adj.* aschgrau, aschfarben.

ashore [ə'ʃɔ:], *adv.* am Land; am Ufer, ans Ufer *or* Land.

ashtray ['æʃtrei], *s.* der Aschenbecher.

Ash Wednesday [æʃ'wenzdei], *s.* der Aschermittwoch.

Asiatic [eiʃi'ætik], *adj.* asiatisch. — *s.* der Asiat.

aside

aside [ə'said], *adv.* seitwärts, zur Seite; abseits.

ask [ɑ:sk], *v.a., v.n.* fragen (*question*); bitten (*request*); fordern (*demand*); einladen (*invite*).

asleep [ə'sli:p], *pred. adj., adv.* schlafend, im Schlaf; eingeschlafen.

asp [æsp], *s.* (*Zool.*) die Natter.

asparagus [æs'pærəgəs], *s.* (*Bot.*) der Spargel.

aspect ['æspekt], *s.* der Anblick, die Ansicht (*view, angle*); der Gesichtspunkt.

aspen ['æspən], *s.* (*Bot.*) die Espe.

asperity [æs'periti], *s.* die Härte; Rauheit.

aspersion [æs'pə:ʃən], *s.* die Verleumdung; Schmähung.

asphalt ['æsfælt], *s.* der Asphalt.

asphyxia [æs'fiksjə], *s.* (*Med.*) die Erstickung.

aspirant [ə'spaiərənt, 'æsp-], *s.* der Bewerber, Anwärter.

aspirate ['æspireit], *v.a.* (*Phon.*) aspirieren. — [—rit] *adj.* aspiriert. — *s.* der Hauchlaut.

aspiration [æspi'reiʃən], *s.* der Atemzug; das Streben (*striving*) ; (*Phon.*) die Aspiration.

aspire [ə'spaiə], *v.n.* streben, verlangen.

ass [æs], *s.* der Esel.

assail [ə'seil], *v.a.* angreifen, anfallen.

assailable [ə'seiləbl], *adj.* angreifbar.

assassin [ə'sæsin], *s.* der Meuchelmörder.

assassinate [ə'sæsineit], *v.a.* meuchlings ermorden.

assassination [əsæsi'neiʃən], *s.* der Meuchelmord, die Ermordung.

assault [ə'sɔ:lt], *v.a.* angreifen, überfallen. — *s.* der Überfall, Angriff.

assay [ə'sei], *s.* die Metallprobe. — *v.a.* (auf Edelmetall hin) prüfen.

assemble [ə'sembl], *v.a., v.n.* versammeln, sich versammeln.

assembly [ə'sembli], *s.* die Versammlung (*assemblage*) ; — line, das laufende Band, das Fließband.

assent [ə'sent], *v.n.* beistimmen (*Dat.*), billigen (*Acc.*). — *s.* die Zustimmung (zu, *Dat.*), Billigung (*Genit.*).

assert [ə'sə:t], *v.a.* behaupten.

assertion [ə'sə:ʃən], *s.* die Behauptung.

assess [ə'ses], *v.a.* schätzen, beurteilen.

assessment [ə'sesmənt], *s.* die Beurteilung, Schätzung, Wertung.

assessor [ə'sesə], *s.* der Beurteiler, Einschätzer, Bewerter, Assessor; der Beisitzer (*second examiner*).

assets ['æsets], *s. pl.* (*Comm.*) die Aktiva; Vorzüge (*personal*).

assiduity [æsi'djuiti], *s.* der Fleiß, die Emsigkeit.

assiduous [ə'sidjuəs], *adj.* fleißig, unablässig, emsig.

assign [ə'sain], *v.a.* zuteilen, anweisen, zuweisen (*apportion*), festsetzen (*fix*).

assignable [ə'sainəbl], *adj.* zuteilbar; bestimmbar.

assignation [æsig'neiʃən], *s.* die Zuweisung; (*Law*) die Übertragung; die Verabredung.

assignment [ə'sainmənt], *s.* die Zuweisung, Übertragung; die Aufgabe.

assimilate [ə'simileit], *v.a., v.n.* assimilieren, angleichen; sich assimilieren, sich angleichen, ähnlich werden.

assist [ə'sist], *v.a., v.n.* beistehen (*Dat.*), helfen (*Dat.*), unterstützen (*Acc.*).

assistance [ə'sistəns], *s.* der Beistand, die Hilfe; die Aushilfe; (*financial*) der Zuschuß.

assistant [ə'sistənt], *s.* der Assistent, Helfer.

assize [ə'saiz], *s.* die Gerichtssitzung; (*pl.*) das Schwurgericht.

associate [ə'souʃieit], *v.a.* verbinden (*link*). — *v.n.* verkehren (*company*); sich verbinden; (*Comm.*) sich vereinigen. — [—iit], *s.* (*Comm.*) der Partner.

association [əsousi'eiʃən], *s.* die Vereinigung, der Bund, Verein; die Gesellschaft; der Verkehr.

assonance ['æsənəns], *s.* (*Phon.*) die Assonanz, der Gleichklaut.

assort [ə'sɔ:t], *v.a.* ordnen, aussuchen, sortieren; —ed sweets, gemischte Bonbons.

assortment [ə'sɔ:tmənt], *s.* die Sammlung, Mischung, Auswahl.

assuage [ə'sweidʒ], *v.a.* mildern, besänftigen, stillen.

assume [ə'sju:m], *v.a.* annehmen; übernehmen, ergreifen.

assuming [ə'sju:miŋ], *adj.* anmaßend; — that, angenommen daß . . ., gesetzt den Fall.

assumption [ə'sʌmpʃən], *s.* die Annahme (*opinion*); Übernahme (*taking up*); Aneignung (*appropriation*); *Assumption of the Blessed Virgin*, Mariä Himmelfahrt.

assurance [ə'ʃuərəns], *s.* die Versicherung; Sicherheit (*manner*).

assure [ə'ʃuə], *v.a.* versichern, sicher stellen, ermutigen.

assuredly [ə'ʃuəridli], *adv.* sicherlich, gewiß.

aster ['æstə], *s.* (*Bot.*) die Aster.

asterisk ['æstərisk], *s.* (*Typ.*) das Sternchen.

astern [ə'stə:n], *adv.* (*Naut.*) achteraus.

asthma ['æsθmə], *s.* das Asthma.

asthmatic [æsθ'mætik], *adj.* asthmatisch.

astir [ə'stə:], *adv.* wach, in Bewegung.

astonish [ə'stɔniʃ], *v.a.* in Erstaunen versetzen, verblüffen.

astonishment [ə'stɔniʃmənt], *s.* das Erstaunen, die Verwunderung; die Bestürzung.

astound [ə'staund], *v.a.* in Erstaunen versetzen, bestürzen.

astounding [ə'staundiŋ], *adj.* erstaunlich, verblüffend.

astral ['æstrəl], *adj.* Stern(en)-, gestirnt.

astray [ə'strei], *pred. adj.*, *adv.* irre; *go* —, sich verirren; (*fig.*) abschweifen.
astride[ə'straid], *pred.adj.*, *adv.* rittlings.
astringent [ə'strindʒənt], *adj.* zusammenziehend.
astrologer [ə'strɔlədʒə], *s.* der Sterndeuter, Astrolog(e).
astrological [æstrə'lɔdʒikəl], *adj.* astrologisch.
astrology [æ'strɔlədʒi], *s.* die Astrologie, Sterndeuterei.
astronaut['æstrənɔːt], *s.* der Astronaut.
astronomer [ə'strɔnəmə], *s.* der Astronom.
astronomical[æstrə'nɔmikəl],*adj.*astronomisch.
astronomy [ə'strɔnəmi], *s.* die Astronomie, Sternkunde.
astute [ə'stjuːt], *adj.* listig, schlau.
astuteness [ə'stjuːtnis], *s.* die Schlauheit, Listigkeit, der Scharfsinn.
asunder [ə'sʌndə], *adv.* auseinander, entzwei.
asylum [ə'sailəm], *s.* das Asyl, der Zufluchtsort (*refuge*); *lunatic* —, das Irrenhaus.
at [æt], *prep.* an; auf; bei; für; in, nach; mit, gegen; um, über; von, aus, zu; — *my expense*, auf meine Kosten; — *all*, überhaupt; — *first*, zuerst; — *last*, zuletzt, endlich; — *peace*, in Frieden; *what are you driving* —? worauf wollen sie hinaus?
atheism ['eiθiizm], *s.* der Atheismus.
atheist ['eiθiist], *s.* der Atheist.
atheistic [eiθi'istik], *adj.* atheistisch, gottlos.
Athens ['æθənz]. Athen, *n.*
Athenian [ə'θiːnjən], *s.* der Athener. — *adj.* athenisch.
athlete ['æθliːt], *s.* der Athlet.
athletic [æθ'letik], *adj.* athletisch.
athletics [æθ'letiks], *s. pl.* die Leichtathletik, Athletik.
Atlantic (Ocean) [ət'læntik ('ouʃən)]. der Atlantik.
atlas ['ætləs], *s.* der Atlas.
atmosphere ['ætməsfiə], *s.* die Atmosphäre.
atmospheric(al) [ætməs'ferik(əl)], *adj.* atmosphärisch. — *s.* (*pl.*) atmosphärische Störungen, *f. pl.*
atoll[ə'tɔl], *s.* die Koralleninsel, das Atoll.
atom ['ætəm], *s.* das Atom.
atomic [ə'tɔmik], *adj.* (*Phys.*) Atom–, atomisch, atomar; (*theory*) atomistisch; — *bomb*, die Atombombe; — *pile*, der Atomreaktor; — *armament*, die atomare Aufrüstung.
atone [ə'toun], *v.n.* sühnen, büßen.
atonement [ə'tounmənt], *s.* die Buße, Sühne, Versöhnung.
atonic [ei'tɔnik], *adj.* tonlos, unbetont.
atrocious [ə'trouʃəs], *adj.* gräßlich, schrecklich, entsetzlich.
atrocity [ə'trɔsiti], *s.* die Gräßlichkeit, Grausamkeit, Greueltat.
atrophy ['ætrəfi], *s.* (*Med.*) die Abmagerung, Atrophie. — ['ætrəfai], *v.n.* absterben, auszehren.

attach [ə'tætʃ], *v.a.* anheften, beilegen, anhängen; (*fig.*) beimessen (*attribute*).
attachment [ə'tætʃmənt], *s.* das Anhaften (*sticking to*, an, *Acc.*); das Anhängsel (*appendage*); die Freundschaft (*to*, für, *Acc.*); die Anhänglichkeit (*loyalty*, an, *Acc.*).
attack [ə'tæk], *v.a.* angreifen. — *s.* die Attacke, der Angriff; (*Med.*) der Anfall.
attain [ə'tein], *v.a.* erreichen, erlangen.
attainable [ə'teinəbl], *adj.* erreichbar.
attainment [ə'teinmənt], *s.* die Erlangung, Erreichung; Errungenschaft; (*pl.*) Kenntnisse, *f. pl.*
attempt [ə'tempt], *s.* der Versuch. — *v.a.* versuchen.
attend [ə'tend], *v.a.*, *v.n.* begleiten, anwesend sein (*be present, at*, bei, *Dat.*); beiwohnen (*be present as guest*); zuhören (*listen to*); bedienen (*customer*); behandeln (*patient*).
attendance [ə'tendəns], *s.* die Begleitung (*accompaniment*); die Anwesenheit (*presence*); die Zuhörerschaft (*audience*); *to be in* —, Dienst tun (*at*, bei); anwesend sein (*be present*).
attendant [ə'tendənt], *s.* der Diener, Wärter.
attention [ə'tenʃən], *s.* die Aufmerksamkeit, Achtung.
attentive [ə'tentiv], *adj.* aufmerksam.
attenuate [ə'tenjueit], *v.a.* verdünnen (*dilute*). — *v.n.* abmagern.
attest [ə'test], *v.a.* attestieren, bezeugen, bescheinigen.
attestation [ætes'teiʃən], *s.* die Bescheinigung; das Zeugnis.
Attic ['ætik], *adj.* attisch, klassisch.
attic ['ætik], *s.* die Dachkammer, die Dachstube.
attire [ə'taiə], *v.a.* ankleiden, kleiden. — *s.* die Kleidung.
attitude ['ætitjuːd], *s.* die Haltung, Stellung (*toward*, zu), Einstellung.
attorney [ə'təːni], *s.* der Anwalt; *Attorney-General*, der Kronanwalt; (*Am.*) der Staatsanwalt; — *at law*, Rechtsanwalt.
attract [ə'trækt], *v.a.* anziehen.
attraction [ə'trækʃən], *s.* die Anziehung; der Reiz (*appeal*); die Anziehungskraft.
attractive [ə'træktiv], *adj.* anziehend, reizvoll.
attribute [ə'tribjuːt], *v.a.* zuschreiben, beimessen. — *s.* [ə'tribjuːt], (*Gram.*) das Attribut, die Eigenschaft.
attributive [ə'tribjutiv], *adj.* (*Gram.*) attributiv; beilegend.
attrition [ə'triʃən], *s.* die Zermürbung, Aufreibung, Reue.
attune [ə'tjuːn], *v.a.* (*Mus.*) stimmen, anpassen (*adapt to*, an, *Acc.*).
auburn ['ɔːbəːn], *adj.* rotbraun.
auction ['ɔːkʃən], *s.* die Auktion, die Versteigerung.
auctioneer [ɔːkʃə'niə], *s.* der Auktionator, Versteigerer.

315

audacious [ɔː'deiʃəs], *adj.* waghalsig, kühn, dreist.

audacity [ɔː'dæsiti], *s.* die Kühnheit (*valour*); Frechheit (*impudence*).

audible ['ɔːdibl], *adj.* hörbar.

audibility [ɔːdi'biliti], *s.* die Hörbarkeit, Vernehmbarkeit.

audience ['ɔːdjəns], *s.* die Audienz (*of the Pope*, beim Papst); (*Theat.*) das Publikum; (*listeners*) die Zuhörer.

audit ['ɔːdit], *s.* die Rechnungsprüfung, Revision. — *v.a.* revidieren, prüfen.

auditor ['ɔːditə], *s.* der Rechnungsrevisor, Buchprüfer.

auditory ['ɔːditəri], *adj.* Gehör–, Hör–.

auditorium [ɔːdi'tɔːriəm], *s.* der Hörsaal, Vortragssaal.

auger ['ɔːgə], *s.* der (große) Bohrer.

aught [ɔːt], *pron.* (*obs.*) irgend etwas (*opp. to* naught).

augment [ɔːg'ment], *v.a.*, *v.n.* vermehren, vergrößern; zunehmen.

augmentation [ɔːgmen'teiʃən], *s.* die Vergrößerung, Erhöhung, Zunahme.

augur ['ɔːgə], *v.a.* weissagen, prophezeien.

August ['ɔːgəst], der August.

august [ɔː'gʌst], *adj.* erhaben.

aunt [ɑːnt], *s.* die Tante.

aurora [ɔː'rɔːrə], *s.* die Morgenröte.

auscultation [ɔːskəl'teiʃən], *s.* (*Med.*) die Auskultation, Untersuchung.

auspices [ɔː'spisiz], *s.* die Auspizien.

auspicious [ɔː'spiʃəs], *adj.* unter glücklichem Vorzeichen, verheißungsvoll, günstig.

austere [ɔːs'tiə], *adj.* streng, ernst, schmucklos.

austerity [ɔːs'teriti], *s.* die Strenge.

Australian [ɔːs'streiljən], *adj.* australisch. — *s.* der Australier.

Austrian [ɔːs'striən], *adj.* österreichisch. — *s.* der Österreicher.

authentic [ɔː'θentik], *adj.* authentisch, echt.

authenticity [ɔːθen'tisiti], *s.* die Authentizität, Echtheit.

author, authoress ['ɔːθə, ɔːθər'es], *s.* der Autor, die Autorin; der Verfasser, die Verfasserin.

authoritative [ɔː'θoritətiv], *adj.* autoritativ, maßgebend.

authority [ɔː'θoriti], *s.* die Autorität, Vollmacht (*power of attorney*); das Ansehen; *the authorities*, die Behörden.

authorization [ɔːθorai'zeiʃən], *s.* die Bevollmächtigung, Befugnis.

authorize [ɔː'θoraiz], *v.a.* autorisieren, bevollmächtigen, berechtigen.

authorship [ɔː'θəʃip], *s.* die Autorschaft.

autobiographical [ɔːtobaiə'græfikl], *adj.* autobiographisch.

autobiography [ɔːtobai'ogrəfi], *s.* die Autobiographie.

autocracy [ɔː'tokrəsi], *s.* die Selbstherrschaft.

autocrat ['ɔːtokræt], *s.* der Autokrat, Selbstherrscher.

autograph ['ɔːtogræf, -grɑːf], *s.* die eigene Handschrift, Unterschrift; das Autogramm.

automatic [ɔːto'mætik], *adj.* automatisch.

automatize [ɔː'tomətaiz], *v.a.* automatisieren, auf Automation umstellen.

automation [ɔːto'meiʃən], *s.* (*Engin.*) die Automation; Automatisierung.

automaton [ɔː'tomətən], *s.* der Automat.

automobile ['ɔːtomobiːl], *s.* der Kraftwagen, das Auto.

autonomous [ɔː'tonəməs], *adj.* autonom, unabhängig.

autonomy [ɔː'tonəmi], *s.* die Autonomie, Unabhängigkeit.

autopsy ['ɔːtopsi], *s.* die Autopsie; Obduktion, Leichenschau.

autumn ['ɔːtəm], *s.* der Herbst.

autumnal [ɔː'tʌmnəl], *adj.* herbstlich.

auxiliary [ɔːg'ziljəri], *adj.* Hilfs-.

avail [ə'veil], *v.n.* nützen, helfen, von Vorteil sein. — *v.r.* — *o.s of a th.*, sich einer Sache bedienen. — *s.* der Nutzen; *of no* —, nutzlos.

available [ə'veiləbl], *adj.* vorrätig, verfügbar, zur Verfügung (stehend).

avalanche ['ævəlɑːnʃ], *s.* die Lawine.

avarice ['ævəris], *s.* der Geiz, die Habsucht, Gier.

avaricious [ævə'riʃəs], *adj.* geizig, habsüchtig, habgierig.

avenge [ə'vendʒ], *v.a.* rächen.

avenue ['ævənjuː], *s.* die Allee; der Zugang.

average ['ævəridʒ], *adj.* durchschnittlich; *not more than* —, mäßig. — *s.* der Durchschnitt; *on an* —, durchschnittlich, im Durchschnitt. — *v.a.* den Durchschnitt nehmen.

averse [ə'vəːs], *adj.* abgeneigt (*to, Dat.*).

aversion [ə'vəːʃən], *s.* die Abneigung, der Widerwille.

avert [ə'vəːt], *v.a.* abwenden.

aviary ['eiviəri], *s.* das Vogelhaus.

aviation [eivi'eiʃən], *s.* das Flugwesen.

aviator ['eivieitə], *s.* der Flieger.

avid ['ævid], *adj.* begierig (*of* or *for*, nach).

avidity [æ'viditi], *s.* die Begierde, Gier (*for*, nach).

avoid [ə'void], *v.a.* vermeiden.

avoidable [ə'voidəbl], *adj.* vermeidlich, vermeidbar.

avoidance [ə'voidəns], *s.* die Vermeidung, das Meiden.

avow [ə'vau], *v.a.* eingestehen, anerkennen (*acknowledge*).

avowal [ə'vauəl], *s.* das Geständnis; die Erklärung.

await [ə'weit], *v.a.* erwarten, warten auf (*Acc.*).

awake(n) [ə'weik(ən)], *v.a.*, *v.n.* *irr.* aufwecken, wecken; aufwachen (*wake up*). — *adj.* *wide awake*, schlau, auf der Hut.

award [ə'wɔːd], s. die Zuerkennung, Auszeichnung; Belohnung (money); (Law) das Urteil. — v.a. zuerkennen; — damages, Schadenersatz zusprechen; verleihen (grant).

aware [ə'wɛə], adj. gewahr, bewußt (Genit.).

away [ə'wei], adv. weg; hinweg, fort.

awe [ɔː], s. die Ehrfurcht; Furcht.

awful ['ɔːful], adj. furchtbar, schrecklich.

awhile [ə'wail], adv. eine Weile, eine kurze Zeit.

awkward ['ɔːkwəd], adv. ungeschickt, unbeholfen, ungelenk; unangenehm (difficult); — situation, peinliche Situation, Lage.

awkwardness ['ɔːkwədnis], s. die Ungeschicklichkeit, Unbeholfenheit.

awl [ɔːl], s. die Ahle, der Pfriem.

awning ['ɔːniŋ], s. die Plane; das Sonnendach.

awry [ə'rai], adj. schief, verkehrt.

axe [æks], s. die Axt, das Beil.

axiom ['æksiəm], s. das Axiom, der Satz, Lehrsatz, Grundsatz.

axiomatic [æksiə'mætik], adj. axiomatisch, grundsätzlich; gewiß.

axis ['æksis], s. die Achse.

axle [æksl], s. die Achse.

ay(e) (1) [ai], adv. ja, gewiß.

ay(e) (2) [ei], adv. ständig, ewig.

azalea [ə'zeiliə], s. (Bot.) die Azalie.

azure ['æʒə, 'eiʒə], adj. himmelblau, azurblau.

B

B [biː]. das B; (Mus.) das H.

baa [baː], v.n. blöken.

babble [bæbl], v.n. schwatzen, schwätzen. — s. das Geschwätz; das Murmeln (water).

babe, baby [beib, 'beibi], s. der Säugling, das Baby, das kleine Kind, das Kindlein.

baboon [bə'buːn], s. (Zool.) der Pavian.

bachelor ['bætʃələ], s. der Junggeselle; (Univ.) Bakkalaureus.

back [bæk], s. der Rücken, die Rückseite. — adj. Hinter-, Rück-; — door, die Hintertür; — stairs, die Hintertreppe. — adv. rückwärts, zurück. — v.a. unterstützen; (Comm.) indossieren; gegenzeichnen; wetten auf (Acc.) (bet on).

backbone ['bækboun], s. (Anat.) das Rückgrat.

backfire ['bækfaiə], s. (Motor.) die Frühzündung; (gun) die Fehlzündung. — [bæk'faiə], v.n. (Motor.) frühzünden; (gun) fehlzünden.

backgammon [bæk'gæmən], s. das Bordspiel, das Puffspiel.

background ['bækgraund], s. der Hintergrund.

backhand ['bækhænd], s. (Sport) die Rückhand; a —ed compliment, eine verblümte Grobheit.

backside [bæk'said], s. (vulg.) der Hintere.

backslide [bæk'slaid], v.n. abfallen, abtrünnig werden.

backward ['bækwəd], adj. zurückgeblieben. **backward(s)** adv. rückwärts, zurück.

backwater ['bækwɔːtə], s. das Stauwasser.

backwoods ['bækwudz], s. pl. der Hinterwald.

bacon ['beikən], s. der Speck.

bad [bæd], adj. schlecht, schlimm; böse (immoral); (coll.) unwohl (unwell); not too —, ganz gut; from — to worse, immer schlimmer; — language, unanständige Worte, das Fluchen; — luck, Unglück, Pech; want —ly, nötig brauchen.

badge [bædʒ], s. das Abzeichen Kennzeichen (mark).

badger (1) ['bædʒə], s. (Zool.) der Dachs.

badger (2) ['bædʒə], v.a. ärgern, stören, belästigen.

badness ['bædnis], s. die Schlechtigkeit, Bosheit, das schlechte Wesen, die Bösartigkeit.

baffle [bæfl], v.a. täuschen, verblüffen. — s. (obs.) die Täuschung; (Build.) Verkleidung; (Elec.) Verteilerplatte.

bag [bæg], s. der Sack, Beutel; die Tasche; shopping —, Einkaufstasche; travelling —, Reisehandtasche. — v.a. einstecken, als Beute behalten (hunt).

bagatelle [bægə'tel], s. die Bagatelle, Lappalie, Kleinigkeit; das Kugelspiel (pin-table ball-game).

baggage ['bægidʒ], s. das Gepäck.

bagging ['bægiŋ], s. die Sackleinwand.

baggy ['bægi], adj. ungebügelt; bauschig.

bagpipe ['bægpaip], s. der Dudelsack.

bagpiper ['bægpaipə], s. der Dudelsackpfeifer.

bail [beil], s. der Bürge; die Bürgschaft; stand —, für einen bürgen; allow —, Bürgschaft zulassen. — v.a. Bürgschaft leisten; — out, (durch Kaution) in Freiheit setzen.

bailiff ['beilif], s. der Amtmann; Gerichtsvollzieher.

bait [beit], s. der Köder. — v.a. ködern, locken (attract).

baiter ['beitə], s. der Hetzer, Verfolger.

baiting ['beitiŋ], s. die Hetze.

bake [beik], v.a., v.n. backen.

baker ['beikə], s. der Bäcker; —'s dozen, 13 Stück.

bakery ['beikəri], s. die Bäckerei.

baking ['beikiŋ], s. das Backen.

317

balance

balance ['bæləns], s. die Waage (scales); die Bilanz (audit); das Gleichgewicht (equilibrium); (Comm.) der Saldo, der Überschuß (profit); die Unruhe (watch). — v.a., v.n. wägen, abwägen (scales); ausgleichen (— up), einen Saldo ziehen (— an account); ins Gleichgewicht bringen (bring into equilibrium).

balcony ['bælkəni], s. der Balkon, der Söller (castle); Altan (villa).

bald [bɔːld], adj. kahl, haarlos; (fig.) armselig, schmucklos.

baldness ['bɔːldnis], s. die Kahlheit (hairlessness); Nacktheit (bareness).

bale (1) [beil], s. der Ballen.

bale (2) [beil], v.n. — out, abspringen; aussteigen.

Balearic Islands [bæli'ærik ailəndz], s. pl. die Balearen, Balearischen Inseln. — adj. balearisch.

baleful ['beilful], adj. unheilvoll.

balk [bɔːk], v.a. aufhalten, hemmen. — v.n. scheuen, zurückscheuen (at, vor).

ball (1) [bɔːl], s. der Ball; die Kugel; — cock, der Absperrhahn; —point pen, der Kugelschreiber.

ball (2) [bɔːl], s. der Ball (dance).

ballad ['bæləd], s. die Ballade.

ballast ['bæləst], s. der Ballast.

ballet ['bælei], s. das Ballett.

balloon [bə'luːn], s. der Ballon.

ballot ['bælət], s. die geheime Wahl, Abstimmung; — -box, die Wahlurne; — -paper, der Stimmzettel. —v. n. wählen, abstimmen.

balm [baːm], s. der Balsam.

balsam ['bɔlsəm], s. der Balsam.

Baltic [bɔːltik], adj. baltisch. — (Sea), die Ostsee; — Provinces, das Baltikum, die Ostsee;

balustrade ['bæləstreid], s. die Balustrade, das Geländer.

bamboo [bæm'buː], s. (Bot.) der Bambus.

bamboozle [bæm'buːzl], v.a. verblüffen; beschwindeln (cheat).

ban [bæn], v.a. bannen, verbannen; verbieten. — s. der Bann, das Verbot.

banal [bæ'næl, 'beinəl], adj. banal.

banality [bæ'næliti], s. die Banalität, Trivialität.

banana [bə'naːnə], s. die Banane.

band [bænd], s. das Band (ribbon etc.); (Mus.) die Kapelle; die Bande (robbers). — v. n. — together, sich verbinden; sich zusammentun.

bandage ['bændidʒ], s. der Verband, die Bandage.

bandit ['bændit], s. der Bandit.

bandmaster ['bændmɑːstə], s. der Kapellmeister.

bandstand ['bændstænd], s. der Musikpavillon.

bandy ['bændi], adj. —legged, krummbeinig. — v.a. — words, Worte wechseln; streiten.

bane [bein], s. das Gift; (fig.) Verderben.

baneful ['beinful], adj. verderblich.

bang [bæŋ], s. der Knall (explosion), das Krachen (clap). — v.n. knallen, krachen lassen. — v.a. — a door, eine Türe zuwerfen.

banish ['bæniʃ], v.a. verbannen, bannen.

banisters ['bænistəz], s. pl. das Treppengeländer.

bank [bæŋk], s. (Fin.) die Bank; das Ufer (river); der Damm (dam). — v.a. einlegen, einzahlen, auf die Bank bringen (sum of money); eindämmen (dam up). — v.n. ein Konto haben (have an account, with, bei).

banker ['bæŋkə], s. der Bankier.

bankrupt ['bæŋkrʌpt], adj. bankrott; zahlungsunfähig; (coll.) pleite.

bankruptcy ['bæŋkrʌptsi], s. der Bankrott.

banns [bænz], s. pl. das Heiratsaufgebot.

banquet ['bæŋkwit], s. das Banquet, Festessen.

bantam ['bæntəm], s. das Bantamhuhn, Zwerghuhn; (Boxing) — -weight, das Bantamgewicht.

banter ['bæntə], v.n. scherzen, necken. — s. das Scherzen, der Scherz.

baptism ['bæptizm], s. die Taufe.

Baptist ['bæptist], s. der Täufer; Baptist.

baptize [bæp'taiz], v.a. taufen.

bar [baː], s. die Barre, Stange (pole); der Riegel; Balken; Schlagbaum (barrier); (fig.) das Hindernis; der Schanktisch (in public house); prisoner at the —, der Gefangene vor (dem) Gericht; call to the —, zur Gerichtsadvokatur (or als Anwalt) zulassen; (Mus.) der Takt. — v.a. verriegeln (door); (fig.) hindern (from action); verbieten (prohibit); ausschließen (exclude).

barb [baːb], s. die Spitze (of wire); der Widerhaken (hook).

barbed [baːbd], adj. spitzig; — remark, die spitze Bemerkung; — wire, der Stacheldraht.

barbarian [baː'bɛəriən], s. der Barbar. — adj. barbarisch.

barbarism ['baːbərizm], s. die Roheit; der Barbarismus.

barber ['baːbə], s. der Barbier, Friseur.

barberry ['baːbəri], s. (Bot.) die Berberitze.

bard [baːd], s. der Barde, Sänger.

bare [bɛə], adj. nackt, bloß; —headed, barhäuptig. — v.a. entblößen.

barefaced ['bɛəfeisd], adj. schamlos.

barely ['bɛəli], adv. kaum.

bargain ['baːgin], s. der Kauf, Gelegenheitskauf; der Handel (trading); das Geschäft; into the —, noch dazu, obendrein. — v.n. feilschen, handeln (haggle) (for, um).

barge [baːdʒ], s. der Lastkahn, die Barke. — v.n. (coll.) — in, stören.

bargee [baː'dʒiː], s. der Flußschiffer, Bootsmann.

baritone ['bæritoun], s. (Mus.) der Bariton.

bark (1) [bɑːk], *s.* die Rinde (*of tree*).
bark (2) [bɑːk], *v.n.* bellen (*dog*); — *up the wrong tree*, auf falscher Fährte sein. — *s.* das Gebell (*dog*).
barley ['bɑːli], *s.* (*Bot.*) die Gerste.
barmaid ['bɑːmeid], *s.* die Kellnerin.
barman ['bɑːmən], *s.* der Kellner.
barn [bɑːn], *s.* die Scheune; — *owl*, die Schleiereule.
barnacle ['bɑːnəkl], *s.* die Entenmuschel; die Klette.
barnstormer ['bɑːnstɔːmə], *s.* der Schmierenkomödiant.
barometer [bə'rɔmitə], *s.* das Barometer.
baron ['bærən], *s.* der Baron, Freiherr.
barony ['bærəni], *s.* die Baronswürde.
baroque [bə'rɔk], *adj.* barock. — *s.* das Barock.
barque [bɑːk], *s.* die Bark.
barracks ['bærəks], *s. pl.* die Kaserne.
barrage ['bærɑːʒ, 'bæridʒ], *s.* das Sperrfeuer (*firing*); das Wehr, der Damm.
barrel ['bærəl], *s.* das Faß (*vat*), die Tonne (*tun*); der Gewehrlauf (*rifle*); die Trommel (*cylinder*); — *organ*, die Drehorgel.
barren ['bærən], *adj.* unfruchtbar, dürr.
barrenness ['bærənnis], *s.* die Unfruchtbarkeit.
barricade [bæri'keid], *s.* die Barrikade. — *v.a.* verrammeln, verschanzen.
barrier ['bæriə], *s.* die Barriere, der Schlagbaum; das Hindernis; (*Railw.*) die Schranke.
barrister ['bæristə], *s.* der Rechtsanwalt, Advokat.
barrow (1) ['bærou], *s.* die Schubkarren, Handkarren; — *boy*, der Höker, Schnellverkäufer.
barrow (2) ['bærou], *s.* (*Archaeol.*) das Hünengrab, Heldengrab.
barter ['bɑːtə], *v.a.* tauschen, austauschen. — *s.* der Tauschhandel.
Bartholomew [bɑː'θɔləmjuː]. Bartholomäus, *m.*; *Massacre of St. Bartholomew's Eve*, Bartholomäusnacht, Pariser Bluthochzeit.
basalt ['bæsɔːlt, bæ'sɔːlt], *s.* der Basalt.
base [beis], *s.* die Basis, Grundlage; der Sockel; (*Chem.*) die Base. — *adj.* niedrig, gemein; (*Metall.*) unedel. — *v.a.* basieren, beruhen, fundieren (*upon, auf*).
baseless ['beislis], *adj.* grundlos.
basement ['beismənt], *s.* das Kellergeschoß.
baseness ['beisnis], *s.* die Gemeinheit, Niedrigkeit.
bashful ['bæʃful], *adj.* verschämt, schamhaft, schüchtern.
basic ['beisik], *adj.* grundlegend.
basin ['beisən], *s.* das Becken.
basis ['beisis], *s.* die Basis, Grundlage.
bask [bɑːsk], *v.n.* sich sonnen.
basket ['bɑːskit], *s.* der Korb.
bass (1) [beis], *s.* (*Mus.*) der Baß, die Baßstimme.

bass (2) [bæs], *s.* (*Zool.*) der Barsch.
bassoon [bə'suːn], *s.* (*Mus.*) das Fagott.
bastard ['bæstəd], *s.* der Bastard.
baste [beist], *v.a.* mit Fett begießen (*roast meat*); (*coll.*) prügeln.
bastion ['bæstiən], *s.* die Bastion, Festung, das Bollwerk.
bat (1) [bæt], *s.* die Fledermaus.
bat (2) [bæt], *s.* der Schläger. — *v.n.* (den Ball) schlagen; (*cricket*) am Schlagen sein (*be batting*).
batch [bætʃ], *s.* der Stoß (*pile*); di Menge (*people*); (*Mil.*) der Trupp.
bath [bɑːθ], *s.* das Bad; (*Am.*) — *robe*, der Schlafrock, Bademantel; — *tub*, die Badewanne.
bathe [beið], *v.n.* baden; *bathing pool*, das Schwimmbad; *bathing suit*, der Badeanzug.
batman ['bætmən], *s.* der Offiziersbursche.
baton ['bætən], *s.* der Stab.
batsman ['bætsmən], *s.* der Schläger (*cricket*).
batten [bætn], *s.* die Holzlatte. — *v.a.* mästen, füttern. — *v.n.* fett werden.
batter ['bætə], *s.* der Schlagteig. — *v.a.* schlagen, zertrümmern; — *ing ram*, (*Mil.*) der Sturmbock.
battery ['bætəri], *s.* die Batterie.
battle [bætl], *s.* die Schlacht; — *cruiser*, der Schlachtkreuzer; — *ship*, das Schlachtschiff. — *v.n.* kämpfen (*for, um*).
Bavarian [bə'vɛəriən], *adj.* bayrisch. — *s.* der Bayer.
bawl [bɔːl], *v.n.* plärren, schreien.
bay (1) [bei], *adj.* rötlich braun.
bay (2) [bei], *s.* die Bucht, Bai; — *window*, das Erkerfenster.
bay (3) [bei], *s.* *keep at* —, in Schach halten, *stand at* —, sich zur Wehr setzen.
bay (4) [bei], *s.* (*Bot.*) der Lorbeer.
bay (5) [bei], *v.n.* bellen, heulen; — *for the moon*, das Unmögliche wollen.
bayonet ['beiənet], *s.* das Bajonett.
bazaar [bə'zɑː], *s.* der Basar.
be [biː], *v.n. irr.* sein, existieren; sich befinden; vorhanden sein; — *off*, sich fortmachen (*move*); ungeniessbar sein (*meat, food*); nicht mehr da sein (— *off the menu*).
beach [biːtʃ], *s.* der Strand, das Gestade.
beacon ['biːkən], *s.* das Leuchtfeuer; der Leuchtturm; das Lichtsignal.
bead [biːd], *s.* das Tröpfchen (*drop*); die Perle (*pearl*); (*pl.*) die Perlschnur; der Rosenkranz.
beadle [biːdl], *s.* (*Univ.*) der Pedell; (*Eccl.*) Kirchendiener.
beagle [biːgl], *s.* der Jagdhund, Spürhund.
beak [biːk], *s.* der Schnabel.
beaker ['biːkə], *s.* der Becher.
beam [biːm], *s.* der Balken (*wood*); der Strahl (*ray*), Glanz. — *v.n.* strahlen.

bean

bean [biːn], *s.* (*Bot.*) die Bohne; *not* ⏌ —, keinen Heller *or* Pfennig.

bear (1) [bɛə], *s.* (*Zool.*) der Bär.

bear (2) [bɛə], *v.a. irr.* tragen, ertragen; gebären (*a child*); hegen (*sorrow etc.*). — *v.n.* — *upon*, drücken auf (*pressure*), Einfluß haben (*effect*); — *up*, geduldig sein.

bearable [ˈbɛərəbl], *adj.* tragbar, erträglich.

beard [biəd], *s.* der Bart. — *v.a.* trotzen (*Dat.*).

bearded [ˈbiədid], *adj.* bärtig.

bearer [ˈbɛərə], *s.* der Träger, Überbringer.

bearing [ˈbɛəriŋ], *s.* das Benehmen, die Haltung (*manner*); (*pl.*) (*Geog.*) die Richtung; *lose o.'s* —s, sich verlaufen; *ball* —s, (*Engin.*) das Kugellager.

bearpit [ˈbɛəpit], *s.* der Bärenzwinger.

beast [biːst], *s.* das Tier; die Bestie.

beastliness [ˈbiːstlinis], *s.* das tierische Benehmen; die Grausamkeit (*cruelty*); die Gemeinheit.

beastly [ˈbiːstli], *adj.* grausam, (*coll.*) schrecklich.

beat [biːt], *s.* der Schlag, das Schlagen; (*Mus.*) der Takt; die Runde, das Revier (*patrol district*). — *v.a. irr.* schlagen; — *time*, den Takt schlagen; — *carpets*, Teppich klopfen. — *v.n.* — *it*, sich davonmachen.

beater [ˈbiːtə], *s.* (*Hunt.*) der Treiber.

beatify [biːˈætifai], *v.a.* seligsprechen.

beau [bou], *s.* der Stutzer, Geck.

beautiful [ˈbjuːtiful], *adj.* schön.

beautify [ˈbjuːtifai], *v.a.* schön machen, verschönern.

beauty [ˈbjuːti], *s.* die Schönheit; — *salon*, der Schönheitssalon; *Sleeping Beauty*, das Dornröschen.

beaver [ˈbiːvə], *s.* (*Zool.*) der Biber.

becalm [biˈkaːm], *v.a.* besänftigen.

because [biˈkɔz], *conj.* weil, da; — *of*, wegen, um … willen.

beck [bek], *s.* der Wink; *be at s.o.'s* — *and call*, jemandem zu Gebote stehen.

beckon [ˈbekən], *v.a.*, *v.n.* winken, heranwinken, zuwinken (*Dat.*).

become [biˈkʌm], *v.n. irr.* werden. — *v.a.* anstehen, sich schicken, passen (*Dat.*).

becoming [biˈkʌmiŋ], *adj.* passend, kleidsam.

bed [bed], *s.* das Bett; Beet (*flowers*); (*Geol.*) das Lager, die Schicht. — *v.a.* betten, einbetten.

bedaub [biˈdɔːb], *v.a.* beflecken, beschmieren.

bedding [ˈbediŋ], *s.* das Bettzeug.

bedevil [biˈdevəl], *v.a.* behexen, verhexen.

bedew [biˈdjuː], *v.a.* betauen.

bedlam [ˈbedləm], *s.* (*coll.*) das Irrenhaus; *this is* —, die Hölle ist los.

Bedouin [ˈbeduin], *s.* der Beduine.

bedpost [ˈbedpoust], *s.* der Bettpfosten.

bedraggle [biˈdrægl], *v.a.* beschmutzen.

bedridden [ˈbedridn], *adj.* bettlägerig, ans Bett gefesselt.

bedroom [ˈbedruːm], *s.* das Schlafzimmer.

bedtime [ˈbedtaim], *s.* die Schlafenszeit.

bee [biː], *s.* (*Ent.*) die Biene; *have a* — *in o.'s bonnet*, einen Vogel haben.

beech [biːtʃ], *s.* (*Bot.*) die Buche.

beef [biːf], *s.* das Rindfleisch; — *tea*, die Fleischbrühe.

beehive [ˈbiːhaiv], *s.* der Bienenkorb.

beeline [ˈbiːlain], *s.* die Luftlinie, gerade Linie; *make a* — *for s.th.*, schnurstracks auf etwas losgehen.

beer [biə], *s.* das Bier; *small* —, Dünnbier, (*fig.*) unbedeutend.

beet [biːt], *s.* (*Bot.*) die Runkelrübe; *sugar* —, die Zuckerrübe.

beetle [biːtl], *s.* (*Ent.*) der Käfer; — *brows*, buschige Augenbrauen.

beetroot [ˈbiːtruːt], *s.* (*Bot.*) die rote Rübe.

befall [biˈfɔːl], *v.a. irr.* widerfahren (*Dat.*). — *v.n.* zustoßen (*happen*, *Dat.*).

befit [biˈfit], *v.a.* sich geziemen, sich gebühren.

befog [biˈfɔg], *v.a.* in Nebel hüllen; umnebeln.

before [biˈfɔː], *adv.* vorn; voraus, voran; (*previously*) vorher, früher; (*already*) bereits, schon. — *prep.* vor. — *conj.* bevor, ehe.

beforehand [biˈfɔːhænd], *adv.* im voraus, vorher.

befoul [biˈfaul], *v.a.* beschmutzen.

befriend [biˈfrend], *v.a.* befreunden, unterstützen (*support*).

beg [beg], *v.a.*, *v.n.* betteln (um, *for*); ersuchen, bitten (*request*).

beget [biˈget], *v.a. irr.* zeugen.

beggar [ˈbegə], *s.* der Bettler.

begin [biˈgin], *v.a.*, *v.n. irr.* beginnen, anfangen.

beginner [biˈginə], *s.* der Anfänger.

beginning [biˈginiŋ], *s.* der Anfang.

begone! [biˈgɔn], *interj.* hinweg! fort! mach dich fort!

begrudge [biˈgrʌdʒ], *v.a.* nicht gönnen, mißgönnen.

beguile [biˈgail], *v.a.* bestricken, betrügen; — *the time*, die Zeit vertreiben.

behalf [biˈhaːf], *s. on* — *of*, um … (*Genit.*) willen; im Interesse von, im Namen von.

behave [biˈheiv], *v.n.* sich benehmen, sich betragen.

behaviour [biˈheivjə], *s.* das Benehmen, Gebaren.

behead [biˈhed], *v.a.* enthaupten.

behind [biˈhaind], *adv.* hinten, zurück, hinterher. — *prep.* hinter.

behindhand [biˈhaindhænd], *adj.*; *adv.* im Rückstand (*in arrears*); zurück (*backward*).

behold [biˈhould], *v.a. irr.* ansehen; er blicken; *lo and* — *!* siehe da!

beholden [biˈhouldən], *adj.* verpflichtet (*to*, *Dat.*).

beholder [biˈhouldə], *s.* der Zuschauer.

behove [bi'houv], *v.a.* sich geziemen, ziemen, gebühren.

being ['bi:iŋ], *pres. part for the time* —, vorläufig, für jetzt. — *s.* das Sein, die Existenz; das Wesen (*creature*).

belated [bi'leitid], *adj.* verspätet.

belch [beltʃ], *v.n.* rülpsen, aufstoßen.

belfry ['belfri], *s.* der Glockenturm.

Belgian ['beldʒən], *adj.* belgisch. — *s.* der Belgier.

belie [bi'lai], *v.a.* täuschen, Lügen strafen.

belief [bi'li:f], *s.* der Glaube, die Meinung.

believable [bi'li:vəbl], *adj.* glaubhaft, glaublich.

believe [bi'li:v], *v.a.*, *v.n.* glauben (*an*, *Acc.*), vertrauen (*Dat.*).

believer [bi'li:və], *s.* der Gläubige.

belittle [bi'litl], *v.a.* schmälern, verkleinern, verächtlich machen.

bell [bel], *s.* die Glocke; Schelle, Klingel; — -*founder*, der Glockengießer; —-*boy*, (*Am.*) — -*hop*, der Hotelpage.

belligerent [bi'lidʒərənt], *adj.* kriegführend. — *s.* der Kriegführende.

bellow ['belou], *v.n.* brüllen. — *s.* das Gebrüll.

bellows ['belouz], *s.* der Blasebalg.

belly ['beli], *s.* der Bauch.

belong [bi'lɔŋ], *v.n.* gehören (*Dat.*), angehören (*Dat.*).

belongings [bi'lɔŋiŋz], *s. pl.* die Habe, das Hab und Gut, der Besitz.

beloved [bi'lʌvd, -vid], *adj.* geliebt, lieb.

below [bi'lou], *adv.* unten. — *prep.* unterhalb (*Genit.*), unter (*Dat.*).

Belshazzar [bel'ʃæzə]. Belsazar, *m.*

belt [belt], *s.* der Gürtel, Gurt; der Riemen; (*Tech.*) Treibriemen; *below the* —, unfair. — *v.a.* umgürten; (*coll.*) prügeln.

bemoan [bi'moun], *v.a.* beklagen.

bench [bentʃ], *s.* die Bank; der Gerichtshof (*court of law*); *Queen's Bench*, der oberste Gerichtshof.

bend [bend], *v.a.*, *v.n. irr.* biegen; beugen; sich krümmen. — *s.* die Biegung, Krümmung, Kurve.

bendable ['bendəbl], *adj.* biegsam.

beneath [bi'ni:θ] *see below.*

Benedictine [beni'dikti:n], *s.* der Benediktiner.

benediction [beni'dikʃən], *s.* der Segensspruch, der Segen; die Segnung.

benefaction [beni'fækʃən], *s.* die Wohltat.

benefactor ['benifæktə], *s.* der Wohltäter.

benefactress ['benifæktris], *s.* die Wohltäterin.

beneficent [be'nefisənt], *adj.* wohltätig.

beneficial [beni'fiʃəl], *adj.* vorteilhaft, gut (*for*, für), wohltuend.

benefit ['benifit], *s.* der Vorteil, Nutzen. — *v.n.* Nutzen ziehen. — *v.a.* nützen.

benevolence [be'nevələns], *s.* das Wohlwollen.

benevolent [be'nevələnt], *adj.* wohlwollend; — *society*, der Unterstützungsverein, — *fund*, der Unterstützungsfond.

Bengali [ben'gɔ:li], *adj.* bengalisch. — *s.* der Bengale.

benign [bi'nain], *adj.* gütig, mild.

bent [bent], *adj.* gebogen, krumm; — *on something*, versessen auf etwas. — *s.* die Neigung, der Hang; — *for*, Vorliebe für.

benzene ['benzi:n], *s.* das Benzol, Kohlenbenzin.

benzine ['benzi:n], *s.* das Benzin.

bequeath [bi'kwi:θ], *v.a.* vermachen, hinterlassen.

bequest [bi'kwest], *s.* das Vermächtnis.

bereave [bi'ri:v], *v.a. irr.* berauben (durch Tod).

bereavement [bi'ri:vmənt], *s.* der Verlust (durch Tod).

beret ['berei], *s.* die Baskenmütze.

Bernard ['bə:nəd]. Bernhard, *m.*; *St.* — *dog*, der Bernhardiner.

berry ['beri], *s.* die Beere.

berth [bə:θ], *s.* (*Naut.*) der Ankerplatz; die Koje. — *v.a.*, *v.n.* anlegen; vor Anker gehen (*boat*).

beseech [bi'si:tʃ], *v.a. irr.* bitten, anflehen.

beset [bi'set], *v.a. irr.* bedrängen, bedrücken, umringen.

beside [bi'said], *prep.* außer, neben, nahe bei; — *the point*, unwesentlich; *quite* — *the mark*, weit vom Schuß.

besides [bi'saidz], *adv.* überdies, außerdem.

besiege [bi'si:dʒ], *v.a.* belagern.

besmirch [bi'smə:tʃ], *v.a.* besudeln.

besom [bi'zəm], *s.* der Besen.

bespatter [bi'spætə], *v.a.* bespritzen.

bespeak [bi'spi:k], *v.a. irr.* bestellen; (*Tail.*) *bespoke*, nach Maß gemacht or gearbeitet.

best [best], *adj.* (*superl. of* **good**) best; — *adv.* am besten. — *s. want the* — *of both worlds*, alles haben wollen; *to the* — *of my ability*, nach besten Kräften; *to the* — *of my knowledge*, soviel ich weiß.

bestial ['bestjəl], *adj.* bestialisch, tierisch.

bestow [bi'stou], *v.a.* verleihen, erteilen.

bet [bet], *s.* die Wette. — *v.a.*, *v.n. irr.* wetten.

betray [bi'trei], *v.a.* verraten.

betrayal [bi'treiəl], *s.* der Verrat.

betrayer [bi'treiə], *s.* der Verräter.

betroth [bi'trouð], *v.a.* verloben.

betrothal [bi'trouðəl], *s.* die Verlobung.

better ['betə], *adj.* (*comp. of* **good**) besser. — *adv. you had* — *go*, es wäre besser, Sie gingen; *think* — *of it*, sich eines Besseren besinnen, sich's überlegen. — *v.a. get the* — *of*, überwinden; *so much the* —, desto or umso besser. — *v.a.* verbessern; — *oneself*, seine Lage verbessern.

betterment [ˈbetəmənt], s. die Verbesserung.

between [biˈtwiːn], adv. dazwischen. — prep. zwischen; unter (among).

bevel [ˈbevəl], s. der Winkelpasser; die Schräge. — v.a. abkanten.

beverage [ˈbevəridʒ], s. das Getränk.

bevy [ˈbevi], s. die Schar (of beauties, von Schönen).

bewail [biˈweil], v.a., v.n. betrauern, beweinen; trauern um.

beware [biˈwɛə], v.n. sich hüten (of, vor).

bewilder [biˈwildə], v.a. verwirren.

bewitch [biˈwitʃ], v.a. bezaubern.

beyond [biˈjɔnd], adv. jenseits, drüben. — prep. über . . . hinaus; jenseits; außer.

biannual [baiˈænjuəl], adj. halbjährlich.

bias [ˈbaiəs], s. die Neigung; das Vorurteil (prejudice). — v.a. beeinflussen.

bias(s)ed [ˈbaiəsd], adj. voreingenommen.

bib [bib], s. der Schürzenlatz; das Lätzchen.

Bible [baibl], s. die Bibel.

Biblical [ˈbiblikəl], adj. biblisch.

bibliography [bibliˈɔɡrəfi], s. die Bibliographie.

bibliophile [ˈbibliɔfail], s. der Bücherfreund.

biceps [ˈbaiseps], s. der Bizeps, Armmuskel.

bicker [ˈbikə], v.n. zanken, hadern.

bickering [ˈbikəriŋ], s. das Gezänk, Hadern, der Hader.

bicycle [ˈbaisikl], (coll.) **bike** [baik], s. das Fahrrad.

bicyclist [ˈbaisiklist], s. der Radfahrer.

bid [bid], v.a., v.n. irr. gebieten, befehlen (Dat.) (order); bieten (at auction); — farewell, Lebewohl sagen. — s. das Gebot, Angebot (at auction).

bidding [ˈbidiŋ], s. der Befehl (order); das Bieten (at auction); die Einladung (invitation).

bide [baid], v.n. irr. verbleiben, verharren (in, by, bei).

biennial [baiˈeniəl], adj. zweijährig, alle zwei Jahre.

bier [biə], s. die Bahre, Totenbahre.

big [big], adj. groß, dick (fat); talking —, großsprecherisch; talk —, prahlen.

bigamy [ˈbigəmi], s. die Bigamie, die Doppelehe.

bigness [ˈbignis], s. die Größe, Dicke.

bigoted [ˈbigətid], adj. bigott, fanatisch.

bigotry [ˈbigətri], s. die Bigotterie.

bigwig [ˈbigwig], s. (coll.) die vornehme Person, der Würdenträger.

bike see bicycle.

bilberry [ˈbilbəri], s. (Bot.) die Heidelbeere.

bile [bail], s. die Galle.

bilge [bildʒ], s. die Bilge, der Schiffsboden; (coll.) Unsinn (nonsense).

bilious [ˈbiljəs], adj. gallig.

bill (1) [bil], s. der Schnabel (bird).

bill (2) [bil], die Rechnung (account); — of exchange, der Wechsel; — of entry, die Zolldeklaration; — of fare, die Speisekarte; (Parl.) der Gesetzentwurf; das Plakat (poster). — v.a. anzeigen.

billboard [ˈbilbɔːd], s. (Am.) das Anschlagbrett.

billet [ˈbilit], s. das Billett (card); das Quartier, die Unterkunft (army).

billfold [ˈbilfould], s. (Am.) die Brieftasche.

billhook [ˈbilhuk], s. die Hippe.

billiards [ˈbiljədz], s. das Billardspiel.

billow [ˈbilou], s. die Woge. — v.n. wogen.

bin [bin], s. der Behälter.

bind [baind], v.a. irr. binden, verpflichten; (Law) — over, zu gutem Benehmen verpflichten.

binder [ˈbaində], s. der Binder, Buchbinder.

bindery [ˈbaindəri], s. die Buchbinderei, Binderwerkstatt.

binding [ˈbaindiŋ], s. der Einband.

binnacle [ˈbinəkl], s. das Kompaßhäuschen.

binocular [biˈnɔkjulə], adj. für beide Augen. — s. (pl.) das Fernglas, der Feldstecher.

binomial [baiˈnoumiəl], adj. binomisch. — s. (pl.) (Maths.) das Binom, der zweigliedrige Ausdruck.

biochemical [baioˈkemikəl], adj. biochemisch.

biochemistry [baioˈkemistri], s. die Biochemie.

biographer [baiˈɔɡrəfə], s. der Biograph.

biographical [baioˈɡræfikəl], adj. biographisch.

biography [baiˈɔɡrəfi], s. die Biographie, die Lebensbeschreibung.

biological [baioˈlɔdʒikəl], adj. biologisch.

biology [baiˈɔlədʒi], s. die Biologie.

biometric(al) [baioˈmetrik(əl)], adj. biometrisch.

biometry [baiˈɔmitri], s. die Biometrie.

biophysical [baioˈfizikəl], adj. biophysisch.

biophysics [baioˈfiziks], s. die Biophysik.

biped [ˈbaiped], s. der Zweifüßler.

biplane [ˈbaiplein], s. (Aviat.) der Doppeldecker.

birch [bəːtʃ], s. (Bot.) die Birke; die Birkenrute, Rute (cane). — v.a. (mit der Rute) züchtigen.

bird [bəːd], s. der Vogel; — of passage, der Wandervogel, Zugvogel; —cage, der Vogelkäfig, das Vogelbauer; — fancier, der Vogelzüchter; —'s-eye view, die Vogelperspektive.

birth [bəːθ], s. die Geburt; — certificate, der Geburtsschein.

birthday [ˈbəːθdei], s. der Geburtstag.

biscuit [ˈbiskit], s. der or das Keks; der Zwieback.

bisect [bai'sekt], *v.a.* entzweischneiden, halbieren.

bisection [bai'sekʃən], *s.* die Zweiteilung, Halbierung.

bishop ['biʃəp], *s.* der Bischof; (*Chess*) der Läufer.

bishopric ['biʃəprik], *s.* das Bistum.

bismuth ['bizməθ], *s.* der *or* das Wismut.

bison ['baisən], *s.* (*Zool.*) der Bison.

bit [bit], *s.* der Bissen (*bite*), das Bißchen (*little* —); das Gebiß (*bridle*); der Bart (*of key*).

bitch [bitʃ], *s.* die Hündin.

bite [bait], *v.a. irr.* beißen. — *s.* das Beißen (*mastication*); der Biß (*morsel*).

biting ['baitiŋ], *adj.* (*also fig.*) beißend, scharf. — *adv.* — *cold*, bitterkalt.

bitter ['bitə], *adj.* bitter.

bitterness ['bitənis], *s.* die Bitterkeit.

bittern ['bitə:n], *s.* (*Orn.*) die Rohrdommel.

bitumen [bi'tju:mən], *s.* der Bergteer, Asphalt.

bivouac ['bivuæk], *s.* (*Mil.*) das Biwak, Lager.

bizarre [bi'za:], *adj.* bizarr, wunderlich.

blab [blæb], *v.a., v.n.* schwatzen, ausplaudern (*give away*).

blabber ['blæbə], *s.* (*coll.*) der Schwätzer.

black [blæk], *adj.* schwarz; — *sheep*, der Taugenichts; — *pudding*, die Blutwurst; *Black Forest*, der Schwarzwald; *Black Maria*, der Polizeiwagen; (*coll.*) die grüne Minna; *Black Sea*, das schwarze Meer.

blackberry ['blækbəri], *s.* (*Bot.*) die Brombeere.

blackbird ['blækbə:d], *s.* (*Orn.*) die Amsel.

blackguard ['blæga:d], *s.* der Spitzbube, Schurke.

blackmail ['blækmeil], *v.a.* erpressen. — *s.* die Erpressung.

bladder ['blædə], *s.* (*Anat.*) die Blase.

blacksmith ['blæksmiθ], *s.* der Grobschmied.

blade [bleid], *s.* die Klinge (*razor*); der Halm (*grass*); *shoulder* —, das Schulterblatt.

blamable ['bleiməbl], *adj.* tadelnswert, tadelhaft.

blame [bleim], *s.* der Tadel, die Schuld. — *v.a.* tadeln, beschuldigen, die Schuld zuschreiben (*Dat.*).

blameless ['bleimlis], *adj.* tadellos, schuldlos.

blanch [bla:ntʃ], *v.n.* erbleichen, weiß werden. — *v.a.* weiß machen.

bland [blænd], *adj.* mild, sanft.

blandish ['blændiʃ], *v.a.* schmeicheln (*Dat.*).

blandishment ['blændiʃmənt], *s.* (*mostly in pl.*) die Schmeichelei.

blandness ['blændnis], *s.* die Milde, Sanftheit.

blank [blæŋk], *adj.* blank, leer; reimlos (*verse*); *leave a* —, einen Raum freilassen; — *cartridge*, die Platzpatrone.

blanket ['blæŋkit], *s.* die Decke; (*coll.*) *a wet* —, ein langweiliger Kerl, der Spielverderber.

blare [blɛə], *v.n.* schmettern.

blaspheme [blæs'fi:m], *v.a., v.n.* lästern, fluchen.

blasphemous ['blæsfiməs], *adj.* lästerlich.

blasphemy ['blæsfəmi], *s.* die Gotteslästerung.

blast [bla:st], *v.a.* sprengen, zerstören. — *s.* der Windstoß (*gust*); der Stoß (*trumpets*); die Explosion (*bomb*); — *furnace*, der Hochofen. — *excl.* (*sl.*) —! zum Teufel!

blasting ['bla:stiŋ], *s.* das Sprengen.

blatant ['bleitənt], *adj.* laut, lärmend; dreist.

blaze [bleiz], *s.* die Flamme (*flame*); das Feuer; der Glanz (*colour etc.*). — *v.n.* flammen; leuchten (*shine*). — *v.a.* ausposaunen, bekannt machen (*make known*).

blazer ['bleizə], *s.* die Sportjacke, Klubjacke.

blazon ['bleizən], *v.a.* verkünden.

bleach [bli:tʃ], *v.a.* bleichen. — *s.* das Bleichmittel.

bleak [bli:k], *adj.* öde, rauh; trübe, freudlos.

bleakness ['bli:knis], *s.* die Öde (*scenery*); Traurigkeit, Trübheit.

bleary ['bliəri], *adj.* trübe; — *eyed*, triefäugig.

bleat [bli:t], *v.n.* blöken.

bleed [bli:d], *v.n. irr.* bluten. — *v.a.* bluten lassen; erpressen (*blackmail*).

blemish ['blemiʃ], *s.* der Makel, der Fehler. — *v.a.* schänden, entstellen.

blench [blentʃ], *v.n.* zurückweichen, stutzen.

blend [blend], *v.a., v.n.* mischen, vermengen; sich mischen. — *s.* die Mischung, Vermischung.

bless [bles], *v.a.* segnen; beglücken; loben.

blessed [blest, 'blesid], *adj.* gesegnet, selig.

blessing ['blesiŋ], *s.* der Segen.

blight [blait], *s.* der Meltau. — *v.a.* verderben.

blind [blaind], *adj.* blind; — *man's buff*, Blinde Kuh; — *spot*, der schwache Punkt. — *s.* die Blende, das Rouleau; *Venetian* —, die Jalousie. — *v.a.* blind machen, täuschen.

blindfold ['blaindfould], *adj.* mit verbundenen Augen.

blindness ['blaindnis], *s.* die Blindheit.

blindworm ['blaindwə:m], *s.* (*Zool.*) die Blindschleiche.

blink [bliŋk], *s.* das Blinzeln. — *v.n.* blinzeln, blinken. — *v.a.* nicht sehen wollen.

blinkers ['bliŋkəz], *s. pl.* die Scheuklappen.

bliss [blis], *s.* die Wonne, Seligkeit.

blissful ['blisful], *adj.* wonnig, selig.

blister ['blistə], *s.* die Blase. — *v.n.* Blasen ziehen, Blasen bekommen.

blithe [blaið], *adj.* munter, lustig, fröhlich.

blitheness [ˈblaiðnis], *s.* die Munterkeit, Fröhlichkeit.

blizzard [ˈblizəd], *s.* der Schneesturm.

bloated [ˈbloutid], *adj.* aufgeblasen, aufgedunsen.

bloater [ˈbloutə], *s.* (*Zool.*) der Bückling.

blob [blɔb], *s.* der Kleks.

block [blɔk], *s.* der Block, Klotz (*wood*); Häuserblock (*houses*); — *letters*, große Druckschrift. — *v.a.* blockieren, hemmen (*hinder*); sperren (*road*).

blockade [blɔˈkeid], *s.* die Blockade.

blockhead [ˈblɔkhed], *s.* der Dummkopf.

blonde [blɔnd], *adj.* blond. — *s.* die Blondine.

blood [blʌd], *s.* das Blut; — *vessel*, das Blutgefäß.

bloodcurdling [ˈblʌdkə:dliŋ], *adj.* haarsträubend.

bloodless [ˈblʌdlis], *adj.* blutlos, unblutig.

bloodthirsty [ˈblʌdθə:sti], *adj.* blutdürstig.

bloody [ˈblʌdi], *adj.* blutig; (*vulg.*) verflucht.

bloom [blu:m], *s.* die Blüte; die Blume. — *v.n.* blühen.

bloomers [ˈbluːməz], *s. pl.* altmodische Unterhosen für Damen.

blooming [ˈbluːmiŋ], *adj.* blühend.

blossom [ˈblɔsəm], *s.* die Blüte. — *v.n.* blühen, Blüten treiben.

blot [blɔt], *s.* der Klecks; Fleck; (*fig.*) der Schandfleck. — *v.a.* beflecken; löschen (*ink*); — *out*, ausmerzen, austilgen; *blotting paper*, das Löschpapier.

blotch [blɔtʃ], *s.* der Hautfleck; die Pustel; der Klecks (*blot*).

blotter [ˈblɔtə], *s.* der Löscher.

blouse [blauz], *s.* die Bluse.

blow (1) [blou], *s.* der Schlag.

blow (2) [blou], *v.a. irr.* blasen; wehen; — *o.'s own trumpet*, prahlen; anfachen (*fire*); — *o.'s nose*, sich schneuzen. — *v.n.* schnaufen, keuchen; — *up*, in die Luft sprengen.

blower [ˈblouə], *s.* das Gebläse; der Bläser.

blowpipe [ˈbloupaip], *s.* das Lötrohr.

blubber [ˈblʌbə], *s.* der Walfischspeck, der Tran. — *v.n.* schluchzen, heulen, flennen.

bludgeon [ˈblʌdʒən], *s.* der Knüppel; die Keule (*club*). — *v.a.* niederschlagen.

blue [bluː], *adj.* blau; schwermütig (*sad*); — *blooded*, aus edlem Geblüte.

bluebell [ˈbluːbel], *s.* (*Bot.*) die Glockenblume.

bluebottle [ˈbluːbɔtl], *s.* (*Ent.*) die Schmeißfliege.

bluestocking [ˈbluːstɔkiŋ], *s.* der Blaustrumpf.

bluff [blʌf], *adj.* grob, schroff. — *s.* der Bluff, die Täuschung, der Trick. — *v.a., v.n.* vortäuschen (*pretend*), bluffen; verblüffen (*deceive*).

blunder [ˈblʌndə], *s.* der Fehler, Schnitzer. — *v.n.* einen Fehler machen.

blunderer [ˈblʌndərə], *s.* der Tölpel.

blunderbuss [ˈblʌndəbʌs], *s.* die Donnerbüchse.

blunt [blʌnt], *adj.* stumpf (*edge*); derb, offen (*speech*). — *v.a.* abstumpfen; verderben (*appetite*).

bluntness [ˈblʌntnis], *s.* die Stumpfheit (*edge*); die Derbheit (*speech*).

blur [bləː], *s.* der Fleck. — *v.a.* verwischen.

blurt [bləːt], *v.a.* — *out*, herausplatzen.

blush [blʌʃ], *v.n.* erröten. — *s.* die Schamröte, das Erröten.

bluster [ˈblʌstə], *s.* das Toben, Brausen. — *v.n.* toben, brausen.

blustering [ˈblʌstəriŋ], *adj.* lärmend, tobend.

boa [ˈbouə], *s.* (*Zool.*) die Boa.

boar [bɔː], *s.* (*Zool.*) der Eber.

board [bɔːd], *s.* das Brett (*wood*); die Tafel (*notice* —); die Verpflegung (*food*); — *and lodging*, die Vollpension; die Behörde, der Ausschuß (*officials*). — *v.a.* — *up*, vernageln, zumachen; — *someone*, verpflegen; — *a steamer*, an Bord gehen; —*ing school*, das Internat, das Pensionat.

boarder [ˈbɔːdə], *s.* der Internatsschüler; der Pensionär.

boast [boust], *v.n.* prahlen, sich rühmen. — *s.* der Stolz (*pride*).

boastful [ˈboustful], *adj.* prahlerisch.

boat [bout], *s.* das Boot; *rowing* —, das Ruderboot; der Kahn.

bob [bɔb], *s.* der Knicks; (*coll.*) der Schilling. — *v.n.* baumeln; springen; *bobbed hair*, der Bubikopf.

bobbin [ˈbɔbin], *s.* die Spule, der Klöppel.

bobsleigh [ˈbɔbslei], *s.* der Bob(sleigh), Rennschlitten.

bodice [ˈbɔdis], *s.* das Mieder, Leibchen.

bodied [ˈbɔdid], *adj. suffix; able-* —, gesund, stark.

body [ˈbɔdi], *s.* der Körper; die Körperschaft (*organisation*).

bodyguard [ˈbɔdigaːd], *s.* die Leibwache.

Boer [ˈbouə], *s.* der Bure.

bog [bɔg], *s.* der Sumpf. — *v.a.* (*coll.*) — *down*, einsinken.

Bohemian [boˈhiːmjən], *s.* der Böhme. — *adj.* böhmisch; künstlerhaft.

boil (1) [bɔil], *v.a., v.n.* kochen, sieden. — *s.* das Kochen; —*ing point*, der Siedepunkt.

boil (2) [bɔil], *s.* (*Med.*) die Beule, der Furunkel.

boisterous [ˈbɔistərəs], *adj.* ungestüm; laut (*noisy*).

boisterousness [ˈbɔistərəsnis], *s.* die Heftigkeit, Lautheit.

bold [bould], *adj.* kühn, dreist; *make* —, sich erkühnen.

boldness ['bouldnis], *s.* die Kühnheit, Dreistigkeit.

Bolivian [bə'livjən], *adj.* bolivianisch. —*s.* der Bolivianer.

bolster ['boulstə], *s.* das Polster, Kissen.

bolt [boult], *s.* der Bolzen, Riegel (*on door*); der Pfeil (*arrow*). — *v.a.* verriegeln (*bar*); verschlingen (*devour*). — *v.n.* davonlaufen (*run away*), durchgehen (*abscond*).

bomb [bɔm], *s.* die Bombe. — *v.a.* bombardieren.

bombard [bɔm'baːd], *v.a.* bombardieren.

bombardment [bɔm'baːdmənt], *s.* die Beschießung.

bombastic [bɔm'bæstik], *adj.* schwülstig, bombastisch (*style*).

bombproof ['bɔmpruːf], *adj.* bombensicher.

bond [bɔnd], *s.* das Band (*link*); die Schuldverschreibung (*debt*); *in* —, unter Zollverschluß; (*pl.*) die Fesseln (*fetters*). — *v.a.* (*Chem.*) binden; (*Comm.*) zollpflichtig erklären (*declare dutiable*).

bondage ['bɔndidʒ], *s.* die Knechtschaft.

bone [boun], *s.* der Knochen; die Gräte (*fish*); — *china*, feines Geschirr, das Porzellan; — *of contention*, der Zankapfel; — *dry*, staubtrocken; — *idle*, stinkfaul; — *lace*, die Klöppelspitze. — *v.a.* Knochen oder Gräten entfernen.

ɔonfire ['bɔnfaiə], *s.* das Freudenfeuer.

bonnet ['bɔnit], *s.* die Haube, das Häubchen.

bonny ['bɔni], *adj.* hübsch, nett.

bony ['bouni], *adj.* beinern, knöchern.

book [buk], *s.* das Buch. — *v.a.* belegen (*seat*); eine Karte lösen (*ticket*); engagieren (*engage*).

bookbinder ['bukbaində], *s.* der Buchbinder.

bookcase ['bukkeis], *s.* der Bücherschrank.

bookie *see* **bookmaker**.

booking-office ['bukiŋfis], *s.* der Fahrkartenschalter; die Kasse (*Theat. etc.*).

book-keeper ['bukiːpə], *s.* der Buchhalter.

book-keeping ['bukiːpiŋ], *s.* die Buchhaltung; *double entry* —, doppelte Buchführung, *single entry* —, einfache Buchführung.

bookmaker ['bukmeikə] (*abbr.* **bookie** ['buki]), *s.* (*Racing*) der Buchmacher.

bookmark(er) ['bukmaːk(ə)], *s.* das Lesezeichen.

bookseller ['bukselə], *s.* der Buchhändler.

bookshop ['bukʃɔp], *s.* die Buchhandlung.

bookstall ['bukstɔːl], *s.* der Bücherstand.

bookworm ['bukwəːm], *s.* der Bücherwurm.

boom (1) [buːm], *s.* der Aufschwung; Boom; (*Comm.*) die Konjunktur; Hausse.

boom (2) [buːm], *v.n.* dröhnen, (dumpf) schallen.

boon [buːn], *s.* die Wohltat.

boor [buə], *s.* der Lümmel.

boorish ['buəriʃ], *adj.* lümmelhaft.

boot [buːt], *s.* der Stiefel, hohe Schuh. — *v.a.* mit dem Stiefel stoßen, kicken.

booth [buːð], *s.* die Bude, Zelle (*Teleph.*).

bootlace ['buːtleis], *s.* der Schnürsenkel, der Schnürriemen.

booty ['buːti], *s.* die Beute.

booze [buːz], *v.n.* (*coll.*) saufen.

boozy ['buːzi], *adj.* (*coll.*) angeheitert, leicht betrunken.

border ['bɔːdə], *s.* der Rand; die Grenze. — *v.a.*, *v.n.* angrenzen (*on*); einsäumen (*surround*).

borderer ['bɔːdərə], *s.* der Grenzbewohner.

bore [bɔː], *v.a.* bohren; langweilen (*be boring*). — *s.* das Bohrloch (*drill-hole*), die Bohrung (*drilling*); der langweilige Kerl (*person*).

boredom ['bɔːdəm], *s.* die Langeweile.

borer ['bɔːrə], *s.* der Bohrer (*drill*).

born [bɔːn], *adj.* geboren.

borrow ['bɔrou], *v.a.* borgen, entlehnen.

borrowing ['bɔrouiŋ], *s.* das Borgen, Entlehnen.

bosom ['buzəm], *s.* der Busen.

boss [bɔs], *s.* der Beschlag, der Buckel; (*coll.*) der Chef.

botanical [bɔ'tænikəl], *adj.* botanisch.

botanist ['bɔtənist], *s.* der Botaniker.

botany ['bɔtəni], *s.* die Botanik.

botch [bɔtʃ], *s.* das Flickwerk. — *v.a.* verderben, verhunzen.

both [bouθ], *adj.*, *pron.* beide, beides; — *of them*, beide. — *conj.* — . . . *and*, sowohl . . . als auch.

bother ['bɔðə], *v.a.* plagen, stören, belästigen; — *it!* zum Henker damit! — *v.n.* sich bemühen. — *s.* die Belästigung, das Ärgernis.

bottle [bɔtl], *s.* die Flasche. — *v.a.* in Flaschen abfüllen.

bottom ['bɔtəm], *s.* der Boden, Grund (*ground*); die Ursache (*cause*); (*Naut.*) der Schiffsboden.

bottomless ['bɔtəmlis], *adj.* grundlos, bodenlos.

bough [bau], *s.* der Zweig, Ast.

boulder ['bouldə], *s.* der Felsblock.

bounce [bauns], *v.a.* aufprallen lassen (*ball*). — *v.n.* aufprallen. — *s.* der Rückprall, Aufprall.

bound (1) [baund], *s.* der Sprung; *by leaps and* —, sehr schnell, sprunghaft. — *v.n.* springen, prallen.

bound (2) [baund], *v.a.* begrenzen, einschränken. — *adj.* verpflichtet; — *to* (*inf.*), wird sicherlich . . .

bound

bound (3) [baund], *adj.* — *for*, auf dem Wege nach.

boundary ['baundəri], *s.* die Grenzlinie, Grenze.

bounder ['baundə], *s.* der ungezogene Bursche.

boundless ['baundlis], *adj.* grenzenlos, unbegrenzt.

bounteous ['bauntiəs], *adj.* freigebig; reichlich (*plenty*).

bounty ['baunti], *s.* die Freigebigkeit (*generosity*); (*Comm.*) Prämie.

bouquet [bu'kei], *s.* das Bukett, der Blumenstrauß; die Blume (*wine*).

bourgeois ['buəʒwaː], *s.* der Bürger; Philister. — *adj.* kleinbürgerlich, philisterhaft.

bow (1) [bau], *s.* (*Naut.*) der Bug; —sprit, das Bugspriet.

bow (2) [bau], *s.* die Verbeugung, Verneigung. — *v.n.* sich verneigen, sich verbeugen. — *v.a.* neigen.

bow (3) [bou], *s.* (*Mus.*) der Bogen; die Schleife (*ribbon*). — *v.a.* streichen (*violin*).

bowel ['bauəl], *s.* der Darm; (*pl.*) die Eingeweide.

bowl (1) [boul], *s.* die Schale, der Napf, die Schüssel.

bowl (2) [boul], *s.* die Holzkugel; (*pl.*) das Rasenkugelspiel, Bowlingspiel. — *v.n.* (*Cricket*) den Ball werfen.

bowler (1) ['boulə], *s.* (*hat*) der steife Hut, die Melone.

bowler (2) ['boulə], *s.* (*Sport*) der Ballmann.

box (1) [bɔks], *s.* (*Bot.*) der Buchsbaum.

box (2) [bɔks], *s.* die Büchse, Dose, Schachtel, der Kasten; (*Theat.*) die Loge; — *office*, die Theaterkasse.

box (3) [bɔks], *s.* der Schlag; — *on the ear*, die Ohrfeige. — *v.n.* boxen.

boxer ['bɔksə], *s.* der Boxer; Boxkämpfer.

Boxing Day ['bɔksiŋ'dei], der zweite Weihnachtstag.

boy [bɔi], *s.* der Junge, Knabe; Diener (*servant*).

boyish ['bɔiiʃ], *adj.* knabenhaft.

boyhood ['bɔihud], *s.* das Knabenalter.

brace [breis], *s.* das Band; die Klammer (*clamp*); — *of partridges*, das Paar Rebhühner; die Spange (*denture*). — *v.a.* spannen, straffen. — *v.r.* — *yourself!* stähle dich!

bracelet ['breislit], *s.* das Armband.

braces ['breisiz], *s. pl.* die Hosenträger.

bracken ['brækən], *s.* (*Bot.*) das Farnkraut.

bracket ['brækit], *s.* die Klammer; *income* —, die Einkommensgruppe. — *v.a.* (ein-)klammern; (*Maths.*) in Klammern setzen.

brackish ['brækiʃ], *adj.* salzig.

brad [bræd], *s.* der kopflose Nagel; — *awl*, der Vorstechbohrer.

brag [bræg], *v.n.* prahlen.

braggart ['brægət], *s.* der Prahlhans.

Brahmin ['braːmin], *s.* der Brahmane.

braid [breid], *s.* die Borte; der Saumbesatz. — *v.a.* (mit Borten) besetzen.

Braille [breil], *s.* die Blindenschrift.

brain [brein], *s.* das Gehirn, Hirn; *scatter-* —*ed*, zerstreut.

brainwave ['breinweiv], *s.* der Geistesblitz.

brake [breik], *s.* die Bremse. — *v.a.* bremsen.

bramble [bræmbl], *s.* der (*Bot.*) Brombeerstrauch.

bran [bræn], *s.* die Kleie.

branch [braːntʃ], *s.* der Ast, Zweig; (*Comm.*) die Zweigstelle, Filiale. — *v.n.* — *out*, sich verzweigen; — *out into*, sich ausbreiten, etwas Neues anfangen; — *off*, abzweigen.

brand [brænd], *s.* der (Feuer) Brand; das Brandmal (*on skin*); die Sorte, Marke (*make*); — *new*, funkelnagelneu. — *v.a.* brandmarken, kennzeichnen.

brandish ['brændiʃ], *v.a.* schwingen, herumschwenken.

brandy ['brændi], *s.* der Branntwein, Kognak, Weinbrand.

brass [braːs], *s.* das Messing; — *band*, die Blechmusik, Militärmusikkapelle; — *founder*, Erzgießer, Gelbgießer; (*sl.*) die Frechheit (*impudence*).

brassiere ['bræsiɛə], *s.* der Büstenhalter.

brat [bræt], *s.* (*coll.*) das Kind, der Balg.

brave [breiv], *adj.* tapfer, kühn. — *v.a.* trotzen, standhalten (*Dat.*). — *s.* der Held, Krieger; der Indianer (*redskin*).

bravery ['breivəri], *s.* die Tapferkeit.

brawl [brɔːl], *s.* der Krawall, die Rauferei. — *v.n.* zanken, lärmen.

brawn [brɔːn], *s.* die Sülze; (*fig.*) die Körperkraft, Stärke.

brawny ['brɔːni], *adj.* stark, sehnig.

bray [brei], *v.n.* iah sagen, Eselslaute von sich geben (*donkey*). — *s.* das Iah des Esels, das Eselsgeschrei.

brazen [breizn], *adj.* (*Metall.*) aus Erz; unverschämt (*shameless*).

brazenfaced ['breiznfeisd], *adj.* unverschämt.

brazier ['breiziə], *s.* der Kupferschmied; die Kohlenpfanne.

Brazil [brə'zil], Brasilien, *n.*; — *nut*, die Paranuß.

Brazilian [brə'ziliən], *adj.* brasilianisch. — *s.* der Brasilianer.

breach [briːtʃ], *s.* die Bresche; der Bruch (*break*); die Verletzung; der Vertragsbruch (*of contract*); der Verstoß (*of, gegen, etiquette etc.*).

bread [bred], *s.* das Brot; *brown* —, das Schwarzbrot; — *and butter*, das Butterbrot.

breadth [bretθ], *s.* die Breite, Weite.

broadcasting

break [breik], *s.* der Bruch (*breach*); die Lücke (*gap*); die Chance (*chance*); *a lucky —*, ein glücklicher Zufall, ein Glücksfall; die Pause (*from work*). — *v.a., v.n. irr.* brechen; — *off*, Pause machen; — *in*, unterbrechen (*interrupt*); — *in*, (*horse*) einschulen, zureiten; — *up*, abbrechen (*school, work*); — *away*, sich trennen, absondern; — *down*, zusammenbrechen (*health*); (*Am.*) analysieren; — auflösen.

breakage ['breikidʒ], *s.* der Bruch, der Schaden (*damage*).

breakdown ['breikdoun], *s.* der Zusammenbruch (*health*); die Panne (*car*); (*Am.*) die Analyse (*analysis*).

breaker ['breikə], *s.* die Brandungswelle, Brandung.

breakfast ['brekfəst], *s.* das Frühstück. *v.n.* frühstücken.

breast [brest], *s.* die Brust.

breath [breθ], *s.* der Atem; der Hauch (*exhalation*); *with bated —*, mit verhaltenem Atem.

breathe [briːð], *v.n.* atmen.

breathing ['briːðiŋ], *s.* die Atmung.

breathless ['breθlis], *adj.* atemlos.

breech [briːtʃ], *s.* der Boden; (*pl.*) die Reithosen, *f. pl.*

breed [briːd], *v.a. irr.* zeugen, züchten (*cattle, etc.*). — *v.n.* sich vermehren. — *s.* die Zucht, die Art (*type*); die Rasse (*race*).

breeder ['briːdə], *s.* der Züchter.

breeding ['briːdiŋ], *s.* die gute Kinderstube (*manners*); die Erziehung; das Züchten (*of plants, cattle etc.*).

breeze [briːz], *s.* die Briese.

breezy ['briːzi], *adj.* windig; lebhaft (*manner*), beschwingt (*tone*).

brethren ['breðrən], *s. pl.* (*obs.*) die Brüder.

Breton [bretn], *adj.* bretonisch. — *s.* der Bretagner, Bretone.

brevet ['brevit], *s.* das Patent.

breviary ['briːviəri], *s.* das Brevier.

brevity ['breviti], *s.* die Kürze.

brew [bruː], *v.a.* brauen. — *s.* das Gebräu, Bräu (*beer*).

brewer ['bruːə], *s.* der Brauer, Bierbrauer.

brewery ['bruːəri], *s.* die Brauerei, das Brauhaus.

briar, brier [braiə], *s.* (*Bot.*) der Dornstrauch, die wilde Rose.

bribe [braib], *v.a.* bestechen. — *s.* das Bestechungsgeld.

bribery ['braibəri], *s.* die Bestechung.

brick [brik], *s.* der Ziegel, Backstein; *drop a —*, eine Taktlosigkeit begehen, einen Schnitzer machen.

bricklayer ['brikleiə], *s.* der Maurer.

bridal [braidl], *adj.* bräutlich.

bride [braid], *s.* die Braut.

bridegroom ['braidgruːm], *s.* der Bräutigam.

bridesmaid ['braidzmeid], *s.* die Brautjungfer.

bridge [bridʒ], *s.* die Brücke. — *v.a.* überbrücken; — *the gap*, die Lücke füllen.

bridle [braidl], *s.* der Zaum, Zügel. — *v.a.* aufzäumen. — *v.n.* sich brüsten.

brief [briːf], *adj.* kurz, bündig, knapp. — *s.* der Schriftsatz, der Rechtsauftrag, die Instruktionen, *f. pl.* (*instructions*). — *v.a.* instruieren, beauftragen; informieren (*inform*).

brigade [bri'geid], *s.* die Brigade.

brigand ['brigənd], *s.* der Brigant, Straßenräuber.

bright [brait], *adj.* hell, glänzend (*shiny*); klug, intelligent (*clever*).

brighten [braitn], *v.a.* glänzend machen (*polish etc.*); erhellen, aufheitern (*cheer*).

brightness ['braitnis], *s.* der Glanz; die Helligkeit; die Klugheit (*cleverness*).

brill [bril], *s.* (*Zool.*) der Glattbutt.

brilliance, brilliancy ['briljəns, -jənsi], *s.* der Glanz, die Pracht.

brim [brim], *s.* der Rand (*glass*); die Krempe (*hat*). — *v.n.* — (*over*) *with*, überfließen von.

brimful ['brimful], *adj.* übervoll.

brimstone ['brimstoun], *s.* der Schwefel; — *butterfly*, der Zitronenfalter.

brindled ['brindld], *adj.* scheckig, gefleckt.

brine [brain], *s.* die Salzsole, das Salzwasser.

bring [briŋ], *v.a. irr.* bringen; — *about*, zustande bringen; — *forth*, hervorbringen; gebären; — *forward*, fördern; anführen; — *on*, herbeiführen; — *up*, erziehen, aufziehen.

brink [briŋk], *s.* (*fig.*) der Rand, — *of a precipice*, Rand eines Abgrundes.

briny ['braini], *adj.* salzig.

brisk [brisk], *adj.* frisch, munter, feurig (*horse*).

brisket ['briskit], *s.* die Brust (eines Tieres).

briskness ['brisknis], *s.* die Lebhaftigkeit.

bristle [brisl], *s.* die Borste. — *v.n.* sich sträuben.

British ['britiʃ], *adj.* britisch.

Britisher, Briton ['britiʃə, 'britən], *s.* der Brite.

brittle [britl], *adj.* zerbrechlich, spröde.

brittleness ['britlnis], *s.* die Sprödigkeit, Zerbrechlichkeit.

broach [broutʃ], *v.a.* anzapfen, anschneiden; — *a subject*, ein Thema berühren.

broad [brɔːd], *adj.* breit, weit; ordinär, derb (*joke*); — *minded*, duldsam, weitherzig.

broadcast ['brɔːdkɑːst], *v.a.* senden, übertragen (*radio*). — *s.* die Sendung, das Programm.

broadcaster ['brɔːdkɑːstə], *s.* der im Radio Vortragende *or* Künstler (*artist*); Ansager.

broadcasting ['brɔːdkɑːstiŋ], *s.* das Senden, der Rundfunk; — *station*, der Sender, die Rundfunkstation.

broadcloth ['brɔːdɔçlɔθ], s. das feine Tuch.

broaden [brɔːdn], v.a. erweitern, verbreitern.

brocade [broˈkeid], s. der Brokat.

brogue [broug], s. der grobe Schuh; der irische Akzent.

broil ['brɔil], v.a. braten, rösten.

broke [brouk], adj. (coll.) pleite.

broken ['broukən], adj. gebrochen; zerbrochen; unterbrochen (interrupted).

broker ['broukə], s. der Makler.

bronchial ['brɔŋkjəl], adj. (Anat.) bronchial, in or von der Luftröhre, Luftröhren-.

bronchitis [brɔŋˈkaitis], s. (Med.) die Luftröhrenentzündung, Bronchitis.

bronze [brɔnz], s. (Metall.) die Bronze, Bronzefarbe.

brooch [broutʃ], s. die Brosche.

brood [bruːd], s. die Brut. — v.n. brüten; grübeln (meditate).

brook (1) [bruk], s. der Bach.

brook (2) [bruk], v.a. ertragen, leiden.

brooklet ['bruklit], s. das Bächlein.

broom [bruːm], s. der Besen; (Bot.) der Ginster.

broth [brɔθ], s. die Brühe; meat —, Fleischbrühe.

brothel ['brɔθəl], s. das Bordell.

brother ['brʌðə], s. der Bruder; — -in-law, der Schwager.

brotherhood ['brʌðəhud], s. die Bruderschaft.

brotherly ['brʌðəli], adj. brüderlich.

brow [brau], s. die Braue, Augenbraue; der Kamm (hill); die Stirn(e) (forehead).

browbeat ['braubiːt], v.a. einschüchtern.

brown [braun], adj. braun; in a — study, in tiefem Nachsinnen.

browse [brauz], v.n. weiden (cattle); stöbern, (durch-)blättern (in books etc.).

Bruin ['bruːin]. Braun, Meister Petz, der Bär.

bruise [bruːz], v.a. quetschen, stoßen; (wund) schlagen. — s. die Quetschung.

Brunswick ['brʌnzwik]. Braunschweig, n.

brunt [brʌnt], s. der Anprall; bear the —, der Wucht ausgesetzt sein, den Stoß auffangen.

brush [brʌʃ], s. die Bürste (clothes); der Pinsel (paint, painting); — stroke, der Pinselstrich. — v.a., v.n. bürsten, abbürsten; — against s.o., mit jemandem zusammenstoßen, streifen (an, Acc.); — up one's English, das Englisch auffrischen; — off, abschütteln.

brushwood ['brʌʃwud], s. das Gestrüpp.

brusque [brusk], adj. brüsk, barsch.

Brussels ['brʌsəlz]. Brüssel, n.; — sprouts, (Bot.) der Rosenkohl.

brutal [bruːtl], adj. brutal, grausam.

brutality [bruːˈtæliti], s. die Brutalität.

brute [bruːt], s. der Unmensch.

bubble [bʌbl], s. die Blase; (fig.) der Schwindel (swindle). — v.n. sprudeln, wallen, schäumen.

buccaneer [bʌkəˈniə], s. der Seeräuber.

buck [bʌk], s. (Zool.) der Bock; (Am. sl.) der Dollar. — v.a. — up, aufmuntern. — v.n. — up, sich zusammenraffen.

bucket ['bʌkit], s. der Eimer, Kübel.

buckle [bʌkl], s. die Schnalle. — v.a. zuschnallen; biegen. — v.n. sich krümmen.

buckler ['bʌklə], s. der Schild.

buckram ['bʌkrəm], s. die Steifleinwand.

buckskin ['bʌkskin], s. das Wildleder.

buckwheat ['bʌkwiːt], s. (Bot.) der Buchweizen.

bucolic [bjuːˈkɔlik], adj. bukolisch, ländlich, Schäfer-.

bud [bʌd], s. (Bot.) die Knospe. — v.n. knospen.

buddy ['bʌdi], s.(coll.Am.) der Freund, Kamerad.

budge [bʌdʒ], v.n. sich rühren, sich regen.

budget ['bʌdʒit], s. das Budget; der Haushaltsplan; der Etat; present the —, den Staatsetat vorlegen. — v.n. voranschlagen (for), planen.

buff [bʌf], adj. ledergelb.

buffalo ['bʌfəlou], s. (Zool.) der Büffel.

buffer ['bʌfə], s. der Puffer.

buffet (1) ['bʌfit], s. der Puff, Faustschlag (blow). — v.a. schlagen, stoßen.

buffet (2) ['bufei], s. das Büffet, der Anrichtetisch.

buffoon [bʌˈfuːn], s. der Possenreißer.

buffoonery [bʌˈfuːnəri], s. die Possen, f. pl.; das Possenreißen.

bug [bʌg], s. (Ent.) die Wanze; (Am.) der Käfer; (coll.) das Insekt.

buggy ['bʌgi], s. der Einspänner.

bugle [bjuːgl], s. (Mus.) das Signalhorn, die Signaltrompete.

bugler ['bjuːglə], s. (Mus.) der Trompeter.

build [bild], v.a., v.n. irr. bauen; errichten; — on, sich verlassen auf (rely on). — s. die Statur, Figur (figure).

builder ['bildə], s. der Bauherr, Baumeister (employer); Bauarbeiter (worker).

building ['bildiŋ], s. das Gebäude, der Bau; — site, der Bauplatz.

bulb [bʌlb], s. (Bot.) der Knollen, die Zwiebel; Dutch —, die Tulpe; (Elec.) die Birne.

bulbous ['bʌlbəs], adj. zwiebelartig; dickbäuchig.

Bulgarian [bʌlˈgɛəriən], adj. bulgarisch. — s. der Bulgare.

bulge [bʌldʒ], s. die Ausbauchung; die Ausbuchtung (in fighting line). — v.n. herausragen, anschwellen.

bulk [bʌlk], s. die Masse, Menge; buy in —, im Großen einkaufen.

bulky ['bʌlki], *adj.* schwer (*heavy*); massig (*stodgy*); unhandlich.

bull (1) [bul], *s.* (*Zool.*) der Bulle, Stier; —'s eye, das Schwarze (*target*).

bull (2) [bul], *s.* (*Papal*) die Bulle, der Erlass.

bulldog ['buldɔg], *s.* der Bullenbeißer.

bullet ['bulit], *s.* die Kugel, das Geschoß.

bulletin ['bulitin], *s.* das Bulletin, der Tagesbericht.

bullfight ['bulfait], *s.* der Stierkampf.

bullfinch ['bulfintʃ], *s.* (*Orn.*) der Dompfaff.

bullfrog ['bulfrɔg], *s.* (*Zool.*) der Ochsenfrosch.

bullion ['buljən], *s.* der Goldbarren, Silberbarren.

bullock ['bulək], *s.* (*Zool.*) der Ochse.

bully ['buli], *s.* der Raufbold, Angeber, Großtuer (*braggart*); der Tyrann. — *v.a.* tyrannisieren, einschüchtern.

bulrush ['bulrʌʃ], *s.* (*Bot.*) die Binse.

bulwark ['bulwək], *s.* das Bollwerk, die Verteidigung.

bump [bʌmp], *s.* der Schlag, der Stoß. — *v.a.* stoßen.

bun [bʌn], *s.* das Rosinenbrötchen; das süße Brötchen; (*hair*) der Knoten.

bunch [bʌntʃ], *s.* der Strauß (*keys*); der Strauß (*flowers*); die Traube (*grapes*). — *v a.* zusammenfassen, zusammenbinden, zusammenraffen.

bundle [bʌndl], *s.* das Bündel.

bung [bʌŋ], *s.* der Spund (*in barrel*).

bungle [bʌŋgl], *v.a.* verpfuschen, verderben.

bungler ['bʌŋglə], *s.* der Stümper.

bunion ['bʌnjən], *s.* die Fußschwiele.

bunk (1) [bʌŋk], *s.* die (Schlaf-)Koje.

bunk (2) [bʌŋk], *s.* (*coll.*) der Unsinn.

bunker ['bʌŋkə], *s.* der Kohlenraum, Bunker.

bunting ['bʌntiŋ], *s.* das Flaggentuch.

buoy [bɔi], *s.* die Boje.

buoyant ['bɔiənt], *adj.* schwimmend; lebhaft, heiter.

buoyancy ['bɔiənsi], *s.* die Schwimmkraft, die Schwungkraft.

burden (1) [bə:dn], *s.* die Bürde, Last. — *v.a.* belasten, beladen.

burden (2) [bə:dn], *s.* der Refrain; der Hauptinhalt.

burdensome ['bə:dnsəm], *adj.* beschwerlich.

bureau [bjuə'rou], *s.* der Schreibtisch; das Büro.

bureaucracy [bjuə'rɔkrəsi], *s.* die Bürokratie.

burgess ['bə:dʒis], *s.* der Bürger.

burglar ['bə:glə], *s.* der Einbrecher.

burglary ['bə:gləri], *s.* der Einbruch, der Diebstahl.

burgomaster ['bə:goma:stə], *s.* der Bürgermeister.

Burgundian [bə:'gʌndiən], *adj.* burgundisch. —*s.* der Burgunder.

Burgundy (1) ['bə:gəndi], das Burgund.

Burgundy (2) ['bə:gəndi], *s.* der Burgunder(-wein).

burial ['beriəl], das Begräbnis; — ground, der Kirchhof, Friedhof; — service, die Totenfeier, Trauerfeier.

burlesque [bə:'lesk], *s.* die Burleske, Posse.

burly ['bə:li], *adj.* dick, stark.

Burmese [bə:'mi:z], *adj.* birmesisch. — *s.* der Birmese.

burn [bə:n], *v.a., v.n. irr.* brennen, verbrennen; — *s.* das Brandmal.

burner ['bə:nə], *s.* der Brenner.

burnish ['bə:niʃ], *v.a.* polieren.

burred [bə:d], *adj.* überliegend; (*Metall.*) ausgehämmert; — over, (*Metall.*) breitgeschmiedet.

burrow ['bʌrou], *s.* der Bau, (*rabbits etc.*). —*v.n.* sich eingraben; wühlen.

burst [bə:st], *v.a., v.n. irr.* bersten, platzen, explodieren (*explode*); — out laughing, laut auflachen; — into tears, in Tränen ausbrechen; — into flames, aufflammen; sprengen (*blow up*). — *s.* der Ausbruch; die Explosion.

bury ['beri], *v.a.* begraben; beerdigen.

bus [bʌs], *s.* der Autobus, Omnibus.

busby ['bʌzbi], *s.* (*Mil.*) die Bärenmütze.

bush [buʃ], *s.* der Busch.

bushel ['buʃl], *s.* der Scheffel.

bushy ['buʃi], *adj.* buschig.

business ['biznis], *s.* das Geschäft; die Beschäftigung, die Tätigkeit (*activity*); Aufgabe, Obliegenheit; der Handel (*trade*); on —, geschäftlich.

businesslike ['biznislaik], *adj.* geschäftsmäßig, nüchtern, praktisch.

businessman ['biznismæn], *s.* der Geschäftsmann.

bust (1) [bʌst], *s.* die Büste.

bust (2) [bʌst], *v.a., v.n.* (*coll.*) sprengen; go —, bankrott machen.

bustard ['bʌstəd], *s.* (*Orn.*) die Trappe.

bustle [bʌsl], *s.* der Lärm, die Aufregung. —*v.n.* aufgeregt umherlaufen; rührig sein (*be active*).

busy ['bizi], *adj.* geschäftig (*active*); beschäftigt (*engaged*, mit, *in*); be —, zu tun haben.

but [bʌt], *conj.* aber, jedoch; sondern. — *adv.* nur, bloß; — yesterday, erst gestern. — *prep.* außer; all — two, alle außer zwei.

butcher ['butʃə], *s.* der Metzger, Fleischer; —'s knife, das Fleischmesser.

butchery ['butʃəri], *s.* die Schlächterei; das Blutbad, das Gemetzel.

butler ['bʌtlə], *s.* der oberste Diener; Kellermeister.

butt [bʌt], *s.* das dicke Ende; der Kolben (*rifle*); der Stoß (*blow*); die Zielscheibe (*target*). — *v.a.* stoßen, spießen.

butter ['bʌtə], *s.* die Butter. — *v.a.* mit Butter bestreichen; — up, schmeicheln (*Dat.*).

butterfly ['bʌtəflai], *s.* (*Ent.*) der Schmetterling.

buttery ['bʌtəri], *s.* die Speisekammer.

329

buttock(s) ['bʌtək(s)], *s.* der Hintere, das Gesäß (*usually pl.*) (*vulg.*).
button [bʌtn], *s.* der Knopf. — *v.a.* — *up*, knöpfen, zumachen.
buttress ['bʌtris], *s.* der Strebepfeiler.
buxom ['bʌksəm], *adj.* drall, gesund.
buy [bai], *v.a. irr.* kaufen.
buzz [bʌz], *s.* das Summen. — *v.n.* summen.
buzzard ['bʌzəd], *s.* (*Orn.*) der Bussard.
by [bai], *prep.* (*beside*) neben, an; (*near*) nahe; (*before*) gegen, um, bei; (*about*) bei; (*from, with*) durch, von, mit; — *the way*, nebenbei bemerkt; — *way of*, mittels. — *adv.* (*nearby*) nahe; nebenan.
by-election ['baiilekʃən], *s.* die Nachwahl; Ersatzwahl.
bygone ['baigɔn], *adj.* vergangen.
bylaw, byelaw ['bailɔ:], *s.* die Bestimmung.
Byzantine [bai'zæntain], *adj.* byzantinisch.

C

C [si:]. das C (*also Mus.*).
cab [kæb], *s.* (*horse-drawn*) die Droschke, der Wagen; das Taxi; —*stand*, der Droschkenhalteplatz; (*Motor.*) der Taxiplatz, Taxistand.
cabaret ['kæbərei], *s.* das Kabarett, die Kleinbühne.
cabbage ['kæbidʒ], *s.* (*Bot.*) der Kohl.
cabin ['kæbin], *s.* die Kabine (*boat*); die Hütte (*hut*); — *-boy*, der Schiffsjunge.
cabinet ['kæbinet], *s.* das Kabinett (*government*); der Schrank (*cupboard*); das kleine Zimmer *or* Nebenzimmer (*mainly Austr.*); (*Rad.*) das Gehäuse; — *maker*, der Kunsttischler.
cable [keibl], *s.* das Kabel (*of metal*), das Seil (*metal or rope*); das Telegramm. — *v.a.* kabeln, telegraphieren.
cablegram ['keiblgræm], *s.* die (Kabel-) Depesche.
cabman ['kæbmən], *s.* der Taxichauffeur.
caboose [kə'bu:s], *s.* die Schiffsküche.
cabriolet [kæbriə'lei], *s.* das Kabriolett.
cackle [kækl], *v.n.* gackern (*hens*); schnattern (*geese*); (*fig.*) schwatzen.
cacophony [kə'kɔfəni], *s.* der Mißklang.
cad [kæd], *s.* der gemeine Kerl, Schuft.
cadaverous [kə'dævərəs], *adj.* leichenhaft.
caddie ['kædi], *s.* der Golfjunge.
caddy ['kædi], *s.* *tea* —, die Teebüchse, Teedose.
cadence ['keidəns], *s.* (*Phonet.*) der Tonfall; (*Mus.*) die Kadenz.
cadet [kə'det], *s.* (*Mil.*) der Kadett.
cadge [kædʒ], *v.a.* erbetteln.

Caesar ['si:zə]. Cäsar, *m.*
Caesarean [si'zɛəriən], *adj.* cäsarisch; — *operation* or *section*, (*Med.*) der Kaiserschnitt.
cafeteria [kæfə'tiəriə], *s.* das Selbstbedienungsrestaurant.
cage [keidʒ], *s.* (*Zool.*) der Käfig; (*Orn.*) das Vogelbauer. — *v.a.* einfangen, einsperren.
cagey ['keidʒi], *adj.* (*coll.*) argwöhnisch, zurückhaltend; schlau.
cairn [kɛən], *s.* (*Archaeol.*) der Steinhaufen, der Grabhügel.
caitiff ['keitif], *adj.* niederträchtig. — *s.* der Schuft.
cajole [kə'dʒoul],*v.a.*schmeicheln(*Dat.*).
cake [keik], *s.* der Kuchen; — *of soap*, das Stück Seife; *have o.'s* — *and eat it*, alles haben. — *v.a., v.n.* zusammenbacken; —*d with dirt*, mit Schmutz beschmiert.
calamity [kə'læmiti], *s.* das Unheil, Unglück; Elend.
calcareous [kæl'kɛəriəs], *adj.* (*Geol.*) kalkartig.
calculate ['kælkjuleit], *v.a.* berechnen.
calculation [kælkju'leiʃən], *s.* die Berechnung.
calendar ['kæləndə], *s.* der Kalender.
calf [kɑ:f], *s.* (*Zool.*) das Kalb; (*Anat.*) die Wade; — *love*, die Jugendliebe.
calibre ['kælibə], *s.* das Kaliber.
calico ['kælikou], *s.* der Kaliko, Kattun.
Caliph ['keilif], *s.* der Kalif.
calk (1) [kɔ:k], *v.a.* beschlagen (*horse*).
calk (2), **caulk** [kɔ:k], *v.a.* (*Naut.*) abdichten.
call [kɔ:l], *v.a., v.n.* rufen, herbeirufen; (*Am.*) antelefonieren, anrufen (*ring up*); (*name*) nennen; — *to account*, zur Rechenschaft ziehen; (*summon*) kommen lassen; — *for*, abholen; *this* —*s for*, das berechtigt zu. — *s.* der Ruf, Anruf; die (innere) Berufung, der Beruf.
callbox ['kɔ:lbɔks] *see* **phone box**.
calling ['kɔ:liŋ], *s.* der Beruf, das Gewerbe (*occupation*).
callous ['kæləs], *adj.* schwielig (*hands*); (*fig.*) unempfindlich, hart, gemein.
callow ['kælou], *adj.* ungefiedert (*bird*); (*fig.*) unerfahren.
calm [kɑ:m], *adj.* ruhig, still; gelassen. — *s.* die Ruhe; (*Naut.*) Windstille. — *v.a.* beruhigen. — *v.n.* — *down*, sich beruhigen, sich legen (*storm etc.*).
caloric [kæ'lɔrik], *adj.* Wärme-, warm; (*Chem.*) kalorisch.
calorie, calory ['kæləri], *s.* die Kalorie.
calumny ['kæləmni], *s.* die Verleumdung.
calve [kɑ:v], *v.n.* kalben, Kälber kriegen.
cambric ['kæmbrik],*s.*der Batist(*textile*).
camel ['kæməl], *s.* (*Zool.*) das Kamel.
cameo ['kæmiou], *s.* die Kamee.
camera ['kæmərə], *s.* (*Phot.*) die Kamera.
camomile ['kæməmail], *s.* (*Bot.*) die Kamille.

camp [kæmp], s. das Lager; Zeltlager. — v.n. sich lagern, ein Lager aufschlagen, zelten.

campaign [kæm'pein], s. der Feldzug. — v.n. einen Feldzug mitmachen; (fig.) Propaganda machen.

camphor ['kæmfə], s. der Kampfer.

camping ['kæmpiŋ], s. die Lagerausrüstung (equipment); das Lagern (activity), das Zelten.

can (1) [kæn], s. die Kanne; die Büchse; watering —, die Gießkanne. — v.a. (Am.) einmachen, einkochen (fruit).

can (2) [kæn], v. aux. irr. können, imstande sein, vermögen.

Canadian [kə'neidiən], adj. kanadisch. — s. der Kanadier.

canal [kə'næl], s. der Kanal; — lock, die Kanalschleuse.

canalize ['kænəlaiz], v.a. kanalisieren, leiten.

cancel ['kænsəl], v.a. widerrufen, absagen (show); aufheben, ungültig machen.

cancellation [kænsə'leiʃən], s. die Aufhebung, Absage, Widerrufung.

cancer ['kænsə], s. (Med., Astron.) der Krebs.

cancerous ['kænsərəs], adj. (Med.) krebsartig.

candelabra [kændi'lɑːbrə], s. der Kandelaber, Leuchter.

candid ['kændid], adj. offen, aufrichtig.

candidate ['kændideit], s. der Kandidat, Bewerber.

candidature ['kændiditʃə], s. die Kandidatur, die Bewerbung.

candied ['kændid], adj. gezuckert, kandiert (fruit).

candle [kændl], s. die Kerze, das Licht.

Candlemas ['kændlməs], (Eccl.) Lichtmeß.

candlestick ['kændlstik], s. der Kerzenleuchter.

candlewick ['kændlwik], s. der Kerzendocht (textile).

candour ['kændə], s. die Offenheit, Aufrichtigkeit.

candy ['kændi], s. (Am.) das Zuckerwerk, (pl.) Süßigkeiten. — v.a. verzuckern.

cane [kein], s. (Bot.) das Rohr, der Rohrstock; Spazierstock. — v.a. (mit dem Stock) schlagen.

canine ['kænain], adj. Hunde-, hündisch; — tooth, der Eckzahn.

canister ['kænistə], s. die Blechbüchse, der Kanister.

canker ['kæŋkə], s. (Bot.) der Brand; (Bot.) der Pflanzenrost; (fig.) eine zerfressende Krankheit.

cannibal ['kænibəl], s. der Kannibale, Menschenfresser.

cannon ['kænən], s. die Kanone, das Geschütz.

canoe [kə'nuː], s. das Kanu.

canon ['kænən], s. (Mus., Eccl.) der Kanon; die Regel; (Eccl.) der Domherr; — law, das kanonische Recht.

canonize ['kænənaiz], v.a. (Eccl.) kanonisieren, heiligsprechen.

canopy ['kænəpi], s. der Baldachin.

cant [kænt], s. die Heuchelei.

can't, cannot [kɑːnt, 'kænɔt] see can (2).

cantankerous [kæn'tæŋkərəs], adj. zänkisch, mürrisch.

cantata [kæn'tɑːtə], s. (Mus.) die Kantate.

canteen [kæn'tiːn], s. die Kantine (restaurant); die Besteckgarnitur (set of cutlery).

canter ['kæntə], s. der Galopp, der Kurzgalopp.

canticle ['kæntikl], s. (Eccl.) der Lobgesang, das Loblied.

canto ['kæntou], s. (Lit.) der Gesang.

canton ['kæntɔn], s. (Pol.) der Kanton, der Bezirk.

canvas ['kænvəs], s. das Segeltuch; (Art) die Malerleinwand; die Zeltplane (tent).

canvass ['kænvəs], v.a., v.n. (Pol.) um Stimmen werben.

canvasser ['kænvəsə], s. (Pol.) der Werber, Stimmensammler.

cap [kæp], s. die Kappe, Mütze; die Haube; der Deckel. — v.a. übertreffen.

capability [keipə'biliti], s. die Fähigkeit.

capable ['keipəbl], adj. fähig (Genit.), imstande (of, zu); tüchtig.

capacious [kə'peiʃəs], adj. geräumig.

capacity [kə'pæsiti], s. der Inhalt, die Geräumigkeit; die Fassungskraft (intellect); die Leistungsfähigkeit (ability); der Fassungsraum (space).

cape (1) [keip], s. (Tail.) der Kragenmantel.

cape (2) [keip], s. (Geog.) das Kap, das Vorgebirge.

caper ['keipə], s. der Sprung, Luftsprung. — v.n. in die Luft springen.

capillary [kə'piləri], adj. haarfein; — tubing, die Haarröhre, die Kapillarröhre.

capital ['kæpitl], s. (Comm.) das Kapital; die Hauptstadt (capital city); — punishment, die Todesstrafe; — letter, der Großbuchstabe. — adj. (coll.) ausgezeichnet, vorzüglich.

capitalize ['kæpitəlaiz], v.a. (Comm.) kapitalisieren; ausnutzen.

capitation [kæpi'teiʃən], s. die Kopfsteuer.

capitulate [kə'pitjuleit], v.n. kapitulieren.

capon ['keipən], s. (Zool.) der Kapaun.

caprice [kə'priːs], s. die Kaprize, Laune.

capricious [kə'priʃəs], adj. launenhaft, eigensinnig.

Capricorn ['kæprikɔːn], s. (Astron.) der Steinbock; tropic of —, der Wendekreis des Steinbocks.

capriole ['kæprioul], s. der Luftsprung.

capsize [kæp'saiz], v.n. umkippen, kentern (boat).

capstan ['kæpstən], s. (Engin.) die Ankerwinde; (Mech.) die Erdwinde; (Naut.) das Gangspill.

capsular ['kæpsjulə], adj. kapselförmig.

capsule ['kæpsjuːl], s. die Kapsel.

captain ['kæptin], s. (Naut.) der Kapitän; (Mil.) der Hauptmann.

331

captious

captious ['kæpʃəs], *adj.* zänkisch, streitsüchtig; verfänglich.
captivate ['kæptiveit], *v.a.* einnehmen, gewinnen.
captive ['kæptiv], *s.* der Gefangene. — *adj.* gefangen.
capture ['kæptʃə], *s.* die Gefangennahme (*men*); Erbeutung (*booty*).
Capuchin ['kæputʃin], *s.* (*Eccl.*) der Kapuziner.
car [ka:], *s.* (*Motor.*) der Wagen; das Auto; (*Am.*) der Eisenbahnwagen.
carafe [kæ'ræf], *s.* die Karaffe, Wasserfläsche.
caravan ['kærəvæn], *s.* die Karawane; der Wohnwagen.
caraway['kærəwei],*s.*(*Bot.*)derKümmel.
carbine ['ka:bain], *s.* der Karabiner.
carbolic [ka:'bɔlik], *adj.* — *acid*, (*Chem.*) die Karbolsäure.
carbon ['ka:bən], *s.* (*Chem.*) der Kohlenstoff.
carbonate ['ka:bəneit], *s.* (*Chem.*) das kohlensaure Salz, Karbonat.
carbonize ['ka:bənaiz], *v.a.* verkohlen. — *v.n.* (*Chem., Geol.*) zu Kohle werden.
carbuncle ['ka:bʌnkl], *s.* (*Min.*) der Karfunkel; (*Med.*) der Karbunkel.
carburettor [ka:bju'retə], *s.* (*Motor.*) der Vergaser.
carcase, carcass ['ka:kəs], *s.* der Kadaver.
card (1) [ka:d], *s.* die Karte, Postkarte; *playing* —, die Spielkarte; *put your —s on the table*, rück mit der Wahrheit heraus!
card (2) [ka:d], *v.a.* krempeln (*wool*); kardätschen (*cotton*).
cardboard ['ka:dbɔ:d], *s.* die Pappe, der Pappendeckel.
cardiac ['ka:diæk], *adj.* (*Med.*) Herz-.
cardinal ['ka:dinl], *s.* (*Eccl.*) der Kardinal. — *adj.* Kardinal-, grundlegend.
cardiogram ['ka:diogræm], *s.* (*Med.*) das Kardiogramm.
cardsharper ['ka:dʃa:pə], *s.* der Falschspieler.
care [kɛə], *s.* die Sorge (*anxiety*, um, *for*); *with* —, mit Sorgfalt, genau; *care of* (*abbr. c/o on letters*) *take* —, sich in acht nehmen. — *v.n.* — *for*, sich interessieren, gern haben.
careen [kə'ri:n], *v.a.* (*Naut.*) kielholen, umlegen.
career [kə'riə], *s.* die Karriere, Laufbahn.
careful ['kɛəful], *adj.* sorgfältig, vorsichtig, umsichtig.
carefulness ['kɛəfulnis], *s.* die Vorsicht, Sorgfalt, Umsicht.
careless ['kɛəlis], *adj.* unachtsam, nachlässig.
carelessness ['kɛəlisnis], *s.* die Nachlässigkeit, Unachtsamkeit.
caress [kə'res], *v.a.* liebkosen, herzen. — *s.* die Liebkosung, die Zärtlichkeit.
caretaker ['kɛəteikə], *s.* der Hausmeister.

careworn ['kɛəwɔ:n], *adj.* abgehärmt, von Sorgen gebeugt.
cargo ['ka:gou], *s.* die Fracht, die Ladung.
caricature [kærikə'tjuə *or* 'kærikətʃə], *s.* die Karikatur. — *v.a.* karikieren, verzerren.
Carinthian [kə'rinθjən], *adj.* kärntnerisch.
carmine ['ka:main], *s.* der Karmin.
carnage ['ka:nidʒ], *s.* das Blutbad.
carnal [ka:nl], *adj.* fleischlich, sinnlich.
carnation [ka:'neiʃən], *s.* (*Bot.*) die Nelke.
carnival ['ka:nivl], *s.* der Karneval.
carnivorous [ka:'nivərəs], *adj.* fleischfressend.
carol ['kærəl], *s. Christmas* —, das Weihnachtslied.
carotid [kə'rɔtid], *s.* (*Anat.*) die Halspulsader.
carousal [kə'rauzəl], *s.* das Gelage, das Gezeche.
carouse [kə'rauz], *v.n.* zechen, schmausen.
carp (1) [ka:p], *s.* (*Zool.*) der Karpfen.
carp (2) [ka:p], *v.n.* bekritteln, tadeln.
Carpathian Mountains [ka:'peiθjən 'mauntinz], die Karpathen, *f. pl.*
carpenter ['ka:pəntə], *s.* der Zimmermann; Tischler.
carpentry ['ka:pəntri], *s.* die Tischlerei, das Zimmerhandwerk.
carpet ['ka:pit], *s.* der Teppich; — *bag*, die Reisetasche.
carriage ['kæridʒ], *s.* der Wagen, Waggon; das Verhalten, die Haltung (*bearing*); (*Comm.*) — *paid*, einschließlich Zustellung; — *way*, der Straßendamm.
carrier ['kæriə], *s.* der Fuhrmann, Fuhrunternehmer.
carrion ['kæriən], *s.* das Aas.
carrot ['kærət], *s.* (*Bot.*) die Mohrrübe; die Karotte.
carry ['kæri], *v.a.* tragen; bringen; führen (*on vehicle*), fahren (*convey*); — *interest*, Zinsen tragen; (*Comm.*) — *forward*, übertragen; — *two* (*in adding up*), zwei weiter; — *on*, weitermachen, fortfahren; — *through*, durchführen, durchhalten; *v.n.* vernehmbar sein (*of sound*); — *on*, weiterarbeiten, weiterexistieren.
cart [ka:t], *s.* der Karren, Frachtwagen.
cartel [ka:'tel], *s.* (*Comm.*) das Kartell.
Carthage ['ka:θidʒ], Karthago, *n.*
carthorse ['ka:θɔ:s], *s.* das Zugpferd.
cartilage ['ka:tilidʒ], *s.* der Knorpel.
carton ['ka:tən], *s.* (*cardboard box*) der Karton, die Schachtel.
cartoon [ka:'tu:n], *s.* die Karikatur; — *film*, der Trickfilm.
cartridge ['ka:tridʒ], *s.* die Patrone.
cartwright ['ka:trait], *s.* der Stellmacher, Wagenbauer.
carve [ka:v], *v.a.* schneiden (*cut*); schnitzen (*wood*), meißeln (*stone*), tranchieren (*meat*).

carver [ˈkɑːvə], *s.* der Schnitzer (*wood*); das Tranchiermesser (*carving knife*).

cascade [kæsˈkeid], *s.* der Wasserfall.

case (1) [keis], *s.* der Kasten, Behälter; das Futteral, Etui (*spectacles*); das Gehäuse (*watch*); die Kiste (*wooden box*); (*Typ.*) der Schriftkasten.

case (2) [keis], *s.* der Fall (*event*); (*Law*) der Rechtsfall, der Umstand (*circumstance*); *in* —, falls.

casement [ˈkeismənt], *s.* der Fensterflügel, das Fenster (*frame*).

caseous [ˈkeisjəs], *adj.* käsig.

cash [kæʃ], *s.* bares Geld; die Barzahlung; — *box*, die Kasse. — *v.a.* einlösen (*cheque*).

cashier [kæˈʃiə], *s.* der Kassierer. — *v.a.* (*Mil.*) entlassen.

cashmere [ˈkæʃmiə], *s.* die Kaschmirwolle (*wool*).

casing [ˈkeisiŋ], *s.* die Hülle; das Gehäuse (*case*); die Haut (*sausage skin*).

cask [ˈkɑːsk], *s.* das Faß.

casket [ˈkɑːskit], *s.* das Kästchen; (*Am.*) der Sarg.

Caspian (Sea) [ˈkæspiən (siː)]. das kaspische Meer.

cassock [ˈkæsək], *s.* die Soutane.

cast [kɑːst], *v.a. irr.* werfen (*throw*); (*Metall.*) gießen; (*Theat.*) besetzen; (*plaster*) formen; — *off*, abwerfen; — *anchor*, ankern; — *o.'s skin*, sich häuten; — *down*, niederschlagen; — *a vote*, die Stimme abgeben. — *s.* der Wurf; (*Metall.*) der Guß; (*Theat.*) die Besetzung der Abguß (plaster). — *adj.* — *iron*, das Gusseisen; — *steel*, der Gußstahl.

castanets [kæstəˈnets], *s. pl.* (*Mus.*) die Kastagnetten, *f. pl.*

castaway [ˈkɑːstəwei], *adj.* weggeworfen; (*Naut.*) schiffbrüchig.

caste [kɑːst], *s.* die Kaste.

caster [ˈkɑːstə], *s.* der Streuer, die Streubüchse; — *sugar*, Streuzucker.

casting [ˈkɑːstiŋ], *s.* (*Metall.*) das Gießen, der Guß.

castle [kɑːsl], *s.* die Burg, das Schloß; (*Chess*) der Turm.

castor (1) [ˈkɑːstə], *s.* (*Zool.*) der Biber.

castor (2) [ˈkɑːstə] *see* **caster**.

castor (3) **oil** [ˈkɑːstər ˈɔil], *s.* das Rizinusöl.

castrate [kæsˈtreit], *v.a.* kastrieren.

castration [kæsˈtreiʃən], *s.* die Kastration.

casual [ˈkæʒuəl], *adj.* zufällig; gelassen (*manner*); gelegentlich; flüchtig.

casualty [ˈkæʒuəlti], *s.* der Unglücksfall; — *ward*, die Unfallstation; (*pl.*) die Verluste, *m. pl.*

cat [kæt], *s.* die Katze; *tom* —, der Kater; — *burglar*, der Fassadenkletterer; —*'s eye*, das Katzenauge, der Rückstrahler; der Reflektor.

cataclysm [ˈkætəklizm], *s.* die Sintflut, die Überschwemmung.

catacomb [ˈkætəkuːm], *s.* die Katakombe.

catalogue [ˈkætələg], *s.* der Katalog, das Verzeichnis. — *v.a.* im Katalog verzeichnen, katalogisieren.

catapult [ˈkætəpult], *s.* die Schleuder (*hand*); (*Mil.*) die Wurfmaschine. — *v.a.* schleudern.

cataract [ˈkætərækt], *s.* der Wasserfall (*water*); (*Med.*) der Star.

catarrh [kəˈtɑː], *s.* (*Med.*) der Katarrh.

catastrophe [kəˈtæstrəfi], *s.* die Katastrophe, das Unglück.

catastrophic [kætəsˈtrɔfik], *adj.* katastrophal, unheilvoll.

catch [kætʃ], *v.a. irr.* fangen, auffangen, fassen; überfallen (— *unawares*, *ambush*); — *a cold*, sich einen Schnupfen zuziehen, sich erkälten; erreichen (*train, etc.*); — *redhanded*, bei frischer Tat ertappen. — *s.* der Fang (*fish*); die Beute (*prey, booty*); der Haken (*hook, also fig.*).

catchpenny [ˈkætʃpeni], *s.* der Flitterkram, Lockartikel. — *adj.* marktschreierisch.

catchphrase, catchword [ˈkætʃfreiz, ˈkætʃwɔːd], *s.* das (billige) Schlagwort.

catechism [ˈkætikizm], *s.* der Katechismus.

categorical [kætiˈgɔrikəl], *adj.* kategorisch, entschieden.

category [ˈkætigəri], *s.* die Kategorie, Klasse, Gruppe, Gattung.

cater [ˈkeitə], *v.n.* Lebensmittel einkaufen; verpflegen; (*fig.*) sorgen (*for, für*).

caterer [ˈkeitərə], *s.* der Lebensmittellieferant.

catering [ˈkeitəriŋ], *s.* die Verpflegung.

caterpillar [ˈkætəpilə], *s.* (*Ent.*) die Raupe; (*Mech.*) der Raupenschlepper.

caterwaul [ˈkætəwɔːl], *v.n.* miauen.

cathedral [kəˈθiːdrəl], *s.* der Dom, die Kathedrale.

Catholic [ˈkæθəlik], *adj.* katholisch. — *s.* der Katholik.

catholic [ˈkæθəlik], *adj.* allumfassend.

Catholicism [kəˈθɔlisizm], *s.* der Katholizismus.

catkin [ˈkætkin], *s.* (*Bot.*) das Kätzchen; *pussy-willow* —, das Palmkätzchen.

cattle [kætl], *s. pl.* das Vieh; — *plague*, die Rinderpest; — *show*, die Viehausstellung.

caucus [ˈkɔːkəs], *s.* die Wahlversammlung; der Wahlausschuß.

caul [kɔːl], *s.* das Haarnetz; (*Anat.*) die Eihaut.

cauldron [ˈkɔːldrən], *s.* der Kessel.

cauliflower [ˈkɔliflauə], *s.* (*Bot.*) der Blumenkohl.

caulk [kɔːk], *v.a.* kalfatern (*see under* **calk** (2)).

causal [ˈkɔːzəl], *adj.* ursächlich.

causality [kɔːˈzæliti], *s.* der ursächliche Zusammenhang; (*Log.*) die Kausalität.

cause [kɔːz], *s.* die Ursache. — *v.a.* verursachen.

causeway [ˈkɔːzwei], *s.* der Damm.

caustic [ˈkɔːstik], *adj.* ätzend; beißend.

cauterize [ˈkɔːtəraiz], v.a. (Med.) ätzen, ausbrennen.

caution [ˈkɔːʃən], s. die Vorsicht (care); die Warnung (warning). — v.a. (Law) ermahnen; warnen.

cautionary [ˈkɔːʃənəri], adj. warnend.

cautious [ˈkɔːʃəs], adj. vorsichtig, behutsam.

cautiousness [ˈkɔːʃəsnis], s. die Vorsicht, Behutsamkeit.

cavalcade [kævəlˈkeid], s. die Kavalkade; (Mil.) der Reiterzug.

cavalry [ˈkævəlri], s. die Kavallerie, die Reiterei.

cave [keiv], s. die Höhle. — v.a. aushöhlen. — v.n. — in, einstürzen, einfallen.

caveat [ˈkeiviæt], s. (Law) die Warnung; der Vorbehalt.

cavern [ˈkævən], s. die Höhle.

cavernous [ˈkævənəs], adj. (Geog., Geol.) voll Höhlen.

caviare [kæviˈaː], s. der Kaviar.

cavil [ˈkævil], v.n. nörgeln (at, über), tadeln (Acc.).

cavity [ˈkæviti], s. die Höhlung.

caw [kɔː], v.n. (Orn.) krächzen.

cease [siːs], v.a. einstellen. — v.n. aufhören.

ceaseless [ˈsiːslis], adj. unaufhörlich.

cedar [ˈsiːdə], s. (Bot.) die Zeder.

cede [siːd], v.a. überlassen. — v.n. nachgeben.

ceiling [ˈsiːliŋ], s. die Decke (room); (Comm.) die Preisgrenze.

celebrate [ˈselibreit], v.a. feiern; zelebrieren.

celebrated [ˈselibreitid], adj. berühmt.

celebration [seliˈbreiʃən], s. die Feier.

celebrity [siˈlebriti], s. die Berühmtheit; der „Star“.

celerity [siˈleriti], s. die Behendigkeit, Schnelligkeit.

celery [ˈseləri], s. (Bot.) der Sellerie.

celestial [siˈlestjəl], adj. himmlisch.

celibacy [ˈselibəsi], s. die Ehelosigkeit; (Eccl.) das Zölibat.

celibate [ˈselibit], adj. unverheiratet.

cell [sel], s. die Zelle.

cellar [ˈselə], s. der Keller; salt —, das Salzfaß.

cellarage [ˈseləridʒ], s. die Kellerei; die Einkellerung (storage).

cellarer [ˈselərə], s. der Kellermeister.

cellular [ˈseljulə], adj. zellartig, Zell-.

Celt [kelt, selt], s. der Kelte.

Celtic [ˈkeltik, ˈseltik], adj. keltisch.

cement [siˈment], s. der Zement, Mörtel. — v.a. auszementieren, verkitten.

cemetery [ˈsemətri], s. der Kirchhof, der Friedhof.

cenotaph [ˈsenotæf or -taːf], s. das Ehrengrabmal, Ehrendenkmal.

censer [ˈsensə], s. (Eccl.) das Weihrauchfaß.

censor [ˈsensə], s. der Zensor.

censorious [senˈsɔːriəs], adj. kritisch, tadelsüchtig.

censure [ˈsenʃə], s. der Tadel, Verweis. — v.a. tadeln.

census [ˈsensəs], s. die Volkszählung.

cent [sent], s. (Am.) der Cent (coin); (Comm.) per —, das Prozent.

centenarian [sentiˈnɛəriən], adj. hundertjährig. — s. der Hundertjährige.

centenary [senˈtiːnəri], s. die Hundertjahrfeier.

centennial [senˈtenjəl], adj. alle hundert Jahre, hundertjährig.

centipede [ˈsentipiːd], s. (Zool.) der Tausendfüßler.

central [ˈsentrəl], adj. zentral.

centralize [ˈsentrəlaiz], v.a. zentralisieren.

centre [ˈsentə], s. das Zentrum, der Mittelpunkt; die Mitte.

centric(al) [ˈsentrik(əl)], adj. (Engin., Maths.) zentral.

centrifugal [senˈtrifjugəl], adj. zentrifugal.

centrifuge [senˈtrifjuːdʒ], s. die Zentrifuge.

centripetal [senˈtripitl], adj. zentripetal, zum Mittelpunkt hinstrebend.

century [ˈsentʃuri], s. das Jahrhundert.

cereal [ˈsiəriəl], adj. vom Getreide, Getreide—. — s. die Kornmehlspeise.

cerebral [ˈseribrəl], adj. Gehirn-.

ceremonial [seriˈmounjəl], adj. feierlich, förmlich (formal). — s. das Zeremoniell.

ceremonious [seriˈmounjəs], adj. feierlich, zeremoniell.

ceremony [ˈserimeni], s. die Zeremonie, die Feier.

certain [ˈsəːtin], adj. sicher, gewiß.

certainty [ˈsəːtinti], s. die Gewißheit.

certificate [səːˈtifikit], s. das Zeugnis, die Bescheinigung.

certification [səːtifiˈkeiʃən], s. die Bescheinigung, Bezeugung.

certify [ˈsəːtifai], v.a. bescheinigen, bezeugen, beglaubigen.

certitude [ˈsəːtitjuːd], s. die Gewißheit.

cerulean [siˈruːljən], adj. himmelblau.

cesspool [ˈsespuːl], s. die Senkgrube.

cessation [seˈseiʃən], s. das Aufhören; (of hostilities) der Waffenstillstand.

cession [ˈseʃən], s. die Abtretung, der Verzicht (of, auf).

chafe [tʃeif], v.a. wärmen, warmreiben; erzürnen (annoy); wundreiben (skin). — v.n. toben, wüten.

chafer [ˈtʃeifə], s. (Ent.) der Käfer.

chaff [tʃaːf], s. die Spreu; die Neckerei (teasing). — v.a. necken.

chaffer [ˈtʃæfə], v.n. handeln, schachern (haggle).

chaffinch [ˈtʃæfintʃ], s. (Orn.) der Buchfink.

chagrin [ʃæˈgriːn], s. der Verdruß, der Ärger.

chain [tʃein], s. die Kette. — v.a. anketten.

chair [tʃɛə], s. der Stuhl; (Univ.) Lehrstuhl. — v.a. vorsitzen (Dat.).

chairman [ˈtʃɛəmən], s. der Vorsitzende.

chalice [ˈtʃælis], s. (Eccl.) der Kelch.

chalk [tʃɔːk], s. die Kreide. — v.a. — up, ankreiden, anschreiben.

chalky [ˈtʃɔːki], adj. (Geol.) kreidig, kreideartig.

challenge [ˈtʃælindʒ], v.a. herausfordern; in Frage stellen (question); anhalten (of a sentry). — s. die Herausforderung; das Anhalten (by a sentry); die Einwendung.

chalybeate [kəˈlibiət], adj. (Med.) eisenhaltig.

chamber [ˈtʃeimbə], s. das Zimmer, die Kammer.

chamberlain [ˈtʃeimbəlin], s. der Kammerherr.

chambermaid [ˈtʃeimbəmeid], s. das Zimmermädchen, Kammermädchen.

chameleon [kəˈmiːljən], s. (Zool.) das Chamäleon.

chamois [ˈʃæmwaː], s. (Zool.) die Gemse.

champagne [ʃæmˈpein], s. der Champagner, der Sekt.

champion [ˈtʃæmpjən], s. der Meister, Verteidiger. — v.a. vertreten (cause); beschützen (person).

chance [tʃaːns], s. der Zufall; die Gelegenheit (opportunity); die Möglichkeit (possibility); take a —, es darauf ankommen lassen; by —, zufällig. — v.a. zufällig tun, geraten; riskieren (risk).

chancel [ˈtʃaːnsəl], s. (Eccl.) der Chor, der Altarplatz.

chancellor [ˈtʃaːnsələ], s. der Kanzler.

chancery [ˈtʃaːnsəri], s. das Kanzleigericht.

chandelier [ʃændəˈliə], s. der Armleuchter, Kronleuchter.

chandler [ˈtʃaːndlə], s. der Lichtzieher; Krämer; (corn merchant) der Kornhändler.

change [tʃeindʒ], s. die Änderung; das Umsteigen (trains); small —, das Kleingeld; die Veränderung; Abwechslung. — v.a. ändern (alter); wechseln (money); umsteigen (trains); eintauschen, umtauschen (exchange); sich umziehen (clothes). — v.n. sich (ver)ändern, anders werden, umschlagen; (Railw.) — for, umsteigen nach.

changeable [ˈtʃeindʒəbl], adj. veränderlich.

changeling [ˈtʃeindʒliŋ], s. der Wechselbalg.

changeover [ˈtʃeindʒouvə], s. der Wechsel; der Umschalter; die Umstellung.

channel [ˈtʃænəl], s. der Kanal. — v.a. leiten, kanalisieren.

chant [tʃaːnt], v.a., v.n. (Eccl.) singen. — s. (Mus.) der Kantus, der liturgische Gesang.

chaos [ˈkeiɔs], s. das Chaos.

chaotic [keiˈɔtik], adj. chaotisch.

chap (1) [tʃæp], s. der Riss (skin etc.). — v.n. Risse bekommen.

chap (2) [tʃæp], s. (usually in pl.) der Kinnbacken.

chap (3) [tʃæp], s. (coll.) der Kerl, der Bursche.

chapel [ˈtʃæpəl], s. (Eccl.) die Kapelle.

chaperon [ˈʃæpəroun], s. die Anstandsdame. — v.a. begleiten, bemuttern.

chaplain [ˈtʃæplin], s. der Kaplan.

chapter [ˈtʃæptə], s. das Kapitel.

char [tʃaː], v.a. verkohlen. — v.n. (coll.) putzen, Hausarbeit verrichten (do housework). — s. (coll.) die Haushilfe, die Hausgehilfin, Putzfrau.

character [ˈkærəktə], s. der Charakter (personality); das Zeichen (sign, symbol); (Maths.) die Ziffer; das Zeugnis (testimonial).

characteristic [kærəktəˈristik], adj. charakteristisch, typisch.

characterize [ˈkærəktəraiz], v.a. charakterisieren, kennzeichnen.

charade [ʃəˈraːd], s. die Scharade, das Silbenrätsel.

charcoal [ˈtʃaːkoul], s. die Holzkohle; — burner, der Köhler.

charge [tʃaːdʒ], v.a. laden, aufladen; (Law) beschuldigen; (Mil.) angreifen; belasten (with a bill); — up to s.o., jemandem etwas anrechnen; verlangen (price). — s. die Ladung, der Auftrag (order); die Aufsicht; to be in —, die Aufsicht haben; (Law) die Beschuldigung, Anklage; das Mündel (of a guardian); (pl.) die Kosten, Spesen.

chargeable [ˈtʃaːdʒəbl], adj. anzurechnend; steuerbar (of objects).

charger [ˈtʃaːdʒə], s. das Schlachtroß.

chariness [ˈtʃɛərinis], s. die Behutsamkeit.

chariot [ˈtʃæriət], s. der Kriegswagen.

charioteer [tʃæriəˈtiə], s. der Wagenlenker.

charitable [ˈtʃæritəbl], adj. wohltätig, mild, mildtätig.

charitableness [ˈtʃæritəblnis], s. die Wohltätigkeit, Milde.

charity [ˈtʃæriti], s. die Güte; Nächstenliebe; Mildtätigkeit (alms); die Barmherzigkeit (charitableness); der wohltätige Zweck (cause); sister of —, barmherzige Schwester.

charlatan [ˈʃaːlətən], s. der Scharlatan, Pfuscher.

charm [tʃaːm], s. der Zauber (magic); der Reiz. — v.a. bezaubern.

chart [tʃaːt], s. (Geog.) die Karte. — v.a. auf der Karte einzeichnen.

charter [ˈtʃaːtə], s. die Urkunde; (Naut.) die Schiffsmiete. — v.a. mieten, chartern, heuern (ship, plane); ein Privileg geben, bevorrechtigen.

charwoman [ˈtʃaːwumən], s. die Putzfrau, Reinemacherin.

chary [ˈtʃɛəri], adj. behutsam; vorsichtig (cautious); sparsam (thrifty).

chase [tʃeis], v.a. jagen, verfolgen. — s. die Jagd (hunt); das Gehege (game preserve).

chaser [ˈtʃeisə], s. der Verfolger (pursuer); die Schiffskanone (gun).

chasm [kæzm], s. die Kluft; der Abgrund.

chassis [ˈʃæsi], s. (Motor.) das Fahrgestell.

chaste [tʃeist], *adj.* keusch, züchtig.
chasten [tʃeisn], *v.a.* züchtigen; reinigen.
chastize [tʃæs'taiz], *v.a.* züchtigen.
chastity [tʃæstiti], *s.* die Keuschheit, Züchtigkeit.
chasuble [tʃæzjubl], *s.* (*Eccl.*) das Meßgewand.
chat [tʃæt], *v.n.* plaudern. — *s.* das Geplauder.
chattel [tʃætl], *s.* (*usually in pl.*) die Habe; *goods and* —*s*, Hab und Gut.
chatter [tʃætə], *v.n.* schwätzen; schnattern. — *s.* das Geschwätz (*talk*).
chatterbox [tʃætəbɔks], *s.* die Plaudertasche.
chatty [tʃæti], *adj.* geschwätzig.
chauffeur [ʃoufə, ʃou'fə:], *s.* (*Motor.*) der Fahrer.
chauffeuse [ʃou'fə:z], *s.* die Fahrerin.
chauvinism [ʃouvinizm], *s.* der Chauvinismus.
cheap [tʃi:p], *adj.* billig.
cheapen [tʃi:pən], *v.a.* herabsetzen, erniedrigen (*value*).
cheapness [tʃi:pnis], *s.* die Billigkeit (*price*).
cheat [tʃi:t], *v.a.*, *v.n.* betrügen. — *s.* der Betrüger.
cheating [tʃi:tiŋ], *s.* das Betrügen; der Betrug.
check [tʃek], *s.* der Einhalt, der Halt; die Kontrolle; das Hindernis (*obstacle*); (*Chess*) Schach; (*Am.*) *see* **cheque.** — *v.a.* zurückhalten, aufhalten (*stop*); überprüfen. — *v.n.* Schach bieten (*Dat.*).
checker *see under* **chequer.**
checkmate [tʃekmeit], *s.* das Schachmatt.
cheek [tʃi:k], *s.* die Wange, die Backe; die Unverschämtheit (*impertinence*). — *v.a.* unverschämt sein *or* handeln (*s.o.*, an jemandem).
cheeky [tʃi:ki], *adj.* frech, unverschämt.
cheer [tʃiə], *v.a.* anfeuern, anspornen; zujubeln; — *up*, aufmuntern. — *v.n.* — *up*, Mut fassen. — *s.* der Zuruf; der Beifallsruf (*acclaim*); *three* —*s*, ein dreifaches Hoch (*for*, auf).
cheerful [tʃiəful], *adj.* fröhlich, froh.
cheerless [tʃiəlis], *adj.* unfreundlich, freudlos.
cheese [tʃi:z], *s.* der Käse; — *straw*, die Käsestange.
cheesecloth [tʃi:zklɔθ], *s.* (*Am.*) das Nesseltuch.
cheeseparing [tʃi:zpɛəriŋ], *adj.* knauserig.
cheesy [tʃi:zi], *adj.* käsig; (*sl.*) schlecht aussehend.
cheetah [tʃi:tə], *s.* (*Zool.*) der Jagdleopard.
chemical [kemikəl], *adj.* chemisch. — *s.* die Chemikalie, das chemische Element; das chemische Produkt.
chemise [ʃi'mi:z], *s.* das Frauenhemd.
chemist [kemist], *s.* der Chemiker; Drogist; Apotheker (*dispenser*).

chemistry [kemistri], *s.* die Chemie.
cheque, (*Am.*) **check** [tʃek], *s.* (*Fin.*) der Scheck.
chequer, **checker** [tʃekə], *s.* das scheckige Muster, Würfelmuster. — *v.a.* würfelig machen, bunt machen.
cherish [tʃeriʃ], *v.a.* hegen, wertschätzen, lieben.
cherry [tʃeri], *s.* (*Bot.*) die Kirsche; — *brandy*, das Kirschwasser.
chess [tʃes], *s.* das Schachspiel; —*man*, die Schachfigur; —*board*, das Schachbrett.
chest [tʃest], *s.* die Truhe (*box*); die Kiste; (*Anat.*) Brust; — *of drawers*, die Kommode.
chestnut [tʃestnʌt], *s.* (*Bot.*) die Kastanie; (*horse*) der Braune. — *adj.* kastanienbraun.
chew [tʃu:], *v.a.* kauen; —*ing gum*, der Kaugummi.
chic [ʃi:k], *adj.* elegant, schick.
chicanery [ʃi'keinəri], *s.* die Schikane, Haarspalterei, Kleinlichkeit.
chicken [tʃikin], *s.* das Huhn, Kücken; — *soup*, die Hühnersuppe.
chickenpox [tʃikinpɔks], *s.* (*Med.*) die Windpocken.
chicory [tʃikəri], *s.* (*Bot.*) die Zichorie.
chide [tʃaid], *v.a. irr.* schelten.
chief [tʃi:f], *s.* der Häuptling (*of tribe*); (*Am. coll.*) der Chef (*boss*). — *adj.* hauptsächlich, Haupt-, oberst.
chieftain [tʃi:ftin], *s.* der Häuptling (*of tribe*); Anführer (*leader*).
chilblain [tʃilblein], *s.* die Frostbeule.
child [tʃaild], *s.* das Kind.
childbirth [tʃaildbə:θ], *s.* die Niederkunft.
childhood [tʃaildhud], *s.* die Kindheit.
childish [tʃaildiʃ], *adj.* kindisch.
childlike [tʃaildlaik], *adj.* kindlich, wie ein Kind.
Chilean [tʃiliən], *adj.* chilenisch. — *s.* der Chilene.
chill [tʃil], *s.* die Kälte, der Frost; die Erkältung. — *v.a.* kalt machen (*freeze*); erstarren lassen (*make rigid*); entmutigen (*discourage*).
chilly [tʃili], *adj.* frostig, eisig, eiskalt.
chime [tʃaim], *s.* das Glockengeläute. — *v.n.* klingen, läuten.
chimera [ki'miərə], *s.* das Hirngespinst, das Trugbild. —
chimney [tʃimni], *s.* der Kamin, der Schornstein; —*pot*, —*stack*, der Schornstein; —*sweep*, der Kaminfeger, Schornsteinfeger.
chimpanzee [tʃimpæn'zi:], *s.* (*Zool.*) der Schimpanse.
chin [tʃin], *s.* (*Anat.*) das Kinn.
china [tʃainə], *s.* das Porzellan; —*ware*, das Küchengeschirr.
chine (1) [tʃain], *s.* das Rückgrat.
chine (2) [tʃain], *s.* (*Geog.*) der Kamm.
Chinaman [tʃainəmən], *s.* (*obs.*) der Chinese.
Chinese [tʃai'ni:z], *adj.* chinesisch. — *s.* der Chinese.
chink [tʃink], *s.* die Ritze, der Spalt.

chip [tʃip], *v.a.* schnitzeln (*wood*); ausbrechen (*stone*); in kleine Stücke schneiden. — *v.n.* — *off*, abbröckeln; — *in*, (*coll.*) sich hineinmischen. —*s.* der Span (*wood*); der Splitter (*glass*, *stone*); (*pl.*) Pommes frites (*pl.*) (*potatoes*).

chiromancy [ˈkaiərɔmænsi], *s.* das Handlesen.

chiropodist [kiˈrɔpədist], *s.* der Fußpfleger.

chirp [tʃəːp], *v.n.* zwitschern (*birds*), zirpen (*crickets*).

chirping [ˈtʃəːpiŋ], *s.* das Gezwitscher (*birds*), das Gezirpe (*crickets*).

chisel—[tʃizl], *s.* der Meißel. — *v.a.* meißeln.

chit [tʃit], *s.* das Stück Papier; (*coll.*) junges Ding; —*chat*, das Geplauder.

chivalrous [ˈʃivəlrəs], *adj.* ritterlich; tapfer (*brave*).

chivalry [ˈʃivəlri], *s.* die Ritterlichkeit (*courtesy*); Tapferkeit (*bravery*).

chive [tʃaiv], *s.* (*Bot.*) der Schnittlauch.

chlorate [ˈklɔːreit], *s.* (*Chem.*) das Chlorsalz.

chlorine [ˈklɔːriːn], *s.* (*Chem.*) das Chlor, Chlorgas.

chloroform [ˈklɔrəfɔːm], *s.* das Chloroform. — *v.a.* chloroformieren.

chocolate [ˈtʃɔkəlit], *s.* die Schokolade. — *adj.* schokoladefarben.

choice [tʃɔis], *s.* die Wahl; Auswahl (*selection*). — *adj.* auserlesen.

choir [ˈkwaiə], *s.* der Chor.

choke [tʃouk], *v.a.*, *v.n.* ersticken; verstopfen (*block*). — *s.* (*Elec.*) die Drosselspule; (*Motor.*) die Starterklappe.

choler [ˈkɔlə], *s.* die Galle; (*fig.*) der Zorn (*anger*).

cholera [ˈkɔlərə], *s.* (*Med.*) die Cholera.

choleric [ˈkɔlərik], *adj.* jähzornig, cholerisch.

choose [tʃuːz], *v.a.* *irr.* wählen, auswählen (*select*).

choosy [tʃuːzi], *adj.* wählerisch.

chop [tʃɔp], *v.a.* abhacken (*cut off*), hacken (*meat*). — *s.* das Kotelett (*meat*).

chopper [ˈtʃɔpə], *s.* das Hackbeil (*axe*); das Hackmesser (*knife*).

choppy [ˈtʃɔpi], *adj.* bewegt (*sea*), stürmisch.

chopstick [ˈtʃɔpstik], *s.* das Eßstäbchen.

choral [ˈkɔːrəl], *adj.* Chor-; — *society*, der Gesangverein.

chorale [kɔˈrɑːl], *s.* (*Eccl.*, *Mus.*) der Choral.

chord [kɔːd], *s.* die Saite; (*Geom.*) die Sehne; (*Mus.*) der Akkord.

chorister [ˈkɔristə], *s.* der Chorknabe (*boy*), Chorsänger.

chorus [ˈkɔːrəs], *s.* der Chor (*opera*); der Refrain (*song*).

Christ [kraist]. Christus, *m.*

christen [krisn], *v.a.* taufen (*baptize*); nennen (*name*).

Christendom [ˈkrisndəm], *s.* die Christenheit.

christening [ˈkrisniŋ], *s.* die Taufe.

Christian [ˈkristjən], *s.* der Christ (*believer in Christ*). — *adj.* christlich; — *name*, der Vorname.

Christianity [kristiˈæniti], *s.* die christliche Religion, das Christentum.

Christmas [ˈkrisməs], *s.* (die) Weihnachten; das Weihnachtsfest; — *Eve*, der heilige Abend.

chromatic [kroˈmætik], *adj.* (*Mus.*) chromatisch.

chrome [kroum], *s.* das Chrom.

chronic [ˈkrɔnik], *adj.* chronisch.

chronicle [ˈkrɔnikl], *s.* die Chronik. — *v.a.* (in einer Chronik) verzeichnen.

chronological [krɔnəˈlɔdʒikəl], *adj.* chronologisch.

chronology [krɔˈnɔlədʒi], *s.* die Chronologie.

chronometer [krɔˈnɔmitə], *s.* das Chronometer.

chrysalis [ˈkrisəlis], *s.* (*Ent.*) die Puppe.

chrysanthemum [kriˈzænθəməm], *s.* (*Bot.*) die Chrysantheme.

chub [tʃʌb], *s.* (*Zool.*) der Döbel.

chubby [ˈtʃʌbi], *adj.* pausbäckig, plump.

chuck [tʃʌk], *v.a.* (*coll.*) — *out*, hinauswerfen. — *v.n.* glucken (*chicken*).

chuckle [tʃʌkl], *v.n.* kichern. — *s.* das Kichern.

chum [tʃʌm], *s.* (*coll.*) der Freund, Kamerad. — *v.n.* (*coll.*) — *up*, sich befreunden (*with*, mit).

chump [tʃʌmp], *s.* der Klotz (*wood*).

chunk [tʃʌŋk], *s.* das große Stück (*meat etc.*).

church [tʃəːtʃ], *s.* die Kirche.

churchwarden [tʃəːˈtʃwɔːdn], *s.* der Kirchenvorsteher.

churchyard [ˈtʃəːtʃjɑːd], *s.* der Friedhof.

churl [tʃəːl], *s.* der Grobian, der grobe Kerl.

churlish [ˈtʃəːliʃ], *adj.* grob, unfein.

churn [tʃəːn], *s.* das Butterfaß. — *v.a.* mischen, schütteln (*butter etc.*); — *up*, aufwühlen (*stir up*).

chute [ʃuːt], *s.* die Gleitbahn.

cider [ˈsaidə], *s.* der Apfelmost.

cigar [siˈgɑː], *s.* die Zigarre; — *case*, das Zigarrenetui.

cigarette [sigəˈret], *s.* die Zigarette; — *holder*, die Zigarettenspitze; — *lighter*, das Feuerzeug.

cinder [ˈsində], *s.* (*usually in pl.*) die Asche (*fire*); die Schlacke (*furnace*).

Cinderella [sindəˈrelə], *s.* das Aschenbrödel, Aschenputtel.

cinema [ˈsinimə], *s.* das Kino.

cinematography [siniməˈtɔɡrəfi], *s.* die Filmkunst.

Cingalese *see* **Singhalese**.

cinnamon [ˈsinəmən], *s.* der Zimt.

cipher [ˈsaifə], *s.* die Ziffer; die Geheimschrift (*code*). — *v.n.* rechnen. — *v.a.* chiffrieren (*code*).

Circassian [səːˈkæsiən], *adj.* tscherkessisch. — *s.* der Tscherkesse.

circle [sə:kl], s. der Zirkel, Kreis; (*social*) Gesellschaftskreis; (*Theat.*) der Rang. — *v.a.* umringen. — *v.n.* umkreisen; sich drehen (*revolve*).

circuit ['sə:kit], s. der Kreislauf; (*Elec.*) der Stromkreis.

circuitous [sə:'kju:itəs], *adj.* weitschweifig, weitläufig.

circular ['sə:kjulə], *adj.* rund, kreisförmig, Rund-; — *tour*, die Rundreise. — ' s. das Rundschreiben (*letter*); der Werbebrief (*advertising*).

circulate ['sə:kjuleit], *v.a.* in Umlauf setzen. — *v.n.* umlaufen, kreisen, zirkulieren.

circulation [sə:kju'leiʃən], s. die Zirkulation, der Kreislauf (*blood*); die Verbreitung, Auflage (*newspaper*); der Umlauf (*banknotes*).

circumcise ['sə:kəmsaiz], *v.a.* beschneiden.

circumference [sə:'kʌmfərəns], s. der Umfang.

circumscribe ['sə:kəmskraib], *v.a.* beschränken, einengen (*narrow down*); umschreiben (*paraphrase*).

circumspect ['sə:kəmspekt], *adj.* umsichtig, vorsorglich.

circumspection [sə:kəm'spekʃən], s. die Umsicht, Vorsicht.

circumstance ['sə:kəmstæns, -sta:ns], s. der Umstand; *pomp and* —, großer Aufmarsch.

circumstantial [sə:kəm'stænʃəl], *adj.* umständlich; zu einem Umstand gehörig; eingehend; — *evidence*, der Indizienbeweis.

circumvent [sə:kəm'vent], *v.a.* überlisten, hintergehen.

circus ['sə:kəs], s. der Zirkus; der Platz.

cirrhus ['sirəs], s. die Federwolke.

Cistercian [sis'tə:ʃən], s. der Zisterzienser (*monk*).

cistern ['sistən], s. die Zisterne, der Wasserbehälter.

citadel ['sitədəl], s. die Zitadelle, die Burg.

citation [sai'teiʃən], s. das Zitat (*Law*) die Zitierung, Vorladung; (*Mil.*) die rühmliche Erwähnung.

cite (sait), *v.a.* zitieren (*quote*); (*Law*) vorladen.

citizen ['sitizən], s. der Bürger, Staatsbürger (*national*); *fellow* —, der Mitbürger.

citizenship ['sitizənʃip], s. das Bürgerrecht, die Staatsangehörigkeit.

citrate ['sitreit], s. (*Chem.*) das Zitrat.

citric ['sitrik], *adj.* (*Chem.*) Zitronen-.

citron ['sitrən], s. die Zitrone. — *adj.* zitronenfarben.

city ['siti], s. die Stadt; die Großstadt; die City. — *adj.* städtisch.

civic ['sivik], *adj.* Stadt-, städtisch (*ceremonial*); bürgerlich.

civil ['sivil], *adj.* zivil; höflich (*polite*); — *engineer*, der Zivilingenieur; — *service*, der Beamtendienst, die Beamtenlaufbahn, der Staatsdienst; — *war*, der Bürgerkrieg.

civilian [si'viljən], s. der Zivilist.

civility [si'viliti], s. die Höflichkeit.

civilization [sivilai'zeiʃən], s. die Zivilisation.

civilize ['sivilaiz], *v.a.* zivilisieren, verfeinern (*refine*).

clack [klæk], *v.n.* klappern (*wood etc.*); plaudern, tratschen.

clad [klæd], *adj.* gekleidet.

claim [kleim], *v.a.* Anspruch erheben (*to, auf*); fordern (*demand*); behaupten (*assert*). — *s.* der Anspruch; die Forderung (*demand*); das Recht.

claimant ['kleimənt], s. der Beanspruchende, Anspruchserheber.

clairvoyance [klɛə'vɔiəns], s. das Hellsehen.

clairvoyant [klɛə'vɔiənt], s. der Hellseher.

clam [klæm], s. (*Zool.*) die Venusmuschel; *shut up like a* —, verschwiegen sein.

clamber ['klæmbə], *v.n.* klettern.

clamminess ['klæminis], s. die Feuchtigkeit, Klebrigkeit.

clammy ['klæmi], *adj.* feucht, klebrig.

clamorous ['klæmərəs], *adj.* lärmend, laut, ungestüm.

clamour ['klæmə], s. das Geschrei, der Lärm. — *v.n.* laut schreien (*for*, nach, *Dat.*)

clamp [klæmp], s. die Klammer, die Klampe. — *v.a.* festklammern.

clan [klæn], s. die Sippe, die Familie.

clandestine [klæn'destin], *adj.* heimlich, verstohlen.

clang [klæŋ], s. der Schall, das Geklirr. — *v.n.* erschallen. — *v.a.* erschallen lassen.

clangour ['klæŋə], s. das Getöse, der Lärm.

clank [klæŋk], s. das Geklirre, das Gerassel (*metal*).

clannish ['klæniʃ], *adj.* stammesbewußt; engherzig (*narrow*).

clap [klæp], *v.a.* schlagen, zusammenschlagen (*hands*). — *v.n.* Beifall klatschen (*Dat.*).

clapperboard ['klæpəbɔ:d], s. (*Film*) das Klappbrett, die Klapptafel; der Klöppel (*beater, in lacemaking*).

claptrap ['klæptræp], s. der billige Effekt, das eitle Geschwätz (*gossip*).

claret ['klærit], s. der Rotwein.

clarification [klærifi'keiʃən], s. die Klarstellung, Aufklärung.

clarify ['klærifai], *v.a.* klarstellen.

clari(o)net [klæri(ə)'net], s. (*Mus.*) die Klarinette.

clarion ['klæriən], s. (*Mus.*) die Zinke, Trompete; — *call*, der laute Ruf.

clash [klæʃ], *v.a.* zusammenschlagen. — *v.n.* aufeinanderprallen, zusammenfallen (*dates*); widerstreiten (*views*). — *s.* (*fig.*) der Zusammenstoß, der Widerstreit.

clasp [kla:sp], *v.a.* ergreifen, festhalten. — *s.* der Haken (*hook*); die Schnalle, die Spange (*buckle, brooch*); — *knife*, das Taschenmesser.

class [klɑ:s], *s.* die Klasse.
classic(al) [ˈklæsik(əl)], *adj.* klassisch.
classics [ˈklæsiks], *s. pl.* die Klassiker, *m. pl.*; die klassische Philologie (*subject of study*).
classification [klæsifiˈkeiʃən], *s.* die Klassifizierung.
classify [ˈklæsifai], *v.a.* klassifizieren.
clatter [ˈklætə], *s.* das Getöse, Geklirr. — *v.a., v.n.* klappern, klirren.
Claus [klɔːz]. Claus, Nicholas, *m.*; Santa —, der heilige Nikolaus, Knecht Ruprecht, Weihnachtsmann.
clause [klɔːz], *s.* (*Gram.*) der Nebensatz; die Klausel (*contract*); (*Law*) der Vertragspunkt.
claw [klɔː], *s.* die Klaue, die Kralle. — *v.a.* kratzen.
clay [klei], *s.* der Ton, Lehm.
clayey [ˈkleii], *adj.* lehmig, tonig.
clean [kliːn], *adj.* rein, reinlich (*habits*); sauber; — *shaven*, glattrasiert. — *v.a.* reinigen, putzen.
cleaner [ˈkliːnə], *s.* die Reinemacherin, die Putzfrau.
cleanliness [ˈklenlinis], *s.* die Reinlichkeit, Sauberkeit.
cleanse [klenz], *v.a.* reinigen.
clear [kliə], *adj.* klar, hell; deutlich (*meaning*); schuldlos (*not guilty*). — *s. in the —,* nicht betroffen, schuldlos. — *v.a.* (*Chem.*) klären; (*Law*) für unschuldig erklären; verzollen (*pass through customs*); springen (über, *Acc.*). — *v.n.* (— *up*), sich aufklären, aufhellen (*weather*).
clearance [ˈkliərəns], *s.* die Räumung; — *sale,* der Ausverkauf; die Verzollung (*customs*).
clearing [ˈkliəriŋ], *s.* die Lichtung (*in wood*); (*Comm.*) die Verrechnung.
clearness [ˈkliənis], *s.* die Deutlichkeit, die Klarheit, Helle.
cleave [kliːv], *v.a. irr.* spalten (*wood*). — *v.n.* sich spalten.
cleaver [ˈkliːvə], *s.* das Hackmesser.
cleek [kliːk], *s.* der Golfschläger.
clef [klef], *s.* (*Mus.*) der Schlüssel.
cleft [kleft], *s.* der Spalt. — *adj.* — *palate,* die Gaumenspalte.
clemency [ˈklemənsi], *s.* die Milde, Gnade (*mercy*).
clement [ˈklemənt], *adj.* mild (*climate*); gnädig (*merciful*).
clench [klentʃ], *v.a.* zusammenpressen; ballen (*fist*).
clergy [ˈkləːdʒi], *s.* (*Eccl.*) die Geistlichkeit.
clergyman [ˈkləːdʒimən], *s.* (*Eccl.*) der Geistliche.
clerical [ˈklerikl], *adj.* (*Eccl.*) geistlich; beamtlich, Beamten-, Büro- (*office*); — *work,* die Büroarbeit.
clerk [klɑːk], *s.* der Schreiber, der Bürogehilfe (*junior*), der Büroangestellte (*senior*); *bank —,* der Bankbeamte.
clever [ˈklevə], *adj.* klug; intelligent; geschickt (*deft*); gewandt; listig (*cunning*).

cleverness [ˈklevənis], *s.* die Klugheit (*intelligence*); die Schlauheit (*cunning*); die Begabung (*talent*); die Geschicklichkeit (*skill*).
clew [kluː] *see* **clue.**
click [klik], *v.a., v.n.* einschnappen (*lock*); zusammenschlagen (*o.'s heels,* die Hacken); schnalzen (*o.'s tongue*); (*sl.*) zusammenpassen (*of two people*). — *s.* das Einschnappen (*lock*); das Zusammenschlagen (*heels*); das Schnalzen (*tongue*).
client [ˈklaiənt], *s.* (*Law*) der Klient; (*Comm.*) der Kunde.
clientele [kliːənˈtel], *s.* die Klientel, die Kundschaft.
cliff [klif], *s.* die Klippe.
climate [ˈklaimit], *s.* das Klima.
climatic [klaiˈmætik], *adj.* klimatisch.
climax [ˈklaimæks], *s.* der Höhepunkt.
climb [klaim], *v.a.* erklettern, erklimmen. — *v.n.* klettern, bergsteigen; (*Aviat.*) steigen. — *s.* der Aufstieg, die Ersteigung.
climber [ˈklaimə], *s.* der Bergsteiger (*mountaineer*); (*Bot.*) die Schlingpflanze.
clinch [klintʃ], *v.a.* vernieten, befestigen; — *a deal,* einen Handel abschließen. — *s.* der feste Griff; die Umklammerung (*boxing*).
cling [kliŋ], *v.n. irr.* sich anklammern, festhalten (*to,* an).
clinic [ˈklinik], *s.* die Klinik.
clinical [ˈklinikl], *adj.* klinisch.
clink [kliŋk], *s.* das Geklirre; (*coll.*) das Gefängnis. — *v.a.* — *glasses,* mit den Gläsern anstoßen.
clinker [ˈkliŋkə], *s.* der Backstein; die Schlacke.
clip (1) [klip], *v.a.* stutzen, beschneiden; lochen (*ticket*).
clip (2) [klip], *v.a.* befestigen. — *s. paper* —, die Büroklammer.
clippings [ˈklipiŋz], *s. pl.* die Abschnitte; die Schnitzel (*waste*); Zeitungsausschnitte, *m. pl.*
cloak [klouk], *s.* der Mantel, der Deckmantel (*cover*). — *v.a.* verbergen.
cloakroom [ˈkloukruːm], *s.* die Garderobe; — *free,* keine Garderobegebühr; (*Railw.*) die Gepäckaufbewahrung.
clock [klɔk], *s.* die (große) Uhr, Wanduhr; — *face,* das Zifferblatt. — *v.n.* — *in,* die Zeitkarte (Kontrollkarte) stempeln lassen, eintreffen (*arrive*).
clockwise [ˈklɔkwaiz], *adv.* im Uhrzeigersinne.
clod [klɔd], *s.* die Erdscholle, der Erdklumpen; (*sl.*) der Lümmel (*lout*).
clog [klɔg], *v.a.* belasten, hemmen, verstopfen. — *v.n.* sich verstopfen. — *s.* der Holzschuh.
cloisters [ˈklɔistəz], *s. pl.* (*Eccl., Archit.*) der Kreuzgang.

close

close [klouz], *v.a.* schließen, verschließen; beenden (*meeting etc.*). — *v.n.* — *in on*, über einen hereinbrechen, umzingeln. — *s.* das Ende, der Schluß; [klous] der Domplatz. — [klous], *adj.* nahe (*near*); knapp (*narrow*); nahestehend, vertraut (*friend*); schwül (*weather*); geizig (*miserly*).

closeness ['klousnis], *s.* die Nähe (*nearness*); die Schwüle (*weather*); die Vertrautheit (*familiarity*).

closet ['klɔzit], *s.* der Wandschrank (*cupboard*); das kleine Zimmer; das Klosett (*W.C.*). — *v.r.* — *o.s. with*, sich mit jemandem zurückziehen, sich vertraulich beraten.

closure ['klouʒə], *s.* der Schluß; der Abschluß (einer Debatte).

clot [klɔt], *s.* das Klümpchen. — *v.n.* sich verdicken, gerinnen; —*ted cream*, dicke Sahne.

cloth [klɔθ], *s.* das Tuch; der Stoff; die Leinwand (*bookbinding*); *American* —, das Wachstuch; — *printing*, der Zeugdruck.

clothe [klouð], *v.a.* kleiden. — *v.r.* sich kleiden.

clothes [klouðz], *s. pl.* die Kleider, *n. pl.*; die Kleidung; die Wäsche (*washing*); — *basket*, der Wäschekorb; — *press*, der Kleiderschrank.

clothier ['klouðiə], *s.* der Tuchmacher (*manufacturer*); der Tuchhändler (*dealer*).

clothing ['klouðiŋ], *s.* die Kleidung.

cloud [klaud], *s.* die Wolke; *under a* —, in Ungnade; —*burst*, der Wolkenbruch. — *v.a.* bewölken, verdunkeln. — *v.n.* — *over*, sich umwölken.

cloudiness ['klaudinis], *s.* die Umwölkung, der Wolkenhimmel.

cloudy ['klaudi], *adj.* wolkig, bewölkt, umwölkt.

clout [klaut], *s.* (*obs.*) der Lappen (*rag*); (*coll.*) der Schlag (*hit*). — *v.a.* schlagen (*hit*).

clove [klouv], *s.* die Gewürznelke (*spice*).

clove(n) [klouv(n)], *adj.* gespalten.

clover ['klouvə], *s.* der Klee; *to be in* —, Glück haben, es gut haben.

clown [klaun], *s.* der Hanswurst. — *v.n.* den Hanswurst spielen.

clownish ['klauniʃ], *adj.* tölpelhaft.

clownishness ['klauniʃnis], *s.* die Derbheit, Tölpelhaftigkeit.

cloy [klɔi], *v.n.* übersättigen, anwidern, anekeln.

club (1) [klʌb], *s.* die Keule (*stick*). — *v.a.* (einen) mit einer Keule schlagen.

club (2) [klʌb], *s.* der Klub, der Verein. — *v.n.* — *together*, zusammen beitragen, zusammensteuern (*contribute jointly*).

club (3) [klʌb], *s.* (*cards*) das Treff, die Eichel (*German cards*).

clubfoot ['klʌbfut], ∴ der Klumpfuß.

cluck [klʌk], *v.n.* glucken (*hen*).

clue [klu:], *s.* der Anhaltspunkt, Leitfaden, die Richtlinie, die Angabe (*crossword*); *no* —, keine blasse Ahnung.

clump [klʌmp], *s.* der Klumpen; die Gruppe.

clumsiness ['klʌmzinis], *s.* die Unbeholfenheit, Ungeschicklichkeit.

clumsy ['klʌmzi], *adj.* unbeholfen, schwerfällig, ungeschickt.

Cluniac ['klu:njæk]. (*Eccl.*) der Kluniazenser.

cluster ['klʌstə], *s.* die Traube (*grapes*), der Büschel. — *v.n.* in Büschen wachsen *or* stehen, dicht gruppiert sein.

clutch [klʌtʃ], *v.a.* ergreifen, packen (*grip*). — *s.* der Griff; (*Motor.*) die Kupplung.

coach [koutʃ], *s.* die Kutsche; der Wagen, der Autobus; der Privatlehrer (*teacher*). — *v.a.* unterrichten, vorbereiten (*for examinations etc.*).

coachman ['koutʃmən], *s.* der Kutscher.

coagulate [kou'ægjuleit], *v.a.* gerinnen lassen. — *v.n.* gerinnen.

coagulation [kouægju'leiʃən], *s.* das Gerinnen.

coal [koul], *s.* die Kohle; — *mine*, das Kohlenbergwerk; die Kohlengrube; — *miner*, der Bergmann.

coalesce [kouə'les], *v.n.* zusammenwachsen, sich vereinigen.

coalescence [kouə'lesəns], *s.* die Verschmelzung.

coalition [kouə'liʃən], *s.* (*Pol.*) die Koalition, das Bündnis.

coarse [kɔ:s], *adj.* grob; gemein (*manner*).

coarseness ['kɔ:snis], *s.* die Grobheit, Unfeinheit.

coast [koust], *s.* die Küste. — *v.n.* (an der Küste) entlangfahren; gleiten, rodeln.

coat [kout], *s.* der Mantel, Rock; die Jacke (*jacket*); das Fell (*animal*); — *of arms*, das Wappenschild; — *of mail*, das Panzerhemd; — *of paint*, der Anstrich. — *v.a.* überziehen, bemalen (*paint*).

coathanger ['kouthæŋə], *s.* der Kleiderbügel.

coating ['koutiŋ], *s.* der Überzug.

coax [kouks], *v.a.* beschwatzen; überreden (*persuade*).

cob (1) [kɔb], *s.* der Gaul.

cob (2) [kɔb], *s.* (*Orn.*) der Schwan.

cob (3) [kɔb], *s.* der (Mais)Kolben (*corn on the* —).

cobble [kɔbl], *v.a.* flicken (*shoes*).

cobbled ['kɔbld], *adj.* mit Kopfsteinen gepflastert.

cobbler ['kɔblə], *s.* der Schuhflicker.

cobble(stone) ['kɔbl(stoun)], *s.* das Kopfsteinpflaster.

cobweb ['kɔbweb], *s.* das Spinngewebe.

cock [kɔk], *s.* (*Orn.*) der Hahn; (*Engin.*) der Sperrhahn, Hahn; — *sparrow*, das Sperlingsmännchen; —*-a-doodle-doo!* kikeriki!

cockade [kɔ'keid], *s.* die Kokarde.

cockatoo [kɔkə'tu:], *s.* (*Orn.*) der Kakadu.

cockchafer [ˈkɔktʃeifə], *s.* (*Ent.*) der Maikäfer.

cockerel [ˈkɔkərəl], *s.* (*Orn.*) der junge Hahn.

cockswain [kɔksn] *see* **coxswain**.

cockle [kɔkl], *s.* (*Zool.*) die Herzmuschel.

cockney [ˈkɔkni], *s.* der geborene Londoner.

cockpit [ˈkɔkpit], *s.* (*Aviat.*) der Pilotensitz, die Kanzel, der Führerraum.

cockroach [ˈkɔkroutʃ], *s.* (*Ent.*) die Schabe.

cocksure [ˈkɔkʃuə], *adj.* zuversichtlich, allzu sicher.

cocoa [ˈkoukou], *s.* der Kakao.

coconut [ˈkoukonʌt], *s.* die Kokosnuß.

cocoon [kəˈkuːn], *s.* der Kokon, die Puppe (*of silkworm*).

cod [kɔd], *s.* der Kabeljau, Dorsch; — *liver oil*, der Lebertran; *dried* —, der Stockfisch.

coddle [kɔdl], *v.a.* verhätscheln, verweichlichen.

code [koud], *s.* das Gesetzbuch, der Kodex; die Chiffre (*cipher*). — *v.a.* chiffrieren, schlüsseln.

codify [ˈkoudifai], *v.a.* kodifizieren.

coerce [kouˈəːs], *v.a.* zwingen.

coercion [kouˈəːʃən], *s.* der Zwang.

coercive [kouˈəːsiv], *adj.* zwingend.

coeval [kouˈiːvəl], *adj.* gleichaltrig, gleichzeitig.

coexist [kouigˈzist], *v.n.* zugleich existieren, nebeneinander leben.

coffee [ˈkɔfi], *s.* der Kaffee; — *grinder*, die Kaffeemühle; — *grounds*, der Kaffeesatz; — *pot*, die Kaffeekanne; — *set*, das Kaffee service.

coffer [ˈkɔfə], *s.* der Kasten, die Truhe.

coffin [ˈkɔfin], *s.* der Sarg.

cog [kɔg], *s.* der Zahn (*on wheel*); — *wheel*, das Zahnrad.

cogency [ˈkoudzənsi], *s.* die zwingende Kraft, Triftigkeit.

cogent [ˈkoudzənt], *adj.* zwingend, triftig.

cogitate [ˈkɔdziteit], *v.n.* nachdenken.

cogitation [kɔdziˈteiʃən], *s.* die Überlegung, das Nachdenken.

cognate [ˈkɔgneit], *adj.* verwandt.

cognisance [ˈkɔgnizəns], *s.* die Erkenntnis; die Kenntnisnahme; (*Law*) die gerichtliche Kenntnisnahme.

cognisant [ˈkɔgnizənt], *adj.* wissend, in vollem Wissen (*of*, *Genit.*).

cognition [kɔgˈniʃən], *s.* die Kenntnis, das Erkennen.

cohabit [kouˈhæbit], *v.n.* zusammenleben.

cohabitation [kouhæbiˈteiʃən], *s.* das Zusammenleben.

coheir [kouˈɛə], *s.* der Miterbe.

cohere [kouˈhiə], *v.n.* zusammenhängen.

coherence [kouˈhiərəns], *s.* der Zusammenhang.

coherent [kouˈhiərənt], *adj.* zusammenhängend.

cohesion [kouˈhiːʒən], *s.* (*Phys.*) die Kohäsion.

coiffure [kwæˈfjuə], *s.* die Frisur, die Haartracht.

coil [kɔil], *s.* (*Elec.*) die Spule; die Windung. — *v.a.* aufwickeln; umwickeln, (auf)spulen. — *v.n.* sich winden.

coin [kɔin], *s.* die Münze, das Geldstück. — *v.a.* münzen, prägen; — *a phrase*, eine Redewendung prägen.

coinage [ˈkɔinidz], *s.* die Prägung.

coincide [kouinˈsaid], *v.n.* zusammenfallen, zusammentreffen.

coincidence [kouˈinsidəns], *s.* das Zusammenfallen, Zusammentreffen; der Zufall (*chance*).

coincident [kouˈinsidənt], *adj.* zusammentreffend.

coke [kouk], *s.* der Koks. — *v.a.* (*Chem.*, *Engin.*) verkoken.

cold [kould], *adj.* kalt; gefühllos, kühl. — *s.* die Kälte (*temperature*); die Erkältung (*indisposition*).

coldish [ˈkouldiʃ], *adj.* kühl.

coldness [ˈkouldnis], *s.* die Kälte (*temperature*); die Kaltherzigkeit (*heartlessness*).

colic [ˈkɔlik], *s.* die Kolik.

collaborate [kəˈlæbəreit], *v.n.* zusammenarbeiten.

collaboration [kələbəˈreiʃən], *s.* die Zusammenarbeit; die Mitwirkung, Mitarbeit (*assistance*).

collaborator [kəˈlæbəreitə], *s.* der Mitarbeiter.

collapse [kəˈlæps], *s.* der Zusammenbruch. — *v.n.* zusammenbrechen (*disintegrate*); zerfallen, einstürzen.

collapsible [kəˈlæpsibl], *adj.* zerlegbar, zusammenlegbar, zusammenklappbar.

collar [ˈkɔlə], *s.* der Kragen; —*bone*, das Schlüsselbein (*Anat.*); der Halsband; (*coll.*) der Priesterkragen; —*stud*, der Kragenknopf. — *v.a.* beim Kragen fassen, ergreifen.

collate [kɔˈleit], *v.a.* vergleichen (*texts etc.*).

collateral [kɔˈlætərəl], *adj.* Seiten-, von beiden Seiten. — *s.* (*Am.*) die Garantie, Bürgschaft.

collation [kɔˈleiʃən], *s.* die Vergleichung, der Vergleich (*texts etc.*); der Imbiß.

colleague [ˈkɔliːg], *s.* der Kollege, die Kollegin.

collect [kəˈlekt], *v.a.* sammeln, zusammenbringen. — *v.n.* sich versammeln. — [ˈkɔlikt], *s.* (*Eccl.*) die Kollekte.

collection [kəˈlekʃən], *s.* die Sammlung.

collective [kəˈlektiv], *adj.* kollektiv, gemeinsam. — *s.* (*Pol.*) das Kollektiv.

collector [kəˈlektə], *s.* der Sammler.

college [ˈkɔlidz], *s.* das Kollegium; das College; die Hochschule, Universität.

collide [kəˈlaid], *v.n.* zusammenstoßen.

collie [ˈkɔli], *s.* der Schäferhund.

collier [ˈkɔliə], *s.* der Kohlenarbeiter; das Kohlenfrachtschiff (*boat*).

collision [kə'liʒən], s. der Zusammenstoß, Zusammenprall.

collocate ['kɔləkeit], v.a. ordnen.

collodion [kə'loudjən], s. (Chem.) das Kollodium.

colloquial [kə'loukwiəl], adj. umgangssprachlich, Umgangs-.

colloquy ['kɔlekwi], s. die Unterredung, das Gespräch (formal).

collusion [kə'lu:ʒən], s. das heimliche Einverständnis, die unstatthafte Partnerschaft; die Verdunkelung.

collusive [kə'lu:ziv], adj. abgekartet.

Cologne [kə'loun]. Köln, n.; eau de —, Kölnisch Wasser.

Colombian [kɔ'lɔmbjən], adj. kolumbisch. — s. der Kolumbier.

colon (1) ['koulən], s. das Kolon, der Doppelpunkt.

colon (2) ['koulən], s. (Med.) der Dickdarm.

colonel [kə:nl], s. (Mil.) der Oberst; --in-chief, der Generaloberst, der oberste Befehlshaber; lieutenant- —, der Oberstleutnant.

colonial [kə'lounjəl], adj. kolonial, aus den Kolonien.

colonist ['kɔlənist], s. der Siedler; Ansiedler.

colonization [kɔlənai'zeiʃən], s. die Kolonisierung, Besiedelung.

colonize ['kɔlənaiz], v.a. besiedeln, kolonisieren.

colonnade [kɔlə'neid], s. die Kolonnade, der Säulengang.

colony ['kɔləni], s. die Kolonie.

colophony [kɔ'ləfəni], s. das Kolophonium (resin).

coloration [kʌlə'reiʃən], s. die Färbung, Tönung.

colossal [kə'lɔsəl], adj. kolossal, riesig, riesenhaft.

colour ['kʌlə], s. die Farbe; (complexion) die Gesichtsfarbe; (paint) die Farbe, der Anstrich; (dye) die Färbung. — v.a. färben; anstreichen (paint house etc.).

colt [koult], s. das Füllen.

columbine ['kɔləmbain], s. (Bot.) die Akelei.

column ['kɔləm], s. die Säule; die Spalte (press); (also Mil.) die Kolonne.

colza ['kɔlzə], s. (Bot.) der Raps.

coma ['koumə], s. (Med.) das Koma, die Schlafsucht.

comb [koum], s. der Kamm. — v.a. kämmen; (fig.) genau untersuchen.

combat ['kʌmbət, 'kɔmbət], s. der Kampf, das Gefecht; in single —, im Duell, Zweikampf. — v.a. kämpfen, bekämpfen.

combatant ['kʌmbətənt, 'kɔmb-], s. der Kämpfer.

comber ['koumə], s. der Wollkämmer.

combination [kɔmbi'neiʃən], s. die Kombination, die Verbindung.

combine [kəm'bain], v.a. kombinieren, verbinden. — v.n. sich verbinden. — ['kɔmbain], s. (Comm.) der Trust, Ring.

combustible [kəm'bʌstibl], adj. verbrennbar; feuergefährlich.

combustion [kəm'bʌstʃən], s. die Verbrennung.

come [kʌm], v.n. irr. kommen; — about, sich ereignen (event); — across, stoßen auf (Acc.); — by (s.th.), ergattern, erwerben; — for, abholen; — forth, forward, hervorkommen, hervortreten; — from, herkommen von, — in, hereinkommen; — off, (of object) loskommen, (succeed) glücken; — out (appear), herauskommen; — to o.s., zu sich kommen; — of age, mündig werden; — to o.'s senses, zur Besinnung or Vernunft kommen; that is still to —, das steht uns noch bevor.

comedian [kə'mi:djən], s. der Komödiant, Komiker (stage).

comedy ['kɔmədi], s. die Komödie, das Lustspiel.

comeliness ['kʌmlinis], s. die Anmut, Schönheit.

comely ['kʌmli], adj. anmutig, schön.

comestible [kə'mestibl], s. (usually pl.) die Eßwaren, f. pl.

comet ['kɔmit], s. der Komet.

comfit ['kʌmfit], s. das Konfekt, die Bonbons.

comfort ['kʌmfət], s. der Trost (solace); der Komfort, die Bequemlichkeit. — v.a. trösten.

comforter ['kʌmfətə], s. der Tröster; (Am.) die Steppdecke.

comfortless ['kʌmfətlis], adj. trostlos, unbehaglich.

comic ['kɔmik], adj. komisch; — writer, humoristischer Schriftsteller. — s. die Bilderzeitung (children's paper).

comical ['kɔmikl], adj. lächerlich, zum Lachen, komisch.

comma ['kɔmə], s. das Komma, der Beistrich; inverted —s, die Anführungszeichen.

command [kə'ma:nd], v.a., v.n. (Mil.) kommandieren; über jemanden verfügen (have s.o. at o.'s disposal). — s. der Befehl.

commandant [kɔmən'dænt], s. der Kommandant, Befehlshaber.

commander [kə'ma:ndə], s. der Befehlshaber.

commandment [kə'ma:ndmənt], s. (Rel.) das Gebot.

commemorate [kə'meməreit], v.a. feiern, gedenken (Genit.).

commemoration [kəmemə'reiʃən], s. die Feier, die Gedächtnisfeier.

commemorative [kə'memərətiv], adj. Gedächtnis-.

commence [kə'mens], v.a., v.n. beginnen, anfangen.

commencement [kə'mensmənt], s. der Anfang, der Beginn.

commend [kə'mend], v.a. empfehlen, loben (praise).

commendable [kə'mendəbl], adj. empfehlenswert.

commendation [kɔmen'deiʃən], s. die
Empfehlung.
commensurable,   commensurate
[kə'menʃərəbl, kə'menʃərit], adj. kom-
mensurabel, entsprechend; angemessen.
comment ['kɔment], v.n. kommen-
tieren (on, zu, Dat.). — s. der Kommentar; die Bemerkung (remark).
commentary ['kɔməntəri], s. der
Kommentar.
commentator ['kɔmənteitə], s. der
Kommentator, Berichterstatter.
commerce ['kɔmə:s], s. der Handel;
college of —, die Handelsschule.
commercial [kə'mə:ʃəl], adj. kommerziell, kaufmännisch, Handels-; —
traveller, der Handelsreisende, Vertreter; — manager, der geschäftliche
Leiter.
commingle [kɔ'miŋgl], v.a. ver-
mischengefühl.
commiserate [kə'mizəreit], v.n. bemitleiden; — with s.o., mit einem
Mitgefühl haben.
commissariat [kɔmi'sɛəriət], s. (Pol.)
das Kommissariat.
commissary ['kɔmisəri], s. der Kommissar. — adj. kommissarisch.
commission [kə'miʃən], s. die Kommission; (Mil.) der Offiziersrang; die
Begehung (of crime); (Law) die
(offizielle) Kommission; der Auftrag,
die Bestellung (order).
commissionaire [kəmiʃən'ɛə], s. der
Portier.
commissioned [kə'miʃənd], adj. bevollmächtigt.
commissioner [kə'miʃənə], s. (Pol.)
der Kommissar, der Bevollmächtigte.
commit [kə'mit], v.a. begehen (do);
übergeben (consign); anvertrauen (entrust). — v.r. sich verpflichten.
committal [kə'mitl], s. das Übergeben;
die Überantwortung.
committee [kə'miti], s. das Komitee,
der Ausschuß.
commodious [kə'moudiəs], adj. bequem, geräumig.
commodity [kə'mɔditi], s. (Comm.) die
Ware, der Artikel.
commodore ['kɔmədɔ:], s. (Naut.) der
Kommodore, der Kommandant eines
Geschwaders.
common ['kɔmən], adj. gewöhnlich
(usual); gemein (vulgar); allgemein
(general); in —, gemeinschaftlich; —
sense, der gesunde Menschenverstand; —
the — man, der kleine Mann. — n. pl.
House of Commons, das Unterhaus.
commoner ['kɔmənə], s. der Bürger;
(Parl.) Mitglied des Unterhauses.
commonness ['kɔmənnis], s. die
Gemeinheit (vulgarity); das häufige
Vorkommen (frequency).
commonplace ['kɔmənpleis], adj. alltäglich. — s. der Gemeinplatz.
commonwealth ['kɔmənwelθ], s. die
Staatengemeinschaft, der Staatenbund; das Commonwealth.

commotion [kə'mouʃən], s. die Er-
schütterung; der Aufruhr; der
Lärm.
communal ['kɔmjunəl], adj. gemeinschaftlich, allgemein; (Pol.) Kom-
munal-.
commune ['kɔmju:n], s. (Pol.) die
Kommune. — [kə'mju:n], v.n. sich
unterhalten.
communicable [kə'mju:nikəbl], adj.
mitteilbar; übertragbar.
communicate [kə'mju:nikeit], v.a. mitteilen; verkünden (proclaim); benachrichtigen. — v.n. in Verbindung
stehen.
communication [kəmju:ni'keiʃən], s.
die Mitteilung; Verlautbarung; die
Verkündigung (proclamation); die
Information; (Elec.) die Verbindung;
(pl.), die Verbindungslinie; —s engineering, Fernmeldetechnik.
communion [kə'mju:njən], s. (Eccl.)
die Kommunion; das heilige Abendmahl; die Gemeinschaft (fellowship).
Communism ['kɔmjunizm], s. (Pol.)
der Kommunismus.
Communist ['kɔmjunist], s. der Kom-
munist. — adj. kommunistisch.
community [kə'mju:niti], s. die Gemeinschaft.
commutable [kə'mju:təbl], adj. um-
tauschbar, auswechselbar.
commutation [kɔmju'teiʃən], s. der
Austausch; (Law) die Herabsetzung
(of sentence).
commutator ['kɔmjuteitə], s. (Elec.)
der Umschalter.
commute [kə'mju:t], v.n. hin und her
fahren, pendeln, mit Zeitkarte fahren
(travel). — v.a. herabsetzen (sentence).
compact ['kɔmpækt], adj. kompakt,
fest; gedrängt (succinct); kurz, bündig
(short).
companion [kəm'pænjən], s. der
Gefährte, die Gefährtin.
companionable [kəm'pænjənəbl], adj.
gesellig, freundlich.
companionship [kəm'pænjənʃip], s. die
Geselligkeit; die Gesellschaft.
company ['kʌmpəni], s. die Gesellschaft; (Mil.) die Kompanie; der
Freundeskreis (circle of friends);
(Comm.) die Handelsgesellschaft;
limited (liability) —, Gesellschaft mit
beschränkter Haftung; public (private)
—, Gesellschaft des öffentlichen
(privaten) Rechtes.
comparative [kəm'pærətiv], adj. ver-
gleichend, relativ. — s. (Gram.) der
Komparativ.
compare [kəm'pɛə], v.a. vergleichen.
— v.n. sich vergleichen lassen.
comparison [kəm'pærisən], s. der
Vergleich; das Gleichnis (simile).
compartment [kəm'pɑ:tmənt], s.
(Railw.) das Abteil; die Abteilung.
compass ['kʌmpəs], s. der Umkreis,
Umfang (scope); (Naut.) der Kompaß; point of the —, der Kompaß-
strich; (Engin.) der Zirkel.

compassion [kəm'pæʃən], *s.* die Barmherzigkeit, das Mitleid, das Erbarmen.
compassionate [kəm'pæʃənit], *adj.*
mitleidig; (*Mil.*) — *leave*, der Son-
derurlaub.
compatibility [kəmpæti'biliti], *s.* die
Verträglichkeit, Vereinbarkeit.
compatible [kəm'pætibl], *adj.* verträglich, vereinbar.
compatriot [kəm'peitriət], *s.* der
Landsmann.
compel [kəm'pel], *v.a.* zwingen, nötigen.
compendium [kəm'pendjəm], *s.* das
Kompendium, die kurze Schrift, die
kurze Darstellung.
compensate ['kɔmpənseit], *v.a.* kompensieren, einem Ersatz leisten.
compensation [kɔmpən'seiʃən], *s.* der
Ersatz, die Wiedergutmachung.
compensatory [kɔmpən'seitəri], *adj.*
ausgleichend, Ersatz-.
compete [kəm'piːt], *v.n.* wetteifern,
konkurrieren.
competence, competency ['kɔmpitəns,
-nsi], *s.* die Kompetenz; Zuständigkeit; Befähigung (*capability*); Tüchtigkeit (*ability*).
competent ['kɔmpitənt], *adj.* kom-
petent; zuständig; fähig (*capable*);
tüchtig (*able*).
competition [kɔmpi'tiʃən], *s.* die Konkurrenz; die Mitbewerbung (*for job*).
competitive [kəm'petitiv], *adj.* Kon-
kurrenz-, konkurrierend.
competitor [kəm'petitə], *s.* (*Comm.*)
der Konkurrent; der Mitbewerber
(*fellow applicant*), Teilnehmer (*sport*).
complacent [kəm'pleisənt], *adj.* selbst-
zufrieden, selbstgefällig.
complain [kəm'plein], *v.n.* sich beklagen (*of*, über, *Acc.*).
complaint [kəm'pleint], *s.* die Klage;
Beschwerde (*grievance*); das Leiden
(*illness*).
complement ['kɔmplimənt], *s.* die
Ergänzung, Gesamtzahl. — [-'ment],
v.a. ergänzen.
complementary [kɔmpli'mentəri], *adj.*
Ergänzungs-, ergänzend.
complete [kəm'pliːt], *adj.* komplett;
voll (*full up*); vollkommen (*perfect*).
— *v.a.* vollenden (*end*); ergänzen
(*make whole*).
completeness [kəm'pliːtnis], *s.* die
Vollendung (*condition*); Ganzheit
(*wholeness*).
completion [kəm'pliːʃən], *s.* die Vollendung (*fulfilment*); die Beendigung
(*ending*); der Abschluß.
complex ['kɔmpleks], *adj.* (*Maths.*)
komplex; kompliziert (*complicated*).
— *s.* der Komplex (*Archit., Psych.*).
complexion [kəm'plekʃən], *s.* die
Gesichtsfarbe; (*fig.*) das Aussehen.
complexity [kəm'pleksiti], *s.* die
Kompliziertheit; die Schwierigkeit.
compliance [kəm'plaiəns], *s.* die
Willfährigkeit, Einwilligung.
compliant [kəm'plaiənt], *adj.* willig,
willfährig.

complicate ['kɔmplikeit], *v.a.* kom-
plizieren, erschweren.
complication [kɔmpli'keiʃən], *s.* die
Komplikation, die Erschwerung.
complicity [kəm'plisiti], *s.* (*Law*) die
Mitschuld.
compliment ['kɔmplimənt], *s.* das
Kompliment. — [-'ment], *v.n.* Kom-
plimente machen.
complimentary [kɔmpli'mentəri], *adj.*
lobend; — *ticket*, die Freikarte.
comply [kəm'plai], *v.n.* einwilligen
(*with*, in, *Acc.*); sich halten (*an, Acc.*).
compose [kəm'pouz], *v.a., v.n.* (*Mus.*)
komponieren; beruhigen (*the mind*);
(*Lit.*) verfassen; (*Typ.*) setzen.
composed [kəm'pouzd], *adj.* ruhig,
gefaßt.
composer [kəm'pouzə], *s.* (*Mus.*) der
Komponist.
composite ['kɔmpəzit], *adj.* zusammengesetzt.
composition [kɔmpə'ziʃən], *s.* (*Mus.
etc.*) die Komposition; Beschaffenheit
Zusammensetzung.
compositor [kəm'pɔzitə], *s.* (*Typ.*) der
Schriftsetzer.
compost ['kɔmpɔst], *s.* (*Agr.*) der
Dünger, Kompost.
composure [kəm'pouʒə], *s.* die Gelassenheit, die Gemütsruhe, die Fassung.
compound [kəm'paund], *s.* (*Chem.*)
die Verbindung; die Zusammensetzung. — *adj.* zusammengesetzt;
kompliziert; (*Comm.*) — *interest*, die
Zinseszinsen. — [kəm'paund], *v.a.*
(*Chem.*) mischen, zusammensetzen.
comprehend [kɔmpri'hend], *v.a.* verstehen (*understand*); einschließen (*include*).
comprehensible [kɔmpri'hensibl], *adj.*
verständlich, begreiflich.
comprehension [kɔmpri'henʃən], *s.*
das Verstehen, das Erfassen; (*Psych.*)
— *tests*, die Verständnisprüfung.
comprehensive [kɔmpri'hensiv], *adj.*
umfassend.
compress [kəm'pres], *v.a.* komprimieren; zusammendrücken (*press together*). — ['kɔmpres], *s.* (*Med.*) die
Kompresse, der Umschlag (*poultice*).
compression [kəm'preʃən], *s.* der
Druck; das Zusammendrücken (*pressing together*); die Kürzung (*abridg-
ment*).
comprise [kəm'praiz], *v.a.* umfassen,
einschließen.
compromise ['kɔmprəmaiz], *v.a.* kompromittieren. — *v.n.* einen Kompromiß schließen. — *s.* der or das Kompromiß.
compulsion [kəm'pʌlʃən], *s.* der
Zwang.
compulsory [kəm'pʌlsəri], *adj.* zwingend; Zwangs-; — *subject*, das
obligatorische Fach.
compunction [kəm'pʌŋkʃən], *s.* die
Gewissensbisse, *m. pl.*
computation [kɔmpju'teiʃən], *s.* die
Berechnung.

compute [kəm'pju:t], *v.a.*, *v.n.* berechnen.

computer [kəm'pju:tə], *s.* die automatische Rechenmaschine.

comrade ['kɔmrid], *s.* der Kamerad.

comradeship ['kɔmridʃip], *s.* die Kameradschaft.

con [kɔn], *v.a.* genau betrachten, studieren; (*ship*) steuern.

concave ['kɔnkeiv], *adj.* (*Phys.*) konkav.

conceal [kən'si:l], *v.a.* verbergen, verstecken.

concealment [kən'si:lmənt], *s.* die Verhehlung, die Verheimlichung (*act of concealing*); *place of* —, das Versteck.

concede [kən'si:d], *v.a.* zugestehen, einräumen.

conceit [kən'si:t], *s.* die Einbildung, der Eigendünkel (*presumption*); (*obs.*) die Idee; (*Lit.*) die (gedankliche) Spielerei.

conceited [kən'si:tid], *adj.* eingebildet, eitel.

conceivable [kən'si:vəbl], *adj.* denkbar; begreiflich (*understandable*).

conceive [kən'si:v], *v.a.*, *v.n.* empfangen (*become pregnant*); begreifen (*understand*).

concentrate ['kɔnsəntreit], *v.a.* konzentrieren. — *v.n.* sich konzentrieren (*on*, auf, *Acc.*). — *s.* (*Chem.*) das Konzentrat.

concentrated ['kɔnsəntreitid], *adj.* konzentriert.

concentration [kɔnsən'treiʃən], *s.* die Konzentration.

concentric [kən'sentrik], *adj.* (*Geom.*) konzentrisch.

conception [kən'sepʃən], *s.* die Vorstellung, der Begriff (*idea*); die Empfängnis (*of a child*).

concern [kən'sə:n], *v.a.* (*affect*) betreffen, angehen; *be concerned with*, zu tun haben (mit, *Dat.*). — *s.* die Angelegenheit (*affair*); die Sorge (*care*, *business*); das Geschäft, das Unternehmen; *cause grave* —, tiefe Besorgnis erregen.

concerned [kən'sə:nd], *adj.* (*worried*) besorgt; (*involved*) interessiert (*in*, an, *Dat.*).

concerning [kən'sə:niŋ], *prep.* betreffend (*Acc.*), hinsichtlich (*Genit.*).

concert ['kɔnsət], *s.* (*Mus.*) das Konzert; Einverständnis.

concerted [kən'sə:tid], *adj.* gemeinsam, gemeinschaftlich.

concertina [kɔnsə'ti:nə], *s.* (*Mus.*) die Ziehharmonika.

concerto [kən'tʃə:tou], *s.* (*Mus.*) das Konzert.

concession [kən'seʃən], *s.* die Konzession (*licence*); das Zugeständnis.

conch [kɔŋk], *s.* die (große) Muschel.

conciliate [kən'silieit], *v.a.* versöhnen.

conciliation [kənsili'eiʃən], *s.* die Versöhnung.

conciliatory [kən'siliətəri], *adj.* versöhnlich.

concise [kən'sais], *adj.* kurz, knapp.

conciseness [kən'saisnis], *s.* die Kürze, Knappheit.

conclave ['kɔnkleiv], *s.* (*Eccl.*) das Konklave.

conclude [kən'klu:d], *v.a.*, *v.n.* schließen, beenden (*speech etc.*); (*infer*) folgern (*from*, aus, *Dat.*); abschließen (*treaty*).

conclusion [kən'klu:ʒən], *s.* der Abschluß (*treaty*); die Folgerung (*inference*); der Beschluß (*decision*).

conclusive [kən'klu:siv], *adj.* entscheidend, überzeugend.

concoct [kən'kɔkt], *v.a.* zusammenbrauen, aushecken.

concoction [kən'kɔkʃən], *s.* das Gebräu, die Mischung.

concomitant [kən'kɔmitənt], *adj.* begleitend; Begleit-, Neben-. — *s.* der Begleitumstand.

concord ['kɔnkɔ:d], *s.* die Eintracht, die Harmonie.

concordance [kən'kɔ:dəns], *s.* die Übereinstimmung; die Konkordanz (*of Bible etc.*).

concordant [kən'kɔ:dənt], *adj.* in Eintracht (mit), übereinstimmend (mit) (*Dat.*).

concordat [kən'kɔ:dæt], *s.* (*Eccl.*, *Pol.*) das Konkordat.

concourse ['kɔnkɔ:s], *s.* das Gedränge (*crowd*).

concrete [kən'kri:t], *s.* (*Build.*) der Beton; (*Log.*) das Konkrete. — *adj.* konkret, wirklich.

concur [kən'kə:], *v.n.* übereinstimmen (*with*, mit, *Dat.*).

concurrence [kən'kʌrəns], *s.* die Übereinstimmung.

concurrent [kən'kʌrənt], *adj.* gleichzeitig (*simultaneous*); mitwirkend (*accompanying*).

concussion [kən'kʌʃən], *s.* (*Med.*) die (Gehirn)Erschütterung.

condemn [kən'dem], *v.a.* verurteilen, verdammen.

condemnable [kən'demnəbl], *adj.* verwerflich, verdammenswert.

condemnation [kɔndem'neiʃən], *s.* die Verurteilung, die Verdammung.

condensate [kən'denseit], *s.* (*Chem.*) das Kondensat, das Ergebnis der Kondensation.

condensation [kɔnden'seiʃən], *s.* die Kondensation; Verdichtung.

condensed [kən'densd], *adj.* (*Chem.*) kondensiert; (*Chem.*, *Engin.*) verdichtet; gekürzt (*abridged*).

condenser [kən'densə], *s.* (*Chem.*, *Engin.*) der Kondensator; (*Elec.*) der Verstärker.

condescend [kɔndi'send], *v.n.* sich herablassen.

condescending [kɔndi'sendiŋ], *adj.* herablassend.

condescension [kɔndi'senʃən], *s.* die Herablassung.

condiment ['kɔndimənt], *s.* die Würze.

condition [kən'diʃən], *s.* der Zustand; Umstand; die Bedingung (*proviso*); der Gesundheitszustand (*physical state*).

conditional [kən'diʃənəl], *adj.* bedingt; unter der Bedingung; konditionell.

conditioned [kən'diʃənd], *adj.* vorbereitet (*for action*); geartet.

condole [kən'doul], *v.n.* Beileid ausdrücken (*with, Dat.*), kondolieren (*with, Dat.*).

condolence [kən'douləns], *s.* das Beileid.

condone [kən'doun], *v.a.* verzeihen.

conducive [kən'dju:siv], *adj.* förderlich, dienlich, nützlich (*to, Dat.*).

conduct [kən'dʌkt], *v.a.* leiten, führen; (*Phys.*) ein Leiter sein; (*Mus.*) dirigieren. — *v.r.* sich aufführen, sich benehmen. — ['kɔndʌkt], *s.* das Benehmen (*behaviour*); — *of a war*, die Kriegsführung.

conductive [kən'dʌktiv], *adj.* (*Elec.*) leitend.

conductor [kən'dʌktə], *s.* der Leiter, Führer (*leader*); (*Phys., Elec.*) der Leiter; (*Am.*) der Schaffner (*train*); (*Mus.*) der Dirigent.

conduit [kʌn-, 'kɔndit], *s.* die Leitung, die Röhre.

cone [koun], *s.* (*Geom.*) der Kegel; (*Bot.*) der Zapfen.

coney ['kouni], *s.* (*Zool.*) das Kaninchen.

confection [kən'fekʃən], *s.* das Konfekt.

confectioner [kən'fekʃənə], *s.* der Zuckerbäcker, Konditor.

confectionery [kən'fekʃənəri], *s.* die Zuckerwaren, *f.pl.* (*sweets*); Konditoreiwaren, *f.pl.* (*cakes*); die Zuckerbäckerei (*sweet shop*); die Konditorei.

confederacy [kən'fedərəsi], *s.* der Bund (*of states*); das Bündnis (*treaty*).

confederate [kən'fedərit], *s.* der Bundesgenosse, der Verbündete. — *adj.* verbündet; — *state*, der Bundesstaat. — [-reit], *v.n.* sich verbünden (*with, mit, Dat.*).

confederation [kənfedə'reiʃən], *s.* das Bündnis (*treaty*); der Bund (*state*).

confer [kən'fə:], *v.a.* verleihen (*degree, title*). — *v.n.* beraten (*with, mit, Dat.*), unterhandeln (*negotiate*).

conference ['kɔnfərəns], *s.* die Konferenz, die Besprechung, die Beratung, Tagung.

confess [kən'fes], *v.a.* bekennen; beichten (*sin*); zugestehen (*acknowledge*).

confession [kən'feʃən], *s.* das Bekenntnis; die Beichte (*sin*); das Glaubensbekenntnis (*creed*).

confessor [kən'fesə], *s.* der Bekenner; *father* —, der Beichtvater.

confidant [kɔnfi'dænt], *s.* der Vertraute.

confide [kən'faid], *v.a.* anvertrauen. — *v.n.* vertrauen (*Dat.*).

confidence ['kɔnfidəns], *s.* das Vertrauen; die Zuversicht; — *trick*, die Bauernfängerei, der Schwindel.

confident ['kɔnfidənt], *adj.* zuversichtlich; dreist (*bold*).

confidential [kɔnfi'denʃəl], *adj.* vertraulich, privat.

confine [kən'fain], *v.a.* einschränken (*hem in*); einsperren; *be —d to bed*, bettlägerig sein.

confinement [kən'fainmənt], *s.* die Einschränkung (*limitation*); das Wochenbett, die Niederkunft (*childbirth*).

confines ['kɔnfainz], *s. pl.* die Grenzen, *f. pl.* (*physical*); die Einschränkungen, *f. pl.* (*limitations*).

confirm [kən'fə:m], *v.a.* bestätigen, bekräftigen (*corroborate*); (*Eccl.*) firmen, konfirmieren.

confirmation [kɔnfə'meiʃən], *s.* die Bestätigung (*corroboration*); (*Eccl.*) die Firmung, Konfirmation.

confirmed [kən'fə:md], *adj.* eingefleischt; unverbesserlich.

confiscate ['kɔnfiskeit], *v.a.* konfiszieren, einziehen, beschlagnahmen.

confiscation [kɔnfis'keiʃən], *s.* die Konfiszierung, die Einziehung, die Beschlagnahme (*customs etc.*).

conflagration [kɔnflə'greiʃən], *s.* der (große) Brand.

conflict ['kɔnflikt], *s.* der Konflikt, der Zusammenstoß. — [kən'flikt], *v.n.* in Konflikt geraten; in Widerspruch stehen.

confluence ['kɔnfluəns], *s.* (*Geog.*) der Zusammenfluß.

confluent ['kɔnfluənt], *adj.* zusammenfließend. — *s.* der Nebenfluß (*tributary*).

conform [kən'fɔ:m], *v.n.* sich anpassen.

conformation [kɔnfɔ:'meiʃən], *s.* die Anpassung.

conformist [kən'fɔ:mist], *adj.* fügsam. — *s.* das Mitglied der Staatskirche.

conformity [kən'fɔ:miti], *s.* die Gleichförmigkeit; *in — with*, gerade so; gemäß (*Dat.*); die Gleichheit (*equality*).

confound [kən'faund], *v.a.* verwirren (*confuse*); vernichten (*overthrow*).

confounded [kən'faundid], *adj.* verdammt, verwünscht.

confront [kən'frʌnt], *v.a.* (*Law*) — *s.o. with*, gegenüberstellen (*put in front of*); gegenüberstehen (*stand in front of*).

confrontation [kɔnfrʌn'teiʃən], *s.* die Gegenüberstellung.

confuse [kən'fju:z], *v.a.* verwirren (*muddle*); bestürzen (*perplex*); verwechseln (*mix up*).

confusion [kən'fju:ʒən], *s.* die Verwirrung, das Durcheinander (*muddle*); die Bestürzung (*astonishment*); die Verlegenheit (*dilemma*).

confutation [kɔnfju:'teiʃən], *s.* die Widerlegung.

confute [kən'fju:t], *v.a.* widerlegen.

congeal [kən'dʒi:l], *v.n.* gefrieren (*freeze*); gerinnen.

congenial [kən'dʒi:niəl], *adj.* geistesverwandt, geistig ebenbürtig, sympathisch.

congeniality [kəndʒi:ni'æliti], *s.* die Geistesverwandtschaft.

conger ['kɔŋgə], *s.* (*Zool.*) der Meeraal.

congest [kən'dʒest], *v.a.* anhäufen, überfüllen.

congestion [kən'dʒestʃən], *s.* die Überfüllung; Stauung; die Übervölkerung (*overpopulation*); (*Med.*) der Blutandrang.

conglomerate [kən'glɔməreit], *v.n.* sich zusammenballen. — [-rit], *s.* das Konglomerat, die Ballung.

conglomeration [kɔnglɔmə'reiʃən], *s.* die Zusammenhäufung, Zusammenballung.

Congolese [kɔŋgo'li:z], *adj.* kongolesisch. — *s.* der Kongolese.

congratulate [kən'grætjuleit], *v.n.* gratulieren (*on*, zu, *Dat.*).

congratulation [kəngrætju'leiʃən], *s.* (*usually pl.*) die Glückwünsche.

congratulatory [kən'grætjuleitəri], *adj.* Glückwunsch-.

congregate ['kɔŋgrigeit], *v.a.* versammeln. — *v.n.* sich versammeln, sich scharen (*round*, um, *Acc.*).

congregation [kɔŋgri'geiʃən], *s.* die Versammlung, die Schar; (*Eccl.*) die Gemeinde.

congregational [kɔŋgri'geiʃənəl], *adj.* (*Eccl.*) Gemeinde-; *Congregational Church*, unabhängige Gemeindekirche.

congress ['kɔŋgres], *s.* der Kongreß.

congruence ['kɔŋgruəns], *s.* (*Geom.*) die Kongruenz.

congruent ['kɔŋgruənt], *adj.* (*Geom.*) kongruent.

congruity [kɔŋ'gru:iti], *s.* (*Geom.*) die Übereinstimmung; die Kongruenz.

congruous ['kɔŋgruəs], *adj.* übereinstimmend, angemessen.

conic(al) ['kɔnik(əl)], *adj.* konisch, kegelförmig; (*Geom.*) — *section*, der Kegelschnitt.

conifer ['kɔnifə], *s.* (*Bot.*) der Nadelbaum.

conjecture [kən'dʒektʃə], *s.* die Mutmaßung, die Annahme. — *v.a.* mutmaßen, annehmen.

conjoin [kɔn'dʒɔin], *v.a.* (*Law*) verbinden.

conjugal ['kɔndʒugəl], *adj.* ehelich.

conjugate ['kɔndʒugeit], *v.a.* (*Gram.*) konjugieren.

conjugation [kɔndʒu'geiʃən], *s.* (*Gram.*) die Konjugation.

conjunction [kən'dʒʌŋkʃən], *s.* (*Gram.*) das Bindewort.

conjunctive [kən'dʒʌŋktiv], *adj.* verbindend; (*Gram.*) — *mood*, der Konjunktiv.

conjunctivitis [kən'dʒʌŋktivaitis], *s.* (*Med.*) die Bindehautentzündung.

conjuncture [kən'dʒʌŋktʃə], *s.* der Wendepunkt; die Krise (*of events*).

conjure ['kʌndʒə], *v.a.* beschwören; — *up*, heraufbeschwören. — *v.n.* zaubern.

conjurer ['kʌndʒərə], *s.* der Zauberer.

connect [kə'nekt], *v.a.* verbinden, in Zusammenhang bringen.

connection, connexion [kə'nekʃən], *s.* die Verbindung, der Zusammenhang.

connivance [kə'naivəns], *s.* die Nachsicht, das Gewährenlassen.

connive [kə'naiv], *v.n.* nachsichtig sein (*at*, bei, *Dat.*); gewähren lassen.

connoisseur [kɔne'sə:], *s.* der Kenner.

connubial [kə'nju:biəl], *adj.* ehelich.

conquer ['kɔŋkə], *v.a.* besiegen (*foe*); erobern (*place*).

conqueror ['kɔŋkərə], *s.* der Eroberer, der Sieger.

conquest ['kɔŋkwest], *s.* der Sieg, die Eroberung.

consanguinity [kɔnsæŋ'gwiniti], *s.* die Blutsverwandtschaft.

conscience ['kɔnʃəns], *s.* das Gewissen; *in all* — wahrhaftig.

conscientious [kɔnʃi'enʃəs], *adj.* gewissenhaft.

conscientiousness [kɔnʃi'enʃəsnis], *s.* die Gewissenhaftigkeit.

conscious ['kɔnʃəs], *adj.* bewußt (*Genit.*)

consciousness ['kɔnʃəsnis], *s.* das Bewußtsein.

conscript [kən'skript], *v.a.* (*Mil.*) einziehen, einberufen. — ['kɔnskript], *s.* (*Mil.*) der Rekrut, der Dienstpflichtige.

conscription [kən'skripʃən], *s.* die allgemeine Wehrpflicht.

consecrate ['kɔnsikreit], *v.a.* weihen, widmen.

consecrated ['kɔnsikreitid], *adj.* geweiht (*Dat.*).

consecration [kɔnsi'kreiʃən], *s.* die Weihe, Einweihung (*of church*); die Weihung.

consecutive [kən'sekjutiv], *adj.* aufeinanderfolgend, fortlaufend.

consecutiveness [kən'sekjutivnis], *s.* die Aufeinanderfolge.

consent [kən'sent], *v.n.* zustimmen, beistimmen (*to*, *Dat.*). — *s.* die Zustimmung, die Einwilligung.

consequence ['kɔnsikwəns], *s.* die Konsequenz; (*Log.*) Folgerung; die Folge; die Wichtigkeit (*importance*).

consequent ['kɔnsikwənt], *adj.* folgend, nachfolgend.

consequential [kɔnsi'kwenʃəl], *adj.* wichtigtuend, anmaßend; (*Log.*) folgerichtig.

consequently ['kɔnsikwəntli], *adv.* folglich, infolgedessen.

conservatism [kən'sə:vətizm], *s.* (*Pol.*) der Konservatismus; die konservative Denkweise.

conservative [kən'sə:vətiv], *adj.* (*Pol.*) konservativ.

conservatoire [kən'sə:vətwa:], *s.* (*Mus.*) das Konservatorium, die Musikhochschule.

conservatory [kən'sə:vətəri], *s.* (*Bot.*) das Gewächshaus.

conserve [kən'sə:v], *v.a.* konservieren, erhalten, bewahren. — *s.* (*fruit*) das Eingemachte.

consider [kən'sidə], *v.a.* betrachten, in Betracht ziehen (*think over*, *look at*); berücksichtigen (*have regard to*); nachdenken über (*Acc.*) (*ponder*).

considerable [kən'sidərəbl], adj. beträchtlich, ansehnlich.

considerate [kən'sidərit], adj. rücksichtsvoll (thoughtful).

consideration [kənsidə'reiʃən], s. die Betrachtung (contemplation); die Rücksicht (regard) (for, auf, Acc.); die Entschädigung (compensation); die Belohnung (reward).

considering [kən'sidəriŋ], prep. in Anbetracht (Genit.).

consign [kən'sain], v.a. überliefern (hand over); übersenden (remit).

consignee [kɔnsai'ni:], s. (Comm.) der Empfänger, der Adressat (recipient).

consigner [kən'sainə], s. der Absender (of goods).

consignment [kən'sainmənt], s. die Sendung (of goods).

consist [kən'sist], v.n. bestehen (of, aus, Dat.).

consistency [kən'sistənsi], s. die Festigkeit, Dichtigkeit; (Chem.) die Konsistenz.

consistent [kən'sistənt], adj. konsequent; — with, übereinstimmend, gemäß (Dat.); (Chem.) dicht, fest.

consistory [kən'sistəri], s. (Eccl.) das Konsistorium.

consolable [kən'souləbl], adj. tröstlich, zu trösten.

consolation [kɔnso'leiʃən], s. der Trost; draw —, Trost schöpfen.

console (1) [kən'soul], v.a. trösten.

console (2) ['kɔnsoul], s. (Archit.) die Konsole.

consolidate [kən'sɔlideit], v.a. befestigen, konsolidieren. — v.n. fest werden.

consolidation [kənsɔli'deiʃən], s. die Befestigung; Festigung, Bestärkung (confirmation).

consonance ['kɔnsənəns], s. (Phonet.) die Konsonanz; der Einklang, die Harmonie.

consonant ['kɔnsənənt], adj. in Einklang (with, mit, Dat.). — s. der Konsonant.

consort ['kɔnsɔ:t], s. der Gemahl, Gatte; die Gemahlin, die Gattin. — [kən'sɔ:t], v.n. verkehren (with, mit, Dat.).

conspicuous [kən'spikjuəs], adj. auffallend, deutlich sichtbar, hervorragend.

conspiracy [kən'spirəsi], s. die Verschwörung.

conspirator [kən'spirətə], s. der Verschwörer.

conspire [kən'spaiə], v.n. sich verschwören.

constable ['kʌnstəbl], s. der Polizist, der Schutzmann.

Constance ['kɔnstəns]. Konstanze f. (name); Konstanz (town); Lake —, der Bodensee.

constancy ['kɔnstənsi], s. die Beständigkeit, Treue.

constant ['kɔnstənt], adj. (Chem.) konstant; treu, beständig.

constellation [kɔnste'leiʃən], s. die Konstellation; das Sternbild.

consternation [kɔnstə'neiʃən], s. die Bestürzung.

constipation [kɔnsti'peiʃən], s. die Verstopfung.

constituency [kən'stitjuənsi], s. der Wahlkreis (electoral district); die Wählerschaft (voters).

constituent [kən'stitjuənt], adj. wesentlich. — s. der Bestandteil (component); (Pol.) der Wähler.

constitute ['kɔnstitju:t], v.a. ausmachen (make up); bilden (form); festsetzen (establish); (Pol.) errichten (set up).

constitution [kɔnsti'tju:ʃən], s. die Konstitution (physique); die Errichtung (establishment); die Beschaffenheit, Natur (nature); (Pol.) die Verfassung.

constitutional [kɔnsti'tju:ʃənəl], adj. körperlich bedingt; (Pol.) verfassungsmäßig.

constrain [kən'strein], v.a. nötigen, zwingen.

constraint [kən'streint], s. der Zwang.

constrict [kən'strikt], v.a. zusammenziehen.

constriction [kən'strikʃən], s. die Zusammenziehung, Beengtheit.

construct [kən'strʌkt], v.a. errichten, bauen, konstruieren.

construction [kən'strʌkʃən], s. die Errichtung, der Bau, die Konstruktion.

constructive [kən'strʌktiv], adj. (Engin.) konstruktiv; behilflich (positive).

constructor [kən'strʌktə], s. der Konstrukteur, der Erbauer (builder).

construe [kən'stru:], v.a. konstruieren, deuten (interpret).

consul ['kɔnsl], s. der Konsul; — -general, der Generalkonsul.

consular ['kɔnsjulə], adj. konsularisch.

consulate ['kɔnsjulit], s. das Konsulat; — -general, das Generalkonsulat.

consult [kən'sʌlt], v.a. konsultieren, zu Rate ziehen; nachschlagen (a book). — v.n. sich beraten (with, mit, Dat.); (Comm.) als Berater hinzuziehen.

consultant [kən'sʌltənt], s. (Med.) der Facharzt; der Berater.

consultation [kɔnsəl'teiʃən], s. die Beratung (advice); die Besprechung (discussion); (Med., Engin.) die Konsultation.

consume [kən'sju:m], v.a. verzehren (eat up); verbrauchen (use up).

consumer [kən'sju:mə], s. der Verbraucher; (Comm.) der Konsument.

consummate [kən'sʌmit], adj. vollendet. — ['kɔnsəmeit], v.a. vollenden, vollziehen.

consummation [kɔnsə'meiʃən], s. die Vollziehung, Vollendung.

consumption [kən'sʌmpʃən], s. (Comm.) der Verbrauch; (Med.) die Schwindsucht.

consumptive [kən'sʌmptiv], adj. (Med.) schwindsüchtig.

contact [′kɔntækt], *v.a.* berühren (*touch*); in Verbindung treten (mit) (*get into touch (with)*). — *s.* (*Elec.*) der Kontakt; die Berührung (*touch*); die Verbindung (*connexion*).

contagion [kən′teidʒən], *s.* (*Med.*) die Ansteckung.

contagious [kən′teidʒəs], *adj.* ansteckend.

contain [kən′tein], *v.a.* enthalten (*hold*); zurückhalten (*restrain*).

container [kən′teinə], *s.* der Behälter.

contaminate [kən′tæmineit], *v.a.* verunreinigen; vergiften.

contemplate [′kɔntəmpleit], *v.a.* betrachten (*consider*). — *v.n.* nachdenken (*ponder*).

contemplation [kɔntəm′pleiʃən], *s.* die Betrachtung (*consideration*); das Sinnen (*pondering*).

contemplative [kən′templətiv], *adj.* nachdenklich, kontemplativ.

contemporaneous [kɔntempə′reiniəs], *adj.* gleichzeitig.

contemporary [kən′tempərəri], *adj.* zeitgenössisch. — *s.* der Zeitgenosse.

contempt [kən′tempt], *s.* die Verachtung; — *of court*, die Gerichtsbeleidigung.

contemptible [kən′temptibl], *adj.* verächtlich, verachtungswert.

contemptibleness [kən′temptiblnis], *s.* die Verächtlichkeit.

contemptuous [kən′temptjuəs], *adj.* höhnisch, verachtungsvoll.

contemptuousness [kən′temptjuəsnis], *s.* der Hohn, der verachtungsvolle Ton, der Hochmut.

contend [kən′tend], *v.n.* streiten; bestreiten, behaupten.

content [kən′tent], *adj.* ·zufrieden. — *v.a.* zufriedenstellen. — [′kɔntent], *s.* (*often pl.*) der Inhalt.

contented [kən′tentid], *adj.* zufrieden.

contentedness, contentment [kən′tentidnis, kən′tentmənt], *s.* die Zufriedenheit.

contention [kən′tenʃən], *s.* der Streit, die Behauptung.

contentious [kən′tenʃəs], *adj.* streitsüchtig (*person*); strittig (*question*).

contest [′kɔntest], *s.* der Streit, Wettstreit, Wettkampf. — [kən′test], *v.a.* um etwas streiten, bestreiten.

context [′kɔntekst], *s.* der Zusammenhang.

contexture [kən′tekstʃə], *s.* (*Engin.*) der Bau, die Zusammensetzung; das Gewebe (*textile*).

contiguity [kɔnti′gju:iti], *s.* die Berührung; die Nachbarschaft.

contiguous [kən′tigjuəs], *adj.* anstossend, anliegend.

continence [′kɔntinəns], *s.* die Mäßigung (*moderation*); die Enthaltsamkeit (*abstemiousness*).

continent (1) [′kɔntinənt], *adj.* enthaltsam, mässig.

continent (2) [′kɔntinənt], *s.* das Festland, der Kontinent.

contingency [kən′tindʒənsi], *s.* der Zufall; die Möglichkeit (*possibility*).

contingent [kən′tindʒənt], *s.* der Beitrag, das Kontingent (*share*). — *adj.* möglich.

continual [kən′tinjuəl], *adj.* fortwährend, beständig.

continuance [kən′tinjuəns], *s.* die Fortdauer.

continuation [kəntinju′eiʃən], *s.* die Fortsetzung.

continue [kən′tinju:], *v.a.* fortsetzen (*go on with*); verlängern (*prolong*). — *v.n.* weitergehen, weiterführen (*of story*).

continuity [kɔnti′nju:iti], *s.* der Zusammenhang, die ununterbrochene Folge, Kontinuität (*Film*); — *girl*, die Drehbuchsekretärin.

continuous [kən′tinjuəs], *adj.* zusammenhängend, ununterbrochen, andauernd.

contort [kən′tɔ:t], *v.a.* verdrehen.

contortion [kən′tɔ:ʃən], *s.* die Verdrehung, Verkrümmung, Verzerrung.

contortionist [kən′tɔ:ʃənist], *s.* der Schlangenmensch.

contour [′kɔntuə], *s.* die Kontur, der Umriß.

contraband [′kɔntrəbænd], *adj.* Schmuggel-, geschmuggelt. — *s.* die Bannware, Schmuggelware.

contract [kən′trækt], *v.a.* zusammenziehen (*pull together*); verengen (*narrow down*); verkürzen (*shorten*); sich eine Krankheit zuziehen (— *a disease*); Schulden machen (— *debts*). — *v.n.* sich zusammenziehen, kürzer werden; einen Kontrakt abschließen (*come to terms*). — [′kɔntrækt], *s.* der Vertrag (*pact*); (*Comm.*) der Kontrakt.

contraction [kən′trækʃən], *s.* die Zusammenziehung; (*Phonet.*) die Kürzung.

contractor [kən′træktə], *s.* (*Comm.*) der Kontrahent; der Lieferant (*supplier*); *building* —, der Bauunternehmer.

contradict [kɔntrə′dikt], *v.n.* widersprechen (*Dat.*).

contradiction [kɔntrə′dikʃən], *s.* der Widerspruch.

contradictory [kɔntrə′diktəri], *adj.* in Widerspruch stehend, widersprechend.

contrarily [′kɔntrərili], *adv.* im Gegensatz dazu, hingegen, dagegen.

contrary [′kɔntrəri], *adj.* entgegengesetzt, *on the* —, im Gegenteil; [kən′trɛəri], widersprechend.

contrast [kən′trɑ:st], *v.a.* einander entgegenstellen, gegenüberstellen. — *v.n.* einen Gegensatz darstellen *or* bilden. — [′kɔntrɑ:st], *s.* der Kontrast (*colours*); der Gegensatz.

contravene [kɔntrə′vi:n], *v.a.* übertreten, zuwiderhandeln (*Dat.*).

contribute [kən′tribju:t], *v.a.* beitragen; beisteuern (*money, energy*).

contribution [kɔntri′bju:ʃən], *s.* der Beitrag.

contributive

contributive, contributory [kǝn'tribjutiv, kǝn'tribjutǝri], *adj.* beitragend, Beitrags-.

contributor [kǝn'tribjutǝ], *s.* der Beitragende, der Spender (*of money*); der Mitarbeiter (*journalist etc.*).

contrite [‘kɔntrait], *adj.* zerknirscht, reuevoll.

contrition [kǝn'triʃǝn], *s.* die Zerknirschung, die Reue.

contrivance [kǝn'traivǝns], *s.* die Vorrichtung, die Erfindung.

contrive [kǝn'traiv], *v.a.* ausdenken, erfinden; fertigbringen (*accomplish*).

control [kǝn'troul], *v.a.* kontrollieren (*check*); die Leitung haben (*have command of*); die Aufsicht führen (*supervise*). — *s.* die Kontrolle; die Aufsicht; die Leitung; (*pl.*) (*Motor.*) die Steuerung; (*Aviat.*) das Leitwerk.

controller [kǝn'troulǝ], *s.* der Aufseher (*supervisor*); der Direktor (*of corporation*); der Revisor (*examiner, auditor*).

controversial [kɔntro'vǝːʃǝl], *adj.* umstritten, strittig.

controversy [‘kɔntrovǝːsi], *s.* die Kontroverse, die Streitfrage.

controvert [‘kɔntrovǝːt], *v.a.* bestreiten, widersprechen (*Dat.*).

contumacious [kɔntju'meiʃǝs], *adj.* widerspenstig, halsstarrig.

contumacy [‘kɔntjumǝsi], *s.* die Widerspenstigkeit (*obstreperousness*); der Ungehorsam (*disobedience*).

contumelious [kɔntju'miːliǝs], *adj.* frech, unverschämt (*insolent*).

contuse [kǝn'tjuːz], *v.a.* quetschen.

conundrum [kǝ'nʌndrǝm], *s.* das Scherzrätsel.

convalescence [kɔnvǝ'lesǝns], *s.* die Gesundung, die Genesung.

convalescent [kɔnvǝ'lesǝnt], *adj.* genesend. — *s.* der Genesende, der Rekonvaleszent.

convene [kǝn'viːn], *v.a.* zusammenrufen, versammeln. — *v.n.* zusammentreten, sich versammeln.

convenience [kǝn'viːniǝns], *s.* die Bequemlichkeit; *at your early* —, umgehend; *public* —, öffentliche Bedürfnisanstalt.

convenient [kǝn'viːniǝnt], *adj.* bequem, gelegen; passend (*time*).

convent [‘kɔnvǝnt], *s.* das (Nonnen)-Kloster.

convention [kǝn'venʃǝn], *s.* die Konvention, der Kongress (*meeting*); der Vertrag (*treaty*); die Sitte (*tradition, custom*).

conventional [kǝn'venʃǝnǝl], *adj.* herkömmlich, traditionell.

conventual [kǝn'ventjuǝl], *adj.* klösterlich.

conversation [kɔnvǝ'seiʃǝn], *s.* die Konversation, Unterhaltung; das Gespräch.

conversational [kɔnvǝ'seiʃǝnǝl], *adj.* gesprächig, umgangssprachlich.

converse (1) [kǝn'vǝːs], *v.n.* sich unterhalten (*with*, mit, *Dat.*).

converse (2) [‘kɔnvǝːs], *adj.* umgekehrt.

conversely [‘kɔnvǝːsli], *adv.* hingegen, dagegen.

conversion [kǝn'vǝːʃǝn], *s.* die Umkehrung (*reversal*); (*Rel.*) die Bekehrung; (*Comm.*) die Umwechslung.

convert [‘kɔnvǝːt], *s.* (*Rel.*) der Bekehrte, die Bekehrte; der Konvertit. — [kǝn'vǝːt], *v.a.* (*Rel.*) bekehren; (*Comm.*) umwechseln.

converter [kǝn'vǝːtǝ], *s.* (*Rel.*) der Bekehrer; (*Metall., Elec.*) der Umformer.

convertible [kǝn'vǝːtibl], *adj.* umwandelbar. — *s.* (*Motor.*) der *or* das Konvertible.

convex [‘kɔnveks], *adj.* (*Phys.*) konvex.

convey [kǝn'vei], *v.a.* transportieren; führen (*bear, carry*); mitteilen (*impart*).

conveyance [kǝn'veiǝns], *s.* die Beförderung (*transport*); das Fuhrwerk (*vehicle*); die Übertragung; (*Law*) das Übertragungsdokument.

conveyancing [kǝn'veiǝnsiŋ], *s.* (*Law*) die legale *or* rechtliche Übertragung.

convict [‘kɔnvikt], *s.* der Sträfling. — [kǝn'vikt], *v.a.* für schuldig erklären.

conviction [kǝn'vikʃǝn], *s.* die Überzeugung; (*Law*) die Überführung, die Schuldigsprechung.

convince [kǝn'vins], *v.a.* überzeugen.

convivial [kǝn'viviǝl], *adj.* gesellig (*sociable*).

conviviality [kǝnvivi'æliti], *s.* die Geselligkeit.

convocation [kɔnvǝ'keiʃǝn], *s.* die Zusammenberufung, Festversammlung; (*Eccl.*) die Synode.

convoke [kǝn'vouk], *v.a.* zusammenberufen.

convolvulus [kǝn'vɔlvjulǝs], *s.* (*Bot.*) die Winde.

convoy [‘kɔnvɔi], *s.* das Geleit, die Bedeckung; (*Mil.*) der Begleitzug. — [kǝn'vɔi], *v.a.* geleiten; (*Mil.*) im Geleitzug mitführen.

convulse [kǝn'vʌls], *v.a.* erschüttern.

convulsion [kǝn'vʌlʃǝn], *s.* der Krampf, die Zuckung.

convulsive [kǝn'vʌlsiv], *adj.* krampfhaft, zuckend.

coo [kuː], *v.n.* girren (*of birds*); *bill and* —, schnäbeln.

cook [kuk], *v.a., v.n.* kochen; (*coll.*) — *the books*, die Bücher(Bilanz)fälschen *or* frisieren. — *s.* der Koch, die Köchin; *too many cooks* (*spoil the broth*), zu viele Köche (verderben den Brei).

cookery [‘kukǝri], *s.* die Kochkunst; — *school*, die Kochschule.

cool [kuːl], *adj.* kühl (*climate*); kaltblütig (*coldblooded*); unverschämt (*brazen*). — *s.* die Kühle. — *v.a.* abkühlen; (*fig.*) besänftigen. — *v.n.* sich abkühlen.

cooler [‘kuːlǝ], *s.* (*Chem.*) das Kühlfaß; (*coll.*) das Gefängnis; (*sl.*) das Kittchen.

coop [ku:p], s. die Kufe; das Faß; *hen* —, der Hühnerkorb. — *v.a.* — *up*, einsperren.

cooper ['ku:pə], s. der Böttcher, der Faßbinder.

cooperate [kou'ɔpəreit], *v.n.* zusammenarbeiten; mitarbeiten, mitwirken.

cooperation [kouɔpə'reiʃən], s. die Zusammenarbeit, die Mitarbeit.

cooperative [kou'ɔpərətiv], *adj.* willig; mitwirkend. — s. die Konsumgenossenschaft, der Konsum.

coordinate [kou'ɔ:dineit], *v.a.* koordinieren, beiordnen. — [-nit], *adj.* (*Gram.*) koordiniert.

coordination [kouɔ:di'neiʃən], s. die Koordinierung.

coot [ku:t], s. (*Orn.*) das Wasserhuhn.

copartnership [kou'pɑ:tnəʃip], s. die Teilhaberschaft; die Partnerschaft in der Industrie.

cope (1) [koup], s. (*Eccl.*) das Pluviale, der Priesterrock; (*Build.*) die Decke.

cope (2) [koup], *v.n.* — *with s.th.*, mit etwas fertig werden, es schaffen.

coping [ˈkoupiŋ], s. (*Build.*) die Kappe; — *-stone* or *copestone*, der Firststein, Schlußstein, Kappstein.

copious ['koupiəs], *adj.* reichlich; wortreich (*style*).

copiousness ['koupiəsnis], s. die Reichhaltigkeit, Fülle.

copper ['kɔpə], s. (*Metall.*) das Kupfer; (*sl.*) der Polizist; (*coll.*) der Penny, das Pennystück. — *adj.* kupfern.

copperplate ['kɔpəpleit], s. der Kupferstich (*etching*); (*Typ.*) die Kupferplatte.

coppery ['kɔpəri], *adj.* Kupfer-, kupfern, kupferfarben (*colour*).

coppice, copse ['kɔpis, kɔps], s. das Unterholz, das Dickicht.

copulate ['kɔpjuleit], *v.n.* sich paaren, begatten.

copulation [kɔpju'leiʃən], s. die Paarung; der Beischlaf (*human*).

copy ['kɔpi], *v.a.* kopieren, abschreiben (*write*); imitieren, nachahmen (*imitate*). — s. die Kopie; *carbon* —, die Durchschrift; Abschrift; die Nachahmung (*imitation*); die Fälschung (*forgery*).

copybook ['kɔpibuk], s. das Heft.

copyist ['kɔpiist], s. der Kopist.

coquet, coquette (1) [kɔ'ket], *v.n.* kokettieren.

coquette (2) [kɔ'ket], s. die Kokette.

coquettish [kɔ'ketiʃ], *adj.* kokett.

coral ['kɔrəl], s. die Koralle. — *adj.* Korallen-.

cord [kɔ:d], s. die Schnur, der Strick (*rope*); (*Am.*) der Bindfaden (*string*); die Klafter (*wood measure*); der Kordstoff (*textile*); *vocal* —, das Stimmband.

cordage ['kɔ:didʒ], s. (*Naut.*) das Tauwerk.

cordial (1) ['kɔ:diəl], *adj.* herzlich.

cordial (2) ['kɔ:diəl], s. der Fruchtsaft (konzentriert), Magenlikör.

cordiality [kɔ:di'æliti], s. die Herzlichkeit.

corduroy ['kɔ:djurɔi], s. der Kordsamt.

core [kɔ:], s. der Kern; das Innere (*innermost part*).

cork [kɔ:k], s. der Kork, der Korken. — *v.a.* verkorken.

corkscrew ['kɔ:kskru:], s. der Korkzieher.

cormorant ['kɔ:mərənt], s. (*Orn.*) der Kormoran, die Scharbe.

corn (1) [kɔ:n], s. das Korn, das Getreide (*wheat etc.*); (*Am.*) *sweet* —, der Mais.

corn (2) [kɔ:n], s. das Hühnerauge (*on foot*).

corned [kɔ:nd], *adj.* eingesalzt; — *beef*, das Pökelrindfleisch.

cornea ['kɔ:niə], s. (*Anat.*) die Hornhaut.

cornel-tree ['kɔ:nəltri:], s. (*Bot.*) der Kornelkirschbaum.

cornelian [kɔ:'ni:liən], s. (*Geol.*) der Karneol.

corner ['kɔ:nə], s. die Ecke; (*Footb.*) der Eckstoß. — *v.a.* in eine Ecke treiben; in die Enge treiben (*force*).

cornered [kɔ:'nəd], *adj.* eckig (*angular*); in die Enge getrieben, gefangen (*caught*).

cornet ['kɔ:nit], s. (*Mus.*) die Zinke, das Flügelhorn; (*Mil.*) der Kornett, der Fähnrich.

cornflower ['kɔ:nflauə], s. (*Bot.*) die Kornblume.

cornice ['kɔ:nis], s. (*Archit.*) das Gesims.

cornucopia [kɔ:nju'koupjə], s. das Füllhorn.

corollary [kə'rɔləri], s. (*Log.*) der Folgesatz; die Folgeerscheinung (*consequence*).

corona [kə'rounə], s. (*Astron.*) der Hof, Lichtkranz.

coronation [kɔrə'neiʃən], s. die Krönung.

coroner ['kɔrənə], s. der Leichenbeschauer.

coronet ['kɔrənet], s. die Adelskrone.

corporal (1) ['kɔ:pərəl], s. (*Mil.*) der Korporal, der Unteroffizier, Obergefreite.

corporal (2) ['kɔ:pərəl], *adj.* körperlich; — *punishment*, die Züchtigung.

corporate ['kɔ:pərit], *adj.* (*Law, Comm.*) als Körperschaft; gemeinschaftlich, einheitlich (*as a group or unit.*)

corporation [kɔ:pə'reiʃən], s. (*Law, Comm.*) die Körperschaft; die Korporation; die Gemeinde (*municipal*); (*sl.*) der Schmerbauch (*stoutness*).

corps [kɔ:], s. das Korps.

corpse [kɔ:ps], s. der Leichnam.

corpulence ['kɔ:pjuləns], s. die Korpulenz, die Beleibtheit.

corpulent ['kɔ:pjulənt], *adj.* korpulent, dick.

Corpus Christi ['kɔ:pəs 'kristi], (der) Fronleichnam, das Fronleichnamsfest.

corpuscle ['kɔ:pʌsl], s. (*Anat.*) das Körperchen.

correct [kə'rekt], *v.a.* korrigieren (*remove mistakes*); verbessern; tadeln (*reprove*); berichtigen (*rectify*). — *adj.* korrekt, tadellos, richtig.

correction [kə'rekʃən], *s.* die Korrektur (*of mistakes*); die Verbesserung (*improvement*); die Richtigstellung (*restoration*); der Verweis (*censure*).

corrective [kə'rektiv], *adj.* zur Besserung. — *s.* das Korrektiv.

correctness [kə'rektnis], *s.* die Korrektheit (*of manner, action etc.*).

corrector [kə'rektə], *s.* der Korrektor (*proof reader etc.*).

correlate ['kɔrileit], *v.a.* in Beziehung setzen, aufeinander beziehen. — [-lit], *s.* (*Log.*) das Korrelat.

correlative [kɔ'relativ], *adj.* in Wechselbeziehung stehend.

correspond [kɔris'pɔnd], *v.n.* korrespondieren (*exchange letters*); entsprechen (*to, Dat.*).

correspondence [kɔris'pɔndəns], *s.* die Korrespondenz; der Briefwechsel (*letters*); die Übereinstimmung (*harmony*).

correspondent [kɔris'pɔndənt], *s.* der Korrespondent (*letter-writer*); der Journalist, Berichterstatter (*newspaper*).

corridor ['kɔridɔ:], *s.* der Korridor; der Gang.

corrigible ['kɔridʒibl], *adj.* verbesserlich.

corroborate [kə'rɔbəreit], *v.a.* bestätigen (*confirm*); bestärken (*strengthen*).

corroboration [kərɔbə'reiʃən], *s.* die Bestätigung, die Bekräftigung.

corroborative [kə'rɔbərətiv], *adj.* bekräftigend.

corrode [kə'roud], *v.a.* zerfressen, zersetzen, ätzen (*acid*).

corrosion [kə'rouʒən], *s.* die Anfressung, Ätzung.

corrosive [kə'rouziv], *adj.* ätzend.

corrugated ['kɔrugeitid], *adj.* gewellt, Well-; — *iron*, das Wellblech; — *paper*, die Wellpappe.

corrupt [kə'rʌpt], *v.a.* verderben (*spoil*); bestechen (*bribe*). — *adj.* korrupt (*morals*); verdorben (*spoilt*).

corruptible [kə'rʌptibl], *adj.* verderblich; bestechlich.

corruption [kə'rʌpʃən], *s.* die Korruption; die Bestechung (*bribery*).

corruptness [kə'rʌptnis], *s.* die Verdorbenheit, der Verfall.

corsair ['kɔ:sɛə], *s.* der Korsar, der Seeräuber.

corset ['kɔ:sit], *s.* das Korsett.

coruscate [kɔrəskeit], *v.n.* schimmern, leuchten.

corvette [kɔ:'vet], *s.* (*Naut.*) die Korvette.

cosine ['kousain], *s.* (*Maths.*) der Kosinus.

cosiness ['kouzinis], *s.* die Bequemlichkeit, die Behaglichkeit (*comfort*).

cosmetic [kɔz'metik], *adj.* kosmetisch. — *s.* (*pl.*) das *or* die (*pl.*) Schönheitsmittel.

cosmic ['kɔzmik], *adj.* kosmisch.

cosmopolitan [kɔzmo'pɔlitən], *adj.* kosmopolitisch, weltbürgerlich. — *s.* der Kosmopolit, der Weltbürger.

Cossack ['kɔsæk], *s.* der Kosak.

cost [kɔst], *v.a. irr.* kosten. — *v.n. irr.* zu stehen kommen. — *s.* die Kosten, *f. pl.* (*expenses*); *at all* —*s*, um jeden Preis.

costermonger ['kɔstəmʌŋgə], *s.* der Straßenhändler.

costly ['kɔstli], *adj.* kostspielig.

costume ['kɔstju:m], *s.* das Kostüm; — *play*, das Zeitstück.

cosy ['kouzi], *adj.* behaglich, bequem.

cot (1) [kɔt], *s.* das Bettchen, Kinderbett.

cot (2) [kɔt], *s.* (*obs.*) die Hütte (*hut*).

cottage ['kɔtidʒ], *s.* die Hütte, das Häuschen.

cottager ['kɔtidʒə], *s.* der Kleinhäusler.

cotton [kɔtn], *s.* die Baumwolle. — *v.n.* — *on to*, (*coll.*) sich anhängen, sich anschließen (*Dat.*); — *on*, folgen können (*understand*).

couch [kautʃ], *s.* die Chaiselongue; der Diwan. — *v.a.* (*express*) in .Worte fassen.

cough [kɔf], *v.n.* husten. — *s.* der Husten; *whooping* —, der Keuchhusten.

council ['kaunsil], *s.* der Rat (*body*); die Ratsversammlung.

councillor ['kaunsilə], *s.* der Rat, das Ratsmitglied; der Stadtrat.

counsel ['kaunsəl], *s.* der Rat (*advice*); der Berater (*adviser*); der Anwalt (*lawyer*). — *v.a.* einen Rat geben, beraten (*Acc.*).

counsellor ['kaunsələ], *s.* der Ratgeber; der Ratsherr; (*Am.*) der Anwalt (*lawyer*).

count (1) [kaunt], *v.a.,v.n.* zählen; — *on s.o.*, sich auf jemanden verlassen. — *s.* die Zählung.

count (2) [kaunt], *s.* der Graf.

countenance ['kauntənəns], *s.* das Gesicht, die Miene. — *v.a.* begünstigen, unterstützen, zulassen.

counter (1) ['kauntə], *s.* der Rechner, der Zähler (*chip*); die Spielmarke; der Zahltisch (*desk*); Ladentisch (*in shop*); Schalter (*in office*).

counter (2) ['kauntə], *adv.* entgegen.

counteract [kauntə'rækt], *v.a.* entgegenwirken (*Dat.*).

counteraction [kauntə'rækʃən], *s.* die Gegenwirkung; der Widerstand (*resistance*).

counterbalance ['kauntəbæləns], *s.* das Gegengewicht. — [-'bæləns], *v.a.* ausbalancieren, ausgleichen.

countercharge ['kauntətʃɑ:dʒ], *s.* die Gegenklage.

counterfeit ['kauntəfi:t, -fit], *s.* die Fälschung (*forgery*); die Nachahmung (*imitation*). — *adj.* gefälscht, falsch.

counterfoil ['kauntəfɔil], s. das Kontrollblatt; der Kupon.

counter–intelligence ['kauntərintelidʒəns], s. die Spionageabwehr.

countermand [kauntə'mɑːnd], v.a. widerrufen.

counterpane ['kauntəpein], s. die Steppdecke.

counterpart ['kauntəpɑːt], s. das Gegenbild, das Gegenstück.

counterplot ['kauntəplɔt], s. der Gegenplan. — v.n. einen Gegenplan machen.

counterpoint ['kauntəpɔint], s. (Mus.) der Kontrapunkt.

counterpoise ['kauntəpɔiz], s. das Gegengewicht. — v.a. das Gleichgewicht halten.

countersign ['kauntəsain], v.a. gegenzeichnen, mitunterschreiben. — s. das Gegenzeichen.

countess ['kauntes], s. die Gräfin.

counting-house ['kauntiŋhaus], s. das Kontor.

countless ['kauntlis], adj. zahllos.

country ['kʌntri], s. das Land. — adj. Land-, ländlich, Bauern-.

county ['kaunti], s. die Grafschaft (British); der Landbezirk (U.S.A.).

couple [kʌpl], s. das Paar. — v.a. paaren, verbinden. — v.n. sich paaren (pair); sich verbinden.

couplet ['kʌplit], s. das Verspaar.

coupling ['kʌpliŋ], s. (Mech.) die Kupplung.

courage ['kʌridʒ], s. der Mut.

courageous [kə'reidʒəs], adj. mutig, tapfer.

courier ['kuriə], s. der Eilbote (messenger); der Reisebegleiter (tour leader).

course [kɔːs], s. der Kurs; der Lauf (time); der Ablauf (lapse of a period etc.); die Bahn (racing track); in due —, zu gegebener Zeit; of —, natürlich.

courser ['kɔːsə], s. das schnelle Pferd.

court [kɔːt], s. der Hof (royal etc.); (Law) der Gerichtshof. — v.a. (a lady) den Hof machen (Dat.); — disaster, das Unglück herausfordern.

courteous ['kəːtiəs], adj. höflich.

courtesan ['kɔːtizən or kɔːti'zæn], s. die Kurtisane, die Buhlerin.

courtesy ['kəːtəsi], s. die Höflichkeit; by — of, mit freundlicher Erlaubnis von.

courtier ['kɔːtiə], s. der Höfling.

courtly ['kɔːtli], adj. höfisch, Hof-.

court-martial [kɔːt'mɑːʃəl], s. das Kriegsgericht.

courtship ['kɔːtʃip], s. das Werben, die Werbung, das Freien.

courtyard ['kɔːtjɑːd], s. der Hof, der Hofraum.

cousin [kʌzn], s. der Vetter (male); die Kusine (female).

cove [kouv], s. die (kleine) Bucht.

covenant ['kʌvənənt], s. (Bibl.) der Bund; (Comm.) der Vertrag.

cover ['kʌvə], v.a. decken, bedecken (table etc.); schützen (protect); — up, bemänteln. — s. die Decke (blanket); der Deckel (lid); der Einband (book); das Gedeck (table); (Comm.) die Deckung; — point, (Cricket) die Deckstellung; under —, (Mil.) verdeckt, unter Deckung; — girl, das Mädchen auf dem Titelblatt (einer Illustrierten).

covering ['kʌvəriŋ], s. die Bedeckung, die Bekleidung (clothing).

coverlet, coverlid ['kʌvəlit, 'kʌvəlid], s. die Bettdecke.

covert ['kʌvəːt], s. der Schlupfwinkel (hideout); das Dickicht (thicket). — adj. verborgen, bedeckt (covered); heimlich (secret).

covet ['kʌvit], v.a., v.n. begehren (Acc.), gelüsten (nach (Dat.)).

covetous ['kʌvitəs], adj. begierig, habsüchtig.

covetousness ['kʌvitəsnis], s. die Begierde, die Habsucht.

covey ['kʌvi], s. der Flug or die Kette (Rebhühner, partridges).

cow (1) [kau], s. die Kuh; — — shed, der Kuhstall.

cow (2) [kau], v.a. einschüchtern.

coward ['kauəd], s. der Feigling.

cowardice ['kauədis], s. die Feigheit.

cower ['kauə], v.n. sich kauern.

cowherd ['kauhəːd], s. der Kuhhirt.

cowl [kaul], s. die Kappe (of monk), die Kapuze (hood).

cowslip ['kauslip], s. (Bot.) die Primel, die Schlüsselblume.

coxswain [kɔksn], s. (Naut.) der Steuermann.

coy [kɔi], adj. scheu, spröde, zurückhaltend.

coyness ['kɔinis], s. die Sprödigkeit.

crab [kræb], s. (Zool.) die Krabbe; — apple, (Bot.) der Holzapfel.

crabbed ['kræbd], adj. mürrisch (temper); unleserlich (handwriting).

crack [kræk], s. der Riß (fissure); der Krach, Schlag; der Sprung; die komische Bemerkung (remark). — adj. (coll.) erstklassig; — shot, der Meisterschütze. — v.a. aufbrechen; aufknacken (nut, safe); — a joke, eine witzige Bemerkung machen. — v.n. — under strain, unter einer Anstrengung zusammenbrechen; bersten (break).

cracked, crackers [krækd, 'krækəz], adj. (coll.) verrückt.

cracker ['krækə], s. der Keks; der Frosch (firework).

crackle [krækl], v.n. knistern, prasseln (fire); knallen, platzen (rocket).

cracknel ['kræknəl], s. die Brezel.

crackpot ['krækpɔt], s. (coll.) der verrückte Kerl.

cradle [kreidl], s. die Wiege. — v.a. einwiegen.

craft [krɑːft], s. die Fertigkeit (skill); das Handwerk (trade); die List (cunning); arts and —s, die Handwerkskünste.

craftsman [′krɑːftsmən], *s.* der (gelernte) Handwerker.

crafty [′krɑːfti], *adj.* listig, schlau.

crag [kræg], *s.* die Klippe.

cragged, **craggy** [krægd, ′krægi], *adj.* felsig, schroff.

cram [kræm], *v.a.* vollstopfen (*stuff full*); (*coll.*) pauken (*coach*). — *v.n.* büffeln.

crammer [′kræmə], *s.* (*coll.*) der Einpauker, Privatlehrer (*tutor*).

cramp [kræmp], *s.* (*Med.*) der Krampf; die Klammer (*tool*). — *v.a.* einengen (*narrow*); verkrampfen.

cramped [kræmpd], *adj.* krampfhaft; eingeengt, beengt (*enclosed*).

cranberry [′krænbəri], *s.* (*Bot.*) die Preiselbeere.

crane [krein], *s.* (*Orn.*) der Kranich; (*Engin.*) der Kran. — *v.a.* — *o.'s neck*, den Hals ausrecken.

crank (1) [kræŋk], *s.* (*Motor.*) die Kurbel; — *handle*, die Andrehwelle; (*Motor.*, *Engin.*) — *shaft*, die Kurbelwelle, die Kurbel.

crank (2) [kræŋk], *s.* der Sonderling, der sonderbare Kauz (*eccentric*).

cranky [′kræŋki], *adj.* sonderbar.

cranny [′kræni], *s.* der Spalt, der Riß; *nook and* —, Eck und Spalt.

crape [kreip], *s.* der Krepp, Flor.

crash [kræʃ], *s.* der Krach; (*Motor.*) Zusammenstoß; (*Aviat.*) Absturz. — *v.n.* krachen (*noise*); stürzen, abstürzen (*fall*).

crass [kræs], *adj.* derb, grob, kraß.

crate [kreit], *s.* der Packkorb (*basket*); die Kiste (*wood*).

crater [′kreitə], *s.* (*Geol.*) der Krater.

cravat [krə′væt], *s.* die breite Halsbinde, das Halstuch (*scarf*); die Krawatte.

crave [kreiv], *v.a.* (dringend) verlangen (*for*, nach, *Dat.*).

craven [kreivn], *adj.* feig, mutlos. — *s.* der Feigling.

craving [′kreivin], *s.* das starke Verlangen.

craw [krɔː], *s.* (*Zool.*) der Vogelkropf.

crawl [krɔːl], *v.n.* kriechen; kraulen (*swim*).

crawling [′krɔːliŋ], *s.* das Kriechen; das Kraulschwimmen.

crayon [′kreiən], *s.* der Farbstift, der Pastellstift.

craze [kreiz], *s.* die Manie; die verrückte Mode (*fashion*).

craziness [′kreizinis], *s.* die Verrücktheit.

crazy [′kreizi], *adj.* verrückt.

creak [kriːk], *v.n.* knarren.

cream [kriːm], *s.* der Rahm, die Sahne; *whipped* —, die Schlagsahne, (*Austr.*) der Schlagobers. — *v.a.* — *off*, (die Sahne) abschöpfen; (*fig.*) das Beste abziehen.

creamery [′kriːməri], *s.* die Molkerei.

creamy [′kriːmi], *adj.* sahnig.

crease [kriːs], *s.* die Falte (*trousers etc.*); — *resistant*, knitterfrei. — *v.a.* falten (*fold*). — *v.n.* knittern.

create [kri′eit], *v.a.* erschaffen, schaffen.

creation [kri′eiʃən], *s.* die Schöpfung.

creative [kri′eitiv], *adj.* schöpferisch.

creator [kri′eitə], *s.* der Schöpfer.

creature [′kriːtʃə], *s.* das Geschöpf.

credence [′kriːdəns], *s.* der Glaube.

credentials [kri′denʃəlz], *s.* *pl.* das Zeugnis, das Beglaubigungsschreiben; die Legitimation (*proof of identity*).

credibility [kredi′biliti], *s.* die Glaubwürdigkeit.

credible [′kredibl], *adj.* glaubwürdig, glaublich.

credit [′kredit], *s.* (*Comm.*) der Kredit; der gute Ruf (*reputation*); das Guthaben (*assets*). — *v.a.* — *s.o. with s.th.*, jemandem etwas gutschreiben; glauben (*believe*).

creditable [′kreditəbl], *adj.* ehrenwert, lobenswert.

creditor [′kreditə], *s.* (*Comm.*) der Gläubiger.

credulity [kre′djuːliti], *s.* die Leichtgläubigkeit.

credulous [′kredjuləs], *adj.* leichtgläubig.

creed [kriːd], *s.* das Glaubensbekenntnis.

creek [kriːk], *s.* die kleine Bucht; das Flüßchen (*small river*).

creel [kriːl], *s.* der Fischkorb.

creep [kriːp], *s.* (*Geol.*) der Rutsch; (*pl.*, *coll.*) *the* —*s*, die Gänsehaut, das Gruseln. — *v.n. irr.* kriechen; (*furtively*) sich einschleichen.

creeper [′kriːpə], *s.* die Schlingpflanze, das Rankengewächs; (*Sch.*) der Kriecher; *Virginia* —, der wilde Wein.

creepy [′kriːpi], *adj.* kriechend; gruselig (*frightening*).

cremate [kri′meit], *v.a.* einäschern.

cremation [kri′meiʃən], *s.* die Verbrennung, Einäscherung.

crematorium, (*Am.*) **crematory** [kreimə′tɔːriəm, ′kremətəri], *s.* das Krematorium.

Creole [′kriːoul], *s.* der Kreole.

crepuscular [kri′pʌskjulə], *adj.* dämmerig.

crescent [′kresənt], *adj.* wachsend, zunehmend. — *s.* der (zunehmende) Mond, die Mondsichel; das Hörnchen.

cress [kres], *s.* (*Bot.*) die Kresse; *mustard and* —, die Gartenkresse.

crest [krest], *s.* der Kamm (*cock*); der Gipfel (*hill*); der Kamm (*wave*); der Busch (*helmet*); das Wappenschild (*Heraldry*).

crestfallen [′krestfɔːlən], *adj.* entmutigt, mutlos, niedergeschlagen.

Cretan [′kriːtən], *adj.* kretisch. — *s.* der Kreter, die Kreterin.

cretonne [′kretən], *s.* die Kretonne.

crevasse [krə′væs], *s.* die Gletscherspalte.

crevice [′krevis], *s.* der Riß.

crew (1) [kruː], *s.* (*Naut.*, *Aviat.*) die Besatzung; (*Naut.*) die Schiffsmannschaft; die Mannschaft (*team*); (*Am.*) — *cut*, die Bürstenfrisur.

crew (2) [kru:] *see* **crow**.

crib [krib], *s.* die Krippe (*Christmas*); die Wiege (*cradle*); (*Sch.*) die Eselsbrücke. — *v.a.* (*Sch.*) abschreiben (*copy*).

crick [krik], *s.* (*in neck*) der steife Hals.

cricket ['krikit], *s.* (*Ent.*) das Heimchen, die Grille; (*Sport*) das Cricket(spiel).

crime [kraim], *s.* das Verbrechen; — *fiction*, die Detektivromane, *m. pl.*

criminal ['kriminəl], *s.* der Verbrecher. — *adj.* — *case*, der Kriminalfall; verbrecherisch (*act*); — *investigation*, die Fahndung.

crimp [krimp], *v.a.* kräuseln (*hair*).

crimson ['krimzən], *adj.* karmesinrot.

cringe [krindʒ], *v.n.* kriechen.

crinkle ['kriŋkl], *v.a., v.n.* kräuseln. — *s.* die Falte.

crinoline ['krinəlin], *s.* der Reifrock.

cripple [kripl], *s.* der Krüppel. — *v.a.* verkrüppeln; lahmlegen (*immobilize*).

crisis ['kraisis], *s.* die Krise, der Wendepunkt; die Notlage.

crisp [krisp], *adj.* kraus (*hair*); knusperig (*bread*); frisch.

criss-cross ['kriskrɔs], *adv.* kreuz und quer.

criterion [krai'tiəriən], *s.* das Kennzeichen, das Kriterium.

critic ['kritik], *s.* der Kritiker; Rezensent (*reviewer*).

critical ['kritikəl], *adj.* kritisch.

criticism ['kritisizm], *s.* die Kritik (*of, an, Dat.*); Rezension, Besprechung (*review*).

criticize ['kritisaiz], *v.a.* kritisieren.

croak [krouk], *v.n.* krächzen (*raven*); quaken (*frog*).

croaking ['kroukiŋ], *s.* das Krächzen, das Gekrächze (*raven*); das Quaken (*frog*).

Croat ['krouæt], *s.* der Kroate.

Croatian [krou'eiʃən], *adj.* kroatisch.

crochet ['krouʃei], *s.* die Häkelei; — *hook*, die Häkelnadel. — *v.a., v.n.* häkeln.

crock [krɔk], *s.* der Topf, der irdene Krug; der alte Topf; (*coll.*) *old* —, der Invalide, Krüppel.

crockery ['krɔkəri], *s.* (*Comm.*) die Töpferware; das Geschirr (*household*).

crocodile ['krɔkədail], *s.* das Krokodil.

crocus ['kroukəs], *s.* (*Bot.*) der Krokus, die Safranblume.

croft [krɔft], *s.* das Kleinbauerngut.

crofter ['krɔftə], *s.* der Kleinbauer.

crone [kroun], *s.* das alte Weib; die Hexe (*witch*).

crony ['krouni], *s.* (*coll.*) *old* —, der alte Freund.

crook [kruk], *s.* der Krummstab (*staff*); der Schwindler (*cheat*). — *v.a.* krümmen, biegen.

crooked ['krukid], *adj.* krumm; (*fig.*) schwindlerisch, verbrecherisch.

crookedness ['krukidnis], *s.* die Krummheit; die Durchtriebenheit (*slyness*).

croon [kru:n], *v.n.* leise singen; (*Am.*) im modernen Stil singen.

crooner ['kru:nə], *s.* der Jazzsänger.

crop [krɔp], *s.* der Kropf (*bird*); die Ernte (*harvest*); der (kurze) Haarschnitt; *riding* —, die Reitpeitsche. — *v.a.* stutzen (*cut short*). — *v.n.* — *up*, auftauchen.

crosier ['krouziə], *s.* (*Eccl.*) der Bischofsstab.

cross [krɔs], *s.* das Kreuz. — *v.a.* (*Zool., Bot.*) kreuzen; überqueren (*road, on foot*); — *s.o.'s path*, einem in die Quere kommen. — *v.n.* überfahren (*übers Wasser*); hinübergehen; — *over*, übersetzen (*on boat or ferry*). — *v.r.* sich bekreuzigen. — *adj.* mürrisch (*grumpy*), verstimmt; *at* — *purposes*, ohne einander zu verstehen; *make* —, verstimmen. — *adv.* kreuzweise; — *-eyed*, schielend; — *-grained*, wider den Strich, schlecht aufgelegt.

crossbow ['krɔsbou], *s.* die Armbrust.

crossbreed ['krɔsbri:d], *s.* die Mischrasse, der Mischling.

cross-examine [krɔsig'zæmin], *v.a., v.n.* (*Law*) ins (Kreuz–)Verhör nehmen.

crossing ['krɔsiŋ], *s.* die Straßenkreuzung; (*Naut.*) die Überfahrt; der Straßenübergang; Kreuzweg.

crossroads ['krɔsroudz], *s.* der Kreuzweg, die Kreuzung.

crossword ['krɔswə:d], *s.* das Kreuzworträtsel.

crotch [krɔtʃ], *s.* der Haken.

crotchet ['krɔtʃit], *s.* (*Mus.*) die Viertelnote; die Grille (*mood*).

crotchety ['krɔtʃiti], *adj.* grillenhaft, verschroben.

crouch [krautʃ], *v.n.* sich ducken (*squat*); sich demütigen (*cringe*).

croup (1) [kru:p], *s.* (*Med.*) der Krupp.

croup (2) [kru:p], *s.* die Kruppe.

crow [krou], *s.* (*Orn.*) die Krähe; das Krähen (*of cock*). — *v.n. irr.* krähen (*cock*).

crowbar ['kroubɑ:], *s.* das Brecheisen.

crowd [kraud], *s.* die Menge (*multitude*); das Gedränge (*throng*). — *v.n.* — *in*, sich hineindrängen, dazudrängen; — *around*, sich herumscharen um (*Acc.*).

crown [kraun], *s.* die Krone (*diadem or coin*); der Gipfel (*mountain*); (*Anat.*) der Scheitel; — *lands*, Krongüter (*n. pl.*), Landeigentum der Krone, *n.*; — *prince*, der Kronprinz; — *of thorns*, die Dornenkrone. — *v.a.* krönen.

crucial ['kru:ʃəl], *adj.* entscheidend, kritisch.

crucifix ['kru:sifiks], *s.* das Kruzifix.

crucify ['kru:sifai], *v.a.* kreuzigen.

crude [kru:d], *adj.* roh, ungekocht, unreif; grob (*manners*), ungeschliffen.

crudity ['kru:diti], *s.* die Rohheit; Grobheit (*manners*).

cruel ['kru:əl], *adj.* grausam.

cruelty ['kru:əlti], *s.* die Grausamkeit.

cruet ['kru:it], *s.* das Salz- *oder* Pfefferfäßchen; das Fläschchen.

cruise [kru:z], *v.n.* (*Naut.*) kreuzen. — *s.* die Seefahrt, die Seereise; *pleasure* —, die Vergnügungsreise (zu Wasser).

cruiser [´kru:zə], *s.* (*Naut.*) der Kreuzer; *battle* —, der Panzerkreuzer.

crumb [krʌm], *s.* die Krume. — *v.a.* zerbröckeln, zerkrümeln.

crumble [krʌmbl], *v.n.* zerfallen, zerbröckeln.

crumpet [´krʌmpit], *s.* das Teebrötchen, das Teeküchlein.

crumple [´krʌmpl], *v.a.* zerknittern (*material*). — *v.n.* — up, zusammenbrechen.

crunch [krʌntʃ], *v.a.* zerstoßen, zermalmen. — *v.n.* knirschen.

crusade [kru:´seid], *s.* der Kreuzzug.

crusader [kru:´seidə], *s.* der Kreuzfahrer.

crush [krʌʃ], *v.a.* zerdrücken; zerstoßen (*pulverize*); drängen (*crowd*); zertreten (*tread down*); (*fig.*) vernichten. — *s.* das Gedränge (*throng*); (*coll.*) have a — on, verknallt sein, in einen verliebt sein.

crust [krʌst], *s.* die Kruste, die Rinde (*bread*). — *v.a.* mit einer Kruste bedecken. — *v.n.* verkrusten.

crustaceous [krʌs´treiʃəs], *adj.* (*Zool.*) krustenartig, Krustentier-.

crusty [´krʌsti], *adj.* krustig, knusperig (*pastry, bread*); mürrisch (*grumpy*).

crutch [krʌtʃ], *s.* die Krücke.

crux [krʌks], *s.* der entscheidende Punkt, der springende Punkt, die Schwierigkeit.

cry [krai], *v.n.* schreien, rufen; weinen (*weep*). — *v.a.* — down, niederschreien. — *s.* der Schrei; der Zuruf (*call*).

crypt [kript], *s.* (*Eccl.*) die Krypta, die Gruft.

crystal [´kristəl], *s.* der Kristall.

crystallize [´kristəlaiz], *v.n.* sich kristallisieren, Kristalle bilden.

cub [kʌb], *s.* (*Zool.*) das Junge. — *v.n.* Junge haben, Junge werfen.

Cuban [´kju:bən], *adj.* kubanisch. — *s.* der Kubaner.

cube [kju:b], *s.* der Würfel; (*Maths.*) — *root*, die Kubikwurzel. — *v.a.* zur Dritten (Potenz) erheben; kubieren.

cubic(al) [´kju:bik(əl)], *adj.* kubisch, zur dritten Potenz.

cubit [´kju:bit], *s.* die Elle.

cuckoo [´kuku:], *s.* (*Orn.*) der Kuckuck.

cucumber [´kju:kʌmbə], *s.* (*Bot.*) die Gurke; *cool as a* —, ruhig und gelassen.

cud [kʌd], *s.* das wiedergekäute Futter; *chew the* —, wiederkauen (*also fig.*).

cuddle [kʌdl], *v.a.* liebkosen, an sich drücken. — *v.n.* sich anschmiegen.

cudgel [´kʌdʒəl], *s.* der Knüttel; *take up the* —s *for*, sich für etwas einsetzen.

cue (1) [kju:], *s.* (*Theat.*) das Stichwort. — *v.a.* einem (*Theat.*) das Stichwort or (*Mus.*) den Einsatz geben.

cue (2) [kju:], *s.* der Billardstock. — *v.a.* (*Billiards*) abschießen.

cuff (1) [kʌf], *s.* die Manschette, der Aufschlag (*shirt*); —*links*, die Manschettenknöpfe.

cuff (2) [kʌf], *s.* der Schlag. — *v.a.* schlagen, puffen.

culinary [´kju:linəri], *adj.* kulinarisch; Küchen-, Eß-, Speisen-.

cull [kʌl], *v.a.* auswählen, auslesen (*from books*).

culminate [´kʌlmineit], *v.n.* kulminieren, den Höhepunkt erreichen.

culpable [´kʌlpəbl], *adj.* schuldig; strafbar.

culprit [´kʌlprit], *s.* der Schuldige, Verbrecher.

cult [kʌlt], *s.* der Kult, die Verehrung; der Kultus.

cultivate [´kʌltiveit], *v.a.* kultivieren; (*Agr.*) anbauen; pflegen (*acquaintance*); bilden (*mind*).

cultivation [kʌlti´veiʃən], *s.* (*Agr.*) der Anbau; die Bildung (*mind*).

culture [´kʌltʃə], *s.* die Kultur, die Bildung.

cumbersome [´kʌmbəsəm], *adj.* beschwerlich, lästig.

cunning [´kʌniŋ], *s.* die List, die Schlauheit. — *adj.* listig, schlau.

cup [kʌp], *s.* die Tasse (*tea*—); der Becher (*handleless*); (*Eccl.*) der Kelch; der Pokal (*sports*); — *final*, das Endspiel. — *v.a.* (*Med.*) schröpfen.

cupboard [´kʌbəd], *s.* der Schrank.

cupola [´kju:pələ], *s.* (*Archit., Metall.*) die Kuppel.

cur [kə:], *s.* der Köter; (*fig.*) der Schurke.

curable [´kjuərəbl], *adj.* heilbar.

curate [´kjuərit], *s.* der Hilfsgeistliche.

curative [´kjuərətiv], *adj.* heilsam, heilend.

curator [kjuə´reitə], *s.* der Kurator, Verwalter, Direktor.

curb [kə:b], *v.a.* zügeln, bändigen. — *s.* der Zaum (*bridle*).

curd [kə:d], *s.* der Rahmkäse, der Milchkäse; (*pl.*) der Quark.

curdle [kə:dl], *v.a.* gerinnen lassen. — *v.n.* gerinnen; erstarren.

cure [kjuə], *s.* die Kur, die Heilung. — *v.a.* kurieren, wieder gesundmachen; einpökeln (*foodstuffs*).

curfew [´kə:fju:], *s.* die Abendglocke (*bells*); das Ausgehverbot, die Polizeistunde (*police*).

curio [´kjuəriou], *s.* die Kuriosität, das Sammlerstück; die Rarität.

curiosity [kjuəri´ositi], *s.* die Neugier; Merkwürdigkeit.

curious [´kjuəriəs], *adj.* neugierig (*inquisitive*); seltsam, sonderbar (*strange*).

curl [kə:l], *v.a.* kräuseln, (in Locken) wickeln. — *v.n.* sich kräuseln. — *s.* die Haarlocke.

curler [´kə:lə], *s.* der Lockenwickler.

curlew [´kə:lju:], *s.* (*Orn.*) der Brachvogel.

curly [´kə:li], *adj.* lockig.

currant [´kʌrənt], *s.* (*Bot.*) die Korinthe, die Johannisbeere.

currency [ˈkʌrənsi], s. die Währung (*money*); der Umlauf (*circulation*).

current [ˈkʌrənt], adj. im Umlauf; allgemein gültig, eben gültig; jetzig (*modern*). — s. (*Elect.*) der Strom; die Strömung (*river*); der Zug (*air*).

curry (1) [ˈkʌri], v.a. gerben (*tan*); — comb, der Pferdestriegel; — favour, sich einschmeicheln.

curry (2) [ˈkʌri], s. das indische Ragout. — v.a. würzen.

curse [kəːs], v.a., — v.n. verfluchen; verwünschen. — s. der Fluch; die Verwünschung.

cursive [ˈkəːsiv], adj. kursiv, Kursiv-.

cursory [ˈkəːsəri], adj. kursorisch, oberflächlich.

curt [kəːt], adj. kurz angebunden (*speech, manner*).

curtail [kəːˈteil], v.a. stutzen, beschränken (*scope*); verkürzen (*time*).

curtain [ˈkəːtin], s. die Gardine; der Vorhang; (*Mil.*) — fire, das Sperrfeuer; — lecture, die Gardinenpredigt; — speech, die Ansprache vor dem Vorhang. — v.a. verhüllen (*hide*); mit Vorhängen versehen (*hang curtains*).

curtness [ˈkəːtnis], s. die Kürze; die Barschheit.

curts(e)y [ˈkəːtsi], s. der Knicks. — v.n. knicksen, einen Knicks machen.

curve [kəːv], s. die Krümmung; (*Geom.*) die Kurve. — v.a. krümmen, biegen. — v.n. sich biegen.

curved [kəːvd], adj. krumm, gebogen.

cushion [ˈkuʃən], s. das Kissen. — v.a. polstern.

custody [ˈkʌstədi], s. die Obhut; Bewachung, Haft.

custom [ˈkʌstəm], s. die Sitte, die Tradition; der Gebrauch, Brauch (*usage*); die Kundschaft (*trade*); (*pl.*) der Zoll (*duty*).

customary [ˈkʌstəməri], adj. gewohnt, althergebracht, gebräuchlich.

customer [ˈkʌstəmə], s. der Kunde, die Kundin.

cut [kʌt], v.a. irr. schneiden; — (*s.o.*) ignorieren; — o.'s teeth, zahnen; this won't — any ice, das wird nicht viel nützen; — both ways, das ist ein zweischneidiges Schwert; — a lecture, eine Vorlesung schwänzen; — short, unterbrechen. — adj. — out for, wie gerufen zu or für; — to the quick, aufs tiefste verletzt; — glass, das geschliffene Glas; — price, verbilligt. — s. der Schnitt (*section*); der Hieb (*gash*); (*Art*) der Stich; — in salary, eine Gehaltskürzung; die Abkürzung, die Kürzung (*abridgement*).

cute [kjuːt], adj. klug, aufgeweckt; (*Am.*) süß, niedlich.

cutler [ˈkʌtlə], s. der Messerschmied.

cutlery [ˈkʌtləri], s. das Besteck (*tableware*); (*Comm.*) die Messerschmiedwaren, f. pl.

cutlet [ˈkʌtlit], s. das Kotelett, das Rippchen.

cut-throat [ˈkʌtθrout], s. der Halsabschneider; — competition, Konkurrenz auf Leben und Tod.

cuttle [kʌtl], s. (*Zool.*) der Tintenfisch.

cyanide [ˈsaiənaid], s. (*Chem.*) zyanidsaures Salz; das Zyanid, die Blausäure.

cyclamen [ˈsikləmən], s. (*Bot.*) das Alpenveilchen.

cycle [saikl], s. (*Geom.*) der Kreis; (*Mus., Zool.*) der Zyklus; (*coll.*) das Fahrrad. — v.n. (*coll.*) radfahren; zirkulieren (*round*, um, *Acc.*).

cyclone [ˈsaikloun], s. der Wirbelwind, der Wirbelsturm.

cyclopaedia [saikloˈpiːdjə] see **encyclopædia**.

cylinder [ˈsilində], s. der Zylinder; die Walze.

cymbal [ˈsimbəl], s. (*Mus.*) die Zimbel, das Becken.

cynic [ˈsinik], s. der Zyniker.

cynical [ˈsinikəl], adj. zynisch.

cypress [ˈsaiprəs], s. (*Bot.*) die Zypresse.

Cypriot [ˈsipriət], adj. zyprisch. — s. der Zypriote.

czar [zɑː], s. der Zar.

Czech, **Czechoslovak(ian)** [tʃek, tʃekoˈslouvæk, tʃekosloˈvækjən], adj. tschechisch. — s. der Tscheche.

D

D [diː]. das D (*also Mus.*).

dab [dæb], v.a. leicht berühren. — s. der leichte Schlag (*blow*).

dabble [dæbl], v.n. sich in etwas versuchen, pfuschen (*in*, in, *Dat.*).

dabbler [ˈdæblə], s. der Pfuscher, Stümper.

dace [deis], s. (*Zool.*) der Weißfisch.

dad, daddy [dæd, ˈdædi], s. der Papa; Vati; daddy longlegs, die Bachmücke, die langbeinige Mücke.

dado [ˈdeidou], s. die Täfelung.

daffodil [ˈdæfədil], s. (*Bot.*) die Narzisse.

dagger [ˈdægə], s. der Dolch; at —s drawn, spinnefeind; look — s, mit Blicken durchbohren.

dahlia [ˈdeiljə], s. (*Bot.*) die Dahlie, die Georgine.

daily [ˈdeili], adj. täglich; Tages-. — s. (*newspaper*) die Tageszeitung; (*woman*) die Putzfrau.

dainties [ˈdeintiz], s. pl. das Backwerk, das kleine Gebäck, das Teegebäck.

daintiness [ˈdeintinis], s. die Feinheit; die Kleinheit; die Leckerhaftigkeit.

dainty [ˈdeinti], adj. fein, klein, zierlich; lecker (*food*).

dairy [ˈdɛəri], s. die Molkerei, die Meierei.

dairyman [ˈdɛərimən], s. der Milchmann; der Senne (*in Alps*).

dais [deis, ˈdeiis], s. das Podium.

daisy ['deizi], s. (Bot.) das Gänseblümchen, das Marienblümchen.

dale [deil], s. das Tal.

dalliance ['dæliəns], s. die Tändelei, Liebelei; Verzögerung.

dally ['dæli], v.n. die Zeit vertrödeln.

dam (1) [dæm], s. der Damm. — v.a. eindämmen, abdämmen.

dam (2) [dæm], s. (Zool.) die Tiermutter.

damage ['dæmidʒ], s. der Schaden; der Verlust (loss); (pl.) (Law) der Schadenersatz. — v.a. beschädigen.

damageable ['dæmidʒəbl], adj. leicht zu beschädigen.

damask ['dæməsk], s. der Damast (textile). — adj. damasten, aus Damast.

dame [deim], s. die Dame (title); (Am.) (coll.) die junge Dame, das Fräulein.

damn [dæm], v.a. verdammen.

damnable ['dæmnəbl], adj. verdammenswert, verdammt.

damnation [dæm'neiʃən], s. die Verdammung, Verdammnis.

damn(ed) [dæm(d)], adj. & adv. verwünscht, verdammt.

damp [dæmp], adj. feucht, dumpfig. — s. die Feuchtigkeit; (Build.) — course, die Schutzschicht. — v.a. dämpfen, befeuchten; — the spirits, die gute Laune verderben.

damsel ['dæmzəl], s. die Jungfer; das Mädchen.

damson ['dæmzən], s. (Bot.) die Damaszenerpflaume.

dance [dɑ:ns], v.a., v.n. tanzen. — s. der Tanz; lead s.o. a —, einem viel Mühe machen.

dandelion ['dændilaiən], s. (Bot.) der Löwenzahn.

dandle [dændl], v.a. hätscheln; schaukeln.

dandy ['dændi], s. der Geck, der Stutzer.

Dane [dein], s. der Däne.

dane [dein], s. great —, die Dogge.

Danish ['deiniʃ], adj. dänisch.

danger ['deindʒə], s. die Gefahr.

dangerous ['deindʒərəs], adj. gefährlich.

dangle [dæŋgl], v.a. baumeln lassen. — v.n. baumeln, hängen.

dank [dæŋk], adj. feucht, naßkalt.

Danube ['dænju:b], die Donau.

dapper ['dæpə], adj. schmuck; niedlich; elegant.

dappled ['dæpld], adj. scheckig, bunt.

Dardanelles, The [dɑ:də'nelz]. die Dardanellen, pl.

dare [dɛə], v.n. irr. wagen; I — say, das meine ich wohl, ich gebe zu.

daredevil ['dɛədevil], s. der Wagehals, der Draufgänger.

daring ['dɛəriŋ], s. die Kühnheit.

dark [dɑ:k], adj. dunkel, finster. — s. die Dunkelheit; shot in the —, ein Schuß aufs Geratewohl, ins Blaue.

darken ['dɑ:kən], v.a. verdunkeln, verfinstern. — v.n. dunkel werden.

darkish ['dɑ:kiʃ], adj. nahezu dunkel.

darkness ['dɑ:knis], s. die Dunkelheit, Finsternis.

darkroom ['dɑ:kru:m], s. die Dunkelkammer.

darling ['dɑ:liŋ], s. der Liebling. — adj. lieb, teuer.

darn (1) [dɑ:n], v.a. stopfen.

darn (2) [dɑ:n], v.a. verdammen.

darn(ed) [dɑ:n(d)], (excl.) verdammt.

darning ['dɑ:niŋ], s. das Stopfen; — needle, die Stopfnadel.

dart [dɑ:t], s. der Pfeil; der Spieß (spear); (pl.) das Pfeilwurfspiel. — v.n. losstürmen, sich stürzen.

dash [dæʃ], v.a. zerschmettern, zerstören (hopes). — v.n. stürzen. — s. der Schlag (blow); die Eleganz; (Typ.) der Gedankenstrich; (Motor.) —board, das Schaltbrett, Armaturenbrett.

dashing ['dæʃiŋ], adj. schneidig.

dastard ['dæstəd], s. der Feigling, die Memme.

dastardly ['dæstədli], adj., adv. feige.

data ['deitə], s. pl. (Science) die Angaben, die Daten.

date (1) [deit], s. das Datum; (Am.) die Verabredung; out of —, vertetal (antiquated), altmodisch (out of fashion). — v.a. datieren; (Am.) ausführen. — v.n. das Datum tragen.

date (2) [deit], s. (Bot.) die Dattel.

dative ['deitiv], s. (Gram.) der Dativ.

daub [dɔ:b], v.a. bekleksen; (coll.) bemalen. — s. die Kleckserei; (coll.) die Malerei.

daughter ['dɔ:tə], s. die Tochter; — -inlaw, die Schwiegertochter.

daunt [dɔ:nt], v.a. einschüchtern.

dauphin ['dɔ:fin], s. der Dauphin.

daw [dɔ:], s. (Orn.) die Dohle.

dawdle ['dɔ:dl], v.n. trödeln, die Zeit vertrödeln.

dawdler ['dɔ:dlə], s. der Trödler, Tagedieb, die Schlafmütze.

dawn [dɔ:n], s. das Morgengrauen, die Morgendämmerung. — v.n. dämmern, tagen.

day [dei], s. der Tag; the other —, neulich; every —, täglich; one —, eines Tages; by —, bei or am Tage.

daybreak ['deibreik], s. der Tagesanbruch.

daytime ['deitaim], s. in the —, bei Tage.

daze [deiz], v.a. blenden (dazzle); betäuben (stupefy).

dazzle [dæzl], v.a. blenden.

deacon ['di:kən], s. (Eccl.) der Diakon.

deaconess ['di:kənes], s. (Eccl.) die Diakonisse.

dead [ded], adj. tot; stop —, plötzlich anhalten; as — as mutton, mausetot; — from the neck up, (coll.) dumm wie die Nacht. — adv. — beat, erschöpft; (Am.) —sure, ganz sicher. — s. in the — of night, in tiefster Nacht; (pl.) die Toten.

deaden [dedn], *v.a.* abschwächen (*weaken*); abtöten (*anæsthetise*).

deadly ['dedli], *adj.* tödlich.

deadness ['dednis], *s.* die Leblosigkeit; Mattheit (*tiredness*).

deaf [def], *adj.* taub; — *and dumb*, taubstumm.

deafen [defn], *v.a.* betäuben.

deafmute ['defmju:t], *s.* der Taubstumme.

deal (1) [di:l], *s.* das Geschäft; die Anzahl; *a fair or square* —, eine anständige Behandlung; *a good* —, beträchtlich; *a great* — *of*, sehr viel; *make a* —, ein Geschäft abschliessen; *it's a* — *!* abgemacht! —, — *!* du liebe Zeit! — *v.a. irr.* austeilen; Karten geben (*cards*); — *a blow*, einen Schlag erteilen. — *v.n. irr.* — *with s.th.*, etwas behandeln.

deal (2) [di:l], *s.* (*Bot.*) das Kiefernholz, die Kiefer; — *board*, das Kiefernholzbrett.

dealer ['di:lə], *s.* der Händler.

dean [di:n], *s.* der Dekan.

dear [diə], *adj.* teuer, lieb (*beloved*); teuer, kostspielig (*expensive*); — *me!* ach, Du lieber Himmel! —, — *!* du liebe Zeit! — *John !* Lieber Hans!

dearness ['diənis], *s.* die Teuerung, das Teuersein.

dearth [də:θ], *s.* der Mangel (*of*, an, *Dat.*).

death [deθ], *s.* der Tod; der Todesfall; — *penalty*, die Todesstrafe; — *warrant*, das Todesurteil.

deathbed ['deθbed], *s.* das Totenbett, Sterbebett.

deathblow ['deθblou], *s.* der Todesstoß.

deathless ['deθlis], *adj.* unsterblich.

debar [di'bɑ:], *v.a.* ausschließen (*from*, von, *Dat.*).

debase [di'beis], *v.a.* erniedrigen, verschlechtern.

debatable [di'beitəbl], *adj.* strittig.

debate [di'beit], *s.* die Debatte. — *v.a., v.n.* debattieren.

debauch [di'bɔ:tʃ], *v.a., v.n.* verführen; verderben.

debauchee [di'bɔ:tʃi:], *s.* der Schwelger, der Wüstling.

debenture [di'bentʃə], *s.* der Schuldschein.

debilitate [di'biliteit], *v.a.* schwächen.

debit ['debit], *s.* die Schuldseite, das Soll (*in account*). — *v.a.* belasten.

debt [det], *s.* die Schuld; *run into* — or *incur* —*s*, Schulden machen.

debtor ['detə], *s.* der Schuldner.

decade ['dekəd, 'dekeid], *s.* das Jahrzehnt; die Dekade.

decadence ['dekədəns], *s.* die Dekadenz, der Verfall.

decalogue ['dekəlɔg], *s.* (*Bibl.*) die zehn Gebote.

decamp [di'kæmp], *v.n.* aufbrechen, ausreißen.

decant [di'kænt], *v.a.* abfüllen, abgießen.

decanter [di'kæntə], *s.* die Karaffe.

decapitate [di'kæpiteit], *v.a.* enthaupten köpfen.

decapitation [di:kæpi'teiʃən], *s.* die Enthauptung.

decay [di'kei], *v.n.* in Verfall geraten. — *s.* der Verfall, die Verwesung.

decease [di'si:s], *s.* das Hinscheiden, der Tod. — *v.n.* sterben, dahinscheiden, verscheiden.

deceit [di'si:t], *s.* der Betrug; die List (*cunning*).

deceive [di'si:v], *v.a.* betrügen.

deceiver [di'si:və], *s.* der Betrüger.

December [di'sembə], der Dezember.

decency ['di:sənsi], *s.* der Anstand; die Anständigkeit, Ehrlichkeit; die Schicklichkeit.

decent ['di:sənt], *adj.* anständig.

decentralize [di:'sentrəlaiz], *v.a.* dezentralisieren.

deception [di'sepʃən], *s.* der Betrug.

deceptive [di'septiv], *adj.* trügerisch.

decide [di'said], *v.a., v.n.* entscheiden; bestimmen (*determine*).

decimal ['desiməl], *adj.* dezimal.

decimate ['desimeit], *v.a.* dezimieren, herabsetzen (*reduce*).

decipher [di'saifə], *v.a.* entziffern (*read*); dechiffrieren (*decode*).

decision [di'siʒən], *s.* die Entscheidung, der Beschluß (*resolution*); die Entschlossenheit (*decisiveness*).

decisive [di'saisiv], *adj.* entscheidend.

decisiveness [di'saisivnis], *s.* die Entschiedenheit.

deck [dek], *s.* (*Naut.*) das Deck; — *chair*, der Liegestuhl. — *v.a.* — (*out*), ausschmücken.

declaim [di'kleim], *v.a.* deklamieren.

declamation [deklə'meiʃən], *s.* die Deklamation.

declamatory [di'klæmətəri], *adj.* Deklamations-, deklamatorisch, Vortrags-.

declaration [deklə'reiʃən], *s.* die Erklärung; die Deklaration.

declare [di'kleə], *v.a.* erklären. — *v.n.* sich erklären.

declared [di'kleəd], *adj.* erklärt, offen.

declension [di'klenʃən], *s.* (*Gram.*) die Deklination, die Abwandlung.

declinable [di'klainəbl], *adj.* (*Gram.*) deklinierbar.

declination [dekli'neiʃən], *s.* (*Phys.*) die Abweichung, Deklination.

decline [di'klain], *v.n.* abweichen (*deflect*); abnehmen (*decrease*); sich weigern (*refuse*); fallen (*price*). — *v.a.* (*Gram.*) deklinieren; ablehnen (*turn down*). — *s.* die Abnahme (*decrease*); der Verfall (*decadence*); der Abhang (*slope*).

declivity [di'kliviti], *s.* der Abhang.

decode [di:'koud], *v.a.* entziffern, dechiffrieren.

decompose [di:kəm'pouz], *v.n.* verwesen; zerfallen, sich zersetzen. — *v.a.* auflösen.

decorate

decorate ['dekəreit], *v.a.* dekorieren (*honour*); ausschmücken (*beautify*); ausmalen (*paint*).

decoration [dekə'reiʃən], *s.* die Dekoration, der Orden (*medal*); die Ausschmückung (*ornamentation*); die Ausmalung (*décor*).

decorator ['dekəreitə], *s.* der Zimmermaler.

decorous ['dekərəs *or* di'kɔːrəs], *adj.* anständig, sittsam.

decorum [di'kɔːrəm], *s.* das Dekorum, das anständige Benehmen.

decoy [di'kɔi], *s.* der Köder (*bait*). — *v.a.* locken, verlocken.

decrease [di'kriːs], *v.a.* vermindern, verringern. — *v.n.* abnehmen. — ['diːkriːs], *s.* die Abnahme, die Verringerung.

decree [di'kriː], *s.* der Beschluß (*resolution*); (*Law*) das Urteil; — *nisi*, das provisorische Scheidungsurteil. — *v.a., v.n.* eine Verordnung erlassen; beschließen (*decide*).

decrepit [di'krepit], *adj.* abgelebt; gebrechlich (*frail*).

decry [di'krai], *v.a.* verrufen; in Verruf bringen.

dedicate ['dedikeit], *v.a.* widmen, weihen, zueignen (*to, Dat.*).

dedication [dedi'keiʃən], *s.* die Widmung, Weihung; die Zueignung.

dedicatory ['dedikeitəri], *adj.* zueignend.

deduce [di'djuːs], *v.a.* schließen (*conclude*); ableiten (*derive*).

deduct [di'dʌkt], *v.a.* abziehen (*subtract*); abrechnen (*take off*).

deduction [di'dʌkʃən], *s.* der Abzug (*subtraction*); die Folgerung (*inference*); der Rabatt (*in price*).

deductive [di'dʌktiv], *adj.* (*Log.*) deduktiv.

deed [diːd], *s.* die Tat, die Handlung (*action*); (*Law*) die Urkunde, das Dokument.

deem [diːm], *v.a.* erachten, halten für.

deep [diːp], *adj.* tief; — *freeze*, die Tiefkühlung; (*fig.*) dunkel. — *s.* die Tiefe (*des Meeres*).

deepen [diːpn], *v.a.* vertiefen. — *v.n.* tiefer werden; sich vertiefen.

deer [diə], *s.* (*Zool.*) das Rotwild, der Hirsch; — *stalking*, die Pirsch.

deface [di'feis], *v.a.* entstellen, verunstalten.

defalcate [di'fælkeit], *v.n.* Gelder unterschlagen.

defamation [defə'meiʃən], *s.* die Verleumdung.

defamatory [di'fæmətəri], *adj.* verleumderisch.

defame [di'feim], *v.a.* verleumden.

default [di'fɔːlt], *v.n.* (vor Gericht) ausbleiben. — *s.* der Fehler (*error*); die Unterlassung (*omission*).

defaulter [di'fɔːltə], *s.* der Pflichtvergessene; (*Law*) der Schuldige.

defeat [di'fiːt], *v.a.* schlagen, besiegen. — *s.* die Niederlage.

defect [di'fekt], *s.* der Fehler, Makel. — *v.n.* abfallen (*desert, from,* von, *Dat.*).

defection [di'fekʃən], *s.* der Abfall.

defective [di'fektiv], *adj.* fehlerhaft, mangelhaft.

defectiveness [di'fektivnis], *s.* die Mangelhaftigkeit, die Fehlerhaftigkeit.

defence [di'fens], *s.* die Verteidigung.

defenceless [di'fenslis], *adj.* wehrlos.

defencelessness [di'fenslisnis], *s.* die Wehrlosigkeit.

defend [di'fend], *v.a.* verteidigen.

defendant [di'fendənt], *s.* (*Law*) der Angeklagte.

defensive [di'fensiv], *adj.* verteidigend. — *s.* die Defensive; *be on the —,* sich verteidigen.

defer [di'fəː], *v.a.* aufschieben (*postpone*). — *v.n.* sich unterordnen, sich fügen (*to, Dat.*).

deference ['defərəns], *s.* der Respekt, die Achtung (*to,* vor, *Dat.*).

deferential [defə'renʃəl], *adj.* ehrerbietig, respektvoll.

defiance [di'faiəns], *s.* der Trotz, die Herausforderung.

defiant [di'faiənt], *adj.* trotzig, herausfordernd.

deficiency [di'fiʃənsi], *s.* die Unzulänglichkeit, der Mangel (*quantity*); die Fehlerhaftigkeit (*quality*).

deficient [di'fiʃənt], *adj.* unzulänglich (*quantity*); fehlerhaft (*quality*).

deficit ['defisit], *s.* das Defizit, der Fehlbetrag.

defile (1) [di'fail], *v.a.* schänden, beflecken.

defile (2) ['diːfail], *v.n.* vorbeimarschieren (*march past*) (an, *Dat.*). — *s.* der Engpaß.

defilement [di'failmənt], *s.* die Schändung.

define [di'fain], *v.a.* definieren, begrenzen; bestimmen (*determine*).

definite ['definit], *adj.* bestimmt (*certain*); klar, deutlich (*clear*); endgültig (*final*).

definition [defi'niʃən], *s.* die Definition, die Klarheit; (*Maths.*) die Bestimmung.

definitive [di'finitiv], *adj.* definitiv, endgültig (*final*); bestimmt (*certain*).

deflect [di'flekt], *v.a.* ablenken (*divert*). — *v.n.* abweichen (von, *Dat.*).

defoliation [diːfouli'eiʃən], *s.* der Blätterfall.

deform [di'fɔːm], *v.a.* verunstalten, entstellen. — *v.n.* (*Metall.*) sich verformen.

deformity [di'fɔːmiti], *s.* die Entstellung; die Häßlichkeit (*ugliness*).

defraud [di'frɔːd], *v.a.* betrügen.

defray [di'frei], *v.a.* bestreiten, bezahlen (*costs*).

deft [deft], *adj.* geschickt, gewandt.

deftness ['deftnis], *s.* die Gewandtheit, die Geschicktheit.

defunct [di'fʌŋkt], *adj.* verstorben. — *s.* der Verstorbene.

defy [di'fai], *v.a.* trotzen (*Dat.*).

degenerate [di'dʒenəreit], *v.n.* entarten; herabsinken (*sink low*). —[-rit], *adj.* degeneriert, entartet.

degradation [degri'deiʃən], *s.* die Absetzung, Entsetzung, Degradierung.

degrade [di'greid], *v.a.* (*Mil.*) degradieren; entwürdigen; vermindern.

degraded [di'greidid], *adj.* heruntergekommen.

degrading [di'greidiŋ], *adj.* entehrend.

degree [di'gri:], *s.* (*Meas., Univ.*) der Grad; (*Univ.*) die akademische Würde; die Stufe (*step, stage*); die Ordnung, die Klasse (*order, class*); by —s, nach und nach, allmählich.

deify ['di:ifai], *v.a.* vergöttern.

deign [dein], *v.n.* geruhen, belieben.

deity [di'iti], *s.* die Gottheit.

dejected [di'dʒektid], *adj.* niedergeschlagen.

dejection [di'dʒekʃən], *s.* die Niedergeschlagenheit.

delay [di'lei], *v.a., v.n.* aufschieben (*put off*); verzögern (*retard*). — *s.* der Aufschub; die Verzögerung.

delectable [di'lektəbl], *adj.* erfreulich, köstlich.

delectation [delek'teiʃən], *s.* die Freude, das Ergötzen (*in*, an, *Dat.*).

delegate ['deligit], *s.* der Delegierte, Abgeordnete; der Vertreter. — ['deligeit], *v.a.* delegieren, entsenden.

delegation [deli'geiʃən], *s.* die Delegation, die Abordnung.

delete [di'li:t], *v.a.* tilgen, (aus-)streichen, auslöschen (*writing*).

deletion [di'li:ʃən], *s.* die Tilgung, die Auslöschung.

deleterious [deli'tiəriəs], *adj.* schädlich.

delf [delf], *s.* das Delfter Porzellan.

deliberate [di'libərit], *adj.* absichtlich (*intentional*); vorsichtig (*careful*); bedächtig (*thoughtful*). — [-reit], *v.n.* beratschlagen, Rat halten. — *v.a.* überlegen, bedenken.

deliberateness [di'libəritnis], *s.* die Bedächtigkeit (*thoughtfulness*); die Absichtlichkeit (*intention*).

deliberation [dilibə'reiʃən], *s.* die Überlegung, die Beratung.

delicacy ['delikəsi], *s.* die Feinheit, Zartheit (*manner*); der Leckerbissen (*luxury food*); die Schwächlichkeit (*health*).

delicate ['delikit], *adj.* fein (*manner*); schwächlich (*sickly*); kitzlig, heikel (*difficult*).

delicious [di'liʃəs], *adj.* köstlich (*food*).

deliciousness [di'liʃəsnis], *s.* die Köstlichkeit.

delight [di'lait], *s.* das Entzücken, das Vergnügen; *Turkish* —, türkisches Konfekt; *take* — *in*, an etwas Gefallen finden, sich freuen (an, über). — *v.a., v.n.* entzücken, erfreuen (*in*, an, *Dat.*).

delightful [di'laitful], *adj.* entzückend, bezaubernd.

delimit [di:'limit], *v.a.* abgrenzen, begrenzen.

delimitation [di:limi'teiʃən], *s.* die Begrenzung, Abgrenzung.

delineate [di'linieit], *v.a.* umreißen, entwerfen, skizzieren (*draft, sketch*); schildern, beschreiben (*describe*).

delineation [dilini'eiʃən], *s.* die Skizze, der Entwurf (*sketch, draft*); die Schilderung (*description*).

delinquency [di'liŋkwənsi], *s.* das Verbrechen.

delinquent [di'liŋkwənt], *adj.* verbrecherisch. — *s.* der Verbrecher, Missetäter (*criminal*).

deliquesce [deli'kwes], *v.n.* (*Chem.*) zergehen, zerschmelzen.

deliquescence [deli'kwesəns], *s.* das Zerschmelzen, die Schmelzbarkeit.

deliquescent [deli'kwesənt], *adj.* leicht schmelzbar (*melting*); leicht zerfliessend (*butter etc.*).

delirious [di'liriəs], *adj.* (*Med.*) phantasierend, wahnsinnig.

delirium [di'liriəm], *s.* (*Med.*) das Delirium; der Wahnsinn (*madness*); das Phantasieren (*raving*); — *tremens*, der Säuferwahnsinn.

deliver [di'livə], *v.a.* abliefern, überreichen (*hand over*); liefern (*goods*); befreien (*free*); erlösen (*redeem*); zustellen (*letters etc.*); entbinden (*woman of child*).

deliverance [di'livərəns], *s.* die Erlösung (*redemption*); die Befreiung (*liberation*); die Übergabe.

delivery [di'livəri], *s.* die Befreiung (*liberation*); (*Med.*) die Niederkunft, Entbindung; der Vortrag (*speech*); die Lieferung, die Zustellung (*goods*); — *man*, der Zustellbote; — *van*, der Lieferwagen.

dell [del], *s.* das enge Tal.

delude [di'lu:d], *v.a.* betrügen, täuschen.

deluge ['delju:dʒ], *s.* die Überschwemmung. — *v.a.* überschwemmen.

delusion [di'lu:ʒən], *s.* die Täuschung, das Blendwerk.

delusive, delusory [di'lu:ziv, di'lu:zəri], *adj.* täuschend, trügerisch.

delve [delv], *v.n.* graben.

demagogic(al) [demə'gɔdʒik(əl)], *adj.* demagogisch.

demagogue ['deməgɔg], *s.* der Demagoge, der Aufrührer.

demand [di'ma:nd], *v.a.* verlangen, fordern. — *s.* die Forderung; das Begehren (*desire*); *on* —, auf Verlangen; *in great* —, viel gefragt; *supply and* —, Angebot und Nachfrage.

demarcate [di:'ma:keit], *v.a.* abgrenzen; abstecken (*field*).

demarcation [di:ma:'keiʃən], *s.* die Abgrenzung; — *line*, die Grenzlinie.

demeanour [di'mi:nə], *s.* das Benehmen.

demented [di'mentid], *adj.* wahnsinnig, von Sinnen, toll.

demerit [di:'merit], *s.* der Fehler.

demesne

demesne [di'mi:n *or* -'mein], *s.* das Erbgut; die Domäne.

demi- ['demi], *prefix.* halb-.

demigod ['demigɔd], *s.* der Halbgott.

demijohn ['demidʒɔn], *s.* der Glasballon.

demise [di'maiz], *s.* der Tod, das Hinscheiden. — *v.a.* (*Law*) vermachen.

demisemiquaver ['demisemikweivə], *s.* (*Mus.*) die Zweiunddreißigstelnote.

demobilize [di:'moubilaiz], *v.a.* demobilisieren.

democracy [di'mɔkrəsi], *s.* die Demokratie.

democratic [demo'krætik], *adj.* demokratisch.

demolish [di'mɔliʃ], *v.a.* demolieren, zerstören, niederreißen.

demon ['di:mən], *s.* der Dämon, der Teufel; *a* — *for work*, ein unersättlicher Arbeiter.

demoniac [di'mouniæk], **demoniacal** [di:mə'naiəkl], *adj.* besessen, teuflisch.

demonstrable [di'mɔnstrəbl], *adj.* beweisbar, nachweislich (*verifiable*).

demonstrate ['demənstreit], *v.a., v.n.* beweisen (*prove*); demonstrieren.

demonstration [demən'streiʃən], *s.* der Beweis (*theoretical*); die Demonstration (*practical*); (*Pol.*) Kundgebung.

demonstrative [di'mɔnstrətiv], *adj.* (*Gram.*) demonstrativ; überschwenglich (*emotional*).

demoralize [di:'mɔrəlaiz], *v.a.* demoralisieren.

demote [di:'mout], *v.a.* (*Mil., official*) degradieren.

demotion [di:'mouʃən], *s.* (*Mil., official*) die Degradierung.

demur [di'mə:], *v.n.* Anstand nehmen; Einwendungen machen (*raise objections*); zögern, zaudern (*hesitate*). — *s.* der Zweifel, der Skrupel.

demure [di'mjuə], *adj.* sittsam, zimperlich (*prim*).

demureness [di'mjuənis], *s.* die Sittsamkeit; die Sprödigkeit (*primness*).

den [den], *s.* die Höhle, Grube; *lion's* —, die Löwengrube.

denial [di'naiəl], *s.* die Verneinung, das Dementi (*negation*); das Ableugnen (*disclaimer*); die Absage (*refusal*).

denizen ['denizən], *s.* der Bürger, der Alteingesessene.

denominate [di'nɔmineit], *v.a.* nennen, benennen (*name*).

denomination [dinɔmi'neiʃən], *s.* die Bezeichnung; der Nennwert (*currency*); (*Rel.*) das Bekenntnis.

denominational [dinɔmi'neiʃənəl], *adj.* konfessionell.

denominator [di'nɔmineitə], *s.* (*Maths.*) der Nenner.

denote [di'nout], *v.a.* bezeichnen, kennzeichnen.

dénouement [dei'nu:mã], *s.* die Entwicklung, die Darlegung, die Lösung.

denounce [di'nauns], *v.a.* denunzieren, angeben; (*Law*) anzeigen.

dense [dens], *adj.* dicht; (*coll.*) beschränkt (*stupid*).

density ['densiti], *s.* die Dichte; — *of population*, die Bevölkerungsdichte.

dent (1) [dent], *s.* die Beule.

dent (2) [dent], *s.* die Kerbe (*in wood*); der Einschnitt (*cut*).

dental [dentl], *adj.* Zahn-; — *studies*, zahnärztliche Studien; — *treatment*, die Zahnbehandlung. — *s.* (*Phonet.*) der Zahnlaut.

dentist ['dentist], *s.* der Zahnarzt.

dentistry ['dentistri], *s.* die Zahnheilkunde.

denude [di'nju:d], *v.a.* entblößen; berauben (*of, Genit.*).

denunciation [dinʌnsi'eiʃən], *s.* die Denunzierung, die Anzeige.

deny [di'nai], *v.a.* verneinen (*negate*); abschlagen (*refuse*); verleugnen (*refuse to admit*).

deodorizer, deodorizer [di:'oudərə, di:'oudəraizə], *s.* der Geruchsentzieher (*apparatus*); der Deodorant.

deodorize [di:'oudəraiz], *v.a.* geruchlos machen.

depart [di'pa:t], *v.n.* abreisen, abfahren (*for*, nach, *Dat.*); scheiden.

department [di'pa:tmənt], *s.* die Abteilung; — *store*, das Kaufhaus.

departmental [di:pa:t'mentl], *adj.* Abteilungs-.

departure [di'pa:tʃə], *s.* die Abreise, die Abfahrt.

depend [di'pend], *v.n.* abhängen, abhängig sein (*upon*, von, *Dat.*); sich verlassen (*upon*, auf, *Acc.*); *that* —*s*, das kommt darauf an.

dependable [di'pendəbl], *adj.* verläßlich, zuverlässig.

dependant [di'pendənt], *s.* das abhängige Familienmitglied (*member of family*); der Angehörige, Abhängige.

dependence [di'pendəns], *s.* die Abhängigkeit (*need*); das Vertrauen, der Verlaß (*reliance*).

dependency [di'pendənsi], *s.* (*Pol.*) die abhängige Kolonie.

dependent [di'pendənt], *adj.* abhängig (*upon*, von, *Dat.*).

depict [di'pikt], *v.a.* schildern, beschreiben.

deplete [di'pli:t], *v.a.* entleeren (*make empty*); erschöpfen (*exhaust*).

depletion [di'pli:ʃən], *s.* die Entleerung.

deplorable [di'plɔ:rəbl], *adj.* bedauernswert, bedauerlich.

deplore [di'plɔ:], *v.a.* beklagen.

deploy [di'plɔi], *v.a.* entfalten. — *v.n.* sich entfalten; (*Mil.*) aufmarschieren.

deployment [di'plɔimənt], *s.* (*Mil.*) das Deployieren; die Entfaltung.

deponent [di'pounənt], *s.* (*Law*) der vereidigte Zeuge. — *adj.* (*Gram.*) (*verb*) der Deponens.

depopulate [di:'pɔpjuleit], *v.a.* entvölkern.

deport [di'pɔ:t], *v.a.* deportieren.

deportation [di:pɔ:'teiʃən], *s.* die Deportation.

deportment [di'pɔ:tmənt], s. die körperliche Haltung (*physical*); das Benehmen (*social*).

depose [di'pouz], v.a. absetzen (*remove from office*); (*Law*) zu Papier bringen (*write down*); schriftlich erklären (*declare in writing*).

deposit [di'pɔzit], s. (*Comm.*) die Anzahlung; (*Geol., Chem.*) der Niederschlag; (*Geol.*) die Ablagerung; (*Comm.*) — *account*, das Depositenkonto. — v.a. (*Geol., Chem.*) absetzen; (*Comm.*) anzahlen, einzahlen.

deposition [di:pə'ziʃən], s. die Niederschrift, die schriftliche Erklärung; die Absetzung (*removal from office*).

depositor [di'pɔzitə], s. (*Comm.*) der Einzahler.

depository [di'pɔzitəri], s. das Lagerhaus.

depot ['depou], s. das Depot, das Lagerhaus (*store*); (*Am.*) der Bahnhof.

deprave [di'preiv], v.a. verderben.

depraved [di'preivd], adj. (moralisch) verdorben.

depravity [di'præviti], s. die Verdorbenheit, die Verworfenheit.

deprecate ['deprikeit], v.a. mißbilligen (*disapprove of*; *Acc.*); sich verbitten.

deprecation [depri'keiʃən], s. die Abbitte; die Mißbilligung (*disapproval*).

depreciate [di'pri:ʃieit], v.a. abwerten, herabwürdigen. — v.n. an Wert verlieren, im Wert sinken.

depreciation [dipri:ʃi'eiʃən], s. die Abwertung; der Verlust (*loss*); (*Pol., Comm.*) die Entwertung.

depredation [depri'deiʃən], s. das Plündern, der Raub.

depress [di'pres], v.a. niederdrücken (*press down*); deprimieren (*morale*).

depressed [di'prest], adj. niedergeschlagen.

depression [di'preʃən], s. das Niederdrücken (*action*); (*Pol.*) die Depression; die Niedergeschlagenheit (*despondency*); das Tief (*weather*).

deprivation [depri'veiʃən], s. der Verlust (*lack*); die Beraubung (*robbery*).

deprive [di'praiv], v.a. berauben (*of*, *Genit.*); wegnehmen (*of*, *Acc.*).

depth [depθ], s. die Tiefe; — *charge*, die Unterwasserbombe; *in the* —*s of night*, in tiefster Nacht; (*Phys.*) — *of focus*, die Tiefenschärfe; *be out of o.'s* —, den Grund unter seinen Füßen verloren haben, ratlos sein (*be helpless*); — *sounder*, das Echolot.

deputation [depju'teiʃən], s. die Deputation, die Abordnung.

depute [di'pju:t], v.a. abordnen, entsenden.

deputize ['depjutaiz], v.n. vertreten (*for*, *Acc.*).

deputy ['depjuti], s. der Abgeordnete, der Deputierte (*delegate*); der Vertreter (*replacement*).

derail [di:'reil], v.a. zum Entgleisen bringen. — v.n. entgleisen.

derailment [di:'reilmənt], s. die Entgleisung.

derange [di'reindʒ], v.a. verwirren, stören.

derangement [di'reindʒmənt], s. die Verwirrung; die Geistesstörung (*madness*).

derelict ['derilikt], adj. verlassen.

dereliction [deri'likʃən], s. das Verlassen; — *of duty*, die Pflichtvergessenheit.

deride [di'raid], v.a. verlachen, verhöhnen.

derision [di'riʒən], s. die Verhöhnung.

derisive [di'raisiv], adj. höhnisch, spöttisch.

derivable [di'raivəbl], adj. ableitbar.

derivation [deri'veiʃən], s. die Ableitung.

derivative [di'rivətiv], adj. abgeleitet. — s. das abgeleitete Wort.

derive [di'raiv], v.a., v.n. ableiten, herleiten.

derogation [derо'geiʃən], s. die Herabsetzung.

derrick ['derik], s. der Ladebaum.

dervish ['də:viʃ], s. der Derwisch.

descant ['deskænt], s. (*Mus.*) der Diskant *or* der Sopran. — [dis'kænt], v.n. sich verbreiten (*on*, über, *Acc.*).

descend [di'send], v.n. hinab- *or* herabsteigen (*go down*); abstammen (*stem from*).

descendant [di'sendənt], s. der Nachkomme.

descent [di'sent], s. der Abstieg (*going down*); der Fall (*decline*); die Abstammung (*forebears*); der Abhang (*slope*); (*Aviat.*) die Landung.

describable [dis'kraibəbl], adj. zu beschreiben, beschreibbar.

describe [dis'kraib], v.a. beschreiben, schildern.

description [dis'kripʃən], s. die Beschreibung; *of any* —, jeder Art.

descriptive [dis'kriptiv], adj. schildernd, beschreibend.

desecrate ['desikreit], v.a. entweihen, entheiligen.

desecration [desi'kreiʃən], s. die Entweihung, die Schändung.

desert (1) ['dezət], s. die Wüste.

desert (2) [di'zə:t], v.a. verlassen, im Stiche lassen. — v.n. desertieren.

desert (3) [di'zə:t], s. (*usually pl.*) das Verdienst.

desertion [di'zə:ʃən], s. (*Mil.*) die Fahnenflucht.

deserve [di'zə:v], v.a. verdienen.

deserving [di'zə:viŋ], adj. verdienstvoll.

design [di'zain], v.a. entwerfen (*plan*); vorhaben (*intend*); bestimmen (*determine*). — s. der Entwurf (*sketch*); der Plan (*draft*); die Absicht, das Vorhaben (*intention*); das Muster (*pattern*).

363

designate

designate ['dezigneit], v.a. bezeichnen (*mark*); ernennen (*appoint*). — [-nit], adj. ernannt; *chairman* —, der künftige Vorsitzende.

designation [dezig'neiʃən], s. die Bestimmung, Ernennung (*appointment*); die Bezeichnung (*mark*).

designer [di'zainə], s. der Zeichner, der Graphiker (*artist*); der Ränkeschmied (*schemer*).

designing [di'zainiŋ], adj. hinterlistig, schlau.

desirable [di'zaiərəbl], adj. erwünscht, wünschenswert.

desire [di'zaiə], s. der Wunsch, die Begierde; das Verlangen, die Sehnsucht (*longing*). — v.a. verlangen, begehren.

desirous [di'zaiərəs], adj. begierig (*of*, *inf.*).

desist [di'zist], v.n. ablassen, aufhören.

desk [desk], s. der Schreibtisch; das Pult; — *lamp*, die Tischlampe *or* Bürolampe.

desolate ['desəlit], adj. verlassen, öde; trostlos (*sad*). — [-leit], v.a. verwüsten (*lay waste*).

desolation [desə'leiʃən], s. die Verwüstung (*of land*); die Trostlosigkeit (*sadness*).

despair [dis'pɛə], v.n. verzweifeln (*of*, an, *Dat.*). — s. die Verzweiflung.

despatch, dispatch [dis'pætʃ], v.a. absenden, befördern (*post*); abfertigen (*send*); erledigen (*deal with*); töten (*kill*). — s. die Abfertigung (*clearance*); die Eile (*speed*); die Depesche (*message*).

desperado [despə'reidou, -'ra:dou], s. der Wagehals, der Draufgänger.

desperate ['despərit], adj. verzweifelt.

desperation [despə'reiʃən], s. die Verzweiflung.

despicable ['despikəbl], adj. verächtlich.

despise [dis'paiz], v.a. verachten.

despite [dis'pait], prep. trotz (*Genit.*, *Dat.*).

despoil [dis'pɔil], v.a. plündern, ausrauben.

despondency [dis'pɔndənsi], s. die Verzweiflung, Verzagtheit.

despondent [dis'pɔndənt], adj. verzagend, verzweifelnd, mutlos.

despot ['despɔt], s. der Despot, der Tyrann.

despotic [des'pɔtik], adj. despotisch.

despotism ['despətizm], s. (*Pol.*) der Despotismus.

dessert [di'zə:t], s. das Dessert, der Nachtisch.

destination [desti'neiʃən], s. die Bestimmung, das Ziel; der Bestimmungsort (*address*); das Reiseziel (*journey*).

destine ['destin], v.a. bestimmen.

destiny ['destini], s. das Geschick; das Schicksal, das Verhängnis (*fate*).

destitute ['destitju:t], adj. verlassen (*deserted*); hilflos, mittellos (*poor*); in bitterer Not (*in great distress*).

destitution [desti'tju:ʃən], s. die Notlage, die bittere Not.

destroy [dis'trɔi], v.a. zerstören (*buildings*); verwüsten; vernichten (*lives*).

destroyer [dis'trɔiə], s. der Zerstörer.

destructible [dis'trʌktibl], adj. zerstörbar.

destruction [dis'trʌkʃən], s. die Zerstörung (*of buildings*), die Verwüstung; die Vernichtung.

destructive [dis'trʌktiv], adj. zerstörend, verderblich.

destructiveness [dis'trʌktivnis], s. die Zerstörungswut, der Zerstörungssinn.

desultory ['dezəltəri], adj. unmethodisch, sprunghaft; oberflächlich (*superficial*).

detach [di'tætʃ], v.a. absondern, trennen.

detachment [di'tætʃmənt], s. die Absonderung (*separation*); (*Mil.*) das Kommando.

detail [di'teil], v.a. im einzelnen beschreiben (*describe minutely*); (*Mil.*) abkommandieren. — ['di:teil], s. die Einzelheit.

detailed ['di:teild], adj. ausführlich; detailliert, ins Einzelne gehend (*report etc.*); [di'teild], (*Mil.*) abkommandiert.

detain [di'tein], v.a. aufhalten, zurückhalten; festhalten (*in prison*).

detect [di'tekt], v.a. entdecken, aufdecken.

detection [di'tekʃən], s. die Entdeckung, die Aufdeckung.

detective [di'tektiv], s. der Detektiv.

detention [di'tenʃən], s. (*Law*) die Haft; die Vorenthaltung (*of articles*).

deter [di'tə:], v.a. abschrecken.

detergent [di'tə:dʒənt], s. das Reinigungsmittel.

deteriorate [di'tiəriəreit], v.n. sich verschlimmern, verschlechtern.

deterioration [ditiəriə'reiʃən], s. die Verschlimmerung.

determinable [di'tə:minəbl], adj. bestimmbar.

determinate [di'tə:minit], adj. festgesetzt, bestimmt.

determination [di'tə:mi'neiʃən], s. die Entschlossenheit (*resoluteness*); die Bestimmung (*identification*); der Entschluß (*resolve*).

determine [di'tə:min], v.a. bestimmen (*ascertain*); beschließen (*resolve*).

deterrent [di'terənt], s. das Abschreckungsmittel.

detest [di'test], v.a. verabscheuen.

detestable [di'testəbl], adj. abscheulich.

detestation [detes'teiʃən], s. der Abscheu (*of*, vor, *Dat.*).

dethrone [di:'θroun], v.a. entthronen, vom Thron verdrängen.

detonate ['di:- *or* 'detoneit], v.n. detonieren, explodieren. — v.a. explodieren, detonieren lassen, zum Detonieren bringen.

detonation [deto'neiʃən], *s.* die Detonation, die Explosion.

detonator ['detoneitə], *s.* der Zünder, die Zündpatrone; (*Railw.*) die Knallpatrone.

detour ['deituə *or* di'tuə], *s.* der Umweg; (*Civil Engin.*) die Umleitung. — *v.n.* (*Am.*) einen Umweg machen. — *v.a.* (*Am.*) umleiten (*re-route*).

detract [di'trækt], *v.a.*, *v.n.* abziehen; schmälern.

detraction [di'trækʃən], *s.* die Schmälerung, die Verleumdung (*slander*).

detractive [di'træktiv], *adj.* verleumderisch.

detractor [di'træktə], *s.* der Verleumder.

detriment ['detrimənt], *s.* der Nachteil, der Schaden.

detrimental [detri'mentl], *adj.* nachteilig; abträglich; schädlich (*harmful*).

deuce (1) [dju:s], *s.* die Zwei (*game*); (*Tennis*) der Einstand.

deuce (2) [dju:s], *s.* (*coll.*) der Teufel.

devastate ['devəsteit], *v.a.* verwüsten, verheeren.

devastating ['devəsteitiŋ], *adj.* schrecklich, verheerend.

devastation [devəs'teiʃən], *s.* die Verheerung, die Verwüstung.

develop [di'veləp], *v.a.* entwickeln. — *v.n.* sich entwickeln; sich entfalten (*prove, turn out*).

developer [di'veləpə], *s.* (*Phot.*) das Entwicklungsmittel.

development [di'veləpmənt], *s.* die Entwicklung.

developmental [diveləp'mentl], *adj.* Entwicklungs-.

deviate ['di:vieit], *v.n.* abweichen.

deviation [di:vi'eiʃən], *s.* die Abweichung.

device [di'vais], *s.* die Vorrichtung (*equipment*); der Kungstgriff (*trick*).

devil [devl], *s.* der Teufel; der Lehrling, Laufbursche (*printer's, lawyer's*); *the — take the hindmost!* der Teufel hol was dann kommt! — *v.n.* in der Lehre sein (*for*, bei, *Dat.*).

devilish ['devəliʃ], *adj.* teuflisch.

devilment, devilry ['devəlmənt, 'devəlri], *s.* die Teufelei, die Teufelslaune.

devious ['di:viəs], *adj.* abweichend; abgelegen; abwegig.

deviousness ['di:viəsnis], *s.* die Abschweifung, Verirrung.

devise [di'vaiz], *v.a.* erfinden (*invent*); ersinnen (*think out*).

deviser, devisor [di'vaizə], *s.* der Erfinder (*inventor*); der Erblasser (*testator*).

devoid [di'vɔid], *adj.* frei (*of*, von, *Dat.*); ohne (*Acc.*).

devolve [di'vɔlv], *v.a.* übertragen (*transfer*); abwälzen (*pass on burden*) (*to*, auf, *Acc.*). — *v.n.* zufallen (*Dat.*).

devote [di'vout], *v.a.* widmen; aufopfern (*sacrifice*).

devoted [di'voutid], *adj.* ergeben (*affectionate*); geweiht (*consecrated*).

devotee [devo'ti:], *s.* der Anhänger; der Verehrer (*fan*).

devotion [di'vouʃən], *s.* die Hingabe; die Aufopferung (*sacrifice*); die Andacht (*prayer*).

devotional [di'vouʃənəl], *adj.* Andachts-.

devour [di'vauə], *v.a.* verschlingen.

devout [di'vaut], *adj.* andächtig, fromm.

devoutness [di'vautnis], *s.* die Frömmigkeit.

dew [dju:], *s.* der Tau.

dewy [dju:i], *adj.* betaut, taufeucht.

dexterity [deks'teriti], *s.* die Gewandtheit, die Fertigkeit.

dexterous ['dekstərəs], *adj.* gewandt, geschickt.

diabetes [daiə'bi:ti:z], *s.* (*Med.*) die Zuckerkrankheit.

diabetic [daiə'betik], *s.* (*Med.*) der Zuckerkranke. — *adj.* zuckerkrank.

diabolic(al) [daiə'bɔlik(əl)], *adj.* teuflisch.

diadem ['daiədem], *s.* das Diadem, das Stirnband.

diæresis [dai'iərəsis], *s.* die Diärese.

diagnose ['daiəg'nouz], *v.a.* diagnostizieren, als Diagnose finden, befinden.

diagnosis [daiəg'nousis], *s.* die Diagnose, der Befund.

diagonal [dai'ægənəl], *adj.* diagonal, schräg. — *s.* (*Geom.*) die Diagonale.

diagram ['daiəgræm], *s.* das Diagramm.

dial ['daiəl], *s.* das Zifferblatt; (*Teleph.*) die Wählerscheibe. — *v.a.*, *v.n,* (*Teleph.*) wählen.

dialect ['daiəlekt], *s.* der Dialekt, die Mundart.

dialectic [daiə'lektik], *s.* (*Phil.*) die Dialektik.

dialektical [daiə'lektikəl], *adj.* dialektisch, logisch.

dialogue ['daiəlɔg], *s.* der Dialog, das Zwiegespräch.

diameter [dai'æmitə], *s.* der Durchmesser.

diametrical [daiə'metrikəl], *adj.* diametral; gerade entgegengesetzt.

diamond ['daiəmənd], *s.* der Diamant; (*Cards*) das Karo.

diaper ['daiəpə], *s.* (*Am.*) die Windel.

diaphragm ['daiəfræm], *s.* (*Anat.*) das Zwerchfell; (*Phys.*) die Membran.

diarrhœa [daiə'riə], *s.* (*Med.*) der Durchfall.

diary ['daiəri], *s.* das Tagebuch, der Kalender.

diatribe ['daiətraib], *s.* der Tadel, der Angriff (*verbal*), die Schmähschrift (*written*).

dibble [dibl], *s.* der Pflanzstock. — *v.n.* Pflanzen stecken, anpflanzen.

dice [dais], *s. pl.* die Würfel (*sing.* **die**). — *v.a.* würfeln, werfen.

dicker

dicker [′dikə], *v.n.* (*Am.*) feilschen, handeln.

dicky [′diki], *s.* das Vorhemd.

dictate [dik′teit], *v.a.*, *v.n.* diktieren, vorschreiben.

dictation [dik′teiʃən], *s.* (*Sch.*) das Diktat.

dictator [dik′teitə], *s.* der Diktator.

dictatorship [dik′teitəʃip], *s.* die Diktatur.

diction [′dikʃən], *s.* die Ausdrucksweise (*speech*).

dictionary [′dikʃənri], *s.* das Wörterbuch.

didactic [di′dæktik], *adj.* lehrhaft, Lehr-.

die (1) [dai], *v.n.* sterben (*of*, an, *Dat.*); — *away*, verebben.

die (2) [dai], *s.* der Würfel (*cube*); die Gießform (*mould*); der Stempel (*punch*); (*Metall.*) das Gesenk (*swage*); — *casting*, der Spritzguß; — *castings*, die Spritzgußteile, Gußteile; — *forging*, das Gesenkschmiedestück.

die (3) [dai] *see under* **dice**.

dielectric [daii′lektrik], *adj.* dielektrisch.

diet (1) [′daiət], *s.* (*Pol.*) der Landtag, Reichstag.

diet (2) [′daiət], *s.* (*Med.*) die Diät. — *v.n.* (*Med.*) eine Diät halten. — *v.a.* (*Med.*) eine Diät vorschreiben.

dietary, dietetic [′daiətəri, daiə′tetik], *adj.* diätetisch.

differ [′difə], *v.n.* sich unterscheiden (*be different from*, von, *Dat.*); anderer Meinung sein (*be of different opinion*).

difference [′difərəns], *s.* (*Maths.*) die Differenz; der Unterschied (*discrepancy*); die Meinungsverschiedenheit (*divergence of opinion*).

different [′difərənt], *adj.* verschieden, verschiedenartig.

differentiate [difə′renʃieit], *v.n.* (*Maths.*) differenzieren; einen Unterschied machen (*between*, zwischen, *Dat.*).

difficult [′difikəlt], *adj.* schwierig, schwer.

difficulty [′difikəlti], *s.* die Schwierigkeit.

diffidence [′difidəns], *s.* die Schüchternheit.

diffident [′difidənt], *adj.* schüchtern.

diffraction [di′frækʃən], *s.* die Ablenkung, (*Phys.*, *Optics*) die Brechung.

diffuse [di′fju:z], *v.a.* ausgießen (*pour*); verbreiten (*spread*). — [di′fju:s], *adj.* verbreitet, weitschweifig (*style*); zerstreut.

diffuseness [di′fju:snis], *s.* die Weitläufigkeit (*style*).

diffusion [di′fju:ʒən], *s.* (*Phys.*) die Diffusion, die Zerstreuung, die Verbreitung.

dig (1) [dig], *v.a. irr.* graben; — *in the ribs*, in die Rippen stoßen. — *v.n.* (*coll.*) wohnen (*live in lodgings*).

dig (2) [dig], *v.a.* (*coll.*) verstehen.

digger [′digə], *s.* der Gräber; (*coll.*) der Australier.

digest [di′dʒest], *v.a.* (*Anat.*) verdauen. — [′daidʒest], *s.* (*Am.*) die Sammlung von Auszügen; (*pl.*) Pandekten.

digestibility [didʒesti′biliti], *s.* die Verdaulichkeit.

digestible [di′dʒestibl], *adj.* verdaulich.

digestion [di′dʒestʃən], *s.* die Verdauung.

digestive [di′dʒestiv], *adj.* Verdauungs-; — *biscuit*, das Kornmehlkeks; — *organs*, die Verdauungsorgane.

digit [′didʒit], *s.* (*Maths.*) die (einstellige) Zahl; der Zahlenwert.

digitalis [didʒi′teilis], *s.* (*Bot.*) der Fingerhut.

dignified [′dignifaid], *adj.* würdig, würdevoll.

dignify [′dignifai], *v.a.* ehren (*honour*); zieren (*decorate*).

dignitary [′dignitəri], *s.* der Würdenträger.

dignity [′digniti], *s.* die Würde.

digress [dai′gres], *v.n.* abweichen, abschweifen.

digression [dai′greʃən], *s.* die Abweichung, die Abschweifung.

digressive [dai′gresiv], *adj.* abschweifend (*style*).

digs [digz], *s. pl.* (*coll.*) das (möblierte) Zimmer, die Wohnung.

dike [daik], *s.* der Graben, der Deich. — *v.a.* eindeichen, eindämmen.

dilapidated [di′læpideitid], *adj.* baufällig.

dilapidation [dilæpi′deiʃən], *s.* die Baufälligkeit, der Verfall.

dilate [d(a)i′leit], *v.a.* erweitern, ausdehnen. — *v.n.* sich ausdehnen; sich auslassen (*speak*) (*on*, über, *Acc.*).

dilation [d(a)i′leiʃən], *s.* die Erweiterung (*expansion*); die Auslassung (*speaking*).

dilatoriness [′dilətərinis], *s.* die Saumseligkeit.

dilatory [′dilətəri], *adj.* zögernd, aufschiebend, saumselig.

dilemma [d(a)i′lemə], *s.* das Dilemma, die Klemme.

diligence [′dilidʒəns], *s.* der Fleiß, die Emsigkeit.

diligent [′dilidʒənt], *adj.* fleißig, arbeitsam.

dilly-dally [′dili′dæli], *v.n.* tändeln, zaudern, Zeit vertrödeln.

dilute [d(a)i′lju:t], *v.a.* (*Chem.*) verdünnen; schwächen (*weaken*).

dilution [d(a)i′lju:ʃən], *s.* die Verdünnung.

diluvial, diluvian [d(a)i′lju:viəl, -iən], *adj.* Diluvial-, des Diluviums; sintflutlich.

dim [dim], *adj.* trübe, unklar; (*Phys.*) abgeblendet. — *v.a.* abdunkeln, abblenden.

dimension [d(a)i′menʃən], *s.* die Dimension, das Maß.

dimensional [d(a)i′menʃənəl], *adj.* dimensional.

diminish [di'miniʃ], *v.a.* vermindern. — *v.n.* sich vermindern.

diminution [dimi'nju:ʃən], *s.* die Verringerung, die Verminderung.

diminutive [di'minjutiv], *adj.* verkleinernd, klein. — *s.* (*Gram.*) das Verkleinerungswort.

dimness ['dimnis], *s.* die Trübheit; die Düsterkeit (*dark*).

dimple [dimpl], *s.* das Grübchen.

dimpled [dimpld], *adj.* mit einem Grübchen.

din [din], *s.* das Getöse, der Lärm.

dine [dain], *v.n.* speisen, essen.

dinginess ['dindʒinis], *s.* die Dunkelheit, die Schäbigkeit.

dingy ['dindʒi], *adj.* dunkel, schäbig.

dinner ['dinə], *s.* das Essen; das Festessen (*formal*); — *jacket*, der Smoking.

dint [dint], *s.* der Nachdruck, der Schlag; *by* — *of*, mittels (*Genit.*).

diocesan [dai'ɔsisən], *adj.* (*Eccl.*) einer Diözese, Diözesan–.

diocese ['daiəsis], *s.* (*Eccl.*) die Diözese.

dip [dip], *v.a.* eintauchen, eintunken; abblenden (*lights*). — *v.n.* (unter)tauchen; sinken; sich flüchtig einlassen (*into*, in). — *s.* die Senke; der Abhang (*slope*).

diphtheria [dif'θiəriə], *s.* (*Med.*) die Diphtherie.

diphthong ['difθɔŋ], *s.* (*Phonet.*) der Diphthong.

diploma [di'ploumə], *s.* das Diplom; *teaching* —, das Lehrerdiplom.

diplomacy [di'plouməsi], *s.* die Diplomatie.

diplomatic [diplo'mætik], *adj.* diplomatisch, taktvoll; urkundlich (*documents*). — *s.* (*pl.*) das Studium der Urkunden.

diplomat(ist) ['diplomæt, di'ploumətist], *s.* (*Pol.*) der Diplomat.

dipper ['dipə], *s.* der Taucher.

dire [daiə], *adj.* fürchterlich, schrecklich; — *necessity*, bittere Not.

direct [d(a)i'rekt], *adj.* direkt, unmittelbar. — *v.a.* leiten (*be in charge of*); hinweisen, hinlenken; den Weg zeigen (*tell the way to*); anordnen (*arrange for*).

direction [d(a)i'rekʃən], *s.* die Leitung (*management*); (*Geog.*) die Richtung, Himmelsrichtung; die Anordnung (*arrangement*, *order*); —*s for use*, die Gebrauchsanweisung.

director [d(a)i'rektə], *s.* der Direktor; der Leiter.

directory [d(a)i'rektəri], *s.* das Adreßbuch; das Telephonbuch.

dirge [də:dʒ], *s.* der Trauergesang.

dirigible ['diridʒibl], *adj.* lenkbar, leitbar.

dirt [də:t], *s.* der Schmutz, der Kot, Dreck. — *adj.* — *cheap*, spottbillig.

dirty ['də:ti], *adj.* schmutzig; gemein (*joke*).

disability [disə'biliti], *s.* die Unfähigkeit, das Unvermögen (*inability*); die Schädigung (*impairment of health*).

disable [dis'eibl], *v.a.* unfähig *or* untauglich machen.

disablement [dis'eiblmənt], *s.* die Versehrung, die Verkrüppelung.

disabuse [disə'bju:z], *v.a.* aufklären, eines Besseren belehren.

disaccustom [disə'kʌstəm], *v.a.* entwöhnen, abgewöhnen.

disadvantage [disəd'vɑ:ntidʒ], *s.* der Nachteil.

disaffection [disə'fekʃən], *s.* die Abneigung; der Widerwille.

disagree [disə'gri:], *v.n.* nicht übereinstimmen, nicht einer Meinung sein.

disagreeable [disə'griəbl], *adj.* unangenehm, verdrießlich; unfreundlich.

disagreement [disə'gri:mənt], *s.* die Uneinigkeit (*disunity*); die Meinungsverschiedenheit (*difference of opinion*).

disallow [disə'lau], *v.a.* nicht gestatten; in Abrede stellen.

disappear [disə'piə], *v.n.* verschwinden.

disappearance [disə'piərəns], *s.* das Verschwinden.

disappoint [disə'pɔint], *v.a.* enttäuschen.

disappointment [disə'pɔintmənt], *s.* die Enttäuschung.

disapprobation [disæpro'beiʃən], *s.* die Mißbilligung.

disapproval [disə'pru:vəl], *s.* die Mißbilligung.

disapprove [disə'pru:v], *v.a.* mißbilligen (*of*, *Acc.*).

disarm [dis'ɑ:m], *v.a.* entwaffnen.—*v.n.* abrüsten.

disarmament [dis'ɑ:məmənt], *s.* die Abrüstung.

disarray [disə'rei], *v.a.* in Unordnung bringen. — *s.* die Unordnung (*disorder*); die Verwirrung (*confusion*).

disaster [di'zɑ:stə], *s.* das Unglück; das Unheil, die Katastrophe.

disastrous [di'zɑ:strəs], *adj.* unheilvoll, schrecklich.

disavow [disə'vau], *v.a.* ableugnen.

disavowal [disə'vauəl], *s.* das Ableugnen.

disband [dis'bænd], *v.a.* entlassen (*dismiss*); auflösen (*dissolve*).

disbar [dis'bɑ:], *v.a.* (*Law*) von der Rechtspraxis ausschließen.

disbelief [disbi'li:f], *s.* der Unglaube (*incredulity*); der Zweifel (*doubt*).

disbelieve [disbi'li:v], *v.a.* nicht glauben; bezweifeln.

disburse [dis'bə:s], *v.a.* auszahlen, ausgeben.

disbursement [dis'bə:smənt], *s.* die Auszahlung, die Ausgabe.

disc [disk], *s.* (*also Med.*) die Scheibe; die Platte (*record*).

discard [dis'kɑ:d], *v.a.* ablegen, beiseite legen, aufgeben.

discern [di'zə:n *or* di'sə:n], *v.a.* unterscheiden; wahrnehmen, bemerken.

discernment [di'sə:nmənt], *s.* die Urteilskraft (*powers of judgment*); die Einsicht.

discharge

discharge [dis'tʃɑːdʒ], *v.a.* entlassen (*dismiss*); abfeuern (*pistol*); abladen, ausladen (*cargo*); bezahlen (*debt*); tun, erfüllen (*duty*). — *s.* die Entladung (*gun*); die Entlassung (*dismissal*); die Bezahlung (*debt*); die Erfüllung (*duty*).

disciple [di'saipl], *s.* (Bibl.) der Jünger; der Schüler.

disciplinarian [disipli'nɛəriən], *s.* der Zuchtmeister.

disciplinary ['disiplinəri], *adj.* disziplinarisch.

discipline ['disiplin], *s.* die Disziplin, die Zucht. — *v.a.* disziplinieren, züchtigen.

disclaim [dis'kleim], *v.a.* verleugnen (*deny*); nicht anerkennen (*refuse to acknowledge*); verzichten (*renounce*).

disclaimer [dis'kleimə], *s.* der Widerruf.

disclose [dis'klouz], *v.a.* eröffnen, enthüllen.

disclosure [dis'klouʒə], *s.* die Eröffnung, die Enthüllung.

discoloration [diskʌlə'reiʃən], *s.* die Entfärbung, Verfärbung.

discomfiture [dis'kʌmfitʃə], *s.* die Verwirrung.

discomfort [dis'kʌmfət], *s.* das Unbehagen; die Beschwerde.

disconcert [diskən'səːt], *v.a.* außer Fassung bringen (*upset*); vereiteln (*frustrate*).

disconnect [diskə'nekt], *v.a.* trennen (*separate*); abstellen.

disconsolate [dis'kɔnsəlit], *adj.* trostlos, untröstlich.

discontent [diskən'tent], *s.* die Unzufriedenheit, das Mißvergnügen. — *v.a.* mißvergnügt stimmen.

discontinuance [diskən'tinjuəns], *s.* die Beendigung (*finish*); das Aufhören (*suspension*); die Unterbrechung (*interruption*).

discontinue [diskən'tinjuː], *v.a.* nicht fortsetzen; unterbrechen (*interrupt*); einstellen.

discord ['diskɔːd], *s.* die Zwietracht (*disagreement*); (Mus.) der Mißklang.

discordance [dis'kɔːdəns], *s.* die Uneinigkeit.

discordant [dis'kɔːdənt], *adj.* uneinig, widersprechend.

discount ['diskaunt], *s.* (Comm.) der Abzug, der Rabatt; *allow a* —, einen Rabatt gewähren; *be at a* —, unbeliebt sein, nicht geschätzt sein; *sell at a* —, unter dem Preis verkaufen. — [dis'kaunt], *v.a.* (Comm.) diskontieren, einen Rabatt gewähren; nur mit Vorsicht aufnehmen (*accept with doubt*).

discountable [dis'kauntəbl], *adj.* diskontierbar, in Abzug zu bringen.

discountenance [dis'kauntinəns], *v.a.* mißbilligen.

discourage [dis'kʌridʒ], *v.a.* entmutigen; abraten (*from*, von, *Dat.*).

discouragement [dis'kʌridʒmənt], *s.* die Entmutigung.

discourse [dis'kɔːs], *v.n.* einen Vortrag halten (*on*, über, *Acc.*); sprechen. — ['diskɔːs], *s.* der Vortrag; das Gespräch, die Rede.

discourteous [dis'kəːtiəs], *adj.* unhöflich.

discourtesy [dis'kəːtəsi], *s.* die Unhöflichkeit.

discover [dis'kʌvə], *v.a.* entdecken.

discovery [dis'kʌvəri], *s.* die Entdeckung.

discredit [dis'kredit], *s.* der üble Ruf; die Schande. — *v.a.* in schlechten Ruf bringen; diskreditieren.

discreditable [dis'kreditəbl], *adj.* schimpflich.

discreet [dis'kriːt], *adj.* diskret, verschwiegen; vorsichtig (*cautious*).

discrepancy [dis'krepənsi], *s.* die Diskrepanz, der Widerspruch; der Unterschied (*difference*).

discretion [dis'kreʃən], *s.* die Diskretion; die Klugheit; der Takt (*tact*); die Verschwiegenheit (*silence*); *at your* —, nach Ihrem Belieben; *use your* —, handle nach deinem Ermessen; handeln Sie nach Ihrem Ermessen.

discretionary [dis'kreʃənəri], *adj.* willkürlich, uneingeschränkt.

discriminate [dis'krimineit], *v.a., v.n.* unterscheiden (*distinguish*); absondern (*separate*).

discriminating [dis'krimineitiŋ], *adj.* scharfsinnig; einsichtig.

discriminatory [dis'krimineitəri], *adj.* einen Unterschied machend; — *legislation*, das Ausnahmegesetz.

discursive [dis'kəːsiv], *adj.* diskursiv, ohne Zusammenhang.

discuss [dis'kʌs], *v.a.* besprechen, erörtern.

discussion [dis'kʌʃən], *s.* die Diskussion, das Gespräch.

disdain [dis'dein], *s.* die Verachtung. — *v.a.* verachten, verschmähen; herabsetzen (*belittle*).

disdainful [dis'deinful], *adj.* geringschätzig, verächtlich.

disease [di'ziːz], *s.* die Krankheit.

diseased [di'ziːzd], *adj.* krank.

disembark [disim'bɑːk], *v.n.* aussteigen, landen. — *v.a.* aussteigen lassen, ausschiffen.

disembarkation [disembɑː'keiʃən], *s.* die Ausschiffung; die Landung.

disenchant [disin'tʃɑːnt], *v.a.* ernüchtern.

disenchantment [disin'tʃɑːntmənt], *s.* die Ernüchterung.

disengage [disin'geidʒ], *v.a.* losmachen, befreien (*release*); freigeben. — *v.n.* (Mil.) sich absetzen.

disengaged [disin'geidʒd], *adj.* frei (*unoccupied*).

disentangle [disin'tæŋgl], *v.a.* entwirren; befreien (*free*).

disentanglement [disin'tæŋglmənt], *s.* die Entwirrung, die Befreiung.

disfavour [dis'feivə], s. die Ungunst, die Ungnade.

disfigure [dis'figə], v.a. entstellen, verunstalten.

disfiguration [disfigjuə'reiʃən], s. die Entstellung, die Verunstaltung.

disfranchise [dis'fræntʃaiz], v.a. das Wahlrecht entziehen (*Dat.*).

disgorge [dis'gɔ:dʒ], v.a. ausspeien.

disgrace [dis'greis], v.a. entehren, Schande bringen. — s. die Ungnade, Schande (*shame*); die Entehrung (*putting to shame*).

disgraceful [dis'greisful], adj. schändlich, entehrend.

disgruntled [dis'grʌntld], adj. verstimmt, unzufrieden.

disguise [dis'gaiz], v.a. verkleiden (*dress*); (*fig.*) verstellen. — s. die Verkleidung; die Verstellung.

disgust [dis'gʌst], s. der Ekel, der Widerwille. — v.a. anekeln; be —ed, sehr ärgerlich sein; be —ed with s. th., etwas verabscheuen.

dish [diʃ], s. die Schüssel (*bowl*); das Gericht (*food*). — v.a. (*coll.*) abtun (*frustrate*); — up, auftragen (*food*).

dishcloth ['diʃklɔθ], s. das Wischtuch; der Abwaschlappen.

dishearten [dis'hɑ:tn], v.a. entmutigen, verzagt machen.

dishevelled [di'ʃevəld], adj. aufgelöst (*hair*); zerzaust (*hair, clothes*).

dishonest [dis'ɔnist], adj. unehrlich.

dishonesty [dis'ɔnisti], s. die Unehrlichkeit.

dishonour [dis'ɔnə], s. die Schande. — v.a. schänden, Schande bringen (über, *Acc.*).

dishonourable [dis'ɔnərəbl], adj. ehrlos, schimpflich.

dishwater ['diʃwɔ:tə], s. das Spülwasser.

disillusion [disi'lu:ʒən], s. die Enttäuschung, die Ernüchterung. — v.a. enttäuschen, ernüchtern.

disinclination [disinkli'neiʃən], s. die Abneigung.

disincline [disin'klain], v.a. abgeneigt machen (*Dat.*).

disinfect [disin'fekt], v.a. desinfizieren.

disinfectant [disin'fektənt], s. das Desinfektionsmittel.

disinfection [disin'fekʃən], s. die Desinfektion.

disingenuous [disin'dʒenjuəs], adj. unaufrichtig, unredlich.

disinherit [disin'herit], v.a. enterben.

disinter [disin'tə:], v.a. exhumieren, ausgraben.

disinterested [dis'intrəstid], adj. uneigennützig.

disinterestedness [dis'intrəstidnis], s. die Selbstlosigkeit, die Uneigennützigkeit.

disjoin [dis'dʒɔin], v.a. trennen.

disjoint [dis'dʒɔint], v.a. zerlegen, zerstücken.

disjointedness [dis'dʒɔintidnis], s. die Zerstücktheit, die Zusammenhangslosigkeit (*style of writing etc.*).

disjunction [dis'dʒʌŋkʃən], s. die Trennung, die Abtrennung.

disjunctive [dis'dʒʌŋktiv], adj. (*Gram.*) trennend, disjunktiv.

disk [disk] *see* **disc.**

dislike [dis'laik], v.a. nicht leiden mögen, nicht gerne haben. — s. die Abneigung (*of*, gegen, *Acc.*).

dislocate ['dislokeit], v.a. verrenken (*bone*); (*fig.*) in Unordnung bringen.

dislocation [dislo'keiʃən], s. (*Med.*) die Verrenkung; die Verwirrung (*traffic etc.*).

dislodge [dis'lɔdʒ], v.a. vertreiben (*drive out*); entfernen (*remove*).

disloyal [dis'lɔiəl], adj. ungetreu; verräterisch.

disloyalty [dis'lɔiəlti], s. die Untreue (*sentiment*); der Verrat (*act*).

dismal ['dizməl], adj. trostlos, traurig (*mood*); düster, trüb (*weather*).

dismantle [dis'mæntl], v.a. niederreißen, zerlegen; abbauen.

dismay [dis'mei], v.a. erschrecken, entmutigen. — s. die Furcht, der Schrecken, die Bangigkeit.

dismember [dis'membə], v.a. zerstückeln.

dismemberment [dis'membəmənt], s. die Zerstückelung, die Aufteilung.

dismiss [dis'mis], v.a. entlassen (*person*); aufgeben (*idea*).

dismissal [dis'misəl], s. die Entlassung; (*Law*) die Abweisung.

dismount [dis'maunt], v.n. vom Pferd absteigen. — v.a. (die Truppen) absteigen lassen.

disobedience [diso'bi:djəns], s. der Ungehorsam.

disobedient [diso'bi:djənt], adj. ungehorsam.

disobey [diso'bei], v.a., v.n. nicht gehorchen.

disoblige [diso'blaidʒ], v.a. verletzen, unhöflich behandeln.

disorder [dis'ɔ:də], s. die Unordnung; der Aufruhr (*riot*). — v.a. verwirren, in Unordnung bringen.

disorderliness [dis'ɔ:dəlinis], s. die Unordentlichkeit.

disorderly [dis'ɔ:dəli], adj. unordentlich (*unsystematic*); aufrührerisch, liederlich.

disorganization [disɔ:gəni'zeiʃən *or* -nai'zeiʃən], s. die Zerrüttung, die Auflösung (*dissolution*).

disorganize [dis'ɔ:gənaiz], v.a. auflösen.

disown [dis'oun], v.a. verleugnen.

disparage [dis'pæridʒ], v.a. verunglimpfen (*slight*); herabsetzen (*minimize*).

disparagement [dis'pæridʒmənt], s. die Herabsetzung.

disparity [dis'pæriti], s. die Ungleichheit.

dispatch [dis'pætʃ] *see* **despatch.**

dispel [dis'pel], v.a. vertreiben, verscheuchen.

dispensable [dis'pensəbl], *adj.* erläßlich, entbehrlich.

dispensation [dispen'seiʃən], *s.* die Austeilung; (*Eccl.*) die Dispensation.

dispensary [dis'pensəri], *s.* die Apotheke.

dispense [dis'pens], *v.a.* ausgeben, austeilen (*distribute*); — *with*, entbehren können, verzichten (auf, *Acc.*).

dispenser [dis'pensə], *s.* der Apotheker, der Pharmazeut.

dispersal [dis'pə:səl], *s.* das Zerstreuen, die Verteilung.

disperse [dis'pə:s], *v.a.* zerstreuen. — *v.n.* sich zerstreuen, sich verteilen.

dispirit [dis'pirit], *v.a.* mutlos machen, entmutigen.

displace [dis'pleis], *v.a.* verlegen, versetzen; (*Phys.*) verdrängen; —*d person*, der Heimatlose, der Verschleppte, der Flüchtling.

displacement [dis'pleismənt], *s.* die Versetzung (*from one place to another*); die Entwurzelung (*uprooting*); (*Phys.*) die Verdrängung; (*Naut.*) das Deplacement.

display [dis'plei], *v.a.* entfalten, ausstellen, zur Schau stellen (*show*). — *s.* die Entfaltung (*showing*), die Schaustellung, Ausstellung (*exhibition*).

displease [dis'pli:z], *v.a.* mißfallen (*Dat.*).

displeased [dis'pli:zd], *adj.* ungehalten (*at*, über, *Acc.*).

displeasure [dis'pleʒə], *s.* das Mißvergnügen, das Mißfallen (— *at*, an, *Dat.*).

disposable [dis'pouzəbl], *adj.* (*Comm.*) disponibel; zur Verfügung stehend.

disposal [dis'pouzl], *s.* die Verfügung (*ordering*), die Übergabe (*handing over*); *at o.'s* —, zur Verfügung; *bomb* —, die Unschädlichmachung der Bomben.

dispose [dis'pouz], *v.a.* einrichten (*thing*); geneigt machen (*person*); — *of*, etwas loswerden (*Acc.*). — *v.n.* anordnen (*ordain*).

disposed [dis'pouzd], *adj.* geneigt; *be well* — *towards s.o.*, jemandem zugeneigt sein *or* wohlwollend gegenüberstehen; *well* —, (in) guter Laune.

disposition [dispə'ziʃən], *s.* (*Psych.*) die Anlage; die Gemütsart (*temperament*); die Anordnung (*sequence*); der Plan, die Anlage (*of book etc.*); die Verfügung (*arrangement*).

dispossess [dispə'zes], *v.a.* enteignen, (des Besitzes) berauben (*Genit.*).

disproof [dis'pru:f], *s.* die Widerlegung.

disproportion [disprə'pɔ:ʃən], *s.* das Mißverhältnis.

disproportionate [disprə'pɔ:sənit], *adj.* unverhältnismäßig.

disprove [dis'pru:v], *v.a.* widerlegen.

disputable [dis'pju:təbl], *adj.* bestreitbar.

disputant ['dispjutənt], *s.* der Opponent, der Disputant.

disputation [dispju'teiʃən], *s.* der gelehrte Streit, die Disputation.

dispute [dis'pju:t], *s.* der Disput, die Meinungsverschiedenheit. — *v.a.*, *v.n.* streiten, verschiedener Ansicht sein; disputieren (*debate*); mit Worten streiten (*argue*).

disqualification [diskwɔlifi'keiʃən], *s.* die Disqualifizierung.

disqualify [dis'kwɔlifai], *v.a.* disqualifizieren, ausschließen.

disquiet [dis'kwaiət], *v.a.* beunruhigen, stören. — *s.* die Unruhe, die Störung.

disquisition [diskwi'ziʃən], *s.* die (lange) Abhandlung *or* Rede.

disregard [disri'gɑ:d], *v.a.* mißachten, nicht beachten. — *s.* die Außerachtlassung, die Mißachtung.

disreputable [dis'repjutəbl], *adj.* verrufen, in üblem Rufe stehend.

disrepute [disri'pju:t], *s.* der schlechte Name, der üble Ruf.

disrespect [disris'pekt], *s.* die Geringschätzung, der Mangel an Respekt. — *v.a.* (*obs.*) mißachten, geringschätzen, respektlos behandeln.

disrespectful [disris'pektful], *adj.* respektlos, unhöflich.

disrobe [dis'roub], *v.a.* entkleiden. — *v.n.* sich entkleiden.

disrupt [dis'rʌpt], *v.a.* abreißen, unterbrechen, stören (*disturb*).

disruption [dis'rʌpʃən], *s.* die Störung, die Unterbrechung (*interruption*); der Bruch.

dissatisfaction [dissætis'fækʃən], *s.* die Unzufriedenheit.

dissatisfied [dis'sætisfaid], *adj.* unzufrieden, unbefriedigt.

dissatisfy [dis'sætisfai], *v.a.* unzufrieden lassen.

dissect [di'sekt], *v.a.* zergliedern, zerlegen; (*Anat.*) sezieren.

dissection [di'sekʃən], *s.* die Zergliederung; (*Anat.*) die Sektion.

dissemble [di'sembl], *v.a.*, *v.n.* heucheln; sich verstellen.

disseminate [di'semineit], *v.a.* verbreiten.

dissemination [disemi'neiʃən], *s.* die Verbreitung.

dissension [di'senʃən], *s.* die Uneinigkeit, der Zwist (*conflict*).

dissent [di'sent], *v.n.* anderer Meinung sein; abweichen (*from*, von, *Dat.*). — *s.* die Abweichung, die abweichende Meinung.

dissenter [di'sentə], *s.* der Dissenter, das Mitglied der Freikirche.

dissertation [disə'teiʃən], *s.* die Dissertation, die Abhandlung.

dissever [di'sevə], *v.a.* trennen (*separate*); zerteilen (*divide*).

dissidence ['disidəns], *s.* die Uneinigkeit.

dissident ['disidənt], *adj.* uneinig, anders denkend.

dissimilar [di'similə], _adj._ unähnlich, ungleichartig.

dissimilarity [disimi'læriti], _s._ die Unähnlichkeit, die Ungleichartigkeit.

dissimulate [di'simjuleit], _v.a._ verhehlen (_conceal_). — _v.n._ sich verstellen, heucheln.

dissimulation [disimju'leiʃən], _s._ die Verstellung, Heuchelei, das Vorgeben (_pretence_).

dissipate ['disipeit], _v.a._ zerstreuen (_spread_); verschwenden (_waste_).

dissipation [disi'peiʃən], _s._ die Zerstreuung, die Verschwendung; die Ausschweifung.

dissociate [di'souʃieit], _v.a._ trennen, lösen. — _v.r._ abrücken (von).

dissociation [disouʃi'eiʃən], _s._ die Trennung; die Dissoziation.

dissolubility [disɔlju'biliti], _s._ die Auflösbarkeit.

dissoluble [di'sɔljubl], _adj._ auflösbar.

dissolute ['disɔlju:t], _adj._ ausschweifend, lose, liederlich.

dissolution [disə'lju:ʃən], _s._ die Auflösung; der Tod (_death_).

dissolvable [di'zɔlvəbl], _adj._ auflösbar, löslich.

dissolve [di'zɔlv], _v.a._ auflösen; lösen. — _v.n._ sich auflösen, zergehen (_melt_).

dissonance ['disənəns], _s._ die Dissonanz, der Mißklang.

dissonant ['disənənt], _adj._ (_Mus._) dissonant; mißhellig (_discordant_).

dissuade [di'sweid], _v.a._ abraten (_from_, von, _Dat._).

dissuasion [di'sweiʒən], _s._ das Abraten.

dissuasive [di'sweisiv], _adj._ abratend.

distaff ['dista:f], _s._ der Spinnrocken (_spinning_); _on the — side_, auf der weiblichen Linie.

distance ['distəns], _s._ die Entfernung; die Ferne (_remoteness_). — _v.a._ hinter sich lassen, sich distanzieren (von, _Dat._.)

distant ['distənt], _adj._ entfernt, fern (_space_); kühl (_manner_).

distaste [dis'teist], _s._ die Abneigung (vor, _Dat._); der Widerwille (gegen, _Acc._).

distasteful [dis'teistful], _adj._ widerwärtig, zuwider.

distastefulness [dis'teistfulnis], _s._ die Widerwärtigkeit.

distemper (1) [dis'tempə], _s._ die Krankheit; die Staupe (_dogs_).

distemper (2) [dis'tempə], _s._ die Wasserfarbe (_paint_). — _v.a._ mit Wasserfarbe streichen.

distend [dis'tend], _v.a._ (_Med._) ausdehnen, strecken. — _v.n._ sich ausdehnen.

distension, distention [dis'tenʃən], _s._ das Dehnen; (_Med._) die Ausdehnung, die Streckung.

distich ['distik], _s._ (_Poet._) das Distichon.

distil [dis'til], _v.a._ destillieren. — _v.n._ (_Chem._) destillieren, herauströpfeln.

distillation [disti'leiʃən], _s._ die Destillierung, (_Chem._) der Destilliervorgang.

distiller [dis'tilə], _s._ der Branntweinbrenner.

distillery [dis'tiləri], _s._ die (Branntwein)brennerei.

distinct [dis'tiŋkt], _adj._ deutlich, klar; — _from_, verschieden von (_Dat._).

distinction [dis'tiŋkʃən], _s._ der Unterschied, die Unterscheidung (_differentiation_); die Auszeichnung (_eminence_).

distinctive [dis'tiŋktiv], _adj._ unterscheidend (_differentiating_); deutlich (_clear_); leicht zu unterscheiden (_easy to distinguish_).

distinctiveness [dis'tiŋktivnis], _s._ die Deutlichkeit (_of voice etc._); die Eigenart, Eigentümlichkeit (_peculiarity_).

distinguish [dis'tiŋgwiʃ], _v.a._ unterscheiden. — _v.r._ — _o.s._, sich auszeichnen.

distinguishable [dis'tiŋgwiʃəbl], _adj._ unterscheidbar.

distinguished [dis'tiŋgwiʃd], _adj._ berühmt, vornehm.

distort [dis'tɔ:t], _v.a._ verdrehen; verzerren, verrenken.

distortion [dis'tɔ:ʃən], _s._ die Verdrehung, Verzerrung; (_fig._) die Entstellung (_of truth etc._).

distract [dis'trækt], _v.a._ abziehen, ablenken (_divert_); stören (_disturb_).

distracted [dis'træktid], _adj._ zerstreut; verrückt (_mentally deranged_).

distraction [dis'trækʃən], _s._ die Ablenkung; die Störung (_disturbance_); _to —_, bis zur Raserei.

distrain [dis'trein], _v.a._ beschlagnahmen, in Beschlag nehmen.

distraint [dis'treint], _s._ die Beschlagnahme.

distress [dis'tres], _s._ die Not, die Trübsal. — _v.a._ betrüben (_sadden_); quälen (_torture_).

distribute [dis'tribju:t], _v.a._ verteilen, austeilen (_among_, unter, _Acc._).

distribution [distri'bju:ʃən], _s._ die Verteilung; die Austeilung (_giving out_); (_Comm._) der Vertrieb.

distributive [dis'tribjutiv], _adj._ (_Gram._) distributiv; — _trades_, die Vertriebsgewerbe.

district ['distrikt], _s._ (_Geog._, _Pol._) der Bezirk; die Gegend (_region_); der Kreis (_administrative_); — _commissioner_, der Kreisbeamte, Kreisvorsteher.

distrust [dis'trʌst], _v.a._ mißtrauen (_Dat._). — _s._ das Mißtrauen (_of_, gegen, _Acc._).

distrustful [dis'trʌstful], _adj._ mißtrauisch (_of_, gegen, _Acc._).

disturb [dis'tə:b], _v.a._ stören (_trouble_); in Unordnung bringen (_disorder_).

disturbance [dis'tə:bəns], _s._ die Störung (_interruption etc._); der Aufruhr (_riot_).

disunion [dis'ju:njən], _s._ die Entzweiung, die Zwietracht.

disunite [disju'nait], _v.a._ entzweien, Zwietracht säen zwischen. — _v.n._ sich trennen.

371

disuse

disuse [dis'ju:z], *v.a.* außer Gebrauch setzen. — [-'ju:s], *s.* der Nichtgebrauch (*abeyance*); die Entwöhnung (*cessation of practice*).

ditch [ditʃ], *s.* der Graben; *dull as —water*, uninteressant, langweilig. — *v.a.* mit einem Graben umgeben (*dig around*); graben.

ditto ['ditou], *adv.* desgleichen, dito.

ditty ['diti], *s.* das Liedchen.

diurnal [dai'ə:nəl], *adj.* täglich.

divan [di'væn], *s.* der Diwan.

dive [daiv], *v.n.* tauchen, springen (ins Wasser); (*Aviat.*) sturzfliegen, einen Sturzflug machen. — *s.* der Hechtsprung (ins Wasser); der Wassersprung; der Kopfsprung; (*Aviat.*) der Sturzflug.

diver ['daivə], *s.* (*Sport, Orn.*) der Taucher.

diverge [dai'və:dʒ], *v.n.* abweichen, auseinandergehen.

divergence [dai'və:dʒəns], *s.* die Abweichung, die Divergenz, Meinungsverschiedenheit.

divergent [dai'və:dʒənt], *adj.* auseinandergehend, abweichend.

divers ['daivəz], *adj. pl.* etliche, verschiedene.

diverse [dai'və:s], *adj.* verschieden, mannigfaltig.

diversify [dai'və:sifai], *v.a.* verschieden machen.

diversion [dai'və:ʃən], *s.* die Zerstreuung; (*Traffic*) die Umleitung.

diversity [dai'və:siti], *s.* die Verschiedenheit; die Ungleichheit (*disparity*).

divert [dai'və:t], *v.a.* ablenken, zerstreuen.

divest [di'vest *or* dai'-], *v.a.* entkleiden, berauben (*of office*, eines Amtes). — *v.r.* — *o.s. of*, auf etwas verzichten (*give up*).

divide [di'vaid], *v.a.* (*Maths.*) dividieren; teilen (*share*); aufteilen (*proportion*); sondern, trennen (*separate*). — *v.n.* sich teilen; (*Maths.*) sich dividieren lassen.

dividend ['dividənd], *s.* (*Comm.*) die Dividende; (*Maths.*) der Dividend.

dividers [di'vaidəz], *s.pl.* der Stechzirkel.

divination [divi'neiʃən], *s.* die Wahrsagung (*prophecy*); die Ahnung.

divine [di'vain], *v.a.* weissagen (*prophesy*); erraten (*guess*). — *adj.* göttlich; (*coll.*) herrlich. —*s.* (*obs.*) der Geistliche (*clergyman*).

divinity [di'viniti], *s.* die Göttlichkeit; die Gottheit (*deity*); die Theologie.

divisibility [divizi'biliti], *s.* (*Maths.*) die Teilbarkeit.

divisible [di'vizibl], *adj.* teilbar.

division [di'viʒən], *s.* (*Maths., Mil.*) die Division; die Teilung (*partition*); die Abteilung (*department*); (*Parl.*) die Abstimmung.

divisor [di'vaizə], *s.* (*Maths.*) der Divisor; der Teiler.

divorce [di'vo:s], *s.* (*Law*) die Scheidung; die Trennung (*separation*). — *v.a.* sich von einem scheiden lassen.

divulge [dai'vʌldʒ], *v.a.* ausplaudern; verraten (*betray*); verbreiten (*spread*).

dizziness ['dizinis], *s.* der Schwindel.

dizzy ['dizi], *adj.* schwindlig.

do [du:], *v.a. irr.* tun, machen; — *o.'s duty*, seine Pflicht erfüllen; — *o.'s bit*, das Seinige leisten; — *o.'s homework*, seine Aufgaben machen; — *a favour*, einen Gefallen erweisen; vollbringen (*accomplish*); — *away with*, abschaffen (*Acc.*); einpacken. — *v.n. this will —*, das genügt; *this won't —*, so geht's nicht; — *without*, ohne etwas auskommen; *how — you — ?* sehr angenehm (*on introduction to people*).

docile ['dousail], *adj.* gelehrig, lenksam, fügsam.

docility [do'siliti], *s.* die Gelehrigkeit, die Fügsamkeit.

dock (1) [dɔk], *s.* (*Bot.*) das Ampferkraut; — *leaf*, das Ampferblatt.

dock (2) [dɔk], *s.* (*Naut.*) das Dock; —*yard*, die Schiffswerft; (*Law*) die Anklagebank. — *v.a.* (*Naut.*) ein Schiff ins Dock bringen.

dock (3) [dɔk], *v.a.* stutzen (*clip*); kürzen (*wages*).

docket ['dɔkit], *s.* der Zettel (*chit*); der Lieferschein.

doctor ['dɔktə], *s.* (*Med.*) der Arzt, der Doktor. — *v.a.* operieren, kastrieren (*a cat etc.*).

doctorate ['dɔktərit], *s.* das Doktorat, die Doktorwürde.

doctrinaire [dɔktri'neə], *s.* der Doktrinär. — *adj.* doktrinär.

doctrinal [dɔk'trainəl], *adj.* Lehr-.

doctrine ['dɔktrin], *s.* die Lehre, die Doktrin.

document ['dɔkjumənt], *s.* das Dokument, die Urkunde.

documentary [dɔkju'mentəri], *adj.* Dokumentar– (*film*); dokumentarisch (*evidence*).

documentation [dɔkjumen'teiʃən], *s.* die Dokumentation, Heranziehung von Dokumenten.

dodge [dɔdʒ], *v.a.* ausweichen (*Dat.*). — *s.* der Kniff.

dodger ['dɔdʒə], *s.* der Schwindler.

doe [dou], *s.* (*Zool.*) das Reh.

doeskin ['douskin], *s.* das Rehleder.

doff [dɔf], *v.a.* abnehmen, ablegen (*clothes*).

dog [dɔg], *s.* der Hund; —*'s ear*, das Eselsohr (*in book*). — *v.a.* verfolgen, auf Schritt und Tritt folgen (*Dat.*) (*follow closely*).

dogfish ['dɔgfiʃ], *s.* (*Zool.*) der Dornhai.

dogged ['dɔgid], *adj.* unverdrossen, zäh.

doggedness ['dɔgidnis], *s.* die Zähigkeit.

doggerel ['dɔgərəl], *s.* der Knüttelvers.

dogma ['dɔgmə], *s.* das Dogma, der Glaubenssatz.

dogmatic [dɔg'mætik], *adj.* dogmatisch.
dogmatism ['dɔgmətizm], *s.* der Dogmatismus.
dogmatize ['dɔgmətaiz], *v.n.* dogmatisieren.
doldrums ['douldrəmz], *s. pl.* die Schwermut, die Depression; (*Naut.*) die Windstillen, *f.pl.*
dole [doul], *s.* das Almosen; die Arbeitslosenunterstützung (*unemployment benefit*); *be on the* —, stempeln gehen, Arbeitslosenunterstützung beziehen. — *v.a.* — *out*, austeilen, verteilen.
doleful ['doulful], *adj.* traurig, bekümmert.
doll [dɔl], *s.* die Puppe.
dollar ['dɔlə], *s.* der Dollar.
dolman ['dɔlmən], *s.* der Dolman.
dolorous ['dɔlərəs], *adj.* (*Lit.*) schmerzlich, schmerzhaft.
dolphin ['dɔlfin], *s.* (*Zool.*) der Delphin.
dolt [doult], *s.* der Tölpel.
doltish ['doultiʃ], *adj.* tölpelhaft.
doltishness ['doultiʃnis], *s.* die Tölpelhaftigkeit.
domain [do'mein], *s.* das Gebiet, der Bereich.
dome [doum], *s.* (*Archit.*) die Kuppel, die Wölbung; der Dom.
domed [doumd], *adj.* gewölbt.
domestic [do'mestik], *adj.* Haus-, häuslich; — *animal*, das Haustier.
domesticate [do'mestikeit], *v.a.* zähmen (*tame*), zivilisieren.
domesticity [domes'tisiti], *s.* die Häuslichkeit.
domicile ['dɔmisail], *s.* das Domizil; der Wohnort.
domiciled ['dɔmisaild], *adj.* wohnhaft (*at*, in, *Dat.*).
dominant ['dɔminənt], *adj.* vorherrschend. — *s.* (*Mus.*) die Dominante.
dominate ['dɔmineit], *v.a.* beherrschen. — *v.n.* herrschen.
domination [dɔmi'neiʃən], *s.* die Herrschaft.
domineer [dɔmi'niə], *v.n.* tyrannisieren.
domineering [dɔmi'niəriŋ], *adj.* überheblich, gebieterisch.
Dominican [do'minikən], *s.* der Dominikaner (*friar*).
dominion [do'minjən], *s.* die Herrschaft (*rule*); das Dominion (*Br. Commonwealth*).
domino ['dɔminou], *s.* (*pl.* —**noes**) der Domino (*mask*); (*pl.*) das Domino (*game*).
don (1) [dɔn], *s.* der Universitätsgelehrte, Universitätsdozent (*scholar*); Don (*Spanish nobleman*).
don (2) [dɔn], *v.a.* anziehen.
donate [do'neit], *v.a.* schenken, stiften.
donation [do'neiʃən], *s.* die Schenkung, die Stiftung; die Gabe (*gift*).
donkey ['dɔŋki], *s.* (*Zool.*) der Esel; — *engine*, die Hilfsmaschine.
donor ['dounə], *s.* der Spender, der Stifter; *blood* —, der Blutspender.

doom [du:m], *s.* die Verurteilung (*judgment*); der Untergang; das jüngste Gericht.
doomed [du:md], *adj.* verurteilt, verdammt (*to*, zu, *Dat.*).
Doomsday ['du:msdei]. der jüngste Tag, der Tag des jüngsten Gerichtes.
door [dɔ:], *s.* die Tür(e); *next* —, nebenan; *out of* —*s*, draußen, im Freien; —*bell*, die Türklingel; —*latch*, die Klinke.
doorman ['dɔ:mæn], *s.* der Türsteher, der Pförtner.
dormant ['dɔ:mənt], *adj.* schlafend; unbenutzt.
dormer window ['dɔ:mə 'windou], *s.* das Dachfenster.
dormitory ['dɔ:mitri], *s.* der Schlafsaal.
dormouse ['dɔ:maus], *s.* (*Zool.*) die Haselmaus.
dose [dous], *s.* (*Med.*) die Dosis. — *v.a.* dosieren.
dot [dɔt], *s.* der Punkt, das Tüpfel. — *v.a.* punktieren; *sign on the* —*ted line*, unterschreiben; — *the i's and cross the t's*, äußerst genau sein.
dotage ['doutidʒ], *s.* die Altersschwäche, das Greisenalter.
dotard ['doutəd], *s.* der alte Dummkopf.
dote [dout], *v.n.* vernarrt sein (*on*, in, *Acc.*).
double [dʌbl], *adj.* (*Maths.*) doppelt; zweideutig (*meaning*); falsch (*false*); — *entry book-keeping*, doppelte Buchführung. — *s.* der Doppelgänger, die Doppelgängerin; *at the* —, im Sturmschritt. — *v.a.* (*Maths.*) verdoppeln; zusammenlegen (*fold in two*). — *v.n.* — *up with pain*, sich vor Schmerzen winden *or* krümmen.
doublet ['dʌblit], *s.* der Wams; — *and hose*, Wams und Hosen; der Pasch (*dice*); (*Ling.*) die Dublette, Doppelform.
doubt [daut], *s.* der Zweifel. — *v.a.* zweifeln (an, *Dat.*); bezweifeln.
doubtful ['dautful], *adj.* zweifelhaft, fraglich (*uncertain*).
doubtless ['dautlis], *adj.* zweifellos, ohne Zweifel.
douche [du:ʃ], *s.* die Dusche.
dough [dou], *s.* der Teig.
doughnut ['dounʌt], *s.* der Krapfen, Pfannkuchen.
doughy ['doui], *adj.* weich, teigig.
douse [daus], *v.a.* begießen, mit Wasser beschütten.
dove [dʌv], *s.* (*Orn.*) die Taube.
dovecote ['dʌvkot], *s.* der Taubenschlag.
dovetail ['dʌvteil], *v.a.*, *v.n.* einpassen; fügen; —*ing*, die Einpassung, die Verzinkung.
dowager ['dauədʒə], *s.* die Witwe (*of noble family*, von Stande).
dowdy ['daudi], *adj.* schlampig, unordentlich, unelegant.
dower ['dauə], *s.* die Mitgift, die Ausstattung.

down

down (1) [daun], *s.* der Flaum, die Daune.

down (2) [daun], *s.* das Hügelland.

down (3) [daun], *adv.* hinunter, herunter; nieder; unter; hinab. — *prep.* herab; hinunter. — *adj.* the — *train*, der Zug aus London. — *v.a.* niederzwingen, hinunterstürzen.

downcast [´daunka:st], *adj.* niedergeschlagen.

downfall [´daunfɔ:l], *s.* der Sturz.

downhill [daun´hil], *adv.* bergab. — [´daunhil], *adj.* abschüssig.

downpour [´daunpɔ:], *s.* der Platzregen.

downright [´daunrait], *adj.* völlig. — *adv.* geradezu.

downward [´daunwəd], *adj.* abschüssig. — *adv.* (also *downwards*) *see* **down**.

dowry [´dauri] *see* **dower**.

doze [douz], *v.n.* dösen, schlummern.

dozen [dʌzn], *s.* das Dutzend.

drab [dræb], *adj.* eintönig; langweilig (*boring*).

draft [dra:ft], *s.* (*Comm.*) die Tratte; der Entwurf (*sketch*); (*Mil.*) das Detachement. — *v.a.* entwerfen (*sketch*); (*Mil.*) abordnen; (*Am.*) einziehen.

drag [dræg], *v.a.* schleppen. — *s.* (*Engin.*) die Schleppbremse, der Dregghaken; der Hemmschuh (*wedge*); —*net*, das Schleppnetz; —*wheel*, das Schlepprad.

dragoman [´drægomən], *s.* der Dolmetscher.

dragon [´drægən], *s.* der Drache.

dragonfly [´drægənflai], *s.* (*Ent.*) die Libelle.

dragoon [drə´gu:n], *v.a.* unterdrücken. — *s.* (*Mil.*) der Dragoner.

drain [drein], *v.a.* entwässern, austrocknen; trockenlegen. — *v.n.* ablaufen, abfließen, auslaufen. — *s.* der Abguß, Abzug, die Gosse (*in street*); (*Engin.*) die Dränage; —*ing board*, das Ablauf- *or* Abwaschbrett; (*Phot.*) —*ing rack*, der Trockenständer; *a* — *on o.'s income*, eine Belastung des Einkommens.

drainage [´dreinidʒ], *s.* die Trockenlegung, die Kanalisierung.

drainpipe [´dreinpaip], *s.* das Abflußrohr; — *trousers*, die Röhrenhosen, *f. pl.*

drake [dreik], *s.* (*Orn.*) der Enterich.

dram [dræm], *s.* der Trunk; Schluck (*spirits*).

drama [´dra:mə], *s.* das Drama, das Schauspiel.

dramatic [drə´mætik], *adj.* dramatisch.

dramatist [´dra:m- *or* ´dræmətist], *s.* der Dramatiker.

dramatize [´dræmətaiz], *v.a.* dramatisieren.

drape [dreip], *v.a.* drapieren, bedecken; einhüllen (*wrap*). — *s.* (*Am.*) der Vorhang.

draper [´dreipə], *s.* der Stoffhändler, der Tuchhändler.

drapery [´dreipəri], *s.* — *department*, die Stoff- *or* Tuchabteilung; die Tuchhandlung (*shop*).

drastic [´dra:stik *or* ´dræstik], *adj.* drastisch, radikal.

draught [dra:ft], *s.* der Zug (*air*); der Tiefgang (— *of ship*); der Schluck (*drink*); der Schlaftrunk (*sleeping* —); — *horse*, das Zugpferd; — *beer*, das Faßbier; —*board*, das Damespielbrett; (*pl.*) das Damespiel.

draw [drɔ:], *v.a. irr.* ziehen (*pull*); zeichnen (*sketch*); anlocken (*attract*); ausschreiben (*cheque*); —*well*, der Ziehbrunnen. — *s.* das Los, die Verlosung (*lottery*); (*Sport*) das Unentschieden.

drawback [´drɔ:bæk], *s.* der Nachteil, die Schattenseite.

drawbridge [´drɔ:bridʒ], *s.* die Zugbrücke.

drawer [´drɔ:ə], *s.* die Schublade; *chest of* —*s*, die Kommode; (*pl.*) die Unterhosen, *f. pl.*

drawing [´drɔ:iŋ], *s.* (*Art*) die Zeichnung; —*board*, das Reißbrett; —*office*, das Zeichenbüro, der Zeichensaal.

drawing room [´drɔ:iŋ rum], *s.* das Wohnzimmer, der Salon.

drawl [drɔ:l], *v.n.* gedehnt sprechen. — *s.* die gedehnte Sprechweise.

drawn [drɔ:n], *adj.* (*Sport*) unentschieden.

dray [drei], *s.* der Rollwagen, der Karren; —*man*, der Kutscher, der Fuhrmann.

dread [dred], *s.* der Schrecken. — *adj.* schrecklich. — *v.n.* fürchten. — *v.n.* sich fürchten (vor, *Dat.*).

dreadful [´dredful], *adj.* schrecklich, furchtbar.

dreadnought [´drednɔ:t], *s.* (*Naut.*) das große Schlachtschiff.

dream [dri:m], *s.* der Traum. — *v.n. irr.* träumen; *I would not* — *of it*, es würde mir nicht im Traum einfallen, ich denke nicht daran.

dreamt [dremt] *see* **dream**.

dreamy [´dri:mi], *adj.* verträumt, träumerisch.

dreariness [´driərinis], *s.* die Öde.

dreary [´driəri], *adj.* traurig, öde.

dredge [dredʒ], *s.* das Schleppnetz. — *v.a.* (*Engin.*) ausbaggern; (*Naut.*) dreggen.

dredger [´dredʒə], *s.* der Bagger, das Baggerschiff; (*Cul.*) die Streubüchse.

dregs [dregz], *s. pl.* der Bodensatz (*in cup etc.*); die Hefe (*yeast*).

drench [drentʃ], *v.a.* durchnässen, tränken.

Dresden [´drezdən]. (*china*) das Meißner Porzellan.

dress [dres], *s.* das Kleid; die Kleidung; *evening* —, die Abendkleidung; *full* —, die Gala(kleidung); — *circle*, erster Rang; —*maker*, die Schneiderin; — *rehearsal*, die Generalprobe; — *shirt*, das Frackhemd; — *suit*, der Frackanzug. — *v.a., v.n.* (sich) anziehen.

dresser ['dresə], s. der Ankleider (valet); der Anrichtetisch (table).

dressing ['dresiŋ], s. (Build.) die Verkleidung; der Verband (bandage); der Verputz (interior decoration); — gown, der Schlafrock, Bademantel; (Theat.) — room, das Künstlerzimmer; Ankleidezimmer; — table, der Toilettentisch.

dressy ['dresi], adj. elegant; modesüchtig.

dribble [dribl], v.n. tröpfeln (trickle); geifern (slaver); (Footb.) dribbeln.

driblet ['driblit], s. die Kleinigkeit, die Lappalie.

drift [drift], s. die Richtung (direction); die Strömung (stream); das Treiben; Gestöber (snow). — v.a. treiben. — v.n. dahintreiben.

drill (1) [dril], v.a. drillen, bohren (bore); (Mil.) exerzieren; (Agr.) eine Furche ziehen; einstudieren (coach). — s. (Mil.) das Exerzieren; (Agr.) die Furche; der Bohrer (tool); — hall, die Übungs- or Exerzierhalle.

drill (2) [dril], s. der Drillich (textile).

drily ['draili], adv. trocken.

drink [driŋk], v.a., v.n. irr. trinken. — s. das Getränk, der Trank (potion); etwas zum Trinken (a —); come, have a —, trinken wir ein Glas (zusammen); strong —, geistiges Getränk.

drinkable ['driŋkəbl], adj. trinkbar; zum Trinken.

drinker ['driŋkə], s. der Trinker, Säufer; der Zecher; der Trunkenbold (drunkard).

drip [drip], v.n. tröpfeln. — s. das Tröpfeln.

dripping ['dripiŋ], s. (Cul.) das Bratenfett, das Schmalz.

drive [draiv], v.a. irr. treiben (sheep etc.); fahren (a car). — v.n. fahren; dahinfahren (— along). — s. die Ausfahrt, Fahrt (trip); die Einfahrt (approach to house).

driving ['draiviŋ], s. das Fahren; — licence, der Führerschein; — school, die Fahrschule; — test, die Fahrprüfung.

drivel [drivl], s. der Geifer; der Unsinn (nonsense). — v.n. Unsinn reden.

driver ['draivə], s. der Fahrer, der Chauffeur; (Railw.) Führer; (Hunt.) der Treiber.

drizzle [drizl], v.n. rieseln; leicht regnen. — s. das Rieseln, der feine Regen, der Sprühregen.

droll [droul], adj. drollig, possierlich.

drollery ['drouləri], s. die Possierlichkeit; die Schnurre.

dromedary ['drʌmədəri or 'drɔm-], s. (Zool.) das Dromedar.

drone (1) [droun], s. das Gedröhn, das Gesumme (noise). — v.n. dröhnen, summen (hum loudly).

drone (2) [droun], s. (Ent.) die Drohne; der Faulpelz (lazybones).

droop [dru:p], v.a. hängen lassen. — v.n. herabhängen; verwelken (flowers); ermatten (tire).

drop [drɔp], s. der Tropfen (liquid); das Fallen (fall). — v.a. fallen lassen; — a brick, eine taktlose Bemerkung machen; — a hint, andeuten, auf etwas hindeuten. — v.n. fallen.

droppings ['drɔpiŋz], s. pl. der Mist, Dünger (of animals).

dropsical ['drɔpsikəl], adj. (Med.) wassersüchtig.

dropsy ['drɔpsi], s. (Med.) die Wassersucht.

dross [drɔs], s. (Metall.) die Schlacke; der Unrat, das wertlose Zeug.

drought [draut], s. die Dürre, die Trockenheit.

drove [drouv], s. die Herde, die Trift (cattle).

drover ['drouvə], s. der Viehtreiber.

drown [draun], v.a. ertränken; überschwemmen (flood); übertönen (noise). — v.n. ertrinken.

drowse [drauz], v.n. schlummern, schläfrig sein.

drowsy ['drauzi], adj. schläfrig.

drub [drʌb], v.a. prügeln.

drudge [drʌdʒ], s. das Packtier; der Sklave, der Knecht.

drudgery ['drʌdʒəri], s. die Plackerei, die Plagerei (hard toil).

drug [drʌg], s. die Droge; die Medizin; das Rauschgift. — v.a. betäuben.

drugget ['drʌgit], s. der (grobe) Wollstoff.

drum [drʌm], s. die Trommel. — v.n. trommeln, austrommeln.

drunk [drʌŋk], adj. betrunken.

drunkard ['drʌŋkəd], s. der Trunkenbold.

drunkenness ['drʌŋkənnis], s. die Trunkenheit.

dry [drai], adj. trocken, dürr; ausgetrocknet, durstig (thirsty). — v.a. austrocknen, trocken machen, dörren. — v.n. trocken werden, trocknen.

dryad ['draiæd], s. die Baumnymphe Dryade.

dryness ['drainis], s. die Trockenheit, die Dürre.

dual ['dju:əl], adj. doppelt; Zwei-.

dub (1) [dʌb], v.a. zum Ritter schlagen; nennen (name).

dub (2) [dʌb], v.a. (Films) synchronisieren.

dubious ['dju:bjəs], adj. zweifelhaft.

ducal ['dju:kəl], adj. herzoglich.

duchess ['dʌtʃis], s. die Herzogin.

duchy ['dʌtʃi], s. das Herzogtum.

duck (1) [dʌk], s. (Orn.) die Ente.

duck (2) [dʌk], v.n. sich ducken, sich bücken; untertauchen (in water).— v.a. untertauchen, ins Wasser tauchen.

duckling ['dʌkliŋ], s. (Orn.) das Entchen.

duct [dʌkt], s. (Anat.) der Kanal; die Röhre.

ductile ['dʌktail], adj. dehnbar; fügsam.

dud

dud [dʌd], *s.* (*Mil.*) der Blindgänger;
der Fehlschlag.
dude [dju:d], *s.* (*Am.*) der Geck.
dudgeon [ˈdʌdʒən], *s.* der Groll, der
Unwille; *in high* —, sehr aufgebracht.
due [dju:], *adj.* gebührend, fällig,
schuldig (*to,Dat.*); angemessen, recht;
this is — *to carelessness*, das ist auf
Nachlässigkeit zurückzuführen. —
adv. direkt, gerade. — *s.* (*pl.*) die
Gebühren.
duel [ˈdju:əl], *s.* das Duell. — *v.n.* sich
duellieren (mit, *Dat.*).
duet [dju:ˈet], *s.* (*Mus.*) das Duett.
duffer [ˈdʌfə], *s.* der Tölpel; (*obs.*)
der Hausierer.
duffle, duffel [ˈdʌfl], *s.* der Düffel, das
Düffeltuch.
dug [dʌg], *s.* die Zitze.
dug-out [ˈdʌg-aut], *s.* der Unterstand,
der Bunker.
duke [dju:k], *s.* der Herzog; *Grand
Duke*, der Großherzog.
dukedom [ˈdju:kdəm], *s.* das Herzogtum.
dull [dʌl], *adj.* fade, langweilig (*boring*);
träge, schwerfällig (*slow to grasp*);
stumpfsinnig (*obtuse*); schal, abgeschmackt (*tasteless*); schwach (*perception*); dumpf (*thud, noise*); matt
(*colour*); trüb, überwölkt (*weather*);
flau (*trade*). — *v.a.* abstumpfen (*senses*).
dullness [ˈdʌlnis], *s.* die Stumpfheit
(*senses*); die Langweile (*boredom*);
die Schwerfälligkeit (*stolidity*); die
Schwäche (*vision etc.*); die Stumpfsinnigkeit (*stupidity*).
dumb [dʌm], *adj.* stumm; (*sl.*) dumm;
—*founded*, verblüfft; —*show*, die
Pantomime; —*bell* (*Gymn.*) die Hantel.
dumbness [ˈdʌmnis], *s.* die Stummheit.
dummy [ˈdʌmi], *s.* der Strohmann
(*cards*); die Kleiderpuppe (*wax
figure*); der Blindgänger (*dud shell*);
der Schnuller (*baby's*).
dump [dʌmp], *v.a.* kippen, abladen;
—*ing ground*, der Abladeplatz. — *s.*
(*Am. coll.*) das Bumslokal.
dumpling [ˈdʌmplin], *s.* der Kloß,
(*Austr.*) der Knödel.
dumps [dʌmps], *s. pl.* der Unmut, der
Mißmut, die Depression.
dumpy [ˈdʌmpi], *adj.* untersetzt, kurz
und dick.
dun (1) [dʌn], *adj.* schwarzbraun.
dun (2) [dʌn], *s.* der Gläubiger. —
v.a. energisch mahnen.
dunce [dʌns], *s.* der Dummkopf.
dune [dju:n], *s.* die Düne.
dung [dʌŋ], *s.* der Dünger. — *v.n.* düngen.
dungeon [ˈdʌndʒən], *s.* der Kerker.
dupe [dju:p], *s.* der Betrogene. — *v.a.*
betrügen.
duplicate [ˈdju:plikeit], *v.a.* verdoppeln; doppelt schreiben *or* ausfüllen
(*write twice*); vervielfältigen (*stencil*).
— [-kit], *s.* das Duplikat.
duplicity [dju:ˈplisiti], *s.* die Falschheit, die Doppelzüngigkeit.
durability [djuərəˈbiliti], *s.* die Dauer-
haftigkeit.

durable [ˈdjuərəbl], *adj.* dauerhaft.
duration [djuəˈreiʃən], *s.* die Dauer,
die Länge (*time*).
duress [djuəˈres], *s.* der Zwang; *under
*—, zwangsweise.
during [ˈdjuəriŋ], *prep.* während.
dusk [dʌsk], *s.* die Dämmerung.
dusky [ˈdʌski], *adj.* dunkel, trüb;
düster.
dust [dʌst], *s.* der Staub. — *v.a.* ab-
stauben (*clean*); bestäuben (*pollinate*);
bestreuen.
dustbin [ˈdʌstbin], *s.* der Mülleimer.
dusty [ˈdʌsti], *adj.* staubig; *not so* —,
(*coll.*) nicht so übel.
Dutch [dʌtʃ], *adj.* holländisch; nieder-
ländisch; — *treat*, auf getrennte Kosten; *double* —, Kauderwelsch, Unsinn.
Dutchman [ˈdʌtʃmən], *s.* der Hol-
länder, der Niederländer.
dutiful [ˈdju:tiful], *adj.* gehorsam,
pflichttreu, pflichtbewußt.
duty [ˈdju:ti], *s.* die Pflicht; die Abgabe
(*tax*); *customs* —, der Zoll; *be on* —,
Dienst haben; (*being*) *on* —, dienstha-
bend; *off* —, dienstfrei; —*free*, zollfrei;
in — *bound*, von Rechts wegen,
pflichtgemäß.
dwarf [dwɔ:f], *s.* der Zwerg. — *v.a.* am
Wachstum hindern (*stunt*); klein
erscheinen lassen (*overshadow*).
dwell [dwel], *v.n.* irr. wohnen (*be domiciled*); verweilen (*remain*).
dwelling [ˈdweliŋ], *s.* die Wohnung; —
place, der Wohnort.
dwindle [dwindl], *v.n.* abnehmen,
kleiner werden.
dye [dai], *v.a.* färben. — *s.* die Farbe;
(*Chem.*) der Farbstoff.
dyeing [ˈdaiiŋ], *s.* das Färben; Fär-
bereigewerbe.
dyer [ˈdaiə], *s.* der Färber.
dying [ˈdaiiŋ], *s.* das Sterben; *the* —,
(*pl.*) die Sterbenden, *pl.* — *adj.*
sterbend.
dynamic [daiˈnæmik], *adj.* dynamisch.
dynamics [daiˈnæmiks], *s. pl.* die
Dynamik.
dynamite [ˈdainəmait], *s.* das Dynamit.
dynamo [ˈdainəmou], *s.* der Dynamo,
die Dynamomaschine.
dynasty [ˈdinəsti], *s.* die Dynastie.
dysentery [ˈdisəntri], *s.* (*Med.*) die Ruhr.
dyspepsia [disˈpepsiə], *s.* (*Med.*) die
Magenverstimmung.
dyspeptic [disˈpeptik], *adj.* mit ver-
stimmtem Magen; schlecht aufgelegt
(*grumpy*).

E

E [i:]. das E (*also Mus.*); *E flat*, Es;
E sharp, Eis; *E minor*, E-moll.

each [i:tʃ], *adj.*, *pron.* jeder, jede, jedes; — *other*, einander; — *one*, jeder einzelne.

eager [ˈiːgə], *adj.* eifrig, begierig.

eagerness [ˈiːgənis], *s.* der Eifer, die Begierde.

eagle [i:gl], *s.* (*Orn.*) der Adler; (*Am.*) das Zehndollarstück.

ear [iə], *s.* das Ohr; —*lap*, das Ohrläppchen; —*phones*, die Kopfhörer; — *piece*, die Hörmuschel; —*drum*, das Trommelfell; — *of corn*, die Ähre.

earl [ə:l], *s.* der Graf.

earldom [ˈəːldəm], *s.* die (englische) Grafschaft.

early [ˈəːli], *adj.* früh, frühzeitig.

earmark [ˈiəmɑːk], *v.a.* kennzeichnen, bezeichnen.

earn [ə:n], *v.a.* verdienen; erwerben.

earnest [ˈəːnist], *s.* der Ernst; der ernste Beweis, das Handgeld; (*Comm.*) die Anzahlung; (*fig.*) der Vorgeschmack. — *adj.* ernst, ernsthaft.

earnings [ˈəːniŋz], *s.* das Einkommen.

earshot [ˈiəʃɔt], *s.* die Hörweite.

earth [ə:θ], *s.* die Erde; der Erdboden (*soil*); der Fuchsbau (*of fox*); *down to* —, praktisch denkend; *move heaven and* —, alles daransetzen; *where on* —, wo in aller Welt.

earthen [ˈəːθən], *adj.* irden, aus Erde; —*ware*, das Steingut.

earthquake [ˈəːθkweik], *s.* das Erdbeben.

earthly [ˈəːθli], *adj.* irdisch.

earthworm [ˈəːθwəːm], *s.* (*Zool.*) der Regenwurm.

earthy [ˈəːθi], *adj.* erdig; irdisch.

earwig [ˈiəwig], *s.* (*Ent.*) der Ohrwurm.

ease [i:z], *s.* die Leichtigkeit (*facility*); die Bequemlichkeit (*comfort*); *feel at* —, sich wie zu Hause fühlen; (*Mil.*) *stand at* —! rührt euch! *ill at* —, unbehaglich. — *v.a.* erleichtern, leichter machen; lindern (*pain*); *v.n.* — *off*, (*Mil.*) sich auflockern.

easel [i:zl], *s.* das Gestell; die Staffelei.

easiness [ˈiːzinis], *s.* die Leichtigkeit, die Ungezwungenheit.

east [i:st], *adj.*, *adv.* Ost-, ostwärts (*direction*). — *s.* der Osten, der Orient.

Easter [ˈiːstə]. das *or* (*n.* or *f. pl.*) die Ostern.

eastern [ˈiːstən], *adj.* östlich; morgenländisch, orientalisch (*oriental*).

easy [ˈiːzi], *adj.* leicht, frei; — *chair*, der Lehnstuhl, Sessel; *stand* —! rührt Euch! *take it* —, nimm's nicht so ernst; es sich (*Dat.*) bequem machen (*make o.s. comfortable*); (*Comm.*) — *terms*, Zahlungserleichterungen; —*going*, gemütlich.

eat [i:t], *v.a.*, *v.n.* irr. essen, speisen (*dine*); fressen (*of animals*); — *humble pie*, sich demütigen; *o.'s hat*, einen Besen fressen; *o.'s words* seine Worte bereuen.

eatable [ˈiːtəbl], *adj.* genießbar, eßbar.

eaves [i:vz], *s. pl.* die Dachrinne, die Traufe.

eavesdrop [ˈiːvzdrɔp], *v.n.* belauschen (*on s.o.*, *Acc.*).

eavesdropper [ˈiːvzdrɔpə], *s.* der Lauscher.

ebb [eb], *s.* die Ebbe. — *v.n.* nachlassen, abebben, abfließen.

ebonize [ˈebənaiz], *v.a.* wie Ebenholz *or* schwarz beizen.

ebony [ˈebəni], *s.* das Ebenholz.

ebullient [iˈbʌljənt], *adj.* aufwallend.

eccentric [ikˈsentrik], *adj.* exzentrisch, überspannt, wunderlich.

eccentricity [eksenˈtrisiti], *s.* die Exzentrizität, die Überspanntheit.

ecclesiastic [ikliːziˈæstik], *s.* der Geistliche. — *adj.* (*also* -ical) geistlich, kirchlich.

echo [ˈekou], *s.* das Echo, der Widerhall. — *v.a.* widerhallen (*resound*); wiederholen (*repeat*).

eclectic [iˈklektik], *adj.* eklektisch. — *s.* der Eklektiker.

eclecticism [iˈklektisizm], *s.* (*Phil.*) der Eklektizismus.

eclipse [iˈklips], *s.* die Verfinsterung, Finsternis (*darkness*); die Verdunklung (*darkening*). — *v.a.* verdunkeln.

ecliptic [iˈkliptik], *s.* die Ekliptik, die Sonnenbahn.

economic [iːkəˈnɔmik], *adj.* ökonomisch, wirtschaftlich.

economical [iːkəˈnɔmikl], *adj.* (*frugal*) sparsam, wirtschaftlich.

economics [iːkəˈnɔmiks], *s.* (*pl.*) die Wirtschaftslehre, die Ökonomie.

economist [iˈkɔnəmist], *s.* der Ökonom der Wirtschaftsfachmann.

economize [iˈkɔnəmaiz], *v.n.* sparen (*on*, mit, *Dat.*); sparsam sein mit (*Dat.*).

economy [iˈkɔnəmi], *s.* die Wirtschaft; *political* —, die Nationalökonomie, Staatswirtschaftslehre.

ecstasy [ˈekstəsi], *s.* die Ekstase, die Entzückung, die Verzückung.

ecstatic [iksˈtætik], *adj.* ekstatisch, verzückt; entzückt (*delighted*).

Ecuadorean [ekwəˈdɔːriən], *adj.* ekuadorianisch. — *n.* der Ekuadorianer.

ecumenical [iːkjuˈmenikəl], *adj.* ökumenisch.

eddy [ˈedi], *s.* der Wirbel, Strudel. — *v.n.* wirbeln.

edge [edʒ], *s.* die Schärfe, die Schneide (*blade*); die Kante (*ledge*); der Rand (*brink*); der Saum (*border*); die Ecke (*corner*); der Schnitt (*book*); die Schärfe (*wit, keenness*); *put an* — *on*, schärfen; *be on* —, nervös sein. — *v.a.* besetzen (*decorate*); umgeben; *double*—*d*, zweischneidig; *two*—*d*, zweischneidig, zweikantig; —*d with lace*, mit Spitze eingefaßt. — *v.n.* sich bewegen; — *forward*, langsam vorrücken; — *off*, sich abseits halten, sich drücken; — *away from*, abrücken.

edgy [ˈedʒi], *adj.* kantig, eckig; (*fig.*) nervös, reizbar.

edible [ˈedibl], *adj.* eßbar.

edict ['i:dikt], *s.* die Verordnung.
edification [edifi'keiʃən], *s.* die Erbauung.
edifice ['edifis], *s.* der Bau, das Gebäude.
edify ['edifai], *v.a.* erbauen.
edit ['edit], *v.a.* herausgeben (*book etc.*).
edition [i'diʃən], *s.* die Ausgabe.
editor ['editə], *s.* der Herausgeber, der Schriftleiter; (*newspaper*) der Redakteur.
editorial [edi'tɔ:riəl], *adj.* Redaktions-. — *s.* der Leitartikel.
editorship ['editəʃip], *s.* die Redaktion; die Schriftleitung.
educate ['edjukeit], *v.a.* erziehen, (heran)bilden.
education [edju'keiʃən], *s.* die Erziehung (*upbringing*); die Bildung (*general culture*); das Bildungwesen, das Schulwesen (*educational system*); *primary* —, die Grundschulung, das Volksschulwesen (*secondary* —, das Mittelschulwesen, das höhere Schulwesen; *university* —, das Hochschulwesen (*system*), die Universitätsbildung (*of individual*); *local* — *authority*, das Schulamt, die Schulbehörde; *Professor of Education*, Professor der Pädagogik; *further*—, *adult* —, weitere Ausbildung, Erwachsenenbildung.
educational [edju'keiʃənəl], *adj.* erzieherisch (*educative*); Bildungs-, Unterrichts- (*for education*); — *attainment*, der Bildungsgrad, die Schulstufe (*grade*); — *facilities*, die Lehrmittel, Bildungs- *or* Schulungsmöglichkeiten, *f. pl.*
education(al)ist [edju'keiʃən(əl)ist], *s.* der Erzieher, der Pädagoge; der Erziehungsfachmann (*theorist*).
eel [i:l], *s.* (*Zool.*) der Aal.
eerie ['iəri], *adj.* gespenstisch, unheimlich.
efface [i'feis], *v.a.* auslöschen, austilgen.
effacement [i'feismənt], *s.* die Austilgung; *self*- —, die Selbstaufopferung.
effect [i'fekt], *s.* die Wirkung; die Folge, das Ergebnis (*consequence*), der Eindruck (*impression*); *of no* —, ohne jede Wirkung; *carry into* —, ausführen; *take* — *from*, vom . . . in Kraft treten. — *v.a.* bewirken (*bring about*).
effective [i'fektiv], *adj.* wirksam (*having an effect*); gültig (*in force*); dienstfähig (*usable*); wirklich (*actual*).
effectual [i'fektjuəl], *adj.* wirksam (*effective*); kräftig, energisch (*strong*).
effectuate [i'fektjueit], *v.a.* bewerkstelligen (*get done*); bewirken (*bring about*).
effeminacy [i'feminəsi], *s.* die Verweichlichung.
effeminate [i'feminit], *adj.* weichlich, verweichlicht.
effervescence [efə'vesəns], *s.* das Aufbrausen, Schäumen.
effervescent [efə'vesənt], *adj.* aufbrausend, aufschäumend.

effete [i'fi:t], *adj.* abgenutzt, erschöpft.
efficacious [efi'keiʃəs], *adj.* wirksam, energisch.
efficacy ['efikəsi], *s.* die Wirksamkeit, die Energie.
efficiency [i'fiʃənsi], *s.* die Tüchtigkeit (*of person*); die Wirksamkeit; die Leistung.
efficient [i'fiʃənt], *adj.* tüchtig; leistungsfähig; wirksam (*drug etc.*).
effigy ['efidʒi], *s.* das Bild, das Abbild.
efflorescent [eflɔ:'resənt], *adj.* aufblühend.
effluent ['efluənt], *adj.* ausfließend.
effluvium [i'flu:viəm], *s.* die Ausdünstung.
effort ['efət], *s.* die Anstrengung, die Bemühung; *make an* —, sich bemühen, sich anstrengen; *make every* —, alle Kräfte anspannen.
effrontery [i'frʌntəri], *s.* die Frechheit (*cheek*); die Unverschämtheit (*impertinence*).
effortless ['efətlis], *adj.* mühelos.
effulgence [i'fʌldʒəns], *s.* der Glanz, das Strahlen.
effulgent [i'fʌldʒənt], *adj.* schimmernd, strahlend.
effusion [i'fju:ʒən], *s.* die Ausgießung; der Erguß (*verse etc.*); der Überschwang.
effusive [i'fju:ziv], *adj.* überschwenglich.
egg [eg], *s.* das Ei; *fried* —, das Spiegelei; *scrambled* —, das Rührei; — *flip*, der Eierpunsch; —*shell*, die Eierschale. — *v.a.* — *on*, anspornen, anreizen.
eglantine ['egləntain], *s.* (*Bot.*) die wilde Rose.
egoism ['egouizm], *s.* der Egoismus.
ego(t)ist ['ego(t)ist], *s.* der Egoist.
egregious [i'gri:dʒəs], *adj.* ungeheuer(-lich).
egress ['i:gres], *s.* der Ausgang, der Ausfluß (*water etc.*).
Egyptian [i'dʒipʃən], *adj.* ägyptisch. — *s.* der Ägypter.
eiderdown ['aidədaun], *s.* die Daunendecke, Steppdecke.
eiderduck ['aidədʌk], *s.* (*Orn.*) die Eidergans.
eight [eit], *num. adj.* acht.
eighteen [ei'ti:n], *num. adj.* achtzehn.
eighty ['eiti], *num. adj.* achtzig.
either ['aiðə], *adj., pron.* einer von beiden. — *conj.* entweder (*or*, oder).
ejaculate [i'dʒækjuleit], *v.a., v.n.* ausstoßen.
eject [i'dʒekt], *v.a.* hinauswerfen; ausstoßen.
ejection [i'dʒekʃən], *s.* die Ausstoßung.
eke [i:k], *v.a.* — *out*, verlängern, ergänzen; — *out an existence*, ein spärliches Auskommen finden.
elaborate [i'læbəreit], *v.a.* ausarbeiten, im einzelnen ausarbeiten. — [-rit], *adj.* detailliert, ausgearbeitet; kunstvoll (*intricate*); umständlich (*involved*).

elaboration [ilæbəˈreiʃən], *s.* die Ausarbeitung (im einzelnen); die Detailarbeit.

elapse [iˈlæps], *v.n.* verstreichen, verfließen (*time*).

elastic [iˈlæstik], *adj.* elastisch. — *s.* das Gummiband.

elasticity [elæsˈtisiti], *s.* (*Phys.*) die Elastizität.

elate [iˈleit], *v.a.* stolz machen; ermutigen.

elated [iˈleitid], *adj.* in gehobener Stimmung.

elation [iˈleiʃən], *s.* der Stolz; die Begeisterung.

elbow [ˈelbou], *s.* (*Anat.*) der Ellenbogen; *at o.'s* —, bei der Hand; — *room*, der Spielraum. — *v.a.* — *o.'s way through*, sich durchdrängen.

elder (1) [ˈeldə], *comp. adj.* älter. — *s.* der Alte, der Älteste; Kirchenälteste.

elder (2) [ˈeldə], *s.* (*Bot.*) der Holunder.

elderly [ˈeldəli], *adj.* älter; alt; ältlich.

elect [iˈlekt], *v.a.* erwählen (*to, zu, Dat.*); auswählen (*choose*). — *adj.* erwählt, auserwählt; *chairman* —, der gewählte Vorsitzende.

election [iˈlekʃən], *s.* die Auswahl (*selection*); (*Pol.*) die Wahlen, *f. pl.*; die Wahl (*choice*); *by(e)* — —, die Bezirkswahl, die Neuwahl; — *broadcast*, eine Radiowahlrede.

electioneering [ilekʃənˈiəriŋ], *s.* das Wahlmanöver, die Wahlpropaganda, der Wahlkampf.

elective [iˈlektiv], *adj.* durch Wahl bestimmt; Wahl-.

elector [iˈlektə], *s.* (*Pol.*) der Wähler; das Mitglied eines Wahlausschusses (*academic etc.*); der Kurfürst (*prince*).

electorate [iˈlektərit], *s.* die Wählerschaft.

electress [iˈlektrəs], *s.* die Kurfürstin (*princess*).

electric(al) [iˈlektrik(əl)], *adj.* elektrisch; *electrical engineer*, der Elektrotechniker; der Student der Elektrotechnik (*trainee*); *electric switch*, der elektrische Schalter; — *razor*, der elektrische Rasierapparat.

electrician [elekˈtriʃən], *s.* der Elektriker.

electricity [ilek- *or* elekˈtrisiti], *s.* die Elektrizität.

electrocution [ilektroˈkjuːʃən], *s.* die Hinrichtung *or* der Unfall (*accidental*) durch Elektrizität.

electron [iˈlektrɔn], *s.* das Elektron.

electroplate [iˈlektropleit], *v.a.* galvanisch versilbern.

electrotype [iˈlektrotaip], *s.* der galvanische Abdruck, die Galvanographie.

elegance [ˈeligəns], *s.* die Eleganz.

elegant [ˈeligənt], *adj.* elegant, fein.

elegy [ˈelidʒi], *s.* (*Lit.*) die Elegie.

element [ˈelimənt], *s.* das Element; der Bestandteil (*component*).

elemental [eliˈmentl], *adj.* elementar.

elementary [eliˈmentri], *adj.* einfach (*simple*); elementar (*for beginners*).

elephant [ˈelifənt], *s.* (*Zool.*) der Elefant.

elevate [ˈeliveit], *v.a.* erheben, erhöhen.

elevation [eliˈveiʃən], *s.* die Erhebung (*lifting*); (*Geom.*) die Elevation; die Erhöhung (*rise*); der Aufriß (*Engin. drawing*).

elevator [ˈeliveitə], *s.* (*Am.*) der Lift, der Aufzug, der Fahrstuhl; (*Agr.*) der Getreideheber.

eleven [iˈlevn], *num. adj.* elf.

elf [elf], *s.* der Elf, der Kobold.

elfin [ˈelfin], *adj.* Elfen-, elfenhaft.

elicit [iˈlisit], *v.a.* herauslocken, entlocken.

eligibility [elidʒiˈbiliti], *s.* die Wählbarkeit.

eligible [ˈelidʒibl], *adj.* wählbar, passend.

eliminate [iˈlimineit], *v.a.* ausschalten, ausscheiden, eliminieren.

elimination [ilimiˈneiʃən], *s.* die Ausschaltung, die Ausscheidung.

elision [iˈliʒən], *s.* (*Phonet.*) die Auslassung, die Weglassung.

elixir [iˈliksə], *s.* das Elixier.

elk [elk], *s.* (*Zool.*) der Elch.

ell [el], *s.* die Elle.

ellipse [iˈlips], *s.* (*Geom.*) die Ellipse.

ellipsis [iˈlipsis], *s.* (*Gram.*) die Ellipse.

elliptic(al) [iˈliptik(əl)], *adj.* (*Gram., Geom.*) elliptisch.

elm [elm], *s.* (*Bot.*) die Ulme.

elocution [eləˈkjuːʃən], *s.* der Vortrag (*delivery*); die Vortragskunst.

elocutionist [eləˈkjuːʃənist], *s.* der Vortragskünstler.

elongate [ˈiːlɔŋgeit], *v.a.* verlängern.

elongation [iːlɔŋˈgeiʃən], *s.* die Verlängerung.

elope [iˈloup], *v.n.* entlaufen, von zu Hause fliehen.

elopement [iˈloupmənt], *s.* das Entlaufen, die Flucht von zu Hause.

eloquence [ˈeləkwəns], *s.* die Beredsamkeit.

eloquent [ˈeləkwənt], *adj.* beredt, redegewandt.

else [els], *adv.* sonst, außerdem, anders; *or* —, sonst . . .; *how* —? wie denn sonst? *nobody* —, sonst niemand; *anyone* —? sonst noch jemand? — *conj.* sonst.

elsewhere [elsˈwɛə], *adv.* anderswo; anderswohin.

Elsinore [ˈelsinɔː], Helsingör, *n.*

elucidate [iˈljuːsideit], *v.a.* erläutern, erklären (*to s.o., Dat.*).

elucidation [iljuːsiˈdeiʃən], *s.* die Erläuterung, die Erklärung.

elude [iˈljuːd], *v.a.* ausweichen, entgehen (*Dat.*).

elusive [iˈljuːsiv], *adj.* schwer faßbar, täuschend.

Elysian [iˈliziən], *adj.* elysisch.

emaciate [iˈmeiʃieit], *v.a.* abmagern, dünn werden.

emaciation [imeiʃiˈeiʃən], *s.* die Abmagerung.

emanate [′eməneit], *v.n.* ausgehen, herrühren (*derive*); ausstrahlen (*radiate*).

emancipate [i′mænsipeit], *v.a.* befreien, emanzipieren.

emancipation [imænsi′peiʃən], *s.* die Emanzipation.

embalm [im′bɑːm], *v.a.* einbalsamieren.

embankment [im′bæŋkmənt], *s.* der Flußdamm, der Eisenbahndamm; die Eindämmung.

embarcation *see* **embarkation.**

embargo [im′bɑːgou], *s.* die Handelssperre.

embark [im′bɑːk], *v.a.* einschiffen. — *v.n.* sich einschiffen; — *upon s.th.*, an etwas herangehen, unternehmen.

embarkation [embɑː′keiʃən], *s.* die Einschiffung.

embarrass [im′bærəs], *v.a.* verlegen machen, in Verlegenheit bringen.

embarrassment [im′bærəsmənt], *s.* die Verlegenheit.

embassy [′embəsi], *s.* (*Pol.*) die Botschaft, die Gesandtschaft.

embed [im′bed], *v.a.* einbetten.

embellish [im′beliʃ], *v.a.* verschönern, ausschmücken; ausmalen (*story*).

embers [′embəz], *s. pl.* die glühende Asche; die Kohlen, *f. pl.*; *Ember Days*, (*Eccl.*) die Quatembertage, *m. pl.*

embezzle [im′bezl], *v.a.* veruntreuen, unterschlagen.

embitter [im′bitə], *v.a.* verbittern.

emblazon [im′bleizn], *v.a.* ausmalen, auf ein Schild setzen.

emblem [′embləm], *s.* das Emblem, das Abzeichen.

emblematic(al) [emblə′mætik(əl)], *adj.* sinnbildlich, symbolisch.

embodiment [im′bɔdimənt], *s.* die Verkörperung.

embody [im′bɔdi], *v.a.* verkörpern.

embolden [im′bouldn], *v.a.* erkühnen, anfeuern, anspornen; *be emboldened*, sich erkühnen.

emboss [im′bɔs], *v.a.* in getriebener Arbeit verfertigen, prägen.

embossed [im′bɔst], *adj.* getrieben, in erhabener Arbeit; gestanzt.

embrace [im′breis], *v.a.* (*fig.*) umarmen, umfassen. — *s.* die Umarmung.

embrasure [im′breiʒə], *s.* die Schießscharte.

embrocation [embro′keiʃən], *s.* die Einreibung (*act*); (*Pharm.*) die Einreibsalbe.

embroider [im′brɔidə], *v.a.* sticken; verzieren, ausschmücken (*adorn*).

embroidery [im′brɔidəri], *s.* die Stickerei; die Verzierung, Ausschmückung (*of story etc.*).

embroil [im′brɔil], *v.a.* verwickeln.

embryo [′embriou], *s.* der Keim; Embryo.

embryonic [embri′ɔnik], *adj.* im Embryostadium, im Werden.

emend [i′mend], *v.a.* verbessern (*text*), berichtigen.

emendation [iːmen′deiʃən], *s.* die Textverbesserung.

emendator [′iːmendeitə], *s.* der Berichtiger.

emerald [′emərəld], *s.* der Smaragd.

emerge [i′məːdʒ], *v.n.* auftauchen, hervortreten, an den Tag kommen.

emergence [i′məːdʒəns], *s.* das Auftauchen, das Hervortreten.

emergency [i′məːdʒənsi], *s.* der Notfall; die kritische Lage; *in case of* —, im Notfalle; — *exit*, der Notausgang; — *landing*, die Notlandung; — *measures*, Notmaßnahmen; — *brake*, die Notbremse.

emery [′eməri], *s.* — *paper*, das Schmirgelpapier.

emetic [i′metik], *s.* das Brechmittel.

emigrant [′emigrənt], *s.* der Auswanderer.

emigrate [′emigreit], *v.n.* auswandern.

emigration [emi′greiʃən], *s.* die Auswanderung.

eminence [′eminəns], *s.* die Anhöhe; die Eminenz, der hohe Ruf (*fame*); die eminente Stellung, die Autorität (*authority*); *Your Eminence*, Eure Eminenz.

eminent [′eminənt], *adj.* eminent, hervorragend.

emissary [′emisəri], *s.* der Abgesandte, der Sendbote.

emission [i′miʃən], *s.* die Aussendung (*sending out*); die Ausstrahlung (*radiation*).

emit [i′mit], *v.a.* aussenden; ausstrahlen; ausströmen.

emolument [i′mɔljumənt], *s.* das (Neben)einkommen, das Zusatzgehalt, das Honorar (*fee*).

emotion [i′mouʃən], *s.* die Rührung, die Bewegung, das Gefühl, die Gemütsbewegung.

emotional [i′mouʃənəl], *adj.* gefühlvoll.

emperor [′empərə], *s.* der Kaiser.

emphasis [′emfəsis], *s.* der Nachdruck.

emphasize [′emfəsaiz], *v.a.* betonen.

empire [′empaiə], *s.* das Reich, das Kaiserreich.

empiric(al) [emp′irik(əl)], *adj.* (*Phil.*) empirisch.

empiricism [em′pirisizm], *s.* (*Phil.*) der Empirizismus.

employ [im′plɔi], *v.a.* benutzen (*thing*); beschäftigen, anstellen (*person*).

employee [im′plɔiiː], *s.* der Angestellte.

employer [im′plɔiə], *s.* der Arbeitgeber.

employment [im′plɔimənt], *s.* die Beschäftigung, die Arbeit.

emporium [em′pɔːriəm], *s.* der Handelsplatz; (*Naut.*) der Stapelplatz; das Warenhaus (*stores*).

empower [em′pauə], *v.a.* bevollmächtigen.

empress [′empres], *s.* die Kaiserin.

emptiness [′emptinis], *s.* die Leere, die Öde.

empty [′empti], *adj.* leer; — *-headed*, geistlos.

enfranchisement

emulate ['emjuleit], v.a. nacheifern (Dat.).

emulation [emju'leifən], s. der Wetteifer, das Nacheifern.

emulous ['emjuləs], adj. nacheifernd, wetteifernd; eifersüchtig (jealous).

emulsion [i'mʌlfən], s. (Pharm.) die Emulsion.

enable [i'neibl], v.a. befähigen; ermächtigen (empower).

enact [i'nækt], v.a. (Pol.) verordnen; verfügen (order); darstellen, aufführen (on stage).

enactment [i'næktmənt], s. die Verordnung.

enamel [i'næml], v.a. emaillieren. — s. die Emaille; (Med.) der Schmelz.

enamour [i'næmə], v.a. verliebt machen.

encamp [in'kæmp], v.n. (sich) lagern, das Lager aufschlagen.

encampment [in'kæmpmənt], s. das Lager.

encase [in'keis], v.a. einschließen, in ein Gehäuse schließen.

encashment [in'kæfmənt], s. (Comm.) das Inkasso, die Einkassierung.

enchain [in'tfein], v.a. in Ketten legen, anketten.

enchant [in'tfɑ:nt], v.a. bezaubern.

enchantment [in'tfɑ:ntmənt], s. die Bezauberung; der Zauber (spell).

encircle [in'sə:kl], v.a. umringen, umkreisen; (Mil.) einkreisen.

encirclement [in'sə:klmənt], s. die Einkreisung.

enclose [in'klouz], v.a. einschließen; einlegen (in letter).

enclosure [in'klouʒə], s. die Einfriedigung; die Beilage, Einlage (in letter).

encompass [in'kʌmpəs], v.a. umfassen, umspannen (comprise).

encore [ɔnkɔ:, ɔŋ'kɔ:], int. noch einmal! —s. die Wiederholung, Zugabe.

encounter [in'kauntə], v.a. treffen; begegnen (Dat.). — s. das Zusammentreffen.

encourage [in'kʌridʒ], v.a. ermutigen; anspornen.

encouragement [in'kʌridʒmənt], s. die Ermutigung; die Förderung (promotion).

encroach [in'kroutf], v.n. eingreifen (interfere); übergreifen.

encroachment [in'kroutfmənt], s. der Eingriff, der Übergriff.

encrust [in'krʌst], v.a. inkrustieren; verkrusten.

encumber [in'kʌmbə], v.a. belasten.

encumbrance [in'kʌmbrəns], s. die Belastung, das Hindernis.

encyclical [en'siklikl], s. das (päpstliche) Rundschreiben, die Enzyklika.

encylopaedia [insaiklo'pi:djə], s. das Lexikon, die Enzyklopädie.

encyclopaedic [insaiklo'pi:dik], adj. enzyklopädisch.

end [end], s. das Ende; der Schluß; das Ziel (aim); die Absicht (intention); in the —, am Ende, letzten Endes; to

that —, zu dem Zweck; put an — to, einer Sache ein Ende machen; make —s meet, sein Auskommen finden; burn the candle at both —s, seine Kräfte verschwenden. — v.a. beenden. — v.n. enden, Schluß machen.

ending ['endiŋ], s. das Ende (of play etc.); (Gram.) die Endung.

endanger [in'deindʒə], v.a. gefährden, in Gefahr bringen.

endear [in'diə], v.a. beliebt machen. — v.r. — o.s. to, sich lieb Kind machen bei.

endearment [in'diəmənt], s. term of —, ein Kosewort.

endeavour [in'devə], v.n. sich bemühen, sich bestreben. — s. das Streben, die Bestrebung, die Bemühung.

endemic(al) [en'demik(əl)], adj. einheimisch; endemisch.

endive ['endiv], s. (Bot.) die Endivie.

endless ['endlis], adj. unendlich, endlos.

endorse [in'dɔ:s], v.a. bestätigen (confirm); beipflichten; (Fin.) indossieren (cheque).

endorsement [in'dɔ:smənt], s. die Bestätigung (confirmation); (Fin.) das Indossament (cheque).

endow [in'dau], v.a. begaben (talents); ausstatten (equip); stiften.

endowment [en'daumənt], s. die Begabung (talents); die Stiftung; — policy, die abgekürzte Lebensversicherung.

endurable [in'djuərəbl], adj. erträglich.

endurance [in'djuərəns], s. die Ausdauer (toughness); die Dauer, Fortdauer (time); das Ertragen (suffering); — test, die Dauerprüfung; (fig.) die Geduldsprobe (patience).

endure [in'djuə], v.a. aushalten, ertragen; leiden (suffer).

endways, endwise ['endweiz, -waiz], adv. mit dem Ende nach vorne; aufrecht (vertical).

enemy ['enəmi], s. der Feind, der Gegner.

energetic [enə'dʒetik], adj. energisch, tatkräftig.

energy ['enədʒi], s. die Energie, die Tatkraft; der Nachdruck (vehemence).

enervate ['enə:veit], v.a. entkräften, schwächen.

enervation [enə:'veifən], s. die Entkräftigung, die Schwächung.

enfeeble [in'fi:bl], v.a. entkräften, schwächen.

enfold [in'fould], v.a. umschließen, umfassen; einhüllen (veil).

enforce [in'fɔ:s], v.a. erzwingen, durchsetzen.

enforcement [in'fɔ:smənt], s. die Erzwingung, die Durchsetzung.

enfranchise [in'fræntfaiz], v.a. freilassen, befreien (emancipate); (Pol.) das Stimmrecht geben.

enfranchisement [in'fræntfizmənt], s. die Befreiung, die Gewährung des Stimmrechts.

engage [in'geidʒ], *v.a.* verpflichten, engagieren (*pledge, bind*); anstellen (*employ*); verwickeln (*in conversation*); *become —d*, sich verloben. — *v.n. in*, sich einlassen in (*Acc.*), sich befassen mit (*Dat.*).

engagement [in'geidʒmənt], *s.* die Verpflichtung (*pledge*); die Verlobung (*betrothal*); die Verabredung (*appointment*); das Gefecht (*with enemy*).

engaging [in'geidʒiŋ], *adj.* freundlich, verbindlich (*smile etc.*); einnehmend.

engender [in'dʒendə], *v.a.* erzeugen, hervorrufen (*cause*).

engine ['endʒin], *s.* die Maschine; der Motor; (*Railw.*) die Lokomotive; *fire —*, die Feuerspritze; *— driver*, (*Railw.*) der Lokomotivführer.

engineer [endʒi'niə], *s.* der Ingenieur (*professional*); der Techniker (*technician*); (*Am.*) der Lokomotivführer (*engine driver*).

engineering [endʒi'niəriŋ], *s.* das Ingenieurwesen; der Maschinenbau; *chemical —*, die chemische Technik *or* Technologie; *civil —*, das Zivilingenieurwesen; *electrical —*, die Elektrotechnik *or* die Elektrotechnologie; *mechanical —*, der Maschinenbau, die Strukturtechnik; *— laboratory*, das technische Labor; *— workshop*, die technische Werkstatt.

English ['iŋgliʃ], *adj.* englisch; britisch. — *s.* die englische Sprache, das Englisch; (*pl.*) *the —*, die Engländer, *m.pl.*

Englishman ['iŋgliʃmən], *s.* der Engländer.

Englishwoman ['iŋgliʃwumən], *s.* die Engländerin.

engrain [in'grein], *v.a.* tief einprägen.

engrave [in'greiv], *v.a.* gravieren, eingravieren (*art*); einprägen (*impress*).

engraver [in'greivə], *s.* der Graveur, der Kupferstecher.

engraving [in'greiviŋ], *s.* der Kupferstich.

engross [in'grous], *v.a.* ganz in Anspruch nehmen, gefangen halten(*mind*).

engulf [in'gʌlf], *v.a.* verschlingen.

enhance [in'hɑːns], *v.a.* erhöhen (*raise*); steigern (*increase*).

enhancement [in'hɑːnsmənt], *s.* die Erhöhung (*pleasure*); die Steigerung (*growth*).

enigma [i'nigmə], *s.* das Rätsel.

enigmatic(al) [enig'mætik(əl)], *adj.* rätselhaft (*puzzling*); dunkel (*obscure*).

enjoin [in'dʒɔin], *v.a.* (an)befehlen (*s.o., Dat.*), einschärfen (*s.o., Dat.*).

enjoy [in'dʒɔi], *v.a.* genießen (*Acc.*); sich freuen (über, *Acc.*). — *v.r. —o.s.*, sich amüsieren.

enjoyable [in'dʒɔiəbl], *adj.* erfreulich, angenehm, genießbar.

enjoyment [in'dʒɔimənt], *s.* der Genuß, die Freude (*of*, an, *Dat.*).

enlarge [in'lɑːdʒ], *v.a.* vergrößern (*premises etc.*); erweitern (*expand*). —

v.n. sich verbreiten (*on* or *upon*, über, *Acc.*).

enlargement [in'lɑːdʒmənt], *s.* die Vergrößerung (*also Phot.*).

enlighten [in'laitn], *v.a.* erleuchten, aufklären (*explain to*).

enlightenment [in'laitnmənt], *s.* (*Eccl.*) die Erleuchtung;(*Phil.*)die Aufklärung.

enlist [in'list], *v.a.* anwerben (*Mil.*); gewinnen (*cooperation*). — *v.n.* (*Mil.*) sich anwerben lassen.

enliven [in'laivn], *v.a.* beleben, aufmuntern.

enmity ['enmiti], *s.* die Feindschaft.

ennoble [i'noubl], *v.a.* adeln; veredeln.

enormity [i'nɔːmiti], *s.* die Ungeheuerlichkeit.

enormous [i'nɔːməs], *adj.* ungeheuer; ungeheuerlich.

enough [i'nʌf], *adj., adv.* genug; ausreichend; *sure —*, gewiß!; *well —*, ziemlich gut.

enquire *see under* **inquire**.

enquiry *see under* **inquiry**.

enrage [in'reidʒ], *v.a.* wütend machen.

enraged [in'reidʒd], *adj.* wütend, entrüstet.

enrapture [in'ræptʃə], *v.a.* in Entzückung versetzen, entzücken (*delight*).

enrich [in'ritʃ], *v.a.* bereichern; (*Chem.*) verbessern.

enrol [in'roul], *v.a.* einschreiben (*inscribe*); (*Mil.*) anwerben. — *v.n.* sich einschreiben; beitreten (*Dat.*).

enrolment [in'roulmənt], *s.* die Einschreibung; *— form*, das Einschreibeformular.

ensconce [in'skɔns], *v.r. —o.s.*, sich niederlassen.

enshrine [in'ʃrain], *v.a.* umhüllen, einschließen (*in*); einen Schrein aufbewahren.

enshroud [in'ʃraud], *v.a.* einhüllen.

ensign ['ensin *or* 'enzən, 'ensain], *s.* (*Naut.*) die Fahne, die Flagge; (*Mil. rank*) der Fähnrich.

enslave [in'sleiv], *v.a.* unterjochen, versklaven.

ensnare [in'snɛə], *v.a.* umgarnen, verführen (*seduce*).

ensue [in'sju:], *v.n.* folgen.

ensure [in'ʃuə], *v.a.* versichern (*assure*); sicherstellen (*make sure*).

entail [in'teil], *v.a.* zur Folge haben, mit sich bringen.

entangle [in'tæŋgl], *v.a.* verwickeln, verwirren (*confuse*).

entanglement [in'tæŋglmənt], *s.* die Verwicklung; die Verwirrung (*confusion*).

enter ['entə], *v.a.* betreten; eintreten; *— o.'s name*, seinen Namen einschreiben. — *v.n.* eintreten (*in*, in, *Acc.*); *— into agreement*, einen Vertrag eingehen; *— on*, sich einlassen in (*Acc.*); *— upon a career*, eine Laufbahn antreten.

enterprise ['entəpraiz], *s.* das Unternehmen; das Wagnis (*daring*); *private —*, das Privatunternehmen; (*Econ.*)

die freie Wirtschaft; *public* —, das staatliche *or* Staatsunternehmen.

enterprising ['entəpraiziŋ], *adj.* unternehmungslustig.

entertain [entə'tein], *v.a.* unterhalten (*amuse*); zu Tisch haben (*person*); hegen (*opinion*).

entertaining [entə'teiniŋ], *adj.* amüsant, unterhaltend.

entertainment [entə'teinmənt], *s.* die Unterhaltung, Vergnügung.

enthral [in'θrɔːl], *v.a.* fesseln, bannen.

enthrone [in'θroun], *v.a.* auf den Thron bringen *or* setzen.

enthusiasm [in'θjuːziæzm], *s.* die Begeisterung; die Schwärmerei.

enthusiast [in'θjuːziæst], *s.* der Enthusiast, der Schwärmer.

enthusiastic [inθjuːzi'æstik], *adj.* enthusiastisch, begeistert, schwärmerisch.

entice [in'tais], *v.a.* locken, anlocken, verlocken (*lure*).

enticement [in'taismənt], *s.* die Lockung.

entire [in'taiə], *adj.* gesamt, ganz; völlig; vollständig (*complete*).

entirety [in'taiəriti], *s.* die Gesamtheit (*totality*); das Ganze (*total*).

entitle [in'taitl], *v.a.* berechtigen; betiteln (*title*).

entitlement [in'taitlmənt], *s.* die Berechtigung.

entity ['entiti], *s.* das Wesen.

entomb [in'tuːm], *v.a.* begraben.

entomologist [entə'mɔlədʒist], *s.* der Entomologe.

entomology [entə'mɔlədʒi], *s.* die Entomologie.

entrails ['entreilz], *s. pl.* die Eingeweide, *n.pl.*

entrain [in'trein], *v.a.* (*Railw., Mil.*) einsteigen lassen. — *v.n.* (*Railw.*) (in den Zug) einsteigen.

entrance (1) [in'entrəns], *s.* der Eingang (*door*); — *fee*, der Eintritt; — *hall*, der Hausflur, die Vorhalle; *university* —, Zulassung zur Universität.

entrance (2) [in'trɑːns], *v.a.* entzücken, hinreißen.

entrant ['entrənt], *s.* (*to school, university etc.*) der (neu) Zugelassene; Teilnehmer.

entrap [in'træp], *v.a.* fangen, verstricken.

entreat [in'triːt], *v.a.* anflehen, ersuchen.

entreaty [in'triːti], *s.* die flehentliche *or* dringende Bitte, (*obs.*) das Ansuchen.

entrench [in'trentʃ], *v.a.* verschanzen, festsetzen.

entrenchment [in'trentʃmənt], *s.* (*Mil.*) die Verschanzung.

entrust [in'trʌst], *v.a.* anvertrauen (*s. th.*); betreuen (*s.o. with*, mit, *Dat.*).

entry ['entri], *s.* das Eintreten, der Eintritt; der Eingang (*house*); (*Comm.*) die Eintragung (*book-keeping*); *double* —, doppelte Buchführung; die Einfuhr (*import*); — *permit*, die

Einreisebewilligung; *no* —, Eintritt verboten!

entwine [in'twain], *v.a.* verflechten, herumwickeln.

enumerate [i'njuːməreit], *v.a.* aufzählen.

enumeration [injuːmə'reiʃən], *s.* die Aufzählung.

enunciate [i'nʌnsieit], *v.a.* aussprechen.

enunciation [inʌnsi'eiʃən], *s.* (*Phonet.*) die Aussprache; die Kundgebung (*declaration*).

envelop [in'veləp], *v.a.* einhüllen, umhüllen.

envelope ['enviloup, 'ɔnvəloup], *s.* die Hülle; der Umschlag, Briefumschlag (*letter*).

enviable ['enviəbl], *adj.* beneidenswert.

envious ['enviəs], *adj.* neidisch (*of s.o.*, auf, *Acc.*).

environment [in'vaiərənmənt], *s.* die Umgebung; (*Geog., Zool.*) die Umwelt.

environs [in'vairənz], *s. pl.* die Umgebung, die Umgegend.

envisage [in'vizidʒ], *v.a.* sich vorstellen.

envoy ['envɔi], *s.* (*Pol.*) der Gesandte, der Bote.

envy ['envi], *s.* der Neid. — *v.a.* beneiden.

epaulette [epɔ:'let], *s.* (*Mil.*) das Achselstück, die Epaulette.

ephemeral [i'femərəl], *adj.* Eintags-, Tages-; eintägig, vergänglich (*transient*).

epic ['epik], *adj.* episch. — *s.* das Epos.

epicure ['epikjuə], *s.* der Epikureer, der Feinschmecker, der Genießer.

epidemic [epi'demik], *s.* die Epidemie.

epigram ['epigræm], *s.* das Epigramm.

epigrammatic [epigrə'mætik], *adj.* epigrammatisch, kurz; treffend (*apt*).

epilepsy ['epilepsi], *s.* (*Med.*) die Epilepsie, die Fallsucht.

epileptik [epi'leptik], *s.* (*Med.*) der Epileptiker.

epilogue ['epilɔg], *s.* der Epilog.

Epiphany [i'pifəni], (*Eccl.*) das Fest der heiligen drei Könige, Epiphanias.

episcopal [i'piskəpəl], *adj.* bischöflich.

episcopate [i'piskəpit], *s.* die Bischofswürde, das Episkopat (*collective*).

episode ['episoud], *s.* die Episode.

epistle [i'pisl], *s.* die Epistel, das Sendschreiben.

epistolary [i'pistələri], *adj.* brieflich, Brief-.

epitaph ['epitɑːf], *s.* die Grabschrift.

epithet ['epiθet], *s.* das Beiwort, die Benennung.

epitome [i'pitəmi], *s.* die Epitome, der Auszug; der Abriß (*summary*).

epitomize [i'pitəmaiz], *v.a.* kürzen; einen Auszug machen von (*Dat.*).

epoch ['iːpɔk], *s.* die Epoche; — *making*, bahnbrechend.

equable ['ekwəbl], *adj.* gleich, gleichmäßig; gleichmütig (*tranquil*).

equal ['iːkwəl], *adj.* gleich, ebenbürtig (*to, Dat.*).

equality [i'kwɔliti], *s.* die Gleichheit, Ebenbürtigkeit.

equalization [i:kwəlai'zeiʃən], *s.* der Ausgleich; — *of burdens*, der Lastenausgleich.

equalize ['i:kwəlaiz], *v.a.* gleichmachen. — *v.n.* (*Footb.*) ausgleichen.

equanimity [i:kwə'nimiti], *s.* der Gleichmut.

equate [i'kweit], *v.a.* (*Maths.*) gleichsetzen.

equation [i'kweiʃən], *s.* die Gleichung.

equator [i'kweitə], *s.* (*Geog.*) der Äquator.

equatorial [ekwə'tɔ:riəl], *adj.* (*Geog.*) äquatorial.

equerry ['ekwəri], *s.* der Stallmeister; diensttuender Kammerherr (*of King*).

equestrian [i'kwestriən], *adj.* beritten; Reit-; — *art*, die Reitkunst.

equidistant [i:kwi'distənt], *adj.* gleich weit entfernt.

equilateral [i:kwi'lætərəl], *adj.* gleichseitig.

equilibrium [i:kwi'libriəm], *s.* das Gleichgewicht.

equine ['ekwain], *adj.* Pferd-, pferdeartig.

equinoctial [i:kwi'nɔkʃəl], *adj.* äquinoktial.

equinox ['i:kwinɔks], *s.* die Tag- und Nachtgleiche.

equip [i'kwip], *v.a.* (*Mil.*) ausrüsten; ausstatten (*furnish*).

equipment [i'kwipmənt], *s.* die Ausrüstung, die Ausstattung; das Zeug.

equitable ['ekwitəbl], *adj.* unparteiisch, gerecht, billig.

equity ['ekwiti], *s.* die Billigkeit, die Unparteilichkeit.

equivalence [i'kwivələns], *s.* die Gleichwertigkeit, die Gleichheit.

equivalent [i'kwivələnt], *adj.* gleichwertig. — *s.* das Äquivalent, der gleiche Wert, der Gegenwert.

equivocal [i'kwivəkəl], *adj.* zweideutig, doppelsinnig, zweifelhaft.

era ['iərə], *s.* die Ära, die Zeitrechnung.

eradicate [i'rædikeit], *v.a.* ausrotten, austilgen, vertilgen.

eradication [irædi'keiʃən], *s.* die Ausrottung, die Vertilgung.

erase [i'reiz], *v.a.* ausradieren.

eraser [i'reizə], *s.* der Radiergummi (*India rubber*).

erasure [i'reiʒə], *s.* die Ausradierung; die Auskratzung (*scratching*).

ere [ɛə], *prep.* (*obs.*) vor. — *conj.* (*obs.*) ehe, bevor.

erect [i'rekt], *adj.* aufrecht, gerade. — *v.a.* aufrichten; errichten (*build*).

erection [i'rekʃən], *s.* die Errichtung (*structure*); die Aufrichtung (*putting up*).

ermine ['ə:min], *s.* der *or* das Hermelin.

erode [i'roud], *v.a.* (*Geog., Geol.*) ausfressen.

erosion [i'rouʒən], *s.* die Erosion.

erotic [i'rɔtik], *adj.* erotisch.

err [ə:], *v.n.* irren.

errand ['erənd], *s.* der Auftrag, Gang; der Botengang; — *boy*, der Laufbursche.

errant ['erənt], *adj.* herumstreifend; *knight* —, fahrender Ritter.

errata *see under* **erratum**.

erratic [i'rætik], *adj.* regellos, unberechenbar, ohne Verlaß.

erratum [e'reitəm, e'rɑ:təm], *s.* (*pl.* **errata** [e'reitə, e'rɑ:tə]) der Druckfehler.

erroneous [i'rouniəs], *adj.* irrig, irrtümlich.

error ['erə], *s.* der Irrtum, der Fehler.

erudite ['erudait], *adj.* gelehrt.

erudition [eru'diʃən], *s.* die Gelehrsamkeit.

erupt [i'rʌpt], *v.n.* ausbrechen.

eruption [i'rʌpʃən], *s.* der Ausbruch.

eruptive [i'rʌptiv], *adj.* Ausbruchs-, ausbrechend.

escalator ['eskəleitə], *s.* die Rolltreppe.

escapade [eskə'peid], *s.* der Streich (*prank*).

escape [is'keip], *v.a., v.n.* entkommen, entgehen, entfliehen.

escapism [is'keipizm], *s.* die Philosophie der Weltflucht.

escapist [is'keipist], *s.* der Weltflüchtling.

escarpment [is'kɑ:pmənt], *s.* die Böschung.

eschew [is'tʃu:], *v.a.* vermeiden.

escort [is'kɔ:t], *v.a.* geleiten; decken (*cover*). — ['eskɔ:t], *s.* (*Mil.*) die Garde, die Deckung; Begleitung (*persons*); (*Mil.*) das Geleit (*conduct*).

escutcheon [is'kʌtʃən], *s.* das Wappenschild.

esoteric [eso'terik], *adj.* (*Phil.*) esoterisch, geheim, dunkel.

espalier [es'pæljə], *s.* (*Mil.*) das Spalier.

especial [is'peʃəl], *adj.* besonder, außergewöhnlich.

espionage ['espiənɑ:ʒ *or* -nidʒ], *s.* die Spionage, das Spionieren.

espouse [is'pauz], *v.a.* (ver-)heiraten; (*fig.*) eintreten (für, *Acc.*).

espy [is'pai], *v.a.* auskundschaften, erspähen.

essay [i'sei], *v.a.* versuchen, probieren. — ['esei], *s.* der Versuch; der Aufsatz, Essay (*composition*).

essayist ['eseiist], *s.* der Essayist.

essence ['esns], *s.* (*Phil., Chem.*) die Essenz.

essential [i'senʃəl], *adj.* wesentlich, wichtig (*important*).

establish [is'tæbliʃ], *v.a.* feststellen, (*ascertain*); gründen (*found*); —*ed Church*, die englische Staatskirche.

establishment [is'tæbliʃmənt], *s.* die Feststellung (*ascertainment*); die Gründung (*foundation*); die Unternehmung, das Geschäft (*business*); (*Mil.*) die Aufstellung, der Bestand; (*Eccl.*) die Staatskirche.

estate [is'teit], *s.* (*Pol.*) der Stand; das Vermögen, das Gut; (*property*) — *duty*, die Vermögenssteuer; — *manager*, der Gutsverwalter; — *agent*, der

Grundstückmakler; *real* —, der Grundbesitz; (*pl.*) Immobilien, *pl.*

esteem [is'ti:m], *v.a.* schätzen (*value*); achten (*respect*). — *s.* die Wertschätzung, die Achtung.

estimable ['estimǝbl], *adj.* schätzenswert.

estimate ['estimeit], *v.a.* schätzen (*evaluate*); berechnen (*calculate*). — ['estimit], *s.* die Schätzung, der Voranschlag.

estimation [esti'meiʃǝn], *s.* die Wertschätzung; die Achtung (*respect*).

Estonian [es'tounian], *adj.* estnisch, estländisch. — *s.* der Este, Estländer.

estrange [is'treindʒ], *v.a.* entfremden.

estrangement [is'treindʒmǝnt], *s.* die Entfremdung.

estuary ['estjuǝri], *s.* die Mündung (*river*); der Meeresarm (*bay*).

etch [etʃ], *v.a.* (*Metall.*) ätzen; (*Art*) radieren.

etching ['etʃiŋ], *s.* (*Art*) die Radierung.

eternal [i'tǝ:nl], *adj.* ewig; immerwährend.

eternity [i'tǝ:niti], *s.* die Ewigkeit.

ether ['i:θǝ], *s.* der Äther.

ethereal [i'θiǝriǝl], *adj.* ätherisch, luftig.

ethical ['eθikl], *adj.* ethisch, sittlich.

ethics ['eθiks], *s. pl.* die Ethik, die Sittenlehre; *professional* —, das Berufsethos.

Ethiopian [i:θi'oupiǝn], *adj.* äthiopisch. — *s.* der Äthiopier.

ethnography [eθ'nɔgrǝfi], *s.* die Ethnographie, die Völkerkunde.

etymology [eti'mɔlǝdʒi], *s.* die Etymologie, die Wortableitung.

eucharist ['ju:kǝrist], *s.* (*Eccl.*) die Eucharistie; das heilige Abendmahl.

eulogize ['ju:lǝdʒaiz], *v.a.* loben, preisen.

euphonium [ju'founiǝm], *s.* (*Mus.*) das Bombardon, Baritonhorn.

euphony ['ju:fǝni], *s.* der Wohlklang.

European [juǝrǝ'piǝn], *adj.* europäisch. — *s.* der Europäer.

euphemism ['ju:fimizm], *s.* der Euphemismus.

euphuism ['ju:fjuizm], *s.* (*Lit.*) die gezierte Stilart.

evacuate [i'vækjueit], *v.a.* evakuieren, räumen.

evacuation [ivækju'eiʃǝn], *s.* die Evakuierung, die Räumung.

evade [i'veid], *v.a.* ausweichen (*Dat.*); entgehen (*escape*, *Dat.*).

evanescent [evæ'nesǝnt], *adj.* verschwindend.

evangelical [i:væn'dʒelikǝl], *adj.* evangelisch.

evangelist [i'vændʒǝlist], *s.* der Evangelist.

evangelize [i'vændʒǝlaiz], *v.a.*, *v.n.* das Evangelium lehren *or* predigen.

evaporate [i'væpǝreit], *v.a.* verdunsten lassen, verdampfen lassen. — *v.n.* (*Chem.*) verdunsten.

evaporation [ivæpǝ'reiʃǝn], *s.* die Verdampfung, die Verdunstung.

evasion [i'veiʒǝn], *s.* die Flucht (*escape*) (*from*, *von*, *Dat.*); die Ausflucht, das Ausweichen.

evasive [i'veiziv], *adj.* ausweichend.

eve, even [i:v], *s.* (*Poet.*) der Vorabend; Abend.

even (2) [i:vn], *adj.* eben, glatt (*smooth*); gerade (*number*); quitt (*quits*); gelassen (*temper*); gleich (*equal*). — *v.a.* — *out*, gleichmachen, ebnen.

even (3) [i:vn], *adv.* gerade, selbst, sogar (*emphatic*); *not* —, nicht einmal; — *though*, obwohl.

evening ['i:vniŋ], *s.* der Abend; — *gown*, das Abendkleid; — *dress*, der Abendanzug; der Smoking (*dinner jacket*); der Frack (*tails*).

evenness ['i:vǝnnis], *s.* die Ebenheit (*of surface*); die Gelassenheit (*of temper*).

event [i'vent], *s.* die Begebenheit, der Vorfall (*happening*); das (große) Ereignis (*state occasion*); *at all* —*s*, auf alle Fälle; *in the* —, im Falle, daß.

eventful [i'ventful], *adj.* ereignisreich.

eventual [i'ventjuǝl], *adj.* schließlich, endlich.

ever ['evǝ], *adv.* je; immer, stets; nur, überhaupt; *for* —, für immer; — *so*, so sehr, sehr; — *since*, seitdem.

evergreen ['evǝgri:n], *adj.* immergrün. — *s.* (*Bot.*) das Immergrün.

everlasting [evǝ'la:stiŋ], *adj.* ewig; dauernd; fortwährend (*continual*).

every ['evri], *adj.* jeder, jeder einzelne (*pl.* alle); — *one*, jeder einzelne; — *now and then*, dann und wann; — *other day*, jeden zweiten Tag; — *day*, alle Tage.

everybody, everyone ['evribɔdi, 'evriwʌn], *s.* jedermann, ein jeder.

everyday ['evridei], *adj.* alltäglich.

everyone *see under* **everybody**.

everything ['evriθiŋ], *s.* alles.

everywhere ['evrihwɛǝ], *adv.* überall.

evict [i'vikt], *v.a.* vertreiben (*eject*); (*Law*) (gerichtlich) kündigen (*Dat.*).

eviction [i'vikʃǝn], *s.* die Kündigung, die Vertreibung.

evidence ['evidǝns], *s.* der Beweis (*proof*); (*Law*) das Zeugnis; *documentary* —, (*Law*) das Beweisstück; (*Law*) *give* —, eine Zeugenaussage machen.

evident ['evidǝnt], *adj.* klar, deutlich (*obvious*); augenscheinlich (*visible*); *self* —, selbstverständlich.

evil ['i:vil], *s.* das Übel, das Böse. — *adj.* übel, böse; — *speaking*, die üble Nachrede.

evildoer ['i:vildu:ǝ], *s.* der Übeltäter.

evince [i'vins], *v.a.* zeigen, dartun, an den Tag legen.

evocation [i:vo'keiʃǝn], *s.* die Beschwörung (*magic*); das Hervorrufen.

evocative [i'vɔkǝtiv], *adj.* hervorrufend, voll Erinnerungen (*of*, *Genit.*).

evoke [i'vouk], *v.a.* hervorrufen (*call forth*); beschwören (*conjure up*).

evolution [i:vǝ'lju:ʃǝn, ev-], *s.* die Entwicklung, Evolution.

evolutionary

evolutionary [i:və'lju:ʃənri], *adj.* Evolutions-, Entwicklungs-.

evolve [i'vɔlv], *v.a.* entwickeln. — *v.n.* sich entwickeln.

ewe [ju:], *s.* (*Zool.*) das Mutterschaf.

ewer ['juə], · *s.* die Wasserkanne.

exact [ig'zækt], *adj.* genau, gewissenhaft, exakt. — *v.a.* fordern; erpressen; eintreiben (*dept.*).

exacting [ig'zæktiŋ], *adj.* genau, anspruchsvoll.

exactitude [ig'zæktitju:d], *s.* die Genauigkeit.

exactly [ig'zæktli], *adv.* (*coll.*) ganz richtig!

exactness [ig'zæktnis], *s.* die Genauigkeit.

exaggerate [ig'zædʒəreit], *v.a.* übertreiben.

exaggeration [igzædʒə'reiʃən], *s.* die Übertreibung.

exalt [ig'zɔ:lt], *v.a.* erhöhen, erheben.

exaltation [egzɔ:l'teiʃən], *s.* die Erhöhung, die Erhebung.

exalted [ig'zɔ:ltid], *adj.* erhaben, hoch.

examination [igzæmi'neiʃən], *s.* die Prüfung; (*Med.*) die Untersuchung; (*Law*) das Verhör, das Untersuchungsverhör; die Ausfragung (*scrutiny*); — *board*, die Prüfungskommission.

examine [ig'zæmin], *v.a.* prüfen; (*Med.*) untersuchen; (*Law*) verhören; ausfragen.

examiner [ig'zæminə], *s.* der Examinator.

example [ig'zɑ:mpl], *s.* das Beispiel; *for* —, zum Beispiel; *set an* —, ein Beispiel geben.

exasperate [ig'zæspəreit], *v.a.* aufreizen; ärgern, aufbringen.

exasperation [igzæspə'reiʃən], *s.* die Entrüstung, die Erbitterung.

excavate ['ekskəveit], *v.a.* ausgraben.

excavation [ekskə'veiʃən], *s.* die Ausgrabung.

exceed [ik'si:d], *v.a.* überschreiten (*go beyond*); übertreffen (*surpass*). — *v.n.* zu weit gehen.

exceeding [ik'si:diŋ], *adj.* (*obs.*) übermäßig, übertrieben.

exceedingly [ik'si:diŋli], *adv.* außerordentlich; äußerst.

excel [ik'sel], *v.a.* übertreffen. — *v.n.* sich auszeichnen (*in*, in, *Dat.*).

excellence ['eksələns], *s.* die Vortrefflichkeit.

excellent ['eksələnt], *adj.* ausgezeichnet, hervorragend.

except [ik'sept], *v.a.* ausnehmen, ausschließen. — *conj.* außer (es sei denn) daß. — *prep.* ausgenommen, mit Ausnahme von (*Dat.*).

exception [ik'sepʃən], *s.* die Ausnahme (*exemption*); der Einwand, Einwurf (*objection*).

exceptionable [ik'sepʃənəbl], *adj.* anfechtbar (*disputable*); anstößig.

exceptional [ik'sepʃənəl], *adj.* außergewöhnlich.

exceptionally [ik'sepʃənəli], *adv.* ausnahmsweise.

excerpt [ik'sə:pt], *v.a.* ausziehen, exzerpieren. — ['eksə:pt], *s.* der Auszug, das Exzerpt.

excess [ik'ses], *s.* das Übermaß; *carry to* —, übertreiben; — *fare*, der Zuschlag; — *luggage*, das Übergewicht.

excessive [ik'sesiv], *adj.* übermäßig, allzuviel.

exchange [iks'tʃeindʒ], *s.* der Austausch; *stock* —, die Börse; *rate of* —, der Kurs; *bill of* —, der Wechsel; der Tausch (*barter*). — *v.a.* wechseln; tauschen (*barter*) (*against*, für, *Acc.*); austauschen (*messages etc.*).

exchangeable [iks'tʃeindʒəbl], *adj.* (*Comm.*) austauschbar.

exchequer [iks'tʃekə], *s.* die Staatskasse; das Finanzamt (*office*); *Chancellor of the Exchequer*, der Schatzkanzler.

excise (1) ['eksaiz], *s.* die Akzise; *customs and* —, das Zollamt, der Zoll; — *officer*, der Zollbeamte, Steuerbeamte.

excise (2) [ek'saiz], *v.a.* (her)ausschneiden.

excision [ek'siʒən], *s.* das Ausschneiden, die Entfernung.

excitable [ik'saitəbl], *adj.* erregbar, reizbar.

excitation [eksi'teiʃən], *s.* (*Phys.*, *Chem.*) die Erregung.

excitement [ik'saitmənt], *s.* die Erregung, Aufregung (*mood*).

exciting [ik'saitiŋ], *adj.* erregend, aufregend, packend (*thrilling*).

exclaim [iks'kleim], *v.a.* ausrufen.

exclamation [eksklə'meiʃən], *s.* der Ausruf (*interjection*); das Geschrei (*shouting*).

exclude [iks'klu:d], *v.a.* ausschließen.

exclusion [iks'klu:ʒən], *s.* der Ausschluß.

exclusive [iks'klu:siv], *adj.* ausschließlich (*sole*); exklusiv (*select*).

exclusiveness [iks'klu:sivnis], *s.* der exklusive Charakter, die Exklusivität.

excommunicate [ekskə'mju:nikeit], *v.a.* (*Eccl.*) von der Kirchengemeinde ausschließen, bannen, exkommunizieren.

excommunication [ekskəmju:ni'keiʃən], *s.* (*Eccl.*) die Exkommunikation, der Bann.

excoriate [eks'kɔ:rieit], *v.a.* häuten; abschälen (*peel*).

excrement ['ekskrimənt], *s.* das Exkrement, der Kot.

excrescence [iks'kresəns], *s.* der Auswuchs.

excretion [eks'kri:ʃən], *s.* die Ausscheidung, der Auswurf.

excruciate [iks'kru:ʃieit], *v.a.* martern, peinigen; *excruciatingly funny*, furchtbar komisch.

exculpate ['ekskʌlpeit], *v.a.* rechtfertigen, entschuldigen.

expenditure

exculpation [ekskʌl'peiʃən], s. die Entschuldigung, die Rechtfertigung.
excursion [iks'kə:ʃən], s. der Ausflug, die Exkursion (*outing*); die Digression (*irrelevance*); der Abstecher (*deviation*).
excusable [iks'kju:zəbl], adj. entschuldbar, verzeihlich.
excuse [iks'kju:s], s. die Entschuldigung. — [-'kju:z], v.a. entschuldigen (*Acc.*), verzeihen (*Dat.*).
execrable ['eksikrəbl], adj. abscheulich.
execrate ['eksikreit], v.a. verfluchen, verwünschen.
execute ['eksikju:t], v.a. ausführen (*carry out*); (*Law*) hinrichten (*kill*).
execution [eksi'kju:ʃən], s. die Ausführung (*of an order*); (*Law*) die Hinrichtung; die Pfändung (*official forfeit*).
executioner [eksi'kju:ʃənə], s. der Henker, der Scharfrichter.
executive [ik'sekjutiv], adj. ausübend, vollziehend (*of power etc.*). — s. (*Pol.*) die Exekutive; (*Comm.*) das Direktionsmitglied.
executor [ik'sekjutə], s. der Testamentsvollstrecker (*of a will*).
exemplar [ig'zemplə], s. das Muster, das Beispiel.
exemplary [ig'zempləri], adj. musterhaft, vorbildlich.
exemplify [ig'zemplifai], v.a. durch Beispiel(e) erläutern.
exempt [ig'zempt], v.a. ausnehmen, befreien, verschonen (*spare*).
exemption [ig'zempʃən], s. die Ausnahme.
exequies ['eksikwiz], s. pl. das Leichenbegängnis, die Totenfeier.
exercise ['eksəsaiz], s. die Übung (*practice*); die körperliche Betätigung (*exertion*). — v.a. üben; — o.'s rights, von seinen Rechten Gebrauch machen; — discretion, Diskretion walten lassen; (*Mil.*) — troops, exerzieren.
exert [ig'zə:t], v.a. ausüben; — pressure, Druck ausüben (*upon*, auf, *Acc.*). — v.r. — o.s., sich anstrengen.
exertion [ig'zə:ʃən], s. die Anstrengung, die Bemühung.
exhale [eks'heil], v.a. ausatmen; aushauchen; ausdünsten.
exhalation [eksha'leiʃən], s. die Ausatmung, die Ausdünstung.
exhaust [ig'zɔ:st], v.a. erschöpfen. — s. (*Motor.*) der Auspuff.
exhaustible [ig'zɔ:stibl], adj. erschöpflich.
exhaustion [ig'zɔ:stʃən], s. die Erschöpfung.
exhibit [ig'zibit], v.a. ausstellen (*display*); zeigen (*demonstrate*). — ['eksibit], s. das Ausstellungsobjekt; (*Law*) das Beweisstück.
exhibition [eksi'biʃən], s. die Ausstellung (*display*); (*Films*) die Vorführung (*showing*); das Stipendium (*scholarship*).

exhibitioner [eksi'biʃənə], s. der Stipendiat.
exhilarate [ig'ziləreit], v.a. aufheitern.
exhilaration [igzilə'reiʃən], s. die Aufheiterung.
exhort [ig'zɔ:t], v.a. ermahnen.
exhortation [egzɔ:'teiʃən], s. die Ermahnung.
exigence, exigency ['eksidʒəns, -si], s. das Bedürfnis, Erfordernis (*necessity*); der dringende Notfall (*emergency*).
exigent ['eksidʒənt], adj. dringend.
exile ['eksail], s. der Verbannte (*person*); das Exil, die Verbannung (*state*). — v.a. verbannen; das Landes verweisen.
exist [ig'zist], v.n. existieren.
existence [ig'zistəns], s. das Dasein, die Existenz.
existent [ig'zistənt], adj. seiend, wirklich, existierend.
existentialism [egzis'tenʃəlizm], s. der Existentialismus.
exit ['eksit], s. der Ausgang; (*Theat.*) der Abgang.
exonerate [ig'zɔnəreit], v.a. entlasten.
exorbitant [ig'zɔ:bitənt], adj. übertrieben, übermäßig.
exorcise ['eksɔ:saiz], v.a. bannen, beschwören.
exorcism ['eksɔ:sizm], s. die Geisterbeschwörung.
exotic [ig'zɔtik], adj. exotisch.
expand [iks'pænd], v.a. erweitern, ausbreiten, ausdehnen. — v.n. sich erweitern (*broaden*); sich ausdehnen (*stretch*).
expansion [iks'pænʃən], s. die Ausdehnung, die Ausbreitung.
expansive [iks'pænsiv], adj. ausgedehnt; Ausdehnungs- (*forces*); (*fig.*) mitteilsam.
expatiate [iks'peiʃieit], v.n. sich verbreiten (*on*, über, *Acc.*).
expatriate [iks'peitrieit], v.a. verbannen.
expect [iks'pekt], v.a. erwarten (*wait for*); glauben (*believe*); hoffen (*hope for*); — a baby, ein Kind erwarten.
expectant [iks'pektənt], adj. schwanger (*with child*); voll Erwartung.
expectation [ekspek'teiʃən], s. die Erwartung, die Hoffnung.
expedience, expediency [iks'pi:diəns, -si], s. die Zweckmäßigkeit, die Schicklichkeit.
expedient [iks'pi:diənt], adj. zweckmäßig, schicklich, ratsam. — s. das Mittel; der Ausweg.
expedite ['ekspidait], v.a. beschleunigen.
expedition [ekspi'diʃən], s. (*Mil. etc.*) die Expedition; die schnelle Abfertigung.
expeditious [ekspi'diʃəs], adj. schleunig, schnell.
expel [iks'pel], v.a. vertreiben, austreiben; (*Sch.*) verweisen (*from*, von, aus).
expend [iks'pend], v.a. ausgeben.
expenditure [iks'penditʃə], s. (*Comm.*) die Ausgabe; der Aufwand (*of energy*).

expense [iks'pens], *s.* die Ausgabe; (*pl.*) die Kosten, Auslagen, Spesen, *f. pl.*

expensive [iks'pensiv], *adj.* teuer, kostspielig.

experience [iks'piəriəns], *s.* die Erfahrung, das Erlebnis. — *v.a.* erfahren.

experienced [iks'piəriənsd], *adj.* erfahren.

experiment [iks'perimənt], *s.* das Experiment, der Versuch. — *v.n.* experimentieren, Versuche machen.

experimental [iksperi'mentl], *adj.* Probe-, probeweise, experimentell.

expert ['ekspə:t], *s.* der Fachmann; der Sachverständige.

expertise [ekspə'ti:z], *s.* die Expertise, die Fachkenntnis.

expertness [iks'pə:tnis], *s.* die Gewandtheit.

expiable ['ekspiəbl], *adj.* sühnbar.

expiation [ekspi'eiʃən], *s.* die Sühnung, die Sühne.

expiration [ekspi'reiʃən], *s.* das Ausatmen; (*fig.*) der Tod; der Ablauf (*time*); die Verfallszeit (*lapse of validity*).

expire [iks'paiə], *v.n.* aushauchen (*breathe*); ablaufen (*run out*); sterben (*die*).

expiry [iks'pairi], *s.* die Ablaufsfrist (*of papers*).

explain [iks'plein], *v.a.* erklären, erläutern.

explanation [eksplə'neiʃən], *s.* die Erklärung, Erläuterung.

expletive [iks'pli:tiv], *s.* das Fluchwort, der Kraftausdruck.

explicable ['eksplikəbl], *adj.* erklärlich, erklärbar.

explication [ekspli'keiʃən], *s.* die Erklärung.

explicit [iks'plisit], *adj.* ausdrücklich, deutlich.

explicitness [iks'plisitnis], *s.* die Deutlichkeit, die Bestimmtheit.

explode [iks'ploud], *v.n.* explodieren; (*Mil.*) platzen (*of a shell*). — *v.a.* explodieren lassen.

exploit [iks'plɔit], *v.a.* ausbeuten; ausnützen (*utilize*). — ['eksplɔit], *s.* die Heldentat, die Großtat.

exploitation [eksplɔi'teiʃən], *s.* die Ausbeutung, die Ausnützung.

exploration [eksplɔ:'reiʃən], *s.* die Erforschung.

explore [iks'plɔ:], *v.a.* erforschen, untersuchen (*investigate*).

explosion [iks'plouʒən], *s.* die Explosion.

explosive [iks'plousiv], *adj.* explosiv. — *s.* der Sprengstoff.

exponent [iks'pounənt], *s.* (*Maths.*) der Exponent; der Vertreter (*of a theory*).

export [iks'pɔ:t], *v.a.* ausführen, exportieren. — ['ekspɔ:t], *s.* der Export, die Ausfuhr.

exporter [iks'pɔ:tə], *s.* der Exporteur, der Ausfuhrhändler, der Exportkaufmann.

expose [iks'pouz], *v.a.* entblößen; aussetzen (*to cold etc.*); bloßstellen (*display*); (*Phot.*) belichten; darlegen (*set forth*); ausstellen (*exhibit*).

exposition [ekspo'ziʃən], *s.* die Aussetzung; die Auslegung (*interpretation*); die Darlegung (*deposition, declaration*); die Ausstellung (*exhibition*).

exposure [iks'pouʒə], *s.* die Aussetzung (*to cold etc.*); die Bloßstellung; (*Phot.*) die Belichtung.

expostulate [iks'pɔstjuleit], *v.n.* zur Rede stellen.

expound [iks'paund], *v.a.* auslegen, darlegen.

express [iks'pres], *v.a.* ausdrücken; zum Ausdruck bringen. — *adj.* ausdrücklich, eilig, Eil-; besonder; — *letter*, der Eilbrief; — *train*, der Schnellzug. — *s.* der Eilzug.

expression [iks'preʃən], *s.* der Ausdruck.

expressive [iks'presiv], *adj.* ausdrucksvoll.

expressly [iks'presli], *adv.* ausdrücklich, besonders.

expropriate [eks'prouprieit], *v.a.* enteignen.

expropriation [eksprouprи'eiʃən], *s.* die Enteignung.

expulsion [iks'pʌlʃən], *s.* die Ausstoßung; der Ausschluß; die Vertreibung (*of a large number*).

expunge [iks'pʌndʒ], *v.a.* austilgen, auslöschen.

expurgate ['ekspə:geit], *v.a.* reinigen.

exquisite [iks'ekskwizit], *adj.* auserlesen, vortrefflich.

extant ['ekstənt, ek'stænt], *adj.* noch vorhanden, existierend.

extempore [eks'tempəri], *adv.* aus dem Stegreif, extemporiert.

extemporize [eks'tempəraiz], *v.a.* extemporieren, improvisieren.

extend [iks'tend], *v.a.* ausdehnen (*boundaries etc.*); ausstrecken (*a helping hand*); verlängern (*time*); bieten (*a welcome*); erweitern (*enlarge*). — *v.n.* sich erstrecken, sich ausdehnen; dauern (*time*).

extensible [iks'tensibl], *adj.* ausdehnbar.

extension [iks'tenʃən], *s.* die Ausdehnung; die Verlängerung (*time*); *university* — *classes*, Abendkurse, *m.pl.* (der Erwachsenenbildung); (*Telephone*) der Apparat.

extensive [iks'tensiv], *adj.* ausgedehnt, umfassend.

extent [iks'tent], *s.* die Ausdehnung, die Weite, die Größe (*size*); *to a certain* —, bis zu einem gewissen Grade; *to the* — *of £x*, bis zu einem Betrage von x Pfund.

extenuate [iks'tenjueit], *v.a.* beschönigen; mildern; *extenuating circumstances*, (*Law*) mildernde Umstände, *m. pl.*

extenuation [ikstenju'eiʃən], *s.* die Beschönigung, die Abschwächung.

exterior [eks'tiəriə], *adj.* äußerlich. — *s.* das Äußere.

exterminate [iks'tə:mineit], *v.a.* ausrotten, vertilgen.

extermination [ikstə:mi'neiʃən], *s.* die Ausrottung, die Vertilgung.

external [eks'tə:nl], *adj.* äußerlich; auswärtig.

extinct [iks'tinkt], *adj.* ausgestorben.

extinction [iks'tinkʃən], *s.* das Erlöschen (*dying*); die Vernichtung (*annihilation*); das Aussterben.

extinguish [iks'tingwiʃ], *v.a.* auslöschen; vernichten (*annihilate*). — *v.n.* auslöschen, ausgehen (*of fire or life*).

extirpate ['ekstə:peit], *v.a.* ausrotten.

extol [iks'toul], *v.a.* preisen, erheben.

extort [iks'tɔ:t], *v.a.* erpressen.

extortion [iks'tɔ:ʃən], *s.* die Erpressung.

extortionate [iks'tɔ:ʃənit], *adj.* erpresserisch.

extra ['ekstrə], *adj.* zusätzlich. — *s.* (*pl.*) die Nebenausgaben, *f. pl.*

extract [iks'trækt], *v.a.* (aus)ziehen (*pull out*). — ['ekstrækt], *s.* (*Chem.*) der Extrakt; der Auszug (*book*).

extraction [iks'trækʃən], *s.* das Ausziehen (*pulling out*); das Zahnziehen (*tooth*); das Verfertigen eines Auszuges (*book*); die Herkunft (*origin*).

extradite ['ekstrədait], *v.a.* (*Pol.*) ausliefern.

extradition [ekstrə'diʃən], *s.* (*Pol.*) die Auslieferung.

extraneous [eks'treiniəs], *adj.* nicht zur Sache gehörig, unwesentlich.

extraordinary [iks'trɔ:dnəri], *adj.* außerordentlich.

extravagance [iks'trævəgəns], *s.* die Extravaganz; die Verschwendung (*waste*).

extravagant [iks'trævəgənt], *adj.* extravagant; verschwenderisch.

extravaganza [ikstrævə'gænzə], *s.* fantastisches Werk, die Burleske, Posse.

extreme [iks'tri:m], *adj.* äußerst (*uttermost*); höchst (*highest*); extrem (*stringent*); letzt (*last*). — *unction*, (*Eccl.*) die Letzte Ölung; *in the* —, äußerst.

extremity [iks'tremiti], *s.* die äußerste Grenze (*limit*); die Notlage (*straits*, *emergency*); (*pl.*) die Extremitäten, *f. pl.*

extricate ['ekstrikeit], *v.a.* herauswinden, herauswickeln (*disentangle*), befreien.

extrude [eks'tru:d], *v.a.* ausstoßen, (*Metall.*) ausziehen.

extrusion [eks'tru:ʒən], *s.* die Ausstoßung; die Ausziehung (*of steel etc.*).

exuberant [ig'zju:bərənt], *adj.* überschwenglich, überschäumend.

exude [ik'sju:d], *v.a.* ausschwitzen; von sich geben (*give out*).

exult [ig'zʌlt], *v.n.* frohlocken.

exultant [ig'zʌltənt], *adj.* triumphierend.

exultation [egzʌl'teiʃən], *s.* das Frohlocken, der Jubel.

eye [ai], *v.a.* ansehen, betrachten. — *s.* das Auge; — *of a needle*, das Nadelöhr; *an* — *for an* —, Aug' um Auge; — *witness*, der Augenzeuge.

eyeball ['aibɔ:l], *s.* der Augapfel.

eyebrow ['aibrau], *s.* die Augenbraue.

eyeglass ['aigla:s], *s.* der Zwicker, Klemmer.

eyelash ['ailæʃ], *s.* die Augenwimper.

eyelid ['ailid], *s.* das Augenlid.

eyesight ['aisait], *s.* die Sehkraft, das Augenlicht.

eyrie ['ɛəri, 'iəri], *s.* der Adlerhorst.

F

F [ef], das F (*also Mus.*).

fable [feibl], *s.* die Fabel; das Märchen.

fabric ['fæbrik], *s.* das Gewebe, der Stoff.

fabricate ['fæbrikeit], *v.a.* herstellen; (*fig.*) fabrizieren; erfinden.

fabrication [fæbri'keiʃən], *s.* (*fig.*) die Erdichtung, die Erfindung.

fabulous ['fæbjuləs], *adj.* fabelhaft; wunderbar.

façade [fə'sɑ:d], *s.* die Fassade.

face [feis], *v.a.* jemandem ins Gesicht sehen (*s.o.*); gegenüberstehen, gegenüberliegen (*lie opposite*, *Dat.*); — *west*, nach Westen gehen (*of house*, *window*). — *v.n.* — *about*, sich umdrehen. — *s.* das Gesicht, (*Poet.*) das Angesicht; — *to* — *with*, gegenüber (*Dat.*); *on the* — *of it*, auf den ersten Blick; *lose* —, sich blamieren; *have the* — *to*, die Frechheit haben etwas zu tun.

facet ['fæsit], *s.* die Facette; der Zug (*feature*).

facetious [fə'si:ʃəs], *adj.* scherzhaft.

facetiousness [fə'si:ʃəsnis], *s.* die Scherzhaftigkeit, die Witzigkeit.

facile [f'æsail], *adj.* leicht.

facilitate [fə'siliteit], *v.a.* erleichtern, leicht machen.

facility [fə'siliti], *s.* die Leichtigkeit (*ease*); die Gewandtheit (*deftness*); die Möglichkeit (*possibility*); (*pl.*) die Einrichtungen, die Möglichkeiten, *f. pl.* (*amenities*).

facing ['feisin], *s.* (*Tail.*) der Besatz, der Aufschlag; (*Build.*) die Verkleidung; (*Mil.*) die Schwenkung, die Wendung.

facsimile [fæk'simili], *s.* das Faksimile.

fact [fækt], *s.* die Tatsache; *as a matter of* —, tatsächlich, in Wirklichkeit; —*s and figures*, der Bericht mit Tatsachen und Zahlen; *in* —, tatsächlich; *in point of* —, in der Tat, in Wirklichkeit.

faction ['fækʃən], *s.* (*Pol.*) die Partei, die Faktion.

factitious [fæk'tiʃəs], *adj.* nachgemacht, künstlich.

factor ['fæktə], *s.* der Faktor; (*Comm.*) der Agent; der Umstand (*fact*).

factory

factory ['fæktəri], *s.* die Fabrik; — *hand*, der Fabrikarbeiter.

factual ['fæktjuəl], *adj.* Tatsachen-, tatsächlich.

faculty ['fækəlti], *s.* (*Univ.*) die Fakultät; die Fähigkeit (*sense*); (*pl.*) die Talente, *n. pl.*, die Begabung; Kräfte *f. pl.*

fad [fæd], *s.* die Grille, die Laune; die Marotte.

faddy ['fædi], *adj.* schrullig.

fade [feid], *v.n.* verschießen (*colour*); verwelken (*flower*); vergehen.

fag [fæg], *v.a.* ermüden. — *v.n.* (*Sch.*) Dienste tun, Diener sein (*for*, für). — *s.* die Plackerei; (*coll.*) die Zigarette; (*Sch.*) der Fuchs, der neue Schüler; — *end*, der Zigarettenstummel; (*Naut.*) das offene Tauende; der letze Rest (*remnant*).

faggot ['fægət], *s.* das Reisigbündel.

fail [feil], *v.a.* im Stiche lassen (*let down*); (*Sch.*) durchfallen (*an examination*, in einer Prüfung. — *v.n.* — *to do*, etwas nicht tun, fehlgehen, scheitern; versagen.

failing ['feiliŋ], *adj.* schwach, versagend. — *s.* der Mangel, Fehler.

failure ['feiljə], *s.* der Fehlschlag; das Versagen (*weakness*); das Nichteinhalten (*non-compliance*); das Durchfallen (*in examinations*); der Versager (*person*).

fain [fein], *adv.* (*obs.*) gern, genne.

faint [feint], *v.n.* in Ohnmacht fallen, ohnmächtig werden. — *adj.* leise, schwach (*noise etc.*); — *hearted*, kleinmütig.

fair (1)′ [fɛə], *adj.* hübsch, schön (*beautiful*); unparteiisch, fair (*impartial*); anständig, angemessen (*equitable*); blond.

fair (2) [fɛə], *s.* der Jahrmarkt (*market*); (*Comm.*) die Messe, die Handelsmesse.

fairness ['fɛənis], *s.* die Schönheit (*beauty*); die Unparteilichkeit, Fairneß (*objectivity*); die Sportlichkeit (*sportsmanship*); die Anständigkeit (*equity*).

fairy ['fɛəri], *s.* die Fee.

faith [feiθ], *s.* der Glaube; die Treue (*loyalty*); das Vertrauen (*trust*).

faithful ['feiθful], *adj.* (*Rel.*) gläubig; treu (*loyal*); ergeben (*devoted*).

faithless ['feiθlis], *adj.* (*Rel.*) ungläubig; treulos, untreu (*disloyal*).

fake [feik], *s.* der Schwindel.

falcon ['fɔ:(l)kən], *s.* (*Orn.*) der Falke.

falconer ['fɔ:(l)knə], *s.* der Falkner.

falconry ['fɔ:(l)kənri], *s.* die Falknerei.

fall [fɔ:l], *v.n. irr.* fallen, abfallen (*leaves*); einbrechen (*night*); sich legen (*wind*); heruntergehen, sinken (*price*); geboren werden (*pigs, lambs*); — *through*, mißlingen, zunichte werden. — *s.* der Fall; (*Am.*) der Herbst (*autumn*); der Abhang (*precipice*); der Verfall (*decay*); der Untergang (*decline*).

fallacious [fə'leiʃəs], *adj.* trügerisch, trüglich, falsch (*assumption etc.*).

fallacy ['fæləsi], *s.* die Täuschung, der Irrtum, Trugschluß.

fallible ['fælibl], *adj.* fehlbar.

falling ['fɔ:liŋ], *s.* das Fallen; — *sickness*, die Fallsucht; — *off*, das Abnehmen (*decrease*); — *out*, der Zwist, der Streit (*disunity*). — *adj.* — *star*, die Sternschnuppe.

fallow ['fælou], *adj.* brach, fahl.

false [fɔ:ls], *adj.* falsch, unrichtig (*untrue*); — *alarm*, der blinde Alarm; — *bottom*, der Doppelboden; — *start*, der Fehlstart; — *step*, der Fehltritt; — *verdict*, das Fehlurteil; — *pretences*, die Vorspiegelung falscher Tatsachen.

falsehood ['fɔ:lshud], *s.* die Lüge, die Unwahrheit.

falseness ['fɔ:lsnis], *s.* die Falschheit; die Unaufrichtigkeit (*insincerity*).

falsify ['fɔ:lsifai], *v.a.* fälschen, verfälschen.

falsity ['fɔ:lsiti] *see* **falseness**.

falter ['fɔ:ltə], *v.n.* straucheln (*stumble*); stammeln (*stammer*).

fame [feim], *s.* der Ruhm; der Ruf; *ill* —, der üble Ruf.

familiar [fə'miljə], *adj.* vertraut, wohlbekannt, intim; gewohnt (*habitual*); *be on* — *terms*, auf vertrautem Fuß stehen.

familiarity [fəmili'æriti], *s.* die Vertrautheit, die Vertraulichkeit (*intimacy*).

familiarize [fə'miljəraiz], *v.a.* vertraut machen, bekannt machen.

family ['fæmili], *s.* die Familie; — *doctor*, der Hausarzt; (*Chem.*) die Gruppe; *be in the* — *way*, in anderen Umständen sein, guter Hoffnung sein, schwanger sein; — *tree*, der Stammbaum.

famine ['fæmin], *s.* die Hungersnot; — *relief*, Hilfe für die Hungernden.

famish ['fæmiʃ], *v.n.* verhungern, hungern; verschmachten.

famous ['feiməs], *adj.* berühmt, wohlbekannt (*for*, wegen).

fan [fæn], *s.* der Fächer (*lady's*); der Ventilator; (*sl.*) der leidenschaftliche Anhänger, der Fan; (*coll.*) Fanatiker (*admirer*). — *v.a.* fächeln; anfachen (*flames*); entfachen (*hatred*). — *v.n.* (*Mil.*) — *out*, sich ausbreiten, ausschwärmen.

fanatic [fə'nætik], *s.* der Fanatiker.

fanatical [fə'nætikəl], *adj.* fanatisch.

fanaticism [fə'nætisizm], *s.* der Fanatismus, die Schwärmerei.

fancier ['fænsiə], *s. pigeon* —, der Taubenzüchter; *bird* —, der Vogelzüchter.

fanciful ['fænsiful], *adj.* schwärmerisch, wunderlich.

fancy ['fænsi], *s.* die Vorliebe (*preference*); die Phantasie; die Laune (*whim*); *take a* — *to*, liebgewinnen. — *adj.* — *dress*, der Maskenanzug, das Kostüm; — *goods*, Galanteriewaren; — *cakes*, Torten, *f.pl.*; das Feingebäck. — *v.a.* denken, gern haben; (*coll.*) — *oneself as*, sich einbilden, man sei; *just* — !, denk doch mal; denk mal an!

fanfare [ˈfænfɛə], s. (Mus.) die Fanfare, der Tusch.

fang [fæŋ], s. (Zool.) der Hauzahn, der Giftzahn (of snake); (Engin.) der Zapfen. — v.a. (Engin.) vollpumpen, aufpumpen und in Tätigkeit setzen.

fanlight [ˈfænlait], s. die Lünette, das Lichtfenster.

fantastic(al) [fænˈtæstik(əl)], adj. fantastisch.

fantasy [ˈfæntəsi], s. (Poet., Mus.) die Phantasie; das Hirngespinst (chimœra).

far [fɑː], adj. weit; fern, entfernt (distant). — adv. — and wide, weit und breit; by —, bei weitem; go too —, zu weit gehen; he will go —, er wird seinen Weg machen; — sighted, weitsichtig.

farce [fɑːs], s. die Farce, die Posse.

fare [fɛə], s. das Fahrgeld; der Fahrpreis (of taxi etc.); der Fahrgast (one travelling in taxi); — stage, die Fahror Teilstrecke; das Essen, die Kost (food); bill of —, die Speisekarte. — v.n. ergehen (Dat.), daran sein.

farewell [fɛəˈwel], interj. lebewohl! — dinner, das Abschiedsessen; — party, die Abschiedsgesellschaft.

farinaceous [færiˈneiʃəs], adj. mehlig, aus Mehl.

farm [fɑːm], s. der Pachthof, der Bauernhof; die Farm; — hand, der Landarbeiter, der Farmarbeiter; — bailiff, der Gutsverwalter. — v.a. bebauen; — out, verpachten. — v.n. Landwirt sein.

farmer [ˈfɑːmə], s. der Bauer, Landwirt; der Pächter (tenant).

farmland [ˈfɑːmlænd], s. das Ackerland.

farmyard [ˈfɑːmjɑːd], s. der Bauernhof, Gutshof.

farrier [ˈfæriə], s. der Hufschmied.

farrow [ˈfærou], s. der Wurf (pigs). — v.n. ferkeln, Junge haben.

farther [ˈfɑːðə], comp. adj., adv. ferner, weiter.

farthest [ˈfɑːðist], superl. adj., adv. fernst, weitest.

farthing [ˈfɑːðiŋ], s. der Farthing, der Heller.

fascinate [ˈfæsineit], v.a. bezaubern, faszinieren.

fascination [fæsiˈneiʃən], s. die Bezauberung; der Reiz, der Zauberbann (spell).

fascism [ˈfæʃizm], s. (Pol.) der Faschismus.

fashion [ˈfæʃən], s. die Mode; out of —, außer Mode; die Art und Weise (manner). — v.a. gestalten, bilden (shape); fully —ed, vollgeformt or geformt, angepaßt.

fashionable [ˈfæʃnəbl], adj. modisch, modern; elegant.

fast (1) [fɑːst], adj. schnell (runner); fest (firm); my watch is —, meine Uhr geht vor; a — woman, eine leichtlebige Frau; — train, der Schnellzug; — and furious, schnell wie der Wind. — adv. fest.

fast (2) [fɑːst], v.n. (Rel.) fasten; (Rel.) — day, der Fasttag.

fasten [fɑːsn], v.a. festbinden, festmachen (fix). — v.n. sich festhalten (on to, an, Dat.).

fastidious [fəsˈtidiəs], adj. wählerisch, anspruchsvoll.

fastidiousness [fəsˈtidiəsnis], s. die anspruchsvolle Art.

fat [fæt], adj. fett; dick (person). — s. das Fett; (Cul.) das Speisefett.

fatal [ˈfeitəl], adj. tödlich (lethal); verhängnisvoll.

fatalism [ˈfeitəlizm], s. der Fatalismus.

fatality [fəˈtæliti], s. das Verhängnis; der Todesfall; der tödliche Unfall.

fate [feit], s. das Schicksal, Geschick; das Verhängnis (doom, destiny).

fated [ˈfeitid], adj. dem Verderben (Untergang) geweiht.

fateful [ˈfeitful], adj. verhängnisvoll, unselig.

father [ˈfɑːðə], s. der Vater; (Eccl.) Pater; — -in-law, der Schwiegervater. — v.a. Vater sein or werden von (Dat.); zeugen (procreate).

fatherland [ˈfɑːðəlænd], s. das Vaterland.

fatherly [ˈfɑːðəli], adj. väterlich; wie ein Vater.

fathom [ˈfæðəm], s. die Klafter. — v.a. ergründen, erforschen.

fatigue [fəˈtiːg], s. die Ermüdung, die Erschöpfung; (Mil.) der Arbeitsdienst. — v.a. ermüden, erschöpfen.

fatling [ˈfætliŋ], s. (Agr.) das Mastvieh.

fatness [ˈfætnis], s. die Beleibtheit (person); die Fettheit (animals).

fatten [fætn], v.a. — up, mästen (animals); fett werden lassen. — v.n. fett werden, sich mästen (an, Dat.).

fatty [ˈfæti], adj. (Chem.) fett, fettig. — s. (coll.) der Dickwanst.

fatuity [fəˈtjuːiti], s. die Albernheit, die Dummheit.

fatuous [ˈfætjuəs], adj. albern, dumm, nichtssagend.

faucet [ˈfɔːsit], s. der Zapfen, der Hahn.

fault [fɔːlt], s. der Fehler; die Schuld; find — with, etwas kritisieren; tadeln; it is my —, es ist meine Schuld; at —, im Irrtum.

faultless [ˈfɔːltlis], adj. fehlerlos, fehlerfrei.

faultlessness [ˈfɔːltlisnis], s. die Fehlerlosigkeit, die fehlerlose Ausführung.

faulty [ˈfɔːlti], adj. fehlerhaft, mangelhaft.

faun [fɔːn], s. (Myth.) der Faun.

fauna [ˈfɔːnə], s. die Fauna, die Tierwelt.

favour [ˈfeivə], s. die Gunst, das Wohlwollen; (Comm.) in — of, zugunsten; do a —, einen Gefallen tun or erweisen; be in —, sehr begehrt sein, in hoher Gunst stehen. — v.a. bevorzugen, begünstigen, wohlwollend gegenüberstehen (Dat.).

favourable [ˈfeivərəbl], adj. günstig, vorteilhaft.

favourite ['feivərit], *s.* der Favorit, der Liebling; der Günstling (*of kings*). — *adj.* Lieblings-, bevorzugt.

fawn (1) [fɔːn], *s.* (*Zool.*) das junge Reh, das Rehkalb; — *coloured*, rehfarben. — *adj.* rehfarben, hellbraun.

fawn (2) [fɔːn], *v.n.* schmeicheln, kriecherisch sein ((*up*)*on*, *Dat.*).

fawning ['fɔːniŋ], *adj.* kriecherisch, kriechend.

fear [fiə], *s.* die Furcht, die Angst; *stand in — of s.o.*, sich vor jemandem fürchten; *for — of*, aus Angst vor (*Dat.*). — *v.a.* fürchten, befürchten.

fearful ['fiəful], *adj.* furchtsam (*full of fear*); furchtbar (*causing fear*).

fearless ['fiəlis], *adj.* furchtlos (*of*, vor, *Dat.*).

fearlessness ['fiəlisnis], *s.* die Furchtlosigkeit.

feasibility [fiːzi'biliti], *s.* die Tunlichkeit, die Möglichkeit.

feasible ['fiːzibl], *adj.* tunlich, möglich.

feast [fiːst], *s.* das Fest, der Festtag; der Schmaus (*good meal*). — *v.n.* schmausen (*upon*, von, *Dat.*). — *v.a.* festlich bewirten.

feat [fiːt], *s.* die Tat, die Heldentat; das Kunststück.

feather ['feðə], *s.* die Feder; *show the white —*, Feigheit an den Tag legen; — *bed*, das Federbett. — *v.a.* federn; — *o.'s nest*, sein Schäfchen ins Trockene bringen.

feature ['fiːtʃə], *s.* der Zug (*characteristic*); der Gesichtszug (*facial*). — *v.a.* charakterisieren; (*Film*) in der Hauptrolle zeigen.

February ['februəri], der Februar.

feckless ['feklis], *adj.* hilflos, unfähig.

feculence ['fekjuləns], *s.* (*Chem.*) der Bodensatz, der Hefesatz.

fecund ['fekənd], *adj.* fruchtbar.

fecundate ['fekəndeit], *v.a.* fruchtbar machen, befruchten.

fecundity [fi'kʌnditi], *s.* die Fruchtbarkeit.

federacy ['fedərəsi], *s.* der Bund, die Föderation.

federal ['fedərəl], *adj.* Bundes-, föderativ.

federalism ['fedərəlizm], *s.* der Föderalismus.

federalize ['fedərəlaiz], *v.a.* verbünden.

federation [fedə'reiʃən], *s.* die Föderation, die Verbündung; (*Pol.*) der Bund.

fee [fiː], *s.* die Gebühr (*official dues*); das Honorar (*of doctor etc.*); (*pl.*) (*Sch.*) das Schulgeld.

feeble [fiːbl], *adj.* schwach, matt; — *minded*, schwachsinnig.

feed [fiːd], *v.a. irr.* füttern; verköstigen (*humans*); unterhalten (*maintain*); zuführen (*into machine, Dat.*); *be fed up with*, etwas satt haben; — *pipe*, die Speiseröhre. — *v.n.* sich nähren (*on*, von, *Dat.*); weiden (*graze*).

feeder ['fiːdə], *s.* der Kinderlatz (*bib*); (*Tech.*) der Zubringer.

feel [fiːl], *v.n. irr.* sich fühlen (*sense*); meinen (*think*). — *v.a.* berühren, betasten (*touch*); empfinden (*be aware of*).

feeler ['fiːlə], *s.* der Fühler; *put out a —*, einen Fühler ausstrecken.

feeling ['fiːliŋ], *s.* das Gefühl; *with —*, bewegt, gerührt (*moved*); grimmig (*in anger*).

feign [fein], *v.a.* vortäuschen, heucheln.

feint [feint], *s.* die Verstellung (*disguise*); die Finte (*fencing*).

felicitate [fi'lisiteit], *v.a.* Glück wünschen (*upon*, zu, *Dat.*), beglückwünschen (*Acc.*).

felicitation [filisi'teiʃən], *s.* die Beglückwünschung, der Glückwunsch.

felicitous [fi'lisitəs], *adj.* glücklich ausgedrückt, gut gesagt (*in speaking*).

felicity [fi'lisiti], *s.* die Glückseligkeit; die glückliche Ausdruckweise (*style*).

feline ['fiːlain], *adj.* Katzen-, katzenartig.

fell (1) [fel], *adj.* grausam; *at one — swoop*, mit einem wilden Schwung.

fell (2) [fel], *v.a.* fällen (*timber*); töten (*kill*).

fell (3) [fel], *s.* das Gebirge, das Felsengelände.

fell (4) [fel], *s.* das Fell, die Haut (*skin*).

fellow ['felou], *s.* der Gefährte, Genosse (*companion*); das Mitglied eines College *or* einer Universität; (*coll.*) der Kerl; *queer —*, seltsamer Kauz; — *feeling*, das Mitgefühl; — *traveller*, der Weggenosse; (*Pol.*) der Mitläufer.

fellowship ['felouʃip], *s.* die Mitgliedschaft (einer Hochschule etc.) (*membership*); die Freundschaft (*friendship*); *good —*, die Geselligkeit.

felly, felloe ['feli, 'felou], *s.* die Radfelge.

felon ['felən], *s.* der Verbrecher.

felonious [fi'louniəs], *adj.* verbrecherisch.

felt [felt], *s.* der Filz.

female ['fiːmeil], *adj.* weiblich. — *s.* (*Zool.*) das Weibchen.

feminine ['feminin], *adj.* weiblich. — *s.* (*Gram.*) das weibliche Geschlecht; das Weibliche.

fen [fen], *s.* das Moor, das Marschland.

fence [fens], *s.* der Zaun, das Staket. — *v.a.* umzäunen, einzäunen (*enclose*). — *v.n.* fechten (*fight with rapiers*).

fencing ['fensiŋ], *s.* die Einzäunung (*fence*); das Fechten (*with rapiers*); — *master*, der Fechtmeister.

fend [fend], *v.a.* — *off*, abwehren, parieren. — *v.n.* — *for oneself*, sich allein behelfen.

fennel [fenl], *s.* (*Bot.*) der Fenchel.

ferment [fəˈment], *v.a.* zur Gärung bringen. — *v.n.* gären, fermentieren. — ['fəment], *s.* das Gärmittel (*also fig.*); (*Chem.*) das Gärungsprodukt.

fermentation [fəmen'teiʃən], *s.* die Gärung.

fern [fəːn], *s.* (*Bot.*) das Farnkraut.

ferocious [fə'rouʃəs], *adj.* wild, grimmig.

ferocity [fəˈrɔsiti], *s.* die Wildheit.
ferret [ˈferit], *s.* (*Zool.*) das Frett, das Frettchen. — *v.a.* — *out*, ausspüren.
ferry [ˈferi], *s.* die Fähre. — *v.a.* — *across*, hinüberrudern, hinüberfahren, übersetzen.
fertile [ˈfəːtail], *adj.* fruchtbar.
fertility [fəːˈtiliti], *s.* die Fruchtbarkeit.
fertilize [ˈfəːtilaiz], *v.a.* befruchten.
fertilizer [ˈfəːtilaizə], *s.* das Düngemittel, der Dünger.
fervent [ˈfəːvənt], *adj.* inbrünstig (*prayer*); heiß (*wish*).
fervid [ˈfəːvid], *adj.* glühend, heiß (*with zeal*).
fervour [ˈfəːvə], *s.* die Inbrunst (*prayer*); die Sehnsucht (*wish*).
fester [ˈfestə], *v.n.* schwären, eitern.
festival [ˈfestivəl], *s.* das Fest, die Festspiele, *n. pl.*
festive [ˈfestiv], *adj.* festlich, Fest-.
festivity [fesˈtiviti], *s.* die Festlichkeit.
festoon [fesˈtuːn], *s.* die Girlande. — *v.a.* behängen, mit Girlanden verzieren, schmücken.
fetch [fetʃ], *v.a.* holen, bringen.
fetching [ˈfetʃiŋ], *adj.* einnehmend.
fetter [ˈfetə], *v.a.* fesseln, binden. — *s.* (*pl.*) die Fesseln, *f. pl.*
feud [fjuːd], *s.* die Fehde.
feudal [ˈfjuːdl], *adj.* feudal, Lehns-.
fever [ˈfiːvə], *s.* das Fieber.
few [fjuː], *adj.* einige; wenige; *a* —, ein paar.
fiancé [fiˈɔnsei], *s.* der Verlobte, Bräutigam.
fiancée [fiˈɔnsei], *s.* die Verlobte, Braut.
fib [fib], *s.* (*coll.*) die Lüge. — *v.n.* (*coll.*) lügen.
fibre [ˈfaibə], *s.* die Fiber, Faser.
fibrous [ˈfaibrəs], *adj.* faserartig.
fickle [fikl], *adj.* unbeständig, wankelmütig.
fiction [ˈfikʃən], *s.* die Erdichtung (*figment*); (*Lit.*) die Romanliteratur.
fictitious [fikˈtiʃəs], *adj.* erdichtet, in der Phantasie.
fiddle [fidl], *s.* (*coll.*) die Geige, Fiedel, Violine. — *v.n.* (*coll.*, *Mus.*) geigen; schwindeln (*cheat*).
fiddlesticks! [ˈfidlstiks], *int.* Unsinn!
fidelity [fiˈdeliti], *s.* die Treue (*loyalty*); Genauigkeit; (*Engin.*) high —, Präzision, High Fidelity.
fidget [ˈfidʒit], *v.n.* unruhig sein.
fidgety [ˈfidʒiti], *adj.* nervös.
fie! [fai], *int.* pfui!
field [fiːld], *s.* das Feld; (*fig.*) das Gebiet; — *glass*, der Feldstecher; (*Hunt.*) — *sports*, die Feldübungen, der Jagdsport. — *v.a.*, *v.n.* abfangen, abpassen (*cricket*).
fiend [fiːnd], *s.* der Unhold, böse Geist; *fresh air* —, ein Freund der frischen Luft.
fiendish [ˈfiːndiʃ], *adj.* teuflisch, boshaft.
fierce [fiəs], *adj.* wild, wütend (*beast*); — *weather*, — *cold*, die grimmige Kälte, der grimmige Winter.

fiery [ˈfaiəri], *adj.* feurig; hitzig.
fife [faif], *s.* (*Mus.*) die Querpfeife.
fifteen [fifˈtiːn], *num. adj.* fünfzehn.
fifth [fifθ], *num. adj.* der fünfte.
fifty [ˈfifti], *num. adj.* fünfzig.
fig [fig], *s.* (*Bot.*) die Feige.
fight [fait], *v.a.*, *v.n. irr.* kämpfen, bekämpfen (*in battle*); raufen (*of boys*). — *s.* der Kampf; die Rauferei.
figment [ˈfigmənt], *s.* die Erdichtung.
figurative [ˈfigjuərətiv], *adj.* bildlich (*style*).
figure [ˈfigə], *s.* die Figur (*body*); die Gestalt, Form (*shape*); (*Maths.*) die Zahl, die Ziffer; *cut a* —, einen Eindruck machen; *a fine* — *of a man!* ein fabelhafter Kerl! — *v.a.* — *out*, ausdenken, ausrechnen. — *v.n.* eine Rolle spielen, rangieren.
figured [ˈfigəd], *adj.* figuriert.
figurehead [ˈfigəhed], *s.* der scheinbare Leiter, die Representationsfigur.
filament [ˈfiləmənt], *s.* der Faden, der Glühfaden (*bulb*).
filbert [ˈfilbəːt], *s.* (*Bot.*) die Haselnuß.
filch [filtʃ], *v.a.* stehlen, klauen.
file [fail], *s.* (*Engin.*) die Feile; (*Mil.*) die Reihe; (*Comm.*) der Aktenstoß, das Aktenbündel, der Ordner; (*pl.*) die Akten, *f. pl.*; *single* —, im Gänsemarsch; *rank and* —, die große Masse; *on the* —, in den Akten. — *v.a.* feilen (*metal*); zu den Akten legen (*papers*); einreichen (*petition*).
filial [ˈfiliəl], *adj.* kindlich.
filibuster [ˈfilibʌstə], *s.* der Freibeuter; (*Am.*) (*Pol.*) die Obstruktion.
filigree [ˈfiligriː], *s.* die Filigranarbeit.
filing [ˈfailiŋ], *s.* (*pl.*) die Feilspäne; das Einheften (*of papers*); — *cabinet*, die Kartei.
fill [fil], *v.a.* füllen; ausfüllen (*place*, *job*); plombieren (*tooth*); — *up*, tanken (*with petrol*). — *s.* das volle Maß; *eat o.'s* —, sich satt essen.
fillet [ˈfilit], *s.* das Filet (*meat*); das Band, die Binde (*band*).
filling [ˈfiliŋ], *s.* die Plombe (*in tooth*); — *station*, die Tankstelle.
filly [ˈfili], *s.* das Füllen.
film [film], *s.* der Film (*cinema*, *Phot.*); die Haut, das Häutchen (*skin*); der Belag (*coating*). — *v.a.* aufnehmen, verfilmen, filmen (*photograph*).
filter [ˈfiltə], *v.a.* filtrieren, filtern. — *v.n.* durchfiltern. — *s.* das Filter.
filth [filθ], *s.* der Schmutz.
filthy [ˈfilθi], *adj.* schmutzig.
filtration [filˈtreiʃən], *s.* das Filtrieren, das Durchsickern.
fin [fin], *s.* (*Zool.*) die Finne, die Flosse.
final [fainl], *adj.* letzt, endlich; endgültig. — *s.* (*Sport*) die Endrunde, das Endspiel.
finale [fiˈnɑːli], *s.* (*Mus.*) das Finale.
finality [faiˈnæliti], *s.* die Endgültigkeit.
finance [fiˈnæns *or* ˈfai-], *s.* die Finanz, das Finanzwesen. — *v.a.* finanzieren.

financial [fi'nænʃəl], *adj.* finanziell, Geld-, Finanz-.

finch [fintʃ], *s.* (*Orn.*) der Fink.

find [faind], *v.a. irr.* finden; — *fault with*, jemanden kritisieren; *all found*, volle Verpflegung (inbegriffen). — *s.* der Fund.

finding ['faindiŋ], *s.* das Finden, der Befund; (*Law*) der Wahrspruch.

fine (1) [fain], *adj.* fein (*delicate*); dünn (*thin*); schön (*beautiful*); scharf (*distinct*); großartig(*splendid*).

fine (2) [fain], *v.a.* zu einer Geldstrafe verurteilen. — *s.* die Geldstrafe.

finery ['fainəri], *s.* der Putz; (*Engin.*) der Frischofen.

finger ['fiŋgə], *s.* der Finger; *have a — in the pie*, die Hand im Spiel haben. — *v.a.* berühren, antasten.

finish ['finiʃ], *v.a.* beenden, fertig machen, vollenden; —*ing touch*, die lezte Hand. — *v.n.* aufhören, enden. — *s.* die Ende (*end*); der lezte Schliff; die Appretur, die Fertigung.

finite ['fainait], *adj.* endlich.

Finn [fin], *s.* der Finne.

Finnish ['finiʃ], *adj.* finnisch.

fir [fə:], *s.* (*Bot.*) die Föhre, die Tanne; — *cone*, der Tannenzapfen.

fire [faiə], *s.* das Feuer; — *brigade*, die Feuerwehr; — *damp*, (*Min.*) schlagende Wetter, *n.pl.*; — *engine*, die Feuerspritze; — *extinguisher*, der Löschapparat, Feuerlöscher; — *escape*, die Rettungsleiter. — *v.a.* brennen (*clay*); anzünden, in Gang setzen (*furnace*); anspornen (*enthuse*); (*coll.*) entlassen (*dismiss*). — *v.n.* feuern (*at*, auf, *Acc.*).

firebrand ['faiəbrænd], *s.* der Aufwiegler.

fireman ['faiəmən], *s.* der Heizer.

fireplace ['faiəpleis], *s.* der Kamin.

fireproof ['faiəpru:f], *adj.* feuerfest.

fireside ['faiəsaid], *s.* der (häusliche) Herd, der Kamin.

firewood ['faiəwud], *s.* das Brennholz.

firework ['faiəwə:k], *s.* (*usually pl.*) das Feuerwerk.

firm [fə:m], *adj.* fest, hart (*solid*); entschlossen (*decided*). — *s.* die Firma.

firmament ['fə:məmənt], *s.* das Firmament, Himmelsgewölbe; der Sternenhimmel.

firmness ['fə:mnis], *s.* die Festigkeit, Entschlossenheit.

first [fə:st], *num. adj.; adv.* erst; zuerst; — *of all*, zuallererst; — *born*, erstgeboren; — *rate*, erstklassig. — *s. from the —*, von Anfang an.

fiscal ['fiskəl], *adj.* fiskalisch, von der Staatskasse, Finanz-.

fish [fiʃ], *s.* der Fisch; *like a — out of water*, nicht in seinem Element; *a queer —*, ein seltsamer Kauz; —*bone*, die Gräte. — *v.n.* fischen; — *for compliments*, nach Lob haschen, nach Komplimenten fischen.

fisherman ['fiʃəmən], *s.* der Fischer.

fishery ['fiʃəri], *s.* der Fischfang.

fishing ['fiʃiŋ], *s.* das Fischen, der Fischfang; — *fly*, die Angelfliege; — *line*, die Angelschnur; — *rod*, die Angelrute; — *tackle*, das Angelgerät.

fishy ['fiʃi], *adj.* (*coll.*) anrüchig, verdächtig.

fissile ['fisail], *adj.* (*Phys.*) spaltbar.

fission ['fiʃ(ə)n], *s.* (*Phys.*) die Spaltung.

fist [fist], *s.* die Faust; *hand over —*, im Überfluß; *tight* —*ed*, geizig.

fisticuffs ['fistikʌfs], *s.* die Schlägerei, das Raufen.

fistula ['fistjulə], *s.* (*Anat.*) die Fistel.

fit (1) [fit], *v.a.* passen, anpassen (*Dat.*); einfügen (— *into s.th.*); — *in*, hineinpassen; — *on a suit*, einen Anzug anprobieren (*Dat.*); — *for a career*, zu einer Laufbahn vorbereiten; — *out*, ausrüsten. — *v.n.* passen, sich fügen (— *into*); — *in*, passen (*in*, zu, *Dat.*). — *adj.* geeignet, fähig (*suitable*); — *to drop*, todmüde; gesund, stark (*healthy*); schicklich (*proper*); (*Sport*) in guter Form.

fit (2) [fit], *s.* der Anfall; *by —s and starts*, ruckweise.

fitful ['fitful], *adj.* launenhaft; unbeständig.

fitness ['fitnis], *s.* die Tauglichkeit (*health*); die Schicklichkeit (*propriety*); die Fähigkeit (*ability*); (*Sport*) die gute Form.

fitter ['fitə], *s.* der Monteur.

fitting, fitment ['fitiŋ, 'fitmənt], *s.* die Armatur; die Montage. — *adj.* passend (*suitable*); geeignet (*appropriate*).

five [faiv], *num. adj.* fünf.

fiver ['faivə], *s.* (*coll.*) die Fünfpfundnote.

fix [fiks], *v.a.* festmachen, befestigen (*make firm*); festsetzen (*a time*); (*Am.*) herrichten, anrichten (*a meal*); — *with a glare or stare*, mit den Augen fixieren, scharf ansehen; — *up* (*coll.*), etwas erledigen (*something*); bedienen (*serve s.o.*). — *s.* (*coll.*) die Klemme, die Schwierigkeit, das Dilemma.

fixture ['fikstʃə], *s.* (*Sport*) die Veranstaltung; das Inventarstück (*furniture*).

fizz [fiz], *v.n.* brausen (*drink*).

fizzle [fizl], *v.n.* zischen (*flame*); — *out*, verebben, ausgehen, zunichte werden; (*Am., coll.*) durchfallen (*fail in school*).

fizzy ['fizi], *adj.* mit Kohlensäure, sprudelnd.

flabbergast ['flæbəga:st], *v.a.* (*coll.*) verblüffen.

flabby ['flæbi], *adj.* schlaff.

flaccid ['flæksid], *adj.* schlapp, schlaff.

flag (1) [flæg], *s.* (*Mil.*) die Flagge; die Fahne; — *officer*, der Flaggoffizier; —*staff*, die Fahnenstange.

flag (2) [flæg], *v.n.* ermatten, erschlaffen.

flag (3) [flæg], *s.* (—*stone*) der Fliesstein, die Fliese. — *v.a.* mit Fliesen auslegen, mit Fliessteinen pflastern.

flagon ['flægən], *s.* die Doppelflasche.

flagrant ['fleigrənt], *adj.* entsetzlich (*shocking*); schamlos (*impudent*).

flail [fleil], *s.* der Dreschflegel.

flair [flɛə], *s.* der Instinkt; (*coll.*) die Nase (*for*, für, *Acc.*).

flake [fleik], *s.* die Flocke. — *v.n.* — *off*, abblättern.

flame [fleim], *s.* die Flamme; (*coll.*) *old* —, die (alte) Liebe, Geliebte(r), die Flamme. — *v.n.* flammen, lodern.

flamingo [flə'mingou], *s.* (*Orn.*) der Flamingo.

flange [flændʒ], *s.* (*Engin.*) der Flan(t)sch.

flank [flæŋk], *s.* die Flanke, die Seite; die Weiche (*of animal*). — *v.a.* flankieren.

flannel [flænl], *s.* der Flanell.

flap [flæp], *s.* die Klappe; das Ohrläppchen (*earlobe*); der Flügelschlag (— *of wings*).

flare [flɛə], *v.n.* flammen, flackern; — *up*, aufbrausen (*in temper*). — *s.* das Aufflammen, das Aufflackern; die Leuchtkugel.

flash [flæʃ], *s.* der Blitz (*of lightning*); das Aufflammen; (*Phot.*) —*light*, das Blitzlicht. — *v.a.* aufflammen lassen, aufblitzen lassen. — *v.n.* aufflammen, aufblitzen.

flashy ['flæʃi], *adj.* großtuend, angeberisch (*bragging*); buntfarbig (*gaudy*).

flask [flɑ:sk], *s.* die kleine Flasche, das Fläschchen.

flat [flæt], *adj.* flach, eben; abgestanden, schal (*drink*); —*footed*, plattfüßig; (*Mus.*) zu tief, vermindert; platt; albern (*conversation*); — *tyre*, die Panne. — *adv.* — *out*, ausgepumpt, erschöpft. — *s.* die Mietwohnung, Wohnung (*lodgings*); (*Mus.*) das B; (*pl.*) das Flachland; (*Theat.*) (*pl.*) die Bühnenbilder.

flatness ['flætnis], *s.* die Flachheit, die Plattheit (*of conversation etc.*).

flatten [flætn], *v.a.* flach machen; glätten (*smooth*).

flatter ['flætə], *v.a.* schmeicheln (*Dat.*).

flattery ['flætəri], *s.* die Schmeichelei.

flaunt [flɔ:nt], *v.a.* prahlen, prunken (*s.th.*, mit, *Dat.*).

flavour ['fleivə], *s.* der Geschmack, die Würze; das Aroma; die Blume (*bouquet of wine*). — *v.a.* würzen.

flaw [flɔ:], *s.* der Riß (*chink*); der Fehler (*fault*).

flawless ['flɔ:lis], *adj.* fehlerlos.

flax [flæks], *s.* (*Bot.*) der Flachs.

flay [flei], *v.a.* schinden, die Haut abziehen (*Dat.*).

flea [fli:], *s.* (*Ent.*) der Floh.

fleck [flek], *v.a.* sprenkeln.

fledge [fledʒ], *v.a.* befiedern; *fully* —*d*, flügge; selbständig.

fledgling ['fledʒliŋ], *s.* der Grünschnabel, der Novize.

flee [fli:], *v.a.*, *v.n. irr.* fliehen, entfliehen (*from*, von, *Dat.*); flüchten (vor, *Dat.*).

fleece [fli:s], *s.* das Vlies. — *v.a.* scheren (*sheep*); ausnützen (*exploit*); berauben.

fleet [fli:t], *s.* die Flotte. — *adj.* (*Poet.*) schnellfüßig.

Fleming ['flemiŋ], *s.* der Flame.

Flemish ['flemiʃ], *adj.* flämisch.

flesh [fleʃ], *s.* das (lebende) Fleisch; die Frucht (*of fruit*).

flex [fleks], *s.* (*Elec.*) die Kontaktschnur.

flexible ['fleksibl], *adj.* biegsam; (*fig.*) anpassungsfähig.

flexion ['flekʃən], *s.* (*Gram.*) die Flexion, die Biegung.

flick [flik], *s.* der leichte Schlag. — *v.a.* leicht schlagen, berühren.

flicker ['flikə], *s.* das Flackern, das Flimmern. — *v.n.* flackern, flimmern.

flight [flait], *s.* (*Aviat.*) der Flug; die Flucht (*escape*); — *of stairs*, die Treppe, Treppenflucht.

flimsy ['flimzi], *adj.* hauchdünn (*material*); schwach (*argument*).

flinch [flintʃ], *v.n.* zurückweichen, zurückzucken (*from*, vor, *Dat.*).

fling [fliŋ], *v.a. irr.* schleudern, werfen. — *s.* der Wurf; *highland* —, schottischer Tanz; *have a last* —, sich zum letzten Mal austoben.

flint [flint], *s.* der Feuerstein.

flippancy ['flipənsi], *s.* die Leichtfertigkeit.

flippant ['flipənt], *adj.* leichtfertig, leichtsinnig, schnippisch.

flirt [flə:t], *v.n.* flirten, liebeln, (*with*, *Dat.*).

flirtation [flə:'teiʃən], *s.* die Liebelei.

flit [flit], *v.n.* hin und her flitzen; huschen.

flitch [flitʃ], *s.* die Speckseite.

flitter ['flitə], *v.n.* flattern.

float [flout], *v.n.* obenauf schwimmen, dahingleiten; —*ing ice*, das Treibeis. — *v.a.* schwimmen lassen; (*Naut.*) flott machen; (*Comm.*) gründen (*a company*); ausgeben (*a loan*). — *s.* das Floß (*raft*); der ausgeschmückte Wagen (*decorated vehicle*).

flock [flɔk], *s.* die Herde (*sheep*). — *v.n.* zusammenlaufen, sich scharen.

floe [flou], *s.* die Eisscholle.

flog [flɔg], *v.a.* peitschen (*whip*); antreiben; — *a dead horse*, sich umsonst bemühen; (*coll.*) verkaufen.

flood [flʌd], *s.* die Flut; das Hochwasser, die Überschwemmung (*flooding*); (*fig.*) die Fülle; — *gate*, die Schleuse. — *v.a.* überfluten, überschütten (*with requests*). — *v.n.* überschwemmen (*of river*).

floodlight ['flʌdlait], *s.* das Flutlicht, Scheinwerferlicht.

floor [flɔ:], *s.* der Boden, der Fußboden; das Stockwerk, der Stock (*storey*); *from the* —, aus dem Plenum; — *walker*, die Aufsicht (*in stores*). — *v.a.* zu Boden strecken, überrumpeln (*surprise*).

flop [flɔp], *v.n.* (*coll.*) hinsinken, hinplumpsen; versagen (*fail*). — *s.* das Hinfallen; der Versager (*play, film etc.*).

Florentine

Florentine ['flɔrəntain], *adj.* florentinisch. — *s.* der Florentiner.

florid ['flɔrid], *adj.* blühend; überladen.

florin ['flɔrin], *s.* das Zweischillingstück.

florist ['flɔrist], *s.* der Blumenhändler.

flotsam ['flɔtsəm], *s.* das Strandgut, Wrackgut.

flounce (1) [flauns], *v.n.* hastig bewegen.

flounce (2) [flauns], *v.a.* mit Falbeln besetzen (*dress*). — *s.* die Falbel (*on dress*).

flounder (1) ['flaundə], *v.n.* umhertappen, unsicher sein.

flounder (2) ['flaundə], *s.* (*Zool.*) die Flunder.

flour ['flauə], *s.* das Mehl.

flourish ['flʌriʃ], *v.n.* blühen; wirken; gedeihen (*thrive*); schnörkeln, verzieren (*in writing*); Fanfaren blasen, schmettern (*trumpets*). — *s.* der Schnörkel; der Trompetenstoß, Tusch (*of trumpets*).

flout [flaut], *v.a.* verhöhnen, verspotten. — *s.* der Hohn, der Spott.

flow [flou], *v.n. irr.* fließen, strömen. — *s.* der Fluß (*of water, goods etc.*); — *of words*, der Redeschwall.

flower ['flauə], *s.* die Blume; die Blüte (*blossom*). — *v.n.* blühen, in Blüte stehen.

flowery ['flauəri], *adj.* gewählt, umständlich, geziert (*style*).

fluctuate ['flʌktjueit], *v.n.* schwanken.

fluctuation [flʌktju'eiʃən], *s.* das Schwanken.

flue [flu:], *s.* der Rauchfang (*of chimney*).

fluency ['flu:ənsi], *s.* das fließende Sprechen, die Geläufigkeit.

fluent ['flu:ənt], *adj.* geläufig, fließend.

fluid ['flu:id], *adj.* fließend, flüssig (*liquid*). — *s.* die Flüssigkeit.

fluke [flu:k], *s.* der glückliche Zufall (*chance*).

flunkey ['flʌŋki], *s.* der Diener, der Bediente.

flurry ['flʌri], *s.* die Unruhe; die Aufregung (*excitement*).

flush (1) [flʌʃ], *s.* das Erröten (*blushing*); die Aufwallung (*of anger*). — *v.a.* nachspülen (*basin*); erröten machen (*make blush*). — *v.n.* erröten.

flush (2) [flʌʃ], *adj.* in gleicher Ebene, eben.

flush (3) [flʌʃ], *v.a.* (*Hunt.*) aufscheuchen.

fluster ['flʌstə], *v.a.* verwirren (*muddle*); aufregen (*excite*).

flute [flu:t], *s.* (*Mus.*) die Flöte; (*Carp.*) die Hohlkehle. — *v.a.* (*Carp., Archit.*) aushöhlen. — *v.n.* (*Mus.*) flöten, Flöte spielen.

flutter ['flʌtə], *v.n.* flattern, unruhig sein. — *s.* die Unruhe.

flux [flʌks], *s.* das Fließen; *be in —*, in der Schwebe sein.

fly [flai], *v.a. irr.* wehen lassen, hissen (*flag*). — *v.n. irr.* (*Aviat.*) fliegen;

fliehen (*escape*); eilen (*hurry*). — *s.* (*Ent.*) die Fliege.

flyleaf ['flaili:f], *s.* das Vorsatzblatt.

flying ['flaiiŋ], *adj.* fliegend, Flug-; — *squad*, das Überfallkommando.

flyover ['flaiouvə], *s.* die Brückenkreuzung, Überführung.

flywheel ['flaiwi:l], *s.* das Schwungrad.

foal [foul], *s.* (*Zool.*) das Füllen. — *v.n.* fohlen.

foam [foum], *s.* der Schaum; — *rubber*, das Schaumgummi. — *v.n.* schäumen.

fob [fɔb], *v.a.* — *off*, abfertigen, abspeisen.

focus ['foukəs], *s.* der Brennpunkt; der Mittelpunkt (*of interest*). — *v.a.* (*Phot.*) einstellen. — *v.n.* — *upon*, sich konzentrieren auf (*Acc.*).

fodder ['fɔdə], *s.* das Futter.

foe [fou], *s.* der Feind.

fog [fɔg], *s.* der Nebel.

fogey ['fougi], *s.* der Kerl, Kauz.

foible ['fɔibl], *s.* die Schwäche, die schwache Seite.

foil (1) [fɔil], *v.a.* vereiteln. — *s.* das Florett (*fencing rapier*).

foil (2) [fɔil], *s.* die Folie; der Hintergrund (*background*).

foist [fɔist], *v.a.* aufschwatzen (*upon, Dat.*).

fold (1) [fould], *v.a.* falten (*clothes etc.*); umarmen (*in o.'s arms*). — *v.n.* schließen, sich falten. — *s.* die Falte (*Geol.*) die Vertiefung.

fold (2) [fould], *s.* die Herde (*sheep*); *return to the —*, zu den Seinen zurückkehren.

folder ['fouldə], *s.* die Mappe (*papers*); das Falzbein.

folding ['fouldiŋ], *adj.* Klapp-; — *chair*, der Klappstuhl; — *door*, die Flügeltür.

foliage ['fouliidʒ], *s.* (*Bot.*) das Laub.

folio ['fouliou], *s.* das Folio, der Foliant.

folk [fouk], *s.* (*also pl.*) die Leute; (*pl.*) (*Am.*) Freunde (*mode of address*).

folklore ['fouklɔː], *s.* die Volkskunde.

folksong ['fouksɔŋ], *s.* das Volkslied.

follow ['fɔlou], *v.a., v.n.* folgen (*Dat.*); — *suit*, dasselbe tun, Farbe bekennen.

follower ['fɔlouə], *s.* der Anhänger (*supporter*); der Nachfolger (*successor*); *camp —*, der Mitläufer.

folly ['fɔli], *s.* die Narrheit; die törichte Handlung (*action*).

foment [fo'ment], *v.a.* anregen (*stimulate*); pflegen (*cultivate*); warm baden.

fond [fɔnd], *adj.* zärtlich, lieb; *be — of*, gern haben.

fondle ['fɔndl], *v.a.* liebkosen.

fondness ['fɔndnis], *s.* die Zärtlichkeit, die (Vor-)liebe.

font [fɔnt], *s.* der Taufstein (*baptismal*).

food [fu:d], *s.* die Nahrung, Speise (*nourishment*); Lebensmittel (*n.pl.*); das Futter (*for animals*); *some —*, etwas zum Essen; — *store*, das Lebensmittelgeschäft.

fool [fu:l], *s.* der Narr, Tor. — *v.a.* zum Narren halten, übertölpeln.

foolish ['fu:liʃ], *adj.* töricht, albern, närrisch (*person*); unsinnig (*act*).

foolscap ['fu:lskæp], *s.* das Kanzleipapier.

foot [fut], *s.* der Fuß; *on* —, zu Fuß; — *board*, das Trittbrett; *put o.'s* — *in it*, eine taktlose Bemerkung fallen lassen, ins Fettnäpfchen treten. — *v.a.* — *the bill*, bezahlen.

footage ['futidʒ], *s.* die Länge in Fuß.

football ['futbɔ:l], *s.* der Fußball.

footbridge ['futbridʒ], *s.* der Steg.

footing ['futiŋ], *s.* die Grundlage, Basis.

footlight ['futlait], *s.* (*usually pl.*) die Rampenlichter, *n. pl.*

footman ['futmən], *s.* der Bediente.

footprint ['futprint], *s.* die Fußstapfe.

footstool ['futstu:l], *s.* der Schemel.

fop [fɔp], *s.* der Geck.

for [fɔ:], *prep.* für (*Acc.*); anstatt (*Genit.*) (*instead of*); *in exchange* —, für, um; — *example*, zum Beispiel; — *heaven's sake*, um Himmels willen; — *two days*, zwei Tage lang; auf zwei Tage; seit zwei Tagen; *now you are* — *it!* jetzt has du's! *as* — *me*, meinetwegen, was mich anbelangt; — *all that*, trotz alledem. — *conj.* denn, weil.

forage ['fɔridʒ], *s.* das Futter. — *v.n.* furagieren.

forasmuch [fɔrəz'mʌtʃ], *conj.* (*obs.*) — *as*, insofern als.

foray ['fɔrei], *s.* der Raubzug.

forbear [fɔ:'beə], *v.a. irr.* vermeiden, unterlassen (*avoid*); sich enthalten (*abstain*). — *v.n.* (geduldig) hinnehmen, ertragen.

forbid [fɔ:'bid], *v.a. irr.* verbieten; *God* —! Gott behüte!

forbidding [fə'bidiŋ], *adj.* abschreckend.

force [fɔ:s], *s.* (*Phys.*) die Kraft; die Macht (*might*); die Gewalt (*brute* —); (*pl.*) die Streitkräfte, *f. pl.*; (*Phys.*) die Kräfte. — *v.a.* zwingen, nötigen.

forceful ['fɔ:sful], *adj.* kräftig, energisch, kraftvoll.

forceps ['fɔ:seps], *s.* (*Med.*) die Zange; die Pinzette.

forcible ['fɔ:sibl], *adj.* heftig, stark (*strong*); gewaltsam (*violent*).

ford [fɔ:d], *s.* die Furt.

fore- [fɔ:], *pref.* Vorder-, vorder.

forebear [fɔ:'beə], *s.* der Vorfahre.

forebode [fɔ:'boud], *v.a.* voraussagen, vorbedeuten.

forecast [fɔ:'ka:st], *v.a.* vorhersagen, voraussagen. — ['fɔ:ka:st], *s.* die Vorhersage.

foreclose [fɔ:'klouz], *v.a.* ausschließen.

forefather ['fɔ:fa:ðə], *s.* der Ahne, der Vorvater.

forefinger ['fɔ:fiŋgə], *s.* (*Anat.*) der Zeigefinger.

forego [fɔ:'gou], *v.a. irr.* vorhergehen.

foreground ['fɔ:graund], *s.* der Vordergrund.

forehead ['fɔrid], *s.* die Stirne.

foreign ['fɔrin], *adj.* fremd; ausländisch.

foreigner ['fɔrinə], *s.* der Fremde, der Ausländer.

foreland ['fɔ:lənd], *s.* das Vorgebirge.

foreman ['fɔ:mən], *s.* der Werkführer, Vorarbeiter.

foremast ['fɔ:ma:st], *s.* (*Naut.*) der Fockmast.

foremost ['fɔ:moust], *adj.* vorderst, vornehmlichst, führend. — *adv.* zuerst; *first and* —, zuallererst.

forenoon ['fɔ:nu:n], *s.* der Vormittag.

forensic [fɔ'rensik], *adj.* forensisch, gerichtsmedizinisch.

forerunner ['fɔ:rrʌnə], *s.* der Vorläufer.

foresail ['fɔ:seil, 'fɔ:səl], *s.* (*Naut.*) das Focksegel.

foresee [fɔ:'si:], *v.a. irr.* vorhersehen.

foreshadow [fɔ:'ʃædou], *v.a.* vorher andeuten.

foreshorten [fɔ:'ʃɔ:tn], *v.a.* verkürzen.

foresight ['fɔ:sait], *s.* die Vorsorge, der Vorbedacht.

forest ['fɔrist], *s.* der Wald; der Urwald (*jungle*).

forestall [fɔ:'stɔ:l], *v.a.* vorwegnehmen, zuvorkommen (*Dat.*).

forester ['fɔristə], *s.* der Förster.

forestry ['fɔristri], *s.* die Forstwissenschaft (*science*); das Forstwesen (*management*).

foretaste ['fɔ:teist], *s.* der Vorgeschmack.

foretell [fɔ:'tel], *v.a. irr.* voraussagen.

forethought ['fɔ:θɔ:t], *s.* der Vorbedacht.

forewarn [fɔ:'wɔ:n], *v.a.* warnen.

forfeit ['fɔ:fit], *s.* das Pfand (*pledge*); die Einbuße (*fine*); (*pl.*) das Pfänderspiel. — *v.a.* verlieren, verwirken.

forfeiture ['fɔ:fitʃə], *s.* die Verwirkung, die Einbuße, der Verlust.

forge [fɔ:dʒ], *v.a.* schmieden (*iron*); fälschen (*falsify*). — *v.n.* — *ahead*, sich vorwärtsarbeiten. — *s.* die Schmiede (*iron*); der Eisenhammer (*hammer*).

forget [fə'get], *v.a., v.n. irr.* vergessen; — *-me-not*, das Vergißmeinnicht.

forgetful [fə'getful], *adj.* vergeßlich.

forgive [fə'giv], *v.a., v.n. irr.* vergeben, verzeihen.

forgo [fɔ:'gou], *v.a. irr.* verzichten; aufgeben.

fork [fɔ:k], *s.* die Gabel; die Abzweigung (*road*). — *v.n.* sich gabeln, sich spalten.

forlorn [fɔ:'lɔ:n], *adj.* verlassen, verloren, elend.

form [fɔ:m], *s.* die Form, die Gestalt (*shape*); die Formalität (*formality*); das Formular (*document*); *in good* —, (*Sport*) in guter Form; *bad* —, gegen den guten Ton; *a matter of* —, eine Formsache. — *v.a.* formen, gestalten (*shape*); bilden (*an association etc. of*, über, *Acc.*).

formal ['fɔ:məl], *adj.* formal, äußerlich; formell.

formality [fɔ:'mæliti], *s.* die Formalität.

formation

formation [fɔːˈmeiʃən], *s.* (*Mil.*) die Formation; (*Geol.*) die Bildung; die Formung; die Aufstellung (*sports team*).

former [ˈfɔːmə], *adj.* früher, vorig.

formidable [ˈfɔːmidəbl], *adj.* schrecklich, furchtbar.

formula [ˈfɔːmjulə], *s.* die Formel.

formulate [ˈfɔːmjuleit], *v.a.* formulieren.

forsake [fɔːˈseik], *v.a.* irr. verlassen, im Stich lassen.

forsooth [fɔːˈsuːθ], *adv.* (*Poet.*) wahrlich, wirklich!

forswear [fɔːˈswɛə], *v.a.* irr. abschwören; — *oneself*, einen Meineid schwören.

fort, fortress [fɔːt, ˈfɔːtris], *s.* das Fort, die Festung.

forth [fɔːθ], *adv.* vorwärts; weiter (*further*); *and so* —, und so weiter (u.s.w.); fort (*away*).

forthcoming [ˈfɔːkʌmiŋ], *adj.* bevorstehend.

forthwith [fɔːθˈwiθ], *adv.* sogleich.

fortieth [ˈfɔːtiəθ], *num. adj.* vierzigst. — *s.* der Vierzigste.

fortification [fɔːtifiˈkeiʃən], *s.* die Befestigung.

fortify [ˈfɔːtifai], *v.a.* befestigen; bestärken.

fortitude [ˈfɔːtitjuːd], *s.* die Tapferkeit.

fortnight [ˈfɔːtnait], *s.* vierzehn Tage, *m. pl.*

fortuitous [fɔːˈtjuːitəs], *adj.* zufällig.

fortunate [ˈfɔːtʃənit], *adj.* glücklich, günstig.

fortune [ˈfɔːtjuːn], *s.* das Glück, das Schicksal; das Vermögen (*wealth*); — *teller*, die Wahrsagerin.

forty [ˈfɔːti], *num. adj.* vierzig.

forward [ˈfɔːwəd], *adj.* vorder (*in front*); voreilig, vorlaut (*rash*); früh (*early*). — *adv.* vorne; — *march!* vorwärts! *carry* —, (*Comm.*) übertragen. — *s.* (*Footb.*) der Stürmer, — *line*, die der Angriff. — *v.a.* weiterleiten, expedieren; (*letter*) *please* —, bitte nachsenden.

forwardness [ˈfɔːwədnis], *s.* die Frühreife; die Voreiligkeit, Dreistigkeit.

fossil [ˈfɔsil], *s.* das Fossil.

foster [ˈfɔstə], *v.a.* nähren (*feed*); aufziehen (*bring up*); — *a thought*, einen Gedanken hegen; — *mother*, die Pflegemutter; — *brother*, der Pflegebruder.

foul [faul], *adj.* schmutzig; faul (*rotten*). — *v.a.* beschmutzen. — *v.n.* (*Footb.*) einen Verstoß begehen. — *s.* (*Footb.*) der Verstoß.

found (1) [faund], *v.a.* gründen, begründen.

found (2) [faund], *v.a.* (*Metall.*) gießen (*cast*).

foundation [faunˈdeiʃən], *s.* das Fundament; die Unterlage; die Begründung, die Gründung (*initiation*); die Stiftung (*establishment*); — *stone*, der Grundstein.

founder (1) [ˈfaundə], *s.* der Gründer, Stifter.

founder (2) [ˈfaundə], *v.n.* scheitern, Schiffbruch erleiden (*on*, an, *Dat.*).

foundling [ˈfaundliŋ], *s.* das Findelkind, der Findling.

foundry [ˈfaundri], *s.* (*Metall.*) die Gießerei.

fount (1) [faunt], *s.* (*Typ.*) der Schriftguss.

fount (2) [faunt] (*Poet.*) *see* **fountain**.

fountain [ˈfauntin], *s.* die Quelle, der Brunnen; der Springbrunnen; — *pen*, die Füllfeder; — *head*, der Urquell.

four [fɔː], *num. adj.* vier; — *-in-hand*, das Viergespann.

fowl [faul], *s.* (*Orn.*) das Huhn, das Geflügel.

fowler [ˈfaulə], *s.* der Vogelsteller, Vogelfänger.

fox [fɔks], *s.* (*Zool.*) der Fuchs; (*fig.*) der listige Kauz, Schlauberger (*cunning fellow*). — *v.a.* (*coll.*) überlisten, täuschen.

fraction [ˈfrækʃən], *s.* (*Maths.*) der Bruch; (*Mech.*) der Bruchteil.

fractional [ˈfrækʃənəl], *adj.* (*Maths.*) Bruch-, gebrochen.

fractionate [ˈfrækʃəneit], *v.a.* (*Chem.*) fraktionieren (*oil*).

fractious [ˈfrækʃəs], *adj.* zänkisch, streitsüchtig.

fracture [ˈfræktʃə], *s.* (*Med.*) der Bruch. — *v.a.* brechen; — *o.'s leg*, sich das Bein brechen.

fragile [ˈfrædʒail], *adj.* zerbrechlich; gebrechlich (*feeble*).

fragment [ˈfrægmənt], *s.* das Bruchstück, das Fragment.

fragrance [ˈfreigrəns], *s.* der Wohlgeruch, Duft.

fragrant [ˈfreigrənt], *adj.* wohlriechend, duftend.

frail [freil], *adj.* gebrechlich, schwach (*feeble*).

frailty [ˈfreilti], *s.* die Schwäche.

frame [freim], *s.* der Rahmen (*of picture*); das Gerüst (*scaffold*); die Form (*shape*). — *v.a.* einrahmen (*a picture*); (*Am.*) in die Enge treiben, reinlegen (*get s.o. wrongly blamed*); (*Comm.*) entwerfen (*a letter*).

framework [ˈfreimwəːk], *s.* der Rahmen (*outline*); das Fachwerk (*construction*).

franchise [ˈfræntʃaiz], *s.* das Wahlrecht.

Franciscan [frænˈsiskən], *s.* der Franziskaner (*friar*).

frank [fræŋk], *adj.* offen, aufrichtig. — *v.a.* frankieren (*letter*). — *s.* der Frankovermerk.

frankincense [ˈfræŋkinsens], *s.* der Weihrauch.

frantic [ˈfræntik], *adj.* wahnsinnig, außer sich.

fraternal [frəˈtəːnəl], *adj.* brüderlich.

fraternity [frəˈtəːniti], *s.* die Bruderschaft; (*Am.*) der Studentenbund, -klub.

fraternize ['frætənaiz], *v.n.* sich verbrüdern, fraternisieren.

fraud [frɔːd], *s.* der Betrug.

fraudulent ['frɔːdjulənt], *adj.* betrügerisch.

fraught [frɔːt], *adj.* voll (*with*, von, *Dat.*).

fray (1) [frei], *v.a.* abnutzen; — *the nerves*, auf die Nerven gehen (*Dat.*).

fray (2) [frei], *s.* der Kampf, die Schlägerei.

freak [friːk], *s.* das Monstrum, die Mißgeburt.

freakish ['friːkiʃ], *adj.* seltsam; grotesk.

freckle [frekl], *s.* die Sommersprosse.

freckled [frekld], *adj.* sommersprossig.

free [friː], *adj.* frei; offen (*frank*); — *trade area*, die Freihandelszone; *of my own* — *will*, aus freien Stücken. — *v.a.* befreien.

freebooter ['friːbuːtə], *s.* der Freibeuter.

freedom ['friːdəm], *s.* die Freiheit; — *of a city*, das Ehrenbürgerrecht.

freehold ['friːhould], *s.* der freie Grundbesitz, der Freigrundbesitz.

freeholder ['friːhouldə], *s.* der (freie) Grundbesitzer.

freeman ['friːmən], *s.* der Freibürger, Ehrenbürger.

freemason ['friːmeisn], *s.* der Freimaurer.

freewheel ['friːˈwiːl], *s.* der Freilauf, das Freilaufrad. — *v.n.* mit Freilauf fahren.

freeze [friːz], *v.a. irr.* gefrieren lassen. — *v.n.* frieren, gefrieren; — *up*, zufrieren.

freight [freit], *s.* die Fracht. — *v.a.* verfrachten.

freighter ['freitə], *s.* (*Naut.*) der Frachtdampfer.

French [frentʃ], *adj.* französisch; — *bean*, die Schnittbohne; — *horn*, (*Mus.*) das Horn.

Frenchman ['frentʃmən], *s.* der Franzose.

Frenchwoman ['frentʃwumən], *s.* die Französin.

frenzied ['frenzid], *adj.* wahnsinnig, außer sich.

frequency ['friːkwənsi], *s.* (*Phys.*) die Frequenz; die Häufigkeit (*of occurrence*).

frequent ['friːkwənt], *adj.* häufig. — [fri'kwent], *v.a.* (häufig) besuchen.

fresh [freʃ], *adj.* frisch, neu; ungesalzen (*water*); (*sl.*) frech; — *water*, das Süßwasser.

fresher, freshman ['freʃə, 'freʃmən], *s.* der Neuankömmling; (*Univ.*) der Fuchs, Anfänger.

fret (1) [fret], *s.* (*Carp.*) das Gitterwerk, Laubsägewerk. — *v.a.* (*Carp.*) durchbrochen verzieren.

fret (2) [fret], *s.* der Verdruß, Ärger. — *v.n.* sich Sorgen machen.

fretful ['fretful], *adj.* verdrießlich, ärgerlich, mißmutig.

fretsaw ['fretsɔː], *s.* (*Carp.*) die Laubsäge.

friar ['fraiə], *s.* (*Eccl.*) der Mönch, Bettelmönch.

friction ['frikʃən], *s.* die Reibung; (*fig.*) die Unstimmigkeit.

Friday ['fraid(e)i]. der Freitag; *Good* —, der Karfreitag.

friend [frend], *s.* der (die) Freund(in).

friendly ['frendli], *adj.* freundlich.

friendship ['frendʃip], *s.* die Freundschaft.

frigate ['frigit], *s.* (*Naut.*) die Fregatte.

fright [frait], *s.* die Furcht, der Schreck, das Entsetzen.

frighten [fraitn], *v.a.* erschrecken (*s.o.*).

frightful ['fraitful], *adj.* schrecklich.

frigid ['fridʒid], *adj.* kalt, frostig; kühl.

frill [fril], *s.* die Krause; die Ausschmückung (*style*).

frilly ['frili], *adj.* gekräuselt, geziert.

fringe [frindʒ], *s.* die Franse (*fringed edge*); der Rand (*edge*, *brink*). — *v.a.* mit Fransen besetzen, einsäumen. — *v.n.* — *on*, grenzen an (*Acc.*).

Frisian ['friːʒən], *adj.* friesisch.

frisk [frisk], *v.a.* (*sl.*) durchsuchen (*search*). — *v.n.* hüpfen (*of animals*). — *s.* der Sprung (*of animals*).

frisky ['friski], *adj.* lebhaft, munter.

fritter ['fritə], *s.* der Pfannkuchen; *apple* —, Äpfel im Schlafrock. — *v.a.* zerstückeln (*cut up*); vertrödeln (*waste*), vergeuden.

frivolity [fri'voliti], *s.* der Leichtsinn, die Leichtfertigkeit.

frivolous ['frivələs], *adj.* leichtsinnig, leichtfertig.

fro [frou], *adv.* *to and* —, auf und ab, hin und her.

frock [frɔk], *s.* der Kittel, das Kleid; (*Eccl.*) die Soutane, Kutte.

frog [frɔg], *s.* (*Zool.*) der Frosch.

frogman ['frɔgmən], *s.* der Tauchschwimmer, Froschmann.

frolic ['frɔlik], *s.* der Scherz; der Spaß. — *v.n.* scherzen, ausgelassen sein.

from [frɔm], *prep.* von; von ... her (*hence*); aus ... heraus (*out of*); von ... an (*starting* —); vor (*in the face of*).

front [frʌnt], *s.* die Stirn; die Vorderseite; (*Mil.*) die Front; *in* — *of*, vor (*Dat.*); — *door*, die Haustür.

frontage ['frʌntidʒ], *s.* die Front, Vorderfront (*of building*).

frontal ['frʌntl], *adj.* Stirn-, Vorder-; (*Mil.*) — *attack*, der Frontalangriff. — *s.* (*Eccl.*) die Altardecke.

frontier ['frʌntjə], *s.* die Grenze; — *police*, die Grenzpolizei.

frontispiece ['frʌntispiːs], *s.* das Titelbild.

frost [frɔst], *s.* der Frost, der Reif.

frostbite ['frɔstbait], *s.* die Frostbeule.

frosted ['frɔstid], *adj.* bereift.

froth [frɔθ], *s.* der Schaum. — *v.n.* schäumen.

frown

frown [fraun], *v.n.* die Stirn runzeln, finster dreinschauen. — *s.* das Stirnrunzeln.

frugal ['fru:gəl], *adj.* frugal, sparsam, einfach.

fruit [fru:t], *s.* die Frucht (*singular*); das Obst (*plural or collective*). — *v.n.* (*Bot.*) Früchte tragen.

frustrate [frʌs'treit], *v.a.* verhindern; vereiteln (*bring to nought*).

fry (1) [frai], *v.a.* braten; *fried potatoes,* Bratkartoffeln, *f. pl.*

fry (2) [frai], *s.* der Rogen (*of fish*); (*fig.*) die Brut, Menge.

frying pan ['fraiiŋpæn], *s.* die Bratpfanne; *out of the — into the fire,* vom Regen in die Traufe.

fuchsia ['fju:ʃə], *s.* (*Bot.*) die Fuchsie.

fudge [fʌdʒ], *s.* weiches Zuckerwerk; (*coll.*) Unsinn!

fuel ['fjuəl], *s.* der Brennstoff, Treibstoff; das Heizmaterial. — *v.a., v.n.* tanken.

fugitive ['fju:dʒitiv], *adj.* flüchtig, auf der Flucht. — *s.* der Flüchtling.

fugue [fju:g], *s.* (*Mus.*) die Fuge.

fulcrum ['fʌlkrəm], *s.* der Stützpunkt, Hebelpunkt.

fulfil [ful'fil], *v.a.* erfüllen; — *a requirement,* einem Gesetz genüge tun.

full [ful], *adj.* voll; vollständig (*complete*); —*time,* hauptberuflich.

fuller ['fulə], *s.* der Walker.

fullness ['fulnis], *s.* die Fülle.

fulsome ['fulsəm], *adj.* widerlich, ekelhaft; übermäßig.

fumble [fʌmbl], *v.n.* tappen (*for,* nach, *Dat.*).

fume [fju:m], *s.* der Rauch, Dunst; der Zorn (*anger*). — *v.n.* zornig sein, wüten (*be angered*).

fun [fʌn], *s.* der Spaß, Scherz; *have —,* sich gut unterhalten, sich amüsieren; *make — of,* zum besten haben.

function ['fʌŋkʃən], *s.* (*also Maths.*) die Funktion; das Amt (*office*); die Feier(lichkeit) (*formal occasion*). — *v.n.* funktionieren (*be in working order*); fungieren (*officiate*).

fund [fʌnd], *s.* der Fonds (*financial*); (*fig.*) die Fülle (*of,* an); *public —s,* die Staatsgelder.

fundamental [fʌndə'mentl], *adj.* grundsätzlich, wesentlich. — *s.* (*pl.*) die Grundlagen, *f.pl.*

funeral ['fju:nərəl], *s.* die Bestattung, Beerdigung.

funereal [fju:'niəriəl], *adj.* wie bei einem Begräbnis, betrübt, traurig.

fungus ['fʌŋgəs], *s.* (*Bot.*) der Pilz; der Schwamm (*mushroom*).

funk [fʌŋk], *s.* (*sl.*) die Angst, Panik. — *v.a.* fürchten.

funnel [fʌnl], *s.* der Trichter.

funny ['fʌni], *adj.* spaßhaft, komisch.

fur [fə:], *s.* der Pelz, das Fell (*coat of animal*); (*Med.*) der Belag (*on tongue*).

furbelow ['fə:bilou], *s.* die Falbel.

furbish ['fə:biʃ], *v.a.* aufputzen.

furious ['fjuəriəs], *adj.* wild, rasend, wütend.

furl [fə:l], *v.a.* (zusammen-)rollen; (*Naut.*) aufrollen.

furlong ['fə:lɔŋ], *s.* ein Achtel einer englischen Meile.

furlough ['fə:lou], *s.* der Urlaub.

furnace ['fə:nis], *s.* der Ofen, Hochofen (*steel*); (*Metall.*) der Schmelzofen.

furnish ['fə:niʃ], *v.a.* ausstatten, versehen (*equip*); möblieren (*a room etc.*).

furnisher ['fə:niʃə], *s.* der Möbelhändler; der Lieferant.

furniture ['fə:nitʃə], *s.* die Möbel, *n. pl.*; die Einrichtung.

furrier ['fʌriə], *s.* der Kürschner.

furrow ['fʌrou], *s.* die Furche (*field*); die Runzel (*brow*). — *v.a.* runzeln (*brow*); Furchen ziehen (*plough up*).

further ['fə:ðə], *comp. adj.*, *adv. see* **farther**. — *v.a.* fördern (*advance*).

furtherance ['fə:ðərəns], *s.* die Förderung (*advancement*).

furthermore ['fə:ðəmɔ:], *adv.* ferner.

furthest ['fə:ðist], *superl. adj.*, *adv. see* **farthest**.

furtive ['fə:tiv], *adj.* verstohlen, heimlich.

fury ['fjuəri], *s.* die Wut; (*Myth.*) die Furie.

furze [fə:z], *s.* (*Bot.*) der Stechginster.

fuse [fju:z], *v.a., v.n.* schmelzen (*melt*); vereinigen (*unite*). — *s.* (*Elec.*) die Sicherung; *blow a —,* eine Sicherung durchbrennen; — *box,* der Sicherungskasten; — *wire,* der Schmelzdraht.

fuselage ['fju:zila:ʒ *or* -lidʒ], *s.* (*Aviat.*) der (Flugzeug-)rumpf.

fusible ['fju:zibl], *adj.* schmelzbar.

fusilier [fju:zi'liə], *s.* (*Mil.*) der Füsilier.

fusion ['fju:ʒən], *s.* die Verschmelzung; die Vereinigung.

fuss [fʌs], *s.* das Getue, die Umständlichkeit; *make a — about,* viel Aufhebens machen.

fussy ['fʌsi], *adj.* übertrieben genau; umständlich; geschäftig (*busy*); — *about,* genau in (*Dat.*).

fusty ['fʌsti], *adj.* moderig, muffig.

futile ['fju:tail], *adj.* nutzlos, vergeblich.

futility [fju:'tiliti], *s.* die Nutzlosigkeit.

future ['fju:tʃə], *s.* die Zukunft. — *adj.* (zu-)künftig.

fuzzy ['fʌzi], *adj.* kraus.

G

G [dʒi:]. das G (*also Mus.*); — *sharp,* das Gis; — *flat,* das Ges; *key of —,* der G Schlüssel, Violinschlüssel.

gab [gæb], s. das Geschwätz; *the gift of the —*, ein gutes Mundwerk.

gabble ['gæbl], v.n. schwatzen.

gable [geibl], s. der Giebel.

gad [gæd], v.n. — *about*, umherstreifen.

gadfly ['gædflai], s. (Ent.) die Bremse.

gag [gæg], s. der Knebel; (sl.) der Witz. — v.a. knebeln.

gaiety ['geiəti], s. die Fröhlichkeit.

gain [gein], v.a. gewinnen, erwerben (earn); — possession, Besitz ergreifen. — s. der Gewinn, Vorteil.

gainful ['geinful], adj. — *employment*, die einträgliche Beschäftigung.

gainsay ['geinsei or gein'sei], v.a. widersprechen (pers., Dat.).

gait [geit], s. das Schreiten, der Schritt, Gang.

gaiter ['geitə], s. die Gamasche.

galaxy ['gæləksi], s. (Astron.) die Milchstraße; (fig.) die glänzende Versammlung.

gale [geil], s. der Sturm.

gall [gɔːl], s. die Galle. — v.a. verbittern, ärgern.

gallant ['gælənt], adj. tapfer (of soldier); gallant, höflich (polite).

gallantry ['gæləntri], s. die Tapferkeit; die Höflichkeit, Galanterie.

gallery ['gæləri], s. die Gallerie.

galley ['gæli], s. (Naut.) die Galeere; (Typ.) — proof, der Fahnenabzug.

gallon ['gælən], s. die Gallone.

gallop ['gæləp], v.n. galoppieren. — s. der Galopp.

gallows ['gælouz], s. der Galgen.

galosh [gə'lɔʃ], s. die Galosche.

galvanic [gæl'vænik], adj. galvanisch.

galvanize ['gælvənaiz], v.a. galvanisieren.

gamble [gæmbl], v.n. um Geld spielen; — away, verspielen. — s. das Risiko.

gambol [gæmbl], v.n. herumspringen.

game [geim], s. das Spiel (play); das Wild, Wildbret (pheasants etc.); fair —, Freiwild, n.; offene Beute, f.

gamecock ['geimkɔk], s. (Orn.) der Kampfhahn.

gamekeeper ['geimkiːpə], s. der Wildhüter.

gammon ['gæmən], s. der (geräucherte) Schinken (bacon).

gamut ['gæmət], s. die Tonleiter.

gander ['gændə], s. (Orn.) der Gänserich.

gang [gæŋ], s. die Bande; die Mannschaft (workmen); — up, eine Bande bilden; — up on s.o., sich gegen jemanden verbünden.

gangrene ['gæŋgriːn], s. (Med.) der Brand; die Fäulnis.

gangway ['gæŋwei], s. die Planke, der Laufgang (on boat); der Durchgang.

gaol, jail [dʒeil], s. das Gefängnis. — v.a. einsperren.

gaoler, jailer ['dʒeilə], s. der Kerkermeister.

gap [gæp], s. die Lücke; die Bresche (breach).

gape [geip], v.n. gähnen, (fig.) klaffen.

garage ['gærɑːʒ or 'gæridʒ], s. die Garage, die Tankstelle.

garb [gɑːb], s. die Tracht, Kleidung.

garbage ['gɑːbidʒ], s. der Abfall; (Am.) — can, der Mülleimer.

garble [gɑːbl], v.a. verstümmeln.

garden [gɑːdn], s. der Garten. — v.n. im Garten arbeiten.

gardener ['gɑːdnə], s. der Gärtner.

gargle [gɑːgl], v.n. gurgeln, spülen.

gargoyle ['gɑːgɔil], s. (Archit.) der Wasserspeier.

garish ['gɛəriʃ], adj. grell, auffallend.

garland ['gɑːlənd], s. der Blumenkranz, die Girlande.

garlic ['gɑːlik], s. (Bot.) der Knoblauch.

garment ['gɑːmənt], s. das Gewand.

garner ['gɑːnə], v.a. aufspeichern (store).

garnet ['gɑːnit], s. der Granat.

garnish ['gɑːniʃ], v.a. ausschmücken, verzieren.

garret ['gærət], s. die Dachkammer.

garrison ['gærisən], s. (Mil.) die Garnison. — v.a. stationieren.

garrulity [gæ'ruːliti], s. die Schwatzhaftigkeit.

garter ['gɑːtə], s. das Strumpfband, das Hosenband; Order of the Garter, der Hosenbandorden.

gas [gæs], s. das Gas; (Am.) see gasoline.

gaseous ['geisiəs], adj. gasförmig, gasartig.

Gascon ['gæskən], s. der Gaskogner.

gasoline ['gæsoliːn], s. (Am.) das Benzin.

gash [gæʃ], s. die Schnittwunde.

gasp [gɑːsp], v.n. keuchen; nach Luft schnappen. — s. das Keuchen, das Luftschnappen.

gastric ['gæstrik], adj. (Anat.) gastrisch; — ulcer, das Magengeschwür.

gate [geit], s. das Tor, der Eingang. — v.a. einsperren, Hausarrest geben (Dat.).

gateway ['geitwei], s. die Einfahrt.

gather ['gæðə], v.a. sammeln, einsammeln (collect); versammeln (assemble). — v.n. entnehmen, schließen (infer); sich versammeln (come together); aufziehen (storm).

gathering ['gæðəriŋ], s. die Versammlung (meeting).

gauche [gouʃ], adj. linkisch, ungeschickt.

gaudy ['gɔːdi], adj. übertrieben, grell, prunkhaft.

gauge [geidʒ], v.a. (Engin.) ausmessen, kalibrieren; eichen (officially). — s. der Maßstab (scale); (Railw.) die Spurweite.

gauger ['geidʒə], s. der Eichmeister.

Gaul [gɔːl], s. der Gallier.

gaunt [gɔːnt], adj. mager; hager.

gauntlet ['gɔːntlit], s. der (Panzer)handschuh.

gauze [gɔːz], s. die Gaze.

gavotte [gə'vɔt], s. (Mus.) die Gavotte.

gay [gei], *adj.* fröhlich, heiter; bunt (*colour*).

gaze [geiz], *v.n.* starren.

gazelle [gə'zel], *s.* (*Zool.*) die Gazelle.

gazette [gə'zet], *s.* die (amtliche) Zeitung; das Amtsblatt.

gear [giə], *s.* das Gerät; (*Mech.*) das Triebwerk; (*Naut.*) das Geschirr; *switch*—, das Schaltgerät; (*Motor.*) der Gang; — *ratio*, die Übersetzung; *differential* —, der Achsenantrieb; *steering* —, die Lenkung (*of car*); — *box*, das Schaltgetriebe, die Gangschaltung; *out of* —, in Unordnung; *in top* —, mit Höchstgeschwindigkeit; *change to bottom* —, auf erste Geschwindigkeit (*or*, auf langsam) einschalten. — *v.a.* — *down*, herabsetzen; (*Engin.*) — *up*, übersetzen; — *to*, anpassen.

gelatine ['dʒeləti:n], *s.* die Gallerte, die Geleemasse.

gem [dʒem], *s.* die Gemme, der Edelstein.

gender ['dʒendə], *s.* (*Gram.*) das Geschlecht.

gene [dʒi:n], *s.* (*Biol.*) das Gen.

geneaology [dʒi:ni'ælədʒi], *s.* die Genealogie; der Stammbaum (*family tree*).

general ['dʒenərəl], *s.* (*Mil.*) der General; *lieutenant*- —, der Generalleutnant — *adj.* allgemein, General-; — *-purpose*, für alle Zwecke; Allzweck-.

generalization [dʒenərəlai'zeiʃən], *s.* die Verallgemeinerung.

generalize ['dʒenərəlaiz], *v.a.* verallgemeinern.

generate ['dʒenəreit], *v.a.* erzeugen; (*Elec.*) Strom erzeugen.

generation [dʒenə'reiʃən], *s.* die Generation (*contemporaries*); das Zeugen (*production*); (*Elec.*) die Stromerzeugung.

generosity [dʒenə'rɔsiti], *s.* die Großmut (*magnanimity*); die Freigebigkeit (*liberality*).

generous ['dʒenərəs], *adj.* großmütig; freigebig (*with gifts*).

Genevan [dʒi'ni:vən], *adj.* genferisch. — *s.* der Genfer.

genitive ['dʒenitiv], *s.* (*Gram.*) der Wesfall, Genitiv.

genial ['dʒi:niəl], *adj.* freundlich, mild.

geniality [dʒi:ni'æliti], *s.* die Freundlichkeit, Leutseligkeit.

genital ['dʒenitəl], *adj.* Zeugungs-. — *s.* (*pl.*) die Geschlechtsteile, Genitalien, *pl.*

genius ['dʒi:niəs], *s.* das Genie; der Genius.

Genoese [dʒenou'i:z], *adj.* genuesisch. — *s.* der Genuese.

Gentile ['dʒentail], *s.* heidnisch; nicht jüdisch.

gentility [dʒen'tiliti], *s.* die Herkunft aus vornehmem Haus, Vornehmheit.

gentle [dʒentl], *adj.* sanft, mild; gelind (*breeze*).

gentlefolk ['dʒentlfouk], *s.* bessere *or* vornehme Leute, *pl.*

gentleman ['dʒentlmən], *s.* der Gentleman, Herr; feiner Herr.

gentleness ['dʒentlnis], *s.* die Milde, Sanftheit.

gentry ['dʒentri], *s.* der niedere Adel.

genuine ['dʒenjuin], *adj.* echt.

genus ['dʒenəs], *s.* (*Biol.*) die Gattung.

geographer [dʒi'ɔgrəfə], *s.* der Geograph.

geographical [dʒi:o'græfikəl], *adj.* geographisch.

geography [dʒi'ɔgrəfi], die Geographie, Erdkunde.

geological [dʒi:o'lɔdʒikəl], *adj.* geologisch.

geologist [dʒi'ɔlədʒist], *s.* der Geologe.

geology [dʒi'ɔlədʒi], *s.* die Geologie.

geometric(al) [dʒi:o'metrik(əl)], *adj.* geometrisch.

geometrist [dʒi'ɔmətrist], *s.* der Geometer.

geometry [dʒi'ɔmətri], *s.* die Geometrie.

geranium [dʒə'reiniəm], *s.* (*Bot.*) die Geranie, das Germaniu.

germ [dʒə:m], *s.* der Keim; (*pl.*) die Bakterien, *f. pl.*

German ['dʒə:mən], *adj.* deutsch. — *s.* der, die Deutsche.

germane [dʒə:'mein], *adj.* zur Sache gehörig, zugehörig.

germinate ['dʒə:mineit], *v.n.* keimen.

Germanic [dʒə:'mænik], *adj.* germanisch.

gerund ['dʒerənd], *s.* (*Gram.*) das Gerundium.

gerundive [dʒe'rʌndiv], *s.* (*Gram.*) das Gerundiv(um).

gesticulate [dʒes'tikjuleit], *v.n.* Gebärden machen, gestikulieren.

gesture ['dʒestʃə], *s.* die Geste; der Gebärde.

get [get], *v.a. irr.* bekommen, (*coll.*) kriegen; erhalten (*receive*); erwischen (*catch up with*); einholen (*fetch*); — *over or across*, klar machen. — *v.n.* gelangen (*arrive*); werden (*become*); — *along*, weiterkommen; — *on or* (*Am.*) *along with s.o.*, mit jemandem auskommen; — *on in the world*, Karriere machen; — *away*, entkommen; — *down to it*, zur Sache kommen; — *in*, hineinkommen; — *off*, aussteigen; *show s.o. where he —s off*, jemandem seine Meinung sagen; (*Sch.*) — *through*, durchkommen (*in examination*); — *up*, aufstehen.

get-up ['getʌp], *s.* das Kostüm; die Ausstattung (*attire*).

Ghanaian [ga:'neiən], *adj.* ghanaisch. — *s.* der Ghanaer.

ghastly ['ga:stli], *adj.* furchtbar, schrecklich.

gherkin ['gə:kin], *s.* (*Bot.*) die Essiggurke.

ghost [goust], *s.* der Geist, das Gespenst.

giant ['dʒaiənt], *s.* der Riese.

gibberish ['dʒibəriʃ], *s.* das Kauderwelsch.

gibbet ['dʒibit], *s.* der Galgen.

gibe [dʒaib], v.n. spotten, höhnen (at, über, Acc.). — s. der Spott, Hohn; die spöttische Bemerkung (remark).

giblets [ˈdʒiblits], s. pl. das Gänseklein.

giddiness [ˈgidinis], s. das Schwindelgefühl.

giddy [ˈgidi], adj. schwindelig.

gift [gift], s. die Gabe, das Geschenk.

gifted [ˈgiftid], adj. begabt.

gig [gig], s. der leichte Wagen; (Naut.) der Nachen, das Gig.

gigantic [dʒaiˈgæntik], adj. riesig, riesengroß.

giggle [gigl], v.n. kichern. — s. das Kichern, Gekicher.

gild [gild], v.a. vergolden; verschönern; —ing the pill, etwas Unangenehmes (die Pille) versüßen.

gill (1) [gil], s. (Biol.) die Kieme.

gill (2) [dʒil], s. das Viertel einer Pinte (0.14 l.).

gilt [gilt], s. die Vergoldung; — edged, mit Goldschnitt; (Comm.) hochwertige or mündelsichere Staatspapiere.

gimlet [ˈgimlit], s. (Carp.) der Handbohrer.

gin [dʒin], s. der Gin, der Wacholderbranntwein; — and tonic, Gin und Tonic.

ginger [ˈdʒindʒə], s. der Ingwer; — haired, rothaarig; — nut, das Ingweror Pfeffernüßchen, Ingwerkeks; — beer, Ingwerbier. — v.a. — up, aufstacheln, anreizen.

gingerbread [ˈdʒindʒəbred], s. der Lebkuchen, Pfefferkuchen.

gipsy [ˈdʒipsi], s. der Zigeuner.

giraffe [dʒiˈraːf], s. (Zool.) die Giraffe.

gird [gəːd], v.a. reg. & irr. (Poet.) gürten.

girder [ˈgəːdə], s. der Balken, Träger.

girdle [ˈgəːdl], v.a. gürten, umgürten; — the earth, die Erde umkreisen.

girl [gəːl], s. das Mädchen.

girlhood [ˈgəːlhud], s. die Mädchenzeit, die Mädchenjahre, n. pl.

girlish [ˈgəːliʃ], adj. mädchenhaft, wie ein Mädchen.

gist [dʒist], s. das Wesentliche.

give [giv], v.a. irr. geben; — out, bekanntgeben, bekanntmachen; — up, aufgeben; — way to, Platz machen. — v.n. sich dehnen, sich strecken (of wood, metal etc.); — in, nachgeben (to, Dat.).

glacial [ˈgleiʃəl], adj. eisig, Gletscher-.

glacier [ˈglæsiə], s. der Gletscher.

glad [glæd], adj. froh, erfreut (at, über, Acc.).

gladden [glædn], v.a. erheitern, erfreuen.

glade [gleid], s. die Lichtung.

glamorous [ˈglæmərəs], adj. bezaubernd, blendend glanzvoll.

glamour [ˈglæmə], s. der Zauber; der Glanz.

glance [glaːns], s. der Blick; at a —, auf den ersten Blick. — v.n. flüchtig blicken.

gland [glænd], s. (Anat.) die Drüse.

glandular [ˈglændjulə], adj. Drüsen-, drüsig.

glare [glɛə], s. der blendende Glanz, das Schimmern; der (scharf) durchbohrende Blick (stare).

glaring [ˈglɛəriŋ], adj. schreiend (of colour); auffallend (obvious).

glass [glaːs], s. das Glas; der Spiegel (mirror); das Wetterglas (barometer); (pl.) die Brille (spectacles).

glassblower [ˈglaːsblouə], s. der Glasbläser.

glassworks [ˈglaːswəːks], s. die Glashütte.

glassy [ˈglaːsi], adj. gläsern.

glaze [gleiz], s. die Glasur. — v.a. glasieren; verglasen.

glazier [ˈgleiziə], s. der Glaser.

gleam [gliːm], v.n. strahlen, glänzen (with, vor, Dat.). — s. der Glanz, das Strahlen.

glean [gliːn], v.a. auflesen; erfahren (learn).

glebe [gliːb], s. das Pfarrgut.

glee (1) [gliː], s. die Freude, Heiterkeit.

glee (2) [gliː], s. (Mus.) der Rundgesang; — club, die Liedertafel.

glen [glen], s. das enge Tal.

glib [glib], adj. glatt, geläufig, zungenfertig.

glide [glaid], v.n. gleiten. — s. das Gleiten.

glider [ˈglaidə], s. (Aviat.) das Segelflugzeug.

glimmer [ˈglimə], s. der Schimmer, Glimmer. — v.n. schimmern, glimmen.

glimpse [glimps], s. der (flüchtige) Blick; catch a —, einen Blick erhaschen. — v.a. flüchtig blicken (auf, Acc.).

glisten [glisn], v.n. glitzern, glänzen.

glitter [ˈglitə], v.n. glänzen, schimmern.

gloaming [ˈgloumiŋ], s. die Dämmerung.

globe [gloub], s. der Globus, der Erdball; die Kugel.

globular [ˈglɔbjulə], adj. kugelförmig.

gloom [gluːm], s. das Dunkel; der Trübsinn, die Traurigkeit.

gloomy [ˈgluːmi], adj. deprimiert, trübsinnig, düster.

glorify [ˈglɔːrifai], v.a. verherrlichen.

glorious [ˈglɔːriəs], adj. herrlich; (Mil.) glorreich.

glory [ˈglɔːri], s. die Herrlichkeit, der Ruhm. — v.n. frohlocken (in, über, Acc.).

gloss [glɔs], s. der Glanz; (Lit.) die Glosse, Anmerkung. — v.a. — over, beschönigen; (Lit.) glossieren, mit Anmerkungen versehen.

glossary [ˈglɔsəri], s. das Glossar, die Spezialwörterliste; das Wörterbuch.

glossy [ˈglɔsi], adj. glänzend.

glove [glʌv], s. der Handschuh.

glow [glou], v.n. glühen. — s. die Glut, das Glühen; Wohlbehagen.

glower [ˈglauə], v.n. — at, feindselig ansehen, anstarren.

403

glue

glue [glu:], *s.* der Leim. — *v.a.* leimen, zusammenleimen.

glum [glʌm], *adj.* mürrisch, finster.

glut [glʌt], *s.* die Überfülle. — *v.a.* überladen, überfüllen.

glutinous [ˈglu:tinəs], *adj.* zähe, klebrig.

glutton [glʌtn], *s.* der Vielfraß.

gluttony [ˈglʌtəni], *s.* die Schwelgerei, Gefräßigkeit.

glycerine [ˈglisəri:n], *s.* das Glyzerin.

gnarled [nɑ:ld], *adj.* knorrig.

gnash [næʃ], *v.a.* knirschen (*teeth*).

gnat [næt], *s.* (*Ent.*) die Mücke.

gnaw [nɔ:], *v.a., v.n.* nagen (an, *Dat.*), zernagen, zerfressen (at, *Acc.*).

gnome [noum], *s.* der Erdgeist, der Zwerg, Gnom.

go [gou], *v.n. irr.* gehen, fahren, laufen; arbeiten (*engine*); verlaufen (*event*); sich erstrecken (*distance*); — *down in the general esteem*, in der Achtung sinken; — *on*, fortfahren; — *mad*, verrückt werden; — *bald*, die Haare verlieren; — *without*, leer ausgehen, entbehren; *let* —, loslassen; — *for*, auf jemanden losgehen; — *in for*, sich interessieren für (*Acc.*); — *all out for*, energisch unternehmen; *a* —*ing concern*, ein gutgehendes Unternehmen; —*ing on for 20*, fast 20 Jahre. — *s.* der Versuch; (*coll.*) *plenty of* —, recht lebhaft, voller Schwung.

goad [goud], *v.a.* anstacheln.

goal [goul], *s.* das Ziel; (*Footb.*) das Tor.

goalkeeper [ˈgoulki:pə], *s.* der Torwart.

goalpost [ˈgoulpoust], *s.* der Torpfosten.

goat [gout], *s.* (*Zool.*) die Geiß, Ziege; *billy* —, der Ziegenbock; *nanny* —, die Geiß.

gobble [gɔbl], *v.a.* verschlingen, gierig essen.

goblet [ˈgɔblit], *s.* der Becher.

goblin [ˈgɔblin], *s.* der Kobold, der Gnom; der Schelm.

go-cart [ˈgouka:t], *s.* der Kinderwagen, Gängelwagen.

God [gɔd], *s.* Gott.

god [gɔd], *s.* der Gott.

godchild [ˈgɔdtʃaild], *s.* das Patenkind.

goddess [ˈgɔdes], *s.* die Göttin.

godfather [ˈgɔdfa:ðə], *s.* der Pate.

godhead [ˈgɔdhed], *s.* die Gottheit.

godless [ˈgɔdlis], *adj.* gottlos, ungläubig.

godmother [ˈgɔdmʌðə], *s.* die Patin.

goggle [gɔgl], *v.n.* glotzen, starren (*stare*). — *s.* (*pl.*) die Schutzbrille.

going [ˈgouin], *s.* das Gehen, das Funktionieren (*of machinery*); *while the* — *is good*, zur rechten Zeit.

gold [gould], *s.* das Gold; (*Fin.*) — *standard*, die Goldwährung.

goldfinch [ˈgouldfintʃ], *s.* (*Orn.*) der Stieglitz.

goldsmith [ˈgouldsmiθ], *s.* der Goldschmied.

gondola [ˈgɔndələ], *s.* die Gondel.

good [gud], *adj.* gut; artig, brav; *for* —, auf immer; *in* — *time*, rechtzeitig; — *and proper*, (*coll.*) wie es sich gehört, anständig; *as* — *as*, so gut wie; — *looking*, hübsch; — *natured*, gutmütig. — *s. for your own* —, in Ihrem eigenen Interesse; *that's no* —, das taugt nichts; (*pl.*) die Güter, *n.pl.*, Waren, *f.pl.*; *goods station*, der Frachbahnhof; *goods train*, der Güterzug; *goods yard*, der Güterstapelplatz.

goodbye [gud'bai], *interj., s.*—! leb wohl! auf Wiedersehen!

goodness [ˈgudnis], *s.* die Güte.

goodwill [gud'wil], *s.* das Wohlwollen; (*Comm.*) die Kundschaft.

goose [gu:s], *s.* (*Orn.*) die Gans.

gooseberry [ˈguzbəri], *s.* (*Bot.*) die Stachelbeere.

gore [gɔ:], *s.* das geronnene Blut. — *v.a.* durchbohren (*pierce, stab*).

gorge [gɔ:dʒ], *s.* die Felsenschlucht (*ravine*); (*Anat.*) die Kehle. — *v.a.* gierig verschlingen.

gorgeous [ˈgɔ:dʒəs], *adj.* prachtvoll, prächtig.

gorse [gɔ:s], *s.* (*Bot.*) der Stechginster.

gory [ˈgɔ:ri], *adj.* blutig.

goshawk [ˈgɔshɔ:k], *s.* (*Orn.*) der Hühnerhabicht.

gosling [ˈgɔzliŋ], *s.* (*Orn.*) das Gänschen.

gospel [ˈgɔspəl], *s.* das Evangelium; *the* — *according to*, das Evangelium des . . .

gossamer [ˈgɔsəmə], *s.* das feine Gewebe; die Sommerfäden.

gossip [ˈgɔsip], *v.n.* klatschen; schwatzen, plaudern. — *s.* der Klatsch; der Schwätzer; die Klatschbase.

Gothic [ˈgɔθik], *adj.* gotisch.

gouge [gaudʒ], *s.* der Hohlmeißel. — *v.a.* aushöhlen, ausstechen.

gourd [guəd], *s.* der Kürbis.

gout [gaut], *s.* (*Med.*) die Gicht.

govern [ˈgʌvən], *v.a., v.n.* (*Pol.*) regieren; beherrschen; (*fig.*) leiten, herrschen.

governable [ˈgʌvənəbl], *adj.* lenkbar, lenksam.

governess [ˈgʌvənis], *s.* die Erzieherin, die Gouvernante.

government [ˈgʌvənmənt], *s.* die Regierung, (*Pol.*) — *benches*, die Regierungssitze; — *loan*, die Staatsanleihe.

governor [ˈgʌvənə], *s.* der Gouverneur, Statthalter.

gown [gaun], *s.* das Kleid (*lady's*); (*Univ.*) der Talar; (*official robe*) die Amtstracht.

grab [græb], *v.a.* packen, ergreifen. — *s.* der Zugriff.

grace [greis], *s.* die Gnade; Gunst (*favour*); die Anmut (*gracefulness*); *Your Grace*, Euer Gnaden; das Tischgebet (*prayer at table*); (*Mus.*) — *note*, die Fermate; *ten minutes'* —, zehn Minuten Aufschub. — *v.a.* schmücken, zieren, ehren.

graceful [ˈgreisful], *adj.* anmutig, reizend; graziös (*movement*).

great

graceless ['greislis], *adj.* ungraziös.
gracious['greiʃəs],*adj.*gnädig,huldreich.
gradation [grə'deiʃən], *s.* die Abstufung, die Stufenleiter.
grade [greid], *s.* der Grad, Rang (*rank*); (*Am.*) (*Sch.*) die Klasse. — *v.a.* sortieren, ordnen.
gradient ['greidiənt], *s.* (*Geog.*) die Steigung; der Steigungswinkel (*angle*).
gradual ['grædjuəl], *adj.* allmählich.
graduate ['grædjueit], *v.n.* promovieren (*receive degree*); — *as a doctor*, als Doktor promovieren, den Doktor machen.— [-djuit], *s.* der Akademiker, Graduierte.
graft (1) [grɑːft], *s.* (*Hort., Med.*) die (Haut)übertragung. — *v.a.* (*Hort., Med.*) übertragen, anheften (*on to*, auf, *Acc.*).
graft (2) [grɑːft], *s.* (*Am.*) der unerlaubte Gewinn; das Schmiergeld; der Betrug (*swindle*).
grain [grein], *s.* das Korn, Samenkorn; das Getreide; das Gran (=0·065 *gramme*); die Maserung (*in wood*); *against the* —, gegen den Strich.
grammar ['græmə], *s.* die Grammatik; — *school*, das Gymnasium.
grammatical [grə'mætikəl], *adj.* grammatisch.
gramme [græm], *s.* das Gramm.
gramophone ['græməfoun], *s.* das Grammophon.
granary ['grænəri], *s.* der (Korn)speicher, die Kornkammer.
grand [grænd], *adj.* groß, großartig; wunderbar; *Grand Duke*, der Großherzog. — *s.* (*Am.*) (*sl.*) 1000 Dollar; (*piano*) der Flügel; *baby* —, der Stutzflügel.
grandchild ['grændtʃaild], *s.* der Enkel, die Enkelin.
grandee [græn'diː], *s.* der spanische Grande.
grandeur ['grændjə], *s.* die Größe, Pracht.
grandfather ['grændfɑːðə], *s.* der Großvater.
grandiloquent [græn'dilokwənt], *adj.* großsprecherisch.
grandmother ['grændmʌðə], *s.* die Großmutter.
grange [greindʒ], *s.* der Meierhof, das Landhaus.
granite ['grænit], *s.* der Granit.
grannie, granny ['græni], *s.* (*coll.*) die Oma.
grant [grɑːnt], *s.* die Gewährung (*of permission etc.*); die Zuwendung (*subsidy*); (*Sch.*) das Stipendium. — *v.a.* geben, gewähren; *take for* —*ed*, als selbstverständlich hinnehmen.
granular ['grænjulə], *adj.* körnig.
granulated ['grænjuleitid], *adj.* feinkörnig, Kristall- (*sugar*).
grape [greip], *s.* (*Bot.*) die Weinbeere; die Traube; — *sugar*, der Traubenzucker; *bunch of* —*s*, Weintrauben, *f. pl.*
grapefruit ['greipfruːt], *s.* die Pampelmuse.

graphic ['græfik], *adj.* (*Art*) graphisch; deutlich, bildhaft, anschaulich.
grapnel ['græpnəl], *s.* (*Naut.*) der Dreganker.
grapple ['græpl], *v.n.* — *with*, raufen, (miteinander) ringen.
grasp [grɑːsp], *v.a.* (mit der Hand) ergreifen, erfassen. — *s.* das Fassungsvermögen, die Auffassung; der Griff (*hand*).
grasping ['grɑːspiŋ], *adj.* habgierig, gewinnsüchtig.
grass [grɑːs], *s.* (*Bot.*) das Gras; der Rasen (*lawn*); — *widow*, die Strohwitwe.
grasshopper ['grɑːshɔpə], *s.* (*Ent.*) die Heuschrecke.
grate (1) [greit], *s.* der Feuerrost, der Kamin.
grate (2) [greit], *v.a.* reiben (*cheese*); schaben, kratzen. — *v.n.* knirschen; auf die Nerven gehen.
grateful ['greitful], *adj.* dankbar.
grater ['greitə], *s.* das Reibeisen; die Reibe (*electrical*).
gratification [grætifi'keiʃən], *s.* die Genugtuung, Befriedigung.
gratify ['grætifai], *v.a.* befriedigen, erfreuen.
grating ['greitiŋ], *s.* das Gitter.
gratis ['greitis], *adv.* gratis, umsonst, frei, unentgeltlich.
gratitude ['grætitjuːd], *s.* die Dankbarkeit.
gratuitous [grə'tjuːitəs], *adj.* frei, freiwillig (*voluntary*); unentgeltlich (*free of charge*); grundlos (*baseless*).
gratuity [grə'tjuːiti], *s.* das Trinkgeld (*tip*); die Gratifikation.
grave (1) [greiv], *adj.* schwer, ernst (*serious*); feierlich (*solemn*). —*s.* (*Mus.*) das Grave.
grave (2) [greiv], *s.* das Grab (*tomb*).
gravel [grævl], *s.* der Kies.
graveyard ['greivjɑːd], *s.* der Friedhof.
gravitate ['græviteit], *v.n.* gravitieren, hinstreben.
gravitation [grævi'teiʃən], *s.* die Schwerkraft.
gravitational [grævi'teiʃənəl], *adj.* (*Phys.*) Schwerkrafts-.
gravity ['græviti], *s.* der Ernst (*seriousness*); (*Phys.*) die Schwere, Schwerkraft.
gravy ['greivi], *s.* die Sauce, Soße; der Saft des Fleisches, des Bratens; — *boat*, die Sauciere.
gray, grey [grei], *adj.* grau.
graze (1) [greiz], *v.n.* weiden.
graze (2) [greiz], *v.a.* streifen (*pass closely*), abschürfen.
grazier ['greiziə], *s.* der Viehzüchter.
grease [griːs], *s.* das Fett; das Schmieröl (*machine*). — *v.a.* einfetten (*pans*); schmieren, einschmieren (*machinery*).
greasy ['griːsi], *adj.* fett, schmierig, ölig.
great [greit], *adj.* groß, bedeutend, wichtig; (*Am.*) wundervoll, wunderbar.

greatcoat ['greitcout], *s.* der Winter-mantel.

great-grandfather [greit'grændfɑ:ðə], *s.* der Urgroßvater.

greatly ['greitli], *adv.* stark, sehr.

greatness ['greitnis], *s.* die Größe, Bedeutung.

greedy ['gri:di], *adj.* gierig; gefräßig (*eater*).

Greek [gri:k], *adj.* griechisch. — *s.* der Grieche.

green [gri:n], *adj.* grün; neu (*new*), frisch (*fresh*).

greengage ['gri:ngeidʒ], *s.* (*Bot.*) die Reineclaude.

greengrocer ['gri:ngrousə], *s.* der Grünwarenhändler, Gemüsehändler.

greenhorn ['gri:nhɔ:n], *s.* der Grün-schnabel.

greenhouse ['gri:nhaus], *s.* das Ge-wächshaus, Treibhaus.

Greenlander ['gri:nləndə], *s.* der Grön-länder.

greet [gri:t], *v.a.* grüßen, begrüßen.

greeting ['gri:tiŋ], *s.* die Begrüßung; (*pl.*) Grüße, *m. pl.*

gregarious [gri'gɛəriəs], *adj.* gesellig.

grenade [gri'neid], *s.* die Granate.

grey *see under* **gray.**

greyhound ['greihaund], *s.* (*Zool.*) das Windspiel, der Windhund.

grid [grid], *s.* (*Elec.*) das Stromnetz; (*Phys.*) die Gitter.

gridiron ['gridaiən], *s.* der Bratrost, das Bratrostgitter.

grief [gri:f], *s.* der Kummer, die Trauer.

grievance ['gri:vəns], *s.* die Klage, Beschwerde.

grieve [gri:v], *v.a.* kränken. — *v.n.* sich grämen, sich kränken (*over*, über, *Acc.*, wegen, *Genit.*).

grievous ['gri:vəs], *adj.* schmerzlich.

grill [gril], *s.* der Rostbraten, Bratrost. — *v.a.* grillieren, rösten (*meat*); verhören (*question closely*).

grilling ['griliŋ], *s.* das Verhör.

grim [grim], *adj.* grimmig, finster.

grimace [gri'meis], *s.* die Grimasse, die Fratze.

grime [graim], *s.* der Schmutz, der Ruß.

grimy ['graimi], *adj.* schmutzig, rußig.

grin [grin], *v.n.* grinsen; (*coll.*) — *and bear it*, mach gute Miene zum bösen Spiel. — *s.* das Grinsen.

grind [graind], *v.a. irr.* zerreiben (*rub*); schleifen (*sharpen*); mahlen (*pulver-ize*); — *o.'s teeth*, mit den Zähnen knirschen. — *s.* (*coll.*) die ungeheuere Anstrengung, die Plackerei.

grinder ['graində], *s.* coffee —, die Kaffeemühle; *knife* —, der Schleifer, Wetzer; der Backzahn (*molar*).

grindstone ['graindstoun], *s.* der Schleif-stein; *keep o.'s nose to the* —, fest bei der Arbeit bleiben.

grip [grip], *s.* der Griff; *lose o.'s* —, nicht mehr bewältigen können (wie bisher); (*Tech.*) der Handgriff (*handle*). — *v.a.* ergreifen, festhalten.

gripe [graip], *v.n.* (*sl.*) meckern.

gripes [graips], *s. pl.* (*Med.*) das Bauch-grimmen, die Kolik.

gripping ['gripiŋ], *adj.* fesselnd (*story*).

grisly ['grizli], *adj.* scheußlich, gräßlich.

grist [grist], *s.* das Mahlgut, Gemah-lene; — *to o.'s mill*, Wasser auf seine Mühle.

gristle [grisl], *s.* der Knorpel.

grit [grit], *s.* das Schrot, der Kies; der Mut (*courage*).

gritty ['griti], *adj.* körnig, kiesig, sandig.

grizzled ['grizld], *adj.* grau, grau-meliert.

groan [groun], *v.n.* stöhnen.

groats [grouts], *s. pl.* die Hafergrütze.

grocer ['grousə], *s.* der Kolonialwaren-händler, Feinkosthändler.

groin [grɔin], *s.* (*Anat.*) die Leiste; (*Archit.*) die Gewölbekante, Rippe.

groom [gru:m], *s.* der Stallknecht (*stables*); (*obs.*) der Junge (*inn*). — *v.a.* schniegeln, bürsten; schön machen.

groove [gru:v], *s.* die Rinne; die Rille (*of gramophone record*). — *v.a.* rillen; furchen (*dig a furrow*).

grope [group], *v.n.* tappen, tasten (*around*, umher).

gross [grous], *adj.* dick (*fat*); plump (*heavy-handed*); grob (*ill-mannered*); — *weight*, das Bruttogewicht; un-geheuer (*error*).

grotto ['grɔtou], *s.* die Grotte.

ground [graund], *s.* der Grund, Boden (*also pl.*); die Ursache (*cause*); — *floor*, das Erdgeschoß. — *v.n.* stranden (*of ship*).

groundwork ['graundwə:k], *s.* die Grundlagen, *f. pl.*

group [gru:p], *s.* die Gruppe. — *v.a.* gruppieren, anordnen.

grouse (1) [graus], *v.n.* (*coll.*) meckern, sich beklagen. — *s.* der Grund zur Klage, die Beschwerde.

grouse (2) [graus], *s.* (*Orn.*) das Birk-huhn, Moorhuhn.

grove [grouv], *s.* der Hain, das Wäld-chen.

grovel [grɔvl], *v.n.* kriechen, schöntun (*Dat.*).

grow [grou], *v.n. irr.* wachsen, sich mehren (*increase*); werden (*become*). — *v.a.* anbauen, pflanzen.

growl [graul], *v.n.* brummen, knurren. — *s.* das Gebrumme, Geknurre.

grown-up [groun'ʌp], *s.* der Erwach-sene. — *adj.* erwachsen.

growth [grouθ], *s.* das Anwachsen (*increase*); das Wachstum (*growing*).

grub [grʌb], *s.* (*Zool.*) die Larve; (*coll.*) das Essen. — *v.n.* — *about*, wühlen.

grudge [grʌdʒ], *s.* der Groll; Neid (*jealousy*). — *v.a.* mißgönnen (*envy*). — *v.n.* — *doing s.th.*; etwas ungerne tun.

gruel ['gru:əl], *s.* der Haferschleim.

gruesome ['gru:səm], *adj.* schauerlich, schrecklich.

gruff [grʌf], *adj.* mürrisch.

grumble [grʌmbl], *v.n.* murren, klagen.

grumbler ['grʌmblə], s. der Unzu-
friedene, Nörgler.

grunt [grʌnt], v.n. grunzen. — s. das
Grunzen.

guarantee [gærən'ti:], v.a. bürgen,
garantieren. — s. die Bürgschaft;
(Comm.) die Garantie.

guarantor ['gærəntɔ:], s. der Bürge;
(Comm.) der Garant.

guard [ga:d], s. die Wache (watch or
watchman); (Railw.) der Schaffner; die
Schutzvorrichtung (protective device);
(fire) —, das Kamingitter; (for
sword) der Stichblatt. — v.a. bewachen; behüten (protect). — v.n. auf
der Hut sein; — against, sich hüten
(vor, Dat.); vorbeugen.

guarded ['ga:did], adj. behutsam,
vorsichtig.

guardian ['ga:djən], s. der Vormund
(of child); der Wächter.

guardianship ['ga:djənʃip], s. (Law)
die Vormundschaft.

Guatemalan [gwæti'ma:lən], adj.
guatemaltekisch. — s. der Guatemal-
teke.

Guelph [gwelf], s. der Welfe.

guess [ges], v.a. raten (a riddle). —
v.n. (Am.) glauben, meinen. — s. die
Vermutung; have a —, rate mal!

guest [gest], s. der Gast; paying —,
der Pensionär.

guffaw [gʌ'fɔ:], s. das (laute) Gelächter.

guidance ['gaidəns], s. die Führung,
Anleitung.

guide [gaid], s. der Führer, Wegweiser,
Reiseführer; (Phot.) die Führung. —
v.a. führen, anleiten.

guided ['gaidid], adj. gelenkt; —
missile, das Ferngeschoß, die Rakete.

guild [gild], s. die Gilde, Zunft, Innung.

guildhall ['gildhɔ:l], s. das Rathaus.

guile [gail], s. der Betrug, die Arglist.

guileless ['gaillis], adj. arglos.

guilt [gilt], s. die Schuld.

guilty ['gilti], adj. schuldig.

guinea ['gini], s. die Guinee (21 shillings); — fowl, das Perlhuhn; — pig,
das Meerschweinchen.

guise [gaiz], s. die Verkleidung (costume); die Erscheinung (appearance).

guitar [gi'ta:], s. (Mus.) die Gitarre.

gulf [gʌlf], s. der Meerbusen, Golf;
der Abgrund (abyss).

gull [gʌl], s. (Orn.) die Möwe.

gullet ['gʌlit], s. (Anat.) der Schlund,
die Gurgel.

gullible ['gʌlibl], adj. leichtgläubig.

gully ['gʌli], s. die Schlucht (abyss).

gulp [gʌlp], v.a. schlucken. — s. der
Schluck, Zug.

gum (1) [gʌm], s. (Bot.) das Gummi.
— v.a. gummieren; (coll.) — up,
verderben (spoil).

gum (2) [gʌm], s. (Anat.) das Zahnfleisch.

gun [gʌn], s. das Gewehr (rifle); die
Kanone (cannon); — carriage, die
Lafette.

gunpowder ['gʌnpaudə], s. das Schieß-
pulver.

gunsmith ['gʌnsmiθ], s. der Büchsen-
macher.

gurgle [gə:gl], v.n. glucksen.

gush [gʌʃ], v.n. sich ergießen; schwärmen.

gusset ['gʌsit], s. (Tail.) der Zwickel.

gust [gʌst], s. der Windstoß.

gut [gʌt], s. (Anat.) der Darm; (pl.) die
Eingeweide, n. pl.; (coll.) der Mut.
— v.a. ausnehmen; ausleeren.

gutter ['gʌtə], s. die Rinne, Gosse.

guttersnipe ['gʌtəsnaip], s. der
Lausbube.

guttural ['gʌtərəl], adj. Kehl-. — s. (Phon.)
der Kehllaut.

guy [gai], s. die Vogelscheuche, die
verkleidete Puppe; (Am.) der Kerl.

guzzle [gʌzl], v.n. schlemmen.

gymnasium [dʒim'neiziəm], s. die
Turnhalle.

gymnastics [dʒim'næstiks], s. pl. das
Turnen; die Gymnastik.

gypsum ['dʒipsəm], s. der Gips; der
schwefelsaure Kalk.

gyrate [dʒaiə'reit], v.n. sich im Kreise
bewegen, sich drehen, kreisen.

H

H [eitʃ]. das H.

haberdasher ['hæbədæʃə], s. der Kurz-
warenhändler.

haberdashery ['hæbədæʃəri], s. die
Kurzwarenhandlung.

habit ['hæbit], s. die Gewohnheit
(custom); force of —, aus Gewohnheit,
die Macht der Gewohnheit; die
Kleidung (costume); riding —, das
Reitkostüm.

habitable ['hæbitəbl], adj. bewohnbar.

habitation [hæbi'teiʃən], s. die Wohnung.

habitual [hə'bitjuəl], adj. gewohnheitsmäßig.

habituate [hə'bitjueit], v.a. gewöhnen.

hack (1) [hæk], v.a. hacken (wood);
treten.

hack (2) [hæk], s. der Lohnschreiber;
der (alte) Gaul, das Mietpferd (horse).

hackle [hækl], v.a. hecheln.

hackney ['hækni], s. — carriage, die
Mietskutsche; das Taxi.

haddock ['hædək], s. (Zool.) der Schellfisch.

haemorrhage ['heməridʒ], s. (Med.)
die Blutung, der Blutsturz.

haemorrhoids ['hemərɔidz], s. pl. (Med.)
die Hämorrhoiden, f. pl.

hag [hæg], s. das alte Weib; die Hexe
(witch).

407

haggard

haggard ['hægəd], *adj.* hager (*lean*); häßlich, abgehärmt.

haggle [hægl], *v.n.* feilschen.

haggler ['hæglə], *s.* der Feilscher.

hail (1) [heil], *s.* der Hagel. — *v.n.* hageln.

hail (2) [heil], *v.a.* (mit einem Ruf) begrüßen; rufen. — *interj.* Heil, willkommen! — *s.* der Zuruf, Gruß.

hair [hɛə], *s.* das Haar; *split* —s, Haarspalterei treiben.

haircut ['hɛəkʌt], *s.* der Haarschnitt.

hairdresser ['hɛədresə], *s.* der Friseur.

hale [heil], *adj.* — *and hearty*, frisch und gesund, rüstig.

half [hɑ:f], *adj.* halb. — *adv.* —baked, unreif; unterentwickelt (*stupid*); (*coll.*) *not* —, und wie! sehr gern. — *s.* die Hälfte; *too clever by* —, allzu gescheit.

halfcaste ['hɑ:fkɑ:st], *s.* der Mischling.

halfpenny ['heipni], *s.* der halbe Penny.

halfwit ['hɑ:fwit], *s.* der Dummkopf.

halibut ['hælibət], *s.* (*Zool.*) der Heilbutt.

hall [hɔ:l], *s.* der Saal; die Halle; der Hausflur (*entrance* —); (*Univ.*) — (*of residence*), das Studentenheim; — *porter*, der Portier.

hallmark ['hɔ:lmɑ:k], *s.* das Kennzeichen.

hallow ['hælou], *v.a.* weihen, heiligen.

Halloween [hælou'i:n]. der Allerheiligenabend.

halo ['heilou], *s.* der Heiligenschein (*of saint*); der Hof (*round the moon*).

hallucination [həlu:si'neiʃən], *s.* die Halluzination.

halt [hɔ:lt], *v.n.* halten, haltmachen; — *! Halt!* zögern (*tarry*), — *s.* (*Railw.*) die (kleine) Haltestelle.

halve [hɑ:v], *v.a.* halbieren.

ham [hæm], *s.* (*Cul.*) der Schinken; (*Anat.*) der Schenkel; — *acting*, das Schmierentheater.

hammer ['hæmə], *s.* der Hammer. — *v.a., v.n.* hämmern; — *away at*, an etwas emsig arbeiten; — *out a problem*, ein Problem zur Lösung bringen.

hammock ['hæmək], *s.* die Hängematte.

hamper (1) ['hæmpə], *s.* der Packkorb.

hamper (2) ['hæmpə], *v.a.* behindern.

hand [hænd], *s.* die Hand; *a fair* —, eine gute Handschrift; der Uhrzeiger (*on watch, clock*); die Seite (*right, left* —); die Karten, *f. pl.* (*card game*); *play a strong* —, starke Karten halten *or* spielen; *on* —, vorrätig, auf Lager; *get out of* —, unkontrollierbar werden. — *v.a.* — *in*, einhändigen, einreichen; — *out*, austeilen; — *over*, übergeben, einhändigen.

handbag ['hændbæg], *s.* die Handtasche.

handbill ['hændbil], *s.* der Zettel, Reklamezettel (*advertising*).

handful ['hændful], *s.* die Handvoll; *to be quite a* —, genug zu schaffen geben; das Sorgenkind.

handicap ['hændikæp], *s.* das Hindernis. — *v.a.* hindern, behindern.

handicraft ['hændikrɑ:ft], *s.* das Handwerk; Kunsthandwerk.

handkerchief ['hæŋkətʃif], *s.* das Taschentuch.

handle [hændl], *s.* der Griff; der Henkel (*pot, vase*). — *v.a.* handhaben (*machine*); behandeln (*person*); anpacken (*problem*).

handlebar ['hændlbɑ:], *s.* die Lenkstange (*bicycle*).

handmaid(en) ['hændmeid(n)], *s.* (*obs.*) die Magd.

handrail ['hændreil], *s.* das Geländer.

handshake ['hændʃeik], *s.* der Händedruck.

handsome ['hænsəm], *adj.* hübsch, schön, stattlich.

handy ['hændi], *adj.* geschickt; — *man*, der Gelegenheitsarbeiter, Mann für alles.

hang [hæŋ], *v.a. reg. & irr.* hängen; aufhängen (*suspend*); — *it!* zum Henker; — *paper*, ein Zimmer austapezieren; — *dog expression*, den Kopf hängen lassen, die betrübte Miene. — *v.n.* hängen; (*coll.*) — *on!* warte einen Moment! — *about*, herumstehen; herumlungern (*loiter*).

hanger-on [hæŋər'ɔn], *s.* der Anhänger, Mitläufer.

hangman ['hæŋmən], *s.* der Henker.

hanker ['hæŋkə], *v.n.* sich sehnen.

Hanoverian [hæno'viəriən], *adj.* hannöversch. — *s.* der Hannoveraner.

hansom ['hænsəm], *s.* die zweirädrige Droschke.

haphazard [hæp'hæzəd], *s.* der Zufall, das Geratewohl.

hapless ['hæplis], *adj.* unglücklich.

happen [hæpn], *v.n.* sich ereignen, passieren; — *to . . .*, zufällig . . .

happiness ['hæpinis], *s.* das Glück; die Glückseligkeit.

happy ['hæpi], *adj.* glücklich, glückselig.

harangue [hə'ræŋ], *s.* die Ansprache. — *v.a.* einsprechen (*auf, Acc.*); anreden.

harass ['hærəs], *v.a.* plagen, quälen.

harbinger ['hɑ:bindʒə], *s.* der Vorbote, Bote.

harbour ['hɑ:bə], *s.* der Hafen. — *v.a.* beherbergen (*shelter*); hegen (*cherish*).

hard [hɑ:d], *adj.* schwer (*difficult*); hart (*tough*); hartherzig (*miserly*); — *up*, in Not, in Geldverlegenheit; — *of hearing*, schwerhörig.

harden [hɑ:dn], *v.a.* härten. — *v.n.* hart werden.

hardiness ['hɑ:dinis], *s.* die Kraft, Stärke; die Rüstigkeit.

hardly ['hɑ:dli], *adv.* kaum.

hardship ['hɑ:dʃip], *s.* die Not, Bedrängnis (*need*); die Beschwerde (*complaint*).

hardware ['hɑːdwɛə], s. die Eisenware(n).

hardy ['hɑːdi], adj. abgehärtet, stark; (Bot.) — annual, ein widerstandsfähiges Jahresgewächs.

hare [hɛə], s. (Zool.) der Hase; — brained, unbedacht, gedankenlos; — lip, die Hasenscharte.

harebell ['hɛəbel], s. (Bot.) die Glockenblume.

haricot ['hærikou], s. (Bot.) — bean, die welsche Bohne.

hark [hɑːk], v.n. horchen.

harlequin ['hɑːlikwin], s. der Harlekin.

harlot ['hɑːlət], s. die Hure.

harm [hɑːm], s. das Leid, Unrecht; do — to, Schaden zufügen (Dat.).— v.a. verletzen (hurt); schaden (damage, Dat.).

harmful ['hɑːmful], adj. schädlich.

harmless ['hɑːmlis], adj. harmlos.

harmonious [hɑːˈmouniəs], adj. harmonisch; einmütig (of one mind).

harmonize ['hɑːmənaiz], v.a. in Einklang bringen. — v.n. harmonieren, in Einklang stehen.

harmony ['hɑːməni], s. (Mus.) die Harmonie; (fig.) der Einklang, die Einmütigkeit.

harness ['hɑːnis], s. der Harnisch. — v.a. anschirren, anspannen (horse); (fig.) nutzbar machen.

harp [hɑːp], s. (Mus.) die Harfe. — v.n. (coll.) — upon, herumreiten auf (Dat.).

harpoon [hɑːˈpuːn], s. die Harpune. — v.a. harpunieren.

harrow ['hærou], s. die Egge, Harke. — v.a. harken, eggen; quälen.

harry ['hæri], v.a. verheeren, quälen.

harsh [hɑːʃ], adj. herb, rauh (rough); streng (severe).

hart [hɑːt], s. (Zool.) der Hirsch.

harvest ['hɑːvist], s. die Ernte; — home, das Erntefest.

hash [hæʃ], v.a. zerhacken; vermischen (mix up). — s. das Hackfleisch; make a — of things, verpfuschen, alles verderben.

hasp [hæsp or hɑːsp], s. der Haken, die Spange.

haste [heist], s. die Hast, Eile (hurry); die Voreiligkeit (rashness).

hasten [heisn], v.n. eilen, sich beeilen.

hasty ['heisti], adj. voreilig.

hat [hæt], s. der Hut; (coll.) talk through o.'s —, Unsinn reden.

hatch (1) [hætʃ], s. die Brut (chickens). — v.a., v.n. (aus-)brüten; aushecken (cunning).

hatch (2) [hætʃ], s. das Servierfenster (for serving food); (Naut.) die Luke.

hatch (3) [hætʃ], v.a. (Art) schraffieren.

hatchet ['hætʃit], s. das Beil, die Axt; bury the —, das Kriegsbeil begraben.

hate [heit], v.a., v.n. hassen; — to ..., nicht ... wollen. — s. der Haß, Widerwille, die Abneigung.

hateful ['heitful], adj. verhaßt (hated); gehässig (hating).

hatred ['heitrid], s. der Haß.

hatter ['hætə], s. der Hutmacher.

haughty ['hɔːti], adj. übermütig (supercilious); hochmütig, stolz (proud); hochnäsig (giving o.s. airs).

haul [hɔːl], v.a. schleppen, ziehen. — s. das Schleppen; (coll.) die Beute.

haulage ['hɔːlidʒ], s. der Schleppdienst, die Spedition.

haunch [hɔːntʃ], s. (Anat.) die Hüfte; der Schenkel (horse); die Keule (venison).

haunt [hɔːnt], v.a. heimsuchen, spuken (in, Dat.); it is —ed, hier spuktes.

have [hæv], v.a. irr. haben, besitzen (possess); erhalten; lassen; — to, müssen; — s.th. made, done, etwas machen lassen.

haven [heivn], s. der Zufluchtsort.

haversack ['hævəsæk], s. der Brotbeutel.

havoc ['hævək], s. die Verwüstung, Verheerung.

hawk (1) [hɔːk], s. (Orn.) der Habicht; der Falke (falcon).

hawk (2) [hɔːk], v.a. hausieren.

hawker ['hɔːkə], s. der Hausierer.

hawthorn ['hɔːθɔːn], s. (Bot.) der Hagedorn.

hay [hei], s. das Heu; — fever, der Heuschnupfen; — loft, der Heuboden; — rick, der Heuschober.

hazard ['hæzəd], s. der Zufall (chance); die Gefahr (danger); das Risiko (risk). — v.a. aufs Spiel setzen, riskieren.

hazardous ['hæzədəs], adj. gefährlich, gewagt.

haze [heiz], s. der Dunst, Nebeldunst.

hazel [heizl], s. (Bot.) die Haselstaude; — nut, die Haselnuß.

hazy ['heizi], adj. dunstig, nebelig.

he [hiː] pers. pron. er; — who, derjenige, welcher, wer.

head [hed], s. der Kopf; die Spitze (of arrow); der Leiter (of firm); (Sch.) der Direktor; die Überschrift (heading); die Krisis (climax); (Pol.) der Führer, das (Staats-)Oberhaupt. — v.a. anführen, führen; (Mil.) befehligen; — v.n. (Naut.) — for, Kurs nehmen auf (Acc.).

headache ['hedeik], s. (Med.) die Kopfschmerzen, m. pl.

headlamp ['hedlæmp], s. der Scheinwerfer.

headphone ['hedfoun], s. (usually pl.) der Kopfhörer.

headstrong ['hedstrɔŋ], adj. halsstarrig.

heady ['hedi], adj. hastig, ungestüm; berauschend (liquor).

heal [hiːl], v.a. heilen. — v.n. (zu)heilen, verheilen.

health [helθ], s. die Gesundheit; — resort, der Kurort; your (good) —! Gesundheit! auf Ihr Wohl! Prosit! (drinking toast).

healthy ['helθi], adj. gesund.

heap [hiːp], s. der Haufen, die Menge. — v.a. häufen, aufhäufen.

hear [hiə]. *v.a.*, *v.n. irr.* hören; erfahren (*learn*); (*Law*) verhören (*evidence*).

hearing ['hiəriŋ], *s.* das Gehör (*auditory perception*); *within —*, in Hörweite; (*Law*) das Verhör.

hearsay ['hiəsei], *s.* das Hörensagen.

hearse [hə:s], *s.* der Leichenwagen.

heart [ha:t], *s.* das Herz; der Mut (*courage*); das Innerste (*core*); *by —*, auswendig; *take to —*, beherzigen; *take — from*, Mut fassen (aus, *Dat.*).

heartburn ['ha:tbə:n], *s.* (*Med.*) das Sodbrennen.

heartfelt ['ha:tfelt], *adj.* herzlich.

hearth [ha:θ], *s.* der Herd.

hearty ['ha:ti], *adj.* herzlich; aufrichtig (*sincere*); herzhaft.

heat [hi:t], *s.* die Hitze, Wärme; die Brunst (*animals*). — *v.a.* heizen (*fuel*); erhitzen (*make hot*).

heath [hi:θ], *s.* die Heide.

heathen [hi:ðən], *s.* der Heide, Ungläubige.

heather ['heðə], *s.* (*Bot.*) das Heidekraut.

heating ['hi:tiŋ], *s.* die Heizung.

heave [hi:v], *v.a. reg. & irr.* heben, hieben. — *v.n.* sich heben und senken.

heaven [hevn], *s.* der Himmel; *good —s!* ach, du lieber Himmel!

heaviness ['hevinis], *s.* die Schwere.

heavy ['hevi], *adj.* schwer; schwerwiegend (*grave*).

Hebrew ['hi:bru:], *adj.* hebräisch. — *s.* der Hebräer, der Jude.

hectic ['hektik], *adj.* hektisch, aufgeregt.

hector ['hektə], *v.a.* tyrannisieren (*bully*). — *v.n.* renommieren, prahlen.

hedge [hedʒ], *s.* die Hecke. — *v.a.* einhegen, einzäunen.

hedgehog ['hedʒhɔg], *s.* (*Zool.*) der Igel.

hedgerow ['hedʒrou], *s.* die Baumhecke.

heed [hi:d], *s.* die Hut, Aufmerksamkeit. — *v.a.* beachten.

heedless ['hi:dlis], *adj.* unachtsam.

heel [hi:l], *s.* die Ferse (*foot*); der Absatz (*shoe*); *take to o.'s —s*, die Flucht ergreifen; (*Am. sl.*) der Lump.

heifer ['hefə], *s.* (*Zool.*) die junge Kuh.

height [hait], *s.* die Höhe, Anhöhe; die Größe (*tallness*); der Hügel (*hill*).

heighten [haitn], *v.a.* erhöhen.

heir [ɛə], *s.* der Erbe (*to, Genit.*).

heiress ['ɛəres], *s.* die Erbin.

heirloom ['ɛəlu:m], *s.* das Erbstück.

helicopter ['helikɔptə], *s.* (*Aviat.*) der Hubschrauber.

hell [hel], *s.* die Hölle. — *interj.* zum Teufel!

hellish ['heliʃ], *adj.* höllisch.

helm [helm], *s.* das Steuer, Steuerruder.

helmet ['helmit], *s.* der Helm.

helmsman ['helmzmən], *s.* (*Naut.*) der Steuermann.

help [help], *v.a.*, *v.n.* helfen (*Dat.*); *I cannot — laughing*, ich muß lachen; *I cannot — it*, ich kann nichts dafür. — *v.r.* — *o.s.*, sich bedienen. — *s.* die Hilfe, Unterstützung.

helpful ['helpful], *adj.* behilflich, hilfreich.

helping ['helpiŋ], *s.* die Portion.

helpless ['helplis], *adj.* hilflos.

helpmate, helpmeet ['helpmeit, -mi:t], *s.* der Gehilfe, die Gehilfin.

helter-skelter ['heltə'skeltə], *adv.* Hals über Kopf.

hem [hem], *s.* der Saum. — *v.a.* (*Tail.*) einsäumen, säumen.

hemisphere ['hemisfiə], *s.* die Halbkugel, Hemisphäre.

hemlock ['hemlɔk], *s.* der Schierling.

hemp [hemp], *s.* der Hanf.

hemstitch ['hemstitʃ], *s.* der Hohlsaum.

hen [hen], *s.* die Henne (*poultry*); das Weibchen (*other birds*).

hence [hens], *adv.* von hier; von jetzt an.

henceforth ['hens'fɔ:θ], *adv.* fortan, von nun an.

henpecked ['henpekd], *adj.* unter dem Pantoffel stehend.

her [hə:], *pers. pron.* sie (*Acc.*), ihr (*Dat.*). — *poss. adj.* ihr.

herald ['herəld], *s.* der Herold. — *v.a.* ankündigen.

heraldry ['herəldri], *s.* die Wappenkunde.

herb [hə:b], *s.* (*Bot.*) das Kraut.

herbaceous [hə:'beiʃəs], *adj.* krautartig.

herbage ['hə:bidʒ], *s.* das Gras; (*Law*) das Weiderecht.

herbal ['hə:bəl], *adj.* krautartig, Kräuter-, Kraut-.

herd [hə:d], *s.* die Herde. — *v.n.* sich zusammenfinden.

here [hiə], *adv.* hier.

hereafter [hiər'a:ftə], *adv.* hernach, künftig. — *s.* die Zukunft; das Jenseits.

hereby [hiə'bai], *adv.* hiermit.

hereditary [hi'reditəri], *adj.* erblich.

heredity [hi'rediti], *s.* (*Biol.*) die Erblichkeit, Vererbung.

heresy ['herisi], *s.* die Ketzerei.

heretic ['heritik], *s.* der Ketzer.

heretofore ['hiətufɔ:], *adv.* zuvor, vormals.

heritage ['heritidʒ], *s.* die Erbschaft.

hermetic [hə:'metik], *adj.* luftdicht.

hermit ['hə:mit], *s.* der Eremit, Einsiedler.

hero ['hiərou], *s.* der Held.

heroic [hi'rouik], *adj.* heldenhaft, heldenmütig.

heroine ['heroin], *s.* die Heldin.

heroism ['heroizm], *s.* der Heldenmut.

heron ['herən], *s.* (*Orn.*) der Reiher.

herring ['heriŋ], *s.* (*Zool.*) der Hering; *red —*, die Ablenkungsfinte, das Ablenkungsmanöver; — *bone*, die Gräte; *pickled —*, der eingemachte Hering.

hers [hə:z], *poss. pron.* ihr, der ihre, der ihrige.

herself [hə:'self], *pers. pron.* sich; sie selbst.

hesitate ['heziteit], *v.n.* zögern, zaudern; unschlüssig sein (*be undecided*).

hesitation [hezi'teiʃən], s. das Zögern, Zaudern; das Bedenken (*delibera-tion*).

Hessian ['heʃən], adj. hessisch. — s. der Hesse.

hessian ['hesiən], s. die Sackleinwand (*textile*).

heterodox ['hetərədɔks], adj. irrgläubig.

heterogeneous [hetəro'dʒi:niəs], adj. heterogen, ungleichartig.

hew [hju:], v.a. irr. hauen.

hexagonal [hek'sægənəl], adj. sechseckig.

hiatus [hai'eitəs], s. die Lücke.

hibernate ['haibəneit], v.n. überwintern.

hibernation [haibə'neiʃən], s. der Winterschlaf.

hiccup ['hikʌp], s. (*usually pl.*) (*Med.*) der Schlucken, Schluckauf.

hickory ['hikəri], s. (*Bot.*) das Hickoryholz.

hide (1) [haid], v.a. irr. verstecken, verbergen. — v.n. irr. sich verbergen; — *and seek*, das Versteckspiel.

hide (2) [haid], s. die Haut (*of animal*), das Fell, (*tanned*) das Leder.

hideous ['hidiəs], adj. häßlich, scheußlich, furchtbar.

hiding (1) ['haidiŋ], s. das Versteck.

hiding (2) ['haidiŋ], s. die Tracht Prügel.

hierarchy ['haiəra:ki], s. die Hierarchie.

higgle [higl] see **haggle**.

higgledy-piggledy ['higldi'pigldi], adv. wüst durcheinander.

high [hai], adj. hoch; erhaben, vornehm; angegangen (*meat*); — *school*, die höhere Schule; — *time*, höchste Zeit; (*Am.*) vergnügliche Zeit; *High Church*, die Hochkirche. — s. (*Meteor.*) das Hoch.

Highness ['hainis], s. die Hoheit (*title*).

highroad, highway ['hairoud, 'haiwei], s. die Haupt- *or* Landstraße.

highwayman ['haiweimən], s. der Straßenräuber.

hike [haik], v.n. wandern, einen Ausflug machen. — s. die Wanderung, der Ausflug.

hilarious [hi'lɛəriəs], adj. fröhlich, lustig, ausgelassen.

hill [hil], s. der Hügel, Berg.

hilt [hilt], s. der Griff.

him [him], pers. pron. ihn, ihm.

himself [him'self], pers. pron. sich; er selbst.

hind [haind], s. (*Zool.*) die Hirschkuh, Hindin.

hinder ['hində], v.a. hindern.

hindmost ['haindmoust], adj. hinterst; *the devil take the* —, den letzten hol der Teufel! nach mir die Sintflut!

hindrance ['hindrəns], s. das Hindernis; (*Law*) *without let or* —, ohne Hinderung.

Hindu [hin'du:], s. der Hindu.

hinge [hindʒ], s. die Angel, der Angelpunkt. — v.n. sich um etwas drehen; von etwas abhängen (on, *Dat.*).

hint [hint], v.n. zu verstehen geben, auf etwas hindeuten (at, auf, *Acc.*), andeuten. — s. die Andeutung, der Fingerzeig.

hip (1) [hip], s. (*Anat.*) die Hüfte.

hip (2) [hip], s. (*Bot.*) die Hagebutte.

hire ['haiə], v.a. (ver-)mieten (*car etc.*); anstellen (*man etc.*). — s. die Miete; der Lohn (*wage*); — *purchase*, der Abzahlungskauf, die Ratenzahlung.

hireling ['haiəliŋ], s. der Mietling.

hirsute ['hə:sju:t], adj. behaart, haarig.

his [hiz], poss. adj. sein, seine. — poss. pron. sein, der seinige, der seine.

hiss [his], v.n. zischen (at, auf, *Acc.*). — s. das Zischen.

historian [his'tɔ:riən], s. der Historiker, der Geschichtsschreiber.

historical [his'tɔrikəl], adj. historisch, geschichtlich.

history ['histəri], s. die Geschichte, die Geschichtswissenschaft.

histrionic [histri'ɔnik], adj. schauspielerisch.

hit [hit], v.a. irr. schlagen, stoßen. — s. der Schlag, der Treffer (*on the target*); (*Am.*) der Schlager, Erfolg (*success*); — *parade*, die Schlagerparade.

hitch [hitʃ], v.a. anhaken (*hook*); anhängen; — *a lift*, — *hike*, per Anhalter fahren. — s. der Nachteil, der Haken.

hither ['hiðə], adv. hierher.

hitherto [hiðə'tu:], adv. bisher.

hive [haiv], s. der Bienenkorb; Bienenstock; — *of bees*, der Schwarm.

hoar [hɔ:], adj. eisgrau, weißlich; — *frost*, der Reif.

hoard [hɔ:d], v.a. hamstern. — s. der Vorrat, Schatz.

hoarding ['hɔ:diŋ], s. die Umzäunung, die Bretterwand; die Reklamewand.

hoarse [hɔ:s], adj. heiser.

hoarseness ['hɔ:snis], s. die Heiserkeit.

hoax [houks], s. der Betrug, die Irreführung; der Schabernack (*in fun*). — v.a. betrügen; foppen (*in fun*).

hobble [hɔbl], v.n. humpeln. — v.a. an den Füßen fesseln.

hobby ['hɔbi], s. das Steckenpferd, Hobby, die Liebhaberei.

hobgoblin [hɔb'gɔblin], s. der Kobold.

hobnail ['hɔbneil], s. der Hufnagel.

hobnailed ['hɔbneild], adj. — *boots*, genagelte Stiefel, m. pl.

hobnob [hɔb'nɔb], v.n. (*coll.*) vertraulich sein.

hock (1) [hɔk], s. (*Anat.*) das Sprunggelenk.

hock (2) [hɔk], s. (*wine*) der Rheinwein.

hod [hɔd], s. (*Build.*) der Trog; der Eimer (*coal*).

hodge-podge see under **hotchpotch**.

hoe [hou], s. die Hacke, Harke. — v.a., v.n. hacken, harken.

hog [hɔg], s. das Schwein. — v.a. verschlingen (*food*); an sich reißen (*grasp*).

hogshead ['hɔgzhed], s. das Oxhoft.

hoist [hɔist], v.a. hissen.

411

hold

hold [hould], *v.a.*, *v.n. irr.* halten (*keep*); enthalten (*contain*); behaupten (*assert*); meinen (*think*); gelten (*be valid*); — *forth*, deklamieren; — *good*, sich bewähren; — *out*, hinhalten (*hope*); (*endure*) aushalten; —*up*, aufhalten. — *s.* (*Naut.*) der Schiffsraum; die Macht (*power*).

holder ['houldə], *s.* der Inhaber, Besitzer.

holding ['houldiŋ], *s.* das Pachtgut (*farm*); der Besitz (*property*); (*Comm.*) der Trust.

hole [houl], *s.* das Loch; die Höhle (*cavity*). — *v.a.* aushöhlen; (*Golf*) ins Loch spielen.

holiday ['hɔlidei], *s.* der Feiertag; der Urlaub (*vacation*); (*pl.*) die Ferien, *pl.*

holiness ['houlinis], *s.* die Heiligkeit.

hollow ['hɔlou], *adj.* hohl. — *s.* die Höhlung; die Höhle.

holly ['hɔli], *s.* (*Bot.*) die Stechpalme.

hollyhock ['hɔlihɔk], *s.* (*Bot.*) die Stockrose.

holocaust ['hɔlokɔːst], *s.* das Brandopfer; die Katastrophe.

holster ['houlstə], *s.* die Pistolentasche, die Halfter.

holy ['houli], *adj.* heilig; *Holy Week*, die Karwoche.

homage ['hɔmidʒ], *s.* die Huldigung; *pay — to*, huldigen (*Dat.*).

home [houm], *s.* das Heim, die Wohnung; die Heimat; *at —*, zu Hause; *Home Office*, das Innenministerium; *— Rule*, (*Pol.*) die Selbstverwaltung.

homer ['houmə] (*Am.*) *see* **homing pigeon**.

homesick ['housmik], *adj.* an Heimweh leidend.

homestead ['houmsted], *s.* der Bauernhof.

homicide ['hɔmisaid], *s.* der Mord (*crime*); der Mörder (*killer*).

homily ['hɔmili], *s.* die Predigt; Moralpredigt.

homing pigeon ['houmiŋ'pidʒən], *s.* die Brieftaube.

homogeneous [hɔmə'dʒiːniəs], *adj.* homogen; gleichartig.

hone [houn], *s.* der Wetzstein. — *v.a.* (*blade, knife*) abziehen.

honest ['ɔnist], *adj.* ehrlich, aufrichtig.

honesty ['ɔnisti], *s.* die Ehrlichkeit.

honey ['hʌni], *s.* der Honig; (*Am.*, *coll.*) Liebling!

honeycomb ['hʌnikoum], *s.* die Honigwabe.

honeymoon ['hʌnimuːn], *s.* die Flitterwochen.

honorarium [ɔnə'rɛəriəm], *s.* das Honorar.

honorary ['ɔnərəri], *adj.* Ehren-, ehrenamtlich.

honour ['ɔnə], *s.* die Ehre; *your —*, Euer Ehrwürden, Euer Gnaden (*title*). — *v.a.* ehren, auszeichnen.

honourable ['ɔnərəbl], *adj.* ehrenwert, ehrenvoll; Hochwohlgeboren (*title*).

hood [hud], *s.* die Kapuze; das akademische Gradabzeichen über dem Talar; (*Hunt.*) die Haube; —*ed falcon*, der Jagdfalke (mit Haube).

hoodwink ['hudwiŋk], *v.a.* täuschen.

hoof [huːf *or* huf], *s.* der Huf (*horse*); die Klaue.

hook [huk], *s.* der Haken; *by — or by crook*, mit allen Mitteln. — *v.a.* angeln, fangen.

hooked [hukd], *adj.* gekrümmt, hakenförmig.

hooligan ['huːligən], *s.* der Rowdy.

hoop [huːp], *s.* der Reifen. — *v.a.* (ein Faß) binden.

hooper ['huːpə], *s.* der Böttcher.

hoopoe ['huːpou], *s.* (*Orn.*) der Wiedehopf.

hoot [huːt], *v.n.* schreien (*owl*); ertönen (*siren*); hupen (*car*).

hooter ['huːtə], *s.* die Sirene (*siren*); die Hupe (*car*).

hop (1) [hɔp], *v.n.* hüpfen, tanzen; —*ping mad*, ganz verrückt.

hop (2) [hɔp], *s.* (*Bot.*) der Hopfen. — *v.a.* (*beer*) hopfen, Hopfen zusetzen (*Dat.*). — *v.n.* Hopfen ernten.

hope [houp], *s.* die Hoffnung. — *v.n.* hoffen (*for*, auf, *Acc.*).

hopeless ['houplis], *adj.* hoffnungslos.

horizon [hə'raizən], *s.* der Horizont.

horizontal [hɔri'zɔntl], *adj.* horizontal, waagrecht.

horn [hɔːn], *s.* das Horn; (*Mus.*) *French —*, das Waldhorn, Horn; (*Motor.*) die Hupe.

hornet ['hɔːnit], *s.* (*Ent.*) die Hornisse.

hornpipe ['hɔːnpaip], *s.* (*Mus.*) der Matrosentanz; die Hornpfeife.

horrible ['hɔribl], *adj.* schrecklich.

horrid ['hɔrid], *adj.* abscheulich.

horrific [hə'rifik], *adj.* schrecklich, schreckenerregend.

horror ['hɔrə], *s.* der Schrecken, das Entsetzen; (*fig.*) der Greuel.

horse [hɔːs], *s.* das Pferd, Roß; *on —back*, zu Pferd.

horseman ['hɔːsmən], *s.* der Reiter.

horsepower ['hɔːspauə], *s.* die Pferdestärke.

horseradish ['hɔːsrædiʃ], *s.* der Meerrettich.

horseshoe ['hɔːsʃuː], *s.* das Hufeisen.

horticulture ['hɔːtikʌltʃə], *s.* der Gartenbau.

hose [houz], *s.* die Strümpfe, *m. pl.* (*stockings*); der Schlauch (*water pipe*).

hosiery ['houʒəri], *s.* die Strumpfwarenindustrie; die Strumpfwaren.

hospitable [hɔs'pitəbl], *adj.* gastlich, gastfreundlich.

hospital ['hɔspitl], *s.* das Krankenhaus.

hospitality [hɔspi'tæliti], *s.* die Gastlichkeit, Gastfreundschaft.

host (1) [houst], *s.* der Gastwirt (*landlord*); der Gastgeber.

host (2) [houst], *s.* (*Rel.*) *angelic —*, die Engelschar; (*Mil.*) das Heer, die Heerschar.

host (3) [houst], *s.* (*Eccl.*) die Hostie.

hostage ['hɔstidʒ], *s.* die Geisel.

hostess ['houstis *or* –tes], *s.* die Gastgeberin; *air* —, die Stewardeß.

hostile ['hɔstail], *adj.* feindlich; feindselig (*inimical*).

hot [hɔt], *adj.* heiß; hitzig (*temperament*); scharf, gewürzt (*of spices*); (*fig.*) heftig, erbittert.

hotchpotch, hodge-podge ['hɔtʃpɔtʃ, 'hɔdʒpɔdʒ], *s.* das Mischmasch.

hotel [ho(u)'tel],*s.*das Hotel,der Gasthof.

hothouse ['hɔthaus], *s.* das Treibhaus.

hound [haund], *s.* (*Zool.*) der Jagdhund. — *v.a.* hetzen.

hour ['auə], *s.* die Stunde; — *hand*, der Stundenzeiger; *for* —*s*, studenlang; *keep early* (*late*) —*s*, früh (spät) zu Bett gehen.

hourglass ['auəglɑːs], *s.* die Sanduhr.

hourly ['auəli], *adj.*, *adv.*, stündlich.

house [haus], *s.* das Haus; (*Comm.*) die Firma. — [hauz], *v.a.* beherbergen, unterbringen.

houseboat ['hausbout], *s.* das Wohnboot.

housebreaking ['hausbreikiŋ], *s.* der Einbruch.

household ['haushould], *s.* der Haushalt.

housekeeper ['hauskiːpə], *s.* die Haushälterin.

housewife ['hauswaif], *s.* die Hausfrau.

housing ['hauziŋ], *s.* die Unterbringung; — *department*, das Wohnungsamt.

hovel ['hɔvl *or* hʌvl], *s.* die Hütte.

hover ['hɔvə *or* 'hʌvə], *v.n.* schweben, schwanken.

how [hau], *adv.* wie; — *do you do?* (*in introduction*) sehr angenehm; — *are you?* wie geht es Ihnen, Dir?

however [hau'evə], *adv.* wie immer, wie auch immer, wie sehr auch. — *conj.* doch, jedoch, dennoch.

howl [haul], *v.n.* heulen. — *s.* das Geheul.

hoyden ['hɔidn], *s.* das wilde Mädchen.

hub [hʌb], *s.* die Nabe (am Rad); — *of the universe*, die Mitte der Welt.

hubbub ['hʌbʌb], *s.* der Tumult, Lärm.

huckaback ['hʌkəbæk], *s.* der Zwillich (*textile*).

huckle [hʌkl], *s.* die Hüfte.

huddle [hʌdl], *v.n.* sich drängen, sich zusammenducken. — *s.* das Gedränge.

hue [hjuː], *s.* der Farbton, die Tönung.

huff [hʌf], *s.* die schlechte Laune, die Mißstimmung.

huffy ['hʌfi], *adj.* mißmutig, übel gelaunt.

hug [hʌg], *v.a.* umarmen. — *s.* die Umarmung.

huge [hjuːdʒ], *adj.* riesig, groß, ungeheuer.

Huguenot ['hjuːgənou *or* –nɔt], *s.* der Hugenotte. — *adj.* hugenottisch, Hugenotten-.

hulk [hʌlk], *s.* (*Naut.*) das Schiffsinnere, der Schiffsrumpf; der schwerfällige Mensch.

hull [hʌl], *s.* die Hülse, Schale; (*Naut.*, *Aviat.*) der Rumpf. — *v.a.* (*Engin.*) hülsen.

hullo! [hə'lou], *interj.* hallo!

hum [hʌm], *v.n.* summen, brummen. — *s.* das Summen, Brummen, Gemurmel (*murmuring*).

human ['hjuːmən], *adj.* menschlich. — *s.* der Mensch.

humane [hjuː'mein], *adj.* menschenfreundlich.

humanity [hjuː'mæniti], *s.* die Menschheit (*mankind*); die Menschlichkeit (*compassion*); (*pl.*) die klassischen Fächer, *n. pl.*, die humanistischen Wissenschaften, *f. pl.*

humanize ['hjuːmənaiz], *v.a.* menschlich oder gesittet machen.

humble [hʌmbl], *adj.* demütig; bescheiden (*modest*); unterwürfig (*servile*). — *v.a.* erniedrigen (*humiliate*).

humbug ['hʌmbʌg], *s.* die Schwindelei (*swindle*); der Schwindler (*crook*); der Unsinn (*nonsense*).

humdrum ['hʌmdrʌm], *adj.* langweilig, eintönig.

humid ['hjuːmid], *adj.* feucht.

humidity [hjuː'miditi], *s.* die Feuchtigkeit.

humiliate [hjuː'milieit], *v.a.* erniedrigen.

humility [hjuː'militi], *s.* die Demut.

humming-bird ['hʌmiŋbəːd], *s.* (*Orn.*) der Kolibri.

humming-top ['hʌmiŋtɔp], *s.* der Brummkreisel.

humorous ['hjuːmərəs], *adj.* humoristisch, spaßhaft, komisch.

humour ['hjuːmə], *s.* der Humor, die (gute) Laune. — *v.a.* in guter Laune erhalten, gut stimmen; willfahren (*Dat.*).

hump [hʌmp], *s.* der Buckel, der Höcker.

hunch [hʌntʃ], *s.* der Buckel; *have a* —, das Gefühl haben.

hunchback ['hʌntʃbæk], *s.* der Bucklige.

hundred ['hʌndrəd], *num. adj. a* —, hundert.

hundredweight ['hʌndrədweit], *s.* der (englische) Zentner.

Hungarian [hʌŋ'gɛəriən],*adj.*ungarisch. — *s.* der Ungar.

hunger ['hʌŋgə], *s.* der Hunger.

hungry ['hʌŋgri], *adj.* hungrig.

hunt [hʌnt], *s.* die Jagd. — *v.a.*, *v.n.* jagen.

hunter ['hʌntə], *s.* der Jäger.

hurdle [həːdl], *s.* die Hürde.

hurdy-gurdy ['həːdigəːdi], *s.* der Leierkasten.

hurl [həːl], *v.a.* schleudern, werfen.

hurly-burly ['həːlibəːli], *s.* der Wirrwarr.

hurricane ['hʌrikin], *s.* der Orkan; — *lamp*, die Sturmlaterne.

hurried ['hʌrid], *adj.* eilig, hastig.

hurry

hurry [ˈhʌri], *v.n.* eilen, sich beeilen; — *to do*, eiligst tun. — *v.a.* beschleunigen. — *s.* die Eile, Hast, Beschleunigung.

hurt [həːt], *v.a. irr.* verletzen; wehetun (*Dat.*); (*verbally*) kränken. — *s.* die Verletzung, Kränkung.

hurtful [ˈhəːtful], *adj.* schädlich, kränkend.

husband [ˈhʌzbənd], *s.* der Mann, Ehemann, Gemahl. — *v.a.* verwalten, sparsam verfahren mit (*Dat.*).

husbandman [ˈhʌzbəndmən], *s.* der Landwirt.

husbandry [ˈhʌzbəndri], *s.* die Landwirtschaft.

hush [hʌʃ], *v.a.* zum Schweigen bringen. — *s.* die Stille; — *money*, das Schweigegeld.

husky (1) [ˈhʌski], *adj.* heiser (*voice*).

husky (2) [ˈhʌski], *s.* (*Zool.*) der Eskimohund.

hussy [ˈhʌzi], *s.* (*coll.*) das Frauenzimmer.

hustings [ˈhʌstiŋz], *s.* die Wahltribüne.

hustle [hʌsl], *v.a.* drängen, stoßen. — *s.* das Gedränge.

hut [hʌt], *s.* die Hütte, Baracke.

hutch [hʌtʃ], *s.* der Trog, Kasten (*chest*).

hybrid [ˈhaibrid], *adj.* Bastard-. — *s.* der Bastard.

hydraulic [haiˈdrɔːlik], *adj.* hydraulisch.

hydrogen [ˈhaidrədʒən], *s.* der Wasserstoff.

hydroelectric [haidrouiˈlektrik], *adj.* hydroelektrisch.

hyena [haiˈiːnə], *s.* (*Zool.*) die Hyäne.

hygiene [ˈhaidʒiːn], *s.* die Hygiene, Gesundheitslehre.

hymn [him], *s.* die Hymne, das Kirchenlied.

hymnal [ˈhimnəl], *s.* das Gesangbuch.

hyper- [ˈhaipə], *prefix.* über-.

hyperbole [haiˈpəːbəli], *s.* die Übertreibung.

hyphen [ˈhaifən], *s.* der Bindestrich.

hypnosis [hipˈnousis], *s.* die Hypnose.

hypochondriac [haipoˈkɔndriæk], *adj.* hypochondrisch. — *s.* der Hypochonder.

hypocrisy [hiˈpɔkrisi], *s.* die Heuchelei.

hypocrite [ˈhipəkrit], *s.* der Heuchler.

hypothesis [haiˈpɔθisis], *s.* die Hypothese.

hypothetical [haipəˈθetikəl], *adj.* hypothetisch, angenommen.

hysteria [hisˈtiəriə], *s.* die Hysterie.

I

I [ai]. das I.
I [ai], *pers. pron.* ich.

ice [ais], *s.* das Eis; — *bound*, eingefroren; (*Naut.*) — *breaker*, der Eisbrecher; (*Am.*) — *box*, der Kühlschrank; — *cream*, das Eis; das Gefrorene. — *v.a.* (*confectionery*) verzuckern; (*cake*) glasieren.

Icelander [ˈaislændə], *s.* der Isländer.

Icelandic [aisˈlændik], *adj.* isländisch.

icicle [ˈaisikl], *s.* der Eiszapfen.

icy [ˈaisi], *adj.* eisig.

idea [aiˈdiə], *s.* die Idee.

ideal [aiˈdiəl], *adj.* ideal. — *s.* das Ideal.

idealize [aiˈdiəlaiz], *v.a.* idealisieren.

identical [aiˈdentikəl], *adj.* identisch, gleich.

identification [aidentifiˈkeiʃən], *s.* die Gleichsetzung, Identifizierung.

identify [aiˈdentifai], *v.a.* identifizieren, gleichsetzen.

identity [aiˈdentiti], *s.* die Identität, Gleichheit.

idiocy [ˈidiəsi], *s.* der Blödsinn.

idiom [ˈidiəm], *s.* das Idiom, die sprachliche Eigentümlichkeit.

idiomatic [idioˈmætik], *adj.* idiomatisch.

idiosyncrasy [idioˈsiŋkrəsi], *s.* die Empfindlichkeit; die Abneigung (gegen, *Acc.*); die Idiosynkrasie.

idle [aidl], *adj.* unnütz (*useless*); müßig, faul (*lazy*). — *v.n.* träge sein.

idleness [ˈaidlnis], *s.* der Müßiggang, die Faulheit.

idiot [ˈidiət], *s.* der Idiot.

idol [aidl], *s.* das Götzenbild; das Idol.

idolatry [aiˈdɔlətri], *s.* die Götzenverehrung.

idolize [ˈaidolaiz], *v.a.* vergöttern, abgöttisch lieben.

idyll [ˈaidil *or* ˈidil], *s.* die Idylle, das Idyll.

idyllic [aiˈdilik *or* iˈdilik], *adj.* idyllisch.

if [if], *conj.* wenn, falls (*in case*); ob (*whether*).

igneous [ˈigniəs], *adj.* feurig.

ignite [igˈnait], *v.a.* entzünden. — *v.n.* zur Entzündung kommen, sich entzünden.

ignition [igˈniʃən], *s.* die Zündung.

ignoble [igˈnoubl], *adj.* unedel, gemein.

ignominious [ignoˈminiəs], *adj.* schimpflich, schmählich.

ignominy [ˈignomini], *s.* die Schande, Schmach.

ignoramus [ignəˈreiməs], *s.* der Unwissende.

ignorance [ˈignərəns], *s.* die Unwissenheit, Unkenntnis.

ignorant [ˈignərənt], *adj.* unwissend.

ignore [igˈnɔː], *v.a.* ignorieren, nicht beachten.

ill [il], *adj.* böse, schlimm (*bad*); krank (*sick*); — *feeling*, die Verstimmung. — *adv.* *at ease*, unbequem, verlegen; *can* — *afford*, kann sich kaum leisten …; —*timed*, zu unrechter Zeit.

illbred [ilˈbred], *adj.* ungezogen.

illegal [iˈliːgəl], *adj.* illegal, ungesetzlich.

illegibility [iledʒiˈbiliti], *s.* die Unleserlichkeit.

illegible [i'ledʒibl], *adj.* unleserlich.
illegitimacy [ili'dʒitiməsi], *s.* die Unehelichkeit, Illegitimität.
illegitimate [ili'dʒitimit], *adj.* illegitim, unehelich.
illicit [[i'lisit], *adj.* unerlaubt.
illiteracy [i'litərəsi], *s.* die Unkenntnis des Schreibens und Lesens, das Analphabetentum.
illiterate [i'litərit], *s.* der Analphabet.
illness ['ilnis], *s.* die Krankheit.
illogical [i'lɔdʒikəl], *adj.* unlogisch.
illuminate [i'lju:mineit], *v.a.* erleuchten; (*fig.*) aufklären.
illuminating [i'lju:mineitiŋ], *adj.* aufschlußreich.
illumination [ilju:mi'neiʃən], *s.* die Erleuchtung; die Erklärung (*explanation*).
illusion [i'lju:ʒən], *s.* die Illusion, Täuschung.
illusive, illusory [i'lju:ziv, i'lju:zəri], *adj.* trügerisch, täuschend.
illustrate ['iləstreit], *v.a.* erläutern; illustrieren (*with pictures*).
illustration [iləs'treiʃən], *s.* die Illustration (*pictorial*); Erläuterung, Erklärung; das Beispiel (*instance*).
illustrious [i'lʌstriəs], *adj.* glänzend, berühmt.
image ['imidʒ], *s.* das Bild; das Ebenbild; die Erscheinung (*appearance*).
imagery ['imidʒəri], *s.* der Gebrauch von Stilbildern (*style*), die Bildersprache.
imaginable [i'mædʒinəbl], *adj.* denkbar.
imaginary [i'mædʒinəri], *adj.* eingebildet, nicht wirklich, vermeintlich.
imagination [imædʒi'neiʃən], *s.* die Einbildung; die Vorstellung; die Phantasie.
imaginative [i'mædʒinətiv], *adj.* erfinderisch, voll Phantasie.
imagine [i'mædʒin], *v.a.* sich vorstellen, sich denken.
imbecile ['imbisail *or* 'imbisi:l], *adj.* schwachsinnig. — *s.* der Idiot.
imbecility [imbi'siliti], *s.* der Schwachsinn.
imbibe [im'baib], *v.a.* trinken; (*fig.*) in sich aufnehmen.
imbroglio [im'brouliou], *s.* die Verwicklung.
imbue [im'bju:], *v.a.* erfüllen, sättigen (*fig.*).
imitate ['imiteit], *v.a.* nachahmen, imitieren.
imitation [imi'teiʃən], *s.* die Nachahmung, Imitation; — *leather*, das Kunstleder.
immaculate [i'mækjulit], *adj.* unbefleckt, makellos.
immaterial [imə'tiəriəl], *adj.* unwesentlich, unwichtig.
immature [imə'tjuə], *adj.* unreif.
immeasurable [i'meʒərəbl], *adj.* unermeßlich, unmeßbar.
immediate [i'mi:djit], *adj.* unmittelbar, direkt, sofortig.

immediately [i'mi:djətli], *adv.* sofort.
immemorial [imi'mɔ:riəl], *adj.* undenklich, ewig.
immense [i'mens], *adj.* unermeßlich, ungeheuer.
immerse [i'mə:s], *v.a.* eintauchen.
immersion [i'mə:ʃən], *s.* das Eintauchen, die Versenkung; — *heater*, der Tauchsieder.
immigrant ['imigrənt], *s.* der Einwanderer.
imminent ['iminənt], *adj.* bevorstehend.
immobile [i'moubail], *adj.* unbeweglich.
immoderate [i'mɔdərit], *adj.* unmäßig.
immodest [i'mɔdist], *adj.* unbescheiden; unsittlich, unanständig (*immoral*).
immodesty [i'mɔdisti], *s.* die Unanständigkeit (*indecency*); Unbescheidenheit (*presumption*).
immolate ['iməleit], *v.a.* opfern.
immoral [i'mɔrəl], *adj.* unsittlich, unmoralisch.
immortal [i'mɔ:tl], *adj.* unsterblich.
immortalize [i'mɔ:təlaiz], *v.a.* verewigen, unsterblich machen.
immovable [i'mu:vəbl], *adj.* unbeweglich (*fig.*).
immunity [i'mju:niti], *s.* die Freiheit, Straffreiheit; Immunität.
immutable [i'mju:təbl], *adj.* unabänderlich; unveränderlich.
imp [imp], *s.* der Knirps, Kobold, kleine Schelm.
impair [im'pɛə], *v.a.* beeinträchtigen; vermindern (*reduce*).
impale [im'peil], *v.a.* aufspießen; durchbohren.
impalpable [im'pælpəbl], *adj.* unfühlbar, unmerklich.
impart [im'pɑ:t], *v.a.* erteilen; verleihen (*confer*); mitteilen (*inform*).
impartial [im'pɑ:ʃəl], *adj.* unparteiisch.
impartiality [impɑ:ʃi'æliti], *s.* die Unparteilichkeit, Objektivität.
impassable [im'pɑ:səbl], *adj.* unwegsam, unpassierbar.
impasse [im'pæs], *s.* der völlige Stillstand.
impassioned [im'pæʃənd], *adj.* leidenschaftlich.
impassive [im'pæsiv], *adj.* unempfindlich.
impatience [im'peiʃəns], *s.* die Ungeduld.
impatient [im'peiʃənt], *adj.* ungeduldig.
impeach [im'pi:tʃ], *v.a.* anklagen.
impeachment [im'pi:tʃmənt], *s.* die Anklage.
impecunious [impi'kju:niəs], *adj.* unbemittelt, mittellos.
impede [im'pi:d], *v.a.* behindern, verhindern.
impediment [im'pedimənt], *s.* das Hindernis.
impel [im'pel], *v.a.* antreiben; zwingen (*force*).

impending

impending [im'pendiŋ], *adj.* bevorstehend, drohend.
impenetrable [im'penitrəbl], *adj.* undurchdringlich, unerforschlich.
impenitent [im'penitənt], *adj.* reuelos, unbußfertig.
imperative [im'perətiv], *adj.* zwingend (*cogent*); dringend notwendig. — *s.* (*Gram.*) der Imperativ, die Befehlsform.
imperceptible [impə'septibl], *adj.* unmerklich.
imperfect [im'pə:fikt], *adj.* unvollständig, unvollkommen; fehlerhaft (*goods etc.*). — *s.* (*Gram.*) das Imperfekt.
imperial [im'piəriəl], *adj.* kaiserlich, Kaiser-, Reichs-.
imperil [im'peril], *v.a.* gefährden; in Gefahr bringen, einer Gefahr aussetzen.
imperious [im'piəriəs], *adj.* gebieterisch.
imperishable [im'periʃəbl], *adj.* unverwüstlich, unvergänglich.
impermeable [im'pə:miəbl], *adj.* undurchdringlich.
impersonal [im'pə:sənəl], *adj.* unpersönlich.
impersonate [im'pə:səneit], *v.a.* verkörpern, darstellen; sich ausgeben als.
impertinence [im'pə:tinəns], *s.* die Anmaßung, Frechheit, Unverschämtheit.
impertinent [im'pə:tinənt], *adj.* anmaßend, frech, unverschämt.
imperturbable [impə'tə:bəbl], *adj.* unerschütterlich, ruhig, gelassen.
impervious [im'pə:viəs], *adj.* unwegsam, undurchdringlich.
impetuous [im'petjuəs], *adj.* ungestüm, heftig.
impetus ['impitəs], *s.* die Triebkraft, der Antrieb.
impinge [im'pindʒ], *v.n.* verstoßen (*on*, gegen); übergreifen (*on*, in).
implacable [im'plækəbl], *adj.* unversöhnlich.
implement ['implimənt], *s.* das Gerät. — [impli'ment], *v.a.* (*Law*) erfüllen, in Wirkung setzen, in Kraft treten lassen.
implementation [implimen'teiʃən], *s.* das Inkrafttreten, die Erfüllung, Ausführung.
implicate ['implikeit], *v.a.* verwickeln.
implicit [im'plisit], *adj.* unbedingt; einbegriffen.
implore [im'plɔ:], *v.a.* anflehen.
imply [im'plai], *v.a.* besagen, meinen; andeuten.
impolite [impə'lait], *adj.* unhöflich, grob.
impolitic [im'pɔlitik], *adj.* unklug, unpolitisch, undiplomatisch.
imponderable [im'pɔndərəbl], *adj.* unwägbar. — *s. pl.* unwägbare, unvorhersehbare Umstände, *m.pl.*
import [im'pɔ:t], *v.a.* einführen, importieren; bedeuten, besagen. —

['impɔ:t], *s.* (*Comm.*) die Einfuhr, der Import; die Bedeutung (*importance, meaning*), Wichtigkeit (*significance*); (*Comm.*) — *licence*, die Einfuhrgenehmigung.)
importance [im'pɔ:təns], *s.* die Bedeutung, Wichtigkeit.
important [im'pɔ:tənt], *adj.* bedeutend, wichtig.
importation [impɔ:'teiʃən], *s.* die Einfuhr.
importune [impɔ:'tju:n], *v.a.* belästigen, angehen, dringend bitten.
impose [im'pouz], *v.a.* aufbürden, auferlegen. — *v.n.* — *upon s.o.*, einen belästigen.
imposition [impə'ziʃən], *s.* die Belästigung; (*Sch.*) die Strafarbeit.
impossible [im'pɔsibl], *adj.* unmöglich.
impostor [im'pɔstə], *s.* der Schwindler, Betrüger.
impotent ['impətənt], *adj.* schwach, machtlos; impotent (*sexually*).
impound [im'paund], *v.a.* beschlagnahmen, in Beschlag nehmen.
impoverish [im'pɔvəriʃ], *v.a.* arm machen.
impoverished [im'pɔvəriʃd], *adj.* verarmt, armselig.
impracticability [impræktikə'biliti], *s.* die Unmöglichkeit, Unausführbarkeit.
impracticable [im'præktikəbl], *adj.* unausführbar.
imprecate ['imprikeit], *v.a.* verwünschen.
impregnable [im'pregnəbl], *adj.* uneinnehmbar, unbezwinglich.
impregnate [im'pregneit], *v.a.* impregnieren; (*Chem.*) sättigen.
impress [im'pres], *v.a.* beeindrucken, imponieren (*fig.*); einprägen, einpressen (*print*). — ['impres], *s.* der Eindruck, (*Typ.*) Abdruck.
impression [im'preʃən], *s.* (*fig.*) der Eindruck; die Auflage (*books*).
impressionable [im'preʃənəbl], *adj.* eindrucksfähig, empfänglich.
impressive [im'presiv], *adj.* ergreifend, eindrucksvoll.
imprint ['imprint], *s.* der Name des Verlags oder Druckers. — [im'print], *v.a.* drucken.
imprison [im'prizn], *v.a.* gefangensetzen, in Haft nehmen.
imprisonment [im'priznmənt], *s.* die Haft; (*Law*) der Arrest.
improbability [imprɔbə'biliti], *s.* die Unwahrscheinlichkeit.
improbable [im'prɔbəbl], *adj.* unwahrscheinlich.
improbity [im'proubiti], *s.* die Unredlichkeit.
impromptu [im'prɔmptju:], *adj., adv.* aus dem Stegreif, unvorbereitet.
improper [im'prɔpə], *adj.* unpassend; unanständig (*indecent*).
impropriety [improu'praiiti], *s.* die Unanständigkeit (*indecency*); die Ungehörigkeit.

improve [im′pruːv], *v.a.* verbessern; (*Hort.*) veredeln. — *v.n.* besser werden, sich bessern; (*Med.*) sich erholen.

improvement [im′pruːvmənt], *s.* die Verbesserung; (*Med.*) die Besserung, der Fortschritt.

improvident [im′prɔvidənt], *adj.* unvorsichtig, nicht auf die Zukunft bedacht.

improvise [′imprəvaiz], *v.a.* improvisieren.

imprudent [im′pruːdənt], *adj.* unklug, unvorsichtig.

impudent [′impjudənt], *adj.* unverschämt.

impugn [im′pjuːn], *v.a.* anfechten, angreifen.

impulse [′impʌls], *s.* der Impuls; der Anstoß.

impulsive [im′pʌlsiv], *adj.* impulsiv.

impunity [im′pjuːniti], *s.* die Straffreiheit.

impure [im′pjuə], *adj.* (*also Metall.*, *Chem.*) unrein, unedel; unsauber.

impute [im′pjuːt], *v.a.* beimessen; zurechnen, die Schuld geben für.

in [in], *prep.* in; an; zu, auf; bei; nach, unter; über; von; mit; — *the morning,* vormittags; — *case,* falls; — *any case,* auf jeden Fall; — *German,* auf deutsch; — *my opinion,* meiner Meinung nach; — *the street,* auf der Straße; — *time,* rechtzeitig. — *adv.* drinnen, innen; herein, hinein; zu Hause.

inability [inə′biliti], *s.* die Unfähigkeit.

inaccessible [inæk′sesibl], *adj.* unzugänglich.

inaccurate [i′nækjurit], *adj.* ungenau.

inaction [i′nækʃən], *s.* die Untätigkeit.

inactive [i′næktiv], *adj.* untätig.

inadequate [i′nædikwit], *adj.* unzulänglich.

inadmissible [inəd′misibl], *adj.* unzulässig.

inadvertent [inəd′vəːtənt], *adj.* unbeabsichtigt; unachtsam.

inadvertently [inəd′vəːtəntli], *adv.* unversehens; versehentlich.

inalienable [in′eiliənəbl], *adj.* unveräußerlich.

inane [i′nein], *adj.* hohl, leer, sinnlos.

inanimate [i′nænimit], *adj.* unbeseelt, leblos.

inanity [i′næniti], *s.* die Leere, Nichtigkeit.

inapplicable [i′næplikəbl], *adj.* unanwendbar; unzutreffend.

inappropriate [inə′proupriit], *adj.* unpassend.

inarticulate [inɑː′tikjulit], *adj.* unartikuliert.

inasmuch [inəz′mʌtʃ], *adv.* insofern (als).

inattentive [inə′tentiv], *adj.* unaufmerksam.

inaudible [i′nɔːdibl], *adj.* unhörbar.

inaugural [i′nɔːgjurəl], *adj.* Inaugural-, Eröffnungs-, Antritts-.

inaugurate [i′nɔːgjureit], *v.a.* einweihen, eröffnen.

inauspicious [inɔː′spiʃəs], *adj.* ungünstig.

inborn [′inbɔːn], *adj.* angeboren.

inbred [′inbred], *adj.* in Inzucht geboren; angeboren, ererbt.

inbreeding [′inbriːdiŋ], *s.* die Inzucht.

incalculable [in′kælkjulabl], *adj.* unberechenbar.

incandescence [inkæn′desəns], *s.* die Weißglut.

incandescent [inkæn′desənt], *adj.* weißglühend.

incantation [inkæn′teiʃən], *s.* die Beschwörung.

incapable [in′keipəbl], *adj.* unfähig (*of doing s.th.,* etwas zu tun).

incapacitate [inkə′pæsiteit], *v.a.* unfähig machen.

incapacity [inkə′pæsiti], *s.* die Unfähigkeit.

incarcerate [in′kɑːsəreit], *v.a.* einkerkern, einsperren.

incarnate [in′kɑːnit], *adj.* eingefleischt; (*Theol.*) verkörpert.

incarnation [inkɑː′neiʃən], *s.* die Verkörperung; (*Theol.*) Menschwerdung.

incautious [in′kɔːʃəs], *adj.* unvorsichtig.

incendiary [in′sendjəri], *adj.* Brandbrennend. — *s.* der Brandstifter.

incense [in′sens], *v.a.* aufregen, erzürnen (*make angry*); (*Eccl.*) beweihräuchern. — [′insens], *s.* (*Eccl.*) der Weihrauch.

incentive [in′sentiv], *adj.* Ansporn-, Anreiz-. — *s.* der Ansporn, Anreiz; (*Comm.*) — *scheme,* das Inzentivsystem, Akkordsystem.

incessant [in′sesənt], *adj.* unaufhörlich, ununterbrochen.

incest [′insest], *s.* die Blutschande.

incestuous [in′sestjuəs], *adj.* blutschänderisch.

inch [intʃ], *s.* der Zoll. — *v.n.* — *away,* abrücken.

incident [′insidənt], *s.* der Vorfall, Zwischenfall; das Ereignis.

incidental [insi′dentl], *adj.* zufällig. — *s.* (*pl.*) zufällige Ausgaben, *f. pl.*; das Zusätzliche, Nebenausgaben, *f. pl.*

incipient [in′sipiənt], *adj.* beginnend, anfangend.

incise [in′saiz], *v.a.* einschneiden, (*Med.*) einen Einschnitt machen.

incision [in′siʒən], *s.* der Einschnitt.

incisive [in′saisiv], *adj.* einschneidend; energisch (*person*).

incite [in′sait], *v.a.* aufreizen, anspornen.

incivility [insi′viliti], *s.* die Unhöflichkeit.

inclement [in′klemənt], *adj.* unfreundlich (*weather, climate*).

inclination [inkli′neiʃən], *s.* die Neigung (*also fig.*).

incline [in′klain], *v.n.* neigen, sich neigen. — [′inklain], *s.* der Neigungswinkel; der Abhang.

include [in′kluːd], *v.a.* einschließen (*contain*); umfassen (*enclose*).

417

including [in'klu:diŋ], *prep.* einschließlich.

inclusive [in'klu:siv], *adj.* einschließlich, mitgerechnet.

incoherent [inko'hiərənt], *adj.* unzusammenhängend.

incombustible [inkəm'bʌstibl], *adj.* unverbrennbar.

income ['inkʌm], *s.* das Einkommen.

incommensurable, incommensurate [inkə'menʃərəbl, inkə'menʃərit], *adj.* unvereinbar, unmeßbar.

incomparable [in'kɔmpərəbl], *adj.* unvergleichlich.

incompatible [inkəm'pætibl], *adj.* unvereinbar.

incompetence, incompetency [in-'kɔmpitəns, -tənsi], *s.* die Inkompetenz; Unzulänglichkeit.

incompetent [in'kɔmpitənt], *adj.* unzuständig, inkompetent; unzulänglich.

incomplete [inkəm'pli:t], *adj.* unvollständig.

incomprehensible [inkɔmpri'hensibl], *adj.* unverständlich.

inconceivable [inkən'si:vəbl], *adj.* unbegreiflich.

inconclusive [inkən'klu:siv], *adj.* unvollständig (*incomplete*); unüberzeugend; ergebnislos.

incongruity [inkɔŋ'gru:iti], *s.* (*Maths.*) die Inkongruenz; (*fig.*) die Unangemessenheit.

incongruous [in'kɔŋgruəs], *adj.* inkongruent; unangemessen.

inconsequent [in'kɔnsikwənt], *adj.* folgewidrig.

inconsequential [inkɔnsi'kwenʃəl] *adj.* inkonsequent (*inconsistent*); unzusammenhängend.

inconsiderate [inkən'sidərit], *adj.* rücksichtslos, unbedachtsam.

inconsistent [inkən'sistənt], *adj.* inkonsequent.

inconsolable [inkən'souləbl], *adj.* untröstlich.

inconstancy [in'kɔnstənsi], *s.* die Unbeständigkeit; Untreue (*fickleness*).

incontestable [inkən'testəbl], *adj.* unanfechtbar, unbestreitbar.

incontinent [in'kɔntinənt], *adj.* unenthaltsam.

incontrovertible [inkɔntro'və:tibl], *adj.* unstreitig, unanfechtbar.

inconvenience [inkən'vi:niəns], *s.* die Unbequemlichkeit, Unannehmlichkeit.

inconvenient [inkən'vi:niənt], *adj.* unangenehm, unpassend.

inconvertible [inkən'və:tibl], *adj.* unveränderlich; (*Comm.*) unumsetzbar.

incorporate [in'kɔ:pəreit], *v.a.* einverleiben (*Dat.*), eingliedern (*Acc.*).

incorporated [in'kɔ:pəreitid], *adj.* (*Am.*) eingetragene Körperschaft, eingetragener Verein.

incorrect [inkə'rekt], *adj.* unrichtig, fehlerhaft; unschicklich, unpassend.

incorrigible [in'kɔridʒibl], *adj.* unverbesserlich.

incorruptible [inkə'rʌptibl], *adj.* unbestechlich.

increase [in'kri:s], *v.a.* vermehren, vergrößern (*size, volume*); steigern (*heat, intensity*); erhöhen (*price*). — *v.n.* sich vermehren, sich erhöhen; wachsen (*grow*). — ['inkri:s], *s.* die Zunahme; der Zuwachs (*family*); die Erhöhung.

incredible [in'kredibl], *adj.* unglaublich.

incredulity [inkre'dju:liti], *s.* die Ungläubigkeit, der Unglaube.

incredulous [in'kredjuləs], *adj.* ungläubig, schwer zu überzeugen.

increment ['inkrimənt], *s.* (*Comm.*) die Zulage, Gehaltserhöhung.

incriminate [in'krimineit], *v.a.* beschuldigen, inkriminieren.

incubate ['inkjubeit], *v.a.* brüten, ausbrüten. — *v.n.* brüten.

incubator ['inkjubeitə], *s.* der Brutapparat.

inculcate ['inkʌlkeit], *v.a.* einprägen.

inculpate ['inkʌlpeit], *v.a.* beschuldigen.

incumbent [in'kʌmbənt], *adj.* (*upon, Dat.*) obliegend, nötig. — *s.* der Pfründner, Amtsinhaber.

incur [in'kə:], *v.a.* auf sich laden, sich zuziehen.

incurable [in'kjuərəbl], *adj.* unheilbar.

incursion [in'kə:ʃən], *s.* der Einfall, Streifzug.

indebted [in'detid], *adj.* verpflichtet, dankbar (*grateful*); verschuldet (*in debt*).

indecent [in'di:sənt], *adj.* unschicklich, unanständig.

indecision [indi'siʒən], *s.* die Unentschlossenheit.

indecisive [indi'saisiv], *adj.* unentschlossen.

indeclinable [indi'klainəbl], *adj.* (*Gram.*) undeklinierbar.

indecorous [indi'kɔ:rəs *or* in'dekərəs], *adj.* unrühmlich, unanständig.

indeed [in'di:d], *adv.* in der Tat, tatsächlich.

indefatigable [indi'fætigəbl], *adj.* unermüdlich.

indefensible [indi'fensibl], *adj.* unhaltbar; unverzeihlich (*unforgivable*).

indefinable [indi'fainəbl], *adj.* unbestimmbar, undefinierbar.

indefinite [in'definit], *adj.* unbestimmt.

indelible [in'delibl], *adj.* unauslöschlich.

indelicate [in'delikit], *adj.* unfein.

indemnify [in'demnifai], *v.a.* entschädigen.

indemnity [in'demniti], die Entschädigung.

indent [in'dent], *v.a.* auszacken, einschneiden.

indenture [in'dentʃə], *s.* der Lehrbrief (*apprentice*); Vertrag.

independence [indi'pendəns], *s.* die Unabhängigkeit, Freiheit.

independent [indi'pendənt], *adj.* unabhängig, frei.

indescribable [indi'skraibəbl], *adj.* unbeschreiblich.

indestructible [indi'strʌktibl], *adj.* unverwüstlich; unzerstörbar.

indeterminable [indi'tə:minəbl], *adj.* unbestimmbar.

indeterminate [indi'tə:minit], *adj.* unbestimmt.

index ['indeks], *s.* (*pl.* **indexes**) das Inhaltsverzeichnis; (*pl.* **indices**) (*Maths.*) der Exponent; — *finger*, der Zeigefinger; (*pl.*) die Finger, Zeiger, *m. pl.* (*pointers*).

India ['indjə], das Indien; — *paper*, das Dünnpapier.

Indian ['indjən], *adj.* indisch; — *ink*, die Tusche. — *s.* der Ind(i)er.

indiarubber ['indjə'rʌbə], *s.* der Radiergummi.

indicate ['indikeit], *v.a.* anzeigen, angeben.

indication [indi'keiʃən], *s.* das Anzeichen, Merkmal, der Hinweis.

indicative [in'dikətiv], *adj.* bezeichnend (für, *Acc.*). — *s.* (*Gram.*) der Indikativ.

indict [in'dait], *v.a.* anklagen.

indictment [in'daitmənt], *s.* die Anklage.

indifference [in'difrəns], *s.* die Gleichgültigkeit.

indifferent [in'difrənt], *adj.* gleichgültig.

indigence ['indidʒəns], *s.* die Armut.

indigenous [in'didʒinəs], *adj.* eingeboren, einheimisch.

indigent ['indidʒənt], *adj.* arm, dürftig.

indigestible [indi'dʒestibl], *adj.* unverdaulich.

indigestion [indi'dʒestʃən], *s.* die Magenbeschwerden, *f. pl.*; die Magenverstimmung.

indignant [in'dignənt], *adj.* empört, unwillig, entrüstet.

indignation [indig'neiʃən], *s.* die Entrüstung, der Unwille.

indignity [in'digniti], *s.* die Schmach, der Schimpf.

indirect [indi'rekt], *adj.* indirekt, mittelbar.

indiscreet [indis'kri:t], *adj.* indiskret, unvorsichtig; unbescheiden (*immodest*); taktlos.

indiscretion [indis'kreʃən], *s.* die Indiskretion, Taktlosigkeit.

indiscriminate [indis'kriminit], *adj.* ohne Unterschied, wahllos, kritiklos.

indispensable [indis'pensəbl], *adj.* unerläßlich, unentbehrlich.

indisposed [indis'pouzd], *adj.* unwohl (*health*); unwillig (*unwilling*).

indisposition [indispə'ziʃən], *s.* das Unwohlsein (*health*); das Abgeneigtsein (*disinclination*).

indisputable [indis'pju:təbl], *adj.* unbestreitbar.

indissoluble [indi'sɔljubl], *adj.* unauflöslich.

indistinct [indis'tiŋkt], *adj.* undeutlich.

indistinguishable [indis'tiŋgwiʃəbl], *adj.* nicht zu unterscheiden, ununterscheidbar.

individual [indi'vidjuəl], *adj.* individuell, persönlich; einzeln (*single*). — *s.* das Individuum, Einzelwesen.

individuality [individju'æliti], *s.* die Individualität.

indivisible [indi'vizibl], *adj.* unteilbar.

Indo-Chinese [indotʃai'ni:z], *adj.* hinterindisch. — *s.* der Hinterind(i)er.

indolent ['indələnt], *adj.* indolent, träge.

Indonesian [indo'ni:ʒən], *adj.* indonesisch. — *s.* der Indonesier.

indoor ['indɔ:], *adj.* im Haus; drinnen (*inside*).

indoors [in'dɔ:z], *adv.* im Hause, zu Hause.

indubitable [in'dju:bitəbl], *adj.* zweifellos, unzweifelhaft.

induce [in'dju:s], *v.a.* veranlassen, bewegen, verleiten (*incite*).

inducement [in'dju:smənt], *s.* der Beweggrund (*cause*); der Anlaß (*reason*); die Verleitung (*incitement*).

induction [in'dʌkʃən], *s.* die Einführung; (*Elec.*) die Induktion.

inductive [in'dʌktiv], *adj.* (*Log.*, *Elec.*) induktiv.

indulge [in'dʌldʒ], *v.a.* nachgeben (*Dat.*); verwöhnen. — *v.n.* — *in*, frönen (*Dat.*).

indulgence [in'dʌldʒəns], *s.* die Nachsicht; das Wohlleben (*Eccl.*) der Ablaß.

industrial [in'dʌstriəl], *adj.* industriell, Industrie-.

industrious [in'dʌstriəs], *adj.* fleißig, arbeitsam.

industry ['indəstri], *s.* die Industrie (*production*); der Fleiß (*industriousness*).

inebriate [i'ni:brieit], *v.a.* berauschen. — [-iit], *adj.* berauscht.

ineffable [i'nefəbl], *adj.* unaussprechlich.

ineffective, ineffectual [ini'fektiv, ini'fektjuəl], *adj.* unwirksam, wirkungslos; unfähig.

inefficiency [ini'fiʃənsi], *s.* die Erfolglosigkeit, Untauglichkeit.

inefficient [ini'fiʃənt], *adj.* untauglich, untüchtig.

ineligible [in'elidʒibl], *adj.* nicht wählbar.

inept [i'nept], *adj.* untüchtig, albern, dumm.

ineptitude [i'neptitju:d], *s.* die Unfähigkeit; die Dummheit (*stupidity*).

inequality [ini'kwɔliti], *s.* die Ungleichheit.

inert [i'nə:t], *adj.* träg.

inestimable [in'estiməbl], *adj.* unschätzbar.

inevitable [in'evitəbl], *adj.* unumgänglich, unvermeidlich.

inexcusable [iniks'kju:zəbl], *adj.* unverzeihlich, unentschuldbar.

inexhaustible [inig'zɔ:stibl], *adj.* unerschöpflich.

inexpedient [iniks'pi:djənt], *adj.* unzweckmäßig, unpraktisch, unpassend.

inexpensive [iniks'pensiv], *adj.* billig, nicht kostspielig.

inexperience [iniks'piəriəns], *s.* die Unerfahrenheit, Naivität.

inexpert [iniks'pə:t], *adj.* ungeübt, unerfahren.

inexpiable [i'nekspiəbl], *adj.* unsühnbar, nicht wieder gut zu machen.

inexplicable [i'neksplikəbl], *adj.* unerklärlich.

inexpressible [iniks'presibl], *adj.* unaussprechlich.

inexpressive [iniks'presiv], *adj.* ausdruckslos.

inextinguishable [iniks'tiŋgwiʃəbl], *adj.* unauslöschlich.

inextricable [i'nekstrikəbl], *adj.* unentwirrbar.

infallible [in'fælibl], *adj.* unfehlbar.

infamous ['infəməs], *adj.* verrufen, abscheulich, berüchtigt.

infamy ['infəmi], *s.* die Schande; Ehrlosigkeit (*dishonour*).

infancy ['infənsi], *s.* die Kindheit, Unmündigkeit; (*fig.*) der Anfang.

infant ['infənt], *s.* das Kind; (*Law*) der Unmündige, das Mündel.

infantry ['infəntri], *s.* die Infanterie.

infatuate [in'fætjueit], *v.a.* betören.

infect [in'fekt], *v.a.* anstecken, infizieren.

infection [in'fekʃən], *s.* (*Med.*) die Ansteckung, Infektion.

infectious [in'fekʃəs], *adj.* (*Med.*) ansteckend.

infer [in'fə:], *v.a.* schließen, herleiten, folgern.

inference ['infərəns], *s.* die Folgerung.

inferior [in'fiəriə], *comp. adj.* geringer; untergeordnet (*subordinate*); schlechter (*worse*).

inferiority [infiəri'ɔriti], *s.* die Inferiorität, Minderwertigkeit.

infernal [in'fə:nəl], *adj.* höllisch.

infest [in'fest], *v.a.* heimsuchen, plagen.

infidel ['infidəl], *adj.* ungläubig. — *s.* der Heide, Ungläubige.

infiltrate ['infiltreit], *v.n.* durchsickern, durchdringen, infiltrieren.

infinite ['infinit], *adj.* unendlich.

infinitive [in'finitiv], *s.* (*Gram.*) der Infinitiv, die Nennform.

infirm [in'fə:m], *adj.* gebrechlich, schwach; siech (*sick*).

infirmary [in'fə:məri], *s.* das Krankenhaus.

infirmity [in'fə:miti], *s.* die Schwäche, Gebrechlichkeit.

inflame [in'fleim], *v.a.* entzünden.

inflammation [inflə'meiʃən], *s.* die Entzündung.

inflate [in'fleit], *v.a.* aufblasen, aufblähen; (*Comm.*) künstlich erhöhen (*values*).

inflation [in'fleiʃən], *s.* die Aufblähung; (*Comm.*) die Inflation.

inflect [in'flekt], *v.a.* (*Gram.*) biegen, flektieren, deklinieren, konjugieren.

inflection [in'flekʃən], *s.* (*Gram.*) die Biegung; (*Phonet.*) der Tonfall.

inflexible [in'fleksibl], *adj.* unbiegsam.

inflexion *see* **inflection**.

inflict [in'flikt], *v.a.* auferlegen (*impose*); beibringen (*administer*).

infliction [in'flikʃən], *s.* die Verhängung, das Beibringen.

influence ['influəns], *v.a.* beeinflussen. — *s.* der Einfluß.

influential [influ'enʃəl], *adj.* einflußreich.

influenza [influ'enzə], *s.* (*Med.*) die Grippe.

inform [in'fɔ:m], *v.a., v.n.* informieren, benachrichtigen; — *against*, jemanden denunzieren.

informal [in'fɔ:məl], *adj.* nicht formell; ungezwungen, zwanglos.

informant [in'fɔ:mənt], *s.* der Angeber.

information [infə'meiʃən], *s.* die Information, Nachricht, Auskunft.

infrequent [in'fri:kwənt], *adj.* selten.

infringe [in'frindʒ], *v.a.* übertreten.

infuriate [in'fjuərieit], *v.a.* wütend machen.

infuse [in'fju:z], *v.a.* einflößen, aufgießen, begießen.

infusion [in'fju:ʒən], *s.* die Eingießung; der Aufguß (*tea*); (*Chem.*) die Infusion.

ingenious [in'dʒi:niəs], *adj.* geistreich, genial.

ingenuity [indʒi'nju:iti], *s.* der Scharfsinn.

ingenuous [in'dʒenjuəs], *adj.* offen, unbefangen, arglos.

ingot ['iŋgət], *s.* der Barren.

ingrained [in'greind], *adj.* eingefleischt.

ingratiate [in'greiʃieit], *v.r.* — *o.s.*, sich beliebt machen, sich einschmeicheln (*with*, bei).

ingratitude [in'grætitju:d], *s.* die Undankbarkeit.

ingredient [in'gri:diənt], *s.* der Bestandteil; die Zutat.

inhabit [in'hæbit], *v.a.* bewohnen.

inhabitant [in'hæbitənt], *s.* der Bewohner; Einwohner.

inhale [in'heil], *v.a.* einatmen.

inherent [in'hiərənt], *adj.* eigen, angeboren (*innate*); in der Sache selbst (*intrinsic*).

inherit [in'herit], *v.a.* erben.

inheritance [in'heritəns], *s.* die Erbschaft, das Erbgut (*patrimony*); (*fig.*) das Erbe.

inhibit [in'hibit], *v.a.* hindern; —*ing factor*, der Hemmfaktor.

inhibition [ini'biʃən], *s.* (*Psych.*) die Hemmung.

inhospitable [inhɔs'pitəbl], *adj.* ungastlich, ungastfreundlich.

inhuman [in'hju:mən], *adj.* unmenschlich.

inhume [in'hju:m], *v.a.* beerdigen.

inimical [i'nimikəl], *adj.* feindlich (gesinnt), feindselig.

inimitable [i'nimitəbl], *adj.* unnachahmlich.

iniquitous [i'nikwitəs], *adj.* ungerecht, schlecht, boshaft.

iniquity [i'nikwiti], *s.* die Ungerechtigkeit (*injustice*); die Schändlichkeit (*shame*).

initial [i'niʃəl], *adj.* anfänglich. — *s.* (*Typ.*) der Anfangsbuchstabe.

initiate [i'niʃieit], *v.a.* einweihen, anfangen.

initiative [i'niʃiətiv], *s.* die Initiative; der erste Anstoß (*impulse*).

injection [in'dʒekʃən], *s.* (*Med.*) die Einspritzung, Injektion.

injudicious [indʒu'diʃəs], *adj.* unbedacht, unbesonnen; übereilt (*rash*).

injunction [in'dʒʌŋkʃən], *s.* die Vorschrift, (*Law*) die gerichtliche Verfügung.

injure ['indʒə], *v.a.* verletzen.

injurious [in'dʒuəriəs], *adj.* verletzend; schädlich (*harmful*).

injury ['indʒəri], *s.* die Verletzung, Verwundung; der Schaden (*damage*).

injustice [in'dʒʌstis], *s.* die Ungerechtigkeit.

ink [iŋk], *s.* die Tinte.

inkling ['iŋkliŋ], *s.* die Ahnung.

inkstand ['iŋkstænd], *s.* das Schreibzeug.

inlaid [in'leid], *adj.* eingelegt.

inland ['inlənd], *adj.* inländisch, Binnen-; — *revenue office*, das Steueramt, Finanzamt.

inlet ['inlit], *s.* (*Geog.*) die kleine Bucht.

inmate ['inmeit], *s.* der Insasse, Bewohner.

inmost ['inmoust], *adj.* innerst.

inn [in], *s.* der Gasthof, das Wirtshaus; *Inns of Court*, die Londoner Rechtskammern, *f. pl.*

innate [in'neit], *adj.* angeboren.

inner ['inə], *adj.* inner; geheim (*secret*).

innings ['iniŋz], *s.* das Daransein (*in Cricket*); die Reihe.

innocence ['inəsəns], *s.* die Unschuld.

innocuous [in'nɔkjuəs], *adj.* unschädlich.

innovate ['inoveit], *v.a., v.n.* als Neuerung einführen, Neuerungen machen.

innovation [ino'veiʃən], *s.* die Neuerung.

innuendo [inju'endou], *s.* das Innuendo, die Anspielung.

innumerable [i'nju:mərəbl], *adj.* unzählig, unzählbar.

inoculate [i'nɔkjuleit], *v.a.* impfen.

inoffensive [ino'fensiv], *adj.* harmlos, unschädlich.

inopportune [in'ɔpətju:n], *adj.* ungelegen.

inordinate [i'nɔ:dinit], *adj.* unmäßig.

inorganic [inɔ:'gænik], *adj.* anorganisch.

inquest ['inkwest], *s.* die gerichtliche Untersuchung (*Law*); *coroner's* —, die Leichenschau.

inquire, enquire [in'kwaiə], *v.n.* sich erkundigen (*after*, nach, *Dat.*), nachfragen.

inquiry, enquiry [in'kwaiəri], *s.* die Nachfrage; — *office*, die Auskunftsstelle.

inquisition [inkwi'ziʃən], *s.* (*Eccl.*) die Inquisition; die gerichtliche Untersuchung.

inquisitive [in'kwizitiv], *adj.* neugierig.

inquisitiveness [in'kwizitivnis], *s.* die Neugier(de).

inroad ['inroud], *s.* der Eingriff, Überfall.

insane [in'sein], *adj.* wahnsinnig.

insanity [in'sæniti], *s.* der Wahnsinn.

insatiable [in'seiʃəbl], *adj.* unersättlich.

inscribe [in'skraib], *v.a.* einschreiben (*enrol*); widmen (*book*).

inscription [in'skripʃən], *s.* die Inschrift.

inscrutable [in'skru:təbl], *adj.* unergründlich, unerforschlich.

insect ['insekt], *s.* das Insekt, Kerbtier.

insecure [insi'kjuə], *adj.* unsicher.

insensate [in'sensit], *adj.* unsinnig (*senseless*); gefühllos..

insensible [in'sensibl], *adj.* unempfindlich; gefühllos.

insensitive [in'sensitiv], *adj.* ohne feineres Gefühl, unempfindlich.

inseparable [in'sepərəbl], *adj.* unzertrennlich, untrennbar.

insert [in'sə:t], *v.a.* einsetzen, einschalten (*add*); inserieren (*in newspaper*).

insertion [in'sə:ʃən], *s.* die Einschaltung (*addition*); die Annonce, das Inserat (*press*).

inside [in'said], *adj.* inner. — *adv.* im Innern. — *prep.* innerhalb. — *s.* das Innere.

insidious [in'sidiəs], *adj.* heimtückisch.

insight ['insait], *s.* der Einblick.

insignia [in'signiə], *s. pl.* die Insignien.

insignificance [insig'nifikəns], *s.* die Geringfügigkeit, Bedeutungslosigkeit.

insignificant [insig'nifikənt], *adj.* unbedeutend, geringfügig.

insincere [insin'siə], *adj.* unaufrichtig.

insincerity [insin'seriti], *s.* die Unaufrichtigkeit.

insinuate [in'sinjueit], *v.a.* zu verstehen geben, andeuten, anspielen auf (*Acc.*).

insinuation [insinju'eiʃən], *s.* der Wink, die Andeutung, Anspielung.

insipid [in'sipid], *adj.* schal, geschmacklos.

insist [in'sist], *v.n.* bestehen (*upon*, auf, *Dat.*).

insistence [in'sistəns], *s.* das Bestehen, Beharren.

insolence ['insələns], *s.* die Frechheit.

insolent ['insələnt], *adj.* frech, unverschämt.

insoluble [in'sɔljubl], *adj.* unlösbar; (*Chem.*) unlöslich.

insolvent [in'sɔlvənt], *adj.* insolvent, zahlungsunfähig, bankrott.

inspect [in'spekt], *v.a.* inspizieren; besichtigen.

inspection [in'spekʃən], s. die Inspektion; Besichtigung.

inspiration [inspi'reiʃən], s. die Inspiration, Erleuchtung, Begeisterung.

inspire [in'spaiə], v.a. inspirieren, begeistern.

instability [instə'biliti], s. die Unbeständigkeit, Labilität.

install [in'stɔ:l], v.a. einsetzen (in office); einbauen.

installation [instə'leiʃən], s. die Einsetzung (inauguration); die Installation.

instalment [in'stɔ:lmənt], s. die Rate; by —s, auf Abzahlung; die Fortsetzung (serial).

instance ['instəns], s. das Beispiel (example); (Law) die Instanz; at my —, auf meine dringende Bitte; for —, zum Beispiel. — v.a. als Beispiel anführen.

instant ['instənt], s. der Augenblick. — adj. gegenwärtig; sofortig; laufend (current month).

instantaneous [instən'teiniəs], adj. augenblicklich, sofortig.

instead [in'sted], adv. dafür, stattdessen; — of, (an)statt (Genit.).

instep ['instep], s. (Anat.) der Rist.

instigate ['instigeit], v.a. aufhetzen, anreizen, anstiften.

instil [in'stil], v.a. einflößen.

instinct ['instiŋkt], s. der Instinkt, Naturtrieb.

institute ['institju:t], s. das Institut. — v.a. einrichten (install); stiften (found).

institution [insti'tju:ʃən], s. die Stiftung (foundation); die Anstalt (establishment).

instruct [in'strʌkt], v.a. unterrichten, unterweisen.

instruction [in'strʌkʃən], s. der Unterricht (in schools etc.); (pl.) die Instruktionen, f. pl.; die Direktive.

instructive [in'strʌktiv], adj. instruktiv, lehrreich.

instrument ['instrumənt], s. das Instrument; Werkzeug (tool).

insubordination [insəbɔ:di'neiʃən], s. der Ungehorsam.

insufferable [in'sʌfərəbl], adj. unerträglich.

insufficient [insə'fiʃənt], adj. ungenügend, unzulänglich.

insular ['insjulə], adj. Insel-; insular (narrow-minded).

insulate ['insjuleit], v.a. absondern (separate); (Elec.) isolieren; insulating tape, das Isolierband.

insult [in'sʌlt], v.a. beleidigen.

insuperable [in'sju:pərəbl], adj. unüberwindlich.

insupportable [insə'pɔ:təbl], adj. unhaltbar (argument); unerträglich (insufferable).

insurance [in'ʃuərəns], s. die Versicherung; — policy, die Police; — premium, die Prämie; — broker, der Versicherungsmakler.

insure [in'ʃuə], v.a. versichern.

insurgent [in'sə:dʒənt], s. der Aufständische, Aufrührer.

insurmountable [insə'mauntəbl], adj. unüberwindlich.

insurrection [insə'rekʃən], s. der Aufstand, Aufruhr; die Empörung.

intact [in'tækt], adj. unversehrt, intakt.

intangible [in'tændʒibl], adj. unberührbar (untouchable); (Log.) abstrakt. — s. pl. (Log.) die Intangibilien, pl.

integer ['intidʒə], s. (Maths.) das Ganze, die ganze Zahl.

integral ['intigrəl], adj. wesentlich; vollständig. — s. (Maths.) das Integral.

integrate ['intigreit], v.a. (Maths.) integrieren.

integration [inti'greiʃən], s. (Maths.) die Integrierung; (fig.) die Integration, das völlige Aufgehen.

integrity [in'tegriti], s. die Rechtschaffenheit, Redlichkeit (probity).

intellect ['intilekt], s. der Geist, Intellekt, Verstand.

intellectual [inti'lektjuəl], adj. intellektuell. — s. der Intellektuelle.

intelligence [in'telidʒəns], s. die Intelligenz; die Nachricht (news).

intelligent [in'telidʒənt], adj. intelligent.

intelligible [in'telidʒibl], adj. verständlich.

intemperance [in'tempərəns], s. die Unmäßigkeit.

intemperate [in'tempərit], adj. unmäßig.

intend [in'tend], v.a. beabsichtigen, vorhaben.

intendant [in'tendənt], s. der Intendant, Verwalter.

intense [in'tens], adj. intensiv, heftig.

intent [in'tent], adj. gespannt, begierig, bedacht (on, auf, Acc.). — s. die Absicht.

intention [in'tenʃən], s. die Absicht.

intentioned [in'tenʃənd], adj. well-, wohlgesinnt.

inter [in'tə:], v.a. beerdigen.

intercede [intə'si:d], v.n. vermitteln (between); sich verwenden (on behalf of, für, Acc.).

intercept [intə'sept], v.a. abfangen, auffangen, hemmen.

intercession [intə'seʃən], s. die Vermittlung, Fürsprache, Fürbitte.

interchange ['intətʃeindʒ], s. der Austausch. — [-'tʃeindʒ], v.a. austauschen.

intercourse ['intəkɔ:s], s. der Verkehr, Umgang.

interdict [intə'dikt], v.a. untersagen, verbieten.

interest ['intrəst], s. das Interesse; die Beteiligung; (Comm.) die Zinsen, m. pl.; compound —, die Zinseszinsen, m. pl. — v.a. interessieren.

interested ['intrəstid], adj. (in, an, Dat.) interessiert; be — in, sich interessieren für.

interesting ['intrəstiŋ], *adj.* interessant.
interfere [intə'fiə], *v.n.* sich einmischen, eingreifen (*in*, in, *Acc.*)
interference [intə'fiərəns], *s.* die Einmischung; (*Rad.*) die Störung.
interim ['intərim], *adj.* vorläufig, Zwischen-.
interior [in'tiəriə], *adj.* innerlich. — *s.* das Innere; das Binnenland; — *decorator*, der Innenraumgestalter, der Innenarchitekt; *Ministry of the Interior*, das Innenministerium.
interjection [intə'dʒekʃən], *s.* die Interjektion; der Ausruf.
interlace [intə'leis], *v.a.* einflechten.
interleave [intə'li:v], *v.a.* durchschießen (*a book*).
interlinear [intə'liniə], *adj.* zwischenzeilig.
interlocutor [intə'lɔkjutə], *s.* der Gesprächspartner.
interloper ['intəloupə], *s.* der Eindringling.
interlude ['intəlju:d], *s.* das Zwischenspiel.
intermarry [intə'mæri], *v.n.* untereinander heiraten.
intermediate [intə'mi:diit],*adj.* Mittel-; (*Sch.*) — *certificate*, das Mittelstufenzeugnis.
interment [in'tə:mənt], *s.* die Beerdigung.
interminable [in'tə:minəbl], *adj.* endlos, langwierig.
intermingle [intə'miŋgl], *v.n.* sich vermischen.
intermission [intə'miʃən], *s.* die Pause, Unterbrechung.
intermit [intə'mit], *v.a.* unterbrechen.
intermittent [intə'mitənt], *adj.* Wechsel-, aussetzend.
internal [in'tə:nl], *adj.* intern, innerlich.
international [intə'næʃənəl], *adj.* international; — *law*, das Völkerrecht.
interpolate [in'tə:poleit], *v.a.* interpolieren, einschalten.
interpose [intə'pouz], *v.a.* dazwischenstellen. — *v.n.* vermitteln (*mediate*).
interpret [in'tə:prit], *v.a.* verdolmetschen; erklären (*explain*); auslegen, interpretieren.
interpretation [intə:pri'teiʃən], *s.* die Auslegung, Interpretation.
interpreter [in'tə:pritə], *s.* der Dolmetscher.
interrogate [in'terogeit], *v.a.* ausfragen, befragen, vernehmen.
interrogation [intero'geiʃən], *s.* die Befragung; (*Law*) das Verhör, die Vernehmung.
interrogative [intə'rɔgətiv], *adj.* (*Gram.*) Frage-, Interrogativ-.
interrupt [intə'rʌpt], *v.a.* unterbrechen; stören (*disturb*).
interruption [intə'rʌpʃən], *s.* die Unterbrechung; Störung (*disturbance*).
intersect [intə'sekt], *v.a.* durchschneiden.

intersperse [intə'spə:s], *v.a.* untermengen, vermischen, einstreuen.
intertwine [intə'twain], *v.a., v.n.* (sich) durchflechten.
interval ['intəvəl], *s.* der Zwischenraum; die Pause; (*Mus.*) das Interval.
intervene [intə'vi:n], *v.n.* eingreifen; als Vermittler dienen (*act as mediator*).
intervention [intə'venʃən], *s.* die Vermittlung, Intervention.
interview ['intəvju:], *v.a.* zur Vorsprache einladen (*a candidate*); interviewen. — *s.* die Vorsprache, das Interview.
intestate [in'testit], *adj.* ohne Testament.
intestines [in'testinz], *s. pl.* (*Anat.*) die Eingeweide, *n. pl.*
intimacy ['intiməsi], *s.* die Vertraulichkeit, Intimität.
intimate ['intimit], *adj.* intim, vertraut, vertraulich. — [-meit], *v.a.* andeuten, zu verstehen geben.
intimation [inti'meiʃən], *s.* der Wink, die Andeutung.
intimidate [in'timideit], *v.a.* einschüchtern.
into ['intu], *prep.* (*Acc.*) in, in … hinein (*towards*).
intolerable [in'tɔlərəbl], *adj.* unerträglich.
intolerance [in'tɔlərəns], *s.* die Unduldsamkeit, Intoleranz.
intonation [into'neiʃən], *s.* (*Phonet.*) die Intonation; (*Mus.*) das Anstimmen, der Tonansatz (*of instruments*).
intoxicate [in'tɔksikeit], *v.a.* berauschen.
intractable [in'træktəbl], *adj.* unbändig, unlenksam.
intransitive [in'trænsitiv *or* in'trɑ:ns-], *adj.* (*Gram.*) intransitiv.
intrepid [in'trepid], *adj.* unerschrocken, furchtlos.
intricacy ['intrikəsi], *s.* die Verwicklung (*tangle*), Schwierigkeit (*difficulty*).
intricate ['intrikit], *adj.* verwickelt, schwierig.
intrigue [in'tri:g], *s.* die Intrige. — *v.n.* intrigieren.
intrinsic [in'trinsik], *adj.* wesentlich; innerlich (*inner*).
introduce [intrə'dju:s], *v.a.* einführen, einleiten (*book etc.*); vorstellen (*person*).
introduction [intrə'dʌkʃən], *s.* die Einführung, das Bekanntmachen; die Einleitung (*preface*); die Vorstellung (*presentation to s.o., Dat.*).
introductory [intrə'dʌktəri], *adj.* einführend.
introspection [intrə'spekʃən], *s.* die Selbstbetrachtung, Introspektion.
introspective [intrə'spektiv], *adj.* nachdenklich, beschaulich.
intrude [in'tru:d], *v.n.* eindringen, sich eindrängen; stören (*be in the way*).
intrusion [in'tru:ʒən], *s.* das Eindringen.

intuition [intju'iʃən], *s.* die Intuition, Eingebung.
intuitive [in'tju:itiv], *adj.* intuitiv, gefühlsmäßig.
inundate ['inʌndeit], *v.a.* überschwemmen.
inure [i'njuə], *v.a.* gewöhnen; abhärten (*harden*).
invade [in'veid], *v.a.* angreifen, einfallen in, *Dat.*).
invalid [in'vælid], *adj.* ungültig (*void*); ['invəlid] krank (*sick*). — *s.* der Kranke, Invalide.
invalidate [in'vælideit], *v.a.* ungültig machen, für ungültig erklären.
invalidity [invə'liditi], *s.* die Ungültigkeit.
invaluable [in'væljuəbl], *adj.* von hohem Wert, wertvoll, unschätzbar.
invariable [in'vɛəriəbl], *adj.* unveränderlich. — *s.* (*Maths.*) die unveränderliche Größe, die Konstante, Unveränderliche.
invasion [in'veiʒən], *s.* die Invasion, der Einfall; Angriff (*of*, auf, *Acc.*).
invective [in'vektiv], *adj.* schmähend. — *s.* die Schmähung.
inveigh [in'vei], *v.n.* schmähen, losziehen (gegen); schimpfen (auf, *Acc.*).
inveigle [in'veigl], *v.a.* verleiten, verführen.
invent [in'vent], *v.a.* erfinden.
invention [in'venʃən], *s.* die Erfindung.
inventor [in'ventə], *s.* der Erfinder.
inventory ['invəntri], *s.* der Bestand, das Inventar; die Liste (*list*).
inverse [in'və:s,'invə:s], *adj.* umgekehrt.
inversion [in'və:ʃən], *s.* die Umkehrung; (*Gram., Maths.*) die Inversion.
invert [in'və:t], *v.a.* umstellen, umkehren. — ['invə:t] (*Chem.*) sugar, der Invertzucker.
invest [in'vest], *v.a.* bekleiden; bedecken; (*Comm.*) investieren, anlegen.
investigate [in'vestigeit], *v.a.* untersuchen, erforschen.
investiture [in'vestitʃə], *s.* die Investitur; die Belehnung.
investment [in'vestmənt], *s.* die Investierung, Kapitalanlage.
inveterate [in'vetərit], *adj.* eingewurzelt, eingefleischt.
invidious [in'vidiəs], *adj.* neiderregend, verhaßt.
invigorate [in'vigəreit], *v.a.* stärken, beleben.
invincible [in'vinsibl], *adj.* unbesiegbar, unüberwindlich.
inviolable [in'vaiələbl], *adj.* unverletzlich.
invisible [in'vizibl], *adj.* unsichtbar.
invitation [invi'teiʃən], *s.* die Einladung.
invite [in'vait], *v.a.* einladen.
invocation [invo'keiʃən], *s.* die Anrufung.
invoice ['invɔis], *s.* die Rechnung, Faktura. — *v.a.* fakturieren.
invoke [in'vouk], *v.a.* anrufen.
involuntary [in'vɔləntri], *adj.* unfreiwillig (*unwilling*); unwillkürlich (*reflex*).

involve [in'vɔlv], *v.a.* verwickeln.
involved [in'vɔlvd], *adj.* schwierig, verwickelt, kompliziert.
invulnerable [in'vʌlnərəbl], *adj.* unverwundbar, unverletzlich.
inward ['inwəd], *adj.* inner(lich). — *adv.* (*also* **inwards**) einwärts, nach innen, ins Innere.
iodine ['aiədain *or* 'aiədi:n], *s.* (*Chem.*) das Jod.
Iraki, Iraqi [i'rɑːki], *adj.* irakisch. — *s.* der Iraker.
Iranian [i'reinjən], *adj.* iranisch. — *s.* der Iranier.
irascible [i'ræsibl], *adj.* jähzornig, aufbrausend.
irate [ai'reit], *adj.* erzürnt, zornig.
ire [aiə], *s.* (*Poet.*) der Zorn.
iridescent [iri'desənt], *adj.* irisierend, schillernd.
iris ['aiəris], *s.* (*Anat.*) die Regenbogenhaut; (*Bot.*) die Schwertlilie.
Irish ['airiʃ], *adj.* irisch, ersisch. — *s.* (*pl.*) *the* —, die Irländer, Iren, *pl.*
Irishman ['airiʃmən], *s.* der Irländer, Ire.
irk [ə:k], *v.a.* verdrießen, verärgern.
irksome ['ə:ksəm], *adj.* lästig, ärgerlich.
iron ['aiən], *s.* (*Metall.*) das Eisen; (*pl.*) die eisernen Fesseln. — *adj.* eisern, Eisen-. — *v.a.* bügeln, plätten; — *out*, schlichten, beilegen.
ironical [ai'rɔnikl], *adj.* ironisch.
ironmonger ['aiənmʌŋgə], *s.* der Eisenhändler.
ironmould ['aiənmould], *s.* der Rostfleck.
irony ['aiərəni], *s.* die Ironie.
irradiate [i'reidieit], *v.a.* bestrahlen.
irrational [i'ræʃənəl], *adj.* (*Log.,Maths.*) irrational; unvernünftig (*without reason*).
irreconcilable [irekən'sailəbl], *adj.* unversöhnlich; unvereinbar (*incompatible*).
irregular [i'regjulə], *adj.* unregelmäßig, gegen die Regel.
irrelevant [i'reləvənt], *adj.* belanglos.
irremediable [iri'mi:diəbl], *adj.* unheilbar; nicht wieder gut zu machen.
irreparable [i'repərəbl], *adj.* unersetzlich.
irrepressible [iri'presibl], *adj.* nicht zu unterdrücken, unbezähmbar.
irreproachable [iri'proutʃəbl], *adj.* untadelhaft, tadellos.
irresistible [iri'zistibl], *adj.* unwiderstehlich.
irresolute [i'rezolju:t], *adj.* unschlüssig, unentschlossen.
irrespective [iris'pektiv], *adj.* ohne Rücksicht (*of*, auf, *Acc.*).
irresponsible [iris'pɔnsibl], *adj.* unverantwortlich.
irretrievable [iri'tri:vəbl], *adj.* unersetzlich, unwiederbringlich.
irreverent [i'revərənt], *adj.* unehrerbietig.
irrevocable [i'revəkəbl], *adj.* unwiderruflich.

irrigate ['irigeit], *v.a.* bewässern.

irritable ['iritəbl], *adj.* reizbar.

irritant ['iritənt], *s.* das Reizmittel.

irritation [iri'teiʃən], *s.* die Reizung, das Reizen; die Erzürnung.

irruption [i'rʌpʃən], *s.* der Einbruch.

island ['ailənd], *s.* die Insel.

isle [ail], *s.* (*Poet.*) die Insel.

isolate ['aisəleit], *v.a.* (*Med.*) isolieren; absondern; (*Chem.*) darstellen.

isolation [aisə'leiʃən], *s.* die Absonderung, Isolierung.

Israeli [iz'reili], *adj.* den Staat Israel betreffend. — *s.* der Israeli.

Israelite ['izreiəlait], *adj.* israelitisch. — *s.* der Israelit.

issue ['isju: *or* 'iʃu:], *s.* der Ausgang, Erfolg (*result*); main —, der Hauptpunkt; die Nachkommenschaft (*children*); die Ausgabe (*edition*); Herausgabe (*publication*). — *v.a.* herausgeben; erlassen (*proclaim*); veröffentlichen (*publish*). — *v.n.* herrühren, stammen (*from*).

isthmus ['isθməs], *s.* die Landenge.

it [it], *pron.* es; with —, damit.

Italian [i'tæljən], *adj.* italienisch. — *s.* der Italiener.

italics [i'tæliks], *s. pl.* (*Typ.*) der Kursivdruck, die Kursivschrift.

itch [itʃ], *s.* das Jucken. — *v.n.* jucken; — *to do s.th.*, (*coll.*) darauf brennen, etwas zu tun.

item ['aitəm], *s.* der Posten (*in bill*); der Programmpunkt (*agenda*); die Einzelheit.

itemize ['aitəmaiz], *v.a.* (*Comm.*) aufführen; verzeichnen.

iterate ['itəreit], *v.a.* wiederholen.

itinerant [i'tinərənt], *adj.* wandernd.

its [its], *poss. adj.* sein, ihr; dessen, deren.

itself [it'self], *pron.* selber, sich; of —, von selbst.

ivory ['aivəri], *s.* das Elfenbein. — *adj.* aus Elfenbein, elfenbeinern.

ivy ['aivi], *s.* (*Bot.*) der Efeu.

J

J [dʒei]. das J.

Jabber ['dʒæbə], *v.n.* schnattern.

Jack [dʒæk]. Hans; *Union* —, die britische Flagge; (*Cards*) der Bube.

jack [dʒæk], *s.* (*Motor.*) der Wagenheber. — *v.a.* — *up*, (*Motor.*) hochwinden.

jackal ['dʒækɔ:l], *s.* (*Zool.*) der Schakal.

jackass ['dʒækæs], *s.* (*Zool.*) der Esel.

jackdaw ['dʒækdɔ:], *s.* (*Orn.*) die Dohle.

jacket ['dʒækit], *s.* das Jackett, die Jacke; *dinner* —, der Smoking;

potatoes in their —*s*, Kartoffeln in der Schale, *f. pl.*

jade [dʒeid], *s.* der Nierenstein.

jaded ['dʒeidid], *adj.* abgeplagt, abgehärmt, ermüdet.

jag [dʒæg], *s.* die Kerbe. — *v.a.* kerben, zacken.

jagged ['dʒægid], *adj.* zackig.

jail *see under* **gaol**.

jailer *see under* **gaoler**.

jam (1) [dʒæm], *s.* die Marmelade, Konfitüre.

jam (2) [dʒæm], *s. traffic* —, die Verkehrsstauung; (*coll.*) *in a* —, in der Klemme. — *v.a.* zusammenpressen (*press together*); (*Rad.*) stören.

Jamaican [dʒə'meikən], *adj.* jamaikanisch. — *s.* der Jamaikaner.

jamb [dʒæm], *s.* der Türpfosten.

jangle ['dʒæŋgl], *v.n.* klirren, rasseln. — *s.* das Geklirr, Gerassel.

janitor ['dʒænitə], *s.* der Portier.

January ['dʒænjuəri]. der Januar.

japan [dʒə'pæn], *s.* lakierte Arbeit. — *v.a.* lackieren.

Japanese [dʒæpə'ni:z], *adj.* japanisch. — *s.* der Japaner.

jar (1) [dʒɑ:], *s.* der Topf, das Glas (*preserves*).

jar (2) [dʒɑ:], *v.n.* offenstehen (*door*); mißtönen, knarren.

jargon ['dʒɑ:gən], *s.* der Jargon.

jasmine ['dʒæzmin], *s.* (*Bot.*) der Jasmin.

jasper ['dʒæspə], *s.* der Jaspis.

jaundice ['dʒɔ:ndis], *s.* (*Med.*) die Gelbsucht; (*fig.*) der Neid (*envy*); —*d outlook*, die Verbitterung, Mißstimmung.

jaunt [dʒɔ:nt], *s.* der Ausflug, Spaziergang. — *v.n.* herumstreifen, spazieren.

jaunty ['dʒɔ:nti], *adj.* leicht, munter, lebhaft.

jaw [dʒɔ:], *s.* (*Anat.*) der Kinnbacken; der Rachen (*animals*).

jay [dʒei], *s.* (*Orn.*) der Häher.

jazz [dʒæz], *s.* die Jazzmusik.

jealous ['dʒeləs], *adj.* eifersüchtig.

jealousy ['dʒeləsi], *s.* die Eifersucht.

jeer ['dʒiə], *v.a., v.n.* spotten, verhöhnen.

jejune [dʒi'dʒu:n], *adj.* nüchtern, trocken.

jelly ['dʒeli], *s.* das Gelee.

jellyfish ['dʒelifiʃ], *s.* (*Zool.*) die Qualle.

jeopardize ['dʒepədaiz], *v.a.* gefährden.

jeopardy ['dʒepədi], *s.* die Gefahr.

jerk [dʒə:k], *v.a.* rucken, stoßen (*push*); plötzlich bewegen (*move suddenly*). — *v.n.* zusammenzucken. — *s.* (*Am. coll.*) der Kerl; der Ruck, Stoß.

jersey ['dʒə:zi], *s.* die Wolljacke.

jessamine ['dʒesəmin], *s.* (*Bot.*) der Jasmin.

jest [dʒest], *s.* der Spaß, Scherz. — *v.n.* scherzen.

jester ['dʒestə], *s.* der Spaßmacher, Hofnarr.

jet

jet (1) [dʒet], *s.* der Strahl, Wasserstrahl; (*Aviat.*) die Düse; — *engine*, der Düsenmotor; — *plane*, das Düsenflugzeug. — *v.n.* hervorspringen.

jet (2) [dʒet], *s.* der Gagat; — *black*, pechschwarz.

jetsam [ˈdʒetsəm], *s.* das Strandgut.

jetty [ˈdʒeti], *s.* der Hafendamm, die Landungsbrücke (*landing stage*).

Jew [dʒu:], *s.* der Jude.

jewel [ˈdʒuəl], *s.* das Juwel, der Edelstein.

jewel(le)ry [ˈdʒuəlri], *s.* der Schmuck; die Juwelen, *n. pl.*

Jewish [ˈdʒu:iʃ], *adj.* jüdisch.

Jewry [ˈdʒuəri], *s.* die Judenschaft, das Judentum.

jiffy [ˈdʒifi], *s.* (*coll.*) der Augenblick.

jig (1) [dʒig], *s.* die Gigue (*dance*).

jig (2) [dʒig], *s.* das Werkzeug (*tool*); —*saw*, die Säge; —*saw puzzle*, das Zusammenlegspiel, -setzspiel.

jilt [dʒilt], *v.a.* sitzen lassen.

jingle [dʒiŋgl], *v.a.* klimpern, klimpern lassen (*coins etc.*). — *s.* das Geklimper.

job [dʒɔb], *s.* die Arbeit, Anstellung; die Stellung; das Geschäft; — *in hand*, die Beschäftigung.

jobber [ˈdʒɔbə], *s.* der Makler, Spekulant (*stock exchange*).

jockey [ˈdʒɔki], *s.* der Jockei, Reiter.

jocular [ˈdʒɔkjulə], *adj.* scherzhaft, lustig.

jocund [ˈdʒɔkənd], *adj.* munter, heiter.

jog [dʒɔg], *v.a.* stoßen, antreiben. — *v.n.* gemächlich traben, trotten. — *s.* der Trott.

join [dʒɔin], *v.a.* verbinden, zusammenfügen; (*club etc.*) beitreten (*Dat.*). — *v.n.* (*rivers*) zusammenfließen (mit, *Dat.*); (*Comm.*) sich vereinigen (mit, *Dat.*).

joiner [ˈdʒɔinə], *s.* der Tischler, Schreiner.

joint [dʒɔint], *s.* (*Anat.*) das Gelenk; das Stück Fleisch, der Braten (*meat*); (*sl.*) das Lokal, die Spelunke. — *adj.* vereint, gemeinsam; (*Comm.*) — *stock company*, die Aktiengesellschaft; — *heir*, der Miterbe.

joist [dʒɔist], *s.* (*Carp.*) der Querbalken.

joke [dʒouk], *s.* der Scherz, Witz.

jollity [ˈdʒɔliti], *s.* die Heiterkeit.

jolly [ˈdʒɔli], *adj.* fröhlich, heiter, lustig.

jolt [dʒoult], *v.a.* schütteln, erschüttern (*shake up*). — *s.* der Stoß.

jostle [dʒɔsl], *v.a.* stoßen, drängen. — *v.n.* drängeln.

jot [dʒɔt], *s.* der Punkt, das Iota. — *v.a.* — (*down*), notieren, niederschreiben.

journal [ˈdʒə:nəl], *s.* die Zeitschrift (*periodical*).

journalism [ˈdʒə:nəlizm], *s.* das Zeitungswesen, der Journalistenberuf.

journalist [ˈdʒə:nəlist], *s.* der Journalist.

journey [ˈdʒə:ni], *s.* die Reise.

joust [dʒu:st], *s.* das Turnier.

jovial [ˈdʒouviəl], *adj.* jovial, freundlich; lustig (*gay*).

joy [dʒɔi], *s.* die Freude.

jubilant [ˈdʒu:bilənt], *adj.* frohlockend.

jubilation [dʒu:biˈleiʃən], *s.* der Jubel.

jubilee [ˈdʒu:bili:], *s.* das Jubiläum.

Judaism [dʒuˈdeiizm], *s.* das Judentum.

judge [dʒʌdʒ], *s.* der Richter. — *v.a.* richten, beurteilen, entscheiden.

judgment [ˈdʒʌdʒmənt], *s.* das Urteil; das Urteilsvermögen (*discretion*), die Urteilskraft.

judicial [dʒu:ˈdiʃəl], *adj.* richterlich, gerichtlich.

judicious [dʒu:ˈdiʃəs], *adj.* klug, scharfsinnig.

jug [dʒʌg], *s.* der Krug.

juggle [dʒʌgl], *v.n.* jonglieren, gaukeln.

juggler [ˈdʒʌglə], *s.* der Jongleur.

Jugoslav *see* **Yugoslav.**

jugular [ˈdʒu:g- *or* ˈdʒʌgjulə], *adj.* Kehl-, Hals-, Gurgel-. — *s.* (*vein*) die Halsader.

juice [dʒu:s], *s.* der Saft.

July [dʒuˈlai], *s.* der Juli.

jumble [dʒʌmbl], *v.a.* zusammenmischen, vermischen. — *s.* das gemischte Zeug; — *sale*, der Verkauf, Ausverkauf gebrauchter Dinge, Ramschverkauf.

jump [dʒʌmp], *v.n.* springen. — *s.* der Sprung.

junction [ˈdʒʌŋkʃən], *s.* (*Railw.*) der Knotenpunkt; die Kreuzung.

juncture [ˈdʒʌŋktʃə], *s.* der (kritische) Zeitpunkt.

June [dʒu:n], *s.* der Juni.

jungle [dʒʌŋgl], *s.* der Dschungel.

junior [ˈdʒu:njə], *adj.* jünger; Unter-.

juniper [ˈdʒu:nipə], *s.* (*Bot.*) der Wacholder.

junk [dʒʌŋk], *s.* (*coll.*) das alte Zeug, alte Möbelstücke, *n. pl.*

junket [ˈdʒʌŋkit], *s.* der Schmaus, das Fest; (*Cul.*) dicke Milch mit Sahne. — *v.n.* schmausen, feiern (*celebrate*).

juridical [dʒuəˈridikəl], *adj.* rechtlich, gerichtlich (*in Court*).

jurisdiction [dʒuərizˈdikʃən], *s.* die Gerichtsbarkeit.

juror [ˈdʒuərə], *s.* der, die Geschworene.

jury [ˈdʒuəri], *s.* die Jury, das Geschworenengericht.

just [dʒʌst], *adj.* gerecht; rechtschaffen (*decent*); gehörig (*proper*). — *adv.* soeben, eben; —*as*, eben als, gerade wie.

justice [ˈdʒʌstis], *s.* die Gerechtigkeit; der Richter (*judge*).

justifiable [ˈdʒʌstifaiəbl], *adj.* zu rechtfertigen, berechtigt.

justify [ˈdʒʌstifai], *v.a.* rechtfertigen.

jut [dʒʌt], *v.n.* — (*out*), hervorragen. — *s.* der Vorsprung.

jute [dʒu:t], *s.* die Jute.

juvenile [ˈdʒu:vənail], *adj.* jugendlich, unreif.

juxtaposition [dʒʌkstəpəˈziʃən], *s.* die Nebeneinanderstellung, Gegenüberstellung.

K

K [kei]. das K.

kale [keil], s. (Bot.) der Krauskohl.

kaleidoscope [kə'laidəskoup], s. das Kaleidoskop.

kangaroo [kæŋgə'ru:], s. (Zool.) das Känguruh.

keel [ki:l], s. der Kiel; on an even —, bei ruhiger See; (also fig.) ruhig. — v.n. — over, umkippen.

keen [ki:n], adj. eifrig (intent); scharfsinnig (perspicacious); scharf (blade).

keenness ['ki:nnis], s. der Eifer; Scharfsinn; die Schärfe (blade).

keep [ki:p], v.a. irr. halten (hold); behalten (retain); führen (a shop); hüten (gate, dog etc.). — v.n. — doing, in etwas fortfahren, — going, weitergehen; — away, sich fernhalten; — in, indoors, zu Hause bleiben; — off, abhalten; sich fernhalten; — out, draußen bleiben; — up, aufrechterhalten. — s. das Burgverlies; der Unterhalt.

keeper ['ki:pə], s. der Hüter, Wärter; Museumsbeamte.

keeping ['ki:piŋ], s. die Verwahrung; in safe —, in guten Händen, in guter Obhut.

keepsake ['ki:pseik], s. das Andenken.

keg [keg], s. das Fäßchen.

ken [ken], s. die Kenntnis; in my —, meines Wissens. — v.a. (Scottish) kennen.

kennel [kenl], s. die Hundehütte.

kerb(stone) ['kə:b(stoun)], s. der Prellstein.

kerchief ['kə:tʃif], s. das Kopftuch, Halstuch.

kernel [kə:nl], s. der Kern.

kettle [ketl], s. der Kessel; — drum, die Kesselpauke.

key [ki:], s. der Schlüssel; (Mus.) die Tonart; die Taste (on piano etc.); — man, eine wichtige Person, Person in einer Schlüsselstellung. — v.a. — (in), einfügen, befestigen.

keyboard ['ki:bɔ:d], s. die Klaviatur; Tastatur (typewriter); — instrument, das Tasteninstrument.

keyhole ['ki:houl], s. das Schlüsselloch.

keystone ['ki:stoun], s. der Schlußstein.

kick [kik], v.a., v.n. mit dem Fuße stoßen or treten; — against s.th., sich wehren. — s. der Fußstoß, Tritt; (Footb.) — off, der Ankick; free —, der Freistoß; penalty —, der Strafstoß, der Elfmeterstoß.

kid (1) [kid], s. (Zool.) das Geißlein, Zicklein; with — gloves, mit Glacéhandschuhen; (coll.) das Kind.

kid (2) [kid], v.a. (Am. coll.) zum Narren haben, aufziehen (tease).

kidnap ['kidnæp], v.a. entführen.

kidney ['kidni], s. (Anat.) die Niere; — bean, die französische Bohne.

kill [kil], v.a. töten; schlachten (animal).

kiln [kiln], s. der Darrofen; der Ziegelofen (tiles, bricks).

kilt [kilt], s. der Schottenrock.

kin [kin], s. die Verwandtschaft; kith and —, die Verwandten, m. pl.

kind [kaind], s. die Art, Gattung, Art und Weise. — adj. freundlich, gütig, liebenswürdig.

kindle [kindl], v.a. anzünden, anfachen.

kindliness, **kindness** ['kaindlinis, 'kaindnis], s. die Güte, Freundlichkeit.

kindred ['kindrid], adj. verwandt.

king [kiŋ], s. der König.

kingdom ['kiŋdəm], s. das Königreich.

kink [kiŋk], s. der Knoten; (coll.) der Vogel, die Grille (obsession etc.).

kinship ['kinʃip], s. die Sippe, Verwandtschaft.

kipper ['kipə], s. der geräucherte Hering.

kiss [kis], v.a. küssen. — s. der Kuß.

kit [kit], s. (Mil.) die Ausrüstung.

kitbag ['kitbæg], s. der Tornister.

kitchen ['kitʃən], s. die Küche; — garden, der Gemüsegarten.

kite [kait], s. der Drache, Papierdrache; fly a —, einen Drachen steigen lassen; (Orn.) der Gabelweih, der (rote) Milan; (sl.) der Schwindler.

kith [kiθ], s. now only in — and kin, die Verwandten, m. pl.

kitten [kitn], s. das Kätzchen.

knack [næk], s. der Kniff, Kunstgriff.

knacker ['nækə], s. der Abdecker (horse).

knapsack ['næpsæk], s. der Rucksack, Tornister.

knave [neiv], s. der Kerl, Schurke; Bube (cards).

knead [ni:d], v.a. kneten.

knee [ni:], s. (Anat.) das Knie.

kneel [ni:l], v.n. irr. knien, niederknien.

knell [nel], s. die Totenglocke.

knick-knack ['niknæk], s. die Nippsache.

knife [naif], s. das Messer. — v.a. erstechen.

knight [nait], s. der Ritter; der Springer (chess).

knit [nit], v.a., v.n. reg. & irr. stricken; knitting needle, die Stricknadel.

knob [nɔb], s. der (Tür)knopf, die Türklinke; der Knorren (wood).

knock [nɔk], v.n. klopfen, schlagen. — s. der Schlag, Stoß.

knoll [noul], s. der kleine Hügel.

knot [nɔt], s. der Knoten; die Schwierigkeit (difficulty).

know [nou], v.a. irr. kennen (be acquainted with); wissen (possess knowledge (of)).

knowing ['nouiŋ], adj. wissend.

knowledge ['nɔlidʒ], s. die Kenntnis (acquaintance with); das Wissen (by

study, information etc.); die Kenntnisse (*of language etc.*).
knuckle [nʌkl], *s.* (*Anat.*) der Knöchel.
— *v.n.* — *under*, sich fügen.
Kremlin [ˈkremlin], *s.* der Kreml.
kudos [ˈkjuːdɔs], *s.* der Ruhm, das
Ansehen.

L

L [el], das L.
label [ˈleibl], *s.* die Etikette, das Schildchen.
labial [ˈleibiəl], *adj.* (*Phonet.*) labial,
Lippen-. — *s.* (*Phonet.*) der Lippenlaut.
laboratory [ləˈbɔrətəri, (*Am.*) ˈlæbərə-
təri], *s.* das Laboratorium, (*coll.*) das
Labor.
laborious [ləˈbɔːriəs], *adj.* mühsam.
labour [ˈleibə], *s.* die Arbeit, Mühe;
Labour Party, die Arbeiterpartei;
(*Med.*) die Geburtswehen, *f. pl.* —
v.n. sich abmühen, leiden; sich
anstrengen.
labourer [ˈleibərə], *s.* der Arbeiter,
Taglöhner.
lace [leis], *s.* die Spitze, Tresse. — *v.a.*
verbrämen (*trim with lace*); zu-
schnüren (*shoe*); stärken (*coffee with
rum etc.*).
lacerate [ˈlæsəreit], *v.a.* zerreißen.
lack [læk], *v.a.* ermangeln (*Genit.*). —
v.n. fehlen (an, *Dat.*). — *s.* der Mangel,
das Fehlen.
lackadaisical [lækəˈdeizikəl], *adj.*
schlaff, (*coll.*) schlapp, unbekümmert.
lackey [ˈlæki], *s.* der Lakai, Diener,
Bediente.
laconic [ləˈkɔnik], *adj.* lakonisch.
lacquer [ˈlækə], *s.* der Lack. — *v.a.*
lackieren.
lad [læd], *s.* der Bursche, Junge.
ladder [ˈlædə], *s.* die Leiter.
lading [ˈleidiŋ], *s.* (*Comm.*) das Laden;
die Fracht; *bill of* —, der Frachtbrief.
ladle [ˈleidl], *s.* der Schöpflöffel, Suppen-
löffel; die Kelle. — *v.a.* aus-
schöpfen, austeilen.
lady [ˈleidi], *s.* die Dame; — *-in-waiting*,
die Hofdame.
ladybird [ˈleidibəːd], *s.* (*Ent.*) der
Marienkäfer.
ladyship [ˈleidiʃip], *s.* (*Title*) gnädige
Frau.
lag [læg], *v.n.* zurückbleiben. — *v.a.*
verkleiden, isolieren (*tank*).
laggard [ˈlægəd], *s.* der Zauderer. —
adj. zögernd, zaudernd.
lagoon [ləˈguːn], *s.* die Lagune.
lair [lɛə], *s.* das Lager (*of animal*).
laird [lɛəd], *s.* der schottische Guts-
herr.

laity [ˈleiiti], *s.* die Laien, *m. pl.*
lake [leik], *s.* der See.
lamb [læm], *s.* (*Zool.*) das Lamm. —
v.n. lammen.
lambent [ˈlæmbənt], *adj.* brennend,
lodernd, strahlend.
lame [leim], *adj.* lahm. — *v.a.* lähmen.
lament [ləˈment], *v.a.*, *v.n.* betrauern,
beweinen. — *s.* das Klagelied, die
Wehklage.
lamp [læmp], *s.* die Lampe; — *-post*,
der Laternenpfahl.
lampoon [læmˈpuːn], *v.a.* schmähen,
lächerlich machen. — *s.* die Schmähschrift.
lamprey [ˈlæmpri], *s.* (*Zool.*) das
Neunauge.
lance [lɑːns], *s.* (*Mil.*) die Lanze. —
v.a. durchbohren; (*Med.*) lancieren.
lancer [ˈlɑːnsə], *s.* (*Mil.*) der Ulan.
lancet [ˈlɑːnsit], *s.* (*Med.*) die Lanzette.
land [lænd], *s.* das Land; das Grundstück (*plot*); — *tax*, die Grundsteuer.
— *v.a.* ans Land bringen, fangen
(*fish*). — *v.n.* landen.
landlord [ˈlændlɔːd], *s.* der Eigentümer,
der Hausherr; Wirt (*pub*).
landmark [ˈlændmɑːk], *s.* der Grenz-
stein, das Wahrzeichen.
landscape [ˈlændskeip], *s.* die Landschaft.
landslide, landslip [ˈlændslaid, ˈlænd-
slip], *s.* der Erdrutsch.
lane [lein], *s.* der Heckenweg, Pfad; die
Gasse; (*Motor.*) die Fahrbahn.
language [ˈlæŋgwidʒ], *s.* die Sprache.
languid [ˈlæŋgwid], *adj.* flau, matt.
languor [ˈlæŋgə], *s.* die Mattigkeit,
Flauheit.
lank [læŋk], *adj.* mager, schlank.
lantern [ˈlæntən], *s.* die Laterne.
Laotian [ˈlauʃən], *adj.* laotisch. — *s.* der
Laote.
lap (1) [læp], *s.* der Schoß.
lap (2) [læp], *s.* das Plätschern (*of
waves*). — *v.a.* auflecken (*lick up*). —
v.n. plätschern.
lapel [ləˈpel], *s.* der Aufschlag (*of
jacket*).
lapidary [ˈlæpidəri], *adj.* lapidarisch;
wuchtig.
lapse [læps], *v.n.* gleiten, fallen; verlaufen (*time*). — *s.* der Verlauf (*time*);
der Fehler (*mistake*); das Verfallen
(*into laziness etc.*).
lapwing [ˈlæpwiŋ], *s.* (*Orn.*) der Kiebitz.
larceny [ˈlɑːsəni], *s.* der Diebstahl.
larch [lɑːtʃ], *s.* (*Bot.*) die Lärche.
lard [lɑːd], *s.* das Schweinefett, Schweineschmalz.
larder [ˈlɑːdə], *s.* die Speisekammer.
large [lɑːdʒ], *adj.* groß; weit; dick, stark.
largesse [lɑːˈdʒes], *s.* die Freigebigkeit
(*generosity*); die Schenkung (*donation*).
lark (1) [lɑːk], *s.* (*Orn.*) die Lerche.
lark (2) [lɑːk], *s.* (*coll.*) der Scherz.
— *v.n.* scherzen.
larkspur [ˈlɑːkspəː], *s.* (*Bot.*) der
Rittersporn.
larva [ˈlɑːvə], *s.* (*Zool.*) die Larve.

larynx ['læriŋks], s. (*Anat.*) der Kehlkopf.

lascivious [lə'siviəs], adj. wollüstig.

lash [læʃ], s. die Wimper (*eye*); die Peitschenschnur (*whip*), der Peitschenhieb (*stroke of whip*). — v.a. peitschen.

lass [læs], s. (*coll.*) das Mädchen.

lassitude ['læsitju:d], s. die Mattigkeit.

lasso [lə'su: *or* 'læsou], s. das Lasso. — v.a. mit einem Lasso fangen.

last (1) [lɑ:st], adj. letzt, vorig, äußerst; *at long* —, endlich.

last (2) [lɑ:st], s. der Leisten (*shoemaking*).

last (3) [lɑ:st], v.n. dauern, anhalten; hinreichen (*be sufficient*).

lastly ['lɑ:stli], adv. zuletzt.

latch [lætʃ], v.a. verschließen.

latchkey ['lætʃki:], s. der Hausschlüssel.

late [leit], adj. spät; verspätet; verstorben, selig (*deceased*); neulich (*recent*); *the train is* —, der Zug hat Verspätung; *of late*, jüngst.

latent ['leitənt], adj. (*Med.*) latent; verborgen.

lateral ['lætərəl], adj. seitlich, Seiten-.

lath [lɑ:θ], s. die Latte.

lathe [leið], s. die Drehbank.

lather ['læðə], s. der Seifenschaum. — v.n., v.a. (sich) einseifen.

Latin ['lætin], adj. lateinisch. — s. das Latein, die lateinische Sprache.

latitude ['lætitju:d], s. die geographische Breite; die Weite (*width*); (*fig.*) der Spielraum (*scope*).

latter ['lætə], adj. letzter; später (*later*). — s. der Letztere.

latterly ['lætəli], adv. neulich, neuerdings.

lattice ['lætis], s. das Gitter. — v.a. vergittern.

Latvian ['lætviən], adj. lettisch. — s. der Lette.

laud [lɔ:d], v.a. loben, preisen.

laudable ['lɔ:dəbl], adj. lobenswert.

laudatory ['lɔ:dətəri], adj. belobend.

laugh [lɑ:f], v.n. lachen; *—ing stock*, der Gegenstand des Gelächters.

laughter ['lɑ:ftə], s. das Lachen, Gelächter.

launch [lɔ:ntʃ], s. die Barkasse. — v.a. vom Stapel lassen.

launching ['lɔ:ntʃiŋ], s. der Stapellauf.

laundress ['lɔ:ndris], s. die Wäscherin.

laundry ['lɔ:ndri], s. die Wäsche (*clothes*); Wäscherei (*place*).

laureate ['lɔ:riit], s. der Hofdichter.

laurel ['lɔrəl], s. (*Bot.*) der Lorbeer.

lavatory ['lævətri], s. das W.C., der Abort, Waschraum; die Toilette; *public* —, die Bedürfnisanstalt.

lavender ['lævəndə], s. (*Bot.*) der Lavendel.

lavish ['læviʃ], adj. freigebig, verschwenderisch. — v.a. vergeuden.

lavishness ['læviʃnis], s. die Freigebigkeit, Verschwendung.

law [lɔ:], s. das Gesetz (*statute*); das Recht (*justice*); die Jura, Jurisprudenz (*subject of study*).

lawful ['lɔ:ful], adj. gesetzlich, gesetzmäßig.

lawless ['lɔ:lis], adj. gesetzlos; unrechtmäßig (*illegal*).

lawn (1) [lɔ:n], s. der Rasen.

lawn (2) [lɔ:n], s. der Batist.

lawsuit ['lɔ:su:t], s. der Prozeß.

lawyer ['lɔ:jə], s. der Advokat, Rechtsanwalt, Jurist.

lax [læks], adj. locker, lax.

laxative ['læksətiv], s. das Abführmittel.

laxity ['læksiti], s. die Schlaffheit, Lockerheit (*of rope etc.*).

lay (1) [lei], v.a. irr. legen; setzen (*put*); stellen (*place*); bannen (*ghost*); — *up*, sammeln. — v.n. legen (*eggs*); wetten (*wager*); — *about one*, um sich schlagen.

lay (2) [lei], s. (*Poet.*) das Lied.

lay (3) [lei], adj. Laien-.

layer ['leiə], s. die Schicht; — *cake*, die Cremetorte.

layman ['leimən], s. der Laie.

laziness ['leizinis], s. die Faulheit.

lazy ['leizi], adj. faul, träge.

lea [li:], s. (*Poet.*) die Aue.

lead (1) [li:d], v.a., v.n. irr. führen, leiten; ausspielen (*cards*). — s. die Führung; (*Elec.*) Leitung.

lead (2) [led], s. das Blei; Bleilot (*plumbline*).

leader ['li:də], s. der Führer; (*Mus.*) der Konzertmeister; der Leitartikel (*leading article*).

leaf [li:f], s. (*Bot.*) das Blatt; (*Build.*) der Türflügel. — v.a. (*coll.*) — *through*, durchblättern.

leafy ['li:fi], adj. belaubt.

league (1) [li:g], s. drei englische Meilen, *f.pl.*

league (2) [li:g], s. das Bündnis (*pact*); *be in* —, verbündet sein; *League of Nations*, der Völkerbund.

leak [li:k], v.n. lecken, ein Loch haben. — s. das Loch; (*Naut.*) das Leck.

leaky ['li:ki], adj. leck.

lean (1) [li:n], v.n. irr.(sich)lehnen (an, *Acc.*), stützen (auf, *Acc.*).

lean (2) [li:n], adj. mager, hager.

leap [li:p], v.n. irr. springen. — s. der Sprung; — *year*, das Schaltjahr.

learn [lə:n], v.a. irr. lernen, erfahren.

learned ['lə:nid], adj. gelehrt.

learning ['lə:niŋ], s. die Gelehrsamkeit.

lease [li:s], s. die Pacht, der Mietvertrag (*of house*). — v.a. (ver)pachten.

leasehold ['li:should], s. die Pachtung.

leash [li:ʃ], v.a. koppeln, anbinden. — s. die Koppel.

least [li:st], adj. wenigst, geringst, mindest, kleinst. — s. *at* (*the*) —, wenigstens, mindestens.

leather ['leðə], s. das Leder. — adj. Leder-, ledern.

leave [li:v], v.a. irr. verlassen (*quit*); lassen (*let*); hinterlassen (*bequeath*). — v.n. Abschied nehmen, abreisen. — s. der Urlaub; der Abschied (*farewell*); die Erlaubnis (*permission*).

leaven [levn], *s.* der Sauerteig. — *v.a.* säuern.

Lebanese [lebə'ni:z], *adj.* libanesisch. — *s.* der Libanese.

lecture ['lektʃə], *s.* die Vorlesung; der Vortrag.

lecturer ['lektʃərə], *s.* (*Univ.*) der Dozent; der Vortragende (*speaker*).

ledge [ledʒ], *s.* der Sims (*window*).

ledger ['ledʒə], *s.* (*Comm.*) das Hauptbuch.

lee [li:], *s.* die Leeseite (*shelter*).

leech [li:tʃ], *s.* (*Zool.*) der Blutegel.

leek [li:k], *s.* (*Bot.*) der Lauch.

leer ['liə], *s.* das Starren; der Seitenblick. — *v.n.* schielen (*at*, auf, nach); starren.

lees [li:z], *s. pl.* der Bodensatz, die Hefe.

left [left], *adj.* link. — *adv.* inks. — *s.* die linke Seite.

leg [leg], *s.* (*Anat.*) das Bein; der Schaft.

legacy ['legəsi], *s.* das Vermächtnis, das Erbe, Erbgut.

legal ['li:gəl], *adj.* gesetzlich.

legality [li'gæliti], *s.* die Gesetzlichkeit.

legatee [legə'ti:], *s.* (*Law*) der Erbe, die Erbin.

legation [li'geiʃən], *s.* die Gesandtschaft.

legend ['ledʒənd], *s.* die Legende, Sage; die Inschrift (*inscription*).

legendary ['ledʒəndəri], *adj.* legendär, sagenhaft.

leggings ['legiŋz], *s. pl.* die Gamaschen.

legible ['ledʒibl], *adj.* leserlich.

legislation [ledʒis'leiʃən], *s.* die Gesetzgebung.

legislative ['ledʒislətiv], *adj.* gesetzgebend.

legislator ['ledʒisleitə], *s.* der Gesetzgeber.

legitimacy [li'dʒitiməsi], *s.* die Gesetzmäßigkeit; (*Law*) die eheliche Geburt (*of birth*).

legitimate [li'dʒitimit], *adj.* gesetzmäßig; (*Law*) ehelich (*child*). — [-meit], *v.a.* für gesetzlich erklären.

legitimize [li'dʒitimaiz], *v.a.* legitimieren.

leguminous [li'gju:minəs], *adj.* Hülsen-; hülsentragend.

leisure ['leʒə], *s.* die Freizeit, Muße.

leisurely ['leʒəli], *adj., adv.* gelassen, gemächlich.

lemon ['lemən], *s.* (*Bot.*) die Zitrone.

lemonade [lemən'eid], *s.* die Limonade.

lend [lend], *v.a. irr.* leihen; —*ing library*, die Leihbibliothek.

length [leŋθ], *s.* die Länge (*extent*); die Dauer (*duration*); *at* —, ausführlich.

lengthen ['leŋθən], *v.a., v.n.* (sich) verlängern.

lengthy ['leŋθi], *adj.* langwierig, lang.

lenient ['li:niənt], *adj.* nachsichtig, milde.

lens [lenz], *s.* die Linse (*optics*); das Objektiv.

Lent [lent], *s.* die Fastenzeit.

lentil ['lentil], *s.* (*Bot.*) die Linse.

leprosy ['leprəsi], *s.* der Aussatz, die Leprakrankheit.

leprous ['leprəs], *adj.* aussätzig.

lesion ['li:ʒən], *s.* die Verletzung.

less [les], *comp. adj., adv.* weniger, kleiner.

lessee [le'si:], *s.* der Pächter, Mieter.

lessen [lesn], *v.a., v.n.* (sich) verringern, vermindern.

lesser ['lesə], *comp. adj.* geringer; kleiner.

lesson [lesn], *s.* die Lehrstunde, Lektion; (*pl.*) der Unterricht; (*Rel.*) der Bibeltext.

lessor ['lesə], *s.* der Eigentümer, Vermieter.

lest [lest], *conj.* damit nicht; aus Furcht, daß.

let [let], *v.a. irr.* lassen; zulassen; vermieten; (*room*), — *down*, blamieren, enttäuschen; *off*, abschießen. — *s. without* — *or hindrance*, ohne Hinderung.

lethal ['li:θəl], *adj.* tödlich.

letter ['letə], *s.* der Brief; der Buchstabe (*character*); — *box*, der Briefkasten; (*pl.*) die Literatur.

letterpress ['letəpres], *s.* die Kopierpresse.

lettuce ['letis], *s.* (*Bot.*) der Salat.

level [levl], *adj.* eben, gleich. — *s.* die Ebene; das Niveau. — *v.a.* ebnen, ausgleichen; (*Build.*) planieren.

lever ['li:və], *s.* der Hebel.

levity ['leviti], *s.* der Leichtsinn.

levy ['levi], *v.a.* erheben (*tax*); auferlegen (*penalty*). — *s.* die Steuer.

lewd [lju:d *or* lu:d], *adj.* liederlich, gemein, unzüchtig.

liability [laiə'biliti], *s.* die Verantwortlichkeit; *limited* —, beschränkte Haftung; die Steuerpflichtigkeit (*to tax*), Zollpflichtigkeit (*to duty*).

liable ['laiəbl], *adj.* haftbar, zahlungspflichtig.

liar ['laiə], *s.* der Lügner.

libel ['laibəl], *s.* die Verleumdung. — *v.a.* verleumden, schmähen.

libellous ['laibələs], *adj.* verleumderisch.

liberal ['libərəl], *adj.* (*Pol.*) liberal; freigebig (*generous*); — *arts*, Geisteswissenschaften, *f. pl.*

liberate ['libəreit], *v.a.* befreien, freisetzen; (*Law*) in Freiheit setzen.

Liberian [lai'biəriən], *adj.* liberisch. — *s.* der Liberier.

libertine ['libəti:n], *s.* der Wüstling.

liberty ['libəti], *s.* die Freiheit; die Erlaubnis (*permission*).

librarian [lai'breəriən], *s.* der Bibliothekar, die Bibliothekarin.

library ['laibrəri], *s.* die Bibliothek.

Libyan ['libjən], *adj.* libysch. — *s.* der Libyer.

licence ['laisəns], *s.* die Genehmigung, Erlaubnis (*permit*); *driving* —, der Führerschein; die Zügellosigkeit (*licentiousness*).

license ['laisəns], *v.a.* genehmigen, bewilligen; *licensing laws*, Ausschanksgesetze, *n. pl.* (*for alcohol*).

licentiate [lai'senʃiit], s. der Lizenziat (degree).

licentious [lai'senʃəs], adj. ausschweifend, liederlich, locker (in morals).

lichen ['laikən, 'litʃən], s. (Bot.) die Flechte.

lichgate ['litʃgeit], s. das Friedhofstor.

lick [lik], v.a. lecken; (Am.) prügeln, verhauen.

lid [lid], s. das Augenlid; der Deckel.

lie [lai], (1) v.n. lügen. — s. die Lüge (untruth).

lie [lai], (2) v.n. irr. liegen; — down, sich legen, hinlegen; sich fügen (fig.).

lieu [lju:], s. in —, an Stelle, anstatt (Genit.).

lieutenant [lef'tenənt], s. der Leutnant.

life [laif], s. das Leben.

lifebelt ['laifbelt], s. der Rettungsgürtel.

lifeboat ['laifbout], s. das Rettungsboot.

lifetime ['laiftaim], s. die Lebenszeit, Zeit seines Lebens.

lift [lift], s. der Aufzug, Fahrstuhl; (coll.) give a — to, mitnehmen (im Auto). — v.a. heben; aufheben (abolish); (coll.) klauen, stehlen.

ligament ['ligəmənt], s. das Band; (Anat.) die Flechse, die Sehne.

ligature ['ligətʃə], s. (Typ.) die Ligatur; die Verbindung.

light [lait], adj. hell, licht; blond (hair); leicht (weight). — s. das Licht; give a —, ein Streichholz geben, Feuer geben. — v.a. irr. beleuchten (room); anzünden (fire). — v.n. irr. — (up), hell werden, leuchten; (fig.) aufleuchten.

lighten [laitn], v.a. erhellen (brighten); erleichtern (ease).

lighter ['laitə], s. das Feuerzeug (smoker's); (Naut.) das Lichterschiff.

lighthouse ['laithaus], s. der Leuchtturm.

lightning ['laitniŋ], s. der Blitz; — conductor, der Blitzableiter; — speed, die Blitzesschnelle.

ligneous ['ligniəs], adj. holzig.

lignite ['lignait], s. die Braunkohle.

like (1) [laik], v.a. gern haben; I — to sing, ich singe gern. — v.n. belieben, wollen; as you —, wie Sie wollen. — s. his —s and dislikes, seine Wünsche und Abneigungen.

like (2) [laik], adj. gleich, ähnlich. — s. his —, seinesgleichen. — prep. gleich, wie; just — him! das sieht ihm ähnlich! feel —, möchte gern; what is it —? wie sieht es aus?

likelihood ['laiklihud], s. die Möglichkeit; Wahrscheinlichkeit (probability).

likely ['laikli], adj. möglich; wahrscheinlich (probable).

liken ['laikən], v.a. vergleichen.

likeness ['laiknis], s. die Ähnlichkeit.

likewise ['laikwaiz], adv. ebenso, gleichfalls, auch.

liking ['laikiŋ], s. die Vorliebe (for, für, Acc.); Neigung (for, zu, Dat.); to my

—, nach meinem Geschmack or Wunsch.

lilac ['lailək], s. (Bot.) der Flieder.

lilt [lilt], v.a., v.n. trällern, summen. — s. die Melodie, Weise.

lily ['lili], (Bot.) s. die Lilie; — of the valley, das Maiglöckchen.

limb [lim], s. das Glied.

limber ['limbə], adj. geschmeidig.

lime (1) [laim], s. der Leim, Kalk (chalk).

lime (2) [laim], s. (Bot.) die Linde (tree); die Limone (fruit); — juice, der Limonensaft.

limestone ['laimstoun], s. der Kalkstein.

limit ['limit], s. die Grenze, das Ende. — v.a. begrenzen, beschränken.

limitation [limi'teiʃən], s. die Begrenzung.

limn [lim], v.a. (Art.) zeichnen, malen.

limp [limp], v.n. hinken. — adj. müde, schlaff.

limpid ['limpid], adj. klar, durchsichtig.

linden ['lindən], s. (Bot.) die Linde.

line (1) [lain], s. die Linie, Eisenbahnlinie (Railw.); die Zeile; der Strich; (Mil.) die Reihe; — of business, die Geschäftsbranche; (Genealogy) die Abstammung; take a strong —, entschlossen auftreten.

line (2) [lain], v.a. füttern (a garment).

lineage ['liniidʒ], s. die Abstammung.

lineament ['liniəmənt], s. der Gesichtszug.

linear ['liniə], adj. linear, geradlinig.

linen ['linin], s. die Leinwand; bed —, die Laken, Bettwäsche. — adj. leinen.

liner ['lainə], s. (Naut.) das Passagierschiff.

linger ['liŋgə], v.n. zögern; verweilen.

lingerie ['lēʒəri:], s. die Damenunterwäsche.

linguist ['liŋgwist], s. der Sprachkundige, Philologe, Linguist.

liniment ['linimənt], s. (Med.) die Salbe.

lining ['lainiŋ], s. das Futter (of garment).

link [liŋk], s. das Glied (in chain); die Verbindung (connexion). — v.a. verbinden, verknüpfen.

linnet ['linit], s. (Orn.) der Hänfling.

linseed ['linsi:d], s. der Leinsamen; — oil, das Leinöl.

lint [lint], s. die Scharpie, das Verbandzeug.

lion ['laiən], s. (Zool.) der Löwe.

lioness ['laiənes], s. (Zool.) die Löwin.

lip [lip], s. (Anat., Bot.) die Lippe (mouth); der Rand (of jug).

lipstick ['lipstik], s. der Lippenstift.

liquefy ['likwifai], v.a., v.n. flüssig machen or werden.

liqueur [li'kjuə], s. der Likör.

liquid ['likwid], adj. flüssig. — s. die Flüssigkeit.

liquidate ['likwdeit], v.a. liquidieren; (Comm.) flüssig machen (assets); bezahlen (pay off).

liquor

liquor ['likə], s. der Alkohol.
liquorice ['likəris], s. die Lakritze.
lisp [lisp], v.n. lispeln. — s. der Sprachfehler, das Anstoßen, Lispeln.
list [list], s. die Liste, das Verzeichnis; (*Naut.*) die Schlagseite.
listen [lisn], v.n. horchen, zuhören.
listless ['listlis], adj. teilnahmslos.
litany ['litəni], s. (*Eccl.*) die Litanei.
literal ['litərəl], adj. buchstäblich.
literary ['litərəri], adj. literarisch, Literatur-.
literature ['litrətʃə], s. die Literatur.
lithe [laið], adj. geschmeidig.
Lithuanian [liθju'einiən], adj. litauisch. — s. der Litauer.
litigate ['litigeit], v.n. einen Prozeß anstrengen, litigieren, prozessieren.
litigation [liti'geiʃən], s. die Litigation, der Prozeß.
litter ['litə], s. (*Zool.*) die Jungen, n. pl.; die Brut; die Sänfte (*carriage*); der Abfall, die Abfälle (*waste paper etc.*). — v.n. (*Zool.*) Junge haben, werfen. — v.a. Abfälle wegwerfen, unsauber machen.
little [litl], adj. klein (*size, value*); gering (*value*); — by —, nach und nach.
liturgy ['litədʒi], s. (*Eccl.*) die Liturgie.
live [liv], v.n. leben; wohnen (*dwell*).
livelihood ['laivlihud], s. der Lebensunterhalt.
liveliness ['laivlinis], s. die Lebhaftigkeit.
lively ['laivli], adj. lebhaft.
liven [laivn], v.a. — up, beleben.
liver ['livə], s. (*Anat.*) die Leber.
livery ['livəri], s. die Livree (*uniform*); — company, die Zunftgenossenschaft.
livid ['livid], adj. bleich, blaß.
living ['liviŋ], s. das Auskommen, der Unterhalt; die Lebensweise; (*Eccl.*) die Pfründe, Pfarrstelle.
lizard ['lizəd], s. (*Zool.*) die Eidechse.
lo! [lou], excl. (*obs.*) sieh, da! siehe!
load [loud], s. die Last, Bürde. — v.a. beladen, belasten. — v.n. laden, aufladen.
loadstone see **lodestone**.
loaf [louf], s. der Laib (*bread*); sugar —, der Zuckerhut. — v.n. herumlungern, nichts tun.
loafer ['loufə], s. der Faulenzer, Drückeberger.
loam [loum], s. der Lehm.
loan [loun], s. die Anleihe. — v.a. leihen.
loath [louθ], adj. unwillig, abgeneigt.
loathe [louð], v.a. verabscheuen, hassen.
loathing ['louðiŋ], s. der Abscheu, Ekel.
loathsome ['louθsəm], adj. abscheulich, ekelhaft.
lobby ['lɔbi], s. die Vorhalle. — v.a. (*Pol.*) einen beeinflußen.
lobe [loub], s. das Läppchen.
lobster ['lɔbstə], s. (*Zool.*) der Hummer.
local ['loukəl], adj. lokal, örtlich. — s. (*coll.*) das Stammgasthaus (*pub*).

locality [lo'kæliti], s. die Lokalität, die Örtlichkeit, der Ort.
localize ['loukəlaiz], v.a. lokalisieren, auf einen Ort beschränken.
locate [lo'keit], v.a. finden (*find*); ausfindig machen.
location [lo'keiʃən], s. die Plazierung (*position*); die Lage; der Standort; on —, auf dem Gelände, auf Außenaufnahme (*film*).
loch [lɔx], s. (*Scot.*) der See.
lock [lɔk], s. das Schloß (*on door*); die Schleuse (*on waterway*); die Locke (*hair*). — v.a. schließen, abschließen (*door*); hemmen (*wheel*). — v.n. sich schließen; — in, ineinandergreifen (*cogs*).
locker ['lɔkə], s. der Schließschrank, das Schließfach.
locket ['lɔkit], s. das Medaillon.
locksmith ['lɔksmiθ], s. der Schlosser.
lock-up ['lɔkʌp], s. der Arrest, die Haftzelle; (*coll.*) die Garage.
locust ['loukəst], s. (*Ent.*) die Heuschrecke.
lodestone ['loudstoun], s. der Magnetstein, Magnet.
lodge [lɔdʒ], v.n. wohnen; logieren (*temporary*). — v.a. beherbergen (*accommodate*); einbringen (*a complaint, protest*). — s. das Haus, das Häuschen; die Loge (*Freemasons*).
lodger ['lɔdʒə], s. der (Unter)mieter.
lodgings ['lɔdʒiŋz], s. pl. das möblierte Zimmer, die Wohnung.
loft [lɔft], s. der Boden, Dachboden.
lofty ['lɔfti], adj. hoch; erhaben; stolz (*proud*).
log [lɔg], s. der Holzklotz, das Scheit; —cabin, —house, das Blockhaus; (*Naut.*) das Log, das Schiffstagebuch. — v.a. (*Naut.*) eintragen.
loggerheads ['lɔgəhedz], s. pl. at —, in Widerspruch, Widerstreit, im Konflikt.
logic ['lɔdʒik], s. die Logik.
logical ['lɔdʒikəl], adj. logisch.
loin [lɔin], s. (*Anat.*) die Lende.
loincloth ['lɔinklɔθ], s. der Lendenschurz.
loiter ['lɔitə], v.n. herumlungern; bummeln.
loiterer ['lɔitərə], s. der Lungerer, Faulenzer.
loitering ['lɔitəriŋ], s. das Herumlungern, Herumstehen, Faulenzen.
loll [lɔl], v.n. herumlungern.
lollipop ['lɔlipɔp], s. das Zuckerwerk, die Süßigkeit; (*fig.*) der Leckerbissen.
loneliness ['lounlinis], s. die Einsamkeit.
lonely ['lounli], (*Am.*) **lonesome** ['lounli, 'lounsəm], adj. einsam.
long [lɔŋ], adj. lang. — adv. — ago, vor langer Zeit; before —, in kurzer Zeit. — v.n. sich sehnen (*for*, nach, *Dat.*).
longitude ['lɔndʒitju:d], s. die Länge; (*Geog.*) der Längengrad.

432

longitudinal [lɔndʒi'tju:dinəl], *adj.* in der geographischen Länge, Längen-.

look [luk], *v.n.* blicken, sehen, schauen (*at*, auf, *Acc.*); — *to it*, dafür sorgen; — *out for*, Ausschau halten nach (*Dat.*); — *out!* paß auf! — *after s.o.*, sich um jemanden kümmern; — *into*, prüfen, untersuchen; — *forward to*, sich freuen (auf, *Acc.*); — *over*, durchsehen. — *s.* der Blick (*glance*); das Aussehen (*appearance*).

looking-glass ['lukiŋglɑ:s], *s.* der Spiegel.

look-out ['lukaut], *s.* der Ausblick; die Ausschau.

loom [lu:m], *s.* der Webstuhl. — *v.n.* in der Ferne auftauchen (*emerge*).

loon [lu:n], *s.* (*Orn.*) der Eisvogel, Eistaucher; (*coll.*) der Narr.

loony ['lu:ni], *adj.* (*coll.*) wahnsinnig, närrisch.

loop [lu:p], *s.* die Schlinge, das Schlingband; (*Railw.*) — *line*, die Schleife.

loophole ['lu:phoul], *s.* der Ausweg, die Hintertür.

loose [lu:s], *adj.* locker, lose; liederlich (*morals*). — *v.a.* lösen.

loosen [lu:sn], *v.a.* auflockern, locker machen.

lop [lɔp], *v.a.* stutzen (*trees*).

lopsided [lɔp'saidid], *adj.* einseitig.

loquacious [lo'kweiʃəs], *adj.* geschwätzig.

loquacity [lo'kwæsiti], *s.* die Schwatzhaftigkeit.

Lord [lɔ:d], *s.* (*Rel.*) the —, Gott der Herr; der Lord (*nobleman's title*); — *Mayor*, der Oberbürgermeister.

lord [lɔ:d], *s.* der Herr.

lordly ['lɔ:dli], *adj.* vornehm, stolz.

lore [lɔ:], *s.* die Kunde.

lose [lu:z], *v.a., v.n. irr.* verlieren; nachgehen (*of timepiece*).

loser ['lu:zə], *s.* der Verlierende.

loss [lɔs], *s.* der Verlust.

lot [lɔt], *s.* das Los; der Anteil (*share*); die Menge (*quantity*); die Partie (*auction*); (*Am.*) das Stück Land.

loth *see* **loath**.

lotion ['louʃən], *s.* das Waschmittel, das Wasser.

loud [laud], *adj.* laut; grell (*colour*).

lounge [laundʒ], *s.* der Gesellschaftsraum; (*Obs.*) die Chaiselongue; — *suit*, der Straßenanzug. — *v.n.* nichts tun, herumlungern, herumsitzen.

louse [laus], *s.* (*Zool.*) die Laus.

lout [laut], *s.* der Tölpel.

lovable ['lʌvəbl], *adj.* liebenswürdig, liebenswert.

love [lʌv], *s.* die Liebe; *for the — of God*, um Gottes Willen; *for —*, um nichts; *not for — nor money*, weder für Geld noch gute Worte, auf keinen Fall. — *v.a.*, *v.n.* lieben; — *to*, gern tun.

lover ['lʌvə], *s.* der Liebhaber, der *or* die Geliebte.

low [lou], *adj.* niedrig; nieder, tief; leise; (*Mus.*) tief; (*spirits*) niedergeschlagen. — *v.n.* muhen (*of cattle*).

lowlands ['loulændz], *s. pl.* die Niederungen, *f. pl.*; die Ebene; das Unterland.

lowliness ['loulinis], *s.* die Demut, Bescheidenheit.

lowness ['lounis], *s.* die Niedrigkeit; Tiefe.

loyal ['lɔiəl], *adj.* treu, ergeben, loyal.

loyalty ['lɔiəlti], *s.* die Treue, Ergebenheit, Loyalität.

lozenge ['lɔzindʒ], *s.* die Pastille; (*Geom.*) die Raute.

lubricant ['lu:brikənt], *s.* das Schmiermittel, Schmieröl.

lubricate ['lu:brikeit], *v.a.* ölen, schmieren.

lucid ['lu:sid], *adj.* klar, deutlich.

lucidity [lu:'siditi], *s.* die Klarheit.

luck [lʌk], *s.* das Glück, der Glücksfall.

luckily ['lʌkili], *adv.* glücklicherweise.

lucky ['lʌki], *adj.* mit Glück gesegnet, glücklich.

lucrative ['lu:krətiv], *adj.* einträglich.

lucre ['lu:kə], *s.* der Gewinn.

ludicrous ['lu:dikrəs], *adj.* lächerlich, komisch.

lug [lʌg], *v.a.* schleifen, zerren; (*burden*) schleppen.

luggage ['lʌgidʒ], *s.* das Gepäck.

lugger ['lʌgə], *s.* (*Naut.*) der Logger, Lugger.

lugubrious [lu:'gju:briəs], *adj.* traurig.

lukewarm ['lu:kwɔ:m], *adj.* lauwarm.

lull [lʌl], *s.* die (Wind)stille. — *v.a.* einlullen, beschwichtigen.

lullaby ['lʌləbai], *s.* das Wiegenlied.

lumbago [lʌm'beigou], *s.* (*Med.*) der Hexenschuß.

lumbar ['lʌmbə], *adj.* (*Anat.*) zu den Lenden gehörig, Lenden-.

lumber ['lʌmbə], *s.* der Kram, das alte Zeug; (*timber*) das Bauholz; — *room*, die Rumpelkammer.

luminous ['lu:minəs], *adj.* leuchtend, Leucht-.

lump [lʌmp], *s.* der Klumpen, Haufen; — *sugar*, der Würfelzucker; — *sum*, die Pauschalsumme. — *v.a.* (*together*), zusammenwerfen.

lumpy ['lʌmpi], *adj.* klumpig.

lunacy ['lu:nəsi], *s.* der Wahnsinn.

lunatic ['lu:nətik], *adj.* wahnsinnig. — *s.* der Wahnsinnige; — *asylum*, das Irrenhaus, die Irrenanstalt.

lunch [lʌntʃ], *v.n.* zu Mittag essen. — *s.* (*also* **luncheon** ['lʌntʃən]) das Mittagessen.

lung [lʌŋ], *s.* (*Anat.*) die Lunge.

lunge [lʌndʒ], *v.n.* stoßen, stürzen. — *s.* der Stoß.

lurch [lə:tʃ], *s. leave in the —*, im Stiche lassen. — *v.n.* taumeln.

lure [luə], *v.a.* locken, ködern (*bait*). — *s.* der Köder (*bait*), die Lockung.

lurid ['ljuərid], *adj.* unheimlich, grell.

lurk [lə:k], *v.n.* lauern.

luscious ['lʌʃəs], *adj.* saftig, süß.

lush [lʌʃ], *adj.* üppig (*vegetation*); übermäßig.

lust [lʌst], *s.* die Wollust, Sucht. —
v.n. gelüsten (*for*, nach, *Dat.*).
lustre ['lʌstə], *s.* der Glanz.
lusty ['lʌsti], *adj.* kräftig, laut.
lute [lu:t], *s.* (*Mus.*) die Laute.
lutanist ['lu:tənist], *s.* (*Mus.*) der
Lautenspieler.
Lutheran ['lu:θərən], *adj.* lutherisch.
— *s.* der Lutheraner.
luxuriate [lʌg'zjuərieit, lʌk'sjuə-], *v.n.*
schwelgen; (*Bot.*) üppig wachsen.
luxurious [lʌg'zjuəriəs, lʌk'sjuə-], *adj.*
üppig; (*rich*) reich ausgeschmückt,
prächtig, luxuriös.
luxury ['lʌkʃəri], *s.* der Luxus, Aufwand.
lymph [limf], *s.* die Lymphe.
lynx [links], *s.* (*Zool.*) der Luchs.
lyric ['lirik], *s.* die Lyrik.
lyrical ['lirikəl], *adj.* lyrisch.

M

M [em]. das M.
macaroon [mækə'ru:n], *s.* die Makrone.
mace [meis], *s.* das Zepter.
macerate ['mæsəreit], *v.a.* abzehren.
machination [mæki'neiʃən], *s.* die
Machenschaft, Ränke, *m.pl.*
machine [mə'ʃi:n], *s.* die Maschine.
mackerel ['mækərəl], *s.* (*Zool.*) die
Makrele.
mackintosh ['mækintəʃ], *s.* der Regenmantel.
mad [mæd], *adj.* verrückt, wahnsinnig.
madam ['mædəm], *s.* (*addr.*) gnädige
Frau.
madden [mædn], *v.a.* verrückt machen.
madman ['mædmən], *s.* der Wahnsinnige.
madness ['mædnis], *s.* der Wahnsinn.
magazine [mægə'zi:n], *s.* die (illu-
strierte) Zeitschrift; (*gun*) der Ladestock; der Lagerraum (*storeroom*).
maggot ['mægət], *s.* (*Ent.*) die Made.
magic ['mædʒik], *adj.* zauberhaft; —
lantern, die Laterna Magica. — *s.* der
Zauber; die Magie, Zauberei.
magician [mə'dʒiʃən], *s.* der Zauberer.
magistracy ['mædʒistrəsi], *s.* die
Obrigkeit (*authority*).
magistrate ['mædʒistr(e)it], *s.* der
Richter.
magnanimity [mægnə'nimiti], *s.* der
Großmut.
magnanimous [mæg'næniməs], *adj.*
großmütig.
magnate ['mægneit], *s.* der Magnat,
Großunternehmer.
magnet ['mægnit], *s.* der Magnet.
magnetic [mæg'netik], *adj.* magnetisch.
magnetize ['mægnitaiz], *v.a.* magnetisieren.

magnificence [mæg'nifisəns], *s.* die
Herrlichkeit.
magnificent [mæg'nifisənt], *adj.* herrlich, großartig.
magnify ['mægnifai], *v.a.* vergrößern
(*make larger*); (*Rel.*) verherrlichen.
magnitude ['mægnitju:d], *s.* die Größe;
order of —, die Größenordnung.
magpie ['mægpai], *s.* (*Orn.*) die
Elster.
Magyar ['mægjɑ:], *adj.* madjarisch.
— *s.* der Magyar, Madjar.
mahogany [mə'hɔgəni], *s.* das Maha-
goni(holz).
maid [meid], *s.* (*Poet.*) das Mädchen;
das Stubenmädchen (*servant*).
maiden [meidn], *s.* (*Poet.*) die Jungfrau,
das Mädchen; — *aunt*, die unverheiratete Tante.
mail (1) [meil], *s.* die Post. — *v.a.*
aufgeben, mit der Post senden.
mail (2) [meil], *s.* (*Mil.*) der Panzer.
maim [meim], *v.a.* verstümmeln,
lähmen.
main (1) [mein], *adj.* hauptsächlich,
Haupt-; (*Railw.*) — *line*, die Haupt-
strecke. — *s.* der Hauptteil; *in the* —,
hauptsächlich; (*Poet.*) das Weltmeer;
(*pl.*) das Hauptrohr, die Hauptleitung.
main (2) [mein], *s. with might and* —,
mit allen Kräften.
mainstay ['meinstei], *s.* die Haupt-
grundlage, Hauptstütze.
maintain [mein'tein], *v.a.* erhalten,
unterhalten (*keep*); behaupten
(*assert*).
maintenance ['meintənəns], *s.* der
Unterhalt, die Unterhaltskosten, *pl.* die
Erhaltung.
maize [meiz], *s.* (*Bot.*) der Mais.
majestic [mə'dʒestik], *adj.* majestätisch, prunkvoll.
majesty ['mædʒəsti], *s.* die Majestät.
major ['meidʒə], *adj.* größer, älter
(*elder brother*); wichtig (*more important*). — *s.* (*Mil.*) der Major; (*Law*)
der Mündige. — *v.n.* (*Am.*) sich
spezialisieren.
majority [mə'dʒɔriti], *s.* die Mehrheit
(*in numbers*); (*Law*) die Mündigkeit;
(*Mil.*) der Majorsrang.
make [meik], *v.a. irr.* machen, schaffen,
herstellen (*produce*); (*coll.*) verdienen
(*money*); *he has made it* (*coll.*) er
hat's geschafft!; — *out*, ausfüllen
(*cheque etc.*); entziffern (*decipher*);
— *up*, erfinden (*invent*); schminken
(*o.'s face*). — *v.n. what do you — of
him?* was halten Sie von ihm? —
s. die Marke.
make-believe ['meikbəli:v], *s.* der
Vorwand. — *adj.* vorgeblich.
maladjustment [mælə'dʒʌstmənt], *s.*
die Unfähigkeit sich anzupassen; die
falsche Einstellung; das Missverhält-
nis.
maladroit [mælə'drɔit], *adj.* ungeschickt, ungewandt.
malady ['mælədi], *s.* das Leiden, die
Krankheit.

Malagasy [mælə'gæsi], *adj.* madagassich. — *s.* der Madagasse.

Malaysian [mə'leiziən], *adj.* malaysisch. — *s.* der Malaysier.

malcontent ['mælkəntent], *adj.* mißvergnügt.

male [meil], *adj.* männlich; — *screw*, die Schraubenspindel. — *s.* der Mann; (*Zool.*) das Männchen.

malefactor ['mælifæktə], *s.* der Übeltäter.

malice ['mælis], *s.* die Bosheit.

malicious [mə'liʃəs], *adj.* boshaft, böswillig.

malign [mə'lain], *v.a.* lästern, verleumden.

malignant [mə'lignənt], *adj.* bösartig.

malignity [mə'ligniti], *s.* die Bösartigkeit.

malinger [mə'lingə], *v.n.* sich krank stellen.

malleable ['mæliəbl], *adj.* (*Metall.*) leicht zu hämmern; (*fig.*) geschmeidig.

mallet ['mælit], *s.* der Schlegel, Holzhammer.

mallow ['mælou], *s.* (*Bot.*) die Malve.

malpractice [mæl'præktis], *s.* das gesetzwidrige Handeln, der Mißbrauch; die Amtsvergehung.

malt [mɔ:lt], *s.* das Malz.

Maltese [mɔ:l'ti:z], *adj.* maltesisch. — *s.* der Malteser.

maltreat [mæl'tri:t], *v.a.* mißhandeln.

mammal ['mæməl], *s.* (*Zool.*) das Säugetier.

man [mæn], *s.* der Mann (*adult male*); der Mensch (*human being*); — *of war*, das Kriegschiff. — *v.a.* bemannen.

manacle ['mænəkl], *s.* die Handschelle. — *v.a.* fesseln.

manage ['mænidʒ], *v.a.* leiten, handhaben, verwalten; *how did you — it?* wie haben Sie's fertiggebracht?

management ['mænidʒmənt], *s.* die Leitung, Führung.

manager ['mænidʒə], *s.* der Leiter, Geschäftsführer, Manager.

mandatary *see* **mandatory**.

mandate ['mændeit], *s.* das Mandat.

mandatory ['mændətəri], *adj.* befehlend, bevollmächtigt, beauftragt. — *s.* der Bevollmächtigte, Beauftragte.

mandrake ['mændreik], *s.* der Alraun.

mane [mein], *s.* die Mähne.

manganese ['mæŋgəni:z], *s.* (*Chem.*) das Mangan.

mange [meindʒ], *s.* die Räude.

manger [meindʒə], *s.* die Krippe.

mangle (1) [mæŋgl], *s.* die Mangel. — *v.a.* rollen; mangeln (*laundry*).

mangle (2) [mæŋgl], *v.a.* verstümmeln (*disfigure*).

mango ['mæŋgou], *s.* (*Bot.*) die Mangofrucht.

manhood ['mænhud], *s.* die Mannbarkeit, das Mannesalter.

mania ['meiniə], *s.* der Wahnsinn, die Manie.

maniac ['meiniæk], *s.* der Wahnsinnige. — *adj.* wahnsinnig.

manifest ['mænifest], *adj.* deutlich, klar, offenbar.

manifestation [mænifes'teiʃən], *s.* die Offenbarung.

manifesto [mæni'festou], *s.* das Manifest.

manifold ['mænifould], *adj.* mannigfach.

manipulate [mə'nipjuleit], *v.a.* manipulieren, handhaben.

mankind [mæn'kaind], *s.* die Menschheit.

manly ['mænli], *adj.* mannhaft, männlich.

manner ['mænə], *s.* die Art, Sitte (*custom*); die Manier (*bearing*); das Benehmen (*behaviour*); (*pl.*) gute Sitten.

mannered ['mænəd], *adj.* gesittet, geartet; manieriert, gekünstelt (*artificial*).

manor ['mænə], *s.* — *house*, das Herrenhaus, Schloß.

manorial [mə'nɔ:riəl], *adj.* des Herrenhauses, herrschaftlich.

manservant ['mænsə:vənt], *s.* der Bediente, Diener.

mansion ['mænʃən], *s.* das (herrschaftliche) Wohnhaus, Herrenhaus.

manslaughter ['mænslɔ:tə], *s.* der Totschlag.

mantelpiece ['mæntlpi:s], *s.* der Kaminsims.

mantle [mæntl], *s.* (*gas*) der Glühstrumpf; (*Tail.*) der Mantel. — *v.a.* verhüllen (*cloak*).

manual ['mænjuəl], *s.* das Handbuch; (*Mus.*) das Handregister. — *adj.* Hand-.

manufacture [mænju'fæktʃə], *s.* die Herstellung, Erzeugung (*production*); (*Comm.*) das Fabrikat (*product*).

manufacturer [mænju'fæktʃərə], *s.* der Fabrikant, Erzeuger.

manure [mə'njuə], *s.* der Dünger; der Mist. — *v.a.* düngen.

manuscript ['mænjuskript], *s.* die Handschrift, das Manuskript.

many ['meni], *adj.* viele; *as — as*, ganze . . . (*emphatically*); — *a*, mancher.

map [mæp], *s.* die Landkarte. — *v.a.* —(*out*), nach der Karte planen.

maple [meipl], *s.* (*Bot.*) der Ahorn.

mar [ma:], *v.a.* verderben.

marauder [mə'rɔ:də], *s.* der Plünderer.

marble [ma:bl], *s.* der Marmor (*rock*); (*pl.*) die Murmel (*game*). — *adj.* marmorn.

March [ma:tʃ]. der März.

march [ma:tʃ], *s.* der Marsch. — *v.n.* marschieren; *steal a — on s.o.*, jemandem zuvorkommen.

marchioness [ma:ʃə'nes], *s.* die Marquise.

mare [mɛə], *s.* (*Zool.*) die Stute.

margin ['ma:dʒin], *s.* der Rand.

marginal ['ma:dʒinəl], *adj.* Rand-, am Rande gelegen.

marigold ['mærigould], *s.* (*Bot.*) die Dotterblume.

marine

marine [mə'ri:n], *adj.* Marine-, See-. — *s.* (*Mil.*) der Seesoldat; *tell that to the Marines!* der Großmutter erzählen.
mariner ['mærinə], *s.* der Seemann.
marital ['mæritəl], *adj.* ehelich.
maritime ['mæritaim], *adj.* Meeres-, See-.
mark [ma:k], *s.* das Zeichen (*sign*); (*Sch.*) die Zensur, Note; (*Comm.*) die Marke; *wide of the* —, auf dem Holzwege. — *v.a.* markieren (*make sign on*); — *my words,* merk dir das! paß auf! (*Comm.*) — *down,* den Preis heruntersetzen; ins Auge fassen (*observe closely*); *a* —*ed man,* ein Gezeichneter.
market [ma:kit], *s.* der Markt. — *v.a.* auf den Markt bringen.
marksman ['ma:ksmən], *s.* der Schütze.
marl [ma:l], *s.* der Mergel.
marmalade ['ma:məleid], *s.* die Orangenmarmelade.
marmot ['ma:mət], *s.* (*Zool.*) das Murmeltier.
maroon (1) [mə'ru:n], *adj.* kastanienbraun, rotbraun.
maroon (2) [mə'ru:n], *v.a.* aussetzen.
marquee [ma:'ki:], *s.* das große Zelt.
marquess, marquis ['ma:kwis], *s.* der Marquis.
marriage ['mærid3], *s.* die Ehe, Heirat; die Hochzeit (*wedding*).
marriageable ['mærid3əbl], *adj.* heiratsfähig.
married ['mærid], *adj.* verheiratet.
marrow ['mærou], *s.* (*Anat.*) das Mark; (*Bot.*) der Kürbis.
marry ['mæri], *v.a.* heiraten; trauen (*perform marriage ceremony*); — *off,* verheiraten (*o.'s daughter*). — *v.n.* sich verheiraten.
marsh [ma:ʃ], *s.* der Morast, Sumpf.
marshal ['ma:ʃəl], *s.* der Marschall.
marshy ['ma:ʃi], *adj.* morastig, sumpfig.
marten ['ma:tin], *s.* (*Zool.*) der Marder.
martial ['ma:ʃəl], *adj.* Kriegs-, kriegerisch.
martin ['ma:tin], *s.* (*Orn.*) die Mauerschwalbe.
martyr ['ma:tə], *s.* der Märtyrer.
martyrdom ['ma:tədəm], *s.* das Märtyrertum, der Märtyrertod.
marvel [ma:vl], *v.n.* staunen (*at,* über, *Acc.*).
marvellous ['ma:v(ə)ləs], *adj.* wunderbar, erstaunlich.
masculine ['mæskjulin], *adj.* männlich. — *s.* (*Gram.*) das Maskulinum, das männliche Geschlecht.
mash [mæʃ], *v.a.* zerquetschen, zerdrücken. — *s.* der Brei.
mask [ma:sk], *v.a., v.n.* maskieren, sich vermummen. — *s.* die Maske.
mason ['meisən], *s.* der Maurer.
masonic [mə'sɔnik], *adj.* freimaurerisch.
masonry ['meisənri], *s.* das Mauerwerk.
masquerade [mæskə'reid], *s.* der Mummenschanz, die Maskerade.
Mass [mæs, ma:s], *s.* (*Eccl.*) die Messe; *Low Mass,* die stille Messe; *High*

Mass, das Hochamt; *Requiem Mass,* die Seelenmesse.
mass [mæs], *s.* die Masse; die Menge. — *v.a., v.n.* (sich) massen, ansammeln.
massacre ['mæsəkə], *s.* das Blutbad.
massive ['mæsiv], *adj.* massiv, schwer.
mast [ma:st], *s.* der Mast. — *v.a.* (*Naut.*) bemasten.
Master ['ma:tə], *s.* (*Univ.*) der Magister; der junge Herr (*before boy's name*).
master ['ma:stə], *s.* der Meister (*of a craft*); der Herr, Arbeitgeber (*employer*); — *key,* der Hauptschlüssel. — *v.a.* meistern, beherrschen.
masticate ['mæstikeit] *v.a.* kauen.
mastiff ['mæstif], *s.* (*Zool.*) der Kettenhund, Mastiff.
mat [mæt], *s.* die Matte.
match (1) [mætʃ], *s.* das Streichholz, Zündholz.
match (2) [mætʃ], *s.* der ebenbürtige Partner (*suitable partner*); *find o.'s* —, seinesgleichen finden; (*Sport*) das Wettspiel, der Wettkampf; Fußballkampf; (*Cricket*) das Cricketspiel. — *v.a., v.n.* passen zu, anpassen; ebenbürtig sein (*be equal*).
matchless ['mætʃlis], *adj.* unvergleichlich, ohnegleichen.
mate (1) [meit], *s.* der Gefährte, Genosse; (*Naut.*) der Maat, Steuermann; (*coll.*) Freund. — *v.n.* sich paaren, sich verheiraten.
mate (2) [meit], *v.a.* (*Chess*) matt setzen.
material [mə'tiəriəl], *s.* das Material, der Stoff. — *adj.* wesentlich (*essential*); materiell (*tangible*).
materialism [mə'tiəriəlizm], *s.* der Materialismus.
maternal [mə'tə:nəl], *adj.* mütterlich.
maternity [mə'tə:niti], *s.* die Mutterschaft; — *ward,* die Geburtsklinik.
mathematical [mæθə'mætikəl], *adj.* mathematisch.
mathematics [mæθə'mætiks], *s.* die Mathematik.
matins ['mætinz], *s.* (*Eccl.*) die Frühmette.
matriculate [mə'trikjuleit], *v.n.* immatrikulieren (lassen).
matrimonial [mætri'mouniəl], *adj.* Ehe-, ehelich.
matrimony ['mætriməni], *s.* die Ehe.
matron ['meitrən], *s.* die Oberschwester, Oberin (*in hospital etc.*); die Matrone (*older woman*).
matter ['mætə], *s.* der Stoff (*substance*); die Sache, der Gegenstand (*subject*); die Angelegenheit (*case*); *printed* —, Drucksache; *what is the* —? was ist los?; *the heart of the* —, des Pudels Kern; *as a* — *of fact,* tatsächlich, ernst gesprochen. — *v.n.* bedeutsam sein, wichtig sein.
mattock ['mætək], *s.* die Haue.
mattress ['mætrəs], *s.* die Matratze.
mature [mə'tjuə], *adj.* reif; (*fig.*) gereift. — *v.a., v.n.* reifen, zur Reife bringen; (*Comm.*) fällig werden.

matured [mə'tjuəd], *adj.* abgelagert.
maturity [mə'tjuəriti], *s.* die Reife;
(*Comm.*) die Fälligkeit.
maudlin ['mɔ:dlin], *adj.* rührselig,
sentimental.
maul [mɔ:l], *v.a.* mißhandeln.
Maundy Thursday ['mɔ:ndi'θə:zd(e)i].
der Gründonnerstag.
mauve [mouv], *adj.* malvenfarbig;
violett.
maw [mɔ:], *s.* (*Zool.*) der Magen.
mawkish ['mɔ:kiʃ], *adj.* abgeschmackt,
sentimental, rührselig.
maxim ['mæksim], *s.* der Grundsatz.
May [mei], *der* Mai.
may (1) [mei], *v.n. aux. irr.* mögen,
können; (*permissive*) dürfen.
may (2) [mei], *s.* (*Bot.*) der Weißdorn.
mayor [mɛə], *s.* der Bürgermeister.
maypole ['meipoul], *s.* der Maibaum.
maze [meiz], *s.* das Labyrinth.
me [mi:], *pers. pron.* (*Acc.*) mich; (*Dat.*)
mir.
mead [mi:d], *s.* der Met.
meadow ['medou], *s.* die Wiese.
meagre ['mi:gə], *adj.* mager, karg
(*lean, poor*); dürftig.
meal (1) [mi:l], *s.* das Mahl, Essen, die
Mahlzeit.
meal (2) [mi:l], *s.* das Mehl (*flour*).
mealy ['mi:li], *adj.* mehlig; — *-mouthed*,
frömmelnd; kleinlaut (*shy*).
mean (1) [mi:n], *v.a. irr.* bedeuten
(*signify*); meinen (*wish to express*);
vorhaben (*intend*).
mean (2) [mi:n], *adj.* mittelmäßig,
Mittel– (*average*). — *s.* die Mitte.
mean (3) [mi:n], *adj.* gemein, niedrig
(*despicable*); geizig.
meander [mi'ændə], *s.* die Windung,
das Wellenmuster. — *v.n.* sich
winden, sich schlängeln.
meaning ['mi:niŋ], *s.* die Bedeutung
(*significance, connotation*); der Sinn.
meaningless ['mi:niŋlis], *adj.* bedeu-
tungslos.
means [mi:nz], *s.* das Mittel; *by all* —,
auf jeden Fall, unbedingt; *by no*
—, keinesfalls; *by–of*, mittels (*Genit.*).
meantime, meanwhile ['mi:ntaim,
'mi:nwail], *s.* die Zwischenzeit.—*adv.*
in der Zwischenzeit, indessen.
measles [mi:zlz], *s.* (*Med.*) die Masern,
f. pl.; *German* —, die Röteln, *m. pl.*
measurable ['meʒərəbl], *adj.* meßbar.
measure ['meʒə], *s.* das Maß; der
Maßstab (*scale*); (*Mus.*) der Takt;
das Zeitmaß.—*v.a.* messen, abmessen.
meat [mi:t], *s.* das Fleisch.
mechanic [mi'kænik], *s.* der Mechaniker.
mechanical [mi'kænikəl], *adj.* mechanisch, automatisch; — *engineering*, der
Maschinenbau.
mechanics [mi'kæniks], *s.* die Mechanik.
medal [medl], *s.* die Medaille, der
Orden.
meddle [medl], *v.n.* sich einmischen
(in, *in, Acc.*).

mediæval, medieval [medi'i:vəl], *adj.*
mittelalterlich.
mediate ['mi:dieit], *v.n.* vermitteln,
intervenieren. — *adj.* mittelbar.
mediator ['mi:dieitə], *s.* der Vermittler.
medical ['medikəl], *adj.* medizinisch,
ärztlich; — *orderly*, der Krankenwärter.
medicate ['medikeit], *v.a.* medizinisch
behandeln.
medicine ['medsən], *s.* die Medizin,
Arznei.
medieval *see* **mediæval.**
mediocre ['mi:dioukə], *adj.* mittelmäßig.
mediocrity [mi:di'ɔkriti], *s.* die Mittel-
mäßigkeit.
meditate ['mediteit], *v.n.* nachdenken,
sinnen.
meditation [medi'teiʃən], *s.* das Sinnen, Nachdenken.
Mediterranean [meditə'reiniən], *adj.*
mittelländisch. — *s.* das Mittelmeer,
mittelländische Meer.
medium ['mi:djəm], *s.* das Medium;
das Mittel (*means*). — *adj.* mittelgroß.
medlar ['medlə], *s.* (*Bot.*) die Mispel.
medley ['medli], *s.* (*Mus.*) das Pot-
pourri; das Gemisch (*mixture*).
meek [mi:k], *adj.* sanft, mild.
meet [mi:t], *v.a., v.n. irr.* treffen (*Acc.*),
sich treffen (mit, *Dat.*), begegnen
(*Dat.*). — *s.* (*Hunt.*) die Jagd.
meeting ['mi:tiŋ], *s.* das Zusammentreffen; die Tagung, Sitzung (*conference*).
melancholy ['melənkɔli], *adj.* melan-
cholisch, schwermütig. — *s.* die
Melancholie, die Schwermut.
mellifluous [me'lifluəs], *adj.* lieblich,
süß (*of sounds*).
mellow ['melou], *adj.* mild, weich,
mürbe (*fruit etc.*); freundlich (*mood*).
— *v.a.* mürbe machen, reifen lassen.
— *v.n.* weich werden.
melodious [mə'loudiəs], *adj.* klangvoll,
wohlklingend, melodisch.
melodrama ['melədra:mə], *s.* das Melodrama.
melody ['melədi], *s.* die Melodie.
melon ['melən], *s.* (*Bot.*) die
Melone.
melt [melt], *v.a., v.n. reg. & irr.* schmelzen.
member ['membə], *s.* das Mitglied (*of
club*); (*Parl.*) der Abgeordnete, das
Glied.
membrane ['membrein], *s.* die Membran; (*Anat.*) das Häutchen.
memento [mi'mentou], *s.* das Andenken.
memoir ['memwa:], *s.* die Denkschrift;
(*pl.*) die Memoiren, *n. pl.*
memorable ['memərəbl], *adj.* denkwürdig.
memorandum [memə'rændəm], *s.* das
Memorandum, die Denkschrift.
memorial [mi'mɔ:riəl], *s.* das Denkmal
(*monument*). — *adj.* Gedenk-, zum
Gedenken, Gedächtnis-.

memory

memory ['meməri], *s.* die Erinnerung; das Gedächtnis (*faculty*); das Andenken (*remembrance*).

menace ['menis], *s.* die Drohung. — *v.a.* bedrohen.

mend [mend], *v.a.* reparieren; verbessern, ausbessern. — *v.n.* sich bessern.

mendacious [men'deiʃəs], *adj.* lügnerisch, verlogen (*lying*).

mendacity [men'dæsiti], *s.* die Lügenhaftigkeit, Verlogenheit.

mendicant ['mendikənt], *adj.* bettlerisch. — *s.* der Bettler.

mendicity [men'disiti], *s.* die Bettelei.

menial ['miːniəl], *adj.* gemein, grob (*job*).

mental [mentl], *adj.* geistig; (*coll.*) geisteskrank.

mention ['menʃən], *v.a.* erwähnen; *don't — it*, gern geschehen! — *s.* die Erwähnung.

mentor ['mentə], *s.* der Ratgeber.

menu ['menjuː], *s.* die Speisekarte.

mercantile ['məːkəntail], *adj.* Handels-, kaufmännisch.

mercenary ['məːsənəri], *adj.* für Geld zu haben, käuflich, feil; materiell eingestellt. — *s.* der Söldner.

mercer ['məːsə], *s.* der Seidenhändler.

mercerised ['məːsəraizd], *adj.* (*Textile*) merzerisiert.

merchandise ['məːtʃəndaiz], *s.* die Ware.

merchant ['məːtʃənt], *s.* der Kaufmann.

merchantman ['məːtʃəntmən], *s.* (*Naut.*) das Handelsschiff, Frachtschiff.

merciful ['məːsiful], *adj.* barmherzig, gnädig.

Mercury ['məːkjuəri]. (*Myth.*) Merkur, *m.*

mercury ['məːkjuəri], *s.* (*Chem.*) das Quecksilber.

mercy ['məːsi], *s.* die Barmherzigkeit, Gnade.

mere (1) [miə], *adj.* bloß, allein.

mere (2) [miə], *s.* der Teich.

meretricious [meri'triʃəs], *adj.* falsch, täuschend.

merge [məːdʒ], *v.n.* aufgehen lassen, verschmelzen (*combine*).

merger ['məːdʒə], *s.* (*Comm.*) die Fusion, Vereinigung, Zusammenlegung.

meridian [mə'ridiən], *s.* der Meridian; (*fig.*) der Gipfel.

merit ['merit], *s.* das Verdienst, der Wert. — *v.a.* verdienen.

meritorious [meri'tɔːriəs], *adj.* verdienstlich.

mermaid ['məːmeid], *s.* die Wasserjungfer, Nixe.

merriment ['merimənt], *s.* die Belustigung, das Fröhlichsein, die Fröhlichkeit.

merry ['meri], *adj.* froh, fröhlich; *— go-round*, das Karussel.

mesh [meʃ], *s.* das Netz; die Masche (*knitting*). — *v.a.* einfangen.

mess (1) [mes], *s.* (*Mil.*) die Offiziersmesse.

mess (2) [mes], *s.* die Unordnung (*disorder*).

message ['mesidʒ], *s.* die Nachricht, Mitteilung, Botschaft.

messenger ['mesindʒə], *s.* der Bote.

Messiah [mi'saiə], *s.* der Messias.

metal [metl], *s.* das Metall.

metallurgy ['metələːdʒi], *s.* die Metallurgie, Hüttenkunde.

metaphor ['metəfɔː], *s.* die Metapher.

metaphorical [metə'fɔrikəl], *adj.* bildlich.

meter ['miːtə], *s.* der Messer, Zähler (*gauge*); (*Am.*) *see* **metre** (1).

methinks [mi'θiŋks], *v. impers.* (*obs.*) mich dünkt, ich meine, mir scheint.

method ['meθəd], *s.* die Methode.

methodical [mi'θɔdikəl], *adj.* methodisch, systematisch.

methylate ['meθileit], *v.a.* (*Chem.*) denaturieren.

metre (1) ['miːtə], *s.* der *or* das Meter (*unit of measurement*).

metre (2) ['miːtə], *s.* (*Poet.*) das Versmaß.

metric ['metrik], *adj.* metrisch (*system of measurement*).

metrical ['metrikəl], *adj.* (*Poet.*) im Metrum, metrisch, Vers-.

metropolis [mi'trɔpəlis], *s.* die Metropole.

metropolitan [metrə'pɔlitən], *adj.* hauptstädtisch. — *s.* (*Eccl.*) der Erzbischof.

mettle [metl], *s.* der Mut (*courage*); *put s.o. on his —*, einen anspornen.

mew [mjuː], *s.* das Miauen (*of cat*). — *v.n.* miauen.

mews [mjuːz], *s. pl.* die Stallung.

Mexican ['meksikən], *adj.* mexikanisch. — *s.* der Mexikaner.

microphone ['maikrəfoun], *s.* das Mikrophon.

mid- [mid], *prefix.* mittel, Mittel-, mittler.

midday [mid'dei], *s.* der Mittag.

middle [midl], *s.* die Mitte, das Zentrum.

middling ['midliŋ], *adj.* (*coll.*) mittelmäßig.

midget ['midʒit], *s.* der Zwerg (*dwarf*).

midnight ['midnait], *s.* die Mitternacht.

midriff ['midrif], *s.* das Zwerchfell.

midshipman ['midʃipmən], *s.* (*Naut.*) der Seekadett.

midwife ['midwaif], *s.* die Hebamme.

mien [miːn], *s.* die Miene.

might [mait], *s.* die Macht, Gewalt.

mighty ['maiti], *adj.* mächtig, stark.

mignonette [minjə'net], *s.* (*Bot.*) die Reseda.

migrate [mai'greit], *v.n.* wandern, migrieren; (*birds*) ziehen.

migratory ['maigrətəri], *adj.* Zug-, Wander-.

Milanese [milə'n:iz], *adj.* mailändisch.
— *s.* der Mailänder.

mild [maild], *adj.* mild, sanft.

mildew ['mildju:], *s.* der Meltau.

mile [mail], *s.* die (englische) Meile.

mileage ['mailidʒ], *s.* die Meilenzahl.

milfoil ['milfɔil], *s.* (*Bot.*) die Schafgarbe (*yarrow*).

military ['militəri], *adj.* militärisch. —
s. das Militär.

militia [mi'liʃə], *s.* die Miliz.

milk [milk], *v.a.* melken. — *s.* die Milch.

milksop ['milksɔp], *s.* die Memme.

milky ['milki], *adj.* milchig; *Milky Way*, die Milchstraße.

mill [mil], *s.* die Mühle; die Spinnerei (*textile*); *rolling* —, das Walzwerk; *run of the* —, gewöhnlich; *through the* —, wohl erfahren, lebenserfahren. — *v.a.* mahlen (*flour*); rollen, walzen (*steel*); rändern (*coins*); —*ed edge*, die Rändelkante. —*v.n.* — (*around*), sich drängen.

miller ['milə], *s.* der Müller.

millet ['milit], *s.* die Hirse.

milliner ['milinə], *s.* die Modistin, Putzmacherin.

millinery ['milinəri], *s.* die Putzwaren, Modewaren, *f. pl.*

million ['miljən], *s.* die Million.

milt [milt], *s.* die Fischmilch; (*Anat.*) die Milz.

mimic ['mimik], *s.* der Mimiker. — *v.a.* nachahmen.

mimicry ['mimikri], *s.* die Nachahmung; (*Zool.*) die Anpassung (*in colour*).

mince [mins], *v.a.* kleinhacken (*meat*); — *o.'s words*, affektiert sprechen; *not* — *o.'s words*, kein Blatt vor den Mund nehmen. — *s.* gehacktes Fleisch; — *pie*, die Dörrobstpastete.

mincemeat ['minsmi:t], *s.* die (gehackte) Dörrobstmischung.

mincing ['minsiŋ], *adj.* affektiert; — *steps*, trippelnde Schritte.

mind [maind], *s.* der Geist, das Gemüt; die Meinung; der Sinn; der Verstand; *what is on your* —? was bedrückt Sie?; *bear in* —, daran denken; *have a* —, Lust haben; *make up o.'s* —, sich entschließen; *with an open* —, unparteiisch. — *v.a.* beachten, achten (auf, *Acc.*). — *v.n. do you* —? macht es Ihnen etwas aus? *never* —, macht nichts; *I don't* —, mir ist's recht, meinetwegen.

minded ['maindid], *adj.* gesinnt, eingestellt.

mine (1) [main], *poss. pron.* mein, meinig.

mine (2) [main], *s.* das Bergwerk (*general*), die Grube (*coal*). — *v.a.* abbauen, graben (*Acc.*, nach, *Dat.*).

miner ['mainə], *s.* der Bergmann, Bergarbeiter; (*coll.*) der Kumpel.

mineral ['minərəl], *s.* das Mineral; (*pl.*) Mineralwasser.

mingle [miŋgl], *v.a.,v.n.* (sich) mischen.

minimize ['minimaiz], *v.a.* (möglichst) klein machen.

mining ['mainiŋ], *s.* die Hüttenkunde (*theory*); der Bergbau.

minion ['minjən], *s.* der Liebling.

minister ['ministə], *s.* (*Pol.*) der Minister; *Prime Minister*, der Ministerpräsident; (*Eccl.*) der Geistliche, Pfarrer. — *v.n.* einen Gottesdienst abhalten; dienen (*to*, *Dat.*).

ministration [minis'treiʃən], *s.* der Dienst, die Dienstleistung.

ministry ['ministri], *s.* das Ministerium (*department of state*); (*Eccl.*) der Beruf *or* das Amt des Geistlichen.

minnow ['minou], *s.* (*Zool.*) die Elritze.

minor ['mainə], *adj.* kleiner, geringer; (*Sch.*) jünger (*after boy's name*). — *s.* (*Law*) der Minderjährige, Unmündige.

minority [mai'nɔriti], *s.* die Minorität (*in numbers*); (*Law*) die Unmündigkeit.

minster ['minstə], *s.* (*Eccl.*) das Münster.

minstrel ['minstrəl], *s.* der Spielmann.

mint (1) [mint], *s.* (*Bot.*) die Minze.

mint (2) [mint], *s.* die Münzstätte. — *v.a.* münzen.

minuet [minju'et], *s.* (*Mus.*) das Menuett.

minute (1) ['minit], *s.* die Minute (*time*); (*pl.*) das Protokoll (*of meeting*). — *v.a.* zu Protokoll nehmen, protokollieren.

minute (2) [mai'nju:t], *adj.* winzig, klein.

minutiae [mi'nju:ʃii], *s.pl.* die Details, *n. pl.,* die Einzelheiten, *f. pl.*

miracle ['mirəkl], *s.* das Wunder.

miraculous [mi'rækjuləs], *adj.* wunderbar; wundertätig.

mirage [mi'ra:ʒ], *s.* die Luftspiegelung, die Fata Morgana.

mire [maiə], *s.* der Schlamm, Kot.

mirror ['mirə], *s.* der Spiegel. — *v.a.* reflektieren, spiegeln.

mirth [mə:θ], *s.* der Frohsinn.

misadventure [misəd'ventʃə], *s.* das Mißgeschick.

misalliance [misə'laiəns], *s.* die Mißheirat, Mesalliance.

misapply [misə'plai], *v.a.* falsch anwenden.

misapprehend [misæpri'hend], *v.a.* mißverstehen.

misapprehension [misæpri'henʃən], *s.* das Mißverständnis.

misappropriate [misə'prouprieit], *v.a.* unrechtmäßig erwerben, unterschlagen.

misbehave [misbi'heiv], *v.n.* sich schlecht benehmen.

miscalculate [mis'kælkjuleit], *v.a.,v.n.* sich verrechnen.

miscarriage [mis'kæridʒ], *s.* das Mißlingen; (*Med.*) die Fehlgeburt.

miscarry [mis'kæri], *v.n.* mißlingen; (*Med.*) fehlgebären.

miscellaneous [misə'leiniəs], *adj.* vermischt.

miscellany

miscellany [mi'seləni], *s.* der Sammelband (*of writers*); die Mischung, das Gemisch.

mischief ['mistʃif], *s.* der Unfug; *out to make* —, darauf aus, Unfug zu stiften; — *maker*, der Unheilstifter.

mischievous ['mistʃivəs], *adj.* boshaft.

misconceive [miskən'si:v], *v.a.* mißverstehen.

misconception [miskən'sepʃən], *s.* das Mißverständnis.

misconduct [mis'kɔndʌkt], *s.* das unkorrekte Verhalten; der Fehltritt.

misconstruction [miskən'strʌkʃən], *s.* die Mißdeutung.

misconstrue [miskən'stru:], *v.a.* mißdeuten.

misdeed [mis'di:d], *s.* die Missetat.

misdemeanour [misdi'mi:nə], *s.* (*Law.*) das Vergehen; die Missetat.

miser ['maizə], *s.* der Geizhals.

miserable ['mizərəbl], *adj.* elend, kläglich (*wretched*); nichtswürdig (*base*).

miserly ['maizəli], *adj.* geizig.

misery ['mizəri], *s.* das Elend, die Not.

misfortune [mis'fɔ:tʃən], *s.* das Unglück.

misgiving [mis'giviŋ], *s.* die Befürchtung, der Zweifel (*doubt*).

misguide [mis'gaid], *v.a.* irreführen, verleiten.

mishap [mis'hæp], *s.* der Unfall.

misinform [misin'fɔ:m], *v.a.* falsch informieren, falsch unterrichten.

misinterpret [misin'tə:prit], *v.a.* mißdeuten.

misjudge [mis'dʒʌdʒ], *v.a.* falsch beurteilen.

mislay [mis'lei], *v.a. irr.* verlegen.

mislead [mis'li:d], *v.a. irr.* verführen, irreführen.

misnomer [mis'noumə], *s.* der falsche Name.

misogynist [mi'sɔdʒinist], *s.* der Weiberfeind.

misplace [mis'pleis], *v.a.* übel anbringen (*remark*); verlegen (*thing*).

misprint [mis'print], *v.a.* verdrucken, falsch drucken. — ['misprint], *s.* der Druckfehler.

misquote [mis'kwout], *v.a.* falsch zitieren.

misrepresent [misrepri'zent], *v.a.* falsch darstellen.

misrule [mis'ru:l], *s.* die schlechte Regierung; die Unordnung (*disorder*).

miss (1) [mis], *s.* das Fräulein.

miss (2) [mis], *v.a.* vermissen (*yearn for*); versäumen (*a train, lesson etc.*); verfehlen (*target*); — *the boat*, den Anschluß verpassen; *be missing,* fehlen.

missal [misl], *s.* (*Eccl.*) das Meßbuch.

misshapen [mis'ʃeipən], *adj.* mißgestaltet.

missile ['misail], *s.* das Geschoß; *ballistic* —, das Raketengeschoß; *guided* —, ferngesteuertes Raketengeschoss.

mission ['miʃən], *s.* die Mission; Sendung; der Auftrag (*task*).

missionary ['miʃənəri], *adj.* Missions-. — *s.* der Missionar.

missive ['misiv], *s.* das Sendschreiben.

misspell [mis'spel], *v.a.* falsch buchstabieren, falsch schreiben.

mist [mist], *s.* der Dunst; Nebel (*fog*).

mistake [mis'teik], *s.* der Fehler. — *v.a. irr.* verkennen.

mistaken [mis'teikn], *adj.* im Unrecht; irrig; *be* —, sich irren.

mistimed [mis'taimd], *adj.* zur Unzeit, unzeitig.

mistletoe ['misltou], *s.* (*Bot.*) die Mistel, der Mistelzweig.

mistress ['mistrəs], *s.* die Herrin; Hausfrau; Geliebte (*paramour*); Lehrerin (*Sch.*).

mistrust [mis'trʌst], *v.a.* mißtrauen.

misunderstand [misʌndə'stænd], *v.a. irr.* mißverstehen.

misuse [mis'ju:z], *v.a.* mißbrauchen.

mite (1) [mait], *s.* (*Zool.*) die Milbe.

mite (2) [mait], *s.* das Scherflein (*coin*); (*coll.*) das Kindchen, das Kerlchen.

mitigate ['mitigeit], *v.a.* mildern.

mitre ['maitə], *s.* die Bischofsmütze, Mitra.

mitten [mitn], *s.* der Fäustling, Fausthandschuh.

mix [miks], *v.a.* mischen, vermischen. — *v.n.* verkehren.

mixed [mikst], *adj. a* — *blessing,* eine fragliche Wohltat.

mizzle [mizl], *v.n.* sprühen, rieseln.

mnemonics [ni'mɔniks], *s.* die Gedächtniskunst.

moan [moun], *v.n.* stöhnen (*wail*); klagen (*complain*). — *s.* (*coll.*) die Klage.

moat [mout], *s.* der Burggraben, Wassergraben.

mob [mɔb], *s.* der Pöbel.

mobility [mo'biliti], *s.* die Beweglichkeit.

mobilize ['moubilaiz], *v.a.* mobilisieren.

mock [mɔk], *v.a.* verspotten (*tease*); täuschen (*mislead*). — *v.n.* spotten. — *s.* der Spott, die Täuschung. — *adj.* Schein-; — *heroic,* komischheroisch.

modal [moudl], *adj.* (*Gram.*) modal, der Aussageweise nach; (*Mus.*) dem Modus nach.

mode [moud], *s.* (*Mus.*) der Modus, die Art; die Mode (*fashion*).

model [mɔdl], *s.* das Modell; das Muster (*pattern*). — *v.a., v.n.* modellieren.

moderate ['mɔdərit], *adj.* mäßig; (*climate*) gemäßigt. — [-reit], *v.a.* mäßigen; abändern.

modern ['mɔdən], *adj.* modern.

modernize ['mɔdənaiz], *v.a.* modernisieren.

modest ['mɔdist], *adj.* bescheiden.

modesty ['mɔdisti], *s.* die Bescheidenheit.

modify ['mɔdifai], *v.a.* abändern, modifizieren.

modish [ˈmoudiʃ], *adj.* nach der neuesten Mode, modisch.
modulate [ˈmɔdjuleit], *v.a.* modulieren.
moil [mɔil], *v.n.* sich plagen.
moist [mɔist], *adj.* feucht.
moisten [mɔisn], *v.a.* befeuchten.
moisture [ˈmɔistʃə], *s.* die Feuchtigkeit.
molasses [moˈlæsiz], *s.* die Melasse.
mole (1) [moul], *s.* (*Zool.*) der Maulwurf.
mole (2) [moul], *s.* das Muttermal (*skin mark*).
mole (3) [moul], *s.* der Seedamm, Hafendamm.
molecular [moˈlekjulə], *adj.* molekular.
molecule [ˈmɔl-, ˈmoulikjuːl], *s.* das Molekül.
molest [moˈlest], *v.a.* belästigen.
mollify [ˈmɔlifai], *v.a.* besänftigen.
mollusc [ˈmɔləsk], *s.* (*Zool.*) die Molluske.
molt *see under* **moult**.
molten [ˈmoultən], *adj.* geschmolzen.
moment [ˈmoumənt], *s.* der Augenblick, Moment (*instant*); die Wichtigkeit (*importance*).
momentary [ˈmouməntəri], *adj.* momentan, einen Augenblick lang.
momentum [moˈmentəm], *s.* das Moment, die Triebkraft.
monarch [ˈmɔnək], *s.* der Monarch.
monarchy [ˈmɔnəki], *s.* die Monarchie.
monastery [ˈmɔnəstri], *s.* das (Mönchs-)kloster.
monastic [məˈnæstik], *adj.* klösterlich.
Monday [ˈmʌndi], *s.* der Montag.
money [ˈmʌni], *s.* das Geld; *ready* —, bares Geld; *make* —, Geld verdienen; — *order*, die Postanweisung.
Mongolian [mɔŋˈgouliən], *adj.* mongolisch. — *s.* der Mongole.
mongrel [ˈmʌŋgrəl], *s.* (*Zool.*) der Mischling.
monitor [ˈmɔnitə], *s.* der Ermahner; (*Rad.*) der Abhörer.
monitoring [ˈmɔnitəriŋ], *adj.* — *service*, der Abhördienst.
monk [mʌŋk], *s.* (*Eccl.*) der Mönch.
monkey [ˈmʌŋki], *s.* (*Zool.*) der Affe.
monomania [mɔnoˈmeiniə], *s.* die Monomanie, fixe Idee.
monopolize [məˈnɔpəlaiz], *v.a.* monopolisieren.
monopoly [məˈnɔpəli], *s.* das Monopol.
monosyllabic [mɔnəsiˈlæbik], *adj.* einsilbig.
monotonous [məˈnɔtənəs], *adj.* monoton, eintönig.
monsoon [mɔnˈsuːn], *s.* der Monsun.
monster [ˈmɔnstə], *s.* das Ungeheuer.
monstrance [ˈmɔnstrəns], *s.* (*Eccl.*) die Monstranz.
monstrosity [mɔnsˈtrɔsiti], *s.* die Ungeheuerlichkeit.
monstrous [ˈmɔnstrəs], *adj.* ungeheuerlich.
month [mʌnθ], *s.* der Monat.
monthly [ˈmʌnθli], *adj.* monatlich, Monats-.

mood [muːd], *s.* die Stimmung, Laune; (*Gram., Mus.*) der Modus.
moodiness [ˈmuːdinis], *s.* die Launenhaftigkeit.
moody [ˈmuːdi], *adj.* launenhaft.
moon [muːn], *s.* der Mond.
moonlight [ˈmuːnlait], *s.* das Mondlicht, der Mondschein.
moonshine [ˈmuːnʃain], *s.* der Mondschein; (*fig.*) Unsinn.
moonstruck [ˈmuːnstrʌk], *adj.* mondsüchtig; verliebt.
Moor [muə], *s.* der Mohr.
moor [muə], *s.* das Moor, Heideland.
moorage [ˈmuəridʒ], *s.* der Ankerplatz.
moorhen [ˈmɔːhen], *s.* (*Orn.*) das Moorhuhn, Wildhuhn.
moorish [ˈmuəriʃ], *adj.* maurisch.
moot [muːt], *v.a.* erörtern, besprechen. — *adj.* a — *point*, ein strittiger Punkt.
mop [mɔp], *s.* der Wischlappen, Mop. — *v.a.* aufwischen (*floor*), wischen (*brow*).
mope [moup], *v.n.* traurig sein.
moral [ˈmɔrəl], *adj.* moralisch (*high principled*); sittlich (*decent*). — *s.* die Moral (*precept*); (*pl.*) die Sitten, *f. pl.*; die Sittlichkeit.
moralize [ˈmɔrəlaiz], *v.n.* moralisieren, Moral predigen (*Dat.*).
morass [moˈræs], *s.* der Morast.
morbid [ˈmɔːbid], *adj.* krankhaft.
more [mɔː], *comp. adj., adv.* mehr; *once* —, noch einmal; *all the* —, umso mehr; *the* — *the better*, je mehr desto besser.
moreover [mɔːˈrouvə], *adv.* zudem, überdies, weiterhin.
morning [ˈmɔːniŋ], *s.* der Morgen, Vormittag; — *coat*, der Cutaway, Frack.
Moroccan [məˈrɔkən], *adj.* marokkanisch. — *s.* der Marokkaner.
Morocco [məˈrɔkou]. Marokko, *n.*
morocco [məˈrɔkou], *s.* der Saffian, das Maroquinleder.
moron [ˈmɔːrɔn], *s.* der Schwachsinnige.
morose [məˈrous], *adj.* mürrisch.
morrow [ˈmɔrou], *s.* (*Poet.*) der Morgen.
morsel [mɔːsl], *s.* der Bissen, das Stück.
mortal [mɔːtl], *adj.* sterblich, tödlich; — *sin*, die Todsünde. — *s.* der Sterbliche, der Mensch.
mortality [mɔːˈtæliti], *s.* die Sterblichkeit.
mortar [ˈmɔːtə], *s.* (*Build.*) der Mörtel; (*Mil.*) der Mörser.
mortgage [ˈmɔːgidʒ], *s.* die Hypothek. — *v.a.* verpfänden; eine Hypothek aufnehmen (auf, *Acc.*).
mortgagee [mɔːgiˈdʒiː], *s.* der Hypothekengläubiger.
mortician [mɔːˈtiʃən], *s.* (*Am.*) *see* **undertaker**.
mortify [ˈmɔːtifai], *v.a.* kasteien (*chasten*); kränken (*humiliate*).
mortise [ˈmɔːtis], *s.* (*Build.*) das Zapfenloch.

mortuary ['mɔ:tjuəri], *s.* die Leichen-halle.

mosque [mɔsk], *s.* (*Rel.*) die Moschee.

mosquito [mɔs'ki:tou], *s.* (*Ent.*) der Moskito.

moss [mɔs], *s.* (*Bot.*) das Moos.

most [moust], *superl. adj.* meist; (*pl.*) die meisten. — *adv.* meist, meistens; höchst (*before adjectives*).

mostly ['moustli], *adv.* meistenteils.

mote [mout], *s.* das Stäubchen.

moth [mɔθ], *s.* (*Ent.*) die Motte.

mother ['mʌðə], *s.* die Mutter; — *-in-law*, die Schwiegermutter; —*-of-pearl*, die Perlmutter.

motherly ['mʌðəli], *adj.* mütterlich.

motion ['mouʃən], *s.* die Bewegung, der Gang; (*Parl.*, *Rhet.*) der Antrag. — *v.a.* bewegen. — *v.n.* zuwinken (*Dat.*).

motive ['moutiv], *s.* das Motiv, der Beweggrund.

motley ['mɔtli], *adj.* scheckig, bunt.

motor ['moutə], *s.* der Motor.

motoring ['moutəriŋ], *s.* das Autofahren, der Autosport.

mottled [mɔtld], *adj.* gescheckt, ge-sprenkelt.

motto ['mɔtou], *s.* das Motto, der Wahlspruch.

mould (1) [mould], *s.* die Form; Guß-form (*casting*); die Schablone. — *v.a.* formen; (*Metall.*) gießen, formen.

mould (2) [mould], *s.* der Schimmel (*fungus*); (*Hort.*) die Gartenerde. — *v.n.* schimmeln.

moulder (1) ['mouldə], *s.* der Bildner; (*Metall.*) der Gießer.

moulder (2) ['mouldə], *v.n.* vermodern.

mouldy ['mouldi], *adj.* moderig, schim-melig.

moult, (*Am.*) **molt** [moult], *v.n.* (*Zool.*) sich mausern.

mound [maund], *s.* der Erdhügel.

mount [maunt], *v.a.* besteigen (*horse*, *hill*); montieren, anbringen (*apparatus*). — *v.n.* sich belaufen (*bill*), betragen. — *s.* (*Poet.*) der Berg.

mountain ['mauntin], *s.* der Berg.

mountaineer [maunti'niə], *s.* der Berg-steiger.

mountainous ['mauntinəs], *adj.* gebirgig.

mourn [mɔ:n], *v.a.*, *v.n.* (be)trauern.

mourner ['mɔ:nə], *s.* der Leidtragende.

mournful ['mɔ:nful], *adj.* traurig.

mourning ['mɔ:niŋ], *s.* die Trauer.

mouse [maus], *s.* (*Zool.*) die Maus.

moustache [mə'stɑ:ʃ], *s.* der Schnurr-bart.

mouth [mauθ], *s.* (*Anat.*) der Mund; (*Geog.*) die Mündung.

movable ['mu:vəbl], *adj.* beweglich, verschiebbar.

move [mu:v], *v.a.* bewegen; (*emotionally*) rühren; den Antrag stellen (*a motion*). — *v.n.* umziehen; über-siedeln (*change residence*).

movement ['mu:vmənt], *s.* die Be-wegung (*motion*); (*Mus.*) der Satz; das Gehwerk (*mechanism*).

movies ['mu:viz], *s. pl.* (*coll.*) das Kino, der Film.

mow [mou], *v.a. irr.* mähen.

much [mʌtʃ], *adj.* viel. — *adv.* sehr, bei weitem; *as — as*, ganze . . .; *as — again*, noch einmal so viel.

mud [mʌd], *s.* der Schmutz, Schlamm.

muddle [mʌdl], *v.a.* verwirren. — *s.* die Verwirrung.

muff (1) [mʌf], *s.* der Muff.

muff (2) [mʌf], *v.a.* verderben (*mar*).

muffin ['mʌfin], *s.* der dünne Kuchen, der Butterkuchen.

muffle [mʌfl], *v.a.* umwickeln; dämp-fen (*a sound*).

muffler ['mʌflə], *s.* das Halstuch; (*Motor.*) der Schalldämpfer.

mug [mʌg], *s.* der Krug; (*coll.*) der Tölpel.

muggy ['mʌgi], *adj.* schwül; feucht (*humid*).

mulatto [mju'lætou], *s.* der Mulatte.

mulberry ['mʌlbəri], *s.* (*Bot.*) die Maulbeere.

mule [mju:l], *s.* (*Zool.*) das Maultier, der Maulesel.

muleteer [mju:li'tiə], *s.* der Maulesel-treiber.

mulish ['mju:liʃ], *adj.* störrisch.

mull (1) [mʌl], *v.a.* würzen (*add spices to*); *mulled wine*, der Glühwein.

mull (2) [mʌl], *v.a.*, *v.n. — over*, überlegen, überdenken.

multifarious [mʌlti'fɛəriəs], *adj.* man-nigfaltig.

multiple ['mʌltipl], *s.* das Vielfache. — *adj.* vielfach.

multiply ['mʌltiplai], *v.a.*, *v.n.* multi-plizieren, (sich) vervielfachen.

multitude ['mʌltitju:d], *s.* die Menge.

multitudinous [mʌlti'tju:dinəs], *adj.* zahlreich, massenhaft.

mumble [mʌmbl], *v.a.*, *v.n.* murmeln.

mummery ['mʌməri], *s.* der Mummen-schanz.

mummy (1) ['mʌmi], *s.* die Mumie.

mummy (2) ['mʌmi], *s.* (*coll.*) die Mutti.

mumps [mʌmps], *s.* (*Med.*) der Ziegen-peter.

munch [mʌntʃ], *v.a.*, *v.n.* kauen.

mundane ['mʌndein], *adj.* weltlich.

municipal [mju'nisipəl], *adj.* städtisch.

municipality [mjunisi'pæliti], *s.* die Stadtgemeinde.

munificence [mju'nifisəns], *s.* die Freigebigkeit.

munificent [mju'nifisənt], *adj.* freige-big.

mural ['mjuərəl], *s.* die Wandmalerei; das Wandgemälde. — *adj.* Wand-.

murder ['mə:də], *s.* der Mord. — *v.a.* ermorden, morden.

murderer ['mə:dərə], *s.* der Mörder.

murderous ['mə:dərəs], *adj.* mör-derisch.

murky ['mə:ki], *adj.* trübe, unklar.

murmur ['mə:mə], *s.* das Gemurmel.

muscle [mʌsl], *s.* (*Anat.*) der Muskel.

muscular ['mʌskjulə], *adj.* (*Anat.*) muskulös, Muskel-.

muse (1) [mju:z], *v.n.* nachdenken, sinnen.

muse (2) [mju:z], *s.* (*Myth.*) die Muse.

museum [mju:'ziəm], *s.* das Museum.

mushroom ['maʃrum], *s.* (*Bot.*) der (eßbare) Pilz.

music ['mju:zik], *s.* die Musik; — **stand**, das Notenpult.

musician [mju:'ziʃən], *s.* der Musiker.

musk [mʌsk], *s.* der Moschus, Bisam.

musket ['mʌskit], *s.* die Muskete, Flinte.

muslin ['mʌzlin], *s.* der Musselin.

mussel [mʌsl], *s.* (*Zool.*) die Muschel.

must [mʌst], *v. aux. irr.* müssen; (*with neg.*) dürfen.

mustard ['mʌstəd], *s.* der Senf.

muster ['mʌstə], *v.a.* mustern. — *v.n.* sich sammeln. — *s.* die Musterung; *pass* —, die Prüfung bestehen.

musty ['mʌsti], *adj.* dumpf, dumpfig, muffig.

mutable ['mju:təbl], *adj.* veränderlich.

mutation [mju:'teiʃən], *s.* die Veränderung; (*Maths., Genetics*) die Mutation.

mute [mju:t], *adj.* stumm. — *v.a.* (*Mus.*) dämpfen. — *s.* (*Mus.*) der Dämpfer.

mutilate ['mju:tileit], *v.a.* verstümmeln.

mutinous ['mju:tinəs], *adj.* aufrührerisch.

mutiny ['mju:tini], *s.* die Meuterei.

mutter ['mʌtə], *v.a., v.n.* murmeln.

mutton [mʌtn], *s.* das Hammelfleisch; — *chop*, das Hammelkotelett.

mutual ['mju:tjuəl], *adj.* gegenseitig.

muzzle [mʌzl], *s.* der Maulkorb (*of dog*); die Mündung (*of rifle*).

my [mai], *poss. adj.* mein.

myrrh [mə:], *s.* die Myrrhe.

myrtle ['mə:tl], *s.* (*Bot.*) die Myrte.

myself [mai'self], *pron.* ich selbst; (*refl.*) mir, mich.

mysterious [mis'tiəriəs], *adj.* geheimnisvoll.

mystery ['mistəri], *s.* das Geheimnis.

mystic ['mistik], *s.* der Mystiker.

mystic(al) ['mistik(əl)], *adj.* mystisch, geheimnisvoll, dunkel.

mystification [mistifi'keiʃən], *s.* die Täuschung, Irreführung.

mystify ['mistifai], *v.a.* täuschen, verblüffen.

myth [miθ], *s.* der Mythos, die Mythe, Sage.

N

N [en]. das N.

nag (1) [næg], *v.a.* nörgeln.

nag (2) [næg], *s.* der Gaul.

nail [neil], *s.* der Nagel. — *v.a.* annageln.

naïve ['naii:v], *adj.* naiv.

naïveté, naïvety [nai'i:vti], *s.* die Naivität, Einfalt.

naked ['neikid], *adj.* nackt.

name [neim], *s.* der Name. — *v.a.* nennen, heißen.

nameless ['neimlis], *adj.* namenlos.

namely ['neimli], *adv.* nämlich.

namesake ['neimseik], *s.* der Namensvetter.

nap [næp], *s.* das Schläfchen. — *v.n.* schlummern, einnicken.

nape [neip], *s.* (*Anat.*) das Genick.

napkin ['næpkin], *s.* die Serviette; Windel (*baby's*).

narrate [nə'reit], *v.a.* erzählen.

narrative ['nærətiv], *s.* die Erzählung, Geschichte.

narrator [nə'reitə], *s.* der Erzähler; (*Rad.*) der Sprecher.

narrow ['nærou], *adj.* eng, schmal; — *gauge*, die Schmalspur; — *minded*, engstirnig.

nasty ['nɑ:sti], *adj.* widerlich, unangenehm.

natal [neitl], *adj.* Geburts-.

nation ['neiʃən], *s.* die Nation, das Volk.

nationality [næʃə'næliti], *s.* die Staatsangehörigkeit, Nationalität.

native ['neitiv], *adj.* einheimisch, eingeboren. — *s.* der Eingeborene.

natural ['nætʃərəl], *adj.* natürlich.

naturalist ['nætʃərəlist], *s.* der Naturforscher.

naturalization [nætʃərəlai'zeiʃən], *s.* die Naturalisierung, Einbürgerung.

naturalize ['nætʃərəlaiz], *v.a., v.n.* naturalisieren, einbürgern.

nature ['neitʃə], *s.* die Natur, das Wesen.

naught [nɔ:t], *s.* die Null.

naughty ['nɔ:ti], *adj.* unartig.

nausea ['nɔ:siə], *s.* (*Med.*) der Brechreiz, das Erbrechen.

nautical ['nɔ:tikəl], *adj.* nautisch, Schiffs-.

naval ['neivəl], *adj.* Marine-.

nave [neiv], *s.* (*Archit.*) das Schiff.

navigable ['nævigəbl], *adj.* schiffbar.

navigate ['nævigeit], *v.a., v.n.* steuern.

navigation [nævi'geiʃən], *s.* die Schiffahrt (*shipping*); das Steuern, die Navigation.

navy ['neivi], *s.* die Flotte, Marine.

Neopolitan [niə'pɔlitən], *adj.* neapolitanisch. — *s.* der Neapolitaner.

near [niə], *adj., adv.* nahe, in der Nähe. — *prep.* nahe (an *or* bei).

nearly ['niəli], *adv.* beinahe, fast.

nearness ['niənis], *s.* die Nähe.

neat [ni:t], *adj.* nett, sauber (*tidy*); rein, unvermischt, pur (*unmixed*).

neatness ['ni:tnis], *s.* die Sauberkeit.

necessary ['nesəsəri], *adj.* notwendig.

necessity [ni'sesiti], *s.* die Not, Notwendigkeit; (*pl.*) das zum Leben Nötige.

neck [nek], *s.* (*Anat.*) der Hals; *stick o.'s* — *out*, es riskieren. — *v.n.* (*Am. sl.*) knutschen.

necklace ['neklis], s. das Halsband, die Halskette.

necktie ['nektai], s. der Schlips, die Krawatte.

need [ni:d], s. die Not, der Bedarf. — v.a. brauchen, nötig haben.

needful ['ni:dful], adj. notwendig.

needle [ni:dl], s. die Nadel. — v.a. (coll.) sticheln, ärgern (annoy).

needy ['ni:di], adj. in Not befindlich, arm, bedürftig.

nefarious [ni'fɛəriəs], adj. nichtswürdig, schändlich.

negative ['negativ], adj. negativ, verneinend. — s. (Phot.) das Negativ; die Verneinung (denial); in the —, verneinend.

neglect [ni'glekt], v.a. vernachlässigen, außer acht lassen. — s. die Vernachlässigung.

neglectful [ni'glektful], adj. nachlässig.

negligence ['neglidʒəns], s. die Nachlässigkeit.

negotiate [ni'gouʃieit], v.a., v.n. verhandeln, unterhandeln.

negotiation [nigouʃi'eiʃən], s. die Unterhandlung.

Negro ['ni:grou], s. der Neger.

neigh [nei], v.n. wiehern.

neighbour ['neibə], s. der Nachbar.

neighbourhood ['neibəhud], s. die Nachbarschaft, Umgebung.

neighbouring ['neibəriŋ], adj. Nachbar-, benachbart.

neighbourliness ['neibəlinis], s. das gute nachbarliche Verhältnis, die Geselligkeit.

neither ['naiðə or 'ni:ðə], adj., pron. keiner (von beiden). — conj. auch nicht; — . . . nor, weder . . . noch.

Nepalese [nepəʹliːz], adj. nepalesisch. — s. der Nepalese.

nephew ['nefju or 'nevju], s. der Neffe.

nerve [nəːv], s. der Nerv; der Mut (courage); die Frechheit (impudence); (pl.) die Angst, Nervosität.

nervous ['nəːvəs], adj. nervös; — of, furchtsam vor (Dat.); ängstlich wegen (Genit.).

nest [nest], s. das Nest; (fig.) — egg, die Ersparnisse, f. pl. — v.n. nisten.

nestle [nesl], v.n. sich anschmiegen.

net (1) [net], s. das Netz. — v.a. (Fische) fangen, ins Netz bekommen.

net (2) [net], adj. netto; ohne Verpackung; — weight, das Nettogewicht.

nettle [netl], s. (Bot.) die Nessel. — v.a. sticheln, ärgern.

neurosis [njuəʹrousis], s. (Med.) die Neurose.

neutrality [njuːʹtræliti], s. die Neutralität.

never ['nevə], adv. nie, niemals; — mind, mach Dir (machen Sie sich) nichts draus!

nevertheless [nevəðəʹles], conj. trotzdem, nichtsdestoweniger.

new [nju:], adj. neu; New Year's Day, der Neujahrstag; New Zealander, der Neuseeländer. — s. (pl.) die Nachrichten, f. pl.

newspaper ['nju:speipə], s. die Zeitung.

next [nekst], adj. nächst. — adv. danach.

nib [nib], s. die Spitze (of pen).

nibble [nibl], v.a., v.n. knabbern, nagen (at, an, Dat.).

nice [nais], adj. fein (scrupulous); nett, angenehm (pleasant).

nicety ['naisəti], s. die Feinheit (of distinction etc.).

nickel [nikl], s. das Nickel; (Am.) Fünfcentstück.

nickname ['nikneim], s. der Spitzname.

niece [ni:s], s. die Nichte.

Nigerian [nai'dʒiəriən], adj. nigerisch. — s. der Nigerier.

niggardly ['nigədli], adj. geizig.

nigh [nai], adj., adv. (Poet.) nahe.

night [nait], s. die Nacht; last —, gestern abend; the — before last, vorgestern abend; at —, nachts.

nightingale ['naitiŋgeil], s. (Orn.) die Nachtigall.

nightmare ['naitmɛə], s. der Alpdruck.

nimble [nimbl], adj. flink; geschickt (deft).

nine [nain], num. adj. neun.

nineteen [nai'ti:n],num. adj. neunzehn.

ninety ['nainti], num. adj. neunzig.

ninth [nainθ], num. adj. neunte.

nip [nip], v.a. zwicken.

nipple [nipl], s. (Anat.) die Brustwarze.

nitrogen ['naitrədʒən], s. (Chem.) der Stickstoff.

no [nou], part. nein — adj. kein. — adv. nicht; — one, niemand.

nobility [no'biliti], s. der Adel.

noble [noubl], adj. edel; großmütig (magnanimous); adlig (well born).

nobody ['noubədi], pron. niemand.

nod [nɔd], v.n. nicken.

noise [nɔiz], s. der Lärm, das Geräusch.

noiseless ['nɔizlis], adj. geräuschlos.

noisy ['nɔizi], adj. laut, lärmend.

nominal ['nɔminəl], adj. nominell.

nominate ['nɔmineit], v.a. nennen (name); ernennen (appoint).

nomination [nɔmi'neiʃən], s. die Nennung, Ernennung.

none [nʌn], pron. keiner, niemand.

nonsense ['nɔnsəns], s. der Unsinn.

nook [nuk], s. die Ecke, der Winkel.

noon [nu:n], s. der Mittag.

noose [nu:s], s. die Schlinge.

nor [nɔ:], conj. auch nicht; neither . . . —, weder . . . noch.

normal [nɔ:məl], adj. normal.

normalize ['nɔ:məlaiz], v.a. normalisieren.

Norman ['nɔ:mən], adj. normannisch. — s. der Normanne.

north [nɔ:θ], s. der Norden. — adj. nördlich.

northerly, northern ['nɔ:ðəli, 'nɔ:ðən], adj. nördlich, von Norden.

Norwegian [nɔ:'wi:dʒən], adj. norwegisch. — s. der Norweger.

nose [nouz], s. (Anat.) die Nase; — dive, der Sturzflug.

nosey ['nouzi], *adj.* (*coll.*) neugierig.
nostalgia [nɔs'tældʒə], *s.* das Heimweh, die Sehnsucht.
nostril ['nɔstril], *s.* (*Anat.*) das Nasenloch.
not [nɔt], *adv.* nicht; — *at all*, keineswegs.
notable ['noutəbl], *adj.* berühmt, wohlbekannt; bemerkenswert.
notary ['noutəri], *s.* der Notar.
notch [nɔtʃ], *s.* die Kerbe. — *v.a.* kerben, einkerben.
note [nout], *s.* die Notiz, der Zettel; (*Mus.*) die Note; die Bedeutung; *take —s*, Notizen machen; *take — of*, zur Kenntnis nehmen. — *v.a.* notieren, aufzeichnen.
notepaper ['noutpeipə], *s.* das Briefpapier.
noteworthy ['noutwə:ði], *adj.* beachtenswert.
nothing ['nʌθiŋ], *pron. s.* nichts; *for —*, umsonst; *good for —*, der Taugenichts.
notice ['noutis], *s.* die Kenntnis (*attention*); die Anzeige (*in press etc.*); Notiz; Bekanntmachung; *give —*, kündigen. — *v.a.* bemerken.
noticeable ['noutisəbl], *adj.* bemerkbar.
notification [noutifi'keiʃən], *s.* die Benachrichtigung, Bekanntmachung.
notify ['noutifai], *v.a.* benachrichtigen, informieren.
notion ['nouʃən], *s.* der Begriff (*concept*); die Idee (*idea*); die Meinung (*opinion*).
notoriety [noutə'raiiti], *s.* der üble Ruf.
notorious [no'tɔ:riəs], *adj.* berüchtigt.
notwithstanding [notwið'stændiŋ], *prep.* ungeachtet (*Genit.*). — *adv.* trotzdem, dennoch. — *conj.* — *that*, obgleich.
nought [nɔ:t], *s.* die Null (*figure 0*); nichts (*nothing*).
noun [naun], *s.* (*Gram.*) das Hauptwort, Substantiv.
nourish ['nʌriʃ], *v.a.* nähren; ernähren.
nourishment ['nʌriʃmənt], *s.* die Nahrung.
Nova Scotian ['nouvə'skouʃən], *adj.* neuschottisch. [Neuschottland]
novel [nɔvl], *s.* (*Lit.*) der Roman. — *adj.* neu; neuartig (*modern*).
novelty ['nɔvlti], *s.* die Neuheit.
November [no'vembə]. der November.
novice ['nɔvis], *s.* der Neuling (*greenhorn*); (*Eccl.*) der, die Novize.
novitiate [no'viʃiit], *s.* die Lehrzeit; (*Eccl.*) das Noviziat.
now [nau], *adv.* nun, jetzt; — *and then*, dann und wann, hin und wieder. — *conj.* — (*that*), da nun.
nowadays ['nauədeiz], *adv.* heutzutage.
nowhere ['nouhwɛə], *adv.* nirgends.
noxious ['nɔkʃəs], *adj.* (*Med., Bot.*) schädlich.
nozzle [nɔzl], *s.* die Düse; (*sl.*) die Schnauze.
nuclear ['nju:kliə], *adj.* (*Phys.*) nuklear, Kern-.
nucleus ['nju:kliəs], *s.* der Kern.

nude [nju:d], *adj.* nackt, bloß.
nudge [nʌdʒ], *v.a.* leicht anstoßen.
nudity ['nju:diti], *s.* die Nacktheit.
nugget ['nʌgit], *s.* der Klumpen.
nuisance ['nju:səns], *s.* die Plage, Lästigkeit; das Ärgernis (*annoyance*).
null [nʌl], *adj.* null und nichtig; ungültig.
nullify ['nʌlifai], *v.a.* annullieren, ungültig machen.
nullity ['nʌliti], *s.* die Ungültigkeit.
numb [nʌm], *adj.* erstarrt, gefühllos. — *v.a.* erstarren lassen.
number ['nʌmbə], *s.* die Zahl, Nummer (*telephone etc.*); die Anzahl (*quantity*); *cardinal —*, die Grundzahl; *ordinal —*, die Ordnungszahl. — *v.a.* nummerieren; zählen (*count*).
numbness ['nʌmnis], *s.* die Erstarrung.
numeral ['nju:mərəl], *s.* (*Gram.*) das Zahlwort.
numerical [nju:'merikəl], *adj.* (*Maths.*) Zahlen-, numerisch.
numerous ['nju:mərəs], *adj.* zahlreich.
numismatics [nju:miz'mætiks], *s.* die Münzkunde.
numskull ['nʌmskʌl], *s.* der Dummkopf.
nun [nʌn], *s.* (*Eccl.*) die Nonne.
nunnery ['nʌnəri], *s.* (*Eccl.*) das Nonnenkloster.
nuptials ['nʌpʃəlz], *s. pl.* (*Lit., Poet.*) die Hochzeit, das Hochzeitsfest.
nurse [nə:s], *s.* die Krankenschwester, Pflegerin; die Amme (*wet nurse*). — *v.a.* pflegen.
nursery ['nə:səri], *s.* das Kinderzimmer; (*Bot.*) die Pflanzschule, Baumschule (*for trees*); — *school*, der Kindergarten.
nurture ['nə:tʃə], *v.a.* nähren, aufziehen.
nut [nʌt], *s.* (*Bot.*) die Nuß; (*Tech.*) die Schraubenmutter; (*Am. coll.*) *nuts*, verrückt.
nutcracker ['nʌtkrækə], *s.* (*usually pl.*) der Nußknacker.
nutmeg ['nʌtmeg], *s.* (*Cul.*) die Muskatnuß.
nutriment ['nju:trimənt], *s.* die Nahrung; (*animals*) das Futter.
nutrition [nju:'triʃən], *s.* die Ernährung.
nutritious [nju:'triʃəs], *adj.* nahrhaft.
nutshell ['nʌtʃel], *s.* die Nußschale; (*fig.*) *put in a —*, kurz ausdrücken.
nymph [nimf], *s.* (*Myth.*) die Nymphe.

O

O [ou]. das O. — *int.* oh!
oaf [ouf], *s.* der Tölpel.
oak [ouk], *s.* (*Bot.*) die Eiche.
oaken ['oukən], *adj.* eichen, aus Eichenholz.

oar [ɔ:], *s.* das Ruder; *put o.'s — in,* sich einmengen.
oasis [ou'eisis], *s.* die Oase.
oath [ouθ], *s.* der Eid; der Fluch (*curse*); *commissioner for —s,* der öffentliche Notar; *take an —,* einen Eid schwören or leisten.
oats [outs], *s. pl.* (*Bot.*) der Hafer; *sow o.'s wild —s,* sich austoben, sich die Hörner ablaufen.
obdurate ['ɔbdjurit], *adj.* halsstarrig.
obedience [o'bi:djəns], *s.* der Gehorsam.
obedient [o'bi:djənt], *adj.* gehorsam.
obeisance [o'beisəns], *s.* die Verbeugung, Ehrfurchtsbezeigung.
obese [o'bi:s], *adj.* fettleibig, beleibt.
obey [o'bei], *v.a., v.n.* gehorchen (*Dat.*).
obituary [o'bitjuəri], *s.* der Nachruf, der Nekrolog.
object ['ɔbdʒikt], *s.* der Gegenstand (*thing*); (*Gram.*) das Objekt; der Zweck (*objective, purpose*). — [əb-'dʒekt], *v.n. — to,* einwenden (*gainsay*); vorhalten (*remonstrate*).
objection [əb'dʒekʃən], *s.* der Einwand.
objectionable [əb'dʒekʃənəbl], *adj.* anstößig.
objective [əb'dʒektiv], *adj.* objektiv, unparteiisch. — *s.* das Ziel (*aim*).
obligation [ɔbli'geiʃən], *s.* die Verpflichtung.
obligatory [o'bligətəri, 'ɔblig-], *adj.* verbindlich, obligatorisch.
oblige [o'blaidʒ], *v.a.* verpflichten; *much obliged,* vielen Dank; *can you — me?* können Sie mir aushelfen?
obliging [o'blaidʒiŋ], *adj.* gefällig, zuvorkommend.
oblique [o'bli:k], *adj.* schräg, schief; (*fig.*) indirekt.
obliterate [o'blitəreit], *v.a.* auslöschen (*extinguish*); vertilgen (*destroy*).
oblivion [o'bliviən], *s.* die Vergessenheit.
oblivious [o'bliviəs], *adj.* vergeßlich.
oblong ['ɔblɔŋ], *adj.* länglich. — *s.* das Rechteck.
obloquy ['ɔbləkwi], *s.* die Schmähung, Schande.
obnoxious [ɔb'nɔkʃəs], *adj.* verhaßt, scheußlich.
obscene [ɔb'si:n], *adj.* anstößig, obszön.
obscenity [ɔb'sen-, ɔb'si:niti], *s.* die Obszönität.
obscure [əb'skjuə], *adj.* dunkel (*dark*); unbekannt (*unknown*).
obscurity [əb'skjuəriti], *s.* die Dunkelheit (*darkness*); die Unbekanntheit.
obsequies ['ɔbsikwiz], *s. pl.* das Leichenbegängnis.
obsequious [ɔb'si:kwiəs], *adj.* unterwürfig.
observance [əb'zə:vəns], *s.* die Befolgung, Beobachtung, das Einhalten (*Law etc.*).
observant [əb'zə:vənt], *adj.* aufmerksam; achtsam.
observation [ɔbzə'veiʃən], *s.* die Beobachtung (*watching*); die Bemerkung (*remark*).

observatory [əb'zə:vətri], *s.* die Sternwarte.
observe [əb'zə:v], *v.a.* beobachten (*watch*); bemerken (*notice, remark on*).
obsession [əb'seʃən], *s.* die Besessenheit, fixe Idee.
obsolete ['ɔbsəli:t], *adj.* veraltet.
obstacle ['ɔbstəkl], *s.* das Hindernis.
obstinacy ['ɔbstinəsi], *s.* die Hartnäckigkeit.
obstinate ['ɔbstinit], *adj.* hartnäckig.
obstruct [əb'strʌkt], *v.a.* hemmen, hindern.
obstruction [əb'strʌkʃən], *s.* das Hindernis, die Hemmung, Verstopfung.
obtain [əb'tein], *v.a.* erhalten, erlangen; bekommen (*get*).
obtrude [ɔb'tru:d], *v.n.* sich aufdrängen. — *v.a.* aufdrängen.
obtrusive [əb'tru:siv], *adj.* aufdringlich.
obtuse [ɔb'tju:s], *adj.* stumpf; dumm (*stupid*).
obviate ['ɔbvieit], *v.a.* vorbeugen (*Dat.*).
obvious ['ɔbviəs], *adj.* klar, offenbar, selbstverständlich.
occasion [o'keiʒən], *s.* die Gelegenheit (*chance*); der Anlaß; die Veranlassung (*cause*). — *v.a.* veranlassen; verursachen (*cause*).
occasional [o'keiʒənəl], *adj.* gelegentlich.
occident ['ɔksidənt], *s.* das Abendland, der Westen.
occult [ɔ'kʌlt], *adj.* geheim, Okkult-.
occupancy ['ɔkjupənsi], *s.* der Besitz, das Innehaben (*holding*).
occupant ['ɔkjupənt], *s.* der Inhaber; der Bewohner (*of house*), Insasse.
occupation [ɔkju'peiʃən], *s.* die Besetzung; (*Mil.*) *army of —,* die Besatzung; der Beruf, die Beschäftigung (*job*); *— with,* das Befassen mit (*Dat.*).
occupy ['ɔkjupai], *v.a.* (*Mil.*) besetzen, in Besitz nehmen; beschäftigen (*engage*); bekleiden (*office*).
occur [ə'kə:], *v.n.* geschehen, sich ereignen; *— to s.o.,* jemandem einfallen.
occurrence [ə'kʌrəns], *s.* das Geschehen, Ereignis, der Vorfall.
ocean ['ouʃən], *s.* der Ozean, die See, das Meer. — *adj.* Meeres-.
octagon ['ɔktəgɔn], *s.* das Achteck.
octagonal [ɔk'tægənəl], *adj.* achteckig.
October [ɔk'toubə], der Oktober.
octogenarian [ɔktodʒi'nɛəriən], *s.* der Achtzigjährige.
ocular ['ɔkjulə], *adj.* Augen-.
oculist ['ɔkjulist], *s.* (*Med.*) der Augenarzt.
odd [ɔd], *adj.* ungerade (*number*); seltsam (*queer*); einzeln (*solitary*). — *s.* (*pl.*) die Wahrscheinlichkeit.
oddity ['ɔditi], *s.* die Seltenheit, Sonderbarkeit.
oddment ['ɔdmənt], *s.* (*pl.*) die Reste, *m. pl.*
ode [oud], *s.* (*Poet.*) die Ode.
odious ['oudiəs], *adj.* verhaßt, widerwärtig.

odium [ˈoudiəm], *s.* der Haß.

odorous [ˈoudərəs], *adj.* duftend, duftig.

odour [ˈoudə], *s.* der Geruch, Duft.

of [ɔv], *prep.* von (*Dat.*); aus (*out of*) (*Dat.*); — *course,* natürlich.

off [ɔf, ɔːf], *adv.* fort, weg; entfernt; *make* —, sich davonmachen; *far* —, weit weg; — *and on,* ab und zu; *well* —, wohlhabend. — *prep.* von (*from*); fort von; entfernt von (*distant from*).

offal [ɔfl], *s.* der Abfall.

offence [oˈfens], *s.* (*Law*) das Vergehen; die Beleidigung (*insult*).

offend [oˈfend], *v.a.* beleidigen (*insult*). — *v.n.* (*Law*) sich vergehen (gegen, *Acc.*).

offensive [oˈfensiv], *adj.* beleidigend (*insulting*); anstößig (*indecent*). — *s.* die Offensive, der Angriff (*against,* auf, *Acc.*).

offer [ˈɔfə], *v.a.* bieten (*auction*); anbieten (*hold out*). — *s.* das Anerbieten; (*Comm.*) das Angebot, der Antrag.

offering [ˈɔfəriŋ], *s.* das Opfer.

office [ˈɔfis], *s.* das Amt; die Stellung (*position*); die Funktion (*duties*); das Büro; (*Eccl.*) der Gottesdienst; *high* —, das hohe Amt; — *bearer,* der Amtswalter.

officer [ˈɔfisə], *s.* (*Mil.*) der Offizier; der Beamte (*functionary*); *honorary* —, der ehrenamtliche Beamte, der Beamte im Ehrenamt.

official [oˈfiʃəl], *adj.* offiziell, amtlich. — *s.* der Beamte.

officiate [oˈfiʃieit], *v.n.* amtieren; fungieren.

officious [oˈfiʃəs], *adj.* zudringlich, (übertrieben) dienstfertig.

offing [ˈɔfiŋ], *s.* (*Naut.*) die hohe See; *in the* —, bevorstehend.

offset [ɔfˈset], *v.a.* (*Comm.*) ausgleichen; (*Typ.*) offset drucken, im Offset drucken; (*fig.*) unschädlich machen, wettmachen. — [ˈɔfset], *s.* (*Comm.*) die Gegenrechnung, der Ausgleich; (*Typ.*) der Offsetdruck.

offshoot [ˈɔfuːt], *s.* der Sprößling.

offspring [ˈɔfspriŋ], *s.* die Nachkommenschaft.

often, (*Poet.*) **oft** [ɔfn, ɔft], *adv.* oft, häufig.

ogle [ougl], *v.a., v.n.* äugeln, beäugeln, glotzen, anglotzen.

ogre [ˈougə], *s.* der Menschenfresser.

oil [ɔil], *s.* das Öl. — *v.a.* einölen, einschmieren.

oilcloth [ˈɔilklɔθ], *s.* das Wachstuch.

ointment [ˈɔintmənt], *s.* die Salbe.

old [ould], *adj.* alt; —*fashioned,* altmodisch.

olive [ˈɔliv], *s.* (*Bot.*) die Olive; *the Mount of Olives,* der Ölberg.

Olympic [oˈlimpik], *adj.* olympisch; *the* — *Games,* die Olympischen Spiele.

omelette [ˈɔmlit], *s.* (*Cul.*) das Omelett, der Eierkuchen.

omen [ˈoumən], *s.* das (böse) Vorzeichen, das Omen.

ominous [ˈɔminəs], *adj.* von schlimmer Vorbedeutung, ominös.

omission [oˈmiʃən], *s.* die Unterlassung; (*Typ.*) die Auslassung.

omit [oˈmit], *v.a.* unterlassen (*leave undone*); auslassen (*leave out*).

omnibus [ˈɔmnibəs], *s.* der Omnibus, der Autobus.

omnipotent [ɔmˈnipətənt], *adj.* allmächtig.

omniscient [ɔmˈnisiənt], *adj.* allwissend.

on [ɔn], *prep.* an; auf; über; vor; bei; zu; nach; um; *call* — (*s.o.*), vorsprechen (bei, *Dat.*); — *fire,* in Flammen; — *condition;* unter der Bedingung (*Comm.*); — *account,* a Konto; — *high,* hoch oben; — *my honour,* auf mein Ehrenwort; — *purpose,* absichtlich; —*sale,* zum Verkauf. — *adv.* weiter, fort (*forward*); gültig, zutreffend (*correct, valid*); *get* —, vorwärtskommen; *get* — *with s.th.,* weitermachen; *get* — *with s.o.,* auskommen (mit, *Dat.*).

once [wʌns], *adv.* einmal; einst (*long ago*); — *more,* nochmals, noch einmal; — *and for all,* ein für alle Mal; *at* —, sogleich; — *in a while,* ab und zu. — *conj.* sobald.

one [wʌn], *num. adj.* ein, eine, ein; — *way street,* die Einbahnstraße. — *pron.* man (*impersonal*). — *s. little* — der Kleine; — *by* —, eins nach dem anderen, einzeln.

onerous [ˈɔnərəs], *adj.* beschwerlich.

onion [ˈʌnjən], *s.* (*Bot.*) die Zwiebel.

onlooker [ˈɔnlukə], *s.* der Zuschauer.

only [ˈounli], *adj.* einzig, allein. — *adv.* nur, bloß. — *conj.* jedoch.

onset [ˈɔnset], *s.* der Angriff (*attack*); der Anfang (*beginning*).

onslaught [ˈɔnslɔːt], *s.* der Angriff, Überfall.

onward [ˈɔnwəd], *adj.* fortschreitend. — *adv.* (*also* **onwards**) vorwärts.

ooze [uːz], *s.* der Schlamm. — *v.n.* träufeln, sickern.

opacity [oˈpæsiti], *s.* (*Phys.*) die Dunkelheit, Undurchsichtigkeit.

opal [oupl], *s.* der Opal.

opaque [oˈpeik], *adj.* (*Phys.*) dunkel, undurchsichtig.

open [oupn], *adj.* offen; offenherzig (*frank*); — *to suggestions,* einem Vorschlag zugänglich. — *v.a.* öffnen; eröffnen (*start*); — *an account,* ein Konto eröffnen. — *v.n.* sich öffnen, sich auftun.

opening [ˈoupniŋ], *s.* das Öffnen; die freie Stelle; die Gelegenheit (*opportunity*). — *adj.* einleitend; — *gambit,* (*Chess*) der Eröffnungszug.

openness [ˈoupənnis], *s.* die Offenheit, Ehrlichkeit (*frankness*).

opera [ˈɔpərə], *s.* (*Mus.*) die Oper; *comic* —, die komische Oper; — *hat,* der Zylinderhut, Klapphut.

operatic [ɔpəˈrætik], *adj.* (*Mus.*) Opern-.

operate ['ɔpəreit], *v.a.*, *v.n.* (*Engin.*) bedienen; (*Med.*) operieren (*on*, *Acc.*).

operation [ɔpə'reiʃən], *s.* (*Med.*, *Mil.*) die Operation; die Bedienung (*of engine etc.*).

operative ['ɔpərətiv], *adj.* wirksam (*effective*). — *s.* der Arbeiter.

opiate ['oupiit], *s.* das Schlafmittel. — *adj.* einschläfernd.

opine [o'pain], *v.n.* meinen.

opinion [o'pinjən], *s.* die Meinung; *in my —*, meiner Meinung nach.

opinionated [o'pinjəneitid], *adj.* von sich eingenommen, selbstgefällig.

opium ['oupjəm], *s.* das Opium.

opponent [ə'pounənt], *s.* der Gegner.

opportune ['ɔpətju:n], *adj.* gelegen, günstig.

opportunity [ɔpə'tju:niti], *s.* die Gelegenheit, Chance; die Möglichkeit.

oppose [ə'pouz], *v.a.* bekämpfen; widerstreiten, entgegentreten (*Dat.*).

opposite ['ɔpəzit], *adj.* entgegengesetzt; gegenüberliegend; gegensätzlich (*contrary*). — *prep.* gegenüber (*Dat.*). — *s.* das Gegenteil.

opposition [ɔpə'ziʃən], *s.* (*Parl.*) die Opposition; der Widerstand.

oppress [ə'pres], *v.a.* unterdrücken.

oppression [ə'preʃən], *s.* die Unterdrückung.

oppressive [ə'presiv], *adj.* drückend, tyrannisch.

opprobrious [ə'proubriəs], *adj.* schändlich, schimpflich.

opprobrium [ə'proubriəm], *s.* die Schande.

optician [ɔp'tiʃən], *s.* der Optiker.

optics ['ɔptiks], *s.* die Optik.

optimism ['ɔptimizm], *s.* der Optimismus.

option ['ɔpʃən], *s.* die Wahl.

optional ['ɔpʃənəl], *adj.* Wahl-, frei, beliebig.

opulence ['ɔpjuləns], *s.* der Reichtum (*an*, *Dat.*), die Üppigkeit.

opulent ['ɔpjulənt], *adj.* reich, üppig.

or [ɔ:], *conj.* oder; noch (*after neg.*); *either . . . —*, entweder . . . oder.

oracle ['ɔrəkl], *s.* das Orakel.

oral ['ɔ:rəl], *adj.* mündlich. — *s.* die mündliche Prüfung.

orange ['ɔrindʒ,] *s.* (*Bot.*) die Orange, Apfelsine.

oration [ɔ'reiʃən], *s.* die feierliche Rede, Ansprache.

orator ['ɔrətə], *s.* der Redner.

oratorio [ɔrə'tɔ:riou], *s.* (*Mus.*) das Oratorium.

oratory ['ɔrətəri], *s.* (*Eccl.*) die Kapelle; (*Rhet.*) die Redekunst.

orb [ɔ:b], *s.* die Kugel; der Reichsapfel; (*Poet.*) der Himmelskörper.

orbit ['ɔ:bit], *s.* (*Astron.*) die Bahn (der Gestirne), Planetenbahn.

orchard ['ɔ:tʃəd], *s.* der Obstgarten.

orchestra ['ɔ:kistrə], *s.* (*Mus.*) das Orchester.

ordain [ɔ:'dein], *v.a.* ordinieren, anordnen; (*Eccl.*) zum Priester weihen.

ordeal ['ɔ:diəl], *s.* die Feuerprobe; Heimsuchung.

order ['ɔ:də], *s.* die Ordnung (*system*); die Verordnung (*command etc.*); (*Mil.*) der Befehl; (*Comm.*) die Bestellung; (*Biol.*) die Ordnung; der Orden (*Eccl.*; *also decoration*); *take (holy) —s*, ordiniert werden, Priester werden; *in — to*, um zu; *in — that*, so daß; *by —*, auf (den) Befehl. — *v.a.* befehlen, verordnen, anordnen; (*Comm.*) bestellen.

orderly ['ɔ:dəli], *adj.* ordentlich, ruhig. — *s.* (*Mil.*) die Ordonanz; (*Med.*) der Gehilfe, Krankenwärter.

ordinal ['ɔ:dinl], *adj.*, *s.* (*number*) die Ordnungszahl.

ordinance ['ɔ:dinəns], *s.* die Verordnung.

ordinary ['ɔ:dinəri], *adj.* gewöhnlich.

ordnance ['ɔ:dnəns], *s.* das schwere Geschütz; (*Mil.*, *Geog.*) — *survey*, die Landesvermessung.

ore [ɔ:], *s.* das Erz, Metall.

organ ['ɔ:gən], *s.* das Organ; (*Mus.*) die Orgel; — *grinder*, der Leierkastenmann.

organic [ɔ:'gænik], *adj.* organisch.

organisation [ɔ:gənai'zeiʃən], *s.* die Organisation.

organise ['ɔ:gənaiz], *v.a.* organisieren.

organism ['ɔ:gənizm], *s.* (*Biol.*) der Organismus.

organist ['ɔ:gənist], *s.* (*Mus.*) der Organist.

orgy ['ɔ:dʒi], *s.* die Orgie.

oriel ['ɔ:riəl], *s.* der Erker; — *window*, das Erkerfenster.

orient ['ɔ:riənt], *s.* der Orient, Osten.

oriental [ɔ:ri'entl], *adj.* östlich.

orifice ['ɔrifis], *s.* die Öffnung, Mündung.

origin ['ɔridʒin], *s.* der Ursprung, die Herkunft.

original [ə'ridʒinl], *adj.* Ursprungs-, ursprünglich; originell (*creative*). — *s.* das Original.

originality [əridʒi'næliti], *s.* die Originalität.

originate [ə'ridʒineit], *v.n.* entstehen, entspringen. — *v.a.* hervorbringen, entstehen lassen.

ornament ['ɔ:nəmənt], *s.* das Ornament; die Verzierung (*decoration*).

ornate [ɔ:'neit], *adj.* geziert, geschmückt.

orphan ['ɔ:fən], *s.* der, die Waise.

orphanage ['ɔ:fənidʒ], *s.* das Waisenhaus.

orthodoxy ['ɔ:θədɔksi], *s.* die Orthodoxie, die Rechtgläubigkeit.

orthography [ɔ:'θɔgrəfi], *s.* die Rechtschreibung.

orthopaedic [ɔ:θə'pi:dik], *adj.* orthopädisch.

oscillate ['ɔsileit], *v.n.* oszillieren, schwingen.

oscillatory ['ɔsileitəri], *adj.* schwingend, oszillierend.

osier ['ouʒjə], *s.* (*Bot.*) die Korbweide.

osprey ['ɔsprei], *s.* (*Orn.*) der Seeadler.

ossify ['ɔsifai], *v.a.* verknöchern; versteinern lassen (*stone*). — *v.n.* verknöchern; versteinern (*stone*).

ostensible [ɔs'tensibl], *adj.* scheinbar, anscheinend, vorgeblich.

ostentation [ɔsten'teiʃən], *s.* die Großtuerei, der Prunk.

ostentatious [ɔsten'teiʃəs], *adj.* großtuerisch, prahlerisch, protzig.

ostler ['ɔslə], *s.* (*obs.*) der Stallknecht.

ostracize ['ɔstrəsaiz], *v.a.* verbannen, ausschließen.

ostrich ['ɔstritʃ], *s.* (*Orn.*) der Strauß.

other ['ʌðə], *adj.* ander. — *pron.*, *s.* *the* —, der, die, das andere.

otherwise ['ʌðəwaiz], *conj.* sonst. — *adv.* andernfalls.

otter ['ɔtə], *s.* (*Zool.*) die Otter.

ought [ɔ:t], *v. aux. defect.* sollte, müßte.

ounce [auns], *s.* die Unze.

our ['auə], *poss. adj.* unser, uns(e)re, unser.

ours ['auəz], *poss. pron.* unsrig, unser, uns(e)re, unser.

ourselves [auə'selvz], *pers. pron.* wir, wir selbst, uns selbst; (*refl.*) uns.

ousel [u:zl], *s.* (*Orn.*) die Amsel.

out [aut], *adv.* aus; draußen (*outside*); außerhalb (*outside, externally*); heraus; hinaus (*outward, away from the speaker*). — *prep.* — *of*, aus, von (*Dat.*).

outer ['autə], *adj.* äußer.

outfit ['autfit], *s.* die Ausrüstung.

outing ['autiŋ], *s.* der Ausflug.

outhouse ['authaus], *s.* das Nebengebäude, der Anbau.

outlaw ['autlɔ:], *s.* der Verbannte, der Vogelfreie.

outlay ['autlei], *s.* (*Comm.*) die Auslagen, die Spesen, *f. pl.*

outlet ['autlit], *s.* der Ausfluß, Abfluß; (*fig.*) das Ventil.

outline ['autlain], *s.* der Umriß, Entwurf. — [aut'lain], *v.a.* skizzieren, umreißen, kurz beschreiben.

outlive [aut'liv], *v.a.* überleben.

outlook ['autluk], *s.* die Aussicht, der Ausblick; die Weltanschauung (*philosophy*).

outlying ['autlaiiŋ], *adj.* außenliegend, außerhalb liegend, entlegen.

outnumber [aut'nʌmbə], *v.a.* an Zahl übertreffen.

outpatient ['autpeiʃənt], *s.* der ambulante Patient.

outrage ['autreidʒ], *s.* die Beleidigung (*insult*); die Gewalttat. — [aut'reidʒ], *v.a.* verletzen, beleidigen, schänden.

outrageous [aut'reidʒəs], *adj.* schändlich, schimpflich, unerhört; übertrieben (*exaggerated*).

outright ['autrait], *adj.* völlig. — [aut'rait], *adv.* gerade heraus, gänzlich.

outrun [aut'rʌn], *v.a. irr.* überholen, einholen.

outset ['autset], *s.* der Anfang.

outshine [aut'ʃain], *v.a. irr.* übertreffen.

outside [aut'said], *adv.* außen, draußen. — ['autsaid], *prep.* außerhalb (*Genit.*).

— *adj.* äußere, außenstehend. — *s.* das Äußere, die Außenseite.

outskirts ['autskə:ts], *s. pl.* die Umgebung, Vorstadt.

outstanding [aut'stændiŋ], *adj.* hervorragend (*excellent*); noch unbeglichen (*unpaid*); unerledigt (*undone*).

outstay [aut'stei], *v.a.* länger bleiben, zu lange bleiben.

outvote [aut'vout], *v.a.* überstimmen.

outward ['autwəd], *adj.* äußere, äußerlich, außerhalb befindlich. — *adv.* (*also* **outwards**) auswärts, nach außen.

outweigh [aut'wei], *v.a.* schwerer wiegen als, überwiegen.

outwit [aut'wit], *v.a.* überlisten.

oval [ouvl], *adj.* oval. — *s.* das Oval.

ovary ['ouvəri], *s.* (*Anat.*) der Eierstock.

ovation [o'veiʃən], *s.* die Huldigung, Ovation.

oven [ʌvn], *s.* der Backofen; (kleine) Schmelzofen.

over ['ouvə], *prep.* über; oberhalb. — *adv.* über; herüber; drüben; — *there*, drüben; hinüber (*across*); vorüber (*past*).

overact [ouvər'ækt], *v.n.* übertreiben.

overawe [ouvər'ɔ:], *v.a.* einschüchtern.

overbalance [ouvə'bæləns], *v.a.* überwiegen. — *v.n.* überkippen.

overbear [ouvə'bɛə], *v.a. irr.* überwältigen.

overbearing [ouvə'bɛəriŋ], *adj.* anmaßend.

overboard ['ouvəbɔ:d], *adv.* über Bord.

overburden [ouvə'bə:dn], *v.a.* überlasten.

overcast [ouvə'ka:st], *adj.* bewölkt.

overcharge [ouvə'tʃa:dʒ], *v.a.* zu viel berechnen (*pers., Dat.*), übervorteien; überladen (*overload*). — *s.* die Übervorteilung; (*Tech.*) der Überdruck.

overcoat ['ouvəkout], *s.* der Mantel; *light* —, der Überzieher.

overcome [ouvə'kʌm], *v.a., v.n. irr.* überwinden.

overdo [ouvə'du:], *v.a. irr.* übertreiben.

overdone [ouvə'dʌn], *adj.* übergar, zu lange gekocht.

overdrive [ouvə'draiv], *v.a. irr.* abhetzen, zu weit treiben. — ['ouvədraiv] *s.* (*Motor.*) der Schnellgang.

overdue [ouvə'dju:], *adj.* überfällig, verfallen.

overflow [ouvə'flou], *v.a., v.n.* überfließen; überfluten (*banks*). — ['ouvəflou], *s.* der Überfluß (*flood*); die Überschwemmung.

overgrow [ouvə'grou], *v.a. irr.* überwachsen, überwuchern. — *v.n.* zu groß werden.

overhang [ouvə'hæŋ], *v.a. irr.* überhängen.

overhaul [ouvə'hɔ:l], *v.a.* überholen. — ['ouvəhɔ:l], *s.* die Überholung.

overhead [ouvə'hed], *adv.* droben; oben (*above*). — ['ouvəhed], *s.* (*pl.*) (*Comm.*) laufende Unkosten, *pl.*

overhear [ouvə'hiə], *v.a. irr.* zufällig hören.

overjoyed [ouvə'dʒɔid], *adj.* entzückt.

overlap [ouvə'læp], *v.n.* überschneiden, zusammenfallen (*dates etc.*). — ['ouvə-læp], *s.* die Überschneidung, das Zusammenfallen.

overload [ouvə'loud], *v.a.* überlasten; (*Elec.*) überladen.

overlook [ouvə'luk], *v.a.* übersehen; verzeihen (*disregard*).

overmuch [ouvə'mʌtʃ], *adv.* allzusehr.

overpay [ouvə'pei], *v.a., v.n.* zu viel bezahlen.

overpopulated [ouvə'pɔpjuleitid], *adj.* übervölkert.

overpower [ouvə'pauə], *v.a.* überwältigen.

overrate [ouvə'reit], *v.a.* überschätzen.

overreach [ouvə'ri:tʃ], *v.a.* übervorteilen.

override [ouvə'raid], *v.a. irr.* überreiten; unterdrücken (*suppress*).

overrule [ouvə'ru:l], *v.a.* nicht gelten lassen, verwerfen.

overseer ['ouvəsiə], *s.* der Aufseher.

oversleep [ouvə'sli:p], *v.n. irr.* sich verschlafen.

overstep [ouvə'step], *v.a.* überschreiten.

overstrain [ouvə'strein], *v.a., v.n.* (sich) zu sehr anstrengen, überanstrengen.

overt ['ouvə:t], *adj.* offenkundig; öffentlich (*public*).

overtake [ouvə'teik], *v.a. irr.* einholen; (*Mot.*) überholen.

overtax [ouvə'tæks], *v.a.* zu hoch besteuern; (*fig.*) überanstrengen (*strain*).

overthrow [ouvə'θrou], *v.a. irr.* umstürzen; (*Pol.*) stürzen. — ['ouvəθrou], *s.* der Sturz.

overtime ['ouvətaim], *s.* Überstunden, *f. pl.*

overture ['ouvətjuə], *s.* die Ouvertüre.

overturn [ouvə'tə:n], *v.a.* umstürzen. — *v.n.* überschlagen.

overweening [ouvə'wi:niŋ], *adj.* eingebildet.

overweight [ouvə'weit], *s.* das Übergewicht.

overwhelm [ouvə'welm], *v.a.* überwältigen.

overwork [ouvə'wə:k], *v.n.* sich überarbeiten.

overwrought [ouvə'rɔ:t], *adj.* übermäßig erregt, aufgeregt, überreizt.

owe [ou], *v.a.* schulden. — *v.n.* verdanken (*be in debt*).

owing ['ouiŋ], *pred. adj.* — *to*, dank (*Dat.*), zufolge (*Dat.*).

owl [aul], *s.* (*Orn.*) die Eule.

own (1) [oun], *v.a.* besitzen (*possess*). — *adj.* eigen.

own (2) [oun], *v.a.* anerkennen (*acknowledge*).

owner ['ounə], *s.* der Besitzer, Eigentümer.

ox [ɔks], *s.* (*Zool.*) der Ochse.

oxidate ['ɔksideit] *see* **oxidise**.

oxide ['ɔksaid], *s.* (*Chem.*) das Oxyd.

oxidise ['ɔksidaiz], *v.a., v.n.* (*Chem.*) oxydieren.

oxtail ['ɔksteil], *s.* der Ochsenschwanz.

oxygen ['ɔksidʒən], *s.* (*Chem.*) der Sauerstoff.

oyster ['ɔistə], *s.* (*Zool.*) die Auster.

ozone ['ouzoun], *s.* (*Chem.*) das Ozon.

P

P [pi:]. das P.

pa [pɑ:], *s.* (*coll.*) Papa, der Vater.

pace [peis], *s.* der Gang, Schritt (*step*); das Tempo (*rate*). — *v.n.* — *up and down*, auf- und abschreiten. — *v.a.* einschulen (*horse*).

Pacific, The [pə'sifik, θə]. der Stille Ozean.

pacific [pə'sifik], *adj.* friedlich, still.

pacify ['pæsifai], *v.a.* Frieden stiften, beruhigen.

pack [pæk], *s.* das *or* der Pack; der Ballen (*bale*); das Rudel (*wolves*); das Spiel (*cards*); das Paket, die Packung. — *v.a.* packen (*a case*); parteiisch zusammensetzen; die Karten schlecht mischen (*cheat at cards*); *packed like sardines*, dichtgedrängt, eingepfercht. — *v.n.* packen; seine Sachen einpacken.

package ['pækidʒ], *s.* der Ballen (*bale*); das Gepäckstück, Paket.

packet ['pækit], *s.* das Paket; (*Naut.*) — *boat*, das Paketboot, Postschiff.

pact [pækt], *s.* der Pakt, Vertrag.

pad [pæd], *s.* das Polster, Kissen; der Notizblock (*writing block*). — *v.a.* auspolstern; *padded cell*, die Gummizelle.

padding ['pædiŋ], *s.* (*Tail.*) das Futter; (*fig.*) die (nichtssagende) Ausfüllung, das leere Geschwätz.

paddle [pædl], *v.a., v.n.* rudern, paddeln. — *s.* das Paddel, (Doppel)ruder, das Schaufelruder; — *steamer*, der Raddampfer.

paddock ['pædək], *s.* der Sattelplatz; das Gehege.

padlock ['pædlɔk], *s.* das Vorhängeschloß, Vorlegeschloß.

pagan ['peigən], *adj.* heidnisch. — *s.* der Heide.

paganism ['peigənizm], *s.* das Heidentum.

page (1) [peidʒ], *s.* der Page (*court attendant*); Hoteljunge (*hotel boy*). — *v.a.* durch Pagen suchen lassen.

page (2) [peidʒ], *s.* die Seite (*of book*). — *v.a.* paginieren (*book*).

pageant ['pædʒənt], *s.* der Aufzug, der Prunkzug; das Schaustück (*dramatic*).

pail [peil], *s.* der Eimer.

pain [pein], *s.* der Schmerz, die Pein; (*pl.*) die Mühe; *go to a lot of* —*s*, sich große Mühe geben. — *v.a.* schmerzen; bekümmern (*mentally*).

paint [peint], *s.* die Farbe (*dye*); die Schminke (*make-up*). — *v.a.* anstreichen, malen.

painter ['peintǝ], *s.* der Maler.

painting ['peintiŋ], *s.* das Gemälde.

pair [pɛǝ], *s.* das Paar; *two* —*s of shoes*, zwei Paar Schuhe; *a* — *of spectacles*, die Brille; *a* — *of scissors*, die Schere. — *v.a.* paaren. — *v.n.* sich paaren.

pajamas [pǝ'dʒɑ:mǝz] *see under* **pyjamas**.

Pakistani [pɑ:ki'stɑ:ni], *adj.* pakistanisch. — *s.* der Pakistaner.

palace ['pælǝs], *s.* der Palast.

palatable ['pælǝtǝbl], *adj.* schmackhaft.

palatal ['pælǝtl], *adj.* (*Phonet.*) palatal, Gaumen-, Vordergaumen-. — *s.* (*Phonet.*) der Gaumenlaut.

palate ['pælit], *s.* der Gaumen.

Palatinate, The [pǝ'lætinit, ðǝ]. die Pfalz, Pfalzgrafschaft.

palaver [pǝ'lɑ:vǝ], *s.* die Unterredung; das Palaver.

pale (1) [peil], *adj.* blaß, bleich.

pale (2) [peil], *s.* der Pfahl; *beyond the* —, unkultiviert.

Palestinian [pælis'tiniǝn], *adj.* palästinisch. — *s.* der Palästiner.

palette ['pælit], *s.* die Palette (*see also* **pallet** (1)).

paling ['peiliŋ], *s.* der Lattenzaun; (*pl.*) der Pfahlbau.

pall (1) [pɔ:l], *s.* das Leichentuch.

pall (2) [pɔ:l], *v.n.* schal werden (*become stale*).

pallet (1) ['pælit], *s.* die Palette (*painter's*); — *knife*, das Streichmesser (*potter's etc.*).

pallet (2) ['pælit], *s.* der Strohsack.

palliative ['pæliǝtiv], *s.* linderndes Mittel; (*fig.*) die Beschönigung.

pallid ['pælid], *adj.* blaß, bleich.

pallor ['pælǝ], *s.* die Blässe.

palm (1) [pɑ:m], *s.* die Handfläche. — *v.a.* — (*off*) *on to s.o.*, an jemanden loswerden, jemandem etwas andrehen.

palm (2) [pɑ:m], *s.* (*Bot.*) die Palme; *Palm Sunday*, Palmsonntag.

palmer ['pɑ:mǝ], *s.* (*obs.*) der Pilger (*pilgrim*).

palmist ['pɑ:mist], *s.* der Handleser, Wahrsager.

palmistry ['pɑ:mistri], *s.* die Handwahrsagerei.

palmy ['pɑ:mi], *adj.* glorreich.

palpable ['pælpǝbl], *adj.* handgreiflich, greifbar, klar.

palpitate ['pælpiteit], *v.n.* klopfen (*of heart*).

palsied ['pɔ:lzid], *adj.* (*Med.*) gelähmt.

palsy ['pɔ:lzi], *s.* (*Med.*) die Lähmung.

paltry ['pɔ:ltri], *adj.* erbärmlich, armselig.

pamper ['pæmpǝ], *v.a.* verwöhnen.

pan (1) [pæn], *s.* die Pfanne. — *v.n.* —

out, sich ausbreiten, sich weiten.

pan (2) [pæn], *v.a.* (*Phot.*) kreisen, im Bogen führen.

panacea [pænǝ'siǝ], *s.* das Universalmittel.

pancake ['pænkeik], *s.* der Pfannkuchen.

pander ['pændǝ], *v.n.* fröhnen (*Dat.*), nachgeben.

pane [pein], *s.* die Glasscheibe.

panel ['pænl], *s.* die Holzfüllung, Täfelung (*in room*); die Liste; die Kommission (*of experts etc.*).

pang [pæŋ], *s.* die Angst, Pein; der Schmerz, Stich (*stab of pain*).

panic ['pænik], *s.* die Panik, der Schrecken.

panoply ['pænǝpli], *s.* (*Poet.*) die Rüstung.

pansy ['pænzi], *s.* (*Bot.*) das Stiefmütterchen; (*sl.*) der Weichling, Feigling.

pant [pænt], *v.n.* keuchen, schwer atmen.

pantaloons [pæntǝ'lu:nz] (*usually abbr.* **pants** [pænts]), *s. pl.* die Unterhosen, Hosen, *f.pl.*

panther ['pænθǝ], *s.* (*Zool.*) der Panther.

pantomime ['pæntǝmaim], *s.* die Pantomime, das Weihnachtsstück.

pantry ['pæntri], *s.* die Speisekammer.

pap [pæp], *s.* der Kinderbrei.

papacy ['peipǝsi], *s.* das Papsttum.

papal ['peipǝl], *adj.* päpstlich.

paper ['peipǝ], *s.* das Papier (*material*); die Zeitung (*daily* —); die Abhandlung (*essay*); — *knife*, der Brieföffner. — *v.a.* tapezieren (*a room*).

paperhanger ['peipǝhæŋǝ], *s.* der Tapezierer.

paperweight ['peipǝweit], *s.* der Briefbeschwerer.

par [pɑ:], *s.* die Gleichheit, das Pari.

parable ['pærǝbl], *s.* die Parabel, das Gleichnis.

parabola [pǝ'ræbǝlǝ], *s.* (*Geom.*) die Parabel.

parabolic [pærǝ'bɔlik], *adj.* parabolisch, gleichnishaft.

parachute ['pærǝʃu:t], *s.* (*Aviat.*) der Fallschirm.

parade [pǝ'reid], *s.* die Parade, der Aufmarsch. — *v.a.* herausstellen; zur Schau tragen (*show off*). — *v.n.* (*Mil.*) vorbeimarschieren.

paradise ['pærǝdais], *s.* das Paradies.

paraffin ['pærǝfin], *s.* das Paraffin.

paragon ['pærǝgǝn], *s.* das Musterkind, Musterbeispiel, Vorbild.

paragraph ['pærǝgrɑ:f], *s.* der Abschnitt, Absatz, Paragraph.

Paraguayan [pærǝ'gwaiǝn], *adj.* paraguayisch. — *s.* der Paraguayer.

parallel ['pærǝlel], *adj.* parallel. — *s.* die Parallele.

paralyse ['pærǝlaiz], *v.a.* lähmen.

paralysis [pǝ'rælisis], *s.* die Lähmung.

paramount ['pærǝmaunt], *adj.* oberst.

paramour ['pærǝmuǝ], *s.* der *or* die Geliebte.

451

parapet

parapet ['pærəpit], *s.* das Geländer, die Brüstung.

paraphrase ['pærəfreiz], *s.* die Umschreibung. — *v.a.* umschreiben.

parasite ['pærəsait], *s.* der Schmarotzer, Parasit.

parasol ['pærəsɔl], *s.* der Sonnenschirm.

parboil ['pɑːbɔil], *v.a.* aufkochen lassen.

parcel [pɑːsl], *s.* das Paket; Bündel (*bundle*). — *v.a.* — *up*, einpacken.

parch [pɑːtʃ], *v.a.* austrocknen.

parchment ['pɑːtʃmənt], *s.* das Pergament.

pardon [pɑːdn], *v.a.* vergeben, verzeihen (*Dat.*); begnadigen (*Acc.*) (*give amnesty*). — *s.* der Pardon, die Verzeihung; — *!*, *I beg your —!* bitte um Entschuldigung; *I beg your —*? wie bitte?

pare [pɛə], *v.a.* beschneiden (*nails*); schälen (*fruit*).

parent ['pɛərənt], *s.* der Vater, die Mutter, (*pl.*) die Eltern, *pl.*

parentage ['pɛərəntidʒ], *s.* die Abkunft, Herkunft.

parenthesis [pəˈrenθisis], *s.* die Parenthese, die Klammer.

parish ['pæriʃ], *s.* das Kirchspiel, die Gemeinde, die Pfarre.

parishioner [pəˈriʃənə], *s.* das Gemeindemitglied.

Parisian [pəˈriziən], *adj.* parisisch. — *s.* der Pariser.

park [pɑːk], *s.* der Park; (*Motor.*) der Wagenpark, Parkplatz. — *v.a., v.n.* parken.

parking ['pɑːkiŋ], *s.* (*Motor.*) das Parken; — *meter*, die Parkuhr, der Parkometer.

parley ['pɑːli], *s.* die Unterredung, Verhandlung. — *v.n.* verhandeln.

parliament ['pɑːləmənt], *s.* das Parlament.

parlour ['pɑːlə], *s.* das Wohnzimmer, die gute Stube; —*maid*, das Dienstmädchen; — *trick*, das Kunststück.

parochial [pəˈroukiəl], *adj.* Pfarr-, Gemeinde-; (*fig.*) engstirnig.

parody ['pærədi], *s.* die Parodie. — *v.a.* parodieren.

parole [pəˈroul], *s.* das Ehrenwort; (*Mil.*) das Losungswort.

paroxysm ['pærəksizm], *s.* der heftige Anfall.

parquet [pɑːˈki], *s.* das Parkett; — *floor*, der Parkettfußboden.

parrot ['pærət], *s.* (*Orn.*) der Papagei.

parry ['pæri], *v.a.* parieren, abwehren.

parse [pɑːs, pɑːz], *v.a.* (*Gram.*) analysieren.

parsimony ['pɑːsiməni], *s.* die Sparsamkeit.

parsley ['pɑːsli], *s.* (*Bot.*) die Petersilie.

parson [pɑːsn], *s.* der Pastor, Pfarrer.

parsonage ['pɑːsənidʒ], *s.* das Pfarrhaus.

part [pɑːt], *s.* der Teil; Anteil (*share*); (*Theat.*) die Rolle; (*Mus.*) die Stimme;

(*Geog.*) die Gegend; *for his —*, seinerseits. — *v.n.* — (*with*), sich trennen (von, *Dat.*); — *company*, auseinandergehen.

partake [pɑːˈteik], *v.n.* teilnehmen, teilhaben (*in*, an, *Dat.*).

partial [pɑːʃl], *adj.* Teil-; parteiisch (*subjective*); — *to*, eingenommen für.

participate [pɑːˈtisipeit], *v.n.* teilnehmen (*in*, an, *Dat.*).

participation [pɑːtisiˈpeiʃən], *s.* die Teilnahme.

participle ['pɑːtisipl], *s.* (*Gram.*) das Mittelwort, Partizip(ium).

particle ['pɑːtikl], *s.* die Partikel, das Teilchen.

particular [pəˈtikjulə], *adj.* besonder (*special*); einzel (*individual*); sonderbar (*queer*); ungewöhnlich; genau. — *s.* (*pl.*) die Details, *n. pl.*, Einzelheiten, *f. pl.*

parting ['pɑːtiŋ], *s.* der Abschied (*taking leave*); der Scheitel (*hair*).

partisan [pɑːtiˈzæn], *s.* der Partisane, Parteigänger.

partition [pɑːˈtiʃən], *s.* die Teilung (*division*); die Scheidewand (*dividing wall*). — *v.a.* teilen; aufteilen (*divide up*).

partly ['pɑːtli], *adv.* zum Teil, teils.

partner ['pɑːtnə], *s.* der Partner; Teilhaber (*in business etc.*).

partnership ['pɑːtnəʃip], *s.* die Partnerschaft.

partridge ['pɑːtridʒ], *s.* (*Orn.*) das Rebhuhn.

party ['pɑːti], *s.* (*Pol.*) die Partei; (*Law*) die Partei, Seite; die Gesellschaft, die Party (*social gathering*); *throw or give a —*, einen Gesellschaftsabend (*or* eine Party) geben; *guilty —*, der schuldige Teil; (*Build.*) — *wall*, die Brandmauer.

Paschal ['pɑːskəl], *adj.* Oster-.

pass [pɑːs], *v.a.* passieren; vorbeigehen (an, *Dat.*); durchlassen (*let through*); (*Law*) — *sentence*, das Urteil fällen. — *v.n.* fortgehen, vergehen, geschehen (*happen*); vorübergehen (*of time*); — *for*, gelten; (*Sch.*) durchkommen (*exam*); *come to —*, sich ereignen. — *s.* der Paß; (*Theat.*) die Freikarte.

passable ['pɑːsəbl], *adj.* gangbar; (*fig.*) leidlich, erträglich.

passage ['pæsidʒ], *s.* der Durchgang (*thoroughfare*); das Vergehen (*of time*); die Seereise; die Stelle (*book*).

passenger ['pæsindʒə], *s.* der Reisende, Passagier; — *train*, der Personenzug.

passer-by ['pɑːsəbai], *s.* der Passant, Vorübergehende.

passing ['pɑːsiŋ], *s.* das Vorbeigehen, das Vorübergehen; (*Parl.*) das Durchgehen; das Hinscheiden (*death*). — *adj.* vorübergehend, zeitweilig.

Passion ['pæʃən], *s.* (*Eccl.*) das Leiden; (*Mus.*) die Passion; — *Week*, die Karwoche; — *flower*, die Passionsblume.

passion ['pæʃən], *s.* die Leidenschaft;

fly into a —, aufbrausen.

passive ['pæsiv], *adj.* passiv. — *s.* (*Gram.*) das Passiv(um).

Passover ['pɑːsouvə], *s.* (*Rel.*) das Passahfest.

passport ['pɑːspɔːt], *s.* der Reisepaß.

past [pɑːst], *adj.* vergangen. — *adv.* vorbei. — *prep.* nach (*time*). — *s.* die Vergangenheit; (*Gram.*) das Imperfekt, Präteritum.

paste [peist], *s.* die Paste, der Brei; der Kleister (*glue*). — *v.a.* kleben, kleistern.

pasteboard ['peistbɔːd], *s.* die Pappe.

pastime ['pɑːstaim], *s.* der Zeitvertreib.

pastor ['pɑːstə], *s.* (*Rel.*) der Seelsorger, Pfarrer.

pastoral ['pɑːstərəl], *adj.* Hirten-, pastoral. — *s.* (*Poet*). das Hirtengedicht.

pastry ['peistri], *s.* (*Cul.*) die Pastete; das Gebäck; — *cook*, der Konditor, Zuckerbäcker.

pasture ['pɑːstʃə], *s.* die Weide, das Grasland. — *v.n.* weiden, grasen.

pasty ['pɑːsti, 'pæsti], *s.* (*Cul.*) die Pastete. — ['peisti] *adj.* teigig.

pat [pæt], *s.* der Klaps; der Schlag (*slap*). — *v.a.* leicht schlagen, streicheln (*gently*).

patch [pætʃ], *v.a.* flicken, ausbessern. — *s.* der Fleck (*mending material*); der Flecken (*land*); (*coll.*) *no — on him*, kein Vergleich mit ihm; nicht zu vergleichen mit ihm.

patent ['peitənt or 'pætənt], *adj.* offen, klar, patent; — *leather*, das Glanzleder. — *s.* das Patent.

patentee [peitən'tiː], *s.* der Patentinhaber.

paternal [pə'təːnəl], *adj.* väterlich.

path [pɑːθ], *s.* der Pfad, Weg, Fußsteig.

pathetic [pə'θetik], *adj.* pathetisch, rührend; armselig.

pathology [pə'θɔlədʒi], *s.* (*Med.*) die Pathologie.

pathway ['pɑːθwei], *s.* der Fußweg, Fußsteig.

patience ['peiʃəns], *s.* die Geduld; die Patience (*card game*).

patient ['peiʃənt], *adj.* geduldig. — *s.* (*Med.*) der Patient.

patrician [pə'triʃən], *adj.* patrizisch. — *s.* der Patrizier.

patrimony ['pætriməni], *s.* das (väterliche) Erbgut.

patriot ['peitriət, 'pætriət], *s.* der Patriot.

patriotism ['peitriətizm, 'pæt-], *s.* die Vaterlandsliebe, der Patriotismus.

patrol [pə'troul], *s.* die Patrouille, Streife. — *v.n.* auf Patrouille gehen.

patron ['peitrən], *s.* der Schutzherr, der Gönner; (*Comm.*) der Kunde; — *saint*, der Schutzheilige.

patronage ['pætrənidʒ], *s.* die Gönnerschaft, Huld.

patronize ['pætrənaiz], *v.a.* besuchen (*frequent*); begünstigen (*favour*).

patronizing ['pætrənaiziŋ], *adj.* herablassend.

patten [pætn], *s.* (*Archit.*) der Sockel; der Holzschuh (*clog*).

patter (1) ['pætə], *s.* das Geplätscher (*rain etc.*). — *v.n.* plätschern.

patter (2) ['pætə], *s.* das Geplauder (*chatter*). — *v.n.* schwätzen.

pattern ['pætən], *s.* das Muster; die Schablone (*in material*).

paucity ['pɔːsiti], *s.* die geringe Anzahl, der Mangel.

paunch [pɔːntʃ], *s.* der Wanst.

pauper ['pɔːpə], *s.* der Arme.

pauperize ['pɔːpəraiz], *v.a.* arm machen, verarmen lassen.

pause [pɔːz], *s.* die Pause. — *v.n.* innehalten.

pave [peiv], *v.a.* pflastern.

pavement ['peivmənt], *s.* das Pflaster; der Bürgersteig, Gehsteig.

pavilion [pə'viljən], *s.* das Gartenhaus; der Pavillon.

paw [pɔː], *s.* die Pfote; die Tatze. — *v.a.* streicheln, betasten.

pawn (1) [pɔːn], *s.* das Pfand. — *v.a.* verpfänden.

pawn (2) [pɔːn], *s.* (*Chess*) der Bauer.

pawnbroker ['pɔːnbroukə], *s.* der Pfandleiher.

pay [pei], *v.a. irr.* zahlen; bezahlen, begleichen (*bill*); — *attention*, aufpassen, Aufmerksamkeit schenken; — *o.'s respects*, Respekt zollen. — *v.n. irr.* sich bezahlt machen, sich lohnen (*it —s to . . .*). — *s.* (*Mil.*) der Sold; (*Comm.*) der Lohn (*wage*), die Bezahlung (*payment*).

payable ['peiəbl], *adj.* zahlbar, zu bezahlen.

payee [pei'iː], *s.* der Empfänger, Präsentant.

payer ['peiə], *s.* der Zahler; (*Comm.*) der Trassat.

payment ['peimənt], *s.* die Bezahlung, Begleichung (*of sum*).

pea [piː], *s.* (*Bot.*) die Erbse (*see also* **peas**(e).

peace [piːs], *s.* der Friede(n); die Ruhe (*restfulness*).

peaceable ['piːsəbl], *adj.* friedlich; friedliebend.

peaceful ['piːsful], *adj.* friedlich, ruhig (*restful*).

peach [piːtʃ], *s.* (*Bot.*) der or (*Austr.*) die Pfirsich.

peacock ['piːkɔk], *s.* (*Orn.*) der Pfau.

peahen ['piːhen], *s.* (*Orn.*) die Pfauhenne.

peak [piːk], *s.* der Gipfel, die Spitze; der Schirm (*of cap*); — *hour*, die Stunde des Hochbetriebs, Hauptverkehrsstunde.

peal [piːl], *v.a.* läuten. — *v.n.* erschallen. — *s.* das Läuten, Geläute.

peanut ['piːnʌt], *s.* (*Bot.*) die Erdnuß.

pear [pɛə], *s.* (*Bot.*) die Birne.

pearl [pəːl], *s.* die Perle; — *barley*, die Perlgraupen, *f. pl.*; *mother of* —, die Perlmutter.

peasant ['pezənt], s. der Bauer.
peasantry ['pezəntri], s. das Bauern-volk, die Bauernschaft.
peas(e) [pi:z], s. pl. pease pudding, der Erbsenbrei, das Erbsenpüree.
peat [pi:t], s. der Torf.
pebble [pebl], s. der Kiesel(stein).
peck (1) [pek], s. der Viertelscheffel (= 9 litres.)
peck (2) [pek], s. das Picken (of hen); (coll.) der Kuß. — v.a. hacken, hauen.
pecker ['pekə], s. die Picke, Haue; keep your — up! Mut bewahren!
peckish ['pekiʃ], adj. hungrig.
pectoral ['pektərəl], adj. Brust-. — s. das Brustmittel.
peculiar [pi'kju:liə], adj. eigenartig, eigentümlich (strange); — to, eigen (Dat.); besonder (special).
peculiarity [pikju:li'æriti], s. die Eigen-tümlichkeit, Eigenartigkeit.
pecuniary [pi'kju:niəri], adj. Geld-, geldlich, finanziell, pekuniär.
pedagogue ['pedəgɔg], s. der Päda-gog(e), Erzieher.
pedal [pedl] s. das Pedal; (Motor.) der Fußhebel. — v.n. radfahren; (coll.) radeln.
pedant ['pedənt], s. der Pedant.
pedantic [pi'dæntik], adj. pedantisch.
pedantry ['pedəntri], s. die Pedanterie.
peddle [pedl], v.a. hausieren.
peddling ['pedliŋ], adj. kleinlich, un-bedeutend.
pedestal ['pedistl], s. der Sockel.
pedestrian [pi'destriən], s. der Fuß-gänger. — adj. Fuß-, Fußgänger-.
pedigree ['pedigri:], s. der Stamm-baum.
pediment ['pedimənt], s. (Archit.) der Ziergiebel.
pedlar ['pedlə], s. der Hausierer.
peel [pi:l], s. die Schale (of fruit). — v.a. schälen. — v.n. sich schälen.
peep [pi:p], v.n. gucken. — s. der (schnelle) Blick, das Gucken; — show, der Guckkasten.
peer (1) [piə], s. (Parl.) der Pair, Lord; der Ebenbürtige (equal).
peer (2) [piə], v.n. gucken, blicken, schauen.
peerage ['piəridʒ], s. der (Reichs)adel.
peeress ['piəres], s. die Gattin eines Pairs.
peerless ['piəlis], adj. unvergleichlich.
peevish ['pi:viʃ], adj. mürrisch.
pe(e)wit ['pi:wit], s. (Orn.) der Kiebitz.
peg ['peg], s. der Pflock (stake); der Holzstift (in wall); clothes —, die Wäscheklammer. — v.a. anpflocken (to ground).
pelican ['pelikən], s. (Orn.) der Pelikan.
pellet ['pelit], s. das Kügelchen.
pell-mell ['pel'mel], adv. durchein-ander.
pelt (1) [pelt], v.a. — with, bewerfen mit, — a person with, werfen nach einem (Acc.). — v.n. strömen (rain etc.); rennen (hasten).
pelt (2) [pelt], s. der Pelz (of animal).

pen (1) [pen], s. quill —, die Feder; fountain —, die Füllfeder; ballpoint —, der Kugelschreiber. — v.a. schrei-ben; verfassen (compose).
pen (2) [pen], s. das Gehege. — v.a. einschliessen (sheep).
penal ['pi:nəl], adj. Straf-; — servitude, die Zuchthausstrafe.
penalize ['pi:nəlaiz], v.a. bestrafen.
penalty ['penəlti], s. die Strafe.
penance ['penəns], s. die Buße.
pence [pens] see under **penny**.
pencil ['pensl], s. der Bleistift; der Stift; (Geom.) der Strahl. — v.a. niederschreiben, notieren.
pendant ['pendənt], s. das Ohrgehänge; (fig.) das Gegenstück.
pendent ['pendənt], adj. hängend, schwebend.
pending ['pendiŋ], adj. in der Schwebe; unentschieden (undecided). — prep. während (during); bis (zu) (until).
pendulum ['pendjuləm], s. das Pendel.
penetrate ['penitreit], v.a. durch-dringen.
peninsula [pi'ninsjulə], s. die Halb-insel.
penitent ['penitənt], s. der Büßer. — adj. bußfertig.
penitentiary [peni'tenʃəri], s. (Am.) das Zuchthaus (prison).
penknife ['pennaif], s. das Taschen-messer.
pennant ['penənt], s. der Wimpel, das Fähnchen.
penniless ['penilis], adj. mittellos, ohne einen Heller Geld, arm.
pennon ['penən] see **pennant**.
penny ['peni], s. (pl. **pence** [pens], **pennies** ['peniz]) der Penny; (Am.) das Centstück; — farthing, das Hoch-rad; — whistle, die Blechpfeife; a pretty —, hübsches Geld.
pension ['penʃən], s. die Pension; das Ruhegehalt. — v.a. (off) pensionieren, in den Ruhestand versetzen.
pensive ['pensiv], adj. nachdenklich.
Pentecost ['pentikɔst], das or (pl.) die Pfingsten.
penthouse ['penthaus], s. das Wetter-dach.
penurious [pi'njuəriəs], adj. unbe-mittelt, arm (poor); dürftig, karg (meagre).
penury ['penjuəri], s. die Not, Armut.
peony ['piəni], s. (Bot.) die Päonie, Pfingstrose.
people [pi:pl], s. pl. das Volk (nation); die Leute, Menschen (pl.). — v.a. bevölkern.
pepper ['pepə], s. der Pfeffer. — v.a. pfeffern.
per [pə:], prep. pro; per; durch; as — account, laut Rechnung.
peradventure [pə:rəd'ventʃə], adv. (obs.) von ungefähr; vielleicht (per-haps).
perambulator [pə'ræmbjuleitə] (abbr. coll.) **pram** [præm], s. der Kinder-wagen.

perceive [pə'si:v], *v.a.* wahrnehmen, merken.

percentage [pə'sentidʒ], *s.* der Prozentsatz (*of interest*); Prozente, *n. pl.*

perceptible [pə'septibl], *adj.* wahrnehmbar, merklich.

perception [pə'sepʃən], *s.* die Wahrnehmung, Empfindung.

perch (1) [pə:tʃ], *v.n.* aufsitzen; sitzen (*of birds*). — *s.* die Stange.

perch (2) [pə:tʃ], *s.* (*Zool.*) der Barsch.

perchance [pə'tʃɑ:ns], *adv.* vielleicht.

percolate ['pə:kəleit], *v.n.* durchsickern, durchtröpfeln.

percolator ['pə:kəleitə], *s.* die Kaffeemaschine.

percussion [pə'kʌʃən], *s.* (*Mus.*) das Schlagzeug.

peremptory ['perəmptəri, pə'remptəri], *adj.* entschieden, bestimmt (*decided*); absprechend.

perennial [pə'reniəl], *adj.* (*Bot.*) perennierend; Dauer-.

perfect ['pə:fikt], *adj.* vollkommen, vollendet, perfekt. — *s.* (*tense*) (*Gram.*) das Perfekt(um). — [pə'fekt], *v.a.* vollenden.

perfection [pə'fekʃən], *s.* die Vollendung, Vollkommenheit; *to* —, vollkommen.

perfidious [pə'fidiəs], *adj.* treulos, untreu; tückisch.

perfidy ['pə:fidi], *s.* die Treulosigkeit.

perforate ['pə:fəreit], *v.a.* durchlöchern, perforieren (*paper*); durchbohren (*pierce*).

perforce [pə'fɔ:s], *adv.* mit Gewalt, notgedrungen.

perform [pə'fɔ:m], *v.a.* ausführen (*carry out*); (*Theat.*) aufführen. — *v.n.* spielen, auftreten (*of actor*).

performance [pə'fɔ:məns], *s.* die Ausführung; Verrichtung (*execution of duty etc.*); (*Theat.*) die Aufführung.

perfume ['pə:fju:m], *s.* das Parfüm; der Duft (*scent*). — *v.a.* parfümieren.

perfunctory [pə'fʌŋktəri], *adj.* nachlässig, oberflächlich, flüchtig.

perhaps [pə'hæps], *adv.* vielleicht.

peril ['peril], *s.* die Gefahr.

period ['piəriəd], *s.* die Periode (*time*); der Zeitraum (*span*); (*Am.*) der Punkt (*full stop*).

periodical [piəri'ɔdikəl], *adj.* periodisch. — *s.* die Zeitschrift.

perish ['periʃ], *v.n.* zugrunde gehen, umkommen.

perishable ['periʃəbl], *adj.* vergänglich; (*leicht*) verderblich (*of food*).

periwig ['periwig], *s.* die Perücke.

periwinkle (1) ['periwiŋkl], *s.* (*Zool.*) die Uferschnecke.

periwinkle (2) ['periwiŋkl], (*Bot.*) das Immergrün.

perjure ['pə:dʒə], *v.r.* meineidig werden.

perjurer ['pə:dʒərə], *s.* der Meineidige.

perjury ['pə:dʒəri], *s.* der Meineid.

permanence, permanency ['pə:mə-

nəns, 'pə:mənənsi], *s.* die Dauer, Beständigkeit.

permanent ['pə:mənənt], *adj.* Dauer-, dauerhaft, beständig; — *wave*, die Dauerwelle.

permeability [pə:miə'biliti], *s.* die Durchdringbarkeit, Durchlässigkeit.

permeable ['pə:miəbl], *adj.* durchdringlich.

permeate ['pə:mieit], *v.a.* durchdringen.

permissible [pə'misibl], *adj.* zulässig, statthaft.

permission [pə'miʃən], *s.* die Erlaubnis.

permit [pə'mit], *v.a.* zulassen, erlauben. — ['pə:mit], *s.* die Erlaubnis; (*official*) die Genehmigung.

permutation [pə:mju'teiʃən], *s.* (*Maths.*) die Permutation.

pernicious [pə'niʃəs], *adj.* verderblich, schädlich, bösartig.

perorate ['perəreit], *v.n.* eine (lange) Rede beschließen.

perpendicular [pə:pən'dikjulə], *adj.* senkrecht. — *s.* die Senkrechte.

perpetrate ['pə:pitreit], *v.a.* begehen (*commit*).

perpetration [pə:pi'treiʃən], *s.* die Verübung, Begehung.

perpetrator ['pə:pitreitə], *s.* der Begeher, Täter.

perpetual [pə'petjuəl], *adj.* (an-) dauernd; ewig.

perpetuate [pə'petjueit], *v.a.* verewigen.

perpetuity [pə:pi'tju:iti], *s.* die Ewigkeit.

perplex [pə'pleks], *v.a.* bestürzen, verblüffen.

perplexity [pə'pleksiti], *s.* die Bestürzung, Verwirrung.

persecute ['pə:sikju:t], *v.a.* verfolgen.

persecution [pə:si'kju:ʃən], *s.* die Verfolgung.

perseverance [pə:si'viərəns], *s.* die Ausdauer, Beharrlichkeit.

persevere [pə:si'viə], *v.n.* beharren (*in*, bei, *Dat.*).

Persian ['pə:ʃən], *adj.* persisch. — *s.* der Perser.

persist [pə'sist], *v.n.* beharren (*in*, auf, *Dat.*).

persistence [pə'sistəns], *s.* die Beharrlichkeit.

person ['pə:sən], *s.* die Person; *in* —, persönlich.

personal ['pə:sənəl], *adj.* persönlich.

personality [pə:sə'næliti], *s.* die Persönlichkeit.

personify [pə'sɔnifai], *v.a.* verkörpern.

personnel [pə:sə'nel], *s.* das Personal; (*Comm.*) — *manager*, der Personalchef.

perspective [pə'spektiv], *s.* die Perspektive. — *adj.* perspektivisch.

perspicacious [pə:spi'keiʃəs], *adj.* scharfsichtig, scharfsinnig.

perspicacity [pə:spi'kæsiti], *s.* der Scharfblick, Scharfsinn.

perspicuity [pə:spi'kju:iti], *s.* die Durchsichtigkeit, Klarheit.

perspicuous

perspicuous [pə'spikjuəs], *adj.* deutlich, klar.

perspiration [pə:spi'reiʃən], *s.* der Schweiß.

perspire [pə'spaiə], *v.n.* schwitzen.

persuade [pə'sweid], *v.a.* überreden.

persuasion [pə'sweiʒən], *s.* die Überredung.

persuasive [pə'sweiziv], *adj.* überzeugend, überredend.

pert [pə:t], *adj.* naseweis, keck.

pertain [pə'tein], *v.n.* (an)gehören (*to Dat.*).

pertinacious [pə:ti'neiʃəs], *adj.* beharrlich, halsstarrig.

pertinacity [pə:ti'næsiti], *s.* die Beharrlichkeit, Halsstarrigkeit.

pertinence, pertinency ['pə:tinəns, 'pə:tinənsi], *s.* die Angemessenheit.

pertinent ['pə:tinənt], *adj.* angemessen, passend.

pertness ['pə:tnis], *s.* die Keckheit, der Vorwitz.

perturb [pə'tə:b], *v.a.* verwirren, stören, beunruhigen.

perturbation [pə:tə'beiʃən], *s.* die Verwirrung, Störung, Beunruhigung.

peruke [pə'ru:k], *s.* die Perücke.

peruse [pə'ru:z], *v.a.* durchlesen.

Peruvian [pə'ru:vjən], *adj.* peruanisch. — *s.* der Peruaner.

pervade [pə'veid], *v.a.* durchdringen.

perverse [pə'və:s], *adj.* verkehrt.

perversion [pə'və:ʃən], *s.* die Perversion.

perversity [pə'və:siti], *s.* die Verdorbenheit, Widernatürlichkeit.

pervert [pə'və:t], *v.a.* verkehren, verderben. — ['pə:və:t], *s.* der Verdorbene, der perverse Mensch.

perverted [pə'və:tid], *adj.* pervers (*sexually*).

pervious ['pə:viəs], *adj.* zugänglich, passierbar; durchlässig.

pessimist ['pesimist], *s.* der Pessimist.

pest [pest], *s.* (*Med.*) die Pest; (*fig.*) die Plage.

pester ['pestə], *v.a.* quälen, auf die Nerven gehen (*Dat.*).

pestiferous [pes'tifərəs], *adj.* verpestend.

pestilence ['pestiləns], *s.* (*Med.*) die Pest, Seuche.

pestle [pesl], *s.* die Mörserkeule.

pet [pet], *s.* das Haustier; der Liebling; — *name*, der Kosename. — *v.a.* liebkosen, streicheln.

petition [pi'tiʃən], *s.* die Bittschrift. — *v.a.* mit einer Bittschrift herantreten an (*Acc.*).

petrel ['petrəl], *s.* (*Orn.*) der Sturmvogel.

petrification [petrifi'keiʃən], *s.* die Versteinerung.

petrify ['petrifai], *v.a.* versteinern; (*fig.*) starr machen, bestürzen; *petrified with fright*, starr vor Entsetzen. — *v.n.* zu Stein werden.

petrol ['petrəl], *s.* das Benzin; (*crude oil*) das Petroleum; — *station*, die Tankstelle.

petticoat ['petikout], *s.* der Unterrock.

pettifogging ['petifɔgin], *adj.* Winkel-, kleinlich, schikanös (*petty*).

pettiness ['petinis], *s.* die Kleinlichkeit.

pettish ['petiʃ], *adj.* verdrießlich.

petty ['peti], *adj.* klein, gering, kleinlich.

petulance ['petjuləns], *s.* die Launenhaftigkeit, Gereiztheit.

petulant ['petjulənt], *adj.* launenhaft.

pew [pju:], *s.* (*Eccl.*) der Kirchensitz; (*coll.*) der Sitz, Stuhl.

pewit ['pi:wit] *see* **pe(e)wit**.

pewter ['pju:tə], *s.* das Zinn; die Zinnwaren, *f. pl.* (*wares*).

pewterer ['pju:tərə], *s.* der Zinngießer.

phantom ['fæntəm], *s.* das Phantom, Trugbild; das Gespenst (*ghost*).

Pharisee ['færisi:], *s.* der Pharisäer.

pharmaceutical [fɑ:mə'sju:tikəl], *adj.* pharmazeutisch.

pharmacy ['fɑ:məsi], *s.* die Apothekerkunst (*dispensing*); die Apotheke (*dispensary*); die Pharmazeutik (*discipline*).

phase [feiz], *s.* die Phase.

pheasant ['fezənt], *s.* (*Orn.*) der Fasan.

phenomenal [fi'nɔminəl], *adj.* außerordentlich, phänomenal.

phenomenon [fi'nɔminən], *s.* das Phänomen.

phial ['faiəl], *s.* die Phiole, das Fläschchen.

philanthropist [fi'lænθrəpist], *s.* der Philanthrop.

philanthropy [fi'lænθrəpi], *s.* die Philanthropie.

philatelist [fi'lætəlist], *s.* der Philatelist, Markensammler.

philately [fi'lætəli], *s.* das Markensammeln, die Philatelie, Briefmarkenkunde.

Philippine ['filipi:n], *adj.* philippinisch.

Philistine ['filistain], *s.* der Philister; (*fig.*) der Spießbürger.

philologist [fi'lɔlədʒist], *s.* der Philologe.

philology [fi'lɔlədʒi], *s.* die Philologie.

philosopher [fi'lɔsəfə], *s.* der Philosoph.

philosophize [fi'lɔsəfaiz], *v.n.* philosophieren.

philosophy [fi'lɔsəfi], *s.* die Philosophie.

phlegm [flem], *s.* das Phlegma (*mood*); (*Med.*) der Schleim.

phlegmatic [fleg'mætik], *adj.* phlegmatisch, gelassen.

phone [foun] *see under* **telephone**.

phonetics [fə'netiks], *s.* die Phonetik.

phosphorescent [fɔsfə'resənt], *adj.* phosphoreszierend, leuchtend.

phosphorus ['fɔsfərəs], *s.* (*Chem.*) der Phosphor.

photograph ['foutəgræf *or* -grɑ:f], *s.* die Photographie, das Lichtbild (*picture*). — *v.a.* photographieren, aufnehmen, (*coll.*) knipsen.

photographer [fə'tɔgrəfə], *s.* der Photograph.

photography [fə'tɔgrəfi], s. die Photographie.

phrase [freiz], s. die Phrase. — v.a. phrasieren, fassen, ausdrücken.

phrenology [fre'nɔlədʒi], s. die Phrenologie, Schädellehre.

phthisis ['θaisis], s. (Med.) die Schwindsucht.

physic ['fizik], s. (obs.) die Medizin, Arznei.

physical ['fizikəl], adj. körperlich (bodily); physikalisch (of physics).

physician [fi'ziʃən], s. der Arzt.

physics ['fiziks], s. die Physik.

physiognomy [fizi'ɔnəmi or -'ɔgnəmi], s. die Physiognomie, die Gesichtsbildung.

physiologist [fizi'ɔlədʒist], s. der Physiolog.

physiology [fizi'ɔlədʒi], s. die Physiologie.

piano(forte) ['pjænou('fɔːti)], s. das Klavier.

pick [pik], v.a. pflücken (flowers); hacken (hack); — up, auflesen; auswählen (select); gewaltsam öffnen (a lock); anfangen (a quarrel). — v.n. why — on me.? warum gerade mich auswählen? — s. die Picke, Spitzhacke (axe); die Auswahl; — of the bunch, (coll.) das Beste von allen.

picket ['pikit], s. die Wache; der Streikposten (of strikers); der Pflock (wood). — v.a. bewachen. — v.n. Wache stehen.

pickle [pikl], s. (Cul.) der Pökel, das Gepökelte; (coll.) die unangenehme Lage (calamity). — v.a. einpökeln.

pickpocket ['pikpɔkit], s. der Taschendieb.

picnic ['piknik], s. das Picknick. — v.n. picknicken.

pictorial [pik'tɔːriəl], adj. illustriert.

picture ['piktʃə], s. das Bild; — book, das Bilderbuch; — postcard, die Ansichtskarte; pretty as a —, bildhübsch; der Film; (pl.) das Kino. — v.a. sich vorstellen.

picturesque [piktʃə'resk], adj. pittoresk, malerisch.

pie [pai], s. (Cul.) die Pastete (savoury); das Törtchen (sweet).

piebald ['paibɔːld], adj. scheckig. — s. der Schecke (horse).

piece [piːs], s. das Stück. — v.a. — together, zusammenflicken (mend), zusammensetzen (compose).

piecemeal ['piːsmiːl], adv. stückweise.

pied [paid] see **piebald**.

pier [piə], s. der Hafendamm; der Pfeiler (column).

pierce [piəs], v.a. durchstechen, durchbohren.

pierglass ['piəglɑːs], s. der Pfeilerspiegel.

piety ['paiəti], s. die Pietät, Frömmigkeit.

pig [pig], s. (Zool.) das Schwein.

pigeon ['pidʒən], s. (Orn.) die Taube.

pigeonhole ['pidʒənhoul], s. das Fach.

pigheaded [pig'hedid], adj. starrköpfig, dickköpfig.

piglet ['piglit], s. (Zool.) das Ferkel.

pigment ['pigmənt], s. das Pigment, der (natürliche) Farbstoff.

pigtail ['pigteil], s. der Haarzopf.

pike [paik], s. (Zool.) der Hecht; die Pike (weapon).

pile (1) [pail], s. der Haufen, Stoß (paper). — v.a. aufhäufen.

pile (2) [pail], s. (Archit.) der Pfahl; Pfeiler (stone).

pile (3) [pail], s. (Text.) der Teppichflausch (carpet), die Noppe (cloth).

piles [pailz], s. pl. (Med. coll.) die Haemorrhoiden, pl.

pilfer ['pilfə], v.a. stehlen, mausen.

pilferer ['pilfərə], s. der Dieb.

pilgrim ['pilgrim], s. der Pilger.

pill [pil], s. (Med.) die Pille.

pillage ['pilidʒ], s. die Plünderung. — v.a. ausplündern.

pillar ['pilə], s. der Pfeiler, die Säule; — box, der Briefkasten.

pillion ['piljən], s. der zweite Sitz, Sozius (motorcycle).

pillory ['piləri], s. der Pranger. — v.a. anprangern.

pillow ['pilou], s. das Kopfkissen.

pilot ['pailət], s. der Pilot; (Naut.) der Lotse. — v.a. (Aviat.) steuern, (Naut.) lotsen.

pimento [pi'mentou], s. (Bot.) der Jamaikapfeffer.

pimp [pimp], s. der Kuppler.

pimple [pimpl], s. der Pickel; (pl.) der Ausschlag.

pin [pin], s. die Stecknadel; (Engin.) der Bolzen, Stift; (skittles) der Kegel. — v.a. — down, festlegen.

pinafore ['pinəfɔː], s. die Schürze, Kinderschürze.

pincers ['pinsəz], s. pl. die Kneifzange, Zange.

pinch [pintʃ], v.a. kneifen, zwicken; (coll.) klauen, stehlen. — v.n. sparen, darben. — s. die Prise (tobacco); at a —, wenn es sein muß.

pine (1) [pain], s. (Bot.) die Kiefer, Föhre.

pine (2) [pain], v.n. — for, schmachten (nach, Dat.), sich sehnen.

pineapple ['painæpl], s. (Bot.) die Ananas.

pinion ['pinjən], s. der Flügel (wing); (Poet.) die Schwinge; (Mech.) das Zahnrad; — shaft, die Ritzelwelle; — spindle, die Zahnradwelle. — v.a. binden, fesseln.

pink [piŋk], adj. rosa. — s. (Bot.) die (rosa) Nelke; (Hunt.) der (rote) Jagdrock; in the — (of condition), in bester Gesundheit, in bester Form.

pinnacle ['pinəkl], s. die Zinne, Spitze; (fig.) der Gipfel.

pint [paint], s. die Pinte (0.57 litre); (beer) der Schoppen.

pioneer [paiə'niə], s. der Pionier. — v.a. bahnbrechend sein, bahnen.

pious ['paiəs], adj. fromm.

pip

pip [pip], *s.* der Obstkern; (*Mil. coll.*) der Leutnantsstern.

pipe [paip], *s.* die Pfeife; (*Engin.*) das Rohr; die Röhre; (*Mus.*) die Pfeife. — *v.a.* pfeifen; durch Rohre leiten.

piping ['paipiŋ], *adj.* — *hot*, kochend heiß.

pipkin ['pipkin], *s.* das Töpfchen.

piquant ['pi:kənt], *adj.* pikant; scharf (*taste*).

pique [pi:k], *s.* der Groll. — *v.a.* reizen.

piracy ['pairəsi], *s.* die Seeräuberei.

pirate ['pairit], *s.* der Pirat, Seeräuber. — [pai'reit], *v.a.* (*fig.*) plagiieren, ohne Erlaubnis drucken (*books*).

pistil ['pistil], *s.* (*Bot.*) der Stempel.

pistol ['pistəl], *s.* die Pistole.

piston ['pistən], *s.* (*Mech.*) der Kolben.

pit [pit], *s.* die Grube; (*Min.*) der Schacht, das Bergwerk; (*Theat., Mus.*) der Orchesterraum; (*Theat.*) das Parterre.

pitch (1) [pitʃ], *s.* der Grad, Gipfel (*height*); (*Mus.*) der Ton, die Tonhöhe (*level*); (*Sport*) das Spielfeld. — *v.a.* werfen; feststecken; (*Mus.*) stimmen; befestigen; (*tent*) (ein Zelt) aufschlagen; — *in*, sich ins Zeug legen.

pitch (2) [pitʃ], *s.* das Pech (*tar*); — *dark*, pechschwarz.

pitchblende ['pitʃblend], *s.* die Pechblende.

pitcher ['pitʃə], *s.* der Krug.

pitchfork ['pitʃfɔ:k], *s.* die Heugabel.

piteous ['pitiəs], *adj.* erbärmlich.

pitfall ['pitfɔ:l], *s.* die Falle.

pith [piθ], *s.* das Mark; (*fig.*) der Kern, das Wesentliche; die Kraft (*strength*).

pithy ['piθi], *adj.* markig, kräftig; prägnant.

pitiable ['pitiəbl], *adj.* erbärmlich.

pitiful ['pitiful], *adj.* erbärmlich (*pitiable*); mitleidig (*sympathetic*).

pitiless ['pitilis], *adj.* erbarmungslos, grausam.

pittance ['pitəns], *s.* der Hungerlohn, das Bißchen, die Kleinigkeit.

pity ['piti], *s.* das Mitleid. — *v.a.* bemitleiden, bedauern.

pivot ['pivət], *s.* (*Mech.*) der Drehpunkt, Zapfen; (*fig.*) der Mittelpunkt, Angelpunkt. — *v.n.* zum Mittelpunkt haben, sich drehen (um).

placard ['plækɑ:d], *s.* das Plakat.

placate [plə'keit], *v.a.* versöhnen.

place [pleis], *s.* der Platz, Ort, die Stelle; — *name*, der Ortsname; (*rank*) der Rang, die Rangstufe. — *v.a.* plazieren (*in a job*); legen, setzen, stellen; — *an order*, einen Auftrag geben.

placid ['plæsid], *adj.* gelassen, sanft, gutmütig.

plagiarism ['pleidʒiərizm], *s.* das Plagiat, das Plagiieren.

plague [pleig], *s.* (*Med.*) die Pest, Seuche; (*fig.*) die Plage. — *v.a.* belästigen, plagen.

plaice [pleis], *s.* (*Zool.*) die Scholle.

plain [plein], *s.* die Ebene, Fläche. — *adj.* eben, flach (*even*); schlicht,

einfach, klar; — *dealing*, ehrliche Handlungsweise; — *speaking*, offenes Sprechen, aufrichtiges Reden; (*Mus.*) — *song*, der einstimmige Chorgesang, die gregorianische Kirchenmusik.

plaintiff ['pleintif], *s.* (*Law*) der Kläger.

plaintive ['pleintiv], *adj.* klagend.

plait [plæt], *s.* der Zopf, die Flechte. — *v.a.* flechten (*hair*); falten.

plan [plæn], *s.* der Plan, Grundriß. — *v.a.* planen, entwerfen.

plane (1) [plein], *v.a.* hobeln (*wood*). — *s.* die Fläche (*surface*); die Stufe (*level*); (*coll.*) das Flugzeug (*aeroplane*).

plane (2) *see* **plane-tree.**

planet ['plænit], *s.* (*Astron.*) der Planet.

plane-tree ['pleintri:], *s.* (*Bot.*) die Platane.

planish ['plæniʃ], *v.a.* (*woodwork*) polieren, glätten.

plank [plæŋk], *s.* die Planke; (*Pol.*) der Programmpunkt.

plant [plɑ:nt], *s.* (*Bot.*) die Pflanze; (*Ind.*) die Anlage, der Betrieb. — *v.a.* anpflanzen, anlegen; — *suspicion*, Verdacht einflößen (*of, against*, gegen, *Acc.*).

plantain ['plæntein], *s.* (*Bot.*) der Wegerich; (*fruit*) der Pisang.

plantation [plæn'teiʃən], *s.* die Pflanzung, Plantage.

plaster ['plɑ:stə], *s.* das Pflaster (*adhesive*); (*Build.*) der Mörtel, der Mauerbewurf; — *cast*, der Gipsabdruck; — *of Paris*, der Stuck, der feine Gipsmörtel. — *v.a.* bepflastern, verputzen; (*fig.*) dick auftragen.

plastic ['plæstik], *adj.* plastisch; (*malleable*) formbar; — *surgery*, plastische Chirurgie. — *s.* der Kunststoff.

Plate, River [pleit, 'rivə] der La Plata Strom.

plate [pleit], *s.* der Teller (*dish*), die Platte, Scheibe; (*coll.*) — *glass*, das Spiegelglas; das Geschirr (*service of crockery*); *gold* —, das Goldgeschirr. — *v.a.* überziehen, versilbern, verchromen.

platform ['plætfɔ:m], *s.* (*Railw.*) der Bahnsteig; die Bühne, das Podium.

platinum ['plætinəm], *s.* das Platin.

platitude ['plætitju:d], *s.* die Plattheit, der Gemeinplatz.

platitudinous [plæti'tju:dinəs], *adj.* nichtssagend.

platoon [plə'tu:n], *s.* (*Mil.*) der Zug.

plaudit ['plɔ:dit], *s.* der Beifall.

plausible ['plɔ:zibl], *adj.* wahrscheinlich, glaubwürdig, einleuchtend.

play [plei], *s.* das Spiel (*game*); (*Theat.*) das Stück. — *v.a., v.n.* spielen.

player ['pleiə], *s.* der Spieler; (*Theat.*) der Schauspieler.

playful ['pleiful], *adj.* spielerisch, spielend.

playground ['pleigraund], *s.* der Spielplatz.

playhouse ['pleihaus], *s.* das Schauspielhaus.

playmate ['pleimeit], *s.* der Spiel-gefährte.

playwright ['pleirait], *s.* der Drama-tiker, Schauspieldichter.

plea [pli:], *s.* die Bitte; das Gesuch; der Vorwand.

plead [pli:d], *v.a., v.n.* plädieren, sich berufen auf; vorschützen (*claim*).

pleasant ['plezənt], *adj.* angenehm, freundlich.

pleasantry ['plezəntri], *s.* das freund-liche Wort, der Scherz (*joke*).

please [pli:z], *v.a., v.n.* gefallen; einen Gefallen tun (*do a favour*); — ! bitte, haben Sie die Güte!; *if you* —, wenn Sie nichts dagegen haben.

pleasing ['pli:ziŋ], *adj.* einnehmend, angenehm.

pleasure ['pleʒə], *s.* das Vergnügen; *at your* —, nach Belieben; *take* — *in*, Vergnügen finden an (*Dat.*).

pleat [pli:t], *v.a.* plissieren. — *s.* die Falte, das Plissee.

pledge [pledʒ], *s.* das Pfand, die Bürg-schaft (*guarantee*); das Versprechen (*promise*). — *v.a.* sich verbürgen, versprechen; zutrinken (*drink to*).

plenary ['pli:nəri], *adj.* Plenar-, voll-ständig.

plenipotentiary [plenipo'tenʃəri], *s.* der Bevollmächtigte.

plenitude ['plenitju:d], *s.* die Fülle.

plenteous, plentiful ['plentiəs, 'plenti-ful], *adj.* reichlich, in Fülle.

plenty ['plenti], *s.* die Fülle.

pleurisy ['pluərisi], *s.* (*Med.*) die Brustfellentzündung.

pliable, pliant ['plaiəbl, 'plaiənt], *adj.* geschmeidig, biegsam.

pliers ['plaiəz], *s. pl.* die Drahtzange.

plight (1) [plait], *s.* die Notlage.

plight (2) [plait], *v.a.* feierlich ver-sprechen.

plod [plɔd], *v.n.* schwerfällig gehen (*walk*); sich plagen (*work hard*).

plot (1) [plɔt], *s.* das Stück Land, der Bauplatz.

plot (2) [plɔt], *s.* das Komplott, die Verschwörung; die Handlung (*book, play etc.*). — *v.a.* aushecken (*ambush etc.*), planen.

plough, plow [plau], *s.* der Pflug. — *v.a.* pflügen; (*coll.*) *be* —*ed*, durch-fallen (*in, in, Dat.*).

ploughshare ['plauʃɛə], *s.* die . Pflug-schar.

plover ['plʌvə], *s.* (*Orn.*) der Kiebitz, Regenpfeifer.

plow *see under* **plough**.

pluck (1) [plʌk], *v.a.* pflücken (*flowers*); rupfen (*feathers*); — *up courage*, Mut fassen.

pluck (2) [plʌk], *s.* (*coll.*) der Mut.

plucky ['plʌki], *adj.* mutig.

plug [plʌg], *s.* (*Elec.*) der Stecker; der Stöpsel (*stopper*); *sparking* —, (*Motor.*) die Zündkerze. — *v.a.* stöpseln, zustopfen (*block*); (*fig.*) betonen, herausstellen (*repeat for advertise-ment*).

plum [plʌm], *s.* (*Bot.*) die Pflaume; (*coll.*) das Beste.

plumage ['plu:midʒ], *s.* (*Orn.*) das Gefieder.

plumb [plʌm], *s.* das Senkblei, Lot; — *-rule*, die Senkwaage. — *adv.* senkrecht, gerade, lotrecht.

plume [plu:m], *s.* die (Schmuck) feder.

plump [plʌmp], *adj.* dick, drall.

plunder ['plʌndə], *v.a., v.n.* plündern. — *s.* die Beute, der Raub.

plunge [plʌndʒ], *v.a., v.n.* unter-tauchen, stoßen, hinabstürzen.

plunger ['plʌndʒə], *s.* der Taucher; (*Engin.*) der Tauchkolben.

pluperfect ['plu:pə:fikt], *s.* (*Gram.*) das Plusquamperfektum.

plural ['pluərəl], *s.* (*Gram.*) der Plural, die Mehrzahl.

plurality [pluə'ræliti], *s.* die Mehrzahl, der Plural.

plus [plʌs], *prep.* plus, zuzüglich.

plush [plʌʃ], *s.* (*Text.*) der Plüsch.

ply [plai], *s.* die Falte (*fold*), Lage (*layer*). — *v.a.* ausüben (*trade*).

plywood ['plaiwud], *s.* das Sperrholz, die Sperrholzplatte.

pneumonia [nju'mouniə], *s.* (*Med.*) die Lungenentzündung.

poach (1) [poutʃ], *v.n.* wildern; — *on*, übergreifen auf.

poach (2) [poutʃ], *v.a.* ohne Schale kochen; *poached eggs*, verlorene Eier, *n. pl.*

poacher ['poutʃə], *s.* der Wilderer, Wilddieb.

pocket ['pɔkit], *s.* die Tasche; — *book*, die Brieftasche; das Taschenbuch; — *money*, das Taschengeld.

pod [pɔd], *s.* (*Bot.*) die Schote.

poem ['pouim], *s.* das Gedicht.

poet ['pouit], *s.* der Dichter.

poetic(al) [pou'etik(l)], *adj.* dichte-risch.

poignancy ['pɔinjənsi], *s.* die Schärfe.

poignant ['pɔinjənt], *adj.* scharf, bei-ßend, schmerzlich.

point [pɔint], *s.* der Punkt (*of remark, sentence*); die Sache; der Zweck; die Spitze (*of pencil etc.*); *make a* —, es sich zur Aufgabe machen; *in* — *of fact*, tatsächlich; *come to the* —, zur Sache kommen. — *v.a., v.n.* spitzen, zuspitzen (*pencil*); — *out*, zeigen, (hin)deuten; — *to*, hinweisen auf; — *the moral*, die Moral erklären.

pointblank ['pɔint'blæŋk], *adj., adv.* schnurgerade, direkt.

pointed ['pɔintid], *adj.* scharf, spitzig, deutlich (*remark*).

pointer ['pɔintə], *s.* der Zeiger; (*fig.*) der Fingerzeig (*hint*).

poise [pɔiz], *s.* das Gleichgewicht; (*fig.*) angemessenes Benehmen, die Grazie. — *v.a.* abwägen; im Gleichgewicht halten. — *v.n.* schweben; —*d for action*, tatbereit.

poison [pɔizn], *s.* das Gift. — *v.a.* vergiften.

459

poke

poke (1) [pouk], *v.a.* schüren (*fire*); stoßen; — *fun at*, sich lustig machen über. — *s.* der Stoß; — *in the ribs*, ein Rippenstoß.

poke (2) [pouk], *s.* der Sack; *a pig in a* —, die Katze im Sack.

poker (1) ['poukə], *s.* der Schürhaken, das Schüreisen.

poker (2) ['poukə], *s.* (*Cards*) das Pokerspiel.

polar ['poulə], *adj.* (*Geog.*) Polar-; (*Phys.*) polar.

polarity [po'læriti], *s.* die Polarität.

Pole [poul], *s.* der Pole.

pole (1) [poul], *s.* (*Geog.*) der Pol.

pole (2) [poul], *s.* die Stange (*rod*); der Pfahl (*upright*).

poleaxe ['poulæks], *s.* die Streitaxt.

polecat ['poulkæt], *s.* (*Zool.*) der Iltis.

polemic [pə'lemik], *s.* die Polemik, der Streit.

police [pə'li:s], *s.* die Polizei. — *v.a.* polizeilich beaufsichtigen.

policeman [pə'li:smən], *s.* der Polizist.

policy (1) ['pɔlisi], *s.* die Politik.

policy (2) ['pɔlisi], *s.* (*Insurance*) die Police.

Polish ['pouliʃ], *adj.* polnisch.

polish ['pɔliʃ], *v.a.* polieren. — *s.* die Politur, der Glanz.

polished ['pɔliʃd], *adj.* glatt (*smooth*); (*fig.*) wohlerzogen, fein (*manners*).

polite [pə'lait], *adj.* höflich.

politeness [pə'laitnis], *s.* die Höflichkeit.

politic ['pɔlitik], *adj.* politisch; schlau (*cunning*).

political [pə'litikəl], *adj.* politisch; staatskundig.

politician [pɔli'tiʃən], *s.* der Politiker, Staatsmann.

politics ['pɔlitiks], *s.* (*sometimes pl.*) die Politik, politische Gesinnung.

poll [poul], *s.* die Wahl (*election*). — *v.n.* abstimmen, wählen, seine Stimme abgeben.

pollard ['pɔləd], *s.* (*Bot.*) der gekappte Baum; (*Zool.*) das hornlose Tier.

pollen ['pɔlən], *s.* (*Bot.*) der Blütenstaub.

pollinate ['pɔlineit], *v.a.* (*Bot.*) bestäuben.

polling ['poulin], *s.* die Wahl, der Wahlgang (*election*); — *station*, das Wahllokal.

pollute [pə'lju:t], *v.a.* verunreinigen.

pollution [pə'lju:ʃən], *s.* die Verunreinigung.

poltroon [pɔl'tru:n], *s.* die Memme.

poly- ['pɔli], *pref.* viel-.

Polynesian [pɔli'ni:ziən], *adj.* polynesisch. — *s.* der Polynesier.

polytechnic [pɔli'teknik], *s.* das Technikum; polytechnische Fachschule.

pomegranate ['pɔm-, 'pʌmgrænit], *s.* (*Bot.*) der Granatapfel.

Pomeranian [pɔmə'reiniən], *adj.* pommerisch. — *s.* der Pommer; der Spitz (*dog*).

pommel [pʌml], *s.* der Sattelknopf; der Knauf (*sword*). — *v.a.* schlagen.

pomp [pɔmp], *s.* der Pomp, das Gepränge.

pompous ['pɔmpəs], *adj.* hochtrabend, prahlerisch; (*manner*) schwerfällig, wichtigtuerisch.

pond [pɔnd], *s.* der Teich.

ponder ['pɔndə], *v.a., v.n.* bedenken, überlegen.

ponderous ['pɔndərəs], *adj.* schwer, schwerfällig.

pontiff ['pɔntif], *s.* der Hohepriester; der Papst.

pontifical [pɔn'tifikəl], *adj.* bischöflich, päpstlich. — *s. pl.* die bischöfliche Amtstracht.

pontificate [pɔn'tifikit], *s.* das (*or* der) Pontifikat. — [-keit], *v.n.* (*coll.*) predigen.

pontoon (1) [pɔn'tu:n], *s.* die Schiffsbrücke, der Brückenkahn.

pontoon (2) [pɔn'tu:n], *s.* (*cards*) das Einundzwanzig, Vingt-et-un.

pony ['pouni], *s.* (*Zool.*) der *or* das Pony.

poodle [pu:dl], *s.* der Pudel.

pooh-pooh [pu:'pu:], *v.a.* verspotten.

pool (1) [pu:l], *s.* die Lache, der Pfuhl.

pool (2) [pu:l], *s.* (*fig.*) der gemeinsame Einsatz (*money, forces etc.*). — *v.a.* zusammenschließen.

poop [pu:p], *s.* (*Naut.*) das Heck, Hinterteil.

poor [puə], *adj.* arm, dürftig; *in* — *health*, bei schwacher Gesundheit; (*fig.*) armselig, schlecht.

pop [pɔp], *v.n.* knallen, explodieren. — *v.a.* (*coll.*) schnell versetzen, verpfänden.

Pope [poup], *s.* (*Eccl.*) der Papst.

poplar ['pɔplə], *s.* (*Bot.*) die Pappel.

poppy ['pɔpi], *s.* (*Bot.*) der Mohn.

populace ['pɔpjulis], *s.* der Pöbel.

popular ['pɔpjulə], *adj.* volkstümlich, beliebt.

popularity [pɔpju'læriti], *s.* die Beliebtheit.

populate ['pɔpjuleit], *v.a.* bevölkern.

population [pɔpju'leiʃən], *s.* die Bevölkerung.

populous ['pɔpjuləs], *adj.* dicht bevölkert.

porcelain ['pɔ:slin], *s.* das Porzellan, das Geschirr.

porch [pɔ:tʃ], *s.* die Eingangshalle, Vorhalle.

porcupine ['pɔ:kjupain], *s.* (*Zool.*) das Stachelschwein.

pore (1) [pɔ:], *s.* die Pore.

pore (2) [pɔ:], *v.n.* sich vertiefen (*over, in*), brüten (*über*).

pork [pɔ:k], *s.* das Schweinefleisch.

porosity [pɔ:'rositi], *s.* die Porosität.

porous ['pɔ:rəs], *adj.* porös.

porpoise ['pɔ:pəs], *s.* (*Zool.*) der Tümmler, das Meerschwein.

porridge ['pɔridʒ], *s.* (*Cul.*) der Haferbrei.

porringer ['pɔrindʒə], *s.* (*Cul.*) der Napf.

port (1) [pɔ:t], *s.* der Hafen.

port (2) [pɔ:t], *s.* der Portwein (*wine*).

portable ['pɔ:təbl], *adj.* tragbar; Koffer- (*radio etc.*).

portcullis [pɔ:t'kʌlis], *s.* das Fallgatter.

portend [pɔ:'tend], *v.a.* vorbedeuten, ahnen lassen.

portent ['pɔ:tent], *s.* die Vorbedeutung.

porter ['pɔ:tə], *s.* (*Railw.*) der Gepäckträger; der Pförtner, Portier (*caretaker, janitor*); das Porterbier (*beer*).

porterage ['pɔ:təridʒ], *s.* der Trägerlohn, die Zustellkosten, *f.pl.*

portfolio [pɔ:t'fouliou], *s.* die Mappe; (*Pol.*) das Ressort; das Portefeuille.

portico ['pɔ:tikou], *s.* (*Archit.*) die Säulenhalle.

portion ['pɔ:ʃən], *s.* die Portion, der Anteil. — *v.a.* aufteilen, austeilen (*share out*).

portliness ['pɔ:tlinis], *s.* die Stattlichkeit (*dignity*); Behäbigkeit (*corpulence*).

portly ['pɔ:tli], *adj.* stattlich (*dignified*); behäbig (*corpulent*).

portmanteau [pɔ:t'mæntou], *s.* der Handkoffer.

portrait ['pɔ:trit], *s.* (*Art*) das Bildnis, Porträt.

portray [pɔ:'trei], *v.a.* im Bilde darstellen, porträtieren; (*fig.*) schildern, darstellen (*describe*).

Portuguese [pɔ:tju'gi:z], *adj.* portugiesisch. — *s.* der Portugiese.

pose [pouz], *s.* die Haltung, Stellung (*of model etc.*). — *v.a.* in Pose stellen; aufwerfen (*question*). — *v.n.* (*as model*) stehen, sitzen; — *as*, posieren, sich ausgeben als (*pretend to be*).

poser ['pouzə], *s.* die schwierige Frage.

position [pə'ziʃən], *s.* die Lage (*situation*); die Stellung (*job*); der Stand, Rang (*rank*); (*Astron., Mil.*) die Position.

positive ['pɔzitiv], *adj.* positiv; (*fig.*) ausdrücklich, sicher (*sure*).

possess [pə'zes], *v.a.* besitzen.

possession [pə'zeʃən], *s.* der Besitz, Besitztum.

possessive [pə'zesiv], *adj.* (*Gram.*) besitzanzeigend, possessiv; (*fig.*) besitzgierig.

possibility [pɔsi'biliti], *s.* die Möglichkeit.

possible ['pɔsibl], *adj.* möglich.

post (1) [poust], *s.* der Pfosten (*pillar*).

post (2) [poust], *s.* die Post (*mail*); der Posten (*job*). — *v.a.* zur Post geben; (*coll.*) einstecken (*letter*).

postage ['poustidʒ], *s.* das Porto; — *stamp*, die Briefmarke.

postal [poustl], *adj.* Post-.

poster ['poustə], *s.* das Plakat.

posterity [pɔs'teriti], *s.* die Nachwelt.

posthumous ['pɔstjuməs], *adj.* hinterlassen, nach dem Tode, postum.

postman ['poustmən], *s.* der Briefträger.

postmark ['poustmɑ:k], *s.* der Poststempel.

post-mortem [poust'mɔ:təm], *s.* – – –

(*examination*), die Obduktion, Leichenschau.

post-office ['poustɔfis], *s.* das Postamt.

postpone [poust'poun], *v.a.* verschieben, aufschieben.

postscript ['poustskript], *s.* die Nachschrift.

postulate ['pɔstjuleit], *v.a.* postulieren, voraussetzen.

posture ['pɔstʃə], *s.* die Positur, Haltung (*of body*).

pot [pɔt], *s.* der Topf; die Kanne (*beer*); (*coll.*) go to —, zugrunde gehen. — *v.a.* einkochen, einmachen; (*fig.*) kürzen.

potash ['pɔtæʃ], *s.* (*Chem.*) die Pottasche.

potassium [pə'tæsiəm], *s.* (*Chem.*) das Kalium.

potato [pə'teitou], *s.* (*Bot.*) die Kartoffel.

potent ['poutənt], *adj.* kräftig, stark, wirksam.

potential [pə'tenʃəl], *s.* das Potential. — *adj.* möglich, potentiell (*possible*).

potter ['pɔtə], *s.* der Töpfer.

pottery ['pɔtəri], *s.* die Töpferei; die Töpferwaren, Tonwaren, *f. pl.* (*goods*).

pouch [pautʃ], *s.* der Beutel.

poulterer ['poultərə], *s.* der Geflügelhändler.

poultice ['poultis], *s.* der Umschlag.

poultry ['poultri], *s.* das Geflügel.

pounce (1) [pauns], *s.* (*obs.*) die Klaue. — *v.n.* — *upon*, herfallen (über, *Acc.*).

pounce (2) [pauns], *s.* das Bimssteinpulver. — *v.a.* (mit Bimsstein) abreiben.

pound (1) [paund], *s.* das Pfund; das Pfund Sterling.

pound (2) [paund], *v.a.* zerstoßen.

poundage ['paundidʒ], *s.* das Pfundgeld, die Gebühr pro Pfund.

pour [pɔ:], *v.a.* gießen, schütten, einschenken. — *v.n.* strömen.

pout [paut], *v.n.* schmollen.

poverty ['pɔvəti], *s.* die Armut.

powder ['paudə], *s.* (*Mil.*) das Pulver; der Puder (*face etc.*). — *v.a.* zu Pulver machen, stoßen; (*face*) pudern.

power [pauə], *s.* die Macht, Gewalt; Kraft; Fähigkeit; — *of attorney*, die Vollmacht; (*Maths.*) die Potenz; (*Elec.*) der Strom; — *house*, — *station*, das Elektrizitätswerk; — *cut*, die Stromstörung.

powerful ['pauəful], *adj.* kräftig, mächtig, einflußreich.

powerless ['pauəlis], *adj.* kraftlos, machtlos.

pox [pɔks], *s.* (*Med.*) die Pocken, *f. pl.*; die Syphilis.

practicable ['præktikəbl], *adj.* ausführbar, tunlich.

practical ['præktikəl], *adj.* praktisch.

practice ['præktis], *s.* die Ausübung (*doing, carrying out*); die Praxis.

practise ['præktis], *v.a.* ausführen, ausüben (*a profession etc.*); üben (*rehearse*). — *v.n.* sich üben.

practised

practised ['præktisd], _adj._ geübt, geschult (in).

practitioner [præk'tiʃənə], _s._ (_Med._) praktischer Arzt; (_Law_) Advokat.

pragmatic [præg'mætik], _adj._ pragmatisch.

prairie ['prɛəri], _s._ die Prärie.

praise [preiz], _v.a._ preisen, loben. — _s._ das Lob.

pram _see under_ **perambulator**.

prance [prɑːns], _v.n._ sich bäumen; (_fig._) sich brüsten (_brag_).

prank [præŋk], _s._ der Streich.

prate [preit], _v.n._ plappern, schwatzen.

prattle [prætl], _v.n._ plaudern, schwatzen. — _s._ das Geschwätz.

prawn [prɔːn], _s._ (_Zool._) die Steingarnele.

pray [prei], _v.n._ beten. — _v.a._ bitten, ersuchen (_beseech_).

prayer [prɛə], _s._ das Gebet.

preach [priːtʃ], _v.a., v.n._ predigen.

preacher ['priːtʃə], _s._ der Prediger.

preamble [priːæmbl], _s._ die Vorrede, der Einleitungsparagraph.

precarious [pri'kɛəriəs], _adj._ unsicher, prekär.

precaution [pri'kɔːʃən], _s._ die Vorsichtsmaßregel.

precede [pri'siːd], _v.a., v.n._ vorausgehen, den Vortritt haben.

precedence ['presidəns _or_ pri'siːdəns], _s._ der Vortritt, Vorrang.

precedent ['presidənt], _s._ der Präzedenzfall.

precept ['priːsept], _s._ die Vorschrift, Regel.

preceptor [pri'septə], _s._ der Lehrer, Lehrmeister.

precinct [pri'siŋkt], _s._ das Gebiet, der Bezirk; (_pl._) die Grenzen, _f. pl._

precious ['preʃəs], _adj._ wertvoll, kostbar; — _metal_, das Edelmetall.

precipice ['presipis], _s._ der Abgrund.

precipitous [pri'sipitəs], _adj._ jäh, abschüssig.

precise [pri'sais], _adj._ genau, bestimmt.

precision [pri'siʒən], _s._ die Präzision, Genauigkeit; (_Engin._) — _tool_, das Präzisionswerkzeug.

precocious [pri'kouʃəs], _adj._ frühreif.

preconceive [priːkən'siːv], _v.a._ vorher denken.

preconceived [priːkən'siːvd], _adj._ vorgefaßt.

preconception [priːkən'sepʃən], _s._ das Vorurteil.

precursor [pri'kəːsə], _s._ der Vorläufer.

predatory ['predətəri], _adj._ räuberisch, Raub-.

predecessor ['priːdisesə], _s._ der Vorgänger.

predestin(at)e [pri'destin(eit)], _v.a._ vorher bestimmen; (_Theol._) prädestinieren.

predicament [pri'dikəmənt], _s._ die Verlegenheit.

predicate ['predikit], _s._ (_Gram._) das Prädikat. — [-keit], _v.a._ behaupten.

predict [pri'dikt], _v.a._ voraussagen, vorhersagen.

prediction [pri'dikʃən], _s._ die Vorhersage (_weather etc._); die Weissagung (_prophecy_).

predilection [priːdi'lekʃən], _s._ die Vorliebe.

predispose [priːdis'pouz], _v.a._ vorbereiten; empfänglich machen.

predominant [pri'dɔminənt], _adj._ vorherrschend.

predominate [pri'dɔmineit], _v.n._ vorherrschen.

pre-eminence [pri'eminəns], _s._ der Vorrang.

prefabricate [pri'fæbrikeit], _v.a._ vorfabrizieren, als Fertigteil herstellen, in der Fabrik herstellen.

prefabrication [priːfæbri'keiʃən], _s._ die Vorfabrizierung.

preface ['prefis], _s._ das Vorwort.

prefatory ['prefətəri], _adj._ einleitend.

prefect ['priːfekt], _s._ der Präfekt.

prefer [pri'fəː], _v.a._ vorziehen.

preference ['prefərəns], _s._ der Vorzug (_Comm._) — _share_, die Vorzugsaktie.

preferment [pri'fəːmənt], _s._ die Beförderung.

prefix ['priːfiks], _s._ die Vorsilbe. — [priːfiks], _v.a._ vorsetzen.

pregnancy ['pregnənsi], _s._ die Schwangerschaft.

pregnant ['pregnənt], _adj._ schwanger.

prejudge [pri'dʒʌdʒ], _v.a._ vorher urteilen, voreilig urteilen.

prejudice ['predʒudis], _s._ das Vorurteil. — _v.a._ beeinträchtigen.

prejudicial [predʒu'diʃəl], _adj._ schädlich.

prelate ['prelit], _s._ (_Eccl._) der Prälat.

preliminary [pri'liminəri], _adj._ vorläufig, Präliminar-. — _s._ (_pl._) die Vorbereitungen, _f. pl._

prelude ['preljuːd], _s._ das Vorspiel.

premature ['premətʃə], _adj._ vorschnell, übereilt, vorzeitig.

premeditate [pri'mediteit], _v.a._ (_Law_) vorher überlegen.

Premier ['premiə], _s._ der Premierminister.

premise (1) ['premis], _s._ (_Log._) die Prämisse; (_pl._) das Haus, Grundstück; die Stätte, der Ort; das Lokal (_inn etc._).

premise (2) [pri'maiz], _v.a._ vorausschicken.

premium ['priːmiəm], _s._ die Prämie.

premonition [priːmə'niʃən], _s._ die Vorahnung.

preoccupation [pri'ɔkjupeiʃən], _s._ die Zerstreutheit.

preoccupied [pri'ɔkjupaid], _adj._ besorgt; zerstreut (_absent-minded_).

preparation [prepə'reiʃən], _s._ die Vorbereitung; Zubereitung (_of meals_).

preparatory [pri'pærətri], _adj._ vorbereitend; — _school_, die Vorschule.

prepare [pri'pɛə], _v.a., v.n._ vorbereiten (_for,_ auf); zubereiten (_meals_).

prepay [priː'pei], _v.a. irr._ vorausbezahlen; (_post_) frankieren.

preponderant [pri'pɔndərənt], *adj.* überwiegend.

preponderate [pri'pɔndəreit], *v.a.*, *v.n.* überwiegen.

preposition [prepə'ziʃən], *s.* (*Gram.*) die Präposition.

prepossess [pri:pə'zes], *v.a.* einnehmen, beeindrucken.

preposterous [pri'pɔstərəs], *adj.* töricht, lächerlich, unerhört.

prerogative [pri'rɔgətiv], *s.* das Vorrecht.

presage [pri'seidʒ], *v.a.* prophezeien. — ['presidʒ], *s.* die Prophezeiung.

prescient ['preʃənt, 'pri:-], *adj.* vorahnend, vorherwissend.

prescribe [pri'skraib], *v.a.*, *v.n.* vorschreiben; (*Med.*) verschreiben, verordnen.

prescription [pri'skripʃən], *s.* die Vorschrift(*precept*); (*Med.*) das Rezept.

presence ['prezəns], *s.* die Gegenwart, Anwesenheit (*attendance*); das Äußere (*appearance*); — *of mind*, die Geistesgegenwart.

present (1) ['prezənt], *adj.* anwesend, gegenwärtig; jetzig. — *s.* (*Gram.*) das Präsens, die Gegenwart; (*time*) die Gegenwart, heutige Zeit.

present (2) [pri'zənt], *v.a.* darstellen (*on stage*); vorstellen (*introduce*); präsentieren (*arms*); schenken, geben (*gifts*). — ['prezənt], *s.* das Geschenk (*gift*).

presentation [prezən'teiʃən], *s.* die Darstellung (*stage*, *art*); die Vorstellung (*introduction*); die Überreichung (*of gift*).

presentiment [pri'zentimənt], *s.* das Vorgefühl, die Vorahnung.

presently ['prezəntli], *adv.* bald, sogleich.

preservation [prezə'veiʃən], *s.* die Erhaltung, Bewahrung.

preservative [pri'zə:vətiv], *s.* das Konservierungsmittel.

preserve [pri'zə:v], *v.a.* bewahren, erhalten; (*fruit*) einmachen. — *s.* (*Hunt.*) das Jagdgehege, Jagdrevier, (*pl.*) die Konserven, *f. pl.*

preside [pri'zaid], *v.n.* (*over*) den Vorsitz führen.

president ['prezidənt], *s.* der Präsident.

press [pres], *v.a.*, *v.n.* drücken (*push*); bügeln, plätten (*iron*); nötigen (*force*); dringend bitten (*entreat*). — *s.* die Presse (*newspapers*, *printing*); der Schrank (*cupboard*); das Gedränge (*crowd*).

pressing ['presiŋ], *adj.* dringend.

pressure ['preʃə], *s.* der Druck.

prestige [pres'ti:ʒ], *s.* das Prestige, Ansehen.

presumable [pri'zju:məbl], *adj.* mutmaßlich, vermutlich.

presume [pri'zju:m], *v.a.*, *v.n.* vermuten; — *on*, sich anmaßen.

presumption [pri'zʌmpʃən], *s.* die Annahme; die Anmaßung (*arrogance*).

presumptive [pri'zʌmptiv], *adj.* mutmaßlich.

presumptuous [pri'zʌmptjuəs], *adj.* anmaßend, dreist, vermessen.

presuppose [pri:sə'pouz], *v.a.* voraussetzen.

pretence [pri'tens], *s.* der Vorwand.

pretend [pri'tend], *v.a.*, *v.n.* vortäuschen, vorgeben.

pretension [pri'tenʃən], *s.* die Anmaßung, der Anspruch (*to*, auf).

pretentious [pri'tenʃəs], *adj.* anspruchsvoll.

preterite ['pretərit], *s.* (*Gram.*) das Präteritum.

pretext ['pri:tekst], *s.* der Vorwand.

pretty ['priti], *adj.* hübsch, nett. — *adv.* (*coll.*) ziemlich.

prevail [pri'veil], *v.n.* vorherrschen, die Oberhand gewinnen.

prevalence ['prevələns], *s.* das Vorherrschen.

prevaricate [pri'værikeit], *v.n.* Ausflüchte machen.

prevent [pri'vent], *v.a.* verhindern.

prevention [pri'venʃən], *s.* die Verhinderung.

preventive [pri'ventiv],*adj.* vorbeugend.

previous [pri'viəs], *adj.* vorhergehend.

prey [prei], *s.* die Beute, der Raub. — *v.n.* rauben, nachstellen.

price [prais], *s.* der Preis, Wert.

priceless ['praislis], *adj.* unschätzbar, unbezahlbar.

prick [prik], *s.* der Stachel, Stich (*stab*). — *v.a.* stechen (*stab*); punktieren (*puncture*).

prickle [prikl], *s.* (*Bot.*) der Stachel.

pride [praid], *s.* der Stolz. — *v.r.* — *o.s.*, sich brüsten, stolz sein (*on*, auf, *Acc.*).

priest [pri:st], *s.* (*Eccl.*) der Priester.

prig [prig], *s.* der eingebildete Tropf; Tugendheld.

priggish ['prigiʃ], *adj.* dünkelhaft, selbstgefällig.

prim [prim], *adj.* steif, spröde.

primacy ['praiməsi], *s.* der, das Primat.

primaeval [prai'mi:vəl], *adj.* Ur-, anfänglich, ursprünglich.

primary ['praiməri], *adj.* erst, ursprünglich; Haupt– (*main*). — *s.* (*pl.*) (*Am.*) die Vorwahlen, *f. pl.* (*Presidential elections*).

prime [praim], *adj.* erst, wichtigst. — *s.* die Blüte, Vollendung, Vollkraft.

primer ['praimə], *s.* das Elementarbuch, die Fibel.

primitive ['primitiv], *adj.* primitiv; ursprünglich (*original*).

primness ['primnis], *s.* die Geziertheit, Steifheit.

primrose ['primrouz], *s.* (*Bot.*) die Primel.

prince [prins], *s.* der Prinz; Fürst (*rank*).

princess [prin'ses], *s.* die Prinzessin.

principal ['prinsipl], *s.* der Direktor (*business*); Rektor (*school etc.*); (*Comm.*) das Kapital; (*Mus.*) der erste Spieler. — *adj.* erst, Haupt-.

principality [prinsi'pæliti], *s.* das Fürstentum.

principle [ˈprinsipl], *s.* das Prinzip, der Grundsatz.

print [print], *v.a.* drucken, abdrucken. — *s.* (*Typ.*, *Art*) der Druck; *out of* —, vergriffen.

printer [ˈprintə], *s.* der (Buch-)drucker.

prior [praiə], *adj.* früher, eher; — *to*, vor (*Dat.*). — *s.* (*Eccl.*) der Prior.

priority [praiˈɔriti], *s.* die Priorität, der Vorrang.

prise [praiz], *v.a.* — *open*, gewaltsam öffnen, aufbrechen.

prism [prizm], *s.* das Prisma.

prison [prizn], *s.* das Gefängnis.

prisoner [ˈprizənə], *s.* der Gefangene, Sträfling.

pristine [ˈpristain], *adj.* ehemalig, vormalig, ursprünglich.

privacy [ˈpraivəsi *or* ˈprivəsi], *s.* die Zurückgezogenheit, Stille.

private [ˈpraivit], *adj.* privat, persönlich, vertraulich (*confidential*). — *s.* (*Mil.*) der Gemeine, Landser.

privation [praiˈveiʃən], *s.* der Mangel, die Entbehrung (*lack*); die Beraubung (*deprivation*).

privilege [ˈprivilidʒ], *s.* das Privileg, Vorrecht. — *v.a.* ausnehmen, privilegieren.

privy [ˈprivi], *s.* der Abtritt, Abort. — *adj.* — *to*, mitwissend; *Privy Council*, der Staatsrat.

prize [praiz], *s.* der Preis, die Belohnung; — *v.a.* hochschätzen.

prizewinner [ˈpraizwinə], *s.* der Preisträger; *Nobel* —, der Nobelpreisträger.

probability [prɔbəˈbiliti], *s.* die Wahrscheinlichkeit.

probable [ˈprɔbəbl], *adj.* wahrscheinlich.

probate [ˈproubeit], *s.* (*Law*) die Testamentsbestätigung.

probation [proˈbeiʃən], *s.* die Bewährung, Bewährungsfrist (*period*).

probationary [proˈbeiʃənəri], *adj.* Bewährungs-.

probe [proub], *v.a.* sondieren, untersuchen. — *s.* die Sonde, Prüfung.

probity [ˈproubiti], *s.* die Redlichkeit, Anständigkeit.

problem [ˈprɔbləm], *s.* das Problem.

problematic [prɔbləˈmætik], *adj.* zweifelhaft, problematisch.

proboscis [prɔˈbɔsis], *s.* (*Ent.*) der Rüssel.

procedure [prəˈsiːdʒə], *s.* der Vorgang, das Verfahren.

proceed [prəˈsiːd], *v.n.* vorgehen, verfahren.

proceeds [ˈprousiːdz], *s. pl.* der Ertrag.

process (1) [ˈprouses], *s.* der Vorgang, Prozeß. — *v.a.* verarbeiten, fertigen.

process (2) [proˈses], *v.n.* in einem Zuge gehen.

procession [prəˈseʃən], *s.* der (feierliche) Umzug, die Prozession.

proclaim [prəˈkleim], *v.a.* (*Pol.*) proklamieren, ausrufen.

proclamation [prɔkləˈmeiʃən], *s.* (*Pol.*) die Ausrufung, Proklamation.

proclivity [prəˈkliviti], *s.* der Hang, die Neigung (*tendency*).

procrastinate [prəˈkræstineit], *v.a.* aufschieben. — *v.n.* zögern, zaudern.

procreate [ˈproukrieit], *v.a.* zeugen, hervorbringen.

procurable [prəˈkjuərəbl], *adj.* zu verschaffen, erhältlich.

procure [prəˈkjuə], *v.a.* verschaffen, besorgen.

prod [prɔd], *v.a.* stoßen.

prodigal [ˈprɔdigəl], *adj.* verschwenderisch, vergeudend; — *son*, der verlorene Sohn.

prodigious [prəˈdidʒəs], *adj.* erstaunlich, ungeheuer.

prodigy [ˈprɔdidʒi], *s.* das Wunderkind.

produce [prəˈdjuːs], *v.a.* erzeugen, produzieren. — [ˈprɔdjuːs], *s.* das Produkt, Erzeugnis.

producer [prəˈdjuːsə], *s.* der Erzeuger; (*Theat.*, *Cinema*) der Regisseur.

product [ˈprɔdʌkt], *s.* das Produkt, Erzeugnis.

production [prəˈdʌkʃən], *s.* die Produktion; die Erzeugung (*industrial*); das Zeigen, Vorweisen (*of documents*); (*Theat.*) die Regie.

productive [prəˈdʌktiv], *adj.* produktiv, schöpferisch (*mind*); fruchtbar (*soil*).

profane [prəˈfein], *adj.* profan; ruchlos.

profanity [prəˈfæniti], *s.* die Profanierung; das Lästern.

profess [prəˈfes], *v.a., v.n.* bekennen, erklären, sich bekennen zu.

profession [prəˈfeʃən], *s.* der (höhere) Beruf; (*Eccl.*) das Bekenntnis; die Beteuerung (*protestation*).

professional [prəˈfeʃənəl], *adj.* beruflich, berufsmäßig.

professor [prəˈfesə], *s.* der (Universitäts) Professor.

professorship [prəˈfesəʃip], *s.* die Professur.

proffer [ˈprɔfə], *v.a.* anbieten (*offer*).

proficiency [prəˈfiʃənsi], *s.* die Tüchtigkeit; (*skill*) die Beherrschung.

proficient [prəˈfiʃənt], *adj.* bewandert, tüchtig; (*in language*) fließend.

profile [ˈproufail], *s.* das Profil.

profit [ˈprɔfit], *s.* der Profit, Gewinn, Nutzen. — *v.n.* Nutzen ziehen. — *v.a.* von Nutzen sein (*Dat.*).

profound [prəˈfaund], *adj.* tief; gründlich (*thorough*).

profuse [prəˈfjuːs], *adj.* reichlich, verschwenderisch.

profusion [prəˈfjuːʒen], *s.* der Überfluß.

progeny [ˈprɔdʒəni], *s.* der Nachkomme; die Nachkommenschaft.

prognosticate [prɔgˈnɔstikeit], *v.a.* vorhersagen.

prognostication [prɔgnɔstiˈkeiʃən], *s.* die Voraussage.

programme, (*Am.*) **program** [ˈprougræm], *s.* das Programm.

progress [ˈprougres], *s.* der Fortschritt. — [prouˈgres], *v.n.* fortschreiten, Fortschritte machen.

progression [pro'greʃən], *s.* (*Maths.*) die Reihe, Progression.

progressive [pro'gresiv], *adj.* fortschrittlich (*modern*); fortschreitend (*continuous*); progressiv.

prohibit [prou'hibit], *v.a.* verbieten.

prohibition [proui'biʃən], *s.* das Verbot.

project [prə'dʒekt], *v.a.* projizieren; entwerfen. — ['prɔdʒekt], *s.* das Projekt, der Plan.

projectile [prə'dʒektail], *s.* das Geschoß.

projection [prə'dʒekʃən], *s.* die Projektion (*film*); der Entwurf (*plan*); der Vorsprung (*jutting out*).

proletarian [prouli'teəriən], *adj.* proletarisch. — *s.* der Prolet(arier).

prolific [prə'lifik], *adj.* fruchtbar.

prolix ['prouliks], *adj.* weitschweifig.

prologue ['proulɔg], *s.* der Prolog.

prolong [prə'lɔŋ], *v.a.* verlängern, prolongieren.

prominent ['prɔminənt], *adj.* prominent, hervorragend.

promiscuous [prə'miskjuəs], *adj.* unterschiedslos (*indiscriminate*); vermischt (*mixed*).

promise ['prɔmis], *v.a.* versprechen. — *v.n.* Erwartungen erwecken. — *s.* das Versprechen.

promissory ['prɔmisəri], *adj.* versprechend; (*Comm.*) — note, der Schuldschein.

promontory ['prɔməntəri], *s.* das Vorgebirge.

promote [prə'mout], *v.a.* befördern; fördern (*foster*).

promotion [prə'mouʃən], *s.* die Beförderung (*advancement*); Förderung (*fostering*); (*Am.*) die Reklame (*publicity*).

prompt [prɔmpt], *adj.* prompt, pünktlich. — *v.a.* (*Theat.*) soufflieren; treiben (*inspire*).

prompter ['prɔmptə], *s.* (*Theat.*) der Souffleur.

promptitude ['prɔmptitju:d], *s.* die Promptheit, Pünktlichkeit.

promulgate ['prɔməlgeit], *v.a.* bekanntmachen, verbreiten.

prone [proun], *adj.* geneigt, neigend.

prong [prɔŋ], *s.* die Zinke, Gabel.

pronominal [pro'nɔminəl], *adj.* (*Gram.*) pronominal.

pronoun ['prounaun], *s.* das Fürwort, Pronomen.

pronounce [prə'nauns], *v.a.*, *v.n.* aussprechen (*words*); feierlich erklären (*proclaim*).

pronunciation [prənʌnsi'eiʃən], *s.* die Aussprache.

proof [pru:f], *s.* der Beweis, die Probe; (*Typ.*) der Korrekturbogen. — *v.a.* (*Engin.*, *Chem.*) impregnieren.

prop [prɔp], *s.* die Stütze, der Stützpfahl. — *v.a.* stützen.

propaganda [prɔpə'gændə], *s.* die Propaganda, Reklame.

propagate ['prɔpəgeit], *v.a.* propagieren; (*Bot.*) fortpflanzen.

propel [prə'pel], *v.a.* forttreiben, vorwärtstreiben.

propeller [prə'pelə], *s.* der Propeller, die Schraube.

propensity [prə'pensiti], *s.* die Neigung, der Hang.

proper ['prɔpə], *adj.* schicklich (*manners*); eigentümlich, eigen (*peculiar*).

property ['prɔpəti], *s.* das Eigentum (*possession*); die Eigenschaft (*quality*).

prophecy ['prɔfisi], *s.* die Prophezeiung, Weissagung.

prophesy ['prɔfisai], *v.a.* prophezeien.

propitiate [prə'piʃieit], *v.a.* versöhnen.

propitiation [prəpiʃi'eiʃən], *s.* die Versöhnung.

propitious [prə'piʃəs], *adj.* gnädig, günstig, geneigt.

proportion [prə'pɔ:ʃən], *s.* das Verhältnis; die Proportion; der Anteil (*portion*); das Ebenmaß (*in art*).

proportionate [prə'pɔ:ʃənit], *adj.* im Verhältnis, verhältnismäßig, proportioniert.

proposal [prə'pouzəl], *s.* der Vorschlag, Antrag.

propose [prə'pouz], *v.a.* antragen, beantragen, vorschlagen. — *v.n.* — to a lady, einen Heiratsantrag machen.

proposition [prɔpə'ziʃən], *s.* der Vorschlag, Antrag; die Idee.

propound [prə'paund], *v.a.* vorlegen, vorbringen (*a theory etc.*).

proprietor [prə'praiətə], *s.* der Eigentümer.

propriety [prə'praiəti], *s.* die Schicklichkeit.

propulsion [prə'pʌlʃən], *s.* der Antrieb.

prorogue [prə'roug], *v.a.* vertagen.

prosaic [prə'zeiik], *adj.* prosaisch, nüchtern.

proscribe [pro'skraib], *v.a.* verbieten, ächten.

proscription [pro'skripʃən], *s.* die Verbannung, das Verbot.

prose [prouz], *s.* die Prosa.

prosecute ['prɔsikju:t], *v.a.* verfolgen; (*Law*) gerichtlich verfolgen, anklagen.

prosecutor ['prɔsikju:tə], *s.* (*public*) der Staatsanwalt; der Kläger.

proselyte ['prɔsəlait], *s.* der Neubekehrte, Proselyt.

prospect ['prɔspekt], *s.* die Aussicht; (*pl.*) die Aussichten, Chancen, *f.pl.* — [prɔs'pekt], *v.n.* suchen (*for*, nach, *Dat.*).

prospectus [prə'spektəs], *s.* der Prospekt.

prosper ['prɔspə], *v.n.* gedeihen, blühen. — *v.a.* segnen.

prosperity [prɔs'periti], *s.* der Wohlstand; der Reichtum; das Gedeihen (*thriving*).

prosperous ['prɔspərəs], *adj.* glücklich, wohlhabend.

prostitute ['prɔstitju:t], *s.* die Prostituierte, Dirne. — *v.a.* erniedrigen.

prostrate ['prɔstreit], *adj.* hingestreckt, niedergeworfen, fußfällig. — [prɔs'treit], *v.a.* niederwerfen.

prosy

prosy ['prouzi], *adj.* prosaisch, weitschweifig, langweilig.

protect [prə'tekt], *v.a.* beschützen.

protection [prə'tekʃən], *s.* der Schutz; die Protektion (*favour*).

protective [prə'tektiv], *adj.* Schutz-, schützend.

protector [prə'tektə], *s.* der Beschützer; (*Engin.*) der Schutz.

protest [prə'test], *v.a., v.n.* protestieren, einwenden. — ['proutest], *s.* der Protest, Einspruch.

Protestant ['protistənt], *adj.* protestantisch. — *s.* der Protestant.

protestation [protes'teiʃən], *s.* die Beteuerung, Verwahrung.

protocol ['proutəkɔl], *s.* das Protokoll.

prototype ['proutotaip], *s.* das Urbild, Modell, der Prototyp.

protract [prə'trækt], *v.a.* in die Länge ziehen; hinausziehen.

protractor [prə'træktə], *s.* der Winkelmesser, Transporteur, die Schmiege.

protrude [prə'tru:d], *v.n.* herausragen, hervorstehen, vordringen.

protuberance [prə'tju:bərəns], *s.* der Höcker, der Auswuchs, die Protuberanz.

proud [praud], *adj.* stolz (*of*, auf, *Acc.*).

prove [pru:v], *v.a.* beweisen. — *v.n.* sich erweisen (*turn out*).

provender ['provində], *s.* das Viehfutter.

proverb ['provə:b], *s.* das Sprichwort.

proverbial [prə'və:biəl], *adj.* sprichwörtlich.

provide [prə'vaid], *v.a., v.n.* vorsehen, versorgen, verschaffen.

provided [prə'vaidid], *conj.* vorausgesetzt.

providence ['providəns], *s.* die Vorsehung.

provident ['providənt], *adj.* vorsorglich.

providential [provi'denʃəl], *adj.* von der Vorsehung bestimmt.

province ['provins], *s.* die Provinz, das Gebiet (*also fig.*).

provincial [prə'vinʃəl], *adj.* ländlich, Provinz-; provinziell.

provision [prə'viʒən], *s.* die Versorgung (*supply*); der Vorrat (*stock*); (*pl.*) die Lebensmittel (*victuals*).

provisional [prə'viʒənəl], *adj.* vorläufig.

proviso [prə'vaizou], *s.* der Vorbehalt.

provocation [provə'keiʃən], *s.* die Herausforderung.

provoke [prə'vouk], *v.a.* herausfordern, provozieren.

prow [prau], *s.* (*Naut.*) der Bug.

prowess ['praues], *s.* die Stärke (*physical*); die körperliche Tüchtigkeit; Tapferkeit.

prowl [praul], *v.n.* herumstreichen.

proximity [prɔk'simiti], *s.* die Nähe.

proxy ['prɔksi], *s.* der Stellvertreter.

prudence ['pru:dəns], *s.* die Klugheit, Vorsicht.

prudent ['pru:dənt], *adj.* klug, vorsichtig.

prudery ['pru:dəri], *s.* die Sprödigkeit.

prudish ['pru:diʃ], *adj.* prüde, spröde, zimperlich.

prune (1) [pru:n], *s.* (*Cul.*) die Backpflaume.

prune (2) [pru:n], *v.a.* beschneiden, stutzen.

Prussian ['prʌʃən], *adj.* preußisch; — *blue*, das Berlinerblau. — *s.* der Preuße.

prussic ['prʌsik], *adj.* blausauer; — *acid*, die Blausäure.

pry [prai], *v.n.* spähen, ausforschen.

psalm [sa:m], *s.* der Psalm.

psychology [sai'kɔlədʒi], *s.* die Psychologie.

pub [pʌb], *s.* das Wirtshaus, die Kneipe.

puberty ['pju:bəti], *s.* die Pubertät, Mannbarkeit.

public ['pʌblik], *adj.* öffentlich. — *s.* das Publikum; die Öffentlichkeit.

publican ['pʌblikən], *s.* der Gastwirt.

publication [pʌbli'keiʃən], *s.* die Veröffentlichung, Herausgabe.

publicity [pʌb'lisiti], *s.* die Werbung, die Reklame; — *manager*, der Reklamechef, Werbeleiter.

publicize ['pʌblisaiz], *v.a.* weithin bekannt machen, publizieren.

publish ['pʌbliʃ], *v.a.* veröffentlichen; verlegen (*books*); —*ing house*, der Verlag.

publisher ['pʌbliʃə], *s.* der Verleger.

pucker ['pʌkə], *v.a.* falten; runzeln (*wrinkle*). — *s.* die Falte.

pudding ['pudiŋ], *s.* der Pudding.

puddle [pʌdl], *s.* die Pfütze. — *v.a.* puddeln (*iron*).

puerile ['pjuərail], *adj.* kindisch, knabenhaft.

puff [pʌf], *v.a., v.n.* puffen, paffen, blasen; —*ed-up*, aufgebläht, stolz. — *s.* der Windstoß; — *pastry*, der Blätterteig.

pug [pʌg], *s.* (*Zool.*) der Mops.

pugnacious [pʌg'neiʃəs], *adj.* kampfsüchtig, kampflustig.

puisne ['pju:ni], *adj.* (*Law*) jünger, Unter-.

puissant ['pwi:sənt], *adj.* mächtig, stark.

puke [pju:k], *v.n.* sich erbrechen.

pull [pul], *v.a., v.n.* ziehen, reißen; zerren. — *s.* der Zug, Ruck.

pullet ['pulit], *s.* (*Orn.*) das Hühnchen.

pulley ['puli], *s.* der Flaschenzug.

pulmonary, pulmonic ['pʌlmənəri, pʌl'mɔnik], *adj.* Lungen-.

pulp [pʌlp], *s.* der Brei; das Fleisch (*of fruit*); das Mark (*marrow*); die Pulpa (*tooth*). — *v.a.* zerstampfen, zu Brei stampfen.

pulpit ['pulpit], *s.* (*Eccl.*) die Kanzel.

pulsate [pʌl'seit], *v.n.* pulsieren, schlagen.

pulse (1) [pʌls], *s.* der Puls.

pulse (2) [pʌls], *s.* (*Bot.*) die Hülsenfrüchte, *pl.*

pulverize ['pʌlvəraiz], *v.a.* zu Pulver stoßen, zerstoßen.

pumice [´pʌmis], s. der Bimsstein.
pump (1) [pʌmp], s. die Pumpe. — v.a.,
v.n. pumpen; ausfragen (question).
pump (2) [pʌmp], s. der Tanzschuh
(dancing shoe).
pumpkin [´pʌmpkin], s. (Bot.) der
Kürbis.
pun [pʌn], s. das Wortspiel. — v.n.
Wortspiele machen.
Punch [pʌntʃ]. das Kasperle; — and
Judy, Hanswurst und seine Frau.
punch (1) [pʌntʃ], v.a. schlagen,
boxen (box). — s. der Schlag (hit);
der Faustschlag (boxing).
punch (2) [pʌntʃ], v.a. lochen (card). —
s. der Pfriem (tool).
punch (3) [pʌntʃ], s. der Punsch (drink).
punchy [´pʌntʃi], adj. kurz, dick,
untersetzt.
punctilious [pʌŋk´tiliəs], adj. sorgfältig, spitzfindig.
punctual [´pʌŋktjuəl], adj. pünktlich.
punctuate [´pʌŋktjueit], v.a. (Gram.)
interpunktieren; (fig.) betonen.
punctuation [pʌŋktju´eiʃən], s. (Gram.)
die Interpunktion.
puncture [´pʌŋktʃə], s. (Motor.) der
Reifendefekt, die Panne; (Med.) die
Punktur, der Einstich. — v.a. (Med.)
punktieren.
pungent [´pʌndʒənt], adj. scharf,
stechend.
punish [´pʌniʃ], v.a. bestrafen (s.o.);
strafen.
punishable [´pʌniʃəbl], adj. strafbar.
punishment [´pʌniʃmənt], s. die Strafe,
Bestrafung.
punt [pʌnt], s. das kleine Boot, Flachboot.
puny [´pjuːni], adj. schwach, winzig.
pup [pʌp], s. der junge Hund; be
sold a —, einen schlechten Kauf
machen. — v.n. Junge werfen.
pupil (1) [´pjuːpil], s. der Schüler.
pupil (2) [´pjuːpil], s. die Pupille (eye).
pupil(l)age [´pjuːpilidʒ], s. die Minder-
jährigkeit (of minor).
puppet [´pʌpit], s. die Puppe, Marionette; der Strohmann (human tool).
puppy [´pʌpi] see pup.
purblind [´pəːblaind], adj. halbblind.
purchase [´pəːtʃis], s. der Kauf, Einkauf. — v.a. kaufen.
pure [´pjuə], adj. pur, rein.
purge [pəːdʒ], v.a. reinigen. — s. die
Reinigung; (Pol.) die Säuberung.
purify [´pjuərifai], v.a. läutern, reinigen.
purl (1) [pəːl], s. die Borte; (knitting)
die Häkelkante.
purl (2) [pəːl], v.n. sich drehen,
wirbeln; (sl.) umkippen.
purl (3) [pəːl], s. das Murmeln, Rieseln
(of brook). — v.n. murmeln, rieseln.
purloin [pəː´lɔin], v.a. stehlen.
purple [pəːpl], adj. purpurn; — patch,
die Glanzstelle. — s. der Purpur.
purport [pəː´pɔːt], v.a. bedeuten, Sinn
haben. — [´pəːpət], s. der Sinn, die
Bedeutung.
purpose [´pəːpəs], s. die Absicht, der
Zweck.

purposeful [´pəːpəsful], adj. zweck-
bewußt, energisch, zielbewußt.
purr [pəː], v.n. schnurren (of cat).
purse [pəːs], s. die Börse, Geldtasche;
das Portemonnaie.
pursuance [pə´sjuːəns], s. (Law) die
Verfolgung, Ausführung.
pursuant [pə´sjuːənt], adj. (Law)
zufolge, gemäß (to, Dat.).
pursue [pə´sjuː], v.a. verfolgen.
pursuit [pə´sjuːt], s. die Verfolgung;
(pl.) die Geschäfte, n. pl.; Beschäftigung.
purvey [pə´vei], v.a. versorgen, liefern.
purview [´pəːvjuː], s. der Spielraum;
das Blickfeld.
push [puʃ], v.a. stoßen, drücken,
schieben, drängen; be —ed for, in der
Klemme sein. — s. der Stoß, Schub,
das Drängen; at a —, wenn absolut
nötig.
pusillanimous [pjuːsi´læniməs], adj.
kleinmütig.
puss, pussy [pus, ´pusi], s. (coll.) die
Katze, das Kätzchen, Miezchen.
put [put], v.a. irr. setzen (set),legen(lay),
stellen (stand); — off, aufschieben,
aus der Fassung bringen (deflect); —
on, anziehen, auflegen; — it on thickly,
es dick auftragen. — v.n. (Naut.) —
in, anlegen.
putrefy [´pjuːtrifai], v.a., v.n. faul
werden (rot), verwesen.
putrid [´pjuːtrid], adj. faul (rotten).
puttee [´pʌtiː], s. (Mil.) die Wickel-
gamasche.
putty [´pʌti], s. der Kitt.
puzzle [pʌzl], s. das Rätsel. — v.a. zu
denken geben (Dat.).
pygmy [´pigmi], s. der Pygmäe.
pyjamas, (Am.) **pajamas** [pi´dʒɑːməz,
pə-], s. pl. der Schlafanzug.
pyramid [´pirəmid], s. die Pyramide.
pyre [paiə], s. der Scheiterhaufen.
pyrotechnics [paiərə´tekniks], s. pl.
das Feuerwerk, die Feuerwerkskunst.
python [´paiθən], s. (Zool.) die Riesenschlange.

Q

Q [kjuː]. das Q.
qua [kwei], conj. als.
quack [kwæk], v.n. quaken; (coll.)
quacksalbern. — s. der Quacksalber.
quadrangle [´kwɔdræŋgl], s. (abbr.)
quad [kwɔd]), das Viereck; der Hof
(in college etc).
quadrant [´kwɔdrənt], s. der Quadrant,
Viertelkreis; (Engin.) der Winkelmesser.
quadrille [kwə´dril], s. die Quadrille,
der Kontertanz.

quadruped

quadruped ['kwɔdruped], *s.* (*Zool.*) das vierfüßige Tier.

quadruple ['kwɔdrupl], *adj.* vierfach.

quaff [kwæf], *v.a.* schlucken. — *v.n.* zechen (*drink heavily*).

quagmire ['kwægmaiə], *s.* der Sumpf.

quail (1) [kweil], *s.* (*Orn.*) die Wachtel.

quail (2) [kweil], *v.n.* verzagen.

quaint [kweint], *adj.* seltsam, wunderlich, eigenartig.

quake [kweik], *v.n.* erzittern, beben.

Quaker ['kweikə], *s.* der Quäker.

qualification [kwɔlifi'keiʃən], *s.* die Befähigung, Qualifikation (*ability*); die Einschränkung (*proviso*).

qualify ['kwɔlifai], *v.a.* befähigen (*make able*); beschränken, mäßigen, qualifizieren (*modify*). — *v.n.* sich qualifizieren, das Studium abschließen.

qualitative ['kwɔlitətiv], *adj.* qualitätsmäßig, Wert-, qualitativ.

quality ['kwɔliti], *s.* die Qualität (*high class*); der Wert (*standard*).

qualm [kwɑ:m], *s.* der Skrupel.

quantitative ['kwɔntitətiv], *adj.* quantitativ.

quantity ['kwɔntiti], *s.* die Quantität, Menge.

quantum ['kwɔntəm], *s.* die Menge; das Quantum; — *theory*, die Quantentheorie.

quarantine ['kwɔrənti:n], *s.* die Quarantäne.

quarrel ['kwɔrəl], *s.* der Streit, Zwist. — *v.n.* streiten, zanken.

quarry (1) ['kwɔri], *s.* der Steinbruch.

quarry (2) ['kwɔri], *s.* die Beute (*prey*).

quart [kwɔ:t], *s.* das Viertelmaß (*1.15 litre*).

quarter ['kwɔ:tə], *s.* das Viertel (*jahr*); (*Arith.*) das Viertel (*also of town*); (*pl.*) das Quartier.

quartermaster ['kwɔ:təma:stə], *s.* (*Mil.*) der Feldzeugmeister.

quartet(te) [kwɔ:'tet], *s.* das Quartett.

quarto ['kwɔ:tou], *s.* das Quartformat.

quartz [kwɔ:ts], *s.* der Quartz.

quash [kwɔʃ], *v.a.* unterdrücken (*suppress*); (*Law*) annullieren.

quaver ['kweivə], *s.* (*Mus.*) die Achtelnote; der Triller (*trill*). — *v.n.* tremolieren, trillern.

quay [ki:], *s.* der Kai, Hafendamm.

queen [kwi:n], *s.* die Königin.

queer [kwiə], *adj.* seltsam, sonderlich.

quell [kwel], *v.a.* unterdrücken.

quench [kwentʃ], *v.a.* löschen; stillen (*thirst*).

querulous ['kweruləs], *adj.* mürrisch, jämmerlich; zänkisch.

query ['kwiəri], *s.* die Frage. — *v.a.* in Frage stellen.

quest [kwest], *s.* das Suchen, Streben; die Suche.

question ['kwestʃən], *s.* die Frage; — *mark*, das Fragezeichen. — *v.a.* fragen, in Frage stellen; ausfragen (*s.o.*).

questionable ['kwestʃənəbl], *adj.* zweifelhaft, fraglich, bedenklich.

queue [kju:], *s.* die Schlange, das Anstellen. — *v.n.* Schlange stehen.

quibble [kwibl], *s.* das Wortspiel, die Ausflucht. — *v.n.* um Worte streiten.

quick [kwik], *adj.* schnell (*fast*); lebendig (*live*).

quicken ['kwikən], *v.a.* beleben, anfeuern.

quicklime ['kwiklaim], *s.* der ungelöschte Kalk.

quicksand ['kwiksænd], *s.* der Flugsand.

quicksilver ['kwiksilvə], *s.* (*Chem.*) das Quecksilber.

quid (1) [kwid], *s.* (*sl.*) das Pfund Sterling.

quid (2) [kwid], *s.* (*Lat.*) etwas; — *pro quo*, Gleiches mit Gleichem.

quiescence [kwi'esəns], *s.* die Ruhe.

quiet ['kwaiət], *adj.* ruhig.

quietism ['kwaiətizm], *s.* der Quietismus.

quietness ['kwaiətnis], *s.* die Ruhe, Stille.

quill [kwil], *s.* der Federkiel, die Feder. — *v.a.* falten, fälteln.

quilt [kwilt], *s.* die Steppdecke.

quince [kwins], *s.* (*Bot.*) die Quitte.

quinine [kwi'ni:n], *s.* (*Med.*) das Chinin.

quinquennial [kwin'kweniəl], *adj.* fünfjährig, fünfjährlich, alle fünf Jahre.

quinsy ['kwinzi], *s.* (*Med.*) die Bräune.

quint [kwint], *s.* (*Mus.*) die Quinte.

quintessence [kwin'tesəns], *s.* die Quintessenz, der Kern, der Inbegriff.

quintuple ['kwintjupl], *adj.* fünffach.

quip [kwip], *s.* die Stichelei; die witzige Bemerkung.

quire [kwaiə], *s.* das Buch Papier.

quirk [kwə:k], *s.* die (unerwartete) Wendung; Spitzfindigkeit.

quit [kwit], *v.a.*, *v.n.* verlassen; weggehen; (*Am.*) aufhören. — *adj.* (*pl.*) (**quits**) quitt, bezahlt.

quite [kwait], *adv.* ganz, völlig.

quiver (1) ['kwivə], *s.* der Köcher.

quiver (2) ['kwivə], *v.n.* erzittern, schauern.

quiz [kwiz], *s.* das Fragespiel, Quizprogramm (*Radio etc.*).

quoit [kɔit], *s.* die Wurfscheibe.

quorum ['kwɔ:rəm], *s.* die beschlußfähige Anzahl.

quota ['kwoutə], *s.* die Quote.

quotation [kwo'teiʃən], *s.* das Zitat; (*Comm.*) der Kostenanschlag, die Notierung.

quote [kwout], *v.a.* zitieren; (*Comm.*) einen Preis zitieren, notieren.

R

R [ɑ:(r)]. das R.

rabbet ['ræbit], *s.* die Fuge, Nute. — *v.a.* einfugen.

rabbi ['ræbai], *s.* (*Rel.*) der Rabbiner.
rabbit ['ræbit], *s.* (*Zool.*) das Kaninchen.
rabble [ræbl], *s.* der Pöbel.
rabid ['ræbid], *adj.* wütend, rasend.
race (1) [reis], *s.* die Rasse; das Geschlecht (*stock*).
race (2) [reis], *s.* das Rennen (*horses etc.*); der Wettlauf (*run*); — *course*, die Rennbahn. — *v.a.*, *v.n.* um die Wette laufen.
racial ['reiʃəl], *adj.* rassisch.
raciness ['reisinis], *s.* das Rassige, die Urwüchsigkeit.
rack [ræk], *s.* die Folterbank; das Reck (*gymnasium*); (*Railw.*) das Gepäcknetz. — *v.a.* recken, strecken; *o.'s brains*, sich den Kopf zerbrechen.
racket (1), **racquet** ['rækit], *s.* der Tennisschläger.
racket (2) ['rækit], *s.* der Lärm (*noise, din*).
racket (3) ['rækit], *s.* (*coll.*) der Schwindel.
racketeer [ræki'tiə], *s.* der Schwindler.
racy ['reisi], *adj.* stark; pikant.
radar, ['reidɑ:], *s.* das Radar.
radiance ['reidiəns], *s.* der Glanz, das Strahlen.
radiant ['reidiənt], *adj.* strahlend.
radiate ['reidieit], *v.a.*, *v.n.* strahlen, ausstrahlen.
radiator ['reidieitə], *s.* der Heizapparat, Heizkörper; (*Motor.*) der Kühler.
radical ['rædikəl], *adj.* (*Pol.*) radikal; gründlich (*thorough*). — *s.* (*Pol.*) der Radikale; (*Phonet.*) der Grundlaut, Wurzellaut.
radio ['reidiou], *s.* das Radio, der Rundfunk.
radioactive [reidiou'æktiv], *adj.* radioaktiv.
radish ['rædiʃ], *s.* (*Bot.*) der Rettich.
radius ['reidiəs], *s.* der Radius, Halbmesser; (*Phys.*, *Maths.*) der Strahl (*line*).
raffle [ræfl], *s.* die Auslosung. — *v.a.* auslosen, ausspielen.
raft [rɑ:ft], *s.* das Floß.
rafter ['rɑ:ftə], *s.* der Dachsparren.
rag (1) [ræg], *s.* der Lumpen.
rag (2) [ræg], *v.a.* necken, zum Besten haben (*tease*).
ragamuffin ['rægəmʌfin], *s.* der Lumpenkerl.
rage [reidʒ], *s.* die Wut, Raserei; die Manie, Mode (*fashion*). — *v.n.* wüten, rasen.
ragged ['rægid], *adj.* zerlumpt; zackig, rauh (*rough*).
ragout [ra'gu:], *s.* (*Cul.*) das Ragout.
raid [reid], *s.* der Streifzug, die Razzia; der Angriff. — *v.a.* überfallen.
rail (1) [reil], *s.* (*Railw.*) die Schiene; *by* —, mit der Eisenbahn.
rail (2) [reil], *v.n.* schmähen; spotten (*Genit.*).
railing ['reiliŋ], *s.* das Geländer, Gitter.
raillery ['reiləri], *s.* die Spötterei, das Schmähen.

railway, (*Am.*) **railroad** ['reilwei, 'reilroud], *s.* die Eisenbahn.
raiment ['reimənt], *s.* (*Poet.*) die Kleidung.
rain [rein], *s.* der Regen. — *v.n.* regnen.
rainbow ['reinbou], *s.* der Regenbogen.
raincoat ['reinkout], *s.* der Regenmantel.
raise [reiz], *v.a.* heben (lift); steigern (*prices*); aufbringen (*army, money*); züchten (*breed*); aufziehen (*children*). — *s.* (*Am.*) die Steigerung, Erhöhung (*salary*).
raisin ['reizin], *s.* (*Bot.*) die Rosine.
rake (1) [reik], *s.* der Rechen (*tool*). — *v.a.* zusammenrechen, harken; bestreichen (*fire at*).
rake (2) [reik], *s.* der Schlemmer (*roué*).
rakish ['reikiʃ], *adj.* liederlich.
rally ['ræli], *v.a.* sammeln, versammeln. — *v.n.* sich versammeln, sich scharen. — *s.* die Massenversammlung, Kundgebung; das Treffen.
ram [ræm], *s.* der Widder; (*Mil.*) die Ramme. — *v.a.* rammen.
ramble [ræmbl], *v.n.* (im Grünen) wandern; herumschweifen; einen Ausflug machen. — *s.* der Ausflug.
rambler ['ræmblə], *s.* der Wanderer (*hiker*); (*Bot.*) die Heckenrose.
ramification [ræmifi'keiʃən], *s.* die Verzweigung, Verästelung (*also fig.*); (*pl.*) Zweige, m. *pl.* (*also fig.*).
ramp [ræmp], *v.n.* sich ranken (*of plants*). — *s.* die Rampe.
rampant ['ræmpənt], *adj.* zügellos, grassierend (*wild*); (*Her.*) sich bäumend.
rampart ['ræmpɑ:t], *s.* der Wall.
ramshackle ['ræmʃækl], *adj.* wackelig, baufällig.
rancid ['rænsid], *adj.* ranzig.
rancour ['ræŋkə], *s.* der Groll, die Erbitterung.
random ['rændəm], *s.* *at* —, aufs Geratewohl. — *adj.* zufällig, Zufalls-.
range [reindʒ], *s.* die Reihe (*row, series*); (*Geog.*) die Bergkette; die Küchenherd (*stove*); (*Mil.*) die Schießstätte (*shooting ground*); die Schußweite, Reichweite (*distance*). — *v.n.* sich reihen; sich erstrecken (*stretch*). — *v.a.* rangieren, anordnen, durchstreifen.
rangefinder ['reindʒfaində], *s.* (*Phot.*) der Entfernungsmesser.
ranger ['reindʒə], *s.* der Förster, Forstgehilfe; (*Mil.*) der leichte Reiter.
rank (1) [ræŋk], *s.* die Klasse; der Rang (*order*); — *and file*, die Mannschaft (*of members*); die Mitgliedschaft, Masse. — *v.n.* sich reihen; gelten.
rank (2) [ræŋk], *adj.* übermäßig, üppig, allzu stark; ranzig (*of fat etc.*).
rankle [ræŋkl], *v.n.* nagen.
ransack ['rænsæk], *v.a.* plündern.
ransom ['rænsəm], *s.* das Lösegeld; *hold to* —, (gegen Lösegeld) gefangen halten. — *v.a.* loskaufen.

469

rant

rant [rænt], *v.n.* wüten; großtun; groß-sprechen.

rap [ræp], *v.a.*, *v.n.* schlagen, klopfen.

rapacious [rə'peiʃəs], *adj.* raubgierig.

rape (1) [reip], *v.a.* vergewaltigen. — *s.* die Vergewaltigung.

rape (2) [reip], *s.* (*Bot.*) der Raps.

rapid ['ræpid], *adj.* rasch, schnell, reißend (*river*). — *s.* (*pl.*) die Strom-schnelle.

rapier ['reipiə], *s.* der Degen; (*fencing*) das Rapier.

rapine ['ræpain], *s.* (*Poet.*) der Raub.

rapt [ræpt], *adj.* entzückt; versunken.

rapture ['ræptʃə], *s.* das Entzücken.

rare (1) [rɛə], *adj.* selten.

rare (2) [rɛə], *adj.* (*meat*) rar.

rarity ['rɛəriti], *s.* die Seltenheit.

rascal ['rɑːskəl], *s.* der Schurke.

rash (1) [ræʃ], *adj.* unbesonnen.

rash (2) [ræʃ], *s.* der Ausschlag (*skin*).

rasher ['ræʃə], *s.* die Speckschnitte.

rasp [rɑːsp], *s.* die Raspel, Feile. — *v.a.*, *v.n.* raspeln; heiser sein (*speech*).

raspberry ['rɑːzbəri], *s.* (*Bot.*) die Himbeere.

rat [ræt], *s.* (*Zool.*) die Ratte; (*fig.*) der Verräter.

ratable ['reitəbl], *adj.* steuerpflichtig.

rate (1) [reit], *s.* das Mass; der Tarif; die Geschwindigkeit (*speed*); Gemein-deabgabe (*tax*); das Verhältnis (*proportion*). — *v.a.* schätzen (*estimate*); (*Am.*) einschätzen, halten für.

rate (2) [reit], *v.a.* schelten (*berate*).

rather ['rɑːðə], *adv.* vielmehr, eher, lieber (*in comparisons*); — *good*, ziemlich gut.

ratification [rætifi'keiʃən], *s.* die Be-stätigung; (*Pol.*) die Ratifizierung.

ratify ['rætifai], *v.a.* bestätigen; (*Pol.*) ratifizieren.

ratio ['reiʃiou], *s.* das Verhältnis.

ration ['ræʃən], *s.* die Ration.

rational ['ræʃənəl], *adj.* Vernunfts-, rationell, vernunftgemäß.

rattle [rætl], *s.* das Geklapper (*noise*); die Klapper (*toy etc.*); *death* —, das Todesröcheln. — *v.a.* klappern, Lärm machen; (*fig.*) aus der Fassung bringen; — *off*, herunterleiern. — *v.n.* rasseln, klappern.

raucous ['rɔːkəs], *adj.* heiser, rauh.

ravage ['rævidʒ], *v.a.* verheeren. — *s.* (*pl.*) die Verheerung, Verwüstung.

rave [reiv], *v.n.* vernarrt sein (*about*, in); schwärmen (*für*).

raven [reivn], *s.* (*Orn.*) der Rabe.

ravenous ['rævənəs], *adj.* gefräßig, gierig.

ravine [rə'viːn], *s.* die Schlucht.

ravish ['ræviʃ], *v.a.* schänden, enthe-hren; (*delight*) entzücken.

raw [rɔː], *adj.* rauh (*rough*); roh (*meat*); jung, grün (*novice*); *a* — *deal*, die unfaire Behandlung.

ray [rei], *s.* (*Phys.*) der Strahl. — *v.n.* strahlen.

ray (2) [rei], *s.* (*Zool.*) der Rochen.

raze [reiz], *v.a.* radieren (*erase*); zer-stören (*destroy*).

razor ['reizə], *s.* der Rasierapparat; — *strop*, der Streichriemen.

re* [riː], *pref.* wieder —, noch einmal, zurück-.

* In the following pages, only those compounds are listed in which the meaning is different from the root word or where no simple stem exists.

reach [riːtʃ], *v.a.* reichen, erlangen (*attain*); reichen (*hand*); erreichen. — *s.* der Bereich, (*fig.*) die Weite.

react [ri'ækt], *v.n.* reagieren (*to*, auf, *Acc.*).

read (1) [riːd], *v.a.*, *v.n. irr.* lesen; an-zeigen (*meter etc.*); — *for a degree*, studieren.

read (2) [red], *adj.* *well*—, belesen.

readable ['riːdəbl], *adj.* gut zu lesen, lesenswert; leserlich (*legible*).

reader ['riːdə], *s.* der Leser; (*Univ.*) der außerordentliche Professor; (*fig.*) das Lesebuch.

readiness ['redinis], *s.* die Bereitschaft, Bereitwilligkeit.

ready ['redi], *adj.* bereit, fertig; prompt; — *money*, das Bargeld.

real [riəl], *adj.* wirklich, wahr, tatsäch-lich; echt; — *estate*, der Grundbesitz.

realistic [riə'listik], *adj.* realistisch.

reality [ri'æliti], *s.* die Wirklichkeit.

realize ['riəlaiz], *v.a.* (*understand*) be-greifen; (*sell*) veräußern; verwirklichen.

realm [relm], *s.* das Reich.

reap [riːp], *v.a.* ernten.

rear (1) [riə], *adj.* hinter, nach-. — *s.* der Hintergrund, (*Mil.*) die Nachhut.

rear (2) [riə], *v.a.* aufziehen, erziehen (*bring up*). — *v.n.* sich bäumen.

reason ['riːzən], *s.* die Ursache, der Grund (*cause*); die Vernunft (*reason-ableness*). — *v.n.* argumentieren, debattieren.

reasonable ['riːzənəbl], *adj.* vernünftig, verständig.

reasonably ['riːzənəbli], *adv.* ziemlich, verhältnismäßig.

rebate ['riːbeit], *s.* der Rabatt.

rebel [rebl], *s.* der Rebell. — [ri'bel], *v.n.* sich empören.

rebound [ri'baund], *v.n.* zurückprallen. —['riːbaund], *s.* der Rückprall.

rebuff [ri'bʌf], *s.* die Abweisung. — *v.a.* abweisen, zurückweisen.

rebuke [ri'bjuːk], *v.a.* zurechtweisen, tadeln. — *s.* der Tadel, die Kritik (an).

rebut [ri'bʌt], *v.a.* zurückweisen.

rebuttal [ri'bʌtl], *s.* die Widerlegung.

recalcitrant [ri'kælsitrənt], *adj.* wider-spenstig, störrisch.

recall [ri'kɔːl], *v.a.* zurückrufen; (*re-member*) sich erinnern.

recant [ri'kænt], *v.a.*, *v.n.* widerrufen.

recapitulate [riːkə'pitjuleit], *v.a.* re-kapitulieren, wiederholen.

recast [riː'kɑːst], *v.a.* neu fassen, umar-beiten.

recede [ri'siːd], *v.n.* zurückgehen; heruntergehen (*prices etc.*).

receipt [ri'si:t], *s.* die Empfangsbestätigung, Quittung. — *v.a.* quittieren.

receive [ri'si:v], *v.a.* erhalten, empfangen; (*Law*) Diebesgut annehmen.

receiver [ri'si:və], *s.* der Empfänger; (*Law*) der Hehler; (*Telephone*) der Hörer; (*Rad.*) der Apparat.

recent ['ri:sənt], *adj.* jüngst, neuest.

recently ['ri:səntli], *adv.* vor kurzem.

reception [ri'sepʃən], *s.* der Empfang.

receptive [ri'septiv], *adj.* empfänglich.

recess [ri'ses], *s.* (*Parl.*) die Ferien, *pl.*; die Pause; die Nische (*nook*).

recession [ri'seʃən], *s.* (*Econ.*) die Rezession, die Baisse.

recipe ['resipi], *s.* (*Cul.*) das Rezept.

recipient [ri'sipiənt], *s.* der Empfänger (*of donation etc.*).

reciprocal [ri'siprəkəl], *adj.* gegenseitig, wechselseitig.

reciprocate [ri'siprəkeit], *v.a., v.n.* erwidern, vergelten.

recital [ri'saitl], *s.* der Vortrag; (*Mus.*) das Solokonzert, Kammerkonzert.

recite [ri'sait], *v.a.* vortragen; (*story*) erzählen, aufsagen.

reckless ['reklis], *adj.* leichtsinnig.

reckon ['rekən], *v.n.* rechnen (*on*, mit, *Dat.*); dafür halten, denken (*think*).

reclamation [reklə'meiʃən], *s.* (*Agr.*) die Urbarmachung; (*fig.*) die Beschwerde, Reklamation.

recline [ri'klain], *v.n.* sich zurücklehnen.

recluse [ri'klu:s], *s.* der Einsiedler.

recognition [rekəg'niʃən], *s.* die Anerkennung.

recognize ['rekəgnaiz], *v.a.* anerkennen (als) (*acknowledge*); erkennen (*know again*).

recoil [ri'kɔil], *v.n.* zurückprallen, zurückfahren.

recollect [rekə'lekt], *v.a.* sich erinnern (an, *Acc.*).

recollection [rekə'lekʃən], *s.* die Erinnerung, das Gedächtnis.

recommend [rekə'mend], *v.a.* empfehlen.

recompense ['rekəmpens], *v.a.* vergelten, entschädigen, belohnen.

reconcile ['rekənsail], *v.a.* versöhnen.

reconciliation [rekənsili'eiʃən], *s.* die Versöhnung.

recondite ['rekəndait], *adj.* dunkel, verborgen, wenig bekannt.

reconnoitre [rekə'nɔitə], *v.a.* auskundschaften.

record [ri'kɔ:d], *v.a.* notieren, eintragen (*enter*), festhalten; aufnehmen (*tape etc.*). — ['rekɔ:d], *s.* die Aufzeichnung (*in writing*); die Schallplatte (*gramophone*); (*Sports*) der Rekord.

recorder [ri'kɔ:də], *s.* der Protokollführer; (*Law*) der Richter; Syndikus, Registrator; (*Mus.*) die Blockflöte.

recount [ri'kaunt], *v.a.* erzählen.

recourse [ri'kɔ:s], *s.* die Zuflucht.

recover [ri'kʌvə], *v.a.* wiedererlangen. — *v.n.* sich erholen.

recovery [ri'kʌvəri], *s.* die Wiedererlangung (*regaining*); (*Med.*) die Genesung, Erholung.

recreation [rekri'eiʃən], *s.* die Erholung.

recrimination [rekrimi'neiʃən], *s.* die Gegenklage.

recruit [ri'kru:t], *v.a.* rekrutieren, anwerben. — *s.* der Rekrut.

rectangle ['rektæŋgl], *s.* das Rechteck.

rectify ['rektifai], *v.a.* richtigstellen; (*Elec.*) gleichrichten, umformen.

rectilinear [rekti'liniə], *adj.* geradlinig.

rectitude ['rektitju:d], *s.* die Aufrichtigkeit.

rector ['rektə], *s.* (*Eccl.*) der Pfarrer; der Rektor, Vorstand (*institution*).

recuperate [ri'kju:pəreit], *v.n.* sich erholen.

recur [ri'kə:], *v.n.* sich wieder ereignen, sich wiederholen.

recurrence [ri'kʌrəns], *s.* die Wiederholung.

red [red], *adj.* rot; — *hot*, glühend heiß.

redbreast ['redbrest], *s.* (*Orn.*) das Rotkehlchen.

redeem [ri'di:m], *v.a.* erlösen.

redemption [ri'dempʃən], *s.* die Erlösung.

redolent ['redolənt], *adj.* duftend.

redound [ri'daund], *v.n.* gereichen, sich erweisen.

redress [ri'dres], *v.a.* abhelfen (*Dat.*); wieder herstellen. — *s.* die Abhilfe.

reduce [ri'dju:s], *v.a.* vermindern, herabsetzen; (*fig.*) degradieren. — *v.n.* (*weight*) abnehmen.

reduction [ri'dʌkʃən], *s.* die Herabsetzung (*price etc.*); die Verminderung (*decrease*); (*Chem.*) die Reduktion.

redundant [ri'dʌndənt], *adj.* überflüssig.

reduplicate [ri:'dju:plikeit], *v.a.* verdoppeln.

reed [ri:d], *s.* (*Bot.*) das Schilfrohr; (*Mus.*) die Rohrpfeife.

reef [ri:f], *s.* das Riff, Felsenriff; (*Naut.*) das Reff.

reek [ri:k], *v.n.* rauchen, dampfen, riechen. — *s.* der Rauch, Dampf, der Gestank.

reel [ri:l], *s.* die Spule, Rolle, Haspel. — *v.a.* — *off*, abrollen; (*fig.*) mechanisch hersagen. — *v.n.* taumeln.

refectory [ri'fektəri], *s.* der Speisesaal; das Refektorium (*in monastery etc.*).

refer [ri'fə:], *v.n.* — *to s.th.*, weiterleiten; überweisen; — *to*, sich beziehen (auf, *Acc.*).

referee [refə'ri:], *s.* der Referent; (*Sport*) der Schiedsrichter.

reference ['refərəns], *s. with* — *to*, in or mit Bezug auf; die Referenz, Empfehlung; Verweisung (*to*, auf); — *library*, die Nachschlagebibliothek; — *index*, das (Nachschlags)verzeichnis.

refine [ri'fain], *v.a.* (*Chem.*) raffinieren; (*manners*) verfeinern; (*products*) läutern, veredeln.

reflect

reflect [ri'flekt], *v.a.* widerspiegeln (*mirror*); ein Licht werfen (auf, *Acc.*). — *v.n.* — *on*, überlegen (*think over*).

reflection, reflexion [ri'flekʃən], *s.* die Überlegung, das Nachdenken; die Spiegelung, Reflexion.

reform [ri'fɔːm], *s.* die Reform, Verbesserung. — *v.a.* reformieren; ['riː'fɔːm] (sich) neu bilden. — *v.n.* sich bessern.

refractory [ri'fræktəri], *adj.* widerspenstig.

refrain (1) [ri'frein], *v.n.* — *from*, sich enthalten (*Genit.*); absehen von (*Dat.*).

refrain (2) [ri'frein], *s.* (*Mus.*, *Poet.*) der Kehrreim.

refresh [ri'freʃ], *v.a.* erfrischen.

refrigerator [ri'fridʒəreitə], *s.* der Kühlschrank.

refuge ['refjuːdʒ], *s.* die Zuflucht.

refugee [refjuː'dʒiː], *s.* der Flüchtling. — *adj.* Flüchtlings-.

refund [riː'fʌnd], *v.a.* ersetzen, zurückzahlen. — ['riː'fʌnd], *s.* die Rückvergütung.

refusal [ri'fjuːzəl], *s.* die Verweigerung.

refuse [ri'fjuːz], *v.a.* verweigern, abschlagen. — *v.n.* — *to*, sich weigern. — ['refjuːs], *s.* der Müll.

refute [ri'fjuːt], *v.a.* widerlegen.

regal ['riːgəl], *adj.* königlich.

regale [ri'geil], *v.a.* bewirten.

regalia [ri'geiliə], *s. pl.* die Kronjuwelen, *n. pl.*; (*fig.*) die Amtstracht, der Amtsschmuck.

regard [ri'gaːd], *v.a.* ansehen (*as*, als); beachten (*heed*); *as* —*s*, was ... betrifft. — *s.* die Hochachtung, Achtung (*esteem*);(*pl.*) die Grüsse,*m.pl.*

regarding [ri'gaːdiŋ], *prep.* bezüglich, mit Bezug auf.

regardless [ri'gaːdlis], *adj.* rücksichtslos, ohne Rücksicht auf.

regency ['riːdʒənsi], *s.* die Regentschaft.

regent ['riːdʒənt], *s.* der Regent.

regiment ['redʒimənt], *s.* (*Mil.*) das Regiment. — [-ment], *v.a.* (*fig.*) regimentieren.

region ['riːdʒən], *s.* die Gegend.

regional ['riːdʒənəl], *adj.* örtlich, lokal, Bezirks-.

register ['redʒistə], *s.* das Register, die Liste. — *v.n.* sich eintragen.

registrar ['redʒistraː], *s.* der Registrator; der Standesbeamte (*births etc.*); der Kanzleidirektor (*institution*).

registry ['redʒistri], *s.* die Registratur.

regret [ri'gret], *v.a.* bereuen, bedauern. — *s.* die Reue; das Bedauern (*in formal apology*); *with* —, mit Bedauern.

regular ['regjulə], *adj.* regelmäßig; (*Am.*) anständig. — *s.* (*Mil.*) der Berufssoldat.

regulate ['regjuleit], *v.a.* regulieren, regeln.

regulation [regju'leiʃən], *s.* die Regelung; die Anordung (*order*).

rehabilitate [riːhə'biliteit], *v.a.* rehabilitieren.

rehearsal [ri'həːsl], *s.* (*Theat.*, *Mus.*) die Probe.

rehearse [ri'həːs], *v.a.* proben, wiederholen.

reign [rein], *v.n.* herrschen, regieren. — *s.* die Herrschaft, Regierung.

rein [rein], *s.* der Zügel, der Zaum.

reindeer ['reindiə], *s.* (*Zool.*) das Ren, Rentier.

reinforce [riːin'fɔːs], *v.a.* betonen, verstärken.

reinforced [riːin'fɔːsd], *adj.* verstärkt; — *concrete*, der Eisenbeton.

reject [ri'dʒekt], *v.a.* ausschlagen, verwerfen.

rejection [ri'dʒekʃən], *s.* die Ablehnung, Verwerfung.

rejoice [ri'dʒɔis], *v.n.* sich freuen.

rejoin ['riː'dʒɔin],*v.a.* wiedervereinigen. — [ri'dʒɔin], *v.n.* erwidern.

rejoinder [ri'dʒɔində], *s.* die Erwiderung.

relapse [ri'læps], *s.* der Rückfall. — *v.n.* fallen, zurückfallen.

relation [ri'leiʃən], *s.* die Beziehung (*connexion*); der, die Verwandte (*relative*); (*pl.*) die Verwandtschaft (*family*).

relative ['relətiv], *adj.* relativ; verhältnismäßig (*in proportion*). — *s.* der, die Verwandte.

relax [ri'læks], *v.n.* sich ausruhen; nachlassen. — *v.a.* entspannen.

relay [ri'lei], *v.a.* (*Rad.*) übertragen. — ['riːlei], *s.* — *race*, der Staffellauf.

release [ri'liːs], *v.a.* freilassen, freisetzen (*prisoner*); freigeben (*news*). — *s.* die Freigabe (*news etc.*); die Freisetzung (*liberation*).

relegate ['religeit], *v.a.* verweisen, zurückweisen.

relent [ri'lent], *v.n.* nachgeben.

relentless [ri'lentlis], *adj.* unerbittlich, unnachgiebig.

relevance ['reləvəns], *s.* die Wichtigkeit.

relevant ['reləvənt], *adj.* wichtig, sachdienlich.

reliable [ri'laiəbl], *adj.* verläßlich, zuverlässig.

reliance [ri'laiəns], *s.* das Vertrauen.

relic ['relik], *s.* das Überbleibsel; das Andenken; (*Eccl.*) die Reliquie.

relief (1) [ri'liːf], *s.* die Erleichterung, Linderung, (*easement*); die Ablösung (*guard etc.*); die Aushilfe (*extra staff etc.*).

relief (2) [ri'liːf], *s.* (*Art*) das Relief.

relieve [ri'liːv], *v.a.* erleichtern; lindern (*pain*); ablösen (*from duty*).

religion [ri'lidʒən], *s.* die Religion.

religious [ri'lidʒəs], *adj.* religiös, gläubig, fromm.

relinquish [ri'liŋkwiʃ], *v.a.* verlassen, aufgeben.

relish ['reliʃ], *v.a.* Geschmack finden an. — *v.n.* schmecken. — *s.* der Geschmack, die Würze.

reluctance [ri'lʌktəns], *s.* der Widerwille, das Zögern.

reluctant [ri'lʌktənt], *adj.* widerwillig, widerstrebend.

rely [ri'lai], *v.n.* sich verlassen (*on*, auf); vertrauen (auf).

remain [ri'mein], *v.n.* bleiben, zurückbleiben, übrigbleiben.

remainder [ri'meində], *s.* der Rest.

remand [ri'mɑ:nd], *v.a.* — *in custody*, in die Untersuchungshaft zurückschicken. — *s.* — *home*, die Besserungsanstalt.

remark [ri'mɑ:k], *s.* die Bemerkung. — *v.a.* bemerken.

remarkable [ri'mɑ:kəbl], *adj.* bemerkenswert, außerordentlich.

remedial [rə'mi:diəl], *adj.* Heil-, abhelfend.

remedy ['remədi], *s.* das Heilmittel, Hilfsmittel. — *v.a.* abhelfen (*Dat.*).

remember [ri'membə], *v.a.* sich erinnern an; — *s.o. to s.o. else*, jemanden von jemandem grüßen lassen.

remembrance [ri'membrəns], *s.* die Erinnerung.

remind [ri'maind], *v.a.* erinnern (*of*, an), mahnen.

reminiscence [remi'nisəns], *s.* die Erinnerung.

remiss [ri'mis], *adj.* nachlässig.

remission [ri'miʃən], *s.* der Nachlaß; (*Rel.*) die Vergebung (*of sins*).

remit [ri'mit], *v.a.* (*Comm.*) überweisen, einsenden; erlassen (*forgive*).

remittance [ri'mitəns], *s.* (*Comm.*) die Rimesse, die Überweisung.

remnant ['remnənt], *s.* der Überrest.

remonstrate ['remənstreit], *v.n.* Vorstellungen machen.

remorse [ri'mɔ:s], *s.* die Reue.

remote [ri'mout], *adj.* fern, entlegen.

removal [ri'mu:vəl], *s.* das Wegschaffen (*taking away*); die Übersiedlung, der Umzug.

remove [ri'mu:v], *v.a.* entfernen. — *v.n.* umziehen. — *s.* (*Sch.*) die Versetzungsklasse; der Verwandtschaftsgrad (*relationship*).

removed [ri'mu:vd], *adj.* entfernt; *cousin once* —, der Vetter ersten Grades.

remuneration [rimju:nə'reiʃən], *s.* die Besoldung, Entlohnung.

rend [rend], *v.a.* reißen, zerreißen.

render ['rendə], *v.a.* leisten (*service*); übersetzen (*translate*); wiedergeben; (*Comm.*) — *account*, Rechnung vorlegen.

rendering ['rendəriŋ], *s.* die Wiedergabe, der Vortrag (*of song etc.*); (*Comm.*) die Vorlage; die Übersetzung (*translation*).

renegade ['renigeid], *s.* der Abtrünnige.

renewal [ri'nju:əl], *s.* die Erneuerung; die Verlängerung (*extension*).

rennet ['renit], *s.* das Lab.

renounce [ri'nauns], *v.a.* entsagen (*Dat.*), verzichten auf (*Acc.*).

renown [ri'naun], *s.* der Ruhm.

rent (1) [rent], *v.a.* mieten, pachten. — *s.* die Miete, Pacht (*of land, farm*).

rent (2) [rent], *s.* der Riß (*tear*).

rental [rentl], *s.* die Miete.

renunciation [rinʌnsi'eiʃən], *s.* die Entsagung, der Verzicht.

repair [ri'pɛə], *v.a.* ausbessern, reparieren. — *s.* die Reparatur; *beyond* —, nicht reparierbar.

reparations [repə'reiʃənz], *s. pl.* (*Pol.*) die Reparationen, Wiedergutmachungskosten, *f. pl.*

repartee [repɑ:'ti:], *s.* die treffende Antwort.

repast [ri'pɑ:st], *s.* die Mahlzeit.

repeal [ri'pi:l], *v.a.* (*Parl.*) aufheben, widerrufen. — *s.* die Aufhebung.

repeat [ri'pi:t], *v.a.* wiederholen.

repent [ri'pent], *v.a.* bereuen.

repercussion [ri:pə'kʌʃən], *s.* der Rückstoß, die Rückwirkung.

repertory ['repətəri], *s.* (*Theat. etc.*) das Repertoire, der Spielplan.

repetition [repi'tiʃən], *s.* die Wiederholung.

replace [ri:'pleis], *v.a.* ersetzen.

replete [ri'pli:t], *adj.* voll, angefüllt.

reply [ri'plai], *v.n.* antworten, erwidern. — *s.* die Antwort.

report [ri'pɔ:t], *v.a., v.n.* berichten. — *s.* der Bericht; (*Sch.*) das Zeugnis; der Knall (*of explosion*).

repose [ri'pouz], *v.n.* ruhen. — *v.a.* setzen (*in*, auf). — *s.* die Ruhe, der Friede.

repository [ri'pozitəri], *s.* die Niederlage, Aufbewahrungsstätte, Fundstätte.

reprehensible [repri'hensibl], *adj.* tadelnswert.

represent [repri'zent], *v.a.* repräsentieren, vertreten.

representative [repri'zentətiv], *adj.* repräsentativ, typisch. — *s.* der Stellvertreter; (*Pol.*) der Repräsentant.

repress [ri'pres], *v.a.* unterdrücken.

reprieve [ri'pri:v], *v.a.* begnadigen. — *s.* die Gnadenfrist.

reprimand [repri'mɑ:nd], *v.a.* verweisen, tadeln. — *s.* der Tadel.

reprint [ri:'print], *v.a.* neu drucken. — ['ri:print], *s.* der Neudruck.

reprisal [ri'praizəl], *s.* die Vergeltungsmaßregel; (*pl.*) die Repressalien, *f. pl.*

reproach [ri'proutʃ], *v.a.* vorwerfen (*Dat.*), tadeln. — *s.* der Vorwurf, Tadel.

reprobate ['reprəbeit], *adj.* ruchlos, verworfen.

reproduce [ri:prə'dju:s], *v.a.* reproduzieren, erzeugen.

reproof [ri'pru:f], *s.* der Vorwurf, Tadel.

reprove [ri'pru:v], *v.a.* tadeln, rügen (*a person*), mißbilligen (*a practice*).

republic

republic [ri'pʌblik], s. die Republik.

repudiate [ri'pju:dieit], v.a. zurückweisen, verwerfen.

repugnant [ri'pʌgnənt], adj. widerwärtig, ekelhaft.

repulse [ri'pʌls], v.a. (Mil.) zurückschlagen; abweisen (s.o.). — s. (Mil.) das Zurückschlagen; (fig.) die Zurückweisung.

repulsive [ri'pʌlsiv], adj. widerwärtig.

reputation [repju'teifən], s. der (gute) Ruf.

request [ri'kwest], v.a. ersuchen. — s. das Ersuchen, Ansuchen, die Bitte.

requiem ['rekwiəm], s. (Eccl.) das Requiem, die Totenmesse.

require [ri'kwaiə], v.a. fordern, verlangen, brauchen.

requirement [ri'kwaiəmənt], s. die Anforderung, das Erfordernis.

requisite ['rekwizit], adj. erforderlich.

requisition [rekwi'zifən], s. (Mil.) die Requisition; die Forderung.

requite [ri'kwait], v.a. vergelten.

rescind [ri'sind], v.a. für ungültig erklären, aufheben.

rescue ['reskju:], v.a. retten. — s. die Rettung.

research [ri'sə:tf], v.n. forschen, Forschung treiben. — s. die Forschung.

resemble [ri'zembl], v.a. ähnlich sein (Dat.), gleichen (Dat.).

resent [ri'zent], v.a. übelnehmen.

resentful [ri'zentful], adj. nachträgerisch; empfindlich (over-sensitive).

resentment [ri'zentmənt], s. die Empfindlichkeit, der Groll (spite).

reservation [rezə'veifən], s. die Reservierung (of seat); der Vorbehalt (doubt).

reserve [ri'zə:v], v.a. reservieren, belegen (seat); (fig.) vorbehalten (o.'s position). — s. die Reserve, die Verschlossenheit (shyness); die Einschränkung (limitation); die Reserven, f. pl. (money).

reside [ri'zaid], v.n. wohnen.

resident ['rezidənt], adj. wohnhaft. — s. der Ansässige.

residual [ri'zidjuəl], adj. übrig bleibend.

residue ['rezidju:], s. der Rückstand, Rest.

resign [ri'zain], v.a. abtreten, aufgeben; (ein Amt) niederlegen. — v.n. abdanken. — v.r. — o.s. to, sich in etwas fügen, zurücktreten.

resignation [rezig'neifən], s. die Resignation, der Rücktritt (from office); die Fügung, Resignation (attitude).

resin ['rezin], s. das Harz.

resist [ri'zist], v.a., v.n. widerstehen, Widerstand leisten (Dat.).

resistance [ri'zistəns], s. der Widerstand.

resolute ['rezəlju:t], adj. entschlossen.

resolution [rezə'lju:fən], s. die Entschlossenheit (determination); die Entscheidung (decision); der Vorsatz, Entschluß (vow).

resolve [ri'zɔlv], v.a. auflösen (solve); beschließen (conclude). — v.n. entscheiden (decide). — s. der Beschluß, die Entscheidung.

resonance ['rezənəns], s. die Resonanz.

resort [ri'zɔ:t], v.n. — to, seine Zuflucht nehmen (zu). — s. seaside —, das Seebad, health —, der Kurort (spa).

resound [ri'zaund], v.n. widerhallen.

resource [ri'sɔ:s], s. das Hilfsmittel; (pl.) die Mittel, n. pl.

respect [ri'spekt], v.a. respektieren, achten; berücksichtigen (have regard to). — s. der Respekt, die Achtung; with — to, mit Bezug auf; in — of, bezüglich (Genit.).

respectability [rispektə'biliti], s. die Anständigkeit; Achtbarkeit.

respective [ris'pektiv], adj. respektiv.

respectively [ris'pektivli], adv. beziehungsweise.

respiration [respi'reifən], s. die Atmung.

respiratory [ris'paiərətri or 'respireitəri], adj. Atmungs-.

respire [ris'paiə], v.n. atmen.

respite ['respit], s. die Frist, der Aufschub.

resplendent [ri'splendənt], adj. glänzend.

respond [ri'spɔnd], v.n. antworten, eingehen (to, auf).

respondent [ri'spɔndənt], s. (Law) der Beklagte.

response [ri'spɔns], s. die Antwort, Aufnahme, Reaktion; (fig.) der Widerhall.

responsibility [rispɔnsi'biliti], s. die Verantwortung, Verantwortlichkeit.

responsible [ri'spɔnsibl], adj. verantwortlich.

responsive [ri'spɔnsiv], adj. empfänglich, zugänglich.

rest (1) [rest], v.n. ruhen, rasten. — s. die Ruhe, Rast; (Mus.) die Pause.

rest (2) [rest], v.n. bleiben (stay); — assured, sei (seien Sie) versichert. — s. der Rest; die übrigen, pl.

restaurant ['restərɑ̃], s. das Restaurant.

restful ['restful], adj. ruhig.

restitution [resti'tju:fən], s. die Wiedergutmachung.

restive ['restiv], adj. unruhig, ruhelos.

restless ['restlis], adj. rastlos, unruhig.

restoration [restɔ:'reifən], s. die Wiederherstellung; (Hist.) die Restauration.

restore [ri'stɔ:], v.a. wiederherstellen.

restrain [ri'strein], v.a. zurückhalten, einschränken.

restraint [ri'streint], s. die Zurückhaltung.

restrict [ri'strikt], v.a. beschränken.

restriction [ri'strikfən], s. die Einschränkung.

restrictive [ri'striktiv], adj. einschränkend.

result [ri'zʌlt], *v.n.* folgen, sich ergeben; (*come about*) erfolgen. — *s.* das Ergebnis, Resultat; (*consequence*) die Folge.

resume [ri'zju:m], *v.a.* wiederaufnehmen; (*narrative*) fortsetzen. — *v.n.* fortfahren.

résumé ['rezjumei], *s.* das Resümee, die Zusammenfassung.

resumption [ri'zʌmpʃən], *s.* die Wiederaufnahme.

resurrection [rezə'rekʃən], *s.* (*Rel.*) die Auferstehung.

resuscitate [ri'sʌsiteit], *v.a.* wiederbeleben.

retail ['ri:teil], *s.* der Kleinhandel, Einzelhandel. — [ri:'teil], *v.a.* im Detail handeln, verkaufen.

retain [ri'tein], *v.a.* behalten.

retainer [ri'teinə], *s.* der Diener; Gefolgsmann; der Vorschuß (*fee*).

retake [ri:'teik], *v.a. irr.* (*Mil.*) wieder erobern; (*Phot., Film*) noch einmal aufnehmen. — *s.* (*Am.*) die Neuaufnahme (*Phot., Film*).

retaliate [ri'tælieit], *v.n.* sich rächen, vergelten.

retard [ri'tɑ:d], *v.a.* verzögern, verlangsamen.

retch [retʃ], *v.n.* sich erbrechen.

retentive [ri'tentiv], *adj.* behaltend, gut (*memory*).

reticent ['retisənt], *adj.* schweigsam, einsilbig.

retina ['retinə], *s.* (*Anat.*) die Netzhaut.

retinue ['retinju:], *s.* das Gefolge.

retire [ri'taiə], *v.n.* sich zurückziehen (*withdraw*); in den Ruhestand treten (*from work*). — *v.a.* pensionieren.

retirement [ri'taiəmənt], *s.* die Pension, der Ruhestand; die Zurückgezogenheit (*seclusion*).

retort [ri'tɔ:t], *s.* (*Chem.*) die Retorte; die scharfe Antwort (*debate*). — *v.n.* scharf erwidern.

retouch [ri:'tʌtʃ], *v.a.* (*Phot.*) retouchieren.

retrace [ri:'treis], *v.a.* zurückverfolgen.

retreat [ri'tri:t], *v.n.* sich zurückziehen. — *s.* der Rückzug (*Mil.*); Zufluchtsort.

retrench [ri'trentʃ], *v.a.* einschränken (*restrict*); verkürzen (*shorten*). — *v.n.* sich einschränken.

retribution [retri'bju:ʃən], *s.* die Vergeltung.

retrieve [ri'tri:v], *v.a.* wieder bekommen, wieder gewinnen.

retriever [ri'tri:və], *s.* (*Zool.*) der Apportierhund, Stöberhund.

retrograde ['retrogreid], *adj.* rückgängig, rückwärts.

retrospect ['retrospekt], *s.* der Rückblick.

retrospective [retro'spektiv], *adj.* rückblickend.

return [ri'tə:n], *v.a.* zurückgeben; erwidern (*reciprocate*); abordnen, entsenden (*to Parl.*); (*figures*) einsenden. — *v.n.* zurückkehren, zurückkommen.

— *s.* die Rückkehr; (*Fin.*) der Gewinn; (*Parl.*) die Entsendung, Mandatierung; (*pl.*) (*figures*) die Einsendung; *by* — *of post*, umgehend, postwendend; — *ticket*, die Rückfahrkarte.

reunion [ri:'ju:niən], *s.* die Wiedervereinigung.

reveal [ri'vi:l], *v.a.* enthüllen, offenbaren (*show*); verraten (*betray*).

reveille [ri'væli], *s.* (*Mil.*) das Wecken, Wecksignal.

revel [revl], *v.n.* schwelgen.

revelation [revə'leiʃən], *s.* die Offenbarung.

revelry ['revəlri], *s.* die Schwelgerei.

revenge [ri'vendʒ], *s.* die Rache, Revanche. — *v.r.* (*also be revenged*) sich rächen (*on*, an, *Dat.*)

revenue ['revənju:], *s.* das Einkommen; *Inland* —, die Steuereinnahmen.

reverberate [ri'və:bəreit], *v.n.* widerhallen.

revere [ri'viə], *v.a.* verehren.

reverence ['revərəns], *s.* die Ehrerbietung, der Respekt; *show* —, Ehrerbietung zollen.

Reverend ['revərənd]. (*abbr.* **Rev.**) (*Eccl.*) *The* —, Seine Ehrwürden; *The Very* —, Seine Hochwürden.

reverent, reverential ['revərənt, revə'renʃəl], *adj.* ehrerbietig.

reverie ['revəri], *s.* die Träumerei.

reversal [ri'və:səl], *s.* die Umkehrung, Umstoßung.

reverse [ri'və:s], *v.a., v.n.* umkehren, umdrehen. — *s.* das Gegenteil (*contrary*); die Kehrseite (*of coin*).

revert [ri'və:t], *v.a., v.n.* umkehren, zurückkehren.

review [ri'vju:], *v.a.* durchsehen, prüfen (*examine*); rezensieren (*book etc.*). — *s.* die Revision; (*Mil.*) die Parade, Truppenmusterung; die Rezension, Besprechung (*book etc.*).

revile [ri'vail], *v.a., v.n.* schmähen.

revise [ri'vaiz], *v.a.* korrigieren (*correct*); wiederholen (*recapitulate*); umarbeiten (*modify*).

revision [ri'viʒən], *s.* die Revision; Korrektur; Umarbeitung; Wiederholung (*recapitulation*).

revolt [ri'voult], *v.n.* sich empören, revoltieren. — *v.a.* empören. — *s.* die Empörung.

revolting [ri'voultiŋ], *adj.* ekelhaft, empörend.

revolution [revə'lju:ʃən], *s.* (*Pol.*) die Revolution; (*Motor.*) die Umdrehung.

revolve [ri'vɔlv], *v.n.* rotieren, sich drehen.

revolver [ri'vɔlvə], *s.* der Revolver.

revue [ri'vju:], *s.* (*Theat.*) die Revue.

revulsion [ri'vʌlʃən], *s.* der Ekel; der Umschwung.

reward [ri'wɔ:d], *v.a.* belohnen (*person*); vergelten (*deed*). — *s.* die Belohnung.

rheumatic [ru:'mætik], *adj.* (*Med.*) rheumatisch.

rheumatism

rheumatism [ˈruːmətizm], *s.* (*Med.*) der Rheumatismus.

rhetoric [ˈretərik], *s.* die Redekunst.

Rhodesian [roˈdiːʃən, -ˈdiːʒən], *adj.* rhodesisch. — *s.* der Rhodesier.

rhododendron [roudoˈdendrən], *s.* (*Bot.*) die Alpenrose.

rhubarb [ˈruːbɑːb], *s.* (*Bot.*) der Rhabarber.

rhyme [raim], *s.* der Reim; *no — nor reason,* sinnlos.

rhythm [riðm], *s.* der Rhythmus.

rib [rib], *s.* (*Anat.*) die Rippe.

ribald [ˈribəld], *adj.* liederlich; (*joke*) unanständig.

ribbon [ˈribən], *s.* das Band.

rice [rais], *s.* der Reis.

rich [ritʃ], *adj.* reich; fruchtbar (*fertile*).

rick [rik], *s.* der Schober.

rickets [ˈrikits], *s.* (*Med.*) die englische Krankheit, die Rachitis.

rickety [ˈrikiti], *adj.* gebrechlich, wackelig, baufällig.

rid [rid], *v.a.* *irr.* befreien, freimachen (*of,* von); — *o.s.,* sich entledigen (*of, Genit.*); *get — of,* loswerden (*Acc.*); *be — of,* los sein (*Acc.*).

riddance [ˈridəns], *s.* die Befreiung, das Loswerden.

riddle (1) [ridl], *s.* das Rätsel (*puzzle*).

riddle (2) [ridl], *s.* das grobe Sieb (*sieve*). — *v.a.* sieben (*sieve*); durchlöchern.

ride [raid], *v.a., v.n.* *irr.* reiten (*on horse*), fahren (*on bicycle etc.*); — *at anchor,* vor Anker liegen. — *s.* der Ritt (*on horse*), die Fahrt (*in vehicle*).

rider [ˈraidə], *s.* der Reiter (*horseman*); der Fahrer (*cyclist etc.*); der Zusatz (*addition*).

ridge [ridʒ], *s.* der Rücken (*edge*); die Bergkette; die Furche (*furrow*). — *v.a.* furchen.

ridicule [ˈridikjuːl], *s.* der Spott. — *v.a.* lächerlich machen.

ridiculous [riˈdikjuləs], *adj.* lächerlich.

rife [raif], *adj.* häufig, weitverbreitet.

rifle (1) [raifl], *s.* die Büchse, das Gewehr.

rifle (2) [raifl], *v.a.* ausplündern.

rift [rift], *s.* der Riß, Spalt, die Spalte. — *v.a.* spalten.

rig [rig], *s.* (*Naut.*) die Takelung; (*fig.*) — *out,* die Ausstattung. — *v.a.* (*Naut.*) (auf)takeln; (*Am.*) fälschen (*fake*); — *out,* ausstatten.

right [rait], *adj.* recht; richtig; wahr; gesund; korrekt; — *hand,* rechtsseitig; *you are —,* Sie haben recht; *that's —,* das stimmt. — *s.* das Recht; *by right(s),* rechtmäßig; *drive on the —,* rechts fahren.

righteous [ˈraitʃəs], *adj.* rechtschaffen, aufrecht.

rightful [ˈraitful], *adj.* rechtmäßig.

rigid [ˈridʒid], *adj.* steif; unbeugsam; streng (*severe*).

rigidity [riˈdʒiditi], *s.* die Steifheit, Unnachgiebigkeit; die Strenge.

rigmarole [ˈrigməroul], *s.* die Salbaderei, das Gewäsch.

rigorous [ˈrigərəs], *adj.* streng; genau.

rigour [ˈrigə], *s.* die Strenge; die Härte.

rill [ril], *s.* (*Poet.*) das Bächlein.

rim [rim], *s.* der Rand, die Felge.

rime [raim], *s.* (*Poet.*) der Reif.

rind [raind], *s.* die Rinde.

ring (1) [riŋ], *s.* der Ring.

ring (2) [riŋ], *s.* der Schall, das Läuten (*bell*); der Anruf (*telephone*); das Geläute (*bells*). — *v.a.* *irr.* läuten, klingeln (*bell*). — *v.n.* läuten; ertönen, tönen (*call, voice*).

ringleader [ˈriŋliːdə], *s.* der Rädelsführer.

rink [riŋk], *s.* die Eisbahn; Rollschuhbahn.

rinse [rins], *v.a.* spülen, waschen. — *s.* das Abspülen.

riot [ˈraiət], *s.* der Aufruhr. — *v.n.* Aufruhr stiften; meutern.

rip [rip], *v.a.* reißen, aufreißen. — *s.* der Riß.

ripe [raip], *adj.* reif.

ripen [ˈraipən], *v.n.* reifen. — *v.a.* reifen lassen.

ripple [ripl], *s.* die Welle, Kräuselwelle (*water*). — *v.n.* kräuseln (*water*); (*Bot.*) riffeln.

rise [raiz], *v.n.* *irr.* aufstehen (*get up*); aufsteigen (*ascend*); anschwellen (*swell*); steigen (*price*). — *s.* die Erhöhung; (*Comm.*) der Anstieg; die Steigerung; Erhöhung (*salary*); der Ursprung (*origin*).

rising [ˈraiziŋ], *s.* der Aufstand (*rebellion*).

risk [risk], *s.* das Risiko. — *v.a.* wagen, riskieren.

rite [rait], *s.* der Ritus.

ritual [ˈritjuəl], *s.* das Ritual.

rival [raivl], *s.* der Rivale, Nebenbuhler. — *adj.* nebenbuhlerisch, konkurrierend. — *v.a.* konkurrieren, wetteifern.

river [ˈrivə], *s.* der Fluß.

rivet [ˈrivit], *s.* die Niete. — *v.a.* nieten.

roach [routʃ], *s.* (*Zool.*) die Plötze.

road [roud], *s.* die Straße; der Weg.

roam [roum], *v.n.* herumstreifen.

roan [roun], *s.* der Rotschimmel (*horse*).

roar [rɔː], *v.n.* brüllen (*animals*); brausen (*storm*). — *s.* das Gebrüll (*animal*); das Getöse, Brausen, Rauschen.

roast [roust], *v.a., v.n.* braten, rösten. — *s.* der Braten.

rob [rɔb], *v.a.* berauben.

robbery [ˈrɔbəri], *s.* der Raub, die Räuberei.

robe [roub], *s.* die Robe.

robin [ˈrɔbin], *s.* (*Orn.*) das Rotkehlchen.

rock [rɔk], *s.* der Felsen, die Klippe. — *v.a.* schaukeln, wiegen. — *v.n.* wackeln, taumeln.

rocket [ˈrɔkit], *s.* die Rakete; (*sl.*) die Rüge. — *v.n.* hochfliegen; hochgehen (*prices*).

rocky [ˈrɔki], *adj.* felsig.

rod [rɔd], s. die Rute; (*fishing*) die Angelrute; die Stange (*pole*).

rodent ['roudənt], s. (*Zool.*) das Nagetier.

roe (1) [rou], s. der Fischrogen.

roe (2) [rou], s. (*Zool.*) das Reh, die Hirschkuh.

rogation [ro'geiʃən], s. das Gebet, die Litanei; *Rogation Sunday*, der Sonntag Rogate.

rogue [roug], s. der Schelm.

role [roul]. s. (*Theat.*, *fig.*) die Rolle.

roll [roul], s. die Liste; — *call*, der Aufruf, die Parade; die Rolle; die Semmel, das Brötchen (*bread*). — *v.a.* rollen; wälzen. — *v.n.* rollen; sich wälzen; sich drehen; schlingen (*ship*); schlenkern (*person*).

roller ['roulə], s. die Rolle; — *bandage*, das Wickelband; — *skates*, die Rollschuhe.

rollick ['rɔlik], *v.n.* herumtollen, lustig sein.

rolling stock ['roulin stɔk], s. (*Railw.*) der Wagenbestand.

romance [rou'mæns], s. die Romanze.

romantic [rou'mæntik], *adj.* romantisch.

romp [rɔmp], s. der Wildfang, das Tollen. — *v.n.* toben.

roof [ru:f], s. das Dach. — *v.a.* decken.

rook (1) [ruk], s. (*Orn.*) die Saatkrähe.

rook (2) [ruk], s. (*Chess*) der Turm.

room [ru:m, rum], s. der Raum, das Zimmer. — *v.n.* (*Am.*) ein Zimmer teilen (*with*, mit).

roomy ['ru:mi], *adj.* geräumig.

roost [ru:st], s. der Hühnerstall. — *v.n.* aufsitzen, schlafen.

root [ru:t], s. die Wurzel. — *v.n.* wurzeln.

rooted ['ru:tid], *adj.* eingewurzelt.

rope [roup], s. das Seil. — *v.a.* anseilen (*in climbing*); (*coll.*) — *in*, verwickeln, hereinziehen.

rosary ['rouzəri], s. (*Rel.*) der Rosenkranz.

rose [rouz], s. (*Bot.*) die Rose.

Rosemary ['rouzməri]. Rosemarie.

rosemary ['rouzməri], s. (*Bot.*) der Rosmarin.

rosin ['rɔzin] *see* **resin**.

rosy ['rouzi], *adj.* rosig.

rot [rɔt], *v.n.* faulen, modern. — s. die Fäulnis, Verwesung; (*coll.*) der Unsinn.

rotate [ro'teit], *v.a.*, *v.n.* (sich) drehen, rotieren.

rote [rout], s. *by* —, mechanisch, auswendig.

rotten [rɔtn], *adj.* faul, verdorben, schlecht.

rotund [ro'tʌnd], *adj.* rundlich, rund.

rough [rʌf], *adj.* rauh, grob; flüchtig, ungefähr (*approximate*); ungehobelt (*ill-mannered*).

roughshod ['rʌfʃɔd], *adj.* rücksichtslos.

round [raund], *adj.* rund. — s. die Runde. — *prep.* (rund) um; um ... herum. — *adv.* (rings)herum; (*around*) ungefähr; etwa (*approximately*).

roundabout ['raundəbaut], s. das Karussel. — *adj.* umständlich.

Roundhead ['raundhed], s. (*Eng. Hist.*) der Puritaner.

rouse [rauz], *v.a.* erwecken.

rout [raut], s. (*Mil.*) die wilde Flucht. — *v.a.* in die Flucht jagen.

route [ru:t], s. der Weg; die Route.

rover ['rouvə], s. der Wanderer, ältere Pfadfinder (*scout*); der Seeräuber (*pirate*).

row (1) [rou], s. die Reihe.

row (2) [rau], s. der Lärm, Streit. — *v.n.* (*coll.*) lärmend streiten, zanken.

row (3) [rou], *v.n.* rudern.

rowdy ['raudi], s. der Raufbold. — *adj.* laut, lärmend.

royal ['rɔiəl], *adj.* königlich.

royalty ['rɔiəlti], s. das Mitglied des Königshauses, die königliche Hoheit; (*pl.*) (*Law*) die Tantieme.

rub [rʌb], *v.a.*, *v.n.* (sich) reiben. — s. die Reibung; die heikle Stelle, das Problem.

rubber (1) ['rʌbə], s. der Gummi; Radiergummi.

rubber (2) ['rʌbə], s. (*Whist*) der Robber.

rubbish ['rʌbiʃ], s. der Abfall, Mist; (*fig.*) der Schund (*book*), der Unsinn (*nonsense*).

ruby ['ru:bi], s. der Rubin.

rudder ['rʌdə], s. das Steuerruder.

ruddy ['rʌdi], *adj.* rötlich.

rude [ru:d], *adj.* roh; grob; ungebildet; unhöflich.

rudiment ['ru:dimənt], s. die Anfangsgründe, die Grundlage.

rue (1) [ru:], s. (*Bot.*) die Raute.

rue (2) [ru:], *v.a.* beklagen, bereuen.

ruff [rʌf], s. die Halskrause.

ruffian ['rʌfiən], s. der Raufbold.

ruffle [rʌfl], *v.a.* zerzausen (*hair*); verwirren (*muddle*). — s. die Krause (*on dress*); die Aufregung.

rug [rʌg], s. die Wolldecke, der Vorleger.

rugged ['rʌgid], *adj.* rauh; uneben.

ruin ['ru:in], s. die Ruine; (*fig.*) der Zusammenbruch. — *v.a.* ruinieren.

rule [ru:l], s. die Regel, Vorschrift; die Herrschaft; *slide* —, der Rechenschieber. — *v.a.* beherrschen; regeln; lin(i)ieren (*draw lines on*). — *v.n.* herrschen (*reign*; *be valid*); lin(i)ieren (*draw lines*); entscheiden (*decide*).

ruling ['ru:lin], s. die Regelung, Entscheidung.

rum (1) [rʌm], s. der Rum.

rum (2) [rʌm], *adj.* (*sl.*) seltsam.

Rumanian [ru:'meinien], *adj.* rumänisch. — s. der Rumäne.

rumble [rʌmbl], *v.n.* poltern, rasseln, rumpeln; (*stomach*) knurren.

ruminate ['ru:mineit], *v.n.* wiederkäuen; nachsinnen.

rummage ['rʌmidʒ], *v.a.*, *v.n.* durchstöbern.

rumour ['ru:mə], s. das Gerücht.

rump [rʌmp], s. der Rumpf, Steiß; — *steak*, das Rumpsteak.

run

run [rʌn], v.n. irr. laufen, rennen;
eilen; verkehren (bus); fließen (flow);
(Theat.) gegeben werden; lauten (text).
— s. der Lauf, das Rennen; (Theat.)
die Spieldauer; in the long —, am
Ende, auf die Dauer.
runaway ['rʌnəwei], adj. entlaufen. —
s. der Ausreißer.
rung [rʌn], s. die Sprosse.
runway ['rʌnwei], s. (Aviat.) die Rollbahn, Startbahn, Landebahn.
rupture ['rʌptʃə], s. (Med.) der Leistenbruch.
rural ['ruərəl], adj. ländlich.
rush (1) [rʌʃ], s. (Bot.) die Binse.
rush (2) [rʌʃ], s. der Ansturm, Andrang;
die Hetze; der Hochbetrieb. — v.n.
stürzen, in Eile sein.
Russian ['rʌʃən], adj. russisch. — s.
der Russe.
rust [rʌst], s. der Rost. — v.n. verrosten.
rustic ['rʌstik], adj. ländlich.
rut (1) [rʌt], s. die Spur; das Geleise.
rut (2) [rʌt], s. (animals) die Brunst.
ruthless ['ru:θlis], adj. grausam, rücksichtslos.
rye [rai], s. (Bot.) der Roggen.

S

S [es], das S.
sable [seibl], s. der Zobel. — adj.
schwarz.
sabotage ['sæbotɑ:ʒ], s. die Sabotage.
— v.a. sabotieren.
sabre ['seibə], s. der Säbel.
sack (1) [sæk], s. der Sack; (coll.) die
Entlassung (get the —). — v.a.
(coll.) entlassen.
sack (2) [sæk], v.a. plündern (pillage).
sack (3) [sæk], s. (obs.) der Weißwein.
sacrament ['sækrəmənt], s. das Sakra-
ment.
sacred ['seikrid], adj. heilig.
sacrifice ['sækrifais], s. das Opfer. —
v.a. opfern.
sacrilege ['sækrilidʒ], s. das Sakrilege,
der Frevel.
sad [sæd], adj. traurig.
sadden ['sædn], v.a. betrüben.
saddle [sædl], s. der Sattel. — v.a.
satteln; (coll.) — s.o. with s.th., einem
etwas aufhalsen.
safe [seif], adj. sicher (secure); wohlbehalten (arrival etc.). — s. der Geldschrank, das Safe.
safeguard ['seifgɑ:d], v.a. beschützen,
garantieren. — s. der Schutz, die
Sicherheit.
safety ['seifti], s. die Sicherheit.
saffron ['sæfrən], s. der Safran. — adj.
safrangelb.

sagacious [sə'geiʃəs], adj. scharfsinnig.
sagacity [sə'gæsiti], s. der Scharfsinn.
sage (1) [seidʒ], s. (Bot.) der, die Salbei.
sage (2) [seidʒ], s. der Weise. — adj.
weise, klug.
sail [seil], s. das Segel. — v.n. segeln,
(Naut.) fahren.
sailor ['seilə], s. der Matrose, Seemann.
Saint [seint, sənt], (abbr. S. or St.)
Sankt (before name).
saint [seint], s. der or die Heilige.
sake [seik], s. for my son's —, um meines
Sohnes willen; for the — of peace, um
des Friedens willen.
salacious [sə'leiʃəs], adj. geil; zotig
(joke).
salad ['sæləd], s. der Salat.
salary ['sæləri], s. das Gehalt.
sale [seil], s. der Verkauf; annual —,
(Comm.) der Ausverkauf.
salesman ['seilzmən], s. der Verkäufer.
salient ['seiliənt], adj. hervorspringend,
wichtig, Haupt-.
saline ['seilain], s. die Salzquelle. —
adj. salzhaltig.
saliva [sə'laivə], s. der Speichel.
sallow ['sælou], adj. blaß, bleich.
sally ['sæli], s. der Ausfall, (fig.)
der komische Einfall. — v.n. ausfallen; — forth, losgehen.
salmon ['sæmən], s. (Zool.) der Lachs.
saloon [sə'lu:n], s. der Salon; (Am.)
das Wirtshaus, die Kneipe.
salt [sɔ:lt], s. das Salz; — cellar, das
Salzfäßchen; (coll.) old —, der alte
Matrose. — v.a. salzen.
saltpetre [sɔ:lt'pi:tə], s. der Salpeter.
salubrious [sə'lju:briəs], adj. gesund
(climate, neighbourhood).
salutary ['sæljutəri], adj. heilsam (lesson,
experience).
salute [sə'lju:t], v.a. grüßen. — s. der
Gruß, (Mil.) Salut.
salvage ['sælvidʒ], s. die Bergung,
Rettung; das Bergegut. — v.a. retten,
bergen.
salvation [sæl'veiʃən], s. die Rettung;
(Rel.) die Erlösung, das Heil.
salve [sælv, sɑ:v], v.a. einsalben; heilen.
— s. die Salbe.
salver ['sælvə], s. der Präsentierteller.
salvo ['sælvou], s. (Mil.) die Salve.
Samaritan [sə'mæritən], s. der Samari-
ter; (fig.) der Wohltäter.
same [seim], adj. der-, die-, dasselbe.
sample [sɑ:mpl], s. die Probe, das
Muster (test, pack etc.). — v.a. probieren; kosten (food).
sampler ['sɑ:mplə], s. das Stickmuster.
sanctify ['sæŋktifai], v.a. heiligen.
sanctimonious [sæŋkti'mouniəs], adj.
scheinheilig.
sanction ['sæŋkʃən], s. (Pol.) die
Sanktion; (fig.) Genehmigung. — v.a.
genehmigen, sanktionieren.
sanctuary ['sæŋktjuari], s. das Heiligtum.
sand [sænd], s. der Sand. — v.a. san-
den, bestreuen; (floors) abreiben.
sandal [sændl], s. die Sandale.

sandwich ['sænwitʃ], s. das belegte (Butter)brot.

sane [sein], adj. gesund (mind); vernünftig.

sanguine ['sæŋgwin], adj. optimistisch.

sanitary ['sænitəri], adj. Gesundheits-, Sanitäts-; — towel, die (Damen)binde.

sanity ['sæniti], s. die Vernunft, der gesunde Menschenverstand; (Law) die Zurechnungsfähigkeit.

Santa Claus [sæntə'klɔːz]. der heilige Nikolaus, Knecht Ruprecht.

sap (1) [sæp], s. der Saft; (fig.) die Lebenskraft.

sap (2) [sæp], v.a. untergraben, schwächen.

sapling ['sæpliŋ], s. (Bot.) das Bäumchen, der junge Baum.

sapper ['sæpə], s. (Mil.) der Sappeur; der Schanzgräber, Pionier.

sapphire ['sæfaiə], s. der Saphir.

sarcasm ['saːkæzm], s. der Sarkasmus.

sarcastic [saː'kæstik], adj. sarkastisch.

sash (1) [sæʃ], s. die Schärpe.

sash (2) [sæʃ], s. — window, das Schiebefenster; — cord, die Fensterschnur.

Satan ['seitən]. der Satan.

satchel ['sætʃəl], s. die Leder(schul)tasche.

sate [seit], v.a. sättigen.

satellite ['sætəlait], s. der Satellit, Trabant.

satin ['sætin], s. (Text.) der Atlas.

satire ['sætaiə], s. die Satire.

satisfaction [sætis'fækʃən], s. die Befriedigung, Zufriedenheit.

satisfactory [sætis'fæktri], adj. befriedigend, genügend; zufriedenstellend.

satisfy ['sætisfai], v.a. befriedigen, sättigen; (fig.) zufriedenstellen.

saturate ['sætʃureit], v.a. (Chem.) saturieren, sättigen.

Saturday ['sætədei]. der Samstag, Sonnabend.

sauce [sɔːs], s. (Cul.) die Sauce, Tunke; (coll.) die Unverschämtheit.

saucepan ['sɔːspæn], s. (Cul.) der Kochtopf.

saucer ['sɔːsə], s. die Untertasse.

saucy ['sɔːsi], adj. (coll.) unverschämt, frech.

saunter ['sɔːntə], v.n. schlendern, spazieren.

sausage ['sɔsidʒ], s. die Wurst.

savage ['sævidʒ], adj. wild. — s. der Wilde.

save [seiv], v.a. retten (life); (Theol.) erlösen; sparen (money); sich ersparen (trouble, labour); aufheben (keep). — v.n. sparen, sparsam sein. — prep., conj. außer, außer daß, ausgenommen.

saving ['seiviŋ], s. das Ersparnis; savings bank, die Sparkasse.

saviour ['seivjə], s. der Retter; (Rel.) der Heiland.

savour ['seivə], s. der Geschmack; die Würze. — v.n. schmecken (of, nach, Dat.).

savoury ['seivəri], adj. schmackhaft. — s. pikantes Vor- or Nachgericht.

saw (1) [sɔː], v.a. sägen. — s. die Säge.

saw (2) [sɔː], s. (obs.) das Sprichwort.

sawyer ['sɔːjə], s. der Sägearbeiter, Säger.

Saxon ['sæksən], adj. sächsisch. — s. der Sachse.

say [sei], v.a. irr. sagen; (lines, prayer) hersagen. — v.n. (Am. coll.) — ! sagen Sie mal! — s. das entscheidende Wort.

saying ['seiiŋ], s. das Sprichwort, der Spruch.

scab [skæb], s. der Schorf, die Krätze.

scabbard ['skæbəd], s. die Degenscheide.

scaffold ['skæfəld], s. (Build.) das Gerüst; das Schafott (place of execution).

scald [skɔːld], v.a. verbrühen; —ing hot, brühheiß.

scale (1) [skeil], s. die Waagschale (balance).

scale (2) [skeil], s. (Mus.) die Skala, Tonleiter.

scale (3) [skeil], s. (Geog. etc.) die Skala, das Ausmaß, der Maßstab; on a large —, im großen (Maßstabe). — v.a. erklettern (climb); — down, im Maßstab verringern.

scale (4) [skeil], s. (fish etc.) die Schuppe. — v.a. schuppen, abschälen (remove —s).

scallop ['skɔləp], s. (Zool.) die Kammuschel.

scalp [skælp], s. (Anat.) die Kopfhaut. — v.a. skalpieren, die Kopfhaut abziehen.

scamp [skæmp], s. (coll.) der Taugenichts.

scan [skæn], v.a. (Poet.) skandieren; (Rad.) absuchen.

scandalize ['skændəlaiz], v.a. empören, verärgern.

scant [skænt], adj. selten; knapp, sparsam.

Scandinavian [skændi'neivjən], adj. skandinavisch. — s. der Skandinavier.

scanty ['skænti], adj. spärlich, knapp.

scapegoat ['skeipgout], s. der Sündenbock.

scar [skaː], s. die Narbe.

scarce [skɛəs], adj. selten, spärlich.

scarcely ['skɛəsli], adv. kaum.

scarcity ['skɛəsiti], s. die Seltenheit, Knappheit.

scare [skɛə], v.a. erschrecken, ängstigen. — s. der Schreck.

scarecrow ['skɛəkrou], s. die Vogelscheuche.

scarf [skaːf], s. der Schal, das Halstuch.

scarlet ['skaːlit], adj. scharlachrot. — s. der Scharlach.

scarp [skaːp], s. die Böschung.

scatter ['skætə], v.a., v.n. (sich) zerstreuen, (sich) verbreiten; streuen.

scavenge ['skævindʒ], v.a. ausreinigen, auswaschen; säubern.

scavenger ['skævindʒə], s. der Straßenkehrer; Aasgeier.

scene

scene [si:n], *s.* die Szene, der Schauplatz; *behind the* —*s*, hinter den Kulissen; — *shifter*, der Kulissenschieber.

scenery [ˈsi:nəri], *s.* die Landschaft (*nature*); (*Theat.*) das Bühnenbild, die Kulissen, *f. pl.*

scent [sent], *s.* der Geruch, Duft, das Parfüm (*perfume*); die Witterung, Fährte (*trail of hunted animal*).

sceptic [ˈskeptik], *s.* der Skeptiker.

sceptre [ˈseptə], *s.* das Zepter.

schedule [ˈʃedju:l, (*Am.*) ˈske-], *s.* der Plan; die Liste; der (Fahr-, Stunden-) plan; (*Law*) der Zusatz (*in documents*). — *v.a.* (*Am.*) einteilen, zuteilen (*apportion*); aufzeichnen.

scheme [ski:m], *s.* das Schema; der Plan; — *of things*, in der Gesamtplanung. — *v.n.* aushecken; Ränke schmieden.

scholar [ˈskɔlə], *s.* der Gelehrte, der Wissenschaftler; der Schuljunge, Schüler; (*Univ.*) der Stipendiat.

scholarly [ˈskɔləli], *adj.* gelehrt.

scholarship [ˈskɔləʃip], *s.* die Gelehrsamkeit (*learning*); das Stipendium (*award*).

scholastic [skoˈlæstik], *adj.* scholastisch. — *s.* der Scholastiker.

school [sku:l], *s.* die Schule. — *v.a.* abrichten; schulen; erziehen.

schoolboy [ˈsku:lbɔi], *s.* der Schüler.

schoolgirl [ˈsku:lgə:l], *s.* die Schülerin.

schoolmaster [ˈsku:lmɑ:stə], *s.* der Lehrer.

schoolmistress [ˈsku:lmistrəs], *s.* die Lehrerin.

schooner [ˈsku:nə], *s.* (*Naut.*) der Schoner.

science [ˈsaiəns], *s.* die Wissenschaft, Naturwissenschaft (*natural* — *s*).

scientific [saiənˈtifik], *adj.* wissenschaftlich, naturwissenschaftlich.

scientist [ˈsaiəntist], *s.* der Gelehrte; Naturwissenschaftler, Naturforscher.

scintillate [ˈsintileit], *v.n.* funkeln, glänzen.

scion [ˈsaiən], *s.* der Sprößling.

scissors [ˈsizəz], *s. pl.* die Schere.

scoff [skɔf], *v.a.* verspotten, verhöhnen. — *v.n.* spotten. —*s.* der Spott, Hohn.

scold [skould], *v.a.* schelten. — *v.n.* zanken.

scoop [sku:p], *v.a.* aushöhlen (*hollow out*); ausschöpfen (*ladle out*). — *s.* die Schippe, Schöpfkelle; (*fig.*) die Sensation, Erstmeldung.

scope [skoup], *s.* der Wirkungskreis, Spielraum.

scooter [ˈsku:tə], *s.* der (Motor)roller.

scorch [skɔ:tʃ], *v.a.* versengen, verbrennen. — *v.n.* versengt werden; (*coll.*) dahinrasen (*speed*).

score [skɔ:], *s.* die Zwanzig; die Rechnung; (*Mus.*) die Partitur; das Spielergebnis (*in game*).

scorn [skɔ:n], *v.a.* verachten. — *s.* der Spott (*scoffing*); die Geringschätzung, Verachtung.

Scot, Scotsman [skɔt, ˈskɔtsmən], *s.* der Schotte.

Scotch [skɔtʃ], *s.* der Whisky.

scotch [skɔtʃ], *v.a.* ritzen; (*fig.*) vernichten.

Scotswoman [ˈskɔtswumən], *s.* die Schottin.

Scottish [ˈskɔtiʃ], *adj.* schottisch.

scoundrel [ˈskaundrəl], *s.* der Schurke.

scour [ˈskauə], *v.a.* scheuern, reinigen.

scourge [skə:dʒ], *s.* die Geißel. — *v.a.* geißeln.

scout [skaut], *s.* der Kundschafter; (*Boy Scout*) der Pfadfinder.

scowl [skaul], *v.n.* finster dreinsehen. — *s.* das finstere Gesicht.

scraggy [ˈskrægi], *adj.* hager, dürr.

scramble [ˈskræmbl], *v.n.* klettern. — *v.a.* verrühren; *scrambled eggs*, das Rührei.

scrap [skræp], *s.* das Stückchen, der Brocken, Fetzen; — *merchant*, der Altwarenhändler. — *v.a.* zum alten Eisen werfen, verschrotten.

scrapbook [ˈskræpbuk], *s.* das Sammelbuch, Bilderbuch.

scrape [skreip], *v.a.,v.n.* (sich) schaben, kratzen; (*coll.*) — *up*, auflesen. — *s.* (*coll.*) die Klemme (*difficulty*).

scraper [ˈskreipə], *s.* der Fußabstreifer.

scratch [skrætʃ], *v.a.,v.n.* kratzen; sich kratzen; (*Sport*) zurückziehen. — *s.* der Kratzer; *come up to* —, seinen Mann stellen.

scrawl [skrɔ:l], *v.a., v.n.* kritzeln (*scribble*); (*coll.*) unleserlich schreiben. — *s.* das Gekritzel.

scream [skri:m], *v.n.* schreien; kreischen. — *s.* der Schrei; (*coll.*) zum Schreien, zum Lachen.

screech [skri:tʃ], *v.n.* schreien, kreischen (*hoarsely*). — *s.* das Gekreisch.

screen [skri:n], *s.* der Schirm (*protection*); (*Cinema*) die Leinwand. — *v.a.* abschirmen (*shade*); (*Film*) durchspielen, vorführen; (*question*) untersuchen; ausfragen.

screening [ˈskri:niŋ], *s.* (*Cinema*) die Vorführung; (*Pol.*) die Befragung, Untersuchung.

screw [skru:], *v.a.* schrauben. — *s.* die Schraube.

screwdriver [ˈskru:draivə], *s.* der Schraubenzieher.

scribble [ˈskribl], *v.a., v.n.* kritzeln, (unleserlich) schreiben. — *s.* das Gekritzel.

scribe [skraib], *s.* der Schreiber.

script [skript], *s.* das Manuskript; (*Film*) das Drehbuch.

scripture [ˈskriptʃə], *s.* die Heilige Schrift.

scroll [skroul], *s.* die Schriftrolle; (*Typ.*) der Schnörkel; die Urkunde (*document etc.*).

scrub [skrʌb], *v.a.* schrubben, reiben, scheuern.

scruff [skrʌf], *s.* (*of the neck*) das Genick.

scruple [skru:pl], *s.* der Skrupel.

scrupulous [ˈskru:pjuləs], *adj.* genau, gewissenhaft; allu bedenklich.

scrutinize [ˈskruːtinaiz], *v.a.* genau prüfen, untersuchen.

scrutiny [ˈskruːtini], *s.* die genaue Prüfung; die Untersuchung.

scuffle [skʌfl], *v.n.* sich raufen. — *s.* die Balgerei, Rauferei.

scull [skʌl], *s.* das kurze Ruder.

scullery [ˈskʌləri], *s.* die Abwaschküche.

scullion [ˈskʌliən], *s.* (*obs.*) der Küchenjunge.

sculptor [ˈskʌlptə], *s.* der Bildhauer.

sculpture [ˈskʌlptʃə], *s.* die Bildhauerei (*activity*); die Skulptur (*piece*).

scum [skʌm], *s.* der Abschaum.

scurf [skəːf], *s.* der Schorf, Grind.

scurrilous [ˈskʌriləs], *adj.* gemein.

scurvy [ˈskəːvi], *s.* (*Med.*) der Skorbut. — *adj.* niederträchtig.

scutcheon [ˈskʌtʃən] *see* escutcheon.

scuttle (1) [skʌtl], *s.* (*Naut.*) die Springluke. — *v.a.* (*Naut.*) ein Schiff zum Sinken bringen, versenken.

scuttle (2) [skʌtl], *s.* der Kohleneimer.

scuttle (3) [skʌtl], *v.n.* eilen (*hurry*).

scythe [saið], *s.* die Sense.

sea [siː], *s.* die See, das Meer.

seal (1) [siːl], *s.* das Siegel, Petschaft. — *v.a.* (be)siegeln.

seal (2) [siːl], *s.* (*Zool.*) der Seehund, die Robbe.

seam [siːm], *s.* der Saum; die Naht; (*Min.*) die Ader, das Flöz; (*Metall.*) die Naht. — *v.a.* einsäumen.

seamstress [ˈsiːmstrəs], *s.* die Näherin.

sear [siə], *v.a.* sengen (*burn*); trocknen; verdorren. — *adj. see* sere.

search [səːtʃ], *v.n.* suchen (*for*, nach, *Dat.*); forschen (*for*, nach, *Dat.*). — *v.a.* untersuchen, durchsuchen (*house, case etc.*). — *s.* die Suche (*for person*); die Untersuchung (*of house etc.*).

searchlight [ˈsəːtʃlait], *s.* der Scheinwerfer.

seasick [ˈsiːsik], *adj.* seekrank.

seaside [ˈsiːsaid], *s.* die Küste, der Strand.

season [siːzn], *s.* die Jahreszeit, Saison; — ticket, die Dauerkarte. — *v.a.* würzen (*spice*). — *v.n.* reifen (*mature*).

seasoning [ˈsiːzniŋ], *s.* die Würze.

seat [siːt], *s.* der Sitz, Sitzplatz, Stuhl. — *v.a.* setzen; fassen (*of room capacity*); be —ed, Platz nehmen.

seaweed [ˈsiːwiːd], *s.* (*Bot.*) der Seetang.

secession [siˈseʃən], *s.* die Loslösung, Trennung, Spaltung.

seclude [siˈkluːd], *v.a.* abschließen, absondern.

seclusion [siˈkluːʒən], *s.* die Abgeschlossenheit.

second [ˈsekənd], *num. adj.* zweit; (*repeat*) noch ein. — *s.* die Sekunde (*time*); (*Sport*) der Sekundant. — *v.a.* sekundieren (*Dat.*), beipflichten; [siˈkɔnd] abkommandieren (*Mil.*).

secondary [ˈsekəndri], *adj.* zweitrangig, sekundär.

secondhand [ˈsekəndhænd], *adj.* antiquarisch, gebraucht.

secrecy [ˈsiːkrəsi], *s.* die Heimlichkeit; *pledge to* —, die Verschwiegenheit.

secret [ˈsiːkrit], *s.* das Geheimnis. — *adj.* geheim.

secretary [ˈsekrətəri], *s.* der Sekretär, die Sekretärin.

secrete [siˈkriːt], *v.a.* ausscheiden, absondern.

secretion [siˈkriːʃən], *s.* die Ausscheidung; (*Med.*) das Sekret.

sect [sekt], *s.* die Sekte.

section [ˈsekʃən], *s.* die Sektion, Abteilung (*department*); der Teil (*part*); Abschnitt (*in book etc.*).

secular [ˈsekjulə], *adj.* weltlich, säkulär.

secure [səˈkjuə], *adj.* sicher, gesichert. — *v.a.* sichern (*make safe*); besorgen (*obtain*).

security [səˈkjuəriti], *s.* die Sicherheit; (*Comm.*) die Garantie, Bürgschaft; (*pl.*) die Staatspapiere, Wertpapiere, *n. pl.*, Aktien, *f. pl.*

sedate [siˈdeit], *adj.* gesetzt, ruhig (*placid*).

sedative [ˈsedətiv], *adj.* beruhigend. — *s.* das Beruhigungsmittel.

sedentary [ˈsedəntri], *adj.* sitzend, Sitz-.

sediment [ˈsedimənt], *s.* der Bodensatz; (*Geol.*) das Sediment.

sedition [siˈdiʃən], *s.* der Aufstand.

seditious [siˈdiʃəs], *adj.* aufrührerisch.

seduce [siˈdjuːs], *v.a.* verführen.

sedulous [ˈsedjuləs], *adj.* emsig, fleißig.

see (1) [siː], *s.* (*Eccl.*) das (Erz)bistum; *Holy See*, der Heilige Stuhl.

see (2) [siː], *v.a., v.n. irr.* sehen; einsehen, verstehen (*understand*).

seed [siːd], *s.* die Saat; der Same (*grain*). — *v.a.* (*Sport*) aussetzen, setzen.

seediness [ˈsiːdinis], *s.* die Schäbigkeit; Armseligkeit, das Elend.

seedy [ˈsiːdi], *adj.* elend; schäbig.

seeing [ˈsiːiŋ], *conj.* — *that*, da doch.

seek [siːk], *v.a. irr.* suchen (*object*). — *v.n.* trachten (*to, infin.*).

seem [siːm], *v.n.* scheinen, erscheinen.

seemly [ˈsiːmli], *adj.* schicklich, anständig.

seer [siə], *s.* der Prophet.

seesaw [ˈsiːsɔː], *s.* die Schaukel.

seethe [siːð], *v.n.* kochen, (*fig.*) sieden.

segment [ˈsegmənt], *s.* (*Geom.*) der Abschnitt.

segregate [ˈsegrigeit], *v.a.* absondern.

segregation [segriˈgeiʃən], *s. racial* —, die Rassentrennung.

seize [siːz], *v.a.* ergreifen, packen (*arrest, grasp*); beschlagnahmen (*impound*).

seizure [ˈsiːʒə], *s.* die Beschlagnahme (*of goods*); (*Med.*) der Anfall.

seldom [ˈseldəm], *adv.* selten.

select [siˈlekt], *v.a.* auswählen; auslesen. — *adj.* auserlesen.

selection [siˈlekʃən], *s.* die Wahl, Auswahl.

self [self], *s.* das Selbst; — *consciousness*, die Befangenheit; — — *denial*, die Selbstverleugnung, Selbstaufopferung.

selfish ['selfiʃ], *adj.* egoistisch, selbstsüchtig.

sell [sel], *v.a. irr.* verkaufen; (*sl.*) — (*s.o.*) *out*, jemanden verraten.

semblance ['semblans], *s.* der Anschein, die Ähnlichkeit.

semi- ['semi], *pref.* halb.

semibreve ['semibri:v], *s.* (*Mus.*) die ganze Note.

semicircle ['semisə:kl], *s.* der Halbkreis.

semicolon ['semikoulən], *s.* der Strichpunkt.

semiquaver ['semikweivə], *s.* (*Mus.*) die Sechzehntelnote.

senate ['senit], *s.* der Senat.

send [send], *v.a. irr.* senden, schicken; — *for*, holen lassen; — *-off*, die Abschiedsfeier.

Senegalese [senigə'li:z], *adj.* senegal-. — *s.* der Senegalese.

senile ['si:nail], *adj.* altersschwach.

senior ['si:njə], *adj.* älter; dienstälter (*in position*).

seniority [si:ni'ɔriti], *s.* der Rangvortritt, das Dienstalter.

sensation [sen'seiʃən], *s.* die Empfindung; Sensation.

sensational [sen'seiʃənəl], *adj.* sensationell.

sense [sens], *v.a.* fühlen, empfinden. — *s.* der Sinn; das Empfinden, Gefühl; *common* —, gesunder Menschenverstand.

senseless ['senslis], *adj.* sinnlos.

sensibility [sensi'biliti], *s.* die Empfindlichkeit.

sensible ['sensibl], *adj.* vernünftig.

sensitive ['sensitiv], *adj.* feinfühlend, empfindlich.

sensitize ['sensitaiz], *v.a.* (*Phot. etc.*) empfindlich machen.

sensual ['sensjuəl], *adj.* sinnlich, wollüstig.

sensuous ['sensjuəs], *adj.* sinnlich.

sentence ['sentəns], *s.* (*Gram.*) der Satz; (*Law*) das Urteil. — *v.a.* verurteilen.

sententious [sen'tenʃəs], *adj.* spruchreich; affektiert.

sentiment ['sentimənt], *s.* die Empfindung, das Gefühl; die Meinung (*opinion*).

sentimental [senti'mentl], *adj.* sentimental, gefühlvoll; empfindsam.

sentinel ['sentinəl], *s.* (*Mil.*) die Schildwache, Wache.

separable ['sepərəbl], *adj.* trennbar.

separate ['sepəreit], *v.a.* trennen. — [-rit], *adj.* getrennt.

separation [sepə'reiʃən], *s.* die Trennung.

September [sep'tembə]. der September.

sequel ['si:kwəl], *s.* die Folge, Fortsetzung (*serial*).

sequence ['si:kwəns], *s.* die Ordnung, Reihenfolge, Aufeinanderfolge.

sequester [si'kwestə], *v.a.* absondern, entfernen.

sere [siə], *adj.* trocken, dürr.

serene [si'ri:n], *adj.* heiter; gelassen, ruhig (*quiet*).

serf [sə:f], *s.* der Leibeigene.

sergeant ['sɑ:dʒənt], *s.* (*Mil.*) der Feldwebel.

series ['siəri:z *or* 'siərii:z], *s.* die Reihe.

serious ['siəriəs], *adj.* ernst, seriös.

sermon ['sə:mən], *s.* die Predigt.

serpent ['sə:pənt], *s.* (*Zool.*) die Schlange.

serpentine ['sə:pəntain], *adj.* schlangenartig, sich schlängelnd.

serrated [se'reitid], *adj.* (*Bot., Engin.*) zackig, gezackt.

serried ['serid], *adj.* dichtgedrängt.

servant ['sə:vənt], *s.* der Bediente, Diener; die Magd, das Mädchen, Dienstmädchen.

serve [sə:v], *v.a., v.n.* dienen (*Dat.*); (*Law*) abbüßen, absitzen (*sentence*); servieren (*food*); (*Tennis*) angeben.

service ['sə:vis], *s.* der Dienst, die Bedienung; (*Mil.*) der Militärdienst; das Service, Geschirr, Porzellan (*china*).

serviceable ['sə:visəbl], *adj.* brauchbar, dienlich, benutzbar.

servile ['sə:vail], *adj.* knechtisch.

servility [sə:'viliti], *s.* die Knecherei.

servitude ['sə:vitju:d], *s.* die Knechtschaft.

session ['seʃən], *s.* die Sitzung; das Studienjahr, Hochschuljahr.

set [set], *v.a. irr.* setzen; stellen (*stand*); legen (*lay*); ordnen (— *out*); — *a saw*, eine Sage schärfen, wetzen; fassen (*stone*); — *fire to*, in Brand setzen; — *aside*, beiseitelegen; — *to music*, vertonen; — *about*, anfangen, sich anschicken; herfallen über (*s.o.*); — *up*, einrichten. — *v.n.* — *forth, forward*, aufbrechen; — *out to*, streben, trachten; (*sun*) untergehen; fest werden (*solidify*). — *s.* der Satz (*complete collection*); die Garnitur (*garments*); der Kreis, die Clique (*circle of people*); (*Theat.*) das Bühnenbild.

settee [se'ti:], *s.* das Sofa.

setter ['setə], *s.* (*Zool.*) der Vorstehhund; *red* —, der Hühnerhund.

setting ['setiŋ], *s.* das Setzen; die Szene (*of play etc.*); der Sonnenuntergang (*of the sun*); (*Typ.*) — *up*, die Auslegung, Aufstellung.

settle (1) [setl], *v.a.* ordnen, schlichten; (*Comm.*) begleichen, bezahlen. — *v.n.* sich niederlassen, siedeln; (*weather*) sich aufklären.

settle (2) [setl], *s.* der Ruhesitz.

settlement ['setlmənt], *s.* (*Comm.*) die Begleichung; die Siedlung (*habitation*).

seven [sevn], *num. adj.* sieben.

seventeen ['sevnti:n], *num. adj.* siebzehn.

seventh [sevnθ], *num. adj.* siebente.

seventy ['sevnti], *num. adj.* siebzig.

sever ['sevə], *v.a.* trennen.

several ['sevərəl], *adj. pl.* verschiedene, mehrere.

severance ['sevərəns], *s.* die Trennung.

severe [si'viə], *adj.* streng.

severity [si'veriti], *s.* die Strenge.

sew [sou], *v.a., v.n.* nähen.

sewage ['sju:idʒ], *s.* das Abfuhrwasser, Kloakenwasser, Kanalwasser.

sewer (1) ['sju:ə], *s.* die Kanalanlage, der Abzugskanal.

sewer (2) ['souə], *s.* der Näher, die Näherin.

sewing ['souiŋ], *s.* das Nähen; — *machine,* die Nähmaschine.

sex [seks], *s.* das Geschlecht.

sexagenarian [seksədʒə'neəriən], *s.* der Sechzigjährige.

sextant ['sekstənt], *s.* der Sextant.

sexton ['sekstən], *s.* (*Eccl.*) der Küster, Totengräber.

sexual ['seksjuəl], *adj.* geschlechtlich, sexuell.

shabby ['ʃæbi], *adj.* schäbig; (*fig.*) erbärmlich.

shackle [ʃækl], *v.a.* fesseln. — *s.* (*usually pl.*) die Fesseln, *f. pl.*

shade [ʃeid], *s.* der Schatten; (*pl.*) (*Am.*) die Jalousien, *f. pl.* (*blinds*). — *v.a.* beschatten; (*Art*) schattieren, verdunkeln.

shadow ['ʃædou], *s.* der Schatten. — *v.a.* verfolgen.

shady ['ʃeidi], *adj.* schattig; (*fig.*) verdächtig.

shaft [ʃɑ:ft], *s.* der Schaft (*handle*); (*Min.*) der Schacht; die Deichsel (*cart*); der Pfeil (*arrow*).

shag [ʃæg], *s.* der Tabak.

shaggy ['ʃægi], *adj.* zottig.

shake [ʃeik], *v.a. irr.* schütteln; rütteln; (*fig.*) erschüttern. — *v.n.* zittern (*tremble*); wanken (*waver*). — *s.* das Zittern, Beben; (*Mus.*) der Triller.

shaky ['ʃeiki], *adj.* zitternd, wankend; rissig, wackelig (*wobbly*); (*fig.*) unsicher (*insecure*).

shall [ʃæl], *v. aux.* sollen (*be supposed to*); werden (*future*).

shallow ['ʃælou], *adj.* flach, seicht. — *s.* die Untiefe (*sea*).

sham [ʃæm], *adj.* falsch, unecht. — *v.a.* vortäuschen.

shambles [ʃæmblz], *s.* die Unordnung; (*fig.*) das Schlachtfeld.

shame [ʃeim], *s.* die Scham (*remorse*); die Schande (*dishonour*); *what a —! * wie schade! — *v.a.* beschämen.

shamefaced ['ʃeimfeisd], *adj.* verschämt.

shameful ['ʃeimful], *adj.* schändlich (*despicable*).

shampoo [ʃæm'pu:], *s.* das Haarwaschmittel. — *v.a.* das Haar waschen.

shamrock ['ʃæmrɔk], *s.* (*Bot.*) der irische Klee.

shank [ʃæŋk], *s.* der Unterschenkel; (*coll.*) *on Shanks's pony,* zu Fuß.

shanty (1) ['ʃænti], *s.* die Hütte.

shanty (2) ['ʃænti], *s. sea —,* das Matrosenlied.

shape [ʃeip], *s.* die Gestalt, Figur, Form. — *v.a.* gestalten, formen. — *v.n.* Gestalt annehmen.

shapely ['ʃeipli], *adj.* wohlgestaltet, schön gestaltet.

share [ʃɛə], *v.a., v.n.* (sich) teilen. — *s.* der Teil, Anteil; (*Comm.*) die Aktie (*in company*).

shareholder ['ʃɛəhouldə], *s.* der Aktionär.

shark [ʃɑːk], *s.* (*Zool.*) der Haifisch, Hai; (*fig.*) der Wucherer (*profiteer*), Hochstapler.

sharp [ʃɑːp], *adj.* scharf; (*fig.*) intelligent. — *s.* (*Mus.*) das Kreuz.

sharpen [ʃɑːpn], *v.a.* schärfen; spitzen (*pencil*).

sharpener ['ʃɑːpnə], *s. pencil —,* der Bleistiftspitzer.

shatter ['ʃætə], *v.a.* zerschmettern. — *v.n.* zerbrechen.

shave [ʃeiv], *v.a., v.n.* (sich) rasieren; abschaben (*pare*). — *s.* die Rasur, das Rasieren.

shavings ['ʃeiviŋz], *s. pl.* die Hobelspäne, *m. pl.*

shawl [ʃɔːl], *s.* der Schal, das Umschlagetuch.

she [ʃiː], *pers. pron.* sie.

sheaf [ʃiːf], *s.* die Garbe.

shear [ʃiə], *v.a. irr.* scheren (*sheep etc.*).

shears [ʃiəz], *s. pl.* die Schere.

sheath [ʃiːθ], *s.* die Scheide.

sheathe [ʃiːð], *v.a.* in die Scheide stecken.

shed (1) [ʃed], *s.* der Schuppen.

shed (2) [ʃed], *v.a. irr.* vergießen (*blood, tears*); ausschütten.

sheen [ʃiːn], *s.* der Glanz.

sheep [ʃiːp], *s.* (*Zool.*) das Schaf.

sheer (1) [ʃiə], *adj.* rein, lauter; senkrecht.

sheer (2) [ʃiə], *v.n.* (*Naut.*) gieren, abgieren.

sheet [ʃiːt], *s.* das Bettuch; das Blatt, der Bogen (*paper*); die Platte (*metal*); — *metal,* — *iron,* das Eisenblech; — *lightning,* das Wetterleuchten.

shelf [ʃelf], *s.* das Brett, Regal; der Sims (*mantel*); (*Geog.*) die Sandbank; (*coll.*) *on the —,* sitzengeblieben.

shell [ʃel], *s.* die Schale (*case*); die Muschel (*mussel*); (*Mil.*) die Bombe, Granate. — *v.a.* schälen (*peas*); bombardieren, beschießen (*town*).

shelter ['ʃeltə], *s.* das Obdach (*lodging*); der Unterstand, Schuppen; der Schutz (*protection*). — *v.a.* Obdach gewähren (*Dat.*); beschützen (*protect*). — *v.n.* sich schützen, unterstellen.

shelve [ʃelv], *v.a.* auf ein Brett legen; (*fig.*) aufschieben (*postpone*).

shelving ['ʃelviŋ], *s.* das Regal.

shepherd ['ʃepəd], *s.* der Schäfer, Hirt.

sheriff ['ʃerif], *s.* der Sheriff.

shew [ʃou] *see* **show**.

shield [ʃiːld], *s.* der Schild. — *v.a.* schützen.

shift [ʃift], *v.a.* verschieben. — *v.n.* die Lage ändern. — *s.* die Veränderung, der Wechsel; (*Industry*) die Schicht.

shifty ['ʃifti], *adj.* unstet; durchtrieben.

shin

shin [ʃin], s. (*Anat.*) das Schienbein.
shindy [ʃindi], s. der Lärm.
shine [ʃain], v.n. irr. scheinen (*sun*); glänzen. — s. der Glanz.
shingle (1) [ʃingl], s. (*Build.*) die Schindel; (*Hair*) der Herrenschnitt.
shingle (2) [ʃingl], s. (*Geol.*) der Kiesel.
shingles [ʃinglz], s. pl. (*Med.*) die Gürtelrose.
ship [ʃip], s. das Schiff. — v.a. verschiffen, (*Comm.*) versenden.
shipping [ʃipin], s. die Schiffahrt; (*Comm.*) der Versand, die Verfrachtung, Verschiffung.
shire [ʃaiə], s. die Grafschaft.
shirk [ʃəːk], v.a. vermeiden, sich drücken (vor, *Dat.*).
shirt [ʃəːt], s. das Hemd.
shirting [ʃəːtin], s. der Hemdenstoff.
shiver [ʃivə], v.n. zittern, beben. — s. der Schauer, Schauder.
shoal [ʃoul], s. der Schwarm; (*Naut.*) die Untiefe.
shock (1) [ʃɔk], v.a. entsetzen; erschrecken; schockieren. — s. der Schock, das Entsetzen.
shock (2) [ʃɔk], s. — of hair, zottiges Haar.
shoddy [ʃɔdi], adj. schlecht, wertlos.
shoe [ʃuː], s. der Schuh. — v.a. beschuhen; (*horse*) beschlagen.
shoelace, shoestring [ʃuːleis, ʃuːstriŋ], s. der Schuhsenkel, (*Austr.*) das Schuhschnürl; on a shoestring, fast ohne Geld.
shoeshine [ʃuːʃain], s. (*Am.*) der Schuhputzer.
shoestring see under **shoelace**.
shoot [ʃuːt], v.a. irr. schießen. — v.n. sprossen, hervorschießen; (*film*) aufnehmen. — s. (*Bot.*) der Sproß.
shooting [ʃuːtin], s. das Schießen; — range, der Schießstand. — adj. — star, die Sternschnuppe.
shop [ʃɔp], s. der Laden, das Geschäft; (*work*) die Werkstatt; (*talk*) — fachsimpeln; — window, das Schaufenster. — v.n. einkaufen.
shopkeeper [ʃɔpkiːpə], s. der Kaufmann, Krämer.
shoplifter [ʃɔpliftə], s. der Ladendieb.
shore [ʃɔː], s. das Gestade, die Küste; die Stütze. — v.a. — up, stützen.
short [ʃɔːt], adj. kurz, klein, knapp; (*curt*) kurz angebunden; — of money, in Geldnot; — knapp werden; —sighted, kurzsichtig; be on — time working, kurz arbeiten. — s. (*Elect.*) (*coll.*) der Kurzschluß (short circuit); (*pl.*) die Kniehose, kurze Hose.
shortcoming [ʃɔːtkʌmiŋ], s. der Fehler, Mangel.
shorten [ʃɔːtn], v.a. verkürzen, abkürzen. — v.n. kürzer werden.
shorthand [ʃɔːthænd], s. die Stenographie; — typist, die Stenotypistin.
shot [ʃɔt], s. der Schuß; (*man*) der Schütze.

shoulder [ʃouldə], s. (*Anat.*) die Schulter. — v.a. schultern, auf sich nehmen, auf die Achsel nehmen.
shout [ʃaut], v.n. schreien, rufen. — s. der Schrei, Ruf.
shove [ʃʌv], v.a. schieben, stoßen. — s. der Schub, Stoß.
shovel [ʃʌvl], s. die Schaufel. — v.a. schaufeln.
show [ʃou], v.a. irr. zeigen; (*fig.*) dartun. — v.n. sich zeigen, zu sehen sein; — off, prahlen, protzen. — v.r. — o.s. to be, sich erweisen als. — s. (*Theat.*) die Schau, Aufführung.
shower [ʃauə], s. der Schauer (rain); (*fig.*) die Fülle, der Überfluß; — (*bath*), die Dusche; take a —(bath), brausen. — v.a., v.n. herabregnen; überschütten.
showing [ʃouiŋ], s. die Vorführung, der Beweis.
showy [ʃoui], adj. protzig, angeberisch.
shred [ʃred], s. der Fetzen; (*fig.*) die Spur (of evidence). — v.a. zerreißen, zerfetzen.
shrew [ʃruː], s. die Spitzmaus; (*fig.*) das zänkische Weib.
shrewd [ʃruːd], adj. schlau, verschlagen, listig.
shriek [ʃriːk], v.n. kreischen. — s. der Schrei, das Gekreisch.
shrift [ʃrift], s. give s.o. short —, mit einem kurzen Prozeß machen.
shrill [ʃril], adj. schrill, gellend, durchdringend.
shrimp [ʃrimp], s. (*Zool.*) die Garnele.
shrine [ʃrain], s. der (Reliquien-)schrein; der Altar.
shrink [ʃrink], v.n. irr. eingehen, einschrumpfen. — v.a. eingehen lassen.
shrinkage [ʃrinkidʒ], s. das Eingehen (fabric); (*Geol.*) die Schrumpfung.
shrivel [ʃrivl], v.n. einschrumpfen, sich runzeln.
shroud [ʃraud], s. das Leichentuch. — v.a. einhüllen.
Shrove [ʃrouv] **Tuesday**, die Fastnacht.
shrub [ʃrʌb], s. (*Bot.*) der Strauch, die Staude.
shrug [ʃrʌg], v.a. (shoulders) die Achseln zucken. — s. das Achselzucken.
shudder [ʃʌdə], s. der Schauder. — v.n. schaudern.
shuffle [ʃʌfl], v.a. (cards) mischen. — v.n. schlürfen, schleppend gehen.
shun [ʃʌn], v.a. meiden.
shunt [ʃʌnt], v.a., v.n. rangieren.
shut [ʃʌt], v.a. irr. schließen. — v.n. sich schließen, zugehen; (*coll.*) — up! halt's Maul!
shutter [ʃʌtə], s. der Fensterladen.
shuttle [ʃʌtl], s. (*Mech.*) das Weberschiff.
shuttlecock [ʃʌtlkɔk], s. der Federball.
shy (1) [ʃai], adj. scheu, schüchtern. — v.n. scheuen (of horses).
shy (2) [ʃai], s. der Wurf.
sick [sik], adj. krank; unwohl, übel; leidend (suffering); (*fig.*) — of, überdrüssig (Genit.).

sicken [sikn], *v.n.* krank werden *or* sein; sich ekeln (*be nauseated*). — *v.a.* anekeln.

sickle [sikl], *s.* die Sichel.

sickness ['siknis], *s.* die Krankheit.

side [said], *s.* die Seite. — *v.n.* — *with*, Partei ergreifen für.

sideboard ['saidbɔːd], *s.* das Büffet, die Anrichte.

sidereal [sai'diəriəl], *adj.* (*Maths.*, *Phys.*) Sternen-, Stern-.

sidewalk ['saidwɔːk] (*Am.*) *see* **pavement**.

siding ['saidiŋ], *s.* (*Railw.*) das Nebengleis.

sidle [saidl], *v.n.* — *up to*, sich heranmachen.

siege [siːdʒ], *s.* die Belagerung.

sieve [siv], *s.* das Sieb. — *v.a.* sieben.

sift [sift], *v.a.* sieben; (*fig.*) prüfen.

sigh [sai], *v.n.* seufzen. — *s.* der Seufzer.

sight [sait], *s.* die Sicht (*view*); die Sehkraft (*sense of*); der Anblick; *at* —, auf den ersten Blick; *out of* —, *out of mind*, aus den Augen, aus dem Sinn; (*pl.*) die Sehenswürdigkeiten, *f. pl.*; —*seeing*, die Besichtigung (der Sehenswürdigkeiten). — *v.a.* sichten.

sign [sain], *s.* das Zeichen; der Wink (*hint*); das Aushängeschild (*of pub*, *shop etc.*). — *v.a.* unterschreiben, unterzeichnen. — *v.n.* winken.

signal ['signəl], *s.* das Signal.

signboard ['sainbɔːd], *s.* das Aushängeschild.

signet ['signit], *s.* das Siegel; — *ring*, der Siegelring.

significance [sig'nifikəns], *s.* die Bedeutung, der Sinn.

significant [sig'nifikənt], *adj.* bedeutend, wichtig.

signify ['signifai], *v.a.* bedeuten (*mean*); anzeigen (*denote*).

silence ['sailəns], *s.* das Schweigen, die Ruhe.

silent ['sailənt], *adj.* still; schweigsam (*taciturn*).

Silesian [sai'liːʃən], *adj.* schlesisch. — *s.* der Schlesier.

silk [silk], *s.* (*Text.*) die Seide.

silkworm ['silkwɜːm], *s.* (*Ent.*) die Seidenraupe.

sill [sil], *s.* die Schwelle; *window* —, das Fensterbrett.

silly ['sili], *adj.* albern, dumm.

silver ['silvə], *s.* das Silber. — *v.a.* versilbern. — *adj.* silbern.

similar ['similə], *adj.* ähnlich.

simile ['simili], *s.* (*Lit.*) das Gleichnis.

simmer ['simə], *v.n.*, *v.a.* langsam kochen.

simper ['simpə], *v.n.* lächeln, grinsen.

simple [simpl], *adj.* einfach; (*fig.*) einfältig.

simpleton ['simpltən], *s.* der Einfaltspinsel, Tor.

simplicity [sim'plisiti], *s.* die Einfachheit; (*fig.*) die Einfalt.

simplify ['simplifai], *v.a.* vereinfachen.

simulate ['simjuleit], *v.a.* nachahmen, heucheln, vortäuschen.

simultaneous [siməl'teinjəs], *adj.* gleichzeitig.

sin [sin], *s.* die Sünde. — *v.n.* sündigen.

since [sins], *prep.* seit (*Dat.*). — *conj.* seit (*time*); weil, da (*cause*). — *adv.* seither, seitdem.

sincere [sin'siə], *adj.* aufrichtig.

sincerely [sin'siəli], *adv. yours* —, Ihr ergebener (*letters*).

sincerity [sin'seriti], *s.* die Aufrichtigkeit.

sine [sain], *s.* (*Maths.*) der Sinus, die Sinuskurve.

sinecure ['sainikjuə], *s.* der Ruheposten, die Sinekure.

sinew ['sinjuː], *s.* (*Anat.*) die Sehne, der Nerv.

sinful ['sinful], *adj.* sündig, sündhaft.

sing [siŋ], *v.a.*, *v.n. irr.* singen; — *of*, besingen.

singe [sindʒ], *v.a.* sengen.

Singhalese [siŋgə'liːz], *adj.* singhalesisch. — *s.* der Singhalese, die Singhalesin.

single [siŋgl], *adj.* einzeln; ledig (*unmarried*); *single-handed*, allein. — *v.a.* — *out*, auswählen.

singlet ['siŋglit], *s.* die Unterjacke.

singly ['siŋgli], *adv.* einzeln (*one by one*).

singular ['siŋgjulə], *adj.* einzigartig, einzig. — *s.* (*Gram.*) die Einzahl.

sinister ['sinistə], *adj.* böse, unheimlich, finster.

sink [siŋk], *v.a. irr.* versenken; (*fig.*) (*differences etc.*) begraben. — *v.n.* versinken; (*Naut.*) sinken, versinken. — *s.* das Abwaschbecken, Ausgußbecken.

sinker ['siŋkə], *s.* der Schachtarbeiter (*man*); (*Naut.*) das Senkblei.

sinuous ['sinjuəs], *adj.* gewunden.

sinus ['sainəs], *s.* (*Anat.*) die Knochenhöhle; die Bucht.

sip [sip], *v.a.* schlürfen, nippen. — *s.* das Schlückchen.

siphon ['saifən], *s.* (*Phys.*) der Heber; die Siphonflasche. — *v.a.* auspumpen.

Sir (1) [sɜː] (*title preceding Christian name*) Herr von... (*baronet or knight*).

sir (2) [sɜː], *s.* Herr (*respectful form of address*); *dear* —, sehr geehrter Herr (*in letters*).

sire [saiə], *s.* der Ahnherr, Vater. — *v.a.* zeugen (*horses etc.*).

siren ['saiərən], *s.* die Sirene.

sirloin ['sɜːlɔin], *s.* das Lendenstück.

siskin ['siskin], *s.* (*Orn.*) der Zeisig.

sister ['sistə], *s.* die Schwester; (*Eccl.*) Nonne; —*in-law*, die Schwägerin.

sit [sit], *v.n. irr.* sitzen. — *v.a.* — *an examination*, eine Prüfung machen.

site [sait], *s.* die Lage, der Platz.

sitting ['sitiŋ], *s.* die Sitzung. — *room*, das Wohnzimmer.

situated ['sitjueitid], *adj.* gelegen.

situation [sitju'eiʃən], *s.* die Lage, Situation; der Posten, die Stellung (*post*).

six

six [siks], *num. adj.* sechs; *be at —es and sevens*, durcheinander, uneinig sein.
sixteen [siks'ti:n], *num. adj.* sechzehn.
sixth [siksθ], *num. adj.* sechste.
sixty ['siksti], *num. adj.* sechzig.
size [saiz], *s.* die Größe, das Maß; (*fig.*) der Umfang.
skate (1) [skeit], *s.* der Schlittschuh. — *v.n.* Schlittschuh laufen.
skate (2) [skeit], *s.* (*Zool.*) der Glattrochen.
skeleton ['skelitən], *s.* das Skelett, Knochengerüst; — *key*, der Dietrich.
sketch [sketʃ], *s.* die Skizze, der Entwurf. — *v.a.* skizzieren, entwerfen. — *v.n.* Skizzen entwerfen.
sketchy ['sketʃi], *adj.* flüchtig.
skew [skju:], *adj.* schief, schräg.
skewer ['skju:ə], *s.* der Fleischspieß.
ski [ski:], *s.* der Schi.
skid [skid], *v.n.* gleiten, schleudern, rutschen, — *v.a.* hemmen, bremsen (*wheel*). — *s.* der Hemmschuh, die Bremse (*of wheel*).
skiff [skif], *s.* (*Naut.*) der Nachen, Kahn.
skilful ['skilful], *adj.* geschickt, gewandt; (*fig.*) erfahren.
skill [skil], *s.* die Geschicklichkeit, Gewandtheit; (*fig.*) die Erfahrung.
skim [skim], *v.a.* abschöpfen, abschäumen.
skimp [skimp], *v.n.* knausern, sparsam sein (*mit, Dat.*).
skimpy ['skimpi], *adj.* knapp.
skin [skin], *s.* die Haut; die Schale (*fruit*); — *deep*, oberflächlich. — *v.a.* häuten, schinden.
skinflint ['skinflint], *s.* der Geizhals.
skinner ['skinə], *s.* der Kürschner.
skip [skip], *v.n.* springen, hüpfen. — *v.a.* (*coll.*) auslassen, überspringen. — *s.* der Sprung.
skipper ['skipə], *s.* (*Naut.*) der Kapitän; (*coll.*) der Chef.
skipping rope ['skipiŋ roup], *s.* das Springseil.
skirmish ['skə:miʃ], *s.* das Scharmützel. — *v.n.* scharmützeln.
skirt [skə:t], *s.* der Rock, Rockschoß (*woman's garment*); der Saum (*edge*). — *v.a.* einsäumen (*seam, edge*); grenzen, am Rande entlang gehen.
skirting (board) ['skə:tiŋ (bɔ:d)], *s.* die Fußleiste.
skit [skit], *s.* die Stichelei, die Parodie, Satire.
skittish ['skitiʃ], *adj.* leichtfertig.
skulk [skʌlk], *v.n.* lauern, herumlungern.
skull [skʌl], *s.* der Schädel; — *and crossbones*, der Totenkopf.
skunk [skʌŋk], *s.* (*Zool.*) das Stinktier; (*coll.*) der Schuft.
sky [skai], *s.* der (sichtbare) Himmel.
skylark ['skailɑ:k], *s.* (*Orn.*) die Feldlerche.
skylarking ['skailɑ:kiŋ], *s.* das Possenreißen, die Streiche.
skyline ['skailain], *s.* der Horizont.
skyscraper ['skaiskreipə], *s.* der Wolkenkratzer.

slab [slæb], *s.* die Platte (*stone*); die Tafel, das Stück.
slack [slæk], *adj.* schlaff (*feeble*); locker (*loose*). — *s.* der Kohlengrus. — *v.n.* nachlassen, locker werden, faulenzen.
slacken [slækn], *v.a., v.n.* locker werden, nachlassen.
slackness ['slæknis], *s.* die Schlaffheit, Faulheit.
slag [slæg], *s.* die Schlacke.
slake [sleik], *v.a.* dämpfen, löschen, stillen.
slam (1) [slæm], *v.a.* zuwerfen, zuschlagen (*door*). — *s.* der Schlag.
slam (2) [slæm], *v.a.* (*Cards*) Schlemm ansagen, Schlemm machen. — *s.* (*Cards*) der Stich.
slander ['slɑ:ndə], *v.a.* verleumden. — *s.* die Verleumdung.
slanderer ['slɑ:ndərə], *s.* der Verleumder.
slang [slæŋ], *s.* der Slang.
slant [slɑ:nt], *s.* die schräge Richtung, der Winkel (*angle*).
slap [slæp], *v.a.* schlagen. — *s.* der Klaps, Schlag.
slapdash ['slæpdæʃ], *adj.* oberflächlich.
slash [slæʃ], *v.a.* schlitzen, aufschlitzen; (*coll.*) (*Comm.*) herunterbringen (*prices*). — *s.* der Hieb, Schlag.
slate [sleit], *s.* der Schiefer. — *v.a.* mit Schiefer decken; (*fig.*) ankreiden, ausschelten (*scold*).
slattern ['slætə:n], *s.* die Schlampe.
slaughter ['slɔ:tə], *v.a.* schlachten; niedermetzeln. — *s.* das Schlachten; das Gemetzel.
slave [sleiv], *s.* der Sklave; — *driver*, der Sklavenaufseher. — *v.n.* — (*away*), sich placken, sich rackern.
slavery ['sleivəri], *s.* die Sklaverei.
slavish ['sleiviʃ], *adj.* sklavisch.
slay [slei], *v.a.* erschlagen, töten.
sled, sledge [sled, sledʒ], *s.* der Schlitten.
sleek [sli:k], *adj.* glatt. — *v.a.* glätten.
sleep [sli:p], *v.n. irr.* schlafen. — *s.* der Schlaf.
sleeper ['sli:pə], *s.* der Schläfer; (*Railw.*) die Bahnschwelle; der Schlafwagen (*sleeping car*).
sleepwalker ['sli:pwɔ:kə], *s.* der Nachtwandler.
sleet [sli:t], *s.* der Graupelregen.
sleeve [sli:v], *s.* der Ärmel; der Umschlag (*of record*); *have up o.'s —*, eine Überraschung bereithalten; *laugh in o.'s —*, sich ins Fäustchen lachen.
sleigh [slei], *s.* der Schlitten; — *ride*, die Schlittenfahrt.
sleight [slait], *s.—of hand*, der Taschenspielerstreich; der Trick.
slender ['slendə], *adj.* schlank, dünn, gering.
slice [slais], *s.* die Schnitte, Scheibe. — *v.a.* in Scheiben schneiden.
slick [slik], *adj.* glatt.
slide [slaid], *v.n. irr.* gleiten, rutschen (*glide*). — *v.a.* einschieben. — *s.* die Rutschbahn; (*Phot.*) das Dia, Diapositiv; — *rule*, der Rechenschieber.

slight [slait], *adj.* leicht (*light*), gering (*small*); (*fig.*) schwach, dünn(*weak*). — *s.* die Geringschätzung, Respektlosigkeit. — *v.a.* mißachten, geringschätzig behandeln.

slim [slim], *adj.* schlank.

slime [slaim], *s.* der Schleim (*phlegm*); der Schlamm (*mud*).

sling [sliŋ], *v.a. irr.* schleudern, werfen. — *s.* die Schleuder; (*Med.*) die Binde: der Wurf (*throw*).

slink [sliŋk], *v.n. irr.* schleichen.

slip [slip], *v.n.* ausgleiten; — *away*, entschlüpfen; — *up*, einen Fehltritt begehen (*err*). — *v.a.* gleiten lassen, schieben. — *s.* das Ausgleiten; (*fig.*) der Fehltritt; der Fehler (*mistake*); der Unterrock (*petticoat*); *give s.o. the* —, einem entgleiten, entschlüpfen.

slipper ['slipə], *s.* der Pantoffel, Hausschuh.

slippery ['slipəri], *adj.* schlüpfrig, glatt.

slipshod ['slipʃɔd], *adj.* nachlässig.

slit [slit], *v.a.* schlitzen, spalten. — *s.* der Schlitz, Spalt.

slither ['sliðə], *v.n.* gleiten, rutschen.

sloe [slou], *s.* (*Bot.*) die Schlehe.

slogan ['slougən], *s.* das Schlagwort.

sloop [slu:p], *s.* (*Naut.*) die Schaluppe.

slop [slɔp], *s.* das Spülicht, Spülwasser.

slope [sloup], *s.* der Abhang, die Abdachung. — *v.n.* sich neigen. — *v.a.* abschrägen.

sloppy ['slɔpi], *adj.* unordentlich, nachlässig.

slot [slɔt], *s.* der Spalt, Schlitz (*slit*); die Kerbe (*notch*); — *machine*, der Automat.

sloth [slouθ], *s.* die Trägheit; (*Zool.*) das Faultier.

slouch [slautʃ], *v.n.* umherschlendern; sich schlaff halten.

slough [slau], *s.* der Morast, Sumpf.

slovenly ['slʌvnli], *adj.* schlampig, schmutzig.

slow [slou], *adj.* langsam; (*Phot.*) — *motion*, die Zeitlupenaufnahme. — *v.n.* — *down*, langsamer fahren *or* laufen.

slow-worm ['slouwə:m], *s.* (*Zool.*) die Blindschleiche.

sludge [slʌdʒ], *s.* der Schlamm, Schmutz.

slug [slʌg], *s.* (*Zool.*) die Wegschnecke; (*Am.*) die Kugel.

sluggish ['slʌgiʃ], *adj.* träg(e).

sluice [slu:s], *s.* die Schleuse. — *v.a.* ablassen (*drain*); begießen (*water*).

slum [slʌm], *s.* das Elendsviertel; Haus im Elendsviertel.

slumber ['slʌmbə], *s.* der Schlummer. — *v.n.* schlummern.

slump [slʌmp], *s.* (*Comm.*) der Tiefstand der Konjunktur; der Preissturz. — *v.n.* stürzen.

slur [slə:], *v.a.* undeutlich sprechen. — *s.* der Schandfleck, die Beleidigung; das Bindezeichen.

slush [slʌʃ], *s.* der Matsch, Schlamm; (*Lit.*) der Kitsch, die Schundliteratur.

slut [slʌt], *s.* die Schlampe.

sly [slai], *adj.* schlau, listig.

smack [smæk], *v.n.* schmecken (*of*, nach, *Dat.*). — *v.a.* schmatzen, lecken. — *s.* der Klaps. — *adv.* (*coll.*) — *in the middle*, gerade in der Mitte.

small [smɔ:l], *adj.* klein; (*fig.*) kleinlich (*petty*); — *talk*, das Geplauder.

smallpox ['smɔ:lpɔks], *s.* (*Med.*) die Blattern, *f. pl.*

smart [smɑ:t], *adj.* schneidig; elegant, schick (*well-dressed*). — *v.n.* schmerzen. — *s.* der Schmerz.

smash [smæʃ], *v.a.* zertrümmern, in Stücke schlagen. — *v.n.* zerschmettern; (*fig.*) zusammenbrechen. — *s.* der Krach.

smattering ['smætəriŋ], *s.* die oberflächliche Kenntnis.

smear [smiə], *v.a.* beschmieren; (*Am. coll.*) den Charakter angreifen, verleumden. — *s.* die Beschmierung, Befleckung.

smell [smel], *v.a. irr.* riechen. — *v.n.* riechen (nach, *Dat.*). — *s.* der Geruch.

smelt (1) [smelt], *v.a.* (*Metall.*) schmelzen.

smelt (2) [smelt], *s.* (*Zool.*) der Stintfisch.

smile [smail], *v.n.* lächeln. — *s.* das Lächeln.

smirk [smə:k], *v.n.* grinsen. — *s.* das Grinsen, die Grimasse.

smite [smait], *v.a. irr.* treffen, schlagen.

smith [smiθ], *s.* der Schmied.

smitten [smitn], *adj.* verliebt.

smock [smɔk], *s.* der Arbeitskittel.

smoke [smouk], *v.a., v.n.* rauchen; räuchern (*fish etc.*). — *s.* der Rauch.

smoked [smoukd], *adj.* — *ham*, der Räucherschinken.

smooth [smu:ð], *adj.* glatt, sanft (*to touch*); (*fig.*) glatt, geschmeidig, wendig. — *v.a.* glätten, ebnen.

smother ['smʌðə], *v.a.* ersticken.

smoulder ['smouldə], *v.n.* schwelen.

smudge [smʌdʒ], *v.a.* beschmutzen. — *v.n.* schmieren, schmutzen. — *s.* der Schmutzfleck, Schmutz.

smug [smʌg], *adj.* selbstgefällig.

smuggle [smʌgl], *v.a.* schmuggeln.

smuggler ['smʌglə], *s.* der Schmuggler.

smut [smʌt], *v.a., v.n.* beschmutzen. — *s.* (*fig.*) der Schmutz.

snack [snæk], *s.* der Imbiß.

snaffle [snæfl], *s.* die Trense.

snag [snæg], *s.* die Schwierigkeit; der Haken.

snail [sneil], *s.* (*Zool.*) die Schnecke.

snake [sneik], *s.* (*Zool.*) die Schlange.

snap [snæp], *v.n.* schnappen (*at*, nach, *Dat.*); (*fig.*) einen anfahren (*shout at s.o.*). — *v.a.* (er)schnappen; (*Phot.*) knipsen. — *s.* (*abbr. for* **snapshot** ['snæpʃɔt]) (*Phot.*) das Photo.

snare [snɛə], *s.* die Schlinge. — *v.a. see* **ensnare**.

snarl [snɑ:l], *v.n.* knurren (*dog*); — *at s.o.*, einen anfahren, anschnauzen.

snatch [snætʃ], *v.a.* erschnappen, erhaschen.

sneak [sni:k], *v.n.* kriechen, schleichen. — *s.* der Kriecher.

sneer [sniə], *v.n.* höhnen, verhöhnen (*at, Acc.*). — *s.* der Spott.

sneeze [sni:z], *v.n.* niesen. — *s.* das Niesen.

sniff [snif], *v.a., v.n.* schnüffeln.

snigger [ˈsnigə], *v.n.* kichern. — *s.* das Kichern.

snip [snip], *v.a.* schneiden, schnippeln.

snipe (1) [snaip], *s.* (*Orn.*) die Schnepfe.

snipe (2) [snaip], *v.n.* schießen.

snivel [snivl], *v.n.* schluchzen (*from weeping*); verschnupft sein (*with a cold*).

snob [snɔb], *s.* der Snob.

snobbish [ˈsnɔbiʃ], *adj.* vornehm tuend; protzig, snobistisch.

snooze [snu:z], *s.* das Schläfchen. — *v.n.* einschlafen, ein Schläfchen machen.

snore [snɔ:], *v.n.* schnarchen. — *s.* das Schnarchen.

snort [snɔ:t], *v.n.* schnaufen; schnarchen (*snore*).

snout [snaut], *s.* die Schnauze, der Rüssel.

snow [snou], *s.* der Schnee. — *v.n.* schneien.

snowdrift [ˈsnoudrift], *s.* das Schneegestöber.

snowdrop [ˈsnoudrɔp], *s.* (*Bot.*) das Schneeglöckchen.

snub [snʌb], *v.a.* kurz abfertigen; (*fig.*) schneiden (*ignore*). — *adj.* — *nosed*, stumpfnasig. — *s.* die Geringschätzung, das Ignorieren.

snuff [snʌf], *s.* der Schnupftabak. — *v.a.* ausblasen (*candle*).

snug [snʌg], *adj.* behaglich; geborgen (*protected*).

so [sou], *adv.* so, also; *not* — *as*, nicht so wie. — *conj.* so.

soak [souk], *v.a.* einweichen, durchtränken. — *v.n.* weichen, durchsickern (*in(to)*, in, *Acc.*). — *s.* der Regenguß.

soap [soup], *s.* die Seife. — *v.a.* einseifen.

soar [sɔ:], *v.n.* sich aufschwingen, schweben.

sob [sɔb], *v.n.* schluchzen. — *s.* das Schluchzen.

sober [ˈsoubə], *adj.* nüchtern. — *v.a., v.n.* — (*down*), (sich) ernüchtern.

sobriety [soˈbraiəti], *s.* die Nüchternheit.

soccer [ˈsɔkə], *s.* (*Sport*) das Fußballspiel.

sociable [ˈsouʃəbl], *adj.* gesellig.

social [ˈsouʃəl], *adj.* sozial, gesellschaftlich. — *s.* die Gesellschaft (*party*).

socialism [ˈsouʃəlizm], *s.* (*Pol.*) der Sozialismus.

socialist [ˈsouʃəlist], *adj.* (*Pol.*) sozialistisch, Sozial-. — *s.* der Sozialist.

society [səˈsaiəti], *s.* die Gesellschaft (*human* —); der Verein (*association*); (*Comm.*) die (Handels)gesellschaft.

sock (1) [sɔk], *s.* der Strumpf.

sock (2) [sɔk], *v.a.* (*sl.*) schlagen, boxen.

socket [ˈsɔkit], *s. eye* —, die Augenhöhle; (*Elec.*) die Steckdose.

sod [sɔd], *s.* der Rasen, die Erde.

sodden [sɔdn], *adj.* durchweicht.

sofa [ˈsoufə], *s.* das Sofa.

soft [sɔft], *adj.* weich, sanft; einfältig (*stupid*).

soften [sɔfn], *v.a.* weich machen, erweichen. — *v.n.* weich werden, erweichen.

soil [sɔil], *s.* der Boden, die Erde. — *v.a.* beschmutzen.

sojourn [ˈsʌdʒən *or* ˈsɔdʒən], *s.* der Aufenthalt. — *v.n.* sich aufhalten.

solace [ˈsɔlis], *s.* der Trost.

solar [ˈsoulə], *adj.* Sonnen-.

solder [ˈsɔldə *or* ˈsɔ:də], *v.a.* löten. — *s.* das Lötmittel.

soldier [ˈsouldʒə], *s.* der Soldat. — *v.n.* dienen, Soldat sein.

sole (1) [soul], *s.* (*Zool.*) die Seezunge.

sole (2) [soul], *s.* die Sohle (*foot*).

sole (3) [soul], *adj.* allein, einzig.

solecism [ˈsɔlisizm], *s.* der Sprachschnitzer.

solemn [ˈsɔləm], *adj.* feierlich.

solemnize [ˈsɔləmnaiz], *v.a.* feiern, feierlich begehen.

solicit [səˈlisit], *v.a.* direkt erbitten, angehen, anhalten (*for*, um).

solicitor [səˈlisitə], *s.* (*Law*) der Anwalt, Rechtsanwalt.

solicitous [səˈlisitəs], *adj.* besorgt.

solid [ˈsɔlid], *adj.* fest; solide; (*fig.*) gediegen; massiv (*bulky*).

solidify [səˈlidifai], *v.a.* verdichten, fest machen. — *v.n.* sich verfestigen.

soliloquy [səˈliləkwi], *s.* das Selbstgespräch, der Monolog.

solitaire [sɔliˈtɛə], *s.* der Solitär; (*Am.*) die Patience.

solitary [ˈsɔlitəri], *adj.* einzeln (*single*); einsam (*lonely*).

solitude [ˈsɔlitju:d], *s.* die Einsamkeit.

solstice [ˈsɔlstis], *s.* die Sonnenwende.

soluble [ˈsɔljubl], *adj.* (*Chem.*) löslich; lösbar.

solution [səˈlju:ʃən], *s.* die Lösung.

solvable [ˈsɔlvəbl], *adj.* (auf)lösbar (*problem, puzzle*).

solve [sɔlv], *v.a.* lösen (*problem, puzzle*).

solvent [ˈsɔlvənt], *adj.* (*Chem.*) auflösend; (*Comm.*) zahlungsfähig. — *s.* das Lösungsmittel.

sombre [ˈsɔmbə], *adj.* düster; schwermütig, traurig.

some [sʌm], *adj.* irgend ein, etwas; (*pl.*) einige, manche; etliche.

somebody [ˈsʌmbɔdi], *s.* jemand.

somersault [ˈsʌməsɔ:lt], *s.* der Purzelbaum.

sometimes [ˈsʌmtaimz], *adv.* manchmal, zuweilen.

somewhat [ˈsʌmwɔt], *adv.* etwas, ziemlich.

somewhere [ˈsʌmwɛə], *adv.* irgendwo(hin).

somnambulist [sɔmˈnæmbjulist], s. der Nachtwandler.

somnolent [ˈsɔmnələnt], adj. schläfrig, schlafsüchtig.

son [sʌn], s. der Sohn; —-in-law, der Schwiegersohn.

song [sɔŋ], s. (Mus.) das Lied; der Gesang; for a —, spottbillig.

sonnet [ˈsɔnit], s. (Poet.) das Sonett.

sonorous [ˈsɔnərəs], adj. wohlklingend.

soon [suːn], adv. bald.

sooner [ˈsuːnə], comp. adv. lieber (rather); früher, eher (earlier), no — said than done, gesagt, getan.

soot [sut], s. der Ruß.

soothe [suːð], v.a. besänftigen.

soothsayer [ˈsuːθseiə], s. der Wahrsager.

sop [sɔp], s. der eingetunkte Bissen; (fig.) die Bestechung (bribe).

soporific [sɔpəˈrifik], adj. einschläfernd.

soprano [səˈprɑːnou], s. (Mus.) der Sopran.

sorcerer [ˈsɔːsərə], s. der Zauberer.

sorceress [ˈsɔːsəres], s. die Hexe.

sorcery [ˈsɔːsəri], s. die Zauberei, Hexerei.

sordid [ˈsɔːdid], adj. schmutzig; gemein.

sore [sɔː], adj. wund, schmerzhaft; empfindlich. — s. die wunde Stelle.

sorrel (1) [ˈsɔrəl], s. (Bot.) der Sauerampfer.

sorrel (2) [ˈsɔrəl], s. (Zool.) der Rotfuchs.

sorrow [ˈsɔrou], s. der Kummer, das Leid, der Gram.

sorry [ˈsɔri], adj. traurig; I am —, es tut mir leid.

sort [sɔːt], s. die Art, Gattung, Sorte. — v.a. aussortieren.

sortie [ˈsɔːtiː], s. (Mil.) der Ausfall.

sot [sɔt], s. der Trunkenbold.

soul [soul], s. die Seele; not a —, niemand, keine Menschenseele.

sound (1) [saund], v.n., v.a. tönen, klingen, erklingen lassen. — s. der Klang, Ton, Laut.

sound (2) [saund], adj. gesund; (fig.) vernünftig (plan etc.); solide.

soup [suːp], s. die Suppe.

sour [sauə], adj. sauer; (fig.) mürrisch.

source [sɔːs], s. die Quelle; der Ursprung (origin).

souse [saus], v.a. einpökeln, einsalzen.

south [sauθ], s. der Süden.

South African [sauθ ˈæfrikən], adj. südafrikanisch. — s. der Südafrikaner.

southern [ˈsʌðən], adj. südlich, Süd-.

sou(th)-wester [sau(θ)ˈwestə], s. (Naut.) der Südwester.

souvenir [ˈsuːvəniə], s. das Andenken.

sovereign [ˈsɔvrin], s. der Herrscher (ruler); das Goldstück (£1 coin). — adj. allerhöchst, souverän.

Soviet [ˈsouviit], adj. sowjetisch. — s. der Sowjet.

sow (1) [sau], s. (Zool.) die Sau.

sow (2) [sou], v.a. irr. säen, ausstreuen (cast).

spa [spɑː], s. das Bad; der Kurort.

space [speis], s. der Zwischenraum (interval); der Raum, das Weltall, der Kosmos (interplanetary); der Platz (room). — v.a. sperren, richtig plazieren.

spacious [ˈspeiʃəs], adj. geräumig.

spade [speid], s. der Spaten; call a — a —, das Kind beim rechten Namen nennen; (Cards) das Pik.

span [spæn], s. die Spanne (time); die Spannweite. — v.a. überspannen (bridge); ausmessen.

spangle [spæŋgl], s. der Flitter. — v.a. beflittern, schmücken.

Spaniard [ˈspænjəd], s. der Spanier.

spaniel [ˈspænjəl], s. (Zool.) der Wachtelhund.

Spanish [ˈspæniʃ], adj. spanisch.

spanner [ˈspænə], s. der Schraubenschlüssel.

spar (1) [spɑː], s. (Naut.) der Sparren.

spar (2) [spɑː], s. (Geol.) der Spat.

spar (3) [spɑː], v.n. boxen.

spare [spɛə], v.a. schonen (save); sparsam sein; übrig haben. — v.n. sparen; sparsam sein. — adj. übrig (extra); mager, hager (lean); Reserve– (tyre etc.).

sparing [ˈspɛəriŋ], adj. sparsam, karg.

spark [spɑːk], s. der Funken; (fig.) der helle Kopf.

sparkle [spɑːkl], v.n. glänzen, funkeln. — s. das Funkeln.

sparrow [ˈspærou], s. (Orn.) der Sperling.

sparrowhawk [ˈspærouhɔːk], s. (Orn.) der Sperber.

sparse [spɑːs], adj. spärlich, dünn.

spasm [spæzm], s. der Krampf.

spasmodic [spæzˈmɔdik], adj. krampfhaft; (fig.) ab und zu auftretend.

spats [spæts], s. pl. die Gamaschen, f.pl.

spatter [ˈspætə], v.a. bespritzen, besudeln.

spatula [ˈspætjulə], s. der Spachtel.

spawn [spɔːn], s. der Laich, die Brut.

speak [spiːk], v.a., v.n. irr. sprechen, reden; — out, frei heraussprechen.

speaker [ˈspiːkə], s. der Sprecher.

spear [spiə], s. der Spieß, Speer, die Lanze. — v.a. aufspießen.

special [speʃl], adj. besonder, speziell, Sonder-.

specific [spiˈsifik], adj. spezifisch, eigentümlich.

specify [ˈspesifai], v.a. spezifizieren.

specimen [ˈspesimən], s. die Probe, (Comm.) das Muster.

specious [ˈspiːʃəs], adj. bestechend, trügerisch.

speck [spek], s. der Fleck.

speckle [spekl], s. der Tüpfel, Sprenkel. — v.a. sprenkeln.

spectacle [ˈspektəkl], s. das Schauspiel, der Anblick; (pl.) die Brille.

spectator [spekˈteitə], s. der Zuschauer.

spectre [ˈspektə], s. das Gespenst.

speculate [ˈspekjuleit], v.n. nachsinnen, grübeln (ponder); spekulieren.

speculative

speculative [ˈspekjulətiv], *adj.* spekulativ; sinnend.

speech [spiːtʃ], *s.* die Rede, Ansprache; das Sprechen (*articulation*); *figure of* —, die Redewendung; *make a* —, eine Rede halten.

speechify [ˈspiːtʃifai], *v.n.* viele Worte machen, unermüdlich reden.

speed [spiːd], *s.* die Eile; die Geschwindigkeit (*velocity*); (*Mus.*) das Tempo. — *v.a.* (eilig) fortschicken. — *v.n.* eilen, schnell fahren; — *up*, sich beeilen.

spell (1) [spel], *s.* der Zauber (*enchantment*). — *v.a.* buchstabieren (*verbally*); richtig schreiben (*in writing*).

spell—(2) [spel], *s.* die Zeitlang, Zeit (*period*).

spellbound [ˈspelbaund], *adj.* bezaubert, gebannt.

spend [spend], *v.a.* irr. ausgeben (*money*); verbringen (*time*); aufwenden (*energy*); erschöpfen (*exhaust*).

spendthrift [ˈspendθrift], *s.* der Verschwender.

spew [spjuː], *v.a.* speien; ausspeien.

sphere [sfiə], *s.* die Sphäre (*also fig.*); (*Geom.*) die Kugel.

spice [spais], *s.* die Würze (*seasoning*); das Gewürz (*herb*). — *v.a.* würzen.

spider [ˈspaidə], *s.* (*Zool.*) die Spinne.

spigot [ˈspigət], *s.* (*Mech.*) der Zapfen.

spike [spaik], *s.* die Spitze, der lange Nagel; (*fig.*) der Dorn. — *v.a.* durchbohren, spießen; (*Mil.*) vernageln (*a gun*).

spill (1) [spil], *v.a.* irr. ausschütten, vergießen; (*Am. coll.*) *the beans*, mit der Sprache herausrücken, alles verraten; *it's no good crying over spilt milk*, was geschehen ist, ist geschehen.

spill (2) [spil], *s.* der Fidibus.

spin [spin], *v.a.* irr. spinnen, drehen, wirbeln. — *v.n.* wirbeln, sich schnell drehen; — *dry*, schleudern. — *s.* die schnelle Drehung; — *drier*, die Wäscheschleuder.

spinach [ˈspinidʒ], *s.* (*Bot.*) der Spinat.

spinal [ˈspainəl], *adj.* Rückgrats-.

spine [spain], *s.* (*Anat.*) die Wirbelsäule; der Rücken (*of book*).

spinney [ˈspini], *s.* das Gestrüpp.

spinster [ˈspinstə], *s.* die (alte) Jungfer; die unverheiratete Dame.

spiral [ˈspaiərəl], *adj.* Spiral-, gewunden. — *s.* (*Geom.*) die Spirale.

spirant [ˈspaiərənt], *s.* (*Phonet.*) der Spirant.

spire [spaiə], *s.* (*Archit.*) die Turmspitze.

spirit [ˈspirit], *s.* der Geist; das Gespenst (*ghost*); der Mut (*courage*); die Stimmung, Verfassung (*mood*); die geistige Getränk (*drink*), (*pl.*) Spirituosen, *pl.*; *in high* —*s*, in guter Stimmung, Laune. — *v.a.* — *away*, entführen, verschwinden lassen.

spiritual [ˈspiritjuəl], *adj.* geistig (*mental*); (*Rel.*) geistlich. — *s.* (*Mus.*) das Negerlied.

spit (1) [spit], *s.* der Spieß, Bratspieß. — *v.a.* aufspießen.

spit (2) [spit], *v.n.* irr. ausspucken. — *s.* die Spucke.

spite [spait], *s.* der Groll; *in* — *of*, trotz (*Genit.*). — *v.a.* ärgern.

spiteful [ˈspaitful], *adj.* boshaft.

spittle [spitl], *s.* der Speichel.

spittoon [spiˈtuːn], *s.* der Spucknapf.

splash [splæʃ], *s.* der Spritzer; *make a* —, Aufsehen erregen. — *v.a.*, *v.n.* spritzen; (*fig.*) um sich werfen (*money etc.*).

splay [splei], *v.a.* ausrenken, verrenken.

spleen [spliːn], *s.* (*Anat.*) die Milz; (*fig.*) der Spleen, die Laune, Marotte.

splendour [ˈsplendə], *s.* die Pracht, der Glanz.

splice [splais], *v.a.* splissen; (*Naut.*) — *the mainbrace*, das Hauptfaß öffnen!

splint [splint], *s.* (*Med.*) die Schiene.

splinter [ˈsplintə], *s.* der Span; der Splitter (*fragment*).

split [split], *v.a.* irr. spalten; (*fig.*) verteilen, teilen (*divide*). — *v.n.* sich trennen; (*coll.*) — *on s.o.*, einen verraten. — *s.* — *second timing*, auf den Bruchteil einer Sekunde. — *s.* die Spaltung.

splutter [ˈsplʌtə], *v.n.* sprudeln. — *s.* das Sprudeln.

spoil [spoil], *v.a.* irr. verderben; (*child*) verwöhnen; (*Mil.*) plündern, berauben. — *v.n.* verderben. — *s.* (*pl.*) die Beute.

spoilsport [ˈspoilspoːt], *s.* der Spielverderber.

spoke [spouk], *s.* die Speiche; die Sprosse.

spokesman [ˈspouksmən], *s.* der Wortführer, Sprecher.

sponge [spʌndʒ], *s.* der Schwamm; — *cake*, die Sandtorte. — *v.a.* mit dem Schwamm wischen. — *v.n.* (*coll.*) schmarotzen (*on, bei, Dat.*).

sponger [ˈspʌndʒə], *s.* (*coll.*) der Schmarotzer (*parasite*).

sponsor [ˈsponsə], *s.* der Bürge (*guarantor*); der Förderer; Pate. — *v.a.* fördern, unterstützen.

spontaneous [sponˈteiniəs], *adj.* spontan, freiwillig.

spook [spuːk], *s.* der Spuk, Geist, das Gespenst.

spool [spuːl], *s.* die Spule. — *v.a.* aufspulen.

spoon [spuːn], *s.* der Löffel. — *v.a.* mit dem Löffel essen, löffeln.

sport [spoːt], *s.* der Sport; (*fig.*) der Scherz. — *v.a.* tragen (*wear*). — *v.n.* scherzen.

spot [spot], *s.* die Stelle, der Ort, Platz; (*stain*) der Fleck; (*fig.*) der Schandfleck (*on o.'s honour*); *on the* —, sogleich; auf der Stelle; *in a* —, (*Am. coll.*) in Verlegenheit; — *cash*, Barzahlung, *f.* — *v.a.* entdecken, finden.

spotted [ˈspotid], *adj.* fleckig, gefleckt; befleckt; pickelig.

spouse [spauz], *s.* der Gatte; die Gattin.

spout [spaut], *v.a.*, *v.n.* ausspeien, sprudeln, sprudeln lassen; (*sl.*) predigen, schwatzen. — *s.* die Tülle (*teapot etc.*); die Abflußröhre.

sprain [sprein], *v.a.* (*Med.*) verrenken. — *s.* die Verrenkung.

sprat [spræt], *s.* (*Zool.*) die Sprotte.

sprawl [sprɔ:l], *v.n.* sich spreizen, ausbreiten.

spray [sprei], *v.a.*, *v.n.* sprühen spritzen. — *s.* die Sprühe; der Sprühregen.

spread [spred], *v.a.*, *v.n. irr.* ausbreiten; verbreiten (*get abroad*); streichen (*overlay with*). — *s.* die Ausbreitung; Verbreitung.

spree [spri:], *s.* das Vergnügen, der lustige Abend, Bummel.

sprig [sprig], *s.* der Zweig, Sprößling.

sprightly ['spraitli], *adj.* munter, lebhaft.

spring [spriŋ], *s.* die Quelle (*water*); der Ursprung (*origin*); der Frühling (*season*); (*Mech.*) die Feder, Sprungfeder, Spirale. — *v.n. irr.* springen (*jump*); entspringen (*originate*). — *v.a. — a surprise*, eine Überraschung bereiten.

springe [sprindʒ], *s.* der Sprenkel.

sprinkle ['spriŋkl], *v.a.* (be)sprengen; (*Hort.*) berieseln.

sprint [sprint], *s.* der Kurzstreckenlauf, Wettlauf.

sprite [sprait], *s.* der Geist, Kobold.

sprout [spraut], *s.* (*Bot.*) die Sprosse, der Sprößling; *Brussels —s*, der Rosenkohl.

spruce (1) [spru:s], *adj.* sauber, geputzt, schmuck.

spruce (2) [spru:s], *s.* (*Bot.*) die Fichte, Rottanne.

spume [spju:m], *s.* der Schaum.

spur [spə:], *s.* der Sporn (*goad*); (*fig.*) der Stachel; der Ansporn, Antrieb; (*Geog.*) der Ausläufer (*of range*). — *v.a.* anspornen.

spurious ['spjuəriəs], *adj.* unecht, falsch.

spurn [spə:n], *v.a.* verschmähen, verachten.

spurt [spə:t], *v.a.* spritzen. — *v.n.* sich anstrengen. — *s.* die Anstrengung.

sputter ['spʌtə], *v.a.* herausprudeln. — *v.n.* sprühen, sprudeln.

spy [spai], *s.* der Spion. — *v.n.* spionieren (*on*, bei, *Dat.*).

squabble ['skwɔbl], *v.n.* zanken. — *s.* der Zank, Streit.

squad [skwɔd], *s.* der Trupp.

squadron ['skwɔdrən], *s.* die Schwadron, das Geschwader.

squalid ['skwɔlid], *adj.* schmutzig, elend, eklig.

squall [skwɔ:l], *s.* der Windstoß.

squalor ['skwɔlə], *s.* der Schmutz.

squander ['skwɔndə], *v.a.* verschwenden, vergeuden.

square [skwɛə], *s.* das Quadrat; der Platz; (*coll.*) der Philister, Spießer. — *v.a.* ausrichten; (*coll.*) ins Reine bringen. — *adj.* viereckig; quadratisch; redlich (*honest*), quitt (*quits*).

squash (1) [skwɔʃ], *v.a.* zerquetschen, zerdrücken (*press together*). — *s.* das Gedränge (*crowd*); der Fruchtsaft (*drink*).

squash (2) [skwɔʃ], *s.* (*Sport*) eine Art Racketspiel.

squat [skwɔt], *v.n.* kauern; sich niederlassen. — *adj.* stämmig, untersetzt.

squatter ['skwɔtə], *s.* der Ansiedler.

squaw [skwɔ:], *s.* die Indianerfrau.

squeak [skwi:k], *v.n.* quieken, quietschen. — *s.* das Gequiek.

squeal [skwi:l], *v.n.* quieken; (*Am. coll.*) verraten, preisgeben.

squeamish ['skwi:miʃ], *adj.* empfindlich, zimperlich.

squeeze [skwi:z], *v.a.* drücken, quetschen. — *s.* das Gedränge.

squib [skwib], *s.* der Frosch (*firework*); (*Lit.*) das Spottgedicht.

squint [skwint], *v.n.* schielen. — *s.* das Schielen.

squire [skwaiə], *s.* der Landedelmann, Junker.

squirrel ['skwirəl], *s.* (*Zool.*) das Eichhörnchen.

squirt [skwə:t], *v.a.* spritzen. — *s.* der Spritzer, Wasserstrahl; (*sl.*) der Wichsel.

stab [stæb], *v.a.* erstechen, erdolchen. — *s.* der Dolchstich, Dolchstoß.

stability [stə'biliti], *s.* die Beständigkeit, Stabilität.

stable (1) [steibl], *adj.* fest, beständig; (*Phys.*) stabil.

stable (2) [steibl], *s.* der Stall.

stack [stæk], *s.* der Stoß (*pile*); der Schornstein (*chimneys*). — *v.a.* aufschichten.

staff [stɑ:f], *s.* der Stab, Stock; (*Mil.*) der Stab, Generalstab; (*Sch.*) der Lehrkörper; das Personal. — *v.a.* besetzen.

stag [stæg], *s.* (*Zool.*) der Hirsch; — *party*, die Herrengesellschaft.

stage [steidʒ], *s.* (*Theat.*) die Bühne; die Stufe, das Stadium (*phase*); (*fig.*) der Schauplatz; *fare —*, die Teilstrecke. — *v.a.* (*Theat.*) inszenieren, abhalten (*hold*).

stagecoach ['steidʒkoutʃ], *s.* die Postkutsche.

stagger ['stægə], *v.n.* schwanken, wanken, taumeln. — *v.a.* (*coll.*) verblüffen (*astonish*); staffeln (*graduate*).

stagnate [stæg'neit], *v.n.* stocken, stillstehen.

staid [steid], *adj.* gesetzt, gelassen.

stain [stein], *s.* der Fleck, Makel. — *v.a.* beflecken; beizen; färben (*dye*).

stained [steind], *adj. — glass window*, buntes Fenster.

stainless ['steinlis], *adj.* rostfrei.

stair [stɛə], *s.* die Stufe, Stiege.

staircase ['stɛəkeis], *s.* das Treppenhaus; die Treppe.

stake [steik], *s.* der Pfahl, Pfosten; Scheiterhaufen; (*Gambling*) der Einsatz; *at —*, auf dem Spiel. — *v.a.* aufs Spiel setzen.

stale [steil], *adj.* abgestanden, schal.

stalemate ['steilmeit], *s.* (*Chess*) das Patt; der Stillstand.

stalk (1) [stɔ:k], *s.* (*Bot.*) der Stengel, Halm.

stalk (2) [stɔ:k], *v.n.* stolzieren, steif gehen. — *v.a.* pirschen (*hunt*).

stall [stɔ:l], *s.* die Bude (*booth*), der Stand (*stand*); (*Eccl.*) der Chorstuhl; (*Theat.*) der Sperrsitz; Parterresitz. — *v.n.* (*Motor.*) stehenbleiben.

stallion ['stæljən], *s.* (*Zool.*) der Hengst.

stalwart ['stɔ:lwət], *adj.* kräftig, stark, verläßlich.

stamina ['stæminə], *s.* die Ausdauer, Widerstandskraft.

stammer ['stæmə], *v.n.* stammeln, stottern.

stamp [stæmp], *s.* der Stempel (*rubber* —); die Marke (*postage*); die Stampfe, Stanze (*die* —). — *v.a.* stempeln; (*Mech.*) stanzen; frankieren (*letters*). — *v.n.* stampfen.

stampede [stæm'pi:d], *s.* die wilde Flucht. — *v.n.* in wilder Flucht davonlaufen.

stand [stænd], *v.n. irr.* stehen. — *v.a.* aushalten, standhalten (*Dat.*). — *s.* der Ständer (*hats etc.*); der Stand (*stall*); (*fig.*) die Stellung.

standard ['stændəd], *s.* der Standard (*level*); (*Mil.*) die Standarte; der Maßstab (*yardstick*). — *adj.* normal.

standing ['stændiŋ], *s.* der Rang, das Ansehen. — *adj.* — *orders*, die Geschäftsordnung; (*Mil.*) die Vorschriften, *f. pl.*, Dauerbefehle, *m. pl.*

standpoint ['stændpɔint], *s.* der Standpunkt (*point of view*).

standstill ['stændstil], *s.* der Stillstand.

stanza ['stænzə], *s.* (*Poet.*) die Stanze, Strophe.

staple [steipl], *s.* das Haupterzeugnis; der Stapelplatz. — *adj.* Haupt-. — *v.a.* stapeln; heften (*paper*).

stapler ['steiplə], *s.* die Heftmaschine.

star [stɑ:], *s.* der Stern; (*Theat. etc.*) der Star. — *v.n.* (*Theat. etc.*) die Hauptrolle spielen.

starboard ['stɑ:bəd], *s.* das Steuerbord.

starch [stɑ:tʃ], *s.* die Stärke (*laundry*). — *v.a.* stärken.

stare [stɛə], *v.n.* starren. — *s.* der starre Blick, das Starren.

stark [stɑ:k], *adj.* völlig, ganz.

starling ['stɑ:liŋ], *s.* (*Orn.*) der Star.

start [stɑ:t], *v.n.* anfangen; aufbrechen; auffahren, aufspringen; stutzen (*jerk*); abfahren (*depart*). — *v.a.* starten (*car etc.*), in Gang setzen. — *s.* der Anfang; (*Sport*) der Start, Anlauf; der Aufbruch (*departure*); *by fits and* —s, ruckweise.

starter ['stɑ:tə], *s.* (*Sport*) der Starter, Teilnehmer (*participant*); das Rennpferd (*horse*); (*Motor.*) der Anlasser.

startle ['stɑ:tl], *v.a.* erschrecken.

starve [stɑ:v], *v.n.* verhungern, hungern. — *v.a.* aushungern.

state [steit], *s.* der Zustand, die Lage;

(*Pol.*) der Staat; (*personal*) der Stand (*single etc.*). — *v.a.* erklären, darlegen.

stately ['steitli], *adj.* stattlich, prachtvoll.

statement ['steitmənt], *s.* die Feststellung; *bank* —, der Kontoauszug.

statesman ['steitsmən], *s.* der Staatsmann, Politiker.

statics ['stætiks], *s.* die Statik.

station ['steiʃən], *s.* (*Railw.*) die Station; der Bahnhof; die Stellung, der Rang (*position*); (*Mil.*) die Stationierung. — *v.a.* (*Mil.*) aufstellen, stationieren; (*fig.*) hinstellen.

stationary ['steiʃənri], *adj.* stationär, stillstehend.

stationer ['steiʃənə], *s.* der Papierhändler.

stationery ['steiʃənri], *s.* das Briefpapier, Schreibpapier; die Papierwaren, *f. pl.*

statuary ['stætjuəri], *s.* die Bildhauerkunst.

statue ['stætju:], *s.* das Standbild.

status ['steitəs], *s.* die Stellung (*rank, position*).

statute ['stætju:t], *s.* das Statut; — *law*, das Landesrecht, Gesetzesrecht.

staunch [stɔ:ntʃ], *adj.* zuverlässig.

stave [steiv], *s.* die Faßdaube (*of vat*); (*Poet.*) die Strophe; (*Mus.*) die Linie. — *v.a.* — *off*, abwehren.

stay [stei], *v.n.* bleiben, verweilen, wohnen. — *v.a.* hindern, aufhalten. — *s.* der Aufenthalt; (*pl.*) das Korsett.

stead [sted], *s.* die Stelle; *in his* —, an seiner Statt.

steadfast ['stedfɑ:st], *adj.* standhaft, fest.

steadiness ['stedinis], *s.* die Beständigkeit.

steady ['stedi], *adj.* fest, sicher; beständig, treu.

steak [steik], *s.* das Steak.

steal [sti:l], *v.a. irr.* stehlen. — *v.n.* sich stehlen, schleichen.

stealth [stelθ], *s.* die Heimlichkeit.

stealthy ['stelθi], *adj.* heimlich, verstohlen.

steam [sti:m], *s.* der Dampf; *get up* —, in Gang bringen *or* kommen; — *boiler*, der Dampfkessel. — *v.n.* dampfen; davondampfen. — *v.a.* dämpfen, (*Cul.*) dünsten.

steed [sti:d], *s.* das Schlachtroß.

steel [sti:l], *s.* der Stahl. — *adj.* stählern. — *v.n.* — *o.s.*, sich stählen.

steep (1) [sti:p], *adj.* steil; (*fig.*) hoch; (*coll.*) gesalzen (*price*).

steep (2) [sti:p], *v.a.* einweichen, sättigen.

steeple [sti:pl], *s.* (*Archit.*) der Kirchturm.

steeplechase ['sti:pltʃeis], *s.* das Hindernisrennen.

steeplejack ['sti:pldʒæk], *s.* der Turmdecker.

steer (1) [stiə], *s.* (*Zool.*) der junge Stier.

steer (2) [stiə], *v.a.* steuern (*guide*).

steerage ['stiəridʒ], *s.* die Steuerung; (*Naut.*) das Zwischendeck.

stellar ['stelə], *adj.* Stern-, Sternen-.

stem (1) [stem], *s.* der Stamm; *(Phonet.)* der Stamm; der Stiel, die Wurzel. — *v.n.* — *from*, kommen von, abstammen.

stem (2) [stem], *v.a.* sich entgegenstemmen *(Dat.)*; *(fig.)* eindämmen.

stench [stentʃ], *s.* der Gestank.

stencil ['stensil], *s.* die Schablone, Matrize; *cut a* —, auf Matrize schreiben.

step [step], *s.* der Schritt, Tritt; *(of ladder)* die Sprosse; *(of stairs)* die Stufe. — *v.n.* treten, schreiten *(stride).* — *v.a. (coll.)* — *up*, beschleunigen.

step- [step], *pref.* Stief- *(brother, mother etc.).*

stereo- ['stiəriou], *pref.* Stereo-.

sterile ['sterail], *adj.* steril.

sterling ['stə:liŋ], *adj.* echt, vollwertig; *pound* —, ein Pfund Sterling.

stern (1) [stə:n], *adj.* streng.

stern (2) [stə:n], *s. (Naut.)* das Heck.

stevedore ['sti:vədɔ:], *s.* der Hafenarbeiter.

stew [stju:], *s. (Cul.)* das Schmorfleisch, das Gulasch.

steward ['stju:əd], *s.* der Verwalter; der Haushofmeister; *(Naut.)* der Steward.

stick [stik], *s.* der Stock, Stecken. — *v.a.* stecken *(insert)*; kleben *(glue).* — *v.n.* stecken, haften bleiben; *(fig., coll.)* — *to s.o.*, zu jemandem halten *(be loyal).*

sticky ['stiki], *adj.* klebrig; *(fig.)* prekär, schwierig *(difficult); come to a* — *end*, ein böses Ende nehmen.

stiff [stif], *adj.* steif; schwer, schwierig *(examination)*; formell *(manner).*

stiffen [stifn], *v.a.* steifen, versteifen. — *v.n.* steif werden, sich versteifen.

stifle [staifl], *v.a., v.n.* ersticken; *(fig.)* unterdrücken.

stigmatize ['stigmətaiz], *v.a.* stigmatisieren, brandmarken.

stile [stail], *s.* der Zauntritt, Übergang.

still (1) [stil], *adj.* still, ruhig. — *adv.* immer noch. — *conj.* doch, dennoch. — *v.a.* stillen, beruhigen.

still (2) [stil], *s.* die Destillierflasche, der Destillierkolben.

stilt [stilt], *s.* die Stelze.

stilted ['stiltid], *adj.* auf Stelzen; *(fig.)* hochtrabend, geschraubt.

stimulant ['stimjulənt], *s.* das Reizmittel. — *adj.* anreizend, anregend.

stimulate ['stimjuleit], *v.a.* anreizen, stimulieren, anregen.

stimulus ['stimjuləs], *s.* der Reiz, die Anregung.

sting [stiŋ], *v.a. irr.* stechen; *(fig.)* kränken, verwunden. — *v.n. irr.* stechen, brennen, schmerzen. — *s.* der Stachel *(prick)*; der Stich *(stab).*

stink [stiŋk], *v.n. irr.* stinken. — *s.* der Gestank.

stint [stint], *s.* die Einschränkung *(limit)*; das Maß, Tagespensum. — *v.a.* beschränken, einschränken.

stipend ['staipend], *s.* die Besoldung, das Gehalt.

stipendiary [stai'pendiəri], *adj.* besoldet, bezahlt.

stipulate ['stipjuleit], *v.a.* festsetzen, ausbedingen.

stir [stə:], *v.a.* rühren, bewegen. — *v.n.* sich rühren. — *s.* die Aufregung; *cause a* —, Aufsehen erregen.

stirrup ['stirəp], *s.* der Steigbügel.

stitch [stitʃ], *v.a.* sticken, nähen. — *s.* der Stich; der stechende Schmerz, der Seitenstich *(pain).*

stoat [stout], *s. (Zool.)* das Hermelin.

stock [stɔk], *s.* das Lager; *in* —, auf Lager; vorrätig; der Stamm, die Familie; *(Fin.)* das Kapital; — *exchange*, die Börse; *(pl.)* die Börsenpapiere, *n. pl.*, Aktien, *f. pl.* — *v.a.* halten, führen.

stockade [stɔ'keid], *s.* das Staket.

stockbroker ['stɔkbroukə], *s. (Fin.)* der Börsenmakler.

stockholder ['stɔkhouldə], *s. (Fin., Am.)* der Aktionär.

stocking ['stɔkiŋ], *s.* der Strumpf.

stocktaking ['stɔkteikiŋ], *s.* die Inventuraufnahme.

stoical ['stouikəl], *adj.* stoisch.

stoke [stouk], *v.a.* schüren.

stoker ['stoukə], *s.* der Heizer.

stole [stoul], *s. (Eccl.)* die Stola; der Pelzkragen *(fur).*

stolid ['stɔlid], *adj.* schwerfällig, gleichgültig.

stomach ['stʌmək], *s.* der Magen; *(fig.)* der Appetit.

stone [stoun], *s.* der Stein; der Kern *(fruit).* — *v.a.* steinigen *(throw* —*at)*; entsteinen *(fruit).*

stony ['stouni], *adj.* steinig; *(sl.)* — *broke*, pleite.

stool [stu:l], *s.* der Schemel, Hocker; *(Med.)* der Stuhlgang.

stoop [stu:p], *v.n.* sich bücken; *(fig.)* sich herablassen.

stooping ['stu:piŋ], *adj.* gebückt.

stop [stɔp], *v.a.* halten, stoppen; aufhören; aufhalten *(halt).* — *up*, verstopfen, versperren *(block)*; *(tooth)* plombieren. — *v.n.* stehen bleiben *(stand)*; sich aufhalten *(stay).* — *s.* der Halt, die Haltestelle *(of bus etc.)*; das Aufhalten, Innehalten *(stoppage)*; das Register *(organ)*; *(Gram.)* der Punkt.

stoppage ['stɔpidʒ], *s.* die Stockung, Hemmung *(hindrance)*; die Arbeitseinstellung *(strike).*

stopper ['stɔpə], *s.* der Stöpsel.

storage ['stɔ:ridʒ], *s.* das Lagern.

store [stɔ:], *s.* der Vorrat, das Lagerhaus, Magazin; *(Am.)* das Kaufhaus; *(fig.)* die Menge *(of anecdotes etc.).* — *v.a.* lagern.

storey ['stɔ:ri], *s.* das Stockwerk.

stork [stɔ:k], *s. (Orn.)* der Storch.

storm [stɔ:m], *s.* der Sturm, das Gewitter.

story ['stɔ:ri], *s.* die Geschichte, Erzählung *(narrative).*

stout [staut], *adj.* fest; stark, kräftig. — *s.* das starke Bier.

stove [stouv], *s.* der Ofen.

stow [stou], *v.a.* verstauen, packen. — *v.n.* — *away*, als blinder Passagier fahren.

stowaway ['stouǝwei], *s.* der blinde Passagier.

straddle [strædl], *v.n.* rittlings sitzen.

straggle [strægl], *v.n.* umherschweifen, streifen; (*Bot.*) wuchern.

straight [streit], *adj.* gerade, offen. — *adv.* — *away*, sofort, sogleich.

straighten [streitn], *v.a.* ausrichten, gerade richten. — *v.n.* sich ausrichten.

strain [strein], *s.* die Anstrengung, Anspannung; (*Mus.*) der Ton, Stil; der Hang. — *v.a.* anstrengen, filtrieren; seihen. — *v.n.* sich anstrengen.

strainer ['streinǝ], *s.* der Seiher, der Filter, das Sieb.

strait [streit], *adj.* eng. — *s.* (*usually pl.*) die Enge, Meerenge.

strand (1) [strænd], *s.* der Strand.

strand (2) [strænd], *s.* die Litze (*of rope, string*).

strange [streindʒ], *adj.* fremd (*unknown*); seltsam (*queer*).

stranger ['streindʒǝ], *s.* der Fremdling, Fremde; der Unbekannte.

strangle [stræŋgl], *v.a.* erdrosseln, erwürgen.

strangulation [stræŋgju'leiʃǝn], *s.* die Erdrosselung, Erwürgung.

strap [stræp], *v.a.* festschnallen, anschnallen. — *s.* der Gurt, Riemen.

strapping ['stræpiŋ], *adj.* stark, stämmig.

strata *see under* stratum.

stratagem ['strætǝdʒǝm], *s.* die List; (*Mil.*) der Plan.

strategy ['strætǝdʒi], *s.* die Strategie.

stratification [strætifi'keiʃǝn], *s.* die Schichtung; (*Geol.*) die Lagerung.

stratum ['streitǝm], *s.* (*pl.* **strata** ['streitǝ]) die Schicht, Lage.

straw [strɔ:], *s.* das Stroh; *that's the last* —, das ist die Höhe!

strawberry ['strɔ:bǝri], *s.* (*Bot.*) die Erdbeere.

stray [strei], *v.n.* irregehen, schweifen; sich verirren. — *adj.* irr, verirrt.

streak [stri:k], *s.* der Strich, der Streifen; (*fig.*) der Anflug.

streaky ['stri:ki], *adj.* gestreift; (*bacon*) durchwachsen.

stream [stri:m], *v.n.* strömen, wehen (*in the wind*). — *s.* die Strömung (*flow*); der Bach (*brook*), der Strom (*river*).

streamer ['stri:mǝ], *s.* der Wimpel, das Band, die Papierschlange.

street [stri:t], *s.* die Straße; —*s ahead*, weit voraus.

streetcar ['stri:tka:], *s.* (*Am.*) *see* tram.

streetlamp ['stri:tlæmp], *s.* die Straßenlaterne.

strength [streŋθ], *s.* die Stärke; die Kraft.

strengthen ['streŋθǝn], *v.a.* stärken; (*fig.*) bekräftigen (*support*).

strenuous ['strenjuǝs], *adj.* anstrengend.

stress [stres], *v.a.* (*Phonet.*) betonen; (*fig.*) hervorheben. — *s.* die Betonung (*emphasis*); der Druck (*pressure*).

stretch [stretʃ], *v.a.* spannen; strecken, ausstrecken; — *a point*, eine Ausnahme machen. — *s.* die Strecke (*distance*); (*coll.*) die Zuchthausstrafe (*penal sentence*).

stretcher ['stretʃǝ], *s.* die Tragbahre.

strew [stru:], *v.a.* streuen, ausstreuen.

strict [strikt], *adj.* streng (*severe*); genau (*exact*).

stricture ['striktʃǝ], *s.* der Tadel, die Kritik; (*pl.*) die kritische Rede.

stride [straid], *v.n.* *irr.* schreiten. — *s.* der Schritt; *take in o.'s* —, leicht bewältigen.

strident ['straidǝnt], *adj.* laut, lärmend, grell.

strife [straif], *s.* der Streit, Zank.

strike [straik], *v.a.*, *v.n.* *irr.* schlagen; abmachen (*bargain*); (*Mus.*) — *up*, anstimmen (*song*), aufspielen (*instrument*); beginnen; — *the eye*, auffallen; streiken, in Streik treten. — *s.* der Streik, die Arbeitseinstellung.

striking ['straikiŋ], *adj.* auffallend.

string [striŋ], *s.* die Schnur; (*Mus.*) die Saite; — *quartet*, das Streichquartett; die Reihe (*series*). — *v.a.* anreihen (*beads etc.*); — *together*, verbinden. — *v.n.* — *along*, sich anschließen.

stringency ['strindʒǝnsi], *s.* die Strenge (*severity*); die Knappheit (*shortage*).

stringent ['strindʒǝnt], *adj.* streng (*severe*); knapp (*short*).

strip [strip], *s.* der Streifen. — *v.a.*, *v.n.* abstreifen, (sich) entkleiden; (sich) entblößen.

stripe [straip], *s.* der (Farb)streifen; die Strieme (*mark on body*). — *v.a.* streifen, bestreifen.

strive [straiv], *v.n.* *irr.* sich bemühen (*for*, um, *Acc.*), streben (*for*, nach, *Dat.*).

stroke (1) [strouk], *v.a.* streicheln.

stroke (2) [strouk], *s.* der Strich (*brush*); der Streich (*sword*); der Stoß (*blow*); (*Med.*) der Schlaganfall.

stroll [stroul], *v.n.* schlendern.

strolling ['strouliŋ], *adj.* — *players*, die Wandertruppe.

strong [strɔŋ], *adj.* stark.

strongbox ['strɔŋbɔks], *s.* die Geldkassette.

strongroom ['strɔŋrum], *s.* der Geldtresor.

strop [strɔp], *s.* der Streichriemen.

structure ['straktʃǝ], *s.* der Bau, Aufbau; die Struktur.

struggle [stragl], *s.* der Kampf, das Ringen. — *v.n.* kämpfen, ringen.

strut [strat], *v.n.* stolzieren.

stub [stab], *s.* der Stumpf, Stummel (*cigarette*). — *v.a.* — *out*, ausmachen, auslöschen (*cigarette etc.*).

stubble [stʌbl], s. die Stoppel, das Stoppelfeld; die (Bart)stoppeln, *f. pl.* (*beard*).

stubborn ['stʌbən], *adj.* eigensinnig, hartnäckig.

stucco ['stʌkou], s. die Stuckarbeit.

stud (1) [stʌd], s. der Hemdenknopf, Kragenknopf (*collar* —). — *v.a.* beschlagen (*nail*); besetzen (*bejewel*).

stud (2) [stʌd], s. das Gestüt (*horses*).

student ['stjuːdənt], s. der Student.

studied ['stʌdid], *adj.* geziert, absichtlich (*deliberate*); gelehrt (*learned*).

studio ['stjuːdiou], s. (*Phot.*) das Atelier; (*Film, Rad.*) das Studio.

studious ['stjuːdiəs], *adj.* beflissen, fleißig; lernbegierig.

study ['stʌdi], *v.a., v.n.* studieren. — s. das Studium; das Arbeitszimmer (*room*); (*Mus. etc.*) die Studie; (*Art*) der Entwurf; die Untersuchung (*investigation*).

stuff [stʌf], s. der Stoff, das Material; (*coll.*) das Zeug (*rubbish*). — *v.a.* stopfen, ausstopfen (*animals*); (*Cul.*) füllen.

stuffing ['stʌfiŋ], s. die Füllung, das Füllsel.

stultify ['stʌltifai], *v.a.* dumm machen.

stumble [stʌmbl], *v.n.* stolpern; — *upon*, zufällig stoßen (auf, *Acc.*).

stumbling ['stʌmbliŋ], s. das Stolpern; — *block*, das Hindernis, der Stein des Anstoßes.

stump [stʌmp], s. der Stumpf. — *v.a.* verblüffen; abstumpfen. — *v.n.* schwerfällig gehen.

stun [stʌn], *v.a.* betäuben, verdutzen.

stunning ['stʌniŋ], *adj.* betörend, fabelhaft, überwältigend.

stunt (1) [stʌnt], *v.a.* am Wachstum behindern, klein halten.

stunt (2) [stʌnt], s. der Trick, das Kunststück; (*Aviat.*) der Kunstflug.

stupefy ['stjuːpifai], *v.a.* betäuben.

stupendous [stjuːˈpendəs], *adj.* erstaunlich.

stupid ['stjuːpid], *adj.* dumm.

stupor ['stjuːpə], s. die Erstarrung, Lähmung (*of mind*).

sturdy ['stəːdi], *adj.* derb, stark, stämmig.

sturgeon ['stəːdʒən], s. (*Zool.*) der Stör.

stutter ['stʌtə], *v.n.* stottern.

sty [stai], s. der Schweinestall.

sty(e) [stai], s. (*Med.*) das Gerstenkorn (*on eyelid*).

style [stail], s. (*Lit.*) der Stil; der Griffel (*stylus*); die Mode (*fashion*); die Anrede (*address*). — *v.a.* anreden.

stylish ['stailiʃ], *adj.* elegant, modern.

suave [sweiv, swɑːv], *adj.* höflich, gewinnend.

sub- [sʌb], *pref.* Unter-.

subaltern ['sʌbəltən], s. (*Mil.*) der Leutnant, Oberleutnant.

subject ['sʌbdʒikt], s. (*Gram.*) das Subjekt; (*Pol.*) der Untertan; der Gegenstand. — *adj.* untertan (*to,*

Dat.); — *to*, abhängig von. — [səbˈdʒekt], *v.a.* unterwerfen (*to, Dat.*); aussetzen (*Dat.*).

subjunctive [səbˈdʒʌŋktiv], s. (*Gram.*) der Konjunktiv.

sublet [sʌbˈlet], *v.a.* in Untermiete vermieten, untervermieten.

sublimate ['sʌblimeit], *v.a.* sublimieren.

submarine ['sʌbməriːn], s. das Unterseeboot.

submission [səbˈmiʃən], s. die Unterwerfung (*subjection*); der Vorschlag (*suggestion*).

submit [səbˈmit], *v.a.* unterwerfen (*subjugate*); vorlegen. — *v.n.* sich beugen (*to, Dat.*).

suborn [sʌˈbɔːn], *v.a.* anstiften; bestechen (*corrupt*).

subpoena [sʌbˈpiːnə], s. (*Law*) die Vorladung.

subscribe [səbˈskraib], *v.a.* unterschreiben. — *v.n.* zeichnen (*to,* zu); abonnieren (*paper*).

subscription [səbˈskripʃən], s. das Abonnement (*to, Genit.*); (*club*) der Beitrag.

subsequent ['sʌbsikwənt], *adj.* folgend.

subservient [sʌbˈsəːviənt], *adj.* unterwürfig.

subside [səbˈsaid], *v.n.* sinken; abnehmen (*decrease*).

subsidence [sʌbˈsaidəns, 'sʌbsidəns], s. das Sinken, Sichsetzen.

subsidiary [sʌbˈsidjəri], *adj.* Hilfs-, Neben-.

subsidize ['sʌbsidaiz], *v.a.* unterstützen (*with money*), subventionieren.

subsidy ['sʌbsidi], s. die Unterstützung, Subvention.

subsist [səbˈsist], *v.n.* leben, existieren.

subsistence [səbˈsistəns], s. das Dasein, Auskommen; der Lebensunterhalt.

substance ['sʌbstəns], s. das Wesen, der Stoff, die Substanz.

substantial [səbˈstænʃəl], *adj.* wesentlich, beträchtlich.

substantiate [səbˈstænʃieit], *v.a.* dartun, nachweisen, bestätigen.

substantive ['sʌbstəntiv], s. (*Gram.*) das Substantiv, Hauptwort. — *adj.* (*Mil.*) effektiv, wirklich.

substitute ['sʌbstitjuːt], *v.a.* ersetzen, an die Stelle setzen. — s. der Ersatzmann, Vertreter.

subterfuge ['sʌbtəfjuːdʒ], s. die Ausflucht.

subtle [sʌtl], *adj.* fein, schlau, subtil.

subtract [səbˈtrækt], *v.a.* abziehen; (*Maths.*) subtrahieren.

suburb ['sʌbəːb], s. die Vorstadt, der Vorort.

subversion [səbˈvəːʃən], s. (*Pol.*) der Umsturz.

subversive [səbˈvəːsiv], *adj.* umstürzlerisch, umstürzend.

subway ['sʌbwei], s. die Unterführung; (*Am.*) die Untergrundbahn.

succeed [səkˈsiːd], *v.n.* erfolgreich sein, Erfolg haben. — *v.a.* nachfolgen (*Dat.*) (*follow*).

success [sǝk'ses], s. der Erfolg.
successful [sǝk'sesful], adj. erfolgreich.
succession [sǝk'sefǝn], s. die Nachfolge.
successive [sǝk'sesiv], adj. der Reihe nach, aufeinanderfolgend.
succinct [sǝk'siŋkt], adj. bündig, kurz.
succour ['sʌkǝ], v.a. beistehen (Dat.), helfen (Dat.).
succulent ['sʌkjulǝnt], adj. saftig.
succumb [sǝ'kʌm], v.n. unterliegen (to, Dat.).
such [sʌtʃ], adj. solch, derartig. — pron. ein solcher; — as, diejenigen, alle die.
suchlike ['sʌtʃlaik], pron. (coll.) dergleichen.
suck [sʌk], v.a., v.n. saugen.
suckle ['sʌkl], v.a. säugen, stillen.
suction ['sʌkʃǝn], s. das Saugen; (Engin.) Saug-.
Sudanese [su:dǝ'ni:z], adj. sudanisch, sudanesisch. — s. der Sudan(es)er.
sudden [sʌdn], adj. plötzlich.
suds [sʌdz], s. pl. das Seifenwasser.
sue [sju:], v.a. gerichtlich belangen, verklagen.
suède [sweid], s. das Wildleder.
suet ['su:it], s. das Nierenfett.
suffer ['sʌfǝ], v.a. ertragen, dulden. — v.n. leiden (from, an).
sufferance ['sʌfǝrǝns], s. die Duldung; on —, nur widerwillig.
suffice [sǝ'fais], v.n. genügen, langen, (aus)reichen.
sufficient [sǝ'fiʃǝnt], adj. genügend, hinreichend.
suffocate ['sʌfǝkeit], v.a., v.n. ersticken.
suffragan ['sʌfrǝgǝn], s. (Eccl.) der Weihbischof.
suffrage ['sʌfridʒ], s. das Wahlrecht, Stimmrecht.
suffuse [sǝ'fju:z], v.a. übergießen, überfließen.
sugar ['ʃugǝ], s. der Zucker; — basin, die Zuckerdose.
suggest [sǝ'dʒest], v.a. vorschlagen, anregen.
suggestion [sǝ'dʒestʃǝn], s. der Vorschlag.
suggestive [sǝ'dʒestiv], adj. zweideutig.
suicide ['sju:isaid], s. der Selbstmord, Freitod.
suit [su:t], s. das Gesuch, die Bitte (request); die Farbe (cards); (Law) der Prozeß; der Anzug (clothes). — v.n. passen (Dat.) (be convenient to); passen zu (look well with). — v.a. anpassen (match).
suitcase ['su:tkeis], s. der Handkoffer.
suitable ['su:tǝbl], adj. passend.
suite [swi:t], s. das Gefolge (following); die Zimmerflucht (rooms); die Reihe (cards).
suitor ['su:tǝ], s. der Brautwerber, Freier.
sulk [sʌlk], v.n. schmollen.
sullen ['sʌlǝn], adj. düster, mürrisch.
sully ['sʌli], v.a. beschmutzen.
sulphur ['sʌlfǝ], s. (Chem.) der Schwefel.

Sultan ['sʌltǝn], s. der Sultan.
Sultana [sʌl'tɑ:nǝ], s. die Sultanin.
sultana [sʌl'tɑ:nǝ], s. (Bot.) die Sultanine.
sultry ['sʌltri], adj. schwül.
sum [sʌm], s. die Summe; (fig.) der Inbegriff. — v.a., v.n. — up, zusammenfassen.
summary ['sʌmǝri], s. die Zusammenfassung, der Auszug. — adj. summarisch.
summer ['sʌmǝ], s. der Sommer; Indian —, der Spätsommer, Altweibersommer, Nachsommer.
summit ['sʌmit], s. der Gipfel, die Spitze.
summon(s) ['sʌmǝn(z)], v.a. (Law) vorladen. — s. (**summons**) die Vorladung.
sump [sʌmp], s. (Motor.) die Ölwanne.
sumptuous ['sʌmptjuǝs], adj. prächtig, mit Aufwand, kostbar.
sun [sʌn], s. die Sonne. — v.r. sich sonnen.
sunburn ['sʌnbǝ:n], s. der Sonnenbrand.
Sunday ['sʌnd(e)i]. der Sonntag.
sundial ['sʌndaiǝl], s. die Sonnenuhr.
sundown ['sʌndaun] see **sunset**.
sundry ['sʌndri], adj. mehrere, verschiedene. — s. (pl.) Gemischtwaren, f. pl.
sunny ['sʌni], adj. sonnig.
sunrise ['sʌnraiz], s. der Sonnenaufgang.
sunset ['sʌnset], s. der Sonnenuntergang.
sunshade ['sʌnʃeid], s. das Sonnendach, der Sonnenschirm (parasol).
super ['su:pǝ], s. (Theat.) der Statist. — adj. (coll.) fein, famos.
super- ['su:pǝ], pref. über-, hinzu-.
superannuation [su:pǝrænju'eiʃǝn], s. die Pensionierung.
superb [su'pǝ:b], adj. hervorragend, herrlich.
supercilious [su:pǝ'siliǝs], adj. hochmütig, anmaßend.
superficial [su:pǝ'fiʃǝl], adj. oberflächlich.
superfluous [su:'pǝ:fluǝs], adj. überflüssig.
superintendent [su:pǝrin'tendǝnt], s. der Oberaufseher.
superior [su:'piǝriǝ], adj. ober, höher. — s. der Vorgesetzte.
superiority [su:piǝri'ɔriti], s. die Überlegenheit.
superlative [su:'pǝ:lǝtiv], s. (Gram.) der Superlativ. — adj. ausnehmend gut.
supermarket ['su:pǝmɑ:kit], s. das Selbstbedienungsgeschäft, SB-Geschäft, der grosse Lebensmittelladen.
supersede [su:pǝ'si:d], v.a. verdrängen.
superstition [su:pǝ'stiʃǝn], s. der Aberglaube.
superstitious [su:pǝ'stiʃǝs], adj. abergläubisch.
supervise ['su:pǝvaiz], v.a. beaufsichtigen, überwachen.

supine [su'pain], *adj.* auf dem Rücken liegend. — ['su:pain], *s.* (*Gram.*) das Supinum.

supper ['sʌpə], *s.* das Abendessen; *Last Supper*, das Heilige Abendmahl.

supplant [sə'plɑ:nt], *v.a.* verdrängen.

supple [sʌpl], *adj.* geschmeidig, biegsam.

supplement ['sʌplimənt], *s.* die Beilage (*paper*); der Zusatz.

supplementary [sʌpli'mentri], *adj.* zusätzlich.

supplier [sə'plaiə], *s.* der Lieferant.

supply [sə'plai], *v.a.* liefern (*s. th.*); beliefern, versorgen (*s.o.*). — *s.* die Versorgung.

support [sə'pɔ:t], *v.a.* unterstützen. — *s.* die Stütze (*prop*); die Unterstützung (*financial aid*).

suppose [sə'pouz], *v.a.* annehmen, vermuten.

supposition [sʌpə'ziʃən], *s.* die Annahme, Vermutung, Voraussetzung.

suppress [sə'pres], *v.a.* unterdrücken.

suppurate ['sʌpjureit], *v.n.* eitern.

supremacy [su'preməsi], *s.* die Überlegenheit (*pre-eminence*); Obergewalt (*power*).

supreme [su'pri:m], *adj.* höchst, oberst.

surcharge [sə'tʃɑ:dʒ], *s.* die Sonderzahlung, der Aufschlag, Zuschlag.

sure [ʃuə], *adj.* sicher; *to be* —, sicherlich; *make* —, sich überzeugen.

surety ['ʃuəti], *s.* (*Law*) die Kaution.

surf [sə:f], *s.* die Brandung.

surface ['sə:fis], *s.* die Oberfläche.

surfeit [sə:fit], *s.* die Übersättigung, das Übermaß. — *v.a.* übersättigen.

surge [sə:dʒ], *v.n.* wogen, rauschen. — *s.* die Woge, das Aufwallen.

surgeon ['sə:dʒən], *s.* (*Med.*) der Chirurg.

surgery ['sə:dʒəri], *s.* (*Med.*) die Chirurgie (*subject*); — *hours*, die Sprechstunde.

surgical ['sə:dʒikəl], *adj.* chirurgisch.

surly ['sə:li], *adj.* mürrisch.

surmise [sə:'maiz], *v.a.* mutmaßen, vermuten. — *s.* die Mutmaßung, Vermutung.

surmount [sə:'maunt], *v.a.* übersteigen; überwinden (*overcome*).

surname ['sə:neim], *s.* der Zuname.

surpass [sə:'pɑ:s], *v.a.* übertreffen.

surplice ['sə:plis], *s.* das Chorhemd.

surplus ['sə:pləs], *s.* der Überfluß.

surprise [sə'praiz], *s.* die Überraschung. — *v.a.* überraschen.

surrender [sə'rendə], *v.a.* übergeben, aufgeben. — *v.n.* sich ergeben. — *s.* die Waffenstreckung, Kapitulation.

surreptitious [sʌrəp'tiʃəs], *adj.* heimlich.

surround [sə'raund], *v.a.* umgeben, einschließen.

surroundings [sə'raundiŋz], *s. pl.* die Umgegend, Umgebung.

survey [sə'vei], *s.* die Übersicht (*of*), die Vermessung. — [sə'vei], *v.a.* überblicken; vermessen.

surveyor [sə'veiə], *s.* der Vermesser, Feldmesser.

survival [sə'vaivəl], *s.* das Überleben.

survive [sə'vaiv], *v.a.*, *v.n.* überleben, überstehen.

susceptibility [səsepti'biliti], *s.* die Empfänglichkeit.

susceptible [sə'septibl], *adj.* empfänglich, empfindlich.

suspect [səs'pekt], *v.a.* verdächtigen. — ['sʌspekt], *adj.* verdächtig. — *s.* die Verdachtsperson, der Verdächtige.

suspend [səs'pend], *v.a.* aufhängen; unterbrechen (*procedure*); einstellen (*work*).

suspense [səs'pens], *s.* die Spannung (*tension*); Ungewißheit (*uncertainty*).

suspension [səs'penʃən], *s.* (*Law*) die Suspension; die Einstellung (*stoppage*); die Aufhängung, Suspension; (*Motor.*) die Federung; — *bridge*, die Kettenbrücke, Hängebrücke.

suspicion [səs'piʃən], *s.* der Verdacht, Argwohn.

suspicious [səs'piʃəs], *adj.* verdächtig; argwöhnisch.

sustain [səs'tein], *v.a.* erleiden (*suffer*); ertragen (*bear*); aufrechterhalten (*maintain*).

sustenance ['sʌstinəns], *s.* der Unterhalt (*maintenance*); die Nahrung (*food*).

suture ['sju:tʃə], *s.* (*Med.*) die Naht.

suzerain ['sju:zərein], *s.* der Oberherr, Oberlehnsherr.

swab [swɒb], *s.* (*Med.*) die Laborprobe, der Abstrich; der Schrubber (*scrubber*). — *v.a.* (*Med.*) eine Probe entnehmen; schrubben (*scrub*).

swaddle [swɒdl], *s.* die Windel.

swaddling ['swɒdliŋ], *adj.* — *clothes*, die Windeln, *f. pl.*

swagger ['swægə], *v.n.* großtun. — *s.* das Großtun, Renommieren.

swallow (1) ['swɒlou], *s.* (*Orn.*) die Schwalbe.

swallow (2) ['swɒlou], *v.a.* schlucken; verschlingen (*devour*).

swamp [swɒmp], *s.* der Sumpf. — *v.a.* versenken (*fig.*) überschütten.

swan [swɒn], *s.* (*Orn.*) der Schwan.

swank [swæŋk], *v.n.* großtun, angeben, aufschneiden. — *s.* der Großtuer.

swap, **swop** [swɒp], *v.a.* eintauschen, tauschen. — *v.n.* tauschen. — *s.* der Tausch.

sward [swɔ:d], *s.* (*Poet.*) der Rasen.

swarm [swɔ:m], *v.n.* schwärmen. — *s.* der Schwarm.

swarthy ['swɔ:ði], *adj.* dunkel, dunkelbraun.

swashbuckler ['swɒʃbʌklə], *s.* der Aufschneider, Angeber, Renommist.

swastika ['swɒstikə], *s.* das Hakenkreuz.

swathe [sweið], *v.a.* einhüllen, einwickeln.

sway [swei], *v.a.* schwenken; beeinflußen. — *v.n.* schwanken, sich schwingen. — *s.* der Einfluß, die Macht.

swear [swɛə], *v.a.*, *v.n. irr.* schwören (*an oath*); fluchen (*curse*).

sweat [swet], *v.n.* schwitzen. — *s.* der Schweiß.

Swede [swi:d], *s.* der Schwede.

Swedish ['swi:diʃ], *adj.* schwedisch.

sweep [swi:p], *v.a.*, *v.n. irr.* fegen, kehren; *a new broom —s clean*, neue Besen kehren gut. — *s.* der Schornsteinfeger (*chimney —*).

sweet [swi:t], *adj.* süß. — *s.* der Nachtisch; (*pl.*) Süßigkeiten, *f. pl.*

swell [swel], *v.a. irr.* anschwellen lassen. — *v.n.* anschwellen. — *adj.*, *adv.* (*Am. sl.*) ausgezeichnet. — *s.* (*sl.*) der feine Kerl.

swelter ['sweltə], *v.n.* vor Hitze vergehen.

swerve [swə:v], *v.n.* abschweifen, abbiegen.

swift (1) [swift], *adj.* schnell, behende, rasch.

swift (2) [swift], *s.* (*Orn.*) die Turmschwalbe.

swill [swil], *v.a.* spülen (*rinse*); (*sl.*) saufen (*drink heavily*). — *s.* das Spülicht (*dishwater*); (*coll.*) das Gesöff.

swim [swim], *v.n. irr.* schwimmen. — *s.* das Schwimmen.

swindle [swindl], *v.a.* beschwindeln. — *s.* der Schwindel.

swine [swain], *s. pl.* die Schweine; (*sing.*) der Schweinehund, das Schwein.

swing [swiŋ], *v.a.*, *v.n. irr.* schwingen, schaukeln. — *s.* der Schwung; die Schaukel.

swipe [swaip], *v.a.* schlagen; (*fig.*) stehlen. — *s.* der Schlag.

swirl [swə:l], *v.a.*, *v.n.* wirbeln (*in air*). — *s.* der Wirbel.

Swiss [swis], *s.* der Schweizer. — *adj.* schweizerisch, Schweizer-.

switch [switʃ], *v.a.* (*Elec.*) — *on*, andrehen, einschalten; — *off*, abschalten; (*fig.*) wechseln, vertauschen (*change*). — *v.n.* umstellen, umschalten. — *s.* (*Elec.*) der Schalter.

switchboard ['switʃbɔːd], *s.* die Telephonzentrale, das Schaltbrett.

switchgear ['switʃgiə], *s.* (*Elec.*) das Schaltgerät, die Schaltung.

swivel [swivl], *v.n.* drehen. — *s.* der Drehring; — *chair*, der Drehstuhl.

swoon [swu:n], *v.n.* in Ohnmacht fallen. — *s.* die Ohnmacht.

swoop [swu:p], *s.* der Stoß. — *v.n.* (herab)stoßen; stürzen; (nieder)-schießen.

swop *see* **swap**.

sword [sɔːd], *s.* das Schwert.

syllable ['siləbl], *s.* die Silbe.

syllabus ['siləbəs], *s.* das Verzeichnis, der Lehrplan.

symbol ['simbəl], *s.* das Symbol, Sinnbild.

sympathetic [simpə'θetik], *adj.* mitfühlend, teilnehmend; sympathisch.

sympathy ['simpəθi], *s.* die Sympathie, das Mitgefühl.

symphony ['simfəni], *s.* (*Mus.*) die Symphonie.

synchronize ['siŋkrənaiz], *v.a.* synchronisieren.

syndicate ['sindikit], *s.* die Arbeitsgruppe, das Syndikat.

synod ['sinəd], *s.* die Synode, Kirchentagung.

synonymous [si'nɔniməs], *adj.* synonym.

synopsis [si'nɔpsis], *s.* die Zusammenfassung, Übersicht.

Syrian ['siriən], *adj.* syrisch. — *s.* der Syrer.

syringe ['sirindʒ], *s.* die Spritze.

syrup ['sirəp], *s.* der Sirup.

system ['sistəm], *s.* das System.

systematize ['sistəmətaiz], *v.a.* ordnen, in ein System bringen.

T

T [ti:]. das T.

tab [tæb], *s.* das Schildchen, der Streifen.

tabard ['tæbəd], *s.* der Wappenrock, Heroldsrock.

tabby ['tæbi], *s.* (*cat*) die getigerte Katze.

table [teibl], *s.* der Tisch; (*Maths.*) die Tabelle, das Einmaleins. — *v.a.* (*Parl.*) einen Entwurf einbringen; (*Am.*) auf die lange Bank schieben.

tablecloth ['teiblklɔθ], *s.* das Tischtuch.

tablemat ['teiblmæt], *s.* der Untersatz.

tablenapkin ['teiblnæpkin], *s.* die Serviette.

tablespoon ['teiblspuːn], *s.* der Eßlöffel.

tablet ['tæblit], *s.* die Tablette (*pill*); die Schreibtafel, der Block (*writing*).

taboo [tə'buː], *s.* das Verbot, Tabu.

tabular ['tæbjulə], *adj.* tabellarisch; wie eine Tafel.

tacit ['tæsit], *adj.* stillschweigend.

taciturn ['tæsitəːn], *adj.* schweigsam, einsilbig.

tack [tæk], *s.* der Stift; der Stich (*sewing*). — *v.a.* nageln; heften (*sew*).

tackle [tækl], *v.a.* (*Naut.*) takeln; (*Footb.*, *fig.*) angreifen; anpacken. — *s.* (*Naut.*) das Takel; (*fig.*) das Zeug; (*Footb.*) das Angreifen.

tact [tækt], *s.* der Takt; das Zartgefühl.

tactics ['tæktiks], *s. pl.* die Taktik.

tadpole ['tædpoul], *s.* (*Zool.*) die Kaulquappe.

taffeta ['tæfitə], *s.* (*Text.*) der Taft.

tag [tæg], *s.* der Anhängezettel; das Sprichwort (*saying*). — *v.a.* anhängen. — *v.n.* — *on to*, sich anschließen.

tail [teil], *s.* der Schwanz; (*fig.*) das Ende; (*pl.*) der Frack (*tailcoat*). — *v.a.* (*Am.*) folgen (*Dat.*).

tailor ['teilə], *s.* der Schneider; —*made*, geschneidert, nach Maß gemacht. — *v.a.* schneidern.

taint [teint], *v.a.* beflecken; verderben (*corrupt*). — *s.* der Fleck.

take [teik], *v.a. irr.* nehmen; bringen, ergreifen (*seize*); erfordern (*require*); — *up*, aufnehmen, beginnen; ertragen (*suffer, tolerate*); — *breath*, Atem holen; — *care*, sich in acht nehmen; — *offence at*, Anstoß nehmen an; — *place*, stattfinden; — *for*, halten für. — *v.n.* wirken (*be effective*); — *to*, Gefallen finden (an, *Dat.*); — *to flight* or *o.'s heels*, sich aus dem Staube machen; — *after*, ähnlich sein.

takings ['teikiŋz], *s.* (*pl.*) die Einnahmen, *f. pl.*

tale [teil], *s.* das Märchen, die Geschichte.

talent ['tælənt], *s.* das Talent, die Begabung.

talented ['tæləntid], *adj.* talentiert, begabt.

talk [tɔːk], *v.a., v.n.* reden, sprechen. — *s.* das Gespräch (*discussion*); der Vortrag (*lecture*); das Reden, Gerede (*speaking*).

talkative ['tɔːkətiv], *adj.* geschwätzig, redselig, gesprächig.

tall [tɔːl], *adj.* hoch (*high*); groß (*grown high*); *a* — *order*, eine schwierige Aufgabe; *a* — *story*, eine Aufschneiderei, das Seemannsgarn.

tallow ['tælou], *s.* der Talg.

tally ['tæli], *v.n.* passen (*match*); stimmen (*be correct*).

talon ['tælən], *s.* die Klaue, Kralle.

tame [teim], *adj.* zahm. — *v.a.* zähmen.

tamper ['tæmpə], *v.n.* hineinpfuschen (*with*, in, *Acc.*).

tan [tæn], *s.* die Lohe; die braune Farbe; der Sonnenbrand (*sun*). — *v.a.* bräunen; (*leather*) gerben; (*fig.*) verbleuen (*beat*).

tang [tæŋ], *s.* der Seetang; (*fig.*) der Beigeschmack.

tangible ['tændʒibl], *adj.* greifbar.

tangle [tæŋgl], *v.a.* verwickeln (*entangle*). — *s.* die Verwirrung, Verwicklung.

tank [tæŋk], *s.* der Tank; (*Mil.*) der Panzer; der Wasserspeicher (*cistern*). — *v.a., v.n.* tanken.

tankard ['tæŋkəd], *s.* der Maßkrug, Bierkrug.

tanner (1) ['tænə], *s.* der Gerber.

tanner (2) ['tænə], *s.* (*sl.*) das Sechspencestück.

tantalize ['tæntəlaiz], *v.a.* quälen.

tantamount ['tæntəmaunt], *adj.* gleich, gleichwertig.

tap [tæp], *v.a.* anzapfen (*barrel*); klopfen; tippen (*on shoulder etc.*); (*fig.*) anpumpen (*for money*). — *s.* der Hahn; der Zapfen (*barrel*); der leichte Schlag (*on shoulder etc.*).

tape [teip], *s.* das Band; *red* —, die Bürokratie, der Bürokratismus; — *measure*, das Bandmaß; — *recorder*, das Tonbandgerät.

taper ['teipə], *v.n.* spitz zulaufen. — *v.a.* spitzen. — *s.* die (spitze) Kerze.

tapestry ['tæpistri], *s.* die Tapete, der Wandteppich.

tapeworm ['teipwəːm], *s.* der Bandwurm.

taproot ['tæpruːt], *s.* die Pfahlwurzel, Hauptwurzel.

tar [tɑː], *s.* der Teer; (*Naut. sl.*) der Matrose. — *v.a.* teeren.

tardy ['tɑːdi], *adj.* träge (*sluggish*), langsam.

tare (1) [tɛə], das Taragewicht, die Tara (*weight*). — *v.a.* auswägen, tarieren.

tare (2) [tɛə], *s.* (*Bot.*) die Wicke.

target ['tɑːgit], *s.* das Ziel; die Zielscheibe (*board*).

tariff ['tærif], *s.* der Tarif.

tarnish ['tɑːniʃ], *v.a.* trüben. — *v.n.* anlaufen.

tarpaulin [tɑː'pɔːlin], *s.* die Persenning.

tarry (1) ['tæri], *v.n.* zögern (*hesitate*); warten (*wait*).

tarry (2) ['tɑːri], *adj.* teerig.

tart (1) [tɑːt], *s.* die Torte.

tart (2) [tɑːt], *adj.* herb, sauer.

tart (3) [tɑːt], *s.* (*sl.*) die Dirne.

Tartar ['tɑːtə], *s.* der Tatar; (*fig.*) der Tyrann.

tartar ['tɑːtə], *s.* (*Chem.*) der Weinstein.

task [tɑːsk], *s.* die Aufgabe, das Tagewerk; *take to* —, zur Rechenschaft ziehen.

tassel [tæsl], *s.* die Quaste.

taste [teist], *v.a.* schmecken; versuchen, kosten. — *s.* die Probe (*tasting*); der Geschmack (*flavour*).

tasteful ['teistful], *adj.* geschmackvoll.

tasteless ['teistlis], *adj.* geschmacklos.

tasty ['teisti], *adj.* schmackhaft.

tatter ['tætə], *s.* der Lumpen. — *v.a.* in Fetzen reißen, zerfetzen.

tattle [tætl], *v.n.* schwatzen. — *s.* das Geschwätz.

tattoo (1) [tə'tuː], *s.* (*Mil.*) der Zapfenstreich, das militärische Schaustück, die Parade.

tattoo (2) [tə'tuː], *v.a.* tätowieren. — *s.* die Tätowierung.

taunt [tɔːnt], *v.a.* höhnen, schmähen. — *s.* der Hohn, Spott.

tavern ['tævən], *s.* die Schenke.

tawdry ['tɔːdri], *adj.* kitschig, flitterhaft.

tawny ['tɔːni], *adj.* braungelb, lohfarbig.

tax [tæks], *s.* die Abgabe, Steuer; Besteuerung (*taxation*). — *v.a.* besteuern; (*fig.*) anstrengen, ermüden (*strain*).

taxi ['tæksi], *s.* das Taxi.

tea [tiː], *s.* der Tee.

teach [tiːtʃ], *v.a., v.n. irr.* lehren, unterrichten.

teacher ['tiːtʃə], *s.* der Lehrer, die Lehrerin.

499

team

team [ti:m], s. (Sport) die Mannschaft; das Gespann (horses); (fig.) der Stab; — spirit, der Korpsgeist.

tear (1) [tɛə], s. der Riß (rent). — v.a. irr. zerreißen (rend).

tear (2) [tiə], s. die Träne.

tearing [ˈtɛəriŋ], adj. — hurry, rasende Eile.

tease [ti:z], v.a. necken (mock); aufrauhen (roughen).

teat [ti:t], s. die Brustwarze, Zitze.

technical [ˈteknikəl], adj. technisch.

technique [tekˈni:k], s. die Technik, Methode.

techy see **tetchy**.

tedious [ˈti:diəs], adj. langweilig, lästig.

tedium [ˈti:diəm], s. der Überdruß, die Langeweile.

tee [ti:], s. (Sport) der Golfballhalter.

teem [ti:m], v.n. wimmeln.

teenager [ˈti:neidʒə], s. der, die Jugendliche; Teenager.

teeth see under **tooth**.

teethe [ti:ð], v.n. Zähne bekommen, zahnen.

teetotal [ti:ˈtoutl], adj. abstinent, antialkoholisch.

teetotaller [ti:ˈtoutlə], s. der Antialkoholiker.

telegram [ˈteligræm], s. das Telegramm.

telephone [ˈtelifoun], s. (abbr. **phone**) das Telephon; – booth, die Fernsprechzelle; — exchange, das Fernsprechamt.

television [teliˈviʒən], s. das Fernsehen; — set, der Fernsehapparat.

tell [tel], v.a. irr. erzählen, berichten (relate); verraten (reveal).

tell-tale [ˈtelteil], s. der Angeber, Zuträger. — adj. sprechend; Warnungs-.

teller [ˈtelə], s. der Zähler; der Kassier (cashier).

temerity [tiˈmeriti], s. die Verwegenheit, Tollkühnheit.

temper [ˈtempə], v.a. vermischen (mix); mäßigen (moderate); (Metall.) härten. — s. die üble Stimmung, Wut, Laune; (Metall.) die Härte.

temperance [ˈtempərəns], s. die Mäßigkeit, Enthaltsamkeit.

temperate [ˈtempərit], adj. gemäßigt, temperiert.

temperature [ˈtemprətʃə], s. die Temperatur.

tempest [ˈtempist], s. der Sturm.

tempestuous [temˈpestjuəs], adj. stürmisch.

temple (1) [templ], s. der Tempel.

temple (2) [templ], s. (Anat.) die Schläfe (side of brow).

temporal [ˈtempərəl], adj. weltlich, zeitlich.

temporary [ˈtempərəri], adj. zeitweilig, vorläufig, provisorisch.

temporize [ˈtempəraiz], v.n. zögern, Zeit zu gewinnen suchen.

tempt [tempt], v.a. versuchen.

temptation [tempˈteiʃən], s. die Versuchung.

ten [ten], num. adj. zehn.

tenth [tenθ], num. adj. zehnte. — s. der Zehnte.

tenable [ˈtenəbl], adj. haltbar.

tenacious [tiˈneiʃəs], adj. zähe, festhaltend, hartnäckig.

tenacity [tiˈnæsiti], s. die Zähigkeit, Ausdauer.

tenancy [ˈtenənsi], s. das Mietverhältnis; die Mietdauer.

tenant [ˈtenənt], s. der Mieter, Pächter.

tench [tentʃ], s. (Zool.) die Schleie.

tend (1) [tend], v.a., v.n. warten, pflegen (nurse).

tend (2) [tend], v.n. neigen, gerichtet sein (be inclined).

tendency [ˈtendənsi], s. die Tendenz, Neigung.

tender (1) [ˈtendə], s. das Angebot (offer); legal —, das Zahlungsmittel. — v.a. einreichen.

tender (2) [ˈtendə], adj. sanft (affectionate); zart, zärtlich, weich (delicate).

tender (3) [ˈtendə], s. (Railw.) der Tender.

tendon [ˈtendən], s. (Anat.) die Sehne, Flechse.

tendril [ˈtendril], s. (Bot.) die Ranke.

tenement [ˈtenimənt], s. die Mietswohnung, die Mietskaserne.

tenet [ˈtenit], s. der Grundsatz (principle); die Lehre (doctrine).

tenfold [ˈtenfould], adj. zehnfach.

tennis [ˈtenis], s. das Tennis.

tenor [ˈtenə], s. (Mus.) der Tenor; der Sinn, Inhalt (meaning).

tense (1) [tens], adj. gespannt; straff (taut).

tense (2) [tens], s. (Gram.) die Zeitform.

tension [ˈtenʃən], s. die Spannung.

tent [tent], s. das Zelt.

tentacle [ˈtentəkl], s. (Zool.) das Fühlhorn, der Fühler.

tentative [ˈtentətiv], adj. versuchend, vorsichtig; (fig.) vorläufig.

tenterhooks [ˈtentəhuks], s. pl. die Spannhaken, m. pl.; be on —, in größter Spannung sein.

tenuous [ˈtenjuəs], adj. dünn, fadenscheinig, spärlich.

tenure [ˈtenjuə], s. der Mietbesitz, die Mietvertragslänge, das Mietrecht; — of office, die Amtsdauer.

tepid [ˈtepid], adj. lau, lauwarm.

term [tə:m], s. der Ausdruck (expression); die Bedingung (condition); der Termin, die Frist (period); (Sch.) das Semester, Trimester; be on good —s with (s.o.), auf gutem Fuß stehen mit. — v.a. benennen, bezeichnen.

terminate [ˈtə:mineit], v.a. beenden, zu Ende bringen. — v.n. zu Ende kommen.

terminus [ˈtə:minəs], s. die Endstation.

terrace [ˈteris], s. die Terrasse.

terrestrial [təˈrestriəl], adj. irdisch.

terrible [ˈteribl], adj. schrecklich, furchtbar.

terrific [təˈrifik], adj. fürchterlich; (coll.) ungeheuer.

terrify ['terifai], *v.a.* erschrecken.

territory ['teritəri], *s.* das Gebiet.

terror ['terə], *s.* der Schrecken.

terse [tə:s], *adj.* bündig, kurz.

tertiary ['tə:ʃəri], *adj.* tertiär.

test [test], *s.* die Prüfung; (*Chem.*) die Probe; — -*tube*, das Reagensglas *or* Reagenzglas. — *v.a.* prüfen.

testament ['testəmənt], *s.* das Testament.

testator [tes'teitə], *s.* der Erblasser.

testicle ['testikl], *s.* (*Anat.*) die Hode.

testify ['testifai], *v.a.* bezeugen.

testimonial [testi'mouniəl], *s.* das Zeugnis.

testimony ['testiməni], *s.* das Zeugnis, die Zeugenaussage (*oral*).

testiness ['testinis], *s.* die Verdrießlichkeit.

testy ['testi], *adj.* verdrießlich, reizbar.

tetanus ['tetənəs], *s.* (*Med.*) der Starrkrampf.

tetchy, techy ['tetʃi], *adj.* mürrisch, reizbar.

tether ['teðə], *s.* das Spannseil; (*fig.*) *at the end of o.'s* —, am Ende seiner Geduld. — *v.a.* anbinden.

text [tekst], *s.* der Text, Wortlaut.

textile ['tekstail], *s.* die Textilware, der Webstoff.

textual ['tekstjuəl], *adj.* textlich, Text-.

texture ['tekstʃə], *s.* das Gewebe, die Struktur.

Thai [tai], *adj.* Thai-, siamesisch. — *s. pl.* die Thaivölker, *pl.*

than [ðæn], *conj.* als (*after comparatives*).

thank [θæŋk], *v.a.* danken (*Dat.*). — *s.* (*pl.*) der Dank.

that [ðæt], *dem. adj.* der, die, das, jener. — *dem. pron.* der, die, das (*absolute, no pl.*) das. — *rel. pron.* der, die, das, welcher, was. — *conj.* daß; damit (*in order* —).

thatch [θætʃ], *v.a.* decken (mit Stroh). — *s.* das Strohdach.

thaw [θɔ:], *v.n.* tauen; auftauen. — *s.* das Tauwetter.

the [ðə, *before vowel* ði], *def. art.* der, die, das. — *adv.* — *bigger* — *better*, je grösser desto *or* umso besser.

theatre ['θiətə], *s.* das Theater; (*fig.*) der Schauplatz.

theatrical [θi'ætrikəl], *adj.* bühnenhaft (*of the stage*); theatralisch; Bühnen-, Theater-.

theft [θeft], *s.* der Diebstahl.

their [ðɛə], *poss. adj.* ihr.

theirs [ðɛəz], *poss. pron.* der, die, das ihrige, der, die, das ihre.

them [ðem], *pers. pron.* sie, ihnen.

theme [θi:m], *s.* das Thema; (*Mus.*) das Thema, Motiv.

then [ðen], *adv.* dann, damals; *by* —, *till* —, bis dahin. — *conj.* dann, denn. — *adj.* damalig.

thence [ðens], *adv.* von da; daher.

theology [θi'ɔlədʒi], *s.* die Theologie.

theorem ['θiərəm], *s.* (*Maths.*) der Lehrsatz, Grundsatz.

theorize ['θiəraiz], *v.n.* theoretisieren.

therapeutics [θerə'pju:tiks], *s. pl.* die Heilkunde.

therapy ['θerəpi], *s.* die Therapie.

there [ðɛə], *adv.* dort, da; dorthin, dahin (*thereto*); — *is*, — *are*, es gibt; *here and* —, hier und da.

thereabout(s) [ðɛərəbaut(s)], *adv.* ungefähr, da herum.

thereafter [ðɛər'ɑ:ftə], *adv.* hernach, danach.

thereby [ðɛə'bai], *adv.* dadurch.

therefore ['ðɛəfɔ:], *adv.* darum, deshalb.

thermal, thermic ['θə:məl, 'θə:mik], *adj.* thermisch; warm; Wärme-.

thermometer [θə'mɔmitə], *s.* das Thermometer.

these [ði:z], *dem. adj. & pron. pl.* diese.

thesis ['θi:sis], *s.* die These; die Dissertation.

they [ðei], *pers. pron. pl.* sie.

thick [θik], *adj.* dick; dicht; (*fig.*) dick befreundet; — *as thieves*, wie eine Diebsbande.

thicken ['θikən], *v.a.* verdicken. — *v.n.* dick werden.

thicket ['θikit], *s.* das Dickicht.

thickness ['θiknis], *s.* die Dicke.

thief [θi:f], *s.* der Dieb.

thieve [θi:v], *v.n.* stehlen.

thigh [θai], *s.* (*Anat.*) der Oberschenkel.

thimble [θimbl], *s.* der Fingerhut.

thin [θin], *adj.* dünn. — *v.a., v.n.* (sich) verdünnen.

thine [ðain], *poss. pron.* (*Poet.*) dein, der, die, das deinige.

thing [θiŋ], *s.* das Ding; die Sache (*matter*).

think [θiŋk], *v.a., v.n. irr.* denken; meinen, glauben.

thinker ['θiŋkə], *s.* der Denker.

third [θə:d], *num. adj.* der, die, das dritte. — *s.* das Drittel.

thirdly ['θə:dli], *adv.* drittens.

thirst [θə:st], *s.* der Durst (*for*, nach). — *v.n.* dürsten.

thirsty ['θə:sti], *adj.* durstig; *be* —, Durst haben.

thirteen [θə:'ti:n], *num. adj.* dreizehn.

thirty ['θə:ti], *num. adj.* dreißig.

this [ðis], *dem. adj.* dieser, diese, dieses. — *dem. pron.* dieser, diese, dieses; dies.

thistle [θisl], *s.* (*Bot.*) die Distel.

thither ['ðiðə], *adv.* dahin, dorthin.

tho' [ðou] *see under* **though.**

thong [θɔŋ], *s.* der Riemen (*strap*); die Peitschenschnur.

thorn [θɔ:n], *s.* (*Bot.*) der Dorn.

thorough ['θʌrə], *adj.* gründlich; völlig (*complete*).

thoroughbred ['θʌrəbred], *s.* das Vollblut, der Vollblüter. — *adj.* Vollblut-.

thoroughfare ['θʌrəfɛə], *s.* der Durchgang (*path*); die Durchfahrt.

those [ðouz], *dem. adj. pl.* die, jene. — *dem. pron. pl.* jene, diejenigen.

thou [ðau], *pers. pron.* (*Poet.*) du.

though [ðou], *conj.* (*abbr.* **tho'**) obgleich, obwohl, wenn auch (*even if*). — *adv.* doch, zwar.

501

thought

thought [θɔːt], *s.* der Gedanke; *also past tense and participle of* think *q.v.*
thoughtful [ˈθɔːtful], *adj.* rücksichtsvoll, nachdenklich.
thoughtless [ˈθɔːtlis], *adj.* gedankenlos.
thousand [ˈθauzənd], *num. adj.* a —, tausend. — *s.* das Tausend.
thrash [θræʃ], *v.a.* dreschen (*corn*); prügeln (*s.o.*).
thread [θred], *s.* der Faden. — *v.a.* einfädeln. — *v.n.* sich schlängeln, sich winden.
threadbare [ˈθredbɛə], *adj.* fadenscheinig.
threat [θret], *s.* die Drohung.
threaten [θretn], *v.a.* drohen, androhen (*Dat.*).
three [θriː], *num. adj.* drei.
threescore [ˈθriːskɔː], *num. adj.* sechzig.
thresh [θreʃ], *v.a.* dreschen (*corn*). — *See also* thrash.
threshold [ˈθreʃould], *s.* die Schwelle (*of door*).
thrice [θrais], *num. adv.* dreimal.
thrift [θrift], *s.* die Sparsamkeit; (*Bot.*) die Grasnelke, Meernelke.
thrill [θril], *v.a.* packen (*grip*). — *v.n.* erschauern, zittern (vor, *Dat.*). — *s.* der Schauer; die Spannung.
thriller [ˈθrilə], *s.* der Thriller, der spannende Roman *or* Film etc.
thrive [θraiv], *v.n.* gedeihen (*also fig.*); (*fig.*) gut weiterkommen, Glück haben.
thriving [ˈθraiviŋ], *adj.* blühend, (*Comm.*) gut gehend.
throat [θrout], *s.* (*Anat.*) der Schlund, die Kehle.
throb [θrɔb], *v.n.* pochen, klopfen.
throes [θrouz], *s. pl.* die Wehen, *f. pl.*; die Schmerzen, *m. pl.*
throne [θroun], *s.* der Thron.
throng [θrɔŋ], *s.* die Menge, das Gedränge. — *v.a., v.n.* drängen.
throttle [θrɔtl], *s.* die Kehle, Luftröhre; (*Mech.*) das Drosselventil; (*Motor.*) open the —, Gas geben.
through [θruː], *prep.* durch (*Acc.*); mittels (*Genit.*) (*by means of*). — *adv.* (mitten) durch.
throughout [θruːˈaut], *prep.* ganz (hin)durch (*space*); während, hindurch (*time*). — *adv.* durchaus, in jeder Beziehung.
throw [θrou], *v.a. irr.* werfen; — *open*, eröffnen. — *s.* der Wurf.
thrush [θrʌʃ], *s.* (*Orn.*) die Drossel.
thrust [θrʌst], *v.a.* stoßen, drängen. — *v.n.* stoßen (*at*, nach); sich drängen. — *s.* der Stoß, Angriff; *cut and* —, Hieb und Gegenhieb.
thud [θʌd], *s.* der Schlag, das Dröhnen, der dumpfe Ton. — *v.n.* dröhnen, aufschlagen.
thumb [θʌm], *s.* (*Anat.*) der Daumen; *rule of* —, die Faustregel; (*Am.*) — *tack* see **drawing pin**. — *a* —*blättern* (*book*); —*a lift*, per Anhalter fahren.
thump [θʌmp], *v.a.* schlagen, puffen. —

v.n. schlagen (*on*, auf; *against*, gegen). — *s.* der Schlag, Stoß.
thunder [ˈθʌndə], *s.* der Donner. — *v.n.* donnern.
thunderstruck [ˈθʌndəstrʌk], *adj.* wie vom Donner gerührt.
Thursday [ˈθəːzdi], der Donnerstag.
Thuringian [θuəˈrindʒiən], *adj.* thüringisch. — *s.* der Thüringer.
thus [ðʌs], *adv.* so, auf diese Weise (*in this way*).
thwart [θwɔːt], *v.a.* vereiteln, durchkreuzen.
thy [ðai], *poss. adj.* (*Poet.*) dein, deine, dein.
thyme [taim], *s.* (*Bot.*) der Thymian.
tic [tik], *s.* (*Med.*) das Zucken.
tick (1) [tik], *s.* das Ticken (*watch*). — *v.n.* ticken.
tick (2) [tik], *s.* (*coll.*) der Kredit, Borg.
ticket [ˈtikit], *s.* die Fahrkarte (*travel*); die Eintrittskarte (*entry*); (*Am.*) der Strafzettel (*driving*).
ticking (1) [ˈtikiŋ], *s.* das Ticken (*of watch*).
ticking (2) [ˈtikiŋ], *s.* (*Text.*) der Zwillich.
tickle [tikl], *v.a., v.n.* kitzeln. — *s.* das Kitzeln.
ticklish [ˈtikliʃ], *adj.* kitzlig.
tidal [taidl], *adj.* Gezeiten-, Ebbe-, Flut-.
tide [taid], *s.* die Gezeiten, *f.pl.*; die Ebbe und Flut. — *v.a.* — *over*, hinweghelfen (über, *Acc.*).
tidiness [ˈtaidinis], *s.* die Sauberkeit, Ordnung.
tidings [ˈtaidiŋz], *s. pl.* (*Poet.*) die Nachricht.
tidy [ˈtaidi], *adj.* nett, sauber, ordentlich. — *v.a.* — *up*, sauber machen.
tie [tai], *v.a.* binden, knüpfen. — *v.n.* (*Sport*) unentschieden sein. — *s.* die Binde, Krawatte; (*Sport*) das Unentschieden.
tier [tiə], *s.* der Rang, die Reihe, Sitzreihe.
tiger [ˈtaigə], *s.* (*Zool.*) der Tiger.
tight [tait], *adj.* fest, eng, dicht (*close*); (*coll.*) betrunken (*drunk*); — *fisted*, geizig (*stingy*). — *s. pl.* die Trikothosen, *f.pl.*
tighten [taitn], *v.a.* festziehen.
tile [tail], *s.* der Ziegel (*roof etc.*); die Kachel (*glazed*). — *v.a.* kacheln, ziegeln.
till (1) [til], *prep., conj.* bis.
till (2) [til], *v.a.* aufbauen, beackern (*land*).
till (3) [til], *s.* die Ladenkasse.
tilt [tilt], *v.a.* kippen, neigen, umschlagen (*tip over*). — *v.n.* sich neigen, kippen, kentern. — *s.* die Neigung.
timber [ˈtimbə], *s.* das Holz, Bauholz.
time [taim], *s.* die Zeit; (*Mus.*) das Tempo, Zeitmaß; *in* —, zur rechten Zeit; *every* —, jedesmal; *what is the* —? wievel Uhr ist es? — *v.a.* zeitlich messen, rechtzeitig einrichten.
timely [ˈtaimli], *adj.* rechtzeitig.

502

timetable ['taimteibl], *s.* (*Railw.*) der Fahrplan; (*Sch.*) der Stundenplan.

timid ['timid], *adj.* furchtsam.

timpani ['timpəni], *s. pl.* (*Mus.*) die Kesselpauken, *f. pl.*

tin [tin], *s.* das Zinn, Weißblech; die Dose, Büchse (*preserved foods*); — *opener*, der Büchsenöffner.

tincture ['tiŋktʃə], *s.* die Tinktur, das Färbungsmittel.

tinder ['tində], *s.* der Zunder.

tinfoil ['tinfɔil], *s.* das Stanniol.

tinge [tindʒ], *v.a.* färben, anfärben. — *s.* die Färbung, leichte Farbe; (*fig.*) die Spur.

tingle [tiŋgl], *v.n.* klingen (*bells*); (*Anat.*) prickeln. — *s.* das Klingen; Prickeln.

tinker ['tiŋkə], *s.* der Kesselflicker. — *v.n.* basteln.

tinkle [tiŋkl], *v.a.* klingeln.

tinsel ['tinsəl], *s.* das Lametta, Flittergold.

tint [tint], *v.a.* färben. — *s.* die Farbe; der Farbton.

tiny ['taini], *adj.* winzig.

tip (1) [tip], *v.a.* kippen; (*coll.*) ein Trinkgeld geben (*Dat.*). — *s.* (*Sport etc.*) (*coll.*) der Tip; das Trinkgeld (*gratuity*).

tip (2) [tip], *s.* die Spitze; das Mundstück (*cigarette*).

tipple [tipl], *v.n.* (viel) trinken, zechen.

tipsy ['tipsi], *adj.* beschwipst.

tiptoe ['tiptou], *s. on* —, auf Zehenspitzen.

tiptop ['tiptɔp], *adj.* (*coll.*) erstklassig.

tirade [ti'reid *or* tai'reid], *s.* der Wortschwall, die Tirade.

tire (1) [taiə], *v.a., v.n.* ermüden.

tire (2) *see under* **tyre**.

tired ['taiəd], *adj.* müde.

tiresome ['taiəsəm], *adj.* langweilig (*boring*); auf die Nerven gehend (*annoying*).

tissue ['tiʃju:], *s.* das Gewebe; — *paper*, das Seidenpapier.

titbit ['titbit], *s.* der Leckerbissen.

tithe [taið], *s.* der Zehnte.

title [taitl], *s.* der Titel, die Überschrift; (*fig.*) der Anspruch (*claim*).

titmouse ['titmaus], *s.* (*Orn.*) die Meise.

titter ['titə], *v.n.* kichern. — *s.* das Kichern.

tittle [titl], *s.* das Tüpfelchen; — *tattle*, das Geschwätz.

titular ['titjulə], *adj.* Titular-.

to [tu], *prep.* zu (*Dat.*), gegen (*Acc.*); bis (*until, as far as*), nach, an, auf; *in order* —, um zu. — [tu:], *adv.* zu; — *and fro*, hin und her.

toad [toud], *s.* (*Zool.*) die Kröte.

toadstool ['toudstu:l], *s.* (*Bot.*) der Giftpilz.

toady ['toudi], *v.n.* kriechen. — *s.* der Kriecher.

toast [toust], *s.* der Toast, das Röstbrot; der Trinkspruch. — *v.a.* toasten,

rösten; trinken auf; — *s.o.*, einen Trinkspruch ausbringen auf einen.

tobacco [tə'bækou], *s.* der Tabak.

toboggan [tə'bɔgən], *s.* der Rodel, der Schlitten. — *v.n.* rodeln, Schlitten fahren.

tocsin ['tɔksin], *s.* die Sturmglocke.

today [tə'dei], *adv.* heute.

toddle [tɔdl], *v.n.* watscheln; abschieben (— *off*).

toddler ['tɔdlə], *s.* (*coll.*) das kleine Kind (das gehen lernt).

toe [tou], *s.* (*Anat.*) die Zehe.

toffee ['tɔfi], *s.* der Sahnebonbon.

together [tə'geðə], *adv.* zusammen.

toil [tɔil], *v.n.* hart arbeiten. — *s.* die schwere, harte Arbeit.

toilet ['tɔilit], *s.* das Anziehen, Ankleiden; die Toilette, der Abort, das Klosett (*lavatory*).

token ['toukən], *s.* das Zeichen (*sign*); der Beweis (*proof*); das Andenken (*keepsake*).

tolerable ['tɔlərəbl], *adj.* erträglich, leidlich.

tolerance ['tɔlərəns], *s.* die Toleranz, Duldsamkeit; (*Tech.*) die Toleranz.

tolerant ['tɔlərənt], *adj.* tolerant, duldsam.

tolerate ['tɔləreit], *v.a.* ertragen, dulden.

toll [toul], *v.a., v.n.* läuten. — *s.* der Zoll; — *gate*, — *bar*, der Schlagbaum.

tomato [tə'mɑ:tou], *s.* (*Bot.*) die Tomate.

tomb [tu:m], *s.* das Grab, Grabmal.

tomboy ['tɔmbɔi], *s.* der Wildfang.

tomcat ['tɔmkæt], *s.* (*Zool.*) der Kater.

tome [toum], *s.* der große Band, (*coll.*) der Wälzer.

tomfoolery [tɔm'fu:ləri], *s.* die Narretei.

Tommy ['tɔmi], *s.* (*Mil.*) (*coll.*) der englische Soldat.

tomorrow [tə'mɔrou], *adv.* morgen; — *morning*, morgen früh; *the day after* —, übermorgen.

ton [tʌn], *s.* die Tonne.

tone [toun], *s.* der Ton, Klang; (*fig.*) die Stimmung (*mood*). — *v.a.* — *down*, abtönen, abstimmen.

tongs [tɔŋz], *s. pl.* die Zange.

tongue [tʌŋ], *s.* (*Anat.*) die Zunge.

tonic ['tɔnik], *s.* das Stärkungsmittel. — *adj.* tonisch, stärkend.

tonight [tu'nait], *adv.* heute abend, heute nacht.

tonnage ['tʌnidʒ], *s.* die Tonnage, das Tonnengeld.

tonsil ['tɔnsil], *s.* (*Anat.*) die Mandel.

tonsilitis [tɔnsi'laitis], *s.* (*Med.*) die Mandelentzündung.

tonsure ['tɔnʃə], *s.* die Tonsur.

too [tu:], *adv.* allzu; zu, allzusehr; auch (*also*).

tool [tu:l], *s.* das Werkzeug, das Gerät; *machine* —, die Werkzeugmaschine.

tooth [tu:θ], *s.* (*pl.* **teeth** [ti:θ]) der Zahn.

toothache ['tu:θeik], *s.* das Zahnweh.

toothbrush ['tu:θbrʌʃ], *s.* die Zahnbürste.

toothpaste ['tu:θpeist], *s.* die Zahnpaste.

top (1) [tɔp], *s.* die Spitze; der Gipfel
(*mountain*); der Wipfel (*tree*); der
Giebel (*house*); die Oberfläche (*surface*); big —, das Zirkuszeltdach; —
hat, der Zylinder. — *v.a.* übertreffen
(*surpass*); bedecken (*cover*).

top (2) [tɔp], *s.* der Kreisel (*spinning* —).

topaz ['toupæz], *s.* der Topas.

tope [toup], *v.n.* zechen, saufen.

toper ['toupə], *s.* der Zecher.

topic ['tɔpik], *s.* das Thema, der
Gegenstand.

topical ['tɔpikəl], *adj.* aktuell (*up to date*).

topmost ['tɔpmoust], *adj.* höchst,
oberst.

topsy-turvy ['tɔpsi 'tə:vi], *adv.* durcheinander, auf den Kopf gestellt.

torch [tɔ:tʃ], *s.* die Fackel; (*Elec.*) die
Taschenlampe.

torment ['tɔ:mənt], *s.* die Qual, Marter.
— [tɔ:'ment], *v.a.* quälen, martern,
peinigen.

tornado [tɔ:'neidou], *s.* der Wirbelsturm.

torpid ['tɔ:pid], *adj.* starr, betäubt;
(*fig.*) stumpfsinnig.

torpor ['tɔ:pə], *s.* die Starre; die
Stumpfheit, Stumpfsinnigkeit.

torrent ['tɔrənt], *s.* der Gießbach, der
(reißende) Strom.

torrid ['tɔrid], *adj.* brennend heiß,
verbrannt.

torsion ['tɔ:ʃən], *s.* die Drehung,
Windung.

tortoise ['tɔ:təs], *s.* (*Zool.*) die Schildkröte.

tortoiseshell ['tɔ:təʃel], *s.* das Schildpatt.

tortuous ['tɔ:tjuəs], *adj.* gewunden.

torture ['tɔ:tʃə], *s.* die Folter; (*fig.*) die
Folterqualen, *f. pl.* — *v.a.* foltern.

Tory ['tɔ:ri], *s.* (*Pol.*) der englische
Konservative.

toss [tɔs], *s.* der Wurf (*of coin, etc.*);
argue the —, sich streiten. — *v.a.*
werfen. — *v.n.* — up, losen.

total [toutl], *adj.* ganz, gänzlich, total.
— *s.* die Gesamtsumme. — *v.a.* sich
(im ganzen) belaufen auf.

totality [tou'tæliti], *s.* die Gesamtheit.

totter ['tɔtə], *v.n.* wanken, schwanken,
torkeln.

touch [tʌtʃ], *v.a.* berühren; anfassen;
(*coll.*) anpumpen (*for money*); — up,
auffrischen. — *s.* die Berührung
(*contact*); (*Mus.*) der Anschlag.

touching ['tʌtʃiŋ], *adj.* rührend, ergreifend.

touchline ['tʌtʃlain], *s.* (*Sport*) der Rand
des Spielfeldes, die Seitenlinie.

touchy ['tʌtʃi], *adj.* empfindlich.

tough [tʌf], *adj.* zäh, widerstandsfähig
(*resistant*); get —, grob werden; —
luck, Pech! — *s.* (*Am. coll.*) der
Grobian.

tour [tuə], *s.* die Tour, Reise; (*Theat.*)
die Tournee. — *v.a.*, *v.n.* touren,
bereisen.

tourist ['tuərist], *s.* der Tourist.

tournament ['tuə- *or* 'tə:nəmənt], *s.* der
Wettkampf, das Turnier.

tout [taut], *v.n.* Kunden suchen,
anlocken. — *s.* der Kundenfänger.

tow [tou], *s.* das Schlepptau. — *v.a.*
ziehen, schleppen.

toward(s) [tu'wɔ:d(z), tɔ:d(z)], *prep.*
gegen; gegenüber; zu . . . hin; auf . . .
zu; für.

towel ['tauəl], *s.* das Handtuch.

towelling ['tauəliŋ], *s.* der Hand-
tuchdrell; *Turkish* —, das Frottiertuch.

tower [tauə], *s.* der Turm, Zwinger. —
v.n. emporragen, hervorragen
(*über*).

towing path ['touə(iŋ) pɑ:θ] *see*
towpath

town [taun], *s.* die Stadt; — *crier*, der
Ausrufer; — *hall*, das Rathaus (*offices*).

townsman ['taunzmən], *s.* der Städter.

towpath ['toupɑ:θ], *s.* der Treidelpfad.

toy [tɔi], *s.* das Spielzeug; (*pl.*) Spiel-
sachen, Spielwaren, *f. pl.*; — *shop*, der
Spielwarenladen. — *v.n.* spielen.

trace [treis], *s.* die Spur. — *v.a.* suchen,
aufspüren; pausen (*through paper*).

track [træk], *s.* die Spur, Fährte (*path*);
(*Railw.*) das Geleis(e).

tract [trækt], *s.* der Traktat (*pamphlet*);
die Strecke (*stretch*).

traction ['trækʃən], *s.* das Ziehen
(*pulling*); (*Tech.*) der Zug.

tractor ['træktə], *s.* der Traktor.

trade [treid], *s.* der Handel (*commerce*);
das Gewerbe (*craft*); — *wind*, der Passatwind; — *union*, die Gewerkschaft.
— *v.a.* — *in*, in Zahlung geben. —
v.n. handeln, Handel treiben; — *in*,
eintauschen.

trademark ['treidmɑ:k], *s.* die (Schutz-)
marke, das Warenzeichen.

tradesman ['treidzmən], *s.* der Lieferant.

traduce [trə'dju:s], *v.a.* verleumden.

traffic ['træfik], *s.* der Verkehr; (*Comm.*)
der Handel; — *light*, die Verkehrs-
ampel.

trafficator ['træfikeitə], *s.* (*Motor.*) der
Winker.

tragedy ['trædʒədi], *s.* die Tragödie,
das Trauerspiel.

tragic ['trædʒik], *adj.* tragisch.

tradition [trə'diʃən], *s.* die Tradition.

traditional [trə'diʃənəl], *adj.* traditionell.

trail [treil], *s.* die Spur, Fährte; (*Am.*)
der Pfad. — *v.a.* ziehen, nachziehen,
schleppen; (*Am.*) nachfolgen (*Dat.*)

trailer ['treilə], *s.* (*Motor.*) der Anhänger; (*Film*) die Voranzeige.

train [trein], *v.a.* ausbilden; (*Sport*)
trainieren, abrichten, dressieren
(*animal*). — *v.n.* (*Sport*) sich vorbereiten; sich ausbilden (*for profession*). — *s.* (*Railw.*) der Zug; (*Mil.*)
der Zug, Transport; die Schleppe
(*bridal gown, etc.*); — *of thought*, die
Gedankenfolge.

training ['treiniŋ], *s.* die Erziehung; Ausbildung; — *college*, das Lehrerseminar, die pädagogische Hochschule.

trait [trei, treit], *s.* der Zug, Wesenszug.

traitor ['treitə], *s.* der Verräter.

tram(car) ['træm(kɑː)], *s.* die Straßenbahn, der Strassenbahnwagen.

trammelled [træmld], *adj.* gebunden, gefesselt.

tramp [træmp], *s.* der Landstreicher, Strolch. — *v.n.* trampeln; (zu Fuß) wandern.

trample [træmpl], *v.a.* niedertrampeln. — *v.n.* trampeln, treten.

tramway ['træmwei], *s.* die Strassenbahn.

trance [trɑːns], *s.* die Verzückung.

tranquil ['træŋkwil], *adj.* ruhig, still, friedlich.

tranquillizer ['træŋkwilaizə], *s.* (*Med.*) das Beruhigungsmittel.

transact [træn'zækt], *v.a.* abmachen; verrichten (*conclude*), erledigen.

transaction [træn'zækʃən], *s.* die Verhandlung, Abmachung, Durchführung.

transcend [træn'send], *v.a.* übersteigen.

transcendental [trænsen'dentl], *adj.* transzendental.

transcribe [træn'skraib], *v.a.* übertragen; umschreiben (*cipher etc.*); abschreiben.

transcription [træn'skripʃən], *s.* die Umschrift; die Abschrift (*copy*).

transept ['trænsept], *s.* (*Archit.*) das Querschiff.

transfer [træns'fəː], *v.a.* versetzen, überführen; übertragen; überweisen (*money*). — *v.n.* verlegt werden. —['trænsfəː], *s.* der Wechsel, Transfer; die Versetzung; Überweisung.

transfigure [træns'figə], *v.a.* verklären.

transfix [træns'fiks], *v.a.* durchbohren.

transform [træns'fɔːm], *v.a.* verändern, umwandeln. — *v.r.* sich verwandeln.

transgress [træns'gres], *v.a.* überschreiten (*trespass on*). — *v.n.* sich vergehen.

transient ['trænsiənt], *adj.* vergänglich.

transit ['trænsit, 'trænzit], *s.* der Durchgang; die Durchfahrt, Durchfuhr (*travel*); (*Comm.*) der Transit. — *v.n.* (*Am.*) durchfahren (*of goods*).

transitive ['trænsitiv], *adj.* (*Gram.*) transitiv.

transitory ['trænsitəri], *adj.* vergänglich, flüchtig.

translate [træns'leit], *v.a.* übersetzen; versetzen (*office*).

translation [træns'leiʃən], *s.* die Übersetzung, die Übertragung.

translucent [trænz'ljuːsənt], *adj.* durchscheinend.

transmission [trænz'miʃən], *s.* die Übersendung, Übermittlung; (*Rad.*) die Sendung; (*Motor.*) die Transmission.

transmit [trænz'mit], *v.a.* übersenden,

übermitteln; (*Rad., T.V.*) übertragen, senden.

transmutation [trænzmju'teiʃən], *s.* die Verwandlung.

transparent [træns'pɛərənt], *adj.* durchsichtig.

transpire [træns'paiə, trænz–], *v.n.* bekannt werden.

transplant [træns'plɑːnt, trænz–], *v.a.* verpflanzen; (*Med.*) übertragen.

transport [træns'pɔːt], *v.a.* transportieren; (*fig.*) entzücken. — ['trænspɔːt], *s.* der Transport; die Versendung (*sending*); (*fig.*) die Entzückung.

transpose [træns'pouz], *v.a.* (*Mus.*) transponieren.

transverse [trænz'vəːs], *adj.* quer; schräg (*oblique*).

trap [træp], *v.a.* in eine Falle führen; ertappen (*detect*). — *s.* die Falle; der Einspänner (*gig*).

trapeze [trə'piːz], *s.* das Trapez.

trapper ['træpə], *s.* der Fallensteller.

trappings ['træpiŋz], *s. pl.* der Schmuck; (*fig.*) die Äußerlichkeiten, *f. pl.*

trash [træʃ], *s.* (*Lit.*) der Schund; der Kitsch; das wertlose Zeug.

trashy ['træʃi], *adj.* wertlos, kitschig.

travail ['træveil], *s.* die Wehen, Sorgen, die Mühe.

travel [trævl], *v.n.* reisen. — *v.a.* bereisen. — *s.* das Reisen; — *agency*, das Reisebüro.

traveller ['trævələ], *s.* der Reisende; (*Comm.*) der Handelsreisende, Vertreter.

traverse ['trævəːs], *adj.* quer. — *s.* die Traverse, der Querbalken. — [trə'vəːs], *v.a.* durchqueren; (*fig.*) durchwandern.

trawl [trɔːl], *v.n.* (mit Schleppnetz) fischen.

trawler ['trɔːlə], *s.* das Fischerboot, der Fischdampfer.

tray [trei], *s.* das Tablett.

treacherous ['tretʃərəs], *adj.* verräterisch; (*fig.*) gefährlich.

treachery ['tretʃəri], *s.* der Verrat.

treacle [triːkl], *s.* der Sirup.

tread [tred], *v.a., v.n. irr.* (be)treten, auftreten. — *s.* der Tritt, Schritt; die Lauffläche (*of a tyre*).

treason [triːzn], *s.* der Verrat.

treasure ['treʒə], *s.* der Schatz.

treasurer ['treʒərə], *s.* der Schatzmeister.

treasury ['treʒəri], *s.* die Schatzkammer; (*U.K.*) *the Treasury*, das Schatzamt, Finanzministerium.

treat [triːt], *v.a.* behandeln; bewirten (*as host*). — *v.n.* (*Pol.*) unterhandeln (*negotiate*). — *s.* der Genuß (*pleasure*).

treatise ['triːtis], *s.* die Abhandlung.

treatment ['triːtmənt], *s.* die Behandlung.

treaty ['triːti], *s.* der Vertrag.

treble [trebl], *s.* (*Mus.*) die Sopranstimme, Knabenstimme, der Diskant; (*Maths.*) das Dreifache. — *v.a.* verdreifachen.

tree

tree [tri:], *s.* (*Bot.*) der Baum.
trefoil [ˈtri:fɔil], *s.* (*Bot.*) der dreiblätt(e)rige Klee; das Dreiblatt.
trellis [ˈtrelis], *s.* das Gitter.
tremble [trembl], *v.n.* zittern. — *s.* das Zittern.
tremendous [triˈmendəs], *adj.* ungeheuer (groß); schrecklich.
tremor [ˈtremə], *s.* das Zittern; (*Geol.*) das Beben; (*Med.*) das Zucken.
trench [trentʃ], *s.* der Graben.
trenchant [ˈtrentʃənt], *adj.* einschneidend, scharf.
trend [trend], *s.* die Tendenz; (*Comm.*) der Trend.
trepidation [trepiˈdeiʃən], *s.* die Angst, das Zittern.
trespass [ˈtrespəs], *v.n.* sich vergehen, übertreten (*law*); — *on*, unbefugt betreten. — *s.* die Übertretung.
tress [tres], *s.* die Flechte, Haarlocke.
trestle [tresl], *s.* das Gestell; — *table*, der Klapptisch.
trial [ˈtraiəl], *s.* die Probe, der Versuch; (*Law*) die Verhandlung, der Prozeß, das Verhör.
triangle [ˈtraiæŋgl], *s.* das Dreieck; (*Mus.*) der Triangel.
tribe [traib], *s.* der Stamm.
tribulation [tribjuˈleiʃən], *s.* die Trübsal, Drangsal.
tribunal [traiˈbju:nəl], *s.* das Tribunal, der Gerichtshof.
tributary [ˈtribjutəri], *adj.* Neben-. — *s.* der Nebenfluß.
tribute [ˈtribju:t], *s.* der Tribut.
trice [trais], *s. in a* —, im Nu.
trick [trik], *s.* der Kniff, Trick. — *v.a.* betrügen.
trickery [ˈtrikəri], *s.* der Betrug.
trickle [trikl], *v.n.* tröpfeln, sickern. — *s.* das Tröpfeln.
tricky [ˈtriki], *adj.* verwickelt; (*fig.*) bedenklich, heikel.
tricycle [ˈtraisikl], *s.* das Dreirad.
tried [traid], *adj.* erprobt, bewährt.
triennial [traiˈeniəl], *adj.* dreijährlich.
trifle [traifl], *v.n.* scherzen, spielen. — *s.* die Kleinigkeit; (*Cul.*) der süße Auflauf.
trigger [ˈtrigə], *s.* der Drücker. — *v.a.* — *off*, auslösen.
trilateral [traiˈlætərəl], *adj.* dreiseitig.
trill [tril], *s.* (*Mus.*) der Triller. — *v.a.*, *v.n.* trillern.
trim [trim], *adj.* niedlich, schmuck; nett (*dress*). — *v.a.* beschneiden; (*Naut.*) — *sails*, einziehen. — *s.* die Ausrüstung; (*Naut.*) das Gleichgewicht.
trimmer [ˈtrimə], *s.* die Putzmacherin; (*fig.*) der Opportunist.
trimmings [ˈtriminz], *s. pl.* (*fig.*) der Kleinkram; (*Tail.*) der Besatz.
Trinity [ˈtriniti], *s.* (*Theol.*) die Dreifaltigkeit, Dreieinigkeit.
trinket [ˈtriŋkit], *s.* das Geschmeide; (*pl.*) Schmucksachen, *f. pl.*
trip [trip], *s.* der Ausflug, die Reise. —

v.a. — *up*, ein Bein stellen (*Dat.*). — *v.n.* stolpern.
tripe [ˈtraip], *s.* die Kaldaunen, *f. pl.*; (*fig.*) der Unsinn.
triple [tripl], *adj.* dreifach.
triplet [ˈtriplit], *s.* der Drilling; (*Mus.*) die Triole; (*Poet.*) der Dreireim.
tripod [ˈtraipɔd], *s.* der Dreifuß.
tripos [ˈtraipɔs], *s.* das Schlußexamen (*Cambridge Univ.*).
trite [trait], *adj.* abgedroschen.
triumph [ˈtraiʌmf], *s.* der Triumph. — *v.n.* triumphieren.
triumphant [traiˈʌmfənt], *adj.* triumphierend.
trivial [ˈtriviəl], *adj.* trivial, platt, alltäglich.
troll (1) [troul], *v.n.* trällern (*hum*); fischen. — *s.* der Rundgesang (*song*).
troll (2) [troul], *s.* der Kobold (*gnome*).
trolley [ˈtrɔli], *s.* der Teewagen (*furniture*); (*Tech.*) die Dräsine, der Karren.
trollop [ˈtrɔləp], *s.* die Schlampe.
trombone [trɔmˈboun], *s.* (*Mus.*) die Posaune.
troop [tru:p], *s.* der Haufe; (*Mil.*) die Truppe, der Trupp. — *v.n.* sich sammeln. — *v.a. Trooping the Colour*, die Fahnenparade.
trophy [ˈtroufi], *s.* die Trophäe, das Siegeszeichen.
tropic [ˈtrɔpik], *s.* (*Geog.*) der Wendekreis; (*pl.*) die Tropen, *f. pl.*
tropical [ˈtrɔpikəl], *adj.* tropisch.
trot [trɔt], *v.n.* traben. — *s.* der Trab, Trott.
troth [trouθ], *s.* (*obs.*) die Treue; *pledge o.'s* —, Treue geloben.
trouble [trʌbl], *s.* die Mühe, Sorge (*worry*); der Kummer (*sadness*); die Störung (*disturbance*). — *v.a.* bemühen (*ask favour of*); bekümmern (*worry*); stören (*disturb*).
troublesome [ˈtrʌblsəm], *adj.* ärgerlich, schwierig, unangenehm.
trough [trɔf], *s.* der Trog; (*Met.*) das Tief.
trounce [trauns], *v.a.* verprügeln.
trouncing [ˈtraunsiŋ], *s.* die Tracht Prügel.
trousers [ˈtrauzəz], *s. pl.* die Hosen, *f.pl.*
trout [traut], *s.* (*Zool.*) die Forelle.
trowel [ˈtrauəl], *s.* die Kelle.
troy(weight) [ˈtrɔi(weit)], *s.* das Troygewicht.
truant [ˈtru:ənt], *s.* (*Sch.*) der Schulschwänzer; *play* —, die Schule schwänzen.
truce [tru:s], *s.* der Waffenstillstand.
truck (1) [trʌk], *s.* (*Rail.*) der Güterwagen; (*Am.*) *see* **lorry**.
truck (2) [trʌk], *s. have no* — *with*, nichts zu tun haben mit.
truculent [ˈtrʌkjulənt], *adj.* streitsüchtig.
trudge [trʌdʒ], *v.n.* sich schleppen.
true [tru:], *adj.* wahr; treu (*faithful*); echt (*genuine*); richtig (*correct*).

506

truffle [trʌfl], s. die Trüffel.

truism ['truːizm], s. der Gemeinplatz, die Binsenwahrheit.

truly ['truːli], adv. yours —, Ihr ergebener.

trump [trʌmp], s. der Trumpf; — card, die Trumpfkarte. — v.a. — up, erfinden, erdichten.

trumpery ['trʌmpəri], s. der Plunder, Schund. — adj. wertlos, belanglos.

trumpet ['trʌmpit], s. (Mus.) die Trompete. — v.a. stolz austrompeten, ausposaunen. — v.n. trompeten.

truncate [trʌŋ'keit], v.a. verstümmeln, stutzen.

truncheon ['trʌnʃən], s. der Knüppel. — v.a. durchprügeln.

trundle [trʌndl], v.n. trudeln; sich wälzen. — v.a. — a hoop, Reifen schlagen.

trunk [trʌŋk], s. der Stamm (tree); der Rüssel (of elephant); der (große) Koffer (chest); — call, das Ferngespräch.

truss [trʌs], s. das Band, Bruchband. — v.a. zäumen, stützen; aufschürzen.

trust [trʌst], v.a., v.n. trauen (Dat.), vertrauen (Dat.); anvertrauen (Dat., Acc.). — s. das Vertrauen; in —, zu treuen Händen, als Treuhänder; (Comm.) der Trust.

trustworthy ['trʌstwəːði], adj. zuverlässig.

truth [truːθ], s. die Wahrheit.

truthful ['truːθful], adj. wahrhaftig.

try [trai], v.a. irr. versuchen (s. th.); (Law) verhören; — on (clothes), anprobieren; — out, ausprobieren. — v.n. versuchen, sich bemühen. — s. der Versuch (attempt); (Rugby) der Try.

Tsar [zɑː], s. der Zar.

tub [tʌb], s. das Faß; die Wanne (bath); (Naut.) das Übungsboot.

tube [tjuːb], s. die Tube (paste etc.); die Röhre (pipe, also Elec.); der Schlauch (tyre); das Rohr (tubing); (Transport) die Londoner Untergrundbahn.

tuberous ['tjuːbərəs], adj. knollenartig, knollig.

tubular ['tjuːbjulə], adj. röhrenförmig.

tuck [tʌk], s. (Tail.) die Falte; (Sch. sl.) der Leckerbissen. — v.a. — up, zudecken; — in, einschlagen. — v.n. (sl.) — in, tüchtig zugreifen.

tucker ['tʌkə], s. (sl.) das Essen.

tuckshop ['tʌkʃɔp], s. der Schulladen.

Tuesday ['tjuːzdi], der Dienstag.

tuft [tʌft], s. der Büschel.

tug [tʌg], v.a. ziehen, zerren. — s. (Naut.) der Schlepper; — of war, das Tauziehen.

tuition [tjuː'iʃən], s. der Unterricht, Privatunterricht.

tulip ['tjuːlip], s. (Bot.) die Tulpe.

tumble [tʌmbl], v.n. purzeln. — s. der Sturz, Fall.

tumbril ['tʌmbril], s. der Karren.

tumid ['tjuːmid], adj. geschwollen.

tumour ['tjuːmə], s. (Med.) die Geschwulst, der Tumor.

tumult ['tjuːmʌlt], s. der Tumult, Auflauf; der Lärm (noise).

tun [tʌn], s. die Tonne, das Faß.

tune [tjuːn], s. die Melodie. — v.a. stimmen; (Rad.) — in (to), einstellen (auf.)

tuneful ['tjuːnful], adj. melodisch.

tuner ['tjuːnə], s. der (Klavier)stimmer.

tunic ['tjuːnik], s. der Kittel.

tuning ['tjuːniŋ], s. das Stimmen; die Abstimmung (also Rad.); — fork, die Stimmgabel.

tunnel [tʌnl], s. der Tunnel. — v.n. graben, einen Tunnel bauen.

turbid ['təːbid], adj. trüb, dick.

turbot ['təːbət], s. (Zool.) der Steinbutt.

turbulence ['təːbjuləns], s. der Sturm, das Ungestüm; (Aviat.) die Turbulenz.

tureen [tjuə'riːn], s. die Suppenterrine, Suppenschüssel.

turf [təːf], s. der Rasen; (Sport) die Rennbahn, der Turf. — v.a. mit Rasen belegen; (sl.) — out, hinausschmeißen.

turgid ['təːdʒid], adj. schwülstig (style).

Turk [təːk], s. der Türke.

turkey ['təːki], s. (Orn.) der Truthahn.

Turkish ['təːkiʃ], adj. türkisch.

turmoil ['təːmɔil], s. die Unruhe, der Aufruhr.

turn [təːn], v.a. wenden, drehen, kehren (to); — down, ablehnen; (coll.) — in, abgeben (hand over); — on, andrehen (tap etc.); — off, ausdrehen; — out, produzieren. — v.n. sich drehen, sich ändern; werden; — on s.o., jemanden verraten (coll.); — out, ausrücken; (coll.) — up, auftauchen. — s. die Drehung, Windung; der Hang; die Reihe; die Nummer (act); it is my —, ich bin an der Reihe.

turncoat ['təːnkout], s. der Überläufer.

turner ['təːnə], s. der Drechsler.

turnip ['təːnip], s. (Bot.) die Rübe.

turnpike ['təːnpaik], s. der Schlagbaum.

turnstile ['təːnstail], s. das Drehkreuz.

turntable ['təːnteibl], s. die Drehscheibe.

turpentine ['təːpəntain], s. der or das Terpentin.

turquoise ['təːkwɔiz or 'təːkɔiz], s. der Türkis.

turret ['tʌrit], s. (Archit.) der Turm, das Türmchen.

turtle [təːtl], s. (Zool.) die Schildkröte; (Orn.) -dove, die Turteltaube.

tusk [tʌsk], s. (Zool.) der Stoßzahn.

tussle [tʌsl], s. der Streit, die Rauferei.

tutelage ['tjuːtilidʒ], s. die Vormundschaft.

tutor ['tjuːtə], s. der Privatlehrer; der Tutor, Studienleiter. — v.a. unterrichten.

twaddle [twɔdl], s. das Geschwätz. — v.n. schwätzen.

twang [twæŋ], s. der scharfe Ton. — v.n. scharf klingen.

tweed [twiːd], s. (Text.) der Tweed.

twelfth [twelfθ], num.adj. zwölft; Twelfth Night, das Fest der Heiligen Drei Könige (6th January).

twelve [twelv], *num. adj.* zwölf.

twenty ['twenti], *num. adj.* zwanzig.

twice [twais], *num. adv.* zweimal, doppelt.

twig [twig], *s.* (*Bot.*) der Zweig, die Rute.

twilight ['twailait], *s.* das Zwielicht, die Dämmerung.

twill [twil], *s.* (*Text.*) der Köper. — *v.a.* köpern.

twin [twin], *s.* der Zwilling.

twine [twain], *s.* der Bindfaden, die Schnur. — *v.a.* drehen, zwirnen. — *v.n.* sich verflechten; sich winden (*plant*).

twinge [twindʒ], *s.* der Zwick, Stich.

twinkle ['twiŋkl], *v.n.* blinzeln, blinken. — *s.* das Zwinkern, der Blick.

twirl [twə:l], *s.* der Wirbel. — *v.a.* schnell drehen, wirbeln.

twist [twist], *v.a.* flechten, drehen; verdrehen. — *s.* die Drehung, Krümmung; das Geflecht; (*fig.*) die Wendung (*sudden change*).

twitch [twitʃ], *v.a.* zupfen, zucken. — *v.n.* zucken. — *s.* das Zucken, der Krampf.

twitter ['twitə], *v.n.* zwitschern; (*fig.*) zittern. — *s.* das Gezwitscher; (*fig.*) die Angst.

two [tu:], *num. adj.* zwei; — -*faced*, falsch.

twofold ['tu:fould], *adj.* zweifach.

tympanum ['timpənəm], *s.* (*Med.*) das Trommelfell.

type [taip], *s.* (*Typ.*) die Type; (*Psych.*) der Typ, Typus. — *v.a., v.n.* tippen; mit der Maschine schreiben.

typewriter ['taipraitə], *s.* die Schreibmaschine.

typhoid ['taifɔid], *s.* (*Med.*) der (Unterleibs)typhus. — *adj.* typhusartig.

typist ['taipist], *s.* der (die) Maschinenschreiber(in).

typhoon [tai'fu:n], *s.* der Taifun.

typical ['tipikəl], *adj.* typisch, charakteristisch.

typography [tai'pɔgrəfi], *s.* die Typographie, Buchdruckerkunst.

tyrannical [ti'rænikəl], *adj.* tyrannisch.

tyranny ['tirəni], *s.* die Tyrannei.

tyrant ['taiərənt], *s.* der Tyrann.

tyre, (*Am.*) **tire** [taiə], *s.* der Reifen.

tyro ['taiərou], *s.* der Anfänger.

Tyrolese [tiro'li:z], *adj.* tirolisch, Tiroler-. — *s.* der Tiroler.

U

U [ju:]. das U.

ubiquitous [ju'bikwitəs], *adj.* überall da, überall zu finden.

udder ['ʌdə], *s.* (*Zool.*) das Euter.

ugly ['ʌgli], *adj.* häßlich.

Ukrainian [ju:'krciniən], *adj.* ukrainisch. — *s.* der Ukrainer.

ulcer ['ʌlsə], *s.* (*Med.*) das Geschwür.

ulcerate ['ʌlsəreit], *v.n.* (*Med.*) schwären.

ulcerous ['ʌlsərəs], *adj.* (*Med.*) geschwürig.

ulterior [ʌl'tiəriə], *adj.* weiter, ferner, weiterliegend.

ultimate ['ʌltimit], *adj.* letzt, endlich, äußerst.

ultimatum [ʌlti'meitəm], *s.* das Ultimatum.

umbrage ['ʌmbridʒ], *s.* der Schatten; *take* —, Anstoß nehmen (an, *Dat.*).

umbrella [ʌm'brelə], *s.* der Schirm, Regenschirm.

umpire ['ʌmpaiə], *s.* (*Sport*) der Schiedsrichter.

umpteen ['ʌmpti:n], *adj.* zahlreiche, verschiedene.

un- [ʌn], *negating pref.* un-, nicht-; *with verbs,* auf-, ent-, los-, ver-; *where a word is not given, see the simple form.*

unable [ʌn'eibl], *adj.* unfähig; *be* —, nicht können.

unaccustomed [ʌnə'kʌstəmd], *adj.* ungewohnt.

unaided [ʌn'eidid], *adj.* allein, ohne Hilfe.

unaware [ʌnə'wɛə], *adj.* unbewußt.

uncertain [ʌn'sə:tin], *adj.* unsicher.

uncle [ʌŋkl], *s.* der Onkel.

unconscious [ʌn'kɔnʃəs], *adj.* bewußtlos; unbewusst.

uncouth [ʌn'ku:θ], *adj.* ungehobelt, roh.

unction ['ʌŋkʃən], *s.* die Salbung (*anointing*); die Salbe; *Extreme Unction,* (*Eccl.*) die Letzte Ölung.

unctuous ['ʌŋktjuəs], *adj.* salbungsvoll.

under ['ʌndə], *prep.* unter. — *adv.* darunter, unten (*underneath*); *pref.* (*compounds*) unter-.

undercarriage ['ʌndəkæridʒ], *s.* (*Aviat.*) das Fahrwerk.

underfed [ʌndə'fed], *adj.* unterernährt.

undergo [ʌndə'gou], *v.a. irr.* durchmachen, erdulden.

undergraduate [ʌndə'grædjuit], *s.* (*Univ.*) der Student.

underground ['ʌndəgraund], *adj.* unterirdisch; — *railway* die Untergrundbahn. — [ʌndə'graund], *adv.* unterirdisch.

underhand [ʌndə'hænd], *adj.* heimlich, hinterlistig.

underline [ʌndə'lain], *v.a.* unterstreichen.

undermine [ʌndə'main], *v.a.* untergraben.

underneath [ʌndə'ni:θ], *adv.* unten, darunter. — ['ʌndəni:θ], *prep.* unter.

undersigned ['ʌndəsaind], *adj.* unterzeichnet. —*s.* der Unterzeichnete.

understand [ʌndə'stænd], *v.a. irr.* verstehen, begreifen.

understatement ['ʌndəsteitmənt], *s.* die zu bescheidene Festellung, Unterbewertung.

undertaker ['ʌndəteikə], *s.* der Leichenbestatter.

undertaking [ʌndə'teikiŋ], *s.* das Unternehmen (*business*); das Versprechen (*promise*).

undertone ['ʌndətoun], *s.* der Unterton.

underwrite [ʌndə'rait], *v.a. irr.* (*Comm.*) versichern.

underwriter ['ʌndəraitə], *s.* (*Comm.*) der Assekurant, Versicherer, Mitversicherer.

undeserved [ʌndi'zə:vd], *adj.* unverdient.

undeserving [ʌndi'zə:viŋ], *adj.* unwürdig.

undignified [ʌn'dignifaid], *adj.* würdelos.

undiscerning [ʌndi'zə:niŋ], *adj.* geschmacklos.

undiscriminating [ʌndis'krimineitiŋ], *adj.* unterschiedslos, unkritisch.

undisputed [ʌndis'pju:tid], *adj.* unbestritten.

undo [ʌn'du:], *v.a. irr.* zerstören (*destroy*); öffnen (*open*).

undoubted [ʌn'dautid], *adj.* zweifellos.

undress [ʌn'dres], *v.a., v.n.* — (sich)ausziehen. — ['ʌndres], *s.* das Hauskleid.

undue [ʌn'dju:], *adj.* unangemessen.

undulate ['ʌndjuleit], *v.n.* wallen, Wellen schlagen.

unduly [ʌn'dju:li], *adv.* ungebührlich, übermäßig.

unearth [ʌn'ə:θ], *v.a.* ausgraben.

unearthly [ʌn'ə:θli], *adj.* überirdisch.

uneasy [ʌn'i:zi], *adj.* unruhig, unbehaglich.

unemployed [ʌnim'plɔid], *adj.* arbeitslos.

unemployment [ʌnim'plɔimənt], *s.* die Arbeitslosigkeit.

unending [ʌn'endiŋ], *adj.* endlos.

uneven [ʌn'i:vən], *adj.* uneben; ungerade.

unexceptionable [ʌnik'sepʃənəbl], *adj.* tadellos.

unexpired [ʌniks'paiəd], *adj.* noch nicht abgelaufen, noch gültig.

unfair [ʌn'fɛə], *adj.* unfair; unehrlich.

unfeeling [ʌn'fi:liŋ], *adj.* gefühllos.

unfit [ʌn'fit], *adj.* (*Mil., Med.*) untauglich, schwach; (*food etc.*) ungenießbar.

unfold [ʌn'fould], *v.a.* entfalten.

unforeseen [ʌnfɔ:'si:n], *adj.* unerwartet.

unfounded [ʌn'faundid], *adj.* grundlos.

unfurnished [ʌn'fə:niʃd], *adj.* unmöbliert.

ungrudging [ʌn'grʌdʒiŋ], *adj.* bereitwillig.

unhappy [ʌn'hæpi], *adj.* unglücklich.

unhinge [ʌn'hindʒ], *v.a.* aus den Angeln heben.

unicorn ['ju:nikɔ:n], *s.* (*Myth.*) das Einhorn.

uniform ['ju:nifɔ:m], *s.* die Uniform. — *adj.* gleichförmig, einförmig.

union ['ju:niən], *s.* die Vereinigung; *trade* —, die Gewerkschaft; *Union Jack*, die britische Nationalflagge.

unique [ju'ni:k], *adj.* einzigartig.

unison ['ju:nisən], *s.* (*Mus.*) der Einklang, die Harmonie.

unit ['ju:nit], *s.* die Einheit (*measure etc.*).

unite [ju'nait], *v.a.* vereinen. — *v.n.* sich vereinen, verbünden.

unity ['ju:niti], *s.* die Einigkeit.

universal [ju:ni'və:səl], *adj.* allgemein.

universe ['ju:nivə:s], *s.* das Weltall.

university [ju:ni'və:siti], *s.* die Universität, Hochschule; — *degree*, der akademische Grad.

unkempt [ʌn'kempt], *adj.* ungekämmt, ungepflegt.

unleavened [ʌn'levənd], *adj.* ungesäuert.

unless [ʌn'les], *conj.* außer, wenn nicht, es sei denn.

unlettered [ʌn'letəd], *adj.* ungebildet.

unlicensed [ʌn'laisənsd], *adj.* nicht (für Alkoholverkauf) lizenziert.

unlike [ʌn'laik], *adj.* ungleich. — ['ʌnlaik], *prep.* anders als, verschieden von.

unlikely [ʌn'laikli], *adj., adv.* unwahrscheinlich.

unlock [ʌn'lɔk], *v.a.* aufschließen.

unmask [ʌn'mɑ:sk], *v.a.* entlarven.

unpack [ʌn'pæk], *v.a., v.n.* auspacken.

unpleasant [ʌn'pleznt], *adj.* unangenehm.

unreliable [ʌnri'laiəbl], *adj.* unzuverlässig.

unremitting [ʌnri'mitiŋ], *adj.* unablässig.

unrepentant [ʌnri'pentənt], *adj.* reuelos.

unrest [ʌn'rest], *s.* die Unruhe.

unsafe [ʌn'seif], *adj.* unsicher.

unscathed [ʌn'skeiðd], *adj.* unversehrt.

unscrew [ʌn'skru:], *v.a.* abschrauben.

unscrupulous [ʌn'skru:pjuləs], *adj.* skrupellos, gewissenlos.

unseat [ʌn'si:t], *v.a.* aus dem Sattel heben; absetzen.

unselfish [ʌn'selfiʃ], *adj.* selbstlos.

unsettle [ʌn'setl], *v.a.* verwirren; (*fig.*) aus dem Konzept bringen.

unsew [ʌn'sou], *v.a.* auftrennen.

unshrinking [ʌn'ʃrinkiŋ], *adj.* unverzagt.

unsophisticated [ʌnsə'fistikeitid], *adj.* naiv, natürlich.

unsparing [ʌn'spɛəriŋ], *adj.* schonungslos.

unstable [ʌn'steibl], *adj.* unsicher; labil.

unstitch [ʌn'stitʃ], *v.a.* auftrennen.

unstop [ʌn'stɔp], *v.a.* aufstöpseln, öffnen (*a bottle*).

unstudied [ʌn'stʌdid], *adj.* ungekünstelt.

unsuccessful [ʌnsək'sesful], *adj.* erfolglos.

unsuspecting [ʌnsə'spektiŋ], *adj.* arglos.

untie [ʌn'tai], *v.a.* losbinden.

until [ʌn'til], *prep., conj.* bis.

untimely [ʌnˈtaimli], *adj.* vorzeitig, unzeitig.

untiring [ʌnˈtaiəriŋ], *adj.* unermüdlich.

unto [ˈʌntu], *prep.* (*Poet.*) zu.

untold [ʌnˈtould], *adj.* ungezählt, unermeßlich.

untoward [ʌnˈtɔːd *or* ʌnˈtouəd], *adj.* unangenehm; widerspenstig (*recalcitrant*).

untrustworthy [ʌnˈtrʌstwəːði], *adj.* unzuverlässig.

unveil [ʌnˈveil], *v.a.* enthüllen.

unwieldy [ʌnˈwiːldi], *adj.* sperrig, schwerfällig.

unwind [ʌnˈwaind], *v.a.* abwickeln.

unwitting [ʌnˈwitiŋ], *adj.* unwissentlich, unbewusst.

unwonted [ʌnˈwountid], *adj.* ungewohnt.

unwrap [ʌnˈræp], *v.a.* auspacken, auswickeln.

unyielding [ʌnˈjiːldiŋ], *adj.* unnachgiebig; hartnäckig.

unyoke [ʌnˈjouk], *v.a.* ausspannen.

up [ʌp], *adv.* auf, aufwärts (*upward*); aufgestanden (*out of bed*); — (*there*), oben; *what's up?* was ist los? — *to*, bis zu; *be — to s.th.*, auf etwas aus sein, etwas im Schilde führen; *it's — to you*, es liegt an dir. — *prep.* auf, hinauf. — *s. ups and downs*, das wechselnde Schicksal, Auf und Ab.

upbraid [ʌpˈbreid], *v.a.* tadeln.

upheaval [ʌpˈhiːvl], *s.* das Chaos, Durcheinander, die Umwälzung.

uphill [ʌpˈhil], *adv.* bergauf(wärts). — [ˈʌphil], *adj.* (an)steigend; (*fig.*) mühsam.

uphold [ʌpˈhould], *v.a.* aufrechterhalten.

upholster [ʌpˈhoulstə], *v.a.* polstern.

upholstery [ʌpˈhoulstəri], *s.* die Polsterung.

upon [ʌˈpɔn] *see on.*

upper [ˈʌpə], *adj.* ober, höher; — *hand*, die Oberhand.

uppish [ˈʌpiʃ], *adj.* anmaßend.

upright [ˈʌprait], *adj.* aufrecht, gerade; (*fig.*) aufrichtig, rechtschaffen.

uproar [ˈʌprɔː], *s.* der Lärm, Aufruhr.

uproot [ʌpˈruːt], *v.a.* entwurzeln.

upset [ʌpˈset], *v.a.* umwerfen; (*fig.*) aus der Fassung bringen. — [ˈʌpset], *s.* das Umwerfen; (*fig.*) die Bestürzung.

upshot [ˈʌpʃɔt], *s.* der Ausgang, das Ergebnis.

upside [ˈʌpsaid], *s.* die Oberseite; — *down*, auf den Kopf gestellt.

upstairs [ʌpˈstɛəz], *adv.* oben, nach oben.

upstart [ˈʌpstɑːt], *s.* der Parvenü, Emporkömmling.

upward [ˈʌpwəd], *adj.* steigend, aufwärtsgehend. — *adv.* (*also* **upwards**) aufwärts; — *of*, mehr als.

urban [ˈəːbən], *adj.* städtisch.

urbane [əːˈbein], *adj.* zivilisiert.

urbanity [əːˈbæniti], *s.* die Bildung, der Schliff.

urchin [ˈəːtʃin], *s.* der Schelm; (*Zool.*) *sea —*, der Seeigel.

urge [əːdʒ], *v.a.* drängen. — *s.* der Drang.

urgent [ˈəːdʒənt], *adj.* dringend, drängend, dringlich.

urine [ˈjuərin], *s.* der Urin.

urn [əːn], *s.* die Urne.

Uruguayan [juːruˈgwaiən], *adj.* uruguayisch. — *s.* der Uruguayer.

us [ʌs], *pers. pron.* uns.

usage [ˈjuːsidʒ], *s.* der (Sprach)gebrauch; die Sitte.

use [juːz], *v.a.* gebrauchen, benutzen. — [juːs], *s.* der Gebrauch, die Benutzung; der Nutzen (*usefulness*).

usher [ˈʌʃə], *s.* der Türhüter, Platzanweiser. — *v.a.* — *in*, anmelden, einführen.

usherette [ʌʃəˈret], *s.* die Platzanweiserin, Programmverkäuferin.

usual [ˈjuːʒuəl], *adj.* gewöhnlich, üblich.

usurer [ˈjuːʒərə *or* ˈjuːʒjuərə], *s.* der Wucherer.

usurp [juːˈzəːp], *v.a.* an sich reißen, usurpieren.

usury [ˈjuːʒjuəri], *s.* der Wucher.

utensil [juːˈtensil], *s.* das Gerät, Werkzeug.

utility [juːˈtiliti], *s.* die Nützlichkeit (*usefulness*); der Nutzen; *public —*, (die) öffentliche Einrichtung.

utilize [juːˈtilaiz], *v.a.* nutzbar machen, ausbeuten, ausnützen.

utmost [ˈʌtmoust], *adj.* äußerst, weitest, höchst. — *s.* das Höchste, Äußerste.

utter [ˈʌtə], *adj.* äußerst, gänzlich. — *v.a.* äußern, aussprechen.

utterly [ˈʌtəli], *adv.* äußerst, völlig.

uvula [ˈjuːvjulə], *s.* (*Anat.*) das Zäpfchen.

V

V [viː]. das V.

vacancy [ˈveikənsi], *s.* die freie Stelle, die Vakanz.

vacant [ˈveikənt], *adj.* frei; leer.

vacate [vəˈkeit], *v.a.* frei machen.

vacation [vəˈkeiʃən], *s.* die Niederlegung (*of a post*); die Ferien, *pl.* (*school*); der Urlaub (*holiday*).

vaccinate [ˈvæksineit], *v.a.* (*Med.*) impfen.

vaccine [ˈvæksiːn], *s.* (*Med.*) der Impfstoff.

vacillate [ˈvæsileit], *v.n.* schwanken.

vacuity [væˈkjuːiti], *s.* die Leere.

vacuous [ˈvækjuəs], *adj.* leer.

vacuum [ˈvækjuəm], *s.* das Vakuum; — *cleaner*, der Staubsauger.

vagabond [ˈvægəbɔnd], *s.* der Landstreicher.

vagary [vəˈgɛəri], *s.* die Laune, Grille.

vagrant ['veigrənt], *adj.* herumstreichend. — *s.* der Landstreicher.

vague [veig], *adj.* vage, unbestimmt, unklar.

vain [vein], *adj.* nichtig, vergeblich, eitel; *in* —, vergebens, umsonst.

vale [veil], *s.* (*Poet.*) das Tal.

valerian [və'liəriən], *s.* (*Bot.*) der Baldrian.

valet ['vælei, 'vælit], *s.* der Diener.

valiant ['væljənt], *adj.* mutig, tapfer.

valid ['vælid], *adj.* gültig, stichhaltig.

valley ['væli], *s.* das Tal.

valuable ['væljuəbl], *adj.* wertvoll, kostbar.

valuation [vælju'eiʃən], *s.* die Schätzung.

value ['vælju:], *s.* der Wert. — *v.a.* wertschätzen, schätzen.

valve [vælv], *s.* (*Mech.*) das Ventil; (*Rad.*) die Röhre.

vamp (1) [væmp], *s.* das Oberleder.

vamp (2) [væmp], *s.* (*Am. coll.*) der Vamp.

vampire ['væmpaiə], *s.* der Vampir.

van [væn], *s.* der Lieferwagen.

vane [vein], *s.* die Wetterfahne.

vanguard ['vænga:d], *s.* die Vorhut, der Vortrupp.

vanilla [və'nilə], *s.* die Vanille.

vanish ['væniʃ], *v.n.* verschwinden.

vanity ['væniti], *s.* die Nichtigkeit; die Eitelkeit (*conceit*).

vanquish ['væŋkwiʃ], *v.a.* besiegen.

vantage ['va:ntidʒ], *s.* der Vorteil; — *point*, die günstige Position.

vapid ['væpid], *adj.* leer, schal.

vapour ['veipə], *s.* der Dunst; (*Chem.*) der Dampf.

variable ['veəriəbl], *adj.* variabel, veränderlich.

variance ['veəriəns], *s.* die Uneinigkeit.

variation [veəri'eiʃən], *s.* die Variation; die Veränderung, Abweichung.

varicose ['værikəs], *adj.* Krampf-, krampfaderig.

variegated ['veərigeitid], *adj.* bunt, vielfarbig.

variety [və'raiəti], *s.* die Mannigfaltigkeit; (*Bot.*) die Varietät, Abart; (*Theat.*) das Varieté, das Varietétheater.

various ['veəriəs], *adj.* verschieden; mannigfaltig.

varnish ['va:niʃ], *s.* der Firnis, der Lack. — *v.a.* mit Firnis anstreichen, lackieren.

vary ['veəri], *v.a.* abändern. — *v.n.* sich ändern, variieren.

vase [va:z], *s.* die Vase.

vassal [væsl], *s.* der Vasall, Lehnsmann.

vast [va:st], *adj.* ungeheuer, groß.

vat [væt], *s.* die Kufe, das große Faß.

vault [vɔ:lt], *s.* das Gewölbe; die Gruft (*grave*); (*Sport*) der Sprung, *pole* —, der Stabhochsprung. — *v.n.* springen.

vaunt [vɔ:nt], *v.a.* rühmen. — *v.n.* prahlen, sich rühmen. — *s.* die Prahlerei.

veal [vi:l], *s.* das Kalbfleisch.

veer [viə], *v.n.* sich drehen.

vegetable ['vedʒitəbl], *s.* das Gemüse.

vegetarian [vedʒi'teəriən], *adj.* vegetarisch. — *s.* der Vegetarier.

vegetate ['vedʒiteit], *v.n.* vegetieren.

vehemence ['vi:əməns], *s.* die Vehemenz, Heftigkeit.

vehicle ['vi:ikl], *s.* das Fahrzeug, Fuhrwerk; (*Motor.*) der Wagen.

veil [veil], *s.* der Schleier. — *v.a.* verschleiern.

vein [vein], *s.* die Ader.

vellum ['veləm], *s.* das feine Pergamentpapier.

velocity [vi'lɔsiti], *s.* die Geschwindigkeit, Schnelligkeit.

velvet ['velvit], *s.* (*Text.*) der Samt.

venal ['vi:nəl], *adj.* käuflich.

vend [vend], *v.a.* verkaufen; —*ing machine*, der Automat.

veneer [və'niə], *s.* das Furnier. — *v.a.* furnieren.

venerable ['venərəbl], *adj.* ehrwürdig.

venerate ['venəreit], *v.a.* verehren.

venereal [və'niəriəl], *adj.* Geschlechts-.

Venezuelan [veni'zweilən], *adj.* venezolanisch. — *s.* der Venezolaner.

vengeance ['vendʒəns], *s.* die Rache.

venison ['venizn *or* venzn], *s.* das Wildpret.

venom ['venəm], *s.* das Gift.

vent [vent], *v.a.* Luft machen (*Dat.*). — *s.* das Luftloch, die Öffnung.

ventilate ['ventileit], *v.a.* ventilieren, lüften.

ventricle ['ventrikl], *s.* (*Anat.*) die Herzkammer.

ventriloquist [ven'triləkwist], *s.* der Bauchredner.

venture ['ventʃə], *s.* das Wagnis, Unternehmen. — *v.a.* wagen, riskieren. — *v.n.* sich erlauben, (sich) wagen.

venue ['venju:], *s.* der Treffpunkt, Versammlungsort.

veracity [və'ræsiti], *s.* die Glaubwürdigkeit, Wahrhaftigkeit.

verbose [və:'bous], *adj.* wortreich, weitschweifig.

verdant ['və:dənt], *adj.* grünend, grün.

verdict ['və:dikt], *s.* das Urteil, die Entscheidung.

verdigris ['və:digri:s], *s.* der Grünspan.

verdure ['və:djə], *s.* das Grün.

verge [və:dʒ], *s.* der Rand, die Einfassung. — *v.n.* grenzen (*on*, an, *Acc.*).

verify ['verifai], *v.a.* bestätigen; (*Law*) beglaubigen.

verily ['verili], *adv.* (*Bibl.*) wahrlich.

veritable ['veritəbl], *adj.* wahr, echt.

vermicelli [və:mi'seli], *s.* die Nudeln, *f. pl.*

vermilion [və'miljən], *s.* das Zinnober (*paint*).

vermin ['və:min], *s. pl.* das Ungeziefer.

vermouth ['və:mu:θ, -mu:t], *s.* der Wermut.

vernacular [və'nækjulə], *s.* die Landessprache. — *adj.* einheimisch.

vernal ['və:nəl], *adj.* frühlingsartig, Frühlings-.

511

versatile ['vəːsətail], *adj.* gewandt; vielseitig.

verse [vəːs], *s.* der Vers; (*Poet.*) die Strophe.

versed [vəːsd], *adj.* bewandert.

version ['vəːʃən], *s.* die Version, Fassung, Lesart; (*fig.*) die Darstellung.

vertebrate ['vəːtibrət], *s.* (*Zool.*) das Wirbeltier. — *adj.* mit Rückenwirbeln versehen.

vertex ['vəːteks], *s.* der Zenit.

vertigo ['vəːtigou], *s.* (*Med.*) der Schwindel, das Schwindelgefühl.

verve [vəːv], *s.* der Schwung.

very ['veri], *adv.* sehr. — *adj.* echt, wirklich,wahrhaftig.

vespers ['vespəz], *s. pl.* (*Eccl.*) der Abendgottesdienst, die Vesper.

vessel [vesl], *s.* das Gefäß (*container*); (*Naut.*) das Fahrzeug, Schiff.

vest [vest], *s.* das Gewand; (*Tail.*) die Weste; das Unterhemd (*undergarment*). — *v.a.* übertragen.

vested ['vestid], *adj.* — *interests*, das Eigeninteresse.

vestige ['vestidʒ], *s.* die Spur.

vestment ['vestmənt], *s.* (*Eccl.*) das Meßgewand.

vestry ['vestri], *s.* (*Eccl.*) die Sakristei.

vetch [vetʃ], *s.* (*Bot.*) die Wicke.

veterinary ['vetərinri], *adj.* tierärztlich; — *surgeon*, der Tierarzt.

veto ['viːtou], *s.* (*Pol.*) der Einspruch, das Veto.

vex [veks], *v.a.* quälen, plagen.

vexation [vek'seiʃən], *s.* die Plage, der Verdruß.

via [vaiə], *prep.* über.

vibrate [vai'breit], *v.n.* schwingen, vibrieren.

vicar ['vikə], *s.* (*Eccl.*) der Pfarrer, Vikar.

vicarious [vi'kɛəriəs], *adj.* stellvertretend.

vice (1) [vais], *s.* das Laster (*immorality*).

vice (2) [vais], *s.* (*Mech.*) der Schraubstock.

vice- [vais], *pref.* Vize-, zweiter (*chairman etc.*).

vicinity [vi'siniti], *s.* die Nachbarschaft, Nähe.

vicious ['viʃəs], *adj.* böse, bösartig.

vicissitude [vi'sisitjuːd], *s.* der Wechsel, Wandel; (*pl.*) Wechselfälle, *m. pl.*

victim ['viktim], *s.* das Opfer.

victuals [vitlz], *s. pl.* die Lebensmittel, *n. pl.*

vie [vai], *v.n.* wetteifern.

Vietnamese [vjetnə'miːz], *adj.* vietnamesisch. — *s.* der Vietnamese.

view [vjuː], *s.* der Anblick, die Aussicht (*panorama*); die Ansicht (*opinion*); die Absicht (*intention*). — *v.a.* betrachten; besichtigen (*inspect*).

vigil ['vidʒil], *s.* die Nachtwache.

vigilance ['vidʒiləns], *s.* die Wachsamkeit.

vigorous ['vigərəs], *adj.* kräftig, rüstig, energisch.

vigour ['vigə], *s.* die Kraft, Energie.

vile [vail], *adj.* schlecht, niedrig.

vilify ['vilifai], *v.a.* beschimpfen, erniedrigen.

villa ['vilə], *s.* das Landhaus, die Villa.

village ['vilidʒ], *s.* das Dorf.

villain ['vilən], *s.* der Schurke.

villainous ['vilənəs], *adj.* niederträchtig.

villainy ['viləni], *s.* die Niedertracht, Schändlichkeit.

vindicate ['vindikeit], *v.a.* behaupten, verteidigen; rechtfertigen (*justify*).

vindictive [vin'diktiv], *adj.* rachsüchtig.

vine [vain], *s.* (*Bot.*) der Weinstock, die Rebe.

vinegar ['vinigə], *s.* der Essig.

vintage ['vintidʒ], *s.* die Weinernte; der Jahrgang (*also fig.*).

vintner ['vintnə], *s.* der Weinbauer, Winzer.

viola [vi'oulə], *s.* (*Mus.*) die Viola, Bratsche.

violate ['vaiəleit], *v.a.* verletzen, schänden.

violence ['vaiələns], *s.* die Gewalt; die Gewalttätigkeit.

violent ['vaiələnt], *adj.* gewalttätig (*brutal*); heftig (*vehement*).

violet ['vaiəlit], *s.* (*Bot.*) das Veilchen. — *adj.* veilchenblau, violett.

violin [vaiə'lin], *s.* (*Mus.*) die Violine, Geige.

viper ['vaipə], *s.* (*Zool.*) die Viper, Natter.

virago [vi'rɑːgou], *s.* das Mannweib.

virgin ['vəːdʒin], *s.* die Jungfrau.

virile ['virail], *adj.* männlich, kräftig.

virtual ['vəːtjuəl], *adj.* eigentlich.

virtue ['vəːtjuː], *s.* die Tugend; *by — of*, kraft (*Genit.*).

virtuoso [vəːtju'ousou], *s.* der Virtuose.

virtuous ['vəːtjuəs], *adj.* tugendhaft.

virulent ['virulənt], *adj.* bösartig, giftig.

virus ['vaiərəs], *s.* (*Med.*) das Gift, Virus.

viscosity [vis'kɔsiti], *s.* die Zähigkeit, Zähflüssigkeit.

viscount ['vaikaunt], *s.* der Vicomte.

viscous ['viskəs], *adj.* zähflüssig, klebrig.

visibility [vizi'biliti], *s.* die Sichtbarkeit, Sicht.

visible ['vizibl], *adj.* sichtbar.

vision ['viʒən], *s.* die Sehkraft; (*fig.*) die Vision (*dream*); die Erscheinung (*apparition*).

visionary ['viʒənri], *s.* der Träumer, (*Poet.*) der Seher. — *adj.* visionär, phantastisch, seherisch.

visit ['vizit], *s.* der Besuch. — *v.a.* besuchen.

visitation [vizi'teiʃən], *s.* die Heimsuchung.

visor ['vaizə], *s.* das Visier.

vista ['vistə], *s.* (*Art*) die Aussicht, der Ausblick.

visual ['viʒjuəl], *adj.* visuell, Seh-.

vital [vaitl], *adj.* lebenswichtig; (*fig.*) wesentlich.

vitality [vai'tæliti], *s.* die Lebenskraft, Vitalität.

vitiate ['viʃieit], *v.a.* verderben, um-stoßen.

vitreous ['vitriəs], *adj.* gläsern, glasar-tig.

vitrify ['vitrifai], *v.a.* verglasen.

vivacious [vi'veiʃəs], *adj.* lebhaft, munter.

viva (voce) ['vaivə ('vousi)], *s.* die mündliche Prüfung.

vivacity [vi'væsiti], *s.* die Lebhaftig-keit.

vivid ['vivid], *adj.* lebhaft.

vixen ['viksən], *s.* (*Zool.*) die Füchsin; (*fig.*) das zänkische Weib.

vizier [vi'ziə], *s.* der Wesir.

vocabulary [vo'kæbjuləri], *s.* das Voka-bular; der Wortschatz.

vocal ['voukəl], *adj.* laut; (*Mus.*) Stimm-, Sing-.

vocation [vo'keiʃən], *s.* die Berufung (*call*); der Beruf (*occupation*).

vociferous [vo'sifərəs], *adj.* schreiend, laut.

vogue [voug], *s.* die Mode.

voice [vɔis], *s.* die Stimme.

void [vɔid], *adj.* leer (*empty*); ungültig, (*invalid*); null and —, null und nich-tig. — *s.* die Leere.

volatile ['vɔlətail], *adj.* flüchtig.

volcanic [vɔl'kænik], *adj.* vulkanisch.

volcano [vɔl'keinou], *s.* der Vulkan.

volition [vo'liʃən], *s.* der Wille.

volley ['vɔli], *s.* (*Mil.*) die Salve; (*Footb.*) der Volleyschuß; (*Tennis*) der Flugball.

volt [voult], *s.* (*Elec.*) das Volt.

voltage ['voultidʒ], *s.* die Spannung.

voluble ['vɔljubl], *adj.* gesprächig, zungenfertig.

volume ['vɔlju:m], *s.* (*Phys.*) das Volumen; der Band (*book*); (*fig.*) der Umfang.

voluminous [və'lju:minəs], *adj.* um-fangreich.

voluntary ['vɔləntri], *adj.* freiwillig. — *s.* (*Mus.*) das Orgelsolo.

volunteer [vɔlən'tiə], *s.* der Freiwillige. — *v.n.* sich freiwillig melden.

voluptuous [və'lʌptjuəs], *adj.* wollüstig, lüstern.

vomit ['vɔmit], *v.a., v.n.* (sich) er-brechen, übergeben.

voracious [vɔ'reiʃəs], *adj.* gierig, ge-fräßig.

vortex ['vɔ:teks], *s.* der Wirbel, Strudel.

vote [vout], *v.n.* (*Pol.*) wählen, abstim-men, die Stimme abgeben. — *s.* (*Pol.*) die Stimme.

voter ['voutə], *s.* der Wähler.

votive ['voutiv], *adj.* (*Eccl.*) geweiht, gelobt; Votiv-.

vouch [vautʃ], *v.a., v.n.* (sich) ver-bürgen, einstehen(für).

voucher ['vautʃə], *s.* der Beleg; (*Comm.*) der Gutschein.

vouchsafe [vautʃ'seif], *v.a.* bewilligen, gewähren. — *v.n.* geruhen, sich herablassen.

vow [vau], *s.* das Gelübde. — *v.a.* schwören, geloben.

vowel ['vauəl], *s.* der Vokal.

voyage ['vɔiidʒ], *s.* die Seereise. — *v.n.* zur See reisen.

vulcanize ['vʌlkənaiz], *v.a.* vulkani-sieren.

vulgar ['vʌlgə], *adj.* gemein, pöbelhaft, ordinär, vulgär.

vulnerable ['vʌlnərəbl], *adj.* verwund-bar, verletzbar.

vulture ['vʌltʃə], *s.* (*Orn.*) der Geier.

W

W ['dʌblju:]. das W.

wabble *see* wobble.

wad [wɔd], *s.* das Bündel (*notes*); der Bausch (*cotton wool*).

waddle [wɔdl], *v.n.* watscheln.

wade [weid], *v.n.* waten, durchwaten.

wafer ['weifə], *s.* die Oblate, die Waffel; (*Eccl.*) die Hostie.

waffle [wɔfl], *s.* (*Cul.*) die Waffel. — *v.n.* (*coll.*) schwafeln.

waft [wæft], *v.a.* wegwehen.

wag (1) [wæg], *v.a.* wedeln, schütteln.

wag (2) [wæg], *s.* der Spaßvogel.

wage (1) [weidʒ], *v.a.* unternehmen; — *war*, Krieg führen.

wage (2) ['weidʒ], *s.* (*often in pl.*) der Lohn.

wager ['weidʒə], *v.a.* wetten. — *s.* die Wette.

waggish ['wægiʃ], *adj.* spaßhaft, mut-willig, schelmisch.

wag(g)on ['wægən], *s.* der Wagen, Güterwagen.

wagtail ['wægteil], *s.* (*Orn.*) die Bach-stelze.

waif [weif], *s.* das verwahrloste Kind; das herrenlose Gut.

wail [weil], *v.n.* wehklagen. — *s.* das Wehklagen, die Klage.

waist [weist], *s.* (*Anat.*) die Taille.

waistcoat ['weiskout, 'weskət], *s.* die Weste, das Wams.

wait [weit], *v.n.* warten; — *for*, warten auf; — *upon*, bedienen. — *v.a.* erwarten.

waiter ['weitə], *s.* der Kellner; *head* —, der Oberkellner, (*coll.*) der Ober.

waiting room ['weitiŋ rum], *s.* das Wartezimmer; (*Railw.*) der Wartesaal.

waive [weiv], *v.a.* aufgeben, verzichten (auf, *Acc.*).

wake (1) [weik], *v.n. irr.* wachen, auf-wachen, wach sein. — *v.a.* aufwecken.

wake (2) [weik], *s.* (*Naut.*) das Kiel-wasser; (*fig.*) die Spur; *in the* — *of*, in den Fußstapfen (*Genit.*).

waken ['weikən], *v.a.* aufwecken. — *v.n.* aufwachen.

walk [wɔ:k], *v.n.* (zu Fuß) gehen. — *s.* der Gang (*gait*); der Spaziergang.

wall [wɔːl], s. die Wand, Mauer.
wallet ['wɔlit], s. die Brieftasche.
wallflower ['wɔːlflauə], s. (Bot.) der Goldlack; (fig.) das Mauerblümchen.
wallow ['wɔlou], v.n. schwelgen; sich wälzen.
walnut ['wɔːlnʌt], s. (Bot.) die Walnuß.
walrus ['wɔːlrəs], s. (Zool.) das Walroß.
waltz [wɔːlts], s. der Walzer.
wan [wɔn], adj. blaß, bleich.
wand [wɔnd], s. der Stab.
wander ['wɔndə], v.n. wandern, durchwandern; (fig.) — from the subject, vom Thema abkommen.
wane [wein], v.n. abnehmen, verfallen.
want [wɔnt], v.a. brauchen, wollen, nötig haben, wünschen. — v.n. mangeln, fehlen. — s. die Not.
wanton ['wɔntən], adj. mutwillig, ausgelassen.
war [wɔː], s. der Krieg.
warble [wɔːbl], v.a., v.n. singen; (Mus.) trillern.
warbler ['wɔːblə], s. (Orn.) der Singvogel.
ward [wɔːd], s. die Verwahrung; das or der Mündel (child in care); (Pol.) der Wahlbezirk; die Station (hospital). — v.a. — off, abwehren.
warden [wɔːdn], s. der Vorstand, Vorsteher; Rektor.
warder ['wɔːdə], s. der Wächter; (in prison) der Wärter, Gefängniswärter.
wardrobe ['wɔːdroub], s. der Kleiderschrank.
ware [wɛə], s. die Ware.
warehouse ['wɛəhaus], s. das Warenlager.
warfare ['wɔːfɛə], s. der Krieg, die Kriegsführung.
warlike ['wɔːlaik], adj. kriegerisch.
warm [wɔːm], adj. warm.
warn [wɔːn], v.a. warnen, ermahnen.
warning ['wɔːniŋ], s. die Warnung.
warp [wɔːp], v.a. krümmen, verziehen (of wood); (fig.) verderben; verzerren, verdrehen. — v.n. sich werfen, krümmen.
warrant ['wɔrənt], s. (Law) der Haftbefehl; — officer, der Unteroffizier; (Comm.) die Vollmacht, Bürgschaft. — v.a. garantieren (vouch for); versichern (assure).
warranty ['wɔrənti], s. (Law) die Gewähr; Garantie.
warren ['wɔrən], s. das Gehege.
warrior ['wɔriə], s. der Krieger.
wart [wɔːt], s. (Med.) die Warze.
wary ['wɛəri], adj. vorsichtig, achtsam (careful).
wash [wɔʃ], v.a., v.n. (sich) waschen; — up, spülen, abwaschen. — s. die Wäsche (laundry).
wasp [wɔsp], s. (Ent.) die Wespe.
waspish ['wɔspiʃ], adj. reizbar, zänkisch, bissig.
wassail [wɔsl], s. das Trinkgelage. — v.n. zechen.
waste [weist], v.a. zerstören, verwüsten;

verschwenden. — adj. wüst, öde. — s. die Verschwendung (process); der Abfall (product); — paper, Makulatur; — paper basket, der Papierkorb.
wasteful ['weistful], adj. verschwenderisch.
watch [wɔtʃ], v.a. bewachen; beobachten (observe); hüten (guard). — s. die Wache (guard); die Uhr, Taschenuhr (time-piece).
watchful ['wɔtʃful], adj. wachsam.
watchman ['wɔtʃmən], s. der Nachtwächter.
water ['wɔːtə], s. das Wasser; (pl.) die Kur; — colour, das Aquarell; — gauge, der Pegel. — v.a. wässern; begießen (flowers).
watercress ['wɔːtəkres], s. (Bot.) die Brunnenkresse.
waterproof ['wɔːtəpruːf], adj. wasserdicht.
watt [wɔt], s. (Elec.) das Watt.
wattle [wɔtl], s. (Bot.) die Hürde.
wave [weiv], s. die Welle; permanent —, die Dauerwelle. — v.n. zuwinken (Dat.); wehen; winken. — v.a. schwenken (handkerchief).
waver ['weivə], v.n. schwanken, unentschlossen sein.
wax [wæks], s. das Wachs, der Siegellack. — v.a. wachsen, bohnern.
waxen [wæksn], adj. aus Wachs, wächsern.
way [wei], s. der Weg (road etc.); die Strecke; Richtung; in no —, keineswegs; (pl.) die Art und Weise; Milky Way, die Milchstraße.
wayward ['weiwəd], adj. eigensinnig.
we [wiː], pers. pron. wir.
weak [wiːk], adj. schwach, kraftlos.
weaken ['wiːkən], v.a. schwächen; v.n. schwach werden.
weakling ['wiːkliŋ], s. der Schwächling.
wealth [welθ], s. der Wohlstand, Reichtum.
wealthy ['welθi], adj. wohlhabend, reich.
wean [wiːn], v.a. entwöhnen.
weapon ['wepən], s. die Waffe.
wear [wɛə], v.a. irr. tragen (clothes). — v.n. — off, sich abtragen, schäbig werden; — out, sich erschöpfen. — s. die Abnutzung.
weariness ['wiərinis], s. die Müdigkeit, der Überdruß.
weary ['wiəri], adj. müde, überdrüssig.
weasel [wiːzl], s. (Zool.) das Wiesel.
weather ['weðə], s. das Wetter. — v.a. überstehen. — v.n. (Geol.) verwittern.
weatherbeaten ['weðəbiːtn], adj. abgehärtet, wetterhart.
weathercock ['weðəkɔk], s. der Wetterhahn; (fig.) wetterwendischer Mensch.
weave [wiːv], v.a. irr. (Text.) weben, — s. das Gewebe.
web [web], s. das Gewebe.
wed [wed], v.a. heiraten; trauen (a couple). — v.n. (sich ver)heiraten.
wedding ['wediŋ], s. die Hochzeit; Trauung (ceremony).

wedge [wedʒ], *s.* der Keil. — *v.a.* keilen.

wedlock ['wedlɔk], *s.* die Ehe.

Wednesday ['wenzd(e)i]. der Mittwoch.

wee [wiː], *adj.* (*Scot.*) winzig, klein.

weed [wiːd], *s.* das Unkraut. — *v.a.* ausjäten, jäten.

week [wiːk], *s.* die Woche.

weep [wiːp], *v.n. irr.* weinen; —*ing willow*, die Trauerweide.

weigh [wei], *v.a.* wiegen, wägen; (*fig.*) abwägen, beurteilen; (*Naut.*) — *anchor*, den Anker lichten. — *v.n.* wiegen.

weighing machine ['weiiŋ mə'ʃiːn], *s.* die Waage.

weight [weit], *s.* das Gewicht; *gross* —, das Bruttogewicht; *net* —, das Nettogewicht.

weighty ['weiti], *adj.* (ge)wichtig; (*fig.*) schwer.

weir [wiə], *s.* das Wehr.

weird [wiəd], *adj.* unheimlich.

welcome ['welkəm], *adj.* willkommen. — *s.* der or das Willkommen. — *v.a.* willkommen heißen, begrüßen.

weld [weld], *v.a.* schweißen.

welfare ['welfɛə], *s.* die Wohlfahrt, soziale Fürsorge.

well (1) [wel], *s.* der Brunnen. — *v.n.* hervorsprudeln.

well (2) [wel], *adv.* gut, wohl; durchaus; — *bred*, wohlerzogen. — *pred. adj.* gesund, wohl.

Welsh [welʃ], *adj.* walisisch. — *s. pl.* die Waliser, *m.pl.*

Welshman ['welʃmən], *s.* der Waliser.

welt [welt], *s.* der Rand, die Einfassung.

welter ['weltə], *s.* die Masse, das Chaos. — *v.n.* sich wälzen.

wen [wen], *s.* (*Med.*) die Schwellung.

wench [wentʃ], *s.* die Magd, das Mädchen.

west [west], *s.* der Westen. — *adj.* (*also* **westerly**, **western** ['westəli, 'westən]) westlich.

Westphalian [west'feiliən], *adj.* westfälisch. — *s.* der Westfale.

wet [wet], *adj.* naß, feucht; — *paint*, frisch gestrichen. — *v.a.* anfeuchten, benetzen, naß machen.

whack [hwæk], *v.a.* durchprügeln. — *s.* die Tracht Prügel, der Schlag.

whale [hweil], *s.* (*Zool.*) der Walfisch.

whalebone ['hweilboun], *s.* das Fischbein.

wharf [hwɔːf], *s.* der Kai.

wharfinger ['hwɔːfindʒə], *s.* der Kaimeister.

what [hwɔt], *rel. & interr. pron.* was; welcher, welche, welches; was für.

what(so)ever [hwɔt(sou)'evə], *rel. pron.* was auch immer. — *adj.* einerlei welche-r, -s, -n.

wheat [hwiːt], *s.* (*Bot.*) der Weizen.

wheedle [hwiːdl], *v.a.* beschwatzen.

wheel [hwiːl], *s.* das Rad; die Umdrehung, Drehung. — *v.a.*, *v.n.* drehen, sich drehen, schieben.

wheelbarrow ['hwiːlbærou], *s.* der Schubkarren.

wheeze [hwiːz], *v.n.* keuchen, schnaufen. — *s.* das Keuchen.

whelp [hwelp], *s.* (*Zool.*) das Junge, der junge Hund. — *v.n.* Junge werfen.

when [hwen], *adv.* (*interr.*) wann? — *conj.* als (*in past*), wenn, während.

whence [hwens], *adv.* woher, von wo.

where [hwɛə], *adv.* wo, wohin; (*interr.*) wo? wohin?

whereabout(s) ['hwɛərəbaut(s)], *adv.* wo, wo etwa. — *s.* (**whereabouts**) der zeitweilige Aufenthalt or Wohnort.

whereas [hwɛər'æz], *conj.* wohingegen, während.

whereupon [hwɛərə'pɔn], *conj.* woraufhin.

wherewithal ['hwɛərwiðɔːl], *s.* die gesamte Habe, das Nötige. — *adv.* (*obs.*) womit.

whet [hwet], *v.a.* wetzen, schleifen.

whether ['hweðə], *conj.* ob.

whey [hwei], *s.* die Molke.

which [hwitʃ], *rel. & interr. pron.* welcher, welche, welches; der, die, das.

whiff [hwif], *s.* der Hauch, Luftzug.

while [hwail], *s.* die Weile, Zeit. — *v.a.* — *away the time*, dahinbringen, vertreiben. — *conj.* (*also* **whilst**) während, so lange als.

whim [hwim], *s.* die Laune, Grille.

whimper ['hwimpə], *v.n.* winseln.

whimsical ['hwimzikəl], *adj.* grillenhaft.

whine [hwain], *v.n.* weinen, wimmern, klagen. — *s.* das Gewimmer, Gejammer.

whinny ['hwini], *v.n.* wiehern.

whip [hwip], *s.* die Peitsche; (*Pol.*) der Einpeitscher. — *v.a.* peitschen.

whir [hwəː], *v.n.* schwirren. — *s.* das Schwirren.

whirl [hwəːl], *s.* der Wirbel, Strudel. — *v.a.*, *v.n.* wirbeln.

whirligig ['hwəːligig], *s.* der Karussel.

whirlpool ['hwəːlpuːl], *s.* der Strudel.

whirr *see* **whir**.

whisk [hwisk], *v.a.* fegen; schlagen; —*away or off*, schnell wegtun (*a th.*), schnell fortnehmen (*a p.*). — *v.n.* — *away*, dahinhuschen. — *s.* der Schläger.

whiskers ['hwiskəz], *s.* der Backenbart, Bart.

whisky ['hwiski], *s.* der Whisky.

whisper ['hwispə], *s.* das Geflüster. *v.a.*, *v.n.* flüstern.

whistle [hwisl], *s.* die Pfeife (*instrument*); der Pfiff (*sound*). — *v.a.*, *v.n.* pfeifen.

whit [hwit], *s.* die Kleinigkeit; *not a* —, nicht im geringsten.

white [hwait], *adj.* weiß; — *lead*, das Bleiweiß; — *lie*, die Notlüge.

whitebait ['hwaitbeit], *s.* (*Zool.*) der Breitling.

whiten [hwaitn], *v.a.* weißen, bleichen.

whitewash ['hwaitwɔʃ], *s.* die Tünche. — *v.a.* reinwaschen.

515

whither ['hwiðə], *adv.* wohin; dahin wo.

whiting ['hwaitiŋ], *s.* (*Zool.*) der Weißfisch; die Schlämmkreide (*chalk*).

whitlow ['hwitlou], *s.* (*Med.*) das Nagelgeschwür.

Whitsun(tide) ['hwitsən(taid)], *s.* (das) Pfingsten; *Whit Sunday*, der Pfingstsonntag.

whittle [hwitl], *v.a.* schnitzen, abschaben.

whiz [hwiz], *v.n.* zischen; (*fig.*) vorbeiflitzen.

who [hu:], *interr. pron.* wer?, welcher?, welche? — *rel. pron.* welcher, welche, welches, der, die, das.

whoever [hu:'evə], *rel. pron.* wer auch immer.

whole [houl], *adj.* ganz, völlig. — *s.* das Ganze.

wholesale ['houlseil], *adv.* im Engros. — *adj.* Engros-, Großhandels-.

wholesome ['houlsəm], *adj.* gesund.

whoop [hu:p], *s.* das Geschrei; — *v.n.* laut keuchen; —*ing cough*, der Keuchhusten.

whortleberry ['hwə:tlbəri], *s.* (*Bot.*) die Heidelbeere.

whose [hu:z], *pron.* wessen, dessen, deren.

whosoever [hu:sou'evə] *see* **whoever**.

why [hwai], *rel. & interr. adv.* warum?

wick [wik], *s.* der Docht.

wicked ['wikid], *adj.* böse, schlecht.

wicker ['wikə], *adj.* Rohr-, geflochten.

wicket ['wikit], *s.* das Pförtchen.

wide [waid], *adj.* weit, breit; (*fig.*) umfangreich, groß, reich(*experience*).— *adv. far and* —, weit und breit; — *awake*, völlig wach.

widen [waidn], *v.a.*, erweitern.

widgeon ['widʒən], *s.* die Pfeifente.

widow ['widou], *s.* die Witwe.

widower ['widouə], *s.* der Witwer.

width [widθ], *s.* die Weite, Breite.

wield [wi:ld], *v.a.* schwingen; — *power*, die Macht ausüben.

wife [waif], *s.* die Frau, Gattin.

wig [wig], *s.* die Perücke.

wild [waild], *adj.* wild.

wilderness ['wildənis], *s.* die Wildnis.

wildfire ['waildfaiə], *s.* das Lauffeuer.

wilful ['wilful], *adj.* absichtlich; vorsätzlich.

wiliness ['wailinis], *s.* die Schlauheit, Arglist.

will [wil], *s.* der Wille; (*Law*) der letzte Wille, das Testament. — *v.n.* wollen. — *v.a.* (*Law*) vermachen, hinterlassen.

willing ['wiliŋ], *adj.* bereitwillig.

will-o'-the-wisp [wiləðə'wisp], *s.* das Irrlicht.

willow ['wilou], *s.* (*Bot.*) die Weide.

wily ['waili], *adj.* schlau, verschmitzt.

wimple [wimpl], *s.* der Schleier.

win [win], *v.a., v.n. irr.* gewinnen, siegen, erringen.

wince [wins], *v.n.* zucken, zusammenzucken.

winch [wintʃ], *s.* die Kurbel, Winde.

wind (1) [wind], *s.* der Wind; der Atem (*breath*); *get* — *of s.th.*, von etwas hören.

wind (2) [waind], *v.a. irr.* winden; wenden, drehen (*turn*); —(*up*), aufziehen (*timepiece*); — *up*, (*business, debate*) beenden. — *v.n.* sich schlängeln, winden.

windfall ['windfɔ:l], *s.* das Fallobst (*fruit*); (*fig.*) der Glücksfall.

windlass ['windləs], *s.* die Winde.

window ['windou], *s.* das Fenster; — *sill*, das Fensterbrett.

windpipe ['windpaip], *s.* (*Anat.*) die Luftröhre.

windscreen ['windskri:n], *s.* (*Motor.*) die Windschutzscheibe.

windshield ['windʃi:ld] (*Am.*) *see* **windscreen**.

windy ['windi], *adj.* windig.

wine [wain], *s.* der Wein; — *merchant*, der Weinhändler.

wing [wiŋ], *s.* der Flügel; (*Poet.*) die Schwinge.

wink [wiŋk], *s.* das Zwinkern; der Augenblick.—*v.n.* blinzeln, zwinkern.

winner ['winə], *s.* der Sieger, Gewinner.

winning ['winiŋ], *adj.* einnehmend.

winsome ['winsəm], *adj.* reizend, einnehmend.

winter ['wintə], *s.* der Winter.

wintry ['wintri], *adj.* winterlich.

wipe [waip], *v.a.* wischen, abwischen.

wire [waiə], *s.* der Draht; (*coll.*) das Telegramm; *barbed* —, der Stacheldraht. — *v.a.* verbinden; (*fig.*) telegraphieren. — *v.n.* telegraphieren.

wireless ['waiəlis], *s.* das Radio. — *adj.* drahtlos.

wirepuller ['waiəpulə], *s.* der Puppenspieler; (*fig.*) der Intrigant.

wiry ['waiəri], *adj.* zäh, stark.

wisdom ['wizdəm], *s.* die Weisheit.

wise [waiz], *adj.* weise, verständig, klug.

wiseacre ['waizeikə], *s.* der Allzuschlaue, Naseweis.

wish [wiʃ], *v.a., v.n.* wünschen. — *s.* der Wunsch.

wistful ['wistful], *adj.* nachdenklich (*pensive*); wehmütig (*sad*).

wit [wit], *s.* der Witz; Geist; Verstand; der witzige Mensch; der Witzbold.

witch [witʃ], *s.* die Hexe, Zauberin.

witchcraft ['witʃkra:ft], *s.* die Zauberkunst, Hexerei.

with [wið], *prep.* mit, mitsamt, bei, durch, von.

withal [wi'ðɔ:l], *adv.* obendrein.

withdraw [wið'drɔ:], *v.a., v.n. irr.* (sich) zurückziehen; widerrufen; abheben (*money from bank*).

withdrawal [wið'drɔ:əl], *s.* der Rückzug; (*Comm. etc.*) die Widerrufung; Abhebung (*bank*).

wither ['wiðə], *v.a.* welk machen. — *v.n.* verwelken; ausdorren, verdorren (*dry up*); (*fig.*) vergehen.

withhold [wið'hould], *v.a. irr.* zurückhalten, vorenthalten.

within [wi'ðin], *prep.* innerhalb; *(time)* binnen *(Genit.).* — *adv.* darin, drinnen.

without [wi'ðaut], *prep.* ohne; *(obs.)* außerhalb *(outside); do* —, entbehren. — *adv.* draußen, außen.

withstand [wið'stænd], *v.a. irr.* widerstehen *(Dat.).*

withy ['wiði], *s.* der Weidenzweig.

witless ['witlis], *adj.* einfältig.

witness ['witnis], *s.* der Zeuge. — *v.a.* bezeugen, Zeuge sein von. — *v.n.* zeugen, Zeuge sein.

witticism ['witisizm], *s.* das Bonmot, die witzige Bemerkung.

witty ['witi], *adj.* witzig, geistreich.

wizard ['wizəd], *s.* der Zauberer.

wizened ['wizənd], *adj.* verwelkt, vertrocknet, runzlig.

wobble [wɔbl], *v.n.* wackeln.

woe [wou], *s. (Poet.)* das Weh, Leid.

wolf [wulf], *s. (Zool.)* der Wolf.

woman ['wumən], *s.* die Frau, das Weib.

womanly ['wumənli], *adj.* weiblich.

womb [wu:m], *s.* der Mutterleib, Schoß; *(Anat.)* die Gebärmutter.

wonder ['wʌndə], *s.* das Wunder. — *v.n.* sich wundern *(be amazed);* gern wissen mögen *(like to know);* sich fragen.

wonderful ['wʌndəful], *adj.* wunderbar.

wondrous ['wʌndrəs], *adj. (Poet.)* wunderbar.

wont [wount], *s.* die Gewohnheit. — *pred. adj.* gewohnt.

won't [wount] = **will not.**

woo [wu:], *v.a.* freien, werben (um).

wood [wud], *s.* das Holz *(timber);* der Wald *(forest).*

woodbine ['wudbain], *s.* das Geißblatt.

woodcock ['wudkɔk], *s. (Orn.)* die Waldschnepfe.

woodcut ['wudkʌt], *s. (Art)* der Holzschnitt.

wooded ['wudid], *adj.* bewaldet.

wooden [wudn], *adj.* hölzern, Holz–.

woodlark ['wudlɑ:k], *s. (Orn.)* die Heidelerche.

woodpecker ['wudpekə], *s. (Orn.)* der Specht.

woodruff ['wudrʌf], *s. (Bot.)* der Waldmeister.

woof [wu:f], *s. (Text.)* der Einschlag, das Gewebe.

wool [wul], *s.* die Wolle; — *gathering,* zerstreut.

woollen ['wulən], *adj.* wollen, aus Wolle.

woolly ['wuli], *adj.* wollig; *(fig.)* unklar, verschwommen.

word [wə:d], *s.* das Wort; *send* —, Botschaft senden. — *v.a.* ausdrücken.

wording ['wə:diŋ], *s.* die Fassung, der Stil.

work [wə:k], *s.* die Arbeit; *out of* —, arbeitslos; das Werk *(opus);* *(pl.)* die Fabrik. — *v.a., v.n.* arbeiten, bearbeiten; *(engine)* funktionieren.

worker ['wə:kə], *s.* der Arbeiter.

workhouse ['wə:khaus], *s.* das Armenhaus.

workshop ['wə:kʃɔp], *s.* die Werkstatt.

world [wə:ld], *s.* die Welt.

worldly ['wə:ldli], *adj.* weltlich, zeitlich.

worm [wə:m], *s. (Zool.)* der Wurm. — *v.a. — o.'s way,* sich einschleichen; — *v.n.* sich einschleichen.

wormeaten ['wə:mi:tn], *adj.* wurmstichig.

worry ['wʌri], *v.a., v.n.* plagen, quälen, sorgen, ängstigen; sich beunruhigen; *don't* —, bitte machen Sie sich keine Mühe. — *s.* die Plage, Mühe, Qual, Sorge *(about,* um, *Acc.).*

worse [wə:s], *comp. adj., adv.* schlechter, schlimmer.

worship ['wə:ʃip], *s.* die Verehrung; der Gottesdienst *(divine* —).

worst [wə:st], *superl. adj.* schlechtest, schlimmst. — *adv.* am schlimmsten *or* schlechtesten. — *s.* das Schlimmste.

worsted ['wustid], *s. (Text.)* das Kammgarn.

worth [wə:θ], *adj.* wert. — *s.* der Wert.

worthy ['wə:ði], *adj.* würdig, wert, verdient.

would [wud] *past tense of* **will,** *q.v.*

wound [wu:nd], *s.* die Wunde. — *v.a.* verwunden.

wraith [reiθ], *s.* das Gespenst.

wrangle [ræŋgl], *v.n.* zanken, streiten. — *s.* der Zank, Streit.

wrap [ræp], *v.a.* einwickeln, einhüllen. — *s. (Am.)* der Mantel *(coat),* Pelz *(fur),* Schal *(stole).*

wrapper ['ræpə], *s.* der Umschlag, die Hülle.

wrath [rɔ:θ], *s.* der Zorn, Grimm.

wreak [ri:k], *v.a. (Lit.)* auslassen, üben.

wreath [ri:θ], *s.* der Kranz.

wreathe [ri:ð], *v.a.* winden, bekränzen.

wreck [rek], *s.* der Schiffbruch; das Wrack *(debris).* — *v.a.* zerstören, zertrümmern, *(fig.)* verderben.

wren [ren], *s. (Orn.)* der Zaunkönig.

wrench [rentʃ], *v.a.* entreißen *(tear from);* verdrehen. — *s.* heftiger Ruck; *(fig.)* der (Trennungs)schmerz.

wrest [rest], *v.a.* zerren.

wrestle [resl], *v.n.* ringen, im Ringkampf kämpfen.

wrestling ['resliŋ], *s.* der Ringkampf.

wretch [retʃ], *s.* der Schuft, Lump *(scoundrel).*

wretched ['retʃid], *adj.* elend.

wriggle [rigl], *v.n.* sich winden, schlängeln.

wring [riŋ], *v.a. irr.* auswinden, ausringen.

wrinkle [riŋkl], *s.* die Hautfalte, Runzel. — *v.a.* runzeln *(brow);* rümpfen *(nose).*

wrist [rist], *s. (Anat.)* das Handgelenk.

wristwatch ['ristwɔtʃ], *s.* die Armbanduhr.

writ [rit], *s.* die Schrift; *(Law)* die Vorladung.

write

write [rait], *v.a., v.n. irr.* schreiben, verfassen.
writer ['raitə], *s.* der Schreiber; (*Lit.*) der Schriftsteller.
writhe [raið], *v.n.* sich winden.
writing ['raitiŋ], *s.* die Schrift; der Stil (*style*).
wrong [rɔŋ], *adj.* falsch, verkehrt; *to be* —, unrecht haben. — *s.* das Unrecht. — *v.a.* Unrecht *or* Schaden tun (*Dat.*).
wrongful ['rɔŋful], *adj.* unrechtmäßig.
wrongheaded [rɔŋ'hedid], *adj.* querköpfig.
wroth [rouθ], *adj.* (*Lit.*) zornig.
wrought [rɔːt], *adj.* (*work*) gearbeitet; — *iron*, das Schmiedeeisen.
wry [rai], *adj.* verkehrt, krumm, schief, verdreht.

X

X [eks]. das X.
X-ray ['eksrei], *s.* (der) Röntgenstrahl.
xylophone ['zailəfoun], *s.* (*Mus.*) das Xylophon.

Y

Y [wai]. das Y, Ypsilon.
yacht [jɔt], *s.* (*Naut.*) die Jacht.
yachtsman ['jɔtsmən], *s.* (*Naut.*) der Segelsportler.
yap [jæp], *v.n.* kläffen.
yard (1) [jɑːd], *s.* der Hof.
yard (2) [jɑːd], *s.* die englische Elle, der Yard.
yarn [jɑːn], *s.* das Garn; (*coll.*) die Geschichte (*tale*).
yarrow ['jærou], *s.* (*Bot.*) die Schafgarbe.
yawl [jɔːl], *s.* (*Naut.*) die Yawl.
yawn [jɔːn], *v.n.* gähnen. — *s.* das Gähnen.
ye [jiː], *pron.* (*obs.*) *see* you.
year [jəː *or* jiə], *s.* das Jahr; *every other* —, alle zwei Jahre.
yearly ['jiəli], *adj., adv.* jährlich.
yearn [jəːn], *v.n.* sich sehnen (nach, *Dat.*).
yeast [jiːst], *s.* die Hefe.
yell [jel], *v.n.* gellen, schreien. — *s.* der Schrei.
yellow ['jelou], *adj.* gelb; (*sl.*) feige.
yelp [jelp], *v.n.* kläffen, bellen. — *s.* das Gebelle.
yeoman ['joumən], *s.* der Freisasse; (*Mil.*) der Leibgardist (*Yeoman of the Guard*).

yes [jes], *adv.* ja; jawohl.
yesterday ['jestəd(e)i], *adv.* gestern; *the day before* —, vorgestern.
yet [jet], *conj.* doch, dennoch. — *adv.* noch, außerdem; *as* —, bisher; *not* —, noch nicht.
yew [juː], *s.* (*Bot.*) die Eibe.
yield [jiːld], *v.a.* hervorbringen, ergeben; abwerfen (*profit*). — *v.n.* nachgeben (*to, Dat.*). — *s.* der Ertrag.
yoke [jouk], *s.* das Joch (Ochsen). — *v.a.* einspannen, anspannen.
yolk [jouk], *s.* das Eidotter.
yon, yonder [jɔn, 'jɔndə], *dem. adj.* (*obs.*) jener, jene, jenes; der *or* die *or* das da drüben.
yore [jɔː], *adv.* (*obs.*) *of* —, von damals; ehedem.
you [juː], *pers. pron.* du, dich, ihr, euch; (*formal*) sie (*in letters*, Du, Dich *etc.*).
young [jʌŋ], *adj.* jung. — *s.* (*Zool.*) das Junge.
your [juə], *poss. adj.* dein, deine, dein; euer, eure, euer; (*formal*) ihr, ihre, ihr (*in letters* Dein, Euer *etc.*).
yours [jɔːz], *poss. pron.* deinig, eurig; der, die *or* das ihrige (*in letters* Deinig, der Ihrige *etc.*).
yourself [juə'self], *pers. pron.* du selbst, Sie selbst; ihr selbst; dich (selbst), euch (selbst) (*in letters* Du selbst; Dich (selbst) *etc.*).
youth [juːθ], *s.* die Jugend.
youthful ['juːθful], *adj.* jugendlich.
Yugoslav [juːgo'slaːv], *adj.* jugoslawisch. — *s.* der Jugoslawe.
Yule, Yuletide [juːl, 'juːltaid], *s.* das Julfest, die Weihnachtszeit.

Z

Z [zed, (*Am.*) ziː]. das Z.
zany ['zeini], *s.* der Hanswurst.
zeal [ziːl], *s.* der Eifer.
zealous ['zeləs], *adj.* eifrig.
zebra ['ziːbrə], *s.* (*Zool.*) das Zebra.
zenith ['zeniθ], *s.* der Zenit, Scheitelpunkt.
zero ['ziərou], *s.* der Nullpunkt, die (Ziffer) Null; — *hour*, die festgesetzte Stunde; festgesetzter Zeitpunkt.
zest [zest], *s.* die Lust; der Genuß; die Würze.
zigzag ['zigzæg], *s.* der Zickzack. — *adj.* Zickzack-.
zinc [ziŋk], *s.* das Zink.
zip(per) ['zip(ə)], *s.* der Reißverschluß (*zip fastener*).
zone [zoun], *s.* die Zone.
zoological gardens [zouə'lɔdʒikəl gɑːdnz], *s.* (*abbr.* zoo [zuː]) zoologischer Garten, der Zoo, Tiergarten.

German Irregular Verbs

Note: *Where a compound irregular verb is not given, its forms are identical with those of the simple irregular verb as listed.*

Infin.	Pres. Indic. 3rd Pers. Sing.	Imperf. Indic.	Imperf. Subj.
backen	bäckt	backte (buk)	backte
befehlen	befiehlt	befahl	beföhle
beginnen	beginnt	begann	begönne
beißen	beißt	biß	bisse
bergen	birgt	barg	bürge
bersten	birst	barst	börste
bewegen	bewegt	bewog	bewöge
biegen	biegt	bog	böge
bieten	bietet	bot	böte
binden	bindet	band	bände
bitten	bittet	bat	bäte
blasen	bläst	blies	bliese
bleiben	bleibt	blieb	bliebe
braten	brät	briet	briete
brechen	bricht	brach	bräche
brennen	brennt	brannte	brennte
bringen	bringt	brachte	brächte
denken	denkt	dachte	dächte
dreschen	drischt	drosch	dräsche
dringen	dringt	drang	dränge
dürfen	darf	durfte	dürfte
empfangen	empfängt	empfing	empfinge
empfehlen	empfiehlt	empfahl	empföhle
empfinden	empfindet	empfand	empfände
erlöschen	erlischt	erlosch	erlösche

Imper.	Past Participle	English
backe	gebacken	bake
befiehl	befohlen	order, command
beginn(e)	begonnen	begin
beiß(e)	gebissen	bite
birg	geborgen	save, conceal
birst	geborsten	burst
beweg(e)	bewogen	induce
bieg(e)	gebogen	bend
biet(e)	geboten	offer
bind(e)	gebunden	tie, bind
bitte	gebeten	request
blas(e)	geblasen	blow
bleib(e)	geblieben	remain
brat(e)	gebraten	roast
brich	gebrochen	break
brenne	gebrannt	burn
bring(e)	gebracht	bring
denk(e)	gedacht	think
drisch	gedroschen	thrash
dring(e)	gedrungen	press forward
	gedurft	be permitted
empfang(e)	empfangen	receive
empfiehl	empfohlen	(re)commend
empfind(e)	empfunden	feel, perceive
erlisch	erloschen	extinguish

German Irregular Verbs

Infin.	Pres. Indic. 3rd Pers. Sing.	Imperf. Indic.	Imperf. Subj.
erschrecken (*v.n.*)	erschrickt	erschrak	erschräke
essen	ißt	aß	äße
fahren	fährt	fuhr	führe
fallen	fällt	fiel	fiele
fangen	fängt	fing	finge
fechten	ficht	focht	föchte
finden	findet	fand	fände
flechten	flicht	flocht	flöchte
fliegen	fliegt	flog	flöge
fliehen	flieht	floh	flöhe
fließen	fließt	floß	flösse
fressen	frißt	fraß	fräße
frieren	friert	fror	fröre
gebären	gebiert	gebar	gebäre
geben	gibt	gab	gäbe
gedeihen	gedeiht	gedieh	gediehe
gehen	geht	ging	ginge
gelingen (*impers.*)	(mir) gelingt	gelang	gelänge
gelten	gilt	galt	gälte
genesen	genest	genas	genäse
genießen	genießt	genoß	genösse
geschehen (*impers.*)	(mir) geschieht	geschah	geschähe
gewinnen	gewinnt	gewann	gewönne
gießen	gießt	goß	gösse
gleichen	gleicht	glich	gliche
gleiten	gleitet	glitt	glitte
graben	gräbt	grub	grübe
greifen	greift	griff	griffe

Imper.	Past Participle	English
erschrick	erschrocken	be frightened
iß	gegessen	eat
fahr(e)	gefahren	travel
fall(e)	gefallen	fall
fang(e)	gefangen	catch
ficht	gefochten	fight
find(e)	gefunden	find
flicht	geflochten	twine together
flieg(e)	geflogen	fly
flieh(e)	geflohen	flee
fließ(e)	geflossen	flow
friß	gefressen	eat (of animals)
frier(e)	gefroren	freeze
gebier	geboren	give birth to
gib	gegeben	give
gedeih(e)	gediehen	thrive
geh(e)	gegangen	go
geling(e)	gelungen	succeed
gilt	gegolten	be worth, be valid
genese	genesen	recover
genieß(e)	genossen	enjoy
	geschehen	happen
gewinn(e)	gewonnen	win
gieß(e)	gegossen	pour
gleich(e)	geglichen	equal, resemble
gleit(e)	geglitten	glide
grab(e)	gegraben	dig
greif(e)	gegriffen	grasp

German Irregular Verbs

Infin.	Pres. Indic. 3rd Pers. Sing.	Imperf. Indic.	Imperf. Subj.
haben	hat	hatte	hätte
halten	hält	hielt	hielte
hangen (v.n.)	hängt	hing	hinge
heben	hebt	hob	höbe
heißen	heißt	hieß	hieße
helfen	hilft	half	hülfe
kennen	kennt	kannte	kennte
klimmen	klimmt	klomm	klömme
klingen	klingt	klang	klänge
kneifen	kneift	kniff	kniffe
kommen	kommt	kam	käme
können	kann	konnte	könnte
kriechen	kriecht	kroch	kröche
laden	lädt	lud	lüde
lassen	läßt	ließ	ließe
laufen	läuft	lief	liefe
leiden	leidet	litt	litte
leihen	leiht	lieh	liehe
lesen	liest	las	läse
liegen	liegt	lag	läge
lügen	lügt	log	löge
mahlen	mahlt	mahlte	mahlte
meiden	meidet	mied	miede
messen	mißt	maß	mäße
mißlingen (impers.)	(mir) mißlingt	mißlang	mißlänge
mögen	mag	mochte	möchte
müssen	muß	mußte	müßte
nehmen	nimmt	nahm	nähme

Imper.	Past Participle	English
habe	gehabt	have
halt(e)	gehalten	hold
häng(e)	gehangen	hang
hebe	gehoben	lift
heiß(e)	geheißen	be called
hilf	geholfen	help
kenn(e)	gekannt	know
klimm(e)	geklommen	climb
kling(e)	geklungen	ring, sound
kneif(e)	gekniffen	pinch
komm(e)	gekommen	come
	gekonnt	be able
kriech(e)	gekrochen	creep
lad(e)	geladen	load
laß	gelassen	let
lauf(e)	gelaufen	run
leid(e)	gelitten	suffer
leih(e)	geliehen	lend
lies	gelesen	read
lieg(e)	gelegen	lie
lüg(e)	gelogen	lie, be untruthful
mahle	gemahlen	grind
meid(e)	gemieden	avoid
miß	gemessen	measure
	mißlungen	fail
	gemocht	wish, be willing
	gemußt	have to
nimm	genommen	take

German Irregular Verbs

Infin.	Pres. Indic. 3rd Pers. Sing.	Imperf. Indic.	Imperf. Subj.
nennen	nennt	nannte	nennte
pfeifen	pfeift	pfiff	pfiffe
preisen	preist	pries	priese
quellen (*v.n.*)	quillt	quoll	quölle
raten	rät	riet	riete
reiben	reibt	rieb	riebe
reißen	reißt	riß	risse
reiten	reitet	ritt	ritte
rennen	rennt	rannte	rennte
riechen	riecht	roch	röche
ringen	ringt	rang	ränge
rinnen	rinnt	rann	rönne
rufen	ruft	rief	riefe
saufen	säuft	soff	söffe
saugen	saugt	sog	söge
schaffen	schafft	schuf	schüfe
scheiden	scheidet	schied	schiede
scheinen	scheint	schien	schiene
schelten	schilt	schalt	schölte
schieben	schiebt	schob	schöbe
schießen	schießt	schoß	schösse
schinden	schindet	schund	schünde
schlafen	schläft	schlief	schliefe
schlagen	schlägt	schlug	schlüge
schleichen	schleicht	schlich	schliche
schleifen	schleift	schliff	schliffe
schließen	schließt	schloß	schlösse
schlingen	schlingt	schlang	schlänge

Imper.	Past Participle	English
nenne	genannt	name
pfeif(e)	gepfiffen	whistle
preis(e)	gepriesen	praise
quill	gequollen	spring
rat(e)	geraten	counsel
reib(e)	gerieben	rub
reiß(e)	gerissen	tear
reit(e)	geritten	ride
renn(e)	gerannt	run
riech(e)	gerochen	smell
ring(e)	gerungen	struggle
rinn(e)	geronnen	flow
ruf(e)	gerufen	call
sauf(e)	gesoffen	drink (to excess)
saug(e)	gesogen	suck
schaff(e)	geschaffen	create
scheid(e)	geschieden	separate
schein(e)	geschienen	appear
schilt	gescholten	scold
schieb(e)	geschoben	shove
schieß(e)	geschossen	shoot
schind(e)	geschunden	skin
schlaf(e)	geschlafen	sleep
schlag(e)	geschlagen	beat
schleich(e)	geschlichen	slink, creep
schleif(e)	geschliffen	slide, polish
schließ(e)	geschlossen	shut, close
schling(e)	geschlungen	wind, devour

German Irregular Verbs

Infin.	Pres. Indic. 3rd Pers. Sing.	Imperf. Indic.	Imperf. Subj.
schmeißen	schmeißt	schmiß	schmisse
schmelzen (v.n.)	schmilzt	schmolz	schmölze
schneiden	schneidet	schnitt	schnitte
schrecken (v.n.)	schrickt	schrak	schräke
schreiben	schreibt	schrieb	schriebe
schreien	schreit	schrie	schriee
schreiten	schreitet	schritt	schritte
schweigen	schweigt	schwieg	schwiege
schwellen	schwillt	schwoll	schwölle
schwimmen	schwimmt	schwamm	schwömme
schwinden	schwindet	schwand	schwände
schwingen	schwingt	schwang	schwänge
schwören	schwört	schwur	schwüre
sehen	sieht	sah	sähe
sein	ist	war	wäre
senden	sendet	sandte or sendete	sendete
singen	singt	sang	sänge
sinken	sinkt	sank	sänke
sinnen	sinnt	sann	sänne
sitzen	sitzt	saß	säße
sollen	soll	sollte	sollte
speien	speit	spie	spiee
spinnen	spinnt	spann	spönne
sprechen	spricht	sprach	spräche
sprießen	sprießt	sproß	sprösse
springen	springt	sprang	spränge
stechen	sticht	stach	stäche
stehen	steht	stand	stände

Imper.	Past Participle	English
schmeiß(e)	geschmissen	hurl
schmilz	geschmolzen	melt
schneid(e)	geschnitten	cut
schrick	(erschrocken)	frighten
schreib(e)	geschrieben	write
schrei(e)	geschrien	cry
schreit(e)	geschritten	stride
schweig(e)	geschwiegen	be silent
schwill	geschwollen	swell
schwimm(e)	geschwommen	swim
schwind(e)	geschwunden	vanish
schwing(e)	geschwungen	swing
schwör(e)	geschworen	swear
sieh	gesehen	see
sei	gewesen	be
send(e)	gesandt *or* gesendet	send
sing(e)	gesungen	sing
sink(e)	gesunken	sink
sinn(e)	gesonnen	meditate
sitz(e)	gesessen	sit
	gesollt	be obliged
spei(e)	gespieen	spit
spinn(e)	gesponnen	spin
sprich	gesprochen	speak
sprieß(e)	gesprossen	sprout
spring(e)	gesprungen	leap
stich	gestochen	prick
steh(e)	gestanden	stand

German Irregular Verbs

Infin.	Pres. Indic. 3rd Pers. Sing.	Imperf. Indic.	Imperf. Subj.
stehlen	stiehlt	stahl	stöhle
steigen	steigt	stieg	stiege
sterben	stirbt	starb	stürbe
stinken	stinkt	stank	stänke
stoßen	stößt	stieß	stieße
streichen	streicht	strich	striche
streiten	streitet	stritt	stritte
tragen	trägt	trug	trüge
treffen	trifft	traf	träfe
treiben	treibt	trieb	triebe
treten	tritt	trat	träte
trinken	trinkt	trank	tränke
trügen	trügt	trog	tröge
tun	tut	tat	täte
verderben	verdirbt	verdarb	verdürbe
verdrießen	verdrießt	verdroß	verdrösse
vergessen	vergißt	vergaß	vergäße
verlieren	verliert	verlor	verlöre
wachsen	wächst	wuchs	wüchse
wägen	wägt	wog	wöge
waschen	wäscht	wusch	wüsche
weichen	weicht	wich	wiche
weisen	weist	wies	wiese
werben	wirbt	warb	würbe
werden	wird	wurde	würde
werfen	wirft	warf	würfe
wiegen	wiegt	wog	wöge
winden (v.a.)	windet	wand	wände

Imper.	Past Participle	English
stiehl	gestohlen	steal
steig(e)	gestiegen	climb
stirb	gestorben	die
stink(e)	gestunken	stink
stoß(e)	gestoßen	push
streich(e)	gestrichen	stroke, touch
streit(e)	gestritten	quarrel, fight
trag(e)	getragen	carry
triff	getroffen	meet
treib(e)	getrieben	drive
tritt	getreten	step
trink(e)	getrunken	drink
trüg(e)	getrogen	deceive
tu(e)	getan	do
verdirb	verdorben (and verderbt)	spoil
verdrieß(e)	verdrossen	grieve
vergiß	vergessen	forget
verlier(e)	verloren	lose
wachs(e)	gewachsen	grow
wäg(e)	gewogen	weigh
wasch(e)	gewaschen	wash
weich(e)	gewichen	yield
weis(e)	gewiesen	show
wirb	geworben	court
werde	geworden	become
wirf	geworfen	throw
wieg(e)	gewogen	weigh
wind(e)	gewunden	wind

German Irregular Verbs

Infin.	Pres. Indic. 3rd. Pers. Sing.	Imperf. Indic.	Imperf. Subj.
wissen	weiß	wußte	wüßte
wollen	will	wollte	wollte
zeihen	zeiht	zieh	ziehe
ziehen	zieht	zog	zöge
zwingen	zwingt	zwang	zwänge

Imper.	Past Participle	English
wisse	gewußt	know
wolle	gewollt	wish, want
zeih(e)	geziehen	accuse
zieh(e)	gezogen	draw, pull
zwing(e)	gezwungen	force, compel

English Irregular Verbs

Infin.	Past Indic.	Past Participle	German
abide	abode	abode	bleiben
arise	arose	arisen	aufstehen
awake	awoke	awoke	aufwecken
be	was, were	been	sein
bear	bore	borne	tragen
beat	beat	beaten	schlagen
become	became	become	werden
beget	begot	begotten	zeugen
begin	began	begun	beginnen
bend	bent	bent	biegen
bereave	bereaved,bereft	bereaved, bereft	berauben
beseech	besought	besought	bitten
bid	bade, bid	bidden, bid	gebieten
bide	bided, bode	bided	verbleiben
bind	bound	bound	binden
bite	bit	bitten	beißen
bleed	bled	bled	bluten
blow	blew	blown	blasen
break	broke	broken	brechen
breed	bred	bred	zeugen
bring	brought	brought	bringen
build	built	built	bauen
burn	burnt, burned	burnt, burned	brennen
burst	burst	burst	bersten
buy	bought	bought	kaufen

Infin.	Past Indic.	Past Participle	German
can (*pres. indic.*)	could	—	können
cast	cast	cast	werfen
catch	caught	caught	fangen
chide	chid	chidden, chid	schelten
choose	chose	chosen	wählen
cleave	cleft, clove	cleft, cloven	spalten
cling	clung	clung	sich anklammern
clothe	clothed, clad	clothed, clad	kleiden
come	came	come	kommen
cost	cost	cost	kosten
creep	crept	crept	kriechen
crow	crowed, crew	crowed	krähen
cut	cut	cut	schneiden
dare	dared, durst	dared	wagen
deal	dealt	dealt	austeilen, handeln
dig	dug	dug	graben
do	did	done	tun
draw	drew	drawn	ziehen
dream	dreamt, dreamed	dreamt, dreamed	träumen
drink	drank	drunk	trinken
drive	drove	driven	treiben
dwell	dwelt	dwelt	wohnen
eat	ate	eaten	essen
fall	fell	fallen	fallen
feed	fed	fed	füttern
feel	felt	felt	fühlen
fight	fought	fought	kämpfen
find	found	found	finden

English Irregular Verbs

Infin.	Past Indic.	Past Participle	German
flee	fled	fled	fliehen
fling	flung	flung	schleudern
fly	flew	flown	fliegen
forbid	forbad(e)	forbidden	verbieten
forget	forgot	forgotten	vergessen
forgive	forgave	forgiven	vergeben
forsake	forsook	forsaken	verlassen
freeze	froze	frozen	frieren
get	got	got	bekommen
gird	girded, girt	girden, girt	gürten
give	gave	given	geben
go	went	gone	gehen
grind	ground	ground	mahlen
grow	grew	grown	wachsen
hang	hung	hung	hängen
have	had	had	haben
hear	heard	heard	hören
heave	heaved, hove	heaved, hove	heben
hew	hewed	hewn, hewed	hauen
hide	hid	hidden, hid	verstecken
hit	hit	hit	schlagen
hold	held	held	halten
hurt	hurt	hurt	verletzen
keep	kept	kept	halten
kneel	knelt	knelt	knien
knit	knitted, knit	knitted, knit	stricken
know	knew	known	kennen, wissen
lay	laid	laid	legen

English Irregular Verbs

Infin.	Past Indic.	Past Participle	German
lead	led	led	führen
lean	leant, leaned	leant, leaned	lehnen
leap	leaped, leapt	leaped, leapt	springen
learn	learned, learnt	learned, learnt	lernen
leave	left	left	lassen
lend	lent	lent	leihen
let	let	let	lassen
lie (= recline)	lay	lain	liegen
light	lit, lighted	lit, lighted	beleuchten
lost	lost	lost	verlieren
make	made	made	machen
may (*pres. indic.*)	might	—	mögen
mean	meant	meant	meinen
meet	met	met	treffen, begegnen
melt	melted	melted, molten	schmelzen
mow	mowed	mown	mähen
must (*pres. indic.*)	—	—	müssen
pay	paid	paid	zahlen
put	put	put	stellen
quit	quit(ted)	quit(ted)	verlassen
—	quoth	—	sagte
read	read	read	lesen
rend	rent	rent	reissen
rid	rid	rid	befreien
ride	rode	ridden	reiten, fahren
ring	rang	rung	klingeln
rise	rose	risen	aufstehen
run	ran	run	laufen

English Irregular Verbs

Infin.	Past Indic.	Past Participle	German
saw	sawed	sawn	sägen
say	said	said	sagen
see	saw	seen	sehen
seek	sought	sought	suchen
sell	sold	sold	verkaufen
send	sent	sent	senden
set	set	set	setzen
shake	shook	shaken	schütteln
shall (*pres. indic.*)	should	—	werden, sollen
shape	shaped	shaped, shapen	formen
shear	sheared	shorn	scheren
shed	shed	shed	vergiessen
shine	shone	shone	scheinen
shoe	shod	shod	beschuhen
shoot	shot	shot	schiessen
show	showed	shown	zeigen
shrink	shrank	shrunk	schrumpfen
shut	shut	shut	schliessen
sing	sang	sung	singen
sink	sank	sunk	sinken
sit	sat	sat	sitzen
slay	slew	slain	erschlagen
sleep	slept	slept	schlafen
slide	slid	slid	gleiten
sling	slung	slung	schleudern
slink	slunk	slunk	schleichen
slit	slit	slit	schlitzen
smell	smelt, smelled	smelt, smelled	riechen

English Irregular Verbs

Infin.	Past Indic.	Past Participle	German
smit	smote	smitten	schlagen
sow	sowed	sown, sowed	säen
speak	spoke	spoken	sprechen
speed	sped, speeded	sped, speeded	eilen
spell	spelt, spelled	spelt, spelled	buchstabieren
spend	spent	spent	ausgeben
spill	spilled, spilt	spilled, spilt	verschütten
spin	spun, span	spun	spinnen
spit	spat	spat	speien
split	split	split	spalten
spread	spread	spread	ausbreiten
spring	sprang	sprung	springen
stand	stood	stood	stehen
steal	stole	stolen	stehlen
stick	stuck	stuck	stecken
sting	stung	stung	stechen
stink	stank, stunk	stunk	stinken
strew	strewed	strewed, strewn	streuen
stride	strode	stridden	schreiten
strike	struck	struck, stricken	schlagen
string	strung	strung	(auf)reihen
strive	strove	striven	streben
swear	swore	sworn	schwören
sweep	swept	swept	kehren
swell	swelled	swollen, **swelled**	schwellen
swim	swam	swum	schwimmen
swing	swung	swung	schwingen
take	took	taken	nehmen

English Irregular Verbs

Infin.	Past Indic.	Past Participle	German
teach	taught	taught	lehren
tear	tore	torn	zerreißen
tell	told	told	erzählen
think	thought	thought	denken
thrive	thrived, throve	thrived, thriven	gedeihen
throw	threw	thrown	werfen
thrust	thrust	thrust	stoßen
tread	trod	trodden	treten
wake	woke, waked	waked, woken woke	wachen
wear	wore	worn	tragen
weave	wove	woven	weben
weep	wept	wept	weinen
will	would	—	wollen
win	won	won	gewinnen
wind	wound	wound	winden
work	worked, wrought	worked, wrought	arbeiten
wring	wrung	wrung	ringen
write	wrote	written	schreiben

Numerical Tables

Cardinal Numbers

0	nought, zero	null
1	one	eins
2	two	zwei
3	three	drei
4	four	vier
5	five	fünf
6	six	sechs
7	seven	sieben
8	eight	acht
9	nine	neun
10	ten	zehn
11	eleven	elf
12	twelve	zwölf
13	thirteen	dreizehn
14	fourteen	vierzehn
15	fifteen	fünfzehn
16	sixteen	sechzehn
17	seventeen	siebzehn
18	eighteen	achtzehn
19	nineteen	neunzehn
20	twenty	zwanzig
21	twenty-one	einundzwanzig
22	twenty-two	zweiundzwanzig
25	twenty-five	fünfundzwanzig
30	thirty	dreißig
36	thirty-six	sechsunddreißig
40	forty	vierzig
50	fifty	fünfzig
60	sixty	sechzig
70	seventy	siebzig
80	eighty	achtzig
90	ninety	neunzig
100	(one)hundred	hundert
101	(a)hundred and one	hundert(und)eins
102	(a)hundred and two	hundert(und)zwei
200	two hundred	zweihundert
300	three hundred	dreihundert
600	six hundred	sechshundert
625	six hundred and twenty-five	sechshundertfünfundzwanzig
1000	(a)thousand	tausend
1965	nineteen hundred and sixty-five	neunzehnhundertfünfundsechzig
2000	two thousand	zweitausend
1,000,000	a million	eine Million
2,000,000	two million	zwei Millionen

Various suffixes may be added to German numerals, the commonest of which are cited in the following examples:

zehnfach	tenfold
dreisilbig	trisyllabic
vierstimmig	four-part (*i.e.* for four voices)
sechsteilig	in six parts

Ordinal Numbers

1st	first	erste (abbr. 1.)
2nd	second	zweite (abbr. 2.)
3rd	third	dritte (abbr. 3.)
4th	fourth	vierte
5th	fifth	fünfte
6th	sixth	sechste
7th	seventh	siebte
8th	eighth	achte
9th	ninth	neunte
10th	tenth	zehnte
11th	eleventh	elfte
12th	twelfth	zwölfte
13th	thirteenth	dreizehnte
14th	fourteenth	vierzehnte
15th	fifteenth	fünfzehnte
16th	sixteenth	sechzehnte
17th	seventeenth	siebzehnte
18th	eighteenth	achtzehnte
19th	nineteenth	neunzehnte
20th	twentieth	zwanzigste
21st	twenty-first	einundzwanzigste
22nd	twenty-second	zweiundzwanzigste
25th	twenty-fifth	fünfundzwanzigste
30th	thirtieth	dreißigste
40th	fortieth	vierzigste
50th	fiftieth	fünfzigste
60th	sixtieth	sechzigste
70th	seventieth	siebzigste
80th	eightieth	achtzigste
90th	ninetieth	neunzigste
100th	hundredth	hundertste
102nd	hundred and second	hundert(und)zweite
200th	two hundredth	zweihundertste
300th	three hundredth	dreihundertste
625th	six hundred and twenty-fifth	sechshundertfünfundzwanzigste
1000th	thousandth	tausendste
2000th	two thousandth	zweitausendste
1,000,000th	millionth	millionste

Fractions etc.

$\frac{1}{4}$	a quarter	ein Viertel
$\frac{1}{3}$	a third	ein Drittel
$\frac{1}{2}$	a half	(ein)halb
$\frac{2}{3}$	two thirds	zwei Drittel
$\frac{3}{4}$	three quarters	drei Viertel
$1\frac{1}{4}$	one and a quarter	ein ein Viertel
$1\frac{1}{2}$	one and a half	anderthalb
$5\frac{1}{2}$	five and a half	fünfeinhalb
$7\frac{2}{5}$	seven and two-fifths	sieben zwei Fünftel
$\frac{15}{20}$	fifteen-twentieths	fünfzehn Zwanzigstel
.7	point seven	0,7 Null Komma sieben